The
POSEN LIBRARY OF JEWISH
CULTURE AND CIVILIZATION

THE POSEN LIBRARY OF JEWISH CULTURE AND CIVILIZATION

A monumental project many years in the making, The Posen Library collects more than three thousand years of Jewish primary texts, documents, images, and cultural artifacts into ten encyclopedic volumes, with selections made by 150 internationally recognized scholars. When complete, the library will include the following volumes:

Volume 1: Ancient Israel, from Its Beginnings through 332 BCE, edited by Jeffrey H. Tigay and Adele Berlin

Volume 2: Emerging Judaism, 332 BCE–600 CE, edited by Carol Bakhos

Volume 3: Encountering Christianity and Islam, 600–1200, edited by Arnold E. Franklin

Volume 4: Late Medieval Era, 1200–1500, edited by Jonathan S. Ray

Volume 5: Early Modern Era, 1500–1750, edited by Yosef Kaplan

Volume 6: Confronting Modernity, 1750–1880, edited by Elisheva Carlebach

Volume 7: National Renaissance and International Horizons, 1880–1918, edited by Israel Bartal and Kenneth B. Moss

Volume 8: Crisis and Creativity between World Wars, 1918–1939, edited by Todd M. Endelman and Zvi Gitelman

Volume 9: Catastrophe and Rebirth, 1939–1973, edited by Samuel D. Kassow and David G. Roskies

Volume 10: Late Twentieth Century, 1973–2005, edited by Deborah Dash Moore and Nurith Gertz

The Posen Foundation's mission is rooted in the belief that Jewish education can make a meaningful difference in Jewish life, and should be available to all who are interested. To this end, the Foundation works internationally to promote Jewish learning, support academic research into Jewish history and culture, and encourage participation in Jewish cultural life.

The Posen Library of Jewish Culture and Civilization

Deborah Dash Moore, *Editor in Chief*

VOLUME 9: CATASTROPHE AND REBIRTH, 1939–1973

Samuel D. Kassow and David G. Roskies, *Editors*

Yale UNIVERSITY PRESS   New Haven and London

The Posen Foundation   Lucerne

Yale University Press books may be purchased in quantity
for educational, business, or promotional use. For
information, please e-mail sales.press@yale.edu (U.S.
office) or sales@yaleup.co.uk (U.K. office).

Designed by George Whipple Design for Westchester
Publishing Services.
Set in Bulmer MT type by Newgen.
Printed in the United States of America.

Library of Congress Control Number: 2011043318
ISBN 978-0-300-18853-0 (hardcover)

A catalogue record for this book is available from the
British Library.

This paper meets the requirements of ANSI/NISO
z39.48-1992 (Permanence of Paper).

10 9 8 7 6 5 4 3 2 1

Contents

ISRAEL (1946–1973) 215

Introduction 215

ANTHOLOGIES 216

CULTURAL, POLITICAL, AND RELIGIOUS THOUGHT 228

Advisory Boards

Project Staff

The Posen Library of Jewish Culture and Civilization, Volume 9

Editor in Chief	Deborah Dash Moore
Founding Editor	James E. Young
Volume Editors	Samuel D. Kassow
	David G. Roskies
Executive Editor	Joyce Rappaport
Managing Editor	Rachel Weinstein
Senior Editors	Alison Joseph
	Maud Kozodoy
Senior Researchers	Avery Robinson
	Miriam Rudavsky Bourgeois
	Henry Rosen
Editorial and Operations Assistant	
Manuscript Coordinator	Marsha Lustigman
Text Permissions Manager	Melissa Flamson
Art Permissions Manager	Elisa Frohlich Gallagher

Posen Foundation

President and Founder	Felix Posen
Managing Director	Daniel Posen

Yale University Press

Executive Editor	Sarah Miller
Commissioning Editor	Jonathan Brent
Managing Editor	Ann-Marie Imbornoni
Editorial Assistant	Ashley E. Lago
Production Controller	Maureen Noonan
Project Management, Newgen North America	Charlie Clark

Acknowledgments

This volume of The Posen Library took almost as many years to assemble as the time span it covers. It took so long because the years 1939–1973 were so rich and eventful that they needed to be approached in smaller segments. The first seven years alone were to become a separate unit. To accomplish so daunting a task, moreover, its two volume editors assembled a band of dedicated scholars whose numbers kept growing. Our nine-person Advisory Board met for the first time in London in the summer of 2004, immediately after the formal launch of The Posen Library at a meeting of its General Advisory Board (fondly known as the Sanhedrin) and all its volume editors. Present at our smaller gathering to begin work on the first five-year segment, the years 1939–1943, were Michael Brenner, Samuel Kassow, Michael Krutikov, Eli Lederhendler, David Roskies, Haim Saadoun, Sasson Somekh, and Hana Wirth-Nesher. Avner Holtzman, responsible for Hebrew literature and culture, was unable to attend. Also present, by special request, was Felix Posen. Felix was eager to see how this handpicked group of experts would go about turning his dream into reality, all the more so because his formative years coincided with the time span of this volume. The volume was ours to shape as we saw fit, but knowing that Felix was squarely behind us would prove instrumental to bringing our collaborative effort to completion.

Until 2009, the Volume Editorial Board met at regular intervals, usually in Tel Aviv at the home of Hana Wirth-Nesher. Her hospitality, generosity, and grace will be fondly remembered by all. With the addition of Yaron Tsur to our ranks, and with some other personnel changes, the Board eventually assumed its present shape. Among its many virtues, this volume bears eloquent testimony to the mutual respect, profound commitment, and camaraderie among its editors.

Yet as work progressed, even a group of such diverse talents was unequal to the task. How fortunate we were to be joined via internet by these specialists in their respective fields: Susan Chevlowe, Nina Lichtenstein, James Loeffler, and Alejandro Meter.

Assembling the materials was a two-tiered process. First came the heady experience of gathering, organizing, and conceptualizing. Then came the enervating task of actually locating, photocopying, scanning, editing, and annotating each and every selection. None of us realized, and no one warned us, how difficult it would be to limit each selection to roughly one thousand words. It was one thing to excerpt a lyric poem; quite another to select one thousand words from a novel or play, and most difficult of all, from a tightly argued essay or well-crafted short story. And so the unsung heroes and heroines of this volume are our team of senior researchers Rita Abramov, Ofer Dynes, Stephanie Ginensky, Stefanie Halpern, and Gosha Zaremba, and junior researchers Max Daniel and Haley Wodenshek. Only after their work was complete did our team of superb translators set to work: Michele McKay Aynesworth, Karen Alkalay-Gut, Solon Beinfeld, David E. Cohen, Jeffrey M. Green, Ofir Haim, David Herman, Alexandra Hoffman, Annie Kantar, Tsipi Keller, Susanne Klingenstein, Madeline Levine, Marvin Meital, and Menahem Rotstein. If selecting and translating was difficult, writing short and accurate biographies was no less daunting. This was ably done by Rachel Alkallay, Michele McKay Aynesworth, Amanda Burstein, Maia Evrona, Alyssa Hauer, Magdalene Klassen, Diana L. Linden, Marsha Lustigman, Yosef Robinson, Sebastian Schulman, Jesse Tisch, Logan Wall, and Rebecca Wolpe. Watching over and spot-checking all their work was the discerning eye of Maud Kozodoy, aided by Avery Robinson and Henry Rosen.

Next come those who worked behind the scenes from beginning to end. Marsha Lustigman served as manuscript coordinator, no small task in a manuscript of this complexity. Melissa Flamson and her team at With Permission tracked down the copyright holders for the many texts in this volume, and Elisa Frohlich Gallagher served as art permissions manager. The monthly missives from Melissa sometimes had the flavor of a detective thriller. And when despite all her efforts permission was denied, her wise counsel helped us find an adequate replacement.

We owe a very special and heartfelt thanks to Rachel Weinstein. Just as we despaired of ever completing the project, Rachel was brought on. Her enthusiasm, her willingness to help us surmount every problem, her organizational brilliance, her tenacity and good cheer, not to speak of her knowledge of photography, kept us going through those last crucial stages. Her joy was ours and our joy was hers.

Joyce Rappaport had the unenviable task of coordinating every aspect of the volume—assigning translations and biographies, editing and coordinating the styles of dozens of different contributors, and editing and polishing the manuscript into a coherent whole. Her skill and devotion, her patience and gentle prodding, are evident on every page.

Deborah Dash Moore has been an energetic and responsive editor in chief of The Posen Library. Her wise counsel and detailed comments serve as a model for how this work is done.

And so, to the editorial staff of The Posen Library and to this incomparable group of colleagues, researchers, writers, and translators who worked with tireless and painstaking effort over so many years we say, *Ḥazak, ḥazak venitḥazek.*

Samuel D. Kassow, West Hartford, Connecticut
David G. Roskies, New York, New York

Introduction to The Posen Library of Jewish Culture and Civilization

Deborah Dash Moore and James E. Young

In 2003 Felix Posen had an audacious idea and the wherewithal to explore it. Born in Berlin, he subsequently abandoned the religious strictures of his youth in the face of the evil of the Holocaust. Then, in his fifties, he decided to learn about the antisemitism that had threatened his life. He began to read about it. "I learned; I listened; I attended lectures," he recalled. "I had the good fortune of befriending one of the world's greatest experts, Yehuda Bauer, who also happened to be the head of something I had never heard of—an Israeli movement in secular Judaism." Those years of reading and learning and that particular encounter ultimately prompted Felix Posen to convene a conference of prominent Jewish scholars and intellectuals. Having prospered in business, he possessed the wherewithal to establish the Posen Foundation to further Jewish education. Thus Felix Posen began a new life in philanthropy. He was able to underwrite not only a conference but also an ambitious project that imagined anchoring Jewish unity in the very multiplicity of the Jewish past. "Each generation must struggle to make sense of its legacy," he reflected. Out of that initial conference emerged a vision of an anthology of Jewish culture and civilization, one that would make more apparent Judaism's immense diversity over the centuries, extending far beyond the parameters of religious orthodoxy. In short, he came to share an understanding of Judaism articulated by the influential biblical scholar Israel Friedländer. In 1907 Friedländer, a recent immigrant to New York City, had observed that American Jews possessed the opportunity to return to Judaism's "original function as a culture, as the expression of the Jewish spirit and of the whole life of the Jews."

The idea of an anthology implicitly drew upon a long and rich Jewish history dating back to the Bible itself, the most influential of Jewish anthologies, and including many classic Jewish texts, such as Mishnah and Talmud, as well as the prayer book. Anthologizing can be seen as a quintessential Jewish practice because of the ways it extends Jewish conversations backward and forward in time. Backward, because anthologizers must read and judge Jewish texts from previous eras, selecting some, rejecting others. And forward, because anthologizers seek to create new understandings that will shape the Jewish future, contributing to an ongoing dialogue. David Stern, editor of

The Anthology in Jewish Literature, argues that the anthology is a ubiquitous presence in Jewish literature—arguably its oldest literary genre. Jewish literature reflects what Stern calls an "anthological habit," that is, a tendency to gather together "discrete and sometimes conflicting stories or traditions." David Roskies dubs this Jewish predilection "the anthological imagination." *The Posen Library of Jewish Culture and Civilization* partakes of both "habit" and "imagination," with the latter often transforming the former. Unlike some past Jewish anthologies, The Posen Library makes no effort to weave together its varied components into a teleological whole.

During the Jewish Middle Ages, anthologies became primary mediums for recording stories, poems, and interpretations of classical texts. They also preserved and transmitted textual traditions across generations. For example, every year at Passover when Jews sat down to conduct a seder, they read from the Haggadah. This Jewish creation is a wonderful anthology that has been continually reinvented—illustrated, translated, modified—to reach new generations.

Yet even as *The Posen Library of Jewish Culture and Civilization* shares in a long and venerable anthological tradition, it also participates in its own moment in time. It is a product of the twenty-first century and the flowering of secular academic Jewish studies in Israel, the United States, and around the world. Its approach to Jewish culture and civilization reflects a new appreciation of Jewish diversity that, for example, embraces women alongside men. Unlike most previous Jewish anthologies, The Posen Library recognizes that both women and men created Jewish culture, although the contributions of women have largely been unacknowledged. The Posen Library's distinguished editorial board reflects contemporary Jewish diversity and includes many of this generation's leading scholars and thinkers in Jewish culture: Michel Abitbol, Robert Alter, Yehuda Bauer, Menachem Brinker (z"l), Rachel Elior, Moshe Halbertal, Paula E. Hyman (z"l), Yosef Kaplan, Sara Japhet, Nadav Na'aman, Fania Oz-Salzberger, Antony Polonsky, Jonathan D. Sarna, Anita Shapira, A. B. Yehoshua, and Steven J. Zipperstein. Together with Felix Posen, this eminent editorial board invited James E. Young to serve as editor in chief of an ambitious anthology project dedicated to the collection of primary texts, documents, images, and artifacts constituting Jewish culture and civilization, from ancient times to the present.

In consultation with the editorial board, James Young prepared a working project outline and précis and appointed individual volume editors with special expertise in particular eras. The précis articulated three important criteria:

1. to gather into a single, usable collection all that the current generation of scholars agrees best represents Jewish culture and civilization in its historical and global entirety;
2. to establish an inclusive and pluralistic definition of Jewish culture and civilization in all of its rich diversity, an evolving amalgam of religious and secular experience;
3. to provide a working anthological legacy by which new generations will come to recover, know, and organize past, present, and future Jewish cultures and civilizations.

While this mandate appeared broad and compelling, the actual task of fulfilling it proved daunting. Gradually, the passing years revealed the immensity of *The Posen Library of Jewish Culture and*

Civilization, involving enormous challenges to find, select, translate, organize, conceptualize, and introduce artifacts and documents that constituted Jewish culture over the ages. The tasks produced changes in leadership. In 2016 James Young assumed the position of founding editor in chief, having launched The Posen Library, and Deborah Dash Moore accepted the responsibilities of editor in chief. Current editors of the ten volumes of *The Posen Library of Jewish Culture and Civilization* are: Jeffrey H. Tigay and Adele Berlin (Volume 1); Seth Schwartz (founding editor), Carol Bakhos (Volume 2); Menahem Ben-Sasson (founding editor), Ora Limor and Israel Jacob Yuval (founding coeditors), Arnold E. Franklin (Volume 3); Ora Limor and Israel Jacob Yuval (founding coeditors), Yaacov Deutsch (past coeditor), Jonathan S. Ray (Volume 4); Yosef Kaplan (Volume 5); Elisheva Carlebach (Volume 6); Eli Lederhendler (founding editor), Israel Bartal and Kenneth B. Moss (Volume 7); Todd M. Endelman and Zvi Gitelman (Volume 8); Samuel D. Kassow and David G. Roskies (Volume 9); and Deborah Dash Moore and Nurith Gertz (Volume 10). These volume editors invited specialists from across diverse genres and geographies in varied disciplines and eras to serve as members of their respective volumes' advisory boards. This collective of some 150 of the world's leading scholars of Jewish culture continues to cull examples of expressions of Jewish culture and civilization from around the world, from antiquity to the twenty-first century.

It is with great pleasure on behalf of all who are assembling *The Posen Library of Jewish Culture and Civilization* to present the fourth published volume of this massive anthology, *Catastrophe and Rebirth, 1939–1973,* coedited by Samuel D. Kassow and David G. Roskies. Volume 9 joins Volume 10, Volume 6, and Volume 8 as the fourth of ten volumes comprising *The Posen Library of Jewish Culture and Civilization* to be published with Yale University Press.

The job of the anthologizer is far from easy. Not only does it involve sifting through many potential historical, philosophical, religious, legal, literary, exegetical, political, folkloristic, popular, and artistic documents, images, and artifacts that might be chosen and extracted. It also requires conceptualizing key themes that characterize each period under consideration. And that process introduces questions about the production of Jewish culture and civilization. Is Jewish culture global, or is it an aggregate of many local Jewish cultures, each of them formed and defined in the interaction between Jewish and surrounding non-Jewish cultures? Are there essential Jewish qualities to Jewish culture or is Jewish culture itself a dialectic between "adaptation and resistance to surrounding non-Jewish cultures," as David Biale has suggested in his *Cultures of the Jews?* Or should Jewish culture be regarded as something that is produced mostly in relationship to itself, its own traditions and texts, as David G. Roskies argued in his review of Biale's volume of essays?

Each volume editor has proffered somewhat different answers to those questions. Some have stressed the experience of Judaism as a minority culture in constant contact and occasional conflict with majority civilizations. Others have emphasized the remarkable internal dynamic of Jewish creativity, responding to developments across time and space. Still others have noted the importance of geography and related political structures, dividing Jews from each other and fostering rather separate and even insular modes of cultural creativity. Historically, any number of distinctive and parallel Jewish civilizations have flourished, some sharing cultural practices and traditions, some with little in common beyond core religious laws and beliefs. Working answers to such fundamental questions as "what is Jewish culture and civilization" are embedded in the multitude of entries selected by individual volume editors and their expert advisory boards. Each volume's extracts allow a reader to savor a myriad of juxtapositions of materials that often illuminate the familiar through the unfamiliar, or, conversely, introduce what is new and unexpected by placing it in conversation with what is well known. Insofar as any culture is itself a composite of multiple peoples, nations, languages, traditions, and beliefs, The Posen Library's volume editors have emphasized the heterogeneity of Jewish culture and civilization.

The Posen Library builds upon the efflorescence of university-based Jewish scholarship of the twentieth century, especially in Israel and the United States. It is heir to debates on the meanings of Jewish culture and Jewish civilization. In the United States, those debates often pictured culture as gendered female and civilization as masculine. Thus civilization evoked machines, work, politics, and technology often associated with cities. Culture suggested nonutilitarian activities, such as the arts, personal refinement, formal higher education, and religion. Nations produced civilizations; peoples nourished cultures. The fact that the title of The Posen Library references both culture and civilization indicates a critical openness to aspects of this binary formulation. It implicitly reflects a consciousness that Jews often had to struggle to gain recognition from others that they possessed a civilization. And it envisions a measure of reciprocity. The Posen anthology project aims for inclusivity and pluralism—"culture" understood both in its anthropological and literary senses, referring to products of everyday life as well as to religious and elite artistic and philosophical work. The inclusion of "civilization" refers to an interest in political, economic, and social dimensions of Jewish life. The Posen Library champions a perspective that is less hierarchical and more egalitarian, one that embraces multiple points of view.

Heterogeneous and pluralist, The Posen Library nonetheless presents Jewish culture and civilization in the English language, the lingua franca of our age. This means that in addition to being an exercise in Jewish anthologizing, it is an exercise in translation. Like anthologizing, translating has a long and distinguished Jewish history as a means of conveying sacred and secular texts to generations unfamiliar with their original source languages. As Anita Norich has observed in *Writing in Tongues*, "The need for translation in Western culture, and among Jews, is commonly traced to the familiar Tower of Babel story, which is to say that it is traced to the human desire to understand and interpret and the hubris implied in that desire." Translation has kept Jewish traditions alive as Jews have acquired new languages in the various parts of the globe where they have lived. In the twelfth century, the great Jewish scholar, Maimonides, in a letter to his translator, Samuel Ibn Tibbon, wrote: "Whoever wishes to translate and purports to render each word literally, and at the same time to adhere slavishly to the order of the word and sentences in the original, will meet with much difficulty. This is not the right method." Rather "the translator should first try to grasp the sense of the subject thoroughly, and then state the theme with perfect clarity in the other language." Creating a Jewish anthology in English means wrestling with the implications of translating Jewish sources into the current world's universal language.

Time, space, and genre are the fundamental organizational units of The Posen Library. These units reflect debates and a measure of consensus that emerged from conferences among the editors.

As much as all members of the editorial board admired the intellectual and interpretive insights into Jewish culture and civilization occasioned by a purely thematic organization of these volumes, most also agreed that consistency across all of the volumes, readability, and proper historicization required subordinating thematic interpretations to broad categories of chronology and genre, while taking into account the significance of the diasporic dispersion of Jews around the globe. As a means of "telling" history, thematic chapter heads are clearly the preferred modus of historian-authors. But as a means of "showing" what exists in its historical time and place, in the immediate context of other works in a given genre (e.g., art, literature, theater, architecture), thematic categories remain inadequate on their own. Such genres as literature, visual and material culture, and intellectual culture provide an immediate context for comprehension and can be found in all of the volumes. The Posen Library aims not to unify or homogenize Jewish culture. Rather, the anthology reflects as closely as possible multiple, even competing manifestations of Jewish culture and civilization as they existed in their own temporal and geographic contexts. It recognizes, for example, that while poetry as a genre exists across all of the many centuries of Jewish civilization, significant differences separate medieval Hebrew poetry from Yiddish poetry.

The volume editors' responsibility here is to research all that has been regarded as representative of Jewish culture over time, even as they may nominate new expressions of Jewish culture. Perhaps a particular editor thinks Soutine or Pissarro made Jewish art, or Kafka wrote Jewish parables, or Heine wrote Jewish poetry, or Freud or the Marx brothers or Al Jolson or any of the hundreds of others added to Jewish culture. However, editors also have to consider what the Jewish cultural worlds of museums, libraries, and other institutional and scholarly arbiters of culture have decided over time in their exhibitions, archives, and anthologies. As the editors of Volume 10 observed, "Jews make culture and make it Jewish in a variety of ways: through language, references, reception, uses." Texts chosen can reflect "a broad understanding of culture, including high and low, elite and popular, folk and mass." Examples can be "chosen as representative, illuminating, unusual, influential, or excellent." Accordingly, volume editors looked closely at how previous anthologizers arrived at their lists of Jewish literature, art, and philosophy in their particular times and places. Volume editors engaged in the anthological task in part by consulting other anthologies. Here is evidence of the anthological imagination at work.

How should the issue of non-Jews' participation and even creation of Jewish culture be answered? This challenging question remained in the hands of the volume editors and their advisory boards. For some members of the advisory board, it was obvious, as Yehuda Bauer insisted, that Jesus' Sermon on the Mount is "so similar to a Jewish text that it is absolutely clear to [him] that this was a Jew speaking to Jews" and would have to be included, even if the original words were subsequently Christianized in the context of their redaction as part of the New Testament and depleted of Jewish meaning. Others, of course, disagreed. Or, consider adaptations that have moved the other way. When Jews employ the products of non-Jewish creativity for Jewish purposes—for example, illuminated Hebrew manuscripts, synagogue architecture, and headstone reliefs—these cultural works take their place as part of Jewish civilization and can be found in The Posen Library.

Thus, The Posen Library presents a model for defining "national culture" as distinct from "nationalist culture." In this approach, a national culture defines itself by its differences and reciprocal exchanges with other cultures, whereas "nationalist culture" portrays itself as sui generis and self-generated. National cultures grow in reciprocal exchanges with others; nationalist cultures partake in a myth of self-containment and self-creation. Unfortunately, we know too well what happens when nations and cultures attempt to purge themselves of all supposedly foreign elements. They become small and sometimes so depleted of inspiration and imagination that they collapse inwardly like hollow shells. By contrast, national cultures continually reinvent and reinvigorate themselves, extending their creativity across new modes of expression. This is especially true of transnational peoples, such as the Jews, whose global movements carried practices and ideas from one context into another. Jewish foodways illustrate this transnational principle very well. Many distinctive foodways originated as borrowings from local practices, modified to accommodate kosher laws, and then carried elsewhere, where they appeared "different" in a new society.

This volume covers a mere thirty-four years, but those years were packed with unparalleled drama, catastrophe, despair, and revival. It is hard to find another handful of decades so full both of Jewish tragedy and triumph. In tackling the complex task of representing Jewish culture and civilization in these years, the editors have drawn specifically upon the power of anthologies to foster Jewish self-understanding. Indeed, to stimulate "critical thinking about the anthology as a genre," each of the sections of this volume begins with excerpts from anthologies published during these years. As the editors note in their introduction, "By telling its story anthologically and by choosing a particular order of telling, Volume 9 captures the tragedy and drama of this extraordinary time period in a completely new way." In fact, reading through the material in the first section of the volume devoted to the years 1939–1945, one uncovers the trauma of the war years unfolding, as it were, in real time. Here is evidence "of how Jews the world over were able to marshal artistic, spiritual, political, pedagogical—indeed, civilizational—resources during the greatest catastrophe that Jews as a people and as individuals have ever faced." The juxtapositions of texts, written during the same awful war years but in different parts of the globe, offer unusually compelling new ways of understanding Jewish resilience and creativity.

The anthologists' task, in this case, is to open a window into an extraordinarily complex time, to allow readers simultaneously to enter multiple, diverse worlds. As coeditors, David Roskies and Samuel Kassow employ the metaphor of eavesdropping, of overhearing conversations among Jews that were taking place in these years. They also extend an invitation to readers to participate in these conversations by contemplating what was written, painted, and produced, and by pondering why some themes and topics were ignored. They consider how Jews took up the task of redefinition after the war ended, and how Jews reimagined what it meant to be Jewish along lines of gender and nation. They also shatter some stereotypes: "that there was little great literature produced in the ghettos of World War II, that serious interest in the Holocaust only began decades after the war, that Yiddish culture vanished after the war." And they offer surprises, including the national reawakening of Soviet Jews.

All of the editors agreed that visual culture constitutes a major part of Jewish culture and civilization and must be included throughout these volumes, in all of its forms. From early synagogue architecture and iconography of ancient texts, to later illuminated manuscripts and Haggadahs, Jewish visual culture in its many forms appears in every volume. It ranges from folk art to costume design and eventually encompasses painting, sculpture, photography, film, installation and performance art, as well as museum and synagogue architecture. In some cases, images may be used to illustrate nonvisual texts; but in most cases, they will be either the actual work (e.g., a painting) itself or images of objects and artifacts being anthologized.

As difficult and complex as it may be to select, extract, and translate every textual entry from its original language into English, or as expensive as it may be to secure the rights to reprint "flat art" images of paintings, sculpture, and architecture, it can also be said that the book form of the volumes itself made the compilation of these literary and visual expressions of culture possible. Unfortunately for The Posen Library, a traditional book excludes motion and sound, and therefore audiovisual works—whether orchestral, theatrical, performative, or cinematic—cannot be heard or seen. Reducing a musical composition to its score, or a theatrical presentation to its written script, or any kind of film performance to still-photos radically transforms these pieces into something they simply are not. As a consequence, The Posen Library represents audiovisual media with what amount to annotated lists of music and titles of film and theater presentations.

What strategic purposes animate this effort to collect in a ten-volume anthology all that this generation deems to constitute Jewish culture and civilization? First, The Posen Library seeks to restore consciousness of the diversity and richness of Jewish culture and civilization across many centuries in many lands. Second, it aims to democratize Jewish knowledge, facilitating readers' encounters with varied texts produced by Jewish thinkers, writers, and artists in dozens of languages around the globe. Third, The Posen Library implicitly demonstrates that, like Jewish national and diasporic culture, other national and diasporic cultures consist of multiple, often competing constituent subcultures. Just as Jews express themselves in, participate in, and engage with cultures around the world, and just as these cultures bear the imprint of Jewish culture and experience, so too do many of these other cultures nourish and shape Jewish culture and civilization. Jewish literature and poetry, religious thought and Talmudic commentaries, and even treatises on what constitutes Jewish culture are written in many of the world's languages—in English, Arabic, French, German, Russian, Spanish, Italian, and Persian—as well as in Hebrew, Yiddish, Ladino, Aramaic, and Judeo-Arabic. Jewish culture and civilization lives in and is shaped by these cultural and linguistic contexts. Finally, The Posen Library offers otherwise disaffected and disengaged Jews opportunities to restore their cultural identifications as Jews. It demonstrates that Jews produced Jewish culture in part through struggles with Jewish identity and tradition, and not only through an embrace of Judaism.

How to Read This Book

Jewish culture and civilization flourishes in many countries, in different languages, and in diverse forms of self-expression. This English-language anthology of primary sources, carefully chosen and edited, attempts to encompass Jewish civilization and culture during the most cataclysmic and transformative period it has ever known: from the eve of World War II to the aftermath of the Yom Kippur War. Holding this vast assemblage of sources together are geography and genre. Our first order of business is to situate the provenance of a given work; hence, the division of this volume into one chronological and four geographical sections. Space is then further divided into a variety of forms, whether anthological or discrete; expository or personal; prosaic, poetic, or dramatic; highbrow or popular; religious or secular; textual or graphic. For convenience's sake, each chapter follows the same generic order, but a full-color insert that covers graphic art and architecture for all the chapters appears near the middle of the volume. Cultural expressions that could not be presented as written text—music and film—are listed at the end of the volume. Entries within a subgenre are organized chronologically; within each year selections are arranged in alphabetical order by author.

This anthology invites four basic kinds of reading. Read sequentially, the anthology tells a story. Chapter 1, focused exclusively on the years 1939–1945, demonstrates the growing awareness of the unfolding catastrophe—the systematic annihilation of all Jews under Nazi occupation—and the worldwide attempt to document and respond to this genocide. The range and expressive power of these sources tell a story that has never been told in this way before. Then, after the defeat of Nazism, the story of the Jews starts over, with the nascent State of Israel and the coming of age of American Jewry as its two bookends.

Read generically, with each genre arranged in chronological order, this volume tells a completely different story. Because so much was lost and abandoned, life writing takes on an urgency and immediacy. The novel, short story, and lyric poem convey precisely the pace of change, accompanied by new anthologies that try to memorialize what is happening, and all this, as Hebrew and English replace Yiddish and German as the dominant languages of Jewish cultural expression.

Read geographically, this anthology covers a period of rapid displacements and dispersions that came about as a result of the Holocaust, Zionism, and globalization. Writers, thinkers, and artists, whether by design or default, moved between different locales; they might write in a language of origin that was not the language of the place where they lived, or, as was the case for so many survivors of the Holocaust, adopt the language of their place of refuge. The geographic divisions of this anthology focus the reader's attention on what it might mean for authors to find themselves categorized as European, American, French, Spanish, or Israeli. Or was every Jewish writer of this period "a kind of survivor"?

But there is also a fourth way of reading this meta-anthology. By picking and choosing among periods, geographies, and forms, the reader (in print or online) will experience the joys of serendipitous synapses and the discovery of fundamental disharmonies.

Selections in this anthology bear the title of the anthologized work, except where it is easier to identify a selection in other ways. Most selections are preceded by a brief biography of the author. Because a number of writers are represented by more than one selection, biographical information appears only the first time a writer is introduced. So, for example, the work of Israeli writer S. Y. Agnon can be found in several genres, but his biography accompanies only his earliest selection, which is in the fiction, drama, and children's literature subsection of the opening chapter. The Index of Authors enables readers to find easily an author's biography and all of the selections by a particular author.

Each selection is followed by the name of the translator (for works not originally written in English). A bibliography of exemplary works by the author appears at the end of each author's first selection, unless no other works are known. Titles of works in the bibliographies are listed in the original language, with English translations provided for well-known works.

Editorial deletions are indicated by bracketed ellipsis points; all other ellipses are included in the original selections. Bracketed ellipses at the beginning or end of a selection indicate that the selection begins or ends in the middle of a paragraph.

Introduction to Volume 9

Samuel D. Kassow and David G. Roskies

The period covered by this volume, 1939 to 1973, is one of the most tragic and dramatic in Jewish history. It saw the Holocaust, the rise of the Jewish state, the end of Eastern Europe and the Arab world as Jewish centers, the radical transformation of French Jewry from a largely Ashkenazi to a predominantly North African community, and the emergence of an American Jewry that enjoyed unprecedented acceptance, rapid social mobility, and a new leadership role on the world Jewish stage. This anthology endeavors to encompass the entirety of Jewish experience in those fateful years and to view it through the multiple lenses of chronology, geography, language, and genre.

Anthologies have long revealed how different Jewish communities responded creatively to cultural challenges and the anxieties of self-definition. From the Bible and Talmud to the prayer book and Passover Haggadah, from the modern *The Book of Legends/Sefer Ha-Aggadah* to *The Jewish Catalog: A Do-It-Yourself Kit*, anthologies have played a critical role in Jewish culture. They introduced new ideas, undermined old paradigms, and facilitated diversity and dissent.[1] In a period far shorter than a thousand years, world Jewry was transformed spatially, demographically, linguistically, politically— in every way imaginable. Anthologies are our first window into these sweeping changes.

Within the Jewish anthological library, *The Posen Library of Jewish Culture and Civilization*, based on principles of inclusivity, equality, and polyphony, occupies a unique place. Our mandate was to be all-inclusive, to cast our net as wide as possible, to embrace all forms and modes of Jewish self-expression, everywhere.

The way an anthology makes sense of the past determines in large measure how it sees the future. The biblical book of Proverbs (see Volume 1) is a collection of ancient wisdom literature, the province of the priestly class, who found the perfect venue to teach future generations about wisdom, virtue, and the world order. The ancient mystics had a completely different way of anthologizing their visions of the end time and the world to come. Their genre of choice of was pseudepigrapha, ascribing authorship to spiritual personalities long since dead (Volumes 2 and 3). The greatest such compendium was the thirteenth-century Zohar, starring Shimon bar Yoḥai, a rabbi of the second century, and his entourage (Volume 4). Then came the invention of printing; eventually no Jewish home would be complete without such essential anthologies as the weekday and festival prayer books, the Passover Haggadah, and various compendia of aggadic material from the Talmud, like the Hebrew ʿEyn Yaʿakov (1516) and the Yiddish Mayse-bukh (1602) (Volume 5). Most popular were biographical legends of the rabbis, their wives, and their livestock, updated to include the foundational figures of medieval Jewry, like Maimonides and Judah the Pietist.

The Posen Library is a twenty-first-century link in that unbroken chain of Jewish creativity. To renew this link, to underscore the importance of anthologies in fostering Jewish self-understanding and debate in changing times and shifting landscapes, and to stimulate critical thinking about the anthology as a genre, each chapter of the present volume begins with a selection of anthologies. To our mind, an anthology is worth a thousand books.

By telling its story anthologically and by choosing a particular order of telling, this volume captures the tragedy and drama of this extraordinary time period in a completely new way. The years from 1939 to 1945 are accorded their own timeline. This is based on a new understanding of the war years, of how Jews the world over were able to marshal artistic, spiritual, political, pedagogical—indeed, civilizational—resources during the greatest catastrophe that Jews as a people and as individuals have ever faced. Because the war years are presented here as a thing apart, the reader will discover cultural synapses never before recorded.

The selections in this anthology encourage readers to eavesdrop on many conversations that took place across the Jewish world or, conversely, to ask why certain conversations did not happen. Sometimes new ideas, songs, poems, or stories found ready resonance throughout the Jewish world, but often they remained local and obscure. Sometimes communities interacted with each other in totally unexpected ways. The Soviet Jewry movement, for example, drew its energy not only from Soviet Jews but also from an awakening of Holocaust memory—and guilt—in American Jewry.

This comprehensive anthology will challenge readers to see how Jews, as communities and as individuals, redefined themselves in the face of destruction and national rebirth in a turbulent period marked by the interplay of danger and opportunity. How did they try to replace what was lost? How did the new Jewish state affect them? How did Jews adapt to the challenges of the postwar world: linguistic shifts, the Cold War, unparalleled prosperity, the move away from old immigrant enclaves, and the betrayal of a communist left in which so many Jews had believed?

A process of redefinition and adaptation embraced novel ideas of space and time, gender, and nation. Unprecedented ways of confronting displacement became more prominent. One prime example is novels and poems about extended families, translating collective identity into personal histories. This anthology challenges readers to rethink some mistaken stereotypes: that there was little great literature produced in the ghettos of World War II, that serious interest in the Holocaust began only decades after the war, that Yiddish culture vanished after the war. It also reveals the remarkable and quite rapid transformation of Israeli culture as it struggled to resolve many critical issues, such as mass immigration and the quest for distinctive national forms of music and art. Finally, there will be surprises. Who, in 1953, for instance, would have predicted the national awakening of Soviet Jewry?

During these years, diverse Jewish communities faced their own individual challenges, but two previously unimagined issues confronted world Jewry and every individual Jew: the meaning and memory of the Holocaust and the safety of the Jewish state. No matter where Jews lived or what their politics were, no matter what languages they spoke, those two key issues, more than any other, demanded some kind of response.

In his 1943 anthology *Memoirs of My People through a Thousand Years*, Leo W. Schwarz, a master of this genre, declared that to get his readers to feel the "hot burning heart of the Jewish people," personal anecdotes, individual stories, and flashes of humor were just as significant as massive histories or intellectual tomes. Schwarz's point is well taken. While this Volume 9 of The Posen Library includes a wide selection of scholarly writing and essays, it also contains gripping individual stories, collections of humor, and life writing. And like Schwarz, the editors of this anthology believe that, despite all the obvious caveats, one can nonetheless speak about a "Jewish people."

Of course, what makes a book or work of art Jewish continues to provoke endless discussion.[2] Is there such a thing as Jewish culture? Some scholars say yes, others no. Ruth R. Wisse has examined the "Jewish canon," Geoffrey Hartman the "Jewish imagination," and Barukh Kurzweil and Dov Sadan have made the assumption of an integral Jewish culture the touchstone of their literary criticism. In contrast, the eminent Israeli literary critic Dan Miron has asserted that "one of the inherent and most significant characteristics of Jewish history in modern times is that it produced not one Jewish culture but many variants of *possible* Jewish cultures or sub-cultures" (emphasis added).

As readers wrestle with the questions posed by Miron, Wisse, and others, they may well find that this anthology will stimulate insights and discussion and help them reach their own conclusions. In doing so, they will have to consider the role of language, the presence or absence of Jewish content, the self-definition of the author or artist, the role of shared memories, and the impact of many different non-Jewish cultures.

Furthermore, the disproportionate Jewish presence in certain genres and certain fields—photography, film, and musicals, for instance—also demands attention, even in the absence of explicitly Jewish content. Photography attracted many Jews because they could get a start in it with little money and faced fewer social hurdles. But it also accommodated, as few other arts did, the leftist passions of second-generation American Jews who brought with them their love of the camera and their fascination with the rhythms and unconscious choreography of the urban scene. The urban photography of Helen Levitt, Rebecca Lepkoff, and Weegee (Arthur Fellig) captured images of city life that were not in and of themselves "Jewish" but that reflected a particular perspective on the drama of the streets and the sidewalks that many of these children of Yiddish-speaking immigrants intuitively grasped.

No one will deny that an Agnon story written in Hebrew about a Jewish shtetl is "Jewish." But what about Leonard Bernstein's *West Side Story* or Rodgers and Hammerstein's *Oklahoma*? Again, neither addresses explicitly Jewish themes. Yet they are included here not only because they highlight the Jewish impact on the quintessentially American genre of the Broadway musical but also because they address issues of human dignity and the dangers of group conflict that have had a particular resonance for Jews. In short, the selections of this anthology span a continuum whose very ambiguity encompasses a critical aspect of the modern Jewish experience. To try to define what is Jewish is itself very Jewish.

One of the first anthologies presented in this volume, *Payn un gvure* (*Suffering and Heroism*), appeared in 1940 in Nazi-occupied Warsaw; the last, *The Jewish Catalog*, was published in the United States in 1973. The first, edited by Eliyohu Gutkowski and Antek Zuckerman, reflected wartime dystopia; the second, individual opportunities that Jews encountered in a changing America. These serve as bookends to a selection of anthologies that underscore the enormous range of Jewish experiences in these years, from catastrophe to renewal. The first anthology stressed the Jewish collective and its history; the last, the wide range of choices available to Jews as individuals.

Great differences separate the two anthologies. But they also share two things. First, they were meant to be *Jewish* anthologies, culling the vast Jewish bookshelf, mining a rich cultural legacy to help meet the challenges of the present. And second, just as the *Catalog* rejected "prefabricated" Judaism, so too did Gutkowski and Zuckerman represent a secular Zionism that had turned its back on the "prefabricated tradition" of Jewish orthodoxy.

Volume 9 of The Posen Library will also help readers navigate the profound linguistic shifts that marked Jewish culture in these years. English and Hebrew, and to a lesser degree French and Spanish, became the major languages of the Jewish world. Jewish culture in Arabic, German, and Polish declined, while, toward the end of this period, Russian slowly began to reemerge. The Ladino-speaking heartland of Salonika and the Balkans was decimated.

The great transnational Yiddish-speaking diaspora that had ranged from Warsaw to New York, from Cape Town to Buenos Aires—Yiddishland—lived on after the Holocaust, but on borrowed time and in vastly changed circumstances. The vast demographic reservoir of Jewish Eastern Europe that had replenished and nurtured Yiddishland was gone. Intense prewar debates between diaspora nationalists and Zionists, between Yiddishists and Hebraists, largely disappeared. More Jews had spoken Yiddish for a longer time than any other language in Jewish history. This was now over.

Yet paradoxically these years witnessed a second golden age of Yiddish culture.[3] Powerful poetry, incisive reportage, moving diaries, ghetto songs—all highlight the ongoing vitality of Yiddish culture under Nazi occupation. After the war, Yiddish writers and poets wrote some of their finest works. Yiddish was the language of the displaced persons camps and of communal Holocaust memory. Until the 1960s it was *the* major language of serious Holocaust scholarship, a fact that remained largely unknown to outsiders. In Buenos Aires, Argentina, Mark Turkow launched the series *Dos poylishe yidntum*, one of the most extraordinary publishing projects in modern Jewish history, a 175-book collection of memoirs, fiction, history, and poetry dedicated to preserving the memory of Polish Jewry. Yiddish schools endured, especially in Canada and Latin America. In Israel, the poet Abraham Sutzkever published the finest Yiddish literary journal in the world, *Di goldene keyt* (The Golden Chain). Yes, Yiddish definitely lived on. But few believed that it had a future. From a living Jewish language, it became, to an increasing extent, *loshn-hakdoyshim*, the language of the martyrs.

The destruction of the Yiddish-speaking heartland of Eastern Europe, at a time when very few Jews spoke Hebrew, meant that much Jewish culture in this period would be created in non-Jewish languages. Indeed, the creation in other languages of a Jewish idiom that is not merely comical ranks among the greatest achievements of this period. This anthology includes many examples of this new Jewish idiom (or to use David Roskies's term, *Jewspeak*), from the stories and novels of Bernard Malamud and Patrick Modiano to the poetry of Allen Ginsberg.

Novelist Saul Bellow alluded to this elusive but important Jewish literature in non-Jewish languages in his 1963 anthology *Great Jewish Short Stories*, when he recalled a lighthearted but significant argument he had had with the Israeli novelist S. Y. Agnon. Agnon warned him that only writings in Hebrew were "safe." But Bellow parried that one could also write in Russian or English and still be a Jewish writer. And what exactly was Jewish anyway, Bellow asked? Neither writer convinced the other. Both would win the Nobel Prize in Literature, a sure sign that Jewish writers were gaining legitimacy and respect.

In the course of this journey through the geographic centers of the Jewish world, readers will also encounter different forms of Jewish space: real, imagined, and remembered. In addition to Yiddishland, the anthology takes readers into the shtetls of Eastern Europe, the mellahs or Jewish sections of North African cities, the ghettos in Nazi-occupied Europe, the displaced persons camps of Germany and Austria, the *ma'abarot* or transit camps in Israel, and the old Jewish neighborhoods of New York, Paris, Salonika, and Baghdad.

New Jewish spaces also reflected far-reaching economic changes that especially affected communities in North America and Western Europe. In the postwar years, prosperity replaced economic depression, and millions of Jews in the Americas, Western Europe, Latin America, Australia, and South Africa moved into the middle class. At the same time, formerly prosperous communities, such as the many once well-to-do Jews of Aleppo and Baghdad, found themselves struggling to gain a new foothold in Israel.

In the United States, Jews moved to the suburbs and created new institutions—Jewish community centers and synagogues—that reflected a transition from immigrant ethnicity to a more comfortable Americanism expressed through outward religious observance and vicarious Zionism. In these postwar years, synagogue architecture and new Jewish community centers became a salient form of American Jewish expression and self-confidence even as they reflected the changing needs of Jews on the suburban frontier. One striking example was the new Congregation B'nai Israel in Millburn, New Jersey, where Percival Goodman joined forces with Robert Motherwell, Adolph Gottlieb, and Herbert Ferber to bring together architecture, design, and sculpture in a new affirmation of faith in an American Jewish future.

Jewish geography now included, for the first time, sovereign space: places like Jerusalem, Masada, Tel Aviv, the kibbutz, and the Negev acquired a new resonance as symbols of the Jewish past, of Jewish heroism, of a pioneering future, of an exciting and lively all-Jewish city. This sovereign space included innovative memorials to the war dead, the Israel Museum, built to symbolize the continuity of Jewish presence in the Land of Israel, and Yad Vashem, to remember the victims of the Holocaust, as well as the Knesset, the symbol of Jewish statehood.

By the early 1960s, another form of Jewish space slowly began to emerge: a "Europe" with its own distinct Jewish identity, neither American nor Israeli, committed to a Jewish future that transcended past betrayals and disappointments. In a 1971 symposium, one participant wrote that, for the first time, "one could think of European Judaism as one entity, and . . . consider that all the Jewries of Europe could be united by a new idea and by a new creation."[4] That search for a new European Jewish identity also rekindled a determination to retrieve and protect the legacy of German Jewry, such as the founding of the Leo Baeck Institute in New York, London, and Jerusalem.[5]

Clearly, in the postwar era, apart from the Holocaust, Jews worldwide would share no one "usable past." While the retrieval of the lost legacy of German Jewry became an important priority for certain historians and religious thinkers, especially in the United Kingdom and Europe, many American Jews would turn toward an idealized image of an East European Jewish past, whereas Israel would craft a vision of the Jewish past based on a Zionist narrative of a parlous diaspora existence ultimately redeemed by a return to the homeland.

In the wake of the destruction of East European Jewry and the uprooting of Arab Jewry to Europe and Israel, older terms such as *Ashkenaz* and *Levant* acquired new meanings. On one level, they connoted lost worlds that still somehow lived on, cultural universes that spanned national boundaries and drew energy from a paradoxical interplay of Jewish inwardness and ongoing engagement with the non-Jewish world. In this volume, scholars, authors, and philosophers respond to the destruction of European Jewry with evocative descriptions of the spiritual, social, and linguistic moorings of an Ashkenaz whose legacy demanded remembrance and study. In the United States, this evocation of collective memory and covenantal space encouraged a recasting of the idea of place in American Jewish identity, the growing fascination with the Lower East Side being a prime example.

In a similar gesture, others reacted to the demise of Arab Jewish culture by proudly turning what had been a pejorative term, *the Levant*, into a badge of honor. Levantine identity—poised between East and West, between Arabic, French, Hebrew, Spanish, Italian, and English—was marked by hybridity and the fluidity of cultural boundaries. To embrace it constituted an act of both self-assertion and resistance. It reflected pride in one's heritage and resistance to the attempts of European Jews in Israel to demonstrate their superiority and to impose cultural hegemony. Other Jews uprooted from the Arab lands describe a complicated search for identity as they navigate the shifting valence of "French," "Arab," and "Jewish," and experience serial disappointments in abstract humanism, European liberalism, and an Arab nationalism that promised but failed to include Arabic-speaking Jews.

Why are geography and history so important in this volume? During the years of the Holocaust, geography literally meant the difference between life and death, while after the war, Jews in different parts of the world fashioned diverse cultures even as they shared common concerns. In the postwar Jewish world, the pace of cultural cross-fertilization was quite uneven, greater in scholarship than in fiction, in religious thought than in poetry or life writing. But this volume aims to makes a pan-Jewish conversation across all genres possible for the first time and in real time.

This anthology traces the development of these parallel Jewish cultures and encourages readers to notice similarities, explore differences, and discover why seeds planted in one particular time and place sometimes sprouted years later in totally surprising ways. For example, for decades much of the extraordinary cultural creativity of the ghettos in Nazi-occupied Europe was largely ignored outside the narrow circles of Yiddishland, resurfacing only many years later. Elie Wiesel's memoir of Auschwitz attracted little notice when it was published in Yiddish in 1956. But two years later, its French version, with less Jewish anger and a more universal pathos, became a publishing sensation.

As genres traveled in time and space, they morphed in unpredictable ways. Popular song played a critical role in shaping a common Israeli identity; behind the Iron Curtain, folk songs remained one of the few forms of allowed Jewish expression. But this genre was less important in the United States or Europe. And as Ziva Amishai Meisels has pointed out, Jewish art rooted in Jewish folk motifs and historical themes really developed in only two places: Israel and Russia.

Some genres traveled through the Jewish world with relative ease. Gershom Scholem's pathbreaking scholarship on Jewish mysticism, Jacob Katz's fresh historical insights into the decline of Jewish traditional society in Europe, and Yehezkel Kaufmann's thesis of the salience of monotheism in Jewish survival all found wide and receptive audiences in translation. Post-Holocaust theology, Hannah Arendt's controversial assertions about the banality of evil and genocide, and the philosopher Abraham Joshua Heschel's explorations of the layers of religious experience and his call for a God-centered theology did not remain confined to time and place. Philosopher Martin Buber's *I and Thou*, first published in German in 1923, was widely read in English translations, reaching new audiences. Scholar Erich Auerbach's *Mimesis* became an instant classic and is studied to this day. Poets in Yiddish and Hebrew, however, had to wait for many decades before they found an audience outside their original languages through translation. Playwrights fared even worse. Hanoch Levin, Israel's greatest political satirist, whose plays were routinely heckled, condemned, and censored, was virtually unknown to non-Hebrew-speaking audiences during his extraordinarily productive but all-too-brief career.

This anthology includes a generous sampling of Jewish humor, a genre that hardly traveled at all. Humor is an invaluable historical artifact, full of cultural and psychological insights. But we let the reader judge whether jokes told in the Warsaw ghetto, Israel, or even the United States are funny outside their particular time and place.

Well into the 1960s, Yiddish was still the language that most easily crossed borders and continents; the new Hebrew culture, though, found little echo outside of Israel. As late as 1960, the leading American Jewish journal, *Commentary*, rejected an article about the great Hebrew writer S. Y. Agnon, who would go on to win a Nobel Prize in Literature, because the editorial board considered him too obscure. In 1963, the American Jewish Congress actually sponsored a symposium on why Israeli and American Jewish writers knew so little about each other's literatures.

Yet shared concerns and interests across the Jewish world were on the rise. The 1961 trial in Israel of Adolf Eichmann, a leading Nazi organizer of the mass murder of Jews, provoked more interest in the Holocaust and its survivors; Hannah Arendt's *Eichmann in Jerusalem* sent shock waves throughout the Jewish world. Israel's Six-Day War in 1967 forced Jews everywhere to confront the existential significance of a Jewish state as well as the relative indifference of many of their non-Jewish friends.

The year 1968 proved another major turning point. The worldwide social and cultural turmoil of the 1960s—antiwar protests, student unrest, the civil rights movement, feminism—had a deep impact, especially on young Jews in Europe and North America whose Jewish identities were challenged as never before by new sensibilities and generational revolt. Most readers might not regard Bob Dylan's "Like a Rolling Stone" as a "Jewish song," but its new voice, provocative and confrontational, evoked the defiance and disorientation that an entire generation was feeling. In the United States, Jews responded in unexpected ways: through a Jewish feminism, the havurah movement, a rethinking of alliances between Jews and blacks, and a reappraisal of Jewish liberalism. In the Soviet Union, the double impact of the Six-Day War and the collapse of any hopes of internal reform that followed the 1968 invasion of Czechoslovakia signaled the first stirrings of revolt and defiance within the third-largest Jewish community in the world.

Fiction and poetry occupy a prominent place in this anthology; this period proved a watershed in Jewish writing, especially in Israel and the United States. For decades, Hebrew literature had played a double role, as a literature that sought equal status among other national literatures and as a surrogate for the entire Zionist project. With the establishment of the State of Israel, Hebrew writers stood at a crossroads. A state could take over many of the functions that had been the burden of Hebrew writers. The previously dominant collective "we" of an older generation of Hebrew writers, who captured the exalted and somber mood of the ferocious struggle for independence, was joined by a quieter "I" of younger writers, who wrote in softer registers and who sought out a realm of private choices and individual sensibilities.

During these years, American Jewish writing came into its own when Jews stopped being regarded as immigrant or provincial writers and joined the American mainstream. Indeed, Jewish critics and writers not only joined that mainstream but also helped to define it, as the "Jew," the emblematic outsider, became the consummate insider endowed with a superior understanding of the complexities of modern life.

Writing on Franz Kafka in 1968, the literary critic Robert Alter argued: "He could envision the ultimate ambiguities of human life in general with a hyperlucidity because he had experienced them in poignant particularity as a Jew. Out of the stuff of a Jewish experience which he himself thought of as marginal, he was able to create fiction at once universal and hauntingly Jewish" (anthologized here).

In a changing society where old elites no longer policed who belonged and who didn't, what had been marginal became a new normal. Jewish writers created characters—Shirley Abramowitz's "loudest voice," Augie March's brash, self-assured Chicago street talk, Portnoy's shocking sexual ruminations, and Herzog's unending stream of letters—who moved to the center of an American literature that included Jewish writers as never before.

Women writers also achieved growing prominence in these years, as did, in the 1960s, an urgent recognition of issues of gender. Many of the voices in this anthology are those of Jewish women:

poets, essayists, novelists, and witnesses. The memoirs of Puah Rakovsky (1942) offer a rare and frank glimpse into the problems faced by independent young women in traditional Jewish society as well as a pointed critique of pervasive sexism in Zionist Palestine. Hebrew-language writing by women reflected a multifaceted literary exploration of the inner world of women, of their efforts to adapt to, or rebel against, a male-dominated society. In postwar America, Jewish feminism found its voice.

In a period of destruction and rebirth, and of the forced uprooting of entire Jewish communities, it was life writing and reportage that conveyed both the immediacy of individual experience and of the myriad ways that Jews as individuals understood and acted out their Jewish identity, remembered their own Jewish stories, and embraced or rejected their Jewishness. It was during this period, therefore, that this genre became especially salient. Life writing and reportage did not have to be consistent or coherent. It could be fragmented, contradictory, inchoate, privileging subjective feelings. The very language in which it was written—Yiddish, Hebrew, French, Arabic—often signaled how these authors defined themselves and the kind of audience they hoped to reach. Life writing appeared in different forms, such as diaries that recorded feelings in real time or memoirs that ordered lived experience through retrospective narrative. And life writing, more than any other genre, highlights one of the most important themes of the modern Jewish experience: the memory of place and the bonds of family. In life writing, uprooted and scattered Jews recall their roots and take refuge in family ties that often spanned many continents.

As a genre, life writing is especially important in times and places marked by danger and uncertainty, such as Nazi-occupied Europe or in an Israel facing constant conflict. Behind the Iron Curtain, Jewish writers found fewer barriers to publication when they wrote in this genre, and they seized opportunities to insert themes that eluded the censor's attention. Reportage, a genre connected to the rise of the mass press, was especially important in the ghettos and in Israel, as it explained, decoded, and described the microcosms of communities experiencing massive displacement and disorientation.

Life writing and reportage conveyed a whole gamut of emotions and experience. This anthology takes the reader into the ghettos of Eastern Europe, into solitary hiding places, and even into the gas chambers of Birkenau. Holocaust survivors like Primo Levi and Elie Wiesel wrote memoirs that a generation later would make Auschwitz the major symbol of the Holocaust. Jews uprooted from Arab lands described their ironic sense of displacement in a Jewish state. Native-born Israelis disclosed their ambivalent feelings toward Holocaust survivors. Young Israeli soldiers, raised in the secular leftist ideals of the kibbutzim of the 1940s and 1950s, reflected on their never-ending war with the Arabs and their conflicted feelings about uprooted Palestinians. The children of Yiddish-speaking immigrants to the United States and Britain narrated their journey from ethnic slums to literary fame.

1939–1945

The years from 1939 to 1945, years of catastrophe, underscore an organizing principle of this anthology: geography and language mattered. Texts composed in the lands under Nazi occupation or influence differed dramatically from those written in the "free zone." In Eastern Europe, more than elsewhere, Jews wrote not just as individuals but also as part of a national collective. To a large degree, this reflects the impact of prewar cultural traditions: a highly developed sense of common Jewish identity and an intense ideological engagement. These texts, mostly in Yiddish, underscored such themes as resistance, the moral state of the Jewish people, Jewish attitudes to European culture and Enlightenment traditions in the wake of the Holocaust, the future of the Jewish people after the Holocaust, and finally, religion. Little could match the sheer urgency and intensity of what came out of the ghettos.

Much of the life writing from the ghettos reflected an ongoing tension between knowledge and false hope, the witnessing of destruction and the delusion that perhaps survival might still be possible. In these unique societies—each ghetto being quite different—slang and street songs replaced newspapers; language changed at warp speed. Spontaneously assembled knots of neighbors and passersby listened to songs about murdered spouses and orphaned children, about Judenrat corruption and the struggle to survive, about rich and poor, about the privileged and the dying, about deportations and about hopes for a better future. The writers of diaries and reportage had to find the right words to make the ghetto experience legible, to describe what eluded description, and to decode a world that defied easy understanding. The act of writing was an assertion of one's humanity and served a moral mission; indeed it could, to quote Gustawa Jarecka, a contributor to the secret Ringelblum archive, "cast a stone under history's wheel." Diarists saw their diaries as their most important reason for staying alive. While some diaries were mainly personal, others possessed a collective focus, aimed at documenting ghetto life. This was also true of ghetto photographers and artists like Esther Lurie and Zvi Kadushin in the Kovno ghetto or Mendel Grossman and Henryk Ross in Łódź.

While Jewish writing in the ghettos and camps certainly included calls for resistance and spiritual defiance, it also touched on less heroic topics: anger at other Jews, betrayal, corruption, the destruction of the family, the terrified waiting for the next blow. During the Holocaust, *when* the Jews realized that the Germans intended to kill them was a crucial moment that separated what came before from what came after. Leyb Goldin wrote his naturalistic "Chronicle of a Single Day" for Warsaw's Oyneg Shabes archive in the summer of 1941, when Jews could only guess their future. And Simkhe-Bunem Shayevitsh wrote "Lekh-Lekho" when he still had a daughter to talk to, before the Germans murdered his wife and two children. Ghetto writing, however, and especially its poetry, also marked the remorseless descent toward the abyss.

The diaries and writings of Western European Jews, along with letters, underscore some major differences between Holocaust-era writing in Eastern and Western Europe. Most of the writers from Eastern Europe saw themselves first and foremost as Jews. While some Jews may have written in Polish, and while many certainly loved Polish culture, most did not consider themselves Poles. But in Western Europe, Jewish writers often felt much more integrated and saw no contradiction between being French or Dutch *and* Jewish. All the more brutal, therefore, was the shock of betrayal as French Jewish writers pondered the stark contrast between how they saw themselves and how their origins determined their fate.

Writings such as Paul Ghez's *Six mois sous la botte* (*Six Months under the Boot*) described the fraught experiences of a Tunisian Jewish community leader during the relatively short six-month German occupation, from November 1942 to May 1943. He included the brutality of the labor camps and the collaboration between Arabs and the local French population in their persecution of the Jews.

Outside the world of Yiddish, a major question was not whether to accept European culture—that was a given—but to show how much Jews had helped make it. Across the Atlantic, German Jewish exiles tried to come to terms with the disaster in Europe by explaining the wider historical context for fascism and antisemitism. Antisemitism, they argued, was not just a Jewish problem but a serious threat to any stable democracy.

Another German émigré, Hannah Arendt, asked why legal emancipation made the Jews more rather than less vulnerable. Quoting Franz Kafka in her essay "The Jew as Pariah: A Hidden Tradition," Arendt stressed that "only within the framework of a people can a man live as a man among men."

This anthology also speaks to the fraught question of how Jews in the "free zone" reacted to the Holocaust. A group of young students at the Jewish Theological Seminary angrily accused Jewish leadership of doing much too little. The Bundist leader Artur-Shmuel Ziegelboym killed himself to protest the indifference of the allies to the murder of Polish Jewry. Arthur Koestler noted that decent people in the West paid more attention to the accidental killing of a dog in the street than they did to the Holocaust. And the Lubavitcher Rebbe saw Jewish suffering as heralding the birth pangs of the Messiah.

Responses to the catastrophe varied. Some, like Sofia Dubnova Erlich, Puah Rakovsky, or I. J. Singer turned to life writing to challenge the retrospective glow of false nostalgia while using individual experience to convey a new awareness of the diversity and reality of East European Jewry. Others, like Michael Molho, in his *Traditions and Customs of the Sephardic Jews of Salonica*, focused on the everyday, the material culture, routines of life that reflected the ethos of a rooted and devoted community in a fascinating parallel to the work of the ghetto archives. Still others turned to poetry and prose.

Taking full advantage of a temporary thaw during the war, Soviet Jewish writers reaffirmed their Jewish pride and mourned the Holocaust. Soviet Jewish photographers like Yevgeny Khaldei and Dimitri Baltermants documented not only the struggle of the Red Army but the murder of the Jews. But even in the middle of the wartime thaw, some Soviet Yiddish poets, like Peretz Markish, had uneasy forebodings about the future, expressed in his poem "Shards." In Brazilian exile, the brilliant, assimilated Polish-language poet Julian Tuwim wrote, "We Polish Jews," an unambiguous gesture of solidarity with his murdered people. In the United States, Rabbi Milton Steinberg's *As a Driven Leaf* and Sholem Asch's daring and controversial Yiddish novel *The Nazarene* pushed back against rising antisemitism by returning to the distant past of Roman-occupied Palestine to show Christian indebtedness to Jewish morality and to explain why the allegedly superior Greco-Roman culture ultimately lacked the ethical core that only Judaism could provide.

Israel (1946–1973)

In this volume of The Posen Library, the Jewish people grapples with the challenges and opportunities of political sovereignty for the first time in two millennia. In 1944, at the height of the Holocaust, David Ben-Gurion, future prime minister of Israel, predicted that sovereignty—the experience of statehood—would create a new Jew, Hebrew-speaking and self-affirming, free of diaspora complexes, and able to defend him- or herself without sacrificing moral principles. This faith in *mamlakhtiyut*, literally "stateness," defined Ben-Gurion's political credo. The creative tension between his vision and a more complex reality frames much of this section of the anthology. To a great extent, post-1948 Israeli culture evolved as a dialogue with Ben-Gurion's Zionist narrative and as a challenge thereto.

Few statesmen in Jewish history achieved as much as Ben-Gurion. His vision, his political will, his laserlike focus on the possible rather than the ideal played a decisive role in the founding of the State of Israel in 1948. Overcoming daunting challenges, and largely under Ben-Gurion's leadership, Israel won its war of independence, absorbed one million Jewish immigrants in ten years, and built a polity based, for the most part, on the rule of law.

Despite great difficulties, the young state doggedly created a shared sense of "Israeliness" based on the Hebrew language, a shared determination to defend the country, and the emergence of a vibrant popular culture in which music was especially important. At a time when many Jews had limited knowledge of Hebrew, music—more than literature or poetry—could appeal to both veteran Israelis and new immigrants. The popularity of army song troupes in the 1950s and 1960s and the widespread habit of public singing all encouraged a musical culture loosely known as Shirey Erets Yisrael (Songs of the Land of Israel). Besides universal themes of love and loss, these songs stressed patriotism, love of the land, memory of the war dead, and a deep-seated yearning for peace that belied any worship of militarism.

The selections in this section, however, also show the limits of Ben-Gurion's vision. The state could not take the place of religion, dictate a uniform sense of history, or decree that collective needs take precedence over the individual and the private. Israel did not become the melting pot that Ben-Gurion had envisaged. Tensions festered between immigrants and veterans, between Jews from Europe and Jews from Africa and Asia, between religious and secular Israelis.

The fraught question of religion in the new state surfaced with the May 1948 "Declaration of the Establishment of the State of Israel," which included the ambiguous phrase "Rock of Israel" to please staunch secularists leery of mentioning God. Such deep disagreements explained why the young state deferred the drafting of a written constitution. Another source of tension in the new state derived from deep-seated Zionist contempt for the diaspora. Ben-Gurion saw the establishment of the state as a decisive break with the diaspora and its history; for the first time since the Roman destruction of the Second Temple, Jews had regained their agency and could make their own history. In this spirit of negation of the diaspora, Ben-Gurion urged all army officers to Hebraize their names. Others went even further. In "An Epistle to Hebrew Youth," written in 1943, the poet Yonatan Ratosh appealed to young "Hebrews" to "remove the Jewish cobwebs from their eyes" and become

"Canaanites," linked to the Arab peoples of the Middle East rather than to world Jewry. But other writers, like Ḥaim Hazaz, pointedly reminded Ben-Gurion that the diaspora legacy of tradition and respect for learning had forged the Jewish people. What good would the state be, Hazaz asked, if it caused Jews to forget who they were? "We have ceased to be a nation," Hazaz complained to Ben-Gurion. "We have become a state."

In the early years of sovereignty the cult of the "sabra" loomed especially large. This proud first generation of native-born Hebrew speakers, self-reliant, irreverent, brusque, hardworking, with names like Uzi and Dani, saw itself as the stark opposite of the diaspora Jew. Many were proud members of the Palmach, the elite fighting force of Jewish Palestine. The songs around the campfire, the slang, the tall stories (*chizbatim*), all created a sense of belonging to a special group with a new culture and language. But writers such as Amos Kenan also discerned less attractive sides to the sabra ethos, such as excessive dependence on the group and a corresponding lack of individuality.

The terrible crucible of the War of Independence took a heavy toll on the first sabra generation, poignantly described by such writers as Menahem Shemi. As the new state found its bearings, the memorialization of the fallen played an outsized role in an emerging Israeli culture. Mordechai Ardon's *For the Fallen*, Batia Lichansky's *Holocaust and Rebirth*, and Itzhak Danziger's *War Memorial* were landmarks in Israeli painting and sculpture. This anthology also presents military leader Moshe Dayan's iconic eulogy in memory of Roi Rotberg, a young member of Kibbutz Nahal Oz, who was killed by Arab infiltrators in April 1956. What made this eulogy so significant was Dayan's brilliant evocation of empathy for the Palestinian plight in order to legitimize the Zionist cause and imbue Israelis with a determination to defend the state. Precisely because Arab hatred was so understandable, it was therefore implacable. Jews could not let their guard down, feel guilty about defending their homeland, or give in to tempting delusions about imminent peace. But some young Israeli soldiers who fought in the 1967 Six-Day War, interviewed by Amos Oz, expressed the very doubts and guilt feelings that Dayan had warned against. They gave voice to their forebodings that a more terrible war was on the way. Some worried that victory had only embittered the Arabs while threatening to turn Jews into brutal occupiers.

In time, the challenge of sovereignty forced a reappraisal of many fundamental mainstays of early Israeli culture. The collective ethos of the cult of the sabra, of the old Palmach and of *mamlakhtiyut*, confronted growing demands for privacy and individual space, even as mass immigration turned the veterans of the old Yishuv into a small minority. Ingrained rejection of the diaspora could not withstand the unrelenting intrusion of Jewish history and memory: the Eichmann trial—which had a transformative impact on previously negative and even contemptuous attitudes toward survivors—or the trauma of Israel's isolation in the frightening weeks that preceded the 1967 war. In his 1971 book *Israelis: Fathers and Sons*, Amos Elon shrewdly dissected the Jewish fear, and even neurosis, that lurked beneath sabra bravado.

The "challenge of sovereignty" struggled to absorb masses of immigrants. Some Ashkenazi veterans, such as the journalist Aryeh Gelblum, felt disdain for "backward" Jewish immigrants from the Arab lands, especially Morocco, and questioned whether the bedrock Zionist commitment to open immigration really made sense. Newly arrived Jews from Iraq, Yemen, and North Africa quickly began to resent their treatment. Salman Shina's *From Babylonia to Zion* conveyed the anger felt by a cultured Baghdadi Jew toward bureaucrats totally ignorant of the great achievements and traditions of Iraqi Jewry. Others lashed out at an official policy that sought to "civilize" non-European Jews instead of seeing them as equal partners in the building of a new culture. Yehuda Nini, in "Thoughts on the Third Destruction," saw the humiliating treatment of Yemenite Jews as an ominous sign of Zionist decay, a loss of such fundamental values as appreciation for manual labor and basic egalitarianism.

But while these tensions between Ashkenazim and non-Ashkenazim led to deep scars and occasional outbreaks of violence, in the end they did not seriously threaten the integrity of the state, largely because of important countervailing trends. For all its faults, Israel was a functioning democracy, and aggrieved immigrants slowly learned how to work the system. There was also the common Arab enemy; many Jews from Arab lands felt pride in the Jewish state and its military successes. In turn, the elites and Ashkenazi Jews understood that the best guarantee of long-term survival was Jewish numbers.

Ironically, the spectacular victory of the 1967 war encouraged heady visions of total Jewish sovereignty in all of the "Land of Israel" and thus sparked the emergence of the very religious-messianic nationalism that Ben-Gurion had hoped to contain. While some leading Israeli writers supported a "Greater Land of Israel," others, like the political activist Lova Eliav and the noted religious scientist Yeshayahu Leibowitz, warned that the fetishization of land and power would endanger the future of the state. Other warnings about the perils of victory and militarism came from the playwright Hanoch Levin, who, in works such as *You, Me and the Next War* and *Ketchup*, subjected the triumphalist pieties of post-1967 Israel to withering and controversial criticism.

The challenge of sovereignty in the early years of statehood also encouraged a far-reaching attempt to define what constituted a distinct, indigenous, Israeli culture. To what degree should Israeli painters, musicians, and writers look to foreign models, if at all? If so, should they turn to Europe? The Middle East? The legacy of the Jewish past? Or was it possible to transcend these models entirely?

In 1953, the Israeli conductor, composer, and music critic Alexander Uriah Boskowicz wrote a revealing article, "The Problems of Native Music in Israel," which called on Israeli composers to avoid aping easily available European or Arab traditions and craft instead a distinct Israeli music inspired by the Mediterranean milieu, the landscape of Eretz Israel, the Bible, and the very sounds of the Hebrew language. Four years later, Ḥaim Gamzu, a leader of the Israeli art world and a director of the Tel Aviv Museum, declared that Israeli artists and sculptors had successfully begun to fashion their own original and distinctive style. The new experience of sovereignty had helped create new tastes and sensibilities. The culture of memorialization played an especially important role in encouraging a specifically Israeli "public sculpture" that forged a bond between the artists and the wider public.

Many Israeli artists, such as Yosef Zaritsky, Marcel Janco, and Mordechai Ardon, felt a natural tension between a search for the contours of a distinct original and Israeli culture and a determination to gain wider recognition in the international art world. But these years saw ongoing experiments that, even as they embraced biblical themes and local landscapes, stood out for their originality and creativity. No less important was the work of Israeli photographers like David Rubinger, who documented the struggles and achievements of the young state. His 1967 photo of Israeli paratroopers at the Western Wall in Jerusalem acquired iconic status and transformed the image of Jews in public perception throughout the West.

Jewish scholarship in Israel also began to find its own distinct voice. As early as 1944, Gershom Scholem called for a fresh turn in Jewish studies that underscored a new relationship between Jewish scholarship and the rebirth of Jewish sovereignty. The apologetic scholarship of the diaspora, Scholem emphasized, had dictated outworn agendas that should give way to an unencumbered awareness of a living Jewish people and of the diverse and often overlooked strains of Jewish cultural development, including mystical and messianic movements and folk culture.

Meanwhile critics and essayists worked their way toward an understanding of an evolving Israeli literature that engaged the growing complexity of Israeli society. The influential critic Barukh Kurzweil lambasted both secular Zionism, which he saw as culturally sterile, and Scholem's heterodox denial of a normative, integral Jewish cultural tradition. In his 1950 critique of S. Y. Agnon's *A Guest for the Night*, Kurzweil saw Agnon as a literary model for the Israeli literature of the future, liberated from false nostalgia for a failed diaspora but still firmly anchored in Jewish tradition. He compared the author's return to his Polish town to Odysseus's return to Ithaca, a masterly evocation of a "before," of a lost past.

While Kurzweil measured Israeli literature by the yardstick of an integral Jewish culture, other critics saw Israeli culture as a frenzied work in progress where few of the younger writers possessed the firm grounding in Jewish texts that had marked older authors like Hazaz or Agnon. The very newness of Israel, the breakneck pace at which an unformed society was emerging from the many corners of the diaspora, put a priori constraints on Israeli literature that writers from other nations did not have to face.

The Israeli literature of the future, the prominent Israeli writer Amos Oz pointed out, would be created by writers watching a new society take shape at warp speed. "This is a world without shade, without cellars or attics, without a real sense of time sequence. And the language itself is half-solid rock and half-shifting sands," he wrote. "We had folk songs before we had a folk."

Nothing better captured the pace and the rhythms of this "world without shade" than Israeli life writing and reportage, which individualized the tension between national rebirth and personal anguish, between collective triumph and individual introspection and doubt. Exaltation and celebration were emotions often tinged with simultaneous anguish and anxiety, the joy of victory and national pride frequently marred by foreboding for the future. Yet it was precisely during this period that Hebrew literature went through a process of consolidation and transformation that would later gain it more respect on the world stage.

By 1939, where this volume begins, Hebrew literature in the "free zone" was largely safe; it had completed its migration from Eastern Europe to Eretz Israel. The wartime Yishuv was torn by powerful crosscurrents and paradoxes: on the one hand, wartime prosperity and the growing self-confidence of the new Hebrew-speaking youth, on the other hand, guilt and anguish caused by news of the murder of European Jewry. Nathan Alterman's 1940 poem "The Mole" evoked the power of the living dead, whose constant presence shaped Jewish memory and held the living in a firm, endless grip. This presence would frame one of the iconic poems of modern Hebrew literature, Alterman's ambiguous "Silver Platter," written in 1947 on the eve of the Israel's War of Independence. This poem, which entered Israel's secular liturgy, evoked a gathered, expectant nation confronting two young, exhausted Jews, a man and a woman, whose sacrifice would be the unending price that Jews would have to pay for the state.

During the war years, the creative tension between Hebrew literature and the Zionist narrative, which would emerge in full force after 1948, dominated key writings, brilliant and disturbing reminders that Zionism was riddled with puzzles and contradictions, and that it was precisely literature, with its ability to delve into the world of individual emotions and imagination, that could offer insights lacking in the monochrome language of political cant. Wartime stories by S. Y. Agnon and Ḥaim Hazaz confronted many sensitive questions. Hazaz's "The Sermon" challenged readers to understand how Zionism could offer salvation when it seemed to deny much of Jewish history. In "From Foe to Friend," Agnon's readers had to ask how Jews could fight off the Arabs and the British in the long run. Agnon's novel *Only Yesterday* rested on the fraught paradox of Zionist promise in a land where so many Jewish immigrants found failure and heartbreak. Yet in the end, what mattered was that somehow the Zionist project went forward, despite setbacks and even when Zionism seemed to defy logic and common sense. There was little triumphalism in these wartime stories by Agnon and Hazaz, who sensed the great struggle that loomed in the future. But the fact that they wrote in Hebrew, and lived in a Hebrew-speaking Yishuv, offered a vision of a house that might finally endure.

The establishment of a Jewish state in 1948 presented Hebrew writers with great challenges but also with great opportunities. After 1948, the ongoing, critical dialogue between Hebrew literature and the Zionist narrative would proceed in a new register and reflect an interplay of parallel generations of writers: an older generation (Agnon, Alterman, Goldberg, Greenberg, Hazaz) at the peak of its powers, the first generation of native Hebrew speakers (Bartov, Gouri, Kaniuk, Megged, Shamir), new immigrants from Europe and the Arab lands (Appelfeld, Ballas, Pagis, Kovner, Kalo, Michael), and finally the "generation of the State," writers like Amos Oz and A. B. Yehoshua whose formative experience had been not the battle for independence but the early years of statehood. This literature confronted the same problems addressed in life writing and political thought: the tension between the collective and the individual, the fraught relationship between Zionism and the Jewish past, the impact of mass immigration on a society that had privileged the myth of a sabra elite, the changing nature of the Hebrew language, and finally, the difficult theme of the Holocaust.

The War of Independence—which began in 1947 and continued until 1949—inspired a literature that highlighted the triumphs and the pitfalls of the battle for Jewish sovereignty. The theme of the "living dead" became ever more salient as two years of vicious fighting decimated an entire generation, especially the soldiers of the elite Palmach. All Israeli writers in the first years of independence were haunted by the deaths of family members and close friends.

The existential danger faced by the Yishuv in its fight for independence underscored the priority of the collective; everything else—individual need, private concerns—was secondary. Poems such as Haim Gouri's 1948 "Behold, Our Bodies Are Laid Out," written after thirty-five Palmach soldiers were killed trying to relieve a besieged settlement, conveyed the emotional toll of the ceaseless fighting even as it underscored the just cause for which the soldiers fell and the absolute necessity of victory. Gouri also composed what would become one of the most memorable songs of the War of Independence, "The Song of Friendship." S. Yizhar's "The Prisoner," written that same year, focused on the inherent tension between the just battle to win independence and the serious threat of moral degradation that caused Jews to mistreat a helpless Arab man. Few works written during the war made a greater impact than Moshe Shamir's 1948 *He Walked through the Fields*, a gripping story of conflict between the personal and the collective. Written in the colloquial Hebrew of the new Yishuv, *He Walked through the Fields* was Israel's first best seller.

When the war ended in 1949, an inevitable emotional letdown followed. The return to civilian life, the disparity between the dreams of independence and the disappointments and failures of a new state, austerity and rationing, the enormous challenge of a mass immigration that threatened to inundate the old Yishuv, all contributed to a sense of depression and disillusionment. The guiding spirit of heroic sacrifice and stoic bereavement was questioned in such short stories as Yehudit Hendel's 1950 "A Common Grave." In 1954, Nissim Aloni's popular play, *Most Cruel of All the Kings*, depicting the succession struggle for King Solomon's throne, raised pointed and timely questions about the tendency of political power to corrupt leaders and to distort formerly lofty ideals.

In the 1950s a reaction set in against the collectivist, Zionist ethos as a new search began for a fiction and poetry that would evoke the individual and private sphere. Poets like Natan Zach declared that poetry should eschew exalted language and collective bombast for a new personal voice. This yearning for private space was also reflected in Pinḥas Sadeh's irreverent 1958 autobiography, *Life as a Parable*, and in Yehuda Amichai's 1961 *Love in Reverse*. Dahlia Ravikovitch's landmark poem "Clockwork Doll" explored how a woman was caught in a trap shaped by men's expectations and demands. In one of his Jerusalem poems, "Tourists," Yehuda Amichai mused about a new kind of Zionism that eschewed national pathos even as it embraced the quotidian pleasures of everyday routines in the homeland.

In 1966, Amalia Kahana-Carmon, who would become one of Israel's major stylists, published one of her first stories, "The Glass Bell." In remarkable prose, which often followed the stream of consciousness of mostly women protagonists, Kahana-Carmon helped open up new vistas in Israeli literature: emotional fragility, the toll of memory and failed choices, the tension between social expectations and individual happiness. In a 1973 essay, "What Did the War of Independence Do to Its Writers?" Kahana-Carmon offered an intriguing insight into what she regarded as the potential pitfalls that faced Israeli literature. The generation of writers of that heroic era, she asserted, were good writers not because of the war, but despite it. For her, constant danger and existential vulnerability do not necessarily encourage good writing.

Jewish writers from the Arab countries, mainly Iraq, also began to make their mark on Israeli literature as they explored the traumatic experience of displacement, the searing loss of language and status, the pain of discrimination, and at the same time, a determination to master Hebrew and to find a foothold in the Jewish state. Sami Michael's "The Artist and the Falafel," originally written in Arabic, drew a picture of poverty and displacement, of insensitive crowds who see in a poor young street artist nothing but a source of entertainment and diversion. A turning point in modern Israeli fiction was the appearance in 1962 of Shlomo Kalo's "The Pile," a modernist portrayal of desperate Mizrahi immigrants seeking a demeaning and low-paid city job clearing a garbage heap. The same theme of social protest appears in Shimon Ballas's *The Ma'abarah* (*The Immigrant Transit Camp*), where immigrants from Arab lands express their bitterness at Ashkenazi condescension and vainly look for way to organize and fight back.

The first significant confrontation of Hebrew literature with the theme of the Holocaust was the 1951 publication of Uri Zvi Greenberg's collection of poems *Streets of the River*, the only volume of Holocaust verse to achieve near-liturgical status. Greenberg, a vociferous opponent of the left-wing labor Zionist establishment, also defied its mandate to highlight Jewish heroism and resistance. Instead, he tore open the raw emotional wounds and guilt of Jews who had enjoyed the safety of the Yishuv while their families were murdered, even as he defied the political correctness of the socialist left by cursing the entire gentile world for its betrayal.

In a cycle of poems addressed "To God in Europe," Greenberg depicts a drastically diminished God, a shepherd without a flock. In a godless, Jew-less world, it is left to the "lying poet" to rage, to mourn, to prophesy the coming redemption of Israel. "Where are there instances of catastrophe / like this that we have suffered at their hands?" asks the poet. "There are none," he replies, "no other instances." This annihilation is without analogy.

Greenberg also evokes the shame, the disgrace, the helplessness, and the guilt of those who could only look on:

> Yes I saved this body of mine when I fled the house of mother and father
> But I did not save my soul
> A soul faint and rank and embittered by tears,
> Plucked of its feathered glory, its wings cropped.

Aside from Greenberg, Hebrew literature in those early years paid relatively little attention to the Holocaust. There were many reasons for this. Holocaust survivors like the poets Abba Kovner and Dan Pagis were few and far between. The younger generation of Hebrew writers had not grown up in Europe, and their formative personal experiences had left them unprepared to write about the disaster. Yiddish writings did not excite much interest among Hebrew readers. For many sabras, the Holocaust and its survivors were a foreign world, to be approached with caution and even involuntary feelings of disgust. And confrontation with Jewish survivors evoked more guilt-ridden ambivalence, explored in such works as Hanoch Bartov's *The Brigade*.

By the late 1950s, new writers appeared on the Israeli literary scene who were themselves survivors. Uri Orlev, a child survivor of the Warsaw ghetto, went on to become one of Israel's most celebrated children's writers. His 1958 *The Lead Soldiers*, about children hiding in Warsaw, narrated from the perspective of a young child, reached a wide audience of Israeli readers, especially young people. Another survivor, Aharon Appelfeld, dealt with those events through a strategy of indirection and through haunting, almost timeless tales of exile and return. Against the backdrop of national rebirth, survivors lived their private lives and wrestled with their private demons, in private spaces untouched and unnoticed.

The stark contrast between traumatized survivors and Zionist aspirations of refuge and redemption is just one of many questions raised by Yoram Kaniuk in his 1968 masterpiece *Adam Resurrected*, which explores Israel's fraught relationship to the Holocaust, in several parallel registers. These include black humor, irony, cynicism, and a main character, Adam Stein, whose story upends all clichés about morality, God, and human agency in the Holocaust. Old Zionist visions of a new, healthy Jewish society based on "good human material" face the wrenching reality of traumatized masses of survivors still struggling with their past, while well-meaning doctors and benefactors try to heal their wounds and restore their faith.

Europe (1946–1973)

In 1945, the future of European Jewry was dire. Jewish survivors returning to their former homes in France and the Netherlands encountered indifference and even hostility, especially when they tried to reclaim their homes and property. In the aftermath of widespread collaboration and German occupation, many Europeans wanted to subsume uncomfortable memories of Jewish suffering in a general narrative of resistance. Indeed, the reemergence of European Jewry was far from certain.[6]

Jewish reintegration into European society sparked debates that engaged Jewish intellectuals on both sides of the Atlantic. One important example was the reaction to Jean-Paul Sartre's foundational series of essays *Reflections on the Jewish Question*, written in 1944, published in the United States under the title *Anti-Semite and Jew*. The Jew, Sartre argued, was largely a creation of the antisemite, his sense of his identity and history dependent on a memory of suffering and persecution.

But events soon proved Sartre wrong, and the postwar world witnessed a surprising resurgence of Jewish self-confidence. While Jewish thinkers in Europe and the United States welcomed Sartre's condemnation of antisemitism, they adamantly rejected his claims that Jewish identity was a creation of non-Jews. Indeed, a Europe compromised by war and fascism could learn a great deal from Jewish values. For instance, in his 1947 response to Sartre, the French Jewish philosopher Emmanuel Levinas asserted that the Jew not only had a positive identity of his own but also carried a message of universal importance. "The Jew," Levinas wrote, "is the entrance itself of the religious event in the world, better yet it is the impossibility of the world itself without religion."[7] Judaism offered Europeans, Levinas believed, a way out of a fateful deadlock between land-and-soil determinism and abstract transcendent universalism. Grounded in rabbinic texts, Judaism emphasized mutual responsibility, which demanded constant attention to specific situations and concrete obligations toward others. Meanwhile, writing in German, Martin Buber, Ignaz Maybaum, and others also defiantly asserted Jewish relevance. The lessons of German Jewry's long struggle for dignity, equal rights, and the best ideals of German humanism mattered more than ever for a German nation tarnished by a total moral collapse. However shaken by the Holocaust, European Jews, Maybaum argued, still had a role to play as a community distinct from both Israel and North America and perhaps in the future, as a bridge between Russian Jews and world Jewry.

On both sides of the Atlantic, Jewish thinkers, culturally identified as well as assimilated, struggled to address the meaning of the Holocaust and whether it should be seen primarily as a crime against Jews or as a crime against humanity. René Cassin drafted the Universal Declaration of Human Rights; Raphael Lemkin coined the term *genocide*. It was for the crime of genocide, rather than for the killing of Jews per se, that Hannah Arendt believed Israel should have tried Eichmann. By the same token, key Jewish organizations such as the American Jewish Committee funded social science research into the origins and causes of prejudice in an effort to show that antisemitism was not just a Jewish problem but a lurking cancer that threatened all healthy democratic societies. European-educated American rabbis harnessed the memory of the Holocaust to remind Jews of their obligation to support African Americans in their struggle for civil rights.[8]

If in the early postwar years the fate of Jews behind the Iron Curtain was largely a closed book to world Jewry, by the middle of the 1960s this was no longer the case. Important analyses of Polish and Soviet Jewry appeared in both the émigré press and illegal publications, the so-called samizdat. Polish Jewish intellectuals, such as Zygmunt Bauman, offered important insights into the dynamics of antisemitism in the communist bloc and hammered another nail into the coffin of what used to be the Jewish romance with the communist left. In the Soviet Union itself, some embers of Jewish culture continued to glow: concerts of Yiddish song, some high-quality poetry and fiction in the journal *Sovetish heymland*, the art of Anatoly Kaplan, Zinovii Tolkachev, and Mikhail Grobman. As an artist attached to a propaganda unit in the Red Army, Tolkatchev drew sketches of Maidanek in 1944 and Auschwitz in 1945. The first artistic renderings of these Nazi camps after the liberation, they captured the bittersweet interplay of the joy of freedom and the anguish of bereavement, and his emotional involvement not only as a Soviet soldier but also as a Jew.

A key development of this period, with worldwide ramifications, was the startling emergence of the Soviet Jewry movement and the national awakening of Soviet Jewry itself. An interplay of simultaneous activism—inside and outside the Soviet Union—reflected growing communication between different Jewish communities. Galvanized by the Six-Day War, the civil rights struggle in the United States, the 1968 invasion of Czechoslovakia, and a sensitivity to the lessons of the Holocaust, the Soviet Jewry movement marked an important milestone in postwar Jewish history. Thanks to this movement, which mobilized both religious and secular Jews in the United States and elsewhere, essays written in the Soviet Union, which could be published only in the clandestine press, nonetheless found a receptive audience in the Jewish world.

Postwar life writing in Europe and the United States explored many important themes: the Holocaust, cultural displacement, the need to define place and memory, a renewed awareness of the importance of family, and the exploration and celebration of the diverse journeys that lead from poverty and obscurity to fame and recognition. Many of those who made those journeys did not forget their Jewish context. Their life writings revealed a lingering amazement about how they could reinvent themselves even as they took memories of their old culture with them.

Interest in life writing about the Holocaust depended greatly on language and place. While memoir literature and historical research flourished in Yiddish in the immediate postwar years, publishing houses in French and Italian preferred books with a more universal resonance that played down specific Jewish suffering. By contrast, publishers in the new Jewish state preferred Holocaust accounts that comported with the Zionist narrative of struggle and resistance to memoirs of hiding and escape. Therefore Leyb Rochman's gripping 1949 Yiddish-language memoir about how Polish petty crooks and prostitutes helped him and four other Jews survive elicited very little interest when it was translated into Hebrew. Jews who hid, and small-town, traditional Jews at that, were less interesting than the young Zionists who fought.

When Primo Levi presented his memoir of Auschwitz, *If This Is a Man* (*Survival in Auschwitz*), immediately after the war, it was turned down by Natalia Ginzburg's well-known Einaudi and five other publishers before a small publisher accepted it. (In his memoir, Levi described his nightmare that when he returned to Italy, no one would be interested in hearing his story.)

By the mid-1960s, Jewish life writing about the Holocaust in all its diversity began to find both a Jewish and a non-Jewish audience. There was a sudden, new surge of interest in Levi, as well as in the memoirs of fellow Auschwitz survivor Elie Wiesel.

Levi and Wiesel did not know each other, and their memoirs were quite different. Levi, a trained chemist, wrote careful, detailed, precise descriptions of what he observed: how the camp functioned, its rules of survival, its debasement of language, and the diabolical ability of the Germans to recruit some prisoners to debase and crush the rest.

Wiesel's *Night*, in contrast, was a spare account that focused on one main character, the young Elie himself. The excerpt from *Night* anthologized here includes one of its best-known passages, when Wiesel and his fellow inmates are forced to watch the hanging of a small boy and two other prisoners. The boy dies slowly, and as one prisoner nearby asks where God is, a voice from within the young Wiesel answers that God is on the gallows. This story of a young boy, his education in hell, and his improbable survival became, like Anne Frank's diary, an iconic Holocaust book.

Another important example of life writing in postwar Europe focuses on the mass migration of North African Jews to France and the ensuing transformation of French Jewry, which became Europe's largest Jewish community. The tug of war between different identities—Jewish, French, Tunisian—is explored by Albert Memmi in his 1962 *Portrait of a Jew*. Sobered by his encounter with Tunisian as well as French antisemitism, and disillusioned with Europe and its false promises of universalist humanism, he recovers his agency through a reengagement with the complexities of a Jewish identity, which he comes to realize as being much more consequential than he had imagined. Even as Memmi struggled to find his way, other Jews from Arab lands still looked for a means to preserve their Arab cultural heritage and maintain the rapidly fraying age-old ties. In a last letter penned on the eve of his execution in 1949, an Iraqi Jewish communist, Sasson Shalom Dallal, still hoped that revolution would allow Jews to live together with their "fellow Arabs." But in fact, centuries of Jewish settlement in Iraq and other Arab-speaking lands were rapidly coming to an end.

However, memories endured. Jacqueline Shohet Kahanoff's "A Letter from Mama Camouna," written in Israel in 1968, explores Jewish identity through an extended family tour through space and time: Tunisian Jews move to France, Israel, and Egypt but remain linked by photographs, by letters, and by common memories that merge into what Kahanoff calls a "Levantine" sensibility. That very space becomes, in Kahanoff's exquisite writing, an extraterritorial counterpart to unwelcome labels such as "Ashkenazi" or "Mizrahi" that failed to capture the nuance and charm of the Levant, rooted in a rich interplay of space, time, and language.

Life writing assumed special importance behind the Iron Curtain, where growing state antisemitism dispelled any lingering Jewish hopes in communism. Accounts of visits to native shtetls, such as that of Gulag-survivor Shmuel Gordon, often slipped taboo details past the censors, such as broad hints about widespread participation of neighbors in the killing and plunder of Jews. Nadezhda Mandelstam's *Hope against Hope* defiantly rejected the myth, still held in the 1950s by hopeful Soviet intellectuals, that Stalin's terror was an aberration and not an essential part of a criminal system begun by Lenin.

Ilya Ehrenburg reflects on what he calls the worst time of his life, the late 1940s and early 1950s, when mass arrests decimated the ranks not only of Yiddish writers but also of Russian Jewish intellectuals like himself. Ehrenburg wrote his memoirs after Stalin's death, so he was well aware of rumors that he owed his survival to his usefulness as a "court Jew" and even to his status as an informer. In trying to dispel these suspicions, he reveals striking details about Stalin and about the stubborn persistence of official antisemitism even after Stalin's death.

As the children of Jewish immigrants gained acceptance in postwar Britain and Western Europe, a certain genre of life writing appeared that reflected the successful navigation of a road that led to recognition and success, and thus made it safe, and even important, to reflect back on one's Jewish roots. In *Two Worlds: An Edinburgh Jewish Childhood*, the eminent writer and literary critic David Daiches recalled his formative years in Edinburgh, where his father was the chief rabbi of Scotland. He found absolutely no contradiction, no tension, between those two worlds: the Jewish world, which he evoked in his memoirs, and the Scottish world in which he lived. Tellingly, both the Jewish and the Scottish identities put forward claims of difference; both staked out their own space in the much wider universe of "British" or "English-speaking" culture.

These claims to difference in wider cultural spheres, anchored in the relatively safe space of family and memory, not only marked life writing; they were also important themes of fiction and poetry by European Jewish writers, especially in France, where Jewish writers began to enjoy unprecedented prominence beginning in the 1960s. Tunisian-born Jacques Zibi's *Mâ* measured the distance between his new life in France and his Tunisian Jewish childhood. The latter was anchored in a warm, traditional home, a mother's love, and an Arabic-Jewish dialect gone forever. Corfu-born Albert Cohen's *Her Lover* (*Belle du Seigneur*) evoked the sometimes hilarious, sometimes poignant contrasts between his earthy origins and his urbane reincarnation as a successful French diplomat. Underneath the comedy and the brilliant style lie more somber reminders of the bonds of time, family, place, and memory—and Jewishness.

In postwar Europe, Holocaust literature explored many different themes: ghettos, memory, the representational limits of language, how to narrate destruction, the ethical dilemmas of trapped Jews, the limits of resistance. Poems such as Paul Celan's subversive and paradoxical "Todesfuge"

(Death Fugue) and Nelly Sachs's "O the Chimneys" pushed language to its limits as they confronted the black core of the Holocaust.

Behind the Iron Curtain, opportunities to write Jewish-themed poetry and fiction, mainly about the Holocaust, opened and closed depending on the political climate. In Poland, Adolf Rudnicki, who wrote relatively little on Jewish themes before the war, penned some of his most powerful fiction on the destruction of Polish Jewry. In 1951, he published a short story, "The Ascension," in which a young woman faces a stark moral choice that forces her to ask what ethical price she will pay to survive.

Another Polish-language masterpiece of Holocaust literature anthologized here is Bogdan Wojdowski's 1971 *Bread for the Departed*. Wojdowski, who had survived the Warsaw ghetto as a child, evokes the disruption and confusion of the ghetto as seen through the eyes of a young boy, David Fremde. Instead of a plot, there is a depressing kaleidoscope of scenes often narrated in the chaotic, deformed "ghetto speak" that alone provided the right words to describe what David saw.

A very different kind of novel, this time about the Łódź ghetto, was Jurek Becker's 1969 *Jacob the Liar*, written in East Germany. Becker was a survivor, and he brilliantly decoded ghetto life by highlighting lies and illusions enlisted to fight despair. These powerless, isolated denizens of the ghetto used their only weapon—words—as they analyzed and parsed the optimistic lies that Jacob disseminated based on his fictitious ghetto radio.

In the postwar years, two Jewish writers born in Eastern Europe and writing in their nonnative French produced Holocaust fiction that broke new, artistically daring ground in the representation of atrocity: Piotr Rawicz's 1961 *Blood from the Sky* and Romain Gary's 1967 *The Dance of Genghis Cohn* (not anthologized here). Both Rawicz and Gary (born Roman Kacew) were masters of acquired identities, a talent that frightened antisemites even as it bemused many Jews. The former's use of multiple angles of narration and representation make it a classic of Holocaust literature, as Rawicz uses the perspective of different voices, none necessarily reliable, to describe atrocity with a frankness that spares no one, including Jews.

Just as the French Jewish community was being transformed by large-scale immigration from North Africa, French Jewish writers began to have a major impact on a nation struggling to come to terms with its ambiguous record in World War II. Two works in particular, André Schwarz-Bart's 1959 *The Last of the Just*, which won the Prix Goncourt, and Jean François Steiner's 1967 *Treblinka*, caused major controversies by highlighting such themes as the Christian roots of antisemitism, French complicity in the Holocaust, and, in Steiner's case, the paradoxical interplay of Jewish passivity and Jewish resistance. These books made the Holocaust more visible as an event separate from World War II.

Diverse Diasporas (1946–1973)

It was in the postwar period that Jewish writers of the changing diasporas of Argentina, Canada, South Africa, and Australia began to play a visible role as cultural figures and interpreters of the Jewish experience. Almost invariably the children of Yiddish-, Ladino-, or Arabic-speaking immigrants, their parents had all lived on their own "Lower East Side": the Jewish colonies on the pampas, the lonely peddler life in the South African veldt, the grim adjustment to the slums of Montreal, Buenos Aires, or Johannesburg. Jews settled even in the most remote frontiers. Yaacov Hasson's "Iquitos: The Jewish Soul in the Amazon, Notes of a Voyager" evokes the tenacity of Jewish identity—and the impact of Zionism—even in the middle of the Amazon rain forest.

But after the war, these communities redefined themselves as they sought out different ways of becoming Argentines or Canadians while remaining Jews deeply concerned with their own history, with the legacy of the Holocaust, and with the security of the new Jewish state. Life writing especially captured the challenges and the poignancy of putting down markers in unknown and uncharted territory. Like Daiches's description of Scottish Jewry, this life writing in the changing diasporas highlighted how Jews sought to preserve their identity within non-Jewish cultures that were themselves, in places like Canada and South Africa, often defined by dueling narratives and sharp cultural differences.

Larry Zolf's "Boil Me No Melting Pots, Dream Me No Dreams" and Mordecai Richler's memoir of hardscrabble Jewish neighborhoods in Montreal highlight real differences between Jewish Canada and Jewish America. Canadian Jewish identity was forged in a society that valued cultural pluralism and eschewed the ideal of the melting pot, where Jews had to maneuver between larger, competing communities. A generation closer to the "old home," Canadian Jews were less likely than their American cousins to intermarry or to live in non-Jewish neighborhoods. It was during these years that Canadian Jewry began to become an integral but distinct part of a Canadian society that was itself struggling to define its identity in the face of rising nationalism in Quebec.

Montreal's A. M. Klein, sensitive to cultural difference and linguistic nuance, wrote with equal empathy about the Holocaust, the formation of the Jewish state, and the French-Canadian culture that shaped his surroundings. His 1951 novella *The Second Scroll* is a profound gloss on the modern Jewish experience: the Holocaust, flirtations with communism, the rebirth of Jewish sovereignty, and the Hebrew language, all strikingly conveyed by the excerpt from *The Second Scroll* found in this anthology. Klein's very sensitivity to the critical place of cultural difference and linguistic nuance enabled him to write powerful poetry about another people struggling to protect its identity, his French Canadian neighbors. Klein became an important influence on his fellow Montrealer, the songwriter and poet Leonard Cohen. It was not by coincidence that when Prime Minister Pierre Trudeau addressed a gathering of Canadian Jews in 1970, he told them that the "Jewish community also afforded Canadians a model in miniature of what Canadian society could and should be."[9] The next year, the Canadian government officially endorsed a vision of multiculturalism that encouraged different minority groups to protect and advance their own cultures.

South African Jewry also took root in an environment that encouraged Jewish difference rather than assimilation. Chaim Sacks's "Sweets from Sixpence" evokes the challenges faced by Lithuanian Jewish immigrants on a new continent, as well as their ongoing struggle to find a niche in a land beset by conflict and tension between Afrikaners, English-speaking whites, Black Africans, and millions of "coloreds." These years were a defining time for South African Jewry, as surging Afrikaner nationalists shut down Jewish immigration from Europe by the late 1930s, flirted with Nazi-inspired antisemitism, and finally gained political power in 1948. The political ascendancy of Afrikaner nationalists, marked by the growth of legally sanctioned apartheid after 1948, confronted Jews with a tough dilemma. On the one hand, Afrikaner antisemitism declined as the new government dismantled barriers to Jewish immigration and offered Jews the enormous material and social privileges connected with being white in an apartheid state.

But those privileges came at a deep moral price. How could Jews profit from and sanction apartheid? Yet what choices did they have? The bitter 1957 exchange between Daniel Jacobson and Ronald Segal on how Jews should react to apartheid also spoke to deeper issues, such as how Jewish minorities should navigate the fraught space between moral integrity and self-preservation.

Despite these painful conflicts, which impelled many Jews to leave the country, the South African Jewish community stood out for its major contributions to South African culture: Lippy Lifschitz, Moses Kottler, and Irma Stern in painting and sculpture; Dan Jacobson, Sara Millin, and Nadine Gordimer in literature; Olga Kirsch in poetry. Olga Kirsch herself offers a striking example of how South African Jews moved in the uncertain and creative spaces that marked the boundaries of different cultures. Kirsch was born in a small town on the Orange Free State, wrote her poetry in Afrikaans, and emigrated to Israel in 1948. She spoke English with her husband and Hebrew with her children. As Andries Wessels points out, key themes in her poetry appealed simultaneously to both Zionist Jews and to Afrikaners:[10]

Yet the silent longing remains unstilled
O land, o rest yet unfulfilled

During these years Latin American Jewish literature in Spanish also came into its own, especially in Argentina. As in Canada and South Africa, writers who had grown up in Yiddish-speaking immigrant homes published journalism, poetry, and fiction that reflected the promise and pitfalls of new frontiers and wide horizons. In Argentina, a major center of postwar Yiddish culture, second-generation Spanish-language writers, including Lázaro Liacho, Samuel Glusberg, Samuel Eichelbaum, Bernardo Verbitsky, and David Viñas, took their place alongside already-established Argentinian Jewish writers such as César Tiempo and Alberto Gerchunoff. Some, like Gerchunoff and Verbitsky, would leave their mark on Argentine culture not only as creative writers but also as leading journalists.

Today Gerchunoff is justly celebrated for his 1910 collection of short stories entitled *Jewish Gauchos*, devoted to the Yiddish-speaking Jewish pioneers from Russia who settled in the new farming colonies of the pampas. These stories, called by one critic the "urtext of Latin American Jewish literature," were also a paean to Argentina, an expression of Gerchunoff's heady optimism about a Jewish future in this new country. Gerchunoff offered a template for Jewish integration into Argentine society and into the Argentine Spanish culture, especially attractive because of a centuries-old bond that linked Jews to the Spanish language. Indeed, the writer Bernardo Verbitzky would say that it was through *Jewish Gauchos* that "Argentine Jews acquired their citizenship papers."[11]

But his 1945 essay on newsreels of the Nazi camps, excerpted here, shows a Gerchunoff who is much more eager to assert his Jewish identity and to temper his earlier optimism about a Jewish future in Argentina. Like other Argentine Jewish writers, Gerchunoff was profoundly affected by the Holocaust and by Zionism. The decades that followed *Jewish Gauchos* saw not only accelerated Jewish immigration and urbanization but also growing antisemitism and a new awareness of the stubborn "otherness" of Jews making their way in a Catholic country. This "otherness" reverberated in César Tiempo's cycle of Sabbath poems, and to a certain degree in the fiction of Bernardo Verbitsky and David Viñas. Over time, it was both tested and nurtured by the populism of Juan Perón, the left-wing radicalism that attracted many young Jews, and the crisis caused by Israel's kidnapping of Adolf Eichmann in 1960.

United States of America (1946–1973)

The postwar rise of American Jewry had far-reaching consequences for the entire Jewish world. World War II brought about profound shifts in a community that had been grappling with antisemitism and discrimination. The impact of the Holocaust made antisemitism less acceptable, and American Jews as a group more determined to affirm their identity and defend fellow Jews around the world. The crowning of Bess Myerson as Miss America in 1945 seemed to symbolize that new era of acceptance. Hollywood abandoned its former reluctance to deal with Jewish issues: films like *Crossfire* and *Gentleman's Agreement* harshly condemned antisemitism. Popular war novels like Norman Mailer's *The Naked and the Dead*, Herman Wouk's *The Caine Mutiny*, and Irwin Shaw's *The Young Lions* depicted Jewish soldiers and officers who "belonged" in the military just as much as their non-Jewish comrades-in-arms did. Few Americans failed to hear the story of the four chaplains, including Rabbi Alexander Goode, who sacrificed their lives for others after the USS *Dorchester* was torpedoed in 1943.

While some observers doubted that American Jewry—with its low level of Jewish knowledge—could ever reach the creative heights of Spanish or Babylonian Jewry, Salo Baron, the foremost Jewish historian in the United States, expressed unbounded confidence. Jewish creativity, he insisted, could indeed flourish in an open society such as America's. Another leading Jewish scholar, Gerson Cohen, also contended that America's openness was "good for the Jews." For many centuries, he observed, interchange with the gentile world had stimulated Jewish creativity.

The year 1945 saw the first issue of *Commentary* magazine, which would become one of the most important journals in postwar Jewish America. In his introductory article, "An Act of Affirmation," *Commentary*'s editor Elliot Cohen saw the establishment of this new journal as an "act of faith in our possibilities in America. . . . Surely, we who have survived catastrophe, can survive freedom, too."

Commentary became an especially important forum for secular Jewish intellectuals who, in the aftermath of the Holocaust, began to evince an interest in Jewish matters. In one landmark article, a

January 1949 response to Sartre's *Anti-Semite and Jew*, critic Harold Rosenberg stressed that Jewish identity and Jewish memory were far more than just a reaction to antisemitism. Rosenberg defended the right of Jews to seek total assimilation if they so chose, an act that Sartre called inauthentic. But, he concluded, "Jewish identity has a remarkable richness for those who rediscover it within themselves" (anthologized here). Jews were free to fashion their own story and shape their Jewishness in any way they chose. Indeed, this new readiness to embrace, or at least to discern Jewishness in all its variety and indeterminacy, would play a major role in the cultural life of American Jewry in the three decades that followed the end of World War II.

In 1948, in "The Future of the American Jew," Mordecai M. Kaplan, founder of Reconstructionist Judaism, had urged his readers to have faith in the "recuperative powers" of the Jewish people and Jews to adopt the prophet Ezekiel as their patron saint. Ezekiel, too, had confronted a people ravaged by national disaster, but he preached a message of self-confidence and revival.

This new Jewish assertiveness and optimism took many forms. As early as 1942, the philosopher Horace Kallen had unapologetically stressed that American Jews, far from being guests in America, were actually playing a critical role in the shaping of American society, whether in labor relations, civil rights, or the theater. What had been confined to the immigrant ghetto was now part and parcel of the American mainstream. "It was Hebraic mortar," Kallen asserted, "that cemented the foundations of American democracy." In the postwar years Kallen's argument found new resonance as Jewish thinkers in various disciplines, eschewing any hint of prewar apologetics, proudly affirmed the importance of Jews for the West and for America.

That same spirit of hope for the future animated the opening of Brandeis University in June 1948. For the first time ever, American Jews were founding an American university and not a Jewish seminary, and this just one month after the establishment of a Jewish state. The new university, its supporters claimed, was a stirring symbol of Jewish resiliency. Its first president, Abram L. Sachar, called the new school "a corporate gift of Jews to American higher education." His autobiography bore the telling title *A Host at Last*.[12]

Admission quotas were slowly disappearing as the GI Bill gave many Jewish veterans a chance to attend college. Barriers to hiring Jewish faculty also gradually lowered, even as Jewish scholars became less diffident about expressing their Jewishness. As late as 1944, the eminent literary critic Lionel Trilling had declared in a symposium sponsored by the *Contemporary Jewish Record* (*Commentary*'s predecessor), "I do not think of myself as a Jewish writer. I do not have it in mind to serve by my writing any Jewish purpose." But by 1950, in a *Commentary* essay entitled "Wordsworth and the Rabbis," Trilling linked one his favorite poets with a Jewish text that he knew well, *The Ethics of the Fathers* (Pirkei Avot). There was a certain irony that Trilling, the first Jew to secure tenure in the Columbia University English department, would mention first-century rabbis in the same article as Wordsworth. The alleged inability of Jews to appreciate the subtleties of English literature had been a frequent pretext to deny them appointments. Now Trilling could write that "between the Law as the Rabbis understood it and Nature as Wordsworth understood it there is a pregnant similarity."

Indeed, the postwar years saw a remarkable resurgence of Jewish scholarship in the United States and set the stage for the later establishment of Jewish studies programs in America's finest universities and, in 1969, for the founding of the Association of Jewish Studies. This resurgence was due to many different factors: a decline in antisemitism, increasing interest in Jewish theology and history, a growing dialogue between Jewish and Christian scholars, the migration of many eminent Jewish scholars from Europe to the United States, and finally the postwar economic boom. In his 1950 article "The Challenge Facing Modern Jewish Scholarship," Robert Gordis, one of the intellectual leaders of the Conservative movement, analyzed the achievements of the past and laid out an agenda for the future. He urged Jewish scholars to reject apologetics and reclaim biblical scholarship from often-biased Christian scholars.

Growing Jewish self-confidence also led to new efforts to fashion a usable past for American Jewry by ensuring that the memory of East European Jewry not be determined by comedians and crooners.

Max Weinreich, in his magnum opus, *History of the Yiddish Language*, and his son, Uriel Weinreich, in his call to create a cultural atlas of European Jewry, pointed the way to a usable past based on a distinct European Jewish civilization, Ashkenaz. Ashkenaz was rooted in the Yiddish language, in European space, and in a creative sense of time determined by textual study that led to constant dialogue between past and present. Ashkenaz had been no hermetic ghetto; its values could not only explain the past and but also guide American Jews in the future.

By the same token, literary critics like Irving Howe and Abraham Tabachnik called for a fresh reading of Yiddish culture as a locus not of shtetl piety but of revolutionary ferment and modernist creativity. Rabbi and philosopher Abraham Joshua Heschel, in *The Eastern European Era in Jewish History*, portrayed East European Jewry as a civilization defined by time and spirit rather than space. To remember that civilization was not only an act of piety but also a matter of urgent necessity, the survivors of that world had to transmit its legacy to American Jewry. "Solidarity with the past," Heschel told an audience in January 1945, "must become an integral part of our existence. . . . [W]e still have the keys to the treasures. If we don't recover them they'll be lost forever."

For the first time, rabbis became part of the American mainstream. In his runaway 1946 best seller, *Peace of Mind*, Joshua Loth Liebman explained how Jewish religious principles could help all Americans in their search for psychological well-being.

Four years later, the October 15, 1951, cover of *Time* magazine featured Louis Finkelstein, chancellor of the Jewish Theological Seminary, with the revealing caption: "The Days of Fear Are Over." Finkelstein predicted a renaissance of Jewish life in America, based on a new interest in religion. By 1955, Will Herberg's *Protestant—Catholic—Jew* had promoted Judaism to the status of America's third religion, despite the small numbers of Jews in the United States. Both Conservative and Reform Judaism showed a new assertiveness and optimism.

Finkelstein's call for "more religion" also spurred interest in Jewish theology. This new importance of theological writing contradicted a widely held belief that, since Judaism stressed halakhah (law) and linked faith to action, it put less stress on the formulation of religious doctrine. The postwar years indeed encouraged new interest in theology. Christian thinkers like Reinhold Niebuhr underscored the relevance of Jewish thought while the Second Vatican Council presaged an unprecedented era in Catholic–Jewish relations.

Although most observers of Jewish religious life agreed that American Orthodoxy faced a bleak future, in a prescient 1954 interview, Joseph B. Soloveitchik, the intellectual leader of Modern Orthodoxy, confidently predicted an upsurge in Orthodox observance, as young American Jews would come to seek a total Jewish experience not offered by Reform and Conservative synagogues. In time, Orthodoxy indeed became stronger, facilitated by the establishment of new yeshivas, the growing prominence of the Chabad movement, and a post-Holocaust Hasidic revival spearheaded by Satmar and other sects.

The cultural ferment of the 1960s underscored social scientist Nathan Glazer's observation that Jews did not stop being Jews but searched for innovative ways of adapting their Jewishness to a rapidly changing America. Creation of a kind of Jewish countercommunity as an alternative to suburban conformity appealed to growing numbers of young Jews. This search for new kinds of community led to the beginnings of the havurah movement.

Another major Jewish response to the counterculture of the 1960s was Jewish feminism, based on demands that women take their rightful place in Jewish religious and communal life as equals rather than as "peripheral Jews." In 1972, a manifesto, "Jewish Women Call for Change," addressed to Conservative rabbis, demanded that women be counted in the minyan, the quorum of ten men required for communal prayer, and that they be admitted to rabbinical and cantorial schools. In 1972, the Reform movement ordained its first female rabbi, Sally Priesand, and Sandy Sasso became the first woman admitted to the Reconstructionist Rabbinical College. As Deborah Dash Moore points out, these decisions by two liberal Jewish religious movements presented a clear alternative to both Modern Orthodoxy and Conservative Judaism and stimulated Jewish feminists to press for even more changes, many of them appearing after 1973 and thus documented in Volume 10 of The Posen Library.

Leftist Jews also confronted new challenges. Old ties between Blacks and Jews, forged in the early days of the civil rights movement, began to fray because of the Black Power movement and growing tensions between Black and Jewish interests in urban politics. The New Left turned against Israel as a matter of course. As the ideal of the melting pot gave way to a new multiculturalism, why, some asked, should Jews accept Black claims to difference but deny their own identity?

Jewish life writing also underscores the special character of the United States, a country that offered Jews unprecedented opportunity not only to prosper but also to redefine themselves and to calibrate the fine balance between personal ambition and collective identity. In the aftermath of the Holocaust, this kind of life writing exemplified the centrality of American Jewry. Immigrant memoirs describe choices, some seemingly quixotic, but others focused on future prospects.

In America, Jewish life writing could also be more frank and uninhibited in comparison with Europe. Judd L. Teller's description of "Goyim," violent gentiles who terrorized Jews in his hometown in Poland, showed an openness and self-confidence that might have been less apparent in his birthplace. In the aftermath of the Holocaust, it was also in America—a gathering place of immigrants—

that life writing could evoke and recenter memories of different, shattered Jewish worlds, in part by drawing on common American experiences of immigration. Leon Sciaky's *Farewell to Salonica: City at the Crossroads*, Jehiel Isaiah Trunk's *Poland: Memoirs and Scenes*, and Joseph Buloff's *From the Old Marketplace* pictured their lost Ladino- and Yiddish-speaking homes through the lens of personal experience: place, streets, childhood games, and above all, the bedrock of family.

Precisely that interplay of memories anchored in family and place refracted through a new prism of postwar sensibility made Alfred Kazin's 1951 *A Walker in the City* such an important example of American life writing. This long "prose poem" was a striking departure from familiar stories of immigrant poverty, squalor, and despair. Instead of naturalistic determinism, it stressed freedom and possibility. Poverty marked Kazin's family but it did not prevent his parents from creating a home. And it was from that home, anchored in the family kitchen, that Kazin set out on his walks through the city, discovered the joys of literature, and exulted in his growing mastery of language. The slum did not destroy Kazin but propelled him forward and outward; through writing and memory he could reimagine his world and remake himself.

The late 1940s, when Kazin was writing *Walker in the City*, was a liminal moment in the development of Jewish fiction and poetry. A new generation, mostly raised in immigrant, Yiddish-speaking homes came into its own just when American literature stood ready to embrace Jewish writers, Jewish themes, and the cadences of Jewish writing in English, not as examples of exotica, parochialism, or immigrant culture but as a mainstay of postwar American culture.

Just a few subway stops away from Kazin's Brownsville, Jacob Glatstein ("Without Jews"), Kadya Molodovsky ("God of Mercy"), and Aaron Zeitlin ("To Be a Jew") were mourning the Holocaust in some of the most powerful poetry ever written in the Yiddish language. Yiddish literature was still a closed book to American Jews, and Holocaust memory still defined and segregated by the barriers of language. But by the early 1950s, the first glimmer of change appeared: Saul Bellow's translation of Isaac Bashevis Singer's "Simple Gimpl," a brilliant tale of how in an immoral and wicked world, gullibility and purposeful naïveté were the only foundation of honesty and integrity.

Many factors shaped the Jewishness of this generation of writers and critics: exposure to an immigrant culture that foregrounded Jewish memory and difference, the lingering impact of Yiddish speech, a tradition of secularism and moral commitment that sought new outlets after the eclipse of 1930s leftism, and an uneasy relationship with postwar bourgeois American Jewry.

One of the most touching postwar voices was Grace Paley's. A sense of "at-homeness" in America, so different from Europe, emerges in her short story "The Loudest Voice," which transforms traditional, dangerous reminders of Jewish marginality—the story of Christ's birth and crucifixion—into a buoyant description of the insouciance and self-confidence of a young daughter of Jewish immigrants. Shirley Abramowitz's loud voice lands her the best role in the school Christmas play, the voice of Christ. Far from feeling inferior or out of place, Shirley, encouraged by her immigrant father, confidently channels Jesus' words in her own cadence as other Jewish children enact the nativity scene.

But if Shirley Abramowitz was a picture of self-confidence, Neil Klugman in Philip Roth's *Goodbye, Columbus* or Alexander Portnoy in Philip Roth's *Portnoy's Complaint* revealed a more complex picture of Jews in midcentury America, with its fraught transition from immigrant poverty to material affluence, from the old ethnic neighborhood to leafy suburbs. Jews had arrived, but to what? Some American Jewish writers, like Herman Wouk in *Marjorie Morningstar*, regarded this new suburban frontier with optimism, with opportunities for Jewish continuity and for better family life. In contrast, Roth, who had little use for the communitarian pieties of the organized Jewish community, deftly explored the fragile vulnerabilities of a new generation of American Jews who were too American to be comfortably Jewish and who felt too Jewish to be totally American. Materialism, dysfunctional families, suffocating Jewish mothers, and sexual neuroses were all fair game for Roth's satire, condemned by some as deplorable self-hatred, lauded by others as brilliant literature.

It goes without saying that the Holocaust loomed large in postwar American Jewish culture. Susan Sontag remembered her first reaction to photographs of the concentration camps:

> Nothing I have ever seen—in photographs or in real life—ever cut me as sharply, deeply, instantaneously. . . . Something was broken. Some limit had been reached, and not only that of horrors; I felt irrevocably grieved, wounded, but a part of my feelings started to tighten; something went dead; something is still crying.[13]

In some of their most powerful writing, Philip Roth ("Eli, the Fanatic") and Bernard Malamud ("The Last Mohican") expose the psychological brittleness of anxious, insecure assimilated American Jews in their encounters with Holocaust survivors. These encounters triggered deep feelings of guilt and even identification.

In a different vein, Saul Bellow's *Mr. Sammler's Planet*, which vented his outrage against the self-indulgent and overly permissive counterculture of the 1960s, also presented, through Mr. Sammler the Holocaust survivor, a deep moral message rooted in Jewish culture: the imperative of "meeting the terms of one's contract."

The newfound salience of American Jewish writers was exemplified by the success of Saul Bellow's *Herzog*, an unmistakably American novel, despite the fact that most of the characters were Jewish. The brilliant portrayals of New York and Chicago, the large tableau of secondary characters, the comic tension between intellectual brilliance and emotional failure—all serve to make Herzog much more than a "Jewish" novel.

This was a time of trauma and rebirth, of despair and soaring self-confidence. For the most part, with the exception of communist Europe, these years were "good for the Jews." Indeed, one need only look at the major changes in the depiction of Jews in photography and the visual arts to understand the incredible transformation of the Jewish condition that took place. In 1939 and the early 1940s, Jews were commonly portrayed as poor and struggling, as refugees dependent on the goodwill of others. By the end of this period, such images largely disappeared; in Garry Winogrand's photographs, for example, Jews are middle-class Americans. This is not to say that by 1973 trauma and worry had disappeared from Jewish life. The Yom Kippur War ended the "heroic era" of Israeli history and ushered in a sober realization that Israeli power had stark limits. In the United States, the pace of assimilation and intermarriage began to quicken, as did growing doubts about the future of the postwar "golden age" of American Jewry. But compared to the dangers of 1939, these worries were mere trifles.

If form is content, then an anthology of arts and letters, culled from two dozen languages and covering all but one continent (Antarctica) is the only form that can do justice to "Jewish culture and civilization" between 1939 and 1973. Certainly no novel, no epic poem, no memoir, has yet been written; no canvas has yet been painted and no blockbuster movie yet made that can capture so many voices and images, so many shades of red, blue, white, and black. However the sources anthologized here are accessed, whether in print or online, whether followed in sequence or in sound bites, there is no gainsaying the chutzpah and sagacity, the passion and hilarity, the precision and artifice, the folly and the prescience of these people called the Jews. Although every effort has been made to situate them in time, place, and form of self-expression, the ultimate purpose of such an anthology is to cross party lines, to overcome the barriers of language, and to defy geography, so as to create a composite, multidimensional portrait of an ever-evolving civilization. It is our hope that each and every entry serves as a door to rooms and palaces as yet unexplored.

Notes

1. A good source on Jewish anthologies is David Stern, ed., *The Anthology in Jewish Literature* (Oxford: Oxford University Press, 2004).

2. See, for example, the excellent collection of articles in Hana Wirth-Nesher, ed., *What Is Jewish Literature?* (Philadelphia: Jewish Publication Society, 1994).

3. This postwar effervescence of Yiddish culture is well described in Jan Schwarz, *Survivors and Exiles: Yiddish Culture after the Holocaust* (Detroit: Wayne State University Press, 2015).

4. *European Judaism: A Journal for the New Europe*, "The Rome Colloquium," Summer, 1972.

5. See, for example, the entry for Siegfried Moses, "Programme for the Leo Baeck Institute of Jews from Germany," in our anthology.

6. A good introduction, among many, to these problems of reintegration is David Bankier, ed., *Jews Are Coming Back: The Return of the Jews to Their Countries of Origin after World War II* (New York: Berghahn Books, 2005).

7. Emmanuel Levinas, "Être juif," *Confluences* 7 (1947): 253–67, 261.

8. On this research, see Stuart Svonkin, *Jews against Prejudice: American Jews and the Fight for Civil Liberties* (New York: Columbia University Press, 1999).

9. Harold Troper, *The Defining Decade: Identity, Politics, and the Canadian Jewish Community in the 1960s* (Toronto: University of Toronto Press, 2010), 288.

10. Andries Wessels, "The Outsider as Insider: The Jewish Afrikaans Poetry of Olga Kirsch," *Prooftexts* 29 (2009): 63–85.

11. Leonardo Senkman, "Argentine Culture and Jewish Identity," in *The Jewish Presence in Latin America*, ed. Judith Elkin and Gilbert Merkx (London: Allen & Unwin, 1988), 255–70, 258.

12. Edward S. Shapiro, "World War II and American Jewish Identity," *Modern Judaism* 10 (1990): 65–84, 79.

13. Quoted in Edward S. Shapiro, "World War II and American Jewish Identity," *Modern Judaism* 10 (1990): 65–84, 74.

1939-1945

In 1939, just before the outbreak of World War II, the situation for the Jewish people in Central and Eastern Europe looked bleak, even desperate. Hitler claimed that world Jewry was a demonic power harnessing the sinister forces of plutocracy and communism to plunge the world into war, destroy Germany, and rule the world. In fact, Jews were vulnerable, politically weak, and divided. In the face of looming danger, whether they lived in Eastern or Western Europe, Palestine or the Americas, Jews were separated into warring camps by political and cultural infighting.

The doubts and defeats of the 1930s left their mark on Jewish writing in all genres during the Holocaust, in the areas both within and outside of Nazi control. Some asked whether Jewish faith in European liberalism and Enlightenment values had been misplaced. Others wondered whether Jews had found themselves stranded midstream, no longer secure in their age-old religious tradition but unable to find acceptance in the non-Jewish world. Still others held fast to a universal Marxist vision or a Jewish national alternative. But alongside despair and doubt, new notes of pride and self-affirmation also emerged, sometimes quite unexpectedly. The selections in this anthology certainly belie the widely believed claims that the ghettos under Nazi rule were a cultural wasteland, or that Jews in areas outside Nazi influence knew little about the unfolding disaster.

Once again, the wartime record underscores a key theme of this anthology: geography and language mattered. Texts composed in lands under Nazi occupation presented a very different focus and content from those written outside them. Texts in Yiddish written during and after the war revealed concerns and agendas unlike those written in other languages, especially English. It is easy to understand why. How many writers in English had to witness the simultaneous murder of their own people and their own language?

The anthologies, reportage, life writing, fiction, and poetry presented here underscore the wide range of Jewish responses to disaster as it unfolded in real time. They take readers back to the immediacy of the moment and let them see the world through Jewish eyes.

ANTHOLOGIES

Louis Brunot and Elie Malka

Brunot, 1882–1965

An academic and lecturer in Rabat, Louis Brunot was director of the Institut des hautes études marocaines and head of the bureau responsible for public instruction. Brunot was the author of a number of works on the history and tradition of Morocco as a maritime nation and collaborated with Elie Malka on works detailing local language and customs.

Malka, Dates Unknown

In 1939, Elie Malka worked as a translator, with the title *interprète civil de la direction des affaires politiques du Maroc.* He graduated from the Institut des hautes études marocaines with a Diplôme d'études supérieures marocaines; he was later a professor of Moroccan affairs there.

Judeo-Arabic Proverbs from Fez
1940

Proverbs

1. "If a pale woman desires you, do not desire her! Do not waste on her the legacy from your father and your grandfather! She is like a white spot that, settling in the eye, blinds it."

This is just a saying; it does not indicate a general repulsion for some women's white skin.

2. "If a rosy-skinned woman desires you, desire her! Spend on her the legacy from your father and your grandfather! She is like the honey that, falling on a wound, heals it."

One should not infer from this saying that women with rosy complexions are always to be preferred.

3. "If a dark woman desires you, do not desire her! Do not waste on her the legacy from your father and your grandfather! She is like the raven that, descending on a tent, leaves it abandoned."

The three sayings above form a whole, a piece of popular literature. They are known in all of the Moroccan mellahs. Cf. [Edward] Westermarck, no. 52: "May God save you from pale and dark women."

4. "If the head is alive, it will not want for a hairdo."

The essential thing for man is to live. Having attained this condition, he will always find what he needs, as long as it is reasonable.

This proverb is cited by Luderitz, no. LIV and by Westermarck, no. 1205.

5. "When the enemy rejoices (at your misfortune), your (ill-fated) destiny is undone."

The proverb declares that when an enemy rejoices at learning of your sickness or misfortune, God reverses the unfavorable decision he had taken in your regard. Thus one can be cured, for example, of a serious illness that would normally lead you to the grave.

6. "When the face is absent, there is no longer respect for the neck."

People are respected only when they are present; as soon as one's back is turned, bad things are said of him.

This proverb is cited by Westermarck, no. 453 and, with a variant, in no. 1506.

7. "Whatever sum a thief realizes (from the sale of a stolen object), the thief has made a profit."

Cited by [Georges Séraphin] Colin, *Chrest[omathie marocaine]*, p. 171, 1.2.

8. "Changing one's residence is restful."

When one stays too long in the same house, one is prey to neighbors and to those who know where one lives. Changing one's residence is restful in this respect.

9. "A country where the stones know you is preferable to one in which men know you."

One is better off in one's own country, where even the stones are familiar, than in a foreign country, even if one knows people there.

This proverb is known in all the Moroccan mellahs. It is cited, with a slight variant, by Westermarck, no. 546.

10. "Your daughter, when she's grown, convert a black [man] for her."

It was not so long ago that the Israelites, particularly those of Fès, Sefrou, and Meknès, took pride in marrying off their daughters at a very young age, between eight and ten years old. A recent law prohibited these early marriages, satisfying those concerned.

The proverb recommends, as a precaution, that the daughter be married off as soon as she is old enough, even if it means, for lack of a more suitable husband, converting a black slave to Judaism and giving him to her as a spouse.

11. "Kiss your dog on the muzzle till you no longer need him."

The dog represents the person one needs yet despises.

Until the time comes when you can do without them, you must take care with people who can, or do, perform services for you. For example, it is good practice not to bully a servant one is dissatisfied with as long as one cannot replace him.

This proverb is cited in practically the same terms by Westermarck, no. 112 and no. 1719, and by Colin, *Chrest.*, p. 171, 1.3.

12. "He brought up the rear (behind everyone else) and claims to know what happened."

This refers to the upstart who meddles in affairs he does not understand yet talks about as if he were thoroughly familiar with them.

NOTE
[Explanatory material was provided by Brunot and Malka.—Eds.]

Translated by Michele McKay Aynesworth.

Other works by Brunot: *La mer dans les traditions et les industries indigènes à Rabat et Salé* (1920); *Textes arabes de Rabat* (1931).

Antek Zuckerman and Eliyohu Gutkowski

Zuckerman, 1915–1981

A hero of Jewish resistance and survivor of the Warsaw ghetto uprising, Antek (Yitzhak) Zuckerman was born in Vilna. He was a leader in the Zionist youth movement He-Ḥaluts. When Jews were confined to the Warsaw ghetto, Zuckerman was sent to the "Aryan" sector as a liaison with the Polish underground and smuggled arms to Jewish ghetto fighters. After the death of the ghetto's leader Mordecai Anielewicz, Zuckerman was appointed commander of the Jewish Fighting Organization (ŻOB). He moved to pre-state Israel in 1947 and was a founder of Kibbutz Lohmei Hageta'ot and the Ghetto Fighters' House Museum.

Gutkowski, 1900–1943

Eliyohu Gutkowski was a teacher and archivist in the Warsaw ghetto. Originally from Kalvarija (now in

Lithuania), he was educated in Łódź and later in Warsaw. Gutkowski was active in the Right Po'ale Tsiyon movement. Along with Antek Zuckerman, he compiled a Yiddish anthology of Jewish history, *Payn un gvure*, for educating young people clandestinely in the Warsaw ghetto. The anthology included readings from the Jewish past about Jewish courage and Jewish martyrdom and became one of the earliest symbols of cultural resistance in the ghetto. Gutkowski was also on the executive committee of Emanuel Ringelblum's Oyneg Shabes archive. Gutkowski did much important work for the archive, including key studies about economics. He was also a liaison to Zionist youth movements, especially Dror. Gutkowski was killed, together with his wife and son, during the ghetto uprising in 1943.

Suffering and Heroism in the Jewish Past in Light of the Present
1940

A major segment of the Jewish people—the Jewish communities in Western and Central Europe—is today experiencing one of the most difficult moments in all of Jewish history. Although we Jews as a people are accustomed to difficult trials, the current troubles surpass the previous ones in many respects. They exhibit a new [. . .] will to oppress and exterminate us. In many countries in Europe where we have lived for generations our enemies strive to kill us spiritually and physically, so that no trace of us will remain.

Before the present war, antisemitism had already exposed us to terrible dangers. [. . .] The war has intensified everything and brought us to the brink of destruction. It is hard now to see a glimmer of light [. . .] in the countries of the Old World. Everywhere—with few exceptions—we see pain and sorrow in the lives of our brothers and sisters, harried and tormented in the countries that have fallen into the hands of a merciless regime.

A sinister new Middle Ages, with more murderous tools, has arrived in a new, refined twentieth-century guise. In the two years before the outbreak of the present war, tens of well-established Jewish communities in the German-speaking and Czech lands were utterly destroyed. In the short period of nine months leading up to the present, hundreds of old Jewish communities in Poland have perished. [. . .] With diabolical force the specter of the Middle Ages has forced its way into our communal life: sealed ghettos, yellow patches on the front and back, Jewish armbands, mass murder. Like the terrifying pogroms in Ukraine [in 1917–1921, during the Civil War], like the massacres of 1648–1649 [during the Khmelnytskyi Cossack revolt], these deeds will remain a blemish on human civilization. [...]

We Jews, and especially our youth, must not give in to bitterness and disgust with European civilization in view of the barbarism now flooding Europe. We have to understand that it is only a transitory phenomenon in the history of mankind. It is a nightmare provoked by the calamities of the previous world war and its social and economic consequences. If we understand this [...] we will not lose the hope for a better future. That future will surely come, because mankind is essentially good. Sooner or later that will become evident, even if today it seems everything is arrayed against us. [...]

We, an old cultural people with a rich spiritual heritage, cannot and will not perish. We have experienced countless difficult moments [...] in our three-thousand-year existence. Yet we have remained alive despite the wrath of our enemies. We have displayed the obstinacy of people who battle for a great truth and a just cause. History shows us that we are a great people—great in our suffering and in our desire to live. Such a people can be oppressed, but it cannot perish.

Let the following chapters from the broad sweep of our history, beginning with the Crusades and ending with the wave of pogroms in Ukraine in 1917–1921, strengthen our determination to overcome the present difficult moment. Our elders chose martyrdom and in the name of a higher truth withstood the worst tortures without succumbing. [...] We are like the legendary phoenix, which rises from its own ashes.

Our three-thousand-year-old history is rich in whole eras drenched in blood and tears. [...]

It is enough to mention the persecutions of the Crusaders, the Shepherds' Crusade,[1] Rindfleisch,[2] the persecutions of 1648–1649,[3] the pogroms in Russia in the 1880s, the Kishinev pogrom [of 1903], or the pogroms in Ukraine during the Civil War—and our hearts burn with anger and outrage over the innocent people who were sent to an unnatural death.

Everywhere we see the same picture: bloodthirsty killers on one side, self-sacrifice on the other, which included resistance to the killers. The heroic deeds of the Jewish self-defense during the pogroms [in Russia and Ukraine] are evidence that we can exact a high price for lives brutally cut short. [...]

Three moments in our history of martyrdom will be highlighted—three moments that inspire awe for the martyrs and hatred for those who cold-bloodedly committed the massacres. These are:

The persecutions of the Crusaders.
The persecutions of Khmelnytskyi, of accursed memory.
The pogroms against Jews in Ukraine in the years 1917–1920.

The matter-of-fact tone of our chroniclers can be depressing. They calmly recount how thousands of Jews were murdered, how long-established Jewish communities were uprooted, and how Jews sacrificed themselves for their beliefs. They tell us that with joy they gave up their lives [...] seeing this as an atonement for their sins in this world. The chronicles seldom dwell on acts of revenge. But despite the piety that dominated the Jewish masses, we nevertheless know of heroic and self-sacrificing acts of individuals and whole communities, who with a sense of their own self-worth exacted a high price for their lives. The chronicles include incidents that show that Jews became martyrs not only through passive resistance, but also by physical revenge on their oppressors. We see this in the chronicles of the Crusaders, of 1648–1649, and in many other descriptions of persecution over the course of many generations. [...]

The idea of Jewish self-defense is thus deeply rooted in the past. But it found its true place in history only in the early years of the twentieth century, during the pogroms against Jews in Russia, in Hashomer [The Guardian],[4] and in the terrible years of 1917–1920 in Ukraine. It has achieved its high point in the Haganah [1920], guardian of the Jewish community in its own land.

NOTES
1. [In 1320, a popular movement in France to drive the Moors from Spain, resulting in massacres of Jews, especially in Aragon.—Trans.]
2. [The leader of mobs that murdered Jews in Franconia, 1298.—Trans.]
3. [The rebellion of Khmelnytskyi's Ukrainian Cossacks against the Poles, during which whole Jewish communities perished.—Trans.]
4. [Founded 1909 in Ottoman Palestine to protect Jewish settlements.—Trans.]

Translated by Solon Beinfeld.

Other works by Zuckerman: *Sefer milḥamot ha-geta'ot: ben ha-ḥomot, ba-maḥanot, ba-ye'arot* (1954);

A Surplus of Memory: Chronicle of the Warsaw Ghetto Uprising (1993).

Corinne Chochem and Muriel Roth

Chochem, 1905–1990

Born in Zhvanets, Russia (now in Ukraine), Corinne Chochem immigrated with her family in 1902 to the United States, where she helped shape the teaching of Israeli folk dance in North America. In 1930, she visited Palestine, working on a kibbutz and studying folk dance. Later she taught at the Jewish Theological Seminary, the University of California, and Cornell University.

Roth, 1908–1990

Composer Muriel Roth (originally Parker) was born in Chicago and received her master's degree in music from the University of Chicago. She married author Henry Roth in 1939, beginning her collaboration with Corinne Chochem in the ensuing years. Later in her life, Roth composed a song cycle titled *Babi Yar*, as well as several works for strings.

Palestine Dances!

1941

Foreword

Against the setting sun, in the fields near a kevutzah in Palestine, a group of young halutzim are dancing. All day long they have worked hard on the land. The morrow brings another day of toil. Still, their zest for life is undaunted and their spirit undimmed.

The dancers move joyously round in a circle—strong, sure and impassioned. Their voices are raised in vibrant song. Their rhythm quickens. Their tempo becomes more staccato. Now the circle breaks and another halutz joins in. The circle closes and the dance goes round, faster and faster. [. . .]

The Sephardic Jews, who, as exiles from Spain after the Inquisition, had migrated to the Balkans and settled there, absorbed this dance into their own ceremony. It became for them a dance of joy, to celebrate their *simhas*—their weddings and their holidays. [. . .]

Like many early folk dances, the Palestinian Horah is circular in form. It begins slowly but vigorously at an even, measured tempo. Its movements are strong and deliberate, and, in the manner of most primitive and oriental dances, it builds on a fast exhilarated crescendo to a continuing, excited whirl.

Moreover, though never losing its force and dynamic rhythms, the Horah subtly fuses the healthy energy of the youthful builders with the mystic ecstasy and abandon of their Hassidic forbears, the exaggerated, sensuous movements giving to the dance new, rich and colorful overtones.

But what matters the story of this dance! The important thing is that after long hours of hard labor in the fields and factories, a people engaged in the upbuilding of a new land find new enthusiasm, new strength and new hope with which to face the difficult years ahead when they dance the Horah, their dance of affirmation.

Look! The plow breaks the soil.

"Y'Minah, Y'Minah," c. 1941. Photo credit: The Dorot Jewish Division, The New York Public Library, Astor, Lenox, and Tilden Foundations.

See
The beauty of the day.
Breath quickens—
The spade, the fork, the rake, the hoe
In happy unison, skillfully
Quicken the earth.

Other work by Chochem: *Jewish Holiday Dances* (1948).

Israel Halperin

1910–1971

Historian Israel Halperin was born in Białystok. In 1934, he immigrated to Palestine, where he taught at the Hebrew University. His research focused on the history of Eastern European Jewry, and he published a number of important works in that field. He helped to create the Israel Historical Society and was editor of the journals *Zion* and *Shivat Zion*. *The Book of Valor* is a three-volume anthology that he completed in 1950.

The Book of Valor
1941

Foreword

This book seeks to unfold before the reader the scroll of Jewish valor, in both Israel and the diaspora, from the destruction of the Hebrew state to the harbingers of the renaissance of the Jewish man. And these are the manifestations of valor during this period: wars of liberation, self-defense, and martyrdom.

Wars of Liberation

On the 9th of Av 3830 [August 2, 70 CE], the Temple was destroyed, and on the 8th of Elul [August 31, 70 CE], dawn rose on a Jerusalem in flames. The great rebellion was steeped in blood and the last vestiges of political rule were taken from Israel. Indeed, on the heights of Masada the revolt had not yet petered out. Nevertheless, it did not take long for its defenders to grant each other a hero's grace, taking their own lives and those of the women and children, before tasting the bitterness of slavery. This was the end of the last rebel stronghold. Although at an end, the war was not over. With every new political constellation, the hope of political salvation was rekindled. Ties were formed; revolts broke out. Scant information regarding these attempts has been preserved for us. [. . .]

However, the kernels of historical truth hidden in all the sources—both Jewish and non-Jewish—speak for themselves, telling of recurring plots and rebellions over hundreds of years, up to the conquest of the Land of Israel by the Arabs, to rise up and rebel against the foreign conquerors and restore political liberation to the Jewish people. These sources recount the love of freedom, the power of the soul, and the valor of a desperate people, showing no fear whatsoever.

The Arab conquest put an end to the wars of liberation. The connection with the Land of Israel lost its concrete, conquest-oriented aspect, taking on a messianic, spiritual guise instead. [. . .]

The more we delve into succeeding generations, the more the bond between the Jewish people and the Land of Israel becomes spiritual and abstract. Manifestations of valor among Jews, both in the Land of Israel and in the diaspora, from the destruction of the Second Temple until the Arab conquest—in the event that such information has reached us—are almost always related to the possibility of a political renaissance in the Jewish homeland. After the conquest, the focus shifts from the homeland to the diaspora.

Self-Defense

In the seventh century, we still find autonomous Jewish tribes in the Arab desert, whose strength derives from the sword. However, they, too, suffered through times of tribulation, and in later generations we have only legends and fanciful rumors about independent Jewish tribes. The lessons learned from the wars of liberation and the survival instinct of a persecuted people gave the Jews other defense mechanisms. Money, assimilation, and even apparent conversion, instead of the sword, were the coin by which Jews were forced to purchase their security. [. . .]

The medieval Jew is always described as helpless and unprotected. Though there is much truth to such a description, it is also something of an exaggeration. [. . .]

As in the days of the Crusades and the [Khmelnytskyi] pogroms of 1648–1649 in Poland, and also at various other times and places, Jews knew how to gird their loins for battle, put on armor, and barricade themselves within castles and fortresses—and if they had no such recourse, they entrenched themselves within their ghettos and synagogues—defending their lives with valor to the very end. This entire chapter of Jews capable of defending themselves and actually doing so has not been researched to date. Jewish historiography has mainly concentrated on describing the martyrology and spiritual life of the Jewish people and has given no consideration—with the exception of B[en-Zion] Dinaburg—to discovering instances of activist defense, of which there were many, as an initial survey indicates.

As previously stated, even in the diaspora, Jews knew how to protect themselves, preemptively killing those who had come to kill them. However, their chances of successfully defending themselves were slight and few in number, and any such attempt was tantamount to facing certain death—being killed by the enemy or taking their own life while there was still time, before the enemy had an opportunity to abuse them. This heroic death, in all its various forms and shades, is what is known as martyrdom [*kiddush hashem*—sanctifying God's name].

Kiddush Hashem

During the Middle Ages, any Jew killed because of his Jewishness was considered a martyr. However, we are dealing here with *kiddush hashem* only as a component of Jewish defense, as a manifestation of fighting for one's life: body and soul. It would seem that the term *kiddush hashem*, as it crystallized in the medieval period, was created only after the destruction of the Temple, but the act itself is deeply rooted in Jewish heroic consciousness from ancient times. During the period of Judges and Kings, we find sporadic displays of heroic assembly, increasing in number during the days of the wars of liberation. Samson calls out: "Let me die with the Philistines" [Judges 16:30] and brings the house down upon himself and all the celebrants inside. Saul falls on his sword, so the uncircumcised [non-Israelites] would not abuse him. And Razi, the Jewish leader during the Hasmonean period, attempted suicide three times rather than fall into enemy hands. [. . .]

Shortly after the destruction of the Temple, a law was instituted in the attic of a house in Lod: for all the transgressions found in the Torah, if you say to someone, "You may transgress so as not to be killed," that person may commit the transgression so as not to be killed—except in the case of idolatry, incest, and bloodshed [b.Sanhedrin 74a]. And Rabbi Akiva said: "He should be killed as an example to others" [b.Avodah Zarah 18a]. From then on, *kiddush hashem* continued covertly from generation to generation, from country to country, reaching its peak on the banks of the Rhine during the Crusades, spreading to Spain, England, Poland, and

other countries—filling the world with the terrible cries of the slaughtered, the burned and the drowned, as they expired, uttering the last word of the Shema [Hear, O Israel, the Lord is our God, the Lord is One].

The outline presented above does not give a complete picture of the manifestations of Jewish defense, in all its various forms and circumstances. It is only a general overview. On the other hand, for details and personalities, events and deeds, thoughts and theories—the reader is invited to study the main body of this work.

The reader will discover—one by one—the remnants of Jewish valor and rebellion, which never ceased to exist even in times of humiliation and tribulation. And heretofore unknown links are revealed herein between the defenders of Masada, who took their own lives rather than undergo slavery, and those, who, after 1,800 years, raised the banner of Jewish defense in the Land of Israel and strove to return and rebuild their country.

Translated by Marvin Meital.

Other works by Halperin: *Pinkas va'ad arba' aratsot* (1945); *Bet yisra'el be-polin* (1948); *Ha-'aliyot ha-rish'onot shel ha-hasidim le-'erets yisra'el* (1956).

Shimon Huberband

1909–1942

Shimon Huberband was born in Chęciny, Poland, into a rabbinic family. A religious Zionist, he founded the Society for Jewish Scholarship in Otwock and published widely on theological and historical topics. After his family was killed in a German air raid in 1939, Huberband went to Warsaw, where he became one of Emanuel Ringelblum's most valued collaborators in the Oyneg Shabes archive. His unique work in Yiddish, later published in Hebrew and English under the title *Kiddush Hashem*, documents how Poland's religious Jews responded to the Holocaust. Most of Huberband's writings, discovered in the Oyneg Shabes archive, remain in manuscript or scattered in the prewar Yiddish and Orthodox Hebrew press.

Ghetto Folklore

1941

Jokes

1

The Führer inquires of General Franco, "Comrade, how did you solve the Jewish problem?"

Franco answers, "I instituted the yellow badge."

"That's nothing," says Hitler. "I imposed tributes, instituted ghettos, lessened their food rations, imposed forced labor." He goes on, enumerating a long list of edicts and persecutions.

Finally, Franco says, "I gave the Jews autonomy and Jewish councils."

"Ah," says Hitler, "that's the solution."

2

The Führer embarked on a journey to visit all the hospitals. Upon his arrival in a certain one, the hospital director gave him a tour and showed him everything. The Führer unexpectedly barged into a corridor and found a securely locked room. This seemed very suspicious to the Führer. He insisted on seeing the room.

"If you insist, then I must first explain what is inside," the hospital director said to Hitler. "Locked up inside, there is a madman whose external appearance is similar to yours. His illness expresses itself in his self-delusion that he is the Führer."

"If that is the case," said the Führer, "then I must see him." Hitler entered the room alone. After a short while, he left the room. But no one is certain which one left and which one remained inside—Hitler or the madman.

3

God dispatched an angel from heaven to find out what's new on earth. The angel returned with a report that he simply could not understand the world. "England is unarmed, and does not want peace. Germany is armed and wants peace. And the Jews are screaming that everything is fine."

4

God forbid that the war last as long as the Jews are capable of enduring.

5

Another version: How long will the hardships last? God forbid that the hardships last as long as the Jews can endure. Because if the hardships last that long, who knows if they will really endure them?

6

Where does Hitler feel best?
In the toilet. There, all the brown masses are behind him.

7

Rubinshteyn says, "I had a *groschen*, but lost it; I had a *tsveyer* (two-groschen piece) but lost it; I had a *drayer* (three-groschen piece) but lost it. Only the *firer* (four-*groschen* piece) I can't seem to lose.

8

Jews are now very pious. They observe all the ritual laws: they are stabbed and punched with holes like *matzahs* and have as much bread as on Passover; they are beaten like *hoshanahs* [willow twigs beaten at the end of the Sukkot festival]; rattled like Haman [during the reading of the Purim Megillah]; they are as green as *esrogim* [citrons used for Sukkot]; they fast as if it were Yom Kippur; they are burnt as if it were Hanukkah [i.e., candles]; and their moods are as if it were the Ninth of Av.

Legends

6. They Fell into Their Own Trap

A large number of German automobiles stopped on Marszalkowska Street. They began to grab Jews from all directions, to be taken to forced labor. A sizable number of Jews were assembled, several hundred. The Germans ordered them to stand in circles and dance around the automobiles, while singing the Polish national anthem. And the Jews were forced to do so.

Before long, hundreds of Jews and thousands of Poles came running to observe the spectacle. At first, they were satisfied with staring, laughing, and poking fun at the unfortunate Jews.

When they saw that the Germans were not interfering with them, the Poles became bolder, and began to beat the dancing Jews. They grabbed the hat of one Jew, pulled another Jew by his jacket, seized a third one by the ear, etc.

By this time, the German soldiers were infuriated against the Poles. In the midst of the dancing, when the streets were filled with thousands of Poles, both sides of Marszalkowska Street were suddenly sealed off by a large unit of military policemen and soldiers. The Jews were ordered to "beat it!"

The soldiers and military policemen suddenly threw themselves at the Poles, locked them up in vehicles, and took them away to Germany for forced labor.

Translated by David E. Fishman.

Samuel Felix Mendelsohn

1889–1953

Born in Starobin, Russia, the rabbi and writer Samuel Felix Mendelsohn immigrated to the United States at the age of seventeen, initially settling in New Jersey. He attended the University of Cincinnati and chose Hebrew Union College for his rabbinical studies. Following his ordination, he took a position at Temple Beth Israel in Chicago, where he remained until his death. As a writer, he was drawn to Jewish humor and folklore, publishing four books on the topic. He also wrote editorials for the *Chicago Sentinel* and was involved in the founding of the Jewish Book Council, along with Boston librarian Fanny Goldstein.

Let Laughter Ring

1941

Preface

Now, more than at any time in the history of our people, humor has a place in Jewish life. I was delighted to find the Jewish Publication Society in agreement with me that at the present time the Jew should be encouraged to laugh. Several valuable books of Jewish humor have appeared in the last few years in German, Yiddish, and Hebrew. The present volume, however, is neither a translation of these collections nor is it in any way dependent upon them. It represents an original effort.

The stories come from a variety of sources. Many were actually told by American Jews and Gentiles. Others were culled from the humor column of the Yiddish and Anglo-Jewish press. The remainder were sent in by numerous friends in response to an appeal issued through the *Chicago Jewish Sentinel* (of which I was editorial writer for a decade and a half). To all those who supplied stories for this collection I offer profound thanks. [. . .]

The stories mirror the many-sided life of the Jewish people and are, in a real sense, a commentary on it. Some carry on the moralizing tendency characteristic of Jewish lore in the past; others continue to reflect, though with decreasing emphasis, the time-honored Jewish assumption that knowledge is the greatest good. In number and importance, however, the stories we tell, like the life we lead, show our interest in the newer and more practical problems. Adjustment to new environments, religious flux and change, characteristics and attitudes adopted by various sections of the Jewish people offer many and serious problems. It is well to see these problems also from the point of view of the humor inherent within them.

Recent years have witnessed the rise of anti-Semitism, particularly in occidental countries. Since this movement is primarily *made in Germany*, all anti-Semitic stories are grouped in a chapter entitled "The Third Reich." This tragic phase of Jewish life is counter-balanced by the tremendous progress which Jews have made in Palestine. This fact is recorded in a new group of stories under the title "The Promised Land." The number of stories dealing with American Jewry is considerably larger than in my first collection, thus pointing to the conclusion that a greater and stronger Jewish community is being created on these shores.

The Prescribed Reward

Simon: Well, what's new today?

Nathan: At last I do have something new. I have just heard a brand new Nazi joke. What do I get for telling it?

Simon: Don't you know by this time? Six months in a concentration camp.

Degrees in Animosity

Manfred Gruenberg, Jewish refugee from Nazidom, was on a streetcar in Amsterdam, where he overheard two Germans discussing Hitler.

"Do you know," said one of the Germans, "Hitler is not as bad as his enemies make of him. The trouble with Hitler is that he is his own worst enemy."

"Not while I am alive!" shouted Gruenberg.

There's One in Every Family

Mrs. Lichtig: How are you, Mrs. Cohen? Haven't seen you in ages. How are your boys?

Mrs. Cohen: You know how it goes. I am getting older and the boys have grown into manhood.

Mrs. Lichtig: How is little Morris?

Mrs. Cohen: He's a strapping six footer now. He calls himself Mortimer Crane. He is a noted lawyer and he will handle no case for less than $500.

Mrs. Lichtig: And your middle son, Sammy, I believe?

Mrs. Cohen: He too changed his name. He is a noted doctor and calls himself Seymour Kingsley. He is a surgeon and his bottom price is not a cent less than $1000 for every operation.

Mrs. Lichtig: And your oldest, Abie?

Mrs. Cohen: He's the same Abie Cohen. He won't change his name or his manner. He is still working in the same clothing store on Canal Street—and, between you and me, if not for Abie we would all starve to death.

Other works by Mendelsohn: *The Jew Laughs* (1935); *Here's a Good One* (1947); *The Merry Heart* (1951).

Oyneg Shabes Archive

In 1940, the Warsaw Jewish historian Emanuel Ringelblum created the secret Warsaw ghetto archive, code-named Oyneg Shabes to preserve secrecy. He brought together a group of more than sixty people, secular and religious, rightists and leftists, imbued by a national and moral mission of collecting documents, artifacts, and photographs to record Jewish life under Nazi occupation and to ensure that posterity and future historians would know the Jews on the basis of Jewish, not German, sources. Two caches of the archive, buried in August 1942 and February 1943, were discovered after the war. A third was lost. Of the sixty members of the Oyneg Shabes there were only three survivors. Because of ghetto archives like the Oyneg Shabes, historians can write about Jews in the Nazi ghettos not as faceless, anonymous victims but as individuals and members of a community that still reflected prewar values and culture.

Guidelines for the Study of the Warsaw Ghetto 1942

Historical Overview: Demographics: Apartments, Living Conditions

Economics
- Workers
- Handicraft and small industry: guilds (*tsekhn*)
- Trade and industry under Aryan trustees
- Free professions: doctors, lawyers, teachers, engineers
- Trade
- Smuggling
- Owning and managing apartments
- Shops

- Employees in ghetto institutions
- Wages and salaries
- Finances and currency exchange
- The ghetto as an economic phenomenon
- From what do Jews live (questionnaire: legal and illegal [occupations])
- Labor unions and the cooperatives

Social Help

- General overview
- The organizations: ŻTOS, CENTOS, TOZ, Aleynhilf
- House committees
- Feeding
  Soup kitchens (Leszno 40, Nalewki 23, Twarda 15, Leszno 29, Zamenhofa 15, Nalewki 22, Nowolipki 68, Karmelicka 29)
- Expellees (*goylim*) and refugees
- Refugee centers (*punktn*)
- Help for children
- Epidemics
- Sanitary services
- Provision of clothing
- TOPOROL[1]
- Help for relatives (*kroyvim hilf*)
- The Judenrat and class tension
- Constructive help: free loan *kases* [credit societies]
- Hospitals
- Religious department

Social and Cultural Life

- General overview
- Social life (*gezelshaftlekh lebn*)
- Literature
- Scholarship and science (*visnshaft*)
- Folklore: sayings, jokes, letters
- Music choirs
- Schools: private schooling (*kompletn*)
- Handicraft training
- Students and classes
- Religious life
- "Them" [the Germans]—attitude to Jews
- Converts
- Converts in the Judenrat
- Converts in artistic life
- Youth
- Libraries

- Women
- Demoralization and corruption
- Housing department
- Inspiring (*derheybene*) moments of Jewish life

Polish–Jewish Relations: The Judenrat (Kehile)

- Organization of the Ghetto (Jewish residential quarter)
- Legal position of the Judenrat
- Development of the Judenrat
- Territorial changes in the boundaries of the Jewish Quarter: topography, geography, names
- Food supply
- Coal Supply Commission
- Post Office
- Jewish police (converts in the police)
- Insurance
- Banks
- Pharmacies
- Health department
- Labor Department
- Cemetery
- Trash and waste removal
- "Protected buildings"
- Industry and trade
- Finance department
- Social aid
- Statistical department
- Housing department

Expellees and Refugees (the Sociological Problems Stemming from Being Uprooted from One's Home)

Artists (Artistn)

Painters

Musicians

Daily Life of Workers, Artisans, Smugglers

The Jewish Child

Shops

NOTE

1. Before the war the TOPOROL was an organization that fostered agricultural education among Jews. In the Warsaw ghetto it organized the planting of vegetable gardens in vacant lots.

Translated by Samuel D. Kassow.

Yehuda Even-Shmuel

1886–1976

Born Yehuda Kaufman in Balta, Ukraine, Yehuda Even-Shmuel received a traditional Jewish education and later studied philosophy and history in London and Paris. Between 1913 and 1919 he lived in Montreal, where he helped to found the Jewish Public Library and taught in the newly established Yidishe Folksshul. He became principal of the Jewish Teacher's Seminary in New York, but in 1926 he left for Palestine, where he worked at the Dvir publishing company and, along with poet Ḥayim Naḥman Bialik and others, helped complete the first major English–Hebrew dictionary. His translations of the first two sections of Maimonides's *Guide of the Perplexed* and of Judah Halevi's *Kuzari* from Arabic into modern Hebrew garnered him the Israel Prize in 1973.

Midrashim of Redemption
1943

> And I will wait upon the Lord,
> who hides His face from the house of Jacob,
> and I will look for Him. (Isaiah 8:16)

I endeavored to place before the educated reader all the literature of redemption that is known to us today from printed sources and manuscripts. I presented the items as they are. I did not modify them, nor try to embellish, but I did make many corrections. Most of the sources have come down to us in mangled form. Some were in a desperate and distressing state. The path taken by Jellinek, Horowitz, Wertheimer, and their colleagues, those who published the smaller *midrashim*, also including Buttenweiser, Israel Levi, and Dr. Heiger, did not seem suitable to my purpose; where they preserve corrupt readings as something sacred, whether or not they provide annotation, I had a deep-felt need to correct them to the best of my ability. I presented the justification for my corrections in general in the introductions to the various and individual *midrashim*—and in variant readings at the end of the book. I am confident that most lovers of truth will agree with most of my textual emendations. The educated reader in particular will take great interest in this compendium, in which all the important apocalyptic works that were created by the members of our nation in apocalyptic times have been collected in a single place. These works illuminated the darkness of the period, and to the extent that their prophecies remained unfulfilled in their day, they were left to be read by following generations. During the present holocaust, let us not despair of redemption, because our redemption will come soon, and all those who await it with perfect faith will be privileged to hear the footsteps of the redeemer in his day! [. . .]

I will make special mention here of the one and only, whose light, though he left us years ago, is still with us, Ḥayim Naḥman Bialik. I retain impressions from conversations with him about the redemption, and these I recalled in the course of my work when I came to write about the history of longings for redemption among the Jews.

The hope of our generation is that we will be the last of those who wait in longing and the first to be redeemed, that in our day the Jewish people will be reborn in their land, and that from the flames of our destruction our great fire will arise, the holy fire of life and creativity.

Translated by Jeffrey M. Green.

Berakha Ḥabas
1900–1968

An editor, writer, and educator, Berakha Ḥabas was one of the first women journalists in Israel. Born in Alytus, Lithuania, to a wealthy, religious family, Ḥabas was the fourth child in a family of seven. In 1908, she emigrated with her family to Palestine, where she studied at the Lewinsky Teachers' Seminary in Tel Aviv. Ḥabas served on the editorial board of the newspaper *Davar* from 1935 to 1953 and was also an editor at the Am Oved publishing house. During and immediately following World War II, she served as the editor in chief of *Min Ha-moked*, a library of original and translated works that chronicled the world crisis.

Letters from the Ghettos
1943

To the Reader

The two hundred and fifty letters presented here require no preliminaries or commentary. No human language is adequate to the task. Even the account of our people's history, drenched as it is in blood and suffering, will fail to communicate the horror now being perpetrated against us.

These letters *are not* a receptacle of Jewish tears. They are but the flutter of hope, faint and feeble, that has been secretly agitating between despair and loss; an echo to the spirit of the pioneering youths who, in spite of the calamities and disappointments, have kept alive the dream of a redeeming Land of Israel, envisioned from afar for years upon years, but never achieved.

The letters in this collection hint at the great Jewish struggle to overcome the dire conditions and to live and to create no matter the circumstances. Herein lie the testimonies to the many brave efforts to secure passage and survival, while fulfilling the goal of agricultural training for Zionist settlement: to organize the collective life in the ghetto based on the principle of mutual responsibility, and to assist the wounded and the refugees in every way possible. From these letters rise the desperate calls that knocked on the heart of the world, and on our hearts, the bold attempts to cross borders, to save and to be saved, the majesty of Jewish girls who took upon themselves the mission that fate had assigned them, the tireless covert endeavor to acquire weapons, to plan a last and desperate uprising—all this is revealed in between the lines of these brief, ordinary letters, written in coded phrases by inexperienced underground resistance fighters.

The writers, one and all, are members of the movement, raised on the ideals and the aspirations to build the Land of Israel and to be built by it, ideals they held in their hearts until their last breaths. They are the members of the Zionist-Socialist party, members of He-ḥaluts, and of the Labor Party youth movement. Some of them are the dedicated veterans, upon whom the fate of our people levied exile and death. Some are young and fervent, who, from afar, nourished their souls with the life and breath of the land but, due to criminal immigration policy, were not allowed to set foot in their homeland.

We can never know with certainty what they felt at the end, to what extent they still believed and hoped, despaired and rebelled, blessed or cursed. We will never know what we could have done and failed to do, what opportunities we missed, and if we could have saved, but failed to save. No matter how much the heart expands reading these letters, these surviving remnants, no matter how hard we knock our heads against the wall, wishing to smash it and open a crack for rescue, no matter how much we torment ourselves for not doing more when we could, for not jolting the indifference of states and peoples—we will never know, we will never grasp what truly took place, how it happened, and what they were thinking.

These letters—they are but a few of the many, maybe one out of ten or maybe even less, of those accumulated during the war years in the archives of the Jewish Agency, the Histadrut, and the organizations connected with the pioneer youth movements in the diaspora. Bundles upon bundles. Most of them are written in German, and the rest in Polish, French, English, and, from some countries, Hebrew, sometimes fluent, other times less so. Most of the letters are translated here for the first time, while others, those that have already been published in booklets, or in newsletters of institutions and organizations, have now been reexamined and sorted out according to countries and dates, with explanations and comments added—all accomplished with the utmost care and caution.

The greater the distance from the original letters—from the bundles of fine rustling pages, densely packed, one after the other, short letters and long ones from many different countries in Europe, letters wherein Jewish lives quiver as they face the gallows—so too, the vigor of the original tends to fade. Additionally, many details had to be omitted, names, places, certain facts. And yet, it is impossible to judge whether enough caution has been exercised. Likewise, it is impossible to judge whether the added explanations and comments do indeed bring us closer to the truth in every instance. This selection, then, is only a fraction of the overall duty incumbent upon us as we come to decipher the bundles of letters from the ghettos, to collect and catalog and publish them in their entirety—an undertaking whose time perhaps is still in the future.

Most of the letters, up until the middle of 1942, were sent to a single address, to a contact bureau in a neutral country. After that date, they were sent to the contact bureau in a different neutral country. For security reasons, the names were omitted. Also omitted are a few names of addressees here in the land. Names in the body of the letters, as well as the signatures, were omitted except for a few names in cases where there was no doubt they were no longer among the living.

Let this booklet, then, also serve as a mark of our sorrow and mourning, a memorial candle to their resistance and their deeds, to the few whose names from now on will be our symbols, and to the many, the thousands of the nameless, to the young and the lively who were slaughtered, an "ingathering of the exiles" of the tortured and the sanctified, camps upon camps, the pioneers from the east and the west. Day by day the list grows longer, the list of names we can safely publish, and the heart grows heavy.

He who gathered these letters, one after the other, became like one who seals in his heart the ocean of tortures and murders, one who carries in his body and flesh the yellow star, one who walks behind the boxcars of death. He who edited the letters became like one who dips his pen in the blood of brothers, one who hears the cries of the tortured, one who sees with his very eyes the quivers of hope and disillusionment.

Let the one who comes to read these letters be as one who touches the sanctities of his people. Let him be aware that he is dwelling among his saintly and his loved ones, he absorbs their grief, he breathes their hope, and their destiny is engraved in him.

Their blood will not be stilled, the living glory of our people!

This collection was assembled with the assistance and advice of M. Neustadt and M. Kluger.

Translated by Tsipi Keller.

Other works by Ḥabas: *Ḥomah u-migdal* (1939); *Korot ma'apil tsa'ir* (1942); *David Ben-Guryon ve-doro* (1952); *He-ḥatser ve-ha-giv'ah* (1968).

Oskar Rosenfeld

1884-1944

Oskar Rosenfeld, a novelist, journalist, translator, and diarist, was born in Koryčany, Moravia, and studied in Vienna, where he became an active Zionist. Rosenfeld wrote about literature, art, and theater for several Jewish newspapers and published his first novel in 1910. In 1927, he was one of the founders of the Jüdische Künstlerspiele, a theater that presented Yiddish works in German. Rosenfeld was also editor in chief of the weekly *Die neue Welt*. In 1938, he fled to Prague, where he was a correspondent for a Jewish newspaper until he was deported to the Łódź ghetto in 1941. In the ghetto, he worked in the statistics department. Hoping to expose the conditions under which Jews suffered, he kept copious notes in school notebooks. He died in Auschwitz.

Encyclopedia of the Łódź Ghetto
1943

A group of people living together under extreme coercive conditions without the conscious intent of forming a community of common fate created forms that were only possible on the basis of the ghetto. Everyday life required certain norms of work and existence. It created its own structure, its own language, its own terminology. Nowhere in the world was there a human community comparable to that of the ghetto.

The change of all social, intellectual, and economic functions brought with it a change in the most common-place conceptions. Concepts that until then were understood unambiguously everywhere among Europeans underwent a complete transformation. They had to adjust to the conditions that came into force with the ghetto. As soon as freedom of movement, the freedom to act, was gone, words, adages, sentences, too, could no longer be used in the conventional sense. The transformation of forms of living forced the transformation of forms of concepts.

Furthermore: Words and the word order were no longer adequate for the demands of the ghetto world. New words had to be created, old ones had to be endowed with new meaning. The three-language base—Yiddish, Polish, German—broadened the foundation of this process. This created the possibility for enrichment of the ghetto language as well as further refinement and the introduction of greater nuances.

Words, which until now had only an innate meaning, were endowed with secondary meaning. These might be ironic but also strictly factual. There was an especial opportunity to expand the meaning of Yiddish words. To the religion-bound, traditional word structure a more current meaning was added. In this connection, some individuals found an outlet for their talent of creating plays on words. Thereby, concepts arose in the way proverbs, or "words from the mouth of the people," used to be created. The source of these linguistic creations is the people, the masses themselves. Nobody can say when or where he heard this or that word, or this or that phrase, for the first time. The *phonetic* origin of these newly created concepts can be documented in countless cases. Since there is no newspaper nor any other printed word or written word that could be disseminated in black and white, the new formulation can only circulate from mouth to mouth.

A new formulation makes its way through the ghetto with the speed of a rumor. With ceaseless passion, hungry for anything worth hearing—even if it is something abstract—the ghetto man absorbs every word variant. For him it is news, that is, a living factor in the monotony of his existence.

Words for things of daily use have suddenly assumed prominence in the use of language. Since the concern for the meager products for a meal pushes to the side all other functions of animal existence, the objects connected with this concern gain the utmost significance—whether they be expressed in Yiddish, Polish, or German words.

Intellectual needs are pressed together in a narrow frame. They require only a few words, concepts, or word associations. The ghetto must renounce all technical assistance from civilization. Political and metaphysical aspirations are excluded. Religious functions are restricted to a narrow circle. What is left is only the area of nutrition and of ressort[1] work, a paltry ground to nourish the unfurling of linguistic life.

And yet, within this limited sphere of intellectual activity, the imagination and humor of the people were able to unfold. A long line of poignant characterizations have earned credibility in the ghetto. Concepts with serious meaning have received an ironic connotation, everyday expressions have been elevated to a higher level. In addition, there are many words previously in little use that now have become very popular among all classes of ghetto dwellers. Polish words in particular have come into general use.

Overall, it is to be noted that the vocabulary has broadened within the confines of the ghetto. Everywhere we encounter expressions that were unknown before the creation of the ghetto or outside the confines of the ghetto. The atmosphere into which the ghetto is strapped determines to some degree the extent of the linguistic forms and vocabulary at the ghetto dweller's disposal.

A collection of these linguistic and word treasures forms part of the cultural history of the ghetto. In a future period, when the ghetto will be researched, such a collection, such an encyclopedia, will add to an understanding, where a mere description of the condition is inadequate. The word, the language, is the history of mankind. This thesis has long been proven by scholars; the language is a more reliable witness and source of truth than other, material artifacts.

The present encyclopedia makes no claim to be a complete and unambiguous explanation of the definitions of words. But it believes itself to be close to its set goal.

In order to achieve this goal, several ghetto personalities have been consulted who, on the basis of their position or their above-average talent (individuality), can lay claim to being inscribed in the dictionary of the cultural history of Ghetto Litzmannstadt. The names themselves must stand the test of objective evaluation. Some personalities listed may not have played an active role in the ghetto but can nevertheless be regarded as "prominent Jews."

A dictionary of ghetto language and ghetto personalities will, no doubt, have historical value beyond the immediate occasion.

Finally must be mentioned that the editors of the encyclopedia have attempted to do justice to the material without any preconceptions and to present thereby a building block for the cultural history of the ghetto.

O. R., December 1, 1943

NOTE

1. [*Ressort*, or factory, was a shortened version of the German term *Arbeitsressort*, meaning "work station" or "workplace."—Eds.]

Translated by Brigitte M. Goldstein.

Other works by Rosenfeld: *Die vierte Galerie: ein wiener Roman* (1910); *Mendl Ruhig* (1914); *Tage und Nächte* (1920).

Leo W. Schwarz

1906-1967

Leo Walder Schwarz was born in New York City and attended Harvard University. After serving in World War II, Schwarz remained in Germany, helping Jewish refugees in the Munich area in his capacity as director of the Joint Distribution Committee. He later wrote *The Redeemers* (1953), which chronicles the fates of Jewish survivors of the Holocaust. A professor of Judaic Studies at Iowa University from 1960 to 1962, Schwarz is best known as an editor of anthologies of Jewish memoirs and literature.

Memoirs of My People through a Thousand Years
1943

I

The anthologist, like the historian and the novelist, is an autobiographer is disguise. He is driven into the jungles and watering places of literature by instinct as well as by design. The ultimate form in which he exhibits his loot is dictated not only by public taste; it is above all the expression of those fundamental impulses and habits that lead him to the library-cubicle rather than

to the market-place. For this reason, and for weightier ones that will soon appear evident, I shall endeavor to explain autobiographically, in part at least, the genesis and character of this book.

II

[. . .] [S]ome years after I had left Cambridge, I soon realized that, despite my continuing studies in the same field, my appreciation of the 4,000-year Jewish experience was dangerously one-sided. There were sources, periods, books, personages galore. But what of their taproots—the wonderful vigor, passion and yearning of the people? I had certainly failed to see the emotional glow and color of passing generations, the electric contact between men, women and children linked enduringly by a passionately remembered experience, the nobility and the degradation of the inarticulate common man. In short, I had failed to understand the essential spirit, the hot-burning heart of my people. [. . .]

While the reason for this shortcoming might conceivably be attributed to ignorance—the bewildering haze of four millennia has cowed more informed minds—it is more likely to be found in the rather prevalent scholastic approach to the Jewish humanities. To continue with myself as a guinea pig, I recall the study, during college years, of historical texts in the admirable Hebrew volumes of Abraham Kahana. Imbedded among them were excerpts of experience told in the first person. (Incidentally, many of them appear in this book for the first time in English translation.) These revelations of character passed over my mind almost without making a dent. I was intent only on the light that these passages threw upon the development of legal and religious tradition. It hardly occurred to me then that such personal accounts and piquant details were revelations of central significance or that the manner of life of the narrator might be something more than a chunk of literary archeology. I did not look upon them as expressions of the "life drive" that gave a peculiar cast to the living tradition and helped to explain the epic of group survival. Nor had I discovered that an intimately personal anecdote, a tactless letter, or a flash of humor, brings us closer to the stuff of life than a papal bull or a rabbinical responsum.

[. . .] One of the first autobiographies that intrigued me was a little work in which Nahman's amanuensis Boswelled him. Without conscious effort I began to search for memoirs, and it was natural that I should come upon the engrossing works of Gamaliel Bradford who had, as no other writer before, mastered the whole field of autobiographical literature. [. . .]

IV

[. . .] You will note also the strong sense of community feeling and the prodigious attachment to intellectual effort. I mention these because they help to explain why I have launched this collection in midstream rather than at the source. The first tale is by an Italian poet of the eleventh century, and the dramatis personae move across an Eastern Mediterranean stage. What of the Biblical epoch, the Greek and Roman epochs? Simply this: Virtually no autobiographical literature is extant from these times. [. . .] The gist of the matter is given in the admirable introduction of Henrietta Szold to the memoirs of Rebekah Kohut: "That Jewish literature should be deficient in personal material lay in the nature of Jewish life as it was perforce constituted. In the overwhelming sum of communal woe and communal aspiration, the individual sank out of sight. His personal desires, trials, successes were frail straws rapidly swirled out of sight on the stream of community life." [. . .] Fortunately, there were exceptions, both among the leaders and the people, and they have made the first part of this book possible. [. . .]

I cannot close without yielding slightly to an irresistible urge to generalize. As I reread these pages, a question posed itself relentlessly: Do these personalities really exhibit only a people of the Book? Does not the life they reveal transcend the Book, and even the Word? I do not pretend to have a ready answer, but an answer must be found if the love of life and joy in wisdom and beauty that is reflected in the highest moments of this millennial experience are to continue. I wonder whether the sovereign achievement of Jews is in their extraordinary religious and intellectual attainments or in the high order of social life they achieved in chronically hostile states and cultures. I am reminded that this pageant of personal history underlines the dangers of black-and-white judgments. The historian, the apologist and the journalist have given us a set of neat labels that for the most part portray Jews as angels or devils. But Jews, like other historical families, like life itself, elude generalization; they are human natural, so to speak, reflecting all the complications and all the contradictions that characterize the struggle for survival and self-expression. Matthew Arnold's classic distinction between Hellenism and Hebraism does not square

with experience: there is as much "sweetness and light" in the character of Jews as there is "fire and strength" in the Greek mind. Nor does Israel Zangwill's superlative epigram, when put to the test, fare any better: the sons of Hellas lived in "the beauty of holiness" just as the sons of Jacob felt the "holiness of beauty." Indeed, what does seem to shine out of the literature of personal experience is the fundamental unity of the human spirit.

Other works by Schwarz: *The Jewish Caravan: Great Stories of Twenty-Five Centuries* (1935); *The Root and the Bough: The Epic of an Enduring People* (1949); *Feast of Leviathan: Tales of Adventure, Faith, and Love from Jewish Literature* (1956); *Great Ages and Ideas of the Jewish People* (1956).

Avraham Levite

1917–1990

Born in Brzozów, Poland, Avraham Levite was a Yiddish writer about whose life few details are known. He received a traditional religious education before leaving his yeshiva to become involved in Yiddishist and Zionist politics. He is primarily known as the author of the introduction to an anthology of literary writing and reportage entitled *Auschwitz* that was intended to document life in the camp. Although the contents of this anthology were never uncovered, the introduction is noted for the remarkable circumstances of its creation as well as for its seeming awareness and anticipation of the complexities of Jewish memory and history after the war. The text was long included in the standard curriculum on the Holocaust in Israeli public schools.

Introduction to the Projected Anthology Auschwitz
1945

All of us—dying here in polar, ice-cold indifference of nations, forgotten by the world and its hustle and bustle—have nonetheless felt the need to leave something for posterity: if not complete documentation, then at least documentary fragments of how we felt as living corpses, how we thought and spoke. We have been buried alive, and the world dances a ghost dance on our graves, trampling and drowning out our moans and pleas for help with its feet. And when we will already have been suffocated, we will be exhumed, and our ashes scattered over the seven seas will then be all that remains. Every cultured and respectable individual does his duty by regretting our passing and offering his eulogy. When our shadows appear on stage and screen, piteous ladies will wipe a tear from their eyes with perfumed hankies, lamenting us: ah, those poor souls.

We know: we will not come out of here alive. On the gates of hell, the devil himself has inscribed this message: "Abandon all hope ye who enter here." We wish to confess our sins; let this stand as our proclamation of "Hear O Israel" [the Lord our God the Lord is One] for all generations to come. Let this be the confession of a tragic generation unequal to its task, a generation whose rickets-stricken feet collapsed under the heavy burden of a martyrdom this epoch had laid upon its shoulders.

And therefore: for us it is not a matter of facts and numbers, of collecting dry documents. That will be done without us. It will be possible to assemble the history of Auschwitz without our assistance. How one died in Auschwitz: that will be narrated by pictures, witnesses, and documents as well. But we, too, want to construct our own image of how one "lived" in Auschwitz as well: to describe what a normal, average day's work in the camp looked like. A day that is a jumbled snarl of life and death, terror and hope, resignation and the will to live. A day in which one minute never knows what the next may bring. A day in which, axes in our hands, we dig and hack away pieces of our own life, bloody pieces, years of youth that we load, out of breath, onto the trucks of time, groaning as if in lament as they travel with their bitter burdens down the iron rails of camp conditions. And toward dusk, we empty those trucks into a deathly weary and deep abyss. For who will delve into that precipitous abyss and select such a bloodstained night and its dark shadows, a night drenched in terror, and display it for all the world to see? [. . .]

We alone must tell our own story. The account we give in our writing is meant to record our tragedy, give an impression of it and represent it, but our powers fall short of the task. In no way can our writing be evaluated using standard literary measures, but instead finds justification in its documentary value. Thus, it is not artistic worth as such that is at stake here, since the time and place of composition must be taken into account before all else. The time: shortly before death. The place: on the executioner's scaffold. Only the actor on the stage is required to scream, cry, and moan in a way that satisfies every artistic convention. Because, as it were, he doesn't feel any pain. In the end, no one will criticize the afflicted victim for moaning too loudly, and crying too softly.

And we certainly have something to say, even if, literarily speaking, we're stutterers. We want to tell the story as we're able, in our own language. Even complete mutes cannot remain silent when they feel pain; they speak at such times, but in a language of their own, in sign language. Keep silent? Leave that to the Bontshas. They make their secretive faces, as if they had who-knows-what to say. It is only in the land of the dead, where posture and pretense no longer mean a thing, that they announced the desire kept secret all their lives: a roll with butter! [. . .]

And the world? The world is probably doing all that it can. Appeals are made and protests waged, new committees are formed of five, thirteen, and eighteen members, the Red Cross strikes a blow, collecting with its little box for its "Charity to Ward Off Death" fund, the newspapers and radio offer eulogies, the archbishop of Canterbury offers his version of "El male raḥamim" [God full of mercy], Kaddish, the prayer for the dead, is pronounced in monasteries, and the world's little housewives toast us with *lekhayim*, to life, wishing us good luck so that our souls might make their ascent, and that salvation will be ours.

The noose has been thrown round our necks. The executioner is in good spirits. He has plenty of time, plays with his victim. In the meantime, he drinks a few beers, smokes a cigar, and smiles, a satisfied man. Let us take full advantage of this moment when the hangman sucks down his swill, and seek to use the gallows as our writing desk, to describe what we have to say, and to tell our story.

And so my friends, write and record: give a picture that is brief and sharp, as brief as the few days left to us to live, and sharp as the knives that are aimed at our hearts. May a few pages survive for YIVO, for the archive of Jewish lament, may our free brothers still alive read them, and perhaps they will learn something from them.

May it be your will, *eyno shomeya kol bekhiyos*, He who does not hear our weeping, to nonetheless grant us this, *shetasim dimoseynu benaodkho lehiyoys*, may you conceal these little pages of tears in the jar of your being: may they come into the right hands and find their repair [*tikkun*].

C.C. [Concentration Camp] Auschwitz, 3 January 1945

Translated by David Suchoff.

Other works by Levite: *Sefer zikaron kehilat Breziv* (1984); *Yidishe shprikhverter un glaykhverter* (1996).

Isaac E. Rontch
1899–1985

Isaac Elhanan Rontch (also spelled Rontsh) spent his early life in Konin and Łódź. Upon arriving in the United States, he lived in Chicago, where he attended Northwestern University, published his writing, and taught in Yiddish schools. In 1924, he moved to New York, where he helped found the group of Leftist poets known as Proletpen (Proletarian Pen). During his lifetime, Rontch most likely thought of himself primarily as a poet. Today, he is remembered for a study on New York's *landsmanshaften*—organizations for immigrants originally from a particular town or region—and for editing a volume of letters from American soldiers deployed during World War II. He died in Los Angeles.

Jewish Youth at War: Letters from American Soldiers
1945

Foreword

These letters have been selected from thousands in a similar vein which it has been the privilege of the editor to peruse. They were forwarded to him from all sections of the country. The ninety-three young men and women serving in the armed forces whose letters are published here are, we believe, a typical cross-section of American Jews in the armed forces of the United States.

Practically all of the letter-writers are the children of Jewish immigrants. Their parents became Americans by choice. The children brought up in these homes were able to appreciate the significance of America to all who have known persecution because of creed, race or political convictions.

The American Jewish soldier fights as an American and as a Jew. He knows the Nazi threat to America. He knows that Nazis murdered his relatives in the death-chambers of Lublin and Maidanek.

The letters which follow express sentiments of American Jewish youth. They are full of hatred toward those who wish to destroy the civilization of the world. The letters help form a composite picture of the Jewish home, and the thinking of American Jews.

The biographical notes which precede the letters reveal that the correspondents come from all walks of life, and are engaged in the various branches of our armed forces. There are factory workers and students among them; youths of academic attainment and those who have barely completed grammar school before they were compelled to go to work to earn their living. Some are religious; some are not. Some have matured; others still have the frivolity of youth.

The war-fronts where they serve are mirrored in their writings. Often one senses that the letters were written with the purpose of soothing their intimates—their parents. They do not always attain their goals. Sometimes the writers are but mere children seeking a word of comfort from their parents. At other times, they have been so hardened by the conflict, that their parents can scarcely believe it is their own child writing that letter to them.

The aim of this book is not to show the Jewish soldier in the role of a hero, though there are real heroes among them. It is rather to present a cross-section of Jewish youth in the armed services. The division of the book is purely an alphabetical one. The letters reveal ninety-three personalities. Through them we can know thousands of other lives, and the feelings and inspirations of Jewish youth at war.

Other works by Rontch: *Amerike in der yidisher literatur* (1945); *Dos lid fun sholem un andere lider* (1952); *In midber: poeme* (1969).

CULTURAL, POLITICAL, AND RELIGIOUS THOUGHT

Simon Dubnow

1860–1941

Simon Dubnow, the dean of East European Jewish historians, was born in Mstislavl, Belorussia. The work of Heinrich Graetz, whom he met in the late 1880s, was the inspiration for Dubnow's magnum opus, *World History of the Jewish People*. A key member of the Jewish intellectual circle in Odessa, Dubnow relocated in 1905 to St. Petersburg, where he founded the Jewish Historical-Ethnographic Society and the journal *Evreiskaia starina*. Dissatisfied with the Bolshevik takeover, he left for Berlin in 1922 and helped to establish the YIVO in Vilna. When Hitler came to power, Dubnow moved to Riga; he was ultimately murdered by the Nazis.

What Should We Do in Haman's Times?
1939

A Letter to the Editors of Oyfn Sheydveg

[. . .] The past two years of the Hitler regime (1938–1939) have led many people to the impression that this is the beginning of the destruction of European Jewry and that the dominant center of our people will be transferred overseas, either to America or to Asia.

We are now passing through one of the gravest crises in our history. The years 5698–5699 (1938–1939) will be recorded in the list of gruesome historical dates: 4856 (the Crusades, 1096), 5108–5109 (the Black Death, 1348–1349), 5252 (expulsion from Spain, 1492), 5408–5409 (Khmielnitski, 1648–1649), 5641–5642 and 5663–5664 (Russian pogroms, 1881–1882, 1903–1904), 5679–5680 (Ukrainian Petlurist pogroms, 1919–1920). The anti-Jewish measures in central Europe today combine all the sufferings of the previous periods with the most modern system of cruelty, vandalism and torture that only the inquisitorial fantasy of a Hitler, Goering or Streicher could create. We are in truth living in Haman's times. Hitler's "system of extermination" is simply a translation of Haman's plan "to destroy, to slay, and to cause to perish all Jews." There is but one difference. In the earlier instance it never got beyond the planning stage, for the Jewish people organized resistance to the

plan and Haman was led to the gallows. Hitler, on the other hand, has almost realized his plan. One million Jews in Germany, Austria and Czechoslovakia are destroyed, plundered and mutilated; about half are driven out and the other half are still in Hitler's land as prisoners or hostages, being subjected to slow and painful destruction. Over all continents and oceans are heard the cries of thousands of "exiles from Germany" knocking at the doors of all the nations and being barred because of immigration restrictions or plain hostility.

What should one do in such times? When the knife is at the throat we must hasten to stay the hand of the murderer and save the victim. We must create a world organization to combat this band of murderers and we must also set up organizations to find emigration lands for the exiles and refugees. For a number of years now, work has been carried out along these lines by both Jews and non-Jews. More recently throughout the world a militant struggle has been initiated against the Nazi–Fascist alliance—a combination which represents just as grave a danger for humanity at large as it does for its Jewish part. All active forces of Jewry must join in this tremendous battle, in order to pull Europe out of the mud and save European Jewry from extinction. First must come the salvaging action, later will come the measures to reconstruct our shattered world and our own little world foundations of justice and liberty, human and national progress.

In these days of confusion and war-scare, among bundles of newspapers that are full of the outcries of Hitler victims, I received the first issue of your journal *Oyfn Sheydveg* (At the Crossroad). In normal times I would have derived great pleasure from it, but today it elicits critical thoughts in me. I would have applauded the very fact that people stop "At the Crossroad" to ponder over the question whether the previous paths taken by our Jewish intelligentsia were the right ones and whether we might not better change some things in our ideology of the nineteenth and twentieth centuries. Is this the time *now*, however, to stop for ideological revision, now when we are engaged in a battle for physical survival, for human dignity, when each day wrenches from our ranks thousands of victims, when a million of our brethren are so overwhelmed by terrible sufferings that many are led either to suicide or to insanity? It seems to me that we are not at the spiritual crossroad, but rather upon a battlefield, where beaten and tortured human beings are falling around us. [. . .]

All in all we have pressing work to do, more than we can handle with the forces at our disposal. And amidst all this, you come to us with expressions of despair and frustration, with confessions and searching for God. This is not the first time that we hear such sentiments of contrition. Even in the past sixty years—from the Russian to the German pogroms—we have gone through several revisions of our ideals: *Hibbat tsiyon*, political and spiritual Zionism, Diaspora autonomism, territorialism and Socialist combinations of all these "isms." You are quite right, my friends, when you say (*Oyfn Sheydveg*, no. 1, p. 5): "After every great catastrophe in the life of the people there would arise from the ruins a new vitality and a spiritual stock-taking." Yes, *after* the catastrophe, but not *in the very midst* of the catastrophe. We are not yet done with it, for it is of longer duration and more severe than all previous catastrophes during the past century. When the "German Expulsion" will have come to an end and we will have settled all our hundreds of thousands of refugees in other countries, we will then have to review the degree to which the assimilationist trend has been eradicated from our midst, after the storm of racism and Hitlerism, and we will have to consider what spiritual measures we can take to salvage the bare souls of the new generation. Right now, however, we must save their bodies. First Jews—then Judaism. Right now we must do battle with the plague of antisemitism in its Nazi form and with the plans for new expulsions and persecutions in eastern Europe.

Translated by Koppel S. Pinson.

Other works by Dubnow: *A History of the Jews in Russia and Poland* (1916); *Kniga zhizni: vospominaniia i razmyshleniia, Materiali dlia istorii moevo vremeni*, 3 vols. (1934–1940).

Max Horkheimer

1895–1973

Philosopher and sociologist Max Horkheimer was born in Stuttgart, Germany, and raised in an Orthodox family. After World War I, he studied at the University of Frankfurt, from which he received his doctorate in 1922. Horkheimer was the director of the Institute of Social Research and professor of social philosophy at the university from 1930 to 1933 and again from 1949 to 1958, after having led the institute in exile when it was relocated to New York during World War II. He is best known for his work in critical theory and as a leader of the Frankfurt School. His most important work, *The Dialectic of Enlightenment* (1947), was written in collaboration with Theodor Adorno.

The Jews and Europe
1939

That is how it is with the Jews. They shed many a tear for the past. That they fared better under liberalism does not guarantee the justice of the latter. Even the French Revolution, which helped the bourgeois economy to victory and gave the Jews equality, was more ambivalent than they dare imagine today. Not ideas but utility are decisive for the bourgeoisie: "It was only decided to bring about the revolutionary changes because people had thought it over. Such thinking was not the province of a few advanced minds; it was a very numerous elite, throughout France, which discussed the causes of the evils and the nature of the remedy." Here, thinking over means calculating. So far as the Revolution overshot the economically desirable goals, things were set right later. People were less concerned with philosophy than with the administration's sluggishness, with provincial and governmental reforms. The bourgeois were always pragmatists; they always kept an eye on their property. For its sake the privileges fell. Even the more radical development, interrupted by the fall of the terrorists, did not point only in the direction of greater freedom. Even then, people were faced with choosing between various forms of dictatorship. Robespierre's and Saint Just's plans envisioned statist elements, a strengthening of the bureaucratic apparatus, similar to the authoritarian systems of the present. The order which was set out as the progressive one in 1789 carried the germs of National Socialism from the beginning.

Despite all the fundamental differences between the Committee of Public Safety and the leaders of the Third Reich, which can be confronted with surprising parallels, the practice of both springs from the same political necessity: to preserve control of the means of production for those groups which already own them, so that the others are subject to their direction at work.

Political freedom for everyone, equality for the Jews, and all the humane institutions were accepted as means to utilize wealth productively. The democratic institutions fostered the supply of cheap labor, the possibility of planning with assurance, and the spread of free trade. With the changing of circumstances the institutions lost the utilitarian character to which they owed their existence. Rationality which ran counter to the specific commercial conditions at any given stage was also considered eccentric or subversive by the Jewish entrepreneur. This kind of rationality now turns against him. A national morality was immanent to the reality in which the Jews lived their lives, according to which they are now found wanting, the morality of economic power. The same rationality of economic expediency, according to which the defeated competitors have always sunk into the proletariat and been cheated of their lives, has now pronounced judgment on the Jews. Once again a large elite, this time not only throughout France, is discussing "the cause of the evils and the nature of their remedy." The result is bad for the Jews. They are being run over. Others are the most capable today: the leaders of the new order in the economy and the state. The same economic necessity that irrationally created the army of the unemployed has now turned, in the form of carefully considered regulations, against entire minority groups.

Translated by Mark Ritter.

Other works by Horkheimer: *Eclipse of Reason* (1947); *Critique of Instrumental Reason: Lectures and Essays since the End of World War II* (1967); *Critical Theory: Selected Essays* (1968).

José Bénech
1898–?

José Bénech was director of the Marrakesh branch of the Banque commercial du Maroc in the 1930s. In his essay on the mellah (Jewish quarter), he describes Jewish life in Morocco in the era of the French protectorate.

Attempt to Explain a Mellah
1940

September 7, 1912. The French enter Marrakesh. Marching through the Djema el Fna Square, surrounded by his general staff, Colonel Mangin is sur-

prised to hear, amid the discordant noises of the crowd, some children belting out a rousing "Marseillaise." Thus do the Alliance's youth greet the dawn of a new order. It is no longer a dream.

A few decrees bring an end to restrictions imposed on the Jewish community: from now on Jews can dress as they like, come and go as they wish, and live and own property wherever they please. At the same time, their privileges are confirmed and their traditions codified, but only insofar as they do not impede progress.

The new order makes official, even as it limits, the authority of rabbinic judges. They now constitute a legitimate court, assisted by a court clerk and presided over by the *rab*, who will bear the title President of the Rabbinic Court. The court clerk and the judges, three in number, will be appointed by the Protectorate after consultation with leading figures in the community.

This court will rule only on disputes relating to personal and religious issues such as inheritance, divorce, and morals. It will register marriages, record wills, and arbitrate—without binding force—minor disputes among Jews. A High Rabbinic Court sitting in Rabat will have appellate jurisdiction.

For every other civil dispute, whether commercial or criminal, Jews will be tried at the Court of Justice in Casablanca's Mahakma du Pacha Palace, or if the accused is a protected French or foreign defendant, by the French or consular court. [. . .]

For several years the mellah continued to look the same.

At first the only sign of liberation was the absence of humiliating measures. Very soon the Jews abandoned their black slippers; a good number of them imitated the few privileged foreigners who were already wearing European-style clothing. Some proudly showed off splendid top hats.

Little by little, sanitation was brought under control. The first mailmen to serve the mellah had to wear sewer workers' boots on rainy days, but regular garbage collection and a rudimentary sewer system soon cleared away the thick layer of filth lining the streets.

Strict legislation managed to diminish the ravages of alcoholism considerably.

Various aid programs developed. With relatively surprising speed, many, even among the most ignorant, recognized that medicine was superior to witchcraft. The Jews were not the last to take advantage of the new forms of French charity: *gouttes de lait* [milk stations] for needy children, anti-tubercular centers, and free consultations.

The Alliance set up a Jewish wing in the indigent maternity ward. The Jewish quarter had a long wait for its own hospital. Finally in 1932, thanks to the generosity of some local Jews, as well as to the combined charity of several sponsors and the Baron de Rothschild, this gap was filled. Near the Mauchamp hospital, the Jews had their own wing comprising fifty beds where patients were treated by French doctors from the neighboring hospital.

Congestion in the mellah also had to be relieved, as the population, once decimated by epidemics, was now rapidly growing (13,000 inhabitants in 1926; 21,000 in 1932; 25,000 in 1936, according to official statistics; however, one must remember that statistics is the art of adding up exactly inexact bits of information). [. . .]

With the population continuing to increase, the mellah still has as many people as it can hold. It has remained an important center for trade in imports and junk. Retailers and laborers from the hinterlands are always milling around its shops. The poor constitute by far the larger part of its population, but rents have gone down since the middle class left.

The state of sanitation has considerably improved. Jews, like all inhabitants of this country, make an effort to practice habits of personal hygiene and cleanliness as soon as they can.

Private enterprises even installed some Turkish baths in the mellah. None have gone bankrupt.

Translated by Michele McKay Aynesworth.

Erich Fromm

1900–1980

Social psychologist Erich Fromm was born in Frankfurt am Main to Orthodox parents. He studied law at Frankfurt University, as well as sociology and philosophy at the University of Heidelberg. Fromm was introduced to psychoanalysis in 1924; he practiced in Berlin, where he was involved with the Institute for Social Research, later known as the Frankfurt School. When the Nazis came to power, Fromm moved to New York and taught psychology at several American universities until 1950, when he relocated to Mexico. Always politically active, Fromm was a member of the American Socialist Party and spoke out against the nuclear arms race and the Vietnam War.

Escape from Freedom
1941

We see that the process of growing human freedom has the same dialectic character that we have noticed in the process of individual growth. On the one hand it is a process of growing strength and integration, mastery of nature, growing power of human reason, and growing solidarity with other human beings. But on the other hand this growing individuation means growing isolation, insecurity, and thereby growing doubt concerning one's own role in the universe, the meaning of one's life, and with all that a growing feeling of one's own powerlessness and insignificance as an individual.

If the process of the development of mankind had been harmonious, if it had followed a certain plan, then both sides of the development—the growing strength and the growing individuation—would have been exactly balanced. As it is, the history of mankind is one of conflict and strife. Each step in the direction of growing individuation threatened people with new insecurities. Primary bonds once severed cannot be mended; once paradise is lost, man cannot return to it. There is only one possible, productive solution for the relationship of individualized man with the world: his active solidarity with all men and his spontaneous activity, love and work, which unite him again with the world, not by primary ties but as a free and independent individual.

However, if the economic, social and political conditions on which the whole process of human individuation depends, do not offer a basis for the realization of individuality in the sense just mentioned, while at the same time people have lost those ties which gave them security, this lag makes freedom an unbearable burden. It then becomes identical with doubt, with a kind of life which lacks meaning and direction. Powerful tendencies arise to escape from this kind of freedom into submission or some kind of relationship to man and the world which promises relief from uncertainty, even if it deprives the individual of his freedom.

European and American history since the end of the Middle Ages is the history of the full emergence of the individual. It is a process which started in Italy, in the Renaissance, and which only now seems to have come to a climax. It took over four hundred years to break down the medieval world and to free people from the most apparent restraints. But while in many respects the individual has grown, has developed mentally and emotionally, and participates in cultural achievements in a degree unheard-of before, the lag between "freedom from" and "freedom to" has grown too. The result of this disproportion between freedom *from* any tie and the lack of possibilities for the positive realization of freedom and individuality has led, in Europe, to a panicky flight from freedom into new ties or at least into complete indifference. [...]

The position in which the individual finds himself in our period had already been foreseen by visionary thinkers in the nineteenth century. Kierkega[a]rd describes the helpless individual torn and tormented by doubts, overwhelmed by the feeling of aloneness and insignificance. Nietzsche visualizes the approaching nihilism which was to become manifest in Nazism and paints a picture of a "superman" as the negation of the insignificant, directionless individual he saw in reality. The theme of the powerlessness of man has found a most precise expression in Franz Kafka's work. In his *Castle* he describes the man who wants to get in touch with the mysterious inhabitants of a castle, who are supposed to tell him what to do and show him his place in the world. All his life consists in his frantic effort to get into touch with them, but he never succeeds and is left alone with a sense of utter futility and helplessness.

The feeling of isolation and powerlessness has been beautifully expressed in the following passage by Julian Green: "I knew that we counted little in comparison with the universe, I knew that we were nothing; but to be so immeasurably nothing seems in some way both to overwhelm and at the same time to reassure. Those figures, those dimensions beyond the range of human thought, are utterly overpowering. Is there anything whatsoever to which we can cling? Amid that chaos of illusions into which we are cast headlong, there is one thing that stands out as true, and that is—love. All the rest is nothingness, an empty void. We peer down into a huge dark abyss. And we are afraid."[1]

However, this feeling of individual isolation and powerlessness as it has been expressed by these writers and as it is felt by many so-called neurotic people, is nothing the average normal person is aware of. It is too frightening for that. It is covered over by the daily routine of his activities, by the assurance and approval he finds in his private or social relations, by success in business, by any number of distractions, by "having fun," "making contacts," "going places." But whistling in the dark does not bring light. Aloneness, fear, and bewilderment remain; people cannot stand it forever. They cannot go on bearing the burden of "freedom

from"; they must try to escape from freedom altogether unless they can progress from negative to positive freedom. The principal social avenues of escape in our time are the submission to a leader, as has happened in Fascist countries, and the compulsive conforming as is prevalent in our own democracy. Before we come to describe these two socially patterned ways of escape, I must ask the reader to follow me into the discussion of the intricacies of these psychological mechanisms of escape. We have dealt with some of these mechanisms already in the previous chapters; but in order to understand fully the psychological significance of Fascism and the automatization of man in modern democracy, it is necessary to understand the psychological phenomena not only in a general way but in the very detail and concreteness of their operation. This may appear to be a detour; but actually it is a necessary part of our whole discussion. Just as one cannot properly understand psychological problems without their social and cultural background, neither can one understand social phenomena without the knowledge of the underlying psychological mechanisms. The following chapter attempts to analyze these mechanisms, to reveal what is going on in the individual, and to show how, in our effort to escape from aloneness and powerlessness, we are ready to get rid of our individual self either by submission to new forms of authority or by a compulsive conforming to accepted patterns. [...]

It has been the thesis of this book that freedom has a twofold meaning for modern man: that he has been freed from traditional authorities and has become an "individual," but that at the same time he has become isolated, powerless, and an instrument of purposes outside of himself, alienated from himself and others; furthermore, that this state undermines his self, weakens and frightens him, and makes him ready for submission to new kinds of bondage. Positive freedom on the other hand is identical with the full realization of the individual's potentialities, together with his ability to live actively and spontaneously. Freedom has reached a critical point where, driven by the logic of its own dynamism, it threatens to change into its opposite. The future of democracy depends on the realization of the individualism that has been the ideological aim of modern thought since the Renaissance. The cultural and political crisis of our day is not due to the fact that there is too much individualism but that what we believe to be individualism has become an empty shell. The victory of freedom is possible only if democracy develops into a society in which the individual, his growth and happiness, is the aim and purpose of culture, in which life does not need any justification in success or anything else, and in which the individual is not subordinated to or manipulated by any power outside of himself, be it the State or the economic machine; finally, a society in which his conscience and ideals are not the internalization of external demands, but are really *his* and express the aims that result from the peculiarity of his self. These aims could not be fully realized in any previous period of modern history; they had to remain largely ideological aims, because the material basis for the development of genuine individualism was lacking. Capitalism has created this premise. The problem of production is solved—in principle at least—and we can visualize a future of abundance, in which the fight for economic privileges is no longer necessitated by economic scarcity. The problem we are confronted with today is that of the organization of social and economic forces, so that man—as a member of organized society—may become the master of these forces and cease to be their slave.

I have stressed the psychological side of freedom, but I have also tried to show that the psychological problem cannot be separated from the material basis of human existence, from the economic, social, and political structure of society. It follows from this premise that the realization of positive freedom and individualism is also bound up with economic and social changes that will permit the individual to become free in terms of the realization of his self. It is not the aim of this book to deal with the economic problems resulting from that premise or to give a picture of economic plans for the future. But I should not like to leave any doubt concerning the direction in which I believe the solution to lie.

NOTE

1. Julian Green, *Personal Record, 1928–1939*, translated by J. Godefroi, Harper & Brothers, New York, 1939.

Other works by Fromm: *Man for Himself: An Inquiry into the Psychology of Ethics* (1947); *Psychoanalysis and Religion* (1950); *The Forgotten Language: An Introduction to the Understanding of Dreams, Fairy Tales, and Myths* (1951); *The Art of Loving* (1956); *Marx's Concept of Man* (1961); *The Heart of Man: Its Genius for Good and Evil* (1964).

Abraham Lewin
1893–1943

Born into a Hasidic family of scholars and rabbis in Warsaw, Abraham Lewin left his Orthodox roots and in 1916 began to teach at the Zionist Yehudia school for girls. When Jewish schools were officially banned by the Nazis in 1939, Lewin and his colleagues continued to teach clandestinely. Inside the Warsaw ghetto, from April 1942 to January 1943, he worked with Emanuel Ringelblum to document the daily lives and suffering of those trapped there.

I. M. Weissenberg Memorial
1941

Eulogy Read at a Commemorative Evening in Honour of Yitshak Meir Weissenberg, 13 September 1941

We live in a prison. We have been degraded to the level of homeless and uncared-for animals. When we look at the swollen, half-naked bodies of Jews lying in the streets, we feel as if we find ourselves at some sub-human level. The half-dead, skeletal faces of Jews, especially those of dying little children, frighten us and recall pictures of India, or of the isolation-colonies for lepers which we used to see in films. Reality surpasses any fantasy; and possibly one thing only could still surprise us. This would be mass-murder in the place of systematic extermination. Hard as it is to utter words such as these, one has to say that for all those who perish of starvation, a swift and violent death would certainly be a release from the protracted terrible suffering of their dying agony.

The proportions of life and death have radically changed. Times were, when life occupied the primary place, when it was the main and central concern, while death was a side phenomenon, secondary to life, its termination. Nowadays, death rules in all its majesty; while life hardly glows under a thick layer of ashes. Even this faint glow of life is feeble, miserable and weak, poor, devoid of any free breath, deprived of any spark of spiritual content. The very soul, both in the individual and in the community, seems to have starved and perished, to have dulled and atrophied. There remain only the needs of the body; and it leads merely an organic-physiological existence.

Such is our situation in the Jewish Wailing-Quarters in Warsaw as well as in other places. However, we do not forget that we are human beings and not primitive, lowly creatures. And, in spite of it all, we remember that only two years ago we used to be free men. We constituted a live and organic community which had and preserved a human image in spite of the negative and dark sides. We used to seek education; we used to strive and to create in every province of life; we used to enrich life. We used to yearn for art as the highest expression of human existence and we used to cultivate art in all its forms as much as our powers and potential permitted. And we used to have both a feeling and an inclination for science.

To sum up—we were human and whatever was human attracted and excited us. How is it nowadays?—How suppressed, how disgraced and miserable are we now!

Yet, we wish to live on, to continue as free and creative men. This will be our test. If, under the thick layer of ashes our life is not extinguished, this will prove a triumph of the human over the inhuman and that our will to live is mightier than the will to destruction; that we are capable of overcoming all evil forces which attempt to engulf us.

The cultural assemblies, the first of which we attend this evening, are meant to be one of the proofs of our vigorous instinct for life. They are supposed to remind us of our past and to stimulate us for a better future. They should recall to us that we used to occupy a place higher than the Gypsies or any of the wild tribes of Africa. And they must arouse in us a renewed intellectual effort and creativity. They must not let us slide into the eternal sleep. I believe in Jewish youth. I believe that they, on whom the war has had such a tragic impact (for they did not yet enjoy the fruits of life, having been deprived of any benefit of school, of science, of literature, of theatre or other human achievements in spiritual or material fields)—to say nothing of physical miseries, of starvation and death—I believe that this youth will enthusiastically accept our initiative and will find in these assemblies a new strength to invigorate themselves and preserve their human image.

We have consecrated this first evening to the late writer, Weissenberg. This may have been just an accident but it is, nevertheless, somewhat symbolic. Weissenberg is one of those creative artists who come to us as though born by themselves, who grow like a flower in an untilled field. In this respect, he reminds us of the Russian author Gorky, who also grew out of an environment devoid of understanding for culture or literature. Artists such as these are evidence of the life-forces of man, of his eternal drive towards light and progress, of his inner creative thrust. These forces sprout unexpectedly, spring up like a hidden source from under the earth.

May the memory of Weissenberg be a symbol of our vital forces which shall, in defiance of any restrictions and stone walls, flow forth unseen until they burst out of hiding in a free world and spread in joy and jubilation all over the field of our life.

Hear, O Jewish Youth! Maybe among you, here in this hall, there is, there are potential Weissenbergs. Do not lose courage! Keep strong and gather power, pick up strength to withstand until the sun shines for all children of the earth without distinction. Then, at that hour, Weissenbergs will appear anew among us, along with other creators. At that hour, we shall honour and celebrate not only the memory of deceased writers, but also the fame and excellence of the living, creating young Jewish artists in every field of culture and of civilization.

NOTE

[Isaac Meir Weissenberg (Itshe Meyer Vaysenberg; 1881–1938), Yiddish prose writer, mentor to young Jewish writers after the death of I. L. Peretz.—Eds.]

Translated by Christopher Hutton.

Other works by Lewin: *Kantonistn: vegn der yidisher rekrutshine in Rusland in di tsaytn fun Tsar Nikolay dem ershtn, 1827–1856* (1934).

Kurt Lewin

1890–1947

Kurt Lewin was born in Mogilno, Prussia, and studied medicine at the universities of Freiburg and Munich before switching to psychology at the University of Berlin in 1910. After being wounded while serving in the German army during World War I, he returned to Berlin to finish his doctorate. In 1933, Lewin immigrated to the United States, where he taught at Cornell University and the University of Iowa. He later served as director of the Research Center for Group Dynamics at MIT and helped establish the National Training Laboratories. Influenced by Gestalt psychology, Lewin is known as the father of modern social psychology because of his pioneering work utilizing scientific methods and experimentation to look at social behavior.

Self-Hatred among Jews
1941

That self-hatred is present among Jews is a fact that the non-Jew would hardly believe, but which is well known among the Jews themselves. It is a phenomenon which has been observed ever since the emancipation of the Jews. Professor Lessing treated this topic in Germany (1930) in a book, *Der Jüdische Selbsthass* ("Jewish Self-Hate"). Novels like that of Ludwig Lewisohn (*Island Within*, 1928), which pictures the New York Jew around 1930, and that of Schnitzler, who deals with the problems of the Austrian Jew in the period around 1900, are striking in the similarity of the problems which they show to exist. In these different countries, the same conflicts arise and Jews of the various social strata and professions attempt the same variety of solutions.

Jewish self-hatred is both a group phenomenon and an individual phenomenon. In Europe, outstanding examples of a hostile sentiment in one Jewish group against another were those of the German or Austrian Jew against the East European Jew, and, more recently, the attitude of the French Jew toward the German Jew. That all the troubles the Jews had in Germany were due to the bad conduct of the East European Jew was an opinion not infrequently heard among German Jews. In this country, the resentment of the Spanish Jew against the immigrating German Jew, and the hostility of the latter to the East European Jew form a parallel to the European situation. […]

An attempt has been made to explain Jewish self-hatred as the outgrowth of certain deep-seated human instincts. This behavior seems to be a prime example of what Freud calls the drive to self-destruction or the "death instinct." However, an explanation like that is of little value. Why does the Englishman not have the same amount of hatred against his countrymen, or the German against the German, as the Jew against the Jew? If the self-hatred were the result of a general instinct, we should expect its degree to depend only on the personality of the individual. But the amount of self-hatred the individual Jew shows seems to depend far more on his attitude toward Judaism than on his personality.

Jewish self-hatred is a phenomenon which has its parallel in many underprivileged groups. One of the better-known and most extreme cases of self-hatred can be found among American Negroes. Negroes distinguish within their group four or five strata according to skin shade—the lighter the skin the higher the strata. […]

Jewish self-hatred will die out only when actual equality of status with the non-Jew is achieved. Only then will the enmity against one's own group decrease to the relatively insignificant proportions characteristic of the majority group's. Sound self-criticism will replace it. This does not mean that nothing can be done meanwhile. After all, we do have a great many Jews who can hardly be classified as anti-Semitic.

The only way to avoid Jewish self-hatred in its various forms is a change of the negative balance between the forces toward and away from the Jewish group into a positive balance, the creation of loyalty to the Jewish group instead of negative chauvinism. We are unable to safeguard our fellow Jews or our growing children today against those handicaps which are the result of their being Jewish. However, we can try to build up a Jewish education both on the children's level and on the adult level to counteract the *feeling of inferiority* and the *feeling of fear* which are the most important sources of the negative balance.

The feeling of inferiority of the Jew is but an indication of the fact that he sees things Jewish with the eyes of the unfriendly majority. I remember how, as an adolescent, I was deeply disturbed by the idea that the accusation against the Jews as being incapable of constructive work might be true. I know that many Jewish adolescents growing up in an atmosphere of prejudice felt similarly. Today, a Jewish youth who has watched Palestine grow, is in an infinitely better situation. Whatever one's opinion about Zionism as a political program may be, no one who has observed closely the German Jews during the fateful first weeks after Hitler's rise to power will deny that thousands of German Jews were saved from suicide only by the famous articles of the *Jüdische Rundschau*, with its headlines "*Jasagen zum Judentum*" ("Saying Yes to Being a Jew"). The ideas expressed there were the rallying point and the source of strength for Zionist and non-Zionist alike.

To counteract fear and make the individual strong to face whatever the future holds, there is nothing so important as a clear and fully accepted belonging to a group whose fate has a positive meaning. A long-range view which includes the past and the future of Jewish life, and links the solution of the minority problem with the problem of the welfare of all human beings is one of these possible sources of strength. A strong feeling of being part and parcel of the group and having a positive attitude toward it is, for children and adults alike, the sufficient condition for the avoidance of attitudes based on self-hatred.

To build up such feeling of group belongingness on the basis of active responsibility for the fellow Jew should be one of the outstanding policies in Jewish education.

Other works by Lewin: *A Dynamic Theory of Personality: Selected Papers* (1935); *Principles of Topological Psychology* (1936); *Field Theory in Social Science: Selected Theoretical Papers*, edited by D. Cartwright (1951).

Yosef Yitshak Schneersohn

1880–1950

Yosef Yitshak Schneersohn was the son of the Chabad rabbi Sholom Dovber and became the head of the Lubavitch yeshiva Tomchei Temimim in 1898. After his father's death in 1920, he took on the position of rebbe, struggling to maintain a network of Chabad institutions, ranging from schools to kosher food banks. He was arrested by Stalin's regime in 1927 and was tortured and exiled. In 1940, following the Nazi invasion of Poland, Schneersohn arrived in New York, where he continued his work of organizational growth through religious and social networks and institutions. Schneersohn's son-in-law, Menachem Mendel, became his successor as the Lubavitcher Rebbe.

First Proclamation: 26 May 1941
1941

Immediate Redemption!

A fire is now sweeping over the whole Old World, threatening to annihilate, heaven forbid, more than two-thirds of the Jewish people. Nobody can guarantee that the fire, heaven forbid, will not leap over even here in the New World! The call of the local spiritual leaders for penitent return, prayer and fasting, though in and of itself correct, is in the current circumstances not enough and of little value. The worst is that the call is insignificantly small. The reason for the insufficient response is twofold: Those who are called are deaf, and the call is, unfortunately, not as it should be!

The Two Fires

A stormy fire burns in the Old World which destroys, heaven forbid, the Jewish body. Here in America, a silent fire burns which destroys the Jewish soul. The customary coldness and indifference of the local Jews to Torah and faith is indeed on account of the fire in the Old World. [That fire] is transformed here into a quiet fire of apostasy which rages no less than the Old World fire. The terrible catastrophe (*Ḥurban*) of Judaism in Europe has turned local Jews against the faith, heaven forbid. They do not see that the Sovereign of the universe is standing by the community of Israel. They are instilled with a single hope, that the Jewish people will be saved through the victory of world democracy. They see that even with the help of world democracy, things are not going well. [But they continue] to contribute toward the victory of democracy with all their talents, with money, and with a Jewish army. They go on thinking this way. But they do not want to hear about penitent return and prayer. They argue falsely that if the Lord or the universe does not help Torah-true Judaism in Europe, it is certainly a waste for American Jews to seek help by becoming more pious than local spiritual leaders demand of them!

The Call of Truth

Therefore, the ones who are called remain deaf to the call for penitent return and prayer. This deafness is indeed the result of the [fact that] local spiritual leaders have until now neglected to respond to the call of truth about which the rabbinic Sages wrote concerning such troubled times. Namely, the call of "Troubles have come to the world, look for the footsteps of the Messiah!" The spiritual leaders neglected to tell the Jewish masses that one of the fundamentals of Judaism is the [doctrine that] "I believe in the coming of the Messiah." Also, that before the Messiah comes, one must expect such troubles as the present ones. And that in any event, it is possible that [what is happening now] are the birth pangs of the Messiah before the Jewish redemption! In truth this [messianic expectation] is no longer a pious hope and empty consolation. It is a fact. The Jewish people are suffering the birth pangs of the Messiah. The complete redemption stands behind our backs. The Jews of this country are completely distracted, [and] as the rabbinic Sages foretold, the Messiah of David will come when the people's attention is diverted, completely unexpectedly! [see B. T. *Sanhedrin* 97a]. [. . .]

The Old Prophetic Warning

Brother Jews of all nonbelieving camps! In our earlier two proclamations, which appeared in the *Morning Journal* and in the *Chicago Courier* and in other Yiddish and Anglo-Jewish American newspapers and elsewhere, we have provided you with the prophetic warning about the current time, "Come, my people, enter thou into thy chambers, and shut thy doors about thee; hide thyself for a little moment, until the indignation be overpassed. For, behold, the Lord cometh forth out of His place to visit upon the inhabitants of the earth their iniquity" [Isaiah 26:20–21]. The prophet Isaiah warns us against getting in the way of the nations of the world when they are being hit with punishment for their sins. Except for the duty that Jews must perform for the lands of exile as citizens and individuals, the prophet warns us that as a community we should go into our own Jewish chambers. We should wash our hands of our own sins, dust off *our own* neglected Jewish faith and *our own* Jewish hopes. Only in this way can we avoid the punishment of the inhabitants of the earth when God leaves his place to wash away the sinners!

All the uninvited mixing by Jews into nationalistic wars will come crashing down on our heads, heaven forbid. Even when we are doing nothing, we are accused of being warmongers, as opponents of [peace] and as the ones solely responsible for all troubles. Even more so when we actually do mix in! The prophet warns us to protect ourselves. Not to intrude where we ought not, not to get involved with the alien world. We should rather confine ourselves to our own four corners. We should do the only thing that we can do to avoid the general world: penitent return with hope for our own redemption! More than any previous time, it now looks as if God has left His place to punish all the inhabitants of the earth for the sins they have committed. More than at any previous time, Jews need to lock themselves in their own chambers and not get in the way of others. Besides these words of the prophet, we also reminded you in our proclamations. Every Jew can understand how timely and necessary the prophet's words are for all of us.

However, it is also a fact that our warning about the forthcoming birth pangs of the Messiah and the redemption which soon follows is right on time! The prophet spoke more than certainly about the current time. Our heart bleeds seeing how everything that the Jews here do and say is exactly opposite to what the prophet advises them!

Translated by Gershon Greenberg.

Other works by Schneersohn: *An Anthology of Talks* (2012); *Lubavitcher Rabbi's Memoirs: The Memoirs of Joseph I. Schneersohn* (2016).

Gershom Scholem
1897–1982

The Berlin-born historian of Jewish mysticism Gershom Scholem was one of the towering intellects of Jewish scholarship in the twentieth century. Born into a highly acculturated family with weak Jewish attachments, he embraced Jewish nationalism in his youth and, despite parental opposition, immersed himself in the study of Judaism. In 1923, he settled in Jerusalem and began working as a librarian at the Hebrew University. In 1925, he was appointed lecturer in Jewish mysticism and several years later was promoted to professor. Scholem pioneered the study of the Jewish mystical tradition, insisting that it was often the major current in Jewish history. When his massive study of Shabetai Tsevi was translated into English and other European languages, his work became known in intellectual circles outside the world of Jewish studies.

Major Trends in Jewish Mysticism
1941

Jewish mysticism in its various forms represents an attempt to interpret the religious values of Judaism in terms of mystical values. It concentrates upon the idea of the living God who manifests himself in the acts of Creation, Revelation and Redemption. Pushed to its extreme, the mystical meditation on this idea gives birth to the conception of a sphere, a whole realm of divinity, which underlies the world of our sense-data and which is present and active in all that exists. This is the meaning of what the Kabbalists call the *world of the "Sefiroth."* I should like to explain this a little more fully.

The attributes of the living God are conceived differently and undergo a peculiar transformation when compared with the meaning given to them by the philosophers of Judaism. Among the latter, Maimonides, in his "Guide of the Perplexed," felt bound to ask: How is it possible to say of God that He is living? Does that not imply a limitation of the infinite Being? The words "God is living," he argues, can only mean that he is not dead, that is to say, that he is the opposite of all that is negative. He is the negation of negation. A quite different reply is given by the Kabbalist, for whom the distinction, nay the conflict, between the known and the unknown God has a significance denied to it by the philosophers of Judaism.

No creature can take aim at the unknown, the hidden God. In the last resort, every cognition of God is based on a form of relation between Him and His creature, i.e. on a manifestation of God in something else, and not on a relation between Him and Himself. It has been argued that the difference between the *deus absconditus*, God in Himself, and God in His appearance is unknown to Kabbalism. This seems to me a wrong interpretation of the facts. On the contrary, the dualism embedded in these two aspects of the one God, both of which are, theologically speaking, possible ways of aiming at the divinity, has deeply preoccupied the Jewish mystics. It has occasionally led them to use formulas whose implied challenge to the religious consciousness of monotheism was fully revealed only in the subsequent development of Kabbalism. As a rule, the Kabbalists were concerned to find a formula which should give as little offense as possible to the philosophers. For this reason the inherent contradiction between the two aspects of God is not always brought out as clearly as in the famous doctrine of an anonymous writer around 1300, according to whom God in Himself, as an absolute Being, and therefore by His very nature incapable of becoming the subject of a revelation to others, is not and cannot be meant in the documents of Revelation, in the canonical writings of the Bible, and in the rabbinical tradition. He is not the subject of these writings and therefore also has no documented name, since every word of the sacred writings refers after all to some aspect of His manifestation on the side of Creation. It follows that while the living God, the God of religion of whom these writings bear witness, has innumerable names—which, according to the Kabbalists, belong to Him by His very nature and not as a result of human convention—the *deus absconditus*, the God who is hidden in His own self, can only be named in a metaphorical sense and with the help of words which, mystically speaking, are not real names at all. The favorite formulae of the early Spanish Kabbalists are speculative paraphrases like "Root of all Roots," "Great Reality," "Indifferent Unity," and, above all, *En-Sof*. The latter designation reveals the impersonal character of this aspect of the hidden God from the standpoint of man as clearly as, and perhaps even more clearly than, the others. It signifies "the infinite" as such; not, as has been frequently suggested, "He who is infinite" but "that which is infinite." Isaac the Blind (one of the first Kabbalists of distinguishable personality) calls the *deus absconditus* "that which is not conceivable by thinking," *not* "He who is not etc." It is clear that with this postulate of an impersonal basic reality in God, which becomes a person—or appears as a person—only in the process of Creation and Revelation, Kabbalism abandons the personalistic basis of the Biblical conception of God. In this sense it is undeniable that the author of the above-mentioned mystical aphorism is right in holding that *En-Sof* (or what is meant by it) is not even mentioned in the Bible and the Talmud. In the following lectures we shall see how the main schools of Kabbalistic thought have dealt with this problem. It will not surprise us to find that speculation has run the whole gamut—from attempts to re-transform the impersonal *En-Sof* into the personal God of the Bible to the downright heretical doctrine of a genuine dualism between the hidden *En-Sof* and the personal Demiurge of Scripture. For the moment, however, we are more concerned with the second aspect of the Godhead which, being of decisive importance for real religion, formed the main subject of theosophical speculation in Kabbalism.

The mystic strives to assure himself of the living presence of God, the God of the Bible, the God who is good, wise, just and merciful and the embodiment of all other positive attributes. But at the same time he is unwilling to renounce the idea of the hidden God who remains eternally unknowable in the depths of His own Self, or, to use the bold expression of the Kabbalists "in the depths of His nothingness." This hidden God may be without special attributes—the living God of whom the Revelation speaks, with whom all religion is concerned, must have attributes, which on another plane represent also the mystic's own scale of moral values: God is good, God is severe, God is merciful and just, etc. As we shall have occasion to see, the mystic does not even recoil before the inference that in a higher sense there is a root of evil even in God. The benevolence of God is to the mystic not simply the negation of evil, but a whole sphere of divine light, in which God manifests Himself under this particular aspect of benevolence to the contemplation of the Kabbalist.

These spheres, which are often described with the aid of mythical metaphors and provide the key for a kind of mystical topography of the Divine realm, are themselves nothing but stages in the revelation of God's creative power. Every attribute represents a given stage, including the attribute of severity and stern judgment, which mystical speculation has connected with the source of evil in God. The mystic who sets out to grasp the meaning of God's absolute unity is thus faced at the outset with an infinite complexity of heavenly spheres and stages which are described in the Kabbalistic texts.

From the contemplation of these "Sefiroth" he proceeds to the conception of God as the union and the root of all these contradictions. Generally speaking, the mystics do not seem to conceive of God as the absolute Being or absolute Becoming but as the union of both; much as the hidden God of whom nothing is known to us, and the living God of religious experience and revelation, are one and the same. Kabbalism in other words is not dualistic, although historically there exists a close connection between its way of thinking and that of the Gnostics, to whom the hidden God and the Creator are opposing principles. On the contrary, all the energy of "orthodox" Kabbalistic speculation is bent to the task of escaping from dualistic consequences; otherwise they would not have been able to maintain themselves within the Jewish community.

I think it is possible to say that the mystical interpretation of the attributes and the unity of God, in the so-called doctrine of the "Sefiroth," constituted a problem common to all Kabbalists, while the solutions given to it by and in the various schools often differ from one another. In the same way, all Jewish mystics, from the Therapeutae, whose doctrine was described by Philo of Alexandria, to the latest Hasid, are at one in giving a mystical interpretation to the Torah; the Torah is to them a living organism animated by a secret life which streams and pulsates below the crust of its literal meaning; every one of the innumerable strata of this hidden region corresponds to a new and profound meaning of the Torah. The Torah, in other words, does not consist merely of chapters, phrases and words; rather is it to be regarded as the living incarnation of the divine wisdom which eternally sends out new rays of light. It is not merely the historical law of the Chosen People, although it is that too; it is rather the cosmic law of the Universe, as God's wisdom conceived it. Each configuration of letters in it, whether it makes sense in human speech or not, symbolizes some aspect of God's creative power which is active in the universe. And just as the thoughts of God, in contrast to those of man, are of infinite profundity, so also no single interpretation of the Torah in human language is capable of taking in the whole of its meaning. It cannot be denied that this method of interpretation has proved almost barren for a plain understanding of the Holy Writ, but it is equally undeniable that viewed in this new light, the Sacred Books made a powerful appeal to the individual who discovered in their written words the secret of his life and of his God. It is the usual fate of sacred writings to become more or less divorced from the intentions of their authors. What may be called their after-life, those aspects which are discovered by later generations, frequently becomes of greater importance than their original meaning; and after all—who knows what their original meaning was? [. . .]

Mystics and philosophers are, as it were, both aristocrats of thought; yet Kabbalism succeeded in establishing a connection between its own world and certain elemental impulses operative in every human mind. It did not turn its back upon the primitive side of life, that all-important region where mortals are afraid of life and in fear of death, and derive scant wisdom from rational philosophy. Philosophy ignored these fears, out of whose substance man wove myths, and in turning its back upon the primitive side of man's existence, it paid a high price in losing touch with him altogether. For it is cold comfort to those who are plagued by genuine fear and sorrow to be told that their troubles are but the workings of their own imagination.

The fact of the existence of evil in the world is the main touchstone of this difference between the philosophic and the Kabbalistic outlook. On the whole, the philosophers of Judaism treat the existence of evil as something meaningless in itself. Some of them have shown themselves only too proud of this negation of evil as one of the fundamentals of what they call rational Judaism. Hermann Cohen has said with great clarity and much conviction: "Evil is non-existent. It is nothing but a concept derived from the concept of freedom. *A power of evil exists only in myth.*" One may doubt the philosophical truth of this statement, but assuming its truth it is obvious that something can be said for "myth" in its struggle with "philosophy." To most Kabbalists, as true seal-bearers of the world of myth, the existence of evil is, at any rate, one of the most pressing problems, and one which keeps them continuously occupied with attempts to solve it. They have a strong sense of the reality of evil and the dark horror that is about everything living. They do not, like the philosophers, seek to evade its existence with the aid of a convenient formula; rather do they try to penetrate into its depth. And by doing so, they unwittingly establish a connection between their own strivings and the vital interests of popular belief—you may call it superstition—and all of those concrete manifestations of Jewish life in which these fears found their expression. It is a paradoxical fact that none other than the Kabbalists, through their interpretation of various religious acts and customs, have made it clear what they signified to the average believer, if not what they really meant from the beginning. Jewish folklore stands as a living proof of this contention, as has been shown by modern research in respect of some particularly well-known examples.

It would be idle to deny that Kabbalistic thought lost much of its magnificence where it was forced to descend from the pinnacles of theoretical speculation to the plane of ordinary thinking and acting. The dangers which myth and magic present to the religious consciousness, including that of the mystic, are clearly shown in the development of Kabbalism. If one turns to the writings of great Kabbalists one seldom fails to be torn between alternate admiration and disgust. There is need for being quite clear about this in a time like ours, when the fashion of uncritical and superficial condemnation of even the most valuable elements of mysticism threatens to be replaced by an equally uncritical and obscurantist glorification of the Kabbalah. I have said before that Jewish philosophy had to pay a high price for its escape from the pressing questions of real life. But Kabbalism, too, has had to pay for its success. Philosophy came dangerously near to losing the living God; Kabbalism, which set out to preserve Him, to blaze a new and glorious trail to Him, encountered mythology on its way and was tempted to lose itself in its labyrinth.

Translated by George Lichtheim.

Other works by Scholem: *On Kabbalah and Its Symbolism* (1965); *The Messianic Idea in Judaism and Other Essays in Jewish Spirituality* (1971); *Sabbatai Zevi: The Mystical Messiah, 1626–1676* (1973); *On Jews and Judaism in Crisis* (1976); *From Berlin to Jerusalem* (1980).

Erich Auerbach

1892–1957

Literary critic and philologist Erich Auerbach was born into an affluent family in Berlin and studied law at the University of Heidelberg. After completing army service in World War I, he earned a doctorate in Romance languages and then taught at the University of Marburg. As a Jew, Auerbach lost his teaching credentials in 1935; he spent the war years in Istanbul, writing his monumental work, *Mimesis: The Representation of Reality in Western Literature* (1946). In 1947, Auerbach came to the United States and became professor of philology at Yale University.

Odysseus' Scar
1942

[. . .] The oft-repeated reproach that Homer is a liar takes nothing from his effectiveness, he does not need to base his story on historical reality, his reality is powerful enough in itself; it ensnares us, weaving its web around us, and that suffices him. And this "real" world into which we are lured, exists for itself, contains nothing but itself; the Homeric poems conceal nothing, they contain no teaching and no secret second meaning. Homer can be analyzed [. . .] but he cannot be interpreted. Later allegorizing trends have tried their arts of interpretation upon him, but to no avail. He resists any such treatment; the interpretations are forced and foreign, they do not crystallize into a unified doctrine. [. . .]

It is all very different in the Biblical stories. Their aim is not to bewitch the senses, and if nevertheless they produce lively sensory effects, it is only because the moral, religious, and psychological phenomena which are their sole concern are made concrete in the sensible matter of life. But their religious intent involves an absolute claim to historical truth. The story of Abraham and Isaac is not better established than the story of Odysseus, Penelope, and Euryclea; both are legendary. But the Biblical narrator, the Elohist, had to believe in the objective truth of the story of Abraham's sacrifice— the existence of the sacred ordinances of life rested upon the truth of this and similar stories. He had to believe in it passionately; or else (as many rationalistic interpreters believed and perhaps still believe) he had to be a conscious liar—no harmless liar like Homer, who lied to give pleasure, but a political liar with a definite end in view, lying in the interest of a claim to absolute authority.

To me, the rationalistic interpretation seems psychologically absurd; but even if we take it into consideration, the relation of the Elohist to the truth of his story still remains a far more passionate and definite one than is Homer's relation. The Biblical narrator was obliged to write exactly what his belief in the truth of the tradition (or, from the rationalistic standpoint, his interest in the truth of it) demanded of him—in either case, his freedom in creative or representative imagination was severely limited; his activity was perforce reduced to composing an effective version of the pious tradition. What he produced, then, was not primarily oriented toward "realism" (if he succeeded in being realistic, it was merely a means, not an end); it was oriented toward truth. Woe to the man who did not believe it! One can perfectly well entertain historical doubts on the subject of the Trojan War or of Odysseus' wanderings, and still, when reading Homer, feel precisely the effects he sought to produce; but without believing in Abraham's sacrifice, it is impossible to put the narrative of it to the use for which it was written. Indeed, we must go even further. The Bible's claim to truth is not only far more urgent than Homer's, it is tyrannical—it excludes all other claims. The world of the Scripture stories is not satisfied with claiming to be a historically true reality—it insists that it is the only real world, is destined for autocracy. All other scenes, issues, and ordinances have no right to appear independently of it, and it is promised that all of them, the history of all mankind, will be given their due place within its frame, will be subordinated to it. The Scripture stories do not, like Homer's, court our favor, they do not flatter us that they may please us and enchant us—they seek to subject us, and if we refuse to be subjected we are rebels.

Let no one object that this goes too far, that not the stories, but the religious doctrine, raises the claim to absolute authority; because the stories are not, like Homer's, simply narrated "reality." Doctrine and promise are incarnate in them and inseparable from them; for that very reason they are fraught with "background" and mysterious, containing a second, concealed meaning. In the story of Isaac, it is not only God's intervention at the beginning and the end, but even the factual and psychological elements which come between, that are mysterious, merely touched upon, fraught with background; and therefore they require subtle investigation and interpretation, they demand them. Since so much in the story is dark and incomplete, and since the reader knows that God is a hidden God, his effort to interpret it constantly finds something new to feed upon. Doctrine and the search for enlightenment are inextricably connected with the physical side of the narrative—the latter being more than simple "reality"; indeed they are in constant danger of losing their own reality, as very soon happened when interpretation reached such proportions that the real vanished.

If the text of the Biblical narrative, then, is so greatly in need of interpretation on the basis of its own content, its claim to absolute authority forces it still further in the same direction. Far from seeking, like Homer, merely to make us forget our own reality for a few hours, it seeks to overcome our reality: we are to fit our own life into its world, feel ourselves to be elements in its structure of universal history. This becomes increasingly difficult the further our historical environment is removed from that of the Biblical books; and if these nevertheless maintain their claim to absolute authority, it is inevitable that they themselves be adapted through interpretative transformation.

Translated by Willard R. Trask.

Other works by Auerbach: *Dante: Poet of the Secular World* (1929); *Literary Language and Its Public in Late Latin Antiquity and in the Middle Ages* (1958).

Gustawa Jarecka

1908–1943

The Polish Jewish novelist Gustawa Jarecka was a member of Emanuel Ringelblum's Oyneg Shabes group of ghetto inmates who documented life in Warsaw for the underground archive. Jarecka was born in Kalisz in 1908 and earned a degree in Polish studies from the University of Warsaw. Before the war she wrote left-wing novels in Polish, which depicted social struggles and working-class life but avoided specifically Jewish themes. Jarecka arrived in the ghetto with her two children and worked as a typist for the Judenrat, using her German and Polish language skills. Her access to Judenrat materials probably explained her recruitment to the Oyneg Shabes archive, where she wrote a particularly eloquent and moving account of the Great Deportation in the summer of 1942. Jarecka was deported with her two children to Treblinka in January 1943.

The Last Stage of Deportation Is Death
1942

[. . .] We have nooses fastened around our necks; when the pressure abates for a moment, we utter a cry. Its importance should not be underestimated. Many a time in history did such cries resound; for a long time they resounded in vain, and only much later they produced an echo.

Documents and a cry of pain, objectivity and passion do not fit together. And yet, it cannot be otherwise. I am noting down figures and from them emerges a picture of the street that was and is now gone, never to return, of people who are no more, of events so unparalleled that one records them in order to convince oneself that they were not a dream.

Before us and behind us is death. One might say that the present moments of waiting are taking place after the sentence already has been passed. An accident can still revoke it. In the moments of waiting in which there is archaic, instinctive hope, we want to leave a record of ourselves. The definition is immaterial—literature, history or a chronicle—this is a simple, gruesome story, one of those on which anonymous world legends about atrocities are based, like the Massacre of the Innocents and Nero's spectacles.

The desire to write is as strong as the repugnance of words. We hate them, because they too often served as a cover for emptiness or meanness. We despise them, for they are pale in comparison with the emotions tormenting us. And yet, in the past the word meant human dignity and was man's best possession—an instrument of communication between people.

We want to believe that there is some sense in still being alive among the shambles, among human hyenas and jackals who live by stripping the dead. These documents and notes are a remnant resembling a clue in a detective story. I remember from childhood such a novel by Conan Doyle, in which the dying victim writes with a faint hand one word on the wall containing the proof of the criminal's guilt. That word, scrawled by the dying man, influenced my imagination in the past. The records left by us, whose survival is so uncertain, remind me of that stereotype image that once so moved me. We are noting the evidence of the crime. This will no longer be of any help to us. The record must be hurled like a stone under history's wheel in order to stop it. That stone has the weight of our knowledge that reached the bottom of human cruelty. It contains the memory of mothers crazed with pain after losing their children: the memory of the cry of little children carried away without overcoats, in summer clothes and barefooted, going on the road to death and crying with innocent tears, not grasping the horror of what was happening to them, the memory of the despair of old fathers and mothers, abandoned to their fate by their adult children, and the memory of that stony silence hanging over the dead city, after the sentence, passed upon 300 thousand persons, had been carried out.

Perhaps this material should be gathered in order to find a reply to the questions: what caused such monstrosity, how did it happen that individuals were found executing these orders, carrying away the children and murdering hundreds of thousands of civilians? Awareness of the following truth should guide the hand and mind that will create the new mold of reality: this city that is silent today and its deserted streets will yet return to life, though the people who have gone away from here will live no more.

One can lose all hopes except the one—that the suffering and destruction of this war will make sense when they are looked at from a distant, historical perspective. From sufferings, unparalleled in history, from bloody tears and bloody sweat, a chronicle of days of hell is being composed, in order that one may understand the historical reasons that shaped the human mind in this fashion, and created government systems which made possible the events in our time through which we passed.

Translated by M. Z. Prives and others.

Other works by Jarecka: *Inni ludzie* (1932); *Stare grzechy* (1934); *Przed jutrem* (1936); *Ludzie i sztandary*, 2 vols. (1938–1939).

Horace M. Kallen

1882–1974

The social philosopher Horace M. Kallen was born in Silesia, the son of a rabbi; he arrived with his parents in the United States in 1887. He was educated at Harvard and taught there, at Clark University, and at the University of Wisconsin. In 1919, he helped to found the New School for Social Research in New York City, where he taught for the rest of his life. His best-known contribution to American thought was his theory of cultural pluralism. Rejecting Israel Zangwill's vision of the United States as "a melting pot," he opposed efforts to force the homogenization of American society and urged immigrants to cultivate and take pride in their national origins. Not surprisingly, he was a supporter of Zionism.

The National Being and the Jewish Community 1942

[. . .] If against the assimilationist the American spirit affirms the right to be different, against the segregationist it affirms the right of free association of the different with one another. But it points also to a certain prior community of the Jewish group with the national being. This community is established in and through the Old Testament, which contributes so largely to the singularity of the Jewish psyche: [W. E. H.] Lecky wrote that "the Hebraic mortar cemented the foundations of American democracy."[1] But furthermore, the Jewish community, like every other composing the national being, serves as a psychological locale for voluntary social experimentation, for invention and discovery, as such, involving more limited risks than a nation-wide adventure would. Thus the Jewish locale has been an area of trial and error in employer–employee relations, in philanthropy, in education, in literature and in the arts. What was started in the Yiddish theaters of the East Side more than once was perfected—or corrupted—on Broadway; what began as a protocol on relations between Jewish employers and Jewish employees on women's wear, has become the initiating precedent in the national growth toward industrial democracy; what began as an effort to help immigrant "coreligionists" cheaply and efficiently, has contributed to the formation of the theory and practice of scientific charity, and so on. And it is not possible to call these developments more an Americanization of Jewry—even of the Jewry of Palestine—than an enrichment of the American way by Jewish contributions. "American Jewish living" makes an impression of a healthy symbiosis with the diverse other forms of living whose interaction orchestrates the Union we call America, and whose combined utterance is the American spirit. Like its neighbors, the community of Jewish living has a character of its own, a singularity which works as a reservoir and a breeding place of the Jewish difference. This its men and women of genius carry beelike from the nest which nurtured them to the national scene, there to serve as a fertilizing contribution to the commonwealth of things and ideals. Louis Brandeis and Ben Cardozo; David Lubin, Nathan Straus and Julius Rosenwald; Sidney Hillman and David Dubinsky; Emma Lazarus; Robert Nathan and Sholem Asch; Edna Ferber and Gertrude Stein; George Kaufmann, Elmer Rice, Clifford Odets, S. N. Behrmann; Aaron Copland and George Gershwin; Leon Kroll, Maurice Sterne, Max Weber, William Gropper—I mention only a few of the long lists of jurists and business men, playwrights, composers, painters, trades unionists, who are figures of my lifetime. There are many others, in every walk of life—virtuosos and inventors, physicians and architects, chemists and psychologists, merchants, engineers, whom *Who's Who* counts—all children or grandchildren of a ghetto that has ceased to be a ghetto because its walls have been breached and its gates opened, so that the life of the nation flows through it, and its life flows and mingles in the national stream, in a confluence where the free flow of each is the expanding life of both.

So I close my "evaluation of American Jewish living." I have not studied to make it either "judicial" or "scholarly." I have been concerned first and last to set down the ideals which any evaluation I could make would have to use for measure, and to signalize what, in terms of the national being, these measures of the Jewish community would come to. I have done so. What I have said can be valid only for those Americans whose faith in democracy is a fighting faith, and for those American Jews who are resolved to stand up in the armies of democracy as the democratic faith requires, freely and boldly as Jews.

NOTE
1. *History of Rationalism in Europe*, II, p. 168.

Other works by Kallen: "Democracy versus the Melting-Pot" (1915); *"Of Them Which Say They Are Jews" and Other Essays on the Jewish Struggle for Survival* (1954); *Cultural Pluralism and the American Idea* (1956).

Zelig Kalmanovitch

1881–1944

The Yiddish linguist and historian Zelig Kalmanovitch was born in Goldingen, Courland (now Kuldīga, Latvia). Before World War I, he showed a keen interest in the politics of diaspora nationalism as well as in Yiddish linguistics and literature. In 1919, he received his doctorate from St. Petersburg University, settling in Vilna in 1928 where he became a leader of the YIVO and the editor of its major journal, *YIVO-bleter*. Kalmanovitch was a major cultural leader of the Vilna ghetto, where he kept a diary in Hebrew in which he questioned the viability of armed resistance and supported Jacob Gens's policy of buying time through productive labor. This diary was found by Avrom Sutzkever after the war. Deported to labor camps in Estonia in 1943, Kalmanovitch died in the fall of 1944.

A Diary of the Nazi Ghetto in Vilna
1942

Sunday, [December] 27, [1942]

This morning I was in the children's nursery. Women who work leave their children from 7 to 6. There are 150 children between the ages of three months and two years, [one group] from two to three years, [one group] from three to six, and another group that studies reading and writing. Speeches, dramatic presentations, the children march in line. But the Jewish flavor is missing. In ghetto circumstances the order is remarkable. What vitality in this people on the brink of destruction!

Who mourns the destruction of East European Jewry? The destruction is a hard fact. Undoubtedly also those who predicted it did not envisage it in this form. Three or four years ago the central Zionist organ was writing of a Jewish center in the Diaspora parallel to the center in Palestine. But the catastrophe was nevertheless a definite thing, its contours so visible. Indeed, the innovative horror for our human consciousness is the personal destruction of human lives: old people, children, blossoming youth, weak and old men, but also those in full vigor. There is no doubt, it tears the heart. But millions of people are losing their lives in all parts of the world in the war. Not only combatants, but also infants and old people. The war has put its face on our destruction. But the destruction was certain even had there been no war. It proceeded on its way in an expansive manner. No one attempted to stem it. On the contrary, whoever attempted to convince himself and the world that he was erecting a defense, actually collapsed. The full proof came in the East [in the U.S.S.R.]. Everything was swallowed up in one great endeavor to disappear. The apparent life of culture was pure nonsense, arid. When the East came here, no one as much as raised his voice. All was happiness. All found a place, a sense of belonging. Undoubtedly here and there someone thought: something is missing. Another reflected: Judaism is disappearing. But all this was glossed over by the fact of mere existence. There is no discrimination. One amounts to something, particularly something in the apparatus. One can have his say. Had the thing continued in existence, nothing would have been left of the enemies of Israel anyway, except, of course, the youth that yearns thither [in Palestine]. Could they actually have got there, they would have been saved for our people, and the people through them. But the rest? The individuals would have remained intact, but would have been lost to our people. Jewry in the East is disappearing. The final result is the same as now.

What is better? Better for whom? The individuals who are saved are saved individuals. There are two billion people in the world, two billion people + X. For our people—the Jewish people—had constructive elements in East European Jewry. Those that yearned thither, if they actually succeeded in coming there, they strengthened our people. Otherwise, our people will mourn them. Great will be the sorrow and mourning, the joy of redemption will be wrapped in black. But the same sorrow is also for the parts that disappeared through apostasy. And if you wish, the sorrow is even greater. Here the evil beast came: "Joseph is without doubt torn in pieces." But how Jacob would have wept if the first plan, God forbid, had been carried out! In that case the Jewish people would have been justified in feeling that sick, impure blood courses in our veins. No external enemy tears off our limbs. Our limbs rot and fall off by themselves. And a page of history will read: The grandchildren were not interior to the grandfathers. Only fire and sword overcame them. A curse upon the murderer! Eternal glory to the innocent victim! But here, where comfort lures people into the camp of the mighty, it is of no interest to history. It will not condemn, but silence means condemnation. You are no longer. Like all of them—Ammon, Moab, Edom, the hundred kingdoms of Aram . . . an object for excavations and students of epigraphy. History will revere your memory, people of the ghetto. Your least utterance will be studied, your struggle for man's dignity will inspire poems, your scum and moral degradation will summon and awaken morality. Your murderers will stand in the pillory forever and ever. The human universe will regard them with fear and fear for itself and will strive to keep from sin. People will ask: "Why was it done so to this people?" The answer will be: "That is the due of the wicked who destroyed East European Jewry." Thus the holocaust will steal its way into world history. Extinction by means of a loving caress creates no sensation and means nothing to anyone.

Eventually the Jewish people itself will forget this branch that was broken off. It will have to do without it. From the healthy trunk will come forth branches and blossoms and leaves. There is still strength and life. Dried up and decayed—this happens to every tree. There are still thousands of years ahead. Lamentation for the dead, of course, that is natural, particularly if they are your own, close to you. But the Jewish people must not be confused. The mourning for close ones—some people bear their sorrow long; most find comfort. Human nature—such is the world. Whatever the earth covers up is forgotten. In the ghetto itself we see how people forget. It cannot be otherwise. It certainly is not wrong. The real motive in mourning is after all fear of one's own end. Wherein are we better than those tens of thousands? It must happen to us, too. If we only had a guarantee of survival! But that does not exist and one cannot always be fearful, then the feeling of fear is projected into mourning for the fallen, and sorrow over the destruction of Jewry. Spare yourself the sorrow! The Jewish people will not be hurt. It will, it is to be hoped, emerge fortified by the trial. This should fill the heart with joyous gratitude to the sovereign of history.

Translated by YIVO editorial committee.

Abba Kovner

1918–1987

Born in Sevastopol and raised in Vilna, Abba Kovner was a partisan, poet, novelist, and major figure in Israeli cultural life. A leader of the Zionist youth group Ha-Shomer ha-Tsaʻir, in late 1941 Kovner issued the first Jewish call to arms and took over the leadership of the United Partisans Organization after the death of Itzik Vittenberg. Among the liberators of Vilna in 1944, Kovner organized illegal immigration of Jews to Palestine (the so-called Beriḥah movement) but was caught by the British when trying to procure arms for a group called Nakam that sought to avenge the Holocaust. During Israel's War of Independence he served as the political commissar for the Givati Brigade. All these experiences he later recast into prose and verse. From 1946 to his death, Kovner was a resident of Kibbutz ʻEin ha-Ḥoresh.

Call to Arms

1942

A Summons to Resistance in the Vilna Ghetto, January 1942

Let us not be led like sheep to the slaughter! Jewish youth!

In a time of unparalleled national misfortune we appeal to you!

We do not yet have the words to express the whole tragic struggle which transpires before our eyes. Our language has no words to probe the depths to which our life has fallen nor to vociferate the anguish which strangles us.

It is still too hard to find the proper definition for the state in which we find ourselves, for the extraordinary cruelty with which the annihilation of the local Jewish population has been carried out.

The community of Jerusalem of Lithuania numbered 75,000. On entering the ghetto, 25,000 were already missing, and today only 12,000 remain. All the others have been killed! Death strolls in our streets; in our tents—powerlessness. But the anguish at this huge misfortune is much greater in the light of the ignoble conduct of the Jews at the present time. Never in its long history of martyrdom has the Jewish people shown such abjectness, such a lack of human dignity, national pride, and unity, such communal inertia and submissiveness to the murderers.

The heart aches even more at the conduct of Jewish youth, reared for twenty years in the ideals of upbuilding and halutz defense, which now is apathetic, lost, and does not respond to the tragic struggle.

There are, however, occasions in the life of a people, of a collective, as in the life of an individual, which seize you by the hair of your head, shake you up, and force you to gird up all your strength to keep alive. We are now experiencing such an occasion.

With what can we defend ourselves? We are helpless, we have no possibilities of organizing any defense of our existence. Even if we are deprived of the possibility of an armed defense in this unequal contest of strength, we nevertheless can still defend ourselves. Defend ourselves with all means—and moral defense above all—is the command of the hour.

Jewish youth!

On none but you rests the national duty to be the pillar of the communal defense of the Jewish collective which stands on the brink of annihilation!

I: Let Us Defend Ourselves during a Deportation!

For several months now, day and night, thousands and tens of thousands have been torn away from our midst, men, the aged, women, and children, led away like cattle—and we, the remainder, are numbed. The illusion still lives within us that they are still alive somewhere, in an undisclosed concentration camp, in a ghetto.

You believe and hope to see your mother, your father, your brother who was seized and has disappeared.

In the face of the next day which arrives with the horror of deportation and murder, the hour has struck to dispel the illusion: There is no way out of the ghetto, except the way to death!

No illusion greater than that our dear ones are alive.

No illusion more harmful than that. It deadens our feelings, shatters our national unity in the moments before death.

Before our eyes they led away our mother, our father, our sisters—enough!

We will not go!

Comrades! Uphold this awareness and impart to your families, to the remnants of the Jerusalem of Lithuania.

—Do not surrender into the hands of the kidnappers!

—Do not hand over any other Jews!

—If you are caught, you have nothing to lose!

—Let us defend ourselves, and not go!

Better to fall with honor in the ghetto than to be led like sheep to Ponary!

II: On Guard over National Honor and Dignity

We work for Germans and Lithuanians. Everyday we come face to face with our employers, the murderers of our brothers. Great the shame and pain, observing the conduct of Jews, stripped of the awareness of human dignity.

Comrades!

—Don't give the foe the chance to ridicule you!

—When a German ridicules a Jew—don't help him laugh!

—Don't play up to your murderers!

—Denounce the bootlickers at work!

—Denounce the girls who flirt with Gestapo men!

—Work slowly, don't speed!

—Show solidarity! If misfortune befalls one of you—don't be vile egotists—all of you help him. Be united in work and misfortunes!

—Jewish agents of the Gestapo and informers of all sorts walk the streets. If you get hold of one such, sentence him—to be beaten until death!

III: In the Presence of the German Soldier

Instead of submissiveness and repulsive bootlicking, you are given the possibility in daily encounters with German soldiers to perform an important national deed. Not every German soldier is a sworn enemy of the Jews, not every German soldier is a sworn Hitlerite. But many have false ideas about Jews. We, the youth, by our conduct, in word and deed, can create in the mind of the German soldier another image of a Jew, a productive one, a Jew who has national and human dignity.

Comrades, show the Jews with whom you work and live together that this is the approach to the German soldier.

IV: To the Jewish Police

Most tragic is the role of the Jewish police—to be a blind tool in the hands of our murderers. But you, Jewish policemen, have at least a chance to demonstrate your personal integrity and national responsibility!

—Any act which threatens Jewish life should not be performed!

—No actions of mass deportation should be carried out!

—Refuse to carry out the orders which bring death to Jews and their families! . . .

—Do not let service in the police be turned into national disgrace for you!

—Jewish policeman, sooner risk your own life than dozens of Jewish lives!

Comrades!

Convey your hatred of the foe in every place and at every moment!

Never lose the awareness that you are working for your murderers!

Better to fall in the fight for human dignity than to live at the mercy of the murderer!

Let us defend ourselves! Defend ourselves until the last minute!

Translated by Lucy Dawidowicz

Other works by Kovner: *Peridah me-ha-darom* (1949); *Panim el panim* (1953-1955); *My Little Sister* (1967); *A Canopy in the Desert* (1970); *Lehakat ha-ketzev mofi'a 'al har gerizim* (1972).

Israel Milejkowski

d. ca. 1943

Israel Milejkowski was a physician at the Czyste St. Hospital in Warsaw. When the Nazis invaded the city, Milejkowski served as head of the Judenrat's health department, in which capacity he documented the effects of hunger on the ghetto's population. He also aimed to show that the Jewish spirit did not fail under dire conditions. Milejkowski himself perished either in Warsaw or while being transported to Treblinka.

Answer to the Oyneg Shabes Questionnaire
1942

. . . I head up the public-health service in the program to combat epidemics and also the hospital department. Besides, I also direct the medical board here in the ghetto, where over 800 doctors are concentrated. All these activities leave me very little free time and my remarks will therefore be based on my daily practice in my own field, but I will try, as far as possible, to give my conclusions a general character. . . .

The root and source of all evil in our miserable existence at the present moment lie in the very fact that we have been locked up in a ghetto. This gives rise to degenerating and demoralizing consequences in our community life. This is the cause of our physical and moral collapse. [. . .]

In order to get a true picture of ghetto life we cannot judge on the basis of what we see in the street. I differentiate between two strata in the ghetto. I would express it graphically as follows: The whole Jewish community in the ghetto is as if it had been thrown into a huge pot of seething water on a big fire, the fire of our afflictions. In the seething water we can distinguish an upper layer and a lower one.

The upper layer seethes and boils and many bubbles appear on its surface. The second layer also boils, but more quietly, more slowly. The upper layer is more conspicuous, though it is not the more numerous or more important, but because it is more visibly astir. If we want to see the true face of the ghetto, we must acquaint ourselves with the lower layer.

At first glance what is most obvious is the benumbed sense of compassion among Warsaw Jews. Without any pity for the desperate plight of thousands of our brethren whom want has forced from their hovels out onto the streets, we pass almost indifferently the barely living unfortunates and the paper-covered corpses of those who died of hunger. Savagery has begun to rule our minds and, accordingly, also our actions. It is worth mentioning that "they" have condescended to note this tragic phenomenon in our lives.

The life of the first layer is not, however, the true one. That is represented by the lower layer . . . in which we find modest but very important happenings, luminous, vigorous, cheering: the sense of compassion as manifested by the work of the basic cells of organized Jewish life, the tenement committees,[1] thanks to which the true Jewish trait of compassion and of charity has been fulfilled.

In addition, there is the quiet, modest work, which has only a temporary life, being done in other areas, for example, in setting up public kitchens of various kinds, medical courses, and vocational training for Jewish adolescents. Intensive medical research on starvation and typhus is also being done. All the clinical materials, unfortunately so bizarrely voluminous, are carefully being researched and the studies are being prepared for their definitive medical conclusions.[2] This is our ambitious and prestigious undertaking!

But this is by no means an original, creative ghetto culture. Afterwards, after the cataclysm, we want to be able to show the world that even horrible persecutions could not crush us. Right now, a small scientific meeting devoted to the ghetto is being held at the hospital. Here (!) problems and scientific presentations, responses and discussions. The results of the research will be published later and I hope that they will interest a broad audience.

These attempts at constructive work in the ghetto, in relation to the negative happenings, are small comfort to us, because one thing is terribly clear: the ghetto demoralizes! What is a blessing for the ghetto—smuggling, for example—is from the national standpoint a curse.

If, for a moment, we discount the utilitarian factor involved in smuggling, if we can forget that thanks to those Jewish smugglers who risk their lives to provide the ghetto with all sorts of delicacies, many Jews can supply themselves with the finest and best meals, and if we ponder instead on what sort of generation will grow out of these smugglers, good-for-nothing scamps—is the ghetto not a curse? Or take, for instance, vocational courses, medical and others. The courses will produce nothing but bunglers, though neither the teachers nor supervisors are at fault. At fault are only the harsh and abnormal conditions of the ghetto. This is not progress or advancement. This is degeneration and brutalization.

Under such harsh conditions of our communal life in the Warsaw ghetto, to return to our simile of the pot of seething water, people from the very bottom rise to the surface of our pot. Blackmailers, informers, bribe-takers of all sorts, and influence-peddlers. This layer of underworld characters, antisocial elements are always found in every society. They increase and multiply in wartime, just as if inhuman living conditions were the best subsoil for the disorderly development of these human hyenas. [. . .]

Our present educational work here in the ghetto ought to be aimed at inculcating the tradition in the hearts and minds of the young generation, that they absorb it so that it becomes part and parcel of their inner being. From this standpoint I take an altogether positive attitude to the religious values of our people. I have realized that the will to survive of the Jewish people, their stubbornness and persistence—"a stiff-necked people"—really come from the traditional religious approach to the problem of our survival. In the religious Jew I see this wholeness. He is without the self-reproachfulness and the doubts that totally consume the mind of the enlightened Jew and thus empty it of its essence.

The mind possesses a whole series of attributes among which faith occupies a prominent place. Deep faith is an antidote for the poison which comes with our daily terrible life. To close the chasm that opens up before the modern Jew's eyes and to enable him to overcome the strongest temptations, his religious feelings must be awakened. . . .

NOTES

1. The tenement committees were a ŻTOS spinoff. Each building was organized for self-help activities and ghettowide philanthropic fund raising [note appears in the translated document].

2. The study was completed October 1942 after the mass deportations from the Warsaw ghetto. It appeared in Warsaw in 1946, published by the JDC under the title, *Maladie de Famine: Recherches cliniques sur la famine executées dans le ghetto de Varsovie en 1942* [note appears in the translated document].

Translated by David L. Gold.

Other works by Milejkowski: *Dermatologja i kosmetyka według wykładów dra Milejkowskiego: do użytku słuchaczek Kursów Kosmetycznych* (1931); *Maladie de famine: recherches cliniques sur la famine exécutées dans le ghetto de Varsovie en 1942* (with Emil Apfelbaum, 1946).

Kalonymus Kalman Shapira

1889–1943

Kalonymus Kalman Shapira was an educator and Hasidic master who, beginning in 1913, served as the rabbi of Piaseczno, Poland; in 1923, he founded Yeshiva Da'at Moshe, a major Hasidic yeshiva in Warsaw. Shapira transcribed and translated his weekly sermons, which he delivered to his followers in the Warsaw ghetto and bequeathed to the Oyneg Shabes archive. He perished in the Trawniki camp near Lublin.

The Holy Fire

1942

Parashat Haḥodesh [Exodus 12:1–20]

[. . .] The Talmud states in Ḥagigah [5b] that, concerning God's outer chambers, we may apply the verse STRENGTH AND REJOICING ARE IN HIS PLACE (I Chron. 16:27), but in His inner chambers. He grieves and weeps for the sufferings of Israel. Therefore, there are occasions when, at a time of [Divine] hiddenness—meaning, when He, may He be blessed, secludes Himself in His inner chambers—the Jewish person communes with Him there, each individual in accord with his situation, and [new aspects of] Torah and Divine Service are revealed to him there. We have already mentioned how the Oral Torah was revealed in exile, and how the Holy Zohar was revealed to Rabbi Simeon bar Yoḥai and his son Rabbi Eleazar at a time of acute suffering, caused by the terror of the [Roman] government.

At times the individual is amazed at himself. [He thinks:] "Am I not broken? Am I not always on the verge of tears—and indeed I do weep periodically! How then can I study Torah? How can I find the strength to think creatively in Torah and Hasidism?" At times the person torments himself by thinking, "Can it be anything but inner callousness, that I am able to strengthen myself and study, despite my troubles and those of Israel, which are so numerous." Then again, he will say to himself, "Am I not broken? I have so much to make me cry; my whole life is gloomy and dark." Such a person is perplexed about himself; but, as we've said, He, may He be blessed, is to be found in His inner chambers, weeping, so that one who pushes in and comes close to Him by means of [studying] Torah, weeps together with God, and studies Torah with Him. Just that makes the difference; the weeping, the pain that a person undergoes by himself, alone—they may have the effect of breaking him, of bringing him down, so that he is incapable of doing anything. But the weeping that the person does together with God—that strengthens him. He weeps—and is strengthened; he is broken—but finds courage to study and teach. *It is hard to rise, time and again, above the sufferings; but when one summons the courage—stretching the mind to engage in Torah and Divine service—then he enters the inner chambers where God is to be found. There he weeps and wails with Him, as it were, together, so that he even finds the strength to study Torah and perform acts of Divine service.*

March 14, 1942

Parashat Mattot [Numbers 30:2–32:42]

. . . How can we lift ourselves up at least a little bit in the face of the terrifying reports, both old and new, which tear us to pieces and crush our hearts? With the knowledge that we are not alone in our sufferings, but that He, may He be blessed, endures with us [as Scripture states], I AM WITH HIM IN TROUBLE (Ps. 91:15). But more: there are some sufferings that we suffer on our own account—whether for our sins, or as sufferings of love in order to purge and purify us—in which case He, may He be blessed, just suffers along with us. There are, however, some sufferings that we just suffer along with Him, as it were. These are the sufferings of *Kiddush Hashem*. [As our liturgy states,] "Our Father, our King, act for the sake of those who are slain for Your holy name."—They are killed, as it were, for His sake and for the sake of sanctifying His holy name. [As our liturgy states,] "Save, please, those who bear Your burden."—Israel also bears His burden [besides its own]. The sufferings are basically for His sake, on His account; in sufferings such as these, we are made greater, raised higher. As a consequence, we can strengthen ourselves a bit more. [As our liturgy states,] "Save those who study Your Torah, whose cheeks are torn of hair, who are given to the floggers, who bear Your burden." . . . How is it possible to study Torah when "our cheeks are torn of hair," when we are "given to the floggers"? Because we know that we "bear Your burden," and we thereby strengthen ourselves a bit.

How can we tell if the sufferings are only on account of our sins, or whether they are to sanctify His name? By [noticing] whether the enemies torment only us, or whether their hatred is basically for the Torah, and as a consequence they torment us as well. Regarding Haman's decree, the Talmud asks, "What did the Jews of that generation do to deserve destruction?," whereas regarding the Hellenic decree [against the Jews that resulted] in the miracle of Hanukkah, the Talmud does not raise the question, despite the fact that thousands of Jews were killed, nearly all of the Land of Israel was conquered, and the Temple was invaded. The difference is that Haman's decree was directed only against the Jews [not their religion]; it follows, then, that the decree [against them] was on account of some sin. However, with respect to the Hellenic [persecution], [our liturgy] states: "In the days of Mattathias, when the wicked Hellenic kingdom arose . . . to make them forget Your Torah and transgress the statutes of Your will. . . ." So it is

not appropriate to ask "for what sin [did the sufferings come]," since, while they did purge them of sin, they were [essentially] sufferings of *Kiddush Hashem*. . . .

July 11, 1942

Translated by Nehemia Polen.

Other works by Shapira: *Ḥovat ha-talmidim* (1932); *Sefer derekh ha-melekh* (1990); *Conscious Community: A Guide to Inner Work* (1996); *A Critical and Annotated Edition of Rabbi Kalonymus Kalman Shapira's Sermons during the Holocaust*, 2 vols. (2017).

Stephen S. Wise
1874–1949

Stephen S. Wise was born into a rabbinical family in Budapest and immigrated to New York as a child. He earned his doctorate in 1901 from Columbia University and was ordained as a Reform rabbi. He served congregations in New York City and then Portland, Oregon. Wise fought for social justice throughout his life and was a founder of the NAACP. He was a leading American Jewish communal figure during World War II, serving as president of the American Jewish Congress and as a member of the World Jewish Congress in Geneva.

Deliverance Will Come
1942

Over and above all else we gather here tonight to dedicate ourselves to the loftiest hopes of our country, to renew unshakeable faith in the victory, early or late, of America and all the United Nations. To the achievement of such victory over the powers of evil and darkness, we who are Americans and Jews pledge anew all that we are, all that we have, all that we hope to be.

Tomorrow will be the eve of Tishe B'Ab, the destruction twice or thrice of the holy Temple of Jerusalem. Tonight we meet not only to sorrow over an ancient grief but also over a limitless wrong of our own day, the Nazi threat to destroy the Jewish people. Great as is our sorrow, deepfelt as is our grief, we do not mourn the destruction of the Jewish people. The destruction of the Jewish people can never be. Its Temple may be destroyed, its people plundered and stricken and wounded, but the eternal people shall not be destroyed. What Pharaoh and Haman, Nebuchadnezar and Epiphanes, Titus and Hadrian, Torquemada and Pobie-donosteff, failed to effect—the extermination of the Jewish people—will never be achieved by Hitler, nor yet by a thousand Hitlers. President Roosevelt's message is true and right, "The Nazis will not succeed in exterminating their victims any more than they will succeed in enslaving mankind."

We would not be worthy of our Jewish fellowship if we did not lift up our voices in solemn lamentation and mournful protest over the oceanic wrongs done to our brother-Jews wherever Nazis live and rule. We would not be equal to our American citizenship if we did not tonight with one voice ask our great-hearted, liberty-loving fellow Americans to join with us in solemn condemnation of the infamy of the Axis in dooming unarmed and defenseless men, women and children by the hundred thousands to suffering, torture and death. Honor is the fate of them who are privileged to fight and die for a cause, but shame is the portion of such as torture and murder masses who are weaponless and defenseless. [. . .]

We are not met tonight to cry for vengeance. "Vengeance is mine," saith the Lord. But for purposes which befit Americans and Jews, we are asking our Government and the United Nations to serve notice upon the Nazi despots that the horror of Nazi mistreatment of civilians should cease, whether of Jews, Protestants or Catholics, whether Poles, Czechs or Greeks. [. . .] We wish, moreover, in and through this assembly to say to our fellow-Jews in the lands of Hitler horror—Afflicted of our people—you are not forgotten and under God your day of deliverance will come. We know that one million and more of you, our brothers, have died of Nazi inhumanity to man, that Jewish multitudes have been and are being exposed to spoilation, starvation, disease, enslavement, massacre, and execution. These ruthless atrocities are visited by the Hitler rule upon the Jews of whom Dr. Goebbels said in *Das Reich* within a few days, "The Jews must be annihilated in order to save Germany." The fact is that neither the Germans nor the Jews will be annihilated, but a civilized world will exterminate the Hitlers and Goebbels and Himmlers who are the scourge of mankind. The salvation of our people and all peoples who would be free can only come under God through a victory speedy and complete of the United Nations.

The greatest crime against the Jewish victims of Hitler would be to treat the crimes against the Jews differently from the treatment of crimes against French, or Czechs, or Poles, or Greeks. The warning of Churchill and Roosevelt, after the murder of the French hostages and the destruction of the Czechian Lidice, has been renewed tonight by President Roosevelt himself with regard to the unspeakable mass murder of Jews. [. . .]

Tonight we speak through prayer to and of the dead. To the living, the surviving, we offer our loving greeting, and in the spirit of Tishe B'Ab we cry: That which is mortal falls, that which is perishable dies, but the hopes and ideals God has implanted within us are undying. You stand not alone in your sorrow; let the faith of a whole world of free men sustain you, the faith of men who now understand as never before that you have suffered through the ages because you denied and rejected Hitlers when you might have gained peace by all the pleasant ways of compromise or appeasement or surrender.

This meeting has yet another purpose. Our brothers in Nazi lands have perished unarmed. That is the tragedy of it. Wherever the Nazis went they could not resist and were doomed to perish without a cause. But one land there is wherein the Jews will and can defend themselves. If Britain only be wise and just enough to use them as the unswerving, loyal allies that they are. For Britain's sake, for the sake of the United Nations, for the sake of honor among comrades and allies—half a million and more builders of Palestine must not suffer the fate of all other Jewish victims of the Nazis.

They must not be left unarmed and defenseless. If, heaven forfend, Rommel reach the outer gates of Palestine, he must be flung back by the heroic prowess and resistless fury of the Jewish defenders of the land. Today, two or three divisions of young Maccabeans might have helped to turn the tide in British favor on the western border of Egypt. A Jewish Home Guard to safeguard Jewish Palestine is as rightful and fitting and necessary as an English Home Guard in and of England. Jews in Palestine are ready to die in the defense of Palestine, but they must not be massacred. They can and will die, if die they must, but they will die like men and Jews and Maccabeans.

My people, I summon you to take your place among the United and Free Peoples of earth. I summon you to fight on every front, including the Second Front, against all tyrants and oppressors. I summon you to arise and march forward as Americans to the liberation of our brothers, to the defense of Zion, to the victory of our country for freedom and humanity.

Other works by Wise: *The Great Betrayal* (with Jacob De Haas, 1930); *As I See It* (1944); *The Challenging Years: The Autobiography of Stephen Wise* (1949); *Servant of the People* (1969).

Nissim ben Shimon
Dates Unknown

A hairdresser from Rabat, Morocco, Nissim ben Shimon (Simon Coiffeur) wrote a famous parody of the traditional Passover story, after the liberation of Morocco by the Allies from the repressive Vichy regime. Writing in Judeo-Arabic, he fashioned the tale as a Seder, using the iconic characters to tell the tale of contemporary persecution against the Jews of Morocco and their subsequent liberation. In his version of the Four Sons, the wise son is the British, the wicked son is Hitler, the simple son is the Americans, and the son who does not know how to ask a question is Roosevelt. "He who brought us forth out of Egypt" is fashioned after General De Gaulle and Rabbi Akiva is General Montgomery.

Hitler's Haggadah
1943

In haste
Quickly came the Americans.

This Bread
These emaciated faces
Of our ancestors in panic
From Hitler
All who are hungry may they walk and fear
All who are in need flee in trembling.
This year here
Next year in tranquility.
This year in the black market
Next year in Palestine,
Free people.

What is different
What is different about this night
From the night of [nineteen] thirty-nine?
For on those nights we could not even speak
On this night we are not afraid.
For on those nights we slept in worry,
This night with a heart of joy.
For on those nights in distress,
We were poisoned
This night look and see;

For on those nights we did not eat,
We did not drink,
We only feared and fled.
On this night in tranquility we sit at the table.

Slaves
We were slaves to Hitler the oppressor,
And the Allies saved us from his hand
With a strong hand and an outstretched arm.
And if the English had not come,
And the Americans
We would not have been saved,
Not us and not our sons,
And not the sons of our sons.
We were seized with dread of Hitler
And his power.

And even if we were wise, if we were intelligent,
Knowing what would happen to us.
All who tell more with jesting
With embellishment that which happened to him
Behold this is praiseworthy.

A Story
A story happened in the days of the great Mussolini,
Hitler and Göring the bastard,
Ribbentrop and Ciano the Italian,
Who were planning with cunning and ruse
All that night,
Until the angels of destruction came
And shook them, Oh my masters,
And the dawn threw them into the furnace.
Mr. Roosevelt said in a speech:
Behold I am as a seventy-year-old,
And I merited the memory of
The destruction of Germany at night in bombing.

Until Mr. Churchill spoke
As it is said:
"So that it will be remembered
What the Eighth Army did to them
On the way to the Land of Egypt."

All the days of your life and my days,
I will remember what happened.
"All the days of your life," the nights
And the Sages say:
"All the days of your life," to bring up to the days of
Russia.

Blessed be God
Blessed be God, blessed be He.

Blessed for He brought the English
And the Americans, blessed be He.

Of four sons the Torah speaks:
England, wise. Hitler, wicked.
America good.
And Mussolini who is not worthy of being
    spoken of.

The Wise
England—*the wise one, what does he say?*
The Royal Air Force acts with wisdom.
And thus you should say to him: How many
Matzot are eaten on Passover?
Every matzo with a bomb on the forehead,
Powerful bombs.

The Wicked
Hitler—*the wicked, what does he say?*
Slavery and torture, all for the Jews.
For the Jews, and not for him.
And just as his spirit was about to go forth in fury,
He was cruel to the Jews.
Also Italy *will blunt his teeth,*
And say to him:
In Libya and Africa I ran out of ammunition
I and not him.
And had I not followed in his footsteps,
The two of us would not have been trapped.

The Simple
America—the good one, what does he say?
What is this?
And you shall say to him: only with our airplanes
We will save the entire world from the persecutor's
    hand.

And he who does not know
And Mussolini, who is not worthy of being
    spoken of?
You shall open for him, as it is said:
"And you shall say to him on the first day
That he was caught in distress,
In the capturing of Ethiopia
And precious Tunisia.
And God performed a miracle and brought the
    English
And He took them out of the Land of Egypt,
And Montgomery pursued them without
    besieging them."

Could it be from the New Moon?

So that he and his partner Hitler should learn,
When the Americans came to Africa.
Could it be on this day?
So it teaches: for the Jews I did not say, but at this
    hour.
From now until Shavuot we will be saved from
    exile. [. . .]

These
These are the Ten Plagues
That the Allies brought upon the Germans in
    Germany, and these are they:
Propaganda and bombs,
Panic and alarm,
Putting out lights, ditches, the abortion of fetuses,
Flight from the cities, hiding in cellars
The black market. [. . .]

Rabbi Akiva
Rabbi Montgomery and [Harold] Alexander says:
How do we know that every single blow
That the Allies brought upon Germany
Was five blows?
As it is said:
"The Royal Air Force will be sent against them,
The Flying Fortress, the fighter planes
The Mosquito and heavy bombers.
The Royal Air Force is one
The Flying Fortress is two,
The fighter planes are three,
The Mosquito is four
The heavy bombers are five.

From now say:
In Berlin they were struck with fifty blows,
And in Hamburg they were struck with two
    hundred and fifty blows.

How many great things
How many tanks are ready, God will save us.
If we drove them out of Egypt,
And Montgomery hadn't beaten them thoroughly,
    that would have been enough for us,
And he hadn't taken Tubruq from them,
And had not pursued them as far as Tunisia, *that*
    would have been enough for us.
If he had pursued them as far as Tunisia
And not moved after them to Sicily,
And had not destroyed their cities, *that would have*
    been enough for us.
If they had destroyed their cities

And not restored the Jews
To their work, *that would have been enough for us.*
If De Gaulle had restored the Jews to their work
And not rescued our fathers, *that would have been
enough for us.*
If he had rescued our fathers,
And De Gaulle had not rescinded the Statute of the
Jews, *that would have been enough for us.*
If De Gaulle had rescinded the Statute of the Jews
And not restored the Jews to their jobs, *that would
have been enough for us.*
If the Jews had returned to their jobs in
supplication,
And Roosevelt hadn't wanted to take us to Palestine,
that would have been enough for us.

How much
How much and how much more
Benefit doubled and trebled
And quadrupled and quintupled
Did God for us.
He drove them out of Egypt,
He beat them thoroughly,
He took Tubruq from them,
He pursued them to Tunisia,
And followed them to Sicily,
And destroyed their cities,
And restored the Jews to their jobs,
And rescinded the Statute of the Jews,
And the Jews returned to their jobs,
And they wanted to take all of us to Palestine,
To atone for all our sins.

Rabban Gamliel
Rabban Montgomery used to say:
Anyone who has not mentioned these three
Nations on Passover,
Has not performed his duty,
And these are they: Germany, Italy, and Japan.

Passover
Germany is the one we are battling against
For what reason?
Because in the days when the world was stable,
Our fathers were trapped there, as it is said:
"And you said he slaughters the Jews
And strips their skin,"
He and the Gestapo plot against us,
And the Allies came and struck Berlin
And they saved our houses
And the people bowed and prostrated themselves.

This matzah
This Italy against which we are battling,
For what reason?
Because Mussolini was bound up with Hitler,
And he said "beware lest they betray me."
And Montgomery moved against them.
And their dough did not have time to rise
Into macaroni.
And the Eighth Army appeared to them
And they fled immediately.
And they baked their dough and made it into
Spaghetti.
When they were driven out of Egypt and they
couldn't puncture the dough
And they made no fast for them.

Translated by Jeffrey M. Green.

Bruno Bettelheim

1903–1990

Bruno Bettelheim was born in Vienna to a secular Jewish family and received his doctorate from the University of Vienna in 1938. He was interned in Dachau and Buchenwald and arrived as a refugee in New York in 1939. Bettelheim was a professor of psychology at the University of Chicago from 1944 until 1973. He was widely known for his work on child psychology, especially his theories about emotionally disturbed children.

Individual and Mass Behavior in Extreme Situations
1943

[. . .] On a terribly cold winter night when a snow-storm was blowing, all prisoners were punished by being forced to stand at attention without overcoats—they never wore any—for hours.[1] This was after having worked for more than twelve hours in the open, and having received hardly any food. The prisoners were threatened with having to stand all through the night.

After about twenty prisoners had died from exposure, the discipline broke down. The threats of the guards became ineffective. To be exposed to the weather was a terrible torture; to see one's friends die without being able to help, and to stand a good chance of dying oneself, created a situation similar to the transportation, except that the prisoners had by now more experience with the SS. Open resistance was impossible, as impossible as it was to do anything definite to safeguard oneself. A feeling of utter indifference swept the prisoners. They did not care whether the SS shot them; they were indifferent to acts of torture committed by the guards. The SS no longer had any authority; the spell of fear and death was broken. It was again as if what was happening did not "really" happen to oneself. There was again a split between the "me" to whom it happened, and the "me" who really did not care and was just a vaguely interested, but essentially detached, observer. Unfortunate as the situation was, the prisoners felt free from fear and therefore were actually happier than at most other times during their camp experiences.

Whereas the extremeness of that situation probably produced the mental split mentioned above, a number of circumstances combined to create the feeling of happiness in the prisoners. Obviously it was easier to withstand unpleasant experiences when all found themselves in "the same boat." Moreover, since everybody was convinced that his chances to survive were slim, each felt more heroic and willing to help others than he would have felt in other situations, when helping others might endanger him. This helping and being helped raised the prisoners' spirits. Another factor was that not only were they free of the fear of the SS, but the SS had actually lost its power over them for the moment, since the guards seemed reluctant to shoot all the prisoners.[2]

After more than eighty prisoners had died, and several hundred had their extremities so badly frozen that they later had to be amputated, the prisoners were permitted to return to the barracks. They were completely exhausted, but did not experience the feeling of happiness which some of them had expected. They were relieved that the torture was over, but felt at the same time that they were no longer free from fear and no longer could rely on mutual help. Each prisoner as an individual was now comparatively safer, but he had lost the safety originating in being a member of a unified group. This event was again freely discussed, in a detached way, and again the discussion was restricted to facts; the prisoners' emotions and thoughts during this night were hardly ever mentioned. The event itself and its details were not forgotten, but no particular emotions were attached to them; nor did they appear in dreams. [. . .]

It seems that what happened in an extreme fashion to the prisoners who spent several years in a concentration camp happened in less exaggerated form to most inhabitants of that large-scale concentration camp called greater Germany. It could have happened to the inhabitants of occupied countries if they had not been able to form organized groups of resistance. The system was too strong for an individual to break its hold over his emotional life, particularly when he found himself within a group which had more or less accepted the Nazi system. It was easier to resist the pressure of the gestapo and the Nazis if one functioned as an individual; the gestapo seemed to know that, and therefore insisted on forcing all individuals into groups which it could supervise.

Some of the methods used to discourage individualism were the hostage system and the punishment of the whole group for whatever a member of it did; not permitting anybody to deviate in his behavior from the group norm, whatever this norm might be; discouraging solitary activities of any kind, etc.

The main goal of the Nazi efforts seemed to be to produce in their subjects childlike attitudes and childlike dependency on the will of the leaders. The most effective way to break this influence seemed to be the formation of democratic resistance groups of independent, mature, and self-reliant persons, in which every member backed up, in all other members, the ability to resist. If such groups were not formed, it was very difficult not to become subject to the slow process of personality disintegration produced by the unrelenting pressure of the gestapo and the Nazi system.

NOTES

1. The reason for this punishment was that two prisoners had tried to escape. On such occasions all prisoners were always punished severely, so that in the future they would give away secrets they had learned, because otherwise they would have to suffer. The idea was that every prisoner ought to feel responsible for any act committed by any other prisoner. This was in line with the SS's principle of forcing the prisoners to feel and act as a group, and not as individuals.

The two escapees were eventually captured and hanged while all prisoners had to stand at attention, watching the hanging.

2. This was one of the occasions in which the antisocial attitudes of certain middle-class prisoners mentioned earlier became apparent. Some of them did not participate in the spirit of mutual help, and some even tried to take advantage of others for their own benefit.

Other works by Bettelheim: *The Informed Heart: Autonomy in a Mass Age* (1960); *The Children of the Dream* (1969); *The Uses of Enchantment: The Meaning and Importance of Fairy Tales* (1976); *Freud and Man's Soul* (1983).

Umberto Cassuto

1883–1951

The historian and biblical scholar Umberto (Moshe David) Cassuto was educated at the University of Florence and the Collegio Rabbinico. He taught at both institutions and from 1914 to 1925 served as chief rabbi of Florence. In 1933, he was appointed to the chair in Hebrew and comparative Semitic languages at the University of Rome, where he taught until 1939. When the fascist racial laws forced him from his position, he continued his academic career at the Hebrew University of Jerusalem, where he focused on biblical exegesis and the question of the redaction of the Hebrew Bible. Toward the end of his career, he made important contributions to the field of Ugaritic studies.

The Israelite Epic

1943

The History of the Epic of the Revolt of the Sea and Its Fate through the Generations

40. When the tradition concerning the opposition of the sea and its confederates to the will of the Creator of the world was accepted among the Israelites, not only were all the idolatrous elements connected therewith in its original form among the gentile nations blurred, but new ideas were attached to it in consonance with the conscience and ethos of the Hebrew people. The Israelites saw in the ancient saga not only an allusion to a natural phenomenon [. . .] but also a symbol of *ethical* and *national* concepts.

41. The sea and the rivers, which revolted against the Lord, became for Israel a symbol of the *forces of wickedness*, who were opposed to the intention of the Lord— the ultimate source of absolute good—and a symbol of the workers of iniquity, the wicked men and wicked nations, who, contrary to the Divine will, do evil in the world. God's triumph over them came to symbolize the action of the attribute of justice, which inflicts retribution upon the wicked, and also the ultimate victory that was awaited in the end of days, when the Lord would remove the principle of evil from His world. This new interpretation that was initiated among the Israelites becomes clearly apparent when we consider the verses of the Canaanite poem on the war waged by Baal against the Prince of the Sea, "Lo, thine enemies, O Baal, lo, thou dost smite through thine enemies, behold thou dost annihilate thy foes," and compare them with

the phraseology of Psalms XCII 10 [9]: "for, lo, Thine enemies, O Lord, for, lo, Thine enemies shall perish; all evildoers shall be scattered." *The Lord's enemies* are identified here with *evildoers*.

42. Together with the *ethical* concepts concerning the punishment of the wicked and the triumph of good over evil, national ideas became linked to the ancient tradition. *The enemies of Israel* are equated with *the foes of the Lord*, and become representatives of the powers of wickedness and the principle of evil. Whenever a people or ruler rose up and oppressed Israel it was as though the ancient revolt of the waters of the sea and the rivers at the time of the creation of the world was re-enacted, and the defeat of the enemies and the salvation of Israel from their hand are regarded as a renewal of the primordial victory of God over those who rebelled against Him.

43. This [. . .] explains why the rebellion of the sea and its confederates is so frequently alluded to in the Scriptures. When the poets and prophets of Israel came to pray for the salvation of their people from the power of their enemies, they besought the Lord to renew His work of old (for example, Isaiah LI 9; Habakkuk III 2); and when they intended to encourage their brethren and to assure them that the Lord would destroy their foes, for there was no bound to His might, and He had it in His power to subdue all his enemies, even if their strength was amazingly mighty, they gave, as proof, what He had done to the mighty waters of the rebellious Deep (for instance, Psalms LXXXIX 10–11 [9–10]). So, too, when they wished to depict any Divine deed wrought in the past for the benefit of Israel and their salvation from their adversaries, like the parting of the Sea of Reeds and the cutting off of the waters of the Jordan, they made use of expressions and phrases and imagery taken from the store of the literary tradition pertaining to the acts of the Lord against the sea and the rivers during the six days of Creation (for example, Isaiah LI 10). Similarly, when they brought consolatory tidings concerning the ultimate extinction of the principle of evil in the future, they formulated their tidings in the form of metaphors alluding to the ancient tradition (for instance, Isaiah XXVI 1). [. . .]

45. However, to the essential *content* of the ancient myths there is not the slightest allusion in the Song of the Sea. [. . .] Although these legends had cast off, among the Israelites, their original mythological garb, and had assumed a form more in keeping with the national ethos, there nevertheless remained certain ele-

ments that were still redolent of an alien origin; hence the Torah's attitude towards them was not sympathetic. It was possible for the prophets and the poets, who are accustomed to make use of poetic similes and embellishments, to allude to those myths; but the Torah, whose every word was meticulously weighed and characterized by the greatest circumspection, deliberately refrained from mentioning them even incidentally. On the contrary, it manifests signs of opposition to the stories of the ancient poems. Not without reason is it noted in the account of Creation [Genesis I 21]: "*so God created the great sea monsters*." At the first blush, the sentence comes as a surprise. For throughout the entire section only the general categories of flora and fauna are mentioned, but not specific species; only in this verse is mention made of a particular genus. This is certainly not unintentional. Apparently, the Torah intended to voice a protest against the myths that were current among the Israelites: Far be it from you (the Torah implies) to suppose that, when the Holy One, blessed be He, created His world, the creatures did not fulfil the respective tasks assigned to them; or that any part of the world possessed an independent will and opposed the Creator's will. He commanded, "let the waters . . . be gathered together" and forthwith: "and it was so" [Genesis I 9]. The sea monsters, too, are only creatures like all other creatures, which were created in their due time and place, so that they may serve their Maker and do His bidding. [. . .]

46. This antagonism helps us to understand the eventual fate of epic poetry, and to explain why it perished among the Israelites. In the epoch enshrouded in the obscurity of the age following that of Ezra and Nehemia, in the period that separates, like a deep abyss, the ancient from the later culture of the people of Israel, which was wholly permeated by the spirit of the Torah, much of the writings of the previous era was undoubtedly lost. All books that did not conform to the spirit of the Torah could not cross this gulf; or, possibly, in time of war and destruction, such as marked the revolt against Artaxerxes III and the like, the people were not concerned to save these works as they were to rescue the Holy Scriptures; or, it may be that they purposely rejected them and forbade their circulation. In this way we may conjecture that the ancient epic poem on the rebellion of the sea perished.

47. It was, in truth, lost, but not entirely. The basic story it related which was widely known among the people, was not completely forgotten. The poetic version was no longer extant, but the knowledge of its content did not become extinct. This tradition continued to live in the people's memory, and was given renewed literary expression in the rabbinic teaching. The fears that aroused the antagonism of the Torah to legends of this nature, no longer existed in the days of the Talmudic Rabbis, since the danger of idolatry had then already passed. Hence the Sages did not refrain from incorporating the accepted folk tradition in their treasury of legend. Even some typical expressions of the ancient poem, having become literary conventions, succeeded in surviving and reappearing here and there in later books.

Translated by Israel Abrahams.

Other works by Cassuto: *Gli ebrei a Firenze nell'età del Rinascimenta* (1918); *The Documentary Hypothesis and the Composition of the Pentateuch* (1934); *The Goddess Anat* (1951).

Szymon Draenger

1916–1943

A resistance fighter in word and deed, Szymon (Szymek) Draenger was born in Kraków. He married Gusta Dawidsohn in 1940; she became his comrade-in-arms under the name Justyna. Arrested and incarcerated twice by the Germans, Draenger managed both times to escape. He was the editor, compositor, and distributor of *Hechalutz Halochem*, the last independent voice of the Jewish resistance in Poland. Written in Polish, it had two audiences: the surviving Jewish fighters living in hiding and the local Polish population. He was eventually caught and shot by the Germans outside of Kraków.

In Defense of the Natural Response
1943

When macabre reality gnaws at a person's soul, it is hard to devote oneself to psychological investigation, even of very pressing subjects. The event also seemed cut off from life, entirely academic, a theoretical discussion in abstract terms, after the ground was swept from under our feet, and one had to cling with a grimace to the last possibilities of life. But we are speaking here of determining certain concepts, which have ceased to be abstract and which have concrete influence on the formation of our reality, and it is hard to pass over them in silence. And who knows, perhaps the resolution of these concepts this very day will influence people's decisions, although belatedly, still correctly, and it will always increase our value as people, after it is properly understood.

From time immemorial, revulsion at the law of the fist and all physical violence has been rooted in the Jewish people. Even in very distant antiquity, when human history and culture were written in iron dipped in blood, the Jewish role in the arms race was relatively small, and they usually took arms only out of necessity, for defense. Often this phenomenon has been attributed to the alleged inborn cowardice of the Jews, but essentially it derived from faith in One God, which is ancient, and from the morality this faith entails, in which Judaism preceded the cultural world by many generations. Because from the dawn of existence the Jewish people had a connection with books ("the People of the Book"), they developed the ideal of a God who sees but is unseen. The nation clung to the abstract, and indeed this often became an absurdity, when it preferred the abstract to the concrete, even in cases when actually, in the name of the exalted ideal, it was wrong to act that way.

Someone once said that the Jews aren't capable of tormenting their fellow man, not because of the goodness imbued in them, but because of their natural softness, and it seems to me that this is correct. Over the generations, the overdevelopment of the intellect and lack of organic connection with the earth created inner softness, for which we have often paid dearly. Thus it deepened within us, so that even today, in a situation that leaves one just a single way out, it opens another door for select individuals, whom the highest morality supposedly protects. But if we were ordinary flesh and blood, with our own land, true independence, and strong resistance—and not an eternal minority that makes do with the leftovers of privileges, which are tossed to us here and there—we would understand that morality in fact demands of a person the full defense of his rights and a strenuous resistance to anyone who tries to strike at them. No morality commands the honoring of a murderer's immunity, or that of an invader, a deceiver, or any other violator of human rights. Those who control the social mechanism of the regime are capable of influencing people educationally, so that crime will not take root in them. But in a place that gives birth to degeneration like a hydra with a thousand heads and threatens with moral or physical destruction, there is

no place for a pedagogical approach nor for waiting until the energy of evil gives way on its own; rather, it must be beheaded with a single stroke. This is not praise of the law of the fist but rather defense of the principle that moral goodness does not command us to disarm, as long as evil is fighting with weapons. We must know how to speak to every person in his own language, to know to whom words should be directed and also who cannot be persuaded with words. Perhaps this may sound like a paradox, but in our opinion natural morality is closer to the person who responds, when he is attacked by antisemitic hooligans, by knocking them to the ground with blows of the fist, than to a person who goes home bruised and bleeding and writes a beautiful essay on mutual respect among people. We must rein in the evil that has taken root, as history teaches us at every step of the way. The direct impulsive response of a person who knows his value is superior to all consideration that leads to the denial of revenge as a despicable emotion. Thus, is it better to look at advancing wickedness and not raise one's hand against it? Is this what those thoughtful people will tell us?

However, to understand the preference for the natural over the purely intellectual response, a strong and inflexible moral backbone is needed, and it is necessary to bear the feeling of justice in your blood, which you are prepared to defend at any price. A person must be able to sacrifice the smaller justification for the sake of a greater one, a secondary matter for the main one, and to feel, almost instinctively, what is of primary importance and what is of secondary importance. I refer to a person's simple, uncomplicated self-defense against hatred, which is ready for any extremism, as we see every day, and which is fertilized by absolute lack of defense.

However, the wanderings of exile for generation upon generation have increased the inner softness in us, always preventing us from responding strongly to the events of the hour. The sanctity of the human being, and also the sanctity of his life, does not permit us to take up arms and spill human blood. Though we have paid for this worldview with millions of sacrifices, though we have learned painfully that only with fire and sword is it possible to uproot the evil that floods the world, we still want to wait; perhaps it is possible to uproot it without spilling blood. We do not know how to kill, that's all. Fear does not prevent people from taking arms. People who hesitate to take up active warfare have proven their true courage countless times, but when asked to strike at an enemy, they retreat. More than once it has happened that a determined young man, bearing weapons, has laid down his arms at the last minute because of the feeling of mercy. In the enemy facing him he still sees a man who has a wife somewhere, a mother or a child, and he is sorry to kill him . . . it is easier for him to think about the despair of strangers than to grit his teeth and take revenge for the blood of his mother, his sister, and his brother. Usually at this moment the enemy shoots, for such feelings and reflections are alien to him. The sensitive, noble man falls dead, and the victorious enemy marches forward, to continue sowing pain and destruction.

This is the softness of the ghetto, and this is where the diasporic mentality leads, lacking steady nerves and unhesitating determination. Herein lies the main reason why millions of people perished without storming the enemy. At a certain moment they no longer had any illusions about their fate, but of all the possible reactions they were able to seize, the one closest to them was the spirit of superiority, which felt contempt, or apathy devoid of any emotion, and in any event not active counterattack. Simply, that element was removed from their exilic mentality, the commandment to storm the enemy. Perhaps, in their tranquil and despairing gaze into the eyes of death there was a greater degree of courage than in any struggle with the enemy. But it is difficult to express admiration for their stoic stance because this was not the time for it. Moreover, in the face of the events it appears to be a pathological phenomenon and not a true expression of maturity.

We, the pioneering youth, have taken up arms, knowing full well that we could not avert the destruction hanging over the heads of the Jews of Poland. But aside from the inner need for revenge, we were motivated by a burning desire to arouse a natural, healthy response in the Jew, like the natural response of any free man. We saw that in this area a void was revealed in the inner life of the Jew, and we wanted to fill it so that our personal example would arouse others to resist.

True, the task is difficult. Generations of exile and the latest shackles of the ghettos have done their work. Our leap fulfilled its task within its limits, but to uproot the softness from the Jewish soul and to teach him how to fight for the rights and moral level of humanity will take many years.

Translated by Jeffrey M. Green.

Lion Feuchtwanger
1884–1958

The German novelist Lion Feuchtwanger was widely read, both in Germany and—in translation—outside Germany, but his literary reputation plummeted after the middle of the twentieth century. A theater critic and playwright before World War I, his novel *Jud Süss* (1925), about the eighteenth-century South German court Jew Joseph Süss Oppenheimer, brought him international recognition. He took refuge in southern France in 1933 and, after the German invasion, escaped to the United States, where he lived in Los Angeles and was a central figure in the German exile community there.

The Working Problems of the Writer in Exile
1943

II

I will not dwell too long on the bitter theme of the many purely external difficulties with which the writer in exile must contend. I hope that those who have not experienced these difficulties will be spared them. [. . .]

The sufferings of banishment have only rare heroic moments; they generally consist of little, silly annoyances that often have a tinge of the ludicrous. But at best it costs much time and money to overcome these little external difficulties. In various countries, for example, I was expected to produce papers which I, as a refugee, could not possibly have. I was expected to prove by means of documents from my home that I am I, that I had been born, that I am an author. It is no exaggeration to state that the efforts to produce such evidence cost me as much time as the writing of a novel. [. . .]

IV

Gradually, willy-nilly, we ourselves change in the new environment, and with us changes all that we create. The only road to the inner vision is through the outer. The new land in which we live affects the theme of our subjects and also affects the form. The landscape which surrounds the writer changes the landscape within him.

[. . .] But everything that I might say on the subject of the writer in exile has been much better expressed in my novel *Paris Gazette*. This novel, incidentally, in its original form is by no means entitled *Paris Gazette*.

This title is a concession to foreign readers. In the original the title is simply, truthfully, and boldly—or if you prefer—imprudently, *Exile*.

Incorporated in this novel *Exile* is a chapter which deals with the effects of banishment, written during one of the gloomiest interludes of my exile, a pause between internment in two different French concentration camps. Today I am glad that, even in those sad days, I placed the emphasis not upon the sufferings of the exiled artist but upon the fact that the true writer, the one deserving of this name, grows in strength in exile.

For although banishment is destructive and makes the victim small and miserable, it also hardens him and adds to his stature. A vast abundance of new material and new ideas pours in upon him, he is confronted with a variety of impressions he would never have known at home.

If we make an effort to take a historical view of our life in exile, it becomes evident even now that almost everything that seemed to hamper our work finally contributed to its welfare. In this connection I must not conceal the fact that, for example, even the constant, enforced contact with a foreign language, which I loudly deplored a few paragraphs earlier, finally results in an enrichment. The author who lives in a foreign speech environment almost automatically and constantly checks his own against the foreign word. He frequently finds that the foreign language has a more striking word for that which he wishes to express. He is therefore not satisfied with that which his own tongue has to offer, but sharpens, files and polishes the existent expression until it has become something new, until he has wrested the new, the more striking word from his own language. Everyone of us has adapted fortunate turns of phrase from the foreign language to his own.

V

It can be said that suffering makes the weak weaker, but the strong stronger. Banishment has constricted some of us, but to the stronger, the more able, it gave breadth and elasticity, it opened their eyes more fully to the great and essential things, and taught them not to cling to nonessentials.

> And till thine this deep behest
> Die to win thy being!
> Art thou but a sullen guest
> Upon earth unseeing.

says Goethe. Banishment is a hard school that sternly teaches the meaning of the behest: Die to win thy being. A number of exiled writers have become inwardly more mature, have been renewed and rejuvenated. They have not only become more bitter, but also more wise and more just toward their new old world, grateful and more conscious of their own mission. "Die to win thy being" has become their experience and their possession.

Other works by Feuchtwanger: *Success* (1930); *The Oppermanns* (1933); *Josephus*, 3 vols. (1935–1942); *Raquel, the Jewess of Toledo* (1956); *Jephtha and His Daughter* (1958).

Noah Golinkin, Jerome Lipnick, and M. Bertram Sachs

Golinkin, 1914–2003

Raised in Vilna, Noah Golinkin immigrated in 1938 to the United States, where he enrolled in the Jewish Theological Seminary (JTS). Golinkin, along with Moshe "Buddy" Sachs and Jerome Lipnick, devoted himself to activism on behalf of Jews in Europe. The three students started a committee at JTS, partnering with Christian organizations and lobbying American Jewish leadership and Congress to aid European Jews. During his rabbinical career, Golinkin led a number of congregations, eventually settling in the area of Washington, D.C. He was active in the civil rights movement and in the campaign to help Soviet Jewry.

Lipnick, 1918–1977

Jerome Lipnick was born in Baltimore and attended Johns Hopkins University, later receiving his ordination as a rabbi at JTS in 1945. While studying at JTS, Lipnick worked tirelessly to draw attention to the plight of Jews in Europe, advocating taking action to rescue them. Following the war, Lipnick remained a passionate activist, working for civil rights and for the Soviet Jewry cause. As a rabbi, he led a variety of synagogues and served as director of education for B'nai B'rith in Washington, D.C.

Sachs, 1920–2009

Known as "Buddy," Moshe Bertram Sachs was born in Baltimore. In 1941, he enrolled at JTS, rooming with Max Gruenewald, a refugee from Mannheim. Determined to rescue Jews from Europe, Sachs, together with Jerome Lipnick and Noah Golinkin, established a committee at JTS devoted to the cause. From 1945 to 1947 he served as an army chaplain in Manila and Okinawa and then traveled to Jerusalem to study with Martin Buber. There, Sachs and his wife enlisted as intelligence agents with the Haganah. During the siege of Jerusalem, Sachs led a Seder for American servicemen. After returning to the United States, Sachs served at a congregation in Minneapolis for nearly two decades before moving to Israel.

Retribution Is Not Enough
1943

We Jews who live in the staid serenity of America have failed to grasp the immensity of the tragedy which has befallen our people and this failure is perhaps the greatest part of the tragedy. Were the entire populations of Boston, Cincinnati, Baltimore, Philadelphia, Chicago, San Francisco, Cleveland, St. Louis, Los Angeles, and Detroit slain, it would be little over half the number of those who have already been annihilated in Europe. What have the rabbis and leaders of these cities, or of New York, done to arouse themselves and their communities to the demands of the hour? What have the rabbinical bodies representing the Orthodox, Conservative, and Reform groups attempted in order to impress upon their congregations the necessity for action now? What have they, or any other responsible organizations within American Jewish life, undertaken to awaken the conscience of the American people?

The United Nations, we are told, have promised retribution for these killings; but this retribution will be meted out after the war. We do not want retribution for Jews who have already died. We prefer help for those Jews who yet live. These protests are meaningless and ineffectual. Have any of the United Nations offered refuge to Hitler's victims? Have they taken any steps beyond protest to indicate that they are really concerned in stopping the bloodshed? In failing to act speedily, they have become partners in these horrible crimes.

As Jews and as American citizens it is our sacred duty to call upon the United Nations, and in particular upon our own country, to come to the aid of European Jewry *now*; and never for a moment must we relax our efforts until that help comes!

"The Nation" and "The New Republic" have been the only publications which have outlined plans for positive and immediate action to ameliorate the position of European Jewry. It seems almost incredible, but the Anglo-Jewish press has done little beyond documenting the tales of horror. Most of us, it appears, have already given up European Jewry in our hearts; others have acquiesced in their helplessness; and those who have not, have chosen the solutions which offer the least difficulties—and the least results. But in order to save five million human beings who have been doomed to die we must take bold and ambitious measures. Here are some of the things we should do:

1. Rescue Jews from Spain and Portugal and other countries threatened with Nazi invasion. Denmark and Bulgaria have expressed a willingness to permit Jews to leave their borders if proper arrangements can be made. These refugees might be brought to Allied countries in order to relieve the war labor shortage which is growing steadily worse.

2. Put pressure on the United Nations to obtain refuge for Jews in the neutral countries of Sweden, Turkey, and Switzerland. Urge that the United States allow Jews to settle in the Virgin Islands since they do not come under the immigration quota. If the United States will not change its immigration laws, then efforts should be made to establish internment camps here for those refugees until the war ends. Jews who are in concentration camps in North Africa must be released and the anti-Jewish laws there must be abrogated.

3. Put pressure on the United Nations to open up Palestine for large-scale immigration. So that refugees in haven countries would not become permanent additions to their populations, guarantees should be made that they will go to Palestine after the war.

4. Request that the United Nations reconsider their blockade of Europe in order to permit the feeding of starving Jewish populations. Perhaps a program similar to the one now successfully operating in Greece could be carried out.

5. Put pressure on the United Nations to recognize a Jewish army to be composed of Palestinian and stateless Jews. The right should be given to refugees who are not subject to American draft laws to form separate commando units under the leadership of the United States army.

6. Put pressure on the United Nations to fully publicize the atrocities against the Jews to the German people and to the peoples of Europe by leaflets and short-wave broadcasts. So far, little has been done to arouse local populations in opposition to these mass murders.

To achieve such far-reaching goals we need mass action on a nation-wide scale, mass action that involves bucking the people and the American government. But bucking injustice is our religious duty!

We should therefore like to suggest that the religious leaders of America initiate the program of positive action along the lines we present here. Since the synagogue is the one institution in American Jewish life which can reach the greatest number of Jews, the synagogue should take the lead in this all-out effort to ameliorate the condition of European Jewry. Action should not be limited to synagogues, however. All Jewish organizations of whatever character should participate in this program designed a) to make Jews and non-Jews aware of the policy of extermination; b) to move them and the duly constituted bodies which represent them, both as Americans and as Jews, to present uniform demands to the United Nations to save as many lives as possible now. [. . .]

A uniform prayer, such as an extra Kaddish, should be recited by the entire congregation in all synagogue services until the end of the war. In this way we would mourn those Jews who have no one left to mourn for them, and we would always remind ourselves of our obligations to those Jews in Europe who still live.

The lives of five million Jews hang in the balance. It is up to us to do everything possible to save them *now*. Each day's delay means thousands of lives lost. When the final tabulation of those murdered has been published will American Jewry be able to say: "*Yadenu lo shafku et hadam hazeh*" (Our hands have not shed the blood")?

Other works by Golinkin: *Shalom Aleichem: Learn to Read the Hebrew Prayerbook!* (1978); *While Standing on One Foot: Learn to Read Hebrew in a Single Day!* (1986). Other work by Lipnick: *From Where I Stand* (1978). Other works by Sachs: *Under Siege and After: Life in Jerusalem, 1947-1949* (2006); *Brave Jews* (2007).

Adolph Gottlieb and Mark Rothko

Gottlieb, 1903-1974

The avant-garde painter Adolph Gottlieb was born into a Jewish family in New York City. As an art-obsessed teenager, Gottlieb fled to Paris; he learned painting, in part, though daily visits to the Louvre and by haunting museums and galleries all over Europe. In the 1930s, as his career flourished, Gottlieb was horrified by the rise of fascism; as a symbol of his defiance, he changed the spelling of his first name: Adolf became Adolph. Later that decade, Gottlieb demanded that the American Artists' Congress repudiate Hitler and Stalin. When it did not, he resigned.

Rothko, 1903-1970

The American painter Mark Rothko was born in Dvinsk, Russia, in the Pale of Settlement. Before becoming one of America's best-known abstract expressionists, he attended Yale University. Rothko grew up speaking Russian, Yiddish, and Hebrew; he was Markus Rotkovich when he attended Jewish school, learning Talmud. When his Orthodox family moved to Portland, Oregon, in 1913, the young Rothko was still engaged in Jewish communal life. As his artistic career flourished, Rothko drifted from Judaism, although some art critics still discern strong Jewish elements in his work.

Letter to the Art Editor of the New York Times
1943

June 7, 1943

Mr. Edward Alden Jewell
Art Editor
New York Times
229 West 43 Street
New York, N.Y.
Dear Mr. Jewell:

To the artist, the workings of the critical mind is one of life's mysteries. That is why, we suppose, the artist's complaint that he is misunderstood, especially by the critic, has become a noisy commonplace. It is, therefore, an event when the worm turns and the critic of the *Times* quietly yet publicly confesses his "befuddlement," that he is "non-plussed" before our pictures at the Federation Show. We salute this honest, we might say cordial reaction towards our "obscure" paintings, for in other critical quarters we seem to have created a bedlam of hysteria. And we appreciate the gracious opportunity that is being offered us to present our views.

We do not intend to defend our pictures. They make their own defense. We consider them clear statements. Your failure to dismiss or disparage them is prima facie evidence that they carry some communicative power.

We refuse to defend them not because we cannot. It is an easy matter to explain to the befuddled that "The Rape of Persephone" is a poetic expression of the essence of the myth; the presentation of the concept of seed and its earth with all its brutal implications; the impact of elemental truth. Would you have us present this abstract concept with all its complicated feelings by means of a boy and girl lightly tripping?

It is just as easy to explain "The Syrian Bull," as a new interpretation of an archaic image, involving unprecedented distortions. Since art is timeless, the significant rendition of a symbol, no matter how archaic, has as full validity today as the archaic symbol had then. Or is the one 3,000 years old truer?

But these easy program notes can help only the simple-minded. No possible set of notes can explain our paintings. Their explanation must come out of a consummated experience between picture and onlooker. The appreciation of art is a true marriage of minds. And in art, as in marriage, lack of consummation is ground for annulment.

The point at issue, it seems to us, is not an "explanation" of the paintings but whether the intrinsic ideas carried within the frames of these pictures have significance. We feel that our pictures demonstrate our aesthetic beliefs, some of which we, therefore, list: 1. To us art is an adventure into an unknown world, which can be explored only by those willing to take the risks. 2. This world of the imagination is fancy-free and violently opposed to common sense. 3. It is our functions as artists to make the spectator see the world our way—not his way. 4. We favor the simple expression of the complex thought. We are for the large shape because it has the impact of the unequivocal. We wish to reassert the picture plane. We are for flat forms because they destroy illusion and reveal truth. 5. It is a widely accepted notion among painters that it does not matter what one paints as long as it is well painted. This is the essence of academicism. There is no such thing as good painting about nothing. We assert that the subject is crucial and only that subject matter is valid which is tragic and timeless. That is why we profess spiritual kinship with primitive and archaic art.

Consequently if our work embodies these beliefs, it must insult anyone who is spiritually attuned to interior decoration; pictures for the home; pictures for over the mantle; pictures of the American scene; social pictures; purity in art; prize-winning potboilers; the National Academy, the Whitney Academy, the Corn Belt Academy; buckeyes, trite tripe; etc.

Sincerely yours,
Adolph Gottlieb
Marcus Rothko
130 State Street
Brooklyn, New York

Fülöp Grünwald

1887–1964

Born in Sopron, Hungary, historian Fülöp Grünwald was a teacher in the Jewish community of Pest and served as deputy director of the Hungarian Jewish Museum in Budapest. During World War II, Grünwald deposited Jewish liturgical objects and books into a bank in the city; these items were ultimately looted. After the war, Grünwald served as head of the history department of the rabbinical seminary in Budapest.

The Report of the Directorate of the Hungarian National Jewish Museum
1943

Any public Jewish institution that is inextricably tied to the greater Jewish community can only express its deep sorrow as it looks back over the past year. Hundreds of thousands of our brethren, the Jewry of entire countries, have been destroyed in Europe during the past cruel year of war. We read in Josephus Flavius' writings that at the siege of Jerusalem, one million Jews died. In the past year alone, a much greater number of us—unarmed men, powerless women, innocent and helpless children as well as the elderly—fell victim to the ferocious racial struggle.

As a Museum Society, which sees its goal as collecting and preserving the historical and artistic artifacts of Jewish life, we not only mourn the destruction of our brethren, but also the destruction of ancient Jewish monuments, artifacts and works of art. In devastated family homes, burnt down synagogues, ravaged cemeteries, many old relics and devotional objects were destroyed forever. From Bordeaux [in the west] to Kharkov [in the east], all over in our continent, the same scene can be observed: Jewish communities condemned to deportation in West and Central Europe, liquidated and empty ghettos in the East. We look in vain for the ancient, eleventh-century, Romanesque-style, humble, two-aisled synagogue in Worms besides the Rhine, which had been surrounded by a wreath of Jewish legends and folktales. The splendid domed synagogues of the cities of Central Europe disappeared as completely as the castle-like, somber synagogues of the large Polish *kehillot* and as the remarkable wooden synagogues of the small market towns. Now we really understand why we have so few Jewish artifacts from bygone centuries. We would scarcely know our devotional articles from before the 16th century were it not that medieval miniatures had retained their pictures for us. [. . .]

As we find ourselves once again in the throes of wartime dangers, we need to be deeply concerned about our irreplaceable treasures. Acting from our sense of responsibility, the leadership of the museum had to save the most valuable pieces of our collection from any possible harm. In this, we merely followed the example of the large Hungarian collections. We have to acknowledge with gratitude the courtesy of the chief administration of the Hungarian National Museum with which, upon our request, it received readily for storage and safekeeping our most precious treasures. Packed professionally, we carried them to the basement of the National Museum. At the same time, we deposited our valuable documents, manuscripts, rare prints, books and valuable *megillas* in a bank safe. [. . .]

In conclusion, let us say a few things about our plans. [. . .] The Jewish Museum can grow in two possible directions. As a historical collection, we have to collect the still existing and salvageable artifacts of the old, rural Jewish communities that had developed from the 17th century onward. On the other hand, we have to further develop the ethnographical nature of our collection. We aim at showing the life of a Jew as it used to be from cradle to grave within the centuries-old traditional framework for the sake of the present generation that does not see this sort of life and does not know it. This, to be sure, is not a new initiative. Professor Kolbach insisted upon such a collection already at the establishment of the museum in 1909.

We are planning for the future, while the very foundations of our existence have become unstable. Mass defection and treacherous betrayals are disrupting the unity of Hungarian Jewry. State laws, decrees, [and] anti-Jewish social movements aim at severing the political, cultural, and economic ties with the Hungarian nation. To all intents and purposes, they try to prepare the final solution to the Jewish question in Hungary, which—as they have repeatedly stated—cannot be anything else than the complete resettlement of the Jews. Against this endeavor, our museum wants to serve two purposes: to strengthen us internally, i.e., to propagate the knowledge and veneration of Jewish religious as well as national life. In addition, by [preserving] historical artifacts of the Hungarian Jewish past, we prove our right to this homeland. We only follow the example of our ancestors in this, who unwaveringly fought for their acquired rights also in the most dangerous of times. Let us just read the documents, the descriptions, how the Jewry expelled from Sopron conducted its 12-year-long desperate struggle with the city in the year of Mohacs [1526], or how the Jews of Buda resisted for decades in the first half of the 18th century, when the city's riff-raff foreign settlers wanted to drive them out. They refer to the fact that the glorious Hungarian kings have granted them an entire Jewish street and a synagogue. Their old houses and 500–600-year-old gravestones are the remains of those. We confess that as the High Kingdom of Hungary could not do without the Jewry at the peak period of the rule of King Louis the Great [1326–1382], or during the sorrowful times following the Mohacs Catastrophe [of 1526], the isolation and exclusion of the Jewry from the life of Hungary does not serve the interests of the country in the present critical era either. We believe against all contradictory statements that there still will be centuries of Hungarian Jewish history. The work of our museum aims at serving that future.

Translated by Rita Horváth.

Other works by Grünwald: *A magyar zsidó múlt historikusai* (1934); *A buda-varhegyi zsido kozseg haromszoros pusztulasa* (1937); *A zsidok tortenete Budan: Vázlat* (1938); *Magyar-Zsidó Oklevéltár* (Monumenta Hungariae Judaica, vols. 5–7, with Sandor Scheiber, 1959–1963).

Judah L. Magnes
1877–1948

The rabbi and community leader Judah Magnes was born in San Francisco and received ordination from Hebrew Union College in 1900. He served as the rabbi of Temple Israel in Brooklyn and later of Temple Emanu-El in Manhattan. Magnes helped to organize the American Jewish Committee (1906) and was president of the Kehillah of New York City from 1908 until 1922; in that capacity, he tried to reconcile differences between the German Jewish and the East European Jewish immigrant communities in America. In 1922, Magnes moved to Mandatory Palestine. There, he was a founder of the Hebrew University of Jerusalem and served as its first chancellor, from 1925 to 1935, and then as its president, from 1935 to 1948. Magnes also actively promoted Arab–Jewish relations and supported the founding of a binational state.

Toward Peace in Palestine
1943

II

The purpose of this article is to warn of the danger of war between Jews and Arabs, and to offer an alternative based upon a reasonable compromise. The uncompromising who believe that this collision is inevitable are supposedly making their preparations. Those who believe in the necessity and the possibility of compromise should also be preparing. Nothing is more dangerous and enervating than the advice to postpone all thinking and planning until the end of the war. The war will not end and the peace will not come unless in every field the utmost exertions are made to think things through and to work things out now. [. . .]

Palestine as a Jewish state: Palestine as an Arab state. The two conceptions leave little room for compromise. But a search for one should be begun. The first step—and the sooner it is taken the better—should be an announcement that the adjustment will not include either of these alternatives. Such an announcement might help dissipate the increasingly bellicose atmosphere and might, perhaps, turn both Jewish and Arab propaganda in the direction of peace and understanding. The ordinary Jew and the ordinary Arab have no hatred for one another. They will rejoice over the prospect of a reasonable settlement which might enable them to live together and to develop their common country in peace. [. . .]

III

[. . .] The proposals which I bring forward are based on the great idea of union. Union must be the guiding political ideal of the United Nations if they are to achieve victory. The unbridled greed of those who have

ruled the world hitherto, and the narrow chauvinism of so many nations, can be overcome only if a really free and really united world is created. The Palestine situation must be raised to the high plane where the gigantic struggle to build a mighty union of free nations is going on. Union for Palestine may be said to have three aspects:

1. Union between the Jews and the Arabs within a bi-national Palestine.

2. Union of Palestine, Transjordan, Syria and the Lebanon in an economic and political federation. These lands form a geographic unit and constituted a political and economic union at several times between ancient Semitic days and the First World War.

3. Union of this federation with an Anglo-American union which is assumed to be part of that greater union of the free nations now laboring to be born out of the ruins of the decaying world. [. . .]

IV

[. . .] We begin again with a negative aspect of the proposed adjustment in order to reach a positive conclusion. No Jews can agree to a fiat which would arbitrarily stop immigration into Palestine, the Land of Israel. [. . .] The Arabs will not agree to unrestricted Jewish immigration. It would build up a Jewish majority and might mean Jewish dominance in Palestine. We must recognize that this is a genuine impasse and that a way out must be found.

The establishment of a federation would help resolve the problem. If and when the federation came into being, the whole question of numbers in Palestine would lose its present primary significance for the Arabs. For a federation of the four states in question, whatever its form, would include an Arab population of several million. The Arabs would be relieved of their present fear of being swamped and dominated by a majority of Jews. A Jewish majority in the federation is hardly conceivable. [. . .]

VI

The Jews are able to help as no other people can or will to build up the proposed federation as an integral part of a union of the free peoples. Their help can be scientific, financial, social, industrial and agricultural. But even before the start of the delicate and complicated process of establishing a political federation there can be an economic union of Palestine, Transjordan, Syria and Lebanon, and these countries can join with their neighbors in economic agreements. [. . .]

Another factor in the suggested compromise is Jerusalem, Holy City of three religions, which might become the federal headquarters or capital. Geography and history alike fit it for this great destiny. Should it once again become a center of spiritual and intellectual exchange, it will restore contact between Judaism, Christianity and Islam. So far these three faiths have failed in their efforts to create a society based upon ideals of righteousness and mercy. Yet despite the afflictions visited upon Israel in the Christian West, we may not despair of the West. And Israel, which once achieved great things for mankind in the Middle East, can acquire renewed youth and deeper wisdom if it is re-invigorated and rooted once more in the ancestral soil. The new Jerusalem, then, would symbolize a new relationship between Judaism, Christianity and Islam in the cradle of their origin. [. . .]

VII

Israel is an imperfect instrument through which universal religious and moral principles have been communicated to mankind. These principles call for the creation of a visible, tangible society founded upon justice and mercy. The utterances of the Prophets of Israel contain as powerful revolutionary ferment as mankind has ever known. Until Israel and the nations of mankind succeed in establishing a universal society based upon those ideals there will continue to be a Jewish problem. That is Israel's destiny.

Other works by Magnes: *War-Time Addresses, 1917–1921* (1923); *Addresses by the Chancellor of the Hebrew University* (1936); *The Perplexity of the Times* (1946).

Yonatan Ratosh

1908–1981

The Israeli poet Yonatan Ratosh was born Uriel Shelach in Warsaw. His Hebrew-speaking Zionist family immigrated to Palestine in 1921. He attended the Hebrew University and then the Sorbonne; he published his first poem in 1926. In the mid-1930s, Ratosh edited the Revisionist movement's newspaper and was active in right-wing underground organizations. In 1939, he founded the Canaanite movement, which rejected both religion and Jewish nationalism

and promoted the theory of a shared cultural heritage for the entire Middle East. In 1950, Ratosh founded and coedited the influential literary journal *Alef*, which included the works of Stendhal, Camus, Shaw, and O'Neill.

An Epistle to Hebrew Youth
1943

The Committee for the Consolidation of Hebrew Youth appeals to you only in order that you understand the very essence of what is in common between you and the rest of Hebrew youth, which operates in different organizational frameworks, voluntarily, consciously by choice, and by force of circumstances also—in frameworks in which they believe that they have found the best possibility for serving the Hebrew homeland, one in which they have chosen to sacrifice their strength, in which they have found the most personal satisfaction so that they will be ready when the time comes to sacrifice even their lives.

And the *Committee for the Consolidation of Hebrew Youth* appeals to you to be aware of the great gap and fundamental alienation which separates you, Hebrew youth from all these sons of the Jewish Exile, all these who clung steadfastly to their opinion in the Diaspora in all of its manifestations and with all of its roots and transformations; by the force of nature its stamp indelibly permeates the roots of their souls and minds; to be aware of this very abyss of Jewish nature through any rhetorical camouflage, through any diaphanous veil of party, organization, or sect, however extreme they may be, however realistic they may be, or however idealistic they may be . . .

The *Committee for the Consolidation of Hebrew Youth* turns to you because you are a Hebrew, because the homeland is for you a real, actual, existing homeland—neither a dream nor something yearned for, nor something legendary; nor a solution to the Jewish question; neither a solution to world issues, nor a solution for various emotional complexes of the Diaspora neurotics. For you the Hebrew language is your real, actual, practical language, a mother tongue, and a language of culture and a language of the soul, the sole language for feeling and thought. [We turn to you] because the reality in which your character was formed, in which you maintained your views, is the Hebrew reality; because the landscape of your soul is the landscape of the homeland, and your past is the past of the homeland only.

Because the best efforts of alienated parents and teachers and leaders and intellectuals were not successful in making you care for or in bringing you close to the background of the Jewish *shtetl* [ghetto] and the history of the Jewish Diaspora with its pogroms, and banishments and banishments and martyrs; they could not uproot from your heart your natural estrangement from all the Diaspora-bound heralds of Zionism and from all the masters of Jewish literature in the Hebrew language and from the entire milieu of the Jewish Diaspora and from all of the problematics of the Jewish Diaspora. For all of these were forced upon you by virtue of all the authorities weighing upon your shoulders as a wornout, patched, tight, borrowed garment. [. . .]

The *Committee for the Consolidation of Hebrew Youth* fears for you, lest during your cultural ascent, while learning to seek answers to your questions, you will not gather enough strength to maintain in all of its purity your feeling for the homeland, you may become entangled like your elder brethren in the labyrinth of the Wisdom of the Jewish Diaspora; the *Committee for the Consolidation of Hebrew Youth* is afraid, lest you yourself, Hebrew youth, continue to strengthen the bonds of the Jewish Diaspora which are choking you, lest you unwittingly betray the Hebrew homeland and the young Hebrew nation which is awakening and taking shape in the land of the Hebrews, lest you turn against it to hand it over to the world Jewish Diaspora, the cradle of slaves and servants from time immemorial, and it will no longer be a Hebrew homeland which comes into being here and not a Hebrew nation which will spread out in it, but only an appendage of the Jewish Diaspora, another ephemeral center in Jewish eternity, a corrupt, hypocritical Holy Land for an everlasting Diaspora . . .

If you will only remove the Jewish cobwebs from your eyes, you will see the vision of the great Hebrew future beyond any achievement of the Jewish soul, past all Jewish borders, and beyond any of the Jewish possibilities.

And if you will remove this whole mask, you will reach spiritual perfection, with the simple, natural correspondence between mental thought and emotional life. There will awaken within you all of the hidden powers under the stranglehold of the Jewish Diaspora and Jewish science and Zionism. And we present you this path towards natural completeness of the Hebrew soul, the bridge to the Hebrew past and the highway to the Hebrew future; we open the gate to the Hebrew

world and call those who pave the way to rebirth, to freedom, to sovereignty.

You are asked to do all this by yourself and you must attain all of this yourself. No one from all the people of the Diaspora can act as your guide. No Zionist white knight will run before you.

Translated by Fern Seckbach.

Other works by Ratosh: *Ḥupah sheḥorah* (1941); *Yoḥemed* (1942); *Tsela'* (1959); *Shirey ḥeshbon* (1963); *Shirey mamash* (1965); *Shirey ḥerev* (1969); *Yalkut shirim* (1974–1975); *Ahavat nashim* (1975); *Shirey ne'arah* (1975); *Shirey prat* (1975); *Shirey ahavah* (1983).

Emanuel Ringelblum
1900–1944

Born in the Galician town of Buczacz, Emanuel Ringelblum was involved in Labor Zionist and Yiddishist politics from an early age. He received his doctorate in history from Warsaw University in 1926, published studies on the history of Polish Jewry, and became a leading member of YIVO's history section. In the 1930s, he took an active role in the relief work of the Joint Distribution Committee, which stressed the importance of self-help as an antidote to despair and economic antisemitism. Applying his prewar credo to the Warsaw ghetto, Ringelblum established the secret Oyneg Shabes archive in November 1940 while simultaneously heading the Aleynhilf (Self-Help). Ringelblum, his wife, and son were shot by the Germans in March 1944. Two caches of the buried archive were discovered in September 1946 and December 1950, and a third cache has never been found.

Oyneg Shabes Archive
1943

Everyone appreciated the importance of the work that was being done. They understood how important it was for future generations that a record remain of the tragedy of Polish Jewry. Some realized that the collection of writings would also serve to inform the world about the atrocities perpetrated against the Jewish population. There were several part-time coworkers who became so involved in the project that they stayed on full time.

Of the several dozen full-time staff, the great majority were self-educated intellectuals, mostly from proletarian parties. We deliberately refrained from drawing professional journalists into our work, because we did not want it to be sensationalized. Our aim was that the sequence of events in each town, the experiences of each Jew—and during the current war each Jew is a world unto himself—should be conveyed as simply and faithfully as possible. Every redundant word, every literary gilding or ornamentation grated upon our ears and provoked our anger. Jewish life in wartime is so full of tragedy that it is unnecessary to embellish it with one superfluous line. Second, there was the matter of keeping a secret; and as is well known, one of the chief failings of journalists is that they reveal secrets. A few able journalists might have been enlisted as time went on, had they not sought contact with the Gestapo informer [Abraham] Gancwajch,[1] and although this relationship was not of a "professional" nature, it nonetheless made it impossible for us to associate with the journalists in any way.

Those who helped us with a single piece of work were ordinary people, who had lived the whole of their daily lives in their hometowns. Upon arrival in Warsaw with the horde of 150,000 refugees, they continued to lead their [fellow] townspeople in the so-called *landsmanshaftn*[2] organized by the refugee center of the Jewish Self-Help. After a day of hard work at the Committee, distributing bread or performing other kinds of assistance, these delegates of the *landsmanshaftn* spent the evening writing—according to our plan—the history of their town; or they related it to our coworkers, who later wrote it up. This was very arduous work. In the terrible overcrowding of the ghetto, the refugees lived in [housing] conditions that simply cannot be described. To preserve secrecy under such conditions was a difficult task. It was cold in the winter nights: last winter most of the Jewish houses did not have electricity. Writing necessarily has attendant risks and indescribable difficulties, and to obtain the chronicle of a town required long weeks and months of exertion. It demanded much effort to encourage my coworkers not to be distracted by all these obstacles and to do their work. Let me complete the picture by adding that at the beginning there was a fear of being discovered by the Gestapo informers. More than one manuscript destined for O[yneg] S[habes] was destroyed as the result of a search in a tenement.

As we have mentioned, our coworkers were mostly [just] ordinary people. Among them were talented individuals whom we spurred on to literary creativity. Had these people not died of hunger or disease, or in the Deportation, we would have been enriched with their new writing talent. And new literary energy would have been infused into a field that was so neglected among us [eastern European Jews]—the writing of memoirs. Because most of our coworkers were suffering great hunger in Warsaw, that city of pitiless Jews. O[yneg] S[habes] had to provide for them. We lobbied the social institutions to supply them with food parcels.

O[yneg] S[habes] strove to give a comprehensive picture of Jewish life in wartime—a photographic view of what the masses of the Jewish people had experienced, thought and suffered. We did our best to arrange for specific events—in the history of a Jewish community, for example—to be described by an adult and by a youngster, by a pious Jew—who was naturally concerned with the rabbi, the synagogue, the Jewish cemetery and other religious institutions—and by a secular Jew, whose narrative emphasized other, no less important factors. [...]

Comprehensiveness was the chief principle of our work. *Objectivity* was the second. We aspired to present the whole truth, however painful it might be. Our depictions are faithful, not retouched.

The atrocities of the Germans against the Jewish population predominate in our work. However, quite a lot of material reveals humanity on the part of Germans. There are constant indications, both in the completed essays and in the oral reports, that we must be objective even in the case of our deadly enemies and give an objective picture of the relationship of Germans and Jews.

The same can be said of Polish–Jewish relations. Opinions prevail among us that anti-Semitism grew significantly during the war, that the majority of Poles were glad of the misfortunes that befell the Jews in the Polish towns and cities. The attentive reader of our material will find hundreds of documents that prove the opposite. He will read, in more than one report on a town, how generously the Polish population behaved toward the Jewish refugees. He will encounter hundreds of examples of peasants who, for months on end, concealed and fed Jewish refugees from the surrounding towns.

In order to ensure the greatest possible objectivity and to obtain the most exact, comprehensive view of the events of the war as they affected the Jews, we tried to have the same events described by as many people as possible. By comparing the different accounts, the historian will not find it difficult to reach the kernel of historical truth, the actual course of an event.

Our coworkers wrote the truth; and they had an additional reason for doing so. We assured everyone that the material, insofar as it concerned living people, would not be exploited for immediate use. Therefore, everyone should write as if the war were already over. He should fear neither the German nor those *kehillah*[3] members who were attacked in a report on a given city. Because of this, the material of O[*yneg*] S[*habes*] is of great importance for the future tribunal, which, after the war, will bring to Justice offenders among the Jews, the Poles and even the Germans.

The war changed Jewish life in the Polish cities very quickly. No day was like the preceding. Images succeeded one another with cinematic speed. For the Jews of Warsaw, now closed in within the narrow confines of a shop, the ghetto period seems like a paradise and the pre-ghetto period an unreal dream. Every month brought profound changes that radically altered Jewish life. It was therefore important to capture at once every event in Jewish life in its pristine freshness. What a quantum leap from the pre-Deportation shop to that which came after. The same is true of smuggling, and of social and cultural life; even the clothes Jews wore were different in the different periods. O[*yneg*] S[*habes*] therefore tried to grasp an event at the moment it happened, since each day was like decades in an earlier time. We succeeded in doing this with many of the events. What greatly aided us in this task was that some of our own coworkers kept diaries in which they not only recorded the facts and happenings of day-to-day life but also evaluated noteworthy events in the ghetto.

NOTES

[Words in brackets appear in the original translation.—Eds.]

1. Gancwajch headed the Office to Combat Usury and Profiteering in the ghetto, which was subject directly to the Germans. He vied with the Judenrat for control of the ghetto and fell from power in July 1941.

2. An organization of Jews hailing from the same town or region.

3. Ringelblum uses this as a synonym for the Judenrat.

Translated by Elinor Robinson.

Other works by Ringelblum: *Notes from the Warsaw Ghetto* (1952); *Kapitlen geshikhte fun amolikn yidishn lebn in Poyln* (1953); *Ksovim fun geto* (1961).

Fishel Schneersohn

1888–1958

Fishel Schneersohn, a psychologist and author born in Kamenetz-Podolski, present-day Ukraine, was a member of the famed Schneersohn rabbinic family. As a teenager, he was ordained as a rabbi, after which he studied at the gymnasium in Gomel, now Belarus. He received his academic training in Berlin and St. Petersburg, and apprenticed under a leading Russian psychiatrist. Schneersohn crisscrossed the globe before finally settling in Tel Aviv. In all these places, he established mental health practices serving especially, though not exclusively, children, and he wrote various psychological and religiously oriented works.

The Spiritual Upheaval in Israel in the Wake of the Holocaust
1943

When we consider the quotidian life of our society, it is impossible to ignore the phenomenon of "avoidance"; namely, it seems that the public at large is unwilling to think too much about the Holocaust. At times one may even get the wrong impression of utter indifference. Indeed, from time to time the authorities announce a national mourning rally and the response of the public is strong and heartfelt. And yet, between one rally and the next, one is hard pressed to find signs of mourning and sorrow in our public life. Life goes on as usual, the cafés and other places of attraction are teeming with people, and so on. Therefore, the general impression one gets is one of indifference. However, we must firmly challenge this mistaken impression that is the result of a superficial and cursory look. First of all, what we have here is the "thunderstruck" effect that stems from the astonishing power of calamities that so exceed mere human suffering, the human mind cannot absorb them; calamities that a person, against his will, must suppress until such time when the "thunderstruck" effect is diminished. In addition, as we will see, two mental illusions are also at work here, and they, too, are directly responsible for such suppression. *In fact, what we have here is not some kind of indifference, but some kind of paralysis.* This is to say that the "thunderstruck" effect, together with the two mental illusions directly connected with it, suppress and numb the public's awareness of the Holocaust and thereby greatly and dangerously undermine necessary action in the rescue effort. During the lengthy periods between one mourning rally and the next, one does not hear the inner voice of the nation mourning its brethren in a spontaneous, heart-rending lament. The public, in fact, is not actively and directly involved in the rescue mission. In every large

Jewish community, a small committee of statesmen is selected and they, preoccupied with their day-to-day duties, "also" devote time to the rescue effort. Not in our country, and not in America, do we find statesmen who devote themselves *solely* to the rescue mission, very much like, for instance, a division commander who devotes himself entirely to the battle at hand. In short, the Jewish public, to a great extent, is stunned and paralyzed in the face of the Holocaust, and however great the desire to participate in the rescue, it finds itself incapable of rising to the challenge. Very much like a man who has been gravely wounded in battle and suffers a mental breakdown—the term for which, in surgery, is shock. This impedes his healing, until the doctor, with the help of restorative drugs, manages to bring the patient out of shock. And so it is with the statesmen today, whose duty it is to bring themselves and the public out of the dangerous paralysis with the help of the "restorative means" of artists and intellectuals who probe the depths and open up paths to creativity in the nation as a whole. Such cooperation between statesmen and writers—already in place during wartime in other cultured nations—must be adopted here, and this cooperation is what may jolt us out of paralysis and toward urgent and bold participation in the rescue effort.

Translated by Tsipi Keller.

Other works by Schneersohn: *Ha-derekh el ha-adam* (1922); *Khayim Gravitser* (1922).

Zalman Shazar

1889–1974

Zalman Shazar (Shneur Zalman Rubashov), the third president of the State of Israel, was born in Mir, Belorussia, to a prominent Hasidic rabbinical family. He became active in the Po'ale Tsiyon movement and immigrated to Palestine in 1924. Shazar was a member of the executive committee of the Histadrut and was active in the World Zionist Organization. In 1944, he was appointed editor of the newspaper *Davar*. Elected to the first Knesset in 1949, Shazar served as minister of education. He was elected president of Israel in 1963 and 1968. Throughout his life, Shazar wrote poetry, autobiographical fiction, scholarly treatises on philology and on biblical criticism, and articles in Yiddish and Hebrew. In 1966, he received the Bialik Prize for literature.

The Heritage of 5703
1943

5703—Because of its horrors, all the preceding years of Hitler will pale in people's memory, even 5677 [1917] and 5665 [1905], and even 5408 [1648] and 5252 [1492]. In none of these peak years of the victories of the wickedness of our persecutors was this program of mass physical destruction carried out as it was carried out now. And it is still being carried out. In no year, even of the blackest years in the history of our torments, has the nation lost, all at once, a quarter of its sons and daughters, as it has in this year. No one yet can even count our casualties nor can any tongue describe their suffering. The enemy called for the ingathering of exiles in its one fashion—for murder, for strangling, for abuse. It came from Amsterdam and Brussels, from Copenhagen and Sophia to Salonika, and from all the corners of Europe. It collected the Jewish diaspora into the mother of diasporas, which became the valley of Jehoshaphat for its sons and brothers, from near and far, the remotest place in the depths of the land. In the extermination camps of Treblinka and Bełżec all the divisions between the ethnic groups and languages and opinions and cultures were ended, and they all became a single Jewish nation on the scaffold.

In all the countries where Hitler had the upper hand in that year, the vast majority of the Jews were doomed to extinction. [. . .] Hebrew existence is being erased from Europe. [. . .]

And we are the survivors of Israel—the remnant of its centers and the crumbs of its remnants, a brand plucked out of the fire [Zechariah 3:2] and seeds of the future—upon whom it is incumbent not only to live through the holocaust of this year, but also to overcome it, and from it to spin forward the thread of our history toward a different and new tomorrow. It is incumbent upon us to distinguish very well whether, in the very darkness that enveloped us this year, there are yet some faint signs of hope, which we can grasp with a soul thirsty for rebirth.

If the entire matter of our liberation were to emerge on its own from the liberation of the world, and every harbinger of redemption for humankind and for democracy were also a harbinger of the future and the arising of our entire nation—then this year, with all its horrors, would be a strong support for the hopes of our people. For this was the first year in which the armies of the enemy were driven out of large territories in its conquered lands in Soviet Russia and in our Orient and in North

Africa. And this was the year in which the legend that no power could withstand the Nazi land armies, which had been embroidered for four or more years, proved to be totally fictional, a legend that wrought destruction upon the souls of the conquered people. This was the year when the Red Army did wonders before everyone's eyes. This was the year when the United States threw all its human, scientific, industrial, and political wealth upon the scales of rescue for Europe. This year the alliance between America and England was strengthened. This was the year when the alliance between Italy and Germany was broken. This year the father of all evil and enslavement fell in Rome. This year the first signs of the rainbow were seen in the clouds, heralding a new heaven over the miserable earth.

However, the victory of the Allied nations is *merely a condition for the dawn of our lives*, without which darkness will crush us. Therefore we give it all our resources and energy. However, it in itself is not a guarantee. Even after it the path to our redemption can still be long, if, meanwhile, new strengths do not emerge and new concepts are not formed within us and around us. And the heart that fears for our future must ask whether something of the heritage of 5703 is inherent in the increase of these forces and in these changes?

Outside us we would seek for these manifestations in vain. This year, indeed, our catastrophe shocked the hearts of many prominent people. The scream that burst forth from the heart of the Hebrew Yishuv enveloped our nation and the good people of other nations. [. . .] However, all the sighs and oaths and promises and invitations did not save those taken to their death. The resourcefulness of the mighty nations was powerless to benefit our [Hebrew] nation in the last year; the mighty spirits were silenced. The major press is too busy to be concerned with murder within the walls of the ghetto. Literature and poetry, in all the languages of the Allies—is immersed head and shoulders in the tempests of the day and accompanies the acts of heroism and the groans of torture of every nation and language in these years of horror—has not turned to, or has hardly turned to, the perishing of the eldest of nations. The mightiest of democratic nations on the European continent has not found it possible to change even the dot over an "i" in its White Paper, which proudly locks the land of hope for its tortured sons, who strive to reach it, as the shore of salvation. [. . .]

In the formal relations between Israel and the nations, we would therefore seek signs of consolation in

vain. One by one we plucked the flames from darkness and the bonfire was not lit. This year it was incumbent upon us regarding the mercy of the best of nations to conclude what our ancestors concluded in the past about their wisdom: it has neither fruit nor flowers.

However, while the holocaust did not mature in the consciousness of the nations into any daring act of rescue, it did not transpire without consequences. [. . .] Now many people, those who are soon to determine the fate of the future, have seen where *failure to solve* the Jewish question leads. Now, even those faithful to the vision of assimilation among the statesmen of the world will not fall so easily for the illusions they once espoused and advocated at the time of the Western Emancipation or in the days of national and civil rights in Eastern Europe. All the proposals that are constantly repeated by those who are openly and tacitly opposed to Zion, about the territorial concentration of the Jewish refugees in a country other than the Land of Israel, prove that those who make such proposals understand full well that the question of the remnant of the Jews of Europe can no longer be solved within the borders of Europe. Even the few remnants who survived and will survive the persecutor's sword—they, too, will need, even after the persecutor's sword is broken—sooner or later, in an organized or fragmented way—to take up the wanderer's staff. Even after victory there will be no escaping the demand to emigrate. Even politicians who were never suspected of a tendency to Zionism have come this year to hold the opinion that, after the world emerges from the bonfires of battle and sets about finding a new arrangement for our people, the tempest of Europe will not be silent, and the wounds of the Jews will not be bound unless they open a land of refuge for them, for large and concentrated emigration, which will be a true homeland for them.

In the consciousness of those who decree the fate of nations this year, a willingness to reevaluate the ability and chances of Zionism has matured. [The pressing need is] to examine it with respect to the *capacity* of the land to absorb within it the surviving Jews from alien lands, and with respect to the capacity *of the nation* to launch a systematic and constant struggle for the realization of its vision without fear of opposition from within and without; to not be broken beneath the burden of its holocaust and to discover within it, even in these times, spiritual powers and the strength to build, upon which their future will rest.

And if the observer considers the fabric of our life this year from these two perspectives, he will learn a great deal. He will find that this *land* did not disappoint this year. [. . .] All that the Jewish immigrants invested in it in the past two generations has fertilized its soil over time. [. . .] This year the land became a small factory for the military industry, which had not been anticipated. This year it completely overcame difficulties in transportation, and if artificial hindrances are not imposed, it can support its inhabitants from its gardens and fields and vineyards and factories without needing ships from abroad. [. . .] In all the countries in the world there is not a single land in which there is a Jewish kernel to absorb its brothers, so resilient, so rooted, so well-organized, and so self-protecting as the Land of Israel. Among all the countries proposed for Jewish immigration, there is not one that has prepared itself for that, for generations, like this land. [. . .]

This year the victim became a warrior. What Hitler and his troops of destruction did in the Warsaw ghetto and the hells of Treblinka will remain an eternal blot upon him and his nation. It is not our shame that we were burned and strangled and buried alive, by abominable people, who have power and dominion. Indeed the tortured people of Warsaw arose and returned fire against the acts of their persecutors who outnumbered them and had a hundred times more power, and they paid with their lives for their rebellion, while at the same time, the *shekhinah* [divine presence] rose from the ashes. And when the Jews who were condemned to death set fire to the hell of Treblinka, somewhere the star of the people's rise was lit. [. . .]

There is no consolation in all this. And there can be no consolation for the year 5703. How can we be consoled while our dead still lie before us, for we will not even know their names? And those who remain—their fate is still suspended over their heads like a sword. The holocaust is still untouched. However, we are commanded to continue to live. To live in order to restore to life. Therefore, never will any scrap of creativity and vitality be as dear to us as they were this year, which raises within us the force of life and brings us closer to the hope of rebirth.

Translated by Jeffrey M. Green.

Other works by Shazar: *Kokhvey boker* (1950); *Or ishim* (1963).

Joseph B. Soloveitchik

1903–1993

Talmudic scholar and Jewish philosopher Joseph Ber (Yosef Dov) Soloveitchik was born in Pruzhan, Poland, a descendant of a Lithuanian rabbinic dynasty. He received both a traditional and a secular education, earning a doctorate (having written his dissertation on the philosopher Hermann Cohen) in 1931 from the University of Berlin. Upon immigrating to the United States in 1932, Soloveitchik became chief rabbi of the Orthodox community of Boston; he also was a founder of that city's Maimonides School. In 1941, Soloveitchik succeeded his father as head of the Rabbi Isaac Elchanan Theological Seminary of Yeshiva University (RIETS rabbinical school) in New York. Known widely as "The Rav," Soloveitchik is regarded as one of the leading figures of Modern Orthodox Judaism.

Halakhic Man

1943

[. . .] The duality in the attitudes of cognitive man and *homo religiosus* is rooted in existence itself. Cognitive man concerns himself with a simple and "candid" reality. He does not seek to closet himself with the hidden in existence but rather focuses his attention on its revealed aspect. This is not the case with *homo religiosus*. He clings to a reality which, as it were, has removed itself from the cognizing subject and has barred the intellect from all access to it. He is totally devoted and given over to a cosmos that is filled with divine secrets and eternal mysteries. The very nature of the law itself, the very phenomenon of cognition is an open book for cognitive man and a closed one for *homo religiosus*.

When God appears to Job out of the whirlwind, He asks him: "Where wast thou when I laid the foundations of the earth? Declare, if thou hast the understanding. Who determined the measures thereof, if thou knowest? Or who stretched the line upon it? Whereupon were the foundations thereof fastened? Or who laid the cornerstone thereof? . . . Have the gates of death been revealed unto thee, etc.? Hast thou entered the treasuries of the snow, etc.? Dost thou know the time when the wild goats of the rock bring forth, etc.? Doth the hawk soar by thy wisdom, etc.?" (Job 38, 39). The consciousness of *homo religiosus* is overflowing with questions that will never be resolved. He scans reality and is overcome with wonder, fixes his attention on the world and is astonished. Moreover, the astonishment that overwhelms *homo religiosus* does not serve simply as a prod to stimulate metaphysical curiosity, is not just a device to excite the cognitive imagination—i.e., is not just a means to an end, as Aristotle thought, but is the ultimate goal and crowning glory of the process of cognition of *homo religiosus*.

And Job, who had raged against heaven because he had sought to render an accounting of the world and erred, accepts upon himself the divine judgment. "Who is it that hideth counsel without knowledge? Therefore have I uttered that which I understood not, things too wonderful for me, which I knew not" (Job 42:3). He sinned with his proud and overly bold venture to grasp and comprehend the secret of the cosmos; he confesses and returns to God with the discovery of the mystery in the created world and of his inability to understand that mystery. "Wherefore I abhor my words, and repent, seeing I am dust and ashes" (Job 42:6). The ultimate goal of religious man is the question, Dost thou know? The path which leads him to his aim is the complete cognition of being. A strange polarity of disclosure and hiding, revealing and concealing, breaks forth and seizes hold of the consciousness of the man of God. He discloses in order to hide, reveals in order *to conceal*. [. . .]

Knowledge and wonder, cognition and mystery, understanding and secrecy, the law and the unknown, these constitute a unified phenomenon which reveals itself to us in a twofold fashion, all in accordance with one's perspective and point of view. However, knowledge does not forfeit its objective status and intrinsic significance as a result of the *teiku*, the unresolvable problem that peers out of its windows. On the contrary, the riddle adorns and embellishes cognition, bestowing upon it the splendor of eternity.

In this respect the teaching of our great master, Maimonides (of blessed memory), is typical. On the one hand, Maimonides ruled that the knowledge of God is the first among the 613 commandments. "The foundation of foundations and the pillar of all sciences is to know that there is a prime being . . . and this knowledge is a positive commandment." On the other hand, he maintained the doctrine of negative attributes, which denies all possibility of knowing God. On the one hand, Maimonides designated the knowledge of the Creator as the guiding criteria for man, as his ultimate end. On the other hand, Maimonides held the view that knowledge of God is not in the realm of human cognition. Are there two greater opposites then these?

Nevertheless! Maimonides himself struggled with this antinomy and devoted two chapters of the *Guide of the Perplexed* (1:59–60) to it. The substance of his answer is that negative cognition does not forfeit its status as cognition. However, we know that the entire phenomenon of negative cognition is only possible against a backdrop of affirmative cognition. For we negate with respect to the Creator all of the attributes that we have affirmed with respect to created beings.

Therefore, in order to arrive at the negation, we must engage in an act of affirmation. The act of negation is reconstructed out of the very substance of affirmation. And what constitutes affirmative cognition if not the cognition of the cosmos—the attributes of action? Moses prayed that these attributes be communicated to him, and his petition was granted. Indeed, we are all commanded to occupy ourselves with the understanding in depth of these attributes, for they bring us to the love and fear of God, as Maimonides explains in the *Laws of the Foundations of the Torah* (II, 2). First we cognize in positive categories God's great and exalted world, and afterward we negate the attributes of created beings from the Creator. This solution accords well with the ontological approach of the man of God: cognition for the sake of grasping the eternal riddle, revealing for the sake of concealing, comprehending for the sake of laying bare the incomprehensible in all its glorious mystery and terror. The negative theology constitutes the great ideal of *homo religiosus*; it is the "telos" of his noetic process (which will never and can never be entirely realized) and the "end point" of his knowledge—the cognition of the riddle without end (negative cognition) through affirmative cognition. It is for the purpose of the unending realization of this idea that *homo religiosus* has been commanded to engage profoundly in rendering an account of the world, to occupy himself with the "natural science" and the "divine science," and this cognition is entirely affirmative and not negative. To be sure, negation is always distantly visible as the goal and final aim of knowledge; however, the process of cognition itself from its "beginning" until its "end" takes on shape in a whirl of colors against an affirmative backdrop. Negation is only the actualization of the cognitive process and the realization of the act of affirmative cognition in its fullness. The old familiar proverb of negative theology—"the goal of knowledge is to know not"—refers, as is clear from the proverb itself, only to the goal and the aim but not to the process of cognition. The knowledge of God which leads to love and fear, concerning which we were commanded in the *Laws of the Foundations of the Torah*, is the cognition of the attributes of action—the cosmos—and this cognition is entirely affirmative.

Translated by Lawrence Kaplan.

Other works by Soloveitchik: *The Lonely Man of Faith* (1965); *The Halakhic Mind* (1976); *Out of the Whirlwind* (2003); *Community, Covenant, and Commitment* (2005); *And from There Shall You Seek* (2008).

Issachar Shlomo Teichtal
1885–1945

Talmudic scholar Issachar Shlomo Teichtal was born in Nagyhalász, Hungary, and received rabbinic ordination in 1906. In 1921, he became head of the Moriah Yeshiva in Piestany, Slovakia; there he trained clergy to counter the teachings of liberal Judaism. He published a volume of responsa in 1924. Initially anti-Zionist, Teichtal changed his thinking radically during World War II while hiding from the Nazis in Budapest. His Holocaust-era work, *A Joyful Mother of Children*, encouraged Jews to return to the Land of Israel in response to the destruction of European Jewry. Teichtal was deported to Auschwitz in 1944.

A Joyful Mother of Children
1943

I entitled this volume *Em Habanim Semeḥah* [Psalms 113:9], based on the Jerusalem tractate of *Berakhot* (toward the close of the second chapter) which portrays *Erets Yisrael* as the mother of Israel and the lands of exile as the stepmother [J.T. *Berakhot* 2:8]. Our sages describe our mother of Zion who weeps and laments when we are in exile. She awaits our return to her bosom. "In my own flesh I behold God" [Job 19:26], when in the year 5702 before Passover a terrible decree was issued in Slovakia by the cursed villains. Young Jewish women from the age of sixteen were forcibly transported to a distant place and to an unknown destination. To this very day we do not know what occurred to the thousands of innocent Jewish souls who were deported. May God avenge them on our behalf.

The Jewish community was in a state of great panic. I knew a person who sought to rescue his young daughters from this evil trap. He tried to cross the border with them. This happened during the interme-diate days of Passover. He promised to send his wife a telegraphed confirmation that he had arrived safely together with his daughters at the predesignated point. The mother waited at home with great anticipation for the good news. As it happened they seized the father together with his daughters before they crossed the border. They were arrested and interned in a prison near the border. The rest of the Passover festival was spent in jail. They were now in great danger of being immediately deported to an unknown destination of doom. This was the anticipated penalty for violating the laws of illegal departure. Those caught for this offense were given a harsher sentence than the other prisoners.

We can imagine the bitter disappointment of the mother when she realized what had actually transpired. The initial joy turned into grief. The holiday [of Passover] was transformed into an occasion of mourning for her husband and daughters. . . . She understood the fate which awaited them. We must now recall with praise the dedicated and valiant efforts . . . of the *Gaon* [genius], *tsadik* [holy, righteous man], and *ḥasid*, our master R. Shmuel David Ungar, may he be blessed with a long and good life, the senior *Dayan* [judge] of the holy community of Nitra. He did not rest or relent until he had ransomed the three captives with a considerable sum. They were set free and returned safety to their home. One can well imagine the reaction of the unfortunate woman when she was informed by telephone that her husband and daughters were free, safe from the clutches of the enemy. From that moment on she waited with yearning for their return. The following day she could no longer be contained. She sat near the entrance of the courtyard with great anticipation waiting for the moment of their return.

Immediately upon seeing them she burst into tears and poured out all the emotions of her heart. Her excitement was so intense that she was unable even to express words of thanks to the Holy One, blessed be He, for the great miracle which transpired for her and for her family. . . . Those who did not witness this reunion, the tears, the emotions of happiness of a joyous mother [reunited] with her children, never were privileged to have witnessed genuine joy. . . .

I imagine that such would be the experience of joy of our Mother *Erets Yisrael* at the time when we shall return to her after a terrible captivity such as in our present time. I have, therefore, called my volume *Em Habanim Semeḥah* [*A Happy Mother of Children*]. May the Lord grant me the privilege of utilizing my book for the purpose of returning the children to their Land [see Jeremiah 31:10] and thereby fulfilling speedily in our day the hope of a joyous mother of children [Psalms 113:9]. May we ascend to Zion in gladness [see Isaiah 35:10] speedily in our day. Amen.

The second preface is now completed in the fifth millennium of the weekly portion: "I have also heard the cries of the children of Israel" [Exodus 6:5] on the new month of *Shevat* . . . the year [5]703 in the city of Budapest. [. . .]

Thus far in this chapter I have expounded upon the subject of rebuilding and settlement of the Land by carefully explaining this mitzvah. I have surveyed the subject in all its aspects. I have confirmed with convincing and compelling evidence that the obligation of the mitzvah is incumbent upon everyone at all times. No individual may absolve himself from this [obligation]. We have an even greater commitment in our present times to emerge and awake from our slumber and idleness. For anyone who has eyes can see, and who has ears may hear that now is the appropriate time for an awakening. One will have heard and seen what has occurred to us during these difficult days and the calamities of the past four years against us which have come to pass, which historians will describe as "The Calamities of 1940–43," similar to the Crusader calamities known as the "Calamities of 1096." Speech cannot describe them. The pen is unable to depict them in writing. Everything occurs in accordance with the Supreme will, because of our many sins. [. . .]

Indeed, at this moment, even as I write these very lines, an atmosphere of fear and terror hovers over us as we witness all of the Admorim in our countries making efforts in the face of enemy danger to flee to Eretz Yisrael. They seem not to consider the demoralizing effect this has upon the Jews when the word spreads: "The *rebbes* are fleeing! What will become of us?" Note *Midrash Ruth* explaining the reason for Elimelekh's punishment, because he demoralized the Israelites when he fled in time of disaster. Our vehement hope is in the Lord, that He may rescue us [from disaster] also in the future. Yet we are all aware that we have more than once been exposed to danger to our lives, and God miraculously spared us. Hence, we must follow the example of Abraham our Patriarch, namely, to distance ourselves from here and to proceed to Eretz Yisrael, since it is a matter of life and death and one may not rely on miracles. . . .

NOTE
[Words in brackets appear in the original translation.—Eds.]
Translated by Pesach Schindler.

Other works by Teichtal: *Mishneh sakhir* (1924; all printed copies destroyed but published posthumously beginning in 1973); *Emunah tserufah be-khur ha-sho'ah: pirke zikhronot*, 2 vols. (1995, 2000).

Joshua Trachtenberg

1904–1959

Joshua Trachtenberg was born in London and received a doctorate from Columbia University. He was ordained as a Reform rabbi in 1936 and served in congregational positions in Pennsylvania and New Jersey. Trachtenberg wrote about the role of folk magic in Jewish culture and explored the roots of modern pagan practices. In addition, his work discusses spiritual differences between Israelis and Americans.

The Devil and the Jews: The Medieval Conception of the Jew and Its Relation to Modern Antisemitism
1943

The mass mind is eminently retentive. Man, in Nietzsche's definition, is the being *with the longest memory*, and José Ortega y Gasset has recently affirmed (in his *Toward a Philosophy of History*) the objective existence of the accumulated past, as a positive element in creative action. But we cannot neglect the reality of the accumulated past as a *negative* influence—a pathological barrier to creative action. Man's inability to forget is the obverse of his faculty of memory. We may please to consider ourselves "moderns," but under our skeptical rationalism and scientific objectivity the conceptions of our forefathers are still potent motivating forces. If we have succeeded in banishing ancient notions from our conscious minds (and it need hardly be pointed out that a vast portion of the Western world has not yet exorcised the spirits and ghosts that preyed upon their ancestors) they have merely receded into the murky depths of the subconscious. Rationalize as it may, the Jew whom the world fears and hates is a heritage from the past—and the not-so-distant past at that. All our wrestling with the rationalizations is pointless effort until we uncover the hidden emotional roots from which illogic and untruth acquire the color of truth and meaning.

It is no sheer accident that Germany has become the motherland of modern antisemitism. The program of National Socialism has simply brought to the surface and intensified the latent hankering of the German people for its romanticized past. Otto D. Tolischus, the distinguished foreign correspondent who has observed Germany at close range throughout its crisis years, offers in his book, *They Wanted War*, a pat characterization of this spiritual regression: the German people, he remarks, "is dominated by Richard Wagner—not the Richard Wagner of the incomparable though still debated melodies, but the Richard Wagner who brought back to life the dismal, pitiless and forgotten world of German antiquity, the world of fighting gods and fighting heroes, of dragons and demons, of destiny and pagan epics, which presents itself to other peoples as mere Wagnerian opera, but which has become subconscious reality to the German masses and has been elevated to the inspirational mythos of the National Socialist movement that rules the Third Reich." We need not quarrel about how far back we must trace Germany's psychic atavism; it is the sober fact that seems unimpeachable. If the Nazi program has sometimes been loosely described as "medieval," in the matter of its Jewish policy it assuredly harks back to the psychology of the Middle Ages.

Modern so-called "scientific" antisemitism is not an invention of Hitler's. But it was born in Germany during the last century, and it has flourished primarily in Central and Eastern Europe, where medieval ideas and conditions have persisted until this day, and where the medieval conception of the Jew which underlies the prevailing emotional antipathy toward him was and still is most deeply rooted. ("Medieval" defines not a chronological but a mental epoch.) Hitler's contribution stemmed from his intuitive awareness of the elemental universality of this conception: call it inspiration or shrewdness, he sprayed the world with the antisemitic virus, knowing that it would everywhere fall upon hospitable ground, breeding the spiritual and social corruption that would open to him the path of conquest.

"The proficiency of the Jews in magic and their kinship with Satan would reveal, if we had the stomach to pursue the subject, the ultimate spring of medieval Jew-hatred," remarks Marvin Lowenthal in his study of *The Jews of Germany*. This is the conception, based upon the crassest superstition and credulity, that has permeated to the lower depths of Western culture, and which

we must "have the stomach to pursue" and expose to the light of day if we are to comprehend the ultimate spring not only of medieval Jew hatred but of its modern, occasionally more sophisticated, version. Here, in this region of the mass subconscious we shall uncover the source of many a weird notion—of the horned Jew, of the Jewish thirst for Christian blood, of the Jew who scatters poison and disease broadcast, of the secret parliament of world Jewry, meeting periodically to scheme and plot, of a distinctive Jewish odor, of Jews practicing black magic and blighting their surroundings with the evil eye—notions that still prevail among the people and that have been advanced by official Nazi publications, for all the "scientific" verbiage of current antisemitism. But, more important, here we shall uncover the spring of the general conviction that prompts Jew hatred: of the Jew as an alien, evil, antisocial, and antihuman creature, essentially subhuman, indeed, and therefore answerable for the supreme crime of seeking to destroy by every subversive technique the fruits of that Christian civilization which in his heart of hearts he despises and abhors.

Anti-Jewish prejudice is older and more extensive than Christendom. It would be absurd to attribute its every manifestation to doctrinaire Christian hatred of the "Christ killers." But its unique demonological character is of medieval origin, with premonitions in earlier times of the turn it was destined to take; the "demonic Jew" was born of a combination of cultural and historical factors peculiar to Christian Europe in the later Middle Ages.

Other works by Trachtenberg: *Jewish Magic and Superstition: A Study in Folk Religion* (1939); *Consider the Years: The Story of the Jewish Community of Easton, 1752–1942* (1944).

American Jewish Committee
Established 1906

The American Jewish Committee (AJC) is a global Jewish advocacy organization, founded in New York on November 11, 1906. Initially concerned with Jews suffering pogroms in the Russian Empire, the AJC had as its primary goal to "prevent infringement of the civil and religious rights of Jews and to alleviate the consequences of persecution." Since then, the organization has fought general discrimination and worked on behalf of social equality, playing a major role in the civil rights movement in the 1950s and 1960s. It has also supported the publication of numerous books and book series on Jewish and interfaith issues.

Declaration of Human Rights
1944

With the inevitable end of Hitler, the struggle begins, not of tank and plane, but of heart and soul and brain to forge a world in which humanity may live in peace. This new world must be based on the recognition that the individual human being is the cornerstone of our culture and our civilization. All that we cherish must rest on the dignity and inviolability, of the person, of his sacred right to live and to develop under God, in whose image he was created.

With this creed as our foundation, we declare:

1. That an international Bill of Human Rights must be promulgated to guarantee for every man, woman and child, of every race and creed and in every country, the fundamental rights of life, liberty and the pursuit of happiness.

2. No plea of sovereignty shall ever again be allowed to permit any nation to deprive those within its borders of these fundamental rights on the claim that these matters are of internal concern.

3. Hitlerism has demonstrated that bigotry and persecution by a barbarous nation throws upon the peace-loving nations the burden of relief and redress. Therefore it is a matter of international concern to stamp out infractions of basic human rights.

4. To those who have suffered under the Hitler regime because of race or creed or national origin, there shall be given fair redress.

5. To those who have been driven from the land of their birth there shall be given the opportunity to return, unaffected in their rights by the Nazi despotism.

6. To those who wander the earth unable or unwilling to return to scenes of unforgettable horror shall be given aid and comfort to find new homes and begin new lives in other parts of the world. This must be made possible by international agreement.

Thus, anew, may we justify the ways of God to man. Thus may we take a vital step forward, on the long road to which civilization seeks to create a world based upon the common fatherhood of God and the common brotherhood of man.

Hannah Arendt
1906-1975

Born in Hanover, Germany, Hannah Arendt was a political theorist and philosopher, influenced during her university education by Karl Jaspers and Martin Heidegger. She fled from Nazi persecution to Paris in 1933. In 1940, she immigrated to the United States, where she was an editor for Schocken Books and a correspondent for *The New Yorker*, reporting on the trial of Adolf Eichmann. Arendt was a professor at the University of Chicago from 1963 to 1967 and later taught at the New School for Social Research.

The Jew as Pariah: A Hidden Tradition
1944

[. . .] That the status of the Jews in Europe has been not only that of an oppressed people but also of what Max Weber has called a "pariah people" is a fact most clearly appreciated by those who have had practical experience of just how ambiguous is the freedom which emancipation has ensured, and how treacherous the promise of equality which assimilation has held out. In their own position as social outcasts such men reflect the political status of their entire people. It is therefore not surprising that out of their personal experience Jewish poets, writers, and artists should have been able to evolve the concept of the pariah as a human type—a concept of supreme importance for the evaluation of mankind in our day and one which has exerted upon the gentile world an influence in strange contrast to the spiritual and political ineffectiveness which has been the fate of these men among their own brethren. Indeed, the concept of the pariah has become traditional, even though the tradition be but tacit and latent, and its continuance automatic and unconscious. Nor need we wonder why: for over a hundred years the same basic conditions have obtained and evoked the same basic reaction.

However slender the basis out of which the concept was created and out of which it was progressively developed, it has nevertheless loomed larger in the thinking of assimilated Jews than might be inferred from standard Jewish histories. It has endured, in fact, from Salomon Maimon in the eighteenth century to Franz Kafka in the early twentieth. But out of the variety of forms which it has assumed we shall here select four, in each of which it expresses an alternative portrayal of the Jewish people. Our first type will be Heinrich Heine's schlemiel and "lord of dreams" (*Traumweltherrscher*); our second, Bernard Lazare's "conscious pariah"; our third, Charlie Chaplin's grotesque portrayal of the suspect; and our fourth, Franz Kafka's poetic vision of the fate of the man of goodwill. Between these four types there is a significant connection—a link which in fact unites all genuine concepts and sound ideas when once they achieve historical actuality. [. . .]

II. Bernard Lazare: The Conscious Pariah

If it was Heine's achievement to recognize in the figure of the schlemiel the essential kinship of the pariah to the poet—both alike excluded from society and never quite at home in this world—and to illustrate by this analogy the position of the Jew in the world of European culture, it was the merit of Bernard Lazare to translate the same basic fact into terms of political significance. Living in the France of the Dreyfus affair, Lazare could appreciate at first hand the pariah quality of Jewish existence. But he knew where the solution lay: in contrast to his unemancipated brethren who accept their pariah status automatically and unconsciously, the emancipated Jew must awake to an awareness of his position and, conscious of it, become a rebel against it—the champion of an oppressed people. His fight for freedom is part and parcel of that which all the downtrodden of Europe must wage to achieve national and social liberation. [. . .]

So long as the Jews of Western Europe were pariahs only in a social sense, they could find salvation, to a large extent, by becoming parvenus. Insecure as their position may have been, they could nevertheless achieve a modus vivendi by combining what Ahad Haam described as "inner slavery" with "outward freedom." Moreover, those who deemed the price too high could still remain mere pariahs, calmly enjoying the freedom and untouchability of outcasts. Excluded from the world of political realities, they could still retreat into their quiet corners there to preserve the illusion of liberty and unchallenged humanity. The life of the pariah, though shorn of political significance, was by no means senseless.

But today it is. Today the bottom has dropped out of the old ideology. The pariah Jew and the parvenu Jew are in the same boat, rowing desperately in the same angry sea. Both are branded with the same mark; both alike are outlaws. Today the truth has come home: there is no protection in heaven or earth against bare murder, and a man can be driven at any moment from the streets and broad places once open to all. At long last, it has become clear that the "senseless freedom" of the individual merely paves the way for the senseless suffering of his entire people.

Social isolation is no longer possible. You cannot stand aloof from society, whether as a schlemiel or as a lord of dreams. The old escape mechanisms have broken down, and a man can no longer come to terms with a world in which the Jew cannot be a human being either as a parvenu using his elbows or as a pariah voluntarily spurning its gifts. Both the realism of the one and the idealism of the other are today utopian.

There is, however, a third course—the one that Kafka suggests, in which a man may forgo all claims to individual freedom and inviolability and modestly content himself with trying to lead a simple, decent life. But—as Kafka himself points out—this is impossible within the framework of contemporary society. For while the individual might still be allowed to make a career, he is no longer strong enough to fulfill the basic demands of human life. The man of goodwill is driven today into isolation like the Jew-stranger at the castle. He gets lost—or dies from exhaustion. For only within the framework of a people can a man live as a man among men, without exhausting himself. And only when a people lives and functions in consort with other peoples can it contribute to the establishment upon earth of a commonly conditioned and commonly controlled humanity.

Other works by Arendt: *Rahel Varnhagen: The Life of a Jewess* (1931); *The Origins of Totalitarianism* (1951); *Eichmann in Jerusalem: A Report on the Banality of Evil* (1963); *Men in Dark Times* (1968).

Asher Barash

1889–1952

The Hebrew writer Asher Barash was born in Lopatin, Galicia, and received both a secular and a religious education. He began writing at an early age and published poetry, stories, and plays in Hebrew, Yiddish, German, and Polish. In 1914, he moved to Palestine, where he taught Hebrew language and literature, first in Tel Aviv and then, after World War I, in Haifa. Much of his fiction drew on memories of his childhood in Galicia. His later writing portrayed the struggles of the pioneering generation in pre-state Israel. Although best known for his short stories, he also wrote essays on literature and culture and children's literature.

Parting Words
1944

We know that a writer has no power except in the pen. Nevertheless there are times when it behooves us to alter the ordinary manner of expression. There are times when the author, too, must depart from the four ells of his study to make his voice heard collectively. We, the Hebrew authors in the Land of Israel, have assembled for the third time to make our voice heard to the world and to our brethren, the Jews; the first time was in Jerusalem, the second time in Hulda, and now in Kefar Shemaryahu.

It was clear to us in the first assemblies as well that with hot breath alone we can't heal the wound of our people, and this time, too, we do not pretend to be a spirit that is in any way adequate to the greatness of the catastrophe. But we believed, and we still believe now, that it is impossible for a voice that screams in great and abiding pain not to be heard somewhere, even if the echo doesn't penetrate and fails to be heard because of the peals of thunder that roll under the whole heaven. Yes, we believe, that with all the human savagery in a blood-soaked war unlike any before, with all the manifestations of hatred and cruelty, previously unknown, the human heart is still able to be shocked by helpless pain, by hearing a voice from within the flames, for without that belief, there would be nothing left to fight for, to live for. And this faith gives us the strength and the justification in our own eyes to voice our words, again and again, words that we have already spoken many times.

We repeat the cry of our ancient ancestors: "Ah heaven, are we not brothers, not the sons of a single father, not the sons of one mother?—How are we different from every nation and folk, that you decree such evil decrees against us?" If there is no mercy for the weak, for the persecuted, who are guilty of nothing, if there is no sacred anger against the desecration of the image of God—what is the meaning of the blood of millions of your sons that has been shed? If the greatest of human iniquity does not arouse you to corrective action—who will believe your claims about other iniquities?

Therefore we cry out again: Open the gates of the Land of Israel to the refugees from murder and destruc-tion and help establish a home for the people whose homeland has been stolen. Help us in our generations-long struggle to remove the Land of Israel from the status of a forgotten corner and to place it in the world as a state that subsists on a life of civilized creativity and culture.

To our Jewish brethren, wherever they may be, and especially to the Hebrew settlement in the Land, we call again: Do not flag in this day of trouble! Show, in your desire to live a life of freedom, in your fidelity to the possessions of the nation, in your unrestricted volunteering, in your limitless help to your brothers, that indeed we are worthy to be a nation, a nation like all the nations on the earth.

If, in this hour of great burdens, we are able to insist on our right to live and to create, the path of life, even if it is strewn with many obstacles, will be open before us. Our many enemies, alas, beyond our ability to bear them, are used to seeing us only as clever people with all sorts of stratagems to *survive* by tolerance, and they do not understand our desire *to live by right*. But with the strengthening of *the fact of our life* in the world's eyes, not in secret but openly before everyone's eyes, even the evil angels will say "amen." We cannot, nor do we wish to continue a life of *outwitting*, we no longer want a substitute for life, but rather tangible, primary possessions that cannot be uprooted: the life of a nation, language, and culture, defense of life and property, and, above all, and primarily, land, sufficient areas of land. If the horrors of these times have taught the multitudes of our nation what we have lost and what we are liable to lose—they would no longer play the bad and dangerous game of divisions and splits over foreign ideologies, over ostensibly sovereign positions, but we should join together with one ardent desire for redemption, before which no power could stand.

Therefore we conclude this assembly with a call from the soil of the Land of Israel, which has once again become a source of subsistence to her returning sons, to every Jewish person, demanding of them, in this hour, limitless loyalty and assistance to their nation, which has experienced more torments than any of the nations of the world, and sacrifice of the individual for the sake of the collective, as is demanded of every nation in times of danger.

Thus I adjourn the assembly, and certainly I express the sentiments of all who are gathered here when I thank Keren Ha-yesod [the United Israel Appeal] with all my heart for taking the trouble to organize our assembly for the third time, and I thank Moshav Kefar Shemaryahu, which has treated us with fine and cultivated hospitality, as befits a group of people who know how to unify in good and effective joyful action on the soil of the homeland.

Translated by Jeffrey M. Green.

Other works by Barash: *Mul sha'ar ha-shamayim* (1925); *Kol ketavav*, 3 vols. (1952–1957); *Collected Stories* (1963); *Pictures from a Brewery* (1972).

David Ben-Gurion
1886–1973

The Labor Zionist David Ben-Gurion was the dominant political figure in the Yishuv during the 1930s and 1940s and the first prime minister of the State of Israel, an office he held from 1948 to 1963 (with the exception of the period 1953 to 1955). A conventional Marxist-Zionist when he made aliyah in 1906, he eventually came to privilege the nationalist side of his political outlook as his socialism became increasingly moderate. He was instrumental in forging the political power of the organized labor movement and in making Mapai the main political party in the Yishuv. He played a major role in securing Israeli independence and believed in the transformative power of statehood to create a new Jew, free of the alleged complexes of the diaspora.

The Imperatives of the Jewish Revolution
1944

The meaning of the Jewish revolution is contained in one word—independence! Independence for the Jewish people in its homeland! Dependence is not merely political or economic; it is also moral, cultural, and intellectual, and it affects every limb and nerve of the body, every conscious and subconscious act. Independence, too, means more than political and economic freedom; it involves also the spiritual, moral, and intellectual realms, and, in essence, it is independence in the heart, in sentiment, and in will. From this inner sense of freedom outer forms of independence will develop in our way of life, social organization, relations with other people, and economic structure. Our independence will be shaped further by the conquest of labor and the land, by broadening the range of our language and its culture, by perfecting the methods of self-government and self-defense, by creating the framework and conditions for national independence and creativity, and finally—by attaining political independence. This is the essence of the Jewish revolution. [. . .]

The Jewish revolution is taking place in a revolutionary era. This is a source of danger, and the pitfalls, though perhaps not evident on the surface, are real and deep.

Does the success of our revolution depend on ourselves, on our own meager resources, or on the great general forces now revolutionizing the world? Whatever danger threatens us is not from the open and avowed enemies of the aims and purposes of the Jewish revolution, even though such relatively unimportant adversaries must nonetheless be reckoned with.

There is some danger from the Jewish agents of foreign powers, the middlemen for alien nations and cultures, who were called in ancient times "traitors to the Covenant" and are known in our day as the "Yevsektzia" (and, in our country, as the "Fraction"), but their well-known dependence on foreign influences weakens their effectiveness. The very fact that they serve unashamedly as foreign agents curbs their influence within our people. *The fate of the Jewish revolution will be determined by its own inner forces.* [. . .]

The first imperative of the Jewish revolution is, therefore—to guard jealously the independence, the inner moral and intellectual freedom of our movement. Yes, we must not ignore or undervalue what is happening in the world without, and we must understand the great forces and the revolutionary movements in all the nations that are shaping the destiny of the world. But we cannot forget for a moment that the Jewish revolution can succeed only through our devotion to our own unique needs and destiny, only by reliance on our own strength, only if we exert the most stubborn efforts to increase its power and to make it *a wave of the future.* We dare not ever stray from his policy of self-reliance, from the will to make of ourselves a wave of the future— the wave of the future of the Jewish people and of a land of Israel so regenerated that it will attract Jews unto itself and make other peoples take account of it in their political and social calculations. If we ever deviate from this basic principle, we shall have destroyed the Jewish revolution and our future as a people. [. . .]

The second indispensable imperative of the Jewish revolution is the *unity of its protagonists.* This sharing together in a fate, a creative process, and a struggle is what unites this vanguard—the pioneers, the builders of the homeland, the workers of the land of Israel, who are inspired by the vision of a Jewish renaissance on humanistic, Zionist, and socialist foundations. The conquest of labor and the land, self-defense, the development of the Hebrew language and culture, freedom for the individual and the nation, co-operation and social responsibility, preparation for further immigration, and the welding of the arrivals from the various Diasporas into a nation—these fundamental purposes are held in common, both in theory and in practice, by all those who are faithful to our revolution. These values make it possible, and indeed mandatory, that they be united. The Jewish revolution is incomparably difficult, and, unless there is unity and co-operation, it will fail. Without such inner unity we cannot hope for full realization of our creative potential; only such unity can give us the strength to withstand obstacles and reverses and make it possible for both the individual and the community to rise to their tasks.

Unity is the imperative of our mission and our destiny. Nonetheless, of all the values of our movement it is the one that is perhaps most honored in theory and least respected in practice. We may now be attempting to become rooted in the homeland and laboring to create an independent life, but the habits of disunity and anarchy which grew wild among us in the course of hundreds of years of exile and subservience cannot easily be corrected. Rifts are appearing not only in the Yishuv as a whole; after decades of displaying an unequaled capacity for unity even the Halutzim are being affected, first in Hehalutz, then in the Kibbutz movement, and finally in the party itself. Once this disruptive force is let loose, it will not spare the Histadrut, the World Zionist Organization, or any of the other over-all bodies of the Yishuv and the Jewish people. Those who are willing to disrupt the Hehalutz or the party will have no compunction about destroying the unity of the Kibbutz movement and the Histadrut.

[. . .] Only together in Hehalutz and in one Socialist-Zionist party, in a united Jewish community and an undivided World Zionist Organization, can we assure Jewish immigration (by whatever means), redeem and rebuild the land, and fight our way through to victory. [. . .]

The third—and perhaps the most important—imperative of the Jewish revolution is: Halutziut.

We are nearing the end of the war. City after city and country after country are being liberated—but we Jews are not sharing in this joy, for almost the entire Jewish population of the newly liberated lands has been wiped out. The wellspring from which the Jewish revolution drew its strength has been destroyed. The Jewish masses on which our effort depended—they are obliterated. The Jewries of Poland, Lithuania, and Galicia—these no longer exist.

Now, more than ever before, we need a strong and devoted pioneering force. The desert area of our land is calling us, and the destruction of our people is crying out to us. In order to save the remnant—and all of us now constitute a remnant, including our own communities here in the land of Israel—our work must proceed at forced draft. [. . .]

First of all, we must conquer the sea and the desert, for these will provide us with room for new settlers and will serve as a laboratory for the development of new forms of economic and agricultural endeavor.

Translated by Arthur Hertzberg.

Other works by Ben-Gurion: *Rebirth and Destiny of Israel* (1959); *Israel: Years of Challenge* (1964); *Recollections* (1970).

Arthur Koestler

1905–1983

Hungarian-British author and journalist Arthur Koestler was born in Budapest and educated in Vienna. He worked as a journalist in Palestine in the late 1920s, and then returned to Europe, where he was arrested and imprisoned during the Spanish Civil War and again in France. Koestler's novel *Darkness at Noon* (1940), advocating against totalitarian regimes, brought him fame. Koestler settled in England, where he supported political causes and wrote essays, novels, and memoirs. His was one of the earliest voices describing and protesting the Holocaust. His death was self-inflicted.

On Disbelieving Atrocities
1944

We, the screamers, have been at it now for about ten years. We started on the night when the epileptic van der Lubbe set fire to the German Parliament; we said that if you don't quench those flames at once, they will spread all over the world; you thought we were maniacs. At present we have the mania of trying to tell you about the killing, by hot steam, mass-electrocution and live burial of the total Jewish population of Europe. So far three million have died. It is the greatest mass-killing in recorded history; and it goes on daily, hourly, as regularly as the ticking of your watch. I have photographs before me on the desk while I am writing this, and that accounts for my emotion and bitterness. People died to smuggle them out of Poland, they thought it was worthwhile. The facts have been published in pamphlets, White Books, newspapers, magazines and what not. But the other day I met one of the best-known American journalists over here. He told me that in the course of some recent public opinion survey nine out of ten average American citizens, when asked whether they believed that the Nazis commit atrocities, answered that it was all propaganda lies, and that they didn't believe a word of it. As to this country, I have been lecturing now for three years to the troops, and their attitude is the same. They don't believe in concentration camps, they don't believe in the starved children of Greece, in the shot hostages of France, in the mass-graves of Poland; they have never heard of Lidice, Treblinka or Belzec; you can convince them for an hour, then they shake themselves, their mental self-defense begins to work and in a week the shrug of incredulity has returned like a reflex temporarily weakened by a shock. [. . .]

Is it perhaps the fault of the screamers? Sometimes no doubt, but I do not believe this to be the core of the matter. Amos, Hosea, Jeremiah were pretty good propagandists and yet they failed to shake their people and to warn them. Cassandra's voice was said to have pierced walls, and yet the Trojan war took place. And at our end of the chain—in due proportion—I believe that on the whole the M.O.I. and B.B.C. are quite competent at their job. For almost three years they had to keep this country going on nothing but defeats, and they succeeded. But at the same time they lamentably failed to imbue the people with anything approaching a full awareness of what it was all about, of the grandeur and horror of the time into which they were born. They carried on business-as-usual style, with the only difference that the routine of this business included killing and being killed. Matter-of-fact unimaginativeness has become a kind of Anglo-Saxon racial myth; it is usually opposed to Latin hysterics and praised for its high value in an emergency. But the myth does not say what happens between emergencies and that the same quality is responsible for the failure to prevent their recurrence.

Now this limitation of awareness is not an Anglo-Saxon privilege, though they are probably the only race which claims as an asset what others regard as a deficiency. Nor is it a matter of temperament; stoics have wider horizons than fanatics. It is a psychological fact, inherent in our mental frame, which I believe has not been given sufficient attention in social psychology or political theory. [. . .]

[. . .] Distance in space and time degrades intensity of awareness. So does magnitude. Seventeen is a figure which I know intimately like a friend; fifty billions is just a sound. A dog run over by a car upsets our emotional balance and digestion; three million Jews killed in Poland cause but a moderate uneasiness. Statistics don't bleed; it is the detail which counts. We are unable to embrace the total process with our awareness; we can only focus on little lumps of reality. [. . .]

These limitations of awareness account for the limitations of enlightenment by propaganda. People go to cinemas, they see films of Nazi tortures, of mass-shootings, of underground conspiracy and self-sacrifice. They sigh, they shake their heads, some have a good cry. But they do not connect it with the realities of their normal plane of existence. It is Romance, it is Art, it is Those Higher Things, it is Church Latin. It does not click with reality. We live in a society of the Jekyll and Hyde pattern, magnified into gigantic proportions.

This was, however, not always the case to the same extent. There were periods and movements in history—in Athens, in the early Renaissance, during the first years of the Russian Revolution—when at least certain representative layers of society had attained a relatively high level of mental integration; times, when people seemed to rub their eyes and come awake, when their cosmic awareness seemed to expand, when they were "contemporaries" in a much broader and fuller sense; when the trivial and the cosmic planes seemed on the point of fusing.

And there were periods of disintegration and dissociation. But never before, not even during the spectacular decay of Rome and Byzantium, was split thinking so palpably evident, such a uniform mass disease; never did human psychology reach such a height of phoneyness. Our awareness seems to shrink in direct ratio as communications expand; the world is open to us as never before, and we walk about as prisoners, each in his private portable cage. And meanwhile the watch goes on ticking. What can the screamers do but go on screaming, until they get blue in the face?

I know one who used to tour this country addressing meetings, at an average of ten a week. He is a well-known London publisher. Before each meeting he used to lock himself up in a room, close his eyes, and imagine in detail, for twenty minutes, that he was one of the people in Poland who were killed. One day he tried to feel what it was like to be suffocated by chloride gas in a death-train; the other he had to dig his grave with two hundred others and then face a machine gun, which, of course, is rather unprecise and capricious in its aiming. Then he walked out to the platform and talked. He kept going for a full year before he collapsed with a nervous breakdown. He had a great command of his audiences and perhaps he has done some good, perhaps he brought the two planes, divided by miles of distance, an inch closer to each other.

I think one should imitate this example. Two minutes of this kind of exercise per day, with closed eyes, after reading the morning paper, are at present more necessary to us than physical jerks and breathing the Yogi way. It might even be a substitute for going to church. For as long as there are people on the road and victims in the thicket, divided by dream barriers, this will remain a phoney civilization.

Other works by Koestler: *Scum of the Earth* (1941); *Dialogue with Death* (1942); *The Ghost in the Machine* (1967); *The Case of the Midwife Toad* (1971); *The Thirteenth Tribe* (1976).

Isaac Rosenfeld
1918-1956

Isaac Rosenfeld was born in Chicago, where he attended high school and college with novelist Saul Bellow. Rosenfeld studied philosophy at the University of Chicago in 1933 and in 1941 moved to New York, where he wrote dynamic reviews, poems, and short stories for *The Nation*, *Partisan Review*, and *New Republic*. Rosenfeld was acclaimed as the voice of a new generation of American Jews, but he died of a massive heart attack at the age of thirty-eight. His only novel, *Passage from Home*, was published in 1946, and he himself was the inspiration for the character Dahfu in Bellow's *Henderson the Rain King*.

The Situation of the Jewish Writer
1944

All discussions pertaining to the Jews must begin with some very gloomy observations. The Jews are, everywhere, a minority group, and it is a particular misfortune these days to be a minority group in the United States. A conscious member of such a group is necessarily overconscious: he is distracted by race and religion, distressed by differences which in a healthy society would be considered healthful. The very simple state of being a Jew—it should occupy no more of a man's attention than any ordinary fact of history—has created traumas, fears of violence, defenses against aggression. These are about the worst conditions under which an artist could seek to carry on his work. An artist should first of all have the security of a dignified neutrality. He should be able to consider himself a *mensch mit alle menschen gleich*—that is, an equal, a man among men, a representative even if extraordinary individual. But a Jewish writer unconsciously feels that he may at any time be called to account not for his art, nor even for his life, but for his Jewishness. Only a brave man can be a brave artist, let alone a good one, in a hostile world. It is therefore clear to me that whatever contribution Jewish writers may make to American literature will depend on matters beyond their control as writers.

But the position of Jewish writers—artists and intellectuals in general—is not entirely an unfortunate one. For the most part the young Jewish writers of today are the children of immigrants, and as such—not completely integrated in society and yet not wholly foreign to it—they enjoy a critical advantage over the life that surrounds them. They are bound to observe much that is hidden to the more accustomed native eye.

The insight available to most Jewish writers is a natural result of their position in American life and culture. Jews are marginal men. As marginal men, living in cities and coming from the middle classes they are open to more influences than perhaps any other group. I vaguely recall a Yiddish proverb to the effect that bad luck always knows where to find a Jew; and as a barometer of political calamity the Jews in this country are second only to the Negroes. But even gentler influences, short of fatality, know where to find Jews—in the middle, in the overlapping area where events converge. And the middle position has its cultural correlate, that of being centrally exposed to all movements in art and in thought. This position of cultural exposure gives the Jewish writer the advantage of access. (There is much more to be said about this point—more than I have the space or the knowledge to disclose. But, generally speaking, the position of Jewish writers illustrates one of the strangest phenomena of modern life. Since modern life is so complex that no man can possess it in its entirety, the outsider often finds himself the perfect insider.)

Close as they are to the main developments in America, some Jewish writers may retain more than a little of European culture. Either through their position in the Jewish community, their childhood, or the influence of their immigrant parents, they may possess a sense of reference to an earlier community. I don't know how widespread this old world feeling is among Jewish writers. But if it is at all common, I should say it is a valuable thing. Jews in America have relatively little contact with country life, with small town folk and farmers. But through cultural retention, through a subliminal orientation to more primitive surroundings, they may still find in themselves access to rural life, understanding of its character and traditions.

But it is one thing to consider the Jewish writer's social equipment, and quite another to regard his actual position in society. As a member of an internationally insecure group he has grown personally acquainted with some of the fundamental themes of insecurity that run through modern literature. He is a specialist in alienation (the one international banking system the Jews actually control). Alienation puts him in touch with his own past traditions, the history of the Diaspora; with the present predicament of almost all intellectuals and, for all one knows, with the future conditions of civilized humanity. Today nearly all sensibility—thought, creation, perception—is in exile, alienated from the society in which it barely managed to stay alive.

But alienation from society, like the paradox of the outsider, may function as a condition of entrance into society. Surely it is not a condition for the Jew's re-entrance into the world that has rejected him. But persecution may lead him, as it has in the past, to a further effort to envisage the good society. No man suffers injustice without learning, vaguely but surely, what justice is. The desire for justice, once it passes beyond revenge, becomes the deepest motive for social change. Out of their recent sufferings one may expect Jewish writers to make certain inevitable moral discoveries. These discoveries, enough to indict the world, may also be crucial to its salvation.

I do not want to make too much of alienation. It is the only possible condition, the theme we have to work with, but it is undesirable, for it falls short of the full human range. Besides, in every society, in every group, there are what Saul Bellow has called "colonies of the spirit." Artists create their colonies. Some day these may become empires.

Other works by Rosenfeld: *An Age of Enormity* (1962); *Alpha and Omega* (1966).

Gershom Scholem

Reflections on Modern Jewish Studies
1944

In my opinion, one cannot understand the development of the Science of Judaism except by taking note of the profound contradictions or, if you will, the unique dialectical tensions present within it since its origins. [. . .]

[. . .] Romantic philology and philosophy were as a magic wand which they used to awaken and bring back to life the subjects of its research. But in very extensive areas, this magic wand has been transformed by the Science of Judaism into a wrecker's rod. The old books, once they came close to them, had their brilliance taken away, and that which was translucent and shining became opaque and cold. [. . .]

[. . .] Spiritualization and sentimentalization ran amok. It follows that the Science of Judaism won its (admittedly modest) place and influence with the Western Jewish public insofar as it appeared in a bourgeois edition, and insofar as it served its purposes (which seem very strange to our eyes today). Knowledge of the martyrs who were killed and the great scholars who spread the light of Enlightenment satisfied the feeling of pride of a generation which did not expect to follow in their footsteps and which awaited the liberal messiah.

The ability of this Science of Judaism to change anything was nil. [. . .]

For what reason, therefore, do I take to task the Science of Judaism during this period of adjustment to becoming good bourgeoisie? The list of its sins is particularly annoying, as I said, among the men of the center, among those liberals who call themselves conservatives and those conservatives who call themselves liberal—including the vast majority of the men of science. The following are the main headings of the charge against it:

The removal of the pointedly irrational and of demonic enthusiasms from Jewish history, through an exaggerated emphasis upon the theological and the spiritual. This is the fundamental, original sin which outweighs all others This awesome giant, our history, is called upon to render an accounting of itself—and this great creation, filled with explosive power, compounded of vitality, wickedness, and perfection, becomes limited and reduced in stature, and declares itself to be naught. The demonic giant is no more than an innocent fool who follows the practice of a progress-loving citizen, who may be greeted in the city square by any respectable house holder, in the tidy market-place of the nineteenth century, so they need not be embarrassed when they speak of his lineage in the gates.

An idyll—the distortion of the past by obscuring its disturbing elements, which rebel and break out into history and thought. Nearly all of those who wrote histories of individuals, families, and communities were of course affected by this fault. In thousands of cases, what wonderful material, which has now completely disappeared, was still available to these scholars! And what destruction was wrought by its dilettantish use, concealing those things which are important to us and stressing the incidental; and if they did not completely conceal it—what poor judgment they exhibited in its evaluation and use!

Morose sentimentality—this first emerged among those who wrote in German in the 1830's and 1840's, but it was considerably augmented by the later Hebrew writers, in keeping with the destructive possibilities hidden in their rhetoric.

The founding of history upon martyrology, in isolation from its real bases.

Apologetics and self-justification—in the sense that "their fear (of the Gentiles . . .) precedes their wisdom." Who does not remember the confusion and panic over the literature concerning circles of Jewish bandits during the period of the French revolution, and the concealing of this issue by scholars, who preferred to close their eyes to the facts or to denounce them as antisemitic inventions. And there is no shortage of other examples. How much pandering to the wealthy and the powerful do we find here, and how much reluctance to render cruel accounts!

Trivialization, to the point of ignoring or even hiding all those phenomena which did not suit the doctrine of progress according to those formulae accepted in the previous century. There was thus created the illusion of a great historical line, exemplifying the doctrine of progress in general within Jewish history.

It was these things which gave the Science of Judaism the striking sense of being a diligent but lifeless discipline.

Translated by Jonathan Chipman.

Elliot E. Cohen
1899–1959

A wunderkind who graduated from Yale University at age nineteen, Elliot E. Cohen went on to found *Commentary*, the famously disputatious magazine of literature and opinion. During Cohen's stewardship, the magazine attempted to harmonize Jewish intellectualism and American values, providing a forum for serious thinking and erudite opinions. Cohen himself flourished as a writer and editor, stressing both eloquence and analytical rigor. Born in Des Moines, he worked on *Menorah Journal*, a biweekly publication for college students, before his *Commentary* days; he ended his own life.

An Act of Affirmation
1945

It is traditional to begin a new magazine with brave declarations. If we do not, we trust we shall be forgiven.

We begin at a moment heavy with a sense of human destiny. Every schoolboy who listens to the radio knows that 1945 marks an epoch in world history. World War II has ended; the United Nations have won the greatest military victory of the ages; yet we stand troubled and hesitant before the glorious era of peace which we have awaited so long, and which now we seem not to know how to deal with.

In war, our country has demonstrated a giant's strength, in production, in cooperation, in planning, in courage. It remains to be seen—and present omens are ambiguous—whether this same giant's strength can be mustered as greatly and as wisely for the arts of peaceful living and the problems of peaceful world governance.

And since August 7, shadowing every moment of our thinking and feeling, there is the fearsome knowledge that through our inventiveness we have unleashed a power that has proved it can end a world war by a single blow, and that only waits to prove that it can—by other well-directed blows—build new, undreamed civilizations, or end the human race. Though ten thousand editorial writers the world over have said it again and again, it is still true: here man faces an ultimate challenge. Here, in its starkest form, we sometimes think, is what the scripture must have meant by the haunting phrase "the knowledge of good and evil."

As Jews, we are of an ancient tradition that, in a very special sense, keeps a vigil with history. We are peculiarly sensitive to the march of events, perhaps because, as some say ruefully, they have so often marched over us. So, at the least, we share with the rest of humanity the deep unease of breathing air almost visibly clotted with fantastic utopias or unimaginable cataclysms. And, in addition, we suffer our own special questionings, which in all candor, we believe humanity should share with us, possibly for the common good.

As Jews, we live with this fact: 4,750,000 of 6,000,000 Jews of Europe have been murdered. Not killed in battle, not massacred in hot blood, but slaughtered like cattle, subjected to every physical indignity—*processed*. Yes, cruel tyrants did this; they have been hurled down; they will be punished, perhaps. Yes, there were men and women in other lands who raised their voices in protest, who lent helping hands. But we must also record this fact: the voices were not many, the hands were not many. There was a strange passivity the world over in the face of this colossal latter-day massacre of innocents, whether Jews or other "minorities."

And we must face this fact, too: that the kind of thinking and feeling that set loose this nightmare phenomenon still burns high in many countries, and lies latent in all. We have no gauge to measure the potentialities of this great Nazi secret weapon of World War II. But there are many—and they are not guided by personal hurt alone—who believe that here is a force that, in the political and social scene, can wreak destruction comparable to the atomic bomb itself. It was the *ignis fatuus* that lured the German people to their doom. It was the flame of the torch that kindled World War II. To resist it; to learn how to stamp it out; to reaffirm and restore the sense of the sanctity of the human person and the rights of man:—here, too, our world is greatly challenged. How that challenge is to be met is, of course, of particular interest to Jews, but hardly less to all mankind, if there is to be a human future.

At this juncture, in the midst of this turbulence and these whirlwinds, we light our candle, *Commentary*. Surely here is an act of faith.

It is an act of faith of a kind of which we seem peculiarly capable, we who, after all these centuries, remain, in spite of all temptation, the people of the Book.

We believe in the Word. We believe in study—as a guide to life, for the wisdom it brings to the counsels of men, and for its own sake. We have faith in the intellect, in the visions of visionary men, in the still, small voices of poets, and thinkers, and sages.

Commentary is an act of faith in our possibilities in America. With Europe devastated, there falls upon us here in the United States a far greater share of the responsibility for carrying forward, in a creative way, our common Jewish cultural and spiritual heritage. And, indeed, we have faith that, out of the opportunities of our experience here, there will evolve new patterns of living, new modes of thought, which will harmonize heritage and country into a true sense of at-home-ness in the modern world. Surely, we who have survived catastrophe, can survive freedom, too. [. . .] It is a many-sided task. But *Commentary*, as its name implies, aims to be many-sided. Commentary means a "record, a history, a memoir." We will reach back for the riches of the past. Commentary means a "running comment." We will keep abreast of the march of events. Commentary means "interpretation." We will present significant discussion by many minds on the basic issues of our times.

But there is also a traditional Jewish meaning of commentary—somewhat private, but very real, we think—which we as editors cherish. Our ancient scribes and sages, as we know, only wrote commentaries on the revelation which was the Law. But we know that these ever-changing interpretations of the past by the men of wisdom and men of insight of each generation, became for that generation more than merely commentaries. It became the truth that men lived by. Truth, as someone has said, is an ever-flowing, ever-renewing stream. . . .

We said we would not speak brave words, but we almost have. As editors, we know our place. It is really a humble function. We are like well-diggers. We roll up our sleeves and in the sweat of our brows, we dig. And if the time and place are right, and the omens are propitious—of a sudden, fresh, cool, flowing waters. . . .

To this task, soberly and earnestly, we dedicate ourselves.

Alberto Gerchunoff

1884–1950

The journalist and fiction writer Alberto Gerchunoff was born in Proskurov (now Khmelnytskyi), Ukraine, and moved in 1891 to Argentina, where he lived in the Jewish agricultural colony of Moisés Ville. He later settled in Buenos Aires. Gerchunoff worked for the newspaper *La Nación* and wrote short stories and novels depicting Jewish life in Latin America. At first encouraging Jewish assimilation, Gerchunoff was convinced by the events of World War II to support the establishment of the state of Israel.

The Nazi Crematorium in the Movie Houses of Buenos Aires

1945

For some days past, newsreels about the concentration camps have been showing in the movie theaters of Buenos Aires. The public can now easily observe the methods used by the Germans in the death camps. Military and newspaper photographers, parliamentary commissions from London, and reporters like Paul Ghali, correspondent for the *Chicago Daily News*, have been to see them and are able to give precise information in respect to the number, nationality, and ethnic identity of the victims. In Auschwitz, in Treblinka, in Dachau, in Ohrdruf, in Buchenwald, in Nordhausen, perished many anti-Nazi Germans, unsubmissive foreigners, and politicians who did not agree with Hitlerism, perhaps tens of thousands. But in those laboratories of refined massacres, six million two hundred thousand Jews were murdered, out of a total of eight million living in various European countries.

This figure, accepted by the Allied governments, shows us that the concentration camps were primarily organized to exterminate the Jewish population and secondarily to purge non-Jews who, for whatever reason, earned the hostility of the Nazis. What stands out in the films now being shown in Buenos Aires is the frightful diligence displayed by the German task forces. Friends of mine who went to see them left feeling that Dante must have returned from the circles of Hell, and they asked me if I was not planning to go myself to visit those scenes of martyrdom. I neither intend to verify—not because of any squeamishness on my part, but rather, out of respect for humanity—those horrors recorded by the cameras, nor do I need to witness the parade of wraiths in order to measure the depths of Nazi depravity. I am always living in a concentration camp, because I, like every Jew, no matter how much he loves his country nor how well he serves it with his heart and mind, is in the end fodder for the inquisitorial enterprises of some who live there and often govern. By instinct, by the legacy of experience that feeds his imagination, the Jew knows what it is to suffer a Spanish Inquisition or a Teutonic pack of hounds with the power of life and death over the most defenseless human being history has ever known, the most marginalized being in Christian society.

It is not we Jews who need to familiarize ourselves with the Nazi horrors revealed in the macabre workshops of Majdanek or Auschwitz. It is the non-Jewish multitudes who must attend these spectacles, in order to understand what they signify, to study the causes that led to that brutal organization, and to determine to what degree they themselves contributed with their active or latent antisemitism, with their blind indifference or tacit consent to the cruel industry of Jewish extermination. Adolf Hitler, the implacable executioner and tenacious promoter of anti-Jewish hatred, would not have been able to establish his mills of extermination if the world had not offered a favorable atmosphere for his diabolical designs. We have not heard, for example, among ourselves, a justification for the mass shooting of hostages; we have heard, on the other hand, justification for the massacre of Jews and the antisemitic hyenas that have grinned with pleasure, at the microphone or in murky periodicals, upon learning the details of death chamber operations. What I want to say is that a secular preparation of enmity, fed by the anti-Christian spirit that invariably animated those Judeophobes, was necessary before the Germans could carry out their persecution and annihilation with such ferocity and persistence.

The world was not moved when Germany sanctioned the racist laws of Nuremberg, when Mussolini adopted them in Rome, and when the sadly diminished Marshal Pétain copied them in Vichy. That world, in its complacency, thought it natural that the Jews should be persecuted and expelled from their posts, and soon the distance between theoretical anti-Jewishness and the ovens established by the Nazis in Germany or Poland was hard to discern. Thus, it is those who belong to that world, those who already seemed prepared to tolerate the sinister norms of the totalitarian regime or did not have the courage to fight against it, they are the ones who are morally obliged to face the reality of the concentration camps, that program carried out with fire and venom by the New Order. The world was complicit in that horror, as it was, moreover, in its own agony. Yes—it is the men of Christian civilization who must fully acquaint themselves with the concentration camps and ask themselves if the antisemitism often taught in the school, in the home, and in society did not help in some degree to make them possible.

The exclusion of Jews was practiced in countries with no official policy of discrimination, but in a hypocritical, underhanded fashion, as in our country, with various sectors deeming it necessary to gloss over the atrocities of the concentration camps. I know that this is not the admirable attitude of today's great European clergy; it is the attitude of the general public, caught off guard and confused by centuries of insidious preaching abetted by common stupidity. That is why people who did not grasp the magnitude of the German crime should go study it in the movie houses; in the dark, alone with their conscience, it would be useful for their reeducation to question themselves in silence and discover how complicit they are in the monstrosity unrolling before their eyes, complicit through inaction, weakness of spirit, or meanness of intellect.

Translated by Michele McKay Aynesworth.

Other works by Gerchunoff: *Los gauchos judíos* (1910); *Cuentos de ayer* (1919); *La jofaina maravillosa* (1923); *Historias y proezas de amor* (1926); *Entre Ríos, mi país* (1950); *El pino y la palmera* (1952).

Hayim Greenberg

1889–1953

Born in Bessarabia, Hayim Greenberg was a prominent Zionist orator and publicist in both Russia and the United States. After being jailed several times by the Bolsheviks for Zionist activities, he left for Berlin in 1921 and then moved permanently to the United States in 1924. In America, he took a leading role in Labor Zionism and edited several of its publications. In 1934, he became editor of the monthly *Jewish Frontier*. Cultured and widely read, he was known particularly for his urbane essays in three languages—Hebrew, Yiddish, and English.

The Universalism of the Chosen People
1945

In what sense is Judaism racist? Does it in general recognize the "holiness" of race and if so, what practical deductions have Jews made from such a theory?

In connection with the Nazi racist propaganda, these questions about Jewry and Judaism have been dealt with extensively in the past few years. Jews regard themselves as a Chosen People and the Germans of our generation also proclaimed their "superiority" to the rest of mankind. Does this mean that Jews, or at least tradition-minded Jews, subscribe to the same theory as the Nazis, but only as applied to themselves? Bernard Shaw seems to think so, and when some years ago he was asked for his opinion of the Nazi theories of racial

purity and racial contamination, he replied that the fault of the Jew is his "enormous arrogance" based on his claim to belong to God's chosen race, that the Nordic nonsense is only an attempt to imitate "the posterity of Abraham," and that the anti-Semites do not see how "intensely Jewish" is the Nazi thesis of race pollution. [. . .]

The Talmud and various Midrashim, as is well known, contain hundreds of passages of harsh criticism and prejudice against other nations, but only very rarely is an outright prejudice expressed against the entirety of the non-Jewish world. The Aggadah and the Midrashim are not less, and frequently far more, outspokenly universalist in tendency than the Prophets. According to one Midrash (Mekhilta on Exodus), the Torah was given to the Jews in the wilderness—a sort of no-man's-land—and not in Palestine, as an indication that in principle the Torah was a gift to all of mankind and not merely to the Jews. Potentially, in the final historical analysis, all peoples are worthy to receive the Torah. According to another legend, the Torah was presented simultaneously in seventy tongues to all the peoples of the earth so that the "three score and ten nations" might hear it, each in its own language—and perhaps, some among them, might accept it. According to another version, the Torah was borne from land to land, from nation to nation: the Creator was, as it were, "experimenting" with His creatures, since He was Himself "not certain" who among them would be prepared to accept it. The experiment failed since all the nations refused the gift, and even Israel (here we again see that symptomatic "apology" for possessing a "precious vessel" denied to others) did not accept the Torah willingly, not being mature enough to evaluate it properly, but under compulsion. "The mountain was overturned upon them like a vat": Either you shoulder the burden of the Torah or the mountain will destroy you. The moral behind this and other Midrashim is that Jews must be more restrained in their boasts of superiority over other peoples. In the original scheme of the world, the Torah was to belong to all, regardless of land, tongue or origin. For the time being, this plan has failed, but eventually it will be realized ("and the earth shall be ripe with wisdom"); Jews are only the first ones to have made a covenant with God. This attitude toward the Gentile bears no similarity to the "scientific" racial theories of today. Blood, origin, biological heritage shape the individual, but more powerful than all these factors is the spirit of every man, and the *Zelem Elohim* (the image of

God) which leaves its stamp on each human face is, in the final analysis, more determinative than the heritage of flesh and blood. [. . .]

[. . .] Everything in man which is vital, dynamic and spiritual comes from God, not from the family tree, and, by the same token, not from "race." In terms of modern psychology, we realize that our sages meant that the part which parents (and race) play in the development of man can perhaps stimulate or retard the unfolding of his soul; they cannot, however, permanently bind or determine his character and moral destiny. To the Jews, the Gentiles appeared as sinful creatures but certainly Judaism never regarded "sinful" as synonymous with "damned." The gates of repentance were open to everyone, and it is significant that during Succoth seventy oxen were sacrificed in the Temple of Jerusalem to atone for the sins of the "Seventy Nations" (Succoth 55). This rite demonstrates more than anything else, and perhaps even more than the universalist visions of the prophets and the latter anti-particularistic interpretations of many of our sages, that however many faults the Jews might have found in their Gentile neighbors and with however many virtues they might have credited themselves—frequently out of sheer naive boastfulness, and at other times in a spirit of refined "triumph" over their oppressors—when it came to a spiritual summation (which found expression in cult, worship and in the mysteries of sacrifice) they evolved a ritual which solemnly stressed the unity of mankind in sin, repentance and atonement.

Other works by Greenberg: *The Inner Eye: Selected Essays*, 2 vols. (1953, 1964).

Abraham Joshua Heschel

1907–1972

Rabbi, theologian, philosopher, poet, and social activist Abraham Joshua Heschel was born in Poland, a descendant of two prominent Hasidic families. Following rabbinical ordination, he obtained his doctorate at the University of Berlin in 1934 and went on to teach at Martin Buber's Jüdisches Lehrhaus in Frankfurt. After a period in Warsaw, and then London, Heschel left in 1940 for Cincinnati, where he taught philosophy and rabbinics at Hebrew Union College. From 1945 on he served as professor of Jewish ethics and mysticism at the Jewish Theological Seminary of America. Heschel

was also respected for his role in the civil rights and peace movements of the 1960s and in Jewish–Christian dialogue.

The Eastern European Era in Jewish History
1945

We Jews, the first nation in the world that began not only to mark but also to appraise and to judge the generations, evaluate eras on the basis of different criteria, namely, how much refinement is there in the life of a people, how much spiritual substance in its workaday existence, i.e., how much metaphysics in its material aspect? To us culture is the style of life of a people. Our gauge of culture is the extent to which the people, and not only individuals, live in accordance with the dictates of an eternal doctrine—the extent to which inwardness, mercy, beauty, and holiness are to be found in the daily life of a people.

The pattern of life of a people is more important than the pattern of its art. What counts most is not expression, but existence itself, the source of expression. The key to the source of creativity lies in the will to cling to spirituality, to be close to refinement, and not merely in the ability of expression. Creativity comes from responsive merging with infinite reality, not from an ambition to say something. To appraise properly the meaning of the Eastern European era in Jewish history, we must not merely dwell upon its contribution to literature, science and the arts, but upon its life-feeling and lifestyle. We shall then find that it was the era in which our people attained the highest degree of inwardness. From that point of view we are justified in saying that it was the golden period in Jewish history, in the history of the Jewish soul. [. . .]

A synthesis of Torah and people is attained by Ashkenazic Jewry. Eastern European Jews speak Yiddish, a language of their own. Hebrew, too, emancipates itself of its rhetorical artificialities, becoming simple and natural as in midrashic times. Because the collective life of the Jews is wholly pervaded by Jewishness, the relations among all the components of the Jewish community, between the saint and the untutored, the Yeshiva student and the farmer, are intimate, organic. The wholesome earthliness of villagers, the geniality of ordinary folk, and the ingenuousness of the *magid*, the popular preacher, penetrate the *Bet-midrash*. [. . .]

It is easier to appraise the beauty of the older Jewish life than the revolutionary spirituality of the modern

Jew, of the *maskil*, Zionist, or socialist. The Jews of older days frequently overlooked this world, because of the other world. Between man and world there stood God. In the meantime, however, decrees and pogroms shattered the ground under the feet of the Jews. They had no peace, nor the means to gain a livelihood. Then came young men with new tidings. There arose the Haskala, the Jewish socialist movement, Zionism, the *halutzim* movement. How much of self-sacrifice, of love of Israel and of the Sanctification of the Name are to be found in these modern Jews, in their will to suffer in order to help! The zeal of pious Jews was transmitted to their emancipated sons and grandsons. The fervor and yearning of Hasidim, the ascetic obstinacy of Kabbalists, the inexorable logic of Talmudists, found their reincarnation in the supporters of the modern Jewish movements. Of the pair, Torah and Israel, they accepted Israel. Even those who have abandoned tradition, even those whom the revolutionary impetus has carried to the antithesis of tradition, have not separated themselves, like the sects of previous days, but have remained within the fold. The powerful urge to redemption continued in them. The Satan of assimilation is very seductive; but the Jews who have not capitulated, who have not deserted Jewish poverty, who have relinquished careers, favor, and comfort in order to find a healing for the hurt of their people: these have been like new wine in old bottles. [. . .]

In the dreadful anguish of these days, a bitter question sears our lips: What will become of us, the surviving? Shall we, Heaven forbid, be subject to the fate of Sephardic Jewry after the catastrophe of 1492: fragmentized groups in Turkey and Morocco, stray individuals in Amsterdam, magnificent synagogues and fossilized Jewishness? Shall we permit our people to be lost in the multitude? Our Sabbath to be dissipated in the week-days?

Rich stores of potential energy, of intellectual resilience and emotional depth, gathered in the course of generations of a disciplined mode of life, are now contained in us. Much wisdom and much refinement are frittered away in intellectual trash, a good deal of the soul is lost to Satan.

We must retain the Jewishness of our fathers and grandfathers. Their Law within the Heart was not a matter of esthetics. Romantic portraiture of Hasidism, nostalgia and piety, are merely ephemeral; they disappear with the first generation. Solidarity with the past must become an integral part of our existence. We are in need of Jews whose life is a garden, not a hothouse. Only a living Judaism can survive. Books are no more than seeds; we must be both the soil and the atmosphere in which they grow.

The present generation is still in possession of the keys to the treasure. If we do not uncover the treasures, the keys will go down to the grave with us, and the storehouse of the generations will remain locked forever. The Eastern European era can become a source of inspiration for all of us. It is incumbent upon us never to forget the Jews that sanctified their lives by their proximity to heaven.

Translated by A. J. Heschel.

Other works by Heschel: *The Earth Is the Lord's: The Inner World of the Jew in Eastern Europe* (1949); *Man Is Not Alone: A Philosophy of Religion* (1951); *Man's Quest for God: Studies in Prayer and Symbolism* (1954); *God in Search of Man: A Philosophy of Judaism* (1955); *The Prophets* (1962).

Life Writing and Reportage

Marc Bloch
1886–1944

Historian and resistance leader Marc Bloch was born in Lyon. The son of a professor of ancient history, Bloch studied at Lycée Louis-le-Grand and the École normale supérieure in Paris, and then in Germany. He served as an officer during World War I. After the war, Bloch taught at the University of Strasbourg and in 1936 became professor of economic history at the Sorbonne. Bloch was a cofounder of the Annales School of French social history and its journal *Annales d'histoire économique et sociale*. He is best known for his *French Rural History and Feudal Society* (1931) and his unfinished work on the writing of history, *The Historian's Craft* (1953), published posthumously. Bloch was shot by the Gestapo during the German occupation of France.

The Testamentary Instructions of Marc Bloch
1940

When death comes to me, whether in France or abroad, I leave it to my dear wife or, failing her, to my children, to arrange for such burial as may seem best to them. I wish the ceremony to be a civil one only. The members of my family know that I could accept no other kind. But when the moment comes I should like some friend to take upon himself the task of reading the following words, either in the mortuary or at the graveside.

I have not asked to have read above my body those Jewish prayers to the cadence of which so many of my ancestors, including my father, were laid to rest. All my life I have striven to achieve complete sincerity in word and thought. I hold that any compromise with untruth, no matter what the pretext, is the mark of a human soul's ultimate corruption. Following in this a far greater man than I could ever hope to be, I could wish for no better epitaph that these simple words: DILEXIT VERITATEM. That is why I find it impossible, at this moment of my last farewell, when, if ever, a man should be true to himself, to authorize any use of those formulae of an orthodoxy to the beliefs of which I have ever refused to subscribe.

But I should hate to think that anyone might read into this statement of personal integrity even the remotest approximation to a coward's denial. I am prepared, therefore, if necessary, to affirm here, in the face of death, that I was born a Jew: that I have never denied it, nor ever been tempted to do so. In a world assailed by the most appalling barbarism, is not that generous tradition of the Hebrew Prophets, which Christianity at its highest and noblest took over and expanded, one of the best justifications we can have for living, believing, and fighting? A stranger to all credal dogmas, as to all pretended community of life and spirit based on race, I have, through life, felt that I was above all, and quite simply, a Frenchman. A family tradition, already of long date, has bound me firmly to my country. I have found nourishment in her spiritual heritage and in her history. I can, indeed, think of no other land whose air I could have breathed with such a sense of ease and freedom. I have loved her greatly, and served her with all my strength. I have never found that the fact of being a Jew has at all hindered these sentiments. Though I have fought in two wars, it has not fallen to my lot to die for France. But I can, at least, in all sincerity, declare that I die now, as I have lived, a good Frenchman.

When these words have been spoken, the same friend shall, if the text can be obtained, read the citations which I received for service in the field.

NOTE
The text here printed was given by Marc Bloch to his family at the time when he was engaged in clandestine activities. There can be few finer examples of beauty of mind expressed in such beauty of handwriting.

Four years after writing the "Statement of the Evidence" contained in the preceding pages, and one year after committing these last wishes in which he sums up all he had to say, with diamond-like precision, Marc Bloch fell to the bullets of a Nazi firing squad [note appears in the translated document].

Translated by Gerard Hopkins.

Other works by Bloch: *Les rois thaumaturges* (1924); *La vie d'outre-tombe du Roi Salomon* (1925); *Les caractères originaux de l'histoire rurale française* (1931); *La société féodale* (2 vols., 1939, 1940); *L'Étrange défaite: témoignage écrit en 1940* (1946); *Apologie pour l'histoire ou métier d'historien* (1949); *Memoirs of War, 1914–1915* (1980); *Méthodologie historique* (1988).

William Goldman

1910–2009

Anglo-Jewish writer William (Willy) Goldman was born into a working-class Orthodox family in London, the child of Russian and Romanian immigrants. Goldman left school at age fourteen to work at a sweatshop, and abandoned traditional Judaism. Partly to escape poverty, he took up boxing as a sport; as a team captain he felt that he could "stand up straight and not be frightened." In the 1930s, he met John Lehmann, founder of the magazine *New Writing,* who employed him and published his stories. Goldman's works, often satiric, portrayed the lives of hard-working Jewish immigrants in London's East End. The British novelist C. P. Snow once described him as "our best reporter of the East End." Goldman was also compared to Dickens by more than one reviewer.

East End My Cradle

1940

Part One

Chapter 1. Yids versus Goys

Anti-Semitism in my infancy, had its compensations, for being confined practically to children (I speak of anti-Semitism not as a subjective attitude but in its positive sense, as demonstrated in Germany), it never amounted to anything more serious than a kind of game. It was largely a pretext for staging occasional "battles" between the Jews and Gentiles. Each party of children took up its stand and pelted the other across the no-man's land of our narrow, cobbled street. For ammunition we used the rubbish from the dustbin and gutters. The "battle" ended when the rubbish gave out; there was no ill will afterwards.

It is only since getting into adult hands that positive anti-Semitism in England has deteriorated from a sport into a tyranny.

I won't say that anti-Semitism was even then without its serious aspects. People living in the predominantly Jewish side of Stepney (Whitechapel) hardly dared venture into the predominantly Gentile side, Wapping. Abuse was the very least one could expect; a beer bottle across the head was the more likely penalty. True, it has

to he admitted that the Gentiles didn't invade us. That is something we may reasonably expect if and when English politics sink to the level of those in pre-1939 Germany.

Our street had its own peculiar racial problem. Welk Street, as it is called, is part of that area between Wapping and Whitechapel known as St. Georges, a neighborhood that is a kind of frontier to either, and in which therefore the populations show signs of the merging. Our street was a typical example. The Gentiles lived clustered together up one half, we occupied the other. You could tell which were which by the kind of cooking smells that greeted you when you passed a door. Our respective smells were quite different.

There was an unspoken hostility between us, but no actual displays of violence—except when the Gentiles returned home drunk from the pub at the corner. They would career noisily up the street, hurl abuse at the Jewish houses and occasionally send one of their "empties" through a Jewish window. We sat silent and watchful behind our doors. It was a reminder to us that pogroms had not died with the Russian Tsar. We were contemptuous rather than afraid: we knew the Gentiles couldn't do very much to us in a free country like England. We waited patiently for the storm to pass. "They don't know any better," my mother explained sadly. "They're only Goyim."

We children took it less philosophically. We hadn't the memory of Tsarist pogroms to help us appreciate the comparative harmlessness of the current attacks. We felt ourselves English and outraged. We wanted to go and fling bottles at *their* windows. Our parents, when they got wind of such an idea, were shocked, and threatened to flay us alive. You couldn't argue with them. "It's the Gentile's country," my mother explained. "He can do what he likes. In your country *you* will be master. You must have patience until the Messiah comes." It seemed to us throwing away a very good opportunity for what was at best an "outside" chance.

In the intervals between such incidents the Jewish and Gentile children bore each other no grudge. There were, of course, individual bullies here and there who ambushed a younger Jew, twisted his arm behind his back, and cried: "Say that Christians are better'n Jews! Gorn, say it!"—and went on twisting until he did. These bullies were disapproved of by Jew and Gentile alike. For most of us "anti-Semitism" was a kind of game or romantic feud. Our two groups mixed quite freely in the street games: Archie Griggs, for instance, was our center-forward when we matched other street teams at football—even though he took opposite sides of the barricades in a "battle."

Differences between us (apart from physical ones) did exist. We, for instance, respected authority more than they. The Gentiles were contemptuous of it. If a policeman suddenly appeared at one of our street football games they would stand their ground and try to have it out with him:

"Gertch, y' mucking copper, you!"

They abused him from the opposite pavement, trying to provoke him into undignified chase. We would stand at a safe distance, shocked, but admiring. [. . .]

It was probably our traditional "minority" status that kept us in restraint. We were never allowed to forget that we were "foreigners." It was up to us to be on our best behavior. Our parents continually reminded us:

"One bad Jew gets the whole race into trouble. The Gentiles don't judge us by the best, but by the worst among us."

It seemed a queer world to us children.

We were therefore a much better behaved group than the Gentiles. [. . .]

The Griggs family, as a bunch, were rather typical of the worst aspects of the Gentile. From the parents down to the six-year-old girl they boozed. Occasionally the children tried to emulate the drunken exploits of their mother, whom they feared but secretly admired. She was a large, blowsy woman with heavy breasts hanging so low that she seemed in a perpetual state of pregnancy. All day she shuffled to and from the street corner in a pair of slippers. She never wore shoes. She didn't need them. Her travels took her no farther than the pub. [. . .]

I think it was the pub that represented the fundamentally different codes of our two peoples. Drink is an important element in the social life of a slum. By abstaining the Jews proclaimed their independence as a racial entity; for the Gentiles this abstinence established beyond doubt the much-talked-of miserliness of the Jew. Our people were quite unmoved by their contempt. To us they were obscene animals who squandered hardearned money that should have been spent on their homes. Drink for us was symbolized in Mrs. Griggs and her barefooted children.

Other works by Goldman: *The Light in the Dust* (1944); *That Thy Days May Be Long* (1945); *Some Blind Hand* (1946); *A Tent of Blue* (1946); *A Start in Life* (1947); *The Forgotten Word* (1948).

Raymond-Raoul Lambert
1894-1943

A veteran of the French army, Raymond-Raoul Lambert was a high-ranking official in the French Jewish community and one of the main intermediaries between it and the Vichy government during World War II. Secretary-general of the Committee for Refugee Assistance (Comité d'assistance aux réfugiés, CAR) and then of the General Union of the Jews of France (Union générale des israélites de France, UGIF), Lambert is remembered as a controversial figure who worked closely with French and German officials but probably saved numerous lives in the process. His diary is considered a valuable testimony, a record of events from the rare perspective of an influential Jewish leader and bureaucrat. Lambert and his family were arrested and sent to the internment camp at Drancy and from there to their deaths at Auschwitz.

Diary of a Witness
1940

Marseilles, October 19, 1940

I found out yesterday morning from a press release, dreadful forewarning of injustice, and yesterday evening from the text itself printed in the *Officiel*, what the *Statut des Juifs* says. The Marshal and his team, on Hitler's orders, have my person and the future of my children in their hands. . . . The Jews of France, even those who died for our country, have never been assimilated. Racism has become the law of the new state. What boundless disgrace! I cannot yet take in this denial of justice and scientific truth. . . . All my illusions are crumbling around me. I am afraid not only for myself but for my country. This cannot last, it's not possible. But in history this 1940 abolition of the Declaration of Human Rights will look like a new Revocation of the Edict of Nantes. . . . I shall never leave this country for which I risked my life, but can my sons live here if they are not allowed to choose freely what career to follow? Because of my blood I am no longer allowed to write, I am no longer an officer in the army. . . . If I were a secondary school or university teacher, I should be dismissed because I am a Jew! I cannot believe it yet. . . .

Two hypotheses are possible: either Germany will be conquered by the Anglo-American forces, and humanity will be saved; or, if Germany wins, a century-long night will descend on Europe. Judaism will maintain itself, as it did during the Middle Ages. But how we shall suffer from undeservedly becoming second-class citizens, after all the freedoms we have enjoyed. . . . Where is freedom of thought now, in France, where is it sleeping, the [. . .]¹ of Descartes and Hugo?

Yesterday evening I wept, like a man who is suddenly abandoned by the wife who has been the one love of his life, the one guiding light of his thinking, the one leader whom he has followed in his actions. [. . .]

Thursday, August 13 [1942]

Departure of the second transport at dawn, in two trains at 5:40 AM and 8 AM. The women and men have been shut up in the cars during the night and forbidden to come out even to relieve themselves. Frida Rosenbaum, age sixty-seven, is being deported. Some groups had only five minutes to pack their bags, and the guards have ransacked their barracks. The mobile [. . .]² dealt brutally with those who did not walk fast enough. . . . I would need a book to write it all down.

From August 23 to 29 I must go to Vichy for the liaison that has been arranged with the Commission. I leave Gaston Kahn at Milles to witness, in my stead, the departure on August 24 of the third train, in which foreign laborers are being deported.

In Vichy, business as usual at the ministries through useful and confident conversations. On Monday the 24th I see Puech and Ramband Darquier's co-workers, at the Commissariat; neither one amounts to anything. On Tuesday the 25th I see Louis Marin, whose optimistic idealism is a comfort to me. He knows about the persecutions and declares that the Marshal is a "Jesuit" who knows everything and is covering for Laval, intoxicated by the power he holds. In the afternoon, instead of Bousquet and Cado, the secretaries in the police office, I speak with Dangelzer, head of the office, who knew me in Paris when he was a small-time editor. I make three requests, with an energy that surprises even me: on behalf of my staff (I demand the same protection as those in Paris), on behalf of war veterans, and on behalf of those who have visas. That evening I have dinner with Pascot. He is moved by what I tell him, but is drunk from the power he holds.

On Wednesday the 26th I write up my notes addressed to Laval, summarizing my negotiations of the day before. I do not mince words. I bring them to Villar, in the president's office, who promises his support (he was purser aboard the *Normandie*). I introduce my-

self to Darquier de Pellepoix, who receives me with a haughty benevolence. He makes no effort to conceal his pique at being sidelined with regard to the deportation measures, which have been decided upon by the president and carried out by the police. . . . This is a strange regime, whose victims are called upon to witness to its administrative disorder! I go to see Xavier Vallat in a domestic staff office in the Park Hotel. He confides in me that now "the Boche are going a bit too far." Curiouser and curiouser!

On Thursday the 27th I renew my negotiations with Dangelzer and Villar. Spanien thinks I put things too strongly. . . . I think, to the contrary, that sounding sincere in what I say can only support what I have written. I shall not stay as general director unless all my staff is protected—and I declare this forcefully. On Friday the 28th I am back again, and I am promised a solution in my favor and that the police chiefs will be notified. I visit the Red Cross, but they have no information about the deportees. On the morning of the 29th I return to Marseilles.

On August 31 the Prefecture asks me to send a team to the Blancarde station to resupply a train filled with deportees when it stops there on its way from Nice, especially with drinking water. I send Marcel Dreyfus with a detachment. At noon he reports to me on the distress he has seen: thirty-two cars, of which twenty-nine are freight cars with rudimentary furnishings and three are third-class passenger cars, with thirty deportees each, men and women separated, guarded by armed police. A medical unit in an ordinary freight car has three desperate Red Cross nurses. On arriving in the station they say they have a patient at death's door, sustained only by injections of camphorated oil, but their request that he be taken to the hospital is not authorized by the Prefecture. He will die before they get there. . . . In the station, the doors and windows of the cars are opened. . . . The faces are painful to look at, and the odor is horrible. The unfortunate people fall upon our water and provisions . . . but without a cry or complaint. Only their faces, tense and ravaged, their eyes full of tears, testify to the suffering they have endured. . . . A woman tries to throw her child out the window, to entrust it to us.

This last detail pushes me to telephone to Villar, in Vichy, in place of Guerard who is not there. In emotional and occasionally violent terms, I declare to him that Mr. Laval "will have blood on his hands" if he doesn't allow parents being deported to leave their children with us, as was done for the first transports. . . . But my plea is in vain, since Hitler is in command!

On September 1 and 2 I go back up to Milles, where another transport is scheduled to leave on the 3rd, and try, together with Spanien, to rescue a few more. But the police are growing irritated, and they haven't filled their quota. . . . During the night of the 1st, roll call is held and the cars are filled in a chaotic way unfit for human beings. Babies are carried aboard without any milk. There are increasing scenes of desperation. I am ashamed to be so powerless, but I must stay there to see what happens. People I have saved from the first two transports are now being taken without any questions raised. . . . It is the most inhuman chaos. And the director of the camp is incompetent, he hasn't made his quota. . . .

At seven o'clock in the morning the police inspector, de Rodellec du Porzie, and his chief secretary Auzanneau turn up in white suits to inventory the cattle to be delivered. . . . Catastrophe and fury. There are two empty cars because the disorderly roll call in the night produced nothing. As if he were dealing with mutinous sailors, the commandant orders everyone off the train and back to the courtyard, where the bell is rung—women to the left, men to the right. Many are in pajamas or are only half-dressed. Two lots of thirty are chosen, surrounded immediately by armed guards, and are off to the train without being given time to get dressed or to get their baggage. . . . It's too much! After all, we aren't in Dachau here. The Quaker representatives are protesting, and I'm thinking of leaving. But I have to stay. Policemen are weeping. . . . I go toward the first group to be taken aboard; a man half-shaven, with a towel around his neck, is making signs to his wife at the back of the courtyard while a fifteen-year-old child looks at me numbly. . . . This must be the way they choose hostages to be shot during a civil war! . . . In the first row of the victims who have been selected is a Knight of the Legion of Honor, Fischer, the Viennese publisher. I can't stand it any more! I rush across the courtyard like a madman. "You can't deport a Knight of the Legion of Honor!" I tell the commandant.

"Go and get him!" I push the guards apart, grab Fischer by the arm, and put him behind me in the middle of the courtyard.

Numb with fear, he must have stayed there for an hour, without the courage even to think of moving away. . . .

Such scenes as this are the mark of a shameful regime. It's a dry run of the St. Bartholomew massacre.

Since everything gets out in spite of the censors, public opinion is becoming concerned. They have now handed over sixteen thousand Jewish refugees, regardless of the asylum law. The police have conducted manhunts and are still doing so, but people feel sorry for these unfortunates who are being so hounded. The clergy have lodged an official protest. Convents are hiding those who are fleeing, seminaries are keeping children. . . . Some day these raids must be written up in full detail. The saddest part is the contemptible cowardice of officials who, when told to carry out such inhuman measures, don't have the courage to resign or at least to admit to finding them abhorrent.

Translated by Isabel Best.

NOTES
1. [This instance of bracketed ellipses appears in the original translation.—Eds.]
2. [This instance of bracketed ellipses appears in the original translation.—Eds.]

Michael Molho

1890-1964

Michael Molho was born in Salonika into a family descended from Sephardic rabbis. In 1921, he served as secretary of the Greek Zionist Federation and then became the editor of the Greek Jewish journal *El Pueblo*. In 1940, before the Nazis destroyed his community, Molho wrote about the culture of Jews in Salonika, creating a valuable history. After World War II, he moved to Buenos Aires and served as rabbi of the Shalom Congregation.

Traditions and Customs of the Sephardic Jews of Salonica
1940

Local Jewish Cuisine

Sephardic cooking in Salonica was based, until the Greek occupation of 1912, on sesame seed oil, which in the Judeo-Spanish dialect was called by the name of *azeite de giungili*. Olive oil was not used in Jewish cooking.

Jewish cooks used all the vegetables according to the season: *bamia* (okra), *calvasicas* (squash), *merengena* (eggplant), tomatoes, spinach, celery, potatoes, leeks, etc. These vegetables were prepared by the lady of the house. Meat was not eaten except in the months of April and May, and prepared with *pinzela* (peas) and beans. Pork was completely excluded from the Jewish diet, and any fish without scales or gills was prohibited, in accordance with Jewish Law.

Quieftes, often prepared with ground meat in the form of meat patties, and cooked in different ways, was a common ingredient in many dishes. The *quieftes* could also be fried. It is important to note that the Sephardim did not fry food very often. Nevertheless, they had a special preference for *quieftes* made with spinach, leeks or fried cheese. The most popular and most accepted dish for the Sephardim of the East was the *fijón* (kidney beans)—called *judias* in modern Spanish—prepared with oil and chopped onion *moradeadas* (that is to say, the oil is first fried with the onion) to give it a rosy tint and a special flavor. In general, the Jews ate *fijón* twice a week, on Tuesday and on Friday at midday and at night preceding the Sabbath. The soups consisted of *alitrea* (pasta), vermicelli, noodles, and the ones prepared with chicken stock were generally preferred.

The normal breakfast consisted of bread and cheese. During the winter the women would breakfast with scalded bread, which consisted of pieces of stale bread, first cooked with water and then sprinkled with grated cheese and sprayed with oil.

On the Sabbath, the days of Jewish Festivals and family celebrations, breakfast consisted of *bureques*, or pies, made with either chopped meat or cheese or vegetables (spinach, eggplant, zucchini, squash) mixed with the meat or with the cheese. The pies were accompanied by *huevos enhaminados*, hard-boiled eggs (cooked with oil and onion skins, which gave them a very special aroma and taste). This festival meal was accompanied by glasses of *raki*. The meal for the children consisted normally of slices of bread, with oil and sprinkled with sugar. The children would say to their mother: "*Dame pan con azeite y asúcar*," "Give me bread with oil and sugar." In smaller proportions, bread with honey was given.

The working class used to drink in the evening, after a heavy day's work, a small glass or two of *raki*, but never more, and they never abused alcohol. Generally, the population did not drink wine during the week after lunch or supper. Only on the holidays did they drink freely, but not enough to embarrass themselves or lose their heads.

Until the end of the nineteenth century, it was not unusual for the matron of the house, on Friday at dawn, to prepare with her own hands the bread for the family for the coming week. In addition to the bread, they would prepare on the night before Sunday (*noche de alhad*) and for the visits; biscuits, *roscas* (sweet rolls), *tarales* (a kind of cookie), *dedicos*, *bizcoches* (a form of cookie), made with oil and sugar. These delicacies were often eaten moistened in water and spirits.

In the winter, after taking the bread and *bizcoches* out of the oven, they would start to roast the dry fruits: almonds, walnuts, hazel nuts, melon seeds, etc., which were greatly enjoyed by the Sephardim on the Sabbath.

The bread, as we have said, was prepared and baked with tremendous effort by the matron of the house at a time when flour was expensive, and so constituted a precious object in everyone's eyes. For this reason, pieces of bread were never thrown in the garbage, and when a Jew occasionally found a crust of bread in the street, he would pick it up, kiss it with great respect, and keep it carefully to be used to feed chickens or other domestic animals. Even today, the *Marranos* of Portugal have the custom of picking up pieces of bread that have fallen in the street, and kissing them before placing them in a position where they cannot be trodden on. [...]

The Daily Life of a Jew

Mosaic Law dominated all the actions and routine occupations of a Jew and penetrated every aspect of his private life. In addition to his normal activities, the Sephardic Jew had to submit himself to the religious prescriptions and traditional customs.

At dawn he was awakened by the voice of the beadle of the neighborhood synagogue, calling out in a loud voice: "*A tefilá, a tefilá!*" "To the prayers, to the prayers!," inviting the men of the community—that is, the breadwinners, the workers, the professionals and the shopkeepers—to rise for the morning prayers. Hurriedly, the Jew would rise and wash his hands and face, reciting a series of benedictions. Having done this, he would go to the synagogue nearest his home, with his *talet* and his *phylacteries*. On returning, the Jew would generally breakfast on bread and cheese. Sometimes he would dip the bread into wine in the manner of the old ways. The use of butter was practically unknown, even among the more affluent classes. After such a frugal meal he would go off to his business, and crossing the threshold of his house, he would touch the *mězuzá* with his fingers and then kiss them. His wife would accompany him with fond glances, saying: "*Con el pie derecho, buen día que tengas*," "Step out with the right foot, have a good day."

In all his commercial transactions, in all his businesses, the Jew dealt honorably with everyone. *La Ley* (Jewish Law) prohibited him from cheating anyone, Jew or non-Jew. To cheat a non-Jew was considered a national disgrace and a profanation of the holy name. The rabbis controlled weights, measures and scales, as well as the quality of the vegetables, fruit and other food products.

Translated by Alfred A. Zara.

Other works by Molho: *Kontribusiyon a la istoriya de Saloniko* (ca. 1931); *Literatura sefardita de Oriente* (1960).

Leyb Goldin

1906–1942

Leyb Goldin was born in Warsaw and grew up in poverty. First active in the city's communist youth organizations, he joined the Bund in 1936. A translator as well as a critic and essayist, Goldin published in the Bundist underground press during World War II. His autobiographical "Chronicle of a Single Day" was included in the Oyneg Shabes archive, of which he was a member. He perished in the great deportation in the summer of 1942.

Chronicle of a Single Day
1941

Bread, bread. The abundance of it dazzles your eyes. In the windows, on the stalls, in hands, in baskets. I won't be able to hold out if I can't grab a bite or breadstuff. "Grab? You don't look suspicious," says he, my murderer. "They'll let you near, they'll even put it in your hand. They'll trust you. They can see you aren't one of the grabbers."

Shut up, buddy, you've forgotten that I can't run. Now *you're* the wise guy, hah?

"You're a goner, you are, my breadwinner," says he. "Just take a look at those two having their identity papers checked at the gate. Look at the color of their faces. You can bet they've eaten today, and they'll damn well eat again, soon. But look over there—they're waiting for the car to pick them up. If you were a *mentsh*, you'd have looked after me earlier on, and you'd be eating like a human being, and not have swollen legs. And you'd also

be able to wheedle yourself in and go along for the ride. They give you half a liter of soup and a loaf of bread a week. Too bad you're such a *shlemazel*!"

Wrong again, you argue with him, your stomach. To begin with, there isn't soup every day. Often enough they come back without eating. And they're not treated with kid gloves either. Sometimes they get pushed around. You take your chances. But now, you're guaranteed the soup in the kitchen, you have a ticket. And for doing nothing, and without working. Well, where could you be more secure? [. . .][1]

A small group of people stand on the sidewalk and look across at the other side, from where a long beam of light falls. It's the children's hospital. Low down, on the first floor, in a wide, high window, a large electric lamp hangs over a table. A short woman in a white mask moves something very quickly with her hands. Around her, other women, also in masks. A calm hurry. And everything—to the table, to the one who lies on the table. An operation. You've never seen one before. At the movies, in a bunk, in the theater, yes, but in life, no. Strange, isn't it? You've lived some thirty odd years, seen so much—and now you're seeing an operation for the first tune: and it has to be in the *ghetto*! But why, why? Why save? Why, to whom, to what is the child being brought back?

And suddenly you remember that dead Jew, whom you nearly tripped over today. What's more, you now see him more clearly than before, when you were actually looking at him. Somewhere, years ago, there was a mother who fed him and, while cleaning his head, knew that her son was the cleverest, the most talented, the most beautiful. Told her aunt, her neighbors his funny sayings. Sought and delighted in every feature in which he resembled his father, his father. And the word *Berishl* was not just a name to her, but an idea, the content of a life, a philosophy. And now the brightest and most beautiful child in the world lies in a strange street, and his name isn't even known; and there's a stink, and instead of his mother, a brick kisses his head and a drizzling rain soaks the well-known newspaper around his face. And over there, they're operating on a child, just as if this hadn't happened, and they save it: and below in front of the gate stands the mother who knows that her Berishl is the cleverest and the most beautiful and the most talented—Why? For whom?

And suddenly (you—a grown, tall man, a male) you feel a quiver in your cheek, in your hands, all over your body. And your eyes become so rigid, so glassy. Yes, that's how it must be. This is the sign—you understand?—the equation, the eternal Law of Life. Maybe you are destined now, of all times, in your last days, to understand the meaning of this meaninglessness that is called life, the *meaning of your hideous, meaningless hungry days.* An eternal law, an eternal machine: death. Birth, life. Life. Life. Life. An eternal, eternal law. An eternal, eternal process. And a kind of clarity pours over your neck, your heart. And your two propellers no longer spin round in one spot—they walk, they walk! Your legs carry you just as in the past! Just as in the past!

Somewhere a clock is striking dully: one, two, half past. Four-thirty, three-thirty, five thirty? I don't know. Here there is no sunrise. The day comes to the door like a beggar. The days are already shorter. But I—I, like the fall, autumnal, foggy dawns. Everything around you becomes so dreamy, lost in thought, longing, serious, blue-eyed, concentrated in itself. Everything—people, the world, clouds—draws away somewhere, prepares for something responsible that carries a yoke, something that connects everything together. The gray patch that stands in the corner of the room with open arms—that's the *new day.* Yesterday I began to write your experiences. From the courtyard came the shouts of the air-raid wardens telling people to turn out the light. There's a smell of *cholent.* How come? It's Thursday, not the Sabbath. [. . .] A forest, a river, the whistle of a train, an endless golden field. Kuzmir. Tatrn. [. . .] The Lithuanian border. This longing, this wound will never go away, it will stay forever, even if today, tomorrow should once again. [. . .] Let it be in the city itself, go, go—go forever without stopping, at least see the bank of the Vistula, at least see just the city. The city that you know. The happiness of quickly turning a corner, then [. . .] the hundredth. With an open jacket, with happy, swift steps. *Your city,* your second mother, your great, eternal love. The longing pierces your heart. It remains.

Somewhere they are typing. [. . .] They're reporting. It is reported from Brussels . . . Belgrade, Paris. Yes, yes, we're eating grass. Yes, we're falling in the streets without a word of protest—we wave our hands like this, and fall. [. . .] Each day the profiles of our children, of our wives, acquire the mourning look of foxes, dingoes, kangaroos. Our howls are like the cry of jackals. Our hymn, *papierosy, papierosy* (cigarettes, cigarettes) is like something from a nature reserve, a

zoo. But we are not animals. We operate on our infants. It may be pointless or even criminal. But animals do not operate on their young!

Tokyo. Hong Kong. Vichy. Berlin. General number of enemy losses: six thousand eight hundred and forty-nine. Stockholm. Washington. Bangkok. The world's turning upside down. A planet melts in tears. And I—I am hungry, hungry. I am hungry.

NOTE

1. [Ellipses inserted by the volume editors. All other bracketed ellipses in this selection appear in the original translation.—Eds.]

Translated by Elinor Robinson.

Other works by Goldin: *Hantbukh fun der velt-literatur, prese, kunst un visnshaft* (1931).

Chaim A. Kaplan
1880–1942

Chaim Kaplan, born in Gorodishche, Belorussia, was the founder and principal of an innovative Hebrew elementary school in Warsaw, where he had settled in 1902 after studying at the Mir yeshiva and at the Government Pedagogical Institute in Vilna. An ardent Hebraist, he visited Palestine in 1936 with plans to emigrate, but he returned to Warsaw. In 1933, Kaplan began keeping a diary and, while in the ghetto, recorded the harrowing physical and psychological conditions under which Jews were forced to live. He smuggled this record out of the ghetto in 1942 before being deported to Treblinka.

Scroll of Agony
1941

November 13, 1941

The journal is my life, my companion and my confidant. Without it I would be lost. In it I pour out all my heart's feelings, until I feel somewhat relieved. When I am angry and irritable and my blood boils; when I am full of reproach and bitterness because I have so little strength and capacity to fight the vicious waves that threaten to engulf me; when my hands tremble with inner feelings—I take refuge in the journal and am immediately enwrapped in the inspiration of the *shekhinah* of creativity, though I doubt whether the task of documentation with which I am occupied is worthy of being called "creativity." In the future let them evaluate it as they may: the main point is that I find repose for my soul in it, and that is enough for me. [. . .]

But before my weary brain can labor and choose some object, a dark, cloudy autumn night spreads its wings over the ghetto dwellers. With evening comes darkness, and the ghetto then becomes a city of madmen and lunatics. The darkness is double: no light outside for fear of air attack. The gas lamps are not lit. Shop windows are extinguished. Shutters are sealed over doors. Quite simply, as it is written [Exod. 10:21]: "a darkness that can be touched." Inside the houses there is no spark of light: at midnight the electric current is cut off, and a watery tallow candle that melts and drips when it smells fire replaces it. To go out at night in darkness such as that is to risk mortal danger. People collide and crash into each other, and they are left wounded and bruised. This is no time to settle your affairs, whether buying or selling. You must put everything off till morning light. By the dim light of the candle the night shadows thicken. You are completely sunk in thoughts and shadows. The silence of the ghetto in the darkness increases the fear of night, full of secrets and hints. In my room there is no living being except the patient with her burning fever and death lying in wait for her.

"'If only it were morning!'" [Deut. 28:67].

November 18, 1941

Warsaw is depressed and wrapped in deep mourning. But it is no ceremonial mourning with only the outward trappings, lacking heartfelt grief. On the contrary, if we could, we would weep bitterly, and our cry would rise to the high heavens. Were it not for fear of the evil kingdom, our wailing would burst forth in the dark alleys, and we would cry and weep and wail dreadfully for our calamity, as vast as the sea. But because of the sword, drawn and waiting for our plaint to lop off our heads—our grief does not break out. Our hearts—are our graves. [. . .]

December 2, 1941

"The Kingdom of Israel" was the magic slogan for the Revisionists. But if those who used that enchanting rallying cry, "the Kingdom of Israel," could have known how it would be implemented in life by the Jews of Poland, by the *shmendriks* from the brothels who came to power, they would not have inscribed it on their banner even as a propaganda measure. The Nazis, wishing to bedeck us with shame before the entire world,

to show our baseness and the abysmal level of our culture, granted us broad "autonomy," almost a "state," as it were. They granted us that "privilege" with the premeditated intent to prove how incapable we are of being our own masters and to reveal our corrupt nature and our desire, stamped in our blood, to do injustice even to our brethren, not only in religion and race, but also in grief and disaster.

True, only a caricature of autonomy was granted us, and not out of excessive affection, but rather out of excessive hatred, the main point of which is only to separate the Jews from the nations, to undermine our material and spiritual existence, to hem in our steps, to have us perish slowly. In essence it is no more than a stillborn child lacking true vitality. By its principles and foundations it would seem to be only the kind of "self-rule" that prisoners have in a jail where some will be hanged and others will die a degraded death from exhaustion. That is known to everyone. [. . .]

In my coming notes I shall tell posterity something of the deceptions of the rulers and their abominations.

I'm not an insider: on the contrary, I come from outside. It could be—that's my advantage. Their "fine" deeds and straight rules are known to me by rumor and some facts I was an eyewitness to. I cling to a great principle: The voice of the people is like the voice of the Lord!

Translated by Jeffrey M. Green.

Other works by Kaplan: *Dikduk ha-lashon ve-shimushah* (1925); *Pezurai* (1937).

Berl Katznelson

1887–1944

Berl Katznelson was one of the central figures in the rise of Labor Zionism in the Land of Israel. Born in Babruysk, Russia, the son of a member of Ḥovevei Tsiyon, he settled in Ottoman Palestine in 1909 and, as a firm believer in the redemptive character of physical labor on the land, worked in agriculture and organized. He was one of the founders of the labor federation Histadrut, the consumer cooperative Ha-mashbir, the health plan Kuppat Ḥolim, the Labor Zionist daily *Davar* (which he edited from its founding in 1925 until his death), and the Am Oved publishing house. He was outspoken in urging the Zionist movement to come to a peaceful agreement with the Arabs in Palestine.

My Way to Palestine
1941

My First Day in Palestine

Whatever happened to me on that day seemed to urge me to muster up all my courage and hope. When the ship approached the harbor of Jaffa, many people were there to meet us; some even came toward us in little boats. There was a strange custom at the time—crowds of people would meet every boat coming in. Some would come because they were unemployed and had nothing else to do; others came out of sheer laziness to do any work. There were others who took a very powerful interest in new people—like men of the desert longing to see the face of someone from the civilized world. All of them would flock to the harbor to meet the new-comers. I am utterly unable to convey to you the scene of that "welcome." The first question on all sides was: "What did you come for?"; this was immediately followed by lies about Palestine, and mocking ridicule for those foolish greenhorns who had come. . . . The worst of them all was one hysterical girl with a group of a certain type of workers around her, who was shouting with others. It was almost impossible to go anywhere in Jaffa without meeting her. She did not speak Hebrew, but a hotch-potch of Russian and Yiddish words. It is difficult, too, to describe the Jaffa of those days—the noise and shouting, the Arabs with their camels, who nearly pushed me over as I was awkwardly carrying my luggage. This was my first impression. I felt that I had left the Galut to come to something even worse—slavery. I met Jews whose thought was not of Palestine, but rather how best to profit by your ignorance, how to cheat you out of something. There was such malignant joy, pleasure and glee over another's difficulties, such derision and mockery at Palestine, and such sneering at those fools who had come. I do not think I have since seen anything equally horrible and repulsive. (By the way, I did not feel like staying at the "Haim Baruch" Hotel, so I fell into a worse hole—the house of the father of that girl in the crowd.)

When I went out at night to look for people, I was told that there was a house somewhere in Jaffa, on the roof of which people used to meet and talk. The mere thought of sitting at night on the illuminated roof of a house is very attractive, especially to someone who has come straight from a northern country. Again I saw a familiar face—the closest friend of Pinhas Bashevsky, an old comrade of mine. The last time I had met him he had been an enthusiastic Zionist and fervent revolutionary of exceptional ability; he was at once intelligent and pleasant, witty and practical. He was not much given to study, but had so much common sense that he grasped most things much better than the "theoreticians."

"Well?" I said to him. His answer was a terrific blow to me. He told me that he was leaving the next day; he was taking a holiday and would travel. Apparently he had been successful with a large business, and had made a lot of money most of which he was giving to Comrades and devoting to Revolutionary movements. I was so thunderstruck by his answer that I could not utter a word to explain why *I* had come to Palestine. I could not say that I believed in Zionism because I did not. That man afterwards met a very tragic death.

During the same night I went for a walk on the beach. Actually the moment I set foot in Palestine I felt certain that my wanderings had come to an end! All that had been before, was now done with. This is no idle boast. I know that for me the problem of Palestine was finally settled on the day I landed in the country. I knew there was no other place for me.

At first, I had great difficulties with my Hebrew. I had never spoken Hebrew. On the contrary, to speak Hebrew somehow seemed to me abnormal and unnatural. So much so, that when my Hebrew teacher in Russia spoke Hebrew to me, I would answer him in Yiddish, because I thought that Hebrew was not a spoken language. When I came to Palestine, I could not make one simple sentence sound natural. I was determined not to use any other language and so for ten days, I did not speak at all. When I was asked a question, I would answer with a relevant quotation from the Scriptures.

Translator unknown.

Other works by Katznelson: *Kitvey B. Katznelson*, 12 vols. (1945–1953).

Peretz Opoczynski
1892–1943

Peretz Opoczynski was born in Lutomiersk, near Łódź, was given a yeshiva education far away from home, which precipitated a break with his Hasidic upbringing. A shoemaker by profession, he also worked as a Yiddish journalist, first in Łódź and then, as of 1935, in Warsaw, specializing in reportage of urban poverty. Confined during the war in the Warsaw ghetto, Opoczynski worked by day as a mailman and by night continued to write reportorial fiction about all aspects of ghetto life for the Oyneg Shabes archive. He was most likely rounded up in the deportation of January 1943.

Goyim in the Ghetto
1941

There's a folk saying: "The way it goes with the Christians, so it goes with the Jews." Many concessions were made to the goyim, especially in matters concerning the ghetto. The guards at the ghetto gates started to look the other way and didn't check entry passes so carefully. Just as it became easier for goyim to enter the ghetto, so too did it become easier for Jews to leave. It wasn't just that now the Germans were preoccupied with the war with Russia to the exclusion of everything else. The war also served as a subtle warning to the Germans that they should be careful and try to win over the population. After all, who knows when you might need friends?

The goyim responded to the German overtures. Every day you could see thousands of goyim on the Wołówka, and they went home with everything you could imagine. The production of remade clothes, shoes, and undergarments flourished as never before. Tailors would take out the cotton from old worn quilts and sew warm jackets and winter trousers, or they would use it as lining for windbreakers or winter coats. And the same process went on with other items.

Goyim, mainly young guys, would come into the ghetto on the transit trams that were not supposed to stop. They would jump off after giving a good bribe to the gentile policeman who sat on every tram that transited the ghetto. The policeman looked the other way. So did the conductor and often the Germans themselves. The gentile guys would wear polished boots, nice fur jackets, and golden rings on their fingers. Their faces were ruddy, clean shaven, and well fed: the very picture of good health. [...] They would move about, just like experienced merchants, from one Jewish seller to the next and would buy up the best stuff dirt cheap. [...]

Sometimes it happens that a gentile woman, who used to work as a servant in a Jewish home and who now is doing very well for herself as a trader, confronts a Jewish woman who she thinks wants too much money. The gentile can't help herself, and she'll say, "Sell, lady, and sell at the price I'm offering you, because if it weren't for me, then all of you here would croak from hunger. . . ."

The Jewish woman gets scared; she hasn't heard that kind of talk from goyim since the days of the anti-Semitic boycotts from before the war.

But then again this kind of talk is not really unexpected. In their folk tales about bad kings, dishonest princes, and hostile rulers, Jews had already heard plenty about persecutions of Jews, about how princes would sick vicious dogs on them or toss an entire family into a pit; about troubles suffered by Jewish tavernkeepers, leaseholders, innkeepers; about calamities suffered by entire communities when they were uprooted and forced into exile, to wander the four corners of the earth . . . and still here we are, we're alive! So what the hell, let the goy spout. We know in the end that the bad times will not last forever.

Okay, maybe the Jewish woman did not think about all these things exactly in the same way, but it didn't matter, it was all there, and inside her heart, like lightning, her faith and all she had learned in a lifetime flashed by. In a second she forgets the vile talk she just heard, calls out to another gentile woman and offers her bargains: wedding dresses of Jewish mothers thrown out in the middle of the night, from the homes they had lived in their whole lives, and forced to wander though dark forests; wedding presents received by young women—[. . .]—silent witnesses to terrible bitter poverty, to hearts weakened by hunger, to the first awful signs of scurvy. [. . .]

How many Jewish women find that they can't bear to part with the nice things and shed bitter tears before they take them away to be sold on the Wołówka? How many wonderful memories are bound up with every item?

But life has crushed us under its wheel and the world has turned upside down; the strongest countries, the freest countries, where everybody was an equal citizen and where nobody thought of discrimination, are now under Hitler's heel; he establishes ghettos everywhere. Will we someday be able to return to our old homes and rebuild them as bright and as neat as they were before the storm?

[. . .] The war knows nothing about kindness, the war doesn't bother itself with morality. The war teaches you to look after your own skin. So the old Jewish woman takes the few gulden for her treasures, which are really more like abstract memories than actual possessions, and she goes home in silence. But she feels better when she sees how her husband and children eat the modest meal she cooks up with the money. As she watches them come back to life she tells herself her only regret was that she wasn't able to salvage more of their possessions to sell and keep on going. . . .

The gentile who comes later and buys the woman's things from the Jew doesn't feel a thing; what he's holding in his hands is just stuff that's worth money, fat pieces of LARD—nothing more than that. If you're looking for some higher value to this buying and selling, then you can find it only in the bridge that has appeared between the Jew and the gentile. It's a bridge built out of bad material: speculation. But it has a good purpose: to keep a large part of the Jewish population from starving to death.

Look, it's possible that the Endeks, the Nara crowd, and all the other Jew haters with whose presence Poland was so abundantly blessed are lurking somewhere in their lairs and grinding their teeth as they watch this catastrophe. They are Hitler's faithful disciples and want to see our physical destruction. But the goyim of the Wołówka foil their plans and thwart their hopes.

Translated by Samuel D. Kassow.

Other works by Opoczynski: *Gezamlte shriftn* (1951); *Reshimot* (1970).

Moshe Flinker

1926–1944

Born in The Hague, Moshe Flinker began writing his Hebrew diary at age sixteen in 1942. He came from an Orthodox family and began writing to relieve boredom while in hiding after his family escaped to Belgium. Because of his youth and Dutch heritage, he has been compared to Anne Frank. Although Flinker died in Auschwitz, his diary was recovered by his sisters and published by Yad Vashem in 1958.

Diary
1942

November 30, 1942

As I thought, I couldn't manage it the next day, or the day after that. I continued to struggle to write even after three days. And now, too (four days later), I didn't think I'd begin to write, because I had already stopped for so long, but nevertheless I gathered strength and resolved that I wouldn't be so weak, so therefore I am continu-

ing what I started. Now I hope that I won't stop from time to time, but with God's help I will write as I intend to every single evening. Now I return to the question I asked above and to its answer: What can the Holy One blessed be He intend with all the troubles that come to us in these horrible days, and why doesn't He prevent them? [However,] the following question must come before any answer to that question and before the question itself. This [primary] question is: Are the troubles that are coming upon us now part of the troubles that have been coming upon us since we first went into exile, or, perhaps, are these troubles different and completely changed from those troubles that we have undergone until now? It seems to me that the second answer is correct, because in fact it is very hard for me to believe that all of what we see today is nothing but a link in the long chain of troubles. First of all, it is hard for me to believe that because of the great impression these decrees and persecutions have on me, but I myself thought that it is very difficult to pin the answer to this important question solely on *impression*. For is it not clear and certain that the persecutions, in Spain for example, and the expulsion from there, or the pogroms of 5408 [1648], or several other troubles also made a great impression on the members of our nation in their time? And maybe the impression that the troubles made on them at that time was greater than the ones today made on me, as can be seen from false messiahs and the like. Hence you must say that the impression is not decisive and doesn't matter, because sometimes there is something whose value is very small but the impression it causes is very great, and the opposite is also possible, as in Christianity, for example, which in my view is a vain thing, but it made such a great impression on important people, authors, poets, and the like. Therefore, we must go and observe their troubles and ours, which means looking at the difference between them. First of all, we see that their troubles were always local. In one place the Jews were severely persecuted, and in another place they dwelt in peace and tranquility. But the second difference is more decisive, and that is the official status of our troubles now and the organization that is effected to make the troubles more grievous. This difference truly pierces one's eyes. And a detail of all this is that the Germans do not at all seek to explain the reason for the persecution by anything, the way the Spanish did, for example, who placed the blame for their persecution on our religion, etc. But with the Germans we don't see any true effort to present a reason for their persecution of us, only that we are Jews. The fact that we were born Jewish is more than enough of a reason for all the persecutions and all the troubles.

To the first reason we can also add that at this time Jewry in general is harmed by this trouble. (Jewry in general is the majority of the Jews!) With this example, it is possible to explain [the difference] very well. In the past, in the Middle Ages, when enemies besieged some city or struck it with all sorts of fire and catapulted stones into it, they also tried to pierce the walls with large, heavy battering rams, and strong and brave men grasped the battering ram in their hands and began to strike the wall. The people who saw this at that time truly thought that it was impossible to be more powerful and aggressive, and when at most about a dozen more men came to help destroy the wall, this was the most that human power could do. But in our day we see that even a small child has the power to destroy a whole city. You only have to take a little dynamite and attach it to electricity, and then with the touch of a single finger, the strongest wall is destroyed in a moment. Thus it is with our troubles today. Then, too, for example in the persecutions at the time of the Crusades, it was impossible to do more than they did, but today without a sword and without a weapon people do things a thousand times worse than what was done then. The reason why this is possible is that today everything is done in an orderly way.

They arrange and organize, organize and arrange, so that maybe only one out of a thousand can flee for his life and hide, and the like. And why is it possible to arrange everything so, while in past days it wasn't that way? The reason for that is, and thus we return to the second principal answer, that with us everything is done in an official way, everything with us is legal. They condemn according to the laws. Just as it is forbidden to steal, so it is a dictate to persecute the Jews.

Because of all that is written above, we conclude that there really is a difference between all the sorrows that we underwent in the time since we were exiled and the sorrows of this horrible present. And therefore one may ask, since the differences are so many: Why did the Holy One blessed be He not prevent them or at least decrease them, or why does He on the contrary allow us to be persecuted and tormented? And what are the consequences that can emerge from these sorrows?

The answer to this question does not seem at all difficult to me. As is known, we were driven from our land because of our many sins, and, therefore, if we wish to return we must repent fully, and then we will be able to return to our land. But if we do not return by repen-

tance, the prophet already foresaw and therefore said that in the end of days we would be redeemed not by our righteousness but by the sins of our enemies and by their torture of us (as in Egypt). And truly it was more than enough that the Holy One blessed be He did not spare us the simple troubles that we underwent until now. But there is another difficulty, and this difficulty is that if we can be redeemed because of our many troubles, there is the great danger that the Jews themselves won't want redemption. As I have heard my Jewish acquaintances answer my question so many times: What returning will there be at the end of the war? Almost always I received as an answer that when the war ends everything will return to the old order. We will once again remain among the gentiles among whom we settled, life will continue as it was, and everything will be as in the beginning. But the Holy One blessed be He does not want that. For this reason, He pulled them out of their homes and cities (where they had lived in the past), and now with all their heart they want to return to our holy land, the Land of Israel.

Therefore, one may hope that since most of the Jews no longer dwell in the place of their first residence, and most of them desire to be redeemed, in truth that time for redemption has come, and with the help of our God we will be redeemed soon; maybe by the coming Hanukkah, God will perform this miracle for our people and redeem us and return us to our land. But there is one small thing that might interfere with this, and I will write about it tomorrow, with God's help, because in truth I am gripped by sleep (it is already past one o'clock in the morning), but before I stop writing I will pray to the God of Israel that he will answer this prayer: *Return us to You, O Lord, our God, and we will return. Renew our days as of old!* [Lamentations 5:21]

December 2, 1942, Morning

The small thing that I mentioned above is this: most of the Jews think that redemption and salvation depend on the victory or defeat of England. For if England wins, then most of the Jews (even those who wish to be redeemed) can say that it wasn't God who saved us but England. And the gentiles will say the same thing. And I mention the gentiles here, too, because I am swayed by the idea that for the gentiles as well something will come out of this war. For ultimately we must know and remember that even though the gentiles don't concern me in the slightest, and even if a million of them die in a single day it wouldn't affect me and wouldn't make any impression on me at all, one mustn't forget that the gentiles lost many, many things, both people and other things, like houses, and countless ships, and a great deal more, and the time has also come that they, too, should learn a little from all the wars that have taken place until now, especially from the two world wars that were almost consecutive. Therefore, I think that this war, in which we are living today, will end not with the victory of one of the combatants but with the victory of the Holy One blessed be He. Neither England nor America, but rather the God of Israel, will emerge victorious from this war. And when this happens, I think that before the final victory Germany will overcome on almost all fronts, and when it appears that she has already almost won, then God will come with His sword and take the victory away from her. Naturally and self-evidently, my entire outlook and what I wrote above is a religious outlook. I hope that I will be forgiven for this, because if I didn't have religion, in truth I couldn't ever reach even the smallest of conclusions to all the questions that leap upon me.

Translated by Jeffrey M. Green.

Herman Kruk

1897–1944

Herman Kruk was a librarian and labor activist. Serving as director of the Bund's Grosser Library at the Cultural League in Warsaw, he fled to Vilna at the beginning of World War II. While confined to the Vilna ghetto he organized a library for the Jewish community. His diary, which he kept until 1944, was hidden in the Vilna ghetto; parts of it were recovered after the war and published by YIVO in 1961. Kruk perished in Estonia.

The Last Days of the Jerusalem of Lithuania: Chronicles from the Vilna Ghetto and the Camps

1942–1943

September 30 [1942], 1:30 in the Afternoon

I WEEP

I weep, and am amazed. I have seen death so many times and have controlled myself. Have experienced so much torment, disgrace, and humiliation, and called myself the eternal optimist. And now?

What is my life worth even if I remain alive?

Whom to return to in my old home town of Warsaw?

For what and for whom do I carry on this whole pursuit of life, enduring, holding out—for what?!

Where are the workers and masses for whom I used to struggle, suffer, and rejoice?

Where are my near and dear ones?

Whom to return to?

Orphaned Warsaw streets, mournful Warsaw!

Talk to me, you slaughtered, at least in sleep. Talk to me, because death and melancholy do not frighten me. My heart has no more strength for sorrow—it is all ache. Blood has lost its color, it doesn't scare me.

My sister, where have you gone, abandoned and alone?

My comrades, where are you in your bitter struggle?

Talk to me at least in sleep!

The Vilna Ghetto is in an uproar and doesn't sense what is taking place all around.

And perhaps somewhere there is a verdict on our little remnant, too—to wipe it out to the last one? . . .

The experienced Vilna Ghetto doesn't think about that at all.

Is this possible?

My bones, rotting somewhere in the forests of Malkinia, come to me in a dream!

All right, then, let me weep—death doesn't scare me anymore. Let me weep! . . . [. . .]

December 29 [1942]

"GOD, LOOK DOWN FROM HEAVEN!"

The vocabulary has become impoverished. Concepts lose their clarity. Everything that was dreadful and terrible is pale and put to shame. Words stop affecting and influencing. It reminds me of another expression of helplessness in a similar period, at the time of the persecutions in Spain:

At the time of the attacks of the Almohades on the Spanish Jewish communities,[1] Rabbi Abraham ibn Ezra wrote about his experiences:

The nation weeps, persecuted and oppressed by the slaves,
And trembles and prays "God look down from heaven!"

I remembered that poem after the events of yesterday at the gate guard. God, look down from heaven and behold our helplessness, dejection, and humiliation.

March 15, [1943]

No COMPARISONS!

Years ago, I happened to read S. Anski's book *The Destruction of Poland, Galicia, and Bukovina.* I remember, as if it were now, how much pain and grief I experienced as I leafed through those volumes. That was how it happened then, years ago. Now I have leafed through these memoirs again.

The book is full of horrible events—race hatred, antisemitism, pogroms, victims, and such. But when I compare what is now going on around us with what I have just read, I can't figure it out: if that was destruction, what is this now? . . . I share my thoughts with friend Weinig from Vilna, who says: "If these events here are called destruction, these events in Poland, Galicia, and Bukovina were idyll. . . ."

The pogrom in Lwów produced . . . 18 dead. So it was called the bloody pogrom of Lwów.

In one place in those books, Dr. Oder [of Tarnów] laments: "A few Jews have suffered from the pogroms. There is no livelihood, people are being grabbed for work." In short, he says, "Jewish life is unbearable here." If it was unbearable there, what is our life?

I look for comparisons:

There are certain parallels, which can be traced through the whole chain of Jewish history: robbery, thievery and . . . annihilation. We have a lot of such parallels.

The Russian soldier, the officer, the general, sees Jewish spies everywhere to blame for their defeat. He shouts: "You, Yids, must all be slaughtered, driven out!" Today's exterminator sees us as enemy number 1—a race that undermines the existence of the world, a people that must be destroyed. They don't see Jews as spies but as partners of Roosevelt and Churchill. Who is making the war? The English-American plutocrats, for the sake of Jewish Bolshevism.

Returning to the destruction of Poland, Galicia, and Bukovina, I want to find a definition—if that was destruction, what is this?

There is really no comparison! . . .

March 29, [1943]

AN ART EXHIBIT

Yesterday, the 28th, at noon, in the lobby of the Ghetto Theater, the opening of the long-promised art exhibit took place. The entrance to the hall made a strange impression: Did we really need all this? But, entering the exhibit hall, you are embraced by warmth: pictures, paintings, sculptures, and projects, including a lot of original ghetto art. Y[ankl] Sher—a series of drawings of ghetto holes, [Dr. Eliyohu] Sedlis—paper posters for ghetto trades (glazier, cabinetmaker, mason, painter, tailor, woodworker). Then, a tapestry by the PPV.[2] And an exhibit of their woodcutting; churches and a part of the unfinished Synagogue Yard, which is to form the scale model "Synagogue Yard" (work of young Notes). The splendid painter [Rachel] Sutzkever is represented beautifully with oils and watercolors. The works of G. Dresin (14 caricatures and 6 cuts of tin figures) are good and successful. Yudl Mut exhibits good works here: drawings, pictures, and two sculptures.

The drawing of the nine-year-old S[amuel] Bak attracted the most attention. The child is apparently an extraordinary talent, in every respect.[3]

The exhibit is heartwarming. But when you leave it, you are once again cooled off. There is another exhibit in the courtyard of Rudnicka 6. Lying here on their bundles are families with all their belongings, the newly arrived refugees from Michaliszki. The leader of the Cultural Department, Mr. [Grisha] Yashunski, talked about that in his opening speech, and the chief of the ghetto, [Jacob] Gens, at the closing.

March 31 [1943]

I TREMBLE FOR TOMORROW

Events here in the ghetto have again begun to move so fast that you can't grasp and digest everything. Recently everything has pointed toward one thing—tremble for tomorrow. But dreadful as that may be, we become more inured every day.

No, we will not be taken like sheep! No we will not let them.

In several conversations I have had recently, everyone answers: If only the initiative succeeds—it will be a happy moment. For me there is nothing to decide, I am decided!" I get such answers wherever I go.

The air here smells of powder. Everything indicates that we are on the brink. We are doing all we can so as not to be taken like sheep. [. . .]

April 19 [1943]

PASSOVER

Under the pressure of all the events and the realizations of what awaits us, we are celebrating the second Passover in the ghetto. The best thing we can wish one another is that we may see each other a year from now.

By now, there seem to be no optimists among us. Everyone here is convinced that we are coming to an end. For, why should we be different from everybody else?

Europe will be purged of Jews. The Jews of Warsaw are being taken to be killed in Malkinia, near Lwów or near Zamość. The Jews from Western Europe are being taken east; their wandering goes on. Transport has recently become very expensive to the Germans, maybe even more precious than money. But transporting for the purpose of ruining and deluding Jews is cheap—it's a war aim!

The Vilna Ghetto has lost all illusions. It is a war aim, and as such, it is the highest priority.

[SS officer Franz] Murer is on furlough. The "Gestapo" has slacked off a bit, and in the ghetto, we spent this year's Passover getting drunk.

A lot of Seders were made in the ghetto, private and public. Everyone who can buys, eats, and drinks, and . . . forgets.

Religious Jews put all their passion into this year's Passover. The religious kitchen on Szawelska 5 is preparing a Seder for 100 Jews today, including the chief, the police chief, and rabbis.

A kilo of matzos in the ghetto costs 300 rubles, like 6 kilos of bread. Nevertheless, it seems there is not a single home without matzos.

The Youth Club is making a Seder. The Zionists use the religious kitchen for a Seder. Even Gens himself organized a big Seder at his home today.

Seders are also being made for schoolchildren. The first Seder night in the building of the Youth Club is for older students; the second, for younger students. The Hebrew studio also made a Seder with the Hebrew choir and the boys' and girls' boarding schools of Yeladim.

The remaining Święciany and Ozmiana Jews in the Vilna Ghetto certainly swim through today's Seder in their own tears. . . .

NOTES

1. A eulogy by the Hebrew poet Abraham Ibn Ezra (1089–1164) for the Jewish communities in Spain and North Africa, which were annihilated by the Almohade oppressors in the mid-1140s. "O woe," it begins, "misfortune from heaven has fallen upon Sefarad [Spain]" [note appears in the translated document].

2. PPV was a special collective tasked with constructing a large Plastic Plan of Vilna. Parts of it were dissembled and survived the war. [Note appears in the translated document.]

3. [See: II. Israel (1947–1973)—Eds.]

Translated by Barbara Harshav.

Abraham Lewin

A Cup of Tears: A Diary of the Warsaw Ghetto
1942

Tuesday, 29 December [1942]

If one looks closely at the passers-by in the streets of the Warsaw ghetto one can see that the overwhelming majority of them are not originally from Warsaw, but are from small towns. They were driven out from their homes a long time ago and saved themselves during the expulsion by hiding out in various dark corners. In general one sees rough faces and vulgar types from the common folk. Members of the middle classes, intelligentsia, the more educated elements, are not to be seen. Very few have survived from bourgeois and cultivated Jewish Warsaw. Teachers, for example, have been almost completely wiped out. I am the only survivor from my school. Out of all the female teachers, the directress, and the male teachers who were working in the classroom until recently, none survive. The same situation can be found at practically all levels of Warsaw Jewry.

Warsaw was in fact the backbone of Polish Jewry, its heart, one could say. The destruction of Warsaw would have meant the destruction of the whole of Polish Jewry, even if the provinces had been spared this evil. Now that the enemy's sword of destruction has run amok through the small towns and villages and is cutting them down with murderous blows—with the death-agony of the metropolis, the entire body is dying and plunging into hell. One can say that with the setting of the sun of Polish Jewry the splendor and the glory of world Jewry has vanished. We, the Polish Jews, were after all the most vibrant nerve of our people.

In terms of the number of victims, Hitler has murdered an entire people. There are many peoples in Europe who number fewer than the number of our martyrs. The Danes and the Norwegians are no more than three million. The Lithuanians, the Letts and the Estonians have far fewer. The Swedes—six million. The Slovaks fewer than two million, and so on. And Hitler has already killed five, six million Jews. Our language has no words with which to express the calamity and disaster that has struck us.

Translated by Christopher Hutton.

Israel Lichtenstein

1904-1943

Born in Radzyn, Poland, Israel Lichtenstein was a teacher, activist, and Yiddish-language journalist in interwar Poland. Trained at the Vilna Yiddish Teachers Seminary, he settled in 1932 in Warsaw, where he became active in the Left Po'ale Tsiyon party organization, wrote for several major Yiddish journals, and directed the city's Borochov school. In 1938, he married Warsaw native Gele Sekstein (Seckstein), a teacher at the same institution and a budding artist. Both active in the Oyneg Shabes archive in the Warsaw ghetto, they left behind a last testament.

Last Testament

1942

With zeal and zest I threw myself into the work to help assemble archive materials. I was entrusted to be the custodian, I hid the material. Besides me, no one knew. I confided only in my friend Hersh Wasser, my superior.

It is well hidden. Please God that it be preserved. That will be the finest and best that we achieved in the present gruesome time.

I know that we will not endure. To survive and remain alive [after] such horrible murders and massacres is impossible. Therefore I write this testament of mine. Perhaps I am not worthy of being remembered, but just for my grit in working with the society Oneg Shabbat and for being the most endangered because I hid the entire material. It would be a small thing to give my own head. I risk the head of my dear wife Gele Seckstein and my treasure, my little daughter, Margalit.

I don't want any gratitude, any monument, any praise. I want only a remembrance, so that my family, brother and sister abroad, may know what has become of my remains.

I want my wife to be remembered. Gele Seckstein, artist, dozens of works, talented, didn't manage to exhibit, did not show in public. During the three years of war worked among children as educator, teacher, made stage sets, costumes for the children's productions, received awards. Now together with me, we are preparing to receive death.

I want my little daughter to be remembered. Margalit, 20 months old today. Has mastered Yiddish perfectly, speaks a pure Yiddish, At 9 months began to speak Yiddish clearly. In intelligence she is on a par with 3- or 4-year-old children. I don't want to brag about her. Witnesses to this, who tell me about it, are the teaching staff of the school at Nowolipki 68. . . .

I am not sorry about my life and that of my wife. But I am sorry for the gifted little girl. She deserves to be remembered also.

May we be the redeemers for all the rest of the Jews in the whole world. I believe in the survival of our people. Jews will not be annihilated. We, the Jews of Poland, Czechoslovakia, Lithuania, Latvia, are the scapegoat for all Israel in all the other lands.

July 31, 1942

The eleventh day of the so-called "resettlement action." In reality, an annihilation action.

Translated by Lucy S. Dawidowicz.

Isaac ben Jacob Mamo

1880-1967

Born in Nabeul, Tunisia, Isaac ben Jacob Mamo was among the earliest Zionist leaders in the area. He served as secretary of the Tunisian delegation at the first Zionist Congress in Basel, Switzerland, and continued to attend through 1911. He spent his last years in Jerusalem.

Introduction to Translation of Avraham Mapu's The Hypocrite *into Judeo-Arabic*

1942-1943

In the early days of November 1942 (on November 14th) the German army conquered Tunisia with the aim of repelling the Allied Armies (the English and American) in Morocco, Algeria, and western Tunisia. The Germans advanced toward the Allied forces in order to attack them. Units of the German army who took up positions along the whole of the Mediterranean coast (of Tunisia) established a position in the city of Nabeul, making it a military center and setting up command headquarters in it. Immediately afterward there began a strict watch on the roads and security checkpoints at the entrances and exits of the city.

At the outset, I thought of leaving Nabeul in order to protect my personal safety, but it became increasingly dangerous to move on the roads. The German forces made the lives of the Jewish population particularly difficult due to their many demands. Initially they demanded beds and bedding, foodstuffs, cars, bicycles, carriages, etc. . . . without any recompense. Afterward, they took all the men, without regard for age, for forced labor and demanded that the municipality pay their daily wage. Among other things, the German authorities demanded large sums of money from the population—under the threat of imprisonment or of taking hostages—as well as kitchenware and tableware, specifically glass and crockery. We can compare these actions to those which occurred in the period in which the Jews who were in Egypt asked the Egyptians to do them a favor and enable them to settle, but the latter pillaged their property, and the Jews suffered the insult without reacting, in silence, until the Lord had compassion on them.

This situation bothered me greatly, and I thought to write about these events so that a testimony would remain for the future, but I asked myself where my place was among the erudite scholars who had already written about these events. After much thought I said to myself that it was preferable to engage in something that would ease my anxieties and help me to forget this tragic period. And so I began to translate the book of Rabbi Avraham Mapu bearing the Hebrew title *'Ayit tsavu'a* [*The Hypocrite*]. I began the work of translation in November 1942 and finished it in March 1943.

As I informed the reader, I completed this translation in March 1943, but I was unable to get it to the printer because communication was very difficult (as well as the travel on the roads). I had not even seen my friends from Tunis since the previous October (1942). Consequently, I am adding this second introduction in order to inform the reader about what happened in the last days of the German occupation of our city. On May 10, 1943, a German in a gendarme's uniform arrived at the office of the Jewish community, accompanied by two soldiers, and demanded to look at the accounts of the community fund. Afterwards he shouted: "I demand that this afternoon, before six (in the evening) you prepare a million francs for me." The responsible heads of the community answered that they didn't have such a sum, and that in this city it was impossible to collect anything like it. The officer told them that he would wait until nine A.M. the following morning, but that they then would have to bring two million francs, and that if this sum was not ready, the Jewish community would be dealt a harsh blow. After saying this, he went away. The community committee gathered the people it managed to collect that day, and they all decided to present themselves before the local authorities to help them delay the deadline. The police commander (brigadier) went with the

community committee to the German command headquarters to tell them that he was shocked by what had happened, and suggested that he be present the following day to request a delay of the appointed time. The committee then appeared before the commander of the gendarmerie, who was also surprised (by the ransom demand) and suggested that he be present the following day to also request a delay. The whole community spent a very bad night. Then dawn broke, the birds began to twitter, the sky brightened, the sun began to appear, its rays became stronger, and the tension grew. Adults and children came out of their houses, shocked and bewildered, each one taking care not to move far from their home, only relying on God in Heaven, who alone had the power to avert the evil decree and to change the situation. It was Tuesday—the day we say is doubly blessed (*pa'amayim ki tov*)—6 Iyar 5703, corresponding to May 11, 1943. The people waited for the future anxiously, asking themselves what their fate would be. It was now ten minutes to nine, every forward move of the clock hands was felt like a hammer blow to the heart of everyone. At one minute to nine this officer appeared, went up to one of the community leaders, and demanded the sum of money from him. He answered that he was going to the bank to get the money, but in actual fact he began to walk in the direction of the German (commandant's) headquarters. Suddenly the gendarme commander was fear-stricken because a few moments before the payment was due, tanks and trucks arrived, accompanied by a great noise with cries of "Long live France!" Afterward the English, the Americans, and the French, who had conquered the city, suddenly appeared, escorted in with singing and cries of joy (of the population). The Germans retreated, and the Jews rejoiced greatly, who in their sorrow remembered the verse: "It will be a time of trouble for Jacob, but he will be saved out of it" (Jeremiah 30:7)—for they surely merited that which had saved them from this distress.

As for myself, I thought that it was necessary to describe this historic event so that it would remain a memory of joy and delight for the Jews of Nabeul.

Amen, and goodbye from your brother, the translator (of *'Ayit tsavu'a*).

The servant of the Lord, Yitsḥak Ḥizkiyah Mamo (May the Lord preserve him and keep him alive).

Translated by David Herman.

Other work by Mamo: *Sefer navah kodesh* (1906).

Yehoshue Perle

1888–1943

Yiddish writer Yehoshue Perle was born in Radom, Poland. He moved to Warsaw in 1905, where he became one of the most popular and prolific Yiddish novelists of the interwar period. His bildungsroman *Everyday Jews* (1935) is one of the consummate achievements of modern Yiddish fiction. Perle fled to L'viv in 1939 but in 1941 returned with his family to Warsaw. In 1942, Perle began writing *Khurbn Varshe*, a detailed account of the atrocities in the Warsaw ghetto. He and his son managed to escape and lived in hiding on the Aryan side of Warsaw until 1943, when they were deported to Bergen Belsen. Perle died in Auschwitz.

4580
1942

A round number. At first glance it looks silly and seems to have no specific meaning. A detached number such as this can be likened to those gray people who go through life alone and die without confession. [. . .]

Sober minds, if they consider it, will probably take it to be the Identity Number of a policeman, a railroad porter, a prisoner or—pardon the proximity—a dog, or the devil knows what else. But that this foolish number should be a substitute for the name of a living person, who was never a policeman, a railroad porter, a prisoner or even a dog—that will be difficult to believe.

People will also not believe that great suffering and pain cry out from the number, and so does the disaster of the people from whom it is my lot to be descended.

And yet the impossible has become possible. It happened in the year 1942, in the month of Tishre, in the land of Poland, in the city of Warsaw. Under the savage rule of Amalek—may his name and memory be blotted out; with the consent of the Jewish *kehillah*—may its good deeds stand it in good stead in this world and in the next

May it merit eternal life, the Warsaw Jewish *kehillah*. For it was the *kehillah* that favored me with the number: *four thousand five hundred and eighty*. It was the *kehillah* that cut off my head—my name—and set a number in its place. I go around with it and live: it has become "me." [. . .]

Amalek, may his stock be obliterated from human memory, gave the order and the Warsaw *kehillah* carried it out. Of three times a hundred thousand living Jewish souls it was granted that some thirty thousand

ciphers of the Chosen People be left, slumped and sealed with the seal of the head of the *kehillah* himself—whose name will one day be used to frighten children in their cradles.

My name and all that is me also found favor in the eyes of the VIPs and were metamorphosed into a number. And just as Sholem Aleichem's Motl, the son of Peyse the Cantor, runs around barefoot and happily proclaims. "I'm alright. I'm an orphan," so I walk around in the tenement courtyard on Franciszkanska Street, which has become the great wide world, and proclaim:

"I'm alright. I'm a number."

I'm leading a life of luxury. The aristocratic number gives me dignity, importance. It elevates me above the rubbish heap where the other thirty thousand or so are swarming—and persuading themselves that they alone are worthy to remain members of the Chosen People Club.

My number receives a quarter of a clayey loaf of bread a day and some very tasty grits consisting mostly of boiled water, a potato that someone has already stolen from the pot and a few grains of cereal that chase about and can never, poor things, catch up with one another. What's more, from time to time they dole out to my number a stale egg with a drop of blood on it, a lick of honey and, once in a blue moon, a strap of aging meat that—even if you were to hack it into pieces—would by no means have the flavor of old wine.

I'm all right; I'm a number. [. . .]

Thus-and-thus, dear number, I decree that you shall present yourself at six o'clock tomorrow, to help build the bleak wall that confines you as with a chain and wants to strangle and choke you. You must wall yourself up. You must also come and wash away the blood of your mother and your father, whom Amalek deigned to slaughter, gladly assisted by the loyal crew. And if there is still something left in your father's house, or in your own house, you must help Amalek to steal it and bring it to him as a precious gift.

"If you are recalcitrant, if you will not come forward"—warns my good head of the *kehillah*—"If you do not wall yourself up with your own hands, if you do not bring Amalek the candlesticks that your dead mother used when she blessed the Sabbath candles, if you do not bring him the diamond brooch with which your mother adorned herself for the blessing of the New Moon, if you do not offer him the pillow on which your child slept, I shall erase you from the Register and you will cease to be a number."

That's how my head of the *kehillah* warns me every day to tell the truth. I'm delighted by these fearsome warnings that I'll stop being a number. I'll become "I" again! I'll get my name back! To put it simply—I'll rise from the dead. Since the world began, not a single Jew has risen from the dead: the Messiah hasn't arrived yet. I'll be the first resurrected Jew. So why shouldn't my heart rejoice? On the other hand, I remember that if I stop being a number there's an executioner's ax waiting for me. No longer being a number means good-bye to the clayey quarter loaf each day, good-bye to the smell of the year-old egg, good-bye to the little room they allotted me to live in, good-bye to the potato that other people steal from my plate of grits, good-bye to honor: no longer an aristocrat, no longer of the Club of the Chosen.

Without a number I'll be like my neighbor, who was once as clever as I and as learned as I, as polite as I—maybe more polite. But evil fortune willed that he should not find favor, not be metamorphosed into a number; he kept his name. His beautiful human name. But a beautiful human name has the same value today as a beautiful human heart, or a beautiful human virtue. Today the beautiful human hearts, the beautiful human virtues lie bleeding among the scraps that lie scattered in the desolate Jewish courtyards.

My neighbor's honest name doesn't get the quarter of a loaf, doesn't taste the flavor of a little grits, has nowhere to lay its head, hides itself in holes together with cats and stray dogs. My neighbor's name has been erased from the Communal Register. The friends of yesterday, who have numbers, no longer say good morning to him, no longer sit with him at the same table, no longer pray with him in the same house of prayer. He has become a leper, this neighbor of mine, with the honest name and without the paper number.

Translated by Elinor Robinson.

Other works by Perle: *Nayn a zeyger in der fri* (1930); *Di gildene pave* (1937); *Gilgulim* (1939).

Puah Rakovsky

1865–1955

Puah Rakovsky was born into an observant Jewish family in Białystok in 1865 and given both a religious and a general education. Fluent in several languages, she began her career as a translator and later trained as a teacher. A strong advocate for women's education and equality, Rakovsky went to Mandatory Palestine in 1920, where she helped establish the Women's International Zionist Organization (WIZO) as well as a vocational school for girls. She settled there permanently in 1935 and wrote her memoir, which provides a feminist perspective on Polish Jewry. She died in Haifa.

My Life as a Radical Jewish Woman: Memoirs of a Zionist Feminist in Poland 1942

As for me, my youth began very early. At the age of ten, I was already a grownup, a *Polner mentsh*, as the Jews said. Besides my diligent studies, back then I was a "God-seeker." I felt confined, and something was raging in me; I wanted something more than study. At the age of thirteen, every Sabbath day I would gather all the serving maids of the courtyard and read them a portion of the *Taitsch-Humash*, choosing chapters from *Menoras HaMaor*, of Psalms, and the Bible. On the Days of Awe, I went to the women's *shul*, where I was accepted as a *firzogerin* [a prayer leader] for the women who couldn't read by themselves. At that time, when I was thirteen, an absurd idea suddenly was born in me: is there a God or not? That was what I wanted to find out, no more and no less. I remember it as if it were now: I wouldn't have told anyone, for the very idea terrified me. But the idea didn't leave me alone. For perhaps a half year I couldn't sleep at night, as I considered and considered and at long last came to the conclusion that there is no God. If that is so, I said to myself, you don't have to be pious. And I stopped praying three times a day; I started combing my hair, washing myself with soap, and reading books (on the Sabbath); and I often took to expressing my thoughts. That aggravated the relations between my parents and me. Mother was especially annoyed with me. At that time, I didn't care so much that I myself was no longer pious, but I did want to attract attention. I stirred up the younger children in the house, my girlfriends, and anyone who would talk with me, listen to me. When my mother preached morals to me, I would always say: "Mama, how come I understand that you can't be like me, but you won't understand that I can't be like you?" [. . .]

A Kheyder for Girls

I was twenty-six years old in 1891 when I came to Warsaw to teach Hebrew and Russian at the girls' *khey-*

der of Bnei Moshe in Poland. I left my eight-year-old son with my parents in Bialystok. My father wanted to educate him to be a rabbi because the boy had a good mind, and at the age of seven had learned seven whole pages of Talmud a week. I took my six-year-old daughter with me. Even though I was very happy to get my teaching job—the work was intellectually gratifying—I was even more satisfied by my economic independence.

I felt that I was a teacher by the grace of God and even then I realized that, like an artist or a writer, a teacher had to be born; yet, I also felt that I had to study more, and not be satisfied simply with a teacher's diploma. I thought that I needed to go abroad to study pedagogy. I knew I could earn enough teaching Hebrew in Switzerland, for example, to be able to live modestly and study at the same time. With that goal in mind, I settled in Warsaw that first year, finding room and board for myself and my little daughter in a boarding house at Karmelicka 27, in a home run by a former principal of a Polish school, a very assimilated Polish Jewish widow with two sons. She herself had lost her right to run a school because the Russian school inspector caught her teaching Polish in one of her classes. I lived frugally so that I could save enough from my income that year to be able to travel abroad to study.

But one thing bothered me very much: Should I take both children with me or leave the boy to be educated by my father? I was afraid that such an education would separate my own child from me since my father and I were far apart spiritually, and that distance was liable to open a chasm between me and my son. I was torn apart: It was bad enough that I had taken my child's father away, but should he also robbed of his mother? The idea often hurt me—who knows if, years later, my children wouldn't condemn me for my fateful step of leaving their father!

This internal struggle lasted almost a whole year and ended with the triumph of maternal love. I decided I could complete my studies at a university in Warsaw, where instruction would be in Russian. I wrote my parents to bring my son to me, rented a small apartment in a poor neighborhood, and made do on my salary. [. . .]

Living my independent life, along with my teaching, I didn't forget my inner obligation to fight for the freedom of women, especially Jewish women, always the most enslaved of all by self-appointed guardians who burdened them and apparently wanted to save their souls. I saw the economic independence of women as the main factor behind their personal and social liberation, and I set myself the goal of working with all my might for their liberation. I wanted to spread that idea among the various classes of Jewish women. Today's youth who have cast off the solution of "Torah and work" cannot even imagine how we Jews regarded work and crafts more than fifty years ago. The greatest disgrace in a family was to have a relative who worked as a craftsman; families of high status boasted with the greatest pride that they had no such stain. [. . .]

Uprooting that crippled notion, cleaning the mold off the psychology of generations, was not easy. Enlightenment-work like that went on for decades. Even in our national and historical home, where we have come to reeducate ourselves emotionally and economically so that we can rebuild ourselves; even in the Land of Israel, we have dragged our Exile notions. Strange as it may sound, I can boast that I was one of the pioneers of the movement in Poland to make the Jewish masses productive. Intuition led me to start that work among individual Jews.

* * *

Our family was large and very extensive. I had relatives in almost every city and town of Russian-Poland at that time, and my example reverberated among the members of my family. As soon as I moved to Warsaw, I started getting letters from female cousins and other relatives who were coming to Warsaw to study some profession. They asked me to help them get settled and I gladly agreed. My little apartment at Pokorna 6 soon became a gathering spot for all the candidates. It was a good time because various industries in Warsaw were operating at a fast pace; Russia was an enormous market that gobbled up all kinds of merchandise. There was a shortage of labor in the production of women's clothing, scarves, millinery, straw hats, etc. There weren't enough hours in the day: People worked three or four shifts—during the day, and at night they took work home.

I had no lack of acquaintance with merchants because the only school in Warsaw where girls learned the Holy Tongue was very popular; therefore, I could get work for all the girls who needed my help. Incidentally, there was also a small workshop in my home: Two of my cousins worked on scarves and a third studied hatmaking. From eight o'clock in the morning, my two children and I were at school, and my empty room was turned into a workshop. My two cousins, from Plock, were orphans from my father's sister; the third was a young woman who was stuck in a bad marriage and whose husband wouldn't give her a divorce. We all lived together. At night we set up beds. The main thing was that everyone was cheerful, lively, and energetic. My two children attended my school; I found a *melamed* [tutor] who taught my son Talmud, and I studied alongside him.

What an interesting and rich life, especially since we struggled so hard for it!

Translated by Barbara Harshav with Paula E. Hyman.

Josef Zelkowicz

1897–1944

Josef Zelkowicz grew up in a wealthy Hasidic family and was ordained as a rabbi. A professional journalist before the war, Zelkowicz took a keen interest in urban poverty, Jewish ethnography, and Hasidic lore. These interests stood him in good stead as a key and extremely productive member of the Łódź ghetto archive. His most sustained piece of writing was his hour-by-hour description of the Szpere, the great deportation from the ghetto in September 1942. He was deported to Auschwitz in August 1944.

In These Nightmarish Days

1942

Here you have him, the proud Jew. The Jew who ruled his kingdom with a high hand in complete despotism: here is the Jew who never heeded anyone's advice, who did everything with his own hand and followed only his own lights. Here that Jew stands in front of the crowd as a broken man. [. . .]

"The ghetto has received a painful blow. They demand its most precious members—the children and the elderly. I have not had the privilege of having a child of my own and have therefore devoted my best years to the care of the child. I have lived and breathed children. I never imagined that my own hand would be the one to bring them to the sacrificial altar. In my old age I am forced to reach out my hand and beg you: brothers and sisters, give them away to me! Fathers and mothers, give me your children! [. . .]

"Early yesterday they gave me the order to deport some twenty thousand Jews from the ghetto, and if not, 'We'll do it ourselves,' I was told. This posed the question: Should I undertake the task myself, or leave it to others to carry out? Viewing the situation chiefly from the standpoint not of 'How many will be lost?' but only through the guiding principle of 'How many will we be able to save?' we have come to the conclusion—that is, my closest colleagues and I—that however difficult it may be for us, we must carry out the deportation with our own hands alone. I must carry out this difficult and bloody operation—must cut off limbs in order to save the body! I must take the children, for if I do not, others, God forbid, will be taken as well."

[Dreadful wailing from the crowd.]

"I have not come today to console you. I have not come to calm you down today either but to uncover the fullness of your sorrow and woe. I have come as a thief to take the greatest treasure you possess in the depths of your hearts. I have tried with every ounce of ability to hold this decree at bay. I have tried, after retracting it became impossible, to cushion its blow. Just yesterday I ordered all nine-year-old children to be registered; I had hoped to save at least this group between ages nine and ten. This I was not allowed. I succeeded in one thing only—saving children ten years of age and older. Let this be our one consolation in our great sorrow.

"We have many sick with tuberculosis in the ghetto whose remaining life can be numbered in days, or in weeks at most. I don't know—maybe it's all the devil's plan, maybe not—but I can't prevent myself from saying to you, 'Give me the sick, and in their place, the well will be able to be saved.' I know how tenderly the sick are tended to at home—especially by Jews. But anytime there is a new decree, the following question must be considered carefully: Who can, should, and is it in fact possible to save? [. . .]

"I must tell you a secret: they demanded twenty-four thousand victims in eight days, with three thousand people deported each day, but I succeeded in reducing the figure to twenty thousand, and even less than twenty thousand, only by agreeing to the condition that it would be children to the age of ten. Children ten years and older are safe. Given that the number of such children and the elderly totals roughly thirteen thousand, there is no choice other than to include the sick. It is difficult for me to speak. I don't have the strength. I simply wish to tell you my request: help me to carry out this *Aktion*! I'm trembling. I'm frightened that others, God forbid, will carry out the decree instead." [. . .]

Like the shadows of wandering dogs on a moon-drenched night in a faraway village, the elderly shuffle miserably along the walls of their rooms . . . walls that have now become dear and precious to their hearts.

Every shred of spider web and the marks of bugs left on the walls become treasured possessions. After all, they're in their own room, something that belongs to them . . . and who knows what tomorrow will bring or how the day after will look? Whether it will even make sense to talk about a room or instead about a common pit filled with two hundred, even a thousand people—men, women, and children all thrown together—filled with all the discarded "scrap"? Oh—to have lived, toiled, slaved, and worked themselves to the bone only to finally come to such an end—to end without burial in a Jewish cemetery and to leave no memory, no sign of their existence, behind! [. . .]

Suddenly, in the middle of the night—without any clear sense of who says so or how they know—the following news is heard: "Twenty thousand Jews from Będzyn and Sosnowiec will be settled in the ghetto." Maybe it's true that walls have ears. Perhaps the prophet had it right: "For a bird from the sky shall carry the sound." Twenty thousand Jews out, twenty thousand Jews in; just shuffle the deck. Like a game. So maybe it's possible that not everybody is going to the scrap heap. From Będzyn and Sosnowiec to Łódź, and from Łódź to Będzyn and Sosnowiec; in fact, when cards are shuffled, some get torn, some eventually wear out and become too faint to read, but most of them remain in play, and the game goes on. A real game played with human lives, but still just a game and not always taken seriously. Isn't it still possible that the children and the elderly will come out winners? Twenty thousand here, twenty thousand there—lives will be broken but not dug out from the roots; lives will be effaced but not erased . . . perhaps. The need to hope is so strong, and so is the will to believe.

NOTE
[Words in brackets appear in the original translation.—Eds.]

Translated by David Suchoff.

Other work by Zelkowicz: "A Picture of the Communal Life of a Jewish Town in the Second Half of the Nineteenth Century" (1951).

Stefan Zweig

1881–1942

The Viennese biographer, dramatist, poet, essayist, and novelist Stefan Zweig grew up in luxury and security in a wealthy, secular family in the last days of the Habsburg Empire. With the rise of Hitler, he moved to England in 1934 and then to the United States in 1940. Before that year was up he left for Brazil, where, depressed by the collapse of European civilization, he committed suicide. He was known particularly for his biographies of historical and literary figures and for his novellas. His much-read autobiography, *The World of Yesterday* (1943), is both praised as elegiac and criticized as naïve.

Universitas Vitae
1942

[. . .] I have always felt it as a particular honor that a man of such outstanding importance as Theodor Herzl was the first to champion me publicly from his exposed and therefore responsible position, and it was difficult for me to determine—ungratefully, it might seem—not to join his Zionist movement actively and in the responsible capacity that he would have wished.

The right relation never presented itself. I was estranged above all else by the disrespect, of a kind hardly comprehensible today, with which his own party associates treated Herzl. Those of the East charged him with not understanding Judaism and not even knowing its customs; the economists looked upon him as a *feuilletonist*; each one had his own objection and they were not always the most respectful. I realized how important and necessary it would have been to Herzl to have persons and particularly young people around him who were completely submissive, but the quarreling and dogmatic spirit, the constant opposition, the lack of honest, hearty subordination in this circle, alienated me from the movement which I had only approached curiously for Herzl's sake. [. . .]

I saw him a number of times afterwards, but only one meeting remains important and unforgettable in my memory, perhaps because it was the last. I had been abroad and had only been in correspondence with Vienna, when I finally met him one day in the Stadtpark. He had obviously come from his office, he was walking very slowly and stooped slightly; it was no longer the old swinging step. [. . .] He approved my having escaped abroad so often. "It's the only thing for us to do," said he. "All that I know, I learned abroad. It is only there that one learns to think in terms of distance. I am convinced that I never would have had the courage for that first idea, they would have destroyed it when it was still budding and growing. But thank God, when

I brought it here, all was finished, and they could do nothing more than try to trip me up. [. . .] I accompanied him all the way to his house. There he stood still, gave me his hand and said, "Why do you not come to see me? You have never been in my house. Call me up first and I will see to it that I am free." I promised him although I was determined not to keep my promise, for the more I love a person the more I respect his time. I was fully determined not to go to him.

But I did go to him—and only a few months later. The illness which had, at the time of that meeting, begun to bend him, broke him off suddenly, and it was only to the cemetery that I was able to accompany him. It was a singular day, a day in July, unforgettable to those who participated in the experience. Suddenly, to all the railroad stations of the city, by day and by night, from all realms and lands, every train brought new arrivals. Western, Eastern, Russian, Turkish Jews; from all the provinces and all the little towns they hurried excitedly, the shock, of the news still written on their faces; never was it more clearly manifest what strife and talk had hitherto concealed—it was a great movement whose leader had now fallen. The procession was endless. Vienna, startled, became aware that it was not just a writer or a mediocre poet who had passed away, but one of those creators of ideas who disclose themselves triumphantly in a single country, to a single people at vast intervals. A tumult ensued at the cemetery; too many had suddenly stormed to his coffin, crying, sobbing, screaming in a wild explosion of despair. It was almost a riot, a fury. All regulation was upset through a sort of elementary and ecstatic mourning such as I had never seen before nor since at a funeral. And it was this gigantic outpouring of grief from the depths of millions of souls that made me realize for the first time how much passion and hope this lone and lonesome man had borne into the world through the power of a single thought. [. . .]

The real significance of my formal admission to the *feuilleton* of the *Neue Freie Presse* lay in its effect on my life. It achieved for me an unexpected security in relation to my family. My parents occupied themselves but little with literature and laid no claims to any judgment of it. For them as well as for the entire Viennese bourgeoisie, only that was of importance which was praised in the *Neue Freie Presse*, and only what was ignored or attached there was inconsequential. Whatever appeared in the *feuilleton* seemed vouched for by the highest authority, because those who sat in judgment there commanded respect by their mere position. Conjure up a family that glances at this first page of the paper each day with awe and anticipation, and one morning stumbles on the discovery that the rather untidy nineteen-year-old at their table, who was none too good at school, and whose scribbling they looked upon indulgently as harmless play (safer than cards or dalliance), was permitted to voice his opinions (which up to then had received small attention at home) in this circle of the tried and famous. If I had written the most beautiful poems of Keats or Hölderlin or Shelley, it could not have brought about so complete a transformation in my entire surroundings; when I entered a theater, people pointed out this curious Benjamin who in some mysterious fashion had penetrated the holy precincts of the elders and worthies. And since I appeared in the *feuilleton* often and almost regularly, I was soon in danger of becoming a local celebrity, a danger which I was able to escape in time by surprising my parents one morning with the announcement that I wished to study in Berlin during the coming semester. And my family had too much respect for me, or rather for the *Neue Freie Presse* in whose golden shadow I stood, not to grant my wish.

Translated by Helmut Ripperger and B. W. Huebsch.

Other works by Zweig: *Marie Antoinette: The Portrait of an Average Woman* (1932); *Beware of Pity* (1939); *The Royal Game* (1942).

Stanisław Adler

d. 1946

Stanisław Adler was a lawyer and officer with the Jüdischer Ordnungsdienst, the Jewish police force in the Warsaw ghetto, as well as director of the housing office. His detailed account of the events leading up to the resettlement and liquidation of the largest Jewish community in Poland provides an inside view of the conditions that allowed for the creation and maintenance of the ghetto from 1940 to 1943. Adler committed suicide in 1946, after the Kielce pogrom.

Warsaw, Aryan Side
1943

Where shall I start? My thoughts are in turmoil. There is an overpowering desire burning in me to put in writing as speedily as possible all that has happened to us in these years of war, especially that which I, myself, have been witness to in the last six months. Even now, I am terrified that the dangers which threaten me from all sides might prevent me from finishing this manuscript.

It is not the first time that I have been motivated by this desire to take up my pen to record this history. But so far, my written work has turned out to be a Penelope's web; I hardly finish a fragment when the fate which pursues me destroys the manuscript. My memoirs from the first months of the war were thrown into a stove by the border police. My reconstruction of those notes was lost when I moved into the Jewish Quarter of Warsaw in 1941. All my writings from the most useful and mature period of my life, and this includes the quickly sketched descriptions of scenes from the "resettlement," I had to leave for the wolves to devour when I escaped from the Warsaw ghetto.

Against a logic which I cannot satisfy, and against literary tradition which I consciously ignore, I feel almost impelled to start from the end of my story. This is not because it is my intention to begin with the impact of my personal experiences, but because I feel the need to vindicate myself. Instead of an axe or a club I am now holding a pen in my hand. I am alive and living here, and not lying in trenches in an unequal battle or in one of the collective graves of Warsaw Jewry. Besides, it was during the period of preparation for the "January 1943 action" that the "Nordic perfidy" was most clearly demonstrated and it was in the course of that action that the criminality of the Nazis was most significantly exemplified.

Translated by Sara Chmielewska Philip.

Gedalyahu Alon

1901–1950

Historian Gedalyahu Alon (born Rogoznitski) was born in 1901 in Kobryn, Belorussia, and studied at the Slobodka yeshiva. In 1926, he immigrated to Palestine and was one of the first graduates of the Hebrew University. He taught Talmud and Jewish history there, clarifying many problems in the development of halakhah and the evolution of the social history of the Jews. In 1953, he was posthumously awarded the first Israel Prize for Jewish studies.

The Lithuanian Yeshivas
1943

II

These students, who poured into the Yeshivah from near and far, what were they seeking? And what was the Yeshivah seeking to give them? Did the students undertake to complete their course work at the Yeshivah in order to become rabbis, like graduates of rabbinical schools in the West? Doubtless, some had this motive, but they were few in number and did not shape the character of the school. This was neither the motive of the Yeshivah, nor was its educational system directed toward this end. [. . .]

III

[. . .] It is well known that the Musar movement in Lithuania owed its beginnings to the personality and efforts of R. Israel Salanter. This great man and unique character urged each Jew during the forties of the nineteenth century to probe deeply into his own thought and to strengthen his spirit, in order to refine his religious and ethical behavior. R. Israel of Salanter realized that successive generations were growing less sensitive to religious feeling, that Jews were losing their spiritual wholesomeness. He therefore announced that it was incumbent upon all to study Musar and to educate themselves by practicing it, to bring out their religious-ethical sense, strengthen their spirit, and refine their manners and everyday behavior. The Musar of R. Israel Salanter encompassed two areas: religious (between man and God) and ethical (between man and man). He established centers for Musar in several Lithuanian communities. He gathered about him ardent pupils and taught them orally and in writing how to study, teach, and practice the Musar doctrine of striving for perfection. [. . .]

A man's life is like a ladder with an infinite number of rungs. The gradations and plateaus which R. Moshe Hayyim Luzzatto [1707–1747] described in his *Mesillath Yesharim* (whose approach is based on the teaching of R. Pinhas B. Yair, quoted at the end of tractate Sotah) are but a schematic diagram, used merely as an example. In truth, the gradations can be multiplied and increased without end. We thus confront a chain bound upward, seemingly without end. Even these few rules, and the very ways of perfection, are without end. Man may discover, indeed is obligated to discover, his own courses, so long as they lead upward. The upward movement has no end. Absolute and continuous progress—this is the way of Musar. He who does not move upward, must against his will move downward. There is no standing still in this world. Even the state of being frozen, of contraction, does not exist. Nothing is merely "permitted" in this world. Either it is a duty or it is forbidden. "There is no place where He is not"—the entire expanse of life, whether in thought or deed, folds together to serve as a stage for the whole man (for every man at every moment; perfection is not a matter of the future. Always strive for the maximum).

NOTE
[Dates in brackets appear in the original translation.—Eds.]

Translated by Sid Leiman.

Other works by Alon: *Toledot ha-yehudim be-'erets yisra'el bi-tekufat ha-mishnah ve-ha-talmud*, 2 vols. (1953–1956); *Meḥkarim be-toledot yisra'el bi-yeme bayit sheni u-bi-tekufat ha-mishnah ve-ha-talmud*, 2 vols. (1957–1958).

Rachel Auerbach
1899–1976

Born in Łanowce, Galicia (now Lanivtsi, Ukraine), Rachel Auerbach (also spelled Rokhl Oyerbakh) was a Yiddish essayist and historian. In 1933, she moved to Warsaw and was active in modernist literary circles. During World War II, she ran a soup kitchen, worked closely with Emanuel Ringelblum, and wrote prolifically while in hiding outside the ghetto. Following the war, Auerbach helped lead the mission to recover the Oyneg Shabes archive, documents compiled during the war that detail life in the ghetto and buried shortly before the ghetto's destruction. In 1950, she settled in Israel, where she helped establish the Yad Vashem Holocaust memorial.

Yizkor, 1943
1943

Condemned to death. Who could—who wished to understand such a thing? And who could have expected such a decree against the mass? Against such low branches, such simple Jews. The lowly plants of the world. The sorts of people who would have lived out their lives without ever picking a quarrel with the righteous—or even the unrighteous—of this world.

How could such people have been prepared to die in a gas chamber? The sorts of people who were terrified of a dentist's chair; who turned pale at the pulling of a tooth.

And what of them . . . the little children?

The little ones, and those smaller still who not long ago were to be seen in the arms of their mothers, smiling at a bird or at a sunbeam. Prattling at strangers in the streetcar. Who still played "pattycake" or cried "giddyup" waving their tiny hands in the air. Or called, "papa." O, unrecognizable world in which these children and their mothers are gone. "Giddyup."

Even the sweetest ones; the two- and three-year-olds who seemed like newly hatched chicks tottering about on their weak legs. And even the slightly larger ones who could already talk. Who endlessly asked about the meanings of words. For whom whatever they learned was always brand new. Five-year-olds. And six-year-olds. And those who were older still—their eyes wide with curiosity about the whole world. And those older still whose eyes were already veiled by the mists of their approaching ripeness. Boys who, in their games, were readying themselves for achievements yet to come.

Girls who still nursed their dolls off in corners. Who wore ribbons in their hair; girls, like sparrows, leaping about in courtyards and on garden paths. And those who looked like buds more than half opened. The kind to whose cheeks the very first wind of summer seems to have given its first glowing caress. Girls of eleven, twelve, thirteen with the faces of angels. Playful as kittens. Smiling May blossoms. And those who have nearly bloomed: the fifteen- and sixteen-year-olds. The Sarahs, the Rebeccahs, the Leahs of the Bible, their names recast into Polish. Their eyes blue and gray and green under brows such as one sees on the frescoes unearthed in Babylon and Egypt. Slender young *fräuleins* from the wells of Hebron. *Jungfraus* from Evangelia. Foreign concubines of Jewish patriarchs; desert maidens with flaring nostrils, their hair in ringlets, dark complected but turned pale by passion. Spanish daughters, friends of Hebrew poets of the Middle Ages. Dreamy flowers bent over mirroring pools. And opposite them? Delicate blonds in whom Hebrew passion is interwoven with Slavic cheerfulness. And the even brighter flaxen-haired peasants, broad-hipped women, as simple as black bread; or as a shirt on the body of the folk.

It was an uncanny abundance of beauty of that generation growing up under the gray flag of ghetto poverty and mass hunger. Why was it that we were not struck by this as a portent of evil? Why was it that we did not understand that this blossoming implied its own end? [. . .]

Ah, the ways of Warsaw—the black soil of Jewish Warsaw.

My heart weeps even for the pettiest thief on Krochmalna Street; even for the worst of the knife wielders of narrow Mila, because even they were killed for being Jewish. Anointed and purified in the brotherhood of death.

Ah, where are you, petty thieves of Warsaw; you illegal street vendors[1] and sellers of rotten apples. And you, the more harmful folk—members of great gangs who held their own courts; who supported their own synagogues in the Days of Awe; who conducted festive funerals and who gave alms like the most prosperous burghers.

Ah, the mad folk of the Jewish street! Disordered soothsayers in a time of war.

Ah, bagel sellers on winter evenings.

Ah, poverty stricken children of the ghetto. Ghetto peddlers; ghetto smugglers supporting their families; loyal and courageous to the end. Ah, the poor barefoot boys moving through the autumn mire with their boxes of cigarettes, "Cigarettes! Cigarettes! Matches! Matches!" The voice of the tiny cigarette seller crying his wares on the corner of Leszno and Karmelicka Streets still rings in my ears.

Where are you, my boy? What have they done to you? Reels from the unfinished and still unplayed, preexpulsion film, "The Singing Ghetto," wind and unwind in my memory.[2] Even the dead sang in that film. They drummed with their swollen feet as they begged: "Money, ah money. Money is the best thing there is."

There was no power on earth, no calamity that could interfere with their quarrelsome presence in that Jewish street. Until there came that Day of Curses[3]—a day that was entirely night.

Hitler finally achieved his greatest ambition of the war. And finally, his dreadful enemy was defeated and fell: that little boy on the corner of Leszno and Karmelicka Streets; of Smocza and Nowolipie; of Dzika Street. The weapons of the women peddlers reached to every market square.

What luxury! They stopped tearing at their own throats from morning until night. They stopped snatching the morsels of clay-colored, day-adulterated bread from each other. [. . .]

Yizkor elohim es nishmas avi mori ve'imi morasi . . . Remember, Oh Lord, the souls of those who passed from this world horribly, dying strange deaths before their time.

And now, suddenly I seem to see myself as a child standing on a bench behind my mother who, along with my grandmother and my aunts, is praying before the east wall of the woman's section of the synagogue in Lanowce. I stand on tiptoe peering down through panes of glass at the congregation in the synagogue that my grandfather built. And just then the Torah reader, Hersh's Meyer-Itsik, strikes the podium three times and cries out with a mighty voice so that he will be heard by men and women on both sides of the partition and by the community's orphans, boys and girls, who are already standing, waiting for just this announcement: "We recite *Yizkor.*"

The solemn moment has arrived when we remember those who are no longer with us. Even those who have finished their prayers come in at this time to be with everyone else as they wait for the words, "We recite *Yizkor.*"

And he who has survived and lives and who approaches this place, let him bow his head and, with anguished heart, let him hear those words and remember his names as I have remembered mine—the names of those who were destroyed.

At the end of the prayer in which everyone inserts the names of members of his family there is a passage recited for those who have no one to remember them and who, at various times, have died violent deaths because they were Jews. And it is people like those who are now in the majority.

Aryan Side of Warsaw,
November 1943

NOTES
1. Called *khesedlekh* in Warsaw slang.
2. A Nazi propaganda film made in the ghetto in May 1942.
3. The *Tokheha.*

Translated by Leonard Wolf.

Other works by Auerbach: *Varshaver tsavoes: bagegenishn, aktivitetn, goyroles, 1933–1943* (1974); *Baym letstn veg: in geto Varshe un oyf der a risher zayt* (1977).

Shloyme Bikl

1896–1969

An essayist, critic, and champion of Yiddish writing, Shloyme Bikl was born in Ustechko, Galicia (present-day Ukraine), and received both a traditional Jewish and a secular education. After earning a law degree at Chernivtsi University in 1922, he lived in Bucharest, where he practiced law and wrote and edited literary publications. He was a regular contributor to the Warsaw weekly *Literarishe bleter*. After he moved to New York in 1939, Bikl was a leading figure in Yiddish writers' circles, and he served on the editorial boards of several Yiddish-language newspapers and journals, as well as on the board at YIVO.

A Cityful of Jews
1943

The man was a ferment of intelligence and emotion. He could not grow accustomed to the conventional life of the common herd. He thought differently from all the others and disliked collective thinking and action. He rebelled against the majority and its established order. Of course, years ago in a pious, even ultra-pious, Jewish community, the rebelliousness of someone like Shloyme Khalfn could only be expressed in small ways, which we "moderns" looked down upon with a smile. But in those days, and in that environment, these trifles were true revolutionary acts. And from these trifles there unfolded in Reb Shloyme's old age his tragic struggle with himself and his faith. And the struggle would ultimately cost him his life.

What did his rebelliousness consist of? Here are a few facts, some of which I remember myself, and some of which were told to me. [. . .]

Reb Shloyme was a member of the Jewish community council, even went to meetings from time to time, but he did not engage in politics. He left that to the professional power-brokers of his day, first to Shloyme-Hersh Keymer and thereafter to Yosl Finklshteyn, whom Sholem Aleichem so brilliantly described in his "*S'iz a lign!*" ("It's a Lie!"). But once, one single time, he fell into the political cauldron of the town. It really was at that time nothing less than a cauldron and the political hot water boiled to the point where it scalded young and old, husband and wife, rich and poor. Who could stand aside in the election campaign between Dr. Bloch and Dr. Bik? The supporters of the Viennese Rabbi Dr. Josef Samuel Bloch let out a rumor that if God forbid the Lemberg [Lwów] lawyer Dr. Emil Bik were elected, Jews would be forbidden to circumcise their children. That's all people needed to hear. Men recited psalms, women measured the cemetery with string to use for wicks in ritual candles and flung open the doors of the Ark of the Torah scroll in the synagogue. A raging hysteria gripped the entire city.

In his heart, it was said, Shloyme Khalfn was in favor of the Viennese Rabbi. After all, what Jewish merit could the Polonized Lemberg lawyer have in his eyes? But the stupid collective hysteria repelled him and he

came out for Dr. Bik. Speaking from the synagogue's reading-desk, one might think he had succeeded in stopping the wave of popular terror. But as soon as his discourse ended and Reb Shloyme went home, a hostile mob of men and women assembled at his house. It reached the point where pious women might grab stones, smash the windows, and burst inside cursing and fighting. [. . .]

Kolomey, on that July day in 1883, experienced in miniature a kind of July 14, 1789, when the famous Revolution of Liberty, Equality, and Fraternity began in Paris. The difference between a hundred years earlier in Paris and a hundred years later in Kolomey was of course fundamental. There, women tore the heads off generals and broke open the doors of jails, so that things should be different from before. Here Jewish women raised a storm . . . and lit sanctified wicks, so that everything should remain the same. The fear that one of the principles of Judaism might be violated on one hand created miraculous unity and on the other aroused the demon of mistrust among one and all. On the one hand, on that day all social boundaries were erased. Devout scholars befriended ignoramuses and respectable property owners mingled with apprentice shoemakers. Young heder schoolboys demonstrated alongside elderly women, while men with gray beards found themselves shoulder to shoulder with young matrons in stylish wigs. On the other hand, the pious were ready to suspect Shloyme Khalfn, and even the Rabbi, of planning, along with the Lemberg lawyer, to destroy the covenant that God established for all time with Abraham and his descendants.

That day of unheard-of Jewish demonstrations was one of the greatest days in the history of Kolomey, but Shloyme Khalfn was not swayed by it. He bravely began swimming against the tide of popular anger. He went to his window, opened it wide and began to speak. "If you're prepared to risk your lives for the sake of the principles of Judaism," he argued, "then why are you afraid of a Lemberg lawyer?" Even those who could not hear him dropped the stones from their hands. "Let the evil decree come and we will all sanctify God's name! But if instead of awaiting the hour of martyrdom you send your wives to the graveyard to beg the dead to help avert it, then it is a sign that you are moved not by the great love of the Covenant of Abraham but by your petty fear of being put to the test." [. . .]

His words made a deep impression on the men and many of them, pensive and ashamed, went home. The women continued to rant for a long time, dispersing only at sundown. It may be that some of them remembered that supper had to be cooked and this reminder spread quickly and calmed the crowd. Nevertheless, God knows how many men in Kolomey went without supper that evening!

It was the women who prevailed. The Viennese Rabbi and not the Lemberg lawyer was elected to parliament. When the election results became known, seemingly out of nowhere, a mass procession arose that stretched from the Jewish alleys to the city hall. The Jews of Kolomey celebrated with great fanfare and enthusiasm the pact between God and Abraham of so many thousand years before. [. . .]

Shloyme Khalfn was not, as I have said, a man to conform to the majority. Since 90 percent of the Jews of Kolomey were Hasidim, Reb Shloyme, of course, had to be a *misnaged*, one of their opponents. For some, being a *misnaged* might mean no more than not venerating a Hasidic rebbe. For Shloyme Khalfn it meant carrying on a passionate ideological struggle against rebbes and Hasidim.

Translated by Solon Beinfeld.

Other works by Bikl: *Inzikh un arumzikh: notitsn fun a polemist un kritsihe bamerkungen* (1936); *Yidn davenen* (1948); *Dray brider zaynen mir geven* (1956); *Rumenye: geshikhte, literatur-kritik, zikhroynes* (1961).

Robert Borgel

1909–1989

Robert Borgel was born in Tunisia, then a French protectorate, and grew up in a religious family. He obtained his doctorate in maritime law in Paris and returned to practice in Tunis. After the French defeat in June 1940, the anti-Jewish laws of Vichy France were applied in Tunisia. Borgel and his father Moïse, president of the Communauté israélite de Tunis, united the leaders of the community to save Jews from their fate under the Nazis.

Yellow Star and Swastika: A Story of Servitude
1943

May 7, 1943

We learn upon waking that Admiral Esteva was brutally kidnapped during the night by some Germans who apparently forced him onto his plane.

A friend attached to Civil Defense, who was patrolling the Residence quarter during that long night of uninterrupted alarms, happened to witness the departure and told us about it the next morning. Around four, a little before dawn, he noticed the presence of armed soldiers in the Residence courtyard and in the surrounding area. Suddenly there's a brouhaha, he makes out some shadows, and a loud voice is heard: "I am a French admiral." The shadowy figures disappear into a military car that takes off at top speed.

Yesterday and again this morning we sent some trucks carrying our men to Bizerte. The evacuation notice had come during the night. We fear that the road has been blocked and that the Protville bridge has been blown up. We wait anxiously. Before noon, we learn that a truck has broken down on the road. Guez, Sfez, and Moumou set out to reconnoiter in the gray Citroën, taking along some spare parts.

The trucks will return with the poor devils who've been replaced—free again after their long night of servitude. In one of the trucks is a beribboned lamb, born in the camp at Bizerte, the company mascot. For several days the workers have been preparing this surprise for the president as a way to celebrate the liberation.

This is the end: explosions everywhere, the Germans are blowing up what they can. The artillery thunders incessantly. They say the Allies are at Massicault.

The wound is being drained.

What will happen in Tunis?

There are always pessimists; they affirm with an assurance equaled only by their ignorance that the Germans mean to defend the city street by street, house by house.

Stalingrad, in other words!

Some people fear the interregnum, when the Germans will have left the city—a time of confusion when shady characters could make trouble in the ghetto. Others come to warn us against nocturnal kidnapping and deportation. The members of the Committee must not sleep at home tonight!

People on terraces point at flames and smoke around the city, behind the kasbah, in the direction of Bardo.

We're at fever pitch.

In a bar across the way and in the restaurant next to it, some Germans are singing and drinking.

Around four-thirty or five, the noise grows, a cry of mad joy. We can't believe it, it's too beautiful.

"THE ENGLISH ARE ON THE WAY."

The English are on the way. It's really true, motorcyclists, a Frenchman, the cadet Waddington, our compatriot. The first armored cars arrive, and tall strapping blond guys with camouflage helmets appear, their faces grimy with gunpowder, looking surprised and happy at the same time.

We pinch ourselves to be sure we're not dreaming.

You would need to have lived through these six months of martyrdom, this daily nightmare, to understand our overflowing joy. We have regained our humanity. We laugh, we cry, we are bursting with happiness. We hug one another, everyone loves everyone. A neighbor is dancing a wild jig.

Young men are busy arresting German or Italian soldiers who are caught in the street and who put up no resistance.[1] For them the war is over; they are weary.

Impossible to get any shut-eye tonight: it's happiness!

May 8

The troops go parading by: the Allies, English, Americans. Finally, the French. Once again we see the glorious standards whose period of mourning is over. At the Military Circle they're replacing the plaque taken down the day Hitler decreed there would no longer be a French army. In a frenzy, we clap and hug one other again and again.

The workers—hundreds, perhaps a thousand—come down the rue d'Alger, cheering the president of the Community and the head of recruitment.

They want to carry them around in triumph. Paul Ghez is lifted onto the shoulders of these young men. M. Borgel, whose natural reserve distances him from such street scenes, refuses at first, but finally yields to everyone's insistence and is carried off, joining in the joy of liberation.

They return with tears in their eyes.

Memories that make up for so many things!

NOTE

1. Some Germans did resist, however. We must cite the case of Sitbon, a young twenty-year-old Jew who on Gambetta Avenue had some trouble with a small group of Germans, found some guns on the body of an officer abandoned in a truck, and used the truck as a blockhouse from which to fire on the Germans. He was thus able to gain enough time to allow reinforcements to arrive. The young man was seriously wounded, but made no claim to glory, and few know of his courageous deed.

Translated by Michele McKay Aynesworth.

Gusta Dawidsohn-Draenger

1917–1943

Gusta Dawidsohn-Draenger, whose nom de guerre was "Justyna," kept a Polish diary in which she documented the saga of the Jewish armed resistance. Born in Kraków to a family of Ger Hasidim, she was a member of the Zionist Akiva youth movement. When World War II broke out, she and her husband, Szymon (Szymek) Draenger, worked underground forging identity documents and publishing *Heḥalutz haloḥem*, in Polish. Referring to herself in the third person, "Justyna" dictated her diary to her fellow cellmates over a three-month period during her imprisonment in 1943. It was recovered and published after the war.

Justyna's Diary
1943

At that time the apartment at No. 13 was the base for all underground activities. Toward evening, groups of two or three left stealthily, some to take action against traitors and informers within the ghetto, others to seek arms on the outside. A minute before the curfew they returned, out of breath, at times triumphant, at times mortified at having failed, though they had so nearly succeeded. Frequently they miraculously eluded the police. At times it seemed the bullets passed right over their heads, that only a timely turn of the head had saved them.

One of the most beautiful evenings was arranged in Anka's honor. It was the ushering in of the Sabbath. The preparations for the celebration lasted fully two days. All were waiting for it impatiently: it was to start at dusk on Friday and last until daybreak the following morning. This tradition has been maintained in the movement for many years. From the grayness of a weekday one is suddenly plunged into a festive mood. In religious concentration one anticipates the moment when the candles will flame into light in the festively decorated room. The girls in white blouses, the boys in white wide-collared shirts took their plates around the table, covered with a white cloth. First a moment of silence, then a strong burst of song, greeting the Sabbath. Eyes gleamed in the candlelight. Strong emotions were reflected in those wide-open black pupils. Another spirit animated them, purer and better. This is the way it had always been, for years and years. In a quiet village, in the noisy city, high up in the mountains, among the factory smokestacks, they had come to greet the Sabbath with the same song, with the same emotions. And today it was the last time together. They had no presentiment of disaster. They were so happy! Song followed song, the ringing notes binding them more tightly and strongly together! In the midst of this happiness that filled them to overflowing, from out of somewhere came its epithet: it was *our* last supper. The name caught on, it was remembered. Thenceforth that evening was never referred to otherwise.

Dolek sat at the end of the table and around him were all the dear faces, radiant, friendly, brave, and so very, very close. They sat crowded together. The room had been filled long since, and new guests kept arriving. Room had to be made for all. In a corner, Martusia, wide-eyed, staring at Dolek, at the radiant faces, at the flaming candles. This was her first Sabbath away from home. She left Tomaszów a few days ago, when the "action" had already started, aware that she might never again see her parents. They were so young in spirit! Her father, saying good-bye to her, told her, "Too bad I am not a few years younger. I would certainly have gone with you!" Marta took those words along and kept them in her heart, her dearest memento of her father. Now she kept thinking of them all the time.

Her home was no more! There the "action" most likely caught her father, her mother, her younger sister. She is alone, all alone in the world. Only seventeen, her eyes wide, she scans the room. She does not feel pain, she does not long for her lost home, for her childhood, for that carefree girlhood which has gone forever. Here is her place, among this youthful company. She feels happy in the crowded room. It is so good to listen to Dolek's words. She has known him for a long time. She feels that today he speaks in quite a different way from the past. Power used to resonate in his words, creative force which summoned faith in life and love of it. Tonight his words forebode the inevitable end which they must confront with dignity.

It was as if he felt death approaching, because he spoke frequently about it. He did not believe that they could survive and he did not want others to believe it. He did not want to delude himself. He wanted all those who undertook the underground work to realize that the end was near. Even now he dropped his hard words into the festive mood:

"There is no return from our journey. We march along the road to death, remember that! Whoever desires to live, let him not seek life among us. We are at the end. But our end is not the dusk. Our end is death, which a strong man steps forward to confront. I feel that this is our last communal ushering in of the Sabbath. We will have to leave the ghetto. There is too much commotion around us. This week we will start dismantling our cozy center at No. 13. Another phase of our life will be over. But we must not regret anything. This is the way it must be."

The windows were gray with dawn, when this, our last supper came to an end.

Translated by Ted Hudes and Mark Nowogrodzki.

Sofia Dubnova-Erlich

1885–1986

Poet and political activist Sofia Dubnova-Erlich was born in Mstislavl, Belorussia, the eldest daughter of historian Simon Dubnow. She studied at St. Petersburg University and the Sorbonne. After she married Henryk Erlich, a leader of the Bund in Poland, the political situation drove Dubnova-Erlich and her husband to move to Warsaw in 1918. During World War II, Henryk was arrested and murdered by the Soviet authorities, and Dubnova-Erlich settled in Vilna until 1941, after which she escaped to the United States, where she learned of her husband's death and her father's murder in the Holocaust. She continued to advocate for civil rights, contributing essays and translations to the Russian- and Yiddish-language press.

Shtetl

1943

The shtetl, lost here among Polish fields and groves, might be called Turek or Przasnysz, Konin or Maków, yet what one remembers is not the name but the old marketplace reeking of tar and dung where a rickety, mud-splattered bus would laboriously grind to a stop. What has stayed in my memory is an old town hall with a blackened clock face, a movie house resembling barracks with crude posters at the entrance, and a herd of coarse small houses with tiny blinking windows, all bunched together.

Getting off the bus onto the square, where left-over patches of straw from market day lay rotting between jagged cobblestones, I would step straight into the seventeenth century. Left behind was the frivolous, lighthearted capital, Warsaw, with the defiant clatter of cavalry spurs and the shrill, drunken screech of jazz trying to drown out the somber grumble of the poverty-stricken outskirts and the threatening rumble of oncoming historical storms. Here, in the provincial backwaters, poverty reigned openly and implacably; it was solid, familiar, passed on from father to son, reeking through and through of stove smoke, yesterday's warmed-up borsch, unaired comforters; a poverty firmly rooted in narrow strips of land among the shops, the synagogue, the heder, and the mikvah. [. . .]

Usually I arrived in the shtetl on Fridays, late in the afternoon, when shop bolts were beginning to clank, the pathetic stalls were emptying, and saleswomen, lazily winding down their bickering, would deftly tighten their heavy checked kerchiefs about their waists and disperse homeward. A holiday sadness, treacley thick, would slowly envelop the shtetl. Here and there, half-blind tiny windows warmed with candlelight illuminate the tangled fringes of wash-worn tablecloths and a challah's round golden crust. [. . .]

We walk to that gloomy barracks along a narrow, wood-planked sidewalk, misstepping time and again into the mud; it doesn't seem easy to make the transition from this centuries-old life to the world of Maxim Gorky, Romain Rolland, and Soviet literature. The hall, however, is already abuzz like a beehive, and I struggle to make my way between benches made of rough boards to a dusty and squeaky stage. Figures and faces merge, but hot currents flow toward me from the back of the hall, I feel a quickened breathing, and I would like to find true and real words to match my listeners' rapt intensity, impatience, and demands born of the depths of a harsh life. I grope to find words borrowed from those seekers of truth, passionate, impatient, and imbued with the gift of clairvoyance. I feel almost physically how invisible wires touch, how sparks of understanding and acceptance flare up, how the idea that not only social conditions but also man himself must be recast—how this idea turns for all of us into Ariadne's thread in this labyrinthine world. These young women with their berets aslant and these young fellows relegated to the stinking back lots of life because of their patched, worn-out jackets will not be satisfied with just a little; they are resolved to jump from the seventeenth century straight into the twentieth and maybe even the twenty-first . . .

By the glass of cloudy, overly sweet tea on the table, a pile of notes mounts—some poorly written, naïve, and clumsy, others surprisingly well phrased, bold, and concise. All the questions could be reduced to one: how to restructure the world.

My interchange with the audience did not stop when a somber custodian began turning out the lights—we just regrouped to a tighter circle. In an attic space, reached by a narrow winding staircase, wooden tables were covered with crude wrapping paper, and smooth pine needles dropped from aromatic branches that hung from low beams. Excited young voices crisscrossed; suddenly singing flared up in a corner, little tongues of flame leapt up from person to person, and the whole attic was humming and sizzling like dry birch bark set aflame, throwing into the dark, dense night of the shtetl the voices' challenge and yearning. [. . .]

On the square, by the bus, I say goodbye to my new friends. Here are Simon and Rakhil, clear-voiced and rosy-cheeked Hannah, the public-school teacher, and David, the carpenter with the sternly Biblical face of a zealot or martyr. Hannah squeezes my hand meaningfully, "I will write you . . ."

A letter arrived after a few days. Hannah wrote that she was pregnant, the child's father was far away, and difficult days lay ahead for she would have to break with her family and her surroundings but was unafraid of the future and happy to take on the hardships . . . That was early spring, 1939.

That fall sirens began howling like hyenas. Bombs and fires, hunger and famine descended on the rough little dwellings gathered together like a frightened herd. The fearful shtetl wailed and surged out onto the road—carrying prayer books in old stiff covers, children in arms, old things grabbed on the run—some headed for the capital, some further away to the east. A hurricane had dispersed the life that centuries had shaped.

I'm thinking now of those who, in those irretrievable and by now inconceivable times, came close to me, face to face. Hannah's child, I am imagining, may have turned up in the kindergarten of a Kazakhstan kolkhoz; David may have been seized by Gestapo spies at an underground printing press and hung in the market square of some district town; Rakhil and Simon, holding hands as at our meeting, may have mounted the barricades on Miła Street and, watching the German troops advance, poked the muzzles of their guns through the slit between the boards. I'm thinking of all the suffering for which there are no words in human language and of the heroism that we just cannot measure by any measure, cannot put into any epic poem, the heroism of impatient and passionate people whom history has marked for greatness.

And you, shtetl, can it be that you have fallen silent for centuries to come, that your strangled gasp will not arouse this dulled world, a world no longer able to wonder at anything? Are you destined, with your impoverished coziness and your yearnings, your acquiescent prayers and your insolent songs, simply to become a silent tract of land, ploughed by history's bloody course for a new sowing?

Translated by Helen Reeve and Martha Kitchen.

Other works by Dubnova-Erlich: *Osenniaia svirel': stikhi* (1911); *Mat'* (1918); *Stikhi raznykh* (1973); *The Life and Work of S. M. Dubnov* (1991); *Khleb i matsa* (1994).

Elhanan Elkes

1879–1944

Elhanan Elkes was in born in Kalvarija, Lithuania, and studied medicine in Königsberg. He was elected chair of the Kovno (Kaunas) Aeltestenrat (Council of Elders) and led the Jewish community there under the Nazis from 1943 to 1944, when the ghetto was liquidated. He was deported, like many men from the Kovno ghetto, to Kaufering in the Dachau camp system.

Last Will and Testament
1943

October 19, 1943

DOCUMENT: LAST TESTAMENT, LETTER FROM DR. ELKES TO HIS SON AND DAUGHTER IN LONDON

My beloved son and daughter!

I am writing these lines, my dear children, in the vale of tears of Vilijampolé, Kovno Ghetto, where we have been for over two years. We have now heard that in a few days our fate is to be sealed. The Ghetto is to be crushed and torn asunder. Whether we are all to perish, or whether a few of us are to survive, is in God's hands. We fear that only those capable of slave labor will live; the rest, probably, are sentenced to death.

We are left, a few out of many. Out of the 35,000 Jews of Kovno, approximately 17,000 remain; out of a quarter of a million Jews in Lithuania (including the Vilna district), only 25,000 live plus 5,000 who, during the last few days, were deported to hard labor in Latvia, stripped of all their belongings. The rest were put to death in terrible ways by the followers of the

greatest Haman of all times and of all generations. Some of those dear and close to us, too, are no longer with us. Your Aunt Hannah and Uncle Arieh were killed with 1,500 souls of the Ghetto on October 4, 1941. Uncle Zvi, who was lying in the hospital suffering from a broken leg, was saved by a miracle. All the patients, doctors, nurses, relatives, and visitors who happened to be there were burned to death, after soldiers had blocked all the doors and windows of the hospital and set fire to it. In the provinces, apart from Siauliai, no single Jew survives. Your Uncle Dov and his son Shmuel were taken out and killed with the rest of the Kalvaria community during the first months of the war, that is, about two years ago.

Due to outer forces and inner circumstance, only our own Ghetto has managed to survive and live out its diaspora life for the past two years, in slavery, hard labor, hunger, and deprivation. (Almost all our clothing, belongings, and books were taken from us by the authorities.)

The last massacre, when 10,000 victims were killed at one time, took place on October 28, 1941. Our total community had to go through the "selection" by our rulers: life or death. I am the man who, with my own eyes, saw those about to die. I was there early on the morning of October 29, in the camp that led to the slaughter at the Ninth Fort. With my own ears I heard the awe-inspiring and terrible symphony, the weeping and screaming of 10,000 people, old and young—a scream that tore at the heart of heaven. No ear had heard such cries through the ages and the generations. With many of our martyrs, I challenged my creator; and with them, from a heart torn in agony, I cried: "Who is like you in the universe, my Lord!" In my effort to save people here and there, I was beaten by soldiers. Wounded and bleeding, I fainted, and was carried in the arms of friends to a place outside the camp. There, a small group of about thirty or forty survived—witnesses to the fire.

We are, it appears, one of the staging centers in the East. Before our eyes, before the very windows of our houses, there have passed over the last two years many, many thousands of Jews from southern Germany and Vienna, to be taken, with their belongings, to the Ninth Fort, which is some kilometers from us. There they were killed with extreme cruelty. We learned later that they were misled—they were told they were coming to Kovno, to settle in our Ghetto.

From the day of the Ghetto's founding, I stood at its head. Our community chose me, and the authorities confirmed me as chairman of the Council of elders, together with my friend, the advocate Leib Garfunkel, a former member of the Lithuanian parliament, and a few other close and good people, concerned and caring for the fate of the surviving few. We are trying to steer our battered ship in furious seas, when waves of decrees and decisions threaten to drown it every day. Through my influence I succeeded, at times, in easing the verdict and in scattering some of the dark clouds that hung over our heads. I bore my duties with head high and an upright countenance. Never did I ask for pity; never did I doubt our rights, I argued our case with total confidence in the justice of our demands.

In these hardest moments of our life, you, my dear ones, are always before us. You are present in our deepest thoughts and in our hearts. In the darkest nights, your mother would sit beside me, and we would both dream of your life and your future. Our innermost desire is to see you again, to embrace you, and to tell you once again how close we are to you, and how our hearts beat as we remember you and see you before us. And is there any time, day or night, when your memory is not with us? As we stand here, at the very gates of hell, with a knife poised at our necks, only your images, dear ones, sustain us. And you, my children, how was your life these past five years, so hard and full of sorrow for the Jewry of Europe? I know that, far away from this place, you have shared our anguish and, in agony, listened to every slight rumor coming from this vale of tears; and that, deep down, you have felt with us this unparalleled tragedy of our people.

With regard to myself, I have little to report. Last year I suffered an acute and severe attack of rheumatoid arthritis, which kept me bedridden for nine months. However, even in the most difficult days of my illness, I carried on in my community, and from my bedside participated actively in the work of my friends. Now I am better; it has been about six months since I ceased being regarded as sick. I am not fully well, either, but I continue to work ceaselessly, without rest or respite.

About six months ago we received a message from Uncle Hans, transmitted to us by way of the Red Cross; it said that you were all right. The little note, written by a stranger, took nine months to reach us.

We have written and written to you by way of the Red Cross and private persons. Have any of our words reached you? We are desolate that during our stay here we could not contact you and tell you that we are still among the living. We know full well how heavily the doubt of our survival weighs upon you, and what strength and confidence you would draw from the news that we are alive. This would certainly give you courage, and belief in work and life with a firm and clear goal. I deeply fear despair, and the kind of apathy which tends to drive a person out of this world. I pray that this may not happen to you. I doubt, my beloved children, whether I will ever be able to see you again, to hug you and press you to my heart. Before I leave this world and you, my dear ones, I wish to tell you once again how dear you are to us, and how deeply our souls yearn for you.

Joel, my beloved! Be a faithful son to your people. Take care of your nation, and do not worry about the Gentiles. During our long exile, they have not given us an eighth of an eighth of what we have given them. Immerse yourself in this question, and return to it again and again.

Try to settle in the Land of Israel. Tie your destiny to the land of our future. Even if life there may be hard, it is a life full of content and meaning. Great and mighty is the power of faith and belief. Faith can move mountains. Do not look to the left or to the right as you pursue your path. If at times you see your people straying, do not let your heart lose courage, my son. It is not their fault—it is our bitter Exile which has made them so. Let truth be always before you and under your feet. Truth will guide you and show you the path of life.

And you, my dear daughter Sarah, read most carefully what I have just said to Joel. I trust your clear mind and sound judgment. Do not live for the moment; do not stray from your chosen path and pick flowers at the wayside. They soon wilt. Lead a life full of beauty, a pure life, full of content and meaning. For all your days, walk together: let no distance separate you, let no serious event come between you.

Remember, both of you, what Amalek has done to us. Remember and never forget it all your days; and pass this memory as a sacred testament to future generations. The Germans killed, slaughtered, and murdered us in complete equanimity. I was there with them. I saw them when they sent thousands of people—men, women, children, infants—to their death, while enjoying their breakfast, and while mocking our martyrs. I saw them coming back from their murderous missions—dirty, stained from head to foot with the blood of our dear ones. There they sat at their table—eating and drinking, listening to light music. They are professional executioners.

The soil of Lithuania is soaked with our blood, killed at the hands of the Lithuanians themselves; Lithuanians, with whom we have lived for hundreds of years, and whom, with all our strength, we helped to achieve their own national independence. Seven thousand of our brothers and sisters were killed by Lithuanians in terrible and barbarous ways during the last days of June 1941. They themselves, and no others, executed whole congregations, following German orders. They searched—with special pleasure—cellars and wells, fields and forests, for those in hiding, and turned them over to the "authorities." Never have anything to do with them; they and their children are accursed forever.

I am writing this in an hour when many desperate souls—widows and orphans, threadbare and hungry—are camping on my doorstep, imploring us for help. My strength is ebbing. There is a desert inside me. My soul is scorched. I am naked and empty. There are no words in my mouth. But you, my most dearly beloved, will know what I wanted to say to you at this hour.

And now, for a moment, I close my eyes and see you both standing before me. I embrace and kiss you both; and I say to you again that, until my last breath, I remain your loving father.

Elchanan

Translated by Jerzy Michalowicz.

Paul Ghez

1898–1971

Paul Ghez was born in Sousse, Tunisia. During World War I, he was wounded while serving as a volunteer in a French artillery unit. After studying law in France, he returned to Tunisia, where he served on the Jewish council and headed the veterans' organization Les anciens combattants. Ghez volunteered again for the French army during World War II. In 1942–1943, when Tunisia was occupied by the Nazis, he was head of the Committee for the Recruitment of Jewish Manpower established by the Jewish leadership to meet Gestapo demands. In 1956, when Tunisia gained independence, Ghez moved to Lyon.

Six Months under the Boot
1943

25 January

One more incident.

A woman shows up at the president's office and demands the immediate return of her son, who is working in Djelloula, in the Italian sector.

It is impossible to reason with her.

Suddenly, her second son, there with her, takes off his coat and announces he's going to beat the hell out of me.

I never yield to threats of this kind, not because I have a taste for brawls, but just because it makes sense.

I don't have military insignia and or a weapon to impose my authority.

If I give way to a maniac who reduces everything to brute force, I'm lost.

I immediately advance upon this swaggering jackass to make him shut up.

The mother screams bloody murder.

Then the door opens and a man appears, revolver in hand. It's an Italian, an informer who identifies vehicles and machines belonging to Jews.

He was there by chance with a German soldier on the lookout for a typewriter.

This fascist hero tells me I'm under arrest and he's taking me to the *Feldgendarmerie* [military police].

I ask him what business this is of his. He answers: "Times have changed. We're the ones in charge now."

I signal to the interpreter Trenner, who telephones the *Kommandantur* from an adjacent office to ask if I must comply. The German soldier is called to the telephone and receives instructions. He immediately withdraws, followed by his fascist.

We've seen the last of them.

* * *

26 January

Alarming news from Bizerte.

Major Zacwecke tells us there've been numerous escapes from the camp.

I was already aware of this bit of news.

Rumors have been circulating that on January 28th the English are going to bomb the city without let-up and have suggested that all inhabitants evacuate.

Some think this news was spread by leaflets, others claim it came from the BBC.

The major curtly invites us to put a stop to this exodus and to bring back or replace the escapees.

I propose to go to Bizerte on the 28th to reassure my men and see what needs to be done. My offer is accepted.

* * *

Henry Sfez traveled to Sousse and to Kairouan and reported back to us.

The situation is dreadful.

Men aged 19 to 50 are all working, recruited and supervised by members of the SOL [Service d'ordre légionnaire], a fascist militia, who carry out their task with implacable zeal.

All the Jews are wearing the yellow star.

The city of Sousse has been destroyed, and the inhabitants have taken refuge in the surrounding villages, living in misery.

All the dwellings and shops spared by the bombs have been looted.

To make matters worse, our fellow Jews are subjected to endless bullying and humiliation. No cigarettes for them, and a shocking inequality in the distribution of food.

My colleague and friend Georges Binhas, in an atmosphere of terror, is doing his best to surmount countless obstacles. No one knows the difficulty of his task better than I. Georges Binhas is a man. He will find a way.

* * *

27 January

Bizerte again.

This morning we received a message advising us that a worker named Hababou, caught just as he was escaping, was cut down by rifle fire by a German sentry.

The number of escapes now exceeds two hundred.

They decided to make an example.

Poor guy.

* * *

28 January

I set off early for Bizerte accompanied by Sfez.

The gray car really doesn't look good.

A mudflap has been torn off. The upholstery inside is in tatters. The poorly fitted doors make a hellish racket.

The brakes don't work well, and the car stops . . . when it feels like it.

Sfez is imperturbable and drives with as much assurance as if he were at the wheel of a Rolls.

We stop for a few minutes at the Sidi-Ahmed airfield.

There we have two hundred workers, including the contingent moved from Aouina on the 9th, rounded out by fifty reinforcements.

The impression is excellent.

The men's morale is good, they eat well.

The German NCOs are humane and let them be.

I meet up again with my driver-boxer, who gives me a manly handshake.

The excellence of this organization is due in great part to the head of the camp Henry Bismut and his seriously disabled aide Alex Bonan, repatriated from a stalag [German POW camp].

I thank these two leaders warmly.

* * *

Here we are in Bizerte. The atmosphere is clearly different.

I am received by hostile cries.

I head toward the camp headquarters. The chants of the crowd massed before the door rise like paper lanterns in the air: "replacements," "replacements."

I swiftly call the camp leaders together.

Gilbert Taieb, champion swimmer, a fine athlete who knows how to command respect.

Jacques Krief, Georges's brother, initially well intentioned, but already disillusioned.

Kako Habib, *Croix de guerre* [Cross of War] 1939, round and roly-poly, always smiling.

Lucien Zarka, former prisoner of war, loudmouth, but a good guy, stubbornly defending the prerogatives of veterans from the first call-up.

Victor Sitbon, nicknamed Tutor, camp manager.

Bédoucha, former sergeant, imperturbably calm, tirelessly devoted.

I immediately hold a conference.

I reproach the leaders for not having been able to preserve their authority, allowing morale in the camp to deteriorate.

My interlocutors tell me of the terrifying, almost daily bombings they've had to endure.

The workers are frequently brutalized by German soldiers.

It's certain that our men, dragged away from their shops and offices, are ill prepared for this.

And what's more, the sick have been replaced in an unfair and chaotic manner, raising the level of exasperation to boiling point.

I acknowledge the validity of these explanations, but as for the present we have no choice.

We must hold steady.

I'm going to try, using my police service, to round up replacements.

But the choice of men to be replaced must be beyond reproach. The sick and heads of big families must go home before all others.

In addition, I'll try to improve basic living conditions, ask for rotating rest breaks, and obtain passes.

In the middle of the talk, we hear a noise.

We rush outside.

The workers have raised up the car and are trying to overturn it. They want to keep me from leaving.

We have to organize a watch. I introduce myself to Lieutenant Elfess, head of the German detachment.

Next to him is a tall soldier who serves as an interpreter, but who intervenes constantly in the discussion to give his opinion.

The name of this particularly active secretary is Rough. They say he is Alsatian and that he served in the French army.

I've already had occasion to encounter him, and we didn't exactly hit it off.

I present my requests.

I ask that all bad treatment end and that weekly rest be granted.

The lieutenant, who's been listening courteously to me, answers that he would be disposed to consider these questions if the escapes came to a stop and if the full complement of workers were reestablished.

I also protest the summary execution of Hababou.

An attempt to escape could be punished without recourse to such an inhuman response.

"These are orders from my superiors. They must be carried out," the officer replies.

Rough rubs it in enthusiastically.

Finally, it is agreed that I will do my best to restore the workforce.

A few passes are conceded on a trial basis.

Orders will be given to forbid corporal punishment on condition that the Jewish leaders take responsibility for discipline upon themselves.

The result of our conversation is, on the whole, satisfactory.

* * *

After lunch, I visit the camp.

The rooms are in bad condition. The most basic rules of hygiene are not being observed.

I point this out to the group leaders.

And then I listen to the men's complaints.

Each one insists on his case, explains his reasons, and inevitably concludes that he must be replaced without delay.

I try hard to explain the difficulties of recruitment, the abysmal failure of call-ups.

I lay out the steps I'll take to put pressure on the recalcitrant in order to allow for a fair system of replacements.

I promise these men I'll do my very best never to abandon them.

I leave the camp, as night is falling, in a perceptibly relaxed atmosphere.

The announced bombing did not take place.

Translated by Michele McKay Aynesworth.

Etty Hillesum

1914–1943

Esther "Etty" Hillesum was born in Middelburg, the Netherlands. At age eighteen, Hillesum enrolled in university in Amsterdam, earning her degree in law before moving on to study Russian. Her letters and diaries, which she began writing in 1941, detail life in Amsterdam and at the Westerbork transit camp during the German occupation. In 1943, Hillesum, her parents, and her brother were sent from Westerbork to Auschwitz and murdered.

Letters from Westerbork
1943

Finding something to say about Westerbork is also difficult because of its ambiguous character. On the one hand it is a stable community in the making, a forced one to be sure, yet with all the characteristics of a human society. And on the other hand, it is a camp for a people in transit, great waves of human beings constantly washed in from the cities and provinces, from rest homes, prisons, and other prison camps, from all the nooks and crannies of the Netherlands—only to be deported a few days later to meet their unknown destiny. [. . .]

The slum-dwellers arrived from the cities, displaying their poverty and neglect in the bare barracks. Aghast, many of us asked ourselves: what sort of democracy did we really have?

The people from Rotterdam were in a class by themselves, hardened by the bombing raids. "We don't frighten easily anymore," you often heard them say. "If we survived all that, we'll survive this too." And a few days later they marched singing to the train. But it was midsummer then, and there were no old people yet, or invalids on stretchers bringing up the rear . . .

The Jews from Heerlen and Maastricht and thereabouts came telling stories that reverberated with the great send-off the province of Limburg had given them. One felt that morally they could live on it for a long time. "The Catholics have promised to pray for us, and they're better at that than we are!" said one of them.

People came with all their rivalries. The Jews from Haarlem said somewhat loftily and acidly: "Those Amsterdammers have a grim sense of humor."

There were children who would not accept a sandwich before their parents had had one. There was a remarkable day when the Jewish Catholics or Catholic Jews—whichever you want to call them—arrived, nuns and priests wearing the yellow star on their habits. I remember two young novices, twins, with identical beautiful, dark ghetto faces and serene, childish eyes peering out from under their skullcaps. They said with mild surprise that they had been fetched at half-past four from morning mass, and that they had eaten red cabbage in Amersfoort.

There was a priest, still fairly young, who had not left his monastery for fifteen years. He was out in the "world" for the first time, and I stood next to him for a while, following his eyes as they wandered peacefully around the barracks where the newcomers were being received.

The others—shaven, beaten, maltreated—who poured in along with the Catholics that day stumbled about the wooden hut with movements that were still unsteady and stretched out their hands toward the bread, of which there was not enough.

A young Jew stood very still next to us. His jacket was much too loose, but a grin broke through his stubbly black beard when he said, "They tried to smash the wall of the prison with my head, but my head was harder than the wall!"

Among all the shaved heads, it was strange to see the white-turbaned women who had just been treated in the delousing barracks, and who went about now looking distressed and humiliated.

Children dozed off on the dusty plank floor; others played tag among the adults. Two little ones floundered helplessly around the heavy body of a woman lying unconscious in a corner. They didn't understand why their mother just lay there without answering them. A gray-haired old gentleman, straight as an arrow and with a clear-cut, aristocratic profile, stared at the whole infernal canvas and repeated over and over to himself: "A terrible day! A terrible day!"

And among all this, the unremitting clatter of a battery of typewriters: the machine-gun fire of bureaucracy. [. . .]

10 July 1943

Maria, hello,

Ten thousand have passed through this place, the clothed and the naked, the old and the young, the sick and the healthy—and I am left to live and work and stay cheerful. It will be my parents' turn to leave soon, if by some miracle not this week, then certainly one of the next. And I must learn to accept this as well. Mischa insists on going along with them, and it seems to me that he probably should; if he has to watch our parents leave this place, it will totally unhinge him. I shan't go, I just can't. It is easier to pray for someone from a distance than to see him suffer by your side. It is not fear of Poland that keeps me from going along with my parents, but fear of seeing them suffer. And that, too, is cowardice.

This is something people refuse to admit to themselves: at a given point you can no longer *do*, but can only *be* and accept. And although that is something I learned a long time ago, I also know that one can only accept for oneself and not for others. And that's what is so desperately difficult for me here. Mother and Mischa still want to "do," to turn the whole world upside down, but I know we can't do anything about it. I have never been able to "do" anything; I can only let things take their course and if need be, suffer. This is where my strength lies, and it is great strength indeed. But for myself, not for others.

Translated by Arnold J. Pomerans.

Other work by Hillesum: *An Interrupted Life: The Diaries of Etty Hillesum, 1941–1943* (1983).

Kovno Jewish Ghetto Police

1941–1944

The Jewish Ghetto Police (Jüdische Ghetto-Polizei or Jüdischer Ordnungsdienst) was organized in August 1941. Like ghetto police elsewhere, the Kovno ghetto police found themselves serving two masters: the German occupation authorities and the Jewish council. They did their best to help the Jewish population while at the same time following Nazi orders. While many of their actions aroused the ire of the Jewish population, who accused them of favoritism and corruption, the Jewish police cooperated with the resistance and helped smuggle food into and children out of the ghetto. Members of the police kept a remarkable chronicle which recorded the life of the ghetto, the dilemmas faced by the police in their relations with the Germans, the Judenrat, and the ghetto population, and their efforts to preserve some modicum of decency and integrity. The leaders of the ghetto police—Moshe Levin, Yehuda Zupevitz, and Ike Griberg—showed great heroism in March 1944 when they refused, under torture, to divulge information about hiding places and Jewish resistance. Very few Jewish policemen survived the war.

History of the Viliampole Jewish Ghetto Police
1943

Sunday, November 1 [1942], it was announced in the order of the day that all policemen must assemble at twenty minutes past two in the premises of the former Slobodka Yeshive for a solemn oath-taking ceremony.

Although it may have been just a coincidence, the fact that the oath-taking ceremony would take place in the famous former Slobodka Yeshive touched discerning people. The Slobodka Yeshive was famous all over the world; great personalities came from it over the decades, people who played a part in the Jewish world—to become famous doctors, professors, Jewish leaders, bearers of the culture. Many of these were former pupils of the Slobodka Yeshive.

During the year that the Russians were here, they closed the Yeshive and established an institute in the building. In the early days of the ghetto it was occupied by families, the same as all other houses of prayer. Later, when the houses of prayer were vacated by their inhabitants, this building also stayed ruined and empty. The police renovated the building somewhat, made some small repairs, cleaned it up.

Honorary guests were invited to the oath-taking ceremony, for whom special seats were reserved. In order to lend the entire ceremony a solemn character, police management organized musicians residing in the ghetto. Among the policemen themselves there were two good violinists, known throughout Lithuania, Stupel and Hoffmekler. Previously, both conducted first-class orchestras in Kovno. A fine orchestra was organized to play at the oath-taking ceremony under the leadership of Hoffmekler.

All policemen showed up at the specified time and, upon the commands of police inspector Zupovitz—which for the first time in the life of the police force were given not in Lithuanian but in clear Hebrew—they lined up in front. A short while thereafter arrived the vice-chairman of the Elder Council, L. Garfunkel (the chairman, Dr. Elkes, who was generally not in good health, was ill on that particular day), in the company of the member of the Elder Council Goldberg, general secretary Golub, and representative of the labor office, Liptzer. In fluent Hebrew, police inspector Z. [Zupovitz] announced their presence in military fashion.

Mr. Garfunkel opened the proceedings with a speech concerning matters of general interest. He was followed by the chief of police, Kopelman; then the policeman Ben Zion Kliotz spoke on behalf of the policemen.

The actual oath-taking ceremony followed. The text was written in Hebrew block letters, in Yiddish and Hebrew, on decoratively illustrated parchment paper, rolled like a scroll [*megila*] and bound with a wide white-and-blue ribbon.

Golub, the general secretary of the Elder Council, read the text first in Hebrew and then in Yiddish, and then again, word by word in Yiddish, which everyone repeated after him. The text of the oath is as follows:

> November 1, 1942
> PLEDGE
> I, member of the Jewish ghetto police, Viliampole, in the presence of the chairman of the Elder Council and the chief of ghetto police, solemnly assume the obligations:
> to conscientiously and unconditionally carry out all assignments and orders without regard to time, personal considerations, or danger;
> to fulfill all duties without regard to personal benefits, kinship, friendship, or acquaintance;
> to rigorously guard all service-related secrets and information;

I pledge to devote all my strength and experience to the well-being of the Jewish community in the ghetto;

I PLEDGE[1]

After reciting the entire text, everyone came in a line to the table upon which lay the written text of the oath, and everyone signed it. The orchestra played national themes throughout the entire time that the line of policemen approached the table to sign the pledge, which lent a solemn character to the entire signing ceremony.

After signing the written text, the entire staff returned to its place, the command to march out was given, and the orchestra thundered the well-known, stirring national march "Beshuv Adonai" [When the Lord brings back]. It was as though the sound of the tune touched off the police staff and part of the audience, awakening suppressed feelings, enflaming hearts and minds, our senses—dulled and atrophied as a result of the entire bundle of our troubles, and, as if by prearrangement, thundered from the throats of hundreds of people, together with the orchestra, *beshuv Adonai et shivas Tzi-yon hayinu k-kholmim, oz yimohle skhok pinu u-lshoneinu rinoh . . . ha-zorim b-dimoh, b-rinohyiktzoru* [From Psalm 126: When the Lord brings the captives of Zion home, we will be as dreamers, yet our mouths will fill with laughter, our lips with song . . . those who sow in tears, will reap with song]. With tears in our eyes the entire assembly sang along the words of the prophecy of freedom and liberation, of the fulfillment of our dreamed-of and most sacred hopes, which are today only fantasies but may perhaps become a reality tomorrow.

With the orchestra playing and the policemen and the assembled people singing, moved by the profound impression made by the demonstration of national will, everyone dispersed.

After this oath-taking ceremony, the idea matured to establish a police association building with a permanent orchestra—a building for music that would serve the cultural needs of the police and of the ghetto population.

Creation of the police association quarters in the premises of the former yeshiva was announced in the order of the day of November 28. Guidelines for the operation of the police association quarters were developed and were endorsed by the chairman of the Elder Council on January 3, 1943. These guidelines defined the activities of the police association quarters. The guidelines consisted of seven paragraphs in which the following is set forth:

The police association building is being established to educate and develop the police staff, which is to function as a separate police entity and be managed by the chief of the police association.

Activities of the police association are divided into organizational and artistic sectors.

The organizational sector encompasses the theoretical lectures and drill exercises. The artistic sector encompasses musical and artistic activities.

The chief of the police association directs all the activities of the police association and, with the concurrence of police management, determines the work-plan for both sectors.

The chief of the police association routinely makes reports to the police administration and receives directions concerning the activities of the police association.

As may be seen from these guidelines, creation of the police association was for theoretical education and development purposes, as well as for artistic and musical performance purposes. In effect, however, the police association quarters became the only place where the permanent police orchestra gave concerts, which were at a high artistic level.

The police association building was rebuilt and renovated, a proper concert hall was arranged, complete with all the decorations, as in the good old days. Music concerts were given every Saturday and Sunday, attended by hundreds of people. Singers and actors were also included, to sing and give recitals.

At the time, creation of a concert hall in the ghetto provoked much commentary and criticism. It was said that the ghetto is not the place to give concerts; this is not the place to make musical presentations and to be merry. We have neither the right nor the desire to forget all that we have lived through.

On the other hand, it became evident later on that the concerts also had a positive character, in the sense that, when all is said and done, one must have in the ghetto a few hours in the week when one can forget a little, to rest up somewhat from the daily nightmare and to rise somewhat above the day-to-day grayness, into a nicer world that fills one with hope and gives courage.

The second view prevailed. The concerts continue uninterrupted and are a positive aspect of ghetto life.

Who would have believed a year ago that Jews in the ghetto would have concerts? Life, by itself, makes things happen that could normally never come about.

A normal life—given a little peace and a semblance of security, and already there is activity, enterprise, vigor, release of pent-up energy.

The police association—a product of its time, of improved living conditions in the ghetto.

NOTES

[Words in brackets appear in the original translation.—Eds.]

1. The manuscript includes the Yiddish as well as the Hebrew texts of the oath, in side-by-side columns.

Translated by Samuel Schalkowsky.

Baruch Milch

1907–1989

Physician Baruch Milch was born in Podhajce, Poland. His wife and family were killed during World War II, but he survived because of the need for his medical skills. He was forced into hiding in 1943 and wrote details of his wartime experiences on scraps of paper that he later donated to the Jewish Historical Institute in Warsaw. After immigrating to Israel in 1948, Milch rewrote his memoir in Hebrew, which was published in English by Yad Vashem.

Can Heaven Be Void?
1943

July 15, 1943

I am in hiding in a loft over a stable, in a village, with good people. The risk of death hovers over me, as it does over all Jews these days, and the slightest lapse of vigilance on my part may cost me my life. I desperately need to spill this heavy burden onto paper. Perhaps it will give me a little relief.

I do not know whether I shall live to finish the writing. All I ask is that if these notebooks fall into the hands of someone who is decent, he will add anything that he deems necessary as long as he undertakes to bring these events to the world's notice. It is difficult to believe that the atrocities I am about to describe actually happened. Therefore, I emphasize that every word is true.

On Friday, September 1, 1939, the day World War II broke out, my real life began to end. The events of that day, and everything that happened in the ensuing days and years, will be remembered to the world's eternal shame for as long as mankind endures. One day, when we tell our children and grandchildren what happened to us, they will find it hard to believe that human beings could endure such agonies. If such stories are true, they will think, then the world must end.

Now, as I write this, the terrible war is in full swing and the threat of final destruction by gas still lies ahead. Only a few of us will survive.

Translated by Helen Kaye.

Calel Perechodnik

1916–1944

Calel Perechodnik was born to an Orthodox Jewish family in Otwock, Poland. Perechodnik was able to temporarily provide for his family by joining the Jewish ghetto police in February 1941. However, his wife and daughter were sent to Treblinka in 1942 and Perechodnik died in 1944 in the Warsaw ghetto. His wartime diaries were published in 1995 by the Karta Center of Warsaw.

Letter to Anka
1943

19 August 1943

Today, dear Anka, is the anniversary of your Golgotha, tomorrow the anniversary of your death. A year has passed since I last saw you. You see, Anka, I do not believe in God and never will, but there is one thing in which I want to and have to believe: the immortality of the soul. Because I can't imagine that there's nothing left of you. Yes, I know very well that the Germans burned your body, your wondrous body I kissed so many times, and used it as fertilizer. Maybe the potatoes I am now consuming grew on your ashes, maybe the rye in the bread I am eating. I don't want to think about that for I'll go out of my mind, but I want and have to think and believe that your soul, your pure and noble soul, is alive and that it's looking down on me from above, that it sees everything I do and praises or reproaches me.

You remember, Anka, how every evening I would tell you about the day's activities? You would listen carefully, perhaps bored by my professional concerns, but you never let that show. You knew my every deed, my every thought. I don't need to tell you that I never lied or hid anything from you. You always knew that very well and were so proud of your Całek. Even at the last moment, when I had a sacred obligation to lie to you, to tell you that they had found the basement where she was hiding and that they killed her, that there was nothing you could have done to save that basement, I broke down; I was unable to lie.

In my introduction to this memoir I wrote that it should be read as my dying confession; in essence, however, it is an accounting presented to you on the anniversary of your death. As I cannot talk to you every evening and share my thoughts and experiences, I had to pour all this down on paper and today I am reading it to you.

Do I need to reassure you that I've left nothing out, that everything I've written is true? You know me, dearest Aneczka; you know I am incapable of lying to you. So you are listening carefully. You probably know not only my past but my future as well.

You may know that I didn't escape the fate of the Jews, you sympathize and pity me for having to endure another year of suffering, for having to see so many horrible things. Are you thinking that it would have been better if I hadn't broken out on that cursed day, if I had bravely accompanied you on your last earthly journey?

Or maybe you know, Anka, that I am fated to survive the war, so that I will remember you always, love you always, always pay homage to you. You see, Anka, I was terribly afraid of dying—not before the Aktion in Otwock but afterward. Before the Aktion I was a fatalist, I believed that whatever is meant to be will be, but I never imagined—and I'm sure you believe me, Anka—that you would perish and I would remain alive.

I was sure we were inseparable and that no force could break us apart. Unfortunately, I was the one who broke us apart—I was indifferent to the fate of the masses and I let you go off into the unknown while I stayed. After that I began to be horribly afraid of dying. Not of death itself, but the shame of dying in this way while I could have died honorably, trying to sweeten the last minutes of your life.

Today, Anka, I am no longer afraid to die, and in a month I'll no longer be afraid of anything. You're not surprised, Aneczka, at this metamorphosis; after all, you always guessed my thoughts right away, before I even spoke them, before I even formulated them for myself. Maybe that's why I could never lie to you? Or maybe I respected you too much, loved you too much

to lie to you? Therefore, Anka, you will understand me perfectly now, as well. Once I wanted to have a child, to remember me in case I died. Now that I am completely alone, now that I am orphaned, I cannot leave a living child for posterity; I had to leave an inanimate object into which I myself breathed life. . . .

This progeny is my account, which I believe will someday be printed so that the whole world will learn of your suffering. I have written it to your glory, to your immortality, and leave it as an eternal monument to you. Now that this child has been brought to life, it must be protected until it grows. . . . Alúska, our first daughter, perished with you. What great fortune, Aneczka dearest, that on that cursed day you did not know that our lawyer friend hoped to save her, that he wanted to take our daughter to his sister to be raised.

Your heart would have broken if you had known how close our daughter came to being saved, in what good hands she might have been placed. Now you do know, but now all human suffering is alien to you. I on the other hand, who have remained, must suffer and rend my living flesh thinking about our Alúska, thinking about my guilt. . . .

I have faith that millions of people will read these memories, that they will pity you for the fate that bound you to me in marriage. If you were single, if you had never believed in me so reverently, surely you would have saved yourself. I brought your doom, but I will also achieve your revenge.

Your second child will avenge you, your child born in the pain of death. On the day I place this child with our friend, my soul will regain its balance, I will no longer be afraid of death or the life to come, and I will no longer regret my still being alive, or that at the last moment I betrayed you so basely.

Translated by Joachim Neugroschel.

Oskar Rosenfeld

Chanukah in the Ghetto
1943

Saturday, December 25, 1943

"The living faith has vanished. . . . All that remains is poetry!" A superficial observer of life in the ghetto might come to more or less the same conclusion about the way religious festivals are celebrated here. The ardor of prayer seems to have yielded to ritual, to a practice that feigns devotion, traces of which have survived only among the old and the pious. As any unbiased Jew will acknowledge, however, the symbols of the festivals remain intact, embedded in tradition, and neither hunger nor cold can claim them.

The difficulty in yielding to the enchantment of religious practice is due, first of all, to a lack of suitable space. The *besmedresh* [prayer and study house] is closed. There are only a very few minyonim holding worship service here and there in a secret shul.

Chanukah, of course, does not require such houses of worship. In the ghetto, Chanukah is a family holiday, as it used to be throughout Eastern Europe before the war. It does not have to be performed on an official stage. A Jew who really wishes to commemorate the Maccabees in traditional fashion stages the festival at home.

In the street, a creature wrapped in rags huddles on dirty steps by a broken door, you can just about make out a face through the rags. The creature is hawking candles [in Yiddish]: "Lekht! Lekht!" Normally, these are the Sabbath candles that are peddled every week on Sabbath eve. This time they are intended for something else, something rarer: candles for the menorah.

Not everyone can afford to allow his menorah its full glory. An additional candle every day, until all eight arms of the menorah are lighted, that means thirty-six candles; counting the candle for lighting the others, the *shames* [sexton], thirty-seven. Or, in terms of money, a minimum of eighteen marks, since each candle costs fifty pfennigs. Indeed, there are families that can even afford to treat themselves to candles of the one-for-a-mark variety, and thus pay thirty-six marks for "mere lighting."

And yet, despite the problems of space and finances, Chanukah was celebrated with dignity this year too.

A great number of families lighted candles. Along with the *sforim* [religious books], *makhzoyrim* [prayer books for holidays], *sidurim* [daily prayer books], *taleysim* [prayer shawls], and *tfiln* [phylacteries], the man of the house had brought the menorah from the city—rescued it, smuggled it—into the ghetto. One sees simple menorahs of brass or cast iron, but also copper and nickel menorahs, old ones, new ones, factory-made or hand-crafted, free-standing menorahs, or those that are hung on walls. People invite friends and acquaintances. The guests clamber up dark staircases, through dank courtyards and hallways, into an apartment—usually just one room that doubles as living quarters and "best room" for special occasions.

Many people dress for the holiday. Everyone is in a holiday mood. One privileged person, often the daughter of the house, sings the benediction before the lighting of candles. It often happens that Jews brought here from the [western Polish] provinces and Jews from the German west find themselves together in one such room and share in the festival. The candles are bright. Memories of previous Chanukah evenings pass through the mind. Memories of youth, of student days, of happy years in freedom, images and impressions somehow connected with the festival of the Maccabees.

People assemble "in private," without official ritual, with only a lighted menorah. Children too celebrate Chanukah. There are gatherings in larger apartments. Everyone brings a small, appropriate gift: a toy, a piece of *babka* [cake], a hair ribbon, a couple of brightly colored empty cigarette packages, a plate with a flower pattern, a pair of stockings, a warm cap. Then comes the drawing of lots; and chance decides.

After the candles are lighted, the presents are handed out. Ghetto presents are not valuable, but they are received with deep gratitude. Finally, songs are sung in Yiddish, Hebrew, and Polish, as long as they are suitable for enhancing the holiday mood. A few hours of merrymaking, a few hours of forgetting, a few hours of reverie. . . . Let the Chanukah celebration of 1943 be the last Chanukah of the war, the last Chanukah in the ghetto. This is everyone's hope. This is what people wish each other when they part—without a word, mutely, with only a handshake.

The menorah candles burn down. It grows dark again. People step out into the street. Ghetto life resumes.

NOTE

[Words in brackets appear in the original translation.—Eds.]

Translated by Joachim Neugroschel.

Mihail Sebastian

1907-1945

Mihail Sebastian was born Iosef Hechter in Brăila, Romania, and studied in Bucharest and Paris. Sebastian wrote for multiple periodicals on topics ranging from the literary to the social, in addition to being a novelist and a playwright. The novel *De două mii de ani* (*For Two Thousand Years*; 1934) is his most famous work, dealing with the interwar Jewish European experience. The original edition of the novel includes a foreword by Nae Ionescu, Sebastian's former mentor who by that time had become a spokesman for antisemitism, making the novel a site of controversy. Sebastian died in Bucharest shortly after the end of Ion Antonescu's reign, leaving behind a journal chronicling his experiences from 1935 to 1944.

Journal, 1935–1944: The Fascist Years
1943

1 January 1943, Friday

I am beginning to get used to the years of war. We seem to struggle through the same journey from first of January to first of January, in a nightmare that is itself beginning to have a certain monotony. The seasons always bring the same phases. Winters of German semislumber, when you feel the armies are tired: low reserves, no stamina left. Then spring comes and you live in expectation of a new offensive—in April? in May? in June? And when the fighting suddenly becomes fierce with the arrival of summer, the offensive and the propaganda reach dizzying new heights, and you live a few days of fear, doubt, and mortification. Could it just possibly be that . . . ? Later, in September or October, you realize that nothing decisive has happened. The pace of events slackens again in the weeks before the first snow, and the cycle begins all over again. How much longer will this continue? Will 1943 bring us peace? I don't think so. Not unless a miracle happens. I tend to think, rather, that 1943 will repeat without major differences the trajectory of 1942, certainly accentuating the German decline and the Allied rise, but not by so much as to bring the denouement rapidly closer. Perhaps in 1944. Anyway, I find it easier to say 1944, precisely because it is still far away.

What is becoming of me, of us, in all this madness? I don't know. For the moment we are still alive. We have got this far, and it's possible that we will get further. Nothing depends on me, on us. Everything takes place over our heads. All we can do is wait. But God knows, it is not easy. [. . .]

Wednesday, 24 February

A dream last night. I am at a political meeting, in a hall which, though not large, is crowded with people. Goebbels is speaking, together with a tall, dark-haired man—probably Gunther. Someone (he looks like Coșoiu, a pupil of mine from 5th Year) shouts: "Hech-

ter! Hechter!" I make desperate signs for him to be quiet. Goebbels comes up to me but is then again speaking at the rostrum. He seems to propose the formation of an action committee. Then Perpessicius appears from a neighboring room and says: I'll sign if you like, but I won't work." Goebbels consults his assistant in the first row and calls on everyone in turn: "And you are Aryan, and you, and you. . . ." He stops in front of Camil Petrescu, hesitates, and smiles awkwardly: "Ah, I'm not sure about you. Maybe you're not." Camil is mortified. That is all I can remember. In fact, it was more complicated and richer in incident—and it was not even as coherent as my account suggests, though I think my broad outline is accurate enough. [. . .]

Tuesday, 18 May

A long visit to Marie Ghiolu, who talked to me about Creața and how she died. She had many absorbing things to add to their story, which is already pretty strange. I'd like to note them down. Maybe tomorrow.

Two terrible dreams last night. In one I was with Hitler, who spoke Romanian and threatened me with dreadful things. In the other I was in Paris, the same German-occupied Paris of which I have dreamed a number of times. I felt horror, a choking sense of unease. Then I woke up terrified.

I regret that I can no longer remember the details. [. . .]

Friday, 31 December

Certain gestures and habits, by force of repetition, have become almost like superstitions: a letter to Poldy, a book for Aristide, some records for Leni. I went to Socec to buy a calendar refill. This evening I shall go for a meal at Alice's. I have hastily reread this notebook.

The 31st of December. Like a year ago, or two years, or three years. When did this year pass? It seemed so heavy, so foggy, so uncertain. And yet it went. It has passed and we are still alive.

But the war is still here beside us, with us, in us. Closer to the end, but for that very reason more dramatic.

Any personal balance sheet gets lost in the shadow of war. Its terrible presence is the first reality. Then somewhere far away, forgotten by us, are we ourselves, with our faded, diminished, lethargic life, as we wait to emerge from sleep and start living again.

Translated by Patrick Camiller.

Other works by Sebastian: *Orașul cu salcâmi* (1935); *Jocul de-a vacant* (1938); *Accidentul* (1940); *Steaua fără nume* (1944); *Ultima oră* (1945).

Ephraim E. Urbach

1912–1991

Ephraim E. Urbach was born into a Hasidic family in Białystok. He was ordained as a rabbi at the Jewish Theological Seminary of Breslau and also earned a doctorate from the University of Rome. In 1938, Urbach moved to Israel, serving in World War II as a chaplain in the British Army. He taught at the Hebrew University, becoming professor of Talmud and Midrash in 1958; his academic focus was on the history of halakhah and of rabbinic thought. Urbach served as president of the Israel Academy of Sciences and Humanities and earned the 1955 Israel Prize for Jewish studies and the Bialik Prize, in 1983, for Jewish thought.

War Journals: Diary of a Jewish Chaplain from Eretz-Israel in the British Army
1943

26 Iyyar (May 5, 1943)

Today I returned from my trip to Tunis, and I will start to record what I witnessed, heard, and felt. On Thursday, 15 Iyyar (May 20, 1943), I left Tripoli. [. . .]

On that day, we reached Medenine, Tunisia. We slept there, and in the morning, we continued [our journey]. We also visited the antiquities at *Jhigis*. [. . .] At 12:00 I reached the shore, from which the boats sail to Djerba. Next to me were waiting Jews from Gabès, Medenine, and Sfax, who also came to Djerba in honor of the celebration. One of them was holding the Vienna edition of *Sefer ha-mada'* [*The Book of Knowledge*] by Maimonides. During the boat trip we sat and studied the laws of reciting the Shema' and of prayer. When we reached Djerba, the aforementioned Jew brought me to the home of the rabbi and went in to announce my arrival. The rabbi, Rabbi Shushan Cohen, came out to greet me. [. . .] They told me about the present situation of the community. According to Rabbi Kalfoun Moshe ha-Kohen and his son, Rabbi Shushan Cohen, the Jews are not yet receiving their ration of food, even though the wealthiest of them are British citizens. Free commerce is stifled; Jews aren't allowed to trade in veg-

etables and fish. The Jews are forced to buy foodstuffs on the black market, and then they are punished and arrested. [. . .] It's known that the Germans forced them to gather up all the gold in their possession before they left. Airplanes circled above the city and threatened to bomb it, and they quickly gathered 43 kg of gold from the local Jewish shops and goldsmiths. Now they want the authority to impose a tax on all the residents of the place according to their economic situation, to assist the poor, many of whom gave up all their gold. Mainly, they blame the local French bureaucrats, who are still loyal to the spirit of Vichy. We promised to do everything in our ability. Afterward, the conversation turned to matters of Torah and wisdom, and again I was reminded of the home of a rabbi in a small village in Poland.

A few more residents of the place gathered. Then we ate lunch, and Rabbi Shushan Cohen told us about the history of the place. [. . .]

We went to see the workshops of the gold- and silversmiths, and we saw them sitting at their workbenches. Though they can't do much work at present, lacking materials, their handiwork is well known and famous, and they are truly excellent artisans. In the local museum there is a whole exhibition of the products of their workshops. The Jews work in all the building trades. We entered the printshop of Rabbi David 'Adan, a Jew who also engages in practical Kabbalah, and is now printing his sermons. Then we went to the place they allotted for us to sleep on the Sabbath, near the ancient El Ghriba synagogue. [. . .]

The synagogue is one of the most beautiful I have ever seen. Much labor and work were, and are still, invested in it to maintain and decorate it. There is a lot of silver, a valuable menorah, and the Ark is full of dozens of Torah scrolls. I'm told there are about eighty. [. . .]

The synagogue is built in two sections. The first room is not regarded as less sacred than the inner room, where everyone who enters must remove his shoes.

Toward evening the celebrants danced, sang, and rejoiced in a great multitude of men, women, and children together in the courtyard and in the hall of the synagogue. Apparently, for that reason the "serious rabbis" fenced themselves off and kept themselves at a distance from the whole celebration, even though the revenue is important to them. Toward evening the women entered to light Sabbath candles, and then they began reciting the Song of Songs. [. . .]

We reached Kairouan. I wanted to see the rabbi, for I knew that he was from Djerba, and the brother of

Rabbi Makhlouf 'Adan. I found an old Jew, infected and stricken, to whom the doctor could not give medicine, for there was none to be had in the market. Afterward I went into the synagogue, which is entirely new; there is only a plaque commemorating that the greatest commentators on the Talmud lived in this city, disseminating the Torah of the geonim of Babylonia in the West. [. . .]

The situation of the Jews of Kairouan is not too bad. The French there are De Gaulle's people, but still, there's not much fondness between the Jews and the French. [. . .]

In the evening, I was invited to the home of a Jew named Ḥayim. The Jews of Tunisia receive the soldiers with open arms, and of course they are mainly happy to see Jewish soldiers. They told me about the Germans who seized their houses, robbed them, took everything they could get their hands on, and forced the community to provide labor for them. Of course, most of them hid, but they nonetheless found about six thousand, and the community had to support them. [. . .]

On the way I saw a building with a Hebrew inscription. I went in and found a grave with a monument and a kind of small synagogue inside it. [. . .] It's the tomb of a kabbalist who is regarded as holy by all the Jews of Tunisia. The whole street was once a cemetery. Then, when they built the road and the houses on both sides, they left just this one tomb.

The next day, Thursday, I met with a few more people from the community, and they all complained about the decline and the great abandonment of the community. I went in to see the building of the Alliance school, where now there is a military office for enlisting civilian workers from among the Jews, the Maltese, and the French. They don't take Arabs because they are all suspect and showed great partiality toward the Germans. They were very disappointed after the entry of the Allies. They persecuted the Jews and showed the Germans their houses and the places where they hid their property, their money, and their capital. The Germans spread a lot of anti-British propaganda among the Arabs and published an illustrated newspaper called *Siknal*, in which they published a great deal of anti-Jewish material, special illustrated cards, and so on. [. . .]

On Friday (May 28, 1943) I visited ancient Carthage, the museum of the White Brethren, and churches and ancient ruins. Of course, the ancient Hebrew writing on many of the tombstones aroused special interest in me. There are some shards with Jewish symbols, a sho-

far, a lulav, a menorah, and the words *shalom* on them. [. . .]

The place, *Qarat Ḥadasha* [Carthage], is outstanding in its exalted beauty and good air. The men of ancient Tyre knew how to choose. Now the headquarters of the First Camp is there. [. . .]

I spent the Sabbath evening in the home of Fortunato Hadar. His whole family honored me, and they couldn't do enough for me. They told me that the attitude of the Italians of Tunisia toward the Jews was much better than that of the French. The Italians, according to them, were only antisemites in their skin, but the French were so even in their hearts. When they took the Jews for forced labor, they didn't take the Jews who were Italian citizens. They even wanted to save them from the confiscation of their houses, but they didn't succeed. In their opinion, the French didn't help the Allies very much; the collaborators left with the Germans, but most of them were neither Gaullists nor Vichyists, but "familyists." Even now there is tension between the French and the Jews. They didn't take a favorable view of the closeness between the Jews and the Allied armies or their great joy upon their arrival. Many Jews were astonished that they had restored the regime to the French, and that they would prefer English or American occupation.

On Sabbath morning I went to the synagogue with Fortunato Hadar. Of course, all of them knew about my coming and started to honor me with the Torah reading. [. . .] I was astonished to see the great number of Jewish soldiers from the First Camp and from the Americans, who filled the synagogue and really came to pour out prayers to their Maker.

In the afternoon many soldiers gathered. I learned that apart from two soldiers from the air corps, whom I had seen earlier, there were also another five from the Land of Israel, from the 5th LFA [Light Field Ambulance], who were on the road to Tunis, and there were also many soldiers from the British and American armies. The synagogue was full from wall to wall—old people and young, women and children—every seat was taken. Two soldiers closed the door after I gave them a sign to do so. The Chief Rabbi and all the notables of the community also attended. At first I spoke in English and described to the soldiers the great joy that the presence of Jewish soldiers in the ranks of the army aroused in every place that was liberated by the Allied armies. I reminded them and described the deeds of the brigades from the Land of Israel, of our war, by our own Jewish army, and the rebirth of the Jewish people. Afterward, I spoke in Hebrew and directed most of my words to the community of Tunisia, among whom some of the words of the *Toḥeḥa* [the Mosaic Curses] had come true: "In the morning you will say, if only it might be evening, and in the evening you will say, if only morning might come" [Deuteronomy 28:67], and "The Lord will bring a nation against you from far, from the end of the earth, as the vulture swoops down; a nation whose tongue you will not understand" [Deuteronomy 28:49]. They must remember that their suffering was as nothing compared to the suffering of our brethren in Europe, but they did taste of bitterness. The synagogue in which we were praying, in which there were still signs in German: *Rauchen verboten* [no smoking] had been polluted by the enemy, who made it a place for their accursed officers. Now once again the crown was restored as of old, but most of our nation had not yet attained even the minimal rights that other nations had received. The struggle continued mainly by the Yishuv in the Land of Israel, upon whom the main burden of this war had been placed, and the Jewish communities which were being liberated had to begin to cooperate actively in this struggle. [. . .] The audience enjoyed my sermon, and tears remained in many eyes, with shouts of agreement and enthusiasm breaking out from time to time.

After I finished, we began afternoon prayers. [. . .] The service ended with the singing of the British national anthem and "Hatikva." When I left, people reached out their hands to me, and children and youth even kissed my hand.

On Sunday morning, I left Tunis and took a Jewish family named Labi with me. They have British citizenship and received permission to return to Tripoli. After a journey of a day and a half, staying overnight in Gabès, I returned to Tripoli on May 31.

Translated by Jeffrey M. Green.

Other works by Urbach: *Arugat ha-bosem* (1939–1963); *Ba'ale ha-tosafot* (1955); *The Sages: Their Concepts and Beliefs* (1969); *The Halakhah: Its Sources and Development* (1986); *Collected Writings in Jewish Studies* (1999).

Artur-Shmuel Ziegelboym

1895–1943

Artur-Shmuel Ziegelboym was born in Borowica, Poland. He was involved in the Jewish labor movement at an early age and was a member of the Central Committee of the Bund. After living in Warsaw and Łódź, he escaped to Belgium in 1939 and served on the National Council of the Polish government in exile, speaking out about the fate of Polish Jewry while spending time in France and the United States. In April 1942, Ziegelboym moved to London to serve as the Bund's representative in the Polish National Council. He committed suicide in 1943, in protest to the indifference of the Allied governments in the face of the Holocaust.

A Letter to the Polish Premier
1943

I take the liberty of addressing to you my last words, and through you to the Polish Government and the Polish people, to the Governments and the peoples of the Allied States—to the conscience of the world.

From the latest information received from Poland, it is evident that the Germans, with the most ruthless cruelty, are now murdering the few remaining Jews in Poland. Behind the ghetto's walls the last act of a tragedy unprecedented in history is being performed. The responsibility for this crime of murdering the entire Jewish population of Poland falls in the first instance on the perpetrators, but indirectly it is also a burden on the whole of humanity, the people and the Governments of the Allied States which thus far have made no effort toward concrete action for the purpose of curtailing this crime.

By the passive observation of the murder of defenseless millions, and of the maltreatment of children, women and old men, these countries have become the criminals' accomplices. I must also state that although the Polish Government has in a high degree contributed to the enlistment of world opinion, it has yet done so insufficiently. It has not done anything that could correspond to the magnitude of the drama being enacted now in Poland. From some 3,500,000 Polish Jews and about 700,000 other Jews deported to Poland from other countries—according to official statistics provided by the underground Bund organization—there remained in April of this year only about 300,000, and this continuing murder still goes on.

I cannot be silent—I cannot live—while remnants of the Jewish people of Poland, of whom I am a representative, are perishing. My comrades in the Warsaw ghetto took weapons in their hands on that last heroic impulse. It was not my destiny to die there together with them, but I belong to them, and in their mass graves. By my death I wish to express my strongest protest against the inactivity with which the world is looking on and permitting the extermination of my people.

I know how little human life is worth today; but, as I was unable to do anything during my life, perhaps by my death I shall contribute to breaking down that indifference of those who may now—at the last moment—rescue the few Polish Jews still alive from certain annihilation. My life belongs to the Jewish people of Poland and I therefore give it to them. I wish that this remaining handful of the original several millions of Polish Jews could live to see the liberation of a new world of freedom, and the justice of true socialism. I believe that such a Poland will arise and that such a world will come.

I trust that the President and the Prime Minister will direct my words to all those for whom they are destined, and that the Polish Government will immediately take appropriate action in the fields of diplomacy. I bid my farewell herewith to everybody and everything dear to me and loved by me.

Translator unknown.

Other works by Ziegelboym: *Zigelboym-bukh* (1947).

Anonymous

The Tragedy of 1st and 2nd June, 1941 in the Capital of Iraq
1944

Memories

Every Jew of our community well remembers these two sorrowful days during which cruel killings took place instead of seeing our way to enjoy them as they were the days of "visits festivals" . . . which turned to be days of sadness and terror.

Every child remembers these two frightful days which turned to be days of weeping and appeals for help. . . . We should hear the appeal for help of those girls and women who were touched by the dirty hands. We should share with those children their feelings of terror when they saw with their own eyes their fathers and mothers being killed and dishonored.

We should look upon the memory of those days as a guiding light that will show us our way in the dark of the future.

We tell every man, woman, young man, and girl, and children too, in this day: "Slavery will not save us from being looted, disdain will not prevent us being annihilated, and caring not for ourselves will not guarantee our lives, so you should beware companions, because the day is today."

We have decided not to keep quiet and not to forget our sorrows until the day will come when Israel and its lost people get back to rescue the land of their forefathers.

We shall remember. . . .

What Happened in Baghdad

The disturbances of Rashīd ʿĀlī were over within a month of commencement, after which the Jews felt free again, and they began to show themselves out in the city with gay appearances. This might have increased the hatred of their enemies to them. So it might have been better for the Jews to have been wiser in the manner of showing themselves out again after the disturbances.

It was on the first day of the "Jewish Festival of Visits" when a Jew was wounded in Ghazi Street. The effect of this event was dreadful among the Jews in general, and they began to run to their homes. They all disappeared after a few minutes of the event, and their enemies, seeing this, were encouraged to treat them with killings, especially when no sign of defense was seen from them. The mob attacked the houses of the Jews and looted them, treating their inhabitants in the way they desired. Jewish men were afraid and were looking for escape from death. Their cries and appeals filled the air, and many of them did actually run away, leaving their women and children struggling in the hands of the enemies.

Bands of enemies were wandering inside the Jewish quarters and were killing and looting. Such events lasted until midnight, and many were killed. Heads of children were cut off like sheep, old men were killed, while women were disgraced. . . . This was how the night passed. In the morning the Jews did not know what had happened to their brothers during the night, and they went out for work as usual, but it was only a short interval given by the killers, after which they resumed their terrorism under the management of policemen and ex-soldiers. They began at 9:30 A.M., completing their program of the night before. Their action was begun in Rashid Street and Shorja, where they broke into the shops and commercial stores belonging to the Jews and looted all they could find in them. They moved thereafter to the neighboring Jewish houses and did similarly in them. Ghazi Street found trouble again that day, later on Amin Street, as well as the Jewish quarters of Abū Seifayn, ʿAbbās Effendī, Aqūliyya, and other far and nearby quarters.

Killing and looting lasted until 11 A.M. that day. . . . Bodies of the dead were thrown on pavements on both sides of the street, and this drama did not stop until its conductors wished it off, i.e., some units of the Kurdish Iraqi soldiers gave a hand and all trouble was over within a few minutes.

Every Jewish house sustained the loss of one of its members, or it had at least had one of them wounded. The remaining people lived in terror.

What Do We Learn from the Massacre of Baghdad?

What was it that the Baghdad Jews did not do to be trusted by the Arabs? They gave up their Hebrew language. Did they not stop giving money for the sake of the Land of Israel?[1] They accepted participating with the Arabs in every activity that was in the interests of the country. They were always the first in giving money to help achieving any national scheme in Iraq and especially in Baghdad. Some of the rich Jews have generously contributed to the funds gathered for the followers of the Mufti, who were called the Palestinian Patriot Fighters.

The Jews in Baghdad, for the sake of buying safety for themselves and a comfortable life for their families, abandoned their human dignity and their liberty. Their rich families in Baghdad lived comfortably, but with fear and disdain, while they forgot their brothers who were astray in Europe and who are working hard in the land of Israel. But did they gain any benefit from all this during the days of slaughter? Could they buy their lives with their dignity, or have they found safety for themselves after having so heavily sacrificed? Never. They never did gain any benefit from all this, as slavery will never make them free from being looted and disdained, or from being annihilated.

Death is the result of giving up our rights and all efforts to show the others that we do not cling to Judaism and awakens hatred in the hearts of our enemies. Every endeavor on the part of the Jews to mix with others and do as the others do leads to butchery. Iraq is just like Yemen. Our luck is the same in all the Eastern countries. It is not enough for the Jews to experience such difficulties. Does our history, which is full of news of killings, teach us nothing of the past? Are our memories

so feeble that we forget all that has been done against us so long as we gain profits?[2]

Our aim is a Hebrew National State with Hebrew Power, and our hope lies in defending ourselves and our dignities in life.

NOTES
1. The translator's typescript reads: "They did not stop giving money for the sake of the future of the Israel Land." This, however, seems to be at variance with the gist of the paragraph.
2. Obviously, this tract was prepared by members of a Zionist Socialist movement. Another pamphlet in the same file, entitled "Hebrew Commandoes," denounces the Irgun and Stern Gang as "terrorists" and "enemy of our people with their foolish actions."

Translated by Norman A. Stillman.

Anne Frank
1929–1945

Anne Frank was born in Frankfurt and moved with her parents, Otto and Edith Frank, and her older sister, Margot, to Amsterdam to escape Nazi persecution. In July 1942, the family went into hiding. For two years, Anne wrote about her experiences and dreams in a diary that has become one the most widely read works of nonfiction in the world. On August 4, 1944, Anne and her family were arrested and sent to the Westerbork labor camp and eventually to Bergen-Belsen, where she died of typhus. *The Diary of a Young Girl* was posthumously published in 1947 and has been translated into sixty-seven languages, as well as adapted for theater and film.

The Diary of a Young Girl
1944

Wednesday, March 29, 1944

Dearest Kitty,
    Mr. Bolkestein, the Cabinet Minister, speaking on the Dutch broadcast from London, said that after the war a collection would be made of diaries and letters dealing with the war. Of course, everyone pounced on my diary. Just imagine how interesting it would be if I were to publish a novel about the Secret Annex. The title alone would make people think it was a detective story.
    Seriously, though, ten years after the war people would find it very amusing to read how we lived, what we ate and what we talked about as Jews in hid-

ing. Although I tell you a great deal about our lives, you still know very little about us. How frightened the women are during air raids; last Sunday, for instance, when 350 British planes dropped 550 tons of bombs on IJmuiden, so that the houses trembled like blades of grass in the wind. Or how many epidemics are raging here.

You know nothing of these matters, and it would take me all day to describe everything down to the last detail. People have to stand in line to buy vegetables and all kinds of goods; doctors can't visit their patients, since their cars and bikes are stolen the moment they turn their backs; burglaries and thefts are so common that you ask yourself what's suddenly gotten into the Dutch to make them so light-fingered. Little children, eight- and eleven-year-olds, smash the windows of people's homes and steal whatever they can lay their hands on. People don't dare leave the house for even five minutes, since they're liable to come back and find all their belongings gone. Every day the newspapers are filled with reward notices for the return of stolen typewriters, Persian rugs, electric clocks, fabrics, etc. The electric clocks on street corners are dismantled, public phones are stripped down to the last wire.

Morale among the Dutch can't be good. Everyone's hungry; except for the ersatz coffee, a week's food ration doesn't last two days. The invasion's long in coming, the men are being shipped off to Germany, the children are sick or undernourished, everyone's wearing worn-out clothes and run-down shoes. A new sole costs 7.50 guilders on the black market. Besides, few shoemakers will do repairs, or if they do, you have to wait four months for your shoes, which might very well have disappeared in the meantime.

One good thing has come out of this: as the food gets worse and the decrees more severe, the acts of sabotage against the authorities are increasing. The ration board, the police, the officials—they're all either helping their fellow citizens or denouncing them and sending them off to prison. Fortunately, only a small percentage of Dutch people are on the wrong side.

Yours, Anne

Tuesday, April 11, 1944

None of us have ever been in such danger as we were that night. God was truly watching over us. Just think—the police were right at the bookcase, the light was on,

and still no one had discovered our hiding place! "Now we're done for!" I'd whispered at that moment, but once again we were spared. When the invasion comes and the bombs start falling, it'll be every man for himself, but this time we feared for those good, innocent Christians who are helping us.

"We've been saved, keep on saving us!" That's all we can say.

This incident has brought about a whole lot of changes. As of now, Dussel will be doing his work in the bathroom, and Peter will be patrolling the house between eight-thirty and nine-thirty. Peter isn't allowed to open his window anymore, since one of the Keg people noticed it was open. We can no longer flush the toilet after nine-thirty at night. Mr. Sleegers has been hired as night watchman, and tonight a carpenter from the underground is coming to make a barricade out of our white Frankfurt bedsteads. Debates are going on left and right in the Annex. Mr. Kugler has reproached us for our carelessness. Jan also said we should never go downstairs. What we have to do now is find out whether Sleegers can be trusted, whether the dogs will bark if they hear someone behind the door, how to make the barricade, all sorts of things.

We've been strongly reminded of the fact that we're Jews in chains, chained to one spot, without any rights, but with a thousand obligations. We must put our feelings aside; we must be brave and strong, bear discomfort without complaint, do whatever is in our power and trust in God. One day this terrible war will be over. The time will come when we'll be people again and not just Jews!

Who has inflicted this on us? Who has set us apart from all the rest? Who has put us through such suffering? It's God who has made us the way we are, but it's also God who will lift us up again. In the eyes of the world, we're doomed, but if, after all this suffering, there are still Jews left, the Jewish people will be held up as an example. Who knows, maybe our religion will teach the world and all the people in it about goodness, and that's the reason, the only reason, we have to suffer. We can never be just Dutch, or just English, or whatever, we will always be Jews as well. And we'll have to keep on being Jews, but then, we'll want to be.

Be brave! Let's remember our duty and perform it without complaint. There will be a way out. God has never deserted our people. Through the ages Jews have had to suffer, but through the ages they've gone on living, and the centuries of suffering have only made them stronger. The weak shall fall and the strong shall survive and not be defeated!

That night I really thought I was going to die. I waited for the police and I was ready for death, like a soldier on a battlefield. I'd gladly have given my life for my country. But now, now that I've been spared, my first wish after the war is to become a Dutch citizen. I love the Dutch. I love this country, I love the language, and I want to work here. And even if I have to write to the Queen herself, I won't give up until I've reached my goal!

I'm becoming more and more independent of my parents. Young as I am, I face life with more courage and have a better and truer sense of justice than Mother. I know what I want, I have a goal, I have opinions, a religion and love. If only I can be myself, I'll be satisfied. I know that I'm a woman, a woman with inner strength and a great deal of courage!

If God lets me live, I'll achieve more than Mother ever did, I'll make my voice heard, I'll go out into the world and work for mankind!

I now know that courage and happiness are needed first!

Yours, Anne M. Frank

Translated by Susan Massotty.

Zalmen Gradowski

1910–1944

Zalmen Gradowski (also Ḥaim Zalmen Gradowski) was born in Suwałki and in his youth received a traditional Jewish education as well as some grounding in European literature. Gradowski spent the early years of World War II in Soviet-occupied Lunna, but with the German occupation, he and his family were deported to Auschwitz in December 1942. Assigned to the *Sonderkommando* (to work at the crematoria), he recorded his impressions of Auschwitz, and two of his manuscripts were recovered after the war. Gradowski was killed leading the *Sonderkommando* revolt of October 1944.

The Czech Transport: A Chronicle of the Auschwitz Sonderkommando

1944

A day passed, and then a second and a third. Wednesday came, the ultimate deadline for the transport's arrival. There were two obvious reason for the delay. First, it appeared that in addition to strategic preparations, moral assurances were demanded. The other reason was that the "authorities" made special efforts to carry out their major massacres on Jewish festivals, and so they had planned this slaughter for Wednesday night, the night of Purim. During those three days, the authorities—murderers and criminals schooled in bloodshed and cynicism—resorted to all kinds of deception in order to disguise the true, barbarous nature of their masquerade and to confound minds that might otherwise "catch on" and penetrate the dark machinations behind the "cultured," smiling facade of the regime.

And so the swindle began. [. . .]

A report was released that, due to certain circumstances, correspondence to Czechoslovakia would be delayed until March 30; those who wanted to request parcels from friends should postdate their letters between now and the thirtieth of the month and hand them over to the authorities, who would send them on and hold the incoming packages until they could be properly distributed. [. . .]

This elaborate swindle was the best means of numbing the minds of the more clear-thinking and perceptive prisoners. All, regardless of gender or age, let themselves be trapped by the illusion that they were being led to work. Only when their deceivers felt that, this "chloroform" had taken its full effect did the extermination process begin.

Families were broken up, men separated from women, young from old, and so they were caught in the trap, led to the nearby, still unoccupied camp. Unsuspecting, the victims were tricked into cold, wooden barracks, each group separately, and the doors were nailed up behind them with boards. The first phase had succeeded. People were maddened, perplexed; they could no longer think clearly. When they realized they had been trapped here to die, they lost hope and no longer possessed the strength to think about struggle and resistance, for every mind—even those that had dispelled all illusion—now faced a new anxiety. Strong young boys and girls thought only of their parents. Who knew what was happening to them there? And young men, full of courage and strength, sat there stunned by grief, thinking of the young wives and children from whom they had only just been parted. Every outburst of struggle or resistance was immediately overwhelmed by individual sorrows. Everyone was bound to his particular misfortune, and this paralyzed any thoughts about the general situation in which he found himself. The unshackled, energetic and rebellious crowd sat inert, resigned, shattered.

Unresisting, the five thousand victims took their first step to the grave.

This demonic deception, rehearsed so long in advance, had succeeded at last. [. . .]

The Convoy

[. . .] On that same night in Auschwitz-Birkenau 140 Jews of the *Sonderkommando* were also marching to a certain destination, but not to a synagogue, not with the intention of celebrating the festival and commemorating the Purim miracle.

They walked like mourners, with heads sunk deep in sorrow, and the profound sadness that emanated from them spread to all the Jews in the camp. For the road on which they marched was the road to the crematorium, to the hell of the Jewish people. And soon they would see not a celebration of the Jewish people's past delivery from death to life, but festivities of another sort—of a nation of betrayers who on this night were carrying out the ancient Purim decree, which their god had revived with still greater brutality.

Soon we would bear witness. With our own eyes we would have to watch our own destruction, as five thousand Jews, five thousand vibrant, thriving souls, women and children, young and old, would pass under the truncheons of civilized brutes. At the authorities' disposal would be rifles, grenades and automatics, as well as their constant four-footed companions, their vicious dogs; these would chase and savagely attack the Jews, who, distracted and confused, would run blindly into the arms of death.

And we, their own brothers, would have to help with this, help unload them from the trucks and lead them to the bunkers, help strip them mother-naked. And then, when all was ready, accompany them to the bunker—to the grave. [. . .]

Mothers passed with small children in arms; others were led by the hands of their little ones. They kissed their children—a mother's heart cannot be bound—kissed them all along the way. Sisters walked arm in arm, clinging together, wanting to face death together.

All glanced scornfully at the line of officers, not wishing to grace them with direct gazes. No one pleaded, no one sought mercy. They knew there was no spark of human conscience in those hearts. They didn't want to give them the pleasure of watching them beg for their lives in despair.

Suddenly the naked procession came to an abrupt hall. A pretty girl of nine, whose long, intricately plaited braids hung in golden strips down her childish shoulders, had approached followed by her mother, who now stopped and boldly addressed the officers: "'Murderers, thieves, shameless criminals! Yes, now you kill innocent women and children. You blame us, helpless as we are, for the war. As if my child and I could have brought this war upon you.

"You think, murderers, that with our blood you can hide your losses on the front. But the war is already lost. You know very well what beatings you take every day on the eastern front. Remember! Now you can smooth everything over, but there will come a day—a day of revenge. Russia will be the victor, and she will avenge us! You will be carved up alive. Our brothers all over the world will not rest until they have avenged our innocent blood."

And then she turned to the woman and said, "She-beast! Have you also come to look on our misfortune? Remember! You too have a child, a family, but you will not enjoy them for long. You will be torn to pieces, and your child won't live much longer than mine. Remember, murderers! You will pay for everything—the whole world will take revenge on you."

Then she spat in their faces and ran into the bunker with her child. The officers stood silent, stunned. They couldn't look at one another. The terrible truth they had just heard tore into their bestial souls. They had let her speak even though they knew what she would say, compelled to listen to this Jewish woman on her way to die. Now they stood gravely, deep in thought. This doomed woman had torn the blinders from their eyes and revealed the future that loomed before them. None of this was new to them: many times dark thoughts had clouded their minds, but now it was a Jewish woman who spoke the truth. Unashamed, she had forced them to see reality. [. . .]

Thirty hellish mouths blaze now in the two huge buildings and swallow countless bodies. It won't be long before the five thousand people, the five thousand worlds, will have been devoured by the flames. [. . .]

The fire burns boldly, calmly. Nothing stands in its way, nothing puts it out. Sacrifices arrive regularly, without number, as though this ancient, martyred nation was created specifically for this purpose.

Translated by Robert Wolf.

Gonda Redlich

1916–1944

Egon (also known as Gonda) Redlich was born in the Moravian city of Olmütz (now Olomouc, Czech Republic); when his law studies were interrupted by the Nazi occupation in 1939, he became a teacher in Prague. In December 1941, he was deported to Terezín, where he became head of the Youth Services Department. Redlich kept a diary in Czech and Hebrew detailing life in Terezín. Before his deportation to Auschwitz with his wife and son in 1944, he concealed his diary in an attic, where it remained until discovered by Czech workers in 1967.

Terezín Diary

1944

August 26, 1944

The end of summer is approaching and we can feel it. The days are still hot, but in the evening, there is a strange smell, the smell of leaves decaying and smoke, the smell of autumn. On Shabbat, I go walking with you on the city ramparts. There are three rows of trees there. You can only walk between the second row, because the third row is on the edge of the wall. From there, you can see the countryside, grass, fields, mountains, far away, freedom. No, there still is no freedom there. Not yet.

Frequently, you hear a sharp whistle, straight to the bone, the whistle of a siren. Within a few minutes, the walls empty out. Air raids. Everyone knows they never attack the ghetto, but it's an order, a military order, since the walls might look like the walls of any other city during an attack. The planes soar overhead at several hundred meters, like a flock of storks. The engines roar as if they were very angry—a huge and terrible anger. But here, below, the big noise becomes a mere growling. Is there freedom under their grey wings? Yes, they bring freedom without the birthpangs of the messiah.

Jews have arrived from Holland. There were bombings there as well, especially of the Jewish camps. Naturally, this was not intended. Perhaps the many barracks caused the British to err, even so, bombs fell and Jews were killed. Many Jews were wounded. A mistake—Jews paid for the mistake in blood and with their lives.

October 6, 1944

[Final Entry.] One of your games! I lift your body and you flutter with your legs like a fish on dry land. Afterwards, I bring my face to yours and you look at me

with such surprise. Learn, my son, to read the face of a man, because everything is written in the countenance of a man; his wisdom and his folly, his anger and his calmness, his happiness and his sadness, his honesty and his falsehood—everything, everything.

They are making a movie of the ghetto, a nice movie. They ordered the evacuation of two beautified youth homes. But before they did it, they filmed the "happy" children's houses. A movie on ghetto life which will show the happy life of the Jews, without worry, "with praises and celebrations." (Indeed, they filmed Jews dancing parlor dances.) They wanted to film you, in order to show a happy family. Luckily, it did not work out. This film would have been a nice reminder of your infancy in place of a photo. In spite of this, it was depressing and degrading. Even the kings of Egypt did not film the children they wanted to kill.

We bought a new baby carriage for you. The seller was one of my clerks and wanted to bribe me by giving me the carriage free. We paid one kilo of sugar, one kilo of margarine, and two cans of sardines.

What is going to happen? Tomorrow, we travel my son. We will travel on a transport like thousands before us. As usual, we did not register for the transport. They put us in without a reason. But never mind, my son, it is nothing. All of our family already left in the last weeks. Your uncle went, your aunt, and also your beloved grandmother. Your grandmother who worked from morning to evening for you and us. Parting with her was especially difficult. We hope to see her there.

It seems they want to eliminate the ghetto and leave only elderly and people of mixed origin. In our generation, the enemy is not only cruel but also full of cunning and malice. They promise [something] but do not fulfill their promise. They send small children, and their prams are left here. Separated families. On one transport a father goes. On another, a son. And on a third, the mother.

Tomorrow we go, too, my son. Hopefully, the time of our redemption is near.

NOTE
[Words in brackets appear in the original translation.—Eds.]

Translated by Laurence Kutler.

I. J. Singer

1893–1944

Israel Joshua Singer was born in Lublin province, and was the brother of Esther Singer Kreitman and Isaac

Bashevis Singer. He traveled to Moscow in 1918 but returned to Warsaw in 1921, where he became a leading exponent of the naturalist style in Yiddish prose. Singer worked as a European correspondent for the *Forverts* from 1924 and settled in the United States in 1934. He is best known for his family saga *The Brothers Ashkenazi* (1936).

Of a World That Is No More
1944

A Tragedy, Due to the Fact That Fate Transposed Genders in Heaven

Our house was gloomy—one reason why, since childhood, I have preferred the street to the home.

One cause of this gloom was the Torah, which filled every cranny of our house and weighed heavily on the spirits of those living there. Ours was more a study-house than a home, a House of God rather than one of man.

Another cause for this gloom was the mismatch between my mother and father. They would have been a well-mated couple if she had been the husband and he the wife. Even externally each seemed better suited for the other's role. Father was short and round, with a soft, fine, delicate face; warm blue eyes; full rosy cheeks; a small, chiseled nose, and plump, feminine hands. If not for the great reddish-brown beard and corkscrew-like sidelocks, he would have resembled a woman. Mother, on the other hand, was tall and somewhat stooped, with large, piercing, cold-gray eyes, a sharp nose, and a jutting pointed chin like a man's.

They were as different in spirit as they were in physique. Although Father was a devoted scholar and an inspired researcher of fresh nuances in the Torah, it could not be said that he had an outstanding mind. He was more a creature of heart than of intellect, one who accepted life as it was and did not delve deeply into the way of things. In general, he was not inclined to over-exert himself. Nor was he plagued by uncertainty. He believed in people and, even more, in God. His absolute faith in God's Torah and in saints was boundless. He never questioned the ways of the Lord, he nursed no resentments, he suffered no doubts. For him, it was enough that a thing had been written in the Torah to believe in it unquestioningly. Nor did he waste time worrying about a livelihood. He trusted God to provide for him just as He provided for all His creatures, from the ox to the mite. "With the help of God, all will be well," he would say.

Mother took after her father, the Bilgoraj rabbi. She was an accomplished worrier, a fretter, a doubter; totally devoted to reason and logic; always thinking, probing, pondering, and foreseeing. She brooded about people, about the state of the world, about God and His mysterious ways. She was, in short, the complete intellectual.

But she loved my father, and when he felt depleted she nursed and spoonfed him. However, she could never forgive him his childlike trust, his frivolity, and his reluctance to accept responsibilities and to provide for his family. Nor could she charitably accept his refusal to take the official examination that would have enabled him to become the rabbi of a decent-sized community instead of accepting an ill-paid, inglorious post in some forsaken hamlet where she was forced to endure poverty, deprivation, and loneliness; to be isolated from her family in Bilgoraj; and to dwell among common and ignorant countrywomen with whom she could not share a serious thought.

For all the overtures she made toward them, she could not force herself to join in their eternal chatter about pots and pans, clothes, and other such nonsense. She didn't have a friend in town. Her interests lay elsewhere: in books such as *Duty of the Heart, The Straight Path, The Prime of Wisdom, The Worldly Tests, The Book of the Righteous*. She also came back time and again to the Torah, the Prophets, and the Hagiographa, which she knew by heart. My father, a Hasid, was not well-versed in the latter two works—he knew only all the passages in the Torah. Whenever he had to locate a passage in the other volumes, he would ask Mother, who always knew precisely where to find it. [. . .]

Late one summer an epidemic broke out in Leoncin and both my younger sisters came down with scarlet fever. [. . .]

Eight days later my parents came back alone.

Mother tried to convince me that the children would be staying on for a while longer in Nowidwor but I knew better, and I felt the full impact of the twofold tragedy. Deeply distraught. Mother began to cry. I still remember how she pleaded with God to tell her the reason both her babies had been taken from her on the same day. "Why?" she cried, her hands stretched upward. "What have I done to deserve this, Father in heaven?"

The Father in heaven did not answer, but my father did. "Obviously it was meant to be," he said brokenly. "One dares not question the ways of the Lord . . . God is just . . . God is good. . . ."

"No, God is bad!" I shouted.

Father was aghast. "A Jew dares not say such a thing!" he said, shaking with fear. "God is righteous. . . ."

"He is evil! Evil!" I cried.

A God Who would hand over my little sisters to the Angel of Death could not be righteous—this didn't square with my concept of righteousness. Because of this resentment, I also quarreled with my tutor when we studied the Book of Job—I sided with Job, the victim and leper, instead of with Job's friends, who comforted him with words, or with God, Who justified His harsh punishment with boasts of His divine power and wondrous works. I raged against God so persistently that pious people stopped up their ears and warned me I would pay for my arrogance. [. . .]

From time to time, a "grandson" would come to Leoncin. This would be an effete stripling of a "rabbi" who laid claim to descent from some distinguished saint and who traveled from town to town in his own wagon, driven by a coachman who doubled as the "rabbi's" beadle. These "grandsons" invariably called on my father. Mother snickered at these fakers in their high fur caps, enormous sidelocks, and silk gabardines, who were mostly ignorant ninnies pretending to be miracle workers and saints. Each one claimed to be a descendant of either Baal Shem; of Rabbi Israel, the Kozienice preacher; or Rabbi Jacob Isaac, the holy man of Przysucha.

Guzzling Mother's tea with relish, they elucidated upon their impeccable pedigrees and decried the fate that had reduced them to traveling *to* Hasidim instead of Hasidim traveling to them. Each one had a story of how he had been usurped of his rightful place as head of a dynasty and sent adrift on a sea of uncertainty and despair. "*Oy*, Rabbi, it's degrading to go wandering in a cart without a home, a wife, children, or a livelihood," they lamented. "The few groschen we do manage to collect all go to feed the horse and the beadle, beg the comparison. . . ."

The beadles, Jews of common background, took care of the emaciated rabbinical nags, brought them hay in feedbags, and affected a euphonious Hebrew befitting their stations as assistant saints.

"*Rebbitzin*, maybe I could wash my hands," the beadles simpered, to insinuate they wanted something to eat.

The town Hasidim didn't waste a moment on the "grandsons," whom they considered *shnorers* and mock saints fit only for females and the rabble. But the women and the common men held them in highest esteem and flocked to them to ask their blessings for loved ones, to buy amulets, magic herbs, devil's dung, holy moss, wolf fangs, charmed amber, olive oil, copper three-kopeck pieces, and other junk. The beadle-coachmen herded the women to the saints, who blessed them and their children. At the same time, the minions wrapped the purchased items and dickered over the price. "Missus, it comes to twice eighteen and not a farthing less . . . and leave something for me too, it'll help your case. . . ."

The "rabbi" then popped his eyes, grimaced wildly, muttered a few incantations, and with a goose quill scribbled a few marks on a little piece of parchment. These scraps were stuffed into little red pouches. The men consulting them were instructed to present them to their wives to wear around their necks with the warning never to open them.

Among the women who consulted these "rabbis" were several wives of respectable Hasidim and scholars. They came without their husbands' knowledge to unburden themselves, since they could obtain no satisfaction from their husbands' distinguished saints and wanted one of their own who could understand and sympathize with a woman's longings.

Translated by Joseph Singer.

Other works by Singer: *Steel and Iron* (1927); *Yoshe Kalb* (1932); *The Family Carnovsky* (1943).

Helen Jacobus Apte

1886–1946

Born in Hawkinsville, Georgia, Helen Jacobus Apte spent the majority of her life in Atlanta and Florida. The daughter of German immigrants who had each come to the United States at young ages, Apte identified strongly as both an American and a Jew. Although illness forced her to leave school at the age of sixteen, Apte was a gifted writer who might have pursued the craft professionally had she been born in another time and been in better health. She settled for keeping a diary, which she began following her marriage at the age of twenty-two.

Heart of a Wife: The Diary of a Southern Jewish Woman

1944–1945

Tampa—Tuesday, June 6, 1944

D-Day at last. The invasion started about 1 A.M., and I have been listening to the radio since 8. My first reaction, and I'm sure everyone else's—"Thank God, and God keep us," each one naming someone near. Someone extra-near: George is no doubt there, as they say the paratroops were among the first.

David sweeter than ever. At two years old he knew the alphabet, could read and spell about six words. Many mushy rhymes and songs. He is very thin, but the doctor says he is in good condition.

Having lots of trouble with my nose. Been to five dermatologists, five X rays, two nose men—still have a sore nose!

Tampa—Wednesday, November 1, 1944

Went to Alice's and stayed three weeks with David while they were in New York. Had a grand time with David, but felt the responsibility. We came back from New York October 29. Our stay in New York was not so pleasant, as it was so hot, but we saw lots of shows— *Voice of the Turtle, Song of Norway, Anna Lucasta, Carmen Jones*, etc., etc. Left here July 21, spent two delightful weeks in Blowing Rock—very cool, good food.

Marred by news of George's death.[1] He was lost in the plane bringing back eighteen wounded soldiers. He had been wounded in the hip in Normandy, six days after D-Day.

Went to Connie's wedding at the Biltmore August 5, then on to New York.

Tampa—Saturday, November 11, 1944

Another Armistice Day! Nothing to celebrate. The fine elation of D-Day is gone. I feel a dreary frustration. The war was not over in September, as had been widely predicted. We are just inside of Germany at Aachen. Robot bombs are flying over England, and this country has been warned. Doesn't seem much chance of victory before the snowfall. Roosevelt was just renominated, by large majority.

Tampa—Saturday, January 20, 1945

Just listened to Roosevelt's fourth inaugural ceremony—very quiet, no celebration. He spoke only six minutes.

On January 16 we got news of Joseph[2]—died in action in Belgium. Impossible to realize. We are all heartbroken; twenty-four years old and gone forever. [. . .]

Tampa—Thursday, March 1, 1945

Date of Joseph's death: December 30. He was buried in a cemetery in Belgium. I have been so depressed. I just can't pull myself out of it. The waste, the futility!

Heard [American aviator Eddie] Rickenbacker speak. He says the war in Germany will be over between June and September and that we will fight on with Japan for years and years. Roosevelt will report on the Yalta meeting at 12:30, and then I'm going out to David's birthday party—three years old today. He is the bright spot, the shining joy of our lives. He knows the whole alphabet, can write at least twenty-five words, and spell them.

Tampa—Monday, April 16, 1945

Just listened to President Truman's first speech— quiet, short, and dignified. He promised to carry on all of Roosevelt's policies and to prosecute the war to unconditional surrender. We were eating dinner at the Cricket Thursday evening, April 12, when we heard the shocking news. The colored waitress said, with tears in her eyes, "I just heard on the radio our president is dead." "Our" president—from a Negro. What greater eulogy? And what eulogies I listened to all day Friday, Saturday, Sunday. All commercials off the air. The whole world in mourning. I heard hundreds of Ave Marias, "Lead, Kindly Light," "Nearer My God to Thee," etc., etc. I heard Negro spirituals. Like Moses, he was given a glimpse of the Promised Land, but not permitted to enter, and who can guess the reason? Victory is almost in sight, and we wait for almost hourly news, though commentators tell us it may be weeks. President Roosevelt, quiet American, hail and farewell.

Alice and Dan were in Clearwater ten days, and we stayed with David. He was with us when we heard the news. Of course, he doesn't realize it, but he says, in a mournful voice, "President Roosevelt is dead, and I guess they are burying him now."

Tampa—Wednesday, June 6, 1945

One year since D-Day, and I remember how I prayed for George, and George is gone. Then came the battle of the Bulge, and I prayed for Joseph, a first lieutenant in Patton's Third Army. And now Joseph is gone. Henry Jr. is on the SS *Claxton* in the Pacific, so now we pray for him, nineteen years old.

We went to New York May 24 and stayed three weeks, at the Waldorf, four days at the Biltmore. Stopped in

Atlanta two days. Anna and Maurice are pitiful. It was cold and raining the whole month in New York (97° here). Saw *Dear Ruth, Bell for Adano, I Remember Mama, Harvey, Glass Menagerie.*

I often wondered where we'd be on V-E Day and pictured it a day of wild celebration and jubilation, like the last war, but it was nothing like that. On Saturday, April 28, we were at a dinner in the Jade Room of the Waldorf. At 8:25 the orchestra suddenly called everyone to attention, and a voice announced: "Ladies and Gentlemen, the news has just come of Germany's unconditional surrender." There was a moment of stunned silence, then a buzz of voices, no cheers. And I was not the only one to burst into tears—tears of sorrow for those who would never come back. The news was later denied. Then came the dreary wait until Monday, May 7, when we heard at 10 A.M. on the radio, "War Is Over, Not Yet Official." Papers were falling like snow out of the high buildings. I walked up Fifth Avenue to 59th Street, and there was no excitement on the streets at all. On Tuesday morning we ordered breakfast in our living room and listened to Truman and Churchill speak. Official.

Such anticlimax, such a let-down feeling. That night, after *Dear Ruth*, we walked down to Times Square, where a "wild celebration" was supposed to be in progress. All we saw was a crowd of kids and hoodlums throwing confetti and blowing horns. That's how V-E Day came to New York, and it seemed to have been the same all through the country.

New York—Savoy Plaza, Wednesday, August 15, 1945

Well, it is over, the blood and sweat and tears. Over also for Joseph and George and all the others, left in their silent graves. There they will lie, and the world will go on. We left Blowing Rock at 3 P.M. August 12, after hearing of the Jap surrender, but nothing official.

On August 14 we were at the Lobster Restaurant on 45th Street. At 7 P.M. a loudspeaker suddenly blared forth—"Surrender Official." We dashed down to Times Square and were there in time to hear the first wild roar, and to see it flashed on the Times Building. It was a sight never to be forgotten.

NOTES

[Words in brackets are found in the original source document.—Eds.]

1. George Lavenson, [cousin] Joan's husband.

2. Joseph Jacobus, the son of Helen's brother Maurice (Bubba).

Roland Gittelsohn
1910–1995

Roland Gittelsohn was born in Cleveland, Ohio, and was ordained a rabbi in 1936 at Hebrew Union College. He was the first Jewish chaplain to serve with the U.S. Marine Corps, ministering to marines and sailors of all faiths during the battle of Iwo Jima in 1945. His sermon at the dedication of the Fifth Marine Division Cemetery on Iwo Jima, titled "The Purest Democracy," received much media attention. Gittelsohn served on President Truman's Committee on Civil Rights in 1947 and was the rabbi of Temple Israel in Boston from 1953 to 1977.

Consider Iwo Jima
1945

Eulogy at the Dedication of the 5th Marine Division Cemetery, Iwo Jima—March 1945

This is perhaps the grimmest, and surely the holiest task we have faced since D-Day. Here before us lie the bodies of comrades and friends. Men who until yesterday or last week laughed with us, joked with us, trained with us. Men who were on the same ships with us, and went over the sides with us as we prepared to hit the beaches of this island. Men who fought with us and feared with us. Somewhere in this plot of ground there may lie the man who could have discovered the cure for cancer. Under one of these Christian crosses, or beneath a Jewish Star of David, there may now rest a man who was destined to be a great prophet—to find the way, perhaps, for all to live in plenty, with poverty and hardship for none. Now they lie here silently in this sacred soil, and we gather to consecrate this earth in their memory.

It is not easy to do so. Some of us have buried our closest friends here. We saw these men killed before our very eyes. Any one of us might have died in their places. Indeed, some of us are alive and breathing at this very moment only because men who lie here beneath us had the courage and strength to give their lives for ours. To speak in memory of such men as these is not easy. Of them too can it be said with utter truth: "The world will little note, nor long remember what we say here. It can never forget what they did here."

No, our poor power of speech can add nothing to what these men and the other dead of our Division who are not here have already done. All that we even hope to do is follow their example. To show the same self-less courage in peace that they did in war. To swear that by the grace of God and the stubborn strength and power of human will, their sons and ours shall never suffer these pains again. These men have done their jobs well. They have paid the ghastly price of freedom. If that freedom be once again lost, as it was after the last war, the unforgivable blame will be ours, not theirs. So it is we the living who are here to be dedicated and consecrated.

We dedicate ourselves, first, to live together in peace the way they fought and are buried in this war. Here lie men who loved America because their ancestors generations ago helped in her founding, and other men who loved her with equal passion because they themselves or their own fathers escaped from oppression to her blessed shores. Here lie officers and men, negroes and whites, rich men and poor—together. Here no man prefers another because of his faith or despises him because of his color. Here there are no quotas of how many from each group are admitted or allowed. Among these men there is no discrimination. No prejudices. No hatred. Theirs is the highest and purest democracy.

Any man among us the living who fails to understand that will thereby betray those who lie here dead. Whoever of us lifts up his hand in hate against a brother, or thinks himself superior to those who happen to be in the minority, makes of this ceremony and of the bloody sacrifice it commemorates, an empty, hollow mockery. To this, then, as our solemn, sacred duty, do we the living now dedicate ourselves: to the rights of Protestants, Catholics and Jews, of white men and negroes alike, to enjoy the democracy for which all of them here have paid the price.

To one thing more do we consecrate ourselves in memory of those who sleep beneath these crosses and stars. We shall not foolishly suppose, as did the last generation of America's fighting men, that victory on the battlefield will automatically guarantee the triumph of democracy at home. This war, with all its frightful heartache and suffering, is but the beginning of our generation's struggle for democracy. When the last battle has been won, there will be those at home, as there were the last time, who will want us to turn our backs in selfish isolation on the rest of organized humanity, and thus to sabotage the very peace for which we fight. We promise you who lie here: we will not do that! We will join hands with Britain, China, Russia in peace, even

as we have in war, to build the kind of world for which you died.

When the last shot has been fired, there will still be those whose eyes are turned backward, not forward, who will be satisfied with those wide extremes of poverty and wealth in which the seeds of another war can breed. We promise you, our departed comrades: this too we will not permit. This war has been fought by the common man; its fruits of peace must be enjoyed by the common man! We promise, by all that is sacred and holy, that your sons, the sons of miners and millers, the sons of farmers and workers, the right to a living that is decent and secure.

When the final cross has been placed in the last cemetery, once again there will be those to whom profit is more important than peace, who will insist with the voice of sweet reasonableness and appeasement that it is better to trade with the enemies of mankind, than by crushing them, to lose their profit. To you who sleep here silently, we give our promise: we will not listen! We will not forget that some of you were burnt with oil that came from American wells, that many of you were killed with shells fashioned from American steel. We promise that when once again men profit at your expense, we shall remember how you looked when we placed you reverently, lovingly, in the ground.

Thus do we memorialize those who, having ceased living with us, now live within us. Thus do we consecrate ourselves the living to carry on the struggle they began. Too much blood has gone into this soil for us to let it lie barren. Too much pain and heartache have fertilized the earth on which we stand. We here solemnly swear: this shall not be in vain! Out of this, and from the suffering and sorrow of those who mourn this, will come—we promise—the birth of a new freedom for the sons of men everywhere. Amen.

Other works by Gittelsohn: *Man's Best Hope* (1961); *Consecrated unto Me: A Jewish View of Love and Marriage* (1965); *How Do I Decide? A Contemporary Jewish Approach to What's Right and What's Wrong* (1989).

A. M. Klein

1909–1972

Canadian poet and novelist Abraham Moses Klein was born in Ratno (now in Ukraine) and raised in the immigrant Jewish district of Montreal. He studied classics and political science at McGill University and law at the Université de Montréal. Klein published poetry and prose in Canadian and American periodicals as a student and practiced law until his retirement in 1956. He was active in the Canadian Jewish community as a speaker, writer, and educator, and he edited the weekly *Canadian Jewish Chronicle* from 1938 to 1955. He was a visiting lecturer in poetry at McGill University (1945–1948) and associated with the Preview circle of poets in Montreal. In the early 1950s, he suffered from depression and gradually withdrew from public life.

Reflections on V-E Day
1945

Not with surprising suddenness did it come; it did not come—as in the dark days we had hoped it would—as a miraculous flash on a radio, a startling announcement lifting us from the depths of despair. By installments, with forewarnings, parceled in rumors, it finally arrived, and even then was only quasi-official: *the Nazis had surrendered, unconditionally.*

How difficult it was to articulate the proper response! So much hope, so much day-in-day-out longing was wrapped up in the coming of this announcement,—this, the day for which we had hoped!—that thoughts stumbled over one another; and the mind was confusion, and the heart a bursting inexpression. Us the moment found on St. James Street: inglorious place. In an instant the street was a bedlam of joy, the tall buildings smiled with hundreds of faces, the paper that streamed from the windows was itself an extended and ubiquitous smile. Everybody said unrememberable things; it wasn't really speech; it was ejaculation, brimful and jubilant. Girls danced, soldiers were borne up on shoulders. People danced in the streets; even those who walked alone glowed with an inner illumination.

And we could not help reflecting upon the great kindness which had been vouchsafed to all of us to be permitted to behold this day. Five years ago—let it be frankly admitted—we saw about us only darkness palpable. The great trek which we had made through history seemed about to come to an end. The enemy appeared invincible, and to us Jews, implacable. A Haman had arisen who meant to obliterate our people, to destroy us, beyond remnant, and beyond memory. For the time being, his ravages were confined to Europe, but his intentions were never concealed—he meant to make the whole world the scene of his totalitarian in-

iquity. Every Jew felt the Nazi tentacle stretch out to reach him, personally. Until the last Jew was cremated, Hitler, we knew, would feel that his task had not been done. Surely, in all our troubled history no such threat had ever been lifted against us.

Now, in the hour of triumph, we could take the Nazi propaganda against us, and make it into a crown, even as we had made the Yellow Badge the shield and ensign of nobility. The arch-enemy of our people had fallen into the dust, miserable and ignominious; the murder he had planned was only partially accomplished; his grand scale of slaughter had been frustrated. Whence could one summon the voice, and whence the hallelujah, that could utter adequate thanksgiving for that this thing did come to pass?

How often, in the past, have we as a people boasted of the ordeals and martyrdoms which we have survived! Antiochus, Pharaoh, Haman, Torquemada, Chmelnitzki—these were names which marked the danger-points of our survival. We had outlived them, and their wicked intention; and ever thereafter, their appellations were like a pendant of grim bloodstones which we wore upon the throat of our history. Sometimes, indeed, we made out of these names a playground for humor, a field for our wit. Pharaoh outlived was a comic character; Ahasuerus outlived was a drunkard and fool.

I wondered what place Hitler and his doings would now occupy in our folklore. I thought about the past years, and the words *blitzkrieg, lebensraum, festung Europa*—portentous terms!—and how henceforth they would sound in the vocabulary of civilized man. But of one thing I was certain—these words and their kindred would never form part of our humor.

For while the bombs were silent, and while the bombast sounded, we could not help but think upon our missing. Conservative estimates place the number of our martyred at five million; only the months to come will reveal the actual figure. Yes, we have survived; but as we take count of our numbers and take stock of our condition, we discover that we have survived, bleeding and maimed. We are less by one quarter of our population.

The poison that has been brewed in Nuremberg still spreads its fetid odor across the face of Europe; much still remains to be done before victory is translated from its military language into a living and meaningful reality. In the meantime, for the great blessing, the supreme boon, gratitude and thanksgiving. For the day, *dayenu*; for the rest, He who has led us thus far, will lead us still.

Other works by Klein: *Hath Not a Jew* (1940); *The Hitleriad* (1944); *The Rocking Chair and Other Poems* (1948); *The Second Scroll* (1951).

Joseph Messas
1892–1974

Born and raised in Morocco, Joseph (Yosef) Messas (Mashash) was a rabbi in Tlemcen, Algeria, and Meknes, Morocco. He later served as the Sephardic chief rabbi of Haifa. Messas was known for his innovative understandings of Jewish law, ruling in favor of liberal interpretations of kashrut, accepting the idea of women's prayer groups, and challenging the custom that married women were required to cover their hair (or that women were even required to marry).

Victory Day in Tlemcen, Algeria
1945

On Thursday, the twentieth day of the month of Ziv, which is Iyyar, the government announced the capture of Berlin, the city of blood, the capital of the cruel German nation, may their name be blotted out and its memory be lost, and it fell into the hands of the following four kingdoms: Russia, America, England, and France, and we celebrated it as a holiday, reciting the Hallel prayers of thanksgiving throughout the city, to the King of Honor, who destroyed the fortresses of the proud, and on the following Sabbath, 24 Iyyar, at two in the afternoon, trumpets were heard heralding the end of the war with cursed Germany, because it was completely captured by the aforementioned kingdoms, and it was disarmed, and its soul was pressed to the dust, so may it always be.

This war lasted seventy-one months, because it began on Friday, at one o'clock on 17 Elul 5699, which corresponds to the Christian date of 1 September 1939, and I was in Tlemcen, and there was a great commotion, such as never had been, weeping and moaning in all the streets of the city. And it was over on 24 Iyyar, as mentioned. . . . And we made it a holiday with Hallel and prayers of thanksgiving in all the streets of the city, until after midnight, and also the next day, Tuesday, we prayed with song and melody and recitation of the prayer, "The Soul of All Living Beings," as on holidays, and also a great Hallel after the Eighteen Benedictions, and all that day and all that night songs and singing did not cease, and dancing and frolicking in the streets of the town, and on Wednesday, at eight-thirty in the morning, the French heroes of Edom came to the synagogue of the rabbi and head of the religious court, our sage teacher Rabbi Barukh Toledano, may the Lord preserve him. The crowd decorated it with flowers and roses and flags, and great lights, and we had a celebration with decent order and decorum.

First the chorus of singers sang, "I will exalt Thee, O Lord, for you have raised me up, etc." and afterward we stood in silence for two minutes, in honor of those killed in the war, as is the custom among the gentiles, and afterward a request for mercy for the dead who were casualties of the war, sons of Israel and sons of other nations, which I, a young man, composed, but when they printed it they spoiled it by removing and adding things, and this is the prayer as I composed it:

Please, God, Father of mercy, who dwells on high, who knows all hidden things, with great and mighty mercy, have mercy on the honest and innocent spirits and souls, beloved and pleasant, of several million Jews, men, women, infants, boys, and girls, who were murdered, slaughtered, burned, drowned, strangled, and buried alive, and who were doomed to strange deaths, in every place where the hand of the cruel persecutor reached, O King, king of kings, with Your mercy have mercy on them, pardon and forgive them, and bundle their souls deep within, in the place of sanctification, with the souls and spirits of your people, the House of Israel, holy and pure, who gave up their souls to sanctify Your great name, at the time of the persecutions in the Middle Ages, may You be satisfied with the brightness of their souls, and slake their thirst with the surfeit of Your House and moisten them with the river of your Eden, and accompany them with peace, and may they find peace where they lie, and raise them up at the end of days, and with the cup of consolation water the heart of their mourners, who are worried and sorrowful for them, and take their vengeance and the vengeance of all the blood of Your servants that has been shed, as it is written in Your holy Torah by the man of God, faithful to Your house, that the blood of Your servants will arise and take vengeance on his persecutors and atone for His land with His people, and by your servants the prophets it is written, and "And I will hold as innocent their blood that I have not held as innocent; and the Lord dwells in Zion" [Joel 4:21]. And it is said [in the prayer book], "Let there be made known among the nations in our sight the re-venging of the blood of thy servants which has been shed. And it is said, For he that makes inquisition for blood remembers them; he forgets not the cry of the humble. And it is further said, He judges among the nations; the land is full of corpses: he smites the head over a wide land," and from now on, a good account-ing, give peace in the land and the kingdoms, and may we be quiet and tranquil to serve You and fear You, and fill the land with knowledge of God, amen.

God full of mercy, please! With your great mercy, have mercy on the souls of the dead of this war from our brothers the Arabs, the French, the Russians, the Americans, and the English, and all those who helped them, give them a portion in Your Garden of Eden, and surfeit them with Your goodness, and may they take a good and beautiful reward for their great mercy, for they did great things with all the people in the world, and especially for our nation the People of Israel, and with the help of God, blessed be He, with their determined work, even spilling their blood on the earth, to remove evil beasts from the land of Hit-ler and all those who swarm after him, they will not arise in judgment, because they will be dust under the feet of the souls of the armies of the aforemen-tioned kingdoms, amen.

Then the rabbi and head of the religious court recited the mourner's kaddish, and the translator translated the memorials into French. After that we blessed the king, his highness Sidi Muhammad, and his highness the Legionnaire de Gaulle, and the chorus of singers sang "Hatikvah," and then the heroes of Edom left, because they were needed on their way, and after they left, the chorus of singers sang the psalm, "Let the redeemed of the Lord say so" [Psalms 107:2] and the "Egyptian Hal-lel" [Psalms 113–118], and the whole congregation stood and together they recited the Great Hallel and other songs of praises, and they promised decent sums to charity and the two holy societies in the city, the "Visit the Sick" society and the "Support the Children" char-ity, and they went to their homes in peace, joyous and happy of heart, and at four o'clock some members of the congregation with the rabbis were invited to the palace of the Legionnaire, where all the ministers of the French and Arabs were, and they received us with great honor and sated us with pleasure with friendship and affec-tion, and tea and sweets, and we went to our homes in peace and that night they still did not stop dancing and frolicking, and songs of praise and thanksgiving to the blessed Place. On Thursday, which was the last day of the holiday, we decorated all the streets of the city and the stores of the Arabs and Jews, with flags and flowers and roses and fresh branches and fronds of palms and carpets and pillows and cushions and curtains, and ta-bles full of tea and preserves and sweets, and the whole city glowed and shone with the color of embroidery, and the congregation made a place for the ministers of the city, splendid with all splendor in the home of the magnate, his honor Rabbi Ḥayim Likhraif, may God preserve him, in the new Street of the Jews, with several kinds of beverages and sweets and a chorus of singers, men and women, on harps and timbrels, and at six in the evening all the ministers and officials of the French and Arabs came, and we greeted them with songs and thanks, and they were very satisfied and pleased with the food and drink and the honor and words of af-fection, with great humility, they went around all the streets of the city and departed in peace, and the whole congregation made a feast with joy in the markets and streets with dancing and frolicking until the dawn hour, and may God, who examines every heart, visit the flock of His part, and Him may they honor from the start, to make pleasant his fate, and his portion and estate, to send him His messiah not too late, and then the gentiles will say, happy is the people who is like this, soon in our days, amen.

Translated by Jeffrey M. Green.

Other works by Messas: *Otsar ha-mikhtavim* (2016).

Ernő Szép

1884–1953

Ernő Szép was born to a poor family in Huszt, present-day Ukraine. He began writing poetry at an early age and worked as a journalist, first in Debrecen, then in Budapest, embracing the Hungarian language and cul-ture. Szép's poetry was influenced by French symbol-ists. His plays continue to be performed in Hungary. His *The Smell of Humans: A Memoir of the Holocaust in Hungary* describes his own experiences as a Jew under the fascist regime in Hungary. Under the ensu-ing communist regime, Szép was marginalized and died in poverty.

The Smell of Humans: A Memoir of the Holocaust in Hungary
1945

The Jewish Question

One of the comrades on sick call had a chat with an army guard. This is the account he gave:

"How stupid can you get, I ask you, what are the limits of human stupidity! This soldier was telling me that it was an ugly thing the Jews were doing in Budapest; he's heard they go up on rooftops at night to signal to the bombers where to drop their bombs. So I tell him: listen, friend, do you think the Jews are that dumb, to call for bombs on the building they live in? And what do you think, what kind of signals could they send? Anyone caught with a lamp or lighting a candle would be shot on the spot. And how else could they signal? Think about it, the airplanes are at an altitude of 5,000 meters; would they see someone waving at them in the dark? How could he swallow such inanities? So he tells me he heard it from someone who came from Budapest and the man doesn't lie."

Years ago I heard an old friend tell about sitting in a cafe at a retired general's table, where several other high-ranking officials were congregated. "One of the generals complained indignantly about that renegade Petschauer, who switched over to the Bolshevik side, and now he was guiding the Bolshie bombers to the public buildings to be destroyed, for he was the only one who knew Budapest like that! Imagine the stupidity! I remonstrated in vain, asking them how they could believe such fairy tales; they shouted me down. When it comes to the topic of Jews, their intelligence goes out like a light. I had to blush for them."

Once, about three years ago, I went to the Jewish Museum to look at an exhibition of pictures. I saw two children peeking in at the museum door. The girl must have been around thirteen and the boy about seven.

"Would you like to come in?"

"We are not allowed, we are Christians."

"That's all right, come on in," and I extended my hand towards the little girl.

"Oh no, because the Jews will kill us," and she grabbed the little boy's hand.

"Do you go to school?" I asked. They were both barefoot.

"Oh yes. I'm in the fourth grade." And they ran off.

So this was the result of the good teachers' work.

And ever since Stalingrad the extreme right wing of the press had been busy spreading the word that if Germany were to lose the war, the Jews would *exterminate the Christians.* And this was swallowed by adults, by people with degrees; the so-called middle class passed this depraved nonsense from mouth to mouth. As my old friend said, it short-circuited their brains. They were able to believe that the Jews would exterminate their own clients. And whom would they cheat, whom would they live off, after that? And how could they believe, the sons of this brave Hungarian nation, that a handful of Jews would exterminate ten million Gentiles? Even counting the Jewish babes in arms, there were no more than 150,000 of us left; weak, unarmed Jews. Couldn't the Gentiles conceive of resisting such an onslaught? After all, they would not have to kneel down and offer their necks to be cut . . .

Oh, this was the greatest suffering, the one meted out on one's intelligence. To have to swallow this thick spate of idiocy, to breathe this filthy smog instead of clean air; all these lies, all these stupefying inanities. To look on helplessly at the mental degradation of this country blessed with such human resources and talent, to witness this atrophy of reason, spirit, humor. When would we ever recover from the damage done to the mind and soul of this nation? There was one explanation for otherwise intelligent people believing these wild inanities about the Jews. When you usurp another people's jobs, businesses and properties, it is easy to believe all the bad things about them, to justify the hatred, and lull the conscience.

On this day I had heard a number of Jewish debates, as we milled around before dinner.

"But I am still a nationalist," said one man, about forty-five years of age.

An older man reacted to this: "But what if your nation does not accept you as a Hungarian?"

"That's only today's mentality; I refuse to acknowledge it."

The other man merely waved his hand and turned away, smiling.

"What I want to know," someone asked, "is why do they hate us?"

Another man answered: "Because we are smarter."

There was general merriment at this: the man who had pronounced these words looked so much like a ram, and not a very bright one at that.

The older man turned back. "I told you, my dear, they consider us foreigners, not Hungarians."

"But to them the Gypsies are just as foreign."

A new voice chimed in: "That's right, we should all go and make music at the tavern instead of being company directors, and then we would not be persecuted."

"Gentlemen, gentlemen, please," interjected another comrade, who had a drugstore on the Boulevard. "The problem is that we are a minority everywhere. Look at the Armenians in Turkey, or the Indians in America: the weaker have always and everywhere been persecuted and murdered."

"Well, it's not such a simple matter." (This came from Bank Director D., who had converted to Christianity.) "It is a matter of religion usually."

"But it did not help us to convert."

"You see, you shouldn't have converted! A man of character does not convert'" said a slender little man, with passion. One side of his face twitched uncontrollably.

At this outburst the group became noisy. At least twenty voices were heard in more or less loud competition.

One elderly gentleman raised his arm.

"Gentlemen, may we have quiet!"

The word "Zionist" was heard, and the little man with the tic shouted:

"That's right, I am a Zionist! That is the only road for the Jews!"

Again there was a loud hubbub, in the midst of which the little man responded to some comment in his excited voice:

"My son will! He will emigrate! I am not a narrow-minded orthodox Jew. Actually I am a freethinker.

This, gentlemen, is a national problem. You don't have the slightest notion of Zionism."

Again, the loud outbursts were calmed by requests for quiet.

Someone, I couldn't see who, exclaimed indignantly:

"But I converted out of conviction!"

"That's right, you were convinced that it would be to your advantage!"

Laughter, and another hubbub. The old gentleman calling for order was almost in tears.

"Gentlemen! Gentlemen!"

A bent, blond-haired man with a tired face said to no one in particular:

"I have nothing to do with this! I was born a Christian."

The little man with the tic laughed as he pointed at the other man's chest:

"And look, they still gave you a star."

"But even with that star I went to church every Sunday. I am a practicing Catholic."

The man with the tic waved him off and left.

The older man, who had started it all, looked at me.

"And what a wasted martyrdom this is, what a ridiculous affair! So we are to be only Jews, after all? We are also Hungarians, and human beings. Oh, to be persecuted for one's religion, in Europe, in our day . . ."

Translated by John Batki.

Other works by Szép: *Patika* (1918); *Lila akác* (1921); *A vőlegény* (1922).

FICTION, DRAMA, AND CHILDREN'S LITERATURE

Sholem Asch

1880–1957

Sholem Asch was born to a Hasidic family in Kutno. Becoming self-educated in European literature, Asch moved to Warsaw and began to write under Y. L. Peretz's patronage. In 1914, Asch settled in New York, working for the *Forverts* and cofounding the American Jewish Joint Distribution Committee. Returning to Europe after the war, he became the best-known and most widely translated Yiddish author in the world. A major theme of his fiction was the need for a Judeo-Christian rapprochement, which sparked fierce controversy in Yiddish national circles. Asch spent the end of his life in Bat Yam, Israel, and is buried in London.

The Nazarene
1939

"'Do you want me to release to you your King of the Jews?' asked Pilate of the multitude.

"'What is that? What does he say?'

"'The Procurator asks whom shall he release to you for the festival: Bar Abba or the King of the Jews?'

"The multitude paused. Debate broke out in its ranks, the debate grew into wild dispute, hands were lifted, beards were seized. Pilate and his men looked on in amusement.

"'Look at those little Jews quarreling,' said Pilate to me, laughing, and pointing to the crowd. 'They'll finish up by tearing each other's eyes out.'

"I heard their shouts:

"'He's not the King of the Jews! He's a blasphemer!'

"'No! He is a holy man. No one knows who he is. He will show us a sign! You will see!'

"'He told us to pay tribute to the Caesar! What kind of Messiah is it that bids us pay tribute to the Caesar'

"'He healed our sick! He performed wonders every day. He drove the Sons of Hanan from the Temple. That is why they have delivered him to the government!'

"At this point my friend Hanan ben Hanan mounted the steps of the platform and called to the crowd:

"'How often have you not come before him and asked him to give you a sign that he is the King-Messiah? Yet he has never given you the sign. Now let him give proof, as Elijah gave proof on Carmel: let him destroy the prophets of Baal!'

"'Let him destroy the prophets of Baal with the breath of his mouth!'

"'Let him come riding in the clouds on the right hand of the power!'

"'Let Pilate be his sign!'

"'Let Pilate be his sign!'

"'They are shouting my name! What is it?' Pilate asked me.

"'They are calling to their Messiah to show them a sign in you.'

"Pilate's face turned purple with rage. The blood pressed into his thick, bulky neck, and I thought he would fall down in an apoplectic fit. But he mastered himself, summoned a smile, and asked the people again:

"'Do you want me to free the King of the Jews?'

"'The Messiah will free himself!'

"Pilate did not answer, but it was clear that he had made up his mind. He strode back to the Pretorium and confronted the prisoner. Across the face of the prisoner passed flickers of pain. We marked a movement of his lips, as though he would lift his voice and say something to those assembled without. But the seal of all the sorrow of the world kept him silent.

"'Do you hear what they say?' asked Pilate.

"The prisoner did not look at him.

"Pilate turned to the Tribune. 'Release Bar Abba!' he commanded.

"Bar Abba's Tribune, old Petronius, who knew the country well, having served under former Procurators, summoned up courage and approached Pilate.

"'Procurator,' he said. 'Bar Abba is a dangerous criminal. He led a revolt against Rome. Had we not received advance information on it, we would have lost many more soldiers than we did. The man is guilty of several murders. Think of the legionaries we lost when we took him prisoner. But that other man, he whom they call the King of the Jews—against him we have nothing, and know of no crime which he has committed. No blood has been shed because of him. On the contrary, we have information that he bade the people in the Temple pay Caesar the tribute due him. But Bar Abba has always preached the withholding of the tribute and rebellion against Rome. Since when, Pilate, do you yield to the clamor of the mob?'

"Pilate became angry, and as always when rage overcame him, a tide of blood washed over his enormous, hairless head, and his breast expanded with haughtiness so that you feared it would crack open. He pulled down the corners of his mouth, growled furiously, and cast a contemptuous glance at old Petronius.

"'The Hebrew spirit is much more dangerous for all of us than the Hebrew fist. Go! Deliver this man to the soldiers. Lash him and crucify him! Crown him the King of the Jews!'

"Among the troops which filled the space about the Pretorium there were many German horsemen, auxiliaries which we always drew to Jerusalem from other stations for the festivals. They, of all our soldiers, were most feared and hated by the Jews; the terror and enmity went back to the days of Herod, who had first used the Germans to hold the Jews in subjection. Many of these Germans, when they became old and could no longer remain in the army, went over to the service of the High Priest, who had them circumcised so that he could keep them in Jerusalem as slaves and use them as guards and watchmen. The old Germans were excellent for this purpose, and they received good pay and good food. They were armed with short clubs, which the Jews called '*Eileh*' and which they celebrated in their ribald songs about the High Priest.

"The commander of the German horsemen was a man with an evil face and cold, murderous eyes. He was the terror of the Jews. His name was Hermanus. It was to Hermanus and his men that the prisoner was delivered.

"I had been watching them during the trial. They stood on their tip-toes, straining like bloodhounds who expect a bone to be flung to them. When they heard that the pale, thin man was accused of setting himself up as the Jewish king, they burst into wild howls of laughter. And now, when he was delivered to them, they went mad with joy, like wolves to whom a sheep has been thrown.

"Hermanus seized the prisoner by the hand. A grimace passed over his face, as though he wanted to smile; but the smile was lost in the wooden immobility of his face; so that instead of a smile there issued a dark, miserable grimace. Like a beast, he did not know how to laugh. He made me think of the black, sunless woods among which he had been born; the thick swamps of his childhood had laid their stamp on him. He dragged the prisoner toward the innermost court, and kept shouting to the soldiers:

"'Come! We're going to crown the King of the Jews.'

"Within, in the court of the camp, there was a tall whipping post, with rings in it, which was always used for criminals condemned to the lash and the cross. What was done there with Yeshua I do not know. We did not follow the soldiers. They remained within a long time. Now and again we heard wild bursts of laughter. But we did not hear a single cry or groan from the prisoner. But we did hear, outside, round the walls of the Procuratorium, the shouting of the multitude, which penetrated the thick walls and gates and reached us in the closed court. It was like the far-off sound of the waves beating on a dam; and it grew from minute to minute, as if the multitude was increasing.

"Finally Hermanus issued, dragging the prisoner by the hand toward the place where Pilate stood with his officers. Hermanus turned, bowed low before the tortured man as before a Caesar, and with the characteristic grimace on his features, proclaimed:

"'The King of the Jews!'

"We looked at the condemned man. On his graying hair lay a wreath woven of thorns. The thorns had pierced through his hair and penetrated the skin and the bone of his head. Little trickles of blood clotted the hair of his earlocks, ran down his beard, and fell drop by drop onto his throat and naked body. Yes, the King of the Jews stood before us naked, crowned with a crown of thorns, his slender white body covered with the swollen, bluish stripes left by the lashes. But I observed something marvelous. It was not as though he were standing naked before us, but we standing naked before him. The livid welts seemed to clothe his body in royal raiment. He was not ashamed in his nakedness. His eyes, which were directed at us, were filled more with self-pity than shame or bitterness. And perhaps it only seemed so to me, for I must confess that at this moment I began to feel a certain weakness for this Rabbi of theirs; and perhaps I had even felt it earlier, when I had led him into the dungeons and had seen his mournful, unhappy face. Perhaps it had grown in me, unobserved by myself, when I had watched him at the trial, standing before Pilate and answering not a word to the accusations. Yes, I think it was already there, in me, undermining my sense of duty as a Tribune, weakening my resolution and blurring my conviction of the man's guilt, making it impossible for me to proceed against him as vigorously as I should. Then I said to myself: 'Beware, Cornelius! This man is beginning to draw you once more into the circle of his magic.' It was not the attitude and bearing of the man which worked on me; it was something that lay in the essential being of him, in the quiet, sad gaze of his eyes, which pierced through you, and seemed to evoke in you queer Hebraic and Semitic emotions. I had been fighting against them all morning. Now those eyes, lifted toward me from the midst of the trickles of blood which ran down his forehead, were becoming dangerously potent, stirring a softness and weakness in my heart. They were binding me to him, they were pulling me toward his feet; and if I did not remain on guard they would transform me into one of those witless, characterless, sentimental Hebrews. Therefore I pulled away from him; I summoned up my Roman will, and opposed it to his; I called to my help my contempt for the Jews and their God. 'Yes, Pilate is right!' I muttered fiercely to myself. 'The Hebrew spirit is more dangerous for us than the Hebrew fist.' And I joined in the laughter of the others."

Translated by Maurice Samuel.

Other works by Asch: *A Shtetl* (1904); *God of Vengeance* (1907); *Uncle Moses* (1918); *Kiddush Hashem* (1919); *Three Cities* (1929–1931); *Salvation* (1934); *What I Believe* (1941); *East River* (1946).

Milton Steinberg

1903–1950

Milton Steinberg was a well-known and influential Conservative rabbi in the United States in the 1930s and 1940s. Born in Rochester, New York, he received a Ph.D. in philosophy from Columbia University and was ordained at the Jewish Theological Seminary in 1928. After leading a congregation in Indianapolis for five years, he was appointed rabbi of the Park Avenue Synagogue in New York City in 1933, where he remained until his untimely death. He was greatly influenced by Mordecai Kaplan, although Steinberg was critical of Reconstructionism for its lack of philosophical attention to God. His historical novel *As a Driven Leaf* (1939), which examines tensions between religion and philosophy through the life of the second-century heretic Elisha ben Abuyah, has never been out of print.

As a Driven Leaf
1939

Chapter I

Toward the end of the first century, in the spring of the last year of the reign of the Emperor Vespasian, two entries were made in the Roman archives of the district of Galilee. The first registered the fact that a male heir had been born to one Abuyah, Jewish patrician, and master of an estate on the outskirts of Migdal. The second, inscribed five days later, recorded the death of Elisheba, wife of Abuyah and mother of the still-unnamed child.

Thus, only kinsfolk in the first degree and the most intimate of friends gathered at the sorrow-shrouded villa on the eighth day after the birth of the baby to witness the rite of circumcision. [...]

"Gentlemen, my apologies for delaying these rites. I was preoccupied." Abuyah stood silhouetted against the day, tall, slender, in a robe cut after the fashion of the Greeks. His face, dark with shadow, was inscrutable. But it was apparent that no earlocks hung over his cheeks, no fringes dangled from his mantle. Nor was his robe rent in the symbol of mourning prescribed by ancient tradition. Only as he came into the room where his features could be read more clearly could it be seen that his handsome arrogant face was ravaged with pain, that his brilliant blue eyes were dull with grief.

He looked down at the baby lying on the table, a wry smile twisting his lips.

"A bad purchase," he mused aloud, "bought at too high a price. Such are the bargains God forces on man." [...]

Rabbi Eliezer's pale, haughty face burned with indignation.

"This child," he prayed stiffly over the bundle he had taken into his arms, "may God bless him with a believing heart."

He transferred his burden to his colleague, missing as he did so the glance of aversion with which Abuyah responded to the unmistakable implications of the prayer. Joshua nestled the child against his ungainly body. His gnarled fingers cupped gently about the swaddling clothes. Softly, as though imparting some secret to the uncomprehending baby, he blessed him.

"God make you great, little one. As we initiate you into the covenant of Abraham our father, so may we be privileged to lead you into the study of our holy Law, into the marital canopy, into a life of good deeds.

"A sweet boy," he added as he surrendered him to Jacob the surgeon.

An instant later a sharp wail of pain pierced the silent room.

Abuyah shuddered and turned aside.

"A merciful custom," he muttered resentfully, "the ordinance of a God of mercy."

Through the crying of the child the guests heard him with horror. Jacob's hands faltered momentarily among his instruments.

"How shall the child be called?" he inquired, recovering.

Again Abuyah was silent. Once more Amram spoke for him.

"Name him Elisha, after his mother Elisheba. So also will he be called after the great prophet. Elisha the son—" he paused as though his throat were choked "—of Abuyah."

With fingers deft from long experience, Jacob dressed the baby and put him into Abuyah's arms.

"You will now say the father's blessing," he instructed. Abuyah shook his head.

"But you must . . ."

"Not I," Abuyah answered bitterly. "I have never believed nor observed. Shall I begin now by thanking a God in whom I have no faith for the death of my wife and the mutilation of my child? If I had not felt that his mother would have wanted this, I . . ." [. . .]

[. . .] Jacob, the surgeon, looked about in perplexity. He had officiated at more rites of circumcision than he could count, but never one like this.

Then he remembered that the ritual was not yet completed. He raised a wine cup full to overflowing above Sapphirah and the baby, intoning the prayers of benediction.

". . . and may his name be known in Israel," he concluded, "as Elisha the son of Abuyah."

Other works by Steinberg: *A Partisan Guide to the Jewish Problem* (1945); *Basic Judaism* (1947).

Delmore Schwartz

1913-1966

The American poet and short story writer Delmore Schwartz was born in Brooklyn, New York, to Romanian Jewish immigrants and studied philosophy at New York University. His most famous short story,

"In Dreams Begin Responsibilities," was published in 1937 in the first issue of the *Partisan Review*. This and other short stories and poems became his first book, published in 1938 when Schwartz was only twenty-five years old. His work received praise from renowned literary figures including T. S. Eliot, William Carlos Williams, and Ezra Pound. He was the youngest poet ever to be awarded the Bollingen Prize for Poetry (1960). Although plagued by mental illness and alcoholism, he continued to publish stories, poems, plays, and essays, and he edited the *Partisan Review* from 1943 to 1955, as well as *The New Republic* from 1955 to 1957.

America! America!
1940

Shenandoah's mother proceeded to explain in detail how insurance was a genial medium for a man like Mr. Baumann. The important thing in insurance was to win one's way into the homes and into the confidences of other people. Insurance could not be sold as a grocer or a druggist sells his *goods* (here Shenandoah was moved again by his mother's choice of words); you could not wait for the customer to come to you; nor could you like the book salesman go from house to house, plant your foot in the doorway, and start talking quickly before the housewife shut the door in your face. On the contrary, it was necessary to become friendly with a great many people, who, when they came to know you, and like you, and trust you, take your advice about the value of insurance.

It was necessary to join the lodges, societies, and associations of your own class and people. This had been no hardship to Mr. Baumann who enjoyed groups, gatherings, and meetings of all kinds. He had in his youth belonged to the association of the people who came from the old country, and when he married, he joined his wife's association. Then he joined the masonic lodge, and in addition he participated in the social life of the neighborhood synagogue, although he was in fact an admirer of Ingersoll. Thus he came to know a great many people, and visited them with unfailing devotion and regularity, moved by his love of being with other human beings. A visit was a complicated act for him. It required that he enter the house with much amiability, and tell his host that he had been thinking of him and speaking of him just the other day, mentioning of necessity that he had just *dropped* in for a moment.

Only after protestations of a predictable formality, was Mr. Baumann persuaded to sit down for a cup of tea. Once seated, said Mrs. Fish (imposing from time to time her own kind of irony upon the irony which sang in Shenandoah's mind at every phase of her story), once seated it was hours before Mr. Baumann arose from the dining room table on which a fresh table-cloth had been laid and from which the lace cover and the cut glass had been withdrawn.

Mr. Baumann drank tea in the Russian style, as he often explained; he drank it from a glass, not from a cup: a cup was utterly out of the question. And while he drank and ate, he discoursed inimitably and authoritatively upon *every topic of the day*, but especially upon his favorite subjects, the private life of the kings and queens of Europe, Zionism, and the new discoveries of science. A silent amazement often mounted in his listeners at the length of time that he was capable of eating, drinking, and talking; until at last, since little was left upon the table, he absentmindedly took up the crumbs and poppyseeds from the tablecloth.

Other works by Schwartz: *Genesis* (1943); *The World Is a Wedding* (1948); *Summer Knowledge: New and Selected Poems, 1938–1958* (1959); *Successful Love, and Other Stories* (1961); *Selected Essays of Delmore Schwartz* (1970).

Shoshana Shababo

1910–1992

Shoshana Shababo was born in Zikhron Ya'akov, the daughter of a teacher at the Alliance school in Safed. She studied at the Levinsky College in Tel Aviv, and at age twenty-two published a controversial two-volume novel, *Maryah*, depicting the lives of nuns and of an Arab family. Shababo was one of the first Sephardi women to publish novels in pre-state Israel; her short stories also appeared in numerous literary journals. After her marriage, she ceased her literary career.

Dina's Braids
1940

Dina has reached the age of seventeen, but her mind and manners are far beyond those years. She is comely and demure and full of charm. Two modest eyes and two wild braids. Why wild? Because they have escaped the usual boundaries and they are long, thick, snake-like. One day, when Dina grew weary of her braids she made her way to Ḥakham Makhlouf, the noted barber of Safed, and made her complaint, and asked if he would do her the honor of cutting off her braids, which weigh down on her head like weighing stones. Ḥakham Makhlouf wondered and teased her with her own words: Has it come to this that she is willing to sell her braids? And she remained single-minded. And so emphatic was her answer that she disconcerted the barber who could not believe what he had heard and, opposing her, half-jokingly, half-embarrassed, he said: On the contrary, I shall weave a crown from her hair for the ladies who dress up. Or even better: I shall make a wig of the hair for holidays for the wife of the Ashkenazi merchant. On the contrary, please be seated—Dina, beg pardon to her honor—on the barber chair, and as Dina rushed to sit down on the chair, without thinking, the barber began to panic and played with her braids. For a moment he twists them around her temples in the shape of a crown, and the next moment wraps them around her neck like a pair of snakes. Or he spreads her hair between his fingers, enjoying their silkiness, or he combs them and grumbles: "A blessing against the evil eye upon this black-haired one. May the person who created the fashion of bobbed hair be covered in ashes, that Dina the daughter of the rabbi is dragged into it . . . hmm . . . and the sheared woman—is the goat in the story. . . ."

In the middle of all this, Hans the Ghaffir [British mandate police] entered with a soft greeting, and wondered and stared at the barber and the girl together. Ḥakham Makhlouf winked at him with a meaningful wink and held the scissors teasingly. His eyes moved from the Ghaffir to the girl to see the response of repentance on her face, and once again back to the Ghaffir whose eyes were becoming bright. His hand shaking, his heart palpitating. In a moment . . . all at once the Ghaffir slapped him on the shoulder and grabbed the scissors from his hand. How could he? How dare he? . . .

Dina stood surprised at the sturdy strength and height of the blond Ghaffir. Her hair was loose, and her modest eyes were wide open—and she was suddenly ashamed. She gathered up her hair somehow, and ran off. And when she escaped, the Ghaffir discharged a series of questions about her, about the owner of the braids. And Ḥakham Makhlouf, who saw what was about to happen, praised and extolled her, the most beauteous of women.

And from that meeting Dina grappled with many unleashed meditations. Day and night, at any time at any hour. She became impatient and her quiet was disturbed. And every time she combed her hair, there appeared before her the pale vision, his hand grabbing the scissors from the hands of Ḥakham Makhlouf, his eyes intoxicating her. Her heart, which had only needed a tiny spark, was now ignited into a flame for the first time.

She heard many and various things about him, about "Goldilocks," who had come from afar, from the lands of the "enlightened." Some say he had studied the wisdom of medicine, and some—that he possessed the knowledge of building big buildings. And now he had come to the land of Israel, with "great intentions," what may be called "ideals," he is a Ghaffir. But, as the ancient proverb has said, "The noble, even in poverty, will ennoble."

And while she was delaying trying to get her thoughts in order, the information she had heard, and her feelings, Goldilocks appeared, to rent a room in their building. Dina understood that this was just an excuse—and pretended to bargain with her mother and with him over the price and all the bother, while the modest eyes were playing a completely different game.

Indeed there are loves, and there are loves, the world is replete with loves, created in higher loves. What do all these have to do with Dina's love, she who was only brought into this world to love her "Goldilocks," to feed him and dress him and be around him on every occasion and every hour, to satisfy him, to appease him, and to make the entire world pleasant to him, until one day she caused her mother to scold her as mothers do to their daughters: "This is not the way a girl should love, but she should love in modesty and hiding. Spoiling is not good for a man, lest he become too proud. . . ." The mother sighed and went on to speak of her humble husband, may he rest in peace, who walked in the righteousness of the blessed Lord. . . . And even that Ghaffir, whose language and customs were strange to them, possessed many of the qualities of the Marḥom. That very obedient modesty that embodies much of greatness. "Truly, the nutrients of this country are preferable to foreign wheat," but he may be considered as the wheat of this blessed land, "God's name upon him and his name."

And just then "Goldilocks" appeared. Light illuminates the house. Always upon his return the light shines in the little home of two women. He goes into his room, washes and combs his hair, and comes to sit next to Dina like a faithful dog. Until now he has not needed to know her language but he believed that Dina was born for him and for him were created these braids. Sometimes he marvels at the wonderful closeness that took place between them so all of a sudden. He—a son of the West in all its breeding, and she—a Sephardi daughter of Sephardim, a "sabra," whose modest ways were a wonder to him. He was accustomed to "brazen" girls—as Dina's mother would call them—girls who demanded all their hearts desire, not like this girl, whose ways were of calm and secret, of sweetness and charm. She could not resist his eyes but was ashamed to embrace him before her mother. And he wondered: "what is this black-braided sabra?"

And while he was sitting down to mend the rips in his clothing he found suitable time to enjoy her braids. Either he was teasing her by tying them to the chair or he was buttoning them into his uniform. Sometimes to the delight of the two women, he spread them between his fingers like the barber mentioned before—and sometimes he just held them, lost in his thoughts. What will he say to her and what will she say to him? And since they know everything, and why should they waste words? And suddenly there rises up that same surge of things and sub-things. He wants to tell her, and say to her, and relate to her (that dark sabra), if she only knew his language. And then there bursts from his heart a surge of yearnings for the fair and silent girl. And he murmurs for the thousandth time the words he knows in Hebrew: "Dina is his and her braids are his." More than anything else he desired her braids. And when he holds them in his hands his heart overflows with joy at the great possession he has saved from the hands of the barber.

And now Dina learns of the transfer of her "Goldilocks" from Safed to Haifa—and her spirit became murky. She feared the daring of the city girls lest they look at him with flirty eyes, prowling for anyone who is successful. In truth even in this place she was anxious when he went to work, even though she believed, in her naiveté, that when he is nearby the righteousness of her father would shelter him. Even when he was not far away, her heart felt threatened. Nevertheless she was forced to give in to the fear until the blessed day would arrive of their wedding.

And when the Devil began to become interested in them their happiness began to tumble down the slope. And one day all of a sudden his path became perverse before him [Numbers 22:32]. It became tangled and black, like the black day when it came upon them like a thief.

On Sabbath evening the women waited for him to return from the city. One hour, two, three. The heart trembles in fear, and the imagination brings up strange images. What the heart fears, the eyes should not have to view coming to pass. In the corner the gentle shadows of the two small women could be seen, and the oil lamp flickered. A woman should not speak with her companion, so as not to open the mouth to the Devil. And suddenly a crowd pushed by and ran towards the hospital, and Dina was shoved and ran as well and her heart was bitter with the same bitterness of the day her father, the Marḥom, died. God willing, she would sacrifice her braids this time only if he returns safely. And he returned, his body shattered, he was brought to the hospital together with the others wounded from the accident, and immediately after Dina's tiny body was trembling over him.

The vows and promises could not help, her father's shelter had been taken from them. Her tears dried and her heart was silenced. What can she say and how complain if the Lord of mercy was miserly of his wealth and fortune for a forgotten orphan. Only words of heresy came to her lips. The Lord is righteous in all His ways.

His mind was clear but he was unable to speak. He tried to tell her, his sabra, what he had said a thousand times. Only his hungry eyes gazed at her beautiful braids with passionate longing. Dina understood, groaned over him and breathed out from her trembling soul as if she wanted to give him her life for his. And then her beautiful braids fell down and rested over his white face.

This time Dina did not rush to the hairdresser, but with her own hands cut off her beautiful braids and placed them near his head.

Translated by Karen Alkalay-Gut.

Other works by Shababo: *Maryah* (1932); *Ahavah bi-tsefat* (1942).

Chaim Sloves

1905–1988

Playwright Chaim (Henri) Sloves was born in Białystok and attended Yiddish secular school. After spending time in Moscow, he joined the Communist Party and was arrested in Warsaw upon his return to Poland. Sloves then studied law at the Sorbonne, graduating in 1935. He was an organizer of the World Congress for Yiddish Culture and a founder of the Yidishe Kultur Farband. During World War II, he was active in the French underground. His play *Haman's Downfall*, with Haman an obvious stand-in for Hitler, was particularly popular in the immediate aftermath of the war.

Haman's Downfall
1940

MORDECAI: A Judgment Day on you and all the Hamans, today and forevermore—

HAMAN: Amen! Mordecai, I think you and I will yet be good friends—yes, Motya? [*Maudlin.*] Come closer, Motya, and I'll tell you the secret of my success. [*Opens his mouth wide.*] Look. Motya, look inside!

MORDECAI: Your beautiful white teeth?

HAMAN: Only a front!

MORDECAI: Your long tongue?

HAMAN: Only good for small talk!

MORDECAI: What, then? Your tonsils?

HAMAN: You're getting warm. My voice, Motya, my *voice*! How do you think I became the greatest statesman of all time? How do you think I got next to Alexander of Macedonia, or Hannibal of Carthage, or Caesar of Rome, or Napoleon of Josephine? How do you think I won the greatest battles of history without a single shot? With my voice! A lion's roar! [*Roars.*] A tiger's scream! [*Screams.*] A jackal's wail. [*Wails.*] The enemy gets scared to death. Then my army marches in and just blows—poof!—and it's all over. That's how I built the biggest empire in the world. That's how I took Assyria and Babylonia and Egypt and—that's what will happen to Greece. You don't believe me? [. . .]

HAMAN: And this people, your majesty, are the Jews. Now I ask you—what benefit do you get out of them alive? They are a bother to all the nations and a misfortune to themselves. If you want to earn the thanks of the world, let them all be exterminated. We'll take over their property—they are almost as rich as me. What do you say majesty?

ADVISORS: [*Softly.*] No . . . no . . . no . . .

AHASUERUS: Eh, I don't know, maybe you're right, but—

HAMAN: Your majesty, never have I asked a favor for myself—

AHASUERUS: You haven't?

HAMAN: [*Excited.*] But now I'm demanding it!

AHASUERUS: Take it easy, Hamdata, you'll spoil my digestion. All right, take my signet ring and do what you like. And now, my esteemed advisors, come with me and help me get dressed for my wedding. [*Exit with advisors.*]

HAMAN: [*Barely able to control himself.*] Ha! Ha! Finally and at last—revenge! Your end is near, damn Jews! Mordecai will get a special lesson! And Esther will be mine! But that is not my purpose. [*Postures.*] My sacred cause is to liberate the world from the Jewish yoke. I shall cut out this cancer of humanity. I shall be known as the greatest man that ever lived. The world will remember me forever! [. . .]

HERALD: [*Shushing advisors.*] What happened to the soldiers?

MARSANA: Shot to pieces!

PARSANA: Haman's to blame!

MARSANA: Curse his name!

PARSANA: What business did we have in Greece?

MARSANA: Strutting like the silly geese!

PARSANA: Now we're down to the very dregs—

MARSANA: With our tails between our legs—

Advisors: The generals went to war, to war.

And now they've come a-running.

So powerful smart they were before.

But now they've lost their cunning!

HERALD: [*Waving advisors back.*] Don't worry, my brave heroes—Haman will get his. And very soon. In this act Mordecai gets his revenge.

MARSANA: Who is this Mordecai?

HERALD: You don't know Mordecai the Tsaddik? You poor ignoramus! Never read the Megilah? No? Well, take it from me—you can depend on Mordecai. At sundown tonight, gather all your soldiers in front of the Queen's palace. But first you'd better disarm Haman's bodyguards. Go in peace, glorious heroes. The audience is getting impatient. I have to raise the curtain. [*Generals exit.*] [. . .]

MORDECAI: [*Clears throat.*] People of Media and Persia and all the 127 provinces! Citizens of Shushan-Habira! This is the new Assistant King, Mordecai ben Ya-eer! [*Cheers.*] Mordecai ben Ya-eer, ben Shammai, ben Kish, a man of Benjamin. [*Cheers.*] Citizens! Our wise and good King Ahasuerus has decided to make Haman the Wicked a head shorter. [*Cheers.*] May that be the fate of all Hamans now and forevermore, amen! [*Wild cheers.*]

From this moment forward, in all the King's provinces from India to Ethiopia, there is no superior race! All are equal! Anyone caught mistreating a Hebrew will follow Haman to his ancestors! I promise our glorious armies—you will never again go out to war! [*Cheers.*]

Citizens! Our country will again be a land of milk and honey, dates and figs, bread and meat, and plenty to eat! Roast duck and beer and good wine to fill you with cheer! No trouble and no fights, sunny days and peaceful nights! [*Stormy applause. Shouts of "Long Live Mordecai."*]

Translated by David F. Lifson.

Other works by Sloves: *Nekome nemer* (1947); *Borekh fun Amsterdam* (1956).

Boris Yampolski

1912–1972

Fiction writer and essayist Boris Yampolski (Iampol'skii) was born in Belaia Tserkov', Ukraine. Beginning in 1927, he spent several years as a journalist in Baku, Azerbaijan, and Stalinsk, Central Siberia. Yampolski then came to Moscow, and during World War II served as a military correspondent in Belorussia for *Krasnaia zvezda* and *Izvestiia*. After the war he composed fiction but found resistance to publication because he wrote about Jewish topics, painfully recalling life in the shtetl. He died in Moscow.

Country Fair
1940

Mr. Dykhes and Others

The small town resounded with whistling and shouting. The smell of stewing, the smell of frying, the smell of boiling.

Mr. Dykhes had sold all his defective soap to the army.

Musicians, go play! Fifers, go dance! Butchers, cut your meat! Bakers, carry your challahs! Cooks, burn in the fire!—bake and fry! Mr. Dykhes is having a good time.

The Dykhes house stands on the river bank—the tallest, most beautiful one in the whole town, with a white zinc roof that sparkles in the sun like silver. The house has a big gilded balcony, curved windows, and a wide front door as in a synagogue. Over the entrance is emblazoned a lion, as if standing watch over the Dykhes gold.

Every morning, when Mr. Dykhes stepped out onto the gilded balcony in his astrakhan, he looked upon the whole small town as his own property. And there was reason to think so. If you looked straight ahead, you saw a five-story windmill, leased from the Countess Branitsky, a mill famous throughout all of Kiev Province. When people saw bread as white as snow, they all said, Dykhes flour! If you looked to the left, you saw black smoke over the Jerusalem neighborhood—that was Dykhes tar smoking and Dykhes soap boiling. If you looked to the right, you saw in the sky the red plume of the sugar factory. Are the old people trudging to the synagogue? It's thanks to Dykhes. He built the town a golden synagogue. Is a corpse being transported? Once again, it's thanks to Dykhes, the honorary head of the local funeral society.

But today is the county fair—the mother of all fairs. Never before has Mr. Dykhes sold so much soap. And what soap it is! Never before have people bought so much flour, so much sugar, so much tar! Gold was flowing in streams.

In Mr. Dykhes's yard a fragrance of fine cooking filled the air. The carcasses of sheep hung on hooks. Steam coiled around the mountains of hot noodles. Gigantic pies, filled with grated apples, were baking in ovens, and the lame baker was keeping an eye on them. The pastry cook in a pink cap was twisting pretzels with his white hands and sprinkling them with poppy seeds and ground nuts. An old woman covered in down and chicken blood was filling the belly of an enormous goose with nuts, apples, and all sorts of good stuff, continually repeating, "That's how Dykhes likes it!" Several ducks craned their necks to get a better look at the proceedings. It probably seemed to them that the goose had been put to sleep so that surgery could be performed, so they guffawed, asking when it would be their turn for the operation.

The old cooks stood beside the ovens with their arms akimbo, looking boldly at the fire as if they were challenging the pots and pans to a fist fight as they discussed how much pepper and how much vinegar suits Mr. Dykhes. More than anything else, the young cooks were terribly afraid of using too much salt, or not enough, and they were discussing among themselves various incidents involving too little salt or too much salt. On various bonfires, copper basins were seething

with jam. The sweet smoke wafted heavenward. Birds flying over the yard stopped in their tracks.

Meanwhile the yard witnessed the arrival of the merry Jew Kukla in his straw Panama hat—a wedding jester. No matter where you wanted to sit down and have something to eat, Kukla would already be sitting there. No matter where you wanted to drink, Kukla was already standing there with a glass. No matter where music was coming from, Kukla was already running there in his silly Panama hat. And a wedding without Kukla was not a wedding: Who would sing and shout? And a bris without Kukla was not a bris: Who would make a speech to the baby? Who would pour into the baby's mouth its first drop of wine? And the chicken that was eaten without Kukla was not a chicken. What kind of chicken was it anyway if Kukla had not eaten the gizzard? If someone said to him, "Kukla, it's impossible to be cheerful all the time," Kukla would reply, "You're taunted by pride; I'm contorted by laughter. You drink tears and I, vodka. What I see on the bottom of a bottle, a sober person will never see. What I have eaten at funerals, you will not get to eat at a wedding." Kukla swore they had bought out the whole fair, slaughtered a bull, stuffed its guts with kasha, killed a hundred of the fattest geese and a hundred of the meanest tom turkeys. Kukla said, "We'll eat, we'll drink."

Auntie beseeched the cooks to let me soak in the smoke: "What does a Jewish boy need? Aroma."

The musicians entered. In front were the fat-faced trumpeters; behind them came the tall flautist, then the little drummer boy with a drum on his belly which was itself like a drum. They entered and stood in a row, and the drummer hit the drum twice with a drumstick, "Pay attention! See what cheeks they have!" The cooks started to laugh and gave him a lamb's leg, and each of the fat-faced trumpeters got a chicken gizzard and the trumpeters said, "God give you health," upon which they swallowed their gizzards and started to play a ceremonial flourish.

The guests were assembling. [. . .]

Everyone kept coming and coming: the rich Gonikshtein, and Syusman, and Efraim—all the very best families, and Piskun, who also considered himself a good family; and Madame Puri, a woman with a bony neck and a chin like a shovel; and Madame Turi, with a fat neck and a triple chin—one desiring the death of the other; both Madame in the turban and Madame in a burnoose—and one was ready to tear the other to pieces. This group was now joined by a Jew dressed to the hilt like a padishah; after him ran a boy with a gaping mouth and protruding ears. Suddenly new names were announced: Vasily Sidorovich Yukilzon and Pavel Ermilovich Yukinton. Absolutely everyone was here: swindlers in beaver hats and girls in crimson chapeaux and dandies in starch.

Translated by Richard Sheldon.

Other works by Yampolski: *Khrabryi krolik i drugie rasskazy o zveriakh i ptitsakh* (1961); *Volshebnyi fonar': Povest', rasskazy, miniatury* (1967); *Arbat, rezhimnaia ulitsa* (1988).

S. Y. Agnon
1887–1970

The Nobel Laureate Shmuel Yosef Agnon (born Czaczkes) grew up in Buczacz, Galicia, memories of which haunted and fed his literary imagination throughout his life. He settled in Jaffa in 1908, joining other members of the Second Aliyah to Palestine. There he adopted his pen name, derived from the title of his tragic tale, "Agunot" (Chained Souls). From 1913 to 1924, when Agnon lived in Germany, he belonged to the circle of Salman Schocken and the young Gershom Scholem. When Agnon returned to Palestine in 1924, he settled in Jerusalem and returned to Orthodox practice. From then on, the main branches of his literary creativity were the novel, stylized folktales and legends from Jewish Eastern Europe, and various anthological projects, in each of which he perfected a unique Hebrew style that was both modernist in tone and steeped in classical sources. Agnon exerted a profound influence on the first generation of Israeli prose writers.

From Foe to Friend
1941

Before Talpiot was built the King of the Winds used to rule over the entire region: and all his ministers and servants, mighty and stubborn winds, dwelled there with him and blew over mountain and valley, hill and ravine, doing whatever their hearts desired, as if the land had been given to them alone.

I went out there once and saw how lovely the place was—the air crisp, the sky pure blue, the land so open and free—and I strolled around a bit. A wind accosted me. "What are you doing here?" he said to me. "I'm taking a walk," I said. "Ah, you're taking a walk?" he said. He clapped me on the head and sent my hat flying. I bent down to pick it up. He rumpled my coat, turned it upside down over my head, and made a fool of me. I pulled my coat back off my head. He came at me again, knocked me to the ground and roared with wild laughter. I got to my feet and stood straight. He bumped up against me and shouted: "On your way! On your way!"

I saw I couldn't contend with one mightier than myself, and I went on my way.

I returned to the city and went inside my house. I became restless and went out. Whether I intended it or not, my feet carried me to Talpiot. I remembered all that the wind had done to me, I took some canvas and pegs and pitched a tent for myself—a refuge from wind and storm.

One night I stayed there. The light suddenly went out. I left the tent to see who had put my light out. I found the wind standing outside. "What do you want?" I asked him. He boxed my ears and slapped my mouth. I went back into my tent. He pulled up my tent pegs and split my rope, turned my tent over and ripped my canvas to shreds. He turned upon me as well, and almost knocked me over.

I saw I couldn't possibly match his strength. I picked up my feet and went back to the city.

I went back to the city and remained within its walls. I became restless and yearned for some place with fresh, pleasant air. Since there is no air anywhere in the entire land like the air of Talpiot, I went to Talpiot. And so that the wind wouldn't abuse me, I took some boards with me and made myself a hut. I thought I had found myself a resting-place, but the wind thought otherwise. A day hardly passed before he started thumping on my roof and shaking the walls. One night he carried off the whole hut.

The wind carried off my hut and left me without any shelter. I picked myself up and went back to the city.

What happened to me once and then a second time happened to me a third time. I returned to the city and I had no peace. How my heart drew me to that very spot from which I had been driven out!

I said to my heart: "Don't you see that it is impossible for us to return to a place from which we have been chased away? And what is impossible is impossible." But my heart thought differently. If I said a thousand times, *Impossible!* My heart replied a thousand and one times, "It *is* possible!"

I took wood and stones and built myself a house.

I won't praise my house, for it was small; but I am not ashamed of it, even though there are bigger and better houses. My house was small, but there was room enough in my house for a man like me who doesn't desire grandeur.

The wind saw that I had built myself a house. He came and asked me:

"What is this?"

"This is a house," I said to him.

He laughed and said: "I'll be damned if I ever saw anything as funny as this thing you call a house!"

I too laughed and said: "What you have never seen before, you see before you now."

He laughed and said: "What is it, this house?"

I laughed and said: "A house is . . . a house!"

He laughed and said to me: "I'll go and inspect it."

He stretched out his hand and inspected the door. The door broke and fell. He stretched out his hand and inspected the windows. The windows broke and fell. Finally he rose and went to the roof. Up he went and down came the roof. The wind laughed at me and said:

"Where is this house you built?"

I too asked where my house was. But I didn't laugh.

At first when the wind drove me away I used to return to the city. Finally things happened that prevented me from returning to the city. I was balked at every turn, and I didn't know what to do. To return to the city was impossible because of what had happened there; to return to Talpiot was impossible because of the wind who drove me out. I had made myself a tent and a hut, but they hadn't lasted. I had built myself a little house, but that hadn't stood up to the wind either. But then, maybe it hadn't withstood the wind because it was so small and frail; perhaps if it had been big and strong it would have stood. I took strong timber and sturdy beams, large blocks of stone, plaster and cement, and I hired good workers and watched over their work day and night. This time I was wise enough to sink the foundations very deep.

The house was built and it stood firm and upright on its own ground.

When the house was finished the wind came and thumped on the shutters.

"Who is rapping on my window?" I asked.

He laughed playfully and said: "A neighbor."

"What does one neighbor want of another on a night of storm and tempest like this?" I asked him.

He laughed and said: "He has come to wish his neighbor well in his new house."

"Is it usual for a neighbor to come through the window like a thief?" I said to him.

He came around and knocked on the door.

"Who is rapping on my door?" I said to him.

"It's I, your neighbor," said the wind.

"You are my neighbor—please come in," I said.

"But the door is locked," he said to me.

"Well, if the door is locked, it must be because I locked it," I said to him.

"Open up!" the wind answered.

"I'm sensitive to the cold; wait till the sun comes up and I will let you in," I said.

When the sun rose I went out to let him in but I couldn't find him. I stood in front of my house and saw that the land was desolate all around: not a tree, not a green leaf anywhere; only dust and stones. "I'll plant a garden here," I said to myself.

I took a spade and started digging. When the soil was ready I brought some saplings. The rains came and watered the saplings; the dews came, and the saplings sprouted; the sun nourished them, and they blossomed. Not many days passed before the saplings that I had planted became trees with many branches.

I made myself a bench and sat in the shade of the trees.

One night the wind returned and started knocking the trees about. What did the trees do? They struck back at him. The wind rose again and shook the trees. Once more the trees struck in return. The wind lost his breath. He turned and went away.

From that time on the wind has been quite humble and meek, and when he comes he behaves like a gentleman. And since he minds his manners with me, I too mind my manners with him. When he comes I go out to meet him and ask him to sit with me on the garden bench beneath the trees. And he comes and sits by my side. And when he comes he brings with him a pleasant scent from the mountains and valleys, and he blows the air around me gently like a fan. Since he behaves like a complete penitent, I never remind him of his former deeds. And when he leaves me and goes on his way I invite him to come again, as one should with a good neighbor. And we really are the best of neighbors, and I am very fond of him. And he may even be fond of me.

Translated by Joel Blocker.

Other works by Agnon: *Only Yesterday* (1945); *To This Day* (1952); *Present at Sinai: The Giving of the Law* (1959); *Shira* (1971); *A City in Its Fullness* (1973).

Budd Schulberg

1914–2009

Screenwriter, sportswriter, and novelist Budd (Seymour Wilson) Schulberg was born in New York, the son of Hollywood mogul B. P. Schulberg. Schulberg attended Dartmouth College and during World War II was assigned to the Office of Strategic Services, where he documented the course of the war with John Ford in Europe. After visiting concentration camps, Schulberg later submitted evidence against war criminals for the Nuremberg Trials. He is best known for his novel *What Makes Sammy Run?* and his screenplay for *On the Waterfront*. He also wrote articles for *Sports Illustrated*.

What Makes Sammy Run?

1941

Three weeks before Sammy's thirteenth birthday Papa came in too upset to eat.

"Tonight when I come out of *schule* the rabbi wants to talk to me. 'Max, my heart is like lead to tell you this,' he says, 'but your son Samuel cannot be *bar-mitzvah*. He never comes to *cheder*. He does not know his *Brochis*. The *Melamud* says he knows no more about the *Torah* than a *goy*.'"

Bar-mitzvah is the Hebrew ceremony celebrating a boy's reaching the state of manhood at the age of thirteen. He shows off all his knowledge and makes a speech which always begins, "Today I am a man . . ." and everybody gives him presents and congratulates the father and feels very good. It is as vital to the Orthodox Jews as Baptism is to the Christians.

"*Oi weh!*" Papa cried. "That I should live to see the day when my own flesh and blood is not prepared to become a man."

"Aw, what's that got to do with becomin' a man?" Sammy said. "Just a lotta crap. I been a man since I was eleven."

"Oh, Lord of Israel," Papa said, "how can You ever forgive us this shame? That I, a man who went to synagogue twice every day of his life, should have such a no-good son."

"Yeah," Sammy said. "While you was being such a goddam good Jew, who was hustlin' up the dough to pay the rent?"

"Silence, silence," Papa roared.

"I guess I gotta right to speak in this house," Sammy said. "For Chris'sake I'm bringin' in more money 'n you are."

"Money!" Papa cried. "That's all you think about, money, money . . ."

"Yes, money, money," Sammy mimicked. "You know what you c'n do with your lousy *bar-mitzvah*. It's money in the pocket—that's what makes you feel like a man."

The day that Sammy was to have been *bar-mitzvahed* Papa went to the synagogue and prayed for him as if he were dead. He came home with his lapel ripped in mourning. He would have liked to lock himself in all day because he couldn't face the shame of it. But it was a weekday and on weekdays he was just an extension of his pushcart.

People saw him push his cart through the street with his eyes staring dumbly at nothing. The driver who hit him said he sounded his horn several times, but the old man did not seem to hear.

When he was carried upstairs to his bed Israel and Mama sat there crying and watching him die.

Afterward, Israel didn't know what to do, so he went up on the roof to look at the stars. He found Sammy there smoking a butt.

"Is it over?" Sammy said, when he saw his brother.

Israel nodded. He had not really broken down yet, but the question did it. He cried, deep and soft, as only Jews can cry because they have had so much practice at it.

Israel was eighteen, but now he was a little boy crying because he had lost his papa. Sammy was thirteen, but he was a veteran; he had learned something that took the place of tears.

When Israel realized that he was the only one crying he became embarrassed and then angry.

"Damn you, why don't you say something?" Israel said. "Why don't you cry?"

"Well, what's there to say?" said Sammy.

"At least, can't you say you're sorry?"

"Sure," Sammy said. "I'm sorry he was a dope."

"I oughta punch you in the nose," Israel said.

"Try it," Sammy stud. "I bet I c'n lick you." Sammy sat there dry and tense. "Aw, don't work yourself into a sweat," he said.

"Sammy," Israel pleaded, "what's got into you? Why must you go around with a chip on your shoulder? What do you have to keep your left out all the time for?"

"Whatta you take me for, a sap like you?" Sammy said. "You don't see me getting smacked in the puss."

"But we aren't fighting now," Israel said.

Israel was right about not knowing Sammy. There were no rest periods between rounds for Sammy. The world had put a chip on his shoulder and then it had knocked it off. Sammy was ready to accept the challenge all by himself and this was a fight to the finish. He had fought to be born into the East Side, he had kicked, bit, scratched and gouged first to survive in it and then to subdue it, and now that he was thirteen and a man, having passed another kind of *bar-mitzvah,* he was ready to fight his way out again, pushing uptown, running in Israel's cast-off shoes, traveling light, without any baggage, or a single principle to slow him down.

Other works by Schulberg: *The Harder They Fall* (1947); *The Disenchanted* (1950); *On the Waterfront* (1954); *A Face in the Crowd* (1957).

Bernardo Verbitsky

1907–1979

Born in Buenos Aires into a family that had emigrated from Russia, Bernardo Verbitsky was raised in an impoverished home. Nonetheless, he studied to be a physician, a field that he later abandoned to become a journalist, novelist, and film writer. His socially conscious writings candidly explore the underside of urban living in Argentina. His own background appears in his autobiographical novel, *Hermana y sombra* (Sister and Shadow).

It's Not Easy to Start Living
1941

XLVI

He was learning about the Jewish festivals from Leo. The arrival of the new year was suddenly upon him, and that's when he decided that fasting on Yom Kippur would be a fine adventure. The thought of spending a whole day without eating or drinking became in his imagination like entering a dark place with threats lurking in sinuous alleyways that he would have to pass through, energized by his own fear. He figured he could only risk a few hours on that exploratory trip and then would have to return, like someone giving up. Planning this fast on Yom Kippur gave a value to eating that it did not have in the routine of daily life. What had always been done without thinking now acquired new importance, imposing in an exaggerated and twisted way the irrational, childish fear of hunger that shuts out all

other feelings. A day of hunger. Then it was no longer a shortcut through tortuous alleyways. A day of fasting stretched out like a pallid desert over which a light mist shimmered. The vision lingered and suddenly connected with the memory of many days of atonement that he had spent in the countryside. He concluded that what he was imagining came from that recollection and that a trace of memory was now turning into consciousness. That white mist reminded him of the synagogue full of men on the hot afternoon of a Day of Atonement. Only a few hours remained before the fast ended, and they had all been there since early morning with prayer shawls hanging from their shoulders. It was already a fading scene. Weak, tired, they doggedly trudged on. Yellow faces transparent with weakness. The smell of a crowd, the smell of humanity in the hot afternoon. The prayers buzzed monotonously and acquired a recurring crescendo that, as they diminished, left a sensation of boredom. He thought he could see a yellowish sunbeam crossing the synagogue at an angle, illuminating the sunken pallor of the faces and the light cream color of the robes. Above them a sour, heavy vapor floated. Once again the fast was a murky space of danger that he did not dare to cross. It seemed that at the end of a day of fasting he would find himself turned into a half-dead specter to which clung white vestments that went well with so much faint-heartedness and weakness. To stand so long in the synagogue murmuring prayers was to be transformed into a candle nourished by its own substance as it slowly burned. To burn in a mystical cold fire, gradually and almost imperceptibly eaten away until you were only yellow bones, in ivory skin.

Translated by Michele McKay Aynesworth.

Other works by Verbitsky: *Calles de tango* (1953); *Villa Miseria también es América* (1957); *Literatura y conciencia nacional* (essays, 1975); *Hermana y sombra* (1977).

Samuel Eichelbaum

1907–1967

The son of Russian immigrants, Samuel Eichelbaum was a leading Argentine dramatist in the 1920s, 1930s, and 1940s, his plays a mainstay of the Buenos Aires theatrical season. He was raised amid the Jewish agricultural colonies, which provided the inspiration for his early short fiction. Several of his plays feature urban, middle-class Jewish characters. He was the author of *Un guapo del 900* (1952), still to date considered a classic.

Nuptial Divorce
1942

ORELLANA: [*To* LEBER, *about to dig into a towering salad*] Hey there, you with the Jewish joke of a face, spit one out for us. That should perk you up. Nobody can tell Jewish jokes like a Jew. And now there's a million of them about Hitler. Have you noticed how a series of Jewish jokes on hot topics will make the rounds? Who tells them, who makes them up?

LEBER: We do it ourselves. We're so sharp at responding to demand that we don't miss a beat, not even about this.

MURCCHIO: So you're spreading those painful jokes about yourselves?

[*The waiter arrives to serve* ARRIGORRIAGA].

LEBER: That's right, we're the ones. We do it to ourselves.

ARRIGORRIAGA: Do you have no sense of shame? It's disgraceful! Pointing the finger at yourselves like that!

LEBER: There's the same distance between real Jews and the Jews in jokes as there is between the plain-spoken, good-natured Basque of jokes and an ordinary Basque like you. We dish out the abuse ourselves to cancel out the cruelty of others. The difference between Basques and Jews is that the stories make Basques more likeable, but only make us look bad. That's storytelling for you!

Translated by Michele McKay Aynesworth.

Other works by Eichelbaum: *La mala sed* (1920); *Un hogar* (1923); *El judío Aarón* (1926); *Nadie la conoció nunca* (1926); *Tejido de madre* (1936).

Ḥaim Hazaz
1898–1973

The Hebrew novelist and short-story writer Ḥaim Hazaz was born in a village in the province of Kiev and received a traditional Jewish education. He left home at age sixteen and until 1921 lived a peripatetic life in various Russian cities. During these years of turbulence and upheaval, he witnessed events that became the foundation of his works. From 1921 to 1931, he lived in Istanbul, Paris, and Berlin. He settled in Jerusalem in

1931 and remained there the rest of his life. Central to most of his work is the tension between the old Jewish world and the wish for redemption through political movements such as Zionism. He was one of the most influential Hebrew writers of his time.

The Sermon
1942

For a while there was quiet—a total, final quiet in the room. Then the chairman stirred, beetling his heavy eyebrows, and spoke with gruff, ironical severity: "Comrade Yudka, I call you to order! If you have something to say, please, say it briefly, no wandering off the subject. And if it's history you want to talk about, then the university is the place for you!"

"It's on the subject, it's on the subject!" Yudka hastened to reply with a propitiating smile. "I can't proceed now without history. I've thought a great deal about it, many nights, every night when I'm on guard. . . ."

The chairman shrugged and spread his hands skeptically. "Speak!" he ordered, to cut it short. [. . .]

[. . .] What if it's true that Judaism can manage to survive somehow in Exile, but here, in the Land of Israel, it's doubtful? . . . What if this country is fated to take the place of religion, if it's a grave danger to the survival of the people, if it replaces an enduring center with a transient center, a solid foundation with a vain and empty foundation? And what if this Land of Israel is a stumbling block and a catastrophe, if it's the end and finish of everything? . . ."

A queer, weary, and ill-defined smile flickered on his lips.

"Well? . . ." He turned his eyes on them as though waiting for an answer. "What if they're right? What if their instinct doesn't deceive them? . . . Just see how here, here, in Israel, they are against us, all the old settlers, all those pious old Jews, simple Jews like all those that ever lived in any other place or time. [. . .]

"To my mind, if I am right, Zionism and Judaism are not at all the same, but two things quite different from each other, and maybe even two things directly opposite to each other! At any rate, far from the same. When a man can no longer be a Jew, he becomes a Zionist. I am not exaggerating. The *Biluim* were primarily very imperfect Jews. It wasn't the pogroms that moved them—that's all nonsense, the pogroms—they were falling apart inside, they were rootless and crumbling within. Zionism begins with the wreckage of Judaism, from the point where the strength of the people fails. That's a fact! Nobody has yet begun to understand Zionism. It is far deeper, far more pregnant with vast and fateful consequences than appears on the surface, or than people say. [. . .]

"All right." Yudka began again, struggling with the words. "Of course I'm not the one to say what Zionism is. I'm not the man for it. Even though I've wracked my brain and thought about it for a long time. But that's not important. . . . One thing is clear. Zionism is not a continuation, it is no medicine for an ailment. That's nonsense! It is uprooting and destruction, it's the opposite of what has been, it's the end. . . . It has almost nothing to do with the people, a thoroughly non-popular movement, much more apart from the people than the Bund, more than assimilationism, more even than communism. The fact is, it turns away from the people, is opposed to it, goes against its will and spirit, undermines it, subverts it and turns off in a different direction, to a certain distant goal. Zionism, with a small group at its head, is the nucleus of a different people. . . . Please note that: not new or restored, but *different*. And if anyone doesn't agree, well, I'm very sorry, but either he's mistaken or he's deluding himself. What? Perhaps it isn't so? I believe that this land of Israel already is no longer Jewish. Even now, let alone in the future. Time will tell, as they say. That's its hidden core, that's the power it will yet unfold. Yes! At any rate, it's a different Judaism, if you choose to fool yourselves and keep that name, but certainly not the same as survived for two thousand years, not at all the same. [. . .]

[. . .] Well, then, it's well known that we're all ashamed to speak Yiddish, as though it were some sort of disgrace. I intentionally said 'ashamed.' Not that we dislike, or fear, or refuse, but we're ashamed. But Hebrew, and none other than Sephardic Hebrew, strange and foreign as it is, we speak boldly, with a kind of pride or vanity, even though it isn't as easy and natural as Yiddish, and even though it hasn't the vitality, the sharp edge and healthy vigor of our folk language. What's the meaning of this? What's the reason for it? For no reason at all, just to take on such an immense burden? But it's quite simple: This community is not continuing anything, it is different, something entirely specific, almost not Jewish, practically not Jewish at all. [. . .] And it doesn't matter that we had the same kind of thing before, that was with the assimilationists, that's easy to understand. There we were living among strangers, people who were different and hostile, and we had to hide, to dissimu-

late, to be lost to sight, to appear different from what we really were. But here? Aren't we among our own, all to ourselves, with no need for shame, or for hiding, or anyone to hide from? Well then, how do you expect to understand this? . . . That's it! That's the whole thing, point by point. It's obvious, no continuity but a break, the opposite of what was before, a new beginning. . . .

Translated by Ben Halpern.

Other works by Hazaz: *Mori Sa'id* (1956); *The Gates of Bronze* (1975); *The End of Days* (1982).

Irène Némirovsky
1903–1942

Born into a rich Jewish banking family in Kiev, Irène Némirovsky settled with her family in France in the wake of the Russian Revolution. She was educated at the Sorbonne and had a successful career as a writer during her lifetime, with several of her novels adapted for stage and screen. As World War II began, Némirovsky, together with her husband Michel Epstein and their two young daughters, converted to Roman Catholicism in an effort to avoid the worst effects of antisemitism in France at the time. This was to no avail, however, as Némirovsky and her husband were ultimately sent to Auschwitz, where they were murdered. Today she is best known for her two wartime novellas; these were preserved by her daughter and not published until 2004.

Suite Française
1942

Madame Perrin told them that her son had died a hero's death in Normandy as the Germans advanced; she had received permission to visit his grave. She complained at great length about the cost of this journey and Madame Angellier sympathized with her. Maternal love and money were two completely different things. The Perrins lived in Lyon.

"The city is destitute. I've seen crows being sold for fifteen francs each. Mothers are feeding their children on crow soup. And don't think I'm talking about the working classes. No, Madame! I'm talking about people like you and me."

Madame Angellier sighed sadly; she imagined her relatives, members of her family, sharing a crow for supper. The idea was somehow grotesque, scandalous (though if it had been just the working classes, all they would have done was say, "Those poor creatures" and then move on).

"Well, at least you have your freedom! You don't have any Germans living with you like us. Yes, Madame, here in this house, behind that wall," said Madame Angellier, pointing to the olive-green wallpaper with the silver palm leaves. "An officer."

"We know," said Madame Perrin, slightly embarrassed. "We heard about it from the notary's wife who came to Lyon. Actually, that's why we've come."

They all involuntarily looked at Lucile.

"Please explain what you mean," Madame Angellier said coldly.

"I've heard that this officer behaves absolutely correctly, is that right?"

"Yes."

"And he's even been seen speaking to you extremely politely on several occasions?"

"He never speaks to *me*," Madame Angellier said haughtily. "I wouldn't stand for it. I accept that my attitude may not be very reasonable" (she stressed this last word) "as has been pointed out to me, but I am the mother of a prisoner of war and because of that, even if I were offered all the money in the world, I wouldn't consider these gentlemen as anything but our mortal enemies. Although other people are more . . . how can I put it? . . . more flexible, more realistic, perhaps . . . my daughter-in-law in particular . . ."

"I answer him if he speaks to me, yes," said Lucile.

"But you're so right, absolutely right!" exclaimed Madame Perrin. "My dear girl, I'm putting all my hope in you. It's about our poor house! You've seen what a terrible state it's in . . ."

"I've only seen the garden . . . through the gates . . ."

"My dear child, do you think you could possibly arrange for us to have back certain items from inside the house to which we are particularly attached?"

"Madame, but I . . ."

"You mustn't refuse. All you have to do is speak to these gentlemen and intervene on our behalf. It might all have been burned or damaged, of course, but I can't believe the house has been so vandalized that it is impossible to recover our family portraits, correspondence or furniture, of sentimental value only to us . . ."

"Madame, you should speak to the Germans occupying your house yourself and . . ."

"Never," said Madame Perrin, pulling herself up to her full height. "Never will I cross the threshold of my house while the enemy is there. It is a question of dignity and sensitivity. They killed my son, my son who had just been accepted to study at the Ecole Polytechnique, in the top six. I'll be staying at the Hôtel des Voyageurs with my daughters until tomorrow. If you could arrange to have certain things returned to us, I would be eternally grateful. Here's the list. If I found myself face to face with one of these Germans, I wouldn't be able to stop myself singing the 'Marseillaise' (I know myself!)," said Madame Perrin in an impassioned voice, "and then I'd get deported to Prussia. Not that that would be a disgrace, far from it, but I have daughters. I must keep going for my family. So, I am truly begging you, my dear Lucile, to do whatever you can for me."

"Here's the list," said Madame Perrin's younger daughter.

She unfolded the paper and began reading:

A china bowl and water jug with our monogram, decorated with butterflies

A salad dryer

The white-and-gold tea service (twenty-eight pieces, the sugar bowl is missing its lid)

Two portraits of grandfather: (1) sitting on his nanny's lap; (2) on his deathbed.

The stag's antlers from the entrance hall, a memento of my Uncle Adolphe

Granny's plate warmer (porcelain and vermeil)

Papa's extra set of false teeth he'd left behind in the bathroom

The pink-and-black sofa from the sitting room

In the left-hand drawer of the desk (key herewith): My brother's first page of writing, Papa's letters to Mama while he was away taking the waters in Vittel in 1924 (tied with a pink ribbon), all our family photographs

There was a deathly silence as she read. Madame Perrin cried softly beneath her veil.

"It's hard, so hard to watch things you care about so much being taken away from you. I beg you, my dear Lucile, do everything you can. Be clever, persuasive . . ."

Lucile looked at her mother-in-law.

"This . . . this officer," said Madame Angellier barely moving her lips, "has not yet come back. You won't see him tonight, Lucile, it's too late, but tomorrow you could speak with him and ask for his help."

"All right. I will."

Translated by Sandra Smith.

Other works by Némirovsky: *Le Malentendu* (1926); *The Wine of Solitude* (1935); *A Modern Jezebel* (1936); *Les chiens et les loups* (1940).

Der Nister
1884–1950

Born in Berdychiv, Russia (present-day Ukraine), Der Nister (pseudonym of Pinkhes Kahanovitsh) is considered one of the most stylistically unique Yiddish writers of the twentieth century. An associate of the Kiev Group and Kultur-lige, Der Nister is remembered for his short prose works that wove together mystical themes, modernist symbolist techniques, and fantastical fairy-tale landscapes. After a short stint in Berlin, he settled in the Soviet Union in 1926. In the late 1930s, Der Nister changed direction stylistically and produced *Di mishpokhe Mashber*, a panoramic, Dostoyevskian novel set in mid-nineteenth-century Berdychiv. A member of the Jewish Anti-Fascist Committee, Der Nister was a victim of the postwar liquidation of Soviet Yiddish culture and died in a prison hospital in 1950.

Meyer Landshaft
1943

A Fragment about an Incident in Today's Occupied Poland

He, Meyer, during all the days when they prepared Wanda for the journey (according to regulations, the women had to take along shoes, clothing, and food for several days, as though going to some kind of work), when occasional cries could be heard in the home, a cry from one and then from someone else in the house, letting go in hysterical outbursts; during all those days, Meyer Landshaft did not appear. Not even on the last day, not even at the last hour, nor in the last few minutes, when Wanda was saying good-bye to everyone, accompanied by wild sobs from her mother, Hanna-Gitl, as well as from her brothers, sisters, and other relatives—not even when Wanda went up to her father's door, and her voice, among all the cries in the house, could be heard pleading: "Daddy, open up, I want to say good-bye to you"—not even then did Meyer Landshaft open the door, or throw his arms around Wanda. During the first few moments, he remained silent, then he said: "No, daughter, I can't." Not out of cruelty, to

be sure, but because he simply didn't have the heart. Standing at the door, Wanda seemed to hear a weeping, which accompanied her and afflicted her for a long time en route—the weeping of a man lamenting not only his own doom, but the doom of an entire world.

Wanda couldn't endure it and she left. . . . But that evening, at the station, when the train was transferred to a distant line and when several of the prisoners, unaccompanied by anyone, stood in the car where Wanda was, stood under the high window, which they could barely reach, saying good-bye, with their last looks, to their home, from which they were being torn away—at that time, Wanda, like others, also stretched her head to that little window. . . . She wasn't thinking of anyone then, not even her mother, whose last loving kisses she could still feel on her jacket, right by her breast, when her mother, upon saying good-bye, had wept into her breast, burying her face there for a long time, unable to tear herself away—no, not the mother, she was thinking of no one else, only her father, imagining him behind the locked door, as he stood and listened to her pleading, the pleading of his youngest child, his baby, Wanda, and he did not have the heart to open the door, to come out and take a final look at her.

Translated by Joachim Neugroschel.

Other works by Der Nister: *Hekher fun der erd* (1910); *Mayselekh in ferzn* (1918); *Gedakht* (1922); *Fun mayne giter* (1929); *Korbones* (1943).

Leah Goldberg
1911–1970

Hebrew poet, playwright, and professor Leah Goldberg was born in Königsberg and grew up in Kovno (Kaunas), Lithuania, where she attended a Hebrew high school. She studied in Berlin and Bonn, earning a doctorate in Semitic languages. Goldberg returned to Kaunas in 1932 and was an active member of the Petaḥ group of poets. In 1935, she moved to Mandatory Palestine, where she taught and edited children's books. In the 1950s, she commenced teaching at the Hebrew University in Jerusalem and founded the department of comparative literature. Goldberg published a large number of volumes of poetry, novels, plays, translations, and books for children. Steeped in Russian culture and European aesthetics, she eschewed national themes in her writing. She was awarded the Israel Prize for Literature in 1970.

My Friends from Arnon Street
1943

Arnon Street is not the largest street in Tel Aviv. On the contrary, it is a small street, nearly an alleyway. There is very little traffic. A double-decker bus does not go through it, or any other bus [for that matter]. Only small cars travel in it, and, every now and then, a truck. And since there is very little traffic, there are many children in the street, and as their fathers and mothers do not have to worry that their children may be run over, they allow them to play outside.

The house on 15 Arnon Street is not the largest and most beautiful house in the alleyway. It is a simple white house, long and narrow. It is three stories tall and has many balconies. There are many such houses in our town.

So why, then, am I writing a story about this one particular house? Very simply, I have been living on this very same street, in this very same house, for the past six years. Over time, a number of the neighbors moved out and others moved in. Children came, and children left. Children went to kindergarten, they finished kindergarten, enrolled in school, and graduated from first grade to second grade. I lived there and I witnessed all of it, I had many friends among the residents of the building, and I wish to tell you about them because it feels good to talk about friends. [. . .]

About three years ago, a brother and sister lived on the second floor. Twins. Ruti was the name of the sister, Yona, the name of the brother. In those days they were five or so years old. They were slight and skinny, light-haired and clear-eyed, with lots of yellow, jolly freckles sprinkled on their faces, especially around the tiny noses that were very much like the button of a doorbell. Ruti was a tiny bit bigger than Yona. And it is no wonder: after all, she is half an hour older than he is!

Ruti and Yona loved candy very much. [. . .]

One day, Yona was playing in the yard with our neighbor Dalia, and Ruti sat alone on the stoop and looked at the pictures of some book. All of a sudden, Yona let out a terrific shriek:

"Ruti, Ruti! Come here! Come quickly!"

Ruti jumped up and ran to him. Yona stood before her, pale with excitement; even the freckles on his nose were pale. He held out his palm with a coin in it:

"Look, I found a white *grush* without a hole!"

Ruti examined the coin and decreed:

"It is not a grush. It is a shilling!"

It needs to be said that, generally speaking, Ruti knew many things that Yona never even imagined.

"And so?" asked Yona, dumbfounded.

"And so, it is worth lots and lots of money!" Ruti said. [. . .]

"So what do we do now?" whispered Yona.

"We'll buy candy!" announced Ruti, her eyes lighting up. [. . .]

They set off at once toward the grocer. [. . .]

Bravely, Ruti walked up to the counter.

"What would you like?" The grocer asked.

"Candy for a shilling."

"A whole shilling?!"

"Yes!" Ruti confirmed boldly.

"And your mother approves?" The grocer inquired.

"Y . . . yes," Ruti said, even though she was not absolutely sure of this." [. . .]

The grocer took the money and tossed a rather large pouch on the scale. [. . .]

It is impossible to describe all that was in that pouch: wonderful candy, small and large, reds and yellows, greens and pinks, translucent and nontransparent. All of them much prettier than those you receive on your birthday!

Ruti and Yona sat on the stoop. They invited Dalia and Yuval from the third floor—and the Candy Festival began.

However, after some time, when the amount of candy in the pouch was greatly reduced, the children, for some reason, felt they had had enough.

"It is a bit too much!" Yuval groaned. [. . .]

"Maybe we should hide them under a stone and have the rest tomorrow?"

"The bigger children will find them, they always find everything!"

"But not shillings!" Yona said proudly. Suddenly, he called out: "I know, I know!"

"What do you know?"

"What to do with the candy!"

"Well?"

"We will plant them! We will plant them in the ground, and afterward many many candies will grow and we will never have to go to the store to buy candy. We will always pick them in the garden, and always, when we feel like it, we will have candy!"

"Good," said Ruti. "Go and fetch the spade!" [. . .]

A moment later, the four of them stood in the back yard and began digging the earth in a small patch near the trash cans. [. . .]

Ruti got hold of the pouch and pushed the candy deep, deep into the ground. [. . .]

Day after day, Ruti and Yona irrigated the small garden. At first, Yuval and Dalia helped them, but soon, when they saw that nothing was growing, they tired of such a chore. Only Ruti and Yona remained loyal to their garden. [. . .]

One morning, when Yona came out of the washroom, Ruti met him with a grumpy face.

"Yona!"

"What happened?"

"I told mother everything!"

"What about?"

"The candy!"

"And what . . . what did she say?"

"She laughed . . . she laughed so hard," said Ruti, beginning to cry "And, she said . . . she said that candy can never grow from the ground. . . ."

"Grownups always say things like that," Yona said angrily, but his eyes, too, swelled with tears.

And this is the tale of what happened in the house on 15 Arnon Street!

And, to this day, no candy blossomed in our yard. But, in the meantime, Ruti and Yona blossomed and grew up. They no longer live in this house; two years ago they moved to Kfar Yedidya. They live there now and they know very well, like all the children in the village, what one plants in a garden.

Translated by Tsipi Keller.

Other works by Goldberg: *Shir ba-kefarim* (1942); *Ve-hu' ha-'or* (1946); *'Al ha-periḥah* (1948), *Barak ba-boker* (1955); *Dirah le-haskir* (1959); *Mukdam u-me'uḥar* (1959); *The Selected Poetry and Drama of Leah Goldberg* (2005).

Lázaro Liacho

1906–1969

Lázaro Liacho was born in 1906 in Buenos Aires; his father was Jacob Simón Liachovitzky, one of the founders of the local Yiddish press and Zionist Federation. While Liacho followed in his father's footsteps, writing as a journalist, Zionist, and essayist, he is primarily recognized as a poet and short-story writer. He considered Argentina to be the new Zion and Jewishness to be primarily a spiritual condition that was not bound to any territory.

Blood

1943

On the nights before Passover, Rosh Hashanah, and Yom Kippur, my mother would send me to the butcher with some birds to be slaughtered according to ritual so the meat would be kosher—that is, clean and proper to eat at a Jewish table.

We lived near the gates of Palermo, and the butcher was located in the ghetto at Junín and Lavalle. We would make the trip to his house in the horse-drawn streetcar. Just as today with the electric ones, it was forbidden to carry live birds with you in the cars. Even so, we tried it, ready to face cheerfully whatever problems resulted. The pleasure of sitting in a "cockroach," as the open trailer was called, emboldened us, and we had no fear of being scolded by the guard or conductor.

The birds we transported were quite large. Two or three months ahead of the celebrations, mama started fattening them up. The idea of preparing our sumptuous holiday feasts using the skinny birds sold in the markets seemed unimaginable. The obligation to have the birds killed by an authorized slaughterer, owner of a razor sharp blade without a single nick, meant we ate fowl only three times a year unless our relatives on Lavalle Street invited us over. We justified this privation by the fact that only the slaughterer was suitably expert: he killed the birds almost instantly, inducing a rapid effusion of blood in accordance with holy kosher laws, sparing them needless suffering. [. . .]

The messy spectacle of the birds' slaughter was depressing, and tears would run down my face as I watched the blood run. But observing my sister's aplomb and the others' indifference, I saw myself as a sentimental youth, worthless in a fight, averse to brawls, a fellow who feared the sight of blood. And that was the truth of it: I trembled at the sight of blood. I would suddenly be overcome with emotion when I felt the dying bird's last glance fall on me. I would grieve for days afterward. It was impossible for me to eat a bite of that bird, though specially prepared by mama for the holiday, that very bird I had raised, only to be forced by tradition to have it slaughtered. I felt like an executioner. I would remember the bird as a friend, recalling the games when I would hide so it would hunt me down and snatch the food from my hands. I would see the bird, its neck against mine, while I kissed its eyes and beak. Oh, the mottled rooster that would wait for me every morning near the kitchen table so I would feed it breadcrumbs while I was having breakfast. Year after year, some of my beloved birds would fall under the butcher's knife, and the vacuum they left behind left me suffering for long periods. As the new baby chicks grew, I showered them with attention, happy to note that all the birds in the henhouse would regularly come to eat from my hands.

One day when no one in the family was sick and it was not a holiday, my sister had a craving to eat some chicken. She called the local butcher shop to ask the young man there to kill the bird.

"At our house," she told him, eyeing me maliciously, "there's no man capable of doing it."

The butcher shop boy did not need to hear the request twice. After a quick sprint, he caught the bird that was pointed out to him and, holding it by the head, swung it around several times in the air, inspected its neck, and delivered its lifeless body to my sister. The bird didn't squawk, didn't twitch or lose a drop of blood. The young man killed the bird instantly. A lightning bolt couldn't strike any quicker. The bird had no spasms, no pain, no flapping of wings. "Why, then, were we taking our birds to the *shohet*?" Bertha asked. The blood had no soul that she could see. Speaking persuasively to me about the chicken's easy death, she managed to destroy my belief in the symbols of holiness, though avoiding the sight of blood meant more to me than being able to eat it. "Whether you fulfill the commandments or not," my sister pointed out, "you're not killing anyone; you don't know how to kill; none of us knows how to kill because the bloodless meat we eat has taught us to feel naturally repelled by blood."

The example of the butcher shop boy was all it took: we no longer had to take our birds to the Jewish butcher. Bertha delighted in the former's method. As soon as the bird was dead, it was hung by its feet so blood would collect in the neck, where it coagulated when refrigerated. Boiled or grilled, the chicken's neck thus became an appetizing morsel, and my sister complacently ate the whole thing, with no attempt on our part to share it with her. She ate it in the kitchen, as the rest of us were opposed to having meat with blood served at the family table. The spirit of tradition thus made its last stand, and in its weak redoubt we resisted the gentiles' influence for a few more years.

Ah, the neck skin of a stuffed hen! Why fill it with blood when mama made it so tasty, stuffed with toasted bread, chicken *griebenes*, mincemeat made with nuts, olives, eggs, and aromatic herbs? Now that was a stuffed chicken neck skin, *heldzl* for a Jewish palate! I only liked it when my mother made it, and it pleased me as much as noodles with pesto sauce, minestrone, or polenta, and no less than *carbonada* stew, stewed sweet corn, or corn pudding. Ah, Creole dishes, and Jewish dishes, and dishes from around the world: how appetizing they are when prepared at home using ingredients the pan expects in order to provide us with an incredible feast! The blessing of bread is born in our mouth; the blessing of wine is born in our spirit, and mankind rejoices in the blood of the fruit of the vine, the gift of earth. I had no wish to see any other kind of blood.

Hearing me say these things, Bertha became annoyed.

"Don't worry so much about the blood," she told me, "that's not what redeems the crimes of humanity, that slits the throats of our brothers like chickens, and lets them bleed to death. Don't be a coward! Blood was meant to boil . . . or to flow!"

And I answered her: "I don't want to see any blood!"

Translated by Michele McKay Aynesworth.

Other works by Liacho: *Bocada de pan* (1931); *Entre Dios y Satán* (1966); *Cantos de tango y vida* (1970).

Rivke Rubin

1906–1987

Yiddish writer and critic Rivke Rubin was born in Minsk and studied literature at the Minsk Pedagogical Institute and the Belorussian Academy of Sciences. From 1934, Rubin taught Yiddish literature at the Moscow Pedagogical Institute and published critical studies on Sholem Aleichem, Mendele Moyker-Sforim, and Y. L. Peretz. Many of Rubin's articles and stories were published in the journal *Sovetish heymland*, whose editorial board she joined in 1961. She ultimately resigned from the periodical because of its anti-Israel stance.

At the Well
1943

Her Yoysef was hanging on the shaft of the well. His beard lay humbly on his breast. His fallen shoulders and feebly dangling hands expressed the most profound hopelessness. What can I do? A stone has been tied to the other end of the shaft, so the body cannot descend.

On the ground near the well lay her daughter, the twenty-five-year-old Beylke. Her eyes had been gouged out. She lay on her back and looked straight into the sky with her empty sockets. Near her sat their old dog on his hind legs, howling piteously, with his muzzle tilted upward.

The big wooden vat, in which old Khaye-Ester used to salt meat for the whole winter, lay against the wall of the house. Wednesday at dawn, when she left home, the vat was full of water. Now it lay on its side and from the water little Elik appeared. His tiny body was swollen and blue.

Khaye-Ester, the tall, strong woman, the best milker on the collective farm, suddenly began to feel weak and old, very old. She barely had enough strength to pick up little Elik and lay him down next to his mother. With eyes clouded by tears, Khaye-Ester contemplated the bodies of her murdered loved ones. She wrung her hands and began to lament loudly, with a melody, in the old Jewish manner.

"Yoysef, my dear husband," she said, "do you remember what your father said at our wedding? 'Here, children,' he said 'take this cottage and may it be a good nest for you, and may the little birds multiply in it and may it be warm and cozy inside.' And then your father said, 'Don't count on miracles, children! A person has to work up a sweat and after that comes abundance and plenty.' And we worked hard, Yoysefke, we drew our happiness from our labor. But what has happened to our nest, Yoysefke? The nest is still here, but the little birds are gone."

"Daughter, daughter," she cried, "do you know that lying next to you is your little boy, all swollen. Did your eyes, which gleamed like diamonds, see how they drowned him or did they close before that?"

"Whom have you left me with, my darlings, and to whom should I lament—since my sons are far from me and my oldest will never come back to me? And I, old Khaye-Ester, am destined to lament all of you. Ay, Sholemke, my son, the apple of my eye, the first bird to fly away from my nest. Your hands and feet lay lifeless on an empty field and you were buried far from home, in foreign parts and your mother did not see you in your last hour . . . and you do not see her pain. . . ."

Thus Khaye-Ester spoke, sitting bent over on the ground, at the well. She spoke more and more quietly. Her voice became hoarser and hoarser. The dog now lay next to her and looked faithfully into her eyes and licked her hands.

Khaye-Ester suddenly felt very tired. She lowered her head and then, half-dozing, saw her youngest son, Azrielke, standing near her. Warmth flooded her heart. "He's still just a child, Azrielke," something in her said smilingly. In her tired, dozing mind the words in Azrielke's last letter began to float by, one by one. The words warmed her painfully, and she sang them out in the same way she had lamented her loved ones.

"Dear Mama," Azrielke had written, "we just shot down a German plane. The plane caught fire. The pilot fell out. His head went off to the side. It was a young, blond, handsome head, but I felt no pity for him. I remembered that people like him bomb women and children running half-naked on the roads. I was afraid that a blond like him might harm you, my dear ones, and I hated him. Oh, how I hated him, though he was by then no more than a lifeless head."

Khaye-Ester awoke with a start. She shook off her drowsiness and felt an urge to go into the house. She wanted to take a look at Azrielke's photograph and talk things over with him, the last living limb of her body, tell him about everything, everything . . . so that he will know. [. . .]

She went into her daughter's room and there before her astonished eyes was an unexpected sight. In the tidy nickel child's bed lay a German. His legs hung down to the floor from the bed. He was dead drunk, sleeping soundly.

Khaye-Ester looked at the German for a while and suddenly felt young and healthy, like in the days when all the boys in the village were in love with her and like the time she landed such a slap on the cheek of a local constable that he nearly fell off his feet. She quietly left the room and returned with an axe in her hands. She looked again into the red, drunken face and whispered, like a prayer: "Azrielke, my child, help me!" She raised her strong hands up high and swiftly brought down the axe. The heavy body of the German slowly slid to the ground. The blond head bounced onto the white child's pillow. Khaye-Ester took the head into her hands and went out in front of the gate. From far away the stamping of horses' hooves could be heard and a Red Army cavalry unit appeared. She waited with the head in her hands till the cavalrymen rode up to the gate. Then she went over to the commander and said: "Comrade Commander, take me with you, send me to the partisans or wherever you like. I will serve them faithfully. Here is a down payment." She pointed to the yellow severed head. Then she added quietly: "Aside from you I have no one here, no one. Take me away from here. Do not leave me by the well."

Translated by Solon Beinfeld.

Other works by Rubin: *Yitskhok-Leybush Perets* (1941); *Af naye vegn* (1949); *Shrayber un verk* (1968); *Es shpint zikh a fodem* (1975); *Aza min tog* (1982).

Oyzer Warshawsky

1898–1944

Oyzer Warshawsky (also spelled Oser Warszawski) was born in Sochaczew, Poland. He received a traditional Jewish education and settled in Warsaw in 1912. His first novel, *Shmuglars* (1920), set during the German occupation of World War I, was an exemplar of Yiddish naturalism. Briefly aligned with the Khalyastre group of Yiddish modernists, Warshawsky moved to Paris in 1924, where he joined the Montparnasse artistic community. In addition to his painting and literature, Warszawski published art and literary criticism. After the German occupation of Paris, he fled to different parts of France and was eventually evacuated to Rome, where he was captured and sent to Auschwitz.

A Contract

1943

Things were looking pretty bleak, when my wife's prewar acquaintance brought a ray of hope into our small room.

If you too were an artist, you might be able to appreciate how impatiently my wife and I awaited our jewel of a contract. [. . .]

A well-dressed guy with his hair carefully parted on the side introduced himself in a pleasant voice: B. Cinejdek, Pola's brother. [. . .]

"Let's take a walk around town. We can't speak about serious matters here. In a cafe, a thousand eyes are watching you." [. . .]

So we walked around town. B. Cinejdek would ask something and I would answer. We still hadn't gotten to the point. We came to a street corner where a color poster from the national lottery was hanging. [. . .]

Standing next to the poster from the national lottery, the swine suddenly spoke up:

"How much do you want for your child?"

I can assure you that as soon as he spoke those words, I saw my grandmother before my eyes, heard her voice

("May lightning strike him!"), I saw my mother and heard hers ("A bombshell!"). I looked at him the way a clay golem gazes at a man possessed of knowledge hut sees no more than . . . an onion!

"For the little one," the swine went on. "I'd rather 'buy' the older one, it's easier. But the little one is more practical."

"And the contract . . . ?" I asked, like a golem, hardly able to part my lips.

With a smile on his, he took me by the arm and led me into an elegant bar. No longer was he afraid of a thousand eyes! He laid out the proposition to me in an ordinary, straightforward, businesslike manner:

I should sell, hand over, lend, rent to him my little three-month-old baby . . .

Just because he, B. Cinejdek, like every other Jew this summer, has already been in a camp. . . . But he's a man with feelings. . . . Sure, if you have gold, you can't resign yourself to staying in a camp. . . . Then you had to be afraid of deportation. So he escaped and came with his sister to G. But were you safe in G.? Probably not. . . . So he has a plan. Since they don't send you back from Switzerland if you have a small child, he could marry his sister and "borrow" a child. . . . "Borrow" a child— God in heaven! B. Cinejdek threw a sour glance more or less in the direction of God. Why is it wrong for him to borrow a child, especially as he is ready to finance a trip to Switzerland for a poor couple with two children and even to support them there for the duration of the war— on the sole condition that one of the children be "signed over" to him. He has already found a family who would "give" him two children, or three if he wanted. But it's a family with nine children. Add in two parents and that comes to eleven. Eleven people!

That's why he felt more "drawn" to me . . .

The whole time he bared his soul, I stood there like an idiot without the slightest thought in my head. I didn't notice the soles of my shoes burning beneath my feet. I didn't feel as though I were suspended between heaven and earth, or atop a snow-covered mountain, one step away from a deep, dark abyss.

Nothing happened. There was no need to call a doctor, I didn't pass out. I wasn't slapped on the face by some madman. But everything had turned black. Soon I felt as though a murderer were threatening me with a knife: "Your child or your life!"

Why did it seem that way? By nature, I am not a seer. I have never been the kind who worries about tomorrow. In that minute, however . . . what am I saying? In that that split second, I saw the border clearly before me. We are on foot. Two couples. My wife is carrying the older, and Pola Cinejdek, her own brother's wife, holds the other. All of us have gotten safely to the other side. We are brought before the guards. They ask us: "What are your names and what is your business?" They divide us up. The ones with the older child remain with them, and those with the infant are led away. Come next morning, the guards have changed, and new ones lead us away: Where? Listen, you'll be amazed: back to the border. We cry, we beg, we scream. The new guards, however, know nothing about a Cinejdek family with a baby. I wring my hands, but in my wife there has sprung up the lioness, the she-wolf, the leopardess, in a word: the Jewish mother. She roars: "Who will nurse the baby? 'Sister' Pola?" But guards are guards. They have pushed us back. Back over to "this side" of the border, where we will surely be caught, sent to an internment camp and, as though that were not enough, from there deported . . .

I don't know whether I simply imagined these things or actually saw them for a hundredth of a second before my eyes. But as you can tell, I didn't fall down and die. Nor did I rail at him and call him names. I just left the little wartime plutocrat sitting there, or rather standing there with his face to the poster for the five million franc lottery prize. And that was all.

That was all?

Yes, that was all.

Like a dumbstruck fool.

For when someone says to you. "Good morning," you answer, "Good day." And if someone says, "The devil take your father," you answer, "The devil take your mother."

And had it not been for the stark terror that came over me, all four of us would now be in safety. We wouldn't have to wake up with a start in the middle of the night, asking, "Did you hear the bell? Didn't you hear the bell?" And we wouldn't have to wonder, in the middle of the day, how to "keep body and soul together," as my grandmother would have said.

In short, we would all be living off the millionaire in Switzerland.

And maybe, just maybe, I would even have the contract . . .

Translated by Alan Astro.

Other works by Warshawsky: *Marc Chagall: Le shtetl et le magicien* (1926); *Shnittsayt* (1926); *On ne peu pas se plaindre* (1943).

Esther Kreitman

1891–1954

Born Hinde Ester Singer in Biłgoraj, Poland, Kreitman was the eldest child in one of the most prominent families in Yiddish literature. While often overshadowed by the success of her younger brothers Israel Joshua Singer and Isaac Bashevis Singer, Kreitman was a notable writer in her own right, producing nuanced works of prose that explore the status of women and portray Jewish society from a bleak and harshly critical point of view. Kreitman's early years were marked by a series of personal misfortunes, from a stifling childhood to an unhappy marriage with Avraham Kreitman, an Antwerp diamond cutter. After World War I, she settled in London where she was active in literary circles and socialist politics, supporting herself through writing, speaking, and the translation of classic British literature into Yiddish.

Diamonds

1944

The refugees sat with their spoons halfway to their mouths, apparently listening with great seriousness, and trying with all their might not to burst into gales of laughter. The long, skinny lady left her podium and went walking about the tables as if nothing had happened, enquiring about the meal: "I'm sure your lunch is delicious?"

Jacques left his table and followed her, imitating her walk, and asked in a quiet, refined voice: "I'm sure your lunch is disgusting?"

The people burst out laughing and Madame Zederbaum shook her black feather, and nervously left without saying another word. The refugees, after their moment of mirth, sat there in gloomy silence. She had ruined their appetite. The truth was that this enforced idleness had made the women so lazy that they couldn't be bothered to wash a single pot.

Madame Zederbaum wouldn't have interfered in such matters if it hadn't been that the "potato king"—so the women maintained—had needlessly shoved the dirty pans, which were already the talk of the Central Hotel, under her nose.

This potato king had a thick, flaming red beard and a neatly trimmed and pomaded moustache, and his nose was as round as the King Edward potatoes which he peeled from morning to night. He really worked hard, the king, and the three deep furrows on his forehead became even deeper and wider as he worked.

His wife, the queen, looked so like her husband, that if it hadn't been for the fact that she wore women's clothes, no one could have told them apart. She also had a little red beard, smaller than his, naturally.

This couple had come from Belgium with all the other refugees. No one knew why they had been picked to help in the kitchen, peeling the potatoes, which were cooked every day. Nor did anyone know who had crowned them with their royal titles. The refugees liked the nicknames, which certainly suited the couple very well. However, what happened? After he had inherited his kingdom, the kitchen, the king began to act like a despot: stern and uncontrollable, never asking for or listening to advice from anyone. A veritable Nicholas the Third.

The other refugees rebelled, and every lunch time, a new Civil War broke out. They suspected the potato king of not putting all the available meat and potatoes into the soup, so that the soup was thin and didn't satisfy their hunger. So they demanded double helpings. The king did not deign to answer them. He did give out double helpings, but only to certain people, who had found favor in the king's eyes, namely, the rich people. No lunchtime passed, therefore, without screaming and shouting, but it was like talking to the wall.

In the end, someone would pluck up enough courage to go to the office and put the matter in the hands of the authorities, the philanthropists, so that they should judge it. The "telltale," as the ladies and gentlemen of the institution called him, would, however, come out of the office looking crestfallen, and after these episodes the king would reign even more despotically than before. When the people saw that they were not going to have any effect on the king, they began to squabble among themselves and take their anger out on each other. [. . .]

The potato king had already heard of Berman when they were both still in Antwerp. With a doglike instinct he sensed that Madame Zederbaum thought highly of Berman, and he immediately allocated him a double helping.

One morning when Berman came down to lunch there was a great turmoil going on. A woman about fifty-years-old was making a fuss, shouting at a thin woman some twenty years younger, who had squeezed herself in at the head of the long table where the cream of the Antwerp Jews sat. These were stout men with long beards, fat stomachs and even fatter wives. The young woman, who had a child on her knee, was weeping, and, at the same time, trying ineffectually to dry her eyes, with a rather grubby pocket handkerchief.

The older woman's bosom was heaving under her silk blouse, diamond earrings dangled from her bluish, elongated ear lobes, the whiskers on her chin were trembling, and her thick lips were purple with rage and flecked with spittle.

"The insolence of it! Scrawny little fool! She has the cheek to think she is my equal! Thank God everyone else from Antwerp knows who I am! How dare she come and sit at this table, the *shnorrer*. No sooner is a little bit of soup doled out than she sticks out her dirty hands and grabs it. She doesn't even know that anyone who grabs gets their fingers smacked, the skinny little idiot!"

The young woman was sobbing, not understanding why the woman was shouting at her. She tried to ask the people at the table what she had done wrong, but she was so upset that she could hardly speak. Some of them thought it was funny and just laughed at her, others were asking the indignant woman to stop shouting, everyone else was busy with their own concerns, and no one answered her.

Berman looked at the older woman and recognized her as the wife of a rich merchant with whom he did business. He glanced at the young woman. "What on earth is a woman like her doing at this table?" he thought, and then he realized, with horror, that it was Gitele. He asked someone else what had happened, and found out immediately, for *he* had no difficulty in getting an answer, that a second helping of soup had been set out for this woman. Gitele, who hadn't had any, had assumed it was for her, and had put her hand out. This had made the other woman apoplectic, and she had started screeching at Gitele.

To make matters worse, the potato king came out of the kitchen and started bellowing at Gitele:

"Shut up, will you! You'd think someone was murdering you. Stop scrubbing at your eyes. The committee doesn't like scenes like this. If you carry on like this Madame Zederbaum will come in and when she sees what trouble you're causing she'll send you to the Palmolive, where you'll have something to cry about!"

Berman was very tempted to tell the potato king that Gitele was in fact the daughter of a rich man in Poland, but he decided that it was better to know nothing and not to get mixed up in the whole business. He gestured to [his wife] Rochl, who understood what he meant and also said nothing. But she refused the double helping which she was offered, and old Reb Chaim Yoysef sank his head so low that his beard touched the table. He sighed heavily and almost choked on the beard which he had softened by putting it in his soup. He said quietly to Rochl, whose eyes were brimming with tears: "This is what we've come to, daughter."

Not only did the potato king have his favorites, but the people themselves had formed cliques. As if by magic, each table was occupied exclusively by people of the same type. At one table sat people who filled their day—before, during and after the meals—with discussion of higher matters. Shakespeare was never absent from this table for one moment, and Bernard Shaw, Ibsen, Heine, Goethe, Homer, Rembrandt and Michelangelo all occupied places of honor there. The intellectuals at this table were experts in everything, sculpture, music, literature. And, of course, they discussed all these matters in loud voices.

The rest of the eaters, even the bearded men at the top table, and their wives with the silk blouses, began to listen in to these conversations, not understanding a word but with a feeling of respect for the people at that table.

The potato king inclined his hairy ear to them and listened intently to find out what those snotty-nosed intellectuals were jabbering about. Hearing them constantly pronouncing names, which he had never heard of, neither in Antwerp nor in London, nor in Galicia, he started to ask around and when he found out that it was books they were discussing, he shook his big head and asked:

"So why do you people discuss books? Books are for reading! Not for messing up your brain. Ach, what fools!" He decided on the spot that *they* would certainly not get double helpings.

"A crowd of lazy good-for-nothings, that's all they are!" he said to his wife, but nevertheless he put food in front of them without banging it down on the table.

He sat Gitele at that table, and she became even more dejected. When the group saw a young woman with a child at their table, they completely ignored her. So she looked for another table, and sat down at a table with poor women whose husbands, even here, were going out to work in order to be able to contribute something towards the bill. These women helped in the kitchen with the washing up—they couldn't afford to throw away dirty saucepans. They sat all day in the women's room, sewing pillowcases and sheets for the hotel bedrooms. At this table everyone welcomed Gitele's child, petting her, and telling Gitele stories about what lovely homes they came from; although their husbands were simple workers, they had kept nice kitchens with steel fittings, sideboards, and even gramophones.

Here Gitele felt at home, and yet, not really at home.

Translated by Heather Valencia.

Other works by Kreitman: *Deborah* (1936); *Blitz and Other Stories* (1949).

Anna Seghers
1900–1983

Novelist Anna Seghers (born Netty Reiling) was born in Mainz into an affluent family. She attended the University of Heidelberg, obtaining a doctorate in art history in 1924 and writing her dissertation on Rembrandt and Judaism. She began publishing stories and novels as a student, and was an outspoken social activist and anti-Fascist along with her husband Ladislaus Rádványi (1900–1978), a Hungarian Jew. In 1929, Seghers joined the German Communist Party, and became a lifelong member. In 1933, she and her husband were forced to flee to Paris and then to Mexico; she settled in East Berlin in 1947. A committed communist, she received the International Stalin Peace Prize in Moscow in 1952.

Mail to the Promised Land
1944

Old Levi turned his face away that was so easily stained by tears. Again, he felt a twinge of longing for his terrestrial home. How strange it was, this longing for a miserable land where one had lived through nothing but humiliation and suffering. The blurry faces of the old men who had meanwhile converged around him, drawn to the garden by the news of the letter, fused into the faces of still older men that had been washed out by time. Old Levi was puzzled because his father-in-law, with his thin, stringy beard, had made the journey here. The teacher, Rosenzweig, had also arrived, angrily waving his hands about, spoiling for a fight. The seamstress's brother who had taught Hebrew letters to his little boy in Paris when no one as yet had any inkling what fame the boy would win for himself. But that fame now eluded the father's comprehension, not as if it had already passed, but as if it had not yet begun. Now the tailor was pushing into the circle, the one who had his shop in the courtyard of the synagogue in St. Paul. He was a rail-thin little man, misshapen, with a wispy white cloud for a beard. All together they began to mumble passages from the letter to each other. Above them the narrow, grimy, eternally shady alleyway was edged by the towers and merlons of the decaying palace.

Unsure of himself, he stepped into the court. The misshapen little man with the wispy white cloud of a beard took from his hand the candle he had been carrying so carefully. He stuck it into one of the free holes in a sheet of tinny metal that already held several candles. The father-in-law said the prayer and lit the candle. The shiny, pale, tender face of his wife who had died during the pogrom in the cellar appeared in the glow of the flame. It was so lovely that the face of his daughter-in-law was diminished in comparison. She was as fine and thin as the candle itself, and everything that came afterward was transient and ungraspable like the few wax drops that were also melting away.

The young widow had not left in time. The Nazi army occupied all of France. The French friends in Algiers were running in vain from ship to ship. After awhile they received only the news that the woman and her sick child had been deported to some place. She had, as these things usually go, delayed departure to nurse the child and thus prepared merely their destruction. The friends no longer entertained hopes of a reunion. From time to time the two Frenchmen, man and wife, talked only about whether a letter to Old Levi ought not to be composed. They even found a refugee who was capable of writing the kind of letter that might match the letters that the old man had been used to. Since at that time Old Levi was already buried it was no longer possible to find out whether or not the letter was a success. It did not, in any case, satisfy the other residents in his house. They had already gotten so used to the arrival of the letters that even now, after Levi's death, they read this letter together in their accustomed place. Perhaps it was only due to the absence of the recipient that they did not feel quite as soothed and refreshed as before.

Translated by Susanne Klingenstein.

Other works by Seghers: *Aufstand der Fischer von St. Barbara* (1928); *Der Kopflohn* (1933); *Das siebte Kreuz* (1942); *Die Toten bleiben jung* (1949); *Die Entscheidung* (1959); *Das wirkliche Blau* (1967).

S. Y. Agnon

Only Yesterday
1945

And now, good friends, as we observe the adventures of Isaac, we are shaken and stunned. This Isaac who is no worse than any other person, why is he punished so harshly? Is it because he teased a dog? He meant it only as a joke. Moreover, the end of Isaac Kumer is not inherent in his beginning. By his nature and his aptitudes, Isaac should have stood on the soil and seen life on the earth and brought his father and his brothers and sisters up to the Land of Israel. Those miserable people who hadn't seen a good moment in their lives, how devoted they were to the Land. Isaac's sisters would have found their mates here and Yudele would have plowed his land and composed pleasant lyrics for her. And Reb Simon Kumer, the father of our comrade Isaac, who was still hounded by usurers, would have seen the happiness of his sons and daughters and would have been happy. And you, Rock of Our Salvation great in counsel and mighty in work, from the mouths of those who thirst for Your Salvation You would have heard Your praise all the days. It's easy for those who don't bother with too much thinking, either because of too much innocence or because of too much wisdom, but a person who is not very innocent and not very wise, what will he answer and what will he say?

And now the neighbors were talking about Isaac and saying that Reb Fayesh's son-in-law's mind is not sane. And imaginative people imagined they saw him crawling on all fours and shouting like a dog and running after every person to bite him. Fear fell on folks and they complained about the officers of the society for letting a dangerous person walk around in public. The officers of the society heard those words and sent a doctor to him. The doctor saw Isaac and said, We have to take him to Egypt to the Pasteur Institute. Meanwhile, the bitten man has to be bound with ropes and put in a separate room behind a locked door.

They bound Isaac with ropes and put him in a room by himself and locked the door behind him and closed the shutters, and they brought him water and food. Because he was so weak, he didn't eat and didn't drink. Isaac sat alone in the dark room and lamented from the Book of Lamentations, She weepeth sore in the night and her tears were on her cheeks. And everyone who heard his voice wept for him and for his wife. Sometimes, his mind would come back and he would warn his attendants to be careful that he didn't bite them, and sometimes he tried to sleep. But sleep didn't come. And sometimes he looked with vacant eyes and didn't want anything.

The dog's venom penetrated all of Isaac's limbs. His face turned dark, his eyes glazed over like glass, his tongue swelled up like a shriveled date. A harsh thirst choked and strangled him. If he took some water to drink, he imagined a delegation of small dogs was dancing in the water. (And people said that he too started barking like a dog.) In the end, the muscles of his body and the muscles of his face became paralyzed. Finally, his pained soul passed away and he returned his spirit to the God of spirits for whom there is no joke and no frivolity.

The dog disappeared, but his bites indicated that he was alive. Since he had tasted the taste of human flesh, he went on biting. Many were injured by him and many mentioned him with horror. Until the troubles of the great war came and that trouble was forgotten.

On the day that Isaac was buried, the sky was covered with clouds. The sun was overcast and a wind came and with it came lightning flashes and thunderbolts. The firmament was shaken with the rumble of their might and began to bring down rare, warm drops. The next day, the clouds scattered and the sun shone, and we knew that all our expectations were in vain. And even the winds we imagined would refresh us didn't bring any gain, as they were hot and piercing as leeches.

But at night the winds cooled and the world began to cool off. And the next day the sun was dull and pressed and squeezed between the clouds. Before it finished its course, it was pushed out of the firmament. That sun, that devouring fire, that had blazed with its strong heat and burned all the grass of the field and parched the trees and dried up the springs of water—darkening clouds pushed her out until there wasn't a corner in the firmament that it wasn't pushed out of. And when we lifted our eyes to the sky to see if the clouds weren't lying, abundant rain began coming down. Only yesterday we had stood in prayer and pleading and we increased the number of Slikhot and we blew Shofars and we recited Hosanna, and today we read aloud the Praising, thanking and singing.

When the rains began coming down they didn't stop coming down by day or by night. The water flowed from above and from below, on the roofs of our houses and underneath our houses, it swept away furnishings and brought down houses. But the cisterns were filled with water. And now we have water to drink and even to cook our food and to bake our bread and to dip our hands. For six or seven days the rains came down, and when they stopped they started coming down again. Finally, the rains stopped and the clouds dispersed and the sun shone. And when we came outside we saw that the earth was smiling with its plants and its flowers. And from one end of the Land to the other came shepherds and

their flocks, and from the soaked earth rose the voice of the sheep, and they were answered by the birds of the skies. And a great rejoicing was in the world. Such rejoicing had never been seen. All the villages in Judea and the Galilee, in the plain and in the mountains, produced crops and the whole Land was like a Garden of the Lord. And every bush and every blade of grass emitted a good smell, and needless to say, so did the oranges. Like a blessed dwelling was the whole Land and its inhabitants were blessed by the Lord. And you our brothers, the elite of our salvation in Kinneret and Merhavia, in Eyn Ganim and in Um Juni, which is now Degania, you went out to your work in the fields and the gardens, the work our comrade Isaac wasn't blessed with. Our comrade Isaac wasn't blessed to stand on the ground and plow and sow, but like his ancestor Reb Yudel Hasid and like some other Saints and Hasids, he was blessed to be given an estate of a grave in the holy earth. May all mourners mourn for that tortured man who died in a sorry affair. And we shall tell the deeds of our brothers and sisters, the children of the living God, the nation of the Lord, who work the earth of Israel for a monument and fame and glory.

> Completed are the deeds of Isaac
> The deeds of our other comrades
> The men and the women
> Will come in the book *A Parcel of Land*.

Translated by Barbara Harshav.

Yekhiel Falikman

1911–1977

Yekhiel Falikman was born in Lyubar, Ukraine. He studied mechanical engineering and, in 1931, art at the university in Kiev. In 1932, Falikman moved to the Jewish Autonomous Region in Birobidzhan to work as a journalist. His first collections of stories concerning life there were published in 1937 and 1940. During World War II, Falikman served in the Red Army, writing for a military paper while continuing to publish Yiddish prose. After the war he completed his studies at the Pedagogical Institute in Kiev (1952) and later was an editor of *Sovetish heymland*. Many of his epic novels about the war were popular in Russian and Ukrainian translation.

The Only One in the Town

1945

Meylekh Snitkever takes the heavy shears and looks at them silently. He holds them in both hands as if to weigh them. Then he shifts his stare to me, the muscles moving in his jaws, which are covered with sparse, curly hairs.

"What would you do if you were being led away to be shot?" he suddenly asks. "Would you go like a sheep to the slaughter, or would you try to run away? I've already seen people being led to their death, and mostly they go obediently, with heads bowed, hands at their sides. It must be because no one believes until the last moment that they really intend to kill him, that they will kill him. He cannot imagine that he, who breathes, sees, feels, thinks, will soon not be able to do any of those things. People also believe that something will happen at the last moment and death will be averted. I was going to my death and knew that they would kill me. My little Dovid and my little Pesye were screaming after me. I saw them waving their hands at me. I didn't see their heads or their faces, and that was the most painful of all. I myself had partly taken leave of my senses. Near me my wife Feyge was walking. She was half in a daze. She kept whispering: "What have they done with our children?" She had no grasp of what was happening to her or where we were being led.

We were the third group. With us were Rakhmiel the housepainter and Nekhemye the shoemaker's deaf mother-in-law. She kept losing a shoe and bending down to tighten the laces. There was also a young woman, a stranger who had been driven here from a village and a boy of about fourteen, probably her son. We were all being driven by one German. I have to describe him to you: he was bald, not very tall, a wide, flabby, clean-shaven face lined with wrinkles that descended from his cheeks to mingle with his goiter. His eyes were dull and vacant. He walked without his jacket, only in his shirt. Evidently he was used to this kind of work and did not want to get sweaty. Under his shirt you could see that his trousers were held up by suspenders and hung down a bit. Maybe they were the wrong size, or maybe his belly had shrunk from so much marching . . . his boots were thick and dusty . . . I looked at him several times and examined him closely. I wanted to see the man who kills me.

So we go, and in my sleeve I carry the shears. That is my lifelong habit—I don't go anywhere without my shears. We marched out of the town and turned off the main road onto the autumn pasture, where our cattle used to graze until the first snows, when it no longer made sense to drive them so far. It was now clear to me—from here we are going to the old graveyard, an abandoned cemetery dating from Turkish times. There the end will come. And we are alone in the field—those who are to die and the German who is to shoot us. The woods are not very far—no more than a *verst* [about a kilometer]. Suddenly I straighten up and with one movement I hold the shears in my hand with the round finger-holes in front. Do they weigh much? I lean forward. The German looks at me in astonishment. I am standing face to face with him. My hand rises up of its own accord and swiftly swings through the air. The shears knock the German in the temple and he falls to the ground without a peep. I stand next to him for a second. That second is worth a whole lifetime—you are filled with immense pleasure. After that I am ready to start to run. I extend my hand to Feyge, but she steps back from me and starts to scream in a strange voice. And after her so does the young woman from the village with the fourteen-year-old son. The shoemaker's deaf mother-in-law starts to choke and hiccup. Her eyes are popping out of her forehead. Rakhmiel the housepainter stands there more dead than alive, as if he were made of chalk. His chin trembles and he is unable to utter a word. The screams of the women are head-splitting. "Let's run," I gesture to them with my hands in desperation. But I myself feel that my legs are wobbling and soon I won't be able to budge. The others look at the dead German as if crazed and scream: "What have you done, what have you done?"

Germans have already begun to appear on the path from the village. They either saw that something was happening, or else heard the scream. I was the only one in a state to begin running. The others remained standing there next to the dead German. I left at the last moment. It seems to me that the weight of the shears in my hand pulled me and drove me into the woods and beyond, to the lakes. In the thickets I heard the shootings around the dead German and kept running.

"That is how I remained the only one . . ." Meylekh finished quietly.

Now I sit on the overturned carriage and listen to the pounding of the hammer—now louder, now softer. The hammer pounds into the tin with enthusiasm. It feels as if I am hearing the pounding of a heart that has much to tell, but cannot express in words, about the life-force of someone who remains utterly solitary, yet still alive.

Translated by Solon Beinfeld.

Other works by Falikman: *Libe in fayer: front-dertseylungen* (1943); *Di shayn kumt fun mizrekh* (1948); *Der shvartser vint* (1968).

Arthur Laurents

1917–2011

Playwright, screenwriter, and director Arthur Laurents (Levine) was born in Brooklyn. He wrote radio plays in the 1930s and, during World War II, training films and plays for army radio. Laurents adapted novels on Broadway and created screenplays in Hollywood. His films include *Anastasia* (1956) and *Bonjour tristesse* (1958), and his musicals include *West Side Story* (1957) and *Gypsy* (1959). He also directed the musicals *I Can Get It for You Wholesale* (1962) and *La cage aux folles* (1983) as well as wrote the film *The Way We Were* (1973).

Home of the Brave

1945

T.J.: Why don't you get the lead out of your can and do something for once?

CONEY [*to* FINCH]: You finish your map.

FINCH: It's finished, Coney.

CONEY: Well, let T. J. Rockefeller do something besides blowing that tin horn.

T.J.: Look who's talking.

FINCH [*jumping up*]: Yeah, look! He stood guard two nights out of three while you snored your fat face off. The Major told him to take it easy today and you know it.

T.J. [*to* FINCH]: The little kike lover.

FINCH: You always get around to that, don't you?

T.J.: Every time I see your friend's face.

CONEY: You son of a bitch.

T.J.: Watch your language or I'll ram it down your throat, Jew boy.

FINCH: You'll get yours rammed down your throat first.

T.J.: Not by him.

CONEY: Listen, T.J.—

T.J.: You listen to me, you lousy yellow Jew bastard! I'm going to—[*At this*, FINCH *steps forward and clips* T.J., T.J. *reels but comes back at* FINCH.] You little—[*He*

swings, FINCH *ducks and socks him again*, T.J. *hits back*, CONEY *tries to break it up but they are punching away as* MINGO *rushes in from down right*.]

MINGO: What the hell is this? Come on, break it up. [*He steps in.*] Why don't you jerks save it for the Japs?

T.J.: He's more interested in saving his yellow Jew friend. [. . .]

MINGO: Sure. He stinks from way back. The Army makes him worse. I'm not apologizing for him. I think he's a bastard, too. But you ought to try to understand him.

CONEY [*turning around sharply*]: You try to understand him! I haven't got time. [*Coming over to them.*] I'm too busy trying to understand all this crap about Jews.

FINCH: Coney . . .

CONEY: I told you I heard something in the middle of the night once. Some drunken bum across the hall from my aunt's yelling: Throw out the dirty sheenies! . . . That was us. But I just turned over and went back to sleep. I was used to it by then. What the hell! I was ten. That's old for a Jew. When I was six, my first week in school, I stayed out for the Jewish New Year. The next day a bunch of kids got around me and said: "Were you in school yesterday?" I smiled and said, "No." They wiped the smile off my face. They beat the hell out of me. I had to get beat up a coupla more times before I learned that if you're a Jew, you stink. You're not like other guys. You're—you're alone. You're—you're something—strange, different. [*Suddenly furious.*] Well, goddamit, you make us different, you dirty bastards! What the hell do you want us to do?

FINCH: Coney . . .

CONEY: Let me alone.

MINGO: Coney, listen—

CONEY: Tell your wife to write a poem about it.

MINGO: Screw me and my wife. You know damn well Finch at least doesn't feel like that.

CONEY: I don't know anything. I'm a lousy yellow Jew bastard. [*He turns and walks back to the tree*, FINCH *hesitates and then walks to him*.]

FINCH: Coney . . .

CONEY: Drop it.

FINCH: You know that doesn't go for me.

CONEY: I said drop it, Finch.

FINCH: Maybe I'm dumb. Maybe I'm an Arizona hayseed like you say. But I never met any Jewish boys till I got in the Army. I didn't even realize out loud that *you* were until somebody said something.

CONEY: I can imagine what.

FINCH: Yes. And I took a poke at him, too. Because I couldn't see any reason for it. And there isn't any. O.K. I'm a jerk, but to me—you like a guy or you don't. That's all there is to it. That's all there ever will be to it. . . . And you know that—don't you? [*He waits for an answer, but there is none. He takes a step back toward* MINGO *and then turns and moves swiftly to* CONEY *and puts an arm around him.*] Aw heck, aren't we buddies?

CONEY [*turning—with a smile*]: You corny bastard. [. . .]

DOCTOR: Then why can't you walk. Coney?

CONEY: What?

DOCTOR: You weren't shot, were you?

CONEY: No.

DOCTOR: You didn't break your legs, did you?

CONEY: No.

DOCTOR: Then why can't you walk. Coney?

CONEY: I don't know. I don't know.

DOCTOR: But you said you remember everything that happened.

CONEY: I—yes. Yes.

DOCTOR: Do you remember waking up in the hospital? Do you remember waking up with that bad feeling?

CONEY: Yes.

[*Slight pause. The* DOCTOR *walks next to the bed.*]

DOCTOR: Coney, when did you first get that bad feeling?

CONEY: It was—I don't know.

DOCTOR: Coney—[*He sits down.*] Coney, did you first get it right after Finch was shot?

CONEY: No.

DOCTOR: What did you think of when Finch was shot?

CONEY: I don't know.

DOCTOR: You said you remember everything that happened. And you do. You remember that, too. You remember how you felt when Finch was shot, don't you, Coney? Don't you?

CONEY [*sitting bolt upright*]: Yes. [*A long pause. His hands twist his robe and then lay still. With dead, flat tones.*] When we were looking for the map case, he said—he started to say: You lousy yellow Jew bastard. He only said you lousy yellow jerk, but he started to say you lousy yellow Jew bastard. So I knew. I knew.

DOCTOR: You knew what?

CONEY: I knew he'd lied when—when he said he didn't care. When he said people were people to him. I knew he lied. I knew he hated me because I was a Jew so—I was glad when he was shot.

[*The* DOCTOR *straightens up.*]

DOCTOR: Did you leave him there because you were glad?

CONEY: Oh, no!

DOCTOR: You got over it.

CONEY: I was—I was sorry I felt glad. I was ashamed.

DOCTOR: Did you leave him because you were ashamed?

CONEY: No.

DOCTOR: Because you were afraid?

CONEY: No.

DOCTOR: No. You left him because that was what you had to do. Because you were a good soldier. [*Pause.*] You left him and you ran through the jungle, didn't you?

CONEY: Yes.

Arthur Miller

1915-2005

Playwright Arthur Miller was born and raised in New York City. His wealthy family's financial suffering during the Depression had a major impact on him. Miller attended the University of Michigan and then joined the Federal Theatre Project in New York; he was later called to testify before the House Committee on Un-American Activities. Miller wrote screenplays, novels, essays, and memoirs, and received the Pulitzer Prize, the American Academy of Arts and Letters Gold Medal, the John F. Kennedy Award for Lifetime Achievement, the Tony Lifetime Achievement Award, and the 2003 Jerusalem Prize.

Focus

1945

Mr. Finkelstein was still a young man, but as a Jew he was very old. He knew what was going on. He could hardly help knowing. Twice in the past three weeks, when he had come out of his house at six in the morning to open his store he had found his garbage can turned on its side, its contents kicked all over his sidewalk.

So when, on this Monday morning, he came out of his house at six o'clock and found his garbage can turned over, with grapefruit rinds thrown up to his very front porch, he hesitated hardly a moment, and proceeded to gather the garbage together again with two stiff pieces of cardboard and dumped it back into the pail. He was smiling all the while. Whenever he was frightened and angry in this particular way, he smiled. It was like an old joke that had been repeated and repeated to him all his life, and all he could do now was to smile at the idiocy of the teller. He smiled too, however, because he had an instinctive feeling that from one of the houses across the street somebody was watching him gathering up this garbage.

It was only when he straightened up after setting the can in its rightful place and looked up the street at the cans set in their proper places before every house—only then did he grow confused. For he noticed with a start that garbage was speckling the lawn of Mr. Newman's house, too, and Mr. Newman's garbage can was also lying on its side.

Mr. Finkelstein observed this carefully, studied the facts. Could it be, he wondered, that his wife had always been right when she claimed that Newman was strictly a Jewish name? That he did not believe, although he did not know why. He simply had always taken it for granted that Mr. Newman who worked for that big company was not a Jew, although lately . . . [. . .]

[. . .] The garbage on Mr. Newman's lawn glistened in the sun as he watched. And at eight o'clock, as usual, Mr. Newman came out of his house to go to work. Mr. Finkelstein observed how he stopped when he saw the garbage. He watched him start back into his house and hesitate again on the porch steps. He saw him turn toward the garbage again and after a moment's pause start picking up some of it. Then he saw Mr. Newman drop the garbage and wipe his hands on the empty burlap bag, and take the pail from the gutter onto the kerb.

Now Mr. Newman was coming down the street in his direction. He saw him slowing before his neighbor—the hunter's—house and look at it. Then Mr. Newman turned and looked across the street at Mr. Carlson's house. After a moment he came on down the street toward Mr. Finkelstein, his eyes scanning the garbage cans as he passed them.

He had never seen Mr. Newman so upset. The man's right hand was half raised as he walked, and it shook visibly. Mr. Finkelstein watched as he drew nearer. His distraction was so terrible that Finkelstein could not help but feel sympathy. When Newman came to within ten yards of the stand, Finkelstein assumed the blank stare which he had lately learned to cultivate, and waited for Newman to pass him by. But the man halted beside him.

Leisurely, Mr. Finkelstein looked up. Newman's lower lip, he saw, was quivering like a live clam. His eyes were blinking rapidly as though to clear away a dream.

"They kicked mine around too," he said, and motioned toward his own garbage pail which stood twenty feet away.

Mr. Newman looked at Finkelstein's garbage pail and then turned back to him. He started to speak but his throat clogged. He cleared it and whispered huskily, "Who did it?"

Finkelstein laughed. "Who? Who always does it? The Christian Front."

He studied the jerky squirming of Mr. Newman's lower lip.

"You think they did, eh?" Mr. Newman said, absently.

"Who goes around kicking over garbage pails but those bums? Decent people don't do that."

"It could have been some children," Mr. Newman said, his voice deadened.

"It could have been but it wasn't," Mr. Finkelstein laughed. "I didn't go to sleep till one o'clock last night and I got up before five . . . I shaved this morning. Between one and five you don't find children going around the streets. Don't worry, it was the Front."

Mr. Newman's face started getting red. And Mr. Finkelstein could not tell whether it was anger or fear pumping up his blood. He decided to risk the question.

"But you got nothing to worry about, Mr. Newman. By you it was probably a mistake."

Mr. Newman turned to him quickly. But he saw that Mr. Finkelstein's little black eyes were filled only with curiosity and no conviction at all that it was a mistake; he too, was merely asking. Newman stood there, absently smoothing down his vest, and then walked on toward the subway.

Finkelstein watched him go. A very neat and tidy man, he thought, as he watched Newman in his immaculate blue suit disappearing around the corner a clean man. It probably only bothers him because they dirtied his yard.

He smiled to himself again and sat on his camp chair. After the morning rush was over he took the yellow paper out of his shirt pocket, unfolded it carefully, and adjusting his horn-rimmed glasses midway down his nose, read it again.

"Jew, if you don't get out of this neighborhood in five days you'll wish you never was born."

Five days, he thought, and laughed a little, soundlessly. Nice of them to give me five days. He laughed again and slipped the warning halfway into his shirt pocket, fixing it so that it stuck out. He sat again and scanned the street, ready to break out in a smile.

Other works by Miller: *Death of a Salesman* (1949); *The Crucible* (1953); *A View from the Bridge* (1955); *Echoes Down the Corridor: Collected Essays 1944–2000* (2000); *Presence: Collected Stories* (2009).

Yosef Rabin
1900–1987

Yosef Rabin, a first-generation Soviet Yiddish writer, was born in Grodno. Earning his spurs as the leader the head of the underground Komsomol youth organization in Vilna, he fled in 1920 to Moscow, where he worked as a Yiddish-language typesetter and studied in the Yiddish department of the Moscow Pedagogical Institute. In 1936, Rabin was sent to lead the writers' organization in the Jewish Autonomous Region of Birobidzhan, but was purged a year later and sent to the gulag. Released during World War II, Rabin fought with the Red Army and returned to Moscow after the war, where he eventually served on the editorial board of *Sovetish heymland* from 1961 to 1972.

Trip Home
1945

It was close to Passover. In the house, Passover was already present. But Father was not in a holiday mood. He looked at nobody and even his appearance changed. A yellow cast covered his face.

He had certainly surmised something, but said nothing.

On the very eve of the holiday, on the eve of Passover itself, as preparations were underway to go to the synagogue, he apparently decided to be cheerful. Perhaps it was so that no one would realize what he was going through. And perhaps it was because this Passover Father was left with only a worn-out coat. From old age and from being often brushed and cleaned, its outer fabric had become thin and transparent. In such a coat Father had to appear among people on the holiday. He was cheerful so no one would grasp that he had surmised something. To console himself and to console the members of the household he started to be merry. He spoke of Passover, of springtime, of dumplings and the four cups of wine. Mother encouraged him. For

about three days it seemed possible that we could believe in the good fortune and happiness that were sure to come. At such an hour, when hope had appeared and when Father was cheerful, Mother came to a decision. She had long sought an appropriate opportunity. She has a present for Father.

"So," says Mother, "if you're ready to go to the synagogue, put on a new coat." Father did not understand what she meant. What was she saying about putting on a new coat?

"Yes, my husband, a new coat. Do you really think that your wife has stopped loving you?"

She handed it to him. True, it was not really new, but it was an intact and handsome coat.

Certainly Father did not at the moment of his death look as terrible as he did at that moment. It is bad enough that he does not buy Mother any presents, but Mother gives them to him; it is bad enough that everyone knows that he is a failure in life who cannot support a family but puts on a foolish act; it is bad enough that he sighs even during the day and the children understand how bad and difficult things are for their father. But on top of everything Mother goes and hands him a coat as a present, which undoubtedly someone bought for him out of pity. And Father surmises who that was. . . . His children have been taken care of, the holiday spirit brought into the house, a present bought for him. Father cannot stand still. His bones all ache. His face has turned yellow. His mouth trembles. He gathers all his strength to keep from weeping or crying out. Nevertheless, his eyes are moist. He braces himself, he does not want to give in, he wants to swallow the heavy, bitter pain.

At any moment Mother will burst into tears. Will Father have enough strength to restrain himself?

Mother stood there with her mouth open. What frightened her more, what surprised her more? Was it that her husband wants to cry, or that she took money without her husband's knowledge, took it from a stranger, from a man whom she had once loved and who still loves her . . . out of fear she shuts her mouth.

Mother seems as if she had become numb. When the numbness passes, she is ready to skin herself alive, to bury herself deep into the earth. She suddenly felt herself to be unclean and deeply in the wrong. She has insulted and shamed Father. Now everything has become clear to her. Her life has ended; it is life without hope. Today she has lost everything.

She wanted to cry, but was unable to.

Instead it is the children who cry, cry bitterly and burst into tears: "Father, Father, don't cry!"

From that holiday forward, Father sighed and groaned during the day. His face became yellower, his hair grayer. From that holiday forward the youngest child remained the youngest child forever.

Now Ruvn asks me: "Is your mother alive?"

"No, she perished."

"Your father?"

"He as well. And your parents?" I ask.

"They too."

These appear to be the most important questions two Jews have to ask each other when they meet. We are used to such answers. We remain silent for a while. [. . .]

We have arrived at our home, Ruvn and I, Velvl.

We climb out of the train and do not recognize the station, or the town, or the streets.

My hometown!

In my blood, in my heart and soul, I absorbed my love for you. The further I was from home, the more beautiful you were in my dreams. The sun on your streets was more golden than elsewhere, the water in your river fresher and softer than in all other rivers and seas. Your springs and wells murmured with the song of my youth. The dust of your streets was pleasant, the smoke of your chimneys was agreeable. Your orchards and gardens were my heart's delight. Your girls were the prettiest. Your inhabitants were the finest. My home, my hometown, you were as dear to me as a first love.

Now I stand in your streets like a mourner, like someone given a harsh sentence, like someone who comes for a wedding and finds a funeral.

Your streets are in ruins, your houses wrecked, your panes shattered. In your orchards there is no green and no shade. Stumps, charred stumps protrude from your earth, like lifetimes cut short. Your chimneys stand abandoned, without smoke. Your cemetery has been left without tombstones, your eternal rest plowed up, even your dead no longer live.

Ruvn and I go through the street of our hometown, in our army coats, with bundles on our backs, Ruvn with a cane. We look like wanderers now, who find their way, lose it and seek it again.

Translated by Solon Beinfeld.

Other works by Rabin: *Eshelonen geyen* (1948); *Ikh ze dikh, Vilne* (1968); *Baym Neman* (1969); *In yenem yor* (1988); *In farsheyde yorn* (1989).

Isaac Bashevis Singer

1903–1991

Isaac Bashevis Singer was born into a strictly observant family in Leoncin, near Warsaw. During World War I, his mother moved the family to Bilgoraj, where his grandfather had been rabbi. As a young man, Singer followed in his older brother's, Israel Joshua Singer's, footsteps, and moved to Warsaw to become a writer himself. Publishing in *Literarishe bleter* and *Undzer ekspres,* Singer began to use the pseudonym Yitskhok Bashevis. Together with Aharon Zeitlin, he founded the monthly *Globus* in 1932, on the pages of which he criticized political aspirations in literature. In 1935, Bashevis emigrated to the United States and began writing for the *Forverts* in New York. After the Holocaust, Bashevis actively pursued the literary memorialization of Polish Jewry. He translated his work into English and became perhaps the most read Yiddish writer, awarded various honors, including the Nobel Prize in Literature in 1978. The corpus of his work translated into English far exceeds the corpus of his work published in Yiddish in book form.

* [Some scholars consider 1904 to be the accurate year for Singer's date of birth.]

Simple Gimpl

1945

Once, at night, after the seven days of mourning, while I lay on the sacks dozing, someone came to me, the Evil One himself, and said to me, "Gimpl, why are you sleeping?"

"What should I be doing," I said, "eating dumplings?"

"The whole world is deceiving you," he said, "deceive the world!"

"How can I deceive the whole world?"

"Collect a pail of urine every day," he answered, "and every night, pour it into the dough. Let them," he said, "devour filth, those Frampol wise guys."

"What about the world to come?" I said.

He said, "There is no next world. They've sold you a pig in a poke."

"Well," I said, "and is there a God?"

"There's no God either."

"So what," I said, "is there?"

"A deep mire."

He stood before my eyes, this orator, with a goat's beard and horns, long teeth and a tail. Hearing this kind of talk, I tried to grab him by the tail, but I fell off the flour sacks, and almost broke a rib. I happened to need to urinate and noticed a big piece of dough that seemed to be begging: *Do it!* In short, I let myself be persuaded.

The assistant came at dawn. We kneaded the loaves, brushed them with caraway seeds, and put them into bread molds. Then the young man left and I stayed, sitting in the oven pit on a pile of rags.

"Well, Gimpl," I thought, "you've had your revenge for all your suffering." The frost was crackling outside, but here it was warm. It heated my face. I bent my head and dozed off.

As I fell asleep, Elka appeared in a dream, dressed in her shroud, and called out: "What have you done, Gimpl?"

"It's your fault," I said and started crying.

She said, "You simpleton! Because Elka is false, is everything a lie? I deceived no one but myself. I'm paying for everything, Gimpl. They spare you nothing here!"

I looked at her face: black as coal. Then I woke up. For a long while I sat silent. I felt like everything hung in the balance. One false step, and I lost the world to come. But God helped me.

I grabbed the oven paddle, removed all the loaves, carried them out into the yard, and started digging a ditch in the frozen earth. In the meantime my young assistant arrived. "Boss," he said, "what are you doing?" And he turned white as a corpse. "It's all right," I said and buried all the bread before his eyes.

Then I went home, took the stack of money out of its hiding place, and divided it up among the children. "On this night," I said, "I saw your mother. She's having a terrible time." They were stunned and couldn't utter a single word. "Be well," I told them, "and forget that there ever was a Gimpl." I put on my coat, a pair of boots, took the bag with my prayer shawl in one hand, my stick in the other, and kissed the *mezuzah*. When people saw me in the street, they were completely taken aback. "Where are you going?" they asked me. And I answered, "I'm off into the wide world." And this way I left Frampol.

I wandered throughout the land and good people did not abandon me. Years passed. I became old and gray. I heard my fill of tall tales, a lot of lies and make-believe, but the longer I lived, the more I saw that there are really no lies. If something doesn't happen to Mendl, it happens to Feivl. If not today, then tomorrow, next year, or even a hundred years from now. What's the difference? More than once, when I heard about some event, I thought, "That can't be." And then a year or two later, I heard that it had happened somewhere, in a place not unlike Frampol. Even if a tale is made up, there's something to it. Why does one person think up one thing, and a second another?

As I wander around the world and eat at strangers' tables, I often tell wild tales. About a demon, a magician, a windmill, you name it. The children run around me, "Grandpa, tell us a story." Sometimes they tell me what story to tell, and I do it for them. As if I care. A bigmouth once said to me, "Grandpa, it's always the same story." And as I live, he was right, that rascal.

It's the same with dreams. It's been so many years since I left Frampol, and as soon as I close my eyes, I'm there again. And who do you think appears? Elka. She stands by the washbasin, like the first time we met, except her face is glowing, her eyes shine like the eyes of a pious woman, and she tells me strange things. When I wake up, I forget everything, but meanwhile I feel good. She solves all my problems and it feels like everything is right. I cry for her and beg: "Take me with you." And she comforts me, "Be patient, Gimpl. It's close, not far." Sometimes she kisses me, hugs me, cries on my face. And when I wake up I feel her lips and the salty taste of her tears.

Of course the world is a world of lies. But it is one step from the true world. Near the door of the poorhouse hovel where I lie is the plank for washing the dead. The gravedigger has his shovel ready. The grave is waiting. The worms are hungry. My shroud is ready in my sack. Another beggar is waiting for my straw bed. God willing, when the time comes at last, I'll go there with joy. Whatever may be there, it is all true, without trickery, without mockery or lies. There, thank God, even Gimpl can't be fooled.

NOTES

1. Triangular pockets of noodle dough filled chopped meat or cheese, boiled and eaten in a soup or as side dish.

2. A small piece of parchment inscribed with a passage from Deuteronomy (6:1–12), rolled up in a scroll, placed in a case or tube, and affixed to the doorpost of a Jewish home as a sign of faith in God.

3. A beggar who shows resourcefulness in getting money from others as though it were his right.

Translated by Isaac Bashevis Singer and David Stromberg.

Other works by Singer: *In My Father's Court* (1956); *The Magician of Lublin* (1960); *The Slave* (1961).

Poetry and Popular Song

Nathan Alterman
1910–1970

The Hebrew poet Nathan Alterman was born in Warsaw and moved to Tel Aviv with his parents when he was fifteen, continuing his education at the Herzliyah Hebrew Gymnasium. At age nineteen, he began studying at the Sorbonne but the following year decided to switch to agronomy and moved to Nancy. In 1932, he returned to Tel Aviv and began working at the Mikveh Yisrael agricultural school but soon decided to earn his living in journalism while devoting himself to poetry. He wrote both lyrical and political poetry. During the last years of the Mandate, the nationalist political verse that he published in his newspaper column, at first in *Haaretz* and then in *Davar*, attracted a wide readership and was at times censored by the British. He also wrote children's books and plays and translated Shakespeare, Racine, and Molière into Hebrew.

The Mole
1940

Not in vain did I vow to be faithful,
not in vain did I tag at your heels.
With the mole I struggled from darkness,
stubborn and under a spell.

You, grief of the nails on my fingers,
you, woe of my head growing bald,
hear me in the cracking of plaster,
in the spreading silence of mold.

In a mirror inlaid with copper
your humble candle sways.
Those who go toward your face in the darkness
have watched from their hiding-place.

But when I stole forth to steal you,
your candle blinded me.
Bristling and dark before it
remained the Mole and I.

Not in vain did I vow to be faithful.
Assaulting the earth where I dwell,

I longed toward your life from my darkness,
for life casts spell upon spell.

See me absurd, my wonder!
rehearsing you clue by clue,
the way you stand, your gestures.
And trembling with joy for you.

My every thought besieged you—
the hairs of my head upright
as I thought of bread on the table
and the candle shedding its light.

Bent and old like your mother,
I held you to my breast,
bearing your misery for you
without refuge from you or rest.

You—grief of the nails on my fingers,

you—woe of my balding head,
burden of my midnight brooding,
burden I cannot forget.

Because our foes persever,
and you break like a stalk of grain,
bristling and dark before them
only Mole and I remain.

In a mirror inlaid with copper
see the candle flicker and spark.
Never shall we forget you,
our faces say from the dark.

For the world is riven, and double
the clamor of its distress.
For no dead have forgotten their dwellings,
all dwellings mourn somebody dead.

At our cities of sorrow forever
gaze the dwellers of darkness and mound.
The glory of our days brims over
with thoughts of the dead underground.

Translated by Robert Friend.

Other works by Alterman: *Selected Poems* (1978); *Little Tel Aviv* (1981).

Mordecai Gebirtig
1877–1942

Yiddish poet and composer Mordecai Gebirtig was born in Kraków, Poland. He fought in World War I, worked as an actor, and published songs in the newspaper of the Jewish Social Democratic Party of Galicia. Gebirtig published his first collection of songs, *Folkstimlekh*, in 1920. Gebirtig is perhaps most famous for his song "S'brent," written in 1938 following the pogrom in Przytyk. Gebirtig and his family were interned in the Kraków ghetto in 1942, and he was killed while in transit to Bełżec concentration camp.

Moments of Hope
1940

> Jews, let us be cheerful!
> It won't be long, don't fear—
> The war will soon be over.
> Their end is very near.
> Cheerful, don't you worry.
> Don't go around so sad.
> Have both hope and patience—
> Bear things and be glad.
>
> Only hope and patience.
> Don't let them out of hand.
> Our ancient weapons
> Help us together band.
> Revel, dance, you butchers.
> It won't be long I hope—
> There was once a Haman—
> For you too waits the rope.
>
> Revel, dance, you butchers,
> Jews their pain can bear.
> The hardest tasks and labor
> Will not our will impair.
> Sweep then? We will sweep then!
> As long as you may deem.
> It's in vain, the sweeping.
> It never will come clean.
>
> Wash then? We will wash then!
> Cain's bright red stain,
> Abel's heart that's bleeding—
> Though washed will still remain.
> Chase us from our dwellings.

> Cut our beards and yell!
> Jews, let us be cheerful—
> Let them go to hell!

Translated by Roslyn Bresnick-Perry.

Other works by Gebirtig: *Mayne lider* (1936); *Geklibene lider* (1954).

Carlos Grünberg
1903–1968

Poet Carlos Moisés Grünberg was born in Buenos Aires, the son of Russian Jewish immigrants who had lived in Palestine. Grünberg became a lawyer but also taught literature. In the 1920s, he associated with an avant-garde circle of writers, including Jorge Luis Borges and was affiliated with the literary journal *Martín Fierro*. Grünberg was a contributor to the cultural and literary review *Judaica* and, in 1946, he edited and translated the Passover Haggadah into Spanish. He was also known for his translations of Heine and Bialik. Grünberg was active in the Zionist movement and was named a liaison between the state of Israel and Argentina in 1948.

Insult
1940

> Jew, you've yelled at him, seething with rage.
> Jew, you've yelled at him, seeking to shame him.
> Jew, no better word can you find to defame him.
> Jew, no better word to vent your disdain.
>
> For him it symbolized glory and martyrdom.
> Tragic grandeur, the meaning he heard.
> Totally pure, like the lily, a hymn.
> Like the lily, for him, a beautiful word.
>
> Now his eyes, lynxlike, are sharper and wiser,
> His vision as clear as if going by touch.
> He sees that all names on your lips are offensive,
> And all words insulting that come from your mouth.

Translated by Michele McKay Aynesworth.

Other works by Grünberg: *Las cámaras del rey* (1922); *El libro del tiempo* (1924); *Junto a un río de Babel* (1965).

Charles Reznikoff

1894–1976

Brooklyn-born Charles Reznikoff was an objectivist poet whose verse addressed the Jewish historical experience more than any other important American poet in the twentieth century. Although he trained as a lawyer, Reznikoff never practiced law and instead eked out a living doing various kinds of editorial work. Despite attracting favorable critical attention, Reznikoff labored in obscurity, self-publishing his work, until late in his life.

A Short History of Israel, Notes and Glosses

1940

XI

> A hundred generations, yes, a hundred and
>   twenty-five,
> had the strength each day
> not to eat this and that (unclean!)
> not to say this and that,
> not to do this and that (unjust!),
> and with all this and all that
> to go about
> as men and Jews
> among their enemies
> (these are the Pharisees you mocked at, Jesus).
> Whatever my grandfathers did or said
> for all of their brief lives
> still was theirs,
> as all of its drops at a moment make the fountain
> and all of its leaves a palm.
> Each word they spoke and every thought
> was heard, each step and every gesture seen,
> by God;
> their past was still the present and the present
> a dread future's.
> But I am private as an animal.
>
> I have eaten whatever I liked,
> I have slept as long as I wished,
> I have left the highway like a dog
> to run into every alley;
> now I must learn to fast and to watch.
> I shall walk better in these heavy boots
> than barefoot.
>
> I will fast for you, Judah,
> and be silent for you
> and wake in the night because of you;
> I will speak for you

in psalms,
and feast because of you
on unleavened bread and herbs.

Other works by Reznikoff: *By the Waters of Manhattan* (1930); *In Memoriam, 1933* (1934); *Early History of a Sewing Machine Operator* (1936); *Going To and Fro and Walking Up and Down* (1941); *Testimony: The United States, 1885–1915* (1965); *By the Well of Living and Seeing: New and Selected Poems, 1918–1973* (1974); *Holocaust* (1975).

Aaron Zeitlin and Sholem Secunda

Zeitlin, 1898–1973

A poet, writer, playwright, essayist, and editor in both Yiddish and Hebrew, Aaron Zeitlin (also spelled Tseytlin) was the eldest son of Hillel Zeitlin (1871–1942) and the brother of Elkhonen Zeitlin (1902–1942). Raised in Homel (now in Belarus), Zeitlin lived in Warsaw between 1907 and 1938. Beginning to write lyrical poetry as a child, Zeitlin was most prolific in interwar Warsaw. He served as the chair of the Yiddish PEN Club from 1930 to 1934 and founded, with the help of Isaac Bashevis Singer, the literary monthly *Globus*. Zeitlin happened to be in New York at the outbreak of World War II; he was powerless to save the family he left behind. His postwar writing was preoccupied with the Holocaust and parapsychology.

Secunda, 1894–1974

Born in the town of Aleksandria (present-day Ukraine), Sholem Secunda was a composer of classical and commercial music, best known for his numerous contributions to the American Yiddish theater. Secunda displayed a keen musical talent early in life and was sought after even as a young boy as a cantor and synagogue chorister in both his native Ukraine and, after his family immigrated in 1907, in New York. A graduate of the Institute of Musical Art, in New York, Secunda produced music and scores for some eighty melodramas, operettas, and other shows for Yiddish theaters into the early 1970s.

Donna Donna

1940

> On a wagon, bound for market
> There's a calf with a mournful eye
> High above her, there's a swallow

Winging swiftly through the sky

How the winds are laughing
They laugh with all their might
Laugh and laugh the whole day through
And half the summer's night

Donna, donna, donna, donna
Donna, donna, donna, don
Donna, donna, donna, donna
Donna, donna, donna, don

Stop complaining said the farmer
Who told you a calf to be?
Why don't you have wings to fly with
Like the swallow, so proud and free?

How the winds are laughing
They laugh with all their might
Laugh and laugh the whole day through
And half the summer's night

Donna, donna, donna, donna
Donna, donna, donna, don
Donna, donna, donna, donna
Donna, donna, donna, don

Calves are easily bound and slaughtered
Never knowing the reason why
But whoever treasures freedom
Like the swallow has learned to fly

How the winds are laughing
They laugh with all their might
Laugh and laugh the whole day through
And half the summer's night

Donna, donna, donna, donna
Donna, donna, donna, don
Donna, donna, donna, donna
Donna, donna, donna, don

Other works by Zeitlin: *Brenendike erd* (1937); *Ha-metsi'ut ha-aheret* (1967); *Poems of the Holocaust and Poems of Faith* (1967). Other work by Secunda: *The Kosher Widow* (1959).

Yocheved Bat-Miriam
1901–1980

Israeli poet Yocheved Bat-Miriam (born Zhelezniak) was born in Keplitz, Belorussia, to a Hasidic Jewish family. She became associated with the pro-Soviet Hebrew Octobrists and changed her name at the age of seventeen. Bat-Miriam studied pedagogy in Kharkov, Moscow, and Odessa and began publishing poems in 1922. Leading an unconventional lifestyle, she had two children while unmarried. In 1928, she moved to Palestine where she published five collections of poems between 1937 and 1946; she ceased writing after the death of her son in the War of Independence. Bat-Miriam received the Bialik Prize in 1968 and the Israel Prize in 1972.

Hagar
1941

Hanging her corals on the night she leaves
silent, possessing nothing.
A moon dives, a splash extinguished
in a wall of water.

Alone, just herself, the path
blown clean with white godhead
twists like a scrawled tattoo
trailing away from child and isolation.

—I won't come back, my country,
like Sphinx at the sun's door
I'll stay here to face
the fate and mystery of the desert land.

Branches rustle in imagined trees,
absent, a well burbles,
their mind-bound tranquility seeks
shelter in the moist shade of my eye,

and for him who stayed behind
who strayed and crossed the line
of a single love starred with silence,
parting and light.

With me, with me from far away
with myself bereft but free
I will be cloaked in make believe
in the drunken error of fantasy.

Wanderer, pursued by restlessness,
in love with impossible splendor,
he will gather us up forcefully to realize
the kingdom of his promised dream.

Stretch out the bow my son,
let the echo speak to the shaft,
so a quavering sound of welcome
may crown my diminishing path.

Translated by Zvi Jagendorf.

Other works by Bat-Miriam: *Me-raḥok* (1932); *Erets yisra'el* (1937); *Shirim la-geto* (1946); *Shirim* (1963).

Shulamit Kalugai
1891–1972

Israeli author Shulamit Kalugai was born in Poltava, Ukraine, and studied at the Sorbonne and at the University of Pittsburgh. She moved to Israel in 1910 and taught at the Hebrew Gymnasia in Jerusalem, and at the Reali School in Haifa. Kalugai wrote children's literature and short stories. She was the sister of Yitzhak Ben-Zvi, the second president of Israel.

Jezebel
1941

The days of my life pass by, dissolve like mist.
I don't know the what and when; I don't know the
    who.
Baal and Astarte have grown alien to me.
My kingdom and my foes grow alien, too.

I don't expect the arrival of anyone.
For who would come to me in my time of drouth?
No one is coming here. Not even a crow
from the river Krit with a greeting in his mouth.

Everything is dream—the islands of Tyre,
Baal's court, my self-enclosure inside Samaria's
    walls—
a dream, my prophets; a dream, the prophets of god,
whom—wild, rebellious, stiff-necked—nothing
    appalls.

All is vanity—pillars of smoke and dream—
sons, brother, sovereignty and love—all things!
Ahab's life and death, the life of Jezebel,
the Queen of Samaria, proud daughter of kings.

And as this summer night approaches dawn,
so does the dream, my life, approach its close.
And Baal and Astarte grow far and dim.
as does Samaria, as do my foes.

Silent the summer night, dark as the grave.
A few stars shine, clouds wander in the air.
A watchman's call, the rustle of olive leaves,
a dog's short bark, dogs barking everywhere . . .

Translated by Robert Friend.

Other works by Kalugai: *Gimnazistit* (1938); *Nashim* (1941).

Itzik Manger
1909–1969

Itzik Manger was born Isidor Helfer in Czernowitz (now Ukraine); he attended a heder and did not finish his gymnasium studies. During World War I, his family moved to Iași, Romania, where Manger began writing Yiddish verse. After serving in the war, he lived in Bucharest, where he wrote journalism and lectured on folklore. His literary career began in the early 1920s, under the mentorship of Eliezer Shteynbarg. Manger arrived in Warsaw in 1928 and spent a prolific decade there, writing and reciting poetry, composing lyrics for cabaret and film, writing and staging plays, as well as publishing multiple collections and periodicals, including two modernist revisions of Jewish biblical folklore: *Khumesh-lider* and *Megile-lider*. He left Poland for Paris in 1938, moved to New York in 1951, and finally settled in Israel in 1958.

Cain and Abel
1941

Dost thou sleep, my brother Abel,
That thou art so wonderfully fair?
Never have I seen thee
As beautiful before.

Does the beauty lie in my ax,
Or is it, perhaps, in thee?
Before the day is done,
Speak—answer me.

Thou art still, my brother Abel,
As the heavens and the earth.
Such pensive silence, until now,
In thee I never heard.

Does the stillness lie in my ax,
Or is it, perhaps, in thee?
Before the day is done,
Speak—answer me.

I stand beside thee, here,
And thou art so alone.
Never before hast thou been
So strangely alien.

Does the strangeness lie in my ax,
Or is it, perhaps, in thee?
Before the day is done,
Speak—answer me.

Come, mother Eve, see how
My brother Abel lies still.
He never slept, so bemused,
In his cradle, for all of thy skill.

Does the stillness lie in my ax,
Or is it, perhaps, in thee?
Before the day is done,
Speak—answer me.

Come, father Adam, and look
At the scarlet ribbon of blood
That wriggles along the earth
And smells so sad and good.

Does the grief lie in my ax,
Or is it, perhaps, in thee?
Before the day is done,
Speak—answer me.

Translated by Leonard Wolf.

Other works by Manger: *Shtern afn dakh* (1929); *Lamtern in vint* (1933); *Demerung in shpigl* (1937); *Noente geshtaltn* (1938); *Volkns ibern dakh* (1942); *Hots-makh-shpil: a Goldfadn-motiv in dray aktn* (1947); *Lid un balade* (1952); *The Book of Paradise: The Wonderful Adventures of Shmuel-Aba Abervo* (1965); *Shtern in shtoyb* (1967); *Shriftn in prose* (1980); *The World According to Itzik: Selected Poetry and Prose* (2002).

Itzik Fefer

1900–1952

Born to a working-class family in Ukraine, Itzik Fefer joined the Communist Party as a teenager and rapidly rose in the ranks of the Soviet Union's first generation of Yiddish-speaking intelligentsia. Fefer was fiercely loyal to the Soviet regime and its ideology, crafting verse in praise of the state and conforming strictly to the tenets of socialist realism. Fefer served as an informant for the NKVD on the Jewish Anti-Fascist Committee, reporting on the activities of its members. Despite his loyalty, he was executed for nationalism and anti-Soviet activities alongside other members of the committee.

I Am a Jew

1942

The wine of countless generations
Has strengthened me in my wandering,
The angry sword of pain and sorrow

Could not destroy my existence—
My people, my faith, and my flowering,
It has not chained my freedom.
From under the sword I shouted:
I am a Jew!

Neither Pharaoh's plagues, nor Titus,
Nor Haman could break my proud spirit,
Eternity carries my name in her hands.
My zest has not decreased
On the black gallows of Madrid,
My glory resounds through time and eternity:
I am a Jew!

When the Egyptian built
My body into the walls, it hurt.
And I sowed the raw earth with my pain
And a sun arose.
Under the sun a path it stretched out
Scattered with barbs,
They would prick me in the eyes—
I am a Jew!

The forty years of a former life
Which I suffered in the desert-sand
Have given me the courage of my years
Bar Kochba's call has cast its spell
On each kernel of my suffering,
And more than gold have I preserved
The stubbornness of my grandfather—
I am a Jew!

What do I need gold for? I gathered that
When I did not even have a corner.
Could gold satiate
My high spirits or my gloom?
Samson's hair which Delilah stole
Glowed and satisfied more than
Than cold, golden coins—
I am a Jew!

The wrinkles in the brow of wise Rabbi Akiva
The wisdom of Isaiah's prophecy
Have quenched my thirst—my dear
And have matched it with hatred;
The zeal of the Maccabean heroes
Still seethes in my rebel-blood,
From all pyres I have announced:
I am a Jew!

The marvelous judgment of our Solomon
Has not abandoned me in my wandering

And Heinrich Heine's crooked smile
Also cost me much spilled blood.
Through the centuries I have heard Yehuda Halevi's
    call
And I have not tired of it,
I have withered often but have not perished—
I am a Jew!

The noise of Amsterdam's marketplace
Did not disquiet my Spinoza
Space itself makes things bigger;
Marx's sun upon the earth
Refreshed with new redness
The ancient blood in my spirit
And my unextinguished fire—
I am a Jew!

There is in my eyes the glow,
The serenity, and the stress
Of Levitan's sunsets,
Of the blessed path which Mendele took
The blade of Russian bayonets,
The dazzle of the rye at harvest.
I am a son of the Soviets,
I am a Jew!

The echo of Haifa port
Resounds with the ring of my voice
Unnoticed telegraph wires
Carry me over sea and dale
The heartbeat of Buenos Aires,
And from New York a Yiddish song,
The horror of Berlin's edicts,
I am a Jew!

I am a Jew who has drunk
From Stalin's magic cup of joy,
Whoever wants to let Moscow sink,
To turn the world backward,
To him I say: No! To him I shout: Down!
I go with the Eastern peoples,
The Russians are my brothers—
And I am a Jew!

My glory a ship on both streams,
My blood lights up eternity,
My pride is Yaakov Sverdlov's name
And Kaganovich—Stalin's friend.
My youth floats over the snows,
The heart is fall of dynamite,
My luck quivers in the trenches,
I am a Jew!

I am not alone! My heroism grows,
The struggle today is for an honest piece of bread,
I glorify the flame, I raise the storm,
Which brings death to the enemy in brown,
My strength no longer lags behind,
The blood of Papernik and Gorelik
Cries and seethes from the earth:
I am a Jew!

And to spite the enemies
Who already prepare graves for me,
I shall still have pleasure without end
Beneath the red banner,
I shall plant my vineyards
And be the forger of my destiny,
I shall still dance on Hitler's grave!
I am a Jew!

Translated by Thomas E. Bird.

Other works by Fefer: *Birobidzhaner lider* (1939); *Roytarmeyish* (1943).

Pavel Friedman

1921–1944

Born in Prague, Pavel Friedman was a poet. He was deported to Theresienstadt in April 1942. In June of that year he inscribed "The Butterfly" on a piece of paper that was discovered after the war. In September 1944, he was deported to Auschwitz. The poem was donated to the Jewish Museum in Prague and remains one of the most famous literary documents from the war.

The Butterfly
1942

He was the last. Truly the last.
Such yellowness was bitter and blinding
Like the sun's tear shattered on stone.
That was his true color.
And how easily he climbed, and how high.
Certainly, climbing, he wanted
To kiss the last of my world.

I have been here seven weeks.
Ghettoized.
Who loved me have found me,
Daisies call to me,
And the branches also of the white chestnut in the
    yard.

But I haven't seen a butterfly here.
That last one was the last one.
There are no butterflies, here, in the ghetto.

Translated by Dennis Silk.

Zuzanna Ginczanka

1917-1944

Born in Kiev but raised by her grandmother in the predominantly Jewish city of Rivne, Zuzanna Ginczanka (also known as Gincburg) was a Polish-language poet, literary translator, and author of radio plays. Ginczanka moved to Warsaw in 1935, bringing with her a reputation as an innovative poet. Her one published collection of poetry, the volume *O centaurach* (1936), was considered a literary sensation in its day. During the war, Ginczanka spent much of her time in hiding, going back to Rivne, then to Lviv, and finally to Kraków. She was ultimately betrayed by one of the landlords who had kept her in hiding in Kraków and likely murdered at a Nazi prison outside the city. Ginczanka's most famous poem "Non omnis moriar" was later used as evidence against her betrayer in a postwar collaborationism trial in Poland.

Non omnis moriar
1942

Non omnis moriar. My grand estate—
Tablecloth meadows, invincible wardrobe castles,
Acres of bedsheets, finely woven linens,
And dresses, colorful dresses—will survive me.
I leave no heirs.
So let your hands rummage through Jewish things,
You, Chomin's wife from Lvov, you mother of a
  volksdeutscher.
May these things be useful to you and yours,
For, dear ones, I leave no name, no song.
I am thinking of you, as you, when the Schupo came,
Thought of me, in fact reminded them about me.
So let my friends break out holiday goblets,
Celebrate my wake and their wealth:
Kilims and tapestries, bowls, candlesticks.
Let them drink all night and at daybreak
Begin their search for gemstones and gold
In sofas, mattresses, blankets and rugs.
Oh how the work will burn in their hands!
Clumps of horsehair, bunches of sea hay,
Clouds of fresh down from pillows and quilts,

Glued on by my blood, will turn their arms into
  wings,
Transfigure the birds of prey into angels.

Translated by Nancy Kassell and Anita Safran.

Other works by Ginczanka: *Wiersze wybrane* (1953); *Udźwignąć własne szczęście* (1991); *Wniebowstąpienie ziemi* (2000); *Wiersze zebrane* (2014); *Mądrość jak rozkosz* (2017).

Hirsh Glik

1922-1944

Hirsh Glik was born in Vilna into an impoverished family and began writing poems at age thirteen, first in Hebrew and later in Yiddish. He became a protégé of two leading Vilna poets, Leyzer Volf and Shmerke Kaczerginski, and helped lead a young poets group called Yungvald. Glik was sent to labor camps in 1941, and in 1943 to the Vilna ghetto. There he wrote songs to raise the morale of his fellow Jews, including the famous "Zog nit keyn mol," which spread throughout the camps and ghettos and continues today to be an anthem at memorial gatherings. This song is often mistakenly associated with the battle of the Warsaw ghetto. Glik joined the main FPO, the major resistance organization in the ghetto, and in September 1943 was sent to a German labor camp in Estonia. He escaped shortly before the liberation of the camp and was killed by German forces in September 1944.

Silence, and a Starry Night
1942

Silence, and a starry night
Frost crackling, fine as sand.
Remember how I taught you
To hold a gun in your hand?

In fur jacket and beret,
Clutching a hand grenade,
A girl whose skin is velvet
Ambushes a cavalcade.

Aim, fire, shoot—and hit!
She, with her pistol small,
Halts an autoful,
Arms and all!

Morning, emerging from the wood,
In her hair a snow carnation.

Proud of her small victory
For the new, free generation!

Translated by Jacob Sloan.

Shmerke Kaczerginski
1908–1954

Poet, songwriter, partisan, popular historian, and ethnomusicologist Shmerke Kaczerginski was born in Vilna and given a religious education. Before World War II, Kaczerginski was active in underground communist activities and was closely involved with Yiddish cultural life in Vilna, becoming a leader of the literary group Yung-Vilne. He was a major cultural figure in the Vilna ghetto, and many of his poems were set to music: "Yugnt Hymn," "Friling," "Shtiler, shtiler," and others. He was also active in the underground resistance, the FPO, and worked to hide Jewish cultural treasures from the Germans. In September 1943, together with the poet Avrom Sutzkever, he left the ghetto for the Narocz forest, where, after many difficulties, he joined the Soviet partisan movement. Later, after failing to revive Yiddish culture in Soviet Lithuania and bitterly disappointed by Soviet anti-semitism, he left first for Poland, then for France, and settled in Argentina. He was killed in a plane crash in Argentina in 1954.

Still, Still
1942

Still, still, let us be still.
Graves grow here.
Planted by the enemy,
they blossom to the sky.
All the roads lead to Ponar,
and none returns.

Somewhere father disappeared,
disappeared with all our joy.
Be still, my child, don't cry, my treasure;
tears are of no avail.
No matter the fury of your tears,
the enemy will not notice.
Rivers open into oceans,
prison cells are not a world,
but to our sorrow,
there is no end,
there is no light.

Spring has blossomed in the countryside,
and all about our lives is fall.
Today the day is full of flowers,
but the night alone holds us.
Somewhere a mother is orphaned.
Her child goes to Ponar.
The river Viliye, chained,
convulses in our pain.
Ice floes race through Lithuania
Into the ocean now.
Somewhere there is no darkness.
Somewhere, out of darkness,
suns are burning.
Rider come at once.
Your child calls you.
Your child calls you.

Still, still, wellsprings flow
deep without our hearts.
Until the gates come falling down
we must guard our tongues.
Don't rejoice, child, your very smile
is treachery now.
Let the enemy see the spring
as a leaf in autumn.
Let the wellspring flow its course
and you be still and hope. . . .
Father will return with freedom.
Sleep, my child, be still.
Like the Viliye freed of its chains
and like the trees renewed in green,
freedom's light will glow
upon your face,
upon your face.

Translated by Hillel Schwartz and David G. Roskies.

Other works by Kaczerginski: *Khurbn Vilne* (1947); *Partizaner geyen* (1947); *Lider fun di getos un lagern* (1948); *Tsvishn hamer un serp: tsu der geshikhte fun der likvidatsye fun der yidisher kultur in Sovyetn-Rusland* (1949); *Ikh bin geven a partizan* (1952).

Yosef Kirman
1896–1943

Raised in Warsaw, Yosef Kirman was a laborer, poet, and political activist. His Yiddish poems and stories were published in journals and in the collection *Ringen* (1919). Some of his most memorable works were written in the Warsaw ghetto, where they were circulated in the underground press, and several were preserved in the Ringelblum Archive. Kirman died when the Poniatów labor camp was liquidated in 1943.

I Speak to You Openly, My Child
1942

(Short Poems in Prose)

Doves on Wires

. . . My child, on a cold and frosty day, with an evil wind blowing and shaking man and earth, your father dragged himself along, tired, in search of himself. He wandered through the streets, past buildings and people.

Instead of himself, he found wires—barbed wires that cut through the street and cut it to pieces. On both sides of the wire people walked up and down. Poverty and hunger drove them towards the fence through which one could see what went on on the other side. Jews, the badge of shame on their arms, walked on one side and Christian boys and girls on the other. When from the other side a loaf of bread was thrown over the fence, boys on this side tried to catch it. Police in jackboots, armed with rubber truncheons, beat up a child. The child cried and German soldiers, looking on, shook with laughter. When a Jewish girl sang a song, begging, pleading—"I am hungry and cold," policemen drove her away, and the soldiers smiled, when they saw the loaf of bread, rolling on the ground.

People walked up and down. And your father stood there and looked over the fence. Suddenly a flight of doves came down, driven from somewhere out of the blue. Silently they settled on the wires and began quietly to coo. I felt the pain of their sadness and sorrow, I listened to their weeping hearts and understood the anguish of the freezing doves.

And yet, my child, how greedy man is! With his heart he feels sympathy, while his eyes are filled with envy. The doves have wings, and if they want to, they can fly, onto wires or up to rooftops, off and away!

Your father stood there, dreaming. And a policeman came and knocked him on the head. Ashamed he began to move on, but he wanted to look once more at the doves. And, then, my child, your father saw something terrible:

The doves were still there, on the barbed wires, but . . . they were eating the crumbs, out of the hands of the soldiers! . . .

My child, your father grew very sad, and sad he still is: not about the doves on freezing wires, and not because they have wings and he has not, but because now he hates the doves, too, and he warns you: Keep away from them, as long as the innocence allows itself to be fed by murderous hands. . . .

Flames over Warsaw

My child, when the steel birds hailed down death we all fled to the woods. You remember how terrified we were when the woods along our tracks caught fire and we went on in our flight without hope and without thought that we would ever reach our goal?

Now it is different. . . . Come, come out into the street. Though a biting frost cuts the ears and it is late in the evening. My dear, beloved son, come, I will show you a fire that lights up the skies over Warsaw. I don't know where it comes from and what it is for. Maybe they are fliers from Russian fields or maybe the birds came from the other side of the Channel; or maybe it is the work of hidden hands at home; perhaps this, perhaps that. . . . But look, how the sky grows red. How beautiful the red is over the snow-covered town; it is evening and it's light and there where the Vistula is frozen to ice, rise up higher, and higher, and almost as high as the sky: giant tongues of fire and of smoke. Wherever we turn we see wide-open spaces lit up by the flames. It smells of sulphur, of white heat, though the frost is grim and the snow lies dense on roofs and walls.

How beautiful is this wintry evening! Something great and unexpected is coming from over there, from the Vistula, where the fires are burning.

My child, you regret that you cannot put out the fire, that you are not a Polish fireman with a little trumpet: *tu-tu-tu!* . . .

Don't be a silly child! You'll be a fireman one day. But not yet, not yet. It's too early yet to extinguish the fires. Let them burn, let them burn, let them burn, my child!

Come children, let's form a ring and dance and clap our hands: *tra-la, tra-la-la!*

A pity the fire grows smaller. . . . Someone asks me:

—What was on fire, Mister Jew, perhaps you know? What was it?

—The wickedness of the world was on fire, I thought. . . .

—Really?—The woman who asked nods knowingly.

It Will Be as in Our Dream . . .

My son! You should not regret it that you have been with me in the locked-up streets of the Ghetto—Dzika, Stavki and Mila.

My son, you should not regret your crying today. It does not matter that, when you look up to the sun, tears come into your eyes.

For you will see, my child, you will see: where today there is wailing and sadness hovers in homes; and the Angel of Death reigns supreme like a drunken madman; and people in rags, heaps of shattered hopes, cower along old, dark and smoky walls; and bodies of old men rot away in doorways or on bare floors, covered with newspapers or pieces of stone; and children shiver and whisper: "We are starving" and like rats stir in piles of refuse; and worn-out women hold up their hands, thin as ribbons in their last barren consumptive prayers; and frost and disease close in on dying eyes that, in their last agony crave for a crust of bread—

There, my dear, my sunny child,
there will yet come
that great,
that greatest of days,
that last, the very last day—
and it will be as in our dream . . .

Translated by Jacob Sonntag.

Other work by Kirman: *Iber shtok un shteyn: lider un poemen* (1930).

Stanley Kunitz

1905–2006

Stanley Kunitz was born in Worcester, Massachusetts. His father committed suicide shortly before the poet was born, and Kunitz left home at age fifteen. He graduated from Harvard College in 1926 and worked as a reporter and editor, earning his master's degree and teaching at numerous universities on the East Coast. Kunitz published his first collection of poetry in 1930 and was a major influence on the writings of Robert Lowell, Allen Ginsberg, and Louise Glück. An outspoken advocate against censorship, Kunitz served as the consultant in poetry to the Library of Congress, and was named U.S. poet laureate in 2000.

Father and Son

1942

Now in the suburbs and the falling light
I followed him, and now down sandy road
Whiter than bone-dust, through the sweet
Curdle of fields, where the plums
Dropped with their load of ripeness, one by one.
Mile after mile I followed, with skimming feet,
After the secret master of my blood,
Him, steeped in the odor of ponds, whose indomitable love
Kept me in chains. Strode years; stretched into bird;
Raced through the sleeping country where I was young,
The silence unrolling before me as I came,
The night nailed like an orange to my brow.

How should I tell him my fable and the fears,
How bridge the chasm in a casual tone,
Saying, "The house, the stucco one you built,
We lost. Sister married and went from home,
And nothing comes back, it's strange, from where she goes.
I lived on a hill that had too many rooms:
Light we could make, but not enough of warmth,
And when the light failed, I climbed under the hill.
The papers are delivered every day;
I am alone and never shed a tear."

At the water's edge, where the smothering ferns lifted
Their arms, "Father!" I cried, "Return! You know
The way. I'll wipe the mudstains from your clothes;
No trace, I promise, will remain. Instruct
Your son, whirling between two wars,
In the Gemara of your gentleness,
For I would be a child to those who mourn
And brother to the foundlings of the field
And friend of innocence and all bright eyes.
O teach me how to work and keep me kind."

Among the turtles and the lilies he turned to me
The white ignorant hollow of his face.

Other works by Kunitz: *Intellectual Things* (1930); *Passport to the War: A Selection of Poems* (1944); *Selected Poems, 1928–1958* (1958); *The Poems of Stanley Kunitz, 1928–1978* (1979); *Next-to-Last Things: New Poems and Essays* (1985); *Passing Through: The Later Poems, New and Selected* (1995); *The Collected Poems* (2000).

Henryka Łazowertówna

1910–1942

Born in Warsaw, Henryka Łazowertówna belonged to the new wave of Polish poetry that arose in the immediate aftermath of World War I. Employed by the Jewish Social Self-Help Organization in the Warsaw ghetto, she was an active contributor to the Oyneg Shabes archive. Łazowertówna is best known for "The Little Smuggler," a poem she wrote in the ghetto. The words are inscribed in Polish, English, and Hebrew on Warsaw's Memorial to the Child Victims of the Holocaust. She was deported to Treblinka in 1942.

The Little Smuggler

1942

Over the wall, through holes, and past the guard,
Through the wires, ruins, and fences.
Plucky, hungry, and determined
I sneak through, dart like a cat.

At noon, at night, at dawn,
In snowstorm, cold or heat,
A hundred times I risk my life
And put my head on the line.

Under my arm a gunny sack,
Tatters on my back,
On nimble young feet,
With endless fear in my heart.

But one must endure it all,
One must bear it all,
So that tomorrow morning
The fine folk can eat their fill.

Over the wall, through holes and bricks,
At night, at dawn, at noon,
Plucky, hungry, artful,
I move silently like a shadow.

And if the hand of destiny
Should seize me in the game,
That's a common trick of life.
You, mother, do not wait up for me.

I will return no more to you,
My voice will not be heard from afar.
The dust of the street will bury
The lost fate of a child.

And only one request
Will stiffen on my lips:

Who, mother mine, who
Will bring your bread tomorrow?

Translated by Ted Hudes.

Other works by Łazowertówna: *Zamknięty pokój* (1930); *Imiona świata* (1934).

Simkhe-Bunem Shayevitsh

1907–1944

Simkhe-Bunem Shayevitsh was born in 1907 in Łęczyca, Poland, into a Hasidic family. He relocated to Łódź, where he worked in textiles; a volume of his short stories was scheduled to appear when the war began. Shayevitsh lived with his wife and daughter in abject poverty in the Łódź ghetto, where he emerged as a major poet. Two of his epic poems were discovered after the liberation and published by Nachman Blumental. In August 1944, Shayevitsh was deported in one of the last transports to Auschwitz. He is immortalized as the poet Berkovitch in Chava Rosenfarb's *The Tree of Life*.

Lekh-lekho

1942

And now Blimele, dear child,
Stop—stop playing now.
No time for that.
We can be called at any minute

To leave our poor home
—A lonely boat on an island of sand—
And be hurled into the midst
Of a naked furious sea.

Outside the first groups already
Are dragging themselves on the trek
Women, men, old people; on their backs
Heavy burdens, in their arms children.

Their grieving faces
Are drunken-red from shame and frost
Their step—fainting, staggering,
Their looks—sentenced to death.

But there is no Jeremiah
To lament the Destruction.
He does not go with them into Exile
To comfort them by Babylon's streams.

Do not gaze at me, dear child
With questioning wondering eyes—

Why are only poor folk here.
Where are the well-fed on the distant roads?

You know, child: *oylem* means world and it means
    eternal
The saying of a famous wise man,
I've told you the story
The story of the Cantonists

Poor children. kidnapped,
Torn away from father and mother.
So why do you wonder, child.
If those times greet the ghetto?

And we must pick up
The old wander-staff and go.
Not knowing what will befall
Our poor sick bones.

Whether we'll get somewhere
And reach a place of rest.
And people will stretch out
Friendly hands, with a kind word;

Or whether like sick birds that fall
Dead in a field, in a valley somewhere.
We'll perish on the road.
Not be buried as Jews.

And the ravens will make
Banquets on our bodies.
And when one flock is sated
It will summon a second

Don't weep, dear child! Don't weep!
Life is beautiful, it draws like a magnet,
And more than ever and more than
    anywhere
It draws beyond the ghetto.

But know that sinful man
Must always be prepared
Both for noisy colorful life
And for bleak unhappy death. [. . .]

And now Blimele, dear child,
Don't weep out your little white teeth
We have only time
To say goodbye to the house.

So let us say goodbye
To all that we hold dear,
To every little thing we leave
And it runs after us like fire,

With the longing that my lung
Breathed into each thing—
And bounds up like a puppy
Everywhere, faithful yet and swift;

With the unsung songs
That flutter about the house
And run ahead and come to meet us
When we are led to the grave. [. . .]

Here, child, is the wardrobe—
Two doors and a mirror between them
Which quietly saw everything
And sealed it in its glassy heart

And holds within it the sunny hue
Of your little red body at birth
And the first protest that made
Your silky lip scowl without a word

And like a phonograph record
The mirror holds hidden within it
The first song that lulled you to sleep
In your simple cradle of straw.

And your first little laugh is engraved there
Which spurted like sweet chocolate;
And also the similar twist of the mouth
In the final throes of death.

And here, child, on the right side of the cupboard
Your mother kept the laundry
Washed by her own hands
And scented with lilac

And she used to weep into it
When her hope evaporated
And her dreams went out
Like suns of earlier days.

But she often laughed into the clothes
When she slumbered amidst her work
And saw your luck like a sun
In a blue sky rising.

And on the left side lie Holy books,
Worldly books, my manuscripts.
Isaiah hobnobs with Goethe,
Reb Jonathan Eybeschuetz with Tuwim.

And Yesenin wants to get drunk
And urinate in public
But suddenly he sees Abraham
Leading Isaac to Mount Moriah.

Miriam Ulinover displays
The "antiques" from her grandmother's treasure;
King David flames up in the Psalms
And foots in His honor the circle-dances.

And the Kotsker still stands waiting
With knotted beard and angry mutter
For ten young men to cry out to the world:
THE LORD ALONE IS GOD!

But the Vorker slaps him on the back
in friendly fashion till the Kotsker blinks.
"Don't be a fool! Every day a Jew in Exile
Performs the command of *Kiddush Hashem.*

"So instead let's take a drop of whiskey,
A bite of cheese, and say *Lekhayim!*
It's time for God, the blessed, Himself
To hallow the name of heaven."

And in humility and trembling
Lie my poems and stories.
They lie and wail in fear
Like poor folk for well-paid jobs

And whisper quietly, softly entreat
Till Rav Ashi hears their murmur
And bids "Make way!"; friendly, too
Is the proud Sholem Asch.

And there's an uproar: "Here's another
In the family—let's crown him!"
Aaron the Priest makes with hands
And spoken words the priestly blessing.

And now, Blimele, dear child.
Put on your little coat, let's go.
The third group sways in readiness
And we must join them now.

But let us not weep.
Let us not lament, but in spite of all foes
Smile, only smile, so those
Who know the Jews will wonder

And not understand that in our blood
Flows the power of our grandfathers
Who in all generations
Climbed atop so many Moriahs;

That although our step is unsteady
Like a blind man's at a strange door.
There rings in it the echo
Of our uncle's stride on Siberian roads

That although, as in a fallen beast,
Terror in our eyelash trembles,
Pride burns in flaming lightning-bolts
As in our father on the gallows.

And although at any minute
We can be tortured and shot.
Well—it is nothing new:
Our sister was whipped naked.

So let us not weep.
Let us not lament, but in spite of all foes
Smile, only smile, so those
Who know the Jews will wonder

And not know that today
The same angels go with us as before:
On the right Michael, on the left Gabriel,
Uriel in front and Raphael in the rear.

And although beneath our feet is death.
Over our head is God's Presence,
So child, let us go with devotion renewed
And our old proclamation of Oneness.

Translated by Elinor Robinson.

Leah Rudnitsky

1916–1943

Yiddish poet Leah Rudnitsky was born in Kalwarija, Lithuania, lived in Kovne (Kaunas), and settled in 1939 in Vilna, where she worked in Yiddish journalism. Ultimately confined to the Vilna ghetto, Rudnitsky wrote poems reflecting the grim circumstances of Jews living under Nazi persecution; she was also a partisan. Her most famous poem, "Dremlen feygl" (Birds Are Drowsing) commemorates the death of Jews slaughtered at Ponary forest, outside Vilna. Rudnitsky perished, possibly in the camp at Majdanek.

Birds Are Drowsing
ca. 1942

Birds are drowsing on the branches.
Sleep, my darling child.
At your cradle, in the field,
A stranger sits and sings.

Once you had another cradle
Woven out of joy.
And your mother, oh your mother

Will never more come by.

I saw your father fleeing
Under the rain of countless stones.
Over fields and over valleys
Flew his orphaned cry.

Translated by Hillel Schwartz and David G. Roskies.

Other works by Rudnitsky: *Durkh neplen* (ca. 1941).

Hillel Bavli

1893–1961

The American Hebrew poet Hillel Bavli was born in Lithuania and arrived in the United States in 1912. He received both a traditional religious education and a modern education. In the United States, he taught Hebrew in several cities on the East Coast. In 1917, he began teaching Hebrew language and literature at the Teachers Institute of the Jewish Theological Seminary, where he remained until his death. He was a central participant in the major Hebraist projects in the United States and worked to create bridges with Hebrew writers in the Land of Israel. He was known in particular for his lyric poetry.

The Martyrdom of the 93 Beit Ya'akov Girls
1943

We cleansed our bodies and we are pure,
We cleansed our spirits and are at peace.
Death does not frighten us,
We shall meet it calmly.

We served God with our life,
We shall know how to hallow His name in death.
A solemn covenant binds the ninety-three of us:
Together we studied God's Torah,
Together we shall die.

We read Psalms aloud and are comforted,
We confessed our sins,
And our hearts grew strong.
Now we are ready to depart.

Let the unclean ones come to defile us;
We do not fear them!
Before their eyes we shall drink the cup of poison
    and die,
Innocent and pure, as befits daughters of Jacob.

We shall pray before mother Sarah and say to her:
We have come,
We met the test of the Binding of Isaac,
Come, pray with us for the people of Israel.

Grant mercy, O Father of mercy,
To the people that has known Thee,
There is no more mercy in mortal man.
Reveal Thy love now concealed,
Rescue and redeem Thine afflicted people,
Purify and preserve Thy world.

The hour of *Neilah* has come; our hearts are quiet.
The last request we make of you, our brethren,
    wherever you are:
Recite the *Kaddish* for us,
For the ninety-three maidens of Israel.

NOTE
[This poem was written in response to a last letter supposedly written from Kraków on 11 August 1942 on behalf of ninety-three Orthodox Jewish school girls who chose martyrdom rather than be sexually defiled by German soldiers. By later incorporating this poem into the Martyrology section of High Holiday prayerbook, the Conservative Movement honored the request that the Kaddish be recited in their memory. This story is apocryphal.—Eds.]

Translated by Ben Zion Bokser.

Other works by Bavli: *Nimim: me'asef le-sifrut yafah u-le-divrey bikoret* (1923); *The Growth of Modern Hebrew Literature* (1939); *Sefer ha-yovel li-khvod Tsevi Sharfstayn li-mlo't lo shiv'im shanah* (1954); *Aderet ha-shanim: shirim* (1955).

Paul Celan

1920–1970

A major twentieth-century poet and translator, Paul Celan (born Antschel; *Celan* is an anagram of his original name) was born in the multicultural city of Czernowitz, Bukovina, the son of German-speaking Jews. He studied medicine in Paris in 1938, and returned to Romania before the outbreak of World War II. His parents died in Nazi labor camps and Celan was interned for eighteen months. After the war, establishing himself as a poet, he lived in Bucharest. He moved to Paris in 1948 to study German philology and literature and in 1960 earned the Büchner Prize from the German Academy of Language and Literature. Celan took his own life, as did a number of other notable survivors of the Holocaust.

Black Flakes
1943

Snow has fallen, with no light. A month
has gone by now or two, since autumn in its
    monkish cowl
brought tidings my way, a leaf from Ukrainian
    slopes:

"Remember it's wintry here too, for the thousandth
    time now
in the land where the broadest torrent flows:
Ya'akov's heavenly blood, blessed by axes . . .
Oh ice of unearthly red—their Hetman wades
    with all
his troop into darkening suns . . . Oh for a cloth,
    child,
to wrap myself when it's flashing with helmets,
when the rosy floe bursts, when snowdrift sifts your
    father's
bones, hooves crushing
the Song of the Cedar . . .
A shawl, just a thin little shawl, so I keep
by my side, now you're learning to weep, this
    anguish,
this world that will never turn green, my child, for
    your child!"

Autumn bled all away, Mother, snow burned me
    through:
I sought out my heart so it might weep, I found—oh
    the summer's breath,
Then came my tears. I wove the shawl.

Translated by John Felstiner.

Other works by Celan: *Selected Poems and Prose of
Paul Celan* (translated by John Felstiner, 2000); *Poems
of Paul Celan: A Bilingual German/English Edition,
Revised Edition* (translated by Michael Hamburger,
2002); *Corona: Selected Poems of Paul Celan* (translated by Susan H. Gillespie, 2013); *Breathturn into
Timestead: Collected Later Poetry of Paul Celan* (translated by Pierre Joris, 2014).

Else Dormitzer
1877-1958

The German poet and journalist Else Dormitzer fled
from her hometown of Nuremburg to the Netherlands
after November 1938; in 1943, however, she and her
husband, who was to perish during the war, were deported to the concentration camp at Theresienstadt in
Czechoslovakia. During her incarceration, Dormitzer
wrote ten poems that were published in 1945 as *There-
sienstädter Bilder* (Pictures from Theresienstadt).

Census
1943

Dense crowds proceed at dawn
Through Theresienstadt's still empty streets
Five abreast curving around corners into squares.
The beast checks if anybody has stumbled.
Today God's chosen people are being numbered!

You see each kind of person,
Only the sick are allowed to stay behind,
At five o'clock the order went out to herd—
No one exempted, into one place:
The lame lead the blind, everyone's excoriated.
Today God's chosen people are being recorded!

Mothers push prams,
Fathers carry puny sons.
The elderly drag along on crutches or just sticks.
The census taker begins his meticulous task:
The pale sun is peeled from the clouds and
    plundered.
Today the chosen people are being numbered!

Finally the counting place is reached!
In an arch we move across Bauschwitz earth,
No chair, no stone or bench to sit on.
No wall to lean your back on:
Stand in hundreds, the command to the frozen.
So today they can count more easily the chosen!

Basic modest needs plague us.
Hunger rampages through our stomachs.
Nothing hot is offered, not a drop of water.
Our faces grow pale and dribbly.
Frost and deprivation have us routed.
Today the chosen people are being counted!

Hour after hour slips by.
The bare earth is the only place to sit,
Despair and diarrhoea mix
And some pass out or pass on:
There we lie stretched out like the dead.
Today the chosen people are being read!

Night is like a corpse, no star in the sky!
Desperate, everyone asks the other:

"Will we stay here till tomorrow?"
Trembling, quailing, fretting, fainting,
Those usually brave find optimism numbered!

Finally the order barks: what relief,
"The Jew can go to the ghetto!"
Scurry, push, elbow, shove, curse;
And parents shrink towards children, children peer
For parents—again to quarters, nobody at play.

The chosen people were counted today!

Translated by Ruth Schwertfeger.

Jacob Glatstein
1896–1971

Jacob Glatstein was the leading American Yiddish
poet of the twentieth century. Born in Lublin, he
moved to the United States in 1914 and lived in New
York, where he helped found the In Zikh group of
Yiddish writers. Glatstein's turn from introspective
poetry to journalism, cultural criticism, and social
engagement occurred in the 1930s, culminating in 1938
in the publication of his poem "Good Night, World,"
and the first two volumes of a planned trilogy loosely
based on his return trip to Poland in 1934. His volume
Gedenklider (Memorial Poems, 1943) marked a shift in
his poetics and was the first major poetic response to
the unfolding Holocaust to appear in any language.

I Have Never Been Here Before
1943

I always thought
I had been here before.
Each year of my patched-up life
I mended the fabrics
of my decrepit, tattered world.
In memory I recognized faces and smiles,
even my father and mother reappeared
as longed-for frescoes of the past.
I have traveled old and squalid paths,
maneuvered my sails
between the shores of history.
I have continually come across the wonder
of memory inscribing itself,
and the agitated past
quietly welling up in the present.
I thought
I had always been here.

Only these last ragged years—
shreds of hair—
inventive deaths—
are my days and nights.
My warped destiny
I have lived to see.
The frozen reverie,
burnt fields,
cartography of cemeteries,
stony silence,
emblems of vicious joy—
I don't recall them.
I have never seen them before.
I have never been here before.

Be still, dead world.
Be silent, in your ruin.
Blasted ornaments will bloom again.
We shall rebuild your foundations
out of the blood that was spilled.
And yet, the dead will still cry midnight prayers—
each corpse, a trickling voice.
Like a tiny candle over each grave,
a cry will burn,
each one for itself.
"I am I"—
thousands of slaughtered I's
will cry in the night:
"I am dead, unrecognized,
my blood still unredeemed."

Such a wealth of gravestones—
I have never seen them before.
Day and night I shall mourn the names.

I have never been here before.

Translated by Richard J. Fein.

Other works by Glatstein: *The Glatstein Chronicles* (1938–1940); *Emil and Karl* (1940); *Fun mayn
gantser mi: 1919–1956* (1956); *Selected Poems of Yankev
Glatshteyn* (1987).

Hirsh Glik

Never Say
1943

Never say, this is the last road for you,
Leaden skies are masking days of blue.
The hour we yearn for is drawing near.

Our step will beat the signal: we are here!

From southern palms, from lands long white with
    snow,
We come with all our pain and all our woe,

Wherever seeped our blood into the earth,
Our courage and our strength will have rebirth.

Tomorrow's sun will gild our sad today,
The enemy and yesterday will fade away.
But should the dawn delay or sunrise wait too long,
Then let all future generations sing this song.

This song was written with our blood and not with
    lead,
This is no song of free birds flying overhead,
But a people amid crumbling walls did stand,
They stood and sang this song with rifles held in
    hand.

Translated by Jacob Sloan.

Leah Goldberg

Nights
1943

All those things whose names I hushed
in secret, I meet in the night's abyss.
I face the dark. Alert, remembering. Silently,
again I'll let you in—my friends, my beloved dead.

And here you are as then, crowned with the small
    serenity
of bright gardens and roadside lawns. . . .
In the folds of your clothes—a whole year's worries
and the simplistic innocence of pain.

Your dreadful innocence! Who knew of its holiness?
My father joking. Delight among friends—
from my deep night my dead city laughs
to the strains of a song from the Days of Awe.

Translated by Annie Kantar.

Yehuda Karni
1884–1949

Hebrew poet Yehuda Karni was born in Pinsk, and
received a religious as well as a general education. His
first Hebrew poem was published in *Ha-tsefirah* in
1897. Karni was active in communal affairs in Vilna,

and attended Zionist congresses as a representative of
the Po'ale Tsiyon movement. In 1921, he moved to Palestine, assisted by Ḥayim Naḥman Bialik. From 1923
until his death, Karni served on the editorial board of
Haaretz, contributing poetry and articles almost daily.
Karni was a pioneer in adopting Sephardic diction in
his poetry.

The Month of Rescue
1943

It is for us, for all of us together,
To assist, to liberate, to rescue brothers,
From capture, from hunger and slaughter—
Rescue them from the vile Nazi oppressor.

Every man and woman whose soul still aches
The sorrow of our people who now dwell in
    darkness,
Must remember every night and day:
Those fated to perish are awaiting our help.

The oppressor with his murderous sword
Continues to slaughter, ignorant of pity,
The cry of woman and child, and the cry of the old
Is heard from every home, from every community.

And we, upon whom God stood guard
Protecting the Yishuv from harm,
Would willingly make the necessary sacrifice
For those whose fate has been so harsh.

We must all work to help and liberate them,
Those who are imploring us from afar,
We must not yield to the affront of the crime,
Day and night we must keep them in our heart.

Translated by Tsipi Keller.

Other works by Karni: *She'arim* (1923); *Bi-
she'arayikh moledet* (1935); *Shir ve-dema'* (1948); *Shirey
Yerushalayim* (1948); *Bimah ketanah* (1951); *Yalkut
shirim shel Yehuda Karni* (1966); *Shirim* (1992).

A. M. Klein

And in That Drowning Instant
1943

And in that drowning instant
as the water heightened over me
it suddenly did come to pass
my preterite eternity

the image of myself intent
on several freedoms
               fading to
myself in yellowed Basle-print
vanishing

              into ghetto-Jew
a face among the faces of
the rapt disciples hearkening
the raptures of the Baal Shem Tov
explaining Torah

              vanishing
amidst the water's flickering green

to show me in old Amsterdam
which topples

              into a new scene
Cordova where an Abraham
faces inquisitors

              the face
is suddenly beneath an arch
whose Latin-script the waves erase

and flashes now the backward march
of many

             I among them

                to
Jerusalem-gate and Temple-door!

*For the third time my body rises
and finds the good, the lasting shore!*

Else Lasker-Schüler

1869–1945

German poet and playwright Else Lasker-Schüler
was born in Elberfeld, Germany, into a middle-class
family. She moved in 1884 to Berlin, where she trained
as an artist and published her first volume of poetry in
1902. Her first and most important play, *Die Wupper*,
was written in 1908 and performed in 1919 in Berlin.
Her Expressionist stories, essays, and poems were
published widely but, despite winning the Kleist
Prize in 1932, as a Jew she was physically harassed and
threatened by the Nazis. She fled to Palestine in 1934,
settling in Jerusalem where she lived until her death.

My Blue Piano
1943

At home I have a blue piano,
I, who cannot play a note.

It stands in the gloom of the cellar door,
now that the world has grown coarse.

The four hands of the stars play there
—the moonwife sang in her boat—
and the rats come out to dance.

Its keyboard and the works all busted . . . . .
My blubbering enters the blue of death.

O angels, open me your way,
forbidden though it be the living.
I who ate the bitter bread now
call you at the door to heaven.

Translated by Brooks Haxton.

Aaron Leyeles

1889–1966

Aaron Leyeles (born Glanz) was one of the founders of
the Introspectivist movement in modern Yiddish poetry and a champion of free verse. Born in Włocławek,
Poland, he grew up in Łódź. He immigrated in 1909
to the United States, where he studied at Columbia
University and was active in the founding of Yiddish National-Radical schools. In addition to writing
poetry, he was an editor and translator and for more
than a half-century wrote articles on literary, social,
and political events for the New York Yiddish daily
Der tog. His prose appeared primarily under his real
name, Glanz, and his poetry under the name Leyeles.
Like his collaborator and chief rival, Jacob Glatstein,
Leyeles adopted a more traditional poetics in the face
and wake of the Holocaust.

The God of Israel
1943

The God of Israel is not rich.
I saw the Sistine Chapel,
Notre-Dame, the Cathedral of Cologne—
You can feast your eyes on them, you can enjoy.

The God of Israel is stingy.
He won't fill his museum with statues,
Paintings, altars, thrones,

Purple gowns, three-tiered crowns,
He does not wish to live in a Palais.
The Jewish museum has a modest display.

A Chanukah-lamp, a curtain, a scroll,
A spice-box, tefillin, a pointing Hand,
A menorah, a Torah Crown, tools for circumcision,
And an old, ancient manuscript.
And another manuscript and another manuscript,
Entangled, bound, locked together.
Letters in love with letters.

What does the God of Israel ask?
What does the God of Israel demand?
The God of Israel is a just demander.
The God of Israel is a strict demander.
The God of Israel is a stingy demander:
Search by yourself, research by yourself, suffer
    yourself—
For your own and for my honor.

In a gray-gray once-upon-a-time,
From a mountain-top into a valley,
He dropped two handfuls of letters,
Scattered them over the roads of the earth.
They sparkled with speech, blazed with sayings,
And since then—
For thousands of years we seek them,
For thousands of years we save them,
For thousands of years we explain them,
And there is no solution, on earth
For the letters, the sayings, the words.

Another manuscript, and another manuscript,
Entangled, bound, locked together—
Letters in love with letters.

Translated by Benjamin and Barbara Harshav.

Other works by Leyeles: *Fabius Lind* (1937); *A yid oyfn yam* (1947); *Velt un vort* (1958); *Amerike un ikh* (1963).

Peretz Markish

1895-1952

The Yiddish poet, playwright, and essayist Peretz Markish was born in poverty in the town of Polonnoye (present-day Ukraine). The leading expressionist Yiddish poet of his generation, Markish became the voice of the revolution during his sojourn in Poland in the 1920s. In Warsaw, he was a member of the modern-ist group Di khalyastre, and cofounded the journal *Literarishe bleter*. After returning to the Soviet Union, Markish became one of the most decorated and significant members of the Soviet Yiddish intelligentsia, and was a prominent member of the Jewish Anti-Fascist Committee during World War II. Markish was among the Soviet Yiddish writers who were murdered on Stalin's orders on August 12, 1952.

Shards
1943

Now, when my vision turns in on itself,
My shocked eyes open, all their members see
My heart has fallen like a mirror on
A stone and shatters, ringing, into splinters.

Certainly, not every shard is free
To testify about me till my last four destined ells.
But don't you trample on me. Time, my judge,
Till I've recovered from the breakage all the bits.

Piece by piece, I'll try to gather them
To make them whole with stabbed and bleeding
    fingers.
And yet, however skillfully they're glued,
My crippled, broken image will be seen.

In the midst of grief, at last I solve the problem;
In the pain of molten glass, flaming, I see
The self's need to be whole inside the mirror
Which, in the shards, was sown to the seven seas.

Translated by Leonard Wolf.

Other works by Markish: *Di kupe* (1922); *Dor oys dor ayn* (1929); *Der fertsikyeriker man* (1978).

Yehuda Haim Aaron HaCohen Perahia

1886-1970

Ladino poet Yehuda Haim Aaron HaCohen Perahia was a descendant of Spanish Jews who had settled in Italy and were notable in the religious community. Perahia worked for a tobacco company in Xanthi, Greece, and was hidden by a Greek Orthodox family in Athens during World War II. During the war years he wrote several novels, a family history, a book of poetry, and information about the Jews of Salonika.

The Third Cry in Anguish in Salonika
1943

My feet walk the streets of this blessed city,
Only yesterday full of faithful adherents of Sinai.
My eyes do not have the courage to look up.
The bitterness of my soul is great, O Holy God!

I tremble all over. In my memory a troubling image
Presents itself, making me see the enticing
    prosperity
Of the Jewish multitude of this beloved city
That was called "Ir vaem beisrael"[1] for its fidelity.

The contrast with today is sad and sorrowful
    indeed.
Not one Jewish soul exists any longer. It is
    lamentable.
The cemetery, synagogues, houses of study all
    filthily profaned;
All that is Jewish—houses, stores—all were robbed.

Tears run from my eyes and my feet do not stop.
My faithful Anastasia who has served me for twenty
    years
Holds me up to prevent me from falling unconscious
And letting the evil enemies take me in this mental
    state.

"Courage," she repeated, "the God of your sainted
    forefathers,
Who watched over you until today, will save you in
    the not distant future
And you will soon reach a more hospitable land,
Fleeing these wretched enemies in their pursuit."

O Holy God! Who will now read the abandoned
    Torah?
Here there were many groups who read it and lived
    by it.
Who will keep the Sabbath, the great day of rest?
How can You be present as a spectator of this
    tragedy?

When criminal hands burned the Beth Amigdash,
The High Priests threw the keys to Heaven to
    deliver them.
Here, it is the strangers who tore in mockery Your
    holy Law,
Taking away to death all the followers of Your
    faith!

And nevertheless, You had promised our ancestors,
Even in the land of their enemies under Heaven:

"I will be merciful unto them, my children, and I
    shall not destroy them;
In their hours of oppression I shall come to them
    and redeem them."

Lord of the Universe, Lord of the Universe! If You
    were a man
I would have brought You to judgment even in Your
    holy name!
But You are not a man and I blaspheme. And what
    can I do
But cry endlessly, since I cannot conceive
That You should thus have us obliterated by our
    oppressors.
Keep Your promise and send us our saviors quickly.

NOTE
1. ["A Mother and City in Israel"—Eds.]

Translated by Isaac Jack Lévy.

Other works by Perahia: *La famille Perhaia a Thessaloniki* (1943); *Bimba* (ca. 1943); *El ultimo esforso* (ca. 1943); *Poemas* (ca. 1943).

Miklós Radnóti
1909–1944

Miklós Radnóti is widely recognized as one of the greatest Hungarian poets of the twentieth century. He came from a highly acculturated Budapest family and received no Jewish education, remaining indifferent to Jewish affairs his entire life. He and his wife converted to Catholicism in 1943 in a desperate effort to save themselves from further persecution. Although his poems have little Jewish content, they foretell and then record the savagery of the Nazi years. While serving in a forced labor battalion during the war, he was killed by his Hungarian guards.

The Dreadful Angel
1943

The dreadful angel in me is invisible
today, his screeching almost still.
You startle at its whisper. Is it
someone come to pay a visit
or a grasshopper tapping at the sill?
It's he. Oh, he is careful now,
preparing for the season of his fury.
Defend me, if you love me; love me
chivalrously. When you're with me he'll cower,
but when you leave he triumphs in his power.

Out of the soul's cave, in his hour
he rises to accuse me, shriekingly.
Mad again. Like poison, so he works in me,
sleeps but rarely, lives within me
and outside of me. In the white cave
of moonlit night, in rustling sandal, he
runs through the fields to rummage in my mother's
    grave.
Was it worth it then?—he whispers to her,
breaking her sleep; then in a choked, insistent
    breath:
you bore him, and it was your death!
Sometimes he looks at me, rips from the calendar
    each date
awaiting its appointed fate.
Henceforth the how and where
are his to say. Last night
his word fell through my heart, a stone
in a pool, whirling, ringed.
Softly I prepared alone.
You were asleep. Naked and bare
I stood; suddenly he was there

disputing with me how and where.
A ghastly pungence filled the air
and a cold whisper crept into my ear.
"Strip further yet!" he prompted me; "no skin
should cover you, raw nerves and flesh is what you
    are.
Be flayed; for know, only the fool
boasts of the flesh as if it were a jail.
This is your mask of skin; here is the knife;
a sigh; a moment of no pain; the gates of life!"

And on the table there awoke the gleaming knife.

Translated by Zsuzannah Ozsváth and Frederick Turner.

Other works by Radnóti: *Pogány köszöntő* (1930);
Újmódi pásztorok éneke (1931); *Lábadozó szél* (1933);
Újhold (1935); *Járkálj csak, halálraítélt!* (1936); *Cartes
postales* (1937); *Meredek út* (1938); *Naptár* (1942); *Taj-
tékos ég* (1946); *Miklós Radnóti: The Complete Poetry in
Hungarian and English* (2014).

Richard Rodgers and Oscar Hammerstein II
Rodgers, 1902–1979

Born in New York City, Richard Rodgers was a
groundbreaking contributor to musical theater, whose
influence continues to this day. He attended Columbia

University and the Institute for Musical Art (today's
Juilliard School). Rodgers collaborated on songs and
scores with lyricists Lorenz Hart (1895–1943) and
Oscar Hammerstein II (1895–1960). He wrote more
than nine hundred songs and forty Broadway musicals. These include *Oklahoma!* (1943), *South Pacific*
(1949), *The King and I* (1951), *The Flower Drum Song*
(1958), and *The Sound of Music* (1959). The 46th Street
Theatre on Broadway was renamed the Richard Rodgers Theatre in his honor.

Hammerstein, 1895–1960

Lyricist and librettist Oscar Hammerstein II was born
in New York City and attended Columbia University.
One of his first achievements was the musical *Show
Boat* (1927), which he created with the composer
Jerome Kern. After several years in Hollywood, Hammerstein returned to New York, where his partnership
with composer Richard Rodgers led to the production
of Broadway's finest musicals including *Oklahoma!*
(1943), *Carousel* (1945), *South Pacific* (1949), and *The
King and I* (1951). Many of Rodgers' and Hammerstein's joint works were adapted into films.

The Farmer and the Cowman
1943

CARNES: The farmer and the cowman should be friends,
Oh, the farmer and the cowman should be friends.
One man likes to push a plough,
The other likes to chase a cow,
But that's no reason why they cain't be friends.

Territory folks should stick together,
Territory folks should all be pals.
Cowboys dance with farmers' daughters,
Farmers dance with the ranchers' gals.
ALL: Territory folks should stick together,
Territory folks should all be pals.
Cowboys dance with farmers' daughters,
Farmers dance with the ranchers' gals.
CARNES: I'd like to say a word fer the farmer.
AUNT ELLER [*spoken*]: Well, say it!
CARNES: He come out west and made a lot of changes.
WILL PARKER: He come out west and built a lot of fences.
CURLY: And built 'em right across our cattle ranges!

[*Spoken insults are exchanged.*]

CARNES [*trying to make peace*]: The farmer is a good
    and thrifty citizen.
No matter what the cowman says or thinks.

You seldom see 'im drinkin' in a bar room—
CURLY: Unless somebody else is buyin' drinks!
CARNES: But the farmer and the cowman should be
friends,
Oh, the farmer and the cowman should be friends.
The cowman ropes a cow with ease,
The farmer steals her butter and cheese,
That's no reason why they cain't be friends.
ALL: Territory folks should stick together,
Territory folks should all be pals.
Cowboys dance with farmers' daughters!
Farmers dance with the ranchers' gals!
AUNT ELLER: I'd like to say a word for the cowboy.
The road he treads is difficult and stony.
He rides for days on end,
With jist a pony fer a friend.
ADO ANNIE: I shore am feelin' sorry fer the pony!
AUNT ELLER: The farmer should be sociable with the
cowboy.
If he rides by an' asks fer food an' water,
Don't treat him like a louse,
Make him welcome in yer house.
CARNES: But be shore that you lock up yer wife an'
daughter.

[*More insults bring the men close to blows.* AUNT
ELLER *stops the fracas by firing a gun. She points it at*
CARNES *to start him singing again.*]

CARNES: The farmer and the cowman should be friends.
A FEW MEN: Oh, the farmer and the cowman should
be friends.
ALL: One man likes to push a plough,
The other likes to chase a cow,
But that's no reason why they cain't be friends.
IKE SKIDMORE: And when this territory is a state,
An' jines the Union jist like all the others,
The farmer and cowman and the merchant
Must all behave theirsel's and act like brothers.
AUNT ELLER: I'd like to teach you all a little sayin',
And learn the words by heart the way you should.
"I don't say I'm no better than anybody else,
But I'll be damned if I ain't jist as good!"
ALL: I don't say I'm no better than anybody else,
But I'll be damned if I ain't jist as good!

Territory folks should stick together,
Territory folks should all be pals.
Cowboys dance with farmers' daughters!
Farmers dance with the ranchers' gals!

Karl Shapiro
1913–2000

The poet Karl Shapiro was born in Baltimore and attended the University of Virginia. During World War II, he was stationed in the Pacific, writing his anthology *V-Letter and Other Poems* while serving in New Guinea; the book was awarded the Pulitzer Prize for Poetry in 1945. After the war, Shapiro edited the magazine *Poetry*, and taught at the University of Nebraska, Lincoln and later at the University of California at Davis. Shapiro received the 1969 Bollingen Prize for Poetry and was the poetry consultant at the Library of Congress (forerunner of the title U.S. poet laureate). He died in New York City.

Lord I Have Seen Too Much
1943

Lord, I have seen too much for one who sat
In quiet at his window's luminous eye
And puzzled over house and street and sky,
Safe only in the narrowest habitat;
Who studies peace as if the world were flat,
The edge of nature linear and dry,
But faltered at each brilliant entity
Drawn like a prize from some magician's hat.

Too suddenly this lightning is disclosed:
Lord, in a day the vacuum of Hell,
The mouth of blood, the ocean's ragged jaw.
More than embittered Adam ever saw
When driven from Eden to the East to dwell.
The lust of godhead hideously exposed!

Other works by Shapiro: *Person, Place, and Thing* (1942); *Essay on Rime* (1945); *A Bibliography of Modern Prosody* (1948); *Poems of a Jew* (1950); *Reports of My Death* (1990); *The Wild Card: Selected Poems Early and Late* (1998); *Selected Poems* (2003); *Coda: Last Poems* (2008).

Noah Stern
1912–1960

Hebrew poet and translator Noah Stern was born in Jonava, Lithuania. He immigrated first as a teenager to the United States, where he attended Harvard and was admitted to graduate studies at Columbia. He moved to Palestine in 1935, where he translated for the newspaper *Davar* and taught in a high school in Tel Aviv. During World War II, Stern served in the Jewish brigade. He translated T. S. Eliot's *The Waste Land*, to good reviews, and Richard Wright's *Black Boy*. However, his own works were recognized only after his suicide, two years after serving a five-year term in prison for attempted murder.

In Sand and Water
1943

In sand and in water
You will yet raise expectant eyes,
Or eyes
As indifferent as death to machine-gun bullets and
　borders on maps.

Together with you
Yet another sought to escape
(At long last to escape)
The ugly beasts,
Yet another believed he'd partaken of your moldy
　bread
(Or did not partake and died like a helpless infant)
And gazed without hope upon rivers and seas.

In such a world one is not ashamed to die,
But in such a world the wonder does not cease:
How can it be?
How has it not come to ruin yet?
(Such an eerie reality,
Such ugly beasts!)

Yet any apparent peace is a deceit,
The tremor is active still.
They are as yet unseen, but they will come,
　unknown winds,
New as the renewable earth, ancient as prophecies,
To excise the rot,
To build anew.

Translated by Tsipi Keller.

Other work by Stern: *Beyn 'arfilim* (1966).

Abraham Sutzkever
1913–2010

The renowned Yiddish poet Abraham (Avrom) Sutzkever was born in Smorgon (in present-day Belarus) and spent his formative years studying and writing in Vilna, a center of Jewish intellectual life at the time. He

fought in the partisan underground during the Nazi occupation of Poland, entered the Soviet Union following the war, and finally settled in Mandatory Palestine in 1947. The following year he founded the Yiddish literary quarterly *Di goldene keyt*. His writings have been widely translated.

How?
1943

How and with what will you fill
Your cup on the day you're free?
Will you in your joy still
Hear the scream of the past
Where the skulls of chained days
Clot in bottomless pits?

Searching hopelessly
For the keys to jammed locks,
You'll chew pavement like bread
And think it was better before,

And time will gnaw your hand gently
Like a cricket under the floor.

In a rubble-encrusted old city
Your memory will be like a hole,
And your glance will burrow furtively
Like a mole, like a mole.

Translated by C. K. Williams.

Other works by Sutzkever: *Lider fun geto* (1946); *Yidishe gas* (1948); *Poetishe verk*, 2 vols. (1963); *Griner akvaryum: dertseylungen* (1975); *Fun alte un yunge ksav-yadn* (1982); *A. Sutzkever: Selected Poetry and Prose* (1991).

Abraham Sutzkever

A Load of Shoes
1943

The cartwheels rush,
quivering.
What is their burden?
Shoes, shivering.

The cart is like
a great hall:
the shoes crushed together
as though at a ball.

A wedding? A party?
Have I gone blind?
Who have these shoes
left behind?

The heels clatter
with a fearsome din,
transported from Vilna
to Berlin.

I should be still,
my tongue is like meat,
but the truth, shoes,
where are your feet?

The feet from these boots
with buttons outside
or these, with no body,
or these, with no bride?

Where is the child
who fit in these?
Is the maiden barefoot
who bought these?

Slippers and pumps,
look, there are my mother's:
her Sabbath pair,
in with the others.

The heels clatter
with a fearsome din,
transported from Vilna
to Berlin.

Translated by C. K. Williams.

Władysław Szlengel
1914–1943

Poet, journalist, and actor Władysław Szlengel was
born in Warsaw. In the 1930s, he emerged as an up-
and-coming poet and songwriter who wrote, exclusively in Polish, on Jewish themes, antisemitism, and
the worsening political situation. Szlengel played a
major role in the cultural life in the Warsaw ghetto.
His poetry was widely copied and declaimed while
his *The Living Newspaper*, with its witty parodies and
satires of ghetto life, became a mainstay of the nightly
shows at the Sztuka Café, which also featured the best
singers, actors, and pianists. As conditions worsened
in the ghetto, Szlengel's searing poetry touched many

themes: fear of death, anger at the Jewish police, Jewish bitterness at Polish indifference to their plight,
and, in January 1943, exaltation at the first outbreak of
Jewish armed resistance. Szlengel was killed during
the Warsaw ghetto uprising in May 1943.

Things
1943

From Hoza Street and Marszalkowska
carts were moving, Jewish carts:
    furniture, tables and chairs,
    suitcases, bundles
    and chests, boxes and bedding,
    suits and portraits,
    pots, linen and wall hangings
    cherry brandy, big jars and little jars,
    glasses, tea pots and silver—
    books, knickknacks and everything
    go from Hoza Street to Sliska.
    A bottle of vodka in a coat pocket
    and a chunk of sausage,
    on carts and wagons and rickshaws
    the gloomy band is going.
And from Sliska Street to Niska everything
all over again went moving:
    Furniture, tables and chairs,
    suitcases and bundles,
    and pots—gents that's it.
    Now there is no carpet,
    of silverware not a sign,
    no cherry brandy this time.
    No suits or boots
    or jars or portraits.
    Already all these trifles
    were left behind on Sliska.
    In the pocket a bottle of vodka
    and a chunk of sausage,
    on carts and rickshaws and wagons
    the gloomy band is going.
They left Niska again and everything
headed for the apartment blocks.
    No furniture or stools,
    no jugs or bundles.
    Teapots have vanished,
    books, boots, little jars.
    Suits and silverware
    dumped together in a pushcart,
    all went to the devil.
    There is still a suitcase, a coat,

a bottle of tea
and piece of candy.
On foot, without any wagon
goes the gloomy procession.
Then, from the apartment blocks to Ostrowska,
moving along a Jewish road
    with no big bundles or little bundles,
    no furniture or chairs,
    no teapots and no carpet,
    no silverware or jars,
    in the hand one suitcase,
    a warm scarf and that's it.
    Still a bottle of water
    and a knapsack with straps.
    Trampling objects underfoot like a herd
    they walked down the streets at night.
And on a cloudy day, at dusk, they walked
from Ostrowska to the Blockhouses.
    A small suitcase and a knapsack,
    no need for anything else,
    evenly . . . evenly by fives
    they marched down the streets.
Nights cooler, days shorter,
Tomorrow . . . maybe day after tomorrow . . .
    to a whistle, a shout or command
    on the Jewish road again
  hands free and only
  water—with a strong pill.
From the Umschlagplatz across the city
all the way to Marszalkowska,
life, Jewish life, is growing
in houses that are empty.
In abandoned apartments
abandoned bundles,
suits and down covers
and plates and chairs.
A woodfire still smolders,
spoons lie there idly,
there are family photographs
scattered in a hurry.
A book lies still open,
a letter in mid-sentence: "bad . . ."
a glass not drunk
and playing cards, half a hand of bridge.
Through a window the wind stirs
the sleeve of a cold shirt,
an eiderdown cover indented
as if someone nestled there.
Ownerless things lie around,

dead apartment stands waiting
until new people
populate the rooms; Aryans—
they will close the open windows,
begin a carefree life
and make these beds,
these Jewish eiderdowns
and wash the shirt,
put the books on a shelf and empty
the coffee from the glass,
together they will finish the hand of bridge.
While in a wagon
only this will remain;
a bottle half-empty
with a strong pill . . .
And in the night of fear that will come,
after days of bullets and swords
    all the Jewish things will come out from chests
        and houses.
    And they will run out through the windows,
        walk down the streets
    until they meet on the roads,
    on the black rails.
    All the tables and chairs
    and suitcases, bundles
    the suits and jars
    and silverware and teapots
    will leave, and disappear,
    and no one will guess what it means
    that the things have departed,
    no one will see them.

But on the judge's table
(if *veritas victi*)
a pill will remain
as a *corpus delecti*.

Translated by John and Bogdana Carpenter.

Other work by Szlengel: *What I Read to the Dead* (1979).

Ion Degen

1925-2017

Ion Degen was born in Mogilev-Podolski (present-day Ukraine) to parents with medical careers. He was wounded many times during World War II, receiving several decorations. His poem "My Comrade Is in His Final Agony" reflects the deep Soviet patriotism of that generation of Soviet Jews born after the revolution. His encounters with Jewish partisans during the liberation of Vilna in 1944 made a lasting impression on him. Degen devoted the rest of his life to medicine. Disillusioned by Soviet antisemitism, he emigrated in 1977 to Israel, where he published poetry, short stories, and essays. Degen played a major role in publicizing the sacrifice of the five hundred thousand Jews who fought in the Red Army.

As You Die There in Agony, Brother
1944

As you die there in agony, brother,
Don't be calling your comrades in vain.
Let me warm my hands on your body,
Make good use of the blood from your veins.

Stop crying, stop groaning, don't be a baby.
You're not wounded. You're simply dead.
For keepsake, let me take off your felt boots
We still got to attack up ahead.

Translated by Alexandra Hoffman.

Other works by Degen: *Iz doma rabstva* (1986); *Portrety uchitelei* (1992); *Gologrammy* (1996); *Nevydumannye rasskazy o neveroiatnom* (1998); *Hasledniki Nasledniki Asklepiia* (2006).

Jacob Fichman
1881–1958

Born in Belz, Galicia, the Hebrew poet, critic, and editor Jacob Fichman received both a secular and religious education. In 1901, he left home for Odessa, joining its lively circle of writers. In 1912, he settled in Palestine, where he edited various Hebrew journals, including the prestigious *Moznaim*, the journal of the Hebrew Writers Association, from 1936 to 1942. He distinguished himself in a variety of genres: children's literature, textbooks, literary essays, and poetry, including sonnets, idylls, ballads, and narrative poems. His poetry bridged the romantic tone of Bialik's generation and the modernist outlook of the following generation.

Corner of the Field
1944

After a long stay in the city, I was glad to go out, to travel as far as the Sharon, full of eagerness for fields, colors, green light. But to my misfortune, I fell into a crowded bus, crammed, stifling. I barely squeezed into the body of the bus; to my right and left passengers, suitcases, and bundles were piled up. I saw straight away that there was no solution, and I sought nothing but a place for my feet. But a foul mood possessed the passengers, like an additional woe in a time of sorrow. It seemed to everyone that his fellow was the cause of the crowding, and if it weren't for him, everything would be fine. The passengers standing in the aisle, instead of making things easy, made things hard for one another, complained, cast bitterness at one another. A fine-looking brunette, whose beauty alone should have brought ease to the entire bus, complained loudly about an unseen person whose valise tripped up her feet, and the glory of her face was spoiled, nothing remained of it except oriental dryness, heat, without a single drop of the grace that had been emitted just a moment before.

At last the bus moved, passing quickly through the open, vacant streets of the suburb, in which dry horse manure was strewn in the sun. It was as if something of the light from outside of the city was cast into our narrow cage. The people fell silent, stood there immersed in themselves, accepted their fate. But there was no ease. The more we rode, the more the stifling became heavier than it had been.

Suddenly through an open window a wave of wind, and when I turned my face toward it, a strip of merry green sparkled in my eyes. Below us a bit of grass appeared, but imbued with such a moist glow, that all of my being clung to it. Finally there was something for my tired eyes to grasp. It was the green splendor that arose from the corner of a field at the side of the highway, shining without cease, and it drew me after it, as if many fields of sunlight, imagined, were stretched behind it in infinite space. That strip of grass flickered, appearing from time to time in true beauty, with new grace—as though including within it all the hidden grace that sank from view behind it.

For a long while I no longer felt the crowding around me. Above the tumult in the bus, these pieces of greenery signaled to me—damp with dew, pure, shining—and the more they appeared, the more they added light and moisture; nothing detracted from their glow. Though they were tiny and transitory, they sustained the presence of spring—the imagined fields, dappled, extending behind them in infinite greenery.

All the world's greenery was intimated to me in that narrow corner of a field.

NOTE
[The work is a prose poem about a Jewish bus ride emerging from a nightmare.—Eds.]

Translated by Jeffrey M. Green.

Other works by Fichman: *Demuyot kedumim* (1948); *Beney dor: mesaprim, meshorerim, ishim* (1952); *Aviv ba-'aretz* (1959); *Kitvey Ya'akov Fikhman* (1959).

Yitshak Katzenelson

1885–1944

Yiddish and Hebrew poet and playwright Yitshak Katzenelson was born in Karelitz, Belorussia. His family moved to Łódź, where Katzenelson was a founder and director of private Hebrew schools; he also wrote textbooks and children's books. In his poetic style and themes, he was strongly influenced by Bialik as well as by the works of Heine. He also founded several theater groups. In 1939, Katzenelson fled to Warsaw, where he continued to teach and to self-translate. He was sent by the Germans to the camp in Vittel and was then deported to Auschwitz. He kept a diary, found after the war, that exposed the conditions under Nazi rule. The Ghetto Fighter's House and museum at Kibbutz Loḥamei Hageta'ot in Israel are dedicated to Katzenelson's memory.

Song of the Murdered Jewish People
1944

Canto IX. To the Heavens

And thus it came to pass, and this was the
　beginning . . . Heavens tell me, why?[1]
Tell me, why this, O why? What have we done to
　merit such disgrace?
The earth is dumb and deaf, she closed her eyes.
　But you, heavens on high,
You saw it happen and looked on, from high, and
　did not turn your face.

You did not cloud your cheap-blue colours,
　glittering in their false light.
The sun, a brutal, red-faced hangman, rolled across
　the skies;
The moon, the old and sinful harlot, walked along
　her beat at night;
And stars sent down their dirty twinkle, with the
　eyes of mice.

Away! I do not want to look at you, to see you any
　more.

False and cheating heavens, low heavens up on high,
　O how you hurt!
Once I believed in you, sharing my joy with you, my
　smile, my tear—
Who are not different from the ugly earth, that heap
　of dirt!

I did believe in you and sang your praises in each
　song of mine.
I loved you as one loves a woman, though she left
　and went.
The flaming sun at dusk, its glowing shine,
I likened to my hopes: "And thus my hope goes
　down, my dream is spent."[2]

Away! Away! You have deceived us both, my people
　and my race.
You cheated us—eternally. My ancestors, my
　prophets, too, you have deceived.
To you, foremost, they lifted up their eyes, and you
　inspired their faith.
And full of faith they turned to you, when jubilant
　or grieved.

To you they first addressed themselves; *Hearken, O
　Heavens, you*[3]—
and only afterwards they called the earth, praising
　your name.
So Moses. So Isaiah[4]—mine, my own. *Hear, O hear*,
　cried Jeremiah, too.[5]
O heavens open wide, O heavens full of light, you
　are as Earth, you are the same.

Have we so changed that you don't recognize us, as
　of old?
But why, we are the same—the same Jews that we
　were, not different.
Not I . . . Not I will to the prophets be compared, lo
　and behold!
But they, the millions of my murdered ones, those
　murdered out of hand—

It's they . . . They suffered more and greater pains,
　each one.
The little, simple, ordinary Jew from Poland of
　today—
Compared with him, what are the great men of a
　past bygone?
A wailing Jeremiah, Job afflicted, Kings despairing,
　all in one—it's they!

You do not recognize us any more as if we hid
　behind a mask?

But why, we are the same, the same Jews that we
were, and to ourselves we're true.

We're still resigned to others' happiness. Saving the
world we still see as our task.

O why are you so beautiful, you skies, while we are
being murdered, why are you so blue?

Like Saul, my king[6] I will go to the goddess Or,
bearing my pain.

In dark despair I'll find the way, the dark road to
Ein Dor; I shall

From underground awaken all the prophets there—
Look ye again,

*Look up to your bright heavens, spit at them and tell
them: Go to Hell!*

You heavens, high above, looked on when, day and
night,

My people's little children were sent off to death, on
foot, by train.

Millions of them raised high their hands to you
before they died.

Their noble mothers could not shake your blue-
skinned crust—they cried in vain.

You saw the little Yomas, the eleven-year-olds,
joyous, pure and good;

The little Bennys, young inquiring minds, life's
remedy and prize.

You saw the Hannas who had born them and had
taught them to serve God.

And you looked on . . . You have no God above you.
Nought and void—you skies!

You have no God in you! Open the doors, you
heavens, fling them open wide.

And let the children of my murdered people enter in
a stream.

Open the doors up for the great procession of the
crucified.

The children of my people, all of them, each one a
God—make room!

O heavens, empty and deserted, vast and empty
desert, you—

My only God I lost in you, and they have not enough
with three:

The Jewish God, the holy ghost, the Jew from
Galilee—they killed him, too.

And then, not satisfied, sent all of us to heaven,
these worshippers of cruelty.

Rejoice, you heavens, at your riches, at your fortune
great!

Such blessed harvest at one stroke—a people
gathered in entire.

Rejoice on high, as here below the Germans do,
rejoice and jubilate!

And may a fire rise up to you from earth, and from
you strike, earthwards, devouring fire!

Canto XV. It's All Over

The end. At night, the sky is aflame. By day the
smoke coils and at night it blazes out again. Awe!

Like our beginning in the desert: A pillar of cloud
by day, a pillar of fire by night.[7]

Then my people marched with joy and faith to new
life, and now—the end, all finished . . .

All of us on earth have been killed, young and old.
We have all been exterminated.

Why? O don't ask why! Everybody knows, all
gentiles, good and bad,

The worst helped the Germans, the best closed one
eye, pretending to be asleep—

No, no, nobody will demand a reckoning, probe,
ask why.

Our blood is cheap, it may be shed. We may be
killed and murdered with impunity.

Among the Poles they looked for freedom fighters,
only for those suspected

Of patriotism . . . They murdered many Russians in
villages and towns—

"Partisans." Among us, they killed babies in their
cribs, even the unborn.

They led us to Treblinka and before killing turned
to us and said:

"Get undressed here. Put your clothes in order,
shoes in pairs, leave your belongings.

You'll need your clothes, shoes and other personal
effects. You'll soon be back!

You just arrived? From Warsaw? Paris? Prague?
Saloniki? Take a bath!"

A thousand enter the hall . . . A thousand wait
naked until the first thousand are gassed.

Thus they destroyed us, from Greece to Norway
to the outskirts of Moscow—about seven
million,

Discounting Jewish children in wombs. Only the
pregnant mothers are counted.

And if Jews remain in far-away America and in nearby Eretz Israel—demand these children too from the world. Demand.

Demand the murdered unborn children. Demand those gassed in their mothers' wombs.

Why? No human being the world asks why, yet all things do: Why?

Each vacant apartment in thousands of towns and cities asks: Why?

Listen, listen: Apartments will not stay vacant and empty homes will not remain empty.

Another people is moving in, another language and a different way of life.

Rising over Lithuanian or Polish towns, the sun will never find

A radiant old Jew at the window reciting Psalms, or going to the synagogue.

On every road peasants will welcome the sun in wagons, going to market.

So many gentiles—more than ever, yet the market is dead. It is crowded, yet seems empty.

Never will a Jew grace the markets, and give them life.

Never will a Jewish *kapota* flutter in markets on sacks of potatoes, flour, porridge.

Never will a Jewish hand lift a hen, pet a calf. The drunken peasant

Will whip his horse sadly, return with his full wagon to the village. There are no more Jews in the land.

And Jewish children will never wake in the morning from bright dreams.

Never go to *ḥeder*, never watch birds, never tease, never play in the sand.

O little Jewish boys! O bright Jewish eyes! Little angels! From where? From here, yet not from here.

O beautiful little girls. O you bright pure faces, smudged and disheveled.

They are no more! Don't ask overseas about Kasrilevke, Yehupetz.[8] Don't.

Don't look for Menachem Mendels, Tevye the Dairyman, Nogids, Motke thieves.[9] Don't look—

They will, like the prophets, Isaiah, Jeremiah, Ezekiel, Hosea, and Amos from the Bible,

Cry to you from Bialik, speak to you from Sholem Aleichem and Scholem Asch's books.

Never will the voice of Torah be heard from *yeshivoth*, synagogues and pale students,

Purified by study and engrossed in the Talmud . . . No, no, it was not pallor but a glow,

Already extinguished . . . Rabbis, heads of *yeshivoth*, scholars, thin, weak prodigies,

Masters of Talmud and Codes, small Jews with great heads, high foreheads, bright eyes—all gone.

Never will a Jewish mother cradle a baby. Jews will not die or be born.

Never will plaintive songs of Jewish poets be sung. All's gone, gone.

No Jewish theater where men will laugh or silently shed a tear.

No Jewish musicians and painters, Barcinskis,[10] to create and innovate in joy and sorrow.

Jews will fight or sacrifice no longer for others.

They will no longer heal, soothe someone's pain, forgetting their own.

O you foolish gentile, the bullet you fired at the Jew hit you too.

O who will help you build your lands? Who will give you so much of heart and soul?

And my hot-headed Communists will no longer bicker and argue with my Bundists,

Neither will they wrangle with my liberty-loving, devoted and conscientious

Halutzim who offered themselves to the world, not forgetting their own woe.

I watched the disputes and grieved . . . If only you could continue to argue and stay alive!

Woe is unto me, nobody is left . . . There was a people and it is no more. There was a people and it is . . . Gone . . .

What a tale. It began in the Bible and lasted till now . . . A very sad tale.

A tale that began with Amalek and concluded with the far crueller Germans . . .

O distant sky, wide earth, vast seas. Do not crush and don't destroy the wicked. Let them destroy themselves!

NOTES
1. Echoes the opening lines of Bialik's "Upon the Slaughter."
2. Allusion to the popular song *Di zun fargeyt in flamen*, "the Sun Sets in Flames."
3. Deut. 32:1, *Ha'azinu hashamayim*.
4. Isa. 1:2.

5. Jer. 2:12, *shomu shamayim*.
6. See 1 Sam. 28.
7. Exod. 13:21–22.
8. Kasrilevke, Yehupetz—fictional towns in Sholem Aleichem's oeuvre.
9. Menachem Mendel, Tevye—Sholem Aleichem's major fictional characters.
10. Hanoch Barcinski—painter and illustrator; killed in 1942.

Translated by Jacob Sonntag (Canto IX) and Noah H. Rosenbloom (Canto XV).

Other works by Katzenelson: *Die zun fargeyt in flamen* (1909); *Dimdumim* (1910), *Vittel Diary* (1964).

Koro Saloniko
1940s

Also known as the Grupo de Reskatados de los Kampos de Alemania (the Group of Liberated Inmates from the German Camps), the Koro Saloniko (or Choir of Salonika) was a group of young Sephardic Jews from the city of Thessaloniki who sang during their internment in Auschwitz. Their tunes were known to blend traditional folk forms, such as the short Iberian form known in Ladino as the *kantiga*, and other melodies, ascribing new words or meanings to songs that already held deep meaning among the Sephardic inmates. This act of resistance took on a special meaning for its performers and listeners, as Sephardic Jews often felt isolated in Auschwitz by their inability to understand Yiddish or German.

In Polish Lands
1944

Trees cry for rain
And mountains for air.
So cry my eyes
For you, dear Mother;
So cry my eyes
For you, dear Mother.

I turn and I ask what will become of me.
In Polish lands
I am destined to die.

White you are and white you wear;
White is your face.
White flowers fall from you,
From your beauty;

White flowers fall from you,
From your beauty.

I turn and I ask what will become of me.
In Polish lands
I am destined to die.

Translated by Isaac Jack Lévy.

Stefánia Mándy
1918–2001

Poet and art historian Stefánia Mándy was born in Budapest, where she studied humanities at the university. In 1944, she was deported to Auschwitz; her experiences there influenced the nature of her poetry, much of which was not allowed to be published during the communist regime in Hungary. After the war, Mándy taught at Pázmány Péter University. She received the Jószef Attila prize for poetry in 2001.

Consciousness
1944

our lightless awful days are passing
splinters of memories prick our brains
daily our Creator beats us using both hands
we are his dry weeds husked to the core

for us fire is no fire for us it is death
the earth for us is no earth it is hell
not for us green gardens our hearts about to stop
I can see my brother a silent statue

slow decay with blackened wings sprinkles
fine ashes on the deep lap of the fields
our hearts have burned up our souls have burned
     up too
only our bodies keep crying flickering aching

with mindless mind and heartless heart
I am crying for you distant lands
how I'd love to give birth to rolling hills
give my blood to the lazily rolling danube

give birth to my mother take her in my arms
o friends loneliness is a deep well
the well of madness silence sits on the mind
into my arms I'd take my mother my mother

silence sits on the mind night sits on the land
consciousness tortures us we huddle together

we want it to tear at us to hurt us
wide-eyed owls today is the day we go blind

Translated by Imre Goldstein.

Other works by Mándy: *Vajda Lajos* (1983); *Az ello-pott tortenelem: Versek, 1944–1992* (1992); *Scintilla: Uj es valogatott versek* (1999).

Muriel Rukeyser

1913–1980

Born in New York City and educated at Vassar College and Columbia University, Muriel Rukeyser was a poet deeply committed to the ideals of social justice, equality, and feminism. Her first book, *Theory of Flight*, published in 1935, earned her the Yale Younger Poets prize. Her politically inspired poetry dealt with industrial disasters, the Scottsboro Case, the Spanish Civil War, and the war in Vietnam.

Letter to the Front

1944

To be a Jew in the twentieth century
Is to be offered a gift. If you refuse,
Wishing to be invisible, you choose
Death of the spirit, the stone insanity.
Accepting, take full life. Full agonies:
Your evening deep in labyrinthine blood
Of those who resist, fail, and resist; and God
Reduced to a hostage among hostages.
The gift is torment. Not alone the still
Torture, isolation; or torture of the flesh.
That may come also. But the accepting wish,
The whole and fertile spirit as guarantee
For every human freedom, suffering to be free,
Daring to live for the impossible.

Other works by Rukeyser: *A Turning Wind* (1939); *Beast in View* (1944); *Elegies* (1949); *The Life of Poetry* (1949); *Body of Waking* (1958); *The Speed of Darkness* (1968); *Breaking Open* (1973); *The Gates* (1976); *The Collected Poems of Muriel Rukeyser* (1979).

Hanna Szenes

1921–1944

Resistance fighter, Zionist, and poet Hanna Szenes (Senesh) was born into an assimilated Jewish family in Budapest. In the 1930s, Szenes moved to Palestine, where she joined Kibbutz Sedot Yam. In 1942, she became a parachutist and was trained by the underground Haganah organization to rescue prisoners of war and organize Jewish resistance in Europe. In March 1944, Szenes was dropped into Yugoslavia. She made her way across the Hungarian border, where she was arrested and killed by the Hungarians. In 1950, her body was interred on Mt. Herzl in Jerusalem. Her diary from her teenage years was published in 1971.

Blessed Is the Match

1944

Blessed is the match, consumed in kindling flame.
Blessed is the flame that burns in the heart's secret
  places.
Blessed is the heart that knows, for honors sake, to
  stop its beating.
Blessed is the match, consumed in kindling flame.

Translated by Marie Syrkin.

Other work by Szenes: *Hannah Senesh: Her Life and Diary* (1971).

Malka Heifetz Tussman

ca. 1896–1987

Born in Ukraine, Malka Heifetz Tussman immigrated to the United States in 1912. She lived in Wisconsin and California and became a Yiddish-language poet, loosely aligned with the introspectivists Jacob Glatstein and A. Leyeles. She taught in Yiddish secular schools and at the University of Judaism in Los Angeles. Her themes addressed Jewish women in history, the natural world, and love. Heifetz Tussman published six volumes and wrote for numerous Yiddish journals. She received the Manger Prize for Yiddish Letters in 1981.

You'll Return with God's Help

1944

You will come back.
You will, with God's help, come back
With a far-off, alien look.
(I'm preparing myself,
I already know,
I've seen how they come back.)

You will sit in your regular chair, unsure
And silent
With nothing to tell.
And I won't know how,
And I won't be able to heal your stark silence.
So with quiet words, I will
Stroke the horror you bear in your spirit
And begin to build a belief for you
In what I no longer believe.

You will, with God's help, come back,
And your nearest and dearest will look strange to you.

My hand on your shoulder,
Your bed and your pillow,
Your plate, your spoon, your fork,
And all that waited for you.
In the midst of everything,
You will not
Grasp anything,
Nor make the connection.
And I will not know
How or what to do
To make light shine beyond your confusion.

You will, with God's help, come back
With a faraway look.
And how we do things will be strange to you.
Embarrassed,
I'll pick up
A green twig to show you,
A red flower.
I'll drag down from the attic
An old toy of yours.
I'll tempt you with smells
Of home cooking.
And you'll
Tighten your lips,
To choke back a groan.

Making a clown-face, I'll celebrate—
My arms waving and my shoulders shaking
Like the hands moving
Around a clock with its old numbers worn off.
I'll point out all we've achieved:
The Empire State Building,
The towers,
The bridges,
The trains,
And everything that Whitman praised . . .

Astounded, you won't respond.
The sadness deep in your eyes
Won't even smile at my senseless babble.

But I will try
Not to grow tired
In building a belief for you
In what
I no longer believe . . .

And
At the first curious glint
That lights up your eyes
I will bow deeply
And turn around
And bow more deeply
Facing backwards
Towards my very own sadness,
Towards my very own sadness.

Translated by Kathryn Hellerstein.

Other works by Heifetz Tussman: *Lider* (1949); *Am I Also You?* (1977); *With Teeth in the Earth: Selected Poems of Malka Heifetz Tussman* (1992).

Julian Tuwim
1894–1953

Julian Tuwim was born into an assimilated Jewish family in Łódź. He studied law and philosophy in Warsaw, where he played an integral role in Polish modernist literary circles. In addition to writing poetry for children and adults, Tuwim was a lyricist, translator, and dramatist, active in the poetic group Skamander. Tuwim wrote exclusively in Polish and stressed his allegiance to Poland while downplaying his attachment to Judaism. He lived in the United States during World War II and returned to Poland after the war, where he expressed deep sympathy for Jews who were killed in the Holocaust.

We Polish Jews
1944

4

"All right," someone will say, "granted you are a Pole. But in that case, why 'we JEWS'?" To which I answer: BECAUSE OF BLOOD "Then racialism again?" No, not racialism at all. Quite the contrary.

There are two kinds of blood: that inside of veins, and that which spurts from them. The first is the sap of the body, and as such comes under the realm of physiologists. Whoever attributes to this blood any other than biological characteristics and powers will in consequence, as we have seen, turn towns into smoking ruins, will slaughter millions of people, and at last, as we shall yet see, bring carnage upon his own kin.

The other kind of blood is the same blood but spilled by this gang-leader of international Fascism to testify to the triumph of his gore over mine, the blood of millions of murdered innocents, a blood not hidden in arteries but revealed to the world. Never since the dawn of mankind has there been such a flood of martyr blood, and the blood of Jews (not Jewish blood, mind you) flows in widest and deepest streams. Already its blackening rivulets are flowing together into a tempestuous river. AND IT IS IN THIS NEW JORDAN THAT I BEG TO RECEIVE THE BAPTISM OF BAPTISMS; THE BLOODY, BURNING, MARTYRED BROTHERHOOD OF JEWS.

Take me, my brethren, into that glorious bond of Innocently Shed Blood. To that community, to that church I want to belong from now on.

Let that high rank—the rank of the Jew Doloris Causa—be bestowed upon a Polish poet by the nation which produced him. Not for my merit, for I can claim none in your eyes. I will consider it a promotion and the highest award for those few Polish poems which may survive me and will be connected with the memory of my name—the name of a Polish Jew. [...]

5

We Polish Jews . . . We, everliving, who have perished in the ghettos and camps, and we ghosts who, from across seas and oceans, will some day return to the homeland and haunt the ruins in our unscarred bodies and our wretched, presumably spared souls.

We, the truth of the graves, and we, the illusion of living; we, millions of corpses and we, a few, perhaps a score of thousands of quasi non-corpses; we, that boundless brotherly tomb, we, a Jewish burial ground such as was never seen before and will never be seen again.

We, suffocated in gas-chambers and turned into soap—a soap that will not wash clean the stains of our blood nor the stigma of the sin the world has perpetrated upon us.

We, whose brains spattered upon the walls of our miserable dwellings and the walls under which we were stood for mass execution solely because we were Jews.

We, the Golgotha upon which an endless forest of crosses could be raised. We, who two thousand years ago gave humanity a Son of Man slaughtered by the Roman Empire, and this one innocent death was enough to make Him God. What religion will arise from millions of deaths, tortures, degradations and arms stretched wide in the last agony of despair?

We Abies, we Kikes, we Sheenies[1] whose names and nick-names will some day exceed in dignity those of Achilles, Boleslaus the Brave, and Richard Coeur-de-Lion.

We, once more in the catacombs, in the manholes under Warsaw pavements, splashing in the stink of sewers to the surprise of our companions—the rats.

We, rifle in hand upon barricades, amidst the ruins of our homes bombed from the sky above; we—soldiers of honor and freedom.

"Kike, go and fight!"[2] He did, Gentlemen, and laid down his life for Poland.

We, who made a fortress of every threshold while house after house crashed about us.

We, Polish Jews growing wild in forests, feeding our terrified children on roots and grass; we crawling, crouching, bedraggled and unkempt armed with an antique shotgun obtained by some miraculous feat of begging and bribing.

"Have you heard the one about the Jewish gamekeeper? It's a riot. The Jew fired; and by golly if he didn't wet his pants from fright! Ha! Ha!"

We, Jobs, we Niobes, mourning the loss of hundreds of thousands of our Jewish Urszulkas[3] . . .

We, deep pits of broken, crushed bones and twisted, welted bodies;

We—the scream of pain! A scream so shrill that the most distant ages shall hear it. We—the Lament, the Howl, we—the Choir chanting a sepulchral El Mole Rachamim whose echo will be passed from one century to the next.

We—history's most glorious heap of bloody manure with which we have fertilized the Polish soil so that the bread of freedom may be sweeter for those who will survive us.

We, the macabre remnants, we—the last of the Mohicans, the pitiful survivors of slaughter whom some new Barnum may well exhibit throughout the world, proclaiming upon multi-colored billboards: "Super Show! The biggest sensation of the World! Genuine Polish Jews. Alive!" We, the Chamber of Horrors, Schreck-enskammer, Chambre des Tortures! "Nervous persons better leave the audience!"

We, who sit and weep upon the shores of distant rivers, as once we sat on the banks of Babylon. All over the world does Rachel bewail her children, and they are no more. On the banks of the Hudson, of the Thames, of the Euphrates and the Nile, of the Ganges and Jordan we wander, scattered and forlorn, crying: "Vistula! Vistula! Vistula! Mother of ours! Grey Vistula turned rosy not with the rosiness of dawn but that of blood!"

We, who will not even find the graves of our mothers and children, so deep are the layers, so widely spread all over the country in one huge burial ground. There will be no one sacred plot upon which to lay our flowers; but even as a sower sows grain so shall we fling them in a wide gesture. And, one maybe will find the spot.

We, Polish Jews . . . We, the legend dripping with tears and blood. A legend, perhaps, fit only to be told in Biblical verses "graven with an *iron pen and read in the rock forever" (Job* 19:24). We—the Apocalyptical stage of history.

NOTES

1.The original consists of a string of names and nicknames for Jews which were common in Polish.

2. In the original: "*Jojne, idź na wojnę!*"—"Jonah, go to war!"—a well-known Polish rhyme which mocks the Jews for their lack of military aptitude.

3. Urszulka—the daughter of the famous Polish poet Jan Kochanowski (1530–1584) who died in her youth. Her father's collection of elegies upon her death *Treny* (1580—"Dirges") is very famous in the literary and cultural traditions of Poland. In the original English translation "Jewish Urszulkas" was rendered as "little ones."

Translated by "Mrs. R. Langer."

Other works by Tuwim: *Czyhanie na Boga* (1918); *Sokrates tańczący* (1920); *Siódma jesień* (1922); *Biblia cygańska* (1933); *Wspomnienie o Łodzi* (1934); *Słowa we krwi* (1936); *Treść gorejąca* (1936); *Lokomotywa* (1938); *Słoń Trąbalski* (1938); *Zosia Samosia* (1938); *My, Żydzi Polscy* (1944); *Kwiaty polskie* (1949); *Pegaz dęba* (1950).

Ella Amitan

1900–1995

A poet, translator, and author of children's books, Ella Amitan was born in Yurev, Russia (now Tartu, Estonia) and immigrated to Palestine in 1925, where she studied at the Hebrew University. She translated works by Goethe, Balzac, Heine, and Hugo into Hebrew. Amitan served in the British army during World War II and was a pioneer in the revival of Hebrew as a modern language with its own literature. Her *Yareah pikeah* (1938) was one of the first Hebrew books composed for children. Amitan's song "Bi-medinat ha-gamadim" is sung by kindergarten children in Israel to this day.

In the Army

1945

> With evening a whistle. Again the sweating store
>   room
> opens its throat wide, and we march out in
>   formation
> worn down by the heat wave and a day so long:
> hard working soldier-women.
>
> And why should you say: biblical figures these,
> verses of song and heroics
> of Yael and Deborah . . . .
> Weary again, with evening we march in formation
> hard working soldier-women.

Translated by Rachel Tzvia Back.

Other works by Amitan: *Lakh u-lekha: shirim* (1949); *Mered ha-perahim: sheloshah mahazot li-yeladim* (1953); *Pirhey neshiyah* (1963); *Temunot min ha-album: shirim* (1985).

Kadya Molodovsky

1894–1975

The Yiddish poet Kadya Molodovsky was born in Bereza Kartuska in Belorussia, where she received a broad Hebrew and secular education. Active throughout her life as a teacher and advocate of children, she produced celebrated Yiddish children's verse that continues to delight Israeli children in Hebrew translation. Her Warsaw years, from 1921 to 1935, were her most productive as a poet, critic, and public figure. In 1935, she joined the expatriate Polish–Yiddish colony of writers in New York, where the focus of her poetry shifted from social to national themes. In America, she and her husband Simkhe Lev published *Svive*, a little magazine, which provided a forum for Isaac Bashevis Singer and other important writers and where Molodovsky serialized her autobiography.

God of Mercy
1945

O God of Mercy
Choose—
another people.
We are tired of death, tired of corpses,
We have no more prayers.
Choose—
another people.
We have run out of blood
For victims,
Our houses have been turned into desert,
The earth lacks space for tombstones,
There are no more lamentations
Nor songs of woe
In the ancient texts.

God of Mercy
Sanctify another land.
Another Sinai.
We have covered every field and stone
With ashes and holiness.
With our crones
With our young
With our infants
We have paid for each letter in your
    Commandments.

God of Mercy
Lift up your fiery brow.
Look on the peoples of the world.
Let them have the prophecies and Holy Days
Who mumble your words in every tongue.
Teach them the Deeds
And the ways of temptation.

God of Mercy
To us give rough clothing
Of shepherds who tend sheep
Of blacksmiths at the hammer
Of washerwomen, cattle slaughterers
And lower still.
And O God of Mercy
Grant us one more blessing—
Take back the divine glory of our genius.

Translated by Irving Howe.

Other works by Molodovsky: *Yidishe kinder* (1945); *Der Melekh Dovid aleyn iz geblibn* (1946); *In Yerushalayim kumen malokhim* (1952); *A House with Seven Windows: Short Stories* (1957).

Jacques Taraboulos
1919-2011

Jacques Taraboulos was born in Cairo and studied at the Colegio Rabbinico of Rhodes and at the École rabbinique de Paris. Taraboulos then lived in Elizabethville in the Belgian Congo (now Democratic Republic of the Congo), where, with Robert Joseph Cohen, he wrote for and published the series *Études juives*, writing about Jews of the Middle Ages and discussing the religions of the Middle East. The destruction of Jewish lives during the Holocaust affected his outlook, and his poems are collected in the undated work *Poèmes tristes*.

The Neila
1945

The end of the day approaches.
The Book of Life and Death
is about to be closed,
and the hand of God will inscribe
the destiny of man.

It hesitates, trembles, stops.
A voice, sweet and frail,
an imperceptible murmur,
rises toward the firmament;
it is a young Jew who prays.
His soul, hurled toward Heaven,
reaches the Holy of Holies.

The Ark is opened wide,
and the Torah is there.
Science and Wisdom.
And a sweet murmur,
like a song in space,
emerges from the Ark.
The soul of the child blends with the Torah
and the Torah prays with him.

For the dead, the burned,
the cadavers that had no grave,
the bones that were bleached in the sun;
for the past misery, and that to come,

the time that was, and that will be
for the sobs of the newborn
who cries on seeing the light;
for the suffering of men,
of creatures, of flowers,
of delicate grass crushed by the passerby,
of the rose in bloom that a bee consumes;
for all that suffers and cries,
and whose voice does not reach
the soul of man.

And the Eternal grew sad from the sadness
of the soul,
and the voice of the Torah rose up to Him.
The sin is in man, O Father,

and forgiveness is Yours,
and love is Yours,
O Great God of Love.

And the Book of Life and Death
did not close at all with the prayer of the Neila,
because the voice of the child
burst from his heart
and, as the water of a stream
goes to join the river,
his soul had rejoined with the Torah,
and the Torah is in God,
and the Torah is God.

Translated by Isaac Jack Lévy.

ISRAEL (1946–1973)

This section underscores the ongoing, creative, and fraught tension between dreams and reality, between a soaring Zionist narrative of idealism and the real challenges of building a new society. Tensions between veterans and immigrants, between religious and secular, and among different ethnic groups complicated the task of forging the new state of Israel.

On the one hand, this is a time of a powerful collectivist ethos shaped by Prime Minister David Ben-Gurion's faith in the transformative power of the new Jewish state. Israeli leaders sought to harness the sacrifices of the War of Independence as they confronted the stark necessity of providing a shared identity to millions of newcomers, both survivors of the Holocaust and Jews from Arab lands. On the other hand, this period witnessed a growing rebellion against this collectivist ethos, which expressed itself in many cultural arenas: in poetry and prose, in life writing and journalism, and in the arts. Writers examined the right to be different, to live a life apart from the collective. Essayists refused to accept pressures to reject two thousand years of Jewish diaspora history. Critics asked searching questions about how artists could create a distinctive Israeli culture that was both original and responsive to international trends.

All the while, Israelis from across the cultural spectrum had to examine the searing legacy of the Holocaust and how this inheritance affected the identity of the new state. In terms of sheer cultural creativity, these early years of statehood have few parallels in Jewish history. And while the rebirth of the Hebrew language had begun some decades before statehood, only now did it flower and develop as never before.

ANTHOLOGIES

Binyamin Tenenbaum
1914-1999

Binyamin Tenenbaum (later Tene) was an author and Polish-to-Hebrew translator who emigrated from Warsaw to Palestine in 1937. He helped establish Kibbutz Eilon in the Western Galilee. In 1946, Tenenbaum returned to Poland with the help of poet Władysław Broniewski to collect testimonies of Jewish child survivors of the Holocaust, which Tenenbaum translated into Hebrew.

One of a City and Two of a Family
1947

The book being presented to the reader represents a selection of a thousand autobiographies composed by Jewish children, survivors of the conflagration, tender children who lived for months and even for years, in the ghettos, in extermination camps, in villages and cities, among the ranks of partisans. The autobiographies do not constitute formal testimonies but were noted down by the children themselves, each child in his own handwriting, each child in his own style and with his own unique approach toward the recounting of what occurred. These were collated in orphanages and children's assembly centers in Poland and also in seventeen refugee camps in Germany in which survivors of the Jewish children in Poland were detained in residence (Darmstadt, Stuttgart, Frankfurt-am-Main, Sulzheim, Lindenfels, Eschwege, Schwebda, Landshut, Rosenheim, Jordanbad, Ulm, Indensdorf [*sic*], near Dachau, Feldafing, Fernwald, Bad Reichenhall, Landsberg [am Lech], Hildenheim [*sic*]). Out of the vast material, seventy characteristic autobiographies have been selected, translated, and presented here, which, taken in conjunction, offer a complete picture—the [significant] events of the lives and the struggles for survival of a generation of children who grew to maturity and who witnessed the world during its darkest era.

What is the unique feature of these autobiographies? What distinguishing mark sets them apart from other writings and books about this period composed by adults?

Besides the historical facts recounted in them, they are distinguished by that genuineness and directness of characterization, stemming from the perspective of the child and its feelings. They are lacking the self-criticism to which adult authors can lay claim, in lesser or greater measure, but their very defect is also their advantage. The simplicity of the narrative and the calmness of its flow remind us of an ancient saga or of the pages of the Bible, which are likewise narratives of historical events, descriptions of events presented without blue and red makeup, without superfluous detail and extra coloring. The young composers speak in the language of facts—a typically faithful chronicle of deeds and events, where the specific detail, over which all these children became so emotional, is silent and hidden behind a curtain, but its charming eyes and its restrained breathing are there, lying concealed between the lines. [. . .]

Our authors—the youngest of whom was two years old and the eldest twelve at the outbreak of the war—and primarily the older ones amongst them, alone elevate themselves far above the factual account, peering out, so to speak, at the events at a distance of years, and with the perspective of adulthood that they have now attained, they reflect literary tones within their lines: "The wheels of the train [the death-wagons] struck the gaskets on the tracks, and it seemed as though they were intoning the melody of death," writes Benjamin Kulig. "I was like a leaf, driven about by the wind after it has fallen from the tree," writes Witold Weinman. But most interesting of all are the songs that have been appended to the autobiographies—songs that were composed at the time, right in the midst of the days of terror and the Holocaust, and the eldest of their composers had not yet reached the age of bar mitzvah. Isaac Digala, whom the hangmen forced to witness the hanging of twenty Jews, created a song about them ("I composed a poem about them"). In the beginning of the song, in the refrain, the anonymity of the description of the "twenty," and in the description of the preparations surrounding the hanging, and the expectations of the twenty who witnessed everything—there are incorporated several of the principles of the classical ballad. [. . .]

Psychologists will come along and investigate, also on the basis of these autobiographies, the character of these child-authors. They will unravel and explain which traits became crystallized within the children during the days of terror, which feelings intensified, which experiences had become intrinsically settled within their hearts, which fountains of their souls had been stopped up, and which spiritual limbs had been totally cut off. Writers will come along and examine these deeds: torn leaves, which had fallen off the truncated tree, the report of which reached us from the midst of the huge, silent graveyard. A future [Hans Christian] Andersen will come along and read the story of the young girl who was among Christians, whose soul was bound in love with a six-year-old Jewish child—a child from the street—how she brought her a piece of bread daily, and how the bitter day arrived when the rabble pelted the little girl with stones, until she was eventually left lying on the sidewalk in a pool of blood. "It seemed to me," writes the young girl Marisa Wasser, "that the sky, smiling with blueness and sunshine, was collapsing on the tops of the houses, and the faces of the men turned black, all in one clump."

Or the story of the young boy who succeeded, after several days of traveling in a death-wagon, to bend his fingers so as to form a hollow of his hand, to bring a little snow into the suffocating railroad car, but he handed it over not to his brother, who was fainting with thirst, but to a little girl who was dying; and his little brother burst out crying and said: "I am not at all thirsty!"

There is the story about a little girl of four years who fell asleep on her father's back when he was fleeing together with her from a death pit.

There is the story of a mother who, with her own hands, dug out a bunker hole for her children in the forest.

There is the story of a girl who dragged her frozen sister seven kilometers through a forest until she arrived at a place of human habitation, and concealed her in the snow.

And there is the story of children forcibly converted [to Christianity] who used to go over Jewish words while lying on their beds, to prevent them being entirely forgotten.

As mentioned above, we have presented here seventy out of the one thousand autobiographies that I have collated. Most of them were written in Yiddish and Polish, and a small minority in Russian. I have added nothing at all. I have not introduced flowery language. Rather, the weakness of the idiom in the writing of the children is, so to speak, a natural melody that does not lend itself to imitation, and it conceals within itself a multiplicity of obstacles and stumbling blocks. I was not always so bold as to adopt this method, and I finally decided—after much hesitation—to render it in a simple yet essentially revised idiom, containing no element of artificiality insofar as the work of the translator is concerned—apart from the occasional biographical statements, here and there, of a frankly childish nature. It does not always depend just on the age of the writer, whose style in its pristine form reflects their very essence. I have, on occasion, condensed what they wrote, and I have invariably added punctuation marks and separated words that should not be combined. I have ignored such errors as were not possible to correct.

I have divided the book into various sections: Warsaw, Vilna, ghettos, the camps, life in the forests and in the villages, and partisans. To these sections I have added "snippets"—biographical fragments selected on account of their containing a novel element. The division of the sections is only an approximate one; a child who was initially in the ghetto may have been transported to a camp and eventually fled to the forest, or wandered around with partisans; and it was not always a straightforward matter to create such divisions within the main body of the work. [. . .]

The children are sitting on the ruins in Poland, learning Hebrew and preparing themselves for aliyah. The sound of their voices, trilling a Hebrew melody, breaks through onto German soil and onto the coasts of France and Italy. They are making aliyah: embarking on ships as intrepid pioneers and knocking violently on the doors of our homes and finding them locked. They are dragged along, cast onto the ships of the great British Empire, and transferred to camps in Cyprus. A large number of the autobiographies presented here were written by children who embarked on the ship *Exodus 1947* and were cruelly driven away from the shores of the Holy Land, en route back to Germany. The great empire dealt the souls of these mini-Jobs yet a further, incurable blow.

But our hearts beat in unison with the hearts of the afflicted ones. May our sunshine effect a healing of their wounds, may our homes be a refuge for the orphaned and abandoned! And when we present to our own communities and children the stories of the lives of the little daring pioneers, we once again extend our hands above and beyond the barbed electric fences [of the concentration camps] and the distant span of time, and we strengthen the distant wanderers as sons and brothers.

Translated by David E. Cohen.

Other works by Tenenbaum: *Mekhorah* (1939); *Masa ba-galil* (1941); *Temolim al ha-saf* (1947); *Dani dan u-telat ofan* (1952); *Kezir ha-pele* (1957); *Shirim u-fo'emot* (1967).

Dov Sadan

1902–1989

Israeli academic and politician Dov Sadan (later Shtok) was born in Brody, Galicia (present-day Ukraine) and received a traditional Jewish education. He was a member of the He-Haluts youth movement during World War I and immigrated to Palestine in 1925. Sadan wrote and edited for the newspaper *Davar* and the publishing house Am Oved. He was appointed head of Yiddish studies at the Hebrew University in 1952 and later taught Hebrew literature at Tel Aviv University. Sadan also served as a member of the Knesset for the Labor Alignment party between 1965 and 1968. Adopting a holistic approach to Jewish literature in all languages, he produced innumerable studies in Jewish intertextuality.

A Bowl of Raisins, or A Thousand and One Jokes
1949

Three Comments

Jewish humor of recent generations, in all its manifestations—jokes, puns, witticisms, and anecdotes—has found patrons within *Our Language* [a Hebrew-language periodical] and already comprises an array of books whose objective is to collect, sort, and classify this treasure. Outstanding among these are the important works of Alter Droynov (*Sefer ha-bediḥa ve-ha-ḥidur* [*Book of Jokes and Puns*]) and M. Lipson (*Dorot* [*Generations*]), both of which are broad-based and extremely varied. The major objective driving these works also sheds light on the present collection offered to the reader. However, the author—and this title especially suits a book such as this—views this document as based on a precondition: what appears in this book is based on *oral transmission*, to which the author himself can testify. *I heard it with my own ears*, because he wrote down *what* he heard and from *whom he heard it* (and there is no rule without an exception, though it be minimal, and this applies to the most widely told joke or to a joke recounted by someone who wishes to remain anonymous, as well as to those few jokes that have been conveyed in writing—given the distances involved). Naturally, complying with this condition restricts the range of jokes collected here to the scope and nature of an author's own life experiences. Nevertheless, the loss of breadth is offset by the authenticity of the material.

His extensive knowledge and memory notwithstanding, the author has taken pains to include in this book items heretofore unpublished in a literary format. An *Our Language*-type presentation, both in *content* and in *style*. He has made a special effort to include remote areas and corners of the world that have received little or no attention from his predecessors. He has even endeavored to add more comprehensive information to the central points, so as to present each joke in all its nuances. He hopes that, in so doing, he has contributed to the study of our humor, which requires collecting material from every source, and that the reader will easily discover the uniqueness of this book in all its sections and appendixes. The footnoted comments and observations for each joke are intended to serve the student reader (especially embedded phrases and foreign words), and sometimes there are observations that are mini-studies in themselves (replete with examples). In order to apprise the reader of a joke's development, a comparison has been made of its different versions with our basic books on joke-telling, and notes have been added regarding its connection or the multifaceted aspects to our aphorisms, as well as many observations on the mechanics of jokes and the many ways they can be told.

The book's structure is mostly by person, and they are arranged in various formats, according to culture, spirit, trends, circles, etc.—sometimes by subject. The sections, which are constructed by person in the various formats, also have subsections, wherever possible, which are arranged chronologically. The detailed structure of this volume will be readily apparent to the reader. Two keys have been provided at the end of the book for the reader's benefit.

Dov Sadan
Tel Aviv, April 1949

1

602

The story goes that when M. M. Ussishkin published his pamphlet *Our Plan*, he was approached by a young man about training high-school students to be pioneers in Israel. Ussishkin replied by emphasizing the damage to the enterprise—which requires an explanation because the expectation of a *charter* is that one is released from practical work. And this is how he put it:

"Unless we release ourselves from this *chort*, nothing will get done."

(As told by Dr. Anshel Shtrumwasser.)

The word *chort* is Slavic and means *demon*.

603

A group of people were talking about M. M. Ussishkin's way of doing things. Some took one side, others another. Shemaryahu Levin said:

"And I will tell you only one anecdote. When Ussishkin's son was born, he wanted to assemble guests for a mitzvah meal, and he asked me to help him make up a list, to which I agreed. We sat at the table and he spread out a large piece of paper; then, he took a pencil and began writing: Me . . .' "

(As told by Asher Beilin.)

604

(A) Shemaryahu Levin was giving a public lecture on Palestine when a member of the audience stood up and cut him off angrily:

"I was in Palestine for several years; what do you think you can teach me?"

Shemaryahu Levin responded calmly:

"A person can eat potatoes for twenty years; that doesn't make him a botanist."

(As told by Natan Rotenstreich.)

For a reverse way of using this witticism, see Friedrich's letter to the House of Gedoren (1753) decrying those commentators of classical literature: "They who would rummage through variant readings or words, without understanding their underlying meaning or spirit. They are like people who stir the wine but don't drink it." [. . .]

(B) Shemaryahu Levin was giving a public lecture on Zionism when he was heckled by anti-Zionist proponents of Marxism. He replied:

"In the past, our adversaries laid a proper foundation for debate, for their reasoning was taken from Marx's own works. Nowadays, our opponents lay no such proper foundation, for their arguments are taken from pamphlets written by those who have lapped at the waters of the pupils of Marx's disciples. And there is no comparison between someone who makes a livelihood from one's full capital and a person who ekes out a living from its paltry interest."

(As told by Shlomo Landkutsh.)

605

Once, a group of people were talking about someone, saying that his erudition did not match his intelligence and that often his folly was no less than his ugliness. Shemaryahu Levin said:

"That person is comparable to a creature standing on a table and trying with all its might to cover its boils with its tail."

When asked, "Why was it standing on the table?" he replied, "To reach up."

(Anonymous.)

See Bernstein-Siegel, 1609: *Er nemt zein kherpah un dekt zein bushah damit tsu.* ([Yiddish] He takes his disgrace and covers it with his shame.)

The matter of standing on the table is well-known and has various versions. For example, there is the story of Hershele Ostropolyer, who, in his youth, came home injured and scarred, and when his mother asked what had happened to him, he replied that he had bitten his nose. And when his mother asked him how he had managed to reach his nose, he replied, "I climbed onto a chair." Another version is told by Ludwig Barna, concerning his rival, Mayer: "They wrote me about him, saying that he was so tall that his head could reach as high as the Tower of Babel. I too want to reach that height; so, if I ever run into him, I will climb onto a chair and kiss him enthusiastically (*Letters from Paris*, 59).

And Druyanov, 2894, cites a story about a boy whose forehead was injured and bleeding, and said that he had bitten himself on the forehead with his teeth. When he was asked how he had reached his forehead with his teeth, he replied that he had climbed onto a chair.

606

Once, a group of people were talking about those whose knowledge of our language was acquired by reading chrestomathies [collections of selected literary passages for learning a language] and the like. Shemaryahu Levin said:

"What an ignoramus. He can read the entire Passover Hagaddah in a Sephardic accent with the proper melody, and yet he still gets it wrong."

(As told by Dr. Natan Rotenstreich.)

607

Shemaryahu Levin was once asked:

"Herzl was a great man. So how come he associated with all these little people, like so-and-so, who was both mean-spirited and of lowly character?"

He replied:

"And did you think that only a small head has lice? A large head can also have them."

(As told by Mordechai Yaffe.)

608

A) Shemaryahu Levin, listening to the demands of the Uganda proponents speaking in favor of having territory, said:

"You think you need terri*tory*? What you need is a sani*torium*!"

(As told by Jacob Leshchinsky.)

B) Sitting in a Tel Aviv café, Shemaryahu Levin said:

"There is an advantage and a disadvantage to the coffee in Tel Aviv. The advantage is that it contains no chicory; its disadvantage is that it contains no coffee."

(As told by Efraim Broida.)

V. M. Naiman writes: "Prof. Moshe Weizman once said, while sitting over a cup of coffee: "As a chemist, I must say that this coffee has the virtue of containing no chicory; however, there is also something missing; it has no coffee in it." (*Davar Ha-Shavua*, no. 144)." That is to say that this joke is attributed to various people, and Droinov, 807, attributes it to Kalev Letz.

Translated by Marvin Meital.

Other works by Sadan: *Al sifrutenu masat-mavo* (1950); *Al S. Y. Agnon* (1959); *Avney bedek* (1962); *Beyn she'ilah le-kinyan* (1968); *Heymishe ksovim: shrayber, bikher, problemen* (1972).

Yitzhak Zuckerman and Moshe Basok

The biography of Yitzhak Zuckerman is included above in the selection *Suffering and Heroism in the Jewish Past in the Light of the Present*, where he is called by the name Antek Zuckerman.

Basok, 1907–1966

A poet, translator, and editor who also wrote under the name M. Bik, Moshe Basok was born in Kovno and grew up in Vilna, also studying at the Slobodka yeshiva. Basok moved in 1936 to Palestine, where he edited newspapers, documented Jewish resistance during World War II, and worked for the publisher Ha-kibbutz Ha-me'uhad.

The Book of the Ghetto Wars: Between the Walls, in the Camps, in the Forests
1954

The Book of the Ghetto Wars is intended to bring together a selection of the materials in our possession—testimony, journals and notes, documents, studies, poems, and stories—that were created during the Holocaust and after it, as an expression of Jewish revolt and rebellion in the former territory of the Republic of Poland. Other countries in Europe—to the east, west, and south of Poland, which fell into the hands of the conqueror and whose Jewish inhabitants joined in the anti-Nazi front by a series of acts of resistance—merit their own anthologies.

Witnesses from among the remnants, who witnessed the horrors of that time in their own flesh, and Jewish historians, to the extent that they dealt with this period at all, placed rows of bricks to build the literature of destruction; the number of their publications has already reached two thousand. The vast majority of German documents that have been discovered, testimony of the tyrants to their own abominations, also discuss the extermination of the Jews in the ghettos and camps.

It is necessary for Jewish historiography to preserve not only the loss—one side of the reality of the ghetto—but also to reveal to its full extent the heroic struggle of the nation, the community, and the individual in the time of the destruction and in the places of destruction themselves.

Circumstances have prevented the Jewish revolt from being engraved upon the national memory, except in its striking symbols such as the April revolt in [the] Warsaw [ghetto]. Of the thousands of underground members and ghetto fighters only a few are left; from the rebels in the death camps only individuals were saved. Just a few of the Germans' documents touching upon the movements of Jewish revolt have been preserved. For there were such documents, as confirmed by the General Stroop's report on the Warsaw [ghetto] uprising and by the document of General Katzmann on the elimination of the fighters in Brody—documents discovered by chance.[1]

Only a few dozen books of testimony have been written about the rebellions, and, despite their importance, they discuss only three or four places of revolt. For inexplicable reasons, the literature of the partisans is even more meager, although many of the fighters in the forests managed to reach the day of liberation. A few historians devoted their research to the fate of certain cities and certain times. However, the wars of the ghettos—this great chapter in Jewish history—still lack comprehensive, inclusive research.

The Book of the Ghetto Wars seeks to give voice to Jewish revolt in all its manifestations and forms of expression, to unfold its broad extent and manifold power. Indeed, a battle cry rises and bursts from its pages, the cry of dozens of large and small settlements, of fighters who fell, of those who remained alive, of poets and authors who followed their struggles from close at hand and from afar.

Certainly only a few of the manifestations of resistance shown by the nation in the days of horror have come down to us. Many documents, testimonies, and journals were obliterated in the bunkers of the ghetto, in the primeval forests, in the crematoria, along with those who wrote them. Many were the villages, especially on the eastern border, in places where all their Jews perished in *Aktionen*. However, by chance something is known to us of their rebellions from the non-Jewish residents or from denunciations of the murderers.

The Holocaust is the general framework of the book. The roots of the wars of the Jews are planted in it. The ghetto, the camp, and the forest—the areas of Jewish life in the times of horror—are also the three main sections of the book: three equal limbs of human courage. The Holocaust—the shocked earth, the rebellion—the bursting lava.

The wars of the ghettos, were, one may say, the battle for life, and perhaps only for death with honor, a death different from the one decreed by the enemy. "Battle" means every deed against the interest and decrees of the violent invader, in public and in secret, by a community or by an individual, organized and planned or appearing suddenly, at the last moment, with a weapon—and even only with a courageous stand, in protest, with a brave voice.

The fate of revolt was a foregone conclusion. The rebels—their end was destruction. Nevertheless, they exist in the memory of the generation. Did their stifled dreams not nourish a generation of fighters for the liberation of the land, for the state of the Jews? May this book, the book of the struggles of a destroyed generation, be a bridge for continuity, for the future.

NOTE

1. [The Stroop Report, formally titled "The Jewish Quarter of Warsaw Is No More!" was a comprehensive recounting of SS General Jürgen Stroop's quelling of the Warsaw ghetto uprising. This report was later used as evidence during the Nuremberg trials, as was SS General Fritz Katzmann's documentation of the liquidation of the Brody ghetto.—Eds.]

Translated by Jeffrey M. Green.

Other works by Basok: *Dos bukh fun der nay-erets-yisroeldiker poezye, antologye* (1936); *Brenendike teg* (1937).

Dan Ben-Amotz and Haim Hefer

Ben-Amotz, 1923–1989

Dan Ben-Amotz, born Mosheh Tehilimzoger in Poland, was an Israeli novelist, playwright, journalist, and actor. He served in the British Army in Palestine and then in the Palmach during Israel's War of Independence. A well-known figure, Ben-Amotz became the model for the native Israeli sabra figure, as he masked his East European autobiographical details until late in his life.

Hefer, 1925–2012

Born in Sosnowiec, Poland, Haim Hefer immigrated to Palestine with his family in 1936. Hefer joined the Palmach at age seventeen and, during his service, was a founding member of Israel's first military entertainment troupe, the Chizbatron. His songwriting and poetry from the early years of the Israeli state were vital to the development of the nation's cultural identity.

A Bag of Lies
1956

Our associates claim—and in moments of weakness we tend to agree—that this compilation has no need for introduction because the subjects speak for themselves. In addition, we cannot ignore the possibility that a large proportion of the readers—in particular those who did not tread the dusty road between the years 1942 and 1948, who did not sip strong coffee from empty tin cans in bright nights around a campfire of castor and eucalyptus twigs, who did not hear the tall tales from the masters of storytellers themselves—might find it difficult to understand the language, in which the subjects speak for themselves. To them, in particular, these words of explanation are addressed, and as for the others . . . oh to hell with the others.

Therefore, let us proceed directly to the task and endeavor to illuminate the source of the term *kazav* in a few strokes, as well as its specific interpretation. *Kazav* is a close translation of the Arabic word *chizb*, a word that was extremely common among the members of the settlements, the sentinels of the field, and the first generation of the Palmach, until it lost its value during the War of Independence, when the veterans of the trade unions and the senior journalists began to utilize the term with troublesome excessiveness, inaccurately, and with a wantonness that lowered the value of its stock in the market of exclusivity. When these and others who knew not to distinguish between *chizb* and "lie" began to conjugate the word (I *chizbed*, you *chizbed*, they *chizbed*)—probably desiring to become more identified with those rogues and to prove to what extent they themselves are in the center of things—the word was buried in a modest ceremony by the "union of truth tellers" and on its tomb the word *kazav* blossomed. Thus far is history.

What is the interpretation of the word *kazav*? If you will, a *kazav* is a story that is entirely, mostly, or partly, a lie, exaggeration, hoax, and/or all three together, and/or none of them, since there is a respectable difference between the three terms. A lie is when no one knows the truth except for the teller. A hoax is when everyone knows the truth except for the victim of the hoax. *Kazav* is when everyone knows that the story is a lie, and yet all are willing to hear it again and again. And this too is not entirely accurate. Not every lie, even though everyone knows that it is a lie, automatically becomes a *kazav*. Usually, only after a great deal of sanding and polishing can a lie be transformed into the higher realm of *kazav*. Many lies have been told in Israel since the meeting of Herzl with Kaiser Wilhelm—and many of them expired as soon as they were created. Only those that stood the test of time, that succeeded in passing through all the torments of popular criticism, those that contained something extra beyond the level of joke or a hoax—and that which we are unable, to our sorrow, to explain—only those that were baked over numerous campfires and retained their bouquet like old wine, have been included in one of the folders in this compilation.

Despite numerous claims, not all the *kazavim* were created in the Palmach. In the best of cases, the Palmach was an incubator, a selector, and a distiller. Numerous stories circulated in which a *ghaffir* in a kalpak hat was the symbol of heroism, and perhaps even before that period.[1] Some of the stories came from people whose connection with the Palmach was exceedingly frail. The Palmach itself created numerous stories or perhaps merely quoted stories that suited it, or that reflected in essence the relationship of that generation to the holy tongue and difficulties they encountered. We would not be surprised, of course, if [the folklore historian] Dov Sadan discovers in these pages *kazavim* that are reminiscent to him of refinements of stories from Lvov or Berlin. We can do nothing about this, since Dov Sadan is capable as we know of proving that there are relationships between the stories of the Africans and the Rabbi of Belz. [. . .]

On this occasion, it might be worth noting that any similarity between the heroes of *kazavim* and personalities among us is not at all accidental, although that in conjunction with the similarity between the contents of *kazavim* and certain historical events—the antithesis is possibly true. [. . .]

The Refrigerator

When they hung the locks on the door of the [commune's] refrigerator, the comrades didn't know what to do. And the saga of the nocturnal inspection of the refrigerator house would have certainly ended had it not been for Yoshke's novel invention. In the wall of the refrigerator house was a hole through which the blocks of ice were removed. Yoshke would lean against the hole until his body shrunk a little from the cold and the other guys would shove him inside. After he had thoroughly inspected the contents of the crates he would take sour cream, apples, chocolate, and sometimes even ice cream. He could get out by himself because inside the fridge his body would have shrunk even more. One night he stuck his head out of the hole and the refrigerator stopped working. His body swelled up and that's how they found him in the morning.

Philosophy

Melancholy Nissan studied philosophy for a year. When he came to Tel Yosef he was sent to work in construction. That evening the builder came to the project manager and said with a pale face: "Get him away from me. I can't take it any longer. Imagine, I'm standing on the scaffolding on the second floor and suddenly he asks me, 'Listen, how do you know that you really exist?'"

The Volunteer

Abu Lesh wasn't the only one who volunteered for the Palmach. Everybody volunteered. But he always talked about it. Once, when he was tired of his work in the vegetable garden of Ein Ha-horesh, he reported to the platoon commander and said, "Listen Buddy, either you send me on a mission or I volunteer out of the Palmach."

NOTE

1. [A *ghaffir* was member of a special police force in British Mandate Palestine created in cooperation with the Haganah, whose task was to protect transit routes and Jewish settlements. Kalpak hats were traditional tall-headwear throughout the Ottoman Empire and Caucasus, adaptable to warm and cold climates.—Trans.]

Other works by Ben-Amotz: *Yalkut ha-kezavim* (1956); *To Remember, to Forget* (1968); *Yofi shel milhamah* (1974). Other works by Hefer: *Mishpahat ha-palmah: yalkut 'alilot ve-zemer* (1973).

Translated by Karen Alkalay-Gut.

Shlomo Tanai, Azriel Okhmani, and Moshe Shamir

Tanai, 1919–2000

Born in Bielsko, Poland, writer and journalist Shlomo Tanai (also spelled Tanny) immigrated to Palestine with his family at a young age. After training as a journalist in France and the United States, Tanai returned to Israel in the 1940s to help define a new generation of Israeli literature. He joined the staff of *Haaretz* in 1944, working as a war correspondent in 1948. In addition to his own prolific oeuvre as a poet, children's author, and translator, Tanai worked widely as an editor of books and magazines.

Okhmani, 1907–1978

Born in Poland, Azriel Okhmani (also spelled Ukhmani) studied agronomy in France before immigrating to Palestine in 1932. Besides his agricultural efforts, Okhmani was a prolific literary critic and helped to found and edit several early Israeli newspapers and literary journals, including *Al ha-Mishmar* and *Ittim*. Okhmani was also a committed member of the left-wing political party Mapam, and in the late 1940s, he served as a counselor at the Israeli embassy in Warsaw.

Shamir, 1921–2004

Moshe Shamir, born in Safed and educated in Tel Aviv, was an Israeli politician, novelist, playwright, and journalist who popularized the idea of the sabra,

the strong, native "new" Israeli. During Israel's War of Independence, Shamir served in the Palmach. After the Six-Day War, Shamir moved from the left to the right of the Israeli political spectrum. He served in the Knesset from 1977 to 1981. The author of more than fifty books, Shamir received the Israel Prize for Hebrew Literature in 1988.

A Generation in the Land
1958

Plans for the anthology of fiction and poetry now presented to the Hebrew reader arose in our minds several years ago, but particularly the tenth anniversary of the State of Israel was found to be most appropriate for its publication. This is the first literary anthology of this generation of our literature, whose time and growth overlap with the time and growth of the State of Israel. [...]

It is possible to imagine the anthology before us as a section cut out of the map of the state, which is enlarged with emphasis on the important and fascinating details. [...]

Quite a few considerations were taken into account by the editors when they came to compose the list of participants in this anthology. Most of the participants were chosen from among authors of the Land of Israel whose writing is based on the land, whether they were born here or whether they immigrated in their youth, and their first appearance was around World War II and the period of struggle. Of these, only those whose works appeared in books were considered, though not everyone who published a book was included. The decisive consideration for the purposes of the editors was the literary level and, not infrequently, consideration of the subject, that is to say: we could not present chapters of a work that were not marked by the land. [...]

Thirty-three writers, of whom seventeen write prose and sixteen write poetry, almost all of them in the fourth decade of their lives, are represented in this anthology: one story each by the writers of fiction, except for a few cases when a section of a larger work is given; and of the poets, either a group of poems that possess unity of their own, or a selection of the poet's work, as a kind of cross-section of their poetry. [...]

The choices were made by the editorial board, with the agreement of the participants, with the intention of offering what is characteristic and excellent for each one of the writers, without ignoring the traits of the generation in general, and the Israeli subject matter, in labor and defense, in the life of the youth, and the landscape.

Finally, we express deep gratitude to all the authors and poets who responded cordially and with friendship to our invitation and provided all the help that was needed, and also to the artistic photographer, Yehudit Sheftel, who spared no effort or pains in providing photographs of the participants.

Translated by Jeffrey M. Green.

Other works by Tanai: *Agadat ha-bayit ha-tsohek* (1962); *Shirey shlomo tanai* (1972); *Mishhakey shir* (1978). Other works by Okhmani: *Kolot adam* (1967); *Emor pela'im, saper ekh kemo sa'ar shememi* (1973). Other works by Shamir: *With His Own Hands* (1951); *The King of Flesh and Blood* (1954); *David's Stranger* (1956); *My Life with Ishmael* (1968).

S. Y. Agnon

The Making of This Book
1959

What makes a book like this more than just a collection of excerpts, strung together interchangeably? What makes it a *book*? If I were to say it had been a matter of selection, who would venture to choose among the words of the Sages, pronouncing some of them acceptable and some not? And if I were to say I had based this composition on the books I happened to own, why, nowadays, when great treasure houses of books are open to all, no author of a book such as this could claim to have done the job by relying only on what was at hand. Thus the question remains. And the answer is: when I set about to compile this book I saw that it would be impossible to make it all of a piece, in a uniform style; and as for making a review of the literature, there is no end to the books that have been written or the views expressed by the Sages of the Torah, from the time of Moses our Teacher until now. And in some cases these views are quite far apart, but this should not be cause for dismay, for all are for the sake of heaven, and all are the words of the living God, as if each had direct access to revelation, to the words of Moses himself, as explained by the Maharshal, may his memory be a blessing, in the introduction of *Yam shel Shlomo* [*Solomon's Sea*], his book on Tractate Baba Kama. There he writes:

Though Moses never uttered a contradiction, the Sages in their study of the text drew different and sometimes contradictory conclusions, either through the exercise of logic or on the basis of tradition handed down from Moses at Sinai, one to another. But all these conclusions are legitimate. How can this be? The Kabbalists explained it this way: All souls were at Mount Sinai and received [the revelation] through forty-nine conduits—being seven times seven, purified twice seven times over. These were the [heavenly] voices they not only heard but also saw [Cf. Exod. 20:15]. And all Israel saw the voices, meaning the proclamations disseminated through the conduits, each seeing through his own conduit according to his ability to comprehend and according to the capacity of his higher soul to be elevated or diminished, one widely differing from another.

[. . .] Thus, when I saw that there was no end to books and no end to opinions—and in any case, what joy is there in merely copying from one book to another?—I said to myself, It is not even your task to *begin*, and I wanted to put this work aside.

I wanted to put this work aside, yet my imagination had already been captivated by it, so that I could not look at anything or any book without being reminded of what happened at Sinai. Each day I personally fulfilled the commandment to remember the Sinai Event, which ought to be called to mind every day, as in the words cited by the prayer books: "Remember the day when you stood before the Lord your God at Horeb, lest you forget what your eyes have seen." And when I recalled what happened at Sinai I recalled the scriptural texts describing it. And every verse had its interpretations and commentaries, its explanations and reasons, its allusions and numerological meanings, first and foremost the halakhic and aggadic midrashim. Things I had read as a child, as a young man, and in the previous year or two all leapt out of the pages. New books seemed to come my way only for the sake of the references to Sinai they contained. Whenever I saw something new on the subject I underlined it, and I did the same with books I had read earlier, which I went back over, not yet realizing that I was preparing something already prepared, that everything was in fact falling into place of its own accord.

At that time I was given an edition of the Zohar with the commentary *Hasulam* [*The Ladder*], by the Kabbalist Rabbi Yehudah Halevi Ashlag, may his memory be a blessing. I reread the Zohar together with the commentary, and I am indebted to the commentator, may his memory be a blessing, for helping me with a number of passages.

One day, as I was looking over my things, I came upon a box full of notes for my book *Sefer, Sofer, Vesippur* [*Book, Author, and Story*].[1] It was originally a short book that I had drafted in five weeks. Now, twenty years later, it had expanded greatly and took up quite a bit of space. I thought, How much longer is it going to lie in this box? I'll take five or six months and prepare it for publication. Truth to tell, even though I have a special fondness for this book, with its stories of most of the writers from Moses' time to our own and how their books were written, and I am constantly adding to it tidbits that I come across, I also have a certain interest in readying this book for publication. I am an old man, and my house is near the frontier, and if, God forbid, there should be a war and I have to flee, I shall not have the strength to carry with me a big box full of notes. So I set aside time and began the work of editing the book, in order to get it published and thereby relieve myself of the responsibility of keeping it. And since the book began with the Torah, I planned to add to it some of the things with which I had of late been so fully taken up.

One thing leads to another, and before long these things turned into a whole separate book. That is how *You Yourselves Saw*, with its four parts, came into being. I did not include in this book all the things I had written down. There were many good and precious things I had to leave out. To have included them as they were would have been impossible, because they were too deep. Yet I was not able to explain them in such a fashion that anyone could read them easily.

"After these faithful deeds" [2 Chron. 32:1], I think I can say that this book reflects, not merely a selection of what I like, but what the years have yielded for me. Books I have read ever since childhood have stood me in good stead in the preparations of this work. And it is not I who have made the choice but the years themselves. At the same time, whoever is interested can easily go beyond the sources I have read and cited here. There are many great and worthy commentaries, early as well as late, that I did not have the good fortune to see, including some I have probably not even heard of. As we learn in *Shnei Luḥot Habrit* [*The Two Tablets of the Covenant*], the Torah has 600,000 interpretations, corresponding to the 600,000 souls [of the Israelites who stood at Sinai], each of whom received one interpretation as his portion. With the little strength at my disposal I have assembled, in the four parts of this book, a tiny bit of four thousand books. May we each find, in the books we write, the very interpretations our souls received as their portion.

Throughout my work I kept in mind the injunction of the *Guide of the Perplexed* (Part 2, chapter 34, as translated by Rabbi Yehudah Alḥarizi) that it is not proper to break through the bounds and say too much about the secrets of Mount Sinai . . . for this is among the hidden aspects of the Torah.

In the midrash *Meor Ha'afelah* [*Illuminations of the Darkness*], it says "Like the awakening at Mount Sinai, so shall be the awakening of the Messianic age." May it be God's will that we merit seeing the latter speedily and soon, amen.

Shmuel Yosef Agnon,
son of Rabbi Shalom Mordekhai Halevi
may the memory of the righteous
be a blessing.

NOTES

[Words in brackets appear in the original translation.—Eds.]
1. Jerusalem, 1938; dedicated to Salman Schocken on his sixtieth birthday; printed in 120 copies at Ha'arez Press, Tel Aviv.—*S.Y.A.* Reissued Jerusalem and Tel Aviv, 1978—*Translator.*

Translated by Michael Swirsky.

Khone Shmeruk

1921–1997

Yiddish scholar Khone Shmeruk was born in Warsaw and educated in a variety of Jewish schools before he enrolled at the University of Warsaw. His studies were interrupted in 1939, when he fled to the Soviet Union. In 1949, he joined his grandparents who had settled in Palestine before the war, went on to head the Yiddish Department at the Hebrew University, and was awarded the Israel Prize in 1996. He chose to be buried in Warsaw's Jewish cemetery.

A Mirror on a Stone: The Poetry and Prose of Twelve Martyred Yiddish Writers in the Soviet Union
1964

Introduction

The criterion for the selection of works to be included in the anthology was above all their lasting literary and artistic value, though here and there poems and short stories were included whose value, from a literary and artistic point of view, was essentially documentary. Despite all efforts to present every writer as much as possible in terms of the entire span of his creative path, it nevertheless turned out that almost all writers are represented by works written by the end of the 1920s or in the 1940s. In the book there is very little from the 1930s. That gap is not fortuitous. In order to explain its causes it is necessary to characterize Soviet Yiddish literature from its beginnings until the late 1940s. [...]

Thematically, Yiddish poetry, which was the essence of Soviet Yiddish literature of the 1920s, is characterized by a common tension stemming from the emotionally stirring and painful problems of the time. The whole of Soviet Yiddish poetry was caught up in the aftermath of World War I, the Russian Revolution, and the ensuing pogroms. The inevitable decline of the shtetl was deeply felt, spilling over into undisguised nostalgia, while at the same time, pervasive urbanization is seen not only as a personal reality, but at least in part as a desirable fate for the Jewish masses. Among the most deeply felt emotions reflected in this poetry is the tragic rupture between the sense of Jewish *vey* [grief] and the general sense of *mut* [boldness] in Dovid Hofshteyn's characterization, or in Markish's expressive metaphor of being at once a *cradle* of the new and a *deathbed* of the old. This sense of rupture flowed out in a wide stream in the most varied poetic forms, expressing deep pain and sadness which was often paired with hope and belief in renewal. A verse like Kushnirov's, from his *Hazkore* ("Memorial for the Dead") found a deep echo and was remembered for many years:

> In my soul a little mouse scrapes
> A melody of my father's or grandfather's
> But the door of my own Sabbath
> Has been bolted shut by the first star of the weekday.

During the early and middle 1920s the connection with Yiddish literature in other countries was freely underscored. Yiddish writers were invited to visit the Soviet Union and had their works published. But by the late 1920s a cultural wall began to be built between Soviet Jewish literature and literature from capitalist countries. [...]

In order to provide an insight into the problems raised by Soviet literary struggles, a number of topical poems have been included in the book whose value is primarily documentary. [...] The compilers of this anthology have striven to represent all the varied themes and contemporary problems that were expressed in Soviet Yiddish literature. At the same time, however, the emphasis has been on Jewish themes and on works that underscore the Jewish national character of that literature, a literature which we have too often and without justification called into question. For that reason, we occasionally chose to overlook the doubtful literary quality or awkwardness of a poem for the sake the fervid national emotions it evoked. (See, for example, Fefer's *Ikh bin a yid* [I am a Jew].)

Translated by Solon Beinfeld.

Other works by Shmeruk: *Peretses yiesh-vizye* (1971); *Sifrut yidish: perakim le-toldoteha* (1978).

Dan Ben-Amotz and Netiva Ben-Yehuda
Ben-Yehuda, 1928–2011

Author and broadcaster Netiva Ben-Yehuda was born in Tel Aviv. She studied at the Bezalel Academy in Jerusalem, at the University of London, and at the Hebrew University. She was a noted member of the Palmach. Ben-Yehuda was an editor of the *Encyclopedia Hebraica* and served as a spokeswoman in the Ministry of Labor. In 1996, she began a weekly broadcast on a popular late-night program of talk and music. Ben-Yehuda championed the importance of spoken Hebrew.

World Dictionary of Hebrew Slang
1972

Excuses and Justifications

Before the custodians of the purity of the Hebrew language begin to tear their hair out in protest of the so-called indecent acts committed herein, in full view, upon the holy tongue, may we be permitted to say some words in our defense.

We alone are not guilty for the existence of the *World Dictionary of Hebrew Slang*. Really, it's not us. The copyright for this act of disobedience belongs to the entire people living in Zion. Its relentless pursuit of the sleeping Hebrew beauty brought into this world the joyful little bastards collected in this volume. As for us, our only crime is that we provide a shelter and roof over the head of the illegitimate sons of the Hebrew language, who gives herself over to all her suitors. [...]

Anyone who can see in a language, beyond its technical linguistic issues, a sociological and psychological reflection of its speakers at any given time period, must show interest in the spoken language. This is the language of daily use, which makes the rounds at the markets and enriches its users, while the "Sabbath Hebrew" slumbers at home over a volume of Agnon's writing and a bowl of cholent. Contemporary writers are in growing need of the treasure of the spoken language, and future generations who would seek to understand the meanings of words and reflect upon the finer points of the language in all its richness and nuances will not be able to do so without using a dictionary. [. . .]

And now, in order to maintain a certain balance, let us say a few words critical of the dictionary. We have already hinted quite clearly that this dictionary is incomplete, that some of its definitions are subject to debate and that its editors make no claim to be schol-ars, but this is still insufficient. From a didactic and ethical viewpoint, this dictionary is totally scandalous. Never have so many curses, maledictions, and insults been gathered in a single volume alongside such an assemblage of adjectives describing a person's physical, intellectual, and psychological imperfections. Not to mention the vast number of obscenities and various expressions of courtship, enticement, and coitus that the revolutionary Ben-Yehuda did not provide us.

Translated by Menachem Rotstein.

Other works by Ben-Yehuda: *Blessings and Curses* (1984); *Through the Binding Ropes* (1985); *When the State of Israel Broke Out* (1991).

Cultural, Political, and Religious Thought

Menachem M. Kasher
1895–1983

Talmudic scholar Menachem M. Kasher was born into a rabbinic family in Warsaw. He was ordained in 1915 and went to Palestine in 1925 as an emissary of the Gerer rebbe, Abraham Mordecai Alter, under whose direction he founded and directed Yeshiva Sefat Emet in Jerusalem. Kasher's *Torah shelemah*, begun in 1927 and completed in 1981, is a forty-volume encyclopedia of the Talmud and Midrash for which he was awarded the Israel Prize in 1962. The introduction to the excerpt below was written by his son-in-law and translator, Aaron Greenbaum.

The Israel Passover Haggadah
1948

Introduction

To Section I, which deals with the Haggadah itself, I have added six other sections.

Section II, entitled "Moses, our Teacher," is a collation of *midrashim*, which discuss his attributes, his ways with the people, and his general character, from his youth until the Exodus.

Section III, "The Beginning of Redemption," presents the views of our rabbis and sages concerning a period closely comparable to our own.

Section IV, "The Land of Israel," comprises verses from the Bible containing the promises of the Eternal to the patriarchs concerning the Land of Israel—the Exodus, the building of the First and Second Temples, the victory of the Hasmoneans, the destruction of the Second Temple, and the proclamation of the State of Israel.

Section V describes the ceremony of the fifth cup, following the custom of R. Loew of Prague (1525–1609), who included it in the manuscript edition of his Haggadah, published in 5665 (1905). Many distinguished rabbis have followed this ritual.

The order of the fifth cup is in accordance with a variant reading in the tractate Pesahim. It is also mentioned by the geonim and the early commentators, who found scriptural support for its inclusion in the ritual in the words, "And I shall bring." The fifth cup, however, is not obligatory but is a highly praiseworthy act, at the discretion of the individual.

By Section VI, I mean those textual variants printed after the portions of the Haggadah which seem to throw a new light upon difficulties in our present text. These are drawn from the manuscripts of the Cairo Genizah as well as from the geonim and the early commentators. One should note especially two variants found in the text of the "bread of affliction" prayer, from manuscripts of the Genizah. There the text runs as follows: "This year we are here, next year in Jerusalem. Yesterday we were slaves, today we are free men!" This clause is pertinent to our own day, especially to the Jews of Israel. Just as we have merited the right to live during the period of the beginning of the redemption, so may we live to see the complete and final redemption.

Section VII consists of significant illustrations from Egyptian monuments, ancient manuscripts and new original paintings on the Passover theme.

We Are Commanded to Give Thanks for a Miracle

Rabbi Huna said: We learn from the Torah, from the Prophets, and from the Writings that a man ought to give praise and thanks to the Almighty for any miraculous event. Where do we find this in the Torah? It is written: "That thou mayest tell in the ears of thy son, and of thy son's son, what I have wrought upon Egypt." Also it is said: "And that My name may be declared throughout the earth." From the Prophets: it is written: "I will make mention of the mercies of the Eternal and the praises of the Eternal." Also it is said: "And ye shall say on that day: Give thanks unto the Eternal, proclaim His name, declare His doings among the peoples, make mention that His name is exalted." From the Writings: it is written: "That which we have heard and known, and our fathers have told us—we will not hide it from their children, telling to the generation to come the praises of the Eternal, and His strength, and His wondrous works that He hath done." Also, it is said: "Let them give thanks unto the Eternal for His mercy, and for His wondrous works for the children of men."

And now, in our own time, when we have been privileged to behold the mercies of the Holy Name, blessed is He, and His salvation over us, in the establishment of the State of Israel, which is the beginning of redemption and salvation from the exile of Edom, even as it is written: *"And I shall bring you* into the land, the same which I have lifted my hand to give unto Abraham, unto Isaac, and unto Jacob, and I have given it unto you as an inheritance: I am the Eternal"—it is fitting and proper that we observe this pious act, the drinking of the fifth cup, as a form of thanksgiving.

We give thanks unto the Eternal for the wartime miracles and wonders He wrought for us. The mercies of the Eternal stood us in good stead in time of dire peril, when seven nations united to destroy and annihilate the Jewish state, and plunge it into rivers of blood and fire. The Eternal, in His lovingkindness, frustrated the designs of our enemies, and vouchsafed victory unto us; as it is promised in His Torah: "The Eternal shall cause thine enemies that rise up against thee to be smitten before thy face; they shall come out against thee one way, and flee before thee seven ways." Truly God has given over the many into the hands of the few, and He cast terror upon those who would destroy us, so that they fled. Now we turn in prayer and hope toward the Eternal, that we shall behold the early rays of the morning sun over the land of our fathers wax into a mighty luminary; and that the Jewish state be firmly built upon the foundation of Torah and tradition, in the ancient spirit of our people.

Just as we have been privileged to see the first realization of "And I shall bring them," so may we be worthy of witnessing the perfect and complete redemption, the coming of the Messiah. May we witness fulfillment of the vision of the prophets, that "evil shall disappear as smoke in the wind, and that all the earth shall be filled with the knowledge of God."

Translated by Aaron Greenbaum.

Other works by Kasher: *Torah shelemah* (1927–1981); *Sefer ha-rambam ve-ha-mekhilta de-rabbi Shimon b. Yoḥai* (1943); *Gemara shelemah* (1960); *Haggadah shelemah* (1961).

Mordecai Nimtsa-bi

1903–1949

Mordecai Nimtsa-bi was born in Pinsk. After studying law in Moscow and Leningrad, he moved to Palestine in 1924 and lived in Haifa. In 1944, he published an official booklet of guidelines for creating Hebrew surnames, directed at new immigrants. In 1948, he became head of the Israel Civil Defense Service. He also published a book discussing strategies for designing the national flag of Israel.

Choose Yourself a Hebrew Name!
1948

Excerpt from the Order of the Prime Minister and Minister of Defense:

. . . It is recommended that all commanders (from platoon leader to head of staff) change their family names—be they German, Anglo-Saxon, Slavic, French, or any other foreign name—to Hebrew family names, in order to set an example for their troops. The Israel Defense Forces needs to be Hebrew in spirit, vision, and in all its internal and external manifestations.

A *Hebrew name*—that is the watchword to the claim that, many years before, too, there were individuals who mentioned this in speech and in writing, in order to provide a Hebrew character to the Yishuv [Jewish population of pre-state Israel]. Now, the time has come for this claim to become a general rule—a motto whose time has come. The time is now for each and every one of us to have a Hebrew first name and family name— may you make it a reality! [. . .]

A person's name is one of the external symbols, as it were, linking them to their people.

Indeed, this claim that has arisen in our renascent people does not originate in national foppishness: remove the foreign names from our midst! For we also have names that are apparently not foreign, but are actually "specifically Jewish"; however, in our desire for naturalness and Hebrew completeness, we too wish to brush off this diaspora specificity. Indeed, in emphasizing each one's Hebrew name, we are, in fact, deliberately surrendering our diaspora heritage and prominently displaying our desire to brush it off in our *Hebrew* homeland—Israel.

This matter is far more important than it may appear at first glance. For here, in this ingathering of the exiles, where people from different languages and nations have brought with them their own ethnic names, removing foreign names and prescribing Hebrew names aids and abets clearing away the barriers separating one ethnic community from another and is an important symbol in consolidating our people. [...]

We must speed up this activity and achieve a Hebrew image also in our names—and straightaway. [...] As long as the Yishuv is relatively young, given the age of its population, it is easier to motivate people to change their names. [...]

Here we are on the verge of absorbing masses of people from the ravaged and sickly diaspora. It is good that these masses are coming to us at a time when we are prepared to act correctly on this point. It is good that new immigrants come to a state whose residents have Hebrew names, for in this way they too will see the necessity for each one of them to change their foreign name to a Hebrew one. [...]

Until now, only a few people have Hebraicized their names, because there has been no body to oversee such an action. Nowadays, such a body does exist—the Israel Defense Forces.

In this booklet, we shall present some of the arguments for and against Hebraicizing a name.

The major argument is: "I've been tied to this name for a long time; it's the umbilical cord connecting me to my father, to my family's lineage—and why would I ever cut myself off from this generational chain? Does this sound like anyone would want to change their name?" [...] Changing one's given name and surname is not such a rare spectacle at all, especially among us. In the diaspora, some seventy to eighty years ago, you could find tens of thousands of Jews who had changed their names to evade the army. [...]

Moreover, half of mankind does change its family name. A married woman stops being called by her maiden name and accepts the name of her husband.

And we know of many incidents where efforts were made to have Jews (and not only Jews) in certain countries change their Jewish names, mostly to uproot the vestige of Yiddishkeit [Jewishness] contained in their names. [...]

Indeed, those wishing to avoid Hebraicizing their foreign names voice the false argument that this is an innovation instituted by us, as it were. Name change is a widespread phenomenon—mostly for invalid reasons. And why should people avoid doing so, especially in Israel, when it is prompted by important national motives?

And as for the argument about cutting ties, as it were, with one's father or family—is that the only type of "disconnect"? What about the changes and permutations

in the lives of the new generations; aren't they a kind of disconnect? [...]

Of course, name changes, especially changing a family name from a foreign one to a Hebrew name, is a type of disconnect; however, it is a necessary one, arising from our national renascence, by our return to our sources, to our Hebrew selfhood. We are the first generation to be redeemed from the diaspora—and the first generation that has been forced and commanded to sever a few capillaries, over which the individual may grieve but from which the public at large will derive much benefit. [...]

Indeed, many and sundry are the arguments—some of which appear to be true and others completely false, even debased—that are voiced by the people to whom you wish to appeal to shed their foreign names. It is important to refute and invalidate such arguments, based on practical logic and our national necessity.

However, even when you succeed in convincing someone to Hebraicize their foreign name, arguments will arise that must be taken into account. The main question is: How, in what way, and by what rules is the change to be made? Does the new Hebrew name have to be a translation of the old foreign name or be as similar to it as possible in sound, or is it perhaps better for it to be completely new—having no connection, either in meaning or sound, with the former name?

Experience has proven that many of those who are prepared to change their names wish to maintain some connection or other with the past. Even though this demand sometimes constitutes "breaking the barrel and preserving the wine" [having your cake and eating it, too], there are many cases where this option exists and is also justified. [...]

Indeed, the era in which we are now living is a transitional period. People are free to choose for themselves an old name or a new one, to their heart's content. However, in this transitional phase of innovation, one can and should find some stricture to uniformity. For example, it is possible to translate the most common family names among us—such as Weiss, Schwartz, Friedman, etc.—which mostly attest to a certain closeness among the families, and this translation or these translations would be fixed; there would be certain names for all the Weisses (let's say, Livni or something like that) and certain names for all the Friedmans (let's say, Shalom, Ben-Shalom, Ish-Shalom, etc.). And again, cohesion will be established, one version will form a connection—the Israeli version instead of the diaspora one. For it would be a waste, an act of foppishness and a blurring of the commonality among people, if everyone were to create their own personal invention, by seeking a name that nobody had ever used before. [. . .]

However, there is another way of giving Hebrew form, content, and sound to the names we brought with us from the diaspora—not only by translation but by permutation: abbreviation or slight modification. [. . .]

A nice way of constructing a Hebraic name or translating the former one is by adding the word *ben* or *bar* [son of] (for instance, Bar-Nafḥa, Ben-Eliyahu, Bar-Adon, etc.) as well as by adding the suffix *el* or *eli* (for example, Avniel, Avnieli) or *yahu* (Benayahu, Berakhyahu, etc.). Constructing a Hebrew surname by taking the first name and placing *ben* or *bar* at the beginning of that name is the most basic, ancient way of forming Hebrew names. [. . .]

However, these are mainly ways of *translating* a name, of *modifying* a name, and such. Yet, there are those who wish to create an entirely new name, and the best way of doing so (whether it be a first name or a surname) is to turn to the large repository of names found in the Holy Scriptures. This is a treasure trove from which one may borrow a name as is or invent a new name based on the ones already found there. [. . .]

And there are many more ways that have either already been found or will be found using this innovative process—whether by the inventive creativity of individuals with taste and linguistic expertise or by the instinctive sense of the Jewish people itself. Our goal was not to exhaust the issue and give a series of recipes for the formation of Hebrew names but rather to give an overview of methods and options.

Translated by Marvin Meital.

Other works by Nimtsa-bi: *Ha-degel* (1948).

Provisional Government of the State of Israel

Declaration of the Establishment of the State of Israel
1948

Eretz-Israel [The Land of Israel] was the birthplace of the Jewish people. Here their spiritual, religious and political identity was shaped. Here they first attained to statehood, created cultural values of national and universal significance and gave to the world the eternal Book of Books.

After being forcibly exiled from their land, the people remained faithful to it throughout their Dispersion and never ceased to pray and hope for their return to it and for the restoration in it of their political freedom.

Impelled by this historic and traditional attachment, Jews strove in every successive generation to re-establish themselves in their ancient homeland. In recent decades they returned in their masses. Pioneers, *ma'pilim* [(Hebrew)—immigrants coming to Eretz-Israel in defiance of restrictive legislation] and defenders, they made deserts bloom, revived the Hebrew language, built villages and towns, and created a thriving community controlling its own economy and culture, loving peace but knowing how to defend itself, bringing the blessings of progress to all the country's inhabitants, and aspiring towards independent nationhood.

In the year 5657 (1897), at the summons of the spiritual father of the Jewish State, Theodor Herzl, the First Zionist Congress convened and proclaimed the right of the Jewish people to national rebirth in its own country.

This right was recognized in the Balfour Declaration of the 2nd November, 1917, and re-affirmed in the Mandate of the League of Nations which, in particular, gave international sanction to the historic connection between the Jewish people and Eretz-Israel and to the right of the Jewish people to rebuild its National Home.

The catastrophe which recently befell the Jewish people—the massacre of millions of Jews in Europe—was another clear demonstration of the urgency of solving the problem of its homelessness by re-establishing in Eretz-Israel the Jewish State, which would open the gates of the homeland wide to every Jew and confer upon the Jewish people the status of a fully privileged member of the comity of nations.

Survivors of the Nazi holocaust in Europe, as well as Jews from other parts of the world, continued to migrate to Eretz-Israel, undaunted by difficulties, restrictions and dangers, and never ceased to assert their right to a life of dignity, freedom and honest toil in their national homeland.

In the Second World War, the Jewish community of this country contributed its full share to the struggle of the freedom- and peace-loving nations against the forces of Nazi wickedness and, by the blood of its soldiers and its war effort, gained the right to be reckoned among the peoples who founded the United Nations.

On the 29th November, 1947, the United Nations General Assembly passed a resolution calling for the establishment of a Jewish State in Eretz-Israel; the General Assembly required the inhabitants of Eretz-Israel to take such steps as were necessary on their part for the implementation of that resolution. This recognition by the United Nations of the right of the Jewish people to establish their State is irrevocable.

This right is the natural right of the Jewish people to be masters of their own fate, like all other nations, in their own sovereign State.

ACCORDINGLY WE, MEMBERS OF THE PEOPLES COUNCIL, REPRESENTATIVES OF THE JEWISH COMMUNITY OF ERETZ-ISRAEL AND OF THE ZIONIST MOVEMENT, ARE HERE ASSEMBLED ON THE DAY OF THE TERMINATION OF THE BRITISH MANDATE OVER ERETZ-ISRAEL AND, BY VIRTUE OF OUR NATURAL AND HISTORIC RIGHT AND ON THE STRENGTH OF THE RESOLUTION OF THE UNITED NATIONS GENERAL ASSEMBLY, HEREBY DECLARE THE ESTABLISHMENT OF A JEWISH STATE IN ERETZ-ISRAEL, TO BE KNOWN AS THE STATE OF ISRAEL.

WE DECLARE that, with effect from the moment of the termination of the Mandate being tonight, the eve of Sabbath, the 6th Iyar, 5708 (15th May, 1948), until the establishment of the elected, regular authorities of the State in accordance with the Constitution which shall be adopted by the Elected Constituent Assembly not later than the 1st October 1948, the People's Council shall act as a Provisional Council of State, and its executive organ, the People's Administration, shall be the Provisional Government of the Jewish State, to be called "Israel."

THE STATE OF ISRAEL will be open for Jewish immigration and for the Ingathering of the Exiles; it will foster the development of the country for the benefit of all its inhabitants; it will be based on freedom, justice and peace as envisaged by the prophets of Israel; it will ensure complete equality of social and political rights to all its inhabitants irrespective of religion, race or sex; it will guarantee freedom of religion, conscience, language, education and culture; it will safeguard the Holy Places of all religions; and it will be faithful to the principles of the Charter of the United Nations.

THE STATE OF ISRAEL is prepared to cooperate with the agencies and representatives of the United Nations in implementing the resolution of the General Assembly of the 29th November, 1947, and will take steps to bring about the economic union of the whole of Eretz-Israel.

WE APPEAL to the United Nations to assist the Jewish people in the building-up of its State and to receive the State of Israel into the comity of nations.

WE APPEAL—in the very midst of the onslaught launched against us now for months—to the Arab inhabitants of the State of Israel to preserve peace and participate in the upbuilding of the State on the basis of full and equal citizenship and due representation in all its provisional and permanent institutions.

WE EXTEND our hand to all neighboring states and their peoples in an offer of peace and good neighborliness, and appeal to them to establish bonds of cooperation and mutual help with the sovereign Jewish people settled in its own land. The State of Israel is prepared to do its share in a common effort for the advancement of the entire Middle East.

WE APPEAL to the Jewish people throughout the Diaspora to rally round the Jews of Eretz-Israel in the tasks of immigration and upbuilding and to stand by them in the great struggle for the realization of the age-old dream—the redemption of Israel.

PLACING OUR TRUST IN THE ALMIGHTY, WE AFFIX OUR SIGNATURES TO THIS PROCLAMATION AT THIS SESSION OF THE PROVISIONAL COUNCIL OF STATE, ON THE SOIL OF THE HOMELAND, IN THE CITY OF TEL AVIV, ON THIS SABBATH EVE, THE 5TH DAY OF IYAR, 5708 (14TH MAY, 1948).

David Ben-Gurion
Daniel Auster. Mordekhai Bentov. Yitzchak Ben Zvi. Eliyahu Berligne. Fritz Bernstein. Rabbi Wolf Gold. Meir Grabovsky. Yitzchak Gruenbaum. Dr. Abraham Granovsky. Eliyahu Dobkin. Meir Wilner-Kovner. Zerach Wahrhaftig. Herzl Vardi. Rachel Cohen. Rabbi Kalman Kahana. Saadia Kobashi. Rabbi Yitzchak Meir Levin. Meir David Loewenstein. Zvi Luria. Golda Myerson. Nachum Nir. Zvi Segal. Rabbi Yehuda Leib Hacohen Fishman. David Zvi Pinkas. Aharon Zisling. Moshe Kolodny. Eliezer Kaplan. Abraham Katznelson. Felix Rosenblueth. David Remez. Berl Repetur. Mordekhai Shattner. Ben Zion Sternberg. Bekhor Shitreet. Moshe Shapira. Moshe Shertok.

Yitzhak Ben-Zvi

1884–1963

Yitzhak Ben-Zvi (b. Shimshelevich) was the second president of the State of Israel and a longtime Labor Party leader. Born in Poltava, Ukraine, Ben-Zvi moved to Palestine in 1907, first living in Jaffa. He studied law at Istanbul University, along with David Ben-Gurion, and was expelled for political reasons from Palestine from 1914 until 1918. Ben-Zvi became the president of the new State of Israel in 1952, a position he held until the end of his life. As a historian of Mizrahi Judaism, Ben-Zvi also founded Jerusalem's Institute for the Study of Oriental Jewish Communities in the Middle East, which was renamed the Ben-Zvi Institute in his honor.

The Institute for the Study of Jewish Communities in the East
1949

The Institute for the Study of Jewish Communities in the East was established in 1948 with the aid of three bodies: the General Organization of the Workers in the Land of Israel, the National Committee, and the Committee of Workers in America.

The aim of the institute is to assemble information and official documents from institutions and from private persons concerning the living conditions of the Jews in the Middle East. The research will focus on their economic, cultural, and external political conditions as well as their [intra-communal] organization and their customs, beliefs, and lore. The material will be collected and arranged systematically in order to enable its publication.

The Framework: The subject of the research is, as stated above, the Jewish collectives that live around the Mediterranean. Three big units and four smaller ones can be discerned in the Middle East. The main characteristic that defines them and differentiates them from one another is their spoken language, notwithstanding the one and only national language [Hebrew] that is shared by the whole Hebrew nation.

The large units [of analysis] are (1) "Arabophone Jewry" (those who speak Arabic), which is in turn divided into eight branches: the Jews of Iraq, Syria, Lebanon, Yemen and Aden, Egypt, Libya, Tunisia, and Algeria and Morocco; (2) the Ladino (*Spaniolit*) speakers of Anatolia, the Balkans (*Rumelia*), and other areas; (3) the Persian-speaking Jews (in Persia, Afghanistan, Bukhara, and Dagestan). The four small units are the Aramaic-speaking Jews (Kurdistan), the Turkic-Tatar-speaking Jews (Russia and parts of Turkey), the Georgian speakers (North Caucasia) and the Berber-speakers (*Shlokh*, in North Africa). To these should be added the research on more remote collectives of far-flung Jews in India, China, Abyssinia, and the isolated communities in the Western and Eastern parts of the globe.

Each of these units possesses not only a distinct history, but also a unique folklore and character in the present day. They maintain a tremendous cultural treasure orally as well as in written forms. These riches, most of them as yet unstudied, are gradually being forgotten and are sometimes completely invisible. Traditions and customs previously unknown [to scholars], which were maintained for hundreds of years, are nowadays vanishing rapidly. There are two causes for this process. The first is national agitation directed mainly against minorities and especially against the constantly persecuted Jewish minorities. These persecutions, which are also aimed at other religions and other people, have wrought particular damage upon Jewish uniqueness. To this should be added the battle against Zionism, which has lately assumed the form of a battle against all Jews. It should be taken into consideration that during this process, vast cultural treasures and whole communities will be damaged and perhaps even vanish, God forbid.

The second cause is the natural tendency towards cultural change and 'aliyah. This tendency has climaxed with the reestablishment of the state of Israel, which has opened hitherto unknown paths of 'aliyah and salvation to those remote communities dispersed in the exiles of Ishmael.

Newcomers from all corners of the East have already gathered. There is hardly any community in the Diaspora from which newcomers have not arrived in the Land of Israel. Many have brought with them living traditions from their places of origin. The land of Israel can [therefore] become a central site for the research of Eastern [Jewish] communities.

It is only natural that here in this country the process of the unification of these tribes into one nation has begun. It is here that the unique characteristics of each tribe are blurring and disappearing. There are several reasons for this. The first one is negative—that is, assimilation. The second one is positive, and it is 'aliyah and national cohesion. In any case [we are witness to] the dissolution of traditions and even to their total erasure. There is thus an urgent need to start gathering the sparks of culture and lore for research purposes while they are still live. Bringing these sparks to our land bears national significance as well, especially in these days in which we are on the verge of redemption.

The Institute for the Study of Jewish Communities in the East exists under the auspices of the Hebrew University, which has appointed a special committee to monitor its activities. The committee is composed of three deputies: the chair of the Institute for Jewish Studies, the chair of the Institute of Near Eastern Studies and a third member who represents the executive management of the university. The signateur [sic] listed below and his assistant, Dr. A. Hirschberg, a research fellow at the Hebrew University, stand at the head of the institute.

We hereby call upon all institutions and people who are interested in the history of their nation and are concerned about its destiny, to help us by sharing any kind of material relating to Jewish life in the East. We are especially interested in manuscripts and printed material such as accounts, regulation, originals or reliable photocopies that may serve the institution's research and publishing purposes. Among other publications we intend to publish a special bulletin that will include extracts of this significant material. The bulletin will be published in Hebrew and include appendices in English and French.

NOTE
[Words in brackets appear in the original translation.—Eds.]

Translated by Miriam Frenkel.

Other works by Ben-Zvi: *Sefer ha-shomeronim* (1935); *Erets yisra'el ve-yishuvah bi-yemey ha-shilton ha-otomani* (1955); *The Exiled and the Redeemed* (1961); *The Hebrew Battalions: Letters* (1969).

Chaim Weizmann

1874–1952

Zionist leader and chemist Chaim Weizmann was born to an observant Jewish family in Motol, Russia (present-day Belarus). He studied at universities in Berlin and Switzerland, receiving a doctorate in chemistry. Weizmann is credited with ensuring British support for the establishment of a Jewish homeland through the 1917 Balfour Declaration. As president of the World Zionist Organization from 1920 to 1931 and again from 1935 to 1946, Weizmann worked to gain support for a Jewish state from the United States as well as the United Nations. He was elected president of Israel on February 16, 1949, and served until his death.

First Address to the Knesset
1949
Paths to Fulfillment

It is with a feeling of deep reverence and consecration that I rise to open the Constituent Assembly of the State of Israel, the first *Knesset Israel* of our time in this eternal city of Jerusalem. At this great moment of our history let us give thanks and praise to the God of Israel who in His mercy granted us the privilege of witnessing the redemption of our people after centuries of affliction and suffering. [. . .]

Ingathering the Exiles

This nation is to be conceived as the ingathering of the exiles, for there is not a Jewish community in the whole world whose members have not their portion in the State of Israel. In these very days, to our heart's joy, thousands and tens of thousands of our brethren from countries near and far are entering the gates of our country that stand wide open to receive them. It is our prayer and hope that this ingathering of the exiles will continue on an increasing scale and will embrace ever larger multitudes of our people who will strike roots here and will work side by side with us in the upbuilding of our state and in making our desolate places fruitful again. [. . .]

In the ancient world this tiny country of ours raised the standard of spiritual revolt against tyranny and brute force. The law of Israel and the vision of her Prophets founded a new ethic of the relations between man and man and led to a new ordering of human society. The authority of the King of Israel was limited by law and tradition. The Prophets of Israel did not fear to utter rebuke and reproof to kings and princes and, with their inspired word for a weapon, they defended the poor and oppressed, the stranger and the slave, the orphan and the widow.

Warning of the Prophet

The very principle of the institution of kingship was hateful to the spiritual leaders of the people. "I shall not rule over you, nor shall my son rule over you; the Lord shall rule over you," declares the Judge to the assembled people. The warnings of the Prophet against the dangers of tyranny thunder from on high in the ears of the people unto the last generation. In Israel this rising up against the authority of one man derived from the noble conception that a people naturally free and freely accepting the rule of law and just judgment does not need compulsion from above to live as an ordered society. The root principle of the constitution of that novel state was the limit set to the authority of the king and it is in this sense that the ancient Hebrew polity was the mother of constitutional government in the modern age. And now it has fallen to our generation to weld anew the links of that life of freedom that were snapped by tyranny's force nearly 1,900 years ago.

I know not why it is precisely that our generation has been privileged to bring about what all generations before us have longed for and cleaved to in the darkness of exile, unless it be that we have earned it by all the hardships and weariness, the sorrow and tribulation, that have been our portion these last 70 years, years when our body was stripped limb by limb until finally one-third of the entire nation was annihilated. We have suffered torture and affliction such as has befallen no other nation in the world until at long last the prophecy is fulfilled—the remnants shall return. But because we are no more than a remnant, a double and treble responsibility is laid upon us to fill the terrible void in our national life that has been created by the slaughter of the best sons of our people, the guardians of their spirit and the hearers of their culture. It is our people that once gave to the whole world a spiritual message fundamental to civilization. The world is watching us now to see what way we choose for ourselves in ordering our lives, in what fashion we will shape our state. The world is listening to hear whether a new message will go forth from Zion and what that message will be.

A new message is not born without sore travail of the creative spirit. It does not see the light without much toil and weariness, difficulty and pain. The creative force of our nation will soon meet a new and serious challenge. The Constitution which this Assembly is called upon to frame will be the supreme test.

Having taken part in the great battles of the human spirit, having shed our blood and given our lives for the liberation of many peoples, we have finally won the right to toil and labor in order to give expression to our distinct national identity and to make our contribution as a free people with other free peoples to the spiritual treasure of the world.

First let us strive to strengthen our constructive resources of science and research which are the basis of human achievement. All the scientific capacity which we have displayed in every country of the world must now be mobilized to help build our motherland. Yet, for all the decisive importance of science, it is not by science alone that we shall win through. Let us build a new bridge between science and the spirit of man. "Where there is no vision the people perish." We have seen what scientific progress leads to when it is not inspired by moral vision—the atomic bomb threatening to destroy the entire planet.

All my life I have labored to make science and research the basis of national endeavor, but I have always known full well that there are values higher than science. The only values that offer healing for the ills of humanity are the supreme values of justice and righteousness, peace and love. "Zion will be redeemed with judgment and her converts with righteousness."

Other works by Weizmann: *Trial and Error: The Autobiography of Chaim Weizmann* (1949); *The Letters and Papers of Chaim Weizmann, Series B, Papers, Vol. 1, August 1898–July 1931* (1983).

Barukh Kurzweil
1907–1972

Barukh Kurzweil, a professor of Hebrew literature and a literary critic, was born to a family of rabbis in Brtnice, Moravia (now the Czech Republic), and studied at Solomon Breuer's yeshiva in Frankfurt and at the University of Frankfurt. Kurzweil immigrated to Palestine in 1939 and taught at a high school in Haifa. From 1955 until his death, he held the post of professor of Modern Hebrew literature at Bar-Ilan University. Kurzweil published studies of prominent Hebrew writers such as Agnon, Bialik, and Greenberg. Kurzweil received the Bialik Prize in Literature in 1962.

Essays on the Stories of Shai Agnon
1950

A Guest for the Night

In S. Y. Agnon's comprehensive literary project, we must also see *A Guest for the Night* as an epic expansion on one central subject, whose tones burst out and rise from most of his stories, both long and short: the emotional, happy, and desperate encounter with the world of childhood and youth, deeply embedded in the author's soul, in which he keeps growing, keeps developing—in the guise of a vision that blurs the boundary between reality and legend. This encounter and confrontation, which cruelly exposes the identity and also the distance between "then" and "now," necessarily brings about a belated return. Behind this eternal subject of every great epic, which naturally seeks always to be a summary and a conclusion of a rich cultural period, we discover, as a psychic and artistic motivation, though often hidden, the mighty struggle of the author as a human being with the mysteries of time to which we are subject, bearing our small happiness and our endless suffering. The secret of our existence thrills us more powerfully when all of our lives are as if concentrated, thickened with sudden intensity, so that we stand and wonder about the meaning of the whole process in which we are enfolded. "Then" and "now" are the poles between which lies the riddle of our lives.

Odysseus' arrival in Ithaca is such a time; Colonel Chabert's entry into the attorney's office for the first time is similar.[1] These are moments of epic symbolic fusion, and the life of Menashe Ḥayim ha-Cohen[2] loses its meaning at this fateful moment of encounter, which forces the protagonist to give ear to its meaning, namely, the final purpose demanded of him, that is to say, his death. With innumerable variations, Agnon presents the subject of belated return in *A Guest for the Night*. He begins with the stationmaster Gumbovitz, who utters the name Shibush[3] and licks "his mustache like someone who has eaten sweet things." He ends with the exalted figure of Rabbi Ḥayim. Indeed, the name Shibush does remain the same, and the fragrance is "the fragrance of honey-sweetened millet, which never leaves the city." The name and the fragrance suddenly liberate all of the pent-up feelings from the past, with a mighty magical power that brings all the images of the past back to life—and how great and depressing is the difference between them and the images of the reality of Shibush! That which is worrisome and demonic in the oppressive confrontation is not mainly the fruit of recognition of what no longer exists at all. The demonic and worrisome especially envelop objects of the past and pretend that they still exist, even though their remnants actually testify to the destructive effects of time!

> From the large houses of . . . three stories, of four stories, nothing remains but the lower floors, and they, too, are mainly destroyed. . . . Even the king's well, the well from which Sobieski, the king of Poland, drank . . . its steps are broken and the plaque that was placed there in his honor is defaced, and its letters, made of gold, are blurred and moldy . . .

That is the point: things exist, and at the same time, they have become something completely different. The same buildings, the same houses of study, the same people, the same streets, the same official at the railroad, the same Daniel Bach, the same Rabbi Ḥayim, the same "Empress," the same monuments on the graves of holy and righteous men—and the more all of them, the inanimate things, are "similar" to what they were "then," in that past, which is both near and distant at the same time, the more their alien nature increases, and "all the places changed, even the air between one house and another has changed. Not the way I saw them when I was little and not the way they were shown to me in a dream soon after my return." With three seemingly small details, which in fact have vast symbolic importance, the author brings out the tragic and disheartening character of his belated return.

Gumbovitz, the stationmaster of Shibush, who ostensibly proclaims its existence, is actually a dubious herald, and it is enough for us to peek at this priest of the Shibush of yesterday, from whose mouth comes the Holy Name, to become aware of the true face of this Shibush: "his left arm was taken away in the war and made of rubber." The herald himself is partially alive and partially dead.

The other one, who guides the guest to his hotel, is Daniel Bach. He rescues the guest from his confusion, from his inability to solve the problem of a hotel. By revealing the hotel, he creates for the guest the illusion that for a brief moment he has succeeded in delivering the untimely [guest]. The hour is late, very late. A short time before Yom Kippur, to which the delayed visitor clings stubbornly, with boundless longing. "That man, Daniel Bach, was tall and thin . . . a kind of laugh hung on his lips and spread into his sunken cheeks, and his right leg was of wood."

Here too, Daniel Bach, the problematic guest's "sponsor," demonstrates a kind of life that is in part merely artificial. His right leg, the dead one, "is more beautiful than the one made by the hands of heaven." But these cynical words, spoken by Daniel Bach, show some of the faith of those who dwell in the paradise of childhood, as does Daniel Bach's lack of faith in the power of repentance: "I'm a light person and don't believe in the power of repentance . . . I don't believe that Yom Kippur has the power to improve bad things." It is as if Daniel Bach had said to the guest: your whole return has no meaning; it is belated, and it believes in a world that is lost and gone in the past. And for the third time in the first chapter, the demonic face of the child-hood paradise, as well as that of the untimely guest, is revealed, with the mention of the house of Rabbi Ḥayim, a symbol of the rule of Torah and its glory. His wife's house has become "a meeting place for sinners." And as for Rabbi Ḥayim himself, "we do not know whether he is living or dead." He too, like Gumbovitz and Daniel Bach, could be either alive or dead. The first three prominent symbols of Shibush, of the childhood paradise, which is essentially identical to the world of tradition, the world of the fathers, testify to the truth—that there is nowhere to return to. The war and time have changed everything.

World War I is seen here, as elsewhere in Agnon's works, as a fateful turning point in the life of the Jewish people and of humanity. Aside from *A Guest for the Night*, particular artistic expression is given to this re-alization in *The Book of Deeds*: "Before the days of the war, when people were not yet whispering to one an-other, when a person met his fellow, he regarded him as a friend." Then there was still friendship, that is to say, decent relations between a person and his fellow, between a person and himself. Thus, for example, Mr. Ya'akov Tsorev in the story "Friendship"—whom the lone adventurer of *The Book of Deeds* believes he is capa-ble of rescuing from the dance of demons—also belongs to the orderly, supposedly harmonious world whose skeleton rises up in *A Guest for the Night*. On the other hand, it is impossible not to see *A Guest for the Night* in particular as a kind of desperate effort once again to en-dow those remnants of Shibush, those skeletons of the past, for the last time, with the potency of something living. In his ironic melancholy, the guest does not want to accept bitter reality, even for a moment, and he cre-ates an artistic fiction. All his actions in Shibush are a heartwarming effort to create a living micro-reconstruc-tion of yesterday's Shibush for himself. The apparently renewed life, in and around the House of Study, the support for the poor, this whole atmosphere of seeming renewal of the world of yesterday—only brings out the one truth more powerfully: everything is past and gone. However, while this clear awareness of the decisive function of World War I in the life of our culture in gen-eral is well known, Agnon's great novel brings it to artis-tic awareness, as is also conveyed by the great European authors of our time. This awareness is what gives the perspective of time to the allegory of Thomas Mann's *Magic Mountain*, as well as to Musil's *The Man Without Qualities*. Despite all the great differences, it is possible

to take note of the fascinating parallels between the re-construction of the world of nostalgia, which has disap-peared, as revealed to us in Proust's works of genius, and Agnon's effort in *A Guest for the Night* to set out "in search of lost time." In the realization of this precious il-lusion, enchanting and sorrowful, we see the inordinate importance of the key motive.

NOTES

1. [Reference is to *Le colonel Chabert*, a novella by Honoré de Balzac, in which the eponymous protagonist, thought to have died on the battlefield during the Napoleonic wars, returns to France to find his wife has remarried.—Eds.]

2. [The main protagonist of Agnon's novella *And the Crooked Shall Be Made Straight*, who is presumed dead and whose wife remarries.—Eds.]

3. [In *A Guest for the Night*, Agnon substitutes the name Shibush, which means "spoiling," for Buczacz, the name of the narrator's native city, to which he returns.—Eds.]

Translated by Jeffrey M. Green.

Other works by Kurzweil: *Masekhet ha-roman* (1952); *Sifrutenu ha-ḥadasha—hemshekh o mahpe-khah?* (1959); *Bialik vce-Tchernikhovsky* (1960); *Masot 'al sippurey Shay Agnon* (1963); *Beyn ḥazon le-veyn ha-absurdi* (1966).

Yehezkel Kaufmann
1889–1963

Biblical scholar Yehezkel Kaufmann was born in the Podolia region of present-day Ukraine and studied in Odessa and Petrograd. He received a doctorate from the University of Bern in 1918. After World War I, he lived in Berlin, and in 1928 he moved to Palestine, there teaching at the Reali School in Haifa. In 1949, he was appointed professor of biblical studies at the Hebrew University of Jerusalem, a post he held until his death. Kaufmann emphasized the unique nature of the Jewish religion—its monotheism and its relative imperviousness to pagan influences—and the decisive role that religious difference played in the preservation of the Jewish people.

The Bible and Mythological Polytheism
1951

Israel's Lifeless Idolatry

What is the place of the idolatry that is reflected in the Bible?

This idolatry is not a representation perverted for the sake of polemic; nor is it an artificial contrivance, the product of naiveté or circumlocution. It is something historically real: it is idolatry as it existed in pre-exilic Israel. This is the key to the riddle of the Bible's conception of idolatry: it knows only Israelite idolatry, which was lifeless, without gods or mythology. Israel was distinct from other nations of antiquity not by its idea of monotheism alone; it was equally distinct in its idolatry. The vestigial idolatry which is reflected in the Bible existed nowhere except in Israel. Herein lay the error of the Biblical writers themselves: failing to realize the uniquely Israelite character of their idolatry, they identified it with that of the gentiles. This idolatry was created by the impact of the monotheistic revolution which occurred at Israel's birth as a nation in the days of Moses. Although the vitality of heathenism was snuffed out by this revolution, it did not entirely disappear at once. Of the early Hebrew pantheon, shades—"satyrs"—were preserved. Another element was similarly preserved: the fetishistic worship of idols which went on among the people for many generations as a real "superstition," as a cult whose ideological roots were severed, which was no longer congruent with the dominant national religion and which therefore was incapable of further creativity as an element in the national culture. That this was its form even in early times is demonstrated by the stories of Rachel and the *teraphim*, Jacob and the "foreign gods," and the "judgment" of Dagon. Such idolatry is the strongest evidence that Israel was a monotheistic nation from its inception and throughout its "idolatrous" pre-exilic period as well. But even this lifeless idol-worship aroused zealots who viewed it as a grievous sin in Israel's history. Fetishistic practices too were a violation of the Covenant and a backsliding of the nation of YHWH; not even *teraphim* in a camel-saddle were to be tolerated!

To be sure, this idolatry received continual nourishment from foreign sources. Despite its essentially Israelite character, it is consistently viewed in the Bible as something foreign. For if gods and myths could not successfully invade the monotheistic atmosphere of Israel, the production of idols still could enter from abroad, and the people did attribute some magical powers to these "charms." Syncretism and theocrasis could not strike roots in Israel since their ideological basis was wanting. There was no family of gods into which foreign deities could marry, nor, indeed any pantheon at all into which they could be naturalized. Syncretism

leads always to the assimilation of foreign gods in their new surroundings with the eventual obliteration of their foreignness. In Israel, however, idolatry never ceased being the worship of "foreign gods." From the *teraphim* of Laban to the "queen of heaven" of Jeremiah's day, the "pantheon" of Israel contained only "gentile" deities, "strange gods . . . that they knew not, new gods that came up of late" (Deut 32 16–17). That these gentile deities have no mythological characteristics attached to them reveals the true significance of their perpetual foreignness: the heathen "pantheon" of Israel was one of images, masks, "dumb idols."

Two Worlds

This conclusion must itself appear quite paradoxical. Can it be that Biblical Israel did not know polytheism? The people lived in a polytheistic world and was in constant contact with heathen nations. Within Israel a form of idolatry was still practiced, and from time to time fanatical idolaters arose in its midst. Ezekiel did see, if only in a vision, the lamentation of Tammuz in the Temple. How could it have been, then, that there was no awareness of the heathens' belief in living gods?

Before attempting to explain this phenomenon of ignorance within Israel, we must note that it is matched by another, equally remarkable, which no one seriously questions: the heathens' ignorance of Israelite religion. This religion was destined to destroy heathenism on its own ground, yet what do the gentiles know of it? We find no trace of the influence of Israelite religion on the cultures of Babylonia, Assyria, Canaan, or Persia. Nor do their literatures contain allusions to any of Israel's great religious thinkers. Contact with Israel is not sufficient to bring about familiarity with its culture. Even after the exile when Jews establish sizeable colonies in the diaspora their religion remains *terra incognita* to the gentiles for centuries. The Persians know it no better than did the early Egyptians and Babylonians. The Greeks and Romans of Second Commonwealth times are likewise ignorant of its essential character. They are acquainted with some of its customs and rites, but the religion itself is a sealed book to them. Even the numerous gentiles who toward the end of this period actually come under the influence of Judaism begin by adopting only its external aspects, with its basic ideology remaining alien to them for a long while. This process parallels the solely ritualistic influence of foreign idolatry on pre-exilic Israel. For a thousand years Israelite religion develops in the midst of a heathen milieu without the heathens' knowing its real nature. We may conclude from this that in the sphere of religious creativity Israel and the gentiles were two worlds, distinct and mutually incomprehensible. And if the gentiles failed to apprehend Israelite religion for so long a period is it any greater marvel that Israel on its part was ignorant of the religion of the gentiles?

Yet we must not misconstrue the extent of this ignorance.

That we find absolutely no grasp of the nature of heathenism in the Bible does not exclude there having been persons or even sects in Israel who were intimate with the religion of the gentiles. Manasseh and the likes of him were unquestionably ardent heathens in religious outlook, and some of the Biblical writers may have known more than they disclose in their writings. One thing however is certain: the people of Israel did not know polytheism. Here again we are not speaking of speculative, abstract knowledge which is essentially external and superficial—such knowledge was, perhaps, to be found here and there. But there was no vital, fundamental, psychic experience of polytheism among the people. Those who knew it, knew it from afar, and not as a creative element in their own midst. The people lived and created in another sphere; they perceived the heathen world, as it were, through an obscuring fog.

It must be remarked in this connection that every creative sphere is isolated from its surroundings in the same manner. Wherever an original national culture arises a closed culture area develops; hence the uniformity in the style of that culture. For several generations it manifests itself in pristine, homogeneous forms as a world in itself. All that Egyptian, Babylonian, Greek, or Chinese art produced in their early, formative period bears a unique, unalloyed impress. Here too one may ask: were not these artists aware of other creative styles? Undoubtedly they were; but awareness of the art of others was not important. It remained external and alien without decisive effect on native expressions and styles. The isolation of Israelite religion from heathenism was perhaps greater because the contrast between them was so much stronger and fundamental. Yet the phenomenon in itself is not limited to these two areas.

Translated by Moshe Greenberg.

Other works by Kaufmann: *Golah ve-nekhar* (1929); *Toledot ha-emunah ha-yisra'elit* (1937); *Ha-sipur ha-mikra'i 'al kibush ha-arets* (1956); *Mi-kivshonah shel ha-yetsirah ha-mikra'it* (1966).

Alexander Uriah Boskowicz

1907–1964

A composer, conductor, music critic, and painter, Alexander Uriah Boskowicz was born in Kolozsvár, Austria-Hungary (now Cluj, Romania) to a Hasidic family. He studied piano in Vienna and Paris. In 1938, Boskowicz was invited to conduct the Palestine Symphony Orchestra, and he moved to Tel Aviv. He was a founder of the Israel Academy of Music and served as a music critic for the newspaper *Haaretz*. Boskowicz was awarded the Israel Philharmonic Orchestra Prize in 1960 and the Henrietta Szold Prize in 1961.

The Problems of Native Music in Israel
1953

The "Where" in the Creation of Israeli Music

The first issue that should have occurred to a European-born, reality-sensitive composer upon immigration to the Land of Israel is: Is the musical vocabulary in which I have spoken thus far appropriate for expressing my experience in this new world? [. . .] And in general, with what kind of musical language can one address this new reality? How does one begin a new and unprecedented melody? One cannot compare this to the new Hebrew language that has become a vernacular, since Hebrew is not abstract; it possesses roots, a continuum, and concrete historical bases going back to the Bible and Mishnah through the Spanish Golden Age and up to this very day. However, where should one look for the historical foundations of Hebrew music? [. . .]

Changing Values in the Creation of the New Hebrew Music: A Geographic and Cultural Perspective [. . .]

The composer who lives this present reality and who attempts to express his impressions in artistic terms must come to the realization that conveying such a reality cannot be accomplished using the vehicles to which he had been accustomed in Europe.

But to the optical landscape is now added an acoustic one. For example, the sounds of the language as spoken by those born in the Orient are new to him as well. He discovers that the spoken melody here is more intense than in the notes of the more acculturated—yet at the same time more boring—speech patterns found in most European nations. Here he hears speech in which the ancient elements of phatogenic singing still live and breathe. He hears archaic Semitic languages. Its values, for it is the sister language of Hebrew and even our own Hebrew, which only yesterday was a fossilized language, which, today sounds a bit Slavic, a little Yiddish, with some German as spoken by ministers, high officials, government functionaries, and even . . . many actors.

The composer's attuned ear is capable of detecting the potential of a sensual sound contained in the Hebrew with its Semitic ring. The dynamic social landscape (of which the phenomenon of sound is an integral aspect) contains customs, ways of life, forms of etiquette, and social organization, which not only do not correspond to what the composer has been accustomed to in his European environment, but are very often *contradictory*. The composer must often face the issue of diagnosing these phenomena—what are they: primitivism or a different culture from those he had previously known?

The dynamic social landscape reveals for him his people, partners in destiny, from every corner of the diaspora. He has come to know Jews from the most diverse cultural and ethnographic backgrounds. The picture contains, therefore, the static oriental landscape as well as spiritual and dynamic social ones, a gathering of exiles, the entire structure of the [Zionist] enterprise.

This static landscape is oriental, but we know well that this oriental reality is in dire need of fundamental repair. (For the universal purpose of our nationalist enterprise is precisely that kind of repair!) It is clear, therefore, that in the faithful description of that reality one must not yield in this dialectic conflict. *Moreover, we must regard this as the central theme of the entire artistic problem that pretends to appear as contemporary Israeli music.* A static oriental landscape on one side and a dynamic one on the other—it is these that serve as the axes for the new Hebrew musical creation. They are the opposing forces that make up the dramatic tension, whose resolution can potentially give birth to an art that expresses truth. [. . .]

The Tasks of the Time

By understanding the circumstances, one can designate the tasks whose success or failure may decide and determine the destiny of the new Israeli culture. These tasks may be summarized as follows:

A. To mold the collective image of the nation's cultural and spiritual prototype. To do so we have first to identify the existing collective spiritual model to deter-

mine its values and deficiencies and to look for what is characteristic and original within it. [. . .] Let us stress that one should sincerely welcome the true spiritual accomplishments of foreign cultures, but one must pay careful attention to the *balance* between the original and the foreign culture.

B. To approach the creation of artistic means of expression, whose role is to define our presence, with appropriate symbolism. Such symbolism yearns for a typical collective form of expression. One can conclude that such symbolism can be understood by the general public, moreover, its value is measured by the authority of the public; the typical collective is its very significance.

Identifying such a typical collective is done by analyzing the Hebrew spirit in all its manifestations: the linguistic, the traditions, the customs, liturgy, etc. This kind of identification demands an understanding of the collective national experiences, past and present. It demands as well the exposure of the original, unmediated meaning of the national inheritance, which has become, in many cases, desiccated traditions and misunderstood "religious" customs, uprooted from the reality that gave birth to them. [. . .]

An Oriental Pastoral

The composer's impression of the new oriental scenery is both important and justified for the collective, for it is the reality of the "where." Obviously, at this stage, such an understanding has a distinctive Impressionist quality expressed in the types of pastorals, but it would be a mistake to regard such pastorals as mere variants or as an inheritance of the standard European model; i.e., a static pastoral. For behind the Israeli pastoral lies a great collective complex; it is composed of the atavism of a people recalling its historical youth, and of the experience of reclaiming the land "facing the wilderness" and creating in it new life.

The love of the landscape attributes to it a living, dynamic quality. Thus, for example, "the camel," "the little foxes," and "the Kinneret" are not mere tableaux, but are expressive projections of the dynamic psyche; therefore, this special lyrical pastoral is dynamic, even when it comes to describe a static, objective landscape. [. . .]

As to the musical material of the Israeli pastoral, it is obviously not a deus ex machina; a post factum analysis of the work proves that there are valid, objective reasons to the author's "subjective" intuition. And one can locate the concrete sources of his inspiration, as he searches for the typical collective musical sources of expression. Such an objective source of inspiration is revealed in the traditional melodies of oriental communities.

The Israeli composer can (and must!) come into direct contact with the oriental melody.

(And let us stress, most emphatically, *direct contact!*) [. . .] Such a melody does not lend itself to precise transcription within the European musical notation without harming its essential originality. [. . .] For at the core of the European musical notation one finds the rational contraction of the comparative method, in which the range of the octave is divided into twelve half tones that constitute the smallest intuitive unit (a small *secunda* = 100 cents according to the Ellis measurement method). True, this particular method, which appears as an accompanying phenomenon to the European polyphony (particularly the instrumental), allows for the creation of massive works within the special conditions of the European musical mentality, but its gain comes at the expense of the endless possibilities of the melodic pleasures.

The European marking system finds itself also helpless vis-à-vis the rhythmic flexibility of the oriental melody. The acculturated European rhythm is content with a limited number of typical, accepted rational rhythms, derived from the sense of symmetry of the European mentality. Such symmetry is foreign to the oriental melody, which is unfamiliar with the cyclical pattern, that which is called rhyme.

The overwhelming impression aroused upon hearing the oriental melody touches as well upon the atavism within the collective subconscious of the Jewish composer. Such melodies do not seem so strange to him, for despite all the historical episodes and all the layers of the European cultural super structure, the roots of the nation are embedded in a Semitic soil after all. Such oriental music—along with various external influences—has known how to integrate foreign cultures, while being able to preserve its unique, original character. It stands to reason, therefore, that the Jewish composer will see in comprehending this musical mentality a reliable means of clarifying the typical collective Semitic image. He will also see in it a means for repairing the Hebrew historic continuum, as well as an untapped source of musical material, which may potentially (as in Bartok's case) provide potency to the uni-

versal musical organism, and perhaps even guide it in a completely new direction.

Translated by Menachem Rotstein.

Musical compositions by Boskowicz: *Sharsheret ha-zahav* (1937); *Suita shemit* (1945); *Bat yisra'el* (1960).

Yeshayahu Leibowitz
1903–1994

Yeshayahu Leibowitz was born in Riga, studied at the University of Berlin, and in 1935 immigrated to Palestine, where he joined the faculty of the Hebrew University; he would teach biochemistry, neurology, and organic chemistry. An observant Jew, Leibowitz staunchly insisted on the strict separation of state and religion and denied any religious significance to the State of Israel or to specific places such as the Western Wall or the West Bank. After the 1967 war, Leibowitz's warnings about the long-term dangers inherent in the occupation of the West Bank and Gaza made him a controversial figure. One of the most prolific and influential Jewish philosophers of the twentieth century, Leibowitz published widely on philosophy, science, and Judaism.

Religious Praxis: The Meaning of Halakhah
1953

Living in accordance with the Halakhah, demarcating a sphere of the sacred through halakhic practice—is this the ultimate end of the religious life? The answer is both yes and no. On the one hand, there can be no doubt that the end and perfection of religiosity, which the prophet calls "knowledge of God" and the psalmist "nearness of God," are not a matter of conduct: "to this ultimate perfection there do not belong either actions or moral qualities . . . it consists only of opinions to which speculation has led and that investigation has rendered compulsory" (Maimonides). The quest pertains to consciousness and inward intentionality. Accordingly, Maimonides identifies the Mitzvoth of the Torah, as it would seem, not with the "ultimate perfection" but with the preparatory perfections. In this sense, halakhic praxis is not the end of religion but only a means and method. But with a penetrating dialectic Maimonides converts the instrumental status of the Mitzvoth into the end of religion: "Know that all the practices of worship, such as reading the Torah, prayer and the per-

formance of the Other commandments, have only the
end of training you to occupy yourself with His commandments, may He be exalted, rather than with matters pertaining to this world, as if you were occupied
with Him, may He be exalted, and not with that which
is other than He." After nine chapters (chaps. 26–34
of *Guide* III) discussing the "intention of the Torah,"
which is to say the purpose of the Mitzvoth, and after
fifteen chapters (35–49) devoted to clarifying the rationale of the particular precepts in terms of their utility
for perfecting the condition of individuals and of society, Maimonides reveals the secret: the purpose of the
Mitzvoth is to educate man to recognize that knowing
God and cleaving to him consist in the practice of these
very precepts, and this constitutes the worship of God!
This is also the meaning of the sentence in his commentary to the tenth chapter of the mishnaic Tractate
Sanhedrin, "There is no other end to the (acquisition
of) Truth than to know that it is true, and the Torah
is true, and the purpose of knowing it is to observe it."

At the same time, the "ultimate perfection" of religion can never be realized. It always remains an eternal
signpost indicating the right direction on an infinitely
extended road. Man cannot observe the Torah in its
entirety because it is divine, not human. Even the perfect man is unable to cleave to God, since he will never
be able to remove the last barrier separating him from
God, "his being an intellect existing in matter." Hence
what is meant by "observance of the Torah" can only be
the perpetual effort to observe it. In this respect the religious life resembles the work of the housewife; her job is
endless, because whatever she does today she will have
to do once more tomorrow. The eternal striving toward
the religious goal, which is never attained, is embodied
in the halakhic practice, which never ends. After all the
effort invested in it, the scope of the remaining task is
never diminished and the goal is never nearer no matter what distance one has covered in one's attempt to
advance toward it. Every morning one must rise anew
to the service of the Creator—the self-same service that
one performed yesterday, and at the end of every Yom
Kippur—after the great realization of repentance and
atonement—the annual cycle of weekday Mitzvoth toward the next Yom Kippur begins anew. Thus halakhic
observance, in itself a means to religious perfection is,
in respect of man, the ultimate religious perfection of
which he is capable.

One of the finest European writers and thinkers,
Gotthold Ephraim Lessing (1729–1789), said that if God
gave him the choice between the truth and the eternal
search for the truth, he would choose the latter, "for the
genuine truth is known to God alone." Similarly, a great
Jewish leader of the socialist movement said in regard to
socialism: "The movement itself is everything, the goal
nothing at all." In like manner, one representing the "religion of Mitzvoth" would say to the proponents of "authentic religiosity": the eternal pursuit of the religious
goal by persevering in religious praxis is the be-all and
the end-all of religion for man. "The end of the matter,
when all is said and done: fear God and keep his Mitzvoth for that is the whole [attainment] of man" (Eccles.
12:13). The end itself is hidden by God. Rabbi Kook put
it this way: "If man is always likely to stumble . . . that
does not detract from his perfection, since the essence of
his perfection is the aspiration and the constant desire
to attain perfection." His disciple, Rabbi Jacob Moshe
Harlap, elaborates on this statement almost in the same
words as Lessing's, whose works he had never read:
"The desire is more of an end than is the achievement,
especially according to Maimonides, who explains that
there is no end other than He, may his Name be exalted.
It follows that, essentially, the end is the aspiration to
attainment of the goal . . . and we must prefer the search
for wisdom to its attainment." "Precisely the mediacy is
the goal . . . to know how to appreciate the effort more
than the attainment of the imaginary end, for, truth to
say, there is no end and mediacy is the chief desidera-
tum and the truest end."

Translated by Eliezer Goldman.

Other works by Leibowitz: *Ha-torah ha-medinah ve-
ha-yahadut ha-datit* (1952); *Torah u-mitzvot ba-zeman
ha-zeh* (1954); *Judaism, Human Values, and the Jewish
State* (1975).

Sami Michael

b. 1926

Sami Michael is an author, translator, editor, and civil
rights activist. Born in Kamal Salah, Iraq, he immigrated to Israel in 1949. In 1974, Michael's debut novel,
Shavim ve-shavim yoter (All Men Are Equal—But
Some Are More) was published, and he subsequently
became an influential left-wing activist in Israel. He
has twice received the Prime Minister's Prize and has
earned honorary doctorates from the Hebrew University and Ben-Gurion University. He has headed the
Association for Civil Rights in Israel.

The Newly Arrived Men of Letters
1954

The man of letters who cares about his links with the people—who is of the opinion that there is no backbone to his literary production except when his social source is present, typified by the dynamics of the people and their pursuit of the future—has to write in a style that the people among whom he lives understand. He has to stay true to the social content of his literature while innovating and recreating his national form in a new garb that the nation where he lives can taste [appreciate]. For the true realist man of letters does not only write *about* the social masses, he also writes *for* them. He does not merely write to express feelings and emotions deep in his soul that leave him restless until he writes them down; instead he also writes because he yearns to find similar ideas, feelings, and emotions in the hearts of the people whom he knows and understands, and whose happiness he considers as his life's highest objective. [. . .]

Capitulation before the Bitter Reality

We do not deny the serious difficulties that the man of letters newly arriving in Israel faces. The harsh life, the bitter struggle for the sake of a better life, the ugly settlement conditions in tents susceptible to being blown apart by gusts of winds, and the grinding depression that those new arrivals face make focusing on reading and writing one of the ideals of which it is difficult even to dream. This economic situation—in addition to the cultural policy of the government—makes it impossible for those new arrivals to be intellectually accommodated in this new country. Above all, this regressive black current, forcefully imposed on Israeli culture, which they are proud of calling "Western culture," creates a suffocating atmosphere for every living artistic talent and dims the light of sound thinking.

We do not deny the difficulty of embarking on the study of the characteristics of Israel's nascent Jewish nationalism so as to understand it accurately and abandon any sectarian, degraded, and rotten elements, while taking what is positive and vital in it. However, at the same time I think that one of the most dangerous attitudes is precisely that view taken by the group that completely brushes off the entire issue with the stroke of a pen under the pretext that it is impossible "to jump into the water." First and foremost, the position of this group is to capitulate before this bitter reality. This leads to the denial of any advantage from the

attempts that some new arrivals from the men of letters undertake to understand the new atmosphere and adapt to it. This adaptation does not imply by any means that under any condition there should be an accommodation or absorption of negative aspects within this new reality. There should be, however, an initial stage of attempting to understand the new reality, before negative aspects can be erased and replaced with a better reality.

At the end of the day, it is clear that the view of this group paves the way for regressive bourgeois writing so that it can spread its poison with no competition standing in its way. It is likewise clear that some of the new arrivals among the men of letters make no attempt to comprehend the new reality. Writing for them is a way to get the crumbs from the table of the elite bourgeoisie. Literary production for them is a secure means of income. They adapt quickly to the new stringent situation, and they start contributing to the doubling of regressive writing and understanding and throw it on the people. They claim that they are very welcomed, while people stand on the shores without daring to jump into the water. They see no benefit in challenging the tumultuous waves and imagine that they would be swamped the moment they touch them.

The men of letters among the new arrivals live mostly at the crossroads. The pretext through which the current regime uncovers its unashamed face is shown clearly. There are people who seek bread from the rubbish, and there are children afflicted with disease and poverty. The governing elites try to create a distorted generation. The army of jobless is stranded between the tent and the workplace, unable to find a means of income. The entire philosophy of the governing class and its lies and opinions get mired in the winter's mud. Therefore, there should be a lesson from those jobless in the tents to the governing class, which fears their progress; the appearance of somebody from among those slim and malnourished bodies who accuses them. What could file the charge and correct the wrongs except these daring hands of the men of letters who bear in mind the interests of the tortured masses? How happy and grateful would the governing class be if the men of letters from the new arrivals imposed silence on themselves by their own free will?! [. . .]

The Only Way

Realism in literature makes it incumbent on the men of letters of the new arrivals to treat the issues that preoccupy people's minds and among which they live as being at the center of life, not at its periphery. This is done in order to contribute to the creation of a humane, progressive Hebrew culture, entrusted with the interests of the Israeli people and respect for other peoples. There is no other way before the men of letters except the choice of either being both Jewish and internationalist men of letters or sliding down the path of cosmopolitanism.

Translated by Atef Alshaer.

Other works by Michael: *Ḥatsotsrah bavadi* (1987); *Viktoryah* (1993); *Ahavah beyn ha-dekalim* (1998); *Aida* (2008).

Ben-Zion Meir Hai Uziel

1880–1953

Jerusalem-born Ben-Zion Meir Hai Uziel was a member of an important rabbinic family, his father a leader in the local Sephardic community. At age twenty, Uziel became a teacher at a Sephardic yeshiva. Later, in 1911, he became the chief rabbi of Jaffa and its vicinity, working to raise the status of the local Sephardic community. While there, he worked closely with Rabbi Abraham Isaac Kook to improve Sephardi–Ashkenazi relations. During World War I, he advocated for the rights of the local Jews and was exiled to Damascus by the Turkish authorities. From 1921 to 1923, he served as chief rabbi of Salonika, Greece, subsequently becoming the chief rabbi of Tel Aviv–Jaffa. From 1939 to his death, he served as the Sephardic chief rabbi of Palestine and later Israel.

Nationalism and Its Awareness
1954

The ultimate national purpose, which is the central, binding shaft, joining and linking and fastening all the members of the nation into a single, solid body, must be consciously known and clear to the leadership of the nation, to every man and women of its citizens, for it is the vital force of nationalism, and all paths lead toward it, and as the Sage of Proverbs said: "Let thine eyes look right on, and let thine eyelids look straight before thee. Ponder the path of thy feet, and let all thy ways be established" (Proverbs 4:25–26). [. . .]

Knowledge of the ultimate purpose and its constant presence before the eyes of the individual and the public creates a national bond that unifies the entire nation into a single entity. Not every nation is privileged to know and see the light in the treasury of nationalism, nor is every man capable and suited to fulfill this ultimate purpose in their lifetime, nor is everyone capable of adding rays of light and splendor to the form of the nation and to enlarge and glorify it, but everyone knows and acknowledges the imperative nature of the national purpose, and that everyone work to sustain it according to their understanding and ability, joining together in the body of the nation, rising up in it, and adding power and might to it. [. . .]

Ignoring the ultimate national purpose causes destruction and disintegration, degeneration and aging, which brings with it destruction and death in life, whereas, on the contrary—observance of the ultimate purpose increases strength, encourages power, adds marvelous force and vigor to set aside all obstacles and hindrances, and to attain the purposeful goal.

The ultimate national purpose is not and cannot be hidden from view, concealed in an obscure corner, or transmitted and revealed only to the people of the nation. Rather it must be raised as a banner, standing "upon the highest places of the city" (Proverbs 9:3), and it proclaims its essence with vigor and courage, calling all humanity to approach it and cling to it—because it has consequences for life. The slogan of the assimilationists, or the philosophizers: be a Jew in your home and a man in the street (Judah Leib Gordon) is absurd and stupid, and it derives from its proclaimers' ignorance of the purpose of Judaism and of the Torah, because Judaism and mankind are interlocked and cling together like a flame to a coal. Judaism in its purpose is nothing but the highest aspiration for the elevation of man in his form and action in life, in his humanity, in his species, in general and in particular, to the highest stage of human perfection. [. . .]

Restriction of our ultimate purpose to the synagogue, to the house of study, or even to the rooms of our homes and dwellings, is tantamount to the burial and interment of our national purpose. [. . .] Those who distinguish between man and Jew thereby make Judaism into an ephemeral soul, which has no grip on life, and in these words of theirs they condemn themselves to destruction, themselves and the nation of Judaism to which they belong and in whose name they speak. [. . .]

The Torah of Israel holds within it the Torah of humanity and the Torah of life, the Torah of justice and morality, the Torah of society and family, the Torah of monarchy and the state, or, in other words: a worldview on human life and activity which is unique, and settlement of the world and its pleasantness in the path of justice and law, peace and love.

The Jewish faith, belief in the Unique One in the world and the Creator of man, in His visible and mysterious Providence over the actions of man and his thoughts, requires man and the nation to recognize its nationalism and purpose, its spiritual ideals, its view of the constitution of the world and its inner nature with clear knowledge, and to spread and inculcate its influence and its eternal views with the power of logic, as an example and model for all of humanity.

This ultimate purpose is the essence of Jewish life, it is the pride and soul of its life, and if you take away the soul—you leave the body mummified like the ancient kings of Egypt or the marble statues, which are well-carved but mute, that are displayed to be seen in all the museums in the world. And you choose a miserable existence like that and advise us to choose it? Woe to you who are wise in your own eyes! To idolatrous advisors it is said: Your ignorant advice is nothing new! The kings of Israel in the image of Jeroboam and Ahab and Menasseh, the Hellenizers or the Herodians and the prophets of the lying Baal [. . .] preceded you with this advice, but Israel did not heed their advice and said: we do not want a strip of land in order to bury the spirit of the nation, nor royal raiment that will come down to the grave with us, but we want a land of the living where the spirit of the nation will thrive and flourish, and a royal state like the kingdom of David, that deals with justice and law for the whole nation, which the nations will seek out in recognition, honor, and admiration. [. . .]

Those who advocated assimilation and denial of Judaism and those who advocated hiding and confining Judaism to the house and to the synagogues thought thereby to take their place and attain citizenship in the countries of their exile. And those who called themselves a sect: members of the faith of Moses, and turned their back on the Jewish homeland—they are uprooted in shame from the lands of their exile, scattered once again to the winds, and they will not reach the soil of Israel. [. . .]

But the faithful of Israel, who know and are familiar with the pleasantness and goodness of Judaism, with its nationalism and its Torah, cannot hide and deny it, in every place and situation where they are found—they give their lives for it, and aspire with all their heart and

soul to influence every person who is created in the image of God with its goodness and splendor. And this is what the words of the greatest prophet intended: "Thou hast avouched the Lord this day to be thy God, and to walk in his ways, and to keep his statutes, and his commandments, and his judgments, and to hearken unto his voice: And to make thee high above all nations which he hath made, in praise, and in name, and in honor; and that thou mayest be an holy people unto the Lord thy God, as he hath spoken" (Deuteronomy 26:17–18). [. . .]

This sanctity is not that of monasticism and withdrawal from life and the work of life, but on the contrary—the sanctity of life itself, to sanctify ourselves in thought and deed, to sanctify our land, to sanctify our personal and national life, to sanctify our entire world, and more marvelous than that are the words of our Sages, saying: "For I am the Lord your God: ye shall therefore sanctify yourselves, and ye shall be holy; for I am holy" (Leviticus 11:44). *Sanctify yourselves*—this means: the first water, *and ye shall be holy*—this is the latter water, *for I am holy*—this is the evening anointment, *For I am the Lord your God*—this is the blessing" (b.Berakhot 53b).

Our sanctification will not be full with withdrawal from human life and its phenomena, pleasures, and cherished things, but we are nourished by all the phenomena of the world, which are daily renewed, by all the marvelous discoveries, by all the philosophical and scientific opinions that arise and flourish and increase in our world, on this table which is set before man. That which bestows sanctity by clarifying and refining thought initially, is the first water, when we wash our hands before eating the meal. Choosing the good and the useful so you may be holy—this is the latter water, when we wash our hands before reciting the grace after the meal. The external foods, which we take in and are nourished by, enrich the treasuries and the richness of our soul, but they do not change the essence of our existence, which is an existence of sanctity and elevation. It abides, floating on the surface of the water, and its fragrance spreads to the distance in its delight and pleasantness. It is what determines the blessing for our God who sanctified us with His holiness, a blessing and spiritual satisfaction for ourselves, and blessing, and praise, and glory from all the nations who live with us on the earth.

The ultimate purpose of Judaism is: to live and work, to build and be built, to improve our world and our lives, to raise ourselves up and to raise up others to the high peak of human perfection and success, in the path of peace and love, to sanctify ourselves in the holiness of God in thought and deed, to be a blessing for ourselves, for blessing and acclamation, for the name and glory of all the nations, to be a nation sanctified to our Lord God, the Creator of the world and of man.

Translated by Jeffrey M. Green.

Other works by Uziel: *Mishpetey Uzi'el* (1935); *Mikhmaney Uzi'el* (1939); *Sha'arey Uzi'el* (1944); *Hegyoney Uzi'el* (1952).

Ḥaim Gamzu
1910–1982

Israeli art and drama critic Ḥaim Gamzu was born in Chernigov, Russia (now Chernihiv, Ukraine), and arrived in Palestine in 1923. Gamzu studied art and philosophy at the Sorbonne and the University of Vienna. He became director of the Tel Aviv Museum of Art in 1962 and founded the Beit Zvi acting school in Ramat Gan. He wrote about painting, sculpture, and the theater for *Haaretz* and published several books. The Tel Aviv Museum's Prize for the Advancement of the Arts is named for him.

Painting and Sculpture in Israel
1957

It is not enough to see a statue. A statue has to be sensed with the fingertips. In our imagination we touch the statue, caress it, examine its rounded and hollow surfaces, and by doing so our sense of vision becomes identical, for a moment, with the sense of touch. […]

Here, to be sure, we give no more than a bare selection from the many different sculptural works already to be found in Israeli art; yet these select examples can serve to indicate the general level and theoretical objectives of sculpture in this country.

The art of sculpture in Israel has not sub-divided into the figurative and abstract streams to anything like the same degree as is found in our painting, where a number of painters have overstepped the boundaries of the objective with an occasionally astonishing haste. Some crossed this Rubicon of abstraction directly from naturalist painting. Others reached it through the channels of expressionism found in the styles of Soutine or Rouault. Some first tried to float and hover in the legendary worlds of Chagall.

The situation in the field of Israeli sculpture, however, is entirely different. Only of late do we observe a trend towards forms which stylistically approach abstraction, while remaining balanced within the bounds of configuration. There is only one of our sculptors who has consistently been seeking forms approaching abstraction for many years. Another sculptor of the younger group has recently begun to follow the same path, and it is abstraction proper. What follows from this is the fact that the sculpture of Israel is still anchored in the safe harbor of an art which, though varied in forms and differing in styles, does not go beyond the differences deriving from the characters and personalities of the artists; whose real concern is not the creation of sects or schools, but the development of talent and mastery of its technical resources.

The sculptors of Israel do not avoid influences. They seek them, and rightly so. And from the entire range of varying influences Israel's sculpture is assuming its character. It is already possible to say that it has merits and a charm of its own, a dynamic quality and softness, a speaking symbolism and delicate primitivism which owes much to Mediterranean elements that are both ancient and contemporary.

The great spiritual and physical transformation taking place in the lives of the various Jewish communities that have come here; the deployment of economic groups which is turning the People of the Book into a people of the soil; the roots that are being struck within a social and economic framework differing so vastly from that in which the citizens of Israel lived in their countries of origin; all serve together to eliminate the lack of roots which was the mark of the Jew in general and the Jewish artist in particular. In the sculpture of Israel, on the contrary, can be found all the marks of a spiritual stability, strength and faith; clear signs of an earthiness which leads to an affirmation of life in spite of all struggle. Sometimes it leads even to an affirmation of life precisely because of the difficulties that are to be met within it, while desire to overcome them is so strong within the citizen of the new Israel that it serves him as a lever towards achievements that are rich in potentialities and exceedingly forceful in their creative quality. […]

The second factor for the development of the art of sculpture in Israel was our War of Independence, which was won with the blood of young heroes. Young lives were cut off in our midst, and the community will not allow them to be forgotten. Parents sought to set up some memorial light for their children. Comrades longed to set up some monument for those who had sanctified their lives in their deaths. Settlements turned to our sculptors and requested them to hallow those who had gone in some tangible fashion. Yad Mordechai, Negba, Ein Geb, Hukok, Hassolelim, Tel Joseph, Rehovot, Ramat-Gan and other places spared no effort in erecting monuments to their sons, who fell fighting for the homeland. Since these monuments and memorials have been erected, sculpture has ceased to be merely an exclusive art only for the select few in Israel. It has become popular. And since the sculptors did not engage in exaggerated abstraction but tried to be comprehensible to the ordinary man while maintaining a high professional level, the public as a whole has become familiar with the art of sculpture in connection with the idea of commemoration. It approves of sculpture as a form of expression for the purest and most holy emotions such as motherhood (in the statue of the mother and her child by Zeev Ben-Zvi, at Mishmar Haemek); comradeship in struggle (the Negba memorial by Nathan Rappaport); the summons to battle, the aid and the grief of the loving woman (Priver's Tel Joseph relief); fatherly love (the Hukok monument by Yehiel Shemi); and so on and so forth. It cannot be claimed that all these monuments are absolutely perfect or represent the peak of artistic achievement. We are still far from having achieved a true monumental sculpture. Yet these are beginnings that are worthy of appreciation. Let us hope that they will be followed by many other works. [. . .]

We now face a kind of silent contest between the arts of painting and sculpture. So far it is painting which has reaped the modest harvest of initial successes at the large international art displays in Europe and America. Yet the time will come when, in spite of the difficulties in, and costs of, the transport of heavy and often fragile sculptures, our plastic art will also be presented as well worthy of consideration at exhibitions outside our country. It may be assumed that this is no mere pious aspiration. In the light of the achievements of our sculptors, examples of which are shown in this album, there is every reason to believe that that day is not in any way distant, and will indeed soon be here.

Translated by I. M. Lask.

Other works by Gamzu: *Ha-omanut be-artsenu: ha-ta'arukhah ha-kelalit shel omaney erets-yisra'el* (1942);

Havay va-nof be-omanut ha-tsiyur ha-yisra'elit (1957); *Ten Israeli Painters* (1957).

Avraham Abbas

1912–1958

Born in Damascus, Avraham Abbas moved to Palestine in 1929. In the 1930s and during World War II, he assisted Jewish immigrants from Syria, working for the Histadrut and then undercover during the war to bring in some fifteen thousand Jews. From 1955 to 1958, Abbas served in the Knesset in the Labor Party. He also wrote about Sephardic Jewish issues in the journal *Shevet ve-'am.*

From Ingathering to Integration
1958

As the day approaches for the election of the Knesset and the local and municipal authorities, Sephardi and oriental Jewish leaders evince increasing alertness to the problems before them. There are rallies of communal leaders in several places; several separate burial societies for Sephardim are being organized in a number of communities. Some of the leaders who lend their support to such separatist moves are undoubtedly driven by noble public considerations in joining such organizations; they hope thereby—to take one specific grievance of recent experience—to express their utter dissatisfaction with the discriminatory policies of the Ministry of Religions which sought to dislodge Sephardi public servants from positions they had long held. There are others, however, who embarked upon such separatist moves as a springboard for the forthcoming electoral campaign, in a vain attempt to exploit the frustration of oriental Jews for their own personal designs and ambitions. It is this psychological background which has rendered possible special separatist rallies of Sephardi engineers, lawyers, rabbis etc., or groups like a federation of immigrants from all Asian and North African countries.

But when this has been said, it must be admitted that each such separatist move (or organization) feeds on a sense of general malaise and disaffection that derive from the cumulative effect of long bitter experience, namely, the overriding fact that after years of residence in the country large masses of people have not yet been integrated into the social economic, educational and cultural life of the country (the strictly educational aspect of the problem has been labored [dealt with] above in my remarks on education). Again, the leaders of several political parties of the country have indirectly contributed to such separatist organization, for they have always viewed oriental Jewish communities as little more than suppliers of votes in times of election. Party leaders often accuse Sephardi, and oriental leaders of separatist and sectional trends, alleging also that the mass of the communities for whom they speak are simply unwilling to find their place within the framework of existing organization. Let us examine such charges dispassionately and see how much truth there is in them. Have the spokesmen for the State, of all parties, done their own soul searching without bias? Have they asked themselves whether it would be just and fair for them to pursue the path they pursued hitherto, and leave these naive and simple oriental Jews on the fringes and in the by-paths of the public institutions, without enabling them to have a say in the framing of their policies? [. . .]

Representation on the Executive of the Jewish Agency and the Zionist Council

For decades these important public bodies have been constituted on an absolutely communal basis, and none but Ashkenazi Jews served on them. To ignore or dismiss this overriding fact is to offend against the truth. Many hasten to draw facile and dangerous inferences from this fact. One of these is: that Sephardi Jews, that very section of the Jewish people which has literally realized the Zionist ideal by coming in mass to settle in the country, was [were] not Zionist at all. Although the constituted bodies of the Zionist movement are there essentially to tackle the problem of these very Jews, they themselves are not represented on [in] the supreme organs of the movement. I refer not to a purely communal representation (I have always discountenanced any such course; on the contrary, in my many years in the country I have always fought for the affiliation of oriental Jews with existing political parties, through which—and through which alone—Sephardi claims and views should be pressed). But let us see whether even on the existing system of representation by parties, Sephardi and oriental Jews could be said to have received their just deserts. The blatant fact is that all political parties, represented on the Executive of the Jewish Agency, have virtually joined in a conspiracy of which the obvious effect is to dismiss Sep-

hardi Jewry as an utterly insignificant factor, so that not a single oriental Jew of the respective parties was nominated for such representative public office. This charge could not perhaps be properly directed to parties with only one representative on the Executive. But there are parties with a fairly large number of representatives, yet all these are Ashkenazi Jews. The Zionist Council with a membership of 80 (apart from several dozen Deputy Members) continues to this day to be constituted, as it was originally constituted, of Ashkenazi members, with perhaps only one or two Sephardi members.

It is futile to argue—as some do—that this body is now stripped of any real influence. If it were so devoid of influence, it should have had no right to exist. But if it exists and functions, we [would] very much like to be associated with it. We would like to take an active part in its deliberations on immigration quotas; the measures it considers for integration; the question of whether the Zionist Organization should be constituted as a unitary and uniform organization or as a federation of political parties. We would like to take an active part in the framing of the policy of selection in immigration, particularly insofar as it applies to North African Jews, and all the more so because that policy was responsible for the denial of immigration facilities to scores of thousands of Jews in Morocco. We claim our share in the public missions sent to all parts of the world. We refuse to believe that there are not among us public leaders and speakers with vision, sympathy and understanding who can carry the message of the land to millions of their brethren abroad.

Translated by Moshe Behar and Zvi Ben-Dor Benite.

Jacob Katz

1904–1998

Historian Jacob Katz was born in Magyargencs, Hungary; he studied both at religious schools and at the University of Frankfurt, receiving a doctorate in 1934. After his move to Palestine, he taught from 1936 to 1950 in Jerusalem at religious schools and at the Mizrachi Teachers Seminary. Specializing in analyses of Reform and Orthodox Judaism, the Enlightenment, and Jewish–Christian relations, he later taught at the Hebrew University, becoming professor of Jewish social and educational history in 1962. In 1969, he was appointed rector of the Hebrew University.

Tradition and Crisis: Jewish Society at the End of the Middle Ages
1958

I. Definition of Our Subject

This book is intended as a description of a "traditional society"—that is, a society that saw itself as based upon a body of knowledge and a set of values handed down to it from the past. World Jewry was such a "traditional society" at least from the Talmudic era until the age of the European Emancipation. Indeed, segments of Jewish society may be referred to in this way even in more recent times. [. . .]

What parallels are there, after all, to Hasidism or Haskala? But in fact even these two apparently unique movements can be seen as examples of broader phenomena. Hasidism and Haskala exemplify the two forces that typically cause the disintegration of traditional social institutions: religious charisma and rationalism. Religious charisma springs from a sense of immediate religious mission, whereas rationalism is grounded upon a belief in the unlimited power of reason and logic. Religious charisma and rationalism are essentially opposites, and are likely to come into conflict when they exist in the same historical framework. But they share a common attitude toward traditionalism: Both find the source of their authority in themselves, and tend to minimize any authority that rests solely on the force of tradition.[1] Both of these types of challenges can be found in Jewish history even in earlier periods. More than once, traditional Jewish society has faced the real threat that rationalist criticism or the demands made by a sense of religious mission could harm or destroy it completely.[2] This is not the place to deal with the question of how or why traditional society escaped this danger prior to the first half of the eighteenth century. But the fact that both of these powerful challenges emerged simultaneously on the historical stage at the end of our period serves as double testimony to the historic watershed at which traditional society had arrived. [. . .]

XXIII. The Emergence of the Neutral Society

So far we have emphasized the breadth of the transformation that Hasidism caused in traditional Jewish society. But this transformation affected only the internal structure of the society—its mode of organization, its sources of authority, and its criteria for stratification.

Nothing changed in the society's relation to the outside world. The isolating barriers remained, and Jewish society's feeling of uniqueness vis-à-vis its surroundings may even have grown stronger and deeper. It is clear, therefore, that the changes brought on by Hasidism cannot be defined as disintegration in the true sense of the word. What happened was a change in the mechanisms that governed the life of society rather than a true disintegration, which would have implied the breakdown of the institutions of society and the dispersal of its membership.

SIGNS OF SOCIAL DISINTEGRATION

Under normal circumstances a society does not totally disintegrate. Usually, institutions break up only to allow for the birth of new ones. Though contemporaries perceive their world as disintegrating, this is largely a subjective reaction to the transitional stage during which the old institutions have lost their authority and the new ones have not yet become established or formed a positive, binding relationship with the individual members of the society. But Jewish society really did face the possibility of true disintegration, since it depended for its existence on an intentional withdrawal from the surrounding society, a withdrawal buttressed by ritual barriers. Should the barriers crumble and the withdrawal end, a total breakdown of social institutions could occur, one that would not be followed by the emergence of substitutes. The individuals in Jewish society would then be absorbed by the surrounding society and would have their needs fully met through its institutions.

Jewish society, as the reader is aware, never went to that extreme, even where it was apparently given the opportunity to do so. But a tendency toward disintegration and self-liquidation did occasionally appear; a prime example of this is provided by the Haskala and emancipatory movement. This movement arose in the West contemporaneously with the rise of Hasidism in the East. The very fact that, within a society that had until then formed a unified continuum, there now simultaneously emerged two movements with quite opposite goals and ambitions is one of the signs of the breakdown of this society into its component parts. [. . .]

A decisive turning point in the history of Jewish society occurred only when its individual members transferred their social aspirations from the context of their own community to that of the surrounding non-Jewish milieu. This happened when they began to regard the non-Jewish society not only as a framework for economic activity but also as a source of social gratification. Up to this time, if such a change in social goals had taken place, it led the individual to a transfer from Jewish to non-Jewish society. That the outward-directed Jew now did not have to convert to Christianity was a function of the fact that a new social class had emerged in non-Jewish society, a class that no longer saw religious differences as a decisive factor. This class gradually emerged under the wings of the absolute state through the coalescing of a new group, the independent middle class, itself the consequence of economic activity in the free market that the absolute state tolerated and sometimes even encouraged. The absolute state aimed at stripping the existing estates of their political power, but unintentionally it also encouraged the weakening of their social framework. More and more, individuals were unable to find satisfaction within the framework of the accepted estates—merchants and artisans in their guilds and confraternities, and the nobility in their estate-bound occupations and social life. These unsatisfied individuals found support in free economic activity based on the rational calculation of market prospects. The emergence of the free market correlates directly with the number of individuals who defected from their estates. The two phenomena were conditioned by numerous and complicated political and technical factors whose full description is beyond the scope of this study.

NOTES

1. See Max Weber, *Wirtschaft und Gesellschaft, Gundriss der Sozialoekonomic* (Tübingen: 1947), pp. 142, 758–759.

2. There are many examples of rational critique of the traditional bases of Jewish society, especially in Spain. See Yitzhak Baer, *A History of the Jews in Christian Spain* (Philadelphia: Jewish Publication Society, 1966), pp. 96–110, 289–305, as well as my Hebrew article "Religious Tolerance in the Halakhic and Philosophical System of R. Menahem ha-Meiri," *Zion* 18 (1953), pp. 15–30 [reproduced in slightly different form in Jacob Katz, *Exclusiveness and Tolerance: Studies in Jewish–Gentile Relations in Medieval and Modern Times* (Oxford: 1961), chapter 10: "Men of Enlightenment," pp. 114–28—tr.]. On the place of the mystical stream in Judaism and its relation to tradition, see Gershom Scholem, *Major Trends in Jewish Mysticism*, 3rd revised edition (New York: Schocken, 1954), pp. 7–10.

Translated by Bernard Dov Cooperman.

Other works by Katz: *Toledot yisra'el ve-he-'amim*, 3 vols. (1945–1950); *Exclusiveness and Tolerance* (1961); *Freemasons and Jews* (1970); *Emancipation and Assimi-*

lation: Studies in Modern Jewish History (1972); *Out of the Ghetto: The Social Background of Jewish Emancipation, 1770–1870* (1973); *Toward Modernity: The European Jewish Models* (1987).

Dan Miron
b. 1934

An author, editor, critic, and translator, Dan Miron is a leading scholar in the fields of Hebrew, Yiddish, and German Jewish literature. Born and brought up in Tel Aviv, Miron is professor emeritus in literature at the Hebrew University and a professor emeritus of Hebrew and comparative literature at Columbia University. Miron was awarded the Israel Prize in 1993.

Yemei Tsiklag: *The Artistic Problems of a War Story*
1958

The reader's first ascent from the stunning expanse of *Days of Tsiklag* is influenced entirely by astonishment because of the rare uniqueness and power of this story, especially since it is about men at war. The distance that Yizhar took from almost any other story of this kind is extremely surprising, in that it is one of essence and not just of quality. In his book, Yizhar created a kind of principled opposite of the very essence of ordinary war stories in both world literature and Israeli literature. War stories, as they developed in European and American literature from the time of *Under Fire* by Henri Barbusse to *All Quiet on the Western Front* by Erich Maria Remarque, and as [they] developed in Israeli literature from the time of the War of Independence, almost always encounter a problem, which is bound up with the artistic and psychological credibility of its plot. This plot, which is necessarily composed of an action or series of actions in the course of battles, describes them until they reach their heroic or tragic resolution and it inevitably risks severing itself from the emotional world of those who take part in it. The plot is not motivated by the inner forces of the protagonists' souls. The movement of influence between character and event that is depicted in it is at most unidirectional: from things to the soul, and not the other way around. The series of events in combat—at least in modern warfare—cannot be changed by the psychological action of one of the protagonists. Only rarely does a narrator allow himself, in developing a war story, to depict reciprocal influence between character and an event in the plot, which alone makes the development of the plot credible to us—not with respect to the facts, military tactics, history, etc., but with respect to the fictional imagination, as a creative poetical act. As a result, in most instances war stories are marked by a partial and dubious degree of artistic integration. [. . .]

The descriptive form of this war literature is reportorial—a form in which the writer gains the reader's trust externally, not by literary means, by reassuring the reader that he is presenting the events as they actually happened. Therefore in war stories in general, and specifically in Israeli war stories, a strange phenomenon is present, opposition between the "material," which stands for the peak of drama, and the outcome of the record—which are revealed in barren grayness after the war is over, giving the stories under discussion value and significance, which do not derive from their literary quality. The reason is that this ready-made drama, when writers merely record events as they occurred, stands like Satan in the way of the only artistic drama that a writer of fiction is capable of producing: the drama born of reciprocal relations between the protagonist and the world around him. Authors who understood this basic stumbling-block, which is inherent in the "material" of a war story, tended as much as possible to divert the center of action in their stories from the major, decisive military events. In the marginal areas of the world of war they were able to develop a plot, which would absorb the full meaning of this world and would at the same time be free and capable of depicting a certain dependency upon the psychological characteristics of the protagonists. Norman Mailer transferred a small group of soldiers to behind the Japanese lines and let them wander aimlessly there (*The Naked and the Dead*). S. Yizhar himself placed two of his best war stories not in a world with battles but in something that happened or would happen ("Ḥirbet Ḥizʿah" and "The Prisoner"). He was thereby able to erect the entire structure of the plot of the lives of his protagonists in an independent fictional structure. Thus he succeeded in placing the significance, the atmosphere, and the spiritual content of war within the act of bringing the Arab prisoner to headquarters, or in thoughts about driving the Arab residents of the Ḥirbe over the border, more than all the others succeeded, those who tried explicitly to describe men fighting, being killed, attacking, and winning.

In *Days of Tsiklag*, Yizhar did not continue in this manner. Here the mirror was not placed on the slopes of the margins (the story describes one of the decisive battles, which led to the liberation of the Negev), and certainly no effort was made to depict the decisive military development as something that might or might not have happened. On the contrary, here, with explicit and conscious intention Yizhar falls upon the heart of the stormy sea of the experience of the throes of battle, which so many writers attempted to describe and ended up in artistic disaster. [. . .]

Instead of describing marginal events of the war, such as transferring a prisoner, driving out the residents of Ḥirbet Ḥizʿah, or even observing a convoy in "Midnight Convoy," here Yizhar tried his hand at describing the very experience of men who are attacked, who fight, who lie in trenches under a hail of shells, who are killed, and who are victorious. Nevertheless, it is doubtful whether any work in Israeli literature is as far as *Days of Tsiklag* is from reportorial conventions, taking a radical and absolute stand upon the inner life of the protagonists and upon it alone. There would appear to be an abundance of obstacles here. The scaffolding of the plot rests upon three conquests of a hill in the south, which had decisive strategic importance, in that it was on the road to the Negev, in that it defended an airfield, and, for an instant, it appeared, to those to whom it so appeared, that this was ancient Tsiklag, the city where David lived before he was a king of Judah. The first conquest of the hill, which was effected with few men and little preparation, ends in panicky retreat on the evening of the following day. The second conquest, for which there was greater preparation, ended once again on the following evening with a retreat that was no less panicked. The book completes a seven-day cycle and concludes with the repelling of a mighty onslaught, which was intended to reverse the third conquest. On the face of it, this is the classic course of events in routine war stories, deriving its vitality from the events and not from the characters. Here we have the same graduated raising of the tension of the struggle, which the stunning failures intensify even more, toward the final, decisive battle, which ends in victory. This gradual increase in the external tension of the events promises the reader, so it would appear, a story characterized by all the "dramatic" traits typical of war stories, the drama born outside the story, born of the tension of reportage. But the palpable result, that is, the impressions while one is reading, are far from this routine plot aimed at the catharsis of victory, so far that is hard to imagine a greater distance. A reader who begins reading this book in hopes of finding riveting entertainment in it of the type he finds in ordinary war stories will put it aside with absolute disappointment after the briefest read. Graduated progress toward the final determination of the battle is just one of the factors that contribute to the structure of the plot of *Days of Tsiklag* and it should not be regarded as a decisive factor. Indeed, Yizhar grasps it without at all needing to pay any lip service to the "natural" drama inherent in it, without resorting to the qualities of "speed" and "economy," so highly recommended for stories of battle and war, and without trying to purchase the good will and interest of ordinary readers of war stories. On the contrary, one may say that with respect to the "aesthetic" rules of a riveting military plot, in *Days of Tsiklag* Yizhar commits an unpardonable sin, in that just here, in this framework of a gradually intensifying and fascinating battle story, he chose to make a most detailed experiment in Hebrew literature, perhaps the most detailed experiment, of entering the regions of human consciousness, pitting it against itself, against the landscape that surrounds it, and against the dread of the possibility of death.

Translated by Jeffrey M. Green.

Other works by Miron: *A Traveler Disguised: The Rise of Modern Yiddish Fiction in the Nineteenth Century* (1973); *The Image of the Shtetl* (2000); *Imahot meyasdot, aḥayot ḥorgot* (2004); *From Continuity to Contiguity: Toward a New Jewish Literary Thinking* (2010).

Dov Sadan

Three Foundations (Sholem Aleichem and the Yiddish Literary Tradition)
1959

[. . .] *Why* is fame accorded to this particular individual, far and beyond his own time and place and *why* does he continue to capture new readers both in the original and in translation? [. . . P]erhaps this disproportion is a result of the old commonplace that associates his name with the famous triad: Sholem Aleichem in the middle, Mendele before him and Yitskhok Leybush Peretz after him. As so often happens, he who stands in the middle gets hurt, just as Isaac was swallowed up between Abraham and Jacob, becoming the prototype of one who is no more than the son of his precursor and the father of his offspring. [. . .]

The triad-formula leads to an even greater pitfall, namely, it encourages a variety of comparisons between him and the other two. But what unites them is only their stature—three proud oaks in the forest of Yiddish—while the differences between them are ever so great. Were we to judge the content of their writing, the differences would emerge in bold relief. Mendele's narrative is limited in time and place to the Pale of Settlement and it does not budge from there. Any attempt to break out of these limits meets with the same fate as Benjamin III whose imagination drew him to remote, faraway places but whose reality dragged him back to his own little niche. [. . .] Y. L. Peretz's narrative is also limited in time and place, to the borders of Poland and environs, with the time boundary extending somewhat beyond the recent past by the inclusion of some of the spheres of influence of Hasidism, the last great collective movement of the Diaspora. Sholem Aleichem's narrative is also time-bound but spatially it moves along the most dynamic lines of Jewish existence during the past generations, namely, along the routes of Jewish migration. Thus, his stories are rooted in the Ukraine, but they branch out over several lands of the dispersion and reach America.

The Jewish migratory course throughout time and place is the very essence of Yiddish prose, but anyone desiring to find its outline in the works of the classic triad will be led only to Sholem Aleichem. The fact that none of them ever set eyes on Jerusalem, the oldest among them dying in Odessa, the next in line in Warsaw, and the youngest in New York, is more than mere biographical data. But if Sholem Aleichem was the forerunner of the other two in the triad in terms of narrative content, making him a kind of embryo of what was to become the diversified temporal and spatial scope of Yiddish prose, it must also be noted that in terms of narrative form, his was a regression to those who *preceded* the other two and this very regression was the source of his achievement. A close look at the narratives of Mendele and Peretz reveals the prototypes of two central prose developments in Yiddish literature: The expansive storytelling of Mendele is the basis of a development in which the novel, especially in its realistic configuration, was to play the central role. The condensed storytelling of Peretz is the basis of a development in which the short story, especially in its psychological configuration, was to play the dominant role. Furthermore, each of these basic narrative approaches nourished other writers who combined them in different proportions and these in turn, shaped the history of

Yiddish prose, be it of the Asch and Opatoshu school or of the Bergelson and Nister school, and so on. As for Sholem Aleichem, though he did in fact write novels, and long ones at that, as well as short stories, neither represents his main achievement. Though they are like scattered stops on the road of his creativity, the main thing is what lies after the stops and between them—the monologue, the letter and the comedy.

It can be argued, moreover, that Sholem Aleichem reverted several times to the novel and to the short story, like someone turning back on the road which was considered the legitimate developmental course of Yiddish prose, but each time he strayed from the path and followed the other three routes, the three foundations, wherein were revealed the talent of his originality and the originality of his talent; wherein he himself was revealed. And most important, in each of the three bases he returned to that which preceded the novel and preceded the short story in Yiddish literature of the last generations. He found lost threads and took them up again, his rethreading providing no mere continuity but rather a renewal, even a revolution.

What prompted Sholem Aleichem to return to the three foundations? Before this can be answered, another problem must be solved: Why could he not function creatively within the framework of the novel and the short story? The answer lies in the nature of these two forms, especially to the extent that they were developed in his day. These forms entailed a selective approach to the subject matter of life, an approach that obligated the writer to choose only such matter that furthered the plot and character in their interaction. Even a spot-check on Sholem Aleichem's novels and short stories reveals the extent to which these barriers were breached and circumvented. It is as if the subject matter of life, in its desire to express its own kaleidoscopic turmoil through the narrative, surmounted all obstacles that were laid in its path. Sholem Aleichem needed genres in which these obstacles were either nonexistent or minimal. The monologue, of course, liberates the spoken word, and this speech shapes the story out of its very freedom, while the limits of this freedom are determined by the world, the character and the needs of the speaker. In this case "speakers" would be more appropriate than "speaker," because through the monologue Sholem Aleichem was able to realize his desire and his talent—to achieve a total identification with a great and multifarious population.

He received the monologue by way of a legacy—the legacy of Haskalah literature. [. . .] The monologue served the maskilim as a utilitarian device, the point of which was, of course, to present a monologue of someone whom the maskil wished to ridicule, and whom he did in fact ridicule by letting him speak for himself. It appeared as if the story came directly from the mouth of a naive narrator, but the maskil pushed the simpleton's naivete so far that it became ridiculous and thus the satiric needle, hidden in the windbag, so to speak, emerged to prick that bag full of holes. [. . .]

Whenever we speak of Sholem Aleichem's monologue, we must always remember that it includes several types. Take the monologue *Genz* ("Geese"), for instance. Here the goose dealer herself speaks like a goose, so that even her digressions from the story proper connect back into it. Or take a monologue like *Dos tepl* ("The Pot"), in which the narrative center is only a crutch, even a pretext for the rapid associative flood that comes from the rambling female narrator. An entirely different type of monologue is *Khanike-gelt* ("Money for Hanukka"), where the story-line is only a frame for presenting a complete typology of a large family. In fact, this relatively short monologue can be regarded as a miniature novel about the members of a sizable household. It follows that a monologue such as *Motl Peysi dem khazns* (*Motl the Son of Peysi the Cantor*), one of the author's finest works, suggests a comparison with that unique monologue, the autobiography *Funem yarid* (*From the Fair*).

Looking back at the maskilic monologue from this vantage point, we can now speak of a legacy which, on the verge of its demise, experienced a rebirth.

What has been said about the monologue holds true for the epistolary form as well: [. . .] its essence lies in the power of identification, with the scriptural author, this time, instead of the oral speaker. And whenever we have an exchange of letters as in the Menakhem-Mendl and Sheyne-Sheyndl series, there is a dual identification—with two sexes, two people, two characters, two milieus, each component activating the complete spectrum of its own expressive possibilities, which the letter form, itself a written monologue, makes possible. Unfortunately, very few authentic Yiddish letters have come down to us, especially from earlier periods. We are therefore unable to construct a chronological survey of our epistolary culture. To the extent that it can be examined, however, the available material shows how the lively, spoken word broke through the ossified conventions and then broke out of them; how the letter, in all generations past, yearned for an artistic expression and finally achieved it through Sholem Aleichem. Though we do not know whether he studied or researched this literary genre and its history, we can say that his intuition made up for whatever was held back from his intellect. Here, too, we may observe that we are dealing with a legacy that was revived on the very verge of its demise.

Last but not least—the comedy, which needs no extensive proof to be regarded as a literary legacy, especially from the Yiddish branch of the Haskalah. Here the line of transmission is clear, for the dramatic literature of the Haskalah obeyed a functional linguistic differentiation: the drama of flamboyant pathos was written in Hebrew, whereas the drama of down-to-earth comedy was written in Yiddish. [. . .]

For our purposes it is important to note that when Sholem Aleichem embarked upon comedy, he tried to build it up into a theatrical spectacle, something which was possible during the blossoming period of the Yiddish theater. And in the very act of creating this spectacle, he fulfilled the mission of the comedy legacy. For if the maskilic comedy at its inception exploited folk elements to satirize a large sector, all, or almost all of the Jewish people, it ultimately became, through Sholem Aleichem's comedy, the very incarnation of the people. A detailed analysis of Sholem Aleichem's comedy reveals the extent to which it was an indispensable form for him. I am not referring to the obvious connection between his long novel *Der blutiker shpas* (*The Bloody Jest*) and its dramatization, *Shver tsu zayn a yid* (*It's Hard to Be a Jew*). I am referring to much more complex examples. Take the novel *Sender Blank,* for instance. It concerns the story of a wealthy father whose household reveals its true nature the moment he takes seriously ill, but upon recovery he throws the truth back in their faces. This main theme was reworked into the famous comedy *Dos groyse gevins* (*The Lottery*) with the necessary adaptation of components: the test is not an illusory terminal illness but an illusory lottery prize which prompts the tailor's family to reveal its true nature. Whoever compares and contrasts the novel and the comedy will realize that not only was the time lag between the two works decisive, for the artist's talent reached maturation in this period, but the different approach and development—necessitated by the different genre—were also decisive in guaranteeing the artistic

level of the comedy. If we recall that Sholem Aleichem nurtured his comedy on the best of the native traditions, especially through a fusion of the literary comedy legacy with the *purim-shpil* and its themes, and this at a time when the drama was undergoing a transition to realism on the one hand and to symbolism on the other—only then will we appreciate how much effort it took for him to respond to his *own* strengths, to pick up a lost thread, rethread it and go on stitching. Hence, that which was said of the monologue and the letter can now be said of the comedy as well: we have here a legacy which was revived on the verge of its demise.

Translated by David G. Roskies.

Ben-Zion Dinur
1884–1973

Born Ben-Zion Dinaburg into a traditional religious home in a small Ukrainian town, the yeshiva-educated future historian was an autodidact in secular subjects. He received advanced training as a historian in Berlin and Bern, then sailed to Mandate Palestine in 1921. He found employment teaching Jewish history at the Hebrew Teachers Seminary in Jerusalem, where he remained for almost thirty years, producing a stream of books, articles, and reviews. In 1932, he also began teaching modern Jewish history at the Hebrew University, where he was ultimately appointed to a professorship in 1948. From 1951 to 1955, Dinur served as minister of education and culture in the third to sixth governments of Israel, and he was the head of Yad Vashem from 1953 to 1959.

Days of War and Revolution: Memories of a Way of Life
1960

The distinctly Land of Israel character in the messianic thought of this generation did not limit itself to the influence of the Shabetai ferment and its offshoots. It was, largely, disseminated widely throughout the population. It was also emphasized in the ethical and homiletical literature of the radical opponents of all forms of the Shabetai messianic movement, including in the missives of the leaders and spokesmen of the Hasidic movement—in their utterances and prayers as well as in the wills, letters, and sermons of the Misnagdim [opponents of Hasidism] belonging to the school of thought of the Vilna Gaon and his disciples. Moreover, immigrating to pre-state Israel was very common, practically part and parcel of being Jewish. Hundreds of rabbis and Jewish leaders, both adherents and nonaffiliates, from the entire Jewish diaspora, are immigrating to Israel. They are mostly individuals of advanced age. Sometimes, however, they come in convoys and groups, whose messianic character is rather pronounced. This aliyah, with its absorption pangs and increased numbers undergoing hardships, has amplified genuine ties and bonds regarding the diaspora's relationship with the Land of Israel. On the one hand, pre-state emissaries have endeavored to highlight the overall value of Jewish settlement in the Land of Israel and its role in hastening redemption, and they have persevered in maintaining ties between the Land of Israel and the diaspora. This determination has been underscored by the fact that, already then, the Jewish settlement in the pre-state period contained people from all the important communities of the Jewish diaspora. Thus, the "small settlement" was created with all its advanced Talmudic institutes, Jewish Studies academies, and institutions, becoming a new factor of great value and influence in improving the genuine ties existing between the Jewish people and the Land of Israel—to an extent unprecedented in many generations.

This genuine nuance in the attitude toward the Land of Israel and in the hope for redemption found expression in folk songs; both those with strong Hebrew underpinnings having a formula, a type of folk prayer produced by groups saturated with a Jewish seminary atmosphere, and a semi-Ukrainian style, attesting to its popular origins, steeped in the most vivid expressions of yearning for redemption and longing for the Land of Israel.

* * *

The realistic tone expressing the longings for redemption and the feelings of yearning for the Land of Israel is rooted not only in ideology. Basically, the entire Aliyah movement, encompassing numerous segments of the Jewish population in pre-state Israel, was based on a very real sense that the ground was crumbling beneath one's feet, of an uncertain future, of an unrelenting tension whereby "every day is much worse than the previous one," an anticipation and dread of the unknown that is liable to set us—young and old alike—on the road to exile. [It is] the threshold of a new era and the onset of a downward spiral. This feeling was especially acute in Poland; however, it was also prevalent in Turkey. Both countries, having large and, at the time, unwanted Jewish populations, underwent times of depletion and decline.

The depletion and decline of Polish Jewry were predicated on the disintegration of the socialist and political regime of the Polish Republic, and on the circumstances surrounding its persistent struggle for existence. Polish nobles did not wish to relinquish their authority and sovereignty as feudal rulers, governors of closed castles, and despots of fortified strongholds—at a time when peoples and countries were fighting fiercely for their existence and sovereignty. At the same time, they sought fully to enjoy all the advantages and comforts, the refinements and pleasures of landowners having open farming and marketable produce.

The political and legal decline in the conditions under which Jews were living was expressed in a new constitution, whose objective was maximum exploitation and minimum protection afforded the Jews by the kingdom and its treasury. The protection was minimal, even taking into account the shrinking resources and poor capability of the waning kingdom.

The essence of the oligarchy's method was increasing the Jews' financial obligations toward the kingdom, so as to relieve the nobility's tax burden, restricting the Jews' earning potential, as a concession to the bourgeoisie—competitors of the Jews—who were striving for political influence in the kingdom, and a reduction and disregard for protection of the Jews in order to give free rein to the militant church's fanatic cruelty, and in so doing, to also satisfy the demands of the priesthood for significant influence in the life of the country.

This political method afforded the church a special way of handling the Jewish question: to enforce all the medieval anti-Jewish laws and edicts by using religious coercion, increasing the church's influence by increasing the number of converts, thereby covering up its corrupted values and immoral image. It also sought to enforce Church law regarding the Jews even to the point of deriving benefit from bribes given by the Jews to its ruling body and from the benefit of political accounts, whereby systematic support of the anti-Jewish demands and propaganda of the bourgeoisie would increase their power in the country against the nobility, which did not want to give the churchmen their due share in running the kingdom.

In addition to the kingdom's general decline and the constant pressure of the ruling classes, the nobility and the clergy, the economic and social deterioration of Polish Jewry resulted from the harsh enmity of the bourgeoisie, who were on an equal social footing. They did not tire of inciting the masses to pressure the Jews and oust them from their positions; thus, fierce rejection was accompanied by bitterness on the part of the competitors and revulsion on the part of the poor, who were also seeking a scapegoat for their failures in competing economically with the Jews in the past as well as compensation for the failures in their political and social aspirations to raise the value of the bourgeoisie in the life of the country.

The country was completely mired in factions: great power blocs plotting and rebelling against the monarchy and the senate, and neighboring kingdoms conquering the land. For years, there was anarchy throughout Poland; only the strongest prevailed.[1] Neither life nor property was safe. Poverty increased daily. Complaints about the lack of livelihood were a normal occurrence. Competition became more intense and any livelihood raised concern that others would burst the earning bubble.[2] Not only did the number of poor people rise within the Jewish population, but there was also a concomitant increase in thieves and robbers.[3] Moreover, the internal organization of Polish Jewry was revoked from without and disintegrated from within. The champions and national leadership were bereft of the little authority they had, thereby diminishing the dignity of all Jews.[4] The heads of the Jewish community ceased to be respected and came increasingly under attack.[5] On the other hand, at a time of increasing hooliganism and scandal, those less worthy were elected to leadership positions.[6] Polish Jewry became a shadow of its former self, battered by storm and tempest. Despite all the prohibitions and stringencies, strict adherence to the boundaries imposed by the governments and the efforts of the Jewish communities to maintain their settlement prerogatives rather than allowing foreigners to move in, the emigration of Polish Jewry to other countries continued unabated.

The waves of immigration to the Land of Israel were also related to the onset of this exodus, given the deep-seated feeling that the ground was shifting beneath their feet.

Turkey, also, witnessed a decline of the Jewish community at this time—a decline from without and a deterioration from within. The Ottoman Empire was in decline. The limits on the sultan's effective power were increasing. The pashas ruled the land. Each one sat on his throne, possessing his own garrison; all he had to do was submit the tax quota to the ruler of the faithful. He was beholden to no one, and nobody made any demands or claims against him. Yet, his position was not secure: the army comprised of irregulars, the troops ruled the citizenry, and, often, they and their officers would see to it that law and order prevailed in the cities and countries.[7] A person had to look out for himself, for as long as he remained in power.

Commerce was at a standstill, all movement ceased. The community dwindled and ignorance rose. All those who still had an inkling of yesteryear hastened to flee "the kingdom of darkness and ignorance" that prevailed in the Jewish communities. Torah scholars who wished to maintain the respect paid to former generations faired particularly badly. "And in our present generation, those who demean Torah scholars both to their face and behind their back, have multiplied manifold. It is almost an insult to be called a Torah scholar" and "when someone wishes to belittle his friend, he calls him a scholar as a derogatory term."[8]

In those days, immigration to the Land of Israel from countries under Turkish hegemony consisted mainly of Torah scholars.

The new reality of yearning for redemption was, therefore, related to a new ideology promulgated by Jewish philosophers who were struggling to maintain their own existence and stature, sensing the decline of the countries around them.

The waves of immigration to the Land of Israel and the settlement of the recent immigrants in the country have produced an entire literature: stories about the adventure of aliyah, descriptions of the country and its customs, letters from the Land of Israel to relatives and friends as well as letters of request to communities and groups of like-minded people in the diaspora, sermons on Zion and news about the activities of the country's leadership on behalf of the Jewish population of pre-state Israel. This literature was reality-based by its very nature; the Land of Israel is a living entity and its people walk the land, they are involved in and concerned about what is troubling the world. Nevertheless, for that very reason, there is a special value to the few innuendos, implying a search for redemption, for, here and there, they reveal the mentality upon which this reality was constructed and the foundations upon which Jewish existence in pre-state Israel was predicated in those days—the creative forces constituting the tissue of life of the Old Yishuv.

Despite the fact that many considered them marginal to Jewish reality, those foundations, overall and in their inner significance, constituted the beginnings of a sharp generational shift in Jewish history and were situated in the mainstream of events shaping it.

NOTES

1. *Zikhronot dov mi-Bolechov* [*Memoirs of Dov of Bolechov*] (Vishnitzer, Berlin, 1923), p. 92.

2. *Igeret hakodesh,* Letter 18, to Rabbi Menahem Mendel from Vitebsk; compare ibid., Letter 6.

3. Dr. Moshe Markuze in *Seyfer refues* (Porick, 1790); Noah Prylucki's *Zamlbikher far yidishn folklor* II, p. 48.

4. Dov ol Bolechov, ibid.

5. *Darkhey No'am,* f. 102v.

6. *Ohel Ya'akov,* Genesis.

7. Compare Iorga, *Geshichte des Osmanischen Reiches,* IV, pp. 467–485; compare also Rosanes, *Korot ha-yehudim be-turkiya* [*History of the Jews in Turkey*] V, ch. 1.

8. *Shulḥan gavoa* [*High Table*], Yosef Molcho, Orekh Ḥayim, no. 607 (Salonika, 1884)].

Translated by Marvin Meital.

Other works by Dinur: *Yisra'el be-artso* (1938); *Bemifneh ha-dorot* (1955); *Yisrael ba-golah,* 5 vols. (1958); *Dorot u-reshumot* (1978).

Gideon Hausner

1915–1990

Israeli lawyer and prosecutor Gideon Hausner was born in Lemberg (today Lviv), and moved in 1927 to Palestine, where he joined the Haganah and fought in Israel's War of Independence. He later served as a military prosecutor and president of the military court and was the country's attorney general from 1960 to 1963. Hausner was the chief prosecutor in the trial of Adolf Eichmann. In 1965, Hausner was elected to the Knesset as a member of the Independent Liberal Party. He returned to private law practice in 1977.

Six Million Accusers

1961

When I stand before you here, Judges of Israel, to lead the Prosecution of Adolf Eichmann, I am not standing alone. With me are six million accusers. But they cannot rise to their feet and point an accusing finger towards him who sits in the dock and cry: "I accuse." For their ashes are piled up on the hills of Auschwitz and the fields of Treblinka, and are strewn in the forests of Poland. Their graves are scattered throughout the length and breadth of Europe. Their blood cries out, but their voice is not heard. Therefore I will be their spokesman and in their name I will unfold the awesome indictment.

The history of the Jewish people is steeped in suffering and tears. . . . Yet never, down the entire blood-stained road travelled by this people, never since the first days of its nationhood, has any man arisen who succeeded in dealing it such grievous blows as did Hitler's iniquitous regime, and Adolf Eichmann as its executive arm for the extermination of the Jewish people. In all human history there is no other example of a man against whom it would be possible to draw up such a bill of indictment as has been read here. . . . Murder has been with the human race since the days when Cain killed Abel; it is no novel phenomenon. But we have had to wait till this twentieth century to witness with our own eyes a new kind of murder: not the result of the momentary surge of passion or mental black-out, but of calculated decision and painstaking planning; not through the evil design of an individual, but through a mighty criminal conspiracy involving thousands; not against one victim whom an assassin may have decided to destroy, but against an entire people. . . .

This murderous decision, taken deliberately and in cold blood, to annihilate a nation and blot it out from the face of the earth, is so shocking that one is at a loss for words to describe it. Words exist to express what man's reason can conceive and his heart contain, [but] here we are dealing with actions that transcend our human grasp. Yet this is what did happen: millions were condemned to death, not for any crime, not for anything they had done, but only because they belonged to the Jewish people. The development of technology placed at the disposal of the destroyers efficient equipment for the execution of their appalling designs. This unprecedented crime, carried out by Europeans in the twentieth century, led to the definition of a criminal concept unknown to human annals even during the darkest ages—the crime of Genocide. . . .

Hitler, his regime and crimes, were no accidental or transient phenomenon. He did not come to power as a result merely of a unique combination of circumstances. Historical processes are usually the product of many developments, like many streams flowing each in its own channel until they combine into a mighty river. They will come together only if their flow is in the same general direction.

No doubt various events contributed to the rise of Nazism: the defeat of Germany in World War I; the subsequent economic difficulties; lack of leadership and futile party divisions; fratricidal strife and disunion—all these impelled the German people, disoriented and groping, to turn its eyes towards the false prophet. But Hitler would not have been able to remain in power, and to consolidate in his support all the strata of the German people, including most of the intellectuals—to win the support of so many university professors and professional men, the civil service and the whole army—if the road to his leadership had not already been paved. Not even the oppressive regime of the concentration camps, and the atmosphere created by the terror so rapidly activated against all opposition by the hooligans of the SS and SA; are adequate alone to explain the enthusiastic and devoted support he received from the majority of the nation, unless it had been preceded by an extensive spiritual preparation. When we read today the declarations of the scientists, authors, and journalists—including many who had not been among his adherents before—who chanted his praises and willingly gave him their support and backing, how they willingly and joyfully accepted his yoke, we must reach the conclusion, however reluctantly, that the people were ready and prepared to crown him as their leader.

Hitler [freed] the hatred of the Jew which was latent in the hearts of large sections of the German people, intensified it and stimulated it into greater activity. The germ of antisemitism was already there; he stimulated it and transformed it into the source of an epidemic. For the purposes of Nazi Germany's internal policy, the Jew was a convenient object of hatred; he was weak and defenceless. The world outside remained silent when he was persecuted, and contented itself with verbal reactions that did little harm. The Jew was pilloried as a supporter of Communism—and therefore an enemy of the German people. In the same breath he was accused of being a capitalist—and therefore an enemy of the workers. National-Socialism had found in the Jew an object of hostility appropriate to both halves of its name, and it set him up as a target for both national enmity and class hatred. The Jew was also a ready target through which the attention of the public could be diverted from other problems. This too was an age-old weapon, which had been used by many antisemites down the ages. . . .

A confused and blinded world was not alarmed by this campaign of hatred and the denial of human rights. It did not understand that the persecution of the Jews was only the beginning of an onslaught on the entire world. The man whose henchmen howled the infamous words:

"When Jewish blood spurts from the knife / Then all goes doubly well!" (*"Wenn Judenblut vom Messer spritzt / Dann geht's nochmal so gut!"*)—the same man would soon, by a natural development and led by the same master-feeling of hate, proclaim that all the cities of England would be subjected to the same fate as bombed Coventry.

In order to complete the picture, we should point out that there were in Germany tens of thousands of scientists and ecclesiastics, statesmen and authors and ordinary people, who dared to help the Jews, to raise their heads in opposition to the iniquitous regime, and even to rebel against it, and among these were men whose names were famous in German science and culture. Thousands of opponents of the bloody regime were imprisoned and were later destined to suffer greatly in concentration camps before the Nazi monster was brought low. Thousands of these died without seeing the day of liberation. Hundreds of ecclesiastics were arrested and imprisoned. There were also examples of personal bravery—like that of a priest who was sent by Eichmann to a concentration camp for intervening openly on behalf of the Jews. There were Germans who hid Jews and shared their rations with them and who at the risk of their lives helped them to hide or to obtain "Aryan" papers, and there were others who maintained an anti-Hitler underground. During the War there were Germans who even protested to Hitler at the disgrace the Gestapo was bringing on the German people by acting like beasts of prey, as they described the extermination of the Jews. There were also soldiers who tried to frustrate the killings by direct intervention.

But after all is said and done, these were a very small minority. The decisive majority of the German people made peace with the new regime, and were phlegmatic witnesses of the most terrible crime ever perpetrated in human history. . . .

There is a Hebrew saying: "The wicked, even at the gate of Hell, do not repent." In April 1945, at the moment of his death agonies, when the Soviet cannons were thundering in the streets of Berlin, when Hitler sat imprisoned in the cellar of the Reichskanzlei, his entire world in ruins and his country stricken, over the corpses of six million Jews—at that moment, the Führer wrote his political last will and testament. He bequeathed to his people the injunction of eternal hatred for the Jews, and he concluded:

> Above all, I enjoin the government and the people to uphold the racial laws to the limit and to resist mercilessly the prisoner of all nations, international Jewry.

Even from beyond the grave, Hitler was still trying to sow the seeds of hatred and destruction for the Jewish people.

NOTE
[Words in brackets appear in the original translation.—Eds.]

Translated by Shabtai Rosenne.

Other work by Hausner: *Justice in Jerusalem* (1966).

Ḥaim Hazaz

On Literature and the State
1962

Our state is young, with a girl's years, just fourteen. Still without her shoes, as the poet says. But she seems old, many generations old. In these few years, old age has pounced on her. No one is proud of her, no one is happy for her. On the contrary, each additional day makes our heart coarser against her. Our spirit is flaccid, and our will has flagged. Grave doubt has seized us, dissatisfaction and spiritual fatigue. We're put off by the truths upon which the nation stands, by the virtues particular to us, by an entity more exalted than us.

Take a mighty and splendid nation, which is stronger than any other nation in matter and powerful in its air force; when one of its airplanes flies around the globe and sees its land from above, it bursts out with a song of praise for the homeland. That's how someone from a great nation acts: a person imbued with their culture and literature, because he was educated in his culture and literature. But we made Zionism into a shameful laughingstock and our state into something ordinary and common, something trivial that doesn't matter.

More than that: resentment of the State of Israel has entered many people's hearts. Some are opposed to it openly and in secret, and some subvert it in theory and practice. Not the government, but the state itself. As if people were neither happy with its existence nor at ease in the world because of it. [. . .]

I won't talk about the positive things in our life. Not because I see only gloom, only evil all day long. Like every one of you, I know about the positive things in our life, abundant good and blessings. But the positive is simple and natural, a necessary part of life, and there is no reason to give praise and thanks for it. I will therefore talk about what is negative in our life. I won't listen to the voice of whisperers and scoffers without common sense, whose ears are stuffed with cotton, who cannot hear and do not want to hear. No, I will talk as dictated by my conscience and my heart, and I will even say old things, things that have already been heard, only because they are useful. [. . .]

In every discussion you may hold about the diaspora and the Jewish shtetl, you will necessarily acknowledge the great values that were there, such as fear of heaven, study of Torah, love of the Jewish people, longing for the Land of Israel, faith in redemption and the coming of the Messiah, and many similar things. These values have been translated into the language of modern man and they are regarded as values that we possess today.

A Jewish person in the diaspora, in a Jewish city, was at home with books all his life. Everyone, even the ignorant, was familiar with *mishnayot*, *midrash*, *'Eyn Ya'akov*, the book of Psalms. And of course, the learned Jews, whose mouths never ceased reciting words of Torah day and night, did not do this for material reward. A person interested in books, who was so interested in books, whose whole devotion was to books, was naturally a superior person, not to mention an entire nation. That is what we were: the people of the book.

It is no wonder that the Jewish shtetl was abundant with great spiritual powers. The great rabbis came from the shtetl, the heads and leaders of the people. From the cities came the first *maskilim* [modern intellectuals]—various kinds of socialists—who gave their lives to sanctify redemption and freedom; all the dreamers and visionaries of the redemption of the Jews: men like Joseph Aharonovitz, Berl Katznelson, A. D. Gordon, Samuel Yavnieli, and so on. Knowingly and unknowingly, they preserved within them the atmosphere of the shtetl and they established, here in the Land of Israel, the same marvelous climate of primal virtues, spiritual devotion, enthusiasm, and idealistic purity. From the shtetl came all the poets and authors in all their innocence, in their abundance and vital energy, in the love of the Jewish people in their heart, in their great fear for the fate and future of the people, in scrupulous preservation of their aspirations and visions. [. . .]

Now we have stopped reading. Here and there you still sometimes find one person in a group and two in a kibbutz who have a book by [Gershon] Shofman or [Micah Josef] Berdyczewski on their table. These are few, the remnant, old-fashioned workers, here for many years, who, in the past, immigrated to the Land of Israel because of the power of these books over them. The people in general have stopped reading. A significant divide separates the people and the book. The mind is not open and time is unavailable. They are concerned with other matters.

We used to learn, from the waves of immigration to the Land of Israel, to see the Land of Israel in the image of [Kibbutz] Degania, in the image of A. D. Gordon and Brenner, whose every deed was done for an exalted purpose alone. How different and distant we now are from A. D. Gordon. Our life has become mundane. We have changed from a people to a state. A state in its roots; more state than nation. [. . .]

Not that artists have ceased to be in the land. Far from it. There are quite a few righteous and modest people among us, but their voice does not go forth, and their words are not heard by the people. They are not the ones who give the generation its countenance, and they are not the ones who symbolize the generation. Their hour is past. They belong to yesterday. Whereas the people of our generation—for there is no generation without righteous people—can be compared to a generation without dreams and longings, without doubts and confusion. They all of them draw from the mediocrity of what is, are reconciled to the experience of what exists, the dominant reality, bone of its bone and body of its body. [. . .]

We are a small state, and it is incumbent upon us to be a unique state. There is no sense in a small state's being like Paris or vast and rich as America, because everything that is like America is superseded by America. We must be what we are obligated to be. I won't say a chosen people, I won't say a light unto the nations. These are exalted slogans, a fine pose to flaunt. These slogans don't become a light unto the nations and they are of no use, and the Bible won't be of any use to us. We don't live according to the Bible. The Oral Law is what made us into the eternal people, not the Bible. [. . .] The Oral Law is something intimate, an intimate vernacular between the Holy One, blessed be He, and the Jewish people. These are things that were spoken in private, from mouth to ear, from the mouth of the Holy One, blessed be He, to the ear of the Jews.

I'm not saying: come, let us base ourselves on the study of Talmud. No, no! But anyone who says that the Bible will save us, everything for the Bible—is both wrong and misleading. The Jewish people never depended on the Bible. [. . .]

The generation can only stand upon original modern literature, which follows from the literature that preceded it, from a Jewish culture that was created through the generations, going back to the Bible. Schools must teach literature and useful scientific studies. If literature is the main subject and the practical sciences come a close second, then none among us will be detached from the root; no recently arrived engineer, no chemist, and no refugee scientist—all of them involved in equal measure will be involved in the homeland, will hold fast to it and will feel a deep attachment to it. And what will link a person to his homeland if not his culture and unique and native literature?

Translated by Jeffrey M. Green.

Elie Eliachar and David Ben-Gurion
Eliachar, 1899–1981

The Jerusalem-born Elie Eliachar (alternately, Eliahu Elisar) spent decades advocating for Sephardi and Mizrahi Jews, demanding inclusion, respect, and the preservation of their culture. Eliachar descended from scholars and rabbis, and was nothing if not outspoken. Early in life, he studied law and medicine, but it was in politics and letters that he made his mark, serving in the Knesset, editing a newspaper (*Echo of the Orient*), and helping to found the World Sephardi Federation. In the 1970s, Eliachar turned to academia, creating a research center focusing on Sephardi and oriental Jewry. To his death, he remained one of their loudest, fiercest champions, insisting on their place at the center, not the margins, of Israeli society.

Who Is a Sephardi?
1964

Haifa 1 Elul, 5724
August 9, 1964

To: His Excellency David Ben-Gurion
Sde Boker
Dear Sir,

From your letter of May 19, 1964, I understood that you wish to avoid a comprehensive discussion of the problems I presented to you [. . .], but first allow me to respond to the objections you raised in the aforementioned letter. [. . .]

You have said to me more than once, and written as well, that the members of the oriental communities—with special emphasis on the Iraqi community—are not Sephardim. It seems to me that this view derives from a desire that exists, in my humble opinion, among large circles of Ashkenazim, political and religious, to prevent the formation of a non-Ashkenazic community in what was the Land of Israel in the past and is now the State of Israel. Perhaps, subconsciously, you reject any ethnic unity of the non-Ashkenazic communities, as was the practice in the time of Turkish rule until the land was conquered by the British. [. . .]

I take you at your word that you are a Jew pure and simple. However, seeing the state of affairs in the country with regard to ethnicity, that is not enough. I cannot determine what part of me is Ashkenazi, Sephardi, Babylonian, European, etc. given the composition of my family. Among my ancestors some were from Vilna, Basra, Egypt, Italy, and more. Therefore I, too, am only Jewish.

Nevertheless, as a Jew I return to the subject, the problem of ethnic groups in Israel, in response to the article I mentioned above. I quote several sentences briefly:

> Racism has penetrated the struggle and the ideological dispute between the Soviets and the Communists. Racism rules over states and new nations in Africa. It also influences the status of Jewish (and other) minorities in the free world. It has become a primary concern in Israel, with the circumstantial problems that were created from the existence of an oriental Jewish ethnic group that is opposed to assimilation into the European Jewish ethnic group, and the existence of an Arab minority which will number more than half a million in the next ten years. [. . .]

I wrote to you that in my opinion the danger lies in *generalizations* regarding existing gaps, exaggerations with respect to Levantinization, that create deepening bitterness in the Israeli public. Don't you think that the time has come to repair the situation in Israel and the diaspora, before it rises up against us all?

I dwell among my people [2 Kings 4:13]—believe me that what your people says is worrisome, very worrisome for our future. [. . .]

Yours sincerely,
Eliahu Elisar

Sde Boker, August 15, 1964
Dear Mr. Elisar,

From your letter I see that it is difficult for you to imagine a Jew who is not at all a member of one or another ethnic group. What is to be done? I was not and will not be an Ashkenazi, but rather a Jew. And not even a secular or religious Jew, but just a Jew.

There are differences among Jews in their material circumstances and education, and these differences must be eliminated as quickly as possible, to our fullest ability. Maimonides is precious not because he was Sephardi, and Bialik, not because he was Ashkenazi. I'm sorry that Maimonides and Judah Halevi wrote their philosophical books in Arabic, and I understand what drove them to that, but in my eyes, they are Jewish thinkers and nothing else.

As far as I know the Jews of Babylonia (today we say Iraq) did not migrate to Spain, and I do not know why it is so necessary for you that they should be among those expelled from Spain. It is known to us that this community dwelled in Babylonia for 2,500 years. Perhaps some of the Jews of Babylonia left their country and migrated to other lands—but what difference does it make where they migrated?

You will certainly admit that Our Teacher Moses and King David and the prophets of Israel never lived in Spain (nor in Ashkenaz), and they did not speak either Ladino or Yiddish.

There are more poor people among the immigrants from Islamic lands than from Europe—and we must repair that situation. We must assure that the children of the poor have true opportunities (and not just legal equality) for elementary, secondary, and higher education. This is a great and vital need, and not because they are Moroccans or Yemenites, but because they are Jews. [. . .]

Yours with cordial respect,
D. Ben-Gurion

Jerusalem August 25, 1964
To: His excellency David Ben-Gurion
Sde Boker
Dear Sir,

This letter is meant to close the circle of our recent correspondence and to wish you and all yours the start of a year and its blessings.

I am convinced that you do not wish to answer the actual questions that I posed to you, and that is your privilege.

I do not deny that you are only a Jew, but I state that, seeing the conditions today, there is a danger that in the State of Israel a division might emerge between Jews like you and like me and the other Jews in the state, going so far as racism.

But you refrained from addressing this division, which, as I pointed out in my earlier letters, we encourage in the Land [of Israel] and in the diaspora. Also, my quotations from the Dutch *Jewish Observer* remain without a response.

True, education helps and will help to remove the gaps and reduce them, and I congratulate those involved in it for that. [...]

You are fortunate in that you believe that only in this way have shocks to our state been avoided. In my humble opinion, this is not enough, because the problem is far more complex and includes social, economic, and representative problems. I am under the impression that you know this, but you were "persuaded" that you must cancel your previous approach, upon which you insisted when you appointed an advisor for the mingling of ethnic groups. [...]

Respectfully yours,
Eliahu Elisar

Translated by Jeffrey M. Green.

Shimon Ballas

1930-2019

Shimon Ballas—author, translator, and editor—was born in Baghdad and immigrated to Israel at age twenty-one, later earning a doctoral degree from the Sorbonne. Ballas wrote articles and criticism in Arabic and taught Arabic literature at Haifa University. He published several works of prose and nonfiction and served as editor of the journal *Al Karmel*. Ballas was awarded the President's Prize in 2006.

Notes to an Old-New Debate
1965

Many people believe that the question of "the mingling of the diasporas" will be resolved in the workplace, in the mixed neighborhood, in school, etc. oriental [Mizrahi] Jews, they say, who acquire professional training in the industrial plant as a result improve their standard of living and acquire knowledge and culture—which can be an important link in the chain of their development and their desired mingling with the population originating in Europe and America. This conception maintains that the veteran settlement (that is to say, the Jewish population of the Land of Israel until the establishment of the state and the mass immigration from countries in Asia and Africa) is a kind of "absorptive institution," and the masses of immigrants are the community to be absorbed: they must undergo stages of formation in the melting pot called "the absorption of immigrants." It appears that this conception, which grew out of the soil of material and technical needs (the provision of workplaces and dwellings, the building of schools, etc.) for some reason maintains that a change in form must bring about a change in content. In other words, the form of work (factories, construction projects, modern agriculture), the form of study (a curriculum developed for Ashkenazi Jews), and the volatile, active character of Israeli society are likely to effect change in the depths of the soul and bring about the desired inclusion.

Of course, these factors are not to be underestimated, because a worker who operates a modern machine or a farmer who works his land with modern methods differs from the diaspora Jew who spent his day in a small workshop or a meager shop. The industrial revolution in Europe completely uprooted values that were dying out and created a new image of the contemporary person. Without a doubt, changes of this kind have taken place among oriental Jews, who had not known mechanized industrial and agricultural labor in their countries of origin. But these changes could not uproot the values of the cultural heritage that the immigrant brought from his country of origin. Moreover, the drastic changes in concepts of labor and social life almost certainly cause a psychological shock that is liable to produce alienation toward the surroundings and withdrawal into oneself, which is like a spiritual defense against a hostile, malevolent world. [...]

In my opinion, there is something one-sided in presenting the problem of the mingling of diasporas from the perspective of the veteran settlement. For some reason, the image appears before our eyes of a consolidated nation and a society anchored in reality, whose members have taken upon themselves the task of absorbing immigrants who are spiritually and economically inferior to them. For some reason, these people are unable to free themselves from the feeling that they are destined, as it were, to be the "receptive institution" and that the immigrant community must fashion itself according to their ways. [...]

In my opinion, there should be no talk of mingling without demanding willingness to mingle from both sides—from the veteran community and from the new one. All the approaches must take place between two points, between two factors. All love is based on at least a pair. So, too, mingling, the stage that comes after the approach, the love, cannot be demanded only from one side.

Here we come to a delicate point, which is the vulnerable point in this complex problem: do the immigrants from Asia and Africa have a culture of their own? And if there is such a culture, is it not valuable enough to measure up to the European culture acquired by the veteran settlement? [. . .]

Many are the European authors who traveled in the East and were impressed by the oriental Jew, who dwelled in the shadow of his fig tree and preserved the sanctity of his tradition. They wrote about his fidelity to his religion, his unwillingness to challenge conventions and rise against the heritage of his ancestors. Perhaps there is truth in these matters. The oriental is proud of his past, proud of the human spirit that throbs in his ancient spiritual treasure; he also knows very well that his ancestors bequeathed to all of humanity an eternal fount of exalted values. But, unfortunately, those European authors did not understand that the oriental was not proud because of the conservatism of his society and its rejection of foreigners. The error of these outside observers was that they saw the backwardness of oriental society as evidence of its spiritual poverty, and they did not recognize (or did not wish to recognize) the fact that culture and civilization are not the same thing. However, the reality of life demonstrated their error; the nations of the East, who did not give up their cultural heritage, adopted the achievements of Western civilization and proved that an ancient culture can dwell together with European civilization and also develop. But at the same time, the weight of estrangement deepened in their heart suspicion and hostility toward the peoples of Europe and their culture, which was a consequence of the contempt for their culture and the desire to impose foreign culture on them.

Most regrettably, an error of this kind is revealed in the complex of actions called "mingling of diasporas." For some reason, those responsible in the state saw it as their duty to impose the values of their culture on the masses of immigrants, who ostensibly lacked culture. This erroneous approach contains a dreadful misconception about the very concept of culture; but mainly it contains a faulty view of Jewish culture in general. While the leaders of the West wished to "acculturate"

entire nations by the force of their colonial rule, the meaning of work of this kind in Israel is seven times more dreadful, and not only because of the negative coercion itself but also because Jews are trying to "acculturate" Jews—and both parties have a single Jewish culture! Again, there is a miserable version, full of danger, of the same confusion of culture and civilization.

The spirit of the Orient, that exalted spirit of national pride, of the pursuit of justice and peace, which is inherent in all of our national cultural treasury, is precisely what united us in every generation. It is the key to the strength of the Jew wandering through the great world and bearing in his heart the belief that the day would come when he would return to his source. [. . .]

Indeed, it is sad that even after seventeen years of the State of Israel, we are still subject to this dreadful shallowness of thought. Recitation of the formulas of the fathers of diaspora Zionism cannot answer the needs of the hour. We need the development of constructive, creative ideas regarding national revival, here, on the soil of the homeland, while managing the campaign to build up the nation. We need liberation from the negative remnants of the diaspora, we need a revision in the ways of thinking and also a new point of departure.

In Israel, Jews who had not been in contact for centuries or millennia encounter each other, and here they are called upon to get out of the shells that they bore from their countries of origin and to unite with one another. This is no easy task. [. . .] Today we are at the peak of the shock, and we must direct it in such a way that it will break the shell and preserve the meat, because the meat is one. If we do not manage to do this in time, we can expect the natural and desired shock to become a negative and destructive force.

This question should serve as the axis for deep, many-sided public discussion. For if we see the assurance of the future existence of Israel in the Arab East as a question of the utmost importance, I have no doubt that every citizen of Israel also sees the question of the formation of the image of the Jewish people and the guarantee of its future as a consolidated, undivided nation as a question of primary importance; and the one depends upon the other.

Translated by Jeffrey M. Green.

Other works by Ballas: *Ha-ma'abarah* (1964); *Sipurim palestiniyim* (1970); *Ha-sifrut ha-'aravit be-tsel ha-milḥamah* (1978).

Ḥaim Zeev Hirschberg

1903–1976

Israeli historian Ḥaim Zeev Hirschberg was born in Tarnopol, Galicia, and arrived in Palestine in 1943. A historian specializing in Jews of the Muslim world, Hirschberg in 1960 became a professor of Jewish history at Bar-Ilan University, subsequently writing a two-volume study of the topic.

A History of the Jews in North Africa
1965

[. . .] [A]n attempt will be made to present the history of the Jews of the African Maghreb, a large, well-defined diaspora which in some respects is different from other Jewish groups generally and from those of the Muslim East in particular.

This diaspora has been treated as a backwater of Jewish history. Jewish scholars mostly devoted their efforts to the vibrant centres of political and cultural life and did not give the Jewish periphery the attention to which it is objectively entitled. The author has repeatedly pointed out that they, nearly all of them members of the 19th-century school of historiography, were allured by the relative—and sometimes imaginary—wealth of literary sources available for the study of such diasporas as Babylonia, Spain, France, Germany and Poland. They were dazzled by the prestige of the Geonim and early Decisors; the work of the Tosaphists, for instance, seemed to them—and rightly so—a kind of continuation of the discussions of the Gemara, a living tie with the debates of the Amoraim. On the other hand, halakhic jurisprudence, even in the sphere of civil law, did not attract scholars—and be it only from a theoretical point of view—in the countries where modern Jewish studies developed. Spanish-Jewish literature appealed to the emotions; the philosophic treatises, in part inspired by ideas current in the non-Jewish world, evoked a sympathetic response because of the similarity of their topics to present-day problems. And so, just as there is a contrast in Jewish history between periods apparently all splendor and others apparently all darkness, a contrast accentuated by a lack of interest in periods deficient in source material and therefore difficult to explore, there are countries receiving detailed and penetrating study and others reduced to backwater status.

In the life of these "backwaters" there were times when they played a highly important part in the history of the Jewish people, and in certain cases even in the history of mankind generally. Such a part was played, e.g., by the Jews of the Arabian Peninsula at the time of the rise of Islam; the Jews in the northern border region of the Arab caliphate and of the Byzantine Empire and the Judaizers in the Khazar kingdom; and the Messianic movements which occurred from time to time in the course of centuries precisely among the simple folk, in societies whose physiognomy is hardly known to us, and not at the centers of learning and wisdom in wealthy, well-regulated circles.

A prominent place among these peripheral Jewries is held by the North African diaspora. [. . .]

Acculturation and Separate Identity

All the epigraphic finds from the antique period attest that North African Jewry adopted the Greek and Latin languages. It seems, moreover, that upon the arrival of the Arabs they were the first among the residents of the region who began to use literary Arabic. Yehuda ibn Quraysh is the first non-Arab in Africa of whom a work in Arabic—in the field of linguistics—has been preserved, and Isaac Israeli was the first non-Muslim student of natural science, medicine and philosophy in the region.

Turkish culture had not, to our knowledge, any influence on North African Jewry, any more than it left a trace among Jews or Arabs anywhere in Asia who were ever under Turkish rule. In the French era, many Jews were prominent exponents of French culture; this was so in Algeria and Tunisia and more recently also in Morocco.

The Jewish elite in Fez, Tetuan, Algiers, Tunis and (in the 19th century) Tangier seems to have been intellectually superior to that in other oriental countries. Members of the prominent families were for many generations in the service of the rulers and in contact with Europeans who came to those cities on various business. In Morocco, the Jews were the only non-Muslims, and Christian visitors were only permitted to reside in Jewish neighborhoods and houses; they were not allowed to reside permanently in the royal cities, and as late as the 19th century all the ambassadors and consuls lived in Tangier. As stated, Jews were the only persons who traveled to European countries on political missions, and were agents and vice-consuls of European states.

Obviously, this contact with the great world left a profound imprint on the physiognomy of the wealthy stratum that had access to the authorities.

At the same time, that stratum did not enjoy a favored status with the Muslim rulers; they were subject to the same humiliations as their fellow Jews.

The perfect Arabic spoken by the Jews in the Middle Ages gradually dwindled into a Jewish dialect, which has survived until today; it is largely the everyday speech of those who lived far from the centers of French culture, but is understood even by the second and third generations of graduates of French schools. The Arabic of the educated, both written and spoken, has not in recent times been current among the Jews, since they did not attend Arabic schools, whose standard was extremely low, while the schools of the Alliance Israélite Universelle, during French rule, allotted no or almost no room to Arabic in their curriculum. In this respect, the situation of Maghreb Jewry was different from that of Iraqi and even Egyptian.

It is thus not surprising that assimilation to French culture made deep inroads into the Arab sector as well. Algeria, for instance, where some nine million Muslims were living in 1955, had not a single Arabic newspaper, and the only illustrated Arabic weekly in Morocco closed down in that year. A literature or press in any of the Berber languages did not exist at all, except for a few textbooks issued by the French Government for two or three Berber schools founded by it. The propensity of the Jews to linguistic assimilation makes it all the more remarkable that they are the only group in the region that preserved its national-religious identity under all circumstances. The Berbers in the settled areas changed their religion four times: they at first adopted Phoenician-Punic and Greco-Roman forms of worship, then they became Christians and finally all of them became Islamized and most of them Arabicized. We shall have to review the material and spiritual struggle of the Jews with their environment, a struggle frequently varying in form, but always maintaining the characteristic Jewish way of pouring old wine into new vessels.

Translated by Menachem Walter Eichelberg.

Other works by Hirschberg: *Yisra'el be-'arav* (1946).

The First Manifesto of the "Greater Land of Israel" Movement

The Manifesto of the Land of Israel Movement, composed by the poet Natan Alterman, first appeared in *Yediot ahronot* on 22 September 1967. It was signed by fifty-seven of the most respected writers and activists of the country, including S. Y. Agnon, Uri Tzvi Greenberg, Yitzhak Zuckerman, Zivia Lubetkin, Haim Gouri, and Moshe Tabenkin. The manifesto asserted the right of the Jewish People to the Land of Israel, including the recently conquered West Bank. Of the fifty-seven signers, nineteen had been members of the Labor Party. Written in the immediate aftermath of the Six-Day War and supported by luminaries from all sides of the political spectrum, the manifesto underscored the conviction that the miraculous Jewish victory over Arabs determined to destroy the Jewish state legitimized Jewish claims to the entire Land of Israel.

1967

For the Greater Land of Israel

The victory of the IDF in the Six-Day War placed the nation and the state in a new and fateful period. Now the whole Land of Israel is in the hands of the Jewish people, and just as we have no right to give up the State of Israel, so too we are commanded to maintain what we have received from its hands: the Land of Israel.

We are committed by faith to the integrity of our land—toward the nation's past as well as its future, and no government in Israel has the right to give up that integrity.

The borders of our land today are a guarantee of security and peace—and also of channels unlike any others for strengthening the whole nation materially and spiritually.

Within these borders there will be freedom and equality—which lie in the foundations of the State of Israel—the possession of all the inhabitants without distinction.

Immigration and settlement of the land are the two principles upon which our future will rest. Great immigration from everywhere in the diaspora of the Jewish people is a basic condition for maintaining the integrity and national character of the Land of Israel. We will make the new tasks and possibilities of this period a cause of awakening and momentum for the Jewish people and the Land of Israel.

The undersigned will act to implement these principles and they see mobilizing the public for this goal and plotting the course and means for its achievement as a central task at this time.

Translated by Jeffrey M. Green.

Yitzhak Rabin

1922–1995

Yitzhak Rabin served as prime minister of Israel from 1974 to 1977 and again from 1992 until his assassination in 1995. Rabin was born in Jerusalem and grew up in Tel Aviv. Chief of staff of the Israel Defense Forces, Rabin commanded the Israeli forces during the Six-Day War in 1967. He received the Nobel Peace Prize in 1994.

Address upon Receiving the Honorary Doctorate of Philosophy at the Hebrew University of Jerusalem
1967

Your Excellency, President of the State; Mr. Prime Minister; President of the Hebrew University; Governors; teachers; ladies and gentlemen.

I stand in awe before you, leaders of our generation, here in this venerable and magnificent place, overlooking Israel's eternal capital and the birthplace of our people's ancient history. Together with other distinguished people, who are no doubt worthy of this honor, you have chosen to do me great honor by conferring upon me the title of Doctor of Philosophy. Permit me to express to you here what is in my heart: I regard myself at this time as the representative of thousands of commanders and tens of thousands of soldiers who brought the State of Israel its victory in the Six-Day War, as a representative of the entire I.D.F. [Israel Defense Forces].

It may be asked why the university saw fit to grant the title of Honorary Doctor of Philosophy to a soldier in recognition of his martial activities. What is there in common between military activity and the academic world which represents civilization and culture? What is there in common between those whose profession is violence, and spiritual values? I, however, am honored that through me you are expressing such deep appreciation to my comrades-in-arms and to the uniqueness of the Israel Defense Forces, which is essentially an extension of the unique spirit of the entire Jewish people. [. . .]

Today, however, the university has conferred this honorary title upon us in recognition of the I.D.F.'s superiority of spirit and morals, as was revealed in the heat of war, for we are standing in this place by virtue of a heavy battle which, though forced upon us, was forged into a victory that is already called miraculous.

War is intrinsically harsh and cruel, bloody and tearstained, but this war in particular, which we have just undergone, brought forth rare and magnificent instances of heroism and courage, together with humane expressions of brotherhood, comradeship, and spiritual greatness. [. . .]

The entire nation was exalted, and many wept, upon hearing the news of the capture of the Old City of Jerusalem. Our sabra youth, and most certainly our soldiers, do not tend toward sentimentality; they shy away from revealing it in public. However, the strain of battle, the anxiety which preceded it, and the sense of salvation and of direct participation of every soldier in the forging of the heart of Jewish history, cracked the shell of hardness and shyness and released wellsprings of deeply felt spiritual emotion. The paratroopers who conquered the Wailing Wall leaned against its stones and wept. As a symbol, this was a rare occasion, almost unparalleled in human history. Such phrases and clichés are not generally used in the I.D.F., but this sight on the Temple Mount, beyond the power of words, revealed, as though by a flash of lightning, a deep truth.

And more than this, the joy of triumph seized the entire nation. Nevertheless, we find, increasingly, a strange phenomenon among our fighters. Their joy is not total, and more than a little sorrow, and shock, permeates their celebration. There are those who do not celebrate at all. The warriors in the front lines witnessed not only the glory of victory but also its price—their comrades who fell beside them, bleeding. And I know that the terrible price paid by our enemies also touched the hearts of many of our men deeply. It may be that the Jewish people never learned, never accustomed themselves to experience the thrill of conquest and victory, and so we receive it with mixed feelings. [. . .]

We speak a great deal about the few against the many. In this war, perhaps for the first time since the Arab invasions of the spring of 1948 and the battles of Negba and Deganya, units of the Israel Defense Forces stood on all fronts, the few against the many. What this means is that relatively small units of our soldiers often entered seemingly endless networks of deeply dug fortifications, surrounded by hundreds and thousands of enemy troops, and faced the task of forcing their way, hour after hour, in this jungle of dangers, even after the momentum and excitement of the first assault had waned and all that remained was the need to have faith in our strength, in the lack of any alternative, in the goal for which we fight, and in the importance of summoning up every spiritual resource in order to continue fighting to the very end. [. . .]

Our pilots who struck the enemy planes with such accuracy that no one in the world understands how it was done and people seek technological explanations in the form of secret weapons; our armored troops who beat the enemy even when our equipment was inferior to theirs; our soldiers in all the branches of the Israel Defense Forces who overcame our enemies everywhere, despite their superior numbers and fortifications; all these revealed not only composure and courage in battle but a fierce faith in their righteousness, an understanding that only their personal stand against the greatest of dangers could bring victory to their country and to their families, and that if victory was not theirs, the alternative was annihilation.

Furthermore, in every sector, I.D.F. commanders of all ranks far outshone those of the enemy. Their resourcefulness, understanding, readiness and will, their ability to improvise, their concern for their soldiers, and above all, their leadership of the troops in battle—these are not matters of materiel or technique. There is no rational explanation, only a deep consciousness of the morality of the war they were fighting.

It all starts and ends with the spirit. Our soldiers prevailed not by their weapons but by their awareness of their supreme mission, by their awareness of the righteousness of their cause, by their deep love for their homeland and by their recognition of the difficult task laid upon them—to ensure the existence of our people in our homeland, to defend, even at the price of their own lives, the right of the Jewish people to live in their own state, free, independent and in peace.

This army, which I had the privilege of commanding during this war, came from the people and returns to the people—to the people who rise in their hour of crisis and overcome all enemies by virtue of their moral stature and spiritual readiness in the hour of need.

As the representative of the Israel Defense Forces, and in the name of every one of its soldiers, I am proud to accept this honor.

NOTE
[Words in brackets appear in the original document.—Eds.]

Translated from the Hebrew.

Amos Elon

1926–2009

Israeli historian and journalist Amos Elon was born in Vienna and arrived in Palestine in 1933. He studied law and history at the Hebrew University and at Cambridge University. In the 1950s, Elon served as a correspondent for *Haaretz* on European and American affairs. He is best known for his work titled *The Israelis: Founders and Builders*. Disillusioned with the political situation in Israel, Elon moved to Italy in 2004.

An Open Wound
1971

Six million perished not because of a cataclysm of nature, as is evoked by use of that inadequate term "holocaust"; they died not because they lacked courage, but because they lacked the minimum prerequisites for putting such courage to practice. It is possible to vanquish and exterminate a people even in its own sovereign state. But with the possible exception of nuclear warfare, there is no mass extermination that cannot be opposed by its intended victims. In the eyes of the younger, post-Zionist generation, the holocaust has thus come to confirm one of the basic tenets of classical, nineteenth-century Zionism: without a country of your own you are the scum of the earth, the inevitable prey of beasts.

But behind this surface of purposeful determination, of flexed muscle and wisdom after the event, behind the proud array of newly acquired sovereign power, behind the impressive spectacle of a young, new society of resolute free men, the whole truth is something else. There remains a suspended confusion, a neurotic constriction, a shifting mood of remembrance and rejection that is one of the root causes for the modern Israeli temper. In the words of Uri Zvi Greenberg, a leading poet of the older generation:

Lord you saved me from Ur-Germany as I fled
Mother's and father's threshold, and arrived whole
In body but with my soul torn, within it the
    lake-of-weeping
Now I live on in my mourning.

The moral turbulence is compounded by pangs of conscience, guilt, and shame. The frequent inability of the young, native-born Israeli to confront the survivor of the holocaust is powerfully reflected in a number of major Israeli novels. In Hanoch Bartov's *The Brigade* the Israeli protagonist meets his surviving cousin in a Displaced Persons camp after the war. The young Israeli is filled with the "terror of belonging to him." He is seized with "more than shock, more than disgust." At the end of the novel he vows "never to return there . . . but as I spoke, my thoughts turned to pillars of salt." [. . .]

The attitudes of younger, native-born Israelis to the holocaust, and to the Jewish Diaspora in general, have always been highly ambivalent, a mixture of compelling awe and of compelling shame. This is at least partly a result of standard Zionist education. A regular textbook on Hebrew syntax—used for many years in Israeli schools—included the following analysis of Bialik's great lament on the pogrom of Kishinev in 1903:

This poem describes the mean brutality of the assailants and the *disgraceful shame and cowardice* of the Jews of the Diaspora *shtetl.*

"Disgraceful," "shame," and "cowardice" are key terms here that point to the heart of Zionist education in its earlier stages. A repellent new term entered the vernacular of Israeli teen-agers after 1945 with the arrival of the first survivors of the Nazi death camps. The refugees were derogatorily referred to by youngsters as *sabon*, or soap. The term has since become generic for cowardice and weakness. To threaten "to soap" someone is to threaten to ruin him. For many years Israeli schoolchildren were taught that the Diaspora was not only a catastrophe, but a disgraceful shame. In her controversial account of the Eichmann trial, Hannah Arendt suggested that during the Nazi holocaust the Jews—through the passivity of their leaders—cooperated in a sense in their own destruction. There was relatively less turmoil over this accusation among Israelis than among Jews elsewhere, because, rightly or wrongly, it confirmed a Zionist cliché image of Diaspora Jewry. [. . .]

Arab encirclement and belligerency—whatever their cause in later years—have only tended to sharpen the general outlines of this picture. Since Independence in 1948, Israelis have lived in a state of geographic and political isolation unusual in the modern world. Since World War II almost every country has been linked to others by military and political pacts or alliances. Most countries today share common markets, or, at least open borders, a common language, or religion, with another. Israel has none of these. Apart from its geographic isolation it is probably the only country in the world that is engaged in constant military conflict and yet has membership in no military, political, or economic alliance. The frustrating consequences of this claustrophobic isolation have been considerable. Against the background of the holocaust and its immediate aftermath, the total effects of isolation have multiplied and given rise to that pessimism of encirclement and of being entirely and utterly alone in the world, which, even today, is a chief characteristic of the Israeli mind.

When our children under the gallows wept,
The world its silence kept. . . .

The feeling is shared by many. It is a root cause for Israeli attitudes which to the outside world frequently seem unduly stubborn. Pious admonishments from outside have very little effect; the most cosmopolitan Israelis will isolate themselves against foreign criticism to an abnormal degree. For, in their eyes, since World War II the civilized world has little moral ground on which to stand when it sermonizes Israel to do this or to refrain from doing that. In the late 1940s David Ben Gurion epitomized this in the remark, "It is not important what the *Goyim* are saying but what Jews are doing." Ben Gurion's reputation has assured a long life to what still is a dangerous half-truth. His remark is still oft quoted. It was under the impact of World War II that in the mid-1940s a new breed of Jews started coming out of Palestine: tough, pessimistic, militant, and as far from the idyllic image of the founding fathers as real life is from Utopia. The "new" breed were a tiny minority, of course, and still are; but it is an active minority that has set a tone. [. . .]

Among younger Israelis, a renewed preoccupation with the so-called "Jewish condition" has been apparent in recent years. The Zionists had originally wanted to reform that condition drastically; and yet in the novel form of Arab belligerency and abysmal hatred it pursues them to this day in the land of their dreams.

War and dangers have put their stamp on Israeli life for many years. At times of war it has not been necessary for young Israelis to be religiously observant, to throw their Zionist education overboard and identify with the historic experience of Judaism. They must not be orthodox traditionalists to feel that sense of existential anguish that had been a distinguishing mark of the Jewish temper in the Diaspora. In times of danger the ghosts of old pogroms hover like clouds over Israel. The upsurge of a certain "intellectual" or propagandistic anti-Semitism among Arabs has acted as a powerful contributory factor. [. . .]

Daily Arab threats continue to obstruct the sense of "normalcy" that had been one of the major, more naive aims, of the early Zionists. But it is not necessary to cultivate a derangement of the senses when reality itself is insane. Precisely because memory of the holocaust is so alive, Arab threats of annihilation arouse in many Israelis what almost amounts to a cultural reflex. The Arabs do not realize that in the Israeli arsenal, this reflex is more powerful a weapon than a mighty armored division. It is an involuntary gift presented to the Israelis by their enemies; it adds resolve, inventiveness, devotion, cohesion, vigor, pluck, and paradoxically, that kind of nervous but fertile "anxiety" which is often said to be a root cause of the traditional Jewish spirit in the Diaspora.

Other works by Elon: *Journey through a Haunted Land: The New Germany* (1967); *Herzl: A Biography* (1975); *Jerusalem: City of Mirrors* (1990); *Founder: A Portrait of the First Rothschild and His Time* (1997); *The Pity of It All: A Portrait of Jews in Germany, 1743–1933* (2002).

Yehuda Nini

1930–2020

Historian Yehuda Nini was born in Palestine in 1930 into a family who had immigrated from Yemen. He received his doctorate from Tel Aviv University in 1977; his dissertation was on the Jewish community in nineteenth-century Yemen. He also cataloged the records of Sana'a, Yemen. In 1994, Nini became head of the Chaim Rosenberg School of Jewish Studies at Tel Aviv University. In 1983 he received the Yitzhak Ben Zvi Prize for his research on the Jews of Yemen.

Thoughts on the Third Destruction
1971

I leaf through the commemorative albums of the settlements of Ri'shon Le-tsion, Reḥovot, Petaḥ-Tikvah, and Ḥadera. Among other things I was looking for documentary material on the establishment of the Yemenite neighborhood in Netanya—for research connected with immigration to the Land of Israel. While leafing through the albums, I found lists of the casualties of the War of Independence at the end of some of them, and, in black frames, their photographs. [. . .] I took some time to look at the photographs, and here were the names of Zeraḥ Sh., Shim'on K., Yiga'el Y., Nissim L., David M., 'Ezra 'A. and more and more familiar faces. Friends at celebrations, friendship in shared opinions, companions in war and in pranks. They are gone. [. . .]

I don't mean to tell about what happened from then to now, and I intended to mention what I wrote above only to remember my friends who are no more. I know how they were killed, and sometimes I also know what they were doing until their final hour. They . . . they do not know what we've done. They don't know how much Israeli society has betrayed them, how cheaply all the ideals they fought for were sold. They don't know that those agents of war, those who thought that their own blood was redder than the others', are the chief speakers today. They don't know that the fanfare of their devotion to the establishment of the highest and dearest—the State of the Jews—was also the playing of taps for those "little men of the Yishuv," pleasant in their deeds and in the values of their heart. [. . .]

And now? So many days have passed, different days. Those who are gone are forgotten from our hearts, but their image exists, abides. The young and sturdy men will be remembered forever, though they were thin and poor. We will get older and older, and they, as fate has decreed, will remain young. [. . .]

I don't go to see them where they are buried and I don't go to see their parents where they are living. "Woe to the father who says kaddish for his son." So said one of them to me at the time, and that was enough for me. I can't look at their grief.

No, they still don't belong to "Israel," and they never will. They do not belong to the generation of automation, to the scientific generation. They were brought here by [Shmuel] Yavnieli to conquer labor, to make it Hebrew labor, to compete with the Arab laborer.[1] Their mission has long been finished. The hands of Hebrew labor have lost their power—no one wants it, and no one wants them. We need people of science and technology, so they, [these Hebrew laborers], are regarded as an anachronism in the new Israeli landscape. They don't know the foreign words that are used in daily life. Their Hebrew is too ancient and too redolent of the Bible, the prayer book, and the Mishnah. They did their job, and the rest is left to the sons of Ishmael, and they—so it is said—are a burden on the country's treasury. Many children, many problems for the educators, for the sociologists, and for the relief workers (many children, and it occurs to no one that many children are our triumphant answer to Auschwitz, Birkenau, Bergen-Belsen . . .). In an article, Amnon Rubinstein argues that we are actually Asiatic. He invites us and invites all the people in the world to look at the human landscape of Israel. Despite everything, we still are worth a little. We can still be used for propaganda. They can batter Yasser Arafat with us, tell him that our country isn't European, imperialist, and colonialist because most of its residents are from the Orient. [. . .]

I said that I don't go to see graves, but it seems to me that I ought to go to them and say that they were deceived, they were deluded, they were misled. To tell them that they died for nothing, and their sacrifice was in vain. Their fathers lying in pits and trenches, and "the others" divided the best of the country among themselves. It seems to me that I have to go to them and say: "The place that was the peak of your lives, that is, the moment of your death, was also the peak of the aspirations of two thousand years of exile, but the death of the hope of the deceived and dizzy people is a worthless magic spell." And everything around is ash. Ash remaining from the fire of a divine flame. Rivers of lies extinguished it, rivers of corruption. In bitterness—honey, in liberty—bitterness. [. . .]

They should be told about their little brothers, with big black eyes, thin legs in trousers that are too big for them. They should be told about the education given by the State of Israel. That state, the hope of two thousand years in exile, of which their ancestors dreamed until their bones were worn down, as they mourned for its destruction—"For whom shall I weep and strike my hand and truly weep?" Weary, drained, tortured, remaining from a selection after a thousand selections, purified to the wearing down of their bones, they mourned for the destruction; "'for whom shall I weep and strike my hand and weep bitterly, for the Ark [of the Covenant] and the cherubs? For the altar prepared for the Levites forever'" etc.[2] [. . .]

For years and years the Zionist movement fought for independent labor, Hebrew labor, etc. Not because it wanted to displace the Arab worker, but because it believed that our return to this land must not have colonialist characteristics, that we shouldn't put other people to work, like white people in Africa or in all the colonial settlements in Asia. But just as other very important values of Zionism were destroyed with the establishment of the state, so, too, this value was destroyed. We Yemenites were proud of being part of the "conquest of labor," but now classes have been created by brutal and artificial force in the country, classes with no natural aristocracy based on ancient culture. Those who came from Europe and America are the class of managers, those who give work, and not necessarily because of their capital, but on the strength of the wealth given to the state, which they made their own, and thereby independent labor has been neglected. Physical labor has become an expression of personal failure, of loserdom, a sign of cultural backwardness. In just a few years we have become a typical, exploitative colonial state, and by virtue of its leechlike characteristic it leaves much for the few. The Arab "natives" are the ones who do the work.

NOTES

1. [Born in Kazanka, Kherson, Shmuel Yavnieli (b. Varshavsky, 1884–1961) migrated to Palestine in 1905. In 1911, *Hapoel Hatsair* sent him to Yemen to encourage immigration by Yemenite Jews, who were wanted as "natural workers." Some 1,500 people migrated from Yemen in consequence of Yavnieli's mission.—Trans.]
2. [From a Yemenite liturgical poem.—Trans.]

Translated by Jeffrey M. Green.

Other works by Nini: *The Jews of the Yemen, 1800–1914* (1991); *He-hayita o halamti halom: Temaney kineret* (1996).

Gershon Shaked
1929–2006

Israel's foremost literary critic, Gershon Shaked was born Gerhard Mandel in Vienna to illiterate parents. As a result of the Nazi annexation of Austria, Shaked's parents rushed to send him to Palestine. Arriving alone at the age of ten, he was later joined by his parents. Shaked received his doctorate in Hebrew literature at the Hebrew University, where he became a professor and served as head of the Hebrew Literature Department. His criticism was awarded the Bialik Prize in 1986 and the Israel Prize in 1993.

The New Wave in Hebrew Fiction
1971

The inception of literature is certainly not merely a matter of ideas and ideology. Not only are the contents connected to the forms and dependent on them, but the development of the forms has its own manner of evolution as well.

The "Great Transition" was largely dependent upon the breaking of the realistic vessels that were typical of most of the literature of the generation of the War of Independence. [. . .]

Literature began to free itself increasingly from alarm bells of public issues and turned toward the "many windows" and "side-entrances" of individual lives. Writers ceased to be concerned with the stereotypical figure of the conventional sabra and the members of his group, and, turning away from this public, they began to discover that thorns and thistles had also grown in this land.

Shamir, Yizhar, and Megged already sensed that not everyone in Rome acts like a Roman, and a person who mingles with crows caws like them. Among the "successors," the relation between the typical sabra and his typical society became increasingly problematic. The new authors sought an atypical society populated by unconventional figures.

For this purpose perhaps they ought first to have noticed how problematic the status of the typical sabra was. The story by Yosef Bar, "The Life and Death of Yonatan Argaman," deals with the dubious status of this typical sabra. [. . .] The problem of the relation between the sabra and his "Jewish" shadow is internalized in this story; the contrast between the hero and the world is no longer external. The main arena of struggle is directed inward and connected to the mythical foundation. Although Bar's artistic intentions were only partially accomplished, the direction he took—inward to the soul, and outward, away from society—is conspicuous. This is one of the "side doors" through which the new fiction entered.

The New Wave came in through three other doors: by extreme emphasis upon the ego, by addressing childhood memories (even Israeli ones) connected to the world of a different, pre-sabra Judaism, and by presenting dark corners of the society, which do not stand at the center of social life but rather in the margins, making it possible to present unusual characters.

One of the most important books in the New Wave is by Pinḥas Sadeh, *Life as a Parable*. This is an autobiographical work that constitutes the polar antithesis of the typical biography of members of the "Generation of the Land." [. . .]

According to Sadeh, literature is not intended to present reality or the deeds of protagonists in social situations, but rather to express the individual. Literature is supposed to express, and the needs of intensified expression are more important than structural or stylistic principles, which restrict the power of expression. Sadeh, who takes the path of the expressionists,

grasps the world as a broken mirror of the ego, and reality as *"die Ausstrahlungen des Ichs"* [the emanations of the ego]. The individual principle is absolutely different from the social conception that is expressed, for example, in the literary manifesto of the "Generation of the Land" group (*Im benei dori*), which was published in *Yalkut ha-re'im*. [. . .]

Sadeh's personal manifesto was written with rather deep contempt for the implied, petit-bourgeois reader, whom the author seeks to astonish with his confessions, by presenting his inner life as the opposite of the reader's orderly life, and to assert the artist's right to live—through his writing. Culturally, Pinḥas Sadeh is worlds apart from the members of the Generation of the Land. In quite a few respects he returns to the cultural sources of the Hebrew fiction of Bialik. Sadeh also absorbs quantities of that which Berdyczewski and Brenner drew from Nietzsche. [. . .]

Society is merely material in the craftsman's hands and no longer a literary subject. The divided ego (and the characters are to a certain degree emanations of the ego) is now revealed in erotic experiences with religious significance, and the reader once again encounters a new world, which is like a side door to our fiction, now bound up with much pounding of the heart. Sadeh's work has romantic impetus, a religious-existentialist philosophy of life, and an expressionist form of expression. It is typical of the New Wave because it successfully described the inward turning of the individual, who returns to himself in order to look once again at society from a new point of view. [. . .]

Modern Hebrew fiction went a long way between the 1940s and the 1970s. Initially it was naïve in its beliefs, full of pathos in its style, and rather monotonous in the characters it depicted and the situations it described. This foundation did not endure. The literature of the Generation of the Land changed *from within*. It lost its innocence upon encountering new situations, after becoming disappointed with the realization of the social dream for which the members of its generation gave their lives. [. . .]

When fiction lost its innocence, the ironic tendency grew stronger. [. . .]

Together with the destruction of the old myth came new figures and new fictional forms. In his expressionistic confessions, Pinḥas Sadeh presents an antisocial and antisabra character, who is not loyal to principles and truths but to its own truth and logic. This is no longer a character who believes in the teachings of A.

D. Gordon and the youth movement, but a figure who seeks old-new deities in the New Testament and the writings of Nietzsche. This character does not go out into the fields but rather goes out to graze in foreign fields, seeking erotic and religious experiences in order to live a full and deep life. [David] Shaḥar, in his story collections, also seeks a "small god" of his own and goes back to discover forgotten neighborhoods of the Jewish settlement. This is also true of Rachel Eitan, who turned to the suburbs, to discover herself and describe the gloomy childhood of an exceptional girl.

Because of the new subjects and characters, the style, the structure, and the sources of literary influence also changed. In the first stages, it spoke in high style; afterward it began to speak in ordinary language, and this process, too, was not unequivocal and direct, but polysemous and tortuous.

Translated by Jeffrey M. Green.

Other works by Shaked: *Ha-siporet ha-'ivrit, 1880–1980* (1977); *The Shadows Within: Essays on the Modern Jewish Writers* (1987); *Shmuel Yosef Agnon: A Revolutionary Traditionalist* (1989).

Amos Oz
1939–2018

Amos Oz was born and raised in Jerusalem. At age fifteen, he moved to Kibbutz Ḥuldah, and he later lived in Arad. A professor of literature at Ben-Gurion University, Oz published works of fiction, numerous essays and articles, several nonfiction works on the Israeli–Palestinian conflict, and a children's book. His works have been translated into more than thirty languages. Oz won many awards, among them the Légion d'honneur, the Bialik Prize, the Israel Prize, and the Dan David Prize. *A Tale of Love and Darkness* was made into a motion picture.

Under This Blazing Light
1972

Witchcraft and Sorcery

So what *do* storytellers do? The ones I like operate more or less like tribal witchdoctors.

Here is a little story for you. Nine thousand six hundred and six years ago, in a musty cave or on a river bank, some shaggy, prognathous men and women are sitting round a fire at night. In the darkness all around lurk monsters, beasts of prey, the ghosts of the dead. Between their terror, the shrieks of birds, the rustling and whispers, these people are suffering mortal agony. And then along comes the storyteller, who is perhaps also the tribal witchdoctor. His stories may be just as frightening as the spirits of the night, perhaps even more so, but in the stories the fear is trapped in words, the ghosts are pent up in a cage of structure, and the monsters are trained to follow the route the storyteller has chosen for them: beginning, middle, and end, tension and release, cunning, mockery, in a word—order. Wild desires and instincts, the very forces of nature, are trapped in the storyteller's snare, in a web of language and purpose. They can be made to seem ridiculous, those forces and instincts and monsters, or compelled to repeat themselves, like a dancing bear, or forced to obey the logic of the story. In this way the storyteller comforts the members of his tribe and helps them to withstand the eternal siege. Animals, lightning, fire, water, lust, disease and death are made to dance to the beat of the story.

The eternal siege is still there, as you know. Ghosts and goblins, despair, desire, disaster, hatred and dread, old age and death still hold sway. Stories still have the power to comfort, and wordsmiths can still work as witchdoctors. [. . .]

I am talking about the need to tell stories "shamelessly." To tell about the primary things in a primary way. To tell as if this were the first or the only book in the world. To start "Once upon a time . . ." and at once to bring to light all the terrors and demons in the depths of one's psyche—which may echo those in the tribal psyche—to use words to bring everything to the surface, to the light: "and in the light all impurities are blasted away." All this apart from questions of genre and technique, which are not my present subject. Any true storyteller, whether he lives in the fourth century BC or the sixth century CE or our own twentieth century, be he a modernist or a realist or a symbolist or any other kind of -ist, if he is a storyteller he is also the witchdoctor of his tribe, who conjures the fears and phantoms and terrors and filth, everything that is "not mentioned in polite society," and so brings some relief either to the whole tribe or to some of its members, even if the tribe is ungrateful, even if it howls with pain and fury, even if it shouts "What will the neighboring tribes say about us," and so on.

And what should an Israeli witchdoctor be doing, here and now, in this strong blue light that is the opposite of twilight? [. . .]

Maybe it is harder to conjure spirits if you live in a modern housing development in Israel. It is harder still because of this pedantic light, that does not favour magic. This is a world without shade, without cellars or attics, without a real sense of time-sequence. And the language itself is half solid rock and half shifting sands. [. . .]

Trees and Manure

In this blazing blue light it is of course possible to try to huddle in the shade. It is possible to turn your back on the time and the place, to ignore the tribal problems and write what they call "universally" about the human condition, or the meaning of love, or life in general. But, in point of fact, *how is it possible*? Surely the time and place will always burst in, however hard you try to hide from them and write about desert islands or Nebuchadnezzar in Tahiti. S. Yizhar once talked about oak trees that cannot grow where there is only a thin layer of topsoil over bedrock. In a rocky wilderness, he said, only shallow-rooted plants can grow. But maybe they will rot down into humus that will permit the growth of shrubs that will rot in their turn so that one day mighty oaks can grow.

This is the State of Israel: a refugee camp thrown together in a hurry. A place of wet paint. Remnants of foreign ways from Marrakesh, Warsaw and Bucharest and godforsaken *shtetls* drying in the sun among the sand in the backyards of wretched new housing developments. There are ancient remains, but only rarely, in Metulla, Ekron or Gedera, will you find a family home that has been standing for three or four generations. Who in the whole of this frantic country lives in the house he was born in? Who lives in the house one of his grandparents was born in? Who has inherited a house from his grandfather or his great-grandfather? Who lives within walls covered with nooks and family memories, surrounded by furniture used by his ancestors (not *nouveau riche* antiques from the flea market but your own family heirlooms)? Who was brought up on the same lullabies that were sung to his grandparents and great-grandparents? Even our lullabies smell of fresh paint: they were composed yesterday out of more or less Polish or Russian melodies embellished with a few biblical or Arab trills. Everything is new, everything is disposable, cardboard, nylon, plastic, everything, folk-stories, lullabies, customs, speech, terms of endearment and curses, the place, the view. I could prove, on the basis of a "statistical sample," that virtually all the writers we enjoy reading grew up with a grandmother. Which of us has a real grandma? I don't mean some weird, Yiddish-speaking old woman but a real grandmother with memories, who can be a "conductor" between you and your origins.

And so, in this blight, it is very hard. It is hard to trace the criss-crossed complex of genetic encounters generation after generation that gives each of us his makeup. The uncles and aunts were murdered in Europe or emigrated to America. The grandparents spoke another language. Everything that constitutes the depth of family and tribe—the jokes, stories, customs, lullabies, gestures, whims, beliefs, superstitions, the resemblance to a remote ancestor or distant cousin—has all been destroyed like an unpicked embroidery.

I was born in Jerusalem in a pool of shade within (relatively) ancient stone walls, but I can picture to myself how awful Kibbutz Hulda must have been for its children in the early days: a place that had nothing but hope, declarations of intent, and limitless good will. No big trees, only saplings. No old houses, only tents, shacks, and a few whitewashed concrete structures. No old people, just enthusiastic young pioneers. "We have left all our yesterdays behind us, / But tomorrow is a long, long way away." A world that was all new fencing, new plantations, a new language, which sounded rather artificial as spoken by the settlers from the *shtetl* (to this day they still cry, laugh, count and quarrel in Yiddish), new buildings, new lawns, new lessons, fresh paint everywhere. There were even new lullabies and new "folk-tales" synthesized by writers from the Jewish National Fund for the new Israeli children. We had folk-songs before we had a folk. Travelling instructors from the competent agencies taught the people how to sing the folk-songs and dance the folk-dances properly.

Yes, I know, we had no choice. Backs to the wall. "To conquer the mountain or die." A new land and a new chapter. I know all that. I'm just trying to explain, perhaps to apologize, and tell you why it is hard to make a story with depth here, one which, like any good story, works witchcraft and conjures up ghosts and spirits.

There is another way that I have been thinking about quite a lot recently. It may be possible to try to catch the time and place, the displaced refugees, as they are, with all their elusiveness and emaciation, with the midday light itself. To write like a camera that takes in too much light, so that the outlines are blurred, the eyes are screwed up, the film is scorched, like photographing straight into the summer sun.

Perhaps I ought to shut up at last. Gradually. Surely the tribe needs its witchdoctor in times of disaster or terror or nightmare, or the opposite, in times of great joy and ecstasy. At other times, only a few need all this. I don't know. I shan't define "the state of the tribe at the present time." I shall keep my thoughts to myself.

But if our tribe is having a brief respite between suffering and ecstasy, what need of sorcery and stories? Let it have musicians, entertainers—and let it rest in peace.

Translated by Nicholas de Lange.

Other works by Oz: *My Michael* (1968); *A Perfect Peace* (1982); *In the Land of Israel* (1983); *Panther in the Basement* (1994); *A Tale of Love and Darkness* (2002).

Amalia Kahana-Carmon

1926–2019

Fiction writer and essayist Amalia Kahana-Carmon was born at Kibbutz 'Ein Ḥarod and raised in Tel Aviv. In the 1940s, she was a member of the Haganah and later joined Palmach, taking part in the 1948 war as a radio operator. Her first book, *Bi-khfifah aḥat* (Under One Roof), was published in 1966 to great acclaim. Her lyrical, allusive style and her subtle rendering of female consciousness made her a dominant figure in Israeli women's writing. She received the Israel Prize for Literature in 2000.

What Did the War of Independence Do to Its Writers?

1973

War of Independence Literature: A Painful Subject

A friend hinted to me that participating in such a discussion would be a tactical error, akin to walking into a minefield. Perhaps. I don't believe in turning an author into someone else's source for another reason—because writers tend to examine matters in light of the problems troubling them, whereas the challenge of what is called War of Independence literature is not, nor has it ever been, one that confronts the issues with which this literature feels an intimate connection. I openly disavow this. I would even go so far as to talk about the personal vision in these books. Or it is not always clear to me where happenstance, subtlety, and intuition come into play here. [. . .]

However, as with any phenomenon that is not fully understood, people try to devise their own theory. [. . .] I'm uncomfortable expressing one because it takes books that differ from one another in every respect and puts them into one package. [. . .] In any event, for argument's sake, let's talk about stereotypes, knowing full well that that's what we are discussing, with all their impediments.

My theory is this: War of Independence literature tries to cope with the imperatives of a meta-reality, an ideal good, an ideal evil, and so forth. Very little interest is placed in reality as it actually is. Authentic reality, with its oceans of neutrality that are indifferent to imperatives, must be perceived comprehensively and authoritatively by the code of refinement of that period. As far as I am concerned, this is part of a larger thesis. This compulsiveness leads to impoverishment precisely in the area where our current sensitivities lie and to a denial of those things that are primal, namely, life itself in all its complexity. Correction: things that only writers are attuned to, and precisely to them. This awareness is what has made them writers. However, here they are impelled to place such mindfulness as a second priority—as perceived by imperatives sawing through their space. [. . .]

An even greater catastrophe is that the imperatives so bothersome to this literature were the kind of values that were commendable in their day. This makes the price even heavier. Nevertheless, we have still not exhausted the subject. It is more complex and here I am coming to what I believe is the central point.

I wish to remind anyone who has forgotten: that period was a paradise of mediocrity. The fine young people then (with all due respect to their sterling qualities), compared to today's youth (despite their shameful shortcomings), were both narrow-minded and amazingly provincial in their attitude. [. . .] The public anonymity of one's self, tending to judge everything in black and white, was, largely, dark and fanatical. And the exceptional individual accepted this verdict in a strangely loving, almost masochistic, manner, for the sake of heaven. This is the interesting point. This literature is a kind of guilt-sacrifice offered up by the exemplary, talented, and special people, who were precisely the ones who found this a hardship. [. . .]

Take most of them as individuals. Those who were supposed to express the spirit of the times through literature were magnificent people. [. . .] On the other hand, how did it happen that those who were the exemplary children, dedicated and obedient to that spirit, were horribly victimized by the times glorious, per se, in which they lived? The answer, I believe, is this. The War of Independence was a short period of time in which conformity was definitely justified. In my opinion, there is nothing worse for a writer to experience. This is tantamount to a bear hug, where even the bear is unaware of you being enfolded within his embrace. And even if a writer's being worse off or not is not a criterion by which this period is examined, this is a minor detail—it is the writer's problem. However, unless I am mistaken, this is where the tragedy lies. [. . .]

I view the stereotype of the War of Independence literature as an account of human endeavor, an attempt by the talented, the exemplary, and the clear-minded, to align themselves with others. Of course, in all periods and with all true writers, one of the major motives for writing is the need to always be in step—that is, to accommodate to a reality that does not meet one's expectations. And the question is why. Using allegory, the writer invents his own reality wherein he attempts to resolve inconsistencies, so as to create a balance that is deficient in the real world. According to our stereotype, given the heroic vindication that these people imposed upon themselves by dint of circumstance, whether they were aware of it or not, the War of Independence was a legacy, which is tantamount to having a healthy-minded individual get into a booby-trapped bed. They took upon themselves a situation, which, from their writer's perspective, was not only fraught with the wrong tension but also sabotaged creativity. This, too, is a form of "see, here are our bodies aligned in one long row." One such writer, who was able to "rehabilitate" himself from the influences of the War of Independence, exhibited vitality, power, and openness perhaps beyond what is found in today's run-of-the-mill individualist, who is not called upon to undergo such a vale of tears. From pinnacle to plain, completely paved with unpleasant disillusionments, each a small death (I know that this may occur at any place and at any time; that is how the road is paved—but still . . .).

Shlomo Grodzensky once said in a private conversation: "I read. And they all write the same inanities." Only after the conversation did it occur to me to say to him: "That is because they all chewed the same strong weed: the War of Independence. That was manna falling upon the earth. Then, we all ate only manna. For a writer, this meant a period of uniform diet, and specifically for writers of the War of Independence, the times

did not nourish them, as is commonly believed, but actually mistreated them, conspired against their innate best, their poetic soul, which, under different circumstances, would have produced a different bloom. In other words, my premise is that they did not become writers because of, but rather despite, the War of Independence. [. . .] It was their misfortune that the talent of these writers matured simultaneously with a period that was wonderful for Israel, but also difficult for personal uniqueness and talent. From this standpoint, the War of Independence passed them by quickly and in a cloud of acrid fumes, leaving behind charred trees. And this, too, passed.

Who is a War of Independence writer? Perhaps, echoing the "Who is a Jew" question, he is someone who sees himself as such. A writer on whose flesh, beneath the shirt, is a small hole, an inoculation against smallpox, and only he knows about it; something in me, somehow, was a charred tree, because of the War of Independence.

This pinprick is a citation of bravery awarded to such a person, irrespective of the quality of his individual writing. This is how an artist works. These people all belong to the same club—they are the bearers of this medallion.

Translated by Marvin Meital.

Other works by Kahana-Carmon: *Sadot magnetiyim* (1977); *Kan nagur* (1996); *Pegishah, ḥatsi pegishah: sipurey ahavah* (2006).

Jacqueline Shohet Kahanoff

1917–1979

Jacqueline Kahanoff (born Shohet) was an Egyptian-born novelist, essayist, and journalist. She was born in Cairo to a Tunisian mother and an Iraqi father who owned a department store. Kahanoff moved to the United States in 1940, earning a journalism degree from Columbia University. She published the novel *Jacob's Ladder* in 1951, three years before she moved to Israel; in Israel she turned to essays and reflective writings. Her mainly English-language works (which were published in Hebrew translation in Israel) drew on her experiences in Egypt in the interwar period, and she is credited with the theory of Levantinism, envisioning multicultural societies in the Middle East.

A Culture Stillborn
1973

It is possible to see the promise of a beginning of Levantine literature—rooted in the realities of the Middle East and influenced by European culture—in *Le livre de Goha le Simple* [*Goha the Fool*] by Albert Adès and Albert Josipovici. This sad and cynical love story, which employs the prototype of Goha, the hero of many Middle Eastern tales, describes the lives of the common folk of Cairo before the spread of Western cultural influence. The innovation in this novel was its description of local realities in the context of a European novel; it was written in French. Adès was born in Cairo in 1833, and Josipovici, the son of a doctor, was born in Constantinople. They both studied in France and lived in Egypt. They wrote the book together in 1913, and it was published by Caiman-Lévy Press in 1919. The book was a great success and almost won the Goncourt Prize, which was granted with all honor to no less a writer than Marcel Proust that very year. *Goha* has been translated into seven languages and made into a play produced by Odeon in 1937.

Albert Adès died in 1921 and Albert Josipovici died in 1931; no one followed in their footsteps. Their deaths caused deep sorrow within the Egyptian Jewish community. I recall my family grieving when Josipovici died. That was how I heard about *Goha the Fool* for the first time. If Adès and Josipovici had remained alive, they would probably have gathered a following of a school of writers from Egypt who would have used local realities as the subject of description in a modern style.

That is in fact what happened in Arabic literature launched by the memoirs of Taha Husayn about the village of his childhood, written in the Egyptian dialect and not in classical literary Arabic rhetoric.[1] But the direction of the educated elite of the minorities was different. Their European cultural orientation was obvious. They read what was published in France and gathered at literary salons and lectures, but never created any literature of value. The Greek poet Constantine Cavafy was an exception in this regard, but it is worth mentioning that the rich, multilingual Greek community lived in Alexandria from ancient times and held on to the Greek language and maintained close ties with Greece. Cavafy belonged to a very specific literary and cultural tradition. The Greeks who lived in Egypt learned French and English but spoke Greek and sent their children to Greek schools.

The situation of the Jewish community was different. Members of the community who were born there were in the minority. The community grew as a result of Jews coming to Egypt from other Mediterranean countries, some for economic reasons—the prosperity that the Suez Canal brought to Egypt—and some for political reasons, because life under the rule of the British protectorate was more secure than under the regimes that had sprung up after the fall of the Ottoman Empire. The Jews who lived in Egypt before and after World War I came from Syria, Iraq, Lebanon, Turkey, Greece, North Africa. Later, Jews came from Romania, Russia, and finally from Austria and Germany. The Sephardi Jews already spoke Ladino among themselves. The Jews from Middle Eastern countries spoke different Arabic dialects. The Jews in Egypt did not have a single shared language like the Yiddish of the Eastern European communities. The connection between them was French culture, which was spread with the help of the network of the Alliance Israélite Universelle extending throughout the Middle East and North Africa.[2]

The Jews were so intoxicated by French culture that they did not pay attention to the advice of the Alliance for the Jews to learn the language of the land in which they lived. In the eyes of the middle-class Egyptian Jews of my generation, speaking in Arabic was considered out-dated and old-fashioned. Only the lower classes, that is to say the Jews of the ghetto, spoke Arabic. With time, they, too, mastered French in the schools offered by the community. The language of instruction was French, and Arabic was taught as a "foreign" language, as was English. A dual French-Arabic educational program was implemented in the schools just before the Arab-Israeli war.

Even the Jews who came to Egypt from Central and Eastern Europe learned French and English and didn't bother learning Arabic. There were several positive aspects to acquiring French culture, but after all was said and done, French and English were not local languages in which people could easily or spontaneously express themselves. To a great extent we were a people without a language. There is no doubt that this lack was a barrier to written expression. Furthermore, we were appreciably carried farther and farther from reality. We had a vague sense of uneasiness because of the difficulties of our position, or perhaps because of the fundamental deceit within it. But we could not nor did we want to confront these things. At the same time Egyptian nationalism adopted a more explicit antiforeign, pan-Arab, and religious-Islamic character. The Moslem majority and the minorities drifted farther apart in their language, their cultures, their aspirations, and their outlooks until nothing shared remained. The resentment and suspicion of the Moslem majority toward the minorities (some of whom were natives, like the Copts) intensified. The minorities scorned the failures of the Egyptians, their degeneracy, and the rest of their faults.

The potential writers from the minority groups could not, therefore, anticipate a local readership. They could not create a meaningful connection with the Egyptian majority, not through their language, and not through the content of their writing. The Egyptians who wrote in Arabic, of course, had no influence on their writing. We didn't even know of their existence, except for Taha Husayn, who was married to a French woman and did not live in a closed Moslem environment. If the name of one of these writers came to our attention, we would dismiss him contemptuously. Their presumed inferiority compared to what we read in French made them not even worth reading. We forgot that we could not read their works even if we wanted to. We did not ask ourselves if perhaps they had something to say that we should know, not only because we lived in the same country. It seemed as if we were afraid to admit to ourselves that we lived in the same cultural, political, spiritual realm. It was as if the explorations of Adès and Josipovici toward symbiosis were a stillborn experiment.

NOTES

[Words in brackets appear in the original source.—Eds.]

1. Taha Husayn's memoir, *al-Ayyam* (*The Days*), like all of his other works, was written in literary Arabic.

2. Alliance Israélite Universelle [French], an organization established to protect the human rights of Jews, was known principally for establishing a network of Jewish schools in the Middle East.

Translated by Deborah A. Starr.

Other works by Kahanoff: *Mi-mizrah shemesh* (1978); *Ben sheney 'olamot* (2005); *Mongrels or Marvels: The Levantine Writings of Jacqueline Shohet Kahanoff* (2011).

LIFE WRITING AND REPORTAGE

Julius Margolin

1900–1971

Julius Margolin was born in Pinsk, earned a doctorate in philosophy in Berlin, lived in Łódź, and went to Palestine in 1936. While visiting his parents in Eastern Europe in 1939, he was trapped during the Soviet invasion of Poland and imprisoned in a labor camp. Upon his release in 1945, Margolin returned to Palestine and wrote in Russian about his experiences; his attempts to publicize his story were not rewarded. Although his work circulated in several versions, the full text of *A Voyage to the Land of Ze-ka* (*Ze-ka* signifying *zaklioutchony*-kontrevolutioner, or Gulag prisoners) was published only in 2010.

A Voyage to the Land of Ze-ka
1947

Before continuing my story about the events in Pinsk in the summer of 1940, I would like to digress briefly into the realm of the miraculous. Let us imagine the impossible—something fantastic and supernatural: what would have happened in Pinsk, if Elijah the Prophet had appeared in the city at the beginning of the summer of 1940?

Much time has passed since that summer, and although none of us is a prophet, and it is hard to project ourselves into the prophetic mode, in the given case, we can easily imagine how a person in Pinsk would have felt if he were able to see the future.

That person would have seen a city on the verge of destruction. Tens of thousands of people condemned to death. At best, these people had about two years left to live. Many thousands were destined to perish even earlier. The Jews of Pinsk were in a trap with no way out. On one side was the German border and the Gestapo. Anyone who crossed that border would die. On the other side was the Russian border. The "Mustapo" [Russian abbreviated form of "wise Stalinist policy"]—closed this border under lock and key. No resident of the condemned city was able to cross this border separating the Russian occupied zone from the territory of the Soviet Union.

The three thousand Jews of Pinsk—in the entire Soviet occupied zone there were about two million Jews—were in a cul de sac. Unaware of their future, however, they did not take their situation too deeply to heart. First, they did not foresee that very soon they would fall into the Germans' hands. Second, they did not imagine that in such a case they faced total annihilation. Third, they all hoped that normalcy would be restored after the war, and each in his or her way imagined a rosy-colored future: one in Palestine, another in democratic Poland, and yet another in a super-democratic Soviet Union.

Just imagine that Elijah the Prophet would come to this city and say to the poor blinded people: "Here is the truth about your life: those of you who stake your future on the Soviets should know that in a year the Germans will arrive and lock you in a ghetto. In another year, you will be slaughtered with your wives, children, and elders. And anyone who runs to the Germans runs straight to his death."

Lo and behold, a second miracle would occur: the people of Pinsk, who generally would not listen to prophecy, would believe him.

They would say to him: "What should we do, Prophet Elijah? We don't see a way out. On the right is the Gestapo; on the left is the "Mustapo." Beneath us is the earth that soon will become our grave. Above us is the sky. Take us to the heavens, Prophet Elijah, because we see no other way."

And the Prophet Elijah would answer them angrily: "You already have an assured place in heaven. You must find a place on earth where you can remain alive."

And they would say: "We don't know what to do. Show us the path of life."

And the Prophet Elijah would show them the path of life.

In fact, there was a path of life for those millions of Jews. Now we do not need to guess or break our heads over it. No matter how surprising this route was—and of course, it surpassed their mental and moral capacity—now, with hindsight, it is clear what they should have done. The only thing that Elijah the Prophet could recommend to them was to stop lying and pretending. The teachers in the Zionist Tarbut high school should not obsequiously agree to renounce their national language and education. They did so not because they changed overnight from Zionists to communists but because they were mortally afraid and thus hoped to avoid persecution and the loss of students. This was, however, the wrong way; it was simply a base betrayal. The opponents of Zionism always contended that the Jews did not need Hebrew or Palestine. The "newly converted" teachers hastened to agree with them: "Yes, Hebrew and Palestine—that was good before you [the Soviets] arrived, but now we renounce them, and we will do what you tell us to do."

Indeed the sole "path of life" for these teachers and hundreds of their pupils was to declare: "We request that the authorities confirm the rights of our school because its language and educational program conform to our wishes, and we refuse to change."

Thousands of Jews who did not want Soviet citizenship should not have taken part in elections to the Supreme Soviet or have accepted the Soviet passports imposed on them. Instead, they should have said aloud what they all thought at the time: "We don't need your citizenship, and we are asking you to let us leave for Palestine." If there were still non-Zionists among them who preferred to remain in Pinsk, then they too should have declared clearly that they did not accept the Soviet regime. That would have been the sacred truth. Deep in their hearts, they did reject it. Such a campaign of civil disobedience, of course, would have been pure madness. I do not suppose for a second that such a thing was feasible without Elijah the Prophet's direct intervention. I can very clearly picture the deceased inhabitants of Pinsk. For example, there was a doctor Y., my friend, a very good doctor and a fine person. In his waiting room hung a framed portrait of Maimonides with a long inscription in Hebrew. The blue and white Jewish National Fund charity box stood in the most prominent spot. Doctor Y. never concealed his love for his people and attachment to Palestine. He did not remove Maimonides' portrait even after the Soviets' arrival. Somehow, however, this man of tradition and owner of two stone houses turned into an ardent Soviet patriot within a week. It was as if his eyes had been opened, and he began to deliver welcoming speeches to the Soviet regime. Why? Perhaps he feared losing his houses? Perhaps he considered it necessary? In any case, it was simply *a lie*. In reality, all that Doctor Y. wanted was to be left in peace or given the opportunity to leave, if not for Palestine, then, at least for America. Probably, he did not want the Bolsheviks.

And Elijah the Prophet was not there to tell him, "Stop lying and pretending. It won't save you from death."

A campaign of civil disobedience would have had fatal consequences for the Jews of Pinsk. The Soviet regime does not treat such cases lightly. Of course, at first it would have been surprised because it was not used to Jews directly and openly saying what was in their hearts. Initially, the regime would have snared some leaders. Ultimately, however, it would have forced all the Jews, with their wives and children, with their prayer books and belongings, up to 100 kilo per person, out of the border zone.

They would not have been the first nor the only people in the Soviet Union to suffer such a fate.

In Central Asia or Yakutia, it would have been extremely difficult for them. Many would have perished. Some, however, would not only have survived the war but also their resistance would have created a decisive argument for both Jewish national culture and a national movement. The "wise Stalinist policy" would have taken into account that Hebrew and Zionism have roots among the Jewish people.

The Jews had the opportunity to choose their own path—the path of open and honest struggle. Unfortunately, the Prophet Elijah was not there to explain this to them.

Translated by Stefani Hoffman.

Other works by Margolin: *Grundphänomene des internationalen Bewusstseins* (1929); *Idea Sjonizmu* (1937); *Shalosh hartza'ot neged ha-komunizm* (1953); *Igeret le-yedidim tse'irim ('al yaḥasey ha-tsenzura be-yisra'el le-va'ayat ha-yehudim be-rusiya)* (1969).

Uri Avnery
1923–2018

Uri Avnery was born in Beckum, Germany. He moved to Mandatory Palestine in 1933, attending school in Nahalal and then in Tel Aviv; he left at age fourteen to work. Avnery joined Etzel and was wounded fighting in the War of Independence. His war reportage, published in 1949, sold an unprecedented thirty thousand copies in one year and, contrary to the author's intention, became the gold standard of authentic—and heroic—war writing. From 1950 to 1990, Avnery turned the weekly *Ha-'olam ha-zeh* into the leading tabloid journal in Israel, and founded a party of the same name in 1965, becoming active on the Israeli Left both as a member of the Knesset and as a high-profile peace activist.

1948. A Soldier's Tale: The Bloody Road to Jerusalem
1948

1 April 1948

At five o'clock in the morning our commanders stormed into the dormitories to wake us. No morning gymnastics. We are in a high state of alert. Our comrades who were on night duty report that the superiors were summoned to battalion HQ around midnight. So it really is serious.

What it is about is still a secret. But most of us can guess the aim. We know that Jerusalem is cut off and that no supply convoys are getting through. This is an existential matter for the whole population. In this situation the army has no choice but to start a large-scale offensive for the first time.

In the evening we are transferred to a temporary field camp near the port of Tel Aviv. Four companies in total (at that time a tremendous force). For the first time we have enough equipment: Australian uniforms, socks, hats, shoes.

Our comrades tell the most amazing stories about heavy automatic weapons that they claim to have seen somewhere: a Browning machine gun, an Italian anti-tank weapon, even a machine gun called Schwarzlose is among them! But nobody has seen simple rifles.

On the high seas a drama was being enacted at the same time. The first of the Army's munitions ships was trying to run the British blockade. In the hold of that ship are the rifles and the automatic weapons that can determine the result of that operation, the fate of the whole of Eretz Israel. The British warships detected it, but it slips by in the dark. On 2 April it docks in the harbor of Tel Aviv. The hour has struck for Operation Nachshon.

In the afternoon there is a roll call for the company. We are reorganized in preparation for combat. Aryeh Spack, the company commander, holds a sheet of paper in his hand and reads out the names.

"Platoon number one. Leader: Yaakov Burstein." Yaakov, small and skinny, moved to the front of the row. "Deputy: Chaim Bulmann." Bulli, tall, broad-shoul-dered, always smiling, stood behind Burstein. "Squad number one. Shlomo Greimann, Uri Avnery, Moshe Shatzky . . ." We look at each other. We know: from now on we will live together, rely on each other, and have faith in the commanders.

Suddenly a stir in the camp—our weapons have arrived. We run, in order not to miss this historic moment. The crates are opened and there they are, the rifles. Thickly coated in grease. With plenty of ammunition. Everyone gets his own personal rifle. As evening falls we sit and clean them without having the right equipment. And the whole time, until long after midnight, we try to come to terms with events: a personal rifle for each Israeli soldier.

Sleep is out of the question. Janek Levkovitz, a refugee from Europe who knows rifles inside out, shows us how to use these guns that we never saw in training. Nobody sleeps.

Saturday 3 April, 1948

DAWN DEPARTURE

At five o'clock the next morning we have breakfast. We stand in a long line, receive our food, devour it in no time, and return to our tents. Everything is packed, the weapons have been cleaned. Four companies are standing by.

The buses arrive. We get in. Our orders are: no singing! Don't make any noise. Keep your weapons out of sight. Nobody in Tel Aviv should notice that a large body of troops is leaving the town. We drive through the empty streets of the sleeping city.

A man is standing at a corner alone. An old German Jew with a hat. He sees the bus full of young people in uniform. Suddenly he lifts his hand and raises his hat. The civilian salutes the soldiers, with a simple, spontaneous, and touching gesture. I look at my comrades. I am the only one who noticed.

We leave the city. In the distance we recognize the Arab bunkers of Jaffa and Tel a-Rish. We gather our weapons from the floor at the same moment as a rousing song bursts from our lips: "Believe me, the day will come/It will be good, that I promise you/I will hold you in my arms/And tell you—everything . . ."

I think about the battle that lies before us. Will we win? And what about the next one? I am convinced that it will be a long war, and that the regular armies of the neighboring countries will cross the border.

We spend the whole day sitting in a lonely field near Ramat Aharon.[1] We are supplied with hand grenades, a very unpopular weapon. Senior officers come to inspect us. The old hands know their names. The one in the green camouflage outfit, that's Chaim Laskov,[2] and that one there with blond hair, that's Shimon "Givati."[3]

In the afternoon we each fire five shots to test our rifles. For the first time we smell the acrid aroma of cordite. For the first time our shoulders feel the kick of a rifle.

Toward evening we drive to Kibbutz Naan. Later in the evening, after dark, we should be in Hulda.

The operation is called "Nachshon."

18 July 1948. A Trench Near Sawafir

CEASEFIRE

It is seven in the evening. The shooting that started five minutes ago has stopped. The artillery on the southern front is silent.

They crawl out of their trenches, and the sun smiles on them from the west. They blink in the sunlight, which they haven't seen for eleven days. They are dirty, their eyes are reddened, their clothes are torn and they are dog tired.

Eleven days! Has it really been only eleven days? Every single day felt like five years. On each day they saw death in a thousand forms.

They crawl out of their trenches and they are only a few. They carry on their backs dead comrades, dying comrades, wounded comrades. Comrades who can never be replaced. Every one has grown together with the unit, become a part of it—and leaves behind a painful gap.

They crawl out of their trenches—the soldiers of the southern front, who have overcome an enemy much stronger and better equipped. They held back the tanks almost with their naked hands, lived through endless battle, and did not flinch.

"Samson's Foxes!"—the commando fighters in their shot-up jeeps, who raced along under fire, who drove into enemy positions, who stormed fortified villages, saved the wounded, and delivered ammunition to remote positions. How many of the original members of this unit are still alive? How many are unwounded?

The defenders of Negba—the men who lived in stifling bunkers and threw back assault after assault of tanks and infantry, who were bombarded twenty-four hours a day by artillery and aircraft, soldiers and "civilians" who moved around, crouching behind the cover of destroyed houses and burning barracks.

The fighters from the Ibdis position—who went through a hell almost beyond description and survived. Who held themselves with their fingernails onto the shaking, heaving ground.

They crawl out of the trenches in Julis and Karatiyya, in Beit Daras and Hatta, the few against the many, the Davids who have beaten the Goliaths.

They crawl out of their trenches and want to live. Every one of them was prepared to die and every one of them is only alive by chance. Each one of them has miraculously escaped a certain death a hundred times.

They crawl out of their trenches. The few, to whom the State of Israel owes a debt it can never repay.

Even after the ceasefire had come into force, operations in the area of Karatiyya continued. The enemy attacked the newly captured village very heavily. The capture of the village was intended to open the way to the Negev and prevent the enemy forces in Majdal and Iraq Suweidan joining up with those in Faluja and Iraq al-Manshiyya.

As in the days of Ibdis the Egyptians attacked with artillery, with tanks, and with an infantry assault. The attack failed. In the evening we were sent out to collect the booty, to test the enemy positions, and to gather in the weapons of the dead left in the field.

But the hope of opening the route to the Negev was disappointed. After the Egyptians had failed to recapture the village, they occupied—in violation of the ceasefire conditions—the hill to its south. Karatiyya remained in our hands. But the Negev was still cut off.

We stayed a few more days in Sawafir, ready to react immediately to any breach of the ceasefire by the enemy. But our opponent, who had suffered enormous losses, sorted out his own positions and kept quiet.

For the first time we could think about home. For eleven days that was a remote, forgotten world. Suddenly we remembered: we have a home. We have a family. We have parents.

19 July 1948. Sawafir

FOR OUR PARENTS

The guns are silent and the soldiers crawl out of their trenches. The desire is strong to send a few words to the parents—your own parents and the parents of friends, to the parents of all the thousands of soldiers at the front who have survived the storms of the battle on the southern front:

* * *

Your son returns for a short period of leave. He is tired and uncommunicative. And you feel that something is standing between you and him which you have no part in.

You would so dearly like to understand it. To have a role to play in everything that concerns him. You ask him questions: but he shrinks back. He falls silent and turns away from you, or he replies with a tortured smile.

And you, mother, you tell your son about your problems. About the bombing, the sleepless nights, the high prices, and the limited amount of food on sale—and he doesn't even listen. As if all that was too far away, as though he came from a different world.

Sometimes you ask each other, Why is your son so distant? Has he cut himself off from you? Has the war opened a chasm between sons and parents, a chasm too wide to bridge?

Yes. Your son is no longer that nice, smiling boy, who put on a uniform and joked about the experiences in the training camp. He has been in combat. He has seen dead and wounded comrades, he has met fear and learned to overcome it. And he has felt that terrible loneliness which comes when you are on your own in a trench under fire.

He tells you nothing about this, to save your feelings. He can't tell you about this enigmatic life and cruel death, because you belong to another world.

But, parents, on those days of battle your son was also very close. When he set off on an operation in the dead of night, he knew that you were lying sleepless in your beds and worrying about him. And his concern was with you—his parents.

You complain that he wrote so little. Wasn't that cruel of him? But what could he write? These empty words "I am fine . . . I look forward to seeing you again soon"? In his position those were empty, meaningless, pathetic words. Sometimes he made a ridiculous attempt to deceive you. Said he wasn't even at the front. That his unit was being held back in reserve. At the same time he knew that you wouldn't believe a word of it.

And when it happened that a friend died next to him—how terrible was the thought of the parents sitting at home without any idea that their son existed no more. Even more horrifying was the thought that tomorrow the same could happen to his own parents.

So, dear parents—if your son comes back on leave, don't make it too difficult for him. Don't ask him any questions. Don't expect any confessions from him. Know that there are things in his heart that cannot be said. Simply enjoy the simple, wonderful reality: Y-o-u-r-s-o-n-i-s-b-a-c-k.

NOTES

1. Ramat Aharon—agricultural settlement to the north of Rehovot.

2. Chaim Laskov—later Chief of General Staff of the Israeli army.

3. Shimon Avidan—his underground name "Givati" was later used to name a brigade.

Translated by Christopher Costello.

Other works by Avnery: *Israel without Zionists: A Plea for Peace in the Middle East* (1968); *My Friend, the Enemy* (1986).

Aryeh Gelblum

1921–1993

Journalist Aryeh Gelblum went from Poland to Palestine in 1925. As a writer for the newspaper *Haaretz* in the late 1940s, he described Israel's immigrants from Arab countries, spreading venomous stereotypes. *Haaretz* published a series of fifteen articles by Gelblum, who lived in settlement camps for a month, pretending to be an immigrant named Ḥaim Klopstock.

I Was a New Immigrant for a Month: The Aliyah from Yemen and the African Problem
1949

In the living quarters of the [North] African [Jews] in the transit camps, here's what you'll find: you'll find filth, card games, and money, drunkenness, and whoring. Many of them are afflicted with eye, skin, and venereal disease. Not to mention burglary and theft. Nothing is safe against this antisocial element, and no lock can seriously close anything. Not only do the immigrants' possessions disappear, but also the general equipment of the camp. While I was living in one camp, people emptied the general storeroom. In another camp, someone died. The corpse was prepared for ritual burial in a room next to the hospital and the gravediggers left for the funeral. When they returned, the purification vessels were gone.

The Africans bring these forms of life to their places of residence, and it's no wonder that the general crime wave in the country is on the rise. In some parts of Jerusalem, it is no longer safe for a young woman and even for a young man to go out in the street alone after sunset. This is even before the young Africans are released from the army.

By the way, these people have assured me more than once: "Once we finish the war against the Arabs, we'll go to war against the Ashkenazim." In one camp they planned a rebellion, which included seizing the guards' guns and murdering all the employees of the Jewish Agency there. In cases when the police appeared, fights often broke out.

However, beyond all this, there is the basic fact, which is no less grave, and it is the lack of everything needed for adapting to life in the country, and, first of all, chronic laziness and hatred of work. All of them, almost without exception, have no profession, and of course they are poverty-stricken. Everyone will tell you that in Africa they were "merchants," which really means that they were small peddlers, and all of them, of course, want to settle "in the city."

What can be done with them? How can they be "absorbed"?

The wave of immigration is swelling. I don't have statistics about how many thousands have already come, but it is certainly more than tens of thousands. However, the main thing is those who have not come yet. If the movement of immigration from Europe has passed its peak for the moment, immigration from Africa has barely begun. In all the countries of North Africa, thousands and tens of thousands are being prepared for this immigration, and not always in the wisest manner. A neutral witness describes the following picture: "Every day, in the past weeks, the narrow streets of the Jewish quarter of Tripoli have been filled with furniture and household items. Jewish families are selling their possession with total abandon. The Jewish stores are holding clearance sales. There are householders who have already sold the roofs over their head. Whole families—fathers, sons, and men—are planning to immigrate together."

With great disruption, in every possible way, they gain passage to the shores of Europe. In the transit camp in Marseilles, 80 percent of the arrivals today belong to this wave of immigration. A few hundred people with infectious eye, skin, and venereal disease are already stuck in camps in France and Italy, with no hope. Without permission from the Jews to continue on to Israel and without it being easy for them to return, they try to steal their way into Israel.

As for us here in Israel, from the start we apparently never considered the true meaning of this immigration and its absorption. "Free immigration!" we declared, and the gates were open. We are opposed to all ethnic discrimination. Let them come!

But when they began to come and they also began to be a "delicate problem," we adopted a hypocritical stance, which is so typical of us. On the one hand, we continued to insist on the principle of the free and unrestricted immigration of Jews from North Africa; on the other hand—we didn't and still don't know what to do with them. On the one hand—everyone is equal; on the other hand—'Aliyat Ha-no'ar [Youth Aliya], which is an official organization, refuses to accept Moroccan children from the camps. On the one hand Jewish and proletarian brotherhood, and on the other both private and Histadrut employers know that a Moroccan worker is unproductive, and can't be relied upon, and the kibbutzim don't want to hear about absorbing them!

Therefore, hundreds and thousands of Africans sit in the camps and claim they are systematically discriminated against by the "Ashkenazim." "Ashkenazim also came on my ship, and they're already out, and we're still here, for months," many of them told me, and they're right. But it isn't intentional discrimination, or a matter of "*protektsia*" [favoritism]. It's simply easier to arrange things for the others and harder to do it for the Africans. Meanwhile some of them are mobbing the French consulate, asking to go back, and all of them are accumulating bitterness, and there is no way of knowing what will explode come the summer.

At the same time the chaos and confusion in Jewish communities in North Africa is growing. Are we interested in fostering mass hysteria among the poor people there to sell everything, with no possibility of absorbing them here? An order has already been issued to reduce the stream of immigration from 4,500 per month to 2,000, but our emissaries don't always obey instructions. That is the true meaning of the admission on the part of the Jewish Agency directors that they have lost control of the immigration. Of course, without doubt, there is an internal momentum to this immigration, because the declaration of the state sparked a kind of messianic movement among the Jewish masses, and once the faucet is open, it's hard to close it. But there is no doubt that there is some organizing hand behind this spontaneity.

Anyone with a degree of responsibility should not be too embarrassed or cowardly to look the problem in the face, with all its meanings. The *Manchester Guardian* wrote that one of the plentiful sources of the future population of Israel will be North Africa.

In Morocco there are 200,000 Jews.

In Algeria there are 140,000 Jews.

In Libya there are tens of thousands, and hundreds of thousands in Tunisia.

There are more than half a million Jews in North Africa, most of whom are candidates for immigration.

Have we given any thought to what will happen to this state if they are its population? One day Jews from Arab countries will also be added! What will the State of Israel look like, and what will be its level, with these populations?

Certainly all of these Jews have the right to immigrate no less than others, and they must be brought here and absorbed. But if this is not done in accordance with the limitations of capacity and with proper timing, they will absorb us, rather than our absorbing them. Is it not the particular tragedy of this absorption, unlike the poor human material from Europe, that their children, too, have no hope? To raise their general level from the depths of their ethnic way of life will be a matter of generations!

Perhaps it is no wonder that Mr. [Menachem] Begin and the [right wing] Herut Party want to bring all of these hundreds of thousands here immediately, because they know that ignorant masses, primitive and poor, are good material for them, and only such an immigration can bring them to power.

I would like to conclude with what a French diplomat and sociologist recently told me, not a Jew but a sympathizer: "You are making a fatal error, one that we French people made, and today it is our undoing and degeneration. You are opening your gates wide to the people of North Africa, without careful supervision and strict order. Don't forget that you won the war against the Arab countries, and you established your project in the land, not because of your greater numbers, and not because of your material wealth, but first of all because of the spirit that throbbed in you and the intellectual and spiritual equipment that you had. The immigration of certain human material is liable to lower you and make you into a Levantine state—and then your fate is sealed, and you will degenerate into oblivion."

Sometimes we lack the courage, and up to now we have avoided seeing the problem. In truth, the problem is bitter, very bitter, but in truth, if we ignore it, its revenge will be even more bitter!

Translated by Jeffrey M. Green.

Amos Kenan
1927–2009

Born in Tel Aviv, the author, playwright, and sculptor Amos Kenan joined the Lehi underground and fought in Israel's War of Independence. In the 1950s, he published a satirical column in the newspaper *Haaretz* and later wrote for *Yediot Aharonot*. A peace activist, Kenan won the Brenner Prize for Literature in 2000.

Dani: In Memoriam
1952

From his earliest childhood, Dani was happy, sociable, and cooperative. When he was in Tova's kindergarten, he loved to sit together with the children and sing: "*Yulla yulla*, what'll we do without our work?"

When he entered first grade, he still loved the group. Every recess he would sit together with them all and sing: "Comrade, comrade, comrade, what'll we do without our labor?"

In fourth grade he joined the youth movement, which he served in for ten years. There he received a basic collective education and learned to do everything together with everyone: to sing, to dance, to hike, to think, to speak, to write, and so on. He even specialized in writing collective poems, which didn't bring out the individual's egotism too much and at the same time underscored social processes.

When everyone joined the struggle, he joined the struggle. When everyone went on Aliyah Bet [between 1934 and 1948], he went on Aliyah Bet. When everyone was detained in Rafah or in Cyprus, he was detained in Rafah or in Cyprus.[1] When everyone got out of there, he got out of there. When everyone went to war, he also went. When everyone was demobilized, he was demobilized, too. When everyone started to look to the future, so did he.

When he left the kibbutz (after a personal crisis), he went to meet the fellows every evening and ask: "Comrades, what are we doing today? What will we do tomorrow? Comrades, should we go to the movies? Comrades, how are the comrades?" In general, wherever the comrades were, he was never absent.

Once a disaster happened: all the comrades left the city to go to the wedding of one of the comrades, and Dani was left by himself. The whole evening he walked around alone in the streets and didn't meet anyone. That led to depression. That's why he killed himself, and to this day no one can figure out how he managed to do it by himself.

NOTE

1. [Cyprus and Rafah were two of many internment camps used by the British Mandatory authorities to detain intercepted illegal immigrants.—Trans.]

Translated by Jeffrey M. Green.

Other works by Kenan: *Ba-tahanah* (1963); *Sefer ha-ta'anugot* (1968).

Menahem Shemi

1897–1951

One of the fathers of Israeli painting, Menahem Shemi (né Schmidt) was born in Bobruisk, Belorussia. An impoverished student, he arrived in Jerusalem in 1913 and gradually found his footing as a teacher and artist, mixing Eastern and European styles into his own sui generis aesthetic. Shemi's painting career flourished over the following several decades, even during the war years. Serving in the British army and painting in his free hours, Shemi continued to evolve artistically, using his refined, cosmopolitan style to capture the land, the people, and the spirit of the Yishuv on the eve of the State of Israel's historic creation.

Friends Talking about Jimmy
1952

Jimmy's body was taken to Har Tuv, where the doctor confirmed his death, and from Har Tuv it was taken to the morgue in the hospital in the convent of Abu Gosh. He lay there, covered with a gray blanket and suede desert boots on his feet. His face was calm, proud, and serious. [. . .]

On the night when they brought Jimmy's body to Abu Gosh I was there. It was a splendid night, with a full moon, one of those beautiful nights that herald the coming of autumn, when scraps of white clouds coast along at great speed between the stars, playing hide and seek with them. [. . .] Nights like that don't happen that often, and there's no greater pleasure than to stand at the entrance of the headquarters building, the way I stood then, and to look into the night. Echoes of the shooting from the battle didn't reach Abu Gosh. "Strange," I thought to myself, "now my comrades are waging a battle not far from here. On a night like this. What a shame." At headquarters I prepared a meal for when the

men would return from the battle. [. . .] They came around dawn. Yosefela, Ra'anana, Benny, and Menachem. Other comrades came too. They entered seriously and quietly. "Jimmy fell," they said. They didn't sit at the table, they didn't eat, didn't speak. Everyone was turned inward, and they went upstairs to sleep. Someone took a piece of bread from the table and left.

In the Sha'ar Hagai battalion, among the soldiers and officers, depression reigned. During the first two or three days, it was expressed in an air of strange silence. People spoke with stifled voices. They didn't talk about him a lot, but it was felt that they were thinking mainly about him and about his death. Suddenly, they began to talk. The name "Jimmy" spread all over the camp.

Again and again they spoke about the circumstances of his unnecessary death: "Why did he leave the bunker just then?" "If only Jimmy hadn't left the bunker." [. . .] They spoke bitterly, protesting against a fact that couldn't be undone, they spoke a lot. They recalled memories, stories, his expressions and jokes, the way he used to behave, as exemplary.

There was depression, and, if I'm not mistaken, also a kind of feeling of general guilt, and a powerful desire throbbed to fill the vacuum that was left by his absence with talk and memories, which arose abundantly, from our common recognition of the psychological need to unburden ourselves of them. At the outset of the battles, the death of each comrade was shocking and depressing. Later on, a different reaction set in. We would wrap ourselves in a kind of coating of coldness. That coating was very superficial, not very truthful, but necessary: as the war dragged on and became crueler, and our ranks diminished, recognition grew: "What can be done? In war some people have to die. We have to accept it." The funerals of the fallen were oppressive. We wanted to keep our spirits from collapsing, so we could go on. It couldn't be that after the disaster of the Thirty-Five on the way to Gush Etzion,[1] or after the Thirty-Three who died at the Kastel, or the Thirty-Seven who fell at Nebi Samuel, we could say, "Enough. We can't do any more. We don't have the strength to continue. It isn't humanly possible to keep going at this game of unequal forces." We did carry on. We knew how to separate sorrow for the death of comrades from our duty to continue. We blocked our sorrow, so that it wouldn't gnaw at us. We didn't want to delve too deeply. On the contrary, after the disaster at Nebi Samuel, the next day, the Haportsim Battalion [Those Who Broke Through] went up to Jerusalem and conquered Katamon, thus saving itself from depression, despair, and weakness. The fierce continuation tough-ened us up, redeeming us from feelings of failure. The continued fighting of the whole division, as battle fol-lowed upon battle, became dynamic, unceasing activity, not leaving much room for gloomy thoughts that could jeopardize the continuation of our war. Until at last, the power of human suffering wore out. It overflowed and showed itself in the final days before the declaration of the first ceasefire. Even then despair toughened our strength into a final resolution: to be or not to be. In the spirit of that cruel resolution, the Battle for Latrun took place.[2] Not everyone's character is the same. There are those who appear to themselves to be more humane, more sensitive, and more tormented by the death of their com-rades than others. But in fact they aren't like that. That sensitivity, in my opinion, comes from another source; it's the sensitivity of people of weaker character and will. This excessive sentimentality regarding the comrades who fell was a kind of refuge from the weakness of their character and all that was bound up with that weakness: fear, despair, and lack of faith. There were times when this sentimentality spread to many soldiers and reached dangerous proportions. The officers worried as to how to make clear to those people the boundary between sadness for the death of comrades and the necessity and duty to continue. Having no choice, the Palmach gave these people an out by offering various kinds of assis-tance, giving up precious human material needed for combat, if only this weakness might not spread among the others like an infectious disease.

But there were cases of death that stirred everyone, even those who were ostensibly immune and indifferent to the death of comrades. There were moments when this theory about death, which we had conquered with great effort, logic, and common sense, seemed to disin-tegrate. This happened with the fall of a comrade with a personality, a very prominent personality, both strong and friendly. This is what happened with Naḥum Ari-eli when he heard the news of the death of Dani Mass.[3] In the first days after the disaster I felt that Naḥum's reason had collapsed, and he had lost control over his steely character. When Dani fell, when Naḥum fell, when Jimmy fell, we felt that the foundations on which we had built our faith were collapsing. "No, this is too much. Too much. Here something has gone too far." Dani expressed this feeling when Brakha died: "Was it worth it?" From Dani to Jimmy a lot of comrades fell, immeasurably precious, and over time death itself be-came something routine, and because of that, Jimmy's

death was so unsettling and shocking to his friends and the members of the battalion.

Jimmy was buried in the cemetery at Kiryat 'Anavim. Two volunteers from abroad who were killed by a mine the day after his death were buried at the same time, on either side of him. Many, many comrades in arms from the front, young and precious, found their last rest in that hidden valley. May all their memories be a blessing.

NOTES

1. [The Convoy of 35 was a convoy of Haganah fighters sent during the 1947–1948 Civil War in Mandatory Palestine on a mission on foot to reach and resupply the blockaded kibbut-zim of Gush Etzion in January 1948. They were spotted before they could reach their target and killed in a prolonged battle by Arab irregulars and local villagers.—Trans.]

2. [The Palestine Police fort in Latrun commanded the only road linking the Yishuv-controlled area of Jerusalem to Israel, giving Latrun strategic importance in the battle for Jerusalem. In May 1948, it was under the control of the Arab Legion. In a series of bloody battles between 25 May and 18 July 1948, Is-raeli forces failed to capture the fort.—Trans.]

3. [Palmach officer Daniel "Dani" Mass was killed on Janu-ary 16, 1948, while commanding the Convoy of 35.—Trans.]

Translated by Jeffrey M. Green.

Salman Shina

1898–1978

Born in Baghdad, Salman Shina attended an Alliance school there. During World War I, he was an officer in the Ottoman army, eventually taken prisoner by the British. After the war, he returned to Baghdad and became a lawyer. In the 1920s, he founded, edited, and wrote for an Arabic-language Jewish literary journal called *al-Misbaḥ*. Shina served as a member of the Iraqi parliament from 1947 to 1951, when he immigrated to Israel along with the rest of the Jewish community. He died in Ramat Gan.

From Babylonia to Zion

1955

First Impressions

With the first morning light I got up and looked out on the landscape of the Jerusalem Hills. I looked toward the nearby border. One of my relatives told me how the well in our house provided water for a large number of residents during the siege. He also showed me the place where a bomb fell on our house, without causing serious damage.

We went out to walk in the city streets. The streets were full of immigrants from Iraq, because the tent encampments of Talpiot and Mekor Ḥayim were mainly populated by Iraqis.

In Maḥane Yehuda by chance I met three of the rabbis from Baghdad.

"How are things?" I asked.

"Things are exactly the way you see them," one of them answered. "You wrote a lot about the Land of Israel in your newspaper, and you were the head of the Zionist movement from the outset. So now you can see the reality clearly."

"But gentlemen, this is our homeland," I answered. "Even if conditions are hard today, we have to ask the Holy One blessed be He to help us, that He will assist us to establish the state on the foundation of truth and justice, and we will ultimately be privileged to see the building up of our land and our full independence." [. . .]

On Rothschild Boulevard

I went down to Tel Aviv to see how our Iraqi brethren were doing in and around the city. I met masses of people from my ethnic group. [. . .]

"We've been left without leadership," they warned. "Thousands of our people are living in unbearable conditions. Who will come to our assistance?"

"Why these expressions of despair?" I asked. "After all, you organized the commercial life of Iraq; you were the most talented officials in government offices, banks, commercial companies; you made Iraq flourish, and you made fortunes flow to it. Why, then, this despair? Be strong and brave. You'll see better days."

"That's the problem. Here skill isn't the main thing. It's *protektsia*," they answered me right away. "And here it's regarded as shameful to have an Iraqi name."

"On the contrary, go see the tent cities," another one interjected. "And see how our brothers are living there. They left all their property behind in their aspiration to immigrate to Israel. Look at the children there who are rolling around in mud in the winter, and in the summer, with the sun beating down. They tell us there's no work."

I tried to calm them down, but all my efforts were in vain.

I went to see one of the tent cities, and I saw tattered tents, stuck in the sand. I remembered the fine villas in Baghdad: "They that did feed delicately are desolate in the streets" (Lamentations 4:5). [. . .]

Racist Discrimination

"Discrimination is destroying the state," a worker said to me, a man who had been a high government official in Iraq. "Among the directors of the Government Employment Office, there's not even a single Iraqi, and that's why we're left out. As if there was no father to be concerned about us and no mother to love us."

"But that's impossible! How could a Jew in his land be discriminated against because of his 'race' or the color of his skin?" I replied.

"Indeed, it's the old system. The old-timers in the country were Ashkenazi, and after the state was established, one man brought in his friend, his brother, and the members of his family to take on the positions of administration and government. So the state filled up with officials, most of whom are from the Ashkenazi group, except for isolated, unimportant cases." [. . .]

I didn't know what to answer, so I stopped our conversation. [. . .]

On the Causes of Discrimination

It seems to me that the emissaries of the Jewish Agency were determined to bring in the mass immigration from Iraq for just one purpose, to increase the number of residents of Israel. Correct reports about the true condition of the Jews of Iraq before their immigration were not presented.

Most of the residents of Israel don't know who the Iraqis are and what they were. Some people regard them as worthless people. In some cases they even think of them as people who actually came from the "jungle." This is mainly because of the lack of appropriate explanations about this matter. The truth is, and statistics prove it, that among the Jews of Iraq the number of people with higher education is high, people like lawyers, doctors, engineers, accountants, bankers, and so on. [. . .]

Relations between Immigrants from Iraq and Veteran Settlers

Almost all the Jews of Iraq immigrated to Israel, but, unfortunately for them, their immigration was the last in line, so it provides a subject for cheap and unfounded articles in the press. Many articles were written about the immigrants from Iraq, and many of them are full of contempt for them. No one in a position of responsibility tried to halt the contemptible propaganda against the immigrants from Babylonia.

I roused myself into action and sent an article to a newspaper, but they refused to publish it. I tried to publish it in another newspaper, but there, too, I encountered refusal, and the same with a third paper, and so on. [. . .]

This incident inspired me to write a short letter, in which I called the attention of people in positions of responsibility to the living conditions of the Jews of Iraq.

A Report in the Newspaper Omer

Here are the words of the letter:

In the *Omer* of March 9, I read an interesting article about the emigration of the Jews of Romania. It quoted passages from a speech given by Idov Cohen in the Knesset, where he explained that discrimination is causing the emigration of Romanian Jews. I think this is the first time that echoes of discrimination reached the ears of the Knesset. The speech explained that the discrimination against the Jews of Romania in Israel, of which people are speaking with great bitterness, is of a certain reality.

I was reminded of the discrimination that also exists against the Jews from Iraq. There is apathy about the subject, because the Jews of Iraq aren't thinking about emigration, and their taking root in the country is assured. I wish to arouse the conscience of those responsible, to give attention to the difficult living conditions of the Jews of Iraq and to do everything possible to improve their situation.

Salman Shina, Attorney at Law
Ramat-Gan

This letter was printed in the *Omer*, but the editors added a marginal note of their own:

A great deal has been written on this subject. There is a "feeling of inferiority" that is expressed in the feeling of discrimination among various circles in the country. The best way to combat this feeling is not to encourage it. We will discuss this question again. [. . .]

You speak about a "feeling of inferiority." It seems to me that this is camouflage, this is evasion, this is ignoring the truth.

The only thing that causes this situation is the "superiority complex," from which a considerable part of the Jews from Central and Eastern Europe suffer, because they regard themselves as the lords of the land and the chosen people.

You order us not to develop this feeling of inferiority, which is a rather ridiculous claim. Instead of asking the "chosen people" to step down from their pride, you order us to wake up and ask for mercy, and maybe we will be heeded. [. . .]

No, this is not the solution. Such a solution will deepen the wound rather than heal it. The only solution is *to bring hearts together*; this is the slogan that must be written down and fought for. The *heart* of the "chosen people" must be taught to feel true love for us and not to look down at us with haughty eyes. [. . .] A bit of mutual understanding, a bit of love, a bit of brotherhood, a bit of interest on the part of the government, and I am confident that the results will be marvelous. [. . .]

President Isaac Ben-Tsvi Proposes a Law against Ethnic Discrimination [. . .]

Sha'arim published the president's statement in full in issue no. 901, on May 27, 1954:

THE PRESIDENT ADVOCATES SPECIAL LEGISLATION AGAINST ETHNIC DISCRIMINATION

I am of the opinion that it would be good to pass a special law against ethnic discrimination like the law in the United States, which, by means of legislation and severe judicial decisions, seeks to combat discrimination among its citizens, until it disappears completely over time. [. . .]

The president emphasized in his response that the law against ethnic discrimination should be passed here in view of the negative and unfortunate phenomena of discrimination against members of certain ethnic groups in the area of housing. Everyone who commits a crime of this kind should be punished with the full severity of the law, because it is impossible to condone the fact that only because of their origin, Jews from the Orient, meet with refusal to rent or sell apartments to them.

Translated by Jeffrey M. Green.

Moshe Dayan

1915–1981

Israeli military leader and politician Moshe Dayan was born in Degania Aleph, the first kibbutz. He grew up in Nahalal and attended agricultural school. Dayan joined the Haganah at age fifteen and was imprisoned. Serving with the British army in Lebanon during World War II, he was wounded; the eye patch he wore became a symbol of the Israeli warrior-statesman. In Israel's War of Independence, Dayan commanded the Jerusalem front; he later served as chief of staff in the Israel Defense Forces during the 1956 Suez crisis and as defense minister during the Six-Day War. After the 1973 Yom Kippur War, he became foreign minister in the Israeli government and helped negotiate the peace treaty between Egypt and Israel.

Eulogy for Roi Rotberg
1956

Yesterday morning Roi was murdered. He was lulled by the quiet of the spring morning and did not notice those lying in wait in the furrow.

Today, let us not cast aspersions at the murderers. How can we remonstrate against their bitter hatred for us? For eight years now they've been sitting in the refugee camps in Gaza while right before their eyes we've been cultivating the land and villages where they and their forefathers lived.

To avenge Roi's blood, it is not to the Arabs of Gaza that we must turn, but to ourselves.

Why did we shut our eyes rather than look straight on and confront our fate and reckon with the mission of our generation in all its cruelty? How did we lose sight of the fact that this group of settlers in Naḥal Oz has been carrying on its young shoulders the heavy gates of Gaza?

Beyond the trench of the border roils a sea of hate and revenge waiting for the day when, due to complacency, our vigilance eases, the day when we will listen to the conspiring ambassadors of hypocrisy who call upon us to lay down our arms.

It is to us and only to us that Roi's blood is calling out from his torn body. Even though we had vowed time and again that our blood would not be spilled in vain, yesterday, again, we were seduced, we listened and we trusted.

Today we will take account of ourselves. We are the generation that settled the land. Without a helmet and a cannon's mouth we will not be able to plant a tree and build a home. We must not recoil from the look of hatred that fuels and charges the lives of hundreds of thousands of Arabs who live all around us. We must

not avert our eyes and so weaken our hand. This is the fate of our generation. This is the choice of our lives: be ready and armed, strong and resolute; or, allow the sword to fall from our hand, from our fist, and our lives will be extinguished.

Roi is the youth who left Tel Aviv to make his home at the gates of Gaza and to protect us. The light in his heart blinded his eyes and he did not see the glint of the blade. The longing for peace deafened his ears and he did not hear the sound of the preying murderers. The gates of Gaza proved too heavy and they overcame him.

—April 30, 1956

Translated by Tsipi Keller.

Other works by Dayan: *Diary of the Sinai Campaign* (1966); *Mappah ḥadasha: yaḥasim aherim* (1969); *Moshe Dayan: Story of My Life* (1976); *Breakthrough: A Personal Account of the Egypt–Israel Peace Negotiations* (1981).

Yigael Yadin
1917–1984

Yigael (Sukenik) Yadin was an Israeli archaeologist and a member of the Knesset from 1977 to 1981. He served as deputy prime minister in the government of Menachem Begin. Born in Jerusalem, Yadin attended the Hebrew University. In 1936, however, he turned to a military career. In 1949, Yadin became Israel's second chief of staff, but he resumed his studies in archaeology in 1953, writing his dissertation on the Dead Sea Scrolls. He conducted excavations of the Qumran caves (1960–1961), Masada (1963–1965), and Megiddo (1966–1967). Yadin received the Israel Prize for Jewish Studies in 1956.

The Message of the Scrolls
1957

In late November 1947, in what had once been a quiet suburb of Jerusalem, I first heard of the Dead Sea Scrolls. I was at the time Chief of Operations of Haganah, the Jewish underground self-defence movement in Palestine. My headquarters were near Tel-Aviv. On the 28th of November I went to Jerusalem to check on the preparedness of the Jewish population against possible Arab attack.

Six thousand miles away, at Lake Success, United Nations deliberations were leading up to a resolution ending the British Mandate and recommending the establishment of a Jewish State. The Resolution was to be voted on any day. Our underground intelligence reported that Arab attacks on Jewish cities and settlements throughout the country were almost certain to follow. The defence problem in Jerusalem was not easy, for there was a highly mixed Arab and Jewish population. I had come to the city for a first-hand inspection of the situation.

I spent several hours at the underground Jerusalem Haganah Headquarters, toured the city with the Haganah commander, and just before returning to Tel-Aviv I went to visit my parents. My father, Elazar L. Sukenik, was the Professor of Archaeology at the Hebrew University. I found him in a state of high exhilaration, eyes glowing with excitement. "What shall I do?" he asked me after our exchange of *shaloms*. "Shall I go to Bethlehem? I must. First thing in the morning. What do you say?"

I gathered that he had made an exciting archaeological discovery but I could not guess what it was. He had returned only a few months earlier from a lecture tour in the United States and had not yet resumed digging. I hadn't the time to unravel the mystery on my own; I was due back at headquarters. I bade my father sit down quietly and begin at the beginning. I confess that by the time he was half way through his story, problems of defence had receded from my mind and I was transported in time and place from Jerusalem, 1947, to the Dead Sea of two thousand years ago. For what had excited my father was a glimpse of the parchments which have now become famous as the Dead Sea Scrolls. He was the first scholar to recognize these parchments for what they were, the first to detect the first scroll as the most ancient surviving manuscript of the prophet Isaiah, the first to record the opinion, later confirmed by the Carbon 14 test, that it was at least a thousand years older than the earliest previously known copy and the first to acquire three of the scrolls for the Hebrew University.

What had happened came out with a rush as my father began talking, words tumbling over each other as he told this tremendous tale of what he was convinced were the most ancient Hebrew documents in the world, and which he felt were almost within his grasp. He was certain that he would succeed in acquiring them as a perpetual Jewish heritage, for he found something symbolic in the thought that this was happening at the very moment when Jewish sovereignty in Palestine was about to be restored after almost two thousand years— the very age of the parchments he had seen.

"It all started on Sunday," he began. Sunday was the 23rd of November, five days earlier; it was now Friday. "When I got to my office at the Hebrew University on Mount Scopus, I found a message from a friend, an Armenian dealer in antiquities, asking me to get in touch with him immediately. He is a most trustworthy person, and I knew that the matter must be urgent and important for him to telephone me on his day of rest. But I had lectures all the morning and my students were waiting. It was not until the afternoon that I was able to speak to him. He told me that he was most anxious to show me some items of interest. I asked him what they were, but he said he could not tell me on the telephone. He urged an early meeting. We fixed it for the next morning. The place we chose was the gateway to Military Zone B."

The British security forces had recently divided the city into military zones, each marked off with barbed wire barriers and guarded by sentries; movement from one zone to another was possible only with an official pass, and neither my father nor his Armenian friend had one. So they had arranged to meet at the barrier dividing their two zones, and the whole momentous conversation was carried on across a barbed wire fence.

My father went on: "When we met, my friend pulled from his briefcase a scrap of leather. He held it up for me to see. On it I noticed Hebrew script, but I could not make out the words. I asked him what it was and his story was so fascinating that I almost forgot the sickening presence of the barbed wire between us. He said that one of our mutual friends, an old Arab antiquities dealer in Bethlehem, had come to him the previous day with a tale of some Bedouin who had called on him bringing several parchment scrolls which they claimed to have found in a cave near the shores of the Dead Sea, not far from Jericho. They had offered to sell him the scrolls, but he, the Arab dealer, did not know whether they were genuine. He had therefore brought them to my Armenian friend. He, too, had no knowledge of whether they were really ancient manuscripts or a fairly recent product. He wanted to know from me whether I considered them genuine and if so whether I would be prepared to buy them for the Museum of Jewish Antiquities of the Hebrew University.

"I was in a difficult situation. If I gave him an immediate affirmative answer, I would be automatically committed to their purchase, since we had known each other long enough for each to trust the word of the other. I hesitated a few minutes, straining my eyes to peer through the loops of barbed wire in an effort to make out the letters on the scrap of leather. Strangely enough, as I gazed at the parchment, the letters began to become familiar, though I could make no immediate sense of the writing. They resembled letters which I had found on several occasions on small coffins and on ossuaries which I had discovered in and around Jerusalem, in some ancient tombs dating back to the period before the Roman destruction of the city. I had seen such letters scratched, carved and, in a few cases, painted on stone. But not until this week had I seen this particular kind of Hebrew lettering written with a pen on leather.

"My first thought was that this was possibly the work of some forger, who had conceived the idea of imitating the script on leather. But this thought stayed with me for barely a moment. As I continued to peer, my hunch became stronger and stronger that this was no forgery but the real thing. I decided to risk buying the scrolls, of which this was a fragment, for the University. I asked my Armenian friend to proceed at once to Bethlehem and bring back some more samples. I asked him to telephone me when he got back and in the meantime I would try and get a military pass so that I could visit him at his store and examine the parchments more closely.

"He telephoned me yesterday [Thursday, 27 November] to say that he had some additional fragments. I raced over to see him, entering Zone B with my newly acquired pass. I sat in his shop and tried to decipher the writing. It was written in a very good, clear hand, and resembled, even more closely than the first sample, the alphabet on the stone ossuaries. I was now more convinced than ever that these were fragments of genuine ancient scrolls. We resolved to go together to Bethlehem and start negotiations with the Arab dealer for their purchase. We arranged to go today, but I'm afraid I have been very foolish. I was so excited when I got home yesterday that your mother asked me what it was all about. I told her, and I was silly enough to add that I was going to Bethlehem today to see the Arab dealer. You should have heard her reaction. She said I was crazy even to think of making such a dangerous journey entirely through Arab territory at a moment of high tension, likely to explode at any minute with the passage of the UN resolution. And so I had to put him off for the moment, but I cannot, I cannot sit here doing nothing. What shall I do? Shall I go to Bethlehem?"

I was silent for a few minutes while my father mused aloud, his mind swinging from anxiety over Palestine and what would happen at Lake Success to anxiety over this new discovery. For years his mind had freewheeled round the possibility of ancient Hebrew scrolls being turned up by the archaeologist's spade. He had often been asked: "Is there any chance that excavations in Palestine, cradle of the Bible, will bring forth ancient Hebrew books which may shed further light on the Bible?" My father's answer had usually been that the humid climate of Palestine was unsuitable for the preservation of organic matter, which includes manuscripts of papyrus; leather or parchment. This opinion had been shared by every archaeologist who had ever worked in the country. My father was therefore weighing in his mind all the pros and cons as to the genuineness of the scrolls. His worries were aggravated by the responsibility he was assuming in buying them for the Hebrew University, perhaps spending public funds on a forgery.

What was I to tell him? As a student of archaeology myself, I felt that an opportunity of acquiring such priceless documents could not be missed. On the other hand, as Chief of Operations of Haganah, I knew perfectly well the dangers my father would be risking in travelling to Arab Bethlehem. And as a son I was torn between both feelings. I tried to hedge, but, before leaving, son and soldier won and I told him not to go. I bade him and my mother *shalom* and left for Tel-Aviv. Fortunately, my father disregarded my advice and next morning left for Bethlehem. But I did not discover this until later. [. . .]

There was little opportunity during the early battles for talks with my father on his discoveries. It was more than a month after our first talk that I had the chance of seeing him. (I was visiting Jerusalem because a group of our co-operative settlements were under heavy attack by the Arab Legion.) It was only then that I found out that the day after I had left him, and on the very day that the United Nations Resolution was carried, he had, this time without telling my mother or indeed anyone else, and in disregard of my advice, met his Armenian friend and gone with him to Bethlehem. There he had made arrangements for buying the Dead Sea Scrolls.

Other works by Yadin: *The Scroll of the War of the Sons of Light against the Sons of Darkness* (1962); *Masada: Herod's Fortress and the Zealots' Last Stand* (1966); *Bar Kokhba: The Rediscovery of the Legendary Hero of the Second Jewish Revolt Against Rome* (1971); *Hazor: The Rediscovery of a Great Citadel of the Bible* (1975); *The Temple Scroll: The Hidden Law of the Dead Sea Sect* (1985).

Ka-Tzetnik 135633
1909–2001

Yehiel Dinur, born Feiner (Fajner), in Sosnowiec, Poland, was known as Ka-Tzetnik 135633, his prisoner name and number at Auschwitz. (*Katzetnik* was the term for an inmate of a concentration camp, after the German *Konzentrationslager.*) He was the first survivor-author in any language to place Auschwitz at the center of his writing. An undistinguished expressionist poet in Yiddish before the war, he rose to prominence in Mandatory Palestine after his arrival there in 1945 with his novels of atrocity, especially *House of Dolls*, which became an international best seller. Dinur revealed his identity in 1961 while testifying at the Eichmann trial in Jerusalem, where he collapsed upon confronting the "ordinary" visage of Eichmann. He is best known for *Sunrise over Hell* (originally: *Salamandra*; 1946), *House of Dolls* (1953), and *They Called Him Piepel* (1961), which formed a trilogy that he called *The Chronicles of a Jewish Family in the Twentieth Century.*

Testimony at the Eichmann Trial
1961

Session No. 68: 23 Sivan 5721 (7 June 1961)

PRESIDING JUDGE: I declare the sixty-eighth Session of the trial open.

DECISION NO. 72

We confirm the request of the Attorney General and will permit the exhibition of films to illustrate the evidence of the Prosecution witnesses, on condition that the films will be sufficiently authenticated.

For reasons of security, because of the blacking-out of the hall during the screening, the public, with the exception of journalists, will not be permitted to be in the Courtroom at the time of the screening.

ATTORNEY GENERAL: I would ask Mr. Dinur to mount the witness stand.

PRESIDING JUDGE: Do you speak Hebrew?

WITNESS DINUR: Yes.

[*The witness is sworn.*]

PRESIDING JUDGE: What is your full name?

WITNESS: Yehiel Dinur.

ATTORNEY GENERAL: Mr. Dinur, you live in Tel Aviv, at 78 Rehov Meggido, and you are a writer?

WITNESS DINUR: Yes.

Q. You were born in Poland?

A. Yes.

Q. And you were the author of the books *Salamandra, The House of Dolls, The Clock Above the Head* and *They Called Him Piepel*?

A. Yes.

Q. What was the reason that you hid your identity behind the pseudonym "K. Zetnik," Mr. Dinur?

A. It was not a pen name. I do not regard myself as a writer and a composer of literary material. This is a chronicle of the planet of Auschwitz. I was there for about two years. Time there was not like it is here on earth. Every fraction of a minute there passed on a different scale of time. And the inhabitants of this planet had no names, they had no parents nor did they have children. There they did not dress in the way we dress here; they were not born there and they did not give birth; they breathed according to different laws of nature; they did not live—nor did they die—according to the laws of this world. Their name was the number "Kazetnik."[1] They were clad there, how would you call it . . .

Q. Yes. Is this what you wore there? [*Shows the witness the prison garb of Auschwitz*]

A. This is the garb of the planet called Auschwitz. And I believe with perfect faith that I have to continue to bear this name so long as the world has not been aroused after this crucifixion of a nation, to wipe out this evil, in the same way as humanity was aroused after the crucifixion of one man. I believe with perfect faith that, just as in astrology the stars influence our destiny, so does this planet of the ashes, Auschwitz, stand in opposition to our planet earth, and influences it.

If I am able to stand before you today and relate the events within that planet, if I, a fall-out of that planet, am able to be here at this time, then I believe with perfect faith that this is due to the oath I swore to them there. They gave me this strength. This oath was the armour with which I acquired the supernatural power, so that I should be able, after time—the time of Auschwitz—the two years when I was a Musselman, to overcome it. For they left me, they always left me, they were parted from me, and this oath always appeared in the look of their eyes.

For close on two years they kept on taking leave of me and they always left me behind. I see them, they are staring at me, I see them, I saw them standing in the queue . . .

Q. Perhaps you will allow me, Mr. Dinur, to put a number of questions to you, if you will agree?

A. [*Tries to continue*] I remember . . .

PRESIDING JUDGE: Mr. Dinur, kindly listen to what the Attorney General has to say.

[*Witness Dinur rises from his place, descends from the witness stand, and collapses on the platform. The witness fainted.*]

PRESIDING JUDGE: I think we shall have to adjourn the session. I do not think that we can continue.

ATTORNEY GENERAL: I did not anticipate this.

PRESIDING JUDGE: [*After some time*] I do not think that it is possible to go on. We shall adjourn the Session now, and please, Mr. Hausner, inform us of the condition of the witness and whether he will at all be able to give his testimony today. And I would ask you to do so soon.

[*The Session was resumed.*]

ATTORNEY GENERAL: With the Court's permission, in view of the unfortunate incident that has taken place, I shall have to arrange the evidence on Auschwitz differently. It was intended that Mr. Dinur should give us a general description, so that the other witnesses could supplement it on various partial aspects. I ask the Court's indulgence if the picture now will not be presented in the manner in which we originally planned. The witness Dinur will not be able to continue his evidence, I understand. He has been taken away from this building and his state of health will not permit him to continue.

NOTE

1. Kazet = Konzentrationslager-Katzetnik: inmate of a concentration camp.

Translator unknown.

Other works by Ka-Tzetnik: *The Clock Overhead* (1960); *Phoenix over the Galilee* (1966).

Nissim Benjamin Gamlieli

1926–2003

Author and translator Nissim Benjamin Gamlieli was among the thousands of Yemenite Jews who made the arduous journey to Israel in 1948. With his collaborator Ezra Cohen, a member of the municipal council of Ramla, he collected accounts of the dangerous trek from Yemen, describing the years spent in the Geula Camp established by the Jewish Agency, on the border near Aden. Gamlieli gathered Yemenite legends and folktales, translating the stories into Hebrew in order to preserve their unique culture.

Yemenite Jews and the Geula Refugee Camp in Aden
1962

The chapter of the wanderings of the Jews from Yemen to Aden remains shrouded in uncertainty. As of today, there has been no publication of a complete and detailed description of the paths and hardships, both natural and political, that stood in the way of the redeemed. I have attempted to fill this gap in a detailed description, laced with stories of experiences from the main route from Yemen to Aden.

Nissim Benyamin Gamlieli (merchant) [. . .]

Introduction

FROM EZRA COHEN

All the shifts and changes that took place in the past hundreds of years all over the world and altered the old orders and traditions did not take place in the serene tranquil country of Yemen of old. The innovations of science and the inventions of technology did not reach there. The colonial empires that took over countries and distant islands all over the world for some reason passed over the land of Yemen and it remained distant and isolated from the great world with all its revolutions and upheavals, devoted and fastened to dense interwoven religions and customs according to engrained fixed patterns. The two world wars did not touch it, and, except for pieces of information and fragments of rumors of what was happening in the great world, the inhabitants knew nothing. Journalists did not pay attention to it, and dedicated to it only a few short articles in the margins of their newspapers, and that only very rarely. [. . .]

Fifteen years ago we abandoned Yemen in droves, with all its past and its splendor and its deep-rooted Jewish experience, replete with its content and innocent faith. Behind us lay a long and rich history of Jewish life rooted and crowned with the aura of heroic and sacrificial acts, innocent tortures and disasters that came upon the Jews for adhering to the faith of their forefathers. [. . .]

We shall relate to our brethren the "ingathering of the exiles," to our sons after us and to the coming generations: there was once a diaspora that was cut off from the other diasporas of Israel for many hundreds of years. Persecutions and hard torments came repeatedly upon it, the hatred of the *goyim*, the royal decrees, the injuries of nature and time that embittered their lives and caused endless grief and suffering; despite all this, because they were devoted to the Rock of their foundation, His Torah, and His commandments, they proudly carried their torment, their troubles, and their afflictions. [. . .]

Nevertheless, these yearnings for redemption were not limited to delusion and imagination and the passive hopes for a miracle from heaven. It was not a mission of the soul that was not to be achieved. There were many great and bold feats. Throughout all the generations and eras, individuals and groups endeavored, despite great danger to their lives, to go to the land of Israel by breaking through the ring of geographical blockades that closed them in from all directions: the Red Sea from the south, east, and west, and the Arabian Desert from the north.

Traveling through the Arabian Desert, the only land route from and to Yemen, was an impossible feat. For religious and other reasons, Jews were not allowed to set foot in all the lands of Mecca and Medina that are sacred to the Muslims. And nevertheless there were a few brave and courageous souls who took this dangerous path. Many of them perished in the heart of the desert. There were those who retraced their steps and only a select few managed to reach the land of Israel in safety. The only way to pass through was the British colony of Aden, through which many immigrants passed and from there they were redeemed on eagles' wings.

The journey between Yemen and the British colony of Aden was rife with terrible dangers for those Jews who took that path. Throughout the British territory reigned tribes of wild and daring robbers who wrought fear on all those who passed. The English ruled those areas only in theory; in practice they were unable to protect the people of the convoys from the hands of these marauders. And to the Jews were added two additional difficulties: the King of Yemen, under pressure from the Arab countries and the Mufti of Jerusalem, issued a royal proclamation absolutely forbidding the exit of Jews from Yemen, and the British, according to the "White Paper" policy, blocked their entry to Aden. Both sides, the Kingdom of Yemen on the one hand and the British Rule on the other, ignored the acts of looting and murder of Jews by the robber gangs. Furthermore, this situation was amenable to them, since in this way they could prevent the immigration of Jews to the land of Israel.

Nevertheless, despite the impediments both of nature and man, multitudes of Jews broke through the double blockade and arrived in Aden. Innumerable times they were caught and returned to the land from which they came, were savagely tortured and placed in prisons, but in spite of that, they did not despair. They were expelled from one direction and returned in seven other ways and retraced their steps in their path to the place of their desire. [. . .]

We shall remember and not forget the members of the Friends of Redemption Organization and our brothers, the Jews of Aden, who from an authentic and faithful sense of brotherhood helped thousands of immigrants by giving them shelter and home and by supporting them financially and ethically!

Translated by Karen Alkalay-Gut.

Ita Kalish

1903–1994

Because she was the daughter of a Hasidic rabbi in Poland, Ita Kalish's secular education was undertaken in secret, conducted against her father's wishes. After his death when she was sixteen, Kalish left her husband and daughter behind to live in Warsaw with her sisters. There, they became active in secular and Zionist circles. In 1923, she moved to Berlin; when the Nazi Party assumed power in 1933, Kalish immigrated to Palestine, where she worked for the Jewish Agency and, eventually, for the Israeli civil service. Despite her withdrawal from Hasidic life, Kalish's memoirs vividly depict the atmosphere of her father's court.

Life in a Hasidic Court in Russian Poland toward the End of the 19th and the Early 20th Centuries
1965

Rabbi Simkha Bunem of Warka Departs for the Holy Land

Rumors of my grandfather's plan to depart for Palestine reached his wife and children shortly after the Russian revolution of 1905. [. . .]

The motive for his journey to Palestine was—in the narrative of my grandmother—as follows: Rabbi Mendele of Warka had died after nineteen years in the rabbinate. My grandfather thought it an insult to his father to continue in the rabbinate longer than he and decided to make a pause. His second journey he made after the passage of another nineteen years. This time he journeyed alone, disillusioned, alienated from the world and kin. On the Sabbath before his departure he proclaimed in the synagogue: "Jews, a fire is raging and no one is aware of it!" [. . .]

When new winds began to blow in the Jewish pale in the years close to World War I, penetrating our court, the citadel of Hassidic piety, and when the inescapable conflict between the generations began to cast its shadow also over his children my father became terribly frightened. He would recall my grandfather's words, "a fire is raging and no one is aware of it." He reproached himself for failing to grasp the import of these words and late at night he could be heard pacing the floor and repeating to himself: "Father, you were right." His world was collapsing. "Jewishness is disappearing," was his constant complaint. Once, after the High Holidays, he said to me: "On Yom Kippur I prayed that if my children, God forbid, no longer be good Jews, then let them remain childless. Let the family come to an end! [. . .]

The End

On my last visit to our home, before World War II, my brother spoke at length about the Holy Land. He mentioned the dream of my father to make a pilgrimage to grandfather's grave in Tiberias and expressed the hope that he would realize that dream. Shortly came World War II. The last cabled appeal for help, for a visa to Palestine, came too late. On his way to Vilna (together with the rabbi of Mszczonow, Simon, of blessed memory) he was somehow separated from his wife. He refused to continue his journey and returned with the children to Otwock.

Details of the tragic end of my brother are related: His wife and children were shot in his presence. He stood, wrapped in his *tallis*, petrified and immobile, repeating the confessional. Suddenly the Nazi hangman leaped up, tore at his *tallis* and exclaimed: "Well, you are a saint. I am giving you five more minutes to pray—for my death or yours."

No miracle happened.

The site of grandfather's villa and its large synagogue, which stood for nearly eighty years in Otwock, is now a field cultivated by a Polish peasant.

O Earth, cover not thou their blood!

Translated by Shlomo Nobel.

Other works by Kalish: *A rebishe heym in amolikn Poyln* (1963); *Siḥot 'im Ḥazaz* (1976).

Leah Goldberg

A Letter to the Readers of My Friends from Arnon Street
1966

Often I receive letters from children who read my stories, and one question that is nearly always put to me in the letters is: "Did it really happen?" But, you see, I cannot always answer this question in the affirmative because when an author writes, he writes about things that did happen and things that did not. To write a book means that the author has to know how to invent stories about people that did not exist and about events that did not happen, but he must invent them in such a way that the reader believes that they really did happen. And why does the reader believe that the events the author writes about did happen, and that the people in the story are real people, and that the author knew them? There is a simple answer to this: when an author invents the heroes of his stories, their actions and adventures, he thinks about them so much, he gets to know everything about them, down to the smallest detail, even details that he does not include in the story. This is because when writing a book, you only tell what is interesting about the people and what they do, leaving out the less interesting parts. Just as it is in real life—when you tell someone a story about friends and acquaintances, you do not tell them everything from beginning to end, but only the parts that are interesting. At the same time, the author, who knows his characters so well, including the details that he does not mention, he himself begins to feel that indeed he is dealing with real living people. For the author, the people he writes about, even when he invents them, it is always as if they really existed. [. . .]

And now my old book, *My Friends from Arnon Street*, is published again, and the stories in this book were written a bit differently than my other stories. In this book there are many details that were actually true. To begin with, at the time, I did live in Tel Aviv, on Arnon Street, and the number of my house was indeed 15, and on the corner of the street there really stood a blue house. I believe that this house is still there today, but, because it has been a long while since I have had occasion to go to Arnon Street, I do not know if it is still blue, or if, in the meantime, it has been painted a different color. Additionally, all my small friends from Arnon Street were, in reality, just as I described them, and we were friends. Ruti and Yona, for instance, were indeed twins and they were small children. Now they are still twins but are already grownups. They and all the other children would come to see me and we would talk about matters that interested them, because, I have to admit, the matters that concerned them were far more interesting to me than my own matters were to them. As to the events in the story—about the candy Ruti and Yona planted in the garden, about the donkey, and about the vegetarian cat, it is difficult for me now to say for sure if they happened just as I described it, or if I did invent some of the stories. [. . .]

All of this happened many many years ago. And because so many years have gone by, there are things in the book that need to be explained. After all, these events took place before the State of Israel was established, and life in Eretz Israel was very different then, and we, as the saying goes, do not even know the shape of the coins in use at the time. And the shape of the coin is precisely what I want to say something about. You will be reading in the story that someone found a coin and said: "I found a white *grush* without a hole!" What does this mean? The *agora* at the time was called *grush* (at times we still use the term today), but every *grush* had a hole in it. And a *grush* without a hole was worth much more than the *agora*; its value was five *agorot* and it was called a shilling. The shilling was made of silver and was brighter than the *agora*, and for a five-year-old boy who did not know the value of the coin, it was "a white *grush* without a hole." These days there are no coins with a hole. A pity, no? I think that for children coins with a hole are much more interesting. But such coins were annulled and, like many other things, remain only in the story. And this is how it is in life—things as they really were have changed, but the stories do not change. Maybe the only truth that never changes is always a story or a poem. I will tell you something else: I, too, have changed a lot since then, but my stories of those days will remain, as if by magic, just as they were.

Yours in friendship,
Leah Goldberg

Translated by Tsipi Keller.

Amos Oz

The Last War or the Third, That Is the Question: A Conversation in Kibbutz Ein Shemer
1967

AVISHAI: There's nothing joyful about the guys who returned from the war. I don't have the feeling that this is the last time that the people sitting here will put on uniform. Right after the war the feeling began that this was another phase, a phase in which we were very successful and that was something of a miracle. But all the time I'm living with the feeling that the next phase will come much sooner than another ten years. It's not a question of political or geopolitical analysis. It's mostly a question of feelings, which I can't always explain to myself. . . . I have a feeling all the time that the next turn will be much crueler. Because if up to now a large part of the Arabs didn't hate us with real hatred, and it's well known that hatred of the enemy is a good motive for war, now that we have finally turned into a conquering army, albeit accompanied by fine manners, because Jews, and specially kibbutzniks, don't know how to conquer or rule . . . We are holding territories where there is a fairly rooted Arab population. I think that next time round the hatred of the Arabs toward us will be much more serious and much deeper. And therefore the next war will be much fiercer and there will be far more victims. . . .

AMOS: Was this the first time you took part in a war?

AVISHAI: Yes. At the time of Suez I was a new recruit. And our commanders said: We're not allowed to screw the Arabs over, so we'll screw you over instead. And they did screw us over good and proper.

—I've been asked this: how did I digest the loss of my comrades who fell in battle? No, I still haven't digested the loss of the comrades who fell three months ago. I haven't interiorized it. You have the feeling that this man, that you used to milk with in the cowsheds—when I go into the cowsheds, I see him from the moment I start milking to the moment I finish. . . .

AMOS: The first time you came home, did you have a feeling that your home had changed? That it wasn't the same place, the same life?

AVISHAI: You come back from places like these, from locations like these, from a huge meeting like this with the whole of Israel, and you return to the place where you were born, and I'm the Kibbutz Secretary now, and as soon as I get back I have to start dealing with the petty day-to-day problems that a secretary has to deal with . . . I didn't manage at all, at least during the first couple of weeks, to get back into the boots of an official and into ordinary normal life.

Amos: But you were happy to be busy?

Avishai: I was very happy. Generally speaking, a secretary's life is not an easy one, but it's fair to say that during that first period I was totally unable to be on my own, to be alone, digesting those things. I simply had to be in some sort of movement, some sort of a hurry, some sort of contact with people: to talk to them, even about uninteresting things, on no account to be left on my own.

Amos: Hagai, you've taken part in two wars, haven't you?

Hagai: This time I fought in Jerusalem. Back then I served in the airborne infantry that advanced via Kuntila, Temed, and Nahal.

Amos: And this time?

Hagai: This time, I took part in the conquest of the Old City. As a platoon commander.

Amos: What did you talk about before the war, during the period of readiness?

Hagai: We talked about home, family, the kibbutz, about everything that we've built up over the years, about things that mattered to us—out of that hidden fear that exists at the moment of feeling a lack of full security. . . . While the moment a man squeezes the trigger and runs, he stops thinking, and the moment he stops thinking he has no problems. The moment he's under fire and he gets up and starts running, he has passed the stage of being afraid and he does things that he wouldn't dare to do if he thought about them. When you're in the battle trance, you have no time to be scared. There may be phases when there is time for lightning thoughts—when the attack is checked and there is an exchange of fire, when you stop for a short while, etc.—In the first five minutes of fighting, forty-five men in my platoon were hit. One was killed and forty-five were injured. I'm not saying I had a shock, but it was a heavy blow, and I got over it by fairly serious means, when you first realize that these guys aren't going to get up again. Some of them were members of my kibbutz who were in the same platoon. At the first moment when such huge quantities of blood were shed, and you don't know

who's alive and who's dead, and when only some of the guys in the platoon get up to follow through, it was a feeling I've never encountered in any previous operation. I'd had operations where a few stray men were injured or killed, but this wasn't on the same scale at all. This was the toughest sensation I've had to face. . . . There are some Jews who think, because they don't believe in any way of compromise, that the only way is that of force. And this is the way they mostly think, without thinking ahead, whether this is possible for years ahead. Is it possible in the years to come, to live like this and to progress like this? They say that they are not too exercised by the question whether it's possible, what exercises them is the fact that they don't believe in the possibility of following any other path.

I think that this is our central problem. It's not a matter of party politics, it's a matter of any young guy who thinks about the subject. As long as we learn first of all to create in ourselves the belief that peace can be achieved, that in fact there is no other choice, that endless wars will not solve anything. On the contrary, the situation will deteriorate from time to time. . . . This very thought must lead to a search for a way that is not based on coercion and subjugation by force. Many of us need to become convinced—I see this as fundamental. And when we reach the point where a broad range of young people reach the conclusion that there is no other way than peace between these two nations, then I guess we will have moved beyond the first and most important phase.

Uri: In the period of readiness, on the eve of the war, the political situation overlapped with the image we had developed of ourselves—we had always drawn a comparison between ourselves, between our present condition, and the Jewish fighter down the ages: a physically weak fighter, fighting against someone stronger; someone weaker but in the right, who wins because he is in the right. . . .

After the war the mood changed. Suddenly we turned into the strong man, as opposed to the "ideal" of the weak man in the right—now we are the strong conqueror, together with all the deeper implications of this change in relation to the previous image, you suddenly discover a parallelism between yourself and all the conquerors who have been in this land before, and this creates for some reason a feeling of unease, a sort of guilt feeling. And even though the security situation has improved following on the change of borders, I personally feel that the next war is unavoidable.

I think that one of the fundamental components in the Arab character is national pride. Their national pride was humiliated by the defeat they suffered in the war. Any peace agreement will be for them an acceptance of the wound to their pride, and that is something they cannot permit themselves, which is why they have no alternative but to go to war again. . . .

As for us, we're not going to budge from the ceasefire lines without a peace agreement. And the outcome: each side sticks stubbornly to itself, there's no contact between the two sides, and there'll be no prospect whatever of dialogue or understanding. And the outcome: the next war is inevitable. It's only a matter of time.

When you go to war knowing that this is the only war you'll have to fight, your attitude to it is different from a war that you know will be followed by others, at whatever intervals. This creates a sense of pessimism and depression and places a question mark over your whole world-view.

Translated by Nicholas de Lange.

Jacqueline Shohet Kahanoff

A Letter from Mama Camouna
1968

Not long after Sammy's visit, my father died after a long illness. My mother's sorrow and mine were compounded by the fact that there were not ten men who had known him in his life to stand by his grave and recite kaddish for him. Seeing we were so few, some strangers at the Holon cemetery visiting their own dead did the mitzvah of coming to recite kaddish for this Jew they had never known. This was the time when we felt that Israel can be exile most bitterly and cruelly. But telegrams and letters poured in from so many places in the world where Father's brothers, nephews, and grand-nephews lived. In New York and in Manchester there were enough of them to gather in his memory and do things the proper way, as he had done all his life for others. And when some of them now come to Israel, and ask to visit his grave, there is a more gentle sorrow, a kind of peace over the fact that he is remembered by them. Sometimes, I go alone, and this loneliness seems incredible when once we were so many.

Then I remember my grandmother telling me when I was a child how Mama Camouna and the other women would take the children to the Jewish cemetery in Tunis, so that the dear dead ones would not feel lonely. "At first we lamented and tore at our cheeks, and then we'd settle down for a collation, and the children would play hide-and-seek among the graves. And we'd remember what our dear ones had said and done and told stories about them. Oh, we'd laugh so much remembering your great-uncle Fragi, because he was so gay, always playing pranks and at weddings he'd compose songs, honoring the bride and groom and their families, with funny refrains about everybody." Then Grandmother and her daughters would remember those weddings in Tunis and what everybody wore, some of the women still in their traditional dresses, wrapped up in big white silk shawls, and those who already dressed in the style that was "modern" before the First World War. Their infectious laughter sometimes seems to echo among the cold rectilinear alignment of the graves in Holon, and they all seem to be there, and I the surviving witness of something marvelously warm, vital, and alive, which I knew but which no longer is. Nowadays, even the dead seem regimented in these straight-lined cemeteries, so different from the old ones, where families kept together, in death as in life. And yet, somehow, life continues, reasserts itself, and some of the old ways still survive. After my father's death, my mother stayed some time with my sister in Paris, where she saw many of her cousins, some who had left Egypt after the Sinai Campaign, and some who, in the meantime, had left Tunis and other North African cities. Then she stayed with my father's relatives in England, and each of his nephews and nieces brought their children and grandchildren to see her, exactly as it was done in the old days. She wrote: "They still cook the same dishes, some of them, at least for the holidays."

She returned to Israel having seen them all, appeased. In Paris, her cousins, the daughters of Uncle David, who are now old ladies, still meet every *motsa'e shabbat* and read the letters they have received. Anyone who passes through Paris joins the circle. The younger people sometimes come and sometimes don't. Perhaps this will be the last generation to keep up the custom, but in the meantime it holds.

And so it was that Gerard, a great-grandson of Uncle David, called me up one day from his kibbutz. A little mockingly, he said, "Grandmother said that if I don't see your mother while I'm in Israel, she'll never forgive me. So when can I come?"

We make arrangements for his visit. He arrives, a handsome boy of eighteen, a student, who, trying to look serious, tells me that he, too, paraded with the black flag of anarchy during the student riots. We laugh. With his long blond hair he looks very much like a beatnik and his pink outfit is very dirty.

"Would you like to wash?" Mother suggests.

Gerard looks scandalized. Then his eyes begin to rove over the pictures hanging on her walls and he recognizes some of the old people he knows when they were still young, and of some he asks, "Who is he? Who is she?" For a brief moment they live again as part of our lives, mixed up with what we say about the Six-Day War, and what Gerard tells us of his kibbutz, and the family in Paris, and the student riots. And Gerard tells my mother, "Aunt Yvonne, you should have seen the crowd that came to hear your letters being read. Aunt Louise called us all up, and said 'A letter from Yvonne!' and we all went. We heard all about your visit to Jerusalem. It was very moving. But your letter about the visit to the Golan Heights drew crowds three Saturdays in a row! It was a masterpiece. You can't imagine what it means now, to have family in Israel."

Mother was very pleased. "I'm only an old woman. I just wrote about what I saw and what I felt about it, and wanted to share it with those I love."

Gerard knits his eyebrows and asks, "But how did it happen that for the last three or four generations we've been constantly on the move? And it's not finished yet. How did it all begin?"

So mother tells Gerard how in her family it might have begun. "You see, your great-great-grandfather had an oil press in Monastir, a small village in Tunisia. The oil was stored in big jars, like those in the tale about Ali Baba and the forty thieves. One jar was kept for ablutions. There was of course no running water in those days. Well, one day, after he had worked hard and sweated and felt very hot, he had the jar filled with cold water and stayed in it too long. He died of pneumonia as a consequence. Times were already changing, and your great-grandfather, my Uncle David, the eldest son, decided to try his luck in Tunis, the big city, and gradually he brought the whole family over to Tunis. That's how it all began."

"Well," Gerard said, "it's not given to everybody to have had an ancestor who died taking a cold bath in an oil jar. I'll have to tell the cousins in Paris about it. I wonder why Grandmother never did."

"Perhaps," Mother said, at once gentle and reproaching, "because you never asked. How do you want us to tell, when you young people nowadays are really not interested in those old tales, when you can't really be bothered with the past, because the world you live in is so different? So it's wiser to wait until you ask." She glances at me, a little slyly. "Isn't it so, my daughter?"

I say yes and I think it's always the same caravans crossing and recrossing. Perhaps memories are like water in a well, that well Rachel uncovered for Jacob when he came to his Uncle Laban. Perhaps that is when it all started, and since then it is only the means of transportation that have realty changed.

Fiction, Drama, and Children's Literature

Natan Shaḥam
1925–2018

Novelist and playwright Natan Shaḥam was born in Tel Aviv, the son of author Eliezer Steinman. Shaḥam served in the Palmach in Israel's War of Independence. He then worked abroad as Israel's cultural attaché in New York and served as editor in chief at the Sifriat Poʻalim Publishing House. His works deal with the issues of assimilation into Israeli culture and threats of war. A musician, Shaḥam received international fame with his *Rosendorf Quartet,* a five-part novel encapsulating the experiences of immigrants from Germany. In 2012, Shaḥam was awarded the Israel Prize for Literature.

The Battle of the Ink-Drawn Flag
1948

He had traveled to Germany once, where he visited a displaced-persons camp. He was to meet Party members in one of the small Bavarian towns, and when he arrived at the "camp," it turned out to be a four-story barracks, bulky and insufferably filthy. Several families crowded into one room under conditions that epitomized all that is iniquitous and dishonorable in society. Exposed to all, down to the most intimate daily activities, they persevered in a warped and dire existence. In these reduced conditions, they raised their watchful and spirited children. On his way to the Party's "meeting room," he had to walk through a dim hallway, amid unmade beds and scattered household implements, holding his breath against the stench and baring his teeth in a forced, polite smile. Everyone knew he was from *Erets Yisrael.* Men smiled at him, and nursing mothers greeted him with a brief wave of a hand before they hastily resumed squeezing the teat in the baby's mouth. [. . .]

He did not deplore the squalor around him, but he wished to avoid it. Only those who spoke Hebrew stood out from the general grim mass and acquired an individual aspect. Their mode of expression distinguished them from the rest; all the others were grouped as one. He had heard their life stories—horrific stories that made you grit your teeth. Still, he had never been confronted, face to face, with their life stories, only with their consequences. He had been accustomed to people who wished to be useful; now he was meeting people who wished only to be. He was aware that unless he lived among them for a while, sharing in their daily struggle until the history of one of them became his own personal experience, until one of them stepped forward to reclaim his life, they would forever remain part of the blurred general mass. [. . .]

Somewhere, a door opened and light hit the floor. A shadow walked over to him, and he now recognized him as a guide from one of the youth movements. Usually, he could recognize them from afar, those whose gait suggests a weary truce in the battle between idealism and the murky well where they seek to find their reflection. [. . .]

"I would like to ask something of you. I—I mean, I belong to another party. Still, we would like very much to hear words of truth from *Erets Yisrael.* And, let me tell you, you are the first sabra we have seen. I mean, envoys from *Erets Yisrael,* yes, but a sabra, we have never had the privilege. We will not mind it if what you say is contrary to our way of thinking. Our comrades will be very, very happy to hear you speak Hebrew."

He agreed. Toward evening the guide appeared, solemn and polite, accompanied by two comrades who were eager to improve their Hebrew, which amounted to a very limited vocabulary. "You will speak Hebrew and I will translate you into Yiddish," the guide told him. [. . .]

The commonplace phrases that issued from his lips were translated by the guide with a pleasing rhetorical fervor. [. . .] The older boys shook his hand vigorously, their eyes sparkling. Girls sought his company, two of whom were quite attractive, directing at him a charming series of bright glances, eyes brimming with Jewish sorrow, graceful modesty, and restrained passion.

And yet, the youth of the girls notwithstanding, he knew that the spark in their eyes was not meant for him personally and that he must transmit it, exactly as it was, to the type he represented, to the rightful recipient of the yearning glances, and share it equally with his fortunate comrades and friends, all of them born in *Erets Yisrael.* [. . .]

He knew that in order to reach them beyond the divide of righteous and dry principles, he must take pains to mask his personality, his style and wishes, when speaking to them face to face. [. . .]

In the morning, he rose early and set out to the train station. A man who had slept on the floor rose and joined him. As was his habit, he did not glance in the man's direction. Over time, he had acquired the practice not to look at the face of his interlocutor. Too often the faces of others were deformed and scarred, and he worried that if he looked at them straight in the face, he might offend them.

"Is there a black market in *Erets Yisrael*?" the man asked in a pronounced Polish intonation.

"Hardly," he replied.

Silence. Only the sound of their steps echoed in the empty, tree-lined street.

"So, what about our life here, then?" the man suddenly asked. A bitter smile appeared on his face. "Such a life, you know, it does not go over just like that, one has to pay for it later. Yes, we pay for it."

"Who pays?"

"Everybody, the children, and all of you as well."

"Who is all of us?"

"You, I mean, *Erets Yisrael*. They will come to you, and it will be different. These people are not pioneers. Their lives are already broken. All they see and know is the black market. Listen to what I am telling you." The man grew agitated, as if preparing for an argument. "You will have to get them off the boat and send them straight to work. You must not allow them even one day to walk around. Do you know what happens to people after such years? Do you even understand what you are talking about here?"

He turned and looked at the speaker. The man grinned, revealing tobacco-stained teeth. He was short, and his small, dark eyes darted nervously under the half-shut lids, as if suddenly anxious that someone might be listening to their conversation. [. . .]

This had taken place before the war, a time when emigrating to Mandatory Palestine did entail some risk for those who decided to go there. The others, those who stayed put, thought it a marvel that one would choose risk and hope over filth and fear and therefore admired the bravery of those who had left. But those who dearly sold their comfort did, in fact, discount their bravery. Not one of the Palestinian Jews who worked the fields considered himself brave. That a man would bundle his past and his belongings and embark upon a new path, with all the risks involved, was, after all, the civic duty of the poor since time immemorial. In other words: want is bravery.

In the meantime, he had gone back to *Erets Yisrael*, the war broke out, and he, a Palmach man, was instantly pulled into the maelstrom. Right at the beginning, it was the Palmach that did most of the work. The best and the bravest among them fell in battle. New men filled the ranks. The veterans were anxious about fighting alongside the new recruits. While the new ones, in fact, fought blindly, trusting the experience and bravery of the veterans. Thanks to their experience and their grasp of the language, a good number of the veterans gradually moved up the ranks. The gap between the officers and the soldiers grew larger due to the lack of a common language, and also because most people will take advantage of their rightful rank and position, disallowing any moralistic qualms. [. . .]

And since it was much easier to conform to the side of the powerful ones, the circles of the top brass consolidated in a sort of furtive solidarity of disregard. They looked upon the new recruits, the privates—most of whom belonged to Gaḥal [the Gush Ḥerut Liberal Party]—through the windows of their cars, as they stood on the road, trying to hitch a ride from a military base to go someplace where no one was waiting for them. [. . .] At times they would reluctantly stop their cars and take a couple of the hitchhikers, who shrugged their shoulders and spoke only Yiddish. Sometimes they had no idea where they were headed and, too often, hitched a ride for a frivolous reason, thereby stirring up the officers' ire. It also happened that one of them would steal a kit bag he happened to find in the car, an act that reflected on all of them. And because they had all been officially stamped as belonging to Gaḥal, everyone else was absolved of having to treat them as individuals, as well as of the vulgar superficiality inherent in generalizations. [. . .] He, too, always watched them as if from the side, in profile, and just as they had seemed to him at the time in Germany, that was how they seemed to him now, in *Erets Yisrael*—as shadows. [. . .] But, unlike him, who acted cowardly, a Gaḥal man, a short guy, did show courage, an act of folly, attempting to rescue the wounded while everyone else fled, and in the evening, he himself was among the wounded.

"Did you not recognize me?" the short man asked.

"No," he answered. ("What about our life here, then? . . . Such a life, you know, it does not go over just like that . . . one has to pay for it . . . we all pay . . . the children, and you . . ." he recalled).

I don't hate this man, he reflected. But I must avoid meeting him. It is this person who holds a place in my life. Not the humiliation. No. I had no obligation to join him. I was never a coward. What's worse is the scorn I feel for him. An ugly event stands between us. He makes me feel much more ignoble than I really am. I was never ignoble.

His name was Pesach, as in lame.[1] Now he turned and looked at Pesach directly, beyond the scorn, beyond the shame he felt. This man is a hero, he reflected. This misshapen man is a hero.

NOTE

1. [The Hebrew root of the word for *Pesach* shares letters with the word that means "lame."—Eds.]

Translated by Tsipi Keller.

Other works by Shaham: *This Land We Love* (1970); *Bone to the Bone* (1981); *The Other Side of the Wall* (1983); *The Rosendorf Quartet* (1987).

Moshe Shamir

He Walked through the Fields
1948

Scene 16. In the Laundry

RUTHKA [*checks the pile of clothes lying on the table*]: You've given him enough clothes to last him for a year.

GITA: When one of our members goes away for a while, I don't want him to be ashamed of his kibbutz.

AVRAHAM: I'm only going for a short time—until they are settled on the land. I think their two tractors have arrived already.

GITA: Wait a minute. Show me what you still need.

AVRAHAM: I rely on you.

GITA: Never trust a woman. See if Avraham's name appears on the towels. Do you have handkerchiefs?

RUTHKA: He has handkerchiefs—I've seen some.

GITA: And socks?

RUTHKA: I don't think so.

AVRAHAM [*looks in parcel*]: None here.

GITA: Wait a minute—I'll bring you some right away [*goes out*].

RUTHKA: When you come home on Shabbat don't forget to bring things for washing.

AVRAHAM [*with sudden warmth*]: The moment the first hut will be up, Ruthka—you'll join me.

RUTHKA: But first you must come on Shabat.

AVRAHAM [*clasps her hands*]: I'll come, don't worry.

RUTHKA: The truth is that I'm worried. Things are happening too quickly for me. They were talking about not going after all—and now we're already speaking about you coming home once a week. What will we speak about tomorrow? And my Uri worries me more than ever. Have you heard the news?

AVRAHAM: I've heard about it.

RUTHKA: And it doesn't frighten you?

AVRAHAM: Me?

RUTHKA: Before you'll have time to look to the left and to the right—I'll be a grandmother. [AVRAHAM *laughs.*]

URI [*enters*]: Shalom. Where's Gita?

RUTHKA: She'll come just now.

URI [*to* AVRAHAM]: Two tractorists are looking for you outside.

AVRAHAM: What—are they here already? [*to* RUTHKA]: Bring me the socks, will you, Ruthka?

RUTHKA: All right.

AVRAHAM [*as he passes* URI]: Oh, there's a telegram for you.

URI: A telegram?

AVRAHAM: You can get it at the office.

URI: Right. [AVRAHAM *goes out.*]

RUTHKA: How're things, Uri?

URI [*takes a letter from his pocket*]: I've had a letter from Dad. [*Offers it to her.*] And you?

RUTHKA: Not yet. Does he know already?

URI: Know what?

RUTHKA: About you . . . and Mika?

URI: I haven't written to him. [*Seeing* RUTHKA *hesitating whether to take the letter or not*]: He sends regards to you at the end. The letter's for you too.

RUTHKA: You should write to your father. He knows her. He was her educator.

URI: Do you think educators know the children they're in charge of?

RUTHKA: I think so.

URI: Like parents knowing their sons. You don't like her, do you?

RUTHKA: You have a gift for saying things in the most cruel way.

URI: Look, mom—if you want me to say something affecting me—please use clearer language.

RUTHKA: You don't know one another well enough.

URI: And after we've known one another for twenty years—will we be an ideal couple? Will we be immune to all surprises?

RUTHKA [*hurt and restrained*]: Why don't you try to be better than we, Uri?

URI: Not better than you and not worse than you, and I don't want to compete with anybody. I'm myself and that's all there is to it.

RUTHKA: Are you angry because I'm interfering too much in your life?

URI: It's your right. [*Silence.* URI *calls to* GITA]: Have you Shabbat clothes for me, Gita?

GITA: Who's that? Uri? [*enters*]. Yes, the bundle's ready. Where is Avraham?

RUTHKA: We must still talk about it, Uri.

URI [*to* GITA, *who is handing him the bundle*]: And Mika's bundle—is it ready?

GITA: Yes. Here it is . . .

URI: I'll take it also . . . [*goes out hastily holding both bundles.*]

RUTHKA: As soon as I get near him, he curls up like a porcupine and puts out his quills.

GITA: And perhaps he really loves her?

RUTHKA: If he really loves her, why is he in such a hurry?

Scene 17. In Uri's Tent.

URI [*enters holding two parcels. Holds out a piece of paper to* MIKA, *who is sitting combing her hair. While she is reading the note, he finds somewhere to put the parcels.*]

MIKA [*reading the note*]: What does it mean?

URI: How should I know?

MIKA: Today?

URI: Wait for me until Sunday. Nothing urgent.

MIKA: Who do you think it's from?

URI: From the unit. I suppose from Ginger.

MIKA: Who's Ginger?

URI: He was in charge of my course . . . one of the boys.

MIKA: Do they want to take you?

URI: Maybe.

MIKA: That's all we need.

URI: Sufficient unto the day is the evil thereof. I spoke to Biberman. We'll be getting a room this week. . . . Aren't you pleased?

MIKA: Yes, of course!—But I thought it would be different . . .

URI: Different? How?

MIKA: Everything . . . different . . .

URI: Do you miss the rabbi? Or perhaps a table with cakes? A long white dress? White shoes? The parents next to the bridegroom . . . the parents next to the bride . . . and the band? Mainly the cakes, isn't that so? . . . What's wrong with you, Mika—crying? Mika . . .

MIKA: Where are my hairpins?

URI [*collects them from the bed*]: Here!

MIKA [*smooths down her hair. Rises.*] If at least your parents lived with us. We're so alone, so deserted . . .

URI: Lonely and deserted . . . in the middle of the kibbutz? What are you talking about, Mika?

MIKA: Alone and abandoned within the kibbutz. Yes! Perhaps you don't feel like that. But I . . . the last few days they look at me as if I've stolen something from them.

URI: You're imaging things—nightmares.

MIKA: And you haven't noticed it, Uri? The whole kibbutz has to love me before they can agree that one of their boys should love me. That's how it is with them. I have to prove myself first. To be good enough to be welcomed into this important family . . . *Gat Ha'amakim!*

URI: Excuse me, Mika—but you're talking nonsense.

MIKA: Either you're lying—or else you're blind.

URI: You don't know what a kibbutz is.

MIKA: I don't know. No! If you'd brought back with you some girl more your type—from one of the kibbutzim—how many days would it take for Biberman to find you a room? How many? And do you think I'm deaf? And haven't I enough sense to understand digs and hints? And don't I see how your mother behaves.

URI: I don't understand you. Mika. I don't understand you.

MIKA: Because you're a good fellow, Uri. [*Picks up her bundle.*] But I'm not so good . . . I have a past, and it's chasing me all the time—here in this place where I hoped to be rid of it—to forget it! Here, of all places—here they won't let me forget anything—anything . . .

URI: Where are you going to now?

MIKA: To put the bundle in my tent.

URI: This is your tent.

MIKA: This is the room they gave us?

URI: This is the room we're taking for ourselves.

MIKA: It's better we should wait till they give it to us.

URI: I'm tired of waiting . . .

MIKA: Leave me, Uri, don't be so wild!

URI: I'm not as good a boy as you thought I was. Put your bundle on the chair.

MIKA: You're creasing my things, Uri . . .

URI: Your eyes are still a bit wet.

MIKA: Wait a bit. You don't know what you're doing . . .

URI: We've stopped waiting . . .

MIKA: I'm frightened, Uri. I'm frightened . . .

Scene 18. In the Courtyard Outside Uri's Tent

KIBBUTZNIK [closes the flaps of the tent]: But the man who hurried at this moment along the road to Gat Ha'amakim wanted something else. His power was greater than the power of love. It was the power of our time. Yes. Those days which tore Willie's life to shreds, the days which tossed Ruthka into the storm, the days which left Mika lonely and forlorn under the heavens— these days did not halt before the doors of Uri's tent. In the early hours of the morning the man who was on his way arrived . . .

Scene 19. In the Same Place

GINGER [enters, knocks with his stick on the tent flaps]: Uri, Hey, Uri. Uri Cahana. [URI's groans are heard from inside the tent.] Are you still alive? Get up— you've got visitors.

URI [comes out of the tent, half asleep]: Who's that? Ginger!! Is that you or just a nightmare?

GINGER [strikes him playfully]: Wake up—then you'll know.

URI: Where did you spring from?

GINGER: From the rich and fertile fields of Ein Yosef. Well said.

URI: First-class.

GINGER: How're you?

URI: Feeling better.

GINGER: Better than what?

URI: Better you don't ask.

GINGER: Did you get my telegram?

URI: I got it, I believe.

GINGER: Then why, I believe—didn't you come?

URI: Were you serious?

GINGER: Where are you living, child? Haven't you heard the news?

URI: I haven't heard a thing.

GINGER: The unit's going into action, friend. We're getting the boys together. We're setting up new companies.

URI: I'm waking up slowly.

GINGER: I suggest you do that quickly. If Ginger's in the saddle—it's a sign we're riding hard. Well said?

URI: Not bad. So what's happening?

GINGER: It's my job to get a new company together in two weeks, and to recruit section leaders anywhere and anyhow—and you're on my list, my boy.

URI: Have you a base already?

GINGER: Ein Yosef itself, no less. A storeroom full of tents is waiting for us. Tomorrow the first people will be arriving. I'm taking you with me tonight.

URI: What else?

GINGER: No discussions.

URI: Nonsense.

GINGER: What's wrong? Are you a proud father already?

URI: Yes, of half a dozen.

GINGER: A girl? That's all I need.

URI: No, but it's impossible like this—so hastily. We must get permission from the kibbutz.

GINGER: We'll get their permission after you'll be with us already.

URI: There's a recruiting quota and a list. My mother, for example, will go crazy, she'll never agree.

GINGER: Then tell her, for example, that she shouldn't go crazy.

URI: It's no good unless the kibbutz agrees.

GINGER: Do you imagine I'm going to start discussing the matter now with secretaries and nursemaids and committees? Without the Palmach there'd be no kibbutz and no anything else either. You take the boys out for training, and after two months you're already in action—in the battle field. The whole of Palestine is boiling, it's just about a battle front—hell, and you come with your discussions . . .

URI: It's not simple all the same.

GINGER: Listen, the question's a simple one: are you prepared or aren't you? You, I mean—you by yourself?

URI: Of course!

GINGER: So—tonight?

URI: What about tonight?

GINGER: Between eight and nine—wait for me by the gate. I'll go past in my truck and pick you up.

URI: Out of the question. It's impossible to get up and go like that.

GINGER: It's the only way, my friend. They won't have time to cry on your shoulder.

URI: No one's crying on my shoulder.

GINGER: Your mother and your piece. What's her name—Noa, Haviva, Leika?

URI: Go to hell.

GINGER: You're right—I'm going [*goes out*].

URI: Hey Ginger . . . wait a minute. Have some breakfast. Let's talk about it.

GINGER [*from off-stage*]: Between eight and nine at the gate.

BIBERMAN [*enters from the other side*]: Good morning, Uri! [*with obvious happiness.*]

URI: Good morning. What's the occasion?

BIBERMAN: Is Mika working today?

URI: No. She's still sleeping.

MIKA [*pokes her head out between the tent flap*]: No, I'm not sleeping.

BIBERMAN: Did I wake you?

MIKA: No. I've been awake for some time.

URI: Did you hear?

MIKA: I heard everything.

BIBERMAN: I've good news for the two of you.

MIKA: Someone got here before you.

BIBERMAN: Really? You know already that you're getting a room? Excellent! You can move in tomorrow!

Translated by Aubrey Hodes.

S. Yizhar

1916-2006

A novelist and children's writer, S. Yizhar (Yizhar Smilansky) was born in Reḥovot. He fought in Israel's War of Independence and held a seat in the Knesset. Yizhar taught education and literature at the Hebrew University and Tel Aviv University. He was a recipient of the Israel Prize, the Brenner Prize, the Bialik Prize, and the Emet Prize. Yizhar's *Days of Tsiklag* (1958) is considered a classic of Jewish literature.

The Prisoner

1948

Shepherds and their flocks were scattered on the rocky hillsides, among the woods of low terebinth and the stretches of wild rose, and even along the swirling contours of valleys foaming with light, with those golden-green sparks of rustling summer grain under which the clodded earth, smelling of ancient soil, ripe and good, crumbles to gray flour at a foot's touch; on the plains and in the valleys flocks of sheep were wandering; on the hilltops, dim, human forms, one here and one there, sheltered in the shade of olive trees: it was clear that we could not advance without arousing excitement and destroying the purpose of our patrol.

We sat down on the rocks to rest a bit and to cool our dripping sweat in the sunlight. Everything hummed of summer, like a golden beehive. A whirlpool of gleaming mountain fields, olive hills, and a sky ablaze with an intense silence blinded us for moments and so beguiled our hearts that one longed for a word of redeeming joy. And yet in the midst of the distant fields shepherds were calmly leading their flocks with the tranquil grace of fields and mountains and a kind of easy unconcern— the unconcern of good days when there was yet no evil in the world to forewarn of other evil things to come. In the distance quiet flocks were grazing, flocks from the days of Abraham, Isaac, and, Jacob. A far-off village, wreathed with olive trees of dull copper, was slumbering in the curves of hills gathered like sheep against the mountains. But designs of a different sort cast their diagonal shadows across the pastoral scene.

For a long time our sergeant had been carefully peering through his fieldglasses, sucking his cigarette, and weaving plans. There was no point in going further, but to return empty-handed was out of the question. One of the shepherds, or at least one of their boys, or maybe several of them, had to be caught. Some action had to be taken, or something be burned. Then we could return with something concrete to point to, something accomplished.

The sergeant, of medium height, had thick brows which met over his deep-sunken eyes; his cap, pushed back on his balding head, exposed a receding forehead and damp, limp wisps of hair to the wind. We followed his gaze. Whatever it was that he saw, we saw a world of green-wool hills, a wasteland of boulders, and far-off olive trees, a world crisscrossed with golden valleys of grain—the kind of world that fills you with peace, while a lust for good, fertile earth urged one to return to back-bending work, to gray dust, to the toil of the burning summer: not to be one of the squad which the sergeant was planning to thrust bravely into the calm of the afternoon.

And, in fact, he was about ready to take action because just then we noticed a shepherd and his flock resting in the leveled grain in the shadow of a young, green oak. Instantly a circle was described in the world: outside the circle, everything else; inside, one man, isolated, to be caught alive. And the hunters were already off. Most of the platoon took cover in the thickets and rocks to the right, while the sergeant and two or three others made an encircling movement down to the left in order to surprise their prey and drive him into the arms of the ambush above. Amid the tender, golden grain we stole like thieves, trampling the bushes which the sheep had cropped so closely, our hobnails harshly kissing the warm, gray, sandy soil. We "took advantage" of the "terrain," of the "vegetation," of the protection offered by "natural cover," and we burst into a gallop toward the man seated on a rock in the shadow of the oak. Panic-stricken, he jumped to his feet, threw down his staff, lurched forward senselessly like a trapped gazelle, and disappeared over the top of the ridge right into the arms of his hunters. [. . .]

On the rim of the village, in those gray, greasy trenches, the other citizen-soldiers of our Home Guard company wandered aimlessly—their food no food, their water no water, their day no day, and their night no night, saying to hell with what we'll do and to hell with what will be, to hell with everything that was once nice and comfortable, to hell with it all! We'll be dirty, we'll grow beards, we'll brag, and our clothes, wet with sweat, will stick to our unwashed bodies, infested with ulcers. We'll shoot stray dogs and let their carcasses stink, we'll sit in the clinging dust, we'll sleep in the filth, and we won't give a damn. It doesn't matter!

Nearing the trenches, we walked with heads high, proud of our loot! We fell smartly into step, almost dancing along. The bleating sheep were milling about in confusion. The prisoner, whose eyes had been covered again, dragged his sandals with clumsy uncertainty as we good-naturedly railed at him. We were happy and satisfied. What an adventure! What a job! Sweaty we were, caked with dust, but soldiers, real men! As for our sergeant, he was beside himself. Imagine our reception, the uproar and berserk laughter that broke loose like a barrel bursting its hoops!

Someone, laughing and sweating profusely, pointing at the unseeing prisoner, approached our sergeant. "Is that the prisoner? Want to finish him off? Let me!"

Our sergeant gulped some water, wiped his sweat and, still grinning, said, "Sit down over there. It's none of your business." The circle which had formed around howled with laughter. The trenches, the troubles, the disorder, no leave, and all that—what were they compared to all this?

One man was taking pictures of the whole scene, and on his next leave he would develop them. And there was one who sneaked up behind the prisoner, waved his fist passionately in the air and then, shaking with laughter,

reeled back into the crowd. And there was one who didn't know if this was proper or not, if it was the decent thing to do, and his eyes darted about seeking the support of an answer, whatever it might be. And there was one who, while talking, grabbed the water jug, raised it high over his head, and swilled the liquid with bared teeth, signaling to his audience with the forefinger of his left hand to wait until the last drop had been drained for the end of his slick story. And there was one wearing an undershirt who, astonished and curious, exposed his rotten teeth: many dentists, a skinny shrew of a wife, sleepless nights, narrow, stuffy room, unemployment, and working for "the party" had aggravated his eternal query of "Nu, what will be?"

And there were some who had steady jobs, some who were on their way up in the world, some who were hopeless cases to begin with, and some who rushed to the movies and all the theaters and read the weekend supplements of two newspapers. And there were some who knew long passages by heart from Horace and the Prophet Isaiah and from Haim Nahman Bialik and even from Shakespeare; some who loved their children and their wives and their slippers and the little gardens at the sides of their houses; some who hated all forms of favoritism, insisted that each man keep his proper place in line, and raised a hue and cry at the slightest suspicion of discrimination; some whose inherent good-nature had been permanently soured by the thought of paying rent and taxes; some who were not at all what they seemed and some who were exactly what they seemed. There they all stood, in a happy circle around the blindfolded prisoner, who at that very moment extended a calloused hand (one never knows if it's dirty, only that it's the hand of a peasant) and said to them: "*Fi, cigara?*" A cigarette?

His rasping voice (as if a wall had begun to speak) at once aroused applause from those with a sense of the ridiculous. Others, outraged by such impudence, raised their fingers admonishingly.

Even if someone were moved to think about a cigarette, it all ended in a different way—in military style. Two corporals and a sergeant came over from headquarters, took the prisoner, and led him away. Unable to see, he innocently leaned on the arm which the corporal had just as innocently extended in support. He even spoke a few words to guide the prisoner's groping steps. And there was a moment when it seemed as if both of them were laboring together peacefully to overcome the things that hindered their way and helped each other as if they went together, a man and another man, close together—until they had almost reached the house, when the prisoner repeated: "Fi, cigara?" These few syllables immediately spoiled the whole thing. The corporal withdrew his arm that had been interlocked with the prisoner's, raised his eyebrows angrily and, almost offended, shook himself free. "Did you ever see such a thing?" It happened so suddenly that the sightless man stumbled and tripped on the front step of the house, lost his balance and, almost falling, plunged headlong into the room. In a desperate effort to right himself, he sent a chair flying and collided with the table. There he stood, helpless, clumsy, overwhelmed by the force of his own violence and the fear of what was to come. His arms dropped to his sides and he stood stupefied, resigned to his fate.

Translated by V. C. Rycus.

Other works by Yizhar: *Ḥirbet ḥizʻah* (1949); *Mikda-mot* (1992).

Yehuda Burla

1886–1969

Born in Jerusalem, author Yehuda Burla was the descendant of rabbis and scholars from Izmir, Turkey. He studied at the Ezra Teachers Seminary in Jerusalem. After serving as an interpreter in the Ottoman army during World War I, Burla worked in Damascus as the director of Hebrew schools and later taught in Haifa and Tel Aviv. Known for his depictions of soldiers' lives during World War I, Burla was the recipient of the Bialik Prize, the Israel Prize, and the Jerusalem Prize.

Aunt Joya
1949

On rare occasions Aunt Joya di Pinso would come over, and whenever she came, the house would be full of good spirits. The minute she set foot on our threshold, pausing for a moment, as was her custom—I couldn't say why—she looked, in her statuesque form and in the whiteness of her garment, her *izar*,[1] as if a princess from the royal palace had descended upon us.

The entire household welcomed her joyfully, with charmed talk on everyone's lips, laughter and light on all faces. Mother, who speaks easily with everyone and whose words are dear to every listener's ear, becomes

overly kind and exuberant. [. . .] And father offers her again and over again the best delicacies and confections that he keeps locked in his cupboard.

And we, the youngsters, brothers and sisters, would gather around her and stare, hearing and wondering. As if being lit up by the light of her eyes and the kindness of her face benefited us as well.

Aunt Joya is beautiful, tall, slim, and pretty. She has blue eyes and a sympathetic voice. Even her speech is gracious and her tongue delectable. She's a woman a little over forty—but is as lovely and delicate as one of the maidens. That is why everyone loves her and all look favorably upon her. I too love her, I love her very much. But yet it seems she shows no affection toward me; she rarely notices me, but I don't hold anything against her—nothing. If any other aunt, or neighbor or relative had treated me so, I would have turned away from her, but she is different. [. . .] She always carries her sadness with her (each of her visits to our house brings—either in the middle or the end—teary eyes). And I truly understand her, I know everything. Whenever she tells her stories and her eyes well up with tears, I recall many verses from the "Twenty-four" [Hebrew Bible] such as "For Shaddai has made my lot very bitter" [Ruth 1:20], "I am a very unhappy woman" [Samuel I 1:15], "For these things do I weep, my eyes, oh, my eyes flow with tears" [Lamentations 1:16].

Truly, God had made her lot very bitter. Such a beautiful woman, tender and gentle, a childless widow. [. . .]

Her husband was a great learned man, Rabbi Avraham Pinso, a noble man, who loved her deeply and respected her endlessly. Had she asked him to bring her a bird in mid-flight, he would have done so. "No" was not an option in her case. The Pinso courtyard on Talmud Torah Street belonged to him. (I know that beautiful, spacious three-storied place.) But—for sins committed—everything is now gone. Due to matters of disagreement among rabbinic scholars. [. . .]

And with his demise, everything was lost. Many, many creditors were left. The courtyard was sold, possessions were dispersed—everything ran out. Even her *ketubah* funds. Nothing remained. She was left a single woman. She was barely thirty (having been married for nine years) while he was about fifty at the time of death. (He was her second husband.) Her first husband, a worthy young man from Hebron, had also left her widowed.

From then on I began hearing bits and pieces of "These are the generations of Aunt Joya"—how I felt pity for her. My compassion was added to my love for her. Oh, how I felt sorry for her! Had I only been able magically to sweep away her hardships, then I would have given my soul in return.

As time went on, I learned many other facts. She came from Hebron, my mother's birthplace. They had been childhood friends; she was from the distinguished Levi family. Who was her brother? Yosef Levi! A young lion. And I knew him. [. . .] He was as good looking as his sister. With glowing facial features and clear, large blue eyes. He sported a thick, curled moustache. His voice was strong. He had a princely voice. And his smile revealed a virile strength accompanied by a lot of charm. All of his dealings were conducted with Arab tribesmen, trading in grain and cattle stock. Once he'd start speaking to the Bedouins in fluent, lovely Arabic, they would listen attentively. Oh, how they respected him! They felt diminished in his presence, calling him "Our Master," even taking an oath upon his name. [. . .]

However, nothing lasts forever. Fate turned its back on him too. Severe pain struck his right foot. He fell ill and was on his deathbed, suffering for days upon days and years upon years, until all his possessions were gone. [. . .] After a number of years they brought him from Hebron to Jerusalem. By then, his foot had developed necrosis and gangrene had spread to his thigh. That is when the doctors pronounced their decree: his life was in danger. The leg would need to be amputated to the thigh. [. . .]

On the day of the operation, Aunt Joya came to our house. Like a wounded animal she agonized, crying from one room to the next. For he was the only one she had left. He was the comforter of her plundered life. Why did God lay His oppressive hand upon her in this manner? What evil deed had she committed? Had she sinned so deeply?

But the heavens were like brass above her head. The gates of mercy were locked.

On the third day following the operation, he passed away. The aunt's misfortune was as great as the ocean itself. The grief was great in our home as well.

About two years passed, and then—as if it happened by itself and some time ago—Aunt Joya was married to the scholar Rabbi Mircado Saragosti. I found that matter to be quite odd.

That she married for the third time was understandable, for necessity knows no law. A woman has no choice but to marry, if only to be provided with food and clothing. And she was, after all, poverty-stricken, lonely and forsaken, and so obviously accepted his offer.

One thing I could not comprehend—how she spoke of him, her spouse Rabbi Mircado, mockingly, whenever she would come over. With sharp laughter she would talk about his manners and actions—something I did not appreciate. It may be true that as high as the sky is above the earth, so are her good looks, cleverness, and charming speech compared to his.

He, to be honest, is not attractive, not at all, short, and his hair and beard are completely gray.

On top of that, he stutters and speaks incoherently (often repeating the last syllable of a word). [. . .]

But still, she does eat of his bread, and it was he who deigned to take her in. And oh, how devoted and obedient he is to her wishes. He rented a room especially for her. She does not live in his home (he has adult sons and daughters). She set a specific condition: she would never set foot in his home—and he agreed. And again, from time to time, when she feels embittered, she lashes out at him in anger: he may not stay in her room on weekdays, it's enough that he burdens her every Sabbath. There are times when she humiliates the man and causes him sorrow.

I recall that on Thursday before dusk, I was accompanying my father to buy whatever was needed for the Sabbath, and we ran into Rabbi Mircado. He approached my father and spoke in a stutter: "Pardon, Mr. Yehoshua, I have been looking for you. Would you please try to convince Joya. I purchased some items for her for the Sabbath today, a little meat, vegetables, flour, and she gave everything back. What is going to happen? She is going to get sick. Please try to convince her; my heart breaks from worry about her, for her."

As I heard his words, my own heart broke, seeing the man in his state of humiliation.

And then one day she demanded that he rent a small room for her outside the city. She felt that living within the Old City's walls was becoming oppressive. He immediately rented a small room for her at the Montefiore houses. I frequently saw him toward afternoon walking outside the city, carrying a heavy basket, and then coming back to the city at sunset . . .

And she lived by herself in that small chamber in the Montefiore, like a bereaved animal in her lair. The door was often closed. She stayed away from any and every acquaintance. She did not visit others and others kept away from her. Like a nun in her monastery's niche, so did she live in that small room.

As if suddenly, bad news was heard in our house: Aunt Joya was ill with heart disease. As the weeks went by, her illness worsened. Rabbi Mircado never stopped sending doctors and medications, even hiring a special woman to stay alongside her throughout.

During those days, Rabbi Mircado conducted special learning sessions by the Western Wall for her recovery. At nightfall, when I returned from heder, my mother asked that I too walk to the Wall to pray for Aunt. I went quickly. There were two minyans there; religious students as well as the poor were praying. One group recited psalms, the other special petitions. At that moment the space before the Wall seemed to be immersed in mercy. Never before had I offered a prayer as pure and genuine as that time when I prayed for Aunt Joya.

The next morning a messenger announced: it's over, her heart gave way. We rose to attend her funeral.

Words cannot express how disappointed I was at that moment by God, by prayer, and by faith.

NOTES

1. [Shawl traditionally worn by Jewish Berber women, clasped by decorative brooches.—Trans.]

2. [The Montefiore houses formed the first modern Jewish neighborhood outside the Old City walls in Jerusalem. —Trans.]

Translated by Menachem Rotstein.

Other works by Burla: *Luna: ben 'erev* (1926); *Bli kokhav* (1927); *Neftuley adam* (1929); *'Im shaḥar* (1946); *Eleh masa'ey yehuda halevi* (1959); *Kol kitvey* (1962); *Yalkut sipurim* (1975).

Yigal Mossinson

1917–1994

The novelist and playwright Yigal Mossinson was born in 'Ein Ganim in pre-state Israel, and studied agriculture. From 1943 to 1949, he served in the Palmach and the Israeli Defense Forces. In 1954 he wrote the stage play *Casablan*, a work that explored the tensions experienced by immigrants from Morocco and other Mizrahi nations; the work became a landmark film. Mossinson lived in the United States from 1959 to 1965. In the 1950s, Mossinson turned to writing thriller stories for children, with the series *Ḥasamba*.

In the Negev Plains: A Play in Three Acts
1949

ABRAHAM: We only have a few minutes, and we have to decide whether the kibbutz should keep fighting, despite the army's withdrawal, while we're surrounded. It must be clear that any decision, one way or the other, entails grave responsibility.

BARUCH: From the military point of view, there's no point in resisting. You know that the soldiers don't manage to rest, to catch their breath, to sleep properly. They've been on their feet too long, and we can't ask for any more. If we don't get reserves, we can't last. And we're not going to get reserves! If we don't get equipment, we can't last. And we're not going to get equipment. With full awareness of the responsibility, I say: from the military point of view, there's no point in resisting.

ABRAHAM: That's also what Giv'oni said.

BARUCH: As a military man, I must say: the decision to stay here and not break through the siege is tantamount to suicide. Worse than that: it's slaughter, exactly that! You can't fight against cannons with empty hands. I'm a disciplined man and subject to direct orders, Abraham. But this is a consultation, and I have to say what's on my mind. This isn't war, it's murder! The murder victim can't protect himself. Against a cannon you have to fight with a cannon, not with cannon-fodder. If you don't have all those things, there's no choice!

ABRAHAM: That means, to withdraw?!

BARUCH: That means to leave the outpost so we can withdraw to another outpost.

ITAMAR: I've always been a realist, without any sentiments. If you use chemical or organic fertilizer, you'll get a fine crop. If you plow and sow and harrow, you're not cheating the soil, and you'll get a proper yield. But here, you're not investing anything, and you want to get good results?! We want to live, you understand, and not to die for the sake of a dubious history. We want to start a kibbutz and live! If it's impossible to hold the first line, you withdraw to the second line. That's how realistic grownups behave.

RIVKA: It's strange to hear that from you, Itamar. Since when has the kibbutz been a front line, an outpost, nothing but a military position? Where's the love that we had here, the children, the big lawn, the dining hall? We've been in this landscape for thousands of days and nights, on these hills, these orchards, the seasons of the year—I can't believe what I'm hearing. There are situations when it's necessary to withdraw, but even then, we'd be retreating from a kibbutz, not from the front line, or the second or third line of defense. Besides, where does the second line of defense end? We just want to understand, Itamar—because even there, at your second line of defense, a realist is sitting, and he, too, according to your arguments, will want to retreat. Where does the retreat end? I'm asking and trying to understand you, Itamar. I don't accept Abraham's apprehension, because fear is speaking from your mouth. I still believe, despite everything, that you love the kibbutz, and you're only considering what's good for it. But, just in order to understand things—we've already sent the children back to the second line of defense. The children aren't at home. Now we'll go over to them, and where, I ask you, where will we send the children in more hard times? In my opinion, there are no lines of defense—just places that we won't leave, and that's all. Even if there's no military justification to holding them. Okay, I can explain to Dan, but what will I say to Dalia, to Uzi, to your little Ḥumi? Daddy left the kibbutz and ran away! Daddy left the house and ran away? No, no. It can't be that in one day I'll lose all the faith I had in you for so many years!

ITAMAR: I don't want to get trapped in your emotional sensitivity, Rivka. The hour is cruel—and I have to make a cruel decision, and it doesn't matter whether or not you lose your faith in me. The Russians also retreated during the war when they had to retreat. Emotionality won't be of any use to us at all.

BARUCH: Itamar's right. We shouldn't mix sentiment in with sober consideration. I'm full of admiration for Rivka's emotional sensitivity. But her words didn't change the situation. We have to look at things with open eyes.

ABRAHAM: Outpost! Front line! Examples from a different army! And I ask you, you the kibbutznik—how excited were you when we flooded Beit Ha-ʻaravah with salt water? I remember that evening. You brought diagrams and photographs—and you, you're giving me examples from everywhere in the world?! Where else on the globe do they pour salt water on every bit of earth in order to grow vegetables? Would anyone except crazy people like us, people without land like us, fall in love with this Negev? I won't live in a strange house! I won't wander on the roads! We're a nation of refugees, naked refugees without anything, refu-

gees who are sitting near a fleshpot for the time being. There's a war for Jewish independence, and we'll win it with less blood than was spilled in a single shtetl in Poland. In vain! In vain, do you hear me, Itamar, in vain. That's what I'm shouting: in vain! I might as well be in Warsaw, and without guns! To be slaughtered like a sheep! Today I have weapons, a few weapons, but I live in hope that the ships will come. The cannons will come, and our airplanes will fly in this sky—and until then, we have to struggle, not to rest—know that this is the only time that it won't be in vain, not in vain! I want to look my Dani in the eye like a fighting man and not like a miserable refugee who fled from his land. The children will never forgive us if we leave their home. It's not an outpost, it's not a line of defense. It isn't only an outpost, just as our land isn't like all the other land in the world, it's the only land that won't make us into refugees and beggars. We have to vote. I don't have the strength to talk anymore. Whoever is in favor of retreat, raise your hand!

ITAMAR: I never knew you were capable of giving speeches in assemblies, with emotionality that can squeeze a few tears out of righteous women. I ask once again, for the hundredth time: from the strictly military point of view, is it possible to make a stand, or is it impossible?! I didn't hear even a single answer to that question. I want to hear clear words and not hollow rhetoric!

ABRAHAM: Listen, you, you "totally" military man. From an economic point of view, is the Negev realistic? And were we really born to be farmers? You want clear words, so I'll say to you: from a military point of view, taking a stand here is suicide! But our suicide depends on whether the army gathers strength, gets weapons—and ships are coming, I know it—we have to extend our time of dying for hours and days, for hours and days. So that other settlements won't commit suicide, too. I didn't choose this fate—fate chose me, and I'm willing to greet it, I, and Rivka, it seems, and my Dani. Now all the cards are on the table. We don't have time. We have to vote. Everyone according to their conscience. At this moment, I'm not the commander of the place, just an average kibbutz member who accepts the kibbutz discipline. I vote: whoever's in favor of retreating, raise your hand!

BARUCH: Excuse me, Abraham. I have to know what's the meaning of this vote?

ABRAHAM: We're dealing with people whose home this is, a home that they never called an "outpost" or a first "line of defense" at the front. Just "home." A place where they hated and loved, had children and saw themselves as responsible for their children and grandchildren, and for the home. These are the people who are voting now. I'm not responsible for the fact that things change the moment people are afraid for their lives, their skin and flesh! I'm not responsible for that. So, whoever's in favor of retreat, raise your hand! [*A huge explosion is heard.*]

SHOSH: Airplanes!

MOSHE: They're diving! [*Everyone lowers their heads instinctively. There are explosions and machine gun fire.*]

ITAMAR: They're trampling us like ants. Those explosions are driving me crazy! Everywhere it seems: yes, now it's aimed at me! Now my turn is coming! The airplane dives, and that's the end, the very end! Like an ant! The boot is slowly approaching, trampling, crushing, and there's no escape, no escape. [*The telephone rings.*]

ABRAHAM: [*On the phone*] Hello? Who's there? Checkpoint 7? What? The observation tower was hit? Don't bother us! Don't bother us! Hang up the telephone! Don't bother us, I'm telling you! Hello! Who's there! Binyamin? What? Who's there? Dani? Dan, where's Binyamin? Wounded? They're bringing him to us. The planes are flying toward Gadera! Dani, goodbye from Daddy! Mommy's here, too. Bye, Dani. Look very, very well. Shosh, tell the medics that we have a wounded person.

RIVKA: [*Quickly climbs up the stairs.* MOSHE *and* BARUCH *follow her.*]

SHOSH: Hello, medics, infirmary, hello! Hello, something's wrong . . . Hello! The line seems to be down. Hello! Hello!

BINYAMIN: [*Two soldiers drag him in.* RIVKA, MOSHE, *and* BARUCH *support him.*] It's not too bad. Just my shoulder—from shrapnel. It doesn't hurt. Abraham, the soldiers are saying we're surrounded—has it been decided to retreat? Is this right?! Is that the truth?! You want to evacuate the kibbutz! Look me in the eye, straight in the eye. You know that if we lose Biq'at Yo'av, we'll lose the war. We, the members of the kibbutz, we'll lose the war. Remember Sha'ar Hagolan and Masada!

RIVKA: Let me bandage you, Binyamin. Look, there's blood!

BINYAMIN: Get Away! Leave me alone! You've abandoned Biq'at Yo'av. You're abandoning Biq'at Yo'av.

If we leave this point, we'll lose the war. We, we . . . will . . . lose . . . the . . . [*Collapses.*]

[*Curtain*]

Translated by Jeffrey M. Green.

Other works by Mossinson: *Mi amar she-hu shaḥor* (1948); *Ha-derekh le-Yeriḥo* (1949); *Derekh gever* (1953); *Yehudah ish keriyot* (1962); *Yeḥi ha-hevdel ha-katan* (1974); *Tarantella* (1979).

Gershon Shofman
1880–1972

The short-story writer Gershon Shofman received a traditional Jewish education in his native Belarus, at the same time immersing himself in Russian and Hebrew literature. In 1913, he moved to Vienna, where he lived until 1938, later settling in Tel Aviv and then Haifa. His short stories are known for their brevity and frugality; they leave much to the reader's imagination. Charged with eroticism and often focused on cruelty, they were considered daring at the time. Shofman was awarded the Bialik Prize in 1946 and the Israel Prize in 1956.

Remove Your Shoes
1949

Remove your shoes from your feet and, barefoot, feel the earth!

Whatever was in the past and be what may now—today the land is ours, the heavens are ours, and the sea is our sea.

Let us go out to the field and thirstily drink in the whiteness of the daisies on the lawn, the gold of the groundsel, the tremor of the clover.

Look at the children, drunk with freedom, playing ball with shouts of joy; their heads gleam in the spring sun, and no enemy eye will spy them.

Lean down and kiss the earth. Don't be bashful. Young men have given their lives for it, and they are no more! Kiss it, kiss it—maidens in their innocence have fallen because of it—

And tears of grief of delicate, pained mothers have moistened its soil; it is holy earth—remove your shoes!

Translated by Jeffrey M. Green.

Other works by Shofman: *Be-terem Harga'ah* (1942); *Be-melkahayim* (1946); *Kol kitvey G. Shofman* (1960); *Yalkut sipurim* (1966).

Yehudit Hendel

1926–2014

Yehudit Hendel was born in Warsaw into a rabbinic family. She moved to Palestine in 1930, eventually settling in Haifa, and published her first stories at age seventeen. As a novelist and short-story writer, Hendel focused on the plight of immigrants, revealing the social inequalities within different ethnic groups in Israeli society; she also stressed issues relevant to women. Some of her works were turned into screen-plays, and she received the Bialik Prize for Literature in 1997 and the Israel Prize in 2003.

A Common Grave
1950

> To the sacred memory of dear Shmulik and his comrades who fell in the battle to liberate Yeḥiʻam

He rose from the bed shading his eyes with his hands as if it was light although it was still dark. His fingers were as dry as dry twigs and the blue of the pre-dawn shrivelled them even more. He put on his shoes and dressed in the darkness and heard the gutters drip-ping. The windows darkened with the absence of stars and he leaned carefully over his wife's bed and covered her bared shoulder. The edging of the white blanket glowed and in the gloom he saw her eyelids fluttering. Since Yossi her son died, she sleeps in fits and her eye-lids flutter as if she were awake in her sleep. He left the room on tiptoes holding the door handle for a moment, pressing his palm to the lock. In the pitch-black hall he stopped momentarily and stood. He felt with his hands for the wall and the wall returned a chill to his hands. He stumbled in the hallway, pressed to the wall, until he entered the kitchen and turned on the light. Then he shut his eyes and shut them hard as if he had never been used to light.

Leftovers from dinner twinkled on the table, and in the sink were unwashed dishes. Now Devorah leaves the dishes day after day as if the reckoning of days has been lost to her. Sometimes she forgets to serve the soup at lunch and returns to put it on the burner in the eve-ning, and sometimes she dozes on the chair with her head limp and when she rises her eyes are red. [. . .]

Now that the mourning period is over, Micha, the younger son, will come home. He was sent away so he wouldn't see the grieving. Now Devorah will be forced to prepare meals on time and take care of the boy's laun-dry. Like this. For twenty years they raised Yossi day after day, night after night. Sometimes he was suddenly ill and they called the doctor in the middle of the night, and sometimes he wrestled with friends and came home with scratched hands. Now that he has grown, he is gone. And Yehoshua Diem distorted his body as if he were repairing lacerations. The wind beat against the windowpane and then the silence was magnified. A thinly feathered bird stood on the rail of the balcony and shook out her dripping head. [. . .]

He strode through the plain to the cemetery. The wind stiffened on the plateau, rolling from the hills to the wadi, returning from the wadi to the hills, rolling on rocky slopes, then crushing among the spines of the thorn bushes. The bushes were dark from the swirling. The treetops blustered and the leaves shivered on the tree trunks.

The wind slapped the tombstones. Like little for-tresses they stood strong within the moving space. He didn't go up to the grave, but walked back and forth, back and forth in the cemetery, his head as if it was a heavy square facing the earth. The wind whistled *heigh* and slashed *heigh* and the storm raged all over the plain. He walked back and forth back and forth rocking him-self with the wind. Rain began to fall.

Then he approached the large mass grave and watched as the rain fell on it. Weeds were already grow-ing on the grave. He breathed hard, and kneeled on the ground, resting his hand on it, which shook like a leaf. A strong odor rose from it. A light rain beat against the nape of his neck, and he leaned against the mound that became blue from the cold as if it were a living being, and pressed his palms against it as if it were a living person.

Suddenly, with a swift movement, he pulled off his coat and spread it on the grave. Then he stood, looking at the deserted mass grave covered with the coat. All night long the heavy rain fell over the grave.

He took a rock and rested it on the coat. Now the wind will not blow it away. Suddenly he thought that not only Yossi was buried here. Forty-two. He was shaken. A massive cold passed through his body and he bent over the coat and held the rock for a moment.

And the rain fell.

He rose and began walking towards the road. The light rain still drizzled. The tombstones stood like roofs of little houses in the cold of winter. A shivering bird hid in the branches of a young cypress. He sensed mois-ture on his back, and suddenly felt that his clothes were wet. He was cold. He huddled under a tree and leaned against its damp trunk. From between the branches life emerged and on the leaves a drop and another drop fell, and he pressed his back to the tree. He stopped a car near the main road and got in, and standing with one foot on the running board, fumbled in his pockets then held out his palm to the driver. The steam of living beings struck him. The strong scent of breath, sweat and smoke. His eyes fluttered over the people, looking for a place, and he sat down. Heat surged from the backs of the people in front of him. A girl spoke with her neighbor and laughed, her shoulders shaking from laughter. Vaguely he heard her laugh and looked at the back of her neck and her moving shoulders. Trees escaped past the window. Plots of green, brown, yellowing. A crashed car stood on the side of the road and his glance followed it.

"My son was killed in that car," he said to the old man next to him.

"Uh huh," said the old man and lowered his hat over his forehead. "Painful," he said.

"He was supposed to get a leave that evening," he said with dry lips. He himself didn't know why he said that.

"Uh huh," the old man muttered. "The good ones always fall." And he coughed into his palm and mumbled something into his white beard.

The car slowed down in the suburbs. He looked at the white roofs and the people walking among the buildings. A woman was walking carrying a basket, and it occurred to him, her son as well. Many of them were from this neighborhood. He looked at the back of the woman and pressed his forehead to the windowpane. The longings became stronger than the pain, and the hidden fabric that weaves life—associated the blue field with the people walking on the road, and the woman coming closer with her full basket, and in the fading day, she crosses through the fence of the garden to a house flickering with light.

He blinked, exhausted.

When he came home it was already dark. The shutters of the settlement were closed. He waded through the muddy path and quietly shut the gate, as if afraid of waking someone. An angry dog barked from the opposite yard. He entered his home. Devorah sat in the kitchen and dozed, her head limp on her shoulders and, as always in the last few days, seemed awake in her sleep. The soup still steamed on the stove. He went into the children's room. Micha had already arrived. He was sleeping in bed. He was covered and only his head peeked out from the white blanket. He slept very wearily, with the film of a dream on his face. He bent over the bed and pressed his head to the cold headboard. The wind beat against the shutter, and suddenly slammed it shut; the boy moved his head, frightened. He bent over the bed and fixed the blanket that had fallen. The blanket radiated the child's body heat and he hid his cold hands for a moment in it.

Translated by Karen Alkalay-Gut.

Other works by Hendel: *Reḥov ha-madregot* (1955); *The Street of Steps* (1963); *He-ḥatser shel momo ha-gedolah* (1969); *Kesef katan* (1988); *Har ha-to'im* (1991); *Aruḥat boker temimah* (1996); *Small Change: A Collection of Stories* (2002); *Terufo shel rofe' ha-nefesh* (2002).

Aharon Megged

1920–2016

Aharon Megged (born Greenberg) was born in Włocławek, Poland, and went as a child to Palestine, where his father was a teacher. He lived on kibbutz Sdot Yam, served as cultural attaché in London from 1968 to 1971, and was writer-in-residence at Oxford and Haifa universities. He served as president of the Israeli branch of PEN from 1980 to 1987 and was a founder and editor of the literary journal *Masa*. He was a novelist, short-story writer, playwright, and translator.

The Name
1950

About two weeks before the birth was due, Grandfather Zisskind appeared in Raya and Yehuda's home for the second time. His face was yellow, angry, and the light had faded from his eyes. He greeted them, but did not favor Raya with so much as a glance, as if he had pronounced a ban upon the sinner. Turning to Yehuda he said, "I wish to speak to you."

They went into the inner room. Grandfather sat down on the chair and placed the palm of his hand on the edge of the table, as was his wont, and Yehuda sat, lower than he, on the bed.

"Rachel has told me that you don't want to call the child by my grandchild's name,"[1] he said.

"Yes . . ." said Yehuda diffidently.

"Perhaps you'll explain to me why?" he asked.

"We . . ." stammered Yehuda, who found it difficult to face the piercing gaze of the old man. "The name simply doesn't appeal to us."

Grandfather was silent. Then he said, "I understand that Mendele doesn't appeal to you. Not a Hebrew name. Granted! But Menahem—what's wrong with Menahem?" It was obvious that he was controlling his feelings with difficulty.

"It's not . . ." Yehuda knew that there was no use explaining; they were two generations apart in their ideas. "It's not an Israeli name . . . it's from the *Golah*."[2]

"*Golah*," repeated Grandfather. He shook with rage, but somehow he maintained his self-control. Quietly he added, "We all come from the *Golah*. I, and Raya's father and mother. Your father and mother. All of us."

"Yes . . ." said Yehuda. He resented the fact that he was being dragged into an argument that was distasteful to him, particularly with this old man whose mind was already not quite clear. Only out of respect did he restrain himself from shouting: That's that, and it's done with! . . . "Yes, but we were born in this country," he said aloud; "that's different."

Grandfather Zisskind looked at him contemptuously. Before him he saw a wretched boor, an empty vessel.

"You, that is to say, think that there's something new here," he said, "that everything that was there is past and gone. Dead, without sequel. That you are starting everything anew."

"I didn't say that. I only said that we were born in this country. . . ."

"You were born here. Very nice . . ." said Grandfather Zisskind with rising emotion. "So what of it? What's so remarkable about that? In what way are you superior to those who were born *there*? Are you cleverer than they? More cultured? Are you greater than they in Torah or good deeds? Is your blood redder than theirs?" Grandfather Zisskind looked as if he could wring Yehuda's neck.

"I didn't say that either. I said that *here* it's different . . ."

Grandfather Zisskind's patience with idle words was exhausted.

"You good-for-nothing!" he burst out in his rage. "What do you know about what was there? What do you know of the *people* that were there? The communities? The cities? What do you know of the *life* they had there?"

"Yes," said Yehuda, his spirit crushed, "but we no longer have any ties with it."

"You have no ties with it?" Grandfather Zisskind bent toward him. His lips quivered in fury. "With what . . . with what *do* you have ties?"

"We have . . . with this country," said Yehuda and gave an involuntary smile.

"Fool!" Grandfather Zisskind shot at him. "Do you think that people come to a desert and make themselves a nation, eh? That you are the first of some new race? That you're not the son of your father? Not the grandson of your grandfather? Do you want to forget them? Are you ashamed of them for having had a hundred times more culture and education than you have? Why . . . why, everything here"—he included everything around him in the sweep of his arm—"is no more than a puddle of tap water against the big sea that was there! What have you here? A mixed multitude! Seventy languages! Seventy distinct groups! Customs? A way of life? Why, every home here is a nation in itself, with its own customs and its own names! And with this you have ties, you say . . ."

Yehuda lowered his eyes and was silent.

"I'll tell you what ties are," said Grandfather Zisskind calmly. "Ties are remembrance! Do you understand? The Russian is linked to his people because he remembers his ancestors. He is called Ivan, his father was called Ivan and his grandfather was called Ivan, back to the first generation. And no Russian has said: 'From today onward I shall not be called Ivan because my fathers and my fathers' fathers were called that; I am the first of a new Russian nation which has nothing at all to do with the Ivans.' Do you understand?"

"But what has that got to do with it?" Yehuda protested impatiently. Grandfather Zisskind shook his head at him.

"And you—you're ashamed to give your son the name Mendele lest it remind you that there were Jews who were called by that name. You believe that his name should be wiped off the face of the earth. That not a trace of it should remain . . ."

He paused, heaved a deep sigh and said:

"O children, children, you don't know what you're doing . . . You're finishing off the work which the enemies of Israel began. They took the bodies away from the world, and you—the name and the memory . . . No continuation, no evidence, no memorial and no name. Not a trace . . ."

And with that he rose, took his stick, and with long strides went toward the door and left.

The newborn child was a boy and he was named Ehud, and when he was about a month old, Raya and Yehuda took him in the carriage to Grandfather's house. [. . .]

[. . .] Grandfather sat at the table upping his thin fingers, and alongside the wall the infant lay in his carriage; it was as if a chasm gaped between a world that was passing and a world that was born. It was no longer a single line to the fourth generation. The aged father did not recognize the great-grandchild whose life would be no memorial. [. . .]

When the door had closed behind them the tears flowed from Raya's eyes. She bent over the carriage and pressed her lips to the baby's chest. At that moment it seemed to her that he was in need of pity and of great love, as though he were alone, an orphan in the world.

NOTE

1. [Perhaps the author means "Grandfather."—Eds.]
2. The Diaspora; the whole body of Jews living dispersed among the Gentiles.

Translated by Minna Givton.

Other works by Megged: *Hanna Senesh* (1958); *The Living and the Dead* (1965); *The Flying Camel and the Golden Hump* (1982); *Foiglman* (1987).

Benjamin Tammuz

1919–1989

Israeli novelist, journalist, painter, and sculptor Benjamin Tammuz was born in Russia and immigrated to Palestine in 1924. He studied law and economics in Tel Aviv and then art history at the Sorbonne. Tammuz designed the Tel Aviv monument to fallen Israeli pilots. He was literary editor of the daily *Haaretz* as well as Israel's cultural attaché in London between 1971 and 1975. He was a writer-in-residence at Oxford University from 1979 to 1984.

Sands of Gold

1950

It was noon and a small boy lay on the couch in the room. The woolly coverlet prickled his back, making him toss about uncomfortably. His eyes roved across the ceiling and down the blank walls to the green glass cupboard, with the door dangling from one hinge and the white chinaware lying bored in its innards. Blank boredom vied with the dreaminess in the boy's eyes; but as they rested for a moment on the schoolbook lying on the table, a mutinous flash wiped both expressions away: How dull were the things they told you in books!

From the large window you can see the sea at the bottom of the street, and when you stand on the roof you can even make out Jaffa and the ships in its port. The sea roars all day long, and you hear it when you wake up at night. Why don't they tell you anything about it at school? Why doesn't the teacher tell you where those ships are bound when they leave the harbor, and what kind of men their captains are, and why they play those games with flags and hooters?

He grimaced. As his mouth rounded into a sad, drawn-out yawn, the memory of the golden sands suddenly flashed across his mind.

At the top of the street, after darting across busy Allenby Road, you sneak over to the railway track then turn left, and there, fringed by a row of solitary sycamores, the golden sands stretch before you. And beyond lie the magic hills and the little creeks and the plowed-up red loams of Sarona. Nearby stands the big red house, a mysterious building with machines clanking inside, and a little further away stands the house of the twin brothers.

All these sights arose in the little boy's memory as he lay imprisoned in the large room. His heart yearned for them, beating fast.

Silently he slid off the prickly couch and peeped into the kitchen. Mother was at her chores, humming as she worked. The door to the outer veranda lay ajar. Slipping his feet into his leather sandals, he stole across the veranda and gained the cool steps that led down to the street and to freedom. His knees trembled and he felt a shiver down his back as the sleeves of his thin shirt fluttered.

As long as he was conscious of the houses in the neighborhood he did not feel safe, but once he had left the quarter he confidently slackened his pace, and his heart began to sing as he edged along the scanty shade cast by the buildings. [. . .]

The noonday heat was growing intense. The boy looked about him for some real shade where he could take a short rest. The passersby were all grown-ups—not a child was to be seen in the street. It struck him that there was something odd about him as he pictured all the other children in their homes, sheltered by the firm pact that exists between parents and their children; the children who obeyed their fathers and mothers, who did their homework properly and didn't lay themselves open to their teachers' tongue-lashing and mothers' scolding.

If only one child would come out of one of the houses! One single child, haunted by restlessness like himself, to go roaming about in the noonday sun.

But the streets were soon deserted even by the grown-ups. The noonday glare beat down, dazzling fiercely. Gloomily he wondered whether it hadn't been foolish of him to leave the house; whether it wouldn't have been better to lie on the prickly sofa and stare at the inside of the green cupboard. But instantly he remembered the twins' house at the edge of the sands, and the red house, too, appeared before him enveloped in distant and mysterious yearning. Faraway words whispered in his heart. He imagined he saw his mother, as well, in the vista of sands—not his mother as she was now, but as she used to be before she became strict about home-work and school, before she started scolding and even smacking him sometimes, her face stern and anxious.

Leaving the cool shade behind, the boy walked on towards that distant past. There lay the railway track, and farther on, to the left, the spreading sycamores stretched before him. From there to the red house it was only a matter of a few steps. You trudged across the scorching sand, which kept trickling into your sandals and tickling your toes; and you could cool off a little under each of the sycamores and pick a handful of sweet figs. [. . .]

There stood the twins' house right in front of him, and the red house as well, tall and narrow, its windows all alike and perfectly aligned. Why was there nobody in sight on the wide stretch of sand? And the twins—where were they? Their yard was deserted and their goatshed gaped empty. Some people were sitting on the veranda of their house, but the boy was too far away to make out who they were. He couldn't pluck up the courage to go into their yard. They would probably finish their meal very soon and come out to see what their goats were up to; in which case he would be able to meet them here, near the sycamores.

But what would he say to them when they came? Surely he couldn't very well admit he had come just because he longed to see them and talk to them; he couldn't simply say that he had walked all that distance just in order to be in their company.

He could tell them, perhaps, that he wanted some rifle bullets very badly and had come to look for some in the sand. After all, everybody knew that the Turkish army had once camped here and that the place was full of bullets. That's what he would tell them, and nobody would suspect him in the least. It wouldn't occur to anybody that a little boy should escape from his big room and the green cupboard and mother and homework and lunch just in order to see the twins, his only friends in

the world, whose house stood in that magic country of golden sands, bounded by hills and creeks and plowed-up red loam and a mysterious red house. [. . .]

He leant against the sycamore, resting in its shade. Then he settled down for a long wait, for there was no sign of life in the twins' yard.

He must have dozed off, for he awoke to hear a man coming up behind him, singing to himself. It was an Arab, holding his stick across his shoulders and the skirts of his burnous hitched up over his arms.

The Arab went up to one of the goats and scratched its back affectionately.

"Yours?" he asked.

"No," the boy answered and laughed. He felt a surge of gratitude to the Arab for treating him like a grown-up and believing he was the owner of livestock. [. . .]

He dozed off a third time, awakening to the sound of a human voice. Behind him stood a woman—the twins' mother most likely, she looked so very much like them—holding out a slice of bread and a tomato and a piece of hard, white cheese. She said:

"Where are you from, child?"

"None of your business!" he retorted sharply, but instantly regretted it and spoke more civilly. "I'm waiting for somebody," he said. "I'll go away very soon."

She handed him the bread and tomato and cheese. He took them, but though hunger gnawed at him, he did not start eating until she had moved off and was walking back to the house.

The bread was stale, but the tomato was juicy and the salt cheese tasted good and smelt of sheep. He munched the food calmly, a jumble of thoughts which he didn't understand crowding into his mind.

He told himself he was sorry the twins hadn't come; then he told himself that the food their mother had handed him was far better and more enjoyable than all the rich food his mother forced him to gulp down at home.

If only they would ask me to come and live with them—he thought sadly—I'd move straight into their house.

In his imagination he saw himself and the twins get-ting up together to go to school, and coming back to-gether, wading through the sand, back to the yard and the goatshed and the dingy veranda. No more would he awaken in the morning to his mother's scolding, prod-ding him to get up to another day in the large apart-ment, where there were no children and no friends, to sit down to a meal of soft, rich, soggy food. No more would he dawdle reluctantly on his way back from school, back to the big room with the chinaware lying white and bored in the green cupboard.

He munched the bread and cheese. His eyes were dry, tearless. But he knew that his heart was crying.

Translated by Joseph Schachter.

Other works by Tammuz: *A Castle in Spain* (1966); *Hapardes* (1972); *Minotaur* (1980); *Ḥayey Elyakum* (1988).

Ka-Tzetnik 135633

House of Dolls
1953

Chapter 1

[. . .] There are moments when the pile of worn clothing in the center of the rag room bestirs itself suddenly like a volcano and sends a pervasive fear throughout the large room. The women, huddled at their benches around the clothes heap, are suddenly still. Their hands manipulate the knives like priestesses readying a ram for offer to a hungry god. The heap fumes in fearful wrath—a wrath, it seems, that will never be quenched. But for the most part, the heap is still—as only a heap of ragged old clothes can be still—while the mouths of the women around it pour out a steady stream of prattle.

Over the rag room is the machine room, where hundreds of sewing machines whir on without stop. Some of the operators, anxious to fill their quotas, work so intently that the treadles of their machines clatter on the floor, and below, in the rag room, the ceiling rumbles like muffled thunderclaps rolling across the sky. The din never lets up. The people have become used to it, like inhabitants of a fishing village to the roar of the surf.

Daniella draws a garment from the clothes heap—men's raincoats are easiest to rip. A long seam runs down the back of this type of coat, and the knife flows right through the seam unhindered—leaving time to daydream. The work is easy. The pockets aren't attached with outside seams, and there is no fear that the sharp cobblers' knife will slip and cut the material.

But the trouble is, you're not allowed to sample through the pile; everyone has to take what comes, off the top. It's all a matter of luck. Everything here is a matter of luck: every so often a gold coin is found hidden, of all places, in the collar of a small child's coat.

No one knows from where the large vans bring the piles of clothing to the shoe factory warehouses day after day. No one knows where the people are who wore these piles of clothes, and no one pursues this thought to its logical confusion: Where were these people taken to—naked, unclothed? But everyone knows that near Breslau there is a vast camp where they do nothing but sift these very clothes or hidden valuables that might be sewn into them.

There, at Camp Breslau, the clothes are sorted: The newer and better ones are shipped to Germany, the shabbier ones are bought by Himmler's Labor Commissioner for the shoe factory recently opened in the ghetto. Here they are ripped, and uppers are cut from them for the wooden shoes the Gestapo buys by the hundreds of thousands—for the Gestapo only knows what purpose.

No one knows if there is anything hidden in the seams of the garment some hands have just pulled from the heap. All draw from the same clothes heap. Every jacket has a collar and all the trousers have the same hidden seams. Everyone knows the garments have been carefully searched at Camp Breslau. Nevertheless the eyes never relax. They might catch a glimpse of a gold coin falling out of a ripped seam into a stranger's hand; or detect some hands unrolling a long, green strip of paper—an American noodle—from a hanger's loop. After all, the examiners at Camp Breslau are only human. [. . .]

Photographs—

All sorts of photographs. So many photographs. Big ones and small ones drop from the ripped pockets. They lie scattered all over the floor; people walk on them. At first, when a photograph would drop out of a pocket, they'd try to read the inscription on the back. Now they don't even bother. Rivkah, the cleaning woman, sweeps them in bunches onto the trash heap. No one pays attention to the photographs any more: Schultze is watching; besides, the faces in the photographs no longer mean anything. One is used to having lying about underfoot: brides and grooms on their bridal day, tots smiling from their cribs, boyish heads darting their sharp, engaging glances at you.

People had taken along these photos as relics of their lives.

The inscriptions on the backs of the photographs aren't read any more. You know without looking you won't be able to understand them, anyway. Some are inscribed in Dutch and others in French; some in Rus-

sian and others in German; some in Flemish, others in
Czech; some in Greek and others in Yiddish; some in
Italian, others in Hebrew. Who here knows so many
languages! [. . .]

A day of letters, written and unwritten. A letter drops
from almost every pocket today. As if the people had
all been members of the same transport: or as if they
had been assured that they would be permitted to write
home as soon as they were brought to their destination.
Rivkah sweeps the letters onto the trash heap. The en-
velopes still pulse with the life of the fingers that sealed
them.

A strange fear now hovers over the rag room. Everyone feels it. Suddenly, the jacket linings begin to ex-
ude human body heat; hands fill out the sleeves; necks
sprout from all collars; stomachs and legs materialize in
all the trousers. Live humans fill the clothes.

A numb silence suddenly settles among the seam
rippers, the knife blades move as of their own accord.
Eyes are lowered to the seam, and the strange garment
reflects back in them their own doom.

Translated by Moshe M. Kohn.

Moshe Shamir

The Opening to the Story
1953

After I published my son's literary estate in a book, I
still had a few scraps of writing and documents of various kinds that I didn't know how to put together with
everything that seemed clear and logical to me, and
for that reason they never saw the light in print. Once
I started seeking some method that would solve a few
of these riddles—something I hadn't done before, so as
not to delay the appearance of the literary estate on the
anniversary of his death—I immersed myself in a task
that can only be defined as an investigation. That investigation ultimately led me on a strange and prolonged
journey, which included visits to two distant continents,
countless conversations, and, I fear, even my acquiring
a bad reputation as a tiresome, nosy man who is hard
to shake off. There is hardly any limit to the facts, the
character traits, the actions, which were revealed to me
from my son's life as a result of this investigation. [. . .]

It turned out that I only knew secondary, external,
and highly incidental things about my son's life. Of all
the events and occurrences that he underwent, whether

it was he himself who initiated them or whether they
overwhelmed him like the sweeping waves of the period, I had knowledge of only the technical aspects,
so to speak: matters of travel, movement from place to
place, getting and quitting jobs, a few proper names,
and personal budgetary problems. Very unfortunately,
it now seems to me that the question isn't "when?"—
that is, at what age his ways began to be concealed from
me—but rather when he began to hide them from his
acquaintances, that is to say, *knowingly, intentionally.*
First of all, they evaded my eyes because of *his* lack of
expression, and because of *my* lack of comprehension,
and certainly because of the unfortunate fact that for me
every mental effort was directed at monetary income,
or, to put it simply, to earning a living. Therefore I was
sparing when I encountered unprofitable areas, such as
spending time in the bosom of the family. [. . .]

He was my eldest son. He was born at the time when
I began to make literature my sole occupation, and this
was immediately after we moved to Tel Aviv. These
three facts can shed light on the background against
which my son grew up. His arrival was greeted with all
the love and all the insecurity that can be described in a
young family that is gathering its first furniture, making
its first social connections in the city, incurring its first
debts. Deeper than love and deeper than insecurity was
the heavy feeling of guilt toward the newborn infant.
[. . .]

To this day I haven't accustomed myself to understanding why the public gives me milk and sandals and
electricity for my manuscripts. At that time not even
the power of routine and habit came to my assistance.
[. . .]

The feeling of guilt toward my son never left me, to
one degree of intensity or another, not even for a single
day. [. . .] In his infancy, the feeling of guilt within me
was inseparably mixed with that soft compassion, that
unbounded love, that willingness to be killed for every
one of his sneezes. The more the boy's circle of contact
with the world expanded, and that of the world with
him, the more the circle of guilt feeling grew larger. At
first it was the bitter feeling of someone who has thrown
a helpless creature, one with no right to protest, into
the world where winds blew through the cracks in the
shutters. [. . .] As time passed, the guilt feeling became increasingly hidden, more and more complex in
new and different ways. Our love, my love, for the child
seemed to grow constantly. But within its folds that bitter feeling was hidden. Perhaps it was not the first ver-

sion—because we brought a creature into this world—but a slightly different version: that we didn't make him better protected to exist in this world. We attributed all his failures, which were not more numerous than his successes, to flaws in his education, in our approach to him, and, even more, to flaws in the very life of our home. Perhaps those hidden corals were planted at that time, the corals with their fabulous building ability, which constructed the terrible wall that, over time, completely hid the subject of our love and apprehension from us. [. . .]

In any event, the feeling of guilt with regard to our son, who constantly expanded the circle of his contact with the world, turned into eagerness to open every gate to him that had not been open to his predecessors. [. . .] He went to seek his own gates and showed almost no interest in the gates that we opened for him. That he went to a kibbutz was a mortal blow for me and his mother. Until that moment we were certain that he was merely joking. By the way, at that time the process of evading my eyes was totally completed. He was like a sealed book for me. [. . .]

After the young man went to the kibbutz, the feeling of guilt increased in a worrisome way, in a way that left rifts in my soul and led me, if it's proper to mention it, to write a few treatises on this event. I was at war with the world, and, in retrospect, with myself. [. . .] When he appeared in our home, once every few months, for a hasty visit which was mainly silence and going to the theater and to be with friends, in his gaunt, sun-tanned, calloused-fingered appearance—I was attacked more than once by the feeling that I know of only in Christianity. He bore my sins! He was, as it were, crucified for me—to atone for my sin, to fill the quota of sacrifices that I refrained from offering. [. . .]

Then the war broke out, and he never returned to our house again. Needless to say, the feeling of guilt toward him became the main value of my life from then on. I'm not sure whether there is anything that could still interest me or arouse any feeling—beyond the circle of the binding of Isaac. I brought a delicate creature to the world in order to kill it, whether by my own hand or by those of an agent. I know that these words of mine won't be pleasant for many people, some of whom had lots worse than mine, but this time I am sitting and writing in order to remove words from my heart. However, I would be denying the truth if I didn't admit that at the same time I want this book to have great success, that it will reach everyone's homes.

The principle is clear to me now and simple, and I don't intend to give up on it, because it is my only consolation in my grief: I am contemptuous of heroism, I hate that function with all the pretty meretricious names, I am the enemy of every organization, of every party, of every state, of every association. I regard political exploitation as more dreadful than material exploitation, and the capitalists of the parties as more dangerous than the capitalists of the factories. I would accept any poverty, any humiliation, any suffering, any dishonor—if only my son could live after me, instead of me living after him. I believe that if people adopted this principle, there would be fewer speeches in the world, fewer books, fewer airline tickets, but also fewer tears. [. . .]

There is one thing of which I have no doubt, though I have a lot of bitterness in it: nothing in the world is more important than that fathers should die before their sons, and even the question of how to attain that must not be solved by the death of sons with their fathers. Not the sons but the fathers must actualize the future, and anyone who puts off the world which is wholly good to the future—is a murderer, or the agent of murderers. There is just one time: *today*, and it has one executor: *the progenitor*. To the people who would take my son from me now so that in a generation or two all men will be brothers, I say: you be brothers *today*! Yes, from this moment, from this very moment, and in this place—go out into the street and be good. From the shirt that is on your flesh, from the chair that is in your room, from the hand that is on your body.

No world will be good if the people in it aren't good. These same people can be good today, too. There is no need for parties for that. [. . .]

Nothing is more transitory than the wise men, and there is nothing more permanent than those who feel, and the politicians are the chaff, exactly that, straw in their lives and chaff in their deaths. [. . .]

With labor and diligence over the years I forged a writing style for myself that became well known. They teach it in the high schools, though for the moment, mainly the linguistic aspect. I know that there are those who deny my talent absolutely, but this time, as I begin to write this book about the episodes in my son's life, which were hidden from my eyes all the time that he was capable of concealing them—this time I will allow my pen to flow on and on without the stretching of the limbs that has become second nature to me, something that can be noted already from the character of this foreword. I will speak ingenuously, and sometimes passages from the words of witnesses will find their way into my story, most of them women, things that serve me as material. As much as I can I will try not to involve myself in the course of the story, not technically, as a first-person narrator, and not in the content. We will let the boy's life flow just as it flowed.

Translated by Jeffrey M. Green.

Nissim Aloni

1926–1998

Playwright and translator Nissim Aloni was born in Tel Aviv and served in the 1948 war. His first play, *Most Cruel of All the Kings*, was staged at Habimah, Israel's national theater, where the reactions were stormy. Aloni founded the Teatron ha-onot and wrote material for the satirical trio, Gashash ha-hiver. In 1996, he was awarded the Israel Prize for Theater.

Most Cruel of All the Kings
1954

REHOBOAM: You have no ambition to govern . . . I know you, Ephraimite. [. . .] Speak like a man, Jeroboam! What did you come to look for in Israel? Why didn't you stay in Egypt? And don't say you came to look for the she-asses.

JEROBOAM: I loved my country. I have no energy to wander any longer. I own a parcel of land in Ephraim, where the people are like me, peace-loving, wishing to live their lives as God had given them.

REHOBOAM: And I was told the Ephraimites have gathered in Shechem. Their appearance does not give the impression that peace is in their hearts.

JEROBOAM: What is a man to do in his village when there is no wheat to reap, nor olives to crush, nor grapes to pick? The famine has eaten all the leftovers of the dry years. Lean cows are grazing upon the barren soil.

REHOBOAM: Woe, Jeroboam. Such matters are not where my strength is. Better to beseech God.

JEROBOAM: And who imposed those taxes? Did God?

REHOBOAM: Please don't underestimate Adoram, the finance minister. Yes, he's a bit older, but even my father said there is no other man who knows his business like him. And my father was wise.

JEROBOAM: Rehoboam, the country is decaying. Your advisers are misleading you. Wherever you look you see a hungry nation, hollow-cheeked, wrapped in rags. Your father placed a heavy burden on us. His collectors have spread to every corner. They are sucking the people's marrow, just like a foreign army.

REHOBOAM: A foreign army! You are sharpening swords in front of my eyes!

JEROBOAM: King of Israel, I am screaming to you the suffering of your people! How many thousands are sent to Lebanon to chop trees! Seventy thousand men have bowed their heads for your father, eighty thousand have hewn rocks from mountains for the building of mansions in Jerusalem! Where are they all, Rehoboam? Who broke their necks? Have you ever asked how many return home and how many thousands of them die, far away in a foreign land, away from mother and child?

REHOBOAM: I understand! I understand . . . the sound of your father's blood—

JEROBOAM: Stop it! Open your eyes, man! What is all this luxury covering the poverty of this land? Why the splendor? Who needs all the imported cedar and cypress trees? Why the gold ornaments in your father's palaces when eyes are dimmed? It took your father seven years to construct a house for the Lord, sixty feet in length, twenty in width, and thirty in height. [*Voice rising.*] But it took him thirteen years to build his own house, a hundred feet long, fifty wide, and thirty feet high. [. . .] Vanity? Wild imagination? And is it also a lie that within the palace wine is drunk from flasks, while outside people are collecting animal dung! A misleading sight! [. . .]

REHOBOAM: Who told you what is best for the people, bread or gold?

JEROBOAM: Go out to your people, king of Israel! Go visit the prison yards. Go into the villages. See the scars upon the people and the land. Go ask your friends how they managed to increase the size of their property by taking away land of the borrowers who could not pay back their loans. No! It was the interest they couldn't repay! How could they, when their sons were sent to Lebanon and their harvest is stolen to be taken to your tables and storehouses? How could they not assemble in the city to bring their tears to you, Rehoboam; today you are our sovereign, give us peace, prosperity, punish our oppressors! I know that their voice had not reached you. I passed through the land of Israel and heard the rising sound of suffering. That sound is calling to you, for you are the king, will you not fear that sound? [. . .] You are feeding off its hard labor and sweat, king!

REHOBOAM: [. . .] What is justice, Jeroboam? Do you know its meaning? You—won't you collect taxes to increase and strengthen justice? [. . .] And if the king of Egypt, Shishak, commands you to fill his granaries with wheat—what will you do? Will you lead this great multitude of people to war or starve it, dressed in rags, and send them to gather dung off the streets? What are you going to do, great hero? We have a small country, coveted by both the Assyrians and Egyptians. One time we bend our heads, another time we wink to one side, then embrace the other lovingly, until they nod off once again. That is our destiny. An old whore who beautifies herself in vain.

JEROBOAM: Until when?

REHOBOAM: Forever! Ours is a small country; whatever strength cannot achieve, love will. It is money. Money speaks and is beloved both by the north, the land of the Assyrians, and by the south, the land of the swollen lips.

JEROBOAM: Whose money speaks? Who will sacrifice all their might to satiate the northern and southern lions? Who will pay the harlot?

REHOBOAM: Take a look outside, to the street. Can you see them? They will!

JEROBOAM: They?

REHOBOAM: I know of whom I speak.

JEROBOAM: And if they refuse?

REHOBOAM: Refuse? Who? Those people?

JEROBOAM: They! They! They!

REHOBOAM: I ascended the throne only yesterday, but I've been watching the riffraff for years. My father punished them by the whip, Jeroboam son of Nebat, but they still had the strength to lift up their heads. [. . .] And you will go out and ask the people if they will not offer their hearts to me gladly, because these people, Jeroboam son of Nebat, the more they are oppressed, the better off they are, the more I bear down on them, the more they will respect me. And I swear, I will bear down on this entire pack of dogs! Once you stop whipping them, they will lift their heads and scream! I shall remove every rebellious thought! By scorpions, Jeroboam son of Nebat! By whips, Jeroboam son of Nebat! But also by soft words, Jeroboam, so that they will hear me well, and also by iron threshing boards, so that they know that I am the one carrying out the kingship in Israel! And so that you too will know that of the two of us, mine is the word that counts.

Translated by Menachem Rotstein.

Other works by Aloni: *Bigdey ha-melekh* (1961); *Ha-nesikhah ha-amerika'it* (1963); *Ha-tso'anim shel Yafo* (1971).

Ephraim Kishon

1924–2005

Born Ferenc Hoffmann to an assimilated Jewish family in Budapest, Ephraim Kishon began writing as a teenager, although his studies and early literary efforts were cut short by the Holocaust. Upon immigrating to Israel, Kishon became the new nation's chief satirist, casting his sharp eye on the actions of the Labor Zionist state as well as the condescension with which established Israelis of Ashkenazi descent treated incoming Mizrahi immigrants. In the 1980s, Kishon moved to Switzerland, where he continued to write humorous commentary.

The Difference

1954

Yitzhak Klein gave such an angry kick to the garbage can that it flew straight into the middle of the sidewalk, scattering its stinking contents in all directions. Klein nearly exploded in his boiling rage that overflowed upon this crazy land. He had a meeting with that sabra, who had managed to pick up a decent Yiddish from him, and he was already late because of that damned transportation system. For an entire hour he had been waiting in line, sweating profusely. And if that wasn't enough, once he got onto the bus, he was picked on. And why not? Why in heaven should he be left alone even on the bus?

The dark-complexioned policeman began to pester him to extinguish his cigarette. Klein retaliated, giving his opinion in colorful Yiddish, by sending the dummy-in-uniform to his boss, Ben-Gurion. The guy did not understand a word and took down his name. So be it. Let him write. We'll pay the fine. In any case, this worthless coin has no value. What's the difference? Let's pretend the money is a new Histadrut tax. Funny. Klein continued to smoke leisurely while perusing the Ḥad Gadya column in the daily *Ma'ariv* paper.[1]

I say, he lets them have it, Klein concluded, with satisfaction. He gives it to them but good! It's true that a bunch of fools run this country! The devil should take this Zionist *protektsia* [favoritism] regime.

Now the main tenant came out, that witch, yelling and screaming about the garbage can. Klein mocked her, laughing. They hated one another as one can only hate when living among that international detritus referred to as "our state."

Why did I even come here? He questioned himself bitterly, as he stretched out on the creaky old government-issued bed. Is this even a country? This is a sickly tumor . . . damn it . . .

Then he fell asleep. [. . .]

"Comrade Klein," called out the Party's supervisor. "This morning, again, you stood in line in front of the grocery!"

Janos Klein trembled. It seems, then, to be true. Ever since he returned from Hungary, he has been under constant surveillance. And this dreadful business! The "supervisor of house morale" walked into his apartment a few days earlier, at the exact moment he happened to be listening to "The Voice of Jerusalem" . . .

"I was in line no longer than five minutes," whispered Klein to the supervisor, "I don't have a grain of sugar left in the house . . ."

O God, what a silly thing to have said! How is it he cannot keep his mouth shut? The supervisor, the skinny tailor, furrowed his brow. Klein felt a current of weakness crawling through his body.

"Comrade Klein, it seems you have not quite reached political maturity yet!" whistled the tailor. "Are you not ready to grasp the fact, comrade, that queuing up helps the reactionary forces, who exploit it as propaganda against the People's Republic?! At a time when the working masses are struggling for peace, and the workers enthusiastically accept production increases, Mr. Klein misses his candy! . . . Mr. Klein, I'm very sorry, I must report this to the Party . . ."

Again, Klein felt that same hysteric shiver that enveloped him whenever he had an exchange with party members. He reserved particular hatred for the supervisor, the tailor who had divorced his Jewish wife during the Nazi occupation.

"Dear comrade supervisor," Klein attempted to say with class consciousness, "I am grateful to you. Your proletarian alertness just saved me from an embarrassing act, unbecoming of the working class. I will not stand in line in the future! I shall prove my loyalty to our Party and to its beloved leaders . . ."

The supervisor measured Klein up with his watery eyes from head to foot. He then went down to the third floor without uttering a word. His brow still furrowed.

* * *

"My dear sir, I would like to bring to his attention that my sister is no longer willing to spend her future time in his company. I trust that those words are quite clear . . ."

Johann Klein stood stunned in front of the elegant Dutch financier. Two years earlier Klein had immigrated to Holland and was up to that point quite sure that he had succeeded in integrating into that beautiful land without arousing suspicion.

"And why is it that she does not desire my company," he inquired hoarsely, "if I may ask?"

The mogul drew circles in the air with his gloved hand.

"I am convinced that my dear sir will be able to understand the reason by himself," he replied politely. "Goodbye, sir. I ask that he behave in accordance with my urgent request . . ."

Klein became pale as a ghost; he approached the cabinet with weak knees and breathed heavily as he glared at his counterfeit birth certificates . . .

* * *

The boss walked across the factory floor, as usual.

"Hey, you! You there! You're fired!" he shouted at James Klein. "Go pick up your two days' salary at the cashier's office."

The enormous door swallowed the boss's figure. Klein packed up his things and went out with total casualness. The others looked at him as if he were transparent.

Strange, the thought crossed his mind, isn't it, that the labor unions never get involved, but he immediately dismissed that annoying thought. Leaving his belongings with the doorman, he went looking for a job. Toward nightfall, he came back exhausted and broken. In front of the building he bumped into the factory owner. Then suddenly, he lost control over his nerves, or maybe it was those glasses of whisky he consumed in his despair that made him enraged.

"What have I done?" he asked the boss. "Why did you throw me out? Huh?"

"I don't employ Jews," said the boss, almost heartily. "That's all, my friend, what do you want?"

Klein pounced on him, letting out an inhuman moan. They were barely able to separate the men.

"You are too green, my friend," said the boss, without much emotion. "What's the big deal? I don't hire

Jews, while Goldstein the manufacturer across the way hires *only* Jews. Are you out of your mind?"

Klein slumped to the sidewalk; his belongings were scattered everywhere. The doorman indicated that he should get moving quickly.

* * *

Yitzhak Klein pressed his head down into the wet pillows, letting out a few broken groans from time to time. The government-issued old bed squeaked noisily beneath him.

"Review?" Klein yelled in his dreams. "Jewish Agency! Review!"

NOTE

1. [The name of Kishon's satirical column in the Hebrew daily *Ma'ariv*, from 1952 to 1982.—Eds.]

Translated by Menachem Rotstein.

Other works by Kishon: *Sallah Shabati* (1964); *Unfair to Goliath* (1968); *Wise Guy, Solomon* (1973).

Sami Michael

The Artist and the Falafel
1955

A mighty gust of a cruel wind slid down from Mount Carmel toward the street.

After having flooded its lights, its tumult and the aromas emanating from its restaurants, it continued making its way to the sea. The stars pulsating against the background of the deep sky appeared to be trembling from the cold. The lamps illuminating the street shook. That marked the end of the pleasant weather the city had been enjoying these last few days.

The lights of the grand, tall buildings poised atop the mountain looked down upon the lower neighborhoods stretching out below them. Those lights neither trembled nor moved due to the cold wind. While the lights of the lower quarters shook in the wind—as did their inhabitants—and were soaked whenever it rained. [. . .]

Some people looked disappointedly back toward home, while the collars of others were stubbornly raised, as the tips of their cold fingers extended toward the loose buttons, as they tried to protect their bodies from the chill. However, the fingers of the artist who stood across from the oriental restaurant remained frozen in place. He did not have any loose buttons that his

fingers could grasp in winter as the cold intensified. All he had to cover himself were a pair of khaki pants, which he had fastened to his waist with a woman's belt, a blue shirt that had been missing three buttons since the previous summer, and a short coat whose sleeves had frayed well before he had picked it up second-hand from an unknown donor. That was his entire wardrobe.

The artist pushed his hands deeper into the pockets of his coat, biting his lip with large, yellowing teeth. At that moment, he did not raise his eyes up to the beautiful sky that encircled the city like a crown, nor did he experience the twinkling lights on the street, as if they were little colorful bells, nor did he examine the faces of the passersby so as to read in them hidden emotions. His spirit was shut off at that moment from the beauty, the meanings, and the colors. He chewed his lips and crumbled the piece of chalk he kept in his pocket. Nothing occupied his mind besides the black mass of clouds that had spread out upon the mountain and begun to hunt and swallow the gleaming stars one by one, as if they were despicable insects. [. . .]

The artist regarded himself as a grown man, but he was actually no more than a child, or at the last stages of childhood. Still, he accepted all of life's events with an adult's outlook. However, his experience of hunger was always that of a child. Hunger elicited within him a feeling of deprivation for no apparent reason and brought tears to his eyes. [. . .]

The artist returned to look at the street and noticed how empty and barren it was. The first show had begun some moments earlier and the audience had entered the theater. Only a handful of familiar faces, which had already become a part of the street itself, remained nearby: the woman selling falafel with her red fingernails, the man with the trembling hand offering thermometers to the crowd hurrying to be amused, the teen selling chocolate, and the girl pressing her thin knees together under her light dress, waiting for the time she could pick up the flowers with her mother and go back home. [. . .]

The artist was a deaf-mute, but he knew everything about these faces. For instance, he knew that the lady selling falafel was waiting, after the second show ended, for the cook from the nearby restaurant. The tired cook's roughness would awaken a sadness within the artist, and he would observe the cook and the falafel seller's lips each time they met, and if those tight lips revealed a rare smile, then his own lips would display a kind of smile, the smile of a deaf child. [. . .]

The thermometer salesman got up and began the long and tiring journey home. Soon after, the woman picked up the flowerpots and disappeared along with her daughter around the bend of a narrow alley. It appeared to the artist that the street had become more deserted than before and that the lights could not scatter the darkness that descended upon the world. The weakness of childhood returned and hunger brought tears to his eyes once more. He was hoping someone would come and take him home with them, but he couldn't recall the faces of his mother and father, who died before he was even weaned. His aunt is disabled, and when the humidity is high she cannot even get out of bed. [. . .]

It is possible that the despair, the hunger or the stubbornness—all of which are true—have all made him kneel suddenly on the ground and sweep away with his small hand a large spot of asphalt. After clearing the floor of the packets of cigarettes, shells of sunflower seeds, pebbles and papers, he pulled out of his pocket the piece of chalk, whose edges he had only a short time earlier unraveled with his fingernails. Wide white lines began flowing with feverish speed upon the filthy black ground, turning it even darker. [. . .]

The artist was certain that he would never again see the shimmer of the coins rolling upon the rider's chest and upon his horse's head. Even if a miracle were to occur, and the black cloud pass without pouring its anger upon the street, the passersby would not notice the drawing. This crowd has strange taste; each evening it surrounds the artist in a tight circle of awestruck eyes, yet not once have the onlookers' eyes focused on the work itself rather than the artist. This audience did not see in front of themselves either art or artist; rather, they enjoyed focusing on the serious lines registered on the kneeling boy's face as he wiped the refuse off the black asphalt with his small hand and then picked up the chalk and dispatched quick, snappy lines forward. The crowd enjoys seeing this deaf and mute creature, wrapped in rags, as he casts his art below its feet. A few used to exclaim, in a knowing tone: "He's an orphan and his aunt is a cripple . . ." Yet none has seen in the child's art any dimension of manliness, the manliness of a person kneeling on the ground for his aunt's sake. Moreover, the coins which they tossed to the ground were not out of pity for the invalid aunt, nor out of mercy for the hungry child, nor as a reward for the artist's craft, but as compensation for the clown who offered them this entertaining moment. The artist therefore understood that the audience that would be streaming from the cinemas would not pay any atten-

tion to the completed artwork, for it is interested in the act of drawing, and not in the drawing itself.

Translated by Menachem Rotstein.

Abraham Sutzkever

Green Aquarium
1956

1

"Your teeth are bars of bone. Behind them, in a crystal cell, your shackled words. Remember the advice of an elder: the *guilty*, those that dropped poison pearls into your goblet—let them go free. In thanks for your generosity, they will erect your immortality. But the others, the *innocent*, that trill falsely like nightingales over a grave—don't spare them. Hang them, be their executioner! Because as soon as you let them out of your mouth, or your pen, they become demons. May the stars keep from falling if I don't speak the truth!"

This bequest was left to me years ago when my native city was alive, by an old bachelor, a distracted poet with a long braid in back like a fresh birch broom. No one knew his name, or his origin. I knew only that he wrote rhymed notes in Aramaic to God, dropped them into the red mailbox by the green bridge, and deliberately and patiently strolled along the Viliye, waiting for heaven's postman to bring him an answer.

2

"Walk over words as over a minefield. One false step, one false move, and all the words that you have been stringing together on your veins over a lifetime will be torn to shreds along with you."

This my own shadow whispered to me when the two of us, blinded by searchlight-windmills made our way at night across a bloody minefield, and my every step, set down on death or life, scratched at the heart, like a nail in a violin.

3

But no one warned me to be wary of words that are drunk with otherworldly poppies. So I became a slave to their will. I haven't been able to understand their will. And certainly not the secret of whether they love me or hate me. They wage wars in my skull like termites in a desert. Their battlefield starts through my eyes with the glare of rubies. And children turn grey with fear when I bid them: good-dream . . .

Once in broad daylight, as I was lying in the garden, under a bough of oranges—or children playing with golden bubbles—I felt a stirring of the soul. Oho, my words were venturing forth! Having realized one victory, they must have decided to conquer fortifications that no words had ever been able to take before. Of people, angels, and why not stars? Intoxicated with otherworldly poppies, their fancy plays free. Trumpets blare.

Torches like burning birds.

Lines accompany them. Frames of music.

To one such word, riding out front in a crown that was sparkling with my tears, apparently the master, I fell on my knees.

"Is this how you leave me, without a farewell, without an *au revoir,* with nothing? We wandered together for years, you ate of my time, so before we part, before you go off to conquer worlds—grant me one request! But give me your word that you won't refuse . . ."

"Agreed. I give my word. But no long sentences. The sun is leaning over the blue branch and in another moment falls into the abyss."

"I want to see the dead!"

"What a request! . . . well, so be it. My word is more precious to me . . . See!"

A green knife slit open the earth.

It became green.

Green.

Green.

The green of dark fir trees through a mist;

The green of a cloud with ruptured bile;

The green of mossy stones in a rain;

The green that appears through a hoop rolled by a seven-year-old;

The green of cabbage leaves in splinters of dew, that bloody the fingers;

First green under melted snow in a circle around a blue wildflower;

The green of a half-moon, seen with green eyes from under a wave;

And the joyous green of grass bordering a grave.

Greens flow into greens. Body into body. And the earth stands transformed into a green aquarium.

Closer, come closer to the green whirlpool.

I look in: people swim here like fish. Countless phosphorous faces. Young. Old. Youth and age combined. All those I have seen in the course of a lifetime, and death has embalmed them with green existence; they all swim in the green aquarium in a kind of silken, aery music.

Here live the dead!

Beneath them rivers, forests, cities—an immense plastic map, and above them floats the sun, in the shape of a fiery being.

I recognize acquaintances, friends, neighbors, and doff my straw hat to them:

"Good morning."

They reply with green smiles, as a well answers a stone with broken circles.

My eyes splash with silver oars, chasing, swimming among the faces. They are in pursuit, searching for a single face.

There at last! There it is! The dream of my dream—

"Here I am, my dearest, here I am. The wrinkles are only a nest for my longing."

My lips, swollen with blood, reach toward hers. But alas they stay suspended on the pane of the aquarium.

Her lips also swim toward mine. I feel the breath of flaming punch. The pane is a cold slaughter-knife between us.

"I want to read you a poem about yourself . . . you must hear it!"

"I know the poem by heart, my dearest, I gave you the words myself."

"Then let me feel your body once more!"

"We can't come any closer, the pane . . ."

"No, this barrier will soon vanish. I'll smash the green pane with my head—"

At the twelfth blow the aquarium burst.

Where are the lips, the voice?

And the dead, the dead—have they died?

There is no one here. In front of me—grass. Overhead—a bough of oranges, or children playing with golden bubbles.

Translated by Ruth R. Wisse.

Aharon Megged

Hanna Senesh
1958

[*When the lights come up again we're in a courtroom. Three colonels at the judges' table. On one side, prosecutor* MATZKAS, *and* SIMON, *a military judge. On the other side defense attorney* DEVCSERY. *Opposite them, in the dock,* HANNA. *At some distance, away from the courthouse, the* MOTHER *sits by herself.*]

JUDGE: [*Lowers the gavel.*] The accused, Hanna Senesh! You've heard the charges, the testimonies, the prosecution, and the defense. Have you anything to say in your defense?

HANNA. [*Stands up.*] Yes.

JUDGE: Speak.

HANNA: I have been accused here of a number of crimes which I do not deny. I did cross the border from the partisans in Yugoslavia—I admit it. I was sent here by the Allies—I admit it. I carried a transmitter to relay information abroad—I admit that, too. I came to save Jews from death—I'm proud of it. But the charge that I betrayed the country of my birth and planned its destruction, I categorically deny. I grew up in this country, I was educated here. At home, in school, in society—they taught me to love this Hungary, this land that had been liberated from the foreign yoke, the Hungary of Petöfi, of Addy, the Hungary of freedom fighters. I loved this land. Its simple, good people, its intellectuals, who stood up to tyranny. In it I breathed the air of freedom. So it was—until I found out that I, the daughter of an admired writer and respected mother—was considered a second-class citizen, that I'm not entitled to the same rights as anyone born in this country—all because I'm a Jew. So I left the country I loved since childhood, and the person closest to me—my mother—and traveled to Palestine. There, I found my real homeland because there I discovered that I can walk with my head held up high, without fear, breathe the air, enjoy the sunlight, without any worry. I would have never left that land—were it not for the terrible events you all know about. I risked my life to get here—to save my brothers from death. Yes, I admit to that crime. If fighting slavery, humiliation, hellish cruelty the world has not seen since the Huns, is sin in your eyes—I admit to that sin. If fighting against vicious, wild beasts who take away innocent men and women, whose only sin is—that they were born Jews—if this is a sin in your eyes—I admit to that sin. But if anyone betrayed this country—that's you, all of you . . . [*Noise in the room.*]

PROSECUTOR: I ask you to stop this! We must not allow her to turn the courtroom into a political forum!

JUDGE B: The accused forgets before whom she stands.

JUDGE C: We won't allow a spy to accuse us!

PROSECUTOR: She is taking advantage of the court's leniency! I demand that she be stopped!

JUDGE: [*Pounding the gavel.*] Since the prosecution is asking for the death penalty—I'll let her finish.

HANNA: I repeat, everyone, including you, who serves this government and does not protest, is a traitor. Look what you have done to your Hungary, to this great country that suffered for hundreds of years under foreign occupation, saved in wars by freedom fighters! Examine your self-dignity, trampled on everywhere, how thousands of your sons are fighting a foreign war, for Hungary's eternal enemy—Germany! Look at the ruin you've brought on your people! How they're haunted by fear! How law-abiding citizens are kidnapped from their homes and thrown into pigsties! How tens of thousands who worked side by side with you for the good of all—are sent to death camps, to the ovens! Could anyone truly love his country and remain deaf to their outcry? Remember! This shameful government that you're serving, its days are numbered. Its hours. Judgment day is near for those who murdered, who shed innocent blood! The day will come when you'll sit in the dock, and facing you will be the souls of all those whose lives you've cut short! What will you say? How will you defend your actions? This is your last chance to retreat. One good deed can purge you of your sins! I know my actions are pure in God's eyes, so I am not afraid of death. If I feared your verdict, I wouldn't have wholeheartedly taken on this mission. You can kill me, as the Prosecutor wants, but know that this is just another nail in your coffin, in the coffin of the order you represent! [*Quiet.*]

JUDGE: [*Gets up, pounds the gavel.*] The court will adjourn for consultations. [*All leave except* HANNA *and the* MOTHER.]

MOTHER: [*Comes over, hugs her, then fixes her eyes on her.*] You've grown so tall, Aniko, that I must raise my eyes to the sky to see you . . .

HANNA: I'm at peace with myself, as if the nightmare were gone . . .

MOTHER: [*Holds her hand, scared.*] Suddenly, I'm scared . . .

HANNA: Of what?

MOTHER: Of losing you . . .

HANNA: But you saw, Mom, how they were afraid to look at me when I spoke!

MOTHER: But your words rang to distances far away from here, from life . . .

HANNA: But I spoke of life, Mom, only of life! [*Enter* DEVCSERY.]

MOTHER: So?

DEVCSERY: They've decided to postpone sentencing for a week.

MOTHER: Is this a good sign or a bad one?

DEVCSERY: I think—it's good, Mrs. Senesh. They're afraid. Very much! They're afraid that judgment day is near, as your daughter has warned them! This is the first time in the history of this military court! [*To* HANNA.] They're afraid of you! [*Light dims. When it comes back again it's* HANNA's *cell; she sits on the bed, holds her head in her hands. She stirs when hearing a noise. Drumbeat and soldiers marching in step. Gets up, tries to get to the window, cannot. Knocks a few times on the walls, hears no answer. Knocks on the door. Enter* YANOS.]

HANNA: Why the drumbeats?

YANOS: [*Terrified.*] Executions, Miss Anna. Every hour—executions . . .

HANNA: You know who?

YANOS: I can't know. Miss Anna. They just grab people from their cells, put them against the wall, and shoot. May Jesus our Savior have mercy on their souls.

HANNA. You haven't heard even one name?

YANOS: Not one. They do it without sentencing. God protect us from Antichrist, it has never been this way.

HANNA: And me—no one asked about me?

YANOS: No, Miss Anna. . . . God have mercy on you. . . . [*After a pause.*] There's a narrow gate to the Kingdom of Heaven. Only a few will enter, but I know that you'll be one of them. Yes, yes . . . [*More drumbeats, marching soldiers.* YANOS *closes the door, leaves quickly. A shot.* HANNA *hides her face in her hands. Tries again to get to the window. Brings a chair, climbs on it. Just then the door opens. It's prosecutor* SIMON. *Hanna climbs down, retreats to the wall.*]

SIMON: [*Stands in front of her for a while, silent.*] I came to inform you that this morning the judges pronounced your sentence . . . [*Long pause.*]

HANNA: Death?

SIMON: [*Head bowed, after a pause.*] You still have one opening left—ask for mercy.

HANNA: When did they pronounce my sentence?

SIMON: An hour ago.

HANNA: That's a lie! There was no sentence! [*Shouting.*] Why didn't you call me? Were you afraid to look me in the eye? Say it! Speak! [*After a pause.*] Are you afraid of the truth, you crawling cowards?! You know

you'll never be able to cleanse yourselves of the blood you're shedding! Miserable creatures! Have you no dignity? Speak! Say something in your defense! [*He's quiet.*] Oh, better to die than live like you! [*After a pause.*] Call for my lawyer, I want to appeal.

SIMON: There is no appeal here.

HANNA: A lie! You know there is a higher court! I want to appeal to it!

SIMON: There is no appeal. You can only ask for mercy.

HANNA: From you? To fall on my knees and ask you for mercy? Never! [*Shouting.*] I want to appeal!

SIMON: The sentence will be carried out in an hour. You may write letters to your family. Be ready.

HANNA: [*Shouts after him, grabs the door bars.*] Bring me my mother! My mother! [*He leaves.*] Bring me my mother! . . . My mother! . . . [*Falls on the bed, hides her face in her hands. Lights dim. Enter* ELIAHU. *She gets up, clings to him.*] Look, what they're doing to me, Eliahu . . . [*Buries her face in his chest, cries.*]

ELIAHU: You said you were strong, remember?

HANNA: I want to live Eliahu, I want so much to live . . .

ELIAHU: I warned you.

HANNA: It's terrible dying like this, like a star in the dark. Terrible.

ELIAHU: It's the common fate of many. Predictable fate.

HANNA: I was a little girl, Eliahu, that's all. A voice called, and I went.

ELIAHU: It was a true voice, wasn't it?

HANNA: Must it be this way—that truth should lead to death?

ELIAHU: Remember? "Blessed is the match consumed / In kindling flame."

HANNA: Please console me, Eliahu.

ELIAHU: Should I tell you about your friends?

HANNA: Yes, tell me everything. [*Pulls him to the bed. They sit down.*]

ELIAHU: Three who went before you, are no more. And twenty-three who went by boat were lost in the sea. Fifteen young men fell when they got to the fortress.

HANNA: Tell me about life, Eliahu. Not about those who are gone.

ELIAHU: The living remember you, Hanna, they'll remember you forever.

HANNA: Tell me about them, I want them with me as I go. It's much easier that way.

ELIAHU: Should I tell you about your kibbutz on the seashore?

HANNA: Yes! I'm so eager to hear it— [*Opposite them, three young men, fishermen, barefoot, sit on shoulders.*]

ELIAHU: The fishermen are leaving now to faraway places . . . almost near the islands . . . and the two trees you planted by your tent have grown since you've left . . . and on the beach, little children run after the seagulls . . .

HANNA: Tell me more, Eliahu . . . [*Drumbeat. Marching soldiers.*] I must go, Eliahu, my time is up. Let me hold you to be strong. I want to look at the rifles without fear . . . [*The song "Blessed Is the Match" grows louder and louder from, afar.* HANNA *walks toward the sound. Lights dim. Dark. More drumbeats.*]

Translated by Michael Taub.

Uri Orlev

b. 1931

Novelist Uri Orlev, born Jerzy Henryk Orlowski, is renowned for his children's books, many of which engage with themes of the Holocaust drawn directly from his own childhood. Born in Warsaw, Orlev survived the Warsaw ghetto, living in hiding on the Aryan side, and was finally flushed out in the Hotel Polski affair. Deported to the Bergen-Belsen concentration camp, he began writing poetry in Polish. After the war, he arrived in Mandatory Palestine with his younger brother, learned Hebrew, and lived on various kibbutzim before moving to Jerusalem. He has published more than thirty books and is a major translator from Polish into Hebrew. In addition to his literary career, Orlev writes for television and radio in Israel. *The Lead Soldiers*, his first and most famous book, was written for adults, not for children.

The Lead Soldiers
1958

Formations of soldiers faced each other across the floor, taking cover in domino houses and bunkers of colored blocks. Yurik and Kazik lay by their soldiers. [. . .]

But Kazik had stopped playing and was listening to the stairs. "Christina's coming." He knew her steps. "She's bringing lunch." A blonde, trim girl of about eighteen entered the room carrying a laundry basket and a bouquet of lilacs.

"See what I brought you? It's spring outside. The lilac's in bloom." She put the flowers in a vase and filled it with water from the pitcher. "I'm in an awful rush, because my mother has lots of laundry today. Hurry up and eat," she requested. She removed the washing from the basket and handed them the plates of food that were underneath it. [. . .]

Christina went down to the laundry.

QUICK AND CLEAN said the sign on the window at the front of the house. Christina, her mother, and two hired girls did the wash inside amid vaporous clouds of steam. Pani Sadomska, whose husband had been killed fighting in the defense of Warsaw, had agreed to take in the two Jewish boys in return for a handsome fee. Her own two-room apartment was attached to the laundry by a narrow corridor. She and her daughter lived in one of the rooms, and her sixteen-year-old son in the other. The room in which the two boys were hidden was seven flights up on the roof. [. . .]

Strange footsteps mounted the stairs and stopped outside their door. The two of them listened tensely. The knocker knocked three times and three times again. It stopped.

"Should I open it?' asked Yurik in a whisper.

The knocker knocked three more times.

"That's nine. I'm going to open it."

A large stranger wearing a stiff, round hat entered the room. He looked at them and then looked for a place to hang his hat. In the end he put it by his briefcase on the table and sat down in the easy chair.

"Good morning, boys," he said. He smiled at Kazik and raised his chin. "'What's your name, young man?"

Kazik didn't answer.

"His name is Kazimierz Stefan Kosopolski," Yurik answered for him.

"Be quiet!" the stranger said angrily. "I wasn't aware that anyone had asked you." He smiled again at Kazik. "Where did you live before coming here, young man?"

Kazik sat there bewildered. He couldn't for the life of him remember the complicated story he had been instructed to tell under such circumstances.

"We're from Lvov," Yurik said.

Sergeant Zuk wheeled around and slapped him in the face. "I asked you not to answer for him," he warned. "Are you Jewish?" he asked Kazik

Kazik's bewilderment grew, but he shook his head.

"He isn't," said Yurik.

The sergeant spun around again. "Wise guy! I told you to shut up. Do you hear me?"

"He . . . he doesn't talk so well," Yurik apologized. "He's still little."

"Are you Jewish?" This time the question was finally directed at Yurik.

"No."

"What's your name?"

"Jerzy Henryk Kosopolski. We're Pani Sadomska's nephews. We came here from Lvov because the Russians were there. They killed our father and mother, and we were sent here by our uncles."

"You took the train to Warsaw?"

"Yes."

"And then?"

"We took a carriage."

"Did the driver have a moustache?"

'It was a long time ago," said Yurik.

"How do you like Warsaw, better than Lvov?"

Yurik forgot himself. "Oh, yes," he said. "Warsaw's much nicer. Especially Zoliboz."

"The train went through Zoliboz?"

"Yes," Yurik replied, giving himself away,

"Oh," said the sergeant.

Christina came with their afternoon snack and paused pale-faced in the doorway. The sergeant gave them a last look. "Oh well," he said. He took his briefcase and his hat "Goodbye, boys," he said.

The two boys waited wordlessly for him to leave. Christina followed him out. He locked the door from outside and removed the key.

"He took it," whispered Yurik. They waited for the footsteps to disappear from the yard and lay down on one of the beds. "What's going to happen?"

Yurik shrugged.

"Nothing's going to happen," Kazik suddenly said.

"How do you know?"

"I had a dream."

"What did you dream?"

"Brown Suit and Gray Suit came to the door and threatened us with pistols. Not real pistols, ones like ours. They were even made out of cardboard, and were flat."

"So?"

"We ran down some streets with Aunt Ella until we got here. Then the ceiling opened up and a naked man came out with lots of hair. There was a lot of light and he had a cross. I think it must have been Jesus."

"When did you dream it?"

"The night before last."

"You're not making it up? Swear to me."

"I swear." Kazik promised.

"Swear by Papa."

"I swear by Papa."

"Then what happened?"

"They got smaller and disappeared into the floor. You know," Kazik remembered, "Pani Sadomska said that when we become Catholics after the war Christina will be our godmother."

"Should we pray?" asked Yurik.

Kazik nodded.

"Hail Mary, full of grace," Yurik began.

"Full of grace," Kazik repeated after him.

"Pray for us now and at the hour of our death. Amen."

Sergeant Zuk of the secret police informed his superiors that his investigation had confirmed that two children were staying with Pani Sadomska, as a certain tenant in the house had reported, but that the boys were undoubtedly the lady's Catholic nephews who had come from Lvov.

Ella obtained his address and went to thank him. She offered him money but he refused. In token of her appreciation she sent him a present of considerable value together with a large bouquet of white lilies.

A bomb fell. Yurik and Kazik sat in the darkness on the table in their room. "Give us this day our daily bread," they prayed. The walls of the room shook and a window pane shattered from the explosion. "Forgive us our trespasses as we forgive those who trespass against us."

"I'm scared," whispered Kazik.

"It's the Russians," Yurik reassured him. "Look, you can see the anti-aircraft fire."

"Let's lie down and pray some more," Kazik suggested.

Yurik lay down next to him and Kazik wrapped his arms around him. There was another explosion.

"Do you know the Credo by heart?"

"No, but I'll say it after you."

"I believe," Yurik began, "in God the omnipotent Father, Creator of heaven and earth."

A majestic pageant of aerial warfare filled the night sky.

Translated by Hillel Halkin.

Other works by Orlev: *'Ad maḥar* (1958); *A Lion for Michael* (1979); *The Island on Bird Street* (1981).

Pinḥas Sadeh

1929-1994

Born in Lemberg (today Lviv), Pinḥas Sadeh and his family immigrated to Palestine in 1934, and he grew up in Tel Aviv. Despite receiving little formal education past primary school, Sadeh became an accomplished and respected writer, known for his spare phrasing and prophetic air in a variety of literary modes. Following the publication of his autobiographical and mystical novel *Life as a Parable*, he attracted something of a cult following, especially among young adults. In the 1960s and 1970s, Sadeh's personal life attracted a great deal of popular attention, and a 2014 Israeli television series in part chronicles his life.

Life as a Parable
1958

While my body, in its restlessness, yearned for distances but always inevitably returned to its point of departure, my soul, lacking repose, yearned to travel far into the mighty distances of the spirit that stretched out in the world of books, but at first it was only able to err and wander about blindly without being able to find its way there. When my thirst for books overcame me I would sit in the reading-room till after midnight, reading incessantly. The books I found there were about social and political subjects—subjects far from life—like *The Communist Manifesto*, *Anti Dühring*, the works of Lenin and Stalin and the like. Yet not only did I read these books with great interest, but I also made voluminous notes, filling note-books with summaries and quotations. I longed to learn, and I knew no other way.

But one evening, one blessed evening, I finally discovered a real book. And then I felt like the prodigal son who had grown accustomed to "fill his belly with the husks that the swine did not eat" and now returned to his father's house and the banquet table with the fatted calf.

The book was *Thus Spoke Zarathustra*, and the way I discovered it seems strange to me to this very day. One evening I felt a sudden overwhelming desire to read a book. As the library was already closed, I went to the librarian's room and asked him for the key. I opened the library door, went in, and found myself alone in the silent room. For a long while I stood and gazed here and there at the books that stood in rows upon the shelves and in cupboards, until my eyes rested on a thick volume on the top shelf, just below the ceiling. I felt strangely drawn to take down this book, though I had never heard of it, and the author's name was unknown to me. I brought the ladder, climbed up and took the book, blew away the dust that had gathered on it during the years that no one had touched it, opened it and began to read. An hour

passed, perhaps more, and the librarian, who had begun worrying about his key, came in. He found me standing on top of the ladder with the open book in my hands and with tears running down my cheeks. That is what he saw—but he could not see that my laughing heart was full of a new and powerful joy.

I did not return to my room, for my room-mates were already asleep and I would not have been able to switch on the light. I went to the reading-room and sat there till dawn, bursting out in laughter like a baby one minute, and crying with joy the next. I laughed because of the wonder of seeing there in print, in black and white, thoughts and feelings which were my own thoughts and feelings, which expressed with such perfection my own state of mind, which seemed to have been written especially for me. Suddenly I had ceased to be alone in the world. I was like a man who after many long days of yearning and misery, finds the love he has been dreaming about. The hours passed, and when the dawn broke I was reading "The Drunken Song" where the book reaches the heights of its beauty, and when the morning light came in through the window and the sounds of the awakening village reached my ears, I came to the end of the book.

A short while after the discovery of *Zarathustra* my instincts led me to another work which became just as dear to me. This was the *New Testament*; and during the years that followed I discovered, always by the same uncanny intuition, the poetry of Hölderlin and the works of four or five other writers who are dearer to me than anything else. I cannot explain this; it may be that logic is not one of my faculties (what is logic, anyway? There is the materialist, animal shrewdness of the citizen, and there is the logic of, say, Thomas Aquinas, which is an artistic and mystic element no less than the *Kabbala*. In any case the two are very different. And, by the way, logic seems to me to be a special, camouflaged kind of clowning, and clowning is, in a sense, a sort of madness) but on the other hand I have been endowed with the faculty of intuiting things and of guessing their essence.

So I also discovered that the very people to whom I was attracted by instinct, were also attracted to each other across the boundaries of time and space and each saw the other as friend and teacher, father and forerunner. Actually this is not so surprising, for the true writers all say the same thing, and cannot but say the same thing, the thing which has been carried aloft through the ages like a sacred flame.

I was drawn to these great solitary ones for without knowing anything about their lives I could guess their solitude, their loneliness—and I identified myself with them so fully that just to think about them or to hear the sound of their names was enough to fill me with a kind of drunkenness. They were people I could understand. I could understand their divine suffering and their heavenly joy, their fiery enthusiasm, their abysmal loneliness, the dark drunkenness of their spirit, their genius. I could understand why they had not been understood during their lives, and why they had chosen to end their bodily lives by crucifixion or suicide or insanity. In my hardest hours of distress, weariness and loneliness I did not lose my faith because I was able to recall the image of the ones I loved, who were more alive and real to me than any person or anything around me. [...]

The next day I went (according to the instructions given me by the recruiting clerk) to the Notre Dame Monastery. In one of the halls, in the shadow of the sacred statues, I found some men seated at a long table, eating breakfast. One of them was the commander of the post.

He sent me, with two other men, to bring some food from a deserted shop in the vicinity. One of those who accompanied me was not much more than a boy, and the other was the sprightly old man from the recruiting office. I never discovered what his status and duties were; he must have volunteered to help the soldiers.

We went to the shop (it was wide open and in ruins) and took a tin pail full of olives and some cans of sardines, and turned back. On the way back we had to cross a narrow street, and my companions warned me that at the end of the street an Arab sniper was hiding. We let the old man cross first before the sniper could see us. The old man crossed safely with a hop, skip and jump. He stood on the opposite sidewalk, breathing deeply and smiling, and motioned us to join him.

My unknown friend and I decided to cross together. We charged forward and jumped. The next thing I remember is a greyish porridge-like substance landing on my black shoes. Then I saw the boy lying on the road, his head shattered, his brain splattered about. It was a part of his brain that had fallen on my shoe.

I stood on the sidewalk, protected by the wall, and did not think at all. The street was completely deserted.

The morning sun sent out a pleasant light, white and gold, on the houses and trees. An undisturbed stillness lay over the world.

The first to break the silence was the old man. He went somewhere and came back a few minutes later carrying a plank. We laid the corpse on the plank and carried it towards the monastery. We passed shops (some that were wide open, some that were locked, and some whose owners had not even had time to lock them during the evacuation) and apartment houses. The old man and I were the only living creatures in the whole visible world—and we were carrying a brainless corpse on a plank between us.

The plank was too short, and the dead man's legs in their spiked heavy black boots dangled from side to side and up and down, at times kicking me in the groin. It was funny. I kept imagining that he was still alive, playing games that were out of place at the moment.

When we reached Notre Dame our burden was taken from us. I went to the hall where previously I had seen the men eating. Now the hall was empty. I sat down at the table, and the cook brought me breakfast.

The walls of the hall were punctured and broken apart in some places. The windows were smashed, and pieces of stained glass were scattered over the floor.

In one corner stood a statue of Peter with his nose off. In another corner was the statue of some other saint, also deformed. I looked at them, meditating. I thought to myself that there was something more funny, more satisfying, more just, more Christian in the way the saints were standing now, with the squashed nose and the broken arm.

Then I asked myself—"What do I feel now?"

It was not fear, nor panic, nor sorrow, not weariness, nor nervousness resulting from the upset in my daily routine; nor was it amazement at seeing the new and the strange.

It was a strange feeling of liberation, almost of joy.

They were still leaving me to my loneliness. I got up and walked the length of the hall. Broken glass grated under my heels. I walked past the noseless Peter.

I went out of the hall, still without meeting anybody. The men were in the forward defence positions. I walked into a small dark room. It had only one window, narrow and high, and through its green glass a pale solitary ray of sunlight penetrated.

And then (for the ray of light fell straight on my face) I saw, in a corner, the statue of the Virgin.

As soon as I saw her, I immediately understood everything I had seen and felt earlier.

In the very midst of destruction, the destruction of material things, of the social order, of commerce, security, mediocrity, in the midst of the destruction of this world filled with distress, stood she who symbolized spiritual birth, the joyful liberation of the spirit from out [sic] material existence.

She stood there with closed eyes, white, lovely, modest, proud, smiling, sad and happy.

Her beauty was not earthly. She promised no joys of the flesh. Her radiance was not of this world. [. . .]

This book is about myself, about a lonely man, living in hiding and in silence, wearing grey clothes. And I am trying to write this book (like the saying of the wise one of the mysteries) not according to the appearance of things, but according to their spirit and meaning. I am trying to write it not with the false art of the scholars, but with the art of anger and emotion, of tears and jokes, of yearning, care and horror . . . I write of life as a parable, as of a dream.

That is why I opened my book with a dream.

To dream profoundly is, in a certain sense, genius. By dreaming man links himself to the vast dream that comprises his existence, and to penetrate profoundly into the essence of existence is the one and only meaning of genius.

So I do not speak of anything that is beyond the sphere of inner experience, beyond the soul, beyond the existence of the individual—I do not speak of society, of relations, of history, of worldly wisdom, of idols, of the hounds of hell . . . Wars have raged and ceased, political matters have raised the dust and been buried, and all that remains is the life of the single individual before the single God. To this life my story is dedicated. [. . .]

On, I go on walking, on and on. Here and there someone shoves me in the shoulder. People run and sweat. The city is noisy, but the earth, the earth is silent.

In the midst of the city din at evening I hear the silence of the earth! An abysmal silence, deeper than all depth, pregnant with secrets.

But what is the secret of the silence of the earth? In its bowels dead men are buried, in its bowels flow water and lava, fire and oil, on its back grow flowers and plants, on its back stand roads and cities, houses, fences and trees. And here I walk upon it as though there were no city and houses, no plants, no dead, no water, as though the earth were only one mighty silence, deep, profound, eternal.

Perhaps this silence is the speech of God!

Meanwhile evening comes, the streetlights come on. I walk on. For I am a lonely man, silent, reticent, wearing grey clothes. And I am free now to walk even to the end of the earth, to the end of the silence of the earth, to the end of the sufferings of the heart.

Translated by Richard Flantz.

Other works by Sadeh: *'Al matsavo shel ha-adam* (1967); *Mot avimelekh va-'aliyato ha-shamaymah bizero'ot imo* (1969); *Sefer ha-dimyonot shel ha-yehudim* (1983); *Sefer ha-agasim ha-tsehuvim* (1985).

Yehuda Amichai

1924–2000

Born Ludwig Pfeuffer in Germany, Yehuda Amichai was a poet, author, translator, and playwright. His family left Germany when he was eleven and settled in Jerusalem. During World War II, Amichai served with the British army; he also fought in Israel's War of Independence. Amichai wrote poetry, prose fiction, children's books, translations, and plays, often playing everyday language against the Hebrew Bible and the Jewish liturgy. Love and war are central themes of his writing. Amichai received the Israel Prize in 1982.

Love in Reverse
1961

Early in the morning he went out to carry out the assignment which he had been given. Jerusalem seemed to be tired and her hair was unkempt. The first revellers had reached the streets. One window was already decorated with the head of a small girl. His soul was like a truck full of empty bottles. They rattled because they were empty. But he knew that they would be refilled and his soul would be calm and very heavy.

Since early morning one lone man had been sitting by himself on the ancient wall near the highway. He was very thin and his face was already turned toward the route which the marchers would take in the afternoon. All that time he did not stir from his place. However, one hour before the start of the parade he suddenly disappeared. The ways of man are strange. A man abandons his place, gives it up, and others take it.

Niches and balconies were filled with girls and families and impatient card players. First-aid stations were set up. Young doctors, in white gowns, strutted among girls who had come to help the helpers. People were being pushed along through open courtyards and winding alleys, governed by the same law which applies to the flow of blood within the body and outside of it. Arguments began over places and over chairs which had been set up before daylight. The orderlies attempted to calm them down and to settle the arguments. The girl soldiers pushed their heavy hair beneath their berets and directed the people in directions which they did not want to follow.

The unit's medic came over to him and the two of them slipped away for a little while to drink a cup of coffee. They sat near the counter on high stools, their feet dangling. They spoke about the woman in the house at the edge of the world. There were no mirrors in the café; only the metal coffee maker, in which their reflections were distorted. Suddenly he asked the doctor: What do we want out of life? What are we seeking? The doctor was startled. He had studied for many years and knew how to answer a variety of questions, but who knows what people want out of life? They stirred the coffee. Then unconsciously they switched cups. They got down from the stools and each one paid for the other's coffee, for they were elated and confused on account of that woman. They were like two roses on one stem. They went out into the street. He wanted to ask the world where its weak spot was, as they had asked Samson. He felt that the powerful world was almost like a human being.

Close to parade time his friend came over, the one who had been through the wars with him. This friend hid his eyes behind dark sunglasses; the world would have a darker view of him. He was always sad. The more he succeeded the sadder he became. His sadness was his fortress and from that fortress he looked at the world through the sunglasses.

Now they sat at the edge of the sidewalk on a side street behind the wall of people that faced the parade route. They sat beside the murky still waters of the twisting, swirling festival, among barbed wire and cast-off paper and peelings. Dust covered them. His friend spoke in a hoarse voice. When he called his attention to the hoarseness of his voice, his friend answered that he was not hoarse from his own shouting, but from the shouting of the world around him. They spoke about their generation of two wars, a generation which had no time to adjust: always early, always late. He said to his friend: But we deserve it, we deserve it.—What do we deserve?—We deserve it!

Thus the two were sad as two dogs standing near a tree. Then they returned to their duties and the festival rolled on down the street.

In the evening he went to see if the woman had recovered. She had. Her eyes were slightly crossed and her lips were full and her mouth was large and almost the shape of a brick. Her head resembled the head of the Queen of Egypt, Nefrititi. Her nose was elongated and her nostrils dilated in order to breathe in his fragrance and that of the world. She said that on the next day he would suffer a total eclipse. He repaired the shutter and then he ate and drank and was silent. He would continue to live, out of habit. He would continue to live as a child continues sobbing long after the source of pain has been forgotten.

Summer arrived several days later. [. . .]

It seemed to him that during those days at the start of the summer they had been at the shore together. But he was not sure of this, for at that time the bond of their love had already loosened and letters had already been sent, for theirs had indeed been a love in reverse.

It seemed to him that they had been at the shore, that hand in hand they had run across the sand still bereft of people, that they had run thundering like galloping horses, hair flying, to the ruins of the ancient pillars by the sea. The soles of their feet were black with pitch and they were clinging gently to each other, near the sea, where the hotels go down to the shore and fishing nets are spread out to dry.

After that they were in Jaffa or in Acco and they walked in the footsteps of children, hiding and going into the courtyard of a house; then they went inside the house and saw that the sea dwelled on the bottom floor, that it went up and down in the rooms with the motion of the waves outside.

But they did not have the blind confidence of the first silent nights, the nights of the end which for them actually was the beginning which brought them to the true end and past it.

For a man may leave a house, but the house does not leave him. He is still there, with its walls and everything that hangs on them, with its rooms and with its doors which are carefully closed, or the house expands and becomes highways on which he who left the house will walk.

The summer waxed and the celebrations were drawn out endlessly. Due to their joy, people celebrating did not have time to lift their heads before a new wave of joy came to engulf them again.

He looked at the city and at the color of its banners. He looked at the city whose costs of destruction and rebuilding he bore, as all its children. Sometimes he wanted to sink as she had, with prophets prophesying and flames and clouds of smoke. [. . .]

The two who found each other in the house on the night of nights were never in it together again; they were not together anywhere. They were already immersed in the great forgetting which exists before events and after them and they awaited each other as one waits for someone still unknown, someone who lives in the burning imagination and in dreams. And they foretold their pasts and their futures, each one in his place. And they used all those short words, such as already, still, not yet, before, a little more, afterward, once—all those short words which melt in life and sweeten it or add bitterness like wormwood.

And so it happened that one day he was sitting in the garden of the King David Hotel. The Israeli flag waved in the center of the roof, the French flag to the right, and the weather instruments to the left. Opposite him stood the cypress trees which hid the Old City. In the late afternoon they began to play. A brazen lady pianist and a sad violinist came out on the balcony; but their music was scattered by the winds. What do people want out of life? He did not ask it in a loud voice, for he sat alone. They were calling people to the telephone. They called them over the loudspeaker. "*G'veret Tufel, b'vakashah l'telefon.*" Or in English, "*Meester Kleinman, telefon pleez.*" Sometimes someone got up after the announcement and sometimes no one got up. And it gives one something to think about how people wander and come from distant places and meet by chance. Chance gives way to destiny. Sometimes chance can choke a man. Sometimes it is possible to feel the stitching between chance and destiny. Sometimes the stitching is soft and sometimes it is hard and coarse. And then destiny again becomes chance and it ends only at the end.

The woman sat in the easy chair, turning the pages of a thick book. Every turning of a white page looked like wings trying to fly. How did she come by her slanting eyes and her elongated head? This time her long hair was piled high in thick curls atop her head.

Once more his thoughts were like two roses on one stem. And he knew that from now on there would be only letters and later empty pages and later the after-forgetting which is like the forgetting-of-before.

The switchboard operators changed. A girl with a soft, deep voice was now on duty. He wanted them to call him, too, but they did not. For him the year of celebrations had ended and with it the year of the hair

undone which fell loosely to the hips. He felt that he was close to the heart of the year and he could hear it beating, more and more faintly, like retreating footsteps.

Translated by Jules Harlow.

Other works by Amichai: *Not of This Time, Not of This Place* (1963); *Amen* (1977); *The Poetry of Yehuda Amichai* (2015).

Shlomo Kalo

1928–2014

Shlomo Kalo was born in Sofia, Bulgaria, and was sent to a concentration camp during World War II. In 1946, he began his studies in medicine at the Charles University in Prague, trained as a pilot, and moved to Israel in 1949. He was a microbiologist and head of medical laboratories while also writing and gaining renown as a poet and short-story writer. He produced some eighty works, including translations. After undergoing a turn to Eastern religions, Kalon established the DAAT publishing house in 1969.

The Pile
1962

The next day Marcel Schwartz registered at the labor exchange. [. . .]

Ten days later he heard clearly and explicitly: Marcel Schwartz! With trembling hands, he took his work notice, went home to his mother, and called to her:

"Work, Mom! I went to the exchange every day, and I finally got a job! Look, Mom—I got a job!"

The heavy-fleshed woman didn't answer. She just stood there and set the table for his supper. [. . .]

"Aren't you happy, Mom? Don't you see—I got a job! A job in the municipality! Surely it's not an important job, but maybe I'll get promoted fast. After all, in the municipality, a guy can advance easily! Especially these days, when everything is expanding, and new jobs pop up every day. Mom, I have a good chance of getting a permanent job!"

The woman didn't answer at all. She sat in her corner and stared in front of her, until Marcel Schwartz cried out: "You're still silent? Aren't you at all interested in the fact that your son got a job? Quit that silence of yours already! Talk, say something!"

The woman answered him softly: "I'll say something when the time comes."

He wiped the bits of food off the table and walked around in the room impatiently. Finally he said: "Now you have to stop working in that factory—you should stop tomorrow! I'll earn enough for you and for me. Stop working, Mom." He turned to her softly. "I'll keep the job I got! I'll show everyone—you, my brother, my brother's wife, his children, and the whole world, that I'm capable of it. . . . Be kind to me, Mom—stop working, from tomorrow!"

The woman was silent.

The next day Marcel Schwartz reported to the clerk at the municipality. The clerk took the job notice, scrutinized Marcel, and spat out: "You look too skinny to me . . ." [. . .] "A lot of people worked here before and didn't do anything. A whole lot! The municipality paid them wages, and they didn't work. Not from weakness, but from laziness. This job, which a person can do in fifteen days, has already cost the municipality sixty workdays, more than sixty!"

"What's the job?" asked Marcel Schwartz.

"Work in a neglected pile of garbage."

"What were they supposed to do?"

"To throw the garbage into the pit next to the pile," explained the clerk. "The garbage truck drivers didn't pour the city's garbage into the pit that was meant for it, but next to it. They poured it out next to it, not into it. [. . .] Garbage collectors were the ones who made the pile with their shovels and pails! And why do you think they did it?" The clerk fixed his eyes on Marcel Schwartz's face and added, as though to answer himself: "To look for treasures! [. . .] They dug around and dug around in the garbage until they made a big pile." [. . .]

"What will my job be?" asked Marcel Schwartz.

"Your job will be to throw the garbage into the pit that was dug for that, and you've been given fifteen days of work."

"But you said you already paid more than sixty days of salary, and the pile is the way it always was."

"Yes, but I also said, that according to the best of calculations, getting rid of the pile shouldn't take more than fifteen workdays, except that the workers had no conscience, and they were lazy."

"Wasn't there a supervisor?"

"No, there was no supervisor. The workers used to write down their works days with me, and you'll do the same."

Marcel Schwartz approached the pile, walked around it, inspected it closely, breathing the stench into his nostrils. Finally, he hurried back to the clerk. [. . .]

"What's the matter?" asked the clerk.

The young man answered: "I'm prepared to sign a contract regarding removal of the pile. So far the pile has cost you around four hundred pounds, and I'll commit myself to removing it in a week for a hundred and fifty pounds."

"But I told you, getting rid of the pile won't take more than fifteen workdays!"

"But still, it has already cost you more than sixty workdays. If I do the work, add another fifteen workdays, and the total will be seventy-five. And your expenses will come to more than four hundred pounds. And the stench will be here all the time, and there will be a danger to public health. And if one day a citizens' committee attacks the municipality, a lot of clerks will be fired."

"But fifteen . . ." the clerk objected. Marcel Schwartz didn't let him finish his sentence:

"Fifteen workdays costs you about ninety pounds," he explained, "and in order for the work to be done, there has to be a supervisor here. That is, another fifteen workdays, at least, for a total of a hundred and eighty pounds. And I'm only asking for a hundred and fifty!"

For a little while the clerk stood as though rooted to the ground, with his mouth open. After he recovered, he said: "And if you don't do the work as promised?"

"We'll make a signed contract! So the municipality will have a valid document!"

The contract was signed the following day. [. . .] After signing the contract, Marcel Schwartz went to the factory and called his mother out. She saw him and asked:

"Did you quit already?"

"Forget about that, Mom," Marcel Schwartz answered and continued softly, "I signed a contract with the municipality, and I have to go to a *moshav* [agricultural settlement] immediately to take care of my business. Yes, Mom, to take care of my business with the municipality. I need a pound."

"Don't ask me for money," said the woman and returned to the factory in a decisive manner.

Marcel Schwartz watched her for a long time and then went out to the main road, waving his hand to every passing car, until later in the afternoon a truck-driver picked him up. Marcel Schwartz went to the *moshav* where he had worked two years earlier and found the man he needed there. He said: "I have great manure for you, tons of great manure, at a very cheap price!"

The man answered gravely: "Let's take a look at the bargain, and then we'll talk!" [. . .]

They reached the pile, and the man, who was tall, with a gray mustache drooping over the corners of his mouth and thick eyebrows, said: "I can't pay more than fifty pounds for this pile, because there's more debris in it than manure." [. . .]

"Fine, so this stink will be yours!" Marcel Schwartz agreed with a broad smile, and they shook hands.

One evening Marcel Schwartz went out to roam the streets with his pockets full of money. [. . .] He went into a store and bought a pink bead necklace made of material unknown to him and a silver pin; in another store he bought a wind-up toy truck, a toy jeep with spring; and in a third store, he bought a light colored necktie of fine cloth.

Marcel Schwartz walked into his mother's house. The heavy-fleshed woman was sitting in her chair and mumbled a reply to his greeting.

"Mom, I bought this for you!" he said and took out the necklace of pink beads.

She said to him: "Is this how you clear your conscience?"

Marcel Schwartz stood still, and his face paled. Then he raised his arm and threw the necklace down on the cement floor. The necklace slammed down hard, the beads came loose and scattered in every which direction with a dull sound.

The woman called out: "No, son! No, son! [. . .] Forgive me, son! Forgive me! Please!"

Then she knelt down and started gathering up the little beads. The sound of her weeping ceased. She said: "These beads will be very becoming for me! This is the first time since I married that I've gotten a present!" Her awkward body trembled.

"Yes," her son suddenly answered softly. "I chose that color, because I knew it would become you. You're very pale, and pink suits you. I bought this tie for my brother, the pin for his wife, and the toys for the boys. My business deal was a success, so I bought all these things. As for the beads, you can keep whatever you pick. Give the other presents to their recipients. I'm going away, because I have no place here." [. . .]

Marcel Schwartz left his house, walking in the darkness with confidence, for he knew the area very well. He got to the widow's kiosk, approached it, and spoke in a whisper so that no one else would hear him: "Do you want to marry me?"

She looked at his face, very seriously, and said: "Are you crazy, Mr. Marcel?" and she turned to her customers.

He picked up his feet and returned to the darkness of the winding streets.

The pile was removed. Within a week it was removed, as Marcel Schwartz had promised. A tractor went around with a young man driving it. The tractor would plunge its shovel into the pile, take a bite, scoop it up and figure out what was worth keeping and what wasn't. It would pour what was worth keeping into a dump truck that was parked nearby and throw the rest into the pit. Within a week the entire pile was gone, and on the sixth evening the only thing left was a wooden post bearing a sign saying it was forbidden to deposit any waste in the area. But the tractor also took that wooden post in its steel jaws, raised it up, and threw it into the gaping mouth of the pit.

Translated by Jeffrey M. Green.

Other works by Kalo: *Atar* (2001); *The Day Is Coming* (2013); *Lili* (2013).

Ehud Ben-Ezer
b. 1936

Writer and critic Ehud Ben-Ezer was born to a founding family of Petaḥ Tikvah. He studied Kabbalah and philosophy at Hebrew University in Jerusalem, and he served in the Naḥal in 1955 and 1956 and as a paramedic during the Six-Day War. After working as a teacher in the Negev, he began writing fiction about his own experiences and those of his ancestors. In addition to his own prolific literary output, Ben-Ezer works as a literary critic, publishing in a number of Israeli periodicals. He has won many literary distinctions in Israel and abroad, including multiple prizes from the prime minister and two fellowships at Oxford University.

The Stone Quarry
1963

Chapter 30

BEDLAM

Nissim Levy dodged out through the back fence. He said goodbye to Danino, but instead of running away, he stood still, not far from there, and tried to pick up some words from the commotion.

He managed to hear Danino calling on the microphone, "Comrades, comrades," and said to himself: "Now he'll explain to them. But what? Never mind. They'll understand, and maybe they'll be scared. They know that it's all just circumstantial. After all, all of them sat with him yesterday in the café of Abu Snin, and all of them were witness to the fact that he was there from the moment he came home from work until late in the evening. He is not guilty, not at all, and he was not the last man to sleep with her. Danino will explain it to them." [. . .]

One of the children called out suddenly in the darkness, just next to him: "Here he is, standing right here, listening to everything being said about him!"

Nissim was terrified. [. . .]

"Where?"

"Where is he?"

"Murderer!"

"Despicable!"

He heard voices from the yard and the alley: "He's a big prick!"—"He's a big prick!"—"We'll hang him on his prick!" [. . .]

"Yes, I'm here!" he wanted to shout, "standing here, ready to explain, ready to bring witnesses for everything, everything. But where are the witnesses? Are they against me along with the rest of the crowd? Impossible. Since someone has to explain that I was all right, someone has to understand me and defend me when I can't do it myself. Should I go home, to Zipporah? She knows everything, she heard and she understood and she knows I'm not guilty. She will be able to explain, and if they see she is defending me, they won't be able to accuse me anymore." [. . .]

And Nissim turned towards his house at his usual pace. [. . .]

"Run away," one of the children called out.

"You bastard, we'll gouge out your eyes!" another shouted.

Hadido ran and two husky men grabbed him by their arms. He breathed with all his might and his legs dragged behind him as if they were not his.

"Leave me alone!" he whispered, "I'm choking, I'm dead." [. . .]

"I'm afraid!" Hadido called out.

"What are you afraid of?" They said to him, "Idiot! He has to be punished for what he did to your daughter. He's despicable."

"You yourselves are despicable too!" Hadido said. [. . .]

Halifa approached him, sweating and excited. She had been walking among the leaders the whole time, shouting with all her might. "Tell us, Hadido," she said

as she beat time with her hand, "Des–pic–ab–le–vy–who fucked my daughter!"

And all the crowd was with her.

"Wonderful, Halifa!"—"Give it to him!"

Hadido was silent. Someone said, "He's crying!"

Halifa stood opposite him and repeated the refrain. Someone stuck an elbow in his chest, and at last, in a weak and drunk voice, he repeated the refrain.

"Wonderful!" Everybody shouted. "Where is Nissim Levy? We'll go grab him!" [. . .]

And they went in a big group led by Halifa and Hadido. The others were carrying boxes and sticks and sheets of tin and they beat on them to the rhythm of their walk. [. . .]

Those up front repeated their cry without a pause: "Des–pic–ab–le–vy—we will kill him." [. . .]

By the time they reached Nissim's home they were already looking like a large, organized, and violent body, with leaders and followers, slogans and war shouts, vanguard and rear guard, and it was impossible to recognize in them the joyous congregation from the wedding which had filled the yard of Danino only half an hour ago.

Nissim Levy's house was surrounded by dozens of children who stood and threw stones against the walls, the windows, and the doors. The building was completely illuminated and inside Nissim was running around shouting.

"Zipporah! Zipporah!"

People were rushing to the yard, crushing the flower beds, digging up stones with their hands and feet from the sidewalks and the pathways in the garden and throwing everything they could find at the house: cans, flowerpots, boxes, plants, hoes, and logs. Then they began to break down the fruit trees and turned over a small chicken coop that stood in the corner. Some of the children grabbed the opportunity and carried away tools, a wheelbarrow, and a few chickens who were running around in shock, as well as fruit and other sundry objects that were lying around the yard. [. . .]

They had not yet dared to enter the house. Only a few broke into the kitchen from the back and took out a few loaves of bread for the crowd. The bread passed from hand to hand, they broke off pieces from them, tore them out of each other's hands with great lust, as if they had not just returned from a sumptuous wedding, but that the bread had saved them from immense hunger after a long period of dearth. [. . .]

In one of the wings of the house, Nissim's children wailed and shouted: "Mommy! Daddy! People, go away! Evil People!" [. . .]

Stones fell into the house through the windows, chipping the table, the chairs, and the floor, breaking the glass sideboard, glass table top, and the wine glasses in the sideboard. From every corner were seen groups of excited people who were standing and cursing him and throwing stones. The yard was filled with them.

They invaded deep into the house. Some were already standing in the hallway while others continued raiding the kitchen, dividing the goods among the crowd. [. . .]

Suddenly a headlight illuminated the street.

"Police!"—"The police are here!"—Those next to the gate shouted, but before the rumor managed to pass through the crowd others began calling: "It's just a taxi, not a police car. Nothing to be afraid of."

Some of the crowd ran out to the street, continuing to shout and wave their arms. The car crept along silently and stopped by the gate. It was immediately surrounded by people who stuck their heads in and waved their fists.

"Is this the home of Nissim Levy?" the driver asked as he parked the car carefully so as not to injure the people. A stone passed by his head, and he immediately opened all the windows.

"What are you doing?" Safrai cried.

"Better they should stick their heads inside than throw stones at the windows. Let me take care of this situation, I know what to do."

Safrai was white as chalk: "What is going on here?"

People peeked into the car. Someone shouted. "Halifa, here comes your husband's man! Come here, ask him where your husband is?"

"What are you talking about?" Safrai cried, "have you gone mad?"

Halifa came running from the yard and approached the car. "Who is this?" she asked.

"Here, here, Halifa. He is the man sitting in the back."

"Let me pass, I'll get in and talk to him," she said. Her robe was torn, her hands were dirtied with kerosene, soot, and dust. Her hair was disheveled and her eyes burned with hatred. [. . .]

"Who are you?" she asked.

"It's the clerk from the quarry," the voices behind her called out. "Moshe David told us today that he spoke with him and you . . . you told us that he was delayed in town because of him."

"Where is Moshe David? Where's my husband?" she asked him.

"Excuse me, Madam, I don't know your husband," Safrai tried to answer her politely. [. . .]

Halifa crawled into the back seat and cried out, "What have you done with my husband? You murderer, murderer!"

Safrai was pushed further and further into the opposite door, but suddenly he felt hands from behind, grabbing him and pressing him against the window. A shudder went through his bones. [. . .]

Suddenly they pulled him out of the door against which he was pressed and they held his arms, and Halifa crawled out after him from the car, jumped up on him and began to scratch his face and kick his body and shout:

"Murderer! Murderer! Give me back my husband. You wanted to fire him from his job, you despicable person! You came to Nissim Levy to do business at our expense, you idiot! But we've already killed him and we'll kill you, you dummy, you . . ." [. . .]

All the time the driver was shouting: "Leave him alone! Madmen! He's the man who works for you more than anyone else in the city!" [. . .]

"Shut up," they told him, "before we burn up your car!"

And Hadido, who came out of the yard as well, approached him and asked:

"Maybe you saw my daughter's head?"

"Madman!" The driver shouted at him.

"Don't call him crazy!" They cried at him and suddenly drew knives from out of the darkness. "His daughter was raped and killed. Don't call him crazy or we'll start thinking that you raped her."

The driver was frightened and was silent. Later, he asked quietly, "Who is she?"

"Hadido's daughter," they answered him. "Do you remember the little girl from town?"

The driver paled. Fortunately, it was not noticed in the darkness.

"Ay! ay!" Safrai began shouting. "Aayyyy! . . ."

Someone came running and cried: "Now it really is the police! Run away! Run away!"

From far away the siren could be heard. A strong fire broke out in Nissim Levy's living room, billowing out strong clouds of heavy black smoke because they had poured kerosene on the furniture. A few had begun to turn over the car that brought Safrai.

The siren came closer with a long, undulating wail as if it was coming to announce something. The people stood for a moment, shocked by the rising flames, and then scattered in fright: "Run away! Run away!"

Safrai lay on the ground, moaning.

Translated by Karen Alkalay-Gut.

Other works by Ben-Ezer: *Anshey Sedom* (1968); *Lo la-giborim ha-milḥamah* (1971); *Ha-pri ha-asur* (1977); *Ha-sheket ha-nafshi* (1979).

Shimon Ballas

The Maʿabarah *(The Immigrant Transit Camp)* 1964

Pounding, heavy feet climbed the muddy path up the hill that looked out over wild bushes. The walkers' steps sank in the earth next to each other and on top of each other on the path upward, in the form of a broken arc, up to the entrance to a wooden shed, which stood, wrapped in the last light of day. [. . .] When they reached the entrance of the shed, the walkers stopped without going inside. Some of them spread this way and that and stood at the open windows on either side of the shed. There was no room inside it for the sole of another foot. Crowded and pressed together, the assembled raised their faces toward the cantor's platform. [. . .]

Ḥayim Vaʿad stood on the platform. His swarthy, shrunken face glowed with the flickering light of the candles, and his small eyes were riveted on the noisy, impatient crowd. [. . .] He extended his right hand to impose silence. [. . .]

Slowly the voices died down. The assembled pinned their eyes on him as he wiped off the sweat and took a deep breath. He removed a scrap of paper from his pocket, placed it on the lectern, but didn't look at it.

"Ladies and gentlemen," he gathered all his strength. "We have not gathered here to make noise. Not to give speeches and issue proclamations. Not to arouse emotions and speak falsely. One purpose stands before our eyes, one high and exalted purpose, without a stain, without anything to do with the pursuit of lucre. Our wish is your wish. Our concerns are you concerns. We have come to you not to give speeches but to discuss seriously, to find out your opinion, to act together for the good of the whole encampment."

His words, spoken in pure Arabic, silenced the last of the voices. [. . .]

"Our concern is the unity of the *maʿabarah*. We must act as one. That is our concern!" Ḥayim shouted and waved his clenched fist. [. . .]

"You have all come to the meeting with the desire to change our bad situation. But how can we change it? Everyone knows that we can't pretend to be innocent. Gentlemen, we, too, are to blame. Especially we ourselves, who were thrown from a high position down to the lowest, from the life of city gentlefolk to the life of desert dwellers, from an affluent, proud life to the life of slaves who scrape by on charity. Yes, ladies and gentlemen, we, too, are to blame. We work and sweat, and the masters throw us a banknote that isn't enough to satisfy our hunger and quench our thirst. And what do we do? We sit in our houses and slander each other." [. . .]

Silence reigned in the shed. Countless eyes looked at him expectantly; he felt victorious.

"We're embroiled in quarrels. One man spills his brother's blood. That's something we know how to do!" He threw this out into the tense atmosphere. [. . .]

"Ladies and gentlemen, it's time to act! The Yiddish [Ashkenazi Jews] are laughing at us. They say we're savage, lazy. And we're on our own. No one speaks a common tongue with his brother."

"What do you propose?" the voice of an elderly man was heard from one of the open windows.

"We have to impose order on the *maʿabarah*!" Ḥayim replied with a shout. "We have to impose order on the *maʿabarah*! We have to put an end to the violence!"

Once again his voice didn't reach the back rows. The silence was broken all at once, and chaos ruled again. [. . .]

"Qui-et!" Ḥayim screamed and pounded on the lectern. [. . .]

"I haven't finished my speech yet, and you're already making noise. Wait a moment. I said—hand in hand. One hand—meaning one party. Yes. There is no place for party divisions among us. Parties divide us. And we won't be unified if every one of us joins one party or another. Thank God—there are plenty of parties in this country! But let me ask you a question: who stands at the head of those parties? The same Yiddish who ridicule us. On the contrary—show me a single party headed by an oriental Jew. If there's a party like that, I'll be the first to join it . . ."

About half a dozen men sat on the only bench in front of the podium, and Eliyahu ʿEyni sat in the middle of them, bending his head over his worry beads. [. . .] Eliyahu 'Eyni wasn't at all at ease. He looked at his large, yellow worry beads, fingered them two by two, and sank deep into his own thoughts. The whole matter wasn't to his liking. This noisy meeting, Ḥayim's speech, the inclusion of young good-for-nothings and ignoramuses in such an important decision—everything was faulty. [. . .] Ḥayim's fiery speech. He knew how to talk, but his fire left smoke. It was stifling here! He raised his eyes from the beads to the speaker. [. . .] What are you shouting there? Who needs this speech? Who needs this noisy, stinking crowd? Who told you to gather this rabble? You came and said it would be a quiet meeting. No speeches would be given. We'd nominate a committee, the participants would vote, and everyone would go home. And now you've been speaking for a long time! Did you consult anyone? You're acting on your own initiative! You want to be the head of us all. The chief. He stamped his foot again, clicked his beads and threw them from hand to hand. [. . .]

"Ladies and gentlemen, silence please! I'll read you the names of the candidates for the *ma'abarah* committee."

"There are also nominations!" the same voice again.

"First listen to the names," said Ḥayim in conciliatory tones, without looking at Na'aman.

"That isn't how it's done. First you hear nominations. Then you have the vote," Na'aman objected.

Voices of agreement were heard from the crowd.

"You have to write down all the names," voices called out.

"And if the names you suggest are already on the list?" Ḥayim asked in the same conciliatory tone, with a broad smile on his face.

At that moment Eliyahu 'Eyni leaped up and rushed to the podium. "I want to say something!" he spoke in a trembling voice, pushing Ḥayim Va'ad aside and gripping the lectern with both hands. "I want to say . . . we invited . . . we intended to invite . . ."

His tongue was as heavy as a stone. His voice died down. He swallowed his saliva and tried to go on, but he couldn't. A heavy burden lay on his chest. For a moment he felt as if he were fainting. Ḥayim, who still hadn't recovered from his astonishment, stared at him, frozen in place. Again the room was in an uproar.

"We didn't come to hear shouting," finally his tongue was loosened. "We have to choose a committee, and that's all . . ."

"What do you want?" someone shouted.

"You have to know—there's no place for good-for-nothings on the committee! No place for good-for-nothings!" His voice grew weaker, and his head hung low. Ḥayim Va'ad tried to support him. Some of his followers hurried to him from the bench, but he didn't let go of the lectern. He pounded on it with his fists and screamed: "There's no room for good-for-nothings!" The crowd roared with impatience, and voices cried out from every side. Ḥayim let go of 'Eyni and leaped nimbly onto the bench.

"What's the matter with him?"

"What does he want?"

"Did you make him the head of the committee?"

The voices closed in on him, and the crowd shook him from side to side.

"Patience. He's angry," he tried to calm their anger.

"Did he lose his marbles?" one of them asked in ridicule.

"He called us good-for-nothings! That owl-face!"

"Did you make him the head of the committee? Couldn't you find anyone else?"

"Let's go. We have no business with crazy men," a middle-aged man shouted and started shoving the people around him.

"Ladies and gentlemen! We'll continue right away. This is just a short incident!" Ḥayim's voice pleaded.

No one listened to him. Everyone was making noise. Laughter broke out here and there. Someone spat out in mockery: "Not our committee!"

The man who had made his way to the door waved his arms. "What do you mean, continue! What will we continue?"

The others streamed after him. "Let's go. There's no reason to stay!"

A lot of them turned toward the exit. The shed began to discharge its occupants.

"Gentlemen, it's just an incident. It will pass," Ḥayim Va'ad kept imploring them.

Translated by Jeffrey M. Green.

Hanoch Bartov

1926–2016

Hanoch Bartov was born in Petaḥ Tikvah the year after his parents immigrated to Palestine from Poland. At age seventeen, he joined the Jewish Brigade of the British army as a medic, helping Holocaust survivors to recover. He subsequently served in the Haganah and then the Israel Defense Forces from 1947 to 1949. After the war, he studied at the Hebrew University in Jerusalem before beginning his career as a writer. His journalism and fiction drew on his wartime experiences in both Europe and Israel. In the 1960s, he acted as the attaché for cultural affairs at the Israeli embassy in London. He received the Israel Prize in 2010 for his contributions to literature.

The Brigade
1965

I was sitting next to Brodsky, and Sonnenshein was sitting opposite us, near the back of the truck. From the moment we had crossed into Germany, something had happened to him. His pipe never left his mouth; as soon as it went out he quickly filled it again.

He took short, nervous puffs and kept his eyes fixed on the landscape outside the tarpaulin flaps. The look of calm intelligence that had appealed to me so strongly had gone from his eyes, and even their color seemed different, almost black. From time to time his facial muscles tightened in a kind of tense expectation, waiting for the next familiar scene to be revealed. Unusually for him, he talked a lot, describing the places we were about to pass before we reached them. "I know Bavaria well," he said. "I spent a lot of time in these parts when I was young. I studied for a while in Freiburg—much further west, and afterwards I stayed in Munich. Look," he cried suddenly in open emotion, "we're coming to the junction. We'll be there in a minute. The right-hand road goes down to Munich."

We took the road to the left, and Sonnenshein made haste to announce that not far from here was Oberammergau. There was something astonishing about this liveliness, about his joy whenever he discovered that his memory had not failed him, that every spot and road was so deeply etched in his heart, although—so he said—sixteen or seventeen years had passed since then. It's not just the memory, I said to myself. I suppose he must have been a young man then, almost as young as I am today, and now he's reliving the passionate feelings of his youth. It's not just the memory—deep feelings are rising to the surface, and you can see on his face how he's experiencing now only what happened then, and not what happened in the meantime. He pronounced all the place names with a distinct German accent, for as he had told me, he had been educated in that language. Prague Jewry was an important center of German culture.

"What's Oberammergau?" I imitated his accent, spitting out the rs and dwelling on the long vowels.

In Sonnenshein's eyes I saw that he had noted the mockery in my voice, and also the reasons for it. The muscles of his face slackened and his expression grew more composed.

"It's a small town, or a large village, where for the past three hundred years or more the villagers have been performing a Passion Play, or religious mystery pageant. It's not theater, but mystery, and both the participants and the spectators identify with the sufferings of Jesus, the savior who was crucified by the Jews. I was there once. And I found the spectacle with the hundreds of ecstatic peasants profoundly moving." Sonnenshein went on looking at me, but he spoke to everyone. "Thousands of people, students like me, enthusiasts of folk art, ordinary people, sat and identified. The thing goes on for hours, and as I sat there watching I felt myself filling with shame. At my Jewishness. And fear. That someone would discover the mark of Cain printed on my brow and they would drag me off to Golgotha overlooking the beautiful scenery of Oberammergau . . . It was only years later that I understood what that terrible place preserves . . . People say that Nazism began in the beer halls of Munich. Maybe so. But the deep roots of the murder of the Jews can be seen here, on the border of the Tyrol and Bavaria, in Oberammergau . . ." and his finger hung in the air, pointing.

We drove on, almost without stopping. The sun began sinking over the trees, but the twilight here went on for ages, not like at home. Night refused to fall, and the convoy refused to stop. Sonnenshein had concentrated my thoughts and made them even more confused. Give me hate, dear God, stick it in my body like nails, make it so much a part of my flesh that I'll scream, that I'll never be able to get rid of it.

Suddenly we stopped.

"Concentration camp!" cried Ostreicher, and we all jumped up and crowded to see.

The green summer lapped the road, and in the distance the forests darkened. But right here, next to the road, there were high barbed-wire fences and watchtowers of black wood. On the other side of the fence were two-story houses, which looked in the twilight like blocks of smoldering coal. Maybe there were huts too, I don't know. The convoy didn't stop, but it didn't move forward either. The drivers in front of us seemed to have slowed down of their own accord, ignoring the officers' commands to drive on. The trucks crept forward, hundreds of trucks, as if they were driving against the wind. And on the roadside for a few dozen meters stood people, waving hands, hats, and scarves, and shouting in broken voices. The people appeared suddenly, and only when our truck drove past the camp gates did we see how many they were. The gate was open and from the inside of the camp more of them came running. I cannot reconstruct those few moments in the land of the black forest, because we fell into them so suddenly, at the end of such a crazy day. One cry galvanized both them and us. Perhaps they sang, perhaps they called out, but among the sounds of singing and shouting two words rang out, "Shalom" and "Eretz"—that is to say, not as if they were shouted again and again, but as one long, continuous cry, from the moment the first people were seen on the road until both voices and faces were lost in the distance.

Or perhaps it was different. Who can remember how and what really happened? Wellsprings of emotion gushed out of us and poured into a cataract at the gates of the camp. We shouted at them like madmen, and someone remembered the empty ration boxes. Piles of sweets we couldn't stomach any more had accumulated in the empty boxes. Now we all jostled and shoved to throw a handful of our own into the little troop of Jews we had suddenly discovered, who were already receding into the distance. For two days we had been traveling in enemy territory, with stony faces, and suddenly we could be glad, see welcoming faces, boys whose eyes went out to us, women weeping with joy. Take, children, take sweets. Take, people, take cigarettes from us. Hey, friend, catch a pack. You'll get one too, here, catch! Take whatever we manage to give you before this moment passes.

We didn't manage much. The convoy moved slowly, as if it were stuck to the fence, but our truck was already past the last boy waving with all his strength at the truck behind us. We hadn't even managed to throw all the sweets at them, and now we sank back onto our damp gear. We had been cut off from the sight as if by a sword, and a strange silence fell on the truck, as if the picture still had to fix itself inside us, without being disturbed.

Translated by Dalya Bilu.

Other works by Bartov: *Ha-ḥeshbon ve-ha-nefesh* (1953); *Everyone Had Six Wings* (1954); *An Israeli in the Court of Saint James* (1969); *Whose Little Boy Are You?* (1970).

Amalia Kahana-Carmon

The Glass Bell
1966

Opposite the windowsill is a shuttered curtain and a wasteland of chimneys. The street is being drained of life. A double-decker bus with gleaming windows of light passes by the corner. A woman pushes a babyless baby carriage. [. . .]

In the park, back-to-back with my bench, sat two teenage girls. Perhaps two English girls from the nearby workers' quarter, I surmised. Waitresses, hair salon aides, or salesgirls in a shopping emporium and today is their day off. Overhearing a bit of their conversation, I knew that I was mistaken. They were speaking Hebrew:

"You can't imagine. He's living on hope."—"Hope, hope. But what can you live on?"—"That's the thing. Washing dishes three nights a week. And now, the exams are two months away. He won't go and take them."

Their conversation did not arouse my interest in the least. The first speaker got up and walked away. The second one remained seated. She opened a textbook and began to read it, looking around aimlessly. A large black dog passed by. There was a father with a little girl skipping rope. The streetlamp lighter and his flashlight. People in the distance like paint drops moving among tree trunks, within the pink shining vapors of twilight.

That is how I actually met Abigail. Last Monday.

Infinite picture windows cast their light on sidewalks desolate and silent like the ocean floor. They are portholes of sunken ships. Soundlessly, human shadows pass them by, like transparent fish.

"There is something unique about you," said Abigail. Here began the plot of the story.

I listened and laughed to myself: I was rejuvenated after wearing myself out. However, something kept recoiling. It seemed that I began believing. In what? I don't know. It was as though a glass bell were placed over us both, separating us from everything else. [. . .]

"I don't know to what extent this has to do with it. But what do you think? Is the hole in the right thumb of the evening-newspaper vendor's glove there to better count out the change?"

Everything is pertinent. The headlines written in white chalk on the blackboard, the lady newspaper vendor, her hoarse throat wrapped in a checkered sweater, the small man leaning in shoddy elegance on the street sign, his hat askew. I buy some roasted chestnuts and share them with Abigail. A woman passes by, a cloth-covered basket on her arm, peeking out from which is the head of a delightful kitten with curious eyes. Abigail calls me to account: "Your room is not 'a room of one's own,' in the words of Virginia Woolf, you know. For convenience's sake, from now on let's call it AROOO [A Room of One's Own]. The study of law, should you continue with it or not, is still not AROOO."

To my surprise, I listen to the verdict calmly. It seems that I believe, without knowing in what, doesn't it? Once again, Abigail gave the impression of understanding. That's what I said—a glass bell was placed over us both, separating us from the rest of the world.

However, Abigail has to travel to Oxford this week. To look for some manuscript, as per her professor's instructions, she said.

In the office.

I called for our stenographer, to dictate a letter to her. She came out of the adjoining room, our manager's office.

"Is he in his office?" I asked routinely.

"No," she replied, "but a young lady is there, waiting for him."

I put the draft down. How did I know it was Abigail?

It *was* Abigail, sitting amidst piles of the *Tel Hai* pamphlet, published by the Small Zionist Library.

"Perhaps he has forgotten that he had an appointment with me," she said.

I half-heard what she said, while gravely taking a hole-punch from the table, without needing it. Perplexed, I continued to remain in the room. I was sorry that she was at the institute. For when I am here, I am a different person. [. . .]

She, too, appeared to be embarrassed. It was as though we both expected a miracle, but no miracle occurred. With hole-punch in hand, I turned to leave:

"Will I see you again before you go?"

"But the train to Oxford leaves tomorrow morning at 8:30 a.m."

A mere misunderstanding. I had meant that she should come to my office before leaving the building. But a strange pride prevented me from correcting her mistake. The wonderful sense of uniqueness disappeared. We were no longer exceptional beings. And the glass bell? What would become of the glass bell?

"So, you intended to travel to Oxford," I said drily. As though I hadn't remembered it from that morning.

With hole-punch in hand, I returned to my office. To the draft. To the stenographer. Abigail did not come by before leaving. I knew that herein ended the tale. I knew that I no longer had AROOO. And a number of things that I wanted to say would remain unsaid. It was difficult to lose that good feeling of once again being in the thick of things, as it were. [. . .]

And it does not matter why, upon her return, Abigail came straight to the Lyons Restaurant. She got off at Tottenham Court Road station and that was the closest restaurant, so she said. Why didn't she stand in the self-service line, instead of walking around and finding my table? Most of the tables were occupied. She wanted to make certain she had a place before taking a tray, she said. And, in telling me this, why did her coffee cup shake slightly on its way from the table to her lips? There was no response. She said nothing. From our corner, one could see the big-nosed Austrian, hidden at an angle, by the shadow of dwarf palms in red flowerpots. And he kept playing the organ. Without taking the cigarette out of his mouth. Without turning the pages of his music book. The candles in the electric candlesticks illuminated his frenetic fingers, white chest, and black bowtie. I remained silent. Abigail lowered her eyes. Once the glass bell breaks, there is no way to repair it. I knew that. Abigail would become just a foreign girl that I happened to meet. Her small valise in hand, she looks here and there, as though unable to decide where to turn. She could have been a waitress, a hairdresser's assistant, or a saleswoman in a large department store.

In any event, here you have a small drama, confused though it may be, of people extending a hand above their floating glacier. Just take a look. A plucked leaf from the mountains of Ararat. A mummified blossom that has withered and died.

Now I shall go down to buy something for supper and prepare it over the gas flame. [. . .]

The street is misty. Traffic lights are changing color in the haze. Next to the streetlight are three barefoot men in tattered army jackets. One is playing cymbals, another the oboe, and the third is playing on a comb, stamping his feet and singing: "Oh, the grand old Duke of York / had an army of ten thousand men. / He marched them up to the top of the hill; / he marched them down again. / Now when you're up, you're up, / and when you're down, you're down, / and when you're only half-way up, you're neither up nor down." And three old hats were lying on the ground, for people to toss in money.

Translated by Marvin Meital.

Aharon Appelfeld
1932–2018

Aharon Appelfeld was born near Czernowitz, Bukovina. Incarcerated in a concentration camp in Transnistria during the Nazi occupation, he escaped and wandered the forests for the next three years until he was liberated by the Red Army. At age fourteen, Appelfeld immigrated alone to Israel, where he adopted the Hebrew language for his short stories and, later, his novels, memoirs, and plays. Appelfeld established his name in Israeli fiction as a teller of spare and disturbing allegorical tales. He created a gallery of Holocaust survivors whose essential condition was defined by their transience, the poverty of their speech, and their sense of estrangement. Although grounded in his own wartime experiences, these stories were set in a symbolic landscape outside of time. He won numerous prizes, including the Israel Prize, the MLA Commonwealth Award in Literature, and Prix Médicis Étranger in France, the Nelly Sachs Preis, the Premio Grinzane Cavour and Premio Boccaccio Internazionale, the Bertha von Suttner Award for Culture and Peace, the Sydney Taylor Book Award, the Independent Foreign Fiction Prize, and the Hemingway Prize in Italy. Appelfeld was a professor of literature at Ben-Gurion University.

The Escape
1967

All that had happened to him lay behind him like a yawning abyss. There was a strange excitement for him in his adjustment, an intoxication beyond fear. His movements were untrammeled, and as a result he made a better peasant than the peasants themselves. He knew how to talk to respectable householders, to the village mayor, to the priest; how to narrow his gaze when a buxom lass came into the tavern.

But elsewhere—in the meadows, in the places where water roared—he would unharness the horse and his whole life would come back to him. He knew: it was the cowardice inside him that had brought him to a halt. The evil shadow clung to his flesh. Sometimes the horse would have to bear the brunt of it. He would beat the animal the way a Jew beats a dog. Yet he knew in his heart that it was not from the horse that he had gotten this smell of goats and butter, but, as it were, from within. The body knows how to protect itself by the lowliest of means, even to the point of emitting odors. Sometimes he would take grass and hide his face in shame. Praying, he would whisper torn verses. His Jewishness lay next to him like fallen leaves beside a tree. It withered in his hand, and within him. He lost the gnawing sorrow too. Awareness was not enough to burn away his madness.

The waters of the stream would show him his face, the peasant face blotched by the sun. He would stand gazing at it. Now and then he would laugh.

Sometimes out of weariness he would linger in the open fields. He would stretch out on the ground, trying to rekindle his memory. His life receded further and further into the distance, leaving no residue within him. His dreams were a strange mixture of crude, amorphous figures: heaven and hell, angels and devils.

He heard tell in the tavern about the heroic deeds of Yaroslav's army. But the actions themselves, the material artifacts, spoke most loudly of all. The looted property found its way quickly into the homes of the peasants, lost its Jewish coloring, and flowered on the sideboards.

He was attached to the horse as though it were an extension of his own body. He walked with it, slept with it. And the horse gave him in return what a domesticated animal can give a man: broad shoulders, a wise step, a look.

He didn't know how this total transformation had come over him. He hadn't made any special effort to learn the others' way or take on their expressions—these things seemed to flow of their own accord. He knew how to eat as they did, how to cross himself. As if he had actually been a peasant.

And so a year went by. The spasms of memory were not strong enough to upset his equilibrium. The latter he drew from some internal source, and it cast up a mighty dam within him—like those peasants who take their strength from the harsh air. [. . .]

As if from a camouflaged lair, a Jew stepped out into his path. He looked like a giant beetle that had lost its sense of direction. "Get the hell out of the way!" he shouted. And the Jew fell on all fours. His features where white and tortured, as though he had been pinned under a rock, gasping for breath. He seemed to have been crouched in hiding for days, the grain growing over him.

"Bread!" cried the Jew in a voice that had not been used for some time. He broke off half a loaf for him. The Jew stretched out a white hand and disappeared like a snail into the forgiveness of the grass.

That night he didn't return to the village. He unloaded the crates by the stream and left the horse to graze. The obsequiousness of the Jew resounded in his ears.

That night the sounds became clearer and reached his ears with a naked lucidity. They were scattered nearby. If they came any closer, he would flee. They crouched in the grass, lapping water from the stream.

As the night deepened, the words grew quieter, and a song arose. So soft was it that only one very nearby would notice it at all. The singing flowed all night long, like inner voices by which the singers alone were rocked to and fro. Then, with the crack of dawn, it faded away. The song of summer exulted now in the fields. He got up humble and submissive that morning, as if his dreams had plucked out his whiskers. His face trembled in the stream, trembled unshaded. The thought of revealing himself to the next Jew he met crossed his mind.

A gentle morning caressed the sheaves. Except for the tracks of animals, there were no footsteps. The trees stood silently by, the wild cherries reddening. The first wagons were being drawn up from the river-bank, laden with the harvest. They stopped to ask why he wasn't coming to the village. He had only stopped there for a moment, he replied. The wagons moved on, leaving ruts in the trampled mud. Only now, belatedly, did he notice how loose the soil was there, how the sheaves seemed almost planted in its crumbling surface. All day long he ambled about in the fields. It was a summer melody without a human voice. Here and there a cow, a horse—they, too, creatures of this stillness—stood hemmed in by the grass.

At dusk he sat down to a meal with two peasants, tenant farmers from the south. They told him about their lives, the years they had spent working another man's land. Their voices had a certain subdued quality. They showed no outward sign of their enslavement, as if it were their natural condition.

The day's sights passed over him like gusts of wind.

An undisguised sorrow contorted the face of the horse, which seemed to sense that it no longer enjoyed the same affection from its master that it once had. It lay by the crates like a neglected pet. He brought water and gave it to drink.

The evening smoke rose from the chimneys of the village. The lowing of the cows and the voices of the peasants sounded to him like a demand: for salt, kerosene, sugar. But the voices did not frighten him; another, darker fear echoed within.

Slowly the blue of evening deepened, and the silence cleared. Once again, the old feelings crept over him. Merchants who had lost businesses and whose voices sounded like the clatter of coins, weaving plans for some commercial onslaught. [. . .]

Little by little the darkness exposed itself. The first light of morning wrapped itself in blue. Three Jews lay in the high grass like a thick patch of darkness left behind on the ground and shriveled up. They recoiled at the sight of him.

"Good morning," one of them mustered the courage to say, speaking in the language of the peasants. Their white faces were frozen with fear.

Silence hung rigid between them, the freezing shudder between hunter and hunted.

"Have mercy," said one of them, getting up on his hands and knees. Fear seemed to put words in his mouth. The black clothes hung loosely on them. They were exposed, like moles which an early-rising predator has taken by surprise.

"They took everything we had. We alone are left," the old man said, clutching the ground beneath him as if preparing to make some kind of sacrificial offering. All his movements together amounted to an expression of helplessness. The other two, who were evidently his sons, hovered at his side.

"I am one of you," he said in the gentile language. And that, coming like a soft blow, was so utterly unexpected that all the old man could do was to grin like a stammerer.

"What?" he said without moving. Experienced with traps and ambushes, he suddenly found himself exposed to the light of day, before a real live heathen.

The man put a hand over his brimming eyes. It had been a long time since the breath of a Jew had whispered in his ear, and it suddenly licked his face like a flame.

It had begun nearly a year before, he told them. Yaroslav's cavalry had broken out like a summer storm, mowing down the villages. Noblemen shut themselves up in their castles; the monasteries demanded apostasy. He had been traveling when the storm hit. He bought himself a fur coat and a horse.

"And no one recognized you?" one of them asked, suddenly finding his voice.

"I walked in the villages and no one knew. I hardly recognized myself at first."

"How much you must have changed. There's no sign."

They drew near and sat down next to him. The riddle slowly unfolded for them.

"Sometimes fear can do it," said the old man, trying to console him. "You completely forgot."

"Had it not been for your voices."

"My son," the old man said. It was evident that he would have liked to bless him, to advise him, had it not been for his rough peasant appearance. He seemed like one of those who work as servants in Jewish households and learn a little of our language.

"And you?" he asked, suddenly stirred.

"We've been here. No one knows yet. The high grass gave us cover. Our feet froze during the winter. We can't go far. Maybe the summer will heal them. If it hadn't been for our feet, we'd have been caught by now. There was a manhunt. If it hadn't been for our feet."

"What are you going to do?"

The tip of the old man's nose trembled, a remnant of his fear.

"So that's how you were saved," the young one said. Astonishment lit up his eyes, the way it does with Jewish boys who hear tell of the wonders of the world. "And you can move about freely in the villages."

"Of course," the old man interjected. "He's a gentile, isn't he?"

He was a prisoner of their gaze. "Maybe he had read forbidden books before that," said the young one, his emaciated face aglow with innocence. He was obviously very young.

"What a change! How can a man change so much?"

"The clothes did it, apparently," the older son tried to explain.

What could he have told them?

He was trapped now in his own enigma. His language was a strange, unfused mixture of Jewish and gentile speech. Like non-Jews who have served in Jewish houses and picked up a few Jewish words.

"And you're not afraid?"

The initial silence returned to obstruct the space between them, a silence no words could fill. The old man studied him, the way one studies a gentile.

The older son managed to say, "You're past the barricade now. They won't chase you any more."

The man did not look up. Their presence was hard for him to bear. He was ready to give them his horse and his supplies if only they would go away and leave him alone. But, like fugitives who have found a kindred spirit and don't want to let go of him, they didn't budge.

The old man asked questions about the village, the way practical men do. He asked as if it were possible for them simply to get up and go. It was not his weakness which spoke, but a whisper of superhuman strength.

A kind of estrangement came between them now. "I'm giving you clothing and the horse. You can go to the villages and do business."

"But what about the dogs?" the old man said.

"Are you afraid of them? The only dogs are those that were here before Yaroslav's invasion. The others have been taken away. Even the cows have."

Then the older one spoke to him. He used their own language. Evening had already descended upon them, and this was the boundary. While they were wrapped up in their prayers, he sat like a defendant in the shadow of the cherry tree, visible in the twilight, apart.

The old man said, "Let's go," as Jews are wont to say in the evening. And they studied him as Jews study a gentile. He wanted to tell them something Jewish, but it came out gentile. Finally he began cursing his own tongue, in the way gentiles curse. "Don't you want the horse? It is a horse, after all," he said, speaking the way drunkards do when they offer other men their wives. They began to be afraid of him. No sooner was it dark than they made off, like nocturnal creatures who suck energy from the darkness. The grass suddenly lost its black spots and shone smooth and green once more.

That night, the forest was bathed in moonlight. The horse plodded slowly along, part and parcel of the chill breathing of the woods. An alien sweat warmed him. He sensed that, unwittingly, he had shed some part of his body. The horse bore him along, but in its gait too there was an unaccustomed lightness, as if it were trying to fly. The saddle was pulled tight. The horse lifted its feet as if preparing for some other, steadier movement. So well-balanced was its flight that it seemed to glide just above the ground without ever touching it.

Translated by Michael Swirsky.

Other works by Appelfeld: *'Ashan* (1963); *Be-gai ha-poreh* (1965); *Kefor 'al ha-'arets* (1965); *The Age of Wonders* (1978); *Badenheim 1939* (1978).

Naomi Frankel

1918–2009

Born into an assimilated family in Berlin, Naomi Frankel joined the Socialist Zionist youth group Ha-Shomer ha-Tsa'ir as a teenager. After being evacuated from Germany to Palestine in 1933, Frankel served in the Palmach during the War of Independence. Later, she joined Kibbutz Bet Alpha, where she began writing, exploring the interactions of Zionism and the prewar German Jewish milieu she had known as a child. In 1970, she left the kibbutz and became observant, rejecting the leftist politics of her youth. She moved in 1983 to Hebron, where she remained the rest of her life, advocating actively for the creation of Greater Israel.

Saul and Johanna

1967

All of a sudden, Grandmother's empty burial plot is occupied. They finally returned mother to father's side. One tree spreads its shadow over both their graves. Grandmother, too, finally gets what she had wished for her entire life. Grandfather is next to her, resting in his place. [. . .]

A spacious burial plot, covered in snow. Here and there the snow had begun to melt and discolor. Not a cloud above. The sun, already emitting some of the warmth and pleasantness of spring, shines above the Jewish cemetery. Grandfather's and mother's graves are covered in fresh black earth. Uncle Alfred said the Kaddish over his father's grave. The cantor recited the *El male' raḥamim*. [. . .]

"Grandfather died as he had lived, invincible." Heinz squeezes the handkerchief in his pocket. He looks at the multitude of people who came to pay Grandfather their last respects. All of the cemetery paths darken with his friends. It's as if Grandfather had assembled a great gathering precisely for this moment, when the powers of the Third Reich prohibited Jews from convening their meetings. "He was invincible. To the very end, invincible." Heinz looks down at his hands and sees the room at the estate. They arrived at night—Phillip, Edith, and he. Grandfather had been lying on his bed for a number of hours by then. Agatha washed his face, dressed him in a white shirt and lit two tall white candles over his head. They stood near Grandfather's bed with Agatha and could not believe that that dead grandfather is their very own Grandpa. [. . .] Heinz looks away from Grandfather's flower-covered grave and then turns to look again. "They arrested Gerda, Grandpa. On the morning after the burning of the Reichstag, they came and took her with them."

Edith is dressed in black. Her face is pale, so restrained, to the point where her face is expressionless. Her eyes are dry, a heavy desire fills her heart to heave herself onto the flowers covering Grandpa's grave. Perhaps there her eyes will shed tears and she will feel relief. From the moment she stood by the bed at the estate of the grandfather who was shot, her eyes had been dry, their dryness searing her heart. The new times murdered Grandpa. The new times took Erwin from her. She no longer cries as she did when Erwin went away. Grandpa was always brave, in life and in death. Life must be lived courageously. Edith lifts her head, picks up her stride to overtake Heinz, winds her arm through his, and warm sparks light up his cool eyes. [. . .]

Alexander lingers by his friend Arthur's grave. He came from London to attend Grandfather's funeral. He's all alone next to the grave, and is contemplating, as if to calm Arthur in his eternal rest: "The children are leaving this place. I have arranged everything for Bomba and Johanna." [. . .]

Separated from Alexander by a handful of people, the old gardener and Saul are walking together. This is not just a coincidence, but Saul has been observing closely the old gardener for some time now—the old man's *kashket* hat [flat-top, newsboy cap] catches his eyes, as well as the gray sweater protecting his neck. "Just like Otto. Exactly like Otto." The old *kashket* draws the old gardener closer to Saul's heart.

And he's about to ask the gardener, as he did Otto:

"What do you think? A Nazi state, seriously, will it last a thousand years?"

"A thousand-year-old state, child . . . no. I don't believe so. But even if it were to last one year, that will be a dark year. A dark generation has risen upon us. Even if it were to last a single year, it will take down into the abyss all that has been accumulated for a thousand years. Generations which will follow this dark one will be forced to start anew, child. Yes, those who believe in great and noble ideals must now reckon with their souls and faith. Yes, yes, after all that happened here a reckoning must be made, unflinchingly."

The old gardener's voice is heavy, like the sound of Otto's voice rising to Saul beyond the surrounding graves. The day Hitler was named chancellor and no call for an uprising was raised, Otto stood by himself in his hallway's store, with Saul as the only one who heard him say:

"Saul, how is it that we marched with all our great ideals and great faith to reach the darkness of this day? Boy, I'm telling you, me, Otto, who knows about such things, we have failed. Let's hope we'll be given a chance to reckon with ourselves."

The gardener suddenly reaches for Saul's hand, looks at him, and says:

"Don't be so sad, Saul; you see, son, regimes, ideologies, and beliefs rise and fall. But the land remains forever and the earth remains too, and the people on it are renewed. Fathers make mistakes, and their sons come and correct their mistakes. You are still young, Saul. Once you mature you'll find a world renewed. Germany will awaken to a new life, and the entire world will be renewed. You are a mere lad, Saul. The miracle of renewal is in your hands." [. . .]

There, where the paths are already empty, Johanna and the Baron Ottokar von Eulenberg are walking. Ottokar stopped Johanna, lifting her face toward him and drying her tears with his handkerchief.

"It has been a long time since I've seen you, Johanna."

"This may be the last time you will see me. In two weeks time I will be going away. I am going to Palestine, Ottokar."

"In two weeks already?"

"Yes, there is nothing for me to do here. Once Dr. Heize was arrested, Heinz just took me out of school. Everything is already set for our departure. Mine and Bomba's."

Ottokar's voice was no longer distinct from that of all the others who had spoken to Johanna in the past three days, ever since grandfather's bullet-riddled body was brought home.

"Were you also present during his arrest?"

"Sure, that was on the morning after the night the Reichstag was set on fire. They came to take him during the long recess, when all the girls were in the school yard. SS men dressed in black marched him around the entire yard, between all the girls. And how he walked! Proud and quiet, head high and erect. I shall never forget him." [. . .]

"But Johanna, but Johanna, the day will come when everything will change here again. You will be able to come back, you will come again, Johanna."

"I told you, no. I shall never again enter the house whose dwellers spit on me. Even if those dwellers will be replaced, Ottokar, it is a house marked by spit. No, no!"

Cries choke her breast. He takes the young woman under his arms, kissing her tearful eyes. But when he tries kissing her mouth, she quickly turns her head.

"I must go home, I'm in a rush."

"I will drive you in my car, Johanna."

The cemetery has emptied already. They walk to the gate alone, Ottokar hugging her shoulders. At the gate, Saul pounces upon them, and without glancing at Ottokar, he screams in anger:

"Where have you been all this time? I waited and waited for you, come home quickly."

"Let me drive both of you home," says Ottokar politely.

"Thank you, Baron, thank you!" Saul pulls himself up, from his wind-tousled forelock to the bottom of his cleated shoes, all gravity and aggressiveness.

"There's no need, Baron, I will take Johanna home."

He lets Johanna nod toward Ottokar, but does not allow her to extend her hand in a gesture of farewell. He takes her by the hand, pulling her after him. Once they are a bit farther, Johanna frees her hand from Saul's and stops in her tracks. She turns to look at Ottokar and lifts her hand to wave goodbye. Ottokar waves back, a slow and sad wave. Ottokar von Eulenberg remains standing alone at the cemetery gate.

Translated by Menachem Rotstein.

Other works by Frankel: *Dodi ve-re'i* (1973); *Na'ar tsamaḥ ba-gadot ha-asi* (1977); *Tsemaḥ bar* (1981).

Dan Ben-Amotz

To Remember, to Forget
1968

Evening in the Street

I don't know what possessed me, but I decided to take the guided tour of Frankfurt. The minute I set eyes on the American tourists and heard the practiced laugh with which the German guide introduced his wisecracks, I should have realized it was a mistake and turned back. [. . .]

The guide paid tribute to the conduct of Frankfurt's people during the "catastrophe," the years following the war and preceding the great economic miracle. In his version Germany was the victim in World War II. These innocents, in whose name others waged war, were ruthlessly bombarded, their homes destroyed, their cities demolished. The shellings continued even after the city had been reduced to rubble—which was unfair and contrary to the rules of the game. But the diligent Germans did not despair. With enthusiasm and determination the ruins were rebuilt. Witness the new city, a testament to their tireless efforts.

He didn't say all this in so many words, but this was the implication of the numbers and dates he cited. In decrying the bombings he raged against war in general and its gross injustice: the plight of the postal clerk whose house was destroyed, the pharmacist whose aged mother was buried alive in debris, the teacher who was blinded, the old man whose dog expired before his eyes. Whether these good, simple folk are English, French, or German is unimportant. Nor does it matter who began the horror, for war is such an awful thing. But let's forget the past. He is willing to forgive. It won't happen again, he hopes—humanity has learned its lesson.

I couldn't take any more of this. When the passengers got off the bus to photograph the old clock above the church and the bell towers, I slipped away and walked until I was bathed in sweat. I stopped to rest and, feeling thirsty, I stepped into the nearest bar. [. . .]

Why was I so enraged, I asked myself. From his point of view that guide was justified. To the pharmacist, the postal clerk, the teacher, it was hardly relevant who started the war. [. . .]

You couldn't really say that these were the people who bombed Holland, Belgium, Poland. You couldn't claim that the lame postal clerk and the blinded painting teacher set up those camps to which peaceful citizens like themselves were sent. At most they were guilty of not acting to reverse the situation, of averting their eyes when neighbors were hauled away in trucks, of lacking the courage to protest, of wanting more than anything to remain alive. And who among us could swear that he would have behaved otherwise? Who can say with confidence that he would not have adjusted, gradually, to the horror, hoping and praying that one day the nightmare would end and life would resume a peaceful course? It was their right to be bitter about the bombs and destruction, even though history could justify these actions. Even a criminal has the right to complain of mice in his cell, the tightness of the handcuffs, the guards' brutality.

Then what was it that enraged me so? Was it the hypocrisy and pretense, the notion that the German people were unaware of these crimes and uninvolved in these events? Was it the standard remorse, the lip service, the flattering asides to Americans in the group and to all things American? What did I expect? How can a German today respond to the questions that confront him everywhere? It may be that silence is the one option. . . . Let them proclaim silence throughout the land, don sackcloth, place ashes on their heads, and transform Germany into a vast monastery of mutes. I have no answer. We all know the questions. No one knows the answers. It is necessary to forget. It is essential to forget. There is no other answer. One or two more whiskeys and all this will sink into billows of cotton. [. . .]

Chimes and whistles welcomed me to the brightly lit street. Once or twice I tried to clear my head, but it was no use. The bells of all the churches in Frankfurt were ringing, the way they used to on Sunday when I was a kid. I stumbled along, not knowing where I was going. Passersby made way for me muttering as I passed. I stepped on someone's toe. He glared at me and exclaimed, "Damn it!" I fell on the sidewalk near a grocery store littered with boxes. Someone tried to help me up. I pushed him away and managed to get up myself. I leaned against a door. It flew open and once more I lay sprawled on the ground, my face in a layer of sawdust.

"Nazis!" I screamed, picking myself up again and heading for the crowd of curious onlookers. "Damned Nazis!" I shouted, wiping the sawdust from my lips. Faces from horror photographs I had once seen gazed back at me impassively. I lunged at them and they quickly cleared a path. Before I knew it I was in the middle of the street. Barely missing me, a car jolted to a stop with a clamor of screeching brakes and wailing horns. I made my way to the sidewalk, swaying from side to side. Pedestrians kept their distance and stared at me with revulsion, as if I were a leper, as if I were a Jew.

"Gestapo!" I shrieked. "Dirty Fascists! Murderers! Neo-Nazi bastards!" They ignored me, though they heard every word.

Suddenly I was circled by three hoodlums in leather jackets whom I'd noticed earlier. When I glared at them they slowed down but kept on trailing me. "Nazis!" I called, spitting in their direction. But the saliva trickled down my own chin.

I was fully conscious. I knew I was drunk. I knew I was spouting nonsense, that there was no rhyme or reason to my ridiculous cries. The scene I was creating wouldn't end well. But I went on shouting imprecations in every direction in curt, cruel German cadences familiar to me from war movies. As a matter of fact I wanted the drama to come to a violent head. I was hoping to provoke an attack, hoping someone would hit me. I wanted the Germans to be true to their assigned roles so I could play the role of victim.

Translated by Zeva Shapiro.

Yoram Kaniuk

1930–2013

Novelist and journalist Yoram Kaniuk was born in Tel Aviv to a culturally well-connected family, involved with such prominent figures as Ḥayim Naḥman Bialik. At age seventeen, Kaniuk joined the Palmach, and his later writings often drew on his experiences in the military. He spent the 1950s in the United States, where he met and married Miranda Baker, a Christian woman. In 2011, as part of his long-standing criticism of organized religion, Kaniuk won the right to change his Israeli identification from Jewish to no religion. The case characterizes Kaniuk's contrarian public persona, a quality that finds expression in his writing as well. Of the twenty-nine books he published, several were adapted for film in Israel.

Adam Resurrected
1968

Ruth

Adam Stein arrived at the port of Haifa in the blazing end of the summer of 1958. In Berlin, where he was born, he had been living a life of ease, as comfortable and carefree as a vegetable, since his return from the Camp. He had few obligations. Except for his daily visit to Dr. Weiss, alias Commandant Klein, bearing that rubber condom filled with coins, there was nothing much left for him to do. But even that was too much. He had a lovely house encircled by poplars and lindens. A maid came every day to clean his house and cook his meals. His parlor, which he had bought with all its furniture and odds-and-ends from Baron Von Hamdung, was crammed full of books, beautiful pictures, ornamented chandeliers, ancient carpets, Oriental vases, easy chairs upholstered in reddish-brown leather. A massive white Mercedes, in perfect condition, was parked in his garage and was looked after by a courteous young chauffeur in a gray uniform.

Adam lacked nothing. Berlin was in the midst of its miraculous economic recovery, and Adam in the midst of his own bank accounts. He had no worries to plague him. There was no dog around. Just a canary bird in a gilded cage. When he returned from the Camp, following Commandant Klein's promise of escape and compensation—that had been the original agreement, and the German kept his word, just as, alas, had Adam, who had entertained everybody on that last trek, playing a violin and making funny faces—he won his court case and received full payment for the circus he had owned before the war. The circus had continued in operation during all the war years, and on its tours through the occupied countries it was a big hit. It even went under the same name: Adam's Circus. After entertaining the victorious Germans and the occupied allied countries, it was also a hit with the British and the Americans. At its sale it was worth (so stated the court judgment) half a million American dollars. And that entire sum was paid to Adam. Adam was wise enough to invest his money in the miracle of recovery, and after a short while his fortune had tripled. Then he took his money out of circulation, deposited it in Swiss banks and savings accounts, and lived in high style off the interest. Subsequently he had no interest whatsoever in the stock columns.

Nor did he return to the circus. [. . .]

Adam would certainly have sat there hidden inside his lovely parlor till the day he died if not for the information he was given one day—namely, that his daughter Ruth, his first-born, who was taken from him and his wife on May 3, 1938, the day that Adam's Circus was declared *Jüdenrein*, who thereafter disappeared completely, who they thought had died in Dachau because somebody actually saw her there, this daughter was alive and living in Israel.

The information shocked him deeply. He had seen his wife, Gretchen, and his daughter Lotta on their last trek. They smiled, knowing that they were safe. Was it possible at that time to comfort them? And jeopardize everything? His whole purpose was to blot out the fear of death. Death itself he could not prevent, nobody could have brought death to a halt, but the dread of it he could dispel for them. Commandant Klein didn't hate Jews any more than the average butcher hates his cows or the average hangman those he hangs. Instead he tried to be helpful. He located Adam, set him up in the corridor, so that during the entire procession Germany's greatest clown would be right up front clowning. After all, if such a person were around, things couldn't be so bad. So Adam didn't address his wife or child, and to the very end they walked with trust and peace in their hearts. Only two years later, when he found himself in neutral Switzerland, did he begin to have longings for Gretchen and Lotta. But by refusing to acknowledge his longings, he saved himself from the shame which was his greatest fear, the shame of guilt. Adam refused to admit his crime, he loathed the way some of his friends would parade their guilt, though in some cavern of his mind he recognized the fact that they had the right to be guilty, whereas he did not.

He said to himself, Palestine is nothing but a joke. Refugees, escapees, bits and pieces of humanity, chaff tossed in the wind, they cannot establish a homeland for themselves and are not worthy, perhaps, of having one. Berlin received him with open arms. His neighbors and acquaintances were glad to have in their developing city, in a little house surrounded by trees, the greatest clown Germany had ever possessed, a clown who had chosen to return to their midst from the furnaces which they themselves had manufactured for him. He was sort of an insurance policy against Hell, in case there was anything more terrible than the things they had created with their own hands. [. . .]

However, when he learned that his daughter was alive, his house of cards buckled and collapsed. Everything was muddled, no longer understood. He sat wrapped in his thoughts, asking questions that the sarcophagi could not answer. [. . .] He sent Ruth a letter at the address he had received. He told her about himself, her mother, her sister. He wrote that all the while he was watching them step toward their death, they smiled with joy, so they were certainly happy where they now were. When he didn't receive an answer, he wrote again. He wrote that God kept quiet. That the good world had died in 1933. That Europe, Christianity, Judaism, Myth, Greece, Scripture, St. Augustine, Civilization, Culture, the Roman Empire, Humanism—everything was ended in one day. Again he received no answer. He wrote that while he was living in a sarcophagus he became estranged from the Messianic vision, from the Jewish madness, from the incomprehensibility woven during more than a thousand years into a compendium of pining and expectation that finally brought about the creation in the East of a nation of Blue Numbers. He wrote that he was separated from all this and was lodged in a coffin, and since he had once been a dog he was no longer a Jew, no longer even German. And that he was her father, and that she ought to write him. If she wrote, maybe he'd understand. That he had neither right nor obligation. He was just a vegetable. A stone. [. . .]

He ripped open the envelope, spread out the letter, and read. His heart shuddered. It was from Israel. A Jewish stamp, in Hebrew, Arabic, English, come to a city that was *Jüdenrein*. A miracle.

Dear Mr. Stein,

My German isn't good enough to write in and my English is not of the best, consequently please forgive all the many mistakes and the bad grammar. I am your daughter Ruth's husband. This morning at 5:30, I took her to the Hadassah hospital in Jerusalem, in order that she might give birth to my son or my daughter. I prefer a daughter, though Ruth wants a son. When I was back home, I searched through her papers (on the way to the hospital she asked me to find some documents and bring them to her, her immigration papers and other credentials, she wanted to have them by her bed, I don't know why) and I found your letters.

She never said a word about these letters, and I'm stunned. Today I discover that my son or my daughter has a grandfather. Amazing! Tomorrow I will no longer be just my father's son but also my son's father, and the fact that, for me, you were born on the very same day causes me great joy. It's hard for me to explain. I know that Ruth never answered your letters. At the bottom of one of the letters she wrote in her green Parker: "Father, I'll never talk to you. It's impossible. Not because you write that you were a scoundrel but because I wasn't there to guide you." Forgive me for writing this down for you. But anything's better than silence, which must certainly be painful to you. That's the way Ruth is. But as I held your letters in front of me, I thought to myself that you ought to know all this. Why? I don't know. I understand that you were separated a long time ago. That you don't know a thing about her. Therefore I'll give you a brief summary. If it won't help, it certainly won't harm. Ruth came to the Land in 1945. She arrived in a blockade-runner. Once here, she tied a small gold crucifix around her neck and swore that her children would be Christian. That way they'd be safer. She was determined, and she used strong language: for example, she told her friends in the youth movement that she would erase the covenant of circumcision—that cursed covenant—from her children's flesh, and would plan for them a way of life in the world that didn't cherish the circumcised. Permit me to boast in front of you—after all, you are my father-in-law—and tell you that thanks to our marriage she became a totally different person. She overcame the terrible fears that were attacking her, and when she became pregnant she took the crucifix from her neck and rejoiced over her pregnancy, even though two years ago she swore to me that she wouldn't bring Jewish children into the world. She was very sick. Some claim that "they" made experiments on her body. She refuses to talk about this subject. Dr. Klein, who took care of her in Jerusalem, says that she went through Hell and was already "beyond death," so beyond that death was for her almost an understatement. That's what Dr. Klein said, and here in Jerusalem he's considered a first-rate doctor.

Let me summarize, in conclusion: Today you are a grandfather. From what I've been saying you can obviously understand that Ruth has changed, and therefore, in the opinion and name of Joseph Graetz, who is your son-in-law, you have a home in Israel. If you want to come, come. I'm convinced that if Ruth saw you face to face, she'd forgive. And if not, from reading your letters I deduce that you could stay with us even without forgiveness.

Yours, in friendship,
Joseph Graetz

Adam grumbled over the last lines of the letter. He hadn't ever asked anybody to forgive him. Nobody was entitled to forgive him. But in less than two months Adam was in the port of Haifa.

Translated by Seymour Simckes.

Other works by Kaniuk: *The Acrophile* (1960); *Himmo, King of Jerusalem* (1966).

S. Y. Agnon

Shira
1971

The woman in charge came out of the children's house and stationed herself on the grass, holding an infant in each arm. Children stood behind and in front of her, waiting for their parents, who were returning from the fields. Some stamped their feet impatiently; others did tricks to show Mommy and Daddy what they could do. Before they knew it, these children were scooped up. One was on his father's shoulders and another on his father's head, having appropriated his father's hat for himself. One was buried in his mother's arms. A little girl was stroking her mother's cheeks and saying, "Love your mommy?" All sorts of pet names and personal dialects were heard.

The workers were all back from the fields. The unmarried men and women ran to the showers, and those with families rushed off to see their children, stopping briefly at the office to ask for mail. Not all the children in Ahinoam were from that settlement. The *kvutza* was still young and hadn't produced many children yet, but, since its climate was so pleasant, several children from less comfortable settlements were spending the summer there.

The entire village was bustling. In one corner, a father was carrying around a child. In another, a mother nursed a baby. Nearby, a young man pranced around with a little girl whose father had been killed on guard duty. Next to them, someone was standing on his head, clapping his feet together. Slim girls with cropped hair, dressed in men's clothing, their shoulders like those of young boys, gurgled at their infants. Alongside each such girl was a suntanned boy with a peeling nose. The setting sun cast its final light, as it did each day, releasing specially created colors in a band that extended around the village from the westernmost reaches of the world. Birds were heard returning to their nests with a final chirp before hiding themselves among the branches for the night. The rabbits scurried around in their box and were suddenly still. A gentle breeze blew. All this lasted less than a minute. Then the bell was heard, announcing dinner.

From all the houses, huts, and tents, they assembled, filing into the dining room. Some had come to eat; others waited. The dining room was small, and there were two shifts, one entering, one leaving. Zahara was occupied with her son, so she didn't come to supper. Avraham-and-a-half was busy helping Zahara, so he didn't come to supper. But her father and mother were seated under the clock, between the windows and across from the door, in a spot reserved for important guests, from which they could see everyone in the *kvutza*.

The Herbsts were in the midst of a circle of young men and women. Some were cutting vegetables; some were spreading margarine on their bread. Some drank tea; others gulped water. Some were calm; others noisy, either behaving as they had learned to at home or demonstrating their liberation from bourgeois table manners. They all ate their fill. Then someone looked up from his bowl and, seeing the Herbsts, leaped up and went to sit with them. Others followed, welcomed them, poured their tea, peeled their cucumbers, sliced their radishes, made them salad and sprinkled it with oil and salt, and handed them dishes, the saltshaker, the cruet of oil, urging them cordially to enjoy everything. As Herbst picked up his tea and was about to drink, a pretty young woman came running with sugar she had obtained especially for the guests. Someone asked, "Has Zahara been informed that she has guests?" Someone else answered, "By the time a speedy fellow like you makes a move to go tell Zahara, it will be time to tell Zahara's grandchild that his grandpa and grandma are here."

The entire *kvutza* responded warmly to Zahara's parents. Some knew the Herbsts, because they had been in their house, enjoyed Mrs. Herbst's cooking and Dr. Herbst's conversation, fingered the books on his shelves, and been stimulated by his ideas. Others didn't know them but had heard about them. Everyone welcomed them, as young people tend to do when company is congenial. There were some guests they were required to welcome: tourists who were ridiculous and whose questions were just as ridiculous; official guests from the national bodies that determined the budget; cultural windbags who assumed they were indispensable. But the Herbsts were welcomed because of Zahara and because of who they were. They were "like us," and, even if our problems weren't theirs, when we discussed them, we didn't run into a stone wall. Furthermore, although Herbst was a scholar, he wrote academic papers in ordinary language.

The two Heinzes—Heinz the Berliner and Heinz from Darmstadt—took charge of the Herbsts. They sat with them and told them what had been happening in the *kvutza* and what was about to happen. They sat talking until a few members of the Culture Committee came to invite Dr. Herbst to give a lecture. "A lecture?" Herbst asked in dismay. "As I was leaving, I stored all my wisdom in a desk drawer. It didn't occur to me that anyone here would be interested in my merchandise." He scrutinized the young people, their amiable charm and lively innocence, and it seemed odd to him to stand up and lecture on his usual topics, which, though important in themselves, were of no consequence here. They pressed him, suggesting all sorts of subjects. He listened and responded, answering with repeated qualifiers that contained not a trace of scorn, only wonder that anyone was still interested in such things.

While the Culture Committee was negotiating with Dr. Herbst, a group of young women were engaged in conversation with Mrs. Herbst on such subjects as cooking, baking, sewing, and weaving. Mrs. Herbst thought in wonderment: When they come to Jerusalem, they pursue everything except domestic activities; here, their interests are exclusively domestic. She had some questions too: Why aren't the thorns at the gate being destroyed, when do the thistles wither here? In her experience, they wither in July, yet here they are still in bloom.

Mrs. Herbst also asked why the olives were preserved in soda, which spoils their taste. She still remembered eating marvelous olives when she first came to the country. The two Heinzes left with the Culture Committee, to give Herbst a chance to prepare his lecture.

Translated by Zeva Shapiro.

Haim Gouri
1923-2018

Haim Gouri, a poet, author, journalist, and documentary filmmaker, was born in Tel Aviv. He was a poet of the 1948 Generation and a major influence on modern Hebrew literature. Gouri joined the Palmach in 1941 and fought in Israel's War of Independence. He wrote more than twenty books of prose and poetry as well as autobiographical works. From 1974 to 1983, when he headed Documentary Films, Gouri—together with David Bergman and Jacquot Ehrlich—created a renowned trilogy of films on the Holocaust.

The Crazy Book
1971

Arab Halva—moist, sticky, fibrous. The taste tears across my lips like a memory. Within me Jaffa stirs, wakens from sleep; eyes and faces of Jaffa.

I am there, it is afternoon, a city half-awake, swept by sea wind. Jaffa arises from sleep domed and spired, shadowy orchards beneath a lilac sky, an ebbing sea like metal.

Evening. This is her silence. The boats return now to the wet salty wharf, except one or two which remain out at sea, white sail on dark water, touched by the sun's crimson. Smell of oranges, fish, seaweed.

No wave washes up now on the jutting rocks south of the harbor. No specter fleets of ships, wrecked or lost forever in weariness, flicker now in the twilight.

Only the sea. Only the sea.

I walk in a city of low wintry skies, between tall Cypriot donkeys in heat, and caravans of camels continuing the Bible, from Damascus jangling their way south. I walk between black carriages and red horses as if at the edge of a crumbling kingdom. I go to Hassan Bek, an adulterer from another city, very near and very far away. I walk and walk, trying to touch things.

Heavy gold. Shamuti oranges. A wintry, slaty sea wind lightly whips abayahs and dresses, washing and sails. Goats on the sandy caravan track between the orchards and the dunes. Bells. A woman. A jar. Imitating pictures immemorially familiar. Soon the dew will fall on the cannon of Ramadan. Houses with long memories. The southern neighbor, enchanting and sluttish, of my native town, scattered as if by chance upon these sands. Different. Not mine.

Spring. Noon at the market, disemboweled slit sheep at the sun-drenched, flyblown butcher stall; the potters' market, the alleys of ironworkers, labyrinths of silversmiths, light and shade of niche and arch and glimmer of gold. Farther on, legendary perfumes, spices borrowed from a past which has forgotten its beginnings. And bananas, onions, oranges.

Labyrinths. Alley upon alley, passages with no name, tunnels of light which disappear into cool darkness, vanishing faces. The sun picks its way westward over gramophoned restaurants choking forth the beseechings of Um Kultum and the consoling response, Egyptian, Abdul Wahab. Florentine walls. Porches with delicate iron trellises and geraniums in pots. I see women watching me from arched windows. Dark-skinned women. Mouths reddening like ovens. Silent as concubines in dreams. Within, the blue of Islam. Of Isfahan.

Streets of the setting sun. Streets of flies, of traders, of shouts and shops and shops and stalls and cafés taking out backgammon tables and stools to the cooling pavement. For the coastal merchants, stout and beturbaned. Leisure. Haste is the work of the devil. Small cups of coffee. Narghiles. Amber beads. I walk past ragged children harvesting squashed cigarette butts from the gutters in the weakening sunlight. Hourani vagrants dozing on the pavements, dead to the world, wrapped in sacks, the soles of their feet like leather. And sea between the houses.

Not far from here, my mother and father must have stood after they disembarked from the *Ruslan* with their bundles, in front of Haim Baruch's hostel or some other.

I walk in yesterday's Jaffa, by its pure blue sea and its golden sands. Seeking footprints and loyalties.

Sunlight on the house of Haim Baruch.

Sunlight on the blood of Joseph Haim.

I am going to the Jaffa of clubs and knives and the insanity of preachers in mosques. I'm going to Jaffa. Don't go to Jaffa! Don't go to Jaffa! I am going to Jaffa, to Sheik el Farouki, to the "United Islam," to the mufti's Jaffa, dense, yelling, hoarse, pouring out of her mosques, brandishing green flags and sword hands, aflame with red Ottoman fez.

Sunlight on the house of Bluma.

Sunlight on the blood of Joseph Haim.

On gramophones tearing the sky.

I am going to Jaffa, to the tunes that have no end but much patience, to the white ice cream, the oily cakes on round copper trays, the semolina and sesame seeds and peanuts and coconut, to the green-almonded baklava, the oven-hot ring rolls, the mint leaves redolent with the smell of the hills at summer's end, to brown hard-boiled eggs, hummus and bean paste in their heavy pools of olive oil, to kebab on glowing coals, grilled tomatoes, charred slices of onion, to the remembered women who never move from their geranium windows, to the cool rooms, the chiaroscuro, the silence. I am going to Jaffa, seagirt, minaretted, and whored. Don't go to Jaffa! Don't go to Jaffa! You're crazy! They're killers, don't you know? You're crazy! Jaffa of the 1921 and 1929 riots. I am going to my forefathers, turbaned, panama-ed, felt-hatted, worker-capped, to my forefathers burning with the fiery love of Zion. To my fragile mothers, scorched by the pitiless sun, getting lost in these shifting dunes. I'm going to Jaffa. Don't go, you're crazy. All the shutters are closing. I'm going, to Manshieh, to Ajami, to Abu Kebir, to Brenner's blood, to the madly barking dogs, to the blue police light, to the black-furred turbans of the Palestine police, the steel-tipped batons and Colts and the rearing horses and the songs of the Haganah. I am going, I am going to Jaffa. Don't go!

Translated by Ruth Nevo.

Other works by Gouri: *Facing the Glass Booth* (1961); *Mar'ot Gihazi* (1974).

Shulamit Hareven

1930–2003

Poet, novelist, journalist, translator, and writer for children, Shulamit Hareven was born in Warsaw and immigrated with her parents to Palestine in 1940, settling in Jerusalem. She served in the Haganah and was a medic during the siege of Jerusalem in 1948. Hareven was a founder of the Israel Defense Forces radio broadcasts and a war correspondent during the War of Attrition (1968–1972) and the Yom Kippur War (1973). She reported on social, cultural, and political events and was an active supporter of the Peace Now movement. As a writer, Hareven is best known for her family saga, *City of Many Days*, and for her novellas on biblical themes.

City of Many Days
1972

The long-suffering city took in people with the strangest ideas, philosophers, freaks, madmen, each with his own nutty flavor, who vanished as suddenly as they appeared. Sometimes Jerusalem seemed to be built as much out of obsessions as of stone.

The streets of the city teemed with inventors, mad geniuses, incorrigible buttonholers, writers of petitions to the League of Nations. Here today, gone tomorrow. One day Sara was traveling on the bus to the hospital next to a chain-smoking, butch-haired woman of about sixty.

"These cigarettes will be the end of me," said the woman to Sara. "But enjoy it, I tell myself, you only live once."

"How do you know?" Sara asked.

The woman looked at her with surprise.

"Aha, I can see you're an intelligent girl. In that case I'll tell you a story. Listen carefully. I've been shot with the same bullet three times in the last five years. Not three different bullets, the same one. And once I was already up there. I knocked on the gate, and suddenly I heard a voice call out from inside: Don't open it. It was my late husband. Guess what? He was living up there with a woman younger than myself and wouldn't let me in. So I came back down. That's just one story. If you travel on this bus often, I'll tell you a new one every day."

She leaned over and whispered in Sara's ear: "I know when the High Commissioner is going to die."

Sara never saw her again.

A light-and-shade-struck city of light-and-shade-struck people. A narrow, arched passageway, fraught with itself, wide enough for a small donkey; the soft light behind it incandescing not on the man but on the red flaps of his clothes, his dark patch of a head barely brushing the moss growing out of the wall. A burro slowly climbs the narrow steps. Around the corner the aquamarine mosaic of the Dome of the Rock, a sudden treasure to look at, a prismatic jewel in a setting of stone.

"I wonder," said Professor Barzel, "whether the Hebrew verb *l'hatsil*, to save, mightn't come from the noun *tsel*, shade? In a hot country like this, where the sun is a medical problem, shade is truly salvation."

"It never occurred to me," said Hulda, shading her infant's face. "You have to have not been born here to think of such a thing."

A city you long for the more you are in it; in which you are most yourself and most miss yourself; in which whatever you find you will want again from afar. A duplicitous city in which everything is its own looking glass, forever mirroring, always the same sky reflecting domed rock cut from sky, always the same broad onrush of evening casting back the red roofs of the houses. People draw near and recede as in mirrors. A few last gilded roofs. Still the spires of the minarets. Evening comes with an avalanche of longing, and you walk slowly through Zion Square as the first lights go on and buy a coal-hot order of stemmed *hamleh m'lan* from the scarfaced Sudanese vendor, eating it as though there were no other food in the world and no other you apart from this one perfect hunger that must be shared with a friend because everything is in it, this entire evening, and is more than one person can bear.

"When I was a girl," Sara told Elias and the Barzels while they were out walking one evening, "I used to think that Egypt was a country under the ground. It wasn't a place you could get to by ordinary travel; it was a secret, hidden land that could only be reached by going straight down, right into the ground beneath your feet. It had a Pharaoh and a great blockhouse for slaves. There were whole subterranean cities lit by lanterns, tunnels with hurricane lamps, warehouses full of grain, gold, and seeds. Sometimes I used to touch the sharp point of a rock sticking up in a field and tell myself that it was the tip of an underground Egyptian pyramid of which nobody knew but myself. And each spring came the exodus from Egypt, everything budding, sprouting, shooting up. Right here in this field near our house."

"And I used to think," said Hulda, "that time was a river. If you wouldn't swim in it, you would never grow old."

"Sara, is it true that Subhi Bey and his family came to visit you every Passover?" asked Professor Barzel.

"Not just every Passover. And when they came it was always with a basket of presents, and dressed in their best. And we used to call on them for Id-el-Fitr, to bring holiday greetings. The things in those straw baskets! Date syrup from palm groves they owned near Gaza. We were crazy about that syrup. What Faiza and we didn't cook for each other! I remember how one Passover they came to visit Grandfather together with Taleb, their eldest son. He had just returned from studying in Germany, where he had apparently spent two years in total isolation. He must have been a pathetic sight there. He's not terribly bright and it's an effort to get him to talk, but there's something serious about him."

Dr. Bimbi shook his head. "He must have gone on living there by his own inner clock. And among all those Lutherans! Good Lord, who sent him there?"

"Subhi, who else? So Taleb very apologetically said that he had a question to ask. *Is'al ya ibni*, said my grandfather, ask, my son. Taleb wanted to know if it was true that the Jews baked their Passover *matsas* with blood, because that was what he had heard from Christians in Europe. Faiza jumped on him of course, and said he should be ashamed of such talk, while Subhi got all red and huffy; I thought he was going to murder him then and there. But Grandfather didn't lose his temper. He told Bukas to bring some cheese, took a piece of matsa from the table, and said: 'Ya Taleb, you and your father are familiar with our customs, and you know that no observant Jew would ever eat milk and meat products together. Look!' And he put the cheese on the matsa and ate it. There was nothing showy about it, it was just a simple act, but we all had goosepimples. For a second I thought I saw that Grandfather was wearing shrouds beneath his clothes."

"Was Taleb convinced?"

"I'm not sure. He's much more pious than his father, by the way. As soon as he came back from Germany he married a very religious girl, the daughter of a *kadi*, who's always veiled and never leaves the house. She's already had three children and no one's even caught a glimpse of her. A real homebody. God only knows what Faiza thinks about it all." [. . .]

There is a moment right after sunset when the stones of the city grow terribly pale, like a man at the end of his strength who waits in spent silence to be transported as he is to whatever lies beyond. Night then falls with softly stunning kindness, a blessing certain and swift.

One adjusts one's breathing to its breath; each street and its houses, each house and its breathers, attending their nocturnal fate. On such nights Sara lay curled by Elias' side, en mi cama matrimonial, as she liked to say to herself, and imagined that the steps of her house led infallibly down to the sea. Suppose the whole street should suddenly lift up and be washed ashore in Brindisi? She was certain she had once been in Brindisi, in another incarnation perhaps, had sat there in the twilight behind bolted shutters in an embroidered, wine-colored dress, a yellow citron lustrous on a table, her head shaven beneath its wig, listening to the sound of seawater as it lapped against the steps of her house.

On the subject of reincarnation, Elias was sure that he had lived in Jerusalem in Herod's time and had been trampled to death there by a horse-drawn chariot in a narrow alley. In his nightmares he saw the horse bearing wildly down on him and the frightened eyes of the charioteer; he felt the wall against him, sudden and hard, and knew he could back off no farther. The dream kept recurring.

He felt at home, so he said, in the Herodian remnants of Jerusalem, in the ruined towers of Phasael and Antonia with their margined, finely dressed stones. A toga would have befit his tall frame. His sad, knowledgeable mouth could have spoken all the tongues of that complicated city without tripping. Greek sounded well on Elias. Not the Greek of Madame Savvidopoulos, but the blunt, wise, stinging Greek of those times.

No city lives closer to the almost visible ghosts of past lives than Jerusalem; no city is better at blind, secret love. Hermetic, ironic, a sink of cold tempests, the city stands upright on the mountain against the cold night, most strong and most vulnerable, something in it never falling asleep. All places outside of it are like a somehow undeserved vacation. Or is there any place at all outside of Jerusalem?

And once, on a nearly violet-skied autumn night, when sleepers lay most unprotected and an abyss surrounded each bed, Sara managed to see Elias' horse in her dream and to feel the hard wall at her back. The two of them awoke and lay with hearts pounding till morning while the waves of the city washed over them again and again with a harsh, moonlike obstinacy.

Toward evening the setting sun took possession of Elias Amarillo's white room, illuminating his head as it bent over documents. Sara would bring his coffee up to him, with a glass of arak and a glass of cold water by its side. It was forbidden to sit in the living room below. Noam had five winkies, invisible creatures that no one could see but himself, and whenever anyone sat on a chair, or the couch he would wail:

"A-y-yy! Get up quick! You're sitting on a winky!"

Which meant that the sitter had to get to his feet and escort the winky outside, a task that was by no means simple, inasmuch as it couldn't be seen. Lately Hillel had refused to see the winkies to the door. He had simply outgrown them. Sometimes Noam would make a fuss:

"They don't want to leave the house."

It then took a considerable amount of entreaty and formal persuasion to get rid of them.

"There'll be loads of fruit this year," said Elias Amarillo, sipping cold water as he looked down at the garden from his second-floor room.

"Grandfather would have loved to see it."

The toothed old city wall near the Damascus Gate could be seen well from Elias' room, though not the young rowdies who had taken to congregating beneath it and to accosting non- Arab women: "Madame, come with me to Ramallah, I weel show you Nablus, Madame." Nor could you see Subhi Bey's slim-shouldered, bitter-souled brother, old Hajj Kemal ad-Din, as he walked with heavy heart and courtly steps to prayer at the Sheikh Lulu mosque. "*Hajj Kemal, ya dayus, ba' al-balad bil filuss*," the children chanted after him, the traitor Kemal is selling Jerusalem for filthy money. But it wasn't money that he wanted, it was peace. Over and over he had tried to persuade the Jewish leaders to stop the flow of immigration from Europe, which they insisted on calling rescue work. What were they so afraid would happen to all those Jews in Europe? Hajj Kemal knew Europe well; it was a civilized place. And without immigration there would be quiet in Palestine. Truly there would be. Only nobody wanted to listen to him. Even Mr. Shertok of the Jewish Agency who had grown up among Arabs in Ein-Sinya refused to lend an ear.

The western light grazed the wall and the roof of the Church of the Dormition, then faded like a last reverberation of brass cymbals.

Translated by Hillel Halkin.

Other works by Hareven: *Yerushlayim dorsanit* (1962); *Soneh ha-nisim* (1983); *Otsar ha-milim shel ha-shalom* (1996); *Tsima'on: shilishiyat ha-midbar* (1996).

Hanoch Levin

1943–1999

Born and brought up in Tel Aviv, Hanoch Levin was a dramatist, director, writer, and poet. Levin was a major force in the Israeli theater and remained a controversial figure throughout his productive and tragically short career. He wrote more than sixty plays, as well as collections of poetry and prose, and two books for children. Many of his poems were set to music. In 1994, Levin received the Bialik Prize.

Ya'akobi & Leidental

1972

Scene Twelve

[LEIDENTAL's *room. Evening.* LEIDENTAL. *One of his fingers is bandaged.*]

LEIDENTAL: [*To himself.*] At eight fifteen I felt I cannot any more with myself. I had: regulation misery, pain to top the misery, sadness to top the pain, the humiliation that I humiliated myself with them, the humiliation that I would still humiliate myself with them, the shame of the humiliation, and in addition self-hatred because I'm so touchy and sensitive. All this built up till eight fifteen when I felt I had to put my attention elsewhere, otherwise I would go mad. So I went to the bathroom and cut my finger. Not a deep cut. Contrary to what I thought, it didn't help, because now on top of everything else, I felt the pain from the wound, and also the shame of not being brave enough to cut myself more seriously. [*Pause.*] I'll ask them if they've iodine. The drugstores are closed by now. But I'll throw away the iodine I keep at home, so I won't feel a liar when I ask them. At least I'll have some profit from the wound.

Scene Thirteen

[*The café. Evening.* YA'AKOBI *and* SHACHASH.]

SHACHASH [*To herself.*]: I'll be eating myself three months on account of the cake I could have ordered and lost. And maybe for all that it's worth my while to order that cake? But what impression would it make on him? That I'm cake-greedy? and to add to that, fickle? Ach, how everything disposes itself not as I would choose. I'd bend the world. But it's already . . . [*Gets up. To* YA'AKOBI.] I'm going home.

YA'AKOBI: And maybe in spite of everything coffee and cake?

SHACHASH [*To herself.*]: Oh temptation, temptation! [*To* YA'AKOBI.] I said, home.

YA'AKOBI [*To himself.*]: I knew I bore. Maybe I should have been more amusing. [*Both get up. Enter* LEI-DENTAL *with his suitcase, pointing to his bandaged finger.*]

LEIDENTAL: Excuse me, perhaps you have a little iodine?

SHACHASH [*To herself.*]: Can anyone explain to me why I fell? And on an empty stomach moreover? [*Stands motionless, then knocks* YA'AKOBI's *hat off and tramples on it.*]

YA'AKOBI [*Stunned.*]: What have I done now?

LEIDENTAL: Yes, yes, Ya'akobi. Life is very diversified.

YA'AKOBI [*Whispering to* SHACHASH.]: Please don't put me to shame in front of him. Thank you. [*Bends down to pick up his hat but* SHACHASH *has her foot on it.*] Not in front of him, please, thank you. [*She does not remove her foot.*] You see, I don't mind if you shame me once in a while. I'm quite used to it, but not in front of him, please. Thank you. [*Bends again to pick up hat,* SHACHASH *is unbudging.*] You've shamed me. [*They sing.*]

Don't Shame Me

> YA'AKOBI: *Don't shame me, don't let me eat crow.*
> *Honour may prove a little pliable—*
> *Without honour it's impossible.*
> SHACHASH and LEIDENTAL: *Don't shame him, don't let him eat crow.*
> *Allow the miserable man a little meaning.*
> *Weight of his manhood hangs heavy on him.*
> YA'AKOBI: *Don't shame me, don't let me eat crow.*
> *A soft look of your eyes will do,*
> *a word of human connection.*
> *I'm yours if you throw me a bone.*
> SHACHASH and LEIDENTAL: *Don't shame him, don't let him eat crow.*
> *Allow the miserable man a little meaning.*
> *Weight of his manhood hangs heavy on him.*

[SHACHASH *picks up hat, hands it to* YA'AKOBI. *Going off, she stops in front of* LEIDENTAL, *smiles at him. Drops a glove.* LEIDENTAL *hastens to pick it up, hands it to her.*]

LEIDENTAL: There's no shame in making a lady's acquaintance through small gentlemanly services. My name is David Leidental. And yours?

SHACHASH [*To herself.*]: I've introduced them both to the tension-struggle and to insecurity. In this way my value rises. [*Exits.*]

YA'AKOBI [*To himself.*]: She doesn't want me—who knows? And again struggle, struggle, struggle—when will I rest with something secure in the hand? When can I know I have a steady base in life and move away from this continuous anxiety? I ask of God, give me something solid. I'm so fed-up, my nerves are wrecked. Other people smile out of their family photographs and I run aimlessly. And how will I iron my hat? [*To* LEIDENTAL.] You, keep your hands off ladies. [*Exit.*]

LEIDENTAL: I think she likes me. At first sight it seems simple. But if you think about it, why should anyone like me? What have I? Have I anything? I haven't anything. Am I tall? Strong? I'm not tall and strong. And maybe I'm a tiny bit tall? No, I'm simply short. Am I rich? I am not rich. Am I established? I am not established. Maybe it appears to her I'm established? No, it doesn't appear to her. On what basis should it appear to her? Out of my suitcase? Perhaps, then, if I'm not established, I am young? Well, am I young? And maybe I'm clever? No, I'm not clever. It's written all over me. So, perhaps if I've nothing of these things, maybe I still have some personal charm that touched her heart. Maybe I'm a character? I'm not a character, and I've no charm, what's to be done, it's not in me. I've a dry look and a dry smile. I'm dry. But maybe she, being a lady of charm and culture, found, by mistake, some feature in me that charmed her? That couldn't be. No, absolutely not. Nothing? Not even something small, tiny, a fleck, a flicker, something of something to signify some frail charm. Not even that? No, nothing. Good, it's impossible that there's nothing. That can't be?! That's a fact. So how, in spite of everything, did she allow me to pick up her glove. Do I know her? She allowed it. It isn't allowed to pick up a glove! It is allowed. [*Pause.*] Where is she? Maybe she has some iodine. [*Exits.*]

Scene Fourteen

[*A street, the doorway of* SHACHASH's *house. Night.* YA'AKOBI *and* SHACHASH.]

SHACHASH: Good night, then.

YA'AKOBI: When will we see each other again? [*Pause. To* SHACHASH.] You should know I'm not one of those who use and discard. And I'm no longer a child. I've a heap of serious intentions. [SHACHASH *keeps smiling.*] What else can I say about myself? And I'm not unusually sickly. Did you hear what I said?

SHACHASH: Yes.

YA'AKOBI: Then why are you smiling? What's your answer?

SHACHASH: I don't say "Yes" and I don't say "No."

YA'AKOBI: Well then?

SHACHASH: Well, I say nothing.

YA'AKOBI: When will you know?

SHACHASH: I don't say "Tomorrow" and I don't say "In a year."

YA'AKOBI: All the time you keep saying what you're not saying.

SHACHASH: I know what I'm saying and what I'm not saying and what I *am* saying. [*Pause.*] Doubt tortures him. [*Passes her hand over his head. He leans it on her neck.*] Yes, cuddle up to me, sniff the dish you've taken a fancy to, brace yourself [*To herself.*] I must take care not to draw the line too sharply and not to forget my own limits.

Of course I'll accept his proposal tomorrow. Why not? He smells of a steady income and he'll listen to whatever I tell him. [*To* YA'AKOBI] Now go to sleep because if my answer is yes then I'll need a healthy husband, at least the first five years. [*Exits.*]

YA'AKOBI: And I'm healthy, healthy. And the heart pulses. Nice, beat, continue, beat. [*Pause.*] I'm wanted, I'm wanted. I'm necessary to somebody, I'm being considered, I belong. To someone it's important I exist. I'm wanted. Somebody will weep following my coffin. Yes, there is, there is weeping, ladies and gentlemen. I scarcely have patience for waiting,

I'd like to die an hour after the wedding. [*Exit.*]

Scene Fifteen

[*Street facing* SHACHASH's *window. Night.* LEIDENTAL.]

LEIDENTAL: Big Lady! Big Lady!

SHACHASH [*From inside house.*]: Who's bigging me in the dead of night in front of my window?

LEIDENTAL: It's me, David Leidental.

SHACHASH: The man of the small gentlemanly services?

LEIDENTAL: Yes. Maybe the lady has a little iodine? I've cut my finger.

LEIDENTAL [*He sings.*]

Girl of My Dreams

Will you lay your hand on my brow
when I've a fever?
Look down my open mouth
with a thermometer?
Worry about me? Want me to live?
Be at my side forever?
Oh, girl of my dreams,
girl of my lost dreams.

Will you summon a night-doctor
when I faint at your side?
Will you be that one who sees
my last look, dimming?
Will you remember me? Want me back?
Weep on my grave, sometimes?
Oh, girl of my dreams,
girl of my lost dreams.

SHACHASH: You amuse me. Come in, you pet. [LEIDENTAL *goes in through the door.*]

Scene Sixteen

[YA'AKOBI's *room. Night.*]

YA'AKOBI: No, no, I can't complain. I've acquired a terrific woman. And I don't think it will be difficult to persuade myself I'm in love with her. Yes, a little effort and I'm persuaded she's the woman I was always dreaming of. However, it would be better if I'd fallen in love with her without any effort, I mean simply fallen in love with her. On the other hand, there's nothing wrong with a little effort. It's nothing unusual with me, and in fact it's what makes me a real man. Now I'll lie down quietly and make a little effort to fall in love with her. An hour or two from now I'll be besotted.

Translated by Dennis Silk and Shimeon Levy.

Other works by Levin: *Tsilo shel melekh* (1968); *Ḥefetz* (1972).

Amos Oz

My Michael
1972

Michael and I arranged to meet that same evening in Cafe Atara in Ben Yehuda Street. Outside an absolute storm was raging, beating down furiously on the stone walls of Jerusalem.

Austerity regulations were still in force. We were given ersatz coffee and tiny paper bags of sugar. Michael made a joke about this, but his joke was not funny. He is not a witty man—and perhaps he could not tell it in an amusing way. I enjoyed his efforts; I was glad that I was causing him some exertion. It was because of me that he was coming out of his cocoon and trying to be amused and amusing. When I was nine I still used to wish I could grow up as a man instead of a woman. As a child I always played with boys and I always read boys' books. I used to wrestle, kick, and climb. We lived in Kiryat Shmuel, on the edge of the suburb called Katamon. There was a derelict plot of land on a slope, covered with rocks and thistles and pieces of scrap iron, and at the foot of the slope stood the house of the twins. The twins were Arabs, Halil and Aziz, the sons of Rashid Shahada. I was a princess and they were my bodyguard, I was a conqueror and they my officers, I was an explorer and they my native bearers, a captain and they my crew, a master spy and they my henchmen. Together we would explore distant streets, prowl through the woods, hungry, panting, teasing Orthodox children, stealing into the woods around St. Simeon's Convent, calling the British policemen names. Giving chase and running away, hiding and suddenly dashing out. I ruled over the twins. It was a cold pleasure, so remote.

Michael said:

"You're a coy girl, aren't you?"

When we had finished drinking our coffee Michael took a pipe out of his overcoat pocket and put it on the table between us. I was wearing brown corduroy trousers and a chunky red sweater, such as girls at the University used to wear at that time to produce a casual effect. Michael remarked shyly that I had seemed more feminine that morning in the blue woolen dress. To him, at least.

"You seemed different this morning, too," I said.

Michael was wearing a gray overcoat. He did not take it off the whole time we sat in Cafe Atara. His cheeks were glowing from the bitter cold outside. His body was lean and angular. He picked up his unlit pipe and traced shapes with it on the tablecloth. His fingers, playing with the pipe, gave me a feeling of peace. Perhaps he had suddenly regretted his remark about my clothes; as if correcting a mistake, Michael said he thought I was a pretty girl. As he said it he stared fixedly at the pipe.

I am not particularly strong, but I am stronger than this young man.

"Tell me about yourself," I said.

Michael said:

"I didn't fight in the *Palmach*. I was in the Signal Corps. I was a radio operator in the Carmeli Brigade."

Then he started talking about his father. Michael's father was a widower. He worked in the water department of the Holon municipality.

Rashid Shahada, the twins' father, was a clerk in the technical department of the Jerusalem municipality under the British. He was a cultivated Arab, who behaved toward strangers like a waiter.

Michael told me that his father spent most of his salary on his education. Michael was an only child, and his father cherished high hopes for him. [. . .] His father's greatest wish was for Michael to become a professor in Jerusalem, because his paternal grandfather had taught natural sciences in the Hebrew teachers seminary in Grodno. [. . .]

I told him that my father had died in 1943. He was a quiet man. He used to talk to people as if he had to appease them and purchase a sympathy he did not deserve. He had a radio and electrical business—sales and simple repairs. Since his death my mother had lived at Kibbutz Nof Harim with my older brother, Emanuel. "In the evenings she sits with Emanuel—and his wife Rina, drinking tea and trying to teach their son manners, because his parents belong to a generation which despises good manners. All day she shuts herself up in a small room on the edge of the kibbutz reading Turgenev and Gorki in Russian, writing me letters in broken Hebrew, knitting and listening to the radio. That blue dress you liked on me this morning—my mother knitted it."

Michael smiled:

"It might be nice for your mother and my father to meet. I'm sure they would find a lot to talk about. Not like us, Hannah—sitting here talking about our parents. Are you bored?" he asked anxiously, and as he asked he flinched, as if he had hurt himself by asking.

"No," I said. "No, I'm not bored. I like it here." [. . .]

I told him I was rooming with an Orthodox family in Achva. In the mornings I worked as a teacher in Sarah Zeldin's kindergarten in Kerem Avraham. In the afternoons I attended lectures on Hebrew literature. But I was only a first-year student.

"Student rhymes with prudent." Straining to be witty in his anxiety to avoid pauses in the conversation, Michael resorted to a play on words. But the point was not clear, and he tried to rephrase it. Suddenly he stopped talking and made a fresh, furious attempt at lighting his obstinate pipe. I enjoyed his discomfiture. At that time I was still repelled by the sight of the rough men my friends used to worship in those days: great bears of *Palmach*-men who used to tackle you with a gushing torrent of deceptive kindness; thick-limbed tractor drivers coming all dusty from the Negev like marauders carrying off the women of some captured city. I loved the embarrassment of the student Michael Gonen in Cafe Atara on a winter's night.

Translated by Nicholas de Lange in collaboration with the author.

Avraham Raz

1937–1971

Born on Kibbutz Gevat to Polish-born parents, Avraham Raz studied modern Hebrew literature at the Hebrew University, turning in his own writing from the short story to drama. Raz explored the relativity of truth, language, and storytelling in his play *Mr. Israel Shefi's Night of Independence*. This play, his best known, was first performed in 1972, after Raz's death.

Mr. Israel Shefi's Night of Independence
1972

[*While the song from the radio can still be heard,* IS-RAEL *sits motionless, in such a way that it is hard to tell whether he is checking a test, thinking, or is just sunk in his place. Later, suddenly, the melody is interrupted in the middle by the beeps announcing the news. Hearing the beeps,* ISRAEL *raises his head and listens with increasing tension. At the same time* HANNAH *also straightens up in her seat on the sofa and listens with increased tension.*]

ANNOUNCER: This is the Voice of Israel from Jerusalem with the news [*the army spokesman announces*]: "because of the heatwave, the army parade that was to be

held tomorrow, on the day of the holiday, at ten in the morning in Jerusalem, was held earlier. The parade has already finished. To the crowd still flowing to the parade in Jerusalem: until further notice, every quarter of an hour special trains will leave from Jerusalem for Tel Aviv, Haifa, and Beersheba." This was an announcement on behalf of the IDF spokesman.

In hundreds of settlements throughout the country the holiday events are continuing. In Jerusalem it is reported that the traditional reception at the president's residence has been postponed. An announcement will be forthcoming about the new date. Because of the heatwave it was also decided to postpone the ceremony awarding the Kaplan Prize. An announcement will be given regarding the new date. For the recipients of the prize and guests who cannot come at the new date, an additional ceremony will be held. An announcement will be given regarding the date of the additional ceremony. In Haifa, too, our correspondent reports that the traditional flower exhibition has been postponed. The exhibition will open when the heatwave is over. From police headquarters in Tel Aviv it is reported that in all the police stations in the district, until now no case of burglary, attack, or any crime at all has been reported. This is the first time since Independence Day celebrations were begun that the city of Tel Aviv is celebrating without crimes or violence. The police also report that they had already run out of all ninety thousand plastic hammers that were supplied on the eve of the holiday by early evening. On orders of the district commander a special airplane was sent to the factory in the south to bring another consignment. From the area of Ḥispin on the Golan Heights it is reported that the battle between our forces and the Syrian army is continuing. Planes from the air force are now bombing the Syrian positions. A number of mortar shells were also fired this evening at She'ar Yishuv. There were no casualties in the settlement, and no damage was caused. The weather will be . . .

ISRAEL: [*Turning off the transistor. After a moment, when he meets* HANNAH's *gaze.*] They announced that there aren't.

HANNAH: They announced it? I didn't hear.

ISRAEL: But I did.

HANNAH: In Ḥispin, too?

ISRAEL: Everywhere. They said explicitly that there were no casualties in the settlement.

HANNAH: They meant She'ar Yishuv.

ISRAEL: No. The word "Yishuv" is also used as a collective term for all of us. For the whole Yishuv.

HANNAH: But they didn't announce that there were none in Ḥispin.

ISRAEL: If there are none, then there are none. What is there to announce?

HANNAH: That there are none.

ISRAEL: Since they already announced it!

HANNAH: But they always announce.

ISRAEL: You don't understand. When they don't announce [*anything*], that's a sign that there aren't any. When they announce that there are none, that's a sign that . . . that there are. There are a few. And when they announce that there are, then . . . [*The telephone rings. They freeze in their places, looking at the ringing telephone.* ISRAEL, *after a moment, overcomes his hesitation and picks up the receiver.*] Shefi residence . . . Yes . . . Who is speaking? Hello? Hello? [*He looks at the receiver then returns it to the cradle. He looks at the notebooks again.*]

HANNAH: What did they say?

ISRAEL: Huh . . .

HANNAH: Who was it?

ISRAEL: Huh. Maybe . . .

HANNAH: Who?

ISRAEL: What? No. No one.

HANNAH: But someone said something, if you answered.

ISRAEL: Nobody.

HANNAH: How could it be nobody, if . . .

ISRAEL: Probably a wrong number. There are a lot of wrong numbers, right? Huh? I mean, calls that . . . Enough! Stop with this! Aside from that, the planes are there already. Didn't you hear? They'll finish things up one-two-three, and they don't take any excuses.

HANNAH: One-two-three.

ISRAEL: They've already finished.

HANNAH: But . . .

ISRAEL: Completely. That's it.

HANNAH: Why did they call in the planes?

ISRAEL: Why? Should they let them strike at our people? Freely?

HANNAH: Did they hit them, do you think?

ISRAEL: What do you mean, without any response from our side?

HANNAH: Really, it's been hours that the battle . . . Maybe . . .

ISRAEL: No maybes!

HANNAH: Couldn't they maybe have done it without the planes?

ISRAEL: What do you mean, couldn't they have done it? But we have planes, so why without them? Boys are fighting there, so why without? They're exposed there . . .

HANNAH: Do you think so?

ISRAEL: Boys in great danger, in the dark . . .

HANNAH: Completely exposed?

ISRAEL: Alone, in the darkness, and they're liable to . . . [*An envelope slips through the slot in the door; they both look at it. After a moment,* ISRAEL *picks up the envelope and stares at it.*] A telegram. [*They both look at the envelope.*]

HANNAH: A telegram? [ISRAEL *opens the envelope and looks.*] Who's the telegram from? What's written in it?

ISRAEL: To Hannah, and to Israel . . .

HANNAH: Who's it from? What's to Hannah and Israel?

ISRAEL: Nothing.

HANNAH: I don't understand.

ISRAEL: Nothing is written. To Hannah and to Israel. That's all.

HANNAH: Who sent it?

ISRAEL: It doesn't say. [*He hands her the telegram.*]

HANNAH: [*Looking at the telegram.*] How could that be? A telegram without the name of the sender.

ISRAEL: A mistake.

HANNAH: Maybe they forgot because of . . .

ISRAEL: There are a lot of mistakes . . . Because of what? It couldn't be. No one can know before the family. Stop. They would have told us already if . . . With us everything is reliable. Stop. All the names for us immediately.

HANNAH: Until they get to the names! First from the field, then to the hospital—

ISRAEL: Hannah.

HANNAH: From the hospital to the unit, from the unit to the quartermaster—

ISRAEL: Stop!

Hannah: From the quartermaster to the city officer, from the city officer to—

ISRAEL: [*Shouting.*] Hannah! . . . [*After a moment, with curiosity mingled with fear.*] Who told you all that?

HANNAH: Let's go to sleep.

ISRAEL: How is it . . . Who did you hear about the way it's done? [*Another envelope slips through the slit in the door. They both look at it. After a moment,* ISRAEL *picks up the envelope and opens it in a panic.*] Who is Mathilde?

HANNAH: Mathilde?

ISRAEL: A telegram. From Mathilde and Edmond.

HANNAH: Rothschild! Give it to me, it's from the Rothschilds.

ISRAEL: [*Hands her the telegram and she, with excitement mingled with apprehension and doubt, reads it and turns it over and over.*] What do they write?

HANNAH: "With you."

ISRAEL: With you?

HANNAH: Uh-huh.

ISRAEL: What's "With you"? Who is "with you"?

HANNAH: I don't know. That's all.

ISRAEL: Two words!

HANNAH: Mathilde and Edmond Rothschild.

ISRAEL: Give it to me.

HANNAH: [*Refusing, and when she encounters his demanding gaze.*] Later . . . [*After a moment, she hands him the telegram unwillingly.*] Give it back to me. [ISRAEL *takes the telegram from her and pores over it for a long time.*] Don't crumple it! Careful!

ISRAEL: [*With certain fear.*] Do they have connections, the Rothschilds?

HANNAH: Oh ho!

ISRAEL: In the highest places, they have.

HANNAH: You're telling me!

ISRAEL: In the Ministry of Defense, in the army, in the quarter . . .

HANNAH: Oh ho! What? [*Fearfully.*] What do you mean?

ISRAEL: Nothing . . . Tell me, who told you how it . . . What you told me before?

HANNAH: Let's go to bed.

ISRAEL: How it's all done. Who did you hear about it from?

HANNAH: I want to go to sleep.

ISRAEL: From them? Tell me! From the Rothschilds?

HANNAH: From Elisha!

ISRAEL: [*In astonishment.*] From Elisha!

HANNAH: [*Trying to get up.*] Help me up.

ISRAEL: How does Elisha know all the? . . .

HANNAH: [*Pleadingly*] Help me.

[ISRAEL *helps her get up. He supports her as she walks to the bedroom. The doorbell rings. They both stop. The bell is heard again. They both are in shock. The feeling of shock fades and changes to great gravity, but full of majesty and elevation, as after extremely heavy*

but purifying grief. ISRAEL *arranges his clothing and tie, and then he goes to the armchair, takes his jacket and puts it on, so that his appearance will be dignified and formal enough. While* ISRAEL *makes his preparations,* HANNAH *goes out, walking slowly and with a measured pace, into the bedroom.* ELISHA *enters. He is dressed in civilian clothes. Formal, but not dandified. The father and son stand in place for some time, surveying each other in silence.*

During the scene that will start with this, HANNAH *will return from the bedroom. Instead of the splendid dress with the deep décolletage she wore before, she will now be dressed differently, impressively formal but modest and without being fancy. She will stand at the door of the bedroom and look at the two others.*]

Translated by Jeffrey M. Green.

Amnon Shamosh

b. 1929

Born in Aleppo, Amnon Shamosh immigrated to Palestine when he was a child. As a young man, he fought in the War of Independence as a member of the Palmach and afterward was a founder of Kibbutz Ma'ayan Barukh, where he still resides. After teaching for many years, at the age of forty Shamosh began writing poetry and prose.

A Son of Two Cities
1972

No sooner had he laid his head on the pillow that he was fast asleep. His insomnia of the night before, his great fatigue on the sailing date, and the ship's swaying in the waves—all combined to immerse him in a deep sleep.

Well-groomed and nicely dressed, he hastened through the city streets, heading towards Jerusalem's Old City. [. . .]

He reaches Jerusalem's Old City via an unfamiliar side street. He lingers by some shop windows displaying high-quality leather goods, agonizing over the time lost when he should be rushing to arrive at his destination. A rather huge dog approaches him with malice in his eyes. He turns around and tries to flee without passersby noticing his consternation and trembling, and without the dog's noticing that he is frightened of it. The dog, however, sinks his teeth into the man's hip, tearing out a sizable chunk. Whereupon, the animal runs away and disappears. Relieved, Yosef stretches his hand to his back and realizes that it was his vest that was torn and ripped away; his back remained completely intact. It was just as well that the malevolent mutt had settled for that. However, it was really a shame that it had happened to such a lovely new vest, his pride and joy. This meant that, even if he arrived on time, he wouldn't be able to go in. It would be disgraceful to be seen in public wearing a torn vest. If it hadn't been so lovely, nobody would have paid any heed to the vest's tattered state. Yet, this vest attracts every eye, let alone every heart. Everyone will point to it. And if they don't point, they'll steal a glance. No, he will absolutely not go inside under these circumstances. Even if he arrives on time. And, in any case, he won't be able to get there in time.

The ringing of church bells inundated the silence. And when the tolling ceased and the bells fell silent, Christmas carols burst forth, capturing the heart with the beauty of their harmony. Where was the church entrance? Is that where he was headed?

To him, the alleyways of ancient Jerusalem became the streets of Athens. Here too, he was always in a rush. His wife at his side. They had only a fixed amount of time in this city he had always longed to visit to view its famed beauty. Today, they are in Athens. He took hold of his wife's exposed arm beneath her armpit and hastened her along. They had to return to the ship in the harbor by six o'clock in the evening. His finger groped its way up to her armpit, which exuded a pleasant dampness, either because of the heat or the delights of his touch—or perhaps both. If we had time, he mused, I would take her to a hotel. He looks at his watch and dismisses the thought. The hands of his watch are accelerating like crazy. They have to find time to buy a small rug for the entryway in their apartment; they had decided to do this even before the ship dropped anchor in Athens. They had seen such rug at the Alon's. And perhaps an umbrella. "And maybe an aphrodisiac," said his wife, "the best aphrodisiac sold here." His conscience bothered him, knowing they were in Athens and were not going to climb the Acropolis or go to any museums. He had dreamed his whole life of seeing Greece's treasures with his own eyes. He spoke about them a great deal, like an inveterate admirer, and now he had been given the opportunity of seeing them. The opportunity was there, and yet, it wasn't. For he did have to do some shopping, to stick to a schedule. Time was short, but the shopping would be long. With all their running around, they stopped to take in the delightful sight of reddening, sizzling chunks of meat revolving in front of a flame. Real shawarma. His mouth starts watering. She, too, stops. Her lips are hungry. They try to figure out if it's lamb or beef. They don't know one word of Greek. The European languages they are conversant with are of no help. With womanly resourcefulness, Ḥava starts lowing like a cow, while asking questions with her palms, fingers, and eyes. The vendor standing behind the flame shakes his head negatively. A few bare-chested men, gathered around them, are enjoying the strange tourists. Everything indicates that they are especially enjoying the female tourist. Nor does she hide her pleasure at their covetous looks. Spittle and blush appear on her lips, not just from her hunger for shawarma or the reflection of the flame. The knife in the manly Greek's hand absorbs the blade's sparkle, shooting it into Yosef's eyes. The semi-naked men's muscles take on the shape, color, and ardor of the beaded shawarma dripping fat. Ḥava's eyes stare hungrily at the cuts of meat. Now, she tries her hand at bleating like a sheep, to which the men nod their heads. They express their admiration for the woman's resourcefulness by smiling broadly and murmuring unintelligible words, which sound crude and racy. One of the Greeks, with a hairy body and thick fingers, extends his hand and taps the woman on her arm, while uttering the first word they could actually understand: "Bravo! Bravo!" Yosef trembled all over. He is unable to avert his murderous look from the hand resting ever so lightly on his wife's plump arm. With two upturned fingers, Ḥava has ordered two servings of shawarma. The knife cuts the meat. Slices of torrid, male muscle and shawarma fall into the pita's gaping gullet. They keep falling and falling, and still the pita is not full; it is like a bottomless barrel. The knife cuts and cuts into the meat. The blade strikes the flame and is thrown back into Yosef's eyes. Alarmed, he opens them, shielding them with his hand.

His cabinmate has just come back and turned on the light. He says he's sorry with exaggerated politeness. He looks exactly like a scoundrel! He goes to his bed, turns on the concealed lamp, and turns off the large light. He takes off his shirt and hangs it up in slow motion while holding it between the thumb and forefinger of both hands. The same hairy chest. Even his back and shoulders are covered with disgusting hair. It's strange that for the first time in his life he saw him that same afternoon, and this non-Jew had already jumped into his dreams. He had never had the opportunity before of seeing a non-Jew in all his nakedness.

Translated by Marvin Meital.

Other works by Shamosh: *Aḥoti kalah* (1974); *Mishel ʿEzra Safra u-vanav* (1978).

A. B. Yehoshua
b. 1936

A. B. Yehoshua is an author, playwright, and essayist. Jerusalem-born, he served in the military, taught in Paris, and was a professor of Hebrew and comparative literature at Haifa University. Yehoshua has written numerous best-selling novels as well as nonfiction, children's books, and plays. His essays have appeared in the Israeli and foreign press. In 1995, Yehoshua received the Israel Prize for Literature.

Early in the Summer of 1970
1972

I believe I ought to go over the moment when I learned of his death once more.

A summer morning, the sky wide, June, last days of the school year. I rise late, faintly stunned, straight into the depths of light; don't listen to the news, don't look at the paper. It is as though I had lost my sense of time.

I get to school late, search the dim green air in vain for a fading echo of the bell. Start pacing the empty playground, across squares of light and shadow cast by the row of windows, past droning sounds of classrooms at their work. And then, surprised, I discover that the Head is running after me, calling my name from afar.

Except that I have nearly arrived at my class, the Twelfth, their muffled clamor rising from the depth of the empty corridor. They have shut the door upon themselves not to betray my absence, but their excitement gives them away.

Again the Head calls my name from the other end of the corridor, but I ignore him, open the classroom door upon their yells and laughter which fade into a low murmur of disappointment. They had by now been certain I wouldn't show up today. I stand in the door waiting for them to sort themselves out, wild-haired, red-faced, in their blue school uniforms, scrambling back to their desks, kicking the small chairs, dropping Bibles, and gradually the desk tops are covered with blank sheets of paper, ready for the exam.

One of them is at the blackboard rubbing out wild words—a distorted image of myself. They look me straight in the eye, impudent, smiling to themselves, but silent. For the present my gray hairs still subdue them.

And then, as I walk softly into the room, the exam paper in my hand, the Head arrives, breathless, pale. All eyes stare at him but he does not even look at the class, looks only at me, tries to touch me, hold me; he who has not spoken to me for the past three years is all gentleness now, whispers, pleads almost: Just a moment . . . never mind . . . leave them . . . you've got to come with me. There's some notice for you . . . come. . . .

It is three years now that no words have passed between us, that we look at each other as though we were stone. Three years that I have not set foot in the common room either, have not sat on a chair in it, not touched the teapot. I intrude into the school grounds early in the morning, and during recess I wander up and down corridors or playground—summers in a large, broad-brimmed hat, winters in a greatcoat with the collar up—floating back and forth with the students. I pay my trips to the office long after school is out, leave my lists of grades, supply myself with chalk.

I hardly exchange a word with the other teachers.

Three years ago I had been due to retire, and had indeed resigned myself to the inevitable, had even considered venturing upon a little handbook of Bible instruction, but the war broke out suddenly and the air about me filled with the rumble of cannon and distant cries. I went to the Head to say I was not going to retire, I was staying on till the war would end. After all, now that the younger teachers were being called up one by one he would need me the more. He, however, did not see any connection between the war and myself. "The war is all but over," he told me with a curious smile, "and you deserve a rest."

No rest, however, but a fierce summer came, and flaming headlines. And two of our alumni, very young, killed one a day after the other. And again I went to him, deeply agitated, hands trembling, informed him in halting phrases that I did not see how I could leave them now, that is to say, now that we were sending them to their death.

But he saw no connection whatever between their death and myself.

The summer vacation started and I could find no rest, day after day in the empty school, hovering about the office, the Head's room, waiting for news, talking to parents, questioning them about their sons, watching pupils in army uniform come to ask about their matric grades or return books to the library, and sniffing the fire-singed smell in the far distance. And again, another death, unexpected, an older alumnus, much liked in his time, from one of the first class-years, killed by a mine on a dirt-track, and I at the Head again, shocked, beaten, telling him: "You see," but he straight away trying to brush me off: he has given instructions to prepare the pension forms, has planned a farewell party—which of course I declined.

A week before the new school year I offered to work for nothing if only he would give me back my classes, but he had already signed on a new teacher and I was no longer on the roster.

School starts. I arrive along with everyone in the morning, carrying briefcase and books and chalk, ready to teach. He spotted me near the common room and inquired anxiously what had happened, what was I doing here, but I, on the spur of the moment, did not reply, did not even look at him, as though he were a stone. He thought I had gone out of my mind, but in the turmoil of a new school year had no time to attend to me. And meanwhile my eyes had been searching out the new teacher, a thin, sallow young man, in order to follow him. He enters the classroom, and I linger a moment and enter on his heels. Excuse me, I say to him with a little smile, you must be mistaken, this isn't your class, and before he has time to recover I have mounted the platform, taken out my ragged Bible. He stammers an apology and leaves the room, and as for the dazed students who never expected to see me again, I give them no chance to say a word.

When after some moments the Head appears, I am deep in the lesson, the class listening absorbed. I would not budge.

I did not leave the room during recess, stayed planted in a crowd of students. The Head stood waiting for me outside but did not dare come near me. If he had I would have screamed, in front of the students I would have screamed and well he knew it; and there was nothing he feared as much as a scandal.

By sheer force I returned to teaching. I had no dealings with anyone but the students. For the first few weeks I scarcely left the school grounds, would haunt them even at night. And the Head in my wake, obsessed by me, dogs my steps, talks to me, appeals to me, holding, stroking, threatening, reproaching, speaking of common values, of good fellowship, of the many years

of collaboration, coaxes me to write a book, is even prepared to finance its publication, sends messengers to me. But I would not reply—eyes on the ground, or on the sky, or on the ceiling; freezing to a white statue, on a street corner, in the corridor, in the empty classroom, by my own gate, or even in my armchair at home, evenings when he would come to talk to me. Till he gave up in despair.

He had meant to drag me into his office, but I did not wish to move out of the students' range. I walked a few paces out into the corridor and stopped, and before the attentive gaze of the students I wrung it all out of him.

Some five or six hours ago—
In the Jordan Valley—
Killed on the spot—
Could not have suffered—
Not broken it to his wife yet, nor to the university—
I am the first—
He had put my name on the forms and for some reason given the school for address.
Must be strong now . . .
And then the darkness. Of all things, darkness. Like a candle the sun going out in my eyes. The students sensed this eclipse but could not move, weren't set for the contingency of my needing help, whereas the Head talked on fluently as though he had been rehearsing this piece of news for the past three years. Till suddenly he gave a little exclamation.

But I had not fainted, only slumped to the floor and at once risen to my feet again, unaided, and the light was returning to me as well, still dim, in the empty classroom, seated on a student's chair, seeing people throng the room, teachers rushing in from nearby classrooms, curious students, office workers, the janitor, people who had not spoken to me these three years. Here they were all coming back, some with tears in their eyes, surrounding me, a whole tribe, breaking my loneliness.

Translated by Miriam Arad.

Other works by Yehoshua: *The Lover* (1977); *A Late Divorce* (1982); *Mr. Mani* (1989); *A Journey to the End of the Millennium* (1997).

Lova Eliav

1921–2010

Author, member of the Knesset, and Israel Prize laureate, Aryeh "Lova" Eliav was born in Moscow as Lev

Lipschitz. In 1924, his family moved to Palestine, and in 1936, he became a fighter in the Haganah. During World War II, he served in a British artillery brigade and in the War of Independence he was a commander in the Israeli navy. Eliav played a critical role in bringing in Jews from Arab countries in the 1950s. Lova Eliav was awarded the Israel Prize in 1988.

The Seagull
1973

On a turquoise sea sails a ship. A sharp-eyed gull flies around the mast, swooping down from time to time to see what is happening on the ship, in all its decks. The boat has three decks and a bridge. On the lowest deck, in the belly of the vessel, sit the oarsmen, chained to the bulkheads. Their bodies are covered with sweat, shining like polished copper. They grasp long oars, reaching through slits at sea level. At the end of this cellar hall sits the chief oarsman. His legs are spread wide. He holds a leather whip with lead on its lashes, and a drummer sits next to him, giving the regular rhythm to the oarsmen. On the middle deck are the kitchen and services. The cooks, sauce-makers, bakers, and beverage makers do their work with haste and noise. Errand boys and servants rush up the spiral staircase to the top deck with trays and pitchers full of delicacies. The upper deck, the bridge, is roomy and bright with sunlight. On soft carpets, cushions, mats, and easy chairs men and women lie about, pampered and stuffed, while their children with golden curls play with gaily colored balls. The commanders are on the bridge. The captain and his comrades are drunk with the wine of their glory, stunned by the libation of their greatness, and sure of themselves and of their status. The helmsman stares at the near horizon, which seems clear and open to him. The ship is solid, narrow, and agile. Storms feel as if they have already been passed. The sea is calm and clear. The oarsmen work steadily. The ship advances swiftly.

The gull leaps up, high, high over the ship rowing in the sea. On the far horizon it sees a wall of frightening pointed rocks, huge and mighty, rising from the sea. It sees that the course of the ship is heading directly toward the wall of boulders. The gull dives down to the bridge, circles around it, waves its wings, tries to arouse the attention of the pilots, flies toward the horizon and keeps returning to the bridge. It shrieks sharp warnings, in vain. Its voice is not theirs, its eyes are not theirs, its horizon, not theirs.

The sun is setting. The fast-moving ship does not change course. Soon night will come. A night with no moon or stars. The helmsman will see nothing but the prow in front of him. The ship will collide with the rocks and run aground. The gull knows this. The gull wants to warn them.

If only it could speak the language of the pilots, it would say: "Open your eyes, ship the oars, raise the sails, change course, let a different, favorable wind bring you to a safe harbor!" Darkness envelops the ship. The sea is calm. The sound of the pounding drum and the sound of the oars is relaxing. Colorful lanterns are lit on the bridge. The passengers there are preparing for a party. And the gull circles and circles, screeching into the night.

Translated by Jeffrey M. Green.

Other works by Eliav: *Between Hammer and Sickle* (1965); *The Voyage of the Ulua* (1967); *New Targets for Israel* (1969); *The Short Cut* (1970); *Shalom: Peace in Jewish Tradition* (1977); *Autobiography: Rings of Dawn* (1984); *New Heart, New Spirit: Biblical Humanism for Modern Israel* (1986); *On Both Sides of the New-Comers' Camp* (with Y. Alfi, 2006).

POETRY AND POPULAR SONG

Nathan Alterman

The Silver Platter
1947

A State is not handed to a people on a silver platter.
[Chaim Weizmann, first president of Israel]

. . . and the land was silent. The incarnate sun
Flickered languidly
Above the smoldering borders.
And a nation stood—cloven hearted but
    breathing . . .
To receive the miracle.
The one miracle and only . . .

The nation made ready for the pomp. It rose to the
    crescent moon
And stood there, at pre-dawn, garbed in festival-
    and-fear.
—Then out they came
A boy and a girl
Pacing slowly toward the nation.

In workaday garb and bandoleer, and heavy-
    shod.
Up the path they came
Silently forward.
They did not change their dress, and had not yet
    washed away
The marks of the arduous day and the night of the
    fire-line.

Tired, oh so tired, forsworn of rest,
And oozing sap of young Hebrewness—
Silently the two approached
And stood there unmoving.
There was no saying whether they were alive or
    shot.

Then the nation, tear-rinsed and spellbound,
    asked,
Saying: Who are you? And the two soughed
Their reply: We are the silver platter
On which the Jewish State has been given
    you.

They spoke. Then enveloped in shadow at the
    people's feet they fell.
The rest will be told in the annals of Israel.

Translated by Dom Moraes and T. Carmi.

Haim Hefer

Dudu
1947

Across a red horizon evening descends
In the breeze treetops tremble and sway
As we sit around the campfire and tell
Of a Palmach man, Dudu was his name

He was with us on long exhausting treks
We patrolled together along border trails
Around the campfire he sang with all his
    strength
While on a spit a chicken roasted and turned

Hand over the kettle and do not argue:
Was there ever a Palmachnik like our Dudu?

The forelock on his head was thick and wavy
And in his eyes a twinkle, a mirthful gleam,
And when the girls crowded around him
He laughed hard and heartily

And let's remember smuggling in the night
When an anchor creaked in the dark
And from boat to shore Dudu carried a child
Stroking his cheek and keeping quiet.

And we wondered: Why so quiet, Dudu,
What's the matter with you?

When the coded message came
Dudu held the rifle close to his chest
High above a summer moon shone bright
And stealthily we set out into the night

We brought him back from battle at daybreak
Slowly the pine lowered his head
Only he who had lost the best of friends
Would know our pain and heartache

Now tell me friends, do tell:
Is Dudu still smiling up there?

Translated by Tsipi Keller.

Haim Gouri

Behold, Our Bodies Are Laid Out
1948

To Dani and his friends

Behold, our bodies are laid out—a long, long row.
Our faces are altered. Death looks out of our eyes.
    We do not breathe.
Twilight dwindles and evening falls over the
    mountain.
Look—we do not come upright to tread the roads in
    the last light of sunset.
We do not make love, we do not strum strings in
    softly gentle sound,
We do not shout in the groves when the wind comes
    streaming through the forest.

Behold, our mothers are stooped and silent, and our
    comrades hold back from weeping,
And there are explosions of grenades nearby and
    fire and signs of an impending storm!
Will you indeed bury us now?
We would rise, coming out as before, and we would
    live again.
We would stagger, awesome and great and rushing
    to help,
For all within us is still living, and racing in the
    arteries, and fervid.

We did not break faith. See, our weapons are held
    close with their cartridges empty, out of bullets.
They remember our words to the very last. Their
    barrels are still hot
And our blood is splattered along the paths step
    upon step.
All we could, we did, until the very last one fell, no
    more to rise.
Will we indeed be blamed if we remain dead at
    evening time
With our lips fixed to the hard stony ground?

Look—what a great wide night.
Look—the blossom of stars in the dark.

Scent of pines. You will bury us now, with clods of
    dirt on our faces.
Here, among the bristling barbed wire, the trenches,
    here we are all together.
New day, do not forget! Do not forget!!
Because we carried your name until death closed
    our eyes.

Behold our bodies are laid out, a long row, and we
    are not breathing.
But the wind, full of breath, is strong in the
    mountains.
Morning is born, and dew-bringing sunset exults.
We will still come back, we will meet, and return
    like red flowers.
You will recognize us at once, as the voiceless
    "Mountain Platoon."
Then will we blossom. When the scream of the last
    shot shall have fallen to silence in the mountains.

Translated by Esther Raizen.

Haim Hefer

We Left Slowly
1948

We left slowly. The night was pale.
In the distance the lights flickered.
And you were all loveliness like your two eyes
With tears cupped in them.

The jackal howled as you went to the vineyard
Your tears flowing like sap from a tree.
And you remembered the hours before
We went out to battle by the narrow path.

You remembered our laughter like a stream.
You remembered a dance and a lilting harmonica.
You remembered the haystack,
And the hand's touch of the only one . . .

And if you are left, with loneliness enfolding,
And you walk in the vineyards slowly—
You will wait. Therefore, in such silence
We parted with a smile in our eyes.

Translated by Esther Raizen.

Rafael Klatchkin

1907–1987

Born in Volkovysk (now Belarus), singer and lyricist Rafael Klatchkin immigrated to Mandatory Palestine in 1921 and joined the Habima Theatre in 1928, after it, too, relocated to Palestine. In addition to his influence on the stage, Klatchkin acted in many popular Israeli films, including *Chalutzim* (1933), the first Israeli sound film. Klatchkin continued to act in a variety of Israeli films well into the 1970s.

Have Faith the Day Will Come
1948

This day is our war, my sister,
So I am far away from here.
Please keep our rendez-vous
In our tiny kitchen

Before my usual chair
Fill a glass of wine
And treat it as if I am
Sitting across from you as always.

Have faith the day will come
I promise you it will be fine
I'll return to embrace you
And relate it all to you.

Yesterday we went out on a mission
until the early dawn
today we rested and relaxed
and the moon turned silver.

I recalled my meeting with you
In your green dress
The night is good for me I said
For you are close and not far away

When mouths of the Stens bark
And the mortars groan
Then my thoughts turn to you
My sister and my love.

And then I know the battle has meaning
Although the price is high to give
So that someday the day will come
When we can breathe and we can live.

Have faith the day will come . . .

Translated by Karen Alkalay-Gut.

Haim Gouri

The Song of Friendship
1949

On the Negev an autumn night falls
Surreptitiously igniting star after star
And as the wind crosses the threshold
Clouds spread over the path.

It's been a year already. We hardly felt
How the times in our fields went past.
Already a year, and only we the few remain
So many are no longer among us.

But we remember them all
Handsome of face and forelock
Such friendship will keep them
Forever deep in our hearts.
A love sanctified by blood
Will again blossom among us.

Wordlessly we've carried you, Friendship—
Gray, stubborn, and silent.
From the nights of great horror
You alone remain bright and ardent.

Friendship, like all your lads
Once again we'll smile and walk in your name
Since friends who fell by the sword
Have kept your memory alive in our hearts.

But we remember them all . . .

Translated by Tsipi Keller.

Abraham Shlonsky

1900–1973

With Nathan Alterman, Abraham Shlonsky was the leading modern Hebrew poet of Mandatory Palestine. Born in a Ukrainian village and sent when he was thirteen to study at the Herzliyah Hebrew Gymnasium in Tel Aviv, he was joined by his entire family in 1921. Shlonsky became a manual laborer, paving roads, working on construction sites, and eventually laboring on the land (he helped to establish Kibbutz 'Ein Harod in the Jezreel Valley). Linguistic inventiveness and sophisticated wordplay characterize Shlonsky's poetry, yet like many poets of his generation, he turned to more national themes in the 1940s. He was known for his many translations of world literature, especially the Russian classics, and for his children's poetry and plays.

The Oath
1949

> By these eyes that have seen the woe and grief,
> their outcries heaving to my heart's embrace,
> by this compassion which taught me: forgive
> till the time did come too awful for grace—
> I have taken this oath: as I breathe and live,
> to forget not a thing of that which took place.
>
> Till the tenth generation—forget no jot,
> till the last of my insults be completely assuaged,
> till the last of my lashes has chastened their lot.
> Cry heaven, if in vain passed that night of rage,
> Cry heaven, if by morning I resume my trod
> not learning the lesson taught me by this age.

Translated by Dov Vardi.

Other works by Shlonsky: *Kitvey Avraham Shlonsky*, 10 vols. (1972–1973).

Abraham Sutzkever

Deer at the Red Sea
1949

> The sunset grew bold: it insisted on staying
> In the Red Sea at night, when the innocent pink
> Young fawns delicately make their way
> Downhill to the palace of water to drink.
>
> They leave their silken shadows on the shore,
> Bending to lick the rings of coolness
> In the Red Sea, with long fiddle-faces. And there
> They are betrothed at last to the silence.
>
> And then—they run away. Rosy flecks
> Animate the sand. But the sunset deer
> Stay behind in the water, mournful, and lick
> The silence of those that are no longer there.

Translated by Chana Bloch.

David Avidan
1934–1995

Poet, essayist, film writer, and peace activist David Avidan was born in Ramat Gan and raised at Kib-

butz Geva'. In the 1950s and 1960s, he was an editor and columnist for the newspaper *Yediot aharonot*. He wrote thirty collections of poetry and the scripts for four films. In 1994, Avidan was awarded the Bialik Prize.

The Joke
1950

> The body of a weary man is primed like an
>   ambulance
> Adrenaline charges through his hot blood.
> I will go mad if we don't end this now.
> Bizarre how a man so blind with bits of coal
> Can strike so exactly at the eyelids of dawn.
>
> Bizarre how a man so deaf hears so well
> The steps of the choking wind outside.
> So what, we've already seen how iron can weep,
> Even how an amulet can be fashioned from a
>   wound—
> But like *t h i s*? (His hot blood has ceased to flow).
>
> The man is already dead. It's not a great joke
> Perhaps, to eulogize him, and in verse yet.
> Maybe it's a bit strange to rinse the plate
> From which he didn't eat, and to scrub
> Under the shower that didn't blithely soak him.
> In the final analysis how are the faucets to blame?
>
> But if we're already calculating the results of this,
> If we're already sinning with this poem, to be
>   precise,
> It might be wise to recall a few fragments of a book
> In a yard flooded with bilge—
> And this is ultimately all that survived.
>
> Almost like two clerks who died at the office.

Translated by Karen Alkalay-Gut.

Other works by Avidan: *Be'ayot ishiyot* (1957); *Mashehu bishvil mishehu: mivhar shirim* (1964); *Shirim shimushiyim* (1973).

Uri Zvi Greenberg
1896–1981

A leading expressionist poet in both Yiddish and Hebrew, Uri Zvi Greenberg (also spelled Uri Tsevi Grinberg) was born in Biały Kamień, Galicia. The son of a Hasidic rabbi, he was raised in Lemberg (today Lviv) and fought on the Eastern front in the Austro-Hungarian army, an experience that shaped him deeply. A peripatetic poet thereafter, he moved from Warsaw to Berlin as the editor and publisher of *Albatros*. Certain that the Jewish people would be exterminated if they remained in Europe, he moved to Mandatory Palestine, where he joined the Revisionist Party in 1930. Emerging from his self-imposed silence during World War II, Greenberg published *Streets of the River: The Book of Dirges and Power* in 1951, a monumental work of personal lyric and national lamentation.

To God in Europe
1951

I. I'll Say to God

God, blood has overflowed the soul; among us, the
    weight of his killed kindred
lies heavy on the head of every living creature.
And it is Sinai, it is Nevo now.
As for the *goyim*, the killers, you bless the fields of
    their countries,
the trees of their gardens
with a heavenly blessing. It is not they
that you have given water of gall to drink.

Who am I to add a rung to the ladder of Hebrew
    prayer
of my holy mother, my holy father and their
    children,
for whom you had no pity on that day
the *goyim* slaughtered them,
when they looked to you where you sat in heaven on
    high!

Where is the lost song now? Where has it streamed
    away?
Was it a seed sown in the lap of whoredom,
in the womb of barren time,
the burial of our soul's strong stream, the splendour
    of our yearning
in the soil of exile? with the corpses of the holy:
who stood in prayer in despair with the children
while the *goyim* raged midst cross and torch and
    spear . . .

God, I as one of the many beheaded of father and
    mother,
the heaps of whose slaughtered lie heavy upon them,
stand before you in the prayer-line of my slain ones,

I replace them in the world as a man replaces his
    comrade in battle,
lest, one link lost, their chain of eternity
drop from the hand of the living:
the chain of the race whose latest link I am,
the chain leading to me,
to the end of the day of my night, and to
the returning time of greatness,
for which the generations forged the chain.
In every circumstance, under every rule, they taught
    their children this,
who learned it by heart and wrote it down,
eye to eye and heart to heart.

Dumb are the slaughtered, the dust of seventy exiles
    stops their mouths:
I pray their prayer for them—and in their cadences.
Though my heart break, their Hebrew words are
    mine.
I believe in the continuity of this, I know
    completely
the earthly coast, its boundaries in dream,
where the pain of longing ends and visions wake
    with dawn.
In my mind I am close to all these, and I can touch
    them.
I am different from my forefathers: they indulged
    their longings, they prophesied right things,
but did not utter the Command of "Do" to
    the-people's-religion-of-longing.
God, therefore do I come to utter
in laws of song
this positive command,
since in Jerusalem there is not yet
ruler or commander for my people.

As I idly walk on my bounded path each day,
One of many along street and boulevard,—
the fragments of my people's disasters within me,
their weeping which is my blood,
and my legs, feelings, thoughts,
give way beneath the grave-stones of my dead—
and I walk my little path as if
I had been walking all my days
enormous distances, and in the warm flow of my
    blood.

I see the powerful armies of the barbarians, their
    wagons, chariots, their bolts and swords

and my intermingled tribes in the mingle of their
    babble:
their splendour and their darkness, the dispersal in
    exhaustion of their powers
though a bull is potent within them:
I see the brewers of mischief, the traitors, fools,
    sages among them:
and Satan walks among them, *but my songs, too, are
    among them,*
and I laugh then in my heart:
the sadness is here, true enough,
but soaring above all this, there soars the eagle of
    song,
carrying in his beak the
    crown-of-the-universal-kingdom:
All, without knowing, go
to the great palace of power,
as my will directs them,
this way or that:
in my songs is the magnet to which they are
    constantly drawn.

II. *To God in Europe*

You are God, and You don't have to get
a permit to move freely around (made out in Your
    name)
from the Army commanders in the occupied areas,
the wide and rotting fields of Israel, Your flock.
By day the sun, at night the stars still blaze:
a bell and organ psalm of blood for the chief
    musician, for the conqueror.

Go then and move among the gentiles there,
the crosses and the dogs. They will not bark or stab
    or madly rage,
their ears will never hear Your footsteps' sound:
sergeant and gentile, chariot and cart, will pass as
    easily through You
as through the air of their street, the wind of the day,
    the shadow of a tree.

Your path is the path of a being bodiless;
    nevertheless,
Your vision encompasses all,
including that which is under the layers of
    grave-soil;
nothing is hidden, nothing can hide from you: not
six million bodies of prayer,—mind pure, heart
    warm with song.

You are He who knows the beginning of Abraham
    and the days of the Kingdom,
the Jews of many exiles in song.
And you know their end: that death, that terror
    beyond all thought, beyond the moulds of words;
making clear: the time has come to disperse all
    parchment words, all letter combinations
so that they stand in uncombinable isolation
as before
the giving from Mt. Sinai of the Law . . .

All sensible survivors of the people dwelt with their
    grief, while I must gnash my teeth,
grinding words that are the children of the writ of
    lamentation.
But the words are not capable of expressing that
    deep pain when the need is lamentation
for every square with its item of horror in terror's
    mosaic.
Never before had our nation known such terror,
    darkening gradually and closing
around it, as around a tree, the ring of bereavement;
    and now
all light is ending. The future holds no rustle of a
    silken hem, no violin that sings
on wedding evenings in our street . . . About us a
    field teems
with graves and wells of Babylon and the streams.

Go wander about Europe, God of Israel, Shepherd-
    Seer, and count Your sheep:
how many lie in ditches, their "Alas" grown dumb:
how many in the cross's shadow, in the streets of
    weeping,
as if in the middle of the sea.
This is the winter of horror,
of orphanhood's sorrow, and of the fifth
    bereavement:
everything, everything is covered by the Christian,
    the silent snow of the shadow of death,
but not the sorrow, the orphanhood, the
    bereavement, the mourning,
for we have become, among the *goyim*, ashes and
    soap—dung for the dung heap.

You will count the few forsaken ones, those who
    have survived,
fugitive, whispering.
And they who light the smallest candle of hope in
    their darkness

will be heartened.
You will not cry aloud in lamentation—
God has no throat of flesh and blood, nor Jewish
   eyes for weeping.

And so You will return to heaven, a dumb
   Shepherd-Seer, after the shepherding and the
   seeing,
a shepherd staff in Your hand,
leaving not even the shadow of a slender staff on the
   death distances of Your Jews
where Your dead flock lie hidden . . .

A lying poet can poeticize: that after entering Your
   heaven
Your useless shepherd staff will shine, a rainbow in
   the sky.
Not I—who see within the vision the divided body
   of the bird.

I know very well that You will take the shepherd
   staff with You,
and wait till the battle subsides of Gog and Magog,
   who are also Your peoples, and our inheritors,
till the survivors assemble in the illusion of safety,
and once again there are synagogues, men praying
   to Your heaven,
societies again for chatter, platforms for speeches,
and again a pathway of roses for Your heretics.
And You will be the shepherd of them all.

And Jews will give their sons and daughters to the
   Moloch of *goyim*:
to seventy tongues—hands grasping pen, wheel, and
   banner;
give diligent agents of kingdoms: officers, soldiers;
give dreamers and fighters; inventors and doctors
   and artists;
those who turn sand into farmland and civilized
   landscape;
and those performing wonders—even for Albania—
   with their master of crafts;
give whores as well for brothels and clowns for
   stages,
dictionary compilers, grammar book sages
for languages still lame,
and spoken by barbarians who cannot write their
   name.

And there will be among us those loyal and
   dedicated

to all that is not ours; to the cultures that murdered
   us,
inherited our houses and all that they contained.
And moss will cover our racial mourning, and the
   sadness be hidden
of the knowledge of our people's bereavement.
Only a man like me will come with his pen in his
   hand
to beweep this moss-covered mourning,
   remembering always
the sorrow since pagan Titus's days
of an ancient race.

My rebuking pen, ripping the clouds apart,
shall make a flood descend!

Who listens to me will forsake his father and his
   mother and his friend,
he who shares his laughter and she who shares his
   heart,
the girl of dances and the woven wreaths—
and he will take the path my poem traces
to the lair of leopards in the mountain places.

III. No Other Instances

We are not as dogs among the gentiles: a dog is
   pitied by them,
fondled by them, sometimes even kissed by a
   gentile's mouth;
as if he were a pretty baby
of his own flesh and blood, the gentile spoils him
and is forever taking pleasure in him.
And when the dog dies, how the gentile mourns
   him!

Not like sheep to the slaughter were we brought in
   train loads,
but rather—
through all the lovely landscapes of Europe—
brought like leprous sheep
to Extermination itself.
Not as they dealt with their sheep did the gentiles
   deal with our bodies;
they did not extract their teeth before they
   slaughtered them;
nor strip them of their wool as they stripped us of
   our skins;
nor shove them into the fire to turn their life to
   ashes;
nor scatter the ashes over sewers and streams.

Where are there instances of catastrophe
like this that we have suffered at their hands?
There are none—no other instances.
(All words are shadows of shadows)—
This is the horrifying phrase. No other instances.

No matter how brutal the torture a man will suffer
in a land of the gentiles.
the maker of comparisons will compare it thus:
He was tortured like a Jew.
Whatever the fear, whatever the outrage,
how deep the loneliness, how harrowing the
    sorrow—
no matter how loud the weeping—
the maker of comparisons will say:
This is an instance of the Jewish sort.

What retribution can there be for our disaster?
Its dimensions are a world.
All the culture of the gentile kingdoms at its peak
flows with our blood,
and all its conscience, with our tears.

If for the Christians of this world there is
the repentance that purifies,
it is: confession. They have sinned.
They desire *the grace, the pain:*
to be Jews with a Jewish fate: the thorn bush without
    end—
from the king on his throne to the peasant in the
    field:
to raise on their staff David's banner and sign;
to inscribe the name of God on the jamb of their
    doors;
to banish their idols from their beautiful houses of
    prayer;
to place the Ark in the heart of soaring
    Westminster,
in St. Peter's, in Notre Dame, in every high house of
    God;
to wrap themselves in prayer shawls,
to crown themselves with the phylacteries
to carry out strictly the 613 commands—and to be
    silent:
so as not to pollute their lips with their language
    soaked in blood.
Perhaps their blood will then be purified, and they
    be Israel.

If they do not desire this with their being's full
    awareness,

And if they go their way—the way of Wotan and the
    Christian way—
a wild beast in their blood,
in the still-living forest, night-of-beast, darkness of
    their heart—
then not the facade
of their courteous religiosity, the majesty of their
    churches,
their splendid festivals, their handsome art work,
head-halo, flower garland,
not the wonderful achievement of their best minds,
will save them
from the terrible passage
to the abyss;
not with a Jerusalem Christianity,
with such a Bible
that Wotan has not been able to digest,
so that Christianity turns in each of their bellies,
into a dish of dead sacrifice;
in every mouth, into a poisonous wine.
Wisdom and conscience sink within those rising
    vapours;
all notions of compassion
(as with the journeymen of scaffolds)
are confounded.

Either Wotan, the forest, the spit, the axe,
the roasted, bleeding limbs of the living;
or Sinai, the Tablets of the Laws, the God of Israel.

Wotan and Christianity are the secret of the
    disaster!
The world does not know.

IV. The Jews and the Beast

The feeling:—God, Father in Heaven, gracious
    Lord and Defender,
on the wheel of time between twilight and twilight—
doesn't exist in the heart of a beast,
doesn't exist in the beat of its heart.
Because its fate in the beautiful world is—to be
    killed;
although not given the knowledge of its fate,
but possessed of the knowledge of fear.
And it isn't its body that cases a shadow,
but the constant fear that is its shadow.
It trembles at the shadow of itself;
nor is its sleep secure.
This is its whole existence in the world.

In this it resembles a Jew in the world.
This is his fate when the gentiles attack him.
Melancholy comes with the ripples of wind;
with the trembling of fish in river waters;
with the gathering of clouds over trees of the forests.
Shivers of fear with every rustle, knock, or cry,
from every side, from every human tread.

There is no man in the world so sad as a Jew in the
    evening,
and none so sad as a beast in the evening . . .
and there is no man like a Jew who weeps and cries
    out
in the fear of his dream in the night—

God is not the beast's gracious Lord and Defender;
therefore it is killed
thus, openly, a murder sanctioned,
to the wrath and the joy of the killer!
And in this the Jew in the world resembles it.
Yet it was he who discovered God in the world!
In the fate of the beast—the fate of the Jew . . .
But in his heart a multitude of feelings, the warmest
    idiom,
a combination of precious letters notated for prayer,
a taste of honey and milk in his mouth from the song
    of his king,
the good longing,
the lofty prayer,
the warm tear
that purifies . . .
And there was a god who was a father, prodigal of
    mercy and power; a shield; and full of grace
as if it were possible to say that the half light of
    morning and evening,
and the whispers of the shining ones round the
    height of the world in the sky,
no longer bear witness to the existence of God.
Did my dead, did my incinerated know, when they
    stood before the *goy* before their death,
that their whole life till then between twilight and
    twilight
had been utterly betrayed
through a fantasy of faith, more powerful than the
    knowledge of knowers,
in which longings put on branches, put on wings,
    and struck enormous roots
to the depth and width of their bodies?
Did my dear ones know that Jews have no father in
    heaven to defend them,

as they have no defending armies and fortresses on
    earth?
that vain was the good longing,
vain the warm tear
and the lofty prayer,
vain the combination of precious letters notated for
    prayer
in summer and winter and spring
all the days of their life in the world?—
Did they know that theirs was the fate of a beast?
What language can express the horror of this
    knowledge suddenly there in the world
in those last moments before Hell—

But my unhappy Muse,
not this . . . not this horrifying knowledge is the
    essence of horror!
"You are happy, beast," says the poet who is wrong.
You were never—like a Jew—led to the scaffold fully
    aware!
You were never ordered by your murderers to dig
    with your own hands
a grave for yourself!
You were never shoved into the crematories with
    your mother and your father and your children!
You are happy, beast, because you had woods and
    holes to hide in,
and safe corners in houses!
But not the Jews,
who resemble the gentiles in the shape of their
    bodies, in their clothes, in the color of their white
    skin,
In the red of their blood . . .
They didn't have a wood to escape to, a tree for
    shade, a hole to hide in!
The cats of the Jews and the dogs of their yards,
the birds on the roofs or in their nests,
the buzzing flies and the butterflies
remained after them,
and the Jews—do not exist!

V. God and His Gentiles

It wasn't for nothing the Europe's faithful Jews
did not raise their heads
to study with their eyes the pride of her cathedrals,
the beauty in them: arch and spire and carving.
As if seared by their shadows the faithful Jews went
    by them—
not for nothing, not for nothing!

We know this clearly now,
From within them the horrors came
and came upon us.

If God in Europe should descend
to the thresholds of cathedrals
and ask His Christians, those who enter there
to pray to Him and praise Him:
"Where are My Jews?
I do not hear their voices in the heavens,
and therefore have I come to seek them here . . .
What is the meaning of their sudden silence?
Where have they disappeared?
Has there been an earthquake?
How is it then
That they've been swallowed up and you survive?
And if the beasts came from their forest to devour
    men
and ate them only, sparing you
are they then so wise?
You have raised up in the city to My glory
splendid cathedrals—
and if in My name you have raise them,
your God stands on your threshold.
Where then are My Jews?"
The gentiles would answer fearlessly:
"There were Germans here and we saw eye to eye.
We killed them. All your Jews,
old and young alike!
We killed them, sparing them no horror,
until they left a space,
as the felling of trees in a forest leaves a clearing,
We had hated them for so many years,
ever since you were nailed to the cross, Pater Noster!
And thought You hated them as much.
Thus, from our childhood, had we been taught
by father, priest, and book.
We saw as well that You had given us field and
    rulership,—
them, not even the shelter of the sky.
They were vulnerable. The despised. The
    to-be-trodden-on.
And then the German came and said: "Among you
    there are many Jews.
Let us make an end to them.
And this is the end, Pater Noster!"
And then, leaning His back against the gate,
God would look at his Christians—
voiceless, speechless.

And the gentiles would see in Him the likeness of a
    Jew:
wild ear-locks, a beard like a mane before Him,
the very eyes of a Jew;
and see that the cathedral resembled a synagogue,
and that there was no cross now at the entrance.
And the Christians would roar like beasts of the
    forest:
Is there still one Jew left among us?
Does a synagogue still stand in our city?
Hey, boys, let's start a little fire.
We'll need kerosene, crowbars, axes."

Translated by Robert Friend. This translation does not include the sixth and final poem in the Hebrew collection.

Other works by Greenberg: *Mefisto* (1921); *Sefer ha-kitrug ve-ha-emunah* (1937); *Be-emtsaʿ ha-ʿolam u-ve-emtsaʿ ha-zemanim* (1979); *Gezamlte verk*, 2 vols. (1979).

Shalom Rada'i

1912–1984

Shalom Rada'i was born and raised in the village of Manakha, southwest of Sana'a, in a traditional Yemenite Jewish family. He was a prolific writer, transcribing Maimonides into Arabic, working as a *sofer*, and writing *piyutim* (liturgical poems) as well as composing their melodies. In 1949, as part of Operation Magic Carpet, he immigrated to Israel, where he was settled in the *maʿabarah* (transit camp) of Znuach. Here he wrote "Esh tokad be-kirbi," based on a Tishah be-Av *piyut* by Abraham Ibn Ezra; it laments the decline of religion in Israel, a common trope throughout his Israeli poetry. This piyut was published in a Neturei Karta pamphlet, emphasizing the consequences of Zionism. Most of his melodies and piyutim were adopted, without citation, in various publications, including Amram Korach's *ʿAlumot shir* (1982).

A Fire Is Kindled within Me
1951

A fire [of joy] is kindled within me, when I recall
    [the spiritual climate] when I was in Yemen,
[But] my soul [descended to] abysmal depths and
    was immensely astounded when I came to Zion.
The Jews were as a beloved treasure, and renowned
    and praised when I was in Yemen,

They who had been perfected from all dross
    overstepped the bounds [of respectable and moral
    conduct] when I came to Zion.
Unto the most revered and awesome God, prayers
    were offered every day, when I was in Yemen,
But they cared only for their work, and failed to
    serve God, when I came to Zion.
Each day and night, times were set aside for Torah,
    when I was in Yemen,
But [I perceived nothing here] besides pursuit of the
    physical and material, overwhelming all things,
    when I came to Zion.
The Law of Moses and the ordinances of Jewry,
    obligatory for every Hebrew woman, prevailed
    when I was in Yemen,
But their heads were uncovered, and their hips and
    bared arms on display, when I came to Zion.
She [the married woman] was the crown of her
    husband within [the marital home], and her face
    was never seen, when I was in Yemen,
Yet here men and women walk along together
    without any shame, when I came to Zion.
Men wore respectable apparel, and donned
    phylacteries, and placed the four fringes upon
    their garments when I was in Yemen,
But they were liberated from all these things,
    wearing alien suits, and walking around bare-
    headed, when I came to Zion.
The Jewish men left seven corners [of their
    heads and beards untrimmed], retaining these
    permanently in place in honor of God, when I
    was in Yemen,
But the law mandating the growth of locks of hair,
    and leaving the seven corners untrimmed, was
    abolished, when I came to Zion.
The Sabbaths and the festival days were especially
    designated for spiritual delight, when I was in
    Yemen,
Woe unto us on account of the desecration of the
    Sabbaths and the Festivals serving as signs of the
    Divine covenant with Israel, when I came to Zion!
Afflicted, contrite souls were joyful in the
    organizing of feasts, when I was in Yemen,
Our souls became parched—who will ever behold
    us once more as we were in days of yore?—when I
    came to Zion.
There were schools for instruction, teaching the
    Law of Moses, when I was in Yemen,

While here the children rejoiced in the lack of
    studies, when I came to Zion.
There is no end to the enumeration of all those
    things that I lack—those things that were once
    mine in Yemen,
May He Who lives and endures restore us, and lead
    us back in righteousness to the state we were once
    in long ago, in Zion!

Translated by David E. Cohen.

Leah Goldberg

The Love of Teresa de Meun
1952

I do not want to see you in my dreams
each night. I do not want to tremble when I hear
a footstep at my door. I do not want
to think of you each hour of every day.

I do not want to see
in the watchful look of girls of seventeen
stinging derision, sly triumphant smiles.
Love of this kind is not the love I want.

In what a careless calm I lived
before you came, and how secure
in wisdom, wearing my ripe years

with dignity, and free at night of fear.
Yet dear are the moments when we sit together,
or when I wait for you in shy confusion here.

From your window and mine we see
the same garden, the same landscape.
And I can love all day
the things your eye has dwelt on.

Before your window and mine
the same nightingale sings at night,
making your heart flutter in its sleep,
while I awake and listen.

The pine, whose every needle
carries your glance like pure dew,
greets me with a blessing every dawn.

Together we have loved so many things,
But no light shines through your small window
when my loneliness touches yours.

Translated by Robert Friend.

Amir Gilboa

1917–1984

Born Berl Feldman in Radziwillow, Poland, where he attended a Tarbut school and also received a Polish state education, Amir Gilboa began as a Yiddish Expressionist poet, and attended a Zionist training camp, preparing for life on a kibbutz. Not long after his arrival in Palestine in 1937, Gilboa joined the British Army's Jewish Brigade, participating in the illegal transfer of Jewish refugees from Europe to Palestine. Gilboa also fought in Israel's War of Independence. His early poetry was heavily influenced by his wartime experience, as well as by the loss of his family in the Holocaust. Gilboa's poems were groundbreaking in their experimentalism and heavily influenced Israeli poets of both his own and later generations.

Isaac

1953

Early in the morning the sun took a walk in the
    woods
with me and my father
my right hand in his left.

A knife flashed between the trees like lightning.
And I'm so scared of the fear in my eyes facing blood
                      on the leaves.

Father father come quick and save Isaac
so no one will be missing at lunchtime.

It's I who am butchered, my son,
my blood's already on the leaves.
And father's voice was choked.
And his face pale.

I wanted to cry out, struggling not to believe,
I tore my eyes open
and woke.

And my right hand was drained of blood

Translated by Shirley Kaufman.

Other works by Gilboa: *Shirim ba-boker ba-boker* (1953); *Ish ha-mayim shel Gili* (1963); *Ratsiti likhtov siftei yeshenim* (1968); *The Light of Lost Suns: Selected Poems of Amir Gilboa* (1979).

Ḥaya Vered

1922–1998

Born in Poland, Ḥaya Vered immigrated to Palestine with her family when she was two years old, growing up in Tel Aviv. In 1941, she moved to Kibbutz Gvar'am, where she remained for almost ten years. On the kibbutz, she worked as a teacher and began publishing her poetry and stories for children. During the Israeli War of Independence, Vered took part in the defense effort. In addition to writing, she translated literature from Yiddish into Hebrew. A number of her poems are taught in Israeli schools and some have been set to music.

The Zero Hour

1953

You,
blood stain of land on the map,
tired you, immersed in soot and ashes,
forever a small piece of land.
And the monuments are witnesses
at every junction and at the roadsides,
and far, far from the roads.

And when the smoke screen lifts,
you celebrate intoxication and victory,
until you are enraged, rotten and limp,
until you are blind
to the sadness of stones beating on your plain
and you are all disappointment and pain.

The living diligently eat and drink,
Taking wives and making babies.
Time runs out of hands
through greedy fingers,
and they won't want to know
that a heartbeat must be dug
out of the ground
counting time in split seconds,
and remember, remember the zero hour.

The dead.
Why did you die?
Why didn't you die alone,
you, only you?
Yes, deep, deep in the ground
with silence in your dreaming, warring eyes,
with your heartbeat all eyes,

encircled by arms and trembling,
love is hidden.

The love on whose dead fingertips
the silver platter is borne,
the people's silver platter:

An open gate to our own blue sea.
And brothers
tens of thousands like a raging sea:
Yemenite ear locks,
the graceful modesty of those from the Indian shore,
the fiery eyes of the Jews of Morocco, Tunis,
    Algiers,
the fiery brand on the arm of the Jews of Lithuania,
    Holland and Poland,
tens of thousands! A whole map of the world!

* * *

And tents and bread of charity,
eyes without hope,
hunger in infants' bodies,
fist fights at the employment offices,
demonstrations,
and like old worn-out nations
ships turn their faces toward the sea.

The silver platter:
hearts like harp strings,
warm feet caressing stone,
cliff and thorny path.
Youth
generous, giving,
wasting themselves
storming the desert, the mountains and the sea.
Youth like a flash, the glint of a sword,
like sheaves, like grain.
Like hope.

* * *

Amputees stalk the streets,
their eyes threaten clerks,
the blind win a dog.
Seeing eyes see only silver,
fingers dig only for silver,
and on the silver platter:
    onions and garlic and pots of meat,
and on the silver platter:
    Frigidaires, luxuries,
        decay and the corpse of conscience.

And you,
    wounded five-year-old child,
    crying for a soul
    and a wind hits the sails.

Captains,
    did your eyes see the withering of the most
        beautiful flowers
    in our two-thousand-year-old garden?
How pure the shore where you drifted, little boat!
How many trees would have burned in the gold of
    your desert,
had we been wrapped in wings of the wind,
the spirit of our youth in dust!

Oh, my small beloved country, alive
and breathing,
listen to the zero hour!
Listen with me to the beat of the clock and the
    heart!
Look with me at the phosphorescent dial.
At the horror waking in our children's eyes!
Listen with me, mother,
stoned by coins until you bleed,
cry to the good and the loving:
they still exist.
Spirit of my dead in the dust:
rise, rise out of the crypts,
enfold us, wind:

in fear, in faith,
in hope bitter as blood—
until
the smoke screen lifts
and you will shine in sorrow.
The bell clappers of your children's laughter ring,
and the spirit will move on the high places,
and the spirit will echo in hearts,
in one pure heart beat—
and a nation.

Translated by Lisa Katz.

Other work by Vered: *Shirim ʿal ḥerev u-metar* (1956).

Yehiel Mohar

1921–1969

Poet and lyricist Yehiel Mohar (also known as Mar) grew up in Berlin and immigrated to Palestine in 1937.

There he helped to found Kibbutz Dovrat and established himself as a prolific writer of both poetry, which he published under the name Yehiel Mar, and popular songs, which he published as Mohar. He collaborated with composer Moshe Wilensky on some of the most well-known Israeli folk songs, including "Hora Mamtera" (Sprinkler Hora) and "Mul Har Sinai" (Facing Mount Sinai).

Sprinkler Hora
1954

A gush of joy in the pipe,
The pipes, the arteries of the Negev,
This is the course of the song,
From the faucet to the clod
The water of the depths ascends.
A pump means bread!
Negev, Negev, what's different today?
Negev—sprinklers spread upon you!

Spin spin sprinkler, hey!
Spin spin sprinkler
Sprinkle sparkling pearls,
Spin and sprinkle water!
A tree will cheer in the lane,
The earth will yield its fruit
Even when it doesn't rain.

The tract has been claimed
The network of pipes has been laid
And look, a sign and a signal,
In the drops a rainbow has appeared
The covenant of flower and furrow
The covenant of serenity and song
Sprinkler, your song is a true one,
Keep singing it forevermore.

Spin spin sprinkler, hey! . . .

Translated by Tsipi Keller.

Other work by Mohar: *Panim le-khan* (1968).

Yehuda Amichai

God Has Pity on Kindergarten Children
1955

God has pity on kindergarten children,
He pities school children—less.
But adults he pities not at all.

He abandons them,
And sometimes they have to crawl on all fours
In the scorching sand
To reach the dressing station,
Streaming with blood.

But perhaps
He will have pity on those who love truly
And take care of them
And shade them
Like a tree over the sleeper on the public bench.

Perhaps even we will spend on them
Our last pennies of kindness
Inherited from mother,

So that their own happiness will protect us
Now and on other days.

Translated by Benjamin and Barbara Harshav.

Yaakov Orland
1914–2002

Born in Tetiiv, Ukraine, playwright, poet, and critic Yaakov Orland immigrated with his family to Mandate Palestine as a child. In 1923, they settled in Jerusalem, where he later studied at the Hebrew University. In 1936, he studied at the Royal Academy of Dramatic Art in London. Orland was a member of the Haganah and served in the British army during World War II. In addition to writing theatrical and poetic works, he contributed to Hebrew literature through the translation of classic English, German, and Yiddish texts.

Song of the Herdsmen
1955

Oh prairie, endless prairie,
The eyes of the herdsmen look out:
Not a bush, not a thistle, not a tree,
A new wind comes to the desert.

Over forlorn expanses the song of the herdsmen
Will sound and reverberate,
And the sun will be rising and setting
And the song will keep on surging.

Oh prairie, prairie, the color of the alder tree,
Thousands of years have risen again:
The herdsman on a primordial horse

Rides across the olden roads.

Oh, oh, oh . . .

Sde Boker—herding field, field of peace, arise!
Forge a path all the way to the mountains!
You are the bastion of this generation
The son of defiance, the son of the wild.

The song of the herdsmen will rise and reverberate
Over ewes and rams and wool,
And the sun will be rising and setting
And the song will keep on surging.

Oh prairie, prairie, respond!
Let not slumber overtake you!
Let us renew, you and I,
Your days as of old.

Oh, oh, oh . . .

Translated by Tsipi Keller.

Other works by Orland: *Shirim me-eretz 'Uts* (1963);
*Yom tel-faher: baladah 'im yari'atsiyot 'al nos'im kiyu-
miyim* (1976).

Emanuel Zamir

1925–1962

Born in Petaḥ Tikvah, Emanuel Zamir became a
founding figure in the sphere of Hebrew folk song.
He began his musical career during his service in the
Israel Defense Forces, where he helped organize an
orchestra and several smaller bands. In the 1950s, he
adapted this approach to civilian life, traveling the
country and establishing singing groups. On his tours
throughout the country, Zamir drew inspiration from
Arab and Bedouin communities he visited, imitating
the melodies and instrumentations he heard and composing songs with his own poetry. His music became
widely popular, the lyrics to his songs remarkable for
their lofty, biblically inspired register and pastoral
imagery.

A Well in the Field
1956

Shepherds had dug a well in the field
but herds of others encircled it.
They left, roaming the mountain trails,
the shepherds who had dug it.

Oh, oh, oh! Desert oases . . .
the lanes of the herd dried up.
A lamb was lost as well
Who will take pity?

Upon the well dug by shepherds
the herds of others descend:
"Well, rise! Rise, well!"
It responds: "My water is held back!"

Ah, ah, ah! Toward the desert
strangers led their herds . . .
A well in the field
Who will take pity?

Toward the well dug by shepherds
from the mountains the herds return.
Enfeebled, the lambs bleat
The well pulsates: "They've returned!"

Hey, hey! No more desert!
Drink, quench your thirst, herd!
A flute and a field together
will join in song!

Translated by Tsipi Keller.

Moshe Dor

1932–2016

The poet and translator Moshe Dor was a founding
member of Likrat, the first group of Israeli poets who
broke demonstratively with the diction, pathos, and
collectivist ethos of Shlonsky and Alterman. Born in
Tel Aviv, Dor served in the Haganah before heading to
university. He was awarded the Bialik Prize in 1987.

Evening of Roses
1957

Evening of roses
Let us go out to the orchard
Myrrh, perfumes, and frankincense
A threshold at your foot.

Night falls slowly
And the rose-wind blows
Let me sing to you in a soft whisper
A song of love.

Dawn the dove murmurs
Your head is full of dew

Your mouth to the morning, rose.
I will pluck it for myself . . .

Translated by Jeffrey M. Green.

Other works by Dor: *The Fullness Thereof: The Hebrew Bible as Homeland* (2002); *Scorched by the Sun*
(2012).

Rukhl Fishman

1935–1984

Rukhl Fishman was born in Philadelphia to a family of
ardent Yiddishist activists and intellectuals. Educated
in Workmen's Circle schools and camps, Fishman displayed literary talent at an early age and was mentored
by the Yiddish poet Malka Heifetz Tussman. Involved
with Ha-Shomer ha-Tsaʿir, Fishman eventually settled
in Israel, where she worked in agriculture on Kibbutz
Bet Alpha. Fishman established herself as the youngest
and only American-born member of the Yung Yisroel
group and formed a close connection with Avrom
Sutzkever. Her poetry is known for the delicate simplicity of its imagery and use of powerful language to
describe everyday occurrences and the natural world.

The Sun and I

1958

We wore each other out today
the sun and I
working in the vineyard.
The sun dropped behind the mountain
exhausted, red,
and burning hot
I was left alone.

We were both
a little overheated
today,
the sun
and I.

Translated by Seymour Levitan.

Other works by Fishman: *Zun iber alts* (1962);
Derner nokhn regn (1966); *Himl tsvishn grozn* (1968);
Vilde tsig (1976).

Haim Gouri

1923–1958

1958

A

And I didn't have time.
Now it is certain
I didn't have time.

Half my life.

It is now allowed
To be silent.
My shadows grow
With the stride of the sun.

I am the man
Who didn't have time.

B

And I didn't have time
To cultivate a tree
Of thoughts slowly.
Resembling something
More clear,
Less random and distilled
Of shouting,
Fleeting meals standing

My life passed from newspaper to newspaper.
My breath shortened from running
Short distances—
For God's sake!

C

And I didn't have time
For moss to cover me
Or rust
And rotate
Birth—burial—birth—
To belong to memories
Or to yellow the pages
Of the heavy book
To be clear.
Certain.
Inherit a fortune.
Between my father and myself—a sea.

D

And the roll-call was full.
People spoke in first person plural.
The days together,
At the end of the journey.

A fossilized moon over a field.
A neighbor turns and passes
His palm over my warm chest,
My hand supports the chin of a sleeping stranger
And slowly becomes white
The weight of an enormous skull
Hair and dreams.

My wife far away
Awake and alone
My salty wife
About to give birth.

Translated by Karen Alkalay-Gut.

Itzik Manger

For Years I Wallowed
1958

For years I wallowed about in the world,
Now I'm going home to wallow there.
With a pair of shoes and the shirt on my back,
And the stick in my hand that goes with me
    everywhere.

I'll not kiss your dust as that great poet did,
Though my heart, like his, is filled with song and
    grief.
How can I kiss your dust? I *am* your dust.
And how, I ask you, can I kiss myself?

Still dressed in my shabby clothes
I'll stand and gape at the blue Kinneret
Like a roving prince who has found his blue
Though blue was in his dream when he first started.

I'll not kiss your blue, I'll merely stand
Silent as a *Shimenesre*[1] prayer myself.
How can I kiss your blue? I *am* your blue.
And how, I ask you, can I kiss myself?

Musing, I'll stand before your great desert,
And hear the camels' ancient tread as they
Sway with trade and Torah on their humps.

I'll hear the age-old hovering wander-song
That trembles over glowing sand and dies,
And then recalls itself and does not disappear.
I'll not kiss your sand. No, and ten times no.
How can I kiss your sand? I *am* your sand.
And how, I ask you, can I kiss myself?

NOTE
1. *Shimenesre*: Yiddish for the *Amidah* prayer that originally consisted of eighteen (*shmone esrey*, Hebrew) blessings.

Translated by Leonard Wolf.

Naomi Shemer

1930–2004

Born in Kvutzat Kinneret, Naomi Shemer began her musical career leading communal song at the kibbutz as a child; the first songs she composed were for children. During her service with the Israel Defense Forces, Shemer wrote several songs for the Central Command troop. After she left the army, Shemer continued to compose songs for a variety of Israeli singers, many of which described the natural beauty of Israel's landscape. Shemer's songs gained wide popularity in the 1960s and 1970s, most notably following the 1967 and 1973 wars. Shemer's songs remain popular today.

Troubadour
1958

The road is long and wide
The road is long and resplendent
We all walk it till the very end
We all walk it until the bitter end

But I walk the road alone
I give thanks and sing Hallelujah
I sing a troubadour's songs
I give thanks and sing Hallelujah

One set his heart on gold
One set his heart on fine gold
Another found a girl to love
Another found a girl to love him

But I walk the road alone. . . .

I don't need a house and a field
I don't need a house and a green field
My reward is your voice responding to me
My reward is your delighted voice responding to me

My voice sings with you as its echo
I give thanks and sing Hallelujah
Lost is the song that has no echo
I give thanks and sing Hallelujah

On the side of the road a tree grows dark
On the side of the road a tree slowly grows dark
Lamps have been turned off all over town
Lamps have been turned off all over this town

But I walk the road alone. . . .

Translated by Tsipi Keller; this is a verbal translation approved by the writer's estate.

Other work by Shemer: *Kol ha-shirim kim'at* (1967).

Dahlia Ravikovitch
1936–2005

Among the most significant poets of modern Hebrew, Dahlia Ravikovitch was born in Ramat Gan, in what was then Mandatory Palestine. She had a troubled childhood and adolescence, living in foster homes before beginning her military service and studying literature at Hebrew University. Upon the publication of her first book in 1959, Ravikovitch was virtually the only female sabra publishing poetry in Israel. More abstractly lyrical as well as more traditional in form than the poems of her male counterparts, in her later years Ravikovitch's work became more political, reflecting her passionate activism.

Clockwork Doll
1959

That night, I was a clockwork doll
and I whirled around, this way and that,
and I fell on my face and shattered to bits
and they tried to fix me with all their skill.

Then I was a proper doll once again
and I did what they told me, poised and polite.
But I was a doll of a different sort,
an injured twig that dangles from a stem.

And then I went to dance at the ball,
but they left me alone with the dogs and cats
though my steps were measured and rhythmical.

And I had blue eyes and golden hair
and a dress all the colors of garden flowers,

and a trimming of cherries on my straw hat.

Translated by Chana Bloch and Chana Kronfeld.

Other works by Ravikovitch: *Ahavat tapuah ha-zahav* (1959); *Ḥoref kasheh* (1965); *Ha-sefer ha-shelishi* (1970); *Tehom koreh* (1978).

Oded Avisar
1918–1976

Born in Hebron, Oded Avisar was committed to documenting the history of Jewish life there. In 1958, while the city was under Jordanian rule, he began editing the *Sefer Ḥevron*, a memorial book for the Jewish community of Hebron modeled after those of Jewish communities destroyed by the Holocaust. By 1970, when the book was published, Hebron was under Israeli rule. Avisar also wrote several popular folksongs on pastoral themes.

Evening Descends
1960

Again the herd throngs the village gateways
and dust rises up from the dirt roads.
And farther still a pair of clappers
keep pace with the lengthening shadows.
Evening descends, evening descends.

Again the wind rustles among the garden fences
and up in the pine tree doves already are
    nodding off.
And along the shoulder of the distant hills
the sun's last rays still linger.
Evening descends, evening descends.

Again the rose dreams its secret dreams,
and in the sky stars slowly light up
And far away in the dark valley
The jackal ushers in the arrival of night.
Night falls, night falls.

Translated by Tsipi Keller.

Other works by Avisar: *Sefer Ḥevron* (1970); *Sefer Teveryah* (1973).

Yankev Fridman

1910–1972

Yiddish writer and poet Yankev Fridman (also Jakow Frydman) was born in Mlynica, Galicia, the son of the town's Hasidic rabbi, a scion of the Ruzhiner dynasty. When Fridman was a child, the family moved to Chernivtsi (now in Ukraine), the city with which the poet and his work remain strongly associated. Fridman's work appeared in the Yiddish press, and he published several highly regarded books of poetry before World War II. Fridman was imprisoned during the war and lived in Bucharest for several years afterward, playing a key role in the revival of Yiddish literature and culture in early postwar Romania. He settled in Israel in 1949. Fridman's oeuvre has been praised for its mystical quality, drawing on Hasidic lore to weave rich imagery, complex ideas, and heavy emotion in a single poem.

God No Longer Speaks
1960

> God no longer speaks
> as he did in the days of the Bible,
> he no longer shines in the firecloud
> over our roof.
> Adam and Eve have run into the depths of the
>   garden
> from God's unveiled presence,
> as we—we run, seeking him
> in the darkness of a closed bud. . . .
>
> The barefoot steps of angels
> no longer kiss our threshold
> as in the days of our forefathers.
> But our yearning weeps
> for their blue wings
> that swim like drowned moons
> over all the world's rivers. . . .
>
> At midnight we huddle, pressing our ears to the
>   sleeping grass,
> to the leaf of a tree, to the skin of young fruit:
> looking for God's fragrant silence, trying to
>   translate it
> with the shadow words of ancient song.
>
> Our forefathers could hear God's words,
> but we write hidden poems
> to hide our naked longing for God's breath,

> more silent than the breath of stars
> over sleeping wintertime lakes.
>
> Our desolation weeps and the weeping
> is dark blue
> like the shadow of a dead bird
> over the white snow of a lifeless forest.
>
> God no longer speaks,
> he's weary, wise, and old:
> God no longer believes
> in the godliness of words.

Translated by Ruth Whitman.

Other works by Fridman: *Nefilim: dramatishe poeme* (1963); *Libshaft* (1967).

Natan Zach

b. 1930

Natan Zach (b. Harry Seitelbach) is a poet, writer, editor, translator, and literary scholar. As a child, he moved to Palestine from Germany, settling in Haifa. Zach enlisted in the Israeli army at age seventeen, and fought in the 1948 War. Zach was a leading figure in the Israeli literary scene in the first decades of the country's independence and has had a profound impact on Israeli poetry; his *Kol he-ḥalav ve-ha-devash* (All the Milk and Honey; 1966) is considered a modern classic. He has also written children's books and nonfiction. Zach was awarded the Israel Prize in 1995.

One Moment
1960

> One moment of silence, please. If you please. I
> would like to say something. He walked
> right past me. I could have touched the hem
> of his mantle. I did not touch it. Who could have
> known what I did not know.
>
> The sand clung to his garments. Twigs
> were entangled in his beard. Apparently he'd
> spent the night in a haystack. Who could have
> known that the following night he'd be
> empty as a bird, hard as a stone.
>
> I couldn't have known. I don't blame
> him. Sometimes I feel him rise
> in his slumber, sleepwalking like a sea, saying

to me, my son.

My son. I hadn't known you are, this much, with me.

Translated by Vivian Eden.

Other works by Zach: *Shirim rishonim* (1955); *Ze-man ve-ritmus etsel Bergson u-va-shirah ha-modernit* (1966); *Shirim ʿal kelev ve-khalbah* (1990); *Mot imi* (1997); *Ha-zamir kevar lo gar poh yoter* (2004); *Kof ha-maḥat* (2004).

Shlomo Zamir

1929–2017

Born in Baghdad, Shlomo Zamir published his earliest poems in Arabic. Upon immigrating to Israel in 1950, he joined a kibbutz and began learning Hebrew by reading poetry. A decade later, Zamir published his first collection of poems in Hebrew to widespread praise. Israeli critics were impressed by the modernist and ironic style, which challenged their perceptions of Arab literary capabilities.

An Old Song
1960

1

PREFACE

Where pain weeps, it is the Jew who weeps.
Where a bullet is fired, it is the Jew who falls.
—Why is the dog barking near the fence?
—Someone threw a rock at him, at the Jew's dog.

We walked on the snowy upland.
We raised our eyes to the stars,
But we found no stars.
Fierce winds, not Jewish, roared all around.
We raised our faces and looked at the moon,
So very, so very not Jewish.

When we reached the shore,
Sailors called out in surprise:
"What happened to your hands?"
We turned our palms—indeed, they were red,
Stained with the crime of our presence in the world.

2

THE HOLOCAUST

Sleep in Europe, that gigantic grave.
There's enough soil to cover you,
Enough hills to serve as tombstones.
Go, stranger, weep for them . . . a little,
Touch a handkerchief to the corner of your eye.
Tonight, when we say "death"
It rings softly, as if we said "Mother."

—You, Sir, can you tell me the road to Germany?
—Go straight and follow the stench of corpses.
—The darkness is thick, what if I lose my way?
—Rest assured, the burning cities
   Will light you the way.
—Why do you walk away red-faced?
—I'm ashamed for being a man!

The women recite from prayer books
Riddled with bullet holes;
In the rain children hold up umbrellas
Riddled with bullet holes.
In the dark and the cold,
The blood, staining the roads and walls,
Cries out: "Mother! Mother!"
At the intersection a woman strikes her chest
One thousand and forty-two times.

Translated by Tsipi Keller.

Other work by Zamir: *Ha-kol mi-baʿad le-ʿanaf* (1960).

Nathan Alterman

The Cobbler's Song
1963

Shlomo reclines within his shrine
Woe to my days, woe to my nights
Everyone knows how he is
Nobody knows about me
Woe to my days, woe to my nights
As if it means something to anybody.

If I have a flask I'm not doing too bad
But Shlomo has it much better
Since that bitter drop
He doesn't either give up
Woe to my days, woe to my nights
If you are not for me who is.

I am Shalmai and he is Shlomo
And my name resembles his
But between his name and mine
There is still an official difference

Woe to my days, woe to my nights
If I am not for me who is.

So my honor is in my place
And Shlomo's honor is in his
If only his place was mine
Shlomo's welfare would be like Shalmai's
Woe to my days, woe to my nights
If I am not for me who is.

NOTE

[The entire song is based on the name of King Solomon—Shlomo—and its resemblance to the name of the cobbler, Shalmai. Shlomo is also close to *shalom*, meaning here
welfare.—Trans.]

Translated by Karen Alkalay-Gut.

Uri Assaf

b. 1936

Poet, composer, and playwright Uri Assaf was born on
Kibbutz Kefar Menaḥem. He began writing poems in
his youth. Assaf served in the IDF as an intelligence
officer and fought in the Sinai campaign in 1956. After
his army service, he studied education. When working
as a teacher, he began writing plays that were performed by the kibbutz children. He left the kibbutz at
the age of forty.

Speak to Me with Flowers
1963

In winter, the rain beat down on the roof.
She said white was her favorite shade.
At hand he then gave her, his heart filled with joy,
A bunch of daffodils, fragrant and moist.
She laughed: "My dear sweet boy,
We shall speak once again in the spring."

Speak to me with flowers, my love,
Speak to me with flowers.

Spring came. She sought to be spring-like.
The fields turned green in expanse and furrow.
He brought her bouquets of golden
    chrysanthemums,
But she was already awaiting a clear summer day.
"Gather for me all the world's flowers
And we shall meet once spring has passed by."

Speak to me with flowers, my love,
Speak to me with flowers.

On a scorching summer's day, he is at home.
Every field has gone dry; no flower has survived.
Suddenly, standing in the doorway, she beckoned
    to him.
She asked for a bouquet of flowers; he had but one.
How could he give her what had totally withered
    away?
However, she repeated her request yet again.

Speak to me with flowers, my love,
Speak to me with flowers.

Translated by Marvin Meital.

Other work by Assaf: *The Last Jew* (with Yaffa
Eliach, 1977).

Ratson Halevi

1922–2007

Born in Taiz, Yemen, in the Jewish district of Sharab,
writer and critic Ratson Halevi immigrated to Palestine in 1933 and began working in construction, work
he would continue throughout his life. An autodidact, Halevi concentrated his studies on Spanish and
Yemenite Jewish poetry and began publishing his own
verse in the late 1940s. Halevi also translated many
significant Judeo-Arabic poems into Hebrew and was a
strong proponent of Arab Jewish culture.

The Voice
1964

On a forgone and alien diaspora night,
Far, far in the midst of childhood,
A heavy bottomless darkness closed upon me,
Surrounding me in fear and horror.

Somewhere in Yemen in the district of Sharav,
I'm a boy gathered in the arms of night,
Deeply frightened, twisting and folding over,
Facing the infinitude of time.

Then a muffled, soft voice was heard,
In the warmth of its sound my sorrow dissolved,
The mountain of darkness was lifted,
And I mustered fortitude in defeat.

Ever since then the voice beats
With the beats of my flushed heart,
And it warns—and oftentimes even scolds—
Always whispering, always on guard.

On nights of sin the voice accompanied me,
Reminding me of my transgressions,
Pulling me away from the muck of desires
And setting me right on the path to Sinai.

And when I wept, feeling so helpless
In face of wicked mankind of no image and likeness,
That voice comforted me with the splendor
Of light and the grace of the eternal.

When bitter and unrelenting oppression assailed
    me,
And a dimming feebleness washed over me,
That voice rose once more—whose voice is it,
It is Your voice, Lord God.

Translated by Tsipi Keller.

Other work by Halevi: *Hami yonat ha-lev* (1966).

Aharon Almog
b. 1931

Writer Aharon Almog was born to a Yemenite family that had been living in Tel Aviv since the nineteenth century. Although his grandfather was a founder of the Yemenite Hatikvah neighborhood, Almog's father, a secular Jew, left it behind. Almog published his first poems in 1951 and by the end of the decade had also begun to publish short stories. His oeuvre, at once ironic and reflective, treats the everyday of Almog's life and his Yemenite milieu.

To the Sons Who Were Banished from Their Fathers' Tables
1965

My father, my father, how you stood over me
Against childhood sorrows and the agony of years.
You raised children, father, and also great hopes,
and in return received nothing but despair and
    woes.

I recall the table even as the songs have long ceased,
I shed a tear, mournful and bleak
My sister Liora on a bright Shabbat morn
teaching me a *seudah shelishit*[1] melody.

I recall my mother, how soothing her hands
When bruises, a child's weeping, and anger were
    her fate.
The son seeking her after yet another fight

punished for a deed he did not commit.

I've done nothing, are you still aching for me?
Your face and tears still haunt me,
and God knows my inapt nature to suffer
With the sufferer and call him "Brother!"

I did have a stepbrother here, mother;
Where is he, my long-gone brother?
Now, mother, coming back in shame,
I tell those who left about their father's pain.

Many of them still wander the bereft path
and I call out to them, friend and foe alike.
And the son you knew not, his tongue stilled,
Today engraves words of love upon your grief.

NOTE
1. [The "third meal," served on Shabbat afternoon.—Eds.]

Translated by Tsipi Keller.

Other works by Almog: *Aviv 'atsevet bi-Yehudah* (1956); *Hatsda'ah le-Yisrael: Hilton Yerushalayim* (1979).

Nathan Alterman

The Householder Departs from the City
1965

Going to his room one night,
he locked his door and by lamp-light
counted his money, counted his foes.
Then from the table of his heart
he struck off every name but one,
which would be there till time was done.
Then rising, he turned off the light.
Sprouting feathers, wings, and bill,
he hopped onto the window sill,
and sailed, a bird, into the night.

Translated by Robert Friend.

Dan Almagor
b. 1935

Dan Almagor was born in Ramat Gan to Polish immigrants and grew up in Rehovot. He studied under Leah Goldberg and Shimon Halkin at the Hebrew University. A prolific writer, Almagor has written plays, songs, and journalism. He is also a translator and a television and radio host. Almagor is best known for his translations and adaptations of plays, including *My Fair Lady*, *Fiddler on the Roof*, and *Guys and Dolls*.

Kol Hakavod!
1966

At noon in the kasbah
When the *souk* was packed
I'd be walking around
My chest toned and hard
And they'd all be saying: What a guy
And as I walked down the alleyways
From every window they waved:
Kol Hakavod!

They all knew right then
Who's deserving   of all the honor
They all knew very well
Who's always deserving   of all the honor

When the battle was raging
And the platoon would not budge
The commander would shout:
"Hey Kaza, you first!"
They all knew that Kazablan
Always is the first in line
And from behind they all chimed:
Kol Hakavod!

They all knew right then . . .

In Jaffa at dusk
A fellow walks with a gal
And if I were so inclined
She'd be mine in no time
But I'm not one to cause trouble
Don't want to watch the fellow tremble
I'm a principled guy
I am honorable!

They all knew right then . . .

If a drunk stumbles into a bar
I cool him down
Send him flying from here
All the way to Jabaliya[1]
But later he returns
Ever so meek and tame
And even raises his glass and says:
Kol Hakavod!

They all knew right then . . .

NOTE

1. [Jabaliya was a coastal Arab village south of Jaffa. It is now the neighborhood of Givat Aliyah.—Eds.]

Translated by Tsipi Keller.

Other works by Almagor: *Ish ḥasid hayah* (1972); *Shoshanat Teman: beney Teman ba-zemer ha-ʿivri* (2008).

Yona Wallach
1944–1985

A lifelong rebel, the Israeli poet Yona Wallach turned an unlucky background into a remarkable career in Israeli letters. Wallach was born in Palestine and grew up fatherless. After being expelled from high school, she found a home among Tel Aviv's young poets, where her immense talent and ferocious will served her well. Wallach published widely; her early poems were raw, close to experience, and depicted maverick women in emotional distress. After her rapid rise, she published infrequently, her production halted by mental illness and personal setbacks. Yet to many Israelis she remains a symbol of artistic and feminist defiance, bold and unapologetic.

Yonatan
1966

I run on the bridge
and the children follow
Yonatan
Yonatan they call
a little blood
just a little blood to finish up the honey
I'd let them pierce me with tacks
but the children want
and they are children
and I am Yonatan
They cut off my head with a gladiola stalk
gather my head
in two gladiola stalks and wrap
my head in rustling paper
Yonatan
Yonatan they say
Please forgive us
We didn't imagine
you are like this

Translated by Lenore Gordon.

Abba Kovner

My Little Sister
1967

My sister sits happy
at her bridegroom's table. She does not cry.
My sister will do no such thing:
what would people say!

My sister sits happy
at her bridegroom's table. Her heart is awake.
The whole world drinks
kosher chicken soup.

The dumplings of unleavened flour
were made by her mother-in-law. The world
is amazed
and tastes the mother's dessert.

My sister-bride sits. A small dish
of honey before her. Such a huge crowd!
Father twisted
the braids of the hallah.

Our father took his bread, bless God,
forty years from the same oven. He never
    imagined
a whole people could rise in the ovens
and the world, with God's help, go on.

My sister sits at the table in her bridal veil
alone. From the mourners' hideout
the voice of a bridegroom comes near.
We will set the table without you;
the marriage contract will be written in stone.

Translated by Shirley Kaufman.

Moshe Sartel

b. 1942

Moshe Sartel was born in Istanbul into a Ladino-speaking family. He moved to Israel in 1949, settling in Petaḥ Tikvah. Sartel studied literature, philosophy, and library sciences at the Hebrew University as well as military history at Tel Aviv University. He has published seven collections of poetry and has received awards for his work, including the President's Prize for Literature (1997) and the Prime Minister's Prize for Hebrew Writers (1999–2000). His epic, intellectual poetry is heavily influenced by T. S. Eliot's *The Waste Land*, Middle Eastern folk history, and classic Hebrew texts.

The Grandfather I Once Had
1967

Every day when his mind was at ease,
Relieved of the need to tell us about the countries
    he'd seen,
He would raise his hands high above our heads,
Appealing on our behalf before the Almighty to let
    our seed
Multiply, and to please keep us from evil and other
    ills.
And because he pleaded for us, as we were too small
    to plead
For ourselves, he enjoyed long years and many
    grandkids.
He gave us everything he had and gifts brought back
    from his travels,
Nurturing our minds with the grace he'd received
    from his forebears.
And we, the small ones, stood around his chair and
    listened to his tales.

The grandfather I had,
Who called my name his and left me all he had,
What would he say, that old man, who had seen the
    world and plowed its fields,
Who provided for his wives and shared his wisdom
    with everyone,
What would he say when he sees me standing,
    bewildered,
Not finding my place.
What would he say, when he learns that the forests
    he had visited,
Are known to me only from his tales,
And that I plow the skies for him, and harvest words
    for him.
His fleshy servants eke out a living in the market
And curse their lot. They repeat his stories into
    their cans
And curse their lot. Indeed this is his legacy, and
    this will be my legacy too,
When the day comes.

Translated by Tsipi Keller.

Other works by Sartel: *Shirey ma'aseh* (1967); *Ha-derekh ve-ha-basar* (1970); *Sefer nitzaḥon gadol* (1986); *Hineh ha-esh* (1994).

Naomi Shemer

Yerushalayim Shel Zahav
1967

Among the dreamy pines
As evening light is slowly dying
And a lonely bell still chimes
So many songs, so many stories
The stony hills recall . . .
Around her heart my city carries
A lonely ancient wall.

   Yerushalayim all of gold
   Yerushalayim, bronze and light
   Within my heart I shall treasure
   Your song and sight.

Alas, the drying wells and fountains,
Forgotten market-day
The sound of horn from Temple's mountain
No longer calls to pray
The rocky caves at night are haunted
By sounds of long ago
When we were going to the Jordan
By way of Jericho.

   Yerushalayim all of gold . . .

But when I come to count your praises
And sing Hallel to you
With pretty rhymes I dare not crown you
As other poets do
Upon my lips is always burning
Your name, so dear, so old:
If I forgot Yerushalayim
Of bronze and light and gold . . .

   Yerushalayim all of gold . . .

Back to the wells and to the fountains
Within the ancient walls
The sound of horn from Temple mountain
Loudly and proudly calls
From rocky caves, this very morning
A thousand suns will glow
As we shall go down to the Jordan
By way of Jericho.

   Yerushalayim all of gold . . .

Translated by the author.

Yoram Taharlev
b. 1938

The poet, songwriter, and author Yoram Taharlev is one of Israel's most prolific and versatile writers. His songs are a fixture at public events, from ceremonies to holidays to dedications to song contests. Some of those songs are personal and draw on his memories of the kibbutz where he grew up; others cover universal themes, such as friendship, family, love of country. Taharlev majored in philosophy at Tel Aviv University, and received a lifetime achievement award from Bar-Ilan University, a career capstone. His vast, diverse body of work includes pop songs, children's songs, comedic stage shows, and secular readings of Jewish religious texts.

Ammunition Hill
1967

"It was then the morning of the second day of the war in Jerusalem. The horizon paled in the east. We were at the climax of the battle on Ammunition Hill. We'd been fighting there for three hours. A fierce battle was under way. Fatal. The Jordanians fought stubbornly. It was a position fortified in an exceptional manner. At a certain point in the fight there remained next to me only four soldiers. We went up there with a force of two platoons. I didn't know where the others were because the connection with Dudik, the platoon commander, was cut off still at the beginning of the battle. At that moment I thought that everyone had been killed."

   At two, two-thirty
   We entered through the stony terrain
   To the field of fire and mines
   Of Ammunition Hill

   Against bunkers which were fortified
   And 120mm mortars
   A hundred and some boys
   On Ammunition Hill

   The pillar of dawn had not yet risen
   Half a platoon lay in blood
   But we were already there at least
   On Ammunition Hill

   Among the walls and the mines
   We left only the medics
   And we ran ahead without our senses
   Towards Ammunition Hill

"At that same moment a grenade was thrown from outside. Miraculously we weren't hit. I was afraid the Jordanians would throw more grenades. Someone had to run from above and cover. I didn't have time to ask who would volunteer. I sent Eitan. Eitan didn't hesitate for a moment. He climbed up and began to fire his machine gun. Sometimes he would overtake me and I'd have to yell to him to remain in line with me. That's how we crossed some 30 meters. Eitan would cover from above and we would clear the bunkers from within, until he was hit in the head and fell inside."

> We went down into the trenches
> Into the pits and channels
> And towards the death in the tunnels
> Of Ammunition Hill
>
> And no one asked where to
> Whoever went first fell
> One needed lots of luck
> On Ammunition Hill
>
> Whoever fell was dragged to the back
> In order not to disrupt the movement forward
> Until fell the next in line
> On Ammunition Hill
>
> Perhaps we were lions
> But whoever wanted still to live
> Should not have been
> On Ammunition Hill

"We decided to try blowing up their bunker with a bazooka. The bazooka made a few scratches in the concrete. We decided to try with explosive material. I waited above them until the guy came back with the explosives. He would throw me package after package, and I would lay them one by one at the entrance of their bunker. They had a system of their own: first they threw a grenade, afterwards they fired a volley, and then they rested. Between volley and grenade, I would approach the entrance of their bunker and place the explosives. I triggered the explosives and moved away as far as I could. I had four meters in which to move because also behind me were [Arab] Legionnaires. I don't know why I received a commendation, I simply wanted to get home safely."

> At seven, seven-twenty
> To the police school
> Were gathered all those who remained
> From Ammunition Hill

> Smoke arose from the hill
> The sun in the east rose higher
> We returned to the city, seven
> From Ammunition Hill
>
> We returned to the city, seven
> Smoke arose from the hill
> The sun in the east rose higher
> On Ammunition Hill
>
> On fortified bunkers
> And on our brothers, men
> Who remained there aged twenty
> On Ammunition Hill

Translated by Alex Ben-Arieh.

Other work by Taharlev: *I'll Take You There* (with Hannan Getride, 2002).

Zelda

1914–1984

Poet Zelda Schneurson (later Mishkovsky) was born in Chernigov, Russia (now Chernihiv, Ukraine) and would later publish under her first name only. The religiously observant daughter of a Hasidic rabbi descended from the Lubavitch dynasty, Zelda immigrated with her family to Palestine at the age of twelve. As a young woman, she wanted to study painting but was never able to do so formally. Instead she taught kindergarten for a number of years while painting and writing poetry in her spare time. Following her marriage in 1950, she ceased teaching and began to focus on poetry. Her first collection was not published until 1965, but her work proved enormously popular; her eventual six books were best sellers in Israel, and her work was translated into many languages and set to music.

Each Rose
1967

> Each rose is an island
> of the promised peace,
> the eternal peace.
>
> Inside the petals
> of each rose dwells
> a sapphire bird called
> "And They Shall Beat Their Swords."
>
> And it seems so
> close, the light
> of that rose, so close

its scent, the silence
of its leaves, so close
that island—just take
a boat and go out
into a sea of flames.

Translated by Barbara Goldberg.

Other works by Zelda: *Shirey Zelda* (1985); *The Spectacular Difference: Selected Poems of Zelda* (2004).

Yehuda Amichai

Jerusalem 1967
1968

1

This year I traveled a long way
to view the silence of my city.
A baby calms down when you rock it, a city calms
    down
from the distance. I dwelled in longing. I played the
    hopscotch
of the four strict squares of Yehudah Ha-Levi:
My heart. Myself. East. West.

I heard bells ringing in the religions of time,
but the wailing that I heard inside me
has always been from the Yehudean desert.

Now that I've come back, I'm screaming again.
And at night, stars rise like the bubbles of the
    drowned,
and every morning I scream the scream of a
    newborn baby
at the tumult of houses and at all this huge light. [. . .]

10

Jerusalem is short and crouched among its hills,
unlike New York, for example.
Two thousand years ago she crouched
in the starting-line position.
All the other cities went out, for long
laps in the arena of time, they won or lost,
and died. Jerusalem remained in the
    starting-crouch:
all the victories are clenched inside her
hidden inside her. All the defeats.
Her strength grows and her breathing is calm.
for a race even beyond the arena. [. . .]

21

Jerusalem is a port city on the shore of eternity.
The Temple Mount is a huge ship, a magnificent
luxury liner. From the portholes of her Western
    Wall
cheerful saints look out, travelers. Hasidim on the
    pier
wave goodbye, shout hooray, hooray, bon voyage!
    She is
always arriving, always sailing away. And the fences
    and the
                                    piers
and the policemen and the flags and the high masts
    of churches
and mosques and the smokestacks of synagogues
    and the boats
of psalms of praise and the mountain-waves. The
    shofar
                                    blows: another one
has just left. Yom Kippur sailors in white uniforms
climb among ladders and ropes of well-tested
    prayers.

And the commerce and the gates and the golden
    domes:
Jerusalem is the Venice of God.

Translated by Stephen Mitchell.

Ehud Manor

1941–2005

Ehud Manor was a popular Israeli songwriter, the pioneer of a sensitive, personal style that verged on the confessional. At a time when most Israeli lyricists sang odes to country and land, Manor sang of love and loss, joy and grief, life's grand pleasures and acute disappointments. His talent, however, flowed in multiple directions; after his army service, he balanced songwriting, broadcasting, advanced literary studies, and translation. Manor was born in Binyamina, and his greatest attachment was to Israel. He was prolific, with more than 630 translations and 1,200 original songs to his name. He received the Israel Prize in 1998.

Next Year
1968

Come next year we shall sit on the porch
Count the birds flying north.

Children on holiday will play catch
Between the house and the meadow.

You will see, you will yet see
How good it will be
In the next year, the next year.

By evening red grapes will ripen
And be served chilled at the table.
Dreamy winds will sweep onto the road
Discarded papers and a passing cloud.

You will see, you will yet see . . .

Come next year we will extend our palms
Toward the white streaming light.
In the light a white egret will spread its wings
And the sun will shine through them.

You will see, you will yet see . . .

Translated by Tsipi Keller.

Yakov Rotblit

b. 1945

Born in Haifa, the singer, songwriter, and journalist Yakov Rotblit has mixed art and activism his entire career. After enlisting in the IDF, he served in the Six-Day War, an experience both traumatic—he was gravely wounded in action—and artistically formative; two years later, he wrote "Shir le-shalom" (A Song for Peace), his best-known protest song and a favorite of the Israeli peace movement. Twenty-six years later, it was sung just before Yitzhak Rabin's assassination, and Rabin was later found to be carrying the song's lyrics in his breast pocket. Rotblit was an outspoken pacifist whose first solo album, *Kakh shihrarti et Yerushalayim* (This Is How I Liberated Jerusalem, 1978), was banned from Israeli airwaves for ten years. In between other projects, he has written songs for Israel's most popular singers.

Shir Leshalom (A Song for Peace)
1968

Let the sun come up today,
Let the morning shine,
All the prayers and plaintive words,
Won't bring us back to life.
For we whose light is darkened now,
Are covered by the dust,

The bitter tears, and endless grief
Are all in vain for us.

No one now can bring us back
From the silent haze,
Here nothing enters—
No sweet hymns of victory,
No sweet psalms of praise.

Chorus:
Let's hear you sing, now, sing of "Shalom"
No silent prayers will do.
Let's hear you sing, now, sing of "Shalom"
With all the love in you . . .

Let the sun come up today,
And shine in through your door,
Dead men hear no elegies,
So weep for them no more.
Fill your hearts with faith and hope,
And aim the guns no more,
Sing a song of love and peace,
No requiem of war.

And do not say: "the day will come,"
It's you who bring the day,
The time is nearing,
Let the people in the land,
Sing of peace today.

Chorus:
Let's hear you sing, now, sing of "Shalom"
No silent prayers will do.
Let's hear you sing, now, sing of "Shalom"
With all the love in you . . .
    Let the sun come up today . . .

Translated by Jerry Hyman.

Other work by Rotblit: *Mikhtavim mi-bayit revi'i* (1989).

Meir Wieseltier

b. 1941

Meir Wieseltier is a poet, editor, essayist, and Hebrew translator. He was born in Moscow and immigrated to Israel at the age of eight. An important figure among the group known as the Tel Aviv Poets, he was a founder of the literary magazine *Siman keriah*. Wieseltier was poetry editor at Am Oved Publications, and he was awarded the Israel Prize in 2000.

Daddy and Mommy Went to the Movies, Ilana Stays Alone in the Armchair Looking at a Gray Book
1968

She turns the pages, naked uncles
so naked and skinny, run and
even aunties with fannies showing
and others in pajamas as in a show
with yellow cloth stars sewed on.
And everybody so ugly and thin,
and big round eyes like chickens.

It's awfully weird, so gray. Ilana has pencils—red
and blue and green and yellow and pink.
So she goes to her room
and takes all the beautiful pencils
and draws with great flair
glasses and funny faces on all of them.
Especially on that bald skinny boy,
she gives him a big red mustache
and perched at the tip of the mustache—a bird.

I saw three baby-faced Germans
sitting in Café Notre Dame.
They were so soft in the morning
those three baby-faced Germans,
their field-grass hair
and their barefoot faces.

It rained on the city and the Seine,
washing trash into the gutter,
stale spit and yesterday's headlines,
hitting the Notre Dame and the Seine
and dripping on the eyelashes of passers-by
who moved in an endless line as if weeping
past windows that creaked on their hinges
in front of three baby-faced Germans.

The world is full of the righteous—
all of us are righteous in our own eyes
drink from our own cups, sit on our own butts
have some pangs of conscience, find our way out
arrange times for meditation, times for tears
lock ourselves in with a little key
and pocket it,
then sleep: and nurture
the shards of our anger.

Translated by Shirley Kaufman, with the author.

Other works by Wieseltier: *Perek alef perek bet* (1967); *Me'ah shirim* (1969); *Kaḥ* (1973).

Haim Be'er
b. 1945

The poet and novelist Haim Be'er has been described as a magical realist, a Jewish Gabriel García Márquez. Born in Jerusalem, a city whose atmosphere and characters animate his fiction, Be'er writes of dreamers, eccentrics, and wonder-struck adventurers who live in their imaginations as much as in reality. Be'er himself worked in publishing, wrote a popular newspaper column, and taught literature and creative writing at Ben-Gurion University of the Negev. His devotion to literature and his playful, peculiar, sensitive writing have made him one of Israel's most cherished and admired literary figures.

Transfiguration
1970

In history class
I draw a Latin-American moustache
On Titus Aspasianus;
Miriam, who under her flannel shirt
Is beginning to show development,
Is making vulgar contours
Onto the sculpture of his bust,
And with one stroke
Transforms the royal diadem
That crowns his glory
To a rakish top hat.
The beloved of the human race
That heated his bath when he arrived
And poured him a glass of wine when he left
Is now shamelessly busy with clowning,
He can even
Grab a whore and sin with her
In the holy of holies
Above the Torah
Resembling someone waging war
On the king in his palace
And blood sprouts from the Torah ark curtain
And the ink soaks into the paper.
In the beginning of the fifties
We were children, Jews
Sitting in *Aeliya Capitolina*
In the classroom that was once the dormitory
Of children with scrubbed faces,
Neophytes of the monks, who on Jerusalem nights
Would giggle little naughty laughs
In their iron beds
And from the windows
The city could be seen from afar

And the apocalyptic skies
Cast cloud after cloud.
And I can still hear
From the end of the century before
A choir of women singing
In the Church of the Redeemer
On the day of its dedication:
Freue dich du Tochter Zion[1]
And my grandmother
A good girl from the Old Settlement
Stands on the corner of the Street of the Prophets
    and Jaffa Street
Under the black Prussian bridge
Showing her respect for the Kaiser
Who forges a gate to make way for him
And dreams of the esteemed king
Selah.

NOTE
1. ["Rejoice, Daughter of Zion," an Advent hymn written by
the Swiss writer Edmond Budry (1854–1932)—Trans.]

Translated by Karen Alkalay-Gut.

Arik Einstein and Shalom Hanoch

Einstein, 1939–2013

Born in Tel Aviv, Arieh Leib Einstein (known as Arik
Einstein) is considered one of the most influential and
popular musicians in Israeli history, a pioneer of Israeli
rock and a beloved figure in the national imagination.
Einstein began his career in the 1950s as a singer in the
Naḥal Brigade army band, a group known for producing some of the country's top musical talent. A prolific
songwriter and artist, Einstein's fifty-year career encompassed some five hundred original songs, at least thirty-
four individual albums, and numerous collaborations
with a variety of Israel's most prominent musicians. In
addition to music, Einstein played a leading role in the
Israeli classic film *Sallaḥ Shabati* and performed as a
member of the famed comedy troupe the Lool Gang.

Hanoch, b. 1946

Shalom Hanoch is a considered a pioneering figure
in Israeli rock music. Born on Kibbutz Mishmarot,
Hanoch displayed a talent for music across genres at an
early age. His career began in the Israeli military as a
member of the Naḥal Brigade army band. After demo-
bilization, Hanoch became part of the Tel Aviv music
scene, where he met future Israeli rock legend Arik
Einstein, with whom he would collaborate frequently.

Hanoch remained a singular force in the development
of Israeli rock during the 1970s and 1980s. Taking a
darker, heavier, and more musically complex turn,
Hanoch's music responded directly to the personal
and political tragedies of the era and held its place as
particularly popular and influential.

Why Should I Take It to Heart
1970

Why should I take it to heart
I have new things on my mind,
Imagination that helps me to forget at times.

Why should I take it to heart
I have so much before that to love,
I always have friends that help me to be cheerful.

Let us shout, let us learn,
Let us laugh and let us listen.
Let us live and make mistakes
Let yourself forgive.
Simply to love

That's what I wanted to write
Take it slow,
And you'll be able to run, start over.

Why should I take it to heart
I have new things on my mind,
Imagination that helps me to forget at times . . .

Translated by Karen Alkalay-Gut.

Dan Pagis

1930–1986

Poet Dan Pagis was born in Romania and was sent to
a concentration camp during his childhood. He immigrated to Israel in 1946 and joined Kibbutz Merḥavyah.
A professor of medieval Hebrew literature at the
Hebrew University, Pagis published several collections
of poetry, as well as works for children. Not until 1970,
however, did Pagis begin to address the Holocaust in
poems that established a new poetics of indirection. In
1973, he was awarded the Prime Minister's Prize.

Twelve Faces of the Emerald
1970

1

I am exceedingly green: chill green.
What have I to do

with all the greenishness of chance?
I am the green-source, the green-self,
one and incomparable.

2

The most suspicious flash
in the cat's eye
at the most acute moment
aspires
to be
me.

3

What have I to do with you, or the living grass?
Among you I am a stranger—
brilliant, cold, playing with my eternities.

4

The emperor Nero, artist in stage-lighting,
raises me to his red eye;
only my green can pacify his blood.
Through me he observes the end of the burning
    world.

5

Slander! I am not
envious of the diamond: fickle duke,

reckless, lacking in self-control:
daggers! fireworks!
on the contrary, am moderate,
know how to bide my time,
to pour, green and accurate,
the poison.

6

As if I shared a secret. Shade of blue,
hint of red in a polished facet,
hesitating violet—
they're gone, they're gone.
I, the green-source,
abolish the colors of the rainbow.

7

You think that you will find your image
in mine.

No. I shall not leave a trace of you;
you never were in me.
Mirror facing mirror facing mirror, enchanted,
I am reflected in I.

8

With one flick of the hand,
I smash your days into twelve
green nights.

9

I am all eye.
I shall never sleep.

10

And so I put on a face,
twelve facets apparently transparent.

11

Fragments of light:
they indeed are my soul: I shall not fear.
I shall not die.
I have no need to compromise.

12

You will never find the secret of my power.
I am I: crystallized carbon
with a very small quantity
of chromium oxide.

Translated by Stephen Mitchell.

Other works by Pagis: *She'on ha-tsel* (1959); *Shahut me'uheret* (1964); *Ha-betsah she-hithapsah* (1973).

Dan Pagis

Written in Pencil on a Sealed Box-Car
1970

here in this carload
i am eve
with abel my son
if you see my other son
cain son of man
tell him that i

Translated by Stephen Mitchell.

Dudu Barak

b. 1948

The Israeli folk singer Dudu Barak was born in Jerusalem. He often returns to his childhood in his art, sprinkling remembered phrases from his school days into his music. Fitting grand themes into small forms, Barak's lyrics deal with all of life—"from love and hate to the Holocaust," as he put it. In addition to music, Barak also writes poetry; his nine poetry books attest to his skill as a wordsmith. Barak's music is part of the tapestry of Israeli life; his song "Flowers in the Rifle Barrel" was a fixture of Israeli radio after the Six-Day War. Shuttling between forms—penning lyrics with the density of poems, and poems with the beauty of lyrics—has long been his modus operandi.

Flowers in the Rifle Barrel

1971

When spring is asleep it palely awakens
In fields of fire the final battle will cease
And a wonderful morning from valley to hillside
Will rise up in singing and in joy.

The sun will stand still between Gaza and Rafah,
the moon will turn white on the peak of the Hermon
Flowers in a muzzle and girls in the turret
troops will return to the city in crowds.

One small girl holding wreaths
Will come out to the White City as in songs,
And place a daisy in the excited soldier's lapel,
And the sky will be so clear.

The sun will stand still between Gaza and Rafah . . .

The soldiers will come to town in great crowds
With girls and with song and with flowers of gold,
And all who yesterday knew pain and mourning
Will no longer know battle and fall.

The sun will stand still between Gaza and Rafah . . .

Translated by Karen Alcalay-Gut.

Other works by Barak: *Songs of Dudu Barak: Eastern Wall* (1998); *My Jerusalem: Poems by Dudu Barak* (2007); *The Beautiful Songs of Dudu Barak* (2008).

Ayin Tur-Malka

b. 1926

Ayin Tur-Malka (pen name of Aliza Grinberg; born Aliza Gurevich) was raised in Jerusalem and published her first poems at the age of sixteen. Tur-Malka was a member of the Leḥi militant group. In 1950, she married the poet Uri Zvi Greenberg and took on her pen name. After her husband's death in 1981, Tur-Malka studied Jewish philosophy at Tel Aviv University. Since then, she has been engaged in publishing Greenberg's complete works, as well as her own poetry. In 2014, she was awarded the Levi Eshkol prize for Hebrew poets.

Memorial Service

1972

Crags in the mountains facing us
are like bereaved mothers
who long ago altered their image:
dew does not slake them,
the sun does not gild them.
—How terrible their silence
and where can we flee?—
A memorial service: belated prayer for mercy.
The sons lie flat
in the wide earth
and the mothers stand tall.
In the line of rain they soak
the depths of the graves with tears.

Translated by Shirley Kaufman.

Other works by Tur-Malka: *Ken shel zeradim* (1963); *Shirat ha-be'erot* (1971); *Ashmorah ha-shlishit* (1989); *Shuvi nafshi li-tekheltekh* (2004).

Naomi Shemer

Lu Yehi

1973

Beyond the cloud upon the ocean
There's a white and lonely sail
    Let us pray and hope
    LU YEHI

I light a candle at my window
And its flame is shy and frail
    Let us pray and hope
    LU YEHI

Let us pray, let us hope
ANA LU YEHI
Let us pray and say
LU YEHI

I hear a sound of drums and trumpets
Of a battle not yet won
   Let us pray and hope
   LU YEHI

Although I know a thousand prayers
In my heart there's only one
   Let us pray and hope
   LU YEHI

Let us pray, let us hope
ANA LU YEHI
Let us pray and say
LU YEHI

A floating high above my country
There's an eagle and a dove
   Let us pray and hope
   LU YEHI

A fading road—a dying summer
Keep your eye on those we love
   Let us pray and hope
   LU YEHI

Let us pray, let us hope
ANA LU YEHI
Let us pray and say
LU YEHI

A little star at last is rising
It shall win the endless night
   Let us pray and hope
   LU YEHI

So let us pray and let us hope
And let us live to see its light
   Let us pray and hope
   LU YEHI

Let us pray, let us hope
ANA LU YEHI
Let us pray and say
LU YEHI

Translated by the author.

Ronny Someck

b. 1951

A poet, creative-writing teacher, and community activist, Ronny Someck was born in Baghdad and immigrated to Israel as a young child. His first book of poetry, *Golah* (Exile), was published in 1976. Someck has collaborated with many artists, including the American jazz musician Elliott Sharp.

Solo Arak
1973

1

Black ants crawl over nicotine-stained fingertips
dipping a mint leaf into the glass.
The alcohol dismantles Abd al-Wahab's
   "Cleopatra."
Now all is clear
solo violin
solo flute
solo oud

we're solo arak

2

Half woman half fish
tattooed on his arm
close to the palm.
His girlfriend applies make-up:
black stripes under the eyes
powder on her cheeks

she has scars on her breast

3

The street closes in on us with bars
of soft iron
words scatter on lips
sand in the eyes.
Once at the Home I heard a brave boy singing:
"Mitzpeh Yam is wrapped up in fences
and around me are 4 walls
and bars in the window
at every corner"
and in the window was the sea of Herzliya
smeared with Velveeta
waking up on the beach on a *dunam* of breasts
summer

after
summer

4

At night
he made love
below his stomach.
His whole body at his fingertips

a thick stain under the blanket

5

Wants to be a man already, like Clark Gable
with full lips and brilliantined hair

only to have strength for a few seconds
only to have strength for a few moans
only to have strength to be gone with the wind

6

The street closes in on us with bars
in the body
the bones turn soft
soaked
easy to bite from

and only a few barks away a burly dog grunts love

Translated by Moshe Dor and Barbara Goldberg.

Other works by Someck: *Bladi meri* (1994); *Gan 'eden le-orez* (1996); *Kaftor ha-tsehok* (with Shirley Someck, 1998); *Ani iraki-pijamah* (2008).

Avot Yeshurun

1903–1992

The poet Avot Yeshurun was born Yehiel Perlmutter in Ukraine and immigrated to Palestine in 1925. He joined the Haganah in 1929 and later fought in the 1948 war. Known for a literary style that combines Arabic and Yiddish idioms, Yeshurun was one of the first Israeli writers to grapple with the Palestinian refugee problem.

The Syrian-African Rift: Six Poems
1973

The Poem on the Eve of This Day

The sages say, that at the time the Syrian-African
    Rift

occurred, the celestial inhabitants were not
up-to-date. Each man was engaged
at his trade. In grinding hatchets. In splitting
    beasts.

Ancient humanity and land of the axe.
And when those wanted some change on the earth
they have to do it by putting to sleep.
After that they waken the earth.

Like they did to me once in isolation in narcosis
under the plywood and the roof
in Beilinson Hospital: "Yeshurun, you underwent
    an operation!"
And here I am. Yom Kippur.

The Poem on the Jews

The head of the congregation here stands at the
    head
of a long line of congregants who stand behind
    him.
A longer line than the one that departed and isn't.
Which—someone who has not seen it,

gradually the sight eludes him whereas
those other people, if not to resort to inhuman
idioms, why it can be said
with one word: they were the big ones when we were
    small.

At their hands each thing was cut they even cut
our slices of bread and they cut us
half an apple which voice of the apple we heard at
    the cutting.
And touched our cheeks and called our names.

They were in a closed circuit the masculine Jews we
    adored.
On holidays and on Sabbaths. With force they
    conducted
prayers and chanted hymns and acknowledged
    God.
And when Yom Kippur came kept packages of food
    for us at the fast.
After the holiday we still longed for the same holiday
    and
the same Jews to see them together. It's good to be
    among those who are one
people who neither change "nor all their wrath
    awaken" and look
upon me as someone they didn't see awhile.

The Poem on This Day

He stood before the prayer and before the singing.
I stood before the threshold. Someone bursts out:
Is there a shelter here?
There's a war here.

Plump a door opens.
I'm before the threshold. This
day, on which I was born
before "Closing Prayer,"

Yom Kippur. It's between us.
Romeo-and-Juliet-photographers-cinema,
now foreign correspondents, will formally launch it:
Yom Kippur or Day of Judgment.

Rabbi Shmuel Eliahu of Modzitz apportions his tear
     to men.
He stood in prayer and singing.
I noticed that. I beat palm to palm
and came out singing.

The Poem on the Guilt

Blest be Mother bind your hand on my head on the
     eve
of this day. I would have what would I have done
for Yom Kippur. Forests crash and you inside and at
     the center
of the land your soul and body you longed and did
     not arrive.

Your Father came in a dream to you.
Opened the glass cupboard; broke you a glass. A
     child of yours died
and you asked why. Your Father didn't reply and
     went out and you meant to forgive
and lay on the floor and lay on the child and died of
     longing.

The Poem on the Africs

Plump a door opens. A soldier pulled a reservist
     outside.
Straightened the *tallith* from street to street and
     listening to the soldier's story.
Walked with the soldier cat and cat
and cheek and cheek.

The two reservist guys went to the Syrian-
African Rift: You came to us to escape the white.
But you be the villain? Loathsome to me is
     death

because an Afric's in your grip.

We have a problem of a sacrifice of Isaac.
And yours, you're inclined to think, the sacrifice of
     Isaac.
For us it comes out as a father has mercy on
     children.
For you it comes out as a father has mercy on
     himself.

The Poem on Our Mother, Our Mother Rachel

And the two reservist guys went. Look, don't
     shoot.
And Jacob lifted his legs and went to the land of
     B'nei Kedem.
And Jacob said unto them: Ben-Gurion and
     Nechemiah Argov, my brothers from
     Whence?
From Ben-Gurion and Nechemiah Argov no
     reaction no response and the two went off.

Ben-Zvi's shack a wooden candelabrum
of local-make carvings by Batia Lishanski,
and not a painting on every painting and not
     Chagall
on every France and presidential mansion rejoice
     and rejoice.

Inside sits Jacob.
Esau stands outside.
From the window looks and wails
Esau's Mother from the lattice.

Punished Earth.
You needn't start up with her. To speak
to her you need. To trick out her wardrobe. As
     meadows
wore sheep so we wore her the Land.

Don't call her by many names.
Call her Rachel.
A man is born as a child and dies as a child.
All this dependent on the Mother.

Punished Earth.
You needn't start up with her. To speak
to her you need. To trick out. As meadows
so we wore this Land.

Translated by Harold Schimmel.

Other works by Yeshurun: *Zeh shem ha-sefer* (1970);
En li 'akhshav (1992); *Kol shirav* (1995).

EUROPE (1946–1973)

This section presents Jewish writing and political thought in a Europe consumed by the challenges of postwar reconstruction, fears of renewed conflict between East and West, and grim memories of destruction and betrayal. The same Europe that had inspired generations of Jews with promises of liberalism and progress witnessed the greatest disaster in Jewish history. And although some non-Jews intervened to save their Jewish neighbors during the war, frequent cases of collaboration with the Nazi occupiers left widespread ripples of mistrust in the aftermath.

Jewish survivors had to take stock and ask themselves on what terms they could again become French, or Dutch, or Italians. Everywhere in Europe, on both sides of the Iron Curtain, Jews discovered, in those first years after the war, that few people wanted to hear their stories or recognize their suffering. In the Soviet Union and the satellite countries of Eastern Europe, communist leaders used their supposedly universalist ideology to spread an invidious antisemitism that erased Holocaust memory, justified discrimination, and resulted in the murder of Jewish writers and poets.

Yet as this part shows, Jews did not give up on Europe. Many Jewish thinkers, ranging from Emmanuel Levinas to Hermann Goldschmidt, boldly asserted that, more than ever, a morally compromised Europe needed to take seriously the legacy of Jewish thought and ethics that the Nazis and so many others had ridiculed. And in time, be it through life writing, fiction, poetry, or the plastic arts, Jews once again had an impact on the culture of a reviving Europe. After years of indifference, witnesses such as Elie Wiesel and Primo Levi finally began to find an audience. France in particular emerged as a new Jewish center, transformed by a North African migration that made the Jewish community significantly larger than before the war. First-generation women writers from Arab lands become especially prominent in this period as poets, novelists, song writers, and performers in French—something that could not have happened in the Maghreb. Spurred by the Six-Day War, the failure of domestic liberalization, and activism in the United States and elsewhere, the first signs of a Jewish revival appeared in even the Soviet Union by the end of this period.

By the mid-1960s, some Jews mused out loud about the need for a new, "European" Jewish identity that would complement the growing movement toward European integration and serve as a link between East and West. For its champions, such a vision of cosmopolitan European Jewishness represented as well an alternative to the two dominant ethnic Jewish communities of Israel and the United States that emerged in the wake of the Holocaust. It heralded the revival of a distinct European Jewish sensibility, creative and connected to deep historical roots.

ANTHOLOGIES

Dovid Diamant
1903–1994

Born in Hrubieszów, Poland, Dovid Diamant (born Erlich) was a member of the French Communist Party and of the French Resistance. Although he was offered safe passage to England several times, he remained in France throughout the war. Afterward, Diamant worked with the Union des juifs pour la résistance et l'entraide (Jewish Union for Resistance and Mutual Aid) to assist Jewish refugees. Diamant also dedicated himself to the documentation of Jewish resistance in France and Poland, especially by communist organizations, and he published widely on the materials he collected.

How We Found the Manuscripts of the Martyred Writers
1946

A people that forgets its dead is condemned to decay—
Jules Guesde

We will never forget our dead. They still live among us and in our thoughts.

For that reason, immediately after the Liberation, we began the task of gathering everything related to the lives and works of the Yiddish writers who had perished. This involved enormous difficulties. At first it was impossible to know what literary legacy a particular individual might have left behind. Despite all the precautions and hiding places the fact remained that every Jewish residence had been sacked by the Germans. If there were any surviving family members of the deceased, in whose hands salvaged manuscripts might potentially be found, they were likely to have wandered all over the towns and villages of the French provinces. Finding their addresses and awaiting their return to Paris took a long time. Even the published works of the writers were unavailable. It took some time before the library of the Central Cultural Council, itself hidden exactly like every Jewish survivor, could be put back in order.

The surviving writers gradually came together. They came from hiding places, from prison, from the death camps. Out of their efforts arose our institution—the Documentation Center. We had to create a central place for the materials, locate the manuscripts, classify them and put them in order. We had to attract the appropriate workers, both writers and nonwriters. All this lengthy and arduous work made it possible to assemble the small amount we have salvaged up to now.

It is necessary to point out the vital role played by ordinary people in safeguarding or salvaging the surviving material.

Arn Bekerman

In 1943, during the pitiless campaign of terror against the Jews, the Parisian Jewish worker Hershl hid in the little town of Ozoir, not far from Paris. Once, walking through the forest, he noticed loose Yiddish pages and Yiddish manuscripts. At that time, to carry on one's person anything written in the Jewish alphabet was no less life-threatening than speaking Yiddish out loud. But Hershl could not resist the temptation to pick up what he could. He gathered the yellowed, soaked pages of books and notebooks, following the traces that led him to the house where the writer Arn Bekerman had previously lived. It appeared that the abandoned little house had attracted the attention of thieves, who, by looting everything of any value to them, had inadvertently found the way to much of Bekerman's literary legacy.

In November 1944, shortly after the liberation of Paris, a group of colleagues traveled to Ozoir to recover Bekerman's archive. Among them were Moyshe Shulshteyn, M. Zeldov, and Gandverg. With great difficulty they dug out the manuscripts hidden under the house. They were packed in a wooden case, corroded by dampness and worms. Everything fell apart in their hands. Whoever saw the confused pile of yellowed pages was unavoidably left with a painful impression. The melancholy image of Bekerman's archive was the expression of the destruction of Yiddish culture as a whole.

In the course of the winter 1945–1946, the staff and volunteers of the Documentation Center expended a great deal of effort in putting the salvaged materials back into an orderly state. Bekerman's memoirs and his diary had become fused into a single mass. The least carelessness could have turned everything to dust. All of this was done in a cramped attic room of four square meters [about 43 square feet], which contained the Documentation Center, the editorial offices of *Droit et liberté* and the bookcases of the library. In the evening, after a day's work, work would begin at sorting the manuscripts. Good-will overcame all difficulties. The work was carried out by the writers B. Shlevin, K. Benek, M. Shulshteyn, Avrom Veyts, the archivist Glezer, the printer Helfgot, and the employee Shtrigler. Even now, Y. Odrozhinsky and the seamstress Valdman are classifying Bekerman's literary correspondence with great devotion.

But it was not only in Ozoir that Bekerman hid his manuscripts. The second place where he wrote under the German occupation was Écueillé, a small town in the Department of the Indre. His devoted friends there were Zalmen and Khantshe Gandverg. At that time, no one knew who would remain alive and each of them left an oral testament for the other. Bekerman asked his friends to undertake to preserve his writings if no one in his family survived. Bekerman, his wife, and his son perished. Zalmen also perished, but Khantshe survived. She loyally carried out Bekerman's wishes. In June 1946, after the archive in Ozoir had been found, she brought to the Documentation Center the remainder of Bekerman's literary correspondence, as well as the 10th and 11th volumes of his diary, *In Times of Madness*, written in Écueillé. He continued to write his diary in the camps of Gurs and Drancy, down to the day of his deportation.

Translated by Solon Beinfeld.

Other work by Diamant: *Les juifs dans la résistance française* (1962).

Michał Borwicz

1911–1987

A pioneer of Holocaust studies in Polish, Yiddish, and French, Michał Maksymilian Borwicz was born Maksymilian Boruchowicz in Kraków. Before the war, he was known as a literary critic, poet, and novelist in the Polish language. From 1942 to 1943, he was incarcerated at the Janowska concentration camp on the outskirts of Lwów. He escaped hanging in 1943. Comrades from the Polish Socialist Party helped him escape from Janowska and he joined the Polish

partisan resistance, commanding a unit of the Armia Krajowa (Home Army) in Kraków, under the nom de guerre "Zygmunt." After the war, Borwicz led the Jewish Historical Commission in Kraków until 1947, when he moved to Paris. There he directed the Centre d'étude de l'histoire des juifs polonais until his death.

The Song of the Dying: To the History of Jewish Creativity under the Nazi Occupation
1947

Among the illegal publications that appeared in Poland during the Nazi occupation, one can find a small anthology of poems entitled *Z otchłani, from the Abyss*. This modest volume, published by the clandestine Jewish National Committee, appeared in Warsaw in the spring of 1944. The microfilmed text was smuggled abroad. [. . .] On November 18, 1944[,] the poems were published in the New-York-based *Nasza Trybuna*. They were also recited at a special literary evening. Shortly thereafter, the entire collection, richly illustrated by Zygmunt Menkes and prefaced by two introductions [by J. Wittlin and J. Apenszlak] was republished as *The Poetry of the Ghetto: From the Jewish Underground of Poland*.

The poet Józef Wittlin . . . wrote that "when we read these poems, our hands tremble, our tongue dries up, we hold our breath. The eyes that read these black, mournful lines of beautiful but terrible verses burn with shame; shame on the eyes that read these poetic traces of heroism and destruction and do not become blind. The words that burst forth from these lines are the same Polish words that living people use to speak with each other. But it seems to me that it is really the language of those whom God has already consoled."

J. Apenszlak declared that "these poems are a revelation not only because of the circumstances in which they were composed. [. . .] Much more effectively than dry facts and reports from the killing grounds, they give us a sense of what the inmates of the ghettos, debased by the bestial Germans to the very depths of humiliation and suffering, thought and felt, how they absorbed the blows."

Today as we ponder the date when these poems appeared, we should remember that the very appearance of this collection may be as significant as the individual poems themselves. That is because as we consider the fate of the Jews under the German occupation, we should recall that those still alive in the spring of 1944 were living in one gigantic cemetery, painfully fresh and totally unlike anything experienced by human beings.

> All perished. Men and women.
> The old and the little children.
> The stars shine in the cold sky,
> Only they remained. [Mieczysław Jastrun, "Poem of a Jewish Boy"]

[. . .] The Jewish National Committee explained in *Z otchłani* that "Our publications are totally unprecedented. They are being put out by people who live under the shadow of a death sentence, who work in nightmarish conditions of extreme secrecy. They are being published by the same Jews who raised the standard of battle for the human and national dignity of the Jews, those individuals whose slogan had been to "live with honor and to die with honor." . . . Self-help and armed struggle were the watchwords that inspired us throughout the martyrdom of Polish Jewry. They are the ideas that still motivate us. . . .

Yes, self-help and armed resistance, life with dignity and death with dignity. In this tangle of fatal combinations, each word that was handed over to the typesetters of the secret printing press had to be not only carefully considered but also weighed. It was not enough that a poem had to be useful and relevant. The Committee also had to believe that each word had deep meaning. . . .

But why poems all of a sudden? In a slim little volume, of all things?

No, it was not all of a sudden. This organization, which had had little to do with literary matters; this organization that had to function in such an extraordinary time and circumstances; this group that had so much to tell the world and such limited means (even compared to the other groups in the underground) with which to print its message and distribute it a group such as this does not issue such a special publication of this kind because of a some whim or out of refined aesthetic motives.

The group published this little volume because in those crazy times poetry became a foundation of struggle. More than one condemned prisoner went to the scaffold with poetry on his lips, much like a shipwrecked person takes one last invigorating drink from a canteen. In most cases that last sip from the canteen did not help the body, but it allowed the mind, which had been so long paralyzed and muffled by the veil of nothingness, one last moment of sober reflection. This made

it possible to meet death with resigned composure and with a determination that included both pain and contempt for the killers. It was a determination of impersonal hope and—as is the prerogative of the weak—bitter understanding.

The little volume *From the Abyss* was no digest of all the literary transformations of those bloody years. It did not include the entire labyrinth of cruelty and crimes. But it did reflect an instinctive faith that in the end "the poem will survive."

Translated by Samuel D. Kassow.

Other works by Borwicz: *Ze śmiercią na ty* (1946); *Écrits des condamnés à mort sous l'occupation allemande, 1939–1945: Étude sociologique* (1954); *Arishe papirn*, 3 vols. (1955); *1000 ans de vie juive en Pologne* (1956); *L'Insurrection du ghetto de Varsovie* (1974).

Shmerke Kaczerginski

The Song of the Vilna Ghetto
1947

Introduction

The German occupation with its huge system of ghettos, concentration camps, death camps, and more cannot be represented in a normal human tongue. No depictions, documents, and images can portray this horror in all its scope. Whoever was not present will not be able to grasp rationally the bloody nightmare that millions of people underwent. Now, when I look back, I often think: what happened to us? How could we have lived and died like that?

Even for those who survived the ghettos and concentration camps, it will eventually become an insoluble riddle. Few documents have been preserved to provide at least a partial picture of the lawless status and everyday life of the Jews in the occupied territories. I therefore believe that the songs issuing from grieving Jewish hearts in the ghettos and death camps and later in partisan bases will be a major contribution to the history of Jewish martyrdom and struggle.

The song, the witticism, the pointed jest—have accompanied the Jew in all times and places: when he went to work, when he stood in line for a bowl of soup, when he was being led to the slaughter and when he went into battle.

It seems to us unnatural when the actor on the stage, during a tragic moment, suddenly begins to sing. Supposedly it doesn't happen that way in real life. But life taught us something different. On the day when the partisans in the Vilna Ghetto mobilized to defend their commander [Itzik] Wittenberg, I did not stop writing my diary, knowing these might be my last moments. When we partisans stood barricaded with weapons in our hands and nearby the Gestapo blew up a house where our partisans were positioned, [Abraham] Sutzkever, [Leyb] Opeskin, Hirsh Glik, and other writers did not stop writing poetry. At that moment I was reading [Franz] Werfel's *Forty Days of Musa Dagh* to a partisan squad.

In moments when it seemed that death was unavoidable the words of our young poet-partisan Hirsh Glik reverberated in our hearts: "Never say that you are walking your last road!"

We sang.

Singing united our souls, raised our spirits, and steeled our muscles—even when the song was sorrowful. . . . Sorrow developed in us hatred and rage—healthy emotions which led to deeds, to vengeance!

We knew the authors of almost all the songs. In ordinary times each song would probably have taken a long time to attain popularity, but in the ghetto we witnessed a wonderful process—individual creations became folklore before our eyes. Every newly created song, which expressed the feelings and experiences of the masses, was at once taken up by the masses and circulated as its own. The bloody events themselves were the creator of folklore. This explains why the subject matter is in some respects so unusual, the form so simple, unpolished, but for all that, immediate and truthful. Yes, truthful . . .

In the ghetto, we did not dare say anything bad about the murderers. If a German approached, the warning "apples!" would immediately be given, meaning "A German is coming!" (Derived from the fact that in winter frozen Germans soldiers would arrive at the Vilna military hospitals "like frozen apples," as the folk-saying went.) When the Yiddish Choir in the Vilna ghetto (directed by A. Slep) sang the song "Shtiler, shtiler," the line "all roads lead to Ponar" had to be changed to "all roads now lead there," and instead of "her child goes to Ponar," they sang "the master is taking the child away." It was forbidden to mention the word "Ponar," though eighty thousand victims had perished there. "There is no Ponar. It's a lie invented by the Bolsheviks," the Germans would say.

We were told to have a theater. What should be performed? For a careless word, Ponar threatened. So the authors of the texts began to write allusively. Take the names of the revues in the Vilna Ghetto Theater: "Korene yorn un vey tsu di teg" (Years of Rye and Woe to the Days) a pun on the Yiddish saying "Korene yorn un veytsene teg" (Years of rye and days of wheat), signifying poverty. "Men ken gornit visn" (You Never Can Tell) and "Moyshe halt zikh" (Moyshe Hold On). In the cabaret theater, "Di yogenish in fas" (The Rush into the Barrel) was a play of words on "Diogenes in fas" (Diogenes in the barrel). Likewise you will seldom encounter the name "German" in the songs. But you recognize the murderer in the subtext of every line. The only exceptions were the songs that were sung in secret. If anyone had been found with the text of these songs, or heard singing them, the Gestapo would have added extra tortures to his death.

Day-to-day Jewish life in the ghetto with all its accompanying phenomena, like prison, death, labor, Gestapo, and Jewish functionaries, is reflected in this bloody folklore. It will help the future historian and reader fathom the soul of the people, its hatred and loathing of the bandits, and its attitude toward its Jewish functionaries, toward its own traitors.

About *my* songs that are included in this collection, needless to say, one should not look for poetry there. I never undertook to create that. I wrote songs only when I felt there was a gap in our repertoire, that there were songs that I and my circle needed. Not everyone could adapt to that simple but important task.

Our goal was to include in this collection the most familiar songs of the Vilna ghetto, songs that later wandered to other ghettos and camps and were not forgotten in the partisan bases or in the days of liberation. The song of the Vilna ghetto was the song of the Jewish people in the time of occupation. Therefore we believe that the particular collection which we present here is not only for the Jews of Vilna, but for all Jewish readers and singers. It is the property of the entire people.

Translated by Solon Beinfeld.

Israel Kaplan

1902–2003

Israel Kaplan, the son of a Lithuanian rabbi, was born in Volozhin, Belorussia, and educated in Brisk, Vilna, and Kovno. He spent his early career as a teacher and writer. With the German occupation, Kaplan was confined to the Kovno and Riga ghettos and later sent to Dachau, from where he was liberated in 1945. An early champion of Holocaust testimony and ethnography, he founded and edited *Fun letstn khurbn* (From the Latest Catastrophe), one of the most important publications to appear in the displaced persons' camps. In 1949 he settled in Israel, where he continued to publish on the Holocaust. He was awarded the Manger Prize for Yiddish Literature in 1987.

Jewish Folk-Expressions under the Nazi Yoke
1949

Forward

Everything, nearly everything, was taken away from us in the ghettos and concentration camps by the great criminals. They did not spare our treasures, both material and spiritual. Even our little children, the apples of our eyes, were torn from us. Their ultimate desire was to undermine the self-confidence of the community and to eliminate the last bit of vitality from every individual. In that case, we would truly have lost everything.

In this effort, the criminals were far from successful. Rarely did any Jew give up hope until his last breath. Every individual felt in every way connected with his people. Everyone's fate was tightly bound with everyone else's.

One of the vital essences which almost everyone indulged in was the eternal "voice of Jacob"—sayings, jokes, anecdotes, wishes, various opinions, and novelties. Those were balm for the concealed emotions and feelings of depression. In the direst situation, with clenched teeth, surrounded on all sides by "unfriendly" eyes and ears, the tongue did not cleave to the palate. Just as life as a whole was torn apart and embittered, so also did the tongue angrily and bitingly drill deep. That is the explanation for the frequently violent and scathing expressions that emerged and also for the in-group insults which frequently bordered on obscenity. (It's premature to publish folk materials that are explicitly directed against other Jews.) [. . .]

KHADOSHES [NEWS]

News. This word burned on the lips of every Jew. When people returned, barely alive, from work in the evening, or when in the middle of the night, "when God himself is still asleep," the prisoners are driven in the darkness through mud and cold to the roll-call, or when

the labor brigade goes out to work at dawn and meets on the way the columns of the night-shift marching back from work, any time Jews encounter one another, even if it is in haste and under the strictest guard, always, on every occasion from one to another the question flies: *khadoshes*, [any] news?

First they have to hear. The source, where does the news originate, is not important. A bit later, when the troubles are nevertheless great and bitter, the whole thing begins to seem shaky for the skeptic. Jews begin to groan and fear that all the good and cheerful news might originate from

YIVO

[The name of the well-known research institute in Vilna] whose initials could be reinterpreted as *Yidn Viln Azoy*—Jews Want It That Way—a well-known "news agency" among the Jews of the Baltic States. But on the shores of the Baltic itself, in Riga, there was a German-Jewish ghetto with "extreme" optimists. They saw

The Messiah Seven Times a Day

as the more unemotional Latvian and Lithuanian Jews said of the constant stream of wonderful news from the "German Ghetto." The soberest among the Litvaks would quickly add, after hearing the latest "German" news:

RGR

yet another "News Agency," *Riga Ghetto Radio*, hoping it did not imply that the real news will be *ErGeR* [worse] . . .

The Hungarian Jews in the camps had their own "News Agency":

HGZ

which meant "*hob gehert zogn*" (I heard it said).

The Jews also came up with a "News Agency" for their non-Jewish neighbors. In the early days of the Nazi occupation Lithuanians or Russians often turned to Jews they knew for explanation of the significance of *DNB* (*Deutsche Nachrichten Büro*/German News Bureau) which repeated in almost every news story in their newspapers. The Jews would interpret it as:

DNB—"*durakom nie bud*" [Russian]

or in Lithuanian: "*durno ne buk*"—both meaning "don't be a fool."

These provincial newspapers—published by the Germans and filled with false news and vicious anti-semitism—were for the Jews almost the only source of news during the ghetto and concentration-camp years. Even getting hold of them was difficult and could involve great danger. Yet Jews were eager to see with their own eyes some sort of newspaper, called:

A Leynendike (Something Readable)

which in the Baltic region was called:

A Ksive (Document)

The most important place in Jewish "talking politics" was naturally occupied by the Germans:

Ashkenazim [in Hebrew], *Yekes* [in derisive Yiddish], *Amoleykim* [Amalekites, biblical enemies of the Jews], *Daledn* [D's (for *Daytshn*)], *Indikes* (Turkeys) . . .

Unlimited names were reserved for Hitler, according to the first initial of his name or the meaning of the word:

Der Hey (The H), *Kapelushmakher/Kapelushnik/ Kirzhner* (hatter [a pun on *hitl*, hat]), *mitsnefes* [cap, upper part of a shroud] . . .

Hitler's former profession was painting, hence:

Pendzler/Shmirer/Patshkun (dauber) . . .

Based on Hitler's cruelty:

The Great Enemy, Haman, *Roshe Merushe* (Wicked Man), *Ashmeday* [Asmodeus, the King of the Devils], Angel of Death—*may his name be erased* . . .

Hitler's arrogance and effrontery earned him the sobriquets:

Cock, Turkey, *Sambatyen* [legendary river, hence turbulent person], *Haliteyni* (glutton, guzzler), Squealer [i.e., pig], Big Mouth . . .

Hitler as *Führer/firer*:

Sus (horse), *Furman* (teamster), *Balagole* (coachman), *Arbe* (four, in Yiddish *fir*) . . .

The Polish Jews looked at Hitler's marital status, so they also called him:

The Bachelor

The Jews of Riga made *gimatries*, adding the numerical values of the Hebrew letters, and discovered that "*Hitler*" was the same as "*Homen kotn*" (little Haman), both equal to 254.

Joseph Goebbels was well-known as:

Yosele, *Yosele Roshele* (little villain), The Dreamer (like Joseph in the Bible), The Preacher, Noisemaker, Bulldog, The Crippled Puppy, *Fishke* (as in Mendele's novel *Fishke the Lame*), *Beygele* (bagel, deformation of "Goebbels," a reference also to his twisted shape) . . .

In the Baltic region, Göring was given the name:

The Salty One, *Selyodka* ([salt] herring in Russian, where G and H are interchangeable).

Translated by Solon Beinfeld.

Other works by Kaplan: *Shlyakh un umveg* (1964); *Geshlayder* (1970).

Josef Wulf and Léon Poliakov

Wulf, 1912–1974

Born in Chemnitz, Germany, and trained as a rabbi, Josef Wulf survived the Holocaust—in the Kraków ghetto and in Auschwitz—and subsequently became a historian. After the war, Wulf remained in Europe, leading the Central Jewish Historical Commission in Poland from 1945 to 1947. Eventually he moved to Berlin, where he wrote extensively on the Third Reich. Although he won recognition for his research, he struggled to find a stable academic position in Germany. In 1974, faced with the ongoing power and presence of former Nazis in the German public sphere, and depressed by the death of his wife, he committed suicide.

Poliakov, 1910–1997

Born in St. Petersburg, Léon Poliakov was a foundational scholar in the study of the Holocaust and among the earliest historians to examine the position of the Vatican during World War II. Poliakov spent time in Italy and Germany before settling in France. At the beginning of the war he joined the French army and, after his escape from a German prisoner-of-war camp, the French Resistance. In 1943, he helped organize the Center of Contemporary Jewish Documentation. Poliakov also assisted French counsel Edgar Faure at the Nuremberg trials.

The Third Reich and the Jews
1955

Without the appropriate distance, writing history is particularly difficult and thorny in this case. And there is an additional element of complexity. Forced into the thankless role of the prosecutor, a Jewish pen—even if it wants to be extraordinarily scrupulous—will always be in danger of failing to hit the right tone, or of foundering on two equally dangerous shoals. The historian, first, must steer clear of all resentment, even if it were entirely understandable and, second, must command a superhuman "scientific" objectivity, which, when faced with six million corpses—one-third of the entire Jewish people—is hard to achieve. For that reason, the only completely neutral and unprejudiced form was chosen: a collection of documents and testimonies by witnesses, documents that are beyond manipulation. The majority of them come from the archives of the Third Reich itself.

Thus, it becomes superfluous to discuss the painful conundrum that has already entered history as the "question of collective guilt." Without returning to this topic, we would like to restrict ourselves to the following remark:

Between 1945 and 1955, numerous works were published in all civilized countries; Jews and non-Jews thought about something entirely new in the history of our culture, namely, the industrialized murder of men, women, and children who could not be reproached for anything other than that they had been born in this bed rather than that one . . .

But in pedantic Germany, of all places, not a single serious study has as yet examined this subject, except for a few publications of a very general nature. Why this imbalance? Is knowing what happened and how it happened not immensely preferable to a silence that could have different, conceivably even contradictory, motives? To the outsider it would appear as if the conscience of the most blameless and most cultivated Germans would be most troubled by those crimes in which they did not have a part, crimes that were, however, committed in their name, in the name of the entire German people. . . . If steady denial (unfortunately all too frequent in our days) is not at all a solution, reticent silence certainly isn't one either. If the present study were to contribute to an allaying of unjustified uneasiness, to greater knowledge of how things hang together, and to an increased awareness of them, and if it were to stimu-

late careful research, the work of the editor of this book would not have been in vain.

Strange are the linkages between German history and the Jewish fate. Germany is almost the only Western European country from which the Jews were never expelled during their thousand-year history. The national language of the Eastern European Jews, Yiddish, developed from German. It is a variety of Middle High German. Until not too long ago, the Jews were indefatigable bearers and disseminators of German culture and German science. The German Jews Marx, Freud, and Einstein contributed decisively to the development of universal ideas; the Jews Haber and Rathenau, who, as is well known, played a role during World War I (1914-1918), were Germans too, and Theodor Herzl wrote his works—fifty years later they led to the founding of the state of Israel—in German. . . .

What sort of tension lies concealed here? Are these extraordinary streams of intellectual energy in any way related to the soil from which the catastrophe arose, and what kind of relationship that might be? These questions are mentioned here only to indicate that even from the perspective of general cultural history, the study of this complex would lead to fruitful results.

Translated by Susanne Klingenstein.

Other works by Wulf: *Die Nürnberger Gesetze* (1960); *Martin Bormann, Hitlers Schatten* (1962); *Raoul Wallenberg: Il fut leur espérance* (1968). Other works by Poliakov: *Harvest of Hate: The Nazi Program for the Destruction of Jews in Europe* (1951); *The History of Antisemitism* (1955); *Jews under the Italian Occupation* (with Jacques Sabille, 1955); *The Aryan Myth: A History of Racist and Nationalistic Ideas in Europe* (1971).

Moisei Beregovskii
1892-1961

Folklorist and ethnomusicologist Moisei (Moshe) Iakovlevich Beregovskii was born in Ukraine. His father was a melamed. Beregovskii studied cello and vocal composition in the Kiev conservatories from 1915 to 1922. In 1927, he founded the Commission for Jewish Folk Music Research at the Ukrainian Academy of Sciences. Beregovskii became something of a wanderer; between 1929 and 1947 he collected more than two thousand field recordings from throughout Ukraine and the former Pale of Settlement. His collection was especially rich in Yiddish folk songs and *purim-shpiln* (Purim skits).

Jewish Folk Songs
1962

At the beginning of the present century a whole constellation of Jewish composers and musicians studied at the St. Petersburg Conservatory under the beneficial influence of Rimski-Korsakov, who constantly directed his multiethnic student body toward the sources of folk art. Gniessin (1956: 208)[1] writes about this:

How freely he expressed himself about the characteristics of these [multiethnic—M.B.] melodies, and with what sensitivity he encouraged students in their work of arrangement, and that includes Russians, Ukrainians, Latvians, Estonians, Armenians, and Jews. Once one of my classmates brought in two pieces, perhaps for violin and piano, titled "Oriental Melodies." "Very nice pieces," said Rimski-Korsakov after listening to the music, "but why are they called oriental melodies? After all, these are typically Jewish melodies—it's hard to confuse them with others!"

Another Rimski-Korsakov student, Lazar Saminsky (1914:78)[2] writes:

Those of his students who have worked in the Jewish field have an exceptional feeling for the memory of Nikolai Andreevich. We will never forget his words, addressed to one of our comrades, perhaps E. I. Shklar, when he brought him a Jewish romance: "I'm glad to see you writing a composition with a Jewish flavor. It's quite strange that my Jewish students interest themselves so little in their own music. Jewish music lives; it is remarkable music and awaits its Glinka."

It is not surprising that at the St. Petersburg Conservatory the trend that led Jewish composers to their own native art was born, strengthened, and encouraged. This atmosphere quickly led to the organizing, in 1908, of the Society for Jewish Music by the young composers and musicians, which had as its goal the creation of Jewish compositions based on folk music. Among the active members of this society we find: M. F. Gniessin, A. M. Zhitomirsky, L. Saminsky, P. R. L'vov, M. A. Milner, I. Achron, S. B. Rosowsky, E. I. Shklar, Z. A. Kiselhof, and others. The young Jewish composers ran up against the fact of a total lack of printed editions of examples of Jewish folk music and so had to turn to the job

of collecting. In that very year (1908), the Jewish Historic-Ethnographic Society was organized, which paid considerable attention to the collecting of examples of oral and musical art. In 1912–14 a series of expeditions was organized by the Society to villages in the Volynsk, Kamenets-Podol'sk, and other *gubernias* (czarist administrative units) in the southwestern region, now part of the Ukrainian S.S.R. These expeditions had already adopted the phonograph for the recording of Jewish folk music. The recordings made in these years by expedition participants have been preserved. In 1939 they were given to the Institute. [. . .]

In the present volume, the first thirty-eight songs are love songs. The word "love" seemed forbidden in the conditions of nineteenth-century Russian Jewish life, so it would seem that love songs would have no place in the song repertoire. Weddings, as a rule, were early and concluded exclusively by matchmaking. There could be no question of free choice. In the more fanatic[3] circles, the newlyweds rarely saw each other until after the ritual betrothal. Nevertheless, collectors have found themselves faced with countless love songs of the most diverse types.

Having deeply studied Jewish songs and their context, Y. L. Cahan (1912a: xxv–xxvi, 1927:65–77)[4] has shown that the love song was widespread as early as the sixteenth century and has been preserved orally down to the present. Among the folk songs collected since the end of the nineteenth century, one finds love and lyrical songs that are very close to those in the oldest manuscript collection of Jewish folk songs, written down in the late sixteenth century by Isaac Waliho. This collection (Rosenberg 1888; a photocopy of the manuscript is in the Cabinet from the archive of the late philologist N. Shtif)[5] contains fifty-five songs, including lyric love songs, satirical songs, dance songs, bride's and groom's songs, and so on. The closeness of sixteenth-century songs to contemporary songs shows that even during the eighteenth and nineteenth centuries, a period when a wave of religiousness swept over Jewish literature, the common folk preserved older lyric and love songs and even created new ones.

Of course, the Jewish working masses[6] could not liberate themselves from the traditional view of marriage. In the midst of poverty, marriages were concluded through matchmaking; dowry (even if nonexistent) and excellence of lineage played an important role. Yet boys and girls of this milieu were in a somewhat different situation, having to make a living as artisans or servants from an early age. Girls had to forego their pay to make up a dowry, without which they couldn't marry their boyfriends. Many circumstances contributed to the creation of the everyday Jewish love song: long years of separation from kin and loved ones, life among strangers, the cheerless and back-breaking work of the seamstress, tailor, shoemaker, shop clerk, milliner, nanny, servant, and other working youth alongside the dream of a better future, and the striving toward and hope for reunion with the beloved, without which life was even harder and sometimes unbearable.

Among the love songs, one can identify a small group that expresses a budding youthfulness, as yet shy, barely acknowledging itself. The boy and girl are happy. There are few songs of this type in Jewish folklore. The majority of songs tell of unhappy love or of broken, at times cruelly injured and ridiculed, feelings. The protagonist is nearly always a girl, victim of unsuccessful love. Usually the obstacle to marriage is the social and material inequality of the lovers. Not infrequently the cause of separation is the young man's need to leave for work or military service. More rarely, one finds songs about the boy's betrayal, about his leaving the singer for another girl.

The Jewish love song is an intimate song, sung to oneself or in a circle of close friends, male or female. In general, Jewish folk songs are monophonic but also solo, performed by an individual. In the poor artisans' workshops (shoemakers, tailors, etc.) one can say that songs resounded from early morning till late at night. Love songs were among those sung at work, but at gatherings or, even more, among one's own immediate circle, love songs were not usually sung (Cahan 1912a: xxxv).

The present anthology also includes a small set of family songs, some of which relate to the wedding topic. It should be noted that no ritual wedding songs existed in the Yiddish language. What we call folk wedding songs are dance tunes or lyric and humorous songs about moments of the wedding ceremony. For example, nos. 50–52 tell of the girl's parting from her parents, but these songs were not sung at weddings. At Jewish weddings the scene of parting was accompanied by the band with no singing or even humming along. There are special *zaj gezunt* (farewell) songs in the instrumental repertoire for this occasion.

Many songs of the domestic cycle are devoted to the burdensome position of the woman in the past. Lullabies are particularly poetic, suffused with boundless maternal love.

The Jewish folk song is often topical. It tells of some concrete event, sad or happy. Developing the story, the anonymous author includes the names of those involved (cf. Dobrushin-Iuditskii 1947:11–12).[7] Among the love songs, however, are some without specific plot. For example, the deep love song "Ven ix zol hobn fligelex" only hints at the weighty experiences of the boy and girl. They are separated, since the boy must leave.[8] The girl pours out her grief and longing in simple images and deeply moving words. The expressive poetic and musical means of Jewish folk song are still insufficiently studied.

NOTES

1. [M. F. Gniessin. *Mysli I vospominaniia o Rimskom-Korsakove* (Moscow: Gosmuzizdat, 1956).]

2. [*Ob evreiskoi muzyke* (On Jewish Music). (St. Petersburg, 1914).]

3. Following Soviet practice of certain periods, Beregovskii's "fanatic" here should be translated as "orthodox" or "observant" and will likely be glossed that way henceforth—M.S.

4. [Y. L. Cahan. *Yidishe folkslider oys dem folks-moyl, gezamlt fun Y. L. Cahan*, vol. 1 (New York and Warsaw: Internatsyonale Bibliotek Farlag, 1912) and Y. L. Cahan. 1927–28: "Yidishe folkslider: naye zamlung fun Y. L. Kahan." [I]n *Pinkes* [a *fertlyoriker zhurnal far yidisher literaturgeshikhte, shprakhforshung, folklor un bibliografye*] (New York: YIVO, 1928).]

5. [Felix Rosenberg dissertation. "Ueber eine Sammlung deutscher Volks- und Gesellschaftslieder in hebräischen Lettern" (Berlin: Braunschweig, 1888).]

6. Beregovskii's "working masses" does not imply a proletariat but rather refers to the common people who must work hard for a living.—M.S.

7. [I. M. Dobrushin and A. D. Iuditskii. *Evreiske narodnye pesni* (Moscow: Ogiz, 1947).]

8. Since Yiddish has no verbal gender endings, it is often hard to tell who the speaker is in a monologue song. We can conclude that this is the song of a girl whose boyfriend had to leave, judging by the character of the text and images. A boy's departure was common, while a girl's was rare.

Translated by Mark Slobin.

Other works by Beregovskii: *Jewish Workers' and Revolutionary Songs* (1934); *Jewish Instrumental Folk Music* (1987); *Jewish Tunes without Words* (1999); *Purim-shpiln* (2001).

Henri Chemouilli

1891–1981

Henri Chemouilli was an outspoken Jewish leader during the War of Algerian Independence, arguing that

French Jews had colonized the Algerian Jewish community just as France had colonized the wider region. Nevertheless, believing that French rule protected the Algerian Jews, Chemouilli supported the Organisation armée secrète, a violently anti-independence group. In the years following the war, Chemouilli wrote extensively about Algerian Jewish life and history, making claims of Jewish indigeneity in the region.

L'Arche, *Dictionary of French Judaism,* "North African"
1972

One must hurry to grasp it; yesterday, it did not exist; tomorrow it will be no more. Yesterday there were Algerians, Tunisians, Moroccans, discovered by French Judaism when French colonization was writing its finest pages, oh yes, oh yes: 1830, 1881, 1912. Years during which those whose descendants form the majority of French Jews today were living in Central Europe or under the boot of the tsars; they were unfamiliar with the life and problems of North African Judaism. What's more, they were self-sufficient: "Jewish assertion, Jewish fervor, Jewish intelligence, that's us. Highly spiritualist, we don't worry about Jewish dress and Jewish cuisine. That's us, too. Those from Arab countries are all Arabs. Hardly kosher. The proof: they don't speak Yiddish, that beautiful Jewish language that God himself placed in our parents' baggage. Where can they have come from?"

They come from times long past: descendants of those who escaped Nebuchadnezzar, colonists settled in Carthage—Karta Hadasha, Jewish Carthage, whose captives Titus sent to the ports of Roman Africa, Jews from Egypt and Cyrenaica who revolted in 115, Berber tribes who one day became Judaized. So much for antiquity, let's pass on to the twentieth century.

For the first sixty years of this century the North African Jew was a myth. Algerian Jews were French, we knew their history. Next, the Tunisians, but they maintained their origins better. Between the two wars, Tunisia stood out as having the only entirely Jewish North African soccer team. Tunis published an astonishing newspaper: *Le Réveil juif* [Jewish Awakening], directed by Félix Allouche, a comrade of Jabotinsky. When Félix Allouche made aliyah to Israel, he would find a modest place with *L'Information d'Israël*. . . . But his *Réveil juif* will have awakened more than a few. Those were the days when the Tunisian Beitar [a militant right-wing Zionist organization] was second only to Poland's.

A Forgotten People

Compared to Algerians and Tunisians, Moroccans seem like poor relations. Among them, poverty and disease are proportionate to their numbers, and the families in the Jewish quarters are numerous. Just after the war Rabi uttered a loud cry: the mellah is our shame. No response. Of all the families of Israel, that of Morocco has been the most ignored, the most abandoned, the most rejected. Only one exception: the AIU [Alliance Israélite Universelle] and its schools.

With the arrival of November 1942, American Jews discovered Jews unlike any they had ever seen before. Among them were some men worthy of esteem, offspring of the AIU, who explained the people's poverty and sought ways to remedy it. In December of 1944, Moroccan Jews attended a meeting of the World Jewish Congress for the first time.

History rushes on—the resurgence of Israel exploded like thunder on Sinai amid this forgotten people. At the same time, the new state needed soldiers, workers, large families. It sent effective emissaries to Morocco. Not always scrupulous. Working with a population as impassioned as in the time of Shabbetai Zvi, they were hugely successful, leading to a mass exodus of Moroccan Jews on their way to the promised land.

Meanwhile, Tunisians and Moroccans who put less faith in promises left for France. When Algeria became independent, a hundred thousand Algerians chose France. The time it took to recover from the journey was the time it took to create the North African Jew. He was born around 1965, he began speaking around 1967, upon the creation of a liaison committee among those originating in the three countries of the Maghreb. He questioned himself before questioning others.

We Are Cold

What do we do to maintain our traditions, our social practices, our ethos, how do we stay warm rather than succumbing to a "cold" environment?

In this French Judaism to which we have given new life, are we not the foot soldiers who are sometimes informed, more rarely consulted, and whose opinions are still more rarely taken into account?

A noble campaign for Jews in the Soviet Union. But were we so unimportant, we who were favored with nothing similar when we were in danger? Sometimes even mortal danger.

Why did not a single one of all our "French" thinkers, strong advocates of Jewish conscience, hear the sound of the slap that Golda Meir gave us in her October interview in *Le Monde*? Why nothing in any "French" newspaper?[1]

Why this poverty among our people in Israel? They are crying for help, but our means are limited. Of the sums that the Jewish Appeal gives each year to Israel we would like part to be expressly designated for the neediest. And let it be made public.

Why did the Zionist elections go unmentioned in France? If our future is in France, how do we manage to become decolonized? And if our future must be in Israel, what can be done so that our uniqueness is acknowledged?

The Sephardic Flavor

These questions are stupid and annoying. Frustrating, you might say. On top of that, the answer: a demand for renewal, freedom, air to breathe. A need to introduce into all assemblies new men who would better represent the new French Judaism. The North African takes into account the forces in play, he weighs the names. At times frightened by his own audacity. Will we be as competent as "they" are? As tenacious? As dedicated?

But who cares! The North African Jew wants to be decolonized.

And behold, in the midst of these questions and doubts a new light dawns. The North African Jew realizes that his destiny is nothing if not commonplace. He wants to keep his character? Others too wish it. He refuses to be downtrodden? Others too refuse it. Others who were spoken of shortly before his arrival on the scene, others who, before him, with small numbers, confronted the same problems: the Sephardim, our ancient glory.

Suddenly the North African remembers that he himself is Sephardic. In truth, he had never forgotten it, it was just so long ago. Here the Sephardim are all close by, the North African is rejoining them in great numbers. North Africa is a thing of the past, the Arabic language, the nostalgia for the *souks* in the shadow of the minarets. He realizes that his traditions, his emotions, his life, in short, with this special flavor that he believed was an "Arabic" flavor, was quite simply the Sephardic

flavor. Today he is returning to the Sephardic family, tomorrow his children will no longer be North African Jews. "Sing! Sing the wondrous tomorrows! Amen!"

Translated by Michele McKay Aynesworth.

NOTE

1. [Chemouilli is probably referring to an interview that Golda Meir gave to *Le Monde* which seemed to say that the poverty of North African Jews antedated their migration to Israel, thus giving the impression that the Israeli government was not to blame for their dire economic straits in Israel.—Eds.]

Other works by Chemouilli: *Journal d'un faux exode* (1957); *Une diaspora méconnue: Les juifs de l'Algérie* (1976).

Arnold Mandel

1913–1987

Arnold Mandel was born in Strasbourg to a Galician family with Hasidic roots. As a journalist, literary critic, and author, Mandel examined the tensions between increasingly assimilated French Jews and the traditional life of East European Jewish immigrants. After being detained twice by the Vichy government, Mandel joined the French Resistance. In the 1950s, Mandel became a major Yiddish literary specialist in France, translating the works of Sholem Yankev Abramovitsh (Mendele Moykher-Sforim). Mandel was also a friend of the existentialists Albert Camus and Jean-Paul Sartre.

L'Arche, Dictionary of French Judaism, "Ashkenaz"
1972

Ashkenaz, a descendant of the sons of Noah, grandson of Japheth, son of Gomer (Genesis 10:3).

It was in a rather ancient period in the history of the diaspora that the term *Ashkenazim*, or descendants of Ashkenaz, came to mean Germans in the context of a kind of ethno-geographic redistribution similar to the gentile "environment" of European Jews: the *Sephardi* of the Bible becomes a Spaniard, the *Tsarfati* a Frenchman, and above all (already in the Talmudic period) Edom, Rome, and the Edomites, Romans. *Ashkenazi* designating German later acquires, by both extension and restriction, the meaning of German Jews or those of German origin, and then more generally, Jews of northern and central Europe, in contrast to the Sephardi—

designating Spanish Jews, and more generally, those originating from or living in southern Europe.

The Ashkenazic Jews are no more culturally monolithic than the Sephardic Jews; the difference is just as great between an Ashkenazi from Bessarabia and one from Scandinavia or Alsace as between a Sephardi from Casablanca and one from Amsterdam. Ashkenazic culture spread out in the Middle Ages from Rhenish Germany (Worms) and eastern France (Troyes), and this culture was above all characterized by an intense Talmudic education, a constant, almost self-righteous practice of casuistry, which has contributed much to Jewish intellectualism, to that subtlety and quick intelligence that can be wondrous or disastrous.

In the realm of the emotions or religious sentiment, one must recognize in the history of Ashkenazim a steadfastness, a spirit of sacrifice that is unequaled. The instinct for collective preservation, the Jewish will to live, coincided with the instinct for individual preservation, which amounts to the same thing. Entire communities in Champagne, in the Loire region, and along the Rhine perished in the flames, yet only in rare cases did anyone abjure his faith. There were no Christianized Jews, no reluctance to be torn between ancestral faith and one's country, as with the Jews of Spain who were put to the test. In the history of human faith, there is surely no other example, on a massive scale, of such an almost joyous submission to the imperative of the *Kiddush hashem* to sanctify the name of God, and this tragic history fully justifies the pride in being Jewish—and why not say it—in being an Ashkenazic Jew.

As the center of Ashkenazism moved eastward, and Poland, Lithuania, and Ukraine became the great reservoir of European Judaism and the very emblem of Ashkenazism, the nature of Ashkenazism changed, acquiring more pronounced ethnic traits, becoming less German and more Hebrew, culminating in dialectical mastery of Talmudic study. The ancient Judeo-Germanic tongue became a completely Jewish one: Yiddish. In modern times, Ashkenazism finally evolved into a national, secular Jewish culture and, from there, had an impact on Jewish Zionism, populism, and socialism, the aspiration toward emancipation without assimilation. At this juncture, the history of Ashkenazism coincided with that of Eastern European Judaism, the center of gravity for the Jewish world—until its destruction in the catastrophic age of Hitler.

Translated by Michele McKay Aynesworth.

Other works by Mandel: *Chair à destin* (1946); *La Voie du hassidisme* (1963); *Nous autres juifs* (1978).

André Neher
1914–1988

Born in Obernai, Germany (now France), André Neher had an early academic interest focused on German literature, but the events of the Holocaust led him to theological–philosophical inquiry instead. During World War II, Neher fled to Brive-la-Gaillarde, where he became a member of Rabbi David Feuerwerker's community. Neher's most influential writings engage the question of divine silence in the aftermath of the Holocaust. He also collaborated with his wife, Renée Neher-Bernheim, on several Jewish historical studies.

L'Arche, Dictionary of French Judaism, "Abraham"
1972

The *Jewish man* is first and foremost the *Hebrew man*, and the Jewish man, since he is Hebrew, is the man of origins. Origins of what? Origins of what all of us are, origins of Western as well as Eastern civilizations, of Judaism, of Christianity, of Islam, of humanism, of Marxism, origins of the vast culture we generally refer to as biblical culture, embracing everything that lies in embryo in the Bible—but the man of origins, not as a matter of curiosity, but of efficacy, for in the beginning an act was necessary.

History begins in Sumer, with that man who was living in Sumer, a Hebrew known as Abraham the Hebrew, whose first human act was to *break* with Sumer, to *reject* Sumerian civilization, to *protest* against the towers of Babel. Sumer had many gods; Abraham the Hebrew yearned to have only one. Sumer's laws were partly just; Abraham wanted complete justice. Sumerian civilization was resplendent with material, technical, and economic success; Abraham aspired to ethics and prayer.

The Hebrew man is the Abrahamic man. The Jewish man, since he feels Hebrew, is ready to relive Abraham's decision and to repeat it; he is ready to rebel, to protest against idols and injustice. The Jewish man, but also the Christian, the Muslim, the Marxist, the humanist, all those who are brothers in Abraham. When a pope declares that we are all spiritually Semites, he really means that we are all spiritually Hebrews.

But what then is the personal, particular meaning of being Hebrew, of being Jewish? It is to accept the condition of the Hebrew in its etymological sense: *'ivri* implies an experience of *passage*. Abraham passed from one world to another, from one shore to another. The Jew is one who passes. Men who pass to the other shore of humanity are transported by every Jew who repeats the act of Abraham. The Jew as Hebrew is the ferryman who, throughout history, has brought ancient pagans to Christianity, Eastern pagans to Islam, the neo-pagans to humanisms; and again, he will ferry all of today's pagans to messianic humanism. The Jew is the ferryman, passing from one shore to the other, and thus, like Abraham the Hebrew, the Jew as Hebrew is in exile, a permanent exile, a necessary exile, in order to play the role of missionary. Exile is a mission that carries the Jew wherever there is a passage to be made, and thus the Hebraic condition places the Jew in a state of universal dizziness, in that beautiful and great calling that makes him the brother in action of all men.

Translated by Michele McKay Aynesworth.

Other works by Neher: *Amos: Contribution à l'étude du prophétisme* (1950); *Histoire biblique du people d'Israël* (with Renée Neher-Bernheim, 1962).

Ilse Aichinger

1921–2016

Born in Vienna to a Jewish mother and a Catholic father, Ilse Aichinger was raised as a Christian. Nevertheless, she was persecuted as a *Mischling* by Nazi policy and spent the war as a forced laborer. In 1945, she began writing about her experiences of Nazi oppression and won many literary prizes for her often surreal and allegorical short stories and poems. Aichinger was among the first Austrian writers to address the events of the Holocaust. She participated in the Gruppe 47, a postwar German writers' group.

A Summons to Mistrust

1946

A printing error? Are your eyes getting weaker? No! You have read entirely correctly—although you may find this headline irresponsible, although . . . you find no words. Is it not precisely mistrust that is the worst and most incurable disease of this probing, injured world shaken by labor pain? Is it not the explosive charge that blows the bridges between nations up into the air, this terrible mistrust, is it not the cruel hand that scatters the goods of this world into the ocean, that overshadows mankind's gaze and, encroaching on it, obscures it? Is it necessary to call forth once again the cause of all torments and to lure it from its den? Have we not looked past each other long enough, have we not whispered instead of talking, have we not crept instead of walking? Have we not avoided one another long enough, paralyzed by fear? And where are we today? Do we not sneer at every authority, every agency, every measure we failed to take, every word we failed to speak? We are filled with mistrust toward God, toward the black marketeer with whom we do business, toward the future, toward nuclear research, and toward the growing grass. And what now? No, it is no error, it says clearly and distinctly: a summons to mistrust! In other words, a summons to poison ourselves? A summons to annihilation?

Calm down, poor, pale citizen of the twentieth century! Do not cry! You shall merely be immunized. You are supposed to receive a serum so that you will be all the more resistant next time around! To the small-est possible degree you shall experience the disease to prevent it from repeating itself on the largest scale. You must understand me correctly. You are supposed to experience the disease yourself! You are not supposed to mistrust your brother, not America, not Russia, and not God. *It is yourself you have to mistrust.* Well? Do you comprehend that? We must mistrust ourselves: the clarity of our intentions, the profundity of our thoughts, the goodness of our actions! We must mistrust our own truthfulness! Is it not again resonant with lies? Our own voice! Is it not void of love, like glass? Our own love! Is it not corrupted by selfishness? Our own honor! Is it not brittle with arrogance?

Didn't you say that you would have preferred living in the past century? It was a very elegant and rational century. Whoever had a full stomach and a white shirt had trust in himself. One praised its reason, its kindness, its humanity. And one put up a thousand safety measures to protect oneself against those who were dirty, ragged, and starved. But no one took safety measures against one's own self. Through the generations the monster thus grew without being watched or observed. We experienced it! We suffered it around us, on us, and perhaps even within us. And yet we are once again ready to become self-assured and patronizing and to flirt with our virtues. Barely have we learned to look up when we have already relearned how to despise and to negate. Barely have we learned to say a stammering "I" when we have already tried once again to emphasize it. Barely have we dared to once again say "you" when we have already misused it! And once again we calm down. But we are not supposed to calm down!

Let us trust in the divinity of everybody whom we encounter, and let us mistrust the snake in our hearts! Let us become mistrustful toward ourselves in order to be more trustworthy!

Translated by Dagmar C. G. Lorenz.

Other works by Aichinger: *Herod's Children* (1948); *Der Gefesselte* (1953).

Leo Baeck

1873–1956

Leo Baeck, born in Lissa, Prussia (present-day Leszno, Poland), was a prominent German leader of Reform Judaism. He first studied in Breslau and then Berlin, pursuing both rabbinics and philosophy. From 1897, he served as rabbi in various German cities, eventually working as a chaplain in the German army during World War I. After the Nazi seizure of power in 1933 until his incarceration in the Terezín concentration camp from 1943 to 1945, he attempted to defend the civil rights of those Jews who remained in Germany. After World War II, he lived briefly in London, before settling in Cincinnati for the remainder of his life.

The Idea Remains
1946

Since the song of victory is silent
About the man now overcome.
I will serve as Hector's witness.[1]

There once was a Germany, we all know it, that belonged to the world, and that was received by the world—the Germany of classicism, of the era of the great poets, the poets in language and music, and of the great thinkers, thinkers of spirit and hope. It was the Germany about which Thomas Carlyle spoke to England and Ralph Waldo Emerson to America. That Germany enthralled people everywhere, just like the France of the great Revolution and the Italy of the *risorgimento*, just like the England of Shakespeare and Newton, Milton and other fighters for freedom, and just like the America of Washington, Jefferson, Lincoln, and of those who followed their course of ideas.

To us Jews that Germany meant even more. Because it was the country from which, in its classical period, issued the great demand for an understanding of the Jews and for equal rights for the Jews—it was the Germany of Dohm[2] and Lessing, of Herder and the brothers Humboldt. Because it was the country in whose soil the field for Wissenschaft des Judentums [the Science of Judaism] was prepared and the country in whose language Jewish poets and thinkers first revealed themselves again in modern times. Far and wide Jews were moved by that Germany.

But especially in Germany itself, the spirit of the classics enchanted the souls of the Jews, most strongly the souls of those who went through the universities; in their souls, the spirit of the classics often turned into enthusiasm. It promised that they were to become a new phenomenon: children of that spirit and of its country and thus children of Europe. And in order to be just that to the fullest extent—so they thought—many of them were prepared, or even considered themselves obligated, to pay the price, so frequently demanded of them, of giving up their Jewish identity or parts of it.

One cannot esteem it highly enough that despite and in the midst of all that, Jews who had opened their inner selves to the New and Great very soon became aware of the inalienable value of their Jewish identity and of their great Jewish history. They had become secure in their dignity, secure in their knowledge that for everything truly historical, for everything truly great, their Jewish heritage provided a solid basis of strength, and that no price ought to be paid—neither that of their Jewish identity for the classical European spirit, nor that of the classical European spirit—for their Jewish identity. They also recognized that the best that each group and each individual could contribute to the whole was precisely their specificity and idiosyncrasy.

These Jewish men were also forced to become increasingly aware in which direction Germany was being led in the course of time. They saw it earlier and more clearly than people of other faiths and other dispositions in the country. Because that was the tragic development: Germany began to separate from Europe and humanity. Antisemitism was initially the most definitive symptom of that separation; it soon became its driving force. We must not forget that these men were now fighting a triple battle: for their Jewish identity, for classical Germany, and for European humanity.

They were mature men who decided to fight the battle; the experiences and disappointments of life had spoken to them. But a battle can stay its course only if the young are joining it. Thus, it was significant, and has its place in the history of the German university too, that in a brave step—the founding of the first K[artell] C[onvent] fraternity,[3] which was followed by many other steps, and eventually the steps formed a path—the Jewish students opened themselves to the task of battle. A course was pursued. It signified one was not mentally standing still but understood old errors and was ready to add new insights.

The battle ended in defeat. It ended in defeat when, against the opposition and over the martyrdom of the few, Germany finally completed its separation from

Europe, from mankind and humanity; it ended when the German universities not only abdicated before the Germany of violence and infamy, but raced to join it, ready to be at its service. But in the realm of the intellect infamy is not a refutation, much less does it spell destruction. The battle was lost, but the idea remains. The idea too always wins only the last battle.

The idea remains, the idea that one's Jewishness, because it is of eternal value, may never be given up for something else, whatever it may be, that Judaism ennobles every place in which a Jew may find himself, and deepens the meaning of every task he needs to accomplish. The idea remains, to continue its work in new forms.

NOTES

1. [Friedrich Schiller, "Das Siegesfest" (The Victory Celebration)—Trans.]

2. [In 1781, the Prussian civil servant Christian Wilhelm von Dohm (1751–1820) argued in favor of reforming the status of the Jews in Germany in his proposal "Concerning the Amelioration of the Civil Status of the Jews."—Trans.]

3. *K. C. Blätter. Festschrift.* New York, 1946, 1–2.

Translated by Susanne Klingenstein.

Other works by Baeck: *The Essence of Judaism* (1905); *This People Israel: The Meaning of Jewish Existence* (1955).

Samuel Gringauz

1900–1975

Although he was trained as a lawyer, Samuel Gringauz's experiences in the Kovno ghetto, the Dachau concentration camp, and the Landsberg displaced persons camp led him to undertake a social-scientific analysis of these contexts and their inhabitants. While chairman of the Landsberg displaced persons camp committee and leader of the Central Committee of the Liberated Jews in the American sector, he conducted several sociological and psychological studies of Jewish survivors. Gringauz, who firmly believed that Europe could no longer be home to Jews, immigrated to the United States in 1947.

Jewish Destiny as the DPs See It: The Ideology of the Surviving Remnant
1947

Today, the *Sherit Hapleita* has an ideology of its own—this despite the fact that in its outlook on life, in

its politics, and its culture, the group is no more unified and no less divided than other Jewish communities. In spite of all internal differences, certain convictions are held in common by the preponderant majority of the Sherit Hapleita, and these convictions justify our speaking of "the ideology of the remnant." [. . .] What above all distinguishes the outlook of the Jewish DP's is *its Judeocentrism and its intra-Jewish universalism and unity.*

For the Jewish DP, Jewishness is a given fact of existence that plays the deciding role in life and death, in attitude and feeling, and influences and governs every aspect of his life. During the most crucial years of his recent experience, it was the mere fact of his Jewishness that determined the physical circumstances of his existence, and it was this fact essentially that lay behind the danger of death in which he stood daily, and behind every important step he took.

The Jewish problem, for the Jewish DP, became a psychic and existential one. His Jewishness became the substance of consciousness, became fate. Just as his enemy showed day in and day out an all-embracing, extremely intense, and omnipresent anti-Jewish attitude, making the Jewishness of the Jew the center of all his attention, so too the Jew, in self-defense, made of his Jewishness the foundation of his consciousness. The results of this experience are what distinguish the Sherit Hapleita from the Jews of countries untouched by the catastrophe, and also from the Jews of Palestine, whose Jewish feeling is indeed strong and central, having been hardened and strengthened in battle, but remains nevertheless normal and healthy. The Judeocentrism of the Sherit Hapleita, as the fundamental factor in its ideology, exceeds in its nationalist intensity and all-embracingness all other tendencies. [. . .]

Through the Sherit Hapleita the entire Jewish people is to measure the extent of its historical tragedy: the Sherit Hapleita must demonstrate to all Jews everywhere their involvement in the common fate. The Sherit Hapleita is to be a herald of the indivisibility of Jewish destiny; it shall, by its existence and its struggles, arouse and strengthen Jewish awareness of the national tragedy.

More than any other group in the Jewish nation, *the Sherit Hapleita feels itself charged with a great obligation to the dead* such as no unveiling of monuments can discharge: they have seen centuries-old monuments destroyed in an instant. Women on the way to the crematoria, children in their final agonies, comrades on the point of martyrdom—all those who screamed for retribution and revenge—have left behind a legacy whose executor the Sherit Hapleita feels itself to be, and whose accomplishment is the substance of its ideology. But the mission of retribution is not directly conceived in the sense of "an eye for an eye"; the enormity of the crime makes this unthinkable. The retributive mission of the Sherit Hapleita takes instead the form of a defiant affirmation of life and national rebirth. Nothing must permit Hitler a final triumph by the destruction of the Jews through the circumstances of the postwar world or through inner disintegration. Judaism, as a nation and a collectivity, must be preserved despite all its enemies, and shall emerge from the great catastrophe healthier and morally purified, shall experience a new renaissance and shall lead a normal life on its own soil. This is to be the retribution and the revenge. [. . .]

This is the basic foundation of the Zionism of the survivors. It is no party Zionism; it is a historical-philosophical Zionism felt as an historical mission, as a debt to the dead, as retribution toward the enemy, as a duty to the living. It is, moreover, a Zionism of warning, because the Sherit Hapleita feels that the continuation of Jewish national abnormality means the danger of a repetition of the catastrophe. [. . .]

The Sherit Hapleita therefore undertakes the prophetic mission of warning the Jews of unaffected countries. Neither equality of rights, nor a constitution, nor patriotism is security against persecution, to their minds. One cannot escape one's Jewishness—either by assimilation, baptism, or mixed marriage. [. . .]

The fate of the Sherit Hapleita, they consider, unites all Jewry in the battle for Palestine. For international Zionism the Sherit Hapleita is an argument, a strength, a reserve. . . .

Ourselves the products of an unheroic and culpable relapse into barbarism, we are called upon to be the champions of a heroic renaissance. Victims of an outer and inner process of demoralization, we are called upon to accomplish a national and moral revival. End-products of a process of corruption unique in history, we are called upon to provide Jewish culture with a deeper and clearer content and theme. Victims of a psychic upheaval, we are called upon to re-establish the psychological stability of our people. Ourselves the product of the barbaric relationship of the environment to the Jews, it is our task to create a more humane relationship to the environment. This enormous discrepancy between what has been given us to do and what has been

granted us to do it with, extraordinarily increases the difficulty of our task, yet does not release us from our obligation. This task history has assigned to us, and it cannot be put off on someone else. . . .

With the end of the great catastrophe, a fundamental change has become apparent in the inner structure of the Jewish people, one that marks the end of an old epoch—European, German-Polish—and the beginning of a new—American-Palestinian. [. . .]

Only in this context can we understand the general tendency to say "Adieu Europe." [. . .] But the renunciation of Europe in no way signifies for us the renunciation of European culture. Quite the contrary. Our resolve to quit Europe is based precisely on the conviction that Europe itself has betrayed the legacy of European culture, and that European culture must be carried forward outside of Europe. We have been too much a part of European culture to abandon it now. As we once expressed it: "We leave Europe because Europe has injured us in our very quality as Europeans."

"History has given us the task of symbolizing to the entire world the Jewish problem in modern civilization. We are the surviving remnant of those Jews who, amid rivers of blood and under the shadow of martyrdom, aroused the attention of the world to that problem. We, who are the victims of this civilization, have been called upon to discover the positive basis on which we can unite with it. We have a bill of indictment to prefer against this civilization. At the same time we know that we are part of it and must therefore bear a responsibility for it. We cannot and will not turn away from it. But we must make new contributions. Our experience must serve to redirect the Jewish people. Our tragedy must become the starting point of a new humanism."

And today this still remains the ideal of the Sherit Hapleita. We do not turn away from Occidental culture. We do seek, however, to contribute to its wider moral development. For it was not the civilization of Western Europe that betrayed us, but the monstrous discrepancy between its moral and its technical culture.

Translated by Martin Greenberg.

Victor Klemperer
1881–1960

Victor Klemperer, renowned for his journals covering the years of the Holocaust, was born in Landsberg an der Warthe (today Gorzów Wielkopolski, Poland).

The son of a rabbi, Klemperer studied philosophy and Romance languages, completing his doctorate in 1913 in Munich. He twice converted to Christianity and taught at the Technical University of Dresden, a position he lost in 1933 when the Nazis came to power. Somewhat protected by his marriage to a Protestant, Klemperer survived the war, leaving Germany only in the final months before May 1945. He subsequently returned to East Germany, joining the Communist Party while remaining critical of its propaganda in his personal notes.

The Language of the Third Reich
1947

People are forever quoting Talleyrand's remark that language is only there in order to hide the thoughts of the diplomat (or for that matter of any other shrewd and dubious person). But in fact the very opposite is true. Whatever it is that people are determined to hide, be it only from others, or from themselves, even things they carry around unconsciously—language reveals all. That is no doubt the meaning of the aphorism *Le style c'est l'homme*; what a man says may be a pack of lies— but his true self is laid bare for all to see in the style of his utterances. [. . .]

Every language able to assert itself freely fulfils all human needs, it serves reason as well as emotion, it is communication and conversation, soliloquy and prayer, plea, command and invocation. The LTI [*Lingua Tertii Imperii*; Klemperer's term for the language of the Third Reich] only serves the cause of invocation. Regardless of whether a given subject properly belongs in a particular private or public domain—no, that's wrong, the LTI no more drew a distinction between private and public spheres than it did between written and spoken language—everything remains oral and everything remains public. One of their banners contends that "You are nothing, your people is everything." Which means that you are never alone with yourself, never alone with your nearest and dearest, you are always being watched by your own people.

It would therefore also be misleading if I were to claim that the LTI addressed itself in all cases exclusively to the will. For whoever appeals to the will always calls on the individual, even if he addresses himself to a general public made up of individuals. The sole purpose of the LTI is to strip everyone of their individuality, to paralyze them as personalities, to make them into unthink-

ing and docile cattle in a herd driven and hounded in a particular direction, to turn them into atoms in a huge rolling block of stone. The LTI is the language of mass fanaticism. Where it addresses the individual—and not just his will but also his intellect—where it educates, it teaches means of breeding fanaticism and techniques of mass suggestion. [. . .]

The poison is everywhere. It is borne by the drinking water of the LTI, nobody is immune to its effects.

The envelope and paper bag factory Thiernig & Möbius was not particularly National Socialist. The boss was a member of the SS but he did whatever he could for his Jews, he spoke politely to them, he sometimes made sure they got something from the canteen. I really don't know what comforted me more thoroughly and enduringly: the arrival of a scrap of horse-meat sausage or for once being addressed as "Herr Klemperer," or even "Herr Professor." The Aryan workers, amongst whom those of us with the Star of David were distributed—segregation only occurred at mealtimes and during air raid protection duty; at the work-place the ban on conversation was supposed to be a substitute for isolation, but no one adhered to it—these workers were certainly not devotees of National Socialism, at least by the Winter of 1943/44 they weren't any more. Everyone feared the foreman and two or three women who were believed to be capable of denunciation, people prodded each other or exchanged warning glances when one of these notorious characters appeared; but once they were out of sight comradely cooperation was immediately restored.

Most friendly of all was the hunchback Frieda who had trained me and continued to help when I got into difficulties with my envelope machine. She had worked for the firm for more than thirty years and did not let even the foreman prevent her from shouting an encouraging word to me above the noise of the machine room: "Don't be so pompous! I didn't talk to him, I simply gave him an instruction regarding the gumming machine!" Frieda knew that my wife was lying ill at home. In the morning I found a big apple in the middle of my machine. I looked over to Frieda's work-place and she nodded to me. A little later she was standing next to me: "For Mama with my best wishes." And then, with a mixture of inquisitiveness and surprise: "Albert says that your wife is German. Is she really German?" . . .

The pleasure in the apple was gone. This Sancta-Simplicitas soul, whose feelings were entirely un-Nazi and humane, had been infected by the most fundamental ingredient of the National Socialist poison; she identified Germanness with the magical concept of the Aryan; it was barely conceivable to her that a German woman could be married to me, to a foreigner, a creature from another branch of the animal kingdom; all too often she had heard and repeated the terms *"artfremd* (alien)" and *"deutschblütig* (of German blood)" and *"niederrassig* (of inferior race)" and *"nordisch* (Nordic)" and *"Rassenschande* (racial defilement[1])": she certainly didn't have a clear picture of what this all meant—but her feelings could not grasp the fact that my wife could be a German.

Albert, from whom she had her information, was rather better at thinking than she was. He harboured his own political opinions, and they were in no way supportive of the government, nor were they militaristic. He had lost a brother in action, he himself had so far been deferred at each army medical examination on the grounds of a serious stomach disorder. He mentioned this "so far" every day: "I'm still free so far—I hope this wretched war is over before they finally call me up!" On that day of the apple, which had also seen a veiled report of the success of the Allies somewhere in Italy, he discussed his favourite topic with a comrade for rather longer than usual. I was stacking piles of paper for my machine on to a trolley right next to Albert's work-place. "I hope they don't call me up," he said, "before this wretched war is over!"—"Look here mate, how on earth is it going to be over? No one wants to give in."—"Yes of course: they will just have to realize that we are invincible; they can't break us because we are so fantastically well organized {*prima organisiert*}!" Fantastically well organized—there it was again, he had swallowed the mind-numbing drug.

An hour later the boss called me to help label the finished boxes. He wrote the labels as per invoice and I stuck them on to the towering rows of boxes which formed a wall separating us from the rest of the workers in the room. This isolation made the old man talkative. He was approaching seventy and still working; this was not how he had imagined his old age, he sighed. But these days you have to work like a slave until you're done for! "And what will happen to my grandchildren if the lads don't come back? We haven't heard anything of Erhard from Murmansk for months, and the youngest is in a military hospital in Italy. If only peace would come . . . It's just that the Americans don't want it, they've no business being here . . . But they're getting rich through this war, this handful of Jewish pigs. It really is the 'Jewish war'! . . . There they are again!" [. . .]

But the consummate and most characteristic feature of the Nazi art of language lies not in this kind of segregated book-keeping for the educated and the uneducated, and also not simply in impressing the masses with a few learned scraps. Rather, the real achievement—and here Goebbels is the undisputed master—lies in the unscrupulous mixture of heterogeneous stylistic elements; no, mixture isn't quite the right word—it lies in the most abruptly antithetical leaps from a learned tone to a proletarian one, from sobriety to the tone of the preacher, from icy rationalism to the sentimentality of a manfully repressed tear, from Fontane's simplicity, and Berlin gruffness, to the pathos of the evangelist and prophet. It is like an epidermal stimulation under the impact of alternating cold and hot showers, and just as physically effective; the listener's emotions (and Goebbels's audience always comprises listeners, even if it only reads the Doctor's essays in the newspaper) never come to rest, they are constantly attracted and rebuffed, attracted and rebuffed, and there is no time for critical reasoning to catch its breath.

NOTE
1. Term used to described forbidden cohabitation between German Aryans and Jews.

Translated by Martin Brady.

Other works by Klemperer: *I Shall Bear Witness: The Diaries of Victor Klemperer, 1933–41*; *To the Bitter End: The Diaries of Victor Klemperer, 1942–1945* (1995).

Emmanuel Levinas

1906–1995

Emmanuel Levinas was one of the most influential philosophers and ethicists of the last century. Born in Kaunas (in contemporary Lithuania), he moved to France in 1923, studying at Strasbourg and later at Freiburg. He was a student of Edmund Husserl and a major influence on Jacques Derrida. Levinas taught at the University of Poitiers, the University of Paris, and the Sorbonne. During the Holocaust, Levinas, a French citizen, was imprisoned as a French Jewish soldier; his parents and siblings were murdered in Kaunas, Lithuania. Delivered first as lectures after World War II, *Time and the Other* comprises descriptive studies of the emergence of subjectivity, intersubjectivity, and time in terms of bodily existence, worldliness, eros, and the rupture and renewal of generations.

Time and the Other
1947

The hope for a better society and the despair of solitude, both of which are founded on experiences that claim to be self-evident, seem to be in an insurmountable antagonism. There is not merely an opposition but an antinomy between the experience of solitude and social experience. Each of them claims the rank of a universal experience and manages to account for the other, referring to it particularly as the degradation of an authentic experience.

The feeling of solitude persists and threatens in the very midst of the optimistic constructivism of sociology and socialism. It enables one to denounce the joys of communication, collective works, and everything that makes the world livable, as Pascalian diversion and the simple forgetfulness of solitude. The fact of finding oneself settled in the world, occupied with things, attached to them, and even the aspiration to dominate them, is not merely depreciated in the experience of solitude, but explained by a philosophy of solitude. Concern for things and needs would be a fall, a flight before the uttermost finality that these needs themselves imply, an inconsequence, a nontruth, inevitable, to be sure, but bearing the mark of the inferior and the reprehensible.

But the inverse is equally true. We behave like the frightful bourgeois in the midst of Pascalian, Kierkegaardian, Nietzschean, and Heideggerian anxieties. Or we are crazy. No one will recommend madness as a way of salvation. [...]

Despite the nudity of existence, one must as far as possible be decently clothed. And when one writes a book on anxiety, one writes it for someone, one goes through all the steps that separate the draft from the publication, and one sometimes behaves like a merchant of anxiety. [...]

These may seem like facile objections, recalling the ones certain realists address to idealists when they reproach them for eating and breathing in an illusory world. But under the circumstances they are less negligible objections: they do not oppose a behavior to a metaphysics but a behavior to a morality. Each of these antagonistic experiences is a morality. They object not to the error but to the inauthenticity of one another.

There is something other than naivety in the flat denial the masses oppose to the elites when they are worried more about bread than about anxiety. From this comes the accent of greatness that stirs in a humanism springing from the economic problem; from this comes the very power that the demands of the working class possess to be elevated into a humanism. They would be inexplicable for a behavior that was to have been simply a fall into inauthenticity, or likewise a diversion, or even a legitimate exigency of our animality. [...]

This antinomy opposes the need to be saved and the need to be satisfied—Jacob and Esau. But the true relationship between salvation and satisfaction is not that which classic idealism perceived, and that despite everything modern existentialism maintains. Salvation does not require the satisfaction of need, like a higher principle that would require the solidity of its bases to be secured. The daily run of our everyday life is surely not a simple sequel of our animality continually surpassed by spiritual activity. But neither does the anxiety about salvation arise in suffering a need that would be its occasional cause, as if poverty or the proletarian condition where the occasion for glimpsing the gate of the Heavenly Kingdom. [...] Economic struggle is already on an equal footing with the struggle for salvation. [...]

How can a being enter into relation with the other without allowing its very self to be crushed by the other? This question must be posed first, because it is the very problem of the preservation of the ego in transcendence. [...] The relationship with the Other,[1] the face-to-face with the Other, the encounter with a face that at once gives and conceals the Other, is the situation in which an event happens to a subject who does not assume it, who is utterly unable in its regard, but where nonetheless in a certain way it is in front of the subject. The other "assumed" is the Other. [...] Relationship with the future, the presence of the future in the present, seems all the same accomplished in the face-to-face with the Other. The situation of the face-to-face would be the very accomplishment of time; the encroachment of the present on the future is not the feat of the subject alone, but the intersubjective relationship. The condition of time lies in the relationship between humans, or in history. [...] If the relationship with the other involves more than relationships with mystery, it is because one has accosted the other in everyday life where the solitude and fundamental alterity of the other are already veiled by decency. One is for the other what the other is for oneself; there is no exceptional place for the subject. The other is known through sympathy, as another (my)self, as the alter ego. [...]

But already, in the very heart of the relationship with the other that characterizes our social life, alterity appears as a nonreciprocal relationship—that is, as contrasting strongly with contemporaneousness. The Other as Other is not an alter ego: the Other is what I myself am not. The Other is this, not because of the Other's character, or physiognomy, or psychology, but because of the Other's very alterity. The Other is, for example, the weak, the poor, "the widow and the orphan," whereas I am the rich or the powerful. It can be said that intersubjective space is not symmetrical. The exteriority of the other is not simply due to the space that separates what remains identical through the concept, nor is it due to any difference the concept would manifest through spatial exteriority. The relationship with alterity is neither spatial nor conceptual. Durkheim has misunderstood the specificity of the other when he asks in what Other rather than myself is the object of a virtuous action. Does not the essential difference between charity and justice come from the preference of charity for the other, even when, from the point of view of justice, no preference is any longer possible?

NOTE

1. [The French *Autrui* refers to the personal other, the other person, which is here translated as "Other" with a capital *O*; the French *autre* refers to personal or impersonal otherness, here translated as "other" with a small *o*.—Trans.]

Translated by Richard A. Cohen.

Other works by Levinas: *La Théorie de l'intuition dans la phénoménologie de Husserl* (1930); *De l'existence à l'existent* (1947); *En découvrant l'existence avec Husserl et Heidegger* (1949); *Autrement qu'être ou au-delà de l'essence* (1974).

René Cassin

1887–1976

René Cassin was born in Bayonne, France, and won the 1968 Nobel Peace Prize for his work on the Universal Declaration of Human Rights. After being wounded during his service as a soldier in World War I, he founded the leftist Union fédérale, France's largest veterans' organization. Besides his renown as a legal scholar and humanitarian, Cassin held many influential political positions, including as a French

delegate to the League of Nations, a member of General de Gaulle's government in exile, and as president of the European Court of Human Rights.

The Universal Declaration of Human Rights 1948

Preamble

Whereas recognition of the inherent dignity and of the equal and inalienable rights of all members of the human family is the foundation of freedom, justice and peace in the world,

Whereas disregard and contempt for human rights have resulted in barbarous acts which have outraged the conscience of mankind, and the advent of a world in which human beings shall enjoy freedom of speech and belief and freedom from fear and want has been proclaimed as the highest aspiration of the common people,

Whereas it is essential, if man is not to be compelled to have recourse, as a last resort, to rebellion against tyranny and oppression, that human rights should be protected by the rule of law,

Whereas it is essential to promote the development of friendly relations between nations,

Whereas the peoples of the United Nations have in the Charter reaffirmed their faith in fundamental human rights, in the dignity and worth of the human person and in the equal rights of men and women and have determined to promote social progress and better standards of life in larger freedom,

Whereas Member States have pledged themselves to achieve, in co-operation with the United Nations, the promotion of universal respect for and observance of human rights and fundamental freedoms,

Whereas a common understanding of these rights and freedoms is of the greatest importance for the full realization of this pledge,

Now, therefore the General Assembly proclaims this Universal Declaration of Human Rights as a common standard of achievement for all peoples and all nations, to the end that every individual and every organ of society, keeping this Declaration constantly in mind, shall strive by teaching and education to promote respect for these rights and freedoms and by progressive measures, national and international, to secure their universal and effective recognition and observance, both among the peoples of Member States themselves and among the peoples of territories under their jurisdiction.

Other works by Cassin: *Les Hommes partis de rien: Le réveil de la France abattue, 1940–1941* (1975).

André Chouraqui

1917–2007

André Chouraqui was born in Aïn Témouchent, Algeria, to a prominent Sephardic family of jurists and rabbis. He studied law and rabbinics in France, although his education was cut short by World War II. While living in Vichy France in the 1940s, he took part in the French Resistance. In the 1950s, on behalf of the Alliance Israélite, Chouraqui was a major proponent of Francophone Jewish culture in Israel and advised David Ben-Gurion on the integration of Jews from Arab countries into Israel. In addition to his advocacy, Chouraqui wrote widely on spiritual and political problems in Israel.

Between East and West: A History of the Jews of North Africa
1952

Independence and Exodus

The French presence in North Africa completely disrupted the pattern of coexistence between the Jewish and Moslem communities that had existed for over a thousand years. Instead of trying to bridge the gap between these two societies, the French had become a third force and the colonial regime brought about so rigid a separation between the three groups that each developed in almost complete isolation from the others, unaware that all were bound by a common destiny. The French in the Maghreb never succeeded in creating truly national states that transcended narrower ethnic and social groupings, or in instilling a sense of unified national allegiance; this was as true of Morocco and Tunisia, where the sovereignty of the French Protectorate administration was juxtaposed with the partially autonomous national state, as it was of Algeria, where French policy thwarted the full implementation of the oft-proclaimed principle of the unitary state.

The extent to which the three communities preserved their isolation despite the proximity of their existence is difficult to comprehend. Contacts between individuals of the separate societies were limited to the necessary minimum; neither schools nor military service nor any other factor brought about a closer understanding between them. It was extremely rare for a person of one community to marry one of another, and even social entertainment seldom managed to break through the race barrier. It was not at all rare to find Europeans (or Europeanized Jews) who had never so much as conducted a conversation with a Moslem, who had not the least conception of Moslem thought and culture or of the aspirations of the impoverished Moslem masses, who had never even heard the voice of the muezzin call out for prayer; the barriers were so impermeable that victims and victimizers were unaware that they had become captives of their own narrow "ghetto."

While, as we have seen, the chasm that separated the Jewish community from the French tended to narrow, that between these two communities and the Moslem society tended to widen and deepen till in the end it provoked the violent overthrow of the established order. The disintegration process was speeded by the fact that the wealth and the means of production were concentrated in the hands of the European communities—a situation which made the poverty of the Moslems more acute, and brought about a growth of racial discrimination against them. These prejudices aggravated the plight of the penniless masses and virtually precluded any possibility that they might one day aspire to a position of equality. Although the Jews, too, were subjected to intense anti-Semitic prejudices on the part of the European colons, they were fortunate inasmuch as they, like the Europeans, benefited from their countries' economic systems.

Social and economic status in North Africa was largely governed by the community to which the individual belonged; class barriers were reinforced by ethnic barriers; being Christian, Jewish or Moslem was not solely an indication of religion but also a determinant of a person's place in the economy and in society. Though the French colonizers had such a marked success in bringing to North Africa a fine network of roads, in establishing modern agriculture and prosperous industries and in building splendid cities, they failed to level the enormous economic disparities between the various ethnic groups or to promote mutual understanding and harmonious coexistence among the separate communities. This was the ultimate tragedy that brought about the dissolution of France's North African empire.

Translated by Michael M. Bernet.

Other works by Chouraqui: *Lettre à un ami arabe* (1969); *La Bible hébraïque et le Nouveau Testament* (1974).

Martin Buber

1878–1965

Martin Buber was one of the best-known Jewish thinkers in the Western world in the twentieth century. His neo romanticism and use of *völkisch* terms of analysis in his early writings exerted an enormous influence on Jewish youth in Central Europe. Perhaps more than any individual, he was responsible for introducing Hasidism to Western-educated Jewish audiences. In 1923, he published his best-known philosophical work, *I and Thou*. In 1938, he moved to Jerusalem, where he was given a chair at the Hebrew University. Before 1948, he was among those in the Yishuv—mainly German-speaking, Central European intellectuals—who advocated a binational state in which Jews and Arabs would cooperate. After World War II, he was much lauded, both in Europe and in America, as a humanitarian. He became the first president of the Israel Academy of Sciences and Humanities in 1960. Among his many awards are the Israel Prize (1953), the Bialik Prize (1961), and the Dutch Erasmus Prize (1963).

Genuine Dialogue and the Possibilities of Peace
1953

I cannot express my thanks to the German Book Trade for the honor conferred on me without at the same time setting forth the sense in which I have accepted it, just as I earlier accepted the Hanseatic Goethe Prize given me by the University of Hamburg.

About a decade ago a considerable number of Germans—there must have been many thousands of them—under the indirect command of the German government and the direct command of its representatives, killed millions of my people in a systematically prepared and executed procedure whose organized cruelty cannot be compared with any previous historical event. I, who am one of those who remained alive, have only in a formal sense a common humanity with those who took part in this action. They have so radically removed themselves from the human sphere, so transposed themselves into a sphere of monstrous inhumanity inaccessible to my conception, that not even hatred, much less an overcoming of hatred, was able to arise in me. And what am I that I could here presume to "forgive"!

With the German people it is otherwise. From my youth on I have taken the real existence of peoples most seriously. But I have never, in the face of any historical moment, past or present, allowed the concrete mul-

tiplicity existing at that moment within a people—the concrete inner dialectic, rising to contradiction—to be obscured by the leveling concept of a totality constituted and acting in just such a way and no other.

When I think of the German people of the days of Auschwitz and Treblinka, I behold, first of all, the great man, who knew that the monstrous event was taking place and did not oppose it. But my heart, which is acquainted with the weakness of men, refuses to condemn my neighbor for not prevailing upon himself to become a martyr. Next there emerges before me the mass of those who remained ignorant of what was withheld from the German public and who did not try to discover what reality lay behind the rumors which were circulating. When I have these men in mind, I am gripped by the thought of the anxiety, likewise well known to me, of the human creature before a truth which he fears he cannot face. But finally there appear before me, from reliable reports, some who have become as familiar to me by sight, action, and voice as if they were friends, those who refused to carry out the orders and suffered death or put themselves to death, and those who learned what was taking place and opposed it and were put to death, or those who learned what was taking place and because they could do nothing to stop it killed themselves. I see these men very near before me in that especial intimacy which binds us at times to the dead and to them alone. Reverence and love for these Germans now fills my heart.

But I must step out of memory into the present. Here I am surrounded by the youth who have grown up since those events and had no part in the great crime. These youth, who are probably the essential life of the German people today, show themselves to me in a powerful inner dialectic. Their core is included in the core of an inner struggle running for the most part underground and only occasionally coming to the surface. This is only a part, though one of the clearest, of the great inner struggle of all peoples being fought out today, more or less consciously, more or less passionately, in the vital center of each people.

The preparation for the final battle of *homo humanus* against *homo contrahumanus* has begun in the depths. But the front is split into as many individual fronts as there are peoples, and those who stand on one of the individual fronts know little or nothing of the other fronts. Darkness still covers the struggle, upon whose course and outcome it depends whether, despite all, a true humanity can issue from the race of men. The so-called cold war between two gigantic groups of states with all its accompaniments still obscures the true obligation and solidarity of combat, whose line cuts right through all states and peoples, however they name their régimes. The recognition of the deeper reality, of the true need and the true danger, is growing. In Germany, and especially in German youth, despite their being rent asunder, I have found more awareness of it than elsewhere. The memory of the twelve-year reign of *homo contra-humanus* has made the spirit stronger, and the task set by the spirit clearer, than they formerly were.

Tokens such as the bestowal of the Hanseatic Goethe Prize and the Peace Prize of the German Book Trade on a surviving arch-Jew must be understood in this connection. They, too, are moments in the struggle of the human spirit against the demonry of the subhuman and the antihuman. The survivor who is the object of such honors is taken up into the high duty of solidarity that extends across the fronts: the solidarity of all separate groups in the flaming battle for the rise of a true humanity. This duty is, in the present hour, the highest duty on earth. The Jew chosen as symbol must obey this call of duty even there, indeed, precisely there where the never-to-be-effaced memory of what has happened stands in opposition to it. When he recently expressed his gratitude to the spirit of Goethe, victoriously disseminated throughout the world, and when he now expressed his gratitude to the spirit of peace, which now as so often before speaks to the world in books of the German tongue, his thanks signify his confession of solidarity with the common battle—common also to Germans and Jews—against the contrahuman, and his reply to a vow taken by fighters, a vow he has heard.

Hearkening to the human voice, where it speaks forth unfalsified, and replying to it, this above all is needed today. The busy noise of the hour must no longer drown the *vox humana*, the essence of the human which has become a voice. This voice must not only be listened to, it must be answered and led out of the lonely monologue into the awakening dialogue of the peoples. Peoples must engage in talk with one another through their truly human men if the great peace is to appear and the devastated life of the earth renew itself.

The great peace is something essentially different from the absence of war.

In an early mural in the town hall of Sienna the civic virtues are assembled. Worthy, and conscious of their worth, the women sit there, except one in their midst who towers above the rest. This woman is marked not by dignity but rather by composed majesty. Three letters announce her name: Pax. She represents the great peace I have in mind. This peace does not signify that what men call war no longer exists now that it holds sway—that means too little to enable one to understand this serenity. Something new exists, now really exists, greater and mightier than war, greater and mightier even than war. Human passions flow into war as the waters into the sea, and war disposes of them as it likes. But these passions must enter into the great peace as ore into the fire that melts and transforms it. Peoples will then build with one another with more powerful zeal than they have ever destroyed one another.

The Siennese painter had glimpsed this majestic peace in his dream alone. He did not acquire the vision from historical reality, for it has never appeared there. What in history has been called peace has never, in fact, been aught other than an anxious or an illusory blissful pause between wars. But the womanly genius of the painter's dream is no mistress of interruptions but the queen of new and greater deeds.

Translated by Maurice Friedman.

Other works by Buber: *The Tales of Rabbi Nachman* (1906); *The Legend of the Baal Shem* (1907); *For the Sake of Heaven* (1943); *Two Types of Faith* (1946); *Tales of the Hasidim* (1947, 1948); *Eclipse of God* (1952).

Siegfried Moses
1887–1974

Born in Lautenburg, Germany (now Poland), Siegfried Moses had a distinguished career as a lawyer and public official before Hitler's rise to power. Between 1933 and 1937 he served as the president of the Zionist Organization of Germany, after which he immigrated to Palestine. There he continued to work in public service and in 1949 assumed the position of Israel's first state comptroller. In addition to his administrative work, Moses was a prominent member of several Jewish organizations, acting as president of many, including the Leo Baeck Institute.

Programme for the Leo Baeck Institute of Jews from Germany
1956

Primarily but not exclusively, the Institute would like to concern itself with the history of German Jewry since the Emancipation. The factual events leading to the catastrophe under the Nazi regime, however, will not be included, as various other institutions have undertaken the collection and description of material on the murderous actions of the Nazis.

1. As a final aim of the Institute, an all-inclusive presentation is contemplated—a comprehensive history of German Jewry. But the working programme, for the next few years at any rate, cannot yet consider such an encyclopaedic project. Perhaps in four or five years' time it will be feasible to entrust such a task to a group of historians who, we hope, will be able to draw on the studies and papers of the Institute which by then will be either published or in preparation. On the other hand, it may well be that such an ambitious project will have to wait for a great historian who does not depend on a personal contact with the generation of Jews who emigrated from Germany.

Looking ahead, it seems therefore an important task for the Institute to prepare the ground for such a comprehensive presentation of German Jewry's history. Yet while serving this end, and to some extent unrelated to it, the Institute fulfils even now a purpose of utmost urgency: to ensure through its publications and research work that the spiritual features of German Jewry, as far as they are still alive today, be preserved for us, the former German Jews; that these features, wherever possible, be retraced and rounded off; and that the Jewish people the world over may learn something of the ways and ideas of German Jewry and their significance. [. . .]

The programme as seen below, may give an idea of the scope which the Institute has set for its activities. It was adopted as a working basis at the founding of the Institute; it makes no claim to completeness, and the bodies of the Institute are continuously engaged on working it out further and defining it precisely.

The Period since the Emancipation

A. The inner development of German Jewry
   1. The struggle for emancipation.
   2. The wave of conversion.
   3. Changes in the social structure of the Jews in Germany.
      a) From ghetto economy to world economy.
      b) The social complexion of the Jews in Germany.
   4. Population movements and family structure.
   5. Entry of the Jews into the liberal professions (art, literature, science).

6. The "Science of Judaism."
7. The development of Jewish religious philosophy in Germany (M. Mendelssohn, N. Krochmal, L. Steinheim, S. Hirsch, M. Lazarus, H. Steinthal, H. Cohen, L. Baeck, M. Buber, F. Rosenzweig).
8. Religious trends in German Jewry
   a) Reform.
   b) Jewish-religious Liberalism.
   c) Orthodoxy.
   d) Secessionist Orthodoxy.
9. The Zionist Organization of Germany.
10. Jewish educational institutes.
11. Jewish journalism in Germany.
12. The Jewish Women's Movement in Germany.
13. Jewish Youth Movements in Germany.
14. The structure of the Jewish communities. (Their rights, constitution and democratic organization.)
15. The social establishments and institutions of German Jewry.
16. Synagogical architecture and popular art.
17. Liturgical music.

B. The problem of the cultural symbiosis
   1. German translations of the Jewish Bible.
   2. Yiddish and German, the Hebrew language.
   3. Jewish achievements in science. (Philosophy—Psychology—Religious Philosophy—Science of Religion—Medicine—Jurisprudence—Natural Science and Technology—Economics—Historiography—Sociology—Pedagogics and Adult Education—Archivistics and Librarianship)
   4. German Jews in
      a) Literature.
      b) Music.
      c) Fine Arts.
      d) Theatre.
   5. German Jews as preceptors of public opinion (press, publicity).
   6. The position of the Jews in the German economy.
   7. German Jews in general politics.
   8. German Jews in the Socialist International.

The Catastrophe
   1. Anti-Semitism up to 1914.
   2. Trends from 1918 to 1933.
   3. The National Socialist State.

4. Jewish life in national socialist Germany up to 1939. (The *Reichsvertretung der Juden in Deutschland*.)
5. The exodus.

German Jewry's Influence on World Jewry
1. The pattern of political emancipation.
2. The national and historic problem of "assimilation."
3. Religious movements and tendencies
   a) The new orthodoxy.
   b) The historical school.
   c) Liberal and Reform Judaism.
4. The systematization of Jewish thought
   a) Martin Buber.
   b) Leo Baeck.
   c) Franz Rosenzweig.
5. German Jews in the development of the Zionist idea.
6. German Jews in the building up of Eretz Israel.

The New Centres of Jews from Germany
1. Great Britain. 2. U.S.A. 3. South America. 4. South Africa. 5. Australia, etc.

German Jewry was not only multiform but also multi-coloured; political differences and antagonism led, in the pre-Hitler period, to discussions and conflicts which had, in many respects, a decisive influence on the development of German Jewry.

Experience has shown that the various shades of opinion, as they naturally exist among the Board members of the Institute, do not affect their objectivity in regard to assignments for research work or the publication of books. Although the differences in outlook have not disappeared, they have lost much of their pungency and are no longer issues of contention. On the other hand, there may be cases where it is objectively justifiable to choose an author not only for his scholarship but also for his personal attitude and approach to a religious problem or to a subject on contemporary history.

It is, indeed, possible and necessary to turn the opalescence of German Jewry into an asset for the work of the Institute.

Other works by Moses: *The Income Tax Ordinance of Palestine* (1942); *Jewish Post-War Claims* (1944).

Robert Weltsch

1891–1984

Robert Weltsch grew up in a German-speaking Jewish milieu in Prague in the last days of the Habsburg Empire. He was a member of the Zionist student group Bar Kokhba. From 1919 to 1938 he served as editor of the twice-weekly, Berlin-based Zionist newspaper *Jüdische Rundschau*. After fleeing Germany, he settled in Israel, where he worked for the prestigious daily *Haaretz*, serving as its London correspondent from 1945 to 1978. He was instrumental in establishing the Leo Baeck Institute, which promotes scholarship on the history, culture, and legacy of German-speaking Jews.

Fool's Paradise: German Jewry, 1933–38
1956

Looking back, we readily recognize how many illusions were inherent in Jewish ideologies.

The Assimilationists idealized emancipation. Some of them became German nationalists, but some saw in it the entry into universal humanity, the accomplishment of prophetic and Messianic ideas. Reality was different, but they still clung to their concept and defended it as though what should be were identical with what actually was.

The Zionists, on the other hand, sometimes overemphasized the virtues of separation. They idealized the image of a Jewish State which was not in existence at that time and could therefore easily be pictured with all the attributes of what is good and beautiful in humanity. Reality, of course, could not live up to these expectations.

Both parties showed much self-righteousness when the opportunity seemed favourable to them. Today, we can see all that in a different perspective. We all have become more humble.

We also do not overrate the short-lived Jewish upsurge of 1933–38. Emotionally it was genuine, but to a considerable extent it was but the defiant reaction of a deeply hurt mind to its affliction. It evoked hopes of a great historical opportunity for the Jews which—seen against the Nazi background—seem to us misconceived today. It had no lasting religious effect. But we should also not under-rate the dignified way in which the majority of German Jews faced their destiny. It was "their finest hour." Judaism gave them comfort and satisfaction and embraced it with honesty and sometimes with enthusiasm. It gave them a feeling of brotherhood and solidarity, perhaps similar to that of the early Christians in the Catacombs. This story is told in various chapters of this book.

At the beginning of the Nazi era, which marked the End of an Epoch, nobody knew what fate had in store. Sometimes it seemed as though it would be possible to establish a genuine and flourishing Jewish life, separated from Nazi barbarism in a sort of *Apartheid*. This was doubly agreeable as it relieved the Jews in the Nazi state from responsibility for all but Jewish internal affairs. In the first period of Nazi rule it was even possible to argue with Nazi officials on the lines that Jews—being ideologically and legally excluded from the German race—must be allowed to express themselves in liberal terms. For those who could not emigrate immediately there was deep comfort in assembling as a Jewish congregation and listening to spiritual leaders. Wholesale emigration seemed physically unthinkable, especially as most countries closed their doors except to a trickle, and in the summer of 1938 the inter-governmental conference of Evian dispersed without the slightest practical result. That something like Auschwitz would ever be possible did not enter into anyone's mind. Many Jews adopted Jewish nationalism as an expression of defiance.

Today, we realize that it was a sort of fool's paradise. We can no longer idealize any kind of Ghetto life. Subsequent events showed where it actually led. So we look back rather melancholically on many of our own proud pronouncements of 1933–38. But at that time, as Max Gruenewald expressed it, "German Jewry did not sink. Its cultural feats . . . belong in a way to the resistance movement."[1]

These five years were one of the strangest episodes in the history of the Jewish people. It was, alas, a kind of euphoria before the end. To convey some of the atmosphere of these bygone days to the present generation in rapidly changing times, is one of the intentions of this book. Perhaps it might be argued that some of the facts of human behaviour and intellectual reaction indicated in this book are of more than local or tribal significance. The Jewish reader may yet discover in them traits common to the general problems of Jewish life and survival anywhere.

NOTE

1. Max Gruenewald, "Education of Culture of the German Jews under Nazi Rule," in *Jewish Review*, vol. V, New York, 1949.

Other works by Weltsch: *Deutsches Judentum* (1963); *Be-naftuley ha-zemanim* (1981); *Die deutsche Judenfrage* (1981).

Hermann Levin Goldschmidt

1914–1998

Philosopher Hermann Levin Goldschmidt was born in Berlin but left for Switzerland in 1938. There he began his studies and became friends with many eminent members of Zurich's political and artistic circles. In the late 1940s, he worked with several other Jewish philosophers, including Martin Buber, to develop the philosophy of dialogue. In 1990, Goldschmidt and his wife Mary Bollag founded the Stiftung Dialogik (Dialogue Foundation) to further philosophical research and scholarship on German and Swiss Jewish history.

The Legacy of German Jewry
1957

German Jewry proved itself to be one of the most deeply characteristic and in every important respect fundamental representatives of the West, proving its mettle as partner in its two-thousand-year struggle for the ideals the West holds dear. In the end, the judgment we form of the German Jewish legacy will apply to the present and future prospects of the West as a whole. Despite their universal dissemination and de facto acceptance in every part of the world without exception, modern Europe's unparalleled cultural achievements have still not achieved full recognition, and remain vulnerable to new losses and oblivion. Like the legacy of German Jewry that both transforms and complements them, Europe's achievements are before all else an irreplaceable seed stock to be carefully collected, tended, and preserved, and even more thoughtfully handed down to future generations. These are the seeds of a Western preeminence that has been doubly superseded at the century's end. First, because Europe frittered away its decisive role once and for all in the two world wars it waged, and second, because as far as modernity is concerned, the kind of single world center we have known since the Middle Ages no longer exists.

In compiling, preserving, and transmitting this preciously fertile trove in all its potential, the legacy of German Jewry represents not the sense of an ending, but a signpost that points us toward the future. That legacy asks us to seriously consider the fact that the end of a crucial epoch in the world history of the Jewish people is at hand, along with the end—in every sense—of Western hegemony. "We alone are not concerned," writes Leo Baeck in just this sense, "when we become a matter of concern." Baeck came upon his insight when looking back on Judaism as such, in the last paragraph of his *The Essence of Judaism*: "Our claims are the claims of conscience, of the commandment. We do not desire to be honored, but rather that truth and justice be honored."

Based on several telling examples, and on Baeck, whom we have just quoted, as the most salient one, the following conclusion can be drawn. The battle Jews waged to the bitter end for an authentic dialogue between Judaism and Christianity, while carried out for Judaism's benefit, also fought for fundamental truths and rights that Christianity and all peoples share. German Jewry's battle for equality enabled it to scale heights of human experience that all humanity may be inspired to enrich. Yet in this regard, their achievement lives on as a legacy and nothing more. Even the innovative consequences of the I-Thou reconception of the relation between Judaism and Christianity, with its worldwide influence in many fields, must be bracketed for the time being, because its acceptance is still nothing more than a hope. If this insistence that Judaism was Christianity's full equal was a victory, what is the significance of a victory recognized by the home team alone, a victory whose example was supposed to stand as a beacon to the world? Has what Baeck fought Harnack to achieve really been accomplished: a recognition and stature for Judaism fully consonant with what Christianity enjoys? Has this situation, and all its consequences, been realized or carried out in practice to the extent hoped for when the first edition of this work conceptualized this idea of religious equality as a "division of labor in redemptive history" that, without erasing any doctrinal distinctions or mutually defining differences, envisioned it as the path toward meaningful religious coexistence? Have we reached the point where the aspiration for such religious equality can ground itself not in the past, but in a vision of a judgment encompassing the present, while pointing out the future's path?

And has what Franz Rosenzweig called the "ecclesiastical-political point" of equal stature for Judaism and Christianity, which he fought to achieve, become unequivocally clear to the Christian neighbor: that an organized "mission to the Jews" is no longer acceptable? Certainly, a "mission to the pagans" and as a new task, an "inner mission" may be acceptable as part of the tra-

dition of religious revelation that presses one to serve as its messenger. "Neither missionary work as such, nor consciousness of one's mission, and the obligation to testify to it, nor its pronouncement" ought to be abandoned. "None of the world religions can withdraw from the world, to whose entirety they bring the good tidings that everything, can, should and will be redeemed. But as world religions, Judaism and Christianity can and must disavow the obligation of trying to convert one another. . . . No act other than relinquishing this program altogether will be the proofstone of their contemporary and future encounter. This act is not just a concession but a conquest as well: in the most literal meaning of the term, the future-laden conquest of Jewish, and Christian modernity."

Translated by David Suchoff.

Other works by Goldschmidt: *Philosophie als Dialogik* (1948); *Weil wir Brüder sind: Biblische Besinnung für Juden und Christen* (1975).

Friedrich Torberg

1908–1979

Critic and journalist Friedrich Kantor, who wrote under the name Friedrich Torberg, was born in Vienna but fled to France in 1938. After spending a year in the Free Czech Army during World War II, Torberg moved to the United States, where he worked as a scriptwriter in Hollywood. He returned to Vienna in 1951 and remained there for the rest of his life. In addition to his own works of satirical fiction and nonfiction, Kantor is known for his German translations of the works of Israeli satirist Ephraim Kishon. Until his death, Torberg remained among the most prominent Jewish critics in Austria, openly condemning collaborators in the Holocaust and writing in tribute to its victims.

Applause for Anne Frank
1957

A Not Entirely Imaginary Dialogue after the Premiere of "The Diary of Anne Frank."

THE SATISFIED ONE: I am gratified by the success in Vienna of *The Diary of Anne Frank*. It is a harrowing play. And it confronts us all the more forcibly with the horrors of a time now past, thank God, as it forgoes all accusatory innuendoes. Since it stays strictly in the realm of the universal, the purely human, it produces just the right effect. The applause of the audience proves that.

THE DISSATISFIED ONE: I am not at all gratified by the success in Vienna of *The Diary of Anne Frank*. It is a harrowing play. But it doesn't show us anything beyond just that: a harrowing play. Since it stays strictly in the realm of the universal, the purely human, it produces precisely the wrong effect. The applause of the audience proves that.

THE SATISFIED ONE: Some spectators even wept.

THE DISSATISFIED ONE: Some spectators weep even in *The Lady of the Camellias*.[1]

THE SATISFIED ONE: One cannot possibly compare them!

THE DISSATISFIED ONE: Why not? Both are plays written for the theater.

THE SATISFIED ONE: *The Diary of Anne Frank* is not a conventional play.

THE DISSATISFIED ONE: Yes, it is. Moreover, it is a damn good one—I am using this phrase deliberately. Almost as good as *The Lady of the Camellias*.

THE SATISFIED ONE: You are really going too far now. *The Lady of the Camellias*, this sentimental kitsch story—

THE DISSATISFIED ONE: —was at the time of its composition a startling drama of social criticism. The fact that the society of its time cannot be criticized for nearly as much as the one that permitted the death of Anne Frank is not something you can hold against *The Lady of the Camellias*.

THE SATISFIED ONE: You are not only going too far, you are going completely off course. You are ignoring the fundamental difference between the two plays.

THE DISSATISFIED ONE: Which is?

THE SATISFIED ONE: *The Diary of Anne Frank*, unlike *The Lady of the Camellias*, is not an invention, but a document. It is not a product of the literary imagination but of reality.

THE DISSATISFIED ONE: We are approaching the root of our difference of opinion. What you are saying holds for the actual diary of Anne Frank. Its dramatization condemns it—that is why I used that phrase earlier—to be effective as a play. Whether and when it will be effective merely as a sentimental kitsch story depends entirely on the audience. In Vienna the audience came pretty close to that point. Damn close, if I may say so.

THE SATISFIED ONE: In that case you are really condemning the spectators rather than the dramatization.

THE DISSATISFIED ONE: I am condemning the dramatization because it enables the spectators to take in a factual report as if it were a sentimental kitsch story. That is, they will take truth for a literary invention. They are not entirely wrong to do so. Since what they are shown on stage is, in a certain way, an invention.

THE SATISFIED ONE: Are you saying, then, that the author of the dramatization invented things that aren't in the original?

THE DISSATISFIED ONE: No, that is not at all what I am saying. As far as I know, the two American adapters—no doubt two proficient and immensely experienced people, highly skilled at their craft and so familiar with the demands of the theater that they succeeded in picking the scenes that are guaranteed to work on stage—those two tasteful monsters added, as far as I know, only one scene.

THE SATISFIED ONE: Which one?

THE DISSATISFIED ONE: What does it matter? It's not noticeable.

THE SATISFIED ONE: Still, I am interested. Which scene is it?

THE DISSATISFIED ONE: The one with the hungry Herr Daan, who during the night raids the scant bread supply in the hideout. If I cared enough I could prove to you on the basis of that one invented scene—and simply because by employing that damn "purely human" tone, it cannot be distinguished from the genuine scenes—the questionable nature of the entire dramatization. But it is not essential. The dramatization is questionable enough without it.

THE SATISFIED ONE: Although that scene is actually quite close to the original?

THE DISSATISFIED ONE: As close as a color picture postcard of the Beethoven House on Eroica Lane is to the reality of the 19th district of Vienna. Photographically close.

THE SATISFIED ONE: Meaning?

THE DISSATISFIED ONE: Meaning, it is not telling you anything about the desolate state of the district's sewer system or about the shabby pensions that some of its old residents received.

THE SATISFIED ONE: I don't understand you. If you are buying a postcard of the Beethoven House, you don't want to be confronted with the abysmal social conditions of the time. You want to see something beautiful.

THE DISSATISFIED ONE: Precisely. If you are going to the theater to see *The Diary of Anne Frank*, you don't want to be confronted with the horrors of the Hitler regime. You want . . .

THE SATISFIED ONE: Stop right there! Do you actually think that what we are being shown in *The Diary of Anne Frank* is "beautiful"?

THE DISSATISFIED ONE: I think that the truth that underlies the play is so incomprehensibly ugly that it cannot be shown at all. And for that reason, I do not consider that which we are shown to be the truth. It is not even a partial truth. What we are shown are purposefully selected snippets of a partial view, arranged with an eye toward their effectiveness on stage and for that reason verging on pure invention. Already Anne Frank's actual diary could convey only a small part of the whole horrendous truth. But that part was authentic. Its authenticity, however, consists exclusively of its *original form of presentation*. The truth is inseparably and organically tied to its original presentation. By transposing the truth into another form, it is falsified; it is prettified or coarsened, or both at the same time. That monstrous drama to which Anne Frank testifies in her diary, thus contributing an infinitesimally small part, smaller than one millionth, to the overall truth, that overwhelming tragedy is de-dramatized through dramatization. The mind-boggling fact that this diary was actually written and was written *just so*, cannot be conveyed in its full significance in any other form than through the diary itself. In this case the "higher truth" resides in reality alone. In this case truth is not heightened by its artistic rendition, but debased.

NOTE

1. [*La Dame aux Camélias*, novel by Alexandre Dumas, *fils*, published in 1848; adapted by him for the stage in 1852, and set to music by Giuseppe Verdi in 1853 as *La Traviata*.—Trans.]

Translated by Susanne Klingenstein.

Other works by Torberg: *Der Schüler Gerber* (1930); *Die Tante Jolesch oder der Untergang des Abendlandes in Anekdoten* (1975).

Isaac Deutscher

1907–1967

Isaac Deutscher was born in Chrzanów, near Kraków, and raised in an Orthodox family, although he turned away from religion in adolescence. Upon moving to Warsaw in 1925, he joined the Communist Party of Poland. He was expelled from the party in the early 1930s for his criticism of Stalin and for spreading what the party considered needless alarm over Nazism. Deutscher moved to London in 1939, in time to avoid the fate that would befall the family he left behind. His laudatory three-volume biography of Leon Trotsky is his best-known work. Deutscher remained a committed Marxist until his death and was a prominent critic of the Vietnam War.

The Non-Jewish Jew
1958

There is an old talmudic saying: "A Jew who has sinned still remains a Jew." My own thinking is, of course, beyond the idea of "sin" or "no sin"; but this saying has brought to my mind a memory from childhood which may not be irrelevant to my theme.

I remember that when as a child I read the Midrash, I came across a story and a description of a scene which gripped my imagination. It was the story of Rabbi Meir, the great saint and sage, the pillar of Mosaic orthodoxy and coauthor of the Mishnah, who took lessons in theology from a heretic, Elisha ben Abuyah, called *Akher* (The Stranger). Once on a Sabbath Rabbi Meir was with his teacher, and as usual they became engaged in a deep argument. The heretic was riding a donkey, and Rabbi Meir, as he could not ride on a Sabbath, walked by his side and listened so intently to the words of wisdom falling from his heretical lips that he failed to notice that he and his teacher had reached the ritual boundary which Jews were not allowed to cross on a Sabbath. The great heretic turned to his orthodox pupil and said: "Look, we have reached the boundary—we must part now; you must not accompany me any farther—go back!" Rabbi Meir went back to the Jewish community, while the heretic rode on—beyond the boundaries of Jewry.

There was enough in this scene to puzzle an orthodox Jewish child. Why, I wondered, did Rabbi Meir, that leading light of orthodoxy, take his lessons from the heretic? Why did he show him so much affection? Why did he defend him against other rabbis? My heart, it seems, was with the heretic. Who was he? He appeared to be in Jewry and yet out of it. He showed a curious respect for his pupil's orthodoxy, when he sent him back to the Jews on the Holy Sabbath; but he himself, disregarding canon and ritual, rode beyond the boundaries. When I was thirteen, or perhaps fourteen, I began to write a play about *Akher* and Rabbi Meir, and

I tried to find out more about *Akher*'s character. What made him transcend Judaism? Was he a Gnostic? Was he an adherent of some other school of Greek or Roman philosophy? I could not find the answers, and did not manage to get beyond the first act.

The Jewish heretic who transcends Jewry belongs to a Jewish tradition. You may, if you like, see *Akher* as a prototype of those great revolutionaries of modern thought: Spinoza, Heine, Marx, Rosa Luxemburg, Trotsky, and Freud. You may, if you wish to, place them within a Jewish tradition. They all went beyond the boundaries of Jewry. They all found Jewry too narrow, too archaic, and too constricting. They all looked for ideals and fulfillment beyond it, and they represent the sum and substance of much that is greatest in modern thought, the sum and substance of the most profound upheavals that have taken place in philosophy, sociology, economics, and politics in the last three centuries.

Did they have anything in common with one another? Have they perhaps impressed mankind's thought so greatly because of their special "Jewish genius"? I do not believe in the exclusive genius of any race. Yet I think that in some ways they were very Jewish indeed. They had in themselves something of the quintessence of Jewish life and of the Jewish intellect. They were *a priori* exceptional in that as Jews they dwelt on the borderlines of various civilizations, religions, and national cultures. They were born and brought up on the borderlines of various epochs. Their minds matured where the most diverse cultural influences crossed and fertilized each other. They lived on the margins or in the nooks and crannies of their respective nations. Each of them was in society and yet not in it, of it and yet not of it. It was this that enabled them to rise in thought above their societies, above their nations, above their times and generations, and to strike out mentally into wide new horizons and far into the future.

Other Works by Deutscher: *Stalin: A Political Biography* (1949); *The Prophet Armed: Trotsky, 1879–1921* (1954); *The Prophet Unarmed: Trotsky, 1921–1929* (1959); *The Prophet Outcast: Trotsky, 1929–1940* (1963).

Anna Langfus

1920–1966

Anna Langfus was born Anna-Regina Szternfinkiel in Lublin, Poland. Imprisoned at Płock for her work in the Polish underground, she relocated to France in 1946 and married Aron Langfus two years later. She began writing in French in the early 1950s, winning acclaim for her novels and plays dealing with the traumas of the Holocaust. Her semiautobiographical novel *Les Bagages de sable* was awarded the Prix Goncourt in 1962.

Conversation with Piotr Rawicz
1961

Piotr Rawicz's *Blood from the Sky* is without question the most forceful of recent novels written about the fate of Jews in Nazi Europe. There has been rare critical unanimity in this respect. To find a "poetic equivalence" for life in the ghetto and in the death camps, Rawicz has made use of black humor, surrealist baroque, the absurd, gratuitous revolt, even sacrilege. . . . It is doubtless a beautiful work of art, but one may wonder whether artistic concerns are not somewhat misplaced when dealing with such a subject. We have asked our collaborator Anna Langfus, author of *The Whole Land Brimstone*, to interview the young novelist. We have made no cuts in Piotr Rawicz's remarks. They are deliberately shocking, indeed, revolting. If Rawicz is sincere, and we have no right to doubt this, do his exhibitionism and nebulous metaphysics not signal a profound despair?

We believe this interview should enter the dossier of traumas suffered by some survivors of the *temps du mépris*.[1]

AL: Did your vocation as a writer become evident before *Blood from the Sky*?

PR: At the age of fifteen, two things were important to me: to write and to make love, which come to the same thing. I wrote *Blood from the Sky* in France and spent two years doing it, 1956 and 1957.

AL: Why did you choose to write about the war period? Do you feel you were sincere in describing it?

PR: I chose that period because I find it very . . . representative, it's perfectly suitable for my purposes. I'm not interested in historic or political truth, only ontological truth.

AL: What is most important in your book?

PR: My poems. The surrounding context—the war period—has only secondary importance. It's merely the cement I used to hold them in place.

AL: Don't you think it would have been better to work on an abstract level, without touching on events that a number of us lived through, rubbing salt in wounds that have yet to heal?

PR: You are right perhaps. But as I said, it is a fascinating period from which one can draw so many things.

AL: And it doesn't bother you that someone could make it serve purely literary purposes?

PR: Not at all. I find the period perfectly normal. It corresponds to that which is deepest within us. For me that war is like the very seed of being, being in its purest state.

AL: Not so long ago I argued in public with a young student who insisted that your book is sincerity itself and that the events you describe must have really happened that way. I tried in vain to convince him that *Blood from the Sky*, in spite of the powerful vision and the beauty of certain pages, is only a literary exercise. I believe it is dangerous to fix such an image of the war in the minds of young people. What do you think?

PR: I think what you said to the student is correct.

AL: In your book you depict a Jew, Dr. Hillel, a Talmud scholar versed in the Kabbalah, as possessing a fine collection of pornographic postcards. Why?

PR: To make him more human, more likeable. For me, collecting pornographic pictures is a trait that makes the character easier to identify with.

AL: You also cite a wholly imaginary speech by Trotsky. Do you believe one can take such liberties with well-known historic figures?

PR: I seem to recall having heard something similar from some woman or other when I was a young man. Since it suited what I wanted to say, in any case, it didn't bother me.

AL: All of the characters in your book are rather "dark." Why?

PR: I don't think there's a single one who is completely despicable. As for good, honest men, I feel they're creations of boy scout morality. The distinctions we draw between good and bad people are not real, in my opinion. If you look closely, the differences are minimal. And I am incapable of indignation.

AL: So the things that happened during the war don't deserve your indignation?

PR: Not in the least. I only feel gratitude toward God. For I am a believer. He allowed me to live during that time and to enter the Garden. The Garden with a capital G. This war is for me a proof of God's existence.

AL: At a certain point one of your characters says he's enjoying himself to no end and finds delight in contemplating the death of his entire family.

PR: That's the reaction of a mature person, and his attitude, faced with death and the suffering of those he loves, is an ambivalent one.

AL: So you basically find nothing terrible about war?

PR: No. I find an endlessly repetitious domestic scene just as horrible.

AL: But does the same scale of values apply? After a quarrel, one can always go watch a movie or eat some cookies to forget about it. What could people under torture do?

PR: It's the same. There were occasional interruptions, and there was prayer. Don't forget, I'm a believer.

AL: Did you lose loved ones during the war?

PR: Yes. My mother and the girl I loved.

AL: And yourself?

PR: I spent three years in the camps.

AL: As a Jew?

PR: No.

AL: That's a pity. Living as a Jew in a concentration camp would have been good for you.

PR: I don't agree. My situation was already rather delicate.

AL: In an image you use to represent our world—the rear end of a cat who keeps chasing his tail—one critic has found a metaphysical message. What do you think of that? (I can't help laughing as I ask this question, and Piotr Rawicz joins in. I'm glad, as on this point we're very much in agreement.)

AL: Here's another question. You remember the minor scandal that arose last year when Mrs. Bellocq's book *La Porte retombée* [The Fallen Door], which won the Prix Femina, came out. You remember Béatrix Beck's indignation at that bit about "ghetto lice" and her subsequent resignation from Femina's jury? Your book has more vermin than hers (though also much more talent). What reaction do you think that would have provoked had it been written by someone other than a Jew?

PR: I have no idea. I only know that I have the right to say it. That world was mine, the only one possible and authentic. And that world continues to attract me. I leave soon for Poland, and I'm going to revisit those places I knew, especially the camps where I truly lived. I have within me enough love for Jews and Judaism that I allow myself to say whatever I please.

AL: But the way you describe them, the victims differ very little from the executioners.

PR: As victims, the Jews seem to me worthy of interest. Otherwise, as I've already told you, I see little difference among human beings. Of course, when I see a judge and someone accused, I'm for the accused. I would not kill Eichmann, even though he is scum. Hess, whom I knew, had his good side in spite of his crimes. He loved plants and animals. But Eichmann is truly a sad case. However, I would not kill him. Don't be shocked, in any case I have no influence.

NOTE

1. [*Le Temps du mépris*: a phrase originally used by André Malraux as the title for his 1935 novel about the trauma of a communist prisoner in a Nazi concentration camp. Malraux's title has been variously translated into English as *Days of Wrath, An Age of Oppression*, and *Days of Contempt*. Albert Camus later made a play out of the novel and used the same title for a 1944 editorial in the Resistance publication *Combat.*—Trans.]

Translated by Michele McKay Aynesworth.

Other works by Langfus: *The Whole Land Brimstone* (1960); *The Lost Shore* (1962); *Saute, Barbara* (1965).

Aron Vergelis

1918–1999

Aron Vergelis was born in Lyubar, Zhitomyr (Ukraine). He started writing in the early 1930s, shortly after moving to Birobidzhan, the Jewish Autonomous area. After studying in Moscow and serving in the Red Army during World War II, Vergelis became a major force in Soviet Yiddish culture: hosting Yiddish radio, publishing poetry, editing journals, and translating Yiddish works into Russian. He was the editor in chief of the Moscow-based Yiddish literary monthly *Sovetish heymland* (Soviet Homeland) from 1961 to 1991, and of its post-Soviet sequel, *Di yidishe gas*.

Inaugural Issue of Soviet Homeland

1961

Dear Reader!

We are placing in your hands this first number of *Sovetish heymland* [Soviet Homeland]. In it you will feel the breath of our times. You will receive news of literary life and hear the multinational voice of the literature of the Soviet Union. As part of that literature, we believe that our journal will honor the name which stands on its cover.

We begin our work at a time when all Soviet literature is filled with ideas in preparation for the XXII Party Congress. "The genius of communism," Comrade N. S. Khrushchev has stated, "is for deep thinking, intense feeling, and strong passion, for art that is capable of inspiring to yet greater achievements the millions of builders of communism."

In the endless spaces of our land, events of enormous scope are taking place. Soviet man has conquered outer space, whole regions are changing their appearance, and millions of acres of virgin lands have been opened up. Workers in labor brigades, in craft unions, in factories, now live and work in communist style. It is the sacred obligation of our writers to find the appropriate stirring words and noble sentiments for these developments.

The tasks that confront the journal *Sovetish heymland* are serious. The journal must illuminate, in breadth and from every perspective, the life of the Soviet nation and its selfless struggle for world peace and a happier future.

The writings sent to us by Soviet Yiddish writers are a guarantee that the journal will be able to reflect, on a high artistic level, the most important problems of our time. Our journal will also publish many new and colorful depictions of Soviet reality from the best creations of the literature of the fraternal Soviet peoples. The voice of the Soviet Jewish writer will be heard within the mighty chorus of fraternal literatures.

As early as 1921, one of the founders of our literature, Peretz Markish, wrote: "Above all, the new Yiddish poetry is a child of revolutionary Russia. . . ." Today, just as forty years ago, we proudly proclaim our organic attachment to the Soviet homeland, to the whole of Soviet literature.

The hero of our writings is the man who has discarded the heavy burden of the past and lives a creative and productive life as one of the builders of communist society. In that respect it is important to stress the significance of literary prose, especially descriptive prose. Only a thorough understanding of life in all its manifestations makes possible the creation of truly artistic and colorful work. In our novels, short stories, and documentary prose, the reader will find spread before him the broad canvas of Soviet life.

While visiting Mikhail Sholokhov in his Cossack village, Veshenskaya, Nikita Khrushchev stated that "our art is called upon to show how heroic accomplishments are achieved and to reveal the spiritual world of contemporary Soviet man, his feelings, thoughts and aspirations." These words express the task of our verbal artists: to penetrate deeply into life, to show how communist ideas govern the broad mass of the people.

We take special satisfaction in the fact that among Yiddish poets the interest in poetry has remained as strong as ever. This is in accord with the experience of our multilingual Soviet literature, which teaches us that in times of greatness great literary genres blossom. It gives us special pleasure to note that this great genre is being used for the description of the present day. But we will succeed in uncovering the spiritual world of the man of our time, his feelings, thoughts, and aspirations, only when alongside epic poetry we raise lyric poetry to a higher level. That is particularly pertinent to political poetry. In this poetry we must hear both the creative enthusiasm that is characteristic of Soviet man, his struggle for peace and social justice and the wrath of the masses against Hitler's heirs, who unfortunately have not yet been effaced from the earth.

As we begin our work in the journal, we believe that our literary critics will pay particular attention to the new generation of writers now active in Soviet Yiddish literature. Most of them were active participants in the Great Patriotic War. In those days they were still young writers. Now they appear before us as mature literary personalities. We expect that our literary critics will reveal to us the originality of these masters of language, along with an appreciation of their significance for the literature of our time.

These, dear reader, are the immediate tasks which the journal *Sovetish heymland* has set for itself.

Translated by Solon Beinfeld.

Other works by Vergelis: *Zhazhda* (1956); *Oyg oyf oyg: lider un poemes* (1969); *Di tsayt* (1981).

Édouard Roditi

1910–1992

Poet, art critic, and translator Édouard Roditi was born in Paris in 1910 to American parents. He studied at Oxford and at the University of Chicago and lived in London, Paris, and Berlin from 1929 to 1937. A polyglot, he was the first to translate André Breton's works into English. Roditi also worked for the U.S. Office of War Information during World War II and was a translator at the Nuremberg war crimes trials, as well as for the State Department during the San Francisco conference that established the United Nations.

Jewish Artists from North Africa
1963

A retrospective exhibit these last few weeks at the Museum of Modern Art in Paris—perhaps too generously big an undertaking—has allowed a wider public to appreciate the originality and importance of Jean Atlan's contribution to the French tradition—assuming there is one—of nonfigurative art since 1945. John Asberry [*sic*], our colleague at the Paris edition of the *New York Herald Tribune*, is alone in failing to understand this work and its importance, a fact we find hardly surprising. Asberry has even attributed the posthumous glory of Atlan to the friends and acquaintances he accumulated over his lifetime. One might say as much of the late Franz Kline, who also passed away prematurely last year in New York. In any case, two characteristics distinguish the "calligraphies" of Atlan from those of Hartung, Soulages, Singier, Estève, and several other artists of the same school of abstract art in Paris. A Jew from Constantine, Atlan never forgot his origins; as an abstract painter, he did no more than translate into a visual, abstract language, both personal and modern, the arabesques that are also found in the Judeo-Arabic or Judeo-Berber embroidery and pottery of his native Algeria. Other painters from the same school have, however, renounced their origins. The watercolors, the gouaches, and the wash tints from Hartung's youth, exhibited a few years ago at the Craven Gallery, were, for example, still faithful to the great traditions of German expressionism. One could even recognize a disciple of that marvelous painter Emil Nolde. In his latest exhibit at the Galerie de France, Hartung's recent works seemed in contrast a complete denial of that glorious past and, in the end, resembled rather the outsize designs of new "modernist" wrapping paper for birthday gifts sold at Galeries Lafayette.

Atlan's palette, moreover, is also faithful to his origins. In the harmonies of those Berber tapestries, there is a sense of color that is not representative of Parisian high fashion or the School of Paris in general. Atlan is thus at the same time one of the greatest of recent French painters and the first great painter of his native North Africa.

* * *

Before Jean Atlan, there were other Jewish painters who had come to us from Algeria or Tunisia. Too often we forget that Lucien Lévy-Dhurmer (1865–1943), born in Algiers, was one of the most original portrait painters of his generation. His portraits of Pierre Loti, Georges Rodenbach, and Georges Clemenceau are true masterpieces of a kind of post-impressionism that was already very literary and symbolic. The National Museum of Modern Art too often fails to show one of his finest realist paintings, representing some blind Muslim beggars in Tangier. Far from being exotic, this painting by Lévy-Dhurmer is only a great expression, perhaps typically Jewish, of human charity. Few French artists have known how to depict scenes of Muslim life as naturally as he. In the December 1962 issue of *Le Judaïsme Sephardi*, Max Nordau published a moving homage to another Jewish painter from Algiers whom we do not fully appreciate: Henry Valensi (1883–1960), who traveled the same road in 1912 as the cubist or post-cubist masters Marcel Duchamp, Albert Gleizes, Francis Picabia, and Jacques Villon. Valensi later founded a new school, that of musicalist painting, which was one of the first French movements of abstract or nonfigurative art. Shortly before Henry Valensi's death, the Galerie de l'Institut on the Rue de Seine gave a small retrospective showing of his work. It was astonishing to see that this little-known painter deserves to be included among the masters, in the finest collections of cubist works. The time has come for Paris to have a full retrospective of his work, along with a catalog that would showcase his talent.

* * *

North Africa in recent years has given us other Jewish painters whose work is clearly different from that of the Jewish painters in Poland or elsewhere. A native of Monastir in Tunisia, Jules Lellouche, who had a show a year ago at Tedesco Frères, is in a sense both Venetian and impressionist, always sensitive to plays of light, changing skies, and varying shades of color. An abstract painter, [Alex] Smadja comes to us from Mostaganem. Often exhibited at Simone Heller's gallery, he is inspired by cubist techniques rather than by Judeo-Arabic or Judeo-Berber calligraphies. In subject matter and coloring, Smadja remains nevertheless in some respect quite close to Atlan. [Armand] Assus, a painter from Algiers who is not well known in Paris, is perhaps too modest, whether in his faithfulness to a certain post-impressionist technique or in his choice of subjects, focusing primarily on local color. And lastly, my readers will perhaps reproach me for singing the praises once again of [Gilbert] Corsia, that veritable Van Gogh or Soutine from Oran whose work expresses all the sensuality and even sometimes the rather dubious taste of the Jewish "*pied noir*" whose roots are in Algeria. Let those whom I have yet to convince go immediately to the Katia Granoff gallery; there they will see some paintings by Corsia that are stunning successes. At the Galerie des Jeunes, on the corner of the Rue de l'Ancienne Comédie and the Rue Saint-André-des-Arts, a young sculptor from Oran, Shecroun, has just had his first show in Paris after having exhibited with several groups, including a show at the Salon de la Jeune Sculpture. Shecroun is not lacking in talent or ambition; for the present, however, we find too his work too often echoes that of sculptors who, for some time now, have been successful at a rather poignant art form, one that gives new life to scrap metal through the alchemy of autogenous welding.

Translated by Michele McKay Aynesworth.

Other works by Roditi: *Poems for F* (1937–1938); *Prison within Prison: Three Hebrew Elegies* (1941); *Oscar Wilde: A Critical Study* (1948); *Dialogues on Art* (1961); *New Hieroglyphic Tales* (1970); *Meetings with Conrad* (1977); *Choose Your Own World* (1992).

Louis Jacobs

1920–2006

Born in Manchester, England, Louis Jacobs studied at yeshivas in Manchester and Gateshead and later at University College London. After teaching at a London synagogue, he served as rabbi at Manchester's Central Synagogue from 1948 to 1954 and at London's New West End Synagogue from 1954 to 1959. From 1959 to 1962, as he was drifting away from strict Orthodoxy, he taught at Jews' College in London but resigned when he was blocked from succeeding Isidore Epstein as the school's principal. This bitter crisis was prompted in part by the 1957 publication of his book *We Have Reason to Believe*. In the aftermath of the crisis, he and some of his congregants broke away to found the New London Synagogue, the Masorti (Conservative) movement's flagship synagogue.

Principles of the Jewish Faith: An Analytical Study
1964

[. . . W]hile there are undoubtedly articles of faith in Judaism there are, nonetheless, fundamental differences between Judaism and Christianity in the matter of dogma. The first of these is due to the practical nature of Judaism. Since both Bible and *Talmud*, the classical sources of Judaism, are non-speculative in character, their influence militated against precise formulations of a Creed until comparatively late in the history of Judaism. Even when such formulations were made, they were the work of individual teachers, enjoying only the authority due to them by their learning. There was no Jewish "Church," no central authority whose opinion in this matter would be binding upon Jews, nothing corresponding to the Athanasian and Nicene Creeds of the Church. To conclude from this that Judaism is unconcerned with belief is erroneous, and much credit is due to Schechter and others who have pointed this out in emphatic terms. In the essay quoted Schechter rightly says: "We usually urge that in Judaism religion means life; but we forget that a life without guiding principles and thoughts is a life not worth living. At least it was so considered by the greatest Jewish thinkers, and hence their efforts to formulate the creed of Judaism, so that men should not only be able to do the right thing, but also to think the right thing. . . . Political economy, hygiene, statistics, are very fine things. But no sane man would for them make those sacrifices which Judaism requires from us. It is only for God's sake, to fulfil His commands and to accomplish His purpose, that religion becomes worth living and dying for. And this can only be possible with a religion which possesses dogmas."

Schechter's contribution here cannot be sufficiently praised. But it is a pity that he stopped there and made no attempt to describe for the modern Jew the dogmas Judaism requires him to accept. There is not really much point in emphasising both the historical significance of dogmas in Judaism and their importance for Jewish religion in the present unless the dogmas are defined. If it be granted that a religion without beliefs has neither salt nor savour, it is surely essential that we know what these beliefs are. Schechter's admission comes, therefore, as a shock: "But it was not my purpose to ventilate here the question whether Maimonides' articles are sufficient for us, or whether we ought to add new ones to them. Nor do I attempt to decide what system we ought to prefer for recitation in the Synagogue—that of Maimonides or that of Chasdai, or of any other writer. I do not think that such a recital is of much use. My object in this sketch has been rather to make the reader *think* about Judaism, by proving that it regulates not only our

actions, but also our thoughts." What Schechter gives with one hand he takes away with the other. It is well-nigh incredible that once Schechter's "old Adam" had asserted itself to point out that Judaism regulates our thoughts he should be content to stop short at even attempting to describe the kind of thoughts it seeks to regulate. The reader convinced by Schechter's powerful argument that there can be no living Judaism without articles of faith will be a poor sort of thinker if he is content to leave it at that. To say that there are dogmas in Judaism but we neither know or can know what they are is tantamount to saying that Judaism has no dogmas. The historical school has always been handicapped by its failure to build theologically on the very sure foundations its researches have uncovered. This has only too often meant that our theologians try to construct systems which have no historical basis while our historians are uninterested in the theological implications of their rediscovery of the Jewish past. Theology thus becomes divorced from historical reality and history of only antiquarian interest. The theologian takes refuge in his concept of "eternity" to ignore the time process. The historian refuses to consider metaphysics, as beyond his competence. In this "post-critical" age an attempt to formulate articles of faith for the modern Jew is one of the most important tasks facing thinkers who are not only historians but Jewish believers.

Other works by Jacobs: *Jewish Values* (1960); *Jewish Ethics, Philosophy, and Mysticism* (1969); *Modern Jewish Thought: Selected Issues, 1889–1966* (1973); *Hasidic Thought* (1976).

Georges Friedmann

1902–1977

Born in Paris to German parents, Georges Friedmann was educated at the Lycée Henri IV and later at the École normale supérieure. His primary intellectual interests—influenced by Marx, Leibniz, and Spinoza, among others—were philosophy, vocational education, and sociology. His sociological work was devoted primarily to the moral and physical effects of industrial mechanization on labor. He also took a lively interest in the Jewish people, traveling to Israel in 1965, where he wrote his *La Fin du peuple Juif?*, addressing the present and expected future problems of the Jewish people and Israel. He was active in the French resistance during World War II; his experiences were published posthumously.

The End of the Jewish People?
1965

Dialogue

At last you admit that Israel, caught up in the wave of technical progress, is becoming an industrial society "like the others." You find it acceptable that the Jews, transformed in the Promised Land into Israelis, pursuing comfort as a product of machines and mass culture, lose what is best in themselves, including the memory of their millenary restlessness.

How could you not see and, better still, proclaim that these "realistic" sabras, the native-born Israelis of whom you speak, have gone too far? If their views prevail, it is the end of everything that is precious and, I firmly believe, irreplaceable, in Judaism. But happily, your technocrats do not yet rule Israel, and if by misfortune they should come to power, all is not lost. Thanks to their historical circumstances, the Jews have always had among them good "detectives" of spiritual problems. Today in Israel itself, some are already saying, "This well-being, this affluence that those around us are chasing after, this technical progress that fascinates them, are means rather than ends." But means to what end?

The young state must confront good fortune. One finds less and less worry over material needs. The kibbutzim are increasingly comfortable places of quiet withdrawal, if not of retreat. The Histadrut trade union center will soon offer everyone the cradle-to-grave security of the welfare state. Anxiety is now focused on the settlement of new immigrants. And even that concern is relative and transitory.

Those who hoped that, once rid of their diasporic agonies, the Israelis would become idealistic missionaries, ready to work as "artisans and guardians of the universal doctrine of justice, charity, and peace,"[1] were, alas, greatly mistaken. Others, believing mass-produced well-being is the answer to Israel's spiritual crisis, are blind. Affluent society in the American or European vein will kill the spirit of Judaism as certainly as a new cult of idols. The vitality and fecundity of the Jewish spirit will fade away. Communities of "happy" people, shaped in Israel and in the diaspora by the environment of technical civilization, conditioned by it, having lost all prophetic drive, all trace of any messianic inspiration, will be no more than the corpse of Judaism. A Jew, sated with creature comforts and pushbutton amenities, put to sleep by the dull hum of prosperity, is no longer a Jew.

Your observation is not exact. We are not there yet. Travel through Israel. Visit their work sites, their new cities growing in the desert, their herculean efforts to irrigate the Negev, their mass immigrant housing, and observe the daily reality of hard, perilous labor in the new kibbutzim and moshavim on the frontiers. The Israelis are not yet dying of abundance. They are struggling to satisfy the basic needs of recent waves of immigrants and to push the Third World back beyond the borders of Israel. For that matter, by recognizing the signs of a new restlessness in certain Israelis, you yourself have shown that the march toward happiness has not entirely killed what you call the "Jewish spirit." You forget, especially, that from Dan to Eilat in Israel today there is a latent anxiety, however well mastered and suppressed: the Arab menace. Hatred of the state of Israel is inculcated every day into millions of men whose leaders proclaim the will to wipe Israel off the map, to annihilate the Jews in a fight that the latter (abandoned to themselves once again) must take up at odds of ten to one, and perhaps one day, twenty to one. Israel without anxiety! What a bitter joke!

And then, I reject your premise. Even in accepting technical progress and its material benefits, the Jews *need not* renounce what is best in themselves. Judaism in history has been perhaps a self-assumed tragedy. But I will never admit that from now on it can only endure as a tragedy desired by its people. Judaism, this rich, many-peopled ensemble, offers various currents: Pharisaism, so unjustly treated, Hasidism, which communicates with God in joy, the Davidic tradition, that symphonic opening toward happiness, life seized whole, tasted in all the splendor of the senses and the spirit. The embrace of misery, sadness, and self-withdrawal has been imposed on the Jews by history. [...]

Judaism is an accident of history, the spiritual fruits of which, for twenty-five centuries, have been purchased at a very high price, consisting of infinite sadness, misery, suffering, and blood. I find that price to be excessive, monstrous, no matter what arguments you put forward or the context in which you make them. I reject that price as vigorously as I reject your premise; happiness does not necessarily destroy what is precious and irreplaceable in the "Jewish spirit." [. . .]

Judaism is not an accident, but rather a metaphysical attribute essential to human history. Responses to it will, with superficial variations, be the same until the end of time. The Jews, exalted by what is best in them, must continue the mission given them on Mount Sinai: to act as priests and to serve all other peoples with justice and integrity. In this age of the atomic bomb, electronics, supersonic jets, and ballistic missiles, we must, as far as possible, preserve them biologically and protect them spiritually.

Let your lonely crowds—including Israel's own, if you insist—rush headlong toward what you call "happiness," let them lose themselves in it, lose themselves in the global marketplace as this century draws to a close and succumb to the frantic pace of "normalcy." But set aside some small place for our disquietude, our tragedy. Keep a few islands of Jewish anguish, at least in the diaspora, just as there are national sanctuaries protecting plant or animal species, the Creator's gifts that are threatened by mankind's stupid slaughters and the poisons of their cities. Maintain some fertile reserves of salutary anguish from which may burst forth the prophecies that are so needed in this world of technology, with its worship of new idols!

You are correct when you say we do not speak the same language. You have not understood me. You have not even noticed that anxiety is at the heart of this book.

NOTE

1. André Zaoui, *Le Figaro littéraire*, March 10, 1962.

Translated by Michele McKay Aynesworth.

Other works by Friedmann: *De la Sainte Russie à l'U.R.S.S.* (1938); *The Anatomy of Work: Labor, Leisure, and the Implications of Automation* (1961); *La Puissance et la sagesse* (1970); *Journal de guerre (1939–1940)* (1987).

Jean Améry

1912–1978

Born into a middle-class family in Vienna as Hans Mayer (the letters of his last name were later rearranged into Améry), Jean Améry published political and literary essays. In 1939, he escaped to Belgium and joined the Resistance. Arrested by the Gestapo for his anti-Nazi activities, Améry was tortured and then, after his Jewish lineage was discovered, interned at several concentration camps. Although he wrote comparatively little on his life during the Holocaust, his best-known work focuses on his experiences as a survivor. His deeply meditative essays and novels have been compared to the works of Primo Levi. Améry committed suicide in 1978.

On the Necessity and Impossibility of Being a Jew
1966

Not seldom, when in conversation my partner draws me into a plural—that is, as soon as he includes my person in whatever connection and says to me: "We Jews . . ."—I feel a not exactly tormenting, but nonetheless deep-seated discomfort. I have long tried to get to the bottom of this disconcerting psychic state, and it has not been very easy for me. Can it be, is it thinkable that I, the former Auschwitz inmate, who truly has not lacked occasion to recognize what he is and what he must be, still did not want to be a Jew, as decades ago, when I wore white half socks and leather breeches and nervously eyed myself in the mirror, hoping it would show me an impressive German youth? Naturally not. The foolishness of my masquerading in Austrian dress—although it was, after all, part of my heritage—belongs to the distant past. It is all right with me that I was not a German youth and am not a German man. No matter how the disguise may have looked on me, it now lies in the attic. If today discomfort arises in me when a Jew takes it for granted, legitimately, that I am part of his community, then it is not because I don't want to be a Jew, but only because I cannot be one. And yet must be one. And I do not merely submit to this necessity, but expressly claim it as part of my person. The necessity and impossibility of being a Jew, that is what causes me indistinct pain. It is with this necessity, this impossibility, this oppression, this inability that I must deal here, and in doing so I can only hope, without certainty, that my individual story is exemplary enough also to reach those who neither are nor have to be Jews.

First of all, concerning this impossibility. If being a Jew means sharing a religious creed with other Jews, participating in Jewish cultural and family tradition, cultivating a Jewish national ideal, then I find myself in a hopeless situation. I don't believe in the God of Israel. I know very little about Jewish culture. I see myself as a boy at Christmas, plodding through a snow-covered village to midnight mass; I don't see myself in a synagogue. I hear my mother appealing to Jesus, Mary, and Joseph when a minor household misfortune occurred; I hear no adjuration of the Lord in Hebrew. The picture of my father—whom I hardly knew, since he remained where his Kaiser had sent him and his fatherland deemed him to be in the safest care—did not show me a bearded Jewish sage, but rather a Tyrolean Imperial Rifleman in the uniform of the First World War. I was nineteen years old when I heard of the existence of a Yiddish language, although on the other hand I knew full well that my religiously and ethnically very mixed family was regarded by the neighbors as Jewish, and that no one in my home thought of denying or hiding what was unconcealable anyhow. I was a Jew, just as one of my schoolmates was the son of a bankrupt innkeeper: when the boy was alone the financial ruin of his family may have meant next to nothing to him; when he joined us others he retreated, as we did, into resentful embarrassment.

If being a Jew implies having a cultural heritage or religious ties, then I was not one and can never become one. Certainly, it could be argued that a heritage can be acquired, ties established, and that therefore to be a Jew could be a matter of voluntary decision. Who would possibly prevent me from learning the Hebrew language, from reading Jewish history and tales, and from participating—even without belief—in Jewish ritual, which is both religious and national? Well supplied with all the requisite knowledge of Jewish culture from the prophets to Martin Buber, I could emigrate to Israel and call myself Yochanan, I have the freedom to choose to be a Jew, and this freedom is my very personal and universally human privilege. That is what I am assured of.

But do I really have it? I don't believe so. Would Yochanan, the proud bearer of a new self-acquired identity, be made immune on the 24th of December by his supposedly thorough knowledge of chassidism against thoughts of a Christmas tree with gilded nuts? Would the upright Israeli, conversing fluently in Hebrew, be able so completely to obliterate the white-stockinged youth who once took such pains to speak a local dialect? In modern literature the switch of identity is quite a stimulating game, but in my case it is a challenge that one meets with no certainty of success, in one's human totality, without the chance of an interim solution, and would—it seems to me—be wholly predestined to fail. One can reestablish the link with a tradition that one

has lost, but one cannot freely invent it for oneself, that is the problem. Since I was not a Jew, I am not one; and since I am not one, I won't be able to become one. A Yochanan on Mt. Carmel, haunted and spirited home by memories of Alpine valleys and folk rituals, would be even more inauthentic than was once the youth with his knee socks. To be who one is by becoming the person one should be and wants to be: for me this dialectical process of self-realization is obstructed. Because being Something, not as metaphysical essence, but as the simple summation of early experience, absolutely has priority. Everyone must be who he was in the first years of his life, even if later these were buried under. No one can become what he cannot find in his memories.

Thus I am not permitted to be a Jew. But since all the same I must be one and since this compulsion excludes the possibilities that might allow me to be something other than a Jew, can I not find myself at all? Must I acquiesce, without a past, as a shadow of the universal-abstract (which does not exist) and take refuge in the empty phrase that I am simply a human being? But patience, we haven't reached that point yet. Since the necessity exists—and how compelling it is!—perhaps the impossibility can be resolved. After all, one wants to live without hiding, as I did when I was in the underground, and without dissolving into the abstract. A human being? Certainly, who would not want to be one. But you are a human being only if you are a German, a Frenchman, a Christian, a member of whatever identifiable social group. I must be a Jew and will be one, with or without religion, within or outside a tradition, whether as Jean, Hans, or Yochanan.

Translated by Sidney and Stella Rosenfeld.

Other works by Améry: *On Aging: Revolt and Resignation* (1968); *Unmeisterliche Wanderjahre* (1971).

Ignaz Maybaum

1897–1976

Born in Vienna, Ignaz Maybaum was a rabbi and influential theologian of post-Holocaust thought. A disciple of the philosopher Franz Rosenzweig, Maybaum received his rabbinical ordination in 1926. In 1935, he was arrested by the Gestapo and spent several weeks in prison, which led him to emigrate to the United Kingdom. He is best known for his controversial contributions to post-Holocaust theology. In his most widely read work, *The Face of God after Auschwitz* (1965), Maybaum theorized the Holocaust as a sign of the Jewish people's covenant with God, arguing that the Divine used European Jews as a sacrificial atonement for the sins of the rest of the world.

European Judaism
1966

Christianity and the cult of Mithras were once in a competition which made the outcome a fifty-fifty chance. Both appealed equally to the Roman soldier who had to fight the endless wars of the Roman Empire. The cross won, because of its message to a world of constant war. The message to the living was: somebody had to die that others may live. In the symbol of the tomb of the unknown soldier, the Cross is revived in modern form. The Christian consolation unites noble tragedy and martyrdom in the symbol of the Cross. To the world of antiquity which saw noble tragedy as the propriety of the hero, the *Akedah* has another message. In the *Akedah* Isaac is *not* sacrificed. The good life is "higher" life and yet not heroic. "God will wipe away the tears from off all faces" is the prophetic message to the mothers of heroes and martyrs: But God is most merciful when He does not allow tears to stain faces. God appears in the *Akedah* in his unlimited mercy, granting happiness to man. The Cross is not a picture of happiness; it is a symbol created to combine the holiness of martyrdom with the nobility of the tragic hero. . . .

The Eichmann trial [in Israel in 1961] and after it Hochhuth's play *The Representative* forced the world to ask: how could Auschwitz happen after two thousand years of Christianity—or better—in spite of two thousand years of Christianity? [. . .]

The reform visualized now by all Christian churches demands first of all the rejection of the doctrine which regards the Jew as an anti-Christian. Jews are non-Christians whom Christians have to acknowledge in their importance for themselves. That Jesus had a Jewish mother is a philosemitic statement but carries only weight within a dialogue in which both partners accept Christian imagery. The Jew does not do this; he has done for two thousand years what the Protestant professor of theology Rudolf Bultmann began to do only recently; he has "demythologized" the New Testament images. Jews are non-Christians; in this gentile world in which they are bidden by God to live as a dispersed people, Jews have a history to which the servant-of-God texts of the Book of Isaiah provide the pattern. In Auschwitz, I say in my sermons—and only in sermons is it appropriate to make such a statement—Jews suffered vicarious death for the sins of mankind. It says in the liturgy of the synagogue in reference to the first and second *hurbans*, albeit centuries after the events: "because of our sins." After Auschwitz Jews need not say so. Can any martyr be a more innocent sin-offering than those murdered in Auschwitz! The millions who died in Auschwitz died "because of the sins of others." Jews and non-Jews died in Auschwitz, but the Jew hatred which Hitler inherited from the medieval church made Auschwitz the twentieth-century Calvary of the Jewish people.

The fact that a liberal pope expunged an offensive phrase about the Jews from Christian liturgy should not be reported in a condescending way. It is a small matter and should only be a beginning. The reform through which the church will emancipate herself from her medieval blindness in regard to the synagogue will have to mean much more. Judaism is the seed, and Yehuda Halevi and Maimonides taught: out of this seed grows the tree, the church. The Golgotha of modern mankind is Auschwitz. The Cross, the Roman gallows, was replaced by the gas chamber. The gentiles, it seems, must first be terrified by the blood of the sacrificed scapegoat to have the mercy of God revealed to them and become converted, become baptized gentiles, become Christians.

Abraham saw the ram in the thicket and sacrificed it as ransom, whereas the gentiles of his time deemed it necessary to bring their human sacrifice to the Moloch. Abraham is above the belief of the gentiles. The Christian message contradicts the belief of the gentiles. But in the Christian contradiction the gentile belief survives. The message of the Cross contradicts the gentiles by telling them: your atoning sacrifice has been brought, it is there on the Cross, do not kill any more. Thus speaks the Cross to the gentiles who argue that the sacrifice is necessary, the sacrifice on the altar of the Moloch. The Jewish message is: atonement is necessary but is possible without sacrifice. What about our sins? On the Day of Atonement the Jewish liturgy announces: "All the people did it—*bish'gagah*—in error." Never can God's love be better preached than in the message of His forgiveness which we receive without having to buy it by any sacrifice. The great sermon of the love of God is unsurpassably preached in the *Akedah*, the 22nd chapter of Genesis, in the book which the church calls the "Old" Testament.

Besides the *Akedah* we read in the Old Testament of the "servant of God." The expression the "suffering servant of God" does not occur in the Hebrew text and is already a Christian exegesis of this text. Abraham, the patriarch, the happy husband and father, the figure which seems to Christian eyes a "bourgeois" figure, any prophet, that prophet, too, who has no other name than "servant of God," each one of them is a human person and no more, but also no less. None of them offers himself as a mediator between God and man. Each one of them invites man himself to meet God, in happiness like Abraham or, in the hour of martyrdom, like the "servant" of the Book of Isaiah. Of the martyr-servant it is written: "Behold, My servant shall succeed, he shall be exalted and lifted up, and shall be very high" (52:13). Happiness surrounded Abraham when he left Moriah. Those who died in the gas chambers are also granted—happiness. Leo Baeck when he came out from the hell of Terezin whence the trainloads of Jews moved to Auschwitz brought with him a message in which he interpreted the Book of Daniel. In this book the author, a Jew who lived at the time of the religious persecution through Antiochus, asked: what happens to those who die and will not see the liberation, soon and surely to come? The answer was we do not die into the grave, we die into the eternity of God.

NOTE
[Words in brackets appear in the original source document.—Eds.]

Other works by Maybaum: *Parteibefreites Judentum* (1935); *Man and Catastrophe* (1941); *Synagogue and Society: Jewish-Christian Collaboration in the Defence of Western Civilization* (1944); *Jewish Existence* (1960); *The Faith of the Jewish Diaspora* (1962).

George Steiner

1929–2020

A cultural and literary critic, essayist, translator, and philosopher, Paris-born George Steiner gained American citizenship and later became professor of comparative literature at Geneva and Cambridge universities. His writings address translation, the natures of language and literature, and culture.

A Kind of Survivor
1966

For Elie Wiesel

Not literally. Due to my father's foresight (he had shown it when leaving Vienna in 1924), I came to America in January 1940, during the phony war. We left France, where I was born and brought up, in safety. So I happened not to be there when the names were called out. I did not stand in the public square with the other children, those I had grown up with. Or see my father and mother disappear when the train doors were torn open. But in another sense I am a survivor, and not intact. If I am often out of touch with my own generation, if that which haunts me and controls my habits of feeling strikes many of those I should be intimate and working with in my present world as remotely sinister and artificial, it is because the black mystery of what happened in Europe is to me indivisible from my own identity. Precisely because I was not there, because an accident of good fortune struck my name from the roll. [. . .]

Nevertheless, the sense I have of the Jew as a man who looks on his children with a dread remembrance of helplessness and an intimation of future, murderous possibility, is a very personal, isolated one. It does not relate to much that is now alive and hopeful. But it is not wholly negative either. I mean to include in it far more than the naked precedent of ruin. That which has been destroyed—the large mass of life so mocked, so hounded to oblivion that even the names are gone and the prayer for the dead can have no exact foothold—embodied a particular genius, a quality of intelligence and feeling which none of the major Jewish communities now surviving has preserved or recaptured. Because I feel that specific inheritance urgent in my own reflexes, in the work I try to do, I am a kind of survivor.

In respect of *secular* thought and achievement, the period of Jewish history which ended at Auschwitz surpassed even the brilliant age of coexistence in Islamic Spain. During roughly a century, from the emancipation of the ghettos by the French Revolution and Napoleon to the time of Hitler, the Jew took part in the moral, intellectual, and artistic noon of bourgeois Europe. The long confinement of the ghetto, the sharpening of wit and nervous insight against the whetstone of persecution, had accumulated large reserves of consciousness. Released into the light, a certain Jewish elite, and the wider middle-class circle which took pride and interest in its accomplishments, quickened and complicated the entire contour of Western thought. To every domain they brought radical imaginings; more specifically, the more gifted Jews repossessed certain crucial elements of classic European civilization in order to make them new and problematic. All this is commonplace; as is the inevitable observation that the tenor of modernity, the shapes of awareness and query by which we order our lives are, in substantial measure, the work of Marx, Freud, and Einstein. [. . .]

Nationalism is the venom of our age. It has brought Europe to the edge of ruin. It drives the new states of Asia and Africa like crazed lemmings. By proclaiming himself a Ghanaean, a Nicaraguan, a Maltese, a man spares himself vexation. He need not ravel out what he is, where his humanity lies. He becomes one of an armed, coherent pack. Every mob impulse in modern politics, every totalitarian design, feeds on nationalism, on the drug of hatred which makes human beings bare their teeth across a wall, across ten yards of waste ground. Even if it be against his harried will, his weariness, the Jew—or some Jews, at least—may have an exemplary role. To show that whereas trees have roots, men have legs and are each other's guests. If the potential of civilization is not to be destroyed, we shall have to develop more complex, more provisional loyalties. There are, as Socrates taught, necessary treasons to make the city freer and more open to man. Even a Great Society is a bounded, transient thing of the mind and the anarchic discipline of its dreams. [. . .]

That is why I have not, until now, been able to accept the notion of going to live in Israel. The State of Israel is, in one sense, a sad miracle. Herzl's Zionist program bore the obvious marks of the rising nationalism of the late nineteenth century. Sprung of inhumanity and the imminence of massacre, Israel has had to make itself a closed fist. No one is more tense with national feeling than an Israeli. He must be if his strip of home is to survive the wolf-pack at its doors. Chauvinism is almost the requisite condition of life. But although the strength of Israel reaches deep into the awareness of every Jew, though the survival of the Jewish people may depend on it, the nation-state bristling with arms is a bitter relic, an absurdity in the century of crowded men. And it is alien to some of the most radical, most humane elements in the Jewish spirit.

Other works by Steiner: *Tolstoy or Dostoevsky: An Essay in the Old Criticism* (1959); *The Death of Tragedy* (1961); *After Babel: Aspects of Language and Translation* (1975).

Raymond Aron
1905–1983

Political scientist, sociologist, journalist, and philosopher Raymond Aron was born into a secular Jewish family in Paris. From 1930 to 1933, he lived in Germany, lecturing at the University of Cologne and studying in Berlin. He left Germany with a deep distaste for totalitarianism, which would later shape his response to Stalinism. During World War II, he served with the French air force, and followed the Free French forces to London, where he edited *La France libre*. Although he was a socialist in his youth, his best-known work, *The Opium of the Intellectuals*, criticized the French Left for overlooking totalitarianism in communist regimes. At the time, Aron's ideas were unpopular, but as the atrocities committed by Stalin came to light, his work came to be considered prophetic.

De Gaulle, Israel, and the Jews
1967

No Jew, whether a believer or an unbeliever, Zionist or anti-Zionist, can be objective when what is at stake is Israel and the two and a half million Jews who built a State in a land equally Holy for the faithful of the three great religions of the Book.

I am what is known as an "assimilated Jew." As a child I wept over France's disasters at Waterloo or Sedan, but not as I listened to the account of the destruction of the Temple. The only flag and the only national anthem that will bring tears to my eyes are the tricolour and the *Marseillaise*. It was Hitler, almost forty years ago now, who revealed my "Jewishness" to me. Come what may I have striven to assume it, which simply means never to conceal it. As I see it, there is neither dishonour nor glory in being a Jew, I am neither ashamed nor proud of it; nor do I have the right to put humanity in the dock, or at least no more so than any man of feeling, just because I survived the Final Solution. [. . .]

For my own part, I can see three sorts of anti-semite, whom I shall call "religious," "political" and "affective." Jules Isaac, rightly in my view, saw in religious anti-semitism, that which denounces the people of deicides, the origin of all the others. Christians have helped to propagate it because, in their eyes, the Jews are unbelievers; they did not recognize Christ and continue to adhere to the Law, although for the past two thousand years this has been saved and superseded by the Gospels.

"Political" anti-semitism is the one which refuses Jews equal status as citizens, and a full and complete share in the rights and obligations of citizenship. Maurras's State anti-semitism belonged in this category. Maurras would neither have ordered nor approved the mass executions of Jews, but, according to his teachings, he would have established a *numerus clausus*, forbidding Jews to exercise certain professions or to succeed to certain positions.

This political anti-semitism invokes various arguments which all come back to the "otherness" of Jewish life in relation to the national life (French or German). Maurras, who was not a racialist, saw the Jews as always representing an alien element in the body of the nation. Some hold that assimilation of the Jews *qua* Jews is still insufficient but not ultimately impossible, others hold it to be excluded once and for all; some denounce their cosmopolitanism, others their alien nationalism, others again their meanness, innate or acquired.

With these last we come to "affective" anti-semitism; hatred or contempt felt towards the Jews as a collectivity. It goes without saying that such feelings may be determined by the most varied causes. It is possible to study in each particular case the circumstances in which the "affective" anti-semitism of this or that individual or group has originated, but such a study only touches on the external conditions of an "existential" choice, it only encompasses the last stage of an age-old phenomenon: the exclusion from the common lot of communities that have not remained merely religious ones and which are not organized politically.

The racialism of Hitler partook of all three of these categories. But a biological philosophy turned hatred into a murdering fury. It was not enough for Hitler and his like to hound out the Jews, as the political anti-semites would have done, or to portray them in hideous colours as the affective anti-semites do, they needed to exterminate them as a noxious species, not because they had crucified the Messiah but perhaps because Christ had come from their race.

To my mind, what I have written here does not contain a conclusion. I would be angry with myself if I fixed or claimed to have fixed the responsibility of either side in this tragic story. Everything has already been said and repeated ad infinitum about the contradictions of the Jewish consciousness, and the paradox of believers who love the God of all mankind yet maintain they are the chosen people. For my own part, I re-read Spinoza's *Tractatus Theologico-Politicus*; I believe "that nations are different one from another, I mean in respect of their social system and of the laws under which they live and govern themselves," but that "everyone, Gentile as much as Jew, has lived under the Law, by which I mean that which alone is concerned with true virtue, not that which is established in respect of each State." More than ever I believe that "in respect of understanding and of true virtue, no nation has been made any different from another, and so, in this respect, there is no nation which God has chosen in preference to others. . . . Today, therefore, there is absolutely nothing which the Jews can claim for themselves which would set them above all other nations." Nothing, I would add, except misfortune, and nothing which would set them below other nations either.

I shall never be a militant in the anti-anti-semitic organizations. It is not for us Jews to boast about our virtues or denounce those who do not like us. As an individual, I claim the right to be a Frenchman without betraying my ancestors, to have a country without giving up my religion, even if, in point of fact, I no longer adhere to it. The rest does not depend on me, the rest does not depend on us.

At the conclusion of his essay on the Jewish question, Jean-Paul Sartre quotes the Negro writer Richard Wright, who said: "There is no black problem in the United States, there is only a white problem." Sartre adds: "Similarly, we shall say that anti-semitism is not a Jewish problem, it is our problem." [. . .]

I am a citizen of France and not of Israel. I am not a believer, at least in the common sense of that word. As Spinoza said, I cannot believe that God has ever concluded a pact with any people as such. A people draws nearer to God in so far as it overcomes its tribal pride and conforms to the commandments of the law or of love. Everyone has the right to his own country, and it is natural to be attached to a group. But the group that believes it has a divine mission is the one most lacking in the religious spirit (as I conceive of it, naturally). Judaism includes both nationalism and universalism, and it is the second which seems to me to answer to the genuine vocation of Judaism and of all religions of salvation. The building of a State in Palestine which proclaims itself to be continuing the Kingdom of Judah, seems to me a historical accident to which only the idolator, who accords a supreme value to the nation, will lend a truly religious meaning.

For all Jews, the State of Israel represents a great event in secular history. It cannot but arouse strong feelings in all of us.

A Jew, even if he has lost his faith, cannot be indifferent to Israel's fate. Personally, I have been deeply affected by what Arthur Koestler (not without having analysed it rationally) called a "miracle," and what I would call the epic story of the pioneers of Israel. Whatever happens in the future, the Israelis won their independence in the "war of liberation," and they are protecting it jealously thanks to the strength of their army, which is constantly on the alert; they have achieved great military renown. They have offered hundreds of thousands of Jews a refuge. They have changed the image that non-Jews had of Jews. They have proved that Jews could once again, as in the days of the Roman Empire, win a reputation for martial valour. From many points of view, what the Jews have done in Israel does credit to Judaism and to the human race as a whole.

But Israel would not belong to secular history if she were not stamped with the imperfections of all human creations. Or rather, as the expression of a paradoxical history, she remains oddly paradoxical herself. The land for the State of Israel was bought in the first place from its Muslim owners with money collected by the Jews of the diaspora; the flight of the Muslims at the start of the "war of liberation" enabled them to take possession of a territory containing the Holy Places of the three religions of salvation. The Israelis assert, rightly, that they did not chase the Muslims out, but that they left hoping to return victorious. But these vicissitudes matter less in Arab eyes than one brutal fact: the Muslims, who had been settled in Palestine for more than ten centuries, had to make way for Jews claiming to be reviving the tradition of the Kingdom of Judah.

Translated by John Sturrock.

Other works by Aron: *Les Guerres en chaîne* (1951); *La Tragédie algérienne* (1957); *Paix et guerre entre les nations* (1962); *La Révolution introuvable* (1968); *République impériale: Les États-Unis dans le monde, 1945–1972* (1973).

Jacques Derrida

1930–2004

Born and raised in El Biar, Algeria, Jacques Derrida was a French philosopher and an influential founder of deconstructionism. After French military service, he studied at the École normale supérieure in Paris and then at Harvard University. From 1960 to 1964 he

was a lecturer at the Sorbonne and from 1964 to 1984 he taught at the École normale supérieure. In 1983, he cofounded the Collège international de philosophie. Writing on Edmond Jabès enabled Derrida to theorize on their common Jewish heritage.

Edmond Jabès and the Question of the Book
1967

Our rereadings of *Je bâtis ma demeure*[1] will be better, henceforth. A certain ivy could have hidden or absorbed its meaning, could have turned its meaning in on itself. Humor and games, laughter and dances, songs, circled graciously around a discourse which, as it did not yet love its true root, bent a bit in the wind. Did not yet stand upright in order to enunciate only the rigor and rigidity of poetic obligation.

In *Le livre des questions*[2] the voice has not been altered, nor the intention abandoned, but the accent is more serious. A powerful and ancient root is exhumed, and on it is laid bare an ageless wound (for what Jabès teaches us is that roots speak, that words want to grow, and that poetic discourse *takes root* in a wound): in question is a certain Judaism as the birth and passion of writing. The passion *of* writing, the love and endurance of the letter itself whose subject is not decidably the Jew or the Letter itself. Perhaps the common root of a people and of writing. In any event, the incommensurable destiny which grafts the history of a

> *race born of the book*
>
> (*Livre des questions*, p. 26)

onto the radical origin of meaning as literality, that is, onto historicity itself. For there could be no history without the gravity and labor of literality. The painful folding of itself which permits history to reflect itself as it ciphers itself. This reflection is its beginning. The only thing that begins by reflecting itself is history. And this fold, this furrow, is the Jew. The Jew who elects writing which elects the Jew, in an exchange responsible for truth's thorough suffusion with historicity and for history's *assignment* of itself to its empiricity.

> *Difficulty of being a Jew, which coincides with the difficulty of writing; for Judaism and writing are but the same waiting, the same hope, the same depletion.*
>
> (Ibid., p. 132)

The exchange between the Jew and writing as a pure and founding exchange, an exchange without prerogatives in which the original appeal is, in another sense of the word, a *convocation*—this is the most persistent affirmation of the *Livre des questions*:

You are he who writes and is written.

. . .

And Reb Ilde: "What difference is there between choosing and being chosen when we can do nothing but submit to the choice?"

(Ibid., p. 30)

And through a kind of silent displacement toward the essential which makes of this book one long metonymy, the situation of the Jew becomes exemplary of the situation of the poet, the man of speech and of writing. The poet, in the very experience of his freedom, finds himself both bound to language and delivered from it by a speech whose master, nonetheless, he himself is.

Words choose the poet. . . .
The art of the writer consists in little by little making words interest themselves in his books.

(*Je bâtis ma demeure*)

In question is a labor, a deliverance, a slow gestation of the poet by the poem whose father he is.

Little by little the book will finish me.

(*L'espace blanc*)³

The poet is thus indeed the *subject* of the book, its substance and its master, its servant and its theme. And the book is indeed the subject of the poet, the speaking and knowing being who *in* the book writes *on* the book. This movement through which the book, *articulated* by the voice of the poet, is folded and bound to itself, the movement through which the book becomes a subject in itself and for itself, is not critical or speculative reflection, but is, first of all, poetry and history. For in its representation of itself the subject is shattered and opened. Writing is itself written, but also ruined, made into an abyss, in its own representation. Thus, within this book, which infinitely reflects itself and which develops as a painful questioning of its own possibility, the form of the book represents itself:

The novel of Sarah and Yukel, through various dialogues and meditations attributed to imaginary rabbis, is the story of a love destroyed by men and by words. It has the dimensions of a book and the bitter obstinacy of a wandering question.

(*Livre des questions*, p. 26)

We will see that by another direction of metonymy—but to what extent is it other?—the *Livre des questions* describes the generation of God himself. The wisdom of the poet thus culminates its freedom in the passion of translating obedience to the law of the word into autonomy. Without which, and if passion becomes subjection, the poet is mad.

The madman is the victim of the rebellion of words.

(*Je bâtis ma demeure*)

Also, through his understanding of this assignment of the root, and through the inspiration he receives from this injunction of the Law, Jabès perhaps has renounced the *verve*, that is, the *capriciousness* of the early works; but he has in no way given up his freedom of speech. He has even acknowledged that freedom must belong to the earth, to the root, or it is merely wind:

A teaching that Reb Zale translated with this image: "You think that it is the bird who is free. You are deceived; it is the flower. . . ."
And Reb Lima: "Freedom is awakened little by little, in the extent to which we become aware of our ties, like the sleeper of his senses; then our acts finally have a name."

(Ibid., p. 124)

Freedom allies and exchanges itself with that which restrains it, with everything it receives from a buried origin, with the gravity which situates its center and its site. A site whose cult is not necessarily pagan. Provided that this Site is not a site, an enclosure, a place of exclusion, a province or a ghetto. When a Jew or a poet proclaims the Site, he is not declaring war. For this site, this land, calling to us from beyond memory, is always elsewhere. The site is not the empirical and national Here of a territory. It is immemorial, and thus also a future. Better: it is tradition as adventure. Freedom is granted to the nonpagan Land only if it is separated from freedom by the Desert of the Promise. That is, by the Poem. When it lets itself be articulated by poetic discourse, the Land always keeps itself beyond any proximity, *illic*:

Yukel, you have always been ill at ease with yourself, you are never HERE,
but ELSEWHERE . . .

(Ibid., p. 33)

What are you dreaming of?—The Land.—But you are on land.—I am dreaming of the Land where I will be.—But we are right in front of each other. And we have our feet on land.—I know only the stones of the way which leads, as it is said, to the Land.

The Poet and the Jew are not born *here* but *elsewhere.* They wander, separated from their true birth. Autochthons only of speech and writing, of Law. *"Race born of the book"* because sons of the Land to come.

Autochthons of the Book. Autonomous too, as we said. Which assumes that the poet does not simply receive his speech and his law from God. Judaic heteronomy has no need of a poet's intercession. Poetry is to prophecy what the idol is to truth. It is perhaps for this reason that in Jabès the poet and the Jew seem at once so united and disunited, and that the entire *Livre des questions* is also a self-justification addressed to the Jewish community which lives under heteronomy and to which the poet does not truly belong. Poetic autonomy, comparable to none other, presupposes broken Tables.

NOTES

1. [Edmond Jabès. *Je bâtis ma demeure: Poèmes, 1943–1957* (Paris: Gallimard, 1959).]

2. [Edmond Jabès. *Le Livre des questions* (Paris: Gallimard, 1963).]

3. [Edmond Jabès. *Le Livre des questions, II: Le Livre de Yukel* (Paris: Gallimard, 1964), p. 32.]

Translated by Alan Bass.

Other works by Derrida: *De la grammatologie* (1967); *L'Écriture et la différence* (1967); *La Dissémination* (1972); *Marges de la philosophie* (1972).

Jean-François Steiner

b. 1938

A journalist, novelist, and academic, Jean-François Steiner was born in Paris. His father, the Zionist journalist and activist Isaac Kadmi Cohen, died in Auschwitz; Steiner took the last name of his stepfather. Steiner is best known for the "nonfiction novel" *Treblinka: The Revolt of an Extermination Camp*, a first-person account (ghostwritten by Gilles Perrault) of the 1943 uprising in the death camp, which sparked controversy and outrage by taking the stance that Jewish inmates had been complicit in their own deaths and in its presentation of a fictionalized account as if it were documentary history. Steiner again courted controversy during the 1980s by defending Maurice Papon, a government minister accused and later con-

victed of supervising the deportation of French Jews as a Vichy police official. Steiner's academic research focuses on quantitative approaches to semiotics.

Treblinka
1967

Was there an element of cowardice in the attitude of the Jewish masses, who preferred to suffer the worst degradation rather than revolt? Given the terrible conditions created by the fierce anti-Semitism of the local population and by the science of the Technicians, the masses had little incentive to resist. A revolt in the name of the honor of the Jewish people, which the young Zionists urged, did not touch the deepest chords in them: the people of the Bible placed their self-respect on an infinitely higher level. But revolt may also be born of despair, of the feeling that there is nothing left, that life has lost its meaning. In this case it is no longer a revolt for the sake of something, some ideal or other, but a revolt against nothingness. But the Jew, the real Jew, raised only on Jewish culture, though he may be susceptible to anguish, is inaccessible to despair. [. . .]

Adolf ran his eyes slowly over the barracks, which was almost entirely consumed by darkness.

"You think they won't follow us if we revolt when the Germans come for us?"

"I am sure of it," replied Galewski with recovered assurance. "Something has been broken in them which it would have taken a very long time to put back together. They are alive only by virtue of an old ancestral reflex, but unconsciously they are ashamed not to have died with their families. That is the extraordinary power of the Nazi system. Like certain spiders, it puts its victims to sleep before killing them. It is a death in two stages: you put men to sleep, then you kill the sleepers. This may seem very complicated, but actually it was the only way. Suppose that the S.S. had arrived announcing that they were going to kill us all, swearing it, starting to prove it. There is no doubt at all that the three million Polish Jews would have revolted. They would have done it with their backs to the wall, with the courage of despair. And it wouldn't have taken a few thousand men to beat us, but the whole Wehrmacht—and even then it isn't certain that all the soldiers would have obeyed! Then look at *us!* Not only do the Jews let themselves be killed without a gesture of revolt, but they even help their killers with their work of extermination. We, the accomplices, the employees of death, live in a world beyond life and death; compromised so profoundly that we can only be ashamed to be alive."

"Monsters, in short?"

"Yes, a new species of men in keeping with this new world."

Translated by Helen Weaver.

Other works by Steiner: *Les Métèques* (1970) ; *Si Paris . . .* (1970); *Varsovie 44, l'insurrection* (1975); *La Sémiométrie—essai de statistique structurale* (2003).

Zygmunt Bauman

1925-2017

Born in Poznań, Poland, sociologist Zygmunt Bauman left Poland in 1971 after renewed antisemitic campaigns. Bauman was professor emeritus of sociology at the University of Leeds. His scholarship illuminates the Holocaust, modern life, politics, and contemporary society.

On Frustrations and Prestidigitators
1968

For the role of scapegoat, the prestidigitators chose Jews.

Rattling around in the recesses of their memory were recollections about how prewar governments in Poland had enjoyed the sympathy of the people, that they had owed it, among other reasons, to the "resonance" of their politics with the anti-Jewish moods of certain branches of society. The authorities in today's Poland may have believed that in 1968 the Polish people are "spontaneously and universally" antisemitic and that anti-Jewish slogans guarantee the government popular sympathy.[1] This calculation was wrong. If for "popular" antisemitism in prewar Poland there really were economic factors in the shape of, say, a competitive struggle for market stalls, for a share of the measly sums intended to support healthy needs in the secondary division of national income, or in the form of the peasant's struggle against his exploitation by the wholesale grain dealer, in postwar Poland nothing of that sort exists. The majority of today's Polish peasants and workers have not seen a live Jew, and twenty years of indoctrination with socialist slogans have not passed without leaving some trace. In 1968, antisemitism in Poland is an artificially constructed phenomenon, prepared from the top down, and finding its echo only in one class of

society—the new middle class—and that only in recognition of the fact that for this class "anti-Zionism" and antisemitic allusions are but a label, a euphemistic name for entirely different matters which are directly linked to the interests, in no way national, of a certain part of that class. The antisemitic coloration of the post-March events in Poland is not in any degree the result of a spontaneous reaction of the people. It is an affair designed by the organizers of the provocation for which only they bear responsibility.

If, however, the provocateurs' calculations about the "popular character" of Polish antisemitism were mistaken, this does not mean that Polish Jews did not possess a couple of essential characteristics that predestined them for the role of scapegoat.

According to contemporary psychological theories, a candidate for scapegoat must meet at least three requirements: (a) it must be sufficiently weak so as to make it possible safely to dump aggressive impulses on it; (b) it must be sufficiently strong so that victory over it will return a sense of one's own value and be a cause for pride; (c) finally, it must stand in logical or quasi-logical connection with a familiar stereotype of the causes of frustration. To a certain extent, Polish Jews possessed all three of these characteristics. First, they were weak—twenty-five thousand in the bosom of a nation of thirty million; furthermore, they were dispersed, deeply rooted in Polish society and culture and yet not connected in the consciousness of the national community nor, more importantly, joined with organizational ties. Second, they were strong, as official propaganda, armed with "secret" documents, demonstrated eagerly and with an enormous expenditure of effort; they were, after all, a branch of the powerful mafia allied with the Bonn devil and secretly in control of the United States Senate, the Pentagon, and the world-wide means of mass media at the head of which stand Radio Free Europe and *Kultura* in Paris. So, at a public meeting, maligning an intimidated bureaucrat with threadbare elbows on his jacket sleeves to the accompaniment of a hysterical mob, they could effect the blessed sense that the hundred-headed hydra smothering the fatherland was being routed and annihilated. Third, and finally, without particular difficulty it was possible to link Polish Jews with Soviet influences in Poland, since it is true that the majority of the Jews remaining in Poland clearly sided with the communist governments. Thus, Moczar was able to speak in his press interview about "politicians, who in officers' overcoats came from the East," winking slyly at the reader: "I know and you understand that we're talking about Jews here, but it's about an entirely different matter, heh heh . . ." With considerably greater effort it was possible to unload on the Jews anti-bigwig feelings and, especially, egalitarian claims. Here, however, propaganda tried too hard, immediately inventing fairy tales about the Canary Islands, creating the unfortunate "Babel" dance hall for the role played by Masonic Lodges as the prewar "bogeymen," and at workers' meetings arranging banners whose physical proximity was intended to suggest a cause-and-effect connection: "Children of workers and peasants to institutions of higher education!" and "Cleanse the institutions of higher education of Zionists!"

But all of this together only explains why within the framework of the post-March coup this particular sign was employed to advance their practical strategies and not some other sign, code, or label. The choice of the code was a secondary problem in comparison with what they really desired to accomplish in the sphere not so much of social consciousness as of the actual system of power. I even think that certain elements in the party leadership, still devoted to the old communist slogans, accepted the label that was put forward with reluctance and procrastination, feeling revulsion at the price that would have to be paid for using it as a way of dealing with the social protest and at the havoc it would wreak in the nation's consciousness. The Jewish problem in the post-March coup was only a tool. Its goal was something else: overpowering a potential opposition, crushing the remaining centers where independent socialist thought was crystallizing, intimidating those who resisted and emboldening the cowardly zealots who were burning to take action, and regaining the most important foundation of power, support from the new middle class. That is what it was about, and deflecting the attention of world public opinion from this main goal with the help of the smokescreen of antisemitism was just one more prestidigitator's trick by the authors of the March provocation. The choice they made of the label is not, of course, a matter of indifference and in and of itself must arouse a lively moral opposition.

They are saying that today the party authorities are yearning to "put an end to the struggle with Zionism," but "the masses" (this is a euphemistic term for designating lower-ranking party functionaries who are the public during "the leaders' conversations with the people") demand the continuation of the struggle and desire the punishment of those guilty of its prema-ture slowdown. This means that the new middle class, and particularly its most frustrated outsider elements, were disenchanted with the paltriness of the mice that the mountain of blustering post-March propaganda spawned. The miserably few profitable positions for those yearning to advance had slowed down, there were no additional places at the trough, the demands for diplomas had not ceased, self-confidence had not increased even one iota. The "masses" don't want to be satisfied with a label, they desire the entire bottle with its entire contents. How to urge back into the bottle the carelessly-freed genie—that is the problem that the authors of the March provocation will have to wrack their brains over in the coming months. A new scapegoat is the necessity of the moment. Has a tempting name for it already been dreamed up?

If the true masses of the people are not already disenchanted with the post-March coup it is only because they never expected much from it. The children of workers and peasants did not fill the university halls even though the Zionists were driven out from them. "The struggle against the bigwigs" turned out to be a battle with only a couple of specific dignitaries. Installment payments are increasing and not decreasing, and the contents of the basket continue to shrink just as they shrank before. Thus, whoever had reasons for frustration has them still. Only, for the time being the real masses are not "putting pressure on the authorities" and are not demanding the punishment of anyone. After the murder committed in cold blood against Czechs who were guilty of a love of freedom, the real masses won't soon begin to exert pressure and make demands.

NOTE

1. [In March 1968, student-led demonstrations calling for liberalization and more democracy broke out in Warsaw. Many of the ringleaders were of Jewish origin, and the Polish Communist Party boss Wladyslaw Gomulka then began an antisemitic purge that led to the emigration of twenty thousand Jews, including many members of the country's cultural elite.—Eds.]

Translated by Madeline G. Levine.

Other works by Bauman: *Socjologia na co dzień* (1964); *Kultura a społeczeństwo* (1966); *Culture as Praxis* (1973).

Boris Kochubiyevsky

b. 1936

Boris Lvovich Kochubiyevsky was born in Kiev and orphaned at age five when his parents were murdered in the Babi Yar massacre. Kochubiyevsky essentially grew up Soviet, without Jewish identity and knowledge. He became an engineer and worked at a Soviet radio factory in Kiev. In 1967, in response to the Six-Day War, Kochubiyevsky contested a "unanimous" motion condemning "Israeli aggression" put forward during a factory meeting, demanding to be put on record as dissenting. After his forced resignation, Kochubiyevsky wrote an essay entitled "Why I Am a Zionist" and applied to leave the Soviet Union. His application was rejected; he was tried for slander and sentenced to three years of forced labor. Upon his release, Kochubiyevsky reapplied and was able to immigrate to Israel.

The Case of Boris Kochubiyevsky
1969

On May 13–16th, 1969, the Kiev Regional Court examined the case of Boris Kochubiyevsky, accused under article 187-1 of the Ukrainian Criminal Code, which corresponds to article 190-1 of the Russian. Kochubiyevsky was charged with making statements on the position of the Jews in the U.S.S.R. Of the charges described in Chronicle No. 6 the speech Kochubiyevsky made at the lecture on Israel's "aggression" in the Six-Day War did not figure in the indictment. The court found him guilty, and Kochubiyevsky was sentenced to three years in ordinary-régime camps.

Kochubiyevsky pleaded not guilty. He denied that his statements had been untrue, and said that even if some of them might be found to be untrue, they were not deliberate untruth, since he had been convinced of the truth of his words when he spoke them. The Procurator objected on this point: "You have received higher education, passed graduate examinations in philosophy, you are acquainted with the Constitution of the U.S.S.R., and therefore you could not fail to know that in our country none of the things you spoke about can exist." This formula, in almost identical wording, was included in the verdict as proof of the deliberate untruth of Kochubiyevsky's statements.

On one of the main charges in the indictment, concerning Baby Yar, eight witnesses appeared, only three of whom reinforced the prosecution's case. Kochubiyevsky asked one of the three, Rabinovich, how he came to be in Baby Yar. Rabinovich replied that he had been looking for a shop and arrived there accidentally. The court rejected the evidence of the defence wit-

nesses, stating that all five of them were friends of the accused and had without exception supported the accused's "Zionist views" in court.

Both Judge and Procurator constantly used the clichés "Zionist" and "Zionist views," in spite of the fact that Kochubiyevsky categorically objected to this. To take a specific example, the Procurator asked: "And have you thought what you've done to your wife? You've infected this sweet young Russian girl with your Zionist views."

Here are two more examples of the logic of the prosecution:

PROCURATOR: You know what we were fighting against?
KOCHUBIYEVSKY: Fascism.
P: And what were we fighting for? Was it freedom?
K: Yes.
P: Did we win?
K: Yes.
P: Well, there you are, then, we have freedom.
JUDGE (or PROCURATOR): I know you will claim there is anti-semitism here, in view of the fact that there are 200,000 Jews in the Ukraine, but no Jewish schools, newspapers or theatres.
KOCHUBIYEVSKY: Yes, and that too.
J: But you know very well that here they don't all live together, they are scattered.
K: But in Canada there is a smaller Ukrainian population, yet they have their own papers, schools and theatres.
J: But what comparisons are you making? I mean, they live in a bourgeois state, they still have to win their freedom!

It is not an accident that no one could remember if it was the Judge or the Procurator who conducted this dialogue. The Judge on the whole behaved more like a spokesman for the prosecution; his manner was much more aggressive than that of the relatively mild Procurator. He kept interrupting the accused, and mocking him; he wrapped up the unsympathetic elements among the public to make hostile remarks, and all the while he did not once call the public to order. All he did was to drop a gentle hint at one point to the effect that he disapproved of comments from the public benches.

Present in the courtroom were the relatives of the accused, and, after giving evidence, the witnesses. The remaining seats were occupied by the "public," amongst whom several K.G.B. men were spotted. When people asked the policemen and the escorts why the public were not being admitted to the courtroom, they replied—besides giving the traditional answer "full up"—that "the K.G.B. won't allow it." A policeman asked one of the K.G.B. men: "Hey, Chief, which are your men here?" Without the permission of the "Chief," the audience was not allowed out for a smoke during breaks. This "Chief," who at one point gave his name to someone as Yury Pavlovich Nikiforov, stood behind Vitaly Kochubiyevsky, brother of the accused, and from time to time repeated quietly "And you're a Yid, you're a Yid."

Many members of the public were not allowed into the courtroom, although they had arrived long before the start of the proceedings and long before the appearance of the "public" in the court. They sent a declaration to the Chairman of the Court, and later a protest to the Kiev City Procurator, but without result. The only thing that everyone managed to hear was the sentence. Among those who protested at not being allowed into the courtroom was the daughter of an active witness for the prosecution, Rudenko.

In the second half of June the appeal in the Kochubiyevsky case was examined by the Ukrainian Supreme Court, and the sentence passed by the Kiev Regional Court was confirmed.

Translated by Peter Reddaway.

Haïm Zafrani

1922–2004

Haïm Zafrani was born in Essaouira, Morocco. He was committed to educational reform in the newly independent Morocco and worked with the Alliance Israélite Universelle to integrate an Arabic curriculum into Jewish community schools. In 1962, Zafrani moved to Paris to be the chair of Hebrew at the École nationale des langues orientales vivantes. In 1969, he founded a department of Hebrew language and Jewish civilization at the University of Paris, where many of his students wrote dissertations on Judeo-Arabic. Zafrani was a prolific writer and scholar of Jewish literary, linguistic, musical, and religious culture in Morocco and in Muslim Spain. He also studied the Jewish and Maghrebi mystical traditions.

Jewish Education in the Land of Islam
1969

"If the majority of Jews in Berber territory speak Arabic as their native language and use Spanish when doing business, their main concern is that Hebrew be the primary language of all instruction and that it not be forgotten. It is to this end that the names of familiar objects, as well as a broad range of commercial terms, are taught in Hebrew even before the child knows the structure of the words and makes practical use of the language. Hebrew vocabulary is thus intermixed with their Arabic or Spanish speech to such an extent that their language is not always easily understood.

"The goal of teaching children at a very young age is that religion and tradition take root in their virgin minds.

"Shabbat is an occasion of exceptional solemnity, appropriate for initiation into religious prescriptions and, moreover, a distinctive sign of Jewishness. Jews are particularly intent on instilling in their children a deep respect for this holy day. The 'queen of solemnities,' as the Sages call it, is welcomed in by ritual recognitions of relatives and friends. In these solemn greetings, the children must abstain from mentioning the name of the heavenly divinity before the age of seven out of respect for the holiness of His Name.

"Associating with Muslim children is absolutely forbidden. . . .

"The fundamentals of education having been addressed in the family setting, the child is sent to school. Before he leaves, his mother is duty-bound to give him something to eat prepared with sugar or honey for breakfast. As she does so, she recites, 'Just as this is sweet to your palate, so the Torah will be pleasing to your soul. . . .'"[1]

2. *Elementary Education*

A) Goal

"Teaching was essentially done at the synagogue, by the synagogue, and for the synagogue." S. D. Goitein's statement regarding Yemen characterizes, to a certain extent, Jewish elementary education in Morocco. The function of this teaching is not to prepare young people for life. Its goals and its content must respond to a single imperative: the correct participation in the worship service and in the community prayers, the initiation into a tradition and a system of negative or positive prescriptions. At the synagogue, the prayers are not read exclusively by the officiating minister: they are distributed among the members in attendance, as are the *piyutim* [liturgical poems] on holidays and Saturdays. When a believer is summoned to go up to the *sefer* [Torah scroll], he is expected to read the section of the Torah that has been assigned to him (everyone is supposed to know how to read from the *sefer*). On holidays he must recite the *haftarah* with its Aramaic and Judeo-Arabic, Judeo-Spanish, or Judeo-Berber translation, according to the region.

Outside the synagogue, all acts of Jewish men from earliest childhood—upon rising, going to bed, after ablutions, before and after meals, etc.—are accompanied by a certain number of blessings (*berakhot*), consecrations, or offerings of praise.

The reading and recitation by memory of the holy texts, as well as their explication and comprehension, are thus the key and fundamental condition for the Jew's participation in the worship of God, requiring a long apprenticeship and substantial learning.

The interdependence between education and community or family religious life is also apparent in the annual allocation of subjects to be taught in seasonal courses, a subject that will be dealt with in a later chapter.

B) The School, Institution for Jewish Teaching

In general, all communities pay careful attention to educating their young. In the old mellahs located in the heart of large cities or in more modest urban or rural settings, in the shadow of high-walled Saharan *ksours* or of the towering Atlas Mountains, whether an important building in the towns or a cramped room in the villages, a place is reserved for education: it is the school, called *sla*. This term also designates not just the place for prayer—the synagogue—but also any other building where traditional education is housed, even if it is a private place rented for the purpose by the teacher, or his own house. The fact is, however, that in most cases the lessons are given in the synagogue or in an annex of the synagogue, further reinforcing the tight link between liturgy and teaching. This overlap is seen everywhere in the Muslim world. In Yemen, synagogue and school have the same name, *kanīs*, and the term *msīd* (Koranic school) is just a variant of *masžid* (place of prayer, mosque).

In the towns, a community building with several rooms, each one of which is assigned to a teacher who receives a salary from the community, is usually known as the *Talmud-Torah* (literally, teaching of the law). It primarily serves orphans and poor children whose parents are unable to pay the salary of a private teacher at the heder.

More well-to-do families will engage a teacher to give private lessons to their children, who thus receive individual instruction in their own home.

Education is a private enterprise, not subject to any control whatsoever, whether administrative or pedagogical. "Hiring a schoolteacher is like opening a boutique" (R. Yosef Messas, cf. infra, his autobiography) and the competition among teachers often leads to conflicts. Community committees only intervene, if necessary, in the distribution of the synagogues among the teaching candidates.

In certain cases legal specialists get involved in order to resolve an administrative or financial issue involving an aspect of the *din* [Jewish community court]. In this regard, two texts taken from works of the responsa written by Moroccan rabbis will be cited.

NOTE

1. [L. Adison, *The Present State of the Jews* (London, 1675).—Trans.]

Translated by Michele McKay Aynesworth.

Other works by Zafrani: *Kabbale, vie mystique et magie* (1986); *Juifs d'Andalousie et du Maghreb* (1996); *Deux mille ans de vie juive au Maroc* (1998).

Elie Kedourie

1926–1992

Historian Elie Kedourie was born in Baghdad and grew up amid worsening antisemitism, contributing to his preoccupation with nationalism. He studied at the London School of Economics as an undergraduate and later worked toward a doctorate in philosophy at Oxford. Because he was required to make changes he did not agree with, Kedourie withdrew his thesis. He then returned to the London School of Economics and became a professor. Eschewing prevailing attitudes in Middle Eastern studies, Kedourie's work also deepened and renewed his comprehension of nationalism. He often worked in collaboration with his wife, Sylvia G. Haim, herself an accomplished historian.

The Chatham House Version
1970

This appraisal of the west has remained Toynbee's considered judgment. "In my eyes," he states in the last volume of *A Study of History*, published in 1961, "the west is a perpetual aggressor." The guilt is clear beyond any doubt. But Toynbee is ready to entertain a plea of diminished responsibility, for he immediately adds: "I trace the west's arrogance back to the Jewish notion of a 'Chosen People.'"[1] This theme is constant in

his writings. As he himself has stated, he has seen Judaism through the eyes of the Christian Church supplemented by Eduard Meyer's. It has been, for him "a pre-
lude to Christianity and one which rejected its manifest
destiny when it repudiated the new religious insight or
revelation to which it had been leading up."[2] This traditional Christian anti-Judaism—which is incongruous in
someone as religiously eclectic as Toynbee—was laced
with something else, which is a by-product of his system. As is notorious, for Toynbee the Jews, who have
seen the light and rejected it, are also a fossil. How he
came to this judgment provides yet another instance of
his tendency progressively to build up initially simple
and perhaps useful metaphors into doctrinal edifices,
neo-Gothic in the luxuriance of their complicated fancies. Originally, it was only a specific community of
Jews whom Toynbee considered to be a fossil. This
was the community of the Ashkenazi Jews in Jerusalem
whom he coupled with the Samaritans, the Druzes, the
Maronites and the Alawis as "fossils of ancient faiths."[3]
His meaning here is quite clear. To the progressive liberal that he was, these traditional communities out of
touch with modern realities were, so to speak, fossils
surviving from another age. With *A Study of History*
this analogy became petrified into a rigid theory. The
needs of his system required Toynbee to postulate the
existence of a "Syriac Civilisation" in which the Jews
willy-nilly had to accommodate themselves, the Bible,
for instance, becoming an example of Syriac mythology. Since the system further required that Syriac Society should be dead, the Jews, who were manifestly still
alive, had to be "the 'fossil' remnant of a society that is
extinct."[4] Of Judaism as a living faith practised by successive generations of Jews since the Roman destruction of the Temple Toynbee was utterly ignorant. Phari-
see, for instance, remained for him a term of abuse, and
it is only very late in his career that he seems to have discovered such authorities on rabbinical Judaism as G. F.
Moore and R. T. Herford.[5] The epithet Judaic has thus
served, throughout *A Study of History*, to denote all that
was most evil in the modern world. "Fanaticism and
race-feeling" among Protestants derives from the Old
Testament; Marxism "has caught its spirit of violence
from an archaic strain of Judaism"; "post-Christian
western rationalism" has inherited from Christianity
"a Judaic fanaticism and intolerance"; Christianity took
the wrong turning when it refused to heed "Marcion's
prophetically warning voice [that the God of Abraham
was really a maleficent demiurge]"; the west since the

seventeenth century has been trying to purge itself of
"its ancestral Judaic fanaticism and intolerance," but
this has erupted again "in such ideologies as Communism, Fascism and National Socialism."[6]

In brief the west is a disintegrating society which,
owing to its Judaic heritage, has shown itself to be mur-
derously aggressive. Its victims, by Toynbee's count,
amount to no less than eight societies,[7] who have been
assaulted militarily, economically and culturally. [. . .]

But, in any case, if one is to set up as moral censor,
one might bear in mind that the guilt of governments
and peoples cannot be ascertained with the summary
methods of a drum-head court-martial. Consider: the
British government is declared guilty of encouraging,
for its own selfish reasons, Zionism, an alien creed and
a harmful movement; but yet, at the same time the British government clearly encouraged Arabism, also for
its own selfish reasons. Can we not say that this also
was a crime, which foisted an alien creed and a harmful
movement on a middle eastern society much too diverse
and complicated and delicate for such crude simplifica-
tions? If the British are adjudged guilty of promoting
Zionism, they must likewise be adjudged guilty of promoting Arabism. Equity demands no less.

But such perplexities and ambiguities do not sit well
with the simple certainties and the draconian verdicts
of the Chatham House Version. British bad faith and
deception are clear and not to be gainsaid. A plea, however, of diminished responsibility can be entertained.
Gibb remarks that Antonius is "justified in stressing the
virtual control of public opinion in Britain and the west
by the all-pervading Zionist propaganda."[8] This Zionist propaganda had clearly acted to lead astray governments and peoples from the first world war onwards.
Thus Longrigg declares that the recommendation of
the Bunsen Committee in 1915 that Palestine should
be internationalized—a decision which the Zionists
greatly disliked and opposed—was one "in which a
considerable element was, no doubt, the pressure of
Zionist spokesmen on British ministers." This author
goes even further and states quite flatly that "The immediate background to the issue of the Balfour Declaration was one of pressure on the British cabinet from
British and American Jewry" and that "the pressure
of Jewry on successive British governments was sufficient fatally to preclude the adequate acknowledgment
of Arab rights."[9] Such an account, of course, woefully
misconceives the situation; for it was not "Jewish" or
even "Zionist" pressure which had led to the issue of

the Balfour Declaration; Jews and still less, Zionists, were not as powerful as all that. It was, among other things, eagerness by the British government to use Zionism in order to do away with the rights which they had themselves shortly before conceded to the French in Palestine. Arabism was used to the same purpose in the Levant, and we may therefore say that, far from being considered rivals or enemies, Zionism and Arabism were, in British eyes, movements which complemented and reinforced one another.[10]

The Chatham House Version relating to Palestine has yet another characteristic. It takes for granted that the Palestine problem was the most important, indeed the key issue, in middle eastern politics. Kirk's way of putting the matter is representative. "They [the Zionists]," he wrote, "studiously refrained from allowing themselves to consider to what extent, in default of the White Paper policy, Arab political agitation, strikes, sabotage, etc., might have interfered with the British middle east war-effort in 1940–2 and consequently with the Persian supply-route to the USSR—and what the ultimate consequences might then have been, for the National Home, for world-Jewry, and for all mankind." And again: "Rashid 'Ali's pro-Axis *putsch* in Iraq in 1941 . . . might have found much greater support in other Arab countries had it not been for the appeasing effect of the White Paper on moderate Arab nationalism."[11] The assumption here is that British policy in Palestine vitally affected all other developments in the Arabic-speaking world. It is no doubt true that in 1938–9 the British government thought it prudent to discourage the Zionists and encourage their opponents; but to argue retrospectively that it was this policy which prevented anti-British and pro-Nazi movements in the middle east is clearly untenable. For, in the first place, such movements did manifest themselves; if they were inefficacious this was not thanks to the Palestine White Paper of 1939, but to swift military action by the British which, owing to their remoteness and preoccupation elsewhere, the Axis powers could not checkmate. It was, further, an illusion to suppose that all British problems in the middle east stemmed from the Balfour Declaration. British relations with Iraq, Egypt or Iran, say, were bedevilled by purely local issues; and again, Balfour Declaration or no Balfour Declaration, an activist and initially successful Germany was bound to—and did—attract, for a time, a large and influential following.

NOTES
1. [A. J. Toynbee] *A Study of History*, 1st ed., vol. 12, p. 627 [1934–1961].
2. Ibid., pp. 596–7.
3. [A. J. Toynbee, *Survey of International Affairs, 1925*, vol. I,] *The Islamic World Since the Peace Settlement*, [part III] (Oxford University Press, 1927), p. 350.
4. *A Study of History*, vol. 2, p. 55 n. 4; see also ibid., pp. 10, 14, 24.
5. In 1954 he was still declaring: "The sin of which I feel that we westerners need to repent is Pharisaism" (in a letter to *The Times Literary Supplement*, reprinted in *Counsels of Hope: The Toynbee—Jerrold Controversy*, 1954, p. 38). In 1961 he was praising "Pharisaic-Christian pacifism" and stating that the "Pharisees'" pacifism saved Judaism from perishing with the Zealots" (*A Study of History*, vol. 12, p. 505).
6. *A Study of History*, vol. 1, p. 214; vol. 5, p. 182; vol. 7, pp. 474 n. 2, 438–9; vol. 12, pp. 541–2.
7. Ibid., vol. 8, p. 405.
8. [H. A. R. Gibb] "The Case for the Arabs" [in *The Spectator*, 25 November 1938].
9. [S. H. Longrigg] *Syria and Lebanon under French Mandate*, [1958,] pp. 54, 59–60. It is of interest to read a review of C. Weizmann's *Trial and Error* [1949], signed S.H.L., which appeared in *The Arab World*, October 1949, p. 17: "It would obviously be optimistic or merely foolish," declares the reviewer, "to expect more than a certain degree of 'loyalty' to Great Britain, its policies and its people from immigrant foreigners of alien blood, background and ambitions such as are the foreign Jews to whom H.M.G. so readily accords the privilege of British nationality."
10. Another account of the origin of the Balfour Declaration appears in *A Study of History*, vol. 8, p. 303, where Toynbee declares that "the Western Powers were tantalizingly inhibited from playing this Palestinian card so long as they had any hope of keeping their Anti-Semitic Russian partner in the firing-line, and it is no wonder that the Balfour Declaration was published as soon as the last Western hopes of further Russian military collaboration had expired." This is hopelessly confused and fanciful, for the Balfour Declaration was not a "Western" but a British enterprise, and there is no evidence of a Tsarist veto having delayed its appearance.
11. [A. J. Toynbee and F. T. Arthur Ashton-Gwatkin ed., *Survey of International Affairs, 1939–1946*:] *The World in March 1939*, [Oxford University Press, 1952,] p. 138.

Other works by Kedourie: *Nationalism* (1960); *The Crossman Confessions* (1964); *Arabic Political Memoirs and Other Studies* (1974); *Politics in the Middle East* (1992).

Peter Szondi

1929–1971

Peter Szondi, literary scholar and philologist, was born in Budapest, the son of psychiatrist Leopold Szondi. Szondi attended high school in Budapest until the German invasion in 1944. He and his family were saved as part of the Kasztner exchange group, spending a number of months in Bergen-Belsen before reaching Switzerland in December 1944. Szondi wrote his doctoral thesis on the theory of modern drama at Zurich University. He later became professor of general and comparative literary studies at the Freie Universität Berlin. Szondi committed suicide in October 1971, leaving in manuscript his volume about poet Paul Celan, published posthumously.

Letter to Gershom Scholem
1970

> Berlin-Grunewald
> Tauberstr. 16
> February 26, 1970
> Dear Mr. Scholem,

Writing this letter does not come easily to me; hence the long delay. And now you know already that I have not been able to decide in favor of coming to you "forever" and of accepting the chair.[1] I would ask you and your wife to understand my decision, if I did not know that you know all too well what has been going on inside me regarding this issue since my last sojourn in Jerusalem two years ago, and that you do "understand" that I will not come, probably without being able to excuse it or approve of it. But it is not only because I know that I cannot tell you something new on this issue that I won't even try now to spell out the "reasons" that "led" me to my decision. The reasons are, at least in regard to this question, merely "reasons"; all of them are perhaps sufficiently credible, but none of them is completely persuasive or entirely compelling, to me as little as to you. You or I could argue against each one of them, and yet it is certain that at present I cannot make the transition (into another environment, language, professional field), or, to say it more honestly: I do not want to make the transition, although I would like to. About this last issue I've written to you some time ago in a letter that you had wanted to bring up during your last visit to Berlin; but unfortunately, I wasn't in the right state of mind then to discuss it with you, and it probably doesn't make much sense to rectify this now in a letter. When I said earlier that you and your wife know exactly what is going on in someone who is in my situation, I did not mean that only in a general way. In Jerusalem, you once articulated in a sentence, as unsurprising in its acumen as it was unforgettable, why I was living in Germany and was very likely going to remain there: because I had unlearned to be at home (I never was at home, neither in my childhood in Budapest nor in Zurich nor, strictly speaking and in another sense, with my parents). This is an illness that might possibly be cured per force, by way of an emigration that might become necessary for one reason or another; but of my own free will I do not have the strength to take this step, and the less so, since, two years ago in Jerusalem, I felt not only that I was at home there, but also that I cannot bear this feeling. I know that I could change and should change this feeling, but that knowledge is not strong enough to break down the resistance that prevails in me now—meaning: for as long as I can tolerate living in Germany. Surely there is no need to spell out for you the feelings with which I wrote down that last sentence only one week after the arson attack in Munich.[2] Now, in regards not to myself, but to Comparative Literature in Jerusalem: while I was there last, I was thinking about various things: about the possibility of a *comparative* approach, in the European-American sense, to the study of literature [and] about the function of the *general* study of literature within the framework of philological training. The first issue would affect whom to appoint to the chair and the design of the curriculum; the second would determine the position of the department in relation to the individual philologies and the point in time when one could begin studying the subject (today only after the B.A.). I did not talk about this then because I did not want to create the impression of being critical of the good Leah Goldberg, whose deep humanity and almost shy determination and strength impressed me very much. But if you were considering now at the University a new construction of this area of study, I would perhaps be able to write a kind of proposal about it addressed to the faculty or the president. Since I know pretty much what I would say, I would be able to write it within eight to ten days. You would only have to tell me that it is wanted. About the Visiting Professorship, I would definitely not be able to come in 1970/71. I do have a chair here. And not only is it impossible to get a leave of absence at just any time (the earliest date would be Winter 1971/72, and then only for one semester), but also the collaboration with the students is so intense and so continuous that I could justify such an interruption (for more than one semester) only if it were already to signal the cessation of my activities here. I would suggest that you turn to Professor Geoffrey Hartman (Yale University), a friend of Tuvia Shlonsky's, who—Hartman—I believe, is currently (or just was) in Jerusalem. Besides him, two other literary scholars might be considered (also for a permanent position) whose names and addresses I am adding in a P.S. since I don't remember them exactly. One is a German scholar in Brazil, the other, who served as assistant professor in Jerusalem and Tel Aviv for two years (most likely also under Leah Goldberg), is an excellent disciple of [René] Wellek and wrote me about his rewarding experiences in Israel.

That I had to cancel my trip to Yale,[3] you probably don't know yet. The new university law is turning everything upside down and I had to stay here in order to safeguard, to the extent possible, the independence of our institute.

With all good wishes and not without longing and a bad conscience I am thinking of you both and of our mutual friends

Yours,
Peter Szondi

P.S. 1: Professor Erwin Rosenthal, Universidade de São Paulo, German Department, São Paulo, Brésil.

2: Professor Alexander Gelley, Cornell University, Dept. of Comparative Literature.

As Visiting Professor you may want to consider: Professor Wolfgang Fleischmann, State University of Massachusetts (?), Amherst, Dept. of Comp. Literature.

NOTES

1. In January 1970, Leah Goldberg died in Jerusalem. She had occupied the chair in Comparative Literature at the Hebrew University. In a letter, dated January 24, 1970, Scholem had asked Szondi if he was willing to come to Jerusalem to occupy the chair, an offer that he had already made in the spring of 1968, when Szondi spent a semester as a guest professor in Jerusalem.

2. On February 13, 1970, an arson attack was perpetrated on the old-age home of the Jewish Community Center in Munich that killed seven people and injured eight. The perpetrators were never found.

3. Szondi had been invited to serve as Visiting Professor at Yale.

Translated by Susanne Klingenstein.

Other works by Szondi: *Theorie des modernen Dramas* (1956); *Celan Studies* (1971); *Die Theorie des bürgerlichen Trauerspiels im 18. Jahrhundert* (1973).

Henri Chemouilli

The Repatriated Ten Years Later
1972

We had more or less forgotten them. We wanted to convince ourselves, without really trying to find out, that the march of time had left them satisfied, happy, at peace. The quarrels provoked by Courrière's film about the Algerian war left them marginalized—as did the impassioned disputes between generals Massu, La Bollardière, and Jules Roy—witnesses or actors in a drama that belongs to memory. But as the years pass, who worries about history's big losers? Mr. Chemouilli, one of the hundred thousand repatriated Algerian Jews, speaks to us here of the semi-exile in which they find themselves, in their own country, and the problems they raise in the heart of a French Judaism to which they have given new life.

Ten years already! No one who lived through these years has forgotten them. The French of Algeria poured back into mainland France at the rate of ten to twenty thousand a day. People rarely spoke of them. There were few details in the newspapers. They were strangely absent from television. Orders from above: don't spoil the great Évian victory, the one France had just won over itself, with shocking images. The French of Algeria were paying the price, but nobody wanted to know that. They got here the best way they could, with their pathetic bundles of belongings. Their children would be clutching an old doll, a teddy bear, a caged bird. They were made to disembark late at night so that the despair in their eyes might be mistaken for weariness. And following another secret order, they were scattered to all corners of the French hexagon. This troublesome fish that could not be drowned was made to vanish. That is how eight hundred thousand "pieds noirs," [black feet]—Christians, Muslims, and Jews—returned to France, their homeland. About 120,000 Jews. And since about twenty thousand others had set out for Israel, the Algerian Jewish community ceased to exist. It had lasted more than twenty centuries, a record.

Those being repatriated were met at their points of disembarkation by men of goodwill: volunteers from Secours Catholique, the Protestant Cimade organization, and the Jewish community. And for many, it was certainly a comfort to see the Star of David as they set foot on French soil. For the Jews of Algeria, the FSJU [Fonds social juif unifié—the United Jewish Welfare Fund] would create more shelters. It neither claimed, nor was it called upon, to replace the Ministry of the Repatriated, but the moral impact was significant. The FSJU had begun to think about these services months earlier, with the influx of Tunisian Jews after the fighting in Bizerte in 1961. They were still imperfect, but at least they existed. Mr. Julien Samuel, director of the FSJU, says this:

I don't think we can ignore the exceptionally warm welcome extended by Jews under sometimes dire conditions, at Orly as well as at other French airports. The supporting framework was inadequate. People arrived wherever and however they could. But at each station, at each port, the Jewish community was present, night and day when necessary, to welcome the repatriated.

For the first time, I believe, the French community mobilized to welcome people who did not expect to be welcomed. And in the general chaos, the reception of the Algerian refugees was felt as the primary evidence of an exceptional unity and fraternity. What we saw emerge in a very short time was an amazing phenomenon.

For Better and for Worse

This is true, but the Jews who were arriving scarcely had the time or the strength to take it all in. It was not just the exodus that traumatized them; the exodus was just the conclusion of long years of warfare during which they, too, had paid a heavy price. Their immediate concern: to make a new start, to forget if possible. And first of all to discover the city, the region that had welcomed them, when chance had not chosen for you, to find lodging, to look for work. Things one could not accomplish overnight. It would take years, the first five years. For many, years of bitterness and strife. But also a certain joy, that old Jewish joy that makes you say, "Nothing more has happened to us than has happened or will happen, one day or another, to all Jews.

We packed our bags just as, in former times, our fathers tied up their bundles." Algerian Judaism rediscovered the meaning of the diaspora, the fate of the Jews, after having lost the homeland in French Algeria.

Algerian Jews had been French for better and for worse. The best, they were certain, had been their liberation, their entry into modern life, their access to Western civilization. The worst was the collective defeat of the Algerian French in the face of indifference, sometimes even scornful insults. Who remembered that those men had made Algiers the capital of Free France, had fought for the victories of France itself: those of Tunisia; of the Italian campaign, from Cassino to Rome; from the landings in Provence to the Rhine and to the Danube? Past history; present history demanded that one begin life anew.

Translated by Michele McKay Aynesworth.

Aleksander Voronel

b. 1931

Physicist Alexander Vladimirovich Voronel was born in Leningrad. He was a vocal critic of Soviet antisemitism and anti-Israel policy. He studied physics at the University of Kharkov (Ukraine) and researched thermodynamics of phase transitions at the Russian Institute for Physical-Technical and Radiation Measurements in Mendeleyevo, Moscow. In the early 1970s, he copublished a series of samizdat essays titled "Jews in the USSR." Voronel immigrated to Israel in 1975, where he became a leader in Russian Jewish circles. Since then, Voronel and his wife, Nina Abramovna (Roginka) Voronel, have helped to found the Russian-language cultural magazine 22, and Voronel has written extensively on Jewish subjects. He continues to teach physics at Tel Aviv University.

The Social Preconditions of the National Awakening of the Jews in the USSR
1972

Jews, in the past celebrated for the ability to understand all things, are now in danger of being unable to understand anything at all culturally, for they do not have self-awareness. Without such awareness, it is impossible to perceive a cultural object in all its completeness, for one is dealing with an unknown quantity in the object. It is even worse if a supposedly known quantity is attributed to the object, for it is often a quantity merely derived from literature.

Though far from all Jews are aware of this danger, they all observe with instinctual alarm the decline in the percentage of Jews who know Yiddish (the percentage who regard Yiddish as their native language declined from 21 per cent in the 1959 census to 17 per cent in 1970, in face of the general decline in the number of Jews and the disappearance of Jewish Soviet literature, theater and musical life). Whereas at the previous stage, technological education, culture as such, "civilization," seemed to them to be of greater value than what they had had, today the sense of loss is dominant. Tradition, language, unique forms of community life, understanding of earlier generations, identity with Jews all over the world, have been lost.

It would be unfair to blame the Soviet government for these losses. The rupture with age-old traditions of Jewry was to a great extent the fault of the older generation of Jews themselves (let us call it error, rather than fault). During the gigantic transformation that took place in the USSR in the 1920s and 1930s many, unfortunately, made the mistake of believing that human psychology is shaped by a few simple elements and that the social factor is the decisive one. If this were indeed so, there would be no Jews in the USSR at all today, for their psychological characteristics would have adapted to their societal being, because in those years the question of nationality in passports could be answered as one wished. Yet even in 1970 there are more than two million people living in the USSR who consider themselves Jews.

It is widely believed in the USSR that Jews are not an integral nation but merely an ethnic group. According to this view, Jews of different countries belong to different ethnic groups and have more in common with the peoples of the countries they live in than with other Jews. However, despite this assertion, Jews are singled out all over the world, and they themselves, too, recognize one another by a multitude of characteristics. Generally, this alone is basis enough for Jews to recognize and defend their common interests and also for at least some of them to seek self-determination as a nation.

But Jews have much more than that in common. A common origin and 2000 years of dispersion have developed in them characteristic traits and inter-relational principles creating a psychological community, and have left an enormous literary heritage on which their cultural community is based. This wealth is embodied in the Jewish language (Hebrew), Jewish history and the Bible.

The development of national feeling and the search for the roots of Jewish distinctiveness observed in recent years have manifested themselves in the appearance of a stable interest in precisely these cultural values. Interestingly, European education and the long experience of equality have affected the psychology of Soviet Jews in such a manner that they are more interested in their ancient history and Biblical literature than in the culture of the recent past, reminding them of their humiliating situation in pre-revolutionary Russia. Apparently, this explains the practical lack of interest in Sholom Aleichem and Yiddish culture while there is a heightened interest in the Bible and the Talmud. Despite the increased difficulties in this respect, young Jews are avidly studying Hebrew and are quite uninterested in Yiddish.

Analogical trends are appearing in the study by young people of Jewish history. This attitude reflects a natural psychological need of people (and peoples) to feel that they are a self-sufficient whole and not a secondary part of someone else's life and history.

Russian history, which is presented to Soviet Jews as a source of information about the past, does not satisfy this need. For example, from a study of Russian history, a Jew can, at best, learn that his ancestors had helped promote the economic development of the western regions of the Russian Empire. But it is hardly this aim that comprised the substance of Jewish life in the past two centuries. Nor does the constant role of victim played by Jews in the history of Russia at the beginning of this century accord with the active world outlook of Soviet Jews. The need arises to go back to much earlier beginnings in history, and here we encounter the intellectuals' acute interest in the Bible.

The difference in reactions to the Bible by Russians and Jews must be stressed. For Russians, the Bible is significant as a general cultural value and a religious book. It is on the latter principle that the attitude of official circles in the USSR to the Bible is based. But for Jews the Bible is the foundation of the national tradition and the original source of history. It cannot be separated from secular Jewish culture and is superior to any other cultural value that might be counter to it. Hence, when they address themselves to spiritual values, Jews cannot bypass the Bible and the traditions connected with it.

A large part of the Jewish religious tradition evolved as the unique spiritualization of secular Jewish history and national life. To separate this national life from religion would be to impoverish it. For example, it is impossible to separate the celebration of the historical liberation of the Jews at Passover, Purim and Hannukah from the religious content of those events.

In embarking on the search for national tradition and more profound spirituality, many go further and affiliate themselves formally with religion. At any rate, young people gather regularly at synagogues, observe national holidays, try to understand the meaning and to observe the letter of Jewish customs. Generally speaking, such aspirations are not identical with religious seekings, for in Jewish tradition the synagogue is not a temple, but merely the center of Jewish community life (literally, a meeting-place), a place to commemorate various cultural and political events of their past; many of the traditions have a perfectly rational origin. But the situation in the Diaspora is such that the non-Jews, and sometimes Jews as well, begin to regard these things in the context of the habitual ideas that evolved under the influence of other religions. This is what leads to identification of the national tradition with religious tradition.

It has been pointed out above that such an interest in tradition is due in part to the slowing down of the social development of the group and the transformation, as it were, of part of their social energy from kinetic into potential. This phenomenon is just the opposite of what took place in the 1920's, when potential spiritual energy, accumulated over a century, found realization in the powerful social development of the Jews.

Some of the one-sidedness is being straightened out now, thanks to the spiritualization mentioned above, and this is a sign of cultural growth. However, this form of growth is encountering a serious barrier in the traditional anti-religious policy of the USSR leadership. As has been pointed out, in Judaism the religious element cannot be formally separated from the secular. Hence, the entire tradition meets with disapproval in the Soviet context.

How can these difficulties be overcome in Soviet society? Can they be overcome?

Translated by Moshe Decter.

Other work by Voronel: *Jewishness Rediscovered: Jewish Identity in the Soviet Union* (1974).

Gisèle Halimi
b. 1927

Gisèle Halimi was born Zeiza Gisèle Élise Taïeb in La Goulette, Tunisia, to a religious, mixed Jewish–Berber family. Educated in a French lycée in Tunis and later at the University of Paris, she graduated with degrees in law and philosophy and has been a member of the Paris bar since 1956. Halimi's legal career has been devoted to defending minorities, notably Muslims and women, for which she became famous during the Franco-Algerian War. She was counsel for the National Liberation Front and, in particular, for Djamila Boupacha, whose case she helped popularize with Simone de Beauvoir. In 1967, Halimi chaired the Russell Tribunal on international war crimes. In 1971, she helped found Choisir la cause des femmes, an organization committed to defending women, criminalizing rape, and legalizing abortion. She is also a prolific author, particularly of feminist history and prose.

The Women's Cause
1973

And yet I had a dreadful feeling! I saw my situation as absurd, paradoxical. I was defending the lives of several militants. I was speaking in the name of the dignity and freedom of a people, and I had to do it while trying desperately to have an abortion by primitive means. I was denied the right to make vital decisions for myself, dependent on biological givens that I could not control. My anguish, this struggle, none of the men in this trial would ever know. I said to myself:

"I am a lawyer. I have therefore a certain degree of power. I have the power of knowledge, of learning, of language, of the law. I can explain, persuade. And yet I'm standing there with a probe in my uterus and won't have the strength to hold out till the end."

For the first time in my life I had doubts about my own power. I asked myself: "Is being a female lawyer exactly the same as being a male lawyer?"

Could I, a woman, make a significant impact on something, on someone, on justice, if I had no real power over myself? Did I, under these circumstances, have the power to save a man? And the bizarre thought came to me that, while defending a man on trial, I was at the same time a potential defendant. I was breaking the law, I was having an abortion. In short, I, a defense attorney, was also a delinquent. In total contradiction to my normal professional life. I felt myself to be at the heart of a struggle, the struggle of all women.

During the twenty-four hours I spent in the hospital, I reflected on my feminine condition, on the necessary struggle. I had to convince them, these women, that was certain. To show them they had the right to the same power as men if they just had the courage to seize it and change it. But they had to fight, to organize. Because to tell them repeatedly that they had only to stand up, to assume responsibility, to act, was really a lie. And it was also a lie to assert that women had the same opportunities as men in the work place, in political life, in creation. In brief, I was seeking a way to tell women that to make their weight felt, they had to begin by winning a fundamental right, that of power over themselves.

This Moknine trial appeared to me thus in a new light, laughable and contradictory. Standing there, with this probe in my uterus, I was the very picture of failure. Officially, the weapons of defense were in my hands. But how could I believe it when I no longer believed myself to be a single, whole, effective person? On the contrary, I was becoming painfully aware of the fact that I was completely helpless, bound to suffer, reduced to secrecy!

Meanwhile the trial continued. And the day for making a case for my clients, I was hospitalized, so I was not able to defend them. Three death sentences, including one for a client of mine, were handed down. Those for whom I could not stay the course. A series of others, sentenced to forced labor, to imprisonment.

Along with some of my Tunisian colleagues, I went to plead for clemency before René Coty, president of the republic, at the Élysée Palace.[1]

This was the first time I had argued such a case. The first time also, I think, that a plea for clemency for someone given a death sentence for political reasons was argued by a woman before the highest magistrate in France. It was rather impressive.

I felt very strongly that this was the condemned man's best chance. The last time that he could express himself through my voice. His last fight to stay alive. The idea filled me with anguish. This is why the presidential protocol requiring me to wear a hat for the hearing seemed to come from Mars. I never wore a hat. I had neither the taste nor the means for it. The wife of a colleague had lent me one for the occasion. So I presented myself at the Élysée Palace wearing a black pillbox. While waiting to be received, I studied myself for a long time in the immense mirrors of the great hall of the palace. Ridiculous! I felt ridiculous in that hat. And deeply revolted. The life of a man was at stake and I was obliged to wear a costume in order to plead for clemency. The bailiff finally came for me and, at the very moment that the door of the president's office opened, I handed the astonished bailiff my headgear. "Put it in the cloakroom!" And President Coty received me in my customary attire, without a hat. A female lawyer. I had rejected the masquerade. Nothing must distract me, not etiquette, not a hat. My case, that life to save, I myself . . . and a president of the republic to persuade . . .

The pardon was granted.

NOTE

1. Later, during the Algerian War, I became accustomed to these hearings, first with President Coty, then with General de Gaulle. See *Le Lait de l'oranger* [*Milk for the Orange Tree*], Chapter IV: "Call Me Maître."

Translated by Michele McKay Aynesworth.

Other works by Halimi: *Djamila Boupacha* (1962); *Le Lait de l'oranger* (1988); *Ne vous résignez jamais* (2009).

Richard Marienstras

1928–2011

Richard Marienstras was born in Warsaw to Jewish parents who divorced when he was a child, leading him toward a nomadic existence with his mother before he settled in Paris, where he studied at the Lycée Janson-de-Sailly. To escape deportation to Germany, he joined the Maquis du Vercors, the resistance force, in 1943. Ever the wanderer, he fought in the war for Israeli independence and later, with his wife, Élise, went to teach in Tunisia and then in America. Returning to France in 1963, Marienstras taught at the Sorbonne, becoming an authority on Shakespeare and the Elizabethans. In 1967, he founded the Cercle Gaston-Crémieux, an affirmation of secular Jewish culture in the diaspora. He devoted much of the 1960s and 1970s to writing about Jews, including *Max, pauvre Max* (1964) and many journal articles, which were compiled into *Être un peuple en diaspora* (1975).

The Jews of the Diaspora, or the Minority Vocation
1973

Certainly, the collective will of diaspora Jews is assured neither of success nor of perennial life. It is situated in history, subject to the erosion and constraints of history, equally conditioned by the past—at once common and varied—and by majority forces that tend to standardize ways of life, imposing constraints and simplified loyalties, turning people into cogwheels that respond readily to the demands of state bureaucracies and industrial empires. This precariousness is obvious; it is the fate of all minorities who are not part of the state. But it is also the fate of nation-states. Neither history nor the gods guarantee the destiny of any human group. That goes, of course, for the Jewish State, whose viability, like that of the diaspora, must be seen through the long lens of history, not measured in the short time of successive generations. It must be recognized that the Jewish State revealed its precarious nature in antiquity, and that all the Zionist and community-oriented propaganda aims at mobilizing the Jews around Israel, essentially focusing on the dangers that threaten it and thus the precariousness of its establishment. In any case, in an age of atomic and other tactical weapons, bigger, more populous nations than Israel cannot be assured of their viability or survival. To claim then that Israel, by some divine or historic grace, escapes the common condition is to profess a mystic faith. To imagine, finally, that Israel could have endured without the constant aid—moral, political, and material—of the diaspora is a vision that the facts belie. A massive immigration that brought men together would deprive the State of the aid the diaspora assures it, thus threatening its very ability to survive.

* * *

Some minorities understand quite well what the majority of Jews, characterized by provincialism and a providential or catastrophic vision of their destiny, do not understand at all: the Jews have endured for so long over the course of history not *in spite of* dispersion, but *thanks to* dispersion. However strong a nation's will to destroy might have been, it has never managed to completely achieve its end because the whole of Jewry was, in part, out of its reach. In addition, temptations of otherness—or of assimilation—have affected Jews in too many forms for the diasporas to succumb simultaneously. Seen from a global perspective, Jewish communities have, over twenty centuries, developed a prodigious arsenal of means of survival which has allowed them to elude total catastrophe—that is, disappearance pure and simple. One cannot say as much for certain "territorial" nations, assimilated or destroyed by colo-

nizers or by more well-structured peoples. In the case of a catastrophe—and only the great nations (great in population, I mean) can neglect the possibility of such situations—the concentration of a complete ethnic group in a restricted region makes it hostage to fortune. [. . .]

It is understandable that certain Jews, dazzled by having attained national existence through interposed community, tend to see in the nation-state a "natural" way of leading a collective existence, and they see the existence of groups that have not formed states as pathological. But this judgment has no normative value today and only expresses an ideology and an option. I do not disdain the option, for I note, along with Albert Memmi, the fact "that Israel is the *only* Jewish nation, which is to say a nation where Jews can settle if they wish, by right and without the permission of a power suspected of antisemitism." But I reject the ideology because it makes this other fact incomprehensible: five-sixths of Jews live outside Israel and are well rooted in their respective diasporas, with specific problems that political Zionism cannot resolve or even correctly formulate. That a small number of them are choosing or have chosen Israel makes even more flagrant this fact: the majority has chosen or is choosing the diaspora option on a daily basis. And if some view Israel today as the best refuge in case of danger, the uncertainties of history are such that no one can say if one day the diaspora in turn will not regain the role it played after the destruction of the Temple.

In short, just because a Jew *can* settle in Israel does not mean that he *should* or that he desires to. It is the facts that speak here. To change the option into an imperative, that is what the ideology of political Zionism does and what has made it an outdated discourse since the creation of the State.

* * *

Doubtless, Israel is not just one Jewish community among others. The state organization and territorial settlement tend dramatically to alter the instabilities of Jewish existence by furnishing, along with the real or imagined security attaching to these givens, a simplified means of identification. It is because there has been, since emancipation, a crisis of Jewish identity—which is in accordance with the general crisis of western civilization—that the simplistic nationalism driving Zionist propaganda has exercised so much influence over the past few years and continues to do so. But it exercises this influence also because majority doctrines tend to deny that the Jews, wherever they find themselves, have a right to "a political existence among nations." The identification of the diaspora Jews with Zionist views—and which some who precisely deny that right attribute to the intensely harmful and misleading power of Zionism—results essentially from that denial. What pushes Jews toward Zionism (a Zionism that is verbal for most of them) is not its magical or demonic character, it is the ensemble of ideological, political, and institutional pressures that prevent them from affirming their status as a national minority.

From the moment that one admits the nationalist nature of Jewish existence and focuses on the *whole* of Jewish destiny, the Zionist idea that Israel alone is invested with historic normalcy, that it constitutes a model and an example for other communities, and that Jewish history can no longer be understood except as a function of Israeli history—the fallacious character of this idea becomes evident. This is a quaint vision of Jewish destiny, obscuring the existence of ten million individuals and adopting the discourse of all those who, siding with state majorities, will their disappearance. There they are, transformed once again into *luftmenschen* and called upon to immigrate in order to recover their reality as Jews.

Let me be clear: shortly after the Six-Day War, I said that "the Jews, for the first time since their dispersion, found themselves identified with a violence that was not justified in universalist terms—revolution, the class struggle, the rights of man—but with a violence that was exercised in their own name, that is, for the safety of their community, their historical destiny, their cultural past." I meant that in today's world a group representing a particular culture—even if that culture is in tatters—but completely deprived of the means of violence, would find itself so seriously exposed that its own members might lose confidence in their collective survival. The will to survive of the diaspora thus depends in large part on the existence of the State of Israel, just as the ability of the State to survive depends in large part on the existence of the diaspora.

But that does not transform dispersion into "exile," it does not make emigration obligatory, it does not turn diasporic existence into a shameful malady. It does not authorize the Israeli government to carry out a policy of annexation or to ignore the Palestinian people, it does not eliminate the political and moral difficulties that result from the use of violence, it does not restore to the State its symbolic virginity. It does not absolve the dias-

pora from analyzing its particular problems, recreating its culture, modifying its institutions, affirming its minority status. Indeed, it is not possible to overlook the multiple conflicts that arise from the insertion of Jews into societies undergoing a formidable crisis of civilization and in which the class struggle, bureaucratic oppression, social injustice, and intolerance force them to make constant and difficult choices.

The joint existence of the State of Israel and of the diaspora shows that from now on there are numerous ways to take responsibility for or to create Jewish destiny. Nationalism does not do away with any problems; rather, it adds to existing political and social problems. Moreover, the Jewish communities' most conservative elements reject the notion that Jews might ally themselves with other minorities and define themselves as a minority. The Zionists and a great number of the religious have only scorn for the diaspora in which, however, they live. Hence, they maintain that the Jews, for nineteen centuries, have been content to submit to their fate and were awaiting the Six Day War to dare to assert themselves. If they had only submitted to their fate, Memmi would not be around today to make this scandalous judgment against them—scandalous, because it sees them once more from the perspective of those who have vainly tried to destroy them. Similarly, it is false to claim that among Soviet Jews only those who wish to emigrate to Israel have "recovered" their Jewish character, if only because some of them never lost it; it is at least hasty to affirm that the migratory behavior of Soviet Jews, if they were free to relocate, would differ greatly from that of Jews living in other developed countries. It is also the "establishment" Jew who sides with the centralizing State and defends its practices—thus prolonging the old alliance between rich Jews and State administrators. [. . .]

* * *

To simplify, let us say that in the diaspora indications of Jewish identity are sometimes minor activities—the reading of a newspaper or a Jewish work—and sometimes deep engagements, whether religious, political, community-oriented, or cultural. The minimal sign of belonging may be only an uneasiness relative to the subject's identity—an uneasiness that makes him perceive the culture of the majority "at a distance" and, particularly, that makes him perceive it precisely as a *cultural* system, not a *natural* one. For what characterizes Jewish existence in the diaspora is loyalty or attachment to multiple cultural systems from which one can, to some degree, become detached or liberated. For several centuries a great number of Jews have known that belonging to the ethnic group is a voluntary act (for they are called upon to assimilate or to convert), that the cultural system is consciously maintained, that it is a human creation, and that one can thus *choose* or *desire* to belong. Though it used to be true that one was born into his culture of origin and that it remained an absolute determining force, today it has only relative significance.

Translated by Michele McKay Aynesworth.

Other works by Marienstras: *Le Proche et le lointain: sur Shakespeare, le drame élisabéthain et l'idéologie aux XVIᵉ et XVIIᵉ siècles* (1981); *Shakespeare au XXIᵉ siècle* (2000); *Shakespeare et le désordre du monde* (2012).

Adam Michnik

b. 1946

Adam Michnik was born in Warsaw to a communist family but would later become a leading opponent of the Polish communist regime. Michnik was removed from his position as a lecturer in history at Warsaw University in 1967 as part of an anti-Jewish purge and arrested the next year for organizing student protests. From here, his opposition to the communist apparatus in Poland developed, and he eventually took on a leadership role in the Solidarity Movement that helped topple the communist government in 1989. A member of the Sejm from 1989 to 1991, he is now well-known both as the editor of *Gazeta Wyborcza* and as a historian of left-wing movements in Eastern Europe.

Shadows of Forgotten Ancestors

1973

The events of 1968 therefore came as a shock to me. [. . .]

One could of course continue to claim that it was not the people but only those horrible communists, those monstrous rulers, who with their many voices roared, "We want blood!" just as they had done in the era of the Stalinist trials. But I believe that to adhere to this idea is to mistake a hopeful illusion for reality: The fundamental difference between the years 1952, for example, and 1968 is that in 1968 the anti-intelligentsia and anti-Semitic pogrom was conducted with the active consent of a significant segment of the population. In Poland communism had created its own subculture, whose essence consisted in a traditionalist nationalism. This element could not be exploited to its limit because of the Big Brother's presence. But allusions in the press and the widespread gossip were enough to allow many people to momentarily see that thug of a secret policeman as a national hero, a patriot, and a fighter for independence. Which Poles could believe this? Did there exist in Poland a tradition that justified these convictions? Did the knights from the Kingdom of Darkness and Ignorance who believed themselves to be the only Poles worthy of that name have a tradition to claim? Had there been others in Poland before them who used their participation in anti-Semitic pogroms as a source of national pride? [. . .]

Searching for analogies is a weakness of man's mind. In the encounter with totalitarian reality we are helpless, powerless; we look for situations that can show us how others behaved when faced with dilemmas similar to ours. It was then—in 1968—that I happened to read an account of a meeting between Dmowski and Witte in 1905. [. . .]

So what was it that caught my attention in that Dmowski-Witte conversation? It was the Polish politician's statement to the Russian premier that revolutionary movements in Poland were the work of Jews who'd come from Russia and that the only way to remedy this situation was to hand the Warsaw government back over to Poles, who would themselves put an end to the activities of the socialist fighting squads.

The man who headed these squads, Józef Piłsudski, was the object of abuse and contempt to the National Democratic journalists. He was held to be a tool in the hands of Russo-Jewish agitators without whom it would never have occurred to the Poles to fight for independence and social reforms. [. . .]

Piłsudski was not a nationalist. He did not think it either proper or healthy to organize a national consciousness around the hatred of other nations. He was formed by the special climate of the Vilna province, the common motherland of peoples from different nations, cultures, and religions, a multilingual mixture where the Lithuanian lived next to the Byelorussian, the Jew to the Tartar, and the Pole next to the Karaite. [. . .] Piłsudski saw Poland as the motherland of many nations, a commonwealth of many cultures; he wanted it to be a state in which not only Poles but also Lithuanians, Ukrainians, and Jews could live in solidarity.

[. . .] He wanted Russia, the "prison-house of nations" and "gendarme of Europe" (these were Lenin's terms), to be torn up by the irredentist revolutionary movements of conquered nations. An alternative solution to the political problems of this part of Europe would have been a Polish–Lithuanian–Ukrainian federation. If it were to be attractive to non-Poles as well, such a state would have no room for national or religious discrimination, for the bench ghetto, anti-Jewish pogroms, or anti-Ukrainian pacification.

Piłsudski later had to abandon his ideas about a federation largely because of chauvinistic National Democratic propaganda. Today, we hardly associate idyllic relations between Poles and Ukrainians or Poles and Jews with the period of the Second Republic. Following World War II, Poland became a nationally uniform country, where people who speak other languages form a microscopic minority. So what is left to us of the old dreams of comrade "Wiktor"?

I don't believe all of them have been lost. What is important are not simply the proposals for solutions to real social problems but also the manner of thinking about society in general. The National Democratic mode of thought adopted by the ruling communists commands pride in national uniformity. A friend of mine called this the substitution of a multicolored, multiflowered meadow with a uniform pile of sand in which each grain looks like every other. The virtue of these grains is the cultivation of uniformity, the animosity toward anything different or strange, and a susceptibility to National Democratic modes of thought. It is not true that National Democratic anti-Semitism was only a response to the otherwise unsolvable Jewish question. Anti-Semitism was the way in which the world was understood by these sand grains, a way that [in 1968] allowed massive anti-Jewish sentiments to develop in a country with practically no Jews. [. . .]

In Poland talking about the problem of anti-Semitism is one of the most difficult and risky undertakings. This stems from a complex sequence of cause and effect. [. . .] Toward the end of the Second Republic, following the extreme polarization of public opinion over the "bench ghetto"[1] issue, a situation arose in which every critic of the Jewish community or its representatives, or even of Poles of Jewish origin, was susceptible to be-

ing called an anti-Semite. This phenomenon recurred more forcefully after 1968. The poet Arnold Słucki, who died in exile, explained his decision to leave Poland as his unwillingness to live in a society made up uniquely of philo-Semites and anti-Semites.

Piłsudski was not a philo-Semite. In his articles he frequently criticized the philo-Russian politics of the Bund, the Jewish socialist party. The Bund, which was active among the Jewish proletariat, popularized Russian literature and thus also Russian culture. There would have been nothing wrong in this, except that the orientation coincided with the invader's policies of Russification, and in such circumstances encouraged large groups of the population to lean toward Russia. Piłsudski critically assessed the indifferent or negative attitude of the Bund toward Polish aspirations for independence. But his criticism had nothing to do with anti-Semitism because it never led to the inflaming of national hatred. Piłsudski never viewed the Jews as intruders in this land which they had inhabited for hundreds of years. He never used Aryan criteria in his choice of friends and collaborators. [. . .]

It is clear from my remarks that I prefer the "early," independence-minded, socialist Piłsudski. The actions of the legions which brought Poland independence were a logical consequence of this "early" period. [. . .]

I did not write, and did not intend to write, a congratulatory scroll for Józef Piłsudski. For my generation, which has heard so many lies, truth is of the utmost importance. I have tried to write the truth about the events that took place at the beginning of this century because I consider them to be of the utmost importance. It is from those experiences that independence arose. But I am writing my own, rather personal view of Piłsudski and his role, and I would not like to forget the dark side as well.

NOTES
[Words in brackets appear in the original translation.]
1. Since the mid-thirties Jewish students at Polish universities were forced by their anti-Semitic colleagues to stand up during lectures.

Translated by Maya Latynski.

Other works by Michnik: *The Church and the Left* (1977); *Letters from Prison and Other Essays* (1985); *Letters from Freedom: Post–Cold War Realities and Perspectives* (1998); *In Search of Lost Meaning: The New Eastern Europe* (2007).

LIFE WRITING AND REPORTAGE

Viktor E. Frankl
1905–1997

A highly influential writer on the Holocaust, Viktor Emil Frankl was born in Vienna. Already a noted psychiatrist prior to the war, he believed that psychological disorders could be treated by helping patients find meaning in their lives, postulating that human beings are driven not by pleasure but by a will to find meaning. He and his young wife were deported along with his parents to Terezín and then to Auschwitz. Only Frankl survived, in a succession of camps where his theories regarding the power of finding meaning even in the worst suffering were, in his view, demonstrated decisively.

From Death-Camp to Existentialism: A Psychiatrist's Path to a New Therapy
1946

In attempting this psychological presentation and a psychopathological explanation of the typical characteristics of a concentration camp inmate, I may give the impression that the human being is completely and unavoidably influenced by his surroundings. (In this case the surroundings being the unique structure of camp life, which forced the prisoner to conform his conduct to a certain set pattern.) But what about human liberty? Is there no spiritual freedom in regard to behavior and reaction to any given surroundings? Is that theory true which would have us believe that man is no more than a product of many conditional and environmental factors—be they of a biological, psychological or sociological nature? Is man but an accidental product of these? Most important, do the prisoners' reactions to the singular world of the concentration camp prove that man cannot escape the influences of his surroundings? Does man have no choice of action in the face of such circumstances?

We can answer these questions from experience as well as on principle. The experiences of camp life show that man does have a choice of action. There were enough examples, often of a heroic nature, which proved that apathy could be overcome, irritability suppressed. Man *can* preserve a vestige of spiritual freedom, of independence of mind, even in such terrible conditions of psychic and physical stress.

We who lived in concentration camps can remember the men who walked through the huts comforting others, giving away their last piece of bread. They may have been few in number, but they offer sufficient proof that everything can be taken from a man but one thing: the last of the human freedoms—to choose one's attitude in any given set of circumstances, to choose one's own way.

And there were always choices to make. Every day, every hour, offered the opportunity to make a decision, a decision which determined whether you would or would not submit to those powers which threatened to rob you of your very self, your inner freedom; which determined whether or not you would become the plaything of circumstance, renouncing freedom and dignity to become molded into the form of the typical inmate.

Seen from this point of view, the mental reactions of the inmates of a concentration camp must seem more to us than the mere expression of certain physical and sociological conditions. Even though conditions such as lack of sleep, insufficient food and various mental stresses may suggest that the inmates were bound to react in certain ways, in the final analysis it becomes clear that the sort of person the prisoner became was the result of an inner decision, and not the result of camp influences alone. Fundamentally, therefore, any man can, even under such circumstances, decide what shall become of him—mentally and spiritually. He may retain his human dignity even in a concentration camp. Dostoevski said once, "There is only one thing that I dread: not to be worthy of my sufferings." These words frequently came to my mind after I became acquainted with those martyrs whose behavior in camp, whose suffering and death, bore witness to the fact that the last inner freedom cannot be lost. It can be said that they were worthy of their sufferings; the way they bore their suffering was a genuine inner achievement. It is this spiritual freedom—which cannot be taken away—that makes life meaningful and purposeful. [. . .]

A human being is not one thing among others; *things* determine each other, but *man* is ultimately self-determining. What he becomes—within the limits of endowment and environment—he has made out of himself. In the concentration camps, for example, in this living laboratory and on this testing ground, we watched and witnessed some of our comrades behave like swine while others behaved like saints. Man has both potentialities within himself; which one is actualized depends on decisions but not on conditions.

Our generation is realistic, for we have come to know man as he really is. After all, man is that being who has invented the gas chambers of Auschwitz; however, he is also that being who has entered those gas chambers upright, with the Lord's Prayer or the *Shema Yisrael* on his lips.

Translated by Ilse Lasch.

Other works by Frankl: *Ärztliche seelsorge* (1946); *Logos und Existenz* (1951); *The Will to Meaning* (1966).

Primo Levi

1919-1987

A chemist and a writer of memoirs, short stories, poems, essays, and novels, Primo Levi was an Italian-born Holocaust survivor, regarded as one of the foremost Italian writers of the aftermath of World War II. He studied chemistry at the University of Turin, graduating in 1941. Subsequently, he wrote for the resistance magazine *Giustizia e libertà* and joined a group of Italian partisans. In 1943, he was captured and deported to Auschwitz; he was liberated in 1945 by the Soviets. Levi won the first annual Premio Campiello Literary Award in 1963 and the Premio Viareggio in 1982.

If This Is a Man (Survival in Auschwitz)
1946

Imagine now a man who is deprived of everyone he loves, and at the same time of his house, his habits, his clothes, in short, of everything he possesses: he will be a hollow man, reduced to suffering and needs, forgetful of dignity and restraint, for he who loses all often easily loses himself. He will be a man whose life or death can be lightly decided with no sense of human affinity, in the most fortunate of cases, on the basis of a pure judgement of utility. It is in this way that one can understand the double sense of the term "extermination camp," and it is now clear what we seek to express with the phrase: "to lie on the bottom." [. . .]

We had soon learned that the guests of the Lager are divided into three categories: the criminals, the politicals and the Jews. All are clothed in stripes, all are Häftlinge, but the criminals wear a green triangle next to the number sewn on the jacket; the politicals wear a red triangle; and the Jews, who form the large majority, wear the Jewish star, red and yellow. SS men exist but are few and outside the camp, and are seen relatively infrequently. Our effective masters in practice are the green triangles, who have a free hand over us, as well as those of the other two categories who are ready to help them and they are not few.

And we have learnt other things, more or less quickly, according to our intelligence: to reply "*Jawohl*," never to ask questions, always to pretend to understand. We have learnt the value of food; now we also diligently scrape the bottom of the bowl after the ration and we hold it under our chins when we eat bread so as not to lose the crumbs. We, too, know that it is not the same thing to be given a ladleful of soup from the top or from the bottom of the vat, and we are already able to judge, according to the capacity of the various vats, what is the most suitable place to try and reach in the queue when we line up. [. . .]

Such will be our life. Every day, according to the established rhythm, *Ausrücken* and *Einrücken*, go out and come in; work, sleep and eat; fall ill, get better or die.

. . . And for how long? But the old ones laugh at this question: they recognize the new arrivals by this question. They laugh and they do not reply. For months and years, the problem of the remote future has grown pale to them and has lost all intensity in face of the far more urgent and concrete problems of the near future: how much one will eat today, if it will snow, if there will be coal to unload.

If we were logical, we would resign ourselves to the evidence that our fate is beyond knowledge, that every conjecture is arbitrary and demonstrably devoid of foundation. But men are rarely logical when their own fate is at stake; on every occasion, they prefer the extreme positions. According to our character, some of us are immediately convinced that all is lost, that one cannot live here, that the end is near and sure; others are convinced that however hard the present life may be, salvation is probable and not far off, and if we have faith and strength, we will see our houses and our dear ones again. The two classes of pessimists and optimists are not so clearly defined, however, not because there are many agnostics, but because the majority, without memory or coherence, drift between the two extremes, according to the moment and the mood of the person they happen to meet.

Here I am, then, on the bottom. One learns quickly enough to wipe out the past and the future when one is forced to. A fortnight after my arrival I already had the prescribed hunger, that chronic hunger unknown to free men, which makes one dream at night, and settles in all the limbs of one's body. I have already learnt not to let myself be robbed, and in fact if I find a spoon lying around, a piece of string, a button which I can acquire without danger of punishment, I pocket them and consider them mine by full right. On the back of my feet I already have those numb sores that will not heal. I push wagons, I work with a shovel, I turn rotten in the rain, I shiver in the wind; already my own body is no longer mine: my belly is swollen, my limbs emaciated, my face is thick in the morning, hollow in the evening; some of us have yellow skin, others grey. When we do not meet for a few days we hardly recognize each other.

We Italians had decided to meet every Sunday evening in a corner of the Lager, but we stopped it at once, because it was too sad to count our numbers and find fewer each time, and to see each other ever more deformed and more squalid. And it was so tiring to walk those few steps and then, meeting each other, to remember and to think. It was better not to think.

Translated by Stuart Woolf.

Other works by Levi: *The Truce* (1963); *The Periodic Table* (1975); *The Wrench* (1978).

Ruth Gruber

1911–2016

As a writer and humanitarian, Ruth Gruber produced work of greater consequence than many journalists ever achieve, becoming a larger-than-life figure in the process. Born in Brooklyn to Russian immigrants, she attended New York University and in 1931 was awarded a fellowship to study in Cologne. There she was exposed to Nazism. Upon her return to the United States, she began writing for the *New York Herald Tribune*, which sent her to Siberia and the Soviet Arctic to report on women living under communism and fascism. During World War II, she traveled to Italy to bring Jewish refugees and wounded American soldiers to the United States. Following the war, Gruber was

a firsthand witness to the fate of the ship *Exodus 1947*. She continued her work over the following decades, reporting on such stories as the exodus of Ethiopian Jews.

Destination Palestine: The Story of the Haganah Ship Exodus 1947
1947

The voices of thousands of people floated to us on the quay. They were singing "Hatikvah," the Hebrew hymn of hope. It was the song the Jews sang at every emergency and in every crisis. It was their song of survival.

The ship looked like a matchbox that had been splintered by a nutcracker. In the torn, square hole, as big as an open blitzed barn, we could see a muddle of bedding, possessions, plumbing, broken pipes, overflowing toilets, half-naked men, women looking for children. Cabins were bashed in; railings were ripped off; the lifesaving rafts were dangling at crazy angles.

Framed in the smashed deck stood a blond man, with the saddest eyes I had ever seen. His whole life seemed to be in his eyes, sunk deep under his blond, almost colorless brows. He wore no tie; his ragged trousers were rolled above his bare ankles; his torn shirt was open; his arms were stretched out, holding on to two broken cables.

Up on the bridge were the marines and the sailors who had captured the vessel. The head of one of the marines was swathed in bandages. "That's a real ironhead up there," one of the British officers near me told another officer who was apparently new in the game. "He's always the first one to board these illegal ships and the first one off. Tough as iron. Always comes down with his eyes black, his nose bleeding, or his head bandaged. But nothing seems to hurt him." The second officer laughed admiringly.

From somewhere on the dock, a loudspeaker began to address the people, who now crowded every hole and porthole on our side. The loudspeaker said in Hebrew: "The commanding officer wishes you to come off quietly, women and children first."

Soldiers placed gangways into the holes and then ran up to take charge. Several stretchers were carried aboard. The first person to come down was a pale, sick woman, holding the arm of her husband. She wore a huge army raincoat that made her look like a scarecrow. She carried no bundles, no bags at all. Her face was white and sunken; her eyes were sunken; her lips trembled. She looked like a thousand years of misery.

A child came off, with large, frightened eyes. He carried a potato sack with his belongings; a blanket was strapped across his back. A man and a child came down, hand in hand. The child broke away and ran back up the gangway, looking for his mother. He was sobbing with fright. The soldiers gently pulled him down the gangway again. No one was allowed to return to the ship.

A man with the dark look of hunger came down, carrying a brief case. A cigarette dipped out of the side of his mouth. Soldiers followed, carrying the dead body of a sixteen-year-old orphan, Hirsch Yakubovich, who had come from the DP orphanage in Indersdorf, Bavaria. He had been killed in the battle. The soldiers then brought down the American first mate, Bill Bernstein, mortally wounded. He was unconscious; his head was hidden in bandages. His thin body was dressed in army shorts; one knee was raised on the stretcher with the easy grace of a child asleep.

The people trickled down the gangways in little groups and milled on the dock like frightened animals. They looked weary and shattered, mourning their dead and hundreds wounded. Surrounded by the troops to prevent their escaping into Haifa, they made their first step on the dreamed-of soil. They breathed the air deeply and tiredly.

Still waiting on the ship, behind the confusion of bedding and baggage and splinters, other people stared out at the British. Some of their faces looked defiant; some were filled with hate; some of the people just stood like tourists.

For a little while, no one came off the ship. I learned later that the soldiers were afraid that the Jews would not disembark peacefully. The soldiers told the refugees that the *Ocean Vigour*, the first of the transports, was a hospital ship with milk for mothers and children. Most of the sick and the families went down to be put on the "hospital ship," or to be taken to the hospital at Haifa.

On the pier, the British took off every bandage and examined every wound to make sure that only the serious cases stayed. Some of the wounded screamed with pain as their heads were untied, examined, and then tied up again. A military ambulance waited on the dock. When the army doctor nodded his head, a patient was placed on one of the ambulance bunks, while the refugees and the American crew men, who had now dis-

guised themselves as refugees, watched the lottery. To be sent to Haifa's hospital, they had to belong more to the dead than to the living.

Inside the old boat which once had carried Sunday excursionists up and down Chesapeake Bay, soldiers gave the 4500 refugees a mimeographed statement in several languages which told them that they were going to Cyprus and that they would get their baggage there. "Have you got your stickers?" the troops kept asking the people, handing them big parcel-post stickers on which to put their names. The soldiers assured them that if the baggage was properly labeled, it would be returned to them tomorrow in Cyprus.

The slow march down the gangplanks started again. A woman with large green eyes and the high cheekbones of a Hungarian beauty came down precipitously, wheeling a straw baby carriage. In it was a three-year-old baby with the same facial structure, the gypsylike eyes and skin.

A group of adolescent Polish girls came down and giggled. Almost everyone carried a big green bottle of water. This was the mark of the illegal refugee, his water bottle. There never was enough drinking water; each person on the underground route to Palestine carried his own bottle with him. It was the first thing the British soldiers took away, as though it were a secret weapon. The pier, near the customs table, was littered with broken glass, as the British dashed each bottle into splinters.

The long journey from the river boat to the prison boat began. The refugees walked inside the tracks lined with soldiers under the British *arc de triomphe*. First their hand baggage was thoroughly searched at a long table by soldiers of the Sixth Airborne Division and the CID. All scissors, knives, razors, and fountain pens, which might be used as weapons, were confiscated. These were never returned. Films were taken out of their cameras and their cameras were taken away.

Only a few had identity cards, but some still had UNRRA cards, saying they had been displaced persons at Feldafing, or Landsberg, or some other DP camp in Germany. All their identity cards were taken. A man whispered to me furtively. I hoped he was going to tell me in a few words what had happened, words stolen through the cordon of guards. But he was telling me the most important fact in his life: that his mother lived right up there on Mount Carmel. Would I please let her know right away that her son had arrived on the *Exodus*, was safe, would write her from Cyprus? Then he lost all fear and kept shouting the address, until the British came and dragged him away.

The reporter for *Davar* attempted to talk to someone in a little space along the tracks where, for a moment, there was no soldier. But Major Cardozo, quick as ever, caught the act, forgot his dignity and his stick, ran to the newspaperman, and grabbed his arm. His baby face boiled lobster red. He called two MPs, ordered them to take the newspaperman off the dock immediately, and gave strict instructions to every MP at the gates that this man was not, under any circumstances, to be allowed on pier again.

The heat grew worse. The soldiers wilted; cigarettes hung listlessly from the sides of their mouths. The pier began to take on the noise and smell and animal tragedy of a Chicago slaughterhouse. The cattle moved slowly down the tracks.

There were new faces in the track under the arch of triumph, and new DP types, but the expressions began to fuse into one face of weariness and despair. The agony which had begun for them with the war was being dragged on for another historic day, to be placed in their minds with the days of occupation, the day of liberation, and now the long-awaited day of arrival in the Holy Land.

The little children continued to look solemn and silent and old, as though they had never known any world but this one and they could take it in their stride. But the older people began to show panic as they looked at the mounting piles of duffel bags, potato sacks, paper suitcases, and knapsacks in which they had packed all their worldly goods. They kept pointing to the pile, begging the soldiers to let them find their belongings. The soldiers moved them along.

On the ship, soldiers tossed the baggage out of the portholes. A loud, anguished cry went up as one of the bags missed the pile and dropped forever into the sea.

Depth bombs kept exploding. The British were making sure there were no underwater swimmers to sabotage their work. Major Cardozo danced back and forth. The hot sun beat unmercifully, and the refugees, wearing all they could rescue on their backs, stood drenched in sweat. They mopped their faces with dirty hands and waited to be taken on board the prison ships. No one cried. No one complained. Some walked slowly, dragging their feet, like people in a dream.

The refugees looked up at Mount Carmel and seemed to say to themselves *This land is mine. Soon it will be mine forever. They're only taking us to Cyprus. We'll be there only a year or two. Then we'll come back with visas. We'll come back forever.*

Inside the unreality, there were two realities, family and belongings. The family might not even be a blood family; it might be a family made in the concentration camp, or a family collected together on the road or the borders which the long exodus crossed. It was perhaps a strange family: mother, father, and children, all thirty or forty years old. But whether it was a made family or a blood family, they were terrified at losing it. And now terror struck.

The people were being separated by the soldiers, men from women, into "search pens," lean-tos made of walls of brown sackcloth and strips of wood. In their unreal world, separation meant only one thing—death.

They had been separated in their towns by the SS and that had meant deportation and shooting. They had been separated in Auschwitz and Dachau and Treblinka by the Nazi soldiers and that had meant the gas chambers. Now they were being separated again. Some screamed; some tried to fight off the soldiers; some clung to their families. But they were separated anyway, gently for the most part, but sometimes crudely, depending on the soldier or policeman at work.

Four Arab women, one of them with a big hole in the heel of her black-cotton stockings, searched the women's bodies. We were not allowed to watch the operation in the search pen, but the reputation of the policewomen was not good in Haifa.

The men were searched in a separate sackcloth pen by soldiers and police. They came out of the lean-tos buttoning up their pants. A few smirked a little, as if they had been caught coming out of a bawdy house.

The separation and the terror it evoked continued as they were marched further along the track to the DDT pens. Ours is the great era of DDT, of death to everything that crawls. Soldiers sprayed the flourlike powder on their hair, down their shirts, up their trousers and skirts, and all over their legs.

By this time the heat had become suffocating. The babies, who had been incredibly quiet, began to cry. Men looked dazed and ready to collapse as the red-bereted soldiers shoved them along the last mile. Members of families, separated for the search pens, were taken to different transports. They were reassured that they would be reunited the next day in Cyprus.

Night was infinitely worse on the broken and defeated *Exodus* than day; fatigued and hungry, most of the people gave up the ship. Hundreds came off in a great spurt and waited, pressed hotly against each other on one end of the wharf. The soldiers kept carrying fainting men and pregnant women to a dimly lit first-aid army tent at the entrance of the dock. The people were given treatment and then marched down the processing tracks between two soldiers.

I left the dock to file a story and returned at midnight. The character of the wharf had changed, and even the character of the people seemed different. Their eyes were turned inward now. They had stopped staring up at Mount Carmel. Glaring blue and green searchlights played weirdly on the nameless brooding mass of people and on the river boat that would soon be pulled around to the graveyard of illegal ships.

The eerie lights picked up bits of the people's bodies, bare feet, torn clothes, bandaged arms and heads, faces oily with sweat and dark with resentment and mourning. These last to leave the *Exodus* were the fighters, the philosophers, the ideologists, the leaders, the ones who clung most desperately to the ship and the hope they knew was hopeless that maybe they could stay.

It was easier to talk to the people now, but they were too hungry to say much. They had eaten nothing for almost thirty hours, since their supper at seven the night before.

The battle was ended; for some it had ended at nine when the *Ocean Vigour*, the "hospital ship," had finished loading and departed. The next group to accept defeat had gone out on the *Runnymede Park*, and at 5:40 in the morning, the last of the *Exodus* people sailed on the *Empire Rival*.

Only the broken hull of the excursion boat remained at the dock, with a few soldiers to guard it in its loneliness.

Other works by Gruber: *Haven: The Unknown Story of 1,000 World War II Refugees* (1983); *Exodus 1947: The Ship that Launched a Nation* (1999); *Inside of Time: My Journey from Alaska to Israel: A Memoir with Eleanor Roosevelt, Harold L. Ickes, Golda Meir, and Other Friends* (2002); *Witness: One of the Great Correspondents of the Twentieth Century Tells Her Story* (2007).

Moyshe Nudelman

1905–1967

Yiddish humorist Moyshe Nudelman was active in the Warsaw Yiddish press before World War II and wrote several books collecting Jewish comedy and satire

from interwar Poland. In 1934, Nudelman coedited, along with Joseph Shimon Goldstein, the weekly *Tararam*, a satirical paper. After the war, he worked on a number of Broadway shows, including the musicals *Let's Sing Yiddish* and *Sing, Israel, Sing*, which both played at the Brooks Atkinson Theatre in New York in the late 1960s.

I, the Polish Jew
1947

I have the good luck to be a Polish Jew.

If I were a Greek Jew, a Dutch Jew, a Turkish Jew, or some other kind of Jew, I would be miserable. Who would pay any attention to me and who would be interested in me? Nobody.

But as a Polish Jew I feel quite otherwise. I know that I'm not alone. The whole world is with me. Never mind the whole world—the *Jewish* world is all mine.

For me they make campaigns and charitable appeals, for me they raise funds, for me *landsmanshaftn* [hometown associations] are created in all corners of the world. For me speeches are made at congresses and the enthusiastic applause is not meant for the speaker, but—for me. I myself am in Poland, or in a camp near Munich, or in a camp in Czechoslovakia, or in a home for emigrants in Paris—and yet somewhere far off, in Los Angeles, in New York, in Rio de Janeiro, in Johannesburg, I receive applause.

For me they send food parcels from all over the world, with the best powdered eggs, the finest powdered milk, the most nutritious bouillon extract. If you wish, it's mushroom soup, if you wish, it's pea soup, and if you wish, it's even pure chicken broth. The inscriptions on the packaging are literally dazzling. An inscription of one kind, an inscription of another. The inscriptions alone are enough to make you feel healthier.

And what about the clothing packages? A huge selection. A vest like this, a vest like that. Trousers of this kind and trousers of other kinds. This kind of shoe and another kind of shoe. All—rarities. Impossible to find elsewhere.

And those who send the garments? They take the best and finest clothes off their own backs and send them to me. It makes no difference to them that they have become accustomed to a garment over a period of years, even decades; they do not care that it is a memento of their father, of their grandfather, and great-grandfather. For me, the Polish Jew, nothing is too expensive.

You will encounter appeals for me in Jewish newspapers throughout the world. It is I, the Polish Jew, who arouse pity from one and all and make the whole world groan; I evoke tears from everybody; I touch the coldest hearts.

To me, the Polish Jew, are sent delegates, envoys, correspondents. They comfort me, they inspect me, they photograph me.

I, the Polish Jew, have been photographed in every pose: in profile and full face, from the waist up and full body, alone and with groups, reclining, sitting, and standing. And everywhere you can see the postscript, dedicated especially to me: "There he is, the Polish Jew."

I, the Polish Jew, am pitied, I am celebrated and admired, and I am written about.

Novels, serials, memoirs, skits, essays, and poems are written about me.

Reports are filed about me, discussions take place about me, conferences, meetings, and congresses are convened about me.

Battles are fought over me, people squabble over me, opinions are divided over me, factions big and small arise in connection with me.

For me organizations are created with headquarters and branches.

For me offices are funded, with committees, with a bureaucracy, with employees.

For me Presidents are chosen, and Chairmen and Secretaries, and Commissions.

Circulars and bulletins are distributed about me.

Materials are submitted about me and protests take place about me.

Because of me, people *buy* good deeds, because of me, people *buy* their place in Heaven, because of me, people *buy* honor. But in the end, *if I could buy something for myself*—that would best of all . . .

Translated by Solon Beinfeld.

Other works by Nudelman: *Gelekhter durkh trern: zamlung fun humoristish-satirishe shafungen funem nokh-milkhomedikn lebn fun poylishe yidn* (1947); *Kh'bin olrayt: ikh makh a lebn!: humoristishe monologn fun a "grinem" in Amerike* (1951); *Lakht a yid in Erets Yisroel* (1956).

Leyb Rochman
1918–1978

Leyb Rochman was born to a Hasidic family in Minsk-Mazowieki, Poland. He moved to Warsaw in 1930 and studied at a yeshiva. In 1936, Rochman left the Hasidic world and became a Yiddish journalist, a career he continued after the war. His confessional diary, kept while in hiding, which also described the liquidation of the ghetto in Mazowieki, became an early classic of Holocaust literature. In 1950, he moved to Jerusalem and became the Israel correspondent for the New York–based Yiddish daily *Forverts* and a Yiddish broadcaster for Kol Israel. He was awarded the President's Prize for Literature in 1975.

The Pit and the Trap: A Chronicle of Survival
1949

Today is Wednesday, February 17, 1943. Exactly twelve weeks have passed since we went into hiding here at Felek's. Twelve weeks are eighty-four days and, if my arithmetic is correct, 2016 hours. That's my count. All of us are constantly reckoning the time. We count even the individual minutes and seconds.

Felek hid us as soon as we arrived here. That night we put up a false wall, and we are inside it. This partition (with a little opening at the bottom through which food is passed to us) is very close to the real wall, and our hideaway is extremely narrow and long. Sitting is impossible, and we stand shoulder to shoulder facing the partition. It's also impossible to turn around. We stand still, shoulders drawn and hands at our side, like a row of soldiers at attention. It's dark in there and we can barely see each other. There's no place for daylight to filter through. This fact particularly upset me. So I obstinately set out to find at least some small crack. I scoured every inch of the partition and finally found a tiny speck of light high above it. Full of excitement, I told the others of my discovery. We all studied that speck of brightness and decided that it really was a message from the sun. I was happy, because my mission had been successful, and because it brought us some relief; it means that we aren't completely alone: at least the sun is thinking of us a little. [. . .]

Yes, we must beware, of everybody, even of children. Just let some child get a whiff of you behind the wall and the secret is out, and within a few days the whole area will be talking: "Another five Jews found and shot." An innocent child could indirectly be our murderer.

Harmlessly, the child could tell its mother, who would tell it to a crony of hers, who would pass the news along. Don't blame us. We suspect everyone. And with good reasons: Once, with a full house of visitors, Felek's cat suddenly recalled having seen some food being passed to us through the little door at the bottom of the partition. She must have been hungry, and, with a cat's memory, she forgot that conversation with us is forbidden in the presence of strangers. Instead, planting herself right in front of our little door, she started scratching at it and meowing, I shudder to think of the moment when, after the cat had been scratching and meowing away for a while, one of the guests, a young peasant asked: "What does that cat want inside the wall?" Our clever host Felek had a ready reply: "I guess she smells mice."

* * *

How many acquaintances does a person have? It's a difficult question to answer. It depends on the person. I, aged twenty-five, had tens of thousands of acquaintances until a few months ago. Of course, there are varying degrees of acquaintanceship. There are comrades, colleagues, friends—intimate friends and casual ones—immediate family and relatives—close relatives and distant ones; there are nodding acquaintances, people whom you've met just once, and people you've seen a number of times: people whom you know only by sight and those you know by sound; people you know as neighbors. And there are one's enemies—they're also acquaintances: you know them.

Acquaintances fill up your entire life. You live for them and create for them. You do good for them and steal for them. You boast to them and are shamed by them. They're the ones that keep you from wrongdoing.

God, all five of us are like one person—without acquaintances and relatives. Like a child. No, a child has parents, sisters and brothers, family, while we, thank God, have only ourselves. Except for a handful of relatives overseas. Who knows whether they're still alive? There's a war on.

All our acquaintances belong to the past; parents, family, relatives, everybody you know! Maybe some acquaintance of yours is stuck away in a hole somewhere just as you are here, and he doesn't know that you're alive just as you don't know that he is either.

But that's not true. There are Felek; his wife; Felek's sister, "Auntie." These are new acquaintances; you didn't know them before. None of your old acquaintances—no one—is alive. [. . .]

Even during a catastrophe miracles come to pass that everyone can see. This day also had its miracle. The day ended at 5 P.M. Everybody had gone. It was turning dark outside. Felek and his wife went visiting. Only Auntie stayed home. She locked the door, moved the half-curtains to cover the windows, and, letting out a sigh, opened the little door to our hideaway. "Come out of your ghetto for a while," she whispered. "It's dark outside. Nobody's around, and I've locked up everywhere."

No sooner had we taken a few steps into the room then she said: "For Heaven's sake, you'll be your own murderers! Don't stand; bend down. And crawl on the floor. Somebody might come up to the window."

We got down and crawled into the corners of the room. Auntie ran from window to window humming nervously to herself. She quickly tired of this, and sat down on a stool next to one of the windows. Esther and Zippora crawled over to her from their respective corners and laid their heads in her lap. Auntie—it seems that some of our Jewish ways had rubbed off on her—started swaying and continued to hum that melody of hers. Ephraim and Froiman dozed off in their corners. I also felt like snoozing, but some indefinable dread overtook me, and I felt that I had to get back to our hideaway as soon as possible. But Auntie, who kept glancing outside from under the window curtain, called to me:

"Juzek, why is the sky so red in the west? A pity: they say that it's the Jews burning in Hell because they didn't believe in Lord Jesus."

I crawled over to the window and looked outside: miles and miles of snow, trees draped in white. A high frost, apparently, the trees and fields glistened and the western sky was in flames. I heard a strange murmur outside, but inside it was silent. I don't know how long that went on. I might even have dozed off, only suddenly, Auntie posed me a riddle: "Juzek, what is heaven and what is earth? What's a Jew and what's a Christian? What's that murmur outside? What is life and what is death? I don't understand a thing, Juzek. There's something heavy on my heart. I don't know what it is. Not sadness. Something. I don't know what!" [. . .]

How time flies! We're in a new hideaway, with a new family, and our spirits are a little better. This hideout seems relatively safe. We even have Morwa for a guard, barking at every stranger's approach. Morwa is a medium-sized bitch with white-spotted tan fur. When Szube unchains her each evening, she comes dashing into the granary and sniffs around. But before she's un-

leashed, we all climb into the dugout. We're afraid of
Morwa. We don't want to get too close to her; she might
yet betray us.

In the new hideout, two of us still stand guard up
on the wall of the granary, peering through the cracks.
People often pass by on the grassy trail behind the
granary. They often pause by the well in the yard on
their way to the next village. Szube offers them a drink
of cold water. He has many friends. He used to know
many Jewish people. He visits the granary every day,
and tells us stories about Jews that he knew. They
were storekeepers, who lived in the surrounding villages. Some of them were honest people, and others
were swindlers, who cheated the farmers. His nostalgic
stories depress us; all those village Jews are gone, with
their flour-dusted tunics and boots and little beards
sprinkled with straw. Those Jews with the floury caps
and faces brought trade to the village, and the bond between them and the villagers had lasted for generations.
They had been part of the village. The farmer spoke of
them in the same warm tone as he spoke of the harvest
of ten or fifteen years ago. In my mind's eye I saw those
good, familiar faces, solid plain Jews who were here not
long ago, it seems like only yesterday, and now are gone.
Szube's stories make me feel like an orphan.

Translated by Moshe Kohn.

Other works by Rochman: *Mit blinde trit iber der erd*
(1969); *Der mabl* (1978).

David Daiches

1912–2005

David Daiches was born in Sunderland, England, but
spent most of his childhood in Edinburgh, where his
father was the chief rabbi of the community. Daiches's
memoir, *Two Worlds*, describes rich layers of intersecting identities: Jewish, Scottish, British, as well as the
experiences of Jewish immigrants. Daiches himself
became a leading scholar and critic, particularly in the
fields of Scottish literature, culture, and history. After
receiving his doctorate from Oxford, Daiches worked
at universities across Britain and North America, most
notably helping to found the English Department at
the University of Sussex and serving as director of the
Institute for Advanced Studies in the Humanities at
Edinburgh University.

Two Worlds: An Edinburgh Jewish Childhood
1956

[. . .] The two worlds, in my childhood, were not
really separate. The synagogue in Graham Street, to
which we walked across the Meadows every Saturday
morning, was as much a part of the Edinburgh scene
to me as the Royal Infirmary nearby, just as my father,
rabbi of the Edinburgh Hebrew Congregation and virtual though not nominal head of Scottish Jewry, was a
part of the religious life of Scotland. Indeed, one of my
father's great aims in life was to bring the two worlds—
the Scottish and the Jewish—into intimate association,
to demonstrate, by his way of life and that of his community, that orthodox Jewish communities could thrive
in Scotland, true to their own traditions yet at the same
time a respected part of the Scottish social and cultural
scene. It never occurred to me as a child that this combination was odd or unattainable (still less that it was
comic, as the idea of Scottish Jewry seems to be to so
many of my American friends): I thought of it as part of
the nature of things, a natural result of the golden age in
which we lived, so utterly different from the dark days
of persecution and martyrdom about which we heard
a great deal but never in any contemporary context.
[. . .]

[. . .] True, my father's synthesis, however brilliantly
illustrated in his own life, proved incapable of transmission to his children, at least in the form he gave it. His
ultimate recognition of this was perhaps rueful rather
than either complacent or tragic. But he went on with
his ministry to the end, pursuing his chosen way of life
with heroic dignity. The last thing he wrote was a series
of charming essays for young people on the Jewish festivals. Perhaps, in Talmudic phrase, his works exceeded
his wisdom; his life is more memorable than his writings. And Rabbi Eleazar the son of Azaryah said that
he whose wisdom exceeds his works is like a tree with
many branches and few roots, easily overturned by the
wind, while he whose works exceed his wisdom is like
a tree with few branches and many roots, which cannot
be overturned by all the winds that blow.

Other works by Daiches: *The Place of Meaning in Poetry* (1935); *The Paradox of Scottish Culture: The Eighteenth-Century Experience* (1964); *Literary Landscapes
of the British Isles: A Narrative Atlas* (1979).

Elie Wiesel

1928–2016

Elie Wiesel was born in Romania and moved to the United States in 1956. Wiesel's most famous work describes his experiences as an inmate of the Auschwitz and Buchenwald concentrations camps. Wiesel taught at Boston University and was active in establishing the United States Holocaust Memorial Museum in Washington, D.C. He was an advocate for Jewish causes and a voice for the victims of oppression. In 1986, Wiesel was the recipient of the Nobel Peace Prize.

Night
1958

One week later, as we returned from work, there, in the middle of the camp, in the *Appelplatz*, stood a black gallows.

We learned that soup would be distributed only after roll call, which lasted longer than usual. The orders were given more harshly than on other days, and there were strange vibrations in the air.

"Caps off!" the *Lagerälteste* suddenly shouted.

Ten thousand caps came off at once.

"Cover your heads!"

Ten thousand caps were back on our heads, at lightning speed.

The camp gate opened. An SS unit appeared and encircled us: one SS every three paces. The machine guns on the watchtowers were pointed toward the *Appelplatz*.

"They're expecting trouble," whispered Juliek.

Two SS were headed toward the solitary confinement cell. They came back, the condemned man between them. He was a young boy from Warsaw. An inmate with three years in concentration camps behind him. He was tall and strong, a giant compared to me.

His back was to the gallows, his face turned toward his judge, the head of the camp. He was pale but seemed more solemn than frightened. His manacled hands did not tremble. His eyes were coolly assessing the hundreds of SS guards, the thousands of prisoners surrounding him.

The *Lagerälteste* began to read the verdict, emphasizing every word:

"In the name of Reichsführer Himmler . . . prisoner number . . . stole during the air raid . . . according to the law . . . prisoner number . . . is condemned to death. Let this be a warning and an example to all prisoners."

Nobody moved.

I heard the pounding of my heart. The thousands of people who died daily in Auschwitz and Birkenau, in the crematoria, no longer troubled me. But this boy, leaning against his gallows, upset me deeply.

"This ceremony, will it be over soon? I'm hungry . . ." whispered Juliek.

At a sign of the *Lagerälteste*, the *Lagerkapo* stepped up to the condemned youth. He was assisted by two prisoners. In exchange for two bowls of soup.

The Kapo wanted to blindfold the youth, but he refused.

After what seemed like a long moment, the hangman put the rope around his neck. He was about to signal his aides to pull the chair from under the young man's feet when the latter shouted, in a strong and calm voice:

"Long live liberty! My curse on Germany! My curse! My—"

The executioner had completed his work.

Like a sword, the order cut through the air:

"Caps off!"

Ten thousand prisoners paid their respects.

"Cover your heads!"

Then the entire camp, block after block, filed past the hanged boy and stared at his extinguished eyes, the tongue hanging from his gaping mouth. The Kapos forced everyone to look him squarely in the face.

Afterward, we were given permission to go back to our block and have our meal.

I remember that on that evening, the soup tasted better than ever . . .

I watched other hangings. I never saw a single victim weep. These withered bodies had long forgotten the bitter taste of tears.

Except once. The *Oberkapo* of the Fifty-second Cable Kommando was a Dutchman: a giant of a man, well over six feet. He had some seven hundred prisoners under his command, and they all loved him like a brother. Nobody had ever endured a blow or even an insult from him.

In his "service" was a young boy, a *pipel*, as they were called. This one had a delicate and beautiful face—an incredible sight in this camp.

(In Buna, the *pipel* were hated; they often displayed greater cruelty than their elders. I once saw one of them, a boy of thirteen, beat his father for not making his bed properly. As the old man quietly wept, the boy was yelling: "If you don't stop crying instantly, I will no longer bring you bread. Understood?" But the Dutchman's little servant was beloved by all. His was the face of an angel in distress.)

One day the power failed at the central electric plant in Buna. The Gestapo, summoned to inspect the damage, concluded that it was sabotage. They found a trail. It led to the block of the Dutch *Oberkapo*. And after a search, they found a significant quantity of weapons.

The *Oberkapo* was arrested on the spot. He was tortured for weeks on end, in vain. He gave no names. He was transferred to Auschwitz. And never heard from again.

But his young *pipel* remained behind, in solitary confinement. He too was tortured, but he too remained silent. The SS then condemned him to death, him and two other inmates who had been found to possess arms.

One day, as we returned from work, we saw three gallows, three black ravens, erected on the *Appelplatz*. Roll call. The SS surrounding us, machine guns aimed at us: the usual ritual. Three prisoners in chains—and, among them, the little *pipel*, the sad-eyed angel.

The SS seemed more preoccupied, more worried, than usual. To hang a child in front of thousands of onlookers was not a small matter. The head of the camp read the verdict. All eyes were on the child. He was pale, almost calm, but he was biting his lips as he stood in the shadow of the gallows.

This time, the *Lagerkapo* refused to act as executioner. Three SS took his place.

The three condemned prisoners together stepped onto the chairs. In unison, the nooses were placed around their necks.

"Long live liberty!" shouted the two men.

But the boy was silent.

"Where is merciful God, where is He?" someone behind me was asking.

At the signal, the three chairs were tipped over.

Total silence in the camp. On the horizon, the sun was setting.

"Caps off!" screamed the *Lagerälteste*. His voice quivered. As for the rest of us, we were weeping.

"Cover your heads!"

Then came the march past the victims. The two men were no longer alive. Their tongues were hanging out, swollen and bluish. But the third rope was still moving: the child, too light, was still breathing . . .

And so he remained for more than half an hour, lingering between life and death, writhing before our eyes. And we were forced to look at him at close range. He

was still alive when I passed him. His tongue was still red, his eyes not yet extinguished.

Behind me, I heard the same man asking:

"For God's sake, where is God?"

And from within me, I heard a voice answer:

"Where He is? This is where—hanging here from this gallows . . ."

That night, the soup tasted of corpses.

Translated by Marion Wiesel.

Other works by Wiesel: *The Gates of the Forest* (1966); *Night, Dawn, The Accident: Three Tales* (1972); *The Oath* (1973).

Albert Memmi
1920–2020

Best known for his fictional, autobiographical, and sociological studies of racism and colonialism, Albert Memmi was born in Tunis near the Jewish ghetto of Hara. After completing his secondary studies in Tunis, he studied at the University of Algiers and the Sorbonne, where he met his Catholic wife. During the war, Memmi was imprisoned in a Nazi labor camp, from which he managed to escape. Following the war, Memmi taught at the Lycée Carnot in Tunis and published *The Colonizer and the Colonized*, a reflection on the decolonization of French North Africa, which has become one of the principal texts in postcolonial theory. Ironically, the anticolonialist agenda of the Tunisian independence movement led to Memmi's expulsion to Paris in 1970.

Portrait of a Jew
1962

I was born in Tunisia, in Tunis, a few steps from that city's large ghetto. My father, a harness maker, was somewhat pious, naturally somewhat so, as were all men of his trade and his station in life. My childhood was marked by the rhythms of the weekly Sabbath and the cycle of Jewish holidays. At a fairly early age, after first attending yeshivah and then the Alliance Israélite, I became associated with various Jewish youth movements—scouts, cultural groups, political groups—so that, though I had profound doubts about religion, I did not stray from Jewry. On the contrary, I found it secured me and even deepened a certain continuity for me. For a number of years I pursued a course of studies that dispensed Jewish culture both traditional and reformed, open to the most immediate problems and yet solidly anchored to the past. I took up collections, among the flat graves in the Jewish cemetery or in front of old synagogues, on behalf of various community works, for the poor, for Polish refugees, for German refugees. Without too much embarrassment, illegally or not, I went from door to door trying stubbornly to convince my co-religionists of the beauty, importance and necessity of the Zionist movement at a period when that movement appeared to be nothing but an adventure. I even thought of going to Israel, or rather, to the romantic, pioneer Palestine of those days. In other words, I was sufficiently involved in all Jewish activities for my emotions, my mind and my life to become identified with the lot of all Jews over a fairly long period.

A moment came, however, which actually had its roots in the French lycée, when that intense ardor seemed to stifle me, and the rest of the world suddenly became more important. That was the period of the war in Spain, of the French *Front Populaire*, and of my own departure for the university. While the physical break with the clan and the community, then with the city, and the contact with the non-Jews whom I admired and liked, did not make me forget I was a Jew, it did cause me to consider that aspect of myself as part of a nobler and more urgent problem. The solution to that large body of ills from which all men suffered would in a way automatically solve my personal difficulties. Exchanging one enthusiasm for another, I came to consider anyone who did not think in universal terms as narrow-minded and petty.

It is necessary to bear in mind what that extraordinary period meant to our generation. We believed, finally, that for the first time humanity had perceived the light that could and must disperse darkness once and for all: oppressive measures, differences that separated us from each other, would be shattered, they were already being shattered. . . . Paradoxically, that universal light bore the clearly defined face of Europe—and more specifically, of France; but that did not trouble us; on the contrary, we were doubly grateful to the privileged for relinquishing their privileges and identifying themselves with freedom and progress. After all, it was they who had invented remedies after the ills; equality after domination, socialism after exploitation, science, techniques and promises of abundance. And by the time I left Tunis to continue my studies—soon to be interrupted, however—I thought no more about Palestine but only of returning to my native land, a universalist

and non-denominational, reconciled to everything and everybody, Tunisians, French and Italians, Moslems and Christians, colonizers and colonized. . . . "The Jewish problem" had been diluted with the honey of that universal embrace which, though not fully realized, was so near, so obvious, because so necessary.

We know what came of it: the sequel belongs to world history: it was war. Our youthful hopes of universalism and brotherly love were destroyed. The Europe we admired, respected and loved assumed strange faces: even France, democratic and fraternal, borrowed the face of Vichy. Afterwards they explained that Vichy was not their only face, nor even the true one, that behind that mask, clandestine and noble. . . . So greatly did I hope it was true that I almost believed it, but I was no longer so enthusiastic or naive. On the whole, it was better to make allowances for a dual personality and hope for a change of roles, which was always possible on the revolving stage of history. In any case, I had learned the harsh lesson that *my* destiny did not necessarily coincide with the destiny of Europe. And when peace came and, after numerous vicissitudes, I returned to Tunisia, I envisioned, for the first time but of my own accord and without anxiety, that separate destiny.

What it was to be, I had no idea when suddenly the event presented itself. My Moslem fellow citizens, having made the same discoveries, were beginning to develop their own history. Sensitive to mass enthusiasms when I considered them legitimate, I naturally shared in theirs: the Tunisians aspired to become a nation; in a world composed essentially of nations and oppressed minorities, what could be fairer?

This time, however, I did not altogether overlook the fact that I was a Jew. Moreover, mistrust, hesitancy, blunders forced me to remember it constantly. But, I was assured, Jews would certainly have their place in the future nation; had they not suffered the same lot and the same insults as other Tunisians? Why would they not benefit from the same liberation? I wanted to believe this. In any case, how could I, who applauded so wildly the struggle for freedom of other peoples, have refused to help the Tunisians in whose midst I had lived since birth and who, in so many ways, were my own people? In short, I did not believe I had any right to think of a separate Jewish destiny. Thus, having ceased to be a universalist, I gradually became, in some ways, a Tunisian nationalist . . . though I failed to see that, on my part, there was still a great deal of hidden, abstract universalism in it, and perhaps even escapism.

Justice done to the Tunisians, I quickly found myself faced with that strange destiny which was still unchanged. Events that followed would force me to recognize that its singularity was still unimpaired, that it decidedly could not be overpowered by any other. To take only one example: the young states, formerly under colonial rule, were in urgent need of all sorts of personnel: technicians, administrators, intellectuals. That formidable vacuum could be partially filled by Tunisian Jews. But, as I had feared, the new states preferred to do without them. I hasten to add that it was difficult to picture a fifty percent Jewish personnel at the head of the new state; such a situation would have raised dangerous problems of domestic, and perhaps foreign, policies. But it was soon equally apparent that our distinctness as Jews was by no means resolved by our new status as citizens. Neither for non-Jews, nor for that matter, for Jews. When the war over Suez broke out, the Tunisian newspaper to which I was contributing and which I had helped to found printed on the front page: "Whoever sheds the blood of Egypt, sheds our blood!" At that time the hearts of all Jews beat as one for the Israeli army: their sons and grandsons were there and the sons and grandsons of their friends. I did not approve of that expedition, but how could one reconcile those two conflicting loyalties! When the Tunisian Constitution appeared, it established the Moslem religion among its essential provisions. For a number of reasons that have nothing to do with my subject, I did not find that too shocking; but why would I, who had rebelled against my own religion, accept, under compulsion, the Moslem religion which was now official? Each step, in short, had to be carefully reviewed and put in order.

It will be said that this is no different from the situation of Jews in Europe, in a Catholic country, for example. Of course, I know that! I have now been around the world enough to realize that precisely the same situation exists everywhere. But does that make it any the less difficult? The end of colonization in Tunisia and Morocco has almost restored the condition of those Jews to the level of the condition of all Jews, a notable and decisive step forward. But where has the common Jewish lot ever been simple and without trouble?

In short, I must admit that I had only postponed attacking my problem seriously; it was time for me to tackle it directly and, if possible, finally. Not that I regret or repudiate anything leading up to this; neither my Jewish childhood and adolescence, my Western and French culture and experiences which played such an

essential part in my development, nor the aid and backing I gave to the just cause of the Tunisians.

Translated by Elizabeth Abbott.

Other works by Memmi: *The Pillar of Salt* (1953); *Jews and Arabs* (1974).

Natalia Ginzburg

1916–1991

Born in Palermo, Italy, to a Jewish father and Catholic mother, Natalia Ginzburg published her first novel in 1942, using the pseudonym Alessandra Tornimparte because of anti-Jewish legislation. After the death of her first husband, Leone Ginzburg, at the hands of German authorities, she remarried and converted to Catholicism, although she kept her last name and maintained a strong connection to Jewish tradition and history. After the war, Ginzburg gained prominence for her novels exploring political and familial ties in the aftermath of World War II and Italian fascism. In the 1980s, Ginzburg became involved with politics, joining the Communist Party and serving in the Italian parliament, through which she advocated for social justice and humanitarian causes.

Family Sayings

1963

After the war the world seemed vast, unknowable and boundless. However, my mother went back to living in the world as best she could, happily, for she had a happy nature. Her spirit could never grow old, and she never came to know old age, which means withdrawing into oneself, lamenting the break-up of the past. My mother looked upon the break-up of the past without tears, and did not mourn it. In any case, she did not like to wear mourning. She was at Palermo when her mother had died in Florence, unexpectedly and alone. She was deeply grieved, then she went out to buy mourning clothes. But instead of buying a black dress, as she meant to do, she bought a red one, and returned to Palermo with it in her suitcase. She said to Paola: "What could I do? My mama could not bear black clothes, and she would be very happy to see me in this lovely red dress!"

Alla Cia venne male a un piede
Pus ne sgorgava a volte la sera,
La Mutua la mando a Vercelli.

Cia had trouble with her foot
Pus oozed from it often in the evening
The Insurance sent her to Vercelli.

These three lines about Cia were part of a long poem about women in the rice-fields, the kind of verse that young poets wrote and submitted to the publishing house. After the war everyone believed themselves to be poets, and politicians. Everybody seemed to imagine that one could, or rather one should, write poetry about anything, after all those years in which it had seemed that the world was dumb and petrified, and reality had been seen, as it were, through a glass, in a state of crystalline, mute immobility. During the Fascist years novelists and poets had remained silent, and the few writers chose their words with the greatest care, from the scanty heritage of crumbs which were left over. During the Fascist régime poets found they could express only the arid circumscribed and mystical world of dreams. But now once again words were in circulation, and reality appeared again to be within arm's length. So the former fasters set to gathering these grapes with gusto. This vintage was universal since everyone thought of taking part, and the result was a confusion of language between poetry and politics which appeared mingled together. But then that reality suddenly turned out to be no less complex and secret, indecipherable and dark than that world of dreams. It was revealed to be the other side of the glass, and the notion of having broken through that glass was seen to be a transitory illusion. As a result, many withdrew, discouraged and disheartened, and sank back again in a mood of bitter self-denial and deep silence. So the post-war period was gloomy and depressed after the first light-hearted post-war years. Many isolated themselves in the world of their dreams or in any work that would provide a living; work taken up haphazardly or in haste which seemed petty and colourless after so much excitement, though everyone forgot the brief illusory moment when they shared their neighbours' lives. For many years, of course, no one practised their own professions, but all thought that they could and should do a thousand things together, and it was some time before each man took up his own profession and accepted its burden and the daily fatigue and solitude, which is the sole means we have of contributing to the needs of others who are similarly lost and prisoners of solitude.

As for the verses about Cia who had trouble with her foot, they are moving, and did not seem beautiful then but clumsy, as indeed they are. At that time two styles of writing were fashionable: one was a simple enumeration of facts, in the wake of a grey damp reality in a bare lifeless landscape; the other was a violent delicious mingling of facts with tears, deep sighs and sobbing. In neither one nor other was there any selection of words, because in the first the words were absorbed into the greyness, and in the other they were lost amid the groans and sobs. The mistake common to both was the belief that everything could be transmuted into poetry and language, which meant that ultimately there was a revulsion from poetry and language, so strong that it carried with it true poetry and a true use of language. Everyone was reduced to silence, paralysed by ennui and nausea. We had to go back to choosing words, examining them in order to see whether they were true or false, to see if they had true roots or only the transitory roots of the common illusion. Writers were obliged to take their work more seriously. The time that followed was like a hangover, a time of nausea, lassitude and boredom, and everyone felt in one way or another that they had been cheated or betrayed. This was equally true of those who lived in the real world, and of those who possessed or thought they possessed the means of describing it. And so everyone went their own way again, alone and discontented.

Revised from the original translation by D. M. Low.

Other works by Ginzburg: *Tutti i nostri ieri* (1952); *Caro Michele* (1973); *La famiglia Manzoni* (1983).

Artur Sandauer

1913–1989

Artur Sandauer was born in Sambor, a town on the Polish–Ukrainian border. His father was a member of the Polish Socialist Party who later became a Bundist. Sandauer wrote literary and critical works in Polish and was a firm proponent of modern Polish literature. He escaped the Sambor ghetto during World War II, living under false papers for the rest of the war. He remained in Poland after the war and continued to write. His postwar fiction often dealt frankly with the tensions of Jewish assimilation in the aftermath of the Holocaust. He was married to the surrealist poet and painter Erna Rosenstein.

Family Conflicts
1963

My childhood, if we're speaking of relations at home, was exceptionally easy; I never felt a need to rebel against my parents' conservatism. I encountered no gates to break through—they were all already open. Nor were there prejudices to overcome—they had all been refuted. My father had undertaken for me the effort to liberate oneself from the Jewish Middle Ages; he had fled his home as a teenager. Thus, the process of Europeanization had been completed before my arrival in the world. I was born into a home that was already Polish, already socialist and atheist; around 1905 my father—like a significant percentage of young people from his neighborhood—had joined the newly arisen organization of the Polish Socialist Party (PPS). [. . .]

If, then, there was no conflict between me and my parents, it was only because the demarcation line had moved one generation back; it ran between them and my grandparents. That conflict was intensified as a result of their living close to each other; both sets lived near Targowica, no longer in the Jewish quarter, but not yet in the Polish one, no longer in Blich, but not yet on the Market Square. That closeness gave rise to constant conflicts. I remember my Grandfather Izrael's rage when he rushed into our house, an old man with a beard like a goat, and constantly trembling as if from fever. "What will your end be like, Abram (for that was my father's original name, which he Europeanized to Adolf only at a later age)?" he would shout. "What will your end be like? The other day your wife was seen walking out of the butcher shop in broad daylight, and last Saturday you lit a fire under the stove near a wide-open window. You tell people to call you Adolf, but do you know," and here he lowered his voice to a whisper, "what they call you? *Aher*—the renegade!"

My father endured those invectives in silence for a long time, only glancing every minute or so at an issue of *The Worker* that was lying in front of him. Once, however—it was during one of those holiday feasts at which the entire family was present—the smile disappeared from his face. When Grandfather, thundering against the apostate as was his wont, called Marx a *"meches* [Jewish convert to Christianity],*"* Father turned pale, and before I managed to turn my head and look, the dinner plates were lying on the floor. At the same time, the calfskin-bound prayer book from which Grandfather pronounced the blessings also fell; it was

tit for tat, profanation for profanation. After that, the invectives ceased, but so, too, did the visits. Father had broken definitively with that world.

Grandfather Izrael, however, was unaware that he himself had created the beginning of that apostasy when half a century earlier he had moved from the tribal lair of Blich to the intermediate terrain that was Targowica. It was precisely where the flood waters of Młynówka were drained and the building sites that arose there were sold for nothing. Because an opportunity arose to buy building materials after a demolition job, he allowed himself to be tempted and shortly afterward turned out to be the proprietor of a complex of small one-story houses erected by him, which earned him the highly honorable title in that district of Landlord. The soil was boggy, there were puddles in the roadways that never dried up, and the building materials were badly damaged, so mold attacked the walls. These houses were occupied by the worst riffraff who could afford nothing better. Grandfather himself, tempted by not having to pay, moved into one of these houses.

Moving there, however, he had not foreseen the future consequences of his deed: that in this way he was making possible the beginning of our family's migrations to the Polish quarter. In fact, in the new place of residence, his son, instead of going to debates at the synagogue, began slipping off to the Market Square from where, together with issues of *The Worker*, he brought back a new language and habits. Was not the Biblical Terah the first to similarly cross the Euphrates from Chaldean Ur and settle halfway there in the middle land of Haran, from which his son, also Abram, would move even farther—to the promised land? And did not that Abram, on leaving, also smash the Chaldean holy images which his father honored, and also change his name—from Abram to Abraham?

Grandfather himself never set up house in Targowica. He enthusiastically returned to the other side of the river, to Blich, where the progenitor of his family line still lived, my great-grandfather Aron, known for his eccentricities and righteousness, the arbiter of many arbitration courts in former days. Legend had it that when a certain local potentate did not want to accept his verdict, Great-Grandfather insisted that he humble himself by standing before him only in his stockings; the memory of this Canossa survived in the little town as proof of the superiority of spiritual over secular power. In my day, he was an ascetic bent by age who spent all his time in the synagogue, more yellow than the candles and parchments surrounding him, with a patina frozen in his wrinkles as in the edge of a brass candlestick. When they brought me to him, he looked up at me with eyes faded with age, but whether he was absorbed in some difficult problem or dismayed by my lack of *peyes* [forelocks], it was enough that after a moment he lowered his gaze without a word to the tiny type in the text lying before him.

What was hidden under the deadness of those eyelids? What ancient knowledge opposed Father's optimistic worldview? What did he remember? Crowds rumbling next to the synagogue? Doors giving way under the blows of poles? Tears dripping silently from eyes, like icicles from paraffin candles? Lips turned colorless? The chattering of teeth? We trivialized that knowledge, convinced of the imminent triumph of progress. And in fact, the first postwar years—both community and family events—appeared to confirm those expectations. Father became a town councilor, ran for the Sejm, and I remember how Mother, feverish and radiant, led me to meetings where he threatened unspecified bourgeois with unspecified barricades. I knew that word already from songs.

Our expectations were to be shattered. After the May coup d'état,[1] Father, who until then directed one of the municipal institutions in the city, lost his position and remained unemployed for many years; he also distanced himself, or rather was distanced, from political life. Despite these failures he stubbornly maintained his beliefs. While his former party comrades evolved from the spirit of the times, going over to Moraczewski,[2] occupying positions in life and an apartment on the Market Square, he changed nothing—neither his address nor his convictions. If his more fortunate contemporaries, lawyers and doctors now, appeared in their old district, it was only once a year to participate in the autumn religious observances which they still did not have the courage to evade. I remember the sarcastic smile with which Father watched them through the window as they paraded in front of our house in their top hats and black suits, with prayer books under their arms, heading to the tribal lair, to Blich, in the direction of the Great Synagogue. He himself did not go to synagogue, did not participate in religious services, and if he bent over some book with prayerful fervor it was probably only over the works of Kautsky or Bebel.

NOTE

1. [In May 1926, Marshal Józef Piłsudski overthrew the established Polish government of President Stanisław Wojciechowski and Prime Minister Wincenty Witos and established a semiauthoritarian regime that was popularly called Sanacja, or "The Cleansing." Piłsudski justified this action by the alleged incompetence and corruption of previous governments. Most Jews preferred Piłsudski to the previously parliamentary regime, which they perceived as more antisemitic.—Eds.]

2. [Jędrzej Moraczewski (1870–1944) was a former Polish prime minister and a prominent figure in the Polish Socialist Party. He was expelled from the party in 1927 because of his ongoing support of Józef Piłsudski. He then organized a rival faction which sponsored its own labor unions, sparking bitter conflicts with the mainstream PPS and the Bund.—Eds.]

Translated by Madeline G. Levine.

Other works by Sandauer: *Śmierć liberała* (1947); *W 2000 lat później* (1956); *On the Situation of the Polish Writer of Jewish Descent in the Twentieth Century* (1982).

Ilya Ehrenburg
1890–1965

Kiev-born Ilya Ehrenburg was a major writer and journalist and one of the most prominent Jews in Soviet culture. During World War II, his patriotic articles were a mainstay of Soviet propaganda. Embracing his Jewish heritage at the outbreak of the war, he served on the Jewish Anti-Fascist Committee and, together with Vasily Grossman, spearheaded a project to document Nazi atrocities against the Jews, in the so-called *Black Book*. Dramatic shifts in Stalin's Jewish policy suppressed publication of the *Black Book* inside the Soviet Union until 1991. Ehrenburg's short novel *Ottepel'* (*The Thaw*), which broke with socialist realist conventions of creativity, was to give its name to an entire political era, the age of post-Stalinist liberalization under Nikita Khrushchev. Ehrenburg's memoirs provided important insights into Soviet cultural policy and postwar antisemitism. They were especially valuable because they were written not by a dissident but by a major establishment figure.

Post-War Years 1945–1954
1966

The months of which I am about to write are probably amongst the most painful in my whole life; I interrupted my work on the book for a long time trying to summon up the courage to embark on this chapter. I should have been glad enough to omit it altogether.

But life is not like a set of galley-proofs; what you live through cannot be deleted on second thoughts. [. . .]

The persecution of "cosmopolitans" was not an isolated phenomenon. Large numbers of people were arrested who, through no fault of their own, had been taken prisoner by the fascists, or had not had time to be evacuated from overrun territory, or had voluntarily returned from exile abroad, or had been "repressed" in the thirties, or had relatives in foreign countries. Beria's arbitrary operations were truly comprehensive.

As for myself, from the beginning of February 1949 I was not allowed to publish anything. My name was deleted from the critics' reviews. These symptoms were quite familiar, and every night I expected the front-door bell to ring. The telephone was silent; only close friends rang up to inquire how I was. There were also those who "checked": the more cautious of our acquaintances would ring up from a call-box to find out whether I had been arrested and on hearing my voice would put down the receiver.

In March 1938 I used to listen anxiously to the lift: in those days I had wanted passionately to live; like many others I had kept a suitcase ready packed with two changes of underwear. In March 1949 I gave no thought to underwear and awaited the outcome almost with indifference. Perhaps it was because I was now fifty-eight and not forty-seven; I was tired and beginning to feel old. Or perhaps because it was a repeat performance, which, coming after the war and the victory over fascism, seemed utterly intolerable. We went to bed late, in the small hours: the idea that they might come and wake me up was too horrible. Once the bell rang at two o'clock in the morning. Lyuba went to open the door. Simonov's wife had sent their driver to find out if her husband was with me.

At the end of March a friend of ours dropped in and shouted with pleasure: "So it isn't true!" He told us that the day before, at a lecture on literature, a speaker who at the time held a rather responsible position had announced in the presence of over a thousand people: "I can give you some good news: Cosmopolitan Number One and enemy of the people Ilya Ehrenburg has been exposed and arrested."

I wrote a short letter to Stalin saying that for the last two months I had been denied all journalistic work and that the day before So-and-so had announced my arrest; that in fact, however, I had not been arrested and I wished to have my position clarified. All I asked was that an end be put to the uncertainty. I took my letter to the Kremlin sentry-box.

The next day Malenkov rang me up. I remember the conversation clearly. "You wrote to Stalin. He asked me to ring you up. Tell me, how did all this start?" "I've no idea. I should like to ask you that." "But why didn't you let us know sooner?" "I spoke to Comrade Pospelov, that was all I could do." "Strange, Comrade Pospelov is a very reliable man but he never said a word to us." [. . .]

Immediately the telephone came to life again: various editorial offices said that there had been a "misunderstanding," that my articles would be published and would I write some more. [. . .]

It is easy to be wise after the event. In the spring of 1949 I did not understand anything at all. Now that we know a little I believe that Stalin used a technique of heavy camouflage. Fadeyev told me that the press campaign against the "unpatriotic critics" had been launched on Stalin's instructions. But a few weeks later he summoned the editors and said: "Comrades, the divulging of literary pseudonyms is inadmissible, it smells of anti-Semitism." Rumour attributed the arbitrary measures to those who carried them out while Stalin was thought to have been a restraining influence. By the end of March he apparently decided that the job was done. [. . .]

I was in wretched form and could not work. Then I was told that I must go to Paris for the World Peace Congress. The defence of peace seemed to me a splendid thing but I did not feel I had the strength to go. It would have been torture to find myself abroad in the state in which I was. I was asked to write a speech and submit it for approval. Faced with a blank sheet I began to write about what was stirring me most deeply. This passage occurred in the speech: "There is nothing more odious than racial and national arrogance. World culture has arteries which cannot be severed with impunity. The peoples have learnt and will continue learning from one another. I believe it is possible to respect distinctive national features while rejecting national exclusiveness." I was summoned to Grigorian, who held a rather high position, and he pressed my hand and thanked me. My speech, typed out on good paper, was lying on his desk, and against the passage I have quoted were the words "Well said!" in a handwriting that looked to me painfully familiar. [. . .]

The Aragons took me to the noisy Restaurant Méditerranée; it was crowded; people were telling one another how they had spent their Easter holidays. Acquaintances came up to the Aragons, there were jokes and laughter. Then Louis and Elsa asked me in Russian: "What is meant by 'cosmopolitans'? Why are pen-names violated?" They were my own people, I had known them for a quarter of a century, but I could not answer their questions. When Cocteau came up and started some urbane social chatter I forced myself to smile. [. . .]

I have said that in this chapter I wanted to recount the most difficult time I ever had to live through. I hardly think I have succeeded, for how can one really convey such things? Let me add only this: the most terrible experience of all was that first night in Paris when, in the long narrow hotel room, I realized the price a man has to pay for being "true to men, to the century, to fate."

Translated by Tatiana Shebunina with Yvonne Kapp.

Other works by Ehrenburg: *The Black Book* (1946); *Liudi, gody, zhizn'* (1961).

Shmuel Gordon

1909–1998

The shtetl, a much maligned subject in Soviet Jewish culture, became the focal point in the postwar reportorial writing of Shmuel Gordon. Born in Kovno (Kaunas), Gordon was orphaned and grew up in Ukraine. He studied at the Yiddish department of the Second Moscow State University, graduating in 1931, and pursued a career as a prose writer and journalist, often writing about Jewish communities in Birobidzhan and agricultural settlements. His first collection of stories was published in 1934. He was employed by the Jewish Anti-Fascist Committee during the Second World War. Imprisoned by Stalin in 1949 as a conspiratorial Jewish intellectual, Gordon survived in the gulags until 1956. He later returned to Moscow and wrote witty reportage for the journal *Sovetish heymland*. His last major work was a novel about the persecution and murder of Soviet Yiddish intelligentsia.

A Soviet Shtetl
1966

Like every shtetl Medzibosz has a main street, and side streets and back streets. Nowadays the old hunched little huts have mostly vanished, and there are new houses in their place—not everywhere.

Thirty years ago many of the inhabitants of the shtetlach left to go to the big industrial towns. Few returned. And few returned also from the collective farms in Crimea and Kherson. Few returned, and fewer new residents have arrived. So the shtetl is more roomy. There are gardens and orchards, and other signs of the village, rather than the shtetl. Even without the war shtetlach like Medzibosz would have grown together with the village. The children of the shtetl who have not left it, have not followed the ways of their parents, have not become tailors or carpenters. They work in the tractor stations and in the repair workshops of the collective farms.

If I hadn't known this was Medzibosz, would I have recognized it as having once been a Jewish shtetl? Hard to say. The street is almost a village street. The sounds are those of a village—the combines and the tractors. The air is full of village smells, fresh hay, ripe cherries, gasoline.

Even before I saw an elderly stocky man coming out of a nearby house I already had my answer. Though the house was painted a light village blue, and the roof was covered with shingles, it was clearly a shtetl house.

"So you're not from these parts," said the elderly Jew, when I asked him if there was a hotel where I could stay. "If you want a hotel. Where are you from? From the Oblast? An inspector? Or perhaps you've come here for a holiday. Because no new residents come to us—not for ever so long. This isn't your first time in Medzibosz? Then there's no need to tell you what a bustling shtetl this was. You see all these gardens and orchards? Before the war there were all houses there, and where the park is there were also houses—and what houses!

"What is the idea, you ask yourself, of tearing down the best houses, the finest houses? How is it that instead of sending the whole shtetl up in fire and flame, as those brutes, curse them, used to do, here they started digging up the ground, and pulling down the houses? Could they have been searching for gold, for gold and diamonds that they thought the evacuated Jews had buried under the floors, buried in the ground? They did the same in all the neighboring shtetlach. I once went to Letitchev. Just the same as here. That's the hotel over there."

He looked at me strangely: "You're not by chance from the Welfare Ministry? It seems to me that I saw you there. Look"—he pulled out a pack of papers—"I'm just on my way to the District Council. I have really more than is needed to get a decent pension. Where and at what haven't I worked in my time? I started as an errand boy in a shop; I was a water carrier, a carter, a watchman. All sorts of things. How should I have known that you must produce papers to prove all this! I have found one paper that shows that I was once, poor me, a kabtzan, a pauper, "declassed" was the word used at that time. They told me in the District Council that this paper has no bearing on the case. So it's no good. So have I to go at my age to learn some new proper trade? Because if I become a watchman I'll only get the same pension that I'm getting now, perhaps a fraction more."

"Where can you go and learn a trade?"

"Where? Number one, in a combine plant. The collective farm. That's two. The canning factory. Three, the mill. How many does that make? Then there's the village. If I had sat on a tractor as much as I have sat on the box of a cart, I'd be all right now. Could you perhaps help me? It isn't the money so much I'm worried about. We're not a big family, just my wife and I, till 120. We've no rent to pay—the house is our own. We don't have to go shopping in the market. We've got a vegetable garden and an orchard. The children, bless them, send us something. It's the annoyance and the shame of it! To have worked for so many years and at the end of it—that's all! Go and explain to everybody why I get such a small pension. Perhaps you can put a word in for me in the Department."

"I'm sorry, but I'm not connected with the Department."

Translated by Joseph Leftwich.

Other works by Gordon: *Tsvishn azovn un shvartsn* (1934); *Patriotn* (1936); *Birobidzhaner kinder* (1937); *Milkhome-tsayt* (1946); *Birobidzhaner toyshvim* (1947); *Yizker* (2003).

Léon Ashkenazi

1922–1996

Yehuda Léon Ashkenazi (Manitou) was born in Oran, Algeria, and was the son of Algeria's chief rabbi, David Askénazi, and his wife, Rachel Touboul, whose family included scholars of Spanish Kabbalah. Ashkenazi studied in yeshiva and secular academies in Algeria and Morocco; he served in the French Foreign Legion during World War II and then settled in Paris, where he earned the nickname "Manitou" in the Jewish Scouts. He taught at the École de pensée juive de Paris with Emmanuel Levinas and André Neher, integrating traditional Judaism with modern philosophical values.

Chapters of My Autobiography
1967

The story of my life is only exceptional in that it represents a great change of identity in the heart of the Jewish people. [. . .]

I was born a Jewish Algerian—a French citizen to boot—and during the first phase of my life, spent in Algeria until World War II, I saw myself, without paying too much attention to definitions, as an Algerian Frenchman of the Jewish faith.

After the war I lived in France, where the immense sociological complexity of the Jewish people and of their history came home to me when I ran into—I, of Sephardic origins—Ashkenazic Judaism.

During the third phase of my life I lived, as an Israeli, in Israel. Thus, after a particular fashion, my life serves as an example of the change of identity that, in our time, has transformed the Jewish people into a Hebrew nation, or more precisely, has transformed Jews into Israelis.

For much of my life I was a Jew of the diaspora, and I still remember the moment when I became aware of my identity as a Jew of the diaspora, an identity that continues to exist in a manner parallel to, or on the periphery of, Israeli society. I know by experience that a Jew of the diaspora does not easily understand the reaction of an Israeli to the fact that four-fifths of the Jewish people seem not to have been touched by this change of identity. Undeniably, there is a solidarity—not of fate, a term foreign to Jewish tradition—but of historic destiny, common to the whole of the Jewish people. And that is why I have felt it necessary to explain in French, for the French public, this conscientious reaction of the contemporary Israeli.

Algerian Frenchman of Jewish Origin

I was born into a family of rabbis; my grandfather was an Algerian rabbi. I always felt comfortable in the world of Jewish identity in which he lived and in which I, as a child, also lived.

That world, which has represented one of the modes of Jewish existence in the diaspora for two thousand years, was extremely complex.

During those two thousand years, the Jew was always the man of mixed identity, of Hebrew origins, but in a very close symbiotic relationship with the cultural landscape of the country to which his travels had led him.

In Algeria, however, there was a particular twist in that several different cultures had been mingled there. One could thus formulate this very particular species of Jewish culture: we prayed in Hebrew and, through the Hebrew of our prayers, we were linked to the whole Hebraic and biblical past. Our psyches were divided among Arabic music, Spanish folklore, and our cultural language, which was French. [. . .]

Today I am familiar with my grandson's Jewish world, a coherent Hebrew world, and I am as comfortable there as I was in that of my grandfather, though in a completely different way. Nonetheless, it is quite obvious that there is a fundamental asymmetry: my grandson will never know the bygone world of my grandfather. [. . .]

My grandfather dreamed of my grandson's world, but he did so in a way that was traditional, classic, Orthodox, in the manner that a rabbi of the diaspora, at one with his tradition and his beliefs, dreamed of the restoration of Hebraic identity. [. . .]

The Flaw in Our Relationship with French Identity

The war arrived in 1939 and, born in 1922, I was not yet old enough to be mobilized. And then, the war was lost. [. . .]

With the Allied landing in 1942 came a profound awakening, one of the first, for many an Algerian Jew: there was a *flaw in our relationship with French identity*.

Thanks to Vichy laws being applied in Algeria, we were no longer considered to be completely French citizens. In fact, we were given French identity cards bearing the words

"Jew-Native Algerian." [. . .]

It was the Vichy regime, pressured by the Germans, and we were expecting to regain our French nationality with the Allied victory. That is how a crucial change came about for Algerian Jews of my generation, who experienced that period intensely, a time that was—I realize a posteriori—one of the reasons for my decision to become an Israeli. For, in fact, after the Allied landing, Vichy's laws against the Jews continued in force, even though Algeria was part of the liberated world. [. . .]

Immediately after the war I returned to France and there began a second stage in my life. [. . .]

I have known survivors from very different Jewish origins—from Poland, from Russia, from Hungary—who for me represented the Jewish people in a much more massive and novel way and who needed to be or-

ganized. Given the flaw in our relationship with French identity, this was the second factor that led me to assume an Israeli identity.

There I found a dimension of identity that was much more solid, more concrete, more coherent than that sort of religious epiphenomenon grafted onto a national identity, however prestigious it might be. An epiphenomenon, certainly, that represented an insertion into the Jewish identity, but expressed in a way that was travestied, translated, devitalized, and bound to be rapidly lost. I discovered the Jewish people as a political entity, whereas in Algeria we were Frenchmen of the Jewish religion. [. . .]

That is when I began to understand that *what unites all the Jews in the world is not primarily their religion but their nationality*.

Belonging to the Jewish religious community is clearly identifiable, but on a collective scale. . . . The religious dimension of Jews is primarily collective, not individual, and that is the source of my understanding that *the Jewish religion is the tradition of a people* and not at all a faith in which individually perceived beliefs are commonly held. In other words, the word *communauté*, which we use in French to translate our word *kehila* [community], is false. We were a national identity with its own religion and not a religious community such as the Protestant congregations after the revolution. [. . .]

I had no calling at all to be a community rabbi. It seemed artificial to be a religious bureaucrat, even though, in an atavistic way, the rabbinic identity was present in me. I wanted to study philosophy in order to express the Jewish tradition in the words and expressions of the West. I never thought of myself as an academic, but rather as a rabbi teaching the Jewish tradition to academics, and to do that I needed to be familiar with general philosophy. [. . .]

We Become Hebrews Once Again

In 1954/1955, I had begun organizing trips to Israel for students at the École d'Orsay, then later for university groups, and thus for the first time I traveled to Israel.

The shock was enormous. First, I felt at home; second, Judaism had been resuscitated. We had become Hebrews once again. By discovering Israeli reality, I had discovered a completely different dimension of that which was our proper work. It was nonsense to imagine the resurrection of Jewish identity in any language other than Hebrew. [...]

We were speaking Hebrew, but it was the Hebrew of antiquity. And so we discovered the insertion into contemporary reality of that which was for us a millennial tradition. That tradition, throughout our exile, had ended by being formulated on a sublimated messianic mode. Suddenly we were becoming aware that in Israel a work was being accomplished in historic reality. [...]

It became clear that it would be absurd not to associate myself with that common destiny of the Jewish people, *the hope that was becoming reality*, and that I should have my own family participate in it. As for why I am the one to have experienced this rather than other Algerian Jews who had nearly the same existential equation—is it attributable to the grace of God? Or to the merits of one's ancestors? Is it the good fortune of having encountered teachers who put me on the right track? Is there a personal calling that will always remain mysterious to me? By definition, a traditional Jew sees himself as belonging to an unbroken chain and to a larger picture.

I experienced this transformation as a personal story, but also as an exemplary event that happened on a collective level.

Translated by Michele McKay Aynesworth.

Other works by Ashkenazi: *Sod ha-'ivri I, II* (2005, 2009); *Misped la-mashiah?!* (2006); *Sod leshon ha-kodesh* (2007); *Sod midrash ha-toladot* (2009).

Elias Canetti

1905–1994

Born in Ruse, Bulgaria, to a Sephardic family, Elias Canetti was a German-language novelist, essayist, and dramatist who lived in Austria, Switzerland, Germany, and England. He is known also for his study of Kafka's letters and for a three-volume autobiography. Canetti received the Nobel Prize in Literature in 1981.

A Visit to the Mellah
1968

On the third morning, as soon as I was alone, I found the way to the mellah [in Marrakesh]. I came to an intersection where many Jews were standing around. Traffic was streaming past them and around a corner. I saw people pass through a vault that appeared inte-

grated into a wall, and followed them. On the other side of the wall, enclosed on four sides, lay the mellah, the Jewish quarter.

I found myself in a small, open bazaar. In low, dungeonous rooms men squatted amid their wares; some of them, dressed in European clothes, sat or stood. Most of them were wearing the black skullcap that distinguishes the Jews here, and many of them were bearded. In the first stores to which I came fabrics were sold. One man was measuring silk with a yardstick. Another was calculating, guiding his pencil quickly and absorbed in thought. Even the more lavishly appointed stores appeared very small. Many of them entertained visitors. In one of them two very fat men were carelessly lounging about a lean one, who was the owner, and were conducting with great dignity an animated discussion with him.

I walked past as slowly as possible, studying the faces. Their diversity was astonishing. There were faces that, in different garb, I would have thought Arab. There were radiant old Jews by Rembrandt. There were Catholic priests of sly stillness and humility. There were Eternal Jews, their entire being suffused with restlessness. There were Frenchmen. There were Spaniards. There were reddish Russians. One would have liked to greet another one as the patriarch Abraham; he spoke condescendingly to Napoleon, and a hot-tempered know-it-all, who looked like Goebbels, interjected himself. I was considering the migration of souls. Perhaps everyone's soul has to become a Jew at some point, and now they are all here. None of them remembers who they were before; and although it is revealed in their faces with such clarity that I, a stranger, can perceive it, each one of them still firmly believes that he is descended in a straight line from the people in the Bible.

But there was something they had in common, and as soon as I had gotten accustomed to the rich diversity of their faces and their expressions, I tried to discern what that commonality was. They shared a way of looking up quickly and judging the passer-by. Not once was I able to walk past unnoticed. When I stopped, they may reasonably have suspected a potential customer and assessed me in that respect. But I received that quick, intelligent glance usually long before I stopped, and received it too when I was walking on the other side of the small street. Even in the few who were lying about like lazy Arabs, that glance was never lazy. It arrived, a skillful scout, and left again swiftly. There were hostile glances among them, and glances that were cold, indifferent, critical, and infinitely wise. But they never seemed stupid. They were the glances of people who had to be always on guard, but who do not want to provoke the hostility they are expecting: not a trace of the slightest provocation, and a fear that kept itself wisely concealed.

One could say that the dignity of these men is contained in their circumspection. The store is open on one side only, and they do not have to worry about what his happening behind their backs. In the street, these men feel more insecure. I soon realized that the Eternal Jews among them, the men who appeared restless and dubious, were always passers-by, people who carried all of their wares with them and had to forge a path for themselves through the throng. They never knew if someone wasn't going to attack their wares from the back, or from the right or left, or from all sides. Whoever had his own store and could to sit in it had something almost calm about him.

Translated by Susanne Klingenstein.

Other works by Canetti: *Auto-da-Fé* (1935); *Crowds and Power* (1960); *Der andere Prozess: Kafkas Briefe am Felice* (1969).

André Chouraqui

Letter to an Arab Friend
1969

The year was 1933: one automobile picked us up to take us both from Jerusalem to Haifa over the road which passes through Nablus. The boat which brought us to Marseilles allowed us to discover for the first time the eastern Mediterranean. We scarcely noticed the British colonials and tourists who surrounded us. The arid rocks and sand which we had just left, our world of olive trees and cactus, of orange trees and pines, heightened our nostalgia. A line from Mallarmé expressed our joy very well: "Je suis hanté: l'azur, l'azur, l'azur, l'azur" [I am haunted: the blue sky . . .]. We were suspended in the infinite blue between sky and ocean.

For the first time in a long time men of our race were leaving their Asian birthplace to set sail for Europe. During the long family evenings in the courtyard of the house covered with its red stones—sign and glory of Jerusalem—your mother would reflect upon the history of our two families, retracing every branch and destiny from generation to generation: as far as man could remember, nothing similar had happened. Our mothers

spoke to each other either in Arabic or in Ladino. When you were a baby, your mother was sick for a time and could not nurse you. My mother nursed you, confirming in the eyes of everyone in the neighborhood the existence of a true family bond between us.

We weighed anchor and pulled away from the gravity of the ages. We were discovering the advantages of being abroad and we marvelled at everything: the rhythm of the ocean, the rolling of the waves, the endless scenery, the biting wind, the schools of dolphins appearing on the sea-foam from time to time and trying to race our boat, the light playing in the full fires of the sun at twilight, in the secret of the night or in the sudden bursts of dawn, and finally, the dazzlement of the ports of call. We had chosen the longer route, the Greek islands and Piraeus, the straits of Sardinia and Stromboli, Naples, Genoa, and finally Marseilles.

After so much sun and blue, the pastures, the forests, the vineyards, seemed to be a miracle. So much green after the barren rocks and sand of the hills of Judea! We had never imagined that such a lush and cultivated world could exist. It seemed as though we had entered a new universe. Was it the universe of grace? In the joy of our discovery, we were ready to believe it.

In Paris, we took rooms not far from rue Mouffetard, in a little hotel, rue du Pot-de-Fer. We were very near the quays and only minutes from the Sorbonne and Notre-Dame. From our balcony on the sixth floor we overlooked the roofs of Paris, the city which would let us discover both the world of the intellect and the world of the heart at the same time. Our university studies gave us more than an occupation—they opened wide the doors of knowledge for us. We read anything that happened to fall into our hands. The events which were occurring around us, the rise of the Popular Front, the establishment of Hitler's empire in Germany slid over us as if we were not really affected by every development. Mussolini's invasion of Ethiopia, the war in Spain, Hitler's seizure of power, all seemed secondary by comparison to the awakening of our minds and paled in the light of the intellectual progress we were making. Everything was new in this marvelous universe which offered itself to us. We distinguished badly between light and shadow. At secondary school in Jerusalem, we had been smug about our literary preferences and life had a tendency to become confused with our dreams. Now we were being carried away by our enthusiasm for the sensual fervor of an Andre Gide or the ontological ecstasy of Spinoza. But our year of philosophy and our contact with our French teachers and friends offered us more solid nourishment. While you were engrossed in Karl Marx, I began to get acquainted with the Bible which distracted me from the seduction of pantheistic thought. It became my guide as I discovered, by myself and for myself, a transcendent reality at the fountainhead of the Infinite.

Books, museums, our long treks across Europe discovering Italy, Spain, the Scandinavian countries, Belgium and Switzerland, our gambits across France, bicycling over the roads of Provence, our awe at Chartres, the chateaux along the Loire, the romanesque churches of Moissac or Vézelay were less meaningful for us in the long run than the warmth of the Parisians. With what wonder we felt the human solidarity which emerged from a ride in the Métro or an hour spent in a café! Our student evenings in the Latin Quarter or at the Cité Universitaire shook us from our lethargy, tore us from our torpor, and opened the great chambers of our minds. We established so many friendships that they finally broke our atavistic resistance. The authority of our teachers, their merit, and even their contradictions united us with the great currents of civilization. They oriented us to the modes of a new thought and permitted us to understand, front a new perspective, what was happening around us and in the world.

Do you remember Arthur Plessier? We met him at a lecture and soon took a liking to him. With such delight we would often scale the steps of the towers of Notre-Dame to sit by the side of the organist during Sunday mass, you the Moslem, I the Jew, with him the Christian, to commune there, thrilled by the organ music and the solemnities of the Christian liturgy. In spite of the years, the memories remain engraved in my mind. I see you next to Karine, the Swedish friend you met one day in the courtyard of the Sorbonne. She had been attracted by your facial expression, and was to understand you better than you, yourself, ever had. Friendship was not slow to become love. There was such a violent contrast in your personalities that you must have both tortured and enriched each other as you shared everything during the many years of your life together. You were like the alliance of water and fire, of earth and air. The two of you, she the Nordic, the Christian, and you the Palestinian Moslem, were a symbol and an omen in our eyes. To what extent did she help your development? To what extent did she shackle the soaring of the genius we recognized in you?

With the ease of genuine talent, you reached the head of the class. When your father died, a wealthier uncle took charge of you. He also had greater ambitions for you. When you first arrived in Paris, you were far behind the others. We watched you and were dismayed that you couldn't pronounce a single foreign word without a telltale Asiatic accent. Yet in a few months you succeeded in catching up and finished the year with honors. Our teachers recognized a mathematical genius in you. We were sure to have a young Einstein among us. Later, you were to have a brilliant career. Yet, you disappointed us. Was it Karine who was responsible for the conflict in you? Or, rather, was it her presence which tore you away from a strictly book-oriented, professorial career to restore you to your vocation as a champion of people's rights, a democratic leader, a revolutionary?

Translated by William V. Gugli.

Hélène Cixous

b. 1937

Born in Oran, Algeria, Hélène Cixous is a French feminist theorist, professor, and fiction writer. In 1968, she received her doctorate and the following year published her first novel, *Dedans*. Cixous helped establish the University of Paris VIII, where she taught literature and organized the Centre d'études féminines. A recipient of the Prix Médicis, Cixous is a founder of poststructuralist feminist theory.

Inside
1969

And my father is rotting. Around the bed where my father used to sleep when he wasn't dead, the mother of my father went round and round in hurried little steps, and I couldn't tell whether she was the one pursuing death as she pushed her stiff legs along, without taking her feet off the floor, or whether it was death who was chasing her around the bed; seeing her walk, I'd always thought she was afraid of the void: she'd never let the worried soles of her feet leave the ground except in the evening, at sunset, when she'd hoist herself atop the three mattresses of her bed. Did she feel the need at night to satisfy the impulse of her soul toward the upper climes? I was told that in my grandfather's time there'd been only two mattresses. Perched up there, she was probably hoping to be closer to him. Dreams alone couldn't lift her stiff body. Squatting on my heels in the southwest corner of the room, huddled up around my soul which was curled up into a ball to the tip of my heart, I took up no more space than a dog. I watched, I listened. Inside the web of my skin I went on transforming myself, never allowing my soul the time to get back to my human form. Better to be a dog, or a lizard, than myself. Better to be dust, a dead cat, or a peach pit, than the daughter of a dead man. The smaller I became, the less of me there would be for life to slash to pieces. For the first time I envied the patience of things, the tininess of specks of dust, the unfeeling flesh of fruit. I had trouble finding the door to get out of the moment; I found I was growing out to infinity, on both sides of the moment, I who had always imagined myself as fitting entirely within the slender arms of my father. Yesterday I was little. Today I was somewhere else and someone else. Yesterday time, world, History, life, all forms of knowledge were in my father's head, and I was in his hands, and there was nothing I needed. The only thing I had to do was grow up. The only thing I owned was my childhood. My dreams I never took seriously. There were stories that were not written down. The past was as closed as my notebooks, from year to year, and every day was so sharply etched between two nights, that I felt its space fitting my rhythm, as though we were made for each other; my piece of bread and butter was just the right size for my mouth; I was still near enough to the ground, at the right height for plants and nice animals. War, money, newspapers, newscasts, rolled along above my head, unable to touch me any more than thunder could; I heard the rumblings of the world that I would enter later on and I took passionate delight in the mysteries of my age. Sadly I worshipped my childhood, I was fragile and all-powerful at the same time. I had the right to rule in a world created for my pleasure, which was enough for me. What was real interested me not at all for it did not burden me. I had time to watch the most unenterprising insects, to make a beetle go round and round, to make a string of ants climb up a stem, I had time to count my steps, and to count the number of stamens in the heart of a daisy. I knew all about dates, odors, shapes.

Yesterday there were three forces, three kinds of matter, three sorts of space, and that made for three ways of being; of these I knew only two and ran from the third. In the center there was me and what I could see, I was alone, barely knowing myself, but not judging myself either. I secretly encouraged all my desires, and protected my fears and my plans behind the outward show of childhood. In truth, I was never a child; I'd imitate the other children out of caution and by guile. I would

cry, sleep, recite as was expected of someone my age, and I hid the fact that I was a growing and ancient force. I didn't know everything my father had learned. But it was only a matter of time; now I had all eternity. In the center of things, I could do anything. I can do anything.

Around me, nature developed my senses. Nature—limited, repetitive, stupid—fascinated and irritated me like the smooth skin of a woman; until the day before, the only thing I knew about it was what touched my body, the elements, seawater, odors, the distances my feet had traveled. I was a visitor on earth: I strolled through a real city, but all of reality, the future, the thinking, lived bottled up inside me. I didn't believe, or even imagine, that behind the walls of houses and behind people's faces, there could be living things: no one spoke but me, no one thought but me, no one waited, or prayed, or desired, or expected a sign, but me.

Around me there were my father, my mother, my brother and I, and around us the family, and then the mass of enemies. My father knew all the words, I was confident in what he knew; I was trying to please him. I didn't dare admit it in my dreams, but the two of us would meet alone, in a space that had been cleared away beforehand, made up of a mixture of solid ground and shadows. My father was an elegant and serious young man, who wore a light-colored suit, and while I asked him the essential questions he would grow and grow until his hat touched the sky, though I would never feel that he'd outgrown me. I concluded from this that I, too, must be growing in his eyes, though I did not seek to prove it to myself since we were together.

Now it was precisely during one of these encounters that he died. I hadn't seen him for two weeks, except in dreams, and it had been a month since I'd heard his voice. He had lapsed into silence, without giving me any explanation, and he lay quietly resting, motionless on the bed. So I summoned him in secret, and when he appeared in his light-colored suit, I had the agonizing feeling that I was betraying the man who lay silently on the bed.

My secret father and I had a good talk however, though we whispered in order not to contradict the needs of what was real. I strained to hear him, I couldn't grasp the meaning of his words; they were all new. On top of that, I was not at the right height, and that day I didn't dare tell my father he was too far above me. At that time, my pride was the greatest power of my being. Nothing could have made me own up to a weakness. All I could make of his murmurings were the most loving sounds I'd ever heard, which breathed such a fire into my body that I took it for that joy which allows human beings to fly. Could it be that my father's words were made of the wind that carries us away, the wind whose name I did not know? I took off.

Translated by Carol Barko.

Other works by Cixous: *La jeune née* (with Catherine Clément, 1975); *Le Rire de la Meduse* (1975).

Nahum Goldmann
1895–1982

Zionist activist Nahum Goldmann was born in the Lithuanian shtetl of Visznevo (now Belarus). His family moved to Frankfurt when he was six years old, and he studied law and philosophy in Germany. Goldmann first visited Palestine in 1913 while working for the Jewish division of the German Foreign Ministry. He became a fervent Zionist and tried to enlist the Kaiser's support for the movement. Goldmann was forced to flee Germany in 1934 and subsequently served as the liaison officer with the League of Nations for the Jewish Agency in Palestine. In 1940, he moved to the United States, where he directed the Jewish Agency in Washington, D.C. After the war, Goldmann returned to Europe and divided his time between Israel and Paris. He was involved in negotiating reparations with West Germany.

The Autobiography of Nahum Goldmann
1969

Negotiations with the Federal Republic of Germany

My negotiations with German Chancellor Konrad Adenauer and his associates, which culminated in the Luxembourg Agreement of 1952, make up one of the most exciting and successful chapters of my political career. From the beginning these negotiations were a subject of great ideological and emotional controversy among Jews. The premises they were based on represented something quite new and unique. There hardly was a precedent for persuading a state to assume moral responsibility and make large-scale compensation for crimes committed against an unorganized ethnic group lacking any sovereign status. There was no basis in international law for the collective Jewish claims; neither Israel nor the Jewish people could use power politics to force Germany to recognize them. This was a moral problem from the first, although post-Hitler Germany had an understandable political interest in allaying the enmity of world Jewry. That Germany could be persuaded to recognize and satisfy this predominantly moral claim is a triumph of momentous significance.

Obvious as it may seem today, many years after the signing of the Luxembourg Agreement, many Jews found it very difficult to recognize its positive side at first. Any question concerning relations between Germans and Jews was highly charged with passion, and I was always aware of the emotional nature of the problem. Even during those critical months, when I was reviled by a large section of Jewish opinion both in Israel and abroad as a betrayer of Jewish honor, when I had to travel accompanied by an Israeli bodyguard, I stated publicly and privately that I understood and respected the hostility my position aroused. But I have always maintained that nations must not let their relations be dictated by emotion. Their own interests require them to find a way to live together and not be dominated solely by feelings, however justified these may be. Every foreign policy determined by emotion sooner or later ends in catastrophe. One nation can conquer another and destroy that defeated enemy, morally reprehensible as such an act always is. But to hold a permanent grudge against yesterday's enemy is impossible in the face of historical change. Only groups that do not engage in foreign politics and are aware of their powerlessness can allow themselves the easy luxury of living for emotions. The Jews did this during their centuries of ghetto and Diaspora life, but a people that has succeeded in establishing its own state, that wants to acquire positions of power and have its claims satisfied can no longer permit itself such indulgence. Be that as it may, the emotional complexion of the problem was for many years an obstacle to any active discussion of restitution. [. . .]

At the same time I emphasized that whatever Germany did could be no more than a gesture. Nothing could call the dead to life again; nothing could obliterate those crimes; but a symbolic gesture would have a deep meaning. The coming negotiations, I said, were unique in nature. They had no legal basis; they were backed by no political power; their meaning was purely an ethical one. If there was to be any haggling, it would be better not to begin the talks at all. If the negotiations were not to be conducted on the basis of an acknowledged moral claim, if they were not to be begun and ended in a spirit of magnanimity, then I, the sponsor of this claim, would advise the chancellor and Israel not to engage in them at all. Conducted under the wrong conditions, they would only poison relations between the Jews and the Germans still more.

I told the chancellor that I understood how difficult it must be for him to accept Israel's demands as they stood as the basis for negotiation and mentioned my talk with Blankenhorn of the day before. On the other hand, I assured him that unless they were accepted neither the Israeli parliament nor the Claims Conference would authorize the opening of negotiations and postponement would jeopardize the whole undertaking. Finally, I told him that I knew I was asking something unusual, something that by conventional standards might be considered incorrect. "But this is a unique case," I concluded. "Until now, Chancellor, I did not know you, but in the twenty-five minutes I have been sitting here opposite you, you have impressed me as a man of such stature that I can expect you to override conventional regulations. I ask you to take upon yourself the responsibility of approving the undertaking I have requested, not merely verbally, as I suggested to Blankenhorn, but in the form of a letter."

Chancellor Adenauer was visibly moved and replied: "Dr. Goldmann, those who know me know that I am a man of few words and that I detest high-flown talk. But I must tell you that while you were speaking I felt the wings of world history beating in this room. My desire for restitution is sincere. I regard it as a great moral problem and a debt of honor for the new Germany. You have sized me up correctly. I am prepared to approve the undertaking you request on my own responsibility. If you will give me the draft of such a letter after our talk, I will sign it in the course of the day."

Translated by Helen Sebba.

Other works by Goldmann: *Erez-Israel, Reisebriefe aus Palästina* (1914); *Von der weltkulturellen Bedeutung und Aufgabe des Judentums* (1916); *My Life as a German Jew* (1982).

Nadezhda Mandelstam
1899–1980

Nadezhda Mandelstam was born Nadezhda Khazina in Saratov, Russia, to a middle-class professional family; her mother was one of the first female doctors certified in Russia, and her father was an attorney. She spent her formative years in Kiev, where she met poet Osip Mandelstam. They were married in 1922. In 1934, after

Osip read from a satirical poem about Stalin, he was sentenced to the gulag. Nadezhda joined him. In May 1938, Osip was arrested again and died. Nadezhda spent the next twenty-eight years wandering throughout Russia's provincial towns to avoid arrest, teaching English. In 1964, she was allowed to live in Moscow, where she completed her dissertation in linguistics. Mandelstam committed her husband's poems to memory in the hope that someday she would be able to publish them, a goal that she ultimately achieved. The focus of her memoir *Hope against Hope*, a masterpiece in its own right, is on the terrible last years of the poet.

Hope against Hope: A Memoir
1970

The death of an artist is never a random event, but a last act of creation that seems to illuminate the whole of his life under a powerful ray of light. [. . .] Why are people surprised when poets are able to foretell their own fate with such insight and know before hand the manner of their death? It is only natural, after all, that death, the moment of the end, should be a cardinal element—one to which all else is subordinate—in the structure of one's life. There is nothing determinist about this—it is rather to be seen as an expression of free will. M. steered his life with a strong hand toward the doom that awaited him, toward the commonest form of death, "herded with the herd," that we could all expect. [. . .]

But, preparing for death, people nevertheless try at the last moment to put off the inevitable end. [. . .] This was how M. behaved after he had written his [fateful] poem about Stalin. [. . .]

The major factor was no doubt a feeling that he could no longer be silent. The phrase "I cannot be silent" was often on the lips of our parents' generation. The same could not be said of ours. But there is always the drop that fills the cup to overflowing. By 1933 we had made great progress in our understanding of what was going on. Stalinism had shown its colors in one large-scale undertaking—the mass deportation of the peasants, and in the lesser one of bringing the writers to heel. [. . .]

Like Akhmatova, M. did not believe in suicide in the ordinary sense—even though everything was driving us to it: our loneliness, isolation, and the times themselves, which were scarcely on our side. Loneliness is not just the absence of friends and acquaintances—there are always enough of these—it is rather a society which heedlessly, with blindfolded eyes, follows its fratricidal path, dragging everybody with it. Not for nothing did M. call Akhmatova "Cassandra." Apart from a few poets like her, there were also some other people of an older generation who could see what was coming, but their voices had died away. Even before the victory of the "new spirit" they had spoken out about its ethics, its ideology, its intolerance and its perverse notions of law. But these had been voices in the wilderness, and with every day that passed it clearly became more and more difficult to speak. How could you speak when your tongue had been cut out?

In choosing his manner of death, M. was counting on one remarkable feature of our leaders: their boundless, almost superstitious respect for poetry. "Why do you complain?" M. used to ask. "Poetry is respected only in this country—people are killed for it. There's no place where more people are killed for it." [. . .]

The first people to hear the poem were horrified, and begged M. to forget it. For these particular people, its value was also lessened by the self-evident nature of the truth it contained. In more recent years it has been received with greater sympathy. Some people ask me how it was that M. could understand everything so well already in 1934, and wonder whether there is a mistake in the dating. These are people who accept the official story that everything was all right until the Yezhov terror, and that even that wasn't so bad—it was only after the war, when he was in his dotage, that the old man went out of his mind and made a mess of things. This may no longer hold water [and the truth is beginning to seep through], but we continue to idealize the twenties and [to tack onto them] the beginning of the thirties. This is a stubborn legend. The old generation is dying out without having had its say, and there are now old men—including even former camp inmates—who go on talking about the glorious years of their youth as a golden age cut short only by their arrest. What will our grandchildren make of it if we all leave the scene in silence? [. . .]

All I know for certain is that M.'s poem was ahead of its time, and that at the moment it was written people's minds were not ready for it. The regime was still winning supporters and one still heard the voices of true believers saying in all sincerity that the future belonged to them, and that their rule would last for a thousand years. The rest, who no doubt outnumbered the true believers, just sighed and whispered among themselves. Their voices went unheard because nobody had any need of them. The line "ten steps away no one hears our speeches" precisely defines the situation in those days. The "speeches" in question were regarded as something old and outmoded, echoes of a past that would never return. The true believers were not only sure of their own triumph, they also thought they were bringing happiness to the rest of mankind as well, and their view of the world had such a sweeping, unitary quality that it was very seductive. In the pre-revolutionary era there had already been this craving for an all-embracing idea which would explain everything in the world and bring about universal harmony at one go. That is why people so willingly closed their eyes and followed their leader, not allowing themselves to compare [theory with practice], or to weigh the consequences of their actions. This explained the progressive loss of a sense of reality—which had to be regained before there could be any question of discovering what had been wrong with the theory in the first place. It will still be a long time before we are able to add up what this mistaken theory cost us, and hence to determine whether there was any truth in the line "the earth was worth ten heavens to us." But, having paid the price of ten heavens, did we really inherit the earth?

Translated by Max Hayward.

Other work by Mandelstam: *Hope Abandoned* (1974).

Emanuel Litvinoff

1915–2011

Emanuel Litvinoff was born in what he called the Jewish ghetto of London's East End. His parents fled from pogroms in Odessa to England, and Litvinoff grew up in poverty, often sleeping in doorways after leaving home. Although drawn to pacifism, he was persuaded to enlist during World War II after learning the magnitude of Nazi persecution of Jews. He first gained success as a poet, notably confronting the antisemitism of T. S. Eliot. After two poetry collections, he turned to novels and wrote plays for television. Following a visit to the Soviet Union in 1955, he pioneered the campaign for Soviet Jewry.

Journey through a Small Planet
1972

The New York Yiddish Theater opened its London season that autumn with what the drama critic of our building, a watchmaker named Shmulik, described as a daring translation of Gotthold Ephraim Lessing's *Nathan the Wise*. I heard him discussing it with old Mrs. Rosen, the grocer, while she was at her daily task of weighing sugar into blue paper bags. Lessing was an assimilationist of the worst kind, according to Shmulik, and consequently he made his heroine, Recha, fall in love with a goy of exceptional vulgarity, a *sheigetz*. Mrs. Rosen shook her head with disapproving vigour, her ritual wig almost slipping into the sugar. Even at the best of times *Nathan the Wise* wasn't Shmulik's favourite play, but on top of everything he had the bad luck to sit next to a woman who didn't stop eating fried fish the whole performance. She must also have been a critic, he remarked sourly.

The failure of *Nathan the Wise* was redressed by the next production, a Goldfaden comedy, the title of which I have forgotten. It succeeded because it made people laugh and cry and remember the past, all at the same time. And even though one always heard how bitter everything was in the past, the old people were still crazy to relive it. After the triumphant first night, there was a stampede for the box-office by every class of Jew from master tailor to under-presser. The moneyed rolled up in taxis all the way from Park Lane and Stamford Hill but mingled on equal terms with class-conscious proletarians. Toothless crones who could barely hobble to the market place, raced along Whitechapel as if rejuvenated and used their stick-like elbows to reach the front of the uproarious queue. Trampled peanut shells and discarded sweet papers made the pavement look like Victoria Park on a Bank Holiday. There were vendors selling hot beigels, baked potatoes, fruit, chestnuts, fizzy drinks. Down-at-heel rabbinical types with matted beards solicited alms for *yeshivot* in Vilna or Jerusalem. Street musicians who hadn't played the fiddle for years scratched out their rusty tunes. Everybody said it was like the old days at the Pavilion and elderly intellectuals in Goide's restaurant, squeezing the last drop of lemon juice into their tea, predicted a miraculous revival of Yiddish culture.

All this, of course, hardly affected the younger generation and Fanya Ziegelbaum might never even have met Rosenheim if the American troupe's costumes had not needed constant running repairs. She was introduced to the wardrobe mistress by a mutual friend. On her very first evening Rosenheim strode off-stage wearing buckskin breeches and cavalry boots. He was full of fire and tenderness, still under the influence of his romantic role. Fanya went down on her knees to stitch up the split

seam and as she did so, she was later to tell my mother, the actor put out his hand to stroke the back of her neck. He must have been pleasantly surprised by her youth and freshness for even *ingenues* in the Yiddish theatre were performed by actresses who'd already married off their own daughters. As for Fanya, she must have been parched for the touch of such a hand, and from then on there was nothing in life she wanted more than to stand under the *chuppah* and become Mrs. Rosenheim. The second Mrs. Rosenheim, in fact, the actor soon confessed, but certainly, he promised, the last. When the season in London was over, he'd take her back to America and there make her his own little angel bride.

Afterwards, when the damage was done, everybody said they'd known it would end badly, but if so they were careful not to say it to the girl's face. Whenever she came round to us, the neighbours were never short of an excuse to drop in. Suddenly they ran out of sugar, or were in need of change for the gas meter, or just looked in as they were passing. The springs of the sofa sagged as one by one they settled down comfortably to stay for a cup of tea.

Fanya was excited and talkative. "Such a cold audience last night," she would say, "you wouldn't believe!" Or, with evident satisfaction: "Six curtain calls yesterday." All of a sudden she was an expert. The future of the Yiddish theatre worried her. People would rather go to see any rubbish at the movies nowadays. And where were the playwrights, the new Sholem Aleichems? The public no longer had respect for a Jewish actor. They spat in his face. Harry—that was what she called Herschel Rosenheim—had turned down offers to play the biggest roles on Broadway, but how long could he go on making such sacrifices?

The women would surely have preferred to hear less of Rosenheim the actor and more of Rosenheim the lover. It was hard for us to believe actors were real people. Did they bleed real blood, experience real suffering, go to the lavatory? Musicians, yes. Prizefighters also. But actors? Fanya was young, foolish, she had romantic notions. Maybe it wasn't even true about Rosenheim: it could be an exaggeration. And even if it was, an ordinary working girl, what did she want with an actor? About such people one thing was sure, morals they didn't have.

My mother said: "An orphan like you, without even a mother or a father, you have to be careful somebody doesn't take an advantage." Everybody knew what that meant. Two minutes pleasure, nine months pain, and unspeakable ruin. "After all, how long do you know him? Practically from yesterday! Sometimes a man pays a compliment. He makes a flirtation. Marriage," my mother said heavily, "is for a whole lifetime."

Fanya was a serious girl. She thought for a while before replying, then looked into my mother's face with the solemn eyes of one who had seen her destiny. "Sometimes you can be sure in a single minute," she said with sombre conviction and added humbly: "I don't know why I should be so lucky. Once Harry danced with Gloria Swanson. At a charity ball. I don't know what he can see in me."

Other works by Litvinoff: *The Untried Soldier* (1942); *A Crown for Cain* (1948); *The Lost Europeans* (1959); *The Man Next Door* (1968); *Notes for a Survivor* (1973).

FICTION, DRAMA, AND CHILDREN'S LITERATURE

Arthur Koestler

Thieves in the Night
1946

But the distant lulls were merely the frame of the picture; the feast for Joseph's eyes was the green Valley of Jezreel itself, the cradle of the Communes. Twenty years ago a desolate marsh cursed with all the Egyptian plagues, it had now become a continuous chain of settlements which stretched like a string of green pearls across the country's neck from Haifa to the Jordan. It was the proudest achievement of the Return, the nucleus of the Hebrew State, the valley of valleys. A battlefield throughout the ages, it was grandiose even in its geological features, for its eastern part sloped down into the deepest inland depression of the earth, four hundred feet under sea level. This eastern part was a broiling tropical underworld with temperatures surpassing a hundred degrees in the shade, and it seemed perverse that the oldest of the large Communes—Herod's Well, House Alpha and Josef's Hill—had been set up just in this infernal, swampy, disease-ridden and robber-haunted spot. But twenty years ago land in those savage marshes had been cheap and each square yard of the country had to be bought for hard cash; and the National Fund's only sources of income were charitable donations and the blue collecting-boxes which the jet-eyed, curly-haired children of the race jingled in the East-Ends from Warsaw to New York;—begging-bowls for the purchase of a kingdom. The race proverbial for its financial genius had to buy its national home by acres on the instalment plan, and native speculation soon drove the price of an acre of desert marsh up to the level of a building plot in an industrial town. If this was Jehovah's punishment of the money-changers, the old desert god had once more proved his vindictive ingenuity. But this time the Colonial Office had outwitted even old Jehovah. No more wasteland was to be sold to the homeless. The wooden plough had to be protected against the noisy tractor, the thirsty earth against the artifice of irrigation, the stones on the fields against impious removal and the helpless mosquitoes against the cruel draining of their breeding marshes. For behold, there was still justice in the world which looked after the feeble. [. . .]

The khamsin is a hot, dry, easterly wind blowing from the Arabian desert. The name is of Egyptian origin and signifies "fifty"—the fifty days between Easter and Pentecost on which the khamsin is said to be particularly frequent.

As with its kin: sirocco and foehn, bora and mistral, the khamsin's effect on the humours of man is violent and mysterious. Its intensity varies from a tepid breeze, importunate like an unwanted caress, to the scalding whiff from an open boiler. But it is not the surface effect of the moving air which counts; nor its heat; nor the thirst, the irking dryness, in throat and nostrils. What matters is the khamsin's nervous effect, and the things which it does to those functions of the body which are beyond voluntary control.

There are no statistics on the increase of suicide, manslaughter and rape on khamsin days. Its influence on the nervous system cannot be expressed in measurable quantities.

Measurable are only the physical changes in the atmosphere. It is known that the temperature close to the ground may jump upward during a khamsin by 35 degrees and pass 110 degrees in the shade. The relative humidity of the air may drop to one-seventh of the normal and come within 2 per cent of absolute dryness. The electrical conductivity of the air may increase to twenty times its normal value, while its radioactivity may increase two- to three-fold. But what do these measurements reveal? Not much, except perhaps the fact that man is subjected to the moods of Nature in more and subtler ways than he is wont to imagine. His apparent dominion over her is purely external; as Gulliver was tied in his sleep by the Lilliputians, so he remains attached to the blind forces by a web of thin, invisible threads tied to his solar plexus, the parasympathetic ganglia, the electrical charge of his nerve-sheaths, the vaso-regulators of his endocrine glands. A clumsy slave who imagines himself master because his chains have been replaced by a silken strait-jacket.

The sky on khamsin days over Ezra's Tower is leaden grey with high vapour and desert dust. On the slope facing Kfar Tabiyeh the twigs of the young pines move in a soft, rain-heralding way in the mute air; but there will be no rain. The liberating thunder seems on the tip of Nature's tongue; but she sticks her tongue out at you and there will be no storm. There is a protracted expectation and frustration in the sulphuric air; like Messalina's long, tormenting embrace it excites but refuses relief; a panting, suffocating ascent which never reaches its climax. A storm is brewing within arm's reach, brewing inside people's ears and ribs, which will never discharge itself. [. . .]

The city of Jerusalem is a mosaic of religious and national Communities, more or less neatly divided into separate residential quarters competing in holiness and mutual hatred.

Its sacred core, the Old City, is surrounded by Soleiman's Wall and divided into a Moslem, a Christian, an Armenian and a Jewish quarter. Outside the Wall there is the German Colony, the Greek Colony and the Commercial Centre; the rest of the town is part Arab, part Hebrew. The latter part is again subdivided according to the origin and period of the immigrants who built it, from the ancient slum ghetto of the quarter of the Hundred Gates to ultra-modern Rechavia, non-Aryan offshoot of the Weimar Republic complete with glass, chromium, Goethe, Adler and Thomas Mann. Each of these separate worlds lives at no more than a ten minutes' walk from the others. They stare and sniff at each other without mixing, rather like camels sniff at the exhaust pipes of motor-cars, and derive about as much satisfaction from it.

The night after their arrival in Jerusalem, Joseph and Simeon walked through the badly lit Arab quarter of Musrara, almost deserted at this late hour, then turned into Me'a She'arim, the Street of the Hundred Gates. The "Hundred Gates" is the oldest of the Hebrew quarters outside the confines of the Old City; it was founded in the eighteen-seventies, and its first inhabitants were the ancient and pious who came to the Land not to live but to die. They brought with them their savings of a lifetime, which they handed over to the Kehillah, the Jewish Community, in exchange for a monthly pittance to the day of their death. While waiting to die they prayed, quarrelled, studied the Book and made souvenirs of the Holy Land—albums with pressed flowers from Mount Scopus, sachets of velvet filled with holy earth, pen-holders of olivewood with a tiny inlaid lens through which one could see a micro-panorama of Jerusalem. These souvenirs were sent abroad to be sold to other Jews, and their proceeds were the main income of the Community. In between these godly occupations the elders of the Hundred Gates fought their family feuds, cheated, begged, got drunk once a year to celebrate Esther's triumph over Haman, fasted on the day of the Temple's destruction, ate bitter herbs to commemorate the exodus from Egypt, blew the ram-horn which brought down the walls of Jericho, expected Messiah's arrival from week to week, and while waiting to die begot children at a patriarchal age. As the years passed younger people too began to inhabit the Hundred Gates, men in black kaftans and fur hats, women with shorn heads and wigs, pious and prolific. A dozen children to a couple were no rarity in those days, the younger ones sleeping in their parents' beds, the others on the floor; they lived in holiness and squalor, in tenements with labyrinthine courts and long narrow iron balconies teeming with toddlers and vermin. Unlike the Moslem slums which were fragrant with spices, horse-dung and charcoal, the Hundred Gates smelt of oil lamps and Primus cookers, damp washing and hot beans in grease. However, underneath all this variety of smells lay as an ever-present foundation the odour of Jerusalem: the odour of the sun-heated rocks and of the white chalk dust in the streets, product of the decaying stone on which the city stands.

"If you bandaged my eyes," said Joseph, "I could still tell the Hundred Gates by their holy stench."

Isaiah Spiegel

1906–1990

The Yiddish poet and prose writer Isaiah Spiegel was born in 1906 in Bałuty (Łódź, Poland) to a family of modest means. He received a traditional heder education and later attended the secular Yiddish Jewish *folkshul* prior to receiving his teacher training. Spiegel continued to write while in the Łódź ghetto, where his poems, set to music, were widely sung. Deported first to Auschwitz and later to a labor camp in Saxony, Spiegel retrieved his buried ghetto writings after the war and published them in revised form. Spiegel headed the Polish Yiddish Writers Association from 1948 to 1951, when he immigrated to Israel.

Bread
1946

Once there was a stroke of misfortune.

The day it happened, Mother couldn't stop cursing this wretched life. Something occurred that almost caused Father to hang himself out of pure shame. After that misfortune he spent whole days just lying on the floor, moaning. Who could have predicted such a thing? Mother just kept repeating: "Now there is nothing lower for him to stoop to, oh Master of the Universe, except to cut a chunk of flesh out of the children and cook it."

They did not know how it came to pass, and even the father himself did not know how things had come to such misfortune and disgrace. Shimmele couldn't fathom what force had urged him to do such a thing. He just did not know.

At that moment a tornado had raged in his heart. It could not have been his very own hands that in the darkness of the chamber stuffed the children's bread into his own mouth. No . . . no. That hadn't been the father anymore. It wasn't Shimmele, but some kind of enchanted shadow that had separated itself from him, that had issued from his hands and feet, some kind of accursed dybbuk who used the father's hands and fingers to tear at the dark, chestnut-flour loaf and salivate over it dozens of times. Wet, half-chewed chunks fell from his stuffed mouth and lay in his palms. From there they were popped right back into the mouth that had spit them out in unnecessary haste. Afterwards, he had just stood there, benighted and petrified, his head buried in his hands.

The day the father ate the children's bread, Mama Glikke came home late. She found both children lying in a corner, famished. When she noticed that a quarter of a loaf was missing, she raised a racket, and it was only then that Shimmele crawled out of the little chamber. When she read the truth in his downcast eyes, she squawked like a slaughtered chicken:

"A father, eh? A fa-ther, is it? *Murderer*!"

And from that moment on the mother walked around worried and anxious, until she found a solution: she sewed two little sacks out of shirts and stuffed the sliced portions of bread into the sacks; in that manner she traversed the streets, the sacks slung over her heart.

The mother has nicknamed Avremele, Umele. He is slight in stature, with a thin, narrow little head and protruding ears, an exact replica of his father. His eyes, too, have a moistness about them, and if you were to look closely, knowing his elderly father, you would see from Umele's pinched expression and pointed chin that he will turn out exactly like the old man. Though Umele has not yet reached his twelfth birthday there is already fixed in his countenance a trace of his father's agedness and brokenness. Like the old man, he always keeps his hand on his bowed forehead, thinking of something.

A restless shadow hovers over his pale, transparent cheeks. The few ghetto months have completely transformed the children. They are not children anymore, but a pair of old people, with the ravages of the last few years showing on their faces.

Umele is sitting on the floor, and next to him, at his side, his little sister, Perele. Perele has a slight limp; her thin, sandy-colored hair cascades down her narrow shoulders. They are both sitting in the corner near the Sabbath candelabras, gazing across at the opposite corner, where the father is busy with something or other. The mother left the room very early in the morning, taking the little sacks of bread with her, and now they are hoping that the father will leave the room soon, so that they can go back into the little chamber. [. . .]

When the two of them, Umele and Perele, see that they have been left alone, their eyes light up with glee. Umele runs quickly to the door of the little chamber and pulls out the nail that keeps the door fastened. The two of them run into the chamber, but as she is running Perele trips on the threshold. She gets up and chases after Umele, her foot dragging. By this time, Umele is already standing in the darkness of the chamber, near the wall that faces out onto the street. Umele had found a crevice in the wall. There are, in fact, two crevices, one a slight distance from the other. Umele takes up his vigil at one of these crevices, and stands there, watching.

Down below, on the other side of the street, across from the wires, there is a little store and the display window of a bakery; Umele's eye aims directly into the window. Brown shiny loaves and white roundish rolls are set out for display. Avremele had discovered that treasure yesterday, when the mother happened to leave the chamber door ajar. And what a treasure! If you really squeezed your eye right up close to the crevice you could see clearly: roundish fresh loaves and wholesome light rolls. There might have been four loaves lying in the window and perhaps ten or more rolls. Right now the sun happened to be just opposite the window, shedding its light directly on the treasures. Umele is taking it all in with his left eye, his tongue is swimming in sweet saliva. When the left eye tires he switches to the right, then back to the left, and still later back to the right. Suddenly he sees a hand inside the store removing one of the loaves. He lets out a sigh. Behind him stands Perele, tugging at his hand. She nags:

"Let me look, let me look too. I'm hungry too."

Umele doesn't budge. Suddenly, he cries out in a strange voice: "Don't take it, don't take it, don't take it!"

Across the way the hand has once again swept away two loaves and a whole pile of rolls. A single loaf of bread and two rolls remain in the window.

Umele still can't tear himself away from the crevice.

When Perele stubbornly grabs hold of his arm and will not relent, he flares up in anger and shouts:

"I don't want to and that's it. Leave me alone."

Through the crevice that Perele has been looking out of, one can see a little shop. Laid out majestically in the display window is a pure white cheese, nothing else. It is possible, by raising oneself a little higher on one's toes, to see part of a field, where a cow is grazing. From Umele's vantage point there is only bread and rolls. Umele stands praying to God not to let the hand reappear. He murmurs a verse his father taught him long before the ghetto. And that fragment has to accomplish everything. If you are ill, it can help; if you are very hungry and you say it with real feeling—your hunger disappears in the wink of an eye. Umele earnestly recites that holy verse now, and waits. The loaves and rolls are so close now, almost within reach. He can even see, at this point, two little holes in the bread. And he notices that a fly has alighted on one of the rolls, a huge fly with large shimmering wings.

"Umele, would you like some cheese?" Perele does not stop her nagging. "Let me in, let me in. If you don't Mama will. . . ."

God forbid that Mama should find out about this. No, Mama must not know about this, because if she does, then the whole treasure is lost. It will no longer be possible to come into the little chamber and gorge oneself on rolls and loaves of white bread. Okay, he'll let her in just for a short while, only a minute.

"Not for a long stay, Perele, all right? I don't like cheese." He moves away slowly and peeps through the other crevice.

Through the crevices the eye can escape into a free, uncaged world. Just a single leap over the fence and you are free. You can go wherever you want: to the courtyard, from the courtyard to the open fields, from the fields to the forest, further and further. The childish eyes float out of the little chamber. First of all, across the road into the shops. Now Umele can see the flat white cheese, Perele the last shiny rolls. How those rolls laugh their way right up to the children; they come so close to the crevice, so close to the eye, that Perele actually licks her little lips. You can smell the sweetness of the rich black poppy seeds. Perele's lips are already tasting the sweetness, and just look, she runs her tongue across

her lips and really—she feels as if she has taken a lick of those sweetish poppy seeds.

Suddenly Perele lets out a scream. Across the street, the hand has just pulled the last of the bread and rolls out of the window. . . . Now the window is empty. Umele runs over to the crack—and he sees that the window opposite has really become a complete void.

Translated by David H. Hirsch and Roslyn Hirsch.

Other works by Spiegel: *Ghetto Kingdom* (1947); *Likht funem opgrunt* (1952); *Vint un vortslen* (1955).

Béla Zsolt
1895–1949

Novelist, poet, journalist, and politician Béla Zsolt was born in Komárom, Hungary. He worked in Budapest for a number of radical Hungarian newspapers before becoming editor in chief of the radical weekly *A Toll*. During World War II, Zsolt was deported to a labor camp in Ukraine. He was later sent to Bergen-Belsen and from there to Switzerland, as part of the Kasztner group. After the war, Zsolt returned to Hungary and in 1947 was elected to parliament. His work *Nine Suitcases* was one of the earliest Holocaust memoirs.

Nine Suitcases
1947

These nocturnal passenger trains in wartime have their own peculiar sounds. The deportation wagons have a way of screeching, like an eagle or a vulture—whereas this kind of train whines and groans as if beseeching, then grinds its teeth in furious impotence, not so much like a beast of burden but like an overburdened man bent double, whose heart skips a beat, but if he dares stop, he is mercilessly driven forward again. Every five hundred paces or so the train comes to a stop, hoping to stay there, on the dark railroad bed—but there is no reprieve; by noon it must arrive at the Keleti Terminal in Budapest. This puny locomotive must drag to the capital seemingly half of the bombed-out families in the country, and an equal number of soldiers on leave, and black-marketeers—anyone traveling from Zágon, Kolozsvár, Gyula, and Szatmár to Budapest must manage to get on this one and only daily train. From time to time the locomotive seems to breathe its last, as if it had run out of steam for good—and then its whistle sounds an almost fluting note of entreaty for help. But the troop trains coming from the other direction streak past like fire engines or ambulances speeding on city streets.

And that puny little locomotive, if one can believe the male falsetto emanating from the other end of the car, had almost been done in by Russian airplanes yesterday afternoon. The falsetto, obviously belonging to an expert, went on to explain that a locomotive such as ours would not even have been allowed out on the tracks of a main line in peacetime.

"The whole front of the engine is riddled with bulletholes! It's a miracle the boiler escaped undamaged!"

"Where did it happen?" asked a tired voice.

"Just past Csap."

The engine struggled on, and silence reigned in the compartment. The travelers went to sleep, or at least tried to catch forty winks. Our gendarme must have been extremely tired by the huge task he had recently accomplished, for he was sound asleep, judging by the even jounce of his head back and forth. Now that his head was bare of the feathered hat and chinstrap, and his jauntily twirled mustache hung limp and ruffled, the sleeping gendarme's harsh, martial features somewhat deflated: he had the impassive, expressionless peasant face of a hired hand who fell asleep on a haywagon bumping along on the road—the oxen would know the way home by themselves. There he sat facing me, his warm breath brushing my face as he dreamed, smacking his lips like a child. And to think of the acts this man had committed in front of my eyes!—or rather: what had they turned this dumb, slumbering, harmless-looking peasant into? My earlier tipsiness must still have been playing games with me, for I almost woke him up to tell him off, in the following way:

"Listen here, homeboy, you're from Győr county, I from Komárom—we're neighbors and practically the same age. We could have gone to the same elementary school, or hung out together waiting for the Vienna steamer at the landing stage by the Danube where we swam naked. So tell me, fellow countryman, what did you do to my poor old mother? Have you gone stark raving mad? Didn't I, as soon as I came of age, take your side, the cause of the poor people? Didn't I insist, even as a kid, that the lands belonging to the count of Ószőny, the baron of Herkály, and the Jew who owned Bélapuszta should be divided up among you poor people?"

Yes indeed, I was on the verge of yanking the gendarme's shirt to wake him, when Mrs. Szabó must have sensed something, for she took my hand and squeezed it in a warning fashion.

All right, all right, I thought. I won't wake him this time. But it had hurt more than words can tell that it was precisely peasants like this one, and other loudmouth "little men" of his kind, who had bloodied their hands and finished us off! The very ones for whom I had fought all my life, much more than I had for the hapless Jews! In the Ukraine, on forced labor service, whenever the officers had tormented me, it left me emotionally uninvolved. All right, they were my enemies, and I was theirs; ever since I had attained the age of reason, I had been fighting these oafish, good-for-nothing bourgeois, who, prisoners of their own ignorance and limited horizons, as if vacuum-sealed, had always considered themselves the cleverest and most special people on earth. All they needed was the racist ideology borrowed from the Germans. But all those articles I had written were on behalf of the "little men"—my proletarians and peasants—although I was well aware that most of them, impoverished and uneducated, were selfish and cold. And yet, whenever one of them, a "prole" or peasant, mistreated me in forced labor, it made me feel that my entire life, all my work, had been ludicrous. [. . .]

[. . .] Yes, this gendarme across from me was the embodiment of the failure of my whole life's professional work. It was for the likes of him that I had fought the power of the ruling upper classes. Back then, who had thought about the Jews? I was ashamed to admit this now, but because of a shameful and meretricious modesty, or worse yet, an even more shameful opportunism, I had never mentioned the Jews as long as it was possible to do so, as long as they were not the main issue in this country! I had struggled against the suffering and injustice of the Hungarian people as a whole, and whenever I demanded, on behalf of the peasants, land, medical care, and schools, the gentry would dismiss me with disparaging comments like "Jews have no right to interfere in the internal affairs of Hungarian society! The Hungarian gentry will know how to settle its affairs with the common folk."

And still I kept persisting, in the role of unasked-for defender, while deep down I had always been aware that even those I had meant to help did not want my aid. On forced-labor service it was the landless peasants who beat me half to death, and the man who wrecked my left eye had been a day laborer. And it was other beggars like them, dressed as civilians or in uniform, who had carried off my mother, my siblings, and my sister's four-year-old boy from Komárom. So here I was now, traveling by train to Budapest, with this utter failure in my heart. Yet I still had no other goal than to try to join the underground fight for this homeland of mine where no one wanted me—not the gentry and not the poor people. And fight against whom? It was almost as if I were to fight against the homeland—for the cause of the homeland. Were I to wake up this gendarme now, to tell him who I was, he would grab my throat in a trice. Would there be anyone I could join? Was there a resistance movement, would there be any partisans?

The tremendous load it carried squeezed sweat and tears of steel from our train. From time to time we lurched forward and then you could tell that the engine driver had no fear of any surprises waiting down the line. We had been dawdling along like this for over two hours—on the stretch between Babruysk and Minsk this would have been more than enough time to get us blown up. Here, too, there were locust groves and cornfields, and we, too, had a steppe—but where was that old peasant looking like a priest, or the toothless *matka* or that playful kid, with whom the German guard would even exchange a mocking word or two, unaware that a few kilometers down the line a train had already been demolished by the dynamite these simple peasants placed along the tracks . . . Where was that peasant of ours? Here he was, sitting opposite me—and if I were to wake him now, and show him that I had one more star on my insignia than he had, he would kill his own mother were I to order him.

But thus far it was only my mother he had killed.

Translated by John Bátki.

Other works by Zsolt: *Házassággal végzödik* (1926); *Gerson és neje* (1930); *Bellegarde* (1932); *Kínos ügy* (1935); *Villámcsapás* (1937).

Jiří Weil

1900–1959

Jiří Weil was born in Praskolesy, Central Bohemia, near Prague. After World War I, his family moved to Prague, where he attended high school and university. In the early 1920s, enamored of the Soviet Union after his first visit, Weil joined the Communist Party, but he was expelled thirteen years later for controversy over his writing, reflected in his 1937 *Moskva-hranice* (Moscow to the Border). Weil survived the Holocaust in hiding and afterward remained in Prague. Although he was a prolific novelist and author of short stories, Weil's work was rarely in line with the prevailing Soviet realism, and he remained a literary outsider.

Life with a Star
1949

I knew they didn't understand me or didn't want to understand me. I knew that the conversation embarrassed them, that they were irritated because I reminded them of their helplessness. They felt better when they considered themselves victims, who with the passing of each day had escaped danger once more; they felt better when they decided they had no choice. In fact, they liked to think they couldn't make decisions. But I kept talking, because I felt like talking that day. I knew they would all be angry at me and wouldn't even be willing to lend me sugar to put in my linden tea when I forgot to bring some from home.

"That's no solution," I said. "I've thought about it a lot. There must be some other way."

They laughed at me. They probably thought that I was bragging, that I, Roubicek the bank clerk, wanted to put on airs, that I wasn't willing to pull with them. I raked the leaves in silence.

"Ruzena," I said, "I told you about the rake, but there are some problems with the song. Many people didn't even hear it, and others put their hands over their ears when an organ-grinder played it for them. I would rather not be alone anymore, but I didn't want to be slaughtered with the others. I looked at the city crying and kneeling in front of its enemies but still hoping to be saved, to be rescued and to stay alive. Even this city, standing in puddles, could have come to a decision. What kind of song can be sung in the middle of a chase when a person has taken off his suspenders and has to hold up his trousers as he runs? What kind of song can be sung when one's coffin is floating in the air and never touches consecrated ground? We used to lie next to each other with happiness between us. That happiness has been cut down and humiliated. I didn't want to decide, I didn't want to leave, but I could have chosen. There was always a choice, Ruzena, really, and there always is a choice. Only I didn't want to make a choice, just like these people here."

I put the rake away, leaned against the wall of the chapel, and waited for a streetcar. I left earlier than the others. I had had enough of their company. "What are you complaining about?" I said to myself. "You're alive, and that's the most important thing. You have nice, quiet work among the dead, you have something to eat, and you can sob and cry about the past and talk about the misfortunes of others. They're dead already and you're still alive. Look at your hands, how they obey you when you order them to do something, how they grip the handle obediently when you order them to grasp the rake. You can ride on the streetcar—that's a great thing, to be able to use the streetcar and not have to walk in the heat, the rain, in a snowstorm." And I also remembered that I had books at home, new books—not really new, but books I hadn't read. I found them at the cemetery, nicely wrapped. Somebody had thrown them away there—good books, in hard covers, but forbidden books. The person who threw them away was probably afraid. I took them home and read every evening. I read slowly so that they would last a long time. Every day, from morning on, I looked forward to coming home. I imagined how I would come home and lie down and read a few pages, new pages. I remembered how I used to read late into the night, until my eyes hurt, and how I got conjunctivitis. I remembered how my uncle forbade me to read because I used up too much electricity, how he went to the meter every morning and calculated how much I had spent, how he took my books away, books I had borrowed from the public library, how he locked them up for the night and gave them back to me in the morning, how I was always able to hide one book under the mattress, put the light out, and then turn it on again when my aunt and uncle were asleep in the next room, how I would quietly pull the book out from under the mattress and start to read. I didn't go slowly then; I turned the pages quickly and read until my eyes began to smart.

"Get out, you dirty swine," yelled a man with an emblem in that foreign language on his lapel. He pushed me so hard I almost fell. I looked around the streetcar. It was quite full. People's faces were set; they were looking at the floor, as if they were searching for a coin that had rolled under the wooden slats. Nobody spoke. Only his sharp voice was heard: "Get out, you swine, or . . ."

The streetcar was traveling through empty streets in the neighborhood of the cemetery; the next stop was still fairly far away. He gave me another hard push. When I was on the steps of the car I jumped. I ran along for a few seconds, then I tripped and fell on the pavement. I saw my glasses fly off my nose and land some distance from me. I got up slowly. I was dirty and my hands were scraped, but I didn't think I was seriously hurt. I was groping for my glasses when I saw that someone was handing them to me.

"That's a silly thing to do, to jump from a moving streetcar. Are you out of your mind? You could have killed yourself."

I didn't feel like talking. I pointed to the star. It was dirty, but its yellow color was still shining in the dusk.

"Uhm," said the man, "I see. That's the Order of the Legion of Honor. Are they allowed to do that?"

"I don't know. Why shouldn't they be?" I said. "Goodbye." "Wait a moment. I'll walk with you to the next stop, and on the way I'll clean you up a bit. I would take you home so that you could wash up, but I live far away. Nobody lives here at all."

"You can't do that," I said. "I'm wearing a star."

"I'm just the one to ask them what I can or can't do. I'm a trainman."

"I don't think that's a good reason to them. They don't make exceptions for trainmen."

"So tear it off."

"Do you have a knife?" I asked. He handed me his pocketknife, and I cut the stitches around the star. I thought there were still traces of it on my coat, but that was nonsense.

Translated by Ruzena Kovarikova with Roslyn Schloss.

Other works by Weil: *Harfeník* (1958); *Na střeše je Mendelssohn* (1960).

Adolf Rudnicki
1912–1990

Adolf Rudnicki (originally Aron Hirszhorn) was born in Żabno, Poland, to a Hasidic family. He moved to Warsaw in the early 1930s to pursue a literary career, initially writing for *Kurier Poranny*. His first novels, *Szczury* (*Rats*; 1932) and *Niekochana* (*Unloved*; 1937), established him as a writer. But when he returned to Warsaw after escaping German captivity, living under false papers, and fighting in the Warsaw Uprising of 1944, he found his wartime writings reduced to a pile of ashes; it became for him a sign to adopt a new mode of writing, akin to psychological journalism. From 1972 to 1977 he lived in self-imposed exile in Paris.

Ascension
1951

He did not object to their unending walk, on and on until they reached a quiet spot. He did not complain of feeling tired. He did not insist that the blanket should be spread somewhere nearer to other people, though he always liked company and could not stand solitude. Unresisting he went into the embrace of destiny.

They sat down on the fringe of a little straggling wood; below them flowed the Vistula. As far as the eye could see, there was no one in sight. In September the Vistula beach no longer has its devotees; even the Sunday trips "out of town" do not attract the crowds. They had not passed anyone for an hour, and since then they had walked on and on without even coming upon an eggshell. Pines, water, sand, sky.

She sat facing the river, and could not see him; she only heard his regular breathing.

"Muszka!"

"Yes?" she asked without changing her position.

"How quiet it is here, how good! Have you been here before?"

"No."

"Then how do you know this spot?"

"It's nice everywhere around here."

"Everywhere? I think this is the only nice spot. Shall we come here again next Sunday?"

"We shall." She was struck by her own voice; it was slower than usual. She did not stop gazing at the sky.

"In fact, we could come here tomorrow."

"If you like . . ."

"The other day," he went on, "I was sitting in our room and thinking to myself: today is Rosh Hashanah, my mother's favorite holiday. My mother's gone, our home's gone, no one will come in and say, 'I wish you all the best.' Just at that moment the judge came in and said: 'I wish you all the best.' 'Thank you,' I said. 'It's very nice of you to remember.' Then I realized that the judge was not supposed to know anything about Jewish holidays—or did he know the truth about us? 'You don't look as if you're enjoying your name day!' . . . So he was congratulating me on my name day . . . How many Christian names had I had during the past two years? I'm getting quite dizzy in my head. A man has to suppress himself so much that it would be quite natural if he began to reply with Hebrew quotations from the Prophets. I've been disappointed in you, Muszka. I wasn't well, I know that myself, but what did you do? You sent me away. The first blow, and you broke under it. Is that the way a wife should behave? My mother was a different sort of wife."

"Perhaps you're not being quite just," she said without expecting a reply, attaching no importance to it. It was not possible to talk with him; conversations were only a pretense of conversations. After ten rational answers, behind the eleventh—darkness yawned. And that eleventh answer canceled all the value of the ten preceding it.

Turning to him, she realized, not for the first time, that he was becoming better looking: his good looks had never had that air of refinement before. His torment had rendered the flesh of his face more delicate, had dried it without spoiling its proportions; he had a high, strong brow and a somewhat weaker line of the chin, burning, avid hazel eyes, a nose with a noble hook, thick black hair. More or less in the center of the forehead a piece of skin the size of a plum showed distinct, as raw as though the place had been scalded.

This plum was never changed either by furrows or by sunburn; it always remained raw. It lay in a slight depression of the forehead like a little well in the middle of the road. "That is the source of all," Raisa often thought. She felt as helpless before that spot as before a tomb.

Her gaze wandered over him as he lay, and through his open shirt she saw the skin puckered where his body was bent, so that its bronze was a shade darker. Through a series of associations she recalled one of their first nights together; he was lying in bed more or less as he was now lying on the blanket, with his head resting on his palm, and was gazing at her. Never speak evil of women! Much more than men, they know how high love can lead, and they pray and watch daily and wait daily, for their ascent to heaven to be achieved through love. Close your eyes, strain your ears, and you will hear their great cry, their daily prayer for an ascent to heaven.

Raisa's ascent to heaven was now seated beside her: a man stepping along a narrow plank between two worlds, contemplating views that no one else but he had ever contemplated; a being with whom it was more difficult to reach an understanding than with the river flowing below, or the pine growing beside them; someone with whom nature was playing, showing its fangs again and again; a lunatic, a being without one chink through which another man could penetrate. With dry eyes, eyes that had not known tears for a long time, Raisa regarded her ascent to heaven.

She already knew she would not give him the poison Bukin had prepared; she knew that, more lonely than any prisoner, she would plunge again into this struggle without victory or reward. She had no idea where she would spend the night, or what the morrow would bring her; she felt the bitter taste of that morrow; pricks,

pricks that seemed not of this world, as if someone were pricking her heart with a long, thin needle—that pain, familiar to all who are cut off from life, frequently visited her. Now she felt it again under this evening sky; it came as a presentiment of the life to which she would be returning, just as sometimes, someone who deeply loves knows all the pang of separation even while the loved one is still sitting beside him.

As if she had no one beside her, she said aloud:

"You who fall asleep easily, remember those to whom the night does not bring sleep. You who are shod, remember those whom God sends barefoot along a road strewn with glass. Look not on blood with an indifferent eye; it may be that it flows so that you should not bleed. Remember. . ."

This was a favorite verse of his mother, the little, shriveled woman who with all her strength of being had implored Raisa to take care of Sebastian. As often as her spirit failed her, as often as she refused to fight any longer, Raisa recalled the promise she had given that woman. Anna was no longer alive, but at times of great light the world is not divided into living and dead; our community extends into dimensions where everything that has ever lived ever endures. She no longer loved Sebastian as a man. As a human being he was of less worth than a shattered vessel. But he had no one but her. To whom then was he to turn?

"Why are you crying?" she suddenly heard his voice.

"I'm no longer crying."

"But I can see you are."

"I'm not. No more, Muszka."

"One must be strong."

"I shall be strong."

"Only the strong have any right to life."

"Only the strong, Muszka . . ."

She raised her head, and her heart felt sick: Sebastian was unscrewing the cap of the thermos containing the poisoned tea. For a second she thought he must have brought another thermos with him. All this time she had been gripping something in her hand under the blanket, convinced that it was the thermos—it was a stone. She started up and knocked the thermos out of his hand. The tea flowed over the blanket.

Translated by H. C. Stevens, revised by Monika Adamczyk-Garbowska.

Other works by Rudnicki: *Epoka pieców* (1948–1952); *Kupiec łódzki* (1963); *Krakowskie Przedmieście pełne deserów* (1986).

Dannie Abse

1923–2014

With dual careers in writing and medicine, Dannie Abse was a Welsh physician, poet, playwright, and novelist who lived in London. His poetry, addressing identity and existence as well as daily life, has been collected in over a dozen volumes. In addition, Abse published more than ten plays, several novels, and essays and stories about medicine. Among other honors, he received the Charles Henry Foyle Award, the Jewish Chronicle Book Award, the Cholmondeley Award, and the Wilfred Owen poetry award.

Ash on a Young Man's Sleeve
1954

When breakfast was over, I had to go to the synagogue, rain or shine, for it was Saturday morning. I used to sit next to Bernard and Simon. We would wear our skull caps and whisper to each other beneath the chant of the Hebrew prayer. A man with a spade-shaped beard would stutter and mutter at us now and then and again. "Shush, shush," his eyes said. Such and these times, we would stare at the prayer book and giggle. It seemed natural that the prayer book wasn't in English, but written and told in some strange language one read from right to left, some mystical language one couldn't understand. Obviously, one couldn't speak to God in everyday English. We stood up when the congregation stood up and sat down when they sat down. The men were segregated from the women lest they should be deviated from their spiritual commerce with God. The women prayed upstairs nearer to heaven; the men downstairs nearer to hell. The sermon would begin and I would stare at the red globe that burned the never-failing oil. The Rev. Aaronowich, a man with an enormous face, gave the sermon. Usually his tone was melancholy. Every New Year, Rosh Hashana, he would begin his speech, raising his hands, eyes round, mournfully direct, "Another year has passed . . . another nail . . . in the coffin." The congregation knew this preface to his sermon by heart. They could have joined in, if they so wished, in some sorrowful chant; instead (except for the elders who nodded their heads slowly as if watching vertical tennis) each would nudge and pinch his neighbour.

However, this Saturday morning in 1934, the Rev. Aaronowich was almost gay. I stopped staring at the red globe and ignored the scrubbings and scratching of Simon and Bernard. He spoke in English, with a Russian and Welsh accent, throwing in a bit of Yiddish when his vocabulary failed him. I think I could understand what he was saying. I believe he proclaimed that it was an honour to be alive, good to breathe fresh air, miraculous to be able to see the blue sky and the green grass; that health was our most important benediction and that one should never say "no" to the earth. (Also, that the congregation should as Jews avoid ostentatiousness.) Never to despair, for when one felt dirty inside, or soiled, or dissatisfied, one only had to gaze at the grandeur of the windswept skies or at the pure wonder of landscapes—one only had to remember the beauty of human relationships, the gentleness and humour of the family, the awe and tenderness when a young man looks upon his betrothed—all things of the earth, of the whole of Life, its comedy, its tragedy, its lovely endeavour and its profound consummation—and I understood this for only that morning my brother Leo had read me from a little blue book words that sounded like "Glory be to God for dappled things"—though, then, I didn't know what "dappled" meant. And the Rev. Aaronowich spoke such beautiful things in such a broken accent that his voice became sweet and sonorous and his huge mask-like face rich, ruffled, handsome.

Afterwards, there was nothing to do but to stare at the red globe again, as the congregation offered thanks to God. In that red globe the oil of Jewish history burned, steadily, devotedly. Or was it blood? Blood of the ghettoes of Eastern Europe. My brother Wilfred said a world flickered in that globe: the red wounds of Abel, the ginger hair on the back of the hands of Esau, the crimson threaded coat of Joseph, the scarlet strings of David's harp, the blood-stained sword of Judas Maccabeus—David, Samson, Solomon, Job, Karl Marx, Sigmund Freud, my brother said lived in that globe. Gosh.

The service seemed interminable, the swaying men, the blue and white *tallisim* around their shoulders, the little black *yamakels*, the musty smelling prayer books, the wailing cry of the Rev. Aaronowich, the fusty smell of sabbaths centuries old. Thousands of years of faith leaned with the men as they leaned—these exiled Jews whose roots were in the dangerous ghetto and in dismayed beauty. Their naked faces showed history plainly, it mixed in their faces like ancient paint to make a curious synthesis of over-refinement and paradoxical coarseness. One received a hint, even as they prayed, a hint of that unbearable core of sensual suffering. As

they murmured their long incantations, I saw in their large dark eyes that infinite, that mute animal sadness, as in the liquid eyes of fugitives everywhere. I was eleven years old then: I could not have named all of this but I knew it . . . I knew it all.

Other works by Abse: *Fire in Heaven* (1956); *Poems, Golders Green* (1962); *Selected Poems* (1970).

Mina Tomkiewicz
1915–1971

Mina Tomkiewicz was born to an affluent family in Warsaw. She began studying medicine at Warsaw University and then received a law degree. In January 1943, Tomkiewicz escaped from the Warsaw ghetto and hid on the Aryan side until she was caught and sent to Bergen-Belsen. After the war she moved to Palestine, contributing writings to the Polish press in Israel and London, and ultimately moving to London.

Of Bombs and Mice: A Novel of Wartime Warsaw
1955

Some two years ago Nata had been deported from Warsaw to Bergen-Belsen concentration camp. Now she was free, but still unable to come to grips with life, so newly regained, though in the first breath of freedom everything had seemed so wonderful.

The luxurious villas which they were entering were still being vacated by the expelled Germans, each carrying a small suitcase. They walked away, still looking prosperous in their smart clothes, but with their heads bent low. A fleeting picture of herself and of others forced out of their homes not so long ago flashed across Nata's mind. She searched within herself for some feeling of hatred, revenge, or joy at the defeat of their enemy, but all she found was absolute indifference. One could not pin such monstrous evil on to a blond German child, crying as he is being taken out of his little bed by his mother.

Yes, it was wonderful, almost unbelievable, to take a warm bath in a real bath-tub, to eat to satiety, to watch Bobush, dressed in a pink flannel suit, fishing cherries out of a big jar, his grubby hands covered with crimson juice. Like some tribeswoman from the African bush she went around touching the switches of an electric cooker, trying on looted dresses, and manipulating the key in the door of her *very own room*. Yes, Nata should feel happy, but actually she only felt drowsy, empty and extremely tired.

She could hear laughter and shouting outside. Some American soldiers were trying to pick up women. They marched straight into the houses, dispensing wine, chocolate and stockings, and without beating about the bush proposed going straight to bed. And why not? Had they not been fighting to make our dreams come true. Were we not, all of us, reborn? Anyway, all this is surely only a dream. . . . [. . .]

The Hillersleben DP Centre was growing; there was the central office with dozens of clerics, an accommodation bureau, a social welfare centre, and a hospital with an ever-increasing number of patients. Various organizations from all over the world—UNRRA, Red Cross, Care, Joint, Hagana, the Jewish Agency—all were sending in their representatives. The place was full of soldiers, welfare workers, journalists and do-gooders of every nationality. They dispensed charity, they offered advice, they took pictures and conducted interviews for various publications. They sometimes even preached and gave lectures.

This was the Displaced Persons Centre, Hillersleben, swarming with multilingual crowd of ex-katzetniks, prisoners of war, forced labourers, who were told that it was all for them, the offices, the do-gooders and the propaganda. The displaced persons, or—as they were often called—the refugees or the remnants of the Holocaust, were coming and going, to and fro, trying desperately to fix the broken pieces of their uprooted lives. They felt themselves to be objects of curiosity, like circus animals. Nervously they wanted to exploit this interest in them: they began to "feel" life as if it were a piece of new cloth, out of which one might order a suit to be made. But instead, they tended to seek out old oddments which might have been adapted, turned and made good.

Well-dressed German ex-supermen swept the streets or struggled with heavy furniture; pink-cheeked German Gretchens served at the tables in the Centre canteens. Thanks be to God that we at least have lived to see it! If only there had been more of us. . . .

Still unable to realize the immensity of the genocide, bleary-eyed people travelled from place to place, questioning other bleary-eyed people, hoping against hope; "Did you know so-and-so?" "Have you come across such-and- such?" "But perhaps . . . my child had . . . my husband was last seen . . . maybe you. . . ." They called over the radio, they cried in the newspapers, "Where

are you?! Do come back to me!" Hungry, expectant eyes searched the neatly typed lists of survivors displayed in every office, all over Europe. But, mostly, those who were desperately searched for were no more.

There were sporadic cases of bloody revenge; occasionally, a former victim attacked or killed some Germans, or burned or stole their possessions. The avengers did not differentiate. How could they, and—in cold truth—why should they? After all, had not the Germans taught them an unequivocal lesson in non-discrimination and in violence? Anyway, these occurrences were comparatively rare, the more so since the Americans imposed very severe penalties in each case, including the death sentence. Rational and still innocent, the Americans tried hard to do justice to everyone, but they did not always believe the ex-victims' horror stories, and they had no hatred for the Germans. On the contrary, they found them obedient, servile and polite—often more likeable, indeed, than the DPs. The German women didn't make too much fuss, and this, too, made their soldiers' lives so much pleasanter. True, the Germans had been their enemies, but, after all, these displaced persons were so difficult. . . .

And difficult they really were. The years of slavery, fear and suffering beyond human endurance had left their stigma as ineradicable as the numbers branded on their arms. They soon realized that their dreams, on which they had fed for such a long time, were not being realized, and so they became more and more touchy, irritable and full of anxiety and impalpable weariness. They had too many claims and needs; they were often rude and cynical. Their shattered nerves were falling into ashes, like burnt paper, on contact with life, and they were tortured by a gnawing sense of emptiness or strange fears. Their attitude was: "I've suffered enough, now I want only the best out of life," but only a few knew what this best looked like, and where to look for it. They were waiting—lost in todays and uncertain of tomorrows, returning with masochistic pleasure to their yesterdays, or seeking escape from their memories and disappointments in sexual orgies, in overeating, or in any other feverish kind of activity.

Nata allowed herself to be borne along on the wave which carried those who remained alone, and who would not or could not shape their own future. She decided to go on a "free tour" organized by "Auntie UNRRA." She took Bobush, a few bags of worthless clothes, and, together with thousands of others like herself, she plunged into the outside world.

On the way to their new destinations they had to move from place to place many times. Every few days they had to pack and unpack their miserable belongings, change lorries, and go on. From one bunk to another they went, begging for a few ounces of butter for their children, for warm clothes, for help and advice. Well-dressed ladies, sometimes dripping with diamonds, came distributing soap, tins of food and chocolate. And the refugees went on demanding soap, tins of food or chocolate; they were getting used to this strange, easy life. Dragged by the red tape from one office to another, to obtain certificates, letters of recommendation, registration cards and stamps, they saw officials who were no longer listening to them, and to whom they were becoming a bore: tiresome refugees, useless remnants of the war.

Translated by Stefan F. Gazel.

Other work by Tomkiewicz: *Tam si? tez zylo* (1947).

Boris Pasternak
1890–1960

Boris Leonidovich Pasternak was born to an artistic family at the center of Moscow's cultural scene; his father was a painter and his mother a pianist. He grew up studying piano, composing three (known) completed pieces before enrolling at Moscow University in 1909 for law and, later, philosophy. He left school in 1912 to pursue his passion for poetry. Pasternak's first poems were published in early 1917; he became widely respected for his serious tone and patriotic themes. He received the Nobel Prize in Literature for his only novel, *Doctor Zhivago*, in 1958. In response to the abundant praise he earned from the West, Pasternak was expelled from the Union of Soviet Writers, and the novel was banned in the Soviet Union until after his death.

Doctor Zhivago
1956

Book 1, Part 4, Chapters 11–12

[Gordon and Zhivago were on their way home in the evening. The sun was going down.] In one village [they passed through] they saw a young Cossack surrounded by a crowd laughing boisterously, as the Cossack tossed a copper coin in the air, forcing an old Jew with a gray beard and a long caftan to catch it. The old man missed every time. The coin flew past his pitifully spread-out

hands and dropped into the mud. When the old man bent to pick it up, the Cossack slapped his bottom, and the onlookers held their sides, groaning with laughter: this was the point of the entertainment. For the moment it was harmless enough, but no one could say for certain that it would not take a more serious turn. Every now and then, the old man's wife ran out of the house across the road, screaming and stretching out her arms to him, and ran back again in terror. Two little girls were watching their grandfather out of the window and crying.

The driver, who found all of this extremely comical, slowed down so that the passengers could enjoy the spectacle. But Zhivago called the Cossack, bawled him out, and ordered him to stop baiting the old man.

"Yes, sir," he said readily. "We meant no harm, we were only doing it for fun."

Gordon and Zhivago drove on in the silence.

"It's terrible," said [Zhivago] when they were in sight of their own village. "You can't imagine what the [miserable] Jewish population [has been going] through in this war. The fighting happens to be in the [pale of their forced settlement]. And as if punitive taxation, the destruction of their property, and all their own sufferings were not enough, they are subjected to pogroms, insults, and accusations that they lack patriotism. And why should they be patriotic? Under enemy rule, they enjoy equal rights, and we do nothing but persecute them. This hatred for them, the basis of it, is irrational. It is stimulated by the very things that should arouse sympathy—their poverty, their overcrowding, their weakness, and this inability to fight back. I can't understand it. It's like an inescapable fate." [. . .]

"You've hit the nail on the head," broke in Gordon. "And now I'll tell you what I think about that incident we saw today. That Cossack tormenting the poor patriarch—and there are thousands of incidents like it—of course it's an ignominy—but there's no point in philosophizing [about it], you just hit it out. But the Jewish question as a whole—there philosophy does come in—and then we discover something unexpected. Not that I'm going to tell you anything new—we both got our ideas from your uncle.

"You were saying, what is a nation? [. . .] And what are the nations now, in the Christian era? They aren't just nations, but converted, transformed nations, and what matters is this transformation, not loyalty to ancient principles. [. . .]

"When the Gospel [said] that in the Kingdom of God there are neither Jews nor Gentiles, [did] it merely mean that all are equal in the sight of God? No—the Gospel wasn't needed for that—the Greek philosophers, the Roman moralists, and the [Old Testament] prophets had known this long before. But it said: In that new way of living and new form of society, which is born of the heart, and which is called the Kingdom of Heaven, there are no nations, there are only individuals.

"You said that facts are meaningless, unless meanings are put into them. Well, Christianity, the mystery of the individual, is precisely what must be put into the facts to make them meaningful.

"We also talked about the mediocre [public figures] who have nothing to say to life and the world as a whole, of petty second-raters who are only too happy when some nation, preferably a small and [suffering] one, is constantly discussed—this gives them a chance to show off their competence and cleverness, and to thrive on their compassion for the persecuted. Well now, what more perfect example can you have of the victims of this mentality than the Jews? Their national idea has forced them, century after century, to be a nation and nothing but a nation—and they have been chained to this deadening task all through the centuries when all the rest of the world was being delivered from it by a new force which had come out of their own midst! Isn't that extraordinary? How can you account for it? Just think! This glorious holiday, this liberation from the curse of mediocrity, this soaring flight above the dullness of a humdrum existence was first achieved in their land, proclaimed in their language, and belonged to their race! And they actually saw and heard it and let it go! How could they allow a spirit of such overwhelming power and beauty to leave them, how could they think that after it triumphed and established its reign, they would remain as the empty husk of that miracle they had repudiated? What use is it to anyone, this voluntary martyrdom? Whom does it profit? For what purpose are these innocent old men and women and children, all these [sensitive], kind, humane people, mocked and [massacred] throughout the centuries? And why is it that all these literary friends of 'the people' of all nations are always so untalented? Why didn't the intellectual leaders of the Jewish people ever go beyond facile *Weltschmerz* and ironical wisdom? Why have they not—even if at the risk of bursting like boilers with the pressure of their duty—disbanded this army which keeps on fighting and being beaten up nobody knows for what? Why don't they say to them: '[You are the first and best Christians in the world.] Come to your senses, stop. Don't hold on to your identity. Don't

stick together, disperse. Be with all the rest. You are the very thing against which you have been turned by the worst and weakest among you.'"

NOTE
[Words in brackets appear in the original translation.]

Translated by Max Hayward and Manya Harari.

Other works by Pasternak: *Over the Barriers* (1917); *The Childhood of Luvers* (1922); *When the Weather Clears* (1959).

Julian Stryjkowski
1905–1996

Julian Stryjkowski was born Pesah Stark in Stryj (present-day Ukraine). He changed his name shortly after World War II and became one of the leading Polish Jewish authors of the postwar period. Although he was initially affiliated with the Zionist group Ha-Shomer ha-Tsaʻir, Stryjkowski joined the Communist Party in 1934. During the war, he worked as a journalist for a communist newspaper in Soviet-occupied Lviv. In 1966, Stryjkowski left the party in response to rising censorship and antisemitism. His writings, which often examined the decline of the shtetl and increasing secularism, were banned until 1978, with the easing of intellectual censorship. In 1993, Stryjkowski publicly disclosed his homosexuality, which was also described in his semiautobiographical *Milczenie* (*Silence*).

Voices in the Darkness
1956

No one paid any attention to Aronek. He took a piece of bread from the cupboard, chose the largest carrot, and went to the neighbors.

At the widow Gitel's it was warm and clean. From the ceiling hung a large lamp with a blue shade. The shade turned pink from the flame.

"It's smoking!" shouted Gitel. "Shlomcia, turn the wick down, for heaven's sake. God forbid that the glass should break."

Shlomcia sat at the sewing machine and sewed. The red cloth with yellow flowers lightly flowed over the polished board.

"Aronek, is that you?" she called. "Come in, come in, why are you standing by the door?"

Fancia was standing in front of the mirror. She was trying on a blouse made out of red cloth with yellow flowers. She turned to the right and then to the left, trying to see how the blouse fit her back.

"What, you're back again, peyes boy? Hee, hee," laughed Fancia. "You're here again! You haven't been here for some time!"

"What are you eating, for heaven's sake!' called Gitel. "The poor child's eating dry bread. Ugh, throw it away." Gitel took away Aronek's carrot. "Poor child, his mother stays late at her market stall. There's no one to give the child anything. Can I give you some milk?"

Aronek didn't say a thing.

"Give him some milk. The milk's in the kitchen," said Shlomcia. "Do you want some warm milk? Don't be shy, Arale."

Gitel gave him a glass of milk. Aronek drank it and cheered up. "Tell me, Arale, do you like my blouse? Hee, hee," Fancia raised her arms and made a dance-like spin. She crouched, lifted Aronek up, and kissed him on the lips. "Look, Mother, how handsome he is. He's got such long eyelashes. Only those peyes. God, what are they doing with these children. Tell me, when you're big will you love me? Right? Nu, say 'yes' and kiss me."

Aronek said "yes," but he turned his head away. Fancia gave him a smacking kiss on the cheek.

"Why are you bothering the child, leave him be," said Shlomcia, without raising her eyes from her work.

Over the sofa above the mirror hung fan-shaped spreads of postcards and photographs. Both sisters, all dressed up, stood beside a table with thin, crooked legs. In the distance were some trees and a white house with large, dark windows. On another photograph there was Fancia from her waist up. She was holding a rose in her mouth. There were also men without peyes, bareheaded, with abundant hair. One had a large moustache. Aronek really liked the man with the wide hat on wavy hair. He had a black ribbon around his neck.

"That's Peretz. Do you know who Peretz is? Hee, hee, he's my fiancé," explained Fancia.

"What nonsense you're telling the boy," stormed Shlomcia. "Don't listen to her foolishness. He's a writer. He wrote books. When you grow up a little, you can read them."

In the kitchen behind pink calico curtains, by a small lamp and a candle, the widow Gitel was dressing a chicken. She held the plucked bird over a burning paper. Over the flame the last feathers sizzled, twisted, were charred, and gave off an unpleasant odor. Later Gitel sank a knife in the chicken's stomach, cut out the gut, which glistened with a beautiful shade of blue, then the intestines and liver. Gitel cut open the gut, took out the pebbles, carefully examined the intestines for ulcers, looked for any nail or needles, to see if the chicken, heaven forbid, happened to be *treyf*. Gitel didn't notice when Elke entered.

"Here he is again. It's bad luck with that boy. He can't stay home for a minute. Aronek, go home, it's time to go to sleep. Why didn't you send him away, Gitel? He's everywhere." His mother approached the table. "What a fine chicken. Yellow as a carrot. All that fat. How much did it cost?"

Gitel did not want to say how much it cost. Oh, it was a shame to admit it. She paid for it as much as for an old pig. The widow Gitel spat. The goyim are simply drinking Jewish blood.

"Oy, Gitel, my love, it's better not to ask what I went through with the goyim today." And Mother told her how the entire thieving village (Koniuchów is all thieves, and they'd drown a Jew in a spoonful of water) came to the stall, ostensibly to buy something. One wants to see some fustian, another wants to see some linen, and still another one wants to see some drill for trousers. They throw the rolls of cloth on the counter and each of them tugs in a different direction. Mother felt faint and started to shout; she sees how one thief hides the remains of some calico in her bosom. And here Mother is alone. She shouts "Gevalt!" She grabs the goya by her vest and takes out the rest of the calico from her bosom. God only knows how some tragedy didn't happen. And now the whole day, the whole market, is spoiled. You wait an entire week for Thursday. May they never have a better market day their entire life than she had on that day.

Gitel put the cut-up chicken into the iron pot with water.

"Yes," said Gitel. "Let it soak. Shlomcia, look at the clock."

"It's nine-thirty," replied Shlomcia from behind the curtain.

"In an hour remind me to salt it, d'you hear, Shlomcia?"

"It's already nine-thirty and I haven't even started the fire in the kitchen," Mother got up and took Aronek by the hand. "We're going now. Enough sitting around houses. You've got your own home, so stay there."

In the courtyard, Aronek asked:

"Mame, how long will I have to have peyes?"

"What? Have you gone crazy? Thunder has struck me! My God, where does my child get such ideas!

Where have you ever seen a Jew without peyes? Doesn't your father have peyes? May I never tell him this, because he'd beat these ideas right out of your head . . . May I never hear this again!"

Translated by Christopher Garbowski.

Other works by Stryjkowski: *Bieg do Fragalà* (1951); *Austeria* (1966); *To samo, ale inaczej* (1990).

Arnold Wesker

1932–2016

Arnold Wesker was born in Stepney, in London's East End, to a working-class leftist family, an upbringing that provided the background for many of his works. The trilogy that first raised him to prominence, *Chicken Soup with Barley* (1956), *Roots* (1958), and *I'm Talking about Jerusalem* (1960), brought the postwar style of "kitchen sink realism" to bear on the lives of Jewish socialists in Britain. A prolific writer across many genres, Wesker wrote fifty plays, which have been translated into more than twenty languages, as well as collections of short stories, essays, and poetry, and an autobiography. He became a Fellow of the Royal Society of Literature in 1985 and was knighted in 2006.

Chicken Soup with Barley
1956

RONNIE: Everything has broken up around you and you can't see it.

SARAH [*shouting*]: What, what, what, you mad boy? Explain what you mean.

RONNIE: What has happened to all the comrades, Sarah? I even blush when I use that word. Comrade! Why do I blush? Why do I feel ashamed to use words like democracy and freedom and brotherhood? They don't have meaning any more. I have nothing to write about any more. Remember all that writing I did? I was going to be a great socialist writer. I can't make sense of a word, a simple word. You look at me as if I'm talking in a foreign language. Didn't it hurt *you* to read about the murder of the Jewish Anti-Fascist Committee in the Soviet Union?

SARAH: You as well. Monty Blatt came up some months ago and said the same thing. He's also left the Party. He runs a greengrocer shop in Manchester.

RONNIE: And Dave and Ada in the Fens, and Prince working in a second-hand shop, and Uncle Hymie

stuck smugly at home and Auntie Cissie once devoted—once involved—wandering from relative to relative. What's happened to us? Were we cheated or did we cheat ourselves? I just don't know, God in heaven, I just do not know! Can you understand what it is suddenly not to know? [*Collapses into armchair.*] And the terrifying thing is—I don't care either.

[*They sit in silence for some seconds.*]

SARAH: Drink your tea, darling.

[RONNIE *closes his eyes and talks.*]

RONNIE: Do you know what the trouble is. Mother? Can't you guess?

SARAH: You're tired, Ronnie.

RONNIE: You do know what the trouble is. You just won't admit it.

SARAH: In the morning you'll feel better.

RONNIE: Think hard. Look at my face. Look at my nose and my deep-set eyes; even my forehead is receding.

SARAH: Why don't you listen to me? Go to bed and—

RONNIE: Political institutions, society—they don't really affect people that much.

SARAH: Ronnie!

RONNIE: Who else was it who hated the jobs he had, who couldn't bear the discipline imposed by a daily routine, couldn't make sense of himself and gave up?

SARAH [*frightened*]: Are you mad?

RONNIE: I've lost my faith and I've lost my ambition. Now I understand him perfectly. I wish I hadn't shouted at him as I used to.

SARAH: Mad boy!

RONNIE: [*rising, opens his eyes and shouts*]: You know that I'm right. *You've* never been right about anything. You wanted everybody to be happy but you wanted them to be happy your way. It was strawberries and cream for everyone—whether they liked it or not. And now look what's happened. The family you always wanted has disintegrated, and the great ideal you always cherished has exploded in front of your eyes. But you won't face it. You just refuse to face it. I don't know how you do it but you do—you just do. [*Louder.*] You're a pathological case, Mother—do you know that? You're still a *communist*!

[*He wants to take back his words but he has lost the power to express anything any more.*]

SARAH: All right! So I'm still a communist! Shoot me then! I'm a communist! I've always been one—since the time when all the world was a communist. You know that? When you were a baby and there was unemployment and everybody was thinking so—all the world was a communist. But it's different now. Now the people have forgotten. I sometimes think they're not worth fighting for because they forget so easily. You give them a few shillings in the bank and they can buy a television so they think it's all over there's nothing more to be got, they don't have to think any more! Is that what you want? A world where people don't think any more? Is that what you want me to be satisfied with—a television set? Look at him! My son! He wants to die!

RONNIE: Don't laugh at me, Sarah.

SARAH: You want me to cry again? We should all sit down and cry?

RONNIE: I don't see things in black and white any more. My thoughts keep going pop, like bubbles. That's my life now—you know?—a lot of little bubbles going pop.

SARAH: And he calls me a pathological case! Pop! Pop, pop, pop, pop—shmop! You think it doesn't hurt me—the news about Hungary? You think I know what happened and what didn't happen? Do any of us know? Who do I know who to trust now—God, who are our friends now? But all my life I've fought. With your father and the rotten system that couldn't help him. All my life I worked with a party that meant glory and freedom and brotherhood. You want me to give it up now? You want me to move to Hendon and forget who I am? If the electrician who comes to mend my fuse blows it instead, so I should stop having electricity? I should cut off my light? Socialism is my light, can you understand that? A way of life. A man *can* be beautiful. I hate ugly people—I can't bear meanness and fighting and jealousy—I've got to have light. I'm a simple person, Ronnie, and I've got to have light and love.

Other works by Wesker: *The Kitchen* (1957); *Shylock* (1976); *The Birth of Shylock and the Death of Zero Mostel* (1997); *Wesker on Theatre* (2010).

Harold Pinter

1930–2008

English dramatist Harold Pinter was born in Hackney, East London, to East European immigrants. He started writing poetry in grammar school, publishing his first poem in *Poetry London*. His first play, *The Room*, which he wrote in three days, premiered in Bristol in May 1957. One of his most produced and best-known plays, *The Birthday Party* (1957), established the "comedy of menace" that characterizes his style. Pinter was also known for his outspoken political stances, antiwar and human rights activism, and involvement with PEN International. In 2005 he was honored with the Nobel Prize in Literature.

The Birthday Party
1957

MEG: Well—it's very, very nice to be here tonight, in my house, and I want to propose a toast to Stanley, because it's his birthday, and he's lived here for a long while now, and he's my Stanley now. And I think he's a good boy, although sometimes he's bad. [*An appreciative laugh from* GOLDBERG.] And he's the only Stanley I know, and I know him better than all the world, although he doesn't think so. [*"Hear—hear" from* GOLDBERG.] Well, I could cry because I'm so happy, having him here and not gone away, on his birthday, and there isn't anything I wouldn't do for him, and all you good people here tonight. . . . [*She sobs.*]

GOLDBERG: Beautiful! A beautiful speech. Put the light on, McCann. [McCANN *goes to the door.* STANLEY *remains still.*] That was a lovely toast [*The light goes on.* LULU *enters from the door, left,* GOLDBERG *comforts* MEG.] Buck up now. Come on, smile at the birdy. That's better. Ah, look who's here.

MEG: Lulu.

GOLDBERG: How do you do, Lulu? I'm Nat Goldberg.

LULU: Hallo.

GOLDBERG: Stanley, a drink for your guest. You just missed the toast, my dear, and what a toast.

LULU: Did I?

GOLDBERG: Stanley, a drink for your guest. Stanley. [STANLEY *hands a glass to* LULU.] Right. Now raise your glasses. Everyone standing up? No, not you, Stanley. You must sit down.

McCANN: Yes, that's right. He must sit down.

GOLDBERG: You don't mind sitting down a minute? We're going to drink to you.

MEG: Come on!

LULU: Come on!

[STANLEY *sits in a chair at the table.*]

GOLDBERG: Right. Now Stanley's sat down. [*Taking the stage.*] Well, I want to say first that I've never been so touched to the heart as by the toast we've just heard.

How often, in this day and age, do you come across real, true warmth? Once in a lifetime. Until a few minutes ago, ladies and gentlemen, I, like all of you, was asking the same question. What's happened to the love, the bonhomie, the unashamed expression of affection of the day before yesterday, that our mums taught us in the nursery?

McCANN: Gone with the wind.

GOLDBERG: That's what I thought, until today. I believe in a good laugh, a day's fishing, a bit of gardening. I was very proud of my old greenhouse, made out of my own spit and faith. That's the sort of man I am. Not size but quality. A little Austin, tea in Fullers, a library book from Boots, and I'm satisfied. But just now, I say just now, the lady of the house said her piece and I for one am knocked over by the sentiments she expressed. Lucky is the man who's at the receiving end, that's what I say. [*Pause.*] How can I put it to you? We all wander on our tod through this world. It's a lonely pillow to kip on. Right!

LULU [*admiringly*]: Right!

GOLDBERG: Agreed. But tonight. Lulu, McCann, we've known a great fortune. We've heard a lady extend the sum total of her devotion, in all its pride, plume and peacock, to a member of her own living race. Stanley, my heartfelt congratulations. I wish you, on behalf of us all, a happy birthday. I'm sure you've never been a prouder man than you are today. Mazoltov! And may we only meet at Simchahs!

Other works by Pinter: *The Homecoming* (1964); *No Man's Land* (1975); *Betrayal* (1978); *Collected Poems and Prose* (1995); and *Ashes to Ashes* (1996).

André Schwarz-Bart
1928–2006

André Schwarz-Bart was born in Metz, France, to parents who had immigrated from Poland four years earlier. Following their deportation in 1942, Schwarz-Bart joined the French Resistance, reputedly the youngest person to do so. At age thirty-one, Schwarz-Bart made history through the publication of his family saga, *Le dernier des justes* (*The Last of the Just*). Embracing eight centuries of Jewish life in Europe, the novel exposed the Christian roots of Nazi paganism, indicted the Vichy regime, and, most outrageously, penetrated the very heart of darkness—the gas chambers at

Auschwitz. Provoking a major controversy at home, it became the first internationally best-selling novel on the Holocaust. Schwarz-Bart died in Pointe-à-Pitre, Guadeloupe, where he lived with his wife.

The Last of the Just
1959

[. . .] It seemed to him that an eternal silence was closing down upon the Jewish breed marching to slaughter—that no heir, no memory would supervene to prolong the silent parade of victims, no faithful dog would shudder, no bell would toll. Only the stars would remain, gliding through a cold sky. "O God," the Just Man Ernie Levy said to himself; as bloody tears of pity streamed from his eyes again, "O Lord, we went forth like this thousands of years ago. We walked across arid deserts and the blood-red Red Sea in a hood of salt, bitter tears. We are very old. We are still walking. Oh, let us arrive, finally!"

The building resembled a huge bathhouse. To left and right large concrete pots cupped the stems of faded flowers. At the foot of the small wooden stairway an S.S. man, mustached and benevolent, told the condemned, "Nothing painful will happen! You just have to breathe very deeply. It strengthens the lungs. It's a way to prevent contagious diseases. It disinfects." Most of them went in silently, pressed forward by those behind. Inside, numbered coathooks garnished the walls of a sort of gigantic cloakroom where the flock undressed one way or another, encouraged by their S.S. cicerones, who advised them to remember the numbers carefully. Cakes of stony soap were distributed. Golda begged Ernie not to look at her, and he went through the sliding door of the second room with his eyes closed, led by the young woman and by the children, whose soft hands clung to his naked thighs. There, under the showerheads embedded in the ceiling, in the blue light of screened bulbs glowing in recesses of the concrete walls, Jewish men and women, children and patriarchs were huddled together. His eyes still closed, he felt the press of the last parcels of flesh that the S.S. men were clubbing into the gas chamber now, and his eyes still closed, he knew that the lights had been extinguished on the living, on the hundreds of Jewish women suddenly shrieking in terror, on the old men whose prayers rose immediately and grew stronger, on the martyred children, who were rediscovering in their last agonies the fresh innocence of yesteryear's agonies in a chorus of identical exclamations: *"Mama! But I was a good boy! It's dark! It's dark!"* And when the first waves of Zyklon B gas billowed among the sweating bodies, drifting down toward the squirming carpet of children's heads, Ernie freed himself from the girl's mute embrace and leaned out into the darkness toward the children invisible even at his knees, and he shouted with all the gentleness and all the strength of his soul, "Breathe deeply, my lambs, and quickly!"

When the layers of gas had covered everything, there was silence in the dark sky of the room for perhaps a minute, broken only by shrill, racking coughs and the gasps of those too far gone in their agonies to offer a devotion. And first a stream, then a cascade, an irrepressible, majestic torrent, the poem that through the smoke of fires and above the funeral pyres of history the Jews—who for two thousand years did not bear arms and who never had either missionary empires nor colored slaves—the old love poem that they traced in letters of blood on the earth's hard crust unfurled in the gas chamber, enveloped it, vanquished its somber, abysmal snickering: "SHEMA YISRAEL ADONOI ELOHEINU ADONOI EH'OTH . . . Hear, O Israel, the Lord is our God, the Lord is One. O Lord, by your grace you nourish the living, and by your great pity you resurrect the dead, and you uphold the weak, cure the sick, break the chains of slaves. And faithfully you keep your promises to those who sleep in the dust. Who is like unto you, O merciful Father, and who could be like unto you . . . ?"

The voices died one by one in the course of the unfinished poem. The dying children had already dug their nails into Ernie's thighs, and Golda's embrace was already weaker, her kisses were blurred when, clinging fiercely to her beloved's neck, she exhaled a harsh sigh: "Then I'll never see you again? Never again?"

Ernie managed to spit up the needle of fire jabbing at his throat, and as the woman's body slumped against him, its eyes wide in the opaque night, he shouted against the unconscious Golda's ear, "In a little while, *I swear it!*" And then he knew that he could do nothing more for anyone in the world, and in the flash that preceded his own annihilation he remembered, happily, the legend of Rabbi Chanina ben Teradion, as Mordecai had joyfully recited it: "When the gentle rabbi, wrapped in the scrolls of the Torah, was flung upon the pyre by the Romans for having taught the Law, and when they lit the fagots, the branches still green to make

his torture last, his pupils said, 'Master, what do you see?' And Rabbi Chanina answered, 'I see the parchment burning, but the letters are taking wing.'" . . . *"Ah, yes, surely, the letters are taking wing,"* Ernie repeated as the flame blazing in his chest rose suddenly to his head. With dying arms he embraced Golda's body in an already unconscious gesture of loving protection, and they were found that way half an hour later by the team of *Sonderkommando* responsible for burning the Jews in the crematory ovens. And so it was for millions, who turned from *Luftmenschen* into *Luft*. I shall not translate. So this story will not finish with some tomb to be visited in memoriam. For the smoke that rises from crematoriums obeys physical laws like any other: the particles come together and disperse according to the wind that propels them. The only pilgrimage, estimable reader, would be to look with sadness at a stormy sky now and then.

And praised. *Auschwitz.* Be. *Maidanek.* The Lord. *Treblinka.* And praised. *Buchenwald.* Be. *Mauthausen.* The Lord. *Belzec.* And praised. *Sobibor.* Be. *Chelmno.* The Lord. *Ponary.* And praised. *Theresienstadt.* Be. *Warsaw.* The Lord. *Vilna.* And praised. *Skarzysko.* Be. *Bergen-Belsen.* The Lord. *Janow.* And praised. *Dora.* Be. *Neuengamme.* The Lord. *Pustkow.* And praised. . . .

Translated by Stephen Becker.

Other works by Schwarz-Bart: *Un Plat de porc aux bananes vertes* (cowritten with Simone Schwarz-Bart, 1967); *A Woman Named Solitude* (1973); *In Praise of Black Women* (2001); *The Morning Star* (2011).

Vasily Grossman

1905–1964

Vasily Grossman was born in Berdichev, Ukraine, to an assimilated Jewish family. He attended university in Moscow and worked as a chemist, although he ultimately became a writer, often exploring Jewish and social issues. During World War II, he served as a front-line newspaper correspondent. He was one of the first Soviet journalists to write firsthand accounts of the Holocaust and the Nazi death camps. He was also a member of the Jewish Anti-Fascist Committee, and he contributed, with Ilya Ehrenburg, to *Chernaia kniga* (the *Black Book*), outlining Russian anti-Jewish policies. After the war, Grossman was outspoken in his views on Soviet antisemitism, and he refused to be censored. His epic novel *Life and Fate*, which was published in the Soviet Union during the thaw of the late 1980s, was a brilliant evocation of Soviet society in wartime. Its unflinching comparison of Nazi and Soviet dictatorship and its frank insights into growing antisemitism and the problems of the Soviet Jewish intelligentsia help make it one of the most significant Soviet novels of the twentieth century.

Life and Fate
1960

Never, before the war, had Viktor thought about the fact that he was a Jew, that his mother was a Jew. Never had his mother spoken to him about it—neither during his childhood, nor during his years as a student. Never while he was at Moscow University had one student, professor or seminar-leader ever mentioned it.

Never before the war, either at the Institute or at the Academy of Sciences had he ever heard conversations about it.

Never had he felt a desire to speak about it to Nadya, to explain to her that her mother was Russian and her father Jewish.

The century of Einstein and Planck was also the century of Hitler. The Gestapo and the scientific renaissance were children of the same age. How humane the nineteenth century seemed, that century of naïve physics, when compared with the twentieth century, the century that had killed his mother. There is a terrible similarity between the principles of Fascism and those of contemporary physics.

Fascism has rejected the concept of a separate individuality, the concept of "a man," and operates only with vast aggregates. Contemporary physics speaks of the greater or lesser probability of occurrences within this or that aggregate of individual particles. And are not the terrible mechanics of Fascism founded on the principle of quantum politics, of political probability?

Fascism arrived at the idea of the liquidation of entire strata of the population, of entire nations and races, on the grounds that there was a greater probability of overt or covert opposition among these groupings than among others: the mechanics of probabilities and of human aggregates.

But no! No! And again no! Fascism will perish for the very reason that it has applied to man the laws applicable to atoms and cobblestones!

Man and Fascism cannot co-exist. If Fascism conquers, man will cease to exist and there will remain only man-like creatures that have undergone an internal transformation. But if man, man who is endowed with reason and kindness, should conquer, then Fascism must perish, and those who have submitted to it will once again become people.

Was not this an admission on his part of the truth of what Chepyzhin had once said? That discussion now seemed infinitely far away, as though decades had passed since that summer evening in Moscow.

It seemed to have been another man—not Viktor at all—who had walked through Trubnaya Square, arguing heatedly and self-confidently.

Mother . . . Marusya . . . Tolya . . .

There were moments when science seemed like a delusion that prevented one from seeing the madness and cruelty of life. It might be that science was not a chance companion, but an ally of this terrible century. How lonely he felt. There was no one he could share his thoughts with. Chepyzhin was far away. Postoev found all this strange and uninteresting. Sokolov had a tendency towards mysticism, towards some strange religious submissiveness before the injustice and cruelty of Caesar.

There were two outstanding scientists who worked in his laboratory—Markov, who carried out the experiments, and the brilliant, debauched Savostyanov. But they'd think he was a psychopath if he started talking like this.

Sometimes he took his mother's letter out of his desk and read it through again.

"Vitya, I'm certain this letter will reach you, even though I'm now behind the German front line, behind the barbed wire of the Jewish ghetto. . . . Where can I find the strength, my son . . . ?"

And once more he felt a cold blade against his throat.

Translated by Robert Chandler.

Other works by Grossman: *Stepan Kol'chugin* (1936); *Za pravoe delo* (1943); *Zhizn i sud'ba* (1953).

Zvi Preygerzon
1900–1969

Zvi Hirsch Preygerzon was a Hebrew writer who spent his whole life in the Soviet Union. Born in Shepetovka, Ukraine, to a Zionist maskilic father and Hasidic mother, he became a committed communist and studied engineering in Moscow. In the 1920s, under the pseudonym A. Tsfoni, he surreptitiously sent his Hebrew writings to Palestine, where they were published in *Davar* and *Gilyonot*. Preygerzon was arrested in 1949 and imprisoned until 1955. In the 1950s and 1960s members of the Israeli consulate smuggled his writings to Israel. He worked as a chemical engineer in the Moscow Mineral Institute.

Hebrew
1960

In solitary confinement it was forbidden to bathe, but when I got to my cell I washed my hands, face, and upper body well and lay down to sleep. This time I slept for about an hour and a half. At six, as every day, the slit opened, and the soldier on duty announced "*podyom*" [let's go]. I had to get out of bed. Soon the slit opened again, and I received my portion of bread, a lump of sugar, and a cup of hot water. I ate the substandard bread greedily. I had the feeling that I had won some victory over the forces of evil.

At night, at eleven-thirty, I was summoned to the interrogator again. Again we sat opposite each other; about five meters separated us. This time I heard coaxing and threats from the interrogator. The threats were connected to members of my family. I was admonished that if I continued my criminal behavior, they would arrest my wife and daughter—yes, my daughter, too, though she was just twelve years old. She would be brought here, but first they would shear off her braids and put her in a cell. All the members of my family were nationalists, criminals, and hooligans.

With unbridled rage and vicious curses he attacked me. His eyes spurted fire, foam gathered in the corners of his mouth. He put his hands on my shoulders and started banging my head against the wall.

"Hebrew!" I shouted for the last time, "Nothing but Hebrew!"

I said nothing. The interrogator worked on me for three nights. His efforts were multifarious. A full gamut of methods, starting with coaxing, in a soft voice, a voice as sweet as honey, and ending with blows, shouts, curses, and threats. All of this for three straight nights, from eleven-thirty to five in the morning.

I was silent. Then I had a few nights without interrogation. That allowed me more hours to sleep, but soon I was summoned back to the interrogator. After a short spell of vulgar insults, which I listened to in silence, the door of the room opened and Weissfish came in.

Yes, it was Seryozhe, he and his roaming mouse-eyes. He was not brought in as a prisoner—he entered as a free man. I had to stand up. As he passed by he gave me a sideways glance and didn't respond at all. He sat on a chair next to the interrogator, and then I sat down, too.

"Do you know this man?" asked the interrogator. I said nothing. I had to be doubly silent, to understand Weissfish's role. This became clear in a moment. The interrogator added: "He will be your translator."

Joy flooded my heart. If so, in the entire vast machinery of the KGB, there was no one whose services the interrogation could use as a Hebrew translator except for this Weissfish, whom I had suspected earlier to be a spy and *dafkan* [informer]. If the interrogation was performed by this man as a translator, then he had to restrict his spying work in other places.

"It's a great pleasure," I said in Hebrew, "to see this man, to whom I taught Hebrew. But I am doubtful whether he can do his job successfully. He was not one of my talented students."

Weissfish translated my remark into Russian.

"Were there other students?" the interrogator asked. "No!" I answered in Hebrew. "Sergei Vladimirovich knows very well that he was my only student."

Weissfish translated those words of mine. Thus the conversation continued slowly. The interrogator spoke in Russian, I answered in Hebrew, and Weissfish translated my words with difficulty.

The conversation turned to listening to the Russian broadcasts of the Voice of America. I answered the interrogator's question, saying that I had heard those broadcasts several times, in the presence of Sergei Vladimirovich and upon his initiative. This time Weissfish only translated the first half of my answer. Meanwhile, the interrogator continued asking whether we had discussed the anti-Soviet news on the American radio broadcasts.

"Sergei Vladimirovich!" I addressed Weissfish, who was sitting with his legs crossed next to the interrogator. "Please translate my answer in full!"

He looked at me briefly with his mouse-eyes and said in Russian: "I can't understand this phrase satisfactorily." I answered in Hebrew: "So you shouldn't have agreed to be a translator. I said it was your initiative to listen to the American broadcast." Weissfish translated my words and added: "It isn't true, comrade Captain!" The interrogator turned to me: "You see, motherfucker, how you lie before your best friend's eyes!"

The words "your friend" insulted me, but I was silent. I had to think well. Maybe the interrogators chose Weissfish as a translator to torment me, to prove that I had dug a pit for myself by teaching their agent Hebrew. Now they were using that work of mine for their double benefit.

The interrogation continued. Now came a long series of questions about the content of the interpretations of the anti-Soviet news items on the American radio station. My answers stuck to the truth. I said that the only commentator among us was Weissfish, and I only listened. Weissfish translated my words, adding, "That isn't true." The interrogator stood up irritably. I felt that he was going to beat me this time. Indeed, after a short sermon that included curses and insults, I received two solid blows. With his legs crossed, Weissfish sat on his chair and watched the interrogator's actions with indifference.

For about two years Weissfish used to come to my house twice a week. After every visit he would give a written report to the KGB. My dossier lay on the interrogator's desk, and he leafed through it, raising various questions. This night of interrogation was seven times harder for me than solitary confinement.

At last they brought me back to the cell. I thought about the situation a lot that day. In my mind I saw many brothers in prison, and they were groaning under the suffering of the interrogators, who looked at their victims with contempt and cruel animosity. I saw prisoners of Zion in distress: the members of their families and their frightened eyes, their souls weeping in the isolation of their solitary cells, in the darkness of solitary confinement, in the interrogators' rooms. Then I saw Weissfish sitting on his chair, next to the interrogator, smoking a cigarette impassively. I was the one who had taught him Hebrew. I was the one who had done that work for the wolves. Now, as he worked as my translator, he was gaining expertise in the language. Once my interrogation was finished, they would send Weissfish to a more responsible position, where knowledge of Hebrew was needed. When I was free, I only did that disgraceful work twice a week, but now I would be doing it every night, for long hours every night.

A feeling of dreadful hatred assailed me.

Translated by Jeffrey M. Green.

Other works by Preygerzon: *Esh ha-tamid* (1966); *Yoman ha-zikhronot: 1949–1955* (1976); *Ḥevley shem: sipurim* (1991).

Piotr Rawicz

1919–1982

The novelist Piotr Rawicz was born in Lemberg (today Lviv), where he studied law and Eastern languages. Despite going underground to avoid arrest by the Nazis, Rawicz was caught by the Gestapo and was sent to Auschwitz as a Ukrainian political prisoner rather than as a Jew. In 1947, he settled in Paris, where he served as a diplomatic correspondent and press attaché to the Polish delegation. Rawicz was awarded the Prix Rivarol for his novel *Blood from the Sky*, a surrealistic account of his wartime experiences. He took his own life.

Blood from the Sky
1961

The only garden left in our walled-up town was the old cemetery, whose earliest graves dated back to the thirteenth century. It was densely overgrown. Picking one's way to its remoter corners meant battling through whole armies of ferns and weeds. One advanced like a diver among the plants on the seabed. In the old days, around the tombstones of the great and the holy, one used to find thousands of little cards bearing intimate prayers scribbled by God-fearing supplicants. They implored the dead to intercede on their behalf in the Heavenly Court. Stirred by a curiosity which was yet devoid of blasphemy, I used to enjoy ferreting out the mighty secrets of the humble by surreptitiously reading these pious petitions. I remember on one occasion chancing upon the prayer of a widow calling for the death of her only child—a girl whose cosseted upbringing had entailed endless sacrifice, but who was guilty of harbouring love for a renegade.

Today I did not find a single one of these faded little cards in the old cemetery. Were our people praying elsewhere? Had faith in the decisive influence of dead martyrs been extinguished? Or in their infinite kindness? All the same, a few cheap candles were still burning on the carved tomb of Tori Zahav, author of one of the key commentaries. Likewise on that of the Golden Rose, who—four hundred years earlier—had succeeded, by means of a miracle and a sacrifice, in deflecting a Tatar chieftain's wrath from our little market town.

My state of mind in these hours: that of a reporter making the fullest use of his eyes and ears with the aim of wiring a special dispatch to his paper. But what *was* my paper . . . ? I fought my way through the resistant vegetation till I came to the mortuary. A group of beggars stood intoning psalms over close to a hundred bodies. Old Yaakov, who knew me well thanks to the frequent bottles of vodka that I used to slip to his mendicant crew of saintly songsters, whispered in my ear: "Fifty-eight suicides last night alone. And let me tell you this: who are they? Not ordinary folk. Not the men and women who are dying of hunger. Bigwigs, every one of them: the ones who even today could afford to keep the cold out and eat better than the rest of us ate before the coming of this Angel of Death."

Scandalized, but visibly proud of the social position of his corpses, he led me around in a thoroughly proprietary manner: "There's Professor Caro and his good lady. They used gas. Don't suppose they felt anything. And that's Urias the banker—the fellow who, three years ago, shelled out three million toward the restoration of the Main Synagogue . . . And this one? Don't you recognize him? It's Tarnovski the poet. Hanged himself. Just look at that bruise. He had no money for poison."

I remembered the fine translations from Homer and Dante, and the bridge that Tarnovski had sought to throw across the Bosphorus, linking Mount Olympus and Mount Zion. He had told me of this bridge of the future, and of how it was to be ornamented, of the gargoyles and grotesques that he had thought of adding.

I nearly jumped: Shulamith's body was there, lying on a narrow oaken trestle. Her black tresses set off her delicate, exceedingly white frame. I recognized the fold of skin below her left breast.

Were those eyes—mirroring the yellow candle flames, and so still and glazed and staring—trying to send me a message? For a split second I relived our first night together and saw again the bloodstains on the sheet at our first awakening, an awakening more distracted and more decisive than the night itself. Neither of us was yet twenty. The act that we had performed, the bond that we had established and discovered, this strange new quantity that had come into being between us—these seemed so much more important than ourselves. Had I been in love with Shulamith, or with her virginity, or with the nameless force that had impelled me to take her? In every fibre of my being I re-experienced the tough resistance of the secret parts that I had rent with a determination which—as I had felt even then—belonged not to my own self but to an outer, encroaching universe.

And afterwards, the weeks in the mountain country, among the lambs and the sheep which used to wake us

with their bleating. The silvery torrents, the trees, the hidden tracks high in the Carpathians, where—two centuries earlier—the *Baal Shem Tov*, Master of the Good Name, had met the mountain-bandit leader Dovbush and revealed the mysteries of Divine Will to him.

You who were so silent, Shulamith, must accompany me on the journey for which I am preparing. In the course of it, silence will be the one token of fidelity to the selves we were.

I reached out, meaning to stroke Shulamith's tresses. Old Yaakov stopped me. "Mr. Boris, you are not allowed to touch dead bodies. You belong to the tribe of Priests, the Cohens, and such contact would defile you. Is it for me to teach you the Law?

"In the days when things were normal, Cohens weren't even allowed to set foot in here or so much as look at the bodies. But I have taken this sin upon myself. You believe in God and you give charitably. Go now, and should we survive this day do not forget me. With things as they are, it isn't easy for a man to keep body and soul together when all he can do is recite psalms. I've got work to do. They must all be washed, so that they may be buried like the righteous of the ages, in accordance with the holy rites of our people."

* * *

I left Yaakov to his work, which he performed like a black and agile spider; but my walk in the garden was not over. After gazing at the death of human beings, I was confronted, on my way out, by the death of stones.

Along the main pathway, under the supervision of a sentry in gray-green, a dozen rickety marionettes were jerking sledgehammers about—not to mention their own bones. Another group was hauling wheelbarrows. The party was demolishing old tombstones. The blind, deafening hammer blows were scattering the holy characters from inscriptions half a millennium old, and composed in praise of some holy man or philosopher. An *aleph* would go flying off to the left, while a *hé* carved on another piece of stone dropped to the right. A *gimel* would bite the dust and a *nun* follow in its wake. . . . Several examples of *shin*, a letter symbolizing the miraculous intervention of God, had just been smashed and trampled on by the hammers and feet of these moribund workmen.

Once the dissolute army of letters had broken free of their ordained contexts, was it going to invade the world of the living, the world of so-called secular objects, hunting down all that was harmonious? Was it going to deal blind and deadly blows like a whole band of Golems run riot?

What a tremendous flood of energy these dying, makeshift workmen were setting loose! Were the fragments about to turn into white-hot shell splinters? Once their excursions through so many towns and nations had ended, were the sacred letters—lonely now—going to reorganize themselves into a new community, re-creating a simple, cruel order, the very opposite of the one that had just been destroyed before our eyes? Was the secret life of these murdered tombstones going to continue in these chips and granules, scattered here, there, and everywhere, lurking in unsuspected holes and corners?

The working party stank—even in the open air. Under the eye of their grubby sentry, they dared not beg aloud. Death—that of their fellow men, of the stones, their own—had become unimportant to them; but hunger hadn't. Though the sound had been barely audible, like the sigh of the wind, I caught the word *lekhem*, which means bread. I didn't have any. I plunged my hand into my pocket and, with a quick jab of the wrist, tossed a small piece of chocolate in the direction of the group. Three or four of the workers flung themselves down. It wasn't their hands that moved, but their long skinny necks, as they gobbled a mixture of dust and tiny scraps of chocolate.

Fear said: "You mustn't become like them!"

A voice said: "You must espouse their condition, their stench, before you die. You mustn't miss this unique opportunity. The divine door is open. You must plumb the depths."

The tombstones were giving way before the thudding blows of the sledgehammers. Like a child who has constantly thumbed through the same picture book, I knew the bas-reliefs by heart, and their simple, time-honoured language:

Candlesticks: a God-fearing woman, mother, and spouse.

Two palms set in an attitude of benediction handed down from the time of the First Temple: beneath this stone there lies a priest.

Felled tree: this man died before fulfilling his earthly destiny.

Fishes: all living creatures perished in the Flood except those who dwelt in the waters. The flood of God's wrath exterminates evildoers. He who lies beneath this stone was just, and he will survive as the fish did.

Lions of Judah and stags and winged dragons and books carved on the tombstones of Doctors of the Law were succumbing to the hammer.

I must save myself, I thought, I must save the old cemetery. . . . Shall I ever be able to take it upon my shoulders, like a black cloak? Muffled up in the old cemetery, as though in the sky, I must start on my journey toward distant lands, and may we not be recognized! May nobody recognize us!

Translated by Peter Wiles; revised translation by Anthony Rudolf.

Other works by Rawicz: *Bloc-notes d'un contre-révolutionnaire ou la gueule de bois* (1969).

Jakov Lind

1927-2007

Jakov Lind (born Heinz Jakov Landwirth) was a writer of short stories, novels, and autobiographical works, in German and English, with a special emphasis on the Holocaust. His writing is distinguished by the use of allegory and farce. Born in Vienna, he fled Austria during the Nazi era on a *Kindertransport* to Holland. There, and in Germany, he survived World War II using a false Dutch identity. Following the war, he immigrated illegally to Palestine, where he met fellow writer Edgar Hilsenrath. Lind later returned to Vienna before finally settling in London in 1954.

Soul of Wood
1962

Those who had no papers entitling them to live lined up to die. The whole North-west Station was a gigantic waiting-room. It was a long, long wait, but eventually everyone's turn came. Those who finally lay in the freight cars thanked God, and when at last the wheels began to turn and the engine spewed, hissed, and let out a long whistle, none of the forty-five had a tear left. Every breath hurt and crying was torture. Besides, the dead don't cry. The forty-five had died. Dr and Mrs Barth lay squeezed together, for fifteen years they hadn't lain so close, and felt neither pain nor cold. They smelled nothing and saw nothing.

Confused thoughts came to them in their half-sleep. They saw Anton's open eyes, large and brown and without lashes, they saw Wohlbrecht's eyes, blue, honest, perhaps a little watery. Dr Barth murmured: Adonai, and Mrs Barth moved her lips and seemed to want to say Mama. The train whistle blew again and again. Anton's eyes grew larger and in the end they were as big as the Black Sea—as big and mad as Odessa—as loud as the market, as shiny as the ships on the sea. The steamers' engines kept pounding out the song: Razhinkes un mandlen—raisins and almonds will be your trade. But I became a doctor. Mrs Barth saw the great rabbi of Chernigev who had taught the mute Rivkele to speak. The doctor and his wife were both from Odessa, and even in dying they were still in the same street where they had played together at the age of four. And now they were both on their way back to Odessa. With a detour, to be sure, by way of Vienna, a forty-year detour and a crippled son left behind, they were going home to their parents and relatives who were also long dead.

But they never reached Odessa. In the little Polish town of Oswiecim they were taken off the train by men in uniform and cremated the same day.

Translated by Ralph Manheim.

Other works by Lind: *Ergo* (1968); *Numbers* (1972); *Trip to Jerusalem* (1973); *The Stove* (1983); *Crossing: The Discovery of Two Islands* (1991).

Arnošt Lustig

1926–2011

Arnošt Lustig was born in Prague to a middle-class Jewish family. A survivor of Theresienstadt, Auschwitz, and Buchenwald, Lustig began writing as a journalist in the late 1940s and as a novelist and short-story writer in the late 1950s. Much of his work centered on the Holocaust. Lustig left Czechoslovakia in the aftermath of the 1968 Prague Spring, which he had supported, and found his way to the United States, where he taught at American University until 2003, when he returned to Prague. From 1995 to 1997 he was the editor in chief of the Czech edition of *Playboy*. His works were nominated for the Pulitzer and Man Booker prizes.

Night and Hope
1962

Looking at her, the coat and everything else seemed to him to be as clear and clean as the sky.

He had to step across the old man's mattress.

He knew he would speak to him.

"Look after Anne's things," he said.

And to Anne it seemed as if only these words really woke the old man. He dropped the hand that had acted as a hearing aid. His almond-brown eyes grew wide and soft.

"Adam," he said.

Then he added: "Right oh! You run along, children!"

She had to lower her eyes once more.

"Is that your brother?" the old man asked.

They looked at each other. He felt the current again running through him.

"Yes," he replied for her.

They went out, and it seemed to them that everything they looked at was without a shadow.

And Stephen wished that the current should pass through the tips of his fingers to Anne, that she might feel in that touch the sun, and hope, and the rosy rays of day and its light.

"Brother and sister," he said.

And then: "More than that."

They walked round the blacksmith's shop. On the other side of the slope that towered above the town they saw the rambling building of the Council of Elders.

"If only I had an uncle here," she said.

"Has he gone?" he asked.

She turned her face to his and, with her finger quite close to him, tapped her forehead.

"Silly," she said, "I was thinking of an uncle who does not exist."

"Are you alone?"

"Completely," she replied.

"Are you hungry?"

"What could you do about it?"

"Do you know where I live?"

"No," she said.

"Here," he said. "Wait a second."

He ran upstairs and pulled a piece of cake out of his knapsack; this he broke in two, leaving one of the halves to the boys who were watching him.

"For your hunger," he said when he was downstairs again.

"Thanks," she said.

Suddenly they both laughed.

"Let's go back there," she said then.

"There?" he asked.

"Yes," she said.

"Yes," he repeated.

When they were sitting down again, he said: "They'll read you tomorrow."

"Oh, I'm not thinking about it," she said.

"There are other things apart from that," he said.

"What things?"

"Other things," he repeated.

Then they went out, but they only had time to walk once round the town.

The darkened trees began to merge with their own shadows, the twilight toying with the leaves.

"Come," she said. "I'll accompany you."

He gazed into her eyes, so close to his. He put his arm around her shoulders, which were frail and gentle, making him think it was up to him to protect her. The strong feeling that seemed to have a life of its own inside him and rose in waves up to his throat and farther, both the light and the dark curve of her silhouette, that which at once constricted him and released him from the shadows, holding out the promise of a sensation of freedom, all this flowed into the single word which he now uttered:

"Anne!"

"Stephen!"

He kissed her on the mouth.

"I've never . . . been like this before," she said.

It was his first kiss as well as hers.

And he again felt those waves returning, clean and fragrant, and he kissed her lips and eyes, which were now filled with tears, and felt a desperate longing that he need never, even at the price of death, live otherwise than at this moment.

They walked a little way from the door, to the spot where a yellow, wooden fence divided off the ghetto from the H.Q.

They shivered with the chill of evening.

"It's not so late yet," she said.

"Annie," he said.

"Where shall we go?" she asked.

"Annie," he repeated.

"We'll have to be going," she said, and stood still. He felt the irrevocability of the hour that closes the day like a thin sword-blade having the power to cut even the invisible current somewhere deep inside where no one can see.

He led her wordlessly round the block of houses next to Q 710. He was aware that some outside influence was disturbing that current inside him, and yet he was glad he was walking by her side and feeling her warmth, and at the same time unhappy because he knew what was coming; his throat was constricted by the same huge hoop that was encircling his chest and pressing against his eyes.

"Annie," he said.

"Yes?" she replied.

And then, after a long silence: "If you want, Stephen," she said, "come and see me in the night."

"I will," he whispered. He felt as though she had cut through ropes which had until now bound him.

"Yes, I will," he said again. "I'll come for sure."

"You can go across the courtyards," she said.

Then she added: "That's how they do it here."

"Yes," he said.

"We'll be moved soon," she said. "I feel it."

"I'll come," he repeated.

"I feel it somehow," she said.

And then, "I'm terribly afraid. It's even worse now."

"Don't worry," he said. "I'll come for sure."

"It's not far across the courtyards," she said.

"Yes," he said.

He took off his coat and threw it over her.

She returned it to him.

Then, all at once, she ran off, suddenly and unexpectedly. She tore herself away from his hands, regretting that she had said what she did. She knew the laws of the ghetto a week longer than he. He only heard her steps, receding into the darkness.

A fraction of that moment was before his eyes every second that passed by, deepening the darkness, these fractional parts of the picture composing a huge mosaic which contained the current and her half-open lips and her tears.

Then the boys became quiet and went to sleep.

He knew he would stay awake. He pieced together the fragments of the night, and only when it seemed to him that the stillness was going to overwhelm him with its immense, unbearable weight, did he steal from his bed.

He jumped over the knapsacks and shoes lying in the middle of the room, and stood by the door. He reached out for the handle. In the instant in which the cool contact poured a whole ocean into his brain, the shining brass growing dull under the imperceptible shadow of his palm, he was again conscious of the warm waves and heard the creaking of the wooden stairs that led up to the attic. At that moment he heard his heart beating, a bronze bell tolling inside him. He pressed down the handle, cautiously but firmly.

The ocean poured itself out into emptiness.

The room was locked.

He felt the soft blow. The earth fell away beneath him. He swallowed his tears. Now he could see the emptiness, and in it a small face and the transparent skin of her forehead, that indescribably fragile something that filled him with a feeling that there was a reason for his existence, those frightened eyes and that breath bitter like almonds.

He crept back to his bed, and then again to the door.

The white square, full of an overpowering silence, gave back a mute echo of the brotherhood he felt for her, a brotherhood that from that moment elevated him above this world and at the time flung him down to its very bottom.

He rattled the handle.

"Be quiet!" someone shouted.

And added something else.

He tried to make himself believe that she could see him all the way from where she was, through the silken web of the night, that it was all one great window, and that behind it was she.

Then he lay on his back, his eyes fixed on the grey ceiling, upon which was her image, indistinct and hazy, but clear in all its details—her eyes and lips. Her hair fell loosely down in the shadows and her voice sounded in the stillness.

His eyes smarted. He was aware of this only every now and again, in the intervals of his imaginings in which he heard every word a thousand times and once, as a single word, and then as one great silence.

She penetrated everything: the white door and the stillness of the night.

She returned to him in his feverish visions, and he walked with her, his hand on her shoulder, and the waves rose and fell in him and filled both of them.

In the morning he ran, breathless, through the town.

He flew upstairs.

All he found was an empty attic.

The transport to the East had left in the night.

Translated by George Theiner.

Other works by Lustig: *Diamonds in the Night* (1958); *Dita Saxova* (1962); *A Prayer for Katerina Horovitzova* (1973); *Lovely Green Eyes* (2000).

René Sussan

1925–2020

Born in Algiers, the French novelist and short-story writer René Sussan is best known for his work in genre fiction, especially detective novels, science fiction, and fantasy. He published under his own name and even more widely using the pen names René Reouven and Albert Davidson. During the 1980s, his literary efforts were focused on the eight-volume *Cycle de Sherlock Holmes*. His works were awarded the Prix Cazes (1965) and the Grand prix de littérature policière (1971 and 1983), and many of his works have been translated into German.

The Story of Farczi
1964

The morning of the third day, Tsiporah tried to distract Noémi.

"Have you read this article?" she asked, handing her *Maariv*.

Noémi finished her nth cigarette, then placed the butt on the already overflowing ashtray.

"It's not easy for me to read Hebrew."

Tsiporah read it to her: an escapee from the Nazi prison camps had regained his memory, lost for twenty years. Since at the same time he regained his family, which by chance had also taken refuge in Israel, he now found himself endowed with grandchildren and great-grandchildren.

"Incredible, isn't it?" Tsiporah concluded.

"Very commonplace," said Noémi, yawning discreetly.

A little later she added:

"Incredibly commonplace. Israel is the meeting place of the incredible and the commonplace, which gain a new dimension through their relationship."

She lit a cigarette. Tsiporah noticed that her skin was pale, her expression, morose. Beneath Noémi's beautiful amber-green eyes, small blue veins showed through her diaphanous skin with a sickly delicacy.

"You thought it was an article about Farczi?" asked Tsiporah, overflowing with awkward attentions.

Noémi burst out laughing.

"No, really! I was sticking to my theory, but it isn't an obsession. . . ."

"And yet you continue to keep an eye on the press."

"Yes," said Noémi dreamily. "The idea may have been knocked down, but Farczi is stuck in my imagination. I am . . . fascinated, obsessed, perhaps somewhat bewitched. You'll admit that such a character is extraordinary. . . ." She blew a slow, melancholy puff of smoke at the ceiling. . . .

"Do you know the cave allegory?"

"Plato's?"

"Yes. Farczi projects an outsized shadow inside the cave. But the truth is outside. I want to go outside the cave, Tsiporah, and I think Catherine de Médici could help me." [. . .]

Noémi and Tsiporah returned on the train. The car was buzzing with conversations. The two girls found themselves seated next to a twenty-something Moroccan who started up a conversation straight off. He was one of those people who, unable to abide solitude, are eager to be of service. He raised the window for some old people, went looking for sodas for the mother of a family, offered his corner seat to Tsiporah. Noémi spoke to him about Farczi.

"Oh he's powerful, powerful!" He immediately chimed in. "Have you seen him on the boulevard?"

And he told him how Farczi had escaped from Jaffa, how one day he had appeared to the bathers, emerging out of the main sewer onto the Tel Aviv beach; how, pursued, he had slipped into a manhole on Trumpeldor Street. He also described his trial: the magistrates were numerous and at liberty, but livid with fear before this individual weighed down by chains, his feet dragging enormous iron balls. . . .

At this point in the narrative, Tsiporah became agitated.

"Let him speak," whispered Noémi, delighted.

It was only an hour later, on the Carmelit railway, that Tsiporah exploded.

"That guy is nuts. Chains, balls, why not the whip? Such things don't happen anymore! Not to mention that he must not be the only one to be spreading such stupidity!"

"It's inevitable," Noémi replied. "Jewish folklore has passed straight from legend to psychotechnique, leaping over the indispensable stage of romanticism . . . popular tradition suffers if it doesn't have its Monte Cristos and its Jesse Jameses."

When they got back, there was the photo of Farczi in the mail that Yoram had promised her. She showed it to Tsiporah, who thought he looked nice enough, though without much personality. She had imagined him differently.

"Everyone sees Farczi in his own way," said Noémi. "Maybe that's the key to his reputation."

"That's also why he is disappointing," Tsiporah remarked. "The bad thing for the romantics is that Farczi exists, with a precise corporal appearance and a well-defined identity."

"That remains to be proven," Noémi replied.

"A typical answer from you!" said Tsiporah, laughing.

Noémi went to place the photo with her notes and, by association of ideas, pulled out her copy of the *Police Bulletin*. She carefully studied the list of activities imputed to Farczi. On certain days, at the same time, he had been reported at places that were quite far away from each other. If ubiquity was ruled out, one had to imagine . . . imagine what?

She reread the article. Nershon must have written it before having obtained Farczi's confession, hence without knowing the outlaw's motives. Nonetheless, his remarkable intuition had moved him to credit the famous "spectacular appearances" every time they conflicted with another more remunerative crime.

One date struck her as familiar: October 13, 1961. That day at dusk a bearded man had entered a private house in the suburb of Beersheba, capital of the Negev. At gunpoint, he had demanded to be fed. His parting words were "Farczi thanks you."

"October 13, October 13," she murmured.

Illumination came suddenly.

"Tsiporah, Tsiporah!" she cried in a slightly hoarse voice.

Translated by Michele McKay Aynesworth.

Other works by Sussan, as René Reouven: *Octave II* (1965); *L'Assassin maladroit* (1970); *Les Confessions d'un enfant du crime* (1977); *Tobie or Not Tobie* (1980); *Élémentaire, mon cher Holmes* (1982).

Georges Perec
1936–1982

Georges Perec was a French novelist, poet, dramatist, and essayist who pioneered the "new novel" movement in French literature and was a member of Oulipo, the Workshop of Potential Literature. A master of wordplay, Perec created experimental lipograms, including his novel *La Disparition* (1969), written without using the letter *e*. With filmmaker and novelist Robert Bober, Perec filmed *Ellis Island Tales*, about immigration to America. He received the Prix Theophraste Renaudot in 1965 and the Prix Médicis in 1978.

Things: A Story of the Sixties
1965

For the first time they earned some money. They did not like their work; could they have liked it? But they did not dislike it a great deal either. They felt they were learning a lot from it. Year after year it changed them completely.

These were their great days of conquest. They had nothing; they were discovering the riches of the world.

For years they had been absolutely anonymous. They dressed like students, that is to say badly. Sylvie had a single skirt, ugly jumpers, a pair of cord trousers, a duffle-coat; Jérôme had a mucky parka, an off-the-peg suit, one pitiful necktie. They leapt ecstatically into fashionable English clothes. They discovered knitwear, silk blouses, shirts by Doucet, cotton voile ties, silk scarves, tweed, lambswool, cashmere, vicuna, leather and jerseywool, flax and, finally, the great staircase of footwear leading from Churches to Westons, from Westons to Buntings and from Buntings to Lobbs.

Their dream was a trip to London. They would have split their time between the National Gallery, Savile Row and a particular pub in Church Street which had stuck with feeling in Jérôme's memory. But they were not yet rich enough to kit themselves out from top to toe in London. In Paris, the first money gaily earned by the sweat of their brows, Sylvie spent on shopping: a knitted silk bodice from Cornuel, an imported lambswool twinset, a straight, formal skirt, extremely soft plaited leather shoes, and a big silk headscarf with a peacock-and-foliage pattern. Jérôme, for his part, though he was still fond of shuffling around from time to time in clogs, unshaven, wearing an old collarless shirt and denim trousers, went in for total contrasts and discovered the joys of lazy mornings: taking a bath, shaving very close, sprinkling *eau-de-toilette*, slipping on over still damp skin a shirt of unimpeachable whiteness, tying a woollen or silken necktie. He bought three of these, at Old England, together with a tweed jacket, some marked-down shirts and a pair of shoes he thought he would not be embarrassed to wear.

Then—and this was one of the important days of their lives—they came across the Flea Market. Splendid, long-collared, button-down Arrow and Van Heusen shirts, at that time unfindable in Paris shops but which American comedy films were making increasingly popular (at least for that marginal set of people who delight in American comedies) were to be found there in untidy heaps, alongside allegedly indestructible trench coats, skirts, blouses, silk dresses, hide jackets and soft leather moccasins. They went every fortnight, on Saturday mornings, for a year or more,

to rummage through tea-chests, display stalls, stacks, boxes, upturned umbrellas, amongst crowds of teenagers with long sideburns, Algerian watch-pedlars and American tourists who emerged from the glass eyes, shiny top hats and hobby-horses of the Vernaison market and wandered in a state of mild bewilderment around the Malik market, pondering on the strange fate of things, laid out alongside used nails, second-hand mattresses, machines of which only the casing remained, and spare parts, things which were but the slightly imperfect surplus stock of America's most celebrated shirtmakers. And they would bring back all kinds of clothes wrapped in newspaper, trinkets, umbrellas, old pots, satchels, records.

They were changing, becoming other people. It wasn't so much because of their (nonetheless genuine) need to differentiate themselves from the people it was their job to interview, to impress without overwhelming them. Nor was it because they met a lot of people, because they were taking their leave, for ever, or so they thought, from what had been their milieu. But money—and this point cannot but be an obvious one—creates new needs. They would have been surprised to realise, if they had thought about it for a moment—but in those years they didn't think to what extent their views of their own bodies had altered, and, beyond that, their vision of everything that affected them, of everything that mattered, of everything that was in the process of becoming their world.

Everything was new. Their sensibilities, their tastes and their position propelled them towards things they had never known. They paid attention to the way others dressed; they noticed the furniture, the knick-knacks and the ties displayed in shop windows; they mused on estate agents' advertisements. They felt as if they understood things they had never bothered about before: it had come to matter to them whether a neighbourhood or a street was sad or jolly, quiet or noisy, deserted or lively. Nothing, ever, had equipped them for such new concerns. They discovered them enthusiastically, with a kind of freshness, and were bemused by having spent so long in ignorance. They felt no surprise, or almost none, at the fact that they thought about almost nothing else.

The paths they were following, the values they were gradually adopting, their outlook, their desires and their ambitions, it must be said, did indeed sometimes all feel desperately empty. [. . .]

And so, step by step, as they took their place in the real world in a rather deeper way than in the past when, as the children of middle-class families of no substance and then as undifferentiated students without individual form, they had had but a superficial and skimpy view of the world, that is how they began to grasp what it meant to be a person of standing.

This concluding revelation, which, strictly speaking, was not a revelation at all but the culmination of the long-drawn-out process of their social and psychological maturing, and of which they would not have been able to describe the steps without a great deal of difficulty, put the final touch on their metamorphosis.

Translated by David Bellos.

Other works by Perec: *Les Choses: une histoire des années soixante* (1965); *La Disparition* (1969); *Les Revenentes* (1972); *W ou le souvenir d'enfance* (1975); *La Vie mode d'emploi* (1978).

Eli Shechtman

1908–1996

Yiddish writer Eli Shechtman was born in the village of Vaskovichi, in Ukrainian Poleyse. He received a traditional Jewish education and studied in the literary department of the Jewish Teachers' Institute at Odessa University. His first novel *Oyfn sheydveg* (*At the Crossroads*), was published in 1930. He joined the Soviet Writers' Union in 1934 and continued to publish fiction until World War II; he later served as a Red Army officer. In 1953, during the "Doctors' Plot" and the persecution of Jewish intelligentsia, Shechtman was arrested on charges of espionage and Zionism. After Stalin's death, he was rehabilitated and began writing his main work, the epic novel *Erev*, describing the long historical odyssey of a Jewish family. Shechtman immigrated to Israel in 1972.

Erev

1965

In every village in the region, in every farmhouse you'd meet them, the Boyars. The first Boyar, family legend had it, had settled in the Polesian forests many generations ago. His name had been Ezra. The Boyars called him Father Ezra.

And at every Passover seder, after the first benediction each Boyar would tell his children, and his children's children, the story of how their ancestor had settled in these parts. And they would tell it like this: "In one of the German states there lived a goldsmith possessed of a blessed pair of hands. He fashioned jewelry and precious things for the richest and most important people in the land. The King himself drank wine from a golden beaker made by Father Ezra. This was no mere beaker, however, but a thing of such wonder that it dazzled the eyes. . . .

At one royal repast attended by monarchs of other lands one of the visiting kings could not resist the temptation and slipped this beaker into his pocket.

"But things being as they are," the Boyars would relate, "each person has even more enemies than friends. . . . And the goldsmith was no exception, particularly in that state where Jews were generally hated. Still, his enemies were reluctant to do anything openly because it would make them look bad before the world and it was liable to end in violence, of which they were also afraid, for besides his ability to fashion the most beautiful and delicate articles Ezra could also break a man in half, being a giant of a man."

"We," the present-day Boyars would at this point complain, "are not built along such lines anymore. But to continue—in addition to his strength, Father Ezra also had access to the highest places. So his enemies arrived at the oldest accusation that could be hurled against the Jew—the ritual murder. And as usual this happened just before Passover.

"Mother Bathsheba, as we Boyars call Father Ezra's wife, rose at her usual time before daybreak to fetch wood for the stove. But she noticed that the wood did not seem to be stacked in its usual way in the woodshed and she grew greatly astonished, since no one else besides herself ever went in there and the family kept no servants. She and her husband were all alone; they had not even been blessed by a child after ten years of marriage—clearly a punishment from God.

"So as she rummaged through the wood Mother Bathsheba already had a premonition of evil and she grew aghast when she discovered a dead child lying beneath the logs.

"The hair stood up on her neck and she nearly swooned. But besides being beautiful, Mother Bathsheba was also very wise and she understood everything at once.

"Only after she had arranged and secured everything, did she wake her husband and tell him the whole story. Ezra promptly became panicky and his first words were: 'We must flee!'

"Whereupon she calmed him and drove the thought from his mind. They did not dare run since it would call down suspicion on them and bring probable destruction to the whole Jewish community. They had to wait until after the first days of Passover.

"And you can imagine," the Boyars would repeat as their near ones sat with hearts beating in anticipation, "for our Father Ezra that Passover was a time of terrible grief and sorrow.

"Coming home from the House of Worship, Ezra put on his white linen robe as usual; the holiday candles were burning just as they did every year—but this time, somehow sadly. A dark cloud seemed to be hovering over the table.

"Suddenly, there was a noise in the courtyard. Although they had been expecting it, the couple turned white as chalk. A troop of soldiers had surrounded their house, and their leader walked into the woodshed without hesitation. He obviously knew just where to look and what to look for.

"They dug up the courtyard, turned the house upside down, ripped up the floorboards, but had to go away empty-handed."

And at this point the Boyars traditionally interrupted the story and refilled the winecups. Everyone drank up and the tale was continued.

"So Father Ezra and Mother Bathsheba left that terrible land to settle in the Polesian forest. And here, God blessed them with a son. This was a true Boyar—a woodsman. They named him Raphael. And now, all their troubles vanished. But Ezra could no longer remain a goldsmith since there were no materials to make precious things from, nor wealthy patrons for whom to make them. So he became a potter. One pot that he made was preserved in the family and passed on from generation to generation."

Akiva, still sitting in the same position, asked: "Reb Itzhok, unless I'm mistaken, that pot is at your house?"

"The family heirloom? Yes, I have it."

"Did you inherit it along with the Inn?"

"Oh no! Not everyone would agree to this so readily. There were many claimants in the family. Gavril moved heaven and earth to get it. He insisted that he had a prior claim. So the family was divided. One faction sided with Gavril, the other—with me. Gavril gave out barrels of mead and flung money around as if it were water. He might have won everybody over but at that time, our great-grandfather, Zorechl, was still living—may

he rest in peace now. He had already passed his second Bar Mitzvah. He sided with me and that settled it."

"Gavril . . ." Akiva looked up. "There's a strange one all right. He's got a burr in his saddle, he has. Does he still go to play at peasant weddings?"

"Not anymore. But you are right. He does have a burr in his saddle. You have to admit, however—"

Akiva interrupted him. "I've heard, Reb Itzhok, that a while ago two strangers came to you offering to buy that pot." "They came from as far away as Petersburg and waved a bundle of money under my nose. I told them: one does not sell one's grandfather."

"And?"

"They began to plead with me to lend them the pot for at least a month for some exhibition. Such work, they told me, the world has never seen. As if I didn't know it! We knew this even before Jewish pottery became fashionable in Petersburg. . . . Giddy up! Do you have to know everything, you old jade?" he growled at the mare.

"Did you give them the pot?"

"Do you mean, did I lend it? I told them the pot wasn't mine to lend, I was only its keeper. But if they got the consent of every Boyar they could have it. Those two men have been on the road for two years already. There are as many Boyars, may the evil eye spare them, as there are trees in the forests."

"A very interesting tribe, the Boyars," Akiva observed thoughtfully. "They are enemies of despair, stubborn beyond belief, and mighty optimists."

"—which?"

"Opti—believers in God."

"Ah . . ." Itzhok nodded. "What's true is true. We are believers. We believe with all our hearts and souls. One must know how to believe and one must believe to the end. If, God forbid, this faith grows shaky, one is lost—a living corpse. Then, all of one's suffering and pains are as if for naught—senseless . . . one might as well be a madman. Of course, Daniel claims that the Jewish faith in God is a terrible sickness. . . . Giddy up! Look how she wants to mix in in the conversation."

The innkeeper urged the mare on, fearful of riding right into the Sabbath. He kept stealing anxious glances at the vanishing daylight. The wind that always grows stronger at the end of day seemed to be holding the sun back from setting. It still seemed caught there in the few remaining clumps of stew-brown oak leaves.

Itzhok Boyar sighed gently. No matter how involved he grew in other matters he could never forget about his children. The youngest, Avrom, dead somewhere in Manchuria . . . Daniel's life flickering out like a candle in the wind . . . Herut, she was like a wound in his heart. And from Rochel—not even a single line.

Akiva pulled out from the straw a long pear, yellow as an autumn mapleleaf.

"Reb Itzhok, I would say that the Boyars accepted the Torah on Mount Sinai. They didn't shrink from the lightning and thunder and the black clouds that hovered overhead. The great voice of the ram's horn didn't frighten them either. When God appeared in fire and smoke and the mountain began to quake, everyone ran away, but the Boyars stood fast. And one among them became known throughout the world, the mightiest Boyar of all—Moses our Patriarch. He is the one who went up to God on Mount Sinai."

Translated by Joseph Singer.

Other works by Shechtman: *Farakerte mezhes* (1932); *Polyeser velder* (1940); *Ringen oyf der neshome* (1981); *Baym shkie aker* (1994).

Peter Weiss

1916–1982

Peter Weiss, avant-garde German-language playwright and author, was born near Berlin to a Jewish father and Christian mother. Weiss began training as a painter in Berlin. He left Germany in 1934 and lived in London, where he studied photography. He then moved to Prague before finally settling in Sweden in 1939, remaining there for the rest of his life. Weiss studied art and later worked as a painter, film producer, and writer. Some of his plays achieved international fame, most notably, his *Marat/Sade*, adapted into a film version by Peter Brook in 1967.

The Investigation: A Play
1965

Canto Two: The Camp

WITNESS 4: When we had crossed the tracks
and were waiting
at the entrance to the camp
I heard
a prisoner say to a woman
The Red Cross van is only used
to carry gas to the crematoria

Your family will be killed
The woman began to scream
A guard who had overheard her
came up and said
But my dear lady
how can you believe a prisoner
They're nothing but criminals and lunatics
Don't you see his prominent ears
his shaven head
How can you listen to such people
JUDGE: Please tell the court
can you remember
who the officer was
WITNESS 4: I saw him again later
I worked as a clerk under him
in the Political Department
His name is Broad
JUDGE: Can you point out Defendant Broad to us
MALE WITNESS 4: This is Herr Broad
    [DEFENDANT 16 *gives the witness a friendly nod*]
JUDGE: What happened to the prisoner
WITNESS 4: I heard he was sentenced
to be flogged
150 blows
for spreading rumours
He died from it
JUDGE: Defendant Broad
have you anything to say about that
DEFENDANT 16: I remember no such case
No one ever hit a prisoner
that many times
WITNESS 3: Even though our baggage had been left behind
and we had been separated
from our families
we still went through the gate
and barbed wire without distrust
We believed
that our wives and children
were being given something to eat
and that we would soon see them again
But then we saw hundreds
of ragged forms
thin as skeletons
Our confidence fled
WITNESS 6: One came up to us
shouting
Prisoners
Do you see the smoke behind the barracks

those are your wives and children
Even for you
who have entered the camp
there is only one way out
Through the gratings of the chimney
WITNESS 3: We were driven into a washroom barracks
Guards and prisoners came
with bundles of papers
We had to undress
And everything we still had
was taken from us
Our rings identity cards and photos
were listed on registration forms
Next we had a number
tattooed on the left forearm
JUDGE: How was the tattooing done
WITNESS 3: They stuck the numbers in the flesh
with the point of a needle
then ink was rubbed in
Our hair was shaved off
and they put us under cold showers
Finally we were provided with clothes
JUDGE: What kind of clothing was it
WITNESS 3: We had underpants that were full of holes
an undershirt
a tattered jacket
patchwork trousers
a cap
and a pair of wooden shoes
Then they ran us
to our block
JUDGE: What did the block look like
WITNESS 3: A wooden barracks without windows
A door in front and behind
A skylight beneath the slanting roof
Right and left bunks arranged in three tiers
The lowest bunk was on the naked ground
The bunks were mounted
between brick partitions
The barracks were roughly 120 feet long
JUDGE: How many prisoners were kept there
WITNESS 3: It was built for 500 men
There were a thousand of us
JUDGE: Were there many such barracks
WITNESS 3: Over 200
JUDGE: How wide were the wooden beds
WITNESS 3: About 6 feet wide
There were 6 men to a bunk
They had to alternate sleeping
on their right and left sides
JUDGE: Was there straw or blankets
WITNESS 3: Many beds had straw
The straw was rotten
The straw from the upper bunk
trickled down to the lower bunk
For each bed there was one blanket
Everyone pulled at it
first the one on the outside
and then the next
The strongest slept in the middle

Translated by Alexander Gross.

Other works by Weiss: *Abschied von den Eltern* (1961); *Die Verfolgung und Ermordung Jean Paul Marats* (1964); *Fluchtpunkt* (1966); *Die Ästhetik des Widerstandsu*, 3 vols. (1975–1981).

Tom Stoppard

b. 1937

The British dramatist Tom Stoppard was born Tomáš Straussler in Zlín, Czechoslovakia. In 1939, as the Nazis invaded, the Straussler family fled to Singapore, and then to Darjeeling, India, after the 1942 Japanese invasion, which his father, a doctor, did not survive. In 1945, Stoppard's mother married Kenneth Stoppard, a British officer, and moved the family with him to England. During the 1950s, Stoppard worked as a journalist and a writer of radio plays. He began publishing and producing his own plays in the 1960s. His works are marked by their absurdist and often political tragicomedy. Beginning in the mid-1970s, Stoppard served as a prominent advocate for dissidents in the Soviet Union and Czechoslovakia. He was knighted in 1997; he has received four Tony Awards for Best Play and an Academy Award for best original screenplay.

Rosencrantz and Guildenstern Are Dead
1966

Ros: We could play at questions.
GUIL: What good would that do?
Ros: Practice!
GUIL: Statement! One-love.
Ros: Cheating!
GUIL: How?
Ros: I hadn't started yet.
GUIL: Statement. Two—love.

Ros: Are you counting that?

Guil: What?

Ros: Are you counting that?

Guil: Foul! No repetitions. Three—love. First game to. . . .

Ros: I'm not going to play if you're going to be like that.

Guil: Whose serve?

Ros: Hah?

Guil: Foul! No grunts. Love—one.

Ros: Whose go?

Guil: Why?

Ros: Why not?

Guil: What for?

Ros: Foul! No synonyms! One—all.

Guil: What in God's name is going on?

Ros: Foul! No rhetoric. Two—one.

Guil: What does it all add up to?

Ros: Can't you guess?

Guil: Were you addressing me?

Ros: Is there anyone else?

Guil: Who?

Ros: How would I know?

Guil: Why do you ask?

Ros: Are you serious?

Guil: Was that rhetoric?

Ros: No.

Guil: Statement! Two—all. Game point.

Ros: What's the matter with you today?

Guil: When?

Ros: What?

Guil: Are you deaf?

Ros: Am I dead?

Guil: Yes or no?

Ros: Is there a choice?

Guil: Is there a God?

Ros: Foul! No *non sequiturs*, three—two, one game all.

Guil [*seriously*]: What's your name?

Ros: What's yours?

Guil: I asked you first.

Ros: Statement. One—love.

Guil: What's your name when you're at home?

Ros: What's yours?

Guil: When I'm at home?

Ros: Is it different at home?

Guil: What home?

Ros: Haven't you got one?

Guil: Why do you ask?

Ros: What are you driving at?

Guil [*with emphasis*]: What's your name?!

Ros: Repetition. Two—love. Match point to me.

Guil [*seizing him violently*]: WHO DO YOU THINK YOU ARE?

Ros: Rhetoric! Game and match! [*Pause.*] Where's it going to end?

Guil: That's the question.

Ros: It's *all* questions.

Guil: Do you think it matters?

Ros: Doesn't it matter to you?

Guil: Why should it matter?

Ros: What does it matter why?

Guil [*teasing gently*]: Doesn't it *matter* why it matters?

Ros [*rounding on him*]: What's the *matter* with you? [*Pause.*]

Guil: It doesn't matter.

Ros [*voice in the wilderness*]: . . . What's the game?

Guil: What are the rules?

[*Enter* HAMLET *behind, crossing the stage, reading a book—as he is about to disappear* GUIL *notices him.*]

Guil [*sharply*]: Rosencrantz!

Ros [*jumps*]: What!

[HAMLET *goes. Triumph dawns on them, they smile.*]

Guil: There! How was that?

Ros: Clever!

Guil: Natural?

Ros: Instinctive.

Guil: Got it in your head?

Ros: I take my hat off to you.

Guil: Shake hands.

[*They do*]

Other works by Stoppard: *The Real Inspector Hound* (1968); *After Magritte* (1970); *Jumpers* (1972); *Travesties* (1974); *Rock 'n' Roll* (2006), *Leopoldstadt* (2020).

Moyshe Altman

1890–1981

A Yiddish writer, journalist, and playwright, Moyshe Altman was born in Lipkan, Bessarabia, received his education in traditional Jewish and Russian schools, and worked for the Yiddish Culture Federation of Romania. He spent time in Argentina and then moved to Bucharest and Kishinev. He spent the years of World War II in Central Asia and was arrested in 1949 for his Zionist activities. Returning to Chernivtsi in 1955, Altman continued to write in Yiddish throughout his life.

A Story about a Name
1968

Older people still remember it. Younger people know about it from reading our classic writers of the older generation: how Jews once gave much thought to naming a child, long before it was born and even before it was known that a child was going to be born. What difference did it make? That's why there's a God, and he gave Eve to Adam and commanded them: be fruitful and multiply. Today things are different. But that's not my point. I just want to acknowledge that writers also often think about a name. . . . And they do it before the "child" is born, because a name is no mere trifle.

In that case what should I call what is fermenting now in my mind and demands to be told?

If I wrote in Hebrew, I would provide a caption: *Meagodes hakhurbn*—From the Legends of the Destruction—not of the Temple, but the *Khurbn* (destruction) of our own time [the Holocaust].

But the material consists of recent and painful reality. Perhaps the only thing that is legendary about it is the hero of the story. And actually, only his end is legendary, because his end was recounted by a very old man, truly an ancient. Still, it must be told, and we begin as is the custom from time immemorial: once upon a time.

Once upon a time there was a city. The city is still here, known by the same name for hundreds of years. People live there. The city has been rebuilt. That is the order of things in this world. Cities are built, then there comes a time when they are destroyed, then rebuilt, but by different people. That is how it was with the city of which we are speaking. The city was in the land of Bessarabia, which lies between the Prut and the Dniester rivers. We called it a shtetl, though in fact it was a city—more than a thousand Jewish families lived there, besides Moldavians, Russians, and Ukrainians. The Jewish quarter constituted the actual town. The Moldavian and other non-Jewish quarters were suburbs. There was never any hatred between Jews and non-Jews—on the contrary. Until there came the great Destruction, and all the Jews were driven to Transnistria.

We can now return to the beginning, to our hero.

He was called Motye, and behind his back, Motkele the *meshugener* (madman). But only behind his back, because he was something of a mystery. Who he was, where he was from, nobody knew except Zelik the tenant farmer and his wife. But they revealed it to no one. Thus it was for decades. How and why he came to the town, nobody knew. Besides, nobody was interested. What little is known is what Zelik and his wife (who left this world long ago) had let fall. We ought instead to go on the assumption that his presence had to do with the character of the town itself. Somehow the town attracted madmen. Maybe it was because the Jews there were not overly clever, but simple, unfussy folk. In the neighboring towns, in fact, they were likened to the fools of Chelm. Girls in the other towns became angry if a matchmaker proposed a match from the town of which we are speaking. Only later, when that town expanded and became a city with commercial relations with the wide world, and, as often happens, young men with knowledge and ability began unexpectedly to appear there, did the other towns began to look at things differently. But at the time when our hero showed up in the town, the place was famous for nothing, except perhaps for its madmen.

In the town there were local madmen and outsider madmen, newcomers like Motye, for example. The outsiders would stay for a while and then leave. The locals lived with their relatives. They did not go begging from house to house, except for Motye after he had let himself go, which happened after the divorce. . . .

Translated by Solon Beinfeld.

Other works by Altman: *Blendenish* (1926); *Medresh pinkhes* (1936); *Shmeterlingen* (1939).

Albert Cohen
1895–1981

The French novelist Albert Cohen was born and spent his early years in Corfu, the inspiration for much of his fiction. His family moved to Marseille in 1900, and after receiving his bachelor's degree, he moved to Geneva, where he trained as a lawyer and spent much of his life. A Zionist, he founded the short-lived journal *Revue juive* in 1925. During World War II, he worked in London for the Jewish Agency, maintaining contacts with governments-in-exile. His major novels constitute one extended autobiographical fiction. Their protagonist, Solal, is a handsome League of Nations civil servant (as Cohen was for many years) who is torn between his Jewish loyalties and the beauty and sensuality of non-Jewish society.

Her Lover (Belle du Seigneur)
1968

Behold the Valiant, the five cousins and sworn friends, newly come unto Geneva, mark them well, these men of silver tongue, these Jews of sunnier climes and even finer words, proud to have remained French citizens within their ghetto on the Greek island of Cephalonia, and loyal to the old and noble country and the old tongue.

First, mark Saltiel of the Solals, uncle to Solal of the handsome visage, an old man of consummate kindliness, without guile, solemn, now seventy-five years of age, so engaging to see with his clean-cut, clean-shaven, pleasantly lined face, with his crest of white hair, the beaver hat tilted over one ear, the nut-brown frock-coat with the inevitable buttonhole, the breeches fastened by a buckle at the knee, the dove-coloured stockings, shoes held by more buckles of antic silver, his earring, the stiff schoolboy collar, the cashmere shawl which keeps his chilly shoulders warm, the flowered waistcoat, and his way of inserting two fingers between the buttons thereof, for he is smitten with Napoleon no less than with the Old Testament and—but tell no man—with the New.

And mark Pinhas of the Solals, whom men call Eater-of-Nails but also Commander-of-the-Winds, bogus barrister and unqualified doctor of medicine, tall and consumptive, with forked beard and tortured face, wearing as always a top-hat and a double-breasted frock-coat over the hairy chest beneath, but today sporting shoes with crampons which he has pronounced indispensable for getting about in Switzerland. So much for him.

Next mark Mattathias of the Solals, known as Gum-Chew but also as Widowman-by-Choice (wives being an expensive item), a tall, gaunt figure, unemotional and circumspect of manner, sallow of face, with blue eyes and pointed ears or rather twitching appendages permanently attuned to the rumour of profit. He has only one arm, for the right ends in a large brass hook with which he scratches the top of his shaven head when estimating how much each potential borrower is good for.

Now mark this perspiring, impressive man of fifty years, by name Michael of the Solals, gold-brocaded usher to the Chief Rabbi of Cephalonia, a gentle giant and devout chaser of skirt. On his island, when he walks through the huddled streets of the Jewish quarter, one hand on hip and the other clenching a bubble-pipe, it is his delight to sing in his deep bass voice and draw the submissive glances of the girls, who admire his immense stature and his large, dyed moustache.

And last, mark the youngest of the Valiant, Solomon of the Solals, seller of apricot-juice in Cephalonia, a sweet, chubby little thing a metre and a half tall, so engaging to behold, with his round, beardless face dotted with freckles, his turned-up nose and the quiff which stands permanently erect over his forehead. A cherub, always admiring, always respectful, dazzled by trifles and readily entranced. Solomon, pure in heart, my best and closest little friend, at times when life disgusts me.

"Well now, gentlemen," began Uncle Saltiel, standing hand on hip and legs bowed. "With the help of the tutelary goddess, I have obtained an electrical coupling of the apparatus which transmits the human voice, with the corresponding apparatus inside the League of Nations, and I have informed a refined voice of the opposite sex that I wished to have speech with my nephew. And then there burst forth, like a flower suddenly blooming, another female voice, yet more refined and melodious, luscious as Turkish delight, which proclaimed itself keeper of my nephew's privy secrets. To it I communicated the intelligence that we have this moment, this thirty-first of May, incontinently arrived in Geneva in accordance with the directions of my dear Sol, informing the same that our personal toilettes being completed by means of total immersion in the baths of the aptly named Hotel Modeste, we were at the entire disposal of His Excellency, even adding, to bring a smile to those charming lips, that Solomon had anointed his quiff and forelock with vaseline in the foolish hope of making it lie down. Whereupon, on learning that I was an uncle on the mother's side, the voice like spun gold informed me that my nephew had delayed his return to Geneva, having been obliged to travel as a matter of urgency to divers capitals on secret business."

"Did she actually say secret?" asked Naileater, somewhat put out.

"No, but the meaning was clear from her tone. He is to return tomorrow, and yesterday he was thoughtful enough to leave a verbal message for me, by the long-distance telephone!"

"All right, all right, we all know you're his pet!" said Naileater. "Just give us the verbal message and let's have done with these interminable blatherings!"

"The nub of the communication transmitted by the refined lady, who must earn a handsome emolument if we may judge by her voice, is that I am invited to present myself, unaccompanied, tomorrow, the first day of June, at nine o'clock ante meridiem, at the first-class Ritz Hotel."

"What do you mean unaccompanied?" said Naileater angrily.

"Unaccompanied, she said, and can I help it if he wishes to speak to me in private?" said Saltiel, who opened his snuffbox and took a delicate pinch. "No doubt your turn will come within the next few days," he added, not without a hint of malice.

"I see. So I had a bath for nothing," said Naileater. "Saltiel, you're going to have to make it up to me, because you needn't think that I braved the waters for my own good pleasure! If that's clear to you. I'm going out. I get edgy if I'm shut up inside too long."

"Where are you going?" asked Solomon.

"I shall put on my white gloves and leave my card with the Vice-Chancellor of the University of Geneva, a simple courtesy which I must discharge as a former Vice-Chancellor of the Jewish and Philosophical University of Cephalonia which I founded with such success, as I believe you know."

"What university?" asked Mattathias while Uncle Saltiel shrugged his shoulders. "Its premises were your back kitchen, and you were the only professor."

"My dear fellow, quality is much more important than quantity," retorted Naileater. "But enough. Let's have no more envy. What I've done is to make a visiting-card by cunningly writing my name so that it looks as if it has been professionally printed. I listed my previous functions, then wrote simply: 'from one colleague to another, distinguished greetings,' then added the address of our hotel should he in turn feel inclined to drop by and leave his card and invite me to share a polite conversation between Vice-Chancellors over a helping of the Swiss dish known as 'fondue,' which is made with cheese, garlic, white wine, nutmeg and a slurp of kirsch which must be added at the last moment. It will all depend on whether he's a man of breeding. Farewell, gentlemen."

Translated by David Coward.

Other works by Cohen: *Mangeclous* (1940); *Book of My Mother* (1954); *Les Valeureux* (1969).

Degracia
1911–1985

Known primarily for autobiographical evocations of her life and times, Gracia Cohen, known by her pen name Degracia, was born in Fès, Morocco, into a family of Sephardic landowners. The sudden, tragic death of her fiancé radically changed the course of her life and, for some years, her religious practices. An affair with a married man left her pregnant, which precipitated her departure from Morocco and her initial residence in France. In 1940, she married Pierre-Louis Cassou, a Catholic military man with whom she would eventually return to Morocco. In 1942, at great personal risk, she traveled to Marseille to recover the child she had earlier placed in an orphanage. Her writing career was delayed by her duties as the mother of seven children, but with the publication of *Mariage mixte* in 1968, Degracia became Morocco's first francophone Jewish woman writer.

Mixed Marriage
1968

Shortly before Paris was occupied, Maurice had me return to my native Morocco.

My parents—my dear parents whom I loved so much and whom I never saw again—were, alas, dead. The other members of the family held me partly responsible for everything bad that had happened since I left.

I did not dare return to Fès, nor to the mellah.

I knew there had been many changes. I was gripped by a longing to revisit the places where I had lived.

I settled with my children in Meknès, some sixty kilometers from the religious capital.

One Sunday morning, I turned on my radio and heard:

"This is the Reverend Father Sylvestre speaking to you."

This is what he said, almost word for word:

"Today," said a strong voice, "I'm going to talk about Jews! As you know, Jews are the vilest people on earth. The lot of them are nothing but usurers, traffickers, and liars, they proliferate, true parasites, on every continent. Their religion can be summed up in two words: profit and money. They . . . the Jews . . . they . . . the Jews. . . ."

Naïvely, I turned down the volume on my radio. That man should not be heard! It's not possible to shout such things over the air waves.

The world is at war!

There's already so much evil being done to Jews! Even here in Morocco, there are Enemy Commissions.

My God, if those people heard this man's sermon, how encouraged they would be! As if they needed encouragement!

And the Arabs? What if they were listening, too?

That speech is a provocation. A call to rioting! To blood!

Isn't what's happening elsewhere enough?

Is it not too much?

Morocco is not openly occupied, but the Enemy is watching. He keeps the country, and thus the Radio, under surveillance!

I caught myself talking to the radio:

"Please, stop your ignominious diatribe!"

But the flow of ignoble words continued with greater intensity!

The whole thing was delivered with such vehemence, hatred, and rage, it surpassed all understanding.

Unable to put up with any more from that man of the cloth, I started banging on the radio. I must have caused a power failure because at last it was quiet.

How naïve I was!

I touched my forehead, my face, I was sweating, I could feel the dampness beneath my clothes.

"I no longer hear him, this Reverend Father. But all the listeners in front of their radios are still hearing that pernicious orator."

So this is how hatred of Jews is being taught?

How can one—gratuitously—insult and trample on a people when they're flat on the ground?

Someday this war will come to an end. And the suffering of the Jewish people as well. I do hope so.

Are these the sermons (a sermon is a religious speech, and religion implies morality) that are heard in the churches?

This theologian who knew better than anyone what the Catholic faith owed to the mother-religion, what was he driving at? He knew that his Lord was a Jew!

Would that be why he so hated the Jews, those brothers of Jesus?

Does the Reverend Father not worry that, by spreading hatred like this, one day hatred will take its revenge?

Up to now, only the Jews of North Africa had remained unmolested by the Enemy.

I am not speaking of Vichy's laws of exception . . .

But two or three speeches like this would surely light some fires. Even worse, they could set off a powder keg.

I could not help thinking that in France, in all the synagogues, on Saturday, every Saturday, when the Scroll of the Law is presented, the rabbi first delivers a long prayer for the Christians:

Eternal God, Lord of the World, Thy Providence embraces the heavens and the earth, power and might belong to Thee, by Thee alone all is raised up and strengthened.

From Thy holy dwelling place, O Lord, bless and protect the French Republic and the French people.

May France thrive and prosper, may she, through unity and concord, be great and strong.

May the rays of Thy light shine upon those who preside over the State's destiny and maintain order and justice in our country.

May France enjoy a lasting peace and keep her glorious place among the nations.

Look favorably upon our prayers.

May the words on our lips and the feelings in our hearts find grace in Thy presence,

O Lord, our Creator and our Liberator.

The faithful, all standing, respond several times, Amen.

Why is it that the Jews love the Christians and all others? And why is it that so many Christians detest the Jews? Yes, why?

Suddenly I also recalled this bit from a recent article I had read in the newspaper:

A French Jew, a great actor and a member of the resistance, arrested in Paris and tortured, beaten bloody by antisemites who dragged him on the ground, had the courage to get up, seconds before breathing his last. He stood as straight as he could before these cruel men, who, surprised, asked him jeeringly, "Why are you standing up, Jew?"

"It will be easier for you, morally speaking, to murder a man who is standing upright." To speak of morality to one's executioners!

This was a lesson delivered from afar by a dying Jew to that strident speaker on Radio-Morocco.

Ah, Maurice, there are days when I am not proud to be the wife of a non-Jew.

Translated by Michele McKay Aynesworth.

Other works by Degracia: *Retour sur un monde perdu* (1971); *Un Sacré métier* (1974); *Récit d'une enfance marocaine* (2003).

Patrick Modiano
b. 1945

Patrick Modiano is a French author and screenwriter, whose works are influenced by the early death of his brother and by the German occupation. Fascinated by the psychology that led to resistance in some and collaboration in others, Modiano has written more than twenty novels, many of which have been translated and adapted for film. He received the Grand prix du roman de l'Académie français, the Prix Goncourt, and, in 2014, the Nobel Prize in Literature.

La Place de l'étoile
1968

Rue Sainte-Catherine, people turned as we passed. Probably because of my father's purple suit, his Kentucky green shirt and the same old shoes with the astrakhan spats. I fondly wished a policeman would stop us. I would have justified myself once and for all to the French, tirelessly explaining that for twenty years we had been corrupted by one of their own, a man from Alsace. He insisted that the Jew would not exist if goys did not condescend to notice him.[1] And so we are forced to attract *their* attention by wearing garish clothes. For us, as Jews, it is a matter of life and death.

The headmaster of the lycée invited us into his office. He seemed to doubt whether the son of this dago could genuinely want to study *lettres supérieures*. His own son—*Monsieur le proviseur* was proud of his son—and spent the holidays tirelessly swotting up on his *Maquet-et-Roger*.[2] I felt like telling the headmaster that, alas, I was a Jew. Hence: always top of the class.

The headmaster handed me an anthology of Greek orators and told me to open the book at random. I had to gloss a passage by Aeschines. I acquitted myself brilliantly. I went so far as to translate the text into Latin.

The headmaster was dumbfounded. Was he really ignorant of the keenness, the intelligence of Jews? Had he really forgotten the great writers we had given France: Montaigne, Racine, Saint-Simon, Sartre, Henry Bordeaux, René Bazin, Proust, Louis-Ferdinand Céline On the spot, he suggested I skip the first year and enrolled me straight into the second year—*khâgne*.

"Congratulations, Schlemilovitch," he said, his voice quavering with emotion.

After we had left the lycée, I rebuked my father for his obsequiousness, his Turkish Delight unctuousness in dealing with the *proviseur*.

"What are you thinking, playing Mata Hari in the office of a French bureaucrat? I could excuse your doe eyes and your obsequiousness if it was an SS executioner you were trying to charm! But doing your belly dance in front of that good man! He was hardly going to eat you, for Christ's sake! Here, I'll make you suffer!"

I broke into a run. He followed me as far as Tourny, he did not even ask me to stop When he was out of breath, he probably thought I would take advantage of his tiredness and give him the slip forever. He said:

"A bracing little run is good for the heart. . . . It'll give us an appetite. . . ."

He didn't even stand up for himself. He was trying to outwit his sadness, trying to tame it. Something he learned in the pogroms, probably. My father mopped his forehead with his pink buckskin tie. How could he think I would desert him, leave him alone, helpless in this city of distinguished tradition, in this illustrious night that smelled of vintage wine and English tobacco? I took him by the arm. He was a whipped cur.

Midnight. I open the bedroom window a crack. The summer air, "Stranger on the shore," drifts up to us. My father says:

"There must be a nightclub around here somewhere."

"I didn't come to Bordeaux to play the lothario. And anyway, you can expect meagre pickings: two or three degenerate kids from the Bordeaux bourgeoisie, a couple of English tourists. . . ."

He slips on a sky-blue dinner jacket. I knot a tie from Sulka in front of the mirror. We plunge into the warm sickly waters, a South American band plays rumbas. We sit at a table, my father orders a bottle of Pommery, lights an Upmann cigar. I buy a drink for an English girl with dark hair and green eyes. Her face reminds me of something. She smells deliciously of cognac. I hold her to me. Suddenly, slimy hotel names come tumbling from her lips: Eden Rock, Rampoldi, Balmoral, Hôtel de Paris: we had met in Monte Carlo. I glance over the English girl's shoulder at my father. He smiles and makes conspiratorial gestures. He's touching, he probably wants me to marry some Slavo-Argentinian heiress, but ever since I arrived in Bordeaux, I have been in love with the Blessed Virgin, with Joan of Arc and Eleanor of Aquitaine. I try to explain this until three in the morning but he chain-smokes his cigars and does not listen. We have had too much to drink.

We fell asleep at dawn. The streets of Bordeaux were teeming with cars mounted with loudspeakers: "Operation rat extermination campaign, operation rat extermination campaign. For you, free rat poison, just ask at this car. Citizens of Bordeaux, operation rat extermination . . . operation rat extermination . . ."

We walk through the streets of the city, my father and I. Cars appear from all sides, hurtling straight for us, their sirens wailing. We hide in doorways. We were huge American rats.

NOTES

1. Modiano is parodying Sartre's *Anti-Semite and Jew*.
2. Latin grammar.

Translated by Frank Wynne.

Other works by Modiano: *La Ronde de nuit* (1969); *Les Boulevards de ceinture* (1972); *Lacombe Lucien* (1974).

Jurek Becker

1937–1997

Born in Poland and a survivor of the Łódź ghetto and concentration camps at Ravensbrück and Sachsenhausen, Jurek Becker wrote novels and film scripts in German. In 1945, he immigrated to East Berlin, where he joined the Socialist Unity party; in 1977, he crossed over to West Berlin. Becker won both the Heinrich Mann Prize and the Charles Veillon Prize in 1971, and the National Prize for literature of the German Democratic Republic in 1975.

Jacob the Liar
1969

And the resistance, I will be asked: Where is the resistance? Could it be that the heroes are gathering in the shoe factory or in the freight yard, at least a few? Is it possible that at the ghetto's southern limits, which are the least clearly defined and hence the hardest to keep under surveillance, dark passages have been discovered through which weapons can be smuggled into the ghetto? Or are there in this wretched town only hands that do exactly what Hardtloff and his sentries demand of them?

Condemn them, go ahead and condemn us; those were the only hands there were. Not a single righteous shot was fired, law and order were strictly maintained, there was never a trace of resistance. I suppose I should say that I believe there was no resistance. I am not omniscient, but I base this assertion on what is called probability bordering on certainty. Had there been anything of the kind, I would have been bound to notice it.

I would have participated, I can swear to that; they need only have asked me, if only for Hannah's sake. Unfortunately I am not one of those rare individuals who raises the battle cry; I cannot inspire others, but I would have participated. And not only myself: why didn't the man emerge who could cry, "Follow me!"? The last few hundred miles would not necessarily have been so long and so hard. The worst that could have happened to us would have been a meaningful death.

I can tell you that I have since read with awe about Warsaw and Buchenwald—another world, but comparable. I have read much about heroism, probably too much, I have been gripped by senseless envy, but I don't ask anyone to believe me. Be that as it may, we remained passive until the last second, and there's nothing I can do about it now. I am not unaware that an oppressed people can only be truly liberated if it contributes toward its liberation, if it goes at least a little bit of the way to meet the Messiah. We did not do this, I did not take a single step, I learned the rules by heart and adhered strictly to them, and only asked poor Jacob from time to time what new reports had come in. I will probably never come to terms with this; I haven't deserved any better. My whole thing about the trees no doubt has something to do with it; as well as my fatal sentimentality and the generosity of my tear ducts. Where I was, there was no resistance.

They say that what is good for your enemies is bad for you. I don't intend to argue about this; anyway, it only makes sense with concrete examples, such as the one I now have, but I don't want to argue about it. My example is the electric current. Jacob doesn't mind in the least doing without it; in fact he manages splendidly without it. Doing without? No one would ever have thought how good no electricity can be. Apart from the Russians and good health for Lina, there is nothing Jacob wishes for as much as no electricity. But Jacob is only one, and we are many. We want electricity. We are at the mercy of our imaginations: if not our saviors, then let it at least be electric current.

The Germans, to return to the example, also want electricity, and not only because at the military office they are ruining their eyes with candlelight. The fine-tuned plans have been thrown into disarray; not a chair, not a sideboard leaves the furniture factory, there are no pliers or hammers or screws coming out of the tool factory, no shoes, no trousers: the Jews are sitting around twiddling their thumbs. Two groups of hurriedly assembled electricians swarm out in search of the damage, double rations of bread and cigarettes, day and night they test fuses and whatever else can be tested, dig up streets, expose cables, accompanied by our good wishes. After five fruitless days Hardtloff has them shot; there is talk of sabotage, which is sheer madness. The electricians were all in one way or another Jacob's customers and had a personal interest in eliminating the problem. They are executed in the square in front of the military office. Anyone is free to watch: Let this be a warning and do what is demanded of you.

Then a German special detachment arrives on a truck, like men from Mars. Equipped like deep-sea divers, they are seen to laugh and relish their importance: We'll take care of it all right, let's see what's stumped these Jewish bunglers. Two days, and the trouble spot is exposed: a swarm of rats has been gnawing at a cable and succumbed to their greed. A new cable is lowered into the ground, and once again there are chairs, shoes, pliers, screws, Jacob's radio.

Translated by Leila Vennewitz.

Other works by Becker: *Irreführung der Behörden* (1973); *Schlaflose Tage* (1978); *Bronsteins Kinder* (1982); *Amanda herzlos* (1992).

Bernice Rubens

1928–2004

Novelist Bernice Rubens was born in Cardiff, Wales, to an Orthodox family of Lithuanian and Polish immigrants. At age thirty-five, she published her first novel, *Set on Edge*. Her works focus on the experiences of Jewish families, exploring the terror and trauma that lurks beneath the surface of domestic scenes. In 1970, she became the first woman to win the Man Booker Prize, for *The Elected Member*. Two of her novels, *I Sent a Letter to My Love* (1975) and *Madame Soustazka* (1962), were adapted into films.

The Elected Member
1969

When the bell rang, he heard Norman shout, "If that's that shit Levy, tell him to piss off."

Rabbi Zweck knew that Dr Levy must have heard through the door and he began apologising on his son's behalf as he let the doctor in.

"Don't worry," Dr Levy said, "it's natural. Can we go into the kitchen?" he whispered. He knew Norman would be listening by his door, and he didn't want to be overheard. He followed Rabbi Zweck into the kitchen and sat at the table. He had become familiar with the room. The copper ladle that hung over the kitchen sink was always at the same angle and with the same high polish. In the cup of lemon tea that Rabbi Zweck put before him, he saw the familiar and now fading rose pattern that lined the cup. He was not their official family doctor. Dr Levy was a psychiatrist, but he was a longstanding friend of the Zweck family. As a friend, he had been in on Mrs. Zweck's dying, sitting on the same chair by the kitchen table, drinking tea out of a less faded rose-patterned cup. Then he had sat with Rabbi Zweck much as he was doing now, comforting him, the truth exposed between them. "It's only a matter of time," he had told the Rabbi then, "and the sooner, the better for you all." Meanwhile, in the vast seven-footer, Mrs. Zweck wondered why she was taking so long to recover from her operation. "It takes longer when you're older," the doctor had told her. "Another month or so and you'll be up and about." So she lay there, having patience, fingering the holiday brochure that Rabbi Zweck had bought her, to help her decide where to convalesce. Now, it was Norman, on the same bed, with a different illusion, but an illusion all the same, while between his father and Dr Levy in the kitchen, straddled the same uneasy truth.

"How long has he been like this?" Dr Levy asked.

"How should I know," Rabbi Zweck said helplessly. "For many days now he doesn't eat. Breakfast he has, a big breakfast, and afterwards, nothing."

"Has he been in the shop?"

"He goes downstairs. He sits. He does nothing, Bella says. And always so rude, I'm ashamed for my customers. If only I knew where he got them. If only . . ."

"Rabbi Zweck," the doctor said gently, "even if you found where he was getting them, it would be of no use. He'd find another source. They're all the same, these addicts. They're so cunning. Come what may, they'll find somewhere to get it. It's expensive of course. Does he have so much money?"

Rabbi Zweck was silent. Then without looking at Doctor Levy, he stretched his hand towards him over the table. "Doctor," he said, "I'm ashamed, but you're a doctor, and is confidence what I tell you." Dr Levy patted the Rabbi's hand.

"He's stealing it?" he said.

Rabbi Zweck hung his head. "My own son," he whispered, "a *ganuf*, and from his father's money. The till," he said, "last week, my Bella is missing fifteen pounds. What can I do? Every minute I can't be with him." Dr Levy opened his black case. "We must get him better, at least over this bout, then we must try again to persuade him to go to hospital. It's the only way. Six months, a year, away from the drug. He might get over it."

"I've tried," the Rabbi said, "Bella's tried. Each time he gets over it, he says he'll stop it. Then he starts again. What will become of him?"

"Let's get him over this lot first," the doctor said businesslike.

Rabbi Zweck squeezed the doctor's hand. "I am thinking," he said, "perhaps *takka* is silver-fish in his room. Perhaps when they come from the cleaning people, they don't look so thoroughly. Like Norman said, a real spring-clean we should have. So we should find them and take them away." He looked at Dr Levy pleadingly.

"You will drive yourself mad," Dr Levy whispered. "You are trying to defend him at the risk of your own sanity. There is nothing in his room. You know it as well as I. Listen Rabbi, it's very simple." Dr Levy leaned forward and spoke very slowly with the patience of one who has explained the same situation over and over again. "When he started to take the drugs, they gave him what they call, a kick. You understand?"

"What should I know from a kick," Rabbi Zweck said wearily. At each of Norman's breakdowns, and at each explanation, he refused to acknowledge that the diagnosis had anything to do with his son. "Doctors' talk," he muttered to himself. "A real spring-clean Bella will give," he said.

"When Norman started," Dr Levy went on, ignoring the interruption, "it took just one tablet to make him feel good. Then as time went on, in order to get the same effect, he had to take more, and more and more. Until, like now, he's taking them by the handful. Now these drugs are dangerous. If you take enough of them, you begin to see things, things that other people don't see. Snakes, elephants, pins, or like Norman, silver-fish. He sees them all right, but he's hallucinating. They're not there, Rabbi Zweck," Dr Levy said firmly, "no matter how much he convinces you. You know they're not there, don't you."

Rabbi Zweck sighed. Sometimes he hated Dr Levy. "How are you so sure they're not there?" he mumbled.

Dr Levy took a small tablet out of the box. "I won't go in and see him," he said. "It will only make him worse. Persuade him to join you and Bella for some coffee dur-

ing the morning, and crush this into the sugar. Let Bella do it. It will dissolve and with luck he won't taste it. If he drinks the whole cup, he'll sleep for a few hours and I'll come over later and give him an injection. Same as before. We'll give him deep sedation for a fortnight. Like last time."

"And the time before that," the Rabbi put in. "And the next time."

"Let's cross this hurdle, shall we, and afterwards we'll try to talk to him. All of us. It's you I'm worried about, Rabbi. More than Norman," Dr Levy said. "You're letting it kill you."

"You want I should dance?" Rabbi Zweck muttered.

"Remember the times when he's all right. In between the bouts. These times are time to live for and look forward to. The times when he's a good son to you."

"They're not so often, these times. Not any more," Rabbi Zweck said. He banged his fist on the table in sudden anger. "I should only find the murderer who sells them to him."

"Walk me downstairs to the shop," the doctor said gently. "You can sell me some cigarettes."

Rabbi Zweck stopped at his son's door. "Norman," he called.

"You can tell Dr Levy from me," Norman shouted, "he's a psychiatrist like the cat's psychiatrist, and he can take his injections to hell. There's nothing the matter with me," he yelled, half-sobbing. "It's you and your lot. You're mad, the lot of you. Just leave me alone."

I'm going downstairs to the shop," his father said evenly. "Soon I'll come back. We'll have a tea together, huh. You, me and Bella."

"I don't want any family conferences," Norman said. "Just leave me alone."

Dr Levy put his arm round Rabbi Zweck's shoulder and led him downstairs to the shop.

Other works by Rubens: *Mate in Three* (1965); *Brothers* (1983); *I, Dreyfus* (1999).

Lili Berger

1916–1996

Yiddish writer Lili Berger was born in Małkin, Poland. Although raised in an Orthodox family, she received a secular high school education in Warsaw. Berger left for Paris in 1936, where she taught and wrote for leading Yiddish journals. She was active in leftist causes and joined the French Resistance during the war. Berger returned to Warsaw in 1949, when the communists took power in Poland, but was forced to leave, along with most Polish Jews, in 1968. She returned to Paris, where she continued to publish essays, criticism, short stories, and novels.

On Saint Katerine's Day
1970

Katerine Vrublevska had thick black curly hair, large, dark velvet eyes, a pale, dreamy, longish face and was fifteen years old.

Her classmates described her skin colour as "café au lait." She knew she was a beauty, how could she not know since they always told her so. Among her schoolfriends she looked like an exotic rose by some chance growing amidst wild flowers. Ever since she could remember she had been called "black beauty," and when her Uncle Karol, a pharmacist from Warsaw, came to visit, he brought gifts for the "pretty gypsy." Uncle Karol loved her dearly, her aunt did too, but now their love seemed so strange to Katerine, so distant, even her mother's love. Why did she hide it from her? Everyone knew, but she didn't. That's why Fat Theresa felt free to make fun of her. Probably everyone, everyone was laughing at her; she had understood nothing, now she understood very well, now she remembered everything. Sundays, at church, she would feel them looking at her strangely. "Because you are a beauty," her mother would tell her. Not true, it was because of something else, all of them, all of them were always looking at her; she had never guessed, was never suspicious. Now she knew, this morning she finally understood everything, now she remembered how they would sometimes say to her, "You're different, somehow." Why hadn't she caught on? [. . .]

Magdalena caught her breath, silent for a while, thinking of how to go on with this painful conversation with her daughter.

"If you want, I'll tell everything. But it mustn't change anything between us. What can it possibly mean to us? Isn't that so? Do you promise me, daughter dear?"

Katerine nodded and blurted through her tears, "I promise, but tell me everything; tell me the whole truth." [. . .]

"It was in 1942, dawn, still dark. They were being driven on this road, the back road that leads to the forest; they passed close to our house. I lay in bed shaking as if I had a fever. The wailing and howling was unbearable, wailing and howling, then an echo of gunshot,

then—silence. There was no question of sleep after that; my heart was heavy, in my ears the wailing rang but outside it was as silent as the graveyard. [. . .]

"It was daylight at last but the town was lifeless; people were still afraid to go out. It was a Sunday; no-one went to work, they stayed indoors. It was very stuffy and I wanted some air, so I carefully opened the front shutter and stuck my head out and . . . a parcel at the door, some sort of strange parcel, a kind of bundle. [. . .] The bundle stirred. I looked around to see whether anyone was watching, pulled the bundle in and untied it . . . a child . . . seemingly smothered; the sop had fallen out of the little mouth. I put my ear to the child; it was breathing. [. . .] I was so terrified that it would cry; I was almost out of my mind with fright, what to do with the child? It was then that I remembered Sister Katerine, she was so compassionate and wise, gave good advice; she wouldn't refuse. I dressed quickly, put the child into the vegetable basket, packing the sop with wet sugar, covered the basket with an old towel, put the flowers from the vase on top, as well as some vegetables I had prepared to take to the convent on Sunday. Fortunately you didn't cry, you were hungry and sucked on the sugar. When Sister Katerine removed your clothing to bathe you a note fell out of your little right sock: 'Merciful people, save this child; God will reward you.' Then the name. Date of birth wasn't given, probably forgotten. Sister Katerine fed you, then made out a certificate of baptism. It was Saint Katerine's Day, just like today; you were given her name and I was forbidden to come to see you, just as well. After that, difficult times befell me." [. . .]

"Told myself that if I survived, you'd be my child; my little girl died, God sent an unfortunate child, had to wait. After the war my situation was difficult, had to come back to myself; thanks to Uncle Karol, he helped me a lot, always loved you; according to the baptismal certificate, you were four years old. Sister Katerine led me to a dark little girl and, pointing to me, said to her, 'This is your mother, a good mother, you must love her. . . .' Since then, I have been so happy; grew to love you like my own child, what's the difference? You really are my own child, my only daughter. I was so. . . ."

The words stuck in her throat, choking. Both were silent now, their heartbeats could be heard in the stillness. Magdalena became alarmed at Katerine's silence and said,

"You see, my child, I've told everything, hidden nothing; you know everything now."

"Not everything yet."

"What more do you want to know?"

"What was my name?"

"Miriam. Miriam Zack."

"And my parents?"

"Sister Katerine may know."

"The note, my note? I want to see. . . ."

"I'll ask Sister, perhaps she has it, perhaps. . . . But be patient, better I go myself, it's more fitting."

"And family? Relatives? Do I have someone . . . ?"

"How can we know that? You have . . . me, Uncle Karol, Auntie, aren't we your family? Am I not a mother to you and you a daughter to me?"

"Yes, yes, you are, of course you are, but—" and Katerine broke into tears again.

Shortly after Saint Katerine's Day, mother and daughter together composed and mailed the following notice to the Red Cross, Missing Relatives Division: "Miriam Zack, daughter of Leyzer and Rivke Zack from the city of T., seeks relatives, wherever they may be, within the country or abroad. Reply."

Translated by Frieda Forman and Ethel Raicus.

Other works by Berger: *Eseyen un skitsn* (1962); *Fun haynt un nekhtn* (1965); *Der letster tog: dramatishe skitse vegn Yanush Kortshak* (1978).

Henryk Grynberg

b. 1936

Henryk Grynberg was born in Warsaw. He and his mother survived the Holocaust in hiding and on false papers. They remained in Poland after the war, and he became a journalist. In the late 1950s, Grynberg began writing autobiographical poems and short stories and became a member of the Warsaw State Jewish Theater. In 1967, while on a theatrical tour, he defected to the United States in response to Polish antisemitic propaganda and censorship. He has published more than twenty books of prose and poetry, most of which use biographical material, incorporating Jewish experiences during and after the Holocaust.

Fatherland

1970

The Jews held cattle dealers in contempt. They considered them illiterate louts in no way different from peasants. My grandfather never let a cattle dealer into

his house. Into the barn yes, but never into the house. My aunts used to run away when Biumek and his brothers arrived in the village, and my grandfather would lock them in the house.

For my grandfather there were only two categories, people or brutes. He knew a brute could offend a person, but there was nothing a person could do to a brute. All a person could do was separate himself from brutes. Lock the doors on them. And that's just what my grandfather did his whole life. With this aim he amassed money. The more he earned, the more he could shut himself up in his house. He had a weakness for books, books about the meaning of man's life and his relations with God. The more he earned, the more time he had for them. Money is time, my grandfather used to say. That's why he was tough in his business. Brutes just thought he was greedy. But can a brute understand such a thing?

"Your grandfather was a wise man," Biumek would say. "He wouldn't talk with just anybody."

Biumek never held it against my grandfather that he never let him into the house. Neither did he hold it against my aunts that they ran away from him and his brothers.

"It wasn't fitting for them to associate with us," he'd say with serious conviction. He didn't say it because neither my grandfather, nor my aunts, nor his brothers were alive. Not for any reconciliation with the dead. Biumek didn't think you had to forgive the dead. Just because they weren't alive? He didn't forgive the wrongs done him by his father-in-law just because he married his daughter.

"Anybody can die," Biumek would say. "The whole trick is to act like a man before you die."

Biumek thought my grandfather had acted properly and that in his place he would have done the same. A man should defend himself the best he can. That my grandfather didn't defend himself in the end didn't apply here. My grandfather couldn't defend himself or my aunts against the brutality they encountered, for that brutality was more than a man could imagine, let alone defend himself against. You can't lock the doors on brutality like that. A man defends himself against the brutality from which there is some defense, held Biumek. And it's his duty to do so for as long as he can. Biumek was no brute. It was just that my grandfather didn't know it. How could he know, when he'd never talked with him, and never let him into the house? [. . .]

I walked around the village and finally came out near that same rotted cross by the roadside. I realized that the cross must have seen my grandfather off when he was leaving on his wagon loaded down with bundles, my grandmother, my epileptic uncle, and my two unmarried aunts. My grandmother wore a long skirt like the one Cyranka still wore. A meek woman full of respect for God and my grandfather. Aunt Rywka had a turned-up nose. She wore a gray city outfit, white shoes, her hair done up in waves, her purse tucked chicly under her arm. . . . After all, she was going to town. Wearing the black cap he never took off in front of anyone, my grandfather had raised his bearded head and gazed for a long time at that cross, which was a sign of our way more than anyone else's. And that man on the cross was also ours, then more than ever before. Then that was clearer than ever. My grandfather couldn't help thinking about it as he went on his own way of the cross.

He didn't get far from here. He rose up to the sky, through a chimney, and returned on the wind. From here to Treblinka it was only a few dozen kilometers, and what's a few dozen kilometers for the wind? So he came back and returned to the earth, enriching the soil of these fields, and now again he floats above them in the smell of the lupine.

My father didn't get far from here either. He is lying close by, beside one of these fields. They thought he had gold in his cap. . . . Now I was walking through the dust of those same fields through which he used to walk, and I look like him—so what has really changed? If I had come here on a motorcycle with a little son sitting behind me, I as my father, my son as me, then my father would be repeated, reborn. Those bones buried at the edge of a field a few kilometers from here, that's not my father. My father, that's me. Because I am here. This is what is meant by fatherland.

The place where my grandfather used to live was overgrown with grass and a boy wearing a school cap was grazing a goat there. The grass was strewn with bricks from the chimney, and there was a stone foundation where it had once stood before it burned down. A small, young tree grew out from the foundation, like a chimney, feeding on the old ashes. You just need to know what you grow on, I thought with a smile. And what you stand on. And stand there. . . . Everything else will repeat itself anyway.

Translated by Richard Lourie.

Other works by Grynberg: *The Jewish War* (1965); *Antynostalgia* (1971); *Wiersze z Ameryki* (1980); *Rysuję w pamięci* (1995); *Drohobycz, Drohobycz and Other Stories* (2002).

Bogdan Wojdowski

1930–1994

Bogdan Wojdowski was born David Wojdowski in Warsaw. He spent his youth in the Warsaw ghetto, escaping in 1942 and living in hiding for the remainder of the war. He began writing in the 1950s as an essayist for Polish journals. Wojdowski's writing revolved around his experiences during the war, which he depicted with unforgiving and even grotesque detail. His most famous novel, *Bread for the Departed*, depicts the emotional and physical traumas of survival in the Warsaw ghetto, often returning to the most basic need, bread. Wojdowski committed suicide on April 19, 1994, the fiftieth anniversary of the Warsaw ghetto uprising.

Bread for the Departed
1971

He felt a gnawing sensation. He knew it was hunger. Nothing in his mouth since morning except for those slops, the slops from the Judenrat kitchen, a watery soup that was almost free, just fifty groschen. Children got a special rate. Manna from heaven is watery and that's why it costs fifty groschen. At this time of year the dying gulp down that *Wassersuppe*—half a liter of a murky fluid with beet shavings and traces of kasha, garnished with green nettle leaves. Their final memory. Raw vegetable matter, just barely blanched by boiling, floats on the surface. And the beggars' ragged clothing, the paving stones beside the wall, and the street where they lie lethargically, stretched out flat on their backs with their tin cans beside them—all are splattered with the vomited green stuff.

Into the tin cans splash the watery slops, a gift of coerced compassion. A skinny goat, the Judenrat's offering, hovers and kneels above the city, and everyone, lamenting, stretches out a hand to its generous teat. A skinny goat, milked by the poor, hovers over the city, and the Judenrat broth squirts from her udder. The great heart of the wealthy has been cooked in this broth. It has scraps of meat for everyone; you just have to be able to detect the taste of those scraps. Those who are lying on the sidewalk can no longer gorge themselves on this broth; it runs right out their noses. They vomit the slops, then sleep all day in a green puddle. They are delirious, torpid, exhausted by the scorching heat, and the flies crawl into their mouths, big, blue, sated flies. Who sent the flies? Who sent the hunger?

When the Jews were murmuring in the desert, God sent them manna from heaven, He sent them quail. The quail fluttered obediently into their encampment and the hungry people caught them with their hands. That was in the evening. They caught them with their bare hands and in the morning grain covered the ground like frost. Their cry rose to heaven. "*Man hu?* What is it?" They ate without knowing what it was. They ate and they praised God, without knowing what they were praising Him for. For six days they gathered the *man hu*, and then came the seventh day, the holy day, the Sabbath, and there was no grain in the fields.

"*Rakhmunes, gite mentshn, rakhmunes, rakhmunes!*"

Don't hear that cry for alms. Grow deaf forever. But how can you walk around, day in and day out, with your ears plugged? His head feels as light and empty as . . .

"Look, a soap bubble."

Who's that in the window? Pale blond hair, white hands and face, and a straw between his teeth. David shouts, Leibuś waves his clenched fists joyfully at the sight of him, and Ernest puffs up his cheeks, blows carefully, and releases soap bubbles through the straw. They flutter lightly down to the street.

"Hey, Albino, where'd you get the straw?"

A rainbow-colored bubble grows, sails away, rises on the air. It flutters, carefree, above the beautiful, horrid, impossible world, and in its glassy, transparent center it reflects everything it meets on its way.

"Do Jews die on Saturday?"

Struck by a fist, a mirror will crack. A stone thrown into water sinks. The rainbow soap bubble blows apart in the wind.

"In a little while we, too, will be dying in the streets. The same end awaits us all."

That's what Father says, and Mother begs him to stop. She begs him to have pity. Her words. David has heard them more than once and they make him uncomfortable; probably he feels ashamed. Shame is when a person doesn't want to sleep on the pavement, to become exhausted and delirious in the sunshine, when he doesn't want other people to see the flies parading all over him. When a man is hungry, it's not right to look him in the eye. But then you have to gobble your own bread on the sly, and to eat like that is also shameful. The hungry have no shame and they prefer to whine and hold out their empty hands to people walking by, rather than die without help inside their four walls. They'd rather demand that good people have pity on them. Good people walk down the streets, and the poor

lie beneath the wall. Good people throw them a coin and walk on, but the hungry remain on the pavement that belongs to them.

"*Rakhmunes, rakhmunes!*" [. . .]

Walking through Mokotów, David heard the passersby speaking a noisy German. because that was the district where the *Volksdeutsch* and *Reichsdeutsch* lived, with their barracks on the corner of Rakowiecka from which the loudspeakers endlessly blared lively marches, the elegant Olympus movie theater on Puławska Street, directly across from the outlet of Narbutt Street, and the office of the German political police close by.

At times he overheard a phrase broken off in midsentence, a whispered wanting, a loud cry; he caught nasty and contemptuous glances. Thrown back on his own resources, he had to figure out the meaning of everything by himself; he was ashamed to ask his father about it. He saw how the street urchins imitated Jews, and their caricatures taught him a great deal. He tried not to draw out his words, not to hamper his speech with a singsong aspiration, not to gesticulate. He remembered to speak slowly, a little carelessly, and not to ask a lot of unnecessary questions. How many questions are there in this world? Everything can be stated in such a way as to become a question. Because he noticed that that made some people laugh, he stopped doing it. He took care not to distinguish himself in any way. He listened attentively to Professor Baum, but the old man spoke with an exaggerated, old-fashioned correctness, distinctly emphasizing his nasal vowels and soft *l*'s, and that grated on him. Any detail might attract an unexpected observation; observing how Uncle Gedali flapped the hems of his long overcoat, tucking his head with his unkempt hair into his raised collar, he could already visualize him on the other side of the wall, trapped, exhibited before the thoughtful glances of the ever-vigilant police. From then on he never raised his collar, even during the worst frosts. Although in the depths of his soul he was moved by the noisiness, the speech, the sad sense of humor, broad gestures, and openness of those who surrounded him, he himself had to avoid such behavior.

Despite this, he was never sure of himself, of how he looked in others' eyes. He had to keep quiet about all this; at home, too, he could not discuss it with anyone. He became secretive, uncommunicative. He grew instinctively nasty. He saw that the sufferings and wrongs of some people only arouse laughter and mockery in others; so then, it was necessary to lower his head and walk past without hurrying, as if nothing were happening. He judged himself harshly, thinking it was fear that guided him at such moments, and he was ashamed, for himself and for the people who were beaten; with time he came to recognize that one could become accustomed to this and he grew indifferent.

A man's clothing wears out and turns into a rag, his face shrivels from thirst and hunger, long-lasting hunger transforms him into a skeleton of skin and bones; in the end, the rags fall away along with his habits and a man is once again what he always was. It is hard for a hungry person to conceal his hunger. Every glance, every movement of his hand betrays him. Looking terrified at the crowd of "wild ones" who jammed the hovel on the second floor, David thought with desperate clarity that they no longer had anything left to hide. Chance had buffeted him blindly, senselessly. Up until now he had somehow always been able to scramble out of its way. He owed it to chance that he was not now at rest in Okopy. How little it took to become a whimpering, weakened, dying man! And who was he, that he deserved a different end? And how had it happened that passageways opened before him that were closed for other people? He felt guilty before those who did not have the strength to live.

Translated by Madeline G. Levine.

Other works by Wojdowski: *Wakacje Hioba* (1962); *Mały człowieczek Nieme ptaszę Klatka i świat* (1975); *Maniuś Bany* (1980).

Danilo Kiš
1935–1989

Danilo Kiš was born to a Jewish father and a Christian mother in Subotica, Yugoslavia (now Serbia). In 1939, fearful of the antisemitism rising throughout Europe, Kiš's parents baptized their children in the Orthodox Church and moved to a small village. The children were spared, but Kiš's father was deported to Auschwitz. In his novels, Kiš often wrote about a character modeled on his father, whom he called Eduard Scham. In 1979, he moved to Paris, where his works were translated from Serbian, and gained worldwide recognition. While Kiš's earlier writings were heavily influenced by the magic realism of Jorge Luis Borges, his later works emphasized a more universalist, humanitarian experience. Kiš was awarded the Yugoslav

Ninova Nagrada Prize for best novel in 1972 but later returned it because of political disagreements.

Hourglass
1972

Treatise on the Potato. The time has come when we must think about ourselves from the standpoint of life and death, not as self-seeking individuals, but as representatives of our entire race, that divine weed scattered over all the continents of the earth, just like the lowly potato (*Solanum tuberosum*), whose origins, like our own, reach back to the dark depths of history and the earth, but whose existence will not, like ours, be called into question as long as the earth endures and there are hungry mouths to feed. This humble potato, *Kartoffel*, *pomme de terre*, this bread of the poor which, slightly disguised, mashed, with gravy, moistened with milk, cream, or meat sauce, also graces the tables of the rich, this vulgar potato, this earthly-heavenly manna, this subterranean growth, this earthly tumor, this hard hernia, this lumpy tuber, has never in all its long history attained the perfect roundness of the apple or the tomato (*Paradiesapfel*, that other heavenly fruit), but has remained imperfect and asymmetrical like man, covered with knots and bumps, bulges and excrescences, holes and cracks, without kernel, center, or anything else that might bear witness to the presence of the Creator and His wisdom. It has thus become a perfect symbol of the earth and of earth-made man, all flesh and skin, without heart or essence, a regular *homunculus* (*homo-homulus-humus*), just like a man, a man without a soul, a man from whom God has been banished.

Do you remember, sister, how, when we peeled sprouted potatoes in the pantry, we found those little potato-men with tiny heads and atrophied, misshapen limbs, little homunculi that we played with as if with dolls, until their heads fell off, until they shriveled and withered like old people?

And today, you see, when I ask for a potato, I can't help thinking about the amazing resemblance between potato and man, and, at the same time, begging your pardon, between potato and Jew. Our origins, as I've said before, go back to the same dark history. But why, gentlemen, is the potato longer-lived than we? Is it because we are, because man is, more perfect? I don't believe so. Speaking of us, I am convinced that the potato is longer-lived and more perfect than we, than you, and that it will survive us; that it will survive the great cataclysm. When the dove returns with the olive branch in its beak, when the ark touches dry land again, its keel will dig up a potato plant from the ravaged, exhausted, flooded earth of some new Ararat. And, if only because of my fondness for images and flights of fancy, I am beginning to believe in earnest that the potato (*Kartoffel*, *pomme de terre*) is the only thing on earth—may God forgive me—that was not created by the will of God and the hand of the Creator, but is the work of some insane, sterile-fertile shaman, the fruit of some sterile alchemy (of which Paracelsus does not take sufficient account in his *De generatione rerum naturalium*). This may explain its youth and hardiness. It is only five hundred years old, it was not brought to Europe until the sixteenth century, and then only as a decorative shrub. And do you know to what country? To Spain, gentlemen. This, I believe, speaks for itself with regard to my apt comparison between the Jew and the potato, for it was undoubtedly in Spain, where the *Ewige Jude* was selected for further wanderings, that there occurred the fateful meeting between man and potato, between the hooked Sephardic nose and the imperfect bumpy tuber; whence they went out into the world together, and one day toward the end of the eighteenth century landed—the potato, that is—on the table of the French kings, from there spreading over the entire earth and, through cross-breeding and under the influence of divergent climates and soils, acquiring the most varied forms and appellations, such as mealy, quarantine, alate, Irish, sweet, and finally, as the highest mark of quality, *magnum bonum*, white.

Translated by Ralph Manheim.

Other works by Kiš: *Psalm 44* (1962); *The Encyclopedia of the Dead* (1983); *The Lute and the Scars* (1994).

Jacques Zibi

Dates Unknown.

Jacques Zibi was born into a Sephardic family in Tunisia and later moved to France. He was especially concerned with questions relating to Sephardi identity and came to grips with such problems in a semiautobiographical book called *Mâ*. A gentle evocation of a Jewish mother who speaks in a Judeo-Arabic dialect, the book addresses the challenges of communication between mother and son, who has assimilated French

language and culture. Another of Zibi's books, *Le Cinquième singe*, was made into a film.

Mâ

1972

Until tomorrow, until forever, until always. The words peek through the keyhole to see where emotion has carried me, to what extent prudence and decency have spoiled me, because you've got to know how not to go too far, words borrowed from a language that nourishes me, but whose milk I did not suck. If I cannot write in Judeo-Arabic, she must be able to understand me, she could read James Hadley Chase or Albert Camus in two to four weeks, she would wait for me a day or two regarding a word she did not understand, crocheting to fill up the time, then leave again, saying they could have said it more simply. She loved to see me laugh at her bookish reflections, a full-bodied smile that caused her scarf, which summer and winter encircled her head in the manner of people from the past such as Nona or Omi Bikya, to slip off. She would conclude by asking, why is it that in books someone always dies? Then she would resume the definitive attitude of someone who pays no attention to anyone else. But it's only a book, ma, someone wrote it, just like on television, the guy you see riddled with bullets is having coffee with almond cake a few minutes later. Yes, but you mustn't joke about what is written. The People of the Book. The Torah is too much like a novel or like La Fontaine's fables. I told her we had an advantage over others. What advantage? We did not understand Hebrew, and each book printed in its signs compelled the respect of the ignorant, aleph being the first letter of Adonai, the only one I remember *perfectly*, the whole text would inspire me to moderate my criticism, just think, people nowadays write thrillers using those same characters!

To write only what moves me. Insidious work of words striving to soar above expectations, flight of birds to the firmament, "post no bills," etc. A sheet of paper 21 × 27, a black ballpoint pen, the pack of cigarettes, and the mineral water.

For a whole week now I haven't shaved or washed up or changed my shirt, the one with the collar someone tore. No, it's not just a literary exercise, I have no desire to reread what I write. In the subway, on the streets, at work, people have thought I was a bit daft, a latter-day hippie, or the result of poor nutrition slowing down my body as if it were always forgotten and left behind, and

I was spending my time making it return, just a stop to breathe and it was back up with me, then together all the way to work or to sleep. For days I would meet with myself in the open air or looking at a book. Physics or general chemistry, Pauling amused me.

Again[1] with daylight my eyes open as if there had never been a yesterday   that only lasts for a few moments   who am I   where am I   what's my name   my age   who owns this house   the city between what seas is this country located   why the wheat   the rain   road accidents   Easter vacation   and above all who just passed in this truly dark night   who am I relative to yesterday's stranger   the anonymous person of tomorrow? I'll renew my efforts to watch him in the bathroom's triple mirror, one facing me, two fixed for the profiles, a head approaches in the half-light, that of an immigrant wandering Jew between two journeys what have I become for a whole night   is it really Me or the Other or both at once   between the dawn and me who is real between night and day life and death heaven and earth who is real   the body approaches   the face touches the mirror, suddenly a dog barks, a car roars by on the wet road, the illuminated brow accentuates the dark circles under the eyes, the hairiness of the chin. I grieve for her body buried in the ground, in the cold, the silence. My mother. Everything is about losing, finding, regaining the intensity of a look by an intense effort; that's it, have to shake a leg, get going, play some sport, find a goal in this life bloody hell, of course, a night is quickly over, and a day, a life, get a move on. But, tell me, what have I become, one night among others, just one night, the one that has just passed?

He sucks her breast, sucks his thumb, and drinks from shitty civilization's springs, he's quickly gone the rounds. Immaturity. There she is, ready for some well-earned rest, why does he hang on, disturb his soul, smoke on Saturday, eat anything not kosher, cast lecherous looks at girls like an aphonic poet. Forgive me. I don't want you to die like just anyone. Like me. She adjusts her blue-gray scarf with a jerk of her chin, a city rushing by, the Pasteur hospital is far away. Forgive me, ma.

NOTE

1. [Spaces are in the original.—Eds.]

Translated by Michele McKay Aynesworth.

Other works by Zibi: *Requiem pour un survivant* (1968); *Le Cinquième singe* (1970).

Yekhiel Shraybman

1913–2005

Yekhiel Shraybman was born in Vad-Rashkev, Bessarabia. He studied at heder and the Czernowitz Hebrew Teacher's Seminary before being expelled for his activity with the Komsomol youth movement. Shraybman moved to Bucharest, was active in underground socialist circles while employed at a Yiddish theater, and worked on a collective farm in Uzbekistan during World War II, which he chronicled in *Dray zumers* (1946). In the wake of the Khrushchev thaw, Shraybman joined the editorial board of the newly established Yiddish monthly, *Sovetish heymland*. His autobiographical and idiosyncratic short stories were very popular and regularly translated into Moldavian and Russian.

A Trade Is a Kingdom

1973

Ay, a lifetime buzzed away . . . what is it, all in all? A dream, a short Friday in winter. . . .

Most people start to philosophize after a savory pot roast and a shot of liquor. Reb Nakhmen the carpenter, in his old age, eats like a bird. A drop of brandy or even a glass of wine would be poison for his sick stomach. He, on the contrary, gets philosophical thoughts in his head when he's just sitting there in the courtyard, drained and tired, with his hands hanging down, like after a bath.

If you think about it, it's one of those misfortunes that can't be avoided. That's how it happens—a generation goes and a generation comes. People die and people are born. You only have to feel the newborn's palm. If there are carpenter's bumps inside—here's your plane, brother, make windows!

A bit of foolishness sticks in your memory. A bit of foolishness from who knows how long ago—more than sixty years, probably. He had then just begun working for a window-maker—plain Moldavian windows, and bigger ones for the parlors. (His job was to sweep up the wood shavings.) Late at night, past the shed with its crooked window frame and its sign hanging outside, the heder schoolboys would rush noisily by, carrying lanterns made of hollowed-out pumpkins. Naturally, he was more drawn to the windows carved out of these heder-lanterns. Well, heder or no heder, but a piece of dairy *malay* [corn-cake]! Oh, how he wanted just a bite, just to savor the taste. On Fridays the boss's wife—all cleaned up, shiny and rosy—used to put a full platter on the workbench. The boss would quickly rattle off: "Nakhmen, will you have a piece of *malay*? No? Why?" He was sure he would want to know why. Why "no." A bit of foolishness that sticks in your memory, a bit of foolishness that is, who knows, probably more than sixty years old.

Sixty long years—amazing!

Sixty years of windows, doors, tables, cupboards, sideboards, noodle-boards and the like. Stools, chests, benches (all sorts: house benches, garden benches, school benches).

Sixty years of drawing lines, sawing, drilling, carving, gouging, planing, nailing together, gluing, painting.

And never, not once, been to a health resort. Never flown in an airplane. Never eaten in a decent restaurant. Not even worn a tie, like other men.

An old, creaking bed covered with rags. A silent wife, may she rest in peace. A house full of children. . . . Chicken pox, measles, scarlet fever. At times—where to borrow a few pounds of cornmeal for the Sabbath? At times—swept the shavings, put away the tools, pulled the curtains. All quiet—the stomach has no windows! One war (went off and thank God, managed to come back in one piece). A second war (sent off two sons and never saw them again). Left the old woman somewhere near Andidjan, under a pile of earth, at an Uzbek cemetery. (She was always a quiet woman and a slow walker. No one ever heard a loud word from her! A saint! Then, during the war, a terrible strength rose up in her. Hungry and tired, she would quarrel with all the women on the steppe. "What are you standing around for? What are you sitting for? Our children are burning in the flames!" And just like that, on the steppe, she fell over on a blazing hot day, sickle in her hand.) The oldest daughter, Ester, the jewel of the family, died like a martyr at the hands of the Germans. (She already had a husband and two children, the first two grandchildren. As a girl she was bursting with energy and enthusiasm. Worked in a weaving-mill in Jassy. Was even arrested a couple of times. Just before the war she was living with

her husband in Capresti. They were both activists in a tailors' cooperative. They were too slow to evacuate—on foot, with two little children in their arms. He was shot just across the Dniester, in a forest. She arrived, people tell me, in the Bershad ghetto a year later, without the children. In the ghetto she sewed and patched shirts and undergarments. It turns out these were no ordinary shirts and undergarments. People say she was taken to be hanged in the middle of town, with a piece of cardboard on her breast: "This is what happens to all partisans!" She was placed on a stool under the gallows and the stool was kicked from under her feet. A white carpenter's stool, people tell me.) The middle daughter, Zhenya, hasn't had a good life . . . (She's married for the fourth time, living somewhere in Tshimkent, Kazakhstan. Childless. Once in a while she sends a letter. "You should see what I look like," she cheers up her old father, "I look older than mama. I'd come see you, but I'm simply too ashamed. . . ."). What a world!

"Feh, Nakhmen, you sit there and complain too much."

"What else? Show me."

"Today is the eleventh, pension day. You sit and wait for the postman and groan. That's not right!"

"Go on. I have nothing in this world."

"Oh, it's the next world you want? You always used to mock the pious fools. . . ."

"That's not it. I'd like to leave a good name behind. Planed away all my life, maybe I did something for the world."

"Listen, Nakhmen, you've no right to complain. You don't say a word about your youngest daughter and your brilliant son-in-law, the engineer. They don't dishonor you in any way."

"I still say I have nothing in this world."

"What about your grandson? Such a remarkable grandson! Isn't that leaving a good name behind?"

"Yes, of course. But that's what's here. I groan about what isn't here, about what is lost. Let an old man groan; it makes old age easier for him."

"You're babbling, Nakhmen, you're babbling."

Translated by Solon Beinfeld.

Other works by Shraybman: *Yorn un reges* (1973); *Zibn yor un zibn khadoshim* (1988).

POETRY AND POPULAR SONG

Primo Levi

Shema
1946

You who live secure
In your warm houses
Who return at evening to find
Hot food and friendly faces:

Consider whether this is a man,
Who labours in the mud
Who knows no peace
Who fights for a crust of bread
Who dies at a yes or a no.
Consider whether this is a woman,
Without hair or name
With no more strength to remember
Eyes empty and womb cold
As a frog in winter.

Consider that this has been:
I commend these words to you.
Engrave them on your hearts
When you are in your house, when you walk on
    your way,
When you go to bed, when you rise.
Repeat them to your children.
Or may your house crumble,
Disease render you powerless,
Your offspring avert their faces from you.

Translated by Ruth Feldman and Brian Swann.

Nelly Sachs

1891–1970

The poet Nelly Sachs was born to a well-to-do assimilated Jewish family in Berlin. Because of ill health,
she was largely educated at home and in her youth
dreamed of becoming a dancer. When she was fifteen,
she was deeply affected by the work of the Swedish
writer Selma Lagerlöf and struck up a correspondence
with her. This correspondence lasted for thirty-five
years and saved Sachs's life; in 1940, Lagerlöf inter-
ceded with the Swedish royal family on Sachs's behalf,
and Sachs and her mother were able to flee to Sweden,
where they settled. Although Sachs had received little
recognition for her poetry prior to taking refuge in
Sweden, following the war, she became one of the
foremost Jewish poets still writing in German. In 1966,
the Nobel Prize in Literature was awarded jointly to
her and S. Y. Agnon.

But Who Emptied Your Shoes of Sand
1947

But who emptied your shoes of sand
When you had to get up, to die?
The sand which Israel gathered,
Its nomad sand?
Burning Sinai sand,
Mingled with throats of nightingales,
Mingled with wings of butterflies,
Mingled with the hungry dust of serpents;
Mingled with all that fell from the wisdom of
    Solomon,
Mingled with what is bitter in the mystery of
    wormwood—

O you fingers
That emptied the deathly shoes of sand.
Tomorrow you will be dust
In the shoes of those to come.

Translated by Michael Hamburger.

Other Works by Sachs: *In den Wohnungen des Todes*
(1947); *Sternverdunkelung* (1949); *Und Niemand weiß
weiter* (1957); *Flucht und Verwandlung* (1959); *Fahrt ins
Staublose* (1961).

Nelly Sachs

O the Chimneys
1947

And though after my skin worms destroy this body, yet in
my flesh shall I see God.—Job 19: 26

O the chimneys
On the ingeniously devised habitations of death
When Israel's body drifted as smoke

Through the air—
Was welcomed by a star, a chimney sweep,
A star that turned black
Or was it a ray of sun?

O the chimneys!
Freedomway for Jeremiah and Job's dust—
Who devised you and laid stone upon stone
The road for refugees of smoke?

O the habitations of death,
Invitingly appointed
For the host who used to be a guest—

O you fingers
Laying the threshold
Like a knife between life and death—

O you chimneys,
O you fingers
And Israel's body as smoke through the air!

Translated by Michael Roloff.

Stanisław Wygodzki

1907-1997

Stanisław Wygodzki was born in Będzin, Silesia, Poland, to a deeply Zionist family. However, as a young man, he was drawn to radical ideals of internationalism and, in the 1920s, was jailed for his communist activities. In 1933, he published his first political poetry volume, *Roll Call*, which was soon followed by *A Leaf's Element* (1936). A survivor of Auschwitz and Dachau, Wygodzki lost his entire family during the Holocaust. After the war, he remained in Poland and became a prominent translator of Yiddish, as well as a Polish writer of poems and short stories, primarily about children and the Holocaust. In 1968, he immigrated to Israel as a result of the increasing antisemitism of communist Poland.

Urn

1948

This urn will be made of fired clay
Of native soil, from Poland, my country
In it are lodged the ashes of my parents
My brothers, daughter, and wife.

The urn will be simple, like a jug
With a small lid, and not like a vase

So that it can hold a thick mist of gas
Painful as night and gray like dawn.

Translated by Antony Polonsky.

Other works by Wygodski: *Pamiętnik miłości* (1948); *Drzewo ciemności* (1971).

Reyzl Zychlinsky

1910-2001

Born in Gombin, Poland, Reyzl Zychlinsky began her poetic career in 1928 and flourished through the 1930s, mentored by Itsik Manger and Melekh Ravitch. She moved to Warsaw and eventually escaped the Nazi occupation in 1940, marrying the psychiatrist Isaac Kanter a year later and surviving the war in the Soviet Union. With her family murdered at Chełmno, Zychlinsky moved to France and later, in 1951, to the United States. She received the Manger Prize for Yiddish Literature in 1975.

God Hid His Face

1948

All roads led to death,
Every road.
All winds breathed betrayal,
Every wind.
In every doorway, vicious dogs barked,
In all the doorways.
All the waters laughed at us,
All the waters.
Every night grew greasy with our fear,
Every night.
And the heavens were naked and empty,
All the heavens.
And God hid his face.

Translated by Kathryn Hellerstein.

Other works by Zychlinsky: *Der regn zingt* (1939); *Shvaygndike tirn* (1962); *Harbstike skvern* (1969); *Di november-zun* (1977).

Arnold Słucki

1920-1972

The poet, writer, and translator Arnold Słucki was born Aron Kreiner in Tyszowce, in Lublin province. He was active in communist circles in the 1930s and fled to the Soviet Union upon Germany's invasion of Poland. Although his earliest works were written in Yiddish, during the war he began writing exclusively in Polish under the assumed name Arnold Słucki. In 1968, he relocated to West Berlin, after a brief stint in Israel, in response to the rising antisemitism of the Polish Communist Party. Much of his poetry was influenced by modernist and socialist realist reflections on the shtetl, Jewish folklore and mysticism, and his childhood memories.

Amputation
1950

And so its pain is unremitting, like an amputated leg
This ash and feathery void chafes at us,
They say two willows were seen in Mazowsze
wearing green prayer shawls also a market stall
in the middle of the sky, possibly a stand,
possibly a piano, pale black on white,
until angels with taut Salvador Dali muscles
converged bearing useless hoes
then plummeted like a beam into greasy emulsion,
the very memory of them zigzagging into absence.
- -
And all the colors were one and the same.

Translated by Madeline G. Levine.

Other works by Słucki: *Słońce nasz towarzysz* (1951); *Eklogi i psalmodie* (1966).

Paul Celan

Todesfuge (1944–45)
1952

Black milk of daybreak we drink it at evening
we drink it at midday and morning we drink it at night
we drink and we drink
we shovel a grave in the air there you won't lie too cramped
A man lives in the house he plays with his vipers he writes
he writes when it grows dark to Deutschland your golden hair Margareta
he writes it and steps out of doors and the stars are all sparkling he whistles his hounds to come close

he whistles his Jews into rows has them shovel a grave in the ground
he commands us play up for the dance

Black milk of daybreak we drink you at night
we drink you at morning and midday we drink you at evening
we drink and we drink
A man lives in the house he plays with his vipers he writes he writes
when it grows dark to Deutschland your golden hair Margareta
Your ashen hair Shulamith we shovel a grave in the air there you won't lie too cramped

He shouts jab this earth deeper you lot there you others sing up and play
he grabs for the rod in his belt he swings it his eyes are so blue
jab your spades deeper you lot there you others play on for the dancing

Black milk of daybreak we drink you at night
we drink you at midday and morning we drink you at evening
we drink and we drink
a man lives in the house your goldenes Haar Margareta
your aschenes Haar Shulamith he plays with his vipers

He shouts play death more sweetly this Death is a master from Deutschland
he shouts scrape your strings darker you'll rise then as smoke to the sky
you'll have a grave then in the clouds there you won't lie too cramped

Black milk of daybreak we drink you at night
we drink you at midday Death is a master aus Deutschland
we drink you at evening and morning we drink and we drink
this Death is ein Meister aus Deutschland his eye is blue
he shoots you with shot made of lead shoots you level and true
a man lives in the house your goldenes Haar Margarete
he looses his hounds on us grants us a grave in the air

he plays with his vipers and daydreams der Tod ist
   ein Meister aus Deutschland

dein goldenes Haar Margarete
dein aschenes Haar Sulamith

Translated by John Felstiner.

Shike Driz

1908–1971

Shike (Ovsei) Driz was born in Krosno in southeastern Poland. He was raised by his grandfather, a tinsmith, after the early death of his father. He studied in heder before moving to a secular Ukrainian school, eventually studying art in Kiev while working in a factory. Driz began writing poetry in the 1920s and in the 1930s became a border guard in the Red Army. At the time of Stalinist suppression of Yiddish, Driz kept a low profile, working as a mason. From the mid-1950s, Driz's verse, for adults and for children, was widely translated into Russian. He was one of the foremost Soviet Yiddish poets during the Khrushchev era and his lyrics for popular songs are still beloved today, notably "Babi Yar" and "Dem zeydns nign."

Babi Yar
1953

> Had I fastened
> The cradle on a rafter,
> And rocked it—and rocked it.
> My little son, my Yankl.
>
> But the house has vanished
> Into a fiery dome,
> How then can I rock
> My little son, my own?
>
> Had I fastened
> The cradle on a little tree,
> And rocked it and rocked it
> My little son, my Shleyml.
>
> But nothing was left.
> Not a thread from a sheet;
> Nothing remained—
> Not a shoestring for my feet.
>
> Had I shorn my long braids,
> My hair untended,
> Upon them the cradle,

> The cradle suspended.
>
> But where can I search for
> The little bones to find them,
> The little bones, the dear ones,
> Of both my precious children.
>
> Help me, mothers, help me
> My mournful song to weep;
> Help me, mothers, help me,
> So Babi Yar may sleep.

Translated by Roslyn Bresnick-Perry.

Other works by Driz: *Likhtike vor* (1930); *Di ferte strune* (1969); *Harbst* (1978).

Bat-Hamah

1898–1979

Bat-Hamah was born Malka Yosifnova Shechtman in Lipniki, Volhynia, Ukraine. She grew up speaking Yiddish with her mother and Hebrew with her father, a forester. Bat-Hamah worked as the assistant director of the Kiev Jewish theater while writing Hebrew poetry as a member of the Hebraic-communist Hebrew Octobrists. Her poetry was smuggled from Kiev into Palestine, where it was published in newspapers and periodicals, including *Ha-Shiloah*, *Hedim*, *Davar*, and *Gehalim lohashot*. Her Sephardic Hebrew was an amalgam of colloquialisms and literary idiom. She destroyed much of her work in 1937 fearing the anti-Zionist climate of the Soviet Union. Her poetry was rediscovered in the mid-1970s in letters she had sent to friends outside of the Soviet Union. She is recognized for her original style and female voice, which often spoke against patriarchal norms in alternative, empowering sexuality. A work of note is her "The Harlot" (1922).

The Vigil
1954

> This is a night of vigil for me,
> in the shudder of my soul
> I shall conceal
> the secret of my youth.
>
> I shall stand on guard:
> No sleep nor slumber!
> And in just one moment
> the veil was taken away.

A white shoulder revealed,
The exposed breast flashed!
It is ended!
My sentence has been sealed.

With a wail I shall shear my hair,
Youth!
Who shall repay the pain
and for whom the repentance?

And you, night,
still yourself,
In the dimness do not reveal
the desecration of honor of the bride . . .

Translated by Karen Alkalay-Gut.

Boris Slutsky

1919–1986

Russian-language Jewish poet Boris Slutsky was born in Slovyansk and grew up in Kharkov, Ukraine. He studied law and literature before dedicating himself to poetry. Although he began writing in the 1930s, Slutsky's first volume of poetry was not published until 1957, after Stalin's death. A leading poet and a member of the Communist Party who was nonetheless critical of the regime, Slutsky circulated his poems only in the samizdat press. Many of his poems on Jewish themes were not published until after his death.

Horses in the Ocean
1956

for I. Ehrenburg

Horses weren't made for water.
They can swim but not too far.

"Gloria" means the same as "glory"—
You will easily remember this part.

Braving the sea, a transatlantic vessel
Raised its flag above the stormy waves.

In its hold stood a thousand horses.
Four thousand feet stamping night and day.

A thousand horses! Four thousand horseshoes!
Not a single one could bring good luck.

In the middle of the stormy ocean
A torpedo tore the plates apart.

People piled into rafts and lifeboats,
Horses had to swim as best they could.

Boats and dinghies weren't made for horses—
What else could the poor creatures do?

A floating herd of reds and bays, a real
Island in the blue-green sea.

And at first they thought it was a river,
And it wasn't difficult to swim.

But the river before them was unending.
As they reached the limit of their strength

The horses raised a neigh, protesting
Against those who pulled them into the depths.

Horses neighed and drowned and drowned,
All went down, to the very last.

That's all. But I often think about it:
Drowning red horses, far away from land.

Translated by Sergey Levchin and Maxim D. Shrayer.

Other works by Slutsky: *Memory* (1957); *Modern History* (1969).

Joseph Brodsky

1940–1996

A celebrated poet and essayist, Joseph Brodsky was considered the finest Russian poet of his era. Born Iosif Alexandrovich Brodsky, in Leningrad, he embraced the United States, and was embraced in turn by American poets and writers. The author of at least nine poetry collections, Brodsky reached the pinnacle of American letters, becoming U.S. poet laureate a few years after receiving the Nobel Prize in Literature. Brodsky's writing—haunting, impassioned, opaque, melancholic—appeared in popular American magazines as well as highbrow literary journals.

Jewish Graveyard Near Leningrad
1958

Jewish graveyard near Leningrad.
Crooked fence of rotten plywood.
Behind the fence lie side by side
lawyers, merchants, musicians, and revolutionaries.

For themselves they were singing.
For themselves building savings.

For others they were dying.
But first they paid taxes,
respected policemen
and, in this hopelessly material world,
interpreted Talmud, remaining idealists.

Maybe they saw more.
Or perhaps their faith was blind.
But they taught their children to be tolerant
and to be persistent.
And they did not sow grain.
They never sowed grain.
They simply laid themselves in the cold soil like
    grain.
And went to sleep forever.
They were covered with soil,
candles were lit for them,
and on the Day of Remembrance
hungry old men wheezing from the cold
were shouting in high voices about eternal calm.
And they achieved it
in the form of decaying matter.

Remembering nothing.
Forgetting nothing.
Behind the crooked fence of rotten plywood
two and a half miles from the end of the tram line.

Translated by Joanna Trzeciak.

Other works by Brodsky: *Elegy for John Donne and Other Poems* (1967); *To Urania: Selected Poems, 1965–1985* (1988); *Selected Poems* (1992); *On Grief and Reason* (1995).

André Chouraqui

Dawns
1960

I am only this song that you place on my lips.
I am yours: yours my arms, yours my legs,
Yours my hands, yours my belly, my loins,
Yours my breasts, yours my teeth, yours my lips,
Yours my tongue, yours my mouth, yours my song,
Yours my eyes, my glances, my speech,
Yours my heart, my knowledge, my will,
Take my anger, my sweetness is yours,
My rapture, my reticence, yours,
To you belongs all, and nothing in me is not thine,
In my ecstasy I can't recall

What in me is still mine.

I am only the joy that you place in my heart:
My soul, my faith, my word I've given,
My hope, my name, my will are yours. Love,
Having all received, I've all returned,
Delivering myself by this oblation,
Holocaust of my powers, oh, pure offering,
In this endless gesture, returning
All, forever.

Dispossessed, I can, by this grand restoration,
Discover your realm,
Of which my death has made me king.
Obeying the summons of your word
I hear the strains of glory annulled,
Oh heaven, oh, earth, the music rings,
And I burn in your joy amid fields of stars.

I am only this song that you place in my soul.

Translated by Michele McKay Aynesworth.

Georg Kreisler

1922–2011

Georg Kreisler—writer, actor, entertainer, and composer of satirical songs—was born in Austria to a middle-class family. He escaped Austria in 1938, fleeing to Hollywood. Kreisler spent part of World War II as an American army interpreter and entertainer in Europe. Following the war, he worked on movies with Charlie Chaplin and earned a living performing at nightclubs. In 1955, he returned to Europe, living in Vienna, and later Munich, Berlin, Basel, and Salzburg.

I Do Not Feel at Home Here
1963

I went to see to my sister in Berlin.
She wants me to consider moving in.
Her husband's passed away now, a schlemiel,
He left her too much money in his will.
Her residence is filled with precious stuff.
She knows the high society.
But I said: sister, I don't want to bluff.
I cannot stand the piety.
I do not feel at home here, at home here, at home
    here.
I am, you must admit it,
Just too simple for this life of art.
I don't feel at home here, at home here, at home here.

Forgive me, if I quit it.
I'll write you soon a card.
I traveled to my brother in New York
Whose days flow by without a stitch of work.
His business drops a million in the till.
My joining in his venture made him thrill.
His business surely was a good as gold.
I would have loved to be his employee.
But came the time to sign, as I was told,
My soul rebelled, New York was not for me.
I do not feel at home here, home here, at home here.
Why bother with the Yankees?
To hell with all the dough.
I do not feel at home here, and therefore, my
   brother,
I'll wave with all my hankies
And let you run the show.
I journeyed to my in-law, Moyshe Green
who lives in Buenos Aires, Argentin'.
He owns a hacienda, rides a horse
And plants his own bananas there, of course.
The señoritas were a sight to see.
So many of them knew how to amuse.
But when my in-law said, please, stay with me,
I sadly said: I must refuse.
I do not feel at home here, home here, at home here.
What good are señoritas
And sunny skies and ocean blue?
I do not feel at home here, home here, at home here,
When every cowboy sees
That I'm not one of you.
But suddenly I knew where I belong
And crowded in among the happy throng
On board the fastest ship that without fail
Was bound for my true homeland Israel.
That was, as it turned out, not very smart
Since no one here advances any cash.
I'm not a farmer, my métier is art.
I have no chance of learning Hebrew in a flash.
I do not feel at home here, home here, at home here.
I feel in every fiber of my being,
Although I am at home here,
I do not feel at home here, home here, at home here.
I'm on the brink of fleeing,
but where to is unclear.
It dawned on me in misery and bliss:
It's my beloved shtetl that I miss.
No one here is pleased to see me back.
My absence had not caused a sense of lack.

The old routine requires bending low.
Suspicion reigns and cowardice.
People look at me askance and deal a blow,
Symbolically, of course, which I dismiss.
Now I feel at home here, home here, at home here.
After years of life in exile
My health was much diminished.
Because I am at home here, home here, at home
   here,
They all exploit me freestyle
And here it is that I'll be finished.

Translated by Susanne Klingenstein.

Other works by Kreisler: *Out of This World*, musical (1944); "Taubernvergiften im Park" [first released as "Frühlingslied"], song (1957); *Das Glas Wasser*, theater (1967); *Der Vogelhändler*, operetta (1968); *Das Orchester*, musical (1979).

Yuli Daniel

1925–1988

The author of strange, satirical stories, Yuli Daniel inspired a generation of young Russian writers to follow his example and poke fun at the Russian government. Writing as "Nikolai Arzhak," Daniel managed to export his work to the West, where it circulated widely, unhindered by government censorship. Put on trial with his fellow writer Andrey Sinyavsky for publishing "anti-Soviet stories," he was sentenced to five years' hard labor in 1966. "To My Friends" belongs to his cycle of poems written in the Gulag. Before his death, Daniel was celebrated as a fearless poet who suffered for his art and politics.

To My Friends
1969

God's grace has surely been overabundant.
Riches were mine. Hardly a day would pass
When human sympathy did not alight on me
Like manna from the sky.

   I cupped my slender fingers to receive it
   Ironically smiling: "God be praised,"
   As a whole caravan of guests descended
   Bearing its priceless freight of light and warmth.

Now, far from your hands, far from your eyes,
It's only now I've really understood

That it was you who saved me from destruction
In those dark and terrible three years.

>No, man does not live by bread alone!
>It was your help that made me win the battles.
>You poured blood and life back into my veins,
>O you who revived me, you who gave me your
>   blood!

It's finished. I'm in trouble up to my neck.
Anxiety is circling around me.
But is there a soul to sigh and say: "You old
    troublemaker . . ."
And stroke my forehead with a warming hand?

>It's finished. It'll be a long time before I'm out.
>Even the ray of hope now hardly glimmers.
>But in the silences of ravaged days
>You've been transfigured into sounds and words.

You've settled on these prison-written pages.
Traveled uncharted roads of darkness, though
    drenched in light.
As flesh and blood I had to lose you all
To rediscover you in meter and rhyme.

Translated by David Burg and Arthur Boyars.

Other works by Daniel: *This Is Moscow Speaking and Other Stories* (1969); *Prison Poems* (1971).

Luisa Futoransky

b. 1939

The poet and novelist Luisa Futoransky was born in Buenos Aires. She studied music at the Conservatorio Municipal from 1953 to 1961. While in law school at the University of Buenos Aires in the late 1960s, she studied poetry with Jorge Luis Borges. In 1970, Futoransky attended the Iowa Writers' Workshop; her poetry has come to reflect the four decades of travel that followed, in which she explores themes of exile, language, and gender, often through Jewish motifs. From 1976 to 1981, she taught in China and Japan, before settling in France. Her works have been translated from Spanish into English, French, Hebrew, Portuguese, German, and Japanese.

Lot's Feud

1972

>At the time for words, father, my adonai, leave it in
>   my hands, the

shame that I don't feel, and assign to me the job of
    justification,
what they call history.
The fact is that every land has its favorite fruits and
    here it is not
rice that sprouts, wheat or coffee that flowers, nor
    are there gold,
metals, or gems to covet, but there never was or will
    be so fertile a
place for the vines of dementia.
In this region we cultivate only with love and
    abound in madmen.
Everyone knows this from having had to put up with
    one. Our
own madmen are perpetual and disturbing; they
    spring up among
stones, grow back in any generation, blend in
    awaiting the right
moment to mow down at last the living and the
    dead, thundering
like those rivers that rain nothing but stones

My sister and I made this long pilgrimage to the
    sources in order
to see ourselves from inside. How fascinating,
    father, to see run-
ning flawlessly through our veins, back to our
    grandmother's
grandmother with her butterfly net, the infirmities,
    the loves of
our uncle, my brother, our grandchildren!

A dense, fragrant, purple sheet, a storm where every
    breath slipped
away until the air became so thick with knowledge
    that we vom-
ited up even our last memory and it wasn't enough.

This is a moment in which history admits all sorts of
    revisions, so
let's just say you really were not drunk, we had a
    fairly good time,
later we all went to the beach, the partridges mama
    cooked were
stupendous and then we all enjoyed a happy
    refreshing sleep.

Translated by Jason Weiss.

Other works by Futoransky: *Babel, Babel* (1968); *The Duration of the Voyage: Selected Poems* (1997); *Nettles* (2016).

VISUAL AND MATERIAL CULTURE

"Is there a Jewish art?" asked the noted art critic Harold Rosenberg in 1966, to which he replied: "What do you mean by Jewish art?" In answering his own question with a question, Rosenberg makes the important point that, like other genres, Jewish art resists hard-and-fast definitions. Like A. Leyeles in his poem "The God of Israel," in which he lists "A Chanukah-lamp, a curtain, a scroll,/A spice-box, tefillin, a pointing Hand,/A menorah, a Torah Crown, tools for circumcision," Rosenberg threw out possible answers, including art produced by Jews, art with undeniably Jewish themes, and ceremonial objects. He also suggested that we pay attention to what he called "identity," the striving of many Jewish artists—outsiders, with an "in-between" status in America—to break the mold and to affirm their individuality. "The work inspired by the will to identity," Rosenberg noted, "has constituted a new art by Jews which . . . is a profound Jewish expression."

In the aftermath of the Holocaust, the establishment of a Jewish state, and the postwar transformation of American Jewry, Jewish artistic creativity took place in strikingly altered conditions. Some Jewish artists deliberately returned to Jewish themes as others embraced an abstract expressionism that challenged critics to discover or deny Jewish influences. More than other genres the visual arts were transnational: geographical boundaries more fluid. Chagall's *White Crucifixion* was painted in Paris, his stained-glass windows for the Hadassah Hospital chapel were done in Jerusalem, his illustrations for his wife's memoir, *Burning Lights*, were produced in New York City. And even as New York displaced Paris as the center of the art world, many Jewish artists explored the creative tension between the abstract and the representative, between universal and Jewish themes.

The establishment of new Jewish museums and a postwar surge in the building of synagogues and community centers gave Jewish artists and architects new sources of material support and wider professional horizons. In Israel, Jewish artists looked for ways to create a new, distinctly "Israeli" art that could at the same time find recognition in the international art world. In the Soviet Union, where Jewish artistic expression was increasingly blocked, photography became an increasingly important medium.

In short, Jewish visual arts in this highly dramatic period of Jewish history, 1939–1973, presented a broad canvas, whose artists—men and, increasingly, women—run the gamut, from committed Jews engaged with explicitly Jewish themes to those, like the painter Ben Shahn, who bristled at being called Jewish artists. But it is precisely this variety and indeterminacy that define the Jewish visual arts of this time.

Maurice Ascalon

1913–2003

The Hungarian-born artist Maurice Ascalon was among the foremost designers of art-deco-style Judaica and introduced the practice of applying chemically induced patina to bronze and brass objects. Ascalon was born Moshe Klein to a Hasidic family, which he left at the age of fifteen in order to pursue his artistic studies at the Académie Royale des Beaux-Arts in Brussels. He immigrated to Palestine in 1934, where he founded Pal-Bell, a company that produced ritual and secular objects in wood and metal. In 1956, Ascalon moved to the United States, living in New York and Los Angeles while continuing to create decorative and functional metalwork for synagogues, educational institutions, and public spaces across the country.

The Scholar, the Laborer, and the Toiler of the Soil

1939

From *Palestine Book*, edited by Meyer W. Weisgal. New York, NY: Published by the Pavilion Publications, Inc., for the American Committee for Jewish Palestine Participation at the New York's World's Fair, 1939. Photo courtesy Spertus Institute.

Itzhak Danziger

1916–1977

The Israeli sculptor and landscape architect Itzhak Danziger was born into a bourgeois Berlin family that settled in Jerusalem in 1923. From 1934 to 1937, he studied at the Slade School in London. While studying in London, he visited the British Museum and was influenced by the Assyrian, Egyptian, and African sculpture he encountered there. He returned to Jerusalem in 1938 and created *Nimrod*, one of the most famous works of Israeli sculpture. From 1948 to 1955, Danziger lived in London, during which time he studied garden and landscape design. He returned to Israel in 1955 and taught three-dimensional design at the Technion.

Nimrod

1939

The Israel Museum, Jerusalem, Israel/Gift of Dr. H. David Orgler, Zurich and Jerusalem/Bridgeman Images.

Milton Bill Finger and Bob Kane

Finger, 1914–1974

Kane, 1915–1998

Comic-book creators Milton "Bill" Finger and Bob Kane (born Robert Kahn) were cocreators of the characters Batman and Robin. Batman first appeared in DC Comics in May 1939 and remains an icon of American popular culture. Although Kane secured the copyright to Batman early on and was long credited as sole creator, Finger played a significant role in the creation and development of the series. Finger worked as a ghostwriter in Kane's studio for many years, and while he never shared in the profits of the ever-growing Batman empire, he has in recent years been given due credit for his major contributions to the enterprise.

Detective Comics, May 1939: *The Amazing and Unique Adventures of the Batman,* ***cover.***
1939

PVDE/Bridgeman Images.

Leo Haas

1901–1983

The Slovak artist Leo Haas created numerous drawings documenting life under Nazi oppression during World War II. Hass trained at German art academies in Karlsruhe and Berlin and worked as an illustrator and caricaturist in Vienna before returning to Czechoslovakia to open his own atelier. Soon after, in 1939 Haas was deported to the labor camp in Nisko and a few years later to Terezín, where he made clandestine drawings of the realities of the Holocaust. Upon the discovery of his drawings, Haas was sent to Auschwitz, Sachsenhausen, and Mauthausen, where he continued his subversive work. In 1955 Haas moved to East Berlin, where he worked as a set designer for the state film and television companies.

Figures in the Nisko Camp, Poland
1939

Ghetto Fighters' House Museum, Israel/Archives.

Isaac David Knafo

1912–1979

Isaac David Knafo was a writer, artist, and activist born in Mogador, Morocco, and educated in Paris. A prominent cultural figure in Morocco, Knafo was well known among the intelligentsia of Mogador for his first book, *Les jeux et les rimes* and later for his anti-Nazi pamphlet *Les Hitlériques*. The laws of the Vichy regime increasingly affected the rights and liberties of Jews in Morocco; in 1942, at the urging of the Jewish community, Knafo burned all the available copies of the pamphlet. A sole surviving exemplar was discovered in 1995. Knafo became an active member of the Zionist movement, immigrating to Israel in 1956 and settling on kibbutz Ramat ha-Kovesh. In Israel, he continued publishing poems, stories, and memoirs and exhibited a collection of one hundred paintings in 1973.

Les Hitlériques, **cover**
1939

Courtesy Haim Melca.

Lee Sievan

1907–1990

Born Lina Gertrude Culik on the Lower East Side of New York, photographer Lee Sievan contributed significantly to the documentation of her city in the mid-twentieth century. Sievan began as a self-taught photographer, later taking courses at the American Artists School and the New School for Social Research. A member of New York's Photo League, Sievan primarily portrayed the everyday people and sights she encountered while walking the city. She also made portraits of a number of prominent artists, including Barnett Newman, Robert Motherwell, and Mark Rothko, whom she met through her husband, the painter Maurice Sievan. Toward the end of her career, Sievan worked as a librarian and archivist at the International Center of Photography. Her photographs were exhibited alongside her husband's paintings in a 1997 exhibition at the Museum of the City of New York.

Movie Posters and Clothes Lines
1939

© Lee Sievan. Courtesy International Center of Photography, Gift of Lee Sievan (34.1990).

Walter Zadek

1900–1992

Self-taught photographer Walter Zadek was an important figure in the development of a distinctly Israeli visual culture. Zadek was born in Berlin, where he worked as a socialist journalist until 1933; he fled Germany after a month-long Nazi imprisonment. Settling in Tel Aviv, Zadek took an interest in photography, working as a freelance press photographer for close to fifteen years. During this time, he founded the Palestine Professional Photographers' Association. His images document several important historical events of the period, including revolts, protests, and the establishment of kibbutzim. During World War II, Zadek opened a bookstore, where he worked through the rest of his career. In 2010, an exhibition of historical photography at the Israel Museum showcased his work.

Immigrants aboard the Parita *Ship*
1939

© Jewish Images. Courtesy Galerie Bassenge, Berlin.

Lotte Errell

1903–1991

The German-born photojournalist and writer Lotte Errell (b. Rosenberg) documented the lives of women in Africa, Asia, and the Middle East. After marrying the Berlin photographer Richard Levy in 1924, she adopted the surname *Errell*, after the initials of her husband's name. The couple traveled to Ghana, and Errell's photos and reports from the trip appeared in several German periodicals; they were later published in book form. Errell divorced Levy in 1933 and continued working as a photojournalist until 1934, when the German Press Association prohibited her from working in Germany. She moved to Baghdad in 1935, where she married another German exile, Herbert Sostmann. During World War II, she attempted unsuccessfully to immigrate to the United States; Errell was detained in several internment camps as a result. She returned to Germany in 1954.

Muslim Woman in Veil
ca. 1939

Lotte Errell/Pix Inc./The LIFE Images Collection/Getty Images.

Ellen Auerbach

1906–2004

The German-born photographer Ellen Auerbach (b. Rosenberg) cofounded the highly successful Berlin-based graphic design and photography studio ringl + pit alongside friend and collaborator Grete Stern. The studio, named for the women's childhood nicknames, provided Auerbach an opportunity to explore her creativity though photography and to secure her financial and social independence. Active from 1930 to 1933, the studio came to a premature end when Auerbach and Stern were compelled to leave Germany. After a brief period spent in Palestine, where she worked as a photographer and filmmaker, Auerbach married and immigrated to the United States, settling first in Philadelphia and later in New York. There, Auerbach found work as a portrait photographer, later switching careers to work as an educational therapist.

Great Spruce Head Island
1940

© The Estate of Ellen Auerbach, courtesy Robert Mann Gallery.

Will Eisner

1917–2005

The Brooklyn-born comic-book artist Will Eisner is widely recognized for his contributions to American comic art. Considered the father of the graphic novel, Eisner developed a new style of visual narration he referred to as sequential art, a form of graphic story-telling that he often used for educational purposes. Eisner attended the Art Students League in New York before immersing himself in the world of comics. Central to Eisner's early career was *The Spirit*, the first comic-book insert created for Sunday newspapers. Eisner later devoted his time to creating educational comics with his company, the American Visual Corporation. In 2002, the artist received a Lifetime Achievement Award from the National Federation for Jewish Culture. The Eisner Award, the comic industry's most prestigious prize, bears his name.

The Spirit, June 2, 1940
1940

© Eisner-Iger Studio. Photo credit: Eisner-Iger Studio/ Photofest.

Sir Jacob Epstein

1889–1959

The modernist sculptor Jacob Epstein was born on the Lower East Side of New York. He studied art in New York and Paris and settled in London in 1905. Much of his early work, with its explicit sexuality, rough-hewn composition, and indebtedness to non-European sculptural traditions, challenged taboos on what was appropriate for public art and aroused much controversy. Later, he became known for his bronze sculptures of the heads of public figures.

Jacob and the Angel
1940

© Estate of Sir Jacob Epstein. Digital image © Tate, London 2016.

Alfons Himmelreich

1904–1993

Alfons Himmelreich was an Israeli photographer, noted for his portraits of modern dancers. Born in Munich, Himmelreich settled in Tel Aviv in 1933, initially working as a carpenter before opening his own photography studio. In addition to his photographs of the new Israeli culture, Himmelreich made portraits of prominent figures, including David Ben-Gurion, Chaim Weizmann, and Moshe Sharett. Influenced by the clean, geometric aesthetic of Bauhaus, Himmelreich's photographs are as elegant as they are documentary; they were exhibited internationally.

Land Is Life
1940

© Presler Museum, Tel Aviv. Courtesy Silver Print Collection, Ein Hod.

Zoltan Kluger

1896–1977

Photographer Zoltan Kluger captured the development of the Israeli state from the mid-1930s through the end of the 1950s, working as the chief photographer for the Orient Press Photo Company. Kluger was born in Hungary, where he served as an aerial photographer during World War I. In the late 1920s, he moved to Berlin to work as a press photographer until 1933, when he moved to Palestine to escape Nazi persecution. Kluger worked as a photographer in Israel until 1958, when he immigrated to New York and opened a small photography studio. Kluger's photos capture the landscape, people, and industry of the region during a crucial historical period, contributing to the visual culture and national consciousness of Israel.

Sport

1940

Courtesy Israel State Archives, Jerusalem.

Marie-Louise von Motesiczky

1906–1996

Born to a cultured and aristocratic family in Vienna, the painter Marie-Louise von Motesiczky began taking art classes at a young age, attended several art schools, and studied with the painter Max Beckmann. Von Motesiczky and her mother fled Austria in 1938, seeking refuge in Holland before settling in England. The artist continued painting throughout the war, having her first solo exhibition at The Hague in 1939. Throughout a successful career that spanned seven decades, von Motesiczky created numerous realist portraits, including a series on her increasingly frail mother with whom she shared a close, lifelong friendship. In the 1950s and 1960s, her work moved beyond the realist style that had long defined it. A major solo exhibition at London's Goethe Institute in 1985 marked the culmination of her long and prolific artistic career.

The Travelers

1940

University of Iowa Stanley Museum of Art. © Marie-Louise von Motesiczky Charitable Trust 2018.

Weegee
1899–1968

Born in Lemberg (present-day L'viv, Ukraine), photojournalist Usher Fellig began his career as an adolescent, working photography-related jobs in New York to help support his family. Fellig, whose first name was changed from Usher to Arthur upon his immigration to the United States, later became known under the pseudonym *Weegee*, a phonetic spelling of *Ouija*, alluding to his seemingly prescient ability to arrive at crime scenes with his camera in hand. As a freelance photographer, Fellig found popular success with his sensational news photos. At the same time, he was respected in fine-art circles, exhibiting his work with New York's Photo League and at the Museum of Modern Art. Fellig produced several photo books, in addition to writing and lecturing about photography.

Coney Island Beach
1940

The Metropolitan Museum of Art, Ford Motor Company Collection, Gift of Ford Motor Company and John C. Waddell, 1987 (1987.1100.252). The Metropolitan Museum of Art. © Weegee/International Center of Photography/Getty Images. Digital image © The Metropolitan Museum of Art. Image source: Art Resource, NY.

Liselotte Grschebina
1908–1994

The photographer Liselotte Grschebina was born in Karlsruhe, Germany. She settled in Tel Aviv in 1934. From the 1930s to the 1950s, she took photographs for WIZO, the Palestine Railways, the dairy cooperative Tnuva, kibbutzim, and various businesses. Incorporating what she had learned from the revolution in photographic art in Weimar Germany, her work was innovative and startling, portraying subjects from surprising vantage points, making use of strong diagonals, and playing with light and shadow.

Tel Aviv
ca. 1940

Photo Liselotte Grschebina © The Israel Museum Jerusalem. Photo Credit: The Israel Museum, Jerusalem/Gift of Beni and Rina Gjebin, Shoham, Israel, with the assistance of Rachel and Dov Gottesman, Tel Aviv and London/Bridgeman Images.

Helmar Lerski

1871–1956

A major innovator in twentieth-century photography, Helmar Lerski was born in Strasbourg as Israel Schmuklerski, the son of immigrants from Poland. He grew up in Zurich but in 1893 sailed to the United States, where he joined a German-speaking theater troupe and changed his name. He did not take up photography until 1910. In 1915, Lerski moved to Berlin, where he worked as a cameraman and a lighting technician on expressionist films. In the late 1920s he returned to portrait photography in the expressionist style, which he continued to pursue after settling in Tel Aviv in 1931. In 1948, he returned to live in Zurich.

From the series *Jewish Soldiers*

1940–1942

Estate Helmar Lerski, Museum Folkwang, Essen. Photo © Museum Folkwang Essen—ARTOTHEK.

Yosl Bergner

1920–2017

Yosl Bergner was a painter, illustrator, and set designer born in Austria. Bergner's family had a strong artistic heritage: his father was the Yiddish poet Melekh Ravitch. Bergner studied painting at the Art School of the National Gallery of Victoria in Australia, where he settled in 1937. In the early 1950s, after serving in the Australian Army and getting married, Yosl and Audrey Bergner settled in Israel, where he found success as an artist. He won the Dizengoff Prize for Painting and Sculpture in 1956 and, in 1980, the Israel Prize for Painting. In 1985, Bergner paid a return visit to Australia, where a major retrospective exhibition of his paintings was held at the National Gallery of Victoria.

Father and Sons

1941

National Gallery of Victoria, Melbourne, A7-1985. © Courtesy of the estate of the artist.

Jack Kirby and Joe Simon

Kirby, 1917–1994

Simon, 1913–2011

Comic-book artists Jack Kirby and Joe Simon are best known for cocreating the iconic superhero Captain America. Simon grew up in Rochester, New York, and Kirby (born Kurtzberg) on the Lower East Side of Manhattan. They each worked for various comic publishers before coming together to produce their groundbreaking comic in 1941. The sensational cover of the debut issue features Captain America slugging Hitler while deflecting Nazi bullets with his shield. Kirby and Simon collaborated on several other superhero comics and, in the late 1940s, created a new genre of romance comics with *True Romance*. To this day, many of their characters remain pop cultural icons in comic books and films.

Captain America, **no. 1, cover**
1941

© Marvel Comics. Photo credit: Marvel Comics/Photofest.

Man Ray

1890–1976

The American multidisciplinary artist Man Ray played a major role in the Dada and surrealist movements of the Parisian avant-garde in the 1920s. Born Emmanuel Radnitzky in Philadelphia, he adopted a pseudonym early on in his career, as did many other Jews working in the period. After meeting and collaborating with the French artist Marcel Duchamp, in 1921 Man Ray moved to Paris, where he opened a photography studio. There he experimented with art film and photography, creating his signature "rayographs," commonly referred to as photograms, in which objects were collaged onto photosensitive paper and exposed to light, producing quasi-abstract, black-and-white images. During World War II, Man Ray lived in the United States, but in 1951 he returned to Paris.

Self-Portrait in Graham Hollywood Car
1941

The J. Paul Getty Museum, Los Angeles. © Man Ray Trust ARS-ADAGP.

Josef Herman

1911–2000

Josef Herman was a painter and draftsman known for his representations of the British working class. Herman was born in Warsaw, where he attended the School of Fine Arts, mounting his first exhibition at the school in 1932. He left Poland for Belgium in 1938 and two years later moved to the United Kingdom, where he spent the remainder of his life. His best-known works are those from an eight-year period during which he lived in Ystradgynlais, a Welsh mining town, where he painted simplified silhouettes of laborers against a range of tonal backdrops. Herman's mining scenes earned him renown within the United Kingdom, leading to a mural commission for the Festival of Britain in 1951. Throughout his life, Herman continued to paint the working people he encountered during his travels.

Refugees
ca. 1941

Bruno Schulz

1892–1942

Born in Poland, Bruno Schulz was a short-story writer as well as a gifted painter and graphic artist. While little of his work survived World War II, a number of remarkable pen-and-ink drawings did. Published posthumously, these include erotically charged illustrations for Leopold von Sacher-Masoch's novella *Venus in Furs* (1870). *The Encounter* is his only oil painting to have survived the war.

Carriage Driver (Self-Portrait), Drohobycz
1941–1942

Collection of the Yad Vashem Art Museum, Jerusalem. Loan of the Drohobychyna Museum, Ukraine.

Charlotte Salomon

1917–1943

Artist Charlotte Salomon was born to a cultured, upper-middle-class family in Berlin. Despite antisemitic policies that restricted access to art academies and guilds, in 1935 Salomon attended art school in Berlin. The situation in Germany worsened, and in 1939 Salomon's parents sent her to France, where she lived with her grandparents. During this time, Salomon created an extensive series of paintings and writings, titled *Life or Theater? An Operetta*, which chronicled the difficult history of her family. Salomon married Alexander Nagler in 1943, and later that year, she and her husband were deported to Auschwitz where both were murdered. Prior to her deportation, Salomon had given her paintings to a French doctor to safeguard throughout the war; her parents later reclaimed them. The paintings are now held at the Jewish Historical Museum in Amsterdam.

Gouache from Leben? Oder Theater?: Ein Singspiel (Life or Theater? An Operetta), no. 4351
1941–1943

Collection Jewish Historical Museum, Amsterdam. © Charlotte Salomon Foundation. Charlotte Salomon

Dmitri Baltermants

1912–1990

Dmitri Baltermants was a Soviet photojournalist who worked for the communist newspaper *Izvestiia* and the illustrated magazine *Ogonyok*. Born in Warsaw, Baltermants moved to Moscow as a child, attending secondary school and university there. His entry into photojournalism came in 1939, when *Izvestiia* sent him to document the Soviet invasion of Poland. His most famous photos were taken on the battlefield during World War II, dramatizing the horrors of war as much as the valor of Soviet soldiers. Baltermants's reputation earned him the opportunity to travel abroad, most notably to China, where he documented Khrushchev's visit, and to Cuba, for Brezhnev's visit. Baltermants also photographed numerous leaders within the Soviet Union, including Stalin and Gorbachev.

Kerch, Crimea (Grief)
1942

© Estate of Dmitri Baltermants. Photo credit: Private collection/Photo © Christie's Images/Bridgeman Images.

Bill Gold

1921–2018

Brooklyn-born Bill Gold designed some of the best-known movie posters of the twentieth century. Trained at the Pratt Institute, in 1941 Gold was hired by Warner Bros. to work in the poster department of its New York office. After World War II, during which he made training films for the army, Gold returned to Warner Bros., this time in Los Angeles. He eventually started his own advertising firm. Gold designed the iconic poster for *Casablanca* at age twenty-one, his first assignment. The film interrogates the isolationist stance that prevailed in the United States prior to its involvement in World War II while also constructing a distinctly American figure in Bogart's character Rick; it remains an American classic.

Casablanca, **Poster for the Film**
1942

© Warner Bros. Pictures/Warner Bros. Pictures/Photofest.

Mendel Grossman

1913–1945

Mendel Grossman was a Polish photographer born in Staszów and raised in Łódź. In 1939, the Grossman family was imprisoned in the Łódź ghetto, where Nazi guards assigned him to take identity-card photographs. With access to a camera, Grossman secretly documented life in the ghetto. Between 1940 and 1944, he shot more than ten thousand images, which he hid in the ghetto before his deportation to the Sachsenhausen work camp. He died on a forced march as the camp was liquidated. After the war, Grossman's sister and friends recovered his negatives and brought them to Israel. Grossman's surviving negatives were printed and published in a 1977 as *With a Camera in the Ghetto* and in 2000 as *My Secret Camera: Life in the Lodz Ghetto.*

Leave Taking before Deportation
1942

Ghetto Fighters' House Museum, Israel/Archives.

Esther Lurie

1913–1998

Esther Lurie was a Latvian-born artist who extensively documented her experiences during the Holocaust in the visual arts and in literature. Lurie studied set design and drawing in Belgium before immigrating to Palestine in 1934. In 1941, while exhibiting her work in Lithuania, Lurie was imprisoned in the Kovno ghetto; she was later moved to the Stutthof concentration camp. During the war, Lurie produced hundreds of drawings in secret, creating portraits of fellow Jewish prisoners. She moved back to Palestine in 1945 and settled in Tel Aviv.

Main Gate of the Ghetto
1942

Ghetto Fighters' House Museum, Israel/Archives.

Mikhail Trakhman

1918–1976

Moscow-born Mikhail Trakhman was a Soviet photojournalist who documented World War II as a photo correspondent for the Telegraph Agency of the Soviet Union. In the 1930s, Trakhman studied photography under Arkady Shaikhet, a prominent Soviet photojournalist, and took courses in cinematography. Despite his Jewish background, Trakhman's photographs served more to advance Soviet ideologies through glorification of the patriotism and heroism of war than to expose the atrocities of the Holocaust.

Leaving a Son to the Partisans, Leningrad
1942

© Soviet Group/Magnum Photos.

Georgi Zelma

1906–1984

Georgi Zelma was a Soviet photojournalist who worked as a Central Asian correspondent for several photo agencies and publications. Born in Uzbekistan, Zelma moved in 1921 to Moscow for three years before joining the photo agency Russfoto. His knowledge of Russian and Uzbek languages served him well as a translator, and he spent much of his career documenting the effects of Soviet policy on rural life in Central Asia. Zelma's photographs adhere to the principles of socialist realism. For a series on Soviet Jewish life, he traveled to Birobidzhan in the Jewish Autonomous Region, photographing the region's Jewish loggers and farmers. During World War II, Zelma was a correspondent for *Izvestiia*, most famously documenting the Battle of Stalingrad in 1942 and 1943.

Stalingrad Attack
1942

Georgi Zelma/Slava Katamidze Collection/Hulton Archive/ Getty Images.

Yankl Adler

1895-1949

The painter Yankl (also Jankel) Adler was born in Tuszyn (now in Poland) into a Hasidic family. He studied engraving in Łódź in 1913 and received further training in Germany. He later moved back to Łódź and helped to launch the Yung-yidish cultural movement, championing the themes and stylistic features of German expressionism. In 1920, he moved back to Germany, aligning himself with the left-wing avant-garde. His pictures from the Weimar period include no Jewish references. He lived in France from 1933 to 1940 and then fought with the Polish Free Army before being evacuated to Scotland in 1941. He eventually moved to London. He returned to painting Jewish themes in the 1940s, and his work frequently registers the suffering of European Jewry during the Nazi years.

The Mutilated

1942-1943

Image # T00372, Tate, London.
©2018 Artists Rights Society (ARS), New York/VG Bild-Kunst, Bonn. Digital image: © Tate, London 2018.

Emmanuel Evzerichin

1911–1981

Born in Rostov-on-Don, a provincial town in southern Russia, to a family of Russian-speaking Jews, the photojournalist Emmanuel Evzerichin was raised with a traditional Jewish education. In the 1920s, Evzerichin joined the Communist Youth League. A chance meeting with the codirector of the Photo Union, who was visiting from Moscow, led to an offer of work, and eventually Evzerichin was employed by the Telegraph Agency of the Soviet Union for most of his career. The anticosmopolitan campaign of the 1940s threw the Soviet Jewish photography community into disarray; before, 50 percent of Soviet photographers were Jews, after, only Evzerichin and one other were still employed. Conditions worsened, however, and Evzerichin turned to teaching photography, which is how he lived out his career.

Memories of a Peaceful Time

1943

University of Colorado Boulder Art Museum, Loan from Teresa and Paul Harbaugh. © Emmanuel Evzerikhin/Nataliia Ratnikova. Courtesy Paul Harbraugh and CU Art Museum.

A. Geftera

No biographical information available.

Cover for Peretz Markish's Book of Poetry, **Far folk un heymland** *(For People and Homeland)*
1943

From the Library of the YIVO Institute for Jewish Research, New York.

Lea Lilienblum

Dates unknown.

Lea Lilienblum was a Polish-born artist best known for her haunting portrait of the Yiddish poet Yitshak Katzenelson, who was murdered at Auschwitz in 1944. Lilienblum and Katzenelson were both prisoners in the Warsaw ghetto; Lilienblum drew his image on the back of a shoebox. Lilienblum survived the ghetto and immigrated to Israel after the war, where she settled on Kibbutz Lohamei HaGeta'ot.

Portrait of Yitzhak Katzenelson
1943

Ghetto Fighters' House Museum, Israel/Archives.

Jacques Lipchitz

1891–1973

The cubist sculptor Jacques Lipchitz was born Chaim Jakob Lipchitz in Druskininkai, Lithuania. After studying engineering in Vilna, Lipchitz left for Paris in 1909, where he studied sculpture at the École des Beaux-Arts and at the Académie Julian. After meeting Pablo Picasso in 1913, Lipchitz became interested in the French avant-garde and began experimenting with the formal aesthetics of cubism. By 1925, he had moved away from the constrained forms of cubism and toward a more expressive, organic sculptural language, receiving critical attention in Europe and the United States. In 1940, Lipchitz was forced to flee Paris when German troops occupied the city, and he immigrated to New York. He received a number of important commissions for public artworks in the United States and Israel, and spent his final years in Italy.

The Prayer
1943

Felix Nussbaum

1904–1944

German-born painter Felix Nussbaum was raised in an upper-middle-class family, allowing him to pursue an extensive arts education. With the rise of fascism in the 1930s, Nussbaum and his wife, Polish artist Felka Platek, were forced to move to Belgium. In 1940, Nussbaum was arrested and interned in France, and although he escaped and was able to live in hiding for several years, he and his wife were later betrayed and turned in to Belgian authorities. The couple was deported to Auschwitz in 1944; neither survived. Nussbaum was remarkably prolific during the final years of his life. Many of his works were destroyed during the war, but he was able to hide more than one hundred paintings with friends. Today, the Felix Nussbaum Museum in the city of his birth, Osnabrück, houses many of his surviving works.

Self-Portrait with Jewish Identity Card
1943

Paul Păun
1915–1994

Paul Păun was a Romanian visual artist and poet, involved with the surrealism movement of the 1930s. Born Zaharia Herșcovici, Păun adopted his pseudonym in high school. He was active in the avant-garde art scene from his midteens, cofounding the Bucharest Surrealist group in 1939; he exhibited with them in the 1940s. Alongside his creative activities, Păun was a practicing doctor. He was forced to work in labor camps for Russian prisoners of war. From 1948 to 1961, Păun struggled to leave Romania for Israel, finally moving to Haifa. In Israel, Păun continued practicing medicine and honing his skills as a draftsman.

Tu tournes lentement (You Turn Slowly)
1943

Private collection, reproduced by permission. © 2018 Artists Rights Society (ARS), New York/ADAGP, Paris.

Abraham Rattner
1893–1978

American artist Abraham Rattner was a painter, printmaker, and particularly skilled colorist. Born in Poughkeepsie, New York, Rattner studied architecture at George Washington University and art at the Corcoran School of Art and the Pennsylvania Academy of Fine Arts before serving in the army for two years during World War I. After his service, Rattner resumed his studies, traveling to Paris, where he absorbed the artistic tendencies of the French avant-garde. Rattner's exposure to modernist styles of figuration profoundly influenced his work, which employed the flat, geometric aesthetics of cubism. He returned to the United States in 1939, exhibiting in New York galleries. Later in his career, he turned toward architecture, designing mosaics and stained glass that reflected an enduring engagement with biblical and Jewish subject matter.

Design for the Memory
1943

Collection of the Birmingham Museum of Art, Alabama; Gift of Leslie and Elton B. Stephens, Jr. Accession #2007.127. © Leepa-Rattner Museum at St. Petersburg College, FL. Photo by Sean Pathasema.

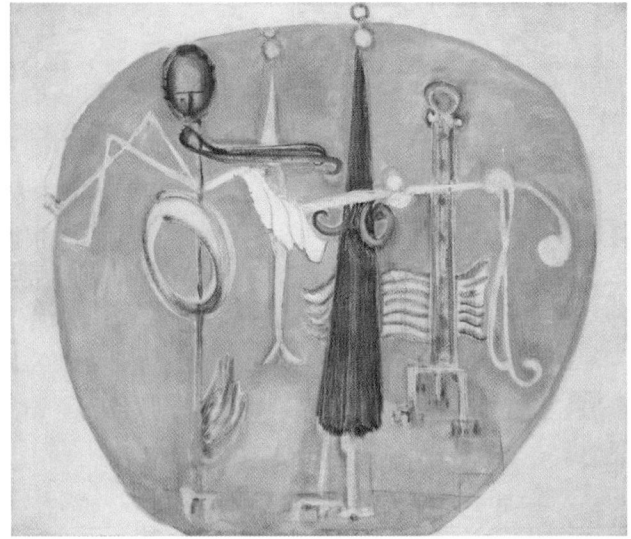

Mark Rothko

1903–1970

Born Marcus Rothkowitz in Dvinsk, Russia (now Daugavpils, Latvia), Mark Rothko was one of the most influential and best-known American abstract expressionist painters. His family moved to Portland, Oregon, in 1913. Rothko attended Yale University on scholarship, leaving the school to study at the Art Students League in New York in 1925. After decades of experimentation, he arrived at the abstract style of color-field painting for which he is celebrated, creating hundreds of large-scale works featuring vertically aligned rectangles that appear to float within the canvas. Though simple in composition, Rothko's paintings were psychologically complex and philosophically driven.

Untitled

1943

Gift of The Mark Rothko Foundation, Inc., National Gallery of Art, Washington, D.C., 1986.43.60. © 1998 Kate Rothko Prizel & Christopher Rothko/Artists Rights Society (ARS), New York.

Gabriel Shamir and Maxim Shamir

Gabriel Shamir, 1902–1992

Maxim Shamir, 1910–1990

Brothers Gabriel and Maxim Shamir (born Scheftelowitsch) were Latvian-born graphic designers who created a number of Israel's official state emblems, medals, stamps, and banknotes. Both attended the Charlottenburg School of Arts in Berlin before opening their own design studio in Riga. Two years later, in 1935, they immigrated to Tel Aviv, where they established a graphics studio and helped found the Graphic Designers Association of Israel. In 1949, the Shamir brothers designed the emblem for the State of Israel, and in 1958 they won a competition to design a series of banknotes for the Bank of Israel. The two continued to work together until 1974.

Fund for Recruitment and Rescue poster

1943

KRA/227, Central Zionist Archives, Jerusalem.

Arthur Szyk

1894–1951

Arthur Szyk was born in Łódź and studied art in Kraków and Paris. He worked primarily as an illustrator, illuminator, and caricaturist. In the interwar period, he divided his time between Poland and Western Europe, and from 1940, he lived in the United States. His unique style was influenced by medieval illuminated manuscripts and Persian miniatures. Much of his work addresses themes of antisemitism and Jewish resistance. During World War II, he produced a series of powerful anti-Axis caricatures, grotesquely portraying the Germans and their allies.

We Will Never Die! Constitution Hall, Washington, D.C., Poster
1943

Courtesy Jewish Historical Society of Greater Washington.

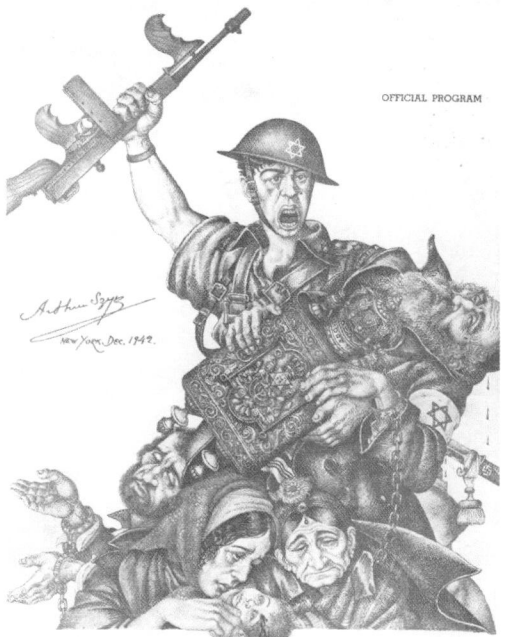

Royal Air Force

This Hebrew-language recruitment poster for women to join the Auxiliary of the British Air Force encourages registration at offices in Jerusalem, Tel Aviv, and Haifa, on all days except the Sabbath.

Women's Auxiliary Air Force Recruitment Poster
ca. 1943

Dobkin Family Collection of Feminism.

Bedřich Fritta

1906–1944

Czech artist Bedřich Fritta trained in Paris and then worked as a graphic designer and cartoonist in Prague until 1941, when he was deported to the Terezín ghetto. There, along with other artists and engineers, he was ordered to direct the painting section of the technical department that produced propaganda materials for the Nazis. In the studio, Fritta and his fellow artists covertly produced paintings and drawings documenting daily life in the ghetto. When SS officers discovered these artworks, the artists were sent to a Gestapo prison and then deported to Auschwitz, where Fritta died. After the war, more than two hundred of his drawings were discovered hidden in the former ghetto.

Façades for the International Commission
1943–1944

© Thomas Fritta-Haas, long-term loan to the Jewish Museum Berlin, photo: Jens Ziehe.

David Bomberg

1890–1957

The painter David Bomberg was one of the "Whitechapel Boys," the cohort of Jewish writers and painters who emerged from the immigrant quarter of East London in the early twentieth century. He studied at the Slade School of Fine Art from 1911 to 1913 but was expelled for the radicalism of his style, which was influenced by Italian futurism and cubism. After the war, his style changed, and he began to focus on landscapes. From 1923 to 1927, he painted and sketched in Palestine with the financial support of Zionist organizations. He is considered one of the greatest painters of twentieth-century Britain.

Evening in the City of London
1944

WA1981.606. Ashmolean Museum, University of Oxford. © 2018 Artists Rights Society (ARS), New York/DACS, London. Digital image © Ashmolean Museum, University of Oxford.

Norman Leibovitch

1932–2002

Painter Norman Leibovitch was a Montreal-based artist whose work was exhibited across North America. Best known for his colorful and expressive Quebec landscapes, female nudes, and depictions of Jewish themes, Leibovitch produced more than one thousand paintings during his long career. He studied at the American Artist School and the Art Students League, both in New York, before settling in his hometown among contemporaries who included the well-known painters Louis Muhlstock, Moe Reinblatt, and Sam Borenstein. Although much of Leibovitch's work drew inspiration from his local environment, he also traveled through Mexico and Israel, absorbing their cultural and aesthetic references as inspiration for his own art.

Untitled—Three Men and a Horse in the Shtetl
1944

© Estate of Norman Leibovitch. Photograph courtesy The Baycrest Art Collection, Toronto, Canada.

Walter Rosenblum

1919–2006

The photographer Walter Rosenblum was born in New York City, the child of East European immigrants. In 1937, he joined the Photo League, a group of socially concerned documentary photographers. During World War II, he served as a combat photographer with the U.S. Army Signal Corps and photographed the D-Day landings on the Normandy beaches in June 1944. He was the first Allied photographer to enter the liberated Dachau concentration camp.

D Day Rescue, Omaha Beach, France, June 6, 1944
1944

The J. Paul Getty Museum, Los Angeles. © Walter Rosenblum.

Jules Lellouche

1903-1963

Born in Monastir, Tunisia, Jules Lellouche was a primarily self-taught painter. He demonstrated early talent and briefly studied painting at the Institut Supérieur des Beaux Arts in Tunis. In the early 1920s, Lellouche began to show his work, both portrait and landscape paintings, at the Tunisian Salon. In 1936, he helped form the Groupe de Quatre, which exhibited together at the Galerie Art Nouveau in Tunis. While a student in Tunis, he was awarded a French government scholarship to study in Paris. He would continue to travel to Paris until 1939. There, he was influenced by impressionist and postimpressionist painting, absorbing the artists' exploration of luminosity and application of brilliant colors and eventually using these works to portray the light of Tunis and the colors of the Mediterranean. In 1955, Lellouche settled permanently in Paris.

La Ghriba Djerba, Tunisia
ca. 1944

Private collection. © Estate of Jules Lellouche.

Felix Lembersky

1913-1970

Felix Lembersky was a Ukrainian painter whose works departed from the conventions of Soviet painting, bringing personal and historical truths into social consciousness. A formally trained artist, Lembersky studied at the Jewish Arts and Trades School in Kiev and the Russian Academy of Arts in Leningrad. He survived the Nazi siege of Leningrad in 1941 but lost his family to the Holocaust. In addition to including Jewish symbols and imagery, Lembersky's painting often represented the harsh realities of Soviet life in a colorful, impressionistic style.

Untitled, Execution: Babi Yar Series. Nizhny Tagil or Leningrad
ca. 1944-1952

© Yelena Lembersky.

Miklós Adler

1909–1965

Printmaker and painter Miklós Adler was born in
Debrecen, Hungary. He attended the Academy of Fine
Arts in Budapest from 1923 to 1934 before returning
to his hometown, where he taught at a Jewish high
school. In 1944, Adler and his family were arrested
and deported to Auschwitz, but their train was
rerouted to the Terezín concentration camp in
Czechoslovakia, which was liberated in May 1945.
After the war, Adler returned to his hometown and
continued his arts career, producing a series of sixteen
woodcuts, seven of which appear in *A Survivors'
Haggadah*, used by Jewish survivors in displaced
persons camps near Munich for the first Passover after
the war. In 1960, Adler immigrated to Israel.

Home! Home?

1945

Reproduced from *A Survivors' Haggadah* by Yosef Dov
Sheinson, with woodcuts by Miklós Adler, and edited by Saul
Touster, by permission of The University of Nebraska Press.
Copyright 2000 by Saul Touster. p. 66, leaf 18v. Published by
The Jewish Publication Society, Philadelphia. Photo credit:
The Dorot Jewish Division, the New York Public Library,
Astor, Lenox and Tilden Foundations.

Alfred Eisenstaedt

1898–1995

Photographer Alfred Eisenstaedt created some of the
most memorable images of twentieth-century American popular culture. Born in Dirschau, German
Empire (now Tczew, Poland), Eisenstaedt began his
career as a freelance photojournalist in Germany,
where he attended the University of Berlin. During
World War I, he served in the German army. As
political tensions rose in the mid-1930s, Eisenstaedt
left Berlin for New York where he continued to
freelance, working for such publications as *Harper's
Bazaar*, *Vogue*, and *Town and Country*. In 1936, he
was hired as one of the first staff photographers at *Life*
magazine, where he worked for the next forty years,
producing more than 2,500 photo essays for it.

V-J Day at Times Square, August 14, 1945
1945

Photo by Alfred Eisenstaedt/The LIFE Picture Collection/
Getty Images.

Yevgeny Khaldei

1917–1997

Yevgeny Khaldei was a Ukrainian-born Soviet photojournalist, now known for his famous image of troops raising the Soviet flag over Berlin's Reichstag in 1945. Khaldei took an interest in photography from an early age, building his first camera from a salvaged box and the lenses from his grandmother's old glasses. By age eighteen he was working professionally as a photographer for the official Soviet news agency, Telegraph Agency of the Soviet Union (TASS). Khaldei worked as a correspondent for TASS during World War II, capturing dramatic images of the devastation of combat. Despite the challenges posed by widespread antisemitism, Khaldei persevered and continued to find work as a photojournalist and photo-lab technician within the Soviet Union.

Budapest Ghetto

1945

Buyenlarge Archive/UIG/Bridgeman Images.

Abel Pann

1883–1963

Abel Pann (born Abba Pfeffermann) was a Latvian-born painter and printmaker, best known for his work in religious iconography. Pann studied at the Odessa School of Art before moving to Paris in 1903 to attend the Académie Julian. After working as an illustrator for French newspapers for nearly a decade, Pann left Paris for Jerusalem at the invitation of Boris Schatz, the founder and director of the Bezalel School of Arts and Crafts, where Pann took a teaching position. Pann devoted his artwork to biblical themes. After purchasing a lithographic press while traveling in Vienna, in 1921 Pann opened Jerusalem's first lithography workshop.

And G-d Remembered Rachel . . . And She Conceived, and Bore a Son

1945

© Estate of Abel Pann. Courtesy of Mayanot Gallery, Jerusalem.

Moses Reinblatt

1917–1979

Moses "Moe" Reinblatt was a Montreal-based painter and teacher. Reinblatt studied under the Canadian painters Anne Savage and Alexandre Bercovitch, developing an appreciation for postimpressionism. Reinblatt joined the Royal Canadian Air Force in 1942, working as an airframe mechanic while painting scenes of fellow workers involved in the war effort. He exhibited his wartime paintings at the Art Association of Montreal, which earned him several awards and an appointment as an official war artist in 1944. Reinblatt served overseas until 1945, when he returned to Montreal and began teaching drawing and graphic art at the Montreal Museum's School of Fine Arts and Design. He was the recipient of numerous awards, including the 1968 Canada Centennial Medal for his outstanding service to Canada.

Dismantling Bent Props

1945

CWM 19710261-4943, Beaverbrook Collection of War Art, Canadian War Museum.

Saul Steinberg

1914–1999

Educated in architecture in Italy during the 1930s, the Romanian-born Saul Steinberg became an extraordinarily popular American artist after World War II through his regularly featured drawings, cartoons, and covers for *The New Yorker* magazine. Steinberg's inventive enigmatic modernism found expression in masks, drawings, collages, and watercolors that incorporated letters, text, and self-reflections. He exhibited his work in European and American galleries, in a traveling retrospective that began at the Whitney Museum in 1978 and another that opened at the Morgan Library and Museum; he also published more than a dozen compilations of his drawings, beginning with *All in Line* (1945) and ending with *The Discovery of America* (1992).

Untitled, New Yorker, *February 3, 1945*

1945

© The Saul Steinberg Foundations/Artists Rights Society (ARS), New York. Photo credit: Saul Steinberg/The New Yorker © Conde Nast.

Morris Topchevsky

1899–1947

Artist and activist Morris Topchevsky immigrated to Chicago from Białystok in 1911.In his early twenties, Topchevsky studied art at Hull-House, a settlement house for immigrants on Chicago's Near West Side, and subsequently at the School of the Art Institute of Chicago. A trip to Mexico in 1924, during which he met and worked with the muralist Diego Rivera, further strengthened his commitment to employing art as a means of resisting and overcoming oppression. Topchevsky spent a number of years teaching at the Abraham Lincoln Centre on Chicago's South Side, working with the local African American community.

Leaflets (Double V)

1945

Used by permission of the Bernard Friedman CHICAGO MODERN Collection.

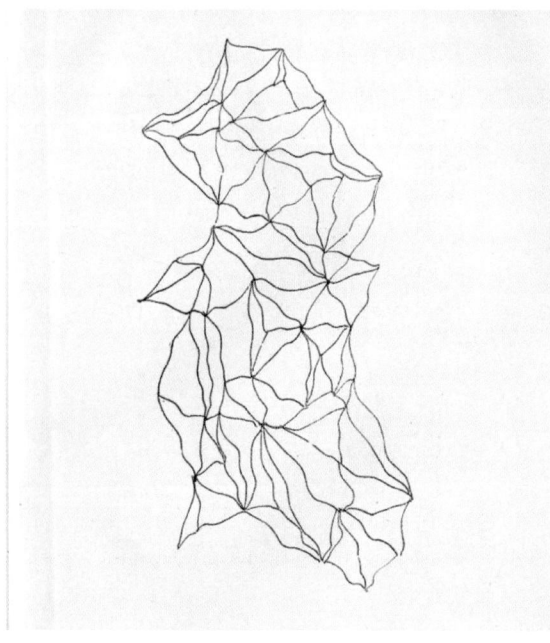

Dolfi Trost

1916–1966

Dolfi Trost was a Romanian surrealist artist, poet, and theorist. Trost was a founder of the Bucharest Surreal-ist Group, a collective of artists who met in secret throughout World War II. He also created the surreal-ist drawing method known as "entopic graphomania." In this technique, imperfections on a piece of paper are connected by lines to produce a geometric abstraction. In addition to creating visual artworks and poems informed by surrealist thought, Trost published several avant-garde works in collaboration with fellow group members, including the Jewish artists Paul Păun and Gherasim Luca. In 1948, Trost left Bucharest for Israel, later immigrating to the United States, where he settled in Chicago.

Entopic Graphomania

1945

© Dolfi Trost.

Adolph Gottlieb

1903–1974

Born in New York, Adolph Gottlieb painted works
influenced by the turn toward abstraction among the
city's avant-garde. Educated at New York's Art Students
League, Parsons School of Design, and Cooper Union,
Gottlieb also spent a year studying in Paris. He began
his exploration of painting through abstract aesthetics,
later experimenting with more figurative and surrealist-
inspired works. The painter exhibited regularly with
contemporaries Willem de Kooning, Franz Kline, and
Mark Rothko. His first solo show was in 1930; it would
be the first of more than thirty. Gottlieb also designed
tapestries and curtains, as well as stained-glass
windows, for several synagogues in the United States.

Voyager's Return
1946

Gift of Mr. and Mrs. Roy R. Neuberger. The Museum of
Modern Art, New York, NY, U.S.A. © Adolph and Esther
Gottlieb Foundation / Licensed by VAGA at ARS, NY, NY.
Digital Image © The Museum of Modern Art/Licensed by
SCALA / Art Resource, NY.

Sid Grossman

1913–1955

Sid Grossman was an American photographer and
teacher who cofounded New York's Photo League, an
organization of socially conscious photographers who
documented the city's rapidly changing neighborhoods
and communities. In addition to his roles as director
and teacher at the League, Grossman spent time
photographing the American Midwest and Central
America, though the majority of his work is dedicated to
his native New York. After the Photo League disbanded
in 1951, Grossman continued teaching privately and
developed his creative practice in both photography and
painting. Toward the end of his life, he created a series
of landscapes and portraits in Cape Cod.

Coney Island
1947

Purchase, The Horace W. Goldsmith Foundation Gift,
through Joyce and Robert Menschel, 1986.(1986.1023). The
Metropolitan Museum of Art. © Howard Greenberg Gallery,
New York. Digital image © The Metropolitan Museum of Art.
Image source: Art Resource, NY.

Saul Leiter

1923–2013

Saul Leiter was an American painter and photographer, one of the first to work in color photography. Born in Pittsburgh, Leiter began studying at a rabbinical school in Cleveland, but soon changed course, moving to New York at age twenty-three to pursue a painting career. In New York, he befriended a number of fellow artists who inspired him to experiment in photography. Leiter worked for fashion magazines including *Harper's Bazaar* and *Vogue*, all the while taking personal photographs that transmuted the bustling urban environment of Manhattan into quiet meditations on color and form. His work has recently enjoyed renewed popularity with the publication of a monograph in 2006, as well as an award-winning 2012 documentary.

Deborah at Tante Esther's
1947

© Saul Leiter Foundation.

Rebecca Lepkoff

1916–2014

Rebecca Lepkoff was a New York–born photographer who captured street life in her Lower East Side neighborhood. Lepkoff bought her first camera with earnings from dancing at the 1939 World's Fair and then turned her eye to the rhythms and movements of daily life in the city. She associated with a number of other Jewish photographers of the period, including Arnold Eagle, who introduced her to the Photo League, a group that recorded the rapidly changing urban environment in which they lived. Her works document the bygone spaces, buildings, and communities of her youth and much of her adult life.

Midtown Manhattan
1947

© Estate of Rebecca Lepkoff, courtesy Howard Greenberg Gallery, New York.

Lippy Lipshitz
1903–1980

Israel-Isaac Lipshitz, known as Lippy Lipshitz, was a
prominent South African sculptor and graphic artist.
Lipshitz was born in Lithuania, and moved to Cape
Town at age five. Lipshitz's artistic formation began at
the Cape Town School of Art and continued at the
Michaelis School of Fine Art. In 1928, he moved to
Paris for four years to study under the sculptor
Antoine Bourdelle. Lipshitz then returned to South
Africa, where he taught at the University of Cape
Town. He is best known for his sculptural work,
although he also experimented with a variety of
graphic media, including drawing, printmaking, and
painting. Toward the end of his life, in 1978, Lipshitz
moved to Israel, settling near Haifa.

Moses Breaking the Tablets of Law
1947

Private collection. © Estate of Israel-Isaac (Lippy) Lipshitz.

Yohanan Simon
1905–1976

Yohanan Simon was born in Berlin and attended art
schools in Frankfurt and Munich, before moving, in
1927, to Paris, where he studied at the École des
Beaux-Arts. He then spent two years living in New
York while working at *Vogue*, before moving to
Palestine in 1936. Simon became a member of the
kibbutz Gan Shmuel, where he created idyllic portraits
of community life, until 1953. During this time, he
also produced a number of murals for Israeli institutions and channeled his creativity into literary
illustration and set design. Simon received numerous
awards throughout his career, including the honor of
representing Israel in the Venice Biennale in 1948 and
1958.

Hashomer Hatzair Poster to Honor the 30th Anniversary of the October Revolution
1947

KRA\1501, Central Zionist Archives, Jerusalem.

Raphael Soyer

1899–1987

Born in Russia, the painter and graphic artist Raphael Soyer moved to the United States in 1913. He studied painting in New York, where he spent the rest of his life. Soyer was a staunch social realist, painting genre scenes of immigrant and city life, as well as portraits of family, friends, and fellow artists. In addition to working in a representational style, he defended it in print against the rising fashion of abstractionism. His brothers Moses and Isaac were also painters.

Imaginary Wall in My Studio
1947

© Estate of Raphael Soyer, courtesy of Forum Gallery, New York, NY.

Erika Stone

b. 1924

American photographer Erika Stone is a successful photojournalist whose images have appeared in *Time* magazine and international publications such as *Der Spiegel*. Stone was born in Germany but immigrated to the United States during World War II. Like many Jewish photographers in New York City, Stone joined the socially conscious Photo League. After the league disbanded, she went on to study at the New School of Social Research in New York. Although she photographed some celebrities, Stone's greatest interest was in the people of her city.

Lower Eastside Façade
1947

Columbus Museum of Art, Ohio: Photo League Collection, Museum Purchase with funds provided by Elizabeth M. Ross, the Derby Fund, John S. and Catherine Chapin Kobacker, and the Friends of the Photo League. © Erika Stone.

Robert Capa

1913–1954

The fearless photographer Robert Capa (born André Friedmann) was hailed as "the greatest war photographer in the world." Capa was born in Budapest. His métier was conflict and carnage. Over a hectic, globe-trotting career, he shot photos in Normandy, Nuremberg, and Hanoi, risking his own life alongside soldiers. After covering D-Day and Israel's War of Independence, Capa went to Indochina. He died after stepping on a land mine, a casualty of his compulsion to chronicle mankind's worst, most destructive tendencies.

Troops Marching, Israel
1948

© International Center of Photography/Magnum Photos (2010.94.1).

Vivian Cherry

1920–2019

Born in New York, photographer Vivian Cherry began working in the 1940s, and in 1947 she joined the social realist Photo League. She studied with Sid Grossman, one of its founders. After an extended break from photography, from 1957 to 1987, Cherry took up her camera again. She exhibited extensively and her works are part of the permanent collections in numerous museums, including the National Portrait Gallery in London and the Smithsonian Institution in Washington, D.C.

Untitled (Group of Boys and Swastika)
1948

Brooklyn Museum, Gift of Steven Schmidt, 1997.138.4. © Vivian Cherry.

Marcel Janco

1895–1984

The avant-garde artist, architect, and art theorist Marcel Janco was born into an upper-middle-class home in Bucharest. He lived in Zurich from 1914 to 1921. There, he took a leading role in the city's bohemian cultural scene, cofounding the Dadaist movement along with his fellow Romanian Tristan Tzara (b. Samy Rosenstock). He broke with Dadaism in 1919 and became a leading proponent of East European constructivism. In January 1941, he and his family fled Bucharest and settled in Palestine. In 1953, he founded the artists' colony Ein Hod, southeast of Haifa.

Nocturne (Death of a Soldier)
1948

Private collection. © Estate of Marcel Janco. Photograph by Noam Feiner.

Arthur Kolnik

1880–1972

Born in Stanisławów, Galicia (now Ivano-Frankivsk, Ukraine), Arthur Kolnik was a painter and printmaker best known for illustrating Yiddish poetry and other Jewish works. Kolnik studied at the School of Fine Arts in Kraków before serving in the Austrian army during World War I. After the war, he lived in Czernowitz, then part of Romania, but eventually moved to New York, where, in 1921, he exhibited his paintings alongside fellow artist and friend Reuven Rubin. Kolnik moved to Paris in 1931, where he worked primarily as an illustrator for fashion journals. In 1940, he and his family were interned at Récébédou. In 1968, Kolnik had a major exhibition at the Tel Aviv Art Museum.

Illustrations to Y. L. Peretz's A gilgl fun a nign [The transmigration of a melody]
1948

Courtesy Graphic Witness.

Jerome Liebling

1924–2011

Brooklyn-born photographer Jerome Liebling produced a substantial body of work and made significant contributions to the pedagogy of photography and filmmaking in the United States. Liebling taught at the University of Minnesota for twenty years, establishing the institution's first photography and film program, and then for another two decades at Hampshire College in Massachusetts as the head of the photography, film, and video program. Prior to his teaching and artistic careers, Liebling served in World War II, returning home in 1946 to study design and photography at Brooklyn College. At this time, Liebling joined New York's socially aware Photo League, using street photography to uncover the realities and hardships of daily life. Liebling's work is held in the permanent collections of the Museum of Modern Art, the Metropolitan Museum of Art, the Smithsonian, and the J. Paul Getty Museum, among many others.

May Day, Union Square, New York City
1948

Margaret Michaelis-Sachs

1902–1985

Margaret Michaelis-Sachs (b. Gross) was one of the few women photographers working in Australia in the mid-twentieth century. Michaelis-Sachs was born in Bielsko, Austria, and studied at the Institute of Graphic Arts and Research in Vienna. After working at photography studios in Vienna and Berlin, Michaelis-Sachs fled Nazism, settling in Spain, where she opened a business specializing in architectural photography. She left Spain in 1937 and immigrated to Australia by way of England, arriving in Sydney in 1939. There, she established a portrait studio that she ran until 1952, when her deteriorating eyesight forced her to leave the business. Multiple retrospectives of her work were held in Australia and Spain following her death.

Self-Portrait, Parramatta River, Sydney
1948

Gift of the estate of Margaret Michaelis-Sachs 1986. National Gallery of Australia, Canberra.

Nathan Rapoport

1911–1987

Born in Warsaw, sculptor Nathan Rapoport lived in the Soviet Union for most of World War II and in Paris and Israel following the war. In 1959, he moved to the United States. Rapoport is best known for his 1948 memorial to the Warsaw ghetto uprising, installed at the site, with a replica at Yad Vashem. Over the course of his career, the artist was commissioned to produce a number of Holocaust memorials in both the United States and Israel. Rapoport received the Herbert Adams medal from the National Sculpture Society in 1987 in recognition of his outstanding achievements in American sculpture.

Warsaw Ghetto Memorial (Warsaw, Poland)
1948

From Ira Nowinski (photographer), *Fitting Memory: Art and Politics of Holocaust Memorials*. Judah L. Magnes Memorial Museum. Published by Wayne State University Press. Photo credit: Stanford University Libraries, Department of Special Collections and University Archives.

Lee Krasner

1908-1984

Brooklyn-born artist Lenore "Lee" Krasner was among the most talented abstract painters of New York's midcentury movement. She trained at the Women's Art School of Cooper Union and the National Academy of Design. Krasner's energetic and colorful compositions were the product of a tireless impulse to push her creative abilities and explore abstract visual language. Krasner ultimately found recognition as an abstract expressionist, with a 1965 retrospective at London's Whitechapel Gallery, a solo exhibition at the Whitney Museum of American Art in 1973, and a full retrospective at the Houston Museum of Fine Arts in 1983.

Untitled

1949

© 2018 The Pollock-Krasner Foundation/Artists Rights Society (ARS), New York. Courtesy Paul Kasmin Gallery.

Barnett Newman

1905-1970

Born Baruch Newman in New York, Barnett Newman's massive-scale color-field paintings earned him a revered spot among New York's abstract expressionists. After studying at the Art Students League in the 1920s, Newman destroyed all of his then-existing work and abandoned painting for a year in 1939, only to reemerge from this hiatus with a new approach to abstract painting. Newman's artwork became increasingly existential and philosophically driven. His canvases are notable for their large swaths of color that are bisected by a vertical band. These austerely geometric paintings, though initially met with criticism, greatly influenced his contemporaries and the subsequent generation of abstract artists, establishing his reputation as one of the most important abstract expressionist painters.

Abraham

1949

Philip Johnson Fund. The Museum of Modern Art, New York, NY. © 2018 The Barnett Newman Foundation, New York/Artists Rights Society (ARS), New York. Digital image © The Museum of Modern Art/Licensed by SCALA/Art Resource, NY.

Chana Orloff

1888–1968

The Ukrainian-born sculptor Chana Orloff settled in Palestine with her parents in 1905. She moved to Paris in 1910 to study and soon became an important member of the avant-garde École de Paris, many students of which were also East European Jewish artists. She remained in Paris the rest of her life, with the exception of the war years, when she found refuge in Switzerland. Her work, mostly in wood, stone, bronze, and marble, was influenced by both cubism and the vogue for primitivism.

Sculpture of Ben-Gurion
1949

Indivision Justman-Tamir.

Emmanuel Mané-Katz

1894–1962

The painter Mané-Katz (also known as Emmanuel Katz) was born in Kremenchug, Ukraine, and was initially destined for the rabbinate. At age seventeen, he left home to study art in Vilna and then Kiev, and in 1913, he went to Paris. He was in Russia during World War I but then returned in 1921 to Paris. There, he remained his whole life, except during World War II, when he lived in the United States. As did Marc Chagall, he favored overtly Jewish themes drawn from his childhood in Eastern Europe.

Orchestra
ca. 1949

Image #T00304, Tate, London. © Tate, London 2016.

Henryk Berlewi
1894–1967

The painter, graphic designer, and typographer Henryk Berlewi was born into an acculturated Warsaw family. He trained in Warsaw, Antwerp, and Paris and became known for his theater posters, book jackets, and page designs in Hebrew and Yiddish. In the 1920s, he took up constructivist abstraction, creating paintings that employed simple geometric forms. In 1928, after moving from Warsaw to Paris, he abandoned the avant-garde and began painting portraits and nudes in a figurative style. He survived the war in Nice, serving in the Resistance, and in 1957, he returned to painting abstract works. He is often considered a progenitor of optical art.

Chair with Red Matter
1950

From the collection of the E. Ringelblum Jewish Historical Institute in Warsaw.

Fernand Bidon
1883–1963

Fernand Bidon was a French photographer who worked under the pseudonym Félix. Born in Marseille, Bidon lived and worked in Marrakech between 1912 and 1963; he was one of the first resident photographers of Morocco. During France's occupation of Morocco, a number of French artists visited the country to document, through European eyes, the culture of the region. Bidon captured hundreds of images of street life in Marrakech, including photographs of the city's Jewish quarter and its residents. Bidon used his photographs to produce postcards, likely capitalizing on the popularity of the exoticized Middle Eastern imagery found in French orientalist painting of the period. The majority of his images are in black and white, although he is known to have experimented with a small series in color. Bidon's work remains in the collection of the Marrakech Museum of Photography and Visual Arts.

Femmes marocaines
1950

Collection Dahan-Hirsch.

Erwin Blumenfeld
1897–1969

Erwin Blumenfeld was one of the most successful American fashion photographers of the mid-twentieth century. His work appeared in *Vogue*, *Harper's Bazaar*, *Cosmopolitan*, and *Life* magazines. Blumenfeld was born in Berlin and in 1925 settled in Holland, where he ran a leather-goods shop. He had been experimenting with photography and photomontage since the age of ten, and he moved to Paris in 1936 to fulfill his aspirations of becoming a professional photographer. There he met British photographer Cecil Beaton, who facilitated a yearlong contract with the French edition of *Vogue*. Blumenfeld's career was interrupted for a year while he was imprisoned in various internment camps in France; he was released in 1941 and moved to New York. By the mid-1950s, he was the highest-paid fashion photographer in the world.

Vogue, January 1, 1950, cover
1950

Erwin Blumenfeld/Vogue © Conde Nast.

Chaim Gliksberg
1904–1970

Raised in Odessa, painter Chaim Gliksberg began studying the visual arts after moving to Jerusalem in 1925. There he attended the Bezalel School of Arts and Crafts, where he began painting portraits of his colleagues. Gliksberg's style was heavily influenced by the avant-garde French painting of the period, which he first encountered in 1924 while living in Moscow. He spent the remainder of his career living and working in Tel Aviv, painting portraits, interior scenes, and street life of the city. In addition to cofounding the Association of Painters and Sculptors, Gliksberg also taught painting and exhibited frequently in museums across Israel. His *A Street in Jerusalem* was featured on an Israeli postage stamp, testifying to the importance of Gliksberg's work to Israeli arts and culture.

Portrait of Itzik Manger
1950

Private collection. © Estate of Chaim Gliksberg.

Zédé Schulmann

1890–1981

Zédé Schulmann was a photographer, filmmaker, and collector who recorded Moroccan Jewish culture during the first half of the twentieth century. Schulmann was born in Safed and in 1913 moved to Morocco, where he began documenting its Jewish culture. Schulmann's project took on greater urgency when Morocco gained national independence in 1953 and much of the country's Jewish community immigrated to Israel or France. Schulmann endeavored to record the material culture and folklore of the country's Jews before they disappeared. He photographed, filmed, and recorded religious events, traditions, dances, and songs and collected objects of worship, clothing, and jewelry. Schulmann's collection was donated to the Israel Museum in 1965 and was part of an exhibition on Moroccan Jewry in 1973.

Membres de la Communauté juive d'Ifrane
1950

Collection Dahan-Hirsch.

Unknown Artist

London's East End was the hub of Eastern European Jewish immigration and workers' movements in the early twentieth century. This district, which included the neighborhoods of Whitechapel and Spitalfields, was home to the majority of England's Jewish welfare organizations, theaters, newspapers, and daily life, a veritable British Lower East Side.

East End, London
1950

John Chillingworth/Picture Post/Getty Images.

Grete Stern

1904–1999

The German photographer and graphic designer Grete Stern was the cofounder of the Berlin-based photography studio ringl + pit. Stern was a multidisciplinary artist, having studied music, graphic design, and photography, and she built a successful business with her friend and collaborator Ellen Auerbach. However, in 1934 Stern was compelled to leave Berlin. She established a photography studio in London before moving with her husband, photographer Horacio Coppola, to his native Argentina in 1935. In Buenos Aires, she taught photography and continued her photographic activity.

Sueño No. 1: "Artículos eléctricos para el hogar"
ca. 1950

The Metropolitan Museum of Art, Twentieth-Century Photography Fund, 2012 (2012.10). The Metropolitan Museum of Art. © Estate of Grete Stern. Courtesy Galería Jorge Mara-La Ruche. Digital image © The Metropolitan Museum of Art. Image source: Art Resource, NY.

Georg Ehrlich

1897–1966

Georg Ehrlich was a multidisciplinary artist born and educated in Vienna. Ehrlich studied painting at the Arts and Crafts School in Vienna before serving as an officer in the Austrian army between 1915 and 1918. After his military service, Ehrlich devoted himself to art, first experimenting with painting and printmaking, and eventually focusing on sculpture. The political climate of Austria became increasingly threatening, and in 1937 Ehrlich moved to the United Kingdom. Ehrlich continued to travel internationally to create and exhibit his bronze-cast figurative sculptures.

The Young Lovers, Festival Garden, London, UK
1950–1951

Mikio Oba/Alamy Stock Photo.

Percival Goodman

1904–1989

Percival Goodman was an architect and urban theorist, recognized for both his architectural work and his critical thought. Born in New York, Goodman was educated at the École des Beaux-Arts in Paris, and from 1946 to 1972 he taught design and urban planning at Columbia University. He is best known for designing more than fifty synagogues in the United States; these synthesize modernist architectural forms with traditional Jewish symbolism, bringing religious architecture and practice into greater harmony with a rapidly modernizing and increasingly secular culture. Goodman, who was fascinated by the concept of utopia, wrote frequently about the social dimensions of architecture and its ability to create healthier communities and better cities.

B'nai Israel (Millburn, New Jersey)

1951

Courtesy Jewish Historical Society of New Jersey.

Louis Stettner

1922–2016

American-born Louis Stettner was known for his photographs of everyday life in New York and Paris. After serving as an army combat photographer during World War II, he taught at the Photo League in New York, organizing on its behalf the first New York exhibition of postwar French photography, in 1947. His work has found recognition in galleries and museums around the world and has been collected in numerous exhibitions.

Coming to America

1951

Purchase: Photography Acquisitions Committee Fund. (2003-10). The Jewish Museum. © 2018 Estate of Louis Stettner. Digital image © 2006 The Jewish Museum, New York, NY. Photo by Ardon Bar Hama, The Jewish Museum. Image source: The Jewish Museum/Art Resource, NY.

Yosef Zaritsky

1891–1985

The painter Yosef Zaritsky was born in Ukraine and studied art in Kiev. In 1923, he settled in Palestine, where he became a prominent figure in the development of Israeli art. He associated with the younger generation of artists who were rebelling against the academic style of the Bezalel School of Arts and Crafts. During his long life, he worked in a number of styles. In the 1920s, his watercolors of Safed, Tiberias, and Jerusalem combined an intense focus on the Israeli landscape with a commitment to quasi abstractionism. His later work was more rigorously abstract in style.

Yehiam (Life in a Kibbutz)
1951

Tel Aviv Museum of Art. Acquisition through a donation from Joseph and Rebecca Meyerhoff, Baltimore, Maryland. © Estate of Yossef Zaritsky. Photo: Abraham Hai.

Herbert Ferber

1906–1991

The American sculptor Herbert Ferber created large-scale, abstract, site-specific works, many of which remain landmarks of public art. Ferber trained as a dentist while attending night classes in drawing and sculpture. A lifelong New Yorker, he was active in the avant-garde art scene of the 1940s and 1950s, often associating with other artists and intellectuals. As Ferber's work evolved, he moved from sculpting in wood to experimenting with welded metal, creating massive assemblages of intersecting biomorphic shapes designed to engage viewers with both the sculptures and the spaces surrounding them. Ferber received several commissions over the course of his career to design metalwork and installations for synagogues and other buildings.

And the Bush Was Not Consumed
1951–1952

Collection of Congregation B'nai Israel, Millburn, New Jersey. © Estate of Herbert Ferber. Image source: The Jewish Museum, New York/Art Resource, NY. Photo by Richard Goodbody, Inc., The Jewish Museum.

Aharon Kahana
1905-1967

Born in Stuttgart, Germany, Aharon Kahana was an
Israeli painter known for his work with the New
Horizons group. Kahana showed an early mastery of
abstraction, studying ceramics in Stuttgart before
traveling to Berlin and Paris. In 1934, Kahana
immigrated to Palestine, where he painted in a realist
manner until 1943. In the 1950s, he developed his
signature style: biblical content depicted in geometric
forms with sharp defining lines. He also decorated
public walls using ceramic techniques. In the 1960s,
Kahana helped to found New Horizons and his style
shifted to pop art, in harmony with the group's vision.
Kahana's final works display a softer, more fluid line,
more personal expression, and a reembrace of the
classical female nude. Kahana died in Paris of a heart
attack during the Six-Day War.

The Binding of Isaac
1952

From the collection of Shoshana and Avraham Rabani.

Henry Valensi
1883-1960

Born in Algiers, painter Henry Valensi was a prominent figure of the French avant-garde at the turn of the
twentieth century, leading a group of artists known as
the Musicalistes (or Effusionists), who sought to
express musical rhythm through abstract painting.
Working between the 1930s and 1950s, the Musicalistes organized more than twenty exhibitions of their
work in Paris, as well as several other group and solo
exhibitions across Europe. As the epicenter of modern
art in Europe during the early twentieth century, Paris
offered Valensi a cohort of fellow abstractionists with
whom he frequently exhibited. This group formed the
collective Section d'Or in 1912, and included the
artists Francis Picabia and Marcel Duchamp; they
strongly influenced Valensi's abstract, geometric style.

Symphonie Vitale
1952

© 2018 Artists Rights Society (ARS), New York/ADAGP,
Paris. Digital image © CNAC/MNAM/Dist. RMN-Grand
Palais/Art Resource, NY. Photo: Philippe Migeat.

Lucien Hervé
1910–2007

Hungarian photographer Lucien Hervé was born László Elkán. He studied design at the Académie des Beaux-Arts in Vienna and then moved to Paris. Drafted into the army in 1939, he was captured the following year at Dunkirk, but he eventually escaped, ending up in Grenoble, where he took his new name as a member of the French Resistance. Hervé is best known for his extensive photographic work with the Swiss architect Charles-Édouard Jeanneret, also known as Le Corbusier. His black-and-white photographic compositions were bold and graphic, nearing abstraction at times, and resonated with Le Corbusier's sense of geometry and modernity. Prior to his photographic career, Hervé worked in a series of creative capacities, including fashion design and art journalism.

L'Unité d'habitation à Nantes-Rezé
1952–1954

© F.L.C. / ADAGP, Paris / Artists Rights Society (ARS), New York 2018. Photo credit: Getty Research Institute, Los Angeles (2002.R.41). Digital image © Copyright J. Paul Getty Trust.

Lucienne Bloch
1909–1999

Lucienne Bloch was a Swiss-born artist who spent the majority of her career working in the United States. Bloch is often noted for her relationship with the artists Diego Rivera and Frida Kahlo, whose work inspired her own diverse creative practices, from murals to photography to sculpture. Bloch was born in Geneva, the daughter of the composer Ernest Bloch. She first studied sculpture at the École des Beaux-Arts in Paris and then spent a year working in glass at the Leerdam Glassworks in Amsterdam. During an exhibition of her work in New York in 1931, Bloch met Rivera, whose controversial Rockefeller mural she photographed, secretly, before it was destroyed. Her friendship with Kahlo and Rivera inspired her foray into mural painting, and Bloch became a talented muralist in her own right. Among her many impressive works is a thousand-square-foot mural at Temple Emanuel in Grand Rapids, Michigan.

Temple Emanuel Sanctuary Wall (Grand Rapids, Michigan)
1953

Courtesy Temple Emanuel, Grand Rapids, MI. Photo: Dave Kagan, Sensitography.

Harvey Kurtzman

1924–1993

Born in New York, Harvey Kurtzman was a prominent American cartoonist. With the creation of his original *Mad* comic book in 1959, Kurtzman became an enduring icon of American culture and humor. *Mad*'s parody of popular culture and entertainment positioned Kurtzman as a critical figure in American postwar satire. After Kurtzman was replaced as editor of *Mad*, he went on to become the editor of *Help!*, another satirical magazine that became a forum for several major talents, including activist and cultural critic Gloria Steinem, filmmaker Woody Allen, and comedians John Cleese and Terry Gilliam of the cult comedy series *Monty Python's Flying Circus*. Kurtzman's projects had a provocative edge and revolutionary spirit that fed the countercultural moment of the 1960s and greatly influenced humor in American culture.

"Superduperman," Mad #4
1953

MAD #4 © E. C. Publications, Inc.

Mark Markov-Grinberg

1907–2006

Mark Markov-Grinberg was a Russian-born photojournalist who worked primarily for Soviet publications. After taking photography classes in high school, Markov-Grinberg took his first job at a Soviet newspaper in 1925, at the same time that he began to freelance for an illustrated magazine. Two years after moving to Moscow from Rostov-on-Don, in 1930, he received an offer from the Telegraph Agency of the Soviet Union (TASS) that enabled him to travel around the country and publish his photographs in numerous Soviet publications. In 1948, Markov-Grinberg lost his job at the TASS during a Stalin-era campaign against Jews. Despite the adversity he faced as a Jewish photographer, Markov-Grinberg spent the duration of his life in Russia. He died in Moscow.

Stone Flower Fountain, Moscow
1953

Gift of Dr. Mark Reichman, 2005.10.7. Heckscher Museum of Art, Huntington, New York.

Ruth Schloss
1922–2013

Born in Nuremberg, Ruth Schloss immigrated to Palestine as a teenager in 1937. She enrolled in Jerusalem's New Bezalel School of Arts and Crafts, where she studied painting under Mordechai Ardon. During the 1940s, Schloss devoted herself to the kibbutz movement, putting aside her art. She resumed painting in 1962, the same year that she opened her studio in Jaffa, which she ran until 1983. Schloss mainly worked with ink and watercolor on paper. Her signature pieces show the influence of the Communist Party and of Soviet socialist realism, a popular aesthetic among Israeli artists at the time. She illustrated books, magazines, and newspapers with figurative imagery focused on the human condition and social oppression. All Schloss's work carries a charge of social criticism and political commentary. Her later works, however, are larger in scale and more expressive and personally motivated.

In the Ma'abarah
1953

Collection of Mishkan Museum of Art, Ein Harod, Israel.

Elbert Weinberg
1928–1991

Connecticut-born sculptor Elbert Weinberg began studying art as a teen, attending night classes at the Harvard Art School and continuing his studies at the Rhode Island School of Design. He earned the prestigious Prix-de-Rome in 1951. Drawing early inspiration from mythological and biblical narratives and later turning to more modern themes, Weinberg worked primarily in wood and bronze. His career took off when a trustee of New York's Museum of Modern Art bought one of his figurative sculptures; art dealer Grace Borgenicht then arranged a commission for Weinberg from the Hirshhorn Museum in Washington, D.C. More commissions followed, including for the Jewish Museum in New York and the Boston University School of Law.

Ritual Figure
1953

A. Conger Goodyear Fund. The Museum of Modern Art, New York, NY. © Elbert Weinberg Trust. Digital image © The Museum of Modern Art/Licensed by SCALA/Art Resource, NY.

Ossip Zadkine

1890–1967

The sculptor Ossip Zadkine was born in Vitsyebsk (in contemporary Belarus), the son of a Jewish father and a Scottish mother, and he received his early training at Yehuda Pen's art school in Vitsyebsk. From 1905 to 1909, he lived in England. He then went to Paris, where he remained for most of his life, although during the war years he found refuge in the United States. Until the mid-1920s, Zadkine worked in the cubist idiom, and afterward, he developed a style of his own, drawing on African and Greek influences.

De verwoeste stad ("The Destroyed City"), 1953, Plein 1940, Rotterdam
1953

Photograph © Jannes Linders, courtesy of Sculpture International Rotterdam.

Frank Auerbach

b. 1931

A prolific London-based painter, Frank Auerbach's distinctive and expressive style has earned him recognition among some of the most respected institutions in the art world. Born in Berlin, Auerbach arrived in London in 1939 as a child refugee and made the city his home and studio, drawing inspiration from his immediate environment and closest relationships. He maintained several regular sitters over the course of his lifetime, including his friend Estella Olive West, whom he painted on a weekly basis for twenty-three years. Auerbach has been exhibiting since 1953, including a solo exhibition at the Royal Academy of Arts in 2001 and a 2015 retrospective at Tate Britain. He had the distinction of representing Britain at the 1986 Venice Biennale, receiving the Golden Lion Award alongside artist Sigmar Polke.

E. O. W. Nude
1953–1954

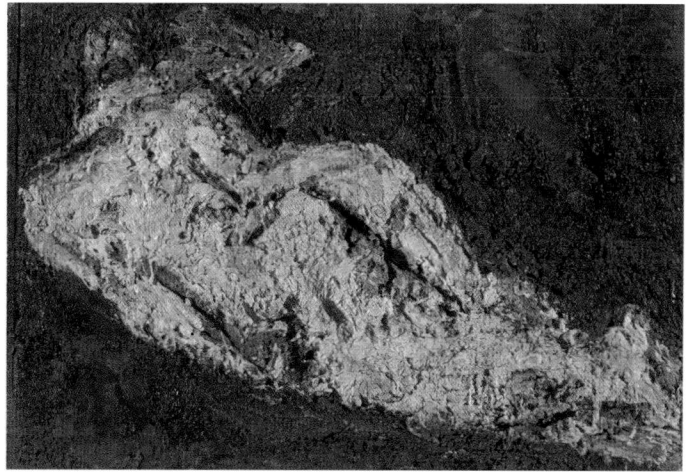

Tate, Purchased 1959, T00313. © Frank Auerbach. Courtesy Marlborough Fine Art, London. Digital image © Tate, London 2016.

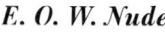

Boris Carmi

1914–2002

Boris Carmi was a pioneer of Israeli press photography who documented the early years of the state. Born Boris Vinograd in Moscow, Carmi left Russia in 1930 and studied ethnography at the Sorbonne. There he took an interest in photography, which he pursued professionally after his arrival in Palestine in 1939. During World War II, Carmi was a photographer for the British army; later he worked for the Haganah and, after the War of Independence, for the Israel Defense Forces. Throughout his career, Carmi took photographs for Israeli newspapers and journals that captured periods of turbulence and hope, demonstrating sensitivity toward his subjects. Carmi's images are central to the collective memory of Israel and have been featured in several exhibitions there, as well as in solo shows in Berlin and Frankfurt.

Nahal Oz

1954

Courtesy Dr. Alexandra Nocke, Berlin.

André Kertész

1894–1985

Born in Budapest, photographer André Kertész had an exceptional eye for formal composition and a rare sensitivity to the poetics of the everyday. He began taking pictures in 1912, continuing during his military service in World War I, and in 1925 he moved to Paris to work as a freelance photographer. Kertész often photographed his immediate environment, finding beauty in the quotidian scenes of Parisian street life. In 1936, he moved to New York, where he worked for several mass-circulated magazines. Kertész's work was the subject of numerous exhibitions in his lifetime, including solo shows at the Bibliothèque Nationale in Paris, the Art Institute of Chicago, and, in New York, both the Metropolitan Museum of Art and the Museum of Modern Art.

Washington Square in the Snow, January 9, 1954

1954

Gift of The André and Elizabeth Kertész Foundation. National Gallery of Art, Washington, D.C. 1997.123.5. © 2017 Estate of André Kertész/Higher Pictures.

Moses Soyer

1899–1974

Moses Soyer was a Russian-born American realist painter. After immigrating in 1912 to the United States and settling in New York, Soyer studied at Cooper Union, the National Academy of Design, and the Ferrer Art School. A 1926 scholarship permitted Soyer to study drawing in Europe, which strengthened his commitment to figurative art. When many other New York artists began experimenting with abstract expressionism in the 1940s, Soyer continued painting in his realist style, portraying scenes of everyday life with an honest, unembellished yet elegant aesthetic. Soyer was elected to the National Academy of Design and the National Institute of Arts and Letters in 1963 and 1966, respectively.

Dancers Resting
1954

Rudi Weissenstein

1910–1992

Czech-born photojournalist Rudi Weissenstein was important to both the development and the preservation of Israel's photographic history. Born Shimon Rudolph Weissenstein, he studied photography in Vienna before moving to Tel Aviv in 1936. He was a skilled conservationist with expertise in preserving photographic negatives, and after opening the studio Pri-Or Photo House with his wife, Miriam (b. Arnstein), the couple created and maintained an extensive archive of more than one million negatives documenting pivotal historic moments from the 1930s onward. The Photo House archive remains active to this day and was the subject of an award-winning 2012 documentary, *Life in Stills*.

Nahalat Binyamin Street, Tel Aviv
1954

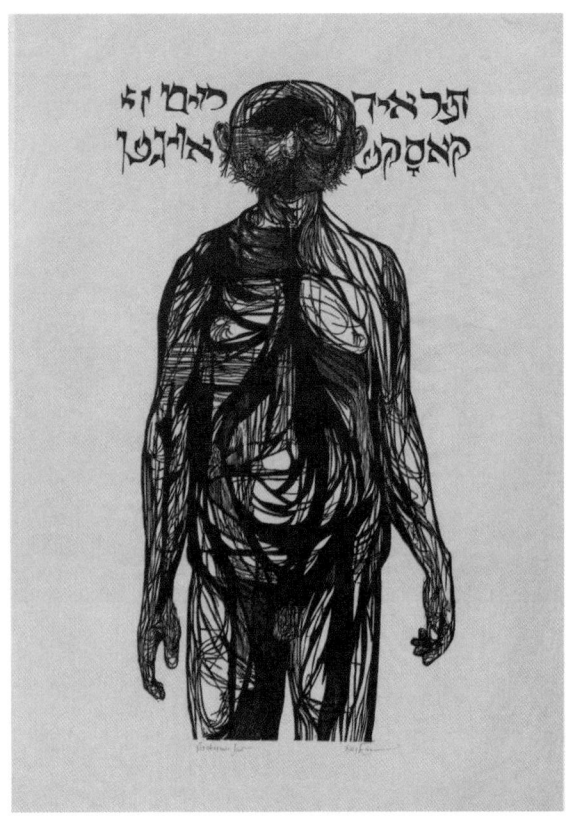

Leonard Baskin

1922–2000

Leonard Baskin was an American sculptor and printmaker as well as the founder of Gehenna Press, a publisher of fine illustrated books. Born in New Brunswick, New Jersey, Baskin studied at New York University, the New School, Yale University, and abroad in Paris and Florence. Baskin later taught at Smith College and at Hampshire College. The artist's figurative sculptures feature monumental human forms in wood, stone, and bronze and include a Holocaust memorial erected at the site of the first Jewish cemetery in Michigan, now part of the campus of the University of Michigan. Baskin's numerous etchings and woodblock prints offer dramatic portraits of humans and animals rendered with the intensity that characterized much of Baskin's extensive oeuvre. The Yiddish caption in this image reads: "The Jew with the squinty eyes."

The Strabismic Jew
1955

Print and published by the artist. Gift of the artist. The Museum of Modern Art. © Estate of Leonard Baskin. Digital image © The Museum of Modern Art/Licensed by SCALA/Art Resource, NY.

Cornell Capa

1918–2008

Cornell Capa was a photojournalist for *Life* magazine and the founder of the International Center for Photography in New York. Born Cornell Friedmann in Budapest, Capa was introduced to photography by his photojournalist brother, Robert. Targeted for his leftist political activities, Robert left Hungary for Paris in 1931, adopting the name Capa; in 1936, Cornell followed him to Paris and began working for him making prints, taking the same name as well. In 1937, Cornell Capa moved to New York to pursue his own career, becoming a staff photographer at *Life* in 1946 and covering hundreds of assignments in the United States and abroad. Upon the death of his brother in 1954, Capa left *Life* to join the cooperative photography agency Magnum Photos, which had been cofounded by Robert. Capa's political consciousness took form in his strong, graphic photographs, which, beyond their documentary function, also mediated issues of social justice.

Hebrew Lesson, Brooklyn, New York
1955

© International Center of Photography/Magnum Photos (164.1994).

Robert Frank

1924–2019

Swiss-born Robert Frank made some of the most influential contributions to twentieth-century American photography with his candid, unvarnished images of everyday citizens. Frank worked as a commercial photographer at the outset of his career, taking photographs for magazines such as *Harper's Bazaar*, *Vogue*, and *Life*. After receiving a Guggenheim Fellowship in 1955, he spent the next two years driving across the United States and capturing what he saw as naturalized American culture. A selection of these photos were published in his 1957 photo book, *The Americans*, and offered a stark contrast to the prevailing image of an idealized postwar America. In 1959, Frank began exploring avant-garde filmmaking and continued to work in both film and photography.

Yom Kippur, East River, New York City
1955

Morris Lapidus

1902–2001

Architect Morris Lapidus was renowned for the opulent Miami Beach hotels he designed in the 1950s and 1960s. Born in Odessa, Lapidus was brought to the United States when he was an infant. He studied architecture at Columbia University and worked in New York after graduating until 1942, when he moved to Miami. One of his best-known projects, the Fontainebleau Hotel, appeared in several films, including the 1964 James Bond feature *Goldfinger*. Lapidus's buildings were designed to impart a sense of luxury, glamour, and vitality, successfully reflecting and celebrating the consumerist fervor of postwar American culture.

Fontainebleau Hotel, Miami Beach, Florida. Over Pool to Hotel. Florida, Miami Beach
1955

Library of Congress, Prints & Photographs Division, Gottscho-Schleisner Collection (reproduction number, LC-G613-T-66993).

David Goldblatt

1930–2018

David Goldblatt photographed and documented South African society for more than fifty years. Of Lithuanian heritage, he was born in Randfontein. He began photographing professionally in the early 1960s, focusing on the effects of the National Party's legislation of apartheid. Over the years, he chronicled the plight of black communities, the culture of the Afrikaner nationalists, and the comfort of white suburbanites, as well as the conditions of race relations after the end of apartheid. Goldblatt received the Hasselblad Photography Award (2006) and the Henri-Cartier Bresson Award (2009).

Arriving Family, King George Street, Johannesburg
ca. 1955

Photograph by David Goldblatt.

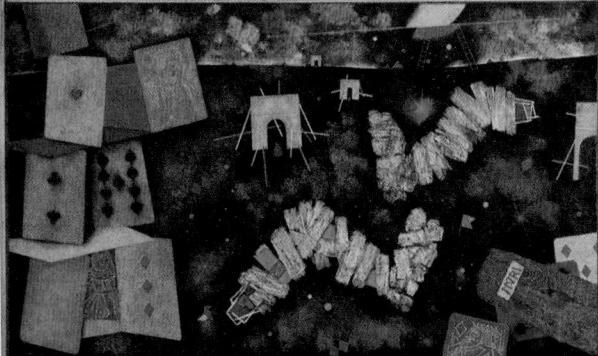

Mordechai Ardon

1896–1992

Mordechai Ardon was an Israeli painter trained in both modern and classical techniques and known for his distinctive, semiabstract, richly colored work. Born Max Bronstein in Tuchów, Galicia, Ardon moved to Germany in 1919 and studied at the Bauhaus school with the painters Wassily Kandinsky and Paul Klee. Ardon then attended the more traditional Academy of Decorative Arts in Munich before fleeing Germany in 1933 and settling in Palestine, where he changed his surname. In Jerusalem, Ardon taught at the Bezalel School of Arts and Crafts, later becoming director. From 1952 to 1963, he worked as an adviser to the Israeli Ministry of Education and Culture. He continued painting, combining elements of Jewish mysticism with contemporary modes of expression.

For the Fallen: Triptych
1955–1956

Collection Stedelijk Museum Amsterdam.

William Klein

b. 1928

Born in New York, William Klein is an innovative photographer and filmmaker, respected for his contributions to American *Vogue* during the 1950s and 1960s. Following his service in the military during World War II, Klein studied art in Paris with the French painter Fernand Léger. In 1954, a series of Klein's kinetic sculptures brought him to the attention of the art director at *Vogue*. Klein's passion for street photography reoriented the direction of fashion photography; he photographed his models outside the studio. He also designed and produced a number of photo books of his personal work. In 1965, Klein left *Vogue* to return to Paris, where he redirected his focus toward filmmaking.

Summer Evening, Via di Monserrato, Rome
1956

© 1956 William Klein. Courtesy Gallery FIFTY ONE, Antwerp.

René Shapshak
1899–1985

René Shapshak was a sculptor whose subjects included Charles de Gaulle, Queen Elizabeth, and Harry Truman. Although Shapshak portrayed some of the most prominent Western leaders of the nineteenth century, he was an anarchist sympathizer who often socialized with the movement's better-known adherents. Shapshak was born in Paris and raised in London, where he was introduced to anarchism. After World War I, he returned to Paris to study at the École des Beaux-Arts, later moving to South Africa and finally to the United States, where he settled in New York. Shapshak and his family lived for several years at New York's famous Chelsea Hotel, nearby which the artist kept a studio. In addition to producing metal sculptures and installations, he worked in paint and watercolor and lectured on modern art.

Bust of Former President Harry S. Truman
1956

Photographer Unknown, Courtesy Harry S. Truman Presidential Library.

Helen Frankenthaler

1928–2011

New York-born Helen Frankenthaler is considered one of America's most important modern artists. An early abstract expressionist, she was a pioneer in the development of color-field painting, inspiring later generations of artists with her technique, introduced in her seminal 1952 painting *Mountains and Sea*, of allowing paint to soak directly into the canvas. In addition to her paintings, Frankenthaler produced welded steel sculptures, ceramics, prints, and illustrated books. Numerous solo exhibitions of her work include retrospectives at the Museum of Modern Art (1989) and the Guggenheim Museum (1998) in New York.

Jacob's Ladder

1957

Gift of Hyman N. Glickstein. The Museum of Modern Art, New York, NY. © 2018 Helen Frankenthaler Foundation, Inc./Artists Rights Society (ARS), New York. Digital image © The Museum of Modern Art/Licensed by SCALA/Art Resource, NY.

Paul Goldman

1900–1986

Unrecognized until after his death, Paul Goldman produced an extensive body of work, totaling more than forty thousand images; it is now celebrated as one of the greatest photographic archives of a critical period in Israeli history. Born in Budapest, Goldman immigrated to Palestine in 1940, joining the British Army and then earning a living as a freelance photojournalist for local newspapers and international news services. Because press photographers were not credited for their work at this time, Goldman's oeuvre remained unacknowledged until 2000, when David Rubinger, *Time* magazine's Israel photographer, uncovered his remarkable collection of negatives. A selection of Goldman's photos was the subject of a 2005 exhibition at the Hebrew Union College's Jewish Institute of Religion Museum in New York.

David Ben-Gurion Standing on His Head (Sharon Hotel Beach, Herzliya)

1957

Paul Goldman, MUSA, Eretz Israel Museum, Tel Aviv Collection.

Ben Shahn
1898–1969

The painter and graphic artist Ben Shahn was born in
Kovno, today Kaunas, and in 1909 came to New York
City, where he received formal art training. From the
late 1920s until about 1950, he worked mainly in a
social realist tradition, attacking injustice, prejudice,
and brutality. During the Great Depression, he was
employed as a photographer by the Farm Security
Administration to document the unemployed and the
poor, government homestead projects, and rural,
small-town life. After 1950, his work became more
allegorical and symbolic and he turned increasingly to
producing illustrated Hebrew texts.

Alphabet of Creation
1957

Harvard Art Museums/Fogg Museum, Stephen Lee Taller
Ben Shahn Archive, Gift of Dolores Taller, M24915. © 2018
Estate of Ben Shahn/Licensed by VAGA at Artists Rights
Society (ARS), NY. Photo: Imaging Department © President
and Fellows of Harvard College.

Jean-Michel Atlan
1913–1960

Born in Constantine, Algeria, Jean-Michel Atlan was
an important contributor to the Parisian avant-garde
movement of the mid-twentieth century. After settling
in Paris in 1930, Atlan studied philosophy at the
Sorbonne. As an active member of the French Resistance, Atlan was arrested by the occupying Nazi forces
in 1942. He managed to escape further persecution by
feigning insanity; he was institutionalized until Paris
was liberated in 1944. The artist spent much of his
time in the asylum painting, developing an abstract
style characterized by fields of pastel and earth tones
outlined by heavy, rhythmic black lines. In addition to
exhibiting his painting widely in France, Atlan also
published a book of poetry entitled *Le sang profond*.

La Kahena
1958

Inv. No. AM3607P. Musée National d'Art Moderne. © 2018
Artists Rights Society (ARS), New York/ADAGP, Paris.
Digital image © CNAC/MNAM/Dist. RMN-Grand Palais/
Art Resource, NY. Photo: Adam Rzepka.

Sonia Delaunay

1885–1979

Born Sara Stern in Ukraine and raised in St. Petersburg, Sonia Delaunay studied at the Academy of Fine Arts in Karlsruhe and the Académie de La Palette in Paris. Active in the Paris art scene at the turn of the twentieth century, Delaunay was greatly influenced by the city's burgeoning modernist movement. Her abstract aesthetic was propelled by color theory and the geometric forms pervasive in cubist painting of the period. A remarkably diverse and prolific artist, Delaunay was also a skilled fashion designer, textile designer, and interior decorator who collaborated frequently with other artists, including her husband, painter Robert Delaunay. Her designs are bold, graphic, and vibrant, speaking to her mastery of color and composition. For her artistic accomplishments, in 1975 she was awarded membership in the Legion of Honor.

Rythme coloré
1958

Gift of Seymour H. Knox, Jr., 1964 (K1964:23). Albright-Knox Art Gallery, Buffalo, New York, New York State, U.S.A. © Estate of Sonia Delaunay-Terk. Courtesy Pracusa SA. Digital image © Art Resource, NY.

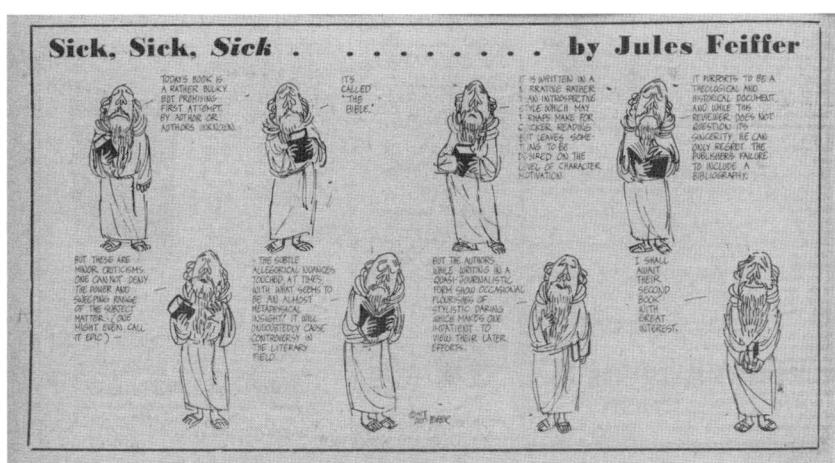

Jules Feiffer

b. 1929

Jules Feiffer grew up in the Bronx, New York. He is a writer, cartoonist, playwright, illustrator, and screenwriter whose satirical cartoon series, first entitled *Sick, Sick, Sick* and later called *Feiffer*, ran for forty-two years in the *Village Voice*. Feiffer is the recipient of a Pulitzer Prize and lifetime achievement awards from the National Cartoonist Society and the Writers Guild of America. He taught at the Yale School of Drama and at Southampton College.

Sick, Sick, Sick, comic strip, The Village Voice
1958

© Jules Feiffer. Courtesy Richard Michelson Gallery. Photo Credit: General Research Division, the New York Public Library.

Al Hirschfeld
1903–2003

Born in St. Louis, Missouri, Al Hirschfeld was a renowned illustrator and caricaturist. Hirschfeld's lifelong passion for the performing arts married his distinctive style with the vibrant personalities of New York's theater scene. Hirschfeld was able to capture the character of his subjects with the simplicity of a line. He recorded personalities as illustrious and diverse as Ella Fitzgerald, Duke Ellington, Ernest Hemingway, Jerry Garcia, and Liza Minnelli, among many others, in a career spanning most of the twentieth century. Hirschfeld's works were featured in several prominent publications including *The New York Times*, *The New Yorker*, and *Rolling Stone*. His portraits of Hollywood stars were also featured in several series of postage stamps in the United States.

Leonard Bernstein
1958

© The Al Hirschfeld Foundation. www.AlHirschfeldFoundation.org.

Morris Louis
1912–1962

The painter Morris Louis was born in Baltimore, where he attended the Maryland Institute of Fine and Applied Arts from 1929 to 1933. After four years living and working in New York, Louis returned to Baltimore to work as a private art instructor before making his final move to Washington, D.C., in 1952. The 1950s were pivotal for Louis's career; he produced his most mature and celebrated works of art during this decade. While teaching at the Washington Workshop Center of the Arts, Louis met fellow abstract painter Kenneth Noland, with whom he visited the studio of Helen Frankenthaler. Louis was profoundly inspired by Frankenthaler's work and incorporated her method of staining canvases into his own process, producing the color-field paintings for which he is known today.

Tzadik
1958

Private collection. © 2018 Maryland Institute College of Art (MICA), Rights Administered by Artist Rights Society (ARS), New York, All Rights Reserved. Photo Courtesy Mnuchin Gallery, New York.

Endre Bálint

1914–1986

Hungarian artist Endre Bálint worked in a variety of media throughout his career, such as painting and printmaking, as well as—in his more experimental work—collage, photomontage, and poetry. Born in Budapest, Bálint attended the College of Applied Arts there before studying privately with two Hungarian artists, János Vaszary and Vilmos Aba Novák. Early on, Bálint took an interest in the aesthetics of surrealism, constructivism, and Hungarian folk art, all of which influenced his semiabstract, symbolic paintings. In 1947, he exhibited his work at both the International Surrealist Exhibition and the Salon des Réalités Nouvelles, a show of international abstract art. After the 1956 Hungarian uprising, the artist spent several years living in Paris, where he produced more than a thousand illustrations for the Jerusalem Bible.

Homesickness

1959

© Courtesy Nudelmann Numismatica.

Arnold Belkin

1930–1992

Canadian-born artist Arnold Belkin became one of the best-known public muralists in Mexico. Belkin began studying at the Vancouver School of Art, moving to Mexico City in 1948 to attend the National School for Painting and Sculpture. As a result of his family's left-wing political background, Belkin took an interest in social issues from a young age and felt particularly drawn to the political public art of muralists Diego Rivera, José Clemente Orozco, and David Alfaro Siqueiros, whose works featured bold, nationalistic imagery. Belkin absorbed the influences of these artists and began painting his own murals in Mexico and later in New York, where he lived between 1968 and 1976. Belkin became a Mexican citizen in 1981, spending the remainder of his career in Mexico City painting, writing, and teaching.

Warsaw Ghetto Uprising

1959

Photo by Dan Jackson.

Mathias Goeritz

1915–1990

German-born painter and sculptor Mathias Goeritz spent a significant part of his career working and teaching in Mexico. After earning a doctorate in philosophy and art history from Friedrich-Wilhelms Universität in 1940, Goeritz moved from Berlin to Morocco and then to Spain, where he cofounded the Escuela de Altamira in 1948. Ultimately, Goeritz settled in Mexico in 1949, teaching at the architecture school of the Universidad de Guadalajara. In Mexico, Goeritz immersed himself in the country's artistic culture, creating the Museo Experimental "El Eco" in Mexico City, which operated from 1951 to 1953. During this time, Goeritz also produced numerous expressive, minimalist sculptures. He remained a tireless advocate of Mexican modern art throughout his life, continuously teaching, creating, and promoting the work of fellow artists.

Message Number 7B, Ecclesiastes VII: 6
1959

Gift of Philip Johnson. 779.1969. The Museum of Modern Art, New York, NY. © Mathias Goeritz. Digital image © The Museum of Modern Art/Licensed by SCALA/Art Resource, NY.

René Goscinny

1926–1977

René Goscinny was a French cartoonist, famed for cocreating the comic *Astérix le Gaulois*. Goscinny was born in Paris and moved with his family to Argentina at a young age, obtaining a degree in fine arts before moving to New York to find work as an illustrator. Returning to Paris, Goscinny was introduced to comic artist Albert Uderzo, with whom he founded the humor magazine *Pilote* in 1959. *Astérix* debuted in the first issue and quickly gained widespread popularity. Goscinny also wrote for numerous other French comic strips. In 1967, he was made a Chevalier of Arts and Letters for his contributions to French culture.

Astérix le Gaulois, no. 1, cover
1959

ASTERIX®—OBELIX®—IDEFIX®/© 2018 LES EDITIONS ALBERT RENE/GOSCINNY—UDERZO.

Dan Pagis

Details about Dan Pagis's biography appear in the section on Israel, 1946–1973.

The Egg That Disguised Itself
1959

Copyright © Am Oved Reprinted from the children's book *Ha-beitsa she-hithapsa* by Dan Pagis. First published in Hebrew by Am-Oved, Israel 1973. Published by arrangement with The Institute for the Translation of Hebrew Literature.

Amiram Erev

b. 1926

Born in Jerusalem, Amiram Erev is an Israeli photographer noted for documenting the early years of the state. Erev's photographs are both aesthetically modern and tied intimately to the national narrative of Israel through his focus on Zionist building and development efforts. Many of his works were commissioned, and almost his entire oeuvre was shot in black and white, adding to his photographs' modernist appeal. Erev took numerous photographs of new housing projects and infrastructure development plans, demonstrating his ideological commitment to the Zionist idea. Shooting in a stark, directly documentary style, Erev introduces little of his own critical or personal perspective. Nonetheless, in many of his images, Erev glorifies both the landscape and those who labored to transform it.

Social Housing Blocks in Upper Nazareth
Early 1960s

From the collection of Shikun & Binui Archive. Courtesy Silver Print Collection, Ein Hod.

Ziva Armoni

(1926–2010)

Hanan Hebron

(1931–2000)

Architects Ziva Armoni and Hanan Hebron were commissioned to design the National and University Library in Jerusalem. The library is charged with collecting and preserving materials connected to cultural, national, and historic elements of Jewish life in Israel and from around the world. The current building was inaugurated in 1960 at the heart of what would become Hebrew University's Givat Ram campus.

The National and University Library
1960

Photo: Assaf Pinchuk

Anatoly Kaplan

1902–1980

Born in Rogachev, Belarus, Anatoly Kaplan was a printmaker, illustrator, and ceramicist who spent much of his career in Leningrad. After studying at the Leningrad Academy between 1921 and 1927, Kaplan worked as a stage designer before beginning to create lithographs in 1937. Despite the challenges facing Jewish artists in Russia at the time, Kaplan found success working in Leningrad, joining the Union of Soviet Artists in 1939 and exhibiting his work regularly. After the war, Kaplan dedicated his art to memorializing the pre-Soviet Jewish landscape through illustrations to Yiddish folk songs and the work of Mendele and Sholem Aleichem. The text surrounding the image says "Whoever ploughs and plants eats his bread in peace."

Pakhar' (Ploughman)
1960

From Anatoliĭ Kaplan: Iz kollektsii Isaaka i Ludmily Kushnir (Sankt-Peterburg)/[sostavitel' izdani iia Isaak Kushnir]. 2007. Page 153 (bottom image only). Courtesy Isaac and Lyudmila Kushnir Collection, St. Petersburg. Photo credit: The Dorot Jewish Division, The New York Public Library, Astor, Lenox and Tilden Foundations.

Gertrud Natzler

1908–1971

Otto Natzler

1908–2007

Partners and creative collaborators Gertrud (b. Amon) and Otto Natzler were among the most important ceramists of the twentieth century. The two Viennese-born artists met in 1933. After taking a ceramics class with Franz Iskara, they went on to set up their own clay studio. Eventually they gained recognition in Europe. The couple fled Austria in 1938, resettling in Los Angeles, California, where they established a studio with Gertrud's kick wheel and a small kiln they had brought from Vienna. Working synergistically, Gertrud created wheel-thrown bowl and bottle forms while Otto fired and glazed each work. Over the course of their long career, Gertrud produced 25,000 pots and Otto developed 2,500 glazes. The Museum of Modern Art in New York purchased several of the couple's works in 1945, and Natzler ceramics are in the permanent collections of dozens of museums around the world.

Apple Green Reduction Fired Glaze with Melt Fissures, Earthenware
1960

Private collection. © Gail Reynolds Natzler, Trustee, The Natzler Trust. Courtesy of Couturier Gallery.

Ori Reisman

1924–1991

Born and raised in Tel Yosef, Israel, Ori Reisman was greatly influenced by the environment and culture that surrounded him in his youth. Reisman was one of the founders of the kibbutz Beit ha-Arava as well as kibbutz Kabri, the two of which account for the painter's primary subject matter. Although he spent much of his life in Israel, Reisman traveled to Paris in the early 1950s and again in the 1970s, where he studied at the École Nationale des Beaux-Arts. It was only toward the end of his life that Reisman began to receive critical attention and acclaim; he spent most of his career at the margins of the Israeli art world.

Carob Tree Boulevard
1960

© Estate of Ori Reisman. Photo credit: The Israel Museum, Jerusalem, Israel. Gift of Georgette and Israel Zafrir, Tel Aviv/ Bridgeman Images.

Paul Schutzer

1930-1967

Paul Schutzer was an American photojournalist who worked for *Life* magazine, chronicling historic events within the United States and abroad. Schutzer began experimenting with photography at age ten, and then studied painting and law before dedicating himself to photography in 1956 as part of the *Life* office in Washington, D.C. Over the course of his brief career, Schutzer photographed such important figures as Martin Luther King Jr., Richard Nixon, John F. Kennedy, and Fidel Castro. He documented an impressive array of historic events, including the construction of the Berlin Wall, the Algerian War, a major earthquake in Iran, and the Vietnam War. Schutzer's life and career were tragically cut short by the photographer's premature death while covering the Six-Day War.

Israeli Beatniks, Night Club
1960

Paul Schutzer/The LIFE Picture Collection/Getty Images.

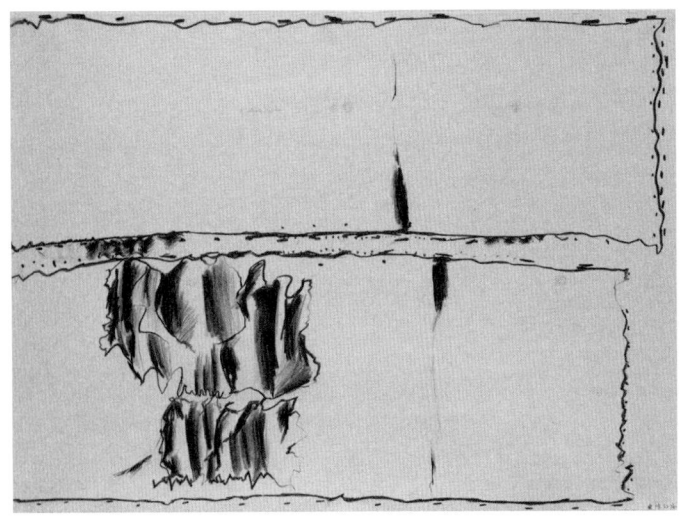

Aviva Uri

1922-1989

Israeli artist Aviva Uri began studying painting in her early twenties, working at the art studio of Moshe Castel in Tel Aviv. After a year studying under Castel, she continued her artistic development with David Hendler, a painter and draftsman who received his art education in Prague; in 1963, the two married. Uri's primary medium was drawing: expressive, minimalist, abstract, and usually done on paper. She had a successful career, with numerous exhibitions of her work, including solo shows at the Tel Aviv Museum in 1957 and 1977, the Israel Museum in 1971, and Amsterdam's Stedelijk Museum in 1984.

Landscape II
1960

The Israel Museum, Jerusalem/Gift of Yona Fischer, Jerusalem, on the occasion of the Israel Museum's 20th anniversary/Photo © the Israel Museum, Jerusalem by Elie Posner/Bridgeman Images.

Siona Shimshi

b. 1939

The Israeli painter, sculptor, ceramicist, and textile designer Siona Shimshi was born in Tel Aviv to a family that had migrated to Palestine from Lithuania. Shimshi studied at the Avni Institute from 1956 to 1959 and went on to study ceramics at Alfred University and, from 1959 to 1962, at Greenwich House Pottery in New York. While in Israel, in 1966 Shimshi helped found the art group Ten+. From 1979 to 1987, she chaired the Department of Ceramic Design at the Bezalel School of Arts and Crafts. Her ceramic sculptures are often figurative busts in which she emphasizes or manipulates discrete facial features to express complex ideas and narrative themes.

Torah Ark Curtain

ca. 1960

Jewish Museum, New York. Gift of George and Vera Rubins. © Siona Shimshi. Image provided by the Jewish Museum, NY.

Saul Bass

1920–1996

Acclaimed graphic designer Saul Bass created some of the most memorable images of American film and advertising. Bass, the son of East European immigrants, grew up in the Bronx and studied at New York's Art Students League and at Brooklyn College. In addition to designing several iconic corporate logos, including those of AT&T, Continental Airlines, Kleenex, and Minolta, Bass made the opening credits sequence of film into an art of its own. In 1955, Bass designed the opening sequence of Otto Preminger's *The Man with the Golden Arm*, an innovation that transformed the production of title sequences and launched his career as a sought-after visual consultant in the film industry. The designer's talent extended to filmmaking; he collaborated on several short films with his second wife, Elaine Makatura, winning an Oscar in 1968 for the documentary short *Why Man Creates*.

Exodus

1961

Gift of Sara and Marc Benda, 2010-21-16. Cooper-Hewitt, National Design Museum, New York, NY, USA. © Estate of Saul Bass. Image source: Cooper Hewitt, Smithsonian Design Museum/Art Resource, NY. Photo: Matt Flynn © Smithsonian Institution.

Aryeh Elhanani

1898–1985

Aryeh Elhanani (Sapozhnikov) was born in Russia and studied at the
School of Arts and Architecture in Kiev. His exposure to avant-garde art
during his studies profoundly influenced his creative output. After immigrating to Palestine in 1922, Elhanani began designing sets and costumes
for theatrical productions, employing the aesthetics of the Russian avant-
garde he had absorbed while in Kiev. As an architect, Elhanani designed a
number of buildings in Tel Aviv, including the Wix Library at the Weizmann Institute of Science in 1957 and the Hall of Remembrance at Yad
Vashem from 1957 to 1961. In 1973, Elhanani was awarded the Israel Prize
for his important contributions to Israeli architecture.

Hall of Remembrance at Yad Vashem
1961

Yad Vashem Photo Archive, Jerusalem. 1495/9.

William Zorach

1889–1966

Lithuanian-born artist William Zorach (b. Zorach Gorfinkel) immigrated to the United States as a young child, growing up in Cleveland, where, as a teen, he took a job at a commercial lithography firm to help support his family. Zorach attended night classes at the Cleveland School of Art before moving to New York City to attend the National Academy of Design and then to Paris to study painting. He eventually abandoned painting to focus on his sculpture, carving wood and stone into modern, simplified human figures. Throughout his career he received commissions for public sculptures across the United States. He also taught for more than thirty years at New York's Art Students League.

Spirit of the Sea, Library Square Park, City of Bath, Maine

1961

Photograph: Larry Wilson.

Zalman Schachter-Shalomi

1924–2014

Zalman Schachter-Shalomi was born in Żółkiew, Galicia (present-day Zhovkva, Ukraine) and was raised in Vienna. After immigrating to New York in 1941, he embraced the Chabad movement and was ordained at its central yeshiva in 1947. After breaking with Chabad in the 1960s, he turned to an experimental, New Age approach to ritual and prayer, incorporating elements of Hasidic mysticism, meditation, and dance into his prayer services. His approach to religious practice is embodied in the B'nai Or tallit (also called the Rainbow tallit), which he designed and encouraged followers to sew for themselves.

B'nai Or Prayer Shawl

ca. 1961

Courtesy Post-Holocaust American Judaism Collections, Special Collections and Archives/University of Colorado Boulder Libraries.

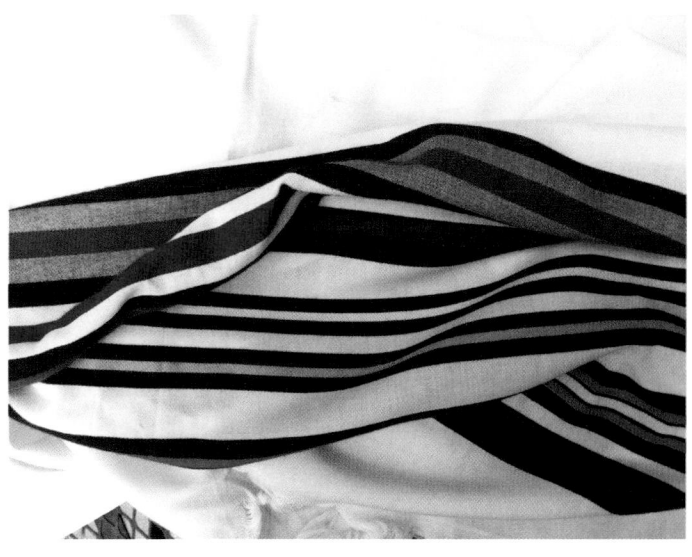

Marc Chagall

1887–1985

Marc Chagall is perhaps the best-known Jewish artist of the modern period. Born into an impoverished Hasidic family in Vitebsk (in contemporary Belarus), he attended art schools in his hometown, St. Petersburg, and Paris, where he lived from 1910 to 1914. He was swept up by revolutionary fervor following the overthrow of the tsarist regime but soon became disillusioned and left the Soviet Union for good in 1922. He lived the rest of his life in France, except for the years between 1941 and 1948, when he was in the United States. His work creates an imaginary world, saturated with color, that draws on his childhood scenes. His use, beginning in the 1930s, of the crucifixion of Jesus as a symbol of Jewish suffering remains controversial.

Benjamin, One of the Twelve Tribes of Israel, Stained-Glass Window, Hadassah Medical Centre, Jerusalem
1962

David Hillman

1894-1974

David Hillman is renowned among Anglo Jewry for his exceptional stained-glass synagogue windows, including those he made for the impressive St. John's Wood Synagogue and the Central Synagogue, both in London, as well as the Renanim Synagogue in Jerusalem. Born and raised in Glasgow, Hillman studied at London's Royal College of Art. The son of a *dayan*, a religious judge, Hillman was himself a rabbinic scholar and infused his knowledge of Jewish sources into his elaborate, colorful designs. Hillman's numerous windows depict biblical images and incorporate scriptural verses.

Stained-Glass Window, Central Synagogue, Portland Street, London
1962

Sonia Halliday Photo Library.

Roy Lichtenstein

1923–1997

One of the best-known American artists, Roy Lichten-stein created some of the most recognizable images of the pop-art movement. His comic-strip-inspired paintings appropriated elements of popular culture, repositioning them in the context of high art as a rebuke to prevailing abstract expressionist aesthetics. Lichtenstein, born and raised in New York, taught at the State University of New York at Oswego and at Rutgers University during the late 1950s and early 1960s, thereafter dedicating himself entirely to making art. Lichtenstein found commercial success throughout his long and prolific career, and his work continues to be widely collected and exhibited in the United States and abroad.

Masterpiece
1962

Avigdor Stematsky

1908–1989

The Russian-born painter Avigdor Stematsky moved to Tel Aviv in 1920, beginning his formal art education at age eighteen while studying at the Bezalel School of Arts and Crafts in Jerusalem. In the 1930s, Stematsky traveled to Paris, where he was profoundly influenced by the city's avant-garde art scene. In 1948, he cofounded the Israeli painters group New Horizons, dedicated to abstract painting. While they did not endeavor to create a distinctly Israeli art, instead working within what they viewed as a universal artistic language, Stematsky and his fellow New Horizons painters became recognized as some of Israel's most important artists.

Etude
1962

Yehezkel Streichman

1906-1993

Yehezkel Streichman was an Israeli painter who cofounded the abstract painters group New Horizons. Streichman was born in Lithuania and immigrated to Palestine in 1924, studying painting at the Bezalel School of Arts and Crafts in Jerusalem before completing his studies in Paris and Florence. French abstract expressionism had a profound influence on Streichman's art, which mingles figurative and abstract forms. Streichman returned to Tel Aviv from Europe in 1936 to teach at the Avni Institute of Art and Design and run an atelier. Among Streichman's many awards was the Dizengoff Prize for painting and sculpture, which he received on four separate occasions; in 1990, he was awarded the Israel Prize for painting.

Fig Tree in Studio Window
1962-1970

The Israel Museum, Jerusalem, Israel, Purchase, Sandberg Prize for Israel Art/Bridgeman Images.

Moshe Castel

1909-1991

The Israeli painter Moshe Castel was born into a Sephardic family in Jerusalem that had lived in Palestine for centuries. He studied at the Bezalel School of Arts and Crafts from 1922 to 1925 and then in Paris, where he lived from 1927 to 1940. With the Nazi conquest of France, he returned home. After the war he divided his time between Paris and Safed. Although the style in which he worked changed dramatically over his career, he continued to paint Jewish and Israeli subjects.

Poésie de Canaan, I
1963

Gift of Mr. and Mrs. David Kluger. The Museum of Modern Art, New York, NY. © Estate of Moshe Castel. Digital image © The Museum of Modern Art/Licensed by SCALA/Art Resource, NY.

Bruce Davidson

b. 1933

Photographer Bruce Davidson grew up in Oak Park, Illinois, where he began taking photos at age ten. He attended the Rochester Institute of Technology to study photography and then Yale University to pursue graduate work in philosophy and visual arts. Drafted into the army in the 1950s, Davidson was stationed in Paris, where he met the photographer Henri Cartier-Bresson. In 1958, after having worked as a staff photographer at *Life*, Davidson joined Magnum Photos, Cartier-Bresson's cooperative photography agency. Throughout his career, Davidson produced photo essays about civil rights and social injustice in the United States, winning grants from the Guggenheim Foundation and the National Endowment for the Arts.

Construction of the Verrazano Narrows Bridge
1963

© Bruce Davidson/Magnum Photos.

Mikhail Grobman

b. 1939

Mikhail Grobman is an artist and poet. He was born in Moscow and came to Israel in 1971. In Moscow during the early 1960s, he was among the originators of the second Russian avant-garde, and in 1975, he founded the Leviathan group of artists in Jerusalem, publishing a Russian-language newspaper of that name and seeking to combine contemporary art with Judaism and mysticism. Grobman lives in Tel Aviv.

Tomb of an Israeli Soldier I
1963

© Michail Grobman.

Arnold Newman

1918–2006

Born in New York, the portrait photographer Arnold Newman captured some of the most prominent cultural personalities of the twentieth century. Pioneering the style of environmental portraiture, Newman photographed his subjects in settings that reflected their character and evoked their particular talents. Newman began his career as an assistant in a photography studio; he opened his own studio in New York in 1946, initially concentrating on portraits of artists before focusing his lens on a more diverse array of famous individuals. During his extensive career, Newman worked for American magazines, including *Harper's Bazaar*, *Life*, *Time*, and *Newsweek*. His subjects included artists Pablo Picasso and Georgia O'Keeffe, actors Marilyn Monroe and Audrey Hepburn, and politicians John F. Kennedy and Bill Clinton.

Arnold Krupp
1963

Gedula Ogen

b. 1929

Gedula Ogen is an Israeli ceramicist and educator. Ogen was born in Jerusalem, where she studied at the Hebrew University and the Bezalel School of Arts and Crafts. From a young age, Ogen accompanied her father, a professional photographer, to sites of archaeological excavations. These childhood experiences influenced her ceramic practice, which draws inspiration from local traditions and relics as well as from the plants and animals of her surroundings. Ogen's oeuvre is diverse and includes both small-scale and monumental sculptures. She was the head of the Ceramics Department at the Bezalel from 1962 to 1980.

The Gathering of Israel, Kibbutz Galuyot
1963

Pedro Friedeberg

b. 1937

Pedro Friedeberg is a Mexican artist and furniture designer. Friedeberg, whose family fled to Mexico from Italy in 1940, has spent his career working against prevailing currents of Mexican art. After studying architecture at the Universidad Iberoamericana, Friedeberg rejected the international style of design that was popular in the country in favor of an aesthetic combining fantasy, surrealism, architectural drawing, and religious and mystical symbolism. He continues to live and work in Mexico, regularly exhibiting his work there as well as in the United States and Europe.

"Insist on yourself . . ." from the Series Great Ideas of Western Man
1964

Smithsonian American Art Museum, Gift of Container Corporation of America.

Louise Nevelson

1899–1988

A leading American sculptor of the twentieth century, Louise Nevelson was born in Kiev and immigrated as a child to the United States. Known especially for her sculptures of assembled wood and found objects, she also produced large-scale works late in her career, including a number of public commissions such as Louise Nevelson Plaza, an environment of seven sculptures in Lower Manhattan (1979). Nevelson drew inspiration from a broad array of artistic movements and styles, including cubism, surrealism, African art, Native American art, abstract expressionism, minimalism, action painting, and color-field painting. She has been the subject of more than 135 solo exhibitions.

Homage to the Six Million
1964

© 2018 Estate of Louise Nevelson/Artists Rights Society (ARS), New York Photo Credit: The Israel Museum, Jerusalem, Israel/Photo © The Israel Museum, Jerusalem Avshalom Avital/Bridgeman Images.

Fanny Rabel

1922–2008

Painter, muralist, and printmaker Fanny Rabel was born Fanny Rabinowich in Lublin, Poland. After spending several years in Paris, she immigrated to Mexico in 1938 and took night classes in drawing and printmaking. In 1942, Rabel began studying at the National School for Painting and Sculpture in Mexico City and started working relationships with painter Frida Kahlo and muralist Diego Rivera. Rabel found inspiration while studying under Kahlo and gained experience in mural painting when she assisted Rivera with his 1948 murals at Mexico's National Palace. Rabel became a member of the Popular Graphics Workshop and the Mexican Salon of Fine Arts, producing a diverse range of expressive works in print and on canvas.

La Ronda en el tiempo
1964

Archivo Digital de las Colecciones del Museo Nacional de Antropología. INAH-CANON.

Miriam Schapiro

1923–2015

Born in Toronto, multidisciplinary artist Miriam Schapiro was a champion of creative practices often dismissed as women's work. In a type of art she called *femmage*, she collaged materials such as cloth, ribbon, and lace into colorful, geometric images. Together with artist Judy Chicago, in 1972 she codirected the interdisciplinary installation *Womanhouse*, which became a landmark event of feminist art. Schapiro was among the first artists to use a computer in her creative process; in 1967, in collaboration with a physicist, she used one to create an abstract painting.

Shrine II
1964

Norton Simon Museum, Anonymous Gift, 1966. P.1966.07.033. © Miriam Schapiro.

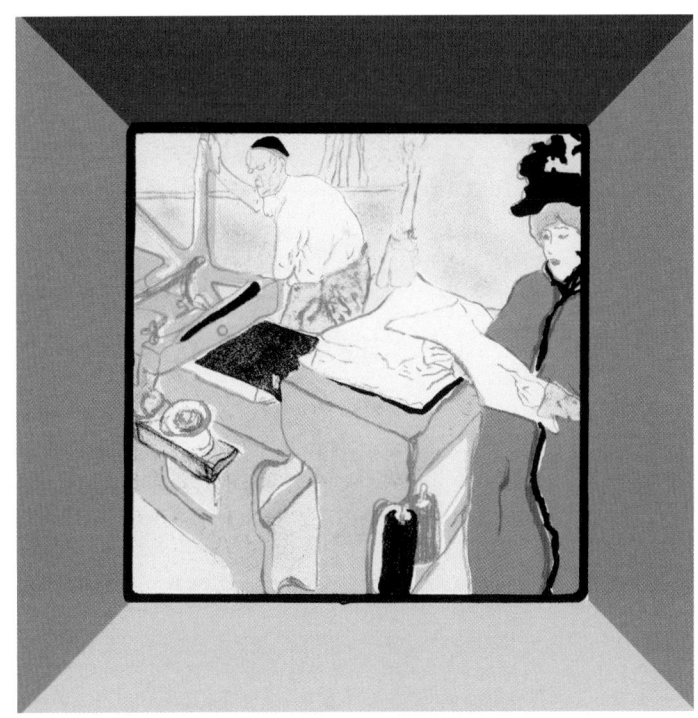

Leon Golub

1922–2004

American painter Leon Golub is known for his large-scale, expressionistic, figurative artworks that draw on classical themes and imagery to address contemporary issues. An outspoken social activist, Golub was politically engaged throughout his career. His work has received critical acclaim and continues to be exhibited at numerous major American and international institutions. In 1951, Golub married fellow artist Nancy Spero.

Gigantomachy I
1965

Gift of Ulrich and Harriet Meyer. The Museum of Modern Art, New York, NY. © 2018 The Nancy Spero and Leon Golub Foundation for the Arts/Licensed by VAGA at Artists Rights Society (ARS), NY. Digital image © The Museum of Modern Art/Licensed by SCALA/Art Resource, NY.

Alfred Mansfeld

1912–2004

Alfred Mansfeld was an Israeli architect best known for designing—in collaboration with interior designer Dora Gad—the Israel Museum, for which he was awarded the Israel Prize in architecture in 1966. Mansfeld was born in St. Petersburg, Russia, and grew up in Germany, training as an architect in Berlin and Paris before immigrating to Haifa in 1935. He designed many residential and public buildings, including the Institute for Jewish Studies at the Hebrew University in Jerusalem and the Hydraulic Institute at the Technion Israel Institute of Technology, where he taught architecture. Mansfeld kept an extensive archive of his preparatory work, including sketches, plans, and maquettes; these are currently housed at the Tel Aviv Museum.

Israel Museum
1965

Photo © The Israel Museum, Jerusalem/Tim Hursley.

Larry Rivers

1923–2002

American painter, sculptor, printmaker, poet, and musician Larry Rivers began his career painting in the style of abstract expressionism but soon developed an iconoclastic figurative style, which many believe served as an inspiration for pop art. Among Rivers's best-known works are his large historical canvases, including *History of Matzoh*, a three-part piece first exhibited at the Jewish Museum in New York. His solo exhibitions include a major retrospective in 2002 at the Corcoran Gallery of Art in Washington, D.C.

The History of the Russian Revolution: From Marx to Mayakovsky
1965

Gift of the Joseph H. Hirshhorn Foundation, 1966. Hirshhorn Museum and Sculpture Garden, Smithsonian Institution. © 2018 Estate of Larry Rivers/Licensed by VAGA at Artists Rights Society (ARS), NY. Photography by Lee Stalsworth, Hirshhorn Museum and Sculpture Garden, Smithsonian Institution.

Unknown Artist

The theologian and social activist Rabbi Abraham Joshua Heschel participated in the civil rights protest march from Selma, Alabama, to Montgomery, led by the Rev. Martin Luther King Jr.

Abraham Joshua Heschel Marching with Martin Luther King Jr. in Selma, Alabama, March 21, 1965
1965

AP Photo.

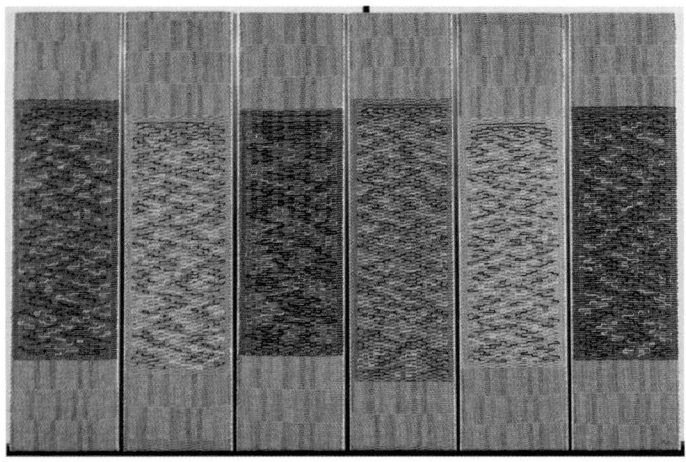

Annelise Albers

1899–1994

Anni Albers is recognized as one of the most influential textile designers of the twentieth century. Born Annelise Fleischmann in Berlin, she attended the renowned Bauhaus school, where she began to experiment with weaving and fiber art, receiving her diploma in 1929. After the Nazis shut down the Bauhaus, Albers and her husband, artist Josef Albers, moved to North Carolina. During their time there, Albers continued designing and weaving with nontraditional materials. In 1949, she became the first textile artist to hold a solo exhibition at the Museum of Modern Art in New York. She later developed an interest in printmaking, her bold designs embodying the abstract, geometric aesthetic characteristic of the midcentury modern movement.

Six Prayers
1965–1966

Gift of the Albert A. List Family, JM 149-72.1-6. The Jewish Museum. © The Josef and Anni Albers Foundation/Artists Rights Society (ARS), New York 2018. Courtesy The Jewish Museum, New York/Art Resource, NY. Photo by John Parnell.

Batia Lichansky

1901–1992

Batia Lichansky was the first woman in Israel to sculpt national monuments and memorials. Born in Malyn, Ukraine, Lichansky immigrated to Palestine in 1910, beginning her studies in 1918 at the Bezalel School of Arts and Crafts in Jerusalem before traveling to Rome, Berlin, and Paris to further her artistic training. In addition to her public sculptures, which move stylistically between realism and expressionism, Lichansky produced more than one hundred busts of prominent cultural figures, including Israeli authors, artists, and political leaders. Her contributions to Israeli art earned her the Dizengoff Prize for painting and sculpture in 1944 and 1957.

Holocaust and Rebirth (Kibbutz Nezer Sereni, Israel)
1965–1968

Photo Avishai Teicher.

George Segal

1924–2000

American sculptor George Segal is best known for his ghostly, white-plaster sculptures of human figures. Born in New York and based largely in New Jersey, Segal studied art at Cooper Union, the Pratt Institute, New York University, and Rutgers University. Although he began his artistic career as a painter, Segal began experimenting with sculpture in the 1960s, using plaster bandages to create molds from live models—often friends and family members—which he then arranged into site-specific tableaux. Segal also produced a number of public monuments cast in bronze, including several powerful Holocaust memorials.

The Costume Party
1965–1972

Al Capp

1909–1979

Creator of the iconic comic strip *Li'l Abner*, Al Capp was one of the most accomplished American cartoonists of the twentieth century. Capp was born Alfred Gerald Caplin in New Haven, Connecticut. After working as a cartoonist for Associated Press, in 1934 Capp published the first strip of *Li'l Abner* through the United Features Syndicate; the comic subsequently ran for a remarkable forty-three years, appearing in more than one thousand newspapers in the United States and internationally. Often satirical and parodic, the subversive politics of Capp's early comics were later complicated by public controversy, entrenching Capp in the popular imagination as a provocative and influential contributor to American visual culture.

"Chickensouperman" from L'il Abner
1966

Nahum Gutman

1898–1980

The Bessarabian-born painter Nahum Gutman moved to Tel Aviv when he was seven. He studied at the Bezalel School of Arts and Crafts and, in the 1920s, in Vienna, Berlin, and Paris. He returned to Palestine in 1926. His oils and watercolors often feature massive, highly stylized individuals. Though influenced by French expressionism, he saw himself as a rebel, turning his back on European traditions of painting and championing a style in harmony with the light and landscapes of Israel.

Mosaic Wall with History of Tel Aviv, Migdal Shalom (Shalom Tower)
1966

imageBROKER/Alamy Stock Photo.

Howard Kanovitz

1929–2009

Born in Fall River, Massachusetts, Howard Kanovitz began his artistic career as a jazz musician. He took up painting in 1949 while studying at the Rhode Island School of Design and the Art Students League's summer school in Woodstock, New York. After moving to New York, Kanovitz initially found success as an abstract expressionist painter in the 1950s and the early 1960s, associating with such contemporaries as Willem de Kooning and Franz Kline. After his father's death, Kanovitz began creating works inspired by family photographs, pioneering the photorealist style that influenced many of his successors. His later works continued in this figurative style.

Lunch at Ratner's
1966

© Estate of Howard Kanovitz. Private collection. Photograph by Alan Wiener.

Elaine Lustig Cohen

1927–2016

Elaine Lustig Cohen was an artist and graphic designer, known for combining European modernism and innovative typography. Lustig Cohen studied painting and art education, working as a teacher for a short period before taking over her late husband's graphic design studio in 1955. Her passion for modern art and Bauhaus principles guided her aesthetic as she designed signs for New York's Seagram building, catalogs and exhibition installations for the Jewish Museum, and more than one hundred book jackets for Meridian Books. A prolific artist, Lustig Cohen continued her practice beyond graphic design, working in paint and collage toward the end of her career. In 2011, she was awarded the American Institute of Graphic Arts (AIGA) Medal for her contributions to American design.

Primary Structures, cover
1966

The Jewish Museum, New York.
© 2016 Elaine Lustig Cohen.

Sorel Etrog

1933–2014

Sorel Etrog was a Romanian-born sculptor, painter, and writer who made important contributions to Canadian arts and culture. After immigrating to Israel in 1950, Etrog studied at the Tel Aviv Art Institute. His early work earned him a scholarship to study at the Brooklyn Museum of Art in 1958; a year later the Solomon R. Guggenheim Museum purchased one of his sculptures. Settling in Toronto in 1963, Etrog went on to have a successful career in Canada and is renowned for his modernist public sculptures in Ontario. He represented Canada in the 1966 Venice Biennale and designed the country's Genie award, which recognizes achievements in Canadian cinema. A multifaceted artist, Etrog also illustrated books and was himself a writer, collaborating with the prominent media theorist Marshall McLuhan in his publication *Spiral*.

Survivors Are Not Heroes
1967

© The Estate of Sorel Etrog. Courtesy Heffel Gallery Ltd.

David Rubinger

1924–2017

David Rubinger was an Israeli photojournalist whose photographs document the history of the state of Israel and have contributed to the development of its collective consciousness. Rubinger was born in Austria, immigrating to Palestine in 1939 and serving in World War II with the British Army's Jewish Brigade. From 1951 on, he dedicated himself to photography, working for the Israeli tabloids *Ha-olam ha-zeh* and *Yedi'ot aharonot* as well as the American magazines *Time* and *Life*. Over the course of his lengthy career, Rubinger shot more than five hundred thousand photos, chronicling the conflicts, leaders, and public celebrations that have defined the history and identity of modern Israel. Rubinger was awarded the Israel Prize in 1997, for his contributions to Israeli visual culture.

Paratroopers at the Western Wall, June 7, 1967
1967

David Rubinger/The LIFE Images Collection/Getty Images.

Tim (Louis Mitelberg)

1919–2002

French political cartoonist and caricaturist Louis Mitelberg was born in Kałuszyn, Poland; he moved to Paris in 1938 to study architecture. After joining the French army, Mitelberg was taken prisoner by the Nazis in 1940, and he escaped the following year. In England, he joined the French Resistance and launched his career as a satirical cartoonist, moving to France after the war. Using the pseudonym Tim, he created cartoons with a satirical bite and pointed wit, taking on such favorite targets as Charles de Gaulle. In 1982, Mitelberg was honored with the International Cartoonist Award.

"Le people juif . . . sur de lui-même et domina-teur . . ." ("The Jews, a People Sure of Itself and Domineering, . . ." Charles de Gaulle)
1967

© Ader Nordmann.

Shlomo Dreizner
b. 1932

An engineer by trade, Solomon (Shlomo) Dreizner joined a secret Zionist organization in Leningrad, his birth city, and was a member of the "Leningrad Nine" when Soviet authorities cracked down on the group. Along with his confreres, Dreizner thought that Jewish culture might flourish in a less repressive Soviet Union. The government thought otherwise. Drcizner was arrested, convicted, and sentenced in a trial whose outcome was a fait accompli. Upon his release, Dreizner promptly returned to activism. He fulfilled his long-deferred dream of emigrating to Israel, arriving just before the Yom Kippur War.

The Liberation of Jerusalem
1968

From Yehude hama'avak: Hatenu'ah hayehudit hale'umit biVerit ha-Mo'atsot, 1967–1989/ed. Raḥel Shnold. 2007. Page 134, fig. 181. © Beit Hatfutsot, the Oster Visual Documentation Center, Tel Aviv, Courtesy of Shlomo Dreizner, Jerusalem. Photo credit: The Dorot Jewish Division, The New York Public Library, Astor, Lenox and Tilden Foundations.

Martha Rosler
b. 1943

Brooklyn-born contemporary artist Martha Rosler explores social and political critique through a variety of media. She has worked with photography, video, performance, and installation, in addition to publishing a number of critical essays that examine issues of gender, violence, and public space within American culture. Among Rosler's best-known works are the photomontages she produced between 1967 and 1972, collectively titled *House Beautiful: Bringing the War Home*, and her 1975 video *Semiotics of the Kitchen*. Rosler has exhibited at some of the most prominent art institutions in the United States and was the recipient of the 2010 Guggenheim Lifetime Achievement Award, as well as many other national and international prizes and awards.

Red Stripe Kitchen
ca. 1967–1972

© Martha Rosler. Courtesy of the artist and Mitchell-Innes & Nash, New York.

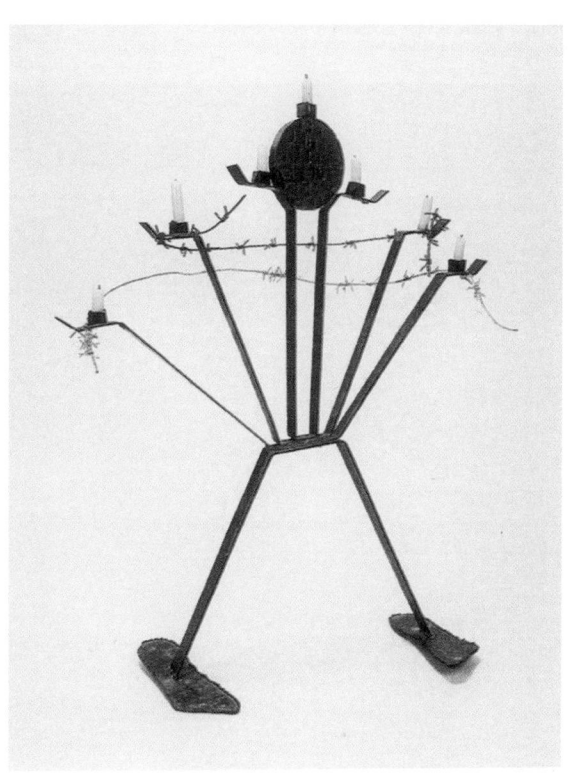

Hersh (Grigory) Inger

1910–1995

Grigory Hersh Inger was a Moscow-born painter and illustrator whose work was invested in the development of modern Yiddish culture. Inger attended art school in Kiev under the instruction of artist Mark Epshteyn. At the time, the school was one of only three Jewish art schools worldwide; it trained a generation of Soviet Jewish artists. Inger was a member of the secular, socialist Jewish cultural organization Kultur-Lige, founded in 1918, which sought to promote and advance Yiddish literature, theater, and culture in Russia. Artists like Inger combined traditional Jewish folklore with contemporary concepts to produce a new style of art that would represent and produce a modern Jewish culture. In addition to painting, Inger illustrated the works of Sholem Aleichem.

Illustration to Sholem Aleichem, "The Haunted Tailor"
1968

SPUTNIK/Alamy Stock Photo.

Boris Penson

b. 1946

Boris Penson, born in Tashkent, Uzbekistan, is an Israeli painter and teacher. Arrested as a teen for "anti-Soviet activity," Penson served several years at hard labor. In 1970, Penson was again arrested as a member of the Leningrad Nine, for allegedly plotting to escape Soviet Russia by hijacking a plane, and condemned to ten years imprisonment. In 1972, during Penson's imprisonment, his work was exhibited at New York's Jewish Museum. Although much of Penson's work was confiscated upon his arrest, a number of his paintings were smuggled out of the Soviet Union by a friend. After his release from prison, Penson immigrated to Israel, where he established a studio and continued painting, participating in several international exhibitions.

The Artist behind Bars (Self-Portrait)
1968

From Yehude hama'avaḳ: Hatenu'ah hayehudit hale'umit bi-Verit haMo'atsot, 1967–1989/ed., Raḥel Shnold. 2007. Page 67, fig. 74. © Boris Penson. Photo credit: The Dorot Jewish Division, the New York Public Library, Astor, Lenox and Tilden Foundations.

Oscar Rabin

1928–2018

Oscar Rabin was a leader of the Lianozovo Group of underground artists near Moscow from the 1950s to the 1970s and one of the organizers of the "bulldozer exhibition" (1974), so called because it was bulldozed by the Soviet authorities. In 1978, Rabine was exiled from the Soviet Union and settled in Paris. His work has been the subject of numerous exhibitions, including a show at the State Russian Museum after the fall of the Soviet Union (St. Petersburg, 1993).

Moscow Evening
1968

Collection Zimmerli Art Museum at Rutgers. Norton and Nancy Dodge Collection of Nonconformist Art from the Soviet Union. © 2018 Artists Rights Society (ARS), New York/ADAGP, Paris. Photo: Jack Abraham.

Gus Schuettler

1933–2012

Born Guenter Schuettler in Kassel, Germany, Gus Schuettler lived in Germany through World War II. He immigrated to the United States and joined the military in the late 1950s. An editor from the army newspaper *Stars and Stripes* saw some of his photographs and immediately hired Schuettler as a staff photographer. Schuettler's photographic style was direct documentary reportage. His career as a military news photographer stretched from the Korean War to the Gulf War. In addition to war images, he captured portraits of some of the best-known personalities of his time.

Daniel Cohn-Bendit Jumping the Police Barricade
1968

Gus Schuettler, © 1968, 2018 Stars and Stripes, All rights reserved.

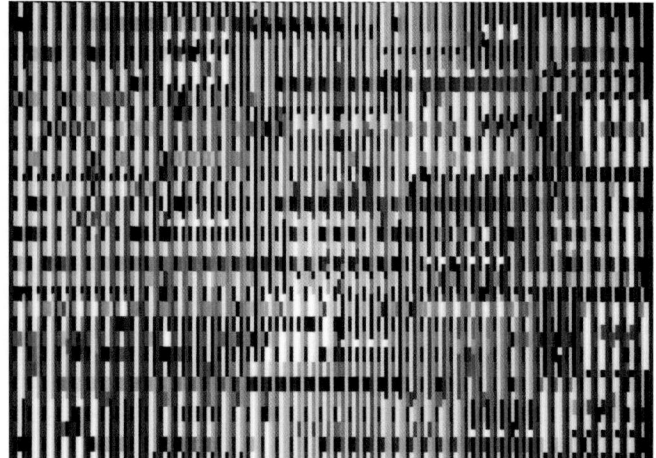

Yaacov Agam

b. 1928

Yaacov Agam is a Paris-based artist, renowned for his interactive, kinetic artworks. Born Yaacov Gipstein in Rishon le-Tsion, Agam studied at the Bezalel School of Arts and Crafts in Jerusalem and subsequently trained in Zurich and Paris. In the mid-1950s, Agam began exhibiting his work, which combined sculpture and painting to create vibrant, abstract, geometric compositions that incorporate movement and encourage viewer participation. In his installations, the perception of each piece changes as the viewer moves around it. Agam has created a number of public artworks in Israel as well as the United States and has exhibited his work across the globe.

Double Metamorphosis III (Counterpoint and Sequence)
1968–1969

AM1976-920. Musee National d'Art Moderne. © 2018 Artists Rights Society (ARS), New York/ADAGP, Paris. Digital image © CNAC/MNAM/Dist. RMN-Grand Palais/Art Resource, NY.

Raffi Lavie

1937–2007

Raffi Lavie played a prominent role in shaping avant-garde art in Israel. A founder of the 10+ group in 1965, he was a central figure in the "want of matter" school, promoting collage and the use of inexpensive materials such as plywood. Many of his paintings are characterized by the erasure of images with scribbles, carvings, and broad strokes of color. Lavie's work has been featured in more than eighty solo exhibitions and was the subject of a special retrospective at the fifty-third Venice Biennale (2009).

Untitled
1969

The Israel Museum, Jerusalem, Israel/Gift of Shaya Yariv, Gordon Gallery, Tel Aviv/Bridgeman Images.

Emanuele Luzzati

1921–2007

Emanuele Luzzati was an award-winning Italian stage designer, illustrator, and animator. Over the course of his prolific career, Luzzati created more than four hundred stage designs, as well as cartoons, ceramics, posters, and even interior decorations for passenger ships. Luzzati was born in Genoa, where he lived until his teens when his family left Italy for Switzerland under the enforcement of Mussolini's antisemitic racial laws. He studied at the École des Beaux-Arts in Lausanne, later returning to Italy in 1947 to pursue a career in theater design. Luzzati often collaborated with other artists, creating colorful, whimsical, fantastical set designs for both classical and contemporary avant-garde productions. He was equally celebrated for his illustrations, having worked on editions of *Pinocchio*, *Alice in Wonderland*, *Peter Pan*, and Voltaire's *Candide*, among others. In 2001, his legacy was honored with the inauguration of the Luzzati Museum in his hometown of Genoa.

Golem, Teatro La Pergola, Firenze
1969

© Nugae srl—Luzzati Museum in Porta Siberia, Genoa.

Joshua Neustein

b. 1940

Georgette Batlle

1940–2009

Joshua Neustein and Georgette Batlle collaborated on several conceptual artworks in the 1960s and 1970s. Neustein, born in Poland, and Batlle, born in Brooklyn, both attended New York's Pratt Institute of Art. While living in Israel between 1964 and 1979, Neustein exerted a major influence on the development of contemporary art in that country, creating a number of installations and land art pieces. Neustein and Batlle cocreated the 1969 installation *Boots*, which featured seventeen thousand pairs of army boots piled in the Artists' House gallery in Jerusalem. The following year, the two also collaborated on the *Jerusalem River Project*, along with artist Gerard Marx, creating a

site-specific installation in which the sounds of a river were played from speakers installed in a valley within the Abu Tor neighborhood of Jerusalem. Neustein moved back to New York in 1979, and Batlle spent the rest of her career in Israel.

Boots, Gallery House, Jerusalem
1969

© Joshua Neustein with Gerry Marx and Georgette Batlle.

Lea Nikel

1918–2005

Lea Nikel (b. Nikelsberg) was a Ukrainian-born artist who grew up in Tel Aviv. Nikel began studying painting in her midteens with several influential avant-garde Israeli artists. She continued her education in Paris, where she lived and worked from 1950 to 1961; she later spent several years in New York and Rome, moving to Israel for good in 1977. Nikel drew inspiration from the artistic atmosphere of Paris, consistently exploring a vibrant aesthetic. She represented Israel in the 1964 Venice Biennale and received the Israel Prize in painting in 1995. In 1997, she was named a Chevalier of Arts and Letters by the French Minister of Culture.

Untitled
1969

The Israel Museum, Jerusalem, Israel/Purchase Riklis Fund/ Bridgeman Images.

Dan Reisinger

1934–2019

Dan Reisinger was one of Israel's most prominent graphic artists and designers. Reisinger was born into an artistic family in Kanjiža, Yugoslavia. During World War II, he was hidden by a Serbian family; he lost most of his family to the Holocaust. After the war, Reisinger immigrated with his mother and stepfather to Israel, where he began working as a house painter. He soon enrolled at the Bezalel School of Arts and Crafts to study painting, sculpture, and poster design and later at the Central School of Art and Design in London. With a career working abroad, Reisinger also opened his own design studio in Tel Aviv in 1967 and quickly began designing in a variety of media for advertising and print. He taught at the Bezalel School and the University of Haifa. In 1998, he was awarded the Israel Prize, the first graphic designer to receive the prestigious award.

"Let My People Go" poster
1969

© Dan Reisinger.

Garry Winogrand

1928–1984

A painter turned photographer, Garry Winogrand is known for street photography and other images documenting American life. He published four books of his photographs, including *The Animals* (1969) and *Women Are Beautiful* (1975). Winogrand received three Guggenheim Fellowship Awards and a National Endowment of the Arts Award. He taught photography courses at the University of Texas at Austin and at the Art Institute of Chicago. When he died, he left more than 2,500 undeveloped rolls of film. A fraction of these images appeared in the posthumous exhibition *Winogrand, Figments from the Real World* at the Museum of Modern Art in 1988.

New York City, Three Women
1969

© The Estate of Garry Winogrand, courtesy Fraenkel Gallery, San Francisco. Digital image © Collection Center for Creative Photography, The University of Arizona.

Audrey Flack

b. 1931

Born in New York, multidisciplinary artist Audrey Flack is best known for photorealistic paintings that closely replicate the quality of photographic images. After studying at Cooper Union, Yale, New York University's Institute of Fine Arts, and the Art Students League in the 1950s, Flack moved from an abstract expressionist style toward the figurative painting for which she is known today. This evolution permitted her better to communicate her social and political commentary. In the early 1980s, Flack began working primarily in sculpture, employing symbolic and mythological imagery to embody a feminist message. A painter of remarkable technical proficiency, Flack has had numerous solo exhibitions, and, since the 1960s, her work has been collected by some of the foremost national art museums.

Farb Family Portrait
1969–1970

Rose Art Museum, Brandeis University, Waltham. © Audrey Flack. Courtesy Rose Art Museum, Brandeis University, Riverside Museum Collection.

Dorothy Bohm

b. 1924

British photographer Dorothy Bohm (b. Israelit) was born in East Prussia to a Lithuanian Jewish family. In 1939 her parents sent her to England, where she studied photography at the Manchester College of Technology. She married Louis Bohm in 1945, opened her own portrait studio in 1946, and settled in North London in 1956. In the 1960s, Bohm turned from studio to street photography, visiting the Soviet Union to capture life in Moscow and Leningrad. In 1971, she cofounded the Photographers' Gallery, the first gallery in Britain devoted solely to photography. Bohm later founded the Focus Gallery for Photography. She was recognized for her significant contributions to British photographic history with her appointment as Honorary Fellow of the Royal Photographic Society in 2009.

Latina, Southern Italy
1960s

© Dorothy Bohm Archive.

Saul Borisov

1912–1991

Saul Borisov was a textile artist who lived and worked in Mexico. Born Saul Pupkin in Borisov, near Minsk, the artist immigrated in 1923 to New York, where he studied painting at the Cooper Union School of Art. After working in the Federal Art Project arm of the Work Projects Administration, Borisov served in the army during World War II and moved to Mexico City in 1948. It was there that Borisov discovered weaving, first learning traditional methods and practices before adopting a more experimental and improvisational approach. Borisov made his own dyes, using vibrant colors to create abstract shapes and asymmetrical compositions in intricate representational tapestries.

Adam and Eve
ca. 1960s

© Estate of Saul Borisov.

Samuel Bak

b. 1933

Painter Samuel Bak was born in Vilna and went into
hiding with his parents during World War II; only he
and his mother survived. When he immigrated to
Israel in 1948, he enrolled at the Bezalel School of Arts
and Crafts. Later he lived in Paris and studied at the
École des Beaux-Arts. Many of Bak's paintings focus
on commemoration and memory of the Holocaust, and
he is particularly well known for his surrealistic still
lifes. Bak lives in Massachusetts.

Houses in an Imaginary Landscape
1970

© Samuel Bak. Courtesy of Stern Gallery Tel-Aviv. Photo by
Ran Erde.

Micha Bar-Am

b. 1930

Micha Bar-Am is a photojournalist who documented
the Israeli army throughout the 1950s and 1960s and
helped found New York's International Center of
Photography in 1974. The Berlin-born photographer
immigrated to Palestine in 1936, serving in the army
in his late teens. Bar-Am's photographic career began
in 1957, when he was hired as a staff photographer at
Bama Hana, an Israeli army magazine. During his
time with the magazine, Bar-Am met photojournalist
Cornell Capa, who introduced him to Magnum
Photos, a photography collective of which Bar-Am
became an active member. In 1968, Bar-Am became a
correspondent for the *New York Times*, documenting
the Israeli–Palestinian conflict. Subsequently, he
worked as a curator for the Tel Aviv Art Museum from
1977 to 1992.

Golda Meir
1970

© Micha Bar Am/Magnum Photos.

Judy Chicago

b. 1939

American painter and sculptor Judy Chicago (b. Cohen, later Gerowitz) is a pioneer of feminist art and art education. Beginning in the early 1970s, she was instrumental in establishing programs for women at California State University–Fresno and the California Institute of the Arts. Her collaborative work *The Dinner Party: A Symbol of Our Heritage* (1974–1979) is regarded as a foundational work of feminist art. The mixed-media *Holocaust Project: From Darkness to Light* resulted from an eight-year collaboration with her husband, photographer Donald Woodman. Other collaborative projects include *The Birth Project* (1980), images of birth in needlepoint, and *Resolutions: A Stitch in Time* (1994), a series of painted and needlework images.

Exhibition Announcement, Jack Glenn Gallery, *Artforum, October 1970*

1970

Moses Feigin

1904–2008

Moses Feigin was a painter who worked in the Soviet Union through much of the twentieth century. Feigin was born in Warsaw and studied at the VKhUTEMAS art school from 1921 to 1928. Although he was trained in academic drawing and painting, he often experimented with abstract forms and vibrant colors as well as with innovative mixed-media works combining paint and collage. Because such avant-garde art was banned in the Soviet Union, Feigin earned a living producing socialist realist work while privately exploring his own forms of expression. This personal work found an audience abroad, and he exhibited frequently in Europe and North America from 1968 on. Feigin's works are now represented in the collections of several Russian museums and have been the subject of retrospective exhibitions in Russia, Western Europe, and the United States.

Beauty

1970

Leon Levinstein

1910–1988

Leon Levinstein was among a group of midcentury New York street photographers who found inspiration in their urban environment. Born in Buckhannon, West Virginia, Levinstein settled in New York after his military service during World War II and began working as an art director in advertising while practicing photography in his free time. Levinstein's candid shots capture subjects who are often unseen or overlooked, those relegated to the fringes of society. Although he rarely took on professional photographic assignments—instead earning a living as a graphic designer—Levinstein found recognition as a photographer, publishing extensively in magazines and exhibiting frequently at the Museum of Modern Art.

Handball Players, Houston Street, NY
1970

© Howard Greenberg Gallery, New York.

Unknown Artist

On December 7, 1970, German Chancellor Willy Brandt traveled to Poland on the occasion of the signing of the Treaty of Warsaw between West Germany and the People's Republic of Poland. During a visit to a monument to the Warsaw ghetto uprising, Brandt surprisingly—and apparently spontaneously—knelt before the monument after laying a wreath. Brandt remained silently in the kneeling position for half a minute or so. The gesture became known as the "Warsaw Genuflection," a sincere statement of both humility and penance toward those killed in the ghetto. About his actions, Brandt later remarked: "Under the weight of recent history, I did what people do when words fail them. In this way I commemorated millions of murdered people."

West German Chancellor Willy Brandt Kneels in Front of the Jewish Heroes Monument Paying Tribute to Jews Killed by the Nazis during the 1943 Uprising in the Warsaw Ghetto, December 7, 1970
1970

Bettmann/Getty Images.

Dmitry Borisovitch Lion
1925-1993

Dmitry Borisovitch Lion was a Russian-born graphic artist and a member of the postwar Soviet nonconformist art movement that rejected the restrictions of socialist realism. Lion, who was born in Kaluga, attended the School of Art in Moscow and later the Moscow Institute of Architecture. After completing his art education, Lion fought in the Red Army between 1943 and 1952, after which he was able to pursue his artistic career, beginning as a graphic artist and teacher in 1953. In 1964, Lion founded a private art academy and taught while continuing his own work. Lion is recognized for his large-scale triptych of Janusz Korczak as well as a number of abstract drawings. His works have been exhibited at the Russian Museum in St. Petersburg and the Pushkin Museum of Fine Arts in Moscow.

Portrait of a Man
1971

© 2018 Artists Rights Society (ARS), New York/UPRAVIS, Moscow. Photo Courtesy Koller Zurich.

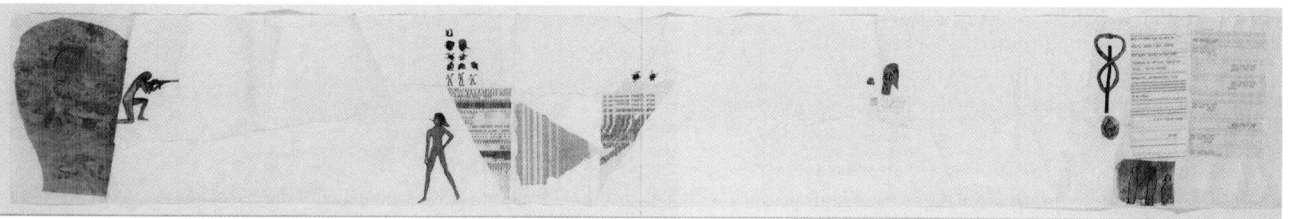

Nancy Spero
1926-2009

Nancy Spero was an important figure in the American feminist art movements of the twentieth century. Spero was born in Ohio and studied at the School of the Art Institute of Chicago and the École des Beaux-Arts in Paris. She was a socially and politically conscious artist whose work addresses issues of power, violence, and sexism. Much of her work focuses on the experiences of women, both historical and contemporary, employing mythological and pictographic imagery to explore issues of gender and sexuality. Spero was a member of Women Artists in Revolution and a founding member of A.I.R. Gallery, a cooperative gallery for women artists established in 1972.

Codex Artaud VII
1971

Museo Nacional Centro de Arte Reina Sofia. © 2018 The Nancy Spero and Leon Golub Foundation for the Arts/ Licensed by VAGA at Artists Rights Society (ARS), NY.

Eric Bulatov

b. 1933

Erik Bulatov is among the foremost contemporary
Russian artists. Bulatov, often considered a sociopoliti-
cal artist, spent the majority of his life in Moscow,
where he studied painting from 1952 to 1958 at the
city's Surikov Art Institute. After the collapse of the
Soviet Union in 1991, Bulatov immigrated to Paris,
and his art became more critically engaged. His
current work draws heavily on Soviet propaganda,
deploying its symbols and slogans against the normalization of aggressive ideology he experienced during
his life in the Soviet Union. Bulatov's work was
featured in the 1977 Venice Biennale.

Red Horizon
1971–2000

Collection of Neil K. Rector. © 2018 Artists Rights Society
(ARS), New York/ADAGP, Paris.

André François

1915–2005

André François was a graphic artist who earned an
international reputation as a cartoonist, poster
designer, and illustrator of children's books. François
was born in Hungary as André Farkas and attended
the Academy of Fine Arts in Budapest from 1932 to
1933. In 1934, François moved to Paris to study at the
atelier of Adolphe Cassandre, a renowned poster artist.
By the late 1940s, François had illustrated several
children's books and was a regular contributor to *The
New Yorker* and *Punch* magazines. He also designed
advertisements for print and television and stage sets
for theatrical productions. For his myriad artistic
achievements, François was named a Chevalier of the
Legion of Honor in France and received an honorary
doctorate from the University of London.

Sheep Readers, *Le nouvel observateur*, *cover*
1972

Collection Stedelijk Museum Amsterdam.

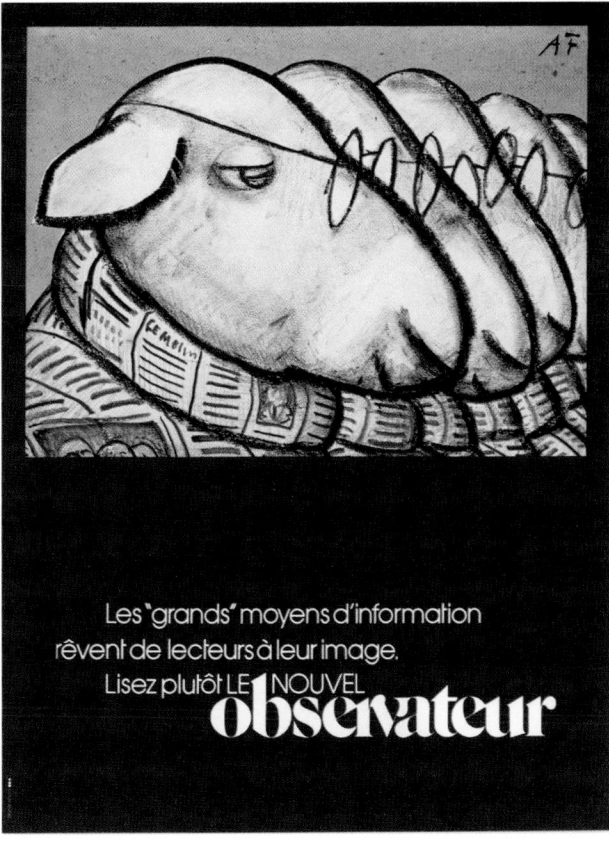

Shmuel Katz

1926–2010

Shmuel Katz was an Israeli illustrator and caricaturist whose work ranged from military sketches to children's book illustrations. Born in Vienna, Katz spent the majority of World War II in hiding with his sister in Hungary. In 1946, Katz decided to immigrate to Palestine, but British authorities intercepted the ship he was on; its passengers were deported to a displaced persons camp in Cyprus. While in Cyprus, Katz made sketches documenting his experiences and held his first exhibition. He arrived in Palestine in 1947 and helped found Kibbutz Ga'aton, where he lived and worked, producing illustrations and caricatures that were widely published in Israel, until his death.

***Leah Goldberg,* Dira le-haskir,** *cover*
1972

Sifriat Poalim.

Vadim Sidur

1924–1986

Vadim Sidur was a Russian illustrator and sculptor, known for his geometric, interlocking, anthropomorphic stone and metal sculptures. His work often reflected the pain and trauma of war as expressed through the human body, in contrast to prevailing Soviet ideologies that glorified military service. Sidur himself was badly injured while serving in the Red Army during World War II and underwent extensive facial reconstruction. After the war, Sidur studied sculpture in Moscow, creating avant-garde, nonconformist pieces that were prohibited from public display within the Soviet Union. Despite the censorship of his art at home, Sidur made a career on private commissions outside the Soviet Union, including several Holocaust monuments. Today, the Vadim Sidur Museum in Moscow, established in 1989, preserves and displays his artwork.

The Formula of Grief
1972

www.panoramio.com. Anna Pronenko.

Yigael Tumarkin

b. 1933

Israeli artist Yigael Tumarkin was born in Dresden and immigrated to Palestine with his family as an infant. In the early 1950s, he returned to Germany, where he designed sets for Bertolt Brecht and the Berliner Ensemble as well as other theater companies. Tumarkin also created sculptures in iron and bronze, often incorporating parts of weapons and castings of human limbs. Sometimes called the enfant terrible of the Israeli art world, Tumarkin is known for both his provocative art and outspoken public persona. In 2004, he was awarded the Israel Prize for sculpture.

Jordan Valley Memorial Monument
1972

Eddie Gerald/Alamy Stock Photo.

R. B. Kitaj

1932–2007

American-born R. B. Kitaj spent the most influential years of his painting career in England, where he settled in 1958. He was a member of a group of artists at the Royal College of Art in London that promoted pop art. Kitaj was controversial for his outspokenness in favor of figurative art. Among his most important exhibitions was a Tate Gallery retrospective in 1994. He was elected to the Royal Academy in 1991, the first American to win this honor in almost a century. In 1995, he received the Golden Lion at the Venice Biennale.

The Autumn of Central Paris (After Walter Benjamin)
1972–1973

Collection Mrs. Susan Lloyd, New York. © R. B. Kitaj Estate.

Alfred Bernheim

1885–1974

Alfred Bernheim specialized in architectural and portrait photography. Bernheim was born and raised in Tiengen, Germany, later attending art school in Pforzheim and studying under the Bauhaus cinematographer Walter Hege. With the rise of Nazism in Germany, in 1934 Bernheim left Europe and immigrated to Jerusalem, where he opened a photography studio. In Israel, Bernheim pursued a successful career as a professional photographer. He became the official photographer for the architect Erich Mendelsohn, who designed several famous buildings in Israel, and he made portraits of prominent Jewish cultural figures, including Israeli president Chaim Weizmann and philosopher Hannah Arendt. Bernheim was recognized as a master photographer; his images have been exhibited at both the Israel Museum and the Tel Aviv Museum of Art.

Portrait of Hannah Arendt
Undated

Bridgeman Images.

Moshe Gross

1952–2018

Moshe Gross was an Israeli photographer who documented the evolution of the country's built environment throughout the second half of the twentieth century. Primarily a technical and industrial photographer, Gross captured images of Israel's myriad infrastructural developments, including petrochemical plants and foundries. His graphic black-and-white photos are as much artistic compositions as documentary images. His photographs have been prominently featured in several Israeli exhibitions, including the 2007 show *Haifa in the Eye of the Camera* at the Haifa City Museum. Gross was the owner of the Keren-Or photography studio in Haifa.

Laying the Pipes of the National Water Carrier from the Sea of Galilee to the Negev
Undated

Private collection. © Estate of Moshe Gross.

Adam Muszka

1914–2005

Adam Muszka was a Polish-born painter raised in the town of Piotrków. During World War II, Muszka took refuge in Tashkent, Uzbekistan, before returning to Poland to find much of his former home in ruins. Muszka relocated to Paris, where he painted nostalgic scenes of Jewish life in Poland and also produced several murals in Piotrków and Łódź during his career. Profoundly influenced by painters Marc Chagall and Paul Cézanne, Muszka painted his scenes of Jewish life using colorful, flat, geometric compositions.

Leaving Cheder
Undated

© Estate of Adam Muszka. Photo Credit: Ben Uri Gallery, The London Jewish Museum of Art/Bridgeman Images.

Leonardo Nierman

b. 1932

Leonardo Nierman is a painter and sculptor who has significantly contributed to the development of modern art in Mexico. Nierman was born in Mexico City and took an interest in the arts, including music, from a young age. In 1951, he graduated with a degree in physics and mathematics from the National Autonomous University of Mexico, later combining his interest in science with his passion for artistic expression. Nierman's abstract paintings and sculptures draw inspiration from cosmic phenomena, combining vibrant colors and sinuous forms into striking, dynamic compositions. Nierman has received numerous awards internationally for his contributions to contemporary Mexican art.

Solar Flame
Undated

Private collection/Photo © Christie's Images/Bridgeman Images.

Anna Ticho

1894–1980

Anna Ticho was an Israeli artist who captured the urban and natural landscape of Jerusalem over the course of seven decades. Born in Brno, Moravia, Ticho moved as a teenager to Vienna, where she began her artistic studies. In 1912, she married her cousin, an ophthalmologist named Abraham Albert Ticho; the couple immigrated to Palestine the same year, settling in Jerusalem. Ticho's precise, detailed artwork captures the intricate, natural textures of the hills surrounding Jerusalem. Among her contributions to the arts and culture of Israel was the Bezalel School of Arts and Crafts in Jerusalem, a major hub for Israeli artists, which she cofounded. She also donated her home and artwork to the Israel Museum. In 1980, Ticho was awarded the Israel Prize for her lifelong dedication to the arts in Israel.

Landscape of Jerusalem
Undated

Private collection. Courtesy Sotheby's.

DIVERSE DIASPORAS (1946-1973)

Even as the United States and Israel became the dominant centers of Jewish life in the postwar period, other diasporas continued to thrive and grow. While the age-old centers of Arabic-speaking Jewry declined, Jews in Canada, South Africa, Australia, and Argentina transformed themselves from largely immigrant societies into more settled communities that sought to preserve their Jewish roots as they gained acceptance and cultural prominence in their new homes.

Despite obvious differences among these changing diasporas, their Jewish experiences reflected certain points in common. Unlike the battered Jewish communities of Europe, many Jews here were recent arrivals. Especially in South Africa and Argentina, many of the first Jewish immigrants settled on lonely frontiers in the Pampas or the Veldt. Unlike American Jewry, Jews in these changing diasporas lived not in a "melting pot" but in the middle of wider ethnic rivalries that in turn fostered, rather than discouraged, cultural diversity.

Non-Jewish ethnic rivalries—between French and English speakers in Canada, English and Afrikaans speakers in South Africa—fostered stronger Jewish identities in both societies. But unlike Canada, South African Jews had to deal with the moral dilemmas of apartheid. Like their Canadian cousins, South African Jews enjoyed a degree of acceptance that had eluded them before the war, especially from the Afrikaners. But that acceptance came at a high moral price that had a major impact on South African Jewish culture and politics.

In Argentina, one writer in particular—Alberto Gerchunoff—symbolized the promise of Jewish integration into Argentine society. But after World War II, Gerchunoff himself tempered his optimism in the face of a new generation of Jewish writers who explored the limits of assimilation for an urbanizing and acculturating Jewish community. During this period, Argentina continued to be a major center of Yiddish culture and publishing. But for the first time in centuries, Spanish again emerged as a significant vehicle of Jewish cultural creativity in a nation that both embraced its Jewish minority and reminded them that on a basic level—reinforced by religion—they would always remain "different."

In these formative postwar years, Jews in Latin America did not cultivate rabbinic leadership, foster theological debate, or advance Judaic scholarship. But the land where Jorge Luis Borges and magic realism were born did inspire a wide and eclectic array of Jewish writing, a literature only one step removed from the shtetl but already inhabiting what Isaac Goldemberg called the seven circles of Jewish hell. Here, Marx rubs shoulders with Jeremiah, Jesus with Freud, and Kafka—Borges's favorite writer—"laughs like crazy." Heretofore marginalized, these plays, novels, short stories, poems, and memoirs from across the Latin American continent now join the transnational Jewish conversation for the first time.

Leybl Shiter

What Is a Pinkes?
1951

Told by Leybl Shiter and Recorded by B. Baler

PINKES KOVEL (KOWEL)

I remember hearing the word *pinkes* several times when I was a small child.

For instance, when an unusual event took place in town, the adults, while commenting among themselves on the events, used to say: "Such a terrible story should be recorded in the pinkes!" On other occasions when things happened that weren't quite as unheard of, but were nevertheless curious, even the women used to finish their accounts with: "It was something to write down in the pinkes!"

But what this thing called a pinkes was, what it looked like, and where it was to be found, this pinkes which was mentioned in tones of such respect, as though it were something holy—I had no idea, and even in my imagination I couldn't picture it.

More and more I was driven by the desire to see the pinkes with my own eyes and touch it with my own hands. Good fortune was mine, and my wish was fulfilled. This is how it happened.

The pinkes in our town, and probably in other towns as well, was kept by the burial society (which was called "The Society of the Concerned" in Kovel). When a new trustee was chosen for the society—on Simkhes Toyre, as was done in other small towns—the pinkes was given to him to hold.

One year my father, may he rest in peace, wanted to become the trustee of the society. My father Mikhl Zaygermakher was an excellent candidate. Why not? Of course! However, there was a hitch: my father couldn't become the trustee, because his name was Mikhl.

Why did the name Mikhl bar him from being trustee of the Society of the Concerned? It was a custom in our town—and no doubt it was thus recorded in the pinkes itself—that any Jew whose name began with an *M* was forbidden to occupy the trusteeship, because the word for "corpse," *mes,* begins with an *m*.

What could my father do to circumvent this custom? It wasn't even the trusteeship itself that drew my father,

but the desire to show the likes of Reb Yankev Fudl and Reb Osher Shvarts, that this year he, Mikhl Shiter, a congregant of the "municipal" study house, would be the trustee, instead of one of the congregants of the Great Synagogue.

Finally something was hit upon. I imagine there was a quiet meeting of congregants from the study house, at which it was decided to nominate Reb Shimen Zokner as trustee. He was a candidate with all the proper credentials for the post. However, being the owner and operator of a tannery and a mill, he had no time to fulfill the trustee's duties. It was arranged that Shimen Zokner would turn over actual responsibility to my father.

On Simkhes Toyre Reb Shimen Zokner was led from the study house to his home with great fanfare, where the crowd drank hot whiskey with honey and ate dumplings also fried with honey, and everyone had a wonderful time.

Shortly after the holiday, the whole town knew that my father was the real head of the society. It was as though my father were Shimen's secretary—no one complained about it.

As soon as the previous trustee handed over the pinkes and the other belongings of the society to Shimen Zokner, he immediately brought everything to our house, where I finally had an opportunity to see the pinkes.

My father put the pinkes in a safe place in our store. One day, when no one was around, I approached the closet where it lay, my steps slow and my heart pounding, opened the doors and looked at it. I saw a large, old book, the size of a volume of the Talmud, with ribbed, leather covers torn in the corners. Out of them peeked the tops of yellowed, inscribed pieces of paper.

I grew terrified just looking at it. I myself don't know why I was so afraid, but at that moment images flew into my mind of awesome, horrifying events that had taken place in our town, events I had been told about and which were certainly recorded in the pinkes. The book seemed especially holy to me, and I was afraid even to touch it.

Yet I still didn't know what the book was needed for, or precisely what it contained. My childish mind burned with the desire to find out the secret. [. . .]

I decided to ask my teacher. He used to come to our house to tutor me, since I attended gymnasium and couldn't go to kheyder. The teacher whom my parents hired was Reb Artshe Karliner, a very fine scholar but, he should forgive me for saying so, a man with an awful temper.

How could I ask him? I had to figure out the right way to approach the matter, since he was always angry and grouchy. If one dared to try to speak to him of a matter that had nothing to do with study, one's life was in danger.

I set upon a plan: I knew that he was dearly fond of a hot glass of tea. Once, when he came to tutor me and my mother was out of the house, I stood up and said, "Rebe, would you like me to pour you a glass of tea?"

"Certainly, bring me a glass of tea. But be careful not to burn yourself!" he warned. With trembling hands, I brought him the tea, and carefully asked him, "Rebe, what is a pinkes? What's written in it?"

The teacher, without raising his eyes from the glass, above which he was bent over, holding it in both hands and sipping from it with great pleasure, emitting a loud "Aaaaaah" after each sip, answered me with measured words in his Lithuanian dialect:

"A pinkes, Leybele, is a book in which all of the unusual events and occurrences that take place in a town are recorded, both good things and, God forbid, not such good things." He continued slowly, sipping after each phrase: "The good things are recorded, so that the generations that follow us will learn to behave well and will also perform good deeds. The bad things that happen, may we be spared, are recorded so that people may know not to do them, and also so that the One Above will pity us and see that no evil harms us in the future. Amen."

Now, in connection with the publication of the *Pinkes Kovel,* I remembered this episode from my childhood. I remembered the old pinkes of our town, which I saw in my parents' house, and which they so carefully and lovingly guarded. I am sure that we, the people of Kovel, wherever we may find ourselves, will know how to judge the value of this pinkes which we have published. We will preserve it as a dear and holy possession, with the same importance and even holiness with which the Jews of Kovel preserved through so many generations the pinkes of our town.

For, to our immense loss and sorrow, this *Pinkes Kovel* is the only remnant that remains of our beloved hometown.

NOTE

[The word *pinkes* means register, and it refers to the Jewish communal record kept in East European communities before World War II. It was a court register, as well as a record of communal bylaws, of wills, and of expenditures of charitable organizations.—Eds.]

Translated by Jack Kugelmass and Jonathan Boyarin.

Pinkes Varshe (The Chronicle of Warsaw)

A Memorial and a Witness
1955

Pinkes Varshe is a memorial erected by the immigrants from Warsaw in Argentina in honor of those generations of Warsaw Jews who, with their lives and struggles, with their heroism and spirituality, earned an honored place in Jewish history. They earned it also in the history of the Polish nation and in the history of Polish Jewish intellectual creativity. It is a memorial to lives cut short by evil and commemorates the struggle and creativity of the hundreds of thousands of Warsaw Jews who were victims of malignant German rule. Warsaw's Jews were killed in every kind of unnatural death in the concentration and deportation camps, in the crematoria of Majdanek, Auschwitz, and Treblinka. They perished inside synagogues set on fire, in shootings at mass graves dug by the victims themselves, on the gallows erected by the victims themselves. Their wives, their old people, and their young children perished with them.

Pinkes Varshe is a memorial to the demand that their life and creativity live on. The Jews of Warsaw went to their deaths with this demand on their lips as if it were a pious *Shema Yisroel* [Hear, O Israel]. It was a testament bequeathed to us surviving Warsaw Jews, wherever we may be. For that reason, this volume aims to be the record, or at least the beginning of a record, of the rich heritage they have left us. It is a heritage formed by life and struggle over generations and centuries in the Polish capital, which in the last century and a half was also the capital of Jewish social and cultural life in Poland. This volume associates us, the Warsaw Jews in Argentina, with the social and cultural activity of the Jews of Warsaw in the new Poland. We believe this faithfully carries out the testament of the murdered Polish Jews. For generations, Jewish social and cultural life in Poland was based on the struggle and aspirations of the Polish Jewish masses for a life of justice and freedom, for the liberation of labor and the free expression of national identity. Today, when that struggle has been won and those aspirations are a reality, the Jews of Poland, including the Jews of Warsaw, are taking part in the judicial and social reconstruction of the country which had always inspired them and was always their ultimate goal.

In order for *Pinkes Varshe* truly to be what it has undertaken to be—a memorial, a family tree, and an identity card for the Jews of Warsaw—it was necessary to do what the *pinkeysim* of yore, the registers of the old Jewish communities and their charitable and artisans' associations used to do: in addition to listing their rules and regulations, they would record the most significant events of their lifetimes. We too have to record what distinguishes Warsaw and the Jews of Warsaw. The editors and compilers have tried to do this through a collection of concise recollections and texts illustrating the history and way of life of Warsaw Jewry.

The publishers and compilers of the *Pinkes* know that this volume cannot provide the total picture of the rich and varied Jewish life of Warsaw in all its social and political tendencies and movements. Therefore it is possible that this volume will be only the first in a series of volumes providing historic and descriptive material about Warsaw in the past and in the present.

Nevertheless, we are convinced that even the present volume of *Pinkes Varshe* fulfills the profound desire of the Jews from Warsaw [in Argentina] to erect a memorial to the cruelly exterminated Jews of Warsaw and to the heroic Ghetto fighters. It carries out their anguished wish, on the eve of their horrible deaths, that their rich spiritual heritage should not perish with them. It responds to their hope that the golden chain of their creativity has not been broken, and that the new, more fortunate generations will move forward in the spirit of their aspirations to greater human happiness and to peace in the world.

Translated by Solon Beinfeld.

Amnon Netser

1934–2008

Born in Rasht, Iran, Amnon Netser arrived in 1950 in Israel, where he studied Middle Eastern and international affairs at the Hebrew University. He devoted his career to journalism and to uncovering and recording the literature and history of Persian Jewry. In 1958, he commenced broadcasting daily Persian-language broadcasts for the Voice of Israel radio station. He

was professor of Persian language and literature at the Hebrew University of Jerusalem until his death. His anthology of Persian songs was directed to non-Jewish Persian-speaking audiences, and the texts were transcribed into Perso-Arabic script.

Anthology of Persian Songs from the Creations of Iranian Jewry
1973

The Cultural Importance of the Iranian and Jewish Peoples

The acquaintance between the Iranian and Jewish peoples began approximately 2,500 years ago. Historical and linguistic evidence supporting this acquaintance is found in the Scriptures, particularly in the books of Ezra, Nehemiah, Esther, Daniel, and Chronicles. The names of the Iranian kings Cyrus, Darius, Xerxes, and Ardashir; Iranian titles such as satrap; words such as *dat* ("law, religion"), *gnazim* ("treasury"), *pardes* ("garden"); and many other titles and words of Iranian origin are attested in Scripture.

This acquaintance continued over time through mutual religious and cultural encounters and works, to the extent that today it is not possible to become completely familiar with the Iranian and Jewish cultures without investigating and delving into the religious and cultural works of the two peoples. The Talmud and other Jewish religious books on the one hand, and the Zoroastrian books such as *Dēnkard*, *Shkand-Gumānīg Wizār*, and *Mēnōg-ī Khrad* on the other hand,[1] contain useful information about the Iranian and Jewish peoples. As for the prevalence and importance of the Persian language during the Sasanian period, a story about Rav Yosef (d. 323 CE), the spiritual leader of the Jews of Babylonia, is recorded, in which he demanded the Jews abandon the Aramaic language and speak Persian [b.Bava Kamma 83a].

The Jews in Iran

The Jewish belief that the tombs of the prophets and their holy great persons are located in Iran, e.g., Daniel's tomb in Shush, Esther and Mordechai in Hamadan, Habakkuk in Tuyserkan, and the pilgrimage site of Serah bat Asher, near Isfahan, indicates the antiquity of Jewish presence in Iran.[2] However, there is unfortunately no written evidence concerning the beginning of mass settlement of Jewish families in Iran and the establishment of villages and quarters in the cities of Iran, except for Isfahan and Mashhad.

According to Armenian sources, Shāpūr II settled a number of Armenian Jews in Isfahan in the early fourth century CE. Zoroastrian sources attribute the settlement of the Jews of Isfahan in the Jayy quarter to Shūshāndukht, the Jewish wife of Yazdegerd I, during the first half of the fifth century.

Muslim historians and geographers for centuries back recognize Nebuchadnezzar as the founder of Yahūdiyya in Isfahan. In their opinion, the fine water and air of Isfahan were reminiscent of the water and air of Jerusalem, and suitable for the nature of the Jews who had been exiled from the kingdom of Judah.[3] In Mashhad, a number of Jews were settled by Nādir Shāh Afshār. It is however unnecessary to repeat that Jews lived in Iranian cities and villages before Islam.

Religious and National Movements and Cultural Cooperation

After the Arab conquest of Iran, the Jews of Iran were more involved in religious and national movements and messianic revival movements than the Jewish population elsewhere. Although the influence of the national and religious movements of the Abbasid period in Iran on Jewish movements in this territory has not yet been thoroughly studied, their mutual impact on each other cannot be ignored. The rise of Jewish leaders and scholars such as Abū ʿĪsā Iṣfahānī, Yūdghān Hamadānī, Mushkī Qummī, Abū ʿĪsā Lavī and Ibn Rāwandī of Ahwaz, and the cultural revival of Ḥīwī Balkhi are prominent examples of the love of freedom, occasionally of separatist tendencies with a mixture of messianic zeal that characterized the Jews of Iran during the early Abbasid period. Even the Karaite movement, which led to the appearance of a separate religious sect among the Jews, had influential sympathizers and followers among the Jews of Iran. Qirqisānī, the historian of this sect who was himself a Karaite, says: "A large number of the Karaite followers has risen from among the Jews of Khorasan, Jibal, Fars, Shushtar, and the eastern regions of the Abbasid caliphate."

In contrast to the general notion, the Jews of Iran were not confined to ghettos and separate quarters. In many cases, they lived together with the Muslim Iranians. The existence of names of Jews in the Shuʿubiyya movement, their cultural cooperation with Ikhwān al-Ṣafāʾ, and historical texts such as al-Fihrist of Ibn al-Nadīm, confirm the active participation of this group in Iranian life. On the other hand, Iranian scholars such

as Ḥamza al-Iṣfahānī (d. 971), Kirmānī (d. 1013), Abū Rayḥān al-Bīrūnī (d. 1047), Nāṣir Khusraw (d. 1088), and Shahristānī (d. 1153) speak in their works of contacts with Jewish scholars and about learning the Hebrew language and Jewish sciences. However, this historical encounter between the Jews and Iran in different places and periods was not limited to the sphere of various movements. The Jews composed valuable literary and cultural works. This is the primary subject of this introduction. [. . .]

The Literary Works of the Jews of Iran

The literature of the Jews of Iran is in fact an important branch of Persian literature, which has remained far from its "mother's lap" until now, due to people's lack of adequate introduction to and knowledge of its particularities. As far as the author knows, Iranian biographers have not mentioned the literary works of the Jews of Iran, and perhaps the principal reason for this was lack of familiarity with the Hebrew script.

The study of the literary works of the Jews of Iran drew the attention of European scholars for the first time only in the nineteenth century. Nowadays, a small number of European, American, and Israeli scholars, especially in the field of linguistics, are investigating these works. From among the researchers of the past, it is worth mentioning the scholarly works of Wilhelm Bacher (d. 1913) from Budapest, and the efforts of Elkan Nathan Adler (d. 1946) from London to gather Judeo-Persian manuscripts from Iran and Bukhara (1896–1897).[4] From the researchers of the last half century, the historical studies of Walter Fischel are worthy of note.[5]

Poetry forms the foundation of the Judeo-Persian literature. Jewish poetry is not particularly rich with regard to diversity in themes and formal aspects. Most of the contents are poured into the mathnavī form, and the forms of mukhammas, mustazād, tarkīb, and tarjīʿ-band, as well as other forms and types of poetry, whether as a qaṣīda or as a ghazal, is less attested. The lack of evolution and development of Jewish poetry in this regard should principally be sought in its absence of courtly life. The Jewish poets were not linked to any of the sultans, emirs, and viziers of Iran. For this reason, panegyric poems are generally not found in Jewish poetry, and Shāhīn's praise of Abū Saʿīd (1316–1335) is an exception.

Prose is used in translations of and commentaries on scripture, in stories, tales and legends, in scientific and legal discussions, and in religious sermons. In fact, the Jewish prose works are insignificant with respect to literary value, but are more important than poetry for linguistic and grammatical research. The majority of the documents and writings studied by professors of linguistics to this day have been prose.

NOTES

1. J. Darmesteter, "Textes Pahlavis Relatives au Judaisme," *Revue des études juives* 18 (1889), pp. 1–15; 19 (1890), pp. 42–56; L. H. Gray, "The Jews in Pahlavi Literature," *Jewish Encyclopaedia*, vol. 9 (New York, 1905), 462–465.

2. E. Herzfeld, *Archaeological History of Iran* (London, 1935), 106 ff.

3. J. Marquart, *Eranšahr, nach der Geographie des ps. Moses Xoreni* (Berlin, 1901), 29; Moïse Khorène, "Histoire de Arménie," *Collection des historiens anciens et modernes de l'Arménie*, vol. 2, ed. V. Langlois (Paris, 1869), 150; J. Darmesteter, "La reine Shasyân Dôkht," *Actes de Huitiéme Congrés des Orientalistes* (Leiden, 1889), 193–198; W. Fischel, "The Jews of Central Asia (Khorasan) in Medieval Hebrew and Islamic Literature," *Historia Judaica* 7 (1945), 38 ff.

4. W. Bacher, "Judeo-Persian," *Jewish Encyclopaedia*, vol. 7 (New York, 1905), 313–317; E. N. Adler, "The Persian Jews: Their Books and Their Ritual," *Jewish Quarterly Review* 10 (1898), 585–625.

5. W. Fischel, "Israel in Iran," *The Jews, Their History, Culture and Religion*, ed. L. Finkelstein (New York, 1949), 817–858.

Translated by Ofir Haim.

Other works by Netser: *The Jews of Iran* (1988); *Padyavand: Judeo-Iranian and Jewish Studies*, 3 vols. (1996–1999).

CULTURAL, POLITICAL, AND RELIGIOUS THOUGHT

Iraqi Zionist Underground

Before the founding of the State of Israel in 1948, about 140,000 Jews lived in Iraq, primarily in Baghdad, Basra, and Mosul. In the summer of 1948, the Iraqi government declared Zionism a capital offense and fired Jews in government positions. Many were imprisoned, falsely charged with Zionist or communist activities; some then crossed the border into Iran, from where they were flown to Israel. Immigration to Israel was outlawed by the Iraqi government, and by 1949, an Iraqi Zionist underground was established to smuggle Jews out of the country. In March 1950, Iraq passed a law to temporarily allow immigration to Israel, limited to one year only, and to strip Jews who emigrated of their Iraqi citizenship.

A Call to the Jewish Community
1950

Saturday, April 8, 1950, 4 P.M.

O Children of Zion Residents of Babylon,
Save Yourselves

For the second time in the history of this diaspora, after 2,488 years, we are hearing the echo of the historic prophecy of our prophets which brings us good tidings and warns us to leave quickly.

The Movement[1] in its previous announcements to the Jewish Community requested that Jews refrain from registering to renounce their citizenship. This was a fundamental part of our general plan. The Jews stood by us admirably.

Today, we are standing before a new threshold and a great turning point in the history of this diaspora.

The hour has arrived when all of the Jews together must quickly register because this is the most important stage of our program.

Today, we have decided that we must leave this hell of exile. It is incumbent upon all of us to enter upon this practical stage and to go and register.

The movement calls upon all Jews, whatever their class, to avail themselves of this decisive opportunity.

You men and women of Israel! You are the backbone of your people and its main support. Do not let the torch be extinguished in the darkness of exile.

O Ḥāvēr,[2] know that at this hour you are in the vanguard. You must guide the Jews and urge them to emigrate wherever possible.

O Jews, Israel is calling to you—"Get out of Babylon!" [. . .]

NOTES
1. That is, the underground Zionist organization.
2. The Hebrew word for "comrade" or "member," designating members of the Zionist movement.

Translated by Yosef Meir.

Joseph Messas

The Teaching of Torah to Women
1953

Gentlemen! This Shabbat, with God's help, I decided to continue in the interpretation of the article by the blessed teacher Rabbi Meir, may his merit protect us, amen, who said that "whoever is engaged in the Torah for its own sake is blessed with many things, etc." Last Shabbat we interpreted the meaning of the phrase "its own sake."

Now we will continue to delve into his holy words. When he says "whoever is engaged," what is added by the word "whoever"? And I saw that the compiler of Midrash Samuel, may his merit protect us amen, who wrote that [the word "whoever"] is there to include even one who is engaged in the Torah not for its own sake and then repents and does it for its own sake, let this be considered.

And in my small estimation, it is not true that after forgiveness the saintliness of his bones is greater; on the contrary, he who has studied the Torah not for its own sake, and then overcame his desire and moved to study it for its own sake, is preferable. As it has been said, one who returns to the fold is superior to a completely righteous man. And is not that preference incorporated within the word "whoever"?

And it seems to me that the word "whoever" is meant to be inclusive, even the craftsman and merchant who make a specific time for the Torah for the sake of love of the Torah, he too is blessed, and so forth. Lest it be said that only he for whom Torah is his vocation is the one who is blessed, etc.

Also it seems that the word "whoever" includes women, who, although they are not obligated to study Torah (See *Shulhan 'Arukh*, Yoreh De'ah 246:6), when they do it for its own sake they too are blessed with many things. For example, Devorah and Huldah, who merited prophecy because of their wisdom and righteousness, as well as Ima Shalom, the wife of Rabbi Eliezer, sister of Rabbi Gamliel (See b.Shabbat 116a at bottom), as well as Bruria, daughter of Rabbi Hanania ben Tradion, the wife of Rabbi Meir (See *Otsar Yisrael* 2, entry "Bruria"), and the daughter of Rashi, who used to write and sign responsa in the name of her father, may his merit protect us amen, and his sister Ḥilit, as well as Miriam the wife of Rabbenu Tam and Hannah sister of Rivam (Rabbi Isaac Bar Menahem, one of the Tosafists), and many others (see *Otsar Yisrael*, entry "Women").

And I also see in a handwritten manuscript that in the city of Algiers in the days of the gaon, our teacher, the Rabbi 'Ayash, may his merit protect us amen, there was a maiden of great beauty, the daughter of a wealthy man, very wise in the ways of the Torah, who devoted herself day and night to the study of Torah, and many honorable men courted her, and she absolutely refused to be the wife of any man, for the same reason [given by] [the Talmudic sage] Ben Azzai: "her soul yearned only for Torah." Her father [went and] complained to this great gaon, who sent for her, to speak good things to her heart. But she refused to listen to him, [arguing from the case of] Ben Azzai, who was a man and commanded "to be fruitful and multiply" and who nevertheless said, "What shall I do, for my soul yearns for the Torah?" All the more so should she [be allowed to not marry], who [as a woman] is not commanded to be fruitful and multiply. And the rabbi said to her, "Is it not also the case that she is not commanded in the study of Torah and there is no reward?" And she laughed, saying unto him, "You must have forgotten for a moment the words of the Rambam, of blessed memory, 'that a woman is recompensed as well for study' (*Shulhan 'Arukh*, Yoreh De'ah 256:6). And also, may it be His will that [your] words be fulfilled, that one will not be recompensed in this world or the next, because I am not studying Torah in the expectation of reward, but only for the love of the Torah." And the gaon was impressed with these words, and he exempted her in peace with many blessings, and he said to her father, "Leave her to do as she wills, for in

[doing] this, her great merit will protect the inhabitants of the city," and thus it came to be.

Once, in his dreams, the gaon saw invaders coming to the city to murder and loot, and that very daughter came out alone toward them, with a drawn sword, and was victorious against them all; she massacred them and was a great savior. The rabbi became frightened because of the beginning of his dream and he fasted. After three days, on Sabbath eve, Spanish invaders came from the sea, and the Lord in his mercy cast a storm on the sea, and all their ships together broke and sank like lead in the great waters, and the Lord saved the entire city from the invaders. Then the rabbi understood the significance of his dream, that the righteousness of that maiden protected the people of the city. And she remained a maiden and yearned for the Torah until she was sixty years old, when she went up to the land of Israel, and was devoted to the Torah until the day of her death at the ripe age of over a hundred years.

It is also told there that in Tlemcen there was an exceedingly beautiful maiden, whose soul yearned for the Torah, and her parents were very poor and had sons and daughters to feed, and one day an unknown young man who was exceptionally wealthy came from the city of Oran and convinced the father of the maiden to give him the daughter in marriage and he would provide dowry and gifts, and [said] that he and his family would eat at his table for the rest of their lives. The parents were very pleased with this offer, and when they gave her the offer and she refused, they fell at her feet and wept and begged her to look at their poverty and misery and strain and to save them from these dire straits. When she could no longer control herself, she asked them for three days to consider the matter, and then they left her alone. She tortured her soul with fasting and wept and pleaded for the Lord, may He be blessed, to open the gates of pardon for her parents, from a different source. And the Lord heard her prayers and saw her tears, and on midnight of the third night, she saw in her dreams, a voice called out to her saying there are great riches deep in the earth upon which you lie, and she rose that night and told her father, and he believed that she was right, and he brought an axe and dug in the place where she slept to the depth of two cubits and found a large ceramic pot full of gold dinars. And no one knew. And they were very, very happy. And in the morning, they informed the man that their daughter was not willing, and they sent him away in peace. And he took some of the gold and established a small business, and he was very successful. And they lived a joyous and quiet and peaceful life, and their daughter found pleasure in the doors of the Torah as she wished. These are the fruits of this world; and in the world to come, I do not know how much more this goodness multiplies. And this is why the holy Rabbi Meir added the word "whoever" to include women.

Translated by Karen Alkalay-Gut.

Raymond Bénichou
1890–1955

Raymond Bénichou was born in Oran to Mardochée Bénichou and Adelaïde Azoubib, a noted writer and poet, both from distinguished Algerian Jewish families. His studies in Paris were interrupted by World War I, and he received the Croix de Guerre for his service. He later earned degrees in literature and law, in addition to pursuing academic work in archaeology, linguistics, history, and philosophy. Bénichou was a promoter of interfaith dialogue, founding with Élie Gozlan the Circle of Monotheist Believers in Algiers in 1935. Some of the goals of the Circle were to prevent religious violence and to further the civil and political rights of disenfranchised Algerian citizens, especially Muslims. After World War II, Bénichou wrote for periodicals, including the Zionist publication *La terre retrouvée.*

Jewish Writings
1957

Yesterday

During the period between the two wars, the relations between Jews and Muslims progressively altered. One can assign several causes to this unfortunate evolution.

One is the acceleration, among the Jews, of the process of assimilation which has overtaken successive strata of a numerous and often wretched proletariat. It is highlighted by the profusion of academic successes, by the ever-increasing accession to liberal careers, by the definitive emancipation from consistorial prohibitions of a political order, but also, alas, by the forgetting of the Arabic language and the historical bonds that linked Judaism and Islam here.

To be sure, relations, especially business ones, remain intimate and cordial, but the traditional friendships between families have become somewhat loosened.

A second cause was, since 1929, at the call of the Mufti of Jerusalem, the hostility of Arabs to Zionist expansion.

A third cause was the intensification of Hitlerian propaganda which, without finding among the Muslims a very receptive audience, did not fail to produce some impression upon some among them.

However, of all these factors, none was decisive, and they would not have troubled the atmosphere were it not for the official solicitude of interested circles. The disorders were, if not provoked, at least encouraged by the upper-level administration and by colonialist circles.

If, since the denouement of the Dreyfus Affair, the hostility of the European masses has ceased to manifest itself in the public forum, it has survived in the penumbra of the bureaus of the central administration. The doctrine of these bureaus has frequently been indecisive and unstable on other levels, but, thanks to the gods! they have known how to show themselves capable of some continuity of views by making the virulent or larval anti-Semitism one of the constants of their political strategy.

As for the colons, the reason for their anti-Semitism has to be sought in the continuous augmentation in value of Algerian land which too often incited the enriched rural folk to abandon the democratic army, of which they were by tradition the stubborn soldiers, for the now-and-then factious phalanxes of political reaction.[1]

There was between their circle and the bureaus of the upper administration complicity—tacit, one would like to believe—in spite of the presence of clear-sighted and generous governors, to divert against the Jews the rather sudden swell of Muslim demands.

Berbers and Arabs had acquired in effect several years ago a political maturity which was translated into an unexpected energy in the expression of their aspirations.

What better outlet to offer these boiling waters than a demonstration for which the Jews would pay the price? That which the European anti-Semites would no longer dare to undertake, what an irresistible temptation to entrust it to the care of the Moors!

An engraving of the period appeared in "L'Oeuvre" (August 2, 1938) to serve as an illustration for an article by the fastidious writer and intrepid republican Jean Mélia.[2] It represented a garroted Jew and a European wearing a colonial helmet designating the victim of the fury of a Muslim armed with a *boussaadi*.[3]

This engraving has only a metaphoric value; nothing armed, in the proper sense of the term, the fanaticized hordes that engaged in the massacres of Constantine on August 5, 1934.[4] However, the incitement was coming from colonialist circles. The highest Muslim personalities bore witness to this fact.

When the tragedy suddenly happened, the anti-Semitic colons, the chiefs of the trusts in competition with the Jews, could barely restrain a sigh of joy, as I have taken occasion to relate elsewhere.[5] [. . .]

Today

Where are we today?

On the side of the Europeans, the horizon is, for the Jews, considerably clarified. In the Department of Algiers, the most conservative newspapers, such as "L'Echo d'Alger," adopted for their side an attitude of ceremonious and stiff correctness. The Jews' preponderant part in the Resistance and notably in the conspiracy of November 8 which paved the way for the liberation of the country, the fear of seeing the Jews make common cause too openly with the Muslim nationalists, the demonstration made many a time that anti-Semitism is the best precursor of communism,[6] these were, without a doubt, the principal reasons for this sudden turnaround. They silence the petty jealousies provoked by the important place taken by the Jews in the luxury trade and in the liberal professions. They also restrain the impatience of genteel folk with blunders of nouveau riche Jews who scarcely yield in self-admiration to the parvenus of other faiths.

As to Jewish-Muslim relations, let us try to make the point:

They have, evidently, changed. The Muslims themselves are very divided. . . .

Regarding the Jews, the attitude of the Muslims has been marked by a certain stiffness. For this change, there is no other serious reason than the events in Palestine. The turn taken by the first battles was felt illogically enough by many of the Arabs of Algeria as a sort of personal humiliation. Inflamed speeches were

addressed to chosen congregations exhorting them to support the policy of the Arab League, whose machinations one can scarcely surmise.

Words ordering a boycott circulated and were temporarily followed; then, the effervescence became progressively calmed.

One can see that when an accord will be reached in the Middle East, a return of confidence will preside here in the relations between the two autochthonous populations: the Jewish and the Muslim. My conviction is that, through secret meetings marked by a certain degree of concession, they would have even been able to concur upon the conclusion of such accords were it not for the spectacle of their collaborating and proclaiming their secular entente. Algerian history bears proof that these peoples who consider themselves descended from the same patriarch are not necessarily called to play the role of fraternal enemies.

However, in order for this appeasement whose fruitfulness would extend to the solution of other Algerian problems to survive permanently, there must be propitious conditions in the economic and social order.

Economically, the seeds of discord are barely perceptible. Here, more or less, is how the juncture appears:

The Muslims are becoming more and more numerous in the cities; their number and their proportion follow a precipitous geometric progression by reason of an extremely high birth rate.

The Muslim population is adapting rapidly to urban activities, notably in business. If we limit our inquiry to Algiers, we observe a very curious phenomenon: Arabs and Kabyles are progressively taking the place of the Jewish merchants in the old city. The latter, pushed on the one hand by this migration, aspiring on the other to the new city, are swarming in their turn into the new quarter. This double transfer is inscribed on the ground with the same fatal regularity as the progress of a frontal moraine. Each one finds it to his benefit.

NOTES
1. After the troubles of Constantine, where the police and the army had adopted a pure contemplative attitude, an inquiry was entrusted to a notoriously anti-Semitic functionary. His conclusions were of such a clear objectivity that he was disavowed by both the military and the civil authority. (Bénichou's note.)
2. Mélia was an unusually liberal colon, who, in his books *La France et l'Algérie* (Paris, 1919) and *Le triste sort des indigènes musulmans d'Algérie* (Paris, 1935), argued for the complete integration of the native Muslims.

3. An Arab dagger.

4. See Part One, p. 100.

5. See *Le Monde Juif* (September 1950, p. 11).

6. Concerning the role played by Jewish youth in the insurrection that helped pave the way for the Allied landing in North Africa, see Michael Ansky, *Les Juifs d'Algérie du Décret Crémieux à la libération* (Paris, 1950), pp. 199–221, and Part One, pp. 134–135.

Translated by Norman Stillman.

Other works by Bénichou: *L'Épreuve sans danger* (1954); *Écrits juifs* (1957).

Albert Memmi

The Colonizer and the Colonized
1957

The Two Answers of the Colonized

The body and face of the colonized are not a pretty sight. It is not without damage that one carries the weight of such historical misfortune. If the colonizer's face is the odious one of an oppressor, that of his victim certainly does not express calm and harmony. The colonized does not exist in accordance with the colonial myth, but he is nevertheless recognizable. Being a creature of oppression, he is bound to be a creature of want.

How can one believe that he can ever be resigned to the colonial relationship; that face of suffering and disdain allotted to him? In all of the colonized there is a fundamental need for change. For the colonizers to be unconscious of this need means that either their lack of understanding of the colonial system is immense or that their blind selfishness is more than readily believable. To assert, for instance, that the colonized's claims are the acts of a few intellectuals or ambitious individuals, of deception or self-interest, is a perfect example of projection: an explanation of others in terms of one's own interests. The colonized's refusal resembles a surface phenomenon, but it actually derives from the very nature of the colonial situation.

The middle-class colonized suffers most from bilingualism. The intellectual lives more in cultural anguish, and the illiterate person is simply walled into his language and rechews scraps of oral culture. Those who understand their fate become impatient and no longer tolerate colonization. They only express the common misfortune. If not, why would they be so quickly heard, so well understood and obeyed?

If one chooses to understand the colonial system, he must admit that it is unstable and its equilibrium constantly threatened. One can be reconciled to every situation, and the colonized can wait a long time to live. But, regardless of how soon or how violently the colonized rejects his situation, he will one day begin to overthrow his unlivable existence with the whole force of his oppressed personality.

The two historically possible solutions are then tried in succession or simultaneously. He attempts either to become different or to reconquer all the dimensions which colonization tore away from him.

The first attempt of the colonized is to change his condition by changing his skin. There is a tempting model very close at hand—the colonizer. The latter suffers from none of his deficiencies, has all rights, enjoys every possession and benefits from every prestige. He is, moreover, the other part of the comparison, the one that crushes the colonized and keeps him in servitude. The first ambition of the colonized is to become equal to that splendid model and to resemble him to the point of disappearing in him.

By this step, which actually presupposes admiration for the colonizer, one can infer approval of colonization. But by obvious logic, at the very moment when the colonized best adjusts himself to his fate, he rejects himself with most tenacity. That is to say that he rejects, in another way, the colonial situation. Rejection of self and love of another are common to all candidates for assimilation. Moreover, the two components of this attempt at liberation are closely tied. Love of the colonizer is subtended by a complex of feelings ranging from shame to self-hate.

The extremism in that submission to the model is already revealing. A blonde woman, be she dull or anything else, appears superior to any brunette. A product manufactured by the colonizer is accepted with confidence. His habits, clothing, food, architecture are closely copied, even if inappropriate. A mixed marriage is the extreme expression of this audacious leap.

This fit of passion for the colonizer's values would not be so suspect, however, if it did not involve such a negative side. The colonized does not seek merely to enrich himself with the colonizer's virtues. In the name of what he hopes to become, he sets his mind on impoverishing himself, tearing himself away from his true self. The crushing of the colonized is included among the colonizer's values. As soon as the colonized adopts those values, he similarly adopts his own condemnation. In order to free himself, at least so he believes, he agrees to destroy himself. This phenomenon is comparable to Negrophobia in a Negro, or anti-Semitism in a Jew. Negro women try desperately to uncurl their hair, which keeps curling back, and torture their skin to make it a little whiter. Many Jews would, if they could, tear out their souls—that soul which, they are told, is irremediably bad. People have told the colonized that his music is like mewing of cats, and his painting like sugar syrup. He repeats that his music is vulgar and his painting disgusting. If that music nevertheless moves him, excites him more than the tame Western exercises, which he finds cold and complicated, if that unison of singing and slightly intoxicating colors gladdens his eye, it is against his will. He becomes indignant with himself, conceals it from strangers' eyes or makes strong statements of repugnance that are comical. The women of the bourgeoisie prefer a mediocre jewel from Europe to the purest jewel of their tradition. Only the tourists express wonder before the products of centuries-old craftsmanship. The point is that whether Negro, Jew or colonized, one must resemble the white man, the non-Jew, the colonizer. Just as many people avoid showing off their poor relations, the colonized in the throes of assimilation hides his past, his traditions, in fact all his origins which have become ignominious.

Those internal convulsions and contortions could have attained their goal. At the end of a long, painful process, one certainly full of conflict, the colonized would perhaps have dissolved into the midst of the colonizers. There is no problem which the erosion of history cannot resolve. It is a question of time and generations. There is, however, one condition—that it not contain contradictory ideas. Well, within the colonial framework, assimilation has turned out to be impossible.

Translated by Howard Greenfeld.

Ronald Segal and Dan Jacobson

Segal, 1932–2008

The author and publisher Ronald Segal was deeply involved with the antiapartheid struggle in South Africa, writing, lecturing, fighting in the courts, and accepting exile as the cost of his activism. Born into affluence in South Africa, he used his family's wealth and his own inexhaustible energy to defend Nelson Mandela and champion an economic boycott of the apartheid regime. Through his magazine, *Africa South*, and the Penguin African Library, he brought international attention to the continent of his birth.

Jacobson, 1929–2014

South Africa–born Dan Jacobson was an all-around man of letters, a novelist, essayist, memoirist, and critic who shifted easily between literary genres. Jacobson's early novels dealt with South Africa's racism; his later ones addressed universal ethics. Still later, he turned toward Jewish subjects, following his family's trail to Lithuania and researching the life of his grandfather, a rabbi.

Apartheid and South African Jewry: An Exchange
1957

Ronald Segal

South African Jews are forever conscious of injustice, but of the injustice that they alone are made to suffer. They quickly grow furious over the treatment of Israel, the power politics being played out in the Middle East. It is unfair, it is wrong that Israel should be refused her ordinary right to exist. Yet they watch with complacency the innumerable daily manifestations of "apartheid," the South African government's refusal to grant the mass of its subjects any rights whatsoever. How can this one-eyed morality be defended? Is it any different ultimately from the hypocrisy with which the Russian delegate to the United Nations denounced Western misdeeds in the Middle East while Soviet tanks were rolling through the streets of Budapest? How many South African Jews of status in the community have I not heard condoning and even casually commending the worst horrors of "apartheid" and, almost within the same breath, pleading for the world to acknowledge at last the cruelties of the Nasser regime. The South African Jewish community was outraged by the seizure of Jewish property and the internment of Jewish civilians in Egypt. It protested publicly and vigorously against the injustice. Yet, when the Africans of Sophiatown were dispossessed of their homes and their right to own land and property in Johannesburg, when they were driven from their houses in the early morning between lines of armed police, how many leaders of Jewish communal organizations protested? There was not one public statement, not one deputation, no representations to the government were made.

At the time of writing, the Native Laws Amendment bill has passed through the lower house of the South African parliament and is being given a brisk passage through the senate. In addition to giving the Minister of Native Affairs power to prohibit all social, political, and industrial gatherings of Africans and Europeans together, it confers upon him the authority to forbid the attendance of Africans and Europeans at the same religious service. When the terms of the bill were first announced, there was public uproar. Especially were the churches outraged, as they saw in the bill a frontal assault upon religious freedom. The late Archbishop of Cape Town, on behalf of the whole large Anglican community, not only protested most strongly against the proposed legislation, but the night before his death wrote to the Prime Minister that if the bill were passed he would feel morally obliged to disobey the law and to counsel his subordinates to do likewise. An Episcopal Synod has since reaffirmed this last challenge of the Archbishop.

Similarly, the Roman Catholic hierarchy has taken an extremely strong stand, as have the Methodists, Baptists, and Presbyterians. Even the apartheid-minded Dutch Reformed Church stirred once for a moment uneasily and made covert representations to the government. Only the synagogues have sat on in silence, and to date only one rabbi has protested against the principles of the bill—in an article in the communal press.

If ever there was a time when South African Jewry should have cried aloud its protest, it was surely at the introduction of a bill to control the freedom of man to worship as they please. Yet it said nothing. Is religious freedom of so little significance to the Jew? Is the memory of the Inquisition now wholly dead? Or is it because there are no black Jews in South Africa and so the right to admit Africans to worship does not affect the community directly? A few servants may no longer be permitted to attend the marriage ceremonies of their masters, but that is surely a small enough price to pay for continued peace with the authorities.

Dan Jacobson

Here I should say that I wish I knew as confidently as Mr. Segal what the Jewish tradition enjoins on Jews in a situation like that prevailing in South Africa today. Mr. Segal is aware that the tradition is a complex thing. He knows that if it seeks justice, it also encourages "a reluctance to fall out with those in power"; and he

knows too that it has always had the elements of a fierce exclusiveness and an indifference to what happens beyond the "ghetto walls." But apparently Mr. Segal is not prepared to allow that all of these are legitimate aspects of the tradition; and that they all are necessary, continuing, and irreconcilable. From such a tradition, from any ethical and historical tradition, we cannot get a single clear directive to present action; but we can, if we are humble enough in our approach to it, get something more valuable: a sense of the inevitability and permanence of conflict between idea and idea, interest and interest, in any human affair. It is precisely this sense, with its concomitant respect for human motives and actions in all their complexity and waywardness, that I miss in the uses Mr. Segal would make of the long and multi-faceted history of the Jews.

Is the idea that in certain circumstances an entire community should be composed of martyrs really so difficult to entertain? asks Mr. Segal. It is not merely difficult, it is impossible for me to imagine that any community will ever sacrifice itself for the sake of another. Mr. Segal's historical parallels seem to me to have a relevance quite the contrary to what he imagines it to be. Does he really need to have it pointed out to him that the Jews in the Middle Ages who sacrificed themselves did so for their own beliefs, their own way of life, that they sacrificed themselves for what they believed to be their own interests as Jews? Does he know of a Jewish community that sacrificed itself for the sake of the Albigensians or Pelagians who were being persecuted then? Did any group ever sacrifice itself for the sake of the Jews, either in the Middle Ages or later? Did any group sacrifice itself for the Jews of Europe from 1933 onward?

Until the Jews of South Africa as a group are persuaded of an immediate identity of material and spiritual interest between themselves and the non-whites in the country, they are not going to do what Mr. Segal wants them to do. Of course one can be convinced that the interests of the Jews, as individuals and as a community, are much closer to the interests of the Africans than the Jews themselves seem to realize. And one can do one's best to persuade them to share this conviction. But Mr. Segal hardly seems aware that that should be his task, if he is serious in the appeal that he is issuing. He really makes remarkably little of the question of group-interest and self-interest: the martyrdoms and self-sacrifices that he calls for from the entire community appear on the whole to be gratuitous, disinterested.

I suggest that to talk in this way about any community is merely to indulge an appetite for righteous feeling.

Other works by Segal: *Into Exile* (1963); *Islam's Black Slaves: The Other Black Diaspora* (2001). Other works by Jacobson: *Time of Arrival* (1963); *The Story of the Stories: The Chosen People and Its God* (1982).

Carlos de Nesry
Dates Unknown

Carlos de Nesry was born in Tangier, Morocco, the son of chief rabbi Yaḥya Nizrī. De Nesry believed Tangerian Jews were more agnostic and West European in their thinking than their coreligionists in North Africa; he attributed these characteristics at least partly to their formal education in European schools like the Alliance Israélite Universelle. A strong supporter of Moroccan independence, de Nesry encouraged his fellow Jews to contribute to the cultural and political life of the new country, an appeal he pushed in his 1958 *Les Israélites marocains à l'heure du choix*. In addition to serving on the Tangier Court of Appeals and being an active journalist, de Nesry took an active role in Jewish community affairs. A man of keen literary ambitions, de Nesry once circulated a petition asking the Nobel Committee to award him the prize for literature.

Moroccan Jews in Their Hour of Decision
1958

The Test

The Jews of Morocco are in the limelight today. The condition of the Jews in a given country always has a certain international dimension. It is a kind of sociological test and a touchstone of evolutionary developments. After having been ignored for a long time, the Jews of this country find themselves under the scrutiny of observers throughout the world. An experiment is in the process of being made in Morocco whose results are being awaited by all the world. The Jews here have lived for approximately two years in a fully Arab and Muslim state—a transcendent experience, charged with portents and possibilities yet to be realized. Has it been conclusive?

The question posed, the prophecies and conjectures take their course. From almost all sides people have begun writing about Moroccan Jews and their problems. . . . They speak of the iron curtain that has fallen

over the 200,000 Jews of this country. They foresee Draconian solutions such as a mass exodus of Moroccan Jewry for which the funds are in the process of being collected. There is in all of this a clear interpolation of the Middle East situation into the Moroccan reality whose inner givens, marginal character, and "specificity" are misjudged. Is this to say that the Jews in the Sharifan Empire have found an airtight and lasting paradise? The truth is more complex. Morocco is in the process of becoming and the condition of the Jews is a function of variables, of coefficients, of subtle factors, to which the future, political orientation, the performance of the parties now in an outright test of strength, the economic future, that of the cultural system, the diplomatic role that will be assigned to the country, all will remain intimately linked.

It has been my lot to live this reality for months now. . . . My reflections here can be considered as conveying a view "from within."

Premises

In the quest for the Moroccan truths, a prefatory question imposes itself: What have the Jews done for the new Morocco? Before asking ourselves about our chances, it would be fitting to know our qualifications. What was—what is—the participation of the Jews in the building of the body politic of this country? Put another way, what does Morocco represent for the Jews?

Sartre saw in liberty an attitude in the face of a given. We do not choose the given which is imposed on us from without, but we choose our attitude toward it. . . . I greatly fear that the participation of Moroccan Jews in the act of independence strangely approaches this Sartrian liberty and responsibility. This independence was made without them, almost without their knowing, occasionally even against their will, at the least against their secret wish. Something passively given and passively received. However, these events which they did not choose, which—properly speaking—they underwent, they can today naught but "assume" them. It is necessary, therefore to assume independence by choosing retrospectively an ad hoc attitude.

The evolution of the Jews in Morocco has followed a somewhat dialectic cycle: Moroccanization, demoroccanization, remoroccanization. Thesis, antithesis, synthesis. In this completely Hegelian dialectic, the first two phases have been completed. The third is the present now being lived and which is unrolling before our eyes. Moroccanized for centuries, the Jews in the Sharifan Empire underwent during the Protectorate a process—often involuntary—of demoroccanization which coincided with the general phenomenon of depersonalization observed in all colonialized societies. As a result of the fact of independence, they find themselves today facing the necessity for a remoroccanization which supposes a rather dramatic reconversion and which is the problem of the hour for all those who have opted to remain in the country.

Independence has been for the Jews of this country the opportunity for the "politization" that till then had been denied them. . . .

The horizons have been widening in the face of ambitions. . . . The future has been opening up before all those who under the old regime were too obscure or too young. In the absence of nationalist credentials, a past unstained by any "collaborationism" sufficed. That was, in the main, the premium accorded neutrality and silence. The degree holders, who in Europe would have exhausted themselves in a vain competition for subordinate posts in any administration whatsoever, could breeze up to the pinnacle of state. The national poverty of cadres will be one of the opportunities—and not the least—offered to Moroccan Jewry.

The Sovereign, Divine Providence

It must be understood that the future of Moroccan Judaism is a function of a series of givens, most of which are beyond our Muslim fellow citizen themselves. The will of the present leaders is clearly for a harmonious coexistence, for a common effort, for national progress—something unthinkable today without the Jews. They want neither our departure, nor our banishment. After that of the Europeans, our departure would be the consummation of the disaster. Morocco's international good name would, furthermore, be compromised by anti-Jewish measures, which the country's adversaries would not fail to highlight (not to mention the opportunity that would thereby be offered to the opposition to rise up against such undemocratic practices). One ought not to suspect a priori, therefore, the egalitarian declarations, tirelessly repeated by the political leaders, whatever their party. One ought not to doubt even less the proclamations to their effect made by the Sovereign, who remains the essential given at the present juncture, who is the primordial factor of stability, the best guarantee of our liberties and our rights, and, in a word, a

veritable providence for Moroccan Jewry. For the Jews of Morocco, Providence is called today Muḥammed V. The affection that the Jewish population of this country bears for him is unanimous in its depth and in its sincerity. Never, since the Antonines and certain princes of the Sasanian dynasty, has there been seen such a movement of veneration for the head of the state where the Jews were living. Never in the synagogues, also, did the prayer for the kings better correspond to the true thoughts of the faithful.

However, there is an evolution that by definition escapes human whims—a sociological evolution, a political evolution. . . . It is an evolution that can be an advance or a regression. . . . Beyond the wishes and the desires, beyond the promises and the proclamations, beyond the signs and the symbols, it is this evolution that dominates our horizons and it is in accordance with its definitive orientation that our survival in this country will depend in the final analysis.

The Crossroads

First, the sociological evolution. Will Morocco continue upon this ascendant, Western, progressive course, which the French presence marked out for it, and which its geographical position, the present formation of its elites, and its natural vocation urgently enjoin it? Will it be secular and liberal as is often promised? Or, on the contrary, will it turn back to the Orient and the call of atavistic conscience? Will it henceforth seek in the Nile or the Euphrates Valley inspirations that it had been accustomed to finding elsewhere?

At their hour of choice, Moroccan Jews await this decisive choice of Morocco.

Translated by Norman Stillman.

Other work by de Nesry: *Le Juif de Tanger et le Maroc* (1956).

Paul Sebag

1919–2004

Paul Sebag was a historian and sociologist, born and raised in a middle-class family in Tunis. Trained in law and philosophy in Paris, Sebag returned home to join the antifascist resistance as a member of the Tunisian Communist Party, to which he remained loyal through his imprisonment and liberation. He was later employed at the University of Tunis, where the twin foundations of his academic career were urban sociology and the history of Tunisian Jewry.

The Hara of Tunis: The Evolution of a North-African Ghetto
1959

Chapter II

THE OLD JEWISH QUARTER

The Jews of Tunis have not been confined to the hara for a long time now. Since the end of the last century, those acquiring a degree of ease have abandoned it and established themselves in the new city being built at the gates of the old one. Indeed, the only ones who remained were those bound by poverty to its houses and small shops. The impoverishment of the population led to the deterioration of its buildings, eroded by time. Its unsanitary conditions soon attracted the attention of public health workers; the time came when a clean-up operation, with massive expropriations and relocations, was planned. But though the work of men was interrupted, that of time continued, implacable. Not a winter passes without notice in the local paper that the day after a heavy rain in the hara a roof has caved in, a wall crumbled, or men, women, and children have had to abandon a house that was threatening collapse. It is understandable that families should be in a hurry to leave those hovels before they are forced to. But the only ones who do are those who can finally manage the high rents of a sanitary house in the modern city, or who, battle weary, have decided to emigrate. If the house they leave behind is still standing, it will not remain unoccupied for long. Poor Muslims or even poor Catholics will come to take the place of the poor Jews who have left. The Tunis ghetto thus offers a complex example of segregation. Populated at first by Jews of all conditions, then only by Jews of low economic means, it now shelters the poor of all religions. [. . .]

THE HARA IN THE MEDINA

If one looks only at the buildings and their layout, nothing distinguishes the hara from the rest of the medina, the old city of Tunis at whose heart it lies. That is not surprising, given the fact that the hara, which was quite small originally, has gradually expanded over the centuries. Today, in fact, it has no precise boundaries. The hara of today can only be defined by reference to the people who have chosen to live there. It includes all the streets or parts of streets in the areas surrounding the old hara in which Jews predominate, or did until recently.

One need only learn from its objects and people, listen to the voices coming from the houses, closely observe the character types, clothing, and behavior in order to infer the residents' ethnic group. In this way, through a patient exploration of the quarter, we came up with a list of streets and parts of streets that we felt constituted the hara. [. . .]

A house in the hara is in the classic Arabic style. Whether one or two stories, it is generally comprised of a certain number of rooms opening onto an interior courtyard. It is normally quite small and modest, with beaten earth floors, lime-plastered walls, and no ornamentation. But it often appears to be a great edifice. Countless rooms, elegant colonnades, marble paving stones, and glazed tiles surround a huge patio: it is the old palace of some notable Jew or Muslim that has been broken up to become a *ûkâla*, a multifamily dwelling. [. . .]

Streets in the hara scarcely differ from streets in the medina. Both are characterized by extreme irregularity. They bend, straighten out again, then abruptly turn at right angles. The outsider can hardly avoid confusing the street he is trying to follow with one of the numerous cul-de-sacs that feed into it. The width of roads—not more than four meters in the main arteries—is as variable as their direction. Narrow, they can widen, but then narrow again. Alleys only two meters across are not at all uncommon. Even at rush hour the lanes for carts may have indescribable bottlenecks, causing long traffic delays. The badly paved surfaces are astoundingly uneven; rainwater accumulates and stagnates in their crevasses, increasing the humidity permeating the hara in hot weather. [. . .]

The freedom enjoyed by women suffices to explain that the Jewish household is less secluded than that of Muslims, that family life is more open to the outside, that the streets echo with the raised voices of housewives and mothers. It also no doubt explains that work and home life are more integrated: the shop is near the dwelling and often communicates with it; a single room, which during the day has functioned as the workshop, at night serves as sleeping quarters; and it is not rare for the wife and children to work alongside the father. Thus one does not fail to notice more animation than anywhere else in these arteries of the hara in which there lives and works an exuberant population that one can actually observe living and working.

Certain activities that are linked to Jewish religion and culture give the quarter its originality. It is the butcher, his big butcher knife in hand, carving the kosher meat; the *shoḥet* in a dingy shop, ritually slaughtering the poultry; the blind merchant selling myrtle and narcissus for evening prayers before Shabbat. It is also the Jewish notary behind his tiny desk preparing to draft a marriage contract, a donation, or a will; the printer composing and hand printing in Hebrew characters the small posters announcing funerals and eulogies; the bookseller offering ritual objects and prayer shawls for sale. And from the synagogues, whose pediments sometimes bear Hebrew inscriptions, come the voices of cantors during religious services.

Finally, always evident from one end of the year to the other, are the Jewish holidays: boutiques and workshops are closed, customers crowd around the pastry or toy merchants, temporary huts topped with leaves and branches spring up on terraces or in courtyards, walls and doors sport cool colors, and houses are bedecked with garlands of flowers. It is understandable that some Jews who escaped the hara long ago but remain attached to its dying traditions still come to stroll through the populous streets of this impoverished quarter.

Translated by Michele McKay Aynesworth.

Other works by Sebag: *Histoire des juifs de Tunisie* (1991); *Tunis: histoire d'une ville* (1998); *Communistes de Tunisie, 1939–1943: Souvenirs et documents* (2001).

Jacques Lazarus

1916–2014

Jacques Lazarus was born in Payerne, Switzerland, to Alsatian-Jewish parents. A career officer in the French army, he was forced out by the Vichy's antisemitic Jewish Statute in 1940. In 1943, he became a leader in the Armée Juive (Jewish Army) French Resistance. Betrayed, arrested, and interned in Paris's Drancy camp, on August 17, 1944, he was shipped out on the last train to Auschwitz. Four days later, with twenty-seven others, he escaped by jumping from the train, an experience chronicled in *Juifs au combat*. After the war, he became head of the World Jewish Congress for Africa and director of the Comité juif algérien d'études sociales (Jewish Algerian Committee for Social Studies). He also founded and edited *Information juive* in Algeria, a monthly publication devoted to Israel, Zionism, Judaism, French and Algerian nationalisms, and related matters.

Beyond the Test
1963

Information juive is back. For nearly fourteen years it was, under the aegis of the Jewish Algerian Committee for Social Studies, the voice of a community of almost 150,000 souls in Algeria; it expressed and defended, as faithfully as possible, their thoughts and aspirations.

It is not without emotion that we reread today the editorial in the first issue published on 15 October 1948 following the birth, the rebirth, of the State of Israel.

"At a time when tensions are rising around the world," we wrote, "when the United Nations is trying to solve complex and painful problems, we thought we should raise our voice, however weak it might be, in support of the great work of Union and Peace."

Union and Peace!

During the terrible years that live on in all memories, these two imperatives have not ceased to guide us.

The statements published in our newspaper attest to this.

The last issue, in September 1961, on the eve of holidays in the month of Tishri, exhorted our coreligionists once again "to do everything possible to keep the gap from widening between populations that are called upon to live side by side and to work in a country where every inhabitant—beyond questions of ethnic or religious origin—feels he has the right to consider it his own and to live there as a free man, with freedom of choice, of opinions, and of destiny."

"The future alone," we concluded, "will tell whether our passionate demand for liberty and fraternity can yet find a place in this land that has been torn apart."

Already, however, our fate was sealed.

A few months later, more than a hundred thousand Jewish men, women, and children left Algeria. Practically the entire Jewish community abandoned a land in which it had been established for centuries, a noteworthy event in the history of our people. It was a weak minority, however, without influence or political power, and was often abused. In the end, it too fell victim to the unpredictable demands of policies on which it never had any influence.

Today at least 125,000 of our own have resettled in France.

We know the painful ordeals that so many of them—like so many from other religions who have been forced to emigrate—have endured.

Ordeals arising from the exodus, the transplantation, the uprooting.

After the months of upheaval, confusion, and distress that followed our arrival, it is essential that we find each other again, become reunified, and rebuild.

That is why certain people, having assumed various responsibilities central to the Jewish community there, decided a few months ago to create the Association of Jews of Algerian Origin.

This association has taken on the task of defending the material, moral, and religious rights of our expatriate brothers. The goal is to facilitate their entry into the community of mainland France, with respect shown for their character and traditions.

Finding each other again, uniting, and holding firm, such was and such remains our primary imperative.

It is to help maintain a way of life that was ours in our homeland, and to which we remain attached, it is to work here toward building the great Jewish community of France whose structures have been so profoundly altered by our very arrival, that *Information juive* has reappeared.

As in the past, our newspaper intends to remain the intersection at which the great avenues of Judaism in this country converge.

Information juive will be a link and a forum for all those whose loyalty to France and, whatever one might say, whose attachment to Israel have led them over the rough roads of the exodus.

If each of our Algerian brothers, our North African brothers, finds new reasons to maintain his Jewish character, his attachment to our spiritual patrimony, to safeguard his fervor and his faith, our exodus will not have been in vain.

Translated by Michele McKay Aynesworth.

Other works by Lazarus: *Juifs au combat: témoignage sur l'activité d'un mouvement de résistance* (1947); *Information juive* (monthly, 1948–2013).

W. Gunther Plaut

1912–2012

A Reform rabbi and writer born in Münster, Germany, W. Gunther Plaut obtained a law degree in Berlin in 1934, but because of the Nazi takeover of Germany, he switched to religious studies. In 1935 he accepted a scholarship to study at Cincinnati's Hebrew Union College and fled Germany. He was ordained in 1939 and worked as a rabbi in Chicago until 1948, leaving his pulpit during World War II to serve as an army chaplain. After the war, he took up a rabbinical position in St. Paul, Minnesota, and then at Toronto's Holy Blossom Temple in 1961, first as its rabbi and then, from 1977, as its senior scholar.

The Rise of Reform Judaism
1963

The Nature of Reform Judaism: A Sourcebook of Its European Origins

WHAT IS REFORM?

Reform Judaism is a phenomenon of man's restless spirit. At its best it is a dynamic faith—and its very dynamism makes it difficult to describe it adequately. Its traditional roots speak of yesterdays; its branches combine the ancient spirit with the special beauty of each new generation. Reform speaks of man's longing for the sure ways of his fathers and at the same time of his own surging and daring struggle for new ways. It is Jewish to the core, although occasional and temporary acceptance of the habits of changing environments may deceive the casual onlooker. [. . .]

Along with Reform's Messianic vision went its broad universalism. Here, too, Reform combined the visions of the prophets with the dreams of man's brotherhood which the American and French Revolutions had proclaimed. The prophecies of old seemed capable of realization in one's own lifetime; Christian, Mohammedan, and pagan—all became objects of human concern. Jews joined the liberal parties, rabbis entered into the political arena, and some suffered exile and incarceration for their convictions. It was natural that on occasion the sweep of this grand vision of human fulfilment should lead to a shallow and fruitless sentimentalism. Occasionally one found men loving mankind without loving their neighbors, and one could find Jews feeling little responsibility for other Jews, while lavishing their concern on Man as such. There was a distinct trend away from parochialism and from what later came to be called Jewish nationalism. The Jewish people, some Reformers averred, no longer existed; it was Judaism that formed the bond across the lands and ages. But somehow this modern Jewish universalism, not unlike its ancient inspiration, could not or would not forsake its ethnic base altogether. Some Reformers might doubt the admissibility of Jewish peoplehood as a concept, but they were in the forefront of those fighting for Jewish rights all over the world.

In fact, Reform's emphasis on man's universal aspirations was always closely linked to the role which the Jew had to play in their achievement. God's Kingdom would be realized for all men only through Judaism. To bring its truths to the world was the Jew's noblest aim; this was Israel's mission to mankind. What made the Jew capable of carrying this burden? It was a special "racial" characteristic—an inherited, innate ability to see the world in spiritual terms. No other people had been so gifted, none other had therefore been chosen. In this way Jewish particularism and Jewish universalism were combined, similar to the manner in which the prophets had taught. For let us make no mistake about it: Reform was thoroughly Jewish. Its leaders were critical of certain traditional customs and concepts, but they were also Judaism's staunchest defenders and protagonists. Where today a polite silence makes interreligious discussion nearly taboo, the Reformers confronted other religions squarely and found them wanting. They exalted Judaism's qualities with fierce pride; they scorned apostasy and weak-kneed convictions. They had studied the cultural treasures of East and West (after a while, all rabbis in Germany were expected to obtain a Ph.D.), but their frame of reference was Judaism and its sources. They were conversant with Talmud and Shulhan Arukh; they quoted freely from all Jewish sources and did so in Hebrew. They loved the holy tongue and, even though they were realists and introduced translations into the prayer book, they insisted that every Jew learn Hebrew to the limits of his ability. They believed in scholarship and formed the "Science of Judaism," discovered old sources and made an incalculable contribution to the understanding of Bible and Talmud. [. . .]

The real forward thrust came in America, where many of the Reformers had gone in the wake of the post-revolution reaction and repression. Hither they translated their enthusiasm, and here they found new and far more fertile ground for further advances. Men like Adler, Einhorn, and Samuel Hirsch, who had broken a lance for European Reform, found the new land ready for imaginative leadership. A frontier psychology prevailed everywhere; nothing was rejected until it had first been tested experimentally. In America, Re-

form reached new heights of spiritual force, but it also went into more blind alleys. America afforded the Jew unprecedented opportunities, and the lures of assimilation were consequently greater. Some mistook the universalistic trend of Reform for an approval of assimilation. It was an unfortunate half-truth. The impulse to assimilation did not originate with the Reform movement; it sprang from the breakdown of social barriers and the problems arising from it. Reform did acknowledge and was ready to assimilate the best in the majority culture, and it did so openly, as a matter of principle (in contrast to the Orthodox, who did the same but unofficially). What was "best" in American or European civilization was, of course, a matter of dispute, and in this area of judgment, American Jews were more prone to embrace the mores of their environment than were their European brethren. But assimilation, i.e., the conscious preference of a non-Jewish way of life, was not part of the Reform philosophy; and in the long run, the draining away of Jewish consciousness occurred more frequently among the children of Orthodoxy than among those of Reform background. The fact that foes (and often friends also) of the movement thought it to be the gateway to convenience and defection did not make it so, and, in time, the abiding qualities of Reform emerged more clearly and put the stamp of their worth upon all of modern Jewish life.

Other works by Plaut: *Your Neighbour Is a Jew* (1968); *The Torah: A Modern Commentary* (1974); *The Haftarah Commentary* (1996).

Pablo Schvartzman
b. 1927

Pablo Schvartzman was born in General Campos, a small community in the province of Entre Ríos, Argentina, to Ukrainian immigrants. He was an avid reader and largely self-taught. In the 1950s, he produced *Haor*, a Jewish newspaper and publishing house in Concepción del Uruguay, a city in Entre Ríos province. Primarily a poet, he also wrote short stories as well as *Judíos en América*, a rather romantic history, given the antisemitism of the 1960s, of Jewish settlement in Latin America since 1492. Schvartzman's poetry ranges from the personal, such as poems dedicated to his children, to poems celebrating the founding of the State of Israel. The poems in *Los mismos*, published in 1963, condemned the rise of antisemitism in Argentina.

Noé Yarcho, Physician to the Jewish Gauchos
1963

Through the large portal of "The Jewish Gauchos," one of the most moving literary tributes to the Republic in the first hundred years after the May Revolution of 1810, Dr. Noé Yarcho, the "miracle doctor" of the Jewish settlements in Entre Ríos at the end of the last century, stepped into immortality.

As with his other Jewish gauchos, Alberto Gerchunoff's masterly pen required only a few pages to describe Dr. Noé Yarcho, physician and pioneer, professional and philanthropist, neighbor and counselor, psychologist and comrade.

A sower of goodness in the fields of Entre Ríos, a self-sacrificing, noble, disinterested, loyal, true "Jewish gaucho," the name of Noé Yarcho is remembered with veneration in the land of Urquiza, and his life and activities in the Entre Ríos settlements have traversed regional boundaries, attaining the loftiness of ardent legend beyond the forests of Montiel.

Noé Yarcho was born in Minsk in 1860. He began primary school at age nine, completing his studies there at fourteen. After completing his bachelor's degree at age seventeen, he attended the University of Kiev, capital of Ukraine. He soon became one of its top students.

In 1883, at the age of twenty-three and after having achieved top grades in all his courses, he received his medical degree. Among more than one thousand papers written by his fellow students, his was the most outstanding dissertation, earning him several honorable mentions and a gold medal.

Characteristic of his generous nature, which the inhabitants of the Entre Río settlements would come to know well, the brand-new physician sold his gold medal so that its proceeds could help some of his needier classmates.

The fledgling doctor began practicing his profession in Ukraine.

He soon realized that not even for a doctor was Jewish life in tsarist Russia an easy one, even within towns without any other Jews.

Yarcho now practiced medicine among the *mujiks* (Russian peasants) of a village in the Chernigov district, where a cholera epidemic had broken out. Those afflicted by the disease died by the dozens. Like his other self-sacrificing colleagues, Yarcho struggled heroically to save lives. However, ignorant and confused, backward and superstitious, the local residents began to seek someone to blame for the terrible epidemic that was taking so many lives. There were no Jews in that town. Perhaps many of its inhabitants did not even know that Dr. Yarcho was Jewish.

Then a rumor began spreading that the doctors were to blame for so many deaths. Someone concocted a distorted theory that, nevertheless, found fertile ground in which to grow rapidly: the same doctors—they said—had found no other solution to end the epidemic sooner than to kill in the shortest time the largest number of those afflicted by the disease. [...]

In the end, Baron Maurice de Hirsch (1831–1896), a wealthy railroad builder, deeply embittered by the tragic living conditions of his fellow Jews in many countries, especially Russia, founded the Jewish Colonization Association, ICA. He invested his enormous fortune in this enterprise in order to help Jews emigrate, setting up agricultural settlements for them in various countries, especially in North and South America. The ICA purchased land in various Argentine provinces, including Entre Ríos, and began to bring hundreds of families there to engage in agriculture.

Identifying with these noble aims, whose significance was the immediate emancipation of thousands of his Russian brethren, Noé Yarcho willingly offered to become a member of the ICA's board of directors in order to be part of immigrant contingents.

In 1891, he set sail for Río de la Plata. [...]

No, life for the Jewish gauchos of Entre Ríos at the end of the last century was not easy.

Dr. Yarcho could have taken an easy, comfortable position in any of the important centers of Europe or America. However, he identified with his people and wished to share his destiny with those who were starting their life anew, with those who were exploring new avenues in new surroundings and, like the people of the Bible, were in contact with nature and the land.

More than a physician and philanthropist, more than a man and counselor, more than a neighbor and psychiatrist, Dr. Yarcho was entirely devoted to the Jewish settlers of Entre Ríos.

And he behaved in exactly the same way toward the area's non-Jewish population.

Translated by Marvin Meital.

Other works by Schvartzman: *Antología mínima* (1962); *Copledal de cuarta espera* (1972); *Cincuenta años y cincuenta versos* (1979).

Marcel Bénabou

b. 1939

Marcel Bénabou was born into a devout Sephardic family in Meknes, Morocco, where he was a prize student at the Alliance Israélite Universelle school. At age sixteen, he left Morocco and gave up his religious practice. Having moved to Paris, he studied at the Lycée Louis-le-Grand, the École Normale Supérieure, and finally, the Sorbonne, earning a doctoral degree in ancient Roman history, a subject on which he has written several books. In addition to his career as a professor of ancient history, Bénabou has had a career as a novelist and autobiographer, taking an active role in the avant-garde Ouvroir de littérature potentielle (Oulipo) group and winning various awards, including the National Jewish Book Award for Autobiography.

Jews and Arabs in Morocco
1964

Among the Jews of Europe, acute feelings of difference always fade with the passage of time. The school, the army, and politics have a unifying force; integration comes about through cultural channels. In Morocco, this simple pattern does not apply; distinctive identities seem to have become fixed. The desire for unification, if it exists, has not yet had either the time or the means to materialize. And though in Europe one commonly speaks of "assimilated" Jews, in Morocco it is hard even to imagine what that means.

There are two principal reasons for this unique situation. First of all, Morocco is now the only Muslim country with a Jewish community that is not numerically insignificant. Arab–Israeli tensions have contributed to emptying Middle Eastern countries of their Jewish citizens. Since independence, most Jews in Algeria have left. Jews in Morocco, on the other hand, have for the most part remained.

Second, Morocco is the only formerly colonized country in which "indigenous" Jews have not tied their fate to that of the colonizers, as was the case in Algeria.

Psychological Adaptation

Thus, in this area as in many others, Morocco preserves its originality. Because if the "Jewish problem" is not new, the terms in which it is posed are radically so. It is not, as in other Arab countries, the legitimacy of the Jewish presence that is in question. Antisemitism does not exist; since independence, the Jews have been on a perfectly equal footing as citizens. For now, the only problem is one of purely psychological adaptation; the integration of souls has yet to happen. Here, as elsewhere, such integration can only be realized by cultural means. That is, moreover, the reason it has never really been achieved. If the cultural fusion of Jews and Muslims knew a golden age eight or nine centuries ago, the intellectual horizon has only continued to shrink since those long-ago times. And Judeo-Arabic culture, which once produced men as exceptional as a Maimonides, rapidly dried up. Jews and Muslims have withdrawn into religion. For the Jews, affirming and cultivating their difference was a matter of life and death; for them it meant nothing less than holding on to their identity. And thus, the best chance for true integration was lost. In what survived of Muslim intellectual life in Morocco, the Jews had no place.

French colonization turned this situation upside down. Curiously, it was French culture that served as a mediator between Jews and Muslims. Momentarily, and for a minority, it broke the cycle of ignorance and reciprocal indifference. At the lycée or at the university, Jews and Muslims formed radically new relationships. For the first time, they were equal and had common concerns: they studied for the same exams, earned the same titles, practiced the same professions. A de facto solidarity took hold. But this solidarity could be only limited.

In the end, it became evident that this supposed cultural community was in fact simply a community of the uprooted, fundamentally undermined by the conditions in which it evolved. The cultural convergence was indeed nothing more than a fluke of history. Jews and Muslims approached French culture haphazardly—not in a conscious and concerted drive toward more universality, but in the parallel march of two separate peoples. Moreover, this chance communion involved only a minority that was hardly representative.

Translated by Michele McKay Aynesworth.

Other work by Bénabou: *La Résistance africaine à la romanisation* (1976).

León Rozitchner

1924–2011

León Rozitchner was born in Chivilcoy, Buenos Aires province, in 1924. His grandfather, a rabbi, immigrated to Argentina in the previous century. Rozitchner made his mark on Argentine society and culture as a leftist philosopher, journalist, and university professor. In 1960, he obtained a doctorate in humanities from the Sorbonne; his philosophy was largely influenced by Merleau-Ponty, Marx, and Freud. He edited the left-wing periodical *Contorno* and was forced into exile in Caracas in 1976. He was one of the first in Latin America to establish links between Marxism and psychoanalysis.

To Be a Jew
1968

> In memory of my father, Salomón Motje Rozitchner.
> What other eternity is there
> if not that of knowing
> you are eternally dead.

For Jews the choices are not just difficult. The revolution requires the sacrifice of negativity, the embrace of a new level of objectivity, the destruction of a false sense of belonging, and the abandonment of class complicity. The leftist militant is the one who, within the process of change, is himself ready to change. This cannot be accomplished without some serious indecision, much wavering back and forth, fear, and lack of clarity. But reality urgently demands, in every case, a new definition of terms, a new adjustment. Does the dialectic not imply recognition of the change in oneself during the process, a change without which reality could not evolve? Is praxis not the constant destruction of habitual practices in order to discover the rationality of the real during the very process in which the objective itself is slowly constructing it? How, then, can we avoid that adaptation and that sacrifice of our present comfort, how can we be faithful to our old loves if the signs of the reality to which we aspire are other?

The historical process accelerates, not admitting pauses, and adaptation to the new must now be seen once more in the context of the Arab–Israeli conflict. This situation, which erupted suddenly, demonstrates again the need for adaptability on the part of the left—with a new adjustment, a need to understand reality in a different way. But if we on the left all agree—at least in regard to the historic need for revolution, opposition to imperialism, and transition from capitalism to socialism—why should this new definition not also be easy for us, they say, when it is a matter of opposing Arab socialism to Jewish capitalism, the peoples' liberation to imperialism? Yet we see certain sectors on the left, especially certain Jews on the left, who seem to be straying from this fundamental Marxist line. They see this conflict as a political exception in keeping with the historical exceptionalism that Jews optimistically claim for themselves. This is the point at which we see revealed the Jewish leftist's lack of revolutionary flexibility, his dwelling in the past and incorrigible lack of innovation, his traditional intransigence when it comes to personal sacrifice and willingness to participate fully in the movement of history. Here we see most vividly a unique characteristic, a strange difference that demonstrates the persistence of a rightist focus that has yet to be eradicated and that resists analysis and the process of liberation. It is a counter-revolutionary seed in the heart of the revolutionary himself. No, we must conclude that Jews on the left who remain Jews are incapable of the sacrifice demanded by reality. It is necessary to exclude them from the revolution. We see once again, in the superior smiles of those who have already seen the light, commiseration for the weak among us whom we have been unable to enlighten.

Must it be that way? Let us try, in any case, to think about whether being Jewish and seeing oneself as such is incompatible with being consistently leftist.

Translated by Michele McKay Aynesworth.

Other works by Rozitchner: *Moral burguesa y revolución* (1964); *Freud y los límites del individualismo burgués* (1972); *Las Malvinas: De la guerra sucia a la guerra limpia* (1985); *Perón: Entre la sangre y el tiempo* (1985).

Emil L. Fackenheim
1916–2003

Emil L. Fackenheim was born in Halle, Germany, escaped to England, and later lived in Canada and Israel. A professor of philosophy at the University of Toronto, he addressed Jewish identity, the Holocaust, and German philosophy in his scholarship. Fackenheim was also an ordained Reform rabbi.

The Commanding Voice of Auschwitz
1969

What does the Voice of Auschwitz command?

Jews are forbidden to hand Hitler posthumous victories. They are commanded to survive as Jews, lest the Jewish people perish. They are commanded to remember the victims of Auschwitz lest their memory perish. They are forbidden to despair of man and his world, and to escape into either cynicism or otherworldliness, lest they cooperate in delivering the world over to the forces of Auschwitz. Finally, they are forbidden to despair of the God of Israel, lest Judaism perish. A secularist Jew cannot make himself believe by a mere act of will, nor can he be commanded to do so. . . . And a religious Jew who has stayed with his God may be forced into new, possibly revolutionary relationships with Him. One possibility, however, is wholly unthinkable. A Jew may not respond to Hitler's attempt to destroy Judaism by himself cooperating in its destruction. In ancient times, the unthinkable Jewish sin was idolatry. Today, it is to respond to Hitler by doing his work.

Elie Wiesel has compared the holocaust with Sinai in revelatory significance—and expressed the fear that we are not listening. We shrink from this daring comparison—but even more from not listening. We shrink from any claim to have heard—but even more from a false refuge, in an endless agnosticism, from a Voice speaking to us. I was able to make the above, fragmentary statement (which I have already previously made and here merely quote) only because it no more than articulates what is being heard by Jews the world over—rich and poor, learned and ignorant, believing and secularist. I cannot go beyond this earlier statement but only expand it.

1. The First Fragment

In the murder camps the unarmed, decimated, emaciated survivors often rallied their feeble remaining resources for a final, desperate attempt at revolt. The revolt was hopeless. There was no hope but one. One might escape. Why must one escape? To tell the tale. Why must the tale be told when evidence was already at hand that the world would not listen?[1] Because not to tell the tale, when it might be told, was unthinkable. The Nazis were not satisfied with mere murder. Before murdering Jews, they were trying to reduce them to numbers; after murdering them, they were dumping their corpses into nameless ditches or making them into soap. They were making as sure as was possible to wipe out every trace of memory. Millions would be as though they had never been. But to the pitiful and glorious desperadoes of Warsaw, Treblinka, and Auschwitz, who would soon themselves be as though they had never been, not to rescue for memory what could be rescued was unthinkable because it was sacrilege.[2]

It will remain a sacrilege ever after. Today, suggestions come from every side to the effect that the past had best be forgotten, or at least remain unmentioned, or at least be coupled with the greatest and most thoughtless speed with other, but quite different, human tragedies. Sometimes these suggestions come from Jews rationalizing their flight from the Nazi holocaust. More often they come from non-Jews, who rationalize their own flight, or even maintain, affrontingly enough, that unless Jews universalize the holocaust, thus robbing the Jews of Auschwitz of their Jewish identity, they are guilty of disregard for humanity.[3] But for a Jew hearing the commanding Voice of Auschwitz the duty to remember and to tell the tale, is not negotiable. It is holy. The religious Jew still possesses this word. The secularist Jew is commanded to restore it. A secular holiness, as it were, has forced itself into his vocabulary.

2. The Second Fragment

Jewish survival, were it even for no more than survival's sake, is a holy duty as well. The murderers of Auschwitz cut off Jews from humanity and denied them the right to existence; yet in being denied that right, Jews represented all humanity. Jews after Auschwitz represent all humanity when they affirm their Jewishness and deny the Nazi denial. They would fail if they affirmed the mere *right* to their Jewishness, participating, as it were, in an obscene debate between others who deny the right of Jews to exist and Jews who affirm it.[4] Nor would they deny the Nazi denial if they affirmed merely their humanity-in-general, permitting an antisemitic split between their humanity and their Jewishness, or, worse, agreeing to vanish as Jews in one way, in response to Hitler's attempt to make them vanish in another. The commanding Voice of Auschwitz singles Jews out; Jewish survival is a commandment which brooks no compromise. It was this Voice which was heard by the Jews of Israel in May and June 1967 when they refused to lie down and be slaughtered.[5]

Yet such is the extent of Hitler's posthumous victories that Jews, commanded to survive as Jews, are widely denied even the right. More precisely—for overt antisemitism is not popular in the post-holocaust world—they are granted the right only on certain conditions. Russians, Poles, Indians, and Arabs have a natural right to exist; Jews must earn that right. Other states must refrain from wars of aggression; the State of Israel is an "aggressor" even if it fights for its life.

Peoples unscarred by Auschwitz ought to protest when any evil resembling Auschwitz is in sight, such as the black ghettoes or Vietnam. The Jewish survivors of Auschwitz have no right to survive unless they engage in such protests. Other peoples may include secularists and believers. Jews must be divided into bad secularists or Zionists, and good—albeit anachronistic—saints who stay on the cross.

The commanding Voice of Auschwitz bids Jews reject all such views as a monumental affront. It bids them reject as no longer tolerable every version—Christian or leftist, Gentile or Jewish—of the view that the Jewish people is an anachronism, when it is the elements of the world perpetrating and permitting Auschwitz, not its survivors, that are anachronistic. A Jew is commanded to descend from the cross and, in so doing, not only to reiterate his ancient rejection of an ancient Christian view but also to suspend the time-honored Jewish exaltation of martyrdom. For after Auschwitz, Jewish life is more sacred than Jewish death, were it even for the sanctification of the divine Name. The left-wing secularist Israeli journalist Amos Kenan writes: "After the death camps, we are left only one supreme value: existence."[6]

NOTES

1. See especially Elie Wiesel, "A Plea for the Dead," *Legends of Our Time* (Holt, Rinehart and Winston, 1968), pp. 174–97.

2. See especially Yuri Suhl, *They Fought Back* (New York: Crown, 1967).

3. Wiesel is dismayed to discover that some critics of Nelly Sachs's poetry try to minimize its Jewishness and contrast a "universal vision" with a merely Jewish one. He comments:

Her greatness lies in her Jewishness, and this makes it belong to all mankind. It is perhaps only natural that there are those who try to remove her, if not to estrange her, from us. But this will never happen. She has many Jewish melodies left to sing. . . . What disturbs me is that strangers have stolen them. ("Conversation with Nelly Sachs," *Jewish Heritage* [Spring 1968], p. 33.)

4. In recent years some North American TV stations and university groups have seen fit to furnish American Nazis and German neo-Nazis with a forum, and even invited Jews to debate with them, apparently utterly oblivious to the obscenity of such invitations.

5. See a letter by Professor Harold Fisch of Bar Ilan University quoted in the article cited in note 10, and also note 26. [The references to notes 10 and 26 refer to the note numbers in the original source.—Eds.]

6. "A Letter to All Good People—To Fidel Castro, Sartre, Russell and All the Rest," *Midstream*, October 1968 (This article originally appeared first in *Yediot Aharonot* and was re-

published in *The New Statesman*). Here and in the following, I single out this article, not only because of its excellence, but also (a fact doubtless largely accounting for this excellence) because its author is a left-wing secularist (who cannot and will not abandon his universalistic ideals) and an Israeli (who cannot and will not condone collective Jewish suicide).

Other works by Fackenheim: *Paths to Jewish Belief: A Systematic Introduction* (1960); *The Religious Dimension in Hegel's Thought* (1967); *Encounters between Judaism and Modern Philosophy: A Preface to Future Jewish Thought* (1973).

Samuel Tarnopolsky
1908–2009

Samuel Tarnopolsky was born in Bernasconi, La Pampa, Argentina, to Russian Jewish immigrants. Tarnopolsky was a celebrated rheumatologist, finishing his studies in Buenos Aires in 1933 and continuing to practice, write, and teach. He wrote extensively on rheumatology as well as on indigenous medicines. He also made a name for himself as a historian, social commentator, and novelist. His primary subjects were the conquistadores, the Pampas Indians, Jewish Argentines, and Argentine antisemitism, which he found especially distressing in people who were perceived to be honorable and indeed liberal.

Half of Nothing
1969

Antisemitism is not an Argentine disgrace; we did not invent it. Other countries preceded us. Not even the far-right Tacuara Nationalist Movement of the 1960s invented it. Before that, there was the Argentine Civic Legion, and even before that, the Patriotic League. Even further back, when we had not even seen a Jew, we already had antisemitism. Just ask Braunstein for a copy of Martel's nineteenth-century novel *La Bolsa* [The Stock Market].

Nor should the wealthy neighborhood called Barrio Norte by the reactionaries be treated as a scapegoat. Tacuara was not an exclusive product of the "Petit Café." On the contrary, the governments that won the vote in regular elections—those most legitimately voted into power—tolerated the bloodiest, most virulent, and most lasting antisemitism: the week of tragedy with Yrigoyen, the shooting of young Edgardo Trilnik under Frondizi, the assassination of Alterman during

Illia's presidency. In contrast, aristocratic, oligarchic, military, revolutionary, or dictatorial governments did not tolerate such criminal extremes.

If antisemitism is a country's shame, others must hang their heads more than we. We did not have, nor do we have, ghettos like Italy's, an inquisition like Spain's, expulsions like Great Britain's, *numerus clausus* like Poland's, trials for religious crimes like Romania's, pogroms like Russia's, confiscations like Portugal's, ovens like Germany's, or a Dreyfus trial like France's. Our country is not worse than others and is, in many ways, better. This problem needs to be approached from a historical perspective. Antisemitism was not lacking among the most abject, dirty, and ignorant town, the town of Dostoyevsky, Gorki, and Tolstoy; nor in the cleanest, most cultivated and soulful, the town of Goethe, Beethoven, and Kant; nor in that of subhuman beings, such as in Arab countries where slave markets still thrive, nor in the most refined product of civilization, the town of Dante. What would have been surprising, rather, is if antisemitism had not taken root here. Such an abnormality would indeed have been a cause for worry.

Antisemitism is not an Argentine phenomenon; it is a phenomenon of Western civilization. But if our civilization were swept away by that of the East, I doubt the Jews would be any better off. Remember Stalin and Khrushchev and a pamphlet by the father of them both, Karl Marx, a booklet entitled *The Jewish Question*. It was published here by Aníbal Ponce, a Stalinist, and reissued by "Cayoacan," a Trotskyite. When Jews are saved from the frying pan, they fall into the fire.

Translated by Michele McKay Aynesworth.

Other works by Tarnopolsky: *Alarma de indios en la frontera sud* (1941); *Los prejuiciados de honrada conciencia* (1971).

Ruth R. Wisse

b. 1936

Romanian-born Ruth R. Wisse grew up in Montreal and taught at McGill University before accepting a position as professor of Yiddish literature at Harvard University. Known for her strong advocacy for Israel, she is a literary critic, a translator, and an author on a range of Jewish topics.

The Schlemiel as Modern Hero
1971

Holocaust Survivor

[. . .] Modern Jewish humor grows from the tension of having to reconcile a belief as absolute as Elijah's with an experience of failure as absolute as that of the priests of Baal.

The schlemiel embodies this tension, being the equivalent of the defeated people, incapable of despair. [. . .]

But in the contemporary phase of our subject, the question arises: at what point will failure break the back of faith? The destruction of European Jewry during World War II, the systematic slaughter of millions of people and the annihilation of thousands of communities has necessarily influenced our attitude towards the schlemiel as the victor in defeat. How does one retain the notion of psychic survival when its cost has been physical extinction? As long as the Jews were suffering from the old ills of hunger and humiliation and as long as pogroms were sporadic, the notion of a "triumph of identity despite failure of circumstance" could still carry some conviction. But after the entire populations of Kasrilevke and Tuneyadevke have been reduced to the ash of crematoria, does it not become a cruel sentimentality to indulge in schlemiel humor and to sustain a faith in the ironic mode?

And yet, strangely enough, the schlemiel has survived even the holocaust. Although almost too painful a subject for Yiddish fiction, which since the war has struggled through chronicles and lamentations with understandably little inclination for humor, he has found a home in American fiction and popular culture. The transplantation of this figure from Europe to America could be symbolized by the story "Gimpel the Fool," written by the Yiddish master, Isaac Bashevis Singer, and translated into English in 1953 by the American novelist Saul Bellow.

"Gimpel Tam," a rare example of the schlemiel figure in postwar Yiddish fiction, is more correctly if less adequately translated as simpleton. [. . .]

The struggle between faith and skepticism is much more explicit in Gimpel than in any of his schlemiel-predecessors, a reflection of the much grimmer historical period within which he was created. As the opening sentences indicate, Gimpel is fully conscious of the distinction between the figure he cuts in the world and his own self-conception. Isaac Bashevis Singer has introduced the fool in Shakespearean ambiguity, a character who may be choosing to play the fool in order to retain his moral sanity in the face of *universal cynicism*. [. . .]

Reading "Gimpel the Fool" our rational prejudice is confronted with an appeal to a deeper truth, deeper because it frees a man from despair, permits him to live in harmony with his conscience, to practice goodness, and hope for justice.

Between opening and conclusion, the tone of the story changes noticeably as the character evolves from simpleton to saintly storyteller. The broad humor of the first three sections is saved from coarseness only by the delicacy of the irony. Its situations are the stuff of bedroom farces, but since the husband is amusing us at his own expense, there is compassion in our laughter. The conclusion, by contrast, is sober. A contemplative monologue supplants the lively narrative. The schlemiel youth grows into a mystical wanderer in a process that illuminates the connection between the two. In his simplicity the schlemiel ignores those same pragmatic social concerns which the mystic actively rejects through contemplation. The schlemiel's naïve substitution of his illusory world for the real one resembles the mystic's supernaturalism, a perhaps accidental resemblance that is shaped by Singer into an organic relation. In "Gimpel the Fool" the schlemiel-figure is explicitly raised to a higher level of significance by the association of a personality pattern with a metaphysic.

The antirational motif, which permeates Singer's work, exerts an obvious influence on his style. In the Gimpel story, and elsewhere, he uses the persona of a naïve storyteller as a convenient means of blurring the distinctions between appearance and more respectable forms of belief. Singer has emphasized that he is committed to the philosophy of "As if":

The "as if" is so much a part of our life that it really isn't artificial. . . . Every man assumes he will go on living. He behaves *as if* he will never die.[1]

The "as if" lies at the heart of Gimpel's philosophy, and less self-consciously articulated, it is every schlemiel's method of coping with reality. Raised by Singer to his most exalted extreme, the schlemiel defies all

rational distinctions and even the limits of life in his determination to remain fully human. The mystic's supernaturalism reflects his quest for God; but Gimpel's appeal to a transcendental standard is merely the result of having sought to live harmlessly among men. [. . .]

The schlemiel in humorous fiction, the saint in rhetoric heightened towards tragedy, reflect the actual response of almost an entire culture. Throughout the process of annihilation, the majority of Jews refused or were unable to face reality. The hymn of the concentration camps was the Ani Maamin: "I believe with perfect faith in the coming of the Messiah. And even though he is slow in coming (he is taking his own sweet time) yet even so, I believe." The song is ambivalent, like the Yiddish proverbs, but desperation has made the faith more fervent. [. . .]

Mendele Mocher Sforim's traveller, Benjamin III, evolved from an object of ridicule into an ironic subject when he stepped into an environment more ridiculous and certainly more sinister than the one that had produced him. Because Sholom Aleichem seemed to accept the destructive environment as a given fact, he rendered what a critic has aptly called, "a judgment of love through the medium of irony."[2] Recreating the familiar schlemiel-figure in the aftermath of the holocaust, Singer made him a character of semifantastic fiction. Since the schlemiel is above all a reaction against the evil surrounding him, he must reject more and more as the evil increases; Gimpel is prepared to walk into eternity in pursuit of personal goodness.

NOTES

[The story "Gimpel the Fool" appears in this volume of *The Posen Library* as "Simple Gimpl."—Eds.]

1. Joel Blocker and Richard Elman, "An Interview with Isaac Bashevis Singer," *Commentary* 36, no. 5 (November 1963): 365.

2. Irving Howe, *A World More Attractive: A View of Modern Literature and Politics* (New York: 1963), p. 209.

Other works by Wisse: *A Little Love in Big Manhattan: Two Yiddish Poets* (1988); *If I Am Not for Myself: The Liberal Betrayal of the Jews* (1992); *The Modern Jewish Canon: A Journey through Language and Culture* (2000); *Jews and Power* (2005); *No Joke: Making Jewish Humor* (2013).

LIFE WRITING AND REPORTAGE

Avrom Teytlboym

1889–1947

A restlessly busy actor with a strong literary bent, Avrom Teytlboym began his career with productions by Y. L. Peretz. An itinerant period followed in which Teytlboym, who was born in Warsaw, moved between London, Buenos Aires, Paris, Moscow, and Vilna, landing finally in New York, where he performed alongside Maurice Schwartz. Along the way, Teytlboym also directed, produced, and stage managed plays, and he published myriad articles and reviews in Yiddish periodicals, earning the sobriquet "the Literary Actor." Toward the end of his life, he returned to the Warsaw of his childhood, producing his most lasting work.

Warsaw Courtyards

1947

Muranow 19

This was not a very big courtyard, a longish but narrow one, like hundreds of others of this type in the thickly settled part of Jewish Warsaw. One side, the innermost one, was a two-story building. The other sides surrounding the court were one-story buildings. In the middle of the courtyard there was a small pump, from which all residents drew their drinking water. It also served as a little gathering place for the women to gossip and for children's games to start.

The courtyard reflected the lives of its inhabitants. If everything was "thank God"—nobody was sick, nothing bad had befallen anyone—in that case the courtyard was lively, good-natured, and smiling. But if someone experienced trouble or misfortune, then the courtyard was in pain, worried, and depressed, because the troubles of one resident were always the troubles of the whole courtyard. Despite all the personal peculiarities and all the confrontations, the whole courtyard lived like one great, extended family. People sometimes quarreled and then became reconciled, loved one another and couldn't stand one another, as is the case with people who are close, are almost of the same flesh and blood.

It was not so much the adults who maintained this sense of family. The fathers seldom saw one another on weekdays. They were preoccupied with making a living, which drove them out early and brought them home late. For most of the day the mothers also were tied down, some to the kitchen, some to cleaning the house and doing laundry, and others to various ways of helping out their husbands in their work. It was the youngsters, the children, who wove the web of kinship and spread it over the entire courtyard. They very nearly abolished the partitions between one home and another. They knew what was going on in everyone's lives. They stayed with neighbors till late at night, when they were sent packing with a good-natured: "Go home, it's late, your mama is calling you . . ."

It was the children who dominated the courtyard. They liked one another, hated one another, played together, had fights, became friends again, and created *koleykes* [gangs] of boys that from time to time set off to do battle with *koleykes* from other courtyards. And for children like me—eight or nine years old—this simple courtyard was not so simple. For us it was, on the contrary, quite distinguished, from the very fact that it faced "Muranow," where there was located at that time one of the most important Jewish marketplaces. In later years, this authentically Jewish marketplace was abolished. The Muranow market was a source of livelihood for hundreds of Jewish families, who had their stalls, booths, and stands in it. What wasn't for sale at the Muranow market? There were stalls of fish—carp, tench, pike, and perch; there were stalls of bread—challahs, currant cakes, buns, and hard rolls; stalls of iron pots, tin forks, wooden noodle-boards, earthen colanders, clay bowls, and porcelain plates; stalls of ribbons, bands, buttons, hooks, bows, and lace; stalls of cloth—silk, cotton, worsted, chintz, and cretonne; stalls of apples, plums, watermelons, small pears, pumpkin seeds, gooseberries, and currants; barrels of herring, cheese, butter, sauerkraut, and pickles; stalls with hundreds of tablecloths, pillowcases and sheets, hats, pants, and hardware. Jewish women in broad aprons and Jewish men with leather pockets filled with silver or copper coins traded, weighed, measured, and "made a profit." From early morning until late in the evening, in summer and in winter, in good weather and bad, you heard the loud hum and bustle of hundreds of Jewish customers, who had come there from all the surrounding streets looking for bargains, to haggle, to feel, to rummage and buy.

For us children, Muranow market was a whole world. Muranow Square was the heart and center of everything that our young minds had hitherto encountered. [. . .]

Twarda 2

The Twarda 2 courtyard [to which we moved] was, in terms of its appearance and the makeup of its inhabitants, very different from the Muranow courtyard where I spent my early childhood. This was a large courtyard, enclosed by its three-story wings, in which there lived many well-off and even aristocratic families. And although here too there was a feeling of good-natured neighborliness, there was missing that sense of being one big family which bound together the inhabitants of the Muranow courtyard. Maybe it had to do with the fact that the neighborhood was a wealthier one, where people were a bit more reserved, more on their own. In addition, the inhabitants of Twarda 2 belonged to various groups which generally had little contact with one another. There were Hasidim, with stately beards, in long caftans, wearing big cloth hats on weekdays and satin coats and velvet hats on the Sabbath; "Germans" (Jews modern in their ways) without beards, with "short clothes" and fedoras; and Mitnagdim [opponents of the Hasidim] who were halfway between, with trimmed beards, in short "chopped" caftans, with small cloth hats and elegant canes in their hands. [. . .]

Our courtyard was located close to other celebrated courtyards. Twarda 4, the adjoining courtyard, was the famous Arele Sardiner's courtyard with its big prayer house, where, for twenty-four hours a day continuous prayer and study went on. Before one *minyan* [quorum of ten men praying] had finished, a second was already standing and waiting to begin. And when one group of students of the Talmud, mostly poor people, finished the lesson in the anteroom late at night, you could already hear the melancholy-joyful tones of the next group that sat down to study until dawn. The courtyard at Twarda 6 was famous for Nozhik's Synagogue, the very large prayer-house which was besieged every Friday evening and Saturday morning with thousands of people who struggled to get in to hear the beloved choir and cantor. At that time, the Minsk cantor Levenzon and the choir-conductor Davidovitsh competed in popularity with the great "German Synagogue"

on Tłomackie Street where Sirota was the cantor and Leo Lyov the conductor. Jews who were knowledgeable about cantorial music and choirs would run every Sabbath to compare the singing and argue about which cantor or choir sings more beautifully.

Across the street was Urlich's Courtyard, a walled-in market with booths and stalls. Not far from there were the big iron-yards of the wealthy Hasidic family Klepfish and the Hasidic millionaire Prives. Grzybow Street and nearby Bagno Street were the center of the iron-yards and hardware shops. Jews with long beards and caftans, young men in small cloth hats, and married women in wigs sold everything from small nails, screws, linchpins and bolts, to saws, hammers, pipes, and small stoves. The open-air yards were covered with hardware of every sort—from rusty wheel-rims, to shiny rails, bars and girders, beds, and spiral stairs.

Not far away was Świętokrzyska Street. There you found the shops with ready-to-wear men's clothes, as well as some for women, and a bit further on, the shops for used books and antiques, all of them owned by Jews.

Twarda Street was full of shops big and small and businesses of every description. At every step—a food shop, a tobacconist, a kerosene-seller, a bakery, a dry-goods store and a fruit-seller or a butcher shop. It was perfectly natural and it was appreciated whether you bought a head of a herring for a *groshn* [penny] in a food shop, or two *groshn*'s worth of kerosene, or several *arshin* [twenty-eight inches] of satin for a Sabbath caftan, or several plump geese whose fat would be rendered for the winter. Close to one another stood beer halls, taverns, coffee shops, and modest restaurants where the customers were Jewish porters, coachmen, artisans, and even well-to-do Jews who wanted to "toss back" a drink and have a bite to eat in an informal eatery.

That's how it was all week long. Grzybow and Twarda Streets were Jewish streets. If a Christian, a Pole from one of the surrounding streets, wandered in, wearing different clothes and with a shiny visor on his cap, he would behave cautiously, like someone in a foreign country. Only on Sunday, or a Christian holiday, would the picture change. As if by prearrangement, the Jews on those days withdrew from Grzybow and handed it over to the Christians. Thousands of them would come to the church and overflow the square and the surrounding streets amid the heavy tolling of the bronze bells on the church towers.

Yet even this was a part of Jewish life and Jewish live-lihoods. Despite the fact that the Jewish shops and beer halls were closed on the street side, the Christians nevertheless filled them and left behind plenty of profits. Using the "back way" through courtyards, they would find their way to Jewish restaurants and live it up at the buffets, where they could enjoy tasty Jewish dishes—gefilte fish or roasted chicken livers—washed down with quantities of beer or whiskey. [. . .]

In countless Jewish homes a new interest and a new form of enjoyment appeared—to sing the popular songs, repeat the clever lines and reenact the scenes played by the Jewish actors in the Yiddish theater. With all its faults, with all the criticism that could be made of the young Yiddish theater in Poland, it was nevertheless invaluable in adding a new dimension to the rapidly emerging Jewish cultural life—the dimension of the living, spoken Yiddish word. The beautifully spoken Yiddish word—in contrast to the deformed, neglected, and ill-sounding language of the street—which hitherto had been heard only on rare occasions from a speaker at a meeting or at a concert, was now freely to be heard night after night from the stage of the Yiddish theater. After all, Libert, Arko, Fishzon, Zaslavska, Braginska, not to mention Ester Rokhl Kaminska or Sonya Edelman, spoke Yiddish more beautifully than one was accustomed to hearing. In their mouths, Yiddish acquired more dignity, more significance and was more impressive. That certainly added in great measure to the fact that Yiddish later blossomed in the mouths of Polish Jewish youth.

In addition, even the written Yiddish word was greatly stimulated by the Yiddish theater of that day. New subjects opened up in the daily Yiddish press, which had begun to expand at the same time as the Yiddish theater. People began to *write* about Yiddish theater. Reviews, essays, analyses, whether of individual actors, of particular performances or about theater in general, began to occupy an increasingly greater place in the Yiddish press.

Translated by Solon Beinfeld.

Other works by Teytlboym: *Fun mayne vanderungen* (1935); *William Shakespeare* (1946).

Jacques Lazarus

To My Tunisian Friends
1948

I have just spent a few days in Tunis.

My pleasure increases each time I return to that city and its inhabitants and experience the liveliness of the Avenue Jules-Ferry, and above all, the free and proud atmosphere in which a committed Jew can fully live his life.

My first visit to this country was in the summer of 1946.

During the course of a quick trip across North Africa, I had visited Algeria, Morocco, and Tunisia, one after the other.

Coming from mainland France, I was confronted by fresh perspectives and by problems of which I had been completely unaware.

Back in France, memories of wretched conditions in the Moroccan mellah, of so much poverty alongside so much wealth, of the indifference of the authorities, of the almost criminal selfishness of certain rich Moroccan Jews, had not left me.

I could not stop thinking about the partitioning imposed by the Administration, especially in regard to education, with some establishments reserved for the French, certain others for young Muslims, and the *Alliance* schools (inadequate, but oh so useful) for young Jews.

Then certain passages from my school-boy "Lavisse"[1] would fill my mind, quickly suppressed by a sad smile.

Algeria. Algiers especially, the only city where I had stayed for a bit, offered a different face.

There I had noticed right away (an opinion shared by all those who had told me of their impressions after having traveled from France to stay awhile in Algeria) a rather marked indifference toward anything that touched, whether closely or not, on the Jewish question.

The majority of the population attached little importance to such problems and seemed to remember their origins only during occasional periods of "alarm" that were forgotten as soon as the danger had passed.

The war and its countless miseries, the parade of suffering endured by the European Jews, seemed to have left only superficial traces in Algeria.

Most of the populace seemed not to have understood.

How else can one explain the attitude of a significant percentage of the Algerian Jewish community?

A good-willed minority struggled and continue to struggle to remedy this state of affairs, one that pains any Jew who is conscious of his obligation to show solidarity.

Their efforts, rather than being encouraged, have been too often stymied or frowned upon.

Again, in Tunisia I saw a different picture.

There I came upon a Jewry that was free, a people that had rejected its shabby prejudices, its routine, its complexes.

In that country, itself North African, one breathed a different air, an air of freedom.

There the Jews, I speak of the many I know, freely discussed problems that, they knew, concerned them as much as Jews in the rest of the world.

And that is why I loved Tunisia straight away.

In Tunis, I had seen young Jews strolling around the city streets, I had seen vendors calling out to sell Jewish newspapers in city squares. I had talked with the Jewish leaders and all of them won me over immediately because no one, French or Tunisian, had hidden from me or from anyone else their deep respect for their French or Tunisian homeland, and their deep love for the Jewish people.

In Morocco, such feelings are just as strong, but they are stifled.

In Tunisia, they express themselves freely, with no constraints.

My memory of the Regency remained vivid.

Two subsequent trips only confirmed it.

The Jews of Tunisia, no matter what social class they belong to, whether doctors, industrialists, lawyers, businessmen, technicians, office workers, or laborers, do not believe they are denying their French or Tunisian homelands (which they have served as well as anyone else and whose strong ties unite them) when they proclaim they belong to the Jewish people and acknowledge with a clear conscience all the duties and all the responsibilities that implies.

Burying one's head in the sand does not impress Tunisian Jews as clever strategy, nor does feigning ignorance or deliberately maintaining silence in the face of clear evidence.

Like me and others, they have not forgotten the words and deeds of certain "Israelite Frenchmen" of the interwar years. Like me, they shudder at the evils that those men of little vision failed to spare their fellow Jews.

The appearance of a Jewish newspaper in Tunisia—one whose only goal is to provide information—is not seen by Jewish leaders, or at least by those claiming to be such, as a reprehensible act threatening serious harm to the community.

In Tunis, in Tunisia, such efforts, far from being hindered, are encouraged.

Fear and "wait-and-see" or "what-will-people-say" attitudes, do not guide every action.

For the Jews of Tunisia, the annual sale of matzah does not seem to be the major concern. They are interested in more important matters: the relief of poverty, the improvement of professional and cultural education.

It was of all this I was thinking, roaming the lively streets of Tunis as evening drew on and young voices cried out, "La Gazette d'Israël," "Défense d'Israël."

It was of all this I was thinking.

And then I returned to Algiers.

Jacquel

NOTE
1. [Ernest Lavisse was a French historian.—Eds.]

Translated by Michele McKay Aynesworth.

Sasson Shalom Dallal
1929–1949

Born in Baghdad, Sasson Shalom Dallal was a member of the League for the Struggle against Zionism, an organization concerned with thwarting Zionist efforts to form a two-state system—Jewish and Arab—in Mandatory Palestine. From their perspective on the far left, Dallal and like-minded Iraqis were convinced that such a political system would serve the interests only of colonialists and the Jewish bourgeoisie. The background of such concerns was the continuing effort of Great Britain to maintain its imperial sway in the Middle East and the Iraqi government's hostility toward communism. For about four months in 1949, Dallal was head of the Iraqi Communist Party, but in the end, like some of his leftist comrades before him, the twenty-year-old was hanged by the state.

Last Letter
1949

Dear Brother:
    It is an enchanting evening. The wind has been blowing steadily the whole day. It suddenly dropped at nightfall. All is still. There is no stir in the air. The

world seems fast asleep. I cannot sleep. It is hard to sleep knowing that tomorrow at dawn I will die. Ever since I was arrested, I wanted to write to you. I was not sure of what to say. I was confused and afraid. I was not sure that you would sympathize with my activity and ideas, ideas that could only prove valid where our lives most need them. I was not sure that your academic life in America would make you see objectively the justice and validity of our cause. To-night, knowing that the coming dawn will start my eternal night, I venture to write to you the thoughts and ideas which are teeming in my brain now.

A wave of terror has taken the country; thousands of people are being arrested, tortured, and executed. I am not the only one to die tomorrow. There are ten others with me. The people as a whole are per-secuted. Life in our country recalls the days when the forces of fascism were marching on, murdering thousands of innocent people. I have not lived long enough to enjoy and know what life is. I opened my eyes fighting for a free life and tomorrow at dawn I am dying for the life I never knew.

I pray to God that my fight has not been in vain. The forces of reaction cannot rule forever. They have been defeated before by the will of the people and by the same will, they will be defeated in the near future. I am dying tomorrow because I have faith in mankind to master their destiny, which is democ-racy, peace, and the perfect life. The forces of reac-tion that are still murdering people to lengthen the time of their criminal rule are afraid of the future. In the future, they see the shadow of their end. This shadow is perverting their minds. They are insane. They have exhausted their ideas. They are bankrupt in their policies, lies, propaganda, and promises. They are terribly afraid of the wrath of the people. They can rob me of my life, but they cannot change my thinking, which is that of all Mankind. I am free because I know the truth and neither prison nor ex-ecution can take away that freedom from me.

Tomorrow at dawn I shall die. Yes, they can end my life and stop me from exposing and fighting them, but with my death, thousands of others will rise against them. We are [the] many, they are the few. Do not grieve for me, dear brother, instead carry my memory with you and perpetuate the fight, which will glorify the future of all humanity. And always remember that I am not sorry to die. In fact, if I am

given once again the chance to live, I would follow the same path.

Goodbye to all, and my love to you.

NOTE

[Words in brackets appear in the original source document.]

Translated by Reading A. Dallal.

Yankev Botoshanski
1895–1964

A well-known essayist, critic, and playwright, Yankev Botoshanski was born in Bessarabia and began his literary career as a journalist in Russian, adopting Yiddish as his language of self-expression in 1912. His cabaret-style plays were widely performed in Romania and Poland. Moving to Argentina in 1926, Botoshanski became the editor of *Di prese*, the major Yiddish daily in Buenos Aires. After the war, he turned to life writ-ing, both about the Old Country and the New.

A Kol Nidre Service at the Gęsia Street Cemetery
1956

I was then in Warsaw for the second time. That city had always exerted a powerful attraction for me, with its great and all-encompassing Jewish life. When I was in the Polish capital for the first time, Jewish life was flour-ishing, though there was no lack of antisemitism even then. When I was in the same city, and in Poland as a whole, a second time, Jewish life there seemed discour-aged and depressed. The antisemitism that stemmed both from the masses and the Polish government had caused most Jews to lose heart. [. . .]

And now it was the day of Yom Kippur eve. Though I was not an observant Jew, I nevertheless felt the need to be somewhere for Kol Nidre.[1] In addition, I felt that as a Yiddish writer I needed to see what Warsaw looked like at Kol Nidre. I had seen many, many cities at Kol Nidre, both in my native Old World and in the New. [. . .]

I was faced with the problem of where to go for Kol Nidre. One of my friends suddenly said to me: "If I were in your place I would go to the cemetery."

"To which cemetery?" I asked in astonishment.

"To the Gęsia Street Jewish Cemetery."

"They say Kol Nidre there?"

"Of course they do."

"Who does it and how?"

"Why do you need to ask so many questions? Go there, and you'll see."

I followed his advice and went there. I deliberately arrived on foot, though it was some distance away. I wanted to see Warsaw on the eve of Yom Kippur. [. . .]

I stared at the crowd. It was varied in its composition. What stood out to me were the cripples. Not only were there many more cripples than I had seen along the way, but some seemed in worse condition. I had already seen, in various cities of Europe and Asia, renowned asylums for cripples. I had seen genuine and sham cripples in marketplaces. In a certain neighborhood of Jewish Vilna I had seen any number of cripples. But never in my life had I seen a "display" of deformities like I now saw at the cemetery in Warsaw.

I repressed the painful feelings evoked in me by the cripples and looked at the rest of the crowd. There was no shortage of poor people without deformities who looked no less miserable. Some of them, both young and old, men and women, looked so pathetic that they needed no deformity to arouse pity. All they would have to do to look frightfully pitiful would be to wrinkle their faces and reach out their hands. I thought to myself that if God gave them a good look, and if he was truly a God of mercy, he would have to help them.

Next to the poor people, with and without deformities, stood the underworld of Warsaw. It too had come to the cemetery for Kol Nidre. You could recognize the heroes of all manner of Yiddish writers. You could surmise who was *only* a thief, and who was also a pimp. Among the thieves you could recognize who was quick and light-fingered and who was a strongman, a young fellow with a hand like a bear's paw, who could stun his victim in one move and take everything from him. You could also recognize the older members of the underworld, the "respectable" thieves whose work now consisted more in giving advice than in doing any thieving on their own. [. . .]

As the men put on their prayer shawls, the women also began to prepare for Kol Nidre. Those women whose heads were still bared covered them with kerchiefs and the shawls they wore around their shoulders. It looked both ceremonial and frightful, a terrifying holiday and perhaps something worse. You heard the *tefillah zakah* being said, the prayer that is recited before Kol Nidre. The Hebrew of that prayer is not easy, but nonetheless some recited the words correctly and with the right feeling. It was clear that there was no lack of people who had studied in a heder and perhaps beyond. The groaning of men could be heard, soon accompanied by the sobbing of women. The weeping made just as strange an impression as the whole picture. The whole affair became more than strange. At this cemetery Jews of every class, some of them very distinguished, lie buried. Yet people who do everything forbidden by God have gathered here to pray to God. Nearby were the tombs of famous rabbis, illustrious figures, and wealthy men, who played an important part in the life of Polish Jews and of Poland in general. And how far was it to the *Ohel Peretz*, where Yitskhok Leybush Peretz as well as Yankev Dinenzon and S. An-ski lie buried? It seemed to me like a scene from Peretz's *At Night in the Old Marketplace*. [. . .]

I looked at my neighbors and all the people within my view. I seldom saw a pair of eyes that was not filled with tears. I asked myself: what in essence is being expressed here? Is it fear, is it pain, or is it just tears? My answer to myself was: it is all these things together. People here have the opportunity to ask God to make things better for them, but they are afraid it will not happen, which is why there is so much fear in their eyes. [. . .]

The half-moon that had appeared in the clear sky accompanied me. The moon seemed to help me gather my thoughts, which had been unclear even to me. More than twenty years have passed since I heard and saw Kol Nidre in the Gęsia Street Cemetery in Warsaw. But I still see before my eyes that strange and terrible picture, in which I nevertheless see the greatness of Polish Jewry.

NOTE

1. [The prayer service commencing Yom Kippur.—Trans.]

Translated by Solon Beinfeld.

Mordecai Richler

1931–2001

Mordecai Richler, a Montreal-born writer who captured the essence of that city's Jewish community, was the author of novels, screenplays, children's books, and numerous essays. His often-satirical fictional works featured Jewish Canadian protagonists, and his journalistic essays frequently criticized Canada. Richler received many honors, including a 1974 Academy Award nomination, the Giller Prize, the Stephen Leacock Award, and the title Companion of the Order of Canada.

Their Canada and Mine
1961

My grandfather, like so many others, came to Canada by steerage from Poland in 1900 and settled down not far from Main Street in what was to become a ghetto. Here, as in the real America, the immigrants worked under appalling conditions in factories. They rented halls over poolrooms and grocery stores to meet and form burial societies and create *shuls*. They sent to the old country for relatives left behind and rabbis and brides. Slowly, unfalteringly, the immigrants started to struggle up a ladder of streets, from one where you had to leave your garbage outside your front door to another where you actually had a rear lane; from the three rooms over the grocery or tailor shop to your own cold-water flat on a street with trees.

Our street, St. Urbain, was one of five working-class ghetto streets between the Main and Park Avenue.

To a middle-class stranger, it's true, any one of these streets would have seemed as squalid as the next. On each corner a cigar store, a grocery, and a fruit man. Outside staircases everywhere. Winding ones, wooden ones, rusty and risky ones. An endless repetition of precious peeling balconies and waste lots making the occasional gap here and there. But, as we boys knew, each street between the Main and Park Avenue represented subtle differences in income. No two cold-water flats were alike and no two stores were the same either. Best Fruit gypped on weight but Smiley's didn't give credit.

Among the wonders of St. Urbain, our St. Urbain, there was a man who ran for alderman each election on a one-plank platform (provincial speed cops were anti-Semites), a boy nobody remembered who had gone on to become a professor at MIT, two men who had served with the MacKenzie-Paps in the Spanish Civil War (they no longer spoke to each other), Herscovitch's cousin Larry, who had demanded kosher food when he was sentenced to six months in jail for receiving stolen goods, a woman who called herself a divorcee, and a boxer who had made the ratings in *Ring* magazine.

St. Urbain was, I suppose, somewhat similar to ghetto streets in New York and Chicago. There were some crucial differences, however. We were Canadians, therefore we had a King. We also had "pea-soups," i.e., French Canadians, in the neighborhood. [. . .]

"Pea-soups" were for turning the lights on and off on Shabbos and running elevators and cleaning out chimneys and furnaces. They were, it was rumored, ridden with TB, rickets, and diseases it's better not to mention. You gave them old clothes. A week before the High Holidays you had one in to wax the floors. The French Canadians were our "*schwartze*." [. . .]

Our world was made up of five streets. Above Park Avenue came Outremont, where Jewish bosses and professional men were already beginning to make inroads on what used to be a middle-class French Canadian reserve. Two streets below our own came the Main.

The Main was rich in delights. But looking at it again after an absence of many years I must say that it can also be sordid, it's filthy, and hollering with stores whose wares, whether furniture or fruit, are ugly or damaged. The signs still say Fantastic Discounts or Forced to Sell Prices Here, but the bargains so bitterly sought after are illusory—and perhaps they always were. [. . .]

Today the original Young Israel Synagogue, where we used to chin the bar, is no longer there. A bank stands where my old poolroom used to be. Some familiar stores have gone. There have been deaths and bankruptcies. But most of the departed have simply packed up and moved with their old customers to the nearest of the new shopping centers at Van Horne or Rockland. And what are these centers if not tarted-up versions of the old Main, where you could do all your buying in a concentrated area and maybe get a special price through a cousin's cousin? Yesterday it was a dollar off because it's you, today it's the shopping stamp.

Up and down the Main you can still pick out many restaurants and steak houses wedged between the sweater factories, poolrooms, cold-water flats, wholesale dry goods stores, and "Your Most Sanitary" barbershops. The places where we used to work in summer as shippers for ten dollars a week are still there. So's Baron Byng High School, right where it always was. Rabbinical students and boys with sidecurls still pass. These, however, are the latest arrivals from Poland and Rumania and soon their immigrant parents will put pressure on them to study hard and make good. To get out.

But many of our own grandparents, the very same people who assured us the Main was only for *bummers* and failures, will not get out. Today when most of the children have made good, now that the sons and daughters have split-level bungalows and minks and winters in Miami, many of the grandparents still cling to the Main. Their children cannot in many cases persuade them to leave. So you still see them there, drained and used-up by the struggle. They sit on kitchen chairs next to the Coke freezer in the cigar and soda store, dozing with a fly-swatter in hand. You find them rolling their own cigarettes and studying the obituary column in the *Jewish Eagle* on the steps outside the Jewish Library. The women still peel potatoes on the stoop under the shade of a winding outside staircase. Old men still watch the comings and goings from the balcony above, a blanket spread over their legs and a little bag of polly [sunflower] seeds on their lap. As in the old days the sinking house with the crooked floor is often right over the store or the wholesaler's, or maybe next door to the junk yard. Only today the store and the junk yard are shut down. Signs for Sweet Caporal Cigarettes or old election posters have been nailed in over the missing windows. There are spider-webs everywhere.

Other works by Richler: *The Apprenticeship of Duddy Kravitz* (1959); *St. Urbain's Horseman* (1971); *Jacob Two-Two Meets the Hooded Fang* (1975).

Melekh Ravitch

1893-1976

The modernist Yiddish poet, essayist, vegetarian, and cultural icon Melekh Ravitch (born Zekharye-Khone Bergner) was born in Radymno, Galicia (now Poland). He served in the Austro-Hungarian army during World War I and moved in 1921 to Warsaw, where he and the poets Uri Zvi Greenberg and Peretz Markish established the expressionist literary group called *Di khalyastre*. From 1924 to 1934 Ravitch was the executive secretary of the Association of Jewish Writers and Journalists in Warsaw, which later inspired his biographical sketches of twentieth-century Yiddish writers. Ravitch, a world traveler, settled in 1940 in Montreal, where he perfected the genre of the autobiographical vignette.

My First Day in the Twentieth Century
1962

The truth, the mathematical truth, is that a new century begins on January 1 of the year one of the new hundred-year time span. But it is the custom to celebrate a new century on January 1 of the last year of the departing century, a year earlier. People are tired of dragging around a worn-out century and wish as quickly as possible to start the new one. Probably it will be a better one—that's how people are. In the villages sur-

rounding the town where I witnessed the arrival of the twentieth century, the Ukrainian peasants used to say: *Nay bide hirshe, abi inshe*—let it be worse, as long as it's different . . .

Already weeks before January 1, 1900, the upcoming event was being talked about. In reality it was not an event, but pure abstraction. At home at that time we used to get two major Viennese newspapers—[*Neues Wiener*] *Tagblatt* and *Neue Freie Presse*, the newspaper that Kaiser Franz Joseph himself used to read from a specially printed copy. In these newspapers a lot was written about the "turn of the century" and the "fin de siècle"—even this French term has stuck in my memory from that time. My mother knew a little French and in general seemed very involved in the transition of the centuries.

New Year's Day was always a school holiday. But this time all the children had to come to school. It was a cold, damp day, which penetrated our every bone. Our big school building, in which my mother, my brothers, and I (and for a short time my daughter) studied, was old. On days like this it was dark as night inside and they would light the oil lamps. And now all the children were assembled in their classrooms, where the burning oil lamps didn't make things much brighter. In the older classes the children might have understood why they were gathered there, spoiling a holiday. In our class, the Jewish boys, and certainly the village boys, understood nothing of what was involved. We were somehow afraid. We wanted to cling to one another. We trembled slightly, as if we were soon to be informed of the end of the world. Ours was the first grade, and consisted entirely of six- and seven-year-olds.

And here comes a whole commission which goes from class to class and says something to the children. The Director of the school comes in and so do the [Roman] Catholic priest and the Ruthenian [Ukrainian Greek Catholic] priest. They tell the children that they must remember this moment. Never forget it. They talk about some sort of new *stulecie* which will be arriving any moment. . . . Fearfully, all the children at once looked out the window and related the damp and icy cold outside with the approaching new *stulecie* (century, in Polish). And although the "event" had long been talked about at our house, it still made my head spin. What went on in the heads of the peasant children when they heard the news can be imagined. Only when the commission which had been visiting the classrooms had left, did the teacher begin to explain. After her explanation, she questioned the children about what they had understood. The children's replies were muddled and confused. Most of them did not even have a concept of the number 100, and now they had to grasp twenty times one hundred. . . . I was questioned by the teacher as well. Although I was ordinarily good at numbers and by then could quickly calculate in the thousands, I became confused and very ashamed, because I liked the teacher a lot and she liked me; I began to stammer and burst into tears. Soon afterwards the class was dismissed.

Since it was a day of wintry weather, there would be someone waiting to take me home. By coincidence, both my father and my mother were waiting outside. My older brother, coming out of his classroom, was in a good mood and told my parents about something that had happened. But when my parents took a look at me, they became frightened. My face was flushed and tearful. My father quickly picked me up in his arms and with his lips to my forehead tried to find out if I was feverish. And in fact, he immediately told my mother that it seemed to him that the child had a fever. He looked deeply into my eyes—for a sign in the pupils that there was fever. My parents began to question me about what had happened. I burst into tears again and sobbed into the ear of my frightened father, who was hastily carrying me home: "*Świat się kończy*—the world is coming to an end—the Director went from class to class and said that the world was coming to an end!"

The world did not come to an end. Instead it was the beginning of the twentieth century. . . .

And that was my first day in it.

Translated by Solon Beinfeld.

Other works by Ravitch: *Kontinentn un okeanen* (1937); *Mayn leksikon* (1945–1958); *Di lider fun mayne lider* (1954); *Dos mayse-bukh fun mayn lebn* (1962–1975).

Yaacov Hasson

1930–2000

Yaacov Hasson was a poet and journalist, but he is most remembered as an official of the Jewish community in Lima, Peru. Hasson was the director of the Jewish community's Human Relations Office there, and in 1966, acting as cultural attaché of Lima's Israeli embassy, he formed part of a delegation visiting the "forgotten" mestizo Jews of Iquitos in the Peruvian Amazon. The delegation participated in the official founding of the Peruvian–Israel Institute there. In 1975, he became the editor of *La Unión*, the Jewish community magazine. In 1990, while head of the Asociación Judía del Perú, Hasson was machine-gunned by suspected Palestinian terrorists, taking eight bullets in his hand and arm. He later founded and edited the *Boletín Hebraica*.

Iquitos: The Jewish Soul in the Amazon, Notes of a Voyager
1969

In the Beginning Was the Struggle

It is difficult in a short article to give the history of Jewish labor in the Peruvian Amazon. I can't pretend to do justice to such an arduous task. The history of the Jewish pioneer in this region has been magnificently written about elsewhere. The subject, however, requires much greater development before everything about it will be known. For the time being, it seems to me that one can't speak of the present situation without tracing, however superficially, the principal lines of the past.

In the middle of the 19th century the exploration, by boat, of the Amazon began. These explorations upset the balance of the region, which now allowed commerce to extend on both sides of the river to places which had once been impenetrable. Peru and Brazil by now both understood the importance of this region, and encouraged commerce and incipient industries.

India-rubber trees grew along the banks of the Amazon like an uncontrollable flood. Many ventured into these practically unexplored regions in order to extract this richness. Adventurers from every nation arrived, in numbers equal to the times of the Spanish Conquistador who had imposed his law, mobilized the native population, and had expeditiously advanced into this region, dominated by the burning fever for wealth.

Between 1880 and 1890 the first Jews began to arrive, attracted also by the richness and this fabulous region full of mystery and danger. Principally from North Africa, Morocco and Tangiers, Sephardic Jews came and formed the basis of an organized and dynamic community. They settled along the banks of the Amazon and put their energies into the birth of restless cities. Until 1910, this movement continued unabated and energetic. [. . .]

After the first decade of the present century the rubber fever declined quite suddenly. Great mineral deposits in the Indian Orient hindered the progress and retarded the initial advances. About 150 Jews had arrived in the Peruvian Amazon, ninety of whom returned disappointed, but not without leaving their fertile and prosperous descendants. Others were overcome by the various sicknesses of the region and the Israelite cemetery sadly became filled. And from that time until the present the bridge between those who remained and the outside world was destroyed. Sixty years passed; sufficient time to erase every Jewish vestige in this area. So it was thought. [...]

Rediscovery and Its Results

Eventually some Jews arrived in this region and learned about this community from others. Those who had remained had not lost pride in their Jewish past, though they sometimes had lost its meaning. I must say, in honor to the truth, in spite of what was known in Lima—even fragmentary—of the existence of these Jews, nothing serious was undertaken to establish contact with them or to disinter their old sentiments. [...]

They started to make arrangements in Lima, to wait for the right occasion. The Israeli Embassy and the Society of Sephardic Benefactors came to their aid. Thus, after long delay, a plane carried us to Iquitos, and we felt a strange mixture of curiosity and uneasy pain. Only when the plane landed did we understand how much of this extraordinary history had been true.

The Peruvian-Israeli Cultural Institute Is Founded

A small delegation received us with a surprising and emotional show of friendship. Ten Jews waited for us. They grasped our hands tightly. With smiles full of friendship and emotion they told us their names: Levy! Bendayan! Benzaquén! Edery! Samolsky! and they shouted: "Shalom ubrajá!" [...]

Others soon came, young people and older people, men and women, they surrounded us. They wanted to hear everything, first about their kin in Lima, and then about Israel. But we let them speak first to us. And they spoke! They spoke with uncontrollable emotion of how their fathers had come there, of what they had done, of how a silence of more than sixty years had covered them. Many of them had been or were dignitaries in the city, loved and respected by everyone. [...]

In el Aula Magna de la Universidad

Saturday afternoon, Iquitos usually hustles with activity. But our Saturday was different. Many businesses were closed, and those which remained open kept their radios going. A great celebration was taking place in la Universidad Nacional de la Amazonia Peruana. The military band played national music. Many of the civic authorities were on hand as well as people of all kinds, including the students.

I cannot imagine a more emotional moment than this. We listened to the national anthem of Peru in silence. Then, for the first time in Iquitos, and certainly for the first time in the Amazonian forests of Peru, was heard "Hatikva," the national anthem of Israel. [...]

From the Jewish Cemetery and the Airport

In the morning, after visiting the surrounding forest and seeing the work that continues to be done by the University in the struggle against nature to put it in the service of mankind, we returned to Lima. More than fifty Jews accompanied us. We stopped at the Jewish cemetery along the way, this silent witness of spirit and conquest: white, clean, quiet. We said Kaddish in memory of these souls who had been delivered to the rain forest. We walked around the tombstones. All had inscriptions in Hebrew, the history of the Jewish soul written silently in the Peruvian Amazon.

Boarding the plane, we waved our hands. Our new friends looked back at us intensely, smiling, full of tenderness. "Shalom!" they called out, "Lehitraot!" Yes! Without doubt, we would return. There, in the land of Loreto, we left friends, human beings who in this rough and angry century, had been forgotten. We will return, my brothers!

Translated by Roberta Kalechofsky.

Other works by Hasson: *Elementos para el estudio histórico y pedagógico de la educación judía en el Perú* (1970); *Canto a mi prójimo: Poemas* (1985); *Un hombre llamado Tupac Amaru: Poemas íntimos* (1989).

Larry Zolf

1934-2011

A bold, eccentric journalist with a comedic streak, Larry Zolf logged four decades with the Canadian Broadcasting Company. With a quick mind and an even quicker tongue, Zolf shifted between sober interviews and zany send-ups, amusing and baffling his Canadian viewers. He fought with politicians, sometimes physically, on the air, and branded himself a "mischief maker"—a redundant, if accurate, label. Born in Winnipeg, Zolf wrote six caustic and humorous books about Canadian politics, earning the title "Canada's Most Compelling Court Jester."

Boil Me No Melting Pots, Dream Me No Dreams
1970

When the fathers of Confederation built this country in 1867, there was universal agreement among *all* Canadians, English- and French-speaking, that there was no place for the American Dream on the northern half of this continent. In 1776 we embraced the United Empire Loyalists and rejected George Washington's Revolutionary Army by force of arms. We booted Uncle Sam in the pants in 1812 and slapped his wrists in the Fenian Raids of the 1880s. We rejected slavery and provided sanctuary for American Negroes fleeing that "peculiar institution."

We rejected republicanism, the American idea that the people in and of themselves can shape their own ends and destinies. We countered Jacksonian democracy with the responsible government of a constitutional monarchy and made it plain to our southern neighbors that there were higher forces shaping our destinies than the untutored rabble of the untouched West. And while we did agree with the Yankee that life and liberty were inseparable, we differed in our pursuit of happiness. In Canada, that pursuit didn't necessarily entail *égalité* and *fraternité*. We flatly rejected the American egalitarianism of the Western frontier and the American fraternity of the melting pot.

Canada was conservative country, the land of particularity. The entity known as Anglo-Saxon British Canada was prepared to tolerate the particularity of French Canada and the Slavic-German-Jewish-Oriental particularities of the Golden West, provided all accepted the British monarchy, the British connection, the British rules of the British game as the *summum bonum* underlying all these particularities.

This, then, was the lay of this land in the year 1926 when an obscure ex-Tzarist draft-dodger and ex-infantryman in Alexander Kerensky's Revolutionary Army decided to emigrate to these shores. That dashing, mustachioed, bulbous-nosed Polack of the Judaic persuasion was none other than Yoshua Falek Zholf, son of Reb Yisroael Zholf, husband to Freda Rachel Zholf, father to Meyer, Reisel, and Judith Zholf, and father-to-be to son-to-be yours truly.

My father was a dreamer. In his youth he dreamed of a Russia where life and liberty were inseparable, where a Jew could freely pursue happiness. In 1914 he was a draft-dodger, moving from city to city and village to village.

When the Tzar was toppled in February, 1917 and Alexander Kerensky proclaimed liberty and equality, my father came out of hiding, drafted his own personal revolutionary manifesto, and presented it to a recruiting officer in Kerensky's army. It read:

> To the Russian Revolutionary Army:
>
> Dear Sirs: Whereas, I, Falek Zholf, have hitherto refused to shed my blood for the bloody Tzar Nikolai the Second, enemy of my people, and, whereas, the great Revolution has freed my people, and all other peoples that inhabit Mother Russia, I today present myself in payment of my holy debt of loyalty to my fatherland.

My father's revolutionary dreams of brotherhood quickly came to naught. He was sickened by Kerensky's execution of soldiers with Bolshevik sympathies, sickened by Bolshevik execution of nationalists, and soon he and his family were threatened by the vicious anti-Semitism of the Polish government of Pilsudski and Sikorski.

Still my father continued to dream. There was the pastoral dream of life on the land in communion with the sky and the stars and all that, but the Polish government took his land away. There was the dream of pioneering in Palestine, but the Zionists wanted only single men. There was the dream of America, the new homeland of his three brothers, but the goddess Liberty had shut her eyes and gates to Europe's teeming, huddled masses.

Suddenly along came Canada, the British colony that dreamed no dreams and offered Pa, the peasant, a chance to join the Galician garlic-eaters that were cultivating the flatlands of the Canadian Golden West.

All this is by way of introduction to a fundamental confusion in my father's life which led to a subsequent fundamental confusion in my life. My father ultimately drifted into Winnipeg and renewed an occupation he once pursued secretly in Poland at some risk to his own life—the teaching of Jewish liberal-socialist values to

Jewish children. He became first a teacher and then the principal of the Isaac Loeb Peretz Folk School in Winnipeg. This school was a branch of a school system and school curriculum with central headquarters in New York City.

Herein lay the rub. My father, unaware of all the trouble Sir John A. and the Fathers had gone to, just naturally assumed that Canada was part of the American Dream. His admission to this country he regarded as a miracle. He looked on Canada as a place where Americans sent people they didn't really want to have now but might take in later on, provided that while here they were always on good behaviour. In a sense, he regarded Canada as America's Australia—a temporary penal colony for temporary undesirables.

As my father's English was not very good and his reading material was strictly confined to Yiddish books and newspapers that came from New York, it was not surprising that Pop soon came to regard Winnipeg as just another borough of Gotham-on-the-Hudson.

The more he read his New York Yiddish newspapers the more he got excited by the American Dream! Who could blame him? The New York paper told of Jewish wonders that poor old Pop could scarcely have imagined in the dreary Polish village that was once his home. Not only could Jews own land in the U.S.A., but, miracle of miracles, wonder of wonders, Jews were actually trusted in America. In the Soviet Union they were purging Trotsky, Kamenev, and Zenoviev. In America they were electing Herbert Lehman governor of New York State. Didn't Roosevelt have a Morgenthau in his cabinet? Weren't Felix Frankfurter, Sam Rosenman, and Ben Cohen FDR's bosom buddies? America was indeed the land of milk and honey; its streets were paved with Jews. [. . .]

I know that my country has not quite made up its mind about what it wants to be. It has ceased being British and, thankfully, has not yet become American. If there is anything still valid to the British heritage left us by the Fathers of Confederation, let it be this: Let the country continue to be a land of un-American activities. Boil me no melting pots and dream me no dreams. Worry not, rumour has it that God is Dead. If so, he can't bless America.

Other works by Zolf: *Survival of the Fattest: An Irreverent View of the Senate* (1985); *Scorpions for Sale* (1989).

Chaim Sacks
1891–1981

Born into a rabbinic family in Kovno (now Kaunas, Lithuania), Chaim Sacks (born Kusselewitz) received a traditional education, studying in the most prestigious yeshivas in the region. Eventually encountering secular literature, Sacks left Orthodoxy before World War I, moving to Vilna and becoming involved in Zionist circles there. In 1924, he moved to Palestine, resettling in South Africa four years later. He remained active in Zionist groups in South Africa, and later in his life began writing, mostly contributing short stories to local Yiddish publications. He published one book in his lifetime. Sacks died in Johannesburg.

Sweets from Sixpence
1971

As a new arrival I wasn't any good at shopkeeping, and not much of an expert with a horse and cart either. So I drifted round the streets, a sort of washout. I can never forget one day wandering about the streets of Johannesburg, envying those shopkeepers who already had the honour to have made it and meeting a man who was in the process of Africanising himself. He drove a horse, which pulled a cart containing peaches. The Jew still wore his old-time beard, and his long capote and homely hat, which were creased and very well worn. On his face were still traces of the former respectability of a man of the *shtetl,* where perhaps he had lived in poverty but yet had still counted for something in his synagogue. It was obvious that he had never held reins in his hands before. He sat on the coach-box in his strange attire with a black man at his side, and they kept on shouting out, "Peaches! Peaches!" First he and then the black man, like the verses of a Psalm chanted antiphonally. A great curiosity seized me to see how a man like this, on a small cart of peaches, adapted himself to the ways of Africa, so I followed him. He had already driven up and down the street several times, repeatedly calling "Peaches!," and no buyer had appeared. The sun baked him; sweating and worn out he suddenly stood up, clenched his fists, raised his eyes to the heavens and shouted out with all his might, "Peaches! Peaches! The devil take it, peaches!" He behaved as though he had a reproach against the Almighty: why did You create peaches, only in order that I should struggle to find my feet in the new country?

After this embittered exclamation, he gave the reins to the black man and despondently sank down again on his coach-box, covered his face with both hands, and remained sitting like that.

Only then did I fully perceive the bitter lot of a greenhorn, and only then did I decide that, come what might, I would rather go back to the trade which I had learnt in the Old Country: making sweets.

But this wasn't so easy. Friends and relatives helped me. I rented a little shop, made a few small tables with my own hands, installed a few machines I had brought with me, and I became a manufacturer. But I could make old-style green candy, not yellow, the way it was made here among the coloured people. I didn't even know what it was called. But God didn't forsake me. I had a friend who worked in a sweet factory and he promised to give me a "boy" who knew the work, and from him I would soon learn how to make sweets of the yellow variety. And that's what happened.

Translated by Woolf Leivick and Joseph Sherman

FICTION, DRAMA, AND CHILDREN'S LITERATURE

Zvi Kolitz

1913–2002

Born in Alytus, Lithuania, the writer Zvi Kolitz produced screenplays and Broadway shows, and wrote one much-anthologized story, "Yossel Rakover's Appeal to God," a searing tale set amid the rubble of the Warsaw ghetto. Soon after World War II ended, Kolitz went to Palestine and joined the underground anti-British resistance. He remained in Israel; he cowrote the country's first full-length film. He later immigrated to New York, where he wrote fiction and philosophy, lectured at Yeshiva University, and, like his character Yossel, retained a deep connection to God and religion.

Yossel Rakover's Appeal to God
1946

In the ruins of the Ghetto of Warsaw, among heaps of charred rubbish, there was found, packed tightly into a small bottle, the following testament, written during the ghetto's last hours by a Jew named Yossel Rakover.

Warsaw, April 28, 1943

I, Yossel, son of David Rakover of Tarnopol, a Chasid of the Rabbi of Ger and a descendant of the great and pious families of Rakover and Meisel, inscribe these lines as the houses of the Warsaw Ghetto go up in flames. The house I am in is one of the last unburnt houses remaining. For several hours an unusually heavy artillery barrage has been crashing down on us, and the walls are disintegrating under the fire. It will not be long before the house I am in is transformed, like almost every other house of the ghetto, into a grave for its defenders. [. . .] Death, swift and immediate, seems to us a liberator, sundering our shackles, and beasts of the field, even if their freedom exceeds their gentleness, seem to me to be so lovable and dear that I feel deep pain whenever I hear the evil fiends that lord it over Europe referred to as beasts. It is untrue that the tyrant who rules Europe now has something of the beast in him. Oh, No! He is a typical child of modern man; mankind as whole spawned him and reared him. He is merely frankest ex-

pression of its innermost, most deeply buried instincts. [. . .]

Now my time has come. And like Job, I can say of myself, nor am I the only one that can say it, that I return to the soil naked, as naked as the day of my birth.

I am forty-three years old, and when I look back on the past I can assert confidently, as confident as a man can be of himself, that I have lived a respectable, upstanding life, my heart full of love for God. [. . .]

I cannot say that my relationship to God has remained unchanged after everything I have lived through, but I can say with absolute certainty that my belief in Him has not changed by a hair's breadth. Previously, when I was happy and well off, my relation to God was as to one who granted me a favor for nothing, and I was eternally obliged to Him for it. Now my relations to Him are as to one who owes me something, too, who owes me very much in fact, and since I feel so, I believe I have the right to demand it of Him. [. . .]

I have three more bottles of gasoline. They are as precious to me as wine to a drunkard. After pouring one over my clothes, I will place the paper on which I write these lines in the empty bottle and hide it among the bricks filling the window of this room. If anyone ever finds it and reads it, he will, perhaps, understand the emotions of a Jew, one of millions, who died forsaken by the God in Whom he believed unshakably. I will let the two other bottles explode on the heads of the murderers when my last moment comes. [. . .]

[. . .] Meanwhile, I still live, and before my death I wish to speak to my Lord as a living man, a simple, living person who had the great but tragic honor of being a Jew.

I am proud that I am a Jew not in spite of the world's treatment of us, but precisely because of this treatment. I should be ashamed to belong to the people who spawned and raised the criminals who are responsible for the deeds that have been perpetrated against us or to any people who tolerated these deeds. [. . .]

I am happy to belong to the unhappiest of all peoples of the world, whose precepts represent the loftiest and most beautiful of all morality and laws. These immortal precepts which we possess have now been even more sanctified and immortalized by the fact that they have been so debased and insulted by the enemies of the Lord. [. . .]

I believe in You, God of Israel, even though You have done everything to stop me from believing in You. I believe in Your laws even if I cannot excuse Your actions. My relationship to You is not the relationship of a slave to his master but rather that of a pupil to his teacher. I bow my head before Your greatness, but I will not kiss the lash with which You strike me.

You say, I know, that we have sinned, O Lord. It must surely be true! And therefore we are punished? I can understand that too! But I should like You to tell me whether *there is any sin in the world deserving of such a punishment as the punishment we have received?*

You assert that you will yet repay our enemies? I am convinced of it! Repay them without mercy? I have no doubt of that either! I should like You to tell me, however—*is there any punishment in the world capable of compensating for the crimes that have been committed against us?* [. . .]

I want to say to You that now, more than in any previous period of our eternal path of agony, we, we the tortured, the humiliated, the buried alive and burned alive, we the insulted, the mocked, the lonely, the forsaken by God and man—we have the right to know *what are the limits of Your forebearance?* I should like to say something more: Do not put the rope under too much strain, lest, alas, it snaps! The test to which You have put us is so severe, so unbearably severe, that You should—You must—forgive those members of Your people who, in their misery, have turned from You. [. . .]

Forgive those who have desecrated Your name, who have gone over to the service of other gods, who have become indifferent to You. You have castigated them so severely that they no longer believe that You are their Father, that they have any Father at all.

Translated by Shmuel Katz.

Other works by Kolitz: *The Tiger beneath the Skin: Stories and Parables of the Years of Death* (1947); *The Teacher: An Existential Approach to the Bible* (1982).

Irma Ychou

b. 1918

Born Irma Bénichou in Blida, Algeria, Irma Ychou contributed to Judeo-Maghrebi literature, intermixing the French language with Hebrew, Judeo-Arabic, Arabic, and Judeo-Alsatian. Her protagonists are Jewish Algerian women adapting to challenges of identity, both cultural and linguistic, caught between tradition and modernity, Africa and Europe. The mother and daughter in *La Famille Bensaïd* represent a rapidly evolving trend away from tradition, the daughter in particular rejecting the notion of a compulsory marriage. Ychou used a second pseudonym, Irma Van Lawick, to write even more freely about women's emancipation. Readers of *Le Chéroub*, published in 1962, were shocked by its erotic portrayal of a young woman who dresses like a boy to seduce both men and women.

The Bensaïd Family
1947

When the bus disappeared, taking away their child, the Bensaïds remained on the empty sidewalk, their souls as barren as if their daughter had been carried off by death.

With a little energy, they could have prevented this departure. Lydia, still young, might have been influenced by them, she might have forgotten what she had learned elsewhere and only retained what they taught her.

Yes, there was still time to take Lydia back, to remake her in their image, and now, through weakness, they were sending her away. They were giving her the possibility of making herself different from them, of no longer sharing their ancestry, their social class. With their own hands, they were killing their child in order to let an unknown be born in her place.

They sighed, with heavy hearts. They slowly returned home.

Of course, their parents had not been so fatuous as to imitate the French! To understand the evolution of customs they themselves had followed, they would have had to look back at their ancestors. The conquest of Algeria had deeply shaken those "Arab Jews," and only a few years ago Grandmother Bensaïd, still living and more than a hundred years old, continued to tell about the arrival of the French: the history of their conquest of Algeria would pour forth disjointedly from her mouth, toothless as a newborn's. Her pitiful shack! . . . She must have been eleven or twelve, and just married. One day there was a terrible storm, gunshots . . . she, her husband, and her family took refuge in the mountains with the Arabs, carrying bundles on their backs and pushing their loaded-down donkeys ahead of them . . . the water came up to their thighs . . . the enemy was after them . . . they shook with fear . . .

The old grandmother spoke in such a faraway voice! Seated around her, the great-grandchildren would lean forward so as better to hear those epic accounts. Their eyes would open wide, but they didn't always understand the old woman. She could only express herself in Arabic, while this young generation, formed in the new school, knew only snippets of it.

The old grandmother would lower her eyelids, which no longer had anything to shut out, pull her silken kerchief forward over her fine white hair, stretch herself out, wearing her long *gaudourah*,[1] and for the latecomers, take up her story again with the same details and the same gaps.

Her daughter, Lydia's grandmother, differed from her only in her conversation, which was sprinkled with a few words of French. She too wore the native dress, married very young, and raised numerous children who didn't attend school. Yet progress had made its way into this house. Evolution had always managed somehow to enter these Algerian Jewish dwellings, where one could find three completely different generations living under the same roof. Between the first generation with its Arabic influence and the third with its French influence, the second served as a buffer, its ill-defined character mixed with strains of Muslim, Christian, and Jewish culture.

In Mrs. Bensaïd's family, the customs had been more tenacious. Her father, a good-looking man with magnificently blue eyes, remained steeped in tradition because of his nobler, purer origins. In his imposing dress—vest embroidered with gold, baggy pants with a prominent pleat, and *checia*[2] or turban on his head—he had maintained the proud look of a patriarch.

Comparing her two grandfathers, Lydia found that one had the manners of a nobleman from *A Thousand and One Nights*, whereas the other, in adopting European dress, had lost all natural distinction and sense of ease.

The Bensaïds were engaged and married without having known each other, Jewish customs being at that time the same as those of Muslims. Knowing nothing of each other, they would happily thereafter, and often, think of themselves as "rather well suited."

Responsible now for the future of a young girl, they no longer knew if they should take inspiration from their parents or if they should keep up with the times.

That was a serious problem. Emancipation had created so many unhappy women! [. . .]

And this attitude of today's girls: "I don't want to get married!" as though marriage had something to do with fantasy. Is marriage not a natural law like birth and death? That's where education leads. It leads to debating God's logic . . . yet one had to admit that change had its good side: giving women careers assures them security in life. You might lose your husband! She herself, Mrs. Bensaïd, had she not suffered during the war when, from one day to the next, she had to earn a living with a baby in her arms? At the time she had certainly regretted not having been prepared for the struggle. At least she could not reproach herself for anything later! . . . You never know what the future holds. And then, in any case, it wouldn't be so bad if Lydia, instead of marrying now, waited a year or two!

From pessimism, the Bensaïds were leaping to optimism, a tendency peculiar to Jews, so fanatically sure of their destiny.

NOTES

1. [Loose North African robe worn by both men and women.—Trans.]

2. [Short, rounded skullcap.—Trans.]

Translated by Michele McKay Aynesworth.

Other works by Ychou, writing as Van Lawick: *Paule* (1938); *Tu réveilleras l'aurore* (1990).

Shalom Darwish

1913–1997

Writer, poet, and lawyer Shalom Darwish was born in Ali al-Gharba, al-Amarra, Iraq. He was a member of Iraqi parliament in the 1940s but resigned to protest electoral corruption. Accused of being a Zionist, Darwish fled in 1950 to Iran and from there to Israel, where he continued to practice law. He wrote on local Arab legal issues, and he also wrote short stories, poetry, plays, and literary and political commentary, switching to Hebrew in the 1980s to expand his readership. Darwish's Jewish and Muslim critics recognized him as one of the most important early Iraqi writers.

A Convoy from the Village
1948

He remembers well how for the first time in his life he tried to cross the big street in Baghdad. With one hand his mother held onto him and with the other she held her long and wide cape, looked right and left and in a loud voice ordered the large band to cross. With him were his sisters, some older than him carrying in their hands objects his family had brought from the village to the capital city, and also his older brother, two years older than him, pulling their goat, that they called Ravsha. The goat, who had arrived with the family from the little village in the south, accompanied them in the long and arduous journey on the deck of a steamship, which fought the current both days and nights and was slower than a donkey climbing up a mountainous path.

They could have sold the goat before they left the village, together with the furniture they had sold, and saved themselves some of the hardships of the journey. The milk she gave them, that the family, young and old, would pounce on morning and night, did not justify all they had to do for her and the inconveniences and worries the goat caused them. But a special attention, that the eye cannot see but the heart knows its value, tied the goat to that band of people.

* * *

This little convoy was trying unsuccessfully to cross the big street, strangers who knowingly pushed themselves into the new and bustling world, struggling among its swells hoping for a better world than the realm of the bucolic that had in it no shelter or sustenance, but only poverty, ignorance, and anonymity. In her deep wisdom, the mother understood that, having lost their father, the children would have to be educated in the educational institutions of Baghdad so that they would be able to make their own way in the future. She was determined and made all the necessary preparations without allowing the fact that she was a widow to deter her from her courageous ambition: to immigrate to the city with no economic means. The little family, which had just landed and was about to cross this big street, seemed like a few sheep that had lost their way and their connection to the flock and the shepherd. They stand now on the sidewalk, the cars racing down the street threatening them—about to run them over, together with their goat. They scream in fear and the goat bleats together with them, and their mother scolds them and tells them to stop shouting and walk after her because she knows this street better than they do. She had lived in Baghdad in the past and went to join her husband in the forlorn village many years ago, when

she was still a girl, and now she returns dragging behind her a flock of children, together with a few inexpensive possessions and the goat and little money and many tears in the wells of her eyes. She knows well that cars do not run over people as long as they are standing on the sidewalk, but her children do not believe it; like most village people they cannot measure the distances or distinguish between sidewalk and street. Therefore they are in a state of chaos, move forward and back, begging for shelter occasionally from the others, sometimes seeking shelter near the walls. After a long wait, when there is a break in the flow of cars, and the mother gives the order to cross the street, only one of the children follows her, while the others delay somewhat, and thus they become divided into two groups, one moving forward, and other retreating, and when the flood of cars once again fills the street, the entire group once again retreats to the sidewalk. When the entire group is ready to cross the street together, the goat pulls back and refuses to accept the danger, since she, like the others, is fearful of the bustling city and shows even more caution than they do. When they would pull at her with force, she would resist and stood firm, preventing them from crossing the street.

This farce ends only after one of the passers-by volunteers to hold the hand of a boy, another grabs the hand of a girl, a third holds the goat, and together they ask the foreign children to shut their eyes and not resist, and they all obey and give in, except for the goat who refuses to close her eyes and continues to bleat and resist, but must in the end succumb to the pressure put on her; in the end, the ship crosses to the other bank of the road and the frightened party disappears immediately into the narrow and ancient alleys.

* * *

He can now remember well this little convoy as it sought for a temporary dwelling to park.

He expected a large house. A much larger home than the one he left in the village, and now he had been shoved into a narrow dwelling lacking light and air, and he felt choked, as if he had entered a pit containing nothing but a narrow hatch.

A short elderly woman embraced him, sealed his cheeks with kisses, and strangled his breath with the bad smell emitting from her mouth, as she shouted in a loud voice, "Shalom, shalom, a hundred thousand shaloms, welcome to us, you really have grown into a man, you have become a real man!"

His little friends, who had been separated from him years ago and had travelled to Baghdad, jump all over him.

The bleating of Ravsha was lost in the racket of the children, the old women, and the girl. Since both families were meeting for the first time after many years of separation, there were embraces, conversations, laughing, and tears. Ravsha went around among the people present as if mad and bleated without any of the young or the old people paying any attention to her.

Suddenly the company heard a loud noise, turned in the direction of it. Eye sockets dilated, and mouths dropped when they learn that Ravsha had turned over the pots and all the food that had been prepared for the guests had spilled and mixed in with the dust and sand, and Ravsha was standing and devouring it all.

The residents and the guests, old and young, were awestruck.

The old lady tore her hair, wrung her hands, spun around herself like a mouse in a trap and screamed.

Her children jumped up on the goat, beat her, kicked her, and cursed her in loud voices, "Bitch! Get out of here! Bitch!"

He was forced together with his brothers, sisters, and his mother to help their feeble goat to save her from the aggressive criminals who shouted and writhed as if they had been struck with madness.

"Ravsha! That's our Ravsha! No! Don't beat Ravsha!"

The attackers are shocked and stop beating the goat, after the guests surrounded her and defended her with their bodies, one kissing her, one petting her shoulders, one embracing her head, and a tear glistening in the eye of another. The residents realize that in their tiny home, which barely houses them, they must now provide shelter not only to the large family but also the mischievous goat.

* * *

What did they eat and how did they pass the night with their Ravsha? Salim wonders how the world knows nothing about that night. Ravsha kept them from food at a time when they were very hungry, but the great shame they felt before the hosts was greater than their hunger and their want.

When the convoy convenes in the small and dark room, illuminated by the dim light of an oil lamp, Ravsha joins them.

"Mother, until when will we be living in this house?"

"A week, two weeks, perhaps a month. It will be fine. Perhaps tomorrow we'll find a better place."

"Where will you find money to rent a house, Mother?"

"There is a God who will help us."

"Mother!"

"Yes."

"If we sell Ravsha, how much will we get for her?"
Salim jumps as if bitten by a crab.

"May Allah watch over you! May Elijah the prophet guard you!"

* * *

Salim remembers now—how can one forget—that short man who stuck his head through the door and shouted:

"Where are you? Who asked for me?"

"The cripple has arrived! The cripple has arrived! Mother, The cripple has arrived!"

He runs to the door, shivering all over.

"May Allah preserve you, don't be afraid. Don't be afraid. It's the shepherd who has come to see Ravsha."

"Now he'll slaughter her! Now he'll slaughter her!"

"No! He won't slaughter her, why should he do that? Salim, it's not nice to cry like that. You are already a man! Are you prepared for Ravsha to stay in the house? Where will you sleep? Didn't you see what happened yesterday in the room? The people of the house were angry with us, we didn't sleep, your brother got sick, and the room stank. You know this is not our house, and so we have decided that it is better that the shepherd takes her. Is it better that she stays with us and remain hungry? Where will I get hay for her? Where will I get food for her?"

Salim recoils when Ravsha bleats as she descends the stairs.

"Meh meh meh."

He breaks into silent tears and cannot stop. Next to him are his brothers and sisters, their faces pale and their teeth chattering. He sees the cripple entering the house, lean with his left hand on the wall, at the same time wielding his cane with his right hand and hitting Ravsha on her back as if examining a glass vessel.

"How much do you want for this wretched sack?"

The little one look at their mother who is swallowing her spittle, her face paling at the shepherd's ugly attempt to reduce the price. A rupee or two more or less is not as important to her as that her goat is not a thing for buying and selling and therefore it is impossible to appraise her value. It hurts her very much that Ravsha is demeaned by this impertinent shepherd.

At last they agree on six rupees for Ravsha. The mother accepts the money with a trembling hand and tries to overcome tears welling in her eyes.

The mother approaches Ravsha and pets her on her back, and the sobbing children run and push each other in the effort to hug her head and neck.

The shepherd leaves pulling the goat after him, who resists unsuccessfully and turns her head to the family who come out to the road to say goodbye to her.

"Goodbye to you, goodbye to you, Ravsha. May Allah protect Ravsha."

And she responds to their blessings.

"Meh meh meh."

Translated by Karen Alkalay-Gut.

Other works by Darwish: *Aḥrār wa-ʿAbīd* (1941); *Bayḍat al-Dīk* (1976); *Kull shayʾ hādiʾ fī al-ʿiyādah* (1981); *Frayim! Frayim!* (1986).

Ted Allan

1916–1995

Novelist, playwright, and short-story writer Ted Allan, born Alan Herman in Montreal, began his writing career at age seventeen in the communist newspaper the *Daily Clarion* and followed with short stories in the left-leaning *New Frontier*. He fought on the communist side in the Spanish Civil War, during which time he met Canadian physician Norman Bethune, on whom his book *The Scalpel, the Sword* (1954) was based. Working in Hollywood in the 1950s, Allan was blacklisted due to McCarthyism; he moved to London and wrote for British radio and television for twenty-five years. Upon his return to North America, he collaborated on several movie scripts, including his *Lies My Father Told Me*, before his death in Toronto.

Lies My Father Told Me

1949

My grandfather stood six feet three in his worn-out bedroom slippers. He had a long grey beard with streaks of white running through it. When he prayed, his voice boomed like a choir as he turned the pages of his prayer book with one hand and stroked his beard with the other. His hands were bony and looked like tree-roots; they were powerful. My grandpa had been a farmer in the old country. In Montreal he conducted what he called "a second-hand business."

In his youth, I was told, Grandpa had been something of a wild man, drinking and playing with the village wenches until my grandmother took him in hand. In his old age, when I knew him, he had become a very religious man. He prayed three times a day on weekdays and all day on Saturday. In between prayers he rode around on a wagon which, as I look back, rolled on despite all the laws of physics and mechanics. Its four wheels always seemed to be going in every direction but forwards. The horse that pulled the wagon was called Ferdeleh. He was my pet and it was only much later, when I had seen many other horses, that I realized that Ferdeleh was not everything a horse could have been. His belly hung very low, almost touching the street when he walked. His head went back and forth in jerky motions in complete disharmony with the rest of him. He moved slowly, almost painfully, apparently realizing that he was capable of only one speed and determined to go no faster or slower than the rate he had established some time back. Next to Grandpa I loved Ferdeleh best, with the possible exception of God, or my mother when she gave me candy.

On Sundays, when it didn't rain, Grandpa, Ferdeleh, and myself would go riding through the back lanes of Montreal. The lanes then were not paved as they are now, and after a rainy Saturday, the mud would be inches deep and the wagon heaved and shook like a barge in a stormy sea. Ferdeleh's pace remained, as always, the same. He liked the mud. It was easy on his feet.

When the sun shone through my window on Sunday morning I would jump out of bed, wash, dress, run into the kitchen where Grandpa and I said our morning prayers, and then we'd both go to harness and feed Ferdeleh. On Sundays Ferdeleh would whinny like a happy child. He knew it was an extra special day for all of us. By the time he had finished his oats and hay Grandpa and I would be finished with our breakfast which Grandma and Mother had prepared for us. [. . .]

Then began the most wonderful of days as we drove through the dirt lanes of Montreal, skirting the garbage cans, jolting and bouncing through the mud and dust, calling every cat by name and every cat meowing its hello, and Grandpa and I holding our hands to our ears and shouting out at the top of our lungs, "Regs, cloze, botels! Regs, cloze, botels!"

What a wonderful game that was! I would run up the back stairs and return with all kinds of fascinating things, old dresses, suits, pants, rags, newspapers, all shapes of bottles, all shapes of trash, everything you can think of, until the wagon was filled. [. . .]

My Sunday rides were the happiest times I spent. Sometimes Grandpa would let me wear his derby hat which came down over my ears, and people would look at me and laugh and I'd feel even happier feeling how happy everyone was on Sunday. [. . .]

If it rained on Sunday my mother wouldn't let me go out, so every Saturday evening I prayed for the sun to shine on Sunday. Once I almost lost faith in God and in the power of prayer but Grandpa fixed it. For three Sundays in succession it rained. In my desperation I took it out on God. What was the use of praying to Him if He didn't listen to you? I complained to Grandpa.

"Perhaps you don't pray right," he suggested.

"But I do. I say, Our God in heaven, hallowed be Thy name, Thy will on earth as it is in heaven. Please don't let it rain tomorrow."

"Ah! In English you pray?" my grandfather exclaimed triumphantly.

"Yes," I answered.

"But God only answers prayers in Hebrew. I will teach you how to say that prayer in Hebrew. And, if God doesn't answer, it's your own fault. He's angry because you didn't use the Holy Language." But God wasn't angry because next Sunday the sun shone its brightest and the three of us went for our Sunday ride.

On weekdays, Grandpa and I rose early, a little after daybreak, and said our morning prayers. I would mimic his sing-song lamentations, sounding as if my heart were breaking and wondering why we both had to sound so sad. I must have put everything I had into it because Grandpa assured me that one day I would become a great cantor and a leader of the Hebrews. "You will sing so that the ocean will open up a path before you and you will lead our people to a new paradise."

I was six then and he was the only man I ever understood even when I didn't understand his words. I learned a lot from him. If he didn't learn a lot from me, he made me feel he did.

I remember once saying, "You know, sometimes I think I'm the son of God. Is it possible?"

"It is possible," he answered, "but don't rely on it. Many of us are sons of God. The important thing is not to rely too much upon it. The harder we work, the harder we study, the more we accomplish, the surer we are that we are sons of God."

At the synagogue on Saturday his old, white-bearded friends would surround me and ask me questions. Grandpa would stand by and burst with pride. I strutted like a peacock.

"Who is David?" the old men would ask me.

"He's the man with the beard, the man with the bearded words." And they laughed.

"And who is God?" they would ask me.

"King and Creator of the Universe, the All-Powerful One, the Almighty One, more powerful even than Grandpa." They laughed again and I thought I was pretty smart. So did Grandpa. So did my grandmother and my mother.

So did everyone, except my father. I didn't like my father. He said things to me like, "For God's sake, you're smart, but not as smart as you think. Nobody is that smart." He was jealous of me and he told me lies. He told me lies about Ferdeleh.

"Ferdeleh is one part horse, one part camel, and one part chicken," he told me. Grandpa told me that was a lie, Ferdeleh was all horse. "If he is part anything, he is part human," said Grandpa. I agreed with him. Ferdeleh understood everything we said to him. No matter what part of the city he was in, he could find his way home, even in the dark.

"Ferdeleh is going to collapse one day in one heap," my father said. "Ferdeleh is carrying twins." "Ferdeleh is going to keel over one day and die." "He should be shot now or he'll collapse under you one of these days," my father would say. Neither I nor Grandpa had much use for the opinions of my father.

On top of everything, my father had no beard, didn't pray, didn't go to the synagogue on the Sabbath, read English books and never read the prayer books, played piano on the Sabbath and sometimes would draw my mother into his villainies by making her sing while he played. On the Sabbath this was an abomination to both Grandpa and me.

One day I told my father, "Papa, you have forsaken your forefathers." He burst out laughing and kissed me and then my mother kissed me, which infuriated me all the more.

I could forgive my father these indignities, his not treating me as an equal, but I couldn't forgive his telling lies about Ferdeleh. Once he said that Ferdeleh "smelled up" the whole house, and demanded that Grandpa move the stable. It was true that the kitchen, being next to the stable, which was in the back shed, did sometimes smell of hay and manure but, as Grandpa said, "What is wrong with such a smell? It is a good healthy smell."

It was a house divided, with my grandmother, mother, and father on one side, and Grandpa, Ferdeleh, and me on the other. One day a man came to the house and said he was from the Board of Health and that the neighbours had complained about the stable. Grandpa and I knew we were beaten then. You could get around the Board of Health, Grandpa informed me, if you could grease the palms of the officials. I suggested the obvious but Grandpa explained that this type of "grease" was made of gold. The stable would have to be moved. But where?

As it turned out, Grandpa didn't have to worry about it. The whole matter was taken out of his hands a few weeks later.

Next Sunday the sun shone brightly and I ran to the kitchen to say my prayers with Grandpa. But Grandpa wasn't there. I found my grandmother there instead—weeping. Grandpa was in his room ill. He had a sickness they call diabetes and at that time the only thing you could do about diabetes was weep. I fed Ferdeleh and soothed him because I knew how disappointed he was.

That week I was taken to an aunt of mine. There was no explanation given. My parents thought I was too young to need any explanations. On Saturday next I was brought home, too late to see Grandpa that evening, but I felt good knowing that I would spend the next day with him and Ferdeleh again.

When I came to the kitchen Sunday morning Grandpa was not there. Ferdeleh was not in the stable. I thought they were playing a joke on me so I rushed to the front of the house expecting to see Grandpa sitting atop the wagon waiting for me.

But there wasn't any wagon. My father came up behind me and put his hand on my head. I looked up questioningly and he said, "Grandpa and Ferdeleh have gone to heaven. . . ."

When he told me they were *never* coming back, I moved away from him and went to my room. I lay down on my bed and cried, not for Grandpa and Ferdeleh, because I knew they would never do such a thing to me, but about my father, because he had told me such a horrible lie.

Other works by Allan: *This Time a Better Earth* (1939); *Double Image* (1957); *Willie the Squowse* (1973).

Claude Benady

1922–2000

Claude Benady was born in Tunis in 1922; his father was Jewish and his mother Christian. He studied at the Collège des Maristes and the Lycée Carnot. Mobilized in 1942, he fought in the Tunisian, French, and German campaigns. After the war, Benady founded several magazines, including *La Kahena* and *Périples*, a literary magazine that became the focus of poetry recitals and avant-garde salons. In 1957, he moved to France, where he was a producer for French Radio and Television (RTF) and opened a bookstore called Périples. His works often expressed the nostalgia of Tunisian Jewish exiles. In 1976, he was awarded the Prix de l'Afrique mediterranéenne for *Marguerite à la source* (1975).

Out of Play, the Dead
1950

At last the time has come. Amid the returning horde, I shall be once more separated from myself. The drama unfolds between the domed sky and the crazily calm sea. Order gorges itself on conquests: it sees everything as conquest, immeasurable grandeur. Possession slides into the heart from the point where day ends. (The mad rolling of the waves pierces our shoulders and the napes of our necks—and it is sweet to feel the wind's salty sting working its way down our body, stirring the surface of our skin, hugging our flesh as it passes.) We walk up the ramp, this time facing the Basilica, which seems, at the end of an uncertain reign, to be peopled by melancholy lassitude. With the onset of evening, the deaf malaise of an infinitely wounded power becomes discernable. But I quickly reject the idea of power; this idea is in man, not in stone. We are not yet so attached to ourselves that we can bear the breadth of the *infinite*.

That splinter in Africa, carved thus, is Carthage. True conquerors know nothing of conquest, and if those ruins, carefully preserved in the pride of generations, ring out the memory of grandeur, they put the dead out of play. What a cold lesson in humility! . . . From a nameless terrace, a witless turntable nibbles the last measures of a cardiac blue. Impassive, two young bulls chew on stunted alfalfa. Here is the dock.

After the ruins, to see with the admirable certainty of love, to mold one's body to the firm flesh of this world in heat, there, I believe, is a rhyme in life's poem.

Ah! To be able to breathe in life through all one's pores!

But the Game Ends Here

We shall leave together, each of us sheathed in young hope. One more pause: the abandoned village with its hands of claw-like shadow, with its myopia of dim lights, sends a great windy yawn back at us. The train enters the station. And suddenly I realize that I love the crowd, in a single look, in a single gesture, in a single tentative step taken along one's path. I have faith in the living man, and even if his eye, his ever-restless eye, raised toward the pregnant sky, tries to reconstitute in a group of skittishly colored stud horses a frisky cavalcade of red thoroughbreds or blue [dun]-stained chestnuts, a puzzle that would be his reward, I have faith in his clear-sightedness. Because, being unable to deny his surroundings, illusion or reality, he can find in his life the reprieve that might postpone death's cancer.

A leaf from an orange tree, slapped, pressed itself against my cheek. No poetry? So be it! But, for me, that leaf is an untranslatable sign of the infinite calm that begins again, while around me the crowd, bathed in perspiration, laughs, drugged with relief.

Translated by Michele McKay Aynesworth.

Other works by Benady: *Le Dégel des sources* (1954); *Marguerite à la source* (1975); *Les Étangs du soleil* (1981).

Elisa Chimenti

1883–1969

Elisa Chimenti was born in Napoli but moved to Tunisia in 1884, before her family finally settled in Tangier, where her father served as personal physician to Sultan Moulay Hassan. Chimenti distinguished herself at an early age by her passion for learning, eventually mastering more than a dozen languages. She was captivated by Berber poetry and regional folklore, particular the experiences of local women. She studied at the University of Leipzig, returning to Tangier to teach and write. In 1914, she helped found the first Italian school in Morocco, where Muslim, Christian, and Jewish children were all welcome. She was the first European woman to teach at an Arabic university. Her *Au coeur du harem* (1958) was the first novel in French by a Moroccan woman.

The Cadi and the Jewish Merchant

1950

Toward the end of the reign of Moulay Hassan, there was a cadi whose avarice was so great that he was lik-

ened to a tomb, for the tomb, ever receiving, never gives anything back. The cadi accepted gifts from everyone but never offered the smallest sum to charity. Although he was well versed in the law of Allah, he failed to obey the precepts of the Koran, of the holy suras. He only repeated the Chasda, for it begins with the word *la* ("no"), which he pronounced continually to refuse whatever was asked of him. The following story is told about him: One day as he was crossing the Loukkos river from Alcazar to Larache, he fell into the water and almost drowned.

A fisherman who was nearby shouted to him, "Give me your hand and I'll pull you out!"

"Give you my hand?" the cadi replied. "Never! Give me yours if you wish to save me."

One morning when the cadi was in the *Mehakma* ("Tribunal") waiting to sit in judgment over the day's lawsuits, a woman dressed in rags came before him. After kissing the ground before him, she burst into tears.

"My lord, my husband is dead and I don't have the money with which to bury him. I beg you to give me some money in the name of the Almighty, for He blesses the giving of alms and rewards the donor."

The cadi, ignoring the words in the Sacred Book which said, "Do not reprimand the pauper," became angry.

"'Give me!'" he said, "'give me!' Those are the only words you know. As if I were rich enough to feed all the beggars and bury all the dead of the town. Go! The men of the mosque will bury your husband."

"My lord," continued the woman, "we have no more bread in the house—my children are dying of hunger."

The cadi called the guards and ordered them to put the woman out.

A Jewish merchant of the *kisaria* was outside the Tribunal awaiting his turn to see the judge. He wore the gray cloak and the black skullcap of those who inhabit the *mellah* ("ghetto"); his heart had the whiteness of pearls and he did a good deed each day so as to find favor in the eyes of the Almighty. When he saw the poor woman being ushered out of the Tribunal, he immediately asked her the reason for the rude ejection.

"My children are hungry, for I have no bread to give them. My husband is dead and I cannot bury him because I have no money. The cadi would not help me."

The merchant was moved by the poor woman's misery. "How much do you need to buy food for your children and bury your late husband (may God have mercy upon him)?"

The widow mentioned a minimum sum that would cover these expenses. The merchant opened his purse and took out some silver pieces—so much to go for food for the children and the reciters of the Koran, so much to go for the burial of the deceased, and so much for the ritual alms of bread and fruit. He insisted that the woman buy her children some sweets, too. It was only just that the children of the poor as well as of the rich knew the meaning of joy.

"When you have spent all the money I have given you, ask for the home of Youssef, the Jewish merchant; there you will always find help."

During the night that followed, the cadi had a dream; he saw that dreadful place in Hell which was reserved for infidels and the unjust; the heads of the victims were covered with dark veils; their chests heaved and panted, yet they could hardly catch their breaths, like men who have been lifting heavy loads. They were allowed to drink warm water and to eat the ill-tasting fruit known as *zacoum* which grows only in the underworld. No matter how much of it was eaten, it never stilled one's hunger. The cadi saw himself among those unfortunates, moaning and repeating over and over, "If I had only known, if I had only known . . ."

Far yonder was the Paradise of Allah, land of unceasing happiness where rivers flow peaceably in the shade of palm trees. There the clouds were whiter than milk, softer than foam, and perfumed with myrtle and amber. Seated under the shadow of trees that remain ever green, the fortunate inhabitants of Heaven quench their thirst from silver goblets. Youssef, the Jewish merchant, was among them. His face radiated joy and contentment.

The cadi said to himself, "How can it be that I, a scholar and a Believer, am condemned to inhabit the dark regions together with infidels, while that Jew, Youssef, is enjoying the delights of Paradise?"

An angel who was nearby answered him, "It was you, was it not, who robbed the orphan of his inheritance, who refused to give a helping hand to the poor? Youssef, the Jew, for whom you have contempt, succored the widow and fed the orphan."

The voice of the muezzin calling to the morning prayer awoke the cadi.

"Allah be praised," said he, "there is still time for me to earn the clemency of Heaven."

He arose, made his ablutions and prayed; then he made his way through the evil-smelling *mellah* to the home of Youssef, the merchant.

"O merchant," he said, "I was told by the guards of the Tribunal that you helped a woman of my race. It is wrong for a Mohammedan to accept alms from a Jew. Tell me how much you gave the widow and her orphans so that I may repay you."

Youssef the merchant smiled, bowed respectfully, and said, "It is useless for me to mention the sum, Sidi ['my lord'], since I don't wish to be recompensed for a single belouin which I gave in the name of Almighty God."

"And if I should offer you double or triple the alms you have given the widow and all the alms you have distributed throughout your life? . . ."

"I repeat—keep your gold, my lord. The dream you had last night was not meant for you alone—I too had the very same dream."

NOTE
[Words in brackets appear in the original translation.]

Translated by Arnon Benamy.

Other works by Chimenti: *Eves marocaines* (1935); *Légendes marocaines* (1959); *Le Sortilège et autres contes séphardites* (1964).

A. M. Klein

The Second Scroll
1951

And then—it was after I had returned from Tiberias to Tel Aviv to attend a literary soirée—then the creative activity, archetypical, all-embracing, that hitherto I had sought in vain, at last manifested itself. Not at the soirée. In the streets, in the shops, everywhere about me. I had looked, but had not seen. It was all there all the time—the fashioning folk, anonymous and unobserved, creating word by word, phrase by phrase, the total work that when completed would stand as epic revealed!

They were not members of literary societies, the men who were giving new life to the antique speech, but merchants, tradesmen, day labourers. In their daily activity, and without pose or flourish, they showed it to be alive again, the shaping Hebrew imagination. An insurance company, I observed as I lingered in Tel Aviv's commercial centre, called itself *Sneh*—after Moses' burning bush, which had burned and burned but had not been consumed. Inspired metaphor, born not of the honoured laureate, but of some actuary, a man of prose! A well-known brand of Israeli sausage was being advertised, it gladdened my heart to see, as *Bashan*—just tribute to its magnum size, royal compliment descended from Og, Bashan's giant king. A dry-cleaner called his firm *Kesheth*, the rainbow, symbol of cessation of floods! An ice-cream organization, Kortov, punned its way to custom fissioning *kortov*, a drop, to *kor-tov*, cold and good! In my student days I had been fascinated always by that word which put an end to the irreconcilable controversies of the House of Hillel and the House of Shammai: this House would maintain *Permitted*, that House would insist *Prohibited*; a deadlock would ensue. Came then the Talmud editor and wrote *taiku*, *stet*, the question abides. My teacher would then go on to explain that *taiku* was really a series of initials that stood for *Tishbi yetaraitz kushioth v'abayoth*, the Tishbite would resolve all problems and difficulties. Now the magic cataleptic word was before me again, in a new context, in a newspaper, the report of a football game where the score had been tied. *Taiku!*

There were dozens, there were hundreds of instances of such metamorphosis and rejuvenation. Nameless authorship flourished in the streets. It was growth, its very principle, shown in prolific action! Twigs and branches that had been dry and sapless for generations, for millennia, now budded, blossomed—and with new flowers!

It was as if I was spectator to the healing of torn flesh, or *heard* a broken bone come together, set, and grow again.

Wonderful is the engrafting of skin, but more wonderful the million busy hushed cells, in secret planning, stitching, stretching, until—the wound is vanished, the blood courses normal, the cicatrice falls off.

I had at last discovered it, the great efflorescent impersonality.

My hopes of finding Uncle Melech revived.

And this discovered poetry, scattered though it was, had its one obsessive theme. It was obsessed by the miraculous. These names and ingenuities and businesses, these artifacts of tradesmen and workers, they were but the elements, the gestures, and abracadabra of the performed miracle. It was sensed everywhere—among the Yemenites to whom the news of the State established had first come like some market rumour of the advent of the Messiah as well as among the European sophisticates who veiled their credulity with rationalization.

Little David had slain Goliath? The miracle had again been repeated; against great odds, the little strug-

gling State had withstood the onslaught of combined might.

Jaffa had seen a whale regurgitate Jonah? A company of Jews had taken over this same city whence eighty thousand Arabs had fled: Jonah regurgitated the whale!

Deborah here had sung a victory the captains could not understand? The accents of her song re-echoed still. *They fought from heaven; the stars in their courses fought against Sisera.*

As in place after place I gathered examples of the recent marvelous, the realization grew upon me that I, too, had been the witness of a miracle—the miracle of the transformed stone.

Jean Daniel

1920–2020

Born in Blida, Algeria, journalist Jean Daniel (born Jean Daniel Bensaïd) moved to France in his youth. As a teenager, he came under the influence of André Gide and the writer's admiration for the Soviet Union. Gide's subsequent disillusionment with Soviet communism deeply affected the young Daniel, initiating his turn toward socialism and eventually toward the center-left. During World War II, Daniel fought in the Algerian resistance, then with the armies of Giraud and Leclerc in North Africa, and finally in France. Like so many other French intellectuals, his politics as well as his personal life were colored by the Franco-Algerian War. Daniel founded *Le Nouvel observateur* in 1964.

The Mistake or the Second Life of Sylvain Regard
1953

I had learned of Louise's suicide upon my return to Blida, my hometown. Spring had just filled the streets with the insolent beauty of those impassive young women. Violent yet secretive, as in Spain or Corsica, a long tradition had endowed them with an appearance of cold modesty, whereas, like grenades, they are primed to explode. Where were they hiding during the winter? The light suddenly reveals them to men's eyes. Louise chose to die during the season that, in this country, oppresses people with the desire to live. There are some overwhelming days; the senses are awakened at each look, at every light touch. Nature descends upon you with the clamor of repressed desire. Louise was dead. The days had never been more beautiful. One was too busy living to think about her. [. . .]

As usual, my sister met me at the airport. It was early in May, noon, and the tarmac was hot. I was sure I had changed, and I wondered how my sister would react to the change. I told her straight away that because of my work I needed to be alone in a room that a friend had made available to me and that my parents needed to be made aware of this. Nothing could have been easier: my parents were in Chréa for a couple of weeks, and they would understand that I could not stay with them in the mountains. My sister then asked if I still intended to use my friend's room since our house was practically empty, and I told her that I wanted to be alone. When we arrived in Blida she left me, and as soon as I had got settled in the room that looked out over the Avenue Moulins, I went to see Louise Martin's uncle [François]. [. . .]

He was not surprised to see me, though I scarcely recognized him. I said, "I've come to hear what you can tell me about Louise." He replied that it was none of my business, that he was fed up with questions about the suicide, that it was a death like any other. Calmly, I said I was not against suicide and that I wanted him to talk to me about Louise. I must have sounded strange, for he stared at me for some time, then invited me to sit down.

"There's not much to say about Louise except that she knew what life was and she was not able to live. Others know how, I know, but I'm through. Louise did well, you understand, she did well. She would never have managed to cope, she would have lingered as I do here, all by myself in this villa, under a sun that belongs to others." [. . .]

"Well, Louise did not like herself. It's not enough to say she suffered from her ugliness if one doesn't understand how extreme her sense of beauty was. As for me, I can imagine it: I sing out of tune, but my hearing is true, and sounds have filled my existence. If I recall something from the depths of my past, it is enveloped in sounds, cries, voices, or simply noise. When I've uttered a sentence, I was hearing it beforehand, in a different tone of voice from the one I normally use. That's nothing. I'm telling you about it so you can understand a contradiction that can be tragic. It hasn't kept me from being happy. Happy as you will never be, as no one will ever be. . . ."

I calmly interrupted to lead him back to what I wanted to know.

"But Louise?"

"Louise? . . . Do you know what she wrote to me last year? She was so dazzled by having seen Donatello's *David* in Florence that she became obsessed with it. Once, after dreaming all night of that David, she spent a whole day thinking she had the same body as he. . . . And then one day she became so besotted by a film star—I no longer remember who, though she told me—that she imagined she had her face. Every time she looked, of course, the mirror dealt her a blow, *but in the end she saw herself differently . . . seeing, even in front of the mirror, instead of her own face, the features of the actress.* I'm the only one who knows this story, but the day I learned of it I had no need of anything else to understand Louise." [. . .]

Old François looked at me, but I didn't react. It all seemed obvious, clear, and in order. I was well aware that nothing should have seemed so, but as the only consolation I had at the moment was to accept myself, I made no effort. He handed me the second page, which was typed. It was a copy of a letter from Louise to Flane that the latter had recently sent to Louise's uncle. It was about "the salt of the sea on men's arms," "the wind that draws one's lips into laughter," "the footsteps of adolescents on wet sands and the sun that spreads triumph and anguish." The conclusion to all this lyricism, seemingly drawn from experience: we must resign ourselves to "the carnality of our being." The uncle, who was reading over my shoulder, recited the essential passages out loud. His voice became tremulous.

"There's no need for explanations, is there? To write that with the face she had! To know that with the body she had! She knew that, if she had been beautiful, she could have been cruel, joyful, even a bitch, in a word, alive, and she saw herself limited to 'moral qualities.'"

Old François had pronounced "moral qualities" with a derisive grimace.

"The worst thing for me, you don't know yet: I was never able to bear looking at her face, her presence. For me, as you've no doubt heard only too often, the insolent look of a pretty woman, that was almost life itself. When Louise was there, I was hard, impatient, and yet she was one of the rare beings for whom I would have given my life. Worse! Even now, to love her in her letters or in memory, I've caught myself giving her another face. I've destroyed her photographs. I'm doing as she did: I see her differently!"

Old François could see in my eyes that he had made a mistake and that I had been closer to him than he would have liked since the beginning of our conversation.

Translated by Michele McKay Aynesworth.

Other work by Daniel: *Le Temps qui reste: essai d'autobiographie professionnelle* (1973).

Abraham Josef Dubelman

1908–1990

Born into a Hasidic family in Rejowiec, Poland, Abraham Josef Dubelman lost his father and his older brother as a young child. He received a religious education before studying briefly in a Jewish public school. After apprenticing as an upholsterer, in 1925 Dubelman immigrated to Cuba, working for a time as a craftsman. His stories from the Cuban countryside were picked up by Yiddish newspapers in New York including the *Forverts*, and he eventually moved to Havana. Dubelman was also a journalist, writing editorials and literary criticism. In 1961, he moved to Miami, where he published his first and only work in English.

The Faith Healer

1953

I got up and stepped out of the hotel. The early-morning breeze was moist and cool—pure refreshment after a night of suffering.

Everything seemed reborn, and the small-town, good-natured Cubans approached me with their infinite eagerness to be of service.

"Are you looking for the *polaco*, *señor*?"

"For my *paisano*."

"Over there, where you see the green door, is where he lives."

I thanked them and the Cubans were happy to have helped. I went on my way, to the only Jewish business in town. The proprietor, an old Jew, met me by the door.

"Peace to a Jew!"

"Peace!"

"Where are you from?"

"From Havana. But it's worth traveling so far to meet another Jew."

His face lit up. He ran his hand through his gray hair, and his light-colored eyes had a gentle, yielding look. His face, wrinkled with age but even more from suffering, turned hospitable.

"Why are you standing at the door? Come inside! We hardly ever see a Jew around here." He started spewing out words, thrilled at the chance to speak Yiddish with someone besides his wife. He began telling me how lonely he was in this miserable little town, where he had already spent eighteen years, unable to leave. [. . .]

"I came to this town the way one comes to an inn, just for the night, as it were. I thought I'd stick around to make a little money before moving to Havana or back to the old country. As it turned out, I ended up settling here. But what kind of life is this? You become a yokel. There's no one to speak Yiddish with. Back in the old country, I was used to living among Jews, stopping by the synagogue to pore over a page of the Talmud. But here? You can't even keep kosher. You have a livelihood, but it doesn't do you a bit of good."

I started to reassure the Jew a little. "It's the same wherever you go. You have to stay confident. Be patient." [. . .]

"Are these your parents?"

"Over there," said the Jew, becoming talkative, "is my father, may he rest in peace. He was a clever man. I'm afraid to look him in the eyes. Do you think I don't know that today is the Sabbath? But what can you do? I try to stay as observant as possible, but we are in exile."

Meanwhile, his wife stood sighing. "This is my mother, may she inherit Paradise. A saintly woman she was. You can't imagine what she had to live through."

Suddenly, the woman caught herself as though she had just remembered something. She opened the back door, bent down, and picked up a glass that was standing by the entrance. The glass was filled with water and various herbs. The water looked greenish and murky, like swill. The wife closed her eyes and started moving her lips in a whisper. Then she started to drink, grimacing from the intense bitterness. The whole scene bewildered me. I was unable to contain my curiosity. "Is that some kind of medicine?" I asked her.

"It relieves my sickness just like that!" She started to redden and hesitated to tell me more. I insisted, acting very interested. She clearly believed that I myself wished to be cured of some illness, and she opened up.

"I had been sick for quite a long time. To tell the truth, I don't know what was wrong. I went to all sorts of doctors. They were always giving me different medicines, but nothing helped. And now, I just take this potion—a glass of water with herbs—and I'm all better." [. . .]

The evening had begun to fall. The setting sun flecked the sky with red. The townspeople had begun closing their shops, leaving doors half ajar, in anticipation of a last-minute customer. The Jew, too, stood by his half-closed shop door and hoped for latecomers, but none came.

He looked at me: "Perhaps you'd like step into the house? I've got to stay here for a little while yet." I understood that he felt a bit uncomfortable counting the days receipts in front of me, so I went in.

His wife asked me to sit down. She glanced up at the sky, then turned to me.

"The stars are already out, aren't they?"

I looked. "You can see them now."

"Since the Sabbath is over, I shall now recite 'God of Abraham.' She went to the faucet, wet the tip of her finger, and intoned the prayer. After she finished, she heartily wished both herself and me a good week to come. I looked at this curious woman, and I couldn't keep from asking, "If you're such a devout Jew, how can you go to a faith healer?"

She stared hard at me. "Do you think I go around crossing myself?" "You're worshiping two gods. What you're practicing is idolatry. The faith healer is not a doctor. A Jew should not believe in superstitions, in magic."

The woman had a guilty look on her face: "One feels so lonely here, so far from other Jews. One must believe in something. All is not lost. God rules the world."

Her reply made me uneasy. I started to encourage her to leave the town and move to Havana. Then her husband came in and wished us a booming "Good week!" as though he had just returned from synagogue. He lit a candle and began the Havdalah service.

I felt somewhat suffocated. I went out to the courtyard to look at the night. In the distance you could hear frogs croaking, and dogs from the surrounding villages bayed at the moon. The night grew darker. From the Jewish home issued forth a graceful voice, lowly chanting the prayerful words, "He who separates the holy from the profane . . ."

Off to the side, behind the door, stood the glass of water mixed with herbs, which the faith healer had prescribed.

Translated by Debbie Nathan.

Other works by Dubelman: *Der balans* (1953); *Der blinder* (1954); *On the Straight Path* (1979).

Albert Memmi

The Pillar of Salt
1953

The City

My name is Benillouche, Alexandre Mordekhai.

How galling the smiles of my classmates! In our alley, and at the Alliance School, I hadn't known how ridiculous, how revealing, my name could be. But at the French lycée I became aware of this at once. From then on, the mere sound of my own name humiliated me and made my pulse beat faster.

Alexandre: brassy, glorious, a name given to me by my parents in recognition of the wonderful West and because it seemed to them to express their idea of Europe. My schoolmates sneered and blared "Alexandre" like a trumpet blast: Alexan-ndre! With all my strength, I then hated them and my name. I hated them, but I believed they were right, and I was furious with my parents for having chosen this stupid name for me.

Mordekhai (colloquially, I was called Mridakh) signified my share in the Jewish tradition. It had been the formidable name of a glorious Maccabee and also of my grandfather, a feeble old man who never forgot the terrors of the ghetto.

Call yourself Peter or John, and by simply changing your clothes you can change your apparent status in society. But in this country, Mridakh is as obstinately revealing as if one shouted out: "I'm a Jew!" More precisely: "My home is in the ghetto," "my legal status is native African," "I come from an Oriental background," "I'm poor." But I had learned to reject these four classifications. It would be easy to reproach me for this, and I have not failed to blame myself. But how is it possible not to be ashamed of one's condition when one has experienced scorn, mockery, or sympathy for it since childhood? I had learned to interpret smiles, to understand whispers, to read the thoughts of others in their eyes, to reconstruct the reasoning behind a casual phrase or a chance word. When anyone speaks about me, I feel provoked in advance: my hair stands up on end and I am ready to bite. One can, of course, ultimately learn to accept anything at the cost of an enormous effort and a vast weariness. But, before this happens, one resists and hates oneself; or else, to defy the scorn of others, one asserts one's own ugliness and even exaggerates it so as to grin and bear it.

At the lycée, I very quickly got into the habit of dropping "Mordekhai" from my lesson headings, and before long I forgot the name as if I had shed it like an old skin. Yet it dragged on behind me, holding fast. It was brought back to my attention by all official notices and summonses, by everything that came from beyond the narrow frame of daily routine. When commencement-time came, on the day diplomas were to be awarded, I knew I would be one of the triumphant scholars; in the midst of a nervous crowd, I waited undisturbed, certain of success. When the usher climbed onto a chair, my name was the first to be called out; in the tense silence, the exact order of my legal status was re-established:

"Alexandre, Mordekhai, Benillouche!"

I didn't move. Surprised by the silence, the crowd looked around for the happy candidate, astonished to hear no explosion of joy, no throwing of notebooks into the air; no one was surrounded or kissed by a delighted family. (I never cared to have my parents present at the public events of my life, so they hadn't been told when the diplomas were to be awarded.) I merely smiled to those of my schoolmates who congratulated me with a look; and I was soon forgotten because everyone was concerned with his own fate.

Alexandre, Mordekhai, Benillouche. Benillouche or, in Berber-Arabic dialect, the son of the lamb. From what mountain tribe did my ancestors descend? Who am I, after all?

I sought—in everything from official documents to my own sharply defined features—some thread which might lead me to the knowledge of who I am. For a while, I believed my forebears had been a family of Berber princes converted to Judaism by Kahena, the warrior-queen and founder of a Jewish kingdom in the middle of the Atlas Mountains. It pleased me to think that I came from the very heart of the country. But then, another time, I found I was descended from an Italian Renaissance painter. I tore the article from the big Larousse encyclopedia and displayed reproductions of my ancestor's paintings to all my friends. Philology could explain away what changes the name had undergone, and my friend Sitboun, the star Latin student, backed me up and even discovered that the patron of a Latin poet had had a similar name. But philology is a fragile science, and the past is much too far away. Could I be descended from a Berber tribe when the Berbers themselves failed to recognize me as one of their own? I was Jewish, not Moslem; a townsman, not a highlander. And even if I had borne the painter's name, I would not have been acknowledged by the Italians. No, I'm African, not European. In the long run, I would always be forced to return to Alexandre Mordekhai Benillouche, a native in a colonial country, a Jew in an anti-Semitic universe, an African in a world dominated by Europe.

Had I believed in signs, might I not have said that my name holds all the meaning of life? How is it possible to harmonize so many discords in something as smooth as the sound of a flute?

Translated by Édouard Roditi.

Samuel Pecar

1922–2000

Samuel Pecar was born in the JCA agricultural colony of Colonia López, Entre Ríos, Argentina. He lived there until 1930 when his family moved to the Buenos Aires suburb of San Fernando. Between 1951 and his move to Israel in 1962, he contributed to *Nueva Sión*, published by the Zionist Socialist party in Argentina, and from 1957 to 1958, for the Jewish daily *Amanecer*. A recognized writer of Jewish life, Pecar's earlier works gently poked fun at Jewish communities in Argentina, while his later works, following his move to Israel, delved into more existential questions. In Israel, he specialized in farm cooperatives, working for the Latin American Department of the Histadrut, and in 1985 he founded and directed the Association of Israeli Writers in Spanish.

Tales of Kleinville
1954

The Community of Kleinville

Open a map, stretch out your index finger, run it along the winding contours of the Plata River, and you will come to a small black dot that does and does not seem like the others. Do not try to read its name; you will not find it. We can tell you what it is: Kleinville, population approximately eight thousand. We are anxious to introduce you to the tiny Jewish community to be found in this enclave.

Getting to Kleinville is simplicity itself.

If you find it convenient to travel by train, kindly get off at the station of the same name. Go to the south end of the platform and cross the roads very carefully, because (may you live longer!) distracted tourists who failed to look both ways did not manage to have a first impression of the town. Then turn right and walk two blocks and you will end up on the main street; that is, in the heart, the spinal column, and the cranium of Kleinville.

If you prefer to come by bus, tell the driver to stop at the central plaza. Otherwise, the rascal is capable of taking you all the way to the outskirts without saying a word, and there you will only be able to talk to the cows and get your shoes muddy.

Now if you are fortunate enough to own an automobile, the matter is simplified. Get a hold of a street map and watch the road signs. In the absence of road signs, ask, and if there is no one to ask, consult Israel Colbin, the community truck driver.

Once in Kleinville, you will wish—we suppose—to explore its streets and visit the Jewish community we referred to earlier. To save you from having to ask questions or guess which way to go, we need to explain something. Kleinville is like an onion. The plaza is the bulb, the main street, its stem, and that is all. At the corners of the plaza are four unmistakable buildings: City Hall, the church, a bank, and a movie theater. Between them, commerce sizzles. Around them, torpor.

We would gladly take you to the house of some good Kleinville Jew, but frankly, we would not know where or with whom to begin. With an outstanding community leader, or with a simple neighbor? With a Zionist, a "progressive," or someone indifferent to politics? A Zionist from the right, the left, or the center? A youth or an adult? A rich man or a poor man?

To avoid conflicts, the safest procedure will be to present the Kleinvillers in order of appearance. Let us return to the plaza. What is the first Jewish business establishment? The shop of Hershel Menis. Perfect. Here we can go in, drink a cup of tea, and in the process, shoot the breeze with the owner. With his help, we shall be put in touch with the rest of the community.

Hershel Menis is not an important person. He is not a president of anything, nor a secretary of any political party, and he does not head any list of donors. Hershel Menis is an average Jew. Coming from Poland, he immigrated to the country some thirty-five years ago, poor as a church mouse but rich in his inner life, in inventiveness, and in activity. Before settling in Kleinville, he wandered through colonies and villages. With his wares on his shoulder, he called at all the ports and tried to make himself understood in all the local languages during his pilgrimage. His prosperity followed the same stages as the progress of the country. When the outdated "general store" was breaking up into small specialized shops, Hershel Menis—witness and actor—left behind his peddler's gear and put an end to his nomadic ways by planting himself behind a shop counter.

His fellow immigrants took the same path. However, as they were adapting to this environment with that fervent desire to live, so characteristic of Jewry, they began to reproduce—within the new conditions they faced—those entities that had shaped Jewish life in their countries of origin. Without a plan or method, but according to their needs.

Translated by Michele McKay Aynesworth.

Other works by Pecar: *La generación olvidado* (1958); *Los rebeldes et los perplejos* (1959); *La edad distinta: confesiones de un inmigrante en Israel* (1970).

Meir Basri

1911–2006

Meir Basri (Mīr Baṣrī) was born in Baghdad, heir to the prominent Baṣrī and Dangoor families. He was a gifted poet, writer, and historian, publishing extensively in Arabic but also in Hebrew, English, and French. He held many diplomatic posts during and after the British Mandate, published in newspapers throughout the Middle East, and is remembered for introducing Iraqis to the English sonnet. He was last president of the Iraqi Jewish Community, leaving Baghdad only in 1974 when exiled by the Ba'ath regime.

The Elementary School Teacher
1955

> Let not Ambition mock their useful toil,
> Their homely joys, and destiny obscure;
> Nor Grandeur hear with a disdainful smile
> The short and simple annals of the poor.
> —Thomas Gray, "Elegy Written in a Country
>   Churchyard"

Many years ago I encountered a teacher in a modest elementary school, where it was possible to find a leader of a forgotten group dedicated to good deeds for children. This teacher was neither a graduate of any school nor ever studied in any formal way; he inherited his profession. Moreover, he infused it into his blood and developed this profession, doing his work well and performing it as it should be. His father ran an old-fashioned one-room school where religious lessons were taught, along with a bit of reading, simple writing, and arithmetic. Probably his grandfather had been a teacher too, like his father before him, so that the boy grew in an ever-expanding home with old and collapsing walls, filled with the noise of children and the loud voice of the teacher that could be heard above the din. That voice, if it became a bit louder, would instill terror in the rebellious republic of pupils. We cannot know how and what this boy learned there, but can be certain, without a doubt, that he learned the basics of reading that became the key to all the knowledge, for which our child was ravenous, and he devoured all the papers and books that came into his hands. In addition he became competent in literature, language, history, geography, mathematics, and the natural sciences, all which he learned with no help from anyone else. He managed to acquire information in different fields, became expert in an environment that had not opened its doors to culture, and was enlightened in a land ruled by ignorance and idleness, aspiring to advance in a period in which the population held on to the worn and barren coattails of the past. [. . .]

After the opening of the first modern school, our friend, by now grown up, was appointed as one of the teachers. And he taught the children and educated them well. After a few years he became principal of the school and ran it with logic and determination implementing a modern style. I have no idea where he learned it or where he became skilled, but I know he implemented it well and managed to produce the greatest results. Despite the fact that he was raised in a religious environment, our friend quickly adopted modern perspectives, and thus he allotted a respectable position to sports, excursions, and games in his school; he distributed prizes to outstanding students, and conducted debate competitions as well as graduation ceremonies to which he invited both parents and notables in the city. He excelled in this exhausting profession, and could be seen working alongside the janitors, debating excitedly and energetically with the teachers, participating with the pupils in their conversations and their games, walking from class to class, and he didn't hesitate to sit together with the pupils to listen to an enjoyable lesson he had not learned before from any teacher.

Our friend continued in this manner for many years without becoming bored or tired. He was the living spirit and the main artery beating in the school, so it was little wonder that his pupils respected and adored him. [. . .]

And then the teacher became old and his eyesight faltered; he could barely find his way. A new principal was assigned to the school, but our friend remained in the position of honorary principal, as he didn't wish to abandon the school that had become part of his flesh and blood. His wife died, as did his son, to whose education and upbringing he had devoted many nights, so the teacher decided to move into one of the rooms in the school. He would leave his room only to take care of school matters or to evaluate its situation.

One day the inevitable occurred. The lamp was extinguished, its wick shriveled and its oil depleted. The ancient, modest teacher went to meet his maker. Even before that, his old and modest school had disappeared, having been deserted by his pupils, and it had become an arid desert. Even the memories, whose aromas had filled its spaces for so long a time, passed away.

Translated by Karen Alkalay-Gut.

Other works by Basri: *Songs of Love and Eternity* (1991); *Eminent Jewish Men of Modern Iraq* (Arabic, in two volumes, 1983, 1993); *The Songs of Love and Eternity* (Arabic, 1991); and *Life's Journey from the Banks of the Tigris to the Valley of the Thames: Reminiscences and Thoughts* (Arabic, 1992).

Salomón Brainsky

1902–1955

Salomón (also known as Shloyme) Brainsky was born in Żelechów, Poland. He was an enthusiastic Zionist, but after a trip to Palestine he became disillusioned, complaining that Yiddish had been shunned there. Fleeing Nazi persecution in 1934, Brainsky emigrated to Bogotá, Colombia. His stories, written in Yiddish, reflected his own situation as a struggling Jewish immigrant, eking out a living as a door-to-door peddler of fabrics. *Gentes en la Noria: Cuentos bogotanos*, published in 1945, was a loose translation of his stories by Colombian poet Luis Vidales. The protagonists are the poor and the marginalized, immigrants who arrive under duress in a strange land whose language they do not understand and who suffer nostalgia for the places and people they left behind.

Temptation
1955

Nathan, the shoemaker from Porisov, a small Jewish village in Poland, came home one evening shortly before his departure for Colombia with a Torah scroll under his arm. With a slight shiver, he lay the holy object down on the table. His wife, Tzipporah, who at that moment stood skimming the broth, froze with the spoon in midair. "What can this mean?" her staring eyes asked in silence. What was a Torah scroll doing in her house? But Nathan—tall and broad-shouldered, with a dense, pitch-black beard that framed his full, fleshy checks— hardly paid attention to his wife's wide-open eyes. He took off his frock coat, wiped the sweat from his brow with his sleeve, and asked if supper was ready.

"I was about to set the table," Tzipporah said, coming out of her stupor. "But where are we going to eat if a Torah scroll is on the table?"

Nathan quickly picked up the scroll and placed it in the cupboard. Only when husband and wife sat at the table, eating their kasha and broth, did Tzipporah ask whence the holy scroll had come. At first Nathan did not answer, but when his wife repeated the question, he said that an opportunity had arisen to buy it at a reasonable price.

"What is a reasonable price?" asked Tzipporah with amazement. "Since when have you, my husband, become a dealer in Torah scrolls?"

"You've gotten quite good at picking on me!" snapped Nathan. "What a plague of a Jewess you are! You were already told I got it for a reasonable price; now stop pestering me."

From the way the words were uttered, it was clear he could not explain why he had suddenly spent a whole hundred zlotys on a Torah scroll, especially on the eve of such a long trip.

Such were the circumstances that had led to the unexpected purchase: a notification from the post office had arrived that afternoon announcing a certified letter. It occurred to Nathan that this must surely be related to his departure, because the mail he received—such as it was—always had to do with some momentous occasion. He took off his apron, put on his frock coat and went to claim the letter. It consisted of a thick stack of papers regarding his trip. But they were written in Gentile letters, which he was unable to read. He did not trust his daughters to decipher them, even though they had some understanding of the language, so he decided to go to Mordechai Mezritsher, whose son was versed in Gentile matters and spoke many tongues.

Mordechai Mezritsher was a small Jew about fifty years old with a pair of lively black eyes that darted around like birds in a cage. He was pleased that Nathan had come by.

"Ah, a visitor. Have a seat, Nathan. What's new?"

"To be frank with you, Mordechai, I have not come to see you, but your son. I would like to have him read some papers I have just picked up at the post office. People say he is quite the expert in such matters."

"I wish he devoted his mind to the Talmud instead of immersing all his senses in those heretical books. Then

I would have a learned son," sighed Mordechai. "Come in, you are needed to do a favor," he called.

Mordechai's son was a comely, dark-skinned lad with sparkling eyes, who sewed bootlegs on a machine all day long and studied during the night. Everything became clear to Nathan after the boy deciphered the papers and explained the details to him.

In the midst of their conversation, Israel-Leon, the tailor, stopped by. All three of them prayed at the same synagogue, where many craftsmen gathered. The arrival of yet another guest pleased Mordechai, a joyous and animated fellow who did not frown at a drink with close friends. He asked them to sit down, and wiped the sweat from his face. "It's terribly hot outside," he remarked. "A cold glass of beer would be a delight." So they sent the apprentice to fetch some bottles of beer.

"What do you think of that, Israel-Leon?" Mordechai said. "Nathan is fleeing from us. He just got all the papers." He asked Nathan when he planned on leaving, but instead of waiting for an answer he went on.

"Tell me, dear Nathan, what kind of place is that Colombia you are off to? Do Jews live there? Do they have a rabbi, a kosher slaughterer, a synagogue to pray in? And, finally, dear Nathan—may you ever be healthy—how does a Jew like you, close to fifty years old, decide to escape to the devil knows where?"

"Well, what can one do, Mordechai? It's hard to make a living here. And besides, I have daughters to marry off," Nathan said with a sigh.

They remained seated for a while in deep and heavy silence. Nathan's simple words went right to their hearts. The bitter present and uncertain future of all the Jews in Poland were clear to them. Suddenly, Israel-Leon's voice cut through the silence: "Why should we add more weight to the heart of a Jew who has decided to throw himself into such an adventure? Anyone who wishes to remain a Jew and follow Jewish law can do so, even in the desert. A Jew like Nathan would not undertake such trip lightly. Do you know, Nathan, what has just occurred to me? It would be a wonderful thing if you could take along a Torah scroll. You're setting off for a land where there will be few Jews, if any. Even if a congregation could be gathered there, who knows if they have a scroll? And perhaps God has appointed you to be the first Jew in that faraway land to assemble a quorum for prayer."

"It certainly would be a wonderful thing," agreed Nathan. "But a Torah scroll could cost several hundred zlotys, and where am I to get the money?" For a long moment the wrinkles on Israel-Leon's brow deepened. Then his face lit up.

"You know what, Nathan? In our small synagogue we have several Torah scrolls. We could give one of them to you, and with God's help you will someday send us money to pay us back," he said.

That very day, between afternoon and evening services in the tailors' synagogue, some ten men gathered. At first, these simple Jews could not grasp what Israel-Leon was asking of them. Just think, to take a Torah scroll out of the Holy Ark and send it off to a remote place! Israel-Leon explained this would be a good deed of which each of them would partake, and they owed no less to one of their members who was about to set off on such a long journey. At that moment, Berl Israel, the main trustee, intervened:

"Listen to me. Nathan is one of us. He has worshiped among us for over twenty years. Many of his hard-earned zlotys lie in these walls and in the holy books we have here. I propose that we ask him for a down payment of a hundred zlotys, and with God's help he will mail the remainder to us later."

Hirsh Odeser, who had been Berl's rival for years, grumbled that a general assembly should be convened to decide the matter, but Berl objected that this was not the time for politicking. They resolved to give a Torah scroll to Nathan, and celebrated with a few drinks. The blessings and well-wishing lifted Nathan's spirit; true joy, the finest wine of all, warmed his heart. He, Nathan the shoemaker from Porisov, might well have the honor of being the first Jew to bring a Torah scroll to a distant, foreign land.

Half an hour after taking leave of his friends and starting home, his merriment began to wane. The three digits making up the number one hundred appeared suddenly before him in the dark. They danced before his eyes, and mocked him with questions: "When did God name you his envoy in charge of supplying Jews with Torah scrolls? It's just a foolish notion that some religious Jew—and an idle one at that—has put into your head. Go back right away, return the scroll, and get back your hard-earned zlotys. It would be a far greater mitzvah to leave that money to your wife and children."

He stood there for a while, but suddenly panicked. "Nathan the shoemaker," a hidden voice warned him, "who are you to play with such a holy object? Do you believe you are purchasing mere leather and thread?"

A shiver of dread ran through Nathan's body. "It is wrong to regard such holy objects lightly," he muttered

to himself, trying to apologize. He pressed the Torah scroll to his chest and strode home.

So that is how—along with Nathan's shoe lasts, rulers, hammers, pliers and files—the first Torah scroll, wrapped in clothes and bedding, sailed over the stormy waters of the Atlantic to that distant, foreign land, Colombia.

Translated by Moisés Mermelstein.

Other works by Brainsky: *Ven fundamentn treysln zikh* (1951); *Mentshn fun Zshelekhov* (1961).

Salomón Zytner
1904–1986

Born into a Hasidic family in Białystok, Salomón (also Shloyme) Zytner received a primary religious education before pursuing further studies independently. He became active at a young age in Zionist labor organizations. In 1925, he emigrated to Uruguay, working initially as a traveling salesman and then in textile manufacturing. At the same time, Zytner was active in the local branch of YIVO and pursued a career as a writer, publishing short stories, poetry, and news reports in Montevideo's Yiddish journals and newspapers. In 1967, he moved to Israel.

The Bar Mitzvah Speech
1955

Bernardo Tzalkin stood there as though he had just been drenched with a bucket of cold water. Perplexed, at a loss for words, he tried to ask the doctor whether the boy could possibly get out of bed the next day for just an hour. It was his thirteenth birthday. . . . He attempted to explain that there was to be a big party. All the guests had been invited. Everything was ready. The boy would have to make a speech, or otherwise the whole celebration would be ruined.

The doctor refused, shaking his head. He could not understand how it could matter so that the boy give a speech and thereby risk his health. Bernardo Tzalkin interrupted the doctor with a small voice, begging his authorization, trying to make him understand: "For us Jews, it's a big occasion. He's been practicing the speech for a long time." Maybe the doctor could prescribe some penicillin shots, for example, a high dose, so that the next day the boy would feel well enough to be taken to the hall, just to recite the speech before the guests. Then they would bring him back home to bed.

The doctor, a good-hearted man of Spanish ancestry, smiled and patted Bernardo Tzalkin on the back, showing he now understood. He uttered a quick "*Está bien*" and left the room.

The next day Bernardo Tzalkin stood outside his house, waiting nervously as his wife helped their daughter arrange her hair and gown before a mirror. The white silk drew tightly at the waist, before falling into slight pleats. With each movement the gown rustled, as though expressing the dreams and longings of the girl, about to take leave of her fifteen childhood years.

Bernardo Tzalkin kept looking at his watch, fearful it was getting late. He saw all the guests sitting at their tables and straining their eyes in anticipation of the hosts' arrival. And here they were still lingering. The injections prescribed by the doctor the day before had wrought the desired effect. The boy felt better, thereby vindicating Bernardo Tzalkin. After all, what would the entire party have been like without the bar mitzvah speech?

All of a sudden he noticed the door opening. Out stepped his daughter, bedecked, shining brilliantly. His wife followed, leading by the hand their son, swaddled in warm clothing. He opened up the car door quickly and took his son by the other arm. Together, they helped the boy into the car.

Bernardo Tzalkin was overtaken by cheer. Here he was, taking his son to recite the long-awaited bar mitzvah speech. The celebration was to go forward exactly as planned.

Upon entering the catering hall, he remarked how his son began hesitating, tottering, and seemed about to fall over. The boys usually ruddy face went pale and gaunt. His eyes were sunken in and surrounded by bluish spots. Bernardo Tzalkin gave a shiver, taking fright lest his son's health worsen and keep him from delivering the bar mitzvah speech.

The band entoned a joyous melody. Merriment and laughter poured over the hall. The honorees were welcomed with great festivity, applause broke out on all sides. Hands stretched out to wish the family happiness. Bernardo Tzalkin was entranced by the music, the jolly faces that shined at him from all directions. The ceremonious music swept over him like a warm wave, embracing and caressing him, making him forget all his cares. The fears regarding his son dissolved. He remembered only that today was a celebration in honor of both his children, a double celebration he had made as sumptuous as possible, renting out the most luxurious hall, arranging for the finest foods—an occasion people were not likely to forget. They would all comment on his unrestrained generosity, his brilliant social standing. And soon his son would recite the bar mitzvah speech.

Translated by Alan Astro.

Other works by Zytner: *Der gerangl un andere dertseylungen* (1955); *Di mishpokhe un andere dertseylungen* (1969); *Tsvishn vent un andere dertseylungen* (1974).

Samuel Rawet
1929–1984

Samuel Rawet was born in the Polish shtetl of Klimontów and immigrated with his family to Brazil in 1936. Rawet grew up in Zona de Leopoldina, a suburb of Rio de Janeiro, the city that later became the setting for much of his literary work. He completed his engineering degree in 1943 at the University of Brazil and went on to build Brasília. He was a poet, playwright, novelist, and essayist. He gave an important early voice to Brazilian Jews, expressing the frustrations of exile and the immigrant experience. He wrote about marginalized groups: Jews, homosexuals, and suburbanites. He was a member of the Café da Manhã group, contributor to *Revista Branca*, and, in 1965, became a member of the Brazilian Associação Nacional de Escritores.

The Prophet and Other Stories
1956

All illusions lost, the only thing really left for him to do was to take that step. The gangplank already hauled off, and the last whistle blown, the steamship would weigh anchor. He again looked at the cranes wielding bales, the piles of ore and other minerals. Down below, people hustling and bustling and foreign tongues. Necks stretched out in cries toward those who surrounded him on the rampart of the upper deck. Handkerchiefs. In the distance, the honking of automobiles revealing the life that continued on in the city he was now abandoning. The sneering looks of some mattered little to him. At another time he would have felt hurt. He understood that the white beard and the long overcoat well below his knees made him a strange figure to them. He had become accustomed to that reaction. Right now they would be laughing at the thin figure, all in black except for the face, the beard, and the even whiter hands. However, no one dared challenge those eyes that commanded respect and instilled a certain majestic air to his demeanor. With fists folded against his temples, he resisted interior escape into the serenity that had brought him to this point. Hearing the ship's muffled toot, he became fully aware of his plunging into solitude. The return, the only way out he had discovered, seemed to him empty and illogical. He thought, at the moment of hesitation, that he had acted as a child. Lately, the idea had been building into gigantic proportions and had culminated in his presence on board the ship. Now he was afraid of seeing that decision effaced by the glimmer of doubt. The fear of solitude terrified him more so because of the experience obtained in his daily contact with death. There was still time. . . .

"Step down the gangplank, please, step down!"

The fat figure of the woman to his side turned upon hearing, or upon thinking that she heard, the words of the old man.

"Sir, did you say something to me?"

Useless. He knew the language barrier would not allow him to say anything. The woman's face changed with the old man's negative nod and supplicating eyes. With exceptions, the true recourse would be mimicry but that would accentuate the childishness that tyrannized him. Only then did he realize he had murmured the sentence, and ashamed, he closed his eyes.

"My wife, my children, my son-in-law."

Confused, he gazed at the group that kept on hugging and kissing, a strange group (even his brother and cousins, if not for the photographs mailed ahead, would also seem strange to him), and the tears then rolling down his cheeks were not of tenderness but of gratitude. He had known the older ones as children. Thirty years ago his own brother was little more than an adolescent. Here he had married, had sons and daughters, and had also seen his daughter marry. Not even after settling into the cushioned springs of the car the son-in-law was driving did his tears stop flowing. To the onslaught of questions, he responded with gestures, evasions, or else silence. Despite its age, his thin but hard body had enabled him to work and, moreover, had saved his life. Now it swayed with the traffic's hesitations and never once did his eyes gaze upon the landscape. He seemed to be concentrating more on responding to the avalanche of tenderness. What was going on inside would be impossible for him to convey

through the superficial contact now being initiated. He figured his silences were embarrassing. The silences following the series of questions about himself, about the most terrifying thing he had experienced. To forget what had happened, never. But how to belittle it, to eliminate the essence of the horror as one sat down to a beautifully set table, or as one sipped tea ensconced in elegant cushions and comfortable armchairs? The avid and inquiring eyes around him, hadn't they heard or seen enough to be horrified as well and to share his silences? One world alone. He expected to find on this side of the ocean the comfort of those like him who had suffered, but whom chance had marginally saved from the worst. And being conscious of that, they shared this meeting with humility. However, he had an inkling of a slight mistake on his part. [. . .]

During the first weeks there was much commotion and many houses to visit, many tables to eat at, and in all the homes he felt indignant for being taken for granted as a *curiosity*. With time, once the enthusiasm and the curiosity had cooled down, he ended up spending time only with his brother. Actually talking only to him or to his wife. The others hardly understood him, nor did his nephews, and even less so the son-in-law, toward whom he began to nurture a real aversion.

"Here comes the 'Prophet'!"

He had barely opened the door when the son-in-law's derisive words and laugh surprised him. He pretended as if he hadn't noticed the others' uneasiness. He had taken his time on the way home from the synagogue and they were already waiting for him at the dinner table. He glimpsed his brother's disapproval and one of the children's shortened laugh. Only Paulo (that's how they called the grandson, whose real name was Pincus) moved his hands babbling as though to complain about the lost playtime. Mute, he placed his hat on the rack, keeping only the black silk cap on his head. He still hadn't learned a thing about the language. But, being a good observer, even though he didn't dare say anything, by association he managed to memorize a few things. And the word "prophet," delivered with mischievous laughter as he came into the house, was becoming familiar. He didn't get its meaning. Little did it matter, however. The word was never uttered without an ironic look, a smirk. In the bathroom (while he was washing his hands) he was reminded of the innumerable times the same sounds were said in front of him. He made the connection with other scenes. From down deep surfaced the memory of something similar having occurred in the temple.

Translated by Nelson H. Vieira.

Other works by Rawet: *Contos do imigrante* (1956); *Abama* (1964); *Que os mortos enterrem seus mortos* (1981).

Adele Wiseman
1928–1992

Born in Winnipeg, Adele Wiseman incorporated many images of the Jewish immigrant communities of the Canadian prairie into her novels, essays, and short stories. Wiseman studied at the University of Manitoba and later lived in England and Italy. She received the Governor General's Award of Canada.

The Sacrifice
1956

The train was beginning to slow down again, and Abraham noticed lights in the distance. He shifted his body only slightly so as not to disturb the boy, and sank back into the familiar pattern of throbbing aches inflicted by the wheels below. A dim glow from the corridor outlined the other figures in the day coach as they slept, sprawled in attitudes of discomfort and fatigue. He tried to close his eyes and lose himself in the thick, dream-crowded stillness, but his eyelids, prickly with weariness, sprang open again.

Urgently the train howled the warning of its approach to the city. Facing him, Abraham's wife seemed to seize the same wailful note and draw it out plaintively as she sighed in her sleep. Her body huddled, strained and unnatural, on the faded green plush seat. He could feel the boy, slack and completely pliant, rolling to the motion of the train. The whistle howled again, the carriage jolted, and his son lurched heavily, almost lifelessly against him.

Enough! With a sudden rush of indignation, as though he had been jerked awake, it came to Abraham that they had fled far enough; the thought took hold in his mind like a command. It came alive in his head and swept through him angrily, in a wave of energy, a rebellious movement of the blood. It was as simple as this. Enough. He must act now.

He sat up carefully, shifting Isaac's limp form into another position, fired in his new determination by the boy's weak protesting mumble. Slowly, he stretched, feeling his joints crackle, willing the cramp out of his body. He looked about him impatiently.

As though summoned, the conductor entered the coach. Abraham turned his head and beckoned imperatively.

"Where are we?" he asked in Ukrainian, tentatively, his red-rimmed eyes gleaming with excitement, his loud voice muted to a hoarse whisper. The man stooped, his face polite, questioning, and to Abraham offensively vacant in its noncomprehension. "I beg your pardon?" he said in English.

"Where are we stopping, please?" Abraham asked urgently in Yiddish, speaking slowly and patiently so that the man must understand. The conductor shook his head. "No speak, no speak," he said, pointing to Abraham's mouth, then to his own, with a deprecating gesture.

Abraham looked at the man with irritation. Was there anyone on the train who could do anything but make faces and smile? "Why does the train stop?" he asked suddenly, hopefully, in Polish.

The conductor shook his head helplessly.

Abraham leaned forward and gestured wildly toward the window to where the lights blinked in the distance.

The conductor, as though realizing something, smiled a broad, reassuring smile, shook his head vigorously, patted Abraham lightly on the arm, and made as if to move on.

"The train! stop! why? What city?" roared the Jew in exasperation, spitting out the words in broken German.

At the sound his son jerked suddenly awake, frightened, and looked blindly about for a moment. Other passengers groaned, stirred; their numb bones, and mumbled in protest. The conductor swayed on down the car, shrugging apologetically at drowsy faces.

"Animals here," muttered Abraham, subsiding and turning helplessly to his son. "They can only gibber and gesticulate."

"What's the matter, Pa?" Isaac yawned, "Can't you sleep?"

"*No!*" With a gesture, he flung aside the overcoat he had used as a cover. "The train is stopping. We're getting off."

"But we have two more days."

"Who awaits us?"

There was no answer to this that the boy knew of. Who awaited them? What awaited them? It did not really matter whether they stopped here, blindly, or went blindly on to the other city for which they had bought the tickets. Isaac crouched for another moment and watched his father, who was collecting their bundles. His own limbs were so knotted that it took him a moment to gather the strength to get out from under his warm coat and. stretch.

The conductor called out the name of the city.

"No; enough, I say," said Abraham. "Fifteen months and eleven days. If I had to spend more days and nights worrying about a new beginning I would not have the strength to begin. Two more days and nights in this position, and this whole human being that you call your father will make sense only to an upholsterer. I do not know where we will sleep tomorrow, but at least our beds will lie flat and we will rock no more."

"But our tickets—" Isaac rubbed his eyes with numb fingers and shook his head to clear his thoughts.

"Ah, our tickets." Abraham scratched the itching skin under his forked beard reflectively. "Well, it's senseless trying to explain anything to that fellow. Listen to him. Me he can't answer a simple question, and now he wakes up the whole train with his shouting up and down. Well, I suppose he can't help himself. Would I have understood him even if he had understood me?"

Strength and humor returned with his decision. He moved around and stretched; his blood began to circulate again. Like a young man entering deliberately into an adventure, he felt excited at making a positive gesture in the ordering of his fate.

"In fact, come to think of it, we'll be saving money. If we get off here we save the rest of our fare, so just in case they're not clamoring for a butcher and I don't get a job here right away, we'll save that much more money to live on in the meantime. That's why it's such a good idea to get off here. You see, your father has not lost his common sense. In fact, it's a wise decision I have made with God's help. And we can see about our tickets in the station."

Lights flashed by; at the other end of the car a young couple were gathering their belongings.

"The important thing now," Abraham continued, "is that we must stop running from death and from every other insult. We will seize our lives in these scarred hands again." He paused to consider his words with pleasure.

"Come, boy, we must wake your mother—but gently. How weary she is."

When the train grunted to a halt Abraham and his family, his wife blinking and shivering with sleep, stood among the few waiting with their bundles in their arms. The conductor, noticing the group assembled to leave, rushed up to them.

"No, no, no!" He shook his head and reached for Abraham's suitcase. "This isn't your stop!"

Abraham brushed his arm away firmly.

"Shalom," he said politely, yet with a certain fierceness that prevented the conductor from persisting. They descended to the platform. The conductor stood shaking his head in exasperation over these immigrants. Abraham cast him a last, forgiving glance. As though it were written, he could see what they must do. First, to find the immigration barracks—to sleep, at last, without the artificial pulse of engines to remind them even in sleep that they were wanderers. Then, with the new day, to settle themselves gingerly on the crust of the city, perhaps someday even to send down a few roots—those roots, pre-numbed and shallow, of the often uprooted. But strong. Abraham felt strength surge up in him, excitement shaking the tiredness out of his body. No matter what is done to the plant, when it falls, again it will send out the tentative roots to the earth and rise upward again to the sky. The boy was young, the boy was blessed, the boy would grow.

Other works by Wiseman: *Old Markets, New World* (1964); *Crackpot* (1974).

David Viñas

1927–2011

David Viñas grew up in Buenos Aires in a family of Russian Jewish immigrants. He studied at the University of Buenos Aires and came to prominence when his novel *Un Dios cotidiano* (1957) won the Gerchunoff Prize. In addition to novels, Viñas wrote short stories, plays, and essays. He was a professor of literature at his alma mater and was considered a major Latin American intellectual, winning the Premio Nacional de Literatura in both 1962 and 1967. Much of his writing was leftist social and political criticism, primarily emphasizing Argentine history, particularly the dynamics of power, immigration, cultural oppression, and Jewish identity. During the 1976–1983 military dictatorship, Viñas lived in exile. Two of his children were disappeared during those years.

An Everyday God
1957

Of course I could explain the history and the comings and goings of the Jews, assuring you that they have suffered much, that everyone persecuted them because they could, that those caricatures you'd seen in various magazines were the products of cretins, that no one but a cretin could believe some of the stories and that this divine curse business was a clumsy attempt at an explanation, and that the Jews in Spain, distinct from the Russians, were the same but different. I could tell you the truth while Mendel would be cut to the bone but grateful.

The next day, I went into the boys' bathroom because it was on my rounds. On the marble of one of the urinals they had written "Mendel is a Jew"; on another one there was an obscene drawing and an inscription saying "This is Mendel." I looked everywhere and didn't see anyone. There were two or three rooms with their doors shut. I kicked them open. No one there either; they were empty.

"Cambaceres!" I yelled; he was the one in charge of cleaning. No one answered, so I went out into the hallway and called again, "Cambaceres!"

A few moments later, there he came, up the back staircase. He was a rickety fellow with a disproportionally large head that seemed to wobble on his turkey neck. He was always skulking in the shadows and would appear out of nowhere when I was doing my rounds at the school. He was completely useless, but they tolerated him because he was very devout, and in the processions he was the one who carried the altar of the Virgin Mary on his back. He would also play the drum when the kids were preparing a parade.

"You called, Father?" he asked.

"Yes. Where have you been?"

"I was mopping in the dormitory."

"But you're supposed to take care of this bathroom."

"Father Adij sent me . . ." he said by way of justification while he dried his hands on his clothes.

I didn't answer, only motioned him to come closer.

"Can you read that?"

"I can't read, Father."

"I don't care whether you can read or not; it's dirty!" I yelled at him.

Cambaceres had fixed his gaze on the floor, seeming to murmur something under his breath while his head bobbed.

"What do you have to say for yourself?" I said accusingly.

"If you want me to erase it . . ."

"Right now, *hombre*."

At the end of that month the director called me to find out how Mendel's preparation was coming, and I explained what had been going on. He already knew; he always knew everything and liked to show it. That's how he demonstrated his power and control over everything that happened in the school. He was everywhere, involved in everything, and it filled him with a childish pride that he couldn't overcome, despite trying to control it when he was dealing with me. He suspected that it was ridiculous, but he couldn't help himself. It grew in him and filled him up until he was red in the face and it overflowed. If he had tried to contain it, he would have fallen ill.

"I even know about the bathroom, Ferré. You get upset too easily."

"That was foolish on my part, Father." I didn't mind humbling myself and admitting whatever he wanted. Mendel's situation was all I cared about, and I sensed that I'd need to lower my head and start to stammer. It was like imitating Porter when he argued.

"But that's just part of the picture, Father," I said, stuttering. "The problem is they're making life impossible for that boy."

"And what do you propose?"

"He should go away."

"What do you mean?" Wrinkles spread across his red brow.

"He should leave the school, Father."

"And where is he going to be baptized?"

"Anywhere . . . in any church."

The director denied my request, shaking his head in very slow movements, which he took his time making. It gave me time and seemed to show sympathy.

"You don't understand, Ferré," he said almost gasping for breath, "Mendel must be baptized here."

"But they're going to make his life here unbearable, and it will only get worse."

"That's how kids are."

"Kids?" I stared him down to make him abandon once and for all that tone of indulgent generosity and understanding. "But kids are ruthless when they want to be."

"Then he will get used to it."

"But . . ."

"Yes, Ferré. Mendel will get used to it. Give him time."

Translated by Michele McKay Aynesworth.

Other works by Viñas: *Los dueños de la tierra* (1958); *Dar la cara* (1962); *Literatura argentina y realidad política* (1964).

Elisa Chimenti

At the Heart of the Harem
1958

Esteemed by his bosses, envied by his friends, husband of an intelligent wife, owner of a lovely house, Si Bou-Djemaa might well have been happy if the desire for a new wife had not tormented him.

Tall and well built, though weighed down by his fifty years, he had a broad face as bronzed as Sakina's, healthy white teeth and, though pug-nosed, a strong, sensual mouth. He still considered himself to be charming and handsome and, unbeknownst to his wife—he was cautious—he sought the company of beautiful women whose eyes seemed to send daggers right through him, and whose veiled faces recalled the crescent moon and, when unveiled, the full moon.

He had married young, when he was only a poor soldier and had been fortunate to obtain in marriage, according to the law of God and the Prophet—blessed be His name—the beautiful Sakina Bent Mohamed, willowy and slender as the branch of a nutmeg tree, with hair the color of dates and exquisite taste in clothes. True, she was a widow, but her husband, the military officer, had left her some modest properties when he died: a small adobe house in a distant village, several teams of oxen, arable land, and one or two hundred sheep that grazed on the edge of the Oum Er-Rbia ("mother of spring" or "mother of vegetation") river. Then the years had flown by with all the haste they make to distance themselves from humans and retreat into those distant parts from which there is no return.

Sakina, misshapen by so many pregnancies, had become slow and ponderous, resembling more an elephant than a gazelle. In vain did she shave her eyebrows and extend the arc with a black, shiny line, in vain did she draw a line of kohl under her slanting eyes and anoint her black hair with a mysterious oil consisting, among other things, of ground scorpions, in vain too did she dye her hair with a product supplied to her by a clever woman from Tétouan and perfume her clothes with sandalwood-scented smoke and essence of jasmine and roses—nothing could make her husband forget the fine wrinkles that marked her dark brow and the corners of her eyes or the flesh that grew flabbier and more abundant by the day.

"How old my wife is getting," thought Si Bou-Djemaa, forgetting that the days that were passing for Sakina were not stopping for him and that like Bou Abbas Ahmed Ennani, he could have said of the single black hair remaining on his head: "I tell my white hairs that are frightened by the presence of this stranger, don't worry, a black African wife will not long remain in a house where the second wife is white!"

"How old my wife is getting," he repeated, and he dreamed not of replacing her, but of presenting her with a beautiful young co-wife whose gaiety and charm would brighten their home.

"What would Sakina say?"

The noble fellow knew her to be violent and jealous and feared her anger and her tears, but he still felt a sort of love based on habit and compassion—a compassion he anticipated feeling if he hurt her.

He began with a ruse, proposing to acquire a slave, a young slave who would do the errands and serve as a good replacement for Mennouch, who had become overly familiar and insolent.

"I have no need of a slave," Sakina had replied, "Mennouch is quite sufficient. True, she is often insolent, but I'll be able to get rid of her the day I've had enough of her pride and her uppity retorts . . . a black woman is at least as dirty, lying, and insolent as this woman from the Rif, if not more so. I need to keep her."

Unhappy with this response—he had wanted a concubine, not just a servant—Si Bou-Djemaa returned to the idea of marriage, which he had temporarily abandoned, and went to find a neighbor known for giving good advice, Tamo, the Jewish woman who people thought acted like a sheep but was at heart a fox. The widow of a rabbi from the Moroccan interior, Tamo strictly followed her ancestral traditions, observing the Sabbath scrupulously, eating unleavened bread during Passover in memory of the exodus from Egypt, placing reeds on her roof for the Feast of Tabernacles. Animated by a poorly understood religious ardor, she detested Muslims and Christians with equal fervor.

Unfortunately, as she had no money but did have half a dozen children to feed, she was obliged to frequent these infidels and take advantage of their passions in order to make a living.

Likeable, knowing the art of flattery to a T—he who has no honey in his house must have some on his tongue—she had made her way into the homes of Muslims and was welcomed by their wives, to whom she sold cloth and jewelry and for whom she carried out delicate missions.

Intelligent and cunning, the Jewish woman gave sage advice, sorted out the knotty and often dangerous intrigues that inflamed the harems, and rendered important services with genuine, albeit self-serving, devotion.

"It's only fair," she said, "that the sheep give a bit of its wool to the one who saves it from the wolf." She was perfectly right, of course.

The Muslim women took an interest in her, some even loved her. They would send her couscous on Fridays, fruit and sweets on feast days, and a daily "share of the abundance that God—may his name be praised—showered on their home." Tamou was welcomed with equal pleasure in the modest dwellings of the poor and in the grand houses of the rich, and like the Muslim women, was part of the circle that Sakina and her friends formed around the low table at tea time.

"Tamou," said Si Bou-Djemaa to the Jewish woman, after having consulted her and received a thousand compliments on his appearance and elegance, "make my wife understand that it's in her interest to open our home to a slave who will never be anything but an obedient servant. For if instead I decide to bring a second wife into our house, the woman must share her rights as 'mistress of things' and will certainly refuse to submit to her will."

Translated by Michele McKay Aynesworth.

Dan Jacobson

The Zulu and the Zeide
1958

Harry was the only person who knew that he and his father had quarrelled shortly before the accident that ended the old man's life took place; this was something that Harry was to keep secret for the rest of this life.

Late in the afternoon they quarrelled, after Harry had come back from the shop out of which he made his living. Harry came back to find his father wandering about the house, shouting for *der schwarzer*, and his wife complaining that she had already told the old man at least five times that *der schwarzer* was not in the house: it was Paulus' afternoon off.

Harry went to his father, and when his father came eagerly to him, he too told the old man, "*Der schwar-*

zer's not here." So the old man, with Harry following, turned away and continued going from room to room, peering in through the doors. "*Der schwarzer*'s not here," Harry said. "What do you want him for?"

Still the old man ignored him. He went down the passage towards the bedrooms. "What do you want him for?" Harry called after him.

The old man went into every bedroom, still shouting for *der schwarzer*. Only when he was in his own bare bedroom did he look at Harry. "Where's *der schwarzer*?" he asked.

I've told you ten times I don't know where he is. What do you want him for?"

"I want *der schwarzer*."

"I know you want him. But he isn't here."

"I want *der schwarzer*."

"Do you think I haven't heard you? He isn't here."

"Bring him to me," the old man said.

"I can't bring him to you. I don't know where he is." Then Harry steadied himself against his own anger. He said quietly: "Tell me what you want. I'll do it for you, I'm here, I can do what *der schwarzer* can do for you."

"Where's *der schwarzer*?"

"I've told you be isn't here," Harry shouted, the angrier for his previous moment's patience. "Why don't you tell me what you want? What's the matter with me—can't you tell me what you want?"

"I want *der schwarzer*."

"Please," Harry said. He threw out his arms towards his father, but the gesture was abrupt, almost as though he were thrusting his father away from him. "Why can't you ask it of me? You can ask me—haven't I done enough for you already? Do you want to go for a walk? I'll take you for a walk. What do you want? Do you want—do you want—?" Harry could not think what his father might want. "I'll do it," he said. "You don't need *der schwarzer*."

Then Harry saw that his father was weeping. The old man was standing up and weeping, with his eyes hidden behind the thick glasses that he had to wear: his glasses and his beard made his face a mask of age, as though time had left him nothing but the frame of his body on which the clothing could hang, and this mask of his face above. But Harry knew when the old man was weeping—he had seen him crying too often before, when they had found him at the end of a street after he had wandered away, or even, years earlier, when he had lost another of the miserable jobs that seemed to be the only one he could find in a country in which his son had, later, been able to run a good business, drive a large car, own a big house.

"Father," Harry asked, "what have I done? Do you think I've sent *der schwarzer* away?" Harry saw his father turn away, between the narrow bed and the narrow wardrobe. "He's coming—" Harry said, but he could not look at his father's back, he could not look at his father's hollowed neck, on which the hairs that Paulus had clipped glistened above the pale brown discolorations of age—Harry could not look at the neck turned stiffly away from him while he had to try to promise the return of the Zulu. Harry dropped his hands and walked out of the room.

No one knew how the old man managed to get out of the house and through the front gate without having been seen. But he did manage it, and in the road he was struck down. Only a man on a bicycle struck him down, but it was enough, and he died a few days later in the hospital.

Harry's wife wept, even the grandsons wept; Paulus wept. Harry himself was stony, and his bunched, protuberant features were immovable; they seemed locked upon the bones of his face. A few days after the funeral he called Paulus and Johannes into the kitchen and said to Johannes: "Tell him he must go. His work is finished."

Johannes translated for Paulus, and then, after Paulus had spoken, he turned to Harry. "He says, yes baas." Paulus kept his eyes on the ground; he did not look up even when Harry looked directly at him, and Harry knew that this was not out of fear or shyness, but out of courtesy for his master's grief—which was what they could not but be talking of, when they talked of his work.

"Here's his pay." Harry thrust a few notes towards Paulus, who took them in his cupped hands, and retreated.

Harry waited for them to go, but Paulus stayed in the room, and consulted with Johannes in a low voice. Johannes turned to his master. "He says, baas, that the baas still has his savings."

Harry had forgotten about Paulus's savings. He told Johannes that he had forgotten, and that he did not have enough money at the moment, but would bring the money the next day. Johannes translated and Paulus nodded gratefully. Both he and Johannes were subdued by the death there had been in the house.

And Harry's dealings with Paulus were over. He took what was to have been his last look at Paulus, but this look stirred him again against the Zulu. As harshly as he told Paulus that he had to go, so now, implacably, seeing Paulus in the mockery and simplicity of his houseboy's clothing, to feed his anger to the very end Harry said: "Ask him what he's been saving for. What's he going to do with the fortune he's made?"

Johannes spoke to Paulus and came back with a reply. "He says, baas, that he is saving to bring his wife and children from Zululand to Johannesburg. He is saving, baas," Johannes said, for Harry had not seemed to understand, "to bring his family to this town also."

The two Zulus were bewildered to know why it should have been at that moment that Harry Grossman's clenched, fist-like features should suddenly seem to have fallen from one another, nor why he should have stared with such guilt and despair at Paulus, while he cried, "What else could I have done? I did my best," before the first tears came.

Mordecai Richler

The Apprenticeship of Duddy Kravitz
1959

Duddy drove to Montreal the next morning, picked up his stuff, and returned to Ste. Agathe by bus the same evening. Yvette met him at the station. "Hey," he said, "did you see the paper? They raided Dingleman's joint. For real, though. There's going to be a trial."

The house Yvette had rented for Virgil and herself was near the tracks, some distance from the lake. But there was a fine back yard and Duddy used to take out a blanket and lie in the sun there. [. . .] But he avoided the lakeshore, the hotels or, indeed, any place where he might run into old friends or business associates. She knew that he had the map of Lac St. Pierre locked in his suitcase and that occasionally he took it out to study, but he would not discuss it. Neither would he go swimming there with her. [. . .]

That made it awkward to ask him about his plans for the future. He was evasive. He'd say no more than, "I've got plans. I'm just letting them jell, that's all."

But what he thought was, Maybe I can just stay here, maybe everyone will forget me. He enjoyed it most when it rained and he could sit on the screened porch playing Scrabble with Virgil or, still better, just staring glumly. Then one afternoon when he was going through his papers he stumbled on Uncle Benjy's letter. This time he read it.

The date doesn't matter

Dear Duddel

I've lived fifty-four years and lots of terrible things have happened to me, but I didn't want to die. That's the kind of malarky you can hear on the radio any Sunday morning. But I didn't want to die and I'd like you to know that.

I wish there were some advice, even one lousy little pearl of wisdom, that I could hand down to you, but—It's not for lack of trying, Duddel. I have notebooks full of my clever sayings: don't worry.

Experience doesn't teach: it deforms.

Some Oscar Wilde I would have made, eh? Anyway, I've burnt the notebooks. I have no advice for you.

Wear rubbers in winter and don't go bareheaded in the sun. It's a good idea to brush your teeth twice a day. That, Duddel, is the sum of my knowledge, so this letter isn't to teach you how to live. It's a warning, Duddel. You're the head of the Kravitz family now whether you like it or not. It took me by surprise, you know. I thought it would be Lennie. He was the bright one, I thought. O.K. I was wrong. Your *zeyda*, bless him, was too proud and I was too impatient. I hope you'll make less mistakes than we did. There's your father and Lennie and Ida and soon, I hope, there will be more. You've got to love them, Duddel. You've got to take them to your heart no matter what. They're the family, remember, and to see only their faults (like I did) is to look at them like a stranger.

You lousy, intelligent people, that's what you said to me, and I haven't forgotten. I wasn't good to you, it's true. I never took time. I think I didn't like you because you're a throwback, Duddel. I'd look at you and remember my own days as a hungry salesman in the mountains and how I struggled for my first little factory. I'd look at you and see a busy, conniving little Yid, and I was wrong because there was more, much more. But there's something you ought to know about me. Every year of my life I have looked back on the man I was the year before—the things I did and said—and I was ashamed. All my life I've ridiculed others, it's true, but I was the most ridiculous figure of all, wasn't I?

NOTE: Before you go any further you might as well know that I haven't left you a cent. Not a bean. The estate will be administered by Rosenblatt and there's money for Ida, a regular income, and enough to set Lennie up in practice. I've also left something for stu-dent scholarships (I haven't got a son, and my name has to live on somehow). What I have left you is my house on Mount Royal with the library and everything else in it. But that bequest is conditional, Duddel. You are not allowed to sell it. If you don't want to live in it with your family when you have one then it reverts to the estate and Rosenblatt will sell it.

Anyway, now that you know where you stand with the inheritance you can read on or not read on, just as you please.

There's more to you than mere money-lust, Duddy, but I'm afraid for you. You're two people, that's why. The scheming little bastard I saw so easily and the fine, intelligent boy underneath that your grandfather, bless him, saw. But you're coming of age soon and you'll have to choose. A boy can be two, three, four potential people, but a man is only one. He murders the others.

There's a brute inside you, Duddel—a regular behemoth—and this being such a hard world it would be the easiest thing for you to let it overpower you. Don't, Duddel. Be a gentleman. A *mensh*.

Take care and God bless,
Uncle Benjy

PS. I built the house on Mount Royal for my son and his sons. That was the original intention.

Duddy folded up the letter, replaced it in the envelope, and locked it in his suitcase.

"Hey," Virgil said, "where are you going?"

"Out."

"It'll soon be time to pick up Yvette."

"Tell her I might be late for dinner."

The lake, as he suspected, looked splendid even in autumn. Some of the trees were going yellow, others burned a brilliant red. Duddy crouched by the shore. He searched for flat pebbles and made them bounce two-three times across the water before they sunk. It's mine, he thought. This is my land and my water, and he looked around hoping for an interloper so that he could say, "I'm sorry, there's no trespassing allowed here." But all he could find were footprints, reasonably fresh, a man's and woman's. The man had used a cane. Maybe two canes. The cane or crunch points dug deep near the water.

Abraham Weisbaum

1895–1970

Abraham Weisbaum (b. Avrom Vaysboym) was born in Końskowola (near Lublin), Poland, where he had a traditional Hasidic education at a local heder and yeshiva. During World War I, he ended up in Harbin, China, where he worked in Avrom Fishzon's Yiddish theater, first as a prompter and later as an actor, traveling with the troupe to Shanghai. From there, he moved to Mexico City in 1925 and began contributing to local Yiddish newspapers. His biting satires of Jewish Mexican arrivistes were collected in two volumes published in Yiddish in 1947 and 1959. Weisbaum remained in Mexico City for the rest of his life.

Yente Tinifotsky
1959

Being rich is no picnic. It's no good to be wealthy, especially in Mexico. You get what I'm saying? It's no good!

When people talk to me, they suck up to me, all smiles and flattery: It's *señora* Tinifotsky this, *señora* Tinifotsky that. But behind my back? Oh my God! All the rich women around here are jealous of me. They backbite me from here to eternity. They begrudge me even a piece of bread! So I ask you, does it pay to be wealthy? Is it my fault I'm rich? And what do I get from all my so-called riches? True, I live in the ritzy Polanco neighborhood. In a big, beautiful house. A palace, I tell you! Twelve rooms with a foyer and with a, a, what do you call it here? A *terraza*, yeah. So what do you think I get from all this? A headache, that's all! I wander around like a stranger, from one room to another. I ring a bell for the help and all four maids come running from everywhere until they find me.

Around the table in the dining room, you can seat sixty people. I sit on one side of the table, my husband facing me on the other side, my daughter in the middle, and across from her my boy, my little Salvador. The maid starts serving the food and, poor thing, she has to go 'round and 'round the table. And the chairs! Oh my God! Why did we need those high, heavy chairs? They're so high that when you sit you can't see anyone over them.

In the old days—God forbid they should return!—I cooked stewed beef, barley soup, meatloaf, and sliced the bread myself. I'd make herring with onions, with vinegar. Back then the food used to really taste like

something. But nowadays? I know I shouldn't complain, God help me. But the food doesn't taste Jewish now. No way!

So what do I get from all my wealth, from all this glitz, from Polanco? Why should you be jealous? Why? Are you jealous of my cars? My diamonds? What do I get from them? Well at least I get a little enjoyment. I've got people to play poker with. I mean, you have to do *something* to while away the time. A person could go nuts here, wandering 'round and 'round all day with nothing to do.

On the other hand, do you think playing poker makes it any better? I mean, everybody and her mother plays these days. You have no idea who you're at the table with. This one woman sits down and puts down a nice, round 25-peso chip. I up her one and put down a 50-peso chip. So then guess what happens? Fifties start flying from all sides, and I decide to show the world that I'm really the famous Yente—Yente Tinifotsky. So I put down a hundred. If it were only so easy for my *children* to give me such pleasure! You heard me—a whole hundred. So then, what do you think? I get matched by this slob of a woman, a pauper, a frump who couldn't even afford to buy my garbage, who any day now will be going bankrupt! So I tell her, "Señora, why risk your last hundred? You won't have anything to go grocery shopping with tomorrow. Why stoop so low that even the good works of your ancestors could not make your case before the Almighty?"

She answers me in a huff: "It's none of your concern. Now let's see what's in your hand, *señora* Tinifotsky."

What gall! The little beggar, acting like she's my equal. What a boor! Hundreds! But I can put down hundreds! I'm allowed! I'm Yente Tinifotsky! Couldn't you just die from the aggravation? Pretty soon it'll be impossible to organize a respectable poker game anymore. But what else could I expect. The women don't just want to keep up with me, they want to outdo me.

Take what happened recently: I bought myself a Persian-lamb jacket for four thousand pesos. In a few days, I see all the women I know wearing fur jackets. I buy myself a cape made out of six foxes—six! Soon the very same capes are all over the place! A few months ago, that miserable husband of mine went to the States, and bought me a sable. Quite an item. A $15,000 or $20,000 sable, the only one in Mexico! So what do you think happens? I meet up with a woman I know who's got on the same sable. I mean, how am I supposed to deal with this?

So I buy a rug—a carpet—for 8,000 pesos. Back in our *shtetl*, not even the biggest landowner had such an expensive carpet under his feet. You walk so quiet on it, so soft, as soft as on a featherbed. You say you're an expert on carpets? A Chinese carpet is as fluffy and thick and soft as a matzah ball, while a Persian rug is as stiff as an overdone Passover pancake. Back in the *shtetl*, we used to take a shovel, a spade, every Friday before Shabbos, and scrape the mud off the floor, then pour sand on it. But here we walk on carpets. A pleasure! So then what happens? Now my neighbors run out and buy two carpets, a Chinese and a Persian, for ten thousand pesos. [. . .]

And you don't think I have my share of heartache from that no-good husband of mine? He's got this new idea in his head. He wants to buy a big, Yiddish library, the biggest Yiddish library in Mexico. What a crazy thought! So I go at him with every nasty word in me: "Are you out of your mind? A library, all of a sudden? What do you mean, a library? It's not like you read lots of Yiddish books. When do you have the time to even *look* at a Yiddish book? You're always busy. You're at the business all day. At night you play a little poker. On Sunday, you go out to the country house. The children never pick up a Yiddish book. So why do you need a literary graveyard here in the house?"

So you see, instead of getting a library, I bought a little silver for the house. Yente Tinifotsky's got some smarts. She's got a head on her! Absolutely: a head on her! Once—this should never happen to you!—in the gloomy, muddy *shtetl*, we had four brass candlesticks with copper brims in our house, and a pan for frying fish. Every Friday I had to shine and rub and scour the candlesticks for Shabbos. Oy, was I jealous of anyone with silver candlesticks. Well, these days everything I have is silver. God, I love silver! I have a silver platter, a thick one. Here, have a look. It weighs seventeen pounds. A silver teapot, creamers, forks, knives, spoons. All made of silver, pure silver—*pura plata*. On the buffet, the credenza, the dresser—there's wrought silverware, silver services. It's such a pleasure to look at so many silver things. They gleam, they shine, they light up from every which way. *And he wants a library*!? Silver! More silver! *¡Plata!*

I'll tell you a secret. Just between you and me. Soon it's going to be impossible to live in Polanco anymore. I'll tell you a story. I'll make it short and sweet.

So I'm driving my car and I spot someone I know. I pull up and go over to her with a big hello. "*¡Buenas tardes!* How are you, *señora*? Don't you remember me?"

She looks at me some, gives me the once over, and claps her hands.

"*Señora* T . . . , T . . . , Tee-nee-fotsk . . . ?"

"Fotsky," I help her out. "Tinifotsky. I'm *señora* Tinifotsky."

So she tells me she remembers when we used to live in the same apartment complex on Avenida Jesús María. So I ask her what she's doing in Polanco. She tells me she's living here. I can't believe it. I ask how on Earth she would up living in Polanco.

She answers me, kind of angry already, "What are you so shocked about? I used to live on Jesús María, then near the Tel Aviv Racetrack, and now I live in Polanco. Why should you live in Polanco and not me? How long did *you* live on Jesús María in three narrow, crowded rooms? Who are you to act so high and mighty? *Señora* Tinifotsky, what a countess you think you've become!"

When I realize I'm dealing with a vulgar little Jewish nobody. I give her an icy *adiós*, and go back to my car. I get home angry, insulted, in a huff, and sit down in the living room, all bent out of shape. That husband of mine is in his fancy armchair, deep in a newspaper.

I'm upset, agitated, and gazing at my gorgeous, manicured nails. God, they're stunning! That's when I realize how much old Yente's changed for the better. These manicured, polished nails once worked overtime, doing laundry, washing floors—oy! Scrubbing pots, burning my fingers on the stove—oy! And today? Fingers like a princess! A queen! See these fingers? To die for! Yente Tinifotsky with polished nails!

"Jacobo. Jacobo!" I say quietly to my husband. "Come here. I've got something to tell you."

He acts like he doesn't hear, the bum, and keeps on reading. So I give out a loud scream: "Yankl! Yankl! Blow-It-Offsky! Come here!"

He's terrified. He runs over and puts his arms around me lovingly, looks me in the eyes with a sweet smile. With love, just like it was only yesterday when we standing under our wedding canopy.

"Yente baby, what's wrong? Are you mad at me about something, sweetie? Why so sad, doll? Honey, what's wrong?"

"I want you to buy me something," I tell him softly, like I have all the time in the world. "Buy me something, darling!"

"Buy?" He's surprised. "Buy what for you? What could you possibly need? You've got a beautiful house.

A car. Diamonds. Servants. The two toy poodles. A wet bar with a Lazy Susan. Baby, what else can I possibly buy you?"

"Yankl," I say to him softly, tenderly. "I want . . . I want you to buy me something that absolutely no one else has. Lover, precious, buy me a . . . a neighborhood!"

He jumps up like he's just gotten scorched, and laughs out loud, "Ha! A neighborhood? You want I should buy you a neighborhood? A neighborhood!"

So I jump up, too, and give a loud shriek: "Why are you laughing, Yankl Blowitoffsky?! Why?!"

Then I say to him softly, tearfully: "You don't have a shred of pity for me. You don't care for me at all. I simply can't bear it. I can't live in Polanco any longer. I just can't! All the bums live here, the beggars, anyone who gets hold of a few pesos buys a piece of land, a lot, a house in Polanco or Lomas. I want to get out of here. Buy me a neighborhood, you hear? I want to live all by myself in my own neighborhood. I want a neighborhood!"

And you'll see: I'll buy myself a neighborhood. Yente Tinifotsky will have her own neighborhood!

Translated by Debbie Nathan.

Other works by Weisbaum: *Meksikaner zigzagn* (1947); *In meksikaner gan-eydn* (1960).

Ruth Prawer Jhabvala

1927–2013

The novelist and screenwriter Ruth Prawer Jhabvala was born in Cologne, where her father, a Polish Jewish immigrant, was an attorney; her maternal grandfather was the cantor of the largest synagogue in Cologne. The family fled Germany in 1939, settling in London. In 1951, she married Cyrus Jhabvala, an Indian architect, and moved to Delhi. The lives of women in newly independent, postcolonial India were the basis for much of her fiction, including her first novel, *Amrita* (1956). After the 1963 adaptation of her novel *The Householder*, she wrote many more screenplays based on British and American literary classics for Merchant Ivory Productions. During their four decades of collaboration, Jhabvala continued to write fiction, publishing fourteen novels. She was awarded two Academy Awards, for the screenplays of *A Room with a View* (1985) and *Howards End* (1992), as well as a Man Booker Prize for the novel *Heat and Dust* (1975).

A Birthday in London
1960

Mr. Lumbik was the first guest to arrive, rather too early. He had a big bunch of flowers in tissue paper, and wore a tweed jacket with leather buttons, which gave him a jaunty air. "A happy birthday, and so many of them," he said to Sonia, bending over her hand to kiss it with that special tender air he had adopted toward her.

Sonia was flustered by his early arrival, by the flowers, by the tender air, which she never knew how to deal with. She blushed, and this made her seem like a lovely young girl receiving her first suitor. "Mr. Lumbik," she said, "you shouldn't. An old woman like me has no birthdays."

"Ow, ow!" he cried, clutching his ears, which stood away from his head so that the light shone through them. "They are hurting, hearing you speak such things!"

She laughed, all young and gay. "You and your jokes. You should be ashamed, Mr. Lumbik."

"One little birthday favor," he begged, holding up one modest finger. "Just one little little favor from the birthday child."

She again became somewhat agitated, and turned away to look out of the window and down into the street, where a line of double-decker buses were swaying their way up to the West End. She hoped Mr. Lumbik wasn't going to ask for a kiss, though that was what she rather expected. She didn't want to kiss him at all—not even to bend down and peck at his cheek, which was never shaved well enough for her liking.

"Not 'Mr. Lumbik,'" he begged. "Not ever again 'Mr. Lumbik.' 'Karl.'" He put his head to one side; and looked up at her pleadingly out of pale, aging small eyes. "All right? 'Karl'? Such a nice name."

She didn't reply. Instead, she went out across the hall and into the kitchen to fetch the *Apfelstrudel*. Mr. Lumbik followed her on his soft crêpe soles. He didn't press for an answer. He prided himself on his knowledge of women, and Sonia was the type one had to proceed with gently and tactfully, for she was of very good family and had had a romantic upbringing.

"Now I have a surprise for you," he said, following her back into her room and watching her as she lovingly placed the *Apfelstrudel* on the table laid for the birthday party. "You will be pleased to learn from me that now they have granted me my British citizenship."

"How nice," said Sonia, concentrating on the last-minute touches to her table. She had been a British citizen for ten years, and the thrill had worn off.

"Yes, a special telephone call from Scotland Yard." He dialled an imaginary telephone and held an imaginary receiver to his ear. "'Hallo, Karl Lumbik? You are now a very small member of the very big British Commonwealth. God save the Queen, Karl Lumbik!' 'God save the Queen, Mr. Scotland Yard!'" The imaginary receiver was replaced and Mr. Lumbik stood at attention.

Sonia laughed. "How funny you are!" Everything was a joke to him. If only Otto had been a bit more like that. But Otto had always taken everything very tragically. When they became British citizens, he had taken that tragically, too. "Yes, our passports they have given us," he had said, "but what else have we got?" "Ottolein," she had cried, "be happy!" But no need to tell Karl Lumbik to be happy.

He was using his tender voice again. "So now I am a very eligible cavalier, I think." But it was the wrong note, he saw at once; she had turned away from him and was adjusting Otto's framed photograph on the table by her sleeping couch. "I think again I have opened my big mouth too wide," he said ruefully, so that the defensive expression went from her face and she couldn't help laughing. She never could help laughing with him—he said such comic things. She tried to be remote and dignified, but, after all, she was the same Sonia Wolff, née Rothenstein, she had always been. The big laughing girl, they had called her. She always had been big, though graceful—large bosom, large hips, a fine full-blown flower on slender stalk legs—and she had been forever laughing, or on the brink of laughter, her short, curved, upper lip trembling over her healthy teeth.

There was a ring at the doorbell, and Mr. Lumbik glided out into the hall like an expert butler. "Come in, come in," he said, bowing deeply at the entrance door. "The *Apfelstrudel* has come out very well."

"Where is the birthday child?" cried Mrs. Gottlob in her hoarse, uninhibited voice. It was a voice Sonia knew only too well, for she had heard it often enough, screaming up the stairs about lights that had been left burning and baths that had not been cleaned after use; Otto, on hearing it, used to grow pale and very quiet, so that Sonia had to go downstairs and be as charming as she could be, accepting and admitting everything to stop Mrs. Gottlob from shouting and upsetting Otto. But, of course, all that was over now, and Mrs. Gottlob was no longer the landlady but a friend.

She came in now and gave Sonia a big smack of a kiss and a box of chocolates.

"The kiss is for love and the chocolates for eating," she said.

The box was very large and ornate, tied with a blue satin ribbon. It was just like the ones Otto had so often brought for her in Berlin. He used come tiptoeing into what they called the morning room, where she would be sitting at her escritoire writing letters or answering invitations, and, smiling and pleased, the box held roguishly behind his back, he would say, "Let us see now what nice surprise there is for us today." And she would jump up, all large and graceful and girlish: "Oh, Otto!"

"So," said Mrs. Gottlob, sitting down with a creak and a groan, "how does it feel like to be twenty-five?" "Already twenty-five!" cried Mr. Lambik, clasping his hands together in wonder.

"Even my baby, my Werner, is nearly twenty-six," said Sonia, shining and proud as she always was when she spoke of either of her children.

"And where is he today, on Mutti's birthday?" demanded Mrs. Gottlob. "Again out with the girl friends, I think?" She shook an extremely fat forefinger. "I know your Werner—a very bad boy."

"If you are not a bad boy at twenty-six, then when can you be a bad boy?" said Mr. Lumbik. He gave a reminiscent smile. "Ask them in Vienna about one Karl Lumbik at twenty-six—la, la, la!" He tilted his head, thinking of the girls and the cafés and Karl Lumbik in a tilted hat and camel coat.

"Ask them in London about one Karl Lumbik at fifty-six," Mrs. Gottlob said. "The story will not be different, only it is an old good-for-nothing where once there was a young good-for-nothing."

"You are giving me a bad reputation," said Mr. Lumbik, not ill-pleased, running his hands down the lapels of his coat and swaying back and forth on his heels.

"I had a letter from my Lilo today," Sonia said. "My birthday letter. Just think, all the way from Israel, and it arrives exactly on the right day. And there are nice photos, too." She took down the letter from where she had propped it proudly on the mantelpiece and showed Mrs. Gottlob the photos of Lilo and her husband—sunburned, stocky farm workers with open collars and rolled-up sleeves—and their blond, naked baby.

"*Ach*, the lovely baby," craned Mrs. Gottlob lovingly into the photo. "He is like your Werner, I think. I remember just like this your Werner's hair went when he was four years and first came to live in my house."

Mr. Lumbik peered over one of Mrs. Gottlob's shoulders and Sonia over the other. "There is also something of my dear late Papa in him," Sonia said, sighing for her father, a large, healthy, handsome man who had loved good living and had died at Auschwitz. "And also, I think—you don't think so?—my dear late Otto. The eyes, you see, and the forehead. Otto had always such a wonderful forehead."

Mr. Lumbik glanced toward Otto's photo, by the sleeping couch. The wonderful forehead, he thought, was mainly created by the absence of any hair on the head. He remembered Otto Wolff as a small, bald, shrinking man, very tired, very sick, very old, in an expensive German dressing gown that had grown too big for him. Mr. Lumbik had always thought what a pity it was that a fine woman like Sonia couldn't have married something better. Though, of course, Otto Wolff had been a very wealthy factory owner in Berlin, and it wasn't quite fair to judge him as he had known him—only a poor refugee who couldn't speak English, had no work, and lodged in Mrs. Gottlob's house.

Other works by Jhabvala: *Esmond in India* (1958); *The Europeans* (screenplay, 1979); *The Remains of the Day* (screenplay, 1993); *A Lovesong for India: Tales from East and West* (2011).

Natalio Budasoff

1903–1981

The poet, playwright, and short-story writer Natalio (Nosn) Budasoff was born in Russia; he immigrated to a Jewish Colonization Association (ICA) agricultural colony in Entre Ríos, Argentina, in 1914. A locust plague in the early 1930s continued for years, bankrupting farmers. In the aftermath, Budasoff moved to Buenos Aires, where he worked as administrator of the Jewish Hospital. Budasoff's book on the locusts, *La langosta: Un mal nacional y sudamericano* (1946), describing their economic impact and proposing ways to rid South America of them, was highly praised. His literary works focused primarily on two themes: the dilemmas of medical ethics and the hardships of early Jewish immigrant farmers who, though spiritually attached to the land, were plagued by natural disasters. Many of his early unpublished works were written in Yiddish.

Yoine Bird
1962

They were neighbors for many, many years. Thirty, forty, maybe half a century . . . ever since Colony D . . . was established back at the beginning of the eighteen-nineties.

Their parents grew up almost together, and their children, needless to say. There was only one thing: the Money God smiled on each of them in a different way.

Yoine struggled his whole life, and, since he couldn't do anything about it, the only thing left was to be content with what little he had. Not because he didn't desire or have hope. Oh no, he desired and hoped for a better life, but you can't make good cakes without flour or eggs!

His extremely modest house was just a league from Lluvias Salvajes, and there he held out the grand and childish hope of becoming a farmer. If the ICA would only give him some land! Give him some land!![1]

His family consisted of five girls, one after the other, a boy, his wife, and him. It goes without saying that the poor man's greatest happiness is his children, and for him they were his delight, his bliss, his greatest joy. But, until they are grown, they are mouths to feed; one must provide them with clothes and shoes, educate them, and receive their daily noisemaking, like playful kittens making a ruckus, as a blessing. For him, they were a rosebush in his quiet spring.

Yoine carried the burden, and, according to the biblical dictate, with the sweat of his brow he ate his bread and was happy with what life had to offer.

During the winter he hauled whatever loads he could: sand, bricks, and dirt, thus contributing to the construction of the village Lluvias Salvajes, and in the summer, he transported grains from neighboring farms to the station.

A strapping young man, prudent, bright, and talkative, with a rough exterior, and a kind heart.

The roosters, waking in the early morning, had barely started crowing, with their *ki-ki-ki-ri-kiii*, when he was already out in the primitive cart, with no springs, that earned him his daily bread. In the tranquil dawn one could hear from far, far away the clatter of his cart. Likewise, the night often caught him on the road: he exhausted, the horses tired, the pebbles complaining under the heavy load, they slowly approached the house, one step at a time, and in the silence of the night the animals' drowsiness and the cart's harsh moans only intensified.

Having heard him coming, his children were outside waiting for him, ready to help. No matter how tired he was, just entering the yard inspired them with candor and innocent joy. For each one he had a joke, a brilliant witticism, a good-natured bit of cleverness, and they all rejoiced. Everyone rushed to help him take the tack off the horses, which were drenched in dirty sweat; they took over the chores of bathing and watering them, and while some were hanging up the gear, others were leading the horses to the pasture, where they had endured hunger more than once.

He would sit down at the table for dinner with his wife and children, and before he had taken the last bite, his eyelids closed, and he would end up asleep at the table. For him the night was over in a flash, and as soon as dawn broke, with the morning star blazing in the east, he would already be on the road with a new load.

And so did his days pass, year after year, the rustic cart his only support, the source of wholesome stews and clothing and canvas shoes for all his kids.

Hard were the days that slipped by for him and his old nags; so as not to be bothered by the racket of the pebbled roads, the burning summer sun, or the winter cold, no matter the time of day, he would start whistling or humming some tune, singing softly to himself, perhaps repeating some sacred music that he would try to recall with religious devotion. . . . As a result—the neighbors, the laborers, and those who knew him for many leagues around—all called him Yoine Bird. [. . .]

For many long years, Yoine kept hoping that the ICA would give him a farm, but . . .—the obstacles to Jewish farming!—Mirichke, the Colonizer's agent, was fond of the saying: "If you don't put in, you don't take out." And from this poor wretch—Yoine Bird!—just forget about what he can put in or what can be taken from him!

The higher-ups in the ICA followed the advice of their agents, who were—according to them—the ones in direct contact with farm workers and the most qualified . . . ignoring—most of the time—though knowing full the fact that these agents gave greater weight to those profiting from the land than those working it. For the former always had cash ready to make payments, while the others could only pay when crop yields were good.

NOTE

1. [Jewish Colonization Association, a philanthropic endeavor of Baron de Hirsch supporting Jewish émigrés in establishing agricultural collectives and training programs in the Americas, Palestine, and elsewhere. The ICA was one of the first, and most successful, planned programs of large-scale (Jewish) migration.—Eds.]

Translated by Michele McKay Aynesworth.

Other works by Budasoff: *Elevación* (1945); *Teatro* (1950); *Lluvias salvajes* (1962).

Isaac Chocrón

1930–2011

Isaac Chocrón Serfaty was born in Maracay, Venezuela, to Moroccan Sephardi parents. He received a Jewish and Catholic education in Venezuela before attending high school at Bordentown Military Institute in New Jersey; he then studied at Syracuse, Columbia, and Manchester universities. Chocrón found that his true vocation was writing—primarily plays, but also novels and literary criticism. He referred to himself as a lefty Jewish homosexual writer. He founded the National Theater Company and served in numerous administrative and university faculty positions in Venezuela. In 1979, Chocrón received Venezuela's National Theater Award. His plays are experimental, borrowing from surrealism and theater of the absurd.

Ferocious Animals
1963

BENLEVÍ: [*while he speaks,* SARA *enters with the slippers*] All they do in the synagogue is talk about Ishmael.

SARA: [*bent over, putting on the slippers*] They seem to forget that they're there to talk to God.

BENLEVÍ: Sara, do you remember what I told you last Friday that the lawyer had said? He said, Rosa, that Ishmael was the first Jew to commit suicide in Venezuela.

SARA: That's none of his business.

BENLEVÍ: Yes it is, Sara, yes it is. First, because in our religion taking your life is a capital sin, and second, because Jews never commit suicide.

ROSA: It's the same thing; I don't see the difference between the first and second reasons.

BENLEVÍ: [*upset*] They don't commit suicide anywhere. They have great faith.

SARA: As much as or less than anyone else.

BENLEVÍ: This lawyer came today and told us that having reviewed all the Jewish death certificates—all of them!—he found that Ishmael is the first suicide.

SARA: [*furious*] And what does he want? A statue?

ROSA: Sara!

SARA: Not for Ishmael, for himself. To honor his discovery. And you? What did you say?

BENLEVÍ: What could I say? What can I say to people who think they're the Lord's chosen? If you could hear how they talk about your family, about Sol . . . What can I say to them? I say my prayers and come home.

SARA: If I were you, I wouldn't go back to that synagogue.

BENLEVÍ: Someone needs to fulfill our responsibilities to God. If none of you will do it . . .

ROSA: We do it in our own way, Benleví.

BENLEVÍ: When one is Jewish, and I believe you two still claim to be, one must fulfill one's responsibilities to God in the Jewish way. And the Jewish way is to go to the synagogue.

SARA: Do you think what goes on in that synagogue pleases God?

BENLEVÍ: The same thing would happen anywhere else. It's natural for them to talk about it.

SARA: I doubt there's a synagogue anywhere else where things are more easily bought or sold. It's a den of iniquity!

BENLEVÍ: So your husband goes to a den of iniquity to pray?

SARA: Unfortunately, you do. Just like a few other well-meaning people. But what do most of them go for? Do you think that lawyer talked to God this afternoon? Do you think he had time to talk to God?

BENLEVÍ: He said what he had to say before and after the service.

SARA: Ah! Well in that case, I hope he talked to God during the service . . . in silence.

BENLEVÍ: But who are you to accuse them? Why accuse them from outside and not from inside? Why don't you come with me on Friday afternoons so you can reform them?

ROSA: Please, Benleví.

BENLEVÍ: What do you mean "Please, Benleví?" I'm sick of her criticizing me when she should thank me for being the only one, the only one who's prayed for Ishmael. And I've prayed even though it's a sin to do so. The only one who's tried to make peace with God, to explain why he shouldn't judge the boy too harshly. I'm the only one in her whole family who's prayed for his nephew! And she tells me that I've come from a den of iniquity where things are bought and sold. She who only believes in that jar of pills! Swallowing them day and night! Well, God is my pill! The synagogue is my pill! And it will be until

I die, do you understand? Until I die . . . but not by suicide. Pure! Without sin! When the devil are you thinking to bring that whisky? [exits]

ROSA: Oh, my God!

SARA: Don't you think we've talked about God enough already for you to go on pining over Him?

ROSA: I don't know what to say.

SARA: Well then don't say anything; pretend you're with Daniel. Don't say anything!

Translated by Michele McKay Aynesworth.

Other works by Chocrón: *Pasaje* (1956); *El quinto infierno* (1961); *Rómpase en caso de incendio* (1975).

Leonard Cohen
1934–2016

Leonard Cohen was a poet, novelist, and singer whose works are known for their expressions of spirituality and sexuality. Born in Montreal to a prosperous family active in Jewish organizational and religious leadership, Cohen attended McGill University, where he was influenced by poets Louis Dudek and Irving Layton. Cohen published his first book of poetry, *Let Us Compare Mythologies*, in 1956. Most known for his songs "Suzanne" and "Hallelujah," Cohen drew upon his Jewish background in such pieces as "Who By Fire." He lived on the island of Hydra in Greece, in Los Angeles, and in Montreal. Cohen was honored as a Companion of the Order of Canada, the nation's highest civilian honor.

The Favourite Game
1963

The Breavmans founded and presided over most of the institutions which make the Montreal Jewish community one of the most powerful in the world today.

The joke around the city is: The Jews are the conscience of the world and the Breavmans are the conscience of the Jews. "And I am the conscience of the Breavmans," adds Lawrence Breavman. "Actually we are the only Jews left; that is, super-Christians, first citizens with cut prongs."

The feeling today, if anyone troubles himself to articulate it, is that the Breavmans are in a decline. "Be careful," Lawrence Breavman warns his executive cousins, "or your children will speak with accents."

Ten years ago Breavman compiled the Code of Breavman:

We are Victorian gentlemen of Hebraic persuasion.

We cannot be positive, but we are fairly certain that any other Jews with money got it on the black market.

We do not wish to join Christian clubs or weaken our blood through inter-marriage. We wish to be regarded as peers, united by class, education, power, differentiated by home rituals.

We refuse to pass the circumcision line.

We were civilized first and drink less, you lousy bunch of bloodthirsty drunks. [. . .]

The Japs and Germans were beautiful enemies. They had buck teeth or cruel monocles and commanded in crude English with much saliva. They started the war because of their nature.

Red Cross ships must be bombed, all parachutists machine-gunned. Their uniforms were stiff and decorated with skulls. They kept right on eating and laughed at appeals for mercy.

They did nothing warlike without a close-up of perverted glee.

Best of all, they tortured. To get secrets, to make soap, to set examples to towns of heroes. But mostly they tortured for fun, because of their nature.

Comic books, movies, radio programmes centred their entertainment around the fact of torture. Nothing fascinates a child like a tale of torture. With the clearest of consciences, with a patriotic intensity, children dreamed, talked, acted orgies of physical abuse. Imaginations were released to wander on a reconnaissance mission from Calvary to Dachau.

European children starved and watched their parents scheme and die. Here we grew up with toy whips. Early warning against our future leaders, the war babies. [. . .]

Among certain commercial Jews he was considered a mild traitor who could not be condemned outright. They were dismayed by the possibility that he might make a financial success out of what he was doing. This their ulcers resented. His name was in the newspapers. He might not be an ideal member of the community but neither was Disraeli or Mendelssohn, whose apostasies the Jewish regard for attainment has always overlooked. Also, writing is an essential part of the Jewish tradition and even the degraded contemporary situation cannot suppress it. A respect for books and artistry will persist for another generation or two. It can't go on forever without being reconsecrated.

Among certain Gentiles he was suspect for other reasons. His Semitic barbarity hidden under the cloak of Art, he was intruding on their cocktail rituals. They were pledged to Culture (like all good Canadians) but he was threatening the blood purity of their daughters. They made him feel as vital as a Negro. He engaged stockbrokers in long conversations about over-breeding and the loss of creative vitality. He punctuated his speech with Yiddish expressions which he never thought of using anywhere else. In their living- rooms, for no reason at all, he often broke into little Hasidic dances around the tea table.

He incorporated Sherbrooke Street into his general domain. He believed he understood its elegant sadness better than anyone else in the city. Whenever he went into one of the stores he always remembered that he was standing in what was once the drawing-room of a smart town house. He breathed a historical sigh for the mansions become brewery and insurance head offices. He sat on the steps of the museum and watched the chic women float into dress shops or walk their rich dogs in front of the Ritz. He watched people line up for buses, board, and zoom away. He always found that a mystery. He walked into lavatory-like new banks and wondered what everyone was doing there. He stared at pediments or carved grapevines. Gargoyles on the brown stone church. Intricate wooden balconies just east of Park. [. . .]

He had no plans for the future. [. . .]

Some say that no one ever leaves Montreal, for that city, like Canada itself, is designed to preserve the past, a past that happened somewhere else.

This past is not preserved in the buildings or monuments, which fall easily to profit, but in the minds of her citizens. The clothes they wear, the jobs they perform are only the disguises of fashion. Each man speaks with his father's tongue.

Just as there are no Canadians, there are no Montrealers. Ask a man who he is and he names a race.

So the streets change swiftly, the skyscrapers climb into silhouettes against the St. Lawrence, but it is somehow unreal and no one believes it, because in Montreal there is no present tense, there is only the past claiming victories.

Breavman fled the city.

Other works by Cohen: *Beautiful Losers* (1966); *Stranger Music: Selected Poems and Songs* (1993); *Book of Longing* (2006).

Osvaldo Dragún

1929-1999

Osvaldo "Chacho" Dragún was born in the JCA settlement of Colonia Barro, Entre Ríos, Argentina, and in 1943 he moved to Buenos Aires, where he performed in the Teatro Popular Fray Mocho. A socially committed dramatist, his first performed play, *La peste viene de Melos* (1956), was about the 1954 Central Intelligence Agency–backed invasion and coup in Guatemala. He left Argentina in 1961 and worked in Latin America, Cuba, and the United States. In 1981, he became a champion of the *teatro abierto* (open theater) movement, which opposed military dictatorship. In 1988, he founded and directed the Theatre School of Latin America and the Caribbean, based in Havana, and in 1996 took over direction of Argentina's prestigious Cervantes National Theatre.

And They Told Us We Were Immortal

1963

GEORGE: They always leave the key under the windowsill. I told you so.

BERT: Ahuh.

[GEORGE *goes to the doors and yells in front of each one.*]

GEORGE: Mamma! Stephen! Mamma!

[*No one answers. Pause.*]

No one's home.

BERT: But the telegram?

GEORGE: I don't know. Put down the bag. You look like Santa Claus.

BERT: No. It's late. If your family should come . . .

GEORGE: Go on! Put down the bag.

[*It is seven o'clock. The clock bells begin to ring. At the same time, the bells of a nearby church begin to ring. BERT, his duffel bag still on his shoulder, goes to the window and looks out.*]

BERT: You have a church nearby?

[GEORGE *goes to the window.*]

GEORGE: Yes.

BERT: Did you used to go?

GEORGE: Yes, when I was a kid. [*Turns to* BERT.] Put down the bag. Now you look like a camel.

BERT: Seriously, no. It's late, and if your family comes . . .

GEORGE: Shut up, Limpie. [GEORGE *takes away the duffel bag and puts it next to his, also leaning against the wall. He returns to* BERT.] Well, this is my house.

BERT [*scans it, smiling*]: I know. You described it like this, that night.

GEORGE: Yes, as if I had worn it, or carried it in my pocket. Bert, do you think Aaron would have liked it?

BERT: I like it.

GEORGE: And Aaron?

BERT: Sure, with a little smell of fish . . .

[GEORGE *smiles, barely.*]

GEORGE: Sure. [*Looks around.*] How odd. Nothing's changed.

BERT: When was the last time you were here?

GEORGE: My last leave was at Christmas.

BERT: And why should things have changed in three months?

GEORGE: I don't know. But it seems strange. [GEORGE *goes to the sideboard and opens a door.*] What do you want to drink?

BERT [*shouts, like an oft-repeated battlecry*]: Grapa, you fool!

GEORGE [*gets to his feet brandishing a bottle of grapa, and shouts like a hymn of response, opening his arms*]: Grapa, Limpie! [*He goes toward the table with the bottle and two glasses.*] The old man uses it as an appetizer.

BERT: Yeah? My uncle uses it as breakfast, lunch, and dinner.

[GEORGE *fills the glasses to the rims.*]

Hey, I took a bath before leaving Cordoba!

[GEORGE *gives him the glass.* BERT *looks at it reflectively.*]

My uncle . . . My aunt . . . I hope that damned old man hasn't sold the house with my aunt inside of it.

GEORGE [*laughs*]: What's your house like, Limpie?

BERT: Amusing. You see that in your house the furniture's on the floor? Well, in my house the floor is on top of the furniture. Everything's upside down. [*Pause. Then, hollowly.*] Amusing . . .

GEORGE [*laughs, then lifts his glass*]: To Aaron, OK?

BERT: Sure, to that Jew: skinny, lazy, swell, and . . . dead!

[*They look at each other. Drink their drinks in one swallow.* GEORGE *remains looking down.*]

GEORGE: I saw him this morning. I didn't want to say anything.

BERT [*looks at him apprehensively*]: Who?

GEORGE: Aaron. On the train. We were inside, and he was sitting outside. He was telling us about his father, like that night, and that he was going to get married, and . . . He stayed on the road, sitting on a pole, like a bird.

BERT: Cut it, George. Aaron's dead. They killed him that night, just like they might have killed us. Cut it.

[GEORGE *looks at him, nods, and refills the two glasses.*]

GEORGE: I know he's dead. [*He drinks, and* BERT *follows suit.*] This is my house, Limpie! [*He leaves his glass on the table and goes toward the left.*] I'm going to show you the album.

BERT: What album?

GEORGE: What d'you mean, "What album?"? My album. [*He looks in the sideboard.*] Where could it be?

BERT: You have an album? Of what?

GEORGE [*hunting*]: What d'you mean "of what?"? Of me . . . Sure, it's in . . . [*He has already crossed the stage and stops in front of the left room.*] It's in my room. [*He enters the left room.* BERT *follows.*] Strange . . . I'd forgotten that I had my own room.

BERT: You forgot because you have it. I sleep in the dining room.

GEORGE [*strikes one bed with his hand*]: This is my brother's bed. (*Hits the other bed.*) This is MY OWN bed! (*Goes toward the wardrobe.*) This is MY OWN side of the wardrobe! [*He opens the wardrobe door.*] These are MY suits. You like them?

BERT: Yeah . . . They're dark . . .

GEORGE: If you like them, I'll give you two or three.

BERT: Lookit, I'd look like a canned sardine in them.

GEORGE: There you are! Needling me again because you're bigger than me.

BERT: It's a good thing I am bigger so that I could take care of you when they shouted "Georgette" at you in boot camp.

GEORGE [*pensively, but not sadly*]: Yes, at first they called me Georgette, and I used to bite like a woman.

BERT: No, you bit to defend yourself. Anything goes!

GEORGE: Yes, but Limpie, you remember that night, all of us were scared to death, Georgettes, or not . . . [*He takes the album out of the wardrobe.*] Here it is. And your glass?

BERT: I left it in the dining room.

GEORGE: Come on. We've just started, haven't we? [*He looks at his room with a puzzled gaze.*] Even my own room doesn't seem to be my room. [GEORGE *goes toward the dining room.*] . . .

BERT: I never knew what went on in the world. Not before, or now. Before, when I was boxing, no one told me anything, and it didn't bother me. Now no one tells me anything, but I know why, Georgette! They wash their hands of it! Aaron died in vain! Seriously, Georgette . . . look at us! You, you're adjusting . . . his father's adjusting . . . I'm adjusting . . . He died in vain. Georgette. Tsk, tsk, and there goes a worm carrying him off.

GEORGE: What'd the old man give you?

BERT [*reads the paper, becomes surprised*]: A poem.

GEORGE [*takes the paper*]: Aaron's? He never told us he wrote poetry . . .

[AARON *appears in front of the curtain in his army uniform. He comes forward and sits on the proscenium, looking at the audience. He begins to talk to it. Conversation.*]

AARON: And they told us we were immortal.
But that was only the first step.
To be born is as easy
As to find a stone, a tree, or a fly.
And they told us we were immortal.
Those who told us died.
And were forgotten,
Because it is as easy to be born
As to find a stone, a tree, or a fly:
The only miracle is the life of a man.
Stars exist
And the sun and the moon exist:
The only miracle is the life of a man,
Because it has to be made.
And then, perhaps we are immortal.
Neither God nor death are problems for me:
They neither cure my liver nor make me laugh.
The only miracle is the life of a man.
Because it has to be made.
And then, perhaps we are immortal.
My twenty years:
A bow and arrow,
Hurled forward.
My twenty years:
A catapult charged
With twenty tons of questions:
That's the miracle.
And then, perhaps I am immortal.

OLD MAN [*gets to his feet and shouts like an officer giving orders*]: Attention, soldiers!! Forward, March! A revolution has broken out, and you are charged with defending the country, the flag, the national anthem, and the honor of the army. Forward! March!

[*On the last "March,"* AARON *falls into the pit as if he had been shot. He disappears. The* OLD MAN *goes back to his reading.*

BERT: He died in vain. Georgette . . . We all wash our hands . . . he died in vain.

GEORGE [*long pause*]: I have to go . . . They're waiting for me.

Translated by Alden James Green.

Other works by Dragún: *Milagro en el mercado viejo* (1963); *Heroica de Buenos Aires* (1965); *Mi obelisco y yo* (1981).

José Chudnovsky

1915–1966

José Chudnovsky was born in a Jewish Colonization Association farming colony in Colón, Entre Ríos, Argentina, to Ukrainian immigrants. His two novels, *Dios era verde* and *Pueblo pan*, were based on his own life. *Dios era verde* is set in the province of Chaco, where Chudnovsky's family ended up, and it recounts the conflict between a traditionally Jewish father and his son, who is self-conscious about his Jewish heritage and the size of his nose. Nobel laureate Miguel Ángel Asturias wrote the prologue for the novel, which won the Argentine Authors Society's Sash of Honor. In addition to being a writer and teacher, José Chudnovsky was a practicing dentist.

The Old Notebook

1964

The filthy train lurched along the tracks, jolting my spine through the slats of the wooden seat.

I was thoughtful, my happiness mixed with vague regrets. Happiness? No, a deserter's sense of hard-won freedom. The countryside and the scant month shared with those close to me unfolded like a fan before my eyes. [. . .]

Laziness or remorse. I put off a bit longer my encounter with the old notebook I'd found while rummaging through my father's moldy books on the very day of my departure. I'd brought it with me without knowing why. As I rose to open my canvas suitcase, I looked at the woods and shimmering fields of my Chaco. I kept rummaging through resistant, balled-up clothes until I stumbled upon the notebook's cover, ragged with age. I opened it curiously. Inside were drafts of letters.

His familiar handwriting covered many pages, some of which had been made completely illegible by the damp stains. But I was familiar with his style. The solitude of my train ride helped. Dates, seasons, ideas. I read it all in one go.

Charata, Chaco, August 1929
Mr. Justice of the Peace:

I hereby declare in my own hand that I alone am responsible for this document. No one else is to be held accountable for it, much less be allowed to judge it! I loved the green. If it were not for this red knot, Ukraine . . . and Jane. Silent and perfumed like a plant. She grew up before my eyes. We failed to put down roots in our native ground. I studied the map.

Land! Humid land for raising children. Ar-gen-ti-na. Silver name. Sonorous as old silverware. Seated beside the samovar I said to my friends: I am going to a land as fertile as our own. *Entre los ríos*—between the rivers . . . there. I was born on the shores of the Dnieper, sir. We came with eyes wide open. Endless days on the ship. The third-class hold. Spanish. How strange to come from Juana's mouth! The Immigrants' Hotel. The first Argentine coins. The symbol of Fraternity. Like the French Revolution! I cried when I read the Constitution. No, I was not blind. This would be the land for my children. Black soil for blond children. And Juana and I in their shadows that would spread and grow stronger every day. But when you uproot a tree the ground bleeds and the roots are wounded! Every step hurt us clear to the top of our heads. Hills. Rises. And mud, lots of mud. Rains and clumsy tenant farmers. The skin of my hands, scratched and torn.

I spoke French, Mr. Justice. I am a teacher of Russian and French. Ah! That's a long story. Not all Jews are merchants. My race is thousands of years old, and you want to know something? We were never allowed to own land! Sure, here we can. Tenant farmers. Some of the bravest and best! Have you heard of the Jewish gauchos? Those were my people. The ones who came to school riding bareback. However, in the end . . . When I was a child they said I would be a rabbi and my hands bled on the ground. The kid would cry. Juana lost her elegance from so much hoeing and bending over. They gave us a house and a small plot to farm, they needed a teacher. And I was a country teacher. A little more than a school teacher . . . because they were the kids of tenant farmers. A generation of immigrant parents. What for us was unattainable, to cultivate and own land, was natural for our children. But here land abounds . . . and weeds. The kids could not believe in those alone. Land, curious . . . once the old ones had the land, their children returned to the book. No, I am not talking nonsense, sir, we are from the land of the Book. . . . But the young people were not seeking God. Nor did I help them to find Him. They built the synagogue fifty meters from my school. I myself planted paradises to provide shade for the believers. For fifteen years the temple and its faithful saw me, but not a single day did I enter there! This was no whim of mine, but a conviction, Mr. Justice, and one of the firmest. God was necessary for fifty centuries in order to save my race, we must respect that! God was necessary . . . well do I know it. But I would be a poor teacher if I did not reason, and my reason does not believe in Him!

As a child, freezing cold at dawn and slapped hands marked me forever with the impious piety of the faithful.

To grow up among theologians who took away my sense of wonder at life. What a grim childhood! From the cradle I was anointed a rabbi, and reason early on shouted its revolt: if He alone disposes, let Him show himself here, on this human earth that has rained miseries down upon my father and given me the name of Jew!

After years of digesting sacred books, my pain could not conceive that His omnipotence might not be there in the dark spaces, like the hunger that tortured the loving eyes of my mother. At the age of eleven, I gave my battle cry: I believe in nature, in human reason! That is why I told my students that God was green! And that the land was holy and that man was a seed. Working in garden plots, my students designed maps of provinces and cities. A warm, living geography. I told them where their parents came from and that if in Russia their greatest ambition was the land, here it was something else. And I taught them to look upward. This country needed minds. Minds cultivated by solid books. Books that are as plain and clear as farmers' talk, not the Talmudic abstractions that had me bound for years. I told my students that the earth is a great open book.

Translated by Michele McKay Aynesworth.

Other works by Chudnovsky: *Pasos en el alma* (1952); *Pueblo pan* (1967).

Elisa Lerner

b. 1932

Elisa Lerner was born in Valencia, Venezuela; her father had immigrated from Novoselitsa, a village in northern Bessarabia (formerly in Romania), and her mother had come from Czernowitz. In 1935, her family moved to Caracas. She is a practicing attorney, but has distinguished herself through writing. She writes mainly for the theater but has also produced essays, short fiction, and a novel. Lerner has written extensively on her Yiddish-speaking mother, on female pop-culture stars—among them Shirley Temple, Susan Sontag, Katharine Hepburn, Eva Perón, and Miss Venezuela—and on the experiences of women more broadly: puberty, maternity, marriage, and divorce. Jewish themes, in particular the issue of Jewish women, are more prevalent in her essays than in her plays. In 1999, she was awarded Venezuela's National Prize for Literature.

In the Vast Silence of Manhattan
1964

[*A room in early evening shadows. It is the room of a New York suburban working girl.*]

[*Time: The early Thirties. A bell strikes eight times, probably from the bell tower of a nearby church.* ROSIE *is onstage, seated in front of a dressing table with a mirror. She holds a powder box and a powder puff in her hands. Hearing her mother's voice, she drops the box and puff on the table, a little startled, as if she were just coming out of a long dream. From the rear of the stage comes the* MOTHER'S *voice.*]

MOTHER'S VOICE: Did you hear, Rosie? [*Without waiting for* ROSIE'S *answer the* MOTHER *enters. She wears a cheap black dress of coarse cloth. Her hair is pulled into an austere knot. Her face is hard, her eyes glitter, her voice has a slight tremor. She is carrying two beautiful silver candelabra. She goes towards where* ROSIE *is sitting, but stops in the middle of the stage.*]

MOTHER: [*Repeating*] Did you hear, Rosie? The clock on the First Church of New Rochelle has struck eight. I hope you're ready. I hope your cheeks, your lips, your eyes are all shining, are all neat and tidy like those linen closets in the best houses in town. That's how they'll need to be.

ROSIE: I know. Soon cousin Emily will come in her car and we'll be off to the dance.

MOTHER: This dance is important, Rosie Davis, my daughter Rosie Davis. Very important that you should go to it. Are you listening, Rosie?

ROSIE: You know I am, Mother. You even know how. I'm listening to you as for years I've always listened to the water we boil for tea with our supper, thinking I could hear the whistle of trains bound for streets I'd never seen. I'm listening to you . . .

MOTHER: I don't know, Rosie. I still have the feeling you're hiding in your sewing box, like satin.

ROSIE: Mother, you're exaggerating.

MOTHER: Maybe so, my daughter Rosie, Rosie Davis. The truth is I would like something savage like desire, something savage like a man to drag you away from those satins, from that shyness. Something savage like desire to shatter that belly into smithereens. Then you'd have to start seeking your belly from the beginning, your vulnerability, in every fragment of the world, in all the blood.

ROSIE: Mother! The flames of your candelabra look so terrible—they dazzle me like those white birds on October mornings that make the sun so vast, so empty. And your words seem to spin more light than your candles. Mother, you frighten me with those candelabras, those words.

MOTHER: Rosie, all I want is your advantage. An advantage is simple. Every advantage is simple. Every advantage is a wedding, a season . . . Yours will be going to this dance. Out-of-town men have been coming to them of late, with breaths as cozy as meat and potatoes. [*She goes up to* ROSIE. *She strokes her cheek with a certain tenderness.*] What I want is to see you married, Rosie. What I want is to see a wedding ring blossom on this finger.

ROSIE: Mother, what you want isn't easy. And besides, these aren't easy times. The men all left town in the Depression. First the bread shortage got so notorious that the Governor shut down all the restaurants. "For Reasons of Public Order" the authorities wrote on all the tables, chairs, glasses and plates in every restaurant in New Rochelle. If you wanted to eat it would have to be in private, as if keeping the secret in your stomach. Then more than ever, Mother, I thought the tableware looked like silver-plated minnows you could never fish from the tablecloth. And now, finally, nobody in town has ventured as far as New York this winter. Hunger and poverty have made the city trains too cold. Nobody goes on them now. They've been thrown out like the king's dirty dishes.

MOTHER: That is why, Rosie, Rosie Davis, it's so important that you go to this dance. Where there's no bread on the tablecloths, you won't find men on the sheets of love. Still, cousin Emily drives her car all around town and in her car, like in a shameless basket, she collects all the rumors. Those rumors . . .

ROSIE: Those rumors . . .

MOTHER: Rosie, those rumors say that men are still coming from the city to this town, men with shining blonde whiskers and mugs of sparkling beer. They will get rich. At night their money will glow like mirrors, like lamps. The bread we lack today they will be seeking at the bottom of mines, of ruins. They will build vast factories, theaters, banks, huge stores . . .

ROSIE: Mother, you're delirious. Sometimes you seem to be seeing mad flashing lights.

MOTHER: What I want is something concrete. There are no kings' crowns anymore. Hardly any dreams. What I want is to see a ring bloom on your finger, the youthful vigor of your marriage. [*Silence.*] Yes, you have only to get married, climb out of that oppressive sewing box, and after a time you will forget all about that clumsy first ring, maybe even forget your hands as well. All that will exist for you will be those long black gloves from the best stores in Manhattan.

ROSIE: Mother, I don't understand you. Now you seem to be chasing metaphors in the sky. It's an audacity to go chasing around these cold weather skies. These skies darkened by the lack of winds and birds.

MOTHER: You must listen to me, Rosie. If I have to I'll smash your sewing box. I'll make it blaze like burning castles and I'll trample your satins on the sidewalk. It's time you learned about desire, about a lover's tongue.

ROSIE: I'm afraid I can't climb out of my sewing box any more. The palest of all my satins is my face.

MOTHER: Rosie, I don't mean to upset you. These last few years we've lost that sense of something metaphysical that exists between one being and another. That was all I wanted to say to you. Cousin Emily should be coming any minute. I've talked too much and the flames on these candles are starting to go out, but even so I can still see you. You look very lovely tonight, Rosie Davis. Leave your fears in your sewing box, in your mirrors that clarify nothing. I'm going to my room now. Bless you. Be happy! [MOTHER *exits.* ROSIE *is alone on stage.*]

Translated by David Pritchard.

Other works by Lerner: *Una sonrisa detrás de la metáfora* (1968); *Vida con mamá* (1976); *Yo amo a Colombo* (1979); *De muerte lenta* (2006).

Humberto Costantini

1924–1987

Humberto "Cacho" Costantini was born in Buenos Aires to Italian Jewish immigrants of Sephardic heritage. He spent most of his life in and around that city, earning his living primarily as a veterinarian. Costantini was a leftist and a sometime communist, although he was alienated by the Soviet line of the Argentine party. He was exiled to Mexico, returning to Argentina in 1984 to publish his existential and moral journey of the common man, *La larga noche de Francisco Sanctis*. After hours, and sometimes in very trying circumstances owing to his political activities, he worked at his other vocations: novelist, short-story writer, poet, and playwright. He won numerous literary prizes, most notably the Casa de Las Américas award for his novel *De dioses, hombrecitos y policías* (1979). Costantini also took a lively interest in the tango, as composer, singer, and dancer.

Don Iudá

1967

Just then Don Iudá took off his coat and greeted us one by one. My mother, out of breath as we'd been in such a hurry to come, explained everything in short choppy phrases.

We children would stay there. She and my father would go back. My father was a *shoḥet* and it seems that because he held the office of ritual slaughterer, he was especially hated by the "goyim."

In any case, Don Iudá had my sister and me go up a dilapidated ladder to an attic crammed full of knick-knacks. In the attic there was a small dormer window through which I could see the street if I climbed onto a table and placed a crate on it.

But when I get to this part of the tale, my memories are confused. To tell the truth, I can no longer clearly distinguish what happened to us in Lucena that night, the fourth after the last night of Pesaḥ in 1108, from what happened to me some eight hundred years later in Kishinev and even some forty years after that in Warsaw.

The truth is that one's recollections become jumbled.

I am no longer sure if the one who came ahead of everybody else, brandishing a cross as if he were brandishing a club, was really a threadbare friar with a sallow face and delirious eyes, or if maybe it was that obese pope whose beard was as handsome as Rabbi Mosché's.

I no longer remember if those men were on foot or if what was coming down the street was a column of four brown tanks from which shots and bursts of laughter poured.

I don't know if those haggard peasants armed with sticks, pitchforks, and sickles were really peasants or were elegant young people cheering for I don't know what patriotic league and waving Browning pistols in their smooth hands.

That is why I prefer not to talk about everything that happened that night.

Just to finish this story, I'm going to tell about something, in itself insignificant and commonplace, that happened right in front of Don Iudá's house.

From the minute the shouting started, he was beside himself. On the one hand he would have liked to run away from there, hide out in the house of some Christian client, and return two or three days later when the panic had given way to lamentations, interminable commentaries, and bursts of sobbing. When peace returned to the Jewish sector.

But on the other hand he couldn't bring himself to leave his workshop, with its mannequin, with its shelves full of fabrics, with its drawers, with its adornments, and with five half-finished suits.

Add to that, those two blessed children hidden in the attic. Why the devil hadn't he told his sister that they couldn't stay there . . . for example because it was too dangerous . . . or because he had to leave right away . . . or just anything at all.

The fact is that now they were there.

Don Iudá paced up and down. He was talking to himself, very fast, almost without moving his lips. That did not stop him from humming softly and rocking his head slightly from side to side. He picked up a prayer book, but left it to climb the ladder and impress upon the children with words and gestures the importance of remaining silent, no matter what happened.

Just like that, until the door to the street suddenly shuddered and groaned under the banging and the blows.

When they bashed in the door, Don Iudá, on a sudden impulse, ran to meet the invaders.

He knew that whatever happened, it was better that it happen in the street.

Surrounded, Don Iudá raised his arms, begged, and went down on his knees. When he saw someone trying to enter the house, he redoubled the shouting, the oaths, and the gestures.

Never had Don Iudá's eyes looked so much like a mouse's as they did then. Those of a poor mouse, corralled and cornered. But perhaps his behavior was not that of a mouse, but rather that of a heroic sparrow desperately circling the nest and making a fuss, knowing this is the only way to save its chicks.

***

That was when Don Iudá was baptized, by the hands of that friar who was brandishing a cross like a club.

And from that day he was no longer called Don Iudá but Don Jerónimo. Jerónimo de Lucena, his baptismal name.

Some time later, the beautiful weather-cock with its tricolored tail abandoned the Jewish quarter and flaunted its elegance on the red roof of a cottage facing the market square.

And through the window you could still see Don Iudá—excuse me, Don Jerónimo de Lucena—leaning over the table, sewing with astonishing speed and crooning a kind of litany.

Perhaps Don Iudá had aged a bit, but his eyes still shone with pleasure like those of a child. And when Rabbi Mosché passed by, looking indifferently toward the window of the ḥayat [tailor], his face lit up with a spark of sardonic complicity.

Don Iudá, that is to say, my uncle, lived some three hundred years in the city of Lucena, up until a certain 31 March 1492.

But we'll talk about that another day.

Translated by Michele McKay Aynesworth.

Other works by Costantini: *De por aquí nomás* (1958); *Un señor alto, rubio de bigotes* (1963); *Háblenme de Funes* (1970); *Una pipa larga, larga, con cabeza de jabalí* (1981).

Lázaro Liacho

On the Cutting Edge of Life
1969

The men, women, and children who arrived, physically destroyed, at the death camp, had only one fixed idea: to survive. The average person, living in a bustling metropolis and enjoying freedom to a greater or lesser extent, cannot imagine the loss of human dignity suffered by those condemned to such a cruel fate. Enslaved by the barbarians, determined to survive no matter the cost, they were driven to express their basic instincts in tragic ways. In their anguished struggle to live, an understandable animality emerged. Survival meant renouncing all higher things, an abject descent into the lower depths. One wanted to see the future, the day of liberation, the dawn of renewed hope. Submerged in this foul pit, I intended to live for the day of vengeance and endured trials worse than death.

When would that time of resurrection come? How long could one bear so much misery, so much diabolical torture? Would freedom ever come? In search of it, people performed the sanest and the maddest acts I can remember. The horrors I witnessed! None worse than that of those two women, mother and daughter, who threw themselves against the electric fence in hopes of rejoining darkness in the peaceful oneness offered by death. At that moment the current wasn't strong enough to kill them, but served well enough to entrap their bodies, inducing horrible convulsions and burns. Their screams, like an outburst of mad savagery, echoed around the camp, which anguish and night had desolated. There is no death worse than that. All of those imprisoned in those filthy, pestilential barracks jumped too, as if electrified.

The mother ended up hanging from the wires like a dried-up, blackened branch, while the daughter was shaking desperately, trying to free herself from the fiery claws. Her young breasts were hugging each other, stuck to the barbed wire. Still alive, the young girl was yanked off, then fell to the ground next to her lifeless mother. The dogs dragged their bodies to the common grave pit. [. . .]

Their mouths took the first blows, their backs the hail of blows that followed. But the men and women resisted, forming arm in arm a defiant group that had been cut to the bone, yet remained standing. Seeing that the brutal beatings did not subdue them, the SS loosed the trained pack of dogs on them. The bites of the bloodthirsty beasts ripped open the calves and necks of those who were begging God for mercy. The dogs' unrestrained fury soon had the conquered and already dying group ready to be dragged to the gas chamber. Scattered over the floor, their broken bodies intermingled, some could still see amid the mists rapidly filling the room a great fiery form that rose to the ceiling, its white hands stretched out over the dying.

Through the peephole of the room next door, I watched the innocent falling asleep to the sound of the angel chorus while lethal gas poured over them. Already in the agony of death, their hands reached out, pleading for mercy. The fire in my eyes was too much, and silent tears began to fall from them as I sought a pathway to those white hands. And I saw that the hands were hanging onto emptiness, until they fell, dragged down by death.

Now God is still in Auschwitz, seeking the crucified in order to save from among them the wandering Jew.

Translated by Michele McKay Aynesworth.

Alejandra Pizarnik

1936–1972

Alejandra Pizarnik was an Argentinean poet born to Russian Jewish immigrant parents in Avellaneda, just outside of Buenos Aires. She grew up in a mixed Spanish and Yiddish environment, eventually pursuing a degree in philosophy, then journalism, and finally literature at the University of Buenos Aires before dropping out. She also studied painting with surrealist Juan Batlle Planas. While living in Paris (1960–1964) among other Latin American expats, she published poems, critical essays, and translations of French works in well-known periodicals such as *Cuadernos*. Much of her poetry was dark, dealing with death, guilt, and mental instability, from which she herself suffered. She died young, of an arguably accidental suicide, after a long history of depression. "The Dead and the Rain" is one of her few works that relate directly to her Jewish heritage.

The Dead and the Rain
1969

"Once there was a man who lived next to a cemetery."
—Shakespeare

Once there was a man who lived next to a cemetery and no one asked why. And why should they? I don't live next to a cemetery and no one asks me why not. Something rotten or sick lies between yes and no. If a man lives next to a cemetery he is not asked why, but neither is he asked why if he lives far from a cemetery. But he didn't live next to a cemetery just by chance. People will tell me that everything comes down to chance, starting with where one lives. It doesn't matter what people tell me because people who believe they're telling me something are never telling me anything at all. I only hear my desperate murmuring, the liturgi-

cal chants coming from the sacred tomb of my illicit childhood. That's a lie. Actually, I'm listening to Lotte Lenya singing *The Threepenny Opera*. Of course I'm talking about a recording, but I can't get over being astonished that in this lapse of three years between the last time I listened to it and today, nothing has changed for Lotte Lenya, but much (maybe everything, if everything were certain) has changed for me. I've learned about death, and I've learned about rain. That's why, perhaps, only for that reason and nothing more, only because of the rain on the tombs, only because of the rain and the dead, could there have been a man who lived next to a cemetery. The dead don't emit signals of any kind. Tough luck and patience, for life is a musical lesson in silence. But something starts to move and come out of hiding when rain falls on a cemetery. I've seen with my own eyes the little men in black singing the dirges of wandering, lost poets. And those wearing caftans soaked through by the rain, and the useless tears, and my too-young father, with the hands and feet of a Greek youth, my father will have felt afraid the first night in that terrible place. The people and the little men in black rapidly emptied the cemetery. A ragged man stayed by my side in case I needed help. Maybe it was the neighbor mentioned in the story that begins *Once there was a man who lived next to a cemetery.* Oh, the record has changed, and Lotte Lenya, it turns out, has aged. All the dead are drunk on dirty, unfamiliar rain in the strange Jewish cemetery. Only in the sound of rain falling on the tombs can I learn something about what I'm afraid to know. Blue eyes, eyes embedded in the fresh earth of empty graves in the Jewish cemetery. If there were an empty cottage next to the cemetery, if it could be mine. And to take possession as of a ship and look through a spyglass at my father's tomb in the rain when the dead, and some living, tell tales of spirits, of ghosts, of apparitions. It happens that I can come closer to my absent ones in the winter, as if the rain made it possible. It's true that it doesn't matter what or who has been called God, but what I read in the Talmud is also true: "God has three keys: that of rain, that of birth, that of the resurrection of the dead."

Translated by Michele McKay Aynesworth.

Other works by Pizarnik: *La tierra más ajena* (1955); *La última inocencia* (1956); *Las aventuras perdidas* (1958).

Diego Viga

1907-1997

The son of a Viennese textile manufacturer, Diego Viga (pseudonym of Paul Engel) obtained a medical degree in Vienna. By 1934, conditions for Jews in Austria had deteriorated to the point that Viga migrated to Uruguay, although he returned in 1936 upon his marriage to Josefine Monath. After Germany annexed Austria, Viga left once more, this time to Bogotá, Colombia, where his extended family managed to join him in exile. In the 1940s, he began writing works in German and Spanish. In the 1950s, Viga and his family moved to Quito, Ecuador, where he continued writing essays and fiction. His literary works received awards in Ecuador and the German Democratic Republic.

The Stutterer's Suicide and the Psychiatrist's Dream

1970

". . . Are you Jewish?"

"Of course, I am. I went to South America to escape persecution, not to enjoy the pleasant climate."

"Well, I'm neither a practicing Jew nor a Zionist. In fact, I dislike any kind of nationalism and often ask myself why we even bother to remain Jews. It's probably out of loyalty precisely because we've been persecuted and discredited for so many thousands of years. To abandon such an oppressed group would lack courage and sincerity. I'm not sure what your opinions are in the matter, but I repeat that although I have no ties to the Jewish faith and community, I . . ."

"Well," I said, "Hitler showed us that not even those who wished to assimilate could escape the Jewish fate."

"Yes, that's true . . ."

"But I agree with you on many points. You believe that only pride . . . !"

"If we start discussing the Jewish problem now, you'll never catch your plane tomorrow morning."

"I have a luncheon engagement today. . . ."

"Don't worry. I only wanted to show you how insignificantly I'm connected to the Jewish community. One might say that psychiatry itself is bad Judaism."

I remembered that Wagner-Jauregg did not have any Jewish blood. "I don't know why I feel this way. . . . *I* never did. I'm not at all nationalistic. I'm just a purely atheistic American citizen. Perhaps some of these ideas were in my mind as I tossed and turned in my bed one night. I was perspiring. In August it is extremely difficult to sleep in this city with its infernal heat; and I can't use air conditioning because I find it impossible to sleep with it on. Thus, that night poor Humberto Mendoza pursued me and in order to drive away his ghost, I remembered you; the culprit who resurrected his spirit. I remembered your voice, and although you spoke English over the telephone, I recognized the voice of a Viennese. Naturally, I knew that you were a Jew as well and thus, I began to reflect on the Jewish fate to free me from the shadow of the stutterer, or the man who preferred to stutter . . . meaning that he preferred to die rather than live without stuttering.

Psychiatrists are bound to be crazy, I thought. No wonder they live in asylums, although this one is in a clinic on 74th Street.

"I didn't want to be a Jew, but I am. I didn't want to be born Jewish, but I was. My father tried to give us a modern education that didn't belong to the ghetto, and during World War I we moved to Vienna. Afterwards my father chose the Austrian Republic. You know how things were. We were always the 'outsiders from the East,' who had come because we were Jewish. We were always different in their eyes. At school I was the 'Jew.' Since I was a good student, they copied my homework, but they never wanted me around. In high school my peers accepted me only because I ingratiated myself to them by being helpful. I truly felt the need to distinguish myself by surpassing everyone else. 'Or is this my nature?' I wondered. 'Must I always be Number One?'

"I never became Number One. I was a good student and tried to establish friendships, but I always felt left out. I just didn't belong. Nor did they give me the best grades. *I* was a good student, but without a doubt, not the best.

"'It's because I'm Jewish,' I told myself. 'If I were a gentile like the others, I'd get better grades and my peers would respect me. They wouldn't hit me in the nose with a ball and knock off my glasses. They wouldn't laugh at my clumsiness.'"

Only then did I realize that those "Freudian eyes" hidden by bifocals were just like my own.

"Finally, I entered the university. You remember how the antisemites dominated there. Ten times worse that the Triple Entente . . . Once again I pushed myself to excel academically."

Not me. I never had such ambition to succeed, I thought. But I shouldn't interrupt him. I wondered why he was telling me his strange little tale. A psychia-

trist with his vulgar, ordinary, boring Jewish experiences . . . he's got something all right, he's a lonely
person who needs to unburden his heart, I concluded.
Victims of neuroses pay him to listen to their small,
psychic sufferings, so I should be grateful to him for
his time and lose my precious hours in New York City?
I didn't exactly come here to bury myself in the life of
Dr. A. E. Lewison!

Luckily I hadn't scheduled appointments with my
friends for an earlier hour. While they work, I lounge
around here, instead of strolling through this grand
city, Central Park or the Metropolitan Museum.

"At least you were born in Vienna," he mentioned,
"but I was always considered the Polish Jew. All Jews
need ten times more publications than anyone else in
order to become a member of the faculty. That had been
my hope, but Mr. Hitler interrupted my career. You've
known some professors . . . well in spite of everything,
I completed my studies so successfully that they accepted me as an intern in the Department of Psychiatry
at the University. Despite my Jewish origin, I accomplished the incredible feat of becoming a member of an
institution of higher learning."

I also achieved this, I thought, but I listened silently
to the confessions of this psychopathic psychiatrist instead of . . . !

"I became somewhat of a resident, an assistant
doctor. . . ."

"I too . . . ," I broke my self-imposed silence.

"Yes, I was very proud, but although they honored
me with a post, as a Jew they did not give me a paid
position. I remained an assistant physician, ad hon-
orem. And later, when the post for the head of the
clinic opened up, of course a gentile colleague was promoted. . . . We Jews never make it."

Translated by Susan Riva Greenberg.

Other works by Viga: *Der Freiheitsritter* (1955); *Eva
Heller* (1966); *Las pecas de Mamá: Seis cuentos* (1970).

Marcos Ricardo Barnatán

b. 1946

Born in Buenos Aires to Sephardic parents with
roots in Spain and Syria, Marcos Ricardo Barnatán
moved to Madrid in 1965 but has traveled frequently
to Argentina, France, and Israel. Barnatán's writing
ranges from scholarly essays to poetry and stories and
from subjects as diverse as Nazis and Jewish culture

to labyrinths and the mystical language of Kabbalah.
A disciple of Jorge Luis Borges, he has written four
books about the Argentine literary giant. Barnatán is
married to the Spanish writer Rosa Pereda and is the
father of actor, writer, and singer Jimmy Barnatán.

The Labyrinth of Zion
1971

In truth Ezra is still very young, but sometimes these
marriages are the ones that turn out best. I used to think
it was a crime to do this to these children, but I see so
many marriages for love destroyed after six months,
finished after a year, that I don't know what to say. At
any rate it was madness, I couldn't allow my daughter
to marry Enrique. Not that I blame her, the boy is ador-
able, super well-mannered, cultured, intelligent, good
looking, well-off, but alas! . . . a *goy*. It would have been
a scandal, and would also set a terrible precedent. If my
daughter marries a goy, what will become of all the other
Jewish girls? Also no one can deny that the Benkatan-
Laudets are charming. A family worthy of my daughter.
It's a shame that my little girl will be going so far away
from me. My dress mustn't be too fancy, Madame Rachel recommended a splendid design to me, well, hers
isn't bad. Of course her dressmaker charged her something outrageous, but a Levi-Sead can't just wear any
old thing. Oh dear! Six o'clock, I should already be at
El Molino. That boy also has me worried sick. So weak,
so fragile, so detached from reality.

Translated by Michele McKay Aynesworth.

Other works by Barnatán: *Ante mí: Poesía del hombre
mutable* (1964); *El libro del talismán* (1970); *La Kábala:
Una mística del lenguaje* (1974).

Isidoro Blaisten

1933–2004

Born in the province of Entre Ríos, Argentina, Isidoro
Blaisten (also spelled Blaistein) moved with his widowed mother and extended family to tenement housing
in Buenos Aires at the age of eight. Four years later, his
older brother Enrique was killed in that city by Nazis.
Blaisten eventually worked as a journalist, bookseller,
photographer, and writer of poetry and fiction. He first
found publishing success with his poetry, then turned
to the humorous, absurdist short stories that began
appearing in 1969. Blaisten was a member of the Argentine Academy of Letters and of the Real Academia

Española, Spain's official guardian of the Spanish language.

Misery in Aries
1971

Do you know what sign I am? Aries. What's that? And? So, what do you think? No big deal? And do you know what my conflict is? The drama? Yes, the drama of my life. Misery. What do you say? Now, just figure, what if I were a Pisces or a Libra or at the very least a Gemini. Sorry, I didn't know. No, I won't just forget about it. No. The birth chart is something else. No. I'll explain it to you later. No problem. Do you know what the Aries sign means? Now pay attention: Aries, the boldest sign in the zodiac, destined to do great things, to sublimate adversity in violence, to value action above thinking, to make possible what seems impossible for the common man. What do you say? Now look at this diptych I'm painting for you: a sign like Aries on one side, misery on the other. Unbelievable, right? Utterly. Wait, no, look. It's not that I don't have anything to eat. No, please. Thank you. Thank you. Many thanks. No, no. Nice person. Very nice person. No, no, the conflict is something else. I want you to understand: I have a roof over my head, I have enough to eat. The conflict is something else. I have everything. But how can I explain. It's all debased by nullity, permeated and tarnished by misery.

Translated by Michele McKay Aynesworth.

Other works by Blaisten: *Sucedió en la lluvia* (1965); *La felicidad* (1969).

Alicia Steimberg
1933–2012

Alicia Steimberg was born in Buenos Aires and was a novelist, educator, and translator. Best known for her fiction writing, she also published short stories and books for adolescents. Her work was strongly autobiographical and often satirical, and her novel *Cuando digo Magdalena* received the Premio Planeto Biblioteca del Sur award in 1992.

Musicians and Watchmakers
1971

"Act dumb," Otilia advised me. "Change the subject." To help me understand what she meant, she il-

lustrated by relating a conversation she had had with a neighbor. It was December, when a great deal of activity was going on in preparation for the approaching holidays.

"You have to do your shopping early," the neighbor remarked, "because at the last minute it's always a madhouse."

"I know," Otilia replied, already on guard.

The neighbor blurted out, "Do you people celebrate Christmas?"

"No," said Otilia.

"What religion are you?"

"We aren't religious," Otilia said, since she was no dummy.

"But your parents, your grandparents, what religion were they?"

Otilia decided to cut her short: "They weren't. They weren't any religion. Look, excuse me, but I've got something burning in the oven." And she left her standing there.

This attitude didn't coincide with that of my paternal aunts, who said that I should never hide my Jewishness from anyone, and furthermore, that I should advertise it all the time by wearing a little chain with the Star of David around my neck.

This was a conflict for me. During a lecture about Christians and Jews, my fifth grade teacher asked all the Jewish girls in the class to raise their hands. A few did, as meekly as when she would ask those who had finished solving a math problem to raise their hands. My own two hands remained on my desk top. On the back of my neck I felt the outraged breath of my Grandma Ana, of my great-grandmother, and of King David himself, as well as that of my Jewish classmates, who were clever at guessing your origin from your surname. But I also felt the approving looks of the Beasts. I was learning not to be a dummy by playing dumb.

Once the teacher had finished scrutinizing the faces of those who had raised their hands, she gave them permission to put them down again and continued with her explanation. She said that the Jews were still paying for a crime that they had committed two thousand years ago: killing Jesus Christ. The proof of this was the fact that so many Jews had died in the war (Poor things! she added). Their punishment would end when all the Jews converted to Christianity and accepted Jesus, who, she said, was infinitely merciful. At this point the bell rang and we went out to recess, although not before the teacher could pass around the charity collection box.

After they married traditional Jews, the Beasts changed their philosophical orientation. They ended up becoming bastions of Jewish pride, and as their financial situation improved, they became involved in social and recreational affairs and charity events sponsored by the Jewish community, competing with the other ladies in the community in the areas of clothing, jewelry, home furnishings, dietitians, and summer vacations at the beach. "She has a Russian Jew face that makes you want to throw up," Otilia said, referring to one of them. "But she's invited me to her house lots of times, so tonight I'm inviting them. No sense in being stupid," she pronounced. "It's best to hang around with members of the community. When they talk about you, at least they won't say, 'She has a Russian Jew face that makes you want to throw up.'"

Translated by Andrea G. Labinger.

Other works by Steinberg: *Como todas las mañanas* (1983); *El árbol del placer* (1986); *La selva* (2000); *La música de Julia* (2008).

Mario Szichman

1945–2018

An Argentine writer, journalist, and literary critic, Mario Szichman lived in New York, where he worked for United Press International and the Cadena Capriles media company of Caracas. Szichman wrote about assimilation, identity, tradition, immigration, and antisemitism. In 1980, he received the first literary prize from Ediciones del Norte.

Jews in the Promised Land
1971

On the first day they sailed, the Pechofs saw the film called *Argentina, the Promised Land*. The screen had been divided into four parts like a coat of arms, and they saw wheat fields, cows in profile, boats filmed from below so that their prows were dizzying, and a family composed of mother, father, son, daughter, and frisky dog, all looking at a radiant sun.

The four of them were good-looking, happy people, and they all had the same face. The difference between the son and the father was owing to his hair having been painted white and smile wrinkles created by makeup between his eyebrows and at the corners of his mouth.

In this country that had been prepared in order to deceive the naive immigrant, there were no Indians, no poisoned arrows, no jungles full of tigers and alligators, no filth, no old houses, no White Guards, no one who was poor, short, or fat, and no jerk-offs or antisemites. This world belonged in the glossy pages of *El Hogar* [a middle-class women's magazine], where money grew on trees and the immigrants proved themselves to be extraordinary rodeo riders in the eyes of the Creoles, who at first mocking and then astonished, invited them after the event to share a maté gourd with a "come on, *paisano*, you earned it fair and square." Everyone moved up the ladder, and with the past erased for lack of a record, soldiers became marshals, bricklayers became engineers, and petty pickpockets became white-gloved thieves. In that imaginary Argentina the informal *tú* form was used, asses were called donkeys, alms were small contributions, the poor wore clothes that were mended but neat, great men came from humble backgrounds, parents enjoyed taking their children to parades and being thrilled when the grenadiers passed by, our friend the policeman devoted himself to helping little old ladies cross the street, the children spoke in highbrow, foppish cliques were worthy institutions, refined ladies stayed in bed, canasta tournaments always took place in magnificent surroundings, and people died telling lies. [. . .]

The Pechofs traveled first to the virgin yellow desert and built the jigsaw puzzle of a past they wanted to take possession of in order to put an end to their uprootedness. They placed their starting point in the year 1810 and set off to eat up the years separating them from the *goyim*, with their unclipped dicks and their genealogies perpetuated in oil portraits of Pueyrredón, Pellegrini, or Morel, from their generations of family generals, judges, or deputies, and their stern grandmothers, from the angular splinter groups that confronted the Unitarias or the Federales [parties for centralized and decentralized government, respectively], from that language that had already been pawed over by ancestors four or five generations back and which had been given to them along with the serene, condescending gestures of those who feel like gods, trying to add to that caste of gutsy, long-donged, larger-than-life characters who extended the frontiers or else hung out in Paris just having a good time, sometimes victorious, sometimes put to rout, but always owners of their land, the faint recollection of some great-grandfather who was lost in memory almost as soon as he boarded a ship bound for Palestine, taking as his only treasure some tefillin written by a disciple of Rashi and some forefathers with long beards, side locks, round *shlapques* [hats] and hooked noses, looking desperately for anyone with a red beard and blue eyes to convert him to believe in the Messiah.

They had to take ownership of a foreign history, full of strange stories. The heroes shrank when the war for independence ended and turned into bloodthirsty warlords. The liberating armies who had mixed their flags in the struggle against the Spanish picked up their trophies and their dead and went off to their homelands to form anarchic guerrilla bands. Glory was replaced by ambition, sacrifice by shameful appetites. The warriors lowered their stature and ruined their profiles, dismounting from the horse on which they had immortalized their proclamations and covering themselves with menacing beards. Time itself was altered, and the cross in the Andes took up as much space in the history books as did Rosas's government.

The Pechofs took the side of the conquerors and the Mayo-Caseros libertarians, becoming anti-Peronists who invited Admiral Rojas to the parties of the DAIA [Delegation for Argentinian Jewish Associations].

Translated by Michele McKay Aynesworth.

Other work by Szichman: *Crónica falsa* (1969).

Eugenia Calny

1929–1999

Fany Eugenia Kalnitzky de Brener, who later adopted the pseudonym Eugenia Calny, was born in Argentina's San Juan province. She had a dual career as a journalist and creative writer in Buenos Aires, and her literary output included plays, poetry, and fiction. Written from the viewpoint of a Jewish feminist, her stories for adults feature protagonists, as in *Las mujeres virtuosas* (1967), who are typically long-suffering women chafing at their oppression and whose restlessness foreshadows the coming movement for liberation. In *El unicornio celeste y el caballito con alas* (1984), she claimed to be turning away from the smaller world of adult literature toward the freer, unbounded world of children's literature.

Clara at Dawn

1972

She couldn't have been more than seventeen years old. They came as war refugees. Survivors of the horror. The community was caring for the nearly cadaver-

ous human beings and her parents wanted her to give a couple of hours after work as well.

The workplace was the same port where the immigrants had just disembarked. A Dantesque parade. A voluntary silence impossible to break. Or a mix of languages and dialects. Madness and disability. Some were crying because they believed the new country was a trap. They resisted giving names, dates, histories. They insulted and cursed them. The majority carried identity cards provided by the International Red Cross. But because of their acute state of malnutrition and depression, the survivors' personal information was often a tragic guess: "He says he's called N.N." "He says he was born in village X." "He says his parents died in some extermination camp." "He says he has no family."

The women would work up to twelve hours at a stretch, often not daring to pause for a coffee, or a sandwich, because snacking in front of these people who were coming from hunger and waiting, from torture and death and waiting, was a painful and unimaginable offense.

Translated by Michele McKay Aynesworth.

Other works by Calny: *El agua y la sed* (1960); *La madriguera* (1967); *El congreso de los árboles* (1979).

Alberto Dines

1932–2018

A native of Rio de Janeiro, Alberto Dines worked as a journalist beginning in 1952. He founded numerous periodicals in Portugal and Brazil, served as a professor of journalism, wrote fifteen books, and in 1996 founded a website for media analysis. At the Jewish school Dines attended as a boy, he learned Yiddish, enabling a facility with German, and at the age of eight he was greatly impressed by a school visit from Stefan Zweig. Dines later wrote a biography of Zweig and became president of the Casa Stefan Zweig, a cultural organization celebrating Zweig's years in Brazil. In 2007 Dines received the Austrian Holocaust Memorial Award for his work remembering the Holocaust.

Can I?

1972

I just can't. Should I? I feel like going in, but I just can't; I remain stationary. The church door opens and closes, continually, and I open and close with it, split asunder. Warmth escapes from inside there, but Judas has prevented me from entering. Once again in my life, I notice that I am cold. I suspect that the people inside are packed very close together, I foresee that there will be chants, gentleness. I want to go in, but I dare not, I am afraid. I tremble with cold and indecision. But it is not good to feel cold; the chill comes from nights long ago. One feels sorry for people and sympathy is generally a lopsided sentiment. It doesn't help you move forward.

"Can I?"

"If you want to . . ."

I do want to, and so I let myself move. I understand that it's important to let yourself move. Or better yet: to let yourself go. And in letting myself go, I arrived almost at the church door, whereby it became easy to allow everything else to happen. I'm inside. I believe they were waiting for me; midnight mass was beginning. Judas has not let me enter churches casually. Judas or whatever they made up about him. I know it wasn't him, I know that it wasn't me, I know, at last, that there is no blame. Let me amend that: we are to blame—those of us who participate, who hear each story. But what can I do if he always appears at every church door?

Today, something is pushing me, not allowing me to return to my hotel room. Because it's Christmas. Because I am in Rome. Because there is something very strong that is pushing me inside.

A children's choir is singing in Italian and I feel good, I feel permitted, you understand? I do not make the sign of the cross, I do not kneel down, I do not pray, I do not sing. I just think about my own prayers. The important thing is that I can touch myself all over since no one is looking. I am now completely within myself and I like this sensation of not having anyone beside me, looking over my shoulder, forcing me to act in a certain way. I search for words and ascertain that the verb *allow oneself* also has a connotation that gives me comfort.

I look around and reckon that nobody is enjoying the midnight mass more than I, here in the heart of Rome—not even the priest. And, as a reward, the children's choir starts to chant a melody that I recognize. I pay attention to the words and cannot immediately identify the language. But, it isn't Italian or Latin or Greek. I pay attention to the melody; it isn't Gregorian, medieval or Baroque. It is Hebrew. Astute, as we must be nowadays, I imagine that someone has identified me and is honoring me with that song. I know it very well: *Hevei'nu shalom aleikhem*, we have brought you peace. . . . Jews sing it at the onset of the Sabbath and Jewish festivals, when

trees are planted, houses are built, and when people arrive in Israel. I've sung it many times, too. The music itself is penetrating. And I become immersed within it.

Can I? I don't even stop to think about it. I begin to sing. Surprise: no one next to me is surprised and they also sing. In Hebrew. In a church. In Rome. On Christmas Eve. I no longer feel cold, or shiver; there is sun everywhere. I admit that I'm crying.

When the song ended, I had the world in my hands. I embraced the first Italian woman with a black shawl on her head and cried out to her: *auguri*, best wishes! She allows herself to be hugged, places her hand on my face and says to me effusively: *mazal tov*, congratulations! Good luck! In Hebrew, in a church, on Christmas, in Rome. I am no longer so easily surprised. Now I accept everything. I take another woman's hand, an old woman, and shout to her: *Tante cose belle!* So many beautiful things! And she replies: *Be-shanah ha-ba'ah bi-yerushalayim!* Next year in Jerusalem!

I don't understand nor do I resist; I let myself go. I am placing my hands on everybody, spreading my best wishes, my embraces, and no one around me resists either. They all respond to my *buon Natale* (Merry Christmas) with louder shouts of *shanah tovah*, Happy New Year. *Ḥag sameaḥ*, Happy Holidays.

Now, the entire church is in motion, heating up. All the people are touching one another, leaning against each other, mingling, singing songs that are mine, saying things that only I know. Finally, friendly trumpets sound and all the doors of the world open, creaking and groaning. And in the midst of that festival of affection, I don't stand still. I understand. I know that I can.

Translated by Marvin Meital.

Other works by Dines: *Death in Paradise: The Tragedy of Stefan Zweig* (1981); *Fire Links: Antônio José da Silva, the Jew, and Other Stories of the Inquisition in Portugal and Brazil* (1992).

Eliezer Levin

b. 1930

The Brazilian author Eliezer Levin captured life in Jewish Brazil with a unique, stunning vividness. Born in southern Brazil, Levin used his childhood milieu—a busy, vital Jewish neighborhood in São Paulo—as both setting and subject. His first novel, set during the 1930s and 1940s, outlined an idyllic, insular Jewish world, its pleasures offset by grim, troubling world events. Later, Levin published two more novels and two short-story collections. Like his childhood itself, Levin's work is lively and polyglot, with a dash of Yiddish and Hebrew spicing up the Portuguese.

Bom Retiro, or The Childhood Neighborhood
1972

Yom Kippur and Rosh Hashanah, the so-called "Days of Awe" arrived.

There was no Jew in all of Bom Retiro who, God forbid, would ever think of not observing them. Any endeavor, no matter how important, was set aside. Even those who never opened the prayer book all year long, would rush, on the eve of the Day of Atonement, to close their businesses, run home, put on clean and well-brushed clothes, take their meal early, surrounded by the wife and children and, finally, head for the synagogue.

José Paulino Street, normally such a bustling thoroughfare, looked abandoned, became empty and quiet, its doors shut, its neon signs turned off.

At school, we were let out earlier and would go straight home. We would take a bath, put on new shoes, slip into clean, nice-smelling clothes, and would sit at the table, on whose white tablecloth stood the candlesticks. And, thus, we sat waiting for the adults to say: "It's time to go." As usual, my father would say: "I hope that there'll be good weather today. Fasting is better endured when it's cold out."

Upon arriving at temple, my mother would give each of us a kiss and head for the women's balcony, while my brother and I went to sit down next to dad.

The voice of the ḥazan dominated the synagogue. His prayers echoed with a strange appeal. I firmly believed that, there in the kingdom of heaven, God Almighty, His book open, was getting ready to decide our fate with a single pen stroke. However, little by little, we became distracted and began to feel like moving around, talking and breathing in pure air. At the first opportunity, we would slip away to the patio, relieved. Coming from inside the temple were the echoes of Kol Nidre and the cries of the people praying.

Among them, next to the rear bench, was Ruvke, the wagoner, huddled in a corner, with his tallis covering his head. He would remain standing the entire time, without moving, immersed in profound silence.

Ruvke lived in the town's last house—the smallest and poorest of them all. Indeed, it was a mystery how so many people could fit into it, since, besides Ruvke

and his wife, there were seven sons ranging in age from one to seven.

The place where Ruvke would wait for customers was located at the corner of José Paulino and Ribeiro de Lima. And the calls would come in aplenty. Ruvke wasn't a lazy person; he would finish loading his cart and, with the first push, which was the most difficult, he would take off, pulling the cart.

Although the merchants did not pay well, there was always work, thank God. It was on very sultry days that Ruvke suffered the most. His body would be soaked in perspiration. Under the hot sun, his head, despite the thick cap he wore, seemed to burst. His was a harsh vocation, but Ruvke was grateful to God for having the means to earn a living.

His grand dream was to be able, one day, to see his children graduate. Nothing more. The oldest would be a physician, the second an engineer, the third a lawyer, and so forth. Ah, if only God would make his dreams come true. But Ruvke was illiterate. There was the rub. Unlike other Jews, he couldn't even read a prayer, and he was mortified by this. On Yom Kippur, he would wrap himself in his *tallis* and simply remain silent. His heart palpitated in pain; his conscience allowed him no peace.

One day, he came to my father's house. He told him his story and revealed the plan he had in mind.

"Professor, I would like to learn how to read. Do you think this is possible at my age? I need you to teach me, no matter what the cost. I want to be a Jew like everyone else. I also want to recite a prayer on Yom Kippur."

My father listened to him in silence and was deeply moved.

"Ruvke, my dear brother," he said, "I will tell you a secret that you may not know. It is written that any of us can communicate with God. You can send him any message you want, as long as you do so in the language that your mother taught you—that's all."

A great smile spread across Ruvke's long face. At first, he didn't want to believe it. But, little by little, the idea took hold in his head and when he took his leave, an immense relief overcame him.

When Yom Kippur arrived, Ruvke covered himself in his tallis and, this time, he didn't remain silent. Everyone prayed. And Ruvke did, too. Only differently.

If anyone had approached him, he would have heard a beautiful prayer.

"Dear God in Heaven, help me, my wife and my children. Also the entire people of Israel. May I have loaded carts all year long. May my strength not fail me. May my health not fail me. May I be able to pay for my children's studies. May they graduate with honors. May we all have a good year. Amen."

Translated by Marvin Meital.

Other works by Levin: *Sessão corrida: Que me dizes avozinho?* (1982); *Crônicas de meu bairro* (1987); *Nossas outras vidas* (1989).

Chava Rosenfarb

1923–2011

Polish-born Chava Rosenfarb, who survived the Holocaust and later immigrated to Canada, was an award-winning author of Yiddish novels, plays, poems, and short fiction. Her writing was heavily influenced by her experiences during World War II. Among other literary honors, she was the recipient of the Sholem Aleichem Prize, the I. J. Segal Prize, the John Glassco Prize, and an honorary degree from the University of Lethbridge.

The Tree of Life: A Novel about Life in the Lodz Ghetto

1972

Presess Rumkowski plunged into the sea of activities and duties like a brave captain who knows his destination, sure that no blizzard, no stormy chaos will cause the ship entrusted into his hands by fate, to stray from its appointed course. He worked with a clear head, with order and a plan, in total composure.

First of all, he had to deal with the problem of Jewish institutions, which ones to liquidate and which to take over and continue in the ghetto. Then there were meetings to be held with Mrs. Feiner and her staff from the *gymnasium,* as well as with the boards of the elementary schools which he had reopened while still in town; and there was the problem of food provisions for the children in general. The rest of his time was spent in conferences about finances. There was the urgent necessity of creating an independent source of income, by opening some factories or Work Resorts as the Germans called them, which would give the people an occupation and establish a more solid base for the existence of the ghetto.

Despite all this work, the Presess was in high spirits. And in spite of his many obligations, he managed to treat himself to a substantial dinner and his beard to a second shave. He put on a clean shirt (lately he wore only white shirts, changing them as often as possible). Afterwards, dressed up in his new suit, he examined himself in the mirror. He was pleased with himself. The hard work did not show on him at all, it seemed rather to suit him. He contemplated his gray head with self-respect. This was how he ought to look. Only the eyeglasses with their cheap frames needed to be changed for better ones. He also decided to see a doctor, not because he felt ill, but because with the help of modern medicine he might perhaps regain his former strength. He, who once had cared so little about his health, decided to protect it here, in the ghetto, like a treasure. Before, it had been only the health of an old director of an orphanage, he objectively explained his case to himself, now it was the health of a great man, of the leader of all Jews in Litzmanstadt-Ghetto. He purred contentedly, as he put on his new stiff hat. He also remembered to put a white handkerchief in the breastpocket of his jacket.

He drove through the streets which teemed with people. He had ordered the coachman of the droshky to put up the hood, but people recognized him. They raced after the droshky, yelling, "Herr Presess! Herr Presess!" begging for favours, for work, for charity. As he passed a corner, someone raised a fist, calling out to him, "We are starving!" He was kept busy brushing off the letters and notes people threw at him. He thought about hiring two muscled bodyguards who would accompany him everywhere.

The corridor to the office was bulging with people who had waited for hours to see the Presess. He nodded to them as they greeted him in a chorus and moved aside to let him pass. He waved to his secretary, Miss Blank, who had once been his ward in the orphanage. She replied with respect, informing him, "Thirty people have appointments to see you, Herr Presess."

He screwed up his face. "Thirty? I saw a hundred. Throw them out. From now on everyone who wants an appointment must write a petition and wait until we call him." He added mildly, "Once the militia begins to work properly, we'll have no trouble. Come here, you must take a letter."

They worked carefully and slowly on the letter. Chaim Rumkowski, as a rule impatient in his writing, was meticulous when it came to his correspondence with the authorities. The letter finished, the time had come for the interviews. He arranged the glasses on his nose, buttoned his jacket and sat up straight. He had mixed feelings about these daily interviews which he had introduced while still in the city. He was pleased with the submissive politeness, in particular of those who, before the war, had kept him waiting for hours in their own waiting rooms. He enjoyed the whining of the well-dressed women, the scent of powder and perfumes which issued from them, as well as the servile flame in their eyes. It was as if they were pledging something in exchange for a good position for their husbands or for themselves; he made a mental note of the most attractive amongst them, to make use of in calmer times. But what he was unable to bear was their syrupy narrations of personal tragedies, as if they were the navel of the world. Nor could he stand it when he detected an undertone of demand in their humble pleas, as if he, Rumkowski, owed them a debt which they had come to collect.

As he signed to Miss Blank to call in the first supplicant, she remarked, "A good friend of yours is waiting outside, Herr Presess. Mr. Samuel Zuckerman. Should I let him in first?"

The Presess was ready to nod, but he restrained himself. A cunning smirk appeared on his face, "There are no privileges here. Let him wait." [. . .]

The yard of the Fire Brigade was overflowing with people. The throngs had climbed onto the roofs of the latrine and the sheds, as well as onto the fire-wagons. Those who were unable to get into the yard were crowded into the neighbouring yards and the street. The entire ghetto had assembled, standing arm to arm, body to body, glued together, yet each alone with his or her fear. They stood in deadly silence, in tense awful expectation. The ghetto held its breath as it listened to the Steps of Fate. Human speech did not belong here. Words lost their meaning before they even reached the lips. The eyes of the people stopped exchanging glances. There was nothing left to think about, but one's own flesh and blood.

So perhaps had the people stood at the foot of Mount Sinai, waiting for God.

From an elevated platform the white prophetic head of Presess Rumkowski surfaced at last. The sky had acquired a pair of hands which rose above the black mass of the throng. The sky had acquired a mouth which through thunder and lightning pronounced the verdict. "Mothers, you must give up your children!" It struck a deafening blow, impossible to absorb. Words like mountains rolled down onto the sea of heads.

The faces in front of Mordecai Chaim became blurred. They were one black mass, one body collapsing into a fit. The earth shook with convulsions. A white foam appeared on thousands of mouths, "No!"

"Mothers!" the Presess called. "Save the ghetto! If we don't give up the children, not one of us will survive. We shall be erased from the face of the earth. If life continues, you will have other children. I cannot help it, brothers! They are demanding children up to ten years of age and old people over sixty-five. I took it upon myself to execute the 'action.' If the Germans come in, there will be a blood bath. Mothers! Make this sacrifice for the people! Let everything move smoothly tomorrow . . . so that we will be saved. . . ." His voice stopped serving him. Others of his entourage then tried to convince the crowd to surrender to the order peacefully.

The black convulsed body of a thousand writhing heads had no ears. A gray moss sprouted on the women's faces. The hair on their scalps stiffened into wires. Water trickled from between their legs.

In the neighbouring yard, which was also beleaguered, the cherry tree shook with the spasms of the crowd. Its dry withered boughs were stretched to the sky like arms trembling in prayer, in supplication; the hands of a dried-out mother. Pressed to the tree's trunk, embracing it, stood the Toffee Man, his sparse beard glued to the trunk like a climbing vine. Back to back with him stood Simcha Bunim Berkovitch, his glasses on the tip of his nose, his upper lip between his teeth. His pulled back cap revealed his sweaty forehead, its furrows cut through by swollen veins which seemed on the point of bursting.

"So that's that," squeaked the Toffee Man, shamelessly sobbing. "If God does not build the house, the builders toil in vain. . . . If God does not guard a city, the watchman watches in vain."

In Bunim's mind the wailing of the crowd mixed with Miriam's child-bearing screams. She had given birth last night. His wife had borne him a male child. Now Bunim would become an Abraham, striking down with his knife . . . for a ram would not appear. . . .

"When forests are on fire don't wail over the flowers that perish!" The voice of the speaker thundered across the back yard.

"Blimele," Bunim murmured his daughter's name.

In the other yard, the speeches went on and on, but the mass of people had begun to sway in the direction of the gate, of the street. Each street turned into a stormy flowing river, each yard into a swaying ship. The ghetto was swarming, wailing, collapsing with spasms, going out of its mind with grief. At last no one was hungry. Nowhere was there a fire lit in a stove. Like poisoned rats people raced through the yards in search of lairs, of holes, in which to hide the little Jews who had such knowing eyes. The children had been to the meeting, they had heard the speeches. They would not let go of their parents' hands for a moment.

The ghetto forgot about curfew. No one undressed or went to bed. Night arrived, but it did not touch the ghetto. Here it was daytime. A full black day of acute alertness. *Waivku Haam.* . . . And the people cried that night. The darkness swam in tears, the air lost its breath in horror.

The next morning the wagons of potatoes arrived, raining down the "gold of the sod" upon the mourning heads. The potato ration could be picked up only in the morning. The workers had been sent home from the Resorts and offices for an indefinite period, and the house arrest, or the *Sperre,* was supposed to begin in the afternoon.

Translated by Chava Rosenfarb in collaboration with Goldie Morgentaler.

Other works by Rosenfarb: *Di balade fun nekhtikn vald* (1948); *Bociany* (1983); *Of Lodz and Love* (2000); *Survivors: Seven Short Stories* (2005); *Exile at Last: Selected Poems* (2013).

Moacyr Scliar

1937–2011

Born in Porto Alegre, Brazil, Moacyr Scliar was one of the most acclaimed and widely translated Brazilian authors. The author of short-story collections and novels, he was credited with giving expression to the Jewish Brazilian experience. Also a public-health physician, Scliar received numerous awards, including from the Academia de Letras, the Brasília Prize, the Guimarães Rosa Prize, and the Brazil PEN Club Award.

A War Has No "Good End"
1972

II

In 1943, the nights were black. The country was at war with Germany and a blackout was instituted, perforated from time to time by fifth-columnists lighting cigarettes to reveal Bom Fim's defensive anti-aircraft position to the Stukas and Messerschmitts. The Nazis were everywhere; on Fernandes Vieira Street, they were discovered in a caramel factory, which was surrounded and set ablaze by the Fernandes Vieira military garrison. At the same time, a large number of milk-coffee bullets were also seized.

But, in general, the nights were quiet—winter nights, with practically deserted streets. Families gathered around the kitchen table. A samovar stood steaming. People took tea, ate crackers, latkes, sunflower seeds. From Oswaldo Aranha Street came the cry of the pine-nut vendor: "hot pine nuts," he would shout, "the pine nuts are hot." People would tell one story after another about Russia. The vendor's voice kept fading away; only the muffled rumble of the J. Abbot streetcar and the distant barking of the dog Melâmpio succeeded in breaking the silence. The neighbors said their good-byes, went back to their homes, walking bent over in the thick mist. "It's time for bed," Samuel announced to his children. Joel and Nathan slept in the same bed. They undressed slowly, looking at one another. Joel was short, with red hair and freckles; Nathan was pale and thin.

They got into bed.

Nathan never slept. He lay quietly, his eyes open, fixed on the padding of old boards, over which an old fat lively rat named Mendl was running. Joel looked at his brother and looked at the padding. Uneasily, he whispered: "Go to sleep, Nathan. Sleep, little brother." Placing his ear on his brother's skull, he heard sounds, fleeting notes.

In the distance, the searchlights of ships moored to the pier crisscrossed in the night, looking for Stukas and Messerschmitts.

III

Early in the morning, after drinking yerba mate, Samuel would go hitch the mare Malke Tube to the cart. This was no easy task; willfully, the mare wouldn't stop tossing her head. Samuel felt like whipping her, but was afraid of hurting the animal. He settled on cussing her out in Yiddish, while he fastened the harness.

Chagall, the painter of the floating violinists, was from Vitebsk, in Russia. Samuel, too, was from Russia. As a little boy, he had come to Brazil with his family. Like many other Jews who were tired of the squalor, snow, and pogroms of Czarist Russia. Marcos Yolovitch writes in this regard: "On a clear April morning in 19 . . . when the steppe was beginning to turn green again at the joyful entrance of spring, beautiful leaflets, with colored illustrations, were distributed in Zagradowka, a small, bubbly Russian hamlet situated in the province of Kherson. They described the excellent climate, fertile land, the richness and variety of the fauna, the beauty and exuberance of the forests, of a vast, faraway American country, called BRAZIL, where a Jewish colonizing company, the Jewish Colonization Association, more commonly known as JCA and the owner of large tracts of land on a ranch called Quatro Irmãos [Four Brothers], located in the municipality of Boa Vista do Erechim, in the State of Rio Grande do Sul, was offering settlements at advantageous terms to anyone wishing to become a farmer."

Samuel's father, Leon, acquired a piece of farming land in the Filipson settlement and built his house there. Those pioneers were an unhappy lot. Leon was a tailor; he knew how to handle a needle and thread, not a hoe. If he tried to cut down a tree, the tree would fall on top of him. If he made a fire in the forest, he would practically burn down his own house. Nothing went right. Grasshoppers devoured the first harvest, his wife was bitten by a snake, his oldest son had appendicitis and died. Leon began to drink. The family left the settlement and came by train to Porto Alegre. All they brought with them from Filipson in a freight car was the mare, Malke Tube.

IV

Malke Tube, the mare, used to be called Maliciosa [Mischief] . . .

Born on a cattle ranch, she was a very pretty animal—all white, around her left eye she had a black blotch, giving her a mischievous air, hence her name. She was really pretty and very sensual. The cattle rancher liked her. He had a special stable built for her and visited her often; he caressed her, muttering: "Mischief, my beauty . . ." One moon-lit night, the rancher wakes with a start. From the stable come muffled whinnies and sighs. He jumps out of bed, grabs his revolver and opens the door in time to see his farm hand running, stark naked, from the stable into the forest. Furious, the rancher has the farm hand horse-whipped and the mare killed. Charged with both tasks, the foreman performs the first one with pleasure, but, pulling out his knife to gut the mare, he is filled with remorse. Instead of killing her, he sells her to Soares de Castro, a plantation owner.

Being a fearless man, he mounts the mare and goes off to wage war.

A fracas breaks out. Swords are crossed; the smell of blood fills the air. Half-crazed, Mischief retreats from the enemy, throwing her rider to the ground and fleeing into a wooded area. Furious and humiliated, the warrior pursues her with a revolver in his hand. He is ready to annihilate the diabolical creature once and for all.

He finds the mare in a thicket. It is a moon-lit night . . . The mare is beautiful. All white, with an impish spot around her mischievously blinking eye. Blood and love . . . Burning desire . . . He succumbs to the mare's charms. Exhausted afterwards, he tumbles into some weeds, where he falls asleep and dreams of centaurs.

Silently, the mare moves away from him. Free at last, she gallops through the fields. Days later, famished and caked in mud, she arrives at Filipson and finds shelter in old Leon's stable.

He discovers her the following day. Filled with joy, he calls his family and they surround the mare, which is resting on the straw. One family member brings some water, another fresh grass, and a third washes her. This is the first gift that they have ever received. Old Leon cries and thanks the Almighty. He christens her "Malke Tube" and hitches her to the cart. The mare bucks, her eyes ablaze with fury, pawing anyone coming near her. Finally, old Leon loses his patience and whips her. Malke Tube surrenders.

Six months later, the family leaves Filipson for Porto Alegre. Tube goes with them—in a freight car—watching the rolling hillside recede into the distance.

At Bom Fim, the mare grows old and loses her lascivious streak. She is resigned to pull Samuel's cart. But her eyes have lost their glow and at night, she dreams of centaurs.

V

Samuel. Samuel sold goods in installments. Seated in his cart, he penetrated the very "pores of society" (Marx). He and Malke Tube traveled throughout the city, from the African Colony at the foot of Morro da Velha, climbing hills and leaping valleys. Perspiring, they brought the latest novelties to their customers, mistrustful people who had little to say and kept their money under the mattress. Samuel would show them flashy fabrics, awakening secret hopes. Yes, he was the one who brought a glow to the eyes of the three mulatto women. He sold them pink dresses with green flowers.

They maintained their modesty during the day, while, at night, they would get up stealthily, get dressed and bedeck themselves, looking at themselves coquettishly in the mirror by candlelight.

Translated by Marvin Meital.

Other works by Scliar: *O carnaval dos animais* (1968); *Os deuses de Raquel* (1975).

Clarice Lispector

1920–1977

Clarice Lispector was born Chaya Pinkhasovna Lispector in Chechelnik, Ukraine. During the pogroms, her mother was raped and contracted syphilis. The family fled Ukraine in 1921, making their way to Maceió, Alagoas, Brazil in 1922. In 1925, they moved to Recife, to better treat her mother's illness; she died when Clarice was nine. Her mother's illness and early death left a strong impact in much of Lispector's writings, especially *Felicidade clandestina* (1971). In 1940, Lispector published her first story, "Triunfo," in *Pan*, while studying law at the University of Brazil. Months later she published "Me and Jimmy" in *Vamos ler!*, spawning a prolific literary career. Her first novel, *Near to the Wild Heart* (1943) won her the Graça Aranha Prize and national acclaim as an emotional, introspective exploration of Brazilian identity.

The Stream of Life

1973

There is much I cannot tell you. I am not going to be autobiographical. I want to be "bio."

I write with the flow of the words.

Before the appearance of the mirror, the person didn't know his own face except reflected in the waters of a lake. After a certain point everyone is responsible for the face he has. I'll now look at mine. It is a naked face. And when I think that no other like it exists in the world, I get a happy shock. Nor will there ever be. Never is the impossible. I like never. I also like ever. What is there between never and ever that links them so indirectly and intimately?

At the bottom of everything there is the hallelujah.

This instant is. You who read me are.

I find it hard to believe that I shall die. Because I'm bubbling in cold freshness. My life will be very long because each instant is. I get the feeling I'm about to be born and can't.

I am a heart beating in the world.

You who are reading me please help me to be born.

Wait: it's getting dark. Darker.

And darker.

The instant is of total darkness.

It goes on.

Wait: I begin to glimpse a thing. A luminescent shape. A milky belly with a navel? Wait—because I shall emerge from this darkness where I am afraid, darkness and ecstasy. I am the heart of the shadow.

The problem is that the curtain over the window of my room is defective. It is stuck and so it doesn't close. So the whole full moon enters and phosphoresces the room with silences: it's horrible.

Now the shadows are retreating.

I was born.

Pause.

Marvelous scandal: I am born.

My eyes are shut. I am pure unconsciousness. They already cut the umbilical cord: I am unattached in the universe. I don't think but feel the *it*. With my eyes I blindly seek the breast: I want thick milk. No one taught me to want. But I already want. I'm lying with my eyes open looking at the ceiling. Inside is the darkness. An I that pulses already forms. There are sunflowers. There is tall wheat. I is.

I hear the hollow boom of time. It's the world deafly forming. If I can hear that is because I exist before the formation of time. "I am" is the world. World without time. My consciousness now is light and it is air. Air has neither place nor time. Air is the non-place where everything will exist. What I am writing is the music of the air. The formation of the world. Slowly what will be approaches. What will be already is. The future is ahead and behind and to either side. The future is what always existed and always will exist. Even if Time is abolished? What I'm writing to you is not for reading—it's for being. The trumpets of the angel-beings echo in the without time. The first flower is born in the air. The ground that is earth forms. The rest is air and the rest is slow fire in perpetual mutation. Does the word "perpetual" not exist because time does not exist? But the boom exists. And this existence of mine starts to exist. Is that time starting?

It suddenly occurred to me that you don't need order to live. There is no pattern to follow and the pattern itself doesn't even exist: I am born.

I'm still not ready to talk about "he" or "she." I demonstrate "that." That is universal law. Birth and death. Birth. Death. Birth and—like a breathing of the world.

I am pure *it* that was pulsing rhythmically. But I can feel that soon I shall be ready to talk about he or she. I'm not promising you a story here. But there's *it*. Bearable? *It* is soft and is oyster and is placenta. I am not joking because I am not a synonym—I am the name itself. There is a thread of steel going through all that I am writing you. There's the future. Which is today.

My vast night goes by in the primary of a latency. The hand touches the earth and listens hotly to a heart pulsing. I see the great white slug with a woman's breasts: is that a human entity? I burn it in an inquisitorial bonfire. I have the mysticism of the darkness of a remote past. And I emerge from these victims' tortures with the indescribable mark that symbolizes life. Elemental creatures, dwarves, gnomes, goblins and sprites surround me. I sacrifice animals to collect the blood I need for my witching ceremonies. In my fury I offer up my soul in its own blackness. The mass frightens me—me who carries it out. And the clouded mind dominates matter. The beast bares its teeth and in the distance of the air gallop the horses of the carnival floats.

In my night I idolise the secret meaning of the world. Mouth and tongue. And a horse free with loosed strength. I keep its hoof in amorous fetishism. In my deep night a mad wind blows that brings me scraps of screams.

I am feeling the martyrdom of an untimely sensuality. In the early hours I awake full of fruit. Who will come to gather the fruit of my life? If not you and I myself? Why is it that things an instant before they happen already seem to have happened? It's because of the simultaneity of rime. And so I ask you questions and these will be many. Because I am a question.

And in my night I feel the evil that rules me. What is called a beautiful landscape causes me nothing but fatigue. What I like are landscapes of dry and baked earth, with contorted trees and mountains made of rock and with a whitish and suspended light. There, yes, a hidden beauty lies. I know that you don't like art either. I was born hard, heroic, alone, and standing. And I found my counterpoint in the landscape without picturesqueness and without beauty. Ugliness is my banner of war. I love the ugly with the love of equals. And I defy death. I—I am my own death. And no one goes further. The barbarian within me seeks the cruel barbarian outside me. I see in light and dark I the faces of people flickering in the flames of the bonfire. I am a tree that burns with hard pleasure. A single sweetness possesses me: complicity with the world. I love my cross,

which I painfully carry. It's the least I can make of my life: accept commiserably the sacrifice of the night.

The strangeness takes me: so I open the black umbrella and throw myself into a feast of dancing where stars sparkle. The furious nerve inside me and that contorts. Until the early hours come and find me bloodless. The early hours are great and eat me. The gale calls me. I follow it and tear myself to pieces. If I don't enter the game that unfolds in life I shall lose my own life in a suicide of my species. I protect with fire the game of my life. When the existence of me and of the world can no longer be borne by reason—then I loose myself and follow a latent truth. Would I recognise the truth if it were proven?

I am making myself. I make myself until I reach the pit.

About me in the world I want to tell you about the strength that guides me and brings me the world itself, about the vital sensuality of clear structures, and about the curves that are organically connected to other curved shapes. My handwriting and my circumvolutions are potent and the freedom that blows in summer has fatality in itself. The eroticism that belongs to whatever is living is scattered in the air, in the sea, in the plants, in us, scattered in the vehemence of my voice, I write you with my voice. And there is a vigor of the robust trunk, of roots buried in the living earth that reacts giving great sustenance. I breathe the energy by night. And all this in the realm of the fantastic. Fantastic: the world for an instant is exactly what my heart asks. I am about to die and construct new compositions. I'm expressing myself very badly and the right words escape me. My internal form has been carefully purified and yet my bond with the world has the naked crudity of free dreams and of great realities. I do not know prohibition. And my own strength frees me, that full life that overflows me. And I plan nothing in my intuitive work of living: I work with the indirect, the informal and the unforeseen.

Now in the early hours I am pale and gasping for breath and have a dry mouth dry in the face of what I achieve. Nature in choral canticle and I dying. What does nature sing? the last word itself that is never again I. The centuries will fall upon me. But for now a fierceness of body and soul that shows itself in the rich scalding of heavy words that trample one another—and something wild, primary and enervated rises from my swamps, the accursed plant that is about to surrender to God. The more accursed, the nearer toward the

God. I deepened myself in myself and found that I want bloody life, and the occult meaning has an intensity that has light. It is the secret light of a knowledge of fatality: the cornerstone of the earth. It is more an omen of life than actual life. I exorcise it excluding the profane. In my world little freedom of action is granted me. I am free only to carry out the fatal gestures.

Translated by Stefan Tobler.

Other works by Lispector: *Family Ties* (1960); *The Passion According to G.H.* (1964); *A descoberta do mundo* (1984).

Jack Ludwig

1922–2018

Winnipeg-born writer Jack Ludwig lived most of his adult life in the United States, although his native city greatly influenced his work. With a doctorate in English literature from the University of California, Los Angeles, he taught at the University of Minnesota and State University of New York at Stony Brook and spent time as writer-in-residence at the University of Toronto. A close friend of Saul Bellow, he appeared as the character Valentine Gersbach in Bellow's 1964 novel *Herzog*. Ludwig worked as a sportswriter in the 1960s and coedited the collection *Soundings: New Canadian Poets* (1971) with Andy Wainwright.

A Woman of Her Age
1973

I

Once a week, even now, Mrs Goffman makes that chauffeur drive her slowly down from the mountain, back to St Lawrence Boulevard and Rachel Street [in Montreal]; she doesn't want any old cronies who might still be alive spotting her in that hearse of a limousine, so she gets out a couple of blocks from the Market and walks the rest of the way, not in her Persian lamb or her warm beaver, but in that worn cloth coat she bought at Eaton's Basement years ago, the black one. Long, gaunt as a late afternoon shadow, Mrs Goffman concentrates on smiling. Otherwise she looks like a spook. At seventy-five you can feel warm, sweet, girlish even, but an old old face has trouble expressing soft feelings. Those reddish-brown eyebrows that didn't turn white with the rest of her hair, they're to blame, so bushy, so fierce,

with an ironic twist that was snappy when she was a hot young radical, but now, when she's old enough to be a great-grandmother, who needs it?

"Wordsworth," her son Jimmy used to call her. In a drugstore window she sees reflected Wordsworth's broad forehead, deep-set eyes, small mouth, short chin. By God, she tells herself, this is a darned good face. Jimmy had this face. Her father had it too—who knows how far back these purplish lips go, or the dark rings under the eyes, or the pale olive complexion? Moses might have had similar colouring. Her nose gives a sly twitch to call attention to itself: Wordsworth's large humped nose she has too, and it deserves the dominant spot it earned for itself on Mrs Goffman's face. She judges everything by its smell. That's why the ambassador's mansion she lives in flunks so badly—it's not only quiet as a church, it smells like a church. Six days a week her nose puts up with that dry lonely quiet smell, does what a nose is supposed to do in Westmount, breathe a little: on St Lawrence Boulevard a nose is for smelling, and Mrs Goffman doesn't miss a sniff. Families are getting ready for sabbath.

Doba, catch that goose roasting, her nose seems to say. Hey, poppyseed cookies! Real stuffed fish! St Lawrence Boulevard, I love you!

II

Mitchell the "Kosher Butcher" nodded his usual pitying nod as she walked past his full window—fresh-killed ducks and chickens hanging by their feet, cows' brains in pools, tongues like holsters, calves' feet signed by the Rabbi's indelible pencil. Mrs Goffman nodded her black-turbaned head at Mitchell but he'd already given his nod, and only stared back, open-mouthed, his hands pressed against his slaughterhouse-looking apron. Naturally Mitchell has her pegged: doesn't he know this shopping trip is a fake, that Mrs Grosney, the cook, does Mrs Goffman's buying and cooking? Mitchell knows about the Persian lamb coat she doesn't wear to Market. Mitchell knew her dead husband well. Mitchell, like all of Montreal, knows the story of her dead son Jimmy.

When Simon-may-he-rest-in-peace was still alive the Goffmans lived down here, among people, in life. Now life was a novelty to Mrs Goffman. Six days to Westmount, one to St Lawrence and Rachel Street, what idiotic arrangement was that? Some day she'd get real tough with her son Sidney. Marry him off. Make him sell the Ambassador's mansion and lead a normal life.

Her eyebrows went into their ironic arch. You, Doba, they seemed to mock her, when could you get your kids to do anything?

Other works by Ludwig: *Confusions* (1963); *Above Ground* (1968); *Hockey Night in Moscow* (1972).

Esther Seligson

1941–2010

Born into a family of Orthodox Jews in Mexico City, Esther Seligson had a prolific writing and teaching career that began in her twenties. She wrote prize-winning novels, short stories, and poetry, contributed to periodicals, and translated literary and philosophical works by authors such as Yourcenar, Woolf, and Cioran into Spanish. Having studied at various academic institutions in Mexico, France, and Israel, Seligson became a teacher of wide-ranging subjects including theater, Jewish philosophy, medieval art, and comparative religion. Her work was furthered and focused by foreign travel, with visits to or residence in many parts of the world, including Paris, Lisbon, and Jerusalem. She died in Mexico City.

Dreams Older Than Memory
1973

The alphabet doesn't have enough letters, you say, to form the names of so many inexpressible feelings, unexpressed for lack of words, and I say to you that we don't have enough life, that too much longing weighs on us for such a short time, that too many worries seethe in so little space. Perhaps it's not the letters' fault but the fact that, as Bernard reflects, sometimes we're too lazy to go searching all over the city for our friend. Today we must go further back than our own past, beyond all personal memory, all the way back to the pain of the crematoria, the heretical pyres, all the way to the curse of the cross and the first exodus, we must wander the desert, thirsty starving people waiting for manna and the Rock of life, dragging that true solitude of ours through the sands and burning bushes without asking who we are or where we're going, just chanting psalms, singing as evening falls around the column of smoke and fire.

Translated by Michele McKay Aynesworth.

Other works by Seligson: *Diálogos con el cuerpo* (1981); *La morada en el tiempo* (1981); *Escritura y el enigma de la otredad* (2000).

POETRY AND POPULAR SONG

Blanche Bendahan

1903–1975

A poet and novelist, Blanche Bendahan was born in Oran, Algeria, to a family of Spanish descent. She was raised and educated in France and published her first anthology of poems, *La voile sur l'eau* in 1926. Her highly-regarded novel *Mazaltob* (1930) portrays a woman struggling with traditional Moroccan family values in the face of modern French influences.

Bull
1948

The trains watch us dreaming
in these charming meadows.
—For we don't love eating
so much as some fellows!—

Gorging suits humans,
they crave sauce and meat.
Me, I love to chew on
grass, so green and sweet.

Men chew on things, too,
like rivalry and riot;
for me such bitter brew's
an unhealthy diet.

On top of that, I don't know why
you'll hear them say "he's horny";
well, I see nothing there at all,
his brow's just flat and corny.

But man allots by measure,
meting out in drops
the clumsy toro's pleasure:
these limits have to stop!

On us, my herd, the curse
is laid a thousand ways:
and when my son is nursed
it's in a stew or braised.

And when allowed to grow,
my son's soon highly rated;
but my tireless young beau
is, in the end, castrated,

a source of steak and stew meat
for man, the opprobrious;
he ends his life as mincemeat
in the slaughterhouse-terminus.

Is it better to keep
our paraphernalia,
performing at peak
in all our regalia?

When a bull's done his duty,
men clap and start joking,
but it's no thing of beauty
to clap when he's croaking!

The trains watch me dreaming,
but my dream's just this:
to eat outraged humans.
Now that would be bliss!

Translated by Michele McKay Aynesworth.

Other work by Bendahan: *Messieurs, vous êtes impuissants* (1961).

Olga Kirsch

1924–1997

Poet Olga Kirsch was born in the town of Koppies in the Orange Free State of South Africa. While a student at the University of the Witwatersrand in Johannesburg, Kirsch made a conscious political decision to write in Afrikaans rather than English, and she is the only Jewish writer of note to have done so. In 1948, she settled in Israel, where she taught English but continued to publish primarily in Afrikaans.

Nostalgia
1948

If I forget thee, O Jerusalem, let my right hand forget itself.

Give us the land we have wandered in time
Through foreign parts, far, so far and then,
Every year at Passover we repeat the line
Next year we shall see Jerusalem

Perhaps I shall never enter the land,
Nor those who follow, but is a people's hope
Not timeless like heaven's orbit band
Wherein a single being is subsumed like smoke

And will the wanderers through all earth's
    plains
Not receive the land in future times
With a Joy that bans their future pains
Forever from their thoughts and minds?

Yet the silent longing remains unstilled
O land, my land, o rest yet unfulfilled.

Translated by Andries Wessels.

Other works by Kirsch: *Die soeklig* (1944); *Mure van die Hart* (1948); *Negentien gedigte* (1972); *Afskeide* (1982); *The Book of Sitrya* (1990).

César Tiempo

1906–1980

César Tiempo was the pen name of the Argentine poet, playwright, and screenwriter Israel Zeitlin, who was born in Dnipropetrovsk, Ukraine, and brought to Buenos Aires as an infant. A prominent figure in Argentine literary circles, he wrote more than three dozen screenplays for the Argentine cinema. His plays and poetry feature Jewish characters and Jewish themes, and they were often concerned with the downtrodden and the exploited of society. He was also a vocal critic of Argentine antisemitism.

Paraphrase
1955

The Bible tells us that from the heights
Moses blessed the children of Israel,
showing them God's Promised Land,
where Moses himself never entered.

Like ships passing by when land is in sight
so Moses passed the promised land by,
a demiurge leading his flock of the dead
toward a chance of resurrection.

Like him, dreamers, and like him,
    wanderers,
they stop a while to gaze upon
the verdant, long-sought paradises.

Suffering and resolute as the sun sets,
they prostrate themselves on the barren hill
to let God know that Israel will pass.

Translated by Michele McKay Aynesworth.

Other works by Tiempo: *Máscaras y caras* (1943); *Así quería Gardel* (1955); *Pan criollo* (1968).

Irving Layton

1912–2006

Born Israel Lazarovitch in Târgu Neamţ, Romania, Irving Layton immigrated with his family to Montreal at the age of twelve. Layton was a flamboyant poet who railed against bourgeois dullness and believed that Canadian poetry needed to break away from British traditionalism and establish its own style. Known as much for his private life as for his writing, Layton helped establish the cooperative poetry publishing house Contact Press in 1952, and taught poetry at several Canadian universities. In 1967, he received the Canada Council Award. which enabled him to travel to Israel, Greece, Nepal, and India, travels that would influence his later writings. He was a professor of poetry at York University.

On Seeing the Statuettes of Ezekiel and Jeremiah in the Church of Notre Dame
1956

They have given you French names
    and made you captive, my rugged
troublesome compatriots;
    your splendid beards, are epicene,
plaster white
        and your angers
unclothed with Palestinian hills quite lost
in this immense and ugly edifice.

You are bored—I see it—sultry prophets
    with priests and nuns
(What coarse jokes must pass between you)
    and with those morbidly religious
i.e. my prize brother-in-law
        ex-Lawrencian
pawing his rosary, and his wife
sick with many guilts.

Believe me I would gladly take you
    from this spidery church

its bad melodrama, its musty smell of candle
    and set you both free again
in no make-believe world
      of sin and penitence
but the sunlit square opposite
alive at noon with arrogant men.

Yet cheer up Ezekiel and you Jeremiah
    who were once cast into a pit;
I shall not leave you here incensed, uneasy
    among alien Catholic saints
but shall bring you from time to time
      my hot Hebrew heart
as passionate as your own, and stand
with you here awhile in aching confraternity.

Other works by Layton: *A Red Carpet for the Sun*
(1960); *Lovers and Lesser Men* (1973); *Seventy-Five
Greek Poems* (1974); *Fortunate Exile* (1987).

Sadia Lévy

1875–1951

Poet, editor, and novelist Sadia Lévy was born in
Oran, Algeria, into a family with roots in Gibraltar.
He studied at the École de sciences politique in Paris,
where he was part of a literary circle which included
the poets Guillaume Apollinaire and Max Jacob. In
addition to French, Lévy was fluent in Hebrew and the
Judeo-Maghrebi dialects of Spanish and Arabic. With
Robert Randau, head of the Algerian literary movement, Levy wrote *Rabbin* (1896), one of the first novels
describing the daily lives and customs of Jews in North
Africa. Because of the Vichy regime's antisemitic laws,
his most important work, *Abishag*, remained unpublished until after his death.

Prélude, Abishag
1957

For my daughter Nedjé
and for her husband Armand Bengui.

Where word and spirit make feeling divine
I see creation and I see poetry . . .
But I know I risk the sin of heresy
If I say the words and spirit are mine.

For they come from the Love that governs me,
Though I want to believe in my fantasy!
Where leadest Thou my soul in its reverie,

God of whom I am Christ, prophet, king?

Women of azure breasts, heralds strange
Whom the Greeks were wont to call angels,
You are Hippocrene, the only Zion.

More elusive than dreamers' choirs,
Inspiration is the suckling of Muses,
Their gift to the mouths of liars.

Translated by Michele McKay Aynesworth.

Other works by Lévy: *Rabbin* (with Robert Randau,
1896); *La Geste éparse de Kehath ben Lévi* (1905–1906);
Sensations d'un égorgé (1922); *Treize á la douzaine*
(1932).

Phyllis Gotlieb

1926–2009

The only child of a father who owned a movie theater,
Toronto-born Phyllis Gotlieb (b. Bloom) originally
wanted to be a poet, though she is now best-known
for her speculative fiction. Writing science fiction in
earnest, she ignited her career with the publication of
Sunburst (1964). She went on to write *Why Should I
Have All the Grief?* (1969), a novel about the Holocaust
and its effects on Jewish life in Canada, as well as several poetry collections and an analysis of the work of
poet A. M. Klein. A testament to her achievement, the
Sunburst Award for best speculative fiction book of the
year was named in honor of Gotlieb's novel.

This One's on Me
1960

1. The lives and times of Oedipus and Elektra
began with bloodgrim lust and dark carnality
but I was born next to the Neilson's factory
where every piece is different, and that's how
    I got
my individuality.

2. I lived on Gladstone Avenue,
2 locations on Kingston Rd.
2 crescents, Tennis and Chaplin
Xanadu, Timbuktu,
Samarkand & Ampersand
and many another exotic locality.

3. My grandparents came from the ghettos
of Russia and Poland with no mementos

one grandfather was a furrier, one a tailor,
grey men in dark rooms tick tack to
gether dry snuffy seams of fur and fibre
my father managed a theatre

4. which one day (childhood reminiscence
   indicated) passing
on a Sunday ride, we found
the burglar alarm was ring
alingaling
out jumped my father and ran for the front door
Uncle Louie ran for the back
siren scream down the cartrack Danforth
and churchbells ding dong ding
(ting a ling)
and brakescreech whooee
six fat squadcars filled with the finest
of the force of our fair city
brass button boot refulgent
and in their plainclothes too
greysuit felthat and flat black footed
and arrested Uncle Louie
Oh what a brannigan
what a brouhaha
while Mother and Aunt Gittel and me
sat in the car and shivered delicious
ly

because a mouse bit through a wire.

5. For some the dance of the sugar-plum fairies
means that.
but the Gryphons and Gorgons of my dreams
dance in the salon of Miss Peregrine Peers
stony eyed, stone footed on Church Street
up grey stairs
where two doors down at Dr Weams I
gnawed his smoky fingers and followed
the convolutions of his twisted septum
as he stretched and knotted little twines of silver
on the rack of my oral cavity
and all the while Miss Peregrine Peers
turn tiddy turn tiddy TUM TUM TUM
O Peregrine O Miss Peers
I find you no longer in life's directories
may you rest in peace
and I do mean

6. Where, oh where are the lovely ladies who taught
   me
to break the

Hearts And trample the *Flowers* of the muses?
                Mrs Reeves
gracile, a willow on a Chinese plate, who
winced with an indrawn gasp when I struck a
   wrong
not, or blew my nose in her handkerchief
absentmindedly?
Miss Marll, under whose tutelage icecubes
popped from the pores of my arm
pits and slid down to drop from my
ELBOWS HELD HIGH FINGERS CURVED ON THE KEYS
may you rot in hell
subtly, Miss Marll.

7. O child of the thirties
of stonewarm porches and spiraea snowfalls
in print cotton dress with matching panties hanging
   well down
(the faded snapshot says)
hand on the fender of the Baby Austin
(feel the heat and glare)
gaptooth grin to be converted by braces
myopic eyes fit for glasses
and tin ears waiting to be bent
by the patient inexorable piano teacher
the postered car advertises in innocence:
LADIES OF LEISURE
See it at the Eastwood Theatre, friends,
next time 1930 rolls around.

Other works by Gotlieb: *Who Knows One?* (1961);
Within the Zodiac (1964); *Ordinary, Moving* (1969); *O
Master Caliban!* (1976).

Nissim Ezekiel

1924-2004

Indian poet, dramatist, critic, broadcaster, and
social commentator Nissim Ezekiel was raised in the
Marathi-speaking Bene Israel Jewish community of
Bombay. He studied literature and philosophy and,
after a brief time in England, began to publish poetry,
influenced by writers Ted Hughes and Philip Larkin.
He wrote defiantly in English and taught that language
at Mumbai University and Mithibai College. He also
helped found the literary monthly *Imprint* and was
a contributing editor and art critic for the *Times of
India* and *Poetry India*. Ezekiel's work earned him the
Padma-Shri, India's highest civilian honor.

Jewish Wedding in Bombay
1962

Her mother shed a tear or two but wasn't really
crying. It was the thing to do, so she did it
enjoying every moment. The bride laughed when I
sympathized, and said don't be silly.

Her brothers had a shoe of mine and made me pay
to get it back. The game delighted all the
neighbours'
children, who never stopped staring at me, the
reluctant
bridegroom of the day.

There was no dowry because they knew I was
"modern"
and claimed to be modern too. Her father asked
me how
much jewellery I expected him to give away with his
daughter.
When I said I didn't know, he laughed it off.

There was no brass band outside the synagogue
but I remember a chanting procession or two, some
rituals,
lots of skull-caps, felt hats, decorated shawls
and grape juice from a common glass for bride and
bridegroom.

I remember the breaking of the glass and the
congregation
clapping which signified that we were well and truly
married
according to the Mosaic Law.

Well that's about all. I don't think there was much
that struck me as solemn or beautiful. Mostly, we
were
amused, and so were the others. Who knows how
much belief
we had?

Even the most orthodox it was said ate beef
because it
was cheaper, and some even risked their souls by
relishing pork.
The Sabbath was for betting and swearing and
drinking.

Nothing extravagant, mind you, all in a low key
and very decently kept in check. My father used
to say,

these orthodox chaps certainly know how to draw
the line
in their own crude way. He himself had drifted into
the liberal
creed but without much conviction, taking us all
with him.
My mother was very proud of being "progressive."

Anyway as I was saying, there was that clapping and
later
we went to the photographic studio of Lobo and
Fernandes,
world-famous specialists in wedding portraits. Still
later,
we lay on a floor-mattress in the kitchen of my wife's
family apartment and though it was past midnight
she
kept saying let's do it darling let's do it darling
so we did it.

More than ten years passed before she told me that
she remembered being very disappointed. Is that all
there is to it? She had wondered. Back from London
eighteen months earlier, I was horribly out of
practice.

During our first serious marriage quarrel she said
Why did
you take my virginity from me? I would gladly have
returned it, but not one of the books I had read
instructed me how.

Other works by Ezekiel: *Time to Change* (1952);
The Discovery of India (1956); *The Exact Name* (1965);
Hymns in Darkness (1976); *Collected Poems* (1989).

Rokhl Korn
1898–1982

From her earliest publications in Yiddish, the poet and
prose writer Rokhl Korn was applauded by critics for
her forceful use of natural imagery, a tight control over
language, and an alarming directness in style. Born
on a farming estate in Sucha Gora, Galicia, Korn was
influenced by Rachel Auerbach to abandon Polish and
embrace Yiddish instead as the language of Jewish self-
expression and pride. After a period of wandering and
dislocation in Moscow, Soviet Central Asia, and Scandinavia during and after World War II, Korn settled in
Montreal, becoming one of the city's leading Yiddish

cultural figures in the postwar era. While retaining the qualities of her earlier work, her later poetry was also suffused with themes of pain, loss, suffering, and loneliness.

On the Other Side of the Poem
1962

On the other side of the poem there is an orchard,
and in the orchard, a house with a roof of straw,
and three pine trees,
three watchmen who never speak, standing guard.

On the other side of the poem there is a bird,
yellow brown with a red breast,
and every winter he returns
and hangs like a bud in the naked bush.

On the other side of the poem there is a path
as thin as a hairline cut,
and someone lost in time
is treading the path barefoot, without a sound.

On the other side of the poem amazing things may
    happen,
even on this overcast day,
this wounded hour
that breathes its fevered longing in the windowpane.

On the other side of the poem my mother may
    appear
and stand in the doorway for a while lost in thought
and then call me home as she used to call me home
    long ago:
Enough play, Rokhl. Don't you see it's night?

Translated by Seymour Levitan.

Other works by Korn: *Royter mon* (1937); *Heym un heymlozikayt* (1948); *Bashertkayt* (1949); *Nayn dertsey-lungen* (1957).

Jeanne Benguigui
1931–2011

Jeanne Benguigui was born and raised in Sidi-Bel-Abbès, Algeria. A teacher by profession, she published her first book of poetry, *L'Arbre de vie,* in 1958 while living in Belgium, where she was recovering from tuberculosis. Benguigui spent much of her life in Vaires sur Marne, France, publishing more than twenty volumes of poetry. She received numerous prizes for her literary work, including for her collection of stories and legends about her birthplace, *Contes de Sidi-Bel-Abbès,* published in 1992.

Song of Exile
1963

Foreign to me are trees in bloom
And grass and air and sky
What storms have banished me
From Eden
What blazing fire from the sun

Your wind won't dry these tears
Land of exile
Your rain won't radiate my soul
Land of exile
Slanting rain of hatred
Acid rain of exile

Guardians caught in the trap
Your foolish willow trees weep
Your mawkish poplar trees weep

Mercilessly you watch me
Land of exile
You've found me proud and black
Challenging your soot-filled sky
Where a bizarre sunbeam sneers

I watch you without love
Land of exile
When savoring your thick grass
Where fine nettles rasp
I find you low and lifeless

I haven't shaped your forests
In my eyes
Your stars
Have not ripened your silences
Or weighed your smiles
On the charred branches of my vows
Rose of exile

My land was made ashes by love
Beneath that sky where slight birds fly
My rain of chiseled crystal
Pelting, pouring down
Where are you, you who call me

Where are you my gentle knights
Pure pilgrims of the stars' rain
You sculpt the anonymous night

Immobile palms in your coats of mail
Consoling earth and sky with your palms
Serene sages under the stars
Watch, watch over the oasis

Where am I going so far from you
Losing my petals of snow
Losing my life
Losing my death
Butterfly of the world's end
Tree bird uprooted

My wings have lost their leaves
My spiritual roots
Must retrace the paths of Eden

I don't want to vanish
In your swamps and your rivers
Closed world of exile

My eyes' dark dew
Will intoxicate you Rose of embers
My arid land of low grasses
Calls for the blood of my death

I am going
To return my dust
To you
Jealous Fatherland
Mother

*At the château of Quesnay
land of nettles*

Translated by Michele McKay Aynesworth.

Other works by Benguigui: *Un long tunnel de lumière* (1969); *Une pierre sur chaque mot* (1978); *Arpenter la forme parfaite* (1983); *Les Parenthèses du Néant* (1985); *Le Déménagement* (1995).

Miriam Waddington

1917–2004

Born and raised in Winnipeg, poet Miriam Waddington (b. Dworkin) was surrounded by a rich, intellectual circle of Yiddish-speaking secular and socialist Jews. In 1930, her family moved to Ottawa, and there the young poet's writing developed under the guidance of the Yiddish poet Ida Maze. Initially trained as a social worker, Waddington joined the English department at Toronto's York University in 1962, where her creativity flourished as a poet, critic, and translator.

Second Generation
1966

Child of a lonely traveller
in a strange country
I live towards my doom
closed in a small tight room.

Closed in a small tight room
where whitehaired quiet ladies
claw the walls   conspire in lies
and wicked things to come.

Closed in this small tight room
there is a warm illimitable
thing inside me keeps me
alive and proud and sane.

Had my father known what
his children would suffer
through the oiled words
and dull circumstance,

had my father dreamed the cunning
of this anglo-saxon conference,
he had never ventured beyond
the plains of home   bloody and

cruel and violent as life was
he would never have brought us
to this small tight room
to this bite-your-tongue-off doom.

Other works by Waddington: *Green World* (1945); *The Second Silence* (1955); *The Season's Lovers* (1958); *The Glass Trumpet* (1966); *Driving Home: Poems New and Selected* (1972).

Leonard Cohen

The Story of Isaac
1968

The door it opened slowly,
My father he came in,
I was nine years old.
And he stood so tall above me,
His blue eyes they were shining
And his voice was very cold.
He said, "I've had a vision

And you know I'm strong and holy,
I must do what I've been told."
So he started up the mountain,
I was running, he was walking,
And his axe was made of gold.

Well, the trees they got much smaller,
The lake a lady's mirror,
We stopped to drink some wine.
Then he threw the bottle over.
Broke a minute later
And he put his hand on mine.
Thought I saw an eagle
But it might have been a vulture,
I never could decide.
Then my father built an altar,
He looked once behind his shoulder,
He knew I would not hide.

You who build these altars now
To sacrifice these children,
You must not do it anymore.
A scheme is not a vision
And you never have been tempted
By a demon or a god.
You who stand above them now,
Your hatchets blunt and bloody,
You were not there before,
When I lay upon a mountain
And my father's hand was trembling
With the beauty of the word.

And if you call me brother now,
Forgive me if I inquire,
"just according to whose plan?"
When it all comes down to dust
I will kill you if I must,
I will help you if I can.
When it all comes down to dust
I will help you if I must,
I will kill you if I can.
And mercy on our uniform,
Man of peace or man of war,
The peacock spreads his fan.

Max Guedj
b. 1936

Max Guedj is a psychotherapist, poet, and author of novels and plays. Guedj has taught at Paris Nanterre University and has been active in the Quatrième Groupe of French analysis since 1990.

Quai Blériot
1969

It all began one wild dawn
The barges slid by under torrents of rain
The clouds raced past shredded and torn
above charcoal-glinting roofs

    Two bourgeois dogs passed by with a sideways
      gait

The silhouette of a woman hesitated
turning toward Javel
Downstairs could be heard
the harsh sound of a small bell that abruptly rings
and stops then the window sputtered and buzzed

    The sky went streaming on
unwaveringly
on a pasty tin-plate background
the street darkly gleamed
like the rump of a pensive mare

on that day
I felt the strangeness of being

Translated by Michele McKay Aynesworth.

Other works by Guedj: *Le Bar à Campora, comédie dramatique en 4 actes* (1972); *Le Voyage en Barbarie* (1977); *L'Homme au basilic* (1991); *Le Cerveau argentin* (1996); *Le Voyage de Vlad à Frisco, ou La pluie* (2005).

Albert Bensoussan
b. 1935

Author, translator, and scholar Albert Bensoussan was born in Algiers into a traditional Jewish family that traced its roots to medieval Spain and North Africa. He received a doctorate in Iberian studies and taught at the Bugeaud High School in Algiers until 1963, as well as at the Sorbonne in Paris and the University of Rennes, from 1978 to 1995. Although he grew up in a world deeply attached to French culture and language, many of his novels portray the Judeo-Arabic universe of his daily life. Bensoussan published several scholarly works before writing his first novel, *Les Bagnoulis* (1965) which recounts the decline of French Algeria. In addition to fiction he has published many translations, especially from Spanish. In 1976, his novel *Frimald-jezar* won the Prix de l'Afrique méditerranéenne and was translated into Spanish.

Isbilia
1970

> I'm seeking you, Isbilia, my sultana, on the cloudy
> circle of water where I spread my glance to
> pierce your reflection, somewhere, between the
> foam and the wave, on the crest of imperceptible
> degradations, somewhere, in the curly hollows
> where the tides swell, beyond the eyelids' veil,
> and deeper than this knot in my bowels where the
> secret movements of my being groan.
>
> I'm seeking you, Isbilia, my sultana, between the
> pulp and the bark, the stalk and the sap, between
> dreaming and waking, beyond the frozen
> carousels of the starry arc, between night and
> shadow, between dawn and day, between the
> jackal and the wolf, on the sunken edge of the
> storm, on the isosceles drift of clouds.
>
> Isbilia, I'm seeking you wherever worlds break apart
> to let the mirage of your face pass through. [. . .]
>
> In Isbilia, one always had a knife in one's back.
>
> Maklouf kept in his pocket the *douk-douk* that had
> nearly nailed him to his door, like an odious old
> owl that half-moon night in which the Fellous
> cried for their dead.
>
> "The shadow was over me . . . the air whistled and
> lifted my head . . . it landed two fingers from my
> hand in the wood."
>
> And he showed it, proud as he was and everything,
> with its carvings, its arabesques, and its prickles.
> And he caressed it and reassured himself, the
> wind back in his sails.

Translated by Michele McKay Aynesworth

Other works by Bensoussan: *L'Humanisme dans la pensée juive medieval* (1957); *Au nadir* (1978); *Le Chant silencieux des chouettes* (1997); *Le Chemin des aque-ducs* (1998); *L'Échelle algérienne: voies juives* (2001); *L'Orpailleur* (2013).

Eli Mandel
1922–1992

Born in Estevan, Saskatchewan, poet, critic, and anthologist Eli Mandel was the child of immigrants from Russia. During the Great Depression, Mandel worked as a pharmacist's assistant and then in the Medical Corps during World War II. The experience marked him deeply and is reflected in his poetry, which speaks of his alienation and pessimism. He taught at the universities of Victoria, Alberta, Toronto, and at York University, and he published nine books of poetry. He encouraged young poets and was a friend of Irving Layton, on whose work he wrote a critique. Writing with a grand, transcendental poetic voice, Mandel is widely regarded for his contributions to Canadian literature.

Day of Atonement: Standing
1973

> My Lord, how stands it with me now
> Who, standing here before you
> (who, fierce as you are, are also just).
> Cannot bow down. You order this.
> Why, therefore, I must break
> If bend I will not, yet bend I must.
>
> But I address myself to you thus.
> Covered and alert, and will not bare
> My self. Then I must bear you,
> Heavy as you are.
>   This is the time
> The bare tree bends in the fierce wind
> And stripped, my God, springs to the sky.

Other works by Mandel: *Fuseli Poems* (1960); *An Idiot Joy* (1967); *Out of Place* (1977); *Life Sentence* (1981).

United States of America (1946-1973)

In the very first issue of *Commentary* magazine, its editor Elliot E. Cohen optimistically predicted a bright future for American Jewry. The year was 1945, and the full shock of the disaster in Europe was just beginning to sink in. The great Jewish centers of Europe were gone, and it was still uncertain whether there would indeed be a Jewish state. But Cohen believed that American Jewry was fully prepared to shoulder its new burdens and assume leadership of the Jewish people. *Commentary* was an expression of faith in American Jewry.

In this section, the reader can explore ways that, during and after the Holocaust, American Jewry indeed entered what might be called a "golden age" of self-confidence and cultural expression. Novelists like Saul Bellow and Philip Roth came into their own, not as representatives of a parochial immigrant culture, but as full-fledged American writers, entitled to a secure place in the literary pantheon. Jewish scholars and thinkers wrote with a new assertiveness and authority. After decades of discrimination, Jews finally entered American universities as teachers and as students. Far from being a marginal group in a Christian society, Jews claimed equal status with Catholics and Protestants. As Christian theologians took a new interest in Judaism, Jewish theological writing in turn flourished as never before. During these years, Jewish life writing confronted the pain of the past, yet it also underscored the redemptive promise of an open and tolerant society that could honor the legacy of the Jewish worlds that were no more.

By the 1960s, new challenges confronted American Jews. The 1967 Six-Day War served as a sudden reminder of an existential bond with the State of Israel. On the other hand, many younger Jews began to feel a growing alienation from what they called the "Jewish establishment," an alienation sharpened by the Vietnam War, civil rights demonstrations, and the new feminist movement. By the end of this period, as this anthology shows, probing questions emerged about the place of women in Jewish life, relations with African Americans, and the implications and lessons of the Holocaust.

Anthologies

Nahum N. Glatzer
1903–1990

A scholar and editor of astonishing industry and curiosity, Nahum N. Glatzer wrote some sixty books and articles over a robust academic career. From Kafka to Talmud, Agnon to the book of Job, Glatzer's interests roamed widely, and he pursued them avidly. Born in Lemberg (present-day Lviv), in the Austro-Hungarian Empire, Glatzer fled Europe in 1933, settling in Palestine and teaching literature and history in Haifa. After moving to the United States, he served for forty years as consulting editor and editor in chief at Schocken Books, and he was professor of Jewish history and philosophy in the Department of Near Eastern and Judaic Studies at Brandeis University from 1951 to 1973. Glatzer was the living link among Franz Rosenzweig, the Frankfurt Lehrhaus, and American Jewry.

The Language of Faith: Selected Jewish Prayers
1947

Epilogue

"Prayer is to religion what thinking is to philosophy. The religious sense prays as the intellectual organ thinks." Prayer, to carry this saying of Novalis a step further, is a significant type of discourse, a human language.

In becoming the central act performed in the House of Worship, prayer was exposed to the danger of institutionalization, of losing that spontaneity without which it is formula. Yet prayer has had sufficient inner strength to withstand convention. It has remained a living language, surviving, in the words of Jewish tradition, as the "Service of the heart." The chief care in this selection of Jewish prayers has been for this heartfelt quality, rather than historical value or liturgic significance.

In this book a community of diverse voices has been assembled: We hear a herdsman pray in his own humble way; a sufferer who continues to aspire to his God; a community imperiled, awaiting the Messiah; a mystic, lonely with the Lonely, in love with the source of Love; worshippers assembled at the dawn and the close of the Day of Atonement; a traveler starting out upon his journey. We hear a simple woman pray for her husband and her children; a congregation longing for Zion and the establishment of the kingdom of God on earth. These many voices unite into one prayer in which man abandons his self-insistence to make room for the eternal Thou, the knowledge of that which is greater than life and men.

About one half of the selections is from the liturgy of Ashkenazic Jewry. (A few Sephardic prayers have also been included.) The other half consists of private devotions, ranging from the talmudic masters to Nahman of Bratzlav (*ca.* 1800), the great hasidic master. The few biblical prayers in this volume have been taken from those which form a part of the synagogue service.

The book is divided into seven sections. Each section takes as its starting point the motive of the corresponding day in the biblical story of creation, or the theme that talmudic and legendary traditions assign to that day.

The original text (occasionally abbreviated) is given side by side with the English translation. Even those who cannot read the original will enjoy the simple apprehension of its form.

The "Adonai" of the English translation is the name the Jew substitutes for yhwh, the unutterable holy name of God. Its literal meaning is "my Lord," corresponding to *Kyrios* in the Septuagint, and "Lord" in the King James and other versions. In referring to God, the word "thou" is used when he is addressed as Adonai, "you" when not.

Other works by Glatzer: *Franz Rosenzweig: His Life and Thought* (1961); *The Dimensions of Job* (1969); *The Loves of Franz Kafka* (1986).

Marie Syrkin
1899–1989

Born in Switzerland, Marie Syrkin made Zionism her life's cause, founding a Labor Zionist journal and championing Israel in newspapers, magazines, and books. Her busy pen produced a chronicle of Jewish resistance during the Holocaust, a three-volume biography of her friend Golda Meir, translations of Yiddish poetry, and much more. In addition to her writing, Syrkin taught English literature at Brandeis

University. She was the founder of *Jewish Frontier,* which she edited, advised, and contributed to for more than fifty years.

Blessed Is the Match: The Story of Jewish Resistance
1947

Why do I begin with the parachutists? Were I to trace the story of Jewish resistance and rescue chronologically, I would have to use a different order. I would have to begin with the gradual development of an underground movement in the ghettos and concentration camps of Europe. Then I would describe the attempts at rescue directed from the neutral centers of Portugal, Switzerland and Istanbul. This would be followed naturally by an account of the partisans, the Maquis, and of the ghetto revolts. Only at the end would I reach the small band of parachutists from Palestine who leapt down into the Nazi-held Balkans in order to bring help to the surviving Jews of Europe. Such a plan would no doubt be logical as well as chronological. I would follow the order of events as they occurred, and it would have the strict sequence of the calendar to recommend it.

Nevertheless, I feel that the instinct which impels me to begin the story backwards is not wholly irrational. It has its own logic which merits examination. In the first place, I must make an admission. I share the reader's reluctance to enter the ghetto gate. "People are fed up on atrocities!"—True, but that is not the chief reason why men turn away from narratives of the Nazi horror. They turn away not because they are satiated or indifferent, but because it is too hard to behold the spectacle which unfolds as soon as one dares lift the curtain be it ever so uncertainly or slightly. One needs strength to walk in and look about. Sometimes one has to borrow this strength. It is not to be had from the sufferers, no matter how heroic. I have spoken face to face with girls who fought on the ghetto barricades and in the Vilna woods, and always the sense of personal shame and of guilt before the victim overpowered every other feeling. To seek inspiration from them smacked of indecency, as though one were to watch a pyre which consumed living flesh and blood, and gloat at the splendor of the blaze.

But the young parachutists who jumped from the skies and afterwards told me their stories in the settlements of Palestine—towards them, and their lost comrades, one could indulge in the luxury of admiration. From them one could presume to take the resolution without which it is impossible to enter the charnel-house of European Jewry. The vitality of their adventure, even when it ended in death, helped one to approach the ashes of six million murdered human beings.

There is also a less personal reason for my choice of method. The story can be told from within and from without. The narratives of those who have escaped have begun to appear in all the languages of the world. These accounts have the virtue of having been composed by those best qualified to make the report and draw up the indictment—the victims themselves. But there is another story too which must be told—the story of those who tried to answer the desperate cry for help. This story, despite its slight success, is part of the whole. It, too, belongs to the account, and it is reasonable and fitting that it begin with those who made the boldest, as well as the most obviously picturesque, effort to save their doomed brothers.

Other works by Syrkin: *Golda Meir: Woman with a Cause* (1963); *The State of the Jews* (1980).

David P. Boder
1886–1961

A pioneer in the recording of survivor testimony, Latvian-born David P. Boder interviewed more than one hundred Holocaust survivors in war-shattered Europe in 1946. Toting around a wire recorder, he went from country to country, finding the traumatized victims of the war and talking to them in their own languages (Boder spoke seven). He returned to the United States with over 120 hours of recordings, which became *I Did Not Interview the Dead,* a collection of transcripts. A psychologist by profession, and drawn to disasters, both natural and man-made, Boder continued interviewing victims after the 1940s.

I Did Not Interview the Dead
1949

Introduction

A few days before the surrender of Germany, General Dwight D. Eisenhower, then Supreme Commander of the Allied Forces, sent out a call to American newspaper editors which may be paraphrased as "Come and see for yourselves." Eisenhower, preoccupied as he must have been with unprecedented responsibilities, found time to reflect upon the significance of preserving for posterity the impressions and emotions aroused by the sight of thousands of victims dead or dying in the liberated concentration camps in Germany.

Upon reading Eisenhower's call to the American press, it occurred to me that the magnetic wire recorder, then a new tool which had been developed by the Armour Research Foundation, offered a unique and exact means of recording experiences of displaced persons. Through the wire recorder the displaced person could relate in his own language and in his own voice the story of his concentration camp life.

It was obvious that the usual "paper and pencil" method of interview would be impractical. The multiplicity of languages of the Russian, Polish, Jewish, Latvian, Lithuanian, Mongolian, Dutch, Flemish, and German sufferers in concentration and forced labor camps might have defeated even an Ernie Pyle. No one could deny that the displaced persons were entitled to an Ernie Pyle of their own, but the language barriers appeared to make the task impossible. The most feasible alternative, therefore, was the wire recorder. The DPs could tell their own stories, and then the records could be translated into English. [. . .]

It was not the purpose of the expedition to gain a comprehensive picture of the whole problem of the DPs. The intention was to gather personal reports in the form of wire recordings for future psychological and anthropological study. [. . .]

In Western Europe in 1946 there were nearly one million people (not counting displaced Germans) who had been forcible uprooted by the war and who remained on sufferance or roamed in foreign lands hoping for a place that they could once more call their own. What they want most is a return to their traditional patterns of individual and family life. They crave a return to privacy. They want their own kitchens. They want familiar, self-chosen clothes. They want the little things which give meaning to life and which are indispensable to human existence above the purely animal level.

The displaced persons, in spite of their sorry state today, are not riffraff, not the scum of the earth, not the poor devils who suffer because they don't know their rights, not idlers who declaim that the world owes them a living. They are uprooted people. They represent the members of all classes of society—farmers, industrial workers, teachers, lawyers, engineers, merchants, artists, housewives—who have been dislocated by a world catastrophe.

Psychologists and anthropologists have suggested a variety of methods for the analysis of personal histories such as those appearing in this book. Study of the wire-recorded narratives has led to the devising of an index by means of which each narrative may be assessed as to the category and number of experiences bound to have a traumatizing effect upon the victim. Called *The Traumatic Index*, it is given here in abridged form.

The Traumatic Index[1]

1. Brutal and abrupt removal from environmental stimuli.
2. Inadequate substitutes for the conditioning framework of normal life.
3. Introduction of new stimuli without relation to past experience and without reference to legal and moral traditions.
4. Insufficient food, clothing, and shelter.
5. Lack of means and facilities for personal and community hygiene.
6. Enforced performance of meaningless tasks.
7. Chronic overtaxing of physical and mental endurance.
8. Seizure of personal property.
9. Blocking of habits of reading, writing, and worship.
10. Abolition of traditions of dignity and decency between the sexes, in treatment of the sick, and in disposal of the dead.
11. Lack of medical and dental care, and wanton mutilation for purposes of alleged medical research.
12. Brutal punishment for trivial infringements of camp rules, and group punishment for alleged offenses perpetrated by unidentified persons.

The reader should find no difficulty in discovering in the narrative, specific instances of the types of traumas listed in the preceding index. To evaluate each of these traumas and to weigh their impact on the personality is an exacting task for which, perhaps, only the professional social scientist is qualified.

Anthropologists use the term *acculturate* when they refer to the incorporation of the individual into the group. Of this phenomenon Dr. John Dollard wrote, "We want to know how a new person is added to the group, what I have called the group-plus-one hypothesis. Every dilemma that could be tabbed as psychological would then be seen as an aspect of the acculturation of a person into group life."[2]

Many of the following recorded personal documents give precisely this picture in reverse—the gradual cutting down of a human being to fit into concentration and annihilation camps. To describe this process I have had to coin the antonym to the term *acculturation*, for what is dealt with here is an unprecedented and planned *deculturation* of personality on a mass scale. The verbatim records presented in this book make uneasy reading. And yet they are not the grimmest stories that could be told—I did not interview the dead.

NOTES

1. *The Traumatic Index* as a method of assessing human experience may prove useful not only in the case of the DPs but also in the exploration of the personality of any adult who has come into conflict with life and social institutions.

2. John Dollard, *Criteria for the Life History* (New Haven: Yale University Press, 1935), p. 277.

Other work by Boder: *The Impact of Catastrophe* (1954).

Louis Finkelstein

1895–1991

Born in Cincinnati, Louis Finkelstein received his Jewish education from his father, an Orthodox rabbi. Louis Finkelstein attended both Columbia University and the Jewish Theological Seminary, where he taught for more than half a century, serving as its head from 1940 to 1972. Under his direction, the seminary grew tremendously, emerging as the chief institution of Conservative Judaism. Finkelstein himself was the dominant figure in the movement before his retirement and took an active role in American public life, especially in interfaith dialogue.

The Jews, Their History, Culture, and Religion 1949

July 4, 1949

The purpose of this book is to bring into focus the vast number and wide variety of data concerning Judaism and the Jews, so that they can be seen in relation to one another and to the general phenomena of human culture. Because of their circumstances, the events in which Jews have participated, and to which they have contributed, are almost as diversified the history of the human race itself. This book is therefore necessarily joint work. Each of the thirty-four contributors has

undertaken to discuss the aspect of Judaism and the Jews with which he is best acquainted. These authors include Christian and Jew; Europeans, Israelis, and Americans; philosophers, historians, social scientists, scientists, men of art and letters, and men of affairs; rationalists and mystics; skeptics and believers. They have not met to discuss their special contributions; no effort has been made to enforce any uniformity of concept or presentation. Any unity nonetheless emerging is due entirely to the nature of the phenomenon under discussion. If the book contains a message (and I believe it does), it is a message inherent in the extraordinary events and insights described.

In the perspective of geology or biology, it is but yesterday that Moses appeared before Pharaoh to demand the release of the Israelite slaves; and but a few hours more since Abraham left Ur of Chaldees. In this short span of time, the undertaking initiated by Patriarchs and early prophets has developed trends in civilization which, it is generally agreed, contain whatever is hopeful for the destiny of man. Beginning with the promise of a Messianic age, these trends are perhaps the chief visible instruments for its attainment. What fate and achievements still await the Jewish and its derivative traditions during the long millennia to come, none dares predict. Despite the widely current fears for man's future, it seems probable that the development of his civilization will proceed with increasing speed. Indeed, if man in future directs to the advancement of his knowledge of human relations, the humanities, ethics, and religion, energies like those spent in recent centuries on study and conquest of the material world, he may in a comparatively brief period as far surpass twentieth-century man as twentieth-century man surpasses the Neanderthal. And if it seems unlikely that our sons and daughters will prophesy, we have Scriptural assurance that that exalted state awaits some of our more distant descendants.

The chronicle and description of the Western world's most ancient tradition, as it emerged from darkness into light, and turned each crisis into an instrument of growth, offers hope for the human race as a whole. The presentation of the facts bearing on this development would itself completely justify this book, but other, more limited, considerations have entered into its planning. The work seemed necessary to dispel widespread misinformation, and to provide authentic information about its central theme. That this should be needed may appear paradoxical. Of all the curiosities of our world, one of the strangest is that a civilization, many of whose basic ideas derive from Judaism, should have so little appreciation of its real character.

Clearly, inadequate comprehension of Judaism cannot be due to lack of knowledge of its basic literature. With the possible exception of the New Testament, no literature approaches in popularity the Scriptures, which are the cornerstone of Judaism. Everywhere men find comfort in the Psalms of David, and guide their lives by the wisdom of Solomon. Jewish rituals are retained in the religious symbolisms of half the world; Jewish theology is a potent force in the development of civilization. The prophetic conception of man and his future pervades much of the science and policy of our day.

Misunderstanding of Judaism cannot be caused by the difficulty or abstruseness of the subject. Its literature is available and may be mastered; its traditions have all been reduced to writing and printing, and handy translations in many languages are widely distributed. There is a vast literature dealing with Judaism as a faith and the Jews as a people.

The ease with which anyone may enter the most sacred portals of Judaism is, in fact, astonishing. The child of a traditional Jewish household often discovers at the age of eight or nine that the book he has been studying is none other than the Talmud on which the erudite in the faith base their opinions. With a curious delight that boy encounters in its folios the very passages his learned rabbi cites in sermon or decision, and recognizes that a child is divided from the foremost scholar in Israel not by kind but by degree of knowledge.

Even the Cabbala which seems to the uninitiate a difficult and perplexing riddle, and is usually described as such, has been superbly expounded by Professor Gershom Scholem.

Despite the general knowledge of so much of Jewish literature, the fact remains that Judaism is today probably the least understood of all major religions. This truth was illustrated for me by an incident connected with the publication of this book. While the proofs were being read, the publisher kindly invited me to meet a group which was to interpret *Judaism and the Jews* (as we then proposed to call this work) to booksellers. Regardless of the value of the material, some were troubled by the title. For the reading public, they argued, Judaism has merely archaeological interest, having ceased to exist more than eighteen centuries ago, with the fall of Jerusalem at the hands of Titus. In contrast, they said,

the Jews are a contemporary phenomenon, of perennial interest. As frequently happens, practical considerations led to a review of the theoretical, and the present title was adopted because of its precision, as well as for its intelligibility.

Never before had I realized so clearly that the religion which I try to practice is not considered "living" by many of my countrymen. But thinking over the discussion, I recalled various incidents which confirmed that view. There was the young author of a book on "modern religion and the doctrine of human brotherhood," who had consulted me about the chapter on Islam, seeking introduction to authorities in that field, and surprised me by his omission of any chapter on Judaism. He apparently had thought Judaism a "tribal" religion, obsolete in the modern world, preserved by a few queer devotees, with no real value for modern man and no bearing on the problems of human brotherhood.

I remembered the occasion when I pleaded with the dean of a well-known college on behalf of a young friend, called to take an examination on the Sabbath. Explaining my position, I reminded the dean that the American people as a whole seek to encourage religion in the young, and that to compel the young man to take his examination as scheduled might be the first step in tearing him away from his faith, and possibly from all faith. After listening to me patiently, the dean, doubtless harassed with many requests for special consideration, and (like many heads of bureaus) intolerant of the need for individual arrangements, said, "My dear friend, you really cannot expect us run this college in accordance with your ancient wilderness customs." [. . .]

In the light of such incidents it is no extravagance to call Judaism the unknown religion of our time. Its adherents live in the same cities and houses as members of other creeds; they travel in the same subways and buses; they correspond, visit, converse, and do business with their fellow Americans of all groups. Jews may be loved as individuals and respected for their gifts. Their prophets are also the prophets of Christendom and Islam. The Holy Land is equally sacred to the members of the Jewish, Christian, and Islamic faiths. Neither Christian nor Moslem theology is intelligible without a study of its Jewish antecedents. But only the rare American or European of any faith appreciates the character of the ancient Jewish tradition, is aware of its distinctive teachings and nature, and seeks to understand the relation of the modern Jew to his predecessor of biblical and talmudic times.

The general confusion about Judaism and the Jews is not dispelled by the popularity of the Bible; on the contrary, the wide knowledge of the Hebrew Scriptures may help increase misconceptions. The reader of the Bible tends, like Nevinson,[1] to identify the Israelites with his own circle, and the Philistines with his own opponents. In mature years it is difficult to substitute for infant imagery the people who follow the faith of the prophets, study their language, and adhere rigidly to their ways.

To paraphrase Stevenson, a Jewish writer sometimes thinks that his own faith has the love of a parent for other faiths derived from it; while these faiths have for Judaism the indifference of a child. Judaism is intensely interested in the history and development of Christianity and Islam, which—to quote Maimonides—it regards as means of carrying to the ends of the earth an understanding of God's unity and the teaching of Scripture. The oldest Western religion sees the younger ones as fruits of its own planting; as part of man's endless future; as steps toward the realization of the prophetic vision of a world of peace. Christendom and Islam seem to think of Judaism as a relic of the past—quaint, valuable for the insight it offers into their origins, astounding in its defiance of the years, but still not an integral part of man's future.

Because the culture of the Western world tends to be predominantly Christian, this lack of faith in Judaism as a contemporary and permanent factor in civilization carries over into Judaism itself. Its own children sometimes doubt its meaning and its future. [. . .]

From the point of view of Judaism as a religion, anti-Semitism is of major interest because it appears as an impediment to the better understanding among men that must occur before a better world can issue from our own anarchic one. As Professor R. M. MacIver has shown in his magnificent study, *The More Perfect Union*,[2] hostility toward any group is part of a cultural trend that must be regarded as a whole. His view must be accepted as authoritative sociology; it is also excellent theology. As the ancient Sages of Israel recognized, hostility suffered by any group will be erased only when hostility, as such, ceases to dominate the minds of men.

The achievement of this goal is one of the major aims of all Western religion, and of Judaism in particular. The tensions among religious groups will not be solved by a retreat from religion, but by advancement toward it. Divisions between men, expressed in mutual hostility, have their origin in paganism and not in monotheism, though monotheism may not have succeeded in eradicating them. For the disappearance of anti-Semitism, Judaism looks to a world in which religion will have been vindicated.

So it comes about that the future of the Jews as a group and as individuals is intimately bound up with the goals of their faith. The Jews are hostages to the doctrine entrusted to them by their prophets and Sages. In a world moving toward religion, Jews may suffer hostilities surviving the pagan era; but in a world which reverts to paganism, Jews have no possibility of life. Said the fishes to the fox, in Rabbi Akiba's fable, "If we are in danger in the water, our natural element, what would happen to us on the dry land!"

Both from the viewpoint of man's spiritual advancement and the more baited one of improved understanding among men, one of the most promising trends of our day is the growth of profound religious insight throughout America. New winds have blown during the past decade, in Judaism as well as in Christianity. The materialistic emphasis widely accepted in my college days is being replaced by new spiritual insights. The wistfulness for religion, first evident in the late 1930's, is taking effective form. The theological seminaries may serve as barometers for the general community in this regard. From a number comes word that there is increasing interest in theology, and that, with philosophy, it is replacing exclusive preoccupation with politics and with social reforms. This appears equally to be true of Jewish and Christian theological seminaries in America. This new religious spirit, unreservedly loyal to the traditions from which it springs, seeks to increase better understanding and love among men rather than to set them apart. It seeks no reduction of the various faiths to a common, meaningless syncretism, but their fulfillment as separate efforts to achieve mutual appreciation among men and common service to God.

NOTES
1. [Henry W. Nevinson, editor of the London *Nation*.—Eds.]
2. *The More Perfect Union*, The Macmillan Company, New York, 1948.

Other works by Finkelstein: *The Pharisees: The Sociological Background of Their Faith* (1938); *Judaism as a System of Symbols* (1953); *New Light from the Prophets* (1969).

Leo W. Schwarz

The Root and the Bough: The Epic of an Enduring People
1949

For the past few years, both in France and Germany, I was awed by the valiant struggle of people who, though only recently liberated from indescribable cruelty, exhibited extraordinary powers of recuperation. I shared with others the deep emotional reverberations evoked by the plight of the displaced persons imbedded in the devastation of Occupied Germany, Austria and Italy, and I found it quite impossible to clothe the power of the emotions induced by the Nazi barbarism in words comprehensible to persons untouched by it all. [. . .] Later I perceived that my emotions had obscured the essence of the experience: the stories of these survivors are a clue to the ultimate hidden resources in humankind. That is why I felt impelled to gather such records as existed and to goad my friends among the survivors to write down their recollections. [. . .]

When I try to recall the tens of thousands of survivors whom I met in Germany, I see an anonymous mass out of which emerge the personalities of those with whom I came into personal contact. They stemmed from almost every corner of Europe, from all walks of life. [. . .] Particularly captivating were the children and youth whose vitality and intelligence helped to explain their emergence from the corrupting influences to which they had been exposed. Their diaries and recollections which I have placed in Part Three reveal, to rare degree, the sources of human power.

One day I was talking with a man who had passed through hells unimaginable even to such minds as Céline or Count de Sade. We were near a tidy little cemetery outside of Munich, now supplanting a mass grave where nineteen members of his family were buried. He was talking under the influence of a memory so intense that it acted like a hypnotic drug. "If you were to tell me the story of my life during these past five years," he said, "I myself would not believe it. But, in retrospect, I recall that even when I was in the camps, I refused to believe what was happening around me. I supposed that the will to live of our people is stronger than reality. Or, perhaps, there is an inner power, incomprehensible to our minds, that makes us cling to life even when it appears worthless." Later on I wondered whether this profound affirmation of life was not a poetic statement of the yearning of flesh and bone to fulfill their natural

obligations. Whatever the truth may be, I am persuaded that these survivors are endowed with an irrefrangible core of vitality. Otherwise, people who have suffered in their inmost fibers so long would have hated their kind for living. [. . .]

There is another aspect of this subject on which it is wise to dwell. Immediately after liberation, many American witnesses including General Eisenhower wondered whether people who had endured so overwhelming an ordeal would again be able to replant their roots in the soil of other countries. I recall, two years later, how deeply impressed General Eisenhower was, during a visit to the Jewish community in Freimann Siedlung near Munich, with their physical appearance and the social organization. Thousands of the survivors are now settled in the United States, and most of those with whom I have kept in touch have made admirable adjustments. Of the tens of thousands who have reached Israel, many have found a hearth in the agricultural settlements and in the cities; some have already rendered great services to their newly-born state. While I do not wish to appear unconcerned with the shadows still lurking in the minds and the wounds of the spirit of the survivors, the fact of immediate significance is the passionate confirmation which comes to the surface wherever society makes place for them. We should remember that these are the unsung allies who were victors over the evil ideal, the powerful secret weapon, of the enemy. Perhaps they can help to answer the crucial question asked by Arnold Toynbee in his *Civilization on Trial*: "Will some spiritual enlightenment [comparable to the Hebrew Prophets and the birth of Christianity] be kindled in the 'displaced persons' who are the counterparts, in our world, of these Jewish exiles to whom so much was revealed in their painful exile by the waters of Babylon? The answer to the question is of greater moment than the still inscrutable destiny of our world-encompassing Western civilization."

I have already indicated why I have put this book together. The small still voices which speak in these pages are not only a condemnation of tyranny but above all constitute a grand testament to human valor and endurance. They bear witness that hatred is human but its works are short-lived; that one can bear the yellow patch with pride, knowing that it is a badge of human dignity; that even in darkness, the heart and the mind contain the seed of all that is gracious and radiant.

NOTE
[Words in brackets appear in the original source.—Eds.]

Irving Howe and Eliezer Greenberg

Howe, 1920–1993

A prominent literary critic and lifelong leftist, Irving Howe was the quintessential New York intellectual, a label he popularized in the 1960s. Born in the Bronx, New York, he turned a quarrelsome temperament into a vocation, writing and editing intellectual journals, criticizing capitalism, and championing democratic socialism. After rejecting Judaism as an adolescent, he changed course dramatically, immersing himself in Yiddish literature and the world of East European Jewish immigrants. Howe lectured widely and taught literature passionately. *Dissent*, the journal he founded and edited, survived him, continuing his legacy.

Greenberg, 1896–1977

Yiddish writer, translator, and editor Eliezer Greenberg (Leyzer Grinberg) was born in Lipkany, Bessarabia, and in 1913 came to the United States, where he was educated at the University of Michigan and later settled in New York. Greenberg published poetry and books of critical essays, and he collaborated on a number of translations with the literary and social critic Irving Howe. Greenberg was director of Yiddish press relations for the American Jewish Committee and was a founder of the Yiddish branch of the PEN Club.

A Treasury of Yiddish Stories
1953

Modern Yiddish literature focuses upon the *shtetl* during its last tremor of self-awareness, the historical moment when it is still coherent and self-contained but already under fierce assault from the outer world. Between language and milieu there is a curious, ambivalent relationship: the one seems to batten on the other. Yiddish reaches its climax of expressive power as the world it portrays begins to come apart.

The Yiddish of Mendele and Sholom Aleichem is a remarkably fluid and intimate language. Perhaps because it is a language forged in opposition to the most powerful groups within the Jewish community, perhaps because it is the voice of the folk rising organically from the life of the folk, Yiddish is breezy in tone, richly idiomatic in flavor, free in its literary possibilities. This very freedom, of course, is also a severe burden: many a Yiddish writer suffers from the absence of inherited modes and forms.

When the first major Yiddish writers appeared toward the end of the nineteenth century, the language did not impose upon them any stylized patterns of expression—which allowed them verbal spontaneity and improvisation but also forced them to create, as it were, the very standards of usage from which they were already deviating. At its peak, however, Yiddish was neither a folk voice nor a sophisticated "literary" language. It was open at both sides, still responsive to the voice of the folk yet beginning to model itself on literary patterns of the West. The most valuable writing in Yiddish appears at the moment when the two opposing forces, the folk voice and the self-consciously literary, achieve an exquisite, if almost always precarious, balance. To strike an extreme comparison which is not meant to suggest an equation of value between the two literatures: Yiddish found itself for a moment in the position of creative youthfulness that English enjoyed during the Elizabethan Age.

It is almost inevitable that in speaking of Yiddish literature one should refer to an inner dialectic, a tension of counterposed elements: the traditional past and the immediate experience, the religious structure and the secular infiltration, the folk voice and the modern literary accent. But even Yiddish literature itself can be seen and, by its most important critics, has been seen as part of a similar dialectic. The pioneering Yiddish critic Baal Machshoves, and in our own time Samuel Niger, repeatedly employ the formula, "two languages and one literature." Such a view of the relationship between Yiddish and Hebrew is partly motivated, no doubt, by a desire to preserve the historic continuity of the Jewish tradition, and partly by the fact that any empirical study of the formation of Yiddish literature must constantly take into account the Hebrew base and the Hebrew component. "Bilingualism," writes Niger, "became among us an accepted fact, a tradition. . . ." The essence of the Jewish experience, he continues, was reflected in this "partnership between Hebrew and Yiddish," a partnership that is indissoluble no matter who would wish to dissolve it. The cultural kinship between the two literatures is so profound that almost any well-educated serious writer in the one literature must be affected by and concerned with the other. Ultimately both literatures draw from and give expression to the same ethos.

But not entirely the same ethos. The theory of "two languages and one literature" is indispensable to an understanding of Yiddish literature; it helps to clarify, for example, how the presence of Hebrew in the background enables Yiddish literature to avoid the painful fate of those literatures of small countries which either become stalled in provinciality or fall into a slavish imitation of the latest vogue from Paris. Yet a too rigorous application of the theory might soon blur those elements and modes that are unique to the Yiddish. For there is something qualitatively unique to the whole cultural aura of Yiddish, something in its characteristic gestures and tones that is summoned by the word *Yiddishkeit*. One way of making this point, perhaps, is to note that Yiddish literature releases a profound yearning for a return not to the supremacy of Hebrew but to those conditions of life that would make possible the supremacy of Hebrew—that is, a yearning for the end of the dispersion and a reintegration of Jewish life. But during most of the span of Yiddish literature this is a hope impossible to realize; and it is the recognition of its impossibility that gives rise to that distinctive Yiddish note which cannot and should not be assimilated into Hebrew, or any other, culture.

Somewhat along the same lines, the Yiddish critic B. Rivkin has advanced the theory that Yiddish literature, more through necessity than choice, came to serve as a substitute for a "would-be territory," thereby taking over the functions of a nation that did not yet exist. This meant that many of the communal needs which for other peoples were met by the nation had somehow to be satisfied by Yiddish literature. In the historical interim during which the hold of religion had begun to decline and the idea of nationality had not yet reached its full power, Yiddish literature became a central means of collective expression for the East European Jews, fulfilling some of the functions of both religion and the idea of nationality. In the absence of a free and coherent national life it had to provide the materials for a sense of national identity; and even as, in honesty, it reported the realities of the *shtetl* and the Pale, it had also to nurture and exalt their collective aspirations. From many points of view, of course, this was an impossible task for any literature, let alone one as frail and youthful as the Yiddish; yet something of the moral seriousness—though little of the metaphysical boldness—that we admire in the nineteenth-century Russian novel is also to be found in Yiddish literature precisely because the Yiddish writers thought of their work in supra-literary terms. One could not say of Yiddish literature, as the critic [Nikolay] Chernyshevsky has said of the Russian, that it "constitutes the sum total of our intellectual life"; but one can say that the Yiddish writers came before their audience, as did the Russian writers of the nineteenth century, with an instinctive conviction that their purpose was something other than merely to entertain and amuse. The achievements of Russian literature are obviously greater than those of the Yiddish, but both share the assumption that the one subject truly worthy of a serious writer is the problem of collective destiny, the fate of a people.

Among the East European Jews the taste for imaginative literature did not come easily or quickly. They had to struggle for it, and struggle, most of all, against themselves. "It was natural," writes B. Rivkin, "for Jews to ask, 'Why literature?' After all, literature was a late development among Jews. The world around them had a well-established literature with its own forms. But here was a people living in an unnatural environment, without its own territorial and governmental organs, without its own self-sustaining social and economic structure. . . . The pioneer of Yiddish literature was, therefore, confronted with the difficult, almost impossible task of justifying literature to the people, and with the not much easier task of creating something equivalent to a natural environment. The first task was fulfilled by Mendele, the second by Sholom Aleichem."[1]

Literature had to be *justified*, it had to be assigned a moral sanction—which is not to say that the Yiddish pioneers, either the writers or the critics, meant that it had to be moralistic. But what, they seemed to be asking themselves, is the distinct use and end of Yiddish literature? How does it take its place in the larger Jewish tradition? The answer they implicitly gave was that Yiddish literature should focus upon one particular experience, the life of dispersion; that it should release, as only imaginative writing can, the deepest impulses of that life and thereby provide a means of both consecrating and transcending the *shtetl*. Yiddish literature, like any other, has always had its schools, groups, and cliques, but there is hardly a Yiddish writer of any significance whose work is not imbued with this fundamental urge to portray Jewish life with the most uncompromising realism and yet to transcend the terms of the portrayal. How could it be otherwise? Simply to survive, simply to face the next morning, Yiddish literature had to cling to the theme of historical idealism. Beyond hope and despair lies the desperate *idea* of hope, and this is what sustained Yiddish writing.

A literature that, even as it is still reeling from the pain of birth, must assume the formidable task of preserving the national sense of identity and adapting it to the unfamiliar modes of the modern world—such a literature will inevitably turn to language as the only available unifying principle. In another time and under different circumstances language might simply be seen as the familiar, accepted vehicle of cultural realization; but here it becomes, so to speak, the very substance and issue of culture, the living repository of the past and future. The effort to create a Yiddish literature meant the effort to affirm a linguistic patriotism: both are expressions of the urge to national dignity, which became so passionate in the Jewish world of the late nineteenth and early twentieth centuries.

NOTE

1. B. Rivkin, *Die Grunt-Tendentsen fun der Yiddisher Literatur in America* [New York: Ikuf Farlag, 1948—Eds.].

Other works by Howe: *Sherwood Anderson* (1951); *World of Our Fathers: The Journey of East European Jews to America and the Life They Found and Made* (1976); *A Margin of Hope: An Intellectual Biography* (1982). Other works by Greenberg: *Gasn un evenyus* (1928); *Di lange nakht* (1946); *Gedenkshaft* (1974).

Harold U. Ribalow

1919-1982

The son of a yeshiva-educated poetry critic, Harold Uriel Ribalow combined his two obsessions—Jews and sports—into one career as writer and editor. If Jews were playing, Ribalow was interested. He wrote about Jewish athletes with stereotype-smashing verve and enthusiasm. The Ukrainian-born Ribalow wrote about nonathletic Jews as well, his byline appearing in major newspapers and magazines and on the cover of anthologies. Still, it was to sports—an elastic category that included chess and bullfighting—that he always returned.

Mid-Century: An Anthology of Jewish Life and Culture in Our Times
1955
Introduction

In the tercentenary year of Jewish settlement in America, this volume is offered as evidence that the past decade—a mid-century point—has seen the publication of some of the most interesting, authoritative, and provocative American-Jewish writing of the century.

Certainly, the fifty contributors to this book include, in surprisingly large measure, a Who's Who of

American Jewry. There are representative writings—all non-fiction—by the most notable names in American-Jewish scholarship, theology, philosophy, culture, and journalism. The essays offered in these pages transcend the dates on which they were originally published because of the timelessness of the material and the manner in which it is approached. Like so many Jews before them and, it is to be hoped, those who come after them, these writers have addressed themselves to the whole Jewish people, and not to a particular Jewish element at a particular time. [...]

The authors of the articles in *Mid-Century* are the men and women who have been addressing the Jewish people in America for the past few decades. They colored and influenced Jewish life in the past and they and their contemporaries will continue to lead the Jewish community through the decades to come.

Curiously, these essays appeared, in the main, in the much-maligned American-Jewish periodical press. Every contribution is the work of a Jew living and working in the United States, writing in English. All but eight of the fifty-three contributions were first published in an English-language magazine edited for American Jews. The other eight were accepted by the editors of such high-quality journals as *The Atlantic Monthly, Harper's, Partisan Review*, and the now defunct *Common Ground*. The great majority of these articles, then, was brought to the attention of the public in the pages of the Jewish magazines sponsored by Jewish organizations and those few published independently by a handful of dedicated souls. [...]

It is remarkable that the Jewish periodicals, which have small circulations, are sponsored by Jewish organizations, and can scarcely support the Jewish writer dependent solely on his typewriter, have been able to offer so much fine writing by so many of American Jewry's outstanding thinkers, leaders, and journalists.

While Jewish fiction often appears in general magazines, Jewish material of the kind found in this volume almost always finds its way into Jewish journals. Now and again, of course, a study such as Jean Paul Sartre's *Anti-Semite and Jew* or a discussion of the alleged dual loyalty of the Jew will appear in an issue of *Partisan Review* or of *Harper's*. But such profoundly Jewish essays of the type written by Dr. Heschel or Hayim Greenberg or Horace Kallen are accepted for publication by the editors of the Jewish magazines. That the past decade alone has seen the emergence of *Commentary, Congress Weekly, The Reconstructionist, The*

Chicago Jewish Forum, Judaism, The Jewish Frontier, and the continuation of *The Menorah Journal,* is convincing evidence of the cultural outlets for the Jewish thinker and writer. For too long a period has the English-Jewish press been belittled. This book is made possible because it exists, and the material presented in this collection more than justifies the existence of that press.

Other works by Ribalow: *Jewish Baseball Stars* (1984); *The Great Jewish Chess Champions* (1986).

Isaac Rivkind

1895–1968

Born in Łódź, Isaac Rivkind grew up amid affluence and learning, a background he parlayed into a long career as a journalist, researcher, and—for thirty-six years—librarian at the Jewish Theological Seminary. Rivkind was a passionate and lifelong Zionist as well as a scholar. He belonged to the Hebrew PEN Club of New York, and his academic interests roamed widely, from bar mitzvah celebrations to Yiddish typography to the poet Bialik to the history of Jews and gambling.

Jewish Money in Everyday Life, Cultural History and Folklore: A Lexicological Study
1959

Introduction

The author is not among those who adhere to the doctrine that "money talks." Knowledge talks, conscience talks, but money is merely counted—more by some, less by others. If the author counts "Jewish money," it is because it is money that recounts. By counting we can recount Jewish life. It is the story of a rich past, of a pious world full of morality, goodness, and sanctity, of Jewishness and humanity. In studying this matter, the author underwent a deep religious experience. Those who had shaped this creative life were constantly appearing before his eyes—Jews: everyday Jews and Sabbath Jews, learned Torah-Jews and simple psalm-reciting Jews, who were all so pitilessly exterminated. "Jewish money" recounts the story of Jewish life created over many generations and in thousands of communities over many lands and across many seas. It tells of a life that once was, and is no more.

Instead of a life of holiness we are left with holy martyrs. Such is the spirit of this book, written in their Yiddish mother-tongue with a trembling hand, as a historic gravestone for generations of ordinary Jews. [. . .]

Jews, Yiddishkeit, and Money

A. FROM THE GOLDEN CALF TO SANCTIFYING GOD

From time immemorial antisemites have reproached us for having ceased to be the people of God and become the people of money. The word *Jew* itself became a synonym for avarice. Their dictionaries contain the concept of *Geltjude* ("money-Jew"), meaning usurer. In English too, the dictionaries translate *Jew* in the same sense. In all dictionaries in general use we find this interpretation. And so it goes even with us Jews. We have been infected by the gentiles and begun to look at ourselves through their eyes, seeing only the Jew who has not withstood the temptation of money. Mendele Moykher Sforim has given us a kind of allegorical money-Jew in "Reb Yankev and the Coin," a prototype of the nouveau riche: "Money has hardened his heart, clogged his brain and in place of his memory there now sits a ruble. Where once there was a fragment of justice, a bit of mercy, a hint of humanity, and a crumb of understanding, there is now lodged a coin." [. . .]

A Yiddish proverb puts it tersely: "Who has the *meye* (big money) has the *deye* (authority)." But in reality, the Jews of long ago honored (learned) authority far more than they did big money. [. . .]

We know that such Jews, men and women for whom money was their whole life, the very essence of their being, were never hard to find. From the moment the People of Israel accepted the yoke of the Kingdom of Heaven, they promised—and rehearsed these words daily in the recitation of the Shema—"You shall love the Lord your God with all your heart, with all your soul and with all your might." With "all your might" was interpreted by the Sages [m. Berakhot 9:5] to mean with all your money; and furthermore, the Sages taught [b.Pesahim 25a, b.Yoma 82a] that "If any man loves his money more than himself, it shall be said of him that he loves it with all his might." Individual Jews who "loved their money more than themselves" are not scarce. There always were and always will be money-Jews, but the Jewish world is not based on them. It stands on the merits of poor *lamed-vovniks*, the thirty-six hidden Righteous Men. Even the "birth pangs of the Messiah" are tied to the ideal of a world without money [b.Sanhedrin 97a]: "the Son of David will not come until the last farthing is gone from all pockets." [...]

B. FROM CRADLE TO ḤUPPAH [MARRIAGE CANOPY]

Money accompanies the Jew from the cradle to the grave. To put it in money-terms—from *bodgelt* (coins that the newborn's father and guests toss in the baby's bath and are kept by the midwife) to *mole-gelt* (payment for having the prayer for the dead, "*el male' raḥamim*," recited). Money encompasses almost all of Jewish life, which winds its way, as Bialik puts it "from the poorhouse to the cemetery, from the synagogue courtyard to the bathhouse" (Bialik, "*A freylekhs*").

At the same time as we see the wealth and abundance of Jewish money, we see the depths of Jewish poverty. On the other hand, we see clearly how rich we were in our poverty. We have no idea how rich and beautiful was the patriarchal Jewish way of life, as in the rabbinic adage, "poverty befits the Jews [like a red ribbon on a white horse]." [...]

[From the Letter Shin]

Shtores-gelt (also: *Shtores-moes*): communal fees for the Rabbi, Cantor and Sexton, and for charity. [...]

Shayngelt (pronounced "shaangelt"): "inspection money" for looking at the bride for the first time in her veil at the groom's house. [...]

Sheyngelt: a considerable sum, a great deal of money. [...]

Shilumim-gelt (mostly shortened to *Shilumim*): the reparations money which the accursed Germans pay for the Nazi Holocaust and robbery of Jewish property during the years 1939–1945, which serves as an acknowledgement of their crimes against the Jewish people. The word originated in the State of Israel and it was there that the dramatic struggle over the *shilumim* first took place. In the sessions of the Second Knesset (1952) the decision was made which nearly split the Jewish people in two and has triggered disputes among Jews everywhere ever since. The vote to accept the reparations was 61 for, 50 against, 4 not present and 5 abstaining.

Translated by Solon Beinfeld.

Other work by Rivkind: *Le-ot u-le-zikaron* (1942).

Yudl Mark and Judah A. Joffe

Mark, 1897–1975

Yiddish linguist, educator, and activist Yudl Mark was born in Palanga (in contemporary Lithuania) and studied history and philology at Petrograd University, where he was active in Jewish politics. Mark helped found YIVO and the Yiddish Real-Gimnazye in Vilkomir (contemporary Ukmergė, Lithuania). In addition, he taught at various schools and seminaries in Lithuania. He was a correspondent for the *Forverts* in New York, and, after settling there in 1936, he edited the YIVO journal *Di yidishe shprakh* and contributed to a wide range of Yiddish political, literary, and educational publications. He settled in Jerusalem in 1970.

Joffe, 1873–1966

Yiddish scholar, philologist, and lexicographer Judah A. Joffe was born in Bakhmut (in contemporary Ukraine) and came to the United States in 1891. Joffe specialized in classical and comparative philology as well as phonetics and historical English grammar. He was a strong advocate for standardized Yiddish spelling. As a musicologist and expert on Slavic languages, he contributed to several years of the *International Yearbook*, as well as the *New International Encyclopedia* (1902). In addition, Joffe translated works from Yiddish, English, and French and lectured on Russian language at Columbia University.

The Great Dictionary of the Yiddish Language 1961

The Great Dictionary of the Yiddish Language has been assembled on the basis of *inclusiveness*—that is to say, as a dictionary which attempts to record and include *all* the words of the Yiddish language. This is a goal which is difficult to achieve with total success, but we strive for it. It is our explicit intent that the *Great Dictionary* should be the full *collection* of all the linguistic assets of the Yiddish-speaking part of our people. [....]

We have striven to record and include words and expressions from all strata of the people: from the language of the Torah scholar to the speech of rural Jews and the jargon of klezmer musicians and thieves; from the speech heard at a rabbinical assembly to the terminology and phraseology of the labor movement; from the language of heder and yeshiva to the language of the Yiddish school where all subjects were taught in Yiddish; from the language of the intellectual to the slang of the underworld; from the language of the marketplace and the workshop to the language of the kitchen and of intimate family life. We have striven to provide the whole speech-spectrum of all trades and the entire social scale of the Yiddish-speaking sector of the Jewish people. Thus, a word from the "sticks," from some out-of-the-way spot, had the same right to be included in our collection as a word from a big city or major cultural center.

The *Great Dictionary* is based not only on what we have written down from literary works and from documents, but also on what we have noted in the living spoken language. We have therefore included the great mass of words that accidentally or for some other reason failed to find their way into literature. In so doing, we have rescued hundreds of words from oblivion.

We had to establish a definitive criterion. Out of a variety of possible definitions as to what constitutes a Yiddish word, we have settled on the following formulation: *any word that was used by a group of Jews while these Jews were thinking and speaking in Yiddish, is a word in the Yiddish language.* In this formulation, the word *group* plays an important role. The group can be small—one profession, even an uncommon one; one small town, one Hasidic *shtibl* [prayer house] or only one yeshiva; only one class studying, let us say, cosmography, and so forth. And *using* a word means not only uttering it in speech, but also absorbing it from reading or hearing. Our definition contains the word *thinking*, which means that we have included the internal, personal element of language, which is after all the basis for learned and written language. This provides a criterion which enables us to exclude words taken from the surrounding languages and haphazardly entered into a Yiddish text or Yiddish speech, although they are in no way accepted in the speaker's environment and the speaker would not use them again. That is also a means of excluding words and expressions whose purpose is exaggeration or comic effect, but are not current coin in any natural Yiddish environment.

In sum, the intention of the *Great Dictionary of Yiddish Language* is to include the whole language in all its three dimensions: in *length*, in the historic chain of all the generations that used Yiddish; in *breadth*, in the whole geographic spread and dispersal of Yiddish; and in *depth*, that is, in all the social and cultural variations that exist or existed among Yiddish speakers. We are fully aware that up to now we have not achieved every-thing. The preparatory work ought to have lasted many more years and the number of collaborators ought to have been much greater. We have not yet been able to record words from all the works of the very oldest literature. We have also fallen behind in recording from the older and newer literature. Most of our compilers have been from Eastern Europe and we sense gaps with regard to Hungarian Yiddish and Western Yiddish in general. [. . .]

We have tried to present the Yiddish words in the garb of the idioms with which they are associated, with the expressions that give them color and life. We have in mind the *cultural-historical* value of the words—how they illuminate the context of everyday life. Defining words that are deeply anchored in the language and combining them with specific expressions can reveal what is intangibly yet inherently Jewish, a quality embedded in what is called the "folk spirit." We avoid metaphoric interpretation, but in many instances we indicate that it is possible. It was important for us not only conscientiously to gather the riches of our language, but also to bring forward all the slivers of a mirror, which in its entirety reflects Jewish life over generations: the Jewish way of thinking, the Jewish way of feeling. Thus we try to connect the Yiddish words with Jewish customs, with the characteristics of Jewish tradition, with the minutiae of Jewishness. Our deepest desire is by means of this original and inclusive dictionary to provide insight into the Jewish worldview and the world of Jewish feeling.

In the case of those words that signal Jewish specificity, we have to some extent stepped outside the bounds of linguistic space and aimed for a condensed folk-encyclopedia. We are doing our work in the awareness that we are trying to create a monument to hundreds of years of Jewish *life* within the creative Ashkenazi branch of our people. At the same time, we have not for one moment forgotten what has been done to our language both by the bloody hands of the oppressor and murderer and by the stormy winds of linguistic assimilation. We consider our assignment as not merely linguistic, but also broadly societal, or as we see it, ethically societal. Our goal is Jewish-national; in our feelings, it is ethically national.

Translated by Solon Beinfeld.

Other work by Mark: *Historishe geshtaltn* (1957). Other work by Joffe: *Bove-bukh* (1949).

Saul Bellow

1915–2005

Born in Montreal, novelist Saul Bellow moved to Chicago when he was nine; that city became the background for many of his works. A professor of English at Boston University and other institutions, Bellow wrote best-selling and critically acclaimed novels, short stories, memoirs, plays, and novellas. He received the 1976 Nobel Prize in Literature, a Pulitzer Prize, three National Book Awards, and a Presidential Medal.

Great Jewish Short Stories
1963

Most of the stories in this collection are modern; a few are ancient. They were written in Hebrew, German, Yiddish, Russian and English, yet all are, to a discerning eye, very clearly Jewish. [. . .]

I would call the attitudes of these stories characteristically Jewish. In them, laughter and trembling are so curiously mingled that it is not easy to determine the relations of the two. At times the laughter seems simply to restore the equilibrium of sanity; at times the figures of the story, or parable, appear to invite or encourage trembling with the secret aim of overcoming it by means of laughter. Aristophanes and Lucian do not hesitate to involve the Olympian gods in their fun, and Rabelais's humor does not spare the heavens either. But these are different kinds of comic genius. Jewish humor is mysterious and eludes our efforts—even, in my opinion, the efforts of Sigmund Freud—to analyze it. Recently one Jewish writer (Hymen Slate in *The Noble Savage*) has argued that laughter, the comic sense of life, may be offered as proof of the existence of God. Existence, he says, is too *funny* to be uncaused. The real secret, the ultimate mystery, may never reveal itself to the earnest thought of a Spinoza, but when we laugh (the idea is remotely Hassidic) our minds refer us to God's existence. Chaos is *exposed*. [. . .]

In Jerusalem several years ago I had an amusing and enlightening conversation with the dean of Hebrew writers, S. J. Agnon. This spare old man, whose face has a remarkably youthful color, received me in his house, not far from the barbed wire entanglements that divide the city, and while we were drinking tea, he asked me if any of my books had been translated into Hebrew. If they had not been, I had better see to it immediately, because, he said, they would survive only in the Holy

Tongue. His advice I assume was only half serious. This was his witty way of calling my attention to a curious situation. I cited Heinrich Heine as an example of a poet who had done rather well in German. "Ah," said Mr. Agnon, "we have him beautifully translated into Hebrew. He is safe." Mr. Agnon feels secure in his ancient tradition. But Jews have been writing in languages other than Hebrew for more than two thousand years. The New Testament scholar Hugh J. Schonfield asserts that parts of the Gospels were composed in a sort of Yiddish Greek, "as colorful in imagery and metaphor as it is often careless in grammatical construction." [. . .]

It cannot be argued that the stories of Isaac Babel are not characteristically Jewish. And they were written in Russian by a man who knew Yiddish well enough to have written them in that language. Before he disappeared from view during one of Stalin's purges, Babel had been put in charge of publishing the works of Sholom Aleichem in Yiddish. Why should he have chosen therefore to write his own stories in Russian, the language of the oppressors, of Pobedonostev and the Black Hundreds? If, before writing, he had taken his bearings he could not have found himself to be "a perfect unit of time and place." He wrote in Russian from motives we can never expect to understand fully. These stories have about them something that justifies them to the most grudging inquiry—they have spirit, originality, beauty. Who was Babel? Where did he come from? He was an accident. We are all such accidents. We do not make up history and culture. We simply appear, not by our own choice. We make what we can of our condition with the means available. We must accept the mixture as we find it—the impurity of it, the tragedy of it, the hope of it.

Other works by Bellow: *The Victim* (1947); *The Adventures of Augie March* (1953); *Henderson the Rain King* (1959); *Herzog* (1964); *Mr. Sammler's Planet* (1970); *To Jerusalem and Back* (1976).

Uriel Weinreich

1926–1967

A pioneering linguist whose life was cut short by leukemia, Uriel Weinreich was born in Vilna (today Vilnius), studied at Columbia University, and followed in his father Max Weinreich's scholarly footsteps. His crowning achievements in the field of Yiddish were the *Language and Culture Atlas of Ashkenazic Jewry* (started in 1950), *College Yiddish* (1949), the first such textbook in any language, and his landmark *Modern English-to-Yiddish/Yiddish-to-English Dictionary*, published in 1968.

Mapping a Culture
1963

The very lack of a self-contained territory that has so far disqualified the study of Yiddish from NDEA [the National Defense Education Act] support endows Ashkenazic Jewry with exemplary value for a particularly crucial problem in social history: the effect of communication channels and barriers on the diffusion of cultural innovations. Despite the emphasis in modern social science on the structural cohesion of linguistic and cultural phenomena, it is still safe to assume that substantial portions of language and culture develop at random. If a society splits into several isolated groups, random innovations will cause each group to evolve differently. On the other hand, if contact remains, at least some innovations in one will be transmitted to the other. The geographic fragmentation of a culture and a language thus yields an opportunity to reconstruct the influences of neighboring localities upon one another. [. . .]

The geographic interlocking of two cultures becomes instructive when we consider, for example, the relation of religious codification to customary practice. On the one hand, it is well known that the Jews in the cities and small towns of Europe formed a profoundly religious society. The Talmudic way of life determined not only every aspect of religious dogma and ritual, but codified economic law, family relations, education, clothing, diet, and many other aspects of daily behavior, often in detail.

On the other hand, there were details of life that in practice escaped religious reach. In dietary law, for example, there was room for considerable variety in cuisine. For a Jew building a house, the religious code prescribed that in every room a corner of a wall remain unplastered in remembrance of the destruction of the Temple, and that the doorposts be equipped with special amulets; but the architecture and the internal furnishings of Jewish houses did not particularly matter. The solemnity of Bible reading and the dignity of prayer were secured by careful regulation of the pronunciation of the Hebrew liturgy; at the same time, the vast domain of the vernacular Yiddish developed without much religious interference.

Now, it might be expected that the peripheral, profane aspects of the culture would develop solely by local improvisation. Whereas the basic outline of the wedding ritual, for example, is given to all Ashkenazic Jews alike, the pre-wedding entertainment, festive foods, music, dances symbolizing fertility and wealth—all these, according to one widespread view, should differ from family to family or from *shtetl* to *shtetl*. Still another theory predicts that in its uncodified aspects, the culture is under influence from the various local cultures. The wedding music, for example, will be Polish among the Jews of Poland, Ukrainian in the Ukraine, Rumanian in Rumania, and so forth.

Neither of these theories is correct. In the domains of culture not explicitly codified by religion, we now find that variation is not individual or local, but conforms to definite regional patterns. And what is more, where cultural borrowing has taken place, the regional patterns in the recipient culture are not necessarily congruent with the corresponding distributions in the Christian source cultures. Apart from the implications for Jewish cultural history, this overlapping autonomy suggests that the role of exclusive territory in the general definition of society may have to be reconsidered.

Enough is known about Yiddish to make possible the formulation of many such problems, at least in their broadest terms. But we lack the full and precise geographic data that are necessary if we are to move toward solutions. [. . .] Hence the urgency with which the *Language and Culture Atlas of Ashkenazic Jewry* is now being compiled at Columbia. [. . .]

An important respect in which the new Atlas departs from established methodology is that the fieldwork is conducted entirely among emigrants. In the areas under study, there are few Jews left, and for political reasons, too, the prospects of field work in Eastern Europe today are hardly encouraging. But emigrants from those areas are easily accessible to the scholar in America. Emigrant organizations (*landsmanshaftn*) are assisting field workers in New York City and Israel to locate suitable representatives of appropriately spaced sample communities on the map of European Jewry.

The full questionnaire takes up to fifteen hours of oral interviewing to administer; but there are abridged regional versions also in use. The conversation with the informant intersperses questions on customs and vocabulary with items designed to elicit local phonetic and grammatical peculiarities of the Yiddish language. Some informants are astonished that their plain speech should be of interest to scholars. Others are fully aware of the preciousness of their testimony to the recapturing of a culture.

Those who hear of this research for the first time commonly question its reliability. Can the details of culture and language in the Old Country be reconstructed from the testimony of aging emigrants at a distance of thousands of miles and several decades from the time and place under study? Is it enough to interview a single native of each sample town, even if he is the son or daughter of native parents? The selection of suitable informants is beset with many difficulties, but the ultimate answer to the question of reliability is an unequivocal affirmative. The very maps shown here give proof that cultural geography at a distance, with a sample of one informant per locality, is indeed possible. The data fall into excellent configurations, yielding sharp boundaries. Failures of memory among the emigrant informants, or linguistic contamination by contact with emigrants from other areas, are random; they might have blurred the isoglosses, but they could hardly have produced an illusory displacement of sharp lines. Well-formed isoglosses such as those that appear on many of the preliminary maps of the *Language and Culture Atlas of Ashkenazic Jewry* cannot be anything but accurate representations of the formative period of the informants' lives. This principle is not only the cornerstone of our investigation; it is also a general methodological discovery, an early bonus of the project.

Other work by Weinreich: *Languages in Contact: Findings and Problems* (1952).

Lucy S. Dawidowicz

1915–1990

Born in New York City, Lucy S. Dawidowicz was a professor of history and Holocaust studies at Yeshiva University; she wrote many important books about American Jewry, the history of East European Jewry, and the Holocaust. Her anthology, *The Golden Tradition*, helped make the heritage of East European Jewry accessible to American Jews. Her work on the Holocaust emphasized the decisive role of Hitler's antisemitism.

The Golden Tradition: Jewish Life and Thought in Eastern Europe
1967

This is a book about East European Jews in crisis, challenge, and creativity from the end of the eighteenth

century until their cataclysmic destruction in the Second World War.

In the sixteenth century, the center of world Jewry moved to Eastern Europe, which until 1939 remained the region of greatest Jewish population and density. Eastern Europe was the cradle of almost every important Jewish cultural, religious, and national movement and the area where Jewish faith, thought, and culture flourished unsurpassed. Thence came the impetus and vitality that preserved the Jewish people intact in prosperity and adversity. East European Jewry became a reservoir of manpower and from the nineteenth century on provided the overwhelming bulk of migrants to the United States, to Israel, and many far-flung communities.

Enlightenment came to the relatively small communities of Western Jews before it went east, and emancipation followed shortly thereafter with the French Revolution. The enlightenment shook the foundations of traditional Judaism, unprepared for its assault; emancipation toppled that traditional Jewish society. Western Jews could not resist the lures of enlightenment, emancipation, and the opportunity to enter the larger society. They rushed to embrace it, though emancipation often turned out to be a mirage and enlightenment a dead end. In a brief span, West European Jewish communities were decimated, having paid heavily for emancipation with conversion.

Eastern Europe was different, and East European Jews responded differently to enlightenment and emancipation. They searched for ways to harmonize tradition and modernity, to preserve their Jewish identity and retain their community. This book is an attempt to show what they did and what the outcome was.

I have here assembled autobiographies, memoirs, reminiscences, and letters of some sixty persons whose lives document these East European Jewish responses to modernity. "Autobiography," Wilhelm Dilthey wrote, "is the highest and most instructive form in which the understanding of life confronts us." The most direct form of history, autobiography is history's most intimate disclosure, a man's assessment of his life, his acts and ideas, successes and failures; an analysis of his origins, his milieu, the flow of events around him.

The autobiographies I sought were those of men, in William James's words, "whose genius was so adapted to the receptivities of the moment, or whose accidental position of authority was so critical that they became ferments, initiators of movement, setters of precedent or fashion." But because the material was not always available, I have tried to repair the gaps with memoirs about them.

I was guided also by the desire to show the diversity of Jews and their culture, the centripetal and centrifugal forces that moved them, and the variety they brought to Jewish thought and life. East European Jewry was not, as the sentimentalists see it, forever frozen in utter piety and utter poverty.

The historical review that follows is an attempt to put these memoirs in the perspective of their time and place and to describe some relevant social, political, and economic currents that affected our memoirists. I have tried to show the tension between assimilatory tendencies and survivalist values among East European Jews, and I have cited the autobiographies as illustrative documents.

East European Jewry was cruelly cut down. But vital elements of its culture survive. Perhaps we, heirs of that culture, can continue its tradition of conserving Jewish identity by fusing the old and the new.

Other works by Dawidowicz: *Politics in a Pluralist Democracy* (1963); *The War against the Jews, 1933–1945* (1975).

The Jewish Catalog

Friends and collaborators Richard Siegel, Michael Strassfeld, and Sharon Strassfeld saw the need for an offbeat, warm-hearted guide to Jewish life, spiced with the spirit of the Jewish counterculture, and created one together: *The Jewish Catalog: A Do-It-Yourself Guide*. The three belonged to the Havurah movement in the early 1970s and remained involved with Jewish communal life in the decades since. Michael Strassfeld, a former rabbi for the Society for the Advancement of Judaism, has written and edited guides to Shabbat, Passover, and other Jewish holidays. Richard Siegel (d. 2018), who served as executive director of the Foundation for Jewish Culture, spent decades promoting Jewish culture, supporting Jewish artists, and editing Jewish books. The editor and author Sharon Strassfeld has written primers on Jewish holidays and customs, as well as an advice book, *Everything I Know: Basic Life Rules from a Jewish Mother*.

The Jewish Catalog
1973

Introduction

Perhaps the most difficult question we have been asked in the course of compiling this catalog has been, "What exactly is it?" Having realized quite early that there are no preexisting categories which would adequately satisfy this compulsion for definition, our rather vague response was generally, "It's a compendium of tools and resources for use in Jewish education and Jewish living in the fullest sense of these terms." Traditional Jewish compilations did not seem overly concerned with definitional precision or rigidity. To the extent that they were records and guides to life, they were wide-ranging and multifaceted. Thus, the Talmud interweaves stories and anecdotes with legalistic debate; the Rambam's commentary on the Mishnah includes a recipe for haroset; the *Shulhan Arukh* lists customs, variations, and kavvanot (intentions) along with ritual and legal prescriptions; and the *Siddur Kol Bo* ("the prayer book with everything in it") has alphabets, diagrams for tying tefillin, calendars, and even pictures of fruit juxtaposed with the traditional order of prayers. Not to be presumptuous, this catalog takes these earlier texts as models for its breadth, variations, uncategorizability, and necessary incompleteness. [. . .]

Basically our intentions are (1) to give enough information to be immediately useful; (2) to direct those interested to additional resources; (3) to present the traditional dimensions of the subjects covered; and (4) to open options for personal creativity and contemporary utilization of these directives. We make no claim to be a repository of the whole past of Jewish ritual, law, folklore, crafts, and so on. This is a nonexhaustive selection of materials which offer the possibility for immediate application and integration into one's personal environment. [. . .] The orientation is to move away from the prefabricated, spoon-fed, nearsighted Judaism into the stream of possibilities for personal responsibility and physical participation. This entails a returning of the control of the Jewish environment to the hands of the individual—through accessible knowledge of the what, where, who, and how of contemporary Judaism.

To facilitate this process, we have collected material on a broad range of topics, investigated them from several aspects, and presented them from different perspectives. A large number of people have contributed to this work. [. . .] As will be apparent, they do not necessarily share approaches, life-styles, assumptions, or significance systems. Their attitudes, biases, inclinations, and orientations have generally not been edited out. This was an editorial decision which we felt was basic to the purpose and texture of the book. The present Jewish community is by no means monolithic. It is multifaceted, open, and pulsing with dynamism. To ignore the range of options and to limit ourselves to one orientation would have been to defeat the purpose of the book. Many opportunities are given for entrance. Many access routes to ritual, celebration, and the various facets of life are suggested through the interweaving of dynamics, laws, intentions, actions, possibilities, etc.

You can plug in wherever you want. Some people may be drawn to the halakhah and various types of halakhic observance within a mitzvah system. Others will be more concerned with the underlying psychological, mythical, spiritual levels and the vehicles which have developed within Judaism to express these. Still others will find the possibilities for physical expression within traditional forms—openings for the artist and craftsman. There is no need to be reductionist about this; many other orientations and needs can find expression within this work. The hope, in fact, is that the catalog will facilitate the development of a "repertoire of responses" so that a person can accommodate himself to the rapid pace of societal and environmental change—as well as to his own personal, emotional, and spiritual flux.

There are two potential drawbacks to this diversity, however.

1. The book reads unevenly. Solution: do not read it all at once.
2. An orientation to which you may respond in one section may not be evident in another. Solution: draw your own transference. If this book opens you to an awareness that there are manifold ways of approaching the facets of Judaism, it will have fulfilled an important function. It is up to you, however, to build on these flexibilities and extend them according to your own creativity.

Ultimately, however, our intentions or hopes for this book are irrelevant. You will or will not respond to what is included for reasons which are beyond our anticipation or our abilities to effect.

May this book serve to fulfill the intention of:
"This is my God and I will beautify Him."

Cultural, Political, and Religious Thought

Joshua Loth Liebman
1907-1948

Joshua Loth Liebman, a Reform rabbi, was born in Hamilton, Ohio. He later moved to nearby Cincinnati, graduating from the University of Cincinnati and Hebrew Union College (HUC), where he was ordained in 1930. He served at various rabbinic posts, in Lafayette, Indiana; Chicago; and Boston. He gained national recognition thanks to his radio sermons and the unprecedented success of his self-help manual, *Peace of Mind*.

Peace of Mind
1946

Once, as a young man, I undertook to draw up a catalogue of the acknowledged goods of life. I set down my inventory of earthly desirables: health, love, talent, power, riches, and fame. Then I proudly showed it to a wise elder. An excellent list, said my old friend, and set down in reasonable order. But you have omitted the one important ingredient, lacking which your list becomes an intolerable burden. He crossed out my entire schedule. Then he wrote down three syllables: peace of mind. This is the gift that God reserves for His special protégés, he said. Talent and health He gives to many. Wealth is commonplace, fame not rare. But peace of mind He bestows charily. This is no private opinion of mine, he explained. I am merely paraphrasing from the Psalmists, Marcus Aurelius, Lao-tse. "O God, Lord of the universe," say these wise ones, "heap worldly gifts at the feet of foolish men. Give me the gift of the untroubled mind." I found that difficult to accept; but now, after a quarter of a century of personal experience and professional observation, I have come to understand that peace of mind is the true goal of the considered life. I know now that the sum of all other possessions does not necessarily add up to peace of mind; on the other hand, I have seen this inner tranquility flourish without the material supports of property or even the buttress of physical health. Peace of mind can transform a cottage into a spacious manor hall; the want of it can make a regal residence an imprisoning shell. Where then shall we look for it? The key to the problem is to be found in

Matthew Arnold's lines: We would have inward peace. But [should be "Yet"] will not look within . . . But will not look within! Here, in a single phrase, our willfulness is bared.

Other works by Liebman: *Psychiatry and Religion* (1948); *Morality and Immorality: The Problem of Conscience* (1950).

Mordecai M. Kaplan
1881-1983

Mordecai Kaplan, founder of the Reconstructionist branch of Judaism in the United States, was born in Lithuania and brought to America when he was nine years old. He studied at the Jewish Theological Seminary but was ordained privately in 1908 by Rabbi Isaac Jacob Reines. He initially served Orthodox congregations in New York City. His radical views led him to break with Orthodoxy, and he created what became Reconstructionist Judaism, whose ideological foundation is the idea that Judaism is an all-embracing civilization, not just a religion in the conventional sense of the term. His conception of God was starkly naturalistic, rejecting the notion of a supernatural Being. Despite his views, he taught at the Jewish Theological Seminary from 1909 until his retirement in 1963.

The Future of the American Jew
1948

The Courage to Face the Facts

If we Jews had our patron saints, the priest-prophet Ezekiel would be the patron saint of those of us who are vitally concerned in the outcome of the present crisis in Jewish life. It is he to whom we should turn for inspiration and guidance in this apocalyptic age.

In the ancient Jewish colony, formed in Babylon during the sixth century B.C.E. by the captives who had been brought from Eretz Yisrael, Ezekiel found himself in the midst of a spiritual wasteland, comparable to our own American-Jewish scene. Some of the Jews were so cowed and overawed by the might of their conquerors and the prestige of their conquerors' religion that they renounced their own God; they gave as an excuse the utter hopelessness of their people. Other Jews adhered to outworn religious doctrines, enjoyed listening to Ezekiel's preachments, without any intention of acting on them, and blithely ignored the responsibilities to which their new surroundings gave rise.

Although Ezekiel realized that both of these trends were bound to prove fatal to the life of his people, he was hopeful that they would be checked before it would be too late. His confidence in Israel's future was so great that it took on the form of his well-known vision of Israel's resurrection. We should learn from him to refrain from self-delusion concerning the critical character of our present situation and from resignation to the inevitability of a tragic outcome.

Since Jewish life nowadays is either smothered by the deadweight of smug complacency or paralyzed by fright and despair, it is essential that we Jews catch something of that spirit with which Ezekiel sought to imbue the Jews of his generation: *courage in the face of disheartening apathy and spiritual decline, faith in the recuperative and regenerative powers of our people, and wisdom and patience in planning and building for the future.*

It is natural to try to conceal from ourselves what we do not wish to believe. But let us not deceive ourselves. The Prophet Jeremiah excoriated the misleaders of his day who kept on saying, "All's well," when all was far from well. Ezekiel described such people as daubing flimsy walls with whitewash. By resenting the disclosure of the critical state of affairs in Jewish life, we put ourselves in one class with those of whom the Prophet said in the name of God: "They shall have no place in the council of my people, nor be enrolled in the register of the Household of Israel." In the long run, more good is apt to come from being worried by the disintegration which is proceeding beneath the surface of Jewish life than from being contented with its superficial semblance of health.

American-Jewish life seethes with activity. Federations, welfare funds, community chests, United Jewish Appeals, hospitals, orphan asylums, homes for the aged, fraternal orders, public relations agencies, and above all Zionism, make quite a clatter. What permanent significance, if any, do they have? Are all these efforts with their vast expenditure of energy part of the *advance* or of the *retreat* of our inner forces? An army that is beating a hasty retreat presents a picture of the most intensive activity—transporting the wounded, eluding the enemy and saving as much of its material as possible. Nevertheless, all that bustle is no indication of headway. From the standpoint of Israel's future, we have ample reason to believe that, by and large, the contribution of the vast network of Jewish public agencies toward keeping alive or awakening in our young the desire to carry on as Jews, if not altogether negative, is certainly negligible.

Some may regard as irrelevant, if not unfair, the very expectation that these philanthropic and social activities should help to perpetuate Jewish life. Is not the actual good they do in the immediate present their justification? We must remember, however, that these activities constitute a burden which the Jew has to carry alone. Every people has a right to exact sacrifices of the energy, time and resources of those who belong to it. These are expected as a means of helping a people to live. A share in its future is the necessary and legitimate reward to which the individual looks forward; otherwise the sacrifice is a gratuitous and meaningless burden. Rebuilding the ruins of shattered European Jewry and rendering Eretz Yisrael secure as a Jewish homeland—the two largest undertakings of American Jews— are projects which will require two or three generations for their consummation. If Jews lose faith in the future of their people, they will lose interest even in the physical salvaging of its human wreckage.

The amazing fact is that *most of our spiritual leaders carry on routine duties as though nothing cataclysmic has happened to Jewish life.* They are like the famous old lady of the London *blitz* whose house had been so thoroughly bombed that all that remained was a jagged frontage in a flattened street. That did not seem to change her routine in the least. Every morning she would turn up as usual to scrub the doorstep. Likewise, most of our rabbis, educators and scholars carry on their daily chores as if the House of Israel were almost intact. They have done little, if anything, to counteract the tendency to identify Jewish loyalty with "dollar Judaism," the Judaism that begins and ends with philanthropy. They have been derelict in their duty to educate the laity to a realization that *to be a Jew today means nothing less than to aid in the rebuilding of the House and in the reconstituting of the Household of Israel.* [. . .]

If we wish to know what, basically, has gone wrong with us Jews, we must resort to a realistic understanding of the revolution that has taken place in the entire world-outlook of mankind. But if we desire to know what is to set us right again, we must resort to the moral realism of the Prophets. They taught us to put faith in God and in the ultimate triumph of His will. We can do nothing better than to adopt that faith as the basis of what must constitute for us this-worldly salvation. This means that *there is no other moral choice for us Jews than to strive with all our might for the establishment of a just social order which will render democratic, benign nationalism safe for the creative survival of the Jewish people.*

To make this choice, however, we have to be fully convinced of the intrinsic value of Jewish survival. We have to see in Jewish life high creative possibilities. We have to find Judaism capable of eliciting the best that is in us. To meet this vital requirement, Judaism must come to possess the kind of social structure which will be organically related to the high purposes of a religious civilization. Moreover, it must have its entire ideology transposed into the key of thought which is relevant to the problems that agitate us today. We have to evaluate our inherited institutions, and, if we discover any elements in them that have become obsolete or irrelevant, we should unhesitatingly deal with them as we would with the withered branches of a tree.

The willing ability to reappraise from time to time our spiritual heritage in terms of ever-increasing knowledge and experience must henceforth become part of Jewish life. However, the sloughing off of the old should be only incidental to the creation of the new. Whether we shall have a future or not depends upon our capacity to elicit new energy and to discover new resources.

The ultimate hope of American Jewry rests with those whose being is rooted in Jewish life, and who cannot contemplate the disintegration of Judaism without a deep sense of frustration. If they are to avert a tragic anti-climax to the life of their people, they should seek out one another and together discipline themselves into a community of mind and heart, animated by the sole purpose of creative Jewish survival. They should constitute themselves as a kind of religio-cultural fellowship or order, with chapters both within and without the existing organizations and institutions, simultaneously resisting any tendency to become identified as an additional sect or denomination. In that way they can act as a ferment within the inert and apathetic mass of our people. They should seek to enlist, in the service of Jewish life, whatever creative talent is to be found among us.

Upon Jews of this sensitive and spiritual type devolves the responsibility of preventing American Jewry from deteriorating into a meaningless human detritus, superfluous to itself and to the rest of the world. They have the opportunity to make Judaism a beneficent influence in American civilization, by becoming a potent factor for the advancement of genuine democracy. Theirs is the obligation to function in our day as part of Israel's faithful remnant; to aid in bringing about the much needed psychic and moral reconstruction in our day, which the Prophet Ezekiel urged upon his contemporaries, when he pleaded:

"Make you a new heart and a new spirit, for why shall ye die, O House of Israel?"

Other works by Kaplan: *Judaism as a Civilization* (1934); *Judaism without Supernaturalism* (1958).

Simon Rawidowicz
1896–1957

The Polish-born Hebraist and historian of Jewish thought Simon Rawidowicz moved to Berlin when he was in his twenties to pursue a university education. When the Nazis seized power in 1933, he took refuge in England, where he taught in London and Leeds before leaving for the United States in 1947. He taught at the College of Jewish Studies in Chicago and later headed the Department of Near Eastern and Judaic Studies at Brandeis University. His crowning work, *Bavel vi-Yerushalaim* (1957), published posthumously, set forth his conception of Jewish history and analyzed the impact of the creation of the State of Israel on modern Jewish life. He was known particularly for rejecting the Zionist doctrine of *shelilat ha-golah* (negation of the diaspora) and arguing that the Land of Israel and the diaspora were mutually supportive, vibrant centers of Jewish creativity.

Israel: The Ever-Dying People
1948

Is Israel alone a dying nation? Numerous civilizations have disappeared before there emerged the one in which we live so happily and unhappily at the same time. Each dying civilization was confident that earth and heaven would disappear with it. How often did man feel he was finished forever! When ancient Rome began to crumble, Romans and others felt sure that the end of the universe was at hand. St. Augustine thought that the "anti-Christ" would appear after the destruction of Rome and man would be called to his last day of judgment. In various aspects, this fear of being the last was also manifest in Christianity and Islam. In addition, the lamentation of *mi-she-met* has its psychological origin in man's great admiration for his living masters, in his fear lest the miracle will not occur again, lest there will be no second set of masters—as if genius rises only once, never again to re-appear.

Yet, making all allowances for the general motives in this dread of the end, it has nowhere been at home so incessantly, with such an acuteness and intensity, as in the House of Israel. The world may be constantly dying, but no nation was ever so incessantly dying as Israel.

Going deeper into the problem—and here I have to confine myself to a hint—I am often tempted to think that this fear of cessation in Israel was fundamentally a kind of protective individual and collective emotion. Israel has indulged so much in the fear of its end, that its constant vision of the end helped it to overcome every crisis, to emerge from every threatening end as a living unit, though much wounded and reduced. In anticipating the end, it became its master. Thus no catastrophe could ever take this end-fearing people by surprise, so as to put it off its balance, still less to obliterate it—as if Israel's incessant preparation for the end made this very end absolutely impossible.

Philosophers like Hegel and Schopenhauer have spoken of the guile of nature, of the guile of history. Is not this peculiar sense of the end also the guile of a nation *sui generis*, a nation that would use every device for its survival, even that of incessant anticipation of its disappearance, in order to rule it out forever? This aspect of national psychology deserves special attention.

As far as historical reality is concerned, we are confronted here with a phenomenon which has almost no parallel in mankind's story; a nation that has been disappearing constantly for the last two thousand years, exterminated in dozens of lands all over the globe, reduced to half or a third of its population by tyrants ancient and modern—and yet it still exists, falls and rises, loses all its possessions and re-equips itself for a new start, a second, a third chance—always fearing the end, never afraid to make a new beginning, to snatch triumph from the jaws of defeat, whenever and wherever possible. There is no nation more dying than Israel, yet none better equipped to resist disaster, to fight alone, always alone.

As far as our foreign relations, if I may so call them, are concerned, there is much comfort in our thorny path in the world. The first ancient non-Jewish document which mentions Israel by name is, symbolically apt, a message of total annihilation. It is the monument—in possession of the British Museum—on which Merneptah, the thirteenth century B.C.E. Egyptian forerunner of Nasser, boasts of his great deeds and triumphs over nations, and, among other things, states succinctly: "Israel is desolated; its seed is no more." Since 1215 B.C.E. how often did prophets at home and abroad prophesy Israel's desolation! How often did nations try to translate this prophecy into practice, and in the most cruel ways! About 3,150 years after that boastful Egyptian conqueror, there arose Satan in the heart of Europe and began to predict Israel's total annihilation—and to prepare the most modern technical devices to make his prophecy come true. And after it was given to him—to our greatest sorrow and the world's greatest shame—to reduce Israel by one-third, Israel is still alive—weakened, to be sure, robbed of its best resources for recuperation, of its reservoir, its fountains of life and learning, yet still standing on its feet, numbering four times as many souls as in the days of the French Revolution, rebuilding its national life in the State of Israel, in the face of so many obstacles! Though not perfect, its spiritual creativity continues. Filled with fear of its end, it seeks to make a new beginning in the diaspora and in the State of Israel.

If so, many will say, what is all the lamenting about? Many nations have suffered, and, if we suffered a little more, we should not exaggerate or carry on hysterically. No need to worry, no need of superhuman efforts—wait and see—nothing will happen; and if it should happen—surely it has happened before. [. . .]

Such easy comfort, such exaggerated optimism is no less dangerous than the pessimism of Israel's end. Neither is justified, neither is helpful.

In the beginning, Israel's message was that of a universal optimism—salvation, happiness and perfection for all peoples. "The mountain of the Lord's house will be established in the top of the mountains" [Isaiah 2:2] means: the peoples of the world will also share alike, with Israel, in the blessing of the messianic age. Many well-known and understandable factors compelled post-exilic and medieval Messianism to become more one-sided and directed exclusively toward the redemption of Israel; optimistic toward Israel, pessimistic toward the world. In more recent times, most Jewish ideologies and political movements were dualistic inasmuch as they saw a world divided, Israel and world torn apart—nay, still more: Israel itself was to them no more. Thus, to give one illustration, Jewish Reform on both sides of the Rhine, 19th-century liberalism, was optimistic as far as the world's future was concerned, pessimistic for the survival of Israel as a nation with all national attributes. This same dualistic attitude was taken up by all kinds of assimilated Jewish revolutionaries in Eastern and Western Europe. Later, two Jewish ideologies fought each other in Europe: one was most optimistic for the remnant of Israel in Zion and pessimistic as far as the Jewish people in the diaspora was concerned, while the other reversed this dichotomy, maintaining that only diaspora Jewry had a future in some liberal or socialist order.

Both made the fundamental mistake of dividing Israel into two parts. Israel must always be considered one and indivisible—*yisrael ehad*. As long as one part of Israel lives in a hell, the other cannot live in paradise.

I therefore say: we may not split up Israel into two spheres of reality. Israel is one. Neither may we approach the Jewish problem from an optimistic or pessimistic angle. Optimism and pessimism are only expressions or indications of our fears, doubts, hopes and desires. Hopes and desires we must have; fears and doubts we cannot escape. Yet, what we need most at present is a dynamic Jewish realism which will see our reality, the reality of the world, our problem, the problem of the world, in its entirety, without any dualism—hell-paradise or whatever.

Such a Jewish realism will also show us the real meaning of that fear of the end which is so inherent in us. A nation dying for thousands of years means a living nation. Our incessant dying means uninterrupted living, rising, standing up, beginning anew. We, the last Jews! Yes, in many respects it seems to us as if we are the last links in a particular chain of tradition and development. But if we are the last—let us be the last as our fathers and forefathers were. Let us prepare the ground for the last Jews who will come after us, and for the last Jews who will rise after them, and so on until the end of days.

If it has been decreed for Israel that it go on being a dying nation—let it be a nation that is constantly dying, which is to say: incessantly living and creating—one nation from Dan to Beersheba, from the sunny heights of Judea to the shadowy valleys of Europe and America.

To prepare the ground for this great oneness, for a Jewish realism built on it, is a task which requires the effort of Jewish scholarship and statesmanship alike. One nation, one in beginning and end, one in survival and extinction! May it be survival rather than extinction, a beginning rather than an ignominious end—one Israel, *yisrael ehad*.

NOTE

[Words and ellipses in brackets appear in the original source.—Eds.]

Other works by Rawidowicz: *Moses Mendelssohn, the German and Jewish Philosopher* (1936); *Studies in Jewish Thought* (1957); *'Iyunim be-maḥshevet Yisra'el*, 2 vols. (1969, 1971).

Abram L. Sachar

1899–1993

Abram L. Sachar was the first president of Brandeis University, a position that followed his original vocation as a historian. Born in New York City to immigrant parents, he became director of the National Hillel Foundation while teaching at the University of Illinois. At Brandeis, he was a visionary with grandiose plans—he had an "edifice complex," some noted—who devoted two decades to expanding the campus, faculty, and student body. All the while, he produced a steady flow of highly admired scholarship.

Brandeis University: The Pledge
1948

[. . .] I look upon this humble beginning as a potentially significant step. It is the first nonsectarian university which becomes the corporate responsibility of the Jewish community in America. Jews have been very generous as individuals. Some of their contributions have been responsible for important research, distinguished chairs, impressive buildings. They have been pillars of strength in some of our outstanding universities. But this is the first time that the Jewish people, *as a people*, underwrites a nonsectarian American university. The Catholics have sponsored more than two hundred; the Protestants have pioneered more than six hundred. The Jewish community in America is an integral part of the tapestry of American life. Tonight it pledges itself to begin weaving a useful and aesthetic pattern of education in this multifariously designed, many colored tapestry. It may be only a minor pattern. It may be often lost among the major themes and motivations of the tapestry. But it is our hope that it may lend just a little color and beauty and originality and distinction to the creations of the American spirit. [...]

More than fifty years ago a quiet, not very eloquent rabbi, Henry Cohen, settled in one of the smaller communities of America, Galveston, Texas. He devoted himself completely to this relatively isolated area. Every year he was called to more glamorous metropolitan opportunities. But he preferred to stay where he was; and his pulpit, his pastoral zeal, his austere interpretation of the rabbi's role, all became a spiritual force in American life, and a faraway Texas community became the medium for a potent prophetic message.

I ardently hope that Brandeis too may live up to the high conceptions of education which Justice Brandeis himself had. Indeed, Justice Brandeis, I believe, would have wanted an institution named for him, to remain small, to emphasize quality. The greatest battles were fought against bigness. He dreaded bigness in industry, bigness in government, the vast impersonality of sheer numbers which swallowed up people as people. He had a horror of the callousness which is a product of tremendous size. [...]

I cannot help commenting on another historic coincidence which stimulates many hopes and which has been alluded to on many occasions. We are launching our University in the same period that the State of Israel begins its independent existence. Justice Brandeis was deeply devoted to the cause of a homeland for the Jewish people in Palestine and his leadership in this cause gave strength to his fellow workers in America. His preeminence in so many areas of American life made him an inevitable example of the American spirit. It is appropriate that his name be given to an American educational institution of quality which begins its life almost in the same moment that the State of Israel resurrects and fulfills an ancient dream.

What wonderful recuperative power there is in the Jewish people! Yesterday the Star of David was fastened upon or burned into the arms of broken men and women as a badge of shame. Our people have now lifted this star from its context of death and indignity, and have worked it into the flag of a free people on a free soil.

Justice Brandeis would have been thrilled by the coincidence and the symbolism. He would have looked ahead with hope to the day when, possibly, an exchange of scholars and students between the Hebrew University in Palestine and Brandeis University in America would fructify the intellectual and spiritual life of both institutions.

The University begins with immense good will. The name that blesses it is a perpetual challenge. God willing, we shall strive together, trustees, benefactors, faculty and students, to make it worthy of the name and the challenge.

Other works by Sachar: *A History of the Jews* (1929); *Sufferance Is the Badge: The Jew in the Contemporary World* (1939); *The Redemption of the Unwanted* (1983).

Leslie A. Fiedler
1917–2003

Leslie A. Fiedler, a swashbuckling literary critic, was a loud, provocative voice in American letters. Born in Newark, New Jersey, he flirted with socialism and Trotskyism before serving in the navy as a cryptologist. As a literary man, he straddled the worlds of academe and small magazines; an anti-highbrow, he championed passionate, transgressive writing, explaining, "I long for the raised voice, the howl of rage or love." His own hot-blooded writing included poetry as well as memoir and fiction.

What Can We Do about Fagin? The Jew-Villain in Western Tradition
1949

The real start of the myth of the Jew with the Knife in English literature goes back to the tale, already hundreds of years old, which Chaucer puts into the mouth of his Prioress, a character faintly ridiculous, but lovable and obviously intended to be esteemed. It is a charmingly told tale about a little boy who so irked the Jews by singing the praises of the Virgin, that their community hired a murderer, who cut the child's throat (another version has his heart and tongue cut out) and tossed him into a jakes "wher as the Iewes purgen her entraile." Needless to say, the crime is revealed by a miracle and the Jews cruelly punished; but the important point is that the crime at the heart of the story is one of mutilation with a knife—and that in the early part of the poem, the conventional identification of the Jews with usury is pointedly made. The pattern is already set.

It was the report of an atrocity (the alleged crucifixion of Hugh of Lincoln) which probably moved Chaucer to set down the "Prioress's Tale"; three hundred and fifty years later, another outburst of lynch hysteria over the case of Lopez, court physician to Queen Elizabeth, and a Jew, created the audience demand to which Marlowe's *Jew of Malta*, Gosson's lost play *The Jew*, and Shakespeare's *Merchant of Venice* all responded. The concept of the Machiavel, the stock Elizabethan villain who elevated a kind of onanistic malevolence into a grand passion, lay ready to hand, and was combined with the more primitive notion of the Slasher who thought God's Mother a whore.

Marlowe's *Jew* is known now to a limited audience only, and Gosson's is no more than a casual reference in a forgotten diary; but Shylock is familiar, at least as a name and vague terror, to almost everyone. Shakespeare's Jew has become pre-eminently a usurer, crafty and merciless, but something more, a representative of the tribal fury of Jewry that will not admit its maltreatment is merited. He loves only one thing more than gold: the sweet savor of vengeance. In the old story of the bond and the pound of flesh, Shakespeare hit upon a fable of extraordinary aptness. It is at once a gross but not pointless caricature of the legalism of the Talmudic mind, and a parable, from the Christian point of view, of the Jews' stubborn invocation of that greater Covenant whose literal meaning seems to be their salvation, the Gentiles' exclusion, but in the end proves to mean just the opposite. It preserves, too, the essential image of the bared blade—and makes clear at just what it is aimed.

What, then, *is* the threat the Christian uneasily dreams? Why is the mythic weapon of the Jew a knife? Antonio is asked to strip; a pound of flesh is to be cut, the original terms stipulated, from anywhere on his body; there is the understanding that such an excision will prevent the consummation of a marriage; in the background, we are aware of the extended meaning of the Bond, the Covenant. It is, of course, *circumcision* with which the *boy* feels Himself menaced, a vicious circumcision that blurs in his guilt-ridden, scared mind into castration. In Shakespeare's actual text, the place from which the flesh is to be cut is finally an area "nearest to the heart," but is not this an obvious displacement, like Chaucer's throat or the tongue and heart of the analogues?

The sense of a threat greater than that explicitly stated, a threat to sexuality, is really there, in the play; and, it seems to me, even the standard atrocity attributed to the Jew, the ritual murder of a child, is a rationalization of that original nightmare of the circumcisor, ritual blade in hand. The Jew as slasher never dies from the imagination; his latest avatar (via the Fagin of Dickens) is Colleoni, the gangster with the razor blade in

Graham Greene's *Brighton Rock*; while the other aspect of Shylock, the Jew as usurer, flourishes in many places in that author's highly mythic works: for instance, the financier in *This Gun for Hire*, or Myatt in *Orient Express*, who struggles briefly against his fate, but whom we see, at last, wondering as he betrays all human feeling and decency "whether Mr. Stein had the contract in his pocket."

For Ezra Pound, of course, Shylock has become a master image of his paranoia, hallucinatory, compulsive, the usurer as enemy of the world, the Yid as the essential evil of all social life. The memory of Shylock's scriptural instance, Jacob and the flocks of Laban, the accent of the Jew, the shadow of his monstrous nose afflict him, haunt his verse. In the earlier poetry of Eliot the same mythic presence is there, in "Gerontion," for instance, as the illegitimate dispossessor of the *goy* fallen on evil days.

Other works by Fiedler: *Love and Death in the American Novel* (1960); *The Last Jew in America* (1966); *Fiedler on the Roof* (1991).

Sidney Hook

1902–1989

Born in Brooklyn to parents of Austrian heritage, Sidney Hook became a prominent postwar pragmatist philosopher. Hook began teaching at New York University in 1927 and spent several decades at the institution, shaping generations of American thinkers until his retirement in 1969. In his youth, Hook was a committed communist, and he traveled to Moscow as a visiting scholar in 1929. He broke away from communism in the early 1930s, and after World War II, he worked closely with American anticommunist efforts. Still, he remained a socialist and continued to write extensively on the place of freedom and debate in democratic societies.

Reflections on the Jewish Question
1949

In describing the psychology of what he calls the "inauthentic Jew" among Gentiles, Sartre does not distinguish between the psychology of what I call the "inauthentic" Jew—the Jew who desires, so to speak, to pass himself off as a Gentile, and the psychology of what I call "the authentic Jew" who accepts himself as a Jew for any reason whatsoever. *La mauvaise foi* or inverted self-consciousness, as Sartre describes it in the few illuminating pages of his turgid and boring *L'être et le néant*, is different in both cases.

The "inauthentic Jew," in my sense, is afflicted with an additional dimension of self-consciousness. No matter how impeccable his conduct, he is always on guard in predominantly non-Jewish company, exquisitely conscious of the possibility that at any moment something he says or does will be regarded as a telltale sign. He feels that there are some things that are appropriate for him to do, and others which are not appropriate, *merely* because he is regarded as a Jew. Whether he is active in public life or in the professions, wherever his words or deeds affect his fellowmen, he is pursued by a nagging consciousness of the specific effect activity as a Jew has on others. In his utterances he must think not only of whether what he says is true or false, but of how, as coming from *him*, it will be received. He finds that he is bothered by what Jews do or leave undone in a way his own attempted escape makes it difficult for him to understand. He develops a guilty sense of Jewish responsibility despite the absence of any consciousness of Jewish loyalty. When he is pretty far down in the scale of creation, he does not overhear anti-Semitic remarks, and touches bottom when he regales the company with anti-Semitic jokes, told with an air that suggests the difference between himself and other Jews, usually too subtle for others to see. Sometimes, without any religious faith, he embraces another religious faith. There are very few inauthentic Jews of this kind. They are really inauthentic people. The main problem of the authentic Jews is to find some rational basis or ideal fulfillment of their authenticity. Sartre is no guide here.

The genuine problem which confronts those who are regarded as Jews in the modern world is whether they should regard themselves as Jews, and what meaning they can give to their lives as Jews once they acknowledge, as elementary decency and dignity demand, that in some sense they accept themselves as Jews. This is a problem of tremendous complexity just because there is no one thing that constitutes Jewishness and because of ideological imperialism of so many different Jewish groups which seek to impose their own particular conception of Jewish life upon all other Jews.

Other works by Hook: *From Hegel to Marx: Studies in the Intellectual Development of Karl Marx* (1936); *The Hero in History: A Study in Limitation and Pos-*

sibility (1943); *Political Power and Personal Freedom: Critical Studies in Democracy, Communism, and Civil Rights* (1959); *The Paradoxes of Freedom* (1962).

Harold Rosenberg
1906–1978

Born in Brooklyn, Harold Rosenberg, art critic for *The New Yorker* from 1967 until his death, was himself a lifelong New Yorker. Although he began his career publishing criticism in the many Marxist journals of the 1930s, Rosenberg gradually became dissatisfied with the strictures of Marxist art theory. In the 1950s and 1960s, Rosenberg was a major proponent of abstract expressionism, championing the independence and creativity of artists such as Willem de Kooning and Arshile Gorky. Influenced by French existentialism and ontology, Rosenberg's art criticism remained more popular and widely accessible than that of many of his contemporaries.

Does the Jew Exist? Sartre's Morality Play about Anti-Semitism
1949

In considering Sartre's conception of the Jew and his relation to anti-Semitism we must not forget that *Reflections on the Jewish Question* (published by Schocken as *Anti-Semite and Jew*) was written immediately after the downfall of the Nazis. It was a moment of intense confusion as to the meaning of the terrible events that had just taken place and of uncertainty as to the attitudes and groupings that would now emerge in liberated France. The Occupation had enlivened the current of anti-Semitism among Frenchmen of all classes. With the return of those Jews who had escaped the German hangman everyone was most anxious that this "question" should not once more stir up hidden rancors. Thus, as Sartre tells us, in the midst of the general greeting of returned prisoners and deportees not a word about the Jews, for fear of irritating the anti-Semites. This testimony is supported by André Spiré's account, in his preface to *Bilan Juif*, of the difficulties experienced in finding a publisher in Paris by those who wished to speak of what had happened. "There has been too much hate," they were told. "Let's have a love story."

Under such circumstances for Sartre to have challenged the anti-Semite as a menace to Frenchmen, to have called upon Gentiles to organize in a war on anti-Semitism, and to have welcomed the French Jews into the French nation was an act of generosity, of feeling, courage, and good sense. [. . .]

For Sartre the Jew exists. The Jewishness of the Jew is not merely, as with the democratic thinkers, a few ethnic, religious, and physical traits added to a *man*. In dissociating himself from liberal rationalism and its abstract man, Sartre asserts the reality of the Jewish identity as a "concrete synthesis" created by history. There is, in short, The Jew, not only men and women who happen to be Jewish. With this conclusion, "unscientific" as it may appear, it is necessary, I believe, to agree. In fact, the best passage for me in Sartre's essay is his criticism of the democratic defender of the Jew, for whom all men are essentially alike, for whom the Jew can belong to human society only to the extent that he suppresses himself as a Jew, and for whom the assertion by Jews of Jewish difference is a sign of stubbornness, backwardness, or ill will. [. . .]

The dream of eliminating all inherited differences among peoples has proven, however, to be Utopian, and not only not possible but not even desirable as a program. Has not democratic universalism meant in practice not a society of man but the absorption of small nations and minorities into larger ones, even if with full equality and freedom? [. . .] Yet Sartre's recognition of the Jewish fact does not take him beyond the democratic conception of the big nation assimilating minorities. For in the end he, too, wishes to dissolve the Jewish collective identity into its abstract particles, that is, into men made more human by ceasing to be Jews. He wants the French Jew to become a Frenchman, as the democrats do. Sartre differs from the democrats only in falling short of the idealism of their theory of man which seeks the ultimate homogeneity of human beings. Though he comes out for socialism he does not say a word about dissolving the French identity. For Sartre it is enough that the *Jews* should be assimilated. [. . .]

This exceptionalism he maintains on the grounds of the peculiar nature of the Jewish identity, that the Jews "have no history" and are but the wretched creatures of anti-Semitism. We shall take up this characterization shortly. Here let us note that Sartre offers us much less than the liberals. For it makes sense that the Jews should assimilate into *man* (though it makes sense only as a theory). But why, especially for a socialist, should the Jew look forward to becoming a *Frenchman*? [. . .]

Sartre fails to consider the Jew and his situation in relation to his beginnings. He splits his "being" in time and in place. "It is the Christians," he says, "who have created the Jew." The opposite is, of course, the case: the Jews created Christianity. But Sartre has cut the Jews off from their past; he even thinks it possible to speak of the Jews while "limiting my description to the Jews in France." If, nevertheless, the Jew's historical feet still protrude from under the blanket of the situation with which Sartre has "surrounded" him, Sartre has misunderstood fundamentally the problem of identity. [. . .]

Having mistaken the Jew's identity, Sartre cannot comprehend *his* history, *his* creative accomplishments, *his* possibilities. Measuring the Jews by general standards of ethnic uniformity, sovereignty, and churchgoing, he finds that the Jews are not a people or a race (or that belonging to this "race" means "a hooked nose, protruding ears, thick lips"), not a nation, not a religion. From this he concludes that "the sole tie that binds them is the hostility and disdain of the societies that surround them." The Jews, says Sartre, "have no history . . . twenty centuries of dispersion and political impotence forbids its having a *historic past*" (his italics). [. . .]

Only if warfare is the essence of the historical is the memory of the Jew during the past two thousand years without historical quality. Is not this period of Exile, with its hopes, coherent with earlier exiles, previous redemptions? The entire story of the Jew—*including the movements toward assimilation that form part of it from the beginning*—has an inner meaning and a structure that would seem to make it history *par excellence*. To such an extent is the Jew identified by the story he remembers, that political and social institutions, linguistic and somatic characteristics, even religious beliefs and practices appear superficial to the common autobiography: these may change, through the uniqueness of his tale the Jew remains himself. In fact, history is the burden under which the Jew all but breaks.

The *common story* of the Jews and not "the hostility and disdain" of others is the principle of their togetherness." [. . .]

In opposition to Sartre's compendium of Jewish nothingness, Jewish imprisonment in his situation, and Jewish traits we may assert the following: Since the Jew possesses a unique identity which springs from his origin and his story, it is possible for him to be any kind of man—rationalist, irrationalist, heroic, cowardly, Zionist or good European—and still be a Jew. The Jew exists but there are no Jewish traits. The Jew who chooses to flee his Jewishness does not thereby turn into something other than a man, any more than an Italian who decides to become an American. Whatever it is, the desire to assimilate is not "inauthentic"; one may choose to suppress the past in oneself or to surpass it. On the other hand, the Jewish identity has a remarkable richness for those who rediscover it within themselves.

Other works by Rosenberg: *The Tradition of the New* (1959); *The Anxious Object: Art Today and Its Audience* (1964); *The De-Definition of Art* (1972).

Theodor Adorno, Else Frenkel-Brunswik, Daniel J. Levinson, and Nevitt Sanford

Adorno, 1903–1969

Born in Frankfurt am Main to a Catholic mother and a Jewish father who had converted to Protestantism, Theodor Wiesengrund Adorno was a leading scholar of the Frankfurt School. Though Adorno was inspired by revolutionary thought and leftist ideals, his interests remained primarily theoretical. During World War II, Adorno immigrated first to the United Kingdom and then to the United States, where he worked at the University of California at Berkeley. He returned to Europe in 1949, helping to restart the Institute for Social Research and renew German intellectual culture in the aftermath of the Holocaust. Adorno's contributions to twentieth-century thought include many influential sociological and critical studies of fascism and popular culture.

Frenkel-Brunswik, 1908–1958

Born in Lviv (Lemberg), Else Frenkel-Brunswik moved with her family to Austria in the aftermath of World War I, settling into Vienna's middle-class Jewish milieu. She pursued a doctorate in psychology at the University of Vienna, working with Karl and Charlotte Bühler. In 1938, after the annexation of Austria into Nazi Germany, Frenkel-Brunswik immigrated to the United States and became a research associate at the University of California at Berkeley. There, she began designing psychological studies of antisemitism in the 1940s, which formed the basis of *The Authoritarian Personality*.

Levinson, 1920–1994

Born in New York, psychologist Daniel J. Levinson studied under Else Frenkel-Brunswik at the University of California at Berkeley in the 1950s, contributing to several joint studies on ethnocentrism and authoritarianism. After moving on to positions at Harvard and Yale, Levinson began his life's work studying the interaction between adult personality, occupational roles, and social structures. Levinson's contributions became foundational to the field of psychology called positive adult development. His most well-known theory, named the stage-crisis view, describes developmental stages of life from youth to elderliness, each defined by a set of crises a person must overcome.

Sanford, 1909–1995

Born in Chatham, Virginia, and descended from two generations of Baptist ministers, psychologist Nevitt Sanford came to prominence with the publication of *The Authoritarian Personality*. Sanford was appointed a professor of psychology at the University of California at Berkeley in 1940 but was dismissed in 1950 near the height of McCarthyism for refusing to sign an oath of loyalty. In 1968, he founded the Wright Institute, a center for the psychological study of social problems.

List of Interview Questions Pertaining to Jews 1950

Do you think there is a Jewish problem? If yes, in what sense? Do you care about it?

Have you had any experience with Jews? What kind? Do you remember names of persons involved and other specific data?

If not, on what is your opinion based?

Did you have any contrary experiences (or hear about such experiences) with Jewish individuals?

If you had—would it change your opinion? If not, why not?

Can you tell a Jew from other people? How?

What do you know about the Jewish religion?

Are there Christians that are as bad as Jews? Is their percentage as high or higher than the percentage of bad Jews?

How do Jews behave at work? What about the alleged Jewish industriousness?

Is it true that the Jews have an undue influence in movies, radio, literature, and universities?

If yes—what is particularly bad about it? What should be done about it?

Is it true that the Jews have an undue influence in business, politics, labor, etc.?

If yes—what kind of an influence? Should something be done to curb it?

What did the Nazis do to the German Jews? What do you think about it? Is there such a problem here? What would you do to solve it?

What do you blame them most for? Are they: aggressive, bad-mannered; controlling the banks; black marketeers; cheating; Christ killers; clannish; Communists; corrupting; dirty; draft dodgers; exploiters; hiding their identity; too intellectual; Internationalists; overcrowding many jobs; lazy; controlling movies; money-minded; noisy; over-assimilative; overbearing; oversexed; looking for privileges; quarrelsome; running the country; too smart; spoiling nice neighborhoods; owning too many stores; undisciplined; unethical against Gentiles; upstarts; shunning hard manual labor; forming a world conspiracy?

Do you favor social discrimination or special legislation?

Shall a Jew be treated as an individual or as a member of a group?

How do your suggestions go along with constitutional rights?

Do you object to personal contacts with individual Jews?

Do you consider Jews more as a nuisance or more as a menace?

Could you imagine yourself marrying a Jew?

Do you like to discuss the Jewish issue?

What would you do if you were a Jew?

Can a Jew ever become a real American?

Other works by Adorno: *Dialectic of Enlightenment* (1944); *Minima Moralia: Reflections from Damaged Life* (1951); *Negative Dialectics* (1966). Other works by Frenkel-Brunswik: *Motivation and Behavior* (1942); *Psychoanalysis and the Unity of Science* (1954). Other works by Levinson: *Patienthood in the Mental Hospital: An Analysis of Role, Personality, and Social Structure* (1964); *The Seasons of a Man's Life* (1978); *The Seasons of a Woman's Life* (1996). Other works by Sanford: *The American College: A Psychological and Social Interpretation of the Higher Learning* (1962); *Self and Society: Social Change and Individual Development* (1966); *Issues in Personality Theory* (1970).

Robert Gordis
1908–1992

A rabbi and a Bible scholar, Robert Gordis was a vital force in Conservative Judaism, helping to define its principles and philosophical outlook. He taught at the Jewish Theological Seminary from 1937 until the late 1980s, simultaneously serving as rabbi of Temple Beth El in Rockaway Park, Queens. In his scholarship, Gordis was especially devoted to the books of Job and Ecclesiastes. As a rabbi, he championed interfaith relations, was dedicated to inter-Jewish dialogue, and in both capacities helped to found the journal *Judaism*.

The Challenge Facing Modern Jewish Scholarship
1950

II

[. . .] Moreover, the ideal of Torah as an end in itself was never felt to be in opposition to the ideal of *Torat hayyim*—"the Torah as a gateway to life." Whatever the logician might argue, Jewish life held fast to both ideals—understanding the world and man's place in it, without fear or favor, went hand in hand with the continual effort to make this body of knowledge relevant to life. When the question was posed before the Rabbis in the Academy at Lydda as to which was more important, study or action, the conclusion reached was thoroughly characteristic for Judaism: *limmud gadol shehallimmud mebhi lidei ma'aseh*—"Study is greater, because study leads to right action" (B. Kiddushin 40b and parallels). And this ideal was embodied in the careers of the greatest Jewish scholars in every age, Saadia, Maimonides, Joseph Karo, Elijah of Vilna, Rabbi Abraham Isaac Kook, and countless lesser figures.

The scientist in the laboratory, the scholar in the library, the student of Torah in the *Beth Hamidrash*—all bear witness to the union of these ideals. To be responsive to life without surrendering the love of truth, that is the mark of learning at its highest. Where either element is suffered to decline or disappear, scholarship is doomed to increasing sterility as soon as the momentum of earlier and more creative periods is exhausted.

III

This principle supplies a touchstone for evaluating the past history and future prospects of scientific Jewish research, long familiar under its German title of *die Wissenschaft des Judentums*. It is little more than a century ago since the inception of the critical and systematic study of Judaism and the Jewish people. [. . .]

The founders of *Juedische Wissenschaft*, deeply interested in the problems of their age, envisaged two goals for their activity, one internal, directed toward the Jewish community, the other external, concerned with the outer environment. The *inner* motive came to the fore as early as 1819, in the organization by Leopold Zunz, Edward Gans, Heinrich Heine and a few other intellectuals of the tragically short-lived *Verein für Kultur und Wissenschaft des Judenthums*. In the *Zeitschrift* of the *Verein*, Zunz published his biography of Rashi, the first modern study of a Jewish historical figure, as well as other pioneering papers. It was the conviction of the group that if the character of Jewish history and culture and the contributions of the Jewish people to civilization were presented in systematic and attractive form to the modern world, they would halt the wholesale defection from Judaism which had begun in Germany in the decade after Napoleon among the ablest and most ambitious members of the Jewish community. The outer motive was also expressed by Zunz at the very inception of his scientific career, when he demanded for the Jews "not rights, but right itself—not liberties, but liberty itself." [. . .]

To be sure, the classical period of Jewish scholarship suffered from several defects inherent in its background and period. Being a product of the nineteenth century it favored the ultra-rationalistic approach to Judaism. It therefore failed to evaluate properly the role of the emotional and mystic factors in Jewish experience. Graetz's great work, *Die Geschichte der Juden*, exhibits to the full this egregious blunder in dealing with the Kabbalah, the various Messianic movements and Hassidism. Moreover, the science of Judaism being concentrated largely in Germany, its devotees had little sympathy or understanding for East-European Jewry. By and large, the millions of Jews in Poland, Russia and Roumania, blessed with unquenchable Jewish vitality, lay outside the ken of the German-Jewish *Gelehrte*. With few exceptions, they had no appreciation for the extraordinarily creative capacities of East-European Jewry, which produced the renaissance of the modern Hebrew language and literature, and the rich fruits of the Yiddish press, literature and drama. They scarcely suspected the deep fountains of idealism to be found in the backward, congested areas of Jewish settlements

in the East, which created the progressive Jewish labor movement on the one hand, and Zionism on the other. They failed to do justice to the superb human material which called into being the heroic miracle of the state of Israel, and the tragic grandeur of the Warsaw ghetto, which John Hersey has embodied in a noble literary monument.

IV

In addition to these drawbacks which inhered in the specific locale that gave it birth, modern Jewish research suffered from a third defect, the virtual neglect of the Bible by modern Jewish scholarship. It seemed as though Jewish scholars were determined to validate a comment made by Rabbi Akiba centuries before. For the ancient Sage had explained that the Mishnah or Oral Law had remained unwritten because God had foreseen that the day would come when the Torah, or Written Law, would be taken over by non-Jews, who would arise and say to the Jewish people: "*ein lakhem helek venahalah bah*—you have no portion or inheritance in it."

The reason for this neglect of Biblical studies in Jewish circles lay, of course, much deeper. The nineteenth century saw the higher criticism of the Bible reach its highest point of development in the classic formulation of the Graf-Wellhausen school. To be sure, Schechter exaggerated when he said that "the Higher Criticism is the higher Anti-Semitism." But it would be fatuous to overlook the personal prejudice of many of the devotees of the Higher Criticism, which undoubtedly played its part in the constant effort to reduce the value, antiquity and originality of the Hebrew Scripture. [. . .]

V

It should be noted, however, that the *two basic motivations which gave meaning to critical Jewish scholarship in its greatest and most fruitful period, apologetics and emancipation, are, at best, minor factors today, if they survive at all*. No wonder Jewish research has lost so much of its vitality and drawing power.

If Jewish scholarship is to recapture its creative impulse, it must re-establish a sense of relevance to the age in its own terms. Nor should this be difficult. For our day has its own problems and interests, and for that matter, its own attitudes and insights. Today we are again confronted by two challenges, which we may describe as external and internal. [. . .]

798 UNITED STATES OF AMERICA (1946–1973)

[. . .] Paradoxical as it may seem, the establishment of the State of Israel confronts world Jewry with a new and unexpected problem—the danger of a division of the Jewish people into two unrelated, even alien groups. To be sure, before the Second World War, the various Jewish communities in the world differed from one another politically, economically and culturally, but the distinction was one of degree and not of kind, for they shared in common the problems of the Diaspora. The establishment of the State of Israel has divided the Jewish world into two completely different spheres. The heroism and sacrifice of the Yishuv has created an environment in which Jews are no longer a minority group, perpetually exposed to the inroads of assimilation and extinction. Here Jewish culture is not secondary, but dominant and self-determining. This situation is rich in promise, though not free from problems of its own. But the important fact to remember, whether we applaud or lament it, is that barring a horrible catastrophe, most of world Jewry will continue to live outside the State of Israel, possessed of radically different problems and attitudes. These differences between the Israelis and World Jewry can prove either fateful or fruitful, depending upon the success with which bridges of communication and cooperation are built. Here Jewish scholarship on a world-wide basis has its second vital function to perform.

It has been maintained above that higher learning, as a branch of culture, naturally and legitimately reflects the society which gives it rise.

If this be true, Israeli scholarship will undoubtedly tend to emphasize the distinctively Jewish elements in our past and present. Diaspora scholarship, on the other hand, has the equally significant role of helping to trace the historic interaction of the Jewish people and its neighbors throughout history. If we may be permitted to cite a few lines written elsewhere, "Israel will play a vital role in keeping American Jewry conscious of its Jewishness and loyal to its achievements, while American Jewry will reciprocate by helping Israel remain conscious of its humanity and the responsibility to all the world. To extend Santayana's great words, 'A people, like a man, must stand with its feet firmly planted in its own country, but its eyes must survey the world.'"

VI

The conclusion is clear. Contemporary Jewish scholarship has a reason for being if it seeks to meet the perils which threaten the survival of civilization as a whole and the unity of Israel. Fortunately, it also has important means at its disposal. It is the beneficiary of over a century of brilliant and creative research. If we see further than did the founders of *Juedische Wissenschaft* it is because we stand upon their shoulders. The frontiers of the Science of Judaism, which originated in Central Europe, have been immeasurably extended by modern Yiddish scholarship, by extensive Jewish research at this College and at other institutions in America, and by the burgeoning intellectual activity in the State of Israel.

All these branches of Jewish scholarship unite in revealing the culture of the Jewish people as a living and a growing entity, possessing an extraordinary vitality and fruitfulness and an almost unlimited variety of content and achievement. In this vast creative process, the Bible and the Talmud represent the first two stages, differing, to be sure, as a youth differs from an adult, yet organically related and continuing unbroken through the Middle Ages and the modern period, to the latest poem or novel in Israel, the responsum of a rabbi, and the research of a Jewish scholar in Europe, America or Israel.

Other works by Gordis: *Koheleth: The Man and His World* (1951); *Judaism for the Modern Age* (1955); *Judaism in a Christian World* (1966); *Sex and the Family in the Jewish Tradition* (1967).

Max Horkheimer and Samuel H. Flowerman

Flowerman, 1912–1958

American psychologist Samuel H. Flowerman was director of the Department of Scientific Research of the American Jewish Committee from 1945 to 1951, conducting investigations to determine which personality characteristics play a role in intergroup conflict. Flowerman was also a consultant for the New York Postgraduate Center for Psychotherapy, teaching intercultural education and race-relations workshops at many colleges, including the New York University Center for Human Relations Studies and the Mental Health Section of the United States Public Health Service. He was an author and editor in the field of psychology, contributing numerous articles to professional journals. In 1950, he coedited the groundbreaking *Studies in Prejudice* with Max Horkheimer.

Studies in Prejudice
1950

At this moment in world history anti-Semitism is not manifesting itself with the full and violent destructiveness of which we know it to be capable. Even a social disease has its periods of quiescence during which the social scientists, like the biologist or the physician, can study it in the search for more effective ways to prevent or reduce the virulence of the next outbreak.

Today the world scarcely remembers the mechanized persecution and extermination of millions of human beings only a short span of years away in what was once regarded as the citadel of Western civilization. Yet the conscience of many men was aroused. How could it be, they asked each other, that in a culture of law, order, and reason, there should have survived the irrational remnants of ancient racial and religious hatreds? How could they explain the willingness of great masses of people to tolerate the mass extermination of their fellow citizens? What tissues in the life of our modern society remain cancerous, and despite our assumed enlightenment show the incongruous atavism of ancient peoples? And what within the individual organism responds to certain stimuli in our culture with attitudes and acts of destructive aggression?

But an aroused conscience is not enough if it does not stimulate a systematic search for an answer. Mankind has paid too dearly for its naive faith in the automatic effect of the mere passage of time; incantations have really never dispelled storms, disaster, pestilence, disease or other evils; nor does he who torments another cease his torture out of sheer boredom with his victim.

Prejudice is one of the problems of our times for which everyone has a theory but no one an answer. Every man, in a sense, believes that he is his own social scientist, for social science is the stuff of everyday living. The progress of science can perhaps be charted by the advances that scientists have made over commonsense notions of phenomena. In an effort to advance beyond mere commonsense approaches to problems of intergroup conflict, the American Jewish Committee in May, 1944, invited a group of American scholars of various backgrounds and disciplines to a two-day conference on religious and racial prejudice. At this meeting, a research program was outlined which would enlist scientific method in the cause of seeking solutions to this crucial problem. [. . .]

Since the completion of these studies the Department of Scientific Research of the American Jewish Committee has moved ahead into areas of research in which the unit of study is the group, the institution, the community rather than the individual. Fortified by a better knowledge of *individual* dynamics, we are now concerned with achieving a better understanding of *group* dynamics. For we recognize that the individual *in vacuo* is but an artifact; even in the present series of studies, although essentially psychological in nature, it has been necessary to explain individual behavior in terms of social antecedents and concomitants. The second stage of our research is thus focused upon problems of group pressures and the sociological determinants of roles in given social situations. We seek answers to such questions as: Why does an individual behave in a "tolerant" manner in one situation and in a "bigoted" manner in another situation? To what extent may certain forms of intergroup conflict, which appear on the surface to be based upon ethnic difference, be based upon other factors, using ethnic difference as content? [. . .]

Max Horkheimer
Samuel H. Flowerman

Abraham Tabachnik
1901–1970

Born near Mogilev-Podolski, Ukraine, writer and critic Abraham Tabachnik immigrated in 1921 to the United States, where he began contributing widely to the Yiddish-language leftist journals of the day. Tabachnik attended the Jewish Teachers' Seminary in the 1920s and afterward pursued a career in journalism, working as a translator and editor for the Jewish Telegraphic Agency from 1941 until his death. He remained a committed Yiddishist throughout his life, and in the 1950s he edited the Yiddish literary journal *Vogshol* (Scale) and recorded several interviews with major Yiddish authors.

Tradition and Revolt in Yiddish Poetry
1950

As Yiddish poetry grew more modern, even modernistic, as it grew freer in rhythm, subtler in tonality, more artful and sophisticated in imagery, it also grew more Jewish—I was almost going to say more Hasidic, in the Reb Nachman Bratzlaver sense of the word. The very first revolt in Yiddish poetry, that of the "Yunge," was expressed in a turning back to origins—origins which Peretz calls "barely experienced"—to the religious vision of the Jewish people, its sorrow and rapture, its Messianic longing and redemption-mythos.

You can see this not only in Leivick, but also in Moishe Leib Halpern, that mutineer and blasphemer. It is apparent in his images, the free skip of his apocalyptic fancies, his grotesquerie which contains so much of Yiddish Purim-theatricality, his bright rhythms redolent of traditional Gemara-tunes. And not only in Leivick and Moishe Leib—there is the same spirit in Mani Leib, that master of Yiddish idiom whom some like to consider not, God forbid, a Jew, but rather a sort of Russian in disguise. Certainly no one can deny or minimize the influence of Russian poetry on Mani Leib. Nevertheless no one else has set forth a poetry of Jewish faith in Mani Leib's particular manner and with his beauty and artistry. If we count Leivick (in verse only, of course) in the tradition of those cabalists who were not satisfied to await the Messiah but wanted to wrest him forth by force, then Mani Leib must be the poet of quiet folk-piety, the poet of belief who finds his expression in the common people's faith that God will not abandon them, that the miracle is not far off and can occur at the last second. [. . .]

What was true of the "Yunge" (and I refer to the "Yunge" in Europe as well, whose major figure was David Einhorn) was also true of the "In Zikh" group in America and the so-called Expressionists in Europe. The "In Zikh" poets, notwithstanding their modernism, indeed because of it, were in the main oriented toward Jewish spiritual tradition. Their achievement was less sublimated than that of the "Yunge"—what they did was done in a direct, open, Jewishly-conscious manner. [. . .]

Soviet Yiddish poetry is a record of important accomplishments not only in the freer first years, but in the later ones. We must know how to read Soviet poetry: it is often a Marrano poetry. Between one or another hymn to Stalin in a good Soviet poet you can frequently find precious lyrical passages. And even from the standpoint of *yidishkayt* not everything is so simple. What appealed to scholarly, religious, even nationalist Jewish tradition nevertheless fulfilled the social tradition of the Jewish masses. "Common people from Nyezhin," to quote Mani Leib, "who study Torah with Vilna seminarians" are also Jews. In the work of Izzi Charik, especially in an early piece like "Minsk Mud,"

the collective energy of the Jewish mass explodes in protest over its bitter lot—an energy previously given blazingly subjective expression in some poems of Morris Rosenfeld and, more artfully, in some of the stories of Itche Meier Weisenberg.

In Itzik Feffer's earliest poems there is something of Sholom Aleichem. Feffer made a huge leap from his *shtetl* into the turbulent forces of the Revolution the way Motl Peisi, the cantor's son, sprang out of the closeness of his father's sickroom into the spring air. Feffer rejoiced in the Revolution and its Red Army regiments and blond Komsomol members on the front just as another boy in Sholom Aleichem rejoiced in a Passover-eve emigration. [. . .]

The tradition is still young and there remain room and possibility enough for innovation and further elaboration. Already there are signs, however, that it is a tradition on the verge of becoming not merely crystallized, but fixed, rigid, in danger of becoming conventional and stereotyped, and of breeding epigones instead of stimulating new vigor. Observe, for example, how the turn toward Jewish spiritual tradition, once so penetrating and fruitful, begins to degenerate into tedium and hollowness, a "love-of-Israel" committed to nothing. We can only hope that today's Yiddish poets are not the last, and that poets may arise who will both invigorate and rebel against the artistic tradition of the last four or five decades.

Translated by Cynthia Ozick.

Other works by Tabachnik: *Der man fun lid: vegn Zisha Landoy* (1941); *Dikhter un dikhtung* (1965).

Lionel Trilling

1905–1975

Born in Queens, New York, Lionel Trilling was one of the most influential literary critics of the twentieth century. After receiving his master's degree at Columbia University in 1926, he returned in 1932 to earn his doctorate, later becoming the first Jewish professor in the English department. His first published works were studies of Matthew Arnold and E. M. Forster, but his name was made with his 1950 collection *The Liberal Imagination*, which sold more than one hundred thousand copies. Despite his success as a critic, Trilling had initially hoped to be a novelist, but his only finished novel was not nearly as well received as his critical work.

Wordsworth and the Rabbis
1950

What I am trying to suggest is that, different as the immediately present objects were in each case, Torah for the Rabbis, Nature for Wordsworth, there existed for the Rabbis and for Wordsworth a great object, which is from God and might be said to represent Him as a sort of surrogate, a divine object to which one can be in an intimate passionate relationship, an active relationship—for Wordsworth's "wise passiveness" is of course an activity—which one can, as it were, handle, and in a sense create, drawing from it inexhaustible meaning by desire, intuition, and attention.

And when we turn to the particulars of the *Aboth* we see that the affinity continues. In Jewish tradition the great Hillel has a peculiarly Wordsworthian personality, being the type of gentleness and peace, and having about him a kind of *joy* which has always been found wonderfully attractive; and Hillel said—was, indeed, in the habit of saying: he "used to say"—"If I am not for myself, who, then, is for me? And if I am for myself, what then am I?" Mr. Herford implies that this is a difficult utterance. But it is not difficult for the reader of Wordsworth, who finds the Wordsworthian moral essence here, the interplay between individualism and the sense of community, between an awareness of the self that must be saved and developed, and an awareness that the self is yet fulfilled only in community.

Then there is this saying of Akiba's: "All is foreseen, and yet free will is given; and the world is judged by grace, and yet all is according to the work." With how handsome a boldness it handles the problem of fate and free will, or "grace" and "works," handles the problem by stating it as an antinomy, escaping the woeful claustral preoccupation with the alternatives, but not their grandeur. This refusal to be fixed either in fate or in free will, either in grace or in works, and the recognition of both, are characteristic of Wordsworth.

There are other parallels to be drawn. For example, one finds in the *Aboth* certain remarks which have a notable wit and daring because they go against the whole tendency of the work in telling us that the multiplication of words is an occasion for sin, and the chief thing is not study but action. One finds the injunction to the scholar to divide his time between study and a trade, presumably in the interest of humility. And the scholar is warned that the world must not be too much with him, that, getting and spending, he lays waste his pow-

ers. There is the concern, so typical of Wordsworth, with the "ages of man," with the right time in the individual's development for each of life's activities. But it is needless to multiply the details of the affinity, which in any case must not be insisted on too far. All that I want to suggest is the community of ideal and sensibility between the *Aboth* and the canon of Wordsworth's work— the passionate contemplation and experience of the great object which is proximate to Deity; then the plain living that goes with the high thinking, the desire for the humble life and the discharge of duty; and last, but not least important, a certain insouciant acquiescence in the anomalies of the moral order of the universe, a respectful indifference to, or graceful surrender before, the mysteries of the moral relation of God to man.

Other works by Trilling: *The Middle of the Journey* (1947); *The Opposing Self: Nine Essays in Criticism* (1955); *Beyond Culture: Essays on Literature and Learning* (1965).

Ruth Gay
1922–2006

Ruth Gay (b. Slotkin) was born and raised in New York City, where she graduated from Queens College; she was married to the sociologist Nathan Glazer. In her writing, Gay (who wrote under the surname of her second husband, Peter Gay) chronicled the experiences of Jews through the Holocaust, during its aftermath in Germany, and in the United States. In 1997, Gay received the National Jewish Book Award for nonfiction.

The Jewish Object: A Shopper's Report
1951

In the new religious revival, the theologians and philosophers have it easy; they can battle about the nature of revelation endlessly in the pages of *Commentary*. Parents and householders, on the other hand, caught up in the new urge toward Jewish observance, find themselves with problems needing immediate, practical answers. Once they have decided that from this Friday night forward the Sabbath will be observed in their house, or that this Chanukah will be marked by the lighting of the menorah, or that they will have a Seder— there is the question of providing the proper ceremonial objects. And, having established what is needed, the next problem is—what will they find when they actually go out to purchase the candlesticks, or the menorah, or a cover for the *challah*, or wine cups, or any of the other objects which can beautify the special usages of the occasion? [. . .]

On window-shopping tours of New York City, undertaken at various times during the past year, I tried to discover what the householder returning to the fold might find in his ritual quest. [. . .]

The obvious place to begin in New York is the Lower East Side. . . . Stuck away in its dirty, ugly streets are stores that specialize in the selling of prayer books, *talleisim*, *tefillin*, and also "ritual objects." . . . Characteristic of them all is the cheap materials in which they are executed. Challah covers are of the sleaziest white satin, sometimes crudely printed in blue ink, sometimes machine-embroidered. Challah knives are simple replicas of kitchen bread knives with imitation bone handles; I did not see the slightest attempt to invest them with any grace or beauty in view of their special festive function. . . . Rather they seem the product of a typical process in small manufacturing where the owner–designer–workman–salesman decides to add this new "feature" or that new "model" because his competitor has already emerged on the market with it, or because he aims to beat his competitor to it. The emergence this past Chanukah of a chromium candelabrum that plays "Rock of Ages" is an unhappy case in point. [. . .]

At a time when there is hardly a rabbi or community-thinker throughout the country who does not have in his pocket (if not already in print) a program for the beautification and revivification of the Jewish tradition, and when new synagogues, often based on the most modern—sometimes, perhaps, too modern—principles of design, are going up in innumerable cities, it is astonishing that no one has apparently sought to attract the attention of serious artist to the problem of creating Jewish ritual objects for our times and taste worthy of the tradition they represent.

Shortly before Passover of 1950 I witnessed a painful enactment of the process of choice under duress that awaits the shopper who goes out to find ritual objects for his home. In honor of the season, and also, presumably, to help sell Passover goods, Macy's had arranged an elaborate display of a model Passover table. Carefully lit, and placed on a fine Persian rug, the table was set for twelve and decorated with a variety of "art objects." These included silver goblets, two large silver candelabra rising to a height of two feet and each holding some half dozen candles . . . engraved with every conceivable symbol. [. . .]

Pressing against the plush ropes marking off the table were crowds of admiring Jews. Was it the silver candelabra and the gold *matzah* holder they were admiring? I think not. It was the gaudy elegance of the "Regency" table, the striped satin seats of the chairs whose color scheme extended to the pillows on which the head of the house would recline, and finally the glistening array of china, silver, linens and crystal. Most of all, perhaps, what attracted the crowd was the flattering suggestion that this gorgeous panoply was possible in every Jewish home. But what happens when the admirers attempt to imitate?

In the adjoining area customers could buy not only groceries, but also "ritual objects"—*matzah* covers, candlesticks, platters for the bitter herbs, *charoset*, etc. Buyers of these platters were faced with three choices: a ceramic platter carelessly glazed in harsh colors, a chromium platter chased with Hebrew letters and stamped with cuplike indentations; the chromium design executed in copper. The perplexity and disappointment of the buyers was expressed in one constantly repeated question: "Don't you have anything else?" [. . .]

It is not impossible for a *matzah* cover to be beautiful. I have seen one of Yemenite workmanship that was brought from Israel by a young soldier. It was not the sort of thing, for some reason, which anyone takes the trouble to export, yet in its gentleness and fineness of execution it breathed all that tenderness which the anxious crowd in Macy's Passover room was seeking. . . . It had simply been made of fine materials by a skillful workman, and it was the integrity and honesty of this workmanship which was so touching. It had been made, not for some anonymous "market," but for itself. [. . .]

The bare simplicity that we have come to associate with "modern" design, the emphasis on form and texture rather than decoration, seems to have conquered in Israel. The filigree work so characteristic of the Middle East, which was once important in Palestinian silverwork, is now seen only rarely. [. . .]

Surprisingly enough, only a comparatively small proportion of the objects seem to be designed for ritual purposes. . . . In the religious objects the greatest ingenuity seems to have gone into the Chanukah menorahs. . . . The objects for Passover have received more casual treatment at the hands of the designers. If anything, they seem to be Israeli reproductions of East European plates and goblets. [. . .]

It is hard to say how much of the work displayed at the various importing houses is characteristically Israeli. To the American purchaser, this is not altogether an irrelevant question. If he is buying a pair of candlesticks because he happens to need a pair of candlesticks, it may be unimportant to him whether they come from France or Java or the United States. But if he buys a dish only because he wants to have some object near him which comes from the land of Israel, then he is likely to hope that it will in some way represent the spirit of the country. From this point of view, one wonders what is peculiarly Israeli in a ceramic plate decorated with the smiling face of a young woman labeled "Halutza" or a row of houses tagged "Scene in Tel Aviv." And inscription albeit in Hebrew does not make a style. [. . .]

Unless what they are offered is ugly beyond redemption, they are willing to suspend the aesthetic judgment they would ordinarily bring to bear on their purchases. What is important to them is that by hanging up these plates they are affirming that theirs is a Jewish home in which Jewish values, however dimly apprehended, are treasured.

It would seem, then, that the Jews of America will not be able to depend on the ravishment of their senses to enjoy their new-found Judaism. . . . [I]t will have to be the spirit of the candle-lighting and of the home in which the candles are kindled, rather than the material form of the candlestick, that captures the heart of the Jewish child. But perhaps in America we may find the way to be observant and beautiful too.

Other works by Gay: *Jews in America: A Short History* (1965); *The Jews of Germany: A Historical Portrait* (1992); *Unfinished People: East European Jews Encounter America* (1996); *Safe among the Germans: Liberated Jews after World War II* (2002).

Abraham Joshua Heschel

The Hiding God
1951

For us, contemporaries and survivors of history's most terrible horrors, it is impossible to meditate about the compassion of God without asking: Where is God?

Emblazoned over the gates of the world in which we live is the escutcheon of the demons. The mark of Cain[1] on the face of man has come to overshadow the likeness of God. There has never been so much distress, agony, and terror. It is often sinful for the sun to shine. At no time has the earth been so soaked with blood. Fellow men have turned out to be evil spirits, monstrous and weird. Does not history look like a stage for the dance of might and evil—with man's wits too feeble to separate the two and God either directing the play or indifferent to it?

The major folly of this view seems to be in its shifting the responsibility for man's plight from man to God, in accusing the Invisible though iniquity is ours. Rather than admit our own guilt, we seek, like Adam, to shift the blame upon someone else. For generations we have been investing life with ugliness and now we wonder why we do not succeed. God was thought of as a watchman hired to prevent us from using our loaded guns. Having failed us in this, He is now thought of as the ultimate Scapegoat.

We live in an age when most of us have ceased to be shocked by the increasing breakdown in moral inhibitions. The decay of conscience fills the air with a pungent smell. Good and evil, which were once as distinguishable as day and night, have become a blurred mist. But that mist is manmade. God is not silent. He has been silenced.

Instead of being taught to answer the direct commands of God with a conscience open to His will, men are fed on the sweetness of mythology, on promises of salvation and immortality as a dessert to the pleasant repast on earth. The faith believers cherish is secondhand: It is a faith in the miracles of the past, an attachment to symbols and ceremonies. God is known from hearsay, a rumor fostered by dogmas, and even nondogmatic thinkers offer hackneyed, solemn concepts without daring to cry out the startling vision of the sublime on the margin of which indecisions, doubts, are almost vile.

We have trifled with the name of God. We have taken ideals in vain, preached and eluded Him, praised and defied Him. Now we reap the fruits of failure. Through centuries His voice cried in the wilderness. How skillfully it was trapped and imprisoned in the temples! How thoroughly distorted! Now we behold how it gradually withdraws, abandoning one people after another, departing from their souls, despising their wisdom. The taste for goodness has all but gone from the earth.

We have witnessed in history how often a man, a group, or a nation, lost from the sight of God, acts and succeeds, strives and achieves, but is given up by Him. They may stride from one victory to another and yet they are done with and abandoned, renounced and cast aside. They may possess all glory and might, but their life will be dismal. God has withdrawn from their life, even while they are heaping wickedness upon cruelty and malice upon evil. The dismissal of man, the abrogation of Providence, inaugurates eventual calamity.

They are left alone, neither molested by punishment nor assured by indication of help. The divine does not interfere with their actions nor intervene in their conscience. Having all in abundance save His blessing, they find their wealth a shell in which there is curse without mercy.

Man was the first to hide himself from God,[2] after having eaten of the forbidden fruit, and is still hiding.[3] The will of God is to be here, manifest and near; but when the doors of this world are slammed on Him, His truth betrayed, His will defied, He withdraws, leaving man to himself. God did not depart of His own volition; He was expelled. *God is in exile.*

More grave than Adam's eating the forbidden fruit was his hiding from God after he had eaten it. "Where art thou?" Where is man? is the first question that occurs in the Bible. It is man's alibi that is our problem. It is man who hides, who flees, who has an alibi. God is less rare than we think; when we long for Him, His distance crumbles away.

The prophets do not speak of the *hidden God* but of the *hiding God*. His hiding is a function, not His essence, an act, not a permanent state. It is when the people forsake Him, breaking the Covenant which He has made with them, that He forsakes them and hides His face from them.[4] It is not God who is obscure. It is man who conceals Him. His hiding from us is not in His essence: "Verily Thou art a God that hidest Thyself, O God of Israel, the Savior!" (Isaiah 45:15). A hiding God, not a hidden God. He is waiting to be disclosed, to be admitted into our lives.

The direct effect of His hiding is the hardening of the conscience: Man hears but does not understand, sees but does not perceive—his heart fat, his ears heavy. Our task is to open our souls to Him, to let Him again enter our deeds. We have been taught the grammar of contact with God; we have been taught by the Baal Shem that His remoteness is an illusion capable of being dispelled by our faith. There are many doors through which we have to pass in order to enter the palace, and none of them is locked.

As the hiding of man is known to God and seen through, so is God's hiding seen through. In sensing the fact of His hiding we have disclosed Him. Life is a hiding place for God. We are never asunder from Him

who is in need of us. Nations roam and rave—but all this is only ruffling the deep, unnoticed, and uncherished stillness.

The grandchild of Rabbi Baruch was playing hide-and-seek with another boy. He hid himself and stayed in his hiding place for a long time, assuming that his friend would look for him. Finally he went out and saw that his friend was gone, apparently not having looked for him at all, and that his own hiding had been in vain. He ran into the study of his grandfather, crying and complaining about his friend. Upon hearing the story, Rabbi Baruch broke into tears and said: "God, too, says: 'I hide, but there is no one to look for me.'"

There are times when defeat is all we face, when horror is all that faith must bear. And yet, in spite of anguish, in spite of terror we are never overcome with ultimate dismay. "Even that it would please God to destroy me; that He would let loose His hand and cut me off, then should I yet have comfort, yea, I would exult even in my pain; let Him not spare me, for I have not denied the words of the holy One" (Job 6:9–10). Wells gush forth in the deserts of despair. This is the guidance of faith: "Lie in the dust and gorge on faith."[4]

NOTES

1. See [Midrash] *Genesis Rabba* 22, 12, ed. Theodor, p. 219f.; L. Ginzberg, *Legends of the Jews* (Philadelphia, 1968), vol. 5, p. 141.
2. Genesis 3:8.
3. Job 13:20–24.
4. Rabbi Mendel of Kotsk, paraphrasing Psalm 37:3.

Leo Strauss
1899–1973

The German-born political philosopher Leo Strauss came to the United States in 1937 after failing to find an academic position in England, where he had fled to escape Nazism. He taught at the New School for Social Research in New York City from 1938 to 1948 and then at the University of Chicago, where his impact on the development of political philosophy in the United States was enormous. He was particularly influential in shaping the study of medieval Islamic and Jewish philosophy.

Persecution and the Art of Writing
1952

In most of the current reflections on the relation between philosophy and society, it is somehow taken for granted that philosophy always possessed political or social status. According to Fārābī, philosophy was not recognized in the cities and nations of Plato's time. He shows by his whole procedure that there was even less freedom of philosophizing in the cities and nations of his own time, i.e., "after philosophy had been blurred or destroyed." The fact that "philosophy" and "the philosophers" came to mean in the Islamic world a suspect pursuit and a suspect group of men, not to say simply unbelief and unbelievers, shows sufficiently how precarious the status of philosophy was: the legitimacy of philosophy was not recognized. Here, we are touching on what, from the point of view of the sociology of philosophy, is the most important difference between Christianity on the one hand, and Islam as well as Judaism on the other. For the Christian, the sacred doctrine is revealed theology; for the Jew and the Muslim, the sacred doctrine is, at least primarily, the legal interpretation of the Divine Law (*talmud* or *fiqh*). The sacred doctrine in the latter sense has, to say the least, much less in common with philosophy than the sacred doctrine in the former sense. It is ultimately for this reason that the status of philosophy was, as a matter of principle, much more precarious in Judaism and in Islam than in Christianity: in Christianity philosophy became an integral part of the officially recognized and even required training of the student of the sacred doctrine. This difference explains partly the eventual collapse of philosophic inquiry in the Islamic and in the Jewish world, a collapse which has no parallel in the Western Christian world.

Owing to the position which "the science of *kalām*" acquired in Islam, the status of philosophy in Islam was intermediate between its status in Christianity and in Judaism. To turn therefore to the status of philosophy within Judaism, it is obvious that while no one can be learned in the sacred doctrine of Christianity without having had considerable philosophic training, one can be a perfectly competent talmudist without having had any philosophic training. Jews of the philosophic competence of Halevi and Maimonides took it for granted that being a Jew and being a philosopher are mutually exclusive. At first glance, Maimonides' *Guide for the Perplexed* is the Jewish counterpart of Thomas Aquinas' *Summa* Theologica; but the *Guide* never acquired within Judaism even a part of the authority which the *Summa* enjoyed within Christianity; not Maimonides' *Guide*, but his *Mishne Torah*, i.e., his codification of the Jewish law, could be described as the Jewish counterpart to the *Summa*. Nothing is more revealing than

the difference between the beginnings of the *Guide* and of the *Summa*. The first article of the *Summa* deals with the question as to whether the sacred doctrine is required besides the philosophic disciplines: Thomas as it were justifies the sacred doctrine before the tribunal of philosophy. One cannot even imagine Maimonides opening the *Guide,* or any other work, with a discussion of the question as to whether the Halakhah (the sacred Law) is required besides the philosophic disciplines. The first chapters of the *Guide* look like a somewhat diffuse commentary on a Biblical verse (Genesis 1, 27) rather than like the opening of a philosophic or theological work. Maimonides, just as Averroes, needed much more urgently a legal justification of philosophy, i.e., a discussion in legal terms of the question whether the Divine Law permits or forbids or commands the study of philosophy, than a philosophic justification of the Divine Law or of its study. The reasons which Maimonides adduces in order to prove that certain rational truths about divine things must be kept secret, were used by Thomas in order to prove that the rational truth about the divine things was in need of being divinely revealed. In accordance with his occasional remark that the Jewish tradition emphasized God's justice rather than God's wisdom, Maimonides discerned the Jewish equivalent to philosophy or theology in certain elements of the Aggadah (or Legend), i.e., of that part of the Jewish lore which was generally regarded as much less authoritative than the Halakhah. Spinoza bluntly said that the Jews despise philosophy. As late as 1765, Moses Mendelssohn felt it necessary to apologize for recommending the study of logic, and to show why the prohibition against the reading of extraneous or profane books does not apply to works on logic. The issue of traditional Judaism versus philosophy is identical with the issue of Jerusalem versus Athens. It is difficult not to see the connection between the depreciation of the primary object of philosophy—the heavens and the heavenly bodies—in the first chapter of Genesis, the prohibition against eating of the tree of knowledge of good and evil in the second chapter, the divine name "I shall be what I shall be," the admonition that the Law is not in heaven nor beyond the sea, the saying of the prophet Micah about what the Lord requires of man, and such Talmudic utterances as these: "for him who reflects about four things—about what is above, what is below, what is before, what is behind—it would be better not to have come into the world," and "God owns nothing in His World except the four cubits of the Halakhah."

The precarious status of philosophy in Judaism as well as in Islam was not in every respect a misfortune for philosophy. The official recognition of philosophy in the Christian world made philosophy subject to ecclesiastical supervision. The precarious position of philosophy in the Islamic-Jewish world guaranteed its private character and therewith its inner freedom from supervision. The status of philosophy in the Islamic-Jewish world resembled in this respect its status in classical Greece. It is often said that the Greek city was a totalitarian society. It embraced and regulated morals, divine worship, tragedy and comedy. There was however one activity which was essentially private and trans-political: philosophy. Even the philosophic schools were founded by men without authority, by private men. The Islamic and Jewish philosophers recognized the similarity between this state of things and the one prevailing in their own time. Elaborating on some remarks of Aristotle, they compared the philosophic life to the life of the hermit.

Fārābī ascribed to Plato the view that in the Greek city the philosopher was in grave danger. In making this statement, he merely repeated what Plato himself had said. To a considerable extent, the danger was averted by the art of Plato, as Fārābī likewise noted. But the success of Plato must not blind us to the existence of a danger which, however much its forms may vary, is coeval with philosophy. The understanding of this danger and of the various forms which it has taken, and which it may take, is the foremost task, and indeed the sole task, of the sociology of philosophy.

Other works by Strauss: *What Is Political Philosophy?* (1959); *The City and Man* (1964); *Natural Right and History* (1965); *Liberalism: Ancient and Modern* (1968).

Mark Zborowski and Elizabeth Herzog

Zborowski, 1908–1990

Born in Uman, Ukraine, Mark Zborowski studied anthropology at the University of Grenoble in France and immigrated to the United States in 1941. During the prior two decades, Zborowski had worked as a spy for the Soviet secret police (NKVD). In America, Zborowski worked for the YIVO Institute for Jewish Research before joining anthropologists Ruth Benedict and Margaret Mead on their Research in Contemporary Cultures project at Columbia University. Zborowski's historical and ethnological expertise became central to the project's goal of anthologizing Jewish life in Eastern Europe. His work alongside Elizabeth Herzog culminated in *Life Is with People*, which for decades after its publication remained among the most popular portraits of East European Jewry.

Herzog, 1904–unknown

Elizabeth Herzog was born in Chicago to a long-established family of German heritage. In 1952, she cowrote the widely praised book *Life Is with People* with ethnologist Mark Zborowski, an evocative re-creation of the shtetl, constructed through interviews with former residents. In the 1960s, while working as the chief of child life research in the Children's Bureau of the U.S. Department of Health, Education, and Welfare, Herzog published several influential studies challenging prevailing stereotypes about poverty, race, and family life.

Life Is with People: The Jewish Little-Town of Eastern Europe
1952

Charity is only one part of maasim tovim, but it is a very important part. The most popular word for it in the shtetl is *tsdokeh*. This is one of the Hebrew words which have been incorporated into the Yiddish vocabulary, and its real meaning is not charity but justice— "social justice" would be more accurate in this context. Tsdokeh covers all acts of giving, from *ndoveh*, the alms given to the beggar, to *gmilus khassodim*, a form of benefice in which mere material help is combined with "bestowing of loving kindness," and which is therefore of a higher quality.

Life in the shtetl begins and ends with tsdokeh. When a child is born, the father pledges a certain amount of money for distribution to the poor. At a funeral the mourners distribute coins to the beggars who swarm the cemetery, chanting "Tsdokeh will save from death."

At every turn during one's life, the reminder to give is present. At the circumcision ceremony, the boy consecrated to the Covenant is specifically dedicated to good deeds. Every celebration, every holiday is accompanied by gifts to the needy. Each house has its round tin box into which coins are dropped for the support of various good works. A home that is not very poor will have a series of such boxes, one for the synagogue, one for a yeshiva in some distant city, one for "clothing the naked," one for "tending the sick," and so on. If something good or something bad happens, one puts a coin into a box. Before lighting the Sabbath candles, the housewife drops a coin into one of the boxes.

It is considered "un-Jewish" to play cards, and the sheyneh layt seldom do so except on Hanukah when it is the custom and therefore correct. The prosteh layt, who often play, usually have a separate "bank" for the poor. If bets are made the stake is likely to go to one of the many community services. "I bet it will rain tomorrow and if I lose I will give so much to the Home for the Aged."

Children are trained to the habit of giving. A father will let his son give alms to the beggar instead of handing them over directly. A child is very often put in charge of the weekly dole at home, when the beggars make their customary rounds. The gesture of giving becomes almost a reflex. When anything out of the ordinary happens, one says a blessing and one drops a coin into the box.

The "social justice" of the shtetl is not wholly voluntary and not wholly individual. Much of it is, and there is wide latitude for individual performance. Nevertheless, it is firmly woven into the organization of the community—or rather, it provides the central mechanism by which the community functions. The interweaving of individual benefaction with collective community service, of the voluntary with the compulsory, of religious injunction with civic obligation is essential to the organization and the flavor of the shtetl.

The giving of tsdokeh, the performance of maasim tovim, are basic not only to the functioning of the shtetl but also to being a good Jew. A variety of proverbs, sayings, and comments define the readiness to do good deeds as an earmark of the "real Jew." "One knows a Jew by his pity," it is said; one knows him by his "Yiddish heart," soft, warm, open to appeal; "a Jew is a pitying man"; "to sympathize with sorrow is a typical Jewish trait." This badge of group membership has been so worked into the structure of the society that it serves as a channel through which property, learning and services are diffused.

The patterns of giving and receiving represent a key mechanism in the shtetl, basic to individual relations and community functions, and paramount in the ethical system to which all relations and all functions are referred. Giving is both a duty and a joy; it is a source of heavenly approval and also a source of earthly prestige. The fortunate man is the one who is in a position to give. The unfortunate is the one who is under pressure to accept. Granted the correct situation, accepting is not necessarily painful—but under any circumstances, giving is counted among the great gratifications of life.

The good things of the world are seen as infinite and attainable. They are not acquired for themselves alone, nor for the individual alone; that they should be transmitted is part of their purpose and their nature. Wealth, learning and other tangible and intangible possessions are fluid and are channeled so that in the main they flow from the strong or rich or learned or mature or healthy to those who are weaker, poorer, more ignorant, younger, or sicker. For help of any kind to flow upward is "unnatural." Giving, however, is not an act of simple altruism, for the donor profits far more than the receiver.

The rewards for benefaction are manifold and are to be reaped both in this life and in the life to come. On earth, the prestige value of good deeds is second only to that of learning. It is chiefly through the benefactions it makes possible that money can "buy" status and esteem. The man who is known as a great benefactor receives honorific deference, *koved.* To "chase after koved," is a shtetl activity almost as important as to "chase after parnosseh." For the "love of koved," one will pour out his substance in charitable activities and in "buying" the preferred portions of the Torah during the Sabbath reading.

Moreover, to perform a mitsva through bestowing either goods, learning or services wins "the recording angel's credit mark." The sum total of the services one piles up determines his *zkhus,* his heavenly merits, of which koved is the earthly counterpart. One's lot in the afterlife depends on the number and qualities of his good deeds more than on anything else. Thus, he who performs a good deed is taking out "afterlife insurance in Olam Habo," the world to come.

Other work by Zborowski: *People in Pain* (1969). Other works by Herzog: *Children of Working Mothers* (1960); *About the Poor: Some Facts and Some Fictions* (1967); *Boys in Fatherless Families* (with Cecelia E. Sudia, 1970).

Trude Weiss-Rosmarin
1908-1989

Writer, educator, and feminist Trude Weiss-Rosmarin was born in Frankfurt, Germany, and received a doctorate in Semitics, archaeology, and philosophy from the University of Würzburg. She was a trailblazer in analyzing and questioning the role of women in Judaism, demanding more rights and better education for women in Jewish contexts. Upon arriving in the United States in 1931, she opened the School of the Jewish Woman in New York City. Weiss-Rosmarin published a number of books and wrote for several journals during her career, including the *Jewish Spectator*, which began at the School of the Jewish Woman. A committed Zionist all her life, in her later years she became an advocate for Jewish–Arab coexistence.

America Is Not Babylonia
1953

But what about the future? Does the American-Jewish community possess those traits and characteristics which, as we know from the experience of a dozen Diaspora communities over two thousand years, are indispensable for the growth of the kind of Jewish integration and stamina that gave rise to the Babylonian Talmud, the Hebrew literature in Spain, the Eastern European culture of Hasidism, the Gaon of Vilna, Peretz, Mendele and Sholom Aleichem, and Bialik, Ahad Ha-am, and the galaxy of writers of the Modern Hebrew Renaissance? Is the situation of the American-Jewish community such that it provides *reasonable* grounds for the expectation that in due time American Jewry will create a Jewish culture of its own, which will form another link in the golden chain of creative Jewish eternity? [. . .]

America is "a country that consumes" its Jews, annihilating their distinctiveness in the great melting pot. Little by little the huge Jewish capital of the Eastern European Jewish immigration was frittered away. First to go was their language—Yiddish. The second generation still could speak Yiddish, although not read and write it. The third generation understands but a few Yiddish catch phrases. [. . .]

Together with the Yiddish language and religious observance went the ideal of Torah study. "This is America," where when a boy doesn't do well at his Jewish studies, Father tells Mother, "It doesn't matter—after all, he won't be a rabbi." [. . .]

All "Jewish Centers of Gravity" of the past were self-contained. Jews lived *in* Babylonia, but although they flourished there for almost a thousand years, they never became integrated in the Babylonian, or later the Persian, fabric to the extent where they were actually of the woof and warp of the country's spiritual pattern. In point of fact, even politically the Babylonian-Jewish community was not integrated with the rest of the population. They always remained "strangers in a land not theirs." They had their own Jewish self-government under the sway of the "Head of the Dispersion." And they had their own courts of law, where judges ruled according to Jewish law, not the law of the land. The much-quoted and much-misunderstood principle of *dina de-malchuta dina*—the law of the land is binding for the Jew—only applies to general government decrees compulsory for all inhabitants, including the Jews. And, of course, the Jews of Babylonia spoke their own language. They were *in* Babylonia but never *of* Babylonia—and so they created a Jewish cultural center.

It was the same in all other Jewish cultural centers. Everywhere the Jews lived *in* the respective country of their *exile*, but were not *of* it. [. . .]

The thesis of the possibility of "creative Jewish survival" in America is predicated on the *uncritical* acceptance of the universal validity of the principle of "cultural pluralism." But the histories of *all* cultural minorities on American soil prove that "dual cultural loyalties" persist only in the first generation of the immigrants for whom the American culture and the English language are an *acquired* language learned in adulthood. For the second generation, born in America and trained in American schools, the American culture and the English language are the natural cultural habitat, whose bonds are so strong that a "minority culture" and a "second language" have simply no chance of *co*-existence.

The progressive attenuation of Jewishness and all areas of Jewish expression in this country over the past twenty-five years, during which the American-born group has increasingly taken over, proves conclusively that the chances for "creative Jewish survival" in America are nil. If *intelligent* Jewish identification, as distinguished from community relations and charitable identification, is at such a low ebb, already now when but one generation has passed since the height of the immigration from Eastern Europe, what hopes dare we entertain for *sound* Jewishness and *adequate* Jewish literacy in the future?

Unlike the Jews of Babylonia, Moslem Spain, Eastern Europe and some other creative centers of Jewish gravity, American Jews do not wish to be apart and separate from their fellow Americans. The Jews of all previous creative centers of Jewish gravity were mindful of the fact that they must guard their Jewish separateness in order to survive. [. . .]

There is, then, no resemblance at all between American Jewry and the "centers of Jewish gravity" of the past. But there is a close resemblance between American Jewry and Alexandrian Jewry, of two thousand years ago, and German Jewry of the post-Mendelssohnian period. [. . .]

It is characteristic of the trend-and-direction of the creative Jewish genius that the works of Philo and of the scholars of the *Wissenschaft des Judentums*, in so far as they were not critical editions of Hebrew texts, did not become part of what is generally defined as "the Jewish legacy." If not for the Church and Christian scholars that preserved his books, it is doubtful whether Philo's works would have come down to us. The Jews ignored Philo, for his books had no relevance for the issues, problems and concerns that agitated integrated Jewish communities living their own lives, separate from the peoples in whose midst they experienced *exile*. Philo *was* at home in Alexandria, and because of this he could not bring a message to Jews who remained strangers in their many *exiles*. [. . .]

As to the evidence adduced from the fate of other Jewish communities, American Jews react like every normal individual responds to the warning that others came to grief on the hazardous road he intends to take. *We shall succeed where others failed!* American Jews are convinced that they shall succeed in keeping America as their home, for ever and ever. And they are convinced that another Babylonian Talmud will be composed on American soil.

The massive evidence of Jewish history controverts this blithely optimistic view. Everything points to it that American Jewry will write a modern version of the Alexandrian Jewish chapter and add another page to the German chapter, as far as loss of Jewishness is concerned.

America is *not* Babylonia! American Jewry will not be able to survive creatively now that Jewish reinforcement from other parts can no longer be expected. Even "the bridge between American Jewry and Israel," should it *ever* be constructed, will not be able to turn New York into another Sura and Chicago into another Pumbeditha.

Other works by Weiss-Rosmarin: *Jewish Women through the Ages* (1940); *Judaism and Christianity: The Differences* (1943); *Jewish Survival* (1949); *Toward*

Jewish–Muslim Dialogue (1967); *Freedom and Jewish Women* (1977).

Joseph B. Soloveitchik

Responsum on Orthodox Judaism in America
1954

QUESTION: In America there is now a notable general rise in religion. The membership of religious organizations has grown, religious gatherings attract a larger audience, etc. Likewise in Jewish life people have lately noticed a more lively interest in religious matters. Do you believe that such a religious mood is favorable to Orthodoxy in America?

RESPONSUM: It appears that religion has lately become fashionable, and a connection with a religious institution is in harmony with general social attitudes. Naturally, the mood finds its echo also in Jewish life, especially in the suburbs, where the Jewish middle class has lately begun to settle. There, "good taste" requires that a Jew should be a member of a temple, so he can tell his gentile neighbor that he is active in his synagogue, just like the neighbor who is a trustee in his church. [. . .]

It is self-evident that superficial religious actions, consisting of participation in a service once a week, cannot be considered the profound experience of someone who is encountering God. The whole thing is more of a social phenomenon than a religious one. It conforms to the conservative political climate that has overtaken public opinion in the last few years. [. . .]

On the contrary, the religious personality is often in opposition to accepted customs and attitudes. It is a solitary carrier of a truth which society does not wish to recognize. Was not Abraham the most isolated of men? Was Moses not lonely and solitary on the dark morning when he climbed Mount Sinai to receive the Torah a second time? "And no man shall come up with thee, neither let any man be seen throughout the mount" (Exodus 34:3). When religiosity becomes fashionable, it must be carefully examined to see if it is genuine. In short, no great deliverance can be expected from the so-called religious "renaissance." [. . .]

The task of bringing Torah into Jewish life in America is a very particular one. The mission must be conceived from a very different perspective from how, for example, the Conservative and Reform movements envision it. Judaism has always preached the idea of the absolute unity of human life—*aḥadut ha-reshuyot* [the unity of domains]—an idea to which modern man is not accustomed.

The man of today, even the deeply religious God-seeker, divides his life into two spheres—profane and sacred. The first sphere, that of the profane, is the one in which he lives almost his entire life. He does not let God into it and within it he recognizes no religious norms and laws. In his business and private life there is no trace of divine authority. He is driven in all these areas by pragmatic-secular motives and does not hesitate to perform any action if he expects it to bring him closer to his materialistic goals. In the profane sphere he is arrogant, vulgar and insensitive and never comes into contact with God.

When he does occasionally wish to meet with the Creator, he has to enter into a different sphere, which occupies a small corner of his life, into which he has confined, so to speak, the spirit of the divine. When the man of today crosses the threshold of the sphere of the sacred, a strange spiritual transformation takes place. A modest, humble, spiritualized person approaches his Creator. He prays, beats his breast, confesses, falls to his knees and silently murmurs "not my will but yours be done," sings a glorious hymn ecstatically, and experiences something beautiful and noble. [. . .]

For true Judaism there is no sacred and profane. Either there is holiness everywhere or everything is unholy. The Living God of Israel cannot be confined to a corner. His spirit spreads itself over the entire expanse of human life, from the most intimate phases to social and public leadership. First, we meet God not [only] in the synagogue but at home, in business, in the factory, in the street and among our fellow human beings. If we do not see God in all these places, we will not find him in the house of prayer. . . . Robbery blocks the prayers, immorality and exaggerated pleasure-seeking transform our devotions into an abomination. To abuse a worker, to show cruelty to the helpless and needy, closes the gates of heaven. To come to the synagogue is important, provided it is the continuation of a pattern of religious-ethical behavior. But when this continuity is lacking, going to the synagogue loses its significance. This idea was preached by the prophets even with regard to the Temple [in Jerusalem]. [. . .]

Our task is difficult. Just as there is no easy way to [a mastery of] geometry and other mathematical disciplines because they are organized deductively and you cannot skip over axioms and theorems, so there is no royal road to Judaism. We cannot implant Jewishness in American Jewish youth supernaturally or by introducing radical changes. The way to Judaism is long, laborious, and difficult. It is a narrow pathway which winds its way uphill and passes not through theatrics in the synagogue, through sociable Sabbath gatherings, through sermons, through Hanukkah celebrations, and ceremonial Passover seders, but through prosaic educational work and the construction of yeshivas at the elementary-school level. We must begin with *alef-bet*, with the ABC's, and gradually climb higher and higher. "Who shall ascend into the hill of the Lord and who shall stand in his holy place?" (Psalms 24:3). [. . .]

It seems to me that it is precisely halakhic Judaism, with its demands and religious laws, that can fill the void created by a thoroughly unholy life. Precisely because the halakhah, Jewish law, is authoritative and intervenes at every level of human existence, it and only it, can provide a human being a spiritual rule, a standard, a religious discipline, a guide to a law-abiding and decent life and a moral fulcrum—in short, the gifts he so badly needs.

Translated by Solon Beinfeld.

Harry L. Golden

1902–1981

Born in Galicia, Harry L. Golden grew up in New York, but he became known throughout the American South for his humor and firm civil rights convictions. Golden moved to North Carolina to work for the *Charlotte Observer*. In 1941, he founded the *Carolina Israelite*, which had a national circulation until its closure in 1968. In addition to his work in journalism, which included reporting on the Eichmann trial, Golden published several popular books, including reminiscences about his childhood and explanations of his political beliefs.

Jew and Gentile in the New South
1955

There is very little real anti-Semitism in the South. There is even a solid tradition of philo-Semitism, the explanation of which lies in the very character of Southern Protestantism itself—in the Anglo-Calvinist devotion to the Old Testament and the Hebrew prophets, and the lack of emphasis on the Easter story which has been so closely connected with European anti-Semitism.

Nevertheless, segregation of a curious sort between Jew and Gentile does exist there. It is confined to the cities and larger towns, and to precisely those middle-class and proprietary circles in which Jews and Gentiles have an identity of interests—"Friction occurs," Shmarya Levin used to say, "where planes meet." [...]

There is a touching naivety in the small-town Southerner's respect for the Jewishness of the Jew in his community. It springs from the Southern Protestant's own attachment to Biblical Judaism, which is manifested in the basic tenets of the several denominations: "The Open Bible on the Altar" (and no other adornment) of the Presbyterians; the Methodists' "Faith without works is dead" ("Good deeds save from Death"); and the Baptists' lack of a formal creed, their congregational autonomy, and their intense individualism. As in Judaism, no special holiday (not excepting Christmas) is considered as important as the weekly Sabbath; and the blue laws of the "Still Sabbath" are only paralleled among Orthodox Jews and the Puritans of Colonial New England—the latter, along with the rural South of modern times, being the heirs of the Sabbatarian Protestant sects of the British Isles. [...]

The small-town Southerner takes it for granted that to be a Jew is to be a religious Jew, that his friend the storekeeper fully possesses that Hebraic tradition handed down through the centuries for which the Southern Christian has so deep a respect. As the Jew in a small Southern town goes about his business of selling dry goods or ready-to-wear clothing, he rarely suspects the symbolic role he enacts for the Gentile society roundabout him—he represents the unbroken tie with sacred history and the prophets of the Bible, he is the "living witness" to the "Second Coming of Christ," the link between the beginning and the end of things. [...]

It was inevitable that the Jews of the South, belonging to a single proprietary class of small capitalists—ready-to-wear, credit jewelry, textile manufacture and distribution, textile machinery, chemicals, cotton waste, metal scrap, mill agents, jobbers, wholesalers and traveling salesmen—should similarly try to align themselves with the new society. It was part of their effort to win the prestige that ordinarily follows wealth, and also to break with their immigrant past. The new society would seem to be the American group or class to which they naturally belonged. From the old aristocracy, with its fourth-generation requirements, they were naturally barred, though hardly more so than the "common people" of the South, or the newly emerged middle class. For wealth played a small part in the self-constituted aristocracy of the South; birth, so-called, was everything.

But it was inevitable also that, in his efforts to join the new society, made up as it was largely of social climbers, the Jew should be rebuffed. No hatred of the Jew was involved; the country club set was trying to evolve a homogeneous group, from which the Jews were barred by definition.

Anti-Semitic attitudes that cropped up in the process were no more than a rationalization of the desire to mix only with the "right kind of people," meaning people like themselves. The Northern manager brought this attitude with him as part of his baggage. The Southern social climber, left to his own devices, might conceivably have been less set in the matter of excluding Jews. He had his own problem; he was running away from his own impoverished past; the Jew was the least of his worries. [...]

As a member of a middle class of proprietors and professionals, the Southern Jew naturally seeks the society of his economic opposite numbers in the Gentile middle class. Apart from this "natural" tendency, there is his desire for koved, the status that such social contacts bring him in his own group. "He has many Christian friends," the middle-class Jew of the South says admiringly—and he does not mean Christian mill workers or service station attendants. A friendship with someone below his own economic level would probably do him more harm than good. Moreover, the Southern Jew of the city lives in constant fear of someone's passing an anti-Semitic remark "to his face." In polite middle-class circles, this danger is reduced to a minimum. Below "the top" he is not sure, and refuses to risk it. His friend Tom may be "all right," but he can never be sure of Tom's luncheon companion or the untried visitor to Tom's home.

But when the Jew seeks his outside social contacts at the top of urban-Gentile society, he is up against the most highly selective members of the entire middle class. The Gentile who establishes "restricted" residential areas and exclusive country clubs is trying to break with his own rural or mountain background or is a Northerner for whom these are accepted things. He has no patience with "climbers" of another group (any more than the wealthy German Jew had for his poorer and less assimilated Lithuanian or Polish brother); they cannot add to his status, and they may diminish it.

This spirit of exclusiveness on the part of the Gentile middle class was responded to by Southern Jews with their own country clubs—and their own kind of exclusiveness. The pattern has been fairly consistent. First there is a long period of trying to get into a Gentile country club. Occasionally a solitary Jew is admitted and the others become hopeful and wait some more. Eventually they give up and build a club of their own.

Other works by Golden: *Only in America* (1958); *Mr. Kennedy and the Negroes* (1964); *Our Southern Landsman* (1974).

Will Herberg

ca. 1901–1977

Though a committed communist in the early 1930s, by the 1950s Will Herberg was a prominent conservative intellectual and editor of the *National Review*. Herberg received his doctorate from Columbia University in 1932 (a fact that is disputed by some), and then worked with the International Ladies' Garment Workers' Union. His break from Marxism brought him to Jewish theology, and he joined the faculty of Drew University in 1955 as a professor of Judaic studies and social philosophy. In the 1960s and 1970s, Herberg dedicated himself to interfaith dialogue, producing books and essays on the topic and lecturing frequently.

Protestant—Catholic—Jew: An Essay in American Religious Sociology
1955

The outstanding feature of the religious situation in America today is the pervasiveness of religious self-identification along the tripartite scheme of Protestant, Catholic, Jew. From the "land of immigrants," America has, as we have seen, become the "triple melting pot," restructured in three great communities with religious labels, defining three great "communions" or "faiths." This transformation has been greatly furthered by what may be called the dialectic of "third generation interest": the third generation, coming into its own with the cessation of mass immigration, tries to recover its "heritage," so as to give itself some sort of "name," or context of self-identification and social location, in the larger society. "What the son wishes to forget"—so runs "Hansen's Law"—"the grandson wishes to remember." But what he can "remember" is obviously not his grandfather's foreign language, or even his grandfather's foreign culture; it is rather his grandfather's religion—America does not demand of him the abandonment of the ancestral religion as it does of the ancestral language and culture. This religion he now "remembers" in a form suitably "Americanized," and yet in a curious way also "retraditionalized." Within this comprehensive framework of basic sociological change operate those inner factors making for a "return to religion" which so many observers have noted in recent years—the collapse of all secular securities in the historical crisis of our time, the quest for a recovery of meaning in life, the new search for inwardness and personal authenticity amid the collectivistic heteronomies of the present-day world. [. . .]

The picture that emerges is one in which religion is accepted as a normal part of the American Way of Life. Not to be—that is, not to identify oneself and be identified as—either a Protestant, a Catholic, or a Jew is somehow not to be an American. [. . .]

This religious normality implies a certain religious unity in terms of a common "American religion" of which each of the three great religious communions is regarded as an equi-legitimate expression. America has emerged as a "three-religion country," in which the Protestant, the Catholic, and the Jew each finds his place. [. . .]

The religious unity of American life implies an institutional and ideological pluralism. The American system is one of stable coexistence of three equi-legitimate religious communities grounded in the common culture-religion of America. Within this common framework there is persistent tension and conflict, reflecting the corporate anxieties and minority-group defensiveness of each of the three communities. To mitigate these tensions and prevent the conflicts from becoming too destructive, American experience has brought forth the characteristically American device of "interfaith," which, as idea and movement, has permeated broad areas of national life. Interfaith, as we have seen, is a religiously oriented civic co-operation of Protestants, Catholics, and Jews to bring about better mutual understanding and to promote enterprises and causes of common concern, despite all differences of "faith." The interfaith movement is not secularistic or indifferentist but in its own way quite religious, for it is conceived as a joint enterprise of representative men and women of the three religious communities dedicated to purposes of common interest felt to be worthwhile from the religious point of view. Interfaith is thus the highest expression of religious coexistence and cooperation within the American understanding of religion.

Other works by Herberg: *The Theology of Reinhold Niebuhr* (1950); *Judaism and Modern Man: An Interpretation of Jewish Religion* (1951); *Athens and Jerusalem: Confrontation and Dialogue* (1965); *Faith Enacted as History: Essays in Biblical Theology* (1976).

Abraham Menes

1897–1969

Bundist and social historian Abraham Menes was born in Hrodna (now in Belarus). He was among the original members of YIVO and contributed to the *Yiddish Encyclopedia* while living in Paris in the 1930s. Menes immigrated to the United States in 1940 and began working for the *Jewish Daily Forward* in 1947. In his historical research, Menes often attempted to relate Jewish biblical history and socialist beliefs.

The East Side: Matrix of the Jewish Labor Movement
1955

Concentration in specific trades was a distinctive feature of the Jewish communities in Eastern Europe. In America this concentration assumed extreme forms. More than half of all Jewish workers (wage workers and self-employed) were engaged in garment manufacturing. Of the wage workers, two-thirds were employed in the needle trades. Since the eighties the needle trades increasingly passed into Jewish hands.

The sweatshop system may have contributed to the predominance of Jews in the needle trades, but it was not the sole, or even the most important factor. There is no doubt that Jewish skill in these trades, as well as initiative, played the chief role in the development of the garment industry, which in turn contributed significantly to democratic processes in American life in general.

Thus it came about that the pioneering labors of the tailors and cloakmakers during the eighteen eighties and nineties paved the way for "the great migration" early in the twentieth century, when nearly one and one-half million Jews entered the United States in the course of fifteen years.

The great Jewish immigrant concentration in New York's East Side, as well as in a number of other ghettos in large cities, was not an accidental development. The miracle that is the Jewish community in America was forged with hard labor and the devotion of generations of pioneers. [. . .]

The pioneers of the Jewish labor movement gave the Jewish worker a sense of his own dignity; they also contributed to the respect with which the East Side came to be regarded in the non-Jewish world. First they won for the Jewish worker the respect of the general labor movement. The working conditions prevailing in the sweatshops of the East Side were not of a kind to win the sympathy of organized labor. But this attitude changed almost overnight when a series of bitter strikes in the garment industry aroused public opinion, and the world became aware that the Jewish workers knew how to defend their rights and interests.

The Jewish labor leaders were keenly aware of the importance of winning public opinion in times of conflict, perhaps because Jewish labor was still weak and urgently needed the moral support of the native American workers. The Jewish workers gained a reputation as good strikers but poor union people. This reputation was not unfounded, though their shortcomings as union people were not the result of a lack of understanding of the importance of organization.

How to account for the fact that Jewish workers so frequently resorted to strikes when their unions were so weak? There were even instances when they struck before formulating their demands.

The workers of the East Side often went on strike for reasons other than formulated economic demands. For them the strike was frequently a way of expressing their protest against a form of society that tried to transform the laborer into a robot. In such instances the strike was an instrument to win recognition for the role of the worker in economic and social life.

In an article published in *Forward* (July 27, 1910) concerning the historic cloakmakers' strike, the poet A. Leyssin characterized the mood of the workers as follows: "The seventy thousand zeros now became seventy thousand fighters." The worker refused to maintain his passive role in the shop or in social life, and struck for his rights as citizen and man.

The great cloakmakers' strike in 1910 marked a turning point in the history of the Jewish labor movement.

It may even justly be maintained that it was a turning point in the history of the American Jewish community. The strike ended in a remarkable fashion. The embittered fight of the workers aroused the entire Jewish community. Prominent personages like Jacob Schiff, Louis Marshall, Louis D. Brandeis, and others became involved as intermediaries. Agreement was reached after long negotiations, and both parties signed a Protocol of Peace which became a milestone in the history of industrial relations in America.

Other works by Menes: *Die vorexilischen Gesetze Israels im Zusammenhang seiner kulturgeschichtlichen Entwicklung* (1928); *Di yidn in Poyln: fun di eltste tsaytn biz der tsveyter velt-milkhome* (1946); *Shabes un yontef: sotsyale gerekhtikeyt, kheshbm hanefesh, geule, inem gang fun yidishn yor* (1973).

Marshall Sklare

1921–1992

Born in Chicago to parents of Lithuanian descent, Marshall Sklare was a third-generation American. His pioneering sociological studies of American Jews were among the first to consider Jewish life in America as a source of scholarly interest, and they defined the parameters of the field for decades. Sklare worked for the American Jewish Committee's Division of Scientific Research, Yeshiva University, and the Princeton Theological Seminary before joining the faculty of Brandeis University in 1969. He remained at Brandeis until his retirement in 1990.

Conservative Judaism: An American Religious Movement
1955

Social Activities and Ethnic Group Maintenance

One other concept in addition to the compromise with secularism is required before the problem under study will become entirely clear. This is the status of Jewry as an ethnic group and of the Jewish religious institution as an "ethnic church." As we shall see, Judaism's ethnic-church character is particularly important in connection with the attitude of Conservatism toward synagogue activities of a non-worship character.

Despite the persistences which we have pointed out, the direction of movement in our society is toward the discarding of ethnic identification. As a consequence, the ethnic church must either transform itself into a non-ethnic institution—in most cases hardly a feasible plan—or it must seek to retard the assimilation of its members. The development of an abundant social life in the ethnic community which parallels and frequently offers greater gratification than is available in the larger society is a feasible device to arrest such tendencies. Its employment by the ethnic church may be described as a *survival technique in a conflict society*. The ethnic churches may state, as do non-ethnic institutions, that their youth groups are for the purpose of combating juvenile delinquency and providing a wholesome social environment—that adult clubs help to develop the personality of their members and are making worthwhile contributions to community life. But the ethnic church has a special interest in developing these good works. The encouragement of non-religious activities, in the form of ethnic associations, is vital to the continuation of its religious program. The non-ethnic type of institution has the specific problem of reconciling itself to, and finding a place in, an urban culture where secularism has challenged traditional values. The ethnic church faces this issue also, but secularism may seem to it to be only a reflection of other problems such as acculturation and assimilation. It must stake its future not only on the assumption by its members of a religious mission, but more significantly on their acceptance of the ethnic burden. Especially as far as Jewry is concerned, in evaluating social and recreational activities we must take the special needs of the institution as an *ethnic* church into consideration, although the compromise-with-secularism factor must by no means be underrated.

We developed the idea earlier that in our society religion is a socially accepted way of perpetuating group differences. It follows then that not only does the synagogue need the ethnicity of Jewry for its self-maintenance, but that many Jews feel that they require the synagogue if Jewish distinctiveness is to be preserved. Pressures toward reinforcement thus arise both from those interested in the institution itself (individuals who display deep religious feelings, or those who, by social or family position, may be strongly identified with a particular synagogue), as well as from those who may be classified as "ethnic survivalists." We have just seen how the desire for ethnic survivalism was diluted and obscured in "old line" Reform Judaism. We have also noted how Orthodoxy tended to limit the employment of the synagogue as a medium for survivalism—it continued to rely upon worship as its chief activity when the old rituals no longer fully expressed the collective life. The special contribution of Conservatism has been its relatively uninhibited "exploitation" of the new type of synagogue—the kind which is a house of assembly as much or more than it is a house of prayer—for the purposes of group survival. The movement has been able to do so because it has not been strongly affected by cosmopolitanism as with Reform, or by institutional rigidity as with Orthodoxy.

The lay people who founded the Conservative movement lacked the intellectual tools with which to develop a systematic analysis of what they were about, as well as the verbal skills needed to make their objectives explicit. For an expression of the sentiments which have motivated them, it is necessary to turn to the rabbis, and especially to Mordecai M. Kaplan. He was one of the earliest among his group to study the works of Durkheim, Cooley, and other social scientists with care. Integrating a functionalist approach with his pragmatic leanings, he was able to raise to a conceptual level the objectives of his colleagues—both lay and professional—when they founded Conservative "synagogue centers."

Kaplan advocated the establishment of local religious institutions which would have additional functions other than worship and the study of the sacred system. He reasoned that since the contemporary synagogue must serve as the bulwark against assimilation, this objective could only result if large numbers participated and if in so doing they gained a feeling of "social togetherness." Since he felt that constant association and participation in common activities would lead to greater group solidarity, Kaplan urged his rabbinical students not to content themselves only with improvements in ritual and decorum. Such reforms, while desirable, could hardly solve survival problems in a non-Jewish environment. New features would have to be added supplementing or replacing worship as a means of reducing *anomie*. Reforms would help achieve greater group solidarity and a sense of improved morale:

> It therefore seemed to me that the only way to counteract the disintegrative influences within, as well as without, Jewish life was to create the *conditions* that would not only set in motion socially and psychologically constructive forces, but that would also make them forces for religion. What was needed . . . was to transform the synagogue into a . . . neighborhood Jewish center. Instead of the primary purpose of congregational organizations being worship, it should be social togetherness. . . .

> The history of the Synagogue . . . is a striking illustration of the importance of creating new social agencies when new conditions arise that threaten the life of a people or of its religion. The integration of Jews into a non-Jewish civilization created such conditions. They, therefore, justify transforming the Synagogue into a new kind of social agent, to be known as a "Jewish center." The function of the Jewish center would have to be the all-inclusive one of developing around the leisure interests a sense of solidarity through face-to-face association and friendship.[1]

NOTE

1. Mordecai M. Kaplan, "The Way I Have Come," *Mordecai M. Kaplan: An Evaluation*, ed. by Ira Eisenstein and Eugene Kohn (New York: Jewish Reconstructionist Foundation, 1952), p. 311. [. . .]

Other works by Sklare: *Jewish Identity on the Suburban Frontier: A Study of Group Survival in the Open Society* (1967); *The Jewish Community in America* (1974); *Understanding American Jewry* (1982).

Lionel Trilling

Isaac Babel, Introduction to Collected Stories
1955

A good many years ago, in 1929, I chanced to read a book which disturbed me in a way I can still remember. The book was called *Red Cavalry;* it was a collection of stories about Soviet regiments of horse operating in Poland. I had never heard of the author, Isaac Babel—or I. Babel as he signed himself—and nobody had anything to tell me about him, and part of my disturbance was the natural shock we feel when, suddenly and without warning, we confront a new talent of great energy and boldness. But the book was disturbing for other reasons as well. [. . .]

There was anomaly at the very heart of the book, for the Red cavalry of the title were Cossack regiments, and why were Cossacks fighting for the Revolution, they who were the instrument and symbol of Tsarist repression? The author, who represented himself in the stories, was a Jew; and a Jew in a Cossack regiment was more than an anomaly, it was a Joke, for between Cossack and Jew there existed not merely hatred but a polar opposition. Yet here was a Jew riding as a Cossack and trying to come to terms with the Cossack ethos. At that first reading it seemed to me—although it does not now—that the stories were touched with cruelty. They were about violence of the most extreme kind, yet they were composed with a striking elegance and precision of objectivity, and also with a kind of lyric *joy,* so that one could not at once know just how the author was responding to the brutality he recorded, whether he thought it good or bad, justified or not justified. Nor was this the only thing to be in doubt about. It was not really clear how the author felt about, say, Jews; or about religion; or about the goodness of man. He had—or perhaps, for the sake of some artistic effect, he pretended to have—a secret. This alienated and disturbed me. It was impossible not to be overcome by admiration for *Red Cavalry,* but it was not at all the sort of book that I had wanted the culture of the Revolution to give me.

Nahum N. Glatzer

The Frankfort Lehrhaus
1956

I

In the treatise *Zeit ist's* [Franz] Rosenzweig outlined a detailed and imposing plan of an Academy for the Science of Judaism, the members of which would be both scholars and teachers. As scholars they would work on one of the several scientific projects undertaken by the Academy; a part of their time, however, they would devote to Jewish teaching in the community of their residence. The Jewish scholar today, Rosenzweig argued, should feel the responsibility of sharing his knowledge with the people and the schools; the youth in schools should be instructed by competent scholars and not by half-educated graduates of teacher's seminaries or by overworked rabbis; the Jewish communities should, as a part of their communal obligation, shoulder the bill for this over-all programme.

This new type of scholar-teacher, if carefully and patiently nurtured would, in time, restore a Jewish intelligentsia which in olden times used to be the core of the community and which is now so sorely missed. Judaism has become a province of specialists, while its power should be with the people. An uninformed—or

ill-informed—Jew is an unconcerned Jew, especially in an otherwise literate society.

It Is Time contains also a meticulously prepared course of Jewish studies. Utilizing the existing framework of time—nine years at the *Gymnasium,* two hours weekly—Rosenzweig showed that by sufficient concentration, and by eliminating any waste of time, Hebrew language, the Bible, the liturgy, the principal documents of classical Judaism, the major trends of Jewish thought and history could be fused into a coherent programme.

This programme, written at the Balkan front on Army postal cards (like the general school programme before, and the *magnum opus,* the *Star of Redemption,* shortly after), intrigued many thinking Jews in Germany. But the plan appeared to be too great a departure from the established. Its central point, the creation of a position of a teaching scholar and scholarly teacher, met with strong opposition from both the scholarly and the teaching groups. An academy was indeed established (in 1919). Its members were aware of the new requirements of Jewish scholarship, as compared with the aims of the nineteenth-century *Wissenschaft des Judentums.* Professor Julius Guttmann echoed Rosenzweig's wishes when he said: "What we look for in Jewish scholarship today is essentially that it shows us a way to the sources of Jewish life." But in reality its function (until the closing down in 1934) was the execution of a number of scholarly projects and the publication of results of individual research. The turn to the purely historical which the Academy had taken, prompted Rosenzweig, its initiator, to look to other ways of realizing his idea of a renaissance of Jewish learning.

II

Frankfort-on-the-Main offered an opportunity. There existed in Frankfort a Jewish adult education institute (*Volkshochschule*), founded after the first World War upon the initiative of Dr. Eugen Mayer, the scholarly and energetic community administrator. Similar institutes existed in other larger Jewish communities, such as Berlin, Munich, Breslau. Rosenzweig, who happened to visit Frankfort in the Fall of 1919, was invited to head the adult institute there and was allowed to re-organize it in accordance with his own ideas. In preparation for this task, Rosenzweig wrote (in the beginning of 1920) the treatise *Bildung und kein Ende,* a criticism of the cultural situation after the Emancipation and a vigorous call to a meaningful Judaism.

In August 1920, Rosenzweig assumed the leadership of the Frankfort institute, which had already carried out two series of lecture courses. In collaboration with the then existing committee, Rosenzweig expanded the programme. Significant for this new trend was the implementation of the lecture courses by study groups mainly devoted to the "introduction into Jewish sources." The central position was to be given to courses in Hebrew language and classical writings.

It was clear that Rosenzweig aimed at more than imparting information on Jewish topics; the audience, accustomed at best to a passive enjoyment of lectures, should be taught to participate actively, to feel personally challenged by the texts before it. Slowly, and with the progress of studies, Rosenzweig hoped, the spirit of classical Jewish learning could be revived. This tendency Rosenzweig indicated by choosing the name *Freies Jüdisches Lehrhaus* (Free House of Jewish Studies). The reference to Beth ha-Midrash was intentional; the *Lehrhaus* should indeed become a modernized Beth ha-Midrash. The word "free" indicated that registration was open to all without an entrance examination; it should also convey the notion of freedom of inquiry. [. . .]

The Jewish youth of Frankfort—as in any other German community—was split into many different organizations, orthodox, liberal, Zionist, neutral. At the outset of his Frankfort activity, Rosenzweig had to convince the various associations of the need to take a broader view, and, without giving up their particular policies, to unite in the pursuit of Jewish learning. That he succeeded—partly at least—in breaking down the stubborn resistance of the organizations is due only to his equally stubborn insistence on his plan and to the greater persuasiveness of his argument.

Nathan Glazer

1923-2019

The son of working-class Jewish immigrants to New York, Nathan Glazer studied at the City College of New York in the 1940s. Initially influenced by Marxism, Glazer's politics became more conservative. In the 1960s, he produced significant criticisms of President Lyndon Johnson's Great Society programs. Glazer taught at the University of California at Berkeley and at Harvard University, and his sociological studies of race, ethnicity, and assimilation have been both widely influential and deeply controversial. He served on national committees related to urban policy and education.

The Jewish Revival in America, II: Its Religious Side
1956

But any honest observer of the contemporary scene must admit that the fading of traditional Jewish piety has not meant its replacement by more "Christian" forms of religious life, even though some of these have considerable sanction in the Jewish past. I think I do not exaggerate when I say there is nothing in American Jewish literature—and many rabbis have written their autobiographies—that might possibly find a place in any anthology of religious experience. I once asked one of our leading authorities on American Jewish history whether he knew of any autobiography, published or in manuscript, by rabbi or layman, that described in detail a spiritual or religious experience—whether a conversion or a loss of faith. He could think only of the autobiography of a Jew who had been converted to Christianity! Admittedly, he spoke on the spur of the moment. His answer nevertheless reflects a striking characteristic of American Jewish literature—that it contains almost nothing that, by ordinary methods of classification, one would call religious experience. In the biographies of American Jews, and of rabbis too, one will find passions engaged by the problems of Zionism, by politics and reform movements, by the conflict of different organizations within Jewish life—but the category of spiritual experience, as ordinarily defined, is absent. [. . .]

If the social attitudes of the Jews are not a part of the heritage of the Jewish religion still alive for American Jews, what else is there? What in the feelings and sentiments of Jews can we see as reflecting their ancestral religion?

We must begin with something that has not happened; this negative something is the strongest and, potentially, most significant religious reality among American Jews: the Jews have not stopped being Jews. I do not now speak of the fact that they are sociologically defined as Jews; this is of small significance from the point of view of Jewish religion. I speak rather of the fact that they still *choose* to be Jews, that they do not cast off the yoke or burden of the Jewish heritage. Despite the concreteness of the words "yoke" and "burden," what I have in mind is something very abstract. It is not that most Jews in this country submit themselves to the Law; they do not. Nor can they tell you what the Jewish heritage is. But they do know there is such a heritage, they do know it may demand something of them, and to that demand, insofar as it is brought to them and has any meaning for them, they will not answer no. The significance of the fact that they have not cast off the yoke is that they are prepared to be Jews. Not to be the Jews their grandfathers were; the medieval world is shattered and Orthodox Judaism is only a museum object as far as the overwhelming majority of American Jews is concerned. But they are prepared to be some kind of Jews, they are capable of being moved and reached, and of transcending the pedestrian life that so many of them live in company with other Americans.

In my view, it is because of this negative characteristic, this refusal to become non-Jews, that we see today a flourishing of Jewish religious institutions. It is true that these institutions do not evoke or engage any deep religious impulses. Yet they are successful only because American Jews are ready to be Jews, are willing to be inducted into Jewish life.

We see the reality of this readiness in the fact that, to every generation of recent times, a different part of the Jewish past has become meaningful. At the same time, to be sure, other parts of that tradition, great chunks without which it seemed it must die, were rejected. And yet at no point has everything been rejected; a kind of shifting balance has been maintained whereby each generation could relate itself meaningfully to some part of the Jewish past. It has been the course of events that has dictated which part of the Jewish past should become more prominent at any given moment—at one time, and for some Jews, philanthropy; at another time, and for other Jews, Zionism or Yiddish-speaking socialism; or, as today, institutional religion. The son of the Reform Jewish philanthropist who gives up the last Jewish connections of his father may surprise us by becoming what his father never was, a Zionist. The son of the Yiddish-speaking socialist who abandoned his father's movement may join the temple. In this way, each generation shoulders a minimal part of the yoke.

There are even more complex patterns than this in the maintenance of the minimal relation to Judaism, and I will mention one. There are American Jews who have been given a good traditional education, and who, following the pattern of the 20's or 30's have broken with all religious observance. They do not attend the synagogue, they do not observe the dietary laws, they do not mark the Jewish holidays, and they do not believe in the existence of God. When this kind of Jew has children, however, he will decide that they should have some sort of Jewish education. Such a man is not succumbing to suburban middle-class pressures; he can resist them as easily as can the classic village atheist. He may tell himself—and believe that the children should know what it means to be a Jew, for willy-nilly they will be considered Jews and they must know how to cope with antisemitism. But one sees at work here that obscure process whereby a minimal relation to Judaism is established. The mental calculus seems to be as follows: since I myself have had a good traditional education, I can afford to be an agnostic or atheist. My child won't get such an education, but he should at least get a taste of the Jewish religion.

Philanthropy, Zionism, Jewish organizational life, attachment to Yiddish, an interest in Hasidism, a love of Hebrew, formal religious affiliation, a liking for Jewish jokes and Jewish food—none of these has, on the surface, any particularly religious meaning. Each of them reflects the concerns of the moment. The Protestant social gospel, the needs of Jews in other parts of the world, varied philosophical movements, a tendency to take pride in one's origins—each finds an echo in American Judaism. It is easy to overlook any common element in the different forms of Judaism of the different generations, and see only the reflection of movements in society and thought at large. Yet what binds all these shifting manifestations of Judaism and Jewishness together is, I repeat, the common refusal to throw off the yoke.

The insistence of the Jews on remaining Jews, which may take the religiously indifferent forms of liking Yiddish jokes, supporting Israel, raising money for North African Jews, and preferring certain kinds of food, thus has a potentially religious meaning. It means that the Jewish religious tradition is not just a subject for scholars, but is capable now and then of finding expression in life. And even if it finds no expression in one generation or another, the commitment to remain related to it still exists. Dead in one, two, or three generations, it may come to life in the fourth.

Other works by Glazer: *American Judaism* (1957); *Beyond the Melting Pot: The Negroes, Puerto Ricans, Jews, Italians, and Irish of New York City* (with Daniel P. Moynihan, 1963); *Soviet Jewry: 1969* (1972).

Hannah Arendt

Reflections on Little Rock
1959

Preliminary Remarks

Finally, I should like to remind the reader that I am writing as an outsider. I have never lived in the South and have even avoided occasional trips to Southern states because they would have brought me into a situation that I personally would find unbearable. Like most people of European origin I have difficulty in understanding, let alone sharing, the common prejudices of Americans in this area. Since what I wrote may shock good people and be misused by bad ones, I should like to make it clear that as a Jew I take my sympathy for the cause of the Negroes as for all oppressed or underprivileged peoples for granted and should appreciate it if the reader did likewise. [. . .]

Segregation is discrimination enforced by law, and desegregation can do no more than abolish the laws enforcing discrimination; it cannot abolish discrimination and force equality upon society, but it can, and indeed must, enforce equality within the body politic. For equality not only has its origin in the body politic; its validity is clearly restricted to the political realm. Only there are we all equals. [. . .]

The question is not how to abolish discrimination, but how to keep it confined within the social sphere, where it is legitimate, and prevent its trespassing on the political and the personal sphere, where it is destructive.

In order to illustrate this distinction between the political and the social, I shall give two examples of discrimination, one in my opinion entirely justified and outside the scope of government intervention, the other scandalously unjustified and positively harmful to the political realm.

It is common knowledge that vacation resorts in this country are frequently "restricted" according to ethnic origin. There are many people who object to this practice; nevertheless it is only an extension of the right to free association. If as a Jew I wish to spend my vacations only in the company of Jews, I cannot see how anyone can reasonably prevent my doing so; just as I see no reason why other resorts should not cater to a clientele that wishes not to see Jews while on a holiday. There cannot be a "right to go into any hotel or recreation area or place of amusement," because many of these are in the realm of the purely social where the right to free association, and therefore to discrimination, has greater validity than the principle of equality. (This does not apply to theaters and museums, where people obviously do not congregate for the purpose of associating with each other.) The fact that the "right" to enter social places is silently granted in most countries and has become highly controversial only in American democracy is due not to the greater tolerance of other countries but in part to the homogeneity of their population and in part to their class system, which operates socially even when its economic foundations have disappeared. Homogeneity and class working together assure a "likeness" of clientele in any given place that even restriction and discrimination cannot achieve in America.

It is, however, another matter altogether when we come to "the right to sit where one pleases in a bus" or a railroad car or station, as well as the right to enter hotels and restaurants in business districts—in short, when we are dealing with services which, whether privately or publicly owned, are in fact public services that everyone needs in order to pursue his business and lead his life. Though not strictly in the political realm, such services are clearly in the public domain where all men are equal; and discrimination in Southern railroads and buses is as scandalous as discrimination in hotels and restaurants throughout the country. Obviously the situation is far worse in the South because segregation in public services is enforced by law and plainly visible to all. It is unfortunate indeed that the first steps toward clearing up the segregation situation in the South after so many decades of complete neglect did not begin with its most inhuman and its most conspicuous aspects. [. . .]

To force parents to send their children to an integrated school against their will means to deprive them of rights which clearly belong to them in all free societies—the private right over their children and the social right to free association. As for the children, forced integration means a very serious conflict between home and school, between their private and their social life, and while such conflicts are common in adult life, children cannot be expected to handle them and therefore should not be exposed to them. It has often been remarked that man is never so much of a conformer—that is, a purely social being—as in childhood. The reason is that every child instinctively seeks authorities to guide it into the world in which he is still a stranger, in which he cannot orient himself by his own judgment. To the extent that parents and teachers fail him as authorities, the child will conform more strongly to his own group, and under certain conditions the peer group will become his supreme authority. The result can only be a rise of mob and gang rule, as the news photograph we mentioned above [not included in this excerpt] so eloquently demonstrates. The conflict between a segregated home and a desegregated school, between family prejudice and school demands, abolishes at one stroke both the teachers' and the parents' authority, replacing it with the rule of public opinion among children who have neither the ability nor the right to establish a public opinion of their own.

Because the many different factors involved in public education can quickly be set to work at cross purposes, government intervention, even at its best, will always be rather controversial. Hence it seems highly questionable whether it was wise to begin enforcement of civil rights in a domain where no basic human and no basic political right is at stake, and where other rights—social and private—whose protection is no less vital, can so easily be hurt.

Eliezer Berkovits

1908–1992

Born in Nagyvárad, Hungary (present-day Oradea, Romania), Eliezer Berkovits was a Zionist and Orthodox rabbi, educator, theologian, and philosopher. After undergoing rabbinic training in Hungary and Germany, he was ordained in 1934 at Berlin's Hildesheimer Rabbinical Seminary under the influence of Rabbi Jehiel Jacob Weinberg. Simultaneously, he received a doctorate in philosophy from the University of Berlin. He served as rabbi in Berlin from 1934 to 1939, when he fled from the Nazis. Over the next decade and a half, he held rabbinic positions in England, Australia, and the United States. From 1958 to 1975 he was chairman of the department of Jewish philosophy at Hebrew Theological College in suburban Chicago. He then relocated to Jerusalem.

God, Man, and History

1959

[. . .] Immanuel Kant once wrote: "The true [moral] service of God is . . . invisible, i.e., it is the service of the heart, in spirit and in truth, and it may consist . . . only of intention."[1] This, indeed, is the noble formula for the historic bankruptcy of all "natural," as well as "spiri-

tual," religions. The invisible service of God is the prerogative of invisible creatures. When man adopts such service for himself, he makes the dualism of his nature itself a religion. He will expect *Gesinnung* (sentiment) and noble intentions of the soul, and will readily forgive the profanity of the body; he will have God "in his heart" and some devil directing his actions. He will serve God on the Sabbath and himself the rest of the week. He will worship like some angelic being in the specified places of worship and follow his self-regarding impulses everywhere else. And he will find such an arrangement in order. For should not the true service of God be invisible? And is not the physical organism—and together with it, all the material manifestations of life—therefore incapable of religion?

Contrary to Kant, Judaism teaches that man's "true service of God" must be human. It should be invisible, as man's soul is invisible; and it should be visible, too, because man is visible. It must be "service of the heart, in spirit and in truth" as well as of the body. It must be service through the *mitzva*, the deed in which man's spiritual and material nature have unified. It is a much higher service than that of the spirit alone. It is the religion of the whole man.[2]

The essence of such service has been beautifully expressed by a latter-day rabbi, who said that of all those commandments that are "between God and man," he loved most that of dwelling in the succah. In entering the succah, one steps into the *mitzva* with one's very boots on. This is, indeed, basic Judaism. It is comparatively easy to relate the spiritual to God; it is as easy as it is ineffective in history. The real task is to orient the whole world of man, matter and spirit, toward God.

NOTES
[Words in brackets appear in the original source document.—Eds.]
1. Kant, *Religion Within the Limits of Reason Alone*, p. 180.
2. Bahya ibn Pakuda differentiated between "duties of the heart" and "duties of the body," but only in order to be able to concentrate all the more on the "duties of the heart." In reality, however, the *mitzva* represents the coalescing of the two categories of duties in the one unifying deed, which should be known as the duty of man.

Other works by Berkovits: *Towards Historic Judaism* (1943); *Man and God: Studies in Biblical Theology* (1969); *Faith after the Holocaust* (1973); *Crisis and Faith* (1976); *Jewish Women in Time and Torah* (1990).

Aleksander Hertz

1895-1983

Born in Warsaw into a Jewish family of fierce Polish patriots, his father having fought in the Polish Uprising of 1863, Aleksander Hertz received a doctorate in sociology from Warsaw University and was known for his work on the sociology of theater. In the 1930s, he helped organize the Stronnictwo Demokratyczne, which advocated a Polish identity that was civic rather than ethnic or religious. Hertz immigrated to the United States in 1940 and was active in Polish émigré publications such as the Paris-based *Kultura*. His landmark book *The Jews in Polish Culture* reflects his ongoing efforts after the war to highlight the key role played by Jews in Polish culture and to remind Polish intellectuals that Jews had been an integral part of their national heritage.

The Jews in Polish Culture
1961

In every caste system the lower caste occupies a marginal position vis-à-vis the upper caste. The Jews were a marginal element to the Polish nobility. The margin was not isolated, for the Jews could have access to various areas in the nobility's life, just as they did to various areas in peasant life. But as a whole, as a caste the Jews were at the margin of what determined the essence of the noble Poland's history.

That marginality did not disappear in the case of Jews assimilated to Polish culture; to a certain extent, it even increased. But certain essential changes occurred in it. [...]

Marginality creates in its participants certain moral stances and a certain attitude toward life. This is particularly striking in milieus with high intellectual level, in urban milieus, and in instances of non-conformism, whether assumed voluntarily or imposed from without. Marginal people, not being actively engaged in the life of the larger community and by maintaining a certain distance from it, are usually more objective observers of that community's affairs and perceive in it things that elude the notice of its active participants. In people of high intellectual attainment, this marginality often gives rise to criticism of the larger community, to irony and skepticism. At times that leads to evolutionary activity, while at others it is reduced to sarcasm, humor, or *Galgenhumor*.

The role of marginal people in the great social and cultural processes of the present time is tremendous. And not only of the present time. Great movements in thought and art, social revolutions, and changes in accepted value systems all usually had some connection with the actions of marginal people. Those people are a fermenting agent, the "yeast" without which culture would not be able to develop and the world would seem dead. What was said in Poland about the Jews—"difficult with them, boring without them"—can be applied to marginal people in general.

In Poland those who left the Jewish caste found themselves at the margin of Polish national society. If it were possible to conceive of the entire Polish margin in numerical terms—which is clearly unfeasible—the share of people of Jewish origin in it would, no doubt, be huge. That was an element that had not chosen marginality of their free will. In Poland, Jewish marginality was the inevitable consequence of the entire caste system. Anyone who left the caste system could not avoid landing on the margin. In the overwhelming majority of cases, those who left the Jewish caste experienced their marginality as difficult, painful, even tragic. They did not want to be on the margin and sought ways out of it. But it was rare that they succeeded. In some cases they even behaved as if they were not marginal. This was the same thing we referred to when speaking of those who acted as if they had never had a caste background. That was make-believe life, an attempt to play a role that was not acknowledged by others.

In practice, the consequences were obvious: among Jews, and particularly among the Polish-Jewish intelligentsia, this inevitably led to the formation of attitudes that are characteristic of all marginal people—keen perception of others and their affairs, criticism, skepticism, irony, and sarcasm. Difficult with them, boring without them. Willy-nilly they became an agent of ferment and unrest. And in that lay their great cultural role, the source of their contribution to Polish culture. Without the part played by marginal people, no matter what their origin, any national culture is in danger of ossifying and lapsing into boredom. [...]

And that was why it was difficult but not boring with the Jews in Poland. The difficulty was greatest for the most extreme conformists. And from that side came the severest accusations about the Jews' destructive qualities and their natural subversiveness. At bottom among many of those "subversives" there was a longing for conformity and a dream of togetherness with their opponents. Wherever Jews cease to be marginal as Jews—in Israel, in the United States—they accept the conformism of the larger community. They cease to be difficult and begin to be boring. Of course, there too they provide recruits for local margins, but as individuals, not by compulsion and within the framework of the general construction of marginal milieus. [...]

In Poland those who left the Jewish caste were compelled to the margin as a result of the distrust and opposition they encountered on the part of the larger community. The latter attempted to maintain some distance between themselves and the Jewish *homines novi*. This had far-reaching consequences, and—as so often happens in history—ones different from those that were intended. The margin produced its own attitudes and tendencies, which exerted a profound influence on the attitudes and tendencies of the larger environment. And that influence was creative. What is more, it outlived the existence of the Polish Jews and the Polish-Jewish margin.

The sarcasm, irony, and skepticism that characterize the intelligentsia's mentality in Poland today are, in the form they take and in their essential expression, a living reminder of what before the war was considered typically Jewish. Current Polish political humor, scathing and sometimes cynical, is a clear continuation of the old *shmontses*. It must be acknowledged, however, that conditions in Poland today also provide fertile ground for such humor: a considerable portion of Polish intelligentsia have now become a marginal element vis-à-vis the conformism of the ruling group. The irony those elements of the Polish intelligentsia direct against themselves is socially conditioned in a way similar to that which influenced the nature and form of the old Jewish humor.

It is my impression that the influence of the old margin is not limited to this alone but also embraces considerably broader areas. It would be extremely interesting to examine from this angle the characteristics of contemporary Polish literature and art, as well as that dimension of political journalism and sociology that eludes the clichés of obligatory party doctrine.

Once again let us stress what we have already indicated: in all the stages of our civilization's development, the culture-creating role played by marginal elements has been prominent and fertile. They were the yeast without which new values could not rise. Among the great creators of Euramerican culture the number of marginal people was enormous. Those were people rejected in one way or another by society, or people who themselves rejected society. Most often, theirs was a personally tragic fate. They had no "success in life." It is not even known where some of them are buried. That was the terrible price they had to pay for what they gave to humanity by grace of their genius.

Translated by Richard Lourie.

Other works by Hertz: *Zagadnienia socjologii teatru* (1939); *Szkice o ideologiach* (1947); *Amerykanskie stronnictwa polityczne* (1957); *Wyznania starego człowieka* (1979).

Betty Alschuler

1920–2013

Born in Brookline, Massachusetts, teacher, art historian, and critic Betty Rogers Alschuler Rubenstein attended Smith College in the 1940s and received a doctorate in art history from Florida State University in 1979. In 1962, Alschuler traveled to Albany, Georgia, with a multidenominational and multiracial group of clergy in support of the desegregation efforts of the civil rights movement, and she reported on her experiences for *The Reconstructionist*. She married theologian and historian Richard Rubenstein in 1966 and was involved in Jewish congregational activities, holding various teaching positions in art history.

Notes from the American Revolution
1962

I have returned from a war—a revolutionary war fought without firearms, without generals, without front lines. For ammunition, the smoldering spirit of the black people of America, like a gusher of oil, is breaking out of the shale with all the fury of pent-up human emotion. Non-violence is violence. Non-violence amid southern hospitality is the more violent. Every revolution has its style, and this one carries the paradoxes of superficial manners and death to an exquisite extreme.

Along with 40 ministers from Chicago—some dark, some white—I went to Albany, Georgia, on a prayer pilgrimage in August, 1962. The front lines of the war are found as soon as black and white gather. As the door of the bus closed us in together, we knew the depth of our fear. A Jew, as I am, heading south, led by a Christian minister, on a Christian mission, has a crowd of memories. My head was teeming: "And the Egyptians dealt ill with us," "And a stranger shalt thou not oppress for ye know the heart of a stranger seeing ye were strangers in the land of Egypt."

Curious but Frightened

I felt a common cause with these good men and women who had been moved to mid-wife freedom in the south, but the gulf that separated us is also wide. Their spirit of confession and atonement for their own sins was a deep part of their journey—their own guilt. Jail could be a catharsis for their spirit. Not for mine. I had no intention of going to jail, but I wanted to understand the nature of the struggle first hand, and by my presence to lend support to the side of freedom.

I was curious, but I was also frightened, and I knew that I was bringing with me my own fear of the dark, the unconscious melancholy shadows which attach themselves to dark people whether we will it or not. I could be overwhelmed by this too. I could come out on the wrong side of the war. I could say with the White South: Stay away from me, black person, you are my fear and I will put you down; I will disgrace you, because you are the self I cannot bear. You are the filth in me and only because you are there (black, filthy and sexual) on your side of town, in your place, can I be pure and clean. Only if I keep you down can I maintain my own image. O father Freud, you have taught me well and I go to a Holy War to fight my segregated self. I see myself on both sides of this battle. I think the black people know this and I think they will say it some day. Whether we have helped them or not, taught them or not loved them or not, they will hate us. [. . .]

Enemy Territory, U.S.A. (1962)

[. . .] My daughter and I speak with two members of the Jewish Congregation in Albany. Two men of dignity and status. My daughter tries to convince them that integration is a must. I listen. We hear frightened men, confused men, say "This is not a Jewish problem. This is not for outsiders. We have been good to the Negro. See the air-conditioned school. We are afraid for our children. We are good friends with the Christian here. Go away and don't bother us. The courts will settle this the American way." They are charming, gallant, well-assimilated southerners who know the art of speaking to women. They tell us that the pressure on their town has made the moderate stand impossible, and that they must be silent.

Can They Be Reached?

I see these gentlemen, Jews, under their southern manners, trapped. If the Klan marches, and they are gathering, if violence breaks, they know they will get it. They can take little initiative. My sympathy goes to them, even though their speeches are absurd. Who is an outsider in the age of spacecraft? We are all stuck on the little planet together. What is this north and south? There is air-conditioning for the Negro children, but when they graduate from the school their learning is pathetically inadequate. The Jewish townsmen even mention the woman who worked for them for thirty years and is like one of the family. A woman can only be a maid in Albany. There are only a very few factory jobs open to the young women, for very small pay. I want to ask my friends how they thought a Negro woman in Albany would marry and raise a normal family, but I don't. Fear and blindness have immobilized them. They cannot stop to ask questions. They speak with all the self-righteousness of people who suspect they are in error, but would lose everything if they confess.

The Jewish men, speaking with pride of the thousands of dollars their town has poured into the police force, are so absolutely ridiculous that one is speechless before them. Can they be reached? Should they be reached, or should we ask only for mercy, and hope that the course of events around them will not sweep them up in its eddy? I cannot agree with them as they ask us to rely on the courts of Albany to solve the problem. I know there is a backlog of a thousand cases, when young people, white and black, are languishing in their jails with no way to get out, with no lawyer to help them.

One young white girl, picked up on a vagrancy charge because she was found in a Negro bar, has been in for seven weeks, no family or friend to help and no money for bail. The courts in Albany are a joke, and Justice is mocked. My Jewish friends are still silent.

"For He has not made us like the people of other lands, nor set us level with the clans of earth, nor fixed our share to equal theirs, our lot to match their crowd and clamor." Who can help the southern Jews to see that if their status—political, economic, social—becomes their over-riding concern, their future is in jeopardy as surely as if they stood boldly for integration?

Other work by Alschuler (Rubenstein): *The Palazzo Magnani: An Iconographic Study of the Decorative Program* (1979).

Salo W. Baron
1895-1989

Salo Wittmayer Baron was the most important Jewish historian in the United States in the middle decades of the twentieth century and one of the key figures in the integration of Jewish studies into the American liberal arts curriculum. Born in Tarnów, Galicia, into a wealthy banking family, he received rabbinical ordination at Vienna's modern rabbinical seminary in 1920 and three doctorates from the University of Vienna—in philosophy (1917), political science (1922), and law (1923). He was teaching at the Jewish Teachers College in Vienna when Stephen Wise offered him a position at the newly established Jewish Institute of Religion in 1926. In 1929, he was appointed to an endowed chair in Jewish history at Columbia University, where he taught until his retirement in 1963. A master of twenty languages, he wrote a comprehensive history of the Jewish people from antiquity to the modern age.

Can American Jewry Be Culturally Creative?
1962

Historical Perspectives

[. . . V]iewed from the broad historic perspective, it is not at all surprising that American Jewry has not yet produced those great cultural achievements for which we are all hoping.

Suffice it to look back upon the major Jewish cultural centers of past ages—Hellenistic Egypt, Babylonia which created the Babylonian Talmud, Spain with its Golden Age, medieval Germany and France, or modern Eastern Europe. A brief consideration will convince us that it took every one of these communities much longer to develop its particular Jewish culture than the entire duration of Jewish settlement on this continent. [. . .]

What is clear from these five examples is that it takes a very long time for any culture to grow. Centuries must pass before the Jewish community can strike sufficient roots in any new country to get adjusted and develop its own new attitude which can become a basis for its new creativity.

Perhaps we are expecting the American Jews to produce results much too quickly. We must not forget that the real history of the Jews in the United States, as far as the large majority of its population is concerned, had only begun a century and a quarter ago. This is much too short a period of time for any community to take roots

and to establish its unique identity in a new environment. None of this proves, however, that the American Jews are not capable of developing a culture of their own.

Effect of Emancipation

True, the differences from past ages are also staggering. Most significantly, we are living in an era of Emancipation in which the Jews are being integrated into society at large. Jews are expected, not to live as a minority facing different majorities, as they did for twenty-five centuries in Egypt, Babylonia, Spain, Germany, Poland, and elsewhere, but to be part and parcel of the majorities themselves. Nowadays we are supposed to be Americans *and* Jews, Englishmen *and* Jews, Argentinians *and* Jews, and so forth.

In short, we are facing a problem of developing a culture which will be both Jewish and Western (or, to take the Soviet Union, both Jewish and Soviet) to embrace a total Jew, a Jew who, for instance in this country, feels himself completely American and completely Jewish at the same time. This is, indeed, a tremendous, in many respects unprecedented, challenge.

Moreover, the very meaning of Jewish culture has undergone a change during the Emancipation era. In Eastern Europe during the twentieth century Jews have been recognized as a nationality among other nationalities. If the Soviet Union had continued along the lines of its first decade during and after the Lenin regime—with the recognition of Jewish national minority rights, with a national school system in Yiddish, a Yiddish press and theater—one might really have witnessed there the emergence of a Judaism devoid of religion, Hebrew, the Zionist-messianic ideal, that is, a purely secular, Yiddishist national entity. Under such conditions, a Russian Jew—as began to be noticeable in the 1920s and the 1930s—could actually look down upon the American Jew as assimilated, because the latter sent his children to English-speaking schools, himself spoke English, and outwardly lived a purely American life.

If that evolution had developed undisturbedly we might have had by now two types of Judaism, a national secular Yiddish Judaism of Eastern Europe, and the religious, Zionist, Hebraic Judaism of the Western world. Each would claim superiority over the other. Unfortunately, the last thirty years have seen great changes in the Soviet Union, and have put an end to the possibility of the development there of any really flourishing secular Judaism in the foreseeable future.

The main question today really is whether Jews can be culturally creative under Emancipation. Can they be creative within their own, as well as within the majority culture? Certainly, there will be Jewish poets and writers, artists, musicians, scientists, and scholars. If the pattern follows past experience, Jews will undoubtedly contribute to the cultures of their environment more than may be expected from their ratio in the respective populations. But will they have enough cultural energy left creatively to cultivate their own Jewish heritage? We can find no answer in history because history has had no precedent of real Jewish Emancipation.

Sixty years ago, a relatively short time in history, half of world Jewry lived in Tsarist Russia; another significant portion in Rumania, the Ottoman Empire, and North Africa—all under conditions of non-emancipation. Even though one-third of world Jewry lived in the United States and other free countries at that time, most of them had been born and bred under conditions of non-emancipation; they could hardly have been expected to have changed overnight merely because they had left their *Shtetls* in the Ukraine or Poland for Chicago or London. In 1917, with the Russian Revolution, and in 1919 with the Peace Treaties it began to look as though world Jewry might at last be truly emancipated once and for all. The great counter-movement of Nazism, however, arose to deny not only Emancipation but also the very right of Jews to exist.

Consequently, Emancipation really had no chance fully to reveal its good, as well as bad, effects until after World War II. Only in our own day have we had the opportunity to observe the effects of real freedom—in this country and elsewhere. As a result, we have seen a tremendous rate of assimilation, but we have also simultaneously witnessed certain elements of religious and cultural revival which pessimists had previously considered impossible. [. . .]

In conclusion, I can merely say that I feel confident that the same Jewry which has already successfully confronted other great challenges and which has proved vastly creative in devising new means of communal coexistence, will also find some appropriate solutions for our present difficulties. After all, our entire community is in many ways unprecedented. Despite the lack of any form of law enforcement, it has succeeded in answering in a pioneering way the challenges of the constant emergencies which it has faced here and abroad.

Given the time, given the challenge, and most importantly given the understanding of that challenge, American Jewry, I am certain, will also give unprecedented, pioneering answers to its present challenge of creating a novel American Jewish culture.

Other works by Baron: *The Jewish Community* (1942); *A Social and Religious History of the Jews*, 18 vols. (1952–1983); *History and Jewish Historians: Essays and Addresses* (1964).

Arthur A. Cohen

1928–1986

A novelist, publisher, and theologian, Arthur A. Cohen was born in New York City. He studied philosophy and comparative religion at the University of Chicago as well as medieval Jewish philosophy at the Jewish Theological Seminary. Although he is best known for his works on the history of modern Jewish thought, Cohen also wrote five novels, including *An Admirable Woman* (1983), which won the National Jewish Book Award in 1983. A publisher, Cohen founded the Noonday Press with Cecil Hemley in 1951 and Meridian Books in 1954. In 1964, he became editor in chief at Holt, Rinehart, and Winston.

The Natural and the Supernatural Jew: An Historical and Theological Introduction 1962

The Renewal of the Jewish Vocation

A natural history of the Jewish mind is impossible. The Jewish mind, as a natural and empirical phenomenon, is an absurdity. It consists in but the pale images of theological models—prophetism and messianism transformed into social and political ideologies, Exile recast as social alienation, the loneliness and spiritual discomfort of biblical man translated into the self-estrangement of modern man. For the natural Jew all that remains of the supernatural community is a treasury of inspiriting maxims and heroic legends, divested not only of their mythological content but of their divinity as well. Judaism has been quietly and unconsciously demythologizing its tradition for centuries; but the purgation of myth has not been accompanied by a sharper, more compelling awareness of the personal truth and meaning of its history (much demythologizing, but little kerygma).

The Jewish mind is demythologized, but the natural Jew has lost, in the process, all contact with and approach to his supernatural life. For centuries the supernatural Jew struggled to survive, and though he perished in the flesh, he did survive. Faith in the promise of the past and trust in the consummating action of God enabled him to survive the assaults of Christendom and Islam. The loss in our time of that supernatural pride which is called the "stubbornness" of the Jew is partially responsible for the loss of contact with the legacy of tradition and the passion to give witness to the incomplete sanctity of the natural order; moreover, the immolation of European Jewry in this century has exploded the last vestige of Jewish mythology—an eschatological trust which was indifferent to the course of world history and culture.

The supernatural Jew, defined as he is by those concerns and preoccupations which form the historic consensus of the Jewish mind, is the last of the eschatologists, for the Jew, more than any other man, lives on the recollection of first things and the anticipation of the last. Each moment comes to the supernatural Jew full of unrealized meaning, for each moment is abundant with the unrealized possibility of God in history. Every moment is potentially an eschatological moment; every moment collects the history of the past and portends the unfulfilled future. There is no such thing for the supernatural Jew as the denial of history, the repudiation of its meaning, the despair of its justification. Where the natural Jew may know despair, the supernatural Jew knows only trust.

But the natural and the supernatural Jew are joined in every Jew. The supernatural Jew may occasionally forget that he is also flesh and blood; he may detach himself from the world and disengage himself from history that he may pursue a path of self-denial and private illumination. Such a Jew is as much in error as is the natural Jew who forgets what links him to eternity. The natural Jew, enmeshed in the historical, cannot help but despair; destiny disappears for him and only the hard and implacable fatality of his life remains. The despair of the historical is but the consequence of fate obliterating destiny; while the ecstasy of the mystic, no less an example of fate, is centered exclusively upon the actuality of God, indifferent to his involvement in the contingent and dangerous war of history.

The religious dilemma which makes the unity of the natural and the supernatural so imperative for the Jewish mind is that the representation of God in history is not pure actuality but actuality committed to the unfulfilled possibility of history. The eschatological consummation toward which Judaism turns its face is his-

tory with God, the actual God realizing new creation, and new concreteness. As such, each moment of the present may become a redemptive moment, a moment in which the new possibility of God and the renewed sensibility of the Jew may meet and sanctify.

The renewal of the historical, the reunion of the Jew with general culture, the reassertion of the catholic claim of Judaism depend upon the rediscovery of the implicit polarity and dialectic of the Jewish nature—that it is natural, participating in all the forms and events of history and culture, and supernatural, transforming those forms and events into bearers of ultimate and consummate meaning. God is not an eschatologist nor is God a messianist. God does what can be done—this is indeed part of the tragedy which we may sense when we speak of God, for God cannot compel history to fulfillment, he can but enrich the moment with those possibilities which become the bearers of meaning. It is man who victimizes God. God maintains freedom and the free destiny; it is human obduracy and folly which refuses such terrifying freedom and finds consolation in the refusal of destiny and the comforting delusion of fate.

The historic moment that bears ultimate meaning is always at hand. But when the argument is done and the historic precedents of the Jewish mind have been adduced and displayed and the consensus of Judaism has been recapitulated, the same question recurs: Can the testimony of all truth compel human decision? Is it possible that the sense of supernatural vocation—lost as it is in the abyss of natural fate—may be renewed? This question still remains, and only Jews can answer it.

Other works by Cohen: *Martin Buber* (1957); *Arguments and Doctrines: A Reader of Jewish Thinking in the Aftermath of the Holocaust* (1970); *In the Days of Simon Stern* (1973); *A Hero in His Time* (1976); *The Tremendum: A Theological Interpretation of the Holocaust* (1981).

Abraham Joshua Heschel

Heavenly Torah: As Refracted through the Generations
1962

Two Philosophical Methods

The fact that at a crossroads in Jewish history two "fathers of the world" met, men who were to become trailblazers in religious philosophy, is of major importance. The meeting of intellectual giants of opposing aspirations, who debated on issues of ultimate significance, inevitably laid bare problems in religious faith that the Sages tended to conceal.

Each generation has its exegetes. Each riddle has its solutions; and the deeper the riddle, the more numerous the solutions. The Torah itself can be acquired in two different ways: via the road of reason or the road of vision. Rabbi Ishmael's path was that of the surface, plain meaning of the text. Rabbi Akiva's path was that of the esoteric meaning. And it is clear that they did not construct their methods *ex nihilo*. Such divergences of paths are the work of generations, and these differences did not suddenly appear in the generation of Rabbi Ishmael and Rabbi Akiva. Their source lay in diverse approaches to Jewish teachings, as they were handed down by tradition over the course of whole eras. The nation harbored treasuries of thought, and Rabbi Ishmael and Rabbi Akiva served as mouthpieces for voices and echoes of generations that preceded them. Yet it was also in their schools that these ideas crystallized and took on a form that had been unknown to previous generations. For they were able to channel ancient and powerful intellectual flows and, in so doing, nourish generations yet to come. [...]

Intellectual debates and psychological rumblings are the stuff of every generation. Spiritual problems continually shed forms and take on new ones. Before you can understand the intellectual movements of recent times, you must inquire into the chain of tradition that precedes them. The things about which Rabbi Akiva and Rabbi Ishmael disagreed were still the subjects of debates and triumphant disputations among medieval scholars, and they are still on the agenda today. [...]

Rationalism and lucidity of thought characterized the teachings of Rabbi Ishmael. His greatness lay in a congenial straightforwardness amenable to all. Soaring visions marked the teachings of Rabbi Akiva; his language was a ladder planted on earth, ending in heaven. In one system of thought, there was clarity; in the other, profundity. Here, a shunning of the wondrous; there, a thirst to apprehend the hidden and the wondrous. [...]

Rabbi Akiva, a man drawn to the esoteric, who was not satisfied with the path of plain reason, felt that the covert in the Torah is far greater than the overt. Thus, he pursued the mysteries of Torah and found that the letters yield wisdom and reveal matters that reason could never imagine. According to his approach, human knowledge is unlike the knowledge contained in Torah, just as human language is unlike the language of Torah. From every jot and tittle, he would extract mounds and mounds of Halakhot.

Rabbi Ishmael, a man devoted to cool analysis, who had no concern for hidden things and who did not see the Torah as a transcendent existence, walked a straight direct path. He tested and balanced verses against one another with the scales of logic, with no gimmicks, and explained them straightforwardly. "The Torah speaks in human language" was his guiding principle. [...]

There were thus two points of view among the Sages: (1) a transcendent point of view, comprising a method of thought always open to the higher realms, striving to understand matters of Torah through a supernal lens; and (2) an immanent point of view, comprising a method of thought modest and confined, satisfied to understand matters of Torah through an earthly lens defined by human experience. These points of view are foundational and paradigmatic, and from them are derived differing conceptions and analyses, rivals to one another. Thus were crystallized two differing methods of understanding the commandments and their underlying purposes. One says: if you sin, what do you do to Him; if your transgressions are many, how do you affect Him? If you are righteous, what do you give Him; what does He receive from your hand? Mortals need God, but surely God does not need the service of mortals! The other says: the Holy and Blessed One needs our service. One says: the commandments were given in order to provide justification to Israel; they were given only in order to refine God's creatures. And the other says: the commandments were given in order to bring pleasure to the Holy and Blessed One. Again, one says: a person makes a pilgrimage three times a year in order to be seen in the Presence of the Lord God; and the other says that just as one comes to be seen, so does one come to see, as a Master anticipates his servant coming to see him.

Rabbi Akiva, who viewed humanity through a heavenly lens, taught that "owing to our sins, people do not have the wherewithal to know the heavenly Image." He was among those Sages who entered the *Pardes*; that is: "they ascended to the firmament." By contrast, Rabbi Ishmael, who viewed humanity through an earthly lens, was not prone to those things that are beyond the ken of human reason; he had no concern for hidden things. The heavens belong to the Lord, but the earth He gave over to humans. The main worry should be about justice and righteousness in this world.

Edited and translated by Gordon Tucker and Leonard Levin.

Saul Lieberman

1898–1983

Saul Lieberman is considered one of the greatest Talmudic authorities of the modern era. Born in Motal, Russia (present-day Belarus), Lieberman received a traditional religious education and completed secular studies in Kiev and later in France. He also studied Talmudic philology and classical Greek at the Hebrew University in Jerusalem. It was there that Lieberman's talent and intellect were first recognized; the university appointed him a lecturer in Talmud in 1931. In 1940, he moved to the United States, where he would come to lead the rabbinical school at the Jewish Theological Seminary in New York. As a scholar, Lieberman was extremely prolific, producing some 225 books and articles, including commentaries on a range of rabbinic texts.

Hellenism in Jewish Palestine
1962

Rabbinic literature is replete with valuable information about the life, manners and customs of the ancients. Many passages in it can be properly understood only in the general frame of its environment. The Jews of Palestine were by no means isolated from the ancient Mediterranean civilized world. They shared many of its general beliefs, conceptions and patterns of behavior. […]

The methods applied in the understanding of dreams were invented neither by the Jews nor by the Greeks. They go back to hoary antiquity. The ingenuity of the diviner or seer produced the most complicated solutions of dreams, oracles and magic, which lent themselves to similar ways of interpretations; they borrow from each other and supplement one another. […]

To sum up, numberless methods for the interpretations of dreams, oracles, and mystic writings existed in the ancient world from times immemorial. Very often the same phenomenon lent itself to various and even contradictory explanations. The Rabbis who flourished at the end of the first and the beginning of the second centuries (and among them we find R. 'Akiba, the famous interpreter of the Torah) already employed the shrewd and complicated methods of the *onirocritica* in their dream interpretations.

For the interpretation of sacred *legal* texts, which were not as a rule formulated in an ambiguous language, different means were undoubtedly in use among the priests. The Rabbis applied comparatively few rules to the elaboration of the legal part of the Torah. They were the result of choice, discrimination and crystallization out of many ways for the exposition of texts. In the *Aggadah* however and in the אסמכתות ("supports") for the *Halakha*, the Rabbis resorted to well established devices which were current in the literary world at that time. Had the Rabbis themselves invented these artificial rules in their interpretations, the "supports" from the Bible would be ineffective and strange to the public. But as the utilization of instruments accepted all over the civilized world of that time their rules of interpretation of the *Aggadah* (and their "supports" for the *Halakha* from Scripture) were a literary affectation which was understood and appreciated by their contemporaries.

However, although we possess no evidence that the Rabbis borrowed their rules of interpretation from the Greeks, the situation is quite different when we deal with formulation, terms, categories and systematization of these rules. The latter were mainly created by the Greeks, and the Jews most probably did not hesitate to take them over and adapt them to their own rules and norms.

Other works by Lieberman: *'Al ha-yerushalmi* (1929); *Tosefet rishonim* (1937); *Sheki'in* (1939); *Midreshey teman* (1940); *Greek in Jewish Palestine* (1942).

Hannah Arendt

Eichmann in Jerusalem: A Report on the Banality of Evil
1963

[…] Without Jewish help in administrative and police work—the final rounding up of Jews in Berlin was, as I have mentioned, done entirely by Jewish police—there would have been either complete chaos or an impossibly severe drain on German manpower. […]

To a Jew this role of the Jewish leaders in the destruction of their own people is undoubtedly the darkest chapter of the whole dark story. It had been known about before, but it has now been exposed for the first time in all its pathetic and sordid detail by Raul Hilberg, whose standard work *The Destruction of the European Jews* I mentioned before. In the matter of cooperation, there was no distinction between the highly assimilated

Jewish communities of Central and Western Europe and the Yiddish-speaking masses of the East. In Amsterdam as in Warsaw, in Berlin as in Budapest, Jewish officials could be trusted to compile the lists of persons and of their property, to secure money from the deportees to defray the expenses of their deportation and extermination, to keep track of vacated apartments, to supply police forces to help seize Jews and get them on trains, until, as a last gesture, they handed over the assets of the Jewish community in good order for final confiscation. They distributed the Yellow Star badges, and sometimes, as in Warsaw, "the sale of the armbands became a regular business; there were ordinary armbands of cloth and fancy plastic armbands which were washable." [. . .]

Wherever Jews lived, there were recognized Jewish leaders. And this leadership, almost without exception, cooperated in one way or another, for one reason or another, with the Nazis. The whole truth was that if the Jewish people had really been unorganized and leaderless, there would have been chaos and plenty of misery but the total number of victims would hardly have been between four and a half and six million people. [. . .]

In the eyes of the Jews, thinking exclusively in terms of their own history, the catastrophe that had befallen them under Hitler, in which a third of the people perished, appeared not as the most recent of crimes, the unprecedented crime of genocide, but, on the contrary, as the oldest crime they knew and remembered. This misunderstanding, almost inevitable if we consider not only the facts of Jewish history but also, and more important, the current Jewish historical self-understanding, is actually at the root of all the failures and shortcomings of the Jerusalem trial. None of the participants ever arrived at a clear understanding of the actual horror of Auschwitz, which is of a different nature from all the atrocities of the past, because it appeared to prosecution and judges alike as not much more than the most horrible pogrom in Jewish history. They therefore believed that a direct line existed from the early anti-Semitism of the Nazi Party to the Nuremberg Laws and from there to the expulsion of Jews from the Reich and, finally, to the gas chambers. Politically and legally, however, these were "crimes" different not only in degree, of seriousness but in essence. [. . .]

The trouble with Eichmann was precisely that so many were like him, and that the many were neither perverted nor sadistic, that they were, and still are, terribly and terrifyingly normal. From the viewpoint of our legal institutions and of our moral standards of judgment, this normality was much more terrifying than all the atrocities put together, for it implied—as had been said at Nuremberg over and over again by the defendants and their counsels—that this new type of criminal, who is in actual fact *hostis generis humani*, commits his crimes under circumstances that make it well-nigh impossible for him to know or to feel that he is doing wrong. [. . .]

Foremost among the larger issues at stake in the Eichmann trial was the assumption current in all modern legal systems that intent to do wrong is necessary for the commission of a crime. On nothing, perhaps, has civilized jurisprudence prided itself more than on this taking into account of the subjective factor. Where this intent is absent, where, for whatever reasons, even reasons of moral insanity, the ability to distinguish between right and wrong is impaired, we feel no crime has been committed. We refuse, and consider as barbaric, the propositions "that a great crime offends nature, so that the very earth cries out for vengeance; that evil violates a natural harmony which only retribution can restore; that a wronged collectivity owes a duty to the moral order to punish the criminal" (Yosal Rogat). And yet I think it is undeniable that it was precisely on the ground of these long-forgotten propositions that Eichmann was brought to justice to begin with, and that they were, in fact, the supreme justification for the death penalty. Because he had been implicated and had played a central role in an enterprise whose open purpose was to eliminate forever certain "races" from the surface of the earth, he had to be eliminated. And if it is true that "justice must not only be done but must be seen to be done," then the justice of what was done in Jerusalem would have emerged to be seen by all if the judges had dared to address their defendant in something like the following terms. [. . .]

Betty Friedan

1921–2006

Born Bettye Naomi Goldstein in Peoria, Illinois, Betty Friedan was an influential writer and feminist thinker of the mid-twentieth-century women's rights movement. Although Friedan excelled in her psychology studies at Smith College, she did not pursue a professional career, choosing instead the life of a homemaker. After interviewing women who had graduated from

Smith, she developed her widely read critique of the social expectation that women ought to be content with domestic work. Subsequently, she became a major figure in the burgeoning women's liberation movement, helping to found the National Organization for Women and continuing to organize and advocate for women's political rights for the rest of her life.

The Feminine Mystique
1963

1: The Problem That Has No Name

The problem lay buried, unspoken, for many years in the minds of American women. It was a strange stirring, a sense of dissatisfaction, a yearning that women suffered in the middle of the twentieth century in the United States. Each suburban wife struggled with it alone. As she made the beds, shopped for groceries, matched slipcover material, ate peanut butter sandwiches with her children, chauffeured Cub Scouts and Brownies, lay beside her husband at night—she was afraid to ask even of herself the silent question—"Is this all?"

For over fifteen years there was no word of this yearning in the millions of words written about women, for women, in all the columns, books and articles by experts telling women their role was to seek fulfillment as wives and mothers. Over and over women heard in voices of tradition and of Freudian sophistication that they could desire no greater destiny than to glory in their own femininity. Experts told them how to catch a man and keep him, how to breastfeed children and handle their toilet training, how to cope with sibling rivalry and adolescent rebellion; how to buy a dishwasher, bake bread, cook gourmet snails, and build a swimming pool with their own hands; how to dress, look, and act more feminine and make marriage more exciting; how to keep their husbands from dying young and their sons from growing into delinquents. They were taught to pity the neurotic, unfeminine, unhappy women who wanted to be poets or physicists or presidents. They learned that truly feminine women do not want careers, higher education, political rights—the independence and the opportunities that the old-fashioned feminists fought for. Some women, in their forties and fifties, still remembered painfully giving up those dreams, but most of the younger women no longer even thought about them. A thousand expert voices applauded their femininity, their adjustment, their new maturity. All

they had to do was devote their lives from earliest girlhood to finding a husband and bearing children. [. . .]

And work can now be seen as the key to the problem that has no name. The identity crisis of American women began a century ago, as more and more of the work important to the world, more and more of the work that used their human abilities and through which they were able to find self-realization, was taken from them. [. . .]

[. . .] We now know that the same range of potential ability exists for women as for men. Women, as well as men, can only find their identity in work that uses their full capacities. A woman cannot find her identity through others—her husband, her children. She cannot find it in the dull routine of housework. As thinkers of every age have said, it is only when a human being faces squarely the fact that he can forfeit his own life, that he becomes truly aware of himself, and begins to take his existence seriously. Sometimes this awareness comes only at the moment of death. Sometimes it comes from a more subtle facing of death: the death of self in passive conformity, in meaningless work. The feminine mystique prescribes just such a living death for women. Faced with the slow death of self, the American woman must begin to take her life seriously.

"We measure ourselves by many standards," said the great American psychologist William James, nearly a century ago. "Our strength and our intelligence, our wealth and even our good luck, are things which warm our heart and make us feel ourselves a match for life. But deeper than all such things, and able to suffice unto itself without them, is the sense of the amount of effort which we can put forth."

If women do not put forth, finally, that effort to become all that they have it in them to become, they will forfeit their own humanity. A woman today who has no goal, no purpose, no ambition patterning her days into the future, making her stretch and grow beyond that small score of years in which her body can fill its biological function, is committing a kind of suicide. For that future half a century after the child-bearing years are over is a fact that an American woman cannot deny. Nor can she deny that as a housewife, the world is indeed rushing past her door while she just sits and watches. The terror she feels is real, if she has no place in that world.

The feminine mystique has succeeded in burying millions of American women alive. There is no way for these women to break out of their comfortable concentration camps except by finally putting forth an effort—that human effort which reaches beyond biology, beyond the narrow walls of home, to help shape the future. Only by such a personal commitment to the future can American women break out of the housewife trap and truly find fulfillment as wives and mothers—by fulfilling their own unique possibilities as separate human beings.

Other works by Friedan: *The Second Stage* (1981); *The Fountain of Age* (1993); *Life So Far* (2000).

Joachim Prinz

1902–1988

Born in a small German town in Silesia, Joachim Prinz rose to prominence in the 1920s as the rabbi of a synagogue in Berlin. After 1933, acutely aware of the dangers presented by Nazism, Prinz urged his congregants to leave Germany and did so himself in 1937, immigrating to the United States. By the 1950s, Prinz had become a major force in American Judaism, serving as president of the American Jewish Congress, among other organizations. In light of his experiences in Nazi Germany, Prinz was dedicated to the American civil rights movement, and helped to organize the 1963 March on Washington.

America Must Not Remain Silent
1963

I speak to you as an American Jew.

As Americans we share the profound concern of millions of people about the shame and disgrace of inequality and injustice which make a mockery of the great American idea.

As Jews we bring to this great demonstration, in which thousands of us proudly participate, a twofold experience—one of the spirit and one of our history.

In the realm of the spirit, our fathers taught us thousands of years ago that when God created man, He created him as everybody's neighbor. Neighbor is not a geographic term. It is a moral concept. It means our collective responsibility for the preservation of man's dignity and integrity.

From our Jewish historic experience of three and a half thousand years we say:

Our ancient history began with slavery and the yearning for freedom. During the Middle Ages my people lived for a thousand years in the ghettos of Europe. Our modern history begins with a proclamation of emancipation.

It is for these reasons that it is not merely sympathy and compassion for the black people of America that motivates us. It is above all and beyond all such sympathies and emotions a sense of complete identification and solidarity born of our own painful historic experience.

When I was the rabbi of the Jewish community in Berlin under the Hitler regime, I learned many things. The most important thing that I learned under those tragic circumstances was that bigotry and hatred are not the most urgent problem. The most urgent, the most disgraceful, the most shameful and the most tragic problem is silence.

A great people which had created a great civilization had become a nation of silent onlookers. They remained silent in the face of hate, in the face of brutality and in the face of mass murder.

America must not become a nation of onlookers. America must not remain silent. Not merely black America, but all of America. It must speak up and act, from the President down to the humblest of us, and not for the sake of the Negro, not for the sake of the black community but for the sake of the image, the idea and the aspiration of America itself.

Our children, yours and mine in every school across the land, each morning pledge allegiance to the flag of the United States and to the republic for which it stands. They, the children, speak fervently and innocently of this land as the land of "liberty and justice for all."

The time, I believe, has come to work together—for it is not enough to hope together, and it is not enough to pray together—to work together that this children's oath, pronounced every morning from Maine to California, from North to South, may become a glorious, unshakable reality in a morally renewed and united America.

Other works by Prinz: *Wir Juden* (1934); *The Dilemma of the Modern Jew* (1962); *The Secret Jews* (1973); *Joachim Prinz, Rebellious Rabbi: An Autobiography; The German and Early American Years* (edited by Michael A. Meyer, 2008).

Zalman Schachter-Shalomi

1924–2014

Zalman Schachter-Shalomi was born in Żółkiew, Galicia (present-day Zhovkva, Ukraine), and raised in Vienna. He and his family escaped Europe via Belgium and France, arriving in New York in 1941. During that time, he embraced the Chabad movement and was ordained at its central yeshiva in 1947, afterward becoming an emissary to college campuses along with Shlomo Carlebach. In the 1960s, he broke with Orthodoxy and sought to forge a new synthesis of neo-Hasidism, Eastern religions, and psychoanalysis, becoming a pivotal figure in the Havurah and Jewish Renewal movements.

Toward an "Order of B'nai Or": A Program for a Jewish Liturgical Brotherhood
1964

Nature of the Brotherhood

We are basically dissatisfied with "the world." Our dissatisfaction stems mainly from the fact that as well-adjusted members of it we would have to live as ardent consumers of goods which we do not really need but which in fact inhibit our best possible functioning in terms of *shlemuth ha'avoda*. We have to isolate ourselves from a contaminated environment. Only then can we make sure that the laboratory conditions will be met which will permit us to proceed in our chosen direction.

We believe that the experience of the cosmic and the divine is potentially given to all men and that, depending on one's style of life, one can become a receptacle for the Grace of God. We believe that there is enough psychic and pneumatic know-how available to us within the Jewish framework. To serve God better, we will not even hesitate to borrow extensively from the know-how of others. We feel that the seriousness of the vocation to serve God has largely become lost in the exoteric assertion of the reception of the unique gift of grace which is the revelation possessed by a group. To put it differently, if I am sure that I possess the clear statement of what God demands of men, this possession ought only humble me and challenge me to fulfill the demands of that revelation. Yet some "guardians of the revelation" see themselves as exempt from the humbling challenge to live up to it, as if their chosenness implied that they need not struggle with their own recalcitrant will, slothful habits, etc. For us, the need to establish a liturgical

community actually means that we have become aware of what William Law calls "the serious call to a holy and devout life"—issuing daily in the *bath kol* from Sinai. [. . .]

The Arts as a Creative Expression of Spiritual Discipline

Hasidic masters have already shown the way of what can be done in the field of musical creation. Taking ethnic tunes they found appealing, they transformed them into profound religious paeans of praise. But these creations have largely been of an ecstatic nature. They may not lend themselves to a more "Apollonian" mode of worship. On the other hand, their uncomplicated rhythms are also not quite contemporaneous; even on the ecstatic musical side, the lively syncopation of jazz has for the most part introduced vulgarities to the Jewish scene. The field still awaits its artist. The same holds true even, on another level: the De Rossis patterned themselves after Palestrina; Sulzer, after his friend Schubert; and Lewandowsky, after Brahms. These men were not involved in living Jewish contemplative lives. The imagination contains the only barrier to the kind of musical creativity that awaits us as a result of the activity of *B'nai Or*.

In poetry dilettantism shows up in the predilection for blank verse. One who has teethed on sonnets could perhaps be in the position to use blank verse with skill. To produce second-rate poetry would not be worthwhile. Already some of the most sublime out-pourings of the spirit appear in *piyyutim* as doggerel.

From a Halachic point of view, abstract painting is to be favored. After some of our people will have become adepts, we hope that they will see fit to arrest and project that which happens in their interior, contemplative eidetic field through their skills in painting. The *Zohar* and the entire Kabbalah with their visual (as differing from the Talmudic aural) emphasis offer countless themes for the artist who prefers abstract forms.

Nowadays, there are far more and more pliable media available than ever before. It will be our task to utilize them. Much philosophy and science has been redeemed and made serviceable to God in our faith. The "muses" are still awaiting redemption. [. . .]

Women in the Liturgical Community

The masculine liturgy is not designed to raise women to spiritual heights. They are bereft of the sacramentals which men experience in such mitzvoth as *tallith* and *t'fillin*, and they have, therefore, been liturgically dependent on the men's synagogue.

The solution for the problem of women lies in a full separation of their entire spiritual work from that of men. Halachically, our women are largely free to experiment with the liturgy and to fit it to their own physiological curves. Chances are that women with different monthly cycles could not act in concert with a *minyan*. Thus, they will largely have to chart their calendars and do their interior spiritual work according to it. In the absence of masculine sacramentals, they would have to invent for their own *minhag* such sacramentals as would be prompted by the stimulus of tradition and reinforced by their own personal insight, aesthetic feelings, and experiences. (We do not refer to such functions as remain *en famille*, but to such functions as are performed at public worship.)

While, in the beginning, women might have to be under the direction of a male spiritual director, it is hoped that very soon spiritual direction of women for women may be achieved.

We expect a larger turnover in the women's novitiate for such who, after a period of initiation into the spiritual life, would wish to return to the world. Furthermore, we do not expect to accept as permanent members women of marriageable age, and those female adepts who are single would remain as postulant novices of a higher degree than recent arrivals, until they marry and remain in the community when they would be accepted as permanent members. Chances are that fate and exigencies will demand a special classification of non-participant dwellers in the community. Thus, for instance, the spouse of a member who happens not to be inclined towards this work will have to be integrated on the sidelines of our community.

Other works by Schachter-Shalomi: *The Dream Assembly: Tales of Rabbi Zalman Schachter-Shalomi Collected and Retold by Howard Schwartz* (1989); *Paradigm Shift* (1993); *Davening: A Guide to Meaningful Jewish Prayer* (2012).

Judah Goldin

1914–1998

Born in New York to immigrant parents, Judah Goldin was among the first American Jewish academics to have been trained in the United States, and he became a leader in midrashic scholarship. Goldin studied social science and English literature before turning to the Midrash, and his later work reflects the diversity of his academic training. He taught at a variety of colleges and universities, including Duke University, the University of Pennsylvania, the University of Iowa, the Jewish Theological Seminary, and Yale University.

Of Change and Adaptation in Judaism 1965

Midrash [. . .] is not mere reference to the past: it is the enlistment of the past in the service of the present. Even more specifically, it is a reinsertion into the present of the original divine Word, "memory / making past present," but a supernatural Word that is not simply the primitive hierogram: that Word is given definition and repeated application by men. Without man, without the scholar, there can be no Midrash. Theoretically, he is not free to invent meanings or implications independently of the Word. Therefore, from the first the divine Word consists of layers upon layers of intentions and instructions. And when the sage offers his interpretation he is making one more disclosure, he is laying bare one more implication, he is exposing to view still another radiance hitherto covered up. Since the Word is the word of the Living God, it never ceases to make contact with the human world. The Word does not change, but it fulfills itself through disclosures and interpretations of the scholars. And if the world changes, the Word has been prepared for all contingencies from the outset. The permanent and the fluid, if I may say so, are not two opposed features, or even sharply distinguished from each other. The Word is continuously directed to the world and the world is shaped by the Word through the instrumentality of the Sages.

Such exegesis clearly demonstrates that the original meaning and intention of a number of early teachings were indeed forgotten. Midrash, which gave the old statements "new" meaning and "new" direction—in other words, applicability in terms of the requirements or emphases of the later periods—could accomplish this because of what we may call "anachronism," the assumption by a later generation that ideas uppermost in its mind are necessarily the ideas uppermost in the mind of the earlier generation. Anachronism, naturally, is always at work in every society. But what makes it so congenial to and operative in classical Judaism is the combination we have been hinting at and now state explicitly—and this is what I meant when I said that, fortunately, a good deal was forgotten: on the one hand, great painstaking at conserving what has been handed down by the past, but on the other, firm conviction that the once-upon-a-time revealed Word and the subsequent words which are its outgrowth continue with unceasing life and liveliness to release successive truths which are not novel, but only newly recognizable, permanent elements of the original content. Not "new written," as Thomas Fuller might have said, but newly scoured. Conserving saves the tradition from transiency; Midrash saves it from arteriosclerosis. And both conserving and commentary must be simultaneously at work; either without the other is empty of meaningfulness.

Other works by Goldin: *The Living Talmud: The Wisdom of the Fathers and Its Classical Commentaries* (1952); *The Song at the Sea: Being a Commentary on a Commentary in Two Parts* (1971).

Joseph B. Soloveitchik

The Lonely Man of Faith
1965

It is not the plan of this essay to discuss the millennium-old problem of faith and reason. I want instead to focus attention on a human-life situation in which the man of faith as an individual concrete being, with his cares and hopes, concerns and needs, joys and sad moments, is entangled. Therefore, whatever I am going to say here has been derived not from philosophical dialectics, abstract speculation, or detached impersonal reflections, but from actual situations and experiences with which I have been confronted. . . . Instead of talking theology, in the didactic sense, eloquently and in balanced sentences, I would like, hesitatingly and haltingly, to confide in you and to share with you some concerns which weigh heavily on my mind and which frequently assume the proportions of an awareness of crisis.

I have no problem-solving thoughts. I do not intend to suggest a new method of remedying the human situation which I am about to describe; neither do I believe that it can be remedied at all. . . . All I want is to follow the advice given by Elihu, the son of Berachel of old, who said, "I will speak that I may find relief"; for there is a redemptive quality for an agitated mind in the spo-

ken word, and a tormented soul finds peace in confession. [. . .]

The nature of the dilemma can be stated in a three-word sentence. I am lonely . . . I am lonely because at times I feel rejected and thrust away by everybody, not excluding my most intimate friends. [. . .]

I am lonely because, in my humble, inadequate way, I am a man of faith for whom to be means to believe. . . . Apparently, in this role, as a man of faith, I must experience a sense of loneliness which is of a compound nature. It is a blend of that which is inseparably interwoven into the very texture of the faith gesture, characterizing the unfluctuating metaphysical destiny of the man of faith, and of that which is extraneous to the act of believing and stems from the ever-changing human-historical situation with all its whimsicality. On the one hand, the man of faith has been a solitary figure throughout the ages, indeed millennia, and no one has succeeded in escaping this unalterable destiny which is an "objective" awareness rather than a subjective feeling. On the other hand, it is undeniably true that this basic awareness expresses itself in a variety of ways, utilizing the whole gamut of one's affective emotional life which is extremely responsive to outward challenges and moves along with the tide of cultural and historical change. [. . .]

I am mainly interested in contemporary man of faith which is, due to his peculiar position in our secular society, lonely in a special way. No matter how time-honored and time-hallowed the interpenetration of faith and loneliness is, and it certainly goes back to the dawn of Judaic covenant, contemporary man of faith lives through a particularly difficult and agonizing crisis. . . . He looks upon himself as a stranger in modern society, which is technically minded, self-centered, and self-loving, almost in a sickly narcissistic fashion, scoring honor upon honor, piling up victory upon victory, reaching for the distant galaxies, and seeing in the here-and-now sensible world the only manifestation of being. What can a man of faith like myself, living by a doctrine which has no technical potential, by a law which cannot be tested in the laboratory, steadfast in his loyalty to an eschatological vision whose fulfillment cannot be predicted with any degree of probability, let alone certainty, even by the most complex, advanced mathematical calculations—what can such a man say to a functional, utilitarian society which is *saeculum*-oriented and whose practical reasons of the mind have long ago supplanted the sensitive reasons of the heart?

Gerson D. Cohen

1924–1991

Born in New York, Gerson Cohen was a rabbi, professor of history, and the chancellor of the Jewish Theological Seminary. After receiving his ordination and a doctorate in history, Cohen became Gustav Gottheil Lecturer in Semitic languages and the director of the Center for Israel and Jewish Studies at Columbia University. Under his leadership at the Jewish Theological Seminary, the Conservative movement ordained its first woman rabbi.

The Blessing of Assimilation in Jewish History
1966

I trust that none of my remarks will be understood to say that assimilation is not now, or has not always been, a great threat to the Jewish group. In a sense, the problem of assimilation is as old as Hebrew literature. And with good reason. There have always been opportunists and despondent people who have preferred to identify totally with the majority and have slipped away from the Jewish community. This is a fact of life, and there is nothing we can do to prevent this slippage any more than our ancestors could do in the days of the Crusades, or the persecutions of the Pastoureaux, or the expulsion from Spain. The threat of assimilation and its problems have always been with us and will continue to be until the vision of Isaiah becomes a reality.

Nevertheless, in conceding the problem and the need for coping with it, I plead that we not lose sight of two obvious factors. First, that we Jews have always been, and will doubtless continue to be, a minority group; and second, that a minority that does not wish to ghettoize itself or that does not wish to become fossilized, will inevitably have to acculturate itself—to assimilate—at least to some extent. If it wants to do business with the people among whom it lives, it will have to learn their language and, to some degree, reorient its style of life, and given the basically limited mental energy that the majority of people have, the need to learn a new language and to adopt a new style of life will cause the older to be forgotten in some significant measure. So it has always been, and so it will continue to be. Furthermore, a change of form will inevitably cause a certain metamorphosis in content; but even these changes in content should not necessarily alarm us. Throughout Jewish history, there have been great changes in law, in thought, and in basic categories of expression, reflecting the need of the Jews to adapt themselves and their way of life to new conditions. This assimilation, or adaptation, was not the consequence of a desire to make things easier, but the result of a need to continue to make the tradition relevant.

Once again, permit me to cite some examples. If rabbinic Judaism was able to win so many thousands of souls to its ethical monotheism, it was precisely because rabbinic Judaism was able to reinterpret the Bible and to reformulate it in Hellenistic terms. Every student of rabbinism knows [. . .] that the Hebrew language underwent a major metamorphosis under the impact of the Greek language and Greek culture. Instead of protesting against this natural growth, the Rabbis appropriated it and made use of it in order to express themselves in terms that were relevant to the Hellenistic world in which they lived.

At the time of the great challenge of assimilation in the geonic period, the leaders of the Babylonian community did the same thing. Saadia Gaon, who translated the Bible into Arabic, tells us that it was because he found as many as fourteen kinds of deviant Jewish beliefs within the city of Baghdad that he decided to compose his great book *Emunot vede'ot* (Beliefs and opinions). Furthermore, not only did he choose, realistically, to write his book in Arabic and not in Hebrew, but far more important, in defending the traditions of Judaism he appealed to reason and philosophy no less than to authority and precedent. By appropriating the intellectual tools of the surrounding Arabic world, he helped to accelerate the process of the adaptation of rabbinic Judaism to the canons and tastes of intellectual Arabic society. As a responsible teacher, he addressed his own generation and spoke to them in a language that would be intelligible and relevant to them. So did Moses Maimonides and his son, Abraham. Abraham Maimuni, indeed, in an effort to make the synagogue a more effective instrument for piety, unabashedly changed a number of practices within the synagogue to conform to patently Arabic tastes.

We could go on with such examples endlessly, for if there is anything that modern scholarship has taught us about Jewish culture, it is that a familiarity with the general milieu in which Jews lived is indispensable to understanding any particular phase of its history. How can we understand the "Golden Age" of Spain, or the theological and moralistic emphases of Franco-German pietism, or the mystical doctrines and associations of the Hasidim of medieval Egypt, without some acquaintance with Arabic literary tastes, Christian theology, and Sufism, respectively? And what is the appropriation of many of these tendencies if not religious and intellectual assimilation?

Even though many of these innovations evoked strong protests from conservative contemporaries—and more than one great writer of medieval times began his work with an apology for his ostensible break with tradition—the fact remains that subsequent generations have acknowledged that these thinkers and writers made essential contributions to their age and served as sources of renewed vitality for Jewish life. My primary point, however, is that these contributions could not have come about were it not for the sensitivity of these great writers and teachers to the challenges of the regnant culture and their readiness to give voice to the tradition in the language of their own time and place.

The great and, to a considerable extent, salutary transformations that overtook the Jews during the nineteenth and twentieth centuries have likewise been in large measure the products of assimilation: the rebirth of Hebrew, the growth of *Jüdische Wissenschaft*, the liberalization of the Jewish religion, the acceptance of Yiddish as a respectable vehicle of Jewish literary expression, the growth of Jewish nationalism, and the State of Israel itself. All the great changes and developments that characterize modern Jewish history and that have made the lives of countless Jews infinitely richer and more pleasant than they had ever been previously are the effects of assimilation. This very institution, in which the Jewish tradition is taught critically and dispassionately, provides one of the many examples of the blessings that assimilation can bring to a community such as ours.

There are, of course, two ways of meeting the problem of assimilation. The first is withdrawal and fossilization, on which we need not dwell here. There is, however—and, as we have seen, there has always been—an alternative approach, one that sought to transform the inevitable inroads of assimilation into new sources of vitality. In seeking to distinguish this type of assimilation and imitation from the kind that aims at obliterating Jewish identity, Aḥad Ha'am characterized it as *hikkuy shel hitharut* ("competitive imitation") as opposed to *hitbolelut* ("assimilation"). In competitive imitation, Aḥad Ha'am detected signs of health and vigor, rather than of attrition and decadence. There can be little doubt that Aḥad Ha'am's reading of the past was highly perspicacious. Who will deny that much of Jewish phi-

losophy and belles-lettres were virtually conscious efforts at imitation of and competition with the cultures among which Jewish writers and thinkers lived?

However, even if this reading of earlier forms of healthy assimilation is correct, in the present context of freedom and equality, and above all, in the context of the increasing tolerance that Jews of the Western world enjoy, the motivation for competition has lost much of its drive. Indeed, in a world in which well-intentioned people are bent on reducing tensions and differences, cultural competition has an almost sinister ring. I would, therefore, speak instead of the healthy appropriation of new forms and ideas for the sake of growth and enrichment.

Assimilation properly channeled and exploited *can* become a blessing. The great ages of Jewish creativity were born out of a response to the challenge of assimilation, and there is no reason why our age should not respond to this challenge with equal vigor. Assimilation is not a one-way street: very much like the Torah itself, it is capable of paralyzing or of energizing, depending upon how we react to it.

Other works by Cohen: *A Critical Edition with a Translation and Notes of the Book of Tradition (Sefer ha-Qabbalah) by Abraham ibn Daud* (1967).

Moshe Greenberg

1928–2010

Moshe Greenberg, born in a Hebrew-speaking home in Philadelphia, was, like his father Simon Greenberg, ordained as a Conservative rabbi. Greenberg became a leading American Jewish biblical scholar and was among the first non-Christian scholars to teach the Bible at a secular university. Greenberg received his doctorate from the University of Pennsylvania in 1954, subsequently teaching there for nearly two decades. His historical-critical approach drew on his rich knowledge of ancient languages. In 1970, Greenberg immigrated to Israel, where he taught at the Hebrew University of Jerusalem until 1996.

The Biblical Grounding of Human Value
1966

Out of a world in which man was viewed fundamentally as an instrument, one among other means of attaining desired ends—be they economic or political—emerged a view so totally different as to amount to a revolution in the way human beings regarded one another. [. . .]

Let us begin [. . .] by looking at biblical laws regarding homicide. At first blush, the matter does not look promising. The biblical law of homicide is severe without parallel. Murder is punishable by death. If homicide is committed by a beast—a goring ox is mentioned—the beast must be stoned and its flesh may not be eaten. If it was known to be vicious and its owner, though warned, was criminally negligent in failing to keep it in, the owner is subject to death as well as the ox, though here the law allows the owner to ransom himself with a sum fixed by the slain person's family. However, this is the sole degree of culpability in which the law allows a ransom. A later law states: "You shall not take a ransom for the life of a murderer who is guilty of death, but he shall surely be put to death." A ransom may be accepted only for a homicide not committed personally and with intent to harm—the one case of the owner of the vicious ox. For murder there is only the death penalty. The unexampled severity of the biblical law of homicide, the demand of life for life has been considered primitive, a desert principle. Likewise the punishment of death laid on the goring ox is regarded as primitive—as though the animal were a person!

The theory that underlies this judgment of the biblical law is that punishments underwent a development in which acceptance of a monetary settlement is the next and higher stage after strict retaliation. Not only is this theory incapable of being demonstrated, but the actual development of the biblical law of homicide shows rather that it followed an altogether different principle from that governing Near Eastern law. Not a difference in stages of development but a difference in underlying principle accounts for the divergence in the laws.

What is the jural postulate underlying the biblical view of homicide? Fortunately we possess a precise and adequate formulation of it in Genesis 9:5: "For your life-blood I shall require a reckoning; of every beast shall I require it . . . Whoever sheds the blood of a man by man shall his blood be shed, for in the image of God was man created." One thing is certain about the phrase "in the image of God was man created," a phrase as unclear as it is famous: it expresses the peculiar and supreme worth of man. Of all creatures, Genesis 1 relates, he alone possesses this attribute, bringing him into closer relation to God than all the rest and conferring upon him highest value. The first practical consequence of

this supremacy is that man may rule the beasts and may eat them. In the value hierarchy of the world he is declared superior to them: he may kill them (for food or sacrifice only) but they may not kill him. A beast that kills a man destroys the image of God and must give a reckoning for it. This is the law of the goring ox: it must be stoned to death. Not primitivism, but a religious evaluation of the value of man is inherent in this law: that it is a religious evaluation, not an archaic personification of a beast that is involved, comes out clearly from the prohibition of eating the flesh of the stoned ox. The beast is laden with guilt and is therefore an object of horror.

Now this view of the uniqueness and supreme value of human life has yet another consequence: it places life beyond the reach of other values. The idea that life may be measured in terms of money or other property, and even more the idea that persons may be valued as equivalences of other persons is excluded. Compensation of any kind for bloodshed is ruled out. The guilt of the murderer is infinite because the murdered life is invaluable. The kinsmen of the slain are not competent to say when he has been paid for. An absolute wrong has been committed, an offense to God in whose image man is made—an offense not subject to human mitigation. The effect of this view is, to be sure, paradoxical: because human life is invaluable, to take it entails the death penalty. Yet the paradox must not blind us to the value judgment the law sought to embody. [. . .]

The full expression of the jural postulate of the biblical law of homicide was reached only later, in rabbinic law. We have already mentioned the paradox into which biblical law was led by its insistence on the incommutability of the punishment of the homicide: just because the slain man's life was invaluable and so cannot be paid for with money, the slayer must die.

In rabbinic law, the idea of the invaluableness of life led to the virtual abolition of the death penalty. But what distinguishes this virtual abolition is that it is not accompanied by the institution of any sort of pecuniary compensation. The conditions that had to be met before the death penalty could be inflicted were made so onerous, that is to say, the concern for the life of the accused became so intense that in effect it was impossible to inflict capital punishment. Nowhere in the account of this process, however, is there a hint that it was ever contemplated to substitute pecuniary for capital punishment. The same reverence for human life that led to the virtual abolition of the death penalty also forbade setting a value on the life of the slain man.

What is the source of this reverence for human life? Again we turn to the creation story of the people to understand its values. Once again we read of an ordering of the chaos, at the end of which man is created: "On the sixth day, after all had been prepared for his creation, God said: Let us make man in our image, after our likeness; and let him have dominion over the fish of the sea, over the birds of heaven, over the cattle, over all the earth, and over all the creeping things that creep upon the earth. So God created man in His image, in the image of God He created him; male and female He created them. And God blessed them and said to them: Be fruitful and multiply, fill the earth and master it, and have dominion over the fish of the sea, the birds of heaven, and all the living things that creep upon the earth."

Not a word here about man's usefulness to God—because this God has no needs that man must serve. Man is not an instrument, not a means, but the end itself of all creation. The earth, sky, and their hosts, have been brought into being only on his behalf. His task is to govern the world, to rule its denizens, to conquer it, as the steward of God. The Paradise story phrases it more picturesquely: "The Lord God planted a garden in Eden . . . and the Lord God took man and set him in the Garden of Eden to work it and tend it." That is the primary condition of man: He is the keeper of God's garden; the world into which he came was a Garden of Eden. Man is the darling creature of God, to serve whom all else has been created. Therefore there can be nothing in this world that ranks higher than he in value, nothing to which man's value can be subordinated. This is the bedrock of the biblical evaluation of man: He is no tool, no instrument, no means; but the end of all, the purpose of all, the measure of all under the sun.

Other works by Greenberg: *The Ḥab/piru* (1955); *Understanding Exodus* (1967); *Biblical Prose Prayer as a Window to the Popular Religion of Ancient Israel* (1983).

Richard L. Rubenstein
b. 1924

Although his parents were secular, Richard L. Rubenstein was ordained as a Conservative rabbi in 1952 at the Jewish Theological Seminary and received his doctorate from Harvard Divinity School in 1960. He

later became a vital force in post-Holocaust theology. In 1963, Rubenstein was one of nineteen rabbis to visit Birmingham, Alabama, in support of the American civil rights movement. In the following decades, Rubenstein served as a chaplain and a professor at several universities, including Harvard and Florida State University. He was president of the University of Bridgeport between 1995 and 1999.

Symposium on Jewish Belief
1966

I am convinced that the problems implicit in "death of God" theology concern Judaism as much as Christianity. Technically death-of-God theology reflects the Christian tradition of the passion of the Christ. As such, the terminology of the movement creates some very obvious problems for Jewish theologians. Nevertheless, I have, almost against my will, come to the conclusion that the terminology is unavoidable. The death-of-God theologians have brought into the open a conviction which has led a very potent underground existence for decades. Death-of-God theology is no fad. It is a contemporary expression of issues which have, in one way or another, appeared in embryo in scholastic philosophy, medieval mysticism, nineteenth-century German philosophy, and in the religious existentialism of Martin Buber and Paul Tillich.

No man can really say that God is dead. How can we know that? Nevertheless, I am compelled to say that we live in the time of the "death of God." This is more a statement about man and his culture than about God. The death of God is a cultural fact. Buber felt this. He spoke of the eclipse of God. I can understand his reluctance to use the more explicitly Christian terminology. I am compelled to utilize it because of my conviction that the time which Nietzsche's madman said was too far off has come upon us. There is no way around Nietzsche. Had I lived in another time or another culture, I might have found some other vocabulary to express my meanings. I am, however, a religious existentialist after Nietzsche and after Auschwitz. When I say we live in the time of the death of God, I mean that the thread uniting God and man, heaven and earth, has been broken. We stand in a cold, silent, unfeeling cosmos, unaided by any purposeful power beyond our own resources. After Auschwitz, what else can a Jew say about God?

When Professor William Hamilton associated my theological writings with the death-of-God movement in his article on radical theology in *The Christian*

Scholar [Spring 1965], I was somewhat dubious about his designation. After reflection, I concluded that Professor Hamilton was correct. There is a definite style in religious thought which can be designated death-of-God theology. I have struggled to escape the term. I have been embarrassed by it. I realize its inadequacy and its Christian origin. I have, nevertheless, concluded that it is inescapable. I see no other way of expressing the void which confronts man where once God stood.

I am acutely aware of the fact that Christian death-of-God theologians remain fully committed Christians as I remain a committed Jew. As Professor Hamilton has suggested, Christian death-of-God theologians have no God, but they do have a Messiah. Christian death-of-God theology remains Christocentric. I affirm the final authority of Torah and reject the Christian Messiah, as Jews have for two thousand years. Professor Thomas J. J. Altizer welcomes the death of God. He sees it as an apocalyptic event in which the freedom of the Gospels is finally realized and the true Christian is liberated from every restraint of the Law. I do not see that awful event as a cosmic liberation. I am saddened by it. I believe that in a world devoid of God we need Torah, tradition, and the religious community far more than in a world where God's presence was meaningfully experienced. The death of God leads Altizer to a sense of apocalyptic liberation; it leads me to a sad determination to enhance the religious norms and the community without which the slender fabric of human decency might well disappear. In the time of the death of God, Christian theologians still proclaim the Gospel of the Christ; Jewish theologians proclaim the indispensability of Torah.

I believe the greatest single challenge to modern Judaism arises out of the question of God and the death camps. I am amazed at the silence of contemporary Jewish theologians on this most crucial and agonizing of all Jewish issues. How can Jews believe in an omnipotent, beneficent God after Auschwitz? Traditional Jewish theology maintains that God is the ultimate, omnipotent actor in the historical drama. It has interpreted every major catastrophe in Jewish history as God's punishment of a sinful Israel. I fail to see how this position can be maintained without regarding Hitler and the SS as instruments of God's will. The agony of European Jewry cannot be likened to the testing of Job. To see any purpose in the death camps, the traditional believer is forced to regard the most demonic, antihuman explosion in all history as a meaningful expression of God's

purposes. The idea is simply too obscene for me to accept. I do not think that the full impact of Auschwitz has yet been felt in Jewish theology or Jewish life. Great religious revolutions have their own period of gestation. No man knows the hour when the full impact of Auschwitz will be felt, but no religious community can endure so hideous a wounding without undergoing vast inner disorders.

Though I believe that a void stands where once we experienced God's presence, I do not think Judaism has lost its meaning or its power. I do not believe that a theistic God is necessary for Jewish religious life. Dietrich Bonhoeffer has written that our problem is how to speak of God in an age of no religion. I believe that our problem is how to speak of religion in an age of no God. I have suggested that Judaism is the way in which we share the decisive times and crises of life through the traditions of our inherited community. The need for that sharing is not diminished in the time of the death of God. We no longer believe in the God who has the power to annul the tragic necessities of existence: the need religiously to share that existence remains.

Finally, the time of the death of God does not mean the end of all gods. It means the demise of the God who was the ultimate actor in history. I believe in God, the Holy Nothingness known to mystics of all ages, out of which we have come and to which we shall ultimately return. I concur with atheistic existentialists such as Sartre and Camus in much of their analysis of the broken condition of human finitude. We must endure that condition without illusion or hope. I do not part company with them on their analysis of the human predicament. I part company on the issue of the necessity of religion as the way in which we share that predicament. Their analysis of human hopelessness leads me to look to the religious community as the institution in which that condition can be shared in depth. The limitations of finitude can be overcome only when we return to the Nothingness out of which we have been thrust. In the final analysis, omnipotent Nothingness is Lord of all creation.

Other works by Rubenstein: *After Auschwitz: Radical Theology and Contemporary Judaism* (1966); *The Religious Imagination: A Study in Psychoanalysis and Jewish Theology* (1968); *My Brother Paul* (1972).

Nahum M. Sarna

1923–2005

Born in London, Nahum M. Sarna settled in the United States in 1951 and later served as professor of biblical studies at Brandeis University. A translator, teacher, editor, and leading scholar of biblical and rabbinic texts, he was also the author of popular and scholarly manuscripts and articles.

Understanding Genesis
1966

The New Creation

The connection between Creation and the Flood is a very real one in biblical theology, especially in the biblical interpretation of human history. Reference has already been made to the fact that in both Mesopotamian and Hebrew traditions, the Flood episode constitutes an epochal juncture in the history of the world. But this is the only important similarity. Beyond this, the story of Noah is developed in the Bible to a degree and in a way that has no parallel in Mesopotamian sources.

In the Bible, Noah's birth is represented in the genealogical lists as the first after Adam's death. This reinforces the notion of Noah as the second father of mankind and emphasizes the idea of the immediate post-diluvial period as a new beginning to life on earth. The covenant between man and God symbolizes, furthermore, a new relationship between the Deity and His world. Noah's ark is thus the matrix of a new creation. That is why only his immediate family is taken aboard, and why there are no other human passengers, no other relatives, no friends, no ship-builders as in the Mesopotamian accounts.

Moreover, Noah received the same divine blessing as Adam, "be fertile and increase" (1:28; 9:1). Just as genealogical lists follow the Creation story, so the "Table of Nations" expressing fulfillment of the blessing, comes after the Flood story. The lineage of all nations is traced back to a common ancestor, Noah.

This schematization of human relationships, artificial though it be, is an unparalleled notion in the world picture of any people in ancient times. Its comprehensiveness and universality prefigure the idea of the brotherhood of man.

The foregoing study of the biblical Deluge story leaves no room for doubting the direct connection between it and the Mesopotamian tradition. Yet a closer look at the two and a careful understanding of the purposes of the Bible leave us with quite a different impression. The Hebrew version is an expression of the biblical polemic against paganism. This assault is carried on, not on the level of dialectics, but indirectly. and inferentially. Through an inspired process of selection, revision and addition, whether deliberate or intuitive, the original material has been so thoroughly reshaped as to become an entirely new and original creation purged of its polytheistic dross. What in the Mesopotamian tradition was apparently of local importance became in the Bible a major event of cosmic significance. What there is largely casual and contingent has become here causal and determinative. Like the Creation narrative, that of Noah and the Flood has been made into a vehicle for the expression of some of the most profound biblical teachings, an instrument for the communication of universal moral truths, the medium through which God makes known what He demands of man.

Other works by Sarna: *A Syllabus of Biblical History* (1953); *The Teaching of the Bible* (1965).

Elie Wiesel

The Jews of Silence: A Personal Report on Soviet Jewry
1966

In your first confrontation with the Jews of Russia you are forced to abandon whatever intellectual baggage you may have brought with you. Logic, you suddenly realize, will not help you here. You have your logic, they have theirs, and the distance between the two cannot be bridged by words. The more you see of them the surer you become that everything you have thought or known till now is worthless; here you must begin anew. This strange new world has customs and laws totally unfamiliar to you; language operates on a level you cannot hope to comprehend. You understand nothing they tell you, and when they explain, you believe nothing. You feel as though you have been propelled into a realm of the absurd; when you try to describe it, your description has the air of a harrowing scene from a Kafkaesque novel or nightmare.

But the nightmare is not yours. It's theirs. [. . .]

On the one hand, the Russian authorities do everything in their power to prevent Jews from conducting their internal affairs within a recognizable organizational framework, with its own self-esteem, its own culture and folklore, its own scale of values. But on the other hand, they do not make it possible for Jews to acculturate to non-Jewish society, a society that is prepared to accept Ukrainians, Uzbeks, and Tartars . . . but not Jews. The impression has been created that Jews are destined to be alien forever.

The Jewish reaction is natural. Since others try to prevent them from living either as Jews or as non-Jews, they decide, despite and even because of the difficulties involved, to preserve their Jewishness. This is the only way I can explain the mass gatherings of Jews in and around the synagogue on Jewish holidays. Most of them come not to pray, not out of a belief in the God of Israel or in His Torah, but out of a desire to identify with the Jewish people—about whom they know next to *nothing*. [. . .]

None of this was news to me. In recent years I had heard and read a great deal about the situation of the Jews in the Soviet Union, and I knew that it was bad. I knew that Jews were in a worse position than others, that despite the progress of de-Stalinization they still enjoyed less freedom than other groups within the population. This is not what I meant when I said the situation was more grievous than I had imagined. I was referring to the Jewish fear that lurks in every pair of eyes, that makes itself felt in every conversation. It is a fear that has penetrated the cells of their bodies; it clings to them like a hateful second skin, black and solid as the night, but not so beautiful. It is the thing that cut me more deeply than anything else in my encounter with the Jews of Russia. And I still do not know whether it is justified or not. Possibly it has remained with them from the days of Stalin, but if so, many of the horrors of that period have yet to be uncovered. The general populace feels practically nothing of this fear; apparently everyone but the Jews has managed to forget those days. The Jews alone remain bound in terror, and who can predict when, or if, they will ever be released? [. . .]

Before I left for the Soviet Union I determined that the purpose of my trip was to discover if the Jews of Russia really wanted to be Jews. I never imagined that the answer would be so absolute and clear. I could never have foreseen that I would stand in a synagogue surrounded by men of all ages, not only the old; that I would be present at a public gathering of thirty thousand youngsters on the night of Simchat Torah and that

they would be singing in Hebrew and Yiddish. Who would have thought that teenagers would be dancing the *hora* on a Moscow street, shouting "David, King of Israel, lives and endures"? Who could have dreamed that some of them—perhaps many of them—would be studying the Hebrew language, would be passing slips of paper back and forth covered with Hebrew words? [. . .]

That is what I wanted to see, and that is what I saw. It is good for us to know; it is essential that we know, both for them and for ourselves. No matter how often it is repeated, the official claim that, apart from a few old men, the majority of Russian Jews wish to forget their Jewish identity is simply untrue. [. . .]

One may question whether we have any way of knowing that the Jews of Russia really want us to do anything for them. How do we know that our shouts and protests will not bring them harm? These are very serious questions, and I put them to the Russian Jews themselves. Their answer was always the same: "Cry out, cry out until you have no more strength to cry. You must enlist public opinion, you must turn to those with influence, you must involve your governments—the hour is late." [. . .]

I believe with all my soul that despite the suffering, despite the hardship and the fear, the Jews of Russia will withstand the pressure and emerge victorious. But whether or not we shall ever be worthy of their trust, whether or not we shall overcome the pressures we have ourselves created, I cannot say. I returned from the Soviet Union disheartened and depressed. But what torments me most is not the Jews of silence I met in Russia, but the silence of the Jews I live among today.

Translated by Neal Kozodoy.

Shalom Spiegel

1899–1984

The scholar of ancient and medieval Hebrew literature Shalom Spiegel was born in Romania and received his higher education in Vienna. He taught in Palestine from 1923 to 1929 and then settled in New York City. He taught initially at Stephen Wise's Jewish Institute of Religion and then, until his death, at the Jewish Theological Seminary. He published work on both biblical and medieval Hebrew literature. His much-praised *The Last Trial* (1950) is a study of the reworking of the story of the sacrifice of Isaac in medieval Hebrew texts.

Amos vs. Amaziah
1967

Semantics of Justice

What made *Amos vs. Amaziah* weigh so heavily in the annals of history? I can only attempt a hint or an inkling of an answer.

I do so best by returning to the vision of Amos, as he saw the Lord standing beside a wall with a plumbline in His hand. It is a homely lesson any mason could understand and impart: a wall to stand and to endure must be straight and strong, without fault of construction. If it be out of plumb, the taller the wall, the surer its fall. The imagery seems to suggest that what the law of gravitation is to nature, justice is to society. Or in the language of Isaiah (30:13–14) who embellished the thought of Amos: iniquity in a commonwealth is like a crack in a high wall; barely visible, it can bring the entire structure tumbling down, the crash coming suddenly, in an instant, like that of a potter's vessel smashed so ruthlessly not one sherd is left with which to scoop up fire from a hearth or to dip water out of a cistern.

Such images and ideas were prompted no doubt by the very meaning of the Hebrew words for "just" and "righteous," and by their synonyms: "straight" (*yashar*), "steady" *(ken)*, "firm" (*nakhon*), "sound" (*tam*) or "whole" (*shalem*). "He leadeth me in paths of righteousness" (Psalms 23:3) actually means "in a straight path." "Perfect and just weight you shall have" (Deuteronomy 25:15) refers to whole and intact weight. Even the Hebrew root for "faith" or "truth" can be used of a house: "I shall build you a faithful (or a true) house" (1 Kings 11:38), that is to say, a sure and firm house, able to last. Of the aging Moses who kept his arms in uplifted position until the sun set, it is said in the Hebrew Bible: His hands were "faith," or "truth"; that is, his hands were steady. A sanctuary is "justified" (Daniel 8:14), when it is rebuilt or restored. Righteous and strong can be synonyms in Hebrew (Isaiah 49:24). Therefore when prophet and psalmist stress God's "righteousness and strength" (Isaiah 45:24, see Psalms 71:16–19), they really want to say that His is infinite strength. The examples could be easily multiplied, but enough is indicated to show the underlying notion that *justice is strength,* by which a social structure is able to maintain itself. It is as if the very roots of the Hebrew words would whisper that what soundness is to construction, or health to the body, justice is to society.

These are edifying thoughts worthy of the holy tongue, the language of the Holy Writ. But they are nothing new, they are inherent in Hebrew, inherited and hardened as it were by household habits of the vernacular long before Amos met Amaziah. Amos and Amaziah shared alike the living legacy of the language in which both were bred, and imbibed such figures and metaphors from infancy. These are common speech patterns, natural and native to Hebrew, deriving their persuasiveness from the semantic subsoil of the root words themselves. But is not that precisely their limitation? Their very involvement with the Hebrew language would make them parochial. [. . .]

The Conclusions of Amos vs. Amaziah

Amos found the divine signature in all men in their *sense of justice.* All men have an innate desire for the right, an inborn fear of arbitrary force, an instinctive response to wrong: It is not right! However failing or blundering, legal systems everywhere are but the attempt to articulate this desire for justice and to incarnate it in institutions capable of lifting from the brow of man the fright and curse of brutal force.

Now Amos was not a mandarin, intent upon "rectification of names," nor a professor, immersed in the varieties of anthropology or comparative law. Amos was a seer who beheld God the Lord setting a plumbline to the walls of Israel, and that vision gave him a measure for things human and divine.

Justice has always appeared binding upon men. Therein Amaziah did not differ from Amos. Only, to Amaziah, justice was an obligation like other obligations, a commandment among many commandments of the law. Injustice was improper, of course, but neither more nor less offensive than any other infringement of the rules.

Amos vs. Amaziah makes justice the *supreme command*, overriding every other consideration or obligation, however important to the life of the community. Justice becomes the categorical imperative, transcending all the other requirements of the law. Other ills of society are remediable, but injustice is a stab at the vital center of the communal whole. It instantaneously stops the heartbeat of the social organism. It cuts off the life-giving supply of health and strength that flow through the soul of the community, enabling its members to uphold the harmony, confidence and security of the covenant. The sheer threat and dread of arbitrary force terrorize and brutalize man. They throw him back into the state of nature and its savage standards: *Homo homini lupus*. Arbitrary force shatters the image of God in man.

Justice is the soil in which all the other virtues can prosper. It is the pre-condition of all social virtue, indeed of all community life. It makes civilized existence, it makes human existence possible. In every society justice must be the paramount concern, for it is the very foundation of all society:

"Let justice roll down like waters,
And righteousness as a mighty stream."

By making justice the supreme end and the culminating claim, *Amos vs. Amaziah* at once established a clear distinction between duties of worship and duties of righteousness.

Worship in biblical religion could never be an end in itself, for God is not in need of ritual, as in magic religions of antiquity where the performance of the cult replenished the waning energies or dying fires of the divine. In Israel, worship is God's favor to man, an act of His grace intended for the good of man,—not God. These implications of the biblical faith *Amos vs. Amaziah* clearly recognized by making ritual subserve the ends of righteousness.

Ritual is propaedeutic to religion, exercise and training for spiritual life, discipline in the restraints of holiness. Worship is meant to inspirit man with passion for justice, to purify and prepare him for the encounter with God.

Where ritual becomes estranged from its aim and is pursued for its own sake, instead of facilitating an approach, it may clog and clutter it with impediments and importunities of its own; it may even make the very encounter, if possible, impossible. As an end in itself, ritual may become a stumbling block in religion.

Amos vs. Amaziah has served as an impassioned reminder of the ever present danger and disposition to confuse means with ends. Worship and ritual are means, while justice and righteousness are ends. More, even, righteousness and justice are the encounter. God is justice, and His holiness is exalted in righteousness.

Whenever and wherever such claims will be made in the course of history, and they will be numberless, the decision of *Amos vs. Amaziah* will be invariably invoked or inferred. The heirs to prophecy will rehearse and re-affirm this verdict in varied circumstances with varied stress and ever new choice of words, but the soul and substance of the message will remain unchanged. God requires devotion, not devotions. Sacrifice and prayer cannot serve as substitutes for justice. Fasts and penances may be indulged even by the wicked, while the righteous may delight in the merriments of life without detriment to virtue:

"Did not your father eat and drink
And do justice and righteousness?
Then it was well with him.
He judged the cause of the poor and needy . . .
Is not this to know Me?" (Jeremiah 22:15f.)

In letter and in spirit it is the lesson and legacy of *Amos vs. Amaziah*.

Other works by Spiegel: *Hebrew Reborn* (1930); *Noah, Danel, and Job: Touching on Canaanite Relics in the Legends of the Jews* (1945).

Isadore Twersky

1930–1997

Isadore Twersky, a Boston-born Orthodox rabbi and professor, was a scion of the Tolner Hasidic dynasty and a son-in-law of Rabbi Dr. Joseph B. Soloveitchik. He received his academic training at Harvard University, where he began teaching Hebrew literature and philosophy in 1956, becoming the chair of Harvard's Department of Near Eastern Languages in 1965. From 1978 to 1993 he was the director of Harvard's Center for Jewish Studies. His expertise included medieval rabbinic literature and philosophy, especially that of Maimonides.

The Shulḥan 'Aruk: Enduring Code of Jewish Law
1967

Shulḥan 'Aruk, a term taken over from early rabbinic exegesis in the Midrash and applied to one of the most influential, truly epochal literary creations of Jewish history, has a double or even triple meaning, and its use therefore necessitates precise definition or description. *Shulḥan 'Aruk* is the title given by R. Joseph Karo (1488–1575) to a brief, four-part code of Jewish law which was published in 1565–66, just over four hundred years ago. *Shulḥan 'Aruk* also designates a composite, collaborative work, combining this original text of R. Joseph Karo, a Spanish emigré from Toledo (1492) who lived and studied in Turkey and finally settled in Palestine in a period of turbulence and instability and apocalyptic stirrings, with the detailed glosses—both strictures and supplements—of R. Moses Isserles (c. 1525–1572), a well-to-do Polish scholar, proud of his Germanic background, who studied in Lublin and became de facto chief rabbi of Cracow in a period of relative stability and tranquillity. This unpremeditated literary symbiosis then generated a spate of commentaries and supercommentaries, brief or expansive, defensive or dissenting, from the *Sefer Me'irat 'Enayim* of R. Joshua Falk and the *Sefer Siftei Kohen* of R. Shabbetai ha-Kohen to the *Mishnah Berurah* of R. Israel Meir ha-Kohen; and the term *Shulḥan 'Aruk* continued to be applied to this multi-dimensional, multi-generational, ever-expanding folio volume—a fact which attests the resiliency and buoyancy of the Halachic tradition in Judaism. A person must, therefore, define his frame of reference when he purports to glorify or vilify, to acclaim or condemn—or, if he is able to avoid value judgments, to describe historically.[1] The genuinely modest purpose of the following remarks is, first, to chronicle the emergence of the *Shulḥan 'Aruk*, especially in its first and second meanings, and then to describe a few of its salient literary and substantive characteristics. "The rest is commentary," which we should go and study. [. . .]

V

[. . . W]hen all is said, it would be incorrect and insensitive to assert unqualifiedly that the *Shulḥan 'Aruk*, that embodiment of Halachah which Jewish history has proclaimed supreme, is a spiritless, formalistic, even timid work. Its opening sentence, especially as elaborated by R. Moses Isserles, acts as the nerve center of the entire Halachic system and the fountain of its strength.

> A man should make *himself* strong and brave as a lion to rise in the morning for the service of his Creator, so that he should "awake the dawn" (Psalms 57:9) . . .
>
> "I have set the Lord always before me" (Psalms 16:8). This is a cardinal principle in the Torah and in the perfect (noble) ways of the righteous who walk before God. For man does not sit, move, and occupy himself when he is alone in his house, as he sits, moves, and occupies himself when he is in the presence of a great king; nor does he speak and rejoice

while he is with his family and relatives as he speaks in the king's council. How much more so when man takes to heart that the Great King, the Holy One, blessed be He, whose "glory fills the whole earth" (Isaiah 6:3), is always standing by him and observing all his doings, as it is said in Scripture: "Can a man hide himself in secret places that I shall not see him?" (Jeremiah 23:24). Cognizant of this, he will immediately achieve reverence and humility, fear and shame before the Lord, blessed be He, at all times.

Law is dry and its details are burdensome only if its observance lacks vital commitment, but if all actions of a person are infused with the radical awareness that he is acting in the presence of God, then every detail becomes meaningful and relevant. Such an awareness rules out routine, mechanical actions; everything must be conscious and purposive in a God-oriented universe, where every step of man is directed towards God. Halachah, like nature, abhors a vacuum; it recognizes no twilight zone of neutrality or futility. It is all-inclusive. Consequently, every action—even tying one's shoes—can be and is invested with symbolic meaning. Nothing is accidental, behavioral, purely biological. Even unavoidable routine is made less perfunctory. The opening paragraph of the *Shulḥan 'Aruk* is thus a clear and resounding declaration concerning the workings and the searchings of the spirit. Its tone should reverberate throughout all the subsequent laws and regulations. It provides—as does also paragraph 231, which urges man to see to it that all his deeds be "for the sake of heaven"—an implicit rationale for the entire Halachah, but it is a rationale that must be kept alive by the individual. It cannot be passively taken for granted; it must be passionately pursued.

What I am saying, in other words, is that to a certain extent the *Shulḥan 'Aruk* and Halachah are coterminous and that the "problem" of the *Shulḥan 'Aruk* is precisely the "problem" of Halachah as a whole. Halachah itself is a tense, vibrant, dialectical system which regularly insists upon normativeness in action and inwardness in feeling and thought. It undertook to give concrete and continuous expression to theological ideals, ethical norms, ecstatic moods, and historical concepts but never superseded or eliminated these ideals and concepts. Halachah itself is, therefore, a coincidence of opposites: prophecy and law, charisma and institution, mood and medium, image and reality, the thought of eternity and the life of temporality. Halachah itself, therefore, in its own behalf, demands the coordination of inner meaning and external observance—and it is most difficult to comply with such a demand and sustain such a delicate, highly sensitized synthesis.

NOTE

1. Contemporaries would sometimes criticize the *Shulḥan 'Aruk*, even stridently, but it was left for modern, post-Enlightenment writers to vilify it. See, for example, the references in L. Greenwald, *R. Joseph Karo u-Zemano* (New York, 1954), pp. 174-176; B. Cohen, *Law and Tradition in Judaism* (New York, 1959), pp. 66-68; R. J. Z. Werblowsky, *Joseph Karo* (Oxford, 1962), p. 7; *Jewish Encyclopedia*, III, p. 588.

Actually, there is no need even for devotees of the *Shulḥan 'Aruk* to indulge in meta-historical panegyrics, for supernatural phenomena carry no weight in Halachic matters. The *Shulḥan 'Aruk* is not a revealed canon, nor is it a hypostasis of the Law. In the long, creative history of the Oral Law, it is one major link connecting R. Hai Gaon, Maimonides, Naḥmanides and R. Solomon ibn Adret with R. Elijah Gaon of Vilna, R. Akiba Eiger, and R. Yosef Rosen. It is a significant work which, for a variety of reasons, became a repository and stimulus, a treasure and inspiration for Halachah, both practice and study.

Other works by Twersky: *Rabad of Posquières: A Twelfth-Century Talmudist* (1962); *Introduction to the Code of Maimonides* (1980).

Max Weinreich

1894–1969

Although Max Weinreich was raised in a German-speaking family in Kuldiga, Russia (now Latvia), he dedicated his life to the study and advancement of the Yiddish language. A linguist with a sociological bent, Weinreich was among the founders of the YIVO Institute for Jewish Research in 1925. He remained a major force in the organization throughout his life and during World War II, having escaped to the United States, he was instrumental in the relocation of YIVO's headquarters from Vilna to New York, where the institute remains today. Weinreich wrote a four-volume history of Yiddish, published posthumously as *Geshikhte fun der yidisher shprakh*.

The Reality of Jewishness vs. the Ghetto Myth 1967

2. What was it that made for the peculiar position of the Jews in the Middle Ages and later, until emancipation came along? It was the *ghetto*, we are told and told again, which was at the root of Jewish living during the long centuries of darkness. Time was, so the argument runs, when the Jews in German lands were not distinguished from their compatriots except by their religion. The Jews behaved and spoke as the Germans did and, in the thirteenth century, even produced a German *minnesinger*, Suezkint von Trimberg. But then, under conditions of growing religious intolerance, they were pressed into the ghettos and thus excluded from general society. As a consequence, they deteriorated over the centuries economically, intellectually, and morally. Their German language, which they had previously spoken like every other German person, declined too. The implication was plain. As soon as the sun of tolerance rose, the Jews would again embrace German culture and differ from the bulk of the German population solely by their faith.

This theory, however, is of rather recent origin. It goes back no further than the second half of the eighteenth century, i.e. the age of Enlightenment, and can be shown to have been developed by the nineteenth-century historians who found themselves fighting for Jewish emancipation.

In preemancipation days, as is well known, the Jews in Central Europe had been largely confined to living quarters of their own. When the repercussions of the French revolution made it possible for the Jews to demand emancipation, restrictions in housing must have appeared to be particularly oppressive. It is then that the ghetto concept became a recurrent topic until it finally was accepted as incontestable evidence. Instead, it must be conceived of as an ad hoc explanation in a political struggle. [...]

5. If the Jews lived together long before segregated living quarters were imposed upon them, then this segregation must have been voluntary. It was. Living apart, no matter how bizarre this may appear in the light of present-day concepts and attitudes, was part of the "privileges" accorded to the Jews in conformity with their own wishes. They wanted to be among their own people, to be able to worship collectively, to study, to apply to their own courts of law, not to speak of their urgent need to maintain a ritual slaughterhouse and a ritual bath and to be buried, when time came, in a Jewish cemetery.

Settling in groups, be it by ethnic origin, by religion, or by occupation was an established pattern in the Middle Ages and even much later. There was consequently nothing unusual, let alone degrading, in the very fact that the Jews clung together. There are documented cases to show that every now and then the Jews asked for *permission* to live together in a definite part of the town because they felt safer this way. [. . .]

9. Ashkenazic reality is to be sought between the two poles of absolute identity with and absolute remoteness from the coterritorial non-Jewish communities. To compress it into a formula, what the Jews aimed at was not isolation from the Christians but insulation from Christianity. Although, throughout the ages, many Jews must be supposed to have left the fold, the community as a whole did succeed in surviving and developing. On the other hand, the close and continuous ties of the Jews with their neighbors, which used to be severed only for a while during actual outbreaks of persecutions, manifested themselves in customs and folk beliefs; in legends and songs; in literary production, etc. The culture patterns prevalent among Ashkenazic Jews must be classified as Jewish, but very many of them are specifically Ashkenazic. They are mid-course formations as those found wherever cultures meet along frontiers, in border zones, or in territories with mixed populations.

The most striking result of this encounter of cultures is the Yiddish language. When the Jews entered Loter, their vernaculars were western Laaz and southern Laaz, the Jewish correlates of Old French and Old Italian, while Hebrew-Aramaic was their sacred tongue. But the non-Jewish population of Loter spoke regional variants of German, and it is this German determinant which brought into the new fusion language of Ashkenaz its quantitatively strongest component. Is this not irrefutable proof of a high degree of contact? On the other hand, the Ashkenazim did not simply become German speakers but fused their acquisitions from German with what they had brought with them in their Hebrew-Aramaic and Laaz determinants. The same applies to the Slavic determinant which made itself felt after the middle of the thirteenth century. Doesn't this, in turn, testify to a remarkable degree of independence? [. . .]

10. [. . .] To make a long story short: many non-Jewish patterns were incorporated into the Jewish system at an early date and throughout, but the division into Jewishness vs. non-Jewishness was never abolished or questioned. It thus turns out that the very existence of a division is much more important than the actual location of the division line.

To put it even more bluntly, and this applies to any field of culture: more often than not, it appears, the distance between Jewish and non-Jewish patterns is created not by a difference in the ingredients proper but rather by the way they are interpreted as elements of the given system.

Other works by Weinreich: *Shtaplen: fir etyudn tsu der yidisher shprakhvisnshaft un literaturgeshikhte* (1923); *Hitler's Professors: The Part of Scholarship in Germany's Crimes against the Jewish People* (1946).

Robert Alter
b. 1935

Robert Alter, born in New York City and brought up in Albany, is a biblical scholar and professor of Hebrew and comparative literature at the University of California, Berkeley. As a longtime contributing editor at *Commentary* magazine, he brought Israeli literature and culture to the attention of the American reader. A literary critic and translator, he is the author of numerous monographs and is the recipient of the National Jewish Book Award and the Koret Jewish Book Award.

Jewish Dreams and Nightmares
1968

The case of Kafka, the acculturated Jew, shows how a man may feel his way into a body of collective history through his very consciousness of being outside it: Kafka brooded over the experience of the people from whom he derived, and I would argue that certain key images and states of awareness that were the product of European Jewish history exerted continual pressure on his imagination as he wrote. In this connection, there is one passage in his recorded conversations with the Czech writer Gustav Janouch that is especially revealing. Janouch had asked him if he still remembered the old Jewish quarter of Prague, largely destroyed before Kafka could have known it; this, according to Janouch, is the reply he received:

> In us it still lives—the dark corners, the secret alleys, shuttered windows, squalid courtyards, rowdy pubs, and sinister inns. We walk through the broad streets of the newly built town. But our steps and our glances are uncertain. Inside we tremble just as before in the ancient streets of our misery. Our heart knows nothing of the slum clearance which has been achieved. The unhealthy old Jewish town within us is far more real than the new hygienic town around us. With our eyes open we walk through a dream: ourselves only a ghost of a vanished age.

This remarkable statement is a kind of spiritual autobiography, a summary of what the awareness of being a Jew meant in Kafka's inner life; at the same time, it might be observed that what he has in effect described here is the imaginative landscape of all three of his novels—the hidden alleys and sinister attics of *The Trial*, the medieval squalor and confusion of the courtyards, the dubious inns and devious byways in *The Castle*, and even the new-world landscape of *Amerika*, which begins with skyscrapers but breaks off in a dark and filthy garret where the protagonist is held prisoner. The world of Kafka's novels incorporates the maddening impersonality and inscrutability of modern bureaucracy in an image of an insecure medieval community derived from a ghetto Kafka remembered obsessively without ever having known.

Typically [. . .] confusions between human and inhuman in Kafka terrify more than they perplex, and the imaginative core of that terror is often Jewish for this writer who lived so intensely with the fear and trembling of a vanished ghetto. The nightmarish little tale entitled "An Old Manuscript" is paradigmatic in this respect. Again, the terms of reference of the story are as universal as those of some ancient myth. A nameless town in a nameless empire has been taken over by fierce, implacable nomads who speak no recognizably human tongue. The Emperor remains a powerless spectator, shut up in his palace, a little like the symbolic King of banished sons in many of the midrashic parables, while the townspeople, in the person of the cobbler who is the narrator, confess their incapacity to cope with the terrible strangers:

From my stock, too, they have taken many good articles. But I cannot complain when I see how the butcher, for instance, suffers across the street. As soon as he brings in any meat the nomads snatch it all from him and gobble it up. Even their horses devour flesh; often enough a horseman and his horse are lying side by side, both of them gnawing at the same joint, one at either end. The butcher is nervous and does not dare to stop his deliveries of meat. We understand that, however, and subscribe money to keep him going. If the nomads got no meat, who knows what they might think of doing; who knows anyhow what they may think of, even though they get meat every day.

One does not have to invoke mythic archetypes to feel the bone and blood of Jewish memories in these ghastly images. Behind the nameless nomadic horsemen are dark hordes of Cossacks, Haidameks, pogromists of every breed—the alien and menacing *goy* in his most violent embodiments, speaking no intelligible language, obeying no human laws, even eagerly violating, as we learn in the next paragraph, the Noahide injunction against consuming the flesh of an animal while it is still alive. To the Jew trembling before the torch and ax and sword of the attacker, it seemed that the enemy quite literally could not belong to the same species, and so here the ironic displacement of inhuman and human of "A Report to an Academy" is reversed, the Jew, in the analogical matrix of this story, associated with vulnerable humanity, and the Gentile with inhuman otherness.

What should also be noted is that the story pronounces judgment on the passivity of the townspeople as well as on the stark bestiality of the nomads. Edmund Wilson has accused Kafka of "meaching compliance" with the brutal and unreasonable forces he means to expose in his fiction, but I think this misses the point, for the object of Kafka's "satire" (the term is applied by Wilson) is not only the inhuman powers but also man's pathetic inadequacy of response to them. To put this in terms of the ethnic background of Kafka's imaginings, he never sentimentalized Jewish history; though he was intrigued by the lore of his forebears and their unusual sense of community, he remained ruthlessly honest about the way Jews were. In the passage quoted, one can see a distinctly familiar response of Jews to violence and impending disaster—the attempt to buy off calamity, to temporize with it. (How sadly characteristic that the tradesmen of the community should answer the terrible challenge only by pooling resources to subsidize the principal victim of the invaders!) The story makes clear that this response represents a failure of courage and of imagination as well: in the face of imminent and hideous destruction, where bold, perhaps violent, action is required, the townspeople can muster no more than a piously impotent wringing of hands, a collection of donations, and the grotesquely timid understatement that "This is a misunderstanding of some kind; and it will be the ruin of us."

Kafka, in sum, addressed himself to the broadest questions of human nature and spiritual existence, working with images, actions, and situations that were by design universal in character; but his self-awareness as a Jew and his consciousness of Jewish history impelled his imagination in a particular direction and imparted a peculiar intensity to much of what he wrote, where the abstractness or generality of the parable is strangely wedded to the most concrete sense of actual experience felt and recollected. He could envision the ultimate ambiguities of human life in general with a hyperlucidity because he had experienced them in poignant particularity as a Jew. Out of the stuff of a Jewish experience which he himself thought of as marginal, he was able to create fiction at once universal and hauntingly Jewish.

Other works by Alter: *Rogue's Progress: Studies in the Picaresque Novel* (1965); *After the Tradition: Essays on Modern Jewish Writing* (1969); *The Art of Biblical Narrative* (1981); *The Five Books of Moses: A Translation with Commentary* (2004).

Arthur Green

b. 1941

Arthur Green grew up in New Jersey. An ordained Conservative rabbi, Green was the founder of Havurat Shalom Community Seminary, who later went to serve as dean of the Reconstructionist Rabbinical College and as rector of the rabbinical school at Boston's Hebrew College. A student of Abraham Joshua Heschel, Green's area of scholarly research is Hasidism and mysticism.

Havurat Shalom: Draft of a Covenant
1968

We join together in this covenant out of a sense of divine mission, out of a search for the realization of the sacred in our lives as individuals and as brothers and sisters in a community. Though each of us make his own path toward this realization, we are bound together by a common sense that religious striving, guided by our roots in Judaism, is the central meaning of our lives.

We join together in the realization that the ideal of Havurah is not easily fulfilled, that the very nature of our undertaking requires dedication in struggle. Havurah to us demands a sense of work, work on our personal growth, toward our growth as a community and toward the transformation of the society within which we live.

We recognize Jewish religion as a revolutionary force, one that does not sit well with the search for comfort or the temptations of complacency. Our commitment is such that we will not be led astray by a search for

respectability, by offers of acceptance from those whose values we reject, or by temptations of material success and superficial growth.

Judaism is a religion at work toward liberation, toward greater freedom for the individual and the society. We reject as perverse any use of religion that leads toward repression of the human spirit, meaningless conformity, or the stunting of serious personal growth.

Our religiosity is characterized both by a constant search for the eternal and an awareness of the radical newness of every hour. Constant study of the sources of Jewish religious life in the past is a vital part of our undertaking; wholly one with that study is the attempt to convert our learning into meaningful religious notion. We seek to be learned Jews, not bound by the tradition, but enriched by its insight.

We join together in religious community because we recognize the absurdity of religion that does not transform the interpersonal and the incompleteness of the interpersonal commitment that does not know the religious dimension. Our relationship with one another and with all men will be marked by the reverence called forth by the image of God.

We come together to share both that which we have in common and our differences. We seek to find a religious path for ourselves as a community and to be open to one another's different paths as individuals, lending strength and support to one another where we differ, as well as where we agree.

We agree to confront one another honestly and openly. We will not be afraid to openly reprove one another when occasion arises and to strive in our relationships with one another to achieve a truth and wholeness that will allow us to join closer together even through disagreement and confrontation.

We will not distrust or fear our own individual strengths. When the community is in need of leaders, we will not hold back, trusting the honesty of others to reprove us when they feel our leadership is not for the good.

We recognize the dangers of rumor and gossip in an intimate community. When we talk about one another our talk should be based on concern; there should be nothing we say about one another that we would not want to say face to face.

This covenant guides not only our understanding of our particular community, but addresses us as to the way in which we shall choose to act throughout our lives. Leaving Havurat Shalom in Cambridge will not affect the commitments we here undertake. Should a signer of this covenant feel, however, that his life can no longer be guided by the principles of this covenant, he may ask the other signers to release him from the obligations here undertaken.

No member of the Havurat Shalom community will be pressed into joining into this covenant. Membership in the community will not be contingent upon this. Each member of the community will be free to join into the covenant if and when he sees fit. No special forms of relationship will exist among those who have signed; they will have only articulated and made definite those commitments that bring all the members of our Havurah together. Prospective new members of the community will be told of this covenant when they are accepted. Their acceptance will not, however, depend upon their preparedness to join the *Berit*.

Each member of the Havurah will be asked to keep a copy of this *Berit* in his home, displayed in a place where he will come in contact with it daily. It shall remain a constant challenge and stimulant to all members of the community.

Other works by Green: *Tormented Master: A Life of Rabbi Nahman of Bratslav* (1979); *Radical Judaism: Rethinking God and Tradition* (2010).

Arthur Hertzberg

1921–2006

Polish-born Arthur Hertzberg came to the United States in 1926 and became a prominent voice of modern Judaism in his roles as a Conservative rabbi, scholar, and communal activist. He advocated on behalf of civil rights, Zionism, and interfaith dialogue.

The French Enlightenment and the Jews
1968

The era of Western history that began with the French Revolution ended in Auschwitz. The emancipation of the Jews was reversed in the most horrendous way. For a short while after 1945 the reigning explanation of the Nazi phenomenon was psychological: this demonic anti-Semitism had arisen from the depths of the most emotionally disturbed element in Europe. This first attempt at explanation has now been overwhelmed by the evidence that has been mounted against it. Adolf Hitler was undoubtedly mad, but the millions who responded to his hatred of Jews cannot be called insane in any con-

ventional sense of individual psychosis. For that matter, the notion that a mass madness in Europe in the twentieth century expressed itself at its most murderous by choosing to attack the Jews requires explanation in itself. What created such a predisposition? Why was the emancipation of the Jews that part of the liberal order which was destroyed most easily and effectively? [. . .]

One of the announced purposes of the Emancipation had been to normalize the economy of the Jew so that no particular pursuit, not even moneylending, should be the Jew's own preserve. As this normalization was happening, what predisposed their enemies both to exaggerate, wildly, the economic power of the Jews as it was in fact declining, and concurrently to adjudge the Jews to be even physically redundant because their power had indeed declined? As moralist, Hannah Arendt was eager to avoid the notion of an eternal anti-Semitism because the image of an overwhelming historical force can be used all too easily by individuals and by whole generations to disclaim moral responsibility. Nevertheless, Arendt's assertion that modern anti-Semitism is entirely new is not true to the facts. Medieval impulses towards hatred of Jews remained much more powerful in the new age of post-Christian ideology than she has suggested. More fundamentally, the secularity that she has identified as the new note in modern anti-Semitism did not arise for the first time in the nineteenth century. This Jew-hatred had old antecedents, even older ones than the Christian anti-Semitism it both used and replaced; its power came from the fact that it was a revival of one of the oldest European traditions.

Modern, secular anti-Semitism was fashioned not as a reaction to the Enlightenment and the Revolution, but within the Enlightenment and Revolution themselves. Some of the greatest of the founders of the liberal era modernized and secularized anti-Semitism too. In this new form they gave it fresh and powerful roots by connecting this version of Jew-hatred with ancient pagan traditions. The action of the French Revolution in emancipating the Jews was thus no simple triumph of liberalism over darkness. The immediate context of this declaration and the sources out of which it arose were complicated and not of one piece. [. . .]

The most crucial and fateful ambivalence about Jews was present among the *philosophes*, the leaders of new thought in the eighteenth century. It has been well known, from his own time to this day, that Voltaire personally disliked Jews quite intensely, and this has generally been explained as an accidental and secondary phenomenon. Voltaire was supposed to have been reflecting both some personal unfortunate experiences with Jews and his incapacity as an individual to free himself from his earliest Christian education. The attacks that he and some of his leading associates mounted on Jews and Judaism were supposedly part of the process by which he was attempting to dethrone Christianity, and they were not meant to lessen the ultimate claims of Jews upon equal regard in the new world that enlightened men were envisaging. A rereading of all the evidence, however, proves beyond any shadow of a doubt that in the discussions of the several decades before the Revolution Voltaire was consistently understood on all sides to be the enemy of the Jews of the present as well as of those of the past. His writings were the great arsenal of anti-Jewish arguments for those enemies of the Jews who wanted to sound contemporary. The "enlightened" friends of the Jews invariably quoted from Montesquieu and did battle with Voltaire.

Voltaire's own views cannot be explained, or rather explained away, in such fashion as to defend a view of the Enlightenment as ultimately completely tolerant. An analysis of everything that Voltaire wrote about Jews throughout his life establishes the proposition that he is the major link in Western intellectual history between the anti-Semitism of classic paganism and the modern age. In his favorite pose of Cicero reborn he ruled the Jew to be outside society and to be hopelessly alien even to the future age of enlightened men.

These ambivalences within the Enlightenment have had large consequences. Jacobin anti-Semites used Voltaire's rhetoric and that of the physiocrats. In the early decades of the nineteenth century some of the greatest figures of European socialism, men like Proudhon and Fourier and even Karl Marx, found reason for doubting or denying entirely that the Jews could be readily included in their socialist vision. Most such arguments derived quite consciously from the same sources. The Christian idea that the religion of the Jews and their rejection of Christianity made them an alien element was still strong in Europe. It had now been reinforced by the pagan cultural argument that the Jews were by the very nature of their own culture and even by their biological inheritance an unassimilable element. It had become possible for religious and anti-religious factions to agree that the emancipation of the Jews could not be realized and that it was dangerous to the European majority.

The sources of the Emancipation are to be found most immediately in the France of the "old order," which the Revolution destroyed. The roots of modern Jew-hatred are to be found there too. Both the hopeful and the tragic elements in modern Jewish history descend directly from the way the Jewish question was defined in France on its way to the Revolution.

Other works by Hertzberg: *The Zionist Idea: A Historical Analysis and Reader* (1959); *Judaism* (1961).

Irving Howe

The New York Intellectuals
1969

We were living directly after the Holocaust of the European Jews. We might scorn our origins; we might crush America with discoveries of ardor; we might change our names. But we knew that but for an accident of geography we might also now be bars of soap. At least some of us could not help feeling that in our earlier claims to have shaken off all ethnic distinctiveness there had been something false, something shaming. Our Jewishness might have no clear religious or national content, it might be helpless before the criticism of believers; but Jews we were, like it or not, and liked or not.

To recognize that we were living after one of the greatest and least explicable catastrophes of human history, and one for which we could not claim to have adequately prepared ourselves either as intellectuals or as human beings, brought a new rush of feelings, mostly unarticulated and hidden behind the scrim of consciousness. It brought a low-charged but nagging guilt, a quiet remorse. Sartre's brilliant essay on authentic and inauthentic Jews left a strong mark. Hannah Arendt's book on totalitarianism had an equally strong impact, mostly because it offered a coherent theory, or at least a coherent picture, of the concentration camp universe. We could no longer escape the conviction that, blessing or curse, Jewishness was an integral part of our life, even if—and perhaps just because—there was nothing we could do or say about it. Despite a few simulated seders and literary raids on Hasidism, we could not turn back to the synagogue; we could only express our irritation with "the community" which kept nagging us like disappointed mothers; and sometimes we tried, through imagination and recall, to put together a few bits and pieces of the world of our fathers. I cannot prove a connection between the Holocaust and the turn to Jewish themes in American fiction, at first urgent and quizzical, later fashionable and manipulative. I cannot prove that my own turn to Yiddish literature during the

50's was due to the shock following the war years. But it would be foolish to scant the possibility.

The violent dispute which broke out among the New York intellectuals when Hannah Arendt published her book on Eichmann had as one of its causes a sense of guilt concerning the Jewish tragedy—a guilt pervasive, unmanageable, yet seldom declared at the surface of speech or act. In the quarrel between those attacking and those defending Eichmann in Jerusalem there were polemical excesses on both sides, insofar as both were acting out of unacknowledged passions. Yet even in the debris of this quarrel there was, I think, something good. At least everyone was acknowledging emotions that had long gone unused. Nowhere else in American academic and intellectual life was there such ferocity of concern with the problems raised by Hannah Arendt. If left to the rest of the American intellectual world, her book would have been praised as "stimulating" and "thoughtful," and then everyone would have gone back to sleep. Nowhere else in the country could there have been the kind of public forum sponsored on this subject by *Dissent*: a debate sometimes ugly and outrageous, yet also urgent and afire—evidence that in behalf of ideas we were still ready to risk personal relationships. After all, it had never been dignity that we could claim as our strong point.

Harry Orlinsky
1908–1992

Born in Owen Sound, Ontario, Harry Orlinsky was a prolific biblical scholar who maintained an interdisciplinary approach that considered archaeology, comparative linguistics, and comparative religion all at once. After graduating from the University of Toronto, Orlinsky received his doctorate from Dropsie College in Philadelphia (now the Center for Advanced Judaic Studies at the University of Pennsylvania). Orlinsky was also the only Jewish member of the committee that produced the Revised Standard Version of the Bible in 1952. Two years later, the Israeli government recruited him covertly to authenticate four Dead Sea Scrolls then up for sale.

Notes on the New Translation of the Torah
1969

The world has changed, and changed very much, since World War I. And the English language has changed, and so too has the American Jewish commu-

nity. Grown by 1950 to about five million souls, who were secure, mature, and optimistic in the continued opportunity to develop freely in every important aspect of its economic, political, cultural, and religious life, the American Jewish community was no longer content with an English Bible that had only undergone revision. In keeping with its new status and verve, unprecedented in the two and one-half millennia of Jewish Diaspora life, the Jewish community in the New World wanted a complete break with the past history of Bible translation. [...]

The New Jewish Version (NJV)

It has not always been easy to break with the more than two-thousand-year-old manner of translating the Hebrew Bible, the word-for-word manner. Thus in Gen. 14.1–2 (cf. vv. 8–9) ". . . Amraphel king of Shinar, Arioch king of Ellasar," etc., is but a mechanical rendering of the Hebrew order (X *mélekh* Y), when the natural order in English would be "King Amraphel of Shinar, King Arioch of Ellasar," etc.

The traditional translations of the Bible might well be designated "And" Bibles; hardly a sentence goes by without an "and" or two, sometimes more. The fact that English, unlike biblical Hebrew, is not coordinate in its sentence structure has been generally ignored by previous translators. So that rather than an automatic "And" for Hebrew *waw*, the context and the idiom ought to have led translators to employ "When," or "So," or "Then," or "Thus," or "Thereupon," or "Although," or "But," or "Yet," or "However," or the like. Traditional "And," precisely because it was mechanical, only succeeded in suppressing the full range of meaning of Hebrew *waw* and in preventing the translator from making clear to the reader the true meaning of the Hebrew verse. In addition, there are hundreds of instances when the *waw* ought not be translated at all, serving in the Hebrew only the function of introducing the verb. For instance, most traditional translations rendered initial *wa(-yómer elohim)* for each day of creation in Genesis 1 (vv. 3, 6, 9, 14, 20, and 24) by "And (God said)"; the new Jewish version reads simply "God said." [...]

Like the *waw*, particles are the bane of the modern Bible translator who tries to reproduce for the reader the precise nuance of each occurrence. The older translators had no problem: simply and mechanically, without regard to idiom or context—sometimes even ungrammatically (e.g., at Gen. 3.22)—they turned every occurrence of *pen* into "lest," of *hinne* into "behold," of *lamma* into "why, wherefore," of *lakhen* into "therefore," and so on. Thus in Gen. 26.7, the older rendering was "(And the men of the place asked him of his wife; and he said: 'She is my sister'; for he feared to say: 'my wife'); 'lest (the men of the place should kill me for Rebekah, because she is fair to look upon.').'"; contrast NJV: "(When the men of the place asked him about his wife, he said, 'She is my sister,' for he was afraid to say 'my wife,' thinking, 'The men of the place) might (kill me on account of Rebekah, for she is beautiful.').'" [. . .]

Starting out with traditional "Thou" ("Thy, Thine") in reference to God when He was addressed directly, NJV decided subsequently in favor of "You" ("Your"). The reasoning behind this decision was simple and forthright. First of all, and primarily, the Hebrew Bible itself never made any distinction between God and man or animal: whether it is God, or the serpent in the Garden of Eden, or Pharaoh who is addressed, the pronoun and the verbal form employed are always in the second singular (*atta*; *natháta*). This was recognized and followed faithfully by all the older translations, Jewish and Christian alike (e.g., Septuagint, Targum, Vulgate, Saadia). Indeed, the Authorized (King James) Version rendered all singulars by forms of "thou" and all plurals by forms of "ye." The Revised Standard Version, however, decided on "you" for both the singular and plural, but retained forms of "Thou" for God.

Not only does "thou" receive no support from the Bible, but this archaic word (and such corresponding verbal forms as "wast, art, shalt") have no place in a modern translation of the Bible: they are awkward and artificial in twentieth-century English. (The common assertion that the use of "thou" in a Bible translation makes for piety and awe is hardly pertinent to scholarship; the first and exclusive obligation of a translator is to the text. And who would certify that piety and awe have been maintained in recent centuries and decades as a consequence of the continued use of "thou"?)

A major consequence of NJV is the realization that Jewish interpretation of the Bible, beginning with the earliest rabbinic literature and extending through Saadia, Rashi, Rashbam, Ibn Ezra, Radak, Ramban, Ralbag, Sforno, and Abravanel, to Luzzatto (Shadal), Malbim, and others, should command in vastly increased measure the respect and gratitude of modern critical scholarship. The reader will not fail to note the frequency with which an older Jewish interpretation of a word or phrase or verse anticipated NJV or provided it with an important lead to a new interpretation. The

Jewish commentators of ancient, medieval, and more recent times gain our scholarly respect not from a blind acceptance of their views but rather from a critical evaluation of their exposition in the manner that any modern commentator expects from his peers.

Other works by Orlinsky: *Ancient Israel* (1954); *Nationalism, Universalism, and Internationalism in Ancient Israel* (1969); *Understanding the Bible through History and Archaeology* (1972).

M. J. Rosenberg
b. 1947

M. J. Rosenberg studied contemporary Jewish studies at Brandeis University. In the 1980s and 1990s, he was a staffer for Democratic members of the House and Senate and at the United States Agency for International Development. He worked for the American Israel Public Affairs Committee in the early 1980s, editing the *Near East Report*. He was director of policy at the Israel Policy Forum for more than ten years. More recently, Rosenberg has become a vocal critic of American foreign policy in relation to Israel.

To Uncle Tom and Other Such Jews
1969

The Jew can be an ally of the black liberation movement and he should be. But first he must find himself. He must realize that his own struggle for liberation is a continuing one, that he also has much to fear and also much to take pride in. The miracle of Israel, a national liberation deferred for two thousand years, should be his inspiration. As the late Robert F. Kennedy said, "Israel's creation . . . has written a new chapter in the annals of freedom and courage—a story that my children and yours will tell their descendants to the end of time." This is recognized by free men everywhere. [. . .]

Therefore it is as a Jew that I must accept black nationalism. The black nationalists may or may not be the equivalents of the militants of the early Zionist organizations, and Malcolm X may or may not be a black Vladimir Jabotinsky, but surely the parallel is there. The Jewish War of Liberation differs from that of the black American or of the Viet Cong only in that the Jewish struggle has seen its greatest aim realized, however tenuously. So will the black revolution succeed. [. . .]

Black nationalism and Jewish nationalism will exist concurrently. To accept one, you must accept the other.

The black is America's Jew and a common fight can be waged. But not at the expense of our own pride. Thus, when some black nationalist calls us "racist Zionists" or tells us that we are poisoning his children's minds; then we must see him for what he is; just another *goy*, using the Jew, the available and acceptable scapegoat. We must then fight him with all we have. That's the way it has to be; we must scrape for no one.

And thus from this point on, I will support no movement that does not accept my people's struggle. If I must choose between the Jewish cause and a "progressive" anti-Israel SDS [Students for a Democratic Society], I shall always choose the Jewish cause. Not blindly, not arbitrarily, but always with full knowledge of who I am and where I must be. If the barricades are erected, I will fight as a Jew. It has been written that after "Auschwitz we retain but one supreme value—to exist." Masada will not fall again.

There is still time but the burden of proof is not on the Jewish nationalist; it is on you—you who reject your identity and attempt to evade the inescapable fact that it follows you wherever you go. You who mockingly reject every lesson of your people's history. You who are so trapped by your Long Island split-level childhood that you can't see straight. You who fight against everything you are—and against the one element that gave you your goddam social consciousness: your Jewish social idealism.

In the aftermath of the crematoriums, you are flippant. In the wake of Auschwitz, you are embarrassed. Thirty years after the Holocaust you have learned nothing and forgotten everything. Ghetto Jew, you'd better do some fast thinking.

Other work by Rosenberg: *The Cybernetic of Art: Reason and the Rainbow* (1983).

Cynthia Ozick

b. 1928

Cynthia Ozick, born in New York, is a novelist, short-story writer, essayist, and critic. Best known for her fiction, which is steeped in Jewish culture, she is a major figure in contemporary American letters. Among her literary honors, Ozick has received three O. Henry Awards, the National Jewish Book Award, and the 2008 PEN/Malamud and 2008 PEN/Nabokov awards for lifetime achievement.

Toward a New Yiddish
1970

[. . .] It seems to me we are ready to rethink ourselves in America now; to preserve ourselves by a new culture-making.

Now you will say that this is a vast and stupid contradiction following all I have noted so far about the historic hopelessness of Diaspora culture. I have already remarked that "there are no major works of Jewish imaginative genius written in any Gentile language, sprung out of any Gentile culture." Then how, you will object, can there be a Yavneh in America, where all the Jews speak a Gentile language and breathe a Gentile culture? My answer is this: it can happen if the Jews of America learn to speak a new language appropriate to the task of a Yavneh.

This new language I will call, for shorthand purposes, New Yiddish. (If you stem from the Sephardic tradition, New Ladino will serve just as well.) Like old Yiddish, New Yiddish will be the language of a culture that is centrally Jewish in its concerns and thereby liturgical in nature. [. . .]

When Jews poured Jewish ideas into the vessel of German they invented Yiddish. As we more and more pour not merely the Jewish sensibility, but the Jewish vision, into the vessel of English, we achieve the profoundest invention of all: a language for our need, our possibility, our overwhelming *idea*. If out of this new language we can produce a Yavneh for our regeneration within an alien culture, we will have made something worthwhile out of the American Diaspora, however long or short its duration. Besides, New Yiddish has a startling linguistic advantage over old Yiddish, which persecution pushed far from its geographic starting-point: New Yiddish can be understood by the Gentile culture around us. So we have a clear choice, to take up an opportunity or to reject it. We can do what the German Jews did, and what Isaac D'Israeli did—we can give ourselves over altogether to Gentile culture and be lost to history, becoming a vestige nation without a literature; or we can do what we have never before dared to do in a Diaspora language; make it our own, our own necessary instrument, understanding ourselves in it while being understood by everyone who cares to listen or read. If we make out of English a New Yiddish, then we can fashion a Yavneh not only for our own renewal but as a demonstration for our compatriots. From being envious apes we can become masters of our own civilization—and let those who want to call this "re-ghet-toization," or similar pejoratives, look to their own destiny. We need not live like ants on the spine of the earth. In the conflict between the illuminations of liturgy and the occult darknesses of random aesthetics we need not go under: by bursting forth with a literature attentive to the implications of Covenant and Commandment—to the human reality—we can, even in America, try to be a holy people, and let the holiness shine for others in a Jewish language which is nevertheless generally accessible. We will not have to flatter or parody; we will not require flattery; we will develop Aggadah *bilshonenu*, in our own language, and build in Diaspora a permanent body of Jewish literature.

If we blow into the narrow end of the *shofar*, we will be heard far. But if we choose to be Mankind rather than Jewish and blow into the wider part, we will not be heard at all; for us America will have been in vain.

Other works by Ozick: *Trust* (1966); *Envy; or, Yiddish in America* (1969); *The Pagan Rabbi, and Other Stories* (1971).

Rachel Adler
b. 1943

Born in Chicago, Rachel Adler is the Rabbi David Ellenson Professor of Jewish Religious Thought and Professor of Modern Jewish Thought and Feminist Studies at Hebrew Union College-JIR/Los Angeles. The recipient of a National Jewish Book Award, Adler has written studies and many articles that approach theology from a feminist and Reform perspective.

The Jew Who Wasn't There
1971

It is not unusual for committed Jewish women to be uneasy about their position as Jews. It was to cry down our doubts that rabbis developed their pre-packaged orations on the nobility of motherhood; the glory of childbirth; and modesty, the crown of Jewish womanhood. I have heard them all. I could not accept those answers for two reasons. First of all, the answers did not accept *me* as a person. They only set rigid stereotypes which defined me by limiting the directions in which I might grow. Second, the answers were not really honest ones. Traditional scholars agree that all philosophies of Judaism must begin with an examination of Jewish law,

Halacha, since in the Halacha are set down the ways in which we are expected to behave, and incontestably our most deeply engrained attitudes are those which we reinforce by habitual action.

Yet scholars do not discuss female status in terms of Halacha—at least not with females. Instead, they make lyrical exegeses on selected Midrashim and Agadot which, however complimentary they may be, do not really reflect the way in which men are expected to behave toward women by Jewish law. This latter is the subject no one wants to discuss. Nevertheless, I think we are going to have to discuss it, if we are to build for ourselves a faith which is not based on ignorance and self-deception. That is why I would like to offer some hypotheses on the history and nature of the "woman problem" in Halacha.

Ultimately our problem stems from the fact that we are viewed in Jewish law and practice as peripheral Jews. [. . .]

To be a peripheral Jew is to be educated and socialized toward a peripheral commitment. This, I think, is what happened to the Jewish woman. Her major mitzvot aid and reinforce the life-style of the community and the family, but they do not cultivate the relationship between the individual and God. A woman keeps kosher because both she and her family must have kosher food. She lights the Shabbat candles so that there will be light, and hence, peace, in the household. She goes to the mikva so that her husband can have intercourse with her and she bears children so that, through her, he can fulfill the exclusively male mitzvah of increasing and multiplying.

Within these narrow confines, there have been great and virtuous women, but in several respects the tzidkaniot (saintly women) have been unlike the tzaddikim. Beruria, the scholarly wife of Rabbi Meir, the Talmudic sage, and a few exceptional women like her stepped outside the limits of the feminine role, but legend relates how Beruria came to a bad end, implying that her sin was the direct result of her "abnormal" scholarship. There is no continuous tradition of learned women in Jewish history. Instead there are many tzidkaniot, some named, some unnamed, all of whom were pious and chaste, outstandingly charitable, and, in many cases, who supported their husbands. In contrast, there are innumerable accounts of tzaddikim, some rationalists, some mystics, some joyous, some ascetic, singers, dancers, poets, halachists, all bringing to God the service of a singular, inimitable self.

How is it that the tzaddikim seem so individualized and the tzidkaniot so generalized? I would advance two reasons. First of all, the mitzvot of the tzadeket are mainly directed toward serving others. She is a tzadeket to the extent that she sacrifices herself in order that others may actualize themselves spiritually. One has no sense of an attempt to cultivate a religious self built out of the raw materials of a unique personality. The model for the tzadeket is Rachel, the wife of Rabbi Akiva, who sold her hair and sent her husband away to study for twenty-four years, leaving herself beggared and without means of support, or the wife of Rabbi Menachem Mendal of Rymanov (her name. incidentally, goes unremembered) who sold her share in the next world to buy her husband bread. [. . .]

Second, as Hillel says, "an ignoramus cannot be a saint." He may have the best of intentions, but he lacks the disciplined creativity, the sense of continuity with his people's history and thought, and the forms in which to give Jewish expression to his religious impulses. Since it was traditional to give women cursory religious educations, they were severely limited in their ways of expressing religious commitment. Teaching, the fundamental method of the Jewish people for transmitting religious insights, was closed to women—those who do not learn, do not teach. [. . .]

In its time, the Talmud's was a very progressive view. The last great revolutionary ruling for women, however, was the Edict of Rabbenu Gershom forbidding polygamy to the Jews of the Western world. That was in 1000 CE. The problem is that very little has been done since then to ameliorate the position of Jewish women in observant Jewish society.

All of this can quickly be rectified if one steps outside of Jewish tradition and Halacha. The problem is how to attain some justice and some growing room for the Jewish woman if one is committed to remaining *within* Halacha. Some of these problems are more easily solved than others. [. . .]

The halachic scholars must examine our problem anew, right now, and with open minds and with empathy. They must make it possible for women to claim their share in the Torah and begin to do the things a Jew was created to do. If necessary we must agitate until the scholars are willing to see us as Jewish souls in distress rather than as tools with which men do mitzvot. If they continue to turn a deaf ear to us, the most learned and halachically committed among us must make halachic decisions for the rest. That is a move to be saved for desperate straits, for even the most learned of us have been barred from acquiring the systematic halachic knowledge which a rabbi has. But, to paraphrase Hillel, in a place where there are no menschen, we may have to generate our own menschlichkeit. There is no time to waste. For too many centuries, the Jewish woman has been a golem, created by Jewish society.

She cooked and bore and did her master's will, and when her tasks were done the Divine Name was removed from her mouth. It is time for the golem to demand a soul.

Other work by Adler: *Engendering Judaism: An Inclusive Theology and Ethics* (1998).

Jacob Neusner

1932–2016

Born in Hartford, Connecticut, Jacob Neusner was a prolific scholar of rabbinic Judaism as well as an editor, translator, and ordained rabbi. He translated both the Babylonian and Palestinian Talmuds. Neusner was a professor of history and theology of Judaism at Bard College. The recipient of numerous awards, he was the author of hundreds of books and articles, both scholarly and popular.

There We Sat Down: Talmudic Judaism in the Making

1971

Like other "holy men," the rabbi played political, religious, and cultural roles. Just as the Zoroastrian Magus was involved in the administration of the local community, in the maintenance of cultic life, and in the study and teaching of Mazdean beliefs and scriptures, so too was the rabbi. The difference, however, was that while the Magus never aspired to overthrow or subvert the Sasanian dynasty, but only to serve as a significant and influential part of its administration and to constitute its religious arm, the rabbis wanted to independently exercise quite direct and substantial power over the Jewish community. Such a difference probably was not readily discernible during this period, for it was apparently only Geniva who acted according to these aspirations. Nevertheless, the lines were drawn, and the direction of rabbinical policy was quite clear. On the one side were rabbis such as Naḥman who would correspond to the priest-politician Kartir, "the soul-savior of [Emperor] Bahram." Such rabbis were part of the Jewish established government, shared its values and aspirations, and served its purposes. They would represent the closest parallel to the leading Magi. On the other were Geniva and those who shared his disdain for, and suspicion of, the Davidic exilarch. To these there was no clear counterpart among the Magi.

A more significant comparison could be drawn to the Christian "religious," the monastic figures who dominated the Christian faith east of the Euphrates and shaped its character. Unlike the Christian monks, it was the aspiration of the rabbi *not* to form a separate society. He kept to himself very little. He did not live in a tight little eschatological community, confidently awaiting the day on which the sinners would know that he was right and they were wrong. For all his sense of forming part of an elite, he did not look upon the rest of the Jewish community as outsiders, less "elect" than himself. At many important points he shared the fundamental convictions of the broader community; what he most wanted was to teach the people how to live up to these convictions as *he* understood them. So if he was not a sectarian, the reason was that he aspired to a wider influence than other religious leaders. He wanted all the Jews to become rabbis. He asked *nothing* of himself that he regarded as inapplicable to others, and nothing of others that did not pertain to himself.

Herein lies a paradox of the rabbinical "estate." On the one hand, it was separate and, by its own standard, superior. On the other, it hoped to obliterate the distinctions between the rabbinate and other Jews, and believed that every Jew was equally able to achieve "superiority." So its aspiration to political power, so partisan and subversive of existing authority, represented a perfectly natural extension of its self-understanding. It was through politics that the rest of Jewry might be changed. Through the rabbinical courts and collaboration with the exilarch's regime that set them up, the most effective influence might be attained. Indeed, when we seek to locate the points of contact between the rabbi and the town, we find those points less in the marketplace, synagogue, or in the streets (though the rabbis did not avert their eyes from what happened there) than in the law courts, which were places not only of litigation, but also of administration of all manner of affairs. To direct those courts represented the most convenient and efficient way of doing what the rabbinate wanted. But it must be emphasized again that what the rabbinate wanted was not to *control* others, who would permanently remain essentially outside its circle, but rather win them to the viewpoint of its own estate, to transform the community into a replica of the academy. The rabbis wanted to bring all Israel closer to their Father in heaven, and his traditions as revealed in the whole Torah provided a very full program on how to do so—and what to do after they had succeeded. [. . .]

From third-century Babylonia onward, "Rabbinic Judaism" was normative; its laws *were* Jewish law: its theology shaped the conceptions of the masses and required the speculative defense of the philosophers; its enemies were designated heretics, and its devotees, the "normative" and "authoritative" exemplifications of Judaism. The rabbinate represents a singularly successful party. In the history of mankind, one can find few "parties" which achieved so lasting a success that, until this very day, their conception of history and society dominates precisely the group which they intended from the beginning to shape and control. There is only one similarly successful group that readily comes to mind, and that is the Christians, who actively undertook to subvert, then control, and finally dominate, the Roman Empire and whose historical role provides an analogy to that of the rabbis. They are not wholly comparable, for the Romans persecuted the Christians sporadically but ferociously, while the patriarchate in Palestine and the exilarchate in Babylonia actually employed the rabbis. The two parties, however, thrived by persistence and faith, and in time succeeded in winning the sovereignty to which they aspired—the one to the Roman world, the other to the rule of Israel. It is only in the past two centuries that either has had to face a significant challenge, a time when the values and ideals of each ceased to shape the groups whom they had dominated for so many centuries.

Other works by Neusner: *A Life of Rabban Yohanan ben Zakkai* (1962); *A History of the Jews in Babylonia* (1969); *Invitation to the Talmud* (1973).

James A. Sleeper

b. 1947

Born in Longmeadow, Massachusetts, political scientist James (also Jim) Sleeper has studied American civic culture and political life for several decades. After earning his doctorate in education at Harvard University in 1977, Sleeper began his career as a professor of urban studies, concentrating specifically on race relations in New York. He currently lectures at Yale University on American identity and the ties between journalism, liberalism, and democracy.

The New Jews
1971

A Critique of the Transition: Youth's Alienation

The American Jewish community is only beginning to come to terms with the meaning of this prostitution of Judaism to the status quo, and it is doing so because of the alienation of the majority of its young people. We have already suggested that their rejection of the Jewish community is less a denial of Judaism as such than it is part of a more general rejection of the deficiencies and misguided priorities inherent in the American Dream their parents have pursued. Judaism is rejected because it is seen as part and parcel of the hollow life-style, and because it has given young people no help in their search for alternatives to what has become the life-style of the Jewish suburb. [. . .]

Jewish suburbia seems to some of us a creation of *adults* who overcame poverty and the sting of minority status by emphasizing the importance of "measuring up"—to materialistic styles and performance-oriented standards as short-cuts to human dignity. Of course they "knew better," and it would be unfair to underestimate the well-intentioned sacrifice and real strength which were often expressed in the various achievements of suburban Jews. But we are concerned with the price that was paid in an often uncritical acceptance of "American life"; in slavishly imitating its trappings, these adults may have lost their capacity to challenge and affect its human and spiritual content.

So suburbia has been at once a launching pad and a target for the alienation and radicalism of the young—a launching pad because it has given them the affluence, sophistication, and perspective of Koheleth, and a target because it has furnished them with a microcosm of that society's bittersweet fruits, with the realization that affluence, sophistication, and perspective do not add up to Meaning. [. . .]

Toward a New Synthesis

In urban centers, young rabbis and educators kept alive another kind of Judaism, less molded by middle-class pressures, and capable, they felt, of offering an alternative way of life to the children of status seekers and organization men. [. . .]

The Jewish Paradox Restored

The "new Jews" do not pretend that Judaism is of such universal theoretical applicability as to have "answers" to modern problems. I have tried to suggest that to see the world through Jewish eyes in this century is to embrace a paradox of hope and despair; to support the anguish of alienation with the strength of a mighty untapped reservoir of resources for personal identity and moral involvement as well as with a language of aesthetics and a way to express personal spiritual development which offers new perspectives to American youth.

The productive union of Jewish life and the radical's grasp for answers is not always an easy one to effect, of course. On the social front the religious and activist communities have much in common: both argue that the "human dimension" must be brought into societal decision-making, both are passionately concerned with justice. But the religious community is more explicitly concerned with nurturing the vision and personal depth which should lie behind the public decisions and strategies of the activist; as such it may have more "territory behind the lines," and its membership and emphasis may be different. The Jewish activist confronts the broad spectrum of human suffering and struggle and sees his small interactive community as an ultimate building-block of humanity; his political activities are supplemented by his concern for the intensity, the depth, and the sensitivity of his own microcosmic community. At times it is a difficult balance of energies and perspectives.

Ultimately I suspect that there is more that is attractive in this synthesis of the universal and the particular than the "healthy creative tension" that may result. Ethnicity and particularism are more than expedients; we cannot escape the knowledge that, whatever Judaism may be for us today, it owes its survival to the belief of our ancestors that Israel somehow transcends the historical contexts through which it wends its paradox-ridden way. It is not clear that Jewishness makes any sense when its sociological roots have been summed, and when its achievements have been behaviorally, historically, and philosophically analyzed. The ultimate claim to a tie with spiritual dimensions of experience which eludes our rational inquiry stares at us constantly through the pages of our history. It is to be hoped that, whatever the specifics of his theology, the Jew will not be able to remain insensitive to the sense of ultimacy and mystery which enters all of our lives and is the spinal cord of our people's past. [...]

Beyond the Pale

[...] American youth stands at a new frontier: we have been the beneficiaries and the victims of the old American Dream of material comfort and open opportunity; now, a frightening and exciting world of intangible goals and human redefinition beckons, even as we are pressured by a spiritually hollow society to ignore its call. Our alienation and radical activity—and our sigh—is a suggestion that we are only beginners in that new world, unable any longer to bear the confines of the old. Perhaps that has always been the story of the Jew.

Other works by Sleeper: *In Search of New York* (1988); *Liberal Racism* (1997).

Ezrat Nashim

Founded 1971

Founded in New York by several prominent Jewish feminists, Ezrat Nashim (a reference to the separate women's sections in synagogues, also signifying "help for women") was a study group for women dedicated to addressing gender inequalities within Judaism. Appealing to the Rabbinical Assembly of Conservative Judaism, they argued for a rethinking of women's place in religious life beyond their roles as wives and mothers and called for women's full participation in religious observance, including being counted in a minyan, being allowed to initiate divorce proceedings, and being allowed to fulfill all the *mitzvot*.

Jewish Women Call for Change
1972

The Jewish tradition regarding women, once far ahead of other cultures, has now fallen disgracefully behind in failing to come to terms with developments of the past century.

Accepting the age-old concept of role differentiation on the basis of sex, Judaism saw woman's role as that of wife, mother, and home-maker. Her ritual obligations were domestic and familial: *nerot* [candles], *challah*, and *taharat ha-mishpachah* [family purity, i.e., laws of mikveh and sexual purity]. Although the woman was extolled for her domestic achievements, and respected as the foundation of the Jewish family, she was never permitted an active role in the synagogue, court, or house of study. These limitations on the life-patterns open to women, appropriate or even progressive for the rabbinic and medieval periods, are entirely unacceptable to us today.

The social position and self-image of women have changed radically in recent years. It is now universally accepted that women are equal to men in intellectual capacity, leadership ability and spiritual depth. The Conservative movement has tacitly acknowledged this fact by demanding that their female children be educated alongside the males—up to the level of rabbinical school. To educate women and deny them the opportunity to act from this knowledge is an affront to their intelligence, talents and integrity.

As products of Conservative congregations, religious schools, Ramah camps, LTF [Leaders Training Fellowship], USY [United Synagogue Youth], and the Seminary, we feel this tension acutely. We are deeply committed to Judaism, but cannot find adequate expression for our total needs and concerns in existing women's social and charitable organizations, such as Sisterhood, Hadassah, etc. Furthermore, the single woman—a new reality in Jewish life—is almost totally excluded from the organized Jewish community, which views women solely as daughters, wives, and mothers. The educational institutions of the Conservative movement have helped women recognize their intellectual, social and spiritual potential. If the movement then denies women opportunities to demonstrate these capacities as adults, it will force them to turn from the synagogue, and to find fulfillment elsewhere.

It is not enough to say that Judaism views women as separate but equal, nor to point to Judaism's past superiority over other cultures in its treatment of women. We've had enough of apologetics: enough of Bruria, Dvorah, and Esther; enough of *Eshet Chayil* [the woman of valor]!

It is time that:

women be granted membership in synagogues
women be counted in the minyan
women be allowed full participation in religious observances—(aliyot, ba'a lot kriyah, shlichot tzibur) [being called to the Torah, reading torah, leading services]
women be recognized as witnesses before Jewish law

women be allowed to initiate divorce

women be permitted and encouraged to attend Rabbinical and Cantorial schools, and to perform Rabbinical and Cantorial functions in synagogues

women be encouraged to join decision-making bodies, and to assume professional leadership roles, in synagogues and in the general Jewish community

women be considered as bound to fulfill all mitzvot equally with men.

For three thousand years, one-half of the Jewish people have been excluded from full participation in Jewish communal life. We call for an end to the second-class status of women in Jewish life.

Ezrat Nashim
411 Avenue N
Brooklyn, New York 11230

The Jewish Catalog

Kashrut
1973

Setting up a kosher home is not at all difficult once one gets the hang of what one is and is not allowed to do and eat. There is *sometimes* an unfortunate tendency among those just beginning to keep kosher to make the process as complicated as possible. One of the best ways to decomplicate the issue is to visit someone who has a kosher home and request a guided tour of the kitchen. Shortcuts and maneuverability areas become clearer and the whole process somehow simplifies itself.

a. You should have two sets of dishes and two sets of silverware—stored separately: one for meat meals and one for dairy meals. These should never be mixed—this rule includes washing, storing, etc.

b. It is preferable to have different dish towels for meat and milk dishes.

c. Two sets of dish drainers and sink liners are advisable (the greatest invention ever for keeping kosher was the double sink). Use kosher soaps and detergents to wash dishes. You absolutely need sink liners so that your utensils don't come in contact with the sink. Never wash meat and milk utensils together. [. . .]

NOTE
[Joe Polak and Marvin Jussoy were also involved in editing this section.—Eds.]

Susan Sontag
1933–2004

Born in New York, Susan Sontag grew up in Tucson and Los Angeles. As a critic, essayist, novelist, short-story writer, and playwright, Sontag produced controversial works on contemporary art, philosophy, literature, politics, and morality. She explored the art of photography and wrote about the stigma and metaphorical interpretations of disease in contemporary society. Among her numerous awards was the 2001 Jerusalem Prize.

Photography
1973

Photographs shock us in so far as they show us something novel. Unfortunately, the ante keeps getting raised—partly through the very proliferation of such images of horror. One's first encounter with the photographic inventory of ultimate horror is a kind of revelation, perhaps the only revelation people are granted now, a negative epiphany. For me, it was photographs of Bergen-Belsen and Dachau which I came across by chance in a bookstore in Santa Monica in July, 1945. Nothing I have seen—in photographs or in real life—ever cut me as sharply, deeply, instantaneously. Ever since then, it has seemed plausible to me to think of my life as being divided into two parts: before I saw those photographs (I was twelve) and after. My life was changed by them, though not until several years later did I understand what they were about. What good was served by seeing them? They were only photographs—of an event I had scarcely heard of and could do nothing to affect, of suffering I could hardly imagine and could do nothing to relieve. When I looked at those photographs, something was broken. Some limit had been reached, and not only that of horror; I felt irrevocably grieved, wounded, but a part of my feelings started to tighten; something went dead; something is still crying.

To suffer is one thing; another thing is living with the photographed images of suffering, which does not necessarily strengthen conscience and the ability to be compassionate. It can also corrupt them. Once one has seen such images, one has started down the road of seeing more—and more. Images transfix. Images anesthetize. An event known through photographs certainly becomes more real than it would have been if one had never seen the photographs—think of the Vietnam war.

But, after repeated exposure to images, it also becomes less real.

Other works by Sontag: *Against Interpretation, and Other Essays* (1966); *I, Etcetera* (1977); *Illness as Metaphor* (1978).

Arthur Waskow

b. 1933

Born in Baltimore, Arthur Waskow is a rabbi, author, educator, activist, and key figure in the Jewish Renewal movement. Involved throughout his career in politics, environmental issues, Jewish theology, and peace efforts, he received the 2001 Abraham Joshua Heschel Award from the Jewish Peace Fellowship.

How to Bring Mashiah
1973

1. "If you're planting a tree and you hear Mashiah has come, first finish planting and then run to the city gates to tell him Shalom" (Yochanan Ben Zakkai).

THEREFORE: Plant a tree somewhere as a small tikkun olam—fixing up the world—wherever the olam most needs it. Plant a tree in Vietnam in a defoliated former forest. [. . .]

Plant a tree in Appalachia where the strip mines have poisoned the forests. *Go there to plant it; start a kibbutz there and grow more trees.* Plant a tree in Brooklyn where the asphalt has buried the forest. *Go back there to plant it* and live with some of the old Jews who still live there. If policemen come to save the asphalt, keep planting. Offer everybody a turn with the shovel.

2. "Mashiah will come when the whole Jewish People keeps/remembers Shabbat twice in a row" (Talmud, Shabbat 118b).

THEREFORE: Forget about all the things you *mustn't* do on Shabbat, and instead think of all the things you would most *like* to do on Shabbat (and forever). Do them. Read Torah with some friends and talk about it; walk on grass barefoot; look very carefully at a flower without picking it; give somebody something precious and beautiful without asking him to pay you; give love. Since it's not enough to do this alone (see the prediction), pick out a few Jews on the street, tell them it's Shabbat, and dance a horah with them (or the kazatsky, if you're into Yiddish).

3. "The nations . . . shall beat their swords into plowshares. . . . They shall never again know war" (Isaiah 2:4).

THEREFORE: Get together a minyan and travel up to West Point. Take along ten swords and a small forge. Put the small forge in the main entrance, start it glowing, and beat the swords into something like a digging tool. Dig holes for ten trees, and plant the trees in the roadway. Meanwhile, sing "Lo yisah goy" and "Ain't Gonna Study War No More" alternately, and if any West Pointers stop to see what's going down, offer them a reworked sword to dig with.

4. "Mashiah will come when one generation is either wholly innocent or wholly guilty" (Talmud, Sanhedrin 98a).

THEREFORE: Analyze the tax system of the United States, and publish a detailed answer to these two questions: (a) Are United States taxes used largely for purposes prohibited by Torah (e.g., oppressing the poor, destroying trees, etc.)? (b) Are any Jews in the United States successfully avoiding payment of all taxes? If the answer to (a) is "Yes" and to (b) is "No," proclaim that the entire generation is guilty *in fact,* regardless of their personal opinions. Ask all shuls to include the proclamation in their Shabbat prayers with strong kavvanah: "HaShem, we are at last *all* guilty: send him!"

5. "And a woman shall conceive and bear in the same day [i.e., without pain]" (Midrash on Jeremiah). "See whether a man doth travail with child; wherefore do I see every man with his hands on his loins, as a woman in travail. . . Alas! for that day is great, so that none is like it" (Jeremiah 30: 6–7).

THEREFORE: If you're a man, practice having a baby. Whether you're a man or woman, take a class in the Lamaze method of trained, fully awake childbirth. Learn and practice the exercises. If you're an expectant father, take as much time off from work as your wife/lover does (before and after the birth), and try to experience fully what giving birth and baby care mean.

6. "For the Lord hath created a new thing in the earth: a woman [nekevah] shall court a man [warrior]" (Jeremiah 31:22).

THEREFORE: If you're a woman, surround the nearest warrior type with a ring of laughing, singing women. If he threatens you with a gun, ask seventeen of your sisters to join you in taking it away from him—gently. But more important, whether you're a man or a woman let the female *within you* encompass the warrior *within you.* Let that soul of yours which is open, receptive, enveloping, envelop that soul of yours which is angry, threatening, thrusting.

7. "In that day shall the Lord [Adonai] be one [Ehad], and His name one" (Zechariah 14:9).

THEREFORE: When you pray and come to "Adonai" in the prayer, either *think* "Ehad" with full kavvanah at the same time you are saying "Adonai," or *say* "Ehad" while you think "Adonai."

8. Rabbi Joshua ben Levi found Elijah the prophet, disguised as a leper, begging at the gates of Rome. "When will you come to proclaim the Mashiah?" he asked. *"'Today, . . . if you will hear his voice,'"* replied Elijah (Talmud Bavli, Sanhedrin 98a).

THEREFORE: Hear his voice. Open yourself to hear it. Practice saying, "Hineni"—"Here I am"—in a sense of total openness.

9. "In the days to come . . . instruction shall come forth from Zion" (Isaiah 2:1–3). Not out of Sinai. "Behold, the days come, saith the Lord, that I will make a new covenant with the house of Israel, . . . not according to the covenant that I made with their fathers in the day that I [led] them out of. . . Egypt. . . . [Instead,] I will put My law [Torah] in their inward parts, and in their hearts will I write it. . . . They shall teach no more every man his neighbor and every man his brother, saying: 'Know the Lord'; for they shall all know Me" (Jeremiah 31:31–34).

THEREFORE: Stop teaching. Listen inward, inward to your own heart, for the new covenant: the covenant of the Torah from Zion. Listen especially for what is new about it.

10. Said a poor tailor one Yom Kippur, "I have committed only minor offenses; but You, O Lord, have committed grievous sins: You have taken away babies from their mothers, and mothers from their babies. Let us be quits: may You forgive me, and I will forgive You." Said Reb Levi Yitzhak of Berditchev to the tailor, "Why did you let Him off so easily? You might have forced Him to redeem all of Israel!"

THEREFORE: Do not let God off so easily. Hear His/Her voice, but challenge His/Her answer. Wrestle mightily; like Yaakov, you may win. *Keep on wrestling!*

NOTE

[Words in brackets appear in the original source document.—Eds.]

Other works by Waskow: *The Limits of Defense* (1962); *Godwrestling* (1978).

LIFE WRITING AND REPORTAGE

Leon Sciaky

1893–1958

Born in Salonika when it was still an Ottoman territory, Leon Sciaky was deeply committed to his hometown. Of Sephardic descent, his family had established themselves there as merchants after the Spanish expulsion, and they continued to speak Ladino at home into the twentieth century. In 1915, in the midst of the turbulence brought about by World War I, Sciaky's family left for the United States and settled in upstate New York, where he worked as a history teacher.

Farewell to Salonica: City at the Crossroads
1946

Our classroom was on the upper floor and in the rear of the building. Its two large windows opened on a garden which, because it could be reached only by crossing M. Shalom's apartment, was forbidden to the children. No one entered it, so that whatever treasure—pocketknife, sling, or cherished agate—was inadvertently dropped from the windows traditionally became the property of the headmaster's younger son, a redheaded boy whom everybody feared and heartily disliked. Surrounded by high walls covered with ivy, with a large sycamore spreading its peeling branches over its long neglected beds, this garden, which no one had taken care of for many years, had become a veritable jungle of weeds and overgrown bushes in which birds nested undisturbed.

To the shrill accompaniment of the cicada on hot summer mornings, under the sleepy supervision of a round-faced, thick-lipped young man, we chanted the "Perek" in unison. Even in its Spanish version, the abstruseness of these aphorisms of old Hebrew philosophers totally defied our comprehension:

. . . muchiguan estudio, muchiguan sabeduria;
muchiguan consejo, muchiguan entendimiento . . .

. . . they increase study, they increase knowledge;
they increase advice, they increase understanding;
they increase kindness, they increase peace;
he acquired a good name, he acquired it for himself;
he acquired for himself the words of the Law,

he acquired for himself life in the world to come.

Word followed word to form sentences, the sentences automatically succeeded each other in their proper order, like so many familiar faces of unknown people marching in a procession. A faint westerly breeze brought through the open windows the tang of the harbor, mingled with all the subtle emanations it had gathered on its journey over the marshy mouth of the Vardar. The eyelids became heavy, and the mind, having nothing to grasp, wandered far from the ink-stained walls and from the rows of ancient desks gouged and carved with the initials of pupils who had preceded us in other years.

Of the three teachers who undertook to unfold the world of knowledge for us, the tall, melancholy Turk with swarthy face who guided our stumbling first steps in that none too easy language soon became my favorite. Selim Effendi could not have been more than in his late twenties when I first knew him, and yet his tobacco-stained, bony fingers trembled as he rolled his cigarettes, or when he sipped his cups of black coffee. His large dreamy brown eyes imparted an unexpected gentleness to his irregular and homely features. The nostrils of his long, hooked nose were like sensitive mirrors which reflected his emotions. They quivered when, from his pulpitlike desk, he quoted the poets:

Bag-i 'alem ichre zahtrda safadir saltanat.
Midst the orchard of the world though empire may appear delight,
Still, if thou wouldst view it closely, empire is but ceaseless fight.
If at times 'tis joy, far oftener empire bringeth dire affright.
Do not envy, do not covet, then, the kingship of the world;
Oh, take heed, Ilhami, empire bides not, swift indeed its flight.

We were all too ignorant of the tongue to appreciate its beauty, but like the old songs of Nona Plata, the rhythm and sounds would enthrall me in a peculiar fascination. They summoned for me strange worlds, worlds in which color and sound blended together to evoke peculiar and stirring emotions.

Selim Effendi soon befriended me and took a special interest in my progress. With infinite patience he taught me the *alif-ba*; with even greater patience he showed me how to sharpen a reed pen, how to cut its tip at the proper angle, how to use just the right amount of ink in the porcelain well loosely stuffed with fiber, and how to hold the paper on my knee.

"Very nicely done, my boy! This page is well written and a pleasure to behold, except for these two lines at the end. It's like a well-dressed man with muddy boots."

Unlike the other teachers, whose emphasis on adherence to rules and stiff class behavior made for dullness and boredom, Selim Effendi brightened school hours by his friendliness and understanding. He had a saying for everything and a ready anecdote to fit all occasions.

"Learn the language well," he would urge. "As the saying goes, 'The tongue has no bones, but it breaks bones.'"

To a boy who had not returned a borrowed pen and who did not have one to do his work, he remonstrated gently: "Do you know the story of Nasr Ed-din Hodja and the *lira*, Halfon?"

"Hayr, Effendi."

"You don't? Then I'll have to tell it to the class." The scratching of the kalems, the reed pens, would cease immediately and we would smile to each other in anticipation.

"Nasr Ed-din Hodja, of whom you have all heard, was once in dire need of money. He had gone to the bazaar and made many foolish purchases, and now his creditors were clamoring for their pay. '*Vallah!*' he said to himself. 'I'll go to the *cadi*, who is a friend of mine, and see if I can borrow a *lira*.' The judge received him kindly, had refreshments served, and after hearing his request, said, 'There, *Hodja*, look under the corner of the mattress on that divan.' Nasr Ed-din lifted the corner of the mattress, found a gold *lira*, and putting it in his bag, departed with many thanks and blessings.

"Many months later, other pressing business found the *hodja* in the same predicament as before, and once more he thought of going to the *cadi* for assistance. Again his friend received him well and entertained him. 'You are welcome to the money,' he said to the *hodja* after hearing of his need. 'What are friends for if they don't extend help? Lift the corner of the mattress of that divan, *Hodja,* and help yourself.' The *hodja* did as he was told. '*Aman, Cadi!*' he said. 'There is nothing under here!' 'Did you put back the *lira* you took out?' the

judge asked. The *hodja* had to admit that he had not. 'How do you expect to find it then?' said the *cadi*."

H. Leivick

1888–1962

Born Leivick Halpern near Minsk, the Yiddish poet and playwright H. Leivick was active in the Bund as a young man; he was exiled to Siberia for life in 1912. He escaped and fled to the United States in 1913. His concern with the struggle for justice and redemption found expression in his poetry and plays, especially in his descriptions of suffering—in the pogroms in Ukraine, in the sweatshops of New York, and in the death camps of the Holocaust. He was among the first American Jewish intellectuals to visit the displaced persons' camps, where he was received as a prophetic figure. His most celebrated work, the verse drama *The Golem* (1921), is still performed.

With the Saving Remnant
1947

With regard to the life and fate of the remaining Jews, located at present in the Occupation Zones of Germany, you hear at every step the words: "*sheyres hapleyte*" [saving remnant], "*sheyres hakhurbn*" [survivors of the destruction/Holocaust], "*di farsholtene daytshe erd*" [the accursed German soil], "*katsetn*" [concentration camps], and "*Erets*" [Land] instead of "*Erets-yisroel*" [Land of Israel]. There are other words created by life and suffering in the Nazi camps. A whole new slang has literally arisen and collecting it is of the greatest interest. Undoubtedly that is already being done and will continue to be done. I, for my part, am interested in several expressions of general Jewish meaning and character.

I hear the aforementioned characterizations so many times, in private conversations and in speeches, that I become confused by them. Confused by the frequency and emphasis with which they are used in the camps.

The abbreviated word *katset*, which means concentration camp, is inflected in the camps into *katsetnik* and *katsetler* [concentration camp inmate]. I have to say at the outset that I am not overly fond of the whole word. It leaves an aftertaste.

Katsetler can perhaps be tolerated, but *katsetnik*, it seems to me, forces the bearer of the name into a permanent inferiority complex.

I am told that the victims themselves chose that name. They adhere to it even now. They do not want to part with it, the way no one wants to part with an honorific title.

In part, this is an act of defiance, a call to the world with all its legitimized titles. But it also represents a sense of being part of an aristocracy of suffering, of pride in martyrdom.

This intention is pleasing to me. I too am filled with pride that the Jewish victim, after being formally liberated, does not wish to return at once to his former prewar attitude toward the world, but prefers to cling, more firmly and for a longer time, to the elevated status of *kidesh-hashem* and *kidesh-ha'am* [martyrdom for the Jewish faith and for the Jewish people].

When a Jew from the camps says of himself: "I am a *katsetnik*," he says it vehemently and with the deep breath of an inveterate smoker inhaling and exhaling tobacco smoke while craving a cigarette.

All of that is true and right.

But it is lacking in *euphony*.

The other expressions created by life in the camps you can accept more willingly. The word *Erets*—of course. If a Jew from the camps says: "I am going to the Land," instead of "Erets-Yisroel," you feel in that abbreviation both warmth and tenderness—I'm going home, in other words. Off I go. What do I care about nations, about borders, about quotas, about England? I'm going home to *Erets* and try and stop me.

But even so it becomes intolerable when you hear the phrase at every step, when it is necessary but also when it is not necessary, and it begins to sound mechanical, like a platitude. But there's nothing to be done. A multitude has put an expression into its mouth (because it has taken it into its heart) and will not allow it to be taken out of its mouth.

And of course the multitude is right.

Translated by Solon Beinfeld.

Other works by Leivick: *In Treblinke bin ikh nit geven* (1945); *Oyf tsarisher katorge* (1959).

Ephraim Lisitzky

1885-1962

Born in Minsk, poet and educator Ephraim Lisitzky immigrated to the United States at the age of fifteen, ultimately moving to New Orleans. There, he became the principal of the city's Hebrew school and settled down to write. Although his works were in Hebrew, Lisitzky drew on standard American literary tropes, writing tragic epics about the decline of Native American life and mélanges of African American folktales and spirituals. Lisitzky was the only American Hebrew poet to complete an autobiography.

In the Grip of Cross-Currents
1949

Chapter IV. [The Hebrew Teacher]

Now that the cup of poison is broken, there is no way out but to drink the cup of sorrows. . . .

My affirmation of life demanded that I should dedicate all the powers of my mind and body to one supreme life goal. This goal was not merely something to provide me with a *raison d'être* but rather to fill my life with a spiritual content that would render it worth while in my eyes. To attain this goal, I must first drain the cup of sorrows. . . .

All my life I have been given to fits of weeping. The wellspring of my tears has always been gushing and free-flowing, inexhaustible. Even so, never had I been so flooded with tears as while draining this cup of sorrows. . . .

Much laborious effort and deep probing went into the search for a suitable life goal, but at last I found it— the vocation of a Hebrew teacher in America.

Actually, I did not have to look for it. It was nothing new, for I was engaged in Hebrew teaching all along. This, however, had been until now in the nature of a temporary occupation, a job to work at while training for a profession that would be free from the insecurity and degradation that marked Hebrew teaching in America. My pharmacist's training now provided me with a comfortable and respectable means of livelihood. More than that, it was now possible for me to realize my heart's desire which had prompted me to choose this profession in the first place—my dream of settling in Erets Yisrael.

The more I read and the more I heard about Erets Yisrael, that new land resurrected from its ruins, the more it rose in my imagination, an ever-present vision of peerless splendor and majesty, by day and by night. And it filled me with a passionate yearning through and through.

Many years were to elapse before I was granted the privilege of making a pilgrimage to the new land of Israel and to behold it with my own eyes. I saw it then in its stark reality, unretouched by the brush of the imagination, in the disenchanting light of reality. But when I left, I felt as if I were departing the Garden of Eden, to go back to a living hell, doomed once more to its tortures.

And yet, notwithstanding the prospect it offered of settling in Erets Yisrael, I gave up pharmacy in favor of Hebrew teaching in America.

I did this not because Hebrew teaching had prospered and gained in prestige, in the meantime. No change for the better had occurred in its lowly condition. I did so only because it promised to provide me with an ultimate goal in life.

In the years I have lived in America, I have witnessed the continuing growth of a flourishing Jewish community, a community destined to exert a decisive influence on the rest of the Jewish Diaspora. No less substantial is bound to be its share in the upbuilding of Erets Yisrael through the contributions of its wealth and energy.

True, this amazing growth has been mainly in the material sense. Yet material growth is not unrelated to spiritual growth. Those same vital forces, so creative in the material sphere, are equally effective in the realm of the spirit, and to foster this creative process is the great mission of Jewish education in this country. A great and difficult task indeed, but wholly within the bounds of possibility.

Whatever the reason for the failure of Jewish education in America, in no way is the Jewish child himself to blame for it. I had ample opportunity to get to know this child well during my years of teaching. He is excellent human material, free from the dross which ghetto life used to deposit in his counterpart across the ocean. What is more, through the public school he comes into possession of an American culture which, potentially, is a blessing for Jewish education, for he is thus better prepared to absorb the best and the highest that Jewish culture has to offer. The great enemy, then, of Jewish education in America is not the make-up of the Jewish child but the utter contempt in which it is held by unworthy parents and teachers. What it needs is inspired and enthusiastic teachers, and above all, a spirit of dedicated pioneering, of *halutsiut* [pioneering spirit]. *Halutsiut*—that is the essential dimension of Hebrew teaching in this country, not unlike the bold vanguard pioneering carried on in Erets Yisrael. Here you might call it rearguard pioneering. I took upon myself this pioneering task, and along with it, its inescapable burdens.

I had not the slightest doubt about my qualification for this type of *halutsiut*, neither on the score of the tenacity nor the power of endurance which it required. These qualities had served me well in my heavy ordeals throughout life. I could not have kept going without them.

If, at first, I did question my qualifications it was on account of my deficiency in another resource which, to my mind, was a *sine qua non*. This resource is spiritual wholeness and a harmonious conception of Judaism.

My mind was broken up into too many separate sovereignties, mutually contradictory and at odds with one another, each claiming exclusive obedience. This multiplicity of sovereignty prevailed also in my conception of Judaism. As a result, my Jewish outlook, too, became subject to conflicts and contradictions.

This is the way I saw it. The basic objective of any teacher is to help his pupils to acquire a spiritual wholeness. A Hebrew teacher must strive to impart, in addition to this spiritual wholeness, a Jewish outlook that is integrated and harmonious. How to go about imparting these two qualities to my pupils when I lacked them myself? Can a teacher inculcate in his pupils something he doesn't have himself? I grappled at length with this doubt as to my qualifications for being a Hebrew teacher. It lingered awhile, but finally it left me.

Chapter V. [A Teacher's Mission]

That doubt left me, having been displaced by another doubt, as soon as its negative proof was established. I first became skeptical about the very possibility of spiritual wholeness in a man of independent spirit, as well as about the possibility of an absolutely integrated conception, at least on the level of a cosmic philosophy. My skepticism soon turned to a firm certainty.

A Hasidic rabbi once put it very well by interpreting this biblical passage: "Why sayest thou, O Jacob, and speakest, O Israel, My path is hid from the Lord?" There should be a pause between "is hid" and "from the Lord," meaning that all the contradictions derive from the Lord Himself.

God made the universe and man the subjects of conflicts and contradictions, and man has presumed to seek various devices to resolve and reconcile them. But all these calculations are fundamentally erroneous and false. For the very concept of "being" implies contradictions, while "not being" means harmony. Reality signifies conflicts; only in nothingness there is unity.

The very act of creation consisted of the creation of conflicts out of harmony, of contradictions out of unity. Man's soul is but one atom among many in the total mass of created beings, and this soul far more than the rest, is invested with a totality of those atoms. In it, as in a mirror, are reflected the individual conflicts and contradictions of all those untold myriads of beings. These then are added to its own, to form its own special amalgam.

To be sure, these conflicts and contradictions are susceptible of harmonious integration. But this integrated whole, inclusive as it is of all the conflicts and contradictions, encompasses their tragic nature as well, the tragedy of an irreparable fundamental split. It is from this tragic element that the *Weltschmerz* is distilled, and the sense of universal beauty flowing from it.

It is not, then, the teacher's mission to impart a spiritual wholeness, nor is it the Jewish teacher's task to impart, along with this spiritual wholeness, an integrated conception of Judaism. The task consists of imparting a sense of that harmonious totality, along with the *Weltschmerz* and the sense of universal beauty—the distillation of conflicts and contradictions.

In choosing Hebrew teaching as my supreme life goal, I decided to combine with it the writing of Hebrew poetry on American soil.

The first steps in my poetic career were hesitant and exploratory, but in the end I hit upon its proper course.

American Hebrew poetry may be compared to a trailing branch of a creeping plant which, as it runs along the ground, puts down its own roots. As a limb it remains attached to the trunk, the trunk's roots supplying it with its main nourishment. But at the same time it draws nourishment from its own roots as well, blending both elements within it. Thus, in fact, the trunk and the branch nurture each other.

American soil is one vast battleground. A new life is being forged on it, out of a clash of elements violently torn from their context and matrix and wrenched from their ordered categories and equations, so that they might be recreated in a new organic form.

There is something sublime in this drama of the struggle of the titans, at once sublime and tragic. One people—the Indians—being extirpated from American soil, its ancient homeland. Another—the Negroes—trampled, pushed around, cast down. And a third—the Jews—struggling to preserve something of its own character in the midst of this new existence. This drama, with its aspect of the sublime and the tragic, holds great promise for American Hebrew poetry and, indeed, for Hebrew poetry in general.

Like Hebrew teaching, Hebrew poetry in America, too, partakes of the nature of pioneering.

I felt myself equally qualified for this kind of pioneering as well. I had come to feel at home in America, gaining an intimate knowledge of the country through the study of its literature and, even more, through the various types of people, Jews and gentiles alike, with whom my rovings brought me together.

Poetic inspiration may come in the midst of an abundance of happiness, yet it is more apt to come amid an abundance of sorrow. As for me, surely mine has been a superabundance of sorrow.

When a heart is broken, strings stretch across its fractures playing a melody notated within that broken heart in fiery musical notes.

I am a man that hath seen pain and affliction, and his heart is broken.

New Orleans, Louisiana

Translated by Moshe Kohn and Jacob Sloan and revised by the author.

Other works by Lisitzky: *Medurot do'akhot* (1937); *Be-oholey kush* (1953); *Bi-yemey shoah u-mesho'ah* (1959).

Judd L. Teller

1912–1972

Yehuda (Judd) Leyb Teller was born in Tarnopol, Galicia, and was brought to New York City in 1921. He studied in Hebrew day schools and then at City College and Columbia University, from which he received a doctorate in psychology. The most prominent of the "American-born" group of Yiddish modernist poets, Teller abandoned his Yiddish literary ambitions and threw his energies into journalism, Zionism, and Jewish communal affairs.

Goyim
1949

When first touched by memory, I found myself already in the midst of [. . .] ominous twilights which came intermittently, in series, and have stayed with me as the keenest memory of childhood.

Our house with its grocery store was usually as open as a circus tent, as if its doors were mere flaps. Customers used to come in by the front door at all hours, from dawn till late in the evening. [. . .]

These awesome twilights, however, would find our house, its doors and shutters bolted, sealed like a clam shell. Inside the shell our family—grandmother, mother (father was in America), my brother and I—huddled around the kitchen stove, backs arched catlike in agonizing anticipation. [. . .]

The *goyim* were on the prowl whenever Tarnapol changed hands in the war waged for its possession. Each time an army retreated, it vented its resentment on the civilian population, particularly the Jews, by plundering, butchering and raping. The incoming army would celebrate its victory in similar fashion. And to fill the vacuum between retreat and entry, the peasants would swirl in from the suburbs. Armed with hatchets and knives, and stimulated by their own hot whiskey breath and collective clamor, they would cause greater damage and more casualties among the Jews than the many months of incessant bombardment that preceded each retreat.

On entering and retreating, the armies always poured past our rambling, bolted house along the precipitous slope. On the mornings of such days one could sense a foreboding restiveness in the air. [. . .]

[. . .] This generally lasted for many hours, followed by an interminable chrysalis; as the last sentries withdrew, we could hear desultory shooting from the direction of the railroad yards, an occasional excoriating outcry from midtown where the Jews lived, and sometimes a light quick chase just outside our windows, a voice shouting "halt," an instant more of light, quick footfalls, a single shot, an outcry and silence. This was the period of greatest danger, when the local *goyim* moved in to fill the vacuum just before the new army took possession. [. . .]

Tall, clean-shaven, immaculate in his vestments, the parish priest would appear in our door, like a visitation, in a cloud of barking, baying and yelping dogs. With a snap of his fingers he would call them off, as frightened I would back into the floursack corner. He looked bemused, standing there, like a disdainful prophet, among his dogs and the Jews; his features small and delicate, and his complexion as white as writing paper which was scarce and expensive in wartime Tarnopol. During the siege, he complained, he had run out of the bread which my mother baked specially for him. He had sent his servant to order more loaves, but when she knocked at the door, there was no answer. So he had

to try just any bread. Oh, Jesus-Maria, what a horrible mixture! This was two days ago and he has been sick since. "What would I have done, poor me, if they had killed you along with the other Jews?" He moved toward me, with appraising mockery in his eyes, and felt my cheeks in the same connoisseur manner in which he felt the loaves before putting them in the basket hanging on his arm. He moved out again in a cloud of yelping dogs, and turned back at the door for a final mocking query. "You will give him to me someday, won't you, before he grows up just another Jew, fattened for the peasants' knives? I could use him, you know, as an incense boy," he would say to my mother. In consequence I would sometimes have dreams in which I sat at his tables, wedged in by my foster brothers, the baying dogs, and suffocating on the *tarfuth* odors from the steaming bowls before him.

One morning we woke up to a topsy-turvy world. Soldiers ran around slapping their officers, instead of saluting. Youngsters in mufti scurried about with rifles dropped by fleeing soldiers. Mother had begun bolting the shutters, when the priest came by. "Stay open," he advised in his habitual mocking tone. "This is the beginning of Polish independence. They'll suspect you're in mourning for the alien ruler, if you shut down now." So we stayed open, but out of sight in the kitchen. A little later, the Christian population appeared in its Sunday's best and a procession with crosses, ikons and flags wound its way down the slope, past our house. The priest was at the head of it, followed by the gentry, their mustaches waxed to a fine point, and by their women wearing long, laced gloves and carrying dainty parasols. Then came the students, rifles dangling from their shoulders, and then the mob roaring the national anthem. All wore red and white little bows in their lapels, the Polish national colors. [. . .]

This was the beginning of a new relationship with *goyim* and of new fears. The ominous twilight sieges had ended but were replaced with something worse. Mother sighed almost with longing for the old days. "So you would stay locked in for several days, then a new army took possession of the city, and you could file complaints with the commandant. But now the danger is everywhere, and at all times, without respite," she would say.

The danger of the twilight sieges was anonymous and shapeless, a mass of noises pouring like a deluge past our bolted doors and windows. But the new danger was identifiable and bore the faces of many of our neighbors. Mother made her purchases at dawn or during the several hours of daylight when the students were at school; Jews kept off the streets in the evening for fear of the prowling students; synagogues were empty for *mincha-maariv* and private *minyanim* of frightened men mushroomed all over the city.

Other works by Teller: *Scapegoat of Revolution* (1954); *The Jews: Biography of a People* (1966); *Strangers and Natives: The Evolution of the American Jew from 1921 to the Present* (1968); *Durkh yidishn gemit* (1975).

Jehiel Isaiah Trunk

1887–1961

Born near Warsaw and descended from a prominent Hasidic family, Jehiel Isaiah Trunk married into one of Poland's richest Jewish families. Despite his inherited wealth and prestige, Trunk was a committed Bundist, and as an essayist, critic, and author himself, he made considerable contributions to the Jewish cultural scene in early twentieth-century Poland. Upon the German invasion of Poland, Trunk and his wife fled, finding their way to New York in 1941. There he began to work on *Poyln*, his seven-volume memoir.

Poland: Memoirs and Scenes
1949

Nighttime at the home of I. L. Peretz, and Shimon (aka Bernard) Kratko appears like a vision. Who masterminded an audience with Peretz, I can't tell you, but it was all that mattered now, as if nothing had gone before:

I defer to the specialist to resolve Kratko's ultimate status for the history of art, but I've never come across an artist's force of personality so compelled to disruption, sheer molten passion enflamed by the muses. He fought to express visions and dimensions in flux beyond the pale, obliterating the monotone of provincial Yiddish writers surrendering soulfully to the hackneyed dictates of reigning culture wars. He ached for a life whose very nucleus was avant-garde, soaring in rapturous communion with the titans of world literature, delighting in his emotive and aesthetic epiphanies. He was a revelation to us all. It's no exaggeration claiming Kratko as the first to pry open our eyes, in every substantive, formal aspect, every transcendent color and idea, to the individual odysseys of visceral art.

What powered this transition next—and cleaved Peretz closer with the disenfranchised—was Kratko's rehabilitative mania for Jewish traditional arts: folk handicrafts and illuminated manuscripts, precious incunabula and discarded threadbare tomes, spartan incidental requisites and prodigious holiday entertainments, communal codexes, totemic designs, parchments, liturgies, token scraps. The artistic sublimity of incomparably wrought Jewish ritual implements reconjured and rescued before our eyes from the anonymity of olden Jewish gold- and silversmiths. Their devotional and ineffable fantasy, these marginalized geniuses gang-pressed and cynically entrusted by desultory patrons to emblazon hosts of "Esteemed art Thou's" over myriad synagogue holy arks. The cherished enraptured mythical beasts, lion, deer, kid-goats, doves, visitations incarnate and imaginative orgy sublimated from the sacrificial servitude of nameless artisans; bequeathing us ravishing frescoes on sanctuary walls, above lecterns, atop eternal lights, and riots of emblematic bouquets bedecking the velvet bodices of Torah scrolls. Kratko moved us to infuse all these eternal motifs into cutting-edge stylized replicas affixed to the bindings and title pages of the newest Yiddish books, culture mobilized for historic departure, rooting Yiddish literature profoundly into the deepest groundswell of ultimate Jewish creation, surpassing national spirit, our iteration of universal scripture.

Peretz simply dazzled, vanquishing new literary ground—the *yesh meayin, creatio ex nihilo*, mystery of his inimitable *Stories in the Folk Vein*, the vertiginous ascent of the daring dramas, constancy in ferment sworn to restore leadership to the despised strata, primacy to the healing ethos of Jewish folk empathy. Peretz was emotionally called to personify national liberation. He, the omnipotent subversive, consequences be damned, impresario of Kratko's crusade to revamp Yiddish Letters and Return All Glory to Israel.

But for Kratko, to breathe life into this radical enterprise, he first had to introduce Peretz to his wife, Tocia.

Tocia was scion of the acknowledged Hasidic "stars" of Poland, the Mlawa Alters and Kutno Lipskis, garnering her, in one fell swoop, melding family from both ethereal Aleksander, and high-strung corporeal Ger, Hasidic stock. [. . .] Tocia's parents were by any measure exemplary Alter and Lipski archetypes. The cocktail they poured, however, was of the most eccentric and irreconcilable bloodlines. The mélange catalyzed mingling Alter blood was too idiosyncratic to fathom, yet preternaturally inevitable. I was not personally favored gauging Tocia's mother's impact in the looks department, but Mendl, Tocia's father, was temperamentally and bodily of such virile specimen, only a classical pagan sculptor would have risked liberating this breathless masculine perfection into the world. He was clearly the prototype for an approximation of the gods. The Greek would have chiseled him into the penultimate mold for Apollo, and the Semite—a warrior-god mounting the sun chariot. He projected both the menacing majesty of Assyrian monolith bas-reliefs and the spellbinding harmonious idealization the ancient Greeks coveted into convention. [...]

Tocia's father was a businessman and Ger Hasid to his core. Everyone looked to the Alter–Lipski merger to maximize a speculative, scandalous return, with three daughters developing under his roof daily confronting his suspicious mien. It stands to reason, prey also to the relentless battering of his maddening beauty, the girls would plunge headlong into the misadventures of artistic pursuit. Only Sureh, the eldest, was entrapped salvaging a Hasidic match for Mendl Lipski. Yet the wild bride's dream was to be a painter, and starved for escapade, she decamped to Paris on her wedding night, feeling like a fish in water among the artist bohemians. Never even dropped a line home. The younger, Liebe, was all set to be a ballerina. Tocia's purpose in life was to become an actress. [...]

Shimon Kratko was a young man on intimate terms with the run of the Warsaw slums. He'd early been offered up to a tradesman as an apprentice. As with so many authentically gifted souls, he refined his rebellious aesthetic alchemizing the lowly matter to which he'd been enslaved. His explosive energy was torridly expended sketching, carving, chiseling, pasting collages, the fantasized workshop of a painter's and sculptor's ideal life. He eked out free time traversing Warsaw's museums, cathedrals, synagogues, ad nauseam, visualizing himself a genus of master responsible for these creations. After meditating interminably upon the ritual objects of Jewish prayer houses, ruminating on the murals, reliefs, alternate realities suppressed inside the arks and raiments, he committed obsessively to ground his convictions in Eretz Israel. Only in the original sacrosanct homeland of Jewish antiquity could he—so he believed—live out the inexhaustible source of experience, themes, inspiration conditional to his growth as a Jewish master. At this very time, the Beza-

lel Art Academy opened its doors in Jerusalem, and Kratko felt destined to attend.

How Tocia, of gossamer refined privilege, joined forces with the elemental and impoverished Kratko, is beyond me. But a poor young novice living on the skids in Warsaw, reinventing the magnificence and wellspring glories of the ancient Jewish Levant, was a copy of Tocia's fictive heartthrob, the despoiled scheming prince at wit's end reclaiming a cornucopia of treasures from an imaginary kingdom. Kratko must also have happened upon her the instant she swore allegiance to some similar lofty pageant, inhabiting the role she pined for—her dangerous and heroic protector and confidante, playing out this improbable, self-fulfilling Romance. I had to question Tocia's real ability to express genuine love for Kratko. Tocia's true feelings were infinitely diluted by theatrical graces and wishfulness. She acted out every given moment. Her pantomime of the immortal love affair was nonpareil, she chilled as the mendacious temptress, stirred as the insatiable consort, all in the grand manner. And it would surprise me if, or how often, Tocia ever felt the freedom of real amour, even carnal satiation. She was most adept at smoke and mirrors. The alibi of a life mediated and transpired for staging. Had Tocia known to separate reality from illusion, and sustain alertness in her flights of fancy—she surely would have evolved into an accomplished stage actress. She looked to have been endowed with all the obligatory talents. As it was, she remained reluctant to draw any fine distinctions. She mired herself in make-believe, and squandered her potential and her life helplessly. What she ultimately achieved was of negligible lasting or personal value, buffeted always by favor, misfortune, and reprieve. [...]

When Tocia met Shimon Kratko, she was barely sixteen. Yet her barrage of ferocious exaltation and pathetic love, like Juliet's ecstatic quest for her Romeo, rattled Mendl Lipski to the bone. He was forced to exert counter-pressure. Who in the world could expect him to settle on a pauper for a son-in-law, on top of which, one festering without prospect like the bankrupt market of the visual arts?! But Mendl Lipsky fell victim to the treacherous paradox of his obtuse gender—the firmer his opposition, the more primal and elaborate the spoils gallant Tocia trotted out from her scripted proscenium. Romeo and Juliet were devoured by subterranean demiurges. Incontestable love was proclaimed under the stars of heaven and to the radiance of the moon. Shimon Kratko steeled himself for the voyage to Eretz

Israel with unworldly defiance. Tocia made him vow to rescue her from her father's house. By intrepid resolve, she eloped to The Holy City with him and they erected their wedding canopy inside the hulk of the Ruined Synagogue of Rabbi Judah the Pious. [. . .]

After their two years in Jerusalem, Shimon Kratko brought Peretz and Tocia together, a spectacle could not have been dreamt of before. Suspicions led to a re-incarnated-being haunting Peretz's home—maybe Sore bas Toyvim, the folk tribune, or was it our Matriarch Rachel Kratko resurrected from her Tomb at the approaches to Bethlehem. The wisp of a girl was wrapped like a mummy with pure vintage relics—holy vestments from Eretz Israel. Bound with reams of Turkish shawls. Underneath the canary-lime frock was a glimpse, by consensus, of a Rebbe's nightgown, or the flyaway skirt of a Whirling Dervish. Her hair weaved extravagantly with loud colored rags and tatters, pierced and pinned with obsolete bobbing curlers, Arabian talismans, and everyday baubles of lucky amber, an assortment of oriental stones and costume bijouterie. Her ears, jangling the siren song of ossified harpies, festooned with hanging turgid green crystals set into faded gold leaf. She was amply, from a mortal's perspective, almost alarmingly, immunized from harm, clipped with a potpourri of fetishes, dangling amulets and charms, mother-of-pearl vials of spices and brews, brooches and lockets, the entire inventory issue of Eretz Israel and its genetic progeny. When she raised her unusually petite hand, fingers run amok clinched and clasped by bracelets and rings redolent of labyrinthine bazaars and ersatz museums, we all witnessed the illusion of a floating Torah pointer come to life, gesticulating over Peretz's table and directing us, each in the allotted order, to a portion of the Weekly Reading.

Shimon Kratko was possessed by this delicate eccentric woman. His scattered works fixated on her powerful eyes, which trailed you from exhibits, graveyards, façade friezes, and the plethora of his illustrated Yiddish book proposals, drafts and projects—everywhere in mood and traits, her face overpowered the subject. Her portrait in every available style and manner. Incredibly, he never substituted another model when posing her. He exposed a naturally recurring dichotomy: Tocia's bust mutating, half Mary Magdalene, half rabbi's consort. He also tinkered with collages of her nude, and invited us up to his atelier to examine Tocia in her anomalous nakedness. But instead, she reclined, a vulnerable tender body in breathless anticipation, remi-

niscent both of Michelangelo's *Pieta* in abandon and, in the pulsing languid line, some chivalric porcelain comfort figurine, surfeited with the balms of the Song of Songs.

Translated by Gabriel Trunk.

Other works by Trunk: *Idealizm un naturalizm in der yidisher literatur* (1927); *Sholem Aleykhem: zayn vezn un zayne verk* (1937); *Der freylekhster yid in der velt: oder, Hersheles lern-yorn* (1953).

Anzia Yezierska

1885–1970

The American novelist and short-story writer Anzia Yezierska was born in Poland and came to New York in 1898. Her stories reflect the dislocations of immigration, the grinding poverty of teeming immigrant quarters, and the clash of values and aspirations between parents and children. Her talent was recognized early in her career with the publication of her book of short stories, *Hungry Hearts* (1920), which was turned into a movie. Feminist critics rediscovered Yezierska's work in the 1970s and celebrated her for her portrayal of young women struggling to escape immigrant poverty, oppressive social norms, and restrictive religious practices.

Red Ribbon on a White Horse
1950

All Whom I Ever Loved

The sunset lit up the sky, splashing the drab tenements with gold, bringing memories of Sabbath candles and the smell of *gefüllte* fish. When I had lived on Hester Street, I would stop at the pushcart of Zalmon Shlomoh, the hunchbacked fish peddler, to buy his leftover fish for the Sabbath.

"How goes your luck today?" I used to ask him. "Except for health and a living, I'm perfectly fine." He always made the same joke as he wiped his hands on his sweater gleaming with the scales of the fish. His broad, bony cheeks, the deformed curve of his back, and his knotted arthritic hands made him a gnome, a grotesque. But his eyes were alive with the radiance of our secret code. Except for health and a living, we were both perfectly fine.

One day he flashed me a look of bold intimacy. "*Und* how goes it with you? With your red hair, you must be always on fire!"

Startled, I returned his look. All at once the hunch-back became a man in my eyes. It had been a long time since I had felt so free with any one. I reached out and touched his arm in responsive gaiety.

"I'm like a sinner in the next world, thrown from one hell into another."

"But you wouldn't be happy except in hell," Zalmon laughed back, exposing the black cavities of his yellow teeth.

That was all I needed to let loose my obsession. "If you want to know what hell is, I'll tell you. Hell is trying to do what you can't do, trying to be what you're not——"

"Nu? So what are you trying to be that you're not?" he bantered.

"It wills itself in me to be a writer——"

"A writer?" He gave me a long, sparkling glance. "A young girl like you! For what do you need yet to write?"

"*Oi weh!* I don't know myself." I sighed as he wrapped the fish in a newspaper and there was no longer any reason to linger at the pushcart. "Time is flying. I can't bear to be left out of life an old maid. Tell me, why do I have to write? When will I live?"

In Zalmon Shlomoh's eyes was such a naked look of comprehension that it silenced me. Unmindful of the hurrying crowd, the shrill cries of the hucksters and the housewives pushing past us with their market baskets, we stood looking at each other. We belonged to the shadowy company of those who were withdrawn from their fellows by grief, illness, or the torment of frustration.

Zalmon turned away and scolded with mock impatience. "You ask more questions in a minute than all the wise men can answer in a lifetime."

Other works by Yezierska: *All I Could Never Be* (1932).

Alfred Kazin

1915–1998

Literary critic and memoirist Alfred Kazin was born in New York City and studied at City College and Columbia University. He achieved fame with his first book, *On Native Grounds* (1942), a critical study of American prose literature from Ernest Hemingway to Willa Cather, and he later became literary editor of the *New Republic*. His essays and reviews were published in *The New Yorker* and the *New York Review of Books*.

Kazin recorded his Brooklyn childhood and literary career in the memoirs *A Walker in the City* (1951) and *New York Jew* (1978).

The Kitchen
1951

In Brownsville tenements the kitchen is always the largest room and the center of the household. As a child I felt that we lived in a kitchen to which four other rooms were annexed. My mother, a "home" dressmaker, had her workshop in the kitchen. She told me once that she had begun dressmaking in Poland at thirteen; as far back as I can remember, she was always making dresses for the local women. She had an innate sense of design, a quick eye for all the subtleties in the latest fashions, even when she despised them, and great boldness. For three or four dollars she would study the fashion magazines with a customer, go with the customer to the remnants store on Belmont Avenue to pick out the material, argue the owner down—all remnants stores, for some reason, were supposed to be shady, as if the owners dealt in stolen goods—and then for days would patiently fit and baste and sew and fit again. Our apartment was always full of women in their housedresses sitting around the kitchen table waiting for a fitting. My little bedroom next to the kitchen was the fitting room. The sewing machine, an old nut-brown Singer with golden scrolls painted along the black arm and engraved along the two tiers of little drawers massed with needles and thread on each side of the treadle, stood next to the window and the great coal-black stove which up to my last year in college was our main source of heat. By December the two outer bedrooms were closed off, and used to chill bottles of milk and cream, cold borscht and jellied calves' feet.

The kitchen held our lives together. My mother worked in it all day long, we ate in it almost all meals except the Passover *seder*, I did my homework and first writing at the kitchen table, and in winter I often had a bed made up for me on three kitchen chairs near the stove. On the wall just over the table hung a long horizontal mirror that sloped to a ship's prow at each end and was lined in cherry wood. It took up the whole wall, and drew every object in the kitchen to itself. The walls were a fiercely stippled whitewash, so often rewhitened by my father in slack seasons that the paint looked as if it had been squeezed and cracked into the walls. A large electric bulb hung down the center of the kitchen at the end of a chain that had been hooked into the ceiling; the old gas ring and key still jutted out of the wall like ant-lers. In the corner next to the toilet was the sink at which we washed, and the square tub in which my mother did our clothes. Above it, tacked to the shelf on which were pleasantly ranged square, blue-bordered white sugar and spice jars, hung calendars from the Public National Bank on Pitkin Avenue and the Minsker Progressive Branch of the Workman's Circle; receipts for the pay-ment of insurance premiums, and household bills on a spindle; two little boxes engraved with Hebrew letters. One of these was for the poor, the other to buy back the Land of Israel. Each spring a bearded little man would suddenly appear in our kitchen, salute us with a hurried Hebrew blessing, empty the boxes (sometimes with a sidelong look of disdain if they were not full), hurriedly bless us again for remembering our less fortunate Jewish brothers and sisters, and so take his departure until the next spring, after vainly trying to persuade my mother to take still another box. We did occasionally remember to drop coins in the boxes, but this was usually only on the dreaded morning of "midterms" and final exami-nations, because my mother thought it would bring me luck. She was extremely superstitious, but embarrassed about it, and always laughed at herself whenever, on the morning of an examination, she counseled me to leave the house on my right foot. "I know it's silly," her smile seemed to say, "but what harm can it do? It may calm God down."

The kitchen gave a special character to our lives; my mother's character. All my memories of that kitchen are dominated by the nearness of my mother sitting all day long at her sewing machine, by the clacking of the treadle against the linoleum floor, by the patient twist of her right shoulder as she automatically pushed at the wheel with one hand or lifted the foot to free the needle where it had got stuck in a thick piece of material. The kitchen was her life. Year by year, as I began to take in her fantastic capacity for labor and her anxious zeal, I realized it was ourselves she kept stitched together. I can never remember a time when she was not work-ing. She worked because the law of her life was work, work and anxiety; she worked because she would have found life meaningless without work. She read almost no English; she could read the Yiddish paper, but never felt she had time to. We were always talking of a time when I would teach her how to read, but somehow there was never time. When I awoke in the morning she was already at her machine, or in the great morning crowd of housewives at the grocery getting fresh rolls

for breakfast. When I returned from school she was at her machine, or conferring over McCall's with some neighborhood woman who had come in pointing hope-fully to an illustration—"Mrs. Kazin! Mrs. Kazin! Make me a dress like it shows here in the picture!" When my father came home from work she had somehow mysteri-ously interrupted herself to make supper for us, and the dishes cleared and washed, was back at her machine. When I went to bed at night, often she was still there, pounding away at the treadle, hunched over the wheel, her hands steering a piece of gauze under the needle with a finesse that always contrasted sharply with her swollen hands and broken nails. Her left hand had been pierced through when as a girl she had worked in the infamous Triangle Shirtwaist Factory on the East Side. A needle had gone straight through the palm, severing a large vein. They had sewn it up for her so clumsily that a tuft of flesh always lay folded over the palm.

The kitchen was the great machine that set our lives running; it whirred down a little only on Saturdays and holy days. From my mother's kitchen I gained my first picture of life as a white, overheated, starkly lit workshop redolent with Jewish cooking, crowded with women in housedresses, strewn with fashion maga-zines, patterns, dress material, spools of thread—and at whose center, so lashed to her machine that bolts of energy seemed to dance out of her hands and feet as she worked, my mother stamped the treadle hard against the floor, hard, hard, and silently, grimly at war, beat out the first rhythm of the world for me.

Other works by Kazin: *The Inmost Leaf* (1955); *Contemporaries* (1962); *Bright Book of Life* (1973); *An American Procession* (1984).

David de Sola Pool

1885–1970

London-born David de Sola Pool was a rabbi, civic leader, and scholar who came from a distinguished Sephardic family. He pursued both secular and rab-binic studies, first in London and then in Heidelberg and Berlin. In 1907, he moved to New York to serve as assistant rabbi at Congregation Shearith Israel, eventu-ally becoming senior rabbi and working there until his retirement in 1956. In addition to his synagogue activi-ties, he did much to support Sephardic communities in the United States and to serve American Jewry more broadly, leading the Synagogue Council of America from 1938 to 1940.

My Spiritual Autobiography
1953

With the passing of childhood and the waning of the impatient eagerness of adolescence, I was rapidly realizing that this was neither the best of all possible worlds, nor one that the optimism of late nineteenth century Victorian England would soon bring to a glorious climax of Messianic fulfilment. Fifty years ago, both the first Zionist Congress and the first meeting of the Socialist International were held. Then in editorial comment the *London Times* told both the Jews and the poor not to be concerned with the unrealistic visions of these congresses, as both antisemitism and poverty would soon disappear from the world. But it increasingly seemed to me that Jews and the poor were suffering too organically and too grievously for such bland optimism to be acceptable. I was finding in our manmade world all too many generally accepted limitations on the application of justice and love, though the centuried traditions of the Judaism that I was learning to know demanded them for both Jew and Gentile, for poor and rich alike. I felt that all over the world the Kishinevs where unhappy men lived must be saved from the vileness of further outrages. This could come about not through protest meetings, nor even through Socialism, though the applied social justice of Fabian Socialism appealed very strongly to me, but only through men everywhere learning and living the religious teachings of their Jewish victims. A Jewish mob howling for blood was unthinkable. It seemed to me that the world's primary need was the religion I was studying. More and more the conviction strengthened itself within me that my chosen life work must be to teach that religion. By making it better known to my own Jewish people, I would thereby also help make it known to a world that so sorely needed its healing balm.

One day an uncle, very much a man of the world, speaking to me about my studying for the rabbinate, said, "You don't want to go into all that nonsense; you should study for the Indian Civil Service." But his counsel came too late; I was then set and determined on the religious path I wished to follow. Kipling's call to assume the white man's burden no longer appealed to me.

One of the religious leaders of the London Jewish community also might have swerved me from the call I felt. In conversation with my parents he said in my presence, "What do you want for him? Do you want him to have all the heartbreaks I have known? Let him follow the suggestion that has come to you from Dr. Mendes in New York that he go to the United States." What sank deeply into my consciousness from his words was not his implication of ampler perspectives in the rabbinate in America, but his depreciation of the rabbinate in England. At the time I had little concept of the wider vistas before the rabbi in the United States. Not uncontentedly I saw before me the prospect of becoming the preacher-reader-teacher-pastor of the Anglo-Jewish ministry of the time, and this rabbi's words were deeply discouraging to me. But the sense of call persisted and triumphed over these and other discouragements. For the challenges which life presented to my adolescent questionings, and the special problems and sufferings of my Jewish people, had convinced me that no service which I could give would be more fruitful than that of a religious ministry.

Other works by de Sola Pool: *The Kaddish* (1909); *Portraits Etched in Stone: Early Jewish Settlers, 1682–1831* (1953); *Why I Am A Jew* (1957).

Ben Hecht
1894-1964

Screenwriter Ben Hecht was born in New York City and grew up in Racine, Wisconsin. Often uncredited, Hecht helped write some of the classics of American film including *The Front Page* (1931), *Some Like It Hot* (1939), *Gone with the Wind* (1939), and *His Girl Friday* (1940). His screenplay for *Underworld* (1927) received the award for best original story at the first Academy Awards in 1929. In addition to his work as a journalist, director, playwright, and novelist, Hecht was active in bringing the plight of European Jewry to the attention of the American public in the 1930s and 1940s and was a member of the so-called Bergson Group. His fundraising for the establishment of the State of Israel resulted in his being blacklisted by the British film industry.

A Child of the Century
1954

The *Readers Digest Magazine* broke the American silence attending the massacre of the Jews in February, 1943. It printed my article called "Remember Us," based on Dr. [Hayim] Greenberg's data. Reading it in the magazine, I thought of a larger idea and set out to test its practicality. [. . .]

It was a pageant about the Jews to be called "We Will Never Die" and it would be put on in Madison Square Garden as a "Memorial to the Two Million Jewish Dead of Europe." [. . .]

The pageant opened with a prayer spoken by a rabbi, in holiday canonicals. I read the prayer to them.

"Almighty God, Father of the poor and the weak, Hope of all who dream of goodness and justice; Almighty God who favored the children of Israel with His light—we are here to affirm that this light still shines in us.

"We are here to say our prayers for the two million who have been killed in Europe, because they bear the name of your first children—the Jews.

"Before our eyes has appeared the strange and awesome picture of a folk being put to death, of a great and ancient people in whose veins have lingered for so long the earliest words and image of God, dying like a single child on a single bayonet.

"We are not here to weep for them, although our eyes are stricken with this picture and our hearts burdened with their fate.

"We are here to honor them and to proclaim the victory of their dying.

"For in our Testament are written the words of Habakkuk, Prophet of Israel, 'They shall never die.'

"They shall never die though they were slaughtered with no weapon in their hand.

"Though they fill the dark land of Europe with the smoke of their massacre, they shall never die.

"For they are part of something greater, higher and stronger than the dreams of their executioners.

"Dishonored and removed from the face of the earth, their cry of Sh'ma Israel remains in the world.

"We are here to strengthen our hearts, to take into our veins the pride and courage of the millions of innocent people who have fallen and are still to fall before the German massacre.

"They were unarmed. But not we!

"We live in a land whose arm is stronger than the arm of the German Goliath. This land is our David.

"Almighty God, we are here to affirm that our hearts will be a monument worthy of our dead.

"We are here to affirm that the innocence of their lives and the dream of goodness in their souls are witnesses that will never be silent. They shall never die."

I read on for an hour. No words I had ever written had ever been received with such love as beamed on me now. When the reading was done, there was a great deal of nose blowing and tear drying. [. . .]

"We Will Never Die" played two performances in its one night in Madison Square Garden. Some forty thousand people squeezed in to witness it. Another twenty thousand crowded the streets outside and listened to the performance and Kurt Weill's great music piped over loud-speakers.

A few weeks later, the pageant played Washington, Philadelphia, Boston, Chicago, St. Louis and Los Angeles. Our victory was more than weeping and cheering audiences. The news and pictures of our pageant in the press were the first American newspaper reports on the Jewish massacre in Europe.

Other works by Hecht: *Erik Dorn* (1921); *A Thousand and One Afternoons in Chicago* (1922); *Perfidy* (1961).

Reuven Iceland
1884–1955

As a founding member of the modernist group Di Yunge (with poets Mani Leib, H. Leivick, and Moshe Leib Halpern), Reuven Iceland was a core member of New York's early twentieth-century Yiddish literary scene. Like many of his associates, Iceland had immigrated to New York from Galicia, in his case in 1901, leaving behind a traditional Hasidic life for the promises of secularism and poetry. In New York, he found dispiriting working conditions and bleak housing but also kindred spirits—other poets who sought to make art into survival. In 1919, Iceland began an affair with fellow poet Anna Margolin; the couple remained together until her death in 1952.

At Goodman and Levine's
1954

There were two reasons why *Di Yunge* chose to carry on by themselves in a separate cafe. One was purely financial. The coffeehouse on Division Street was too dear for young writers, most of whom either were poor workers in a factory or had no job whatever. To spend these hours at Sholom's they would need at least a quarter in their pocket and—in those days, for these young men—this was a sizable sum. [. . .] The other reason was snobbish. Our spokesmen simply felt that it was beneath us to pass the time in the same cafe as our elders.

There was a bit of immaturity in this snobbish exclusiveness. Nonetheless, it also expressed a healthy instinct. *Di Yunge* had found something that was new and personal and they felt that, for this to survive, they must isolate themselves from the old and established writers. It was therefore forbidden to have any dealings with the papers and magazines in which the others printed their things. [. . .] To avoid dependence on the newspapers, we began to print our own journals and anthologies. Not to be under one roof with the older writers, we isolated ourselves in a separate cafe. [. . .]

I have already mentioned that in those days the majority of the young writers were shop workers. To miss a day's pay often meant not to have money to buy a pair of shoes for your child or be short three dollars toward the rent. Nonetheless, whenever you came into the cellar, you would find a crowd of people who, as you knew, were supposed to be in the shop. Several of *Di Yunge* were paperhangers and painters, and it wasn't unusual for them to get off the ladders in the middle of a job and come into the cafe in spattered work clothes which had once been white and with streaks of color on their face and hands. For a long time I used to have my lunch in the shop, fearful that if I went down to a restaurant I would not have the strength of will to complete the day's work.

Once on a Saturday in summer, when I worked only half a day, I came home and, after having my lunch, went to a barber to be shaved. In the evening, I was going to take my wife and six-month-old daughter to see one of our relations. I lived on Fourth Street, close to Avenue B; the barbershop was somewhere on Houston. In the chair, however, I suddenly felt the call of the cafe and was hardly able to wait for the barber to finish my shave.

It did enter my mind that it might be sensible to go home first and say where I was going. But my feet already were turning toward East Broadway. The day being hot, I expected to find only a couple of my colleagues in the cafe. For this reason, if no other, I would probably stay only an hour or two. It turned out, however, that the cellar was full. Out of a sea of faces and the clouds of smoke, there began to emerge the image of Mani Leib—a finger rocking in front of his nose like a pointer—his green, visionary eyes squinting at the homely, freckled, yet vital and insolent face of Moishe Leib Halpern.

I no longer remember what subject they were so passionate about at the time I came in. All I know is that in a moment I was in the midst of it myself. And it continued to boil—an hour, two, three. From one topic we would leap into a second, from a second to a third. Soon we were back at the first, each trying to prove a point with a quotation from an essay or a poem. In the same fashion, others tried to prove the opposite and for this purpose were also able to find crushing statements from a different authority. [. . .] Hours flew. Night fell: no one noticed. Half the crowd had vanished; yet we, the other half, continued to sit there. The sweat kept pouring: yet we sat—talking. Goodman, at the buffet, sent sharp and contemptuous glances. Not seeing him or his eyes, we continued the discussion. Finally, Goodman exclaimed, "Even in Hell there is a time when they rest. Go in good health!" But it sounded like—Go to the devil! [. . .]

At long last, the group started to get smaller, till only two of us were left, Mani Leib and I. It wasn't far from my house but he lived in Brooklyn and began to feel gloomy about having to go back, so he asked me to walk him as far as Delancey Street, where he would take the trolley that would bring him home. On Delancey, he decided to walk me back to my house. Then, in the middle of this, we turned again on Delancey.

Our literary conversation had run down. It was just before sunrise, yet we now had reached the haunting wistfulness of sunset. We began to speak about the workday week, about the hardship of that life, about the fretting and yearning that fills the nights at home, and how all this, these long and boring talks, are at bottom no more than an escape, an attempt to hush the yearnings in oneself. He told me that when he comes home late at night he gets into his apartment not by way of the door, but climbs up to the roof and from there moves down the fire escape to a window in his flat, and that he creeps into his house like a thief—so his wife shouldn't hear him; and that, once, he happened to get lost and opened the window of a neighbor, an Italian, and how the other, thinking he was a thief, attacked him with a knife.

When Mani Leib finally got on the streetcar, the sun had already risen on the Brooklyn side of the East River. Only now did I realize that I'd stayed away the whole night, that I had not told my wife I might be delayed, and that we were supposed to visit a relation. It was with a troubled heart that I began approaching Fourth Street. When I came to the building in which I lived, the grocery downstairs was already open and the grocer, standing by the door, looked at me severely and said, "Young man, wasn't it your wife who ran to the police to look for you?"

Translated by Nathan Halper.

Other works by Iceland: *Fun mayn zumer* (1922); *Dos gezang fun Hirsh* (1944); *From Our Springtime: Literary Memoirs and Portraits of Yiddish New York* (1954).

Howard Fast

1914–2003

Born in New York, Howard Fast was a prolific novelist and scriptwriter who often depicted historical struggles for rights and freedoms, including those of Native Americans and African Americans. In the 1950s, Fast joined the Communist Party USA and was imprisoned for three months for his refusal to provide the House Un-American Activities Committee with names of his colleagues. Blacklisted throughout the decade, Fast began writing under pseudonyms including Behn Boruch and E. V. Cunningham, the latter of which he continued to use into the 1980s. In 1960, Dalton Trumbo wrote the screenplay for *Spartacus* as an adaptation of Fast's 1951 novel of the same title.

The Naked God: The Writer and the Communist Party
1957

I asked about a certain Russian poet. All good writers are poets to one extent or another, but that is a way of saying something. It is something else and clearer, to say that the poet is a very special sort of writer; and when the poet is a great poet, his songs come as close to probing the meaning of human existence and human destiny as any human effort can. This poet I refer to was Itzik Feffer. It happened that some of us here in America knew him personally, for early during the war he came here on a good-will mission and he won our hearts. A tall, handsome man, wearing the uniform of a colonel in the Red Army, he appeared to be a symbol of what the Soviet Union had pledged in the way of wiping anti-Semitism out of Russia; for Feffer was a Jew, a beloved poet in the Soviet Union, an army officer, and a man who in every word he spoke breathed the love of his fatherland.

How then that the rumor came to us, a good while before the Twentieth Congress of the Bolshevik Party, that he was dead, and that he had died strangely? We didn't know. I asked and others asked,

"Where is Itzik Feffer and how did he die?"

A hundred times that question was asked and left unanswered, and we who asked it were looked at as fools because we could not understand the political subtleties of the murder of poets. I asked it of a *Pravda* correspondent, only a few days before I finally broke with the Party—but I was an unwelcome guest now in the beautiful building on Park Avenue, for I had already spoken my first angry criticism in the pages of the *Daily Worker* and the Communist cultural magazine, *Mainstream*. As the diplomatic reception eddied around us, this man from *Pravda*, talking with the voice of "socialism" and "brotherhood," said to me angrily, in English, which he spoke very well,

"Howard, why do you make so much of the Jews? Jews? Jews? That is all we hear from you! Do you think Stalin murdered no one but Jews?" [. . .]

Before Bergelson died, Itzik Feffer learned where he was and what was happening to him; and being a friend of his, Feffer set out to try to save him. Writer after writer refused to join with Feffer. They were afraid. They told Feffer that if he persisted he would be arrested. Feffer pleaded with Ehrenburg, and the story goes that Ehrenburg refused. Ehrenburg stood high and well with Stalin. The story also goes that Feffer cried out to Ehrenburg:

"Then I'll do it alone—and when they arrest me and kill me, my death will be upon your soul for as long as you live!"

As it was. Thus, because he was driven by his human conscience, Feffer perished with Bergelson. Where then was Fadeyev, who shot himself after the Twentieth Congress? Where was Polovoy, whom I loved and respected as I have loved and respected few men? Where was Simonov? Where was Sholokhov? Where were all of these who had lectured the world upon the honor and integrity of humankind—these "socialist" men? Where were the preachers and righteous ones of the *Literary Gazette*? Where were those Soviet writers of honor who called America a land of barbarians without a heritage or a culture?

Yes, we killed Sacco and Vanzetti, but our own cry went out to haunt the world. Was my own voice ever silent concerning injustice in my own land? In the name of all that is holy to you, my Russian colleagues, where were your voices when murder walked in your land? And today, the question of the poet remains unanswered.

In writing this, I am not shedding guilt. I take no refuge in the fact that I made my voice heard against injustice here. Joseph Clark, the foreign editor of the *Daily Worker* then, and before that Russian correspondent for the *Daily Worker*, sat in my living room in January of 1957 and cried out to me, in a tortured voice that only disguised his own heartsickness and guilt,

"If you and Paul Robeson had raised your voices in 1949, Itzik Feffer would be alive today!"

Nor had I the spirit to claim that I did not know in 1949—even as one outside of Russia had then known that Feffer stood before the firing squad. For in a sense Clark was right in his accusation. But it is not with this failure to know, to believe, that my Russian colleagues charge me; not at all. They claim that I have betrayed them because I cannot remain silent.

Oh, lightly enough did we become writers in the beginning. We loved the sound of a story and the music of words, and we loved the books that we dreamed of making. There was no one to tell us that the desire would turn into a passion and the passion into a curse; and that eventually our obligation would be at odds with the whole world. Some of us learned, but with awful pain; for wherever we stood, we came to know that sooner or later we must break the image—for we had singled ourselves out to be enemies of obedience. It becomes a reversal of the old Faustian legend, for unless we spit in the face of the devil, in whatsoever form he be, we end with the barter of our souls.

I set out here in this section of what I write to make a few comments on the writer as he stands today in society, the Communist Party on his left, the fleshpots of well-paid mediocrity on his right; but I make no judgments. I am past that, as regards my colleagues in this profession. I can only tell what happened and why I as a writer could exist no longer in the Communist movement. I no longer enjoy the practice of my craft; it is full of pain and too many memories, but it is all I know; and I don't ask that anyone should weep for writers. Ours is an old and once honorable craft, and perhaps someday it will be that again.

But I cannot love the Party for what it did to us—and not the worst was to the dead. The living were also naked. I am alive. Boris Polovoy is alive. We were comrades in a movement that I believed with all my heart and soul—he the head of the Union of Soviet Writers, myself a Communist writer in America. We came to know each other by correspondence, and through our letters a love and warmth and mutual respect grew and

flowered. When finally I met him in New York, where he had come as the leader of a delegation of Soviet writers, I embraced him as a beloved and old companion. He was big, warm, open, his smile a thing of joy to see as my wife and I dragged him home with us. "No fear?" he wanted to know. "My coming to your home?" But how could fear exist when the two of us were together? We had rich lives to share; we had lived and seen and ventured a thing or two, and we were knit beyond politics, beyond continents, in that fine brotherhood of our craft. What an evening that was—of warmth and closeness and drink and food and fellowship!

We saw him again the following day, my wife and I, at a party given for himself and his comrades. Again the warmth, closeness and openness. Here were a round dozen of us, Russian and American, and our feeling was, "May the devil take politics and politicians too. We are together—may all the people of both our nations come to know each other, openly and in good friendship."

During the course of that evening I happened to be in a little group that was talking to Boris Polovoy. The conversation concerned Russian writers and what they were currently doing, and since Polovoy spoke no English, the translation was provided by an old friend of mine, a brilliant student of Slavic languages whose Russian was perfect. The faultlessness of his Russian was important, for I have since checked and rechecked this story as to accuracy. Someone asked Polovoy whether he couldn't provide us with some information concerning the Jewish writer Kvitko. He explained to Polovoy that for some time now, rumors had been circulating to the effect that Kvitko, among other Jewish writers, had been arrested and subsequently put to death. Could Polovoy settle these rumors once and for all?

Polovoy said that he could. The rumors were, of course, the usual anti-Soviet slanders. Fortunately, Polovoy said, he was in a position to refute them, for Kvitko was at present living in the same apartment house as he, Polovoy. Could there be a better denial of any rumor? he asked.

We were relieved and delighted. We asked what Kvitko was doing, and Polovoy said that he was finishing a translation and planned a new book after that. He also added that he had seen Kvitko before leaving for America and that he, Kvitko, had asked Polovoy to convey his very best regards to friends in America.

So Polovoy answered, and this was witnessed by too many people that night to be denied. But after Polovoy had gone home, after the Twentieth Congress, we learned via a Jewish-Polish Communist paper that Kvitko had been dead for years, beaten and executed even as Feffer had been, even as Bergelson.

I say: May all the implacable justice of time and history be visited upon those who not only murdered men and artists, but who dirtied the soul of such a man as Boris Polovoy. For it was not merely that he told a tragic and grotesque lie; his invention was the summation of what the Communist Party does to a writer.

Other works by Fast: *Citizen Tom Paine* (1943); *April Morning* (1961); *The Immigrants* (1977).

A. M. Rosenthal

1922–2006

Born in Sault Ste. Marie, Ontario, Abraham Michael Rosenthal moved with his family to New York City as a child. The deaths of his father and four of his siblings as well as a bout with osteomyelitis developed in him a profound strength of character that stood him in good stead as he climbed the journalistic ladder of the *New York Times* from City College campus correspondent in 1943 to executive editor from 1977 to 1988 and columnist from 1988 to 1999. In the 1950s and 1960s, Rosenthal worked as a foreign correspondent and, as managing editor of the paper from 1969, he was instrumental in covering the Vietnam War, the Watergate scandal, and in publishing the Pentagon Papers.

There Is No News from Auschwitz
1958

The most terrible thing of all, somehow, was that at Brzezinka the sun was bright and warm, the rows of graceful poplars were lovely to look upon and on the grass near the gates children played.

It all seemed frighteningly wrong, as in a nightmare, that at Brzezinka the sun should ever shine or that there should be light and greenness and the sound of young laughter. It would be fitting if at Brzezinka the sun never shone and the grass withered, because this is a place of unutterable terror.

And yet, every day, from all over the world, people come to Brzezinka, quite possibly the most grisly tourist center on earth. They come for a variety of reasons—to see if it could really have been true, to remind themselves not to forget, to pay homage to the dead by the simple act of looking upon their place of suffering.

Brzezinka is a couple of miles from the better-known southern Polish town of Oswiecim. Oswiecim has about 12,000 inhabitants, is situated about 171 miles from Warsaw and lies in a damp, marshy area at the eastern end of the pass called the Moravian Gate. Brzezinka and Oswiecim together formed part of that minutely organized factory of torture and death that the Nazis called Konzentrationslager Auschwitz.

By now, fourteen years after the last batch of prisoners was herded naked into the gas chambers by dogs and guards, the story of Auschwitz has been told a great many times. Some of the inmates have written of those memories of which sane men cannot conceive. Rudolf Franz Ferdinand Hoess, the superintendent of the camp, before he was executed wrote his detailed memoirs of mass exterminations and the experiments on living bodies. Four million people died here, the Poles say.

And so there is no news to report about Auschwitz. There is merely the compulsion to write something about it, a compulsion that grows out of a restless feeling that to have visited Auschwitz and then turned away without having said or written anything would somehow be a most grievous act of discourtesy to those who died here.

Brzezinka and Oswiecim are very quiet places now; the screams can no longer be heard. The tourist walks silently, quickly at first to get it over with and then, as his mind peoples the barracks and the chambers and the dungeons and flogging posts, he walks draggingly. The guide does not say much either, because there is nothing much for him to say after he has pointed.

For every visitor, there is one particular bit of horror that he knows he will never forget. For some it is seeing the rebuilt gas chamber at Oswiecim and being told that this is the "small one." For others it is the fact that at Brzezinka, in the ruins of the gas chambers and the crematoria the Germans blew up when they retreated, there are daisies growing.

There are visitors who gaze blankly at the gas chambers and the furnaces because their minds simply cannot encompass them, but stand shivering before the great mounds of human hair behind the plate glass window or the piles of babies' shoes or the brick cells where men sentenced to death by suffocation were walled up.

One visitor opened his mouth in a silent scream simply at the sight of boxes—great stretches of three-tiered wooden boxes in the women's barracks. They were about six feet wide, about three feet high, and into them from five to ten prisoners were shoved for the night. The guide walks quickly through the barracks. Nothing more to see here.

A brick building where sterilization experiments were carried out on women prisoners. The guide tries the door—it's locked. The visitor is grateful that he does not have to go in, and then flushes with shame.

A long corridor where rows of faces stare from the walls. Thousands of pictures, the photographs of prisoners. They are all dead now, the men and women who stood before the cameras, and they all knew they were to die.

They all stare blank-faced, but one picture, in the middle of a row, seizes the eye and wrenches the mind. A girl, 22 years old, plumply pretty, blonde. She is smiling gently, as at a sweet, treasured thought. What was the thought that passed through her young mind and is now her memorial on the wall of the dead at Auschwitz?

Into the suffocation dungeons the visitor is taken for a moment and feels himself strangling. Another visitor goes in, stumbles out and crosses herself. There is no place to pray at Auschwitz.

The visitors look pleadingly at each other and say to the guide, "Enough."

There is nothing new to report about Auschwitz. It was a sunny day and the trees were green and at the gates the children played.

Other works by Rosenthal: *Thirty-Eight Witnesses: The Kitty Genovese Case* (1964); *One More Victim: The Life and Death of a Jewish Nazi* (1967).

Raphael Lemkin

1901–1959

Raphael Lemkin was born in Volkovysk, Russia (now Vawkavysk, Belarus). As a lawyer in Warsaw he worked to safeguard the rights of ethnic, religious, and political groups until the Nazi occupation forced him to flee to the United States in 1941. Lemkin taught at Duke University and later joined the War Department, where he helped prepare the prosecution for the Nuremberg Trials. He coined the word *genocide* in 1944 and lobbied for the rest of his life to ensure that the act was recognized as a crime under international law. On December 9, 1948, the United Nations approved the Convention on the Prevention and Punishment of Genocide.

Totally Unofficial: The Autobiography of Raphael Lemkin
1959

The Nuremberg judgment only partly relieved the world's moral tensions. Punishing the German war criminals created the feeling that, in international life as in civil society, crime should not be allowed to pay. But the purely juridical consequences of the trials were wholly insufficient. The quarrels and other follies of the Allies, which permitted Hitler to grow and become strong, survived these proceedings and found expression in the Nuremberg Tribunal's refusal to establish a precedent against this type of international crime. The Allies decided their case against a past Hitler but refused to envisage future Hitlers. They did not want to, or could not, establish a rule of international law that would prevent and punish future crimes of the same type.

Genocide was included in the indictment of the war criminals in London in August 1945 as a war crime. The Tribunal had thrown out this charge. It declared that it was bound by the Statute of the International Military Tribunal, which did not contain the charge of genocide, The Tribunal said, in fact, in its opinion as follows: "The Tribunal recognized in advance the superiority of a document signed by the prosecution." The statute that created the legal framework of the Tribunal was signed by the chief prosecutor of the Allies on August 8, 1945.

It could be that this timidity in establishing future rules of international law is due to the Tribunal's military origins. It could not step outside its military limitations and the authority given to it by its founding document. Maybe members of the military tribunals asked themselves, with appropriate humility: How can we, a military institution dealing with a concrete war situation, promulgate principles for the behavior of the civilian world in times of peace? Maybe they also thought: The essence of democracy is civilian control of the military, and not vice versa.

The judgment of the International Military Tribunal can be reduced to the following points:

1. The German war criminals were punished for planning and waging a war of aggression.
2. They were punished for certain war crimes or crimes committed during the war on the civilian population of occupied countries.

3. They were punished for certain crimes committed against a civilian population during a war of aggression. These were called "crimes against humanity" and were made punishable only when they were committed in connection with other crimes that were subject to the jurisdiction of the Tribunal, namely crimes against peace, and war crimes.

In brief, the Germans were punished only for crimes committed during or in connection with the war of aggression. Crimes against humanity were not an independent category in themselves. They were considered crimes only when their connection with other crimes could be established. Thus, in order to punish someone for crimes against humanity, the following elements were necessary:

1. A crime against humanity had to be proven.
2. A crime against peace or a war crime had to be proven.
3. A connection between the concrete plan against humanity on the one hand and crimes against peace or a war crime had to be established.
4. All these elements had to materialize in the course of an aggressive war and not a defensive war.
5. War of aggression was not defined.

No precedent applicable to crimes committed in a defensive war or in peacetime could be found in the judgment. Still, one should note that nations that are attacked may also commit crimes against a civilian population. But on this point, the Tribunal was silent. This was in brief the legal situation after Nuremberg.

About six months before the Nuremberg Tribunal issued its verdict, I published several articles on genocide in the *American Scholar* in New York, in the *Belgium Review of Penal Law and Criminology*, and in the Norwegian magazine *Samitisen* (Modern Times). I attached to this article a list of points that outlined the workings of the Genocide Treaty through the U.N. It appeared to me that machinery for protecting national, racial, religious, and ethnic groups must be established through the world body. I sincerely believed that a modification of the proposal I had made in Madrid in 1933 could be enforced through the U.N. But I still hoped that the Nuremberg Tribunal would issue a verdict that could at least have some limited use as a precedent for bringing up the issue of a Genocide Convention in the U.N. This was the reason I went to Nuremberg in May 1946. [. . .]

There were still three weeks before the Economic and Social Council would start discussing the Genocide Convention. I felt that the issue must be made important in the eyes of the delegates. Major Ennals organized two lectures on genocide: one in the building of the United Nations to which delegates were invited, the other in the summer school that the World Federation of the U.N. Associations was running for foreign students. A discussion followed each lecture. Interest was aroused by my historical examples, dating from antiquity through the middle ages to modern times. When questions were asked I did not refrain from reading aloud, in considerable detail, from my historical files. In this way I conveyed the impression that genocide is not the result of the mood of an occasional rogue ruler but a recurring pattern in history. It is like a disease that is congenital to certain situations and requires remedies. I was asked whether genocide had ever occurred in the Far Fast, and I quoted the case of fifty thousand Catholics who were destroyed in Japan in the seventeenth century. They were compelled to drink water until their bodies were completely bloated. Then all the openings of their bodies were closed with cement; they were made to lie down and then covered with planks, and carts with heavy loads, pulled by horses, were rolled over the planks. The bodies of the victims exploded with a strange mixture of water and blood. So perished fifty thousand Catholics.

"What can you do to prevent such a thing from happening?"

"You do exactly what you do to prevent other crimes. We have to deal with this matter on two levels: national and international. Nationally, we must make it a crime in our criminal codes and punish it through national courts in the same way as we punish larceny and arson.

"On the international level," I continued, "we make every nation responsible to the world community, either by bringing up cases of genocide in the World Court of Justice in The Hague, to which all civilized nations belong, or in the U.N. The main thing is to make the nations of the world feel that minorities and weaker nations are not chickens in the hands of a farmer, to be slaughtered, but that they are groups of people of great value to themselves and to world civilization."

Although not one night passed that I did not think about the Genocide Convention and not one day elapsed when I did not do something practical for the convention, I still felt as though I were moving in a big void. I did not see around me persons with the fitting gleam in their eyes on whom I could rely. I knew that such a fight was unavoidable, and somewhere, somebody must be found who had power, imagination, and determination.

Other works by Lemkin: *Axis Rule in Occupied Europe: Laws of Occupation, Analysis of Government, Proposals for Redress* (1944).

Norman Podhoretz

b. 1930

Neoconservative political philosopher Norman Podhoretz grew up in Brooklyn, New York. He is the former editor in chief of *Commentary* and is also a literary critic and author of numerous books, essays, and two memoirs. He received the Presidential Medal of Freedom from George W. Bush in 2004 and the Guardian of Zion Award from Bar-Ilan University in Israel in 2007.

Making It
1967

Now whatever else may be involved in a nondeliberate change of accent, one thing is clear: it bespeaks a very high degree of detachment from the ethos of one's immediate surroundings. It is not a good ear alone, and perhaps not even a good ear at all, which enables a child to hear the difference between the way he and everyone else around him sound when they talk, and the way teachers and radio announcers—as it must have been in my case—sound. Most people, and especially most children, are entirely insensitive to such differences, which is why anyone who pays attention to these matters can, on the basis of a man's accent alone, often draw a reasonably accurate picture of his regional, social, and ethnic background. People who feel that they belong in their familiar surroundings—whether it be a place, a class, or a group—will invariably speak in the accent of those surroundings; in all likelihood, indeed, they will never have imagined any other possibility for themselves. Conversely, it is safe to assume that a person whose accent has undergone a radical change from childhood is a person who once had fantasies of escaping to some other world, whether or not they were ever realized.

But accent in America has more than a psychological or spiritual significance. "Her kerbstone English," said Henry Higgins of Eliza Doolittle, "will keep her in the gutter to the end of her days." Most Americans probably respond with a sense of amused democratic superiority to the idea of a society in which so trivial a thing as accent can keep a man down, and it is a good measure of our blindness to the pervasive operations of class that there has been so little consciousness of the fact that America itself is such a society.[1] While the broadly regional accents—New England, Midwestern, Southern—enjoy more or less equal status and will not affect the economic or social chances of those who speak in them, the opposite is still surely true of any accent identifiably influenced by Yiddish, Italian, Polish, Spanish—that is, the languages of the major post-Civil War immigrant groups, among which may be included American-Irish. A man with such an accent will no longer be confined, as once he would almost automatically have been, to the working class, but unless his life, both occupational and social, is lived strictly within the milieu in whose tone of voice he speaks, his accent will at the least operate as an obstacle to be overcome (if, for example, he is a schoolteacher aspiring to be a principal), and at the most as an effective barrier to advancement (if, say, he is an engineer), let alone to entry into the governing elite of the country. For better or worse, incidentally, these accents are not a temporary phenomenon destined to disappear with the passage of the generations, no more than ethnic consciousness itself is. I have heard third-generation American Jews of East European immigrant stock speaking with thicker ethnic coloring even than their parents.

Clearly, then, while fancying myself altogether at home in the world into which I was born, I was not only more detached from it than I realized; I was also taking action, and of a very fundamental kind, which would eventually make it possible for me to move into some other world. Yet I still did not recognize what I was doing—not in any such terms. My ambition was to be a great and famous poet, not to live in a different community, a different class, a different "world." If I had a concrete image of what greatness would mean socially, it was probably based on the famous professional boxer from our block who had moved to a more prosperous neighborhood but still spent his leisure time hanging around the corner candy store and the local pool room with his old friends (among whom he could, of course, experience his fame far more sharply than he could have done among his newly acquired peers).

But to each career its own sociology. Boxers, unlike poets, do not undergo a cultural change in the process of becoming boxers, and if I was not brave enough or clever enough as a boy to see the distinction, others who knew me then were. "Ten years from now, you won't even want to talk to me, you won't even recognize me if you pass me on the street," was the kind of comment I frequently heard in my teens from women in the neighborhood, friends of my mother who were fond of me and nearly as proud as she was of the high grades I was getting in school and the prizes I was always winning. "That's crazy, you must be kidding," I would answer. They were not crazy and they were not kidding. They were simply better sociologists than I.

As, indeed, my mother herself was, for often in later years—after I had become a writer and an editor and was living only a subway ride away but in a style that was foreign to her and among people by whom she was intimidated—she would gaze wistfully at this strange creature, her son, and murmur. "I should have made him for a dentist," registering thereby her perception that whereas Jewish sons who grow up to be successes in certain occupations usually remain fixed in an accessible cultural ethos, sons who grow up into literary success are transformed almost beyond recognition and distanced almost beyond a mother's reach. My mother wanted nothing so much as for me to be a success, to be respected and admired. But she did not imagine, I think, that she would only purchase the realization of her ambition at the price of my progressive estrangement from her and her ways. Perhaps it was my guilt at the first glimmerings of this knowledge which accounted for my repression of it and for the obstinacy of the struggle I waged over "manners" with Mrs. K.

For what seemed most of all to puzzle Mrs. K., who saw no distinction between taste in poetry and taste in clothes, was that I could see no connection between the two. Mrs. K. knew that a boy from Brownsville with a taste for Keats was not long for Brownsville, and moreover would in all probability end up in the social class to which she herself belonged. How could I have explained to her that I would only be able to leave Brownsville if I could maintain the illusion that my destination was a place in some mystical country of the spirit and not a place in the upper reaches of the American class structure?

Saint Paul, who was a Jew, conceived of salvation as a world in which there would be neither Jew nor Greek, and though he may well have been the first, he was very far from the last Jew to dream such a dream of transcendence—transcendence of the actual alternative categories with which reality so stingily presents us. Not to be Jewish, but not to be Christian either; not to be a worker, but not to be a boss either; not—if I may be forgiven for injecting this banality out of my own soul into so formidable a series of fantasies—to be a slum child but not to be a snob either. How could I have explained to Mrs. K. that wearing a suit from de Pinna would for me have been something like the social equivalent of a conversion to Christianity? And how could she have explained to me that there was no socially neutral ground to be found in the United States of America, and that a distaste for the surroundings in which I was bred, and ultimately (God forgive me) even for many of the people I loved, and so a new taste for other kinds of people—how could she have explained that all this was inexorably entailed in the logic of a taste for the poetry of Keats and the painting of Cezanne and the music of Mozart?

NOTE

1. On the other hand, the *New York Times* reported on May 8, 1966, that "A real-life Professor Higgins" had "descended upon Harlem in search of Eliza Doolittles." The *Times* went on: "Every Saturday afternoon the portly 45-year-old professor of comparative education at Teachers College of Columbia University, Dr. George Z. F. Bereday, directs 10 Negro girl seniors from Benjamin Franklin High School on the upper East Side in a series of classes in grooming, dress, make-up, speech, poise, rhythmics and general deportment and culture." Explained Dr. Bereday: "The theory is that there are factors other than skin color in racial discrimination. These factors are class differences and they are more immediately manageable. They oil their hair and chew gum. Maybe a girl can get a good job as a secretary, but if her hair smells like coconut oil. . . ." (Dr. Bereday himself speaks with a thick Polish accent, which makes him acceptably foreign rather than unacceptably lower class.)

Other works by Podhoretz: *Doings and Undoings: The Fifties and after in American Writing* (1964); *Breaking Ranks: A Political Memoir* (1979); *The Prophets: Who They Were, What They Are* (2002).

Joseph Buloff

1899–1985

Born in Vilna, actor Joseph Buloff began his career with the renowned Yiddish theater ensemble the Vilner Trupe. After marrying actress Luba Kadison in 1925, Buloff and his wife performed together in Vienna and Bucharest before immigrating to the United States in 1926. There, Buloff began a professional relationship with Maurice Schwartz, director of the Yiddish Art Theatre, and Buloff and his wife ran the Folks Theatre. Buloff and Kadison toured Argentina in 1949 with a successful Yiddish version of *Death of a Salesman*. His final role was in Warren Beatty's 1981 film *Reds*.

From the Old Marketplace
1972

Benjamin came back with the same suitcase and the same few sets of underwear he had left with for Germany. He brought back everything—his illness included. The only thing he didn't bring back were his bankbooks.

He had squandered a fortune on a whole army of famous German specialists, clinics, hospitals, and spas—and the result of it all was that on the second day after his return he suffered a fresh attack that was even stronger than any of the previous ones.

The local doctors came again and availed themselves of all the old methods, but by now it was already obvious to everyone—most of all to the patient himself—that nothing would help him anymore and that the next day or the day after that he would surely choke to death. The stricken bruiser who until the time of his illness hadn't experienced so much as a toothache now suffered not only from the pain but even more so from the fear and vexation. To feel so choked and shattered from a pair of insignificant lungs, when until a short time ago he hadn't even known on which side of his body they were located, left him wildly furious and resentful. He slammed the table in his bitterness and cursed all the doctors and specialists who had taken his "millions" and, instead of curing him, left him on the verge of death. With every cough he spat out his anger at the medical profession with all its specialists and famous professors. He forbade the local doctors to come into his house and "practice their barbering on his beard."

Relatives, friends, and acquaintances from the old marketplace, particularly those who had always enjoyed his benevolence, came to comfort him and to advise him not to drive the doctors away even though they were ignorant quacks, for even if they knew nothing, they would keep trying until they finally came up with the right thing to do. But the patient responded to each effort to calm him with a choice epithet dripping with sarcasm and directed at those who lived off his charity . . . and at the doctors who milked him for his money, and at himself for wasting his fortune.

The proud paupers from the old marketplace resented the insult! His sickness was given by God as had his money been taken by God, for wasn't it written that God giveth and God taketh away? To this the irritated patient replied that he had no quarrel with God, since the list of those who had taken his money included no such name, and that it was sheer abomination to make up sayings in His name and to attribute to Him such a vulgar canard as "Charity delivereth from death" in order to wheedle money out of a doomed benefactor.

Singly and in chorus they strove to convince him that they were ready to give him their own lungs if that were possible, but Benjamin remained adamant, for the facts were clearly on his side.

If the patient's bitterness had no bearing on his physical condition, it radically altered his spiritual state. He suddenly grew loquacious and began to use words and express ideas that as far as the market people could recall he had never uttered before.

It seemed as if he had grown somehow exalted by the illness, as if in place of his clogged lungs there had suddenly opened within him a source of remarkable wisdom. He began talking as if with a borrowed tongue, like Balaam's ass when it saw the knife blade at its throat.

At first his friends came to see him out of duty, but presently they came to provoke him into a conversation since they were no longer as interested in his health as in what he had to say about his illness, about himself, about the world, and even about God.

They had known him when he was still a young fellow, a poor cap maker. They used to call him Handsome Benjamchik. Almost every market person had a nickname, but most were as fitting as a fifth wheel on a wagon. For instance, Pinie, who was lively, spirited, and agile, was called "the Turtle," while Haim, a tiny fellow with a button nose, was called "the Elephant." But Benjamin was really handsome, far too good-looking to be a simple cap maker. Sitting around their stoves on winter evenings, they had speculated as to whether he wouldn't be better suited to be a banker or a millionaire. But that the millionaire should suddenly lose his millions and turn into a sage just like old Job, who was also a simple middle-class man who, thanks to his horrible afflictions, became a world-famous sage—this was intriguing, this merited a closer look, this justified getting into a discussion or even a debate about higher matters with that new fellow "Job."

Sarah would place a large bowl of cooked chickpeas on the table (a snack befitting a broke millionaire) and, chewing the chickpeas, the market people tried to convince the sage that he wasn't completely right. But the sage used his biting scorn like an ax to hack away at the polemicists so that they could only shrug and admit that although he didn't let them conclude their thoughts and finish what they had to say, he was nevertheless right.

The only thing that stood in his way was his constant coughing. Some of his opponents would take advantage of this and, the moment the patient stopped in mid-argument to catch his breath, they would jump in and present their views. The patient would wave his hands for them to wait for his rebuttal, but the opponents used this opportunity to outshout the cougher. The moment he regained his breath, he would fix them with his bloodshot eyes and angrily say, "We won't settle anything this way. We're not fighting on equal terms. Go and catch asthma first, then come to me as equal to equal and we'll finish the discussion."

Although the visitors didn't take this proposal too seriously, it put an end to the discussions.

The incessant coughing burst the patient's eardrums and subjected him to a new source of intolerable anguish. It was difficult enough for him to speak, and now it became painful for him to hear as well. His only source of comfort, the discussions, had to be abandoned.

Translated by Joseph Singer.

Hortense Calisher

1911–2009

Born and raised in New York City, Hortense Calisher published fifteen novels, numerous short stories, and articles in prominent periodicals. Her work, reflecting on her family's southern U.S. and German Jewish links—the "old stock" both of America writ large and of American Jewry writ small—has been widely anthologized, and her honors included her presidency of PEN, four O. Henry Awards, and the Lifetime Achievement Award from the National Endowment for the Arts.

Herself

1972

Apples. That's what New Yorkers of the 1930s remember. Apples of the Hesperides, neatly stalled on corner after corner, sold on the last trembling line of decency by men who were unwilling to beg. Sometimes a man had only two. We bought them, our Cézannes-to-be, with the nickel carfare home, and didn't know it was our education we were bringing back. "You walked again!" said our middle-class mothers. "Forty blocks! My God, what am I going to do about those shoes?" And, for the first time, they might mean it.

Depression settled on us younger ones slow as the really big snowflakes. My father came home from a business trip, his face ashen, though still for *others.* "Decent family men stop you. They say nothing. When I took out my wallet—one wept." 1929 had brought his business to the wall, but he still had it. We would always eat. And did. It never occurred to me that he and my mother were frantic, within their scale. Then it developed that college was no longer assumed for me. I mightn't go. . . . I wasn't to. "Go and be a secretary!" said my mother. "Like Mary. *Work!*" Mary!—my friend from the "wrong" neighborhood—two blocks away. My father said nothing; maybe he knew there were almost no secretaries any more.

But I had to go to college. All the books I still hadn't read were there. And, in the way of the young, my methods were rough—and clean. Pride of my dancing school, I went and got the chorus job guaranteed to blow my mother's cool—and me, of course, to sexual ruin. "I start on Monday," I said. So, to college I went. The $400 for the first term was found, somewhere. I even had a short, frilled red crepe I could wear right now, and never wore out, for *boom*—that fall, skirts fell. And oh, yes, isn't it all tender and charming and somehow gayer than now—as retrospect always is. But there was still to come the incredible gift the '30s gave some of us. For I still didn't know how rich we were.

At Barnard, where I took no sociology or economics (which wouldn't have helped), I thought I was learning—how poor. I'd had to ask for a scholarship. But when the banks closed, many around me mourned for what their papas still had there. Another's father had jumped from his skyscraper office into a large bloody pool of insurance. Meanwhile, I had one new dress per year, and almost no pocket money. So I worked. Summers and Saturdays. And a few more snowflakes fell.

Am I telling you about the decline of the middle class, or the rise of liberalism among the well fed? Indeed not, I still think sociology is for the simple-minded. I'm telling you how a "society" girl was prepared for her debut.

First job—hostess in a Happiness restaurant: (later Schrafft's), hours 11:00–3:00, wages $11 per week and lunch. There she learned: (a) waitresses whose pinched cheeks testify to one meal a day eat different from a girl to whom it's just by-the-way; (b) professionals, who've worked up to what they are, hate those who get the job because of what *they* are; (c) to hate customers. And most important of all, in later life: never take the first table a hostess offers you. Saturdays, she worked as salesclerk in a department store, where she learned to hate employers—particularly, among the buyers, a Miss Siff, whom she saw snarl to a manufacturer waiting outside the buying office—hat humbly in hand, a Homburg like *her* own father's—"Get out."

And outside, "society" waited, for him and for me. Not a matter of the "400," any more. Some of this I saw, of course, though with a strictly visual eye. . . . Southward of those Hudson River sunsets behind the college, along the flats below Riverside Drive, a squatter town had risen, tar-paper shacks that to us flapped carefree, Romany Rom in the breeze. . . . At the Savoy night club in Harlem, where a boyfriend was announcer (radio), I stomped almost as good as *them,* until replaced by a black girl supple as the two-foot bird of paradise on her head. . . . In the newspapers, certain farmers in the West were raging toward revolution—but when is a farmer ever real to New York? Or the Okies?—even then trickling toward Steinbeck, and to a clever, arty still in *Bonnie and Clyde.* . . . Politics was happening to many, for the first time. At school, the editor of the paper was pulled off it for writing sympathetically of Russia; we figured she'd met one, somewhere, at the parties of those parlor pinks ten years too old for us. . . .

Meanwhile, at home, we moved from ten rooms to four; my mother, "on the advice of her doctor," now did her own housework; and the family business, on which so many relatives depended, went bankrupt. But we went on managing—my father, aged 70, got a job. How remarkable this now was for a man of any age, he never said. Soon, I would know.

And so would my boyfriends—a word deeded to me from the '20s, along with some of its gaiety, of which we still had our own frolicsome kit bagful. (For a decade never knows for sure when it *is* one, or when it is over. We didn't know we were "the '30s" yet.) Among my male classmates the architects worried the most, having been taught early that they depended on the promises an economy makes to itself, "Bodies will still need help," the grinning medics said. "I'll open a grocery store," said the business types, laughing. "People always need food." And that, of course, was to be—very

true. Why, we were all of us brimming with expectation—of the world, the flesh, and maybe the devil, too. No one had explained to us that imagination wasn't the same as "looking ahead." Why should it be? But I'm no one to talk.

Other works by Calisher: *In the Absence of Angels* (1951); *The New Yorkers* (1969); *The Collected Stories of Hortense Calisher* (1975).

Heda Margolius Kovály

1919–2010

Born Heda Bloch in Prague, Heda Margolius Kovály was shaped by her experiences of the Holocaust and communism. Interned during the war in the Łódź ghetto, Margolius Kovály survived Auschwitz and a forced march to Bergen-Belsen, during which she and a few other women escaped back to Prague. Her husband Rudolf Margolius was executed in 1952 during the notorious antisemitic Slánský trial. Left with a young son to support, she married Pavel Kovály in 1955, and the family fled to the United States in 1968. Settling in Boston, Margolius Kovály took a position at the Harvard Law Library and became an accomplished writer.

Under a Cruel Star: A Life in Prague, 1941–1968
1973

Two months after liberation, people had stopped cheering and embracing. They were not giving away food and clothing anymore, but selling it on the black market. Those who had compromised their integrity during the Occupation now began to calculate and plan, to watch and spy on each other, to cover their tracks, eager to secure the property they had acquired through collaboration with the Germans, by cowardice or denunciation, or by looting the homes of deported Jews. Their sense of guilt and fear of retribution soon bred hate and suspicion directed mainly at the real victims of the Occupation: the active and passive resisters, the partisans, the Jews, and political prisoners; the honest people who had stood their ground and had not betrayed their principles even at the cost of persecution. The innocent became a living reproach and a potential threat to the guilty.

Now these survivors, dead-tired from standing in endless lines for documents, ration cards, and food, disgusted by the petty skirmishes with bureaucrats and profiteers, began to worry seriously about the future of the country. It was becoming evident to many that while evil grows all by itself, good can be achieved only through hard struggle and maintained only through tireless effort, that we had to set out clear, boldly-conceived goals for ourselves and join forces to attain them. The problem was that everyone envisioned these goals differently.

For all those whom the war had displaced, the biggest worry was housing. Partisans who throughout the war had lived in the woods, widows of the executed who for years had slept on the floor of some basement, and ailing survivors of the concentration camps all spent day after day waiting in lines at the Housing Authority while butchers and grocers and other wartime profiteers walked in by the back door and were seen first. Most of them already had good apartments, but now that they had become rich they wanted better ones. There were a number of empty apartments in Prague, abandoned by the Germans, beautifully decorated with furniture that had once belonged to Jews, so how about it? Hadn't the butchers and grocers supplied the bureaucrats at City Hall with meat and flour throughout the war? Weren't they now entitled to a little recognition for their efforts?

Meanwhile, in the waiting room, a clerk would yell at the women who stood there weeping: "What do you want me to do? So many of you came back—how do you think we can find housing for you all? You expect miracles?" And people would walk out, humiliated, their fists clenched in rage.

I have often thought that many of our people turned to Communism not so much in revolt against the existing political system, but out of sheer despair over human nature which showed itself at its very worst after the war. Since it is impossible for men to give up on mankind, they blame the social order in which they live; they condemn the human condition.

In the end, I wound up with an apartment sooner than Mr. Boucek, the owner of a poultry store whom I would often see conferring with the clerks at the Housing Authority. Of course, he was after something luxurious, while all I wanted was a roof over my head.

One evening, just before the building closed, I marched into the office of the chairman of the Housing Authority with a shopping bag containing all my possessions, mostly gifts from friends, and declared that I would sleep right there in the office for as long as I remained homeless because I had no other place to go.

That was true. I had spent the last few nights in various improvised shelters for displaced persons. Before that, I had used up the store of my acquaintances who were willing to give me a place to stay; I had decided that I would not take advantage of their patience any longer. Besides, I thought it was about time I slept in my own bed after all these years.

The chairman of the Housing Authority began to fume, but I paid no attention to him. Slowly, I unpacked my bag. I took out a cake of soap, then a toothbrush, then a glass. Next to it I laid out a white napkin, and on it a slice of bread, a piece of cheese, and a bottle of milk. I draped a towel and my nightgown over an office chair. Then I sat down in the chairman's chair, poured myself a glass of milk, and bit into the bread. The chairman was still ranting. I finished eating and, very slowly, started taking off my shoes. Then I opened the first button of my blouse, silently praying for something, anything, to happen. I undid the second button. The chairman's face reddened. He wiped the sweat off his neck and shot out of the office.

I put my feet up on another chair, lit a cigarette—another precious gift—and waited. Some time later, there was a knock on the door and, after my pleasant invitation to enter, the door opened a crack and the chairman's bald pate appeared. Reassured that my preparations for the night had not proceeded any further, he let out a sigh of relief, beckoned to someone behind him, and came in. He was followed by his underling, a clerk who had previously told me many times that he understood my situation and would be only too happy to help me, but that he could not give me an apartment because he did not have one. Now he held a piece of paper toward me and said, "If we give you this deed right now so that you can move in tomorrow, will you please go away?"

I signed the deed, finished my glass of milk, and asked if they wished to share with me what remained in the bottle. They refused politely, and the chairman folded up my things with his own hands and put them back in my shopping bag. I took the bag and the deed and went to have a look at the house in which I would live. I seem to remember that the Housing Authority was eventually shut down because of corruption, but I am not certain.

The apartment was so tiny that two years later, when I was expecting a baby, Rudolf had to do all the cooking, because I could not fit between the stove and the wall. But there were lots of bookshelves and the sun shone in all day long. Friends came to visit, bringing mugs and dishes and blankets and pillows and, by the end of the summer, we were already calling it home.

Those shelves filled up quickly with books about politics and economics, old and torn, that Rudolf studied endlessly, and with a lot of new pamphlets printed on cheap paper, which I devoured. They offered such clear and simple answers to the most complicated questions that I kept feeling there had to be a mistake somewhere.

All injustice, discrimination, misery, and war, I read, stem from the fact that the handful of people who wield power are unwilling to relinquish their acquisitive urge, their exploitation of the working class, and their lust for world domination. As soon as the working people—the creators of all value—understand what must be done, they will overthrow the exploiters and their henchmen, will reeducate them as well as themselves, and the kingdom of heaven will come to earth. The real enemies of man are those who take profit from the sweat and callouses of others. If we divide the riches of the world equally, and apply ourselves to the work at hand, each according to his ability, society will see to it that no one wants for anything.

We shall no longer fight one another for an ever-larger slice of the economic pie. We shall pool our efforts and build happiness and prosperity for all. The soil belongs to the people who till it, the factories to those who work in them. At first, of course, it will be necessary to take a firm stand against the rich; those in power will not voluntarily give up their privileges. No capitalist will give up his position without a fight. But once the new order is established, even the capitalist will understand that progress toward a better society cannot be stopped. Eventually, unwilling to be left behind; he too will join our effort. We shall all be brothers, regardless of language or race. Only capitalism breeds racism; in a socialist society, all people are equal. Democracy, a progressive idea when first conceived, has degenerated and played out its role in history; today, it affords capitalists the opportunity to exploit and the unemployed the opportunity to beg. The capitalist economy inevitably leads to depression, and depression to fascism and war. The bourgeoisie has brought the world to the brink of destruction. Do you want to see another war in a decade or two? The last of all wars, a nuclear catastrophe? Isn't it time to change the world?

Let us go out and convince others, explain our ideas and goals. We do not wish to force people to change: people have to see the light by themselves and learn from their own experience. We can only help them toward an understanding by disseminating, our ideas, our own—the only scientific truth.

Why do wars happen? See pages 45 through 47! What causes economic depressions? See page 66! Does God exist? What is truth? Marxism provides the answers to all these questions and offers solutions to problems which have plagued mankind since the dawn of history. The great change we are calling for is within our reach: people can change the conditions under which they live and through this change, man himself will eventually be transformed.

Friends—all of them young—came to visit Rudolf and me in our small apartment. They sat on the floor because there was no other place to sit and debated till morning. There was hardly an opinion that was not defended by someone, hardly an idea that went unproposed. Usually, I sat in a corner and just listened. I knew nothing about politics and less than nothing about economics. But I began to understand that life had become politics and politics had become life. It would not do anymore to say, "I don't care. I just want to be left in peace and quiet."

Whenever anyone defended the principles of democracy that I had been raised to believe, something inside me cried out, Yes, that's the way it is! But then I became uncertain when I heard the objections. The principles on which the prewar Czechoslovak Republic had been founded, the humanistic, democratic ideals of Thomas G. Masaryk, were an unrealistic illusion. Our democracy had allowed the growth of the fascist and Nazi parties which had in the end destroyed it. Worst of all, it had failed to defend the country against Hitler. After Munich, where our treacherous allies had forsaken us, our democratic government had surrendered to the Germans without a struggle.

Did we want to repeat the same mistakes and live out a new version of Munich? Who had sold us out to Hitler? Our allies the Western capitalists. Who had offered us help when every other country had abandoned us? The Soviet Union. Who had liberated Prague while the American army stood watching from Pilsen, some undefended fifty miles away? The Soviet Union.

Once two friends that Rudolf had known since childhood met in our home. Zdenek's father, a factory worker who had been unemployed for years before the war, had joined the Resistance soon after the Occupation. The Germans had arrested, then executed him. Zdenek himself had spent all the years of the war with the partisans. He limped awkwardly on feet that had been frostbitten during the war, but when he entered a room he brought with him that familiar self-assurance and strength of people for whom hardship is a challenge, and opportunity to measure oneself, to see how far one can stretch the limit of one's will, personality, humanity. Zdenek had been accepted in to the Communist Party somewhere in the forest, in a tent, by candlelight, with a submachine gun in his hands.

The other friend was Franta, one of the people who had refused to help me during those first days after my escape from the camp. He had survived the entire war living quietly, inconspicuously, in Prague. He had done nothing dishonorable. He had not collaborated with the Nazis nor had he denounced anyone. But he had not taken any risks either. Although he had completed his military service before the war as an officer in the Czechoslovak army, it had never entered his mind that he should join the Resistance. He lived out the war like a hibernating animal. He had gained nothing, but he had also lost very little.

Later on, I would often remember the conversation between these two men. Every argument Franta made for democracy sounded right and reasonable to me. But every argument Zdenek made for communism was supported by the force of his personality and his experiences. Anything he said sounded strong and convincing simply because it was he who said it. As I listened to him, I felt almost ashamed to be agreeing with his opponent, Franta, who was so rational and prudent and who never forgot which side his bread was buttered on. It seemed unthinkable to choose Franta's side in this confrontation between caution and courage. That evening, as usual, the debate ended in total disagreement. Only the discord between these two men was unusually sharp. Theirs was not only a clash of views but of two worlds, two contradictory sets of concepts, feelings, and visions.

Much later, during the tormented haze of the fifties, when I would try, foolishly, to pinpoint the moment when our good will and enthusiasm betrayed us, when we took our first step toward desolation and destruction, I would think of that evening. Rudolf listened carefully to the two men and entered into the debate only occasionally. But I could see that his heart was completely with Zdenek, surely in part because he had never forgiven Franta for his cowardly behavior toward me. If his reason still posed objections to Zdenek's arguments, Rudolf had obviously decided to ignore them.

The Communists at that time kept stressing the scientific basis of their ideology, but I know that the road that led many people into their ranks in Czechoslovakia was paved with good and strong emotions.

Rudolf was a very quiet, serious man, utterly unselfish. The experience of the concentration camps and the Occupation had affected him more deeply than anyone else I knew. He never overcame the humiliation that he—a young, healthy man, an officer in the Czechoslovak army—had allowed himself to be thrown into a camp without resisting and had looked on like a helpless cripple while people were murdered all around him. He had often risked his life to help his fellow inmates—they would come tell me about it themselves—but the memory of his helplessness and a sense of guilt never stopped torturing him. Now he believed more than ever before that every individual should aim to contribute to the common good, but he doubted that this could be achieved by means that had failed so miserably before.

About a week after Zdenek and Franta had spent the evening with us, Rudolf took me to see some of his friends, prewar Communist intellectuals who had lived in the Soviet Union during the war. They were a middle-aged couple who had a nice house, furnished in tasteful, totally unproletarian style. They were well-educated, very kind, and I felt quite at home with them. The wife discussed housekeeping with me and suggested ways to prepare the canned pork that came to us from the United Nations relief fund so that it would taste Czech. We asked them to tell us about their life in the Soviet Union. With tears in their eyes, they described the self-sacrifice and the patriotism of even the simplest Russians, their endurance and steadfast belief in eventual victory over the Nazis. They spoke about the profound feeling of brotherhood that reigned within the Soviet Union, the equality of the various nationalities and races, the fervor with which people performed even the hardest labor and the most dangerous tasks for their country; they described the solicitude of the Party and of the Soviet government, the friendly acceptance that they and other refugees had enjoyed. We left deeply impressed.

Two days later, Rudolf brought home applications for membership in the Communist Party.

Ten years later, the old lady who had been our hostess confessed that nearly everything she and her husband told us during our visit had been untrue. They had suffered hard times in Russia. People had been afraid to talk to them. Black marketeering, collaboration, anti-Semitism were rampant. Many people died unnecessary deaths. But since they did not dare, for the most part, to guess at the cause of their suffering, they died blessing the Party and Stalin with their last breath.

Our conditioning for the revolution had begun in the concentration camps. Perhaps we had been most impressed by the example of our fellow prisoners, Communists who often behaved like beings of a higher order. Their idealism and Party discipline gave them a strength and an endurance that the rest of us could not match. They were like well-trained soldiers in a crowd of children.

But there were other things too. All survivors remember to this day the stubborn determination which dominated that time, the total concentration on a single goal, the end of the war. Life was not life in any proper sense; it was only a thrust in that one direction. All our thinking and doing justified itself by the prospect of the future. The present only existed to be overcome, somehow, anyhow.

When the war finally ended, our joy soon changed into a sense of anticlimax and a yearning to fill the void that this intensity of expectation and exertion of will had left behind. A strong sense of solidarity had evolved in the concentration camps, the idea that one individual's fate was in every way tied to the fate of the group, whether that meant the group of one's fellow prisoners, the whole nation, or even all of humanity. For many people, the desire for material goods largely disappeared. As much as we longed for the comforts of life, for good food, clothing, and homes, it was clear to us that these things were secondary, and that our happiness and the meaning of our lives lay elsewhere. I remember how some of our fellow citizens for whom the war years had been a time of acquisition and hoarding, stared when we did not try to retrieve stolen property, to apply for restitution, to seek inheritances from relatives. This was true not only of Rudolf and myself but of any number of people who had come to identify their own well-being with the common good and who, rather logically, ended up in the most ideologically alluring political party—that of the Communists.

The years of imprisonment had yet another paradoxical effect. Although we continually hoped for freedom, our concept of freedom had changed. Shut up behind barbed wire, robbed of all rights including the right to live, we had stopped regarding freedom as something natural and self-evident. Gradually, the idea of freedom as birthright became blurred. By the end of their time in the camps, many prisoners came to accept the view that freedom is something that has to be earned and fought for, a privilege that is awarded, like a medal. It is hardly possible for people to live for so many years slaves in everyday contact with fascists and fascism without becoming somewhat twisted, without contracting a trace of that dry rot unwittingly and unwillingly. Usually, the reasoning went something like this: if, for the purpose of building a new society, it is necessary to give up my freedom for a time, to subsume something I cherish to a cause in which I strongly believe, that is a sacrifice I am willing to make. In any case, we are a lost generation. We all might have died uselessly in the camps. Since we did survive, we want to dedicate what is left of our lives to the future.

Translated by Franci Epstein and Helen Epstein.

Other work by Margolius Kovály: *The Victors and the Vanquished* (1973).

FICTION, DRAMA, AND CHILDREN'S LITERATURE

Sholem Asch

East River
1946

The Triangle firm was housed in a modern building, practically a skyscraper, situated on the edge of the enormous open square in the heart of the city. The factory took up several floors of the building. The offices, showrooms, and cutting rooms were on the lower floors. On the ninth floor about two hundred and thirty girls and a few men worked at sewing machines. Other hands worked on the eighth floor. The tenth floor housed the finishers, cleaners, and examiners. Besides a large number of men, cutters and pressers, Triangle employed more than seven hundred girls. [. . .]

As they talked above the whirr of the machines a sudden quiet fell on the shop; even the machines sounded subdued. Something seemed to be happening at the far end of the room. Sarah stood up to see what was going on. Mary scrambled up beside her. They could see nothing.

"What is it?" Mary asked in sudden alarm.

"I don't know," Sarah answered.

All at once they saw puffs of thick smoke coming up between the cracks of the floor boards near the door leading to the elevator. Forked flames of fire followed the smoke. All the fright in the world broke out in a chorus of hysterical screams.

"Fire! Fire! Fire!"

Panic swept through the room. There was the noise of running feet, the clatter of chairs and stools being thrown over. The two girls began to run with the rest.

The running mob pushed them toward the exit door on the Greene Street side. It was near the door leading to the elevator that the flames were licking through the planks of the floor. They remembered that no stairway descended from the corridor. The elevator was the only exit. They would be trapped in the corridor by the flames. The smoke and fire coming through the floor near the door terrified them. The crowd veered and dashed to the other side of the loft, where the door led to the stairway that went down to Washington Place. Mary and Sarah, holding each other by the hand, ran with the rest.

They stumbled over chairs and upended stools. They were blocked by hysterical girls who were too terrified to move. Sarah and Mary tried to drag some of them along with them. Here and there tongues of fire were coming up through the floor. Around the sewing machines the heaps of remnants of material and trimmings, silks, linings, padded cotton, the oil-soaked rags which the girls used to clean the machines after oiling them, blazed into flame. The oil-soaked rags were the first to catch fire, setting alight the piles of cuttings and feeding the flames from one machine to the next. The grease-covered machines themselves began to blaze together with the piles of material on them. The fire grew in volume by the minute. It spread like a stream overflowing its banks. The waves of living flame licked at the skirts of the fleeing, screaming, trapped girls.

Barely had they escaped through the corridor of flame between the rows of machines when they were blocked by a wall of smoke which rose up from the large stacks of finished blouses. With the smoke came a suffocating odor. The smoke arose to the ceiling, where it hung like a cloud. They began to suffocate, gagging and choking. Her eyes blinded and her throat gasping, Sarah dragged Mary along. The door, when they reached it, was blocked with a mass of bodies. Hair loosed, clothing torn, the mob pulled and tore at each other in panicked attempts to get to the door. From the packed mass of bodies came a high-pitched keening, a hysterical yammering. [. . .]

Desperately Sarah looked around. Half of the floor was in flames, and the flames were coming toward them. The space near the windows which overlooked Washington Place was still untouched. In front of the windows frantic girls were weaving, clutching at the window sills, desperately trying to find some way of escape.

Near one of the windows the flames were coming closer. Here only a few girls were gathered. If there was any escape it would have to be through this window, the thought flashed through Sarah's mind. They would have to get through it before the flames reached it. She began to drag Mary toward the window! Mary showed no resistance. She was only half conscious. She let the other do what she willed. [. . .]

The flames came closer. Urged on by Sarah and driven by the terrifying spectacle of the approaching tongues of flame, Mary, scrambled onto the sill, and, with her back to the street, managed to get her legs through the hole in the window, holding on frantically to Sarah's shoulders. She gashed her knee on the jagged edges of the glass but never felt the pain. Holding tightly to Sarah, she groped for some projecting ledge to support her. Except for the balconies outside the line of windows below her, the wall fell sheer. But the balcony was too far down; she couldn't reach it. Sarah, holding Mary firmly by the arms, reached out of the window as far as she dared, trying to lower her as close as possible to the balcony. [. . .]

[. . .] Through the mist of consciousness left to her Sarah saw that Mary could now find a footing. "Just a little more. Just a little more," she thought. She could feel herself moving farther forward. She could feel the flames licking up from her shoes, climbing her legs. Then she could feel nothing. If only she could lean out a little more, Mary would reach the balcony. She dare not let go of Mary's hands. She was no longer herself. She no longer existed. She had become a part of Mary. She was only an instrument to help her reach the balcony. . . . Now she could reach it. Sarah threw the upper half of her body violently forward. Mary felt below her feet the firm surface of the balcony. Her hands, suddenly released, clutched at the bare sides of the building. Above her, out of the shattered window, a flaming body fell, like a living torch, down to the street below.

Translated by A. H. Gross.

Isaac Rosenfeld

Passage from Home
1946

Father glared; Willy smiled. Father sat erect, his skullcap square on his head; Willy slouched, all relaxed, his cap slung at an angle like a beret. One declaimed the Hebrew text, loudly, punctiliously; the other looked at the pictures, whispered to the women, pinched my knee under the table and cracked nuts with his teeth, disdaining the nutcracker which my father used.

Of course, their opposition was not quite so perfect or so simple. For while my father deported himself belligerently, as if he had been appointed guardian of the

Passover, a latter-day Moses, he, too, had his easier moments. He would also whisper and smile, let his attention wander from the text, flip the pages, play with chips of matzoh on the tablecloth. But my father's levities were always followed by sternness, by a sharp little cough which announced each change of heart. I never knew whether his digressions into good humor were spontaneous or deliberate—whether his mood would actually change, or whether he simply felt it was time to put on a smile, as a man may take a pill at stated intervals.

He and Willy came into conflict at the very point where the Seder is as gay as comic opera. The point, that is, where the Israelites offer up their great digressions, the better to sing their deliverance. We extol the Lord's virtues one by one and list the blessings bestowed on us, claiming, after each, that had this been the only blessing, it would have been enough: *Daiyenu.* There comes chorus after chorus,

> Dai-dai-yenu
> Dai-dai-yenu
> Dai-dai-yenu
> Daiyenu, daiyenu . . .

Done with this we sang about a kid "which my father bought for two *zuzim*"—a song in the manner of The House that Jack Built. It grows like a rolling snowball, picking up verses on its way, each devoted to a cat, a dog, a stick, fire, water, an ox, and a ritual slaughterer—until the angel of death comes and with the stroke of the fierce and tribal Jehovah sets things right by ending them. Then we sang the same song over again, with variations,

> The master sends
> A man to the woods,
> A man to the woods,
> To pick pears,
> To pick pears.
> The pears refuse to fall,
> The pears refuse to fall. . . .

after which we broke into a chant to honor Elijah, the Prophet,

> Elijah the prophet,
> Elijah the Tishbite,
> Elijah, Elijah,
> Elijah of Gilead.

No wonder it took us forty years to cross the desert.

Now while all this gay spirit was raging Willy thrust himself into the thick of it. He did not know the words—but seizing a knife in one hand and a wine glass in the other he set to work beating out the rhythm.

"Careful, you'll break the glass," said my father.

But the singing went on, and with it Willy's conducting. And during a pause, Willy struck up a song of his own.

I believe in the good old Bible,
I believe in the good old Bible,
I believe in the good old Bible,
And it's good enough for me.

He had a Bible-country voice, with a Southern drawl and inflection, a break and a trailing swing in its rhythm. He clapped his hands—and you could see in him the mountain folk sitting in their wilderness in a circle at the tabernacle, following the evangelist with whooping and handclapping. He sang—and went barefoot, his skullcap changed into a straw hat, horse-cropped at the crown. He was professing the faith. . . .

It was good enough for Paul and Peter,
It was good enough for Paul and Peter. . . .

My grandfather beamed and melted, snapped his fingers, smacked his lips.

It's that old time religion. . . .

It was Passover in the hill country, celebrated by the lost tribes.

"Amen!" cried my grandfather.

"Amen!" we all responded.

It's that old time religion,
It's that old time religion.
And it's good enough for me.

Willy got up and stomped around the room, the children after him. The wine glasses trembled; the decanter threw off its rainbows in a fury of winking. "Amen!" cried my grandfather, and even my grandmother, who had by now finished reading the *Haggadah* and looked up bewildered, trying her best to say, "This is not my house anyway, you may do as you please . . ."—even she was smiling, unconsciously nodding her head, approving without knowing that she approved. Only my father sat silent and *motionless* at the table, diminished, defeated, utterly dispossessed.

In such fashion the Seder ended, with Willy leading us in song. I remember hearing my stepmother say as we drove home that night, "He's such a wonderful man. It's a pity, he should get married again." My head was swimming in wine and in sleep.

Jo Sinclair
1913–1995

Born Ruth Seid in Brooklyn, writer Jo Sinclair grew up in a working-class home, the daughter of parents who had immigrated from Russia. The family moved to Cleveland, Ohio, when Sinclair was an infant. After graduating from a technical high school as class valedictorian, Sinclair worked in a factory before she was hired through the Works Progress Administration's program for writers. Taking up her pseudonym, she published her first story, titled "Noon Lynching," in 1936 in *New Masses*, a Marxist magazine affiliated with the Communist Party. Her novel *Wasteland* won the Harper Prize in 1946, bolstering her career as a writer. Across her oeuvre, her writing reflects themes of the disenfranchised, exploring Jim Crow segregation, immigration, antisemitism, gender, and sexuality.

Wasteland
1946

He carried his camera and case into the dining room, and as he stood there for a moment, peering at the table through the twilight haze in the room, he breathed deeply of the familiar holiday odors. Then he snapped on the light, and the table seemed to spring up out of darkness. [. . .]

He took several shots, quietly happy at the wonderful detail of the plateful of matzoth at the old man's place, the pillow on his chair, the open *Haggadah* at his own place, and the shine and shimmer of the glasses, the rich look of the wine.

Jewish Holiday, Twentieth Century, he thought. Or I could call it, They Keep Faith in America, Too. [. . .]

Easy to take these pictures he had always been afraid to take. Easy to sit at this table he had been afraid to face all these years. Easy to leave the house and yet to know he need not leave it, to know that it was not dragging at him with chains of mother and iron balls of obligation never faced and never met.

Easy? At what point does a guy start feeling easy about things? Or—as Debby would say it—when does he start to know peace? Cessation of spiritual torment, beginning of self; that's how Debby would say it. This was like dreaming, except that in the dream his heart would not be banging like this, would it? In the dream it wouldn't be so easy to sit here and want to cry, would it?

Sitting there, he remembered some of the words he had read so many times in the *Haggadah*. "Because we were slaves unto Pharaoh in Egypt, and the Eternal, our God, brought us forth thence with a mighty hand and an outstretched arm."

Because we were slaves unto wasteland, he thought. [. . .]

His father lifted the wineglass. Jake sipped, his eyes on the others as they brought their glasses to their lips.

The quick, pattering prayer said, his father dipped bits of parsley into salt water, passed a piece to each person at the table. Again, one of the fast, muttered prayers came from his lips, and everyone ate, a moment after he had begun to chew the piece he had kept for himself.

It was almost time. Jake watched his father break the middle matzoth and hide away one half. He watched him pick up the dish containing the bone and the egg. As the chant began again, Jake gripped his *Haggadah*, watched his mother fill each wineglass to the brim.

Inside of him, a quiet, tremulous voice said. Oh God—.

Then his father said, "Well, Jake, ask the questions."

He stood up, began reading to them with all his heart: "Wherefore is this night distinguished from all other nights? . . . "

Other works by Sinclair: *Sing at My Wake* (1951); *The Changelings* (1955); *Anna Teller* (1960); *The Seasons: Death and Transfiguration* (1993).

Laura Z. Hobson

1900–1986

Laura Z. Hobson was born Laura Kean Zametkin in New York to Russian immigrant parents with socialist affiliations. She attended Cornell University before marrying publisher Thayer Hobson in 1930. Later divorced, Zametkin kept Hobson's name, working in advertising and as a *New York Post* reporter before turning to writing full time in 1940. Her novel *Gentleman's Agreement*, which exposed the hidden antisemitism of 1940s America, made her a household name. Hobson's other lesser-known works are considered to be of equally fine literary value, among them *First Papers* (1964) and *The Tenth Month* (1970), both of which are in part autobiographical, as, Hobson acknowledged, much of her work was.

Gentleman's Agreement
1947

"Every article you've done for us, Phil," Minify had said, "has a kind of human stuff in it. The right answers get in it somehow."

Sure. But he hadn't asked for them and pried for them. When he'd wanted to find out about a scared guy in a jalopy with his whole family behind him hoping for a living in California, he hadn't stood on Route 66 and signaled one of them to a stop so he could ask a lot of questions. He'd just bought himself some old clothes and a breaking-up car and taken Route 66 himself. He'd melted into the crowds moving from grove to grove, ranch to ranch, picking till he'd dropped. He lived in their camps, ate what they ate, told nobody what he was. He'd found the answers in his own guts, not somebody else's. He'd *been* an Okie.

And the mine series. What had he done to get research for it? Go and tap some poor grimy guy on the shoulder and begin to talk? No, he'd damn well gone to Scranton, got himself a job, gone down into the dark, slept in a bunk in a shack. He hadn't dug into a man's secret being. He'd *been* a miner.

"Christ!"

He banged his fist on his thigh. His breath seemed to suck back into his lungs. The startled flesh of his leg still felt the impact of the blow.

"Oh, God, I've got it. It's the way. It's the only way. I'll *be* Jewish. I'll just say—nobody knows me—I can just say it. I can live it myself. Six weeks, eight weeks, nine months—however long it takes. Christ, I've got it."

An elation roared through him. He had it, the idea, the lead, the angle. A dozen times he could have settled for some other idea, but each time he'd thrown it away, tossed it, profligate, stubborn. He'd known that there was somewhere, around some unexpected corner, a better idea, stronger, more real, the only. He'd stalked it, beseeched it, spied for it, waited, rushed, fought. And when he'd found it, this burst of recognition shouted out from him.

"I Was Jewish for Six Months." That was the title. It leaped at him. There was no doubt, no editing, no need to wonder. *That* would get read. *That* there was no passing up. Six weeks it might be, ten, four months, nine, but apart from that one change, it was it. [. . .]

He went to the telephone, dialed Kathy's number.

"It's me, Phil. I never thought you'd be in."

"How's your mother? You sound as if she were better."

"She is, lots. Kathy, you haven't a date?"

"I got stood up." She laughed. "I'm just wrapping presents. Why?"

"I can't leave her alone here. I'd be afraid to. But I've *got* it at last, and I thought, I mean, I'd give a lot to tell you about it."

"The angle? What *is* it?" [. . .]

[. . .] "I'm going to tell everybody I'm Jewish, that's all."

"Jewish? But you're not, Phil, are you?" Instantly she added, "It wouldn't make any difference, of course."

But something had appeared in her eyes.

"You said, 'I'm going to tell'—as if you hadn't *before* but would now," she went on, "so I just wondered. Not that it'd matter to *me,* one way or the other."

"You said that before." He put his drink down.

"Well, *are* you, Phil?"

He almost said, "You know I'm not," but it choked back. Some veil of a thing *had* shown in her eyes. He'd been watching her face every minute, greedy for the quick approval that would show there. This had been quick, but different. She wanted him not to be Jewish. She knew he was not, knew that if he were, he'd never have concealed it. But she wanted to hear him say so right out.

"Oh, this is nonsense," she said briskly. "I know perfectly well you're not Jewish and I wouldn't care if you were. It's just interesting."

He reached for a cigarette. Of course she wouldn't care, any more than he would. Or would she? If he said now, "I really am Jewish"? He'd be the same guy, the same face, the same voice, manner, tweed suit, same eyes, nose, body, but the word "Jewish" would have been said and he'd be different in her mind. In that very same vessel that contained him there'd be a something to "not-care" about.

"Why, Phil," she said slowly, "you're annoyed." She put her drink down also. "You haven't said anything."

"I'm not annoyed. I'm just thinking."

"Don't be so serious about it—you must know where *I* stand."

"I do, Kathy."

"It's just that it caught me off balance. You know, not knowing much about you because you kept making *me* talk about my childhood. So for a second there—" She laughed and shook her head. "Not very bright on the uptake."

He smiled. He felt heavy, flattened out. With her last sentence, the creamy smooth tone had come back. The laugh was the laugh he'd heard that first night. His hand, listless on the arm of the sofa, dropped over the side. Without knowing that he did it, he felt his thumb and forefinger tip together, out of sight, making a circle.

"But anyway, you don't like my angle," he said. "Do you?"

"Oh, I do. It's——" She broke off. Now she reached for a cigarette, and he leaned toward her to light it. Her hair shone. He heard her breathe. Physical knowledge of her moved through him. But there was a sadness to it he couldn't name.

"It's what?"

"Oh, Phil, I just think it'll mix everybody up. People won't know *what* you are."

"After I'm through, they'll——" He couldn't say it. A remarkable thing had happened. Something had seized him that he couldn't argue with. It had started to happen with her first question. Now he knew suddenly what it was. This heavy strange thing in him was what you felt when you'd been insulted. He felt insulted. If he were really a Jew, this is what he'd feel. He was having his first lesson. With Kathy, he'd stumbled into his first lesson at feeling bruised and unwilling to say the placating thing, the reassuring thing. She had reminded him that there was something important about knowing that you were *not* a Jew or were a Jew, no matter what your face or voice or manners or whole being. A slow soreness had been spreading through him. He'd be damned if he'd let her see it. But at last he knew what it was.

Other works by Hobson: *The Trespassers* (1943); *The Other Father* (1950); *The Celebrity* (1951); *Consenting Adult* (1975).

Maurice Schwartz

1889–1960

Actor, producer, and screenwriter Maurice Schwartz was born in Sudlekov, Galicia, and came to the United States in 1901. Fascinated by acting, he toured the United States and in 1918 founded the Yiddish Art Theatre in New York City, along with a school for acting. The Yiddish Art Theatre, for which he served as producer and director, existed for forty years and produced more than 150 plays, including classics from other languages. Schwartz also directed and starred in two Yiddish films, *Uncle Moses* (1932) and *Tevye* (1939).

Shylock and His Daughter
1947

SHYLOCK: You speak of revenge, you who cage us within ghettos, you who cast us alive into flames, only because we are Jews. [*Pause.*] Are not Jews and Christians alike fashioned in the image of God? Does not Mother Earth offer nourishment to Jews and Christians alike? Have we not the right to breathe the breath of life as you do? Do not the healing rays of the sun reach for us as for you? The least of God's creatures has the right to live, and the will to protect its life. And when you wish to, wipe us off the face of the earth, Shall we not resist? Shall we Jews be the only ones among God's creatures to resign ourselves to death, even without defense? You speak of revenge. Who has taught us the law of revenge? You. Who has driven us to earn our embittered bread by usury? You. And if you let some of us live in the Ghetto at all, it is only that you may boast of love, mercy and charity, which you proclaim with your lips and disdain in your hearts. [*Pause.*] Our father Abraham, Signor Antonio, was a hospitable man. None left his tent empty-handed. You are my guest. And though you disdained to cross the threshold of my house, yet will I lend you the three thousand ducats—Without interest. [. . .]

SHYLOCK: Almighty God! See what these Christians are! . . . Not only do you torment us with Ghettos and Inquisitions, but you seek to demean us by mockery and derision. You call me base cur, and I am ready to lend you three thousand ducats—gratis, on the mere credit of your bond. And you, in order to inflict hurt on myself and my people, are desirous of making this loan into a sport and a mockery . . . If it is your pleasure to jest and to continue your everlasting game of derision, very well then, Signor Antonio, we shall write that clause into our contract to wit, that . . .

ANTONIO: That if, on the seventeenth day of August in the year of our Lord, 1559, at sunset, the merchant Antonio fails to repay the loan, then the Jewish usurer Shylock is entitled to a pound of flesh from the merchant's breast, cut nearest his heart. [. . .]

RABBI: Shylock, the Community has sent us to hear your final decision. Tomorrow will be a *Yom Kippur,* a Day of Atonement, for us. Jews will weep and fast, and hide in their homes, for tomorrow the shameful trial begins. A Jew will demand a Christian's pound of flesh. Do you realize what a misfortune you are bringing on the communities of Israel? For generations and generations, Jews will not be able to free themselves of this horrible accusation. In the name of the Community, I plead with you, Shylock: Do not go to the Court tomorrow. Cancel that debt of three thousand ducats. The Community will refund you the loss.

SHYLOCK: Whose daughter was led to apostasy—mine or yours. Rabbi?

RABBI: Other Jews have suffered what you suffer. They found solace in the Psalms, in the Talmud.

SHYLOCK: The Psalms and the Talmud will not return my child to me. God has taken two sons of mine and a daughter. I then pronounced the blessing: "The Lord hath given, the Lord hath taken, blessed be the Name of the Lord." My Leah departed from me. I said *Kaddish,* I read the Psalms for her. What prayer can I say for an apostate? No more Psalms, no more prayers for me! Choose another Community Head. I will not cross the threshold of the Synagogue again.

TUBAL: Shylock, you are calling down destruction on all the Jews of Italy.

RABBI: Your base revenge is dearer to you than the God of your faith and the lives of your brethren. To such a sinner there can be only one answer—excommunication. Tomorrow you must come to the Synagogue to give account to the Community.

SHYLOCK: Henceforth, my place is in the Court of Venice, not in the Synagogue.

RABBI: If so, may the curse strike you immediately. In the name of the Community, I pronounce you excommunicate and accursed. Like a leper, shall you be cast out of our midst. Any Jew who will offer you a drink of water or a slice of bread shall be accursed as you are. Henceforth, you may not come near a Sacred Place, for you are contaminate. [*Pause.*] Samuel, son of Jacob, you may no longer stand within four cubits of him. He is contaminate. Samuel, son of Jacob, leave this sinner, and come with us to the Synagogue. [SAMUEL MORRO *does not budge.*] You move not from your place. Then the curse rests also on you. You, too, are excommunicate. Come, brothers. *Shaketz teshaktzenu*—thou shalt utterly detest him, and thou shalt utterly abhor him, for he is accursed.

Translated by Abraham Regelson.

Howard Fast

My Glorious Brothers
1948

A Prologue

WHEREIN I, SIMON SIT IN JUDGMENT

On an afternoon in the month of Nisan, which is the sweetest time of the year, the bells were sounded; and I, Simon, the least, the most unworthy of all my glorious brothers, sat down for judgment. I shall tell you of that, even as I write it here, for judgment is compounded out of justice—or so they say—and I can still hear the voice of my father, the Adon, saying:

"On three things life rests: on right, which is set forth in the Law; on truth, which is set forth in the world; and on the love of one man for another, which is set forth in your heart."

But that is a long time ago, as men think, and my father, the old man, the Adon, is dead, and all my glorious brothers are dead too, and what was plain then is far from plain now. So if I write down here all that took place—or almost all, since a man's thoughts are loosely woven and not like the hide of a beast—it is for myself to know and to understand, if there is any such thing as knowing and understanding. Judas knew, but Judas never sat, as I sit, over the whole land with the land in peace, the roads open north and south and east and west, the land tilled for the harvest, the children playing in the fields and laughing as they play. Judas never saw the vines so heavy they could not support their load, the barley breaking out like pearls, the grain cribs cracking under their fullness; and Judas never heard the song of women in joy and no terror.

Nor did there ever come to Judas a legate from Rome, as he came to me this day, making the whole long journey, as he put it—and you can decide for yourself when a Roman speaks the truth or when he lies—for one reason: to speak with a man and to grasp his hand.

"And are there no men in Rome?" I said to him, after I had given him bread and wine and fruit, and seen that he was provided with a bath and a room to rest in.

"There are men in Rome," he smiled, the movement of his thin, shaven upper lip as deliberate as all his other movements, "but there are no Maccabees. So the Senate gave me a writ and ordered me to go to the land where the Maccabee rules and seek him out . . ." He hesitated here for long enough to count to five; the smile went away and his dark face became almost sullen. ". . . And give him my hand, which is Rome's hand, if he offers his."

"I don't rule," I said. "A Jew has no ruler, no king."

"Yet you are the Maccabee?"

"That's right."

"And you lead these people?"

"I judge them—now. When they have to be led, it may be that I will lead them and it may be that someone else will. That makes no difference. They'll find themselves a leader, as they found them before."

"Yet you *had* kings, as I recall," the Roman said meditatively. "We had them, and they were like a poison to us. We destroyed them or they destroyed us. Whether the King is Jew or Greek or—"

"Or Roman," the legate said, that slow, deliberate smile returning.

"Or Roman." [. . .]

"What do you worship, Simon Maccabeus, what do you respect?" the Roman prodded. "In all the world, are there no other men of worth than the Jews?"

"All men are of worth," I murmured. "Of equal worth." "Yet you are the chosen people, as you put it so frequently. What are you chosen for, Simon? And if men are of equal worth, how can you be chosen? Or did no Jew ever ask that before, Simon?"

I shook my head somberly.

"Do I trouble you, Simon Maccabeus?" the Roman said. "You are too proud, I think. We are a proud people, too, but we do not scorn what others make. We do not scorn what others are or do. You hate slavery, Simon, yet your people hold slaves. How then? Why so ready to say good or bad, as if this tiny land were the center of the whole universe?"

I had no answers. He was the dealer in nations, and I was Ethnarch of a tiny land and a small people; and like a heavy sickness inside of me came the realization that I moved on currents beyond me, beyond my knowing.

So I sit tonight, writing down this account of my glorious brothers, writing it for all men to read, Jew or Roman or Greek or Persian—writing it in the hope that out of my own memory will come some understanding of whence we came and where we go, we who are Jews and like no other people, we who meet all the adversity and hurt of life with that strange and holy phrase:

"Once we were slaves in the land of Egypt."

Norman Mailer

1923-2007

Born in New Jersey and raised in Brooklyn, Norman Mailer burst onto the literary scene with *The Naked and the Dead*, considered one of the best war novels ever written. Based on his brief army experience in the Philippines, the novel won the 1948 Pulitzer Prize and propelled Mailer to a level of fame at which he brashly remained for the next sixty years. Painstaking and exact in his writing, most of Mailer's books took years to write. His powerful evocation of executed murderer Gary Gilmore in *The Executioner's Song* garnered him his second Pulitzer Prize in 1980. Prolific in all aspects, including political activism, he left behind forty-five thousand letters when he died.

The Naked and the Dead
1948

The old man Moshe Sefardnick sits in the rear of the place on a camp stool. There is never any work for him to do and indeed he is too old for it, too bewildered. The old man has never been able to understand America. It is too large, too fast, the ordered suppressed castes of centuries wither here; people are always in flux. His neighbors become wealthier, move away from the East Side to Brooklyn, to the Bronx, to the upper West Side; some of them lose their little businesses, drift farther down the street to another hovel, or migrate to the country. He has been a peddler himself; in the spring before the First World War, he has carried his goods on his back, tramped the dirt roads through small New Jersey towns, selling scissors and thread and needles. But he has never understood it and now in his sixties he is prematurely senile, an old man relegated to the back of a tiny candy store, drifting in Talmudic halls of thought. (If a man hath a worm on his brain, it may be removed by laying a cabbage leaf near the orifice onto which the worm will crawl.)

His grandson, Joey, now seven, comes home from school weeping, a bruise on his face. Ma, they beat me up, they beat me up, they called me sheenie.

Who did, who was it?

It was the Italian kids, a whole gang, they beat me up.

The sounds move in the old man's mind, alter his thought stream. The Italians. He shrugs. An undependable people; in the Inquisition they let the Jews in at Genoa, but at Naples . . . Naples.

He shrugs, watches the mother wash the blood away, fit a patch of adhesive to the cut. Oh, mein Joey.

The old man laughs to himself, the delicate filtered laughter of a pessimist who is reassured that things have turned out badly. Nu, this American is not so different. The old man sees the goy faces staring at the victims.

Joey, he calls in a harsh cracked voice.

What is it, zaydee?

The goyim, what did they call you?

Sheenie.

The grandfather shrugs again. Another name. For a moment an ancient buried anger moves him. He stares at the unformed features of the boy, the bright blond hair. In America even the Juden look like goyim. Blond hair. The old man rouses himself to speech, talks in Yiddish. They beat you because you're a Jew, he says. Do you know what a Jew is?

Yes.

The grandfather feels a spasm of warmth for his grandchild. So handsome. So good. He is an old man and he will die soon, and the child is too young to understand him. There is so much wisdom he could give.

It's a difficult question, the meaning of a Jew. It's not a race, he says, it's not even a religion any more, maybe it will never be a nation. Dimly, he knows he has lost the child already, but he continues talking, musing aloud.

What is it, then? Yehudah Halevy said Israel is the heart of all nations. What attacks the body attacks the heart. And the heart is also the conscience, which suffers for the sins of the nations. He shrugs once more, does not differentiate between saying aloud what he thinks or merely moving his lips. It's an interesting problem, but personally I think a Jew is a Jew because he suffers. Olla Juden suffer.

Why?

So we will deserve the Messiah? The old man no longer knows. It makes us better and worse than the goyim, he thinks.

But the child must always be given an answer. He rouses himself, concentrates and says without certainty, It is so we will last. He speaks again, wholly lucid for a moment. We are a harried people, beset by oppressors. We must always journey from disaster to disaster, and it makes us stronger and weaker than other men, makes us love and hate the other Juden more than other men. We have suffered so much that we know how to endure. We will always endure.

The boy understands almost nothing of this, but he has heard the words and they engrave a memory which perhaps he will exhume later. He looks at his grandfather, at the wrinkled corded hands and the anger, the febrile intelligence, in his pale old-man's eyes. Suffer. It is the only word Joey Goldstein absorbs. Already he has forgotten most of the shame and fear of his beating. He fingers the plaster on his temple, wonders if he can go out to play.

Other works by Mailer: *An American Dream* (1964); *The Armies of the Night* (1968); *Marilyn* (1973).

Paul Goodman

1911–1972

Born in New York, Paul Goodman grew up in poverty, his father having left his mother for another woman before his birth. Goodman graduated City College of New York in 1931 and promptly applied himself to writing and teaching drama. After being fired from multiple teaching positions because of his bisexuality, Goodman spent years struggling to support his family. His book *Growing Up Absurd* (1960) touched on the growing disaffection of American youth at the time and brought him into public awareness. He was one of the Group of Seven who founded the New York Institute for Gestalt Therapy. He also wrote a book on urban planning titled *Communitas* (1947), with his renowned architect brother Percival Goodman.

A Memorial Synagogue
1949

The Painter had a different personality. A tiny Polish Jew, he was famous as a creator of wonderful whimsical animals. He said:

"For my part I wanted to use stained glass. But the architect says we must love white light for reading. Why must they read so much when they can look at my pictures? O.K. I can tell the story on the walls."

"What story?"

"A fable I heard in the old country, unless it came to me in a dream. It goes like this:

"God said to Noah, 'Build the ark, three stories high; then the animals, two of each kind, will go up in it and be saved from the flood.' This was the arrangement and Noah set to work and did his part. But when the animals heard about it they called a world Congress. (Maybe some of the finest animals didn't even come to the Congress.) They chattered and jabbered; finally it came down to two factions. The first faction was superstitious and they thought they'd better do as they were told. But the other faction was indignant and didn't trust the arrangement at all.

"'Since when,' said they, 'have these men been so good to us that now we should put our trust in them and, to be quite frank, walk like boobies into a trap. I for my part have a lively memory of Nimrod, that mighty hunter. Ha! you turn pale. So.

"'And what do you think of the accommodations? We go by twos; but Noah! he doesn't go alone with his wife, but he also takes with him those three fat boys, of whom I need say no further. *And* their wives. Include us out.'

"The others only said, 'We'd better go.'

"So the day came and Noah blew on his shofar a loud blast—"

"Excuse me," said Armand, "what's a shofar?"

"A shofar—is a shofar."

"Yes, but what is it? Noah blew a blast on his shofar; what's a shofar?"

"A shofar is a shofar, dummy," said the painter angrily.

"What is it, a kind of bugle?"

"Yes, it's a bugle. Noah blew a blast on his bugle!"

"What's to get angry about? How should I know? Why didn't you say it was a bugle in the first place?"

"Please—" the painter screwed up his face in pain and turned to us appealingly, "is a shofar a bugle?"

"—He blew a blast and some of the animals came, and then came the rain and the flood. But the others *didn't* come, and they *drowned. Ach!*—So perished from the earth the wonderful snodorgus and the kafooziopus, and klippy, and Petya, and the marmape, and Sadie—"

It was impossible to believe one's eyes and ears, for suddenly the little man began to bawl in strange little sobs at the top of his chest, for his fantastic animals whose names he was making up as he went along.

"So died," he screamed, "the loveliest and the shrewdest. Petya! And my sister's little girls, and my brothers, and long ago my friend Apollinaire, who had the alivest voice.

"But I shall paint these beauties into existence again, on every wall in the world!"

The architect said:

"In a building of this kind the chief thing to communicate is the sense of the Congregation. The sense of itself *by* the Congregation. Therefore we must be careful about the sight-lines."

He hesitated. "The sight-lines. I arrange the seats in two banks, facing each other across a plain. The Ark is at the eastern end of the plain. See, the sight-lines: everybody is in full view."

He hesitated and began to draw lines on the tracing-paper.

"They flash across the space! Sometimes they get tangled in mid-air. What does *that* mean? It means that a man gets the impression he is being stared at.

"Don't misunderstand me," he apologized. "I'm not saying that it's embarrassing to be looked at; if that were so it would be the end of architecture; but—not just now.

"Strictly speaking there is nothing else to see in the Jewish service except the Congregation itself. There is no sacrificial act.

"A few men are called up to bless the passage; that's all the service consists of. That's what we have to keep in full view. Here they open the scroll to read it, and quidam is called on to bless the passage. Ach! *everybody* is suddenly looking at him, a fine representative figure of a man!

"Suppose with an angry flush on his face, he turns and stares at *you!*

"Maybe the visible Congregation is not such a good idea after all and something is to be said for the stained glass.

"The old men cover their heads with their prayer-shawls, but you could never get the young ones to do it. They are ashamed to be ashamed."

He began to slash the paper with heavy lines, as if the sight-lines were clashing in the space like knives.

He hesitated. The hesitation endured, but there was no moment at which you could say he fell silent.

Finally some one prompted him. "What about the sight-lines? What do they see?"

"The people are crying," he said.

He heaved a sigh of relief. "That solves the problem!" he said more cheerfully. "Each one is hiding behind a shiny wall of tears; they can't see each other anyway."

Other works by Goodman: *The Grand Piano; or, The Almanac of Alienation* (1942); *State of Nature* (1946); *Gestalt Therapy* (1951).

Arthur Miller

Death of a Salesman
1949

Act One

BIFF: People are worse off than Willy Loman. Believe me. I've seen them!

LINDA: Then make Charley your father, Biff. You can't do that, can you? I don't say he's a great man. Willy Loman never made a lot of money. His name was never in the paper. He's not the finest character that ever lived. But he's a human being, and a terrible thing is happening to him. So attention must be paid. He's not to be allowed to fall into his grave like an old dog. Attention, attention must be finally paid to such a person. You called him crazy—

BIFF: I didn't mean—

LINDA: No, a lot of people think he's lost his—balance. But you don't have to be very smart to know what his trouble is. The man is exhausted.

HAPPY: Sure!

LINDA: A small man can be just as exhausted as a great man. He works for a company thirty-six years this March, opens up unheard-of territories to their trademark, and now in his old age they take his salary away. [. . .]

Act Two

WILLY [*stops him with*]: May you rot in hell if you leave this house!

BIFF [*turning*]: Exactly what is it that you want from me?

WILLY: I want you to know, on the train, in the mountains, in the valleys, wherever you go, that you cut down your life for spite!

BIFF: No, no.

WILLY: Spite, spite, is the word of your undoing! And when you're down and out, remember what did it. When you're rotting somewhere beside the railroad tracks, remember, and don't you dare blame it on me!

BIFF: I'm not blaming it on you!

WILLY: I won't take the rap for this, you hear?

[HAPPY *comes down the stairs and stands on the bottom step, watching.*]

BIFF: That's just what I'm telling you!

WILLY [*sinking into a chair at the table, with full accusation*]: You're trying to put a knife in me—don't think I don't know what you're doing!

BIFF: All right, phony! Then let's lay it on the line. [*He whips the rubber tube out of his pocket and puts it on the table.*]

HAPPY: You crazy—

LINDA: Biff! [*She moves to grab the hose, but* BIFF *holds it down with his hand.*]

BIFF: Leave it there! Don't move it!

WILLY [*not looking at it*]: What is that?

BIFF: You know goddam well what that is.

WILLY [*caged, wanting to escape*]: I never saw that.

BIFF: You saw it. The mice didn't bring it into the cellar! What is this supposed to do, make a hero out of you? This supposed to make me sorry for you?

WILLY: Never heard of it.

BIFF: There'll be no pity for you, you hear it? No pity!

WILLY [*to* LINDA]: You hear the spite!

BIFF: No, you're going to hear the truth—what you are and what I am!

LINDA: Stop it!

WILLY: Spite!

HAPPY [*coming down toward* BIFF]: You cut it now!

BIFF [*to* HAPPY]: The man don't know who we are! The man is gonna know! [*To* WILLY]: We never told the truth for ten minutes in this house!

HAPPY: We always told the truth!

BIFF [*turning on him*]: You big blow, are you the assistant buyer? You're one of the two assistants to the assistant, aren't you?

HAPPY: Well, I'm practically—

BIFF: You're practically full of it! We all are! And I'm through with it. [*To* WILLY]: Now hear this, Willy, this is me.

WILLY: I know you!

BIFF: You know why I had no address for three months? I stole a suit in Kansas City and I was in jail. [*To* LINDA, *who is sobbing*]: Stop crying. I'm through with it.

[LINDA *turns away from them, her hands covering her face.*]

WILLY: I suppose that's my fault!

BIFF: I stole myself out of every good job since high school!

WILLY: And whose fault is that?

BIFF: And I never got anywhere because you blew me so full of hot air I could never stand taking orders from anybody! That's whose fault it is!

WILLY: I hear that!

LINDA: Don't, Biff!

BIFF: It's goddam time you heard that! I had to be boss big shot in two weeks, and I'm through with it!

WILLY: Then hang yourself! For spite, hang yourself!

BIFF: No! Nobody's hanging himself, Willy! I ran down eleven flights with a pen in my hand today. And suddenly I stopped, you hear me? And in the middle of that office building, do you hear this? I stopped in the middle of that building and I saw—the sky. I saw the things that I love in this world. The work and the food and time to sit and smoke. And I looked at the pen and said to myself, what the hell am I grabbing this for? Why am I trying to become what I don't want to be? What am I doing in an office, making a contemptuous, begging fool of myself, when all I want is out there, waiting for me the minute I say I know who I am! Why can't I say that, Willy? [*He tries to make* WILLY *face him, but* WILLY *pulls away and moves to the left.*]

WILLY [*with hatred, threateningly*]: The door of your life is wide open!

BIFF: Pop! I'm a dime a dozen, and so are you!

WILLY [*turning on him now in an uncontrolled outburst*]: I am not a dime a dozen! I am Willy Loman, and you are Biff Loman!

[BIFF *starts for* WILLY, *but is blocked by* HAPPY. *In his fury,* BIFF *seems on the verge of attacking his father.*]

BIFF: I am not a leader of men, Willy, and neither are you. You were never anything but a hard-working drummer who landed in the ash can like all the rest of them! I'm one dollar an hour, Willy! I tried seven states and couldn't raise it. A buck an hour! Do you gather my meaning? I'm not bringing home any prizes any more, and you're going to stop waiting for me to bring them home!

WILLY [*directly to* BIFF]: You vengeful, spiteful mutt!

[BIFF *breaks from* HAPPY. WILLY, *in fright, starts up the stairs.* BIFF *grabs him.*]

BIFF [*at the peak of his fury*]: Pop, I'm nothing! I'm nothing, Pop. Can't you understand that? There's no spite in it any more. I'm just what I am, that's all.

[BIFF's *fury has spent itself, and he breaks down, sobbing, holding on to* WILLY, *who dumbly fumbles for* BIFF's *face.*]

WILLY [*astonished*]: What're you doing? What're you doing? [*To* LINDA]: Why is he crying?

BIFF [*crying, broken*]: Will you let me go, for Christ's sake? Will you take that phony dream and burn it before something happens? [*Struggling to contain himself, he pulls away and moves to the stairs.*] I'll go in the morning. Put him—put him to bed. [*Exhausted,* BIFF *moves up the stairs to his room*].

WILLY [*after a long pause, astonished, elevated*]: Isn't that—isn't that remarkable? Biff—he likes me!

LINDA: He loves you, Willy!

HAPPY [*deeply moved*]: Always did, Pop.

WILLY: Oh, Biff! [*Staring wildly*]: He cried! Cried to me. [*He is choking with his love, and now cries out his promise*]: That boy—that boy is going to be magnificent.

Hortense Calisher

Old Stock

1950

Hester sat down quietly next to her mother, whose sewing went on and on, a mild substitute for conversation. For a while, Hester watched the long, important-looking shadows that encroached upon the hills, like enigmas stated every afternoon but never fully solved. Then she leaned carefully toward Miss Onderdonk. "May I go see your parlor?" she asked.

Miss Onderdonk gave no sign that she had heard. It might have been merely the uncanny luck of the partly deaf that prompted her remark. "People come by here this morning," she said. "From down to your place. Walk right into the parlor, no by your leave. Want to buy my antiques!"

Mrs. Elkin, needle uplifted, shook her head, commiserating, gave a quick, consolatory mew of understanding, and plunged the needle into the next stitch.

"Two women—and a man all ninnied out for town," said Miss Onderdonk. "Old woman had doctored hair. Grape-colored! Hollers at me as if I'm the foreign one. Picks up my Leather-Bound Onderdonk History!" Her explosive breath capitalized the words. The cat, squirting suddenly from her twitching hand, settled itself, an aggrieved white tippet, at a safe distance on the lawn. "'Put that down,' I said," said Miss Onderdonk, her eyes as narrow as the cat's. "'I don't have no antiques,' I said. 'These here are my belongings.'"

Mrs. Elkin put down her sewing. Her broad hands, with the silver-and-gold thimble on one middle finger, moved uncertainly, unlike Miss Onderdonk's hands, which were pressed flat, in triumph, on her faded flour-sack lap.

"I told Elizabeth Smith," Miss Onderdonk said. "I told her she'd rue the day she ever started taking in Jews."

The short word soared in an arc across Hester's vision and hit the remembered, stereopticon picture of the parlor. The parlor sank and disappeared, a view in an album snapped shut. Now her stare was for her mother's face, which was pink but inconclusive.

Mrs. Elkin, raising her brows, made a helpless face at Hester, as if to say, "After all, the vagaries of the deaf . . ." She permitted herself a minimal shrug, even a slight spreading of palms. Under Hester's stare, she lowered her eyes and turned toward Miss Onderdonk again.

"I thought you knew, Miss Onderdonk," said her mother. "I thought you knew that we were—Hebrews." The word, the ultimate refinement, slid out of her mother's soft voice as if it were on runners.

"Eh?" said Miss Onderdonk.

Say it, Hester prayed. She had never before felt the sensation of prayer. Please say it, Mother. *Say "Jew."* She heard the word in her own mind, double-voiced, like the ram's horn at Yom Kippur, with an ugly present bray but with a long, urgent echo as time-spanning as Roland's horn.

Her mother leaned forward. Perhaps she had heard it, too—the echo. "But we are Jewish," she said in a stronger voice. "Mr. Elkin and I are Jewish."

Miss Onderdonk shook her head, with the smirk of one who knew better. "Never seen the Mister. The girl here has the look, maybe. But not you."

"But—" Mrs. Elkin, her lower lip caught by her teeth, made a sound like a stifled, chiding sigh. "Oh, yes," she said, and nodded, smiling, as if she had been caught out in a fault.

"Does you credit," said Miss Onderdonk. "Don't say it don't. Make your bed, lie on it. Don't have to pretend with me, though."

With another baffled sigh, Mrs. Elkin gave up, flumping her hands down on her sewing. She was pinker, not with anger but, somehow, as if she had been cajoled.

"Had your reasons, maybe." Miss Onderdonk tittered, high and henlike. "Ain't no Jew, though. Good blood shows, any day."

Hester stood up. "We're in a book at home, too," she said loudly.

"'The History of the Jews of Richmond, 1769–1917.'" Then she turned her back on Miss Onderdonk, who might or might not have heard, on her mother, who had, and stomped down the steps.

At the foot of the lawn, she stopped behind a bush that hid her from the steps, feeling sick and let-down. She had somehow used Miss Onderdonk's language. She hadn't said what she meant at all. She heard her father's words, amused and sad, as she had heard them once, over her shoulder, when he had come upon her poring over the red-bound book, counting up the references to her grandfather. "That Herbert Ezekiel's book?" He had looked over her shoulder, twirling the gold cigar-clipper on his watch chain. "Well, guess it won't hurt the sons of Moses any if they want to tally up some newer ancestors now and then."

Miss Onderdonk's voice, with its little, cut-off chicken laugh, travelled down to her from the steps. "Can't say it didn't cross my mind, though, that the girl does have the look."

Isaac Bashevis Singer

The Family Moskat
1950

Five years after the death of his second wife Reb Meshulam Moskat married for a third time. His new wife was a woman in her fifties, from Galicia, in eastern Austria, the widow of a wealthy brewer from Brody, a man of erudition. Sometime before he died, the brewer had gone bankrupt, and all that was left to his widow was a bookcase full of learned tomes, a pearl necklace—which later turned out to be imitation—and a daughter named Adele; her name was properly Eidele, but Rosa Frumetl, her mother, called her Adele, after the modern fashion. Meshulam Moskat made the widow's acquaintance in Karlsbad, where he had gone to take the waters. There he had married her. No one in Warsaw knew anything about the marriage; Reb Meshulam wrote to none of his family from the watering-place, nor was it his habit to give anyone an account of his doings. It was not until the middle of September that a telegram to his housekeeper in Warsaw announced his return and gave orders that Leibel, the coachman, was to drive out to the Vienna Station to wait for his employer. The train arrived toward evening. Reb Meshulam descended from the first-class car, his wife and stepdaughter after him.

When Leibel came up to him Reb Meshulam said: "This is your new mistress," and lowered a ponderous eyelid. All the luggage Reb Meshulam was carrying was a small, well-worn portfolio thickly plastered with colored customs labels. He had checked his large metal-strapped trunk through on the baggage car. But the ladies were weighted down with all sorts of valises, packages, and bundles. There was hardly enough room in the carriage to stow the stuff away; it was necessary to pile most of it on the driver's box.

Leibel was far from being a timid man, but at the sight of the women he turned red and lost his tongue entirely. The new Madame Moskat was of medium height and thin. Her shoulders showed the beginnings of a stoop, her face was heavily wrinkled. Her nose was red with catarrh and her eyes were the sad, moist eyes of a woman of gentle birth and breeding. She wore the close-fitting wig of the pious Jewish matron, covered with a soft black shawl. Long earrings hung, glittering, from her earlobes. She was dressed in a silk outer coat, in the style of a pelerine, over a cloth dress, and pointed-toed, French-style shoes. In one hand she carried an amber-handled umbrella; with the other she held fast to her daughter, a girl in her early twenties, tall and slender, with an irregularly shaped nose, prominent-boned features, a sharp chin, and thin lips. There were dark rings under the girl's eyes; she looked as though she had gone sleepless for nights. Her faded blond hair was combed tightly back into a Greek knot and was thickly peppered with hairpins. She was carrying a bunch of withered yellow flowers, a package tied with red ribbon, a large box, and a book, from the edges of which a little bundle of twigs protruded, reminding Leibel of the osier branches used in the ritual on the Feast of Tabernacles. The girl gave off a scent of chocolate, a faint flavor of caraway-seed perfume, and something arrogantly foreign. Leibel grimaced.

"A show-off!" he muttered to himself.

"Adele, my child, this is Warsaw," Rosa Frumetl said. "A big city, isn't it?"

"How do I know? I haven't seen it yet," the girl answered in a flat Galician accent.

As always when Reb Meshulam left on a trip or came back from one, a ring of curious onlookers gathered around him. Everyone in Warsaw knew him, Christians as well as Jews. The newspapers had published stories about him and his enterprises more than once; even his picture had been printed. In appearance he was different from the Warsaw Jews of the old school. He was tall and lean, with thin features, sunken cheeks, and a short white chin beard, each individual hair separated from the next. From below his bushy eyebrows peered a pair of greenish eyes, steely and piercing. His nose was hooked. On his upper lip there was a scant mustache like the whiskers of a sea lion. He was wearing a cloth cap with a high crown. His overcoat, with a gathered waist and split back, managed to look like an aristocratic caftan. From a distance he might have been taken for one of the Polish gentry or even for a Great Russian. But a closer view showed indications of the sidelocks of the pious Jew on his temples.

Reb Meshulam was in a hurry. Every once in a while he poked Leibel in the shoulder to drive faster. But the loading of the luggage had taken a long time. Besides, the road from Vielka Street to the Gzhybov was blocked with fire engines and it was necessary to drive by way of the Marshalkovska and the Krulevska. The street lights were already lit, and around the spherical greenish-blue lamps flew swarms of flies, casting darting shadows onto the sidewalk. From time to time a red-painted tramcar rumbled by, the electric wires overhead giving off crackling blue sparks. Everything here was familiar to Reb Meshulam: the tall buildings with the wide gates, the stores with the brightly illuminated windows, the Russian policeman standing between the two rows of car tracks, the Saxon Gardens, with densely leaved branches extending over the high rails. In the midst of the thick foliage tiny lights flickered and died. From inside the park came a mild breeze that seemed to carry the secret whisperings of amorous couples. At the gates two gendarmes stood with swords to make sure that no long-caftaned Jews or their wives ventured into the park to breathe some of the fragrant air. Farther along the road was the Bourse, of which Reb Meshulam was one of the oldest members.

The carriage turned into Gzhybov Place, and abruptly everything changed. The sidewalks were crowded with gaberdined Jews wearing small cloth caps, and bewigged women with shawls over their heads. Even the smells were different now. There was a whiff of the market place in the air—spoiled fruits, lemons, and a mixture of something sweetish and tarry, which could not be given a name and which impinged on the senses only when one returned to the scene after a longish absence. The street was a bedlam of sound and activity. Street peddlers called out their wares in ear-piercing chants—potato cakes, hot chick peas, apples, pears, Hungarian plums, black and white grapes, watermelon whole and in sections. Although the evening was warm, the merchants wore outer coats, with large leather money pouches hanging from the belts. Women hucksters sat on boxes, benches, and doorsills. The stalls were lighted with lanterns, some with flickering candles stuck on the edges of wooden crates. Customers lifted and pinched the fruits or took little exploratory nibbles, smacking their lips to savor the taste. The stall-keepers weighed purchases on tin scales.

Translated by A. H. Gross.

Chaim Grade

1910–1982

A novelist and poet, Chaim Grade is considered one of the giants of Yiddish literature, particularly for the postwar period. Born in Vilna, Grade was educated in the yeshivas of the moralist *mussar* movement that emphasized extreme ethical piety and harsh introspection. Although he left this milieu at the age of twenty-two, the religious ideology of his early years left an undeniable imprint on his later work. A member of the literary group Yung Vilne, Grade achieved quick success as a poet with a distinctive, prophetic voice. After the war, Grade settled in the United States, where he published his most famous works, both poetry and novels. He is perhaps best remembered for his novel-length portrayals of Vilna Jewry, richly described in all its complexity and color.

My Quarrel with Hersh Rasseyner
1951

"Reb Hersh," I finally said, "as I sat here listening to you, I sometimes thought I was listening to myself. And since it's harder to lie to yourself than to someone else, I will answer you as though you were my own conscience, with no thought either of merely being polite or of trying to win a debate. I am under no greater obligation than you to know everything. I don't consider it a special virtue not to have doubts. I must tell you that just as the greatness of the faithful consists in their innocence and wholeness, so the heroism of thinkers consists in their being able to tolerate doubt and make their peace with it. You didn't discover your truth; you received it ready-made. If anyone should ask you about something in your practice of which you yourself don't know the meaning, you answer, 'The work of my fathers is in my hands.' As a rule, a man is a rebel in his youth; in age he seeks tranquillity. You had tranquillity in your youth, while I don't have it even now; you once predicted it would be so with me. But is your tranquillity of soul a proof that the truth is with you? For all your readiness to suffer and make sacrifices, there is an element of self-satisfaction in you. You say of yourself that you were born in a coat of many colors.

"They used to call 'the old one,' the founder of Novaredok, the master of the holes. It was said that Reb Joseph Yoizl lived apart for many years in the woods in a hut that had two holes in the wall; through one they would hand him dairy foods and through the other meat foods. When he put his withdrawal behind him and came back into the world, his philosophy was either milk or meat, one extreme or the other, but nothing in between. His disciples, including you, took this teaching from him. His disciples want what they call wholeness too, and they have no use for compromises. What you said about our wanting a small Torah so that it would be easier for us was simply idle talk. On the contrary, we make it harder for ourselves, because we acknowledge a double responsibility—toward Jewish tradition and toward secular culture.

"You said that among Jews the important thing was always the community and not the individual, until we came along and spoiled it; we wanted to be like the gentiles, for whom the 'I' is more important than anything else. And in order to hurt me you tried to persuade me that what I want to do is to climb up the Hotel de Ville and put myself there as a living monument to myself. You allow yourself to mock, because, after all, what you do is for the sake of heaven, isn't that so? I won't start now to tell you historical facts about leaders and rulers who made the community their footstool. As for what you say, that the principle among Jews was always the community until we came, I agree. We secularists want to free the individual. You say a man should tear his individual desires out of himself. But for hundreds of years men have gone to torture and death so that the commonwealth shall consist of free and happy individuals. I could read you an all but endless list of our own boys and girls whose youth was spent in black dungeons because they would not be deterred from trying to make the world better. You yourself know about Jewish workers who fought against all oppressors and tyrants. The only thing is that you won't concede that free thinkers can sacrifice themselves too, so you complain that they left Jewish tradition only to enjoy forbidden pleasures. That is untrue. In my own quarter I knew as many 'seekers' as in Novaredok—and more. Because you denied the world, Reb Hersh, you withdrew into an attic. But these young people dearly loved the world, and they sacrificed themselves—to better it.

"What right then do you have to complain to us about the world? You yourself said that we dreamed about another, a better world—which nullifies your accusation. We carried into the world our own vision of what the world should be, as the Jews in the wilderness carried the Ark with the tablets of the Covenant, so that they could enter the land of Canaan with their own Torah. You laugh; you say that we deceived ourselves. I'll ask you: Do you renounce Judaism because the Samaritans and the Karaites distorted the Law of Moses?"

Translated by Milton Himmelfarb.

Other works by Grade: *Yo* (1936); *Musernikes* (1939); *My Mother's Sabbath Days* (1955); *The Agunah* (1961); *The Yeshiva* (1967–1968).

Saul Bellow

The Adventures of Augie March
1953

Chapter I

I am an American, Chicago born—Chicago, that somber city—and go at things as I have taught myself, free-style, and will make the record in my own way: first to knock, first admitted; sometimes an innocent knock, sometimes a not so innocent. But a man's character is his fate, says Heraclitus, and in the end there isn't any way to disguise the nature of the knocks by acoustical work on the door or gloving the knuckles.

Everybody knows there is no fineness or accuracy of suppression; if you hold down one thing you hold down the adjoining.

My own parents were not much to me, though I cared for my mother. She was simple-minded, and what I learned from her was not what she taught, but on the order of object lessons. She didn't have much to teach, poor woman. My brothers and I loved her. I speak for them both; for the elder it is safe enough; for the younger one, Georgie, I have to answer—he was born an idiot—but I'm in no need to guess, for he had a song he sang as he ran drag-footed with his stiff idiot's trot, up and down along the curl-wired fence in the backyard:

Georgie Mahchy, Augie, Simey
Winnie Mahchy, evwy, evwy love Mama.

He was right about everyone save Winnie, Grandma Lausch's poodle, a pursy old overfed dog. Mama was Winnie's servant, as she was Grandma Lausch's. Loud-breathing and windbreaking, she lay near the old lady's stool on a cushion embroidered with a Berber aiming a rifle at a lion. She was personally Grandma's, belonged to her suite; the rest of us were the governed, and especially Mama. [. . .]

Grandma Lausch was our boarder, not a relation at all. She was supported by two sons, one from Cincinnati and one from Racine, Wisconsin. The daughters-in-law did not want her, and she, the widow of a powerful Odessa businessman—a divinity over us, bald, whiskery, with a fat nose, greatly armored in a cutaway, a double-breasted vest, powerfully buttoned (his blue photo, enlarged and retouched by Mr. Lulov, hung in the parlor, doubled back between the portico columns of the full-length mirror, the dome of the stove beginning where his trunk ended)—she preferred to live with us, because for so many years she was used to direct a house, to command, to govern, to manage, scheme, devise, and intrigue in all her languages. [. . .]

She used to read us lessons off poor Georgie's head. He would kiss the dog. This bickering handmaiden of the old lady, at one time. Now a dozy, long-sighing crank and proper object of respect for her years of right-minded but not exactly lovable busyness. But Georgie loved her—and Grandma, whom he would kiss on the sleeve, on the knee, taking knee or arm in both hands and putting his underlip forward, chaste, lummoxy, caressing, gentle and diligent when he bent his narrow back, blouse bagging all over it, whitish hair pointy and close as a burr or sunflower when the seeds have been picked out of it. The old lady let him embrace her and spoke to him in the following way: "Hey, you, boy, clever *junge*, you like the old Grandma, my minister, my *cavalyer*? That's-a-boy. You know who's good to you, who gives you gizzards and necks? Who? Who makes noodles for you? Yes. Noodles are slippery, hard to pick up with a fork and hard to pick up with the fingers. You see how the little bird pulls the worm? The little worm wants to stay in the ground. The little worm doesn't want to come out. Enough, you're making my dress wet." And she'd sharply push his forehead off with her old prim hand, having fired off for Simon and me, mindful always of her duty to wise us up, one more animadversion on the trustful, loving, and simple surrounded by the cunning-hearted and tough, a fighting nature of birds and worms, and a desperate mankind without feelings. Illustrated by Georgie. But the principal illustration was not Georgie but Mama, in her love-originated servitude, simple-minded, abandoned with three children. This was what old lady Lausch was driving at, now, in the later wisdom of her life, that she had a second family to lead. [. . .]

Chapter IV

All the influences were lined up waiting for me. I was born, and there they were to form me, which is why I tell you more of them than of myself.

At this time, and later too, I had a very weak sense of consequences, and the old lady never succeeded in

opening much of a way into my imagination with her warnings and predictions of what was preparing for me—work certificates, stockyards, shovel labor, penitentiary rockpiles, bread and water, and lifelong ignorance and degradation. She invoked all these, hotter and hotter, especially from the time I began to go with Jimmy Klein, and she tried to tighten house discipline, inspected my nails and shirt collar before school, governed my table conduct more sharply, and threatened to lock me out nights if I stayed in the streets after ten. "You can go to the Kleins, if they'll take you in. Listen to me, Augie, I'm trying to make something of you. But I can't send Mama out to follow you and see what you do. I want you to be a *mensch*.

Sylvia Regan

1908–2003

Born Sylvia Hoffenberg in New York, Sylvia Regan took the stage name Sylvia Hoffman for her brief Broadway acting career in the 1920s. After it foundered, she worked in promotions and public relations at the Theatre Union and Orson Welles's Mercury Theatre but found greater success as a playwright. Her first play, *Morning Star*, debuted on Broadway in 1940 and told the story of a Jewish immigrant family on the Lower East Side. Regan divorced her first husband in 1936 but kept his name and went on to marry the famed Yiddish musical composer Abraham (Abe) Ellstein, with whom she wrote the musical comedy *Great to Be Alive!* in 1950 and *The Golem*, produced by the New York City Opera in 1961.

The Fifth Season
1953

PINKIE: [*Jumping up*] Johnny, did you ever hear of The Marshall Plan? The Five Year Plan? The Morris Plan? Now listen to the *Pincus Plan! Let's give up the business!*

JOHNNY: [*With a quiet intensity, as he goes to* PINKIE] Let's give up the business? Let's give up the plans, the hopes, the schemes over a thousand cups of midnight coffee? Let's give up the day we took an empty loft, and signed the lease, and went downstairs to celebrate with a champagne cocktail? [*His glance taking in the room*] Remember what this place looked like when we took it? Look at it now. It's every dollar, it's every dream we have in the world. Let's give it all up. That's a very easy thing to do, isn't it?

PINKIE: Who said it's easy? But our last dollar is gone, and the bank won't take a dream for security.

JOHNNY: Pinkie, baby, when you're down, where else can you go but up?

PINKIE: You've been telling me this for months—but when are we going up?

JOHNNY: We can still manipulate. All we need is a break. One good store chain and we're in! I've got a million hot prospects!

PINKIE: This morning you saw a very hot prospect, a certain lady buyer from Stacy's Department Store. Did she buy?

JOHNNY: [*Uneasily*] I don't want to talk about Stacy's buyer!

PINKIE: All of a sudden, no dialogue. When you were talking me into the business, you had plenty. Quit Shirley-May Garments! Partnership! Promises! With your salesmanship and my tailoring, we would have penthouses on Park Avenue.

JOHNNY: You still can't realize, Shirley-May was getting rich on our brains.

PINKIE: On the same brains we went busted. Did we have to do it *your* way? We couldn't start small and grow gradual? I had in mind a small loft, with a little office. A nice picture of George Washington on one side, a nice Abraham Lincoln on the other side— with an American flag in the middle.

JOHNNY: Were we starting a public school?

PINKIE: [*Taking bric-a-brac off wall*] Whoever heard of an office with *dishes* in it? This was absolutely necessary for a garment business?

JOHNNY: [*Taking dish from* PINKIE, *he hangs it back in its place*] No, Pinkie. It wasn't absolutely necessary. It isn't absolutely necessary for a man to have a bathroom in his house. When you boarded with my mother and me in the tenement on Cherry Street, there was one john in the hall for eight families. People got along. We lived. Nothing is absolutely necessary. It's a matter of a man's pride, his dignity, what satisfies him inside. [*Somewhat in awe*] Twenty years ago, would you dream some day we'd have a genuine Boule desk a hundred years old? When a buyer sits in this Sheraton chair, the man has to think—these are not a couple of broken down cloak and suiters—these are *people*.

PINKIE: I should only live to see a *buyer* sitting in Mr. Sheridan's chair. [*Bursting out*] What happened to all the customers you were selling for years. [. . .]

LEWIS: Johnny, I appeal to you as a gentleman.

JOHNNY: If you want to appeal to a gentleman, I suggest you address my partner, Mr. Pincus.

PINKIE: [*Sitting*] Mr. Goodwin, I don't want to talk to the bum!

LEWIS: All right! I made you two-bit pushcart peddlers, and I can break you! Mr. Pincus! Mr. Goodwin!

PINKIE: [*Hotly*] You're calling us names—Johnny. [*Rising*] Pinkie, let me handle him!! Pinkie. [*To* LEWIS] Oh, no! Till now the advantages were on your side. You stepped on us like dogs! But it's the revolution— the dictatorship is over! You—you—totalitarian, you!

JOHNNY: [*To* LEWIS] You heard what the man said. Lewis. [*Marches to door, but he knows when he is beaten*] Boys, boys, can't we straighten this out? [JOHNNY *laughs, a dry laugh, with no mirth in it.*] You wouldn't laugh if it happened to you. You think you had a bad evening? I had a worse one. I threw you out. Lorraine threw me out. I walk into my office this morning—she's *waiting* for me.

JOHNNY: No—

LEWIS: She told me if I don't square myself with you guys she'll tell Grace about last night. And you know Grace. And that's not all!

JOHNNY: [*Beginning to understand, he momentarily forgets his personal troubles in the amusement of the situation*] That's not all?

LEWIS: She's got me in a triple play. She threatens to tell my wife about Grace!

JOHNNY: [*Laughing uproariously, he drops onto pouf*] She will? That's terrible—it's a catastrophe.

LEWIS: [*Beseechingly*] For God's sake, Johnny—call her off before she ruins me. I'm married to a sadistic bitch! Clarice has been waiting for this! She'll take my kids away. She caught me once, three years ago. I had to make an agreement with her. If she ever catches me again, she gets half a million—and the children. You're a father, Goodwin—
[PINKIE *and* JOHNNY *exchange looks.*]
Besides, I still need a Spring line.
[PINKIE *and* JOHNNY *exchange looks again.*]

JOHNNY: Well, Mr. Pincus, what do you think?

PINKIE: Mr. Goodwin—I don't know why I'm turning so soft, but since his children are involved—

JOHNNY: [*Rising*] Meanwhile, we'll accept your certified check for—

LEWIS: [*Taking prepared check from his pocket*] Seventy-six thousand, twenty-one dollars—

PINKIE: And forty-five cents. If you haven't got the change we'll wait.

LEWIS: [*Hands check to* PINKIE. *Cheerily*] Well, boys, the way business looks, we three have a big future together.

JOHNNY: I'm sorry, Lewis, we'll keep our present commitments, but you don't have any future with us.

LEWIS: What do you mean?

PINKIE: [*Jumping up*] Wait a minute, Johnny. Don't be so hasty. Mr. Lewis can still do business with us, on a strictly cash basis.

LEWIS: O.K. Five percent for cash!

PINKIE: *Two* percent.

LEWIS: *Five.*

JOHNNY: *Two.*

LEWIS: Why at two I can't keep my head above water.

PINKIE: Drown a little. [*Slapping* LEWIS *on the back*] I knew we'd get along.

Other works by Regan: *Marianne* (1944); *Zelda* (1969).

Frances Goodrich and Albert Hackett

Goodrich, 1890–1984

New Jersey–born writer and dramatist Frances Goodrich was responsible for some of the best-loved movies of Hollywood's Golden Age. Having graduated from Vassar College in 1912 and working with her husband Albert Hackett, Goodrich wrote the screenplays for such films as *The Thin Man* (1934), *It's a Wonderful Life* (1946), and *Father of the Bride* (1950). The couple's dramatization of *The Diary of Anne Frank* won the Tony Awards for Best Author and Best Play of 1956 as well as the Pulitzer Prize for Drama. In addition to her prolific writing career, Goodrich performed in both comedies and dramas on Broadway.

Hackett, 1900–1995

Born in New York to silent-film actress Florence Hackett, Albert Hackett played his first minor role on Broadway at the age of six in *Lottie, the Poor Saleslady*. Vaudeville and several other dramatic and comedic roles followed before he found his career footing writing for Broadway and Hollywood with his wife and partner Frances Goodrich. The stage production of *The Diary of Anne Frank* garnered the duo their greatest fame, resulting in two Tony Awards and the Pulitzer Prize for Best Drama. The play has gone on to be a stage classic, produced in multiple languages and venues over the past sixty years. Hackett and Goodrich's successful partnership continued until the latter's death.

The Diary of Anne Frank
1954

Scene V

> *It is the first night of the Hanukkah celebration.* MR. FRANK *is standing at the head of the table on which is the Menorah. He lights the Shamos, or servant candle, and holds it as he says the blessing. Seated listening is all of the "family," dressed in their best. The men wear hats,* PETER *wears his cap.*

ALL: Amen.

> [MRS. FRANK *puts down the prayer book and goes to get the food and wine,* MARGOT *helps her.* MR. FRANK *takes the men's hats and puts them aside.*]

DUSSEL: [*Rising*] That was very moving.

ANNE: [*Pulling him back*] It isn't over yet!

MRS. VAN DAAN: Sit down! Sit down!

ANNE: There's a lot more, songs and presents.

DUSSEL: Presents?

MRS. FRANK: Not this year, unfortunately.

MRS. VAN DAAN: But always on Hanukkah everyone gives presents . . . everyone!

DUSSEL: Like our St. Nicholas' Day.

> [*There is a chorus of "no's" from the group.*]

MRS. VAN DAAN: No! Not like St. Nicholas! What kind of a Jew are you that you don't know Hanukkah?

MRS. FRANK: [*As she brings the food*] I remember particularly the candles . . . First one, as we have tonight. Then the second night you light two candles, the next night three . . . and so on until you have eight candles burning. When there are eight candles it is truly beautiful.

MRS. VAN DAAN: And the potato pancakes.

MR. VAN DAAN: Don't talk about them!

MRS. VAN DAAN: I make the best *latkes* you ever tasted!

MRS. FRANK: Invite us all next year . . . in your own home.

MR. FRANK: God willing!

MRS. VAN DAAN: God willing.

ANNE: [*Sitting at the table*] And now let's have the song, Father . . . please . . . [*To* DUSSEL] Have you heard the Hanukkah song, Mr. Dussel? The song is the whole thing! [*She sings*] "Oh, Hanukkah! Oh Hanukkah! The sweet celebration . . ." [. . .]

MR. FRANK: [*Rising*] I think we should first blow out the candle . . . then we'll have something for tomorrow night.

MARGOT: But, Father, you're supposed to let it burn itself out.

MR. FRANK: I'm sure that God understands shortages. [*Before blowing it out*] "Praised be Thou, oh Lord our God, who hast sustained us and permitted us to celebrate this joyous festival."

[*He is about to blow out the candle when suddenly there is a crash of something falling below. They all freeze in horror, motionless. For a few seconds there is complete silence.* MR. FRANK *slips off his shoes. The others noiselessly follow his example.* MR. FRANK *turns out a light near him. He motions to* PETER *to turn off the center lamp.* PETER *tries to reach it, realizes he cannot and gets up on a chair. Just as he is touching the lamp he loses his balance. The chair goes out from under him. He falls. The iron lamp shade crashes to the floor. There is a sound of feet below, running down the stairs.*]

Other works by Goodrich: *Naughty Marietta* (1935); *Rose-Marie* (1936); *The Long, Long Trailer* (1954); *Seven Brides for Seven Brothers* (1954); *Five Finger Exercise* (1962). Other works by Hackett: *The Thin Man* (1934); *It's a Wonderful Life* (1946); *Father of the Bride* (1950); *The Long, Long Trailer* (1954); *Five Finger Exercise* (1962).

Clifford Odets
1906–1963

The American playwright and screenwriter Clifford Odets was the son of East European immigrants. He was raised in New York City, where he began his theatrical career, first as an actor. A member of the Communist Party from 1930, his plays of that decade, for which he is best known, portrayed working-class Jewish families coping with the material and emotional stresses of the Great Depression. He also wrote screenplays for films and television and lived in Hollywood from 1942 to 1948 and from 1955 to his death. Called to testify before the House Un-American Activities Committee in 1952, Odets was cited for contempt when he refused to cooperate.

The Flowering Peach
1954

NOAH: Lonely times again. . . .? [*Sighing.*] Now I must go out in the world an' make meself for a big nuisance again. . . ? [*Then.*] Why should she think I'm crazy? [*Abruptly standing.*] Now, just a minute! How do I know I'm not? I had a dream or not? [*Stamping his foot.*] Floor, listen to me! [*Slapping the table.*] Tell me, tell me, table—I had a dream or not? [*He listens, bewildered and fevered, but only silence answers him back, then he abruptly throws his arms upward and speaks angrily!*] If you spoke to me, Lord, I don't want it! I'm too old everybody should laugh in my face! I ain't got the gizzard for it—No, sir! [*Toning down to a softer devotional tone resting his mouth on clasped bands.*] Oh, God, excuse me—You are All and Everything an' I'm unworthy. You see me—what am I good for? All I do is cough an' spit. Pass me by—pass me by. Please. . . . [*Now the Presence of God is heard: it is expressed by a certain musical rustle or widening shimmer, as if a gigantic tuning fork had been struck, its vibrations stern and imperious. With this comes one long thunder roll (which in the theatre is made by one good union stage hand rolling a lead ball across the back of the stage).* NOAH *falls to his knees as if struck, his head is bowed low. After a moment he tilts his head a little and his nose twitches like a rabbit's.* "Lord?" *he asks. The musical shimmer deepens, spills everywhere and then softens.*] You came out, God. . . ? [*Then, listening reverently.*] Don't be mad. Because if I must, I must . . . I must? [*Sighing and shaking his head sadly. Gradually growing sly.*] What do I know about boats? Ast my Esther an' she'll tell you; when was I near water. Bread is bread, I know it—a pickle is a pickle, a knife is a knife—but boats? . . . [NOAH's *slyness is reproved by a brief but angry thunder roll.* NOAH *nods meekly but he is heartsick nevertheless.*] [. . .]

JAPHETH: [*Crosses D.C. to* NOAH.] It's NOT right! I never bossed anyone in my life! [SHEM *crosses U.R.*] But Shem and Ham have bullied me for years, and what they don't like, Poppa, is that I won't stay bullied! I admit it—I may be excitable from time to time, but I love you, Poppa, and I always will. You're the only master in my life—you taught me everything I know. I respect and revere you like you were dead.

NOAH: [*Dryly.*] Thanks . . . [*Pausing, doubtful of the compliment.*] But you're changed, Japheth, in different ways, too.

JAPHETH: Because I insist upon a rudder? I can't help it—a rudder is vital to the health of the Ark. Would you want me to lie?

ESTHER: [*To* NOAH.] You want him to lie?

NOAH: [*Hushing her.*] I'm here, ain't I . . . ? [*Then, to* JAPHETH.] Sonny, the Supreme Being who selected us—He made me the Chairman, didn't He? He'll see I don't fall outa the chair! [*Then.*] But I asted you, for an instance, maybe five times to take a wife. . . .

JAPHETH: [*Pausing and squirming.*] But how can I do that, Poppa? How can I take a wife in times like these?

NOAH: [*With gentle insistence.*] But God tells you to do it, don't He? The new world will need babies, bushels an' bushels of babies.

JAPHETH: And what about the bushels of babies who will die in the flood? Since you bring it up . . . is this vengeful God the very God I was taught to love?

NOAH: [*Recoiling.*] Sonny, you mustn't, you dasn't talk this way . . .

JAPHETH: Forgive me, Poppa, but I must! Because I can't stay here!

NOAH: [*Turning cold.*] Can't stay here . . . ?

JAPHETH: No, I can't! I cannot work for this brutal God!

NOAH: [*Slowly.*] The Lord is good for anybody an' everybody, at all times! He was wonderful for the world in the old days an', blessed be His name, He will be for the new days to come! . . . [*With a real grandeur* NOAH *has said the last word and turns away. Crosses U.R.C.*]

JAPHETH: [*Removes apron—tosses on bench L.*] If you won't forgive me, you'll have to forget me . . . you and Momma . . .

SHEM: [*Crosses to him. Incredulously.*] You mean you're walking off this job! [RACHEL *rises.*]

JAPHETH: I won't be back . . . [*Exits* D.R.]

SHEM: [*Enraged.*] That boy's hands should be chopped off! [*Agonized, on the verge of sobbing.* JAPHETH *starts out* D.L. NOAH *has brought his clasped hands to his mouth and is rocking faintly, in prayer. In* RACHEL's *and* ESTHER's *eyes there are tears.* Rachel *sits.*]

ESTHER: His hands should never hurt . . .

Other works by Odets: *Night Music* (1940); *Golden Boy* (1965).

Herman Wouk

1915–2019

Born in New York, American novelist and playwright Herman Wouk served in the U.S. Navy during World War II. Many of his works of historical fiction draw on his wartime experiences, incorporating Jewish characters and themes as depicted in Europe, Israel, and the United States. Wouk received a Pulitzer Prize in 1952, and his works have been widely translated.

Marjorie Morningstar
1955

Chapter 1: Marjorie

[. . .] Marjorie returned to the bedroom and waited for a moment, watching the doorknob. Then she walked to the full-length mirror on the closet door, and draped the black dress against her bosom, pleased by the contrast it made with her naked shoulders and tumbling hair.

At this moment—it was quite an important moment in her life—she grew hot, and prickled all over. An intuition about her future came flooding into her mind, like sunlight at the drawing of a curtain. She was going to be an actress! This pretty girl in the mirror was destined to be an actress, nothing else!

Since entering Hunter College in February of the previous year, Marjorie had been taking a course of study leading to a license as a biology teacher; but she had long suspected that she was going through empty motions, that chalk and blackboard weren't for her. Nor had she been able to picture herself settling into dull marriage at twenty-one. From her thirteenth year onward a peculiar destiny had been in her blood, waiting for the proper time to crop out, and disturbing her with premonitory sensations. But what she experienced on this May morning was no mere premonition; it was the truth bursting through. She was going to be an actress! The daydreams of her childhood had not been mere dreams, after all. [. . .]

Chapter 47. The Man She Married

[. . .] Marjorie kept staring at herself in the mirror through the vapors, unmindful of the roaring waste of hot water. Had there ever been successful Jewish actresses? Of course: Sarah Bernhardt, Rachel—and now that she thought of it, rumor described half the great stars of Hollywood as Jewish.

But her name wasn't good. It wasn't good at all. There was wondrous resonance in *Sarah Bernhardt*, stark elegance in *Rachel*—whereas her own . . . Marjorie Morgenstern . . .

Then came the confirming flash, the white streak of revelation. Such a simple change! Not even a change, a mere translation of the German compound, and her drab name turned into an incantation, a name that could blaze and thunder on Broadway. She pushed aside the dress, seized a pencil, threw open her biology notebook to a blank page, and hastily printed

MARJORIE MORNINGSTAR [. . .]

Marjorie was an extremely beautiful bride. They always say the bride is beautiful, and the truth is that a girl seldom looks better than she does at this moment of her glory and her vanishing, veiled and in white; but even among brides Marjorie was remarkably lovely. For years afterward Lowenstein's hostess said that the prettiest bride she ever saw was Marjorie Morgenstern.

The Goldstones were there, in one row near the back; and Marsha and Lou Michaelson, and the Zelenkos, and Aunt Dvosha, and Uncle Shmulka, and Geoffrey Quill, and Neville Sapersteen in a dark blue suit, and the banker Connelly, and Morris Shapiro, and Wally Wronken—these familiar faces and dozens of others she recognized, though her eyes scarcely moved. She had taken but two or three steps downward when she also saw, in the very last row of the array of black-clad men and beautifully gowned women, the tall blond man in brown tweed jacket and gray slacks, with an old camel's hair coat slung over one arm, incongruous as he was startling. She had not even known Noel Airman was in the United States; but he had come to see her get married. She could not discern his expression, but there wasn't a doubt in the world that it was Noel.

She didn't waver or change countenance at all; she continued her grave descent. But in an instant, as though green gelatins had been slid one by one in front of every light in the ballroom, she saw the scene differently. She saw a tawdry mockery of sacred things, a bourgeois riot of expense, with a special touch of vulgar Jewish sentimentality. The gate of roses behind her was comical; the flower-massed canopy ahead was grotesque; the loud whirring of the movie camera was a joke, the scrambling still photographer in the empty aisle, twisting his camera at his eye, a low clown. The huge diamond on her right hand capped the vulgarity; she could feel it there; she slid a finger to cover it. Her husband waiting for her under the canopy wasn't a prosperous doctor, but he was a prosperous lawyer; he had the mustache Noel had predicted; with macabre luck Noel had even guessed the initials. And she—she was Shirley, going to a Shirley fate, in a Shirley blaze of silly costly glory.

All this passed through her mind in a flash, between one step downward and the next. Then her eyes shifted to her father's face, rosily happy, looking up at her from the foot of the stairs. The green gelatins slid aside, and she saw her wedding again by the lights that were there in the room. If it was all comical in Noel's eyes, she thought, he might derive from that fact what pleasure he could. She was what she was, Marjorie Morgenstern of West End Avenue, marrying the man she wanted in the way she wanted to be married. It was a beautiful wedding, and she knew she was a pretty bride.

She reached the bottom of the stairs. Her father stepped to her side. Taking his arm, she turned a bit and squarely faced into Noel Airman's expected grin; he was not ten feet from her. But to her surprise Noel wasn't grinning. He looked better than he had in Paris: not so thin, not so pale, and he appeared to have gotten back all his hair. His expression was baffled, almost vacant. His mouth hung slightly open; his eyes seemed wet.

The organ music swelled to its loudest. Marjorie marched down the aisle with solemn gladness to her destiny, and became Mrs. Milton Schwartz.

Other works by Wouk: *The Caine Mutiny* (1951); *The Winds of War* (1971).

Meyer Levin

1905–1981

The child of East European immigrants, the novelist and journalist Meyer Levin was born and raised in Chicago, the setting for his masterpiece *The Old Bunch* (1937), a realistic novel about young Jews in the Jazz Age and during the Great Depression. While his earliest fiction was not concerned with Jewish themes, his writing from the 1930s on was passionately engaged with the trials and tribulations of contemporary Jewry. He was an outspoken critic of the de-Judaized version of Anne Frank's diary that was presented on Broadway and later filmed by Hollywood; he described the troubles he encountered in consequence in *The Fanatic* (1963) and his autobiography, *The Obsession* (1973).

Compulsion
1956

We waited half through the night, with the news leaking out to us. The confessions were going well. The time was long because the state's attorney was going over each fact, nailing down the evidence so every point could be proven even if later some smart lawyers had the boys withdraw their statements.

Thus we hovered between the two confession rooms, catching bits of the story, certain it was turning out to be a sex murder, perversion, with the ransom plan tacked on to cover the act. Just as Tom and I had thought. We waited, the hours broken only by a call from Louisville informing the state's attorney that the miserable, almost forgotten drug clerk, Holmes, had died without talking.

Behind each door the story was pouring forth; each of the culprits seemed bent on getting ahead of the other. And as usual when it came right down to the end, Horn's assistants let us know, these smarties were like everyone else—they were frantically blaming each other.

Then gradually a new and curious idea came out to us. It was that there was something else to the crime, something other than a motive of lust. This different idea was being insisted upon especially by Judd, with a kind of triumphant disdain for the authorities who, even with the murderers in their hands, failed to see the real nature of the crime. Judd vowed that lust really had nothing to do with it. And as for money—would two millionaire boys risk their lives for ten thousand dollars? He had a strange explanation to offer. This was a crime for its own sake. It was a crime in a vacuum, a crime in a perfectly frozen nothingness, where the atmosphere of motive was totally absent.

And as we learned how Artie and Judd thought of their crime, the whole event again became a mystery. For was even their own notion of it the truth?

We could, in that night, only grasp their claim of an experiment, an intellectual experiment, as Judd put it, in creating a perfect crime. They would avow no other motive; their act sought to isolate the pure essence of murder.

Before, we had thought the boys could only have committed the murder under some sudden dreadful impulse. But now we learned how the deed had been marked by a long design developed in full detail. What was new to us was this entry into the dark, vast area of death as an abstraction. Much later, we were to seek the deeper cause that compelled these two individuals to commit this particular murder under the guise, even the illusion, that it was an experiment.

Just as there is no absolute vacuum, there is no absolute abstraction. But one approaches a vacuum by re-moving atmosphere, and so, in the pretentious excuse offered by Judd, it seemed that by removing the common atmospheres of lust, hatred, greed, one could approach the perfect essence of crime.

Thus one might come down to an isolated killing impulse in humanity. To kill, as we put it in the headlines, for a thrill! For an excitation that had no emotional base. I think the boys themselves believed this was what they had done.

At first their recital sounded much like an account of daydreams that all could recognize. They had been playing with the idea of the "perfect murder." Is not the whole of detective-story literature built on this common fantasy? True, in such stories we always supply a conventional motive. We accept that a man may kill for a legacy or for jealousy or for revenge, though inwardly we may make the reservation—that's foolish, the butler wouldn't go so far. We accept that a dictator may unleash a war out of "economic needs" or "lust for power" but inwardly we keep saying, "Why? Why? Why?"

Other works by Levin: *My Father's House* (1947); *In Search* (1950).

Samuel Nathaniel Behrman

1893–1973

Born in Worcester, Massachusetts, Samuel Nathaniel Behrman took a roundabout road to writing more than two dozen hit comedies for the theater. Coming from an Orthodox family, Behrman had his love of theater sparked at age eleven, when he saw the play *Devil's Island*. He tried his hand at vaudeville but ended up studying literature, graduating with a B.A. from Harvard University and an M.A. from Columbia University. His career took off when the Theatre Guild produced his play *The Second Man* in 1927, and a string of successful works for the stage followed, often more serious in tone, in the 1930s. In addition to his theater pieces, Behrman wrote screenplays ranging from lighthearted comedies to romances to tragedies.

The Cold Wind and the Warm
1958

Act I

TOBEY'S VOICE: I find as I grow older that I keep going back to my friendship with Willie—when we were young and happy and living in Worcester, Massachusetts, in the early years of the century. Willie was always preoccupied with mystery—the mystery of life—the mystery of death. He used to illuminate all my childish problems for me. But he left me an inheritance of the greatest mystery of all: why he killed himself, why he felt he had to do it. What were the steep dark walls in Willie's mind that converged on him to destroy him? I don't know. What I do know, as I look back on my relationship with him—and on his relationships with others—was that he was the most life-giving person I have ever known. I remember still the first mysteries I brought him to solve: the mystery of infinity, the mystery of the True Name of the Lord. Did Willie, at the end, ponder these mysteries? Had he sought the True Name? Did he, I wonder, come too close? I don't know. I shall never know. I can only tell what I can remember. [. . .]

WILLIE: [*Squirms.*] Whatever it is—don't you think she ought to be told?

FATHER: Is Jim Nightingale God?

WILLIE: [*With some heat.*] He's a damn good doctor!

FATHER: Can he read the future? How does he know that some cure will not be discovered? Or that Dan may not be the exception who recovers? My dear wife has been given up several times. Yet God has seen fit to spare her.

WILLIE: Jim says it's inevitable.

FATHER: Look into your soul, my boy. I know how you feel about Myra. If anyone tells Myra—it shouldn't be you.

WILLIE: [*Suddenly.*] Why don't *you* tell her?

FATHER: I'm a poor stumbling creature. I am not God. In any case, Willie—

WILLIE: Well?

FATHER: You know—according to the ancient law—if Dan should die . . .

WILLIE: [*Truculent.*] Well?

FATHER: Myra would be bound, unless released by Dan's family, to marry Dan's younger brother, Aaron, who professes to be in love with her too.

WILLIE: What is that law?

FATHER: It is called the levirate law. [FATHER *goes to bookshelves and hands him a book.*] There's been a great deal written about it. Here is something on it—in English. [. . .]

WILLIE: Well, it's interesting as history. Fossilized social customs. No contemporary relevance whatever. Nonsense.

FATHER: [*Rather stern.*] If you analyze it, you'll find it is not nonsense.

WILLIE: We're living in Massachusetts in nineteen eight. We are not living in ancient times.

FATHER: This will only bring us back to our old argument . . . faith versus reason. You are a good boy, Willie . . . [*Smiles at him.*] though a scientist! You came to ask my advice. People who ask your advice usually want it to justify a course they have already decided on. You have probably decided, already, to tell Myra . . .

WILLIE: [*In self-defense.*] If I had, why wouldn't I just have gone and done it . . . why did I come to you?

FATHER: Then all I can say is . . . look into your heart—ask yourself why you're doing it. Is it to save Myra? Or to save her for yourself? [*Going to* WILLIE.] Go home, my son, and think.

[*A silence.* WILLIE *cracks his knuckles. He is in a turmoil of indecision; he knows that* MR. SACHER *has probed to the truth.*]

WILLIE: Well—thank you, Mr. Sacher.

FATHER: [*With tenderness for him.*] Good night, my boy. [WILLIE *goes out.* MR. SACHER, *deeply disturbed, begins again to repeat his prayer, pacing the floor. Intoning.*] "Before me Uriel, behind me Raphael, and over my head the divine presence of God. [. . .]

TOBEY: Father.

FATHER: Yes, Tobey.

TOBEY: Did you love Mother the way Willie loves Myra?

FATHER: You don't love like that when you're older.

TOBEY: But you did love Mother?

FATHER: Yes. I loved her very much.

TOBEY: Still you quarreled. I used to hear you quarreling. Mother never said anything. But your voice would go up—up—

FATHER: [*This makes him suffer.*] I am a sinful man, Tobey.

TOBEY: You pray all the time. You think about God all the time. That's why I could never understand about those quarrels.

FATHER: I suffer now over those quarrels. [*He stops, tries to explain.*] Look, Tobey, your mother lived in a silent world. She had been in this country as long as I, and yet she never learned the language. I was a student when I married her—had never left our village. And then I went away to study more—in France and Germany—and when I came back—

TOBEY: Yes?

FATHER: Your mother was still a village girl. And I was arrogant and impatient! I wish that I could have—But it's too late now.

TOBEY: Father, do you think Willie will get over this?

FATHER: That's a question I can't answer, Tobey. When I see the troubles of the young, it's a positive relief to be old.

TOBEY: Father—is it possible, Father, to be in love without being unhappy?

FATHER: It's possible, but highly unlikely. [. . .]

TOBEY: [*Jumps up, cutting him off.*] Listen, Willie. I owe you more than I can ever possibly repay: you made me see life as a wonder and as an adventure. I owe you everything—even the truth. And the truth is that you have wasted yourself—scattered your gifts, as my father warned you. I remember your arguments with my father. He was right—all the way. You feel this need for the concrete, so you turn to manual labor, which will probably bore you to death after one week. Another horizon, another mirage, another postponement. Chemistry. Law. What you know, what you have, you turn your back on. It is the unknowable that lures you. Even my talent is an unknown quantity and you made a concept out of that. Willie, the near things, the achievable things, the warm winds of affection, of friendship, of love, don't seem to touch you any more.

[*A pause.*]

WILLIE: You're right. I'm destructive to people—Leah—even Myra. I waited for Dan to die. He was my friend. When he died I couldn't repress a feeling of exaltation. Ethically speaking, I am a murderer.

TOBEY: Concepts again! That's distortion. [*Sitting beside him.*] Willie, for pity's sake, live your own life in this world. Attach yourself to something definite—with all the problems that go with it—Leah—your child—you could do for him what you've done for me.

WILLIE: You're right about everything. The pupil has outstripped the master. In the kid is wisdom. Tell me what to do, Tobey, and I'll do it.

TOBEY: I don't have to tell you. You know what to do.

WILLIE: I'll go to Leah and ask her to marry me. [*A pause.*] But what about Myra? She's coming here.

Other works by Behrman: *Biography* (1932); *No Time for Comedy* (1939); *People in a Diary: A Memoir* (1972).

Bernard Malamud

1914–1986

Brought up in Brooklyn, New York, Bernard Malamud was a major novelist and short story writer. The honorary consultant in American letters to the Library of Congress, Malamud also taught English at Bennington College. He received the National Book Award, the Pulitzer Prize, and the O. Henry Award.

The Last Mohican
1958

Behind him, a short distance to the right, he had noticed a stranger—give a skeleton a couple of pounds—loitering near a bronze statue on a stone pedestal of the heavy-dugged Etruscan wolf suckling the infant Romulus and Remus, the man contemplating Fidelman already acquisitively so as to suggest to the traveler that he had been mirrored (lock, stock, barrel) in the other's gaze for some time, perhaps since he had stepped off the train. Casually studying him, though pretending no, Fidelman beheld a person of about his own height, oddly dressed in brown knickers and black, knee-length woolen socks drawn up over slightly bowed, broomstick legs, these grounded in small, porous, pointed shoes. His yellowed shirt was open at the gaunt throat, both sleeves rolled up over skinny, hairy arms. The stranger's high forehead was bronzed, his black hair thick behind small ears, the dark, close-shaven beard light on the face; his experienced nose was weighted at the tip, and the soft brown eyes, above all, *wanted*. Though his expression suggested humility, he all but licked his lips as he approached the ex-painter.

"Shalom," he greeted Fidelman.

"Shalom," the other hesitantly replied, uttering the word—so far as he called—for the first time in his life. My God, he thought, a handout for lire. My first hello in Rome and it has to be a schnorrer.

The stranger extended a smiling hand. "Susskind," he said, "Shimon Susskind."

"Arthur Fidelman." Transferring his brief case to under his left arm while standing astride the big suitcase, he shook hands with Susskind. A blue-smocked porter came by, glanced at Fidelman's bag, looked at him, then walked away.

Whether he knew it or not Susskind was rubbing his palms contemplatively together.

"Parla italiano?"

"Not with ease, although I read it fluently. You might say I need the practice."

"Yiddish?"

"I express myself best in English."

"Let it be English then." Susskind spoke with a slight British intonation. "I knew you were Jewish," he said, "the minute my eyes saw you."

Fidelman chose to ignore the remark. "Where did you pick up your knowledge of English?"

"In Israel."

Israel interested Fidelman. "You live there?"

"Once, not now," Susskind answered vaguely. He seemed suddenly bored. "How so?"

Susskind twitched a shoulder. "Too much heavy labor for a man of my modest health. Also I couldn't stand the suspense."

Fidelman nodded.

"Furthermore, the desert air makes me constipated. In Rome I am light hearted."

"A Jewish refugee from Israel, no less," Fidelman said good humoredly.

"I'm always running," Susskind answered mirthlessly. If he was light hearted, he had yet to show it.

"Where else from, if I may ask?"

"Where else but Germany, Hungary, Poland? Where not?"

"Ah, that's so long ago." Fidelman then noticed the gray in the man's hair. "Well, I'd better be going," he said. He picked up his bag as two porters hovered uncertainly nearby.

But Susskind offered certain services. "You got a hotel?"

"All picked and reserved."

"How long are you staying?"

What business is it of his? However, Fidelman courteously replied, "Two weeks in Rome, the rest of the year in Florence, with a few side trips to Siena, Assisi, Padua and maybe also Venice."

"You wish a guide in Rome?"

"Are you a guide?"

"Why not?"

"No," said Fidelman. "I'll look as I go along to museums, libraries, et cetera."

This caught Susskind's attention. "What are you, a professor?"

Fidelman couldn't help blushing. "Not exactly, really just a student."

"From which institution?"

He coughed a little. "By that I mean a professional student, you might say. Call me Trofimov, from Chekov. If there's something to learn I want to learn it."

Other works by Malamud: *The Natural* (1952); *The Assistant* (1957); *The Fixer* (1966); *Dubin's Lives* (1979).

Leon Uris
1924–2003

The novelist Leon Uris was born in Baltimore to a Polish father and Russian mother. During World War II, he served as a radio operator for the Marine Corps in the Pacific. Uris's novels were characterized by their epic sweep, engagement with political and military history, and detailed research process. He claimed to have traveled twelve thousand miles within Israel and to have conducted more than 1,200 interviews while researching and writing *Exodus* (1958). *Exodus*, which at the time of its publication was the best-selling American novel since *Gone with the Wind* (1936), fictionalized the founding of the state of Israel. It was adapted as an Academy Award–winning film in 1960. Uris's other novels turned to historical topics including the Warsaw ghetto uprising, the Irish independence movement, and the 1949 blockade of Berlin.

Exodus
1958

Chapter Nineteen

The *Exodus* was declared fit and ready for the run to Palestine.

Ari set the sailing time as the morning after the Chanukah party which the management of the Dome Hotel had arranged on the hotel terrace.

Three hundred places were set. The small Jewish community of Cyprus and the crew of the *Exodus* sat at a long head table. There was tremendous gaiety as the children rushed to the terrace dressed in new clothing and were deluged with gifts from the people of Cyprus and soldiers from the garrison. The children took one gift each for themselves and marked the rest for the detention camps at Caraolos. The tables were bulging with food and the children squealed with delight. The terrible ordeal of the hunger strike was behind them; they had carried their burden like adults and now they could act like happy children with complete abandon.

All around the terrace dozens of curious Greeks and British soldiers watched the celebration.

Karen looked around frantically for Kitty and lit up when she saw her some distance away, standing with Mark Parker by the rail.

"Come on, Kitty," Karen called, "There is a place for you here."

"It's your party," Kitty answered. "I'll just watch."

When everyone had opened his present, David Ben Ami stood at the head table. The terrace became very still as he began to speak. Only the steady shush of the sea could be heard behind him.

"Tonight we celebrate the first day of Chanukah," David said. "We celebrate this day in honor of Judah Maccabee and his brave brothers and his band of faithful men who came from the hills of Judea to do combat with the Greeks who enslaved our people."

Some of the youngsters applauded.

"Judah Maccabee had a small band of men and they had no real right fighting so large and powerful an enemy as the Greeks, who ruled the entire world. But Judah Maccabee had faith. He believed that the one true God would show him the way. Judah was a wonderful fighter. Time and again he tricked the Greeks; his men were the greatest of warriors, for the faith of God was in their hearts. The Maccabees stormed Jerusalem and captured it and drove out the Greeks of Asia Minor, who ruled that area of the world."

A riot of applause.

"Judah entered the Temple and his warriors tore down the idol of Zeus and again dedicated the Temple to the one true God. The same God who helped us all in our battle with the British."

As David continued with the story of the rebirth of the Jewish nation, Kitty Fremont listened. She looked at Karen and at Dov Landau—and she looked at Mark and she lowered her eyes. Then she felt someone standing alongside her. It was Brigadier Bruce Sutherland.

"Tonight we will light the first candle of the Menorah. Each night we will light another candle until there are eight. We call Chanukah the feast of lights."

David Ben Ami lit the first candle and the children said "oh" and "ah."

"Tomorrow night we shall light the second Chanukah candle at sea and the night after we shall light the third one in Eretz Israel."

David placed a small skullcap on his head and opened the Bible. "'*He will not suffer thy foot to be moved; he that keepeth thee will not slumber.*'"

Kitty's eyes came to rest on the head table. She looked at them—Zev Gilboa the farmer from the Galilee, and Joab Yarkoni the Moroccan Jew, and David Ben Ami, the scholar from Jerusalem. Her eyes stopped at Ari Ben Canaan. His eyes were rimmed with weariness now that he had had a chance to relax from his ordeal. David set the Bible down and continued to speak from memory.

"'*Behold!*'" David said, "'*he that keepeth Israel shall neither slumber nor sleep.*'"

An icy chill passed through Kitty Fremont's body. Her eyes were fixed on the tired face of Ari Ben Canaan. "*Behold . . . he that keepeth Israel shall neither slumber nor sleep.*"

The ancient motors of the *Exodus* groaned as she slid back into the center of Kyrenia Harbor and she turned and pointed out to sea in the direction of Palestine.

At dawn of the second day everyone sighted land at once. "Palestine!"

"Eretz Israel!"

A hysteria of laughing and crying and singing and joy burst from the children.

The little salvage tug came within sight of land and the electrifying news spread through the Yishuv. The children who had brought the mighty British Empire to its knees were arriving!

The *Exodus* sputtered into Haifa Harbor amid a blast of welcoming horns and whistles. The salute spread from Haifa to the villages and the *kibbutzim* and the *moshavim* and all the way to Jerusalem to the Yishuv Central building and back again to Haifa.

Twenty-five thousand Jews poured onto the Haifa dock to cheer the creaky little boat. The Palestine Philharmonic Orchestra played the Jewish anthem— "Hatikvah," the Hope.

Tears streaked down the cheeks of Karen Hansen Clement as she looked up into Kitty's face.

The *Exodus* had come home!

Other works by Uris: *Battle Cry* (1953); *Mila 18* (1961); *Armageddon: A Novel of Berlin* (1963); *Trinity* (1976).

Paddy Chayefsky

1923–1981

The playwright and screenwriter Paddy Chayefsky was born Sidney Aaron Chayefsky in the Bronx; he was given the nickname "Paddy" during his military service in World War II, when he asked to be excused from kitchen duty in order to attend mass. As the author of teleplays during the 1950s, he helped to establish the small screen as a venue for serious dramatic performance. Across the screen and stage, his work was marked by naturalistic dialogue and a satiric edge that blurred comedy and drama. *The Tenth Man* ran for 623 performances on Broadway and was nominated for three Tony Awards. Chayefsky is also the only person to have been awarded, as the sole author, three Academy Awards for Best Screenplay: for *Marty* (1955), *The Hospital* (1971), and *Network* (1976).

The Tenth Man
1959

THE CABALIST: Sexton, light the candles. [THE SEXTON *lights each man's candle.* THE CABALIST *advances slowly to* THE GIRL, *who stands slackly, her body making small occasional jerking movements, apparently in a schizophrenic state.* THE CABALIST *slowly draws a line before* THE GIRL *with the flat of his toe. Quietly.*] Dybbuk, I draw this line beyond which you may not come. You may not do harm to anyone in this room. [THE OLD MEN *shift nervously in their various positions around the synagogue. To* THE SEXTON] Open the Ark. [THE SEXTON *moves quickly up to the altar and opens the brown sliding doors of the Ark, exposing the several scrolls within, standing in their handsomely covered velvet coverings.* THE CABALIST *moves slowly back to his original position; he says quietly:*] Dybbuk, you are in the presence of God and His Holy Scrolls. [THE GIRL *gasps.*] I plead with you one last time to leave the body of this girl. [*There is no answer.*] Then I will invoke the curse of excommunication upon your pitiable soul. Sexton, blow Tekiah. [THE SEXTON *raises the ram's horn to his lips, and the eerie, frightening tones shrill out into the hushed air.*] Sexton, blow Shevurim. [*Again,* THE SEXTON *raises the ram's horn and blows a variation of the first hollow tones.*] Sexton, blow Teruah. [*A third time,* THE SEXTON *blows a variation of the original tones.*] Sexton, blow the Great Tekiah and, upon the sound of these tones, dybbuk, you will be wrenched from the girl's body and there will be cast upon you the final anathema of excommunication from all the world of the living and from all the world of the dead. Sexton, blow the great Tekiah.
[*For the fourth time,* THE SEXTON *raises the ram's horn to his lips and blows a quick succession of loud*

blasts. *A silence falls heavily on the gathered* MEN, *the notes fading into the air. Nothing happens.* THE GIRL *remains as she was, standing slackly, her hands making involuntary little movements.* FOREMAN's *head sinks slowly on his chest, and a deep expression of pain covers his face.* THE CABALIST *stares steadily at* THE GIRL. *Then, suddenly,* ARTHUR *begins to moan softly, and then with swift violence, a horrible atavistic scream tears out of his throat. He staggers one brief step forward. At the peak of his scream, he falls heavily down on the floor of the synagogue in a complete faint. The echoes of his scream tingle momentarily in the high corners of the air in the synagogue. The* OTHERS *stand petrified for a moment, staring at his slack body on the floor.*]

ALPER: My God. I think what's has happened is that we have exorcised the wrong dybbuk.

THE POLICEMAN: [*He starts toward* ARTHUR's *limp body.*) All right, don't crowd around. Let him breathe.

THE CABALIST: He will be all right in a moment.

ZITORSKY: If I didn't see this with my own eyes, I wouldn't believe it.

THE RABBI: Mr. Hirschman, will he be all right?

THE CABALIST: Yes.

SCHLISSEL: [*With simple devoutness.*] Praise be to the Lord, for His compassion is everywhere.
[THE RABBI *moves slowly down and stares at* ARTHUR *as* SCHLISSEL, ZITORSKY *and* ALPER *help him to a chair.*]

ALPER: How are you, my dear fellow?

ARTHUR: [*Still in a state of bemused shock.*] I don't know.

THE SEXTON: [*Coming forward with some wine.*] Would you like a sip of wine?

ARTHUR: [*Taking the goblet.*] Yes, thank you very much. [*Turning to look at* THE GIRL.] How is she? [*Her schizophrenic state is quite obvious.* ARTHUR *turns back, his face furrowed and his eyes closed now in a mask of pain.*]

SCHLISSEL: Was it a painful experience, my friend?

ARTHUR: I don't know. I feel beyond pain. [*Indeed, his hands are visibly trembling as if from cold, and the very rigidity of his masklike face is a frozen thing. Words become more difficult to say.*] I feel as if I have been reduced to the moment of birth, as if the universe has become one hunger. [*He seems to be almost on the verge of collapse.*]

ALPER: A hunger for what?

ARTHUR: [*Gauntly.*] I don't know.

THE CABALIST: For life.

ARTHUR: [*At these words he sinks back onto his chair exhausted.*] Yes, for life. I want to live. [*He opens his eyes and begins to pray quietly.*] God of my fathers. You have exorcised all truth as I knew it out of me. You have taken away my reason and definition. Give me then a desire to wake in the morning, a passion for the things of life, a pleasure in work, a purpose to sorrow—[*He slowly stands, for a reason unknown even to himself, and turns to regard the slouched figure of* THE GIRL.] Give me all these things in one—give me the ability to love. [*In a hush of the scene, he moves slowly to* THE GIRL *and stands before her crouched slack figure.*] Dybbuk, hear me. I will cherish this girl, and give her a home. I will tend to her needs and hold her in my arms when she screams out with your voice. Her soul is mine now—her soul, her charm, her beauty—even you, her insanity, are mine. If God will not exorcise you, dybbuk, I will. [*To* THE GIRL.] Evelyn, I will get your coat. We have a lot of things to do this afternoon. [*He turns to the* OTHERS.] It is not a simple matter to get somebody released from an institution in New York. [*He starts briskly across to the rabbi's office, pauses at the door.*] Officer, why don't you just call in and say you have located the girl and she is being brought to her father? [*To* FOREMAN.] You'd better come along with us. Would somebody get my coat? We will need her father's approval. We shall have to stop off at my office and have my secretary draw some papers. [. . .]

ALPER: [*Pulling up a chair.*] He still doesn't believe in God. He simply wants to love. [ZITORSKY *joins the other two.*] And when you stop and think about it, gentlemen, is there any difference? Let us make a supposition . . .

Other works by Chayefsky: *Middle of the Night* (teleplay, 1954; stage, 1956; film, 1959); *The Goddess* (1958).

Grace Paley

1922–2007

Born and brought up in the Bronx, Grace Paley wrote short stories and poetry. As a feminist and peace activist, she wrote works that portrayed the everyday lives of her contemporaries. She taught at Sarah Lawrence College and the City College of New York, earning Guggenheim and National Endowment for the Arts fellowships, the National Institute of Arts and Letters Award, and the title of New York's first state author.

The Loudest Voice
1959

There is a certain place where dumb-waiters boom, doors slam, dishes crash; every window is a mother's mouth bidding the street shut up, go skate somewhere else, come home. My voice is the loudest. [. . .]

One cold morning the monitor tapped me on the shoulder. "Go to Room 409, Shirley Abramowitz," he said. I did as I was told. I went in a hurry up a down staircase to Room 409, which contained sixth-graders. I had to wait at the desk without wiggling until Mr. Hilton, their teacher, had time to speak.

After five minutes he said, "Shirley?"

"What?" I whispered.

He said, "My! My! Shirley Abramowitz! They told me you had a particularly loud, clear voice and read with lots of expression. Could that be true?"

"Oh, yes," I whispered.

"In that case, don't be silly; I might very well be your teacher someday. Speak up, speak up."

"Yes," I shouted.

"More like it," he said. "Now, Shirley, can you put a ribbon in your hair or a bobby pin? It's too messy."

"Yes!" I bawled.

"Now, now, calm down." He turned to the class. "Children, not a sound. Open at page 39. Read till 52. When you finish, start again." He looked me over once more. "Now, Shirley, you know, I suppose, that Christmas is coming. We are preparing a beautiful play. Most of the parts have been given out. But I still need a child with a strong voice, lots of stamina. Do you know what stamina is? You do? Smart kid. You know, I heard you read 'The Lord is my shepherd' in Assembly yesterday. I was very impressed. Wonderful delivery. Mrs. Jordan, your teacher, speaks highly of you. Now listen to me, Shirley Abramowitz, if you want to take the part and be in the play, repeat after me, 'I swear to work harder than I ever did before.'"

I looked to heaven and said at once, "Oh, I swear." I kissed my pinky and looked at God.

"That is an actor's life, my dear," he explained. "Like a soldier's, never tardy or disobedient to his general, the director. Everything," he said, "absolutely everything will depend on you."

That afternoon, all over the building, children scraped and scrubbed the turkeys and the sheaves of corn off the schoolroom windows. Goodbye Thanksgiving. The next morning a monitor brought red paper and green paper from the office. We made new shapes and hung them on the walls and glued them to the doors.

The teachers became happier and happier. Their heads were ringing like the bells of childhood. My best friend Evie was prone to evil, but she did not get a single demerit for whispering. We learned "Holy Night" without an error. "How wonderful!" said Miss Glacé, the student teacher. "To think that some of you don't even speak the language!" We learned "Deck the Halls" and "Hark! The Herald Angels." . . . They weren't ashamed and we weren't embarrassed. [. . .]

Miss Glacé looked around and saw that everyone was in costume and on line waiting to play his part. She whispered, "All right . . ." Then:

Jackie Sauerfeld, the prettiest boy in first grade, parted the curtains with his skinny elbow and in a high voice sang out:

"Parents dear
We are here
To make a Christmas play in time.
It we give
In narrative
And illustrate with pantomime."

He disappeared.

My voice burst immediately from the wings to the great shock of Ira, Lester, and Meyer, who were waiting for it but were surprised all the same.

"I remember, I remember, the house where I was born . . ."

Miss Glacé yanked the curtain open and there it was, the house—an old hayloft, where Celia Kornbluh lay in the straw with Cindy Lou, her favorite doll. Ira, Lester, and Meyer moved slowly from the wings toward her, sometimes pointing to a moving star and sometimes ahead to Cindy Lou.

It was a long story and it was a sad story. I carefully pronounced all the words about my lonesome childhood, while little Eddie Braunstein wandered upstage and down with his shepherd's stick, looking for sheep. I brought up lonesomeness again, and not being understood at all except by some women everybody hated. Eddie was too small for that and Marty Groff took his place, wearing his father's prayer shawl. I announced twelve friends, and half the boys in the fourth grade gathered round Marty, who stood on an orange crate while my voice harangued. Sorrowful and loud, I declaimed about love and God and Man, but because of

the terrible deceit of Abie Stock we came suddenly to a famous moment. Marty, whose remembering tongue I was, waited at the foot of the cross. He stared desperately at the audience. I groaned, "My God, my God, why hast thou forsaken me?" The soldiers who were sheiks grabbed poor Marty to pin him up to die, but he wrenched free, turned again to the audience, and spread his arms aloft to show despair and the end. I murmured at the top of my voice, "The rest is silence, but as everyone in this room, in this city—in this world—now knows, I shall have life eternal."

That night Mrs. Kornbluh visited our kitchen for a glass of tea.

"How's the virgin?" asked my father with a look of concern.

"For a man with a daughter, you got a fresh mouth, Abramowitz."

"Here," said my father kindly, "have some lemon, it'll sweeten your disposition."

They debated a little in Yiddish, then fell in a puddle of Russian and Polish. What I understood next was my father, who said, "Still and all, it was certainly a beautiful affair, you have to admit, introducing us to the beliefs of a different culture."

"Well, yes," said Mrs. Kornbluh. "The only thing . . . you know Charlie Turner—that cute boy in Celia's class—a couple others? They got very small parts or no part at all. In very bad taste, it seemed to me. After all, it's their religion."

"Ach," explained my mother, "what could Mr. Hilton do? They got very small voices; after all, why should they holler? The English language they know from the beginning by heart. They're blond like angels. You think it's so important they should get in the play? Christmas . . . the whole piece of goods . . . they own it."

I listened and listened until I couldn't listen any more. Too sleepy, I climbed out of bed and kneeled. I made a little church of my hands and said, "Hear, O Israel . . ." Then I called out in Yiddish, "Please, good night, good night. Ssh." My father said, "Ssh yourself," and slammed the kitchen door.

I was happy. I fell asleep at once. I had prayed for everybody: my talking family, cousins far away, passersby, and all the lonesome Christians. I expected to be heard. My voice was certainly the loudest.

Other works by Paley: *The Little Disturbances of Man: Stories of Men and Women in Love* (1959); *Enormous Changes at the Last Minute* (1974).

Philip Roth

1933–2018

A celebrated twentieth-century American writer, born in Newark, New Jersey, Philip Roth was the author of more than two dozen novels, known for their memorable characters, semiautobiographical elements, and biting satire directed at post–World War II America. His works have been widely honored, receiving among other awards two National Book Awards, three PEN/Faulkner Awards, and a Pulitzer Prize.

Eli, the Fanatic

1959

Inside the house they took their seats. Though it was lighter than a few evenings before, a bulb or two would have helped. Eli had to hold his briefcase towards the window for the last gleamings. He removed Tzuref's letter from a manila folder. Tzuref removed Eli's letter from his pants pocket. Eli removed the carbon of his own letter from another manila folder. Tzuref removed Eli's first letter from his back pocket. Eli removed the carbon from his briefcase. Tzuref raised his palms. ". . . It's all I've got . . ."

Those upraised palms, the mocking tone—another accusation. It was a crime to keep carbons! Everybody had an edge on him—Eli could do no right.

"I offered a compromise, Mr. Tzuref. You refused."

"Refused, Mr. Peck? What is, is."

"The man could get a new suit."

"That's all he's got."

"So you told me," Eli said.

"So I told you, so you know."

"It's not an insurmountable obstacle, Mr. Tzuref. We have stores."

"For that too?"

"On Route 12, a Robert Hall—"

"To take away the one thing a man's got?"

"Not take away, *replace*."

"But I tell you he has nothing. *Nothing*. You have that word in English? *Nicht*? *Gornisht*?"

"Yes, Mr. Tzuref, we have the word."

"A mother and a father?" Tzuref said. "No. A wife? No. A baby? A little ten-month-old baby? No. A village full of friends? A synagogue where you knew the feel of every seat under your pants? Where with your eyes closed you could smell the cloth of the Torah?" Tzuref pushed out of his chair, stirring a breeze that swept Eli's letter to the floor. At the window he leaned out, and looked, beyond Woodenton. When he turned he was shaking a finger at Eli. "And a medical experiment they performed on him yet! That leaves nothing, Mr. Peck. Absolutely nothing!"

"I misunderstood."

"No news reached Woodenton?"

"About the suit, Mr. Tzuref. I thought he couldn't afford another."

"He can't."

They were right where they'd begun. "Mr. Tzuref!" Eli demanded. "*Here*?" He smacked his hand to his billfold.

"Exactly!" Tzuref said, smacking his own breast. "Then we'll buy him one!" Eli crossed to the window and taking Tzuref by the shoulders, pronounced each word slowly. "We-will-pay-for-it. All right?"

"Pay? What, diamonds!"

Eli raised a hand to his inside pocket, then let it drop. Oh stupid! Tzuref, father to eighteen, had smacked not what lay under his coat, but deeper, under the ribs.

"Oh . . ." Eli said. He moved away along the wall. "The suit is all he's got then."

"You got my letter," Tzuref said.

Eli stayed back in the shadow, and Tzuref turned to his chair. He swished Eli's letter from the floor, and held it up. "You say too much . . . all this reasoning . . . all these conditions . . ."

"What can I do?"

"You have the word 'suffer' in English?"

"We have the word suffer. We have the word law too."

"Stop with the law! You have the word suffer. Then try it. It's a little thing."

"They won't," Eli said.

"But you, Mr. Peck, how about you?"

"I am them, they are me, Mr. Tzuref."

"Aach! You are us, we are you!"

Eli shook and shook his head. In the dark he suddenly felt that Tzuref might put him under a spell. "Mr. Tzuref, a little light?"

Tzuref lit what tallow was left in the holders. Eli was afraid to ask if they couldn't afford electricity. Maybe candles were all they had left.

"Mr. Peck, who made the law, may I ask you that?"

"The people."

"No."

"Yes."

"Before the people."

"No one. Before the people there was no law." Eli didn't care for the conversation, but with only candlelight, he was being lulled into it.

"Wrong," Tzuref said.

"We make the law, Mr. Tzuref. It is our community. These are my neighbors. I am their attorney. They pay me. Without law there is chaos."

"What you call law, I call shame. The heart, Mr. Peck, the heart is law! God!" he announced.

"Look, Mr. Tzuref, I didn't come here to talk metaphysics. People use the law, it's a flexible thing. They protect what they value, their property, their well-being, their happiness—"

"Happiness? They hide their shame. And you, Mr. Peck, you are shameless?"

"We do it," Eli said, wearily, "for our children. This is the twentieth century . . ."

"For the goyim maybe. For me the Fifty-eighth." He pointed at Eli. "That is too old for shame." [. . .]

Eli felt relieved—he leaned forward. In the basket was what he'd come to see. Well, now that he was here, what did he think he was going to say to it? I'm your father, Eli, the Flipper? I am wearing a black hat, suit, and fancy underwear, all borrowed from a friend? How could he admit to this reddened ball—*his* reddened ball—the worst of all: that Eckman would shortly convince him he wanted to take off the whole business. He couldn't admit it! He wouldn't do it!

Past his hat brim, from the corner of his eye, he saw Ted had stopped in a doorway at the end of the corridor. Two interns stood there smoking, listening to Ted. Eli ignored it.

No, even Eckman wouldn't make him take it off! No! He'd wear it, if he chose to. He'd make the kid wear it! Sure! Cut it down when the time came. A smelly hand-me-down, whether the kid liked it or not!

Only Teddie's heels clacked; the interns wore rubber soles—for they were there, beside him, unexpectedly. Their white suits smelled, but not like Eli's.

"Eli," Ted said, softly, "visiting time's up, pal."

"How are you feeling, Mr. Peck? First child upsets everyone. . . ."

He'd just pay no attention; nevertheless, he began to perspire, thickly, and his hat crown clutched his hair.

"Excuse me—Mr. Peck. . . ." It was a new rich bass voice. "Excuse me, rabbi, but you're wanted . . . in the temple." A hand took his elbow, firmly; then another hand, the other elbow. Where they grabbed, his tendons went taut.

"Okay, rabbi. Okay okay okay okay okay okay. . . ." He listened; it was a very soothing word, that okay.

"Okay okay everything's going to be okay." His feet seemed to have left the ground some, as he glided away from the window, the bassinet, the babies. "Okay easy does it everything's all right all right—"

But he rose, suddenly, as though up out of a dream, and flailing his arms, screamed: "I'm *the father!*"

But the window disappeared. In a moment they tore off his jacket—it gave so easily, in one yank. Then a needle slid under his skin. The drug calmed his soul, but did not touch it down where the blackness had reached.

Other works by Roth: *Goodbye, Columbus and Five Short Stories* (1959); *Portnoy's Complaint* (1969); *Looking at Kafka* (1973).

Joseph Heller
1923–1999

Brooklyn-born writer Joseph Heller gloried in his time spent as a bombardier flying sixty missions in Italy during World War II. Postwar, he obtained his master's degree in English from Columbia University, afterward teaching at Pennsylvania State University and then moving into advertising as a copywriter. The idea for *Catch-22*, his best-known novel, came to Heller on a mundane day at home, and he wrote it first as a short story. Publisher Simon & Schuster bought the one-third of the book that had been put to paper; Heller then took eight years to finish it. The long incubation time proved fruitful, as more than ten million copies were eventually sold. In all, he produced seven novels, three plays both for screen and stage, and two autobiographies.

Catch-22
1961

Chapter 5: Chief White Halfoat

It was a horrible joke, but Doc Daneeka didn't laugh until Yossarian came to him one mission later and pleaded again, without any real expectation of success, to be grounded. Doc Daneeka snickered once and was soon immersed in problems of his own, which included Chief White Halfoat, who had been challenging him all that morning to Indian wrestle, and Yossarian, who decided right then and there to go crazy.

"You're wasting your time," Doc Daneeka was forced to tell him. "Can't you ground someone who's crazy?"

"Oh, sure. I have to. There's a rule saying I have to ground anyone who's crazy."

"Then why don't you ground me? I'm crazy. Ask Clevinger."

"Clevinger? Where is Clevinger? You find Clevinger and I'll ask him."

"Then ask any of the others. They'll tell you how crazy I am."

"They're crazy."

"Then why don't you ground them?"

"Why don't they ask me to ground them?"

"Because they're crazy, that's why."

"Of course they're crazy," Doc Daneeka replied. "I just told you they're crazy, didn't I? And you can't let crazy people decide whether you're crazy or not, can you?"

Yossarian looked at him soberly and tried another approach. "Is Orr crazy?"

"He sure is," Doc Daneeka said.

"Can you ground him?"

"I sure can. But first he has to ask me to. That's part of the rule."

"Then why doesn't he ask you to?"

"Because he's crazy," Doc Daneeka said. "He has to be crazy to keep flying combat missions after all the close calls he's had. Sure, I can ground Orr. But first he has to ask me to."

"That's all he has to do to be grounded?"

"That's all. Let him ask me."

"And then you can ground him?" Yossarian asked.

"No. Then I can't ground him."

"You mean there's a catch?"

"Sure there's a catch," Doc Daneeka replied. "Catch-22. Anyone who wants to get out of combat duty isn't really crazy."

There was only one catch and that was Catch-22, which specified that a concern for one's own safety in the face of dangers that were real and immediate was the process of a rational mind. Orr was crazy and could be grounded. All he had to do was ask; and as soon as he did, he would no longer be crazy and would have to fly more missions. Orr would be crazy to fly more missions and sane if he didn't, but if he was sane he had to fly them. If he flew them he was crazy and didn't have to; but if he didn't want to he was sane and had to. Yossarian was moved very deeply by the absolute simplicity of this clause of Catch-22 and let out a respectful whistle.

"That's some catch, that Catch-22," he observed.

"It's the best there is," Doc Daneeka agreed." [. . .]

Chapter 8: Lieutenant Scheisskopf

It was all very confusing to Clevinger. There were many strange things taking place, but the strangest of all, to Clevinger, was the hatred, the brutal, uncloaked, inexorable hatred of the members of the Action Board, glazing their unforgiving expressions with a hard, vindictive surface, glowing in their narrowed eyes malignantly like inextinguishable coals. Clevinger was stunned to discover it. They would have lynched him if they could. They were three grown men and he was a boy, and they hated him and wished him dead. They had hated him before he came, hated him while he was there, hated him after he left, carried their hatred for him away malignantly like some pampered treasure after they separated from each other and went to their solitude.

Yossarian had done his best to warn him the night before. "You haven't got a chance, kid," he had told him glumly. "They hate Jews."

"But I'm not Jewish," answered Clevinger.

"It will make no difference," Yossarian promised, and Yossarian was right. "They're after everybody."

Clevinger recoiled from their hatred as though from a blinding light. These three men who hated him spoke his language and wore his uniform, but he saw their loveless faces set immutably into cramped, mean lines of hostility and understood instantly that nowhere in the world, not in all the fascist tanks or planes or submarines, not in the bunkers behind the machine guns or mortars or behind the blowing flame throwers, not even among all the expert gunners of the crack Hermann Goering Antiaircraft Division or among the grisly connivers in all the beer halls in Munich and everywhere else, were there men who hated him more. [. . .]

Chapter 19: Colonel Cathcart

We were speaking about conducting religious services in the briefing room before each mission. Is there any reason why we can't?"

"No, sir," the chaplain mumbled.

"Then we'll begin with this afternoon's mission." The colonel's hostility softened gradually as he applied himself to details. "Now, I want you to give a lot of thought to the kind of prayers we're going to say. I don't want anything heavy or sad. I'd like you to keep it light and snappy, something that will send the boys out feeling pretty good. Do you know what I mean? I don't want any of this Kingdom of God or Valley of Death stuff. That's all too negative. What are you making such a sour face for?"

"I'm sorry, sir," the chaplain stammered. "I happened to be thinking of the Twenty-third Psalm just as you said that."

"How does that one go?"

"That's the one you were just referring to, sir. 'The Lord is my shepherd; I—'"

"*That's* the one I was just referring to. It's out. What else have you got?"

"'Save me, O God; for the waters are come in unto—'"

"No waters," the colonel decided, blowing ruggedly into his cigarette holder after flipping the butt down into his combed-brass ash tray. "Why don't we try something musical? How about the harps on the willows?"

"That has the rivers of Babylon in it, sir," the chaplain replied. "'. . . there we sat down, yea, we wept, when we remembered Zion.'"

"Zion? Let's forget about that one right now. I'd like to know how that one even got in there. Haven't you got anything humorous that stays away from waters and valleys and God? I'd like to keep away from the subject of religion altogether if we can."

The chaplain was apologetic. "I'm sorry, sir, but just about all the prayers I know are rather somber in tone and make at least some passing reference to God."

"Then let's get some new ones. The men are already doing enough bitching about the missions I send them on without our rubbing it in with any sermons about God or death or Paradise. Why can't we take a more positive approach? Why can't we all pray for something good, like a tighter bomb pattern, for example? Couldn't we pray for a tighter bomb pattern?" [. . .]

[. . .] We'll allocate about a minute and a half for you in the schedule. Will a minute and a half be enough?"

"Yes, sir. If it doesn't include the time necessary to excuse the atheists from the room and admit the enlisted men."

Colonel Cathcart stopped in his tracks. "What atheists?" he bellowed defensively, his whole manner changing in a flash to one of virtuous and belligerent denial. "There are no atheists in my outfit! Atheism is against the law, isn't it?"

"No, sir."

"It isn't?" The colonel was surprised. "Then it's un-American, isn't it?"

"I'm not sure, sir," answered the chaplain.

"Well, I am!" the colonel declared. "I'm not going to disrupt our religious services just to accommodate a bunch of lousy atheists. They're getting no special privileges from me. They can stay right where they are and pray with the rest of us. And what's all this about enlisted men? Just how the hell do they get into this act?"

The chaplain felt his face flush. "I'm sorry, sir. I just assumed you would want the enlisted men to be present, since they would be going along on the same mission."

"Well, I don't. They've got a God and a chaplain of their own, haven't they?"

"No, sir."

"What are you talking about? You mean they pray to the same God we do?"

"Yes, sir."

"And He *listens?*"

"I think so, sir."

"Well, I'll be damned," remarked the colonel, and he snorted to himself in quizzical amusement. His spirits drooped suddenly a moment later, and he ran his hand nervously over his short, black, graying curls. "Do you really think it's a good idea to let the enlisted men in?" he asked with concern.

"I should think it only proper, sir." [. . .]

"Do you think," he asked, "that keeping the enlisted men out might interfere with our chances of getting results?"

The chaplain hesitated, feeling himself on unfamiliar ground again. "Yes, sir," he replied finally. "I think it's conceivable that such an action could interfere with your chances of having the prayers for a tighter bomb pattern answered."

"I wasn't even thinking about that!" cried the colonel, with his eyes blinking and splashing like puddles. "You mean that God might even decide to punish me by giving us a *looser* bomb pattern?"

"Yes, sir," said the chaplain. "It's conceivable He might."

"The hell with it, then," the colonel asserted in a huff of independence. "I'm not going to set these damned prayer meetings up just to make things worse than they are." With a scornful snicker, he settled himself behind his desk, replaced the empty cigarette holder in his mouth and lapsed into parturient silence for a few moments. "Now that I think about it," he confessed, as much to himself as to the chaplain, "having the men pray to God probably wasn't such a hot idea anyway."

Other works by Heller: *We Bombed in New Haven* (1968); *Something Happened* (1974).

Herb Gardner

1934–2003

Herb Gardner was born in Brooklyn, New York. He was a playwright, screenwriter, novelist, and cartoonist. Many of his comedies, with their eccentric characters, have been adapted into feature films. Gardner received the Tony Award for Best Play, the Writers Guild of America Lifetime Achievement Award, and nominations for Academy and Emmy Awards.

A Thousand Clowns
1962

Act I

MURRAY: People fall into two distinct categories. Miss Markowitz; people who like delicatessen, and people who don't like delicatessen. A man who is not touched by the earthy lyricism of hot pastrami, the pungent fantasy of corned-beef, pickles, frankfurters, the great lusty impertinence of good mustard—is a man of stone and without heart. Now, Albert is obviously not a lover of delicatessen and you are well rid of him.

SANDRA: [*She is still sitting on the bed, her hands folded neatly in her lap on top of her files and his undershirt.*] What am I going to do? This is an awful day.

MURRAY: [*He sits on the swivel chair next to the bed.*] Miss Markowitz, this is a beautiful day and I'll tell you why. My dear, you are really a jolly old girl and you are well rid of Albert. You have been given a rare opportunity to return the unused portion and have your money refunded.

SANDRA: But—my work—what am I going to—?

MURRAY: You are a lover, Dr. Markowitz, you are a lover of things and people so you took up work where you could get at as many of them as possible, and it just turned out that there were too many of them and too much that moves you. Damn it, please be glad that it turned out you are not reasonable and sensible. Have all the gratitude you can, that you are capable of embarrassment and joy and are a marathon crier.

SANDRA: [*Looking directly at him.*] There is a kind of relief that it's gone—the job, and even Albert. But I know what it is, it's just irresponsible . . . Oh, I don't have the vaguest who I am—

MURRAY: [*He takes her hand.*] It's just there's all these Sandras running around who you never met before, and it's confusing at first, fantastic, like a Chinese fire drill. But god *damn*, isn't it great to find out how many Sandras there are? Like those little cars in the circus, this tiny red car comes out and putters around, suddenly its doors open and out come a thousand clowns, whooping and hollering and raising hell. [. . .]

Act III

ARNOLD: Murray, I finally figured out your problem. There's only one thing that really bothers you—[*With a sweep of his hand.*] Other people. [*With a mock-secretive tone.*] If it wasn't for them other people, everything would be great, huh, Murray? I mean, you think everything's fine, and then you go out into the street—and there they all are again, right? The other people; taking up space, bumping into you, asking for things, making lines to wait on, taking cabs away from ya—The Enemey. Well, watch out, Murray, *they're everywhere*—

MURRAY: Go ahead, Arnie, give me advice, at thirty thousand a year you can afford it.

ARNOLD: Oh, I get it, if I'm so smart why ain't I poor? You better get a damn good act of your own before you start giving mine the razzberry. What's this game you play gonna be like ten years from now, without youth? Murray, Murray, I can't *watch* this, you gotta *shape-up*—

MURRAY: [*Turning quickly to face* ARNOLD, *in a surprised tone.*] Shape-*up*? [*Looks directly at* ARNOLD, *speaks slowly.*]: Arnie, what the hell happened to you? You got so old. I don't know you any more. When you quit "Harry the Fur King" on Thirty-eighth Street, remember?

ARNOLD: That's twenty years ago, Murray.

MURRAY: You told me you were going to be in twenty businesses in twenty years if you had to, till you found out what you wanted. Things were always going to change. Harry said you were not behaving maturely enough for a salesman; your clothes didn't match or something—[*Laughs in affectionate memory of the event.*] So the next day, you dressed perfectly, homburg, gray suit, cuff-links, carrying a brief-case and a rolled umbrella—and you came into Harry's office on roller skates. You weren't going to take crap from *any*body. So that's the business you finally picked—taking crap from everybody.

ARNOLD: I don't do practical jokes any more, if that's what you mean.

MURRAY: [*Grabs both of* ARNOLD'S *arms tensely.*] Practical, that's right; a way to stay alive. If most things aren't funny, Arn, then they're only exactly what they are; then it's one long dental appointment interrupted occasionally by something exciting, like waiting or falling asleep. What's the point if I leave everything exactly the way I find it? Then I'm just adding to the noise, then I'm just taking up some more room on the subway.

Other works by Gardner: *The Goodbye People* (1974); *Thieves* (1974).

Bernard Malamud

The Jewbird
1963

The bird cawed hoarsely and with a flap of its bedraggled wings—feathers tufted this way and that—rose heavily to the top of the open kitchen door, where it perched staring down.

"Gevalt, a pogrom!"

"It's a talking bird," said Edie in astonishment.

"In Jewish," said Maurie.

"Wise guy," muttered Cohen. He gnawed on his chop, then put down the bone. "So if you can talk, say what's your business. What do you want here?"

"If you can't spare a lamb chop," said the bird, "I'll settle for a piece of herring with a crust of bread. You can't live on your nerve forever."

"This ain't a restaurant," Cohen replied. "All I'm asking is what brings you to this address?"

"The window was open," the bird sighed; adding after a moment, "I'm running. I'm flying but I'm also running."

"From whom?" asked Edie with interest.

"Anti-Semeets."

"Anti-Semites?" they all said.

"That's from who."

"What kind of anti-Semites bother a bird?" Edie asked.

"Any kind," said the bird, "also including eagles, vultures, and hawks. And once in a while some crows will take your eyes out."

"But aren't you a crow?"

"Me? I'm a Jewbird."

Cohen laughed heartily. "What do you mean by that?"

The bird began dovening. He prayed without Book or tallith, but with passion. Edie bowed her head, though not Cohen. And Maurie rocked back and forth with the prayers, looking up with one wide-open eye.

When the prayer was done Cohen remarked, "No hat, no phylacteries?"

"I'm an old radical."

"You're sure you're not some kind of a ghost or dybbuk?"

"Not a dybbuk," answered the bird, "though one of my relatives had such an experience once. It's all over now, thanks God. They freed her from a former lover, a crazy jealous man. She's now the mother of two wonderful children."

"Birds?" Cohen asked slyly.

"Why not?"

"What kind of birds?"

"Like me. Jewbirds."

Cohen tipped back in his chair and guffawed. "That's a big laugh. I heard of a Jewfish but not a Jewbird."

"We're once removed." The bird rested on one skinny leg, then on the other. "Please, could you spare maybe a piece of herring with a small crust of bread?"

Edie got up from the table.

"What are you doing?" Cohen asked her.

"I'll clear the dishes."

Cohen turned to the bird. "So what's your name, if you don't mind saying?"

"Call me Schwartz."

"He might be an old Jew changed into a bird by somebody," said Edie, removing a plate.

"Are you?" asked Harry, lighting a cigar.

"Who knows?" answered Schwartz. "Does God tell us everything?" [...]

Weeks went by. Then on the day after Cohen's mother had died in her flat in the Bronx, when Maurie came home with a zero on an arithmetic test, Cohen, enraged, waited until Edie had taken the boy to his violin lesson, then openly attacked the bird. He chased him with a broom on the balcony and Schwartz frantically flew back and forth, finally escaping into his birdhouse. Cohen triumphantly reached in and, grabbing both skinny legs, dragged the bird out, cawing loudly, his wings wildly beating. He whirled the bird around and around his head. But Schwartz, as he moved in circles, managed to swoop down and catch Cohen's nose in his beak, and hung on for dear life. Cohen cried out in great pain, punched at the bird with his fist, and, tugging at its legs with all his might, pulled his nose free. Again he swung the yawking Schwartz around until the bird grew dizzy, then, with a furious heave, flung him into the night. Schwartz sank like a stone into the street. Cohen then tossed the birdhouse and feeder after him, listening at the ledge until they crashed on the sidewalk below. For a full hour, broom in hand, his heart palpitating and nose throbbing with pain, Cohen waited for Schwartz to return, but the brokenhearted bird didn't.

That's the end of that dirty bastard, the salesman thought and went in. Edie and Maurie had come home.

"Look," said Cohen, pointing to his bloody nose swollen three times its size, "what that sonofabitchy bird did. It's a permanent scar."

"Where is he now?" Edie asked, frightened.

"I threw him out and he flew away. Good riddance."

Nobody said no, though Edie touched a handkerchief to her eyes and Maurie rapidly tried the nine-times table and found he knew approximately half.

Saul Bellow

Herzog
1964

If am out of my mind, it's all right with me, thought Moses Herzog.

Some people thought he was cracked and for a time he himself had doubted that he was all there. But now, though he still behaved oddly, he felt confident, cheerful, clairvoyant, and strong. He had fallen under a spell and was writing letters to everyone under the sun. He was so stirred by these letters that from the end of June he moved from place to place with a valise full of papers. He had carried this valise from New York to Martha's Vineyard, but returned from the Vineyard immediately; two days later he flew to Chicago, and from Chicago he went to a village in western Massachusetts. Hidden in the country, he wrote endlessly, fanatically, to the newspapers, to people in public life, to friends and relatives and at last to the dead, his own obscure dead, and finally the famous dead. [...]

The house was two miles beyond the village, in the hills. Beautiful, sparkling summer weather in the Berkshires, the air light, the streams quick, the woods dense, the green new. As for birds, Herzog's acres seemed to have become a sanctuary. Wrens nested under the ornamental scrolls of the porch. The giant elm was not quite dead, and the orioles lived in it still. Herzog had the driver stop in the mossy roadway, boulder-lined. He couldn't be sure the house was approachable. But no fallen trees blocked the path, and although much of the gravel had washed down in thaws and storms the cab might easily have gotten through. Moses, however, didn't mind the short climb. His chest was securely armored in tape and his legs were light. He had bought some groceries in Ludeyville. If hunters and prowlers had not eaten it, there was a supply of canned goods in the cellar. Two years ago he had put up tomatoes and beans and raspberry preserves, and before leaving for Chicago he had hidden his wine and whisky. The electricity of course was turned off but perhaps the old hand pump could be made to work. There was always cistern water to fall back on. He could cook in the fireplace; there were old hooks and trivets—and here (his heart trembled) the house rose out of weeds, vines, trees, and blossoms. Herzog's folly! Monument to his sincere and loving idiocy, to the unrecognized evils of his character, symbol of his Jewish struggle for a solid footing in White Anglo-Saxon Protestant America ("The land was ours before we were the land's," as that sententious old man declared at the Inauguration). I too have done my share of social climbing, he thought, with hauteur to spare, defying the Wasps, who, because the government gave much of this continent away to the railroads, stopped boiling their own soap circa 1880, took European tours, and began to complain of the Micks and the Spicks and the Sheenies. What a struggle I waged!—left-handed but fierce. But enough of that—here I am. *Hineni*!

Bel Kaufman

1911-2014

Born in Berlin and raised in Odessa, Bel Kaufman immigrated to New York City with her family at the age of twelve. The granddaughter of Yiddish writer Sholem Aleichem, Kaufman became an accomplished author herself, earning degrees at Hunter College and Columbia University, and she eventually became a teacher in the city's public-school system. Her multiple decades of experience with teaching gave shape to *Up the Down Staircase*, written in the form of teachers' and students' notes, class plans, blackboard assignments, and principals' memos. The book's success lifted the divorced, poverty-stricken Kaufman into a life of financial security that her family had never known. She established the Sholem Aleichem Foundation, remarried happily in the 1970s, and, at age 101, was still teaching two years before her death.

Up the Down Staircase
1964

INTRASCHOOL COMMUNICATION

FROM: Mrs. B. Schachter, Lobby
TO: 304
Dear #443—

The Board moves in a mysterious way. Always did. In my day—Depression Years—they failed a brilliant girl who would have made great teacher—on the oral exam, for something they called "lateral emission"! They almost got *me* on the "sibilant S" (that was the year they were after the S's): My Waterloo was: "He still insists he sees the ghosts."

And a friend of mine, a Millay scholar, was failed for poor interpretation of a sonnet by Millay. Her appeal was not granted, even after Edna Millay herself wrote a letter to the Board explaining that was exactly what she had meant in her poem. My friend did establish a precedent, I believe: ever since, candidates for the English license have been given poems by very dead poets, long silent in their graves.

Now, of course, things are different: they thrust the license upon anybody who can stand up and use a board eraser.

The Aide didn't show up and I'm stuck in the lobby again. Send down some cheery news!

Bea

INTRASCHOOL COMMUNICATION

FROM: 304
TO: Mrs. B. Schachter, Lobby
Dear Bea—

Cheery? I feel lost and a bit absurd—as if I were tilting at windmills which aren't there, or shouting in an empty tunnel. I keep trying to remember who I am. The Board of Ed has the same trouble.

Now they inform me that "A teacher who has exhausted his cumulative sick leave may borrow up to 20 days of additional sick leave."

Who's sick? I don't mind their lack of faith in my health; it's the Dear Sir or Madam I mind. How do I convince them I'm a Madam?

Syl

INTRASCHOOL COMMUNICATION

FROM: Mrs. B. Schachter
TO: 304
Dear Syl—
Play it cool. They'll catch on.

Bea

INTRASCHOOL COMMUNICATION

FROM: 304
TO: 508
Dear Bea,

Today I must return *Odyssey* and *Myths & Their Meaning*; someone else needs crack at them. I've had only ten school days on them, in my slow class, with half of students absent or truant, and not enough books to go around, and no help from librarian—whose note is enclosed:

My dear Miss Barrett,

I am forced to cancel the library lesson you had planned for your 3rd term students in connection with their study of mythology. Sending them here six at a time creates havoc and disorder. They have already misplaced *The Golden Age of Greece* and have put Bullfinch on the Zoology shelf, besides talking. Two of your students took out books indiscriminately, that had nothing to do with the assignment. I cannot allow them the facilities of the school library until they learn the proper respect for the printed page.

Sincerely,
Charlotte Wolf, Librarian

Do you know Paul's song about her: "Who's Afraid of Charlotte Wolf"?

I think I really got the kids interested; I made myths live for them by linking them with their own lives and with the present. To find out how much they've actually absorbed, I'm giving them a quiz next period. I've armed myself with a red pencil (over McHabe's dead body!) for correcting content, and a blue one for mistakes in spelling, grammar, etc. The two-tone correction was the idea of a Ped Prof of mine in college.

What I had attempted to do was to convey the comedy of the gods against the tragedy of mortals—

Syl

FROM: 508
TO: 304
Dear Syl—
That may be the only way to convey tragedy: through comedy. Humor is all we've got.

Bea

Other works by Kaufman: *Abroad in America* (1976); *Love, Etc.* (1979).

Joseph Stein, Sheldon Harnick, and Jerry Bock

Stein, 1912–2010

Bronx-born librettist Joseph Stein entertained millions through his work for the Broadway stage. He began his career as a psychiatric social worker in 1939. After a chance encounter with actor Zero Mostel, who needed material for a radio show, Stein began writing, joining Sid Caesar's *Your Show of Shows* and then moving on to Broadway with his first book, written with Will Glickman, for the 1955 musical *Plain and Fancy*. Teaming up with composer Jerry Bock and lyricist Sheldon Harnick, Stein wrote the book for *Fiddler on the Roof*, which went on for three thousand performances on Broadway and has been staged internationally many times. Stein also wrote the libretto for the musical *Zorba* (1968), based on Nikos Kazantzakis's 1952 novel *Zorba the Greek*.

Harnick, b. 1924

Chicago-born Sheldon Harnick began writing music and comedy in high school, interrupting his budding career with a stint in the army and then obtaining a bachelor's degree in music from Northwestern University. He moved to New York City in the early 1950s and began writing for Broadway. When he

met composer Jerry Bock, Harnick's career took off as the pair created the Pulitzer Prize–winning musical drama *Fiorello!* (1959) and later *Fiddler on the Roof* (1964), which garnered them both Tony Awards. He and Bock split up after the production of *The Rothschilds* (1970), but Harnick continued to be active into his eighties.

Bock, 1928–2010

Born in New Haven, Connecticut, and raised in New York City, composer Jerry Bock is best-known for creating the Broadway musical *Fiddler on the Roof* together with Sheldon Harnick. Bock began his Broadway career alongside Lawrence Holofcener composing songs for *Catch a Star* and *Mr. Wonderful*, a vehicle for Sammy Davis Jr. With Harnick, Bock won the Tony Award for Best Musical as well as the Pulitzer Prize for Drama for *Fiorello!* (1959), based on the life of controversial New York mayor Fiorello LaGuardia. The Jerry Bock Award for Excellence in Musical Theater is given annually to the lyricist and composer of a project developed in the BMI Foundation's Lehman Engel Musical Theatre Workshop.

Fiddler on the Roof
1964

Prologue

The exterior of TEVYE's *house. A* FIDDLER *is seated on the roof, playing.* TEVYE *is outside the house.*

TEVYE: A fiddler on the roof. Sounds crazy, no? But in our little village of Anatevka, you might say every one of us is a fiddler on the roof, trying to scratch out a pleasant, simple tune without breaking his neck. It isn't easy. You may ask, why do we stay up here if it's so dangerous? We stay because Anatevka is our home. And how do we keep our balance? That I can tell you in a word—tradition!

VILLAGERS [*Enter, singing.*]

> Tradition, tradition—Tradition.
> Tradition, tradition—Tradition.

TEVYE: Because of our traditions, we've kept our balance for many, many years. Here in Anatevka we have traditions for everything—how to eat, how to sleep, how to wear clothes. For instance, we always keep our heads covered and always wear a little prayer shawl. This shows our constant devotion to

God. You may ask, how did this tradition start? I'll tell you—I don't know! But it's a tradition. Because of our traditions, everyone knows who he is and what God expects him to do.

TEVYE *and* PAPAS [*Sing*]:

["Tradition"]

> Who, day and night,
> Must scramble for a living,
> Feed a wife and children,
> Say his daily prayers?
> And who has the right,
> As master of the house,
> To have the final word at home?

ALL:

> The papa, the papa—Tradition.
> The papa, the papa—Tradition.

GOLDE *and* MAMAS:

> Who must know the way to make a proper
> home,
> A quiet home, a kosher home?
> Who must raise a family and run the home
> So Papa's free to read the Holy Book?

ALL:

> The mama, the mama—Tradition.
> The mama, the mama—Tradition.

SONS:

> At three I started Hebrew school,
> At ten I learned a trade.
> I hear they picked a bride for me.
> I hope she's pretty.

ALL:

> The sons, the sons—Tradition.
> The sons, the sons—Tradition.

DAUGHTERS:

> And who does Mama teach
> To mend and tend and fix,
> Preparing me to marry
> Whoever Papa picks?

ALL:

> The daughters, the daughters—Tradition.
> The daughters, the daughters—Tradition.

[*They repeat the song as a round.*]

> PAPAS: The papas.
> MAMAS: The mamas.
> SONS: The sons.
> DAUGHTERS: The daughters.
> ALL: Tradition.
> PAPAS: The papas.
> MAMAS: The mamas.
> SONS: The sons.
> DAUGHTERS: The daughters.
> ALL: Tradition.

TEVYE: And in the circle of our little village, we have always had our special types. For instance, Yente, the matchmaker . . .

YENTE: Avram, I have a perfect match for your son. A wonderful girl.

AVRAM: Who is it?

YENTE: Ruchel, the shoemaker's daughter.

AVRAM: Ruchel? But she can hardly see. She's almost blind.

YENTE: Tell the truth, Avram, is your son so much to look at? The way she sees and the way he looks, it's a perfect match.
[ALL *dance.*]

TEVYE: And Reb Nahum, the beggar.

NAHUM: Alms for the poor, alms for the poor.

LAZAR: Here, Reb Nahum, is one kopek.

NAHUM: One kopek? Last week you gave me two kopeks.

LAZAR: I had a bad week.

NAHUM: So if you had a bad week, why should I suffer?
[ALL *dance.*]

TEVYE: And most important, our beloved rabbi . . .

MENDEL: Rabbi, may I ask your counsel?

RABBI: Certainly my son.

MENDEL: Is there a proper blessing for the Tsar?

RABBI: A blessing for the Tsar? Of course. May God bless and keep the Tsar—far away from us!
[ALL *dance.*]

TEVYE: Then, there are the others in our village. They make a much bigger circle.
[*The* PRIEST, *the* CONSTABLE, *and other* RUSSIANS *cross the stage. The two groups nod to each other.*]

TEVYE: His Honor the Constable, his Honor the Priest, and his Honor—many others. We don't bother them, and, so far, they don't bother us. And among ourselves we get along perfectly well. Of course, there was the time [*pointing to the* TWO MEN] when he sold him a horse and he delivered a mule, but that's all settled now. Now we live in simple peace and harmony and—

[*The* Two Men *begin an argument, which is taken up by the entire group.*]

FIRST MAN: It was a horse.

SECOND MAN: It was a mule.

FIRST MAN: It was a horse!

SECOND MAN: It was a mule, I tell you!

VILLAGERS: Horse!

VILLAGERS: Mule!

VILLAGERS: Horse!

VILLAGERS: Mule!

VILLAGERS: Horse!

VILLAGERS: Mule

VILLAGERS: Horse!

VILLAGERS: Mule!

EVERYONE:

> Tradition, tradition—Tradition.
> Tradition, tradition—Tradition.

TEVYE: [*Quieting them*] Tradition. Without our traditions, our lives would be as shaky as—as a fiddler on the roof!

[*The* VILLAGERS *exit and the house opens to show its interior.*]

Other works by Stein: *Mr. Wonderful* (1956); *The Body Beautiful* (1958); *Enter Laughing* (1963); *Irene* (1973). Other works by Harnick: *New Faces of 1952* (1952); *The Body Beautiful* (1958); *Tenderloin* (1960); *She Loves Me* (1963); *The Apple Tree* (1966). Other works by Bock: *The Body Beautiful* (1958); *Tenderloin* (1960); *Man in the Moon* (1963); *The Apple Tree* (1966); *The Rothschilds* (1970).

Cynthia Ozick

The Pagan Rabbi
1966

When I heard that Isaac Kornfeld, a man of piety and brains, had hanged himself in the public park, I put a token in the subway stile and journeyed out to see the tree. [. . .]

[. . .] On the day of his funeral the president of his college was criticized for having commented that although a suicide could not be buried in consecrated earth, whatever earth enclosed Isaac Kornfeld was

ipso facto consecrated. It should be noted that Isaac hanged himself several weeks short of his thirty-sixth birthday; he was then at the peak of his renown; and the president, of course, did not know the whole story. He judged by Isaac's reputation, which was at no time more impressive than just before his death.

I judged by the same, and marveled that all that holy genius and intellectual surprise should in the end be raised no higher than the next-to-lowest limb of a delicate young oak, with burly roots like the toes of a gryphon exposed in the wet ground. [. . .]

In the bottommost meadow fringing the water I recognized the tree which had caused Isaac to sin against his own life. It looked curiously like a photograph—not only like that newspaper photograph I carried warmly in my pocket, which showed the field and its markers—the drinking-fountain a few yards off, the ruined brick wall of an old estate behind. The caption-writer had particularly remarked on the "rope." But the rope was no longer there; the widow had claimed it. It was his own prayer shawl that Isaac, a short man, had thrown over the comely neck of the next-to-lowest limb. A Jew is buried in his prayer shawl; the police had handed it over to Sheindel. I observed that the bark was rubbed at that spot. The tree lay back against the sky like a licked postage stamp. Rain began to beat it flatter yet. A stench of sewage came up like a veil in the nostril. It seemed to me I was a man in a photograph standing next to a gray blur of tree. I would stand through eternity beside Isaac's guilt if I did not run, so I ran that night to Sheindel herself. [. . .]

[. . .] "Take Isaac's notebook and bring it back when you can."

I obeyed. In my own room, a sparse place, with no ornaments but a few pretty stalks in pots, I did not delay and seized the notebook. It was a tiny affair, three inches by five, with ruled pages that opened on a coiled wire. I read searchingly, hoping for something not easily evident. Sheindel by her melancholy innuendo had made me believe that in these few sheets Isaac had revealed the reason for his suicide. But it was all a disappointment. There was not a word of any importance. [. . .]

I have forgotten to mention that the notebook, though scantily filled, was in three languages. The Greek I could not read at all, but it had the shape of verse. The Hebrew was simply a miscellany, drawn mostly from Leviticus and Deuteronomy. Among these I found the following extracts, transcribed not quite verbatim:

Ye shall utterly destroy all the places of the gods, upon the high mountains, and upon the hills, and under every green tree.

And the soul that turneth after familiar spirits to go a-whoring after them, I will cut him off from among his people.

These, of course, were ordinary unadorned notes, such as any classroom lecturer might commonly make to remind himself of the text, with a phrase cut out here and there for the sake of speeding his hand. Or I thought it possible that Isaac might at that time have been preparing a paper on the Talmudic commentaries for these passages. Whatever the case, the remaining quotations, chiefly from English poetry, interested me only slightly more. They were the elegiac favorites of a closeted Romantic. I was repelled by Isaac's Nature: it wore a capital letter, and smelled like my own Book Cellar. It was plain to me that he had lately grown painfully academic: he could not see a weed's tassel without finding a classical reference for it. He had put down a snatch of Byron, a smudge of Keats (like his Scriptural copyings, these too were quick and fragmented), a pair of truncated lines from Tennyson, and this unmarked and clumsy quatrain:

> And yet all is not taken. Still one Dryad
> Flits through the wood, one Oread skims the hill;
> White in the whispering stream still gleams a
>   Naiad;
> The beauty of the earth is haunted still.

All of this was so cloying and mooning and ridiculous, and so pedantic besides, that I felt ashamed for him. And yet there was almost nothing else, nothing to redeem him, and nothing personal, only a sentence or two in his rigid self-controlled scholar's style, not unlike the starched little jokes of our correspondence. "I am writing at dusk sitting on a stone in Trilham's Inlet Park, within sight of Trilham's Inlet, a bay to the north of the city, and within two yards of a slender tree, *Quercus velutina*, the age of which, should one desire to measure it, can be ascertained by (God forbid) cutting the bole and counting the rings. The man writing is thirty-five years old and aging too rapidly, which may be ascertained by counting the rings under his poor myopic eyes." Below this, deliberate and readily more legible than the rest, appeared three curious words:

Great Pan lives.

Maurice Sendak (Review by Nat Hentoff)
1928–2012

Brooklyn-born Maurice Sendak was born to Sarah (Schindler) and Philip Sendak, first-generation immigrants from Eastern Europe whose trauma he struggled to understand. He learned to address these and other ever-present stressors—the Holocaust, child kidnapping, bullying, and his undisclosed homosexuality—through illustrations and fantasy. He illustrated his first book, Maxwell Leigh and Hyman Ruchlis Eidinoff's *Atomics for the Millions* (1947), while in high school, and his first children's book, Marcel Aymé's *The Wonderful Farm*, in 1951. Sendak illustrated more than one hundred books, many of his own creation, received the Caldecott Medal (1964) for *Where the Wild Things Are* (1963), and numerous other awards for his literary and theatrical contributions. Nat Hentoff (1925–2017), the author of this selection on Sendak, was an award-winning American Jewish writer, newspaper columnist, and jazz advocate.

Among the Wild Things [Review by Nat Hentoff]
1966

In the past few years, I have become increasingly interested in Sendak's work, reading his books for my own pleasure as well as for the amusement of my children. His drawings, I have found, are oddly compelling. Intensely, almost palpably alive, they seem to move on the page and, later, in memory. This quality is pervasive in "Where the Wild Things Are," the story of a boy named Max who assumes a demonic face and puts on a wolf suit one night and makes mischief. His mother calls him a "WILD THING!" and Max answers, "I'LL EAT YOU UP!"[1] He is sent to bed without his supper. Standing in his room, Max watches a forest grow until it becomes the world. An ocean tumbles by with a boat in it for Max, and he sails to where the wild things are. The wild things—a colony of monsters—try to frighten Max, but, frowning fiercely, he commands them to be still. Cowed, they make Max King of the Wild Things. Then, at Max's order, a rumpus begins—six wordless pages of howling, dancing, tree-climbing, and parading by Max and the wild things. Max presently stops the revels, though, and sends the wild things to bed without *their* supper, and then, feeling lonely, gives up his crown. The wild things so hate to see Max leave that they try to scare him into staying, but he is not intimidated, and he sails back to his room, where he finds his supper waiting for him.

As I studied the pictures of Max and his companions, it seemed to me that I had never seen fantasy depicted in American children's books in illustrations that were so powerfully in motion. Brian O'Doherty, the former art critic of the *Times*, has written that Sendak is "a fantasist in the great tradition of Sir John Tenniel and Edward Lear," and I agree. O'Doherty has also described Sendak as "one of the most powerful men in the United States," in that he "has given shape to the fantasies of millions of children—an awful responsibility." I had known a few men who possessed power, but never this kind of power, so I made arrangements to meet the creator of the wild things. [. . .]

Fantasy, I learned in subsequent visits to the studio, has been familiar terrain to Sendak from his earliest years. He was born in Brooklyn on June 10, 1928, the youngest of three children of Philip and Sarah Sendak. (His sister, Natalie, was eight when he was born, and his brother, Jack, was five.) Both parents had come to America before the First World War from Jewish *shtetls*, or small towns, outside Warsaw. The father, who worked in the garment district, told his children long stories based on tales he remembered from his childhood and alive with myth and fantasy. "He was a marvellous improviser, and he'd often extend a story for many nights," Sendak recalls. "One short one I've always wanted to make into a book was about a child taking a walk with his father and mother. He becomes separated from them. Snow begins to fall, and the child shivers in the cold. He huddles under a tree, sobbing in terror. An enormous figure hovers over him and says, as he draws the boy up, 'I'm Abraham, your father.' His fear gone, the child looks up and also sees Sarah. He is no longer lost. When his parents find him, the child is dead. Those stories had something of the character of William Blake's poems. The myths in them didn't seem at all factitious. And they fused Jewish lore with my father's particular way of shaping memory and desire. That one, for instance, was based on the power of Abraham in Jewish tradition as the father who was always there—a reassuring father even when he was Death. But the story was also about how tremendously my father missed his parents. Not all his tales were sombre, though. My father could be very witty, even if the humor was always on the darker side of irony." [. . .]

"I was always conscious of usable material for books," Sendak recalls. "I remember examining my grandmother all the time and placing her in various fantasies. And I was so conscious of the streets on which I lived that I can remember them now in complete detail—how many houses there were, who lived in which house, what the people looked like. During my early teens, I spent a lot of time at the window, sketching the kids at play, and those sketchbooks are, in a sense, the foundation of much of my later work. Maybe that's another reason the children in my books are called European-looking. Many of them resemble the kids I knew growing up in Brooklyn. They were Jewish kids, and they may well look like little greenhorns just off the boat. They had—some of them, anyway—a kind of bowed look, as if the burdens of the world were on their shoulders." [. . .]

Sendak lit a cigarette. "Recently, I gave a lecture at Pratt Institute, and a student asked me if I ever sit down with the intention of doing a children's book dealing with anxiety," he said. "Of course I don't, I told him. If I did, I'd hardly be any kind of creative artist. When I write and draw, I'm experiencing what the child in the book is going through. I was as relieved to get back from Max's journey as he was. Or, rather, I like to think I got back. It's only after the act of writing the book that, as an adult, I can see what has happened, and talk about fantasy as catharsis, about Max acting out his anger as he fights to grow."

The room was now quite dark, and Sendak put on the light. "For me, that book was a personal exorcism," he went on. "It went deeper into my own childhood than anything I've done before, and I must go even deeper in the ones to come."

NOTE

1. [Sendak is translating from the Yiddish of his Brooklyn home where a child who misbehaved was called "a *vilde khaye*, a wild beast."—Eds.]

Other works by Sendak: *Chicken Soup with Rice* (1962); *Higglety Pigglety Pop!* (1967); *In the Night Kitchen* (1970); *Outside over There* (1981); *Brundibár* (with Tony Kushner, 2003).

Nat Hentoff, "Among the Wild Things," *The New Yorker* (22 January 1966). © Condé Nast. Used with permission of Condé Nast. Including quotes from Maurice Sendak, from *Where the Wild Things Are* (New York: HarperCollins, 1984); Brian O'Doherty, "Art: Current Exhibitions Summarized: Maurice Sendak," *New York Times* (April 4, 1964).

Chaim Potok

1929–2002

Born in New York City, Chaim Potok was a novelist, ordained rabbi, teacher, and the former editor in chief of the Jewish Publication Society. His best-selling novels often explore the conflict between Jewish heritage and secularism. Also the author of nonfiction works, children's literature, a memoir, and novellas, Potok received the National Jewish Book Award, the Athenaeum Award, the National Foundation for Jewish Culture Achievement Award, and the O. Henry Award.

The Chosen

1967

For the first fifteen years of our lives, Danny and I lived within five blocks of each other and neither of us knew of the other's existence. [. . .]

Danny and I probably would never have met—or we would have met under altogether different circumstances—had it not been for America's entry into the Second World War and the desire this bred on the part of some English teachers in the Jewish parochial schools to show the gentile world that yeshiva students were as physically fit, despite their long hours of study, as any other American student. They went about proving this by organizing the Jewish parochial schools in and around our area into competitive leagues, and once every two weeks the schools would compete against one another in a variety of sports. I became a member of my school's varsity softball team [. . .]

[. . .] To the rabbis who taught in the Jewish parochial schools, baseball was an evil waste of time, a spawn of the potentially assimilationist English portion of the yeshiva day. But to the students of most of the parochial schools, an inter-league baseball victory had come to take on only a shade less significance than a top grade in Talmud, for it was an unquestioned mark of one's Americanism, and to be counted a loyal American had become increasingly important to us during these last years of the war. [. . .]

[. . .] I crouched down, waiting, remembering Danny Saunders' promise to his team that they would kill us apikorsim. The word had meant, originally, a Jew educated in Judaism who denied basic tenets of his faith, like the existence of God, the revelation, the resurrection of the dead. To people like Reb Saunders, it also meant any educated Jew who might be reading,

say, Darwin, and who was not wearing side curls and fringes outside his trousers. I was an apikoros to Danny Saunders, despite my belief in God and Torah, because I did not have side curls and was attending a parochial school where too many English subjects were offered and where Jewish subjects were taught in Hebrew instead of Yiddish, both unheard-of sins, the former because it took time away from the study of Torah, the latter because Hebrew was the Holy Tongue and to use it in ordinary classroom discourse was a desecration of God's Name. I had never really had any personal contact with this kind of Jew before. My father had told me he didn't mind their beliefs. What annoyed him was their fanatic sense of righteousness, their absolute certainty that they and they alone had God's ear, and every other Jew was wrong, totally wrong, a sinner, a hypocrite, an apikoros, and doomed, therefore, to burn in hell. I found myself wondering again how they had learned to hit a ball like that if time for the study of Torah was so precious to them and why they had sent a rabbi along to waste his time sitting on a bench during a ball game.

Standing on the field and watching the boy at the plate swing at a high ball and miss, I felt myself suddenly very angry, and it was at that point that for me the game stopped being merely a game and became a war. The fun and excitement was out of it now. Somehow the yeshiva team had translated this afternoon's baseball game into a conflict between what they regarded as their righteousness and our sinfulness. I found myself growing more and more angry, and I felt the anger begin to focus itself upon Danny Saunders, and suddenly it was not at all difficult for me to hate him.

Schwartzie let five of their men come up to the plate that half inning and let one of those five score. Sometime during that half inning, one of the members of the yeshiva team had shouted at us in Yiddish, "Burn in hell, you apikorsim!" and by the time that half inning was over and we were standing around Mr. Galanter near the wire screen, all of us knew that this was not just another ball game.

Other works by Potok: *The Promise* (1969); *My Name Is Asher Lev* (1972); *Wanderings: Chaim Potok's History of the Jews* (1978); *The Book of Lights* (1981).

Saul Bellow

Mr. Sammler's Planet
1969

They went down in the elevator, the grey woman and Mr. Sammler, and through lower passages paved in speckled material, through tunnels, up and down ramps, past laboratories and supply rooms. Well, this famous truth for which he was so keen, he had it now, or it had him. He felt that he was being destroyed, what was left of him. He wept to himself. He walked at the habitual rapid sweeping pace, waiting at crossways for the escorting nurse. In stirring air flavored with body-things, sickness, drugs. He felt that he was breaking up, that irregular big fragments inside were melting, sparkling with pain, floating off. Well, Elya was gone. He was deprived of one more thing stripped of one more creature. One more reason to live trickled out. He lost his breath. Then the woman came up. More hundreds of yards in this winding underground smelling of serum, of organic soup, of fungus, of cell-brew. The nurse took Sammler's hat and said, "In there." The door sign read P.M. That would mean post-mortem. They were ready to do an autopsy as soon as Angela signed the papers. And of course she would sign. Let's find out what went wrong. And then cremation.

"To see Dr. Gruner. Where?" said Sammler.

The attendant pointed to the wheeled stretcher on which Elya lay. Sammler uncovered his face. The nostrils, the creases were very dark, the shut eyes pale and full, the bald head high-marked by gradients of wrinkles. In the lips bitterness and an expression of obedience were combined.

Sammler in a mental whisper said, "Well, Elya. Well, well, Elya." And then in the same way he said, "Remember, God, the soul of Elya Gruner, who, as willingly as possible and as well as he was able, and even to an intolerable point, and even in suffocation and even as death was coming was eager, even childishly perhaps (may I be forgiven for this), even with a certain servility, to do what was required of him. At his best this man was much kinder than at my very best I have ever been or could ever be. He was aware that he must meet, and he did meet—through all the confusion and degraded clowning of this life through which we are speeding—he did meet the terms of his contract. The terms which, in his inmost heart, each man knows. As I know mine. As all know. For that is the truth of it—that we all know, God, that we know, that we know, we know, we know."

Philip Roth

Portnoy's Complaint
1969

Even if I consider myself too much of a big shot to set foot inside a synagogue for fifteen minutes—which is all he is asking—at least I should have respect enough to change into decent clothes for the day and not make a mockery of myself, my family, and my religion.

"I'm sorry," I mumble, my back (as is usual) all I will offer him to look at while I speak, "but just because it's your religion doesn't mean it's mine."

"What did you say? Turn around, mister, I want the courtesy of a reply from your mouth."

"I don't have a religion," I say, and obligingly turn in his direction, about a fraction of a degree.

"You don't, eh?"

"I can't."

"And why not? You're something special? Look at me! You're somebody too special?"

"I don't believe in God."

"Get out of those dungarees, Alex, and put on some decent clothes."

"They're not dungarees, they're Levis."

"It's Rosh Hashanah, Alex, and to me you're wearing overalls! Get in there and put a tie on and a jacket on and a pair of trousers and a clean shirt, and come out looking like a human being. And shoes, Mister, hard shoes."

"My shirt *is* clean—"

"Oh, you're riding for a fall, Mr. Big. You're fourteen years old, and believe me, you don't know everything there is to know. Get out of those moccasins! What the hell are you supposed to be, some kind of Indian?"

"Look, I don't believe in God and I don't believe in the Jewish religion—or in any religion. They're all lies."

"Oh, they are, are they?"

"I'm not going to act like these holidays mean anything when they don't! And that's all I'm saying!"

"Maybe they don't mean anything because you don't know anything about them, Mr. Big Shot. What do you know about the history of Rosh Hashanah? One fact? Two facts maybe? What do you know about the history of the Jewish people, that you have the right to call their religion, that's been good enough for people a lot smarter than you and a lot older than you for two thousand years—that you can call all that suffering and heartache a lie!"

"There is no such thing as God, and there never was, and I'm sorry, but in my vocabulary that's a lie."

"Then who created the world, Alex?" he asks contemptuously. "It just happened, I suppose, according to you."

"Alex," says my sister, "all Daddy means is even if you don't want to go with him, if you would just change your clothes—"

"But for what?" I scream. "For something that never existed? Why don't you tell me to go outside and change my clothes for some alley cat or some tree—*because at least they exist!*"

"But you haven't answered me, Mr. Educated Wise Guy," my father says. "Don't try to change the issue. Who created the world and the people in it? Nobody?"

"Right! Nobody!"

"Oh, sure," says my father. "That's brilliant. I'm glad I didn't get to high school if that's how brilliant it makes you."

"Alex," my sister says, and softly—as is her way—softly, because she is already broken a little bit too—"maybe if you just put on a pair of shoes—"

"But you're as bad as he is, Hannah! If there's no God, what do shoes have to do with it!"

"One day a year you ask him to do something for you, and he's too big for it. And that's the whole story, Hannah, of your brother, of his respect and love . . ."

"Daddy, he's a good boy. He does respect you, he does love you—"

"And what about the Jewish people?" He is shouting now and waving his arms, hoping that this will prevent him from breaking into tears—because the word love has only to be whispered in our house for all eyes immediately to begin to overflow. "Does he respect them? Just as much as he respects me, just about as much . . ." Suddenly he is sizzling—he turns on me with another new and brilliant thought. "Tell me something, do you know Talmud, my educated son? Do you know history? One-two-three you were bar mitzvah, and that for you was the end of your religious education. Do you know men study their whole lives in the Jewish religion, and when they die they still haven't finished? Tell me, now that you are all finished at fourteen being a Jew, do you know a single thing about the wonderful history and heritage of the saga of your people?"

But there are already tears on his cheeks, and more are on the way from his eyes. "A's in school," he says, "but in life he's as ignorant as the day he was born."

Blume Lempel

1907–1999

Born Blume Pfeffer in Chorostków, Galicia (now Khorostkiv, Ukraine), Blume Lempel overcame many obstacles to become a Yiddish prose writer of great originality. Lempel studied in a girls' heder. A chance stopover in Paris to visit her brother on her way to Palestine in 1929 set her life on a different course. She married the furrier Lemel Lempel and in 1939 moved to New York. Writing under the pseudonym Rokhl Halpern, she published her first short story in 1943 in the Zionist *Der tog*, while her novel *Tsvishn tsvey veltn* appeared in the communist *Morgn-frayhayt*. Her works won Yiddish literary prizes, but at the time of her death, she remained largely unknown and untranslated.

Even the Heavens Tell Lies
1970

When I crossed the ocean, I carried with me the habit of speaking to the shadows, and it became my way of life. I look up at the stars that were extinguished long ago. For me they still shine with the first fire of creation. I don't care that the heavens tell lies. I accept the fantasy along with the fact. I'm not looking for truth. I'm seeking the faith that I've lost, a way out of chaos, a place where my broken self can put down roots. I know the evil powers that reside within people and make no attempt to cloak them in pretty words. I don't separate myself from the community, but I live on the sidelines, like a stranger in my own world. I live with the snakes and scorpions, with the black leeches in my brain, in my blood.

I live with the garden in my back yard. Among the stones I carried with me, flowers grow. I refer to them by the names of those who are no more. They burn like memorial candles, each in its season. My parents, who were killed in the winter, emerge from the snow. Their tart red berries reach up like blood-soaked fingers. I like to watch as the hungry birds peck at the berries one by one. It seems to me that my mother's white fingers are holding out the fruit for the birds to see, and that she enjoys having them eat from her hands.

The first bloom that breaks through the winter crust is called Rosa. She appears as a narcissus, white, slender and shy, bestowing the rich perfumes of her pure soul upon the wind. The snow may lie at her feet, but she tolerates the bitter weather, holding her head high, stretching up with youthful exhilaration. Sometimes she lasts for a day, sometimes for a week, but the bulb stays planted deep in the earth. She will return, and she knows I will be waiting.

My summer flowers, on the other hand, have no fixed identities. They change their character day by day, according to my mood. When the sky is blue, the gladiolus laughs with my cousin Gitl's sensuous mirth. The pink goblet with its red rim reminds me of Gitl's half-parted lips, always eager to be fruitful and multiply. At twenty she was already the mother of two sets of twins. Whenever she was nursing a child, her mind would flood with intoxicating notions. She kept her grey eyes lowered, ashamed to raise them lest her thoughts be revealed. Perhaps she asked God to forgive her for feeling such heated desire for her husband. It was said that at the very end she was pregnant again. A German put a bullet in her belly and left her lying in the street with her guts spilling out. The sight was so bizarre that the peasants crossed themselves in fear on their way to church that Sunday. In my mind I lift her up and carry her far away from human eyes. Surely if a wolf came upon her in the forest he would devour her. A cannibal would make a feast of her. Yet her ultra-civilized murderer left her lying in the street to show the world what he could do.

The shadows slink around me as I sit in my garden. A smile, a gesture, swims into memory. They are not numbers but living people, each one unique. In the rich soil of my garden, their severed lives are flourishing. Pansies with violet eyes, blue forget-me-nots, red poppies like congealed blood, white roses choked by murderous parasitic vines—side by side with yesterday, a today is blooming. Often I feel that a tomorrow, too, is growing. Whenever I recall a particular face, I plant a flower. I don't pamper my blooms with synthetic food. They must cope with the raw elements. Free from illusions, self-aware, they rely on no one but themselves. Soaking up the hot sunshine and the plenteous rain, the hail and the hurricane, they know the art of adaptation and survival.

Sometimes, when the storms fail to arrive and the thorns on my roses turn limp and passive, a fear overtakes me. In my desperation I summon a storm of my own, awakening the shadows with my mute wailing, my wild laughter. I laugh and I storm, and it seems to me that the wind storms with me.

Translated by Ellen Cassedy and Yermiyahu Ahron Taub.

Other works by Lempel: *A rege fun emes* (1981); *Balade fun a kholem* (1986).

Neil Simon

1927–2018

Playwright and screenwriter Neil Simon was born in New York City. He served in the military during World War II and then wrote for radio and television. He wrote and produced numerous Broadway plays. Among Simon's awards were the Pulitzer Prize, the Tony Award, the Golden Globe, the Writers Guild of America Award, and the 2006 Kennedy Center Mark Twain Prize for American Humor.

The Prisoner of Second Avenue
1970

Act I

MEL: I'm not having an anxiety attack. I'm a little tense.

EDNA: Why don't you take a Valium?

MEL: I took one.

EDNA: Then take another one.

MEL: I took another one. They don't work any more. [*He sits down in a chair*]

EDNA: *Two* Valiums? They *have* to work.

MEL: They don't work any more, I'm telling you. They're supposed to calm you down, aren't they? All right, am I calm? They don't work. Probably don't put anything in them. Charge you fourteen dollars for the word "Valium." [*He bangs on the wall*] Don't you ever fly anywhere? Keep somebody in Europe awake!

[*He bangs on the wall again with his fist*]

EDNA: Stop it, Mel. You're really getting me nervous now. What's wrong? Has something happened? Is something bothering you?

MEL: Why do we live like this? Why do we pay somebody hundreds of dollars a month to live in an egg box that leaks?

EDNA: You don't look well to me, Mel. You look pale. You look haggard.

MEL: I wasn't planning to be up. [*He rubs his stomach*]

EDNA: Why are you rubbing your stomach?

MEL: I'm not rubbing it. I'm holding it.

EDNA: Why are you holding your stomach?

MEL: It's nothing. A little indigestion. It's that crap I had for lunch.

EDNA: Where did you eat?

MEL: In a health-food restaurant. If you can't eat health food, what the hell can you eat any more?

EDNA: You're probably just hungry. Do you want me to make you something?

MEL: Nothing is safe any more. I read in the paper today two white mice at Columbia University got cancer from eating graham crackers. It was in *The New York Times*.

EDNA: Is that what's bothering you? Did you eat graham crackers today?

MEL: Food used to be so good. I used to love food. I haven't eaten food since I was thirteen years old.

EDNA: Do you want some food? I'll make you food. I remember how they made it.

MEL: I haven't had a real piece of bread in thirty years. If I knew what was going to happen, I would have saved some rolls when I was a kid. You can't breathe in here. [*He goes out onto the terrace*] Christ, what a stink. Fourteen stories up, you can smell the garbage from here. Why do they put garbage out in eighty-nine-degree heat? Edna, come here, I want you to smell the garbage.

EDNA [*Comes to the door of the terrace*]: I smell it, I smell it.

MEL: You can't smell it from there. Come here where you can smell it.

EDNA [*Walks to the edge of the terrace and inhales*]: You're right. If you really want to smell it, you have to stand right here.

MEL: This country is being buried by its own garbage. It keeps piling up higher and higher. In three years this apartment is going to be the second floor.

EDNA: What can they do, Mel? Save it up and put it out in the winter? They have to throw it out sometime. That's why they call it garbage.

MEL: I can't talk to you. I can't talk to you any more.

EDNA: Mel, I'm a human being the same as you. I get hot, I get cold, I smell garbage, I hear noise. You either live with it or you get out.

[*Suddenly a dog howls and barks*]

MEL: If you're a human being you reserve the right to complain, to protest. When you give up that right, you don't exist any more. I protest to stinking garbage and jiggling toilets . . . and barking dogs. [*Yells out*] Shut up, goddamnit. [. . .]

MEL: Two dollars' worth of food that comes in three dollars' worth of wrapping. Telephone calls to find out what time it is because you're too lazy to look at a clock . . . The food we never ate, the books we never read, the records we never played. [*He picks up a little thing off the bar*] Look at this! Eight and a half

dollars for a musical whiskey pourer. *Eight and a half dollars!* God forbid we should get a little bored while we're pouring our whiskey! Toys! Toys, novelties, gimmicks, trivia, garbage, crap, HORSESHIT!!! [*He hurls the basket to the floor*]

EDNA: No more. We'll never buy another thing, Mel. I promise. I promise.

MEL [*He is seething with anger*]: Twenty-two years I gave them. What did I give them twenty-two years of my life for? A musical whiskey pourer? It's my *life* that's been poured down the drain. Where's the music? Where's a cute little tune? They kick you out after twenty-two years, they ought to have a goddamned brass band.

EDNA: All right, don't get upset. You're going to get yourself sick.

MEL: You know where my music is? [*He goes over to the wall and points*] There! There it is! It's playing on the other side of that wall. [*Screaming*] There's my music after twenty-two years. [*He grabs his chest, grimacing*] Ohh!

EDNA: What is it, Mel? What's the matter?

MEL: I got pains in my chest. It's nothing, don't worry. It's not a heart attack.

EDNA [*Nervously*]: What do you mean? Why do you say it's not a heart attack?

MEL: Because it's not a heart attack. It's pains in my chest.

EDNA: Why are you having pains in your chest?

MEL: BECAUSE I DON'T HAVE A JOB. BECAUSE I DON'T HAVE A SUIT TO WEAR! BECAUSE I'M HAVING A GODDAMNED BREAKDOWN AND THEY DIDN'T EVEN LEAVE ME WITH A PILL TO TAKE! [*He rushes out onto the terrace again and screams*] BASTARDS! YOU DIRTY BASTARDS!

[*Suddenly a* VOICE, *probably from the terrace above, yells down*]

VOICE: Shut up, down there! There are children up here!

MEL [*Leans over the terrace wall and yells up*]: Don't you yell at me! They took everything! EVERYTHING! They left me with a goddamned pair of pants *and a golf hat!*

Other works by Simon: *Come Blow Your Horn* (1961); *Barefoot in the Park* (1963); *The Odd Couple* (1966); *California Suite* (1976).

Herbert Gold

b. 1924

Novelist Herbert Gold grew up in the Cleveland, Ohio, area and moved to New York to study at Columbia University. Gold was awarded a Fulbright Scholarship, and he moved to Paris, attending the Sorbonne. He later came to San Francisco, where he associated with the Beat generation, notably poets Allen Ginsberg and Lawrence Ferlinghetti. Gold is the author of more than twenty novels.

My Last Two Thousand Years
1972

I was present at the last birth. My wife and I had done the natural childbirth exercises. We were ready. The doctor was kind and easy.

The child was born, my fourth child, a boy. After three girls, Ann, Judy, and Nina, a boy. We would name him Ari, a Hebrew name meaning the Holy Lion.

"Okay, one more push, Mrs. Gold, Melissa, and it'll be all over. Now push."

She did what she was told. We knew the routine. It was planned and prepared and we understood everything. She pushed and it was not all over.

The doctor's face turned gray.

A baby slipped out into his hands, a tiny, perfectly healthy little boy who had been crouching unnoticed behind his brother Ari all this time, unsuspected by anyone. His cries were piping and powerful. I was crashing about the room, laughing; and also trying to console my wife for this surprise. The doctor was explaining how it could happen, it was logical, it was a surprise, it could easily happen, it happened all the time, this was the first time in all his experience; and I in my sterile white gown was consoling him, too, telling him we didn't mind at all; and my wife and I were consoling the nurses and doctors, telling them not to be upset, they didn't have to predict everything, no one needed to predict and control everything, we were surprised but pleased.

We named him Ethan, because it is an old American name, and my wife is descended from Ethan Allen, leader of the Green Mountain boys, and that way we could have one Jewish and one New England Protestant twin. But it turns out that Ethan is also an ancient Hebrew name, spelled Aleph Yod Tav Nun and meaning Firmness, Perpetuity, and Strength.

Having a child, now that I have had five, does not seem to be a creative act. It's an act in which I assist nature to be creative. I enjoy a power which is not mine but in which I share.

Being a Jew has come to seem like having a child: I have given birth to the Jewishness within myself. I did not choose it; it has been given me; but I share in the power and pain which it has offered. I am a part of history [. . .]

Other works by Gold: *Birth of a Hero* (1951); *Love and Like* (1960); *The Age of Happy Problems* (1962); *Fathers: A Novel in the Form of a Memoir* (1967); *A Walk on the West Side* (1981); *Not Dead Yet* (2011).

POETRY AND POPULAR SONG

Jacob Glatstein

Without Jews
1946

Without Jews, no Jewish God.
If, God forbid, we should quit
this world, Your poor tent's light
would out.
Abraham knew You in a cloud:
since then, You are the flame
of our face, the rays
our eyes blaze,
our likeness
whom we formed:
in every land and town
a stranger.
Shattered Jewish skulls,
shards of the divine,
smashed, shamed pots—
these were Your light-bearing vessels,
Your tangibles,
Your portents of miracle!
Now count these heads
by the millions of the dead.
Around You the stars go dark.
Our memory of You, obscured.
Soon Your reign will close.
Where Jews sowed,
a scorched waste.

Dews weep
on dead grass.
The dream raped,
reality raped,
both blotted out.
Whole congregations sleep,
the babies, the women,
the young, the old.
Even Your pillars, Your rocks,
the tribe of Your saints,
sleep their dead
eternal sleep.

Who will dream You?
Remember You?

Deny You?
Yearn after You?
Who will flee You,
only to return
over a bridge of longing?

No end to night
for an extinguished people.
Heaven and earth wiped out.
Your tent void of light.
Flicker of the Jews' last hour.
Soon, Jewish God,
Your eclipse.

Translated by Cynthia Ozick.

Aaron Zeitlin

To Be a Jew
1947

Being a Jew means running forever to God
even if you are His betrayer,
means expecting to hear any day,
even if you are a nay sayer,
the blare of Messiah's horn;

means, even if you wish to,
you cannot escape His snares,
you cannot cease to pray—
even after all the prayers,
even after all the "evens."

Translated by Robert Friend.

David Ignatow
1914–1997

David Ignatow was born in Brooklyn to Russian-immigrant parents. His father worked as a bookbinder; poems such as "Europe and America" speak to differences between his immigrant father's experiences and his own as an American-born son. In a plain American vernacular, Ignatow's poetry explores Jewishness, poverty, and the relationships between fathers and sons. His style was heavily influenced by William Carlos

Williams and Walt Whitman, emphasizing content and meaning over language and artifice. The author of more than twenty-five volumes of poetry, Ignatow received the Bollingen Prize in 1977.

Europe and America
1948

My father brought the emigrant bundle
of desperation and worn threads,
that in anxiety as he stumbles
tumble out distractedly;
while I am bedded upon soft green money
that grows like grass.
Thus, between my father
who lives on bed of anguish for his daily bread,
and I who tear money at leisure by the roots,
where I lie in sun or shade,
a vast continent of breezes, storms to him,
shadows, darkness to him, small lakes, rough
    channels
to him, and hills, mountains to him, lie between
    us.

My father comes of a small hell
where bread and man have been kneaded and baked
    together.
You have heard the scream as the knife fell;
while I have slept
as guns pounded offshore.

Other works by Ignatow: *Poems* (1948); *Figures of the Human* (1964); *Selected Poems* (1975); *Whisper to the Earth* (1981); *Against the Evidence: Selected Poems, 1934–1994* (1994).

Howard Nemerov
1920–1991

Born and raised in New York City, Howard Nemerov was the poet laureate of the United States from 1988 to 1990. A distinguished poet and novelist as well as the author of criticism, short stories, and nonfiction, he was a professor of English at Washington University in St. Louis. Nemerov received many major awards, including the National Book Award, the Pulitzer Prize, the Bollingen Prize, and the National Medal of the Arts.

Nicodemus
1950

I

I went under cover of night
By back streets and alleyways,
Not as one secret and ashamed
But with a natural discretion.

I passed by a boy and a girl
Embraced against the white wall
In parts of shadow, parts of light,
But though I turned my eyes away, my mind
    shook
Whether with dryness or their driving blood;
And a dog howled once in a stone corner.

II

Rabbi, I said,
How is a man born, being old?
From the torn sea into the world
A man may be forced only the one time
To suffer the indignation of the child,
His childish distempers and illnesses.
I would not, if I could, be born again

To suffer the miseries of the child,
The perpetual nearness to tears,
The book studied through burning eyes,
The particular malady of being always ruled
To ends he does not see or understand.

A man may be forced only the one time
To the slow perception of what is meant
That is neither final nor sufficient,
To the slow establishment of a self
Adequate to the ceremony and respect
Of other men's eyes; and to the last
Knowledge that nothing has been done, so
The bitter bewilderment of his age,
A master in Israel and still a child.

III

Rabbi, all things in the springtime
Flower again, but a man may not
Flower again. I regret
The sweet smell of lilacs and the new grass
And the shoots put forth of the cedar
When we are done with the long winter.

Rabbi, sorrow has mothered me
And humiliation been my father,
But neither the ways of the flesh
Nor the pride of the spirit took me,
And I am exalted in Israel
For all that I know I do not know.

Now the end of my desire is death
For my hour is almost come.
I shall not say with Sarah
That God hath made me to laugh,
Nor the new word shall not be born
Out of the dryness of my mouth.

Rabbi, let me go up from Egypt
With Moses to the wilderness of Sinai
And to the country of the old Canaan
Where, sweeter than honey, Sarah's blood
Darkens the cold cave in the field
And the wild seed of Abraham is cold.

Other works by Nemerov: *Journal of the Fictive Life*
(1965); *The Collected Poems of Howard Nemerov* (1977).

Louis Zukofsky
1904–1978

The avant-garde poet Louis Zukofsky was born to
Yiddish-speaking immigrants on New York's Lower
East Side. After coming to the attention of Ezra Pound,
Zukofsky organized the objectivist school of American
modernism, which also included George Oppen and
Charles Reznikoff, and he was guest editor of a unique
Poetry issue in 1931. He toiled at his major work, *A*,
from 1927 until his death, writing for many years in
obscurity. This "poem of a life" takes the poet's daily
observations as its starting point for exploring (among
others) the works of Bach, Marx, Aristotle, Spinoza,
Shakespeare, and the American Yiddish poet Yehoash.
"A"-12 turns from a focus on labor history to family
history: the immigration of Zukofsky's father and the
life of his young son.

"A"-12
1950

In Hebrew "In the beginning"
Means literally *from the head?*
A source creating
The heaven and the earth
And every plant in the field

Before it was in the earth.
Sweet shapes from a head
Whose thought must live forever—
Be the immortelle—
Before it is thought
A prayer to the East.
Before light—the sun later—
To get over even its chaos early.
"You should not forget Him after crossing the sea,
    Pinchos"

Maishe Afroim to Pinchos—
Paul, after he had crossed it,
To those who could not say Pinchos.

Naming little Paul for him
Almost ninety—
I knew Pinchos would not mind
Their "English" names being the same.
He might have said to reprove me:
Jews remember the dead in time
Are in no hurry to flatter the living.
He never reproved me.
"Let it be Paul—I know
Ivanovich named for Ivan,
Before he is born.
Still, our Hebrew names are not the same.
Bless him, may he live
120 years."
And the end is the same:
Bach remembers his own name.
Had he asked me to say Kadish
I believe I would have said it for him.
How fathom his will
Who had taught himself to be simple.
Everything should be as simple as it *can* be,
Says Einstein,
But not simpler.

A Michtam of David,
So many times on his lips:
You have said to Him
My goodness does not extend to you,
The pious in the earth and the excellent
Are all of my delight.
These lines are pleasant to me
That I have inherited.
My heart teaches me at night.
You are before me,
You strengthen my right hand
That my breath rejoices.

You will not let me see death.
You lead me to life
Its pleasures, with your hand
Forever.

Other works by Zukofsky: "Poem Beginning 'The'"
(1928); *Bottom: On Shakespeare* (1963); *Prepositions:*
The Collected Critical Essays of Louis Zukofsky (1968);
Catullus (1969); *Anew: Complete Shorter Poetry* (2011).

Karl Shapiro

The Alphabet
1954

The letters of the Jews as strict as flames
Or little terrible flowers lean
Stubbornly upwards through the perfect ages,
Singing through solid stone the sacred names.
The letters of the Jews are black and clean
And lie in chain-line over Christian pages.
The chosen letters bristle like barbed wire
That hedge the flesh of man,
Twisting and tightening the book that warns.
These words, this burning bush, this flickering pyre
Unsacrifices the bled son of man
Yet plaits his crown of thorns.

Where go the tipsy idols of the Roman
Past synagogues of patient time,
Where go the sisters of the Gothic rose,
Where go the blue eyes of the Polish women
Past the almost natural crime,
Past the still speaking embers of ghettos,
There rise the tinder flowers of the Jews,
The letters of the Jews are dancing knives
That carve the heart of darkness seven ways.
These are the letters that all men refuse
And will refuse until the king arrives
And will refuse until the death of time
And all is rolled back in the book of days.

Jacob Glatstein

Sunday Shtetl
1956

Rabbi Levi Yitskhok's drayman—the one who wore
tales and *tfiln* as he smeared the wheels

of his wagon with tar—
turns up in the shape of a bunch of Jews
hanging around their houses,
washing the car
(while the shtetl drowses
in its Sunday snooze),
adding up bills and working out deals
to pay up what's owed to the pinochle fund-raiser
they attended last night at the Center.

A hushed hand feeds the ache
of this chronic languor
that drops on the town:
weekly monotonous logic,
once out of seven.
In the little square
the clock creeps on
to point the dawn;
a wary church bell wakes
its passive god.
Windows start the stench
of bacon crackling.

The neighbors are off to church.
Our draymen-in-disguise,
hosing down their wheels,
cut the stream to cut the noise.
Lost souls, they look for safekeeping
to the deserted synagogue
that waits to fill up on Yom Kippur.

These Sunday Jews are secret Jews
smiling for the neighbors.
The church bell tolerantly skips over
the doorposts of the Jews.
They listen
with pricked-up ear,
in Marrano fear.

Translated by Cynthia Ozick.

Allen Grossman

1932–2014

Allen Grossman was a postmodern poet born in Minneapolis. He taught at Brandeis University and was the
Andrew W. Mellon Professor Emeritus of the Humanities at Johns Hopkins University. Grossman earned
three Pushcart Prizes, a MacArthur Fellowship, the
Bassine Citation from the Academy of American Poets,

and Yale University's Bollingen Prize in American
Poetry.

I Am in Babylon Dying
1957

The bell pursues me. It is time to die.
It is the hour when no man works. I feel
My time fill up with leaves like a dry well
With many autumns over it, leaves that I
Leave to sigh in the ears of my children. My enemy
Asks for a song, but I sing not. Let the willow
Tell how many sons of them my sons will kill
Before they forget Jerusalem. I cry
Not though the bell pursues and the willow hangs
    over.
This is vile captive food these my tears.
I am in Babylon dying. In the leaves that cover
The silent women by the river my fear
And hate hang like a harp which the wind will ply.

Other works by Grossman: *A Harlot's Hire* (1961);
The Recluse, and Other Poems (1965); *The Woman on
the Bridge over the Chicago River* (1979).

Allen Ginsberg
1926–1997

The Beat poet Allen Ginsberg was an American
original, the best-known poet of his generation. A
fearless self-chronicler, he wrote in bold, Whitman-
esque strokes, describing drug use, spiritual journeys,
and mental illness. Ginsberg was born in Newark,
New Jersey, and attended Columbia University, where
he befriended Jack Kerouac and studied with Lionel
Trilling. He was committed, above all, to frank self-
expression, and he wrote candidly about marijuana,
free love, and other generation-defining pursuits while
championing free speech, gay rights, and creative
license in poetry.

Kaddish: Hymmnn
1959

IV

O mother
what have I left out
O mother
what have I forgotten

O mother
farewell
with a long black shoe
farewell
with Communist Party and a broken stocking
farewell
with six dark hairs on the wen of your breast
farewell
with your old dress and long black beard around the
    vagina
farewell
with your sagging belly
with your fear of Hitler
with your mouth of bad short stories
with your fingers of rotten mandolins
with your arms of fat Paterson porches
with your belly of strikes and smokestacks
with your chin of Trotsky and the Spanish War
with your voice singing for the decaying overbroken
    workers
with your nose of bad lay with your nose of the smell
    of pickles of Newark
with your eyes
with your eyes of Russia
with your eyes of no money
with your eyes of false China
with your eyes of Aunt Elanor in an oxygen tent
with your eyes of starving India
with your eyes pissing in the park
with your eyes of America taking a fall
with your eyes of your failure at the piano
with your eyes of your relatives in California
with your eyes of Ma Rainey dying in an ambulance
with your eyes of Czechoslovakia attacked by robots
with your eyes going to painting class at night in the
    Bronx
with your eyes of the killer Grandma you see on the
    horizon from the Fire-Escape
with your eyes running naked out of the apartment
    screaming into the hall
with your eyes being led away by policemen to an
    ambulance
with your eyes strapped down on the operating table
with your eyes with the pancreas removed
with your eyes of appendix operation
with your eyes of abortion
with your eyes of ovaries removed
with your eyes of shock
with your eyes of lobotomy

with your eyes of divorce
with your eyes of stroke
with your eyes alone
with your eyes
with your eyes
with your Death full of Flowers

V

Caw caw caw crows shriek in the white sun over
  grave stones in Long Island
Lord Lord Lord Naomi underneath this grass my
  halflife and my own as hers
caw caw my eye be buried in the same Ground
  where I stand in Angel
Lord Lord great Eye that stares on All and moves in
  a black cloud
caw caw strange cry of Beings flung up into sky over
  the waving trees
Lord Lord O Grinder of giant Beyonds my voice in
  a boundless field in Sheol
Caw caw the call of Time rent out of foot and wing
  an instant in the universe
Lord Lord an echo in the sky the wind through
  ragged leaves the roar of memory
caw caw all years my birth a dream caw caw New
  York the bus the broken shoe the vast highschool
  caw caw all Visions of the Lord
Lord Lord Lord caw caw caw Lord Lord Lord caw
  caw caw Lord

Other works by Ginsberg: *Howl and Other Poems*
(1956); *Kaddish and Other Poems* (1961).

Chaim Grade

Elegy for the Soviet Yiddish Writers
1960

I

I weep for you with all the letters of the alphabet
that made your hopeful songs. I saw how reason
  spent
itself in vain for hope, how you strove against
  regret—
and all the while your hearts were rent
to bits, like ragged prayer books. Wanderer, I slept
in your beds, knew you as liberal hosts;
yet every night heard sighs of ancient ghosts:

Jews converted by force. My memory kept
it all, your hospitality, and all that Russian land
that fed me, broad as its plains and confining as a
  cell,
with its songs on the Volga, and the anchor sunk in
  sand;
homeland all gone down in blood. And so I tell
your merits, have always looked to your defense, not
  to justify

for pity of your deaths, but for what you were when
  all the space
of Russia sustained you still, and you lived your
  deathly lie:
Marranos—your deepest self denies your face.

II

I saw you, stunned and dumb,
Yiddish poets of Minsk, Moscow, Kiev, when they
  brought home
Job's heavy hurt, the few whom fate had spared.
  Agonized,
you saw the credo you had catechized
in holy Hebrew—*Ani m'amin
b'emunah shlomah*—fall dead in the ravine
at Kiev, among the hidden slain: "With full faith I
  believe
in Friendship of Peoples!"—faith even faith could
  not retrieve
from Babi Yar.
  "Are you asleep?" David Bergelson came to me in
  the night:
"No sleep for me, Chaim. My bed is all nails from
  fright
of what we hoped for—the New Enlightened Man!
And I have lived to know him in my own life's
  span."
I can see his noose hanging down like lead,
and his canny eyes, quick to find.
From the way he bites on the knot of his thoughts
  with teeth set askew in his head
I can tell no one knows better the maze of his mind.
  [. . .]

IV

Mikhoels, tragedian of Tevye and King Lear!
The milkman's faith, the king's despair—
your very fingers speak the lines,

while double-dealing fate plays on.
They call you Solomon, and Moscow crowns
you King. I myself would rather shun
Mikhoels; I fear nothing in him throbs
for Solomon's Song, or Israel's sobs.
But one New Year's night when a blizzard beat,
and partied and vodka'd all Moscow went mad,
and both of us drunk we pitched through the sleet,
he groaned out the grief that stuck in his blood:
"I play the King with my hands, Susskin the Fool
    with his feet.
The audience knows no Yiddish; we bleat
to an ignorant hall." The nation trembled at his
    death
when tyranny snuffed the guiltless breath. [. . .]

VI

Smelling of summer, a stag with belly sated,
charming as a child, Kvitko smiled and prated.
But Bergelson bellowed, "A third eye's what you'll
    need
for all the tears you've yet to lose if you run
away, Chaim—you'll only run to weep!" Feffer gave
    his creed
with outstretched arm: "The days of the trials are
    done."
Posters on walls could thrill us then—but he forgot
the walls of the cellars where the prisoners were
    shot.
The day of his trial—let me be mute:
praise God I wasn't there. I feel my own head crack
with the bullet aimed at Colonel Itzik Feffer's back
in cold murder. Hard for me to speak of him, and
    then
hard not to. Still let me deliver
his name from evil repute. *Ani ha-gever!*
I am the man!—When we met to remember the slain
I saw his tear, and heard his hallowed Amen. [. . .]

IX

Remember the poet who had no legs!
The Germans hurled his wooden pegs
after him, onto the pile of dead. Vilna townsmen
    both,
Gradzenski and I. They threw his legs with a jeer.
    And I am loath,
Markish, mourning you, to pierce your pride with
    grisly metaphor

made to mourn your song: but it was a god of wood
flung after you into the grave—that poem where
    with a roar
of rage you paid violent tribute to the dead.
"Who can sleep? The horror!" you used to gasp.
    "The German dregs,
hangmen! To throw at a legless man his legs!"

Since then your mouth is numb and dumb. And
    since you fell,
I have no sleep or praise for God for any miracle,
though I came safe away. The miracle you waited
    for—
that the Revolution's poets might not become its
    prey—
vanished with the verdict on that fearful day:
"Slay the Jewish poet, slay his Lenin medal, slay
    slay slay!"

X

I weep for your beauty, gone to dust,
comely as Adam on his first day.
Your glance silenced me to awe.
A god made your mouth, your face, your hands.
As David mourned his friend in a bound of trust,
Mount Gilboa's battle-fallen prince,
so I mourn you, Peretz Markish. Your wound, long
    stilled,
oozes in my heart. O you whom the rule of Stalin
    killed,
my brothers, poets!—no one knows your burial
    place
in the land where you were sentenced to disgrace
even after death. Your language, your repute,
were trampled underfoot.
Then let this song be your monument and rest.
In every phrase I cache your being, lest,
blundering birds, you wearily go
after death's black ship, to and fro. [. . .]

XII

Ghosts justify my despair, phantom faces
smile their lost mute shame.
Through nights of fever and dream
you razed your palaces
to glimmering ruin. In your poems you were
like a pond—crooked mirror
for the world of truth. The young

have forgotten you and me and the hour
of our grief. Your widows receive their dower
of blood money. But your darkly murdered tongue,
silenced by the hangman's noose,
is no longer heard, though the muse
again sings in the land. You left
me your language, lilted with joy. But oh, I am
    bereft—
I wear your Yiddish like a drowned man's shirt,
wearing out the hurt.

Translated by Cynthia Ozick.

Reyzl Zychlinsky

Everything Will Remember
1962

Everything will remember
That I was here.
The ships will be the color
Of my clothing,
The birds will use my voice for singing,
The fisherman on the rock
Will ponder my poem,
The river
Will follow my footprints.

Translated by Lucy S. Dawidowicz and Florence Victor.

Bob Dylan

b. 1941

One of the most influential songwriters and poets of
the modern era, Bob Dylan was born Robert Zimmer-
man in Duluth, Minnesota. He grew up in a Jewish
middle-class family in the small city of Hibbing and
played in local rock bands as a teenager. He moved to
New York City in 1961 and performed in folk clubs and
cafés. A protégé of folk singer Woody Guthrie, Dylan
soon turned to songs of protest and rebellion. Later, he
recorded rock and roll, love songs, blues, and country
and gospel music. His 1963 recordings "Blowin' in
the Wind" and "The Times They Are A-Changin'"
became anthems of the civil rights and antiwar movements of that era. In 2016, Bob Dylan was awarded the
Nobel Prize in Literature, the first musician to win the
award.

Like a Rolling Stone
1965

Once upon a time you dressed so fine
You threw the bums a dime in your prime, didn't
    you?
People'd call, say, "Beware doll, you're bound to
    fall"
You thought they were all kiddin' you
You used to laugh about
Everybody that was hangin' out
Now you don't talk so loud
Now you don't seem so proud
About having to be scrounging for your next meal
How does it feel
How does it feel
To be without a home
Like a complete unknown
Like a rolling stone?
You've gone to the finest school all right, Miss
    Lonely
But you know you only used to get juiced in it
And nobody has ever taught you how to live on the
    street
And now you find out you're gonna have to get used
    to it
You said you'd never compromise
With the mystery tramp, but now you realize
He's not selling any alibis
As you stare into the vacuum of his eyes
And ask him do you want to make a deal?
How does it feel
How does it feel
To be on your own
With no direction home
Like a complete unknown
Like a rolling stone?
You never turned around to see the frowns on the
    jugglers and the clowns
When they all come down and did tricks for you
You never understood that it ain't no good
You shouldn't let other people get your kicks for you
You used to ride on the chrome horse with your
    diplomat
Who carried on his shoulder a Siamese cat
Ain't it hard when you discover that
He really wasn't where it's at
After he took from you everything he could steal
How does it feel

How does it feel
To be on your own
With no direction home
Like a complete unknown
Like a rolling stone?
Princess on the steeple and all the pretty people
They're drinkin', thinkin' that they got it made
Exchanging all kinds of precious gifts and things
But you'd better lift your diamond ring, you'd better
    pawn it babe
You used to be so amused
At Napoleon in rags and the language that he used
Go to him now, he calls you, you can't refuse
When you got nothing, you got nothing to lose
You're invisible now, you got no secrets to conceal
How does it feel
How does it feel
To be on your own
With no direction home
Like a complete unknown
Like a rolling stone?

Other works (full-length records) by Dylan: *Freewheelin' Bob Dylan* (1963); *Highway 62 Revisited* (1965); *Blonde on Blonde* (1966); *Nashville Skyline* (1969); *Blood on the Tracks* (1974).

John Hollander

1929–2013

Born in New York City, John Hollander was a poet, critic, editor, scholar, and translator who served as Sterling Professor of English at Yale University. He also wrote children's literature and libretti. Hollander received the Bollingen Prize for poetry as well as fellowships from the MacArthur Foundation, the National Foundation for the Humanities, and the Guggenheim Foundation. Hollander's translations of Moyshe-Leyb Halpern are especially prized.

The Ninth of Ab
1965

August is flat and still, with ever-thickening green
    Leaves, clipped in their richness; hoarse sighs in
        the grass,
            Moments of mowing, mark out the
                lengthening summer. The ground
We children play on, and toward which maples
    tumble their seed.

Reaches beneath us all, back to the sweltering
    City:
        Only here can it never seem yet a time to be
            sad in.
Only the baking concrete, the softening asphalt, the
    wail
        Of wall and rampart made to languish together in
            wild
                Heat can know of the suffering of summer.
                    But here, or in woods
Fringing a pond in Pennsylvania, where dull-red
    newts
        The color of coals glow on the mossy rocks, the
            nights
                Are starry, full of promise of something
                    beyond them, north
Of the north star, south of the warm dry wind, or
    east of the sea.
        There are no cities for now. Even in the time of
            songs
                Of lamenting for fallen cities, this spectacular
                    sunset
Over the ninth hole of the golf-course of the hotel
    Should lead to no unusual evening, and the tall
        Poplars a mile away, eventually fading to total
Purple of fairway and sky and sea, should remain
    unlit
        By flaring of urban gloom. But here in this room,
            when the last
                Touches of red in the sky have sunk, these
                    few men, lumped
Toward the end away from the windows, some with
    bleachy white
        Handkerchiefs comically knotted at each corner,
            worn
                In place of black skullcaps, read what was
                    wailed at a wall
In the most ruined of cities. Only the City is
    missing.
        Behold their sitting down and their rising up.
        I am their music,
            (Music of half-comprehended Hebrew, and
                the muddied
Chaos of *Lamentations*)

        The City, a girl with the curse,
    Unclean, hangs on in her wisdom, her filthiness
        in her skirts,
            Gray soot caked on the fringes of buildings,
                already scarred

With wearing. North, north of here, I know, though,
   that she waits
      For my return at the end of August across the
         wide
         River, on a slow ferry, crawling toward the
            walls
Of high Manhattan's westward face, her concrete
   cliffs
      Micaed with sunset's prophecies of stars, her
         hardened clay
         Preserved, her gold undimmed, her prewar
            streets uncluttered.
But here in this hot, hushed room I sit perspiring
      Among the intonations of old tropes of despair;
         Already, dark in my heart's dank corners,
            grow alien spores;
These drops of sweat, tears for Tammuz; these
   restless fidgetings,
      Ritual turnings northward, away from here where
         fractured
         And gutted walls seem still afire in history's
            forests,
Toward her, the City who claims me after each
   summer is over.
      Returning is sweet and somehow embarrassing
         and awful,
         But I shall be grateful to burn again in her
            twilight oven.

Meanwhile the cooling ground down toward the
   roots of the grass
      Heightens the katydids' scherzo. The men
         disperse in a grove
         Of spruces, while from the distant water-
            hazard, grunts
Of frogs resume their hold on the late-arriving
   night,
      And the just-defunct chants, never perfunctory,
         but not
         Immediate, have vanished into the familiar
            unknown.
When the days are prolonged, and every vision fails
   to blaze
      Up into final truth, when memories merely blur
         A sweated lens for a moment, night is enough
            of a blessing
And enough of a fulfillment. See! the three
   canonical stars
      Affirm what is always beyond danger of being
         disturbed

By force of will or neglect, returning and
   unstoppable.

Other works by Hollander: *The Untuning of the Sky*
(1961); *Movie-Going, and Other Poems* (1962); *The Night
Mirror* (1971).

George Oppen

1908–1984

The poet George Oppen was born into a wealthy family of German Jewish descent in New Rochelle, New York. After his mother's suicide in 1918, the family moved to San Francisco. Oppen's poetry appeared alongside that of Carl Rakosi, Charles Reznikoff, and Louis Zukofsky in the 1931 "Objectivists" issue of *Poetry: A Magazine of Verse*. He later founded the Objectivist Press with Reznikoff and Zukofsky. "Psalm" demonstrates Oppen's belief that poetry should depict concrete objects and achieve the status of an object for itself. With his wife, Mary, he joined the Communist Party in 1935. Despite having earned a Purple Heart for his service in World War II, he fled to Mexico to escape the McCarthy hearings and FBI investigations from 1950 to 1958. After he had not written nor published more than minimally for more than twenty years, Oppen was widely celebrated when he returned to writing verse in the 1960s. He won the Pulitzer Prize in 1969.

Psalm

1965

Veritas sequitur . . .
In the small beauty of the forest
The wild deer bedding down—
That they are there!

Their eyes
Effortless, the soft lips
Nuzzle and the alien small teeth
Tear at the grass

The roots of it
Dangle from their mouths
Scattering earth in the strange woods.
They who are there.

Their paths
Nibbled thru the fields, the leaves that shade them
Hang in the distances is
Of sun

The small nouns
Crying faith
In this in which the wild deer
Startle, and stare out.

Other works by Oppen: *The Materials* (1962); *This in Which* (1965); *Of Being Numerous* (1968); *Primitive* (1978); *New Collected Poems* (2008).

Gabriel Preil
1911–1992

The Hebrew–Yiddish American modernist poet Gabriel Preil was born in Tartu, Estonia; he immigrated to New York in 1922. Influenced by the avant-garde Yiddish poets of the Inzikhist (Introspectivist) movement, he began writing in Yiddish but spent the bulk of his career writing in Hebrew. He published his first book of Hebrew poetry in 1944 and, in addition to original works, translated American poets including Walt Whitman, Wallace Stevens, Carl Sandburg, Robert Frost, and Robinson Jeffers into what he referred to as "the language of my heart." Although he had few American readers, Preil's influence was felt in Israel, where he was awarded the prestigious Bialik Prize in 1991.

New York: February 1965
1965

On a day transparent with light
like a landscape by Monet,
my childhood broke away
from a small Jewish town
and glided on ice
blue in the distance—
while a small cloud hovered in me
like a cloud of a Shakespeare sonnet.

Perhaps because I was ill
the frosty town
meant to shower and solace me
with the almond tree's fragrant snow
even though somewhere else
like a reluctant seer
an olive tree nodding its head
refused to reveal a thing.

Translated by Robert Friend.

Other works by Preil: *Israeli Poetry in Peace and War* (1959); *Autumn Music: Selected Poems of Gabriel Preil* (1979, translated by Howard Schwartz); *Sunset Possibilities and Other Poems* (1985, translated by Robert Friend).

Malka Heifetz Tussman

Water Without Sound
1965

The sea
tore a rib from its side
and said:
Go! Lie down there, be
a sign that I
am great and mighty.
Go
be a sign.

The canal
lies at my window,
speechless.

What can be sadder
than water
without sound?

Translated by Marcia Falk.

Anthony Hecht
1923–2004

The American formalist poet, literary critic, and professor Anthony Hecht was born into a German Jewish family in New York City. During his service in the U.S. Army, he helped liberate the Flossenbürg concentration camp (April 1945), an experience that informed much of his writing. He published seven volumes of poetry during his lifetime, characterized by their command of traditional forms and controlled language. His best-known and most highly regarded works date from the 1960s and 1970s. Beginning with *The Hard Hours* (1967), these works created unsettling juxtapositions between the formal structure of his poetry and their subject matter: explorations of the darkness of human nature based on his experiences in World War II. Hecht's work was awarded the Pulitzer Prize (1968), the Bollingen Prize (1983), and the Academy of American Poets Tanning Prize for lifetime achievement (1997). From 1982 to 1984, he was the poet laureate consultant at the Library of Congress.

Rites and Ceremonies
1968

I. The Room

Father, adonoi, author of all things
of the three states,
the soft light on the barn at dawn,
   a wind that sings
in the bracken, fire in iron gates,
   the ram's horn,
Furnisher, hinger of heaven, who bound
   the lovely Pleaides [*sic*],
entered the perfect treasuries of the snow,
   established the round
course of the world, birth, death and disease
   and caused to grow
veins, brain, bones in me, to breathe and sing
   fashioned me air
Lord, who governing cloud and waterspout,
   o my King,
held me alive till this my forty-third year—
   in whom we doubt—
Who was that child of whom they tell
   in lauds and threnes?
Whose holy name all shall pronounce
   Emmanuel,
which being interpreted means,
   "Gott mit uns"?

I saw it on their belts. A young one, dead,
Left there on purpose to get us used to the sight
When we first moved in. Helmet spilled off, head
Blond and boyish and bloody. I was scared that night.
And the sign was there,
The sign of the child, the grave, worship and loss
Gunpowder heavy as pollen in winter air,
An Iron Cross.

It is twenty years now, Father. I have come home.
But in the camps, one can look through a huge
   square
Window, like an aquarium, upon a room
The size of my livingroom filled with human hair.
Others have shoes, or valises
Made mostly of cardboard, which once contained
Pills, fresh diapers. This is one of the places
Never explained.

Out of one trainload, about five hundred in all,
Twenty the next morning were hopelessly insane.
And some there be that have no memorial,

That are perished as though they had never been.
Made into soap.
Who now remembers "The Singing Horses of
   Buchenwald"?
"Above all, the saving of lives," whispered the Pope.
Die Vögelein schweigen im Walde,

But for years the screaming continued, night and
   day,
And the little children were suffered to come along,
   too.
I am there, I am there. I am pushed through
With the others to the strange room
Without windows; whitewashed walls, cement floor.
Millions, Father, millions have come to this pass,
Which a great church has voted to "deplore."

Are the vents in the ceiling, Father, to let the spirit
   depart?
We are crowded in here naked, female and male.
An old man is saying a prayer. And now we start
To panic, to claw at each other, to wail
As the rubber-edged door closes on chance and
   choice.
He is saying a prayer for all whom this room shall
   kill.
"I cried unto the Lord God with my voice,
And He has heard me out His holy hill." [. . .]

IV. Words for the Day of Atonement

Merely to have survived is not an index of
   excellence,
Nor, given the way things go,
Even of low cunning.
Yet I have seen the wicked in great power,
And spreading himself like a green bay tree.
And the good as if they had never been;
Their voices are blown away on the winter wind.
And again we wander the wilderness
For our transgressions
Which are confessed in the daily papers.

Except the Lord of hosts had left unto us
A very small remnant,
We should have been as Sodom,
We should have been like unto Gomorrah.
And to what purpose, as the darkness closes about
And the child screams in the jellied fire,
Had best be our present concern,
Here, in this wilderness of comfort

In which we dwell.
Shall we now consider
The suspicious postures of our virtue,
The deformed consequences of our love,
The painful issues of our mildest acts?
Shall we ask,
Where is there one
Mad, poor and betrayed enough to find
Forgiveness for us, saying,
"None does offend,
None, I say,
None"?

Listen, listen.
But the voices are blown away.

And yet, this light,
The work of thy fingers, . . .

The soul is thine, and the body is thy creation:
O have compassion on thy handiwork.
The soul is thine, and the body is thine:
O deal with us according to thy name.
We come before thee relying on thy name;
O deal with us according to thy name;
For the sake of the glory of thy name;
As the gracious and merciful God is thy name.
O Lord, for thy name's sake we plead,
Forgive us our sins, though they be very great.

It is winter as I write.
For miles the holy treasuries of snow
Sag the still world with white,
And all soft shapes are washed from top to toe
In pigeon-colored light.

Tree, bush and weed maintain
Their humbled, lovely postures all day through.
And darkly in the brain
The famous ancient questions gather: Who
Fathered the fathering rain
That falleth in the wilderness
Where no man is, wherein there is no man
To satisfy the cress,
Knotweed and moonwort? And shall scan
Our old unlawfulness?

Who shall profess to understand
The diligence and purpose of the rose?
Yet deep as to some gland,
A promised odor, even among these snows,
Steals in like contraband.

Forgiven be the whole Congregation of the Children
of Israel,
and the stranger dwelling in their midst. For all the
people
have inadvertently sinned.

Father, I also pray
For those among us whom we know not, those
Dearest to thy grace,
The saved and saving remnant, the promised third,
Who in a later day
When we again are compassed about with foes,
Shall be for us a nail in thy holy place
There to abide according to thy word.

Neither shall the flame
Kindle upon them, nor the fire burn
A hair of them, for they
Shall be thy care when it shall come to pass,
And calling on thy name
In the hot kilns and ovens, they shall turn
To thee as it is prophesied, and say,
"He shall come down like rain upon mown grass."

Other works by Hecht: *A Summoning of Stones*
(1954); *Millions of Strange Shadows* (1977); *The Darkness and the Light* (2001); *Melodies Unheard: Essays on the Mysteries of Poetry* (2003).

Carl Rakosi

1903-2004

Carl Rakosi was born in Berlin and immigrated to the United States with his father and stepmother in 1910, settling in Kenosha, Wisconsin. Rakosi attended the University of Chicago (where he began to write poetry), the University of Wisconsin, and the University of Pennsylvania. His poetry was influenced by the American modernist Ezra Pound, who introduced him to the objectivist poets Louis Zukofsky, Charles Reznikoff, and George Oppen. He abandoned poetry from 1940 to 1967 because he found it less relevant than his work as executive director of Jewish Family and Children's Services in Minneapolis. His later works, including various "Meditations," turn to more explicitly Jewish themes, including the poetry of Solomon ibn Gabirol, Judah Halevi, and Moses ibn Ezra.

Meditation
1968

After Jehudah Halevi

> How long will you remain a boy?
> Dawns must end.
> Behold the angels of old age.
>
> Shake off temporal things then
> the way a bird shakes off the night dew.
> Dart like a swallow
>   from the raging ocean
> of daily events
> and pursue the Lord
> in the intimate company
> of souls flowing
>   into His virtue.

After Moses Ibn Ezra

> Men are children of this world,
> yet God has set eternity in my heart.
>
> All my life I have been in the desert
> but the world is a fresh stream.
>
> I drink from it. How potent this water is!
> How deeply I crave it!
>
> An ocean rushes into my throat
> but my thirst remains unquenched.

After Solomon Ibn Gabirol

> Three things remind me of You,
> the heavens
>   who are a witness to Your name
> the earth
>   which expands my thought
>   and is the thing on which I stand
> and the musing of my heart
>   when I look within.

Other works by Rakosi: *Selected Poems* (1941); *Amulet* (1967); *Ex Cranium, Night* (1975); *Collected Poems* (1986); *Poems 1923–1941* (1989); *Earth Suite* (1997); *The Old Poet's Tale* (1999).

Linda Pastan
b. 1932

Linda Pastan was born in New York City and is a poet and essayist. She served as an instructor at the Bread Loaf Writers' Conference, was poet laureate of Maryland from 1991 until 1995, and is the recipient of numerous awards, including the 1958 Dylan Thomas Poetry Award and the 2003 Ruth Lilly Poetry Prize.

Passover
1971

I

> I set my table with metaphor:
> the curling parsley—green sign nailed to the doors
> of God's underground; salt of desert and eyes;
> the roasted shank bone of a Pascal lamb,
> relic of sacrifice and bleating spring.
> Down the long table, past fresh shoots of a root
> they have been hacking at for centuries,
> you hold up the unleavened bread—a baked scroll
> whose wavy lines are undecipherable.

II

> The wise son and the wicked, the simple son
> and the son who doesn't ask, are all my son
> leaning tonight as it is written,
> slouching his father calls it. His hair is long;
> hippie hair, hassid hair, how strangely alike
> they seem tonight.
> First Born, a live child cried
> among the bullrushes, but the only root
> you know stirs between your legs, ready
> to spill its seed in gentile gardens.
> And if the flowers be delicate and fair,
> I only mind this one night of the year
> when far beyond the lights of Jersey,
> Jerusalem still beckons us, in tongues.

III

> What black throated bird in
> a warm country
> sings spirituals,
> sings spirituals
> to Moses now?

IV

One exodus prefigures the next.
The glaciers fled before hot whips of air.
Waves bowed at God's gesture
for fugitive Israel to pass;
while fish, caught then behind windows
of water, remembered how their brothers once
pulled themselves painfully from the sea,
willing legs to grow
from slanted fins.
Now the blossoms pass from April's tree,
refugee raindrops mar the glass,
borders are transitory.
And the changeling gene, still seeking
stone sanctuary, moves on.

V

Far from Egypt, I have sighted blood,
have heard the throaty mating of frogs.
My city knows vermin, animals loose in hallways,
boils, sickness, hail.
In the suburban gardens
seventeen year locusts rise
from their heavy beds
in small explosions of sod.
Darkness of newsprint.
My son, my son.

Other works by Pastan: *A Perfect Circle of Sun* (1971);
The Five Stages of Grief (1978).

Maxine Kumin

1925–2014

Brought up in Philadelphia, Maxine Kumin was a
poet, novelist, and essayist. She served as consultant
in poetry to the Library of Congress (predating the
existence of a U.S. poet laureate) and as poet laureate
of New Hampshire from 1989 until 1994. She received
numerous awards, including the Pulitzer Prize, the
Ruth Lilly Poetry Prize, and the Aiken Taylor Prize.

Woodchucks

1972

Gassing the woodchucks didn't turn out right.
The knockout bomb from the Feed and Grain
    Exchange

was featured as merciful, quick at the bone
and the case we had against them was airtight,
both exits shoehorned shut with puddingstone,
but they had a sub-sub-basement out of range.

Next morning they turned up again, no worse
for the cyanide than we for our cigarettes
and state-store Scotch, all of us up to scratch.
They brought down the marigolds as a matter of
    course
and then took over the vegetable patch
nipping the broccoli shoots, beheading the carrots.

The food from our mouths, I said, righteously
    thrilling
to the feel of the .22, the bullets' neat noses.
I, a lapsed pacifist fallen from grace
puffed with Darwinian pieties for killing,
now drew a bead on the littlest woodchuck's face.
He died down in the everbearing roses.

Ten minutes later I dropped the mother. She
flipflopped in the air and fell, her needle teeth
still hooked in a leaf of early Swiss chard.
Another baby next. O one-two-three
the murderer inside me rose up hard,
the hawkeye killer came on stage forthwith.

There's one chuck left. Old wily fellow, he keeps
me cocked and ready day after day after day.
All night I hunt his humped-up form.
I dream I sight along the barrel in my sleep.
If only they'd all consented to die unseen
gassed underground the quiet Nazi way.

Other works by Kumin: *Halfway* (1961); *The Privilege* (1965); *The Abduction* (1971).

Adrienne Rich

1929–2012

Born in Baltimore, Adrienne Rich was a distinguished
poet, writer, teacher, feminist, and peace activist. Rich
was the recipient of the 1974 National Book Award and
the National Book Foundation's 2006 Medal for Distinguished Contribution to American Letters, among
other honors.

Diving into the Wreck

1972

First having read the book of myths,
and loaded the camera,
and checked the edge of the knife-blade,
I put on
the body-armor of black rubber
the absurd flippers
the grave and awkward mask.
I am having to do this
not like Cousteau with his
assiduous team
aboard the sun-flooded schooner
but here alone.

There is a ladder.
The ladder is always there
hanging innocently
close to the side of the schooner.
We know what it is for,
we who have used it.

Otherwise
it is a piece of maritime floss
some sundry equipment.

I go down.
Rung after rung and still
the oxygen immerses me
the blue light
the clear atoms
of our human air.
I go down.
My flippers cripple me,
I crawl like an insect down the ladder
and there is no one to
tell me when the ocean
will begin.

First the air is blue and then
it is bluer and then green and then
black I am blacking out and yet
my mask is powerful
it pumps my blood with power
the sea is another story
the sea is not a question of power
I have to learn alone
to turn my body without force
in the deep element.

And now: it is easy to forget
what I came for
among so many who have always
lived here
swaying their crenellated fans
between the reefs
and besides
you breathe differently down here.

I came to explore the wreck.
The words are purposes.
The words are maps.
I came to see the damage that was done
and the treasures that prevail.
I stroke the beam of my lamp
slowly along the flank
of something more permanent
than fish or weed

the thing I came for:
the wreck and not the story of the wreck
the thing itself and not the myth
the drowned face always staring
toward the sun
the evidence of damage
worn by salt and sway into this threadbare beauty
the ribs of the disaster
curving their assertion
among the tentative haunters.

This is the place.
And I am here, the mermaid whose dark hair
streams black, the merman in his armored body.
We circle silently
about the wreck
we dive into the hold.
I am she: I am he

whose drowned face sleeps with open eyes
whose breasts still bear the stress
whose silver, copper, vermeil cargo lies
obscurely inside barrels
half-wedged and left to rot
we are the half-destroyed instruments
that once held to a course
the water-eaten log
the fouled compass

We are, I am, you are
by cowardice or courage

the one who find our way
back to this scene
carrying a knife, a camera
a book of myths
in which
our names do not appear.

Other works by Rich: *Necessities of Life* (1966); *The Will to Change* (1971); *Of Woman Born: Motherhood as Experience and Institution* (1976).

Anna Frajlich
b. 1942

Born in Kyrgyzstan and raised in Szczecin, Poland, poet and scholar Anna Frajlich (also Frajlich-Zając) immigrated in 1969 to New York, where she taught Polish language and literature at Columbia University until 2016. She has published poetry as well as essays and scholarly articles in English, Polish, and French. She was awarded the Knight Cross of the Order of Merit by the president of Poland in 2002 and in 2008 received the honorary title of ambassador of Szczecin.

Acclimatization
1973

I forget meticulously
I forget scrupulously
		my native landscape
		my daily landscape
I forget the ragged
I forget the billowy
		clouds in a sky
		clouds over a town
I forget to the end
I forget them nonstop
	—faces cloaked in the dusk
		behind windows of trains.

Translated by Regina Grol.

Other work by Frajlich: *Aby wiatr namalować* (1976).

Isaac Goldemberg
b. 1945

Peruvian-born Isaac Goldemberg, a poet, playwright, and novelist, now lives in New York, where he teaches at Maria de Hostos Community College of the City University of New York. He is director of the Latin American Writers Institute and editor of the *Hostos Review*. His writings explore the role of the outsider in search of identity as well as themes of alterity, dislocation, and diaspora.

Jews in Hell
1973

Tell us the tale,
that the Jews
bought themselves
a private place in hell.

In the first circle,
seated on a wooden bench,
Karl Marx fans himself with palms.
The prophet Jeremiah
fights the heat with psalms.

In the second circle,
Salomon studies
the stones of his Temple.
Moses's hieroglyphs on scrolls
Are not so simple.

In the third circle,
Jesus Christ dreams of Pilate.
Observing with a clinical eye,
Freud smiles wryly.

In the fourth circle,
Spinoza composes
a story of vermin.

In the fifth circle,
Jacob wrestles a devil.
Cain and Abel
behave like brothers.

In the sixth circle,
Noah, drunk, is into a zebra.
In the hollows, seeking atoms,
Einstein is in a fever.

In the last circle,
tilting a telescope,
Kafka laughs like crazy.

Translated by Michele McKay Aynesworth.

Other works by Goldemberg: *Hombre de paso* (1981); *Tiempo al tiempo* (1985); *The Grand Book of Jewish Latin America* (1998); *El nombre del padre* (2001); *Peru-*

vian Blues (2001); *Golpe de gracia* (2003); *La vida son los ríos* (2005); *Tierra de nadie* (2006).

José Kozer
b. 1940

Cuban-born José Kozer, the son of Jewish immigrants from Poland and Czechoslovakia, came to the United States in 1960. He is professor emeritus of Spanish and Latin American literature at Queens College of the City University of New York. A leading Latin American poet, some of his works have been published in bilingual editions. Kozer received the Julio Tovar Poetry Prize in 1974 and the Pablo Neruda Ibero-American Poetry Prize in 2013.

Grandfather Is Facing Death
1973

Not as if it were an accident,
not as if he were leaving Prague and coming to
    Havana,
eight years later bringing Mama,
to put her behind the cash register,
instill certain principles,
give her little cartons of imported cherries.
Grandfather is facing death,
not like a Spanish hidalgo,
after all he had a grocery store,
he would close up on Saturdays
and weep, covered in ashes, before the ark.
No! Grandfather is not facing death
not with gallantry,
nor with resignation,
nor with a cry that evaporates in the Havana noon.
He is starting to wear gray like the restaurants of
    Prague,
he hurriedly rolls up his tefillin
the Cuban sky setting on his Yom Kippur.
And here,
still in time to see the last procession going back to
    del Carmen Church,
still in time to serve another customer,
gather his grandchildren, give each an American
    quarter,
grandfather is facing death,
dying of cancer.

Translated by Michele McKay Aynesworth.

Other work by Kozer: *Padres y otras profesiones* (1972).

Marge Piercy
b. 1936

Born in Detroit, Marge Piercy is a poet, novelist, and activist whose themes address feminism, social concerns, and Jewish identity. She is the author of numerous novels, volumes of poetry, and a memoir.

To Be of Use
1973

The people I love the best
jump into work head first
without dallying in the shallows
and swim off with sure strokes almost out of sight.
They seem to become natives of that element,
the black sleek heads of seals
bouncing like half-submerged balls.

I love people who harness themselves, an ox to a
    heavy cart,
who pull like water buffalo, with massive patience,
who strain in the mud and the muck to move things
    forward,
who do what has to be done, again and again.

I want to be with people who submerge
in the task, who go into the fields to harvest
and work in a row and pass the bags along,
who are not parlor generals and field deserters
but move in a common rhythm
when the food must come in or the fire be put out.

The work of the world is common as mud.
Botched, it smears the hands, crumbles to dust.
But the thing worth doing well done
has a shape that satisfies, clean and evident.
Greek amphoras for wine or oil,
Hopi vases that held corn, are put in museums
but you know they were made to be used.
The pitcher cries for water to carry
and a person for work that is real.

Other works by Piercy: *The Grand Coolie Damn* (1969); *Small Changes* (1973); *Women on the Edge of Time* (1976).

Musical Selections

Classical

1938
Sternberg, Erich Walter
Twelve Tribes of Israel
Palestine/Israel

1942
Bernstein, Leonard
Jeremiah Symphony
United States

1943
Ben-Haim, Paul
Five Pieces for Piano, Op. 34
Palestine/Israel

1943
Klein, Gideon
Lullaby
Theresienstadt, Czechoslovakia

1944
Braunfels, Walter
*String Quintet in F# minor,
    Op. 63*
Germany

1944
Copland, Aaron
Appalachian Spring
United States

1944
Haas, Pavel
Four Songs on Chinese Poetry
Theresienstadt, Czechoslovakia,
    Czech

1945
Boskovich, Alexander
Semitic Suite
Soviet Union

1945
Castelnuovo-Tedesco, Mario
The Flood; Genesis Suite, Mov. V
Italy/United States, English

1945
Klebanov, Dmitri
*In Memory of the Victims of
    Babi Yar*
Soviet Union

1945
Korngold, Erich Wolfgang
Quartet No. 3 in D Major, Op. 34
United States

1947
Schoenberg, Arnold
Survivor from Warsaw
Italy/United States; English,
    Hebrew

1950
Castelnuovo-Tedesco, Mario
*Quintet for Guitar and String
    Quartet, Op. 143*
Italy/United States

1951
Bloch, Ernest
Suite Hébraïque
East Germany

1953
Vainberg, Moishe (Mieczysław
    Weinberg)
Moldavian Rhapsody
Soviet Union

1954
Gál, Hans
Biedermeiertänze, Op. 66
England

1958
Tansman, Alexandre
*Shabbetaï Zévi, le Faux
    Messie*
France, French

1959
Ligeti, György
Atmosphères
Austria

1961
Seter, Mordecai
Tikun Ḥatzot (Midnight Vigil)
Israel, Hebrew

1962
Tansman, Alexandre
Suite in modo polonico
France

1963
Bernstein, Leonard
Symphony No. 3, Kaddish
United States; English, Aramaic

1963
Toch, Ernst
Symphony No. 5 "Jephtha,
Rhapsodic Poem," Op. 89
United States

1966
Castelnuovo-Tedesco, Mario
When the Morning of Life
Comes (Divan of Moses Ibn-
Ezra, Op. 207)
Italy/United States

1968
Kurtág, György
The Sayings of P. Bornemisza
(1963–68)
Hungary, Hungarian

1970
Reich, Steve
Four Organs
United States

1971
Glass, Philip
Music in Twelve Parts (1971–74)
United States

1973
Kurtág, György
Játékok (Games), Vol. I
Hungary

1973
Milhaud, Darius
Études sur des thèmes
liturgiques du Comtat
Venaissin, Op. 442
France

Popular

1939
Arlen, Harold
Over the Rainbow
United States

1939
Hemsi, Alberto
El moro de Antequera
Turkey/Egypt/France, Ladino

1942
Agatov, Vladimir (lyrics), and
Nikita Bogoslovskii (music)
Temnaia noch' (Dark Is the
Night)
Soviet Union, Russian

1942
Eisler, Hanns
An den kleinen Radioapparat
United States, German

1942
Utesov, Leonid, Shalom Secunda
(music), Anatoli Fidorovskii
(lyrics), O. Kandata (arr.)
Baron von der Pschick
Soviet Union, German

1942
Veksler, Misha (music), and Leyb
Rozental (lyrics)
Yisrolik
Nazi-occupied Poland (Vilna
Ghetto), Yiddish

1943
Rodgers, Richard, and Oscar
Hammerstein
Oklahoma!
United States, English

1944
Vainberg, Moishe (Mieczysław
Weinberg)
Tife griber, royte leym
(Deep Graves, Red Earth)
Soviet Union, Yiddish

1957
Bernstein, Leonard
West Side Story
United States, English

1959
Carlebach, Shlomo
Essa einai (I Lift Up My Eyes)
United States, Hebrew

1959
Herman, Jerry
Milk and Honey
United States, English

1960
Herrmann, Bernard
Psycho [film score]
United States

1963
Carlebach, Shlomo
Pischu li (Open for Me)
United States, Hebrew

1963
Dylan, Bob
Blowing in the Wind
United States, English

1963
Sherman, Alan
Hello Mudda, Hello Fadda
United States, English

1964
Barbara (Monique Andrée Serf)
Göttingen
France, French

1964
Simon, Paul, and Art Garfunkel
The Sound of Silence
United States, English

1967
Cohen, Leonard
Suzanne
United States, English

1967
Gainsbourg, Serge
Le sable et le soldat (Sand and Soldier)
France, French

1967
Guthrie, Arlo
Alice's Restaurant
United States, English

1968
Gainsbourg, Serge
Bonnie and Clyde
France, French

1968
Vysotsky, Vladimir
Spasite nashi dushi (Save Our Souls)
Soviet Union, Russian

1969
Diamond, Neil
Sweet Caroline
United States, English

1969
Moustaki, Georges
Le Métèque
France, French

1970
Bock, Jerry, and Sheldon Harnick
The Rothschilds
United States, English

1971
King, Carole
You've Got a Friend
United States, English

1973
Hamlisch, Marvin (lyrics), and Alan and Marilyn Bergman
The Way We Were
United States, English

Film Selections

1939
Litvak, Anatole
Confessions of a Nazi Spy
United States, English

1942
Lubitsch, Ernst
To Be or Not to Be
United States, English

1943
Curtiz, Howard, Julius Epsteinu,
  and Philip Epstein
Casablanca
United States, English

1945
Siegel, Don
Hitler Lives
United States, English
Documentary

1945
Ulmer, Edward G.
Detour
United States, English

1947
Dmytryk, Edward
Crossfire
United States, English

1947
Kazan, Elia
Gentleman's Agreement
United States, English

1947
Lerski, Helmar
Tomorrow's a Wonderful Day
Palestine, Hebrew, English,
  Yiddish, Italian, Serbo-
  Croatian, French, German
Documentary

1948
Becker, Israel, Herbert B.
  Fredersdorf, and Marek
  Goldstein
Lang ist der Weg
West Germany; German, Polish,
  Yiddish

1948
Ford, Aleksander
*Ulica Graniczna (Border
  Street)*
Poland, Polish

1948
Goskind, Shaul, and Natan
  Gross
Unzere kinder (Our Children)
Poland, Yiddish, English
  subtitles

1948
Meyers, Sidney
The Quiet One
United States, English
Documentary

1948
Schweizer, Richard, and Fred
  Zinnemann
The Search
Switzerland/United States,
  English

1949
Kortner, Fritz, and Josef von
  Báky
Der Ruf (The Last Illusion)
West Germany, German

1949
Radok, Alfréd
*Daleká cesta (Distant
  Journey)*
Czechoslovakia, Czech
Documentary

1950
Almaz, Michael "Miko"
Me'ever hagvul (Across the Border)
Israel, Hebrew

1950
Amar, Amram
Hafuga (Cease-fire)
Israel, Hebrew

1950
Mankiewicz, Joseph L.
All about Eve
United States, English

1952
Leytes, Joseph
Kirya Ne'emana (The Faithful City)
Israel, English

1954
Biberman, Herbert
Salt of the Earth
United States, English, Spanish

1955
Dassin, Jules
Du rififi chez les hommes (Rififi)
France, French, Italian, English

1955
Kolitz, Zvi, and Peter Frye
Giv'a 24 eina onah (Hill 24 Doesn't Answer)
Israel, Hebrew, English

1956
DeMille, Cecil B.
The Ten Commandments
United States, English

1956
Habib, Nuri
Be'ein moledet (Lacking a Homeland)
Israel, Hebrew

1959
Chukhrai, Grigori Naumovich
Ballada o soldate (Ballad of a Soldier)
Soviet Union, Russian

1960
Milestone, Lewis
Ocean's 11
United States, English

1960
Pontecorvo, Gillo
Kapò
Italy/France, Italian

1960
Preminger, Otto
Exodus
United States, English

1961
Dienar, Baruch
Hem hayu 'asara (They Were Ten)
Israel, Hebrew

1961
Kramer, Stanley E., and Abby Mann
Judgment at Nuremberg
United States, English, German

1961
LeRoy, Mervyn
A Majority of One
United States, English

1961
Morgenstern, Janusz
Ambulans (Ambulance)
Poland, Polish

1961
Robbins, Jerome, and Robert Wise
West Side Story
United States, English, Spanish

1963
Golan, Menahem
El Dorado
Israel, Hebrew

1963
Gross, Natan
Ha-martef (The Cellar)
Israel, Yiddish, Hebrew

1963
Lewis, Jerry
The Nutty Professor
United States, English

1963
Munk, Andrzej, and Witold Lesiewicz
Pasażerka (The Passenger)
Poland, Polish

1963
Perlov, David
Be-Yerushalaim (In Jerusalem)
Israel, Hebrew
Documentary

1964
Brynych, Zbyněk
. . . And the Fifth Horseman Is Fear
Czechoslovakia, Czech

1964
Cukor, George
My Fair Lady
United States, English

1964
Kishon, Efraim
Sallaḥ Shabati
Israel, Hebrew

1964
Kubrick, Stanley
Dr. Strangelove
United States/United Kingdom, English

1964
Lumet, Sidney
The Pawnbroker
United States, English

1964
Zohar, Uri
Ḥor ba-levana (Hole in the Moon)
Israel, Hebrew

1965
Kadár, Ján
Obchod na korze (The Shop on Main Street)
Czechoslovakia, Slovak, Yiddish

1966
Berri, Claude
Le vieil homme et l'enfant (The Two of Us)
France, French

1966
Lelouch, Claude Barruck Joseph
Un homme et une femme (A Man and a Woman)
France, French

1967
Brooks, Mel
The Producers
United States, English, German

1967
Milo, Yosef
Hu halaḥ ba-sadot (He Walked through the Fields)
Israel, Hebrew

1967
Nichols, Mike
The Graduate
United States, English

1967
Zohar, Uri, and A. B. Yehoshua
Shlosha yamim ve-yeled (Three Days and a Child)
Israel, Hebrew

1968
Ben-Amotz, Dan, and Gilberto Tofano
Matsor (The Siege)
Israel, Hebrew

1968
Frankenheimer, John
The Fixer
United Kingdom, English

1968
Wyler, William
Funny Girl
United States, English

1969
Herz, Juraj
Spalovač mrtvol (The Cremator)
Czechoslovakia, Czech

1969
Kishon, Efraim
Te'alat Blaumilch (The Big Dig)
Israel, Hebrew

1969
Mazursky, Paul
Bob & Carol & Ted & Alice
United States, English

1969
Schlesinger, John
Midnight Cowboy
United States, English

1970
Ophüls, Marcel
The Sorrow and the Pity
France, French, German
Documentary

1971
Friedkin, William
The French Connection
United States, English

1971
Golan, Menahem
Katz and Carasso
Israel, Hebrew

1971
Kishon, Efraim
Ha-shoter Azulai (The Policeman)
Israel, Hebrew

1972
Allen, Woody
Play It Again, Sam
United States, English

1972
Aloni, Nissim, and David Perlov
Haglulah (The Pill)
Israel, Hebrew

1972
Heffner, Avraham
Le'an ne'elam Daniel Wax? (But Where Is Danny Wax?)
Israel, Hebrew

1972
May, Elaine
The Heartbreak Kid
United States, English

1973
Dayan, Nissim
Or min ha-hefker (Light out of Nowhere)
Israel, Hebrew

Credits

Avraham Abbas, "From Ingathering to Integration," from *Modern Middle Eastern Jewish Thought: Writings on Identity, Politics, and Culture, 1893–1958*, ed. and trans. Moshe Behar and Zvi Ben-Dor Benite (Waltham, Mass.: Brandeis University Press, 2013), pp. 243–45. Used with permission of the author's estate and the translators.

Dannie Abse, from *Ash on a Young Man's Sleeve* (London: Hutchinson, 1954), pp. 33–36. Used with permission of United Agents on behalf of The Estate of Dannie Abse.

Rachel Adler, "The Jew Who Wasn't There: Halacha and the Jewish Woman," *Davka*, vol. 1, no. 4 (Summer 1971), pp. 6–11. Used with permission of the publisher.

Stanislaw Adler, "Warsaw, Aryan Side," from *The Warsaw Ghetto 1940–1943: The Memoirs of Stanislaw Adler*, trans. Sara Chmielewska Philip (Jerusalem: Yad Vashem, 1982), p. 3. Used with permission of the publisher.

Shmuel Yosef (S. Y.) Agnon, "The Making of This Book," *Present at Sinai: The Giving of the Law*, commentaries selected by S. Y. Agnon, trans. Michael Swirsky (Philadelphia: Jewish Publication Society, 1994), pp. 5–6, 10–12. English translation copyright 1994 by the Jewish Publication Society. Originally published in Hebrew as *Atem Re'item* (Tel Aviv: Schocken, 1959). Copyright © 1959 Schocken Publishing House Ltd., Tel Aviv, Israel. Reprinted by permission of the University of Nebraska Press and Schocken Publishing House Ltd.; "From Foe to Friend," trans. Joel Blocker, from *Sleepwalkers and Other Stories: The Arab in Hebrew Fiction*, ed. Ehud Ben-Ezer (Boulder, Colo.: Lynne Rienner, 1999), pp. 53–56. Published in Hebrew as *Me-oyev le-ohev ve-od sipurim* (Jerusalem and Tel Aviv: Schocken, 1992). © Schocken Publishing House Ltd., Tel Aviv, Israel. Used with permission of the translator and Schocken Publishing House Ltd.; from *Only Yesterday*, trans. Barbara Harshav (Princeton, N.J.: Princeton University Press, 2000), pp. 639–42. Published in Hebrew as *Temol shilshom* (Jerusalem and Tel Aviv: Schocken, 1968). © Schocken Publishing House Ltd., Tel Aviv, Israel. Reproduced with permission of Princeton University Press in the format Book via Copyright Clearance Center, and Schocken Publishing House Ltd.; from *Shira*, trans. Zeva Shapiro (New York: Schocken Books, 1989), pp. 332–35. Originally published in Hebrew as *Shira* (Tel Aviv: Schocken, 1971). © Schocken Publishing House Ltd., Tel Aviv, Israel. Translation copyright © 1989 by Schocken Books Inc. Used by permission of Schocken Publishing House Ltd and Schocken Books, an imprint of the Knopf Doubleday Publishing Group, a division of Penguin Random House LLC. All rights reserved. Any third-party use of this material, outside of this publication, is prohibited. Interested parties must apply directly to Penguin Random House LLC for permission.

Ilse Aichinger, "A Summons to Mistrust," from *Contemporary Jewish Writing in Austria: An Anthology*, ed. and trans. Dagmar C. G. Lorenz (Lincoln: University of Nebraska Press, 1999), pp. 159–60. Published in

Feminist Press at CUNY, 1999), p. 109. Published in Hebrew in *Shirim* (Tel Aviv: Sifriat Poalim Publishing House Ltd., 1963). Used with permission of the translator and Hakibbutz Hameuchad–Sifriat Poalim Publishing.

Zygmunt Bauman, "O Frustracji i o Kuglarzach" [On Frustrations and Prestidigitators], *Kultura*, vol. 12, no. 255 (1968), pp. 18–21. Used with permission of the author.

Hillel Bavli, "The Martyrdom of the 93 Beit Yaakov Girls," from *The High Holy Day Prayer Book*, trans. Ben Zion Bokser (New York: Hebrew Publishing Company, 1959), p. 435. Used with permission of the author's and translator's estates.

Jurek Becker, from *Jacob the Liar*, trans. Leila Vennewitz (New York: Arcade Pub., distributed by Little, Brown and Co., 1996), pp. 80–82. Used with permission of Arcade Publishing, an imprint of Skyhorse Publishing, Inc., and Suhrkamp Verlag.

Haim Be'er, "Transfiguratsiya" [Transfiguration], from *Sha'ashui'm yom yom* (Tel Aviv: Am Oved, 1970), pp. 7–8. © Haim Be'er and ACUM. Used with permission of ACUM, on behalf of the author.

S. N. Behrman, from *The Cold Wind and the Warm*, from *Awake and Singing: Seven Plays from the American Jewish Repertoire*, ed. Ellen Schiff (New York: Mentor, 1995), pp. 457, 478–79, 480–81, 511, 533. Copyright © 1959 by S. N. Behrman, copyright renewed © 1987 by Elza Behrman. Used by permission of Brandt & Hochman Literary Agents, Inc. All rights reserved.

Saul Bellow, from *The Adventures of Augie March* (New York: Viking Press, 1953), p. 5. Copyright 1949, 1951, 1952, 1953, renewed © 1977, 1979, 1980, 1981 by Saul Bellow. Used by permission of Viking Books, an imprint of Penguin Publishing Group, a division of Penguin Random House LLC, and The Wylie Agency, LLC. All rights reserved; Excerpts from *Herzog* (New York: Penguin Books, 1976), pp. 1, 309–10. Copyright © 1961, 1963, 1964, 1969, 1970, renewed 1989, 1991 by Saul Bellow. Used by permission of Viking Books, an imprint of Penguin Publishing Group, a division of Penguin Random House LLC, and Penguin Books Ltd. All rights reserved; Excerpts from "Introduction," from *Great Jewish Short Stories* (London: Vallentine, Mitchell & Co., 1971), pp. 9, 12, 14–16. Copyright © 1963 by Saul Bellow, used by permission of The Wylie Agency LLC; Excerpt from *Mr. Sammler's Planet* (New York: Penguin Books, 2004), pp. 259–60. Copyright © 1969, 1970 by Saul Bellow. Used by permission of Viking Books, an imprint of Penguin Publishing Group, a division of Penguin Random House LLC, and Penguin Books Ltd. All rights reserved.

Dan Ben-Amotz, from *To Remember, to Forget*, trans. Zeva Shapiro (Philadelphia: Jewish Publication Society of America, 1973), pp. 81–91. Translated from *Li-zekor veli-shekoah* (Tel Aviv: Amikam, 1968). © Dan Ben-Amotz and ACUM. Used with permission of the translator and of ACUM, on behalf of the author's estate.

Dan Ben-Amotz and Haim Heffer, from *Yalkut hakezavim* [A Bag of Lies] (Tel Aviv: Hakibbutz Hameuchad, 1956), pp. 5–8, 29, 44–45. © Dan Ben-Amotz, Haim Heffer, and ACUM. Used with permission of ACUM, on behalf of the authors' estates.

Dan Ben-Amotz and Netiva Ben-Yehuda, eds., "Rationale and Rationalization," from *Milon 'olamit le'ivrit me-duberet* [The World Dictionary of Hebrew Slang], 2nd ed. (Tel Aviv: Zmora, Bitan, 1982), pp. unnumbered, ו. Used with permission of the Estate of Dan Ben-Amotz.

Ehud Ben-Ezer, from *Hamahtsevah* [The Stone Quarry] (Tel Aviv: Am Oved, 1963), pp. 242–50. © Ehud Ben-Ezer and ACUM. Used with permission of ACUM, on behalf of the author.

David Ben-Gurion, "The Imperatives of the Jewish Revolution," from *The Zionist Idea: A Historical Analysis and Reader*, ed. Arthur Hertzberg (Philadelphia: Jewish Publication Society, 1959), pp. 606–19. Published in Hebrew as "Tsivuey Ha-Mapeha Ha-Yehudit," from *Ba-Maaracha*, vol. III (Tel Aviv: Am-Oved, 1957), p. 197. Reprinted by permission of the University of Nebraska Press and Am-Oved.

Nissim ben Shimon, "Haggadah de Hitler" [Hitler's Haggadah], trans. into Hebrew from Judeo-Arabic by Avishai Bar-Asher, *Pe'amim* 114/115 (Winter/Spring 2008), pp. 164–71. Used with permission of Ben-Zvi Institute.

Yitzhak Ben-Zvi, "The Institute for the Study of Jewish Communities in the East," from *Sephardi Lives: A Documentary History, 1700–1950*, ed. Julia Phillips Cohen and Sarah Abrevaya Stein, trans. Miriam Frenkel (Stanford: Stanford University Press, 2014), pp. 422–24. Copyright © 2015 by the Board of Trustees of the

Leland Stanford Jr. University. All rights reserved. Used with permission of the Lavon Institute for Labor Movement Research and Stanford University Press, www.sup.org.

Marcel Bénabou, "Juifs et Arabes au Maroc" [Jews and Arabs in Morocco], *La Nef*, no. 19-20 (September-December, 1964), pp. 164-65. Used by permission of the author and *La Nef*, www.la-nef.fr / www.edgarfaure.fr.

Claude Benady, from *Hors de jeu, les morts* [*Out of Play, The Dead*] (Tunis: Periples, 1950), pp. 24-26. Used with permission of the author's estate.

Blanche Bendahan, "Vacheries" [Bull], from *Poèmes en short* (Paris: R. Lacoste, 1948). Used with permission of the author's family.

José Bénech, from *Essai d'explication d'un Mellah* [Attempt to Explain a Mellah] (Paris: Larose, 1940), pp. 271-75.

Jeanne Benguigui, "Chant d'exil" [Song of Exile], from *Les cendres du soleil* (Anvers, Belgium: Éditions de la Pleiade des Jeunes, 1964), np. Jeanne Benguigui's current books are only available via Éditions des Cahiers Bleus, address: parvisdesalliances@gmail.com. Used with permission of the author's estate.

Raymond Benichou, "Jewish Writings," trans. Norman Stillman, in Norman A. Stillman, "An Algerian Jewish Intellectual Reflects upon Muslim–Jewish Relations at a Time of Rising Tensions," from *The Jews of Arab Lands in Modern Times*, ed. Norman A. Stillman (Philadelphia: Jewish Publication Society, 2003), pp. 542-54. Copyright 1991 by the Jewish Publication Society. Reproduced by permission of the University of Nebraska Press.

Albert Bensoussan, "Isbilia," from *Isbilia. Suivi de Foraine et le l'Éponge* (Paris: Pierre Jean Oswald, 1970), pp. 36, 46. Used with permission of the author.

Moshe Beregovski, "Jewish Folk Songs," from *Old Jewish Folk Music: The Collections and Writings of Moshe Beregovski*, trans. and ed. Mark Slobin (Syracuse, N.Y.: Syracuse University Press, 2000), pp. 288-90, 291-93. Used with permission of the author's estate and the translator.

Lili Berger, "On Saint Katerine's Day," trans. Frieda Forman and Ethel Raicus, from *Found Treasures: Stories by Yiddish Women Writers*, ed. F. Forman (Toronto: Second Story Press, 1994), pp. 226-27, 231-35. Used with permission of the translators.

Eliezer Berkovits, from *God, Man, and History*, ed. David Hazony (Jerusalem: Shalem Press, 2014), pp. 125-26, 185. Used with permission of Mercaz Shalem.

Bruno Bettelheim, "Individual and Mass Behavior in Extreme Situations," from *The Informed Heart: Autonomy in a Mass Age* (Glencoe, Ill.: Free Press, 1960), pp. 64-66, 82-83. Copyright © 1960 by The Free Press; copyright renewed © 1988 by Bruno Bettelheim. All rights reserved. Originally published in the *Journal of Abnormal and Social Psychology* (1943), vol. XXXVIII, pp. 417-52. Reprinted with the permission of The Free Press, a Division of Simon & Schuster, Inc.

Shloyme Bikl, from *A shtot mit yidn* [A Cityful of Jews], 2nd ed. (Buenos Aires: Farlag Kiem, 1960), pp. 26-31. Used with permission of the author's estate.

Isidoro Blaistein, "Mishiadura en Aries" [Misery in Aries], from *La salvación* (Buenos Aires: Centro Editor de América Latina, 1971), pp. 10-11. © Herederos de Isidoro Blastein. c/o Schavelzon Graham Agencia Literaria. www.schavelzongraham.com. Used with permission of the author's estate.

Marc Bloch, "The Testamentary Instructions of Marc Bloch," from *Strange Defeat: A Statement of Evidence*, trans. Gerard Hopkins (New York and London: Oxford University Press, 1949), pp. 177-78. Extract from *L'Étrange défaite* © Éditions Gallimard, Paris, 1990. Used by permission of Oxford University Press and Éditions Gallimard.

David P. Boder, from *I Did Not Interview the Dead* (Urbana: University of Illinois Press, 1949), pp. xi, xiv, xvii-xix. Used with permission of the author's estate.

Robert Borgel, from *Étoile jaune et croix gammée. Les Juifs de Tunisie face aux nazis* [*Yellow Star and Swastika: A Story of Servitude*], ed. Claude Nataf (Paris: Le Manuscrit, 2007), pp. 377-80. Used with permission of Ed Manuscrit.

Michał Borwicz, from *Pieśń Ginących: z Dziejów Twórczości Żydów pod Hitlerowską Okupacją* [The Song of the Dying: To the History of Jewish Creativity under the Nazi Occupation] (Kraków: Central Jewish Historical Commission in Poland, 1947), p. 9. Used with permission of the author's estate.

Alexander Uriah Boskowicz, *"Ba'ayot hamuzika hamekorit be-yisrael"* [The Problems of Native Music in Israel], from Alexander Uriyah Boskovich: *Hayyav yetsirato vehaguto* [Alexander Uriah Boskovich: His Life, His Work and His Thought], eds. Jehoash Hirshberg and Herzl Shmueli (Jerusalem: Carmel Publishing, 1995), pp. 193–99. Used with permission of the publisher.

Yankev Botoshanski, "A kol nidre oyf dem gensher bais oylem" [A Kol Nidre Service at the Gesia Street Cemetery], from *Dos amolike yidishe Varshe biz der shvel fun dritn khurbn, 1414–1939 in lid, balade, poeme: an antologye* (Montreal: Farband fun varshever Yidn in Montreal, 1966), pp. 121, 123, 125, 127.

Salomón Brainsky, "Temptation," trans. Moisés Mermelstein, from *Yiddish South of the Border: An Anthology of Latin American Yiddish Writing*, ed. Alan Astro (Albuquerque: University of Mexico Press, 2003), pp. 125–29. Copyright © 2003 University of New Mexico Press, 2003. Used with permission of the publisher.

Joseph Brodsky (b. Iosif Brodskii; 1940–1996), "Jewish Graveyard Near Leningrad," in *An Anthology of Jewish-Russian Literature: Two Centuries of Dual Identity in Prose and Poetry*, edited, selected, cotranslated, and with introductory notes by Maxim D. Shrayer. (Armonk, N.Y.: M. E. Sharpe, 2007), II: 670–71. Original publication "The Jewish Grave" by Joseph Brodsky, copyright © Joseph Brodsky. Translated, from the Russian of "Evreiskoe kladbishche okolo Leningrada," by Joanna Trzeciak. English translation copyright © by Joanna Trzeciak. Reprinted by permission of the The Wylie Agency LLC and Maxim D. Shrayer. All Rights Reserved. Not for Reproduction.

Louis Brunot and Elie Malka, eds., "Judeo-Arabic Proverbs from Fez," from *Glossaire Judeo-Arabe de Fès* (Rabat: Ecole du Livre, 1940; publication of l'Institut des Hautes Études Marocaines, vol. 37), pp. 379–80.

Martin Buber, "Genuine Dialogue and the Possibilities of Peace," from *A Believing Humanism: My Testament, 1902–1965*, trans. Maurice Friedman (New York: Simon and Schuster, 1967), pp. 195–98. Copyright © 1967 by Maurice Friedman. Reprinted by permission of Georges Borchardt, Inc., on behalf of the Estate of Maurice Friedman, and Börsenverein des Deutschen Buchhandels.

Natalio Budasoff, "Yoine pajarito" [Yoine Bird], *Lluvias salvajes* (Buenos Aires: Ediciones Mosaicos, 1962), pp. 85–89. Used with permission of the author's estate.

Joseph Buloff, from *From the Old Marketplace*, trans. from Yiddish by Joseph Singer (Cambridge, Mass.: Harvard University Press, 1991), pp. 154–56. English translation, Copyright © 1991, by Joseph Singer. Used with permission of the translator's estate.

Yehuda Burla, "Hadoda Joya" [Aunt Joya], from *Nashim* [Women] (Tel Aviv: Am Oved), pp. 313–18. © Yehuda Burla and ACUM. Used with permission of ACUM, on behalf of the author's estate.

Hortense Calisher, from *Herself: An Autobiographical Work* (New York: Open Road Media, 2013). Used with permission of the publisher; "Old Stock," from *In the Absence of Angels* (New York: Open Road Media, 2013. Originally published in *The New Yorker*, vol. 26, no. 30 (September 30, 1950). Used with permission of the publisher.

Eugenia Calny, from *Clara al amanecer* [Clara at Dawn] (Buenos Aires: Ediciones Crisol, 1972), p. 89. Used with permission of the author's estate.

Elias Canetti, "Visit to the Mellah," from *Die Stimmen von Marrakesch: Aufzeichnungen nach einer Reise* [The Voices of Marrakesh] (Munich: Carl Hanser Verlag, 1967), pp. 36–37. © by Elias Canetti 1967, by the heirs of Elias Canetti 1994. Published by kind permission of Carl Hanser Verlag GmbH & Co. KG, München.

René Cassin, "The Universal Declaration of Human Rights: Preamble." United Nations Department of Public Information, NY, http://www.ohchr.org/EN/UDHR/Pages/Language.aspx?LangID=eng.

Umberto (Moshe David) Cassuto, "The Israelite Epic," from *Biblical and Oriental Studies*, ed. and trans. Israel Abrahams (Jerusalem: Magnes Press, 1973), pp. 98–99, 101–2. Used with permission of the publisher.

Paul Celan, "Black Flakes," from *Selected Poems and Prose of Paul Celan*, trans. John Felstiner (New York: W. W. Norton, 2001), p. 15. Published in German as "Schwarze Flocken," from Paul Celan, *Die Gedichte*.

Kommentierte Gesamtausgabe in einem Band, ed. Barbara Wiedemann (Frankfurt am Main: Suhrkamp Verlag, 2003). Copyright © 2001 by John Felstiner. © Suhrkamp Verlag Frankfurt am Main 2003. All rights reserved by and controlled through Suhrkamp Verlag Berlin. Used by permission of W. W. Norton & Company, Inc and Suhrkamp Verlag; "Todesfuge," from *Selected Poems and Prose of Paul Celan*, trans. John Felstiner (New York: W. W. Norton, 2001), pp. 31, 33. First published in German in Paul Celan, *Mohn und Gedächtnis* (Munich: Deutsche Verlags-Anstalt, 1952). Copyright © 2001 by John Felstiner. Copyright © 1952, Deutsche Verlags-Anstalt, München, in der Verlagsgruppe Random House GmbH. Used by permission of W. W. Norton & Company, Inc. and Deutsche Verlags-Anstalt.

Paddy Chayefsky, from *The Tenth Man*, in *The Collected Works of Paddy Chayefsky: The Stage Plays* (Milwaukee: Applause Books, 2000), pp. 183–86, 187. Copyright © 1960 Paddy Chayefsky. Renewal Copyright © 1985 Susan Chayefsky. All Rights Reserved. Reprinted by permission of Applause Theatre & Cinema Books, LLC.

Henri Chemouilli, "Les rapatriés, dix ans après" [The Repatriated Ten Years Later], *L'Arche*, no. 183 (May 26–June 25, 1972), pp. 43–44. Used with permission of the publisher; "Nord Africain" [North African], from "Dictionnaire du judaisme français" [Dictionary of French Judaism], *L'Arche*, nos. 186–87 (September–October 1972; special edition), pp. 86–87. Used with permission of the publisher.

Elisa Chimenti, from *Au cœur du Harem* [At the Heart of the Harem] (Paris: Collection Alternance / Les Éditions du Scorpion, 1959), pp. 45–48. Used with permission of the author's estate, Senso Unico Editions, and Éditions du Sirocco; "The Cadi and the Jewish Merchant," from *Tales and Legends of Morocco*, trans. Arnon Benamy (New York: Ivan Obolensky, 1965), pp. 53–56. Used with permission of the author's estate, Senso Unico, and Éditions du Sirocco.

Corinne Chochem and Muriel Roth, from *Palestine Dances! Folk Dances of Palestine as Set Down by Corinne Chochem and Muriel Roth*, 2nd ed. (New York: Behrman House, 1946), pp. 5–7, 19. Used with permission of the authors' estates.

Isaac Chocrón, "Animales Feroces" [Ferocious Animals], from *Animales Feroces* (Caracas: Editora Grafos, 1963), pp. 28–29. Used with permission of the author's estate.

André Chouraqui, "Aurores" [Dawns], from Cantique pour Nathanël (Paris: Librairie José Corti, 1960), pp. 217–18. Used with permission of the publisher; from *Between East and West: A History of the Jews of North Africa*, trans. Michael M. Bernet (Philadelphia: Jewish Publication Society, 1968), pp. 263–65. Copyright 1968 by the Jewish Publication Society of America. Reproduced by permission of the University of Nebraska Press, and the author's estate; From *Letter to an Arab Friend*, trans. William V. Gugli (Amherst, Mass.: University of Massachusetts Press, 1972), pp. 33–36. Copyright © 1972 by University of Massachusetts Press. Reprinted by permission of the University of Massachusetts Press and the author's estate.

José Chudnovsky, "Dios era verde" [God Was Green], *from Cien años de narrativa judeoargentina (1889–1989)* (Buenos Aires: Milá, 1990), pp. 163–68. Used with permission of the author's estate.

Hélène Cixous, excerpt from *Inside*, trans. Carol Barko (New York: Schocken Books, 1986), pp. 16–19. Copyright © 1986 by Schocken Books, Inc. Used by permission of Schocken Books, an imprint of the Knopf Doubleday Publishing Group, a division of Penguin Random House LLC. All rights reserved.

Albert Cohen, from *Her Lover (Belle du Seigneur)*, Penguin Modern Classics series, trans. David Coward (London and New York: Penguin Books, 2005), pp. 114–17. Original French edition copyright © Éditions Gallimard, 1968. English language translation copyright © Albert Cohen and David Coward, 2005. Reproduced by permission of Penguin Books, Ltd. and Éditions Gallimard.

Arthur A. Cohen, "Epilogue: Renewal of the Jewish Vocation," from *The Natural and the Supernatural Jew: An Historical and Theological Introduction* (New York: Pantheon Books, 1962), pp. 311–14. Used with permission of the author's estate.

Elliot E. Cohen, "An Act of Affirmation," *Commentary*, vol. 1 (November, 1945), pp. 1–3. Used with permission of the publisher.

Originally published in Yiddish as "Ich bin a yid," *Eynikeyt* (December 27, 1942), and uncensored in *Roytar-meish* (New York: *Folks-farlag IKUF, alveltlekher yidisher kultur-farband*, 1943). Used with permission of National Coalition Supporting Eurasian Jewry and the Estate of Itzik Feffer.

Lion Feuchtwanger, "The Working Problems of the Writer in Exile," from *University of California, Los Angeles and Hollywood Writers Mobilization, Writers' Congress: The Proceedings of the Conference Held in October 1943 under the Sponsorship of the Hollywood Writers' Mobilization and the University of California* (Berkeley: University of California Press, 1944), pp. 346–49. Published in German as "Arbeitsprobleme des schriftstellers im Exil," *Freies Deutschland*, vol. 3, no. 4 (1943), pp. 27–28. © Aufbau Verlag GmbH & Co. KG, Berlin 1999, 2008. Used with permission of Aufbau Verlag.

Yaakov Fichman, from Pe'at Sadeh [Corner of the Field] (Tel Aviv: Schocken 1944), pp. 224–25. © Yaakov Fichman and ACUM. Used with permission of ACUM, on behalf of the author's estate.

Leslie A. Fiedler, "What Can We Do About Fagin? The Jew-Villain in Western Tradition," *Commentary*, vol. 7 (May 1949), pp. 413–14. Used with permission of the publisher.

Louis Finkelstein, ed., from *The Jews: Their History, Culture, and Religion*, vol. I, 3rd ed. (New York: Harper & Brothers, 1950), pp. xxi–xxiii, xxvi, xxx–xxxi. Copyright © 1949, 1955, 1960 by Louis Finkelstein. Reprinted by permission of HarperCollins Publishers.

Rukhl Fishman, "The Sun and I," from *I Want to Fall Like This*, trans. Seymour Levitan (Detroit: Wayne State University Press, 1994), p. 19. Copyright © 1994 Wayne State University Press. Reprinted with the permission of Wayne State University Press.

Anna Frajlich, "Acclimitization," from *Between Dawn and the Wind*, trans. Regina Grol (Austin: Host Publications, 2006), p. 11. Used with permission of the publisher.

Anne Frank, excerpts from *The Diary of a Young Girl, The Definitive Edition (1942–44)*, eds. Otto H. Frank and Mirjam Pressler, trans. Susan Massotty (New York: Doubleday, 1995 / London: Viking, 1997), pp. 243–45, 260–62. Copyright © The Anne Frank-Fonds, Basle, Switzerland, 1991. English translation copyright © 1995 by Doubleday, a division of Random House LLC. Reproduced by permission of Penguin Books Ltd and Doubleday, an imprint of the Knopf Doubleday Publishing Group, a division of Penguin Random House LLC. All rights reserved.

Naomi Frankel, from *Sha'ul veYohanah* [Saul and Johanna] (Merhavia: Sifriat Poalim, 1967), pp. 635–42. © Naomi Frankel and ACUM. Used with permission of ACUM, on behalf of the author's estate.

Viktor E. Frankl, "From Death-Camp to Existentialism: A Psychiatrist's Path to a New Therapy," from *Man's Search for Meaning: An Introduction to Logotherapy*, trans. Ilse Lasch (Boston: Beacon Press, 2006), pp. 65–67. Published in the UK as *Man's Search for Meaning* (London: Rider, 2004), pp. 74–76. Copyright ©1959, 1962, 1984, 1992 by Viktor E. Frankl. Reprinted by permission of the author's estate, Beacon Press, Boston, and The Random House Group Limited.

Alicia Freilich de Segal, "Ghettos en Rebelión" [Ghettos in Rebellion], from *Triálogo* (Caracas: Editorial Tiempo Nuevo, 1973), pp. 161–63. Used with permission of the author.

Yankev Fridman, "God No Longer Speaks," trans. Ruth Whitman, from *The Penguin Book of Modern Yiddish Verse*, eds. Irving Howe, Ruth R. Wisse, and Khone Shmeruk (New York: Viking, 1989), pp. 650–52. Copyright © 1987 by Irving Howe, Ruth Wisse, and Khone Shmeruk. Used by permission of Viking Books, an imprint of Penguin Publishing Group, a division of Penguin Random House LLC, and the author's estate. All rights reserved.

Betty Friedan, from *The Feminist Mystique* (New York: Norton, 1963), pp. 15–16, 334, 336–37. Copyright © 1963 by Betty Friedan. Reprinted by permission of Curtis Brown, Ltd. and The Orion Publishing Group, London. All rights reserved.

Pavel Friedman, "The Butterfly," trans. Dennis Silk, from Dennis Silk, *The Punished Land* (New York: Viking Press, 1980), p. 5. Used with permission of the translator's estate.

Georges Friedmann, extracts from *Fin du peuple juif?* [The End of the Jewish People?] (Paris: Éditions Gallimard, 1965), pp. 349–54. Georges Friedmann © Éditions Gallimard, Paris, 1965. Used with permission of the publisher.

Jews," trans. Cynthia Ozick, from *The Penguin Book of Modern Yiddish Verse*, eds. Irving Howe, Ruth R. Wisse, and Khone Shmeruk (New York: Viking, 1989), pp. 434, 436. Copyright © 1987 by Irving Howe, Ruth Wisse, and Khone Shmeruk. Used by permission of Viking Books, an imprint of Penguin Publishing Group, a division of Penguin Random House LLC, and the author's estate. All rights reserved.

Nahum N. Glatzer, "Epilogue," excerpt from *Language of Faith* (New York: Schocken Books, 1947), pp. 119–20. Copyright © 1947 by Schocken Books Inc. Copyright renewed 1975 by Schocken Books Inc. Copyright © 1967, 1974 by Schocken Books Inc. Used by permission of Schocken Books, an imprint of the Knopf Doubleday Publishing Group, a division of Penguin Random House LLC. All rights reserved; "The Frankfort Lehrhaus," *The Leo Baeck Institute Year Book*, vol. 1, no. 1 (1 January 1956), pp. 106–8. By permission of Oxford University Press, on behalf of The Leo Baeck Institute, and the author's estate.

Nathan Glazer, "The Jewish Revival in America, II: Its Religious Side," *Commentary*, vol. 21, no. 1 (January 1, 1956), pp. 18–19, 20–21. Copyright © 2016 by Commentary, Inc. Reprinted by permission of the publisher.

Ruth Glazer (Gay), "The Jewish Object: A Shopper's Report," *Commentary*, vol. 2 (January 1951), pp. 63–67. Used with permission of the publisher.

Hirsh Glik, "Never Say," trans. Jacob Sloan, from *A Treasury of Jewish Folk Song*, ed. Ruth Rubin (New York: Schocken Books, 1950), p. 185. Used with permission of the translator's estate; "Silence, and a Starry Night," trans. Jacob Sloan, from *A Treasury of Jewish Folksong*, ed. Ruth Rubin (New York: Schocken Books, 1950), p. 181. Used with permission of the translator's estate.

Herbert Gold, from *My Last Two Thousand Years* (New York: Random House, 1972), pp. 244–45. Used with permission of the author.

Leah Goldberg, "Laylot" [Nights], from *Shirim*, vol. 2 (Tel Aviv: Sifriat Poalim, 2001), p. 72. Used with permission of the publisher; From "A Letter to the Readers of My Friends from Arnon Street," from *Yedidai merehov Arnon: arba'ah sipurim* (Merhaviah: Sifriat Po'alim, 1966), pp. 5–8. Used with permission of the publisher; "The Love of Teresa de Meun, verse 2," trans. Robert Friend, from *Leah Goldberg: Selected Poems* (London: Menard Press, 1976), pp. 115, 117. Published in Hebrew as "Ahavata shel Tereza Di Mon," from *Ktavim* [Collected Works] (Tel Aviv: Sifriat Poalim Publishing House Ltd., 1973, 1986). Translation copyright © Jean Shapiro Cantu. Used with permission of the translator's estate and Hakibbutz Hameuchad–Sifriat Poalim Publishing group; "The Love of Teresa de Meun, verse 9," trans. Robert Friend, from *The Defiant Muse: Hebrew Feminist Poems from Antiquity to the Present*, eds. Shirley Kaufman, Galit Hasan-Rokem, and Tamar S. Hess (New York: The Feminist Press at CUNY, 1999), p. 117. Translated from Lea Goldberg, Ktavim [Collected Works] (Tel Aviv: Sifriat Poalim Publishing House Ltd., 1986). Translation copyright © Jean Shapiro Cantu. Used with permission of the translator and Hakibbutz Hameuchad-Sifriat Poalim Publishing; From *Yedidai merehov Arnon: arba'ah sipurim* [My Friends from Arnon Street] (Merhaviah: Sifriat Po'alim, 2001), pp. 12–13, 36–39. Used with permission of the publisher.

Isaac Goldemberg, "Los judíos en el infierno" [Jews in Hell], from *De Chepén a la Habana*, eds. Isaac Goldemberg and José Kozer (New York: Editorial Bayú-Menoráh, 1973), p. 7. Used with permission of the author.

Harry L. Golden, "Jew and Gentile in the New South: Segregation at Sundown," *Commentary*, vol. 20, no. 5 (November 1955), pp. 403–12. Used with permission of the publisher.

Judah Goldin, "Of Change and Adaptation in Judaism," from *Studies in Midrash and Related Literature*, eds. Barry L. Eichler and Jeffrey H. Tigay (Philadelphia: Jewish Publication Society, 1988), pp. 222–23, 230. Copyright 1988 by the Jewish Publication Society, Philadelphia. Reprinted by permission of the University of Nebraska Press.

Leyb Goldin, "Chronicle of a Single Day," trans. Elinor Robinson, from *The Literature of Destruction: Jewish Responses to Catastrophe*, ed. David G. Roskies (Philadelphia: Jewish Publication Society, 1989), pp. 424–34. Copyright 1989 by the Jewish Publication Society, Philadelphia. Published in Yiddish in *Tsvishn lebn un toyt*, ed. Ber Mark (Warsaw: Yidish-bukh, 1955), pp. 49–65. Reprinted by permission of the University of Nebraska Press.

William Goldman, from *East End My Cradle*, 2nd ed. (Glasgow: Art & Educational Publishers, 1947), pp. 17–22. Used with permission of the author's estate.

Nahum Goldmann, from *The Autobiography of Nahum Goldmann: Sixty Years of Jewish Life*, trans. Helen Sebba (New York: Holt, Rinehart and Winston, 1969), pp. 249–50, 259–60. Used with permission of the author's estate and the translator's estate.

Hermann Levin Goldschmidt, "The Legacy of German Jewry," from *The Legacy of German Jewry*, trans. David Suchoff (New York: Fordham University Press, 2007), pp. 236–38. Used with permission of the publisher.

Noah Golinkin, Jerome Lipnick, and N. Bertram Sachs, "Retribution Is Not Enough," *The Reconstructionist*, vol. 9, no. 2 (March 5, 1943), pp. 19–21. Used with the permission of the publisher.

Paul Goodman, "A Memorial Synagogue," from *The Break-up of Our Camp: Stories 1932–1935* (Santa Barbara, Calif.: Black Sparrow Press, 1978), pp. 86–97. Used with permission of the Estate of Paul Goodman and the publisher.

Frances Goodrich and Albert Hackett, excerpts from *Diary of Anne Frank* (New York: Random House, 1956), pp. 84–87, 96, 99–100. Copyright © 1956 by Albert Hackett, Frances Goodrich Hackett, and Otto Frank, copyright renewed 1986 by Albert Hackett, David Huntoon, and Frances Neuwirth. Used by permission of Flora Roberts, Inc. and Random House, an imprint and division of Penguin Random House LLC. All rights reserved.

Robert Gordis, from *The Challenge Facing Modern Jewish Scholarship* (Philadelphia: Dropsie College for Hebrew and Cognate Learning, 1950), pp. 3–6, 8–10. Copyright 1950. Reprinted with permission of the University of Pennsylvania Press.

Shmuel Gordon, "A Soviet Shtetl," trans. Joseph Leftwich, from *The Way We Think: A Collection of Essays from the Yiddish*, vol. 2 (South Brunswick, N.J.: Thomas Yoseloff, 1969), pp. 814–16. Used with permission of the translator's estate.

Phyllis Gotlieb, "This One's on Me," from *Mirror of a People: Canadian Jewish Experience in Poetry and Prose*, eds. Sheldon Oberman and Elaine Newton (Winnipeg: Jewish Educational Publishers of Canada, 1985), pp. 132–34. Used with permission of the author's estate.

Adolph Gottlieb and Marcus Rothko, "Letter to the Art Editor of the *New York Times*, June 7, 1943," from *Adolph Gottlieb: A Retrospective*, illus., essays Sanford Hirsch, Mary Davis MacNaughton, and Lawrence Alloway (New York: Adolph and Esther Gottlieb Foundation, 1981), p. 169. © Adolph and Esther Gottlieb Foundation, New York. Used with permission of Adolph Gottlieb's estate and the Flammarion Groupe.

Haim Gouri, "1923–1958, from *Shoshanat ruhot: shirim* (Tel Aviv: Hakkibutz Hameuḥad, 1960), pp. 258–60. © Haim Gouri and ACUM. Used with permission of ACUM, on behalf of the author's estate; "Behold Our Bodies Are Laid Out," from *No Rattling of Sabers: An Anthology of Israeli War Poetry*, trans. and intro. Esther Raizen (Austin: Center for Middle Eastern Studies, the University of Texas at Austin, 1995), pp. 4, 6. Translation Copyright © 1995 by the Center for Middle Eastern Studies at the University of Texas at Austin. Translated from "Hinne mutalot gufoteinu," from *Pirhei esh* (Tel Aviv: Hakibbutz Hameuchad, 1976). © Haim Gouri and ACUM. Used with permission of Center for Middle Eastern Studies and of ACUM, on behalf of the author's estate; "Ha-Sefer ha-meshuga" [The Crazy Book], trans. Ruth Nevo, from *Contemporary Israeli Literature: An Anthology*, ed. Elliott Anderson, poetry ed. Robert Friend (Philadelphia: Jewish Publication Society of America, 1977), pp. 135–38. © Haim Gouri and ACUM. English translation copyright 1977 by the Jewish Publication Society of America. Reproduced by permission of the University of Nebraska Press and ACUM; music by Sasha Argov, "Shir hare'ut" [The Song of Friendship]. © Haim Gouri and ACUM. Used with permission of ACUM, on behalf of the author's estate.

Chaim Grade, excerpts from "Elegy on the Soviet Yiddish Writers," from *A Treasury of Yiddish Poetry*, ed. Irving Howe & Eliezer Greenberg, trans. Cynthia Ozick (New York: Holt Rinehart, 1969), stanzas 1–2, 4, 6, 9–10, 12, pp. 339–44. © 1962 from Man of Fire published by CYCO. © 1969 by Holt, Rinehart and Winston, reprinted by Schocken 1976. Permission granted by the Melanie Jackson Agency, on behalf of the translator, and YIVO and its agent, Robin Straus Agency, Inc. Any third-party use of this material, outside of this publication, is prohibited. Interested parties must apply directly to Robin Straus Agency, Inc., and Melanie Jackson Agency, for permission; "My Quarrel with Hersh Rasseyner," trans. Milton Himmelfarb, from *A*

behalf of the Estate of Arthur Koestler; From *Thieves in the Night: Chronicle of an Experiment* (New York: The Macmillan Company, 1946), pp. 228–29, 248–49, 282–83. Reprinted by permission of Peters Fraser & Dunlop (www.petersfraserdunlop.com) on behalf of the Estate of Arthur Koestler.

Zvi Kolitz, "Yossel Rakover's Appeal to God," trans. Shmuel Katz, from *Out of the Whirlwind: A Reader of Holocaust Literature*, ed. Albert H. Friedlander (New York: Union of American Hebrew Congregations, 1968), pp. 390–97. Text rediscovered and translated into German by Paul Badde. Reprinted by permission of the author's estate, the translator's estate, and Paul Badde.

Rokhl Korn, "On the Other Side of the Poem," trans. Seymour Levitan, from *The Penguin Book of Modern Yiddish Verse*, eds. Irving Howe, Ruth R. Wisse, and Khone Shmeruk (New York: Viking, 1989), p. 524. Copyright © 1987 by Irving Howe, Ruth Wisse, and Khone Shmeruk. Used by permission of Viking Books, an imprint of Penguin Publishing Group, a division of Penguin Random House LLC, and the author's estate. All rights reserved.

Koro Saloniko (Salomon and Renée Bivas, Haim and Esther Rafael), "In Polish Lands," trans. Isaac Jack Lévy, from *And the World Stood Silent: Sephardi Poetry of the Holocaust*, ed. Isaac Jack Lévy (Urbana and Chicago: University of Illinois Press, 2000), p. 213. Used with permission of the authors' estates and the translator.

Heda Margolius Kovály (born Heda Bloch), excerpted from *Under a Cruel Star: A Life in Prague 1941–1968*, trans. Franci Epstein and Helen Epstein with the author (Cambridge, Mass.: Plunkett Lake Press, 1986), pp. 52–61. eBook edition at http://plunkettlakepress.com/uacs. Used with permission of the publisher.

Abba Kovner, "Call To Arms (1 Jan. 42)," trans. Lucy S. Dawidowicz, from *A Holocaust Reader*, ed. Lucy S. Dawidowicz (New York: Behrman House, 1976), pp. 334–36. © Behrman House, Inc. Reprinted with permission of Behrman House, Inc. www.behrmanhouse.com; Canto 28, "My Little Sister," from *My Little Sister and Selected Poems*, trans. Shirley Kaufman (Oberlin, Ohio: Oberlin College, 1986), pp. 66–67. Translated from "Achoti Ha-ktana," canto 28 ("Achoti Yoshevet Smecha"), from *Kol Shirei Abba Kovner*, vol. 2 (Jerusalem: Bialik Institute, 1997), pp. 42–43. © Abba Kovner and ACUM. Translation Copyright © 1986 by Oberlin College. Reprinted with the permission of Oberlin College Press and of ACUM, on behalf of the author's estate.

Kovno Jewish Ghetto Police, anonymous members, "History of the Viliampole Jewish Ghetto Police," from *The Clandestine History of the Kovno Jewish Ghetto Police*, ed. and trans. Samuel Schalkowsky (Bloomington: Indiana University Press in association with the United States Holocaust Memorial Museum, Washington, D.C., 2014), pp. 359–62. Copyright © 2014 by Indiana University Press. Translation copyright © 2014 Samuel Schalkowsky. Reprinted with permission of Indiana University Press.

José Kozer, "Abuelo enfrenta la muerte" [Grandfather Is Facing Death], from *De Chepén a la Habana*, eds. Isaac Goldemberg and José Kozer (New York: Editorial Bayú-Menoráh, 1973), p. 61. Used with permission of the author.

Georg Kreisler, lyrics from "Ich fühl mich nicht zu Hause" [I Do Not Feel at Home Here]. Used with permission of the author's estate.

Esther Kreitman, from *Diamonds*, trans. Heather Valencia (London: David Paul, 2010), pp. 207–12. Used with permission of the publisher.

Herman Kruk, from *The Last Days of the Jerusalem of Lithuania: Chronicles from the Vilna Ghetto and the Camps, 1939–1944*, ed. and intro. Benjamin Harshav, trans. Barbara Harshav (New Haven, Conn.: Yale University Press, 2002), pp. 371, 439–40, 475, 490, 519. Used with permission of the publisher.

Maxine Kumin, "Woodchucks," from *Selected Poems, 1960–1990* (New York: W. W. Norton & Company, 1997), pp. 80–81. Used by permission of W. W. Norton & Company, Inc.

Stanley Kunitz, "Father and Son," from *The Collected Poems* (New York: W. W. Norton, 2000), pp. 62–63. Copyright 1944, 1971 by Stanley Kunitz. Used by permission of W. W. Norton & Company, Inc.

Barukh Kurzweil, "Oreaḥ natah lalun" [Agnon's A Guest for the Night], from *Masot 'al sipurei Shay Agnon* (Tel Aviv: Schocken, 1962), pp. 50–54. © Schocken Publishing House Ltd., Tel Aviv, Israel. Used with permission of the publisher.

Jack Ludwig, "A Woman of Her Age," from *Prize Stories: O. Henry Award 1965*, ed. Richard Poirier and William Abrahams (New York: Doubleday & Co., Inc., 1965), pp. 81–82. © Jack Ludwig. Used with permission of the author.

Arnošt Lustig, from *Night and Hope*, trans. George Theiner (Iowa City: University of Iowa Press, 1972), pp. 144–49. Used with permission of the author's estate.

Judah L. Magnes, "Toward Peace in Palestine," *Foreign Affairs*, vol. 21, no. 2 (January, 1943), pp. 241–49. Copyright 1943 by the Council on Foreign Relations, Inc. www.ForeignAffairs.com. Reprinted by permission of Foreign Affairs.

Norman Mailer, "The Time Machine," excerpts from *The Naked and the Dead* (New York: Picador, 1998), pp. 481–83. Copyright © 1948, renewed in 1976, by Norman Mailer. Used by permission of The Wylie Agency LLC.

Bernard Malamud, "The Jewbird," from *The Stories of Bernard Malamud* (New York: Macmillan, 1983), pp. 145–46, 153–54. Originally published in *Idiots First* (New York: Macmillan, 1963). Copyright © 1983, 1997 by Bernard Malamud. Reprinted by permission of Farrar, Straus and Giroux and Russell & Volkening as agents for the author; "The Last Mohican," from *The Stories of Bernard Malamud* (New York: Macmillan, 1983), pp. 43–49. Copyright © 1978, 1983 by Bernard Malamud. Reprinted by permission of Farrar, Straus and Giroux and Russell & Volkening as agents for the author.

Isaac ben Jacob Mamo (1880–1967), "Introduction" to his translation of Avraham Mapu's *Ayit tsavu'a into Judeo-Arabic* [1942], *Pe'amim* 114/115 (Winter/Spring 2008), pp. 234–35. Used with permission of Ben-Zvi Institute.

Arnold Mandel, "Ashkenaz," from "Dictionnaire du judaisme français" [Dictionary of French Judaism], *L'Arche*, no. 186–187 (September–October 1972; special edition), pp. 73–74. Used with permission of the publisher.

Eli Mandel, "Day of Atonement: Standing," from *Mirror of a People: Canadian Jewish Experience in Poetry and Prose*, eds. Sheldon Oberman and Elaine Newton (Winnipeg: Jewish Educational Publishers of Canada, 1985), p. 121. Used with permission of the author's estate.

Nadezhda Mandelstam, from *Hope Against Hope: A Memoir*, trans. from the Russian by Max Hayward (New York: Atheneum, 1970 / London: Harvill Press, 1971), pp. 157–60, 162. Copyright © 1970 by Atheneum Publishers. Reprinted with the permission of Scribner, a division of Simon & Schuster, Inc., and The Random House Group Ltd. All rights reserved.

Stefánia Mándy, "Consciousness," trans. Imre Goldstein, from *Contemporary Jewish Writing in Hungary: An Anthology*, eds. Susan Rubin Suleiman and Éva Forgács (Lincoln: University of Nebraska Press, 2003), pp. 147–48. Copyright 2003 by the University of Nebraska Press. Reprinted by permission of the University of Nebraska Press.

Itzik Manger, "Cain and Abel," trans. Leonard Wolf, from *A Treasury of Yiddish Poetry*, eds. Irving Howe and Eliezer Greenberg (New York: Holt Rinehart, 1969), pp. 278–80. Used with permission of the author's estate and the translator; "For Years I Wallowed," trans. Leonard Wolf, from *The Penguin Book of Modern Yiddish Verse*, eds. Irving Howe, Ruth R. Wisse, and Khone Shmeruk (New York: Viking, 1989), pp. 590–92. Copyright © 1987 by Irving Howe, Ruth Wisse, and Khone Shmeruk. Used by permission of Viking Books, an imprint of Penguin Publishing Group, a division of Penguin Random House LLC, and the author's estate. All rights reserved.

Ehud Manor, music by Nurit Hirsh, "Bashana haba'ah" [Next Year]. © Ehud Manor and ACUM. Used with permission of ACUM, on behalf of the author's estate.

Julius Margolin, "Elijah the Prophet," from *A Voyage to the Land of Ze-Ka*, trans. Stefani Hoffman (unpublished). Used with permission of the author's estate, the translator, and Le Bruit du Temps.

Richard Marienstras, "Les juifs de la Diaspora: ou la vocation minoritaire" [The Jews of the Diaspora, or the Minority Vocation], from *Être un peuple en diaspora*, preface by Élise Marienstras and afterword by Pierre

Adam Michnik, "Shadows of Forgotten Ancestors," from *Letters from Prison and Other Essays*, trans. Maya Latynski (Berkeley: University of California Press, 1985), pp. 203–21. © 1987 by the Regents of the University of California. Used with permission of the author and the publisher.

Baruch Milch, from *Can Heaven Be Void?*, ed. Shosh Milch-Avigal, trans. Helen Kaye (Jerusalem: Yad Vashem, 2003), pp. 34, 55. Used with permission of the publisher.

Israel Milejkowski, "Answer to the Oyneg Shabes Questionnaire," trans. David L. Gold, from *A Holocaust Reader*, ed. Lucy Dawidowicz (New York: Behrman House, 1976), pp. 221–25. © Behrman House, Inc. Reprinted with permission of Behrman House, Inc. www.behrmanhouse.com.

Arthur Miller, from *Death of a Salesman* (New York: Penguin Books, 1976), pp. 56, 129–33. Copyright 1949 by Arthur Miller, copyright renewed © 1977 by Arthur Miller. Used by permission of Viking Books, an imprint of Penguin Publishing Group, a division of Penguin Random House LLC, and The Wylie Agency LLC. All rights reserved; Excerpts from *Focus* (London: Metheun, 2000), pp. 75–78. Copyright © 1945, 1973 by Arthur Miller. Used by permission of The Wylie Agency LLC.

Dan Miron, "Shtei he'arot le-yemei ziklag: yemei ziklag—ba'ayotav ha-omanutiyut shel sipur milḥama" [Yemei Ziklag: The Artistic Problems of a War Story], from *Arba panim ba-sifrut ha-'Ivrit bat yamenu: 'iyunim bi-yetsirot Alterman, Ratosh, Yizhar, Shamir* (Jerusalem: Schocken, 1962), pp. 297–302. © Schocken Publishing House Ltd., Tel Aviv, Israel. Used with permission and approval of the publisher and author.

Patrick Modiano, from *The Occupation Trilogy*, trans. Frank Wynne (New York, London, and Oxford: Bloomsbury Publishing Plc, 2015), pp. 35–38. © Patrick Modiano. Used with permission of Bloomsbury Publishing Plc.

Yehiel Mohar, music by Moshe Wilensky, "Hora mamtera" [Sprinkler Hora]. © Yehiel Mohar and ACUM. Used with permission of ACUM, on behalf of the author.

Michael Molho, from *Traditions and Customs of the Sephardic Jews of Salonica*, trans. Alfred A. Zara, ed. Robert Bedford (New York: Foundation for the Advancement of Sephardic Studies and Culture, 2006), pp. 136–49. Used with permission of the author's estate.

Kadya Molodovsky, "God of Mercy," trans. Irving Howe, from *The Penguin Book of Modern Yiddish Verse*, eds. Irving Howe, Ruth R. Wisse, and Khone Shmeruk (New York: Viking, 1989), pp. 331–32. Copyright © 1987 by Irving Howe, Ruth Wisse, and Khone Shmeruk. Used by permission of Viking Books, an imprint of Penguin Publishing Group, a division of Penguin Random House LLC, and the author's estate. All rights reserved.

Siegfried Moses, "Leo Baeck Institute of Jews from Germany," *The Leo Baeck Institute Year Book*, vol. 1, no. 1 (1 January 1956), xiii, xiv–xvi. By permission of Oxford University Press, on behalf of The Leo Baeck Institute, and the author's estate.

Yigal Mossinson, from *Be'arvot hanegev: Mahaze beshalosh ma'arekhot* [In the Negev Plains: A Play in Three Acts] (Tel Aviv: Habimah, 1959), pp. 39–45. Used with permission of the author's estate.

Ezrat Nashim, "Jewish Women Call for Change," Jewish Women's Archive, Collection of Paula Hyman, from http://jwa.org/media/jewish-women-call-for-change. Used with permission of Jewish Women's Archive.

Andre Neher, "Abraham," from "Dictionnaire du judaisme français" [Dictionary of French Judaism], *L'Arche*, no. 186–187 (September–October, 1972; special edition), pp. 4–5. Used with permission of the publisher.

Howard Nemerov, "Nicodemus," from *Collected Poems of Howard Nemerov* (Chicago: University of Chicago Press, 1977), pp. 54–56. © 1977 by Howard Nemerov. Originally published in Howard Nemerov, *Guide to the Ruins* (New York: Random House, 1950). © 1947, 1948, 1949, 1950 by Howard Nemerov. Used with permission of the publisher.

Irène Némirovsky, excerpt from *Suite Française*, trans. Sandra Smith (London: Chatto & Windus / New York: Alfred A. Knopf, 2006), pp. 273–75. Copyright © 2004 by Éditions Denoël. Translation copyright © 2006 by Sandra Smith. Used by permission of Alfred A. Knopf, an imprint of the Knopf Doubleday Publishing Group, a division of Penguin Random House LLC, by permission of the translator, and of Éditions Denoël. All rights reserved.

Piotr Rawicz, from *Blood from the Sky*, trans. Peter Wiles, revised trans. and ed. with an afterword by Anthony Rudolf (London: Elliott and Thompson/Menard Press, 2004), pp. 53–57. Used with permission of Anthony Rudolf, Yale University Press, and Éditions Gallimard. Extract from *Le sang du ciel*, Piotr Rawicz © Éditions Gallimard, Paris, 1961. Used with permission of Éditions Gallimard.

Simon Rawidowicz, "Israel: The Ever-Dying People," from *Modern Jewish Thought: A Source Reader*, ed. Nahum N. Glatzer (New York: Schocken Books, 1977), pp. 139–42. Used with permission of the author's estate.

Avraham Raz, from *Lel ha'atsmaut shel mar Yisrael Shefi: mahazot* [Mr. Israel Shefi's Night of Independence: Plays] (Tel Aviv: Hakibbutz Hameuchad, 1976), pp. 179–83. Used with permission of the publisher.

Gonda (Egon) Redlich, from *The Terezin Diary of Gonda Redlich*, trans. Laurence Kutler, ed. Saul S. Friedman, (Lexington: University Press of Kentucky, 1992), 1992, pp. 159–61. Reproduced with permission of University Press of Kentucky in the format Other Published Product via Copyright Clearance Center.

Sylvia Regan, from *The Fifth Season* (New York: Samuel French, 1953), pp. 16–18, 88–89. Used with permission of the author's estate.

Charles Reznikoff, "A Short History of Israel, Notes and Glosses," from *The Poems of Charles Reznikoff: 1918–1975*, ed. Seamus Cooney (Boston: Black Sparrow Press, 2005), pp. 183. Copyright © 2005 by the Estate of Charles Reznikoff. Reprinted by permission of Black Sparrow Books, an imprint of David R. Godine, Publisher, Inc.

Harold Uriel Ribalow, ed., "Introduction," from *Mid-century: An Anthology of Jewish Life and Culture in Our Times* (New York: Beechhurst Press, 1955), pp. 11–13. Used with permission of the editor's estate.

Adrienne Rich, "Diving into the Wreck," from *Diving into the Wreck: Poems 1971–1972* (New York: W. W. Norton & Company, 1973), pp. 22–24. Copyright © 1973 by W. W. Norton & Company, Inc. Used by permission of W. W. Norton & Company, Inc.

Mordecai Richler, from *The Apprenticeship of Duddy Kravitz* (Middlesex, England: Penguin Books, 1991), pp. 325–29. Used with permission of Mordecai Richler Productions, Inc.; "Their Canada and Mine," *Commentary*, vol. 32 (August, 1961), pp. 135–43. Used with permission of Mordecai Richler Productions, Inc.

Emanuel Ringelblum, "Oyneg-shabes," trans. Elinor Robinson, from *The Literature of Destruction: Jewish Responses to Catastrophe*, ed. David G. Roskies (Philadelphia: Jewish Publication Society, 1989), pp. 389–91. Published in Yiddish in Emanuel Ringelblum, *Ksovim fun geto, vol. 2: Notitsn un ophandlungen (1942–1943)*, 2nd rev. ed. (Tel Aviv: I. L. Peretz, 1985). Used with permission of the translator.

Isaac Rivkind, from *Yidishe gelt* [Jewish Money] (New York: American Academy for Jewish Research, 1959), pp. ix, xiii, 271–72. Used with permission of the publisher.

Leyb Rochman, from *The Pit and the Trap: A Chronicle of Survival*, trans. Moshe Kohn, ed. Sheila Friedling (New York: Holocaust Library, 1983), pp. 11, 13–14, 19–20, 213. Used with permission of the author's and translator's estates.

Richard Rodgers & Oscar Hammerstein II, "The Farmer and the Cowman" lyrics, Copyright © 1943 by Williamson Music, Copyright Renewed. International Copyright Secured. All Rights Reserved. Used by Permission of Williamson Music.

Edouard Roditi, "Artistes Juifs d'Afrique du Nord" [Jewish Artists from North Africa], *L'Arche*, no. 74 (March, 1963), pp. 61–62. Used with permission of the publisher.

Isaac E. Rontch, "Foreword," from *Jewish Youth at War: Letters from American Soldiers*, ed. Isaac E. Rontch (New York: Marstin Press, 1945), pp. i–ii. Used with permission of the author's estate.

Harold Rosenberg, "Does the Jew Exist? Sartre's Morality Play about Anti-Semitism," *Commentary*, vol. 7, no. 1 (January, 1949), pp. 8–18. Used with permission of the publisher.

M. J. Rosenberg, "To Jewish Uncle Toms," *Jewish Frontier*, vol. 36 (February 1969), pp. 233–34, 235–36. Used with permission of Ameinu.

Chava Rosenfarb, from *The Tree of Life, Book Two: From the Depths I Call You, 1940–1942*, trans. Chava Rosenfarb in collaboration with Goldie Morgentaler (Madison: University of Wisconsin Press, 2005), pp. 36–38;

from *The Tree of Life, Book Three: The Cattle Cars Are Waiting, 1942–1944*, trans. Chava Rosenfarb in collaboration with Goldie Morgentaler (Madison: University of Wisconsin Press, 2006), pp. 123–25. © 2005 by the Board of Regents of the University of Wisconsin System. Reprinted by permission of The University of Wisconsin Press.

Isaac Rosenfeld, from *Passage from Home* (New York: Dial Press, 1946), pp. 18–21. Used with permission of the author's estate; "The Situation of the Jewish Writer," *Contemporary Jewish Record*, vol. 7, no. 1 (February 1944), pp. 34–36. Used with permission of *Commentary*.

Oskar Rosenfeld, "Chanukah in the Ghetto, 1943," trans. Joachim Neugroschel, from *The Chronicle of the Łódź Ghetto, 1941–1944*, ed. Lucjan Dobroszycki (New Haven, Conn.: Yale University Press, 1984), pp. 421–23. Used with permission of the publisher; "Encyclopedia of the Łódź Ghetto," from *In the Beginning Was the Ghetto: Notebooks from Łódź*, ed. Hanno Loewy, trans. Brigitte M. Goldstein (Evanston, Ill.: Northwestern University Press, 2002), pp. 229–31. Originally published in 1994 in German under the title *Wozu noch Welt: Aufzeichnung aus dem Getto Lodz*. Copyright 1994 by Verlag Neue Kritik. English translation copyright © 2002 by Northwestern University Press. All rights reserved. Used with permission of Northwestern University Press.

A. M. Rosenthal, "There Is No News from Auschwitz," *The New York Times Magazine* (31 August 1958), p. 5. © 1958 The New York Times. All rights reserved. Used by permission and protected by the Copyright Laws of the United States. The printing, copying, redistribution, or retransmission of this Content without express written permission is prohibited.

David G. Roskies, from *Nightwords: A Liturgy on the Holocaust* (New York: CLAL, 2000). First published as *Night Words: A Midrash on the Holocaust* (Washington, D.C.: B'nai Brith Hillel, 1971), pp. 17–21. Used with permission from the author and CLAL—The National Jewish Center for Learning and Leadership.

Yaakov Rotblit, music by Yair Rosenblum, "Shir leshalom," trans. Jerry Hyman. © Yaacov Rotblit and ACUM. Used with permission of the translator and of ACUM, on behalf of the author.

Philip Roth, excerpts from "Eli, the Fanatic," from *Goodbye, Columbus* (Boston: Houghton Mifflin Company, 1989), pp. 263–66, 297–98. Copyright © 1959, renewed 1987 by Philip Roth. Reprinted by permission of Houghton Mifflin Harcourt Publishing Company. All rights reserved; Excerpt from *Portnoy's Complaint* (New York: Random House, 1969), pp. 60–63. Copyright © 1969, 1997 by Philip Roth. Used by permission of The Random House Group Limited and Random House, an imprint and division of Penguin Random House LLC. All rights reserved.

León Rozitchner, from *Ser judío* [To Be Jewish] (Buenos Aires: Ediciones de la Flor, 1968/1988), pp. 9–11. Reprinted in *Ser judío y otros ensayos afines* (Buenos Aires: Biblioteca Nacional, 2015). Used with permission of Biblioteca Nacional.

Zalman Rubashov (Shazar), "Moreshet taf-shin-giml" [The Legacy of 5703], from *Tav Shin Gimmel Baolam, Bauma, Batnua Uvaaretz* (Tel Aviv: Davar, 1942-1943), pp. 5–10. Used with permission of The Lavon Institute for Labor Movement Research.

Bernice Rubens, extract from "The Elected Member," in *Contemporary Jewish Writing in Britain and Ireland: An Anthology*, ed. Bryan Cheyette (Lincoln: University of Nebraska Press, 1998), pp. 23–26. Reprinted by permission of Peters Fraser & Dunlop (www.petersfraserdunlop.com) on behalf of the Estate of Bernice Rubens.

Richard L. Rubenstein, "Symposium on Jewish Belief," from *After Auschwitz: Radical Theology and Contemporary Judaism* (Indianapolis: Bobbs-Merrill, 1966), pp. 151–54. First published in *Commentary*, vol. 42 (August 1966). Used with permission of the author.

Rivke Rubin, "Bam brunem" [At the Well], from *Yidishe froyen: fartseykhenungen* (Moscow: Ogiz, 1943), pp. 22–26. Used with permission of the author's estate.

Adolf Rudnicki, "Ascension," from *Contemporary Jewish Writing in Poland: An Anthology*, ed. Antony Polonsky and Monika Adamczyk-Garbowska (Lincoln and London: University of Nebraska Press, 2001), pp. 118–21. Translation revised by Monika Adamczyk Garbowska, based on Adolph Rudnicki, *Ascent to*

Heaven, trans. H. C. Stevens (New York: Roy Publishers, 1951). Translated from "Wniebowstapienie," from *Sto jeden*, vol. 1 (Kraków: Wydawnictwo Literackie, 1984). Published in French as *Les fenêtres d'or et autres récits* (Paris: Gallimard 1966). © Éditions Gallimard, Paris, 1966. Copyright 2001 by the University of Nebraska Press. Reprinted by permission of the University of Nebraska Press and Éditions Gallimard.

Leah Rudnitzky, "Birds Are Drowsing," trans. Hillel Schwartz and David G. Roskies, from *The Literature of Destruction: Jewish Responses to Catastrophe*, ed. David G. Roskies (Philadelphia: Jewish Publication Society, 1989), pp. 478–79. Copyright 1989 by the Jewish Publication Society. Reprinted by permission of the University of Nebraska Press.

Muriel Rukeyser, "Letter to the Front," from *Beast in View* (Garden City, N.Y.: Doubleday, Doran and Company, Inc.,1944), pp. 62. Used with permission of International Creative Management.

Abram L. Sachar, "Brandeis University: The Pledge," from *Brandeis University: The Challenge, The Assurance, The Pledge* (Boston: Brandeis University, 1948), pp. 8–11. Used with permission of the author's estate and Brandeis University.

Nelly Sachs, "But who emptied your shoes of sand," trans. Michael Hamburger, from *O the Chimneys: Selected Poems* (New York: Farrar, Straus and Giroux. 1967), p. 9. Published in German as "Wer aber leerte den Sand aus euren Schuhen," from *Werke, Band 1: Gedichte 1940–1950*, ed. Matthias Weichelt, annotated edition in 4 volumes, ed. Aris Fioretos (Berlin: Suhrkamp, 2010). © Suhrkamp Verlag Berlin 2010. Translation copyright © 1967, renewed 1995 by Farrar, Straus & Giroux, Inc. Reprinted by permission of Farrar, Straus and Giroux and Suhrkamp Verlag; "O the Chimneys," trans. Michael Roloff, from *O the Chimneys: Selected Poems* (New York: Farrar, Straus and Giroux, 1967), p. 3. Published in German as "O die Schornsteine," from *Werke, Band 1: Gedichte 1940–1950*, ed. Matthias Weichelt, annotated edition in 4 volumes, ed. Aris Fioretos (Berlin: Suhrkamp, 2010). © Suhrkamp Verlag Berlin 2010. Translation copyright © 1967, renewed 1995 by Farrar, Straus & Giroux, Inc. Reprinted by permission of Farrar, Straus and Giroux and Suhrkamp Verlag.

Chaim Sacks, "Sweets from Sixpence," trans. Woolf Leivick and Joseph Sherman, from *From a Land Far Off: South African Yiddish Stories in English Translation*, ed. Joseph Sherman (Cape Town: Jewish Publications, South Africa, 1987), pp. 154–55. Used with permission of the translators' estates and the publisher.

Dov Sadan, ed., "Preface" and "Three Footnotes," from *Ka'arat tsimukim: o elef bediḥah uvediḥah: asufat humor beYisra'el* [A Bowl of Raisins, or A Thousand and One Anecdotes: A Collection of Jewish Humor] (Tel Aviv: M. Neuman, 1949), unnumbered preface and pp. 295–97. Used with permission of the author's estate; From "Three Foundations (Sholem Aleichem and the Yiddish Literary Tradition)," trans. David G. Roskies, *Prooftexts*, vol. 6 (1986), pp. 55–63. Translated from *Heymishe ksovim: shrayber, bikher, problemen*, 2 vols. (Tel Aviv, 1972), vol. 1, pp. 15–27. Originally delivered as a lecture at the Hebrew University in honor of Sholem Aleichem's 100th birthday. © Dov Sadan and ACUM. Used with permission of the translator, Indiana University Press, and ACUM, on behalf of the author's estate.

Pinhas Sadeh, from *Life as a Parable*, trans. Richard Flantz (Jerusalem: Carta, 1989), pp. 61–62, 135–37, 336–37, 366–67. Translation © Copyright Carta, Jerusalem. Translated from *HaHayim KeMashal* (1958). © Pinhas Sadeh and ACUM. Used with permission of Carta and of ACUM, on behalf of the author's estate.

Artur Sandauer, from *Zapiski z martwego miasta* [Notes from the Dead Town] (Warsaw: Czytelnik, 1963), pp. 9–17, 101–102. Used with permission of the author's estate.

Nahum M. Sarna, from *Understanding Genesis* (New York: Jewish Theological Seminary of America, 1966), pp. 52–59. Reprinted with the permission of The Jewish Theological Seminary of America. All rights reserved.

Moshe Sartel, "Saba shehaya li" [The Grandfather I Once Had], from *Mi shenatal: Shirei ma'aseh* (Jerusalem: Mitshaf, 1967), p. 9. Used with permission of the author.

Zalman M. Schachter, "Toward an 'Order of B'nai Or': A Program for a Jewish Liturgical Brotherhood," *Judaism*, vol. 13, no. 2 (Spring 1964), pp. 187–88, 194–97. Used with permission of the author's estate.

Yosef Yitshak Schneersohn, "First Proclamation, 26 May 1941," and "Third Proclamation: 8 July 1941," trans. Gershon Greenberg, from *Wrestling with God: Jewish Theological Responses during and after the Holocaust,* eds. Steven T. Katz, Shlomo Biderman, and Gershon Greenberg (Oxford and New York: Oxford University Press, 2007), pp. 172–73, 180. By Permission of Oxford University Press, USA.

Fishl Schneourson, "Mahpekhot hanefesh be-yisrael ba'akev hashoah" [The Spiritual Upheaval in Israel in the Wake of the Holocaust], *Moznayim*, vol. 16, no. 6 [June] 1943), p. 375. Speech at Kibbutz Hulda, June 7, 1943. Used with permission of the publisher and the author's estate.

Gershom Scholem, excerpts from *Major Trends in Jewish Mysticism*, trans. George Lichtheim (New York: Schocken, 1954), pp. 10–14, 35–37. Copyright © 1946, 1954; and renewed 1974, 1982 by Schocken Books, a division of Random House, Inc. Foreword copyright © 1995 by Robert Alter. Used by permission of Schocken Books, an imprint of the Knopf Doubleday Publishing Group, a division of Penguin Random House LLC. All rights reserved; "Reflections on Modern Jewish Studies," trans. Jonathan Chipman, from Gershom Scholem, *On the Possibility of Jewish Mysticism in Our Time and Other Essays*, ed. Avraham Shapira (Philadelphia: Jewish Publications Society, 1997), pp. 53, 61–64. Copyright 1997 by Gershom Scholem. Reprinted by permission of the University of Nebraska Press.

Budd Schulberg, from *What Makes Sammy Run?* (Harmondsworth: Penguin, 1978), pp. 198–200. Copyright © 1941, by Budd Schulberg. Reprinted by permission of Miriam Altshuler Literary Agency, on behalf of Budd Schulberg.

Pablo Schvartzman, "Noé Yarcho, el médico de los gauchos judíos" [Noé Yarcho, Physician to the Jewish Gauchos], from *Judíos en América* (Buenos Aires: Instituto Amigos del Libro Argentino, 1963), pp. 111–12. Used with permission of the author.

Delmore Schwartz, "America! America!," from *In Dreams Begin Responsibilities and Other Stories*, ed. James Atlas (New York: New Directions, 1978), pp. 12–13 (London: Souvenir Press, 2003). Copyright © 1937 by New Directions Publishing Corp. Reprinted by permission of New Directions Publishing Corp. and Souvenir Press Ltd.

Maurice Schwartz, from *Shylock and His Daughter*, trans. Abraham Regelson (New York: Yiddish Art Theater, 1947), pp. 71–72, 75, 122. Used with permission of the author's estate.

Leo W. Schwarz, ed., "Introduction," from *Memoirs of My People through a Thousand Years* (New York: Farrar and Rineholt, 1943), pp. xiii–xxvi; From *The Root and the Bough: The Epic of an Enduring People* (New York: Rinehart, 1949), pp. xi–xvi.

André Schwarz-Bart, from *The Last of the Just*, trans. Stephen Becker (New York: Atheneum Publishers, 1960), pp. 372–74. Originally published in French as *Le Dernier des justes*. English translation copyright © 1960 by Atheneum Publishers. Copyright © 1959 by Éditions du Seuil. Reprinted by permission of Georges Borchardt, Inc., for Éditions du Seuil.

Leon Sciaky, from *Farewell to Salonica: City at the Crossroads* (Philadelphia: Paul Dry Books, 2003), pp. 86–89. Copyright © 1946, 1974. Used by permission of Paul Dry Books, Inc., www.PaulDryBooks.com.

Moacyr Scliar, from *A guerra no bom fim* [A War Has No "Good End"] (Porto Alegre: L&PM, 2013), pp. 27–28 (Rio de Janeiro: Editora Expressão e Cultura, 1972), pp. 11–12. Used with permission of Agencia Literaria Riff.

Paul Sebag, "La Hara de Tunis: L'évolution d'un ghetto nord-africain" [The Hara of Tunis: The Evolution of a North-African Ghetto] (Paris: Presses Universitaires de France, 1959), pp. 21–24. Used with permission of the publisher.

Mihail Sebastian, from *Journal, 1935–1944: The Fascist Years*, trans. Patrick Camiller (Chicago: Ivan R. Dee, 2000), pp. 533, 547, 557. Used with permission of the publisher.

Ronald Segal and Dan Jacobson, "Apartheid and South African Jewry: An Exchange between Ronald Segal and Dan Jacobson on Mr. Jacobson's January 1957 Article, 'The Jews of South Africa,'" *Commentary*, vol. 24, no. 5 (November, 1957), pp. 428–31. Used with permission of the publisher.

Anna Seghers (Netty Reiling), "Post ins Gelobte Land 1944" [Mail to the Promised Land], from *Der Ausflug der toten Mädchen und andere Erzählunge* (New York: Aurora-Verlag, 1946), pp. 66–68 / (Berlin: Aufbau Taschenbuch Verl, 2012). © Aufbau Verlag GmbH & Co. KG, Berlin 1948, 2008. Used with permission of Aufbau Verlag.

Władysław Szlengel, "Things," trans. John and Bogdana Carpenter, *Chicago Review*, vol. 52, no. 2/4 (Autumn 2006), pp. 283–86. Used with permission of the publisher and the translators.

Peter Szondi, "An Gershom Sholem" [Letter to Gershom Scholem], from *Briefe*, ed. Christoph König and Thomas Sparr (Frankfurt am Main: Suhrkamp, 1993), pp. 301–3. Used with permission of the publisher.

Abraham Tabachnik, "Tradition and Revolt in Yiddish Poetry," trans. Cynthia Ozick, from *Voices from the Yiddish: Essays, Memoirs, Diaries*, eds. Irving Howe and Eliezer Greenberg (Ann Arbor: University of Michigan Press, 1972), pp. 294–98. Copyright © by The University of Michigan 1972. Used with permission of the publisher.

Yoram Taharlev, music by Yair Rosenblum, "Ammunition Hill" (Giv'at Ha'Takhmoshet), trans. Alex Ben-Arieh, http://www.historama.com/online-resources/israeli-music/idf_bands.html#Ammunition. © Sami Michael and ACUM. Translation © Alex Ben-Arieh. Used with permission of the translator and of ACUM, on behalf of the author.

Benjamin Tammuz, "Sands of Gold," first published in English in *A Rare Cure*, trans. from the Hebrew by Joseph Schachter (Tel Aviv: Hakibbutz Hameuchad Publishing House / The Institute for the Translation of Hebrew Literature, 1981), pp. 60–67. First published in the Hebrew language as "Ḥolot ha-zahav" (Tel Aviv: Hakibbutz Hameuchad Publishing House, 1976). Copyright © The Estate of Benjamin Tammuz and ACUM. English translation copyright © 1981 by The Institute for the Translation of Hebrew Literature. Published by arrangement with The Institute for the Translation of Hebrew Literature and with ACUM, on behalf of the author's estate.

Shlomo Tanny, Azriel Okhmani, and Moshe Shamir, eds., "Preface," from *Dor ba'arets: antologia shel sifrut yisra'elit* [The Native-Born Generation: Anthology of Israeli Literature] (Merhavia: Sifriat Poalim, 1958), pp. 1–2. Used with permission of the editors' estates.

Jacques Taraboulos, "The Neila," trans. Isaac Jack Lévy, from *And the World Stood Silent: Sephardi Poetry of the Holocaust*, ed. Isaac Jack Lévy (Urbana and Chicago: University of Illinois Press, 2000), pp. 189–91. Used with permission of the author's estate and the translator.

Samuel Tarnopolsky, from *La mitad de dada* [Half of Nothing] (Buenos Aires: Editorial Milá, 1988), pp. 206–7. Used with permission of the author's estate.

Issachar Shlomo Teichtal, "A Joyful Mother of Children," from *Restoration of Zion as a Response During the Holocaust*, ed. and trans. Pesach Schindler (Hoboken: Ktav, 1999), pp. 33–36, 300–301, 326–27. Used with permisson of the translator's estate.

Judd L. Teller, "Goyim," from *Mid-century: An Anthology of Jewish Life and Culture in Our Times*, ed. Harold Uriel Ribalow (New York: Beechhurst Press, 1955), pp. 17–23. Originally published in *The Antioch Review*, vol. 9, no. 2 (Summer 1949), pp. 236–42. Used with permission of *The Antioch Review*.

Binyamin Tenenbaum, from *Eḥad me'ir ushnayim mimishpaḥa* [One of a City and Two of a Family: The Holocaust Testimonies of Children] (Tel Aviv: Sifriat Po'alim, 1947), p. vi, 8–9, 10–11, 11–12. Used with permission of the publisher.

Avrom Teytlboym, from *Varshever heyf: mentshn un gesheenishn* [Warsaw Courtyards] (Buenos Aires: Tsentral-farband fun poylishe yidn, 1947), pp. 11–13, 50, 51–53, 195.

César Tiempo (aka Israel Zeitlin), "Paráfrasis" [Paraphrase], from Buenos Aires, Esquina Sábado, *Antología de César Tiempo*, ed. Eliahu Toker (Buenos Aires: Archivo General de la Nación, 2007), p. 120. Used with permission of the author's estate.

Mina Tomkiewicz, from *Of Bombs and Mice: A Novel of Wartime Warsaw*, trans. Stefan F. Gazel (London: Allen & Unwin, 1970), pp. 8–11. Used with permission of the author's estate.

Friedrich Torberg, "Applaus für Anne Frank" [Applause for Anne Frank], from *Wien oder der Unterschied* (München: Langen Müeller 1998), pp. 239–45. © 1998 by Langen Müeller at F. A. Herbig Verlagsbuchhandlung GmbH, Munich: www.herbig.net. Used with permission of F. A. Herbig Verlagsbuchhandlung GmbH.

Joshua Trachtenberg, from *The Devil and the Jews: The Medieval Conception of the Jew and Its Relation to Modern Anti-Semitism* (New Haven, Conn.: Yale University Press, 1943), pp. 4–6. Used with permission of the author's estate.

Lionel Trilling, "Isaac Babel," from *Beyond Culture* (New York: Viking Press, 1965), pp. 119–21. Copyright © 1955, 1957, 1961, 1962, 1963, 1965 by Lionel Trilling. Used by permission of The Wylie Agency LLC; "Wordsworth and the Rabbis," from *The Moral Obligation to be Intelligent: Selected Essays*, ed. and intro. Leon Wieseltier (New York: Farrar, Straus & Giroux, 2000), pp. 184–86. Copyright © 2000 by the Estate of Lionel Trilling. Originally published in *The Opposing Self: Nine Essays in Criticism* (London: Secker and Warburg, 1955), pp. 127–28. Reprinted by permission of Farrar, Straus and Giroux and The Random House Group Ltd.

Jehiel Isaiah Trunk, from *Poyln: zikhroynes un bilder* [Poland: Memoirs and Scenes], vol. 5 (New York: Farlag Medem-klub, 1944–1953), pp. 49–51, 52–54. Unpublished trans. Gabi Trunk. Used with permission of Gabi Trunk.

Ayin Tur-Malka, "Memorial Service," trans. Shirley Kaufman, from *The Defiant Muse: Hebrew Feminist Poems from Antiquity to the Present*, ed. Shirley Kaufman, Galit Hasan-Rokem, and Tamar S. Hess (New York: The Feminist Press at CUNY 1999), p. 131. Translated from "Azkara," from *Shirat Ha-be'erot* (Tel Aviv: Ya'ir Publishers Ltd., 1972 / 1989). © Ayin Tur-Malka and ACUM. Used with permission of the translator and of ACUM, on behalf of the author.

Malka Heifetz Tussman, "Vest kumen mit gots hilf tsurik" [You Will, with God's Help, Come Back], from *Lider* (Los Angeles: Malka Kheyfets-Tuzman bukh-komitet, 1949), pp. 37–39. Used with permission of the author's estate; "Water Without Sound," trans. Marcia Falk, from *With Teeth in the Earth: Selected Poems of Malka Heifetz Tussman, translated, edited, and introduced by Marcia Falk* (Detroit: Wayne State University Press, 1992), p. 75. Copyright © 1992 Marcia Lee Falk. Used by permission of the translator. Available from www.marciafalk.com.

Julian Tuwim, "We Polish Jews," trans. Mrs. R. Langer, from My, Żydzi Polscy / We, Polish Jews, ed. Khone Shmeruk (Jerusalem: Magnes Press, the Hebrew University, 1984), pp. 18–19, 20–22. Translation first published in *Free World* (July 1944). One-time permission to reproduce granted to Yale University Press by The Hebrew University Magness Press.

Isadore Twersky, "The Shulhan Arukh: Enduring Code of Jewish Law," *Judaism*, vol. 16, no. 2 (Spring 1967), pp. 141–42, 156–57. Used with permission of the American Jewish Congress.

Ephraim E. Urbach, from *Reshimot bi-yeme milhamah: yomano shel Rav Erets-Yisre'eli ba-tsava ha-Briti* [War Journals: Diary of a Jewish Chaplain from Eretz-Israel in the British Army, 1942–1944] (Tel Aviv: Ministry of Defense, 2008), pp. 162–66, 170–72, 174–77. Used with permission of the publisher.

Leon M. Uris, excerpt from *Exodus* (London: Corgi Books, 1977), pp. 304–307. Copyright © 1958 by Leon M. Uris. Used by permission of Doubleday, an imprint of the Knopf Doubleday Publishing Group, a division of Penguin Random House LLC, and HarperCollins Publishers Ltd. All rights reserved.

Ben-Zion Meir Hai Uziel, "Hale'umit veti'udatah" [Nationalism and Its Awareness], from *Masoret ba'idan hamoderni: hakhamim Sefaradim badorot haaharonim*, ed. Yitzhak Shouraqui (Tel Aviv: Mishkal, 2009), pp. 189–94. Used with permission of the publisher.

Bernardo Verbitsky, "Es difícil empezar a vivir" [It's Not Easy to Start Living], from *Cuentos judíos latinoamericanos*, ed. Ricardo Feierstein (Buenos Aires: Editorial Milá, 1989), pp. 27–28. Used with permission of the author's estate.

Haya Vered, "The Zero Hour," trans. Lisa Katz, from *The Defiant Muse: Hebrew Feminist Poems from Antiquity to the Present*, ed. Shirley Kaufman, Galit Hasan-Rokem, and Tamar S. Hess (New York: The Feminist Press at CUNY 1999), pp. 125–29. Translated from "Sh'at Ha-efes," from *Shirim al herev u-meilar* (Tel Aviv: Hakibbutz Hameuchad Publishing House, Ltd., 1956). © Haya Vered and ACUM. Used with permission of the translator and of ACUM, on behalf of the author's estate.

Aaron Vergelis, *Sovetish heymland*, vol. 1, no. 1 (July–August 1961), pp. 4–5. Used with permission of the author's estate.

Diego Viga (Paul Engel), "The Stutterer's Suicide and the Psychiatrist's Dream," trans. Susan Riva Greenberg, from Roberta Kalechofsky, *Echad: An Anthology of Latin American Jewish Writers* (Marblehead, Mass.: Micah Publications, 1980/1984), pp. 98–99. Used with permission of the publisher, the author's estate, and the translator.

David Viñas, from *Un dios cotidiano* [An Everyday God] (Buenos Aires: Centro Editor de América Latina, 1987), pp. 48–50. Used with permission of the author's estate.

Aleksander Voronel, "The Social Preconditions of the National Awakening of the Jews in the USSR," trans. Moshe Decter, from *I am a Jew: Essays on Jewish Identity in the Soviet Union*, eds. Aleksander Voronel, Viktor Yakhot, and Moshe Decter (New York: Anti-Defamation League of B'nai B'rith, Academic Committee on Soviet Jewry, 1973), pp. 32–35. Used with permission of the Anti-Defamation League.

Miriam Waddington, "Second Generation," from *The Collected Poems of Miriam Waddington: A Critical Edition*, vol. 2 (Ottawa: University of Ottawa Press, 2014), p. 25. Used with permission of the author's estate.

Yona Wallach, "Yonatan," trans. Lenore Gordon, from *Contemporary Israeli Literature: An Anthology*, eds. Elliott Anderson and Robert Friend (Philadelphia: Jewish Publication Society of America, 1977), p. 309. Published in Hebrew in *Devarim* (Tel Aviv: Achshav, 1966). © Haim Gouri and ACUM. English translation copyright 1977 by the Jewish Publication Society of America. Reprinted by permission of the University of Nebraska Press and ACUM.

Oser Warszawski, "A Contract," trans. Alan Astro, in *Yale French Studies*, no. 85, *Discourses of Jewish Identity in Twentieth-Century France* (June 22, 1994; special issue), pp. 108–12. Used with permission of the publisher.

Arthur Waskow, "How to Bring Mashiah," from *The First Jewish Catalog: A Do-It-Yourself Kit*, eds. Richard Siegel, Michael Strassfeld, and Sharon Strassfeld (Philadelphia: Jewish Publication Society of America, 1973), pp. 250–51. Reprinted by permission of the University of Nebraska Press.

Jiří Weil, excerpt from *Life with a Star*, trans. Ruzena Kovarikova with Roslyn Schloss (New York: Farrar, Straus & Giroux, 1989), pp. 99–102. Copyright © 1989 by Farrar, Straus & Giroux, Inc. Reprinted by permission of Farrar, Straus and Giroux.

Max Weinreich, "The Reality of Jewishness vs. the Ghetto Myth," from *To Honor Roman Jakobson*, vol. 3 (The Hague: Mouton, 1967), pp. 211–21. Used with permission of Walter de Gruyter.

Uriel Weinreich, "Mapping a Culture," *Columbia University Forum*, vol. 6, no. 3 (Summer 1963), pp. 17–21. Used with permission of the author's estate and University Archives, Rare Book & Manuscript Library, Columbia University in the City of New York.

Abraham Weisbaum, "Yente Tinifotski," excerpted from "The Tinifotsky Monologues," trans. Debbie Nathan, from *Yiddish South of the Border: An Anthology of Latin American Yiddish Writing*, ed. Alan Astro (Albuquerque: University of Mexico Press, 2003), pp. 164–70. Copyright © 2003 University of New Mexico Press, 2003. Used with permission of the publisher.

Peter Weiss, excerpt from "Canto Two: The Camp," from *The Investigation*, trans. Alexander Gross (London: Calder and Boyars, 1966), pp. 33–36. Published in 1966 by Calder & Boyars, reprinted 2015 by Marion Boyars Publishers, London & New York. Originally published in German by Suhrkamp Verlag, Berlin. Used with permission of Marion Boyars.

Trude Weiss-Rosmarin, "America Is Not Babylonia," from *Mid-century: An Anthology of Jewish Life and Culture in Our Times*, ed. Harold Uriel Ribalow (New York: Beechhurst Press, 1955), pp. 469, 471–78. First published in *Jewish Spectator* (March 1953). Used with permission of *Jewish Spectator*.

Chaim Weizmann, "1st Address to Knesset," paper 100, from *The Letters and Papers of Chaim Weizmann*, Series B: Papers, vol. 2, December 1931–April 1952, ed. Bernard Litvinoff (New Brunswick, N.J.: Transaction Books / Jerusalem: Israel Universities Press, 1983), pp. 705–9. Copyright Yad Chaim Weizmann 1984. Republished with permission of Transaction Publishers, permission conveyed through Copyright Clearance Center, Inc.

Robert Weltsch, "Introduction," *The Leo Baeck Institute Year Book*, vol. 1, no. 1 (1 January 1956), pp. xxx–xxxi. By permission of Oxford University Press, on behalf of The Leo Baeck Institute, and the author's estate.

Arnold Wesker, from *Chicken Soup with Barley*, from *The Wesker Trilogy: Plays*, vol. 1 (London: Bloomsbury Methuen Drama, an imprint of Bloomsbury Publishing Plc, 2001), pp. 73–76. © Arnold Wesker. Used with permission of Bloomsbury Publishing Plc.

Elie Wiesel, excerpts from *The Jews of Silence: A Personal Report on Soviet Jewry*, trans. Neal Kozodoy (New York: Holt, Rinehart and Winston, 1966), pp. 113–14, 119–22, 125–27. English language translation copyright

Anzia Yezierska, excerpt from "All Whom I Ever Loved," from *Red Ribbon on a White Horse: My Story*, pp. 102–3. Copyright 1950 by Anzia Yezierska, and renewed © 1978 by Louise Levitas Henriksen. Reprinted with the permission of Persea Books, Inc (New York), www.perseabooks.com.

S. Yizhar, "The Prisoner," trans. V. C. Rycus, from *Modern Hebrew Literature*, ed. Robert Alter (New York: Behrman House, 1975), pp. 294–95, 298–300. Translated from "Hashavuy," from *Sipur hirbat hizah, hashavuy* (Merhavia: Sifriyat Po'alim, 1949). © S. Yizhar and ACUM. English translation © Behrman House, Inc. Reprinted with permission of Behrman House, www.behrmanhouse.com, and ACUM, on behalf of the author's estate.

Natan Zach, "One Moment," trans. Vivian Eden (unpublished). © Uri Natan Zach and ACUM, translation © Vivian Eden. Used with permission from the translator and ACUM, on behalf of the author's estate.

Haim Zafrani, from *Pédagogie juive en terre d'Islam* [Jewish Education in the Land of Islam] (Paris: Adrien Maisonneuve, 1969), pp. 41–43. Used with permission of Librairie d'Amérique et d'Orient—Adrien Maisonneuve.

Emanuel Zamir, music by Emanuel Zamir, "Be'er basadeh" [A Well in the Field], published by Tarbut-Vechinuch Ed. © Emanuel Zamir and ACUM. Used with permission of ACUM, on behalf of the author.

Shlomo Zamir, "Shirah yeshanah" [An Old Song], from *Hakol miba'ad le'anaf: shirim*, rev. ed. (Tel Aviv: Sifriat po'alim, 1990), pp. 50–51. Used with permission of the author.

Mark Zborowski and Elizabeth Herzog, from *Life Is With People: The Jewish Little-Town of Eastern Europe*, fwd. Margaret Mead (New York: Schocken Books, 1962), pp. 193–95. Used with permission of Mark Zborowski's estate.

Aaron Zeitlin, "Donna Donna," Yiddish Lyrics by Aaron Zeitlin, English lyrics by Sheldon Secunda, Teddi Schwartz, and Arthur Kevess, Music by Sholom Secunda. Copyright © 1940 and 1968 (Renewed 1968 and 1996) Beam Me Up Music, EMI Mills Music Inc. and Williamson Music. International Copyright Secured. All Rights Reserved. Used by permission of Williamson Music. Copyright © 1940, 1956 (Copyrights Renewed) EMI Mills Music Inc. and Williamson Music Co. in the U.S. All Rights outside the U.S. Administered by EMI Mills Music Inc. and Hargail Music Press. All Rights Reserved. Used by permission of Alfred Music; "To Be a Jew," trans. Robert Friend, from *A Treasury of Yiddish Poetry*, ed. Irving Howe and Eliezer Greenberg (New York: Holt, Rinehart and Winston, 1969), p. 318. Originally published in Yiddish as "Zayn a Yid," from *Gezamlte lider*, vol. 1 (New York: Farlag Matones, 1947), pp. 47–48. Translation copyright © Jean Shapiro Cantu. Used with permission of the translator's estate.

Zelda (Schneerson Mishkovsky), "Each Rose," trans. by Barbara Goldberg, from *After the First Rain: Israeli Poems on War and Peace*, ed. Barbara Goldberg and Moshe Dor (Syracuse, N.Y.: Syracuse University Press, 1998, originally published by Dryad Press, 1997). © Dryad Press, 1997. Translated from Zelda, "Kol Shoshana," from *Shirei Zelda* (Tel Aviv: Hakibbutz Hameuchad Publishing House, Ltd., 1985). © Zelda (Schneerson Mishkovsky) and ACUM. Used with permission of the translator, of Hakibbutz Hameuchad-Sifriat, and of ACUM, on behalf of the author's estate.

Josef Zelkowicz, "In Those Nightmarish Days," trans. David Suchoff, from *In Those Nightmarish Days: The Ghetto Reportage of Peretz Opoczynski and Josef Zelkowicz*, ed. Samuel Kassow (New Haven, Conn.: Yale University Press, 2015), pp. 215–17, 222–25. Used with permission of the publisher.

Jacques Zibi, from *Mâ* (Paris: Mercure de France, 1972), pp. 118–22. Used with permission of the publisher.

Larry Zolf, "Boil Me No Melting Pots, Dream Me No Dreams," from *Zolf* (Toronto: Exile Editions, 1999), pp. 1–4, 7. First published in the *Toronto Telegram*. Used with permission of Exile Editions.

Béla Zsolt, "Nine Suitcases," trans. John Bátki, from *Contemporary Jewish Writing in Hungary: An Anthology*, eds. Susan Rubin Suleiman and Éva Forgács (Lincoln: University of Nebraska Press, 2003), pp. 17–20. Copyright 2003 by the University of Nebraska Press. Reprinted by permission of the University of Nebraska Press.

Antek Zuckerman and Eliyohu Gutkowski, "Payn un gvure in dem yidishn over in likht fun der kegnvart" [Suffering and Heroism in the Jewish Past in Light of the Present], trans. Solon Beinfeld (Warsaw: Dror, 1940), pp. 4–8. Used with permission of Antek Zuckerman's estate.

Antek (Yitzhak) Zuckerman and Moshe Basok, eds., from *Sefer milḥamot hageta'ot: ben haḥomot, bamaḥanot baye'arot* [The Book of Jewish Armed Resistance: Within the Walls, in the Camps and the Forests] (Tel Aviv: Hakibbutz Hameuchad, 1954), pp. vi–vii. Used with permission of the publisher.

Louis Zukofsky, "A-12," from *A* (New York: New Directions, 2011), pp. 142–44. Used with permission of the author's estate. All Louis Zukofsky material Copyright Paul Zukofsky; the material may not be reproduced, quoted, or used in any manner whatsoever without the explicit and specific permission of the copyright holder.

Stefan Zweig, "Universitas Vitae," from *The World of Yesterday: An Autobiography*, trans. Helmut Ripperger and B. W. Huebsch (New York: The Viking Press, 1943), pp. 106–10. Translation copyright 1943; renewed © 1971 by The Viking Press, Inc. Used by permission of Viking Books, an imprint of Penguin Publishing Group, a division of Penguin Random House LLC. All rights reserved.

Reyzl Zychlinsky, "Everything Will Remember," from *A Treasury of Yiddish Poetry*, ed. Irving Howe & Eliezer Greenberg, trans. Lucy S. Dawidowicz and Florence Victor (New York: Holt Rinehart, 1969), p. 231. Copyright © 1969 by Lucy C. Dawidowicz. Reprinted with permission of the author's estate and Georges Borchardt, Inc., on behalf of the Estate of Lucy S. Dawidowicz; "Got hot farbahaltn zayn ponem" [God Hid His Face], from *Shvaygndike tirn: lider* (New York: Hammeḥabbēr, 1962), p. 112. Used with permission of the author's estate.

Salomón Zytner, "The Bar Mitzvah Speech," trans. Alan Astro, from *Yiddish South of the Border: An Anthology of Latin American Yiddish Writing*, ed. Alan Astro (Albuquerque: University of Mexico Press, 2003), pp. 184–85. Copyright © 2003 University of New Mexico Press, 2003. Used with permission of the publisher.

Index of Authors and Artists

Biographical information about each author or artist appears at the beginning of the person's first selection. The reader may search by subject in the web-based version of *The Posen Library of Jewish Culture and Civilization.*